To my good friend, Judge P. C. Rao

with my warm regards
and good wishes

Tommy Koh, editor-in-chief
May 2007

SINGAPORE
THE ENCYCLOPEDIA

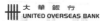

Cover pictures: *1 The Merlion. 2 Performance by The Arts Fission Company. 3 President S.R. Nathan. 4 Traditional batik sarong. 5 Public housing flats at Bukit Gombak. 6 Vanda Miss Joaquim, the national flower. 7 Lantern at Tan Si Chong Su Temple. 8 Clifford Pier, c. 1960. 9 Minister Mentor Lee Kuan Yew. 10 The Istana. 11 Coloured rice flour art (rangoli), part of Deepavali decorations. 12 Mardan Mamat, golfer. 13 Minaret of Malabar Mosque. 14 Bugis Street. 15 Statue of Sir Stamford Raffles near Singapore River. 16 Shophouse facade. 17 Lim Fei Shen, dancer. 18 Old Parliament House, arts venue. 19 Esplanade—Theatres on the Bay. 20 Choo Hoey, conductor. 21 PSA International container terminal. 22 Yusof Ishak, first president of Singapore. 23 Ang Peng Siong, swimmer. 24 Figurines at Sri Srinivasa Perumal Temple. 25 Georgette Chen, self-portrait. 26 State crest, Istana gates. 27 Southern lion dance. 28 Macaws at Jurong BirdPark. 29 Pan Shou, calligrapher and poet. 30 Ong Teng Cheong, fifth president of Singapore. 31 Stefanie Sun, singer. 32 Serangoon Road. 33 Performance by Dance Ensemble Singapore. 34 Ceramic wall panel depicting rubber tapping, Keppel Railway Station. 35 The Bandstand at Singapore Botanic Gardens. 36 Dick Lee, singer and songwriter. 37 Workhorse Afloat, play by TheatreWorks. 38 Elgin Bridge, Singapore River. 39 Ornamental detail, Thian Hock Keng Temple. 40 National Day celebrations. 41 Stained-glass window, St George's Church. 42 Singapore Expo Mass Rapid Transit station. 43 Tiger Balm brand label. 44 Fountain of Wealth, Suntec City. 45 Ee Peng Liang, philanthropist. 46 Poster for Speak Mandarin campaign. 47 Tailfin, Singapore Airlines.*

SINGAPORE
THE ENCYCLOPEDIA

SINGAPORE: THE ENCYCLOPEDIA

Editor-in-Chief
TOMMY KOH

General Editors
TIMOTHY AUGER • JIMMY YAP • NG WEI CHIAN

Picture Editor
SNG SIOK AI

Editorial Team
IBRAHIM TAHIR • KIM LEE • ONG MAY ANNE
JEREMY E. TAYLOR • SHAN WOLODY

Copy Editors
ANJANA CHANDRA • JANICE A. FUNG • JUDITH HOLMBERG • LEOW AIK JIANG
GEETHA MENON • BERNARD PEREIRA • HIREN PHUKAN • DIANA SAW • HARRY TAN
TAN BAH BAH • BERNICE TANG • LIM SIEW CHING

Studio Manager
ANNIE TEO

Project Design Manager
TAN SEOK LUI

Designers
LISA DAMAYANTI • FELICIA WONG • PASCAL CHAN

Production Manager
SIN KAM CHEONG

EDITIONS DIDIER MILLET

Publisher
DIDIER MILLET

General Manager
CHARLES ORWIN

First published in 2006 by Editions Didier Millet in association with the National Heritage Board

EDITIONS DIDIER MILLET
121 Telok Ayer Street
#03-01
Singapore 068590
www.edmbooks.com

NATIONAL HERITAGE BOARD
MICA Building
140 Hill Street
#03-02
Singapore 179369

Colour separation by SC Graphic Technology Pte Ltd
Printed and bound in Singapore by Tien Wah Press

Reprinted 2006

ISBN: 981-4155-63-2

ACKNOWLEDGEMENTS

In creating this encyclopedia, we were assisted by many people. Some helped by giving expert advice, while others pointed us in the right direction or to the right people. Another group of people reviewed entries after they were written. Many people helped to verify the information contained herein. This volume could not have been produced without them.

The following assisted in drawing up the list of entries, as well as, in some cases, also writing them. Prominent among them is legal and history scholar Dr Kevin Tan of Equilibrium Consulting, who not only gave advice from an early stage, but wrote a wide range of entries on law, history, and other topics. We would also like to acknowledge the assistance of: Associate Professor Nicholas Aplin, National Institute of Education • Associate Professor Peter Borschberg, Department of History, National University of Singapore • Professor S. Gopinathan, Vice-Dean, Centre for Research in Pedagogy and Practice, National Institute of Education • Mr Idris Rashid Khan Surattee, Singapore Press Holdings • Assistant Professor Kho Ee Moi, Humanities and Social Studies Education Academic Group, National Institute of Education • Mr Kwa Chong Guan, Institute of Defence and Strategic Studies • Associate Professor Albert Lau, Department of History, National University of Singapore • Associate Professor John Miksic, Southeast Asian Studies Department, National University of Singapore • Associate Professor Vineeta Sinha, Department of Sociology, National University of Singapore • Ms Helen Doreen Tan, Humanities and Social Studies Education Academic Group, National Institute of Education • Associate Professor Shandre M. Thangavelu, Department of Economics, National University of Singapore • Associate Professor Tan Eng Chye, Dean, Faculty of Science, National University of Singapore • Associate Professor Tan Ern Ser, Department of Sociology, National University of Singapore • Ms Wang Luan Keng, The Raffles Museum of Biodiversity Research • Associate Professor Peter Wilson, Department of Economics, National University of Singapore • Associate Professor Wong Yunn Chii, Department of Architecture, National University of Singapore • Associate Professor Wong Poh Poh, Department of Geography, National University of Singapore

Getting a preliminary list of entries is one thing. Deciding which individuals should be included and who should be excluded was also a difficult task. A group of experts in their fields gave us valuable advice and helped refine the list of artists, musicians, theatre practioners, photographers and the like. We wish to thank:
Mr Ahmad Mashadi, Senior Curator, Singapore Art Museum • Mr Chong Wing Hong, Specialist Writer, *Lianhe Zaobao* • Mdm Goh Soo Khim, Artistic Director, Singapore Dance Theatre • Mr Eric Goh Wee Seng • Assistant Professor Ho Chee Kong, Music Associate Director, Yong Siew Toh Conservatory of Music • Mr Koh Buck Song • Mr Nelson Kwei • Mr Lee Weng Choy, Artistic Co-Director, The Substation • Dr Leong Liew Geok • Ms Lim Fei Shen, Head of Studies (Curriculum Development and Projects), Nanyang Academy of Fine Arts • Ms Angela Liong, Artistic Director, The Arts Fission Company • Mr Benjamin Loh • Mr Raphaël Millet • Mr Ong Keng Sen, Artistic Director, TheatreWorks • Ms Teresa Pee • Ms Lindy Poh, Balkenende Chew & Chia • Mr T. Sasitharan, Director, The Theatre Practice • Dr K.K. Seet, Department of English Language and Literature, National University of Singapore • Mr Venka Purushothaman, Dean, Faculty of Performing Arts and Integrated Studies, LASALLE-SIA College of the Arts • Ms Bridget Tracy Tan, Nanyang Academy of Fine Arts • Dr Eleanor Tan Ai Ling, Senior Lecturer (Music Department), Nanyang Academy of Fine Arts • Ms Hannah Tan • Mr Paul Tan • Mr Tan Lip Seng • Associate Professor Kelly Tang, Visual and Performing Arts, National Institute of Education • Mr David P.C. Tay • Mr Bernd Michael Teichmann, Head, School of Dance, Nanyang Academy of Fine Arts • Ms Jennifer Tham, Music Director, Singapore Youth Choir Ensemble Singers • Professor Edwin Thumboo, Department of English Language and Literature, National University of Singapore • Mr Kelvin Tong, Boku Films • Assistant Professor Valerie Wee, Department of English Language and Literature, National University of Singapore • Professor Jan Uhde, Fine Arts/Film Studies, University of Waterloo, Ontario, Canada • Ms Yvonne Ng Uhde, Editorial Board, *KINEMA* • Dr Victor Valbuena, School of Film and Media Studies, Ngee Ann Polytechnic • Mr Eric Watson, Senior Lecturer, School of Music, Nanyang Academy of Fine Arts • Professor Yu Chun Yee, Artistic Advisor, Nanyang Academy of Fine Arts

After the entries were written, they were given over to a group of experts who read through and commented upon them. We are grateful for the efforts of:
Mr Barry Desker, Director, Institute of Defence and Strategic Studies • Mr K. Kesavapany, Director, Institute of Southeast Asian Studies • Mr Kishore Mahbubani, Dean, Lee Kuan Yew School of Public Policy • Professor A. Mani, Dean of International Cooperation—

Research, Ritsumeikan Asia Pacific University, Oita, Japan • Mr Dinesh Naidu • Ms Pushpalatha Naidu, Senior Executive (Heritage and Asia), National Library Board • Ms Elaine Ng, Deputy Director (Performing Arts), National Arts Council • Associate Professor Euston Quah, Head, Division of Economics, Nanyang Technological University • Mr Peter Schoppert, McKinsey & Company • Mr Samuel Dorai Singam • Professor Tan Cheng Han, Dean, Faculty of Law, National University of Singapore • Associate Professor Tan Tai Yong, Department of History, National University of Singapore • Mr Tan Tarn How, Senior Research Fellow, Institute of Policy Studies • Mr Teo Han Wue, Executive Director, Art Retreat • Mr Robin Tomlin, Vice-Chairman (Asia), UBS AG • Associate Professor Wong Yunn Chii, Department of Architecture, National University of Singapore.

The entries were further checked by an important group of people who ensured that the information in the book was current and accurate. Their efforts have been invaluable in making this encyclopedia authoritative. We would like to thank:
Assistant Professor Choy Keen Meng, Division of Economics, School of Humanities and Social Sciences, Nanyang Technological University and Ms Lau Siew Kheng, former librarian at the Ministry of Foreign Affairs.

Staff from the National Archives of Singapore, the National Museum of Singapore, National Library Board and Preservation of Monuments Board have also made very significant contributions to this volume by checking facts:
National Archives of Singapore: Mrs Ang-Low Kia Hiang • Mr Paul Chan Eng Chwee • Ms Yvonne Chan • Ms Julia Chee • Ms Chew Hui Min • Mr Foong Park Meng • Ms Elaine Goh • Ms France Goh • Ms Khoo Gim Soon • Ms Koh Yock Hong • Mrs Kwek-Chew Kim Gek • Ms Grace Li Weixuan • Ms Ruth Lim • Mr Lim Guan Hock • Mdm Lim Lay Jean • Mrs June Lin • Ms Michelle Low Mei-Fun • Ms Lye Soo Choon • Mr Ng Sek Hiong • Mrs Ng Yoke Lin • Ms Noridah Jamaluddin • Mr Ong Wei Meng • Mr Pitt Kuan Wah • Dr Phang Lai Tee • Mrs Rahmah Saini • Ms Sharina Md Shariff • Ms Stella Clare Wee • Mr Jeremy Tan Zhong Yang • Ms Grace Tang Pei Pei • Ms Michelle Tay Hui Wen • Ms Elaine Yam • Mrs Yap-Wong Wai Fey • Ms Claire Yeo Ching Yui • Mr Ian Yeo Tian Chiang • Ms Yeo Seow Ling • Ms Joanne Yip Oi Toh • Mdm Zainah Arshad
National Library Board: Ms Ang Seow Leng • Ms Azizah Sidek • Mr Chan Fook Weng • Mr Joshua Chia • Ms Fauziah Hassan • Mr Heirwin Mohd Nasir • Ms Gracie Lee • Ms Makeswary Periasamy • Mr Muhamad Ashif Padili • Ms Judy Ng • Ms Nor-Afidah Abdul Rahman • Mr Ong Eng Chuan • Mr Alexander Ong • Mdm Ramlah Hashim • Mr Timothy Pwee • Ms Bonny Muliani Tan • Ms Yashodha Devi Nadarajan
National Museum of Singapore: Ms Chung May Khuen • Mr Iskander Mydin • Ms Cheryl-Ann Low • Ms Lee Chor Lin • Mr Ng Ching Huei • Ms Tamilselvi Muthu • Ms Sim Wan Hui • Mr Tan Boon Hui • Mr Jason Toh • Ms Katrina Van Dinter • Ms Vidya Murthy • Ms Wong Hong Suen
Preservation of Monuments Board: Mr Wan Meng Hao

The following contributed in other ways with help, advice, suggestions, and comments:
Mr Aidil Mohamed Idris • Mr Ismaeil Al-Khatib • Professor Syed Farid Alatas, Department of Sociology, National University of Singapore • Ms Ang Thing Sing, Manager (Planning), National Arts Council • Mr Anuar Mohamed, Teater Ekamatra • Associate Professor Geoffrey Benjamin, General Studies Unit, Nanyang Technological University • Ms Sarah Benjamin • Mr Don Bosco • Ms Duriya Aziz • Mr Chan Cheow Thia • Mr Kannan Chandran, Journalist, *The Straits Times* • Dr Chee Heng Leng, Asia Research Institute • Mr Cheng Wei Yeow, Executive Officer (Library), Singapore Federation of Chinese Clan Associations • Ms Alice Chia, Assistant Manager (Singapore Writers' Centre), National Book Development Council • Mr Chia Hwee Pheng, President, Singapore Literature Society • Ms Chua Ai Lin • Professor Chua Beng Huat, Department of Sociology, National University of Singapore • Ms Chua Beng Hwee, Deputy Director, Centre for the Arts, National University of Singapore • Mr Chua Chim Kang, Editor, Local News Desk, *Lianhe Zaobao* • Ms Dale Edmonds • Mr Fang Weicheng • Ms Fong Poh Ling, Senior Manager, Locations and Facilities, MediaCorp • Ms Foong Woei Wan, Journalist, *The Straits Times* • Ustaz Ghouse Khan Suratee • Dr Denise Gimpel, Department of Cross-Cultural and Regional Studies, University of Copenhagen • Associate Professor Robbie Goh, Department of English Language and Literature, National University of Singapore • Ms Harziana, Sriwana • Ms Ho Sheo Be • Associate Professor Husain Mutalib, Department of Political Science, National University of Singapore • Mr Theo Kamsma, Vrije Universiteit, Amsterdam, The Netherlands • Associate Professor Khoo Hoon Eng, Medical Education Unit, Yong Loo Lin School of Medicine, National University of Singapore • Mr Aun Koh, Deputy Director (Visual and Literary Arts) National Arts Council • Assistant Professor Koh Hock Kiat,

Asian Languages and Cultures, National Institute of Education • Mr Kok Heng Leun, Artistic Director, Drama Box • Ms Lim Boon Tan, Executive Director, Singapore Federation of Chinese Clan Associations • Mr Sharaad Kuttan • Dr M.S. Shri Lakshmi • Mr Samuel Lee • Ms Rebecca Lim • Ms Shirley Lim, Assistant Vice-President, Editorial Services, English and Malay Newspapers Division, Singapore Press Holdings • Mr Lim Cheng Tju • Associate Professor Sharen Liu, Head, Division of Electronic and Broadcast Media, School of Communication and Information, Nanyang Technological University • Ms Felicia Low, Lee Wei Song School of Music • Ms Louise Mak, Manager (Literary Arts), National Arts Council • Ustaz Mohamed Ibrahim Mohamed Kassim • Ms Josephine Mok, Programme Manager, National Book Development Council of Singapore • Ms Lily Ng, Personal Assistant to Professor Tommy Koh, Ministry of Foreign Affairs • Mr Noor Effendy Ibrahim, Artistic Director and Producer, Teater Ekamatra • Ms Terri Lena Oh, National Parks Board • Ms Pearl Pang, Girls' Brigade Singapore • Ms Pang Cheng Lian, Special Assistant to United Overseas Bank Chairman, United Overseas Bank • Dr Joseph Peters • Mr Phan Ming Yen, Director, Artistic Development, The Arts House • Dr Phua Kai Hong, Department of Community, Occupational and Family Medicine, National University Hospital • Associate Professor Euston Quah, Head, Division of Economics, School of Humanities and Social Sciences, Nanyang Technological University • Associate Professor Quah Sy Ren, Deputy Head, Division of Chinese, School of Humanities and Social Sciences, Nanyang Technological University • Dr Rajesh Rai, Visiting Fellow, South Asian Studies Programme, National University of Singapore • Associate Professor Ananda Rajah, Department of Sociology, National University of Singapore • Ms Indrani C. Rajaram, Chief Scientific Officer, Pollution Control Department, National Environment Agency • Ravindran Drama Group • Professor Peter Reeves, Head, South Asian Studies Programme, National University of Singapore and Director, Centre for Language Studies, National University of Singapore • Mr T.K. Sabapathy • Mr Seow Choke Meng, Singapore Press Holdings • Mr Dashim Shah, Singapore Jain Religious Society • Mr Shen Shi'an, Chief Editor/HOD, Web Department and Library Department (Dharma Propagation Division), Kong Meng San Phor Kark See Monastery • Ms Sophie Siegel • Ms Sandra Sin, Executive Secretary, Singapore Soka Association • Mr Pasha Siraj • Mr Ziggy Soh Yew Peng, School of Film and Media Studies, Ngee Ann Polytechnic • Mr Suryakenchana • Ms Adeline Tan, Assistant Manager (Programmes), Centre for the Arts, National University of Singapore • Ms Adeline Tan, Personal Assistant to the Director, National Museum of Singapore • Professor Bernard Tan Tiong Gie, Department of Physics, National University of Singapore • Ms Kaylene Tan, Director, spell#7 • Ms Winnie Tan, Corporate Affairs, Standard Chartered Bank • Mr Tan Chin Pei • Mr Tan Jin Buck, Supervisor (Marine & Climatology), Business Technical Services Department, Meteorological Services Division, National Environment Agency • Dr Tan Kim Huat, Dean of Studies, Trinity Theological College • Ms Tay Lee San, Senior Scientific Officer, Pollution Control Department, National Environment Agency • Ms Joanne Teo, Scripteasers • Ms S. Thenmoli, President, Agni Koothu • Dr Colleen Kim Thomas, Singapore General Hospital • Mr John Ting, A.I.M. & Associates 402 • Mr Toh Hsien Min, *Quarterly Literary Review of Singapore* • Mr Jolovan Wham, Executive Director, Humanitarian Organisation for Migration Economics (H.O.M.E.) • Mrs Wee-Leong May Lai, Manager (Research/Sports Museum), Market Research Analysis, Communications and Knowledge Group, Singapore Sports Council • Mr Benjamin K.L. Wong, Maritime and Port Authority of Singapore • Professor John Wong, Dean of Medicine, National University of Singapore • Dr Wong Meng Voon • Mr X'Ho • Ms Yap Yien Li • Mr Ying Peian and Ms Goh Beng Choo, Grassroots Book Room • Ms Elaine Yeo • Professor Brenda Yeoh, Department of Geography, National University of Singapore • Mr Yeow Kai Chai, Journalist, *The Straits Times* • Associate Professor Yong Li Lan, Department of English Language and Literature, National University of Singapore • Dr Yu Weijie, Dean, School of Performing Arts, Nanyang Academy of Fine Arts • Mr Victor Yue

Acknowledgement is due to the National Arts Council for funding the research behind the entries on Chinese popular music and Indian classical music.

Thanks also go to the following:
Ms Dorothy Ng, Corporate Communications Assistant Manager, National Museum of Singapore, as project Secretariat • Ms Melissa Cheah, Assistant Manager, Branding and Corporate Communications, Ms Karen Goh, Assistant Director, Audience Development and Industry Promotion, Ms Cheryl Koh, Audience Development and Industry Promotion, of Corporate Communications and Industry Promotion, National Heritage Board

Thanks are due to those who have very kindly helped with the provision of photos from archives and personal collections. Special thanks go to Ms Jean Chen, Acting Head, Archives Reference Services, Ms Noridah Jamaluddin, Assistant Archivist, Archives Services and Ms Wong Wee Hon, Head, Archives Reference of the National Archives of Singapore. The other organizations, groups and individuals are:
Abdul Aleem Siddique Mosque: Mr Mohamed Nassir • **Action for AIDS (Singapore)**: Mr Paul Toh, Executive Director • **ACTION Theatre**: Ms Azizah Ibrahim,

Administrator • **Agni Koothu**: Ms S. Thenmoli, President • **Ai Tong School**: Mdm Elis Tan Lee Ching, Second Vice-Principal • **Aidah Bridal** • **Alliance Entertainment**: Ms Adeline Lim • **Anglo-Chinese School (Independent)**: Dr Ong Teck Chin, Principal and Ms Fanny Tan, Deputy Principal • **The Arts Fission Company**: Ms Angela Liong, Artistic Director, Mr Firdaus Arman, Assistant Manager and Ms Aisha Amrin, Administrator • **Asia Pacific Breweries**: Ms Josephine Lee and Ms Shirley Poo • **Asian Civilisations Museum**: Ms Jennifer Quong, Executive, Marketing and Corporate Communications, Ms Jean Tan, Curatorial Department and Mr Ken Chua, Image Request Officer • **Asian Women's Welfare Association**: Ms Florence Tang, Volunteer Coordinator, TEACH ME Services, Ms Rachel Tang • **Aspidistra Fly**: Mr Ricks Ang and Ms April Lee • **Astreal and Wallwork Records**: Mr Nick Chan • **Automobile Association Singapore**: Ms Catherine Tan, Assistant Manager • **Banyan Tree Hotels and Resorts**: Ms Gladys Ng, Assistant Manager, Partnership Program and colleagues • **Bee Cheng Hiang Hup Chong Foodstuff**: Ms Fion Yeo Gek Dian, Operations Executive, Sales and Marketing • **Boku Films**: Mr Leon Tong • **Canadian International School**: Mr Brian Tucker and Ms Ida Betryl Cecil • **Cathay Organisation**: Ms Jennifer Wee • **Centrestage Consultants**: Mrs Annie Lee • **Chartered Semiconductors Manufacturing**: Ms Khor Hwee Eng, Marketing Communications • **Chevron Oronite**: Mr Jan Lee, Marketing Communications Manager, Asia-Pacific • **Chinatown Heritage Centre**: Ms Karen Toh, Assistant Marketing Manager • **Chinese Heritage Centre**: Mr Ang Cher Kiat, Assistant to Director • **Chinese Opera Institute**: Ms Bai Shuping • **Chinese Theatre Circle**: Mr Leslie Wong, Chairman • **Chung Cheng High School**: Mr Tan King Ming • **Civil Aviation Authority of Singapore**: Ms Connie Lee and colleagues • **ComfortDelGro**: Ms Tammy Tan • **Creative Technology** • **Dance Ensemble Singapore**: Mr Chua Teow Khee • **Donaldson & Burkinshaw**: Mr Tan Bok Hoay and Mr Twang Kern Zern • **Drama Box**: Ms Nicole Lim, Administrative Manager • **ECNAD**: Ms Wee Sheau Theng, Production Artist • **Editions Didier Millet (Kuala Lumpur)**: Mr Martin Cross and colleagues • **Electrico**: Mr Desmond Goh and Mr Daniel Sassoon • **Eng Leong Medallic Industries**: Ms Lisa Dass, Marketing Manager • **Eng Wah Organisation**: Ms Vivien Ong, Sales & Marketing Manager • **Er Woo Amateur Musical & Dramatic Association**: Ms Ng Lee Eng • **ExxonMobil Asia-Pacific**: Ms Selene Chan, Community Relations and Refinery Public Affairs Advisor • **Flip Media**: Mr Ian Yap • **Frontier Danceland**: Ms Low Mei Yoke • **The Fullerton**: Ms Regina Eng, Marketing Communications Manager and colleagues • **Gan Eng Seng School**: Mr Victor Giam Chong Guan, Principal • **Girl Guides Singapore**: Ms Jillien Foo, Communications and Shop Executive • **Genome Institute of Singapore** • **Haw Par Corporation**: Ms Jezamine Lee, Corporate Communications Manager • **Health Promotion Board**: Ms Liew Shin Dee, Senior Executive, Resource Development Services Department • **Home Nursing Foundation**: Mr Tan Boon Leng, Corporate Relations Executive • **Housing & Development Board**: Mr Julian Lim Thong Nan and Ms Pearl Peh Sze Min • **Hwa Chong Institution**: Mr Joseph Tan Chye Liang • **Hyflux**: Ms Martha Ng, Administrator, Corporate Communications • **Immigration and Checkpoints Authority**: Mr Kong Yong Sin, Senior Public and Internal Communications Executive and colleagues • **Imperial War Museum**: Mr Thomas Eaton • **Institute of Bioengineering and Nanotechnology**: Ms Adeline Goh, Head, Corporate Communications • **Institute of Contemporary Arts Singapore**: Ms June Yap • **Institute of Molecular and Cell Biology**: Mr Joshua Woo • **Institute of Technical Education**: Ms Yong Tsuey Ling • **J Team Productions**: Ms Hazel Wong, Head, Artiste Management • **Jewish Welfare Board** • **Khong Guan Biscuit Factory**: Mr Andrew Tan Tiong Par, Export Manager • **Kim Eng Securities**: Ms Molly Tay • **Konica Minolta**: Ms Mabel Lim • **Kwong Wai Siew Peck San Theng** • **Land Transport Authority**: Ms Sham Chong, Ms Lim Wee Leng and Mr Ken Chong • **Leung Kai Fook Medical Company**: Mr Jimmy Leong Sin Fook, Business Development Manager • **Lee Kuan Yew School of Public Policy**: Ms Jileen Tan, Personal Assistant to Dean • **M1**: Ms Clara Koh Ei-Linn, Senior Executive, Corporate Communications • **Makansutra**: Ms Jie Huijuan • **MakanTime.com**: Mr Yeo Thian-Hoe • **Malay Heritage Centre**: Mr Marah Hoessein Salim, General Manager and staff • **Masjid Alkaff Kampung Melayu**: Mr Idham Othman, Executive Officer, Admin and Operations • **MediaCorp Raintree Pictures**: Ms Chan Pui Yin • **MediaCorp Studios**: Ms Audrey Khee Siong Lian, Manager, Studios Business Division, Ms Joyce Ong, Marketing Assistant, Marketing and Distribution and Ms Tan Ai Wah, Artist Management • **Methodist Archives & History Library**: Mr Earnest Lau and Ms Jenny Ng, Research Assistant • **Ministry of Community Development, Youth and Sports**: Ms Ho Chee Har, Assistant Manager/Communications and International Relations Division • **Ministry of Defence**: Ms Deborah Ong, Public Relations Branch • **Ministry of Education**: Ms Linda Tan, Personal Assistant to Minister • **Ministry of the Environment and Water Resources**: Mr Andy Yeo, Corporate Communications • **Ministry of Finance**: Mdm Leela Pokkan • **Ministry of Foreign Affairs**: Mr Daniel James Chee • **Ministry of Home Affairs**: Ms Charlotte Loh, Public Communications Executive • **Ministry of Law**: Ms Joann Tan, Corporate Communications Officer • **Ministry of Manpower**: Ms Serene Chua, Corporate Communications Officer •

The Editors

7

CONTRIBUTORS

NAA. AANDEAPPAN Chairman, Association of Singapore Tamil Writers
AMITAV ACHARYA Deputy Director, Institute of Defence and Strategic Studies
NICHOLAS APLIN Associate Professor, Physical Education and Sports Science, National Institute of Education
MARIA PIETER AQUILIA Asssociate Professor, School of Communication and Information, Nanyang Technological University
MUKUL ASHER Professor, Lee Kuan Yew School of Public Policy, National University of Singapore
AZHAR IBRAHIM Lecturer, Asian Languages and Cultures, National Institute of Education
TIMOTHY BARNARD Associate Professor, Department of History, National University of Singapore
KEVIN BLACKBURN Lecturer, Humanities and Social Studies Education, National Institute of Education
PETER BORSCHBERG Associate Professor, Department of History, National University of Singapore
PESI CHACHA Parsi Zoroastrian Assocation of Southeast Asia
GLORIA CHAN Writer
LENA CHAN Deputy Director, Biodiversity Centre, National Parks Board
SIMON CHAN Ernest Lau Professor of Systematic Theology, Trinity Theological College
CHANG TOU LIANG Writer
CHEAH JIN SENG Senior Consultant, National University Hospital
JULIA CHEE Assistant Director, Records Management, National Archives of Singapore
JEAN CHEN Acting Head, Archives Reference, National Archives of Singapore
CHEW HUI MIN Assistant Archivist, Audio Visual Archives, National Archives of Singapore
ROSALIND CHEW SEOW LUNG Associate Professor, Nanyang Technological University
CHEW SOON BENG Professor, Division of Economics, Nanyang Technological University
ERNEST CHEW Associate Professor, University Scholars Programme, National University of Singapore
CHIA WEI KHUAN Associate Professor, Music Unit, Visual and Performing Arts, National Institute of Education
CHIANG MING SHUN Pastor-in-Charge, Aldersgate Methodist Church
CHIN SEE CHUNG Director, Singapore Botanic Gardens, National Parks Board
CHON SHI JIAO Assistant Archivist, Archives Services, National Archives of Singapore
CHOU LOKE MING Professor, Department of Biological Sciences, National University of Singapore
CYNTHIA CHOU Associate Professor, Department of Cross-Cultural Studies, University of Copenhagen, Denmark
CHOY KEEN MENG Assistant Professor, Division of Economics, Nanyang Technological University
CHUA BENG HUAT Professor, Department of Sociology, National University of Singapore
CHUA SOO PONG Director, Chinese Opera Institute
CHUNG MAY KHUEN Curator, National Museum of Singapore
GEORGE H. CROY Writer
GOH EK MENG Orchestra Librarian (Resources), Singapore Chinese Orchestra
EUGENE I. DAIRIANATHAN Deputy Head, Music Unit, Visual and Performing Arts, National Institute of Education
TANIA DE ROSARIO Writer
IMELDA DIAMSE-LEE Correspondent, The Catholic News
IAN DICKERSON Writer, United Kingdom
GERARDINE DONOUGH-TAN Writer
MANESH DUTT Bengali Association Singapore
MARK EMMANUEL Senior Tutor, Department of History, National University of Singapore
BRIAN FARRELL Associate Professor, Department of History, National University of Singapore
CYRIL FERNANDO Singapore Sinhala Association
TILMAN FRASCH Research Fellow, Asia Research Institute
SUSAN GALLAGHER Writer
JOHN GEE Writer
CHERIAN GEORGE Assistant Professor, Divison of Journalism and Publishing, Nanyang Technological University
ELAINE GOH Assistant Director, Archives Services, National Archives of Singapore
FRANCE GOH Archivist, Archives Services, National Archives of Singapore
ROBBIE GOH Associate Professor, Department of English Language and Literature, National University of Singapore
WILLIAM GWEE Writer
KARL HACK Lecturer, Department of History, The Open University, United Kingdom
HADIJAH RAHMAT Associate Professor, Malay Language and Culture, National Institute of Education
HASEENAH KOYAKUTTY Visiting Public Diplomacy Fellow, Institute of Defence and Strategic Studies
DEREK HENG THIAM SOON Assistant Professor, Department of History, Ohio State University, USA
MICHAEL HILL Geography Department, Francis Holland School, London, United Kingdom
JOSHUA HO HOW HOANG Senior Fellow, Institute of Defence and Strategic Studies
MARK HONG Visiting Research Fellow, Institute of Southeast Asian Studies
HUANG JIANLI Associate Professor, Department of History, National University of Singapore
IBRAHIM TAHIR Writer
ISKANDER MYDIN Senior Curator, National Museum of Singapore
ARUNAJEET KAUR Writer
K. KESAVAPANY Director, Institute of Southeast Asian Studies
KHAIRUDIN ALJUNIED Writer
KEVIN KHOO Research Assistant, Archives Services, National Archives of Singapore
KOH BUCK SONG Author, How Not to Make Money: Inside Stories from Singapore's Commercial Affairs Department
KOH YOCK HONG Research Assistant, Archives Services, National Archives of Singapore
KWOK KIAN CHOW Director, Singapore Art Museum
KWOK KIAN WOON Associate Professor, Division of Sociology, Nanyang Technological University
LAI AH ENG Senior Research Fellow, Institute of Policy Studies
LAM PENG ER Senior Research Fellow, East Asian Institute
THEODORA LAM Department of Geography, National University of Singapore
ALBERT LAU Associate Professor, Department of History, National University of Singapore
LEE CHER LENG Associate Professor, Department of Chinese Studies, National University of Singapore
LEE CHEUK YIN Associate Professor, Department of Chinese Studies, National University of Singapore
LEE CHOR LIN Director, National Museum of Singapore
LEE GEOK BOI Author, The Syonan Years
LEE HUI MIN Writer

IOLA LENZI Author, *Museums of Southeast Asia*
LEONG CHEE CHIEW Chief Operating Officer, National Parks Board
LEONG LIEW GEOK Author and editor
LEONG WAI TENG Senior Lecturer, Department of Sociology, National University of Singapore
SUSAN LEONG Writer
LEOW AIK JIANG Writer
GRACE LI Assistant Archivist, Audio Visual Archives, National Archives of Singapore
MARGARET LIANG Consultant, World Trade Organization/Trade Issues, Ministry of Foreign Affairs
LIEW WOON YIN Director General, Intellectual Property Office of Singapore
HAZEL LIM Writer
IRENE LIM Author, *Secret Societies of Singapore*
JON LIM Writer
KELVIN LIM Collection Manager, Raffles Musuem of Biodiversity and Research
SHARON LIM Writer
LIM KIM LIAN Department of Economics, National University of Singapore
LIM KIM SENG Author, *Vanishing Birds of Singapore*
LIM TECK PENG Director, Centre for the Development of Christian Ministry, Trinity Theological College
EDMUND LIM WEE KIAT Teaching Fellow, Humanities and Social Studies Education, National Institute of Education
JUNE LIN Senior Archivist, Archives Services, National Archives of Singapore
GRETCHEN LIU Author, *Singapore: A Pictorial History*
LO YUET KEUNG Assistant Professor, Department of Chinese Studies, National University of Singapore
RACHEL LO Writer
SIMON LONGMAN Director, Streetscape, National Parks Board
BERNARD LOO Assistant Professor, Institute of Defence and Strategic Studies
CHERYL-ANN LOW Curator, National Museum of Singapore
SHAWN LUM Assistant Professor, Natural Science and Science Education, National Institute of Education
MAAROF SALLEH Director General, Centre for Contemporary Islamic Studies
ANNE MARKEY MAHBUBANI Writer
A. MANI Dean of International Cooperation—Research, Ritsumeikan Asia Pacific University
KALYANI K. MEHTA Associate Professor, Department of Social Work, National University of Singapore
GOPINATH MENON Adjunct Associate Professor, School of Civil and Environmental Engineering, Nanyang Technological University
ELAINE MEYERS Author, *Convent of the Holy Infant Jesus: 150 years in Singapore*
JOHN MIKSIC Associate Professor, Southeast Asian Studies Programme, National University of Singapore
RAPHAËL MILLET Author, *Singapore Cinema*
PAT D'ROSE MONKMAN Public Relations and Promotions Manager, Eurasian Association
MUKHLIS ABU BAKAR Assistant Professor, Malay Language and Culture, National Institute of Education
NAGAH DEVI Department of Sociology, National University of Singapore
NARAYANAN GANAPATHY Assistant Professor, Department of Sociology, National University of Singapore
ASHA MELWANI NATHIRMAL Writer
NEO PENG FU Assistant Professor, Department of Chinese Studies, National University of Singapore
PETER NG Director, The Raffles Museum of Biodiversity Research
TISA NG Author, *Ong Teng Cheong*
NG BENG YEONG Head and Senior Consultant, Department of Psychiatry, Singapore General Hospital
NG CHING HUEI Curatorial Officer, National Museum of Singapore
NG WEI CHIAN Writer
NG YOKE LIN Head, Audio Visual Archives, National Archives of Singapore
NOORMAN ABDULLAH Writer
OH CHIN WEE Writer
ONG MAY ANNE Author, *Five: The CapitaLand Story*
ALEXANDER ONG Reference Librarian
OOI GIOK LING Associate Professor, Humanities and Social Studies Education, National Institute of Education
A. PALANIAPPAN Writer
GAVIN PEEBLES Author, *Economic Growth and Development in Singapore*, United Kingdom
ALEXIUS PEREIRA Assistant Professor, Department of Sociology, National University of Singapore
BERNARD PEREIRA Sub-Editor, *TODAY*
JOSEPH PEREIRA Author, *Legends of the Golden Venus*
PHUA CHEE SENG Pastor, Chen-Li Presbyterian Church
LINDY POH Writer
ROBERT POWELL Author, *Singapore: Architecture of a Global City*
VENKA PURUSHOTHAMAN Dean, Faculty of Performing Arts and Integrated Studies LASALLE-SIA College of the Arts
TIMOTHY PWEE Senior Reference Librarian
JON QUAH Professor, Department of Political Science, National University of Singapore
JUNELI RAI Writer
NITIN DAS RAI Writer
SRINIVAS RAI Writer
JÜRGEN RUDOLPH Author, *Reconstructing Identities. A Social History of the Babas in Singapore*
VISWA SADASIVAN Writer
CHITRA SANKARAN Assistant Professor, Department of English Language and Literature, National University of Singapore
SATHIAVATHI CHINNIAH South Asian Studies Programme, National University of Singapore
PETER SCHOPPERT Writer
K.K. SEET Senior Lecturer, Department of English Language and Literature, National University of Singapore
K.F. SEETOH Makansutra
SAMUEL SEOW Samuel Seow Law Corporation
RODOLFO SEVERINO Visiting Senior Research Fellow, Institute of Southeast Asian Studies
SIM WAN HUI Curator, National Museum of Singapore
BILVEER SINGH Associate Professor, Department of Political Science, National University of Singapore
KIRPAL SINGH Associate Professor of Literature, School of Economics and Social Sciences, Singapore Management University

VINEETA SINHA, Assistant Professor, Department of Sociology, National University of Singapore
FELIX SOH Deputy Editor, *The Straits Times*
ELI SOLOMON Writer, Hong Kong
SURIANI SURATMAN Assistant Professor, Department of Malay Studies, National University of Singapore
LEO SURYADINATA Director, Chinese Heritage Centre
TAMILSELVI MUTHU Curator, National Museum of Singapore
BONNY MULIANI TAN Reference Librarian
BRIDGET TRACY TAN Director, Gallery and Theatre, Nanyang Academy of Fine Arts
JEREMY TAN Research Assistant, Archives Services, National Archives of Singapore,
KEVIN TAN President, Singapore Heritage Society
LEO TAN Director, National Institute of Education
PETER TAN Senior Lecturer, Department of English Language and Literature, National University of Singapore
RIA TAN Author, *Chek Jawa Guidebook*
TAN BOON HUI Assistant Director (Public and International Programming), National Museum of Singapore
TAN KHEE GIAP Associate Professor, Division of Banking and Finance, Nanyang Technological University
ALAN TAN KHEE JIN Associate Professor, Faculty of Law, National University of Singapore
TAN PUAY YOK Assistant Director, Research, National Parks Board
TAN SIOK SUN Author, *Goh Keng Swee: A Portrait*
TAN TAI YONG Associate Professor, Department of History, National University of Singapore
TAN TARN HOW Senior Research Fellow, Institute of Policy Studies
TAN TECK MENG Professor, School of Accountancy, Singapore Management University
TAN TIAN HUAT, ANDREW Senior Lecturer, Defence Studies, King's College London, UK
TAN WEE KIAT Advisor, National Parks Board
NICOLE TAN WEE LEE Writer
TAN WEE LIANG Lee Kong Chian School of Business, Singapore Management University
TAN WOAN SHIN Writer
GRACE TANG Assistant Archivist, Archives Services, National Archives of Singapore
NICHOLAS TANG Senior Fellow, Centre for Research Pedagogy and Practice, National Institute of Education
TAY KHENG SOON Adjunct Professor, Department of Architecture, National University of Singapore
MALCOLM TAY Writer
JEREMY E. TAYLOR Writer, Australia
TEOH ENG SOON Author, *Orchids of Asia*
S.P. THINNAPPAN Visiting Fellow, South Asian Studies Programme, National University of Singapore
MARGARET THOMAS Director, Special Duties, News, Radio and Print, MediaCorp
SUJIN THOMAS Journalist, *The Straits Times*
EDWIN THUMBOO Professorial Fellow, Department of English Language and Literature, National University of Singapore
SENAKA TIRANAGAMA President, Singapore Sinhala Association
JASON TOH Assistant Curator, National Museum of Singapore
SUSAN TSANG Writer
TORSTEN TSCHACHER Research Scholar, South Asian Studies Programme, National University of Singapore
AMINA TYABJI Lecturer, Department of Economics, National University of Singapore
KATRINA VAN DINTER Curatorial Officer, National Museum of Singapore
ROY VARGHESE Writer
A.M. VENTHAN Writer
VIDYA MURTHY Researcher, National Museum of Singapore
K.C. VIJAYAN Journalist, *The Straits Times*
WAN MENG HAO Executive Secretary, Preservation of Monuments Board
WANG LUAN KENG Research Officer, The Raffles Museum of Biodiversity Research
WANG RUNHUA Professor and Chairman, Department of Chinese Linguistics and Literature, Yuan Ze University, Taiwan
SAMUEL WANG Pastor, Jurong Christian Church
VADI PVSS Artistic Director, Miror Theatre and Advisor, Ravindran Drama Group
ANN ELIZABETH WEE Former Head, Department of Social Work, National University of Singapore
DANIEL WEE Vicar, Light of Christ City Church
STELLA WEE Outreach Services Executive, National Archives of Singapore
VIVIENNE WEE Associate Professor, Department of Applied Social Studies, City University of Hong Kong, Hong Kong SAR
WEE YEOW CHIN Author, *Ferns of the Tropics*
JENNIFER WIDJAYA Assistant Archivist, Records Management, National Archives of Singapore
EUGENE WIJEYSINGHA Author, *The Eagle Breeds a Gryphon*
SHAN WOLODY Writer
ALFRED WONG Chairman, AWP Pte Ltd
JOHN WONG Professor, East Asian Institute
WONG CHEE WAI Writer
WONG CHIN SOON Writer
WONG HONG SUEN Assistant Curator, National Museum of Singapore
WONG TUAN WAH Director, Conservation, National Parks Board
WONG SIN KIONG Deputy Head, Department of Chinese Studies, National University of Singapore
WONG YUNN CHII Associate Professor, Department of Architecture, National University of Singapore
NADIA H. WRIGHT Author, *Respected Citizens: The History of Armenians in Singapore and Malaysia*, Australia
GRACIE XIANG Assistant Archivist, Audio Visual Archives, National Archives of Singapore
JIMMY YAP Writer
DANNY YEO CHIN WEI Lecturer, School of Humanities, Ngee Ann Polytechnic
YEO SEOW LING Assistant Archivist, Records Management, National Archives of Singapore
BRENDA YEOH Professor, Department of Geography, National University of Singapore
YI YAN Senior Executive Officer, Singapore Federation of Chinese Clan Associations
JOANNE YIP Research Assistant, Archives Services, National Archives of Singapore
YUNG SAI-SHING Associate Professor, Department of Chinese Studies, National University of Singapore, Singapore
ZARINAH MOHAMED Writer
ZHOU YANFEI Writer

NOTES ON USAGE

In looking up entries, it will help the reader to be familiar with the conventions used in this encyclopedia in regard to the order in which the entries are arranged, as well as the style in which people's names are given.

Alphabetization

All the entries in the book have been arranged alphabetically, letter by letter. The articles 'the' and 'a' are either dropped or moved to the end of the heading. For example, an entry on the newspaper, *The Straits Times*, appears as 'Straits Times, The', and can be found under S.

In alphabetizing, titles such as 'Sir', 'Major' or 'Lieutenant-General' are disregarded although they appear in the entry header. The entry on Air Chief Marshall Sir Robert Brooke-Popham is listed as 'Brooke-Popham, Air Chief Marshall Sir Robert', but his rank and title are disregarded in determining the order in which the entry appears.

Entry headings that start with numerals appear alphabetically as if the number were spelled out. The movie *12 Storeys* appears in the letter T, as if the number 12 were given as 'Twelve'.

Personal names

Names are listed in the form in which they are commonly known. Chinese names appear as they are used in Singapore. Ambassador Chan Heng Chee is listed as 'Chan Heng Chee', not 'Heng Chee, Chan'. Musician Dick Lee is listed as 'Lee, Dick' rather than 'Lee Peng Boon, Dick' or 'Lee, Dick Peng-Boon'. Sir Stamford Raffles is listed as 'Raffles, Sir Stamford', rather than 'Raffles, Sir Thomas Stamford Bingley'. Commas affect the order: 'Lee, Dick' precedes 'Lee Boon Yang'.

Tamil and Malay names do not have surnames. Entries on people with Tamil or Malay names are listed according to given names. Thus, former president Yusof Ishak comes under Y while Cabinet minister Tharman Shanmugaratnam is listed under T. The terms 'bin' and 'binte' for Malay names and 's/o' and 'd/o' for Tamil names are omitted.

For Japanese names, the encyclopedia uses the Japanese convention of having the surname first. This does not affect the order in which they appear in the encyclopedia. However, readers will need to be aware that when an entry refers to Shinozaki Mamoru, Shinozaki is the surname.

Cross references

In the text there are numerous cross references so that readers can find related information elsewhere in the book. If a word, term or phrase is set in SMALL CAPS, this means that there is an entry under this heading in another part of the book. Related entries are sometimes referred to at the end of entries.

Currency

The dollar sign ($) in this encyclopedia refers to various dollars, depending on the period, as follows:

- Most of the 19th century: the silver dollar
- 1897–1904: both the Straits dollar and the silver dollar
- 1904–38: the Straits dollar exclusively
- 1938–42: the Malayan dollar
- 1942–45: the Japanese military dollar
- 1945–50: the Malayan dollar
- 1950–67: the Malayan and British Borneo dollar
- 1967–present: the Singapore dollar

ABBREVIATIONS

BA	Bachelor of Arts
BAcc	Bachelor of Accountancy
BAO	Bachelor of Arts in Obstetrics
BArch	Bachelor of Architecture
BBA	Bachelor of Business Administration
BCom	Bachelor of Commerce
BEng	Bachelor of Engineering
BScSoc	Bachelor of Social Science
CBE	Commander of the Order of the British Empire
ChB	Bachelor of Surgery
CMG	Companion, Order of St Michael and St George
DCh	Doctor of Surgery
DLitt	Doctor of Literature, Doctor of Letters
FACP	Fellow, American College of Physicians
FACS	Fellow, American College of Surgeons
FAHA	Fellow, Australian Academy of the Humanities
FAIA	Fellow, American Institute of Architects
FAMS	Fellow, Academy of Medicine, Singapore
FASA	Fellow of the Australian Society of Accountants
FCA	Fellow, Institute of Chartered Accountants
FCGP	Fellow, College of General Practioners
FICA	Fellow, Institute of Chartered Accountants in England and Wales
FICE	Fellow, Institution of Civil Engineers
FICS	Fellow, International College of Surgeons
FIEE	Fellow, Institution of Electrical Engineers
FIEM	Fellow, Institution of Engineers, Malaysia
FIES	Fellow, Institution of Engineers, Singapore
FIMechE	Fellow, Institution of Mechanical Engineers
FRACO	Fellow, Royal Australian College of Ophthalmologists
FRACOG	Fellow, Royal Australian College of Obstetricians and Gynaecologists
FRACP	Fellow, Royal Australasian College of Physicians
FRACS	Fellow, Royal Australasian College of Surgeons
FRAIA	Fellow, Royal Australian Institute of Architects
FRCGP	Fellow, Royal College of General Practitioners
FRCOG	Fellow, Royal College of Obstetricians and Gynaecologists
FRCP	Fellow, Royal College of Physicians, London
FRCPA	Fellow, Royal College of Pathologists of Australia
FRCPE	Fellow, Royal College of Physicians, Edinburgh
FRCPGlas	Fellow, Royal College of Physicians and Surgeons of Glasgow
FRCPSGlas	Honorary Fellow, Royal College of Physicians and Surgeons of Glasgow
FRCS	Fellow, Royal College of Surgeons of England
FRCSE	Fellow, Royal College of Surgeons of Edinburgh
FRCSGlas	Fellow, Royal College of Physicians and Surgeons of Glasgow
GCMG	Knight Grand Cross, Order of St Michael and St George
ICPAS	Institute of Certified Public Accountants of Singapore
LLB	Bachelor of Laws
LLM	Master of Laws
LMS	Licentiate in Medicine and Surgery
LRCP	Licentiate, Royal College of Physicians, London
LRSM	Licentiate, Royal Schools of Music
MA	Master of Arts
MD	Doctor of Medicine
MAppSc	Master of Applied Science
MArch	Master of Architecture
MBA	Master of Business Administration
MBBS	Bachelor of Medicine and Bachelor of Surgery
MBE	Member of the Order of the British Empire
MIES	Member, Institution of Engineers Singapore
MMed	Master of Medicine
MPA	Master of Public Administration
MRCOG	Member, Royal College of Obstetricians and Gynaecologists
MRCP	Member, Royal College of Physicians, London
MRCPE	Member, Royal College of Physicians, Edinburgh
MRCPI	Member, Royal College of Physicians of Ireland
MRCS	Member, Royal College of Surgeons of England
OBE	Officer of the Order of the British Empire
PhD	Doctor of Philosophy
RIBA	Royal Institute of British Architects

INTRODUCTION

This encyclopedia consists of over 2,500 entries written by more than 200 authors on a vast range of topics. It covers Singapore's history, geography, economy, laws, politics, arts, culture, entertainment, architecture, food and natural history. Also covered are Singapore's political, legal, education and healthcare systems. Companies, clubs and associations, housing estates, significant historical events, festivals and customs also have their place in the book.

The encyclopedia covers events that have been significant in the development of Singapore's national identity. These are shared memories or shared stories which have entered the national consciousness. They include politically significant events such as Separation and Confrontation, or emotionally charged disasters such as the Bukit Ho Swee fire, the MI 185 Silk Air crash or the Nicoll Highway collapse.

Individuals profiled in the encyclopedia run the entire gamut. They include artists, musicians, actors, politicians, businessmen, entrepreneurs, soldiers, priests, pastors, *ulema*, civil servants, entertainers, ambassadors, judges, sportsmen, and even murderers.

In such an ambitious undertaking, the first hurdle was getting a comprehensive list of all possible entries. Thanks to the advice of experts, it was possible to compile a list of entries that we felt adequately covered the various topics and categories. Creating the initial list was hard. Later deciding what or who to include and leave out was just as difficult.

We have attempted to use objective criteria to justify the inclusion of individuals. For artists, writers, musicians and theatre practitioners, we have used the Cultural Medallion as the initial criterion for inclusion. However, to ensure that we did not miss out other individuals who might be worthy, we have turned to panels of experts. Being awarded significant National Day honours such as the Meritorious Service Medal or being admitted into the Distinguished Service Order was another criterion for inclusion.

Companies featured in the encyclopedia are here because they are historically significant. Some may not be large, but they are household names in Singapore. To ensure a representative selection, companies listed in the Straits Times Index have been included in the book.

In a work of this nature, subjectivity cannot be eliminated altogether—even the attempt to find objective criteria for inclusion has a subjective element.

Of course, in allocating space, we have attempted to give priority to the more important entries. However, importance is in the eye of the beholder. In fact, a few entries are relatively long by virtue of the fact that they are intrinsically more interesting than others, even though they may not perhaps be the more significant in the larger scheme of things.

No one person can be a specialist in all aspects of Singapore. This book represents the collective wisdom of a large team of experts in various fields, and this is its major strength.

The Editors

While every effort has been made to verify the information in this publication, no book is perfect. As this is the first edition, we welcome your feedback as regards factual errors or omissions. Constructive contributions should be addressed by e-mail to: **singapedia@edmbooks.com.sg**

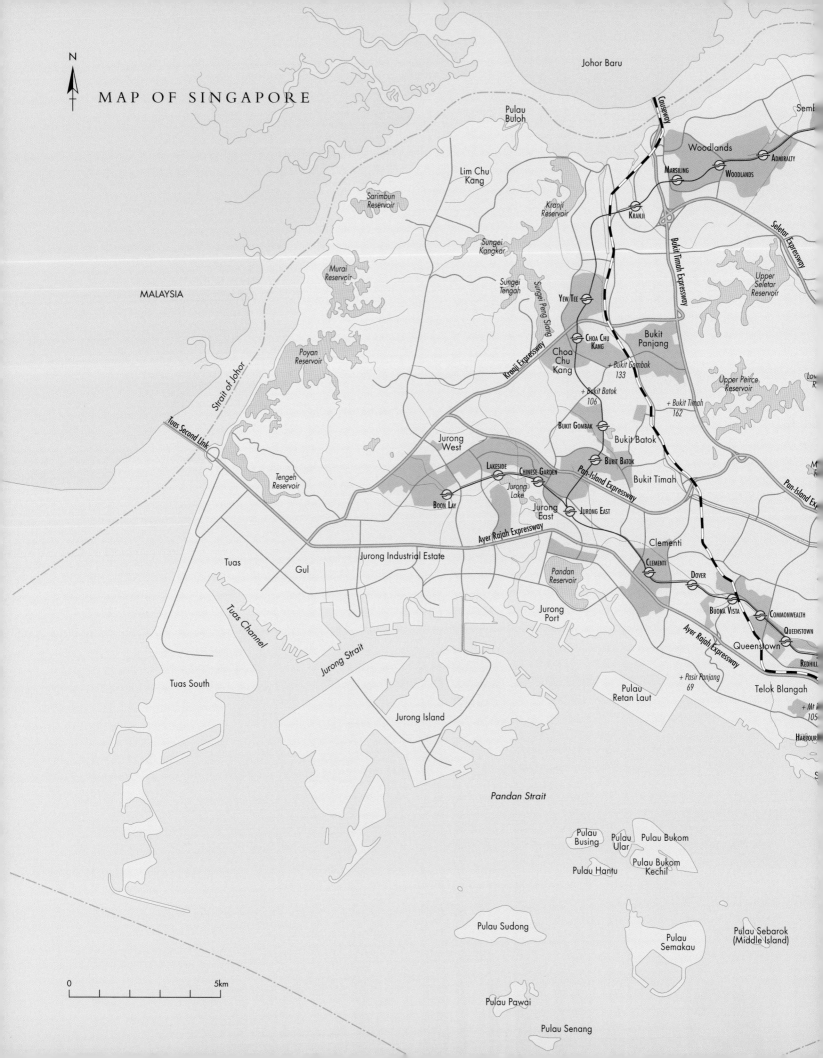

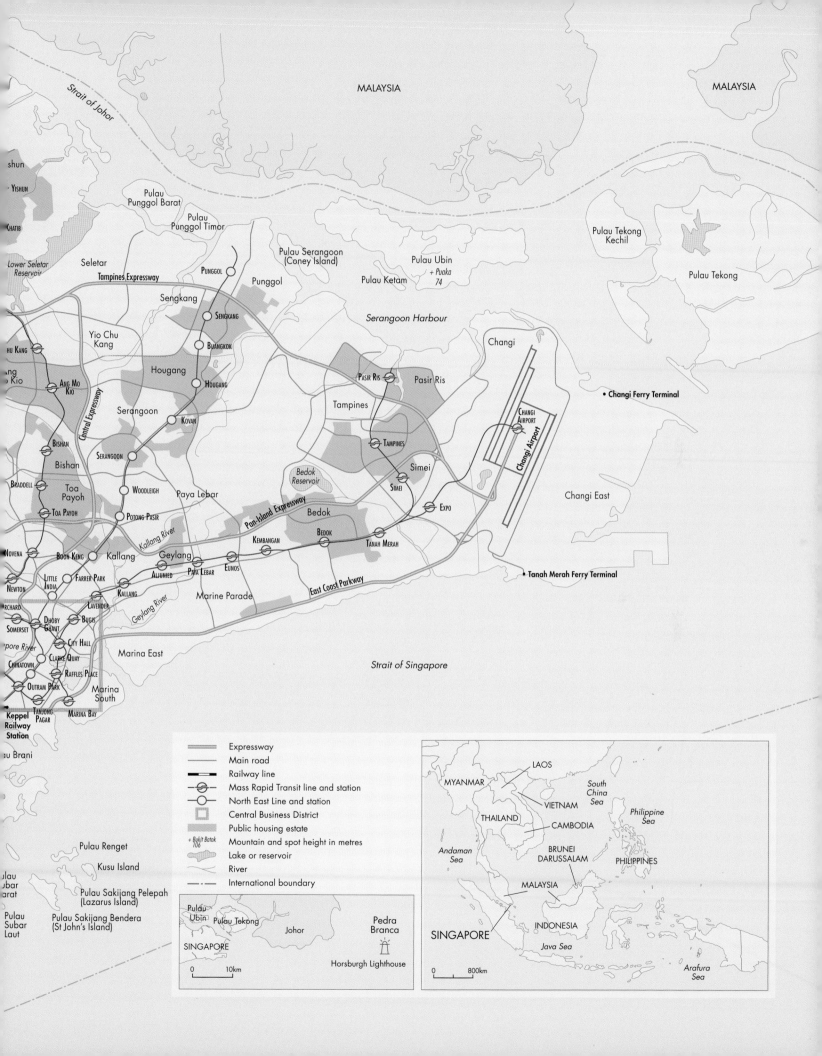

MALAYSIA

MALAYSIA

Strait of Johor

shun
· YISHUN

· KHATIB

Pulau
Punggol Barat

Pulau
Punggol Timor

Pulau Serangoon
(Coney Island)

Pulau Ubin
Pulau Ketam
+ Puaka
74

Pulau Tekong
Kechil

Pulau Tekong

Lower Seletar
Reservoir

Seletar

PUNGGOL

Punggol

Changi

Changi Ferry Terminal

Tampines Expressway

Sengkang

SENGKANG

Serangoon Harbour

Yio Chu
Kang

BUANGKOK

PASIR RIS

Pasir Ris

hu Kang

Hougang

Changi
Airport

ng
Kio

ANG MO
KIO

HOUGANG

Tampines

Changi Airport

Central Expressway

Serangoon

KOVAN

BISHAN

SERANGOON

TAMPINES

Simei

Bishan

WOODLEIGH

Paya Lebar

SIMEI

BRADDELL

Toa
Payoh

Bedok
Reservoir

Changi East

TOA PAYOH

POTONG PASIR

EXPO

Pan-Island Expressway

Bedok

NOVENA

BOON KENG

Kallang River

Kembangan

BEDOK

BEDOK

TANAH MERAH

LITTLE
INDIA

FARRER PARK

Kallang

Geylang

ALJUNIED

PAYA LEBAR

EUNOS

Tanah Merah Ferry Terminal

NEWTON

KALLANG

RCHARD

LAVENDER

Geylang River

Marine Parade

East Coast Parkway

SOMERSET

DHOBY
GHAUT

BUGIS

pore River

CITY HALL

CLARKE QUAY

CHINATOWN

RAFFLES PLACE

Marina East

Strait of Singapore

OUTRAM PARK

Marina
South

TANJONG
PAGAR

MARINA BAY

Keppel
Railway
Station

u Brani

	Expressway
	Main road
	Railway line
⊖	Mass Rapid Transit line and station
○	North East Line and station
▢	Central Business District
	Public housing estate
+ Bukit Batok 106	Mountain and spot height in metres
	Lake or reservoir
	River
—·—·—	International boundary

Pulau Renget

Kusu Island

LAOS

MYANMAR

South
China
Sea

Pulau Sakijang Pelepah
(Lazarus Island)

VIETNAM

Philippine
Sea

ulau
ubar
arat

THAILAND

CAMBODIA

Pulau Sakijang Bendera
(St John's Island)

Andaman
Sea

BRUNEI
DARUSSALAM

Pulau
Subar
Laut

Pulau
Ubin Pulau Tekong

Johor

Pedra
Branca

PHILIPPINES

SINGAPORE

MALAYSIA

SINGAPORE

0   10km

Horsburgh Lighthouse

INDONESIA

Java Sea

0   800km

Arafura
Sea

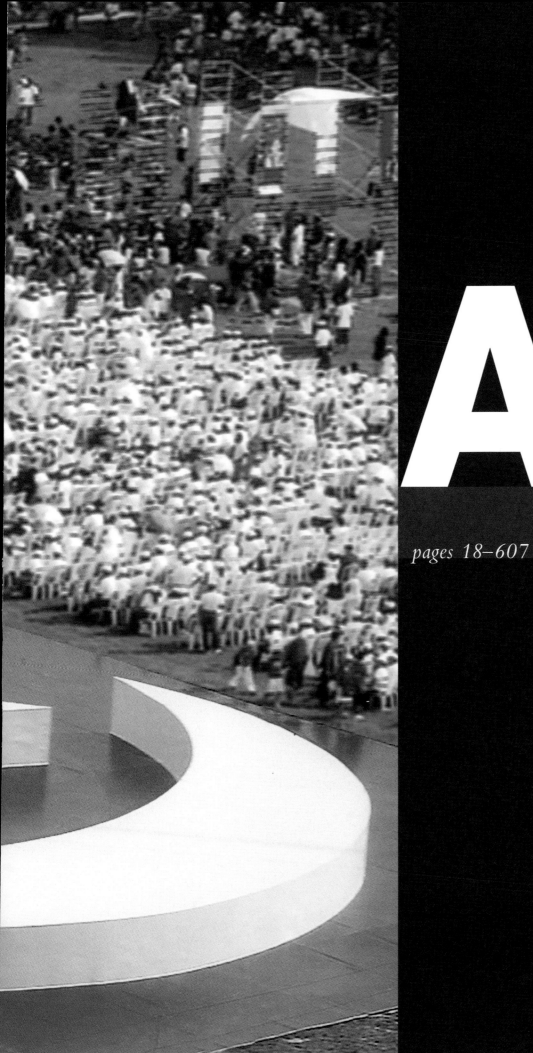

A TO Z

A

Maulana Abdul Aleem Siddique

Abdul Ghani Abdul Hamid

Abdul Ghani Abdul Hamid:
Lalang (2000).

Abdul Aleem Siddique, Maulana (1892–1954) Islamic scholar. Born in Meerut, India, to a pious family, Maulana Abdul Aleem Siddique was an exceptionally intelligent child, said to have memorized the Qur'an at four and delivered his first sermon when he was nine. After completing his religious education, he travelled almost continuously for 40 years. His journeys were documented by AHMAD MOHAMED IBRAHIM in his book about Abdul Aleem, *The Roving Ambassador of Peace*. Abdul Aleem came to Singapore in 1930 and founded the All-Malaya Missionary Society (now known as JAMIYAH). In 1949, he called upon MALCOLM MACDONALD, then Singapore's commissioner-general, to discuss issues of solidarity amongst religions. This meeting paved the way for the setting up of the Inter-Religious Organisation in the same year. He also initiated the foundation of a mosque in Telok Kurau: the Abdul Aleem Siddique Mosque was established in 1954.

Abdul Gaffoor Mosque Originally a wooden structure, the mosque was erected by Shaik Abdul Gaffoor Shaik Hyder on Dunlop Street in 1859. The land between Dunlop Street and Mayo Street is part of the Dunlop Street Mosque Endowment. Shaik Abdul Gaffoor, as one of the trustees of the endowment, directed the building of SHOPHOUSES on the land. He then collected the income generated from the shophouses and applied it to the construction of the

Abdul Aleem Siddique: the mosque established and named in his honour.

brick mosque. Building began in 1907. In 1910, when the new mosque was partially completed, the old wooden building was pulled down. The brick mosque was restored in 2003, and was the first mosque to be presented with the Architectural Heritage Award by the URBAN REDEVELOPMENT AUTHORITY.

Above the main door of the mosque there is an elaborate sundial. The sundial—unique in the Islamic world—is decorated with Arabic calligraphy, denoting the names of the 25 prophets of Islam. The yellow-and-green colour scheme, the intricate decoration, and the blend of Islamic and European architecture, make this mosque distinct. It was gazetted as a national monument in 1979.

Abdul Ghani Abdul Hamid (1933–) Artist, poet and author. Abdul Ghani Abdul Hamid received his formal education from Telok Kurau Malay School, Telok Kurau English School and, later, Raffles Institution. He started writing in 1948. His published books include *Jalinan Rasa* (Bonds of Feelings) (1964), *Mata dan Hati* (Eye and Heart) (1972), *Delima Merah di Jari Manis* (Red Ruby On a Ring Finger) (1977), *Desa ini Hatiku* (This City is My Heart) (1985), *Nota* (Note) (1988), *An Artist's Note* (1991), *Harun, Seorang Penulis* (Harun, A Writer) (1994), *Tawajuh* (Orientation) (1997), *Wak Cantuk* (1997), *A Journey With No End* (1998), and *Sepanjang Jalan Ini* (The Journey Thus Far) (1998). He has written several plays, including *Enrique Anak Melayu* (Enrique the Malay Child) (1994).

Abdul Ghani is a founding member of the Singapore Malay Artists Association or Angkatan Pelukis Aneka Daya (APAD). Being both an artist and a cultural commentator, he produced an illustrated book in English, a documentation of Islamic-inspired art in Singapore, entitled *The Mosque, The Art* (2002). He has participated in several art exhibitions at home and abroad. He also co-authored a biography of the late composer Zubir Said, *Mengenang Pak Zubir* (Remembering Pak Zubir) (1988), with Sulaiman Jeem. In 1998, he received two prestigious awards, the Tun Seri Lanang Award and the Southeast Asia Write Award. He was awarded the CULTURAL MEDALLION in 1999.

Abdul Halim Haron (1972–) Sportsman. Abdul Halim Haron won a gold medal in the men's bantamweight (65 kg) body-building at the 2002 Asian Games in Busan, Korea, despite having to juggle two jobs before the games (as despatch rider by day, and part-time bouncer at night).

Abdul Halim began competing in the welterweight category and won a bronze medal at the 2000 Asian Championships, and the Singapore National title in 2001. He later switched to the lower weight cat-

Abdul Gaffoor Mosque

egory for a better chance of winning an international medal. For his achievements in Busan, he was inducted into the SINGAPORE SPORTS COUNCIL HALL OF FAME.

Abdul Rahman, Sultan (1780–c. 1831) Malay royal. Abdul Rahman was the son of Sultan MAHMUD of the Johor-Riau kingdom. After Sultan Mahmud's death in 1812, Abdul Rahman's succession to the throne was backed by the powerful BUGIS Yang di-Pertuan Muda (regent), Raja Jafar. Abdul Rahman devoted his time to religion and the company of religious men. Unhappy that he had not been installed with the traditional regalia and *nobat* (royal orchestra)—the latter withheld from him by his late father's widow, Engku Puteri—he withdrew to Terengganu in the early 1820s. There, he married a sister of the Yang di-Pertuan (ruler) of Terengganu. The Yang di-Pertuan later became Sultan Ahmad of Terengganu. Through marriage, the Johor-Riau and Terengganu ruling courts became linked.

After the Dutch forcibly secured the *nobat* from Engku Puteri, Abdul Rahman was formally installed as sultan in 1823, nearly a decade after his father's death. In the wake of the installation, news was received in the Johor-Riau court of an impending division of the Johor-Riau kingdom between the EAST INDIA COMPANY (EIC) and the Dutch. The court despatched an envoy to the Dutch governor-general in Batavia to check on developments. The Dutch confirmed the division of the Johor-Riau kingdom between themselves and the EIC under the terms of the ANGLO-DUTCH TREATY of March 1824. Abdul Rahman was also informed that, as a result, he would lose Johor and Pahang, which would come under the EIC's allotment, or sphere of influence.

Abdul Rahman fell ill and died in August 1832. His son, Tengku Besar, succeeded him as sultan with the title Sultan Muhammad Syah.

See also MALAY ROYALTY.

Abdul Rahman, Temenggong (unknown –1825) Malay royal. Abdul Rahman was the Dato Temenggong Sri Maharaja of Johor from 1806. He was one of the signatories to the 19th-century agreements which allowed the EAST INDIA COMPANY (EIC) to establish a trading post in Singapore.

Sultan MAHMUD (reigned 1762–1812) conferred the office of *temenggong* on Abdul Rahman after it had been refused by Abdul Rahman's uncle Engku Muda. *Temenggong* has been traditionally translated as 'chief of police'. Abdul Rahman was a distant cousin of, and related by marriage to, Tengku HUSAIN SHAH. Husain Shah was the older son of Sultan Mahmud and was bypassed for succession to the throne in favour of his younger half-brother, also named Abdul Rahman (*see* Sultan ABDUL RAHMAN).

Abdul Rahman's domains initially included Singapore, a number of islands in the northern part of the Riau Archipelago and part of the Malay Peninsula. He set up a village with some of his followers in Singapore in the first decade of the 19th century. In 1824, his followers on the island numbered between 6,000 and 10,000, which included the people in his kampong in Singapore and his ORANG LAUT followers.

Abdul Rahman met Sir STAMFORD RAFFLES in January 1819 in Singapore and signed a provisional agreement with him allowing the EIC to set up a trading post in Singapore. This agreement was formalized by a treaty signed on 6 February 1819 between Abdul Rahman, Raffles, and Tengku Husain, whom Raffles recognized as sultan.

In subsequent agreements, Abdul Rahman and Sultan Husain gave up more of their rights to, and received monetary payments from, the EIC. In 1823, Abdul Rahman received a sum of money from the EIC to move his kampong from the Singapore River to Telok Blangah.

On 3 August 1824, EIC official JOHN CRAWFURD negotiated a new treaty whereby Abdul Rahman and Sultan Husain fully ceded Singapore and adjacent islands to the EIC in exchange for cash. Abdul Rahman died in 1825. His son Daeng Ibrahim became the next *temenggong,* but not until 1841.

See also MALAY ROYALTY.

Abdul Rahman, Tunku (1903–1990) Malaysian politician. The first prime minister of Malaya and then Malaysia, Tunku Abdul Rahman played a key role in the formation of Malaysia and Singapore's eventual separation from it. A prince of the state of Kedah, Tunku Abdul Rahman Putra Al-Haj, popularly known just by his royal title 'Tunku', was born of a Siamese mother on 8 February 1903 as the 20th child of

Tunku Abdul Rahman: at work in the 1950s.

Sultan Hamid Halim Shah, the 24th ruler of Kedah.

He began his formal education in Alor Star, where he was sent to a Malay, and then an English, school, before continuing his studies in Bangkok and Penang. Granted a state scholarship, he was admitted to St Catharine's College, Cambridge University, where he read law and history, graduating with a bachelor of arts degree in 1925. The following year, he continued his study of law at the Inner Temple in London but returned to Malaya in 1931 without qualifying as a barrister-in-law. After serving for a time as a district officer in the Kedah civil service, he retook his Bar examination in London in 1938, but his plans were interrupted by the outbreak of war in Europe and he was summoned home. Two years later war was to reach Malaya also.

The Tunku soon became well known for foiling, in December 1941, the efforts of a retreating British convoy taking his father, the sultan, to safety in Penang; he 'abducted' and removed his father to a place of safety within the state instead. During the war, he intervened on behalf of Malays and Chinese arrested by the Japanese; he took part in welfare and relief efforts, including refugee work; and immediately after the war ended, he played a part in preventing a take-over of Alor Star by the largely Chinese-led MALAYAN PEOPLE'S ANTI-JAPANESE ARMY, the armed wing of the communist resistance—this would have led to serious communal clashes.

To complete his law studies, the Tunku went back to Britain in December 1946, and in 1949, on his third attempt, finally qualified for the Bar. After returning to Malaya that year, he served in the Kedah legal service but was then transferred to Kuala Lumpur, where he became a deputy public prosecutor.

The Tunku became increasingly involved with the United Malays National Organization (UMNO), the main Malay nationalist party. In 1949, he accepted the chairmanship of the Kedah branch of UMNO. After an internal party crisis in August 1951 led to the resignation of its

president, Dato Onn bin Jaafar, who had suggested that non-Malays be admitted as associate members, the Tunku was persuaded by close friends led by Abdul Razak, an assistant state secretary in Pahang, to accept nomination for the post. Elected UMNO's second president, the Tunku remained at its head for the next 20 years.

Unlike Dato Onn, the Tunku believed that UMNO should be exclusively Malay, convinced as he was that the racial groups in Malaya would be better served if each had its own political party. But, like the former president, he realized that the races would have to demonstrate some sense of national unity before the British would concede independence. When branch leaders of UMNO and the Malayan Chinese Association forged an informal electoral alliance to contest the Kuala Lumpur municipal election, the Tunku gave them his support. In February 1952, the 'Alliance' defeated their main rival, the new Independence of Malaya Party led by Dato Onn. Expanding the grouping into a fully fledged Alliance Party by including the Malayan Indian Congress in 1955, the Tunku led the Alliance to its first federal electoral victory in July 1955, winning 51 out of 52 seats.

In December 1955, with this mandate, the Tunku, now chief minister, met CHIN PENG, leader of the MALAYAN COMMUNIST PARTY, for talks at Baling in Kedah. Although negotiations failed over the Tunku's demand for an unconditional communist surrender, his firm handling of the communists enhanced his stature (*see* EMERGENCY). And in the London constitutional talks from January to February 1956 and in May 1957, his demand that the schedule for Malaya's independence be accelerated was heeded (*see* MERDEKA). On 31 August 1957, the Tunku became the first prime minister of an independent FEDERATION OF MALAYA.

Tunku Abdul Rahman's next major achievement was the formation of Malaysia, an enlarged federation created by the merger with Singapore, Sabah and Sarawak. Though the origins of the scheme lay in

Tunku Abdul Rahman: with Lee Kuan Yew, left, at Paya Lebar Airport, 1962.

Tunku Abdul Rahman

British wartime plans to set up a post-war 'dominion of South East Asia' made up of their territories in the region, progress had been slow. Preoccupied with the task of attaining independence, the Tunku had previously rejected MERGER overtures from successive chief ministers of Singapore, DAVID MARSHALL and LIM YEW HOCK. But in May 1961, the Tunku changed his mind and proposed the formation of an enlarged federation. He was apparently persuaded by concerns that Singapore, with its Chinese majority, might come under pro-communist control and so threaten Malaya; he considered a Singapore inside the federation less dangerous than one outside it. There was also the further attraction of gaining the three Borneo territories—Sarawak, North Borneo, and Brunei—from the British, who were preparing to decolonize there also. The addition of the non-Chinese from the Borneo territories would help to counterbalance Singapore's Chinese majority in the enlarged federation. The Federation of Malaysia—comprising Malaya, Singapore, Sabah (as British North Borneo was renamed) and Sarawak—was formed on 16 September 1963.

But while he successfully dealt with the Philippines' claims over Sabah and blunted Indonesia's 'Crush Malaysia' campaign, the Tunku was less effective in establishing the Alliance Party's control over Singapore. The PEOPLE'S ACTION PARTY government had been returned in an election held in Singapore five days after the formation of Malaysia, despite the Tunku's personal intervention on behalf of the rival SINGAPORE ALLIANCE PARTY at the polls. After Singapore's participation in the FEDERAL ELECTION (1964) resulted in escalating political and communal tensions—there were RACE RIOTS in Singapore in July and September 1964—the Tunku made an abortive attempt to disengage Singapore from Malaysia. In August 1965, as Sino-Malay tensions threatened to

Munshi Abdullah Abdul Kadir

Munshi Abdullah Abdul Kadir: the scholar (right) and his translation of Hikayat Binatang *(1846).*

get out of control, he took the fateful decision to cast Singapore out of the Federation (*see* SEPARATION).

Four years later, on 13 May 1969, after UMNO had lost ground in Malaysia's general election, race riots broke out in Kuala Lumpur. An emergency was declared, and the Constitution temporarily suspended. Held by some to be responsible for the crisis, the Tunku resigned as prime minister in September 1970, in favour of his deputy, Tun Abdul Razak.

After leaving high office, Tunku Abdul Rahman served as secretary general of the Organization of Islamic Conference in Jeddah and initiated the setting up of the Islamic Development Bank. Upon returning to Malaysia in 1974, he took up journalism and wrote a column in *The Star* newspaper. In later years he was somewhat critical of the government of Malaysian prime minister Mahathir Mohamad.

Tunku Abdul Rahman died on 6 December 1990.

Abdul Samad (dates unknown) Doctor. Abdul Samad was Singapore's first Malay doctor and a prominent member of the Malay-Muslim community in the 1920s. He studied medicine locally and graduated from the KING EDWARD VII COLLEGE OF MEDICINE. He was involved with the Persekutuan Islam Singapore (Muslim Association of Singapore) but viewed the association's efforts in helping poorer Malays as inadequate. Together with other leading Malays in Singapore such as MOHAMMAD EUNOS ABDULLAH and Tengku Kadir, Abdul Samad founded the Muslim Institute in 1921. The Muslim Institute focused on education and helped Malay schoolchildren coming from Peninsular Malaysia to find accommodation in Singapore. Not much is known about his medical practice. He is best remembered for his instrumental role in forming the Kesatuan Melayu Singapura (The Singapore Malay Union), the first Malay political organization on the island, in 1926. It provided support to the first Malay member of the Straits Settlements Legislative Council, Mohammad Eunos Abdullah. Little else is known of Abdul Samad's later career.

Abdullah Abdul Kadir, Munshi (1796–1854) Scholar, teacher and author. Munshi Abdullah Abdul Kadir's two major works, *Kisah Pelayaran Abdullah* (The Story of Abdullah's Voyage) and *Hikayat Abdullah* (Abdullah's Story), are important sources for the social history of 19th-century Singapore.

Born in Kampung Pali, Malacca, in 1796 (1797 by some accounts) to Yemeni and Tamil parents, Abdullah proved to be linguistically gifted with a talent for writing. At an early age, Abdullah memorized a major portion of the Qur'an and mastered Arabic, TAMIL, Hindi and MALAY. There are

also indications that he picked up at least one of the Chinese dialects.

Abdullah first found work copying documents for the British. A few years after the arrival of Sir STAMFORD RAFFLES in 1819, Abdullah was appointed his secretary and interpreter. He also tutored Raffles in the Malay language, and is credited with having familiarized Raffles with many aspects of Malay society and culture. In addition, he also taught Malay to Indian soldiers as well as American and British missionaries, earning the title 'Munshi' (teacher or educator) in the process.

The *Hikayat Abdullah* is Abdullah's defining achievement. The autobiography, completed in 1843 and published in multiple editions, is valuable for its detailed accounts of figures contributing to the development of early colonial Singapore. His writing on the founding of Singapore shifts the emphasis away from Raffles towards the efforts of Colonel WILLIAM FARQUHAR and Sir JOHN CRAWFURD—both of whom he termed 'rajas'—to establish the island as a commercial centre.

In the same volume, Abdullah is especially critical of Sultan ALI ISKANDAR SHAH, whom he held responsible for the backwardness of the Malays. He felt that the MALAY ROYALTY, riven by power struggles, had been corrupted by decadent behaviour, and that elements in the life of common Malays, including many of their traditions and beliefs, were impeding social progress. The British were seen by Abdullah to be a civilizing influence.

Abdullah also wrote accounts of his voyages to Kelantan and Jeddah, and these writings are among the earliest examples of Malay travel writing. In *Kisah Pelayaran Abdullah ke Kelantan* (1838) (The Story of Abdullah's Journey to Kelantan), Abdullah described his journey to the northern Malay states (Kedah, Kelantan, Perlis and Terengganu) and the problems faced by their societies. Abdullah's sentiments regarding British rule were repeated in this work, where he suggests that the peace and prosperity brought by the British to the Malays in Singapore should be an ideal which the rulers of these states would do well to follow.

In addition to being a writer, Abdullah was also a translator and poet, and is the earliest-known Muslim in Southeast Asia to have translated the Gospels into Malay. Owing to these translations and his close association with Christian missionaries, he was nicknamed 'Abdullah Padri' ('Pastor Abdullah'). He was also referred to less kindly by some Malays as '*boneka*' ('puppet') and '*tali barut*' ('collaborator'). Historians have been divided in their opinion with regard to Abdullah's true attitude toward CHRISTIANITY, with one camp alleging that Abdullah died a Christian, and another arguing that Abdullah maintained his faith in Islam despite his engagement with

Christian texts and individuals. Yet another camp has seen Abdullah's translation of the Gospels as a covert attempt to right 'deviations' inherent in Christianity.

Less controversially, Abdullah edited, translated and published Malay and Sanskrit classics such as the SEJARAH MELAYU (Malay Annals) (1835), *Hikayat Pandja Tanderan* (1835) (a Sanskrit text) and *Kitab Adat Segala Raja-raja Melayu Dalam Segala Negeri* (1837) (The Book of Customs of Malay Kings from All Lands). He co-published *Vocabulary of the English and Malay Languages* (1820) with renowned preacher Claudius Henry Thomsen.

Abdullah was also a prolific poet. His first poem 'Syair Singapura Terbakar' (Poem on a Fire in Singapore) (1830), reveals the deplorable living conditions in early Singapore and the circumstances that led to a major fire.

Abdullah died in Jeddah en route to Mecca. The Abdullah School for Malay children at KAMPONG GLAM was established in his memory in 1856. The school was in operation until World War II, but it is not known when it closed down.

Abdullah Tarmugi (1944–) Politician. Born in Singapore, Abdullah Tarmugi was educated at Raffles Institution and the University of Singapore, where he obtained a bachelor of social science (honours) degree. He joined the government service and worked in the Planning Department. In 1972, he obtained a post-graduate diploma in urban studies from the University of London. In 1980, Abdullah joined The STRAITS TIMES as a leader/feature writer and went on to become an associate news editor. From 1984 to 1993, he was research manager at SINGAPORE PRESS HOLDINGS. In 1984, he contested his first election and was elected MEMBER OF PARLIAMENT for Siglap constituency. He held various posts in the Cabinet, including minister for community development (1996–2002) and deputy Speaker of Parliament (1989–93). He was elected SPEAKER OF PARLIAMENT in 2002.

Abingdon Tunnels Underground ammunition bunker in Changi, located at Abingdon and Cosford Roads. The only remaining bunker among those built by the British military for its 15-inch guns (also known as 'Monster Guns') just before WORLD WAR II to protect Singapore against sea attacks, the magazines of the bunker stored 15-inch shells for one of the three guns and their installations which made up the Johor Battery.

When the guns were about to fire, the shells would be moved out of their racks and hoisted up mechanically into the breech of the gun. Each shell weighed about 879 kg, or the weight of a small car, had a range of 34 km, and could be fired at the rate of two shells per minute. The 15-inch gun was directly above the ammunition bunker, which was three

storeys deep. The bunkers containing the ammunition for the other guns were about 500 m apart and also had their guns directly above them. The other two 15-inch guns were to the north of the Abingdon Tunnels site. Today one of the runways of CHANGI AIRPORT runs over the position of the northernmost bunker.

All the 15-inch guns of the Johor Battery were controlled by Changi Fire Command, which, from the top of Changi Hill, directed their fire as well as the firing of smaller 9.2-inch and 6-inch guns. Two 15-inch guns of the Johor Battery were able to turn around and fire on the Japanese attacking Singapore from Malaya. They fired into JOHOR BAHRU and later at enemy troops during the BATTLE OF BUKIT TIMAH. However, the 15-inch gun on top of Abingdon Tunnels could not turn more than 180 degrees. It had been mounted on an older Mark I casing instead of the Mark II casing of the other two guns, which could turn 290 degrees.

The guns were dismantled before the British surrendered in 1942. All the underground bunkers, except the one at Abingdon Road, were removed for the expansion of Changi Airport. The Abingdon bunker had been sealed by the British when they withdrew their forces from Singapore in 1971, but was rediscovered by the Prisons Department in 1991 when they were excavating the site prior to its redevelopment. In 2002, it was marked as a historic site, with a life-sized replica of a 15-inch gun erected on top of the remains of the bunker.

Abisheganaden, Alex (1926–) Singer and musician. A student of renowned guitarist John Williams, Alex Abisheganaden founded the Singapore Classical Guitar Society in 1967 and the National University of Singapore Guitar Ensemble, of which he is honorary conductor. He is also the father of jazz singer JACINTHA ABISHEGANADEN and the brother of classical musician PAUL ABISHEGANADEN. For his contributions to music, he was awarded the CULTURAL MEDALLION in 1988 and the COMPASS Meritorious Award in 1998.

Abisheganaden, Jacintha (1958–) Singer and actress. Jacintha Abisheganaden co-founded the THEATREWORKS company in 1985 and headlined several big productions such as *Beauty World* (1988), *Fried Rice Paradise* (1991) and the Australian production of *Cats* (1993).

Abisheganaden is the daughter of guitarist ALEX ABISHEGANADEN and enjoyed a musical childhood. She entered the music scene in 1976 when she and her trio, Vintage, won the TV talent competition, *Talentime*. After graduating from the University of Singapore with an honours degree in English literature, she released her first pop album, *Silence*, in 1983. She went

on to release three more albums—*Tropicana* (1986), *Dramamama* (1991) and *My Life* (1997). She has starred in TV shows such as *Mum's Not Cooking* (1993) and *My Grandson The Doctor* (1996).

In 1999, Abisheganaden switched to recording jazz albums produced by local record label Groove Note. Following the release of her jazz debut, *Here's To Ben* (1999), influential American audio magazine, *The Absolute Sound*, proclaimed that her voice far surpassed that of American jazz singer Diana Krall. Her three jazz releases so far have sold over 100,000 copies worldwide.

Abisheganaden, Paul (1914–) Musician. One of Singapore's pioneer practitioners of Western classical music, Paul Abisheganaden graduated from Raffles College and pursued singing and conducting studies at London's Guildhall School of Music. He founded and conducted the Singapore Chamber Ensemble, one of Singapore's earliest music groups to play Western classical music. He was also principal of Victoria School and the Teacher's Training College. He was made a Member of the Order of the British Empire (MBE) in 1956. Abisheganaden has led choruses of up to 4,500 voices. His book, *Notes Across the Years* (2005), is an anecdotal account of professional and amateur musical life in Singapore. He is the brother of musician ALEX ABISHEGANADEN.

ABN AMRO Oldest foreign bank in Singapore. ABN AMRO is the product of a merger between the Algemene Bank Nederland (ABN) and the Amsterdam-Rotterdam (Amro) Bank in 1991, which led to the formation of one of the largest banking groups in the world, with approximately US$500 billion in global assets and employing more than 100,000 professional staff worldwide.

Its roots in the region, however, date back to 1826 when it opened its first office in Batavia (Jakarta) as a branch of the Netherlands Trading Society (NTS). NTS was founded in March 1824 on the initiative of King William I in The Hague, with the task of expanding commercial relations, opening up new trade channels, as well as financing business ventures in the Dutch East Indies. In 1830, the Dutch colonial governor introduced the 'plantation system' under which the native population was compelled to pay taxation in kind (chiefly tea, coffee, sugar and rubber). NTS acted as state banker, merchant and shipping agent. It sold and shipped the products the Dutch government obtained through this system.

By 1850, NTS even owned a number of plantations and was so successful in its business ventures and financing business that it acquired the nickname 'Kompenie Ketjil' or 'Little Company', after the older and more established Dutch East India

Abdullah Tarmugi

Alex Abisheganaden: with the National University of Singapore Guitar Ensemble.

Jacintha Abisheganaden

Paul Abisheganaden

ABN AMRO: premises of its predecessor, the Netherlands Trading Society, at the junction of Cecil Street and D'Almeida Street, 1915.

Abu Bakar Pawanchee

Acupunture

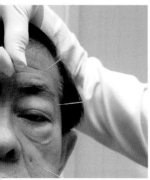

Company. As part of this policy, an NTS branch—a predecessor of what is one of the oldest banks in Singapore—was opened in Singapore on 1 May 1858. NTS' first Singapore premises were originally located at Boat Quay, before moving to Collyer Quay in 1865. In 1902, the bank moved to the corner of Cecil and D'Almeida streets, known as 'the Dutch corner' because it housed a number of Dutch companies. Four buildings were constructed on this site, but they had to be vacated due to extensive renovations of the Singapore harbour front.

NTS and Twentsche Bank merged in October 1964 to become Algemene Bank Nederland, or ABN. In 1991, ABN and Amro merged. Later, all of the bank's operations were moved to 63 Chulia Street, which houses both the Singapore branch and the bank's Asia-Pacific regional office.

In October 1999, ABN AMRO Singapore was awarded Qualifying Full Bank status (*see* BANKING) by the Monetary Authority of Singapore, and the bank expanded its corporate banking franchise to include consumer banking. With the liberalization of the retail financial scene in Singapore, ABN AMRO offered its customers a variety of retail services ranging from car and housing loans to wealth management products such as deposits, unit trusts and insurance.

Abu Bakar, Sultan (1833–1895) Malay royal. At age 29, Abu Bakar succeeded his father, Temenggong Daeng Ibrahim, after the latter's death in 1862. Abu Bakar developed the territory of Johor he inherited from his father, turning the village of Johor Baru into the administrative centre of his new kingdom and recruiting officials who were born and educated in Singapore. During his early rule, rising gambier and pepper prices contributed to the prosperity of his kingdom. Abu Bakar became more powerful than any other Malay chief in the peninsula at the time. He intervened in the Pahang civil war, and as a reflection of his status, the Malay chiefs of Negeri Sembilan agreed to refer disputes among themselves to him. In 1885, he was recognized as sultan of Johor by the British. Sultan Abu Bakar continued to maintain close links with the British in Singapore while safeguarding his independence. He made several overseas trips to Java, China, Japan and Europe, where he met ruling monarchs. He died in 1895 after an illness.

Abu Bakar Pawanchee (1917–1993) Civil servant and diplomat. Born in Penang, Abu Bakar Pawanchee was educated at the Penang Free School, Raffles College, Singapore, and St John's College, Cambridge University. He joined the civil service after graduation and eventually became permanent secretary of the Ministry of Commerce and Industry (1958–61). In 1961, he was appointed

Sultan Abu Bakar

Singapore's first senior trade and cultural representative to Jakarta, and was awarded the MERITORIOUS SERVICE MEDAL in 1963 for his part in promoting two-way trade between Singapore and Indonesia. From 1963 to 1965, he was permanent secretary of the Ministry of Finance.

After SEPARATION, Abu Bakar became the Ministry of Foreign Affairs' first permanent secretary and was appointed Singapore's first permanent representative to the UNITED NATIONS. He returned from New York in 1966 and continued to serve as permanent secretary of foreign affairs until he retired in 1967. He then returned to Malaysia where he became deputy chairman of the Malaysian Rubber Exchange (1967–80).

Action for AIDS Volunteer organization. Action for AIDS (AFA) was formed in 1988 to raise awareness of HIV-AIDS and to offer assistance to victims of the disease. The organization provides medical subsidies, legal assistance and social support to patients and their relatives. Action for AIDS also organizes community outreach programmes in vernacular languages, anonymous HIV testing, counselling, and AIDS conferences. It publishes a journal, *The ACT*, and is involved in AIDS research.

ACTION Theatre Theatre company. ACTION Theatre was founded in 1987 by Thai-born Ekachai Uekrongtham to develop and present new works. It has achieved a reputation for staging plays that explore contemporary issues in an imaginative manner. These include plays which tackled the subjects of singlehood, materialism and identity in *Confessions of Three Unmarried Women* (1987), *Six Lonely Oysters* (1994), *Block Sale* (1996), and *How Do You Know You're Chinese?*. *Mail Order Brides & Other Oriental Take-Aways* (1998), about Internet match-making, was the first Singaporean play to be staged in New York.

Its most famous production was *Chang & Eng: The Musical* (2000), which became Singapore's longest-running homegrown musical and the first English-language musical to be staged in China. In 1999, ACTION Theatre received the Excellence of Singapore Award in recognition for 'being among the best in their area of activity in Asia or in the world'. Its productions of Desmond Sim's *Autumn Tomyam* and David Auburn's *Proof* were each named Play of the Year at the DBS Life! Theatre Awards in 2002 and 2003 respectively.

See also ENGLISH THEATRE.

acupuncture Alternative medical technique which has gained a level of acceptance in Singapore. Acupuncture is the practice of inserting thin needles through the skin at specific points on the body to control pain and other symptoms. It is perhaps also the best-known form of TRADITIONAL CHINESE MEDICINE, which has been generating much interest in the Western medical community. The World Health Organisation has recognized acupuncture as a valid type of alternative medicine.

Acupuncture has always had a place in Singapore, where the majority of the population is Chinese. But it is only in more recent times that the practice has been accorded more serious official attention. The first Acupuncture Research Clinic was set up by the Ministry of Health in 1995 in the Ang Mo Kio community hospital. A preliminary study found that acupuncture is safe and appears to relieve pain and stiffness—for example in stroke patients—and improves mobility.

Adelphi Hotel One of Singapore's three best-known hotels in earlier times (the others being RAFFLES HOTEL and HOTEL DE L'EUROPE). It opened in 1863 and was owned by Jewish trader Sir MANASSEH MEYER until Armenians Arathoon Sarkies and Eleazar

Action for AIDS: awareness-raising poster.

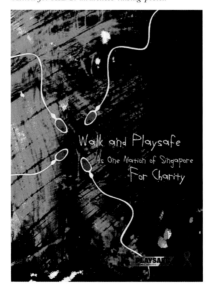

Adelphi Hotel: photographed c. 1910.

Johannes acquired it in 1903. The hotel occupied several locations but by 1905 it had settled into a SWAN & MACLAREN-designed building located at the corner of North Bridge Road and Coleman Street.

The Adelphi Hotel was the venue of a lunch held by the Foreign Correspondents' Association of Southeast Asia on 27 May 1961. It was at this lunch that Tunku ABDUL RAHMAN first mooted the idea of MERGER.

The hotel was closed and the building demolished in the mid-1980s to make way for The Adelphi, a shopping complex containing many shops specializing in high-end audio products.

Administration of Muslim Law Act The Administration of Muslim Law Act (AMLA) makes provisions for regulating Muslim affairs. The first legal guidelines can be traced to the colonial period. Before he left Singapore in 1823, Sir STAMFORD RAFFLES stipulated, among other matters, that 'in all cases regarding the ceremonies of religion, and marriages, and the rules of inheritance, the laws and customs of the Malays will be respected'. Before Independence in 1965, the Mohammedan Ordinances regulated Muslim life. Enacted in 1966, AMLA does not define Muslim law but regulates and governs the three bodies that it established: the MAJLIS UGAMA ISLAM SINGAPURA, SYARIAH COURT, and REGISTRY OF MUSLIM MARRIAGES.

Administrative Service Elite branch of the civil service. Administrative Service officers are the links between the Cabinet and the rest of the civil service. They are concerned with policy, constructive long-term thinking, directing the business of government departments, preparing new legislation and assisting ministers in the conduct of Parliamentary business. In 1934, the Straits Settlements Civil Service was established and contained certain posts previously included in the Malayan Civil Service (reserved solely for candidates of European descent). However, few locals were appointed to the highest administrative posts. With the establishment of Singapore's own Public Service Commission under the Public Service Commission Ordinance 1949, the Singapore Administrative Service was established in 1950. The first appointments of UNIVERSITY OF MALAYA graduates (three in all) were made that year.

Adnan Saidi, Lieutenant (1915–1942) War hero. Born in Kajang, Selangor, Adnan Saidi received an English education at Pekan Sungei Ramal School. Upon graduation, he taught at his alma mater for over a year. In 1933, he joined the MALAY REGIMENT and was named its best recruit a year later. He was promoted rapidly: sergeant (1936); sergeant-major (1937); and second lieutenant (1939). Upon graduation from officer cadet school, he was made leader of the 7th Platoon, C Company. In late 1941, Adnan was posted to Singapore.

During the BATTLE OF PASIR PANJANG, also known as the Battle at Opium Hill or Battle at Bukit Chandu, a numerically superior Japanese force met with fierce resistance from Adnan and C Company who were entrusted to the defence of Pasir Panjang Ridge. On 14 February 1942, the Japanese finally succeeded in overwhelming the soldiers of C Company and Adnan himself was captured. According to one eyewitness account, Adnan was hung upside down and bayoneted, and his throat was slit many times.

Adult Education Board The Council for Adult Education was formed in 1950 to coordinate the activities of various voluntary adult education organizations. It was succeeded by the Adult Education Board, established in April 1960 by the passing of the Adult Education Board Ordinance (Lembaga Gerakan Pelajaran Dewasa Ordinance).

The board was an autonomous institution charged with promoting adult education in Singapore. It comprised a full-time chairman, a part-time deputy chairman and nine part-time members. These members represented a variety of interests, including those of educational institutions and the trade union movement. The chairman was assisted by a full-time director, who, with a deputy director and five assistant directors, was responsible for carrying out the board's programmes.

The board organized both part-time and full-time courses, primarily held in the evening on the premises of day schools. Supplementary classes were held at weekends. Courses ranged from primary, secondary and pre-university education, to language, commercial, vocational, cultural, recreational and general knowledge subjects. The wide variety proved popular, and there was an average of 31,000 students enrolled monthly in 1978.

The Adult Education Board merged with the Industrial Training Board in 1979 to form the Vocational and Industrial Training Board, which was in turn succeeded by the INSTITUTE OF TECHNICAL EDUCATION in 1992.

Agency for Science, Technology and Research Statutory board. The National Science and Technology Board was set up in 1991 to raise the standards of science and technology in Singapore. In 2001, it was reorganized and, in 2002, renamed the Agency for Science, Technology and Research (A★STAR).

A★STAR focuses on encouraging and promoting scientific research, and nurturing talent for a KNOWLEDGE-BASED ECONOMY. It consists of five divisions. Aside from a corporate planning and administration division, the Biomedical Research Council is in charge of biomedical research and development in the public sector; the Science and Engineering Research Council promotes public sector R&D in electronics, infocommunications, chemicals and general engineering; the A★STAR Graduate Academy promotes science scholarships and other programmes to develop skilled manpower; and Exploit Technologies, formerly NSTB Holdings, is A★STAR's commercialization unit, which helps to transform technologies into marketable products and applications.

A★STAR works with a five-year budget of $5 billion. Of this, about $500 million is spent each year to fund several research institutes and centres. It employs over 2,000 researchers who do work on molecular biology, genetics, nano-technology, bioinformatics and medicine. In 2003, the biomedical research institutes moved into the Biopolis at ONE-NORTH.

agency houses The history of agency houses is an integral part of the story of Britain's colonial expansion in South and Southeast Asia. Merchants played an important role in sustaining and augmenting Britain's commercial interests. Singapore became, in the 19th century, a key trade centre. Goods were brought here, unloaded, and then redistributed. This attracted commercially minded European merchants who set up agency houses. These dealt initially with the

Lieutenant Adnan Saidi

Agency houses: godown of agency house Gilfillan Wood & Co.

of three days during which payment had to be made. Slowly, the agency houses expanded their interests and were soon acting as bill brokers, bankers, freighters, insurance agents and ship owners. For example, the highly successful German-operated BEHN MEYER AND CO. had interests in many shipping lines.

The invention of steamships, electric telegraphy, and the emergence of other trading posts such as Hong Kong in the mid-19th century, altered the way the agencies functioned. Further, the linking of the Malay states by railway offered Singapore agency houses new opportunities. Guthrie & Co., for instance, started operations in Penang in 1902.

An important aspect of managing trade was the development of the banking system, which allowed for the transfer of vast sums of money into the island. This influx of revenue allowed for the development of cash crops such as RUBBER in Malaya. Before major banks established a branch network in Singapore and Malaya, the merchant houses often acted as their agents.

While many agency houses survived, some closed and a few others became absorbed into bigger establishments. Over time, they were converted into partnership firms and occasionally changed hands when a member retired or died. Some became public companies.

In time, the agency houses began to operate on behalf of governments. They involved themselves in public activities such as the support of schools and churches, and were represented in the Legislative Council. The Straits Settlements Association started by them in 1868 was robust in its stand on free trade and the Colonial Office in London had to first deal with the association when it sought to levy import taxes and duties. Their successors continued to safeguard the agencies' commercial interests in the early 20th century, protesting against any moves that conflicted with their notions of free trade.

After World War II, the agency houses faced increased competition from Japan and rising nationalism especially in the Malay states. Some suffered physical damage in the war—the offices of Guthrie & Co. in south Boat Quay were bombed, and most of the company's records were destroyed during the occupation.

trans-shipment of goods for commission. They were at the top of the trading system in which the middlemen, shopkeepers and other indigenous traders operated.

Other factors leading merchants to open agencies in Singapore included the end of the EAST INDIA COMPANY's monopoly in India in 1814, and in China in the 1830s. By 1834, the bulk of British trade, especially with China, was in the hands of private traders. The oldest agency house in Singapore was established by Scotsman ALEXANDER JOHNSTON in 1819. He was followed by ALEXANDER GUTHRIE who came from South Africa in 1821 and set up what came to be known as GUTHRIE & CO. In 1823, SYME AND CO. was set up. By 1846, there were 43 merchant houses, 20 of them British-owned. With the opening of the Suez Canal in 1869, trade surged, and in the last part of the 19th century British trading houses faced growing competition from the Dutch, French and Germans.

The function of the agency houses changed over time. Initially, they acted as an intermediary between the West and the East. Connected closely to Western markets and factories, they imported manufactured goods into the region and shipped back local goods for a small commission. When the goods arrived in Singapore, part would be given to the Chinese middlemen on a basis that included both barter and credit. This system could not last long: the middlemen were not always prompt, and in 1835, the Singapore merchants decided to trade with cash. In cases of credit, they would use promissory notes and allow a grace period

Agni Kootthu: scene from the play 1915.

Agni Kootthu Tamil and English theatre company founded in 1991 by S. Thenmoli. Its name means 'Theatre of Fire'. The group is a pioneer of experimental TAMIL THEATRE. Apart from Tamil plays, Agni Kootthu has also staged Tamil translations of Mandarin plays by KUO PAO KUN and HAN LAO DA. Its Artistic Director, ELANGOVAN, has translated, written and directed all the plays staged by the group. Controversy surrounded the group when they staged Talaq (Divorce), a play about an Indian Muslim woman caught in an abusive marriage. It was first performed in Tamil in 1998, but an attempt to restage the play in English and Malay two years later gave rise to complaints from religious groups, and a licence was not issued by the Public Entertainment Licence Unit.

agriculture In 1819, Sir Stamford Raffles despatched a gardener from Bencoolen to plant clove and NUTMEG trees on the slopes of Bukit Larangan (Forbidden Hill, now FORT CANNING). The crops flourished and Raffles allocated 48 acres of adjoining land as a botanic garden. He worked closely with Dr Nathaniel Wallich of the Calcutta Botanic Garden and hoped that his experimental garden would form the foundation of Singapore's agricultural prosperity.

Many Europeans were deceived into thinking that the soil was very fertile on account of the lush forests. In 1836, a group of enthusiasts formed the Singapore Agricultural and Horticultural Society to experiment with crops. Nutmeg was the most popular, and by the 1850s its cultivation had become a sort of mania. However, disease struck the plantations, and by the mid-1860s, only one plantation remained. The next most popular crop was COCONUTS but these grew best in the sandy soil of the east coast, in the Katong area. SUGAR cane proved disastrous, as did coffee, cotton, cinnamon, cloves and indigo.

The main crops that flourished were PEPPER AND GAMBIER, farmed mainly by the Chinese. The two crops were complementary since the waste from gambier provided much-needed nutrients and fertilizer for the pepper, which tended to exhaust the

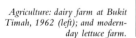

Agriculture: dairy farm at Bukit Timah, 1962 (left); and modern-day lettuce farm.

soil very quickly. Gambier production reached its peak in the 1850s, when there were about 800 gambier and pepper plantations on the island.

By the late 1850s, even the gambier and pepper planters were abandoning their fields. The intense farming of these two crops, and the slash-and-burn method of clearing the land, led to much leaching and exhaustion of the soil. Many of these farmers moved to Johor, where they would repeat the same cycle. Planting gambier and pepper was a hazardous occupation as plantation workers were often subject to attacks by TIGERS which roamed the jungles of Singapore until the early 20th century.

For a decade or two, there was little new agricultural enterprise on the island. Many planters continued to struggle on with their coffee, cocoa and coconut crops. It was not until the arrival of HENRY RIDLEY, the new director of the SINGAPORE BOTANIC GARDENS, that another cash crop—RUBBER—was introduced and grown on a large scale. Rubber continued to be the main cash crop grown in Singapore until the 1950s. However, increased demands on land in Singapore subsequently made it far more economical to grow rubber in Malaya.

By the 1960s, with the push towards industrialization, the importance of Singapore's agricultural sector diminished. There were pockets of vegetable, poultry and pig farming throughout the island, but these were not on a large scale. Most of the produce was consumed locally and there was never enough for export. In the 1980s and 1990s, technology was employed to expand agricultural production, especially in vegetable farming. Hydroponic systems were introduced, minimizing the use of land. Today, very little traditional agriculture is practised in highly urbanized Singapore.

ah ku Polite term of address in Cantonese for a Chinese prostitute in colonial Singapore. Abject poverty and desperate hunger brought women to Singapore from the coastal regions of southeast China. They were sold or kidnapped and brought to the NANYANG (Southern Seas) to work as sex providers in a predominantly single, male, immigrant society. The vast majority of *ah ku* in Singapore came from Guangdong province. They were found at all levels of the occupational hierarchy, providing sexual services to the rich in the exclusive enclaves of Smith Street, and as *xian shui mei* (salt-water girls), who rowed out to entertain foreign sailors and men on lighters, junks and steamers in the port. Shophouse signs with *heung* (Cantonese for 'fragrance') or *lau* ('building') at the end usually indicated a Chinese brothel. Some Teochew *ah ku* from the Swatow region had to acquire basic Cantonese to avoid unease or resistance from some of their working-class Cantonese clients.

At the turn of the 20th century, a com-

Ah ku: *Chinese prostitute.*

mon *ah ku* could be sold for $20–$50. The price escalated to $150–$500 as demand increased due to the dramatic growth in Chinese immigration.

Ahmad Ibrahim (1927–1962) Trade unionist and politician. Born in Penang, Ahmad Ibrahim was educated at the Bayan Lepas Malay School in Penang, the Francis Light School and the Penang Free School for secondary education in English. After World War II, he joined the Singapore Naval Base fire department as a watch-room operator and became a clerk. Active in the trade union movement, he became the first branch secretary of the All-Singapore Fire Brigade Employees Union in 1948; he was later elected vice-chairman of the central executive committee of the Naval Base Labour Union, and became honorary adviser to the Singapore Traction Company Employees' Union in 1957.

Ahmad joined the PEOPLE'S ACTION PARTY (PAP) and became a member of its central executive committee as assistant secretary-general. In the LEGISLATIVE ASSEMBLY ELECTION (1955), he was fielded by the PAP at Sembawang and won. He was re-elected under the PAP banner in the LEGISLATIVE ASSEMBLY ELECTION (1959) and was appointed minister for health, becoming the first Malay to hold a ministerial appointment in self-governing Singapore.

In a Cabinet reshuffle in September 1961, Ahmad exchanged portfolios with K.M. BYRNE and became minister of labour. Confronted by mass strikes engineered by radicalized workers, he stood firm and played a key role in the deregistration of the communist-infiltrated SINGAPORE TRADES UNION CONGRESS and cracked down on left-wing operators in the Works Brigade. He was a supporter of multi-racialism and spoke out against what he saw as Chinese chauvinism.

Ahmad was in poor health after 1958. He visited London for a medical consultation in June 1962, and on his return to

Singapore, died on 21 August of that year aged only 35. His was among the briefest of political careers within the PAP. His death eliminated the PAP's absolute parliamentary majority, leaving it with 25 seats, the same number as the opposition.

A state funeral was ordered by the Yang di-Pertuan Negara, YUSOF ISHAK. Ahmad Ibrahim was buried at the Bidadari Cemetery. The road Jalan Ahmad Ibrahim was named after him, as was the Ahmad Ibrahim Secondary School and the library at the Muslim orphanage school off Aljunied Road.

Ahmad Jaafar (1919–) Songwriter. Born and raised in Sumatra, Ahmad Jaafar is often regarded as the 'father of modern Malay pop'. He came to Singapore in 1946 and composed many songs for films. His first job was as a saxophonist with the Cecil Wilson Band at GREAT WORLD Amusement Park. He founded and led the famous Rayuan Kencana Orchestra in the 1950s. He also headed the Singapore Broadcasting Corporation orchestra until 1980. His songs 'Ibu' (Mother), 'Bunga Tanjung' (Cape Flower) and 'Selamat Hari Raya' (Happy Hari Raya) are enduringly popular. A cover version of the song 'Ibu' was recorded by the first winner of SINGAPORE IDOL, Taufik Batisah, in his album *Blessings*.

Ahmad has received many awards such as the Public Service Medallion, the CULTURAL MEDALLION, the Distinguished Achievement Award and the Gold Premier Award. In 2005, he was given the Lifetime Achievement Award by the Composers' and Authors' Society of Singapore (COMPASS).

Ahmad Mattar (1940–) Politician and academic. Ahmad Mattar was educated at Geylang English School, Raffles Institution and then at the University of Singapore, where he obtained a PhD in applied acoustics. He joined the the University of Singapore as assistant lecturer in 1964. In the 1972 general election, he contested the

Ahmad Jaafar

Ahmad Ibrahim: speaking at St Michael's Road Market, 1960.

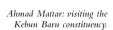

Leng Kee seat on the PEOPLE'S ACTION PARTY ticket, and won. He rose through the government ranks, serving in several capacities including parliamentary secretary to the Ministry of Education (1972–77), minister for social affairs and minister-in-charge of Muslim affairs (1977–93) and minister for the environment (1985–93). He retired from the Cabinet in 1993 and from Parliament in 1996. He has served as a member of the World Supreme Council for Mosques and in 1981 became founding chairman of MENDAKI, a position he held until 1993.

Ahmad Mohamed Ibrahim (1916–1999) Lawyer, academic and diplomat. Tan Sri Datuk Professor Ahmad Mohamed Ibrahim was educated at Victoria Bridge School, Raffles Institution and Raffles College. In 1935, he won the prestigious QUEEN'S SCHOLARSHIP which allowed him to read law at St John's College, Cambridge University where he graduated with first class honours. He was called to the Bar at Middle Temple in 1941, and joined the Straits Settlements Legal Service upon his return to Singapore. After World War II, he became a magistrate and subsequently district judge. On 1 May 1947, he was appointed a lecturer in law at Raffles College. From 1949 to 1955, Ahmad was in private practice but also served on the Municipal Commission, Rural Board and Legislative Council. In 1955, he rejoined the Legal Service, and by February 1957, was senior Crown counsel. On 25 June 1959, he was appointed state advocate-general of Singapore. When Singapore attained independence, the office became that of attorney-general.

Ahmad Mohamed Ibrahim: inspection of student guard-of-honour at Gan Eng Seng School, 1964.

Ahmad was awarded the MERITORIOUS SERVICE MEDAL in 1962. In 1967, he retired from the Legal Service and was appointed Singapore's ambassador to Egypt. Later he joined the UNIVERSITY OF MALAYA and was appointed professor (1969–72), dean of the Faculty of Law (1972–83) and professor emeritus (1984). He then became founding dean of the law faculty at the International Islamic University Malaysia (1983–99)—the faculty was named after him in 2000.

Ahmadiyya Movement established in India by Mirza Ghulam Ahmad (1835–1908), who claimed—though there are differences of opinion among sub-sects—to be the Prophet of the Age. In 1889, he laid down the foundation of his community, which was subsequently known as the Ahmadiyya Muslim Jamaat. Since its inception, its objective was to renew ISLAM, but after Mirza's death, the movement split into two sub-sects, the Ahmadiyya Muslim Community and the Lahore Ahmadiyya Movement. Both sub-sects, however, support their belief by using an allegorical interpretation of references in Islamic literature relating to the return of Jesus. Muslim scholars contend that the founder's claim of prophethood violates a basic tenet of Islam—that Muhammad is the last prophet.

The Ahmadiyya movement claims a worldwide membership of 200 million. The Ahmadiyya Muslim Mission was established in Singapore in 1935. It currently has about 220 active members. A public debate in the 1940s between an Ahmadi cleric, Ghulam Husin, and an Islamic religious teacher, Syed Ahmad Dahlan al-Husaini, caused many to recant their Ahmadi beliefs. On 19 October 1960, a mass rally was held in Geylang to counter Ahmadi teachings. It was organized by four major Muslim bodies: MUHAMMADIYAH, PERGAS, JAMIYAH and the Muslim Advisory Board. They jointly declared that Ahmadiyyah is not part of the Sunni Islam. A fatwa (religious ruling) by MAJLIS UGAMA ISLAM SINGAPURA, issued on 23 June 1969, declared that followers of the group are not considered Muslim. They are not subject to the ADMINISTRATION OF MUSLIM LAW ACT.

Ahmadis have their own place of worship, Masjid Taha (Taha Mosque), at Onan Road. In general, the group's relationship with the Muslim community has been peaceful and followers are free to practise their beliefs.

Ai Tong School One of six schools managed by the SINGAPORE HOKKIEN HUAY KUAN, which took over its management in 1927. Ai Tong School began in 1912 as a boys' school at the Methodist Church in Boon Tat Street. The enrolment was 30. In 1950, the boys were joined by girls from Ai Hwa School, which then became defunct. Relocating several times over the years as student numbers grew, Ai Tong is now at

Al-Abrar Mosque

Bright Hill Drive. It is a SPECIAL ASSISTANCE PLAN SCHOOL where pupils take Chinese and English as a first language. In keeping with the Hokkien Huay Kuan's goals of preserving and promoting Chinese culture, the school has programmes for students to practise *guzheng* (Chinese zither), *wushu* (martial arts), Chinese dance and Chinese calligraphy.

Al-Abrar Mosque This mosque in Telok Ayer Street was built by the Chulia community, most of whom used to live in Chinatown (*see* CHULIAS). Also known as Koochoo Palli (literally 'hut mosque' in Tamil), it was originally a thatched hut. It became one of the main Indian Muslim mosques, and between 1850 and 1855, a brick mosque was built on the site of the original building, spanning the width of three shophouses. It has two minarets and a distinctive street facade. It was gazetted as a national monument in 1974.

Al Imam Islamic reformist magazine, published between 1906 and 1908, that was modelled on the reformist publication *al-Manar*, which was published by Rashid Rida in Cairo. Established on 23 July 1906 by a group that included four prominent Muslim intellectuals and personalities of the time—Sheik TAHIR JALALUDDIN (its first editor), SYED SHEIK ALHADI, Haji Abbas Mohd Taha and Sheik Salim al-Kalali (its director for the first two years). Published monthly, it was printed by Matbaah Melayu Tanjung Pagar and, later, Al-Imam Printing Company Ltd. It was written in Malay, but many Arabic words and expressions were used as its audience comprised mainly those who had undergone religious education. The magazine was available in Malaya and was distributed in Sumatra as well.

Al Imam was published primarily to condemn traditional practices and institutions of the Muslim world on the premise that they were largely un-Islamic and were remnants of the pre-Islamic past. In particular, the magazine singled out the corrupt lifestyles and values of the ruling elite, and the outdated teaching methods of the conservative ulema (scholars). While primarily concerned with religion, the magazine also touched on political, economic and social issues of the Malays. *Al Imam* ceased publication on 25 December 1908.

Al-Khatib, Umar Abdullah (1907–1997) Islamic scholar and teacher. Born in Hadramaut, South Yemen, Umar Abdullah Al-Khatib had memorized the Qur'an when he was only nine. Educated by scholars in Hadramaut, he became proficient in Arabic and its sub-disciplines such as grammar, logical analysis and rhetoric. He also learned Qur'anic exegesis, Hadith (sayings and doings of the Prophet Muhammad), doctrine, and jurisprudence in all four Sunni schools. He specialized in the SHAFI'I SCHOOL. He was offered the position of judge when he was just 27 but in deference to the elder scholars, he declined. This reticence was to be a hallmark of his career—he continually shunned publicity and status.

Al-Khatib migrated to Singapore in 1935 and initially worked in a company owned by the al-Haddad family. In the mid-1960s, he left for Saudi Arabia. He stayed there for about ten years, teaching in Mecca and Medina. In recognition of his scholarship, he was given a special room in which to teach in the Grand Mosque at Mecca.

On his return to Singapore in 1976, Al-Khatib began teaching. His students came from all walks of life and included SYED ISA MOHAMAD SEMAIT, mufti of Singapore, and Syed Abdillah Ahmad al-Jufri, former president of PERGAS.

As the teacher for a whole generation of ulema (scholars), he significantly shaped Islamic education and opinion. His works on jurisprudence have been published posthumously.

Alatas, Syed Hussein (1928–) Academic and scholar. Syed Hussein Alatas was born in Java to a Malayan tea trader of Yemeni descent. He graduated in political and social sciences from the University of Amsterdam and returned to Malaya, where he headed the Research Section of Dewan Bahasa dan Pustaka (Institute for Language and Literature). He later returned to Amsterdam and earned his PhD in political and social sciences in 1963. From 1963 to 1967, he was the head of the Cultural Division at the University of Malaya's Department of Malay Studies. He then served as professor of Malay Studies at the National University of Singapore from 1967 to 1988. In 1988, he was appointed the vice-chancellor of the University of Malaya. From 1995 to 1999, he served at Universiti Kebangsaan Malaysia (National University of Malaysia), initially as professor at the Centre for General Studies and later at the Department of Anthropology and Sociology. In 1999, he was appointed principal research fellow at the Institute of the

Malay World and Civilisation, Universiti Kebangsaan Malaysia.

Alatas' widely published writings address issues on religion, development, corruption and politics. He often combines academic duties and political activism—he was a founding member of Parti Gerakan Rakyat Malaysia (a Malaysian political party). In his book, *The Myth of the Lazy Native* (1977), he debunked the colonial belief that Malays are inherently lazy and backward. He argued that this fallacy has even affected the Malay self-image. In order to correct this, he wrote profusely in the 1970s and 1980s about the need for Malays to become 'Men of Excellence'. This gave birth to the idea of the 'New Malay'. Politicians and thinkers in both Malaysia and Singapore picked up on this idea and developed it. His other major works include *Thomas Stamford Raffles: Schemer or Reformer?* (1972), *Modernisation and Social Change In Southeast Asia* (1972), *Kita Dengan Islam* (Us and Islam) (1972), *Islam dan Sosialisma* (Islam and Socialism) (1976) and *Intellectuals In Developing Societies* (1977).

Alexandra Barracks Buildings near Alexandra Road built and used by the British army during the colonial period. Roads leading to the barracks bear names reflecting their association with the British military, such as Hyderabad, Cornwall, Berkshire, Royal, Winchester, Canterbury and York. Among the most prominent of the old buildings is Eton Hall, formerly a school for the children of officers living in the barracks, and named after Eton College in the United Kingdom. Its motto, 'Manners Makyth Man'—which, in fact, follows closely the motto of Winchester College and not Eton—is emblazoned over the entrance.

Alexandra Barracks was built on a former gambier plantation originally to house Indian soldiers from the 5th Bengal Light Infantry Regiment who arrived in Singapore in 1914—part of the regiment mutinied in 1915 in what became known as the SEPOY MUTINY. The original barrack buildings were demolished between 1935 and 1940. In their place, large two-storey bungalows, with extensive gardens and plenty of space for servants' quarters, were built to house senior British military personnel up to the level of general. During

Alexandra Barracks: military housing on the former barracks site.

Alexandra Hospital: as it appeared in the 1950s.

the Japanese Occupation, the buildings were converted into Japanese medical officers' quarters. From 1945 until the British military withdrawal from Singapore in 1971, Alexandra Barracks was once again reserved for senior British military personnel.

Alexandra Hospital The history of Alexandra Hospital dates back to 1938 when it was built by the British armed forces to serve the medical needs of the troops and their families. Known as the British Military Hospital, it was then the largest and best-equipped military hospital outside the United Kingdom. With the advent of war, the 32 Company Royal Army Medical Corps occupied the hospital. In February 1942, Japanese troops massacred around 200 hospital personnel and patients (*see* box). In 1971, as part of the process of British military withdrawal from the region, the hospital was transferred to the Singapore government for a token sum of $1, and reopened as a general hospital, serving the population in the western part of Singapore (*see* HOSPITALS).

In 2000, Alexandra Hospital became a member of the National Healthcare Group, one of the two clusters under the Ministry of Health. It is now a 400-bed hospital, serving both private and subsidized patients. It provides international inpatient services, catering to the medical and personal needs of foreign patients. In 2005, Alexandra Hospital was accredited by the Joint Commission International.

Alexandra Hospital massacre Massacre of the staff and patients of the British Military Hospital (present-day ALEXANDRA HOSPITAL) by Japanese troops. In the final days of the fall of Singapore in 1942, Japanese soldiers from the 18th Division killed about 200 staff members and patients in retaliation for being fired at by Indian troops on the hospital grounds. After they captured the hospital on the afternoon of 14 February, the Japanese soldiers went on an orgy of violence. They first bayoneted a British officer, Lieutenant Weston, who was carrying a white flag, and killed Corporal Holden of the British 2nd Loyals while he was lying on the operating table. The soldiers then rounded up about 200 patients and staff, putting them into servants' quarters before bayoneting them to death. The young Japanese officers who carried out the massacre were later tried by their superiors and executed. During the Japanese Occupation, Alexandra Hospital was used by the Japanese forces.

The hospital continued to be used by the British military after the war, until the British withdrew their troops from Singapore in 1971. It was then transferred to the Singapore government.

Alfian Sa'at

Aliman Hassan

Alfian Sa'at (1977–) Author, poet, playwright and theatre practitioner. Alfian's first work, *One Fierce Hour* (1998), was published while he was a medical student. The more mature and substantial *A History of Amnesia* (2001) has many politically driven poems and several pieces inspired by Malay folklore. *History* was one of the 'ten notable books' (fiction) selected by the judges for the 2001 Kiriyama Book Prize. *Corridor: Twelve Short Stories* (1999) won a Commendation Award in the 1998 Singapore Literature Prize for Fiction.

Alfian has written more than two dozen plays in English and Malay. They include *Causeway* (1998), a satire on Malaysia–Singapore relations, *Minah & Monyet* (Minah & Monkey) (2003) and *Mengapa Isa?* (Why Jesus?/Why the **I**nternal **S**ecurity **A**ct?) (2004). His *Landmarks: Asian Boys Vol 2* (2004) won the 2005 Life! Theatre Awards for Best Script. Alfian edited *Bisik* (*Whisper*): *An Anthology of Singapore Malay Drama* (2003). In 2001, he won the Golden Point Award for Poetry and was the NATIONAL ARTS COUNCIL's Young Artist Award for Literature. He discontinued medical studies in 2002, despite having only one more year to complete. Since 2003, Alfian has been resident playwright of W!LD RICE Theatre Company.

Alhambra Cinema. Located in Beach Road, the Alhambra was built in 1907 and was owned by Tan Cheng Kee, who also owned the Marlborough theatre next to it. One of the pioneer cinemas in Singapore, the Alhambra was the first to screen 'talkies' in the early 1930s. After Tan's death in 1939, United Exhibition Syndicate took over the Alhambra. It was acquired by Shaw Organisation in the 1950s and renamed New Alhambra. It underwent extensive renovations in 1966 but was later demolished to make way for Shaw Towers, which was completed in 1974.

Ali Iskandar Shah, Sultan (c. 1824–1877) Malay royal. Ali Iskandar Shah was ten years old when his father, Sultan HUSAIN SHAH of Singapore, died in Malacca in 1835. Five years later, Ali moved to Singapore, where the East India Company (EIC) administration recognized his right to his late father's property in Singapore but not to the title of sultan. Ali petitioned the EIC government

Alhambra: cinema entrance (right), and tickets.

in Calcutta for recognition as sultan but without success. In 1855, Ali accepted a settlement with Temenggong Daeng Ibrahim, where the latter acknowledged Ali's claim to the title of sultan. In return, Ali gave up his claim to Johor except for Kesang, a small area in Muar. Ali died in Malacca.

See also MALAY ROYALTY.

Aliman Hassan (1932–) Teacher, poet and author. Aliman Hassan attended the Kota Raja Malay School before continuing his education at Sultan Idris Training College, Perak. He joined the teaching service and, later, MAJLIS UGAMA ISLAM SINGAPURA. Some of his poems are published in anthologies such as *Puncak Sembilan* (Nine Pinnacles) (1975), *Singapore Writing* (1977), *Puisi-puisi Nusantara* (Poems of Nusantara) (1981) and *Tiga Warna Bertemu* (Meeting of Three Colours) (1987). His literary commentary, *Sekadar Pengisi Ruang* (To Fill Space) and his first novel, *Empat* (Four), were published in 1993 and 2002 respectively. Aliman is also active in the literary organization ASAS 50, KESATUAN GURU-GURU MELAYU SINGAPURA (Singapore Malay Teachers Union) and LEMBAGA BIASISWA KENANGAN MAULUD (Prophet Muhammad's Birthday Memorial Scholarship Fund). He was given the Tun Seri Lanang Award in 2001 by the Malay Language Council of Singapore.

Aljunied family The earliest Arab clan to have settled in Singapore. Syed Muhammad Harun Aljunied arrived from Palembang, Sumatra in 1819. His nephew, SYED OMAR ALI ALJUNIED joined him soon after. Syed Omar was the one who expanded the family's wealth, and was known for his philanthropy. His cousin, Syed Ali (son of Syed Muhammad) financed the building of four wells to ensure the community's supply of drinking water. Syed Omar's grandson, Syed Abdul Rahman, built Madrasah Aljunied on land owned by his grandfather, which was originally used as a burial ground. The madrasah was opened in 1927.

The Aljunieds were the first ARABS to systematically shift their business interests entirely to real estate, a move which was later emulated by other Arab families. The early Aljunied pioneers were prominent religious and social figures in the Singapore community. Some family members are still engaged in business and real estate, while others have taken up other professions. Aljunied Road was named after the family.

Aljunied, Syed Omar Ali (unknown–1852) Businessman and philanthropist. Syed Omar Ali Aljunied arrived in Singapore in 1819 from Palembang with his uncle, Syed Mohammad Harun Aljunied. They settled in KAMPONG GLAM and were prominent traders and businessmen. Syed Omar traded in spices and cloth, and he bought large amounts of land. He was known as a phil-

Alkaff family: the Arcade, built by the family between Raffles Place and Collyer Quay in 1909.

anthropist who gave to various charitable and religious causes. He donated land for the building of the first mosque in Singapore in 1820, the OMAR KAMPONG MELAKA MOSQUE. He also gave land for the Pauper's Hospital in 1844, which later became TAN TOCK SENG HOSPITAL. He owned a large plot of land between Victoria Street and Rochor Canal. This was originally used as an Arab-Muslim burial ground, which was named after him.

Alkaff family The Alkaff family hail from Hadramaut, Yemen. The first Alkaff to arrive in Singapore was Syed Shaik Alkaff, a trader. He came in 1852 and traded between the Dutch East Indies (Indonesia) and India. His elder brother, Syed Mohamed Abdul Rahman Alkaff, had built a profitable trading empire and Shaik Alkaff inherited his brother's wealth. He continued trading and ploughed his profits into properties in Singapore. Real estate soon became his primary business. By 1888, the family was rich enough to buy a large piece of land in the heart of the city at Collyer Quay. In 1909, they built The Arcade at Raffles Place. This was sold to the Woh Hup Group in the 1970s. They also bought a piece of land on two hills near Telok Blangah Road: this is the site of ALKAFF MANSION. The Alkaff family was probably the largest landowner among the Arab families in Singapore. The family built the famous Alkaff Gardens, which were opened in 1929. The park, located off Macpherson Road, had a lake with rowboats, landscaped paths and trees, and was a scenic place for picnics. The gardens were sold in 1949 to make way for housing, with all traces of the park disappearing by 1964. The early Alkaffs were involved in the social and political affairs of Hadramaut. Like the other Arab families, the Alkaffs remitted large amounts of money to support their families and charitable institutions there.

Alkaff Mansion In 1918, a wealthy trader and philanthropist from Yemen named Syed Abdul Rahman Alkaff built a large mansion on Bukit Jagoh (now part of MOUNT FABER). He chose the site for its cool air and spectacular views. Extensive gardens surrounded the mansion and were used for lavish parties.

The ALKAFF FAMILY sold the mansion after World War II. In 1990, the mansion was leased to HOTEL PROPERTIES LIMITED and converted into a restaurant called Alkaff Mansion, which specialised in serving the Dutch–Indonesian *rijstafel*. It was also a popular venue for wedding receptions. In 2003, the restaurant ceased operations.

The gardens (not to be confused with Alkaff Gardens) are now part of Telok Blangah Hill Park, popular with local residents, including wedding couples having their photos taken. The Terrace Garden is the main feature, providing a 360-degree view of Singapore. Bougainvilleas have been planted on the terraces, and shade for picnickers is provided by tall trees.

Allen, Christopher (1933–2004) Theatre director and actor. Born in Bombay and educated in Britain, Christopher Henry Rothwell Allen came to Singapore in 1954 to work for a shipping company. He joined the Stage Club, Singapore's first English-language amateur theatre company. Founded in 1945 by British servicemen, the company comprised mainly British expatriates. Allen became club president in 1970, and again in 1976, 1978–80 and 1983.

Allen distinguished himself as an actor in Stage Club plays such as *Night of the Iguana* (1977), *There's a Girl in My Soup* (1978), *Pygmalion* (1979), *Boeing Boeing* (1979), *Witness for the Prosecution* (1980), and *Habeas Corpus* (1981). He played a dame in many of the club's Christmas pantomimes. As a director, his affinity for both classical and contemporary plays—he directed Tennessee Williams' *Night of the Iguana* (1977), Alan Ayckbourn's *Table Manners* (1979) and *Living Together* (1980)—brought a range of drama to Singaporean audiences. This exposure led to attempts by Singaporean directors and companies to indigenize theatre in the 1980s. Allen was

Allgreen Properties: Great World City, its flagship investment property.

awarded the CULTURAL MEDALLION for Theatre in 1983. He eventually returned to live in the United Kingdom.

See also ENGLISH THEATRE.

Allen & Gledhill Law firm founded in 1902 by Rowland Allen and John Joseph Gledhill. Allen was admitted to the Singapore Bar in 1895, and became a partner of Joaquim Brothers in 1898. When the partnership dissolved in 1902, Allen went into partnership with Gledhill, at the time a legal assistant in the firm. The firm of Allen & Gledhill then took over the practice of Joaquim Brothers in Singapore and Malacca. Allen & Gledhill has grown into one of the largest law firms in Singapore. In 2000, it formed a joint law venture with global firm Linklaters.

Allgreen Properties Incorporated as Allgreen Investments in May 1986, Allgreen Properties Limited was listed on the Singapore Exchange in May 1999. It is the local property arm of the Kuok Group, whose principal activities are property development and investment, construction, project and property management, and trading in building materials.

Allgreen's property portfolio includes residential space, commercial office space, retail space, serviced apartments and a hotel. As at the end of 2005, the company had a land bank of 3.4 million sq ft of attributable gross floor area for residential development, both on freehold and leasehold land. Its investment property portfolio includes the wholly owned flagship Great World City. Its other investment properties are owned through a 55.4 per cent stake in Cuscaden Properties, which owns the 546-room Traders Hotel, Tanglin Mall and Tanglin Place. The company is also engaged in construction, project management and sourcing of building materials through its wholly-owned subsidiaries—Leo Property Management, Wyndham Construction and Wyndham Supplies.

In 2005, Allgreen Properties reported a net profit of $63.3 million on a turnover of $317.6 million.

Alliance Française Institution promoting French language and culture. The Alliance Française de Singapour was founded by a group of French-speaking residents headed by Paul Clerc in 1949. At the time, it had only 20 students and 50 members. In 1962 there were 350 students learning French, and by 2006, almost 3,500 students, mostly Singaporeans. Its new premises at Sarkies Road were inaugurated in 1995. The Alliance Française in Singapore is one of 1,085 Alliances Françaises worldwide. Its mission is not only to be a premier French language school but also to serve as a cultural centre, bringing together events from France and Singapore. Dr SHAW VEE MENG became president in 1983.

Alsagoff family The Alsagoff family were from the Hejaz (in present-day Saudi Arabia), but they also had close links with the branch of the family in Hadramaut, Yemen. Syed Abdul Rahman Alsagoff and his son, Syed Ahmad, came to Singapore in 1824, having established a spice trade in Malacca. Syed Abdul Rahman traded in spices and travelled between Java, Sumatra and Celebes. In 1848, they established Alsagoff & Co. When Syed Abdul Rahman died, Syed Ahmad managed the business. Syed Ahmad's marriage to Raja Siti, daughter of Hajjah Fatimah, enhanced the family fortune as he took over Hajjah Fatimah's considerable business operations after her death. Syed Ahmad also had a successful business arranging the HAJ for pilgrims in Southeast Asia.

His son, Syed Mohamed, succeeded him. Syed Mohamed's close ties with the Johor royal family allowed him to expand the family business, and it reached its peak between 1879 and 1888. Sultan ABU BAKAR bestowed upon him a large estate in Kukup, Johor. He had plantations of rubber, sago, and pineapples in Kukup and even issued his own currency there. He bought property in Singapore, including the RAFFLES HOTEL building. In 1904, Syed Mohamed founded the Muslimin Trust Fund Association (MTFA). Madrasah Alsagoff, built in 1912, stands on WAKAF land endowed by him. When he died, he left a will that stipulated that income from the *wakaf* should go towards charitable causes such as the distribution of food for the poor in Singapore and Hadramaut, the maintenance of the HAJJAH FATIMAH MOSQUE and the maintenance of Muslim

Alkaff family: postcard of the Alkaff Gardens, located in the Sennett Estate from 1929 to 1949.

Christopher Allen

Alsagoff family: staff of Alsagoff and Co.

The American Club

Amusement parks: tea-cup ride in one of the last-surviving parks, Kallang Wonderland, 1970s.

orphanages. His nephew, Syed Abdul Rahman Taha Alsagoff, continued his business and tradition of philanthropy.

Syed Abdul Rahman, being partly of BUGIS royal descent, was known as Engku Aman ('Engku' is a form of address for Bugis royalty and 'Aman' is short for 'Rahman'). He built up his wealth by establishing his own company, S.A.T. Alsagoff Landowners and Estate Developers in 1915. He was the president of the MTFA, which at that time undertook the task of caring for orphans. This initiative led to the establishment of the orphanages Darul Ihsan Lilbanin (for boys) and Darul Ihsan Lilbanat (for girls). Engku Aman Road is named after him.

The Alsagoff family was also active in local politics in Singapore. Syed Mohamed Ahmad was a member of the Municipal Board of Commissioners in 1883. His son Syed Ahmad, his nephew Syed Umar, and Syed Umar's son, Syed Ibrahim were appointed justices of the peace at various times. Syed Ibrahim Umar arrived in the 1920s from Mecca and eventually took over the family business. He was a founding member of the Muslim World League (Rabita al-Alam al-Islami) and served as Saudi honorary consul-general for Singapore and the Federation of Malaya. The Alsagoffs also founded the newspaper, *Warta Melayu* (Malay Newspaper), which was published from 1930 to 1941.

Amallathasan (1939–) Poet. Born in Kuala Kubu Baru, Selangor, Amallathasan has written over 1,500 poems on a wide range of themes. His work has been published in Singapore, Malaysia and India. Closely associated with the founder-editor of TAMIL MURASU, GOVINDASAMY SARANGAPANY, he supported the reformist ideals espoused in Sarangapany's editorials and columns.

Amallathasan works in a traditional style and in 2005, he published two volumes of poetry—*Pullangkuzhal* (Flute) and *Tamizhar Thalaivar Tamizhavel* (Tamizhavel, Leader of the Tamils). He was chairman of the Association of Singapore Tamil Writers

(1987–2005) and initiated the Tamizhavel Award for Tamil writers.

Amallathasan wrote lyrics for the songs 'Alaiyaadum Kadal Melae' ('On the Sea with Dancing Waves'), which received special mention in a 1975 song-writing contest for Singapore's four official languages, and 'Singapore Enum Pothilae' ('When You Say Singapore'), which was composed and sung by S. Gunasegaran and received the first prize in the National Day Song Contest (2005).

See also TAMIL LITERATURE.

Ambo Sooloh, Haji (c. 1891–1963) BUGIS businessman and community leader. Ambo Sooloh traded in pepper and gambier and had plantations in Sumatra and Borneo. He was active in the Malay community and, in 1926, co-founded the Kesatuan Melayu Singapura (KMS) (Singapore Malay Union) with Tengku Abdul Kadir. When MOHAMMED EUNOS ABDULLAH died in 1934, Ambo Sooloh replaced him on the Legislative Council and took over as president of KMS. Under his leadership, KMS continued to cooperate with the government, offering mild criticism of official policies towards Malays, and not allying itself with the more extreme radicals. He was appointed justice of the peace in 1927, and helped to establish UTUSAN MELAYU in 1932.

Ambrose, James (1909–1992) Judge. James Walter Davy Ambrose was educated at the Penang Free School where he won the QUEEN'S SCHOLARSHIP to read law at Oxford University. In 1935, he was called to the Bar at the Inner Temple. He moved to Singapore, and was appointed the assistant official assignee in 1936. He was posted to Malacca in the same capacity in 1939, and became magistrate and assistant district judge of Malacca in 1940.

After World War II, Ambrose served as deputy public prosecutor for Negri Sembilan and Malacca. Between 1947 and 1952, he was successively senior assistant registrar of the Supreme Courts of Ipoh, Penang and Kuala Lumpur. In 1955, he was appointed district judge in Singapore and then commissioner of estate duties (1957). Ambrose was elevated to the Bench as PUISNE JUDGE in 1958. Suffering from arthritis, he retired in 1968, before reaching the constitutional retirement age for judges in Singapore.

American Chamber of Commerce The American Chamber of Commerce (AmCham) in Singapore has its origins in the American Association, formed in 1917 by a group of businessmen to serve the interests of American businesses. This association lasted until the late 1960s. By then, American investments in Singapore had grown substantially, especially as the economy became more industry-based. Many oil-exploration, refining, and heavy industrial

manufacturers as well as financial institutions were creating a bigger presence, and a new organization was needed. A meeting with the US Embassy in 1969 led to the formation of an American Business Committee under the auspices of the American Association. It was not until 1973 that a separate, independent body was created. Called the American Business Council (ABC), it was registered as a trade society and employers' group, with an office at the US Trade Center at Yen San Building, Orchard Road.

In 1983, the ABC decided that one of its responsibilities was to foster a positive attitude toward American businesses operating in Singapore. Members were encouraged to support American cultural events, such as the New York Philharmonic Orchestra performances and the American Classical Film Festival. The good response led to the formation of the Cultural Affairs Program, which won the Friend of the Arts Award from the National Arts Council on many occasions.

In December 1992, the Board of Governors decided to upgrade the business council into a Chamber of Commerce. On 15 September 1993, ABC officially became the American Chamber of Commerce, whose mission is to promote the interests of members in Singapore and the region by providing advocacy, business information and networking opportunities. The group has more than 1,400 members, many of whom serve in 22 active committees.

American Club, The Established in September 1948, The American Club is located at Scotts Road. It has expanded beyond the original building with its Scotts Road frontage to a much larger presence with rear access from Claymore Hill. The club is one of several community organizations under the umbrella of the American Association of Singapore, set up in 1917, and it houses the offices of the other bodies under the association. The club provides social and community service activities, and its membership in 2005 included some 60 nationalities.

amusement parks In the 1920s and 1930s three entertainment parks were opened in Singapore—NEW WORLD, Happy World (later renamed GAY WORLD) and GREAT WORLD.

The New World amusement park opened in 1923. Located on Kitchener Road, it was built by brothers Ong Boon Tat and Ong Peng Hock. Within three months, it had made a name for itself as a venue for boxing and wrestling contests, variety shows and opera performances. Located in Kim Seng Road, Great World Amusement Park was founded by Lee Choon Seng shortly after the opening of New World. It was then bought by SHAW BROTHERS and Ong Peng Hock. Shaw

Brothers subsequently became its sole owner. Happy World, located on Mountbatten Road, was started by George Lee in 1937.

Although each had its own unique features, the three 'worlds' were similar in many ways. Decked out in bright lights, with blaring music and gaudy surroundings, they provided fun and games for the whole family. *Getai*, or open-air stages, were used for acts such as comic skits, talent contests and song-and-dance items, while the restaurants were favoured for weddings and other celebrations. Sporting events such as boxing and wrestling were also popular. The stalls sold everything from household wares and textiles, to groceries, sports goods, and food and beverages. There were also the ubiquitous gaming stalls and gambling dens, as well as carnival rides.

In the 1950s, as other forms of entertainment gained popularity, the 'worlds' began a slow decline, and have all been demolished, although Great World is recalled in the name of Great World City, a shopping mall built on the same site.

Anderson, Sir John (1852–1924) Businessman. Born in London, John Anderson came to Singapore with his parents in 1859 and was educated at Raffles Institution before joining the civil service. In 1871, he left to become a clerk in BOUSTEAD & COMPANY. Early in 1876, Anderson joined GUTHRIE & CO. as an assistant, and quickly rose to become a partner and, later, director of the firm. By then, he was a prominent figure in the business world, playing a major role in the development of Malaya's RUBBER industry. Anderson was also very active in the public affairs of Singapore. He spoke fluent Malay, was a member of the Volunteer Fire Brigade, and from 1886, served various terms as a member of the Singapore Legislative Council. During his years of public service, Anderson was best known for chairing the Opium Commission. In 1912, he received a knighthood in recognition of his years of public service. He returned to London in the same year.

Anderson, Sir John (1858–1918) Colonial official. Sir John Anderson was governor of the Straits Settlements (1904–11), after Sir FRANK SWETTENHAM. He was lauded for beginning a new order of things in Malaya and is remembered for his municipal housing policy. The creation of back lanes between city tenements gave much needed space for movement and helped curb the prevailing high death rates due to unsanitary conditions caused by overcrowding. He was responsible for the expropriation of the Tanjong Pagar dock as he firmly believed in the future of the port and advocated that the government should acquire it. This was a starting point in a number of public improvements to strengthen Singapore's

Sir John Anderson (1858–1918)

commercial competitiveness which included the construction of the railway to Johor as well as the completion of the VICTORIA MEMORIAL HALL in October 1905.

Anderson was also credited with fixing the value of the Straits dollar (*see* CURRENCY), which served as a steadying influence for trade. Anderson was also responsible for various changes in the civil service. He initiated the practice of appointing civil servants to the judicial Bench. During his administration, he officially opened the bridge named after him at the mouth of the Singapore River.

Ando Kozo (dates unknown) Director of Medical Services in Singapore and Malaya during the JAPANESE OCCUPATION. In 1912, Dr Ando Kozo graduated from Singapore's King Edward VII Medical School (*see* KING EDWARD VII COLLEGE OF MEDICINE). He had a hospital in Middle Road in the heart of the pre-war Japanese community's business district, and was elected president of the Singapore section of the British Medical Association's Malaya Branch. In 1937, the local Singapore medical association named its golf trophy after Ando, who was a keen golfer.

According to local doctors TJ DANARAJ, KHOO OON TEIK, and J. B. Van Cuylenburg, who worked during the Japanese Occupation, Ando was a kind man who knew most of the senior staff in the hospitals from his pre-war days, and 'helped them whenever it was possible for him to do so'. With the closure of King Edward VII College of Medicine during the Japanese Occupation, he helped medical undergraduates who had had their studies interrupted by the war. He also played a role in setting up the Marei Ika Daigaku (Malaya Medical College) in Singapore, to take the place of the College of Medicine during the Japanese Occupation.

Ang, Andrew (1946–) Judge. Andrew Ang was educated at the University of Singapore where he graduated with an LLB in 1971. He subsequently went to Harvard Law School to pursue a masters degree on a Ford Foundation Scholarship. Ang then returned to teach at the University of Singapore's Faculty of Law, and left for private practice three years later. He joined the firm of LEE & LEE and rose to become senior partner and head of its corporate and banking department. Chambers' global directory, *The World's Leading Lawyers* (2002 and 2003 editions) named him one of the two lawyers in the top tier of banking and finance practice in Singapore. In 2000, Ang was awarded the Public Service Medal. He was for many years external examiner of the Faculty of Law, National University of Singapore. Ang has held directorships in the Land Transport Authority, Isetan (Singapore) and Keppel Corporation. On 15 May 2004, he was appointed JUDICIAL COMMISSIONER and was elevated to judge of the Supreme Court on 15 May 2005.

Ang, Belinda (1954–) Judge. Educated at the Methodist Girls' School, Belinda Ang read law at University College of Wales in Aberystwyth. In 1978, she was called to the Bar at Middle Temple. She then went on to do a masters degree in law at University College London where she graduated with distinction in 1979. On her return to Singapore, Ang joined the firm of Godwin and Co., and became a partner within five years (1985). She then left to establish Ang and Partners with Loo Dip Seng and Goh Kok Leong. From 1985 to 2002, Ang was shipping partner of the firm and developed a formidable reputation as a shipping lawyer. On 1 February 2002, she was appointed JUDICIAL COMMISSIONER and in January 2003, she was made a judge of the Supreme Court.

Ang, Sunny (1939–1967) One of Singapore's most famous criminals, convicted on 18 May 1965 for the murder of bar waitress Jenny Cheok Cheng Kid, whose body was never found. The prosecution alleged that on 27 August 1963, Sunny Ang had hired a sampan (small boat) to

Sunny Ang: hanged in 1967 for the murder of his girlfriend during a diving trip.

Ang Chwee Chai

Ang Kok Peng

Ang Peng Siong

Ang Mo Kio: new town development, the first to incorporate five-room flats in a slab block.

bring him and Cheok to Sisters Islands south of Singapore, ostensibly to collect corals; but the real motive was murder—she was heavily insured. Ang was bankrupt whereas Cheok had been insured for a total of $450,000 with several insurance companies. Some of Cheok's policies were renewed on the morning of her death, although Ang's were not. The beneficiaries were Ang's mother and Cheok's estate.

Ang had helped Cheok to don the diving gear and let the novice diver descend alone. When she failed to surface, he did not go down to search for her. Moreover, he filed the insurance claims less than 24 hours after her disappearance. One of Cheok's flippers was later found with the heel strap cut in two places by a sharp instrument. The prosecution relied entirely on circumstantial evidence. The jury found Ang guilty of murder and he was sentenced to death. He was unsuccessful in applying for leave to appeal to the PRIVY COUNCIL and was hanged on 6 February 1967.

Ang Chwee Chai (1910–1995) Photographer. An early member of the PHOTOGRAPHIC SOCIETY OF SINGAPORE (PSS) and its precursor, the Singapore Camera Club, Ang Chwee Chai was a recipient of the Public Service Star (1964) and CULTURAL MEDALLION (1983). He was the second president of the PSS (serving 15 terms), honorary president of both the Singapore Malay Photographic Society and the Nanyang University Photographic Society. Noted for his colour slides and cine films, Ang received the Honorary Excellence Distinction from the International Federation of Photographic Art (FIAP). He also chaired the Photographic Art Advisory Committee of the Ministry of Culture in the 1980s. The Photographic Society of Singapore conferred an Honorary Fellowship on Ang and named a memorial award after him.

Ang Kok Peng (1927–1997) Academic, politician and diplomat. Born in Taiping, Perak, Ang Kok Peng was educated at the University of Malaya, where he obtained his BSc (1950), MSc (1952) and PhD

(1955) in chemistry. He was awarded the Raffles College Scholarship (1947–50) and the Queen's Fellowship (1956–57 and 1959–60). In 1952, Ang joined the Department of Chemistry of the University of Malaya and rose to the rank of professor in 1976, specializing in anti-pollution research. He was head of the department from 1971 to 1988.

In 1968, Ang was appointed Singapore's first ambassador to Japan, a position he held until 1971. In 1972, he won the Crawford seat under the People's Action Party banner and was appointed minister of state for communications (1972–74) and then minister of state for health (1974–76). He retired from politics in 1988.

Ang was president of the Singapore National Academy of Science (1978–92) and chairman of the People Scholarship Fund, of which he was founder.

Ang Mo Kio Seventh 'new town' developed by the HOUSING & DEVELOPMENT BOARD (HDB). It covers an area of some 640 ha of undulating terrain bounded by Lorong Kinchir in the south, Serangoon Garden Estate in the east and Yio Chu Kang in the north. Ang Mo Kio is laid out in six neighbourhoods, each with between 4,000 and 6,000 housing units. There is a 24-ha town centre in the heart of the town. Ang Mo Kio is unique among HDB estates because it was the first one with five-room flats in a slab block rather than in a point block. There are almost 48,000 flats in Ang Mo Kio housing over 164,000 residents.

'Ang Mo Kio' means 'Red Hair Bridge' in Hokkien. Local lore has it that the name refers to the bridge built by John Turnbull Thomson while he was surveying the area in the 1840s. 'Ang mo kwee' is the Hokkien term for 'red-haired devils', a colloquial term to describe Westerners, and it was thought that they named Thomson's bridge after him—the bridge built by the 'red-haired devil'. However, maps that pre-date Thomson's arrival in Singapore record the name of the area as 'Amokiah'.

Ang Mo Kio-Thye Hua Kwan Hospital Rehabilitation and geriatric care hospital. Patients at this hospital do not require the facilities of an acute general hospital. Most suffer from stroke and need relatively less complicated treatment. Hence, the hospital's main role is to offer rehabilitative care to help patients recuperate and regain their functional abilities.

In 2002, the management of the hospital was transferred to two voluntary welfare organizations—Thye Hua Kwan Moral Society and Chee Hoon Kog Moral Promotion Society which, in turn, invited the HINDU ENDOWMENTS BOARD and JAMIYAH to come on board as shareholders. The hospital caters for both private and subsidized patients (*see* HOSPITALS).

Ang Peng Siong (1962–) Sportsman. National swimmer and two-time Olympian, Ang Peng Siong recorded the world's best time (22.69 sec) for the 50-m freestyle in 1982. Unfortunately, that was before the event was officially recognized in the Olympics. A repeat of the feat in Seoul (1988), when the event was finally introduced to the Games, would have given him a bronze medal.

The son of 1964 judo Olympian Ang Teck Bee, Peng Siong made his international debut in 1978 at the Asian Games at age 16. He represented Singapore at the Olympics in Los Angeles (1984) and Seoul (1988). In Los Angeles, he won the consolation final of the 100-m freestyle in a national record of 51.09 sec. His medal haul includes a gold at the Asian Games in New Delhi in 1982 and a bronze at the Asian Games in Seoul in 1986. He was named Sportsman of the Year (1982, 1983, 1984) by the Singapore National Olympic Council, and was inducted into the SINGAPORE SPORTS COUNCIL HALL OF FAME.

In 1982, he won the gold medal at the US Nationals in 22.69 sec. Since 2000, he has been a regular at the World Masters event, one of the world's most important swimming competitions. In 2002, at the age 40, he clocked 24.64 sec for the 50-m freestyle at the World Masters in Christchurch, which was just two seconds off his time when he was 20.

He has been the head coach of the Singapore swimming team at various Southeast Asian (SEA) Games, Asian Games, Commonwealth Games and Olympic Games, and joined the Board of Governors of the SINGAPORE SPORTS SCHOOL.

Anglicans Anglicanism first arrived in Singapore with settlers from the British East India Company in 1819. It was the usual practice for English settlers, many of them members of the Church of England (the Anglican Church), to establish churches to accommodate their devotions, and as early as 1823, Sir Stamford Raffles earmarked the land on which ST ANDREW'S CATHEDRAL now stands as a site for the building of a church. It was not until nearly 11 years later, however, that construction began. In the meantime, an Anglican priest, the Rev Robert Burn, had arrived in 1826 and was conducting services in the Mission Chapel belonging to the London Missionary Society (at Bras

ANGLICANS: BISHOPS OF SINGAPORE	
1909–27	Charles James Ferguson-Davie
1927–41	Basil Colby Roberts
1941–49	John Leonard Wilson
1949–61	Henry Wolfe Baines
1961–66	Cyril Kenneth Sansbury
1966–82	Joshua Chiu Ban It
1982–2000	Dr Moses Tay Leng Kong
2000–	Dr John Chew Hiang Chea

Source: Anglican Diocese of Singapore

Anglicans: Bishop Leonard Wilson, right, with Dr Chelliah and Canon R.K.S. Adams.

Basah Road). This represented the founding of the Anglican Church in Singapore. St Andrew's Cathedral was finally completed in 1837 and named after the patron saint of Scotland.

Because of the size of the area under the purview of the See of Calcutta, and the corresponding administrative challenges, a Diocese of Singapore, Labuan and Sarawak was formed in 1855 as a missionary diocese of the Archdiocese of Canterbury. In 1881, the Right Rev George Frederick Hose was appointed as its first bishop. By 1909, the diocese was reorganized as the Diocese of Singapore with the Right Rev Charles Ferguson-Davie as the first bishop of Singapore. In 1966 the church had its first local bishop, the Right Rev Joshua Chiu Ban It (*see* table).

In 1996, the Province of South East Asia was established, comprising the Dioceses of Singapore, West Malaysia, Sabah and Kuching, with the then Bishop of Singapore, the Most Rev Dr Moses Tay, appointed as the first provincial archbishop.

Since its early days, the Anglican Church in Singapore has been active in social welfare work and in education. In 1842, the first girls' school in Singapore, ST MARGARET'S GIRLS' SCHOOL, was founded, and in 1914, ST ANDREW'S SCHOOL; both

Anglicans: Stained glass at St George's Church.

were under the Anglican umbrella. St Andrew's Junior College was established in 1976. In 1913, the first diocesan clinic was opened in Chinatown and in 1923, St Andrew's Mission Hospital for women was set up in Erskine Road.

Today, there are nine Anglican schools in Singapore and the church fulfils a social welfare role through St Andrew's Mission Hospital, clinics, several care centres, homes for the aged, childcare centres and kindergartens. The diocese also runs a crisis relief response arm, the Anglican Crisis Relief Outreach and Support, Singapore (ACROSS), to cope with regional emergencies.

The Diocese of Singapore encompasses not just Singapore, but also the Archdeaconry of Thailand and the Deaneries of Indonesia, Cambodia, Vietnam, Laos and Nepal.

In Singapore, there are 26 parishes across the island with services in many languages and Chinese dialects and a total membership of about 18,000. After St Andrew's Cathedral, the biggest parishes are the Church of Our Saviour in Queenstown, St John's-St Margaret's in Dover Road and the Chapel of Resurrection in Potong Pasir.

Anglo-Chinese School Also known by the abbreviation 'ACS', the group of Anglo-Chinese Schools comprises the primary schools ACS Primary and ACS (Junior); secondary schools ACS (Barker Road) and ACS (Independent); Anglo-Chinese Junior College; and ACS (International) which offers secondary and post-secondary education.

Founded as a boys' school on 1 March 1886 by Bishop William Fitzjames Oldham of the American Methodist Mission, ACS began with 13 pupils in a small shophouse at Amoy Street. In the following year, owing to an increase in enrolment, the school moved to Coleman Street, which was the location of the first Methodist Chapel. In subsequent years, as ACS continued to expand, it moved into a series of different premises, including Cairnhill and Barker Road. The latter was the first school campus in Singapore to have an Olympic-sized swimming pool.

By 1977, ACS had split into the two primary schools, a secondary school, and the junior college at Rochester Park. Following the government's intitiative to allow schools which excelled academically to be run as INDEPENDENT SCHOOLS, ACS was renamed ACS (Independent) in 1988. ACS (Independent) moved to premises in Dover Road in 1992. After lobbying from alumni, however, a second secondary school was maintained at the Barker Road campus, and is known as ACS (Barker Road).

In 2006, ACS (Independent) became the first school in Singapore to offer the International Baccalaureate Programme as

part of the INTEGRATED PROGRAMME. In the same year, girls were admitted for the first time to the school, but only after completing four years of secondary education in other schools. A private school, ACS (International), was opened in January 2005, and accepts an intake of local and international students. ACS (International) students take the International General Certificate of Secondary Education in their fourth year, then go on to take a two-year International Baccalaureate diploma.

ACS maintains a strong alumni network through its Old Boys' Association. A number of leaders from the fields of politics, business, sports, music and drama are ACS alumni, including former deputy prime minister of Singapore Dr GOH KENG SWEE; President S.R. NATHAN; Cabinet ministers NG ENG HEN, VIVIAN BALAKRISHNAN and THARMAN SHANMUGARATNAM; opposition politician and member of Parliament CHIAM SEE TONG; and national swimmer ANG PENG SIONG.

Anglo-Dutch Treaty Treaty settling territorial and trade disputes between Britain and the Netherlands in Asia. It is also known as the Treaty of London. Under this treaty, BENCOOLEN was ceded to the Dutch, MALACCA was ceded to the British, and Dutch objections to the British settlement in Singapore were withdrawn.

Britain's objective in negotiations was to ensure a secure passage to China and freedom to trade in as much of Southeast Asia as possible. The Dutch, on the other hand, sought to preserve their own monopoly. The trade provisions of the treaty did not have a lasting effect. However, the agreement to divide insular Southeast Asia politically endured, even though there was no historical basis to it. The treaty is responsible for the fact that Malaysia and Singapore were historically in the British sphere of influence; while Indonesia was in the Dutch sphere.

The settlement of Singapore was initially not a priority for the negotiators. Indeed, the British EAST INDIA COMPANY would have preferred to keep Fort

Anglicans: Rev Joshua Chiu Ban It, first local Anglican bishop.

Anglo-Chinese School: school emblem at the old Amoy Street site (top), and Barker Road premises.

Anson by-election: J.B. Jeyaretnam on a victory tour.

Marlborough (Bencoolen, present-day Bengkulu in Sumatra) even though it was neither strategically located nor profitable. While willing to cede Singapore, the British refused to deliver it directly to the Dutch and would only consent to return it to the Sultan of Johor from whom they had originally taken it.

The treaty provided for mutual conferment of most favoured nation status in the East. Neither party would impose any duties on trade goods more than double what they imposed on their own nationals. Treaties with third parties to restrict each other's trade were also prohibited. British access to the Spice Islands (present day Moluccas) was granted but the Dutch reserved their monopoly rights there. With respect to territorial disputes in Southeast Asia, the Malay Peninsula would be under the British while Sumatra, the Karimun Islands and all islands south of the Strait of Singapore would belong to the Dutch. Neither party would make any treaties with rulers or states in the other's sphere. Notably, despite its size, Borneo was not covered by this treaty.

Signed in London on 17 March 1824, the treaty was ratified by the British Parliament on 30 April 1824 and by the Dutch on 2 June 1824.

Arab Street: one of many textile shops in the area.

Angullia family Ebrahim Mohamed Salleh Angullia came to Singapore from Surat, India around 1838 and started an import-export business. The business prospered and was managed subsequently by his son, Eusof Ebrahim Angullia, grandson Mohamed Salleh Eusoff Angullia and great-grandson Ahmad Mohamed Salleh Angullia. Mohamed Salleh Eusoff established a WAKAF (endowment) in 1898. He bequeathed his properties in Selegie Road, Wilkie Road and in the Rochore area to be part of the *wakaf*. The funds were distributed to social and charitable causes in Singapore, Mecca, Medina, Baghdad and Randir, India. The Angullia *wakaf* is one of the largest in Singapore. The family also founded a number of mosques in Singapore, such as the Angullia Mosque in Serangoon Road, which was built in 1890. In 1934, another Angullia Mosque was built in Orchard Road but was demolished in 1988.

annual wage supplement A single annual payment supplementary to an employee's total annual wage. It is subject to negotiation and mutual agreement between employer and employees or their trade unions. The annual wage supplement (commonly referred to by its abbreviation 'AWS') is often equivalent to a month's pay, and so is often known colloquially as the '13th month bonus'. Employers may negotiate with employees or trade unions to reduce the supplement if business is exceptionally poor, making it an important component of the flexible wage system proposed for Singapore.

Anson by-election Landmark by-election in which the PEOPLE'S ACTION PARTY'S (PAP) monopoly of Parliament was broken. Since the 1950s, Anson had been a hotly contested constituency. In 1979, C.V. DEVAN NAIR, then secretary-general of the NATIONAL TRADES UNION CONGRESS (NTUC), contested a by-election in the Anson constituency to fill the vacancy left by the death of the PAP's P. Govindaswamy. Nair retained this seat during the 1980 general election but had to resign it when he was elected Singapore's third president in October 1981. On 31 October 1981, a by-election was held to fill the vacancy. The two contestants were the PAP's Pang Kim Hin and J. B. JEYARETNAM of the WORKERS' PARTY. In the first opposition party victory in more than 13 years, Jeyaretnam garnered 7,012 votes or 51.93 per cent of the valid votes cast, to become MEMBER OF PARLIAMENT for Anson. He retained his seat in the 1984 general election but was forced to vacate it in 1986 due to a criminal conviction.

Various explanations have been advanced for the loss of Anson. The PAP might have miscalculated in choosing Pang to face an opposition heavyweight. Some felt that he did not connect effectively with

the working-class constituents, and failed to use Anson's grassroots leaders in his campaign. Some Anson residents, particularly those living in Blair Plain, saw the election as an opportunity to express discontent over the fact that they had not been given priority for Housing & Development Board flats when their old homes were demolished for a new Port of Singapore Authority container complex.

Anwarul Haque (1939–) Sportsman. Anwarul Haque began representing Singapore in hockey in 1957. In 1960, he was on the Singapore team that triumphed 1–0 over the New Zealand Olympic hockey team—the same one which had routed Singapore four years earlier at the Melbourne Olympics. He was an Olympian (Tokyo, 1964) and Asian Games representative (Jakarta, 1962; Bangkok, 1970).

Two years after representing Singapore at the Asian Games in Jakarta, Anwarul joined the Malaysian team—which at the time included Singapore—in Tokyo for the 1964 Olympics. But he fell victim to a selection policy that left him on the sidelines throughout the competition.

Though success eluded Singapore at the 1970 Asian Games, and goalkeeper Anwarul endured an injury, his performances were internationally recognized. He was nominated for the Asian All-Stars team, though the tour never materialized; and he was presented with a Merit Award by the Singapore National Olympic Council. Anwarul played for Singapore in the 1971 Southeast Asian Peninsular (SEAP) Games—which later came to be known as the Southeast Asian (SEA) Games—when hockey was introduced for the first time. Singapore took the silver medal behind Malaysia's gold.

Anwarul became a lawyer, and president of the SINGAPORE CRICKET CLUB.

APEC *See* ASIA-PACIFIC ECONOMIC COOPERATION.

Apsaras Arts Indian classical dance company. Founded by Sri Lankan immigrant artistes Sathyalingam and his wife Neila, Apsaras Arts has been in operation since 1977. Besides being involved in the annual CHINGAY parades, Apsaras Arts also promotes Indian dance through participation in local television programmes and community centre performances. Despite being well known for its semi-classical dance performances, the company places emphasis on mastering the classical dance form, Bharathanatyam.

Arab Street Located in the KAMPONG GLAM area, which was designated by Sir Stamford Raffles as a Muslim settlement, Arab Street was named after the Arab traders who were among the first to arrive in Singapore, and mainly sold textiles and spices there. The street also attracted Indian Muslim merchants, who specialized in the textile and jewellery trades. These trades continue in the street to this day. Because many Javanese also settled in the same area, the Chinese called this street 'Javanese Street'.

Arabs Almost all Arabs in Singapore trace their origins to Hadramaut, Yemen. Commonly known as 'Hadramis', they were distinguished by the enterprising traits of establishing business networks and propagating Islam in Southeast Asia. Hadramis settled in the KAMPONG GLAM area, as directed by the 1822 city plan drawn up by Lieutenant Phillip Jackson.

Among the earliest Hadramis to arrive were two wealthy merchants from Palembang in Sumatra, Syed Mohammed Harun Aljunied and his nephew, SYED OMAR ALI ALJUNIED. Other families, such as the Alkaff, Alsagoff and Bamadhaj arrived later (see ALJUNIED FAMILY, ALKAFF FAMILY and ALSAGOFF FAMILY). Many of the Arab families came to Singapore after having lived for several generations in the Dutch East Indies (present-day Indonesia). They had made their wealth in Indonesia and were familiar with the customs and language of the Malays. They thus integrated easily with the Malays in Singapore.

By the late 1860s, prominent Hadramis had assumed important roles within society, such as justices of the peace, philanthropists, municipal commissioners, as well as religious leaders. They also owned properties, many of which were transformed into public charitable trusts (see WAKAF). MADRASAHS, such as Madrasah Alsagoff Al-Arabiah, and mosques, such as OMAR KAMPONG MELAKA MOSQUE, were built upon these trusts.

The wealth of the Hadramis was severely diminished by the Rent Control Act enacted by the British in 1947 which imposed restrictions on the renting of properties. In 1966, the Land Acquisition Act empowered the government to acquire land for urban renewal. This further reduced Hadrami property ownership. Though their economic influence has waned, Hadramis such as SYED ISA MOHAMAD SEMAIT (Mufti of Singapore), Syed Abdillah al-Jufri (former president of PERGAS), and Umar Alkhatib (scholar and teacher) have played key roles as religious leaders in post-Independence Singapore.

The Arab Association of Singapore (Al-Wehdah Al-Arabiah Bi-Singhafura), established in 1947, seeks to protect the interests of the Hadramis and promote awareness of their language as well as culture and identity. According to the census of 2000, there were just over 7,000 Arabs in Singapore, but according to unofficial estimates by the Arab Association, the number is closer to 10,000. This disparity is due to the fact that some Arabs are classified as Malays in official documentation.

Arasu, V.T. (1926–) Journalist. Born V. Thirunavukkarasu in India, Arasu distinguished himself as a journalist, editor, and proponent of the Tamil language. He came to Singapore in 1951 with five years' experience in journalism, and joined the leading Tamil daily, TAMIL MURASU, as a sub-editor. Arasu's columns had a loyal following. He played a prominent role in the cultural and educational movements of the 1950s and 1960s under the guidance of Tamil Murasu editor GOVINDASAMY SARANGAPANY. Arasu left Tamil Murasu in 1958 to join the civil service as an information officer (Tamil) when preparations were under way to make Tamil one of Singapore's official languages. He edited Tamil current affairs weeklies Kannottam and Kannadi (Mirror) alongside other publications from the Ministry of Culture, where he also served as the head of the Media Relations Department.

In 1989, he returned to Tamil Murasu as chief editor, updating the paper's design and overseeing an increase in circulation. When the paper was struggling due to increased costs he was instrumental in its sale to SINGAPORE PRESS HOLDINGS to ensure its continuity and growth. He was chairman of the HINDU ADVISORY BOARD (1984–86) and president of the Tamil Language and Cultural Society (1984–98). He was also chairman of the Tamil Language Council—a national organization supported by the government for the promotion of Tamil—from its launch in 1999 until 2005.

Arasu was the co-author of Singapore: an Illustrated History, 1941–1984 (1984). Arasu has also been awarded the Efficiency Medal (1985) and the Public Service Medallion (PBM) (1999); and the Association of Singapore Tamil Writers honoured him with the Tamizhavel Award (2005).

arbitration A form of alternative dispute resolution. Since the early 1990s, the Singapore JUDICIARY has promoted arbitration as an important and effective form of commercial dispute resolution.

The two primary laws governing arbitration are the Arbitration Act (for domestic arbitration) and the International Arbitration Act (IAA). Arbitrators—who need not be legally trained—preside. The main advantages of arbitration are: the relative flexibility and informality of the proceedings; the experience and knowledge of arbitrators selected; the finality of the decision reached; the privacy of the proceedings; the confidentiality of the award; party autonomy; and the parties' ability to control the proceedings.

An arbitration is 'international' if at least one party has a registered place of business outside Singapore; or if the place of arbitration, the place where the contract is to be performed, or the place with which the subject matter of the dispute is most closely connected, is outside the state where the parties have their place of business. It is also 'international' if the parties expressly agree that the subject matter of the arbitration agreement relates to more than one country.

The IAA adopts the Model Law on International Commercial Arbitration adopted by the United Nations Commission on International Trade Law (UNCITRAL) on 21 June 1985). The Singapore International Arbitration Centre (SIAC) has its own Arbitration Rules that are largely based on UNCITRAL Arbitration Rules and the Rules of the London Court of International Arbitration.

In May 2001, the SIAC Domestic Arbitration Rules were enacted to cater for the increase in the number of cases being referred for arbitration and to give the SIAC greater supervision over the activities of arbitrators.

archaeological sites See box.

architecture See box.

Area Licensing Scheme and Restricted Zone
Singapore implemented the world's first road pricing scheme on 2 June 1975; it was applied to the Central Business District (CBD), which became known also as the Restricted Zone. To enter the zone during the morning rush hours on weekdays and Saturdays, cars and taxis had to buy and display area licences ($3 for a daily licence and $60 for a monthly licence) on their windscreens. To encourage more efficient use of cars, car and taxi pools (a driver and three passengers) were given free entry into the Restricted Zone. Police manned the entry points demarcated by gantry signs and noted down the licence plate numbers of vehicles violating the scheme.

The Area Licensing Scheme went through many revisions to accommodate changing traffic patterns. The restricted zone was enlarged to 720 ha, up from 670 ha, and the licence fees were adjusted four times. In 1989, all vehicles except emergency vehicles were required to purchase area licences—car and taxi pool exemptions

V.T. Arasu: with Tamil Murasu newspaper.

Area Licensing Scheme and Restricted Zone: gantry in the CBD, 1975.

Armenian Church

were withdrawn. The hours of operation were extended to include the evening rush hours in 1989 and eventually to the whole working day in 1994. The Area Licensing Scheme was replaced by the ELECTRONIC ROAD PRICING system in 1998.

Armed Forces Council Body set up for the administration of matters relating to the SINGAPORE ARMED FORCES. The Armed Forces Council (AFC) was established in 1972 under the Singapore Armed Forces Act, and is chaired by the defence minister. Other members include any minister assigned to assist the principal defence minister, the permanent secretary (or secretaries) of the MINISTRY OF DEFENCE, the chief of defence force, the chief of army, the chief of air force, the chief of navy, and up to four more members appointed by the president. In appointing members or revoking their membership, the president acts in concurrence with the prime minister's advice.

The AFC also has legal responsibilities. The council can call for summary trials of senior officers. The chairman of the AFC may appoint a Senior Disciplinary Committee consisting of at least three AFC members to carry out summary trials of officers who are of or above the rank of brigadier-general, as well as summary trials of colonels in certain circumstances. The AFC also has the power to quash or substitute findings or sentences by a disciplinary officer, and to order retrials. The appointment of key legal personnel such as the judge advocate general; director, Legal Services of the Singapore Armed Forces; military prosecutors and registrars for the Military Court of Appeal or subordinate military courts is done by the AFC.

Armenian Church Located on Hill Street, the church's full name is the Armenian Apostolic Church of St Gregory the Illuminator, but is popularly known as the Armenian Church. The ARMENIANS were the first Christian community to erect a permanent place of worship in Singapore. Though never large, the community was prosperous.

Armenian Church: tombstone of Nanajan (Anna) Sarkies, wife of prominent Armenian Johannes Shanazar Sarkies.

In 1834, application was made for land on which to build a church and a lease was granted for a site at the foot of Fort Canning. The church was built at a cost of 5,058 Spanish dollars, half donated by Singapore Armenians, a quarter from Armenians in India and Java and the remaining sum from Chinese merchants and other residents. The consecration was celebrated on 26 March 1836.

The church is a fine example of the work of GEORGE D. COLEMAN, the first British-trained architect to practise in the settlement, and one of Singapore's most outstanding classical buildings. The design bears the hallmarks of originality in conception and sensitivity to the tropical environment which Coleman exercised in all of his work. Its most striking features are developed from the Greek cruciform plan. The tower and spire were added in c. 1853, when the roofline may have been altered from the original dome shape to the present hipped form.

A gazetted national monument since 6 July 1973, the building was fully restored in the early 1990s.

Armenians The Armenians were one of the first minorities to settle in Singapore. None of the community came from Armenia itself, but were descendants of Armenians forcibly taken to Persia (present-day Iran) by Shah Abbas I in the early 1600s. From 1820, these descendants came directly to Singapore from Persia, or first spent time in India or elsewhere in Southeast Asia.

The Armenian community in Singapore remained tiny. In 1823, Armenians accounted for a mere 16 out of Singapore's population of 10,683. By 1845, there were 63 Armenians and in 1881 the total was 76. The community increased gradually, but never surpassed 100 at any one time, a figure reached in the 1920s and in 1947.

Of the 670 Armenians who lived in Singapore from 1820 to 2004, only 184 remained for over 25 years, yet they left a legacy out of all proportion to their numbers. Deeply religious, they were conducting church services in the early 1820s, and in 1835 they constructed the first permanent Christian church in Singapore: the Armenian Apostolic Church of St Gregory the Illuminator (*see* ARMENIAN CHURCH). Until 1938, a resident priest who was sent out from Iran looked after the spiritual needs of the Armenian community.

In the early years, most Armenians lived in the vicinity of Commercial Square and Hill Street, but later moved to Oxley Hill and further afield. Splendid homes including CATCHICK MOSES' residence, the Pavilion on Oxley Hill; Buitenzorg off Paterson Road; Eskbank in Tanglin; Mount Narcis off Tanjong Pagar Road and Zetland House on Armenian Street, were owned by Armenians. None of these properties is still standing.

archaeological sites After their arrival in Singapore in 1819, the British recorded the discovery of numerous archaeological remains: brick ruins, Chinese and local ceramics, and Chinese coins dating from the Tang and Song dynasties on Fort Canning Hill; a large inscription in a script which has been palaeographically dated to the 9th–14th centuries at the mouth of the SINGAPORE RIVER; and an earthen rampart about 5 m wide, 3 m high and approximately 1.5 km long, flanked by a natural stream in the plain and a dry artificial ditch which ran uphill. Almost all these remains were quickly obliterated as the new settlement grew. The only other remnants of life on the island prior to Raffles' arrival which attracted attention during the colonial period were some gold ornaments found in 1928 during the construction of a reservoir on FORT CANNING.

Archaeological research began in earnest in 1984. Seven sites with evidence of 14th-century activity have been excavated between the Singapore River and Stamford Road, the seaward edge of the PADANG, and the inland side of Fort Canning Hill. The ancient settlement within these boundaries covered approximately 85 ha.

The PHC and EMP sites
Between 1984 and 1994, excavation was limited to sites in Fort Canning Park. In the ten years which followed, the pace of excavation increased. Parliament House Complex (PHC) and Empress Place (EMP) along the north bank of the Singapore River were excavated in 1994–95 and 1998. Colombo Court, across High Street from PHC, was also investigated.

PHC and EMP were on or near the 14th-century riverbank. Large quantities of 14th-century artefacts including pottery, metal, glass, and organic remains such as bones and tortoise shell were recovered. A unique find at EMP was a lead statue of a man riding a horse (*see* PRE-MODERN HISTORY). Besides Chinese coins, a few metal coins from late 13th-century Sri Lanka (*1*) were also found, demonstrating

1

2

that Singapore had commercial links with the island as well as with India, Indonesia, and China.

Vietnamese and Thai ceramics of the 15th century from PHC and EMP provide further evidence of the wide reach of ancient Singapore's trade. At EMP a substantial quantity of late Ming porcelain was recovered (2), proving that the settlement was not completely abandoned until about 1600.

OPH, SCC, STA and FTC excavations

In 2003 and 2004, three more sites were examined. At Old Parliament House (OPH) little controlled excavation was possible due to construction work. Coordination with the PUBLIC WORKS DEPARTMENT and the contractors, however, made it possible to obtain a large amount of artefacts with reasonably good information on their provenance.

The other two sites excavated were SINGAPORE CRICKET CLUB (SCC) and ST ANDREW'S CATHEDRAL (STA). At SCC only a small excavation was permitted, but the results were significant. At STA it was possible to work for nearly 12 months. This project was completed in mid-September 2004. A large quantity of data was obtained from this site. STA was the first site that was excavated near the probable location of the OLD LINES of Singapore that formed the northern boundary of the 14th-century settlement.

Each of the seven 14th-century sites has unique characteristics. Fort Canning (FTC) has yielded many rare or unique objects. In addition to the gold ornaments found in 1928, several other artefacts support the idea that the legend of BUKIT LARANGAN (Forbidden Hill) is not a myth, but a folk memory of an actual centre of royal power.

Analysis of the finds

Analysis of glass from Fort Canning indicates that it consists of two different types, both of which are probably of Chinese origin. One category consists of over 10,000 coiled beads (3). Shards of vessels, fragments of bangles and globules belong to a separate category. The vessels are particularly complex in design. Although early Chinese glass-making was not known for its technical sophistication, it is likely that a small but highly specialized glass-making workshop developed somewhere in southern China during the Song–Yuan period, perhaps in Quanzhou. In the

14th century, these shards were recycled on Fort Canning, perhaps in a palace workshop where bangles were produced.

Unique specimens of Chinese porcelain of the late Yuan Dynasty (1300–67) have also been recovered at FTC. One of these is a white bowl with underglaze blue or black decorations consisting of Chinese characters for compass directions (4). Although literary descriptions of such bowls exist, no example with Chinese characters (and degree marks) has yet been recorded. The compass was used by mariners of the Yuan period, but was also employed by FENG SHUI masters (geomancers).

At OPH, the full range of 14th-century items typical of ancient Singapore riverside sites was recovered,

4

including Malay and Chinese ceramics, Chinese coins, and fragments of 14th-century Javanese red burnished ware.

Notable features of the OPH site included a high proportion of 'small-mouthed jars' (5) probably designed to carry liquid mercury. Eleven of these vessels were recovered intact, and are the first 14th-century items to be found whole in Singapore. Some particular specialized activity involving these jars or their contents must have been conducted on or near OPH. Had it been possible to conduct more direct investigation, it might have been possible to make some determination of what this activity may have been.

Another item worthy of note is a highly corroded iron blade. X-rays of the object failed to prove conclusively that what appears to be a sinuous blade was in fact, designed to be so shaped; this may simply be the result of the corrosion process. It seems that the blade was meant to be the business end of a spear rather than a *keris* (traditional Malay dagger).

At SCC, in addition to ceramics typical of other 14th-century Singapore sites, copper or copper-alloy objects were recovered. Some appear to be finished products. Others are Song Dynasty Chinese coins (6) which were shipped to Southeast Asia by the ton. Although by 1300 these coins had become the legal tender of the Javanese kingdom of MAJAPAHIT, and were probably also used in this way in Singapore, many of them were destined to be recycled rather than used as currency. Evidence of this at SCC consists of some distorted coins, a fragment of a crucible with residue adhering to it which has not yet been analyzed, and a fragment of a stone trough.

Other interesting items found at SCC were fragments of intricate glass bangles, and beads including a black-and-white cylindrical example, a moulded white bead, and several beads of a hard red stone (probably carnelian).

At STA, hundreds of volunteers responded to an appeal for assistance. As a result, it was possible to excavate about 80 per cent of an area affected by a construction project which began in April 2004.

The churchyard had been disturbed by various activities during the colonial era. In some areas, remains of brick buildings, debris from

6

the construction of the cathedral, and 19th- and 20th-century refuse including a number of rifle and pistol bullets were found in dense concentrations. This excavation demonstrated that this area was occupied in the 14th century. Another new type of artefact excavated is a carved stone with a human head at one tip, and a point at the other (7). Similar stone pins have been found in northwest Malaysia and northeast Sumatra. The use of these artefacts is unknown. The discovery of one complete and one fragmentary example of these pins enables us to note that the local culture of this 14th-century port shared many similarities with ports at the north end of the Strait of Malacca.

It is now possible to conclude that much of the area within the boundaries of the 14th-century settlement was in fact utilized for occupation-related activities. It is not, however, possible to identify specific areas used for warehouses, dwellings, or workshops, with the possible exception of a charcoal concentration near the glass globules found on Fort Canning.

7

ARCHAEOLOGICAL SITES

National Museum of Singapore

Bras Basah Park

Christian cemetery

Fort gate

Keramat Iskandar Shah

Fort Canning excavation site

Pancur Larangan

Stamford Road

BUKIT LARANGAN (FORT CANNING HILL)

St Andrew's Cathedral

Coleman Street

Fire director's residence

Hill Street

North Bridge Road

St Andrew's Road

Connaught Drive

Colombo Court

Singapore River

Parliament House Complex

High Street

Singapore Cricket Club

Old Parliament House

Pulau Saigon

Empress Place

0   500 m

Singapore Stone

■ Ancient earthen wall

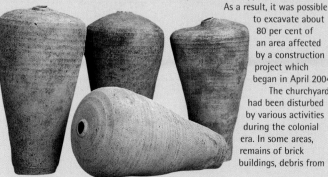

3

5

architecture: from founding to self-government

Following the establishment by the East India Company of a trading post in Singapore, it was not long before migrants from all over Asia and Europe made an architectural imprint on the island. Those from China erected religious buildings, among the earliest of which were the FUK TAK CHI TEMPLE (1824) and the THIAN HOCK KENG TEMPLE (1839–42). Indian and Arab migrants built mosques and temples including the NAGORE DURGHA Indian Muslim shrine (1828–30) (*1*) and the JAMAE MOSQUE (1830–35). A Malay

businesswoman founded the HAJJAH FATIMAH MOSQUE (1845–46). Hindu temples sprang up, including SRI MARIAMMAN TEMPLE (1843) and SRI SRINIVASA PERUMAL TEMPLE (1855). These temples followed the traditions of the migrants' countries of origin, and then, as now, there was little that was markedly 'Singaporean' about them.

Singapore's first 'architects'

Singapore's first 'architect' in the modern sense was GEORGE D. COLEMAN, who designed a house for John Argyle Maxwell (1826–27), which later served in turn as the Court House, the Legislative Assembly Building and (from 1965 to 1997) Parliament House (*see* OLD PARLIAMENT HOUSE AND ANNEXE). Coleman's finest work was the ARMENIAN CHURCH. The influence of Coleman was profound and his advice on urban planning crucial to Sir STAMFORD RAFFLES' memorandum to the town committee on 4 November 1822 recommending an orthogonal planning grid, with continuous walkways (*see* FIVE-FOOT WAY). Coleman's apprentice, D. L. McSwinney was the designer of the CATHEDRAL OF THE GOOD SHEPHERD

(1843–46) (*2*). The first major Anglican church was St Andrew's (*see* ST ANDREW'S CATHEDRAL): the original building was by Coleman, but the one standing today (*3*) was designed by Colonel Ronald MacPherson in the Gothic/Early English style, and consecrated in 1862. Several French Catholics made an indelible mark on Singapore's religious architecture. For example, Brother Lothaire designed the centre block of ST JOSEPH'S INSTITUTION (1865–67) (*4*); the curved wings were the work of Father Charles Benedict Nain, who also designed the Gothic-revival chapel of the CONVENT OF THE HOLY INFANT JESUS (1890). Most religious buildings of the time echoed the Classical- or Gothic-revival styles of Europe, albeit on a generally smaller scale.

Shophouses

Perhaps the most important building type associated specifically with Singapore and peninsular Malaya from the earliest colonial days is the terraced shophouse, of which a key feature is the 'five-foot way'. Closely related to the shophouse is the terraced townhouse. See SHOPHOUSES.

Symbols of the colonial era

As the 19th century moved on, and the STRAITS SETTLEMENTS became a Crown Colony administered from London, Singapore became the administrative headquarters of 'British Malaya', and more and more important economically. The government enclave in the city became more clearly defined with the building of the Town Hall (1856–62) (*5*), designed by John Bennett (*see* VICTORIA CONCERT HALL AND VICTORIA THEATRE). Nearby was built the EMPRESS PLACE building (1864–67) (*6*), designed by Major J. F. A. McNAIR of the Public Works Department. The prevalent architectural language of British imperial power was neoclassical, of which McNair was the foremost exponent in late 19th-century Singapore. He designed the governor's official residence, Government House (1867–69) (*7*), now the ISTANA, residence of the President of Singapore. McNair also designed Raffles Library and Museum (1886–87), now the NATIONAL MUSEUM OF SINGAPORE (*8*).

Philanthropic merchants

Much economic power within Singapore lay with leading members of the Chinese community, and the 19th century saw the emergence of prominent entrepreneurs, some of whom were great philanthropists. For example, the Tan Tock Seng pauper hospital (1844) was funded by TAN TOCK SENG, a successful Hokkien merchant. The money to build the TAN SI CHONG SU temple (1876) (*9*) was donated by TAN KIM CHING and TAN BENG SWEE. Another philanthropist, GAN ENG SENG, funded the OLD THONG CHAI MEDICAL INSTITUTION (1892) while TAN YEOK NEE built a Chinese courtyard house in Clemenceau Avenue (1885), used today as a business education campus. Philanthropy was not a Chinese monopoly.

Arab traders played a significant role: the ALSAGOFF FAMILY, for instance, endowed the Madrasah Alsagoff (1912) in Kampong Glam. For the benefit of the Jewish community, the CHESED-EL SYNAGOGUE (1905) was funded by MANASSEH MEYER.

Corinthian capital.

Neoclassical

After some outbreaks of Victorian-style eclecticism, the neoclassical held sway so far as commercial buildings were concerned. The classically ornamented JINRICKSHA STATION (1903) (*10*), a prominent landmark on a triangular site at Tanjong Pagar Road, was designed by Samuel Tomlinson and D.M. Craik for the MUNICIPAL COMMISSION. Both public and commercial commissions were undertaken by the most prominent architectural practice of the time, SWAN & MACLAREN, who in 1899 designed the extensions to RAFFLES HOTEL (*11*), opened by the SARKIES BROTHERS in 1886. The same firm were the architects for TAO NAN SCHOOL (1910) (*12*), SULTAN MOSQUE (1924–28), the second Hongkong and Shanghai Bank (1922) (*13*), and other buildings in the Raffles Place area no longer standing. Keys and Dowdeswell were

the architects of the Classical-style FULLERTON BUILDING (1928) while the Municipal Building, later renamed CITY HALL (1926–29) (*14*), was designed by A. Gordon and F.D. Meadows. Classicism lingered on for a few years more: Frank Dorrington Ward of the Public Works Department was responsible for the Hill Street Building (1934–36) (*see* MICA BUILDING) and for what has been described as the 'last example of British imperial architecture in Singapore', the old SUPREME COURT building (1937–39) (*15*). A gradual shift from Palladian themes can already be detected in the Municipal Commission's CENTRAL FIRE STATION (1909), and in ST GEORGE'S CHURCH (1911) designed by William Henry Stanbury R.E., clearly influenced by the Arts and Crafts tradition.

Modern architecture

The modernist idiom arrived in Singapore in the 1930s. The SINGAPORE IMPROVEMENT TRUST (SIT) was formed in 1927 and its Tiong Bahru Estate (1936–54) (*16*) was distinctly modern in character. A link between the Arts and Crafts movement and modernism was provided by FRANK BREWER, with houses at Ridout Road and the Dalvey Estate (1934);' Brewer later designed the CATHAY BUILDING (1939) (*17*), Singapore's first 'skyscraper. D.S. Petrovich, working for SWAN & MACLAREN, was responsible for the design of the KEPPEL RAILWAY STATION (1932–37) (*18*); Frank Dorrington Ward showed that he too could turn his hand to modernist design with CLIFFORD PIER (1933) (*19*) and KALLANG AIRPORT (1937). Modern architecture was embraced by local architects. Ho Kwong Yew, working for Chung and Wong, was responsible for the house of Aw Boon Par (1930); his design for the Chee Guan Chiang House (1938) was decidedly modern in its language.

Black-and-whites

Many more prosperous members of colonial society lived in 'black-and-white' houses, so-called because of their visual reference to the Tudor-style half-timbering reminiscent of prosperous English suburbs between the world wars, but adapted to tropical conditions. Some later colonial houses showed more than a hint of Art Deco, as did later shophouses. *See* BLACK-AND-WHITE HOUSES.

Towards self-government

British architectural practices returned to Singapore after the end of World War II. PALMER AND TURNER designed MACDONALD HOUSE for the Hongkong and Shanghai Bank; the same firm's Bank of China Building (1953–54) (*20*) was amongst the first tower blocks constructed post war; and the SIT also resumed work, with flats at Sago Street (1948), Prinsep Street (1948) and Towner Road (1952). The slightly smaller jobs were handled by Van Sitteven and Partners (responsible for the now-replaced LIDO THEATRE, amongst other works) and James Ferrie and Partners, responsible for the original American Club (since replaced) and high-rise apartments in Balmoral Road. The local practitioners were led by Ng Keng Siang, responsible for the ASIA INSURANCE building (1953) (*21*), the NANYANG UNIVERSITY campus (1956), a multi-storey apartment block along

Orchard Road referred to as Ngee Ann Kongsi (now demolished) and most of the larger projects from the Chinese developers. Others were Ho Kwong Yew and Sons, Chan and Wong, and Wong Foo Nam. A significant number of young Singaporean architects assumed important roles in the profession after their education overseas (there was no tertiary training available in Singapore at that time). Among them were Ang Keng Leng, who progressively replaced Ng Keng Siang as the service provider to the rich Chinese businessmen when Ng gradually retired from active practice.

A distinctive building designed by a Chinese partner in SWAN & MACLAREN, C. Y. Koh, and a good example of the architecture of its era, remains standing to this day at Fullerton Road. It used to be the headquarters of the Port of Singapore 'Waterboat Office' (1953) and is now a restaurant, but the original form of the building has been maintained (*22*).

architecture: a new nation

A significant event in the development of Singapore's architectural profession was the formation of the Society of Malayan (later Malaysian) Architects (SMA), of which Ng Kheng Siang was the first president in 1958/59. After separation from Malaysia, the SMA was renamed Singapore Institute of Architects. Its input to planning decisions contributed to the

modernization of Singapore by updating regulatory requirements, paving the way for the development of modern buildings. It also helped establish a fully fledged architectural faculty at the National University of Singapore. In the 1960s, a number of local firms developed their practices, producing designs for medium-sized projects such as schools, churches and housing, some of them reflective of the Singapore identity—despite frugal budgets. The NATIONAL THEATRE (1964) (1) by ALFRED WONG Partnership, and the NTUC Conference Hall (1964) (2) by the Malayan Architects Co-partnership, were expressions of national pride and aspirations appropriate to the time.

Industrialization and change

A symbol of Singapore's new economy was provided by a local firm, Architects Team 3, with their Jurong Town Hall (1970) (3). Design Partnership was successful with its proposal for the People's Park Complex (1973) (4), and followed this with the Woh Hup Complex (1973), later renamed the GOLDEN MILE COMPLEX (5). Pearl Bank Apartments (1976) (6) was an experimental housing project by Tan Cheng Siong of Archurban Architects Planners, who also did the Pandan Valley Condominium (1976–79). During this period the face of Singapore was being changed dramatically not only by major schemes in the city centre, but by large-scale rehousing projects in new towns and housing estates (see PUBLIC HOUSING).

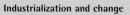

International names

When the Urban Redevelopment Authority started major redevelopment of the central area, large parcels of land—created, under the Land Sale Policy of 1967, by amalgamating small shophouse lots—became available to corporate investors such as major banks, who had already entered the age of globalization and had seen signature commercial buildings overseas, in cities such as New York and Chicago. These were images no corporate client could ignore. Many hired international designers, as did several international hotel chains. Such design concepts might not have been accepted if proposed by homegrown architects, who did not yet have the track records demanded for such projects. The trend was signalled by the appointment of I.M. Pei as designer of the OCBC Centre (1976) (7). He was also the designer of Raffles City (1984–86) (8).

John Portman was the architect of Marina Square (1984–86) (9), which included three hotels with an internal atrium—a Portman trademark. In the 1980s, the Hitachi Towers/Caltex House complex (1993) (10) was designed by Murphy Jahn Architects. SINGAPORE INDOOR STADIUM was the work of Kenzo Tange, also design consultant for UOB

Condominiums

In land-scarce Singapore, condominiums have been a significant channel for architectural expression. An early example of the genre was Pandan Valley (1976–79), by Archurban Architects Planners. More recent condominiums produced by local practices include Nassim Jade (1997) by Chan Sau Yan, which achieved a remarkable sense of privacy for a

densely populated island. Paterson Edge (1999) by Mok Wei Wei, is an example of work by a younger generation of Singaporean architects. Foreign practitioners in this field have included the American architect Paul Rudolph and the Archiplan team, with The Colonnade (1985) (15). Moshe Safdi and Associates were design consultants for The Habitat (1984) (16). As in past times, expatriate architects, such as the Australian Kerry Hill, have put down roots in Singapore. Lincoln Modern (2003) is by Penang-born Chan Soo Khian. One Moulmein Rise (17) is by WOHA Architects.

Competitions

Right from the early days, the Singapore Institute of Architects has promoted the idea of competitions based on workable requirements with qualified assessors. The result has been some outstanding buildings, which uplifted architectural design in Singapore. The earliest example was the competition for the NTUC Conference Hall, followed by the Science Centre (Raymond Woo), and the PUB Headquarters Building, now known as Singapore Power Building (Group 2 Architects: Tan Puay Huat and Ong Chin Bee). More recently, a competition was held in 2000 for two MRT stations: the future Museum station (WOHA Architects) promises to be an outstanding piece of urban architecture. In 2002 Arc Studios won an important competition for the design of a public housing development at Duxton Plain.

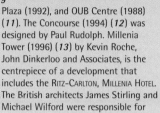

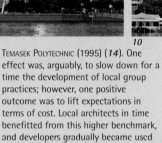

9

10

12

13

Plaza (1992), and OUB Centre (1988) (*11*). The Concourse (1994) (*12*) was designed by Paul Rudolph. Millenia Tower (1996) (*13*) by Kevin Roche, John Dinkerloo and Associates, is the centrepiece of a development that includes the RITZ-CARLTON, MILLENIA HOTEL. The British architects James Stirling and Michael Wilford were responsible for

TEMASEK POLYTECHNIC (1995) (*14*). One effect was, arguably, to slow down for a time the development of local group practices; however, one positive outcome was to lift expectations in terms of cost. Local architects in time benefitted from this higher benchmark, and developers gradually became used to more realistic budgets.

14

11

18

19

20

21

22

Modern worship

The years since independence have produced several notable religious buildings. The Church of the Blessed Sacrament (*18*), designed by Y. G. Dowsett and officially opened in 1965, complemented Queenstown's expansion as Singapore's first satellite town. Its iconic feature is the roof. Masjid Darul Aman (1986) (*19*) was designed by the Housing & Development Board. Chee Tong Temple (1986) (*20*) by Akitek Tenggara is a modern reinterpretation of the traditional Chinese temple. More recent examples include The Church of St Mary of the Angels (2003) (*21*), by WOHA Architects. Assyafaah Mosque (2004) (*22*) was designed by Tan Kok Hiang of FORUM Architects.

Icons of today

A global city needs visual icons. Major recent public buildings include The ESPLANADE–THEATRES ON THE BAY (1994–2002) (*23*), a collaboration between DP Architects

and Michael Wilford of the UK. British architect Norman Foster's first project in Singapore was the Expo MRT Station (2001) (*24*), which he followed with the new SUPREME COURT BUILDING (2005). Completed in the same year were the

NATIONAL LIBRARY (*25*), designed by Kenneth Yeang of T.R. Hamzah & Yeang International (Malaysia), and the SINGAPORE MANAGEMENT UNIVERSITY, by KNTA Architects and Edward Cullinan.

23

24

25

Armenians: wedding party after the turn of the 20th century.

Army: the Singapore Army on manoeuvres.

Armenian businessman relinquished his interests in Singapore and emigrated. As well as trading, Armenians established legal firms, notably Joaquim Brothers; photographic studios including the Photo Stores; and jewellery and watchmaking businesses.

However, it is with RAFFLES HOTEL that Armenians are synonymous. Founded in 1887 by Tigran and Martin Sarkies, the hotel earned international fame under the management of Tigran, followed by Aviet Sarkies and finally Martyrose Arathoon. After the shock bankruptcy of SARKIES BROTHERS in 1931, the hotel left Armenian hands.

Other Armenian-owned hotels included the Pavilion Hotel and Bowling Alley, the ADELPHI HOTEL (run by Arathoon Sarkies and Eleazar Johannes), the SEA VIEW HOTEL, the Grosvenor and the Oranje Hotel. The Oranje was the last hotel connected to Armenians, and after 1963 became known as Stamford House.

Several Armenians made their mark on Singapore's development. Prominent lawyer Joaquim P. Joaquim served on the Municipal Commission for nearly 16 years, and was elected president in 1887. In the 1890s, he was appointed to the Legislative Council and was made deputy consul-general for the United States. George G. Seth rose through the civil service to become SOLICITOR-GENERAL in 1920. Catchick Moses founded *The Straits Times* newspaper in 1845, and Gregory Galastaun founded the Armenian newspaper *Usumnaser* in 1849. Agnes Joaquim bred the orchid VANDA MISS JOAQUIM, selected as Singapore's national flower in 1981.

The small size of the Armenian community meant it was not demographically viable. Lacking potential spouses within their community, Armenians married non-Armenians. Intermarriage, which began in the 1850s, led to assimilation. This, compounded by deaths, few new migrants, emigration and the emergence of a new Singapore in the 1950s, led to the decline of the community. By 2005, the last of the Persian Armenians had left Singapore, leaving about a dozen residents who were close descendants. However, the arrival of other Armenians who were posted to Singapore on business from America, Europe and Australia engendered the beginning of a new Armenian community.

Surnames associated with the Persian Armenian community in Singapore include: Anthony, Apcar, Arathoon, Aviet, Catchatoor, Carapiet, Chater, Constantine, Edgar, Gabriel, Galstaun, Galistan, Gregory, Hacobian, Joaquim, Johannes, Mackertoom, Manuk, Martin, Michael, Moses, Paul, Phannous, Sarkies, Seth, Stephens and Zechariah. The anglicized spellings were adopted by the families themselves. The names of Armenian Street, Sarkies Road, Galistan Avenue and St Martin's Drive are reminders of this early community.

As highly respected members of Singapore society, Armenians played an active role in social and civic life. Isaiah Zechariah represented the Armenian merchants in the first Chamber of Commerce in 1837. Others served on boards, committees and the Municipal Commission. In 1895 two of Singapore's eight municipal commissioners were Armenian: Aristarkies Moses and Joaquim P. Joaquim.

Armenians initially made their name as traders, merchants, brokers and commission agents. Pioneering merchants exported regional produce and imported manufactured goods. In the 1830s, Armenian merchants were responsible for reopening trade with Borneo, and had cornered the antimony market. From the 1850s to the 1880s, Armenians dominated the OPIUM trade in Singapore.

Aristarkies Sarkies established the first Armenian business firm in 1820; subsequently, more than 60 trading firms were founded by Armenians. Some were one-man operations, a few were financial disasters, while others such as Sarkies and Moses (1840–1914) were icons of old Singapore. Later firms, including Edgar Brothers (1912–68), and Stephens Paul & Company (1896–1941), became large multinational companies. In 1983, the last Persian

Army The origins of the Singapore Army lie in the formation of the Singapore Volunteer Rifles in 1854. In the 1950s, the nature of the force changed, following moves towards independence from Britain. In 1957, the Singapore Infantry Regiment (SIR) was established, and by the time Singapore joined the Federation of Malaysia, there were two SIR battalions. In November 1964 and June 1965, during CONFRONTATION, 2SIR was deployed in Johor and saw action against Indonesian commando infiltrators. Between November 1964 and April 1965, 1SIR was sent to Sabah to counter Indonesian incursions. NATIONAL SERVICE was introduced in 1967, and the Enlistment Act in 1970 provided for 30 or 24 months of full time military service depending on rank. In 2004, this was reduced to 24 months regardless of rank. Life-long reservist obligations (up to age 50 for officers and 40 for other ranks) continue.

The army conducts a large proportion of its training overseas in countries such as Brunei and Australia. It places emphasis on the use of simulators due to the lack of training space and the built-up nature of Singapore's land area. Development of the army has been sustained throughout the decades since Independence in 1965, and hence Singapore has a very modern army. In 2005, the Army had 46,000 regular and conscript soldiers, as well as an additional 280,000 in the active reserves, all of whom could be mobilized in six hours using a system of both 'open' and 'silent' MOBILIZATION. The bulk of the Singapore Army's fighting capability lies with its Operational Commands which comprise mainly Operationally Ready National Servicemen. They kept trained and ready.

By 2005, the army had several combined arms divisions as well as a rapid deployment force. It had significant armour capabilities, comprising 450 Centurion Main Battle Tanks and AMX-13 light tanks, as well as 1,547 armoured personnel carriers, such as M-113, Commando, AMX-10, and locally-produced BIONIX armoured fighting vehicles. Its artillery capability consisted of a mixture of light and heavy artillery, such as 169 pieces of 155-mm howitzers, including the locally made FH88, FH2000 and PRIMUS self-propelled types; light howitzers, such as 37 LG1 towed 105-mm types; and a range of 81-mm, 120-mm and 160-mm mortars. The Army also deploys sophisticated mortar-locating radars, such as the AN/TPQ types. Anti-tank missile capabilities revolve around modern types, such as Milan, Armbrust and Spike. During the 1990s, the army undertook a programme known as Army 21, whereby it developed relatively light but potent forces capable of quick deployment. Improvements have been made to logistical support as well as to command, control and reconnaissance capabilities.

The Arts Fission Company: site-specific performance of Urban Sanctuary *in 2000.*

arowana (*Scleropages formosus*) Also known as the 'golden dragonfish', the arowana is not native to Singapore but is valued as an ornamental fish. Its slender body, large reflective scales and a pair of stiff barbells at the tip of its lower jaw make it resemble a Chinese dragon, and it is thus believed by some to be capable of warding off evil and bringing good fortune. The arowana can be seen in the rivers and lakes of Malaysia, Indonesia and Thailand. It grows to 90 cm and is a voracious predator of small fish. It is an internationally protected species, and only captive-bred arowanas can be legally traded.

art *See* box.

Artists Village, The Registered as a non-profit society in February 1992, The Artists Village was founded by artist TANG DA WU in 1988 at 61-B Lorong Gambas, a converted chicken farm off Ulu Sembawang. Tang resided there with his then wife, artist-illustrator Hazel McIntosh, and their son. With his brother Tang Dahon, he turned The Artists Village into Singapore's first notable art colony and commune—the precursor of the artist-run studio-residences that later proliferated. The Artists Village established a reputation for its open house sessions, installations and performances and came to represent vanguard and alternative art in Singapore, developing the concept of the 'artist collective'. At one time, it had some 35 artists living there, working there or having project affiliations with it, including Vincent Leow, Wong Shih Yaw, Amanda Heng, Baet Yoke Kuan, Zai Kuning, Koh Nguang How and Tang Mun Kit.

The artists were evicted from the former chicken farm in March 1990. The group then began operating without a physical office or studio space, but continues to organize and participate in events and exhibitions. The goals of The Artists Village are 'to promote contemporary art and to bring about a better understanding of contemporary art practices and their contribution to society'.

Arts Fission Company, The Dance company. Founded in 1994 by choreographer Angela Liong and visual artist Chandrasekaran S., it made its debut in 1995 at the Festival of Asian Performing Arts with the multimedia production *Mahabharata: A Grain of Rice*. Under Liong's direction, it is known for its cross-disciplinary interests and site-specific dance theatre in public spaces, such as *Urban Sanctuary* (2000) at a gondola track on Centennial Tower's 35th floor, and *Borrowed Scenery* (2002) in collaboration with sculptor HAN SAI POR for the Yogyakarta Arts Festival. In 2003, it presented a revised *Shadowhouses* as the opening act of the Laokoon Festival in Hamburg. *12 SMS Across the Mountains*, its collaboration with Korean group Dance Theatre CcadoO, premiered at the Seoul International Dance Festival in 2005.

Arts House, The Arts venue. Also known as the Old Parliament House, it is Singapore's oldest government building. A $15 million facelift transformed it into a centre for arts lovers, which opened in March 2004. Arts festivals and exhibitions, films, theatre, dance, open air concerts and fashion shows are on the multidisciplinary centre's list of events. (*See also* OLD PARLIAMENT HOUSE AND ANNEXE)

Arts Theatre of Singapore One of the oldest Mandarin theatre troupes in Singapore, Arts Theatre of Singapore was founded in 1955 by a group of 16 *huaju* (spoken drama) enthusiasts. Known at that time as Singapore Amateur Players (SAP), the group enjoyed the support of activists in the Chinese high schools' drama societies. Its first production was *Sun Rise* by Cao Yu in 1955; and for the next decade the group staged three to four productions a year, of major plays from Europe, China, Singapore and other Asian countries. From 1973, it produced several original plays, voicing concern about a wide range of social issues. These included *The Second Run*, *Maggot*, *Who Is Our People*, *Do Not be Muddle-Headed*, *Uncle Ah Tien*, *A Nightmare*, *Dream of a Secretary* and others. In the 1980s, APS continued to present foreign plays and new local plays.

In 1993, SAP switched its focus to children's theatre. In 1995, Singapore Amateur Players was re-structured as Arts Theatre of Singapore. Since 1998, it has organized the National Short Play Competition.

See also CHINESE THEATRE.

Arya Samaj Hindu reform movement started by Swami Dayanand Sarasvati. The Swami planted the seeds of the movement in 19th-century India as an effort to reform HINDUISM, which had been affected by the growing influence of rites and rituals not considered truly part of the religion. Drawing upon the teaching of the Vedas and the Upanishads, he clarified his thinking in his book, *The Light of Truth*, to explain in simple language the basic tenets of Hinduism. He drew upon his learning of scriptures. He also started schools known as Anglo Vedic Schools. However, his movement was confined to the Punjab, Uttar Pradesh, Bihar and other Hindi-speaking provinces in India.

The Swami's followers who settled in Singapore, established Arya Samaj in 1927 in a shophouse in Rowell Road. The Arya Samaj decries idol worship and believes in Vedic teaching. It allows followers of other religions to embrace Hinduism by going through an initiation ceremony.

The movement's present building at Syed Alwi Road was opened in 1963 by Mollamal Sachdev, whose family gave generously to the building fund. The place used to see large gatherings on Sundays but the numbers have declined with the opening of the SHREE LAKSHMINARAYAN TEMPLE. The building is used as a community hall for weddings and other traditional celebrations such as DEEPAVALI and HOLI. The Arya Samaj has started teaching Hindi at its premises through the DAV Hindi School.

Asahi Isohi, Count (dates unknown) Controller of enemy aliens in Singapore, Malaya and Sumatra during the Japanese Occupation. Count Asahi Isohi was in charge of civilian internment camps from 1942 to 1943. He was also director custodian of enemy property and secretary of the Singapore Municipality. His headquarters was in Singapore. Asahi came from a Japanese aristocratic background, was educated at Harrow School and Cambridge University and worked as a Japanese consul to Singapore in the pre-war days. He was an interpreter at the 15 February 1942 surrender of Singapore at the FORD MOTOR FACTORY.

Asahi was considered a benevolent commandant by many of the civilian internees in CHANGI PRISON. They described him helping out with food and

arowana

The Arts House

art The genesis of modern art in Singapore can be traced to the late 1930s. An important event was the formation of the Society of Chinese Artists in 1936, its initial membership primarily made up of alumni of art academies in Shanghai, including CHEN CHONG SWEE and Tchang Ju Chi. The society went beyond the promotion of Chinese ink painting—an earlier emphasis in the ethnic Chinese cultural circle—to include a broad range of oil and watercolour practices. It also believed in the communicative and educational functions of art. Two years later, Singapore's first major art school, the NANYANG ACADEMY OF FINE ARTS (NAFA)—modelled on the Chinese art academies—was established. This concentration of activities is regarded as the beginning of a Nanyang School movement in Singapore art, the impetus for modern art here.

Beginnings of the Nanyang School
LIM HAK TAI, an art educator from Xiamen (Amoy) Art Academy, was the founding principal of NAFA. Trained in painting and crafts in Fuzhou (Foochow), he later taught at Xiamen Art Academy and Jimei Teachers' Training College in Xiamen. As Huang Suibi and Yang Gengbao (founders of the Xiamen Art Academy) first studied Western art in the Philippines, the subsequent founding of NAFA in Singapore under Lim Hak Tai delineated an early East and Southeast Asian nexus in modern art. Tchang Ju Chi, Huang Pao Fang and Chong Pai Mu joined the NAFA teaching staff in 1940, and Wu Tsai Yan and See Hiang Tuo the following year. Tay Long, who would later own art materials suppliers Straits Commercial Art, an

important gathering place for local artists, was among the first batch of NAFA graduates.

Xu Beihong, Portrait of Lim Hak Tai, *1939.*

New art of Malaya
Lim understood Singapore's potential as an international arts hub. He articulated that Nanyang ('South Seas', i.e. Southeast Asia)—particularly Singapore, which was at the crossroads of Europe and Asia and a commercial centre for the region, and enriched by complex ethnic identities—would help mediate cultures of East and West. Lim advocated a 'new art of Malaya'. The art discourse then was also linked to developments in China, Indonesia, the Malayan Peninsula and India. Influential artists included Xu Beihong (who visited Singapore on five occasions between 1919 and 1942), and Lee Man Fong (active in both Indonesia and Singapore).

Singapore's art scene was influenced by European artists who visited Singapore in the 1930s. Among them were Russian artist Dora Gordine, British painter Eleanor

Watkins and Austrian sculptor Karl Duldig. The Belgian artist Adrien-Jean Le Mayeur held three exhibitions in Singapore between 1933 and 1941; these had a tremendous impact on pioneering Singapore artists and stimulated travel to Bali in the 1950s.

Russian artist, Dora Gordine, Indian Head, *1930–35 (above). Belgian artist, Adrien-Jean Le Mayeur,* Pollok with magazines, *(left).*

Multicultural art
The development of art in Singapore was interrupted by World War II, but resumed soon after the Japanese surrender. The first multicultural art society—the Singapore Art Society, based in the British Council building—was inaugurated in 1949. Founding members included artist LIU KANG, Richard Walker (the art superintendent of government English schools before the war), Suri Mohyani (a founding member of the Society of Malay Artists inaugurated in the same year), and CARL GIBSON-HILL (director of the Raffles Library and Museum, predecessor of the NATIONAL MUSEUM OF SINGAPORE).

Liu Kang, Artist and Model, *1954 (above). Richard Walker,* Self-portrait, *undated (left).*

Bali Field Trip
It was in the 1950s that the Nanyang School, or NANYANG STYLE, reached a high point. The era is exemplified by leading artists such as Chen Chong Swee, Liu Kang, CHEN WEN HSI and CHEONG SOO PIENG. They were so popular that the Singapore Art Society organized two joint exhibitions of their works within a single year. The four artists went together to Bali in 1952; they travelled across Java and met artists in Surabaya before arriving at Bali, where they also visited Le Mayeur. The artists were in search of a mode of visual expression that was particular to Southeast Asia.

Bali was a rich visual source and also revealed to them the ritualistic, experiential and decorative nature of Southeast Asian art. Images of Bali provided both the inspiration and sources which enabled the artists to crystallize new visual ideas in their search for a new artistic language. This was most obvious in the case of Cheong Soo Pieng, who later said that Bali made him think about colour technique. His unique synthesis of highly stylized and decorative forms with traditional structural forms in Chinese ink, coupled with his sensitive modelling and emphatic silhouettes, made him the most innovative of the

Cheong Soo Pieng, Untitled, *1959 (top).* Chen Wen Hsi, Grazing, *1965 (above).*

pioneer artists in pictorial techniques. He later experimented with a wide range of art-making, from impasto effects and mixed media to Chinese ink on cotton.

Golden years of the Nanyang School
The 1950s was a truly exciting period in Singapore art. The Bali Field Trip marked a high point in Nanyang art, providing further stylistic inspiration. There were further multicultural art activities; batik became a new medium of expression; there was a wave of Europe-bound and returning local artists and a concurrent tendency towards social realism.

In the 1950s, Georgette Chen arrived on the scene. Chen taught at the Nanyang Academy of Fine Arts from 1954 until her retirement in 1981. She encouraged students to break new ground. In her own landscape, still-life and portrait paintings, she would apply the same sensitivity towards every detail of her subject, often in a

setting of harmonious colours. The landscape commonly has a light, cheerful and atmospheric quality, capturing the sunny airiness of tropical scenery; and her still-lifes are a celebration of simple joy and festive spirit.

Georgette Chen, The Temple, *1964.*

Social realism

The EQUATOR ART SOCIETY, founded in 1956, is often associated with social realism—realist art used for social or political comment—although it was more of a confluence of Singapore's own tradition of realist art and the exchange of artistic aesthetics from China. The society was also, to some extent, a reaction to the emerging formalism—concern of technique over social value—of the 1950s. Artists active in the realist genre during this time included Chua Mia Tee, Lim Yew Kuan, Lee Boon Wang and Lai Kui Fang.

Lim Yew Kuan and five other artists, Seascape, *1966 woodcut (upper left).* *Chua Mia Tee,* National Language Class, *1950 (lower left).*

The decline of social realism

The MODERN ART SOCIETY, which organized its inaugural exhibition in 1963, was a reaction to the social realists of the previous decade. The group's spokesperson Ho Ho Ying lamented that while in the initial years of the Equator Art Society there were a few artists with a strong foundation in realism, the realist works of the society in general were merely documentary and lacking in creativity. The Modern Art Society, which included founding members Ng Yat Chuan, TAY CHEE TOH and WEE BENG CHONG, proclaimed that realism had passed its golden age and fauvism and cubism were declining; any attempt to recover past glory would be in vain.

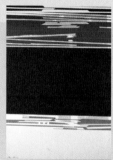

Wee Beng Chong, Painting, *1979 (upper right).* *Ho Ho Ying,* Composition, *1974 (lower right).*

In the footsteps of the pioneers

Between 1961 and 1970, the Ten Men Art Group—led by artist and Chung Cheng High School art teacher Yeh Chi Wei—visited the Malay Peninsula, Java, Bali, Thailand, Cambodia, Sarawak, Sabah, Brunei and Sumatra, still in search of the Nanyang Style. Among the group were Choo Keng Kwang, LIM TZE PENG and Seah Kim Joo.

Choo Keng Kwang, Streetside Coiffure, *undated.*

Pluralism

The 1960s was a period of new blood. A group of Europe- and America-bound artists included TEO ENG SENG, THOMAS YEO, NG ENG TENG, GOH BENG KWAN and ANTHONY POON. These 'Second Generation' artists imbibed aesthetics in their formative training—as had the pioneer artists—and created a significant impact upon their return in the late 1960s and 1970s. Also in the 1960s, a new Malay artist group was initiated by Abdul Ghani Hamid and Marhaban Kasman. The group's name in Malay, Angkatan Pelukis Aneka Daya, or Association of Artists of Various Resources, aptly captured the pluralism of the Singapore art scene in the 1960s and 1970s.

Thomas Yeo, Green Symphony, *1999 (upper right).* *Ng Eng Teng,* Mother and Child, *1974 (lower right).*

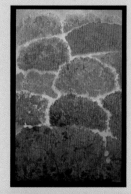

Expansion and experimentation

The notion of 'various resources' also anticipated new experiments in art in the context of a cultural and information environment rapidly transformed by new delivery channels, experiences and visual language brought about by multimedia technology. While painting remained the predominant art form, three-dimensional or time-based works, including installations and performances, became popular among younger artists. The most influential practitioner in this expanded field of art was TANG DA WU, whose installation and performance art in the late 1970s and 1980s, along with The ARTISTS VILLAGE group he founded in 1987, were a focal point for new experiments. At its height, The Artists Village (also a venue) attracted some 35 artists to live and work in its rented bungalow in Sembawang. Artists associated with the group included Wong Shih Yaw, Jailani Kuning, Vincent Leow, Amanda Heng, Tang Mun Kit, Lim Poh Teck, Faizal Fadil, Koh Nguang How and Baet Yeok Kwan.

Faizul Fadil, Study of Three Thermos Flasks, *1991 (top).* *Lim Poh Teck,* In Progress, *1992 (above).*

Multi-ethnic and multimedia

Another group of note in the 1980s was 'Trimurti', so known because of their joint multimedia exhibition of the same title in 1988; members included Salleh Japar, Goh Ee Choo and S. Chandrasekaran. The three artists, ethnically Malay, Chinese and Indian respectively, chose the Hindu composite of Brahma, Vishnu and Shiva—symbolizing creation, preservation and dissolution—to show that different cultural and religious backgrounds could co-exist harmoniously. With multimedia works, the artists created an 'energy' space intended to capture a total experience beyond the visual world.

Chandrasekaran, Visvayoni, *1988 (left).* *Goh Ee Choo,* Untitled, *1992 (above).*

The further development of art infrastructure, including the establishment of the LASALLE–SIA COLLEGE OF THE ARTS in 1972, the National Museum Art Gallery in 1976 (which became the SINGAPORE ART MUSEUM in 1996), institutional and corporate collections, and involvement in international exhibitions, biennales, research and publication projects, have helped reinforce the position of visual arts in the cultural life of Singapore. The development of art history here, with its unique linkages with broader Asian and international aesthetics, has contributed to Singapore's multi- and inter-cultural dynamism.

medical supplies, intervening to assist them against some of the brutalities of his subordinates and helping several civilian internees to work outside Changi Prison for the Singapore Municipality. Asahi, in cooperation with Marquis Yoshichika Tokugawa, who was president of the Raffles Museum and the Botanic Gardens in Syonan-to (Singapore), and E.J.H. Corner, assistant director of the Botanic Gardens, was instrumental in saving the valuable historical and scientific records on Malaya and Singapore held at the Raffles Museum and other locations. (*See* NATIONAL MUSEUM OF SINGAPORE.)

ASAS 50 Malay literary movement. ASAS 50 is an abbreviation of 'Angkatan Sasterawan 50'. It was formed in 1950 by 19 writers led by MUHAMMED ARIF AHMAD, MASURI S.N. and Hamzah Hussein. By 1952, it had attracted more than 100 members, many of whom were teachers, writers, journalists and people from the film industry. They eschewed 'art for art's sake', and chose instead to use literature as a means of pressing for independence from British colonial rule, and of highlighting social issues and injustices. The theme of most of their works was the common man's daily struggle for a decent life. Notable examples are works from short-story writer Keris Mas and poets Masuri S.N. and Usman Awang. Other themes explored by ASAS 50 included the plight of workers (such as seamen and plantation workers) and their frequent strikes, the impact of war, poverty, and prostitution. ASAS 50 wrote to the colonial government demanding better jobs and housing for everyone.

ASAS 50 has continued to be active in the promotion of Malay literature. In 2006, it organized the Sayembara Noktah Putih short story and poetry writing competition.

ASEAN *See* ASSOCIATION OF SOUTHEAST ASIAN NATIONS.

ASEAN Free Trade Area The ASSOCIATION OF SOUTHEAST ASIAN NATIONS Free Trade Area (AFTA) was established at the 4th ASEAN Summit in Singapore in 1992 to eliminate tariff barriers among its members. Its aim is to integrate the ASEAN economies into a single production base and create a regional market exceeding 500 million people, making ASEAN a more attractive destination for large-scale direct investment from

inside and outside the region.

A critical step in this direction is the liberalization of trade in the region. The Common Effective Preferential Tariff (CEPT) Scheme is a cooperative arrangement among ASEAN member countries to reduce intra-regional tariffs and remove non-tariffs barriers over a 15-year period commencing 1 January 1993. The original goal of the scheme was to reduce tariffs on all manufactured goods to between 0 and 5 per cent by the year 2008. This was later moved forward, first to 2003, then later to 2002.

The target year of 2002 applied to the six original signatories to the CEPT-AFTA: Brunei, Indonesia, Malaysia, the Philippines, Singapore and Thailand. The new ASEAN members such as Cambodia, Laos, Myanmar and Vietnam also committed to the acceleration of AFTA but on a different timetable. By 2004, 98.6 per cent of the products in the CEPT Inclusion List (IL) of the original signatories had been brought down to the 0–5 per cent tariff range. For the new ASEAN member countries, 79.1 per cent of the products traded in the region had been moved into the IL and tariffs on 69.9 per cent of these items had been brought down to the 0–5 per cent band.

Since the inception of CEPT-AFTA, intra-ASEAN exports have grown at a faster rate than ASEAN's total exports. AFTA is important because it makes ASEAN more competitive at a time when both China and India are expanding rapidly and posing a great challenge to ASEAN.

ASEAN Regional Forum A security forum established in 1994 for the Asia–Pacific region. Its original membership included the member nations of ASEAN (the ASSOCIATION OF SOUTHEAST ASIAN NATIONS), the United States, China, Australia, New Zealand, Canada and Russia. The ASEAN Regional Forum (ARF) is based on the principle of 'cooperative security', which implies that security is best achieved through dialogue as a way of building mutual confidence and trust. The ARF brought together former Cold War adversaries, such as Russia and the US, China and Russia, China and India, and Vietnam and Thailand. The ARF was conceptualized by Singapore and adopted by ASEAN.

Some initial steps towards confidence-building have been undertaken, such as the exchange of defence policy statements, the publication of defence White Papers on a voluntary basis, and meetings of heads of national defence colleges. But more advanced confidence-building measures, such as advance notification of military exercises, or non-deployment of troops within 100 km of national borders, have not yet been undertaken by the ARF, partly because of lingering conflicts in the region, and more generally because of concerns about sovereignty. The ARF is

ASEAN Sculpture Garden

gradually moving from confidence-building to preventive diplomacy.

The ARF's main contribution has been the engagement of China, Japan, India and the US. Initially, China was concerned that the US could use the ARF to raise the Taiwan issue, or that ASEAN would use the ARF to internationalize its territorial disputes with China in the South China Sea. China soon realized that the ARF gave it an opportunity to engage its neighbours and reassure them about China's intentions. The US was initially worried that the multilateral security approach represented in the ARF would undercut the rationale for its bilateral alliances in the region. However, it too came to accept the ARF as a necessary element of the regional security architecture which would complement, rather than compete with, its bilateral relationships in the region.

ASEAN Sculpture Garden An area located in Fort Canning Park where sculptures from the ASEAN region are displayed. The ASEAN Sculpture Garden was launched following an ASEAN Sculpture Symposium in 1982. At the gathering, five members of the Southeast Asian grouping were asked to donate a work to the park to commemorate the region's unity and promote a sense of community among its sculptors. Each of the 5-m tall sculptures displayed in the park is intended to reflect the commitment of member nations to forging closer ties with each other. The works are *Unity* by Indonesia, *Taning Sari* by Malaysia, *Fredesvinda* by the Philippines, *Concentration* by Thailand and *Balance* by Singapore sculptor NG ENG TENG.

Asia–Europe Foundation A non-profit foundation, the mission of the Asia–Europe Foundation (ASEF) is to advance mutual understanding, deeper engagement and continuing collaboration among the people of Asia and Europe, through greater intellectual, cultural and people-to-people exchanges between the two regions. It does so through a range of programmes, confer-

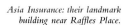

ences and workshops at the civil society level. These activities focus on promoting policy debate and strategic thinking on themes of inter-regional importance, enhancing cross-cultural dialogue and professional exchanges among young artists and other cultural practitioners, and building bridges through youth education and cooperation among future leaders. The programmes draw participants from a variety of backgrounds, including academics, officials, journalists, students, artists, and members of think-tanks and non-government organizations.

ASEF was launched in Singapore in February 1997 by members of the Asia–Europe Meeting (ASEM)—seven from the ASSOCIATION OF SOUTHEAST ASIAN NATIONS plus China, Japan and Korea, and 15 from the European Union, plus the European Commission. Following a proposal by then Singapore Prime Minister GOH CHOK TONG, the first ASEM Summit was held in Bangkok in March 1996. Since then, summit-level meetings have been held every two years. In 2004, membership expanded to include ten new members from the European Union, as well as Cambodia, Laos and Myanmar. Singapore-based ASEF is the only existing ASEM institution. The executive director position alternates between an Asian and a European, beginning with veteran Singaporean diplomat, Tommy Koh. After six years in a heritage house in Nassim Hill, ASEF moved to Kent Ridge to become part of a cluster of international organizations and think-tanks at Heng Mui Keng Terrace.

Asia Insurance Incorporated on 11 July 1923, Asia Insurance Company Limited is one of the oldest local insurance companies. It was originally set up to offer general insurance for local businesses. In 1948, it set up its life assurance company in Singapore, followed by the commencement of its operations in Malaya in 1959. The group has since expanded its presence to Brunei, Taiwan, Myanmar, China and Vietnam.

Despite adopting what is considered by many industry watchers as a conservative approach to asset management, Asia Insurance was the first Asian general insurer outside of Japan to be awarded the highest rating of 'A+' by the international rating agency, Standard & Poor's. The group has an asset base of about $444 million with shareholders funds of $215 million in 2004. Though one of the smaller insurers in Singapore, it is also generally regarded as one of the strongest covering Singapore and Malaysia. Both Asia Insurance and its sister company, The Asia Life Assurance Society Limited, are subsidiaries of Asia General Holdings Ltd, which has interests in life and general insurance, property and investment holdings.

The property arm of Asia Insurance in Singapore is the developer and manager of several residential projects and commercial buildings such as Asia Garden, Asia Insurance Building, and Asia Chambers; and it is owner-manager of Hotel Asia at Scotts Road.

The company's office building was once the tallest in Southeast Asia: the Asia Insurance Building was officially opened on 10 December 1955 by the governor of Singapore, Sir Robert Brown Black. This distinctive, 19-storey, art-deco building was designed by Ng Keng Siang. It still stands at Finlayson Green, but was sold in 2006.

Asia Pacific Breweries Maker of Tiger Beer. Asia Pacific Breweries (APB) was formed in 1931 as Malayan Breweries, a joint venture between FRASER & NEAVE and the Dutch brewers Heineken. It established Singapore's first brewery and launched the Tiger Beer brand in 1932. It added Anchor Beer to its product range in the 1940s, as well as SP Lager in Papua New Guinea in the 1950s. *Time for a Tiger,* the title of the 1956 first novel of British author ANTHONY BURGESS, is a reference not to the wild cat but to the beer.

Reflecting its regional aspirations, the company was renamed Asia Pacific Breweries Limited in 1990. By 2006, APB operated 29 breweries in ten countries— Singapore, Malaysia, Thailand, Vietnam, Cambodia, China, New Zealand, Papua New Guinea, India and Sri Lanka.

Group sales for the financial year 2005 were $1.44 billion. The company oversees a portfolio of over 40 beer brands including Tiger Beer, Anchor Beer, Baron's Strong Brew and ABC Extra Stout, as well as the international brew, Heineken. Besides its flagship Tiger Beer, another homegrown brand, Anchor, is brewed and sold in Singapore, Malaysia, Vietnam, Cambodia and southern China. APB brews and markets Heineken in six countries: Singapore, Malaysia, China, New Zealand, Thailand and Vietnam. The brewer offers a range of other brands in overseas markets: in Shanghai, it offers the REEB brand, and a Tiger variant named Tiger Crystal that caters to an increasing demand for light beers; in New Zealand, it offers brands such as Tui, Export Gold and Monteith's; in Vietnam, Bivina and Amber Stout; in Thailand, Cheers; and in Papua New Guinea, APB's range—which includes SP Lager, South Pacific Export Lager and Niugini Ice Beer—has gained over 90 per cent of the market.

Asia–Pacific Economic Cooperation The Asia–Pacific Economic Cooperation (APEC) inter-governmental grouping was formed in 1989 to facilitate TRADE and economic cooperation within the Asia–Pacific community. Singapore is one of 12 founding members. The number of members has since expanded to 21. It operates on the basis of non-binding commitments and open dialogue. Decisions made within APEC are reached by consensus, and commitments are undertaken on a voluntary basis.

APEC has played an important role in forging and speeding up liberalization of global as well as regional trade and investment. Key to achieving APEC's vision are the Bogor Goals, adopted by the leaders at their 1994 meeting in Bogor, Indonesia, which outlined the targets of achieving free and open trade and investment in the Asia Pacific by 2010 for industrialized economies and 2020 for developing economies.

In addition, APEC plays the role of ensuring the safe and efficient movement of goods, services and people across borders in the region through policy alignment and economic and technical cooperation. During the 2004 meeting in Santiago, Chile, APEC leaders, led by Singapore, agreed to focus on maritime and port security as a key counter-terrorism priority.

Asia Research Institute The Asia Research Institute (ARI) was established in July 2001 at the NATIONAL UNIVERSITY OF SINGAPORE (NUS) as one of NUS' strategic initiatives to make the university an important research hub. Scholars at ARI engage the social sciences and especially the interdisciplinary frontiers between and beyond disciplines. ARI has a team of full-time researchers and also provides support for doctoral and post-doctoral research, conferences, workshops, seminars and study groups. Its research clusters are organized around the following themes: The Changing Family in Asia; Asian Migration; Cultural Studies in Asia; Religion and Globalization in Asian Contexts; Southeast Asia–China Interactions; and Asian Cities.

Asian Civilisations Museum See box.

Asian dollar bond market Debt market launched in 1971 for instruments denominated in foreign currencies and listed on the SINGAPORE EXCHANGE. Listed debt issues include Euro–Asian bonds floated simultaneously and listed on Asian and European bourses. While the first debt issuers were mainly Singapore GOVERNMENT-LINKED COMPANIES, the market has since extended to multinational corporations, banks, governments and international organizations.

Asian dollar market Asian equivalent of the Eurodollar Market. It was established in 1968 in Singapore, when the government gave approval for the local branch of Bank of America to borrow deposits of non-residents based in foreign currencies, and use them to finance corporate activities in Asia. The Asian dollar market (ADM) is therefore primarily an international money and capital market for foreign currencies.

Asia Pacific Breweries: an early label for Tiger Beer.

Asian Civilisations Museum Though founded in 1997, the Asian Civilisations Museum (ACM) traces its roots to the 1887 British-established Raffles Library and Museum and its collections (*see* NATIONAL MUSEUM OF SINGAPORE). The concept to devolve the old National Museum into three separate institutions was proposed in 1991 by Brigadier-General GEORGE YEO, who was minister for information at the time. The mission of the newly formed ACM was to highlight the diverse cultures which influenced the development of Singapore: Chinese, Malay, Indian, and Islamic/West Asian. At the museum's official opening at EMPRESS PLACE in 2003, Ambassador-at-Large Professor Tommy Koh said 'it reflects who we are and where we came from'.

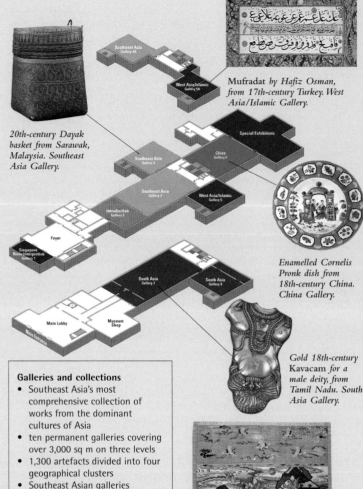

Mufradat *by Hafiz Osman, from 17th-century Turkey. West Asia/Islamic Gallery.*

20th-century Dayak basket from Sarawak, Malaysia. Southeast Asia Gallery.

Armenian Street
The first home of the ACM was in Armenian Street, in what was originally the TAO NAN SCHOOL. This building was constructed in 1910 in a style described as 'Eclectic Classical'. It was renovated in 1994–96, and the museum moved in during the following year. Later, after the bulk of the collection moved to Empress Place, the process began of dedicating the Armenian Street site to the documentation and display of

Peranakan, or Straits Chinese, culture and history. The ACM (Armenian Street) was scheduled to re-open as the Peranakan Museum in 2008.

Enamelled Cornelis Pronk dish from 18th-century China. China Gallery.

Empress Place
In 2003, the ACM moved to much larger and newly renovated premises in Empress Place. This landmark building was initially constructed in 1867 to house the colonial government offices. Located on a bend near the mouth of the Singapore River, the area is historically significant as the landing site of Sir Stamford Raffles in 1819. The building

was designed by colonial engineer J.F.A. MCNAIR and built by convict labour. Laid out symmetrically along a central axis, the building combined Neo-Palladian Classical elements with tropical features such as a wide shaded porch and timber louvred shutters. Three major extensions were added in 1880, 1904–09 and 1920.

Beginning in 1997, a six-year extension and renovation project prepared the building for its role as the new home of the ACM, offering state-of-the-art conservation technology, historically evocative 19th-century architecture and views of the city and river.

The galleries are clustered into the four main regions which shaped the establishment of modern Singapore—China, South Asia, West Asia/Islamic and Southeast Asia (the majority of the 19th-century artefacts from the original Raffles Museum are found in this latter section).

Gold 18th-century Kavacam *for a male deity, from Tamil Nadu. South Asia Gallery.*

Galleries and collections
- Southeast Asia's most comprehensive collection of works from the dominant cultures of Asia
- ten permanent galleries covering over 3,000 sq m on three levels
- 1,300 artefacts divided into four geographical clusters
- Southeast Asian galleries include: Prehistory, The Malay World
- China galleries include: The Patriarchal Family, The Imperial System
- South Asia galleries include: Medieval India, Stone Sculptures
- West Asia/Islamic galleries include: Islam as a Way of Life, Islamic Art

Eight Immortals on silk hanging from China, c. 1600. China Gallery.

Its operation is subject to the approval of the MONETARY AUTHORITY OF SINGAPORE, and a separate bookkeeping entity known as the Asian Currency Unit is used. Most of the funds come from external or non-resident sources such as central banks, multinational companies and those seeking a stable location for the deposit of cash. Developmental projects in the region can be financed with the surplus funds which the ADM provides to financial institutions. The ADM has a large volume of inter-bank and non-bank loans (*see* Chart 1). It has been recently strengthened by increased lending to East Asia as well as Europe. The ADM is one of the largest off-shore financial markets in the world; its assets have grown from US$30 million in 1968 to a record high of US$582 billion in December 2004, before a slight dip in early 2005 (*see* Chart 2).

Asian financial crisis The Asian financial crisis erupted in July 1997, with a number of Asian countries experiencing sharp declines in the values of their currencies, stock markets, and other asset prices. The crisis threatened these countries' financial systems, and disrupted their real economies, accompanied by large contractions in credit and economic activity that created a social and political crisis alongside a financial one in some afflicted nations.

The crisis began in Thailand as a result of intense speculation that the baht was over-valued. This led to the floating of the currency on 2 July 1997, and it immediately fell by 15 per cent. The contagion spread rapidly to other Asian countries, which were vulnerable to an erosion of competitiveness after the devaluation of the baht. In addition, unnerved by economic events in Latin America, Western investors lost confi-

dence in securities in East Asia and began to pull money out, which compounded the crisis. In September 1998, Malaysia pegged its currency to the US dollar as part of capital controls to shield its economy from the effects of the crisis.

The countries most affected by the crisis were Indonesia, Korea and Thailand. The Thai stock market dropped 75 per cent in 1997, and Finance One, its largest finance company, collapsed. The South Korean economy demonstrated strong macroeconomic fundamentals but was burdened by non-performing loans in the banking sector. The excess debt situation led to major business failures and takeovers. By the end of November 1997, the Seoul stock exchange had fallen by more than 15 per cent. Indonesia's rupiah crisis began in July but intensified in November 1997. Companies that had borrowed in US dollars had to face higher debt servicing costs due to the decline of the rupiah. That, coupled with steep price hikes for food staples, led to riots throughout the country. The Indonesian economy contracted by 13.5 per cent of GDP in 1997.

Despite distress in the region, Singapore emerged without serious damage. Although the stock and property markets took a beating, the economy performed well under the circumstances. Nonetheless, Singapore's annual GDP growth rate fell from 8.3 per cent in 1997 to -1.4 per cent in 1998. The economy rebounded in 1999 with 7.2 per cent GDP growth.

Asian Women's Welfare Association

Established in 1970, and registered as a charity in November 1984, the Asian Women's Welfare Association (AWWA) seeks to provide a comprehensive range of services for the disadvantaged from infancy to old age. It aims to improve their well-being and equip them with useful skills. Members must be female and resident in Singapore. AWWA provides homes for the elderly and runs family service centres. The centres are run by professionally trained social workers and counsellors, but much of the work is done by AWWA volunteers.

Association of Banks in Singapore, The

The Association of Banks in Singapore (ABS) was formed in 1973 after Singapore and Malaysia ended the interchangeability agreement on their currencies and each issued its own currency. ABS membership is voluntary and is open to both local and foreign banks licensed by the MONETARY AUTHORITY OF SINGAPORE (MAS) to operate in Singapore. As of 30 April 2006, the ABS had 106 ordinary and seven associate members who are involved in a wide spectrum of financial and banking activities, ranging from major global giants to smaller financial niche service providers.

The role of the ABS is to represent and further the interest of its member banks, set standards of good practice and upgrade the expertise of the Singapore banking sector. The association holds regular consultations with the MAS to discuss industry issues and promote a sound financial system. It also provides input for legislation and guidelines relating to the financial industry, and helps establish common ground for member

Asian Women's Welfare Association: morning exercise session.

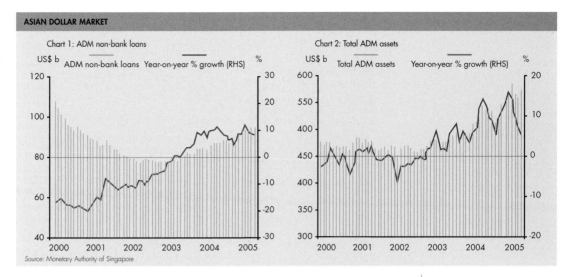

banks to reconcile differing opinions and support projects of mutual benefit. The association liaises with institutions and trade associations, such as the SINGAPORE EXCHANGE, the Real Estate Developers Association and the CONSUMERS ASSOCIATION OF SINGAPORE, who use banking and financial services extensively. ABS also works closely with MAS to support Singapore's continuing ambition to become a premier financial centre within the Asia–Pacific region.

Association of Muslim Professionals

Malay/Muslim self-help group and non-profit organization. The Association of Muslim Professionals (AMP) was formed against the backdrop of a number of issues in the 1980s which thrust the Malay/Muslim community into the spotlight, such as the questioning of Malay loyalty in the army, the perceived lack of Malay voters' support for the government and the change in the long-held policy of automatic tuition-fee waiver for all Malay tertiary students. A core group of Muslim professionals organized the National Convention of Singapore Malay/Muslim Professionals in 1990 to discuss the future directions of the Malay/Muslim community. The convention, attended by over 500 professionals, endorsed the creation of an independent and non-partisan organization to help solve the problems of the community through the mobilization of those who are more successful.

AMP was incorporated on 10 October 1991 as a company limited by guarantee and was registered as a charitable organization on 19 October. Its long-term vision is to develop Malay/Muslims into a 'model Muslim minority community'. AMP has four core areas of activity—social action, education, training and research—that work towards accelerating the development of the community. It runs various programmes and schemes in educational enrichment, work-skills training and family-life coaching. In 2000, AMP mooted the

idea of a 'collective leadership' in which non-political and independent leaders could represent the views of the community, complementing the role of Malay members of Parliament. This proposal however, was rejected by the government and was subsequently dropped by AMP.

Association of Small & Medium Enterprises

Non-governmental, non-profit body founded in 1986 by a group of entrepreneurs to support the national pro-enterprise drive initiated during Singapore's 'Second Industrial Revolution'. The objectives of the association (also known as ASME) include advancing the interests of SMALL- AND MEDIUM-SIZED ENTERPRISES in general, strengthening their bonds with the government and motivating entrepreneurs. It offers training programmes and seminars, networking events, and presents Entrepreneur of the Year and Singapore Promising Brand awards.

Association of Southeast Asian Nations

Formed in 1967, the Association of Southeast Asian Nations (ASEAN) originally consisted of five countries—

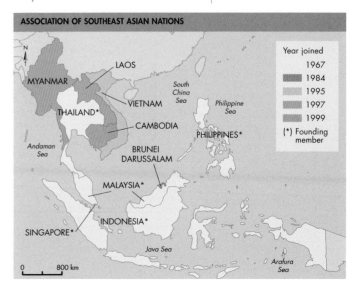

Indonesia, Malaysia, the Philippines, Singapore and Thailand. ASEAN has since been expanded to include Brunei, Vietnam, Laos, Myanmar and Cambodia.

ASEAN was founded at a time when the war in Vietnam was spreading into Cambodia and when various countries in the region were facing communist insurgencies. Singapore helped to form ASEAN because Singapore wanted to create a regional framework for cultivating stable and productive relations with its neighbours.

ASEAN solidarity has had concrete benefits for Singapore. In October 1978, Australia announced a new International Civil Aviation Policy which restricted the operations of Southeast Asian airlines, including Singapore Airlines. Singapore sought ASEAN support for its position and the bilateral disagreement escalated into an Australia versus ASEAN dispute. In the end, Australia backed down.

ASEAN was also an important platform for Singapore to mobilize diplomatic opposition to Vietnam's invasion of Cambodia in 1978, and its subsequent occupation. Singapore was part of the ASEAN team campaigning to free Cambodia from the twin evils of rule by the Khmer Rouge and occupation by a foreign country.

Economically, ASEAN has been through two phases. In the 1970s and 1980s, ASEAN's idea of economic cooperation consisted of allocating a large industrial project to each member-country, the products of which would be protected from competition. Being a free market economy, Singapore was unenthusiastic about such schemes, although it reluctantly went along with the rest of ASEAN. In the early 1990s, however, faced with growing competition from a rising China and from other economic groups, ASEAN moved towards regional economic integration instead.

Thus, Singapore strongly supported Thailand in its push for economic integration, which led to the 1992 agreement on an ASEAN FREE TRADE AREA. Singapore has been a strong proponent of regional integration and of stronger regional institutions ever since. Singapore also pushed the concept of e-ASEAN—using information and communications technology as a means of integration. In 2003, Prime Minister Goh Chok Tong proposed the ASEAN Economic Community as the next stage in Southeast Asian integration.

Beyond economics, ASEAN, particularly Singapore, took a leading role in one of the region's most successful endeavours in regional cooperation—the collective mobilization against SARS (*see* SEVERE ACUTE RESPIRATORY SYNDROME) in 2003 — and in the international response to the December 2004 earthquake and tsunami.

Singapore has been at the forefront of ASEAN's efforts to engage partners outside the region. It provided much of the intellectual underpinning of the ASEAN REGIONAL FORUM for security dialogue and cooperation in East Asia and it influenced the eventual shape of the ASEAN-driven EAST ASIAN SUMMIT. Singapore also initiated the idea of a free trade arrangement between ASEAN and Australia, and between ASEAN and New Zealand. It set the tone for ASEAN's positive response to China's proposal for an ASEAN–China free trade area and led ASEAN's move to reach out to India.

Association of Women for Action and Research

Also known as AWARE, the association was formed in November 1985 as a voluntary organization made up of women concerned with women's rights in the home and workplace. AWARE has three main areas of focus: support, research and advocacy. It strives to raise awareness of women's and men's rights and responsibilities. It runs seminars which seek to educate and empower women on their rights and provides counselling, legal assistance and support for women. It also runs a helpline. Past presidents of AWARE include former nominated members of Parliament KANWALJIT SOIN and Braema Mathi.

attorney-general *See* LEGAL SYSTEM.

Attorney-General's Chambers

A colonial-era government building that is part of the new Parliament House complex, the 19th-century building, gazetted a national monument on 14 February 1992, has been through several rounds of renovation to suit changing requirements and architectural tastes. The core of the building is far older than its early 20th-century Edwardian facade. The first building on the site was the one-storey Court House annexe, built c. 1839. This was later either replaced by, or enlarged into, a two-storey building that housed the Government Printing Office. In 1906, funds were approved for its substantial rebuilding.

The PUBLIC WORKS DEPARTMENT occupied the building from the late 1960s to 1976, and it was subsequently renovated to become the Attorney-General's Chambers. The building was vacated in 1992 so that it could be restored and incorporated into the new Parliament House complex.

Auditor-General's Office

The Auditor-General's Office is responsible for auditing and reporting on the accounts of all departments and offices of the government, the PUBLIC SERVICE COMMISSION (PSC), the Legal Service Commission, the SUPREME COURT, all SUBORDINATE COURTS and PARLIAMENT. The auditor-general is appointed by the president, acting on the advice of the prime minister (who must consult the chairman of the PSC). The term of office is six years but reappointment is possible for further six-year terms.

Automobile Association of Singapore: motorcycle formerly used for emergency service patrol.

To ensure independence, the auditor-general may be removed from office only by the president, and only under certain conditions. The president must receive and concur with the advice of the prime minister. The latter may not tender such advice unless the auditor-general is no longer able to discharge his functions or is guilty of misbehaviour; otherwise such advice requires the concurrence of a tribunal consisting of the CHIEF JUSTICE and two other judges of the Supreme Court nominated for that purpose by the chief justice. Furthermore, the auditor-general's remuneration cannot be altered to his disadvantage during his term of office.

In addition to his general duties, the auditor-general has to inform the president of any proposed government transaction which, to his knowledge, is likely to draw on reserves not accumulated by the government during its current term of office.

Automobile Association of Singapore

The beginnings of the Automobile Association can be traced to 1905, when a body was created in London, initially to help motorists avoid police 'speed traps'.

The first 'auto car' arrived in Singapore in 1896. By 1907, however, automotive technology had developed significantly, the numbers of motorists had increased and it was clear that they needed organizing. In March of that year, the Singapore Automobile Club was born. In January 1932, the club became part of the newly formed Automobile Association of Malaya. In March 1952, with the number of Singapore motorists growing rapidly, it parted company with its Malayan counterpart to become the Automobile Association of Singapore (AAS). By the 1970s, its emergency breakdown service, which had started in 1948 with one mechanic on a motorcycle, was handling 30,000 calls annually. By 2005, the AAS had over 80,000 members.

autonomous schools Government or government-aided schools that have greater autonomy and more funds than mainstream schools to enable them to provide a wider range of programmes. They differ from INDEPENDENT SCHOOLS in their limited autonomy. Owing to the elitism associated with independent schools, the government subsequently set up autonomous schools, which adhere to broad education policies set by the MINISTRY OF EDUCATION (MOE). Admission is based on merit and class size is the same as that of other government and government-aided schools. Autonomous schools, however, may charge an additional school fee of between $3 and $15 per month to cover the costs of the enhanced educational programmes offered.

In 1994, there were only six autonomous schools: Anderson Secondary, Bukit Panjang Government High, Convent of the Holy Infant Jesus Secondary (Toa Payoh), Dunman High School, River Valley High School and VICTORIA SCHOOL. This increased to 25 by 2006. Autonomous schools have not only maintained high standards, but have made use of their autonomy to introduce new ideas and so spearhead improvements in the system. The MOE, therefore, decided in 2000 to expand the number of autonomous schools to 30–40 in the coming years, representing some 25 per cent of all secondary schools.

avian flu *See* BIRD FLU.

Aw Boon Haw (c. 1882–1954) Businessman, banker and philanthropist. Aw Boon Haw was born in Rangoon, Burma, although the year is uncertain.

The Aw brothers inherited a small pharmacy, Eng Aun Tong, from their father in 1908. The brothers opened their first shop in Bangkok in 1911 and their Singapore shop in 1923. Three years later, Aw moved his headquarters to Singapore.

Together with his brother Boon Par, Aw Boon Haw built an Asia-wide business empire, marketing pharmaceutical products under the trademark Tiger Brand, the principal product of which was TIGER BALM, an ointment marketed as a remedy for headaches, stomach aches, coughs, colds, rheumatism and insect bites. He became known as the 'Tiger Balm King'. He established the well-known HAW PAR VILLA (also known as Tiger Balm Gardens) in Singapore and Hong Kong, and built 26 mansions around Asia.

In 1929, Aw began publishing Chinese daily newspaper SIN CHEW JIT POH in Singapore. This was followed by other papers in Swatow (present-day Shantou), Amoy (Xiamen) and Hong Kong. By 1939, he had started 12 newspapers in eight East Asian cities.

On 4 February 1950, Aw Boon Haw and other HAKKA merchants established Chung Khiaw Bank in Singapore with Aw as its first chairman. He owned the world's largest private exhibition of jade and was also a generous philanthropist, donating initially 25 per cent and later 50 per cent of Eng Aun Tong's profits to charity.

Aw had four wives, seven sons and two daughters. He died on 4 September 1954 in Honolulu while journeying back to Singapore following an operation in Boston. He was cremated in Honolulu and his ashes were taken to Hong Kong.

Axe Brand Universal Oil Medicated oil made from a blend of eucalyptus, menthol, camphor and other essential oils. Axe Brand Universal Oil is manufactured and distributed by Leung Kai Fook Medical Company, a company founded in 1928 by Leung Yun Chee, who arrived in Singapore from Shunde, China, in the 1920s.

With savvy advertising and marketing, Leung sold large quantities of his medicated oil and business flourished. After World War II, Leung built the six-storey Leung Kai Fook Building on South Bridge Road. He died in 1971 and his son Heng Keng succeeded to the leadership of the company. Today, Axe Brand Universal Oil is sold in over 40 countries. In 1986 the company ventured into the hospitality business in China.

Azahari revolt In December 1962, the leader of Brunei's dominant political party, the Partai Rakyat Brunei (PRB), Sheik Ahmad Mahmud Azahari (1929–) led a revolt against the British in protest against British plans to include Brunei in the soon-to-be-formed Federation of Malaysia. Azahari had long advocated a union of the North Borneo states—which would have included Sabah, Sarawak and Brunei—instead, and he supported Indonesian President Sukarno's Maphilindo concept of close ties between all the Malay states. The PRB was at the forefront of opposition to Tunku ABDUL RAHMAN and Malaysia and garnered increased support as such, accusing the Tunku of colonialism, racism and self-serving ambition.

Azahari's and the PRB's opposition to the Federation of Malaysia coincided with the BARISAN SOSIALIS' objection to a merger as well. In 1962, while on a visit to Singapore, Azahari was introduced to the Barisan's leader, LIM CHIN SIONG, by SAID ZAHARI. This meeting was later cited as part of a conspiracy between the PRB, the Barisan and Sukarno to instigate the Brunei revolt in an effort to jettison the Federation. Brunei's Sultan Omar Ali Saifuddin was originally non-committal about Malaysia but later declared that he found the proposition attractive.

The revolt broke out on the morning of 8 December 1962. Azahari was then in Manila and it was left to the PRB's secretary-general Jasin Affandy to proclaim the independence of the Unitary State of North Borneo (Negara Kesatuan Kalimantan Utara). The rebels failed to capture the sultan and the British authorities brought in the GURKHAS and Highlanders to deal with Azahari's forces. By 11 December, the revolt was crushed and

Axe Brand Universal Oil: advertisement, 1930s.

Sukarno was widely thought to be responsible for instigating and planning it. In January 1963, with British troops heavily deployed along the Indonesian border, Sukarno announced a campaign to confront the British over the forced inclusion of the North Borneo states in the Federation of Malaysia. The campaign was known as Konfrontasi (CONFRONTATION).

Azman Abdullah (1963–) Sportsman. A bodybuilder who won Singapore's first Mr Universe title in 1993, Azman Abdullah was twice named Sportsman of the Year (1993, 1994) by the Singapore National Olympic Council. He is also a three-time Southeast Asian (SEA) Games gold medallist (Jakarta, 1989; Manila, 1991; Singapore, 1993). At the age of 30, he won the World Games middleweight (under 80 kg) title in Holland. He followed this with a victory in the light-heavyweight category of the World Championships in Seoul, turning professional at the end of 1993.

Azman entered the SINGAPORE SPORTS COUNCIL HALL OF FAME, but was also a source of controversy. He lost the opportunity in 1994 to achieve his ambition of becoming Mr Olympia by suddenly announcing he would quit the sport, a decision he reversed two months later. Disappointed at being awarded second place in the Coca-Cola/*The Sunday Times* Annual Sports Star Awards, he returned his trophy and cash prize. Following a failed lawsuit soon after, he remained out of the limelight for six years.

Azman returned to international competition in 2003 at 40, winning a bronze medal at the SEA Games in Vietnam. In 2005, he became assistant national coach but continued to compete internationally.

Axe Brand Universal Oil

Aw Boon Haw

Azman Abdullah

B

Babas *See* PERANAKANS.

Babu Sahib, Moulavi (1929–2001) Cleric and community leader. Born in India, Moulavi Babu Sahib came to Singapore in 1947 to help in his uncle's business. In 1950, he was inspired to further his understanding of Islam after attending a lecture delivered by ABDUL ALEEM SIDDIQUE. In 1957, he travelled back to India to seek a formal Islamic education.

Babu returned to Singapore in 1964, becoming involved in JAMIYAH and other associations such as DARUL ARQAM, MENDAKI, the ASSOCIATION OF MUSLIM PROFESSIONALS (AMP) and the Inter-Religious Organisation (IRO). He became a member of the Appeals Board of MAJLIS UGAMA ISLAM SINGAPURA (MUIS) (1970–76), and served as a member of the Fatwa Committee of MUIS (1975–76). Among the many awards he received were the Allamah Sir Muhammad Iqbal Centenary Medal for Islamic Scholarship, and the Meritorious Service Award from MUIS (1994).

Babu was the author of *Know Islam* and *The Law of Inheritance in Islam*. However, the majority of his written works—mainly translations and commentaries on classical Islamic texts—were never published. Perhaps his greatest work was his translation of and commentary on the theological poem *Jawharat al-Tawhid* (Pearls of Monotheism). Babu laboured over this extensive work for three decades, finally publishing it under the auspices of MUIS as *The Tenets of Islam* in 2000.

Badang Malay legend recorded in the SEJARAH MELAYU (Malay Annals). Badang was a slave who became a hero. He lived in Saluang and spent his days toiling over his master's land and catching fish. However, he always found his traps filled with fish bones and half-eaten fish. Suspecting that someone had been eating his catch, he decided to trap the culprit, who turned out to be a river spirit. He attacked it with a parang (a Malay knife), but the spirit, fearing for its life, begged for mercy. He promised to grant Badang any wish if he spared its life. Badang agreed, on condition that the spirit granted him superhuman strength. To acquire this, he had to consume the vomit of the spirit. He subsequently used this new-found strength to win his release from his master.

Upon hearing of Badang's strength, Seri Rama Wira Kerma, a 14th-century ruler of TEMASEK, summoned him. After displaying his strength and skills, he was appointed chief commander. In one of his feats of strength, Badang threw an enormous stone from a hill. It landed at the mouth of the SINGAPORE RIVER. In the 19th century, the SINGAPORE STONE was found in that vicinity.

When news of Badang's strength reached distant lands, champions were sent to challenge him. The King of Kalinga in India sent Nadi Bijaya Pikrama, a fierce wrestler, while the noblemen of Perlak sent Benderang. Badang emerged victorious from both contests, and eventually lived in Temasek until his death.

Baha'i Religion founded by Bahá'u'lláh (1817–92). Baha'i literally means 'follower of the *Bahá'u'lláh*' (Glory of God). The religion advocates unity, and that the world's religions are successive stages in the revelation of God's will and purpose for humanity. The faith is based on fundamental principles which include: acceptance of the unity of humanity, and being of service to mankind; recognition of the divine origin and the essential oneness of all the world's great religions; gender equality; elimination of extremes of wealth and poverty, and seeking spiritual solutions to economic problems; compulsory universal education; recognition that true religion works in harmony with science; and maintenance of a sustainable balance between nature and technology.

The Baha'i faith was introduced into Singapore in 1950 by Dr K.M. Fozdar (1898–1958) and his wife, Shirin Fozdar (1905–92). The Fozdars, who were born into the Baha'i faith, had been active in community and humanitarian work in India, working particularly with the Harijans (untouchables). In 1950, they volunteered to move to Singapore to establish the Baha'i faith. Dr Fozdar, who was then a medical officer in the state railways, resigned from his post, and the couple left India for Singapore. The first local Spiritual Assembly in Southeast Asia was formed in Singapore in 1952. Today, the Baha'i community comprises over 2,000 members in five local spiritual assemblies. Baha'i marriage is recognized by Singapore law, with the Registrar of Marriages appointing solemnizers. Since 1957, the Baha'is have had an exclusive cemetery site in Choa Chu Kang.

bahara 'Bahara' is a Malay word meaning 'load'; it can also denote an indefinite measure of weight. According to R.J. Wilkinson, author of *A Malay–English Dictionary (Romanised)*, it may have been equal to about 460 pounds but this is uncertain. In Malaya, one *bahara*—equivalent to three PICUL or 300 KATI—equalled 400 pounds (just over 180 kg).

Bahau JAPANESE OCCUPATION resettlement scheme. Bahau was designed as a means of moving people out of Singapore so that they could cultivate food crops in Malaya, thus alleviating food shortages in Singapore. The scheme's Japanese name was Fuji-Go (Fuji Village). Organized by Bishop Adrian Devals of the Catholic Church and the Japanese-sponsored Eurasian Welfare Association, the settlement, located at Bahau, in the Malayan state of Negri Sembilan, was intended for Eurasian and Chinese Catholics, EURASIANS of other Christian denominations, and Europeans from neutral countries such as Switzerland. The first settlers left Singapore in December 1943. The settlers did not have the necessary farming skills or equipment. Many died of diseases such as MALARIA, dysentery and beri-beri. The resettlement scheme was a failure.

See also ENDAU.

Bai Yan (1918–) Actor. Born in Jiangsu, China, Bai Yan is the stage name adopted by Yan Boyuan. He came to Singapore with the Silver Moon Song and Dance Troupe in 1939, which also featured his wife Ye Qing. A versatile actor, director, dancer and magician, Bai Yan's heyday was in the 1950s in AMUSEMENT PARK theatres, when audiences packed the house night after night. Although the performances featured mainly Mandarin songs, the troupe also presented skits and dances. Bai Yan also produced and directed Mandarin drama classics, such as *Lei Yu* (Thunderstorm), *Yuan Ye* (Wilderness), *Ah Q Zheng Chuan* (Story of Ah Q), and *New Year's Sacrifice*.

When the Ministry of Defence set up its Music and Dance Company in 1972, Bai Yan was appointed as its first trainer in comedy sketches, magic and dance. From 1985 to 1996, he was a television drama actor for the SINGAPORE BROADCASTING CORPORATION and later the TELEVISION CORPORATION OF SINGAPORE.

bak chor mee Popular hawker dish. Also known as minced meat noodles, this dish originated from Chaozhou in south China. Egg noodles are boiled and then tossed in a sauce made with chilli paste, lard, sesame oil, soy sauce and a dash of vinegar. This is

Bai Yan

Bak chor mee

Bahau: the first batch of settlers leaves Singapore, December 1943.

usually topped with boiled minced pork, Chinese mushrooms, fishcake slices, bean sprouts and fishballs.

bak kut teh Popular hawker dish. 'Bak kut teh' literally means 'pork rib tea'. This is a dish of pork ribs brewed with herbs, garlic and pepper over a low fire. The result is soft and tender ribs served in a peppery soup. It was traditionally a common breakfast dish that was served with a bowl of steamed rice, you cha kway (dough sticks) and a soy sauce and chilli dip. However, bak kut teh is eaten around the clock these days, and is especially popular as a suppertime dish.

Baker, Maurice (1920–) Academic and diplomat. Born in Alor Star, Kedah, Maurice Baker was educated at the Anglo-Chinese School, Ipoh; Raffles College, Singapore (1941); and King's College, London (on a QUEEN'S SCHOLARSHIP), where he graduated with an honours arts degree in English (1951). While in London, Baker became a founding member of the MALAYAN FORUM and president of the Malayan Students' Union (1948–51). On his return to Singapore, he taught briefly at Victoria School. In 1955, he became a lecturer in English literature at the University of Malaya and, in 1971, became the head of English language and literature (1971–77) at the same university (by this time the University of Singapore).

In 1967, Baker was appointed Singapore's first high commissioner to India (1967–69). His other diplomatic positions included high commissioner to Malaysia (1980–88) and ambassador to the Philippines (1977–79). Baker was also chairman of the National Theatre Trust; president, Malayan Staff Association; and director, Kim Eng Holdings Ltd and Sime Singapore. In 1987, Baker was awarded the MERITORIOUS SERVICE MEDAL.

Balakrishnan, Vivian (1961–) Doctor and politician. Vivian Balakrishnan was educated at the Anglo-Chinese School, National Junior College and the National University of Singapore (NUS), where he obtained an MBBS on a PRESIDENT'S SCHOLARSHIP. He later obtained a masters degree in ophthalmology at NUS (1991). Balakrishnan then joined NUS as a lecturer, and subsequently as a senior lecturer and associate professor.

Bak kut teh

Between 1993 and 1995, he worked at Moorfields Eye Hospital in London. In 1995, he returned to Singapore and was appointed consultant ophthalmologist at the Singapore National Eye Centre (SNEC). In January 1999, he became medical director of the SNEC, and was subsequently appointed chief executive officer of Singapore General Hospital (2000–01).

In 2001, Balakrishnan entered politics on the People's Action Party ticket, becoming member of Parliament for Holland-Bukit Panjang GROUP REPRESENTATION CONSTITUENCY (GRC). In 2006, he was returned unopposed as a member of Parliament for Holland–Bukit Timah GRC.

Balakrishnan was appointed minister of state for national development (2002–04); minister of state for trade and industry (2003–04); senior minister of state for trade and industry (2004–05); second minister for trade and industry (2005–06); minister for community development, youth and sports (2005–); and second minister for information, communications and the arts (2006–).

balance of payments Statistical record of economic transactions between domestic residents (households, firms and government) and foreigners. The external accounts include the current account balance, and the capital and financial account balance. The summation of the two account balances is known as the overall balance of payments (BOP). This balance is measured by changes in the official reserve assets, or MONETARY AUTHORITY OF SINGAPORE (MAS) holdings of foreign currency assets. Foreign exchange intervention operations and swap operations by the MAS facilitate the conversion of export earnings and other receipts into Singapore's official foreign reserves (OFR).

Singapore's overall BOP has been positive in each year since 1966 (with the exception of 2001), thus allowing for a continuous accumulation of foreign reserves. After turning positive in the mid-1980s, the current account surplus rose from 12 per cent during the period 1988–97 to over 20 per cent of gross national income (GNI) between 1998 and 2005, while the capital and financial account deficit correspondingly rose from 7 per cent of GNI (1993–97) to 17 per cent in 2005, reflecting larger capital outflows due to lower investor confidence in the region in the wake of the ASIAN FINANCIAL CRISIS as well as increased outward investments by Singaporean companies. The BOP surplus also increased from an average 6.6 per cent of GNI in the 1980s to around 10 per cent of GNI between 1990 and 1997. However, after the 1997 Asian financial crisis, the BOP surplus fell to a low of 3.3 per cent of GNI between 1998 and 2002. In 2005, the BOP surplus surged to 10.5 per cent of GNI ($20.4 billion), reflecting a rise in current account surplus, which was under-

Joseph Balestier: Balestier Road, named after the first US consul to Singapore, has several buildings of architectural interest.

pinned by a turnaround in the external environment and a strong export recovery.

In line with these developments, strong upward pressures were exerted on the Singapore dollar. Institutional factors such as sizeable fiscal surpluses and reduced liquidity as a result of contributions to the CENTRAL PROVIDENT FUND also placed further strain on the exchange rate. As a result, the MAS's intervention to dampen the Singapore dollar's appreciation contributed to a build-up of OFR. In the post-crisis period from 1998 to 2002, however, the rate of OFR accumulation slowed to around $4.6 billion per year from $10.1 billion in 1990–97. During this period, the frequency and intensity of external shocks increased, and the Singapore dollar came under speculative pressures. But MAS intervention again prevented any sharp devaluation of the Singapore dollar exchange rate.

Maurice Baker

Balestier, Joseph (c. 1785–unknown) Merchant and diplomat. Joseph Balestier was originally appointed United States consul to Riau by President Andrew Jackson. Arriving in Singapore in 1834, Balestier remained on the island due to the significant trade opportunities that existed here. In 1837, he became the first US consul in Singapore. Although he did much to promote American trade in Singapore, his meagre income forced him to go into business for himself. He acted as an agent for US shipping firms, traded in various goods and established a sugar plantation near what is now Balestier Plain.

He was married to Maria Revere, daughter of Paul Revere—the hero of the American Revolution and a bellmaker. Maria commissioned a bell for ST

Vivian Balakrishnan

BALANCE OF PAYMENTS					
Year	Current account balance (A)	Capital and financial account balance (B)	Net errors and omissions (C)	Overall balance (A+B+C)	Official reserves (Net)*
1970	-1750.8	532.6	1,783.0	564.8	-564.8
1980	-3,345.6	3,388.3	1,376.6	1,433.8	-1,433.8
1990	5,659.5	7,115.2	-2,881.9	9,892.5	-9,892.5
1997	26,617.8	-16,554.6	1,792.5	11,855.7	-11,855.7
2000	20,557.0	-9,817.0	1,096.0	11,835.0	-11,835.0
2005	55,372.6	-33,718.0	-1,257.9	20,396.7	-20,396.7

NOTE: Figures are in $'000. *Increase in assets indicated by minus (-) sign.
Source: Economic Survey of Singapore (various issues)

ANDREW'S CATHEDRAL in 1843. This bell is the only Revere Bell outside the US and is now at the National Museum of Singapore.

After Maria died in 1847, Balestier's health deteriorated, and he returned to the US the following year. He later recovered and was appointed US special agent to Brunei (1849). Retiring in 1852, he returned again to the US. Balestier Road is named in his honour.

Ballas, Jacob (1921–2000) Stockbroker. Born to a poor family, Jacob Ballas became a very successful stockbroker and in 1958, founded brokerage J. Ballas & Co. (later, Vickers Ballas and Co.). In 1962, he became chairman of the Malayan Stock Exchange. From 1964 to 1967, he was chairman of the Malaysia and Singapore Stock Exchange. Ballas was also a philanthropist who donated to charitable causes, as well as suppporting the Jewish community and his alma mater, St Andrew's School, where many Jewish boys studied. Though Ballas died in 2000, his trust fund continues to benefit charities, the Jewish community and Singapore society, funding the development of the Ballas Community Centre next to the MAGHAIN ABOTH SYNAGOGUE. The Jacob Ballas Children's Garden in the SINGAPORE BOTANIC GARDENS has been named in his memory.

See also STOCKBROKING and SINGAPORE EXCHANGE.

banana money Popular term for currency used during the JAPANESE OCCUPATION. The name came from the banana-tree motif on the $10 note. Notes produced early in the occupation had serial numbers while the ones produced later did not. As inflation spiralled during the war years, the term came to be applied to worthless currency in general. In September 1945, when the British returned to Singapore, banana money was demonetized, leaving hundreds of thousands of people penniless. More recently, banana money notes have become popular with collectors.

bangsawan A form of MALAY THEATRE. The word 'bangsawan' is thought to be derived from two words, 'bangsa' (people) and 'wan' (noble), thus 'noble people'. The origin of *bangsawan* can be traced to an all-male troupe, the Wayang Parsi or Mendu in Penang in 1870. A repertoire of well-

S.T. Bani

Banana money

Bangsawan: Putera Iskandar Jauhari, staged by Sri Anggerik Bangsawan.

known stories from the Middle East and India performed in the Hindustani language made the troupe popular with audiences. They were soon to be seen at large events and at state and royal functions. In 1885, a Penang businessman, Mamak Pushi, bought all the production paraphernalia from the group, which had become defunct, and started his own professional troupe, Pushi Indera Bangsawan. The new troupe followed the theatrical traditions of the Mendu, but now performed in the Malay language and included women in its cast. It toured major cities in Malaya, ending up in Singapore before heading to Batavia (now Jakarta) where it was sold to another owner.

The development of *bangsawan* in Singapore may be considered in four stages: the introduction of the art form with the arrival of Pushi Indera Bangsawan (1885–1902); its golden era (1903–35); decline (1936–77); and revival (from 1978).

The *bangsawan* became very popular, especially among the Malay community. Performances were staged in theatres such as Happy World (Geylang), NEW WORLD (Jalan Besar) and GREAT WORLD (Kim Seng Road). Its decline began in the mid-1930s, with the introduction of new forms of entertainment such as cinema and radio, and accelerated after World War II, when many of the *bangsawan* actors joined the flourishing Malay film industry. In 1955, the *bangsawan* was revived in radio plays, and was still being broadcast into the 1990s.

After a long absence, the *bangsawan* was performed in 1978 during an arts festival. This was the beginning of its revival in Singapore. It was again performed in theatres and special programmes were made for television. Although the *bangsawan* is not performed as regularly as it was, the tradition is kept alive by a few theatre groups, in particular the Sri Anggerik Bangsawan.

Bani, S.T. (1934–1985) Trade unionist and politician. S.T. Bani was a member of the People's Action Party (PAP) and came to

prominence as an impressive and well-spoken leader of the Business and House Employee Union. During the 1959 general election, he contested and won the seat in Thomson constituency.

In 1960, Bani sensed that the pro-Communist faction within the PAP was winning the power struggle and decided to switch sides. In mid-August 1961, a left-wing committee of the Singapore Trades Union Congress representing 82 unions announced the formation of the Singapore Association of Trade Unions (SATU) with the Singapore General Employees' Union at its heart and Bani as chairman. The split within the PAP in 1962 saw Bani being expelled from the party. He joined the newly-formed BARISAN SOSIALIS (BS) and stood against PAP stalwart K.M. BYRNE in the Crawford constituency during the General Election (1963). Bani defeated Byrne by just 193 votes. The BS, backed by the unions, and especially SATU, tried to block merger with the Federation of Malaya but failed. Shortly after MERGER was achieved, the Malaysian authorities carried out a number of operations to round up suspected communists.

Bani was detained under Operation Pechah (*see* OPERATION COLD STORE) on 8 October 1963 and was released in 1966. He resigned from BS and moved to Malaysia.

Bani Buang (1929–1996) Theatre director and drama producer. Bani Buang was a member of Pemuda Baru Sandiwara (literally, 'New Youth Drama'), an early local MALAY THEATRE group in Singapore, and another theatre group Cahaya Timor Sandiwara (Light of the East Drama). He was active in Perkumpulan Seni (Arts Village), a Malay cultural group formed in 1956. He directed many of the plays staged by this association. His earlier plays were very much influenced by the BANGSAWAN style though he experimented with new techniques in his later plays. Some of his major works are: *Lela Satria* (1960), *Ribut* (Storm), *Corak Dunia* (Earth Design)

(1962), *Gerbang Neraka* (Gate to Hell) (1967), *Rashomon* (1971), *Hamlet* (1980) and *Sang Rajuna Tapa* (1981). He also directed the first Malay musical, *Gema Seni* (Echo of the Arts). He joined state broadcaster Radio Television Singapore in 1973, and became synonymous with the Malay television dramas (*sandiwara*). He was awarded the CULTURAL MEDALLION in 1983.

banking The Union Bank of Calcutta was the first bank to be set up in Singapore in 1840. While this bank has become a mere footnote to history, many other banking institutions which set up during the early years of Singapore became household names, not only in Singapore but also globally. They include the MERCANTILE BANK (later taken over by Hong Kong and Shanghai Bank, now HSBC), Chartered Bank (now the STANDARD CHARTERED BANK), International Banking Corporation (an ancestor of today's CITIBANK), and Nederlandsche Handel-Maatschappij (an ancestor of ABN AMRO).

The first local bank, Kwong Yik Bank, was set up to serve Chinese businesses in

Banking: banking hall of the Hongkong and Shanghai Bank, 1920s (top); automated teller machines in a shopping mall, 2006.

1903, but was wound up a decade later. A number of other similar banks, however, were amalgamated to form the OVERSEA-CHINESE BANKING CORPORATION (OCBC), whose growth was to mirror that of Singapore's entrepôt trade, interrupted only briefly by World War II.

The 1970s saw a new era in commercial banking in Singapore. The authorities started issuing two classes of banking licences: a full licence which allowed institutions to provide a full range of banking services; and a restricted licence, under which banks were allowed to provide the full range of banking services, except for taking in savings deposits and fixed deposits below $250,000. Banks with restricted licences could operate only from a single location. Their offices were generally in the commercial downtown district, at RAFFLES PLACE, SHENTON WAY or Robinson Road. These provisions were aimed at attracting foreign banking institutions, while at the same time safeguarding the local retail banks from market saturation. Since 2001, restricted banks were renamed 'wholesale banks'.

As the growth of the ASIAN DOLLAR MARKET continued to attract foreign commercial banks to Singapore, in 1973 the MONETARY AUTHORITY OF SINGAPORE (MAS) introduced a third type of banking licence—the offshore licence (*see* box). MAS has been relaxing its restrictions on the sector since 1978, opening the domestic banking market sector to offshore banks, and intensifying competition in the process.

Some foreign banks only operate representative offices in Singapore. These offices do not engage in banking per se, but serve as regional listening posts and liaise between potential Singapore customers and their head offices. Many representative offices have in due course upgraded, becoming wholesale or offshore banks.

The table illustrates two main developments in the Singapore banking scene. There has been a sharp increase in the number of foreign banks following the opening up of the banking industry to a greater number of wholesale and offshore banks. There has also been a reduction in the number of domestic banks, falling from 11 to five over the period 1970–2006. This is a result of local mergers promoted by the government to enhance the competitive-

Year	Domestic	Foreign			Total
	Full	Full	Restricted/wholesale	Offshore	
1970	11	26	—	—	37
1971	11	25	6	—	42
1973	11	25	12	7	55
1980	13	23	13	42	91
1985	13	23	14	79	129
1990	13	22	14	87	136
1995	12	22	14	92	140
2000	8	23	16	93	140
2004	5	23	37	50	115
2006	5	24	34	45	108

BANKING: COMMERCIAL BANKS IN SINGAPORE

Source: Monetary Authority of Singapore, Annual Report (various issues)

ness of Singapore banks, locally and in the region, following similar trends on the global banking scene.

This consolidation started in earnest in 1998 with the takeover of Tat Lee Bank by Keppel Bank, which in turn was acquired by OCBC in 2001. The Post Office Savings Bank (POSB) (*see* POSBANK) merged with the Development Bank of Singapore (DBS BANK) in 1998, while UNITED OVERSEAS BANK (UOB) successfully acquired the OVERSEAS UNION BANK (OUB) group in 2001. Of the 11 local banks that were originally doing business in 1970, five remain: OCBC, DBS, UOB, the Bank of Singapore and Far Eastern Bank.

As part of the liberalization of the banking sector, in 1999 the MAS introduced a Qualifying Full Bank (QFB) licence. This allows certain foreign banks to expand in Singapore. The aim was to promote a more competitive environment and spur the upgrading of local banks. The licence regulates the number of branches and off-site ATMs. QFBs are allowed to have up to 15 service locations (branches or off-site ATMs), share ATMs among themselves and provide debit services using the EFTPOS (electronic funds transfer at point of sale) network. In 2006, ABN AMRO Bank NV, BNP Paribas, Citibank, HSBC, Maybank and Standard Chartered Bank had QFB licences. By the end of 2005, all of them except BNP Paribas had linked their ATM networks.

Banyan Tree Operator of spas and resorts. Banyan Tree Hotels & Resorts is a Singaporean brand that has achieved international recognition. The company was founded in 1994 by HO KWON PING and his wife Claire Chiang, and caters to high-end tourists looking for a sense of romance, adventure and intimacy. With the help of Ho's brother, an architect, Banyan Tree developed an abandoned tin mine in Phuket, Thailand, into a 94-villa boutique resort. Each villa has its own private pool and tropical spa; an innovation at the time, these design elements have since been copied by other resort operators. The name Banyan Tree stems from the founders' memories of their days spent in their home on Lamma Island in Hong Kong—they lived at Yung Shue Wan, or, Banyan Tree Bay.

Bani Buang

Banyan Tree: beachfront villa in the Maldives.

offshore banking Much of the banking activity in Singapore is carried out offshore through the Asian dollar market (ADM) or Asian Currency Units (ACU) of financial institutions based in Singapore. ACUs essentially borrow and lend in non-Singapore dollars or foreign currencies.

In 1968, Singapore created the ADM—the counterpart of the eurodollar market—when it allowed the Singapore branch of the Bank of America to borrow and lend in offshore currencies. This was the first step in achieving the country's objective of developing into a leading financial centre. To stimulate the development of the ADM, the government also granted ACUs preferential tax and regulatory treatment. The opening up of the banking sector to more foreign players through the issue of more restricted, wholesale and offshore licences also paved the way for growth in the ADM, which expanded from a market capitalization of US$30 million in its inaugural year of 1968 to US$582 billion by the end of 2004, or about 61.6 per cent of total financial assets in Singapore.

Banyan Tree established boutique resorts in other exotic destinations—including several World Heritage sites in Maldives, Seychelles, Indonesia and China—with plans for more in Sri Lanka, Bahrain, Dubai, Greece, Morocco, Barbados and Mexico. It also operates the Angsana chain of resorts and spas, which offers more affordable choices for young families and professionals. Banyan Tree also operates a chain of 50 spas and 53 retail galleries in 19 countries. In 2006, Banyan Tree listed on the Singapore Exchange.

The Banyan Tree resorts are built using indigenous materials and employ landscape and architectural designs that blend in with the existing environment. Banyan Tree has set up a Green Imperative Fund to help the conservation of wildlife and habitats in areas such as Thailand, Maldives and Seychelles.

Baptists The first group of Baptists in Singapore came from Shantou (Swatow), China. They joined a group of Presbyterian Christians who came from the same place and worshipped at the Tekka Church (later the Singapore Life Church).

On 5 December 1937, a group of more than 30 Baptists formed the first Baptist church here, the Oversea-Chinese (Swatow) Baptist Church of Singapore. They would meet at a private house in Orchard Road. In 1955, new premises were found for the church, which was then renamed the

Gopal Baratham: Sayang (1991).

Thomson Road Baptist Church. On 7 July 1949, another church was established: the Oversea-Chinese (Cantonese) Baptist Church of Singapore. This eventually became the Kay Poh Road Baptist Church.

After China closed its doors to foreign missionaries, the Foreign Mission Board of the Southern Baptist Convention of the United States reassigned missionaries to other parts of the world. In 1950, Lora Clement, together with Dorcas Lau from Hong Kong, were sent to Singapore. Pastors and missionaries from Hong Kong, Taiwan and the US followed. They helped the Baptist churches here to grow and by 1970, the churches had 1,487 members.

The Singapore Baptist Convention, a voluntary association, was formed in 1974 to facilitate cooperation among these churches, and provide a platform for the members to work together on social service projects. The Baptist Golden Age Home, Baptist Community Care, Baptist Theological Seminary and Baptist Bookstore are among the organizations affiliated to the Convention, which also has 32 Baptist churches with a total membership of about 7,000. Some Baptist churches, however, are not members of the Convention.

Baratham, Gopal (1935–2002) Neurosurgeon and author. Gopal Baratham graduated in medicine from the University of Malaya, Singapore. After completing neurological studies at London Hospital, he worked at the Department of Neurosurgery, University of Edinburgh for three years before returning to Singapore in 1972. He worked in several hospitals and was head of neurosurgery at Tan Tock Seng Hospital from 1984 until 1987, when he left for private practice.

Baratham's first works were collections of short stories—*Figments of Experience* (1981; reissued as *Love Letter and Other Stories* in 1988) and *People Make You Cry* (1988). He published three novels. *A Candle Or The Sun*, completed in 1985, was rejected by publishers in Singapore because it was considered too political, with a plot revolving around a conspiracy by a religious group. It was eventually published in London in 1991 and was given the Commendation Award by the National Book Development Council of Singapore in 1992. Believing his work deserved the top prize, Baratham rejected the award. *Sayang* (1991) deals with a group involved in sex, drugs, and religion. Baratham's third novel, *Moonrise, Sunset* (1996), is a murder mystery, again linked to sex. *Memories that Glow in the Dark* (1995), his third collection, comprises 14 short stories most of which address sexual themes. Baratham's short stories are collected together in *City of Forgetting* (2001). Ironically, Baratham achieved bestselling author status with a non-fiction work—*The Caning of Michael Fay* (1994), a critique of the caning and imprisonment of the American teenager, MICHAEL FAY, for vandalism in Singapore.

Barisan Socialis: supporters on their way to a rally in 1963.

At the time of his death in 2002 from pneumonia, he was working on the autobiographical *Beads in the Sutra,* and *Poppy*, the sequel to *Moonrise, Sunset.* Baratham received the Southeast Asia Write Award in 1991.

Barisan Sosialis Political party. The Barisan Sosialis (BS)—meaning Socialist Front—was established in 1961 by left-wing former members of the PEOPLE'S ACTION PARTY (PAP), and was led by LEE SIEW CHOH. It was the main opposition party in self-governing Singapore before Independence.

After the PAP's rise to power in 1959, radical leftists within the PAP became unhappy with the faction led by the more moderate LEE KUAN YEW, and they subsequently broke away to form the new party. The BS was accused by the PAP of being a front for communism, a charge which members of the party vehemently denied. The party's platform included opposition to merger with the Federation of Malaya; it was feared that the staunchly anti-communist Malayan government would proscribe the party and detain its members. In February 1963, many BS members were arrested during OPERATION COLD STORE and detained under the INTERNAL SECURITY ACT.

Even so, the BS managed to win 13 of the 51 seats contested during the GENERAL ELECTION (1963). More BS members were arrested following the election for alleged communist and subversive activities. Among those detained were many key members of the BS, including CHIA THYE POH, who became Singapore's longest-serving political detainee. After Singapore's separation from Malaysia in 1965, several BS members resigned from Parliament. The BS had decided it would abandon Parliament and take the fight 'to the streets'. This was a serious tactical error. In the by-elections that followed, voters ignored the BS' calls to cast blank ballots, and the PAP won all contested seats. By the 1968 general election, there would be no opposition member of Parliament. This state of affairs would last for 13 years.

The BS failed to have any impact on subsequent general elections even though its leader, Lee Siew Choh, continued to campaign. In 1988, the BS was dissolved,

Baptists: Thomson Road Baptist Church (right); Christmas celebrations at the Oversea-Chinese Baptist Church in 1952.

E.W. Barker: presenting Outward Bound awards.

and its members, led by Lee, joined the WORKERS' PARTY. Lee was appointed a NON-CONSTITUENCY MEMBER OF PARLIAMENT following the general election of 1988.

Barker, E.W. (1920–2001) Lawyer and politician. Edmund William (also popularly known as 'Eddie') Barker studied at the Anglo-Chinese Paya Lebar Continuation School and then Serangoon English School before being admitted to Raffles Institution. He excelled both in the classroom and on the sports field, and was elected head prefect in 1938. It was at Raffles Institution that Barker came to befriend both LEE KUAN YEW and Kwa Geok Choo (later Lee's wife).

In 1939, Barker entered Raffles College. He won the Exhibition in his first year there, and the College Scholarship in his second year. Barker also became the college's athletics champion and captain of its rugby team.

The Japanese invasion interrupted Barker's education, and it was not until 1946 that he returned to Raffles College to complete his studies. In 1946, he won the QUEEN'S SCHOLARSHIP and proceeded to St Catherine's College, Cambridge, to read law. The many friends that Barker made at both Raffles College and Cambridge—including Lee Kuan Yew, Kwa Geok Choo, Tun Abdul Razak (later to be Malaysia's deputy prime minister and subsequently prime minister) and Raja Azlan Shah (later to be lord president of Malaysia)—would make him an invaluable member of the People's Action Party in later years.

Barker returned to Singapore in 1950, and was called to the Bar in 1951. He joined the firm of BRADDELL BROTHERS. In 1956, he was invited to join the firm of LEE & LEE, which had been established by his old friends Lee and Kwa. A week before the GENERAL ELECTION (1963), GOH KENG SWEE and Lee suggested to Barker that he enter politics.

Barker stood as a candidate in the Tanglin constituency and won. He was also

elected to replace Sir GEORGE OEHLERS as speaker of the Legislative Assembly in the same year. On 1 November 1964, Barker joined Lee's Cabinet as minister for law. By this time, Singapore was already part of Malaysia. But it was the separation of Singapore from the federation that was to see Barker in his most important role. Indeed, Barker emerged, along with Goh Keng Swee, as a key player on the Singapore side of the negotiations leading to SEPARATION. Barker was trusted by both Lee and his Malaysian friends, particularly Tun Abdul Razak—a key decision-maker on the Malaysian side of the negotiations.

Lee asked Barker to draft the Separation Agreement towards the end of July 1965. On 6 August that year, Barker travelled to Kuala Lumpur to finalize arrangements with the Malaysians. It was Barker who was responsible for the final draft of the agreement, and it was he and Goh who first signed this document on behalf of the Singapore delegation. At one point, Razak asked Barker if Lee would sign once the Malaysians had done so. Barker assured him, as 'an old friend', that Lee would do so. Afterwards, Lee thanked Barker for this 'bloodless coup'. In the aftermath of Separation, Barker was kept busy with legal matters, especially the urgent need to draft a workable Constitution for Singapore. He would also continue to serve Singapore as minister for national development (1965–75), home affairs (1972), environment (1975–79), science and technology (1977–81) and labour (1983); LEADER OF THE HOUSE (1968–84); president of the Singapore National Olympic Council (1970–90); chairman of the Bukit Turf Club (1989–94); and chairman of the Singapore Stock Exchange (1989–93). His life-long friendship with the Sultan of Johor also proved important for Singapore–Malaysia relations.

Barker was a popular politician. Given his friendship with Lee, he felt able to criticize and contradict him when in government. On his side, Lee has acknowledged his 'debt' to Barker, and has praised Barker's sense of duty. In 1988, Barker retired from politics. In 1990, he was admitted into the ORDER OF NILA UTAMA (First Class).

bar-top dancing Dancing by clubbers on bar counters. Until 2003, Singapore had placed restrictions on bar-top dancing on grounds that it could turn rowdy and that clubbers' safety could be endangered. In November 2001, the National Crime Prevention Council established an Advisory Panel on Licensing to study the issue of bar-top dancing; and in March 2003, it recommended that the restriction be lifted. It was indeed lifted, on 1 August 2003. In his 2003 National Day Rally Speech, Prime Minister Goh Chok Tong stated that the introduction of bar-top dancing signalled a shift in the mindset of

Bar-top dancing: Coyote Ugly bar in Mohamed Sultan Road.

Singaporeans from strait-laced Victorianism to a more relaxed and open-minded stance. At midnight on 31 July 2003, the first legal bar-top dancing took place simultaneously at three bars in Singapore: Coyote Ugly, Devils Bar and 37 The Bar.

Pubs and bars wishing to introduce bar-top dancing were required to apply for a Live Entertainment Licence costing $140 per month for bars holding fewer than 200 people and $210 per month for larger bars. Moreover, bar tops had to be specially strengthened with steel and concrete to withstand the weight of the clubbers, and railings had to be installed for their safety.

Batam One of the largest islands of the Indonesian archipelago, part of the Riau province. Two-thirds the size of Singapore, it used to be home to some 100,000 ORANG LAUT, a fishing community which relies on the sea for its livelihood, and farmers. Things changed when the Indonesian government earmarked the island for industrial, tourism and trade purposes in the 1970s. It became the support base for the state-owned Pertamina oil company and its offshore oil exploration, and in 1971, a presidential decree designated Batam as an industrial zone. In 1978, Batam was established as a bonded area, and in 1989, it was declared a free-trade zone.

To Singaporeans, Batam is a popular destination for recreation. It is a 35-minute ferry ride from the Tanah Merah Ferry Terminal. As a tourist destination, Batam is to Singapore what Macau or Shenzhen is to Hong Kong—a getaway which is both convenient and affordable. There are six international-standard golf courses, large shopping malls, seafood restaurants, two

Batam: two-storey kelong converted into business centre.

Batik: Melancholy, batik painting by Seah Kim Joo (left); detail of traditional batik sarong, 1930s.

Battle Box: recreation of wartime military command centre.

marinas, numerous nightclubs and lounges, hotels and resorts, bowling alleys and seasports facilities. Visitors can also visit the 6-ha Duta Maitreya Buddhist monastery, or the Galang and Rempang islands south of Batam. Linked by a bridge to the main island, they have good beaches and an abundance of marine life.

batik Dyeing method used to decorate fabrics. 'Batik' also refers to the cloth that has been dyed using this process. The technique involves the application of melted wax—according to a pattern—on parts of a plain cotton cloth. The cloth is then dyed. Only the unwaxed parts of the cloth take the colour. The cloth is then boiled to remove the wax. This process is repeated with different dyes and wax patterns, eventually producing a colourful cloth with intricate designs.

Batik gained prominence in Southeast Asia during the 18th and 19th centuries, but may have originated much earlier. Sir Stamford Raffles, when he was based in Java, was the first European to study this art. He described the batik process and included illustrations of batik patterns in his *History of Java*.

In Singapore, batik is used most frequently to decorate the sarong (long skirt-like garment) worn by MALAYS, PERANAKANS and the JAWI PERANAKANS. Although the use of batik has declined over the years, men—of all races—sometimes wear batik shirts for formal occasions.

Artists have transformed batik into a contemporary art form through the use of synthetic pigments and modern techniques. Prominent artists who use batik are SARKASI SAID, Jaafar Latiff, TAY CHEE TOH, Seah Kim Joo and Chieu Shuey Fook. Acrylic and oil paintings on canvas may be done in the style of batik, for example, *Artist And Model*, by LIU KANG.

Battle Box This labyrinth of bomb-proof underground bunkers on FORT CANNING Hill served as Lieutenant-General ARTHUR PERCIVAL's command centre. It was the largest military operations complex in Singapore and was part of the MALAYA COMMAND headquarters during WORLD WAR II. The Japanese took over the site, and it became the headquarters of Lieutenant-General KAWAMURA SABURO. The public can now visit its 22 rooms, listen to simulated bomb blasts and air raid sirens, and view life-like wax figurines of British soldiers.

Battle of Bukit Timah World War II battle on 10–11 February 1942, by which means the Japanese took a commanding position over Bukit Timah Road, a short distance from Singapore town. Maintaining control of the 162-m-high Bukit Timah Hill, a jungle-covered nature reserve in the centre of the island, was essential if the defenders were to hold nearby storage areas. Advancing from the west, the Japanese attacked on the afternoon of the 10th, securing Bukit Timah Village that day and the hill early on the 11th. The Japanese High Command then air-dropped an invitation to the British to surrender. Instead, the defenders made a counter-attack. After it failed, Japanese tanks drove down Bukit Timah Road on the 12th, almost reaching Chinese High School. Lieutenant-General ARTHUR PERCIVAL responded by pulling his forces back to a new perimeter line around Singapore town, for a desperate final defence.

Battle of Pasir Panjang World War II battle. Japanese forces made their first landing on Singapore on 8 February 1942. The Japanese encountered fierce allied resistance for the next three days but by 12 February had succeeded in pushing back all defenders to a final perimeter around Singapore town, stretching from Pasir Panjang to Kallang.

The British perimeter spanned 45 km. At the point where it crossed Bukit Timah Road, the perimeter was less than 2.7 km from Orchard Road. However, the Japanese chose to focus the full weight of their attacking capabilities at Pasir Panjang Ridge as it provided direct passage to key military installations in the Alexandra area. The final stand against Japanese forces by the MALAY REGIMENT at Pasir Panjang Ridge was one of the fiercest and most heroic battles waged by defenders of Singapore and is most deserving of honourable mention.

On 12 February, Malay Regiment positions were arranged in a 'box' formation around Pasir Panjang Ridge, with Reformatory Road (now Clementi Road) held by A and C Companies of the 1st Battalion. In spite of continual pressure from enemy mortar and artillery fire, the 1st Battalion held the line until the night when they were finally ordered to retrograde to positions nearer to the Alexandra area between Ayer Rajah Road and the Gap Ridge (now Kent Ridge). In the morning of 13 February, Japanese forces attempted to break through the line held by A Company. A Company sustained a concentration of accurate artillery fire resulting in the deaths of company commander, Captain Horsburgh and two platoon commanders, Lieutenants G.D. Haggit and H.N.D. Russell.

C Company, positioned along the southeast of Reformatory Road, also engaged the army around this time. Despite considerable casualties, the company held their ground. During this Japanese attack, Private Yacob Bidin, a member of a C Company Bren Gun Team won the Military Medal for taking out an enemy mortar position.

In the evening, Brigade Headquarters ordered a general withdrawal after dusk and the 1st and 2nd Battalions took up fresh positions at the Alexandra Brickworks and other areas in Buona Vista. Company positions in the early morning of 14 February had B Company covering the two approaches to Buona Vista Village (Pasir Panjang Road and Buona Vista Road); C Company holding the ridge above the Opium Factory and D Company occupying the beaches at Labrador. One Japanese wave of attack focused on the coastal roads and was successful in punching through B Company positions at the Buona Vista Village road junction. Although B Company suffered heavy casualties in this battle, the Japanese attack was delayed long enough for the Malay Regiment to erect a second line of defence at Labrador. By late evening, the Malay Regiment managed to halt the Japanese

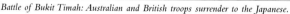

Battle of Bukit Timah: Australian and British troops surrender to the Japanese.

Batu Berlayar: 19th-century drawing of the rock, also known as Lot's Wife; unknown artist, 1845–50.

advance to reach Keppel Harbour via Pasir Panjang Road and Buona Vista Road.

On the same day and almost simultaneously, Japanese forces attempted to take Bukit Chandu or 'Opium Hill' situated on Pasir Panjang Ridge, a position otherwise identified militarily as Point 226. Faced with fierce resistance from Malay Regiment positions on Bukit Chandu, Japanese soldiers attempted subterfuge and disguised themselves as Indian troops in a move to infiltrate the area. Malay Regiment officers Lieutenant ADNAN SAIDI and Lieutenant Abbas saw through the ruse and waited for the enemy to come within close range before repelling the Japanese effort. Two hours later, the Japanese attempted a frontal assault and used the whole force of their crack unit, the 18th Division, against the defenders. Lieutenant Adnan personally manned a Lewis gun and exposed his position frequently to inspire his men to engage the enemy. Although Lieutenant Adnan was subsequently heavily wounded in the battle, he led by example and persevered while ordering his platoon to fight to the very end. It is believed that after the Japanese overran Malay Regiment positions, the body of Lieutenant Adnan was repeatedly bayoneted, hung from a nearby rubber tree and refused a proper burial.

The Japanese gained control of Pasir Panjang Ridge with the whole city within range of Japanese artillery.

Batu Berlayar Pillar of rock that protruded from the water at Labrador Point. Batu Berlayar means 'sail rock' in Malay. An English map drawn in 1709 marks the feature as Lot's Wife—a name derived from a biblical story. The Chinese name for the rock, *long ya men*, means 'dragon's tooth' (*see* LONGYAMEN). The pillar was blown up by the British in 1848 in order to widen a shipping lane. In the early 19th century, the spot was named Singki Point, which may be a corruption of the toponym Sengkir Strait—the name given to the waterway

between Blakang Mati (SENTOSA) and Brani islands. The name Singki may have been derived from a perpetuation of the original toponym in one of the dialects spoken by boat-dwellers living in the strait's vicinity in the early 19th century.

Bedok Area in the east of Singapore. 'Bedok' is a very old name long associated with this part of Singapore. In de Eredia's map of Singapore dating from 1604, a river called Sune Bodo (Sungei Bedok or Bedok River) is indicated. Most locals believe that 'Bedok' is an anglicized spelling of the Malay word 'bedoh'—the large drum used for calling Muslims to prayer or to sound the alarm. Bedok was the fifth new town developed by the HOUSING & DEVELOPMENT BOARD, with development commencing in April 1973. The area of the new town is bounded by Bedok Reservoir Road, Kaki Bukit Avenue 1, New Upper Changi Road, Bedok South Road and Simei Avenue. It covers an area of almost 940 ha and contains a mix of residential and industrial buildings. In 2005, there were some 60,000 flats in the town, housing around 187,000 residents.

Bee Cheng Hiang Famous manufacturer of *bak kwa* (barbecued meat). It is common to see long queues outside Bee Cheng Hiang outlets—especially in Chinatown—during CHINESE NEW YEAR. Bee Cheng Hiang is also known for its meat floss, Chinese sausages, mooncakes and other dried Chinese delicacies.

Bedok: new town first developed in the 1970s.

One of the most recognizable brands in Singapore, Bee Cheng Hiang was founded by Teo Swee Ee who started hawking his *bak kwa* from a pushcart in Chinatown in 1933. But it was only during the 1980s, after the business was corporatized, that it took brand recognition seriously. The company invested $1.2 million to set up a research and development department to enhance its product lines and create new products to meet market demand. Bee Cheng Hiang runs a total of 113 outlets, with 30 outlets in Singapore and 83 overseas outlets in Malaysia, China, Hong Kong, Taiwan, Indonesia and the Philippines. The company's staff strength has grown to 1,000 in the region.

Behn, Meyer & Co. Early trading company and multinational. Behn, Meyer and Co. was established in 1840 as a trading company by two young Germans from Hamburg: Theodor August Behn (1816–86) and Valentin Lorenz Meyer (1817–1901). Behn arrived in Singapore on 5 July 1839. He capitalized on the poor relations between Britain and China on account of the Opium Wars and the consequent embargo on British trading ships. Using neutral German ships, Behn managed to bring Bombay cotton into China. With the profits from this venture, he was able to strike out on his own in partnership with his soon-to-be brother-in-law, Valentin Meyer (the two young men had met in a private boarding school in Germany and had become fast friends). Shortly after Behn established the company, he sent for Meyer to come out to Singapore to join him. The date on which Meyer arrived in Singapore—1 November 1840—was declared the official date on which the firm of Behn, Meyer and Company was founded. The company initially traded in tropical produce such as coconut oil, copra, pepper, camphor, and rattan; and later moved into shipping and insurance. It expanded into Penang, the Philippines, Siam (Thailand) and the Dutch East Indies (Indonesia). The company developed into one of the biggest shipping agents and trading houses in Southeast Asia. After surviving two world wars, Behn Meyer is today a group of companies operating in Germany, Singapore, Malaysia, Thailand, Indonesia, Vietnam, Myanmar, Cambodia and Jamaica. Its parent company, Behn Meyer (D) Holding AG and Co. (formerly known as Arnold Otto Meyer), is based in Hamburg.

Bencoolen Pepper-trading centre established by the British EAST INDIA COMPANY on Sumatra in 1684. It was the base for Sir STAMFORD RAFFLES when he established a trading port in Singapore in 1819. It is now known as Bengkulu.

In 1684, the Dutch expelled the British from Banten (west Java), Southeast Asia's major pepper port (*see* PEPPER AND GAMBIER).

Bee Cheng Hiang: market leader in bak kwa *(barbecued meat).*

Bengalis: alpona, *floor artworks using ground rice, are made for festivals.*

Bengawan Solo: founder Anastasia Liew.

Frank J. Benjamin

At the time, pepper was an extremely valuable commodity, and was considered a strategic resource in Europe. The British then established a new outpost at Bencoolen on the western coast of Sumatra, where a significant proportion of the pepper sold in Banten was actually grown.

Bencoolen controlled a coastal strip 500 km in length. However, the colony's location was far removed from the main trading routes through the Strait of Malacca. It was also difficult to supply, unattractive to immigrants and plagued by disease and earthquakes.

In 1816, other than Penang, Bencoolen was Britain's only foothold in Southeast Asia. Raffles was sent there as lieutenant-governor of Bencoolen in 1818. Almost immediately, he began to plan for the establishment of a settlement at the southern end of the Strait of Malacca, in the belief that Bencoolen had no long-term potential.

While four of Raffles' children were born in Bencoolen, three died there at an early age while his infant daughter Ella was sent back to England. Raffles set out from Bencoolen for England on 2 February 1824. However, on his first night at sea, a fire broke out on the ship—the *Fame*—and the vessel sank. Raffles and his wife managed to get back to shore in a lifeboat. As so few ships called at Bencoolen, they were unable to leave again until 10 April. They finally reached England on 20 August 1824.

In March 1824, Raffles had learned that a final settlement had been reached with the Dutch regarding the division of territory in Sumatra and Malaya. According to the ANGLO-DUTCH TREATY of that year, Singapore and Malacca were ceded to the British, and Bencoolen to the Dutch. The outpost of Bencoolen is commemorated in Singapore in the name of Bencoolen Street.

Bencoolen Mosque Located on Bencoolen Street, it was built in 1845 largely with funds contributed by SYED OMAR ALI ALJUNIED. Historically, it was attended predominantly by the Indian Muslim community associated with the HANAFI SCHOOL. A redevelopment project that involved the mosque, and the addition of commercial premises and residential apartments, was completed in 2004 at a cost of $35 million. The mosque was considerably expanded and can accommodate about 1,200 people, as compared to 600 previously.

Bendemeer House In 1840, well-known local merchant HOO AH KAY (WHAMPOA) purchased a piece of land in SERANGOON ROAD and turned it into one of the most beautiful gardens in Singapore, which he called Nansheng Gardens. After Whampoa's death, the property was sold in 1895 to Seah Liang Seah who demolished Whampoa's house and built a new home which he named 'Bendemeer'. In 1962, the

Bendemeer House: *in 1960, just prior to demolition.*

house and property were acquired by the HOUSING & DEVELOPMENT BOARD and the house was pulled down.

Bengalis People from what used to be the state of Bengal in northeast India. Bengal has since been partitioned into the Indian state of West Bengal, and the independent country of Bangladesh. In the 19th century, Bengalis came to work in the Straits Settlements in the clerical and health inspection services. Some set up their own businesses as traders and shopkeepers. There were also professionals, mainly doctors and lawyers, who either joined the government service or set up their own practice. A prominent early Bengali was businessman Annukul Chander. In 1920, he became the first Indian to be made a justice of the peace. Chander Road is named after him. In the early 20th century, Singapore and Malaya also provided a refuge for Bengali revolutionaries who were pursued by the British.

For a long time, there were too few Bengalis to form a real community. It was only just before the World War II that a leader emerged. S.C. GOHO, a prominent Bengali lawyer, formed a group of Indian volunteers named 'The Indian Passive Defence Force' to look after the interests of Bengalis.

After the end of World War II, many Bengalis began arriving in Singapore—some from India but most from Malaya, attracted by the remuneration available and the expansion of the education service. A few came with the British army and stayed on.

The Bengali Association Singapore was formed in 1956 and its initial membership was 50 families. The aim of the association was to encourage cultural, social and other activities of interest to its members.

Bengalis: *dancing girls and violinist, c. 1910.*

The size of the community grew significantly from the early 1970s as Singapore began its INDUSTRIALIZATION programme. More and more professionals, such as naval architects, university lecturers, doctors, bankers, managers, and business leaders began to arrive. Many of them joined the Bengali Association. The association now has about 400 families as members.

Students have been given the option to study Bengali as a MOTHER TONGUE at GCE 'O'-level (since 1990) and 'AO'-level (since 1991). The option to take it as a subject at the Primary School Leaving Examination became available in 1993. A part-time Bengali school, BLLS School, was formed in 1994 by the Bangla Language and Literary Society (Singapore), to offer lessons to its members.

Singapore also has a population of Bengali speakers from Bangladesh, a significant source of FOREIGN WORKERS. This is a transient group of people who work for a few years in Singapore before returning to Bangladesh.

Bengawan Solo Confectionery company. Famous for its *kueh-kueh* (sticky cakes), tarts and other pastries, Bengawan Solo was founded by Anastasia Liew in 1979. Liew came to Singapore in 1973 from Indonesia, where she had learned her baking skills from her mother and other relatives.

At first she entertained friends and relatives with her Indonesian specialities; their fame spread through word of mouth, and before long she began to receive orders for them. Baked in her flat, they even appeared on the shelves of some supermarkets and emporiums. However, word of this unlicenced home-baking business reached officials from the Ministry of the Environment, who put a stop to it. The incident prompted Liew to set up the very first Bengawan Solo Cake Shop in Marine Terrace.

With demand increasing and new outlets opening every year, Liew set up a central kitchen. After relocating the central bakery several times, Bengawan Solo finally invested $6 million and shifted production to a 2,300 sq m factory in Woodlands in November 1997. It employs more than 400 employees and operates 38 retail outlets, which sell over 100 varieties. Popular favourites include coconut-flavoured *kueh lapis* cakes and pineapple tarts.

Benjamin, Frank J. (1934–) Jewish community leader and businessman. Frank J. Benjamin was educated at St Mary's in Bombay (present-day Mumbai) and St Andrew's School in Singapore. He started working for Getz Brothers, but founded his own firm of FJ BENJAMIN in 1959. During the firm's first decade, it dealt mainly in novelties and photographic equipment. In 1969, it ventured into fashion, acting as the local distributor for Australia's AMCO and Parisian label Lanvin. Benjamin opened the first stand-alone Lanvin boutique in Singapore in 1975. This was followed by a Gucci boutique in Australia (1987); the Asia franchise for Guess (1992); the Guess boutique in Hong Kong (1994); and the Manchester United Football Club franchise in Singapore (1999). Benjamin is also active in the Jewish community; he was appointed president of the Jewish Welfare Board and founder-editor of *Shalom*.

Benjamin Sheares Bridge Singapore's first viaduct. It was officially opened in 1982. The bridge spans Marina Bay and links the eastern and western sections of the East Coast Parkway. It is also the first bridge to be named after a former president (*see* SHEARES, BENJAMIN). It is 1.8 km long and was built by Japanese contractor, Sato Kogyo, which also constructed the East Coast Parkway. The viaduct, made of pre-stressed concrete, rises approximately 20 m above the ground and is built on reclaimed land. Since 1995, the Singapore Armed Forces Recreation Association has organized the annual combined Sheares Bridge Run and Army Half Marathon, attracting an average of 65,000 participants. The full length of the bridge is part of the route.

Bennett, Lieutenant-General Gordon (1887–1962) Henry Gordon Bennett was Australia's most controversial WORLD WAR II commander. He joined the army at the age of 21, and had an eventful military career in World War I, being wounded at Gallipoli. He returned to the fray and in the years that followed acquired a reputation for courageous leadership—and for having a somewhat prickly personality.

The fact that the chief of the general staff, General Sir C.B.B. White, when pressed, informed Bennett that he had 'certain qualities and certain disqualities' for an active command, goes some way to explaining why, when World War II began, Bennett was not given a divisional command until September 1940: the following year he led the 8th Division to Malaya, where, in common with his British counterparts, he was unsuccessful in thwarting the Japanese invasion.

Bennett escaped from Singapore on the night of the surrender, 15 February 1942. With an aide, a staff officer, and some planters serving with the volunteer forces, Bennett commandeered a sampan at gunpoint and slipped across the Malacca Strait to Sumatra. Ultimately they reached Java, from where Bennett flew to Melbourne, arriving on 2 March 1942.

This escape, although adventurous, has been the subject of controversy. Bennett claimed later that he had valuable knowledge of Japanese fighting methods that would be of use to the Australian army. A court of enquiry and a Royal Commission after the war found that his conduct was not justified, and he was not given another

field command. After the war, Bennett took up farming near Sydney.

Berita Harian Malay newspaper, launched on 1 July 1957. A Sunday edition, *Berita Minggu*, was launched on 10 July 1960. It is owned by SINGAPORE PRESS HOLDINGS.

Initially produced in Kuala Lumpur and distributed throughout Malaya, the Roman-script paper was a rival to UTUSAN MELAYU, a Jawi-script (modified Arabic script) daily. It featured articles translated from the English-language newspaper, THE STRAITS TIMES. In 1959, Abdul SAMAD ISMAIL, who had joined *The Straits Times* the year before, was appointed editor to reverse the trend of plummeting circulation. He began to develop the paper's identity, with an emphasis on Malay language, literature and culture.

After SEPARATION in 1965, it was decided that the paper should have more Singapore content and therefore a Singapore office was opened. However, after the split of the Straits Times Press (Malaya) Berhad Group in 1972, and the incorporation of Straits Times Press (Singapore) Pte Ltd in 1973, the paper began to take on a distinct Singaporean identity. The paper has become a source of Malay leadership—many of its journalists and editors have moved into politics and become members of Parliament. They include Mohamad Maidin Packer Mohd, Hawazi Daipi and Zainul Abidin Rasheed.

The average daily circulation of 20,000 copies in 1971 has risen to over 58,000 copies with the weekend edition reaching up to 66,000 copies—covering more than 80 per cent of the Malay-Muslim households in Singapore. An Internet version, *cyBerita*, was launched in 1996.

Beurel, Father Jean-Marie (1813–1872) Priest and missionary. Father Jean-Marie Beurel, a member of the MEP (Paris Foreign Missions Society), arrived from France in 1839 and took charge of the Catholic community in 1840. At that time, the only place of worship in Bras Basah Road was a chapel already too small for its congregation. Beurel obtained from the government a piece of land on the other side of the road and built the CATHEDRAL OF THE GOOD SHEPHERD, which was officially opened on 6 June 1847 and still stands.

Beurel placed great emphasis on Catholic education. When the church was completed, he started raising funds to build Catholic schools and looked for dedicated people to run them. He approached two famous teaching congregations in France: the Brothers of St John Baptist de la Salle (La Salle Brothers) and the Infant Jesus (IJ) Sisters. To speed up negotiations with these congregations, he left Singapore for France in October 1850, returning in May 1852 with six La Salle brothers and five IJ sisters.

Benjamin Sheares Bridge

Lieutenant-General Gordon Bennett

However, Bishop Jean Baptiste Boucho, who worked in the Mission in the Straits Settlements, insisted on opening schools in Penang first. He retained three of the brothers in Penang, and sent the rest to Singapore to open a school for boys in the old chapel, in 1852. This was ST JOSEPH'S INSTITUTION, for which new premises were completed in 1857, and which is now the SINGAPORE ART MUSEUM. On 5 February 1854, the IJ sisters opened a school in Victoria Street, in a house bought for them by Father Beurel: this school became the CONVENT OF THE HOLY INFANT JESUS (the premises later became the site for CHI-JMES).

Beurel also helped build the CHURCH OF ST JOSEPH in Bukit Timah, the CHURCH OF THE NATIVITY OF THE BLESSED VIRGIN MARY in Upper Serangoon Road, and the CHURCH OF ST PETER AND ST PAUL in Queen Street.

Father Beurel also ministered to Chinese migrants, convicts and British soldiers. He explored the south of Johor and some of the Riau islands with a view to expanding the Church there. Due to illness, he returned to France in 1868 and died on 3 October 1872. A memorial plaque to Beurel—considered the founder of Catholicism in Singapore—can be seen at the Cathedral of the Good Shepherd.

Bey Hua Heng (1959–) Photographer. Bey Hua Heng was the recipient of the National Arts Council Young Artist Award

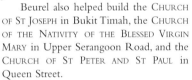

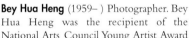

Berita Harian

Father Jean-Marie Beurel

(Photography) in 1993. He is an associate of the Royal Photographic Society, United Kingdom, and has also received the artist's 'Distinction award' (AFIAP) from the International Federation of Photographic Art. The organizer of numerous photography events and initiatives, Bey was the chairman of Boon Lay Community Centre Photographic Club (1996–2000).

Bey Soo Khiang, Lieutenant-General
(1955–) Chief of Defence Force. Bey Soo Khiang was a SINGAPORE ARMED FORCES Overseas Scholar who studied at Cambridge University, where he earned a first-class honours (1977) and a master's degree (1981). He also did a postgraduate degree at Harvard (1988). He was a pilot and commanding officer of the aviation squadron (1980), head of Air Intelligence, head of Air Operations, and commander of Paya Lebar Air Base (1991–92). Bey was chief of Air Force (1992–95) before taking the top job of CHIEF OF DEFENCE FORCE in 1995, the first person who was not from the Army to assume this position. He retired from the armed forces as lieutenant-general in 2000, and joined Singapore Airlines as executive vice-president (Technical). He received the MERITORIOUS SERVICE MEDAL (Military) in 2000.

Bhaskar, K.P. (1925–) Dancer, choreographer and teacher. K.P. Bhaskar is founder and artistic director of the Nrityalaya Aesthetics Society and Bhaskar's Arts Academy. He studied the Indian classical traditions of *kathakali* and *kathak* as well as Manipuri dance, trained in *kandyan* dance in Sri Lanka, and learned ballet from a Russian ballerina. After working with dancer-choreographer Uday Shankar on the film *Kalpana* (1948), he joined Gemini Studios in Chennai as assistant dance director. While travelling to Australia in 1952, he settled in Singapore and set up Bhaskar's Academy of Dance; his wife SANTHA BHASKAR joined him in 1955. In 1962, he was awarded the MERITORIOUS SERVICE MEDAL. That same year, he co-formed the Singapore Kathakali Yogam, the only troupe to perform and teach *kathakali* in the country until it was closed in 1975.

Santha Bhaskar: dancing at Merdeka Day celebrations at the Happy World Stadium, 1959.

Bhumiband: the group receiving an award at the Anugerah Planet Muzik, 2005.

K.P. Bhaskar: peacock dance, Victoria Theatre, 1952.

Bhaskar, Santha (1939–) Dancer, choreographer and teacher. A 1990 CULTURAL MEDALLION recipient, Santha Bhaskar is chief choreographer of the Nrityalaya Aesthetics Society and Bhaskar's Arts Academy. Having studied the Indian classical traditions of *bharatanatyam*, *kathakali* and *mohiniattam* in her native Kerala, she joined her dancer-husband K.P. BHASKAR in Singapore in 1955, teaching and choreographing at his Bhaskar's Academy of Dance. She staged and danced in one of the academy's earliest cross-cultural successes, *Liang Shanbo and Zhu Yingtai* (1958), an Indian-dance adaptation of a Chinese folktale. Open to experimenting with different modes of expression, she brought together Indian and Thai dance in *Manohra* (1996), a dance-drama that premiered at the SINGAPORE ARTS FESTIVAL and was also performed in India in 1998.

Bhumiband Malay popular music group. Bhumiband got its name from the Sundanese word for 'house'. The group was started by Indonesian Dimas Santoso, who lived in Singapore for a number of years. The seven-piece group released its debut album, *Suara Dunia* (Voice of The World), in 2004. Their musical influences include alternative rock, rap and even pop. In the Anugerah Planet Muzik 2005, an award ceremony held in Singapore, the band won Best New Group/Duo, Best Singapore Album and Best Singapore Song.

Bidadari Cemetery Multi-religious burial ground. It was opened on 1 January 1908 after the Bukit Timah Cemetery, then the only Christian cemetery in Singapore, had been closed the year before. The name 'Bidadari' is derived from the Sanskrit word *widyadari* (literally, 'nymph' or 'fairy'). Over the years, the Bidadari Cemetery, located at the junction of Upper Serangoon Road and Upper Aljunied Road, became a multi-ethnic, multi-religious site where Roman Catholics, Protestants, and Muslims of different nationalities were buried. There was

also a small area for Hindus. Before it was closed in 1973, the cemetery was also used for military burials, and served as the resting place for prominent individuals such as community leader LIM BOON KENG and English sailor Augustus Podmore Williams, upon whose life JOSEPH CONRAD based his novel, *Lord Jim*.

Under the government's Master Plan 1998, the cemetery grounds were slated for the development of public housing and other facilities. Clearance of the cemetery also facilitated the construction of a road interchange at the junction of Braddell Road and Bartley Road, as well as the construction of Woodleigh MRT Station on the North–East Line.

Exhumation of the estimated 143,000 graves, undertaken by the Housing & Development Board, commenced in December 2001. The exhumation is to be completed by the end of 2006. The CHOA CHU KANG COLUMBARIUM serves as the resting place for cremated remains from the Bidadari Cemetery and elsewhere. Remains from Muslim graves were exhumed and reinterred at Pusara Abadi Muslim Cemetery, Choa Chu Kang (see PUSARA AMAN AND PUSARA ABADI).

A piece of land the size of four basketball courts has been set aside for the Bidadari Memorial Garden at Vernon Park. It commemorates the lives of 20 people, originally buried at Bidadari Cemetery, who are considered significant to Singapore's history, including LIM BOON KENG, R.A.J BIDWELL and AHMAD IBRAHIM. There is also a board commemorating the civilians who died in the 1915 Indian Army Mutiny (see SEPOY MUTINY) and the 33 who died in the 1954 plane crash at KALLANG AIRPORT. The old gates of the cemetery have been placed at the entrance to the garden. The gates bear the lion emblem of the Singapore Municipal Council.

Bidwell, R.A.J. (1869–1918) Architect. Born in London, Regent Alfred John Bidwell was trained as an architect. In the early 1890s, he was working for the London County Council. He later moved to Malaya and served in the Public Works Department in Kuala Lumpur. He soon gained a reputation for designing handsome government buildings. In 1897, he left the colonial service and joined the firm of SWAN & MACLAREN where he became part-

Bidadari Cemetery: entrance gates, now moved.

R.A.J. Bidwell: designed Stamford House.

ner in 1899. By the time he left Swan & Maclaren to establish his own practice in 1911, he was the most important architect in Singapore. His work included RAFFLES HOTEL, GOODWOOD PARK HOTEL (formerly the TEUTONIA CLUB), the CHESED-EL SYNAGOGUE in Oxley Rise, Stamford House, the Lai Chun Yuen Opera House in Trengganu Street, the joining of VICTORIA THEATRE to the old Town Hall (later known as the VICTORIA MEMORIAL HALL) and the design of the Hebrew School. He was also responsible for several large private houses, including Glencaird, one of four which were built on the White House Park Estate off Stevens Road. He died on 7 April 1918 and was buried at BIDADARI CEMETERY.

BigO Singapore-based periodical. *BigO* (Before I Get Old) was launched in September 1985. Relying largely on volunteer writers, *BigO* publisher Michael Cheah and editors Philip Cheah and Stephen Tan first began the magazine in black-and-white photocopied form before introducing a professionally printed colour version in 1990. With a monthly circulation of some 8,000–12,000 copies, it kept readers in touch with both the international and local music scenes, and was the only publication of its kind to focus strongly on local independent music, which it promoted through features, interviews with bands and CD compilations of demo songs sent to the magazine.

Compilations such as the New School Rock series and BigO Singles Club series raised awareness of independent rock bands such as AWOL, Force Vomit and The PADRES. The Padres' 'Radio Station' from the first *Singles Club* CD was played by renowned radio DJ John Peel on the BBC World Service. Peel called the song one of the best releases of 1993.

In the early 2000s, *BigO* ceased publishing its print edition and moved its content to the Internet. Its focus also changed, with less emphasis on music and more on local and international politics.

BIL International Singapore-based hotel and investment company. Formerly known as Brierley Investments, BIL International was incorporated in New Zealand in 1961 by Sir Ronald Brierley, and is an international investment company with a global portfolio and some 85,000 shareholders. The initial focus of the company was to acquire substantial shareholdings in public companies in New Zealand and Australia. But by the 1980s, the portfolio had expanded to numerous global investments with shareholdings in more than 300 global companies. In the late 1980s, BIL began to realign its strategy by focusing on a smaller number of assets with a core of trading subsidiaries and associated companies.

Following the Asian economic crisis in 1997, the Board initiated a review of corporate philosophy and investment strategy. This led to the write-down of asset values, disposal of a number of investments, the reduction of bank debt, a new management team and a new strategic focus for the company. In 1999, its domicile was transferred to Bermuda. It moved its global head office to Singapore and switched its primary stock listing from New Zealand to Singapore in 2000. The company subsequently changed its name from Brierley Investments to BIL International Limited in December 2001. BIL's primary role is that of an active investor with strategic holdings and active investment management aimed at extracting and maximising shareholder value, and is headed by Malaysian tycoon Quek Leng Chan, who is also the chairman of the Hong Leong Group in Malaysia. By 2006, BIL's focus was primarily on hotels and resorts development. Its wholly-owned subsidiary, the Thistle Hotels group, owned or managed about 50 hotels in Britain and was the largest hotel operator in the city of London. The company was also listed on the New Zealand and London exchanges. It reported a net profit of US$87 million on revenues of US$344 million for the financial year 2005. Its substantial stakeholders included Mr Quek's investment vehicles such as Camerlin Holdings, Hong Leong Malaysia and the Guoco Group.

bilingualism Policy designed to promote fluency in two languages. This policy required children to learn two languages: English and a MOTHER TONGUE, which could be Malay, Mandarin or Tamil. The government introduced compulsory bilingual education for all students in 1966. From 1969, all students had to take a second language in their school certificate level examinations. Since 1979, a pass in a second language is required for admission to pre-university.

English remains the working language in Singapore and the medium of instruction in schools. It is dominant because it is the language of global business, science and technological research. However, mother tongue languages are also taught so that students in Singapore can appreciate and retain their cultural identity and roots.

Since the introduction of the bilingualism policy, more people have become fluent in English, and the proportion of people who are bilingual has also risen. More members of the Chinese community now also use Mandarin, rather than dialects such as HOKKIEN and CANTONESE.

However, there continue to be difficulties with implementation of the bilingualism policy. A substantial number of children find the required mastery of two languages difficult. There have been numerous reviews to address these concerns, and to develop more differentiated curricula and effective pedagogies.

Bintan Island in the Riau Archipelago, and part of Indonesia. In the SEJARAH MELAYU, or Malay Annals, Bintan is significant because Sri Tri Buana stopped there first after leaving Palembang. The island was ruled by a queen, Sakidar Shah, who adopted Sri Tri Buana as her son, and invented the *nobat*—a collection of musical instruments including a 'drum of sovereignty', which became a key part of the royal regalia and a necessary object used in the installation of all subsequent Malay rulers. TEMASEK, by contrast, is depicted in the Malay Annals as having no ruler and no residents at that time. From Bintan, Sri Tri Buana moved to the apparently uninhabited island of Temasek and founded Singapura.

Chinese ceramics dating from the 13th through to the 15th centuries have been found along the Bintan River. Historical sites along the Riau River date from the 17th through to the 19th centuries.

The island of Bintan has acquired new economic importance to Singapore in recent years. A Framework Agreement on Regional Economic Cooperation was signed between Indonesia and Singapore in 1990, which promotes investment within the Riau region, of which Bintan is part. The development of Bintan Industrial Estate followed. The Asian strategies of some international companies have involved establishing a regional headquarters in Singapore, while outsourcing manufacturing activities to either Bintan or nearby BATAM.

BigO: supporter of local music and musicians.

Bintan: recently developed Bintan Industrial Estate.

Bionix: armoured personnel carrier.

The greatest foreign investment on Bintan has been in the tourist sector. The island, only a short ferry trip away, is a favourite weekend spot for Singaporeans, and its attractions have been promoted jointly by the Singaporean and Indonesian tourism authorities.

See also GROWTH TRIANGLE.

Bionic Boy (1977) Film directed by Filipino Leody M. Diaz. This co-production between the Philippines, Malaysia and Singapore was initiated by Filipino Bobby A. Suarez, director and scriptwriter of *They Call Her...Cleopatra Wong* (1978). The action movie starred ten-year-old tae kwon do champion Johnson Yap from Singapore in the lead role, along with an international cast. Inspired by blaxploitation movies like *Willie Dynamite* and the television series *The Six Million Dollar Man*, it was meant for an international audience and was shot in English. The young protagonist of the film was to return the following year in a sequel titled *Dynamite Johnson* (1978) (also known as *The Return of Bionic Boy*), playing alongside Marrie Lee of *They Call Her...Cleopatra Wong* fame.

Bionix Armoured personnel carrier. Bionix is the first project jointly developed by the SINGAPORE ARMED FORCES, the DEFENCE SCIENCE AND TECHNOLOGY AGENCY and Singapore Technologies Kinetics (ST Kinetics). It was completed in 1997 and comes in two versions—the IFV 25 and the IFV 40/50. 'IFV' stands for 'Infantry Fighting Vehicle'. The Bionix IFV 25 can carry 10 men, and has a thermal gun-sight, which allows it to identify targets in the dark and through smoke screens. A stabilized two-man turret system enables it to fire while moving.

The Bionix IFV 40/50 carries 11 soldiers, and is armed with a 40-mm automatic grenade launcher, a 1.27-mm heavy machine-gun weapon station and a 7.62-mm machine gun.

Both versions have enhanced armour protection and hydro-pneumatic suspen-

sion which enable them to traverse rough terrain, and cross streams and rivers at high speed. Despite a weight of between 21.5 tons and 22.9 tons, the Bionix can reach a top speed of 70 km per hour.

For its work in developing the Bionix, ST Kinetics became the first local company to be awarded the Defence Technology Prize by the Ministry of Defence.

biotech Singapore demonstrated an early interest in the biotech sector when it welcomed the British pharmaceutical firm Glaxo to its shores in 1982. However, it was not until the early 1990s that the government identified the biotech cluster as a fourth pillar of growth within MANUFACTURING, alongside electronics, chemicals and engineering.

Through the ECONOMIC DEVELOPMENT BOARD, the government attracted biotech investors and talent by offering tax breaks, grants and other financial incentives. In October 2003, the government opened Biopolis, the epicentre of biomedical research in Singapore. The 185,000-sq-m complex can house about 2,000 workers in five publicly-funded biomedical research institutes and the research laboratories of major biotechnology and pharmaceutical companies.

The industry's high growth in Singapore is attributed to factors including the regulatory framework for the protection of Intellectual Property Rights, an environment that is conducive for research and development, a skilled workforce, and the availability of venture funding for business start-ups. Pharmaceutical multinationals such as GlaxoSmithKline, Merck and Pfizer have made Singapore their global manufacturing hub.

The manufacturing output of the Biomedical Sciences industry was $15.8 billion in 2004, an increase of 33 per cent over 2003. It currently contributes about 5 per cent to gross domestic product. The government plans to transform Singapore into a global focal point for life-sciences research and manufacturing activities, setting an output target of $25 billion to be achieved by 2015.

Several world-famous names in the biomedical industry have come to work in Singapore, including Edison Liu, former director of the Division of Clinical Sciences at the National Cancer Institute in the United States; British biochemistry pioneer Alan Colman, one of the creators of the cloned sheep Dolly; cancer researcher Yoshiaki Ito and his team from Kyoto University; and Nobel Prize-winning molecular biologist Sydney Brenner.

bird flu Viral respiratory disease affecting poultry and other birds. The disease is caused by the type A influenza virus. The H5N1 strain of the type A influenza virus has been known to affect humans and is the

most deadly. In 1997 in Hong Kong, of the 18 people seriously infected with the H5N1 strain, six died.

A bird flu outbreak began in January 2004 in Vietnam and Thailand. The spread of the H5N1 strain devastated poultry farms in many Southeast Asian countries. By the end of 2005, millions of birds had been culled in an effort to limit the spread of the virus and to prevent the onset of a pandemic. According to the World Health Organization (WHO), by July 2006 there had been 231 human cases worldwide with 130 deaths since the outbreak—an alarmingly high rate of mortality. Most of the people infected were in close contact with diseased birds. Person-to-person transmission is limited, though researchers believe that the H5N1 strain virus may mutate and make this kind of transmission possible. It is believed that the 1918 'Spanish Flu' pandemic that caused up to 40 million deaths worldwide, started out as a form of bird flu.

According to the WHO, a bird flu pandemic is imminent. The Ministry of Health (MOH) has outlined a national strategy to deal with bird flu. The strategy comprises three main areas: establish a surveillance system to detect the import of the virus, limit the damage when the first pandemic wave hits, and immunization when a vaccine becomes available.

The surveillance strategy formulated by the MOH is designed to detect the first cases or clusters of influenza in humans and animals, and to detect new strains of viruses. It involves community surveillance (compiling reports from polyclinics and hospitals), laboratory surveillance, hospital surveillance, veterinary surveillance through the Agri-Food and Veterinary Authority (AVA), and external surveillance (monitoring outbreaks regionally and internationally).

The AVA has taken precautions to prevent the disease from entering Singapore, one of which is the suspending of the import of live birds from countries affected by bird flu. Imported eggs and poultry consignments are routinely sampled and tested for the virus. As a further precaution, the AVA has intensified surveillance of poultry slaughterhouses, where workers are required to protect themselves with masks and adhere strictly to hygiene practices.

In August 2004, when the bird flu virus was detected on a poultry farm in Kelantan, Malaysia, the AVA banned all imports of poultry (including eggs) from the country. The ban was lifted after six weeks.

The MOH has implemented the Disease Outbreak Response System. It serves as a frame of reference for responses of increasing intensity according to predefined alert levels. For example, Alert Green means that the threat to public health is low and there are no new viral outbreaks in the world. Alert Orange means that the pandemic is underway and the

Bionic Boy (1977)

infection has become a human disease with widespread person-to-person transmission.

Antiviral medication, as shown in research, is effective in the early treatment of influenza. The MOH is maintaining a stockpile of antiviral medication to be used in an outbreak. The use of antiviral medication is also expected to reduce flu-related complications that would otherwise require hospitalization. It is thus seen as an important strategy to prevent medical services from being overwhelmed.

birds *See* box.

birth and death rates *See* DEMOGRAPHY.

Bishan New town. Bishan is built on the grounds of the former Peck San Theng Chinese Cemetery, one of the largest burial grounds in Singapore. In 1870, the Kwong Wai Siew Association established a temple and cemetery named Peck San Theng— Bishan Ting or Bishan Pavilion (*see* KWONG WAI SIEW PECK SAN THENG). This was exhumed in 1979 to make way for the HOUSING & DEVELOPMENT BOARD (HDB) new town of Bishan.

The town is circumscribed by Ang Mo Kio Avenue 1, Upper Thomson Road and Braddell Road, with Bishan Road cutting across it. One of the most outstanding features of Bishan new town is its 52-ha Bishan Park, a huge recreational space frequented by residents of Bishan and neighbouring Ang Mo Kio. The town is not very large and is divided into two neighbourhoods, one on each side of Bishan Road. In 2005 there were around 19,000 flats in the estate. Bishan's proximity to amenities such as Bishan Park, the Bishan MRT station and schools such as Raffles Institution, Raffles Junior College and Catholic High School, makes its HDB residential properties highly sought-after.

Black, Sir Robert Brown (1906–1999) Colonial official. Sir Robert Brown Black served in the administration of Britain's colonies for more than 30 years. During World War II, he spent several years in a Japanese prison camp in Malaya. After the war ended, he returned to the colonial service and served in North Borneo and Hong Kong before moving to Singapore. Taking over the mantle from Governor Sir JOHN NICOLL in 1955, Black was thrust straight into a confrontation with the first elected chief minister of Singapore, DAVID MARSHALL. In July 1955, Marshall demanded the appointment of four assistant ministers. When Black refused, Marshall threatened to resign unless Singapore was granted immediate self-government, pointing to the anomaly of a British governor in a self-governed Singapore. The British feared that Marshall's departure would pave the way for a more radical and irresponsible government. So it was immediately ruled that

Black should act on the chief minister's advice. It was also agreed that constitutional talks (*see* MERDEKA) would be held after the Assembly had been in existence for one year instead of allowing it to run to its full term.

Marshall aimed to secure full internal self-government for Singapore, but the British rejected his proposal and Marshall resigned on his return to Singapore in June 1956. He was replaced as chief minister by LIM YEW HOCK, whose government was weak and hastily assembled. As part of a general campaign of counter subversion, Lim dissolved seven communist-front organizations in 1956. When Lim led the second all-party delegation to London to discuss the issues of self-government, he was well-received. Black and the Colonial Office found it easier to deal with Lim, and the 1957 negotiations achieved a degree of success to spur Singapore on to the next constitutional conference in London in 1958. In 1957, WILLIAM GOODE took over the governorship from Black.

black-and-white houses Mock Tudor houses, built between the end of the 19th century and World War II. The design of these residences was much influenced by the Arts and Crafts and art deco movements. Typically, they were two-storey buildings with large verandahs—sometimes up to three of them—on the upper floor, with a car or carriage porch below the projecting upper-floor verandah. The ground floor contained an entrance hall with a stairway. Rooms on the upper floor were arranged between continuous verandahs running along both the front and back of the house. Often the main building was linked to an out-house. The house was topped with a pitched roof, with wide eaves acting as very effective sunshades.

In the 1930s, Mock Tudor gave way to the 'tropical art deco' style which favoured a more streamlined design and flat roofs.

Most of these houses were built by government departments (such as the Public Works Department) and larger commercial firms. Today, most of the black-and-white houses—so named on account of the way the exterior was painted, often with a 'half-timbered' effect—are owned and managed by the state, although there are still a few in private hands.

black-spotted sticky frog (*Kalophrynus pleurostigma*) A frog that dwells in leaf-litter. In 1990, zoologists Kelvin Lim and Peter Ng found tadpoles living in the cup-shaped leaves of a PITCHER PLANT (*Nepenthes ampullaria*). The specialized leaves of pitcher plants contain a liquid containing an enzyme, which helps the carnivorous plant digest insects that have drowned in the liquid. The pair of zoologists observed that these tadpoles were unharmed by this enzyme. The tadpoles were not feeding on insects that had drowned in the pitchers, but

Black-and-white houses: typically in spacious grounds.

Black-spotted sticky frog

obtained nutrition from their own yolk sacs.

The frog is rare in Singapore but can be spotted in the BUKIT TIMAH NATURE RESERVE. It can grow up to 6 cm and secretes a sticky substance, probably to deter predators.

Blackmore, Sophia (1857–1945) Australian Methodist missionary. She was the first woman missionary sent by the Methodist Women's Foreign Missionary Society to Singapore, arriving in July 1887. She served for 40 years. During that time, she set up the METHODIST GIRLS' SCHOOL (MGS) and the Fairfield Methodist Girls' School, and helped develop the first Baba Malay (PERANAKAN) Church.

Her first project, the Tamil Girls' School, opened in August 1887 in a two-room shophouse at 33 Short Street. Classes were attended by nine daughters of Tamil businessmen, who provided the sole teacher's monthly salary and donated furniture. Enrolment eventually reached 100, and the school moved to Middle Road. It was renamed the Methodist Girls' School in the 1890s. Younger brothers of the students—including future president BENJAMIN SHEARES and future Methodist bishop T.R. Doraisamy—were allowed to attend classes at the school.

Sophia Blackmore is commemorated in the address of the MGS site since 1992, Blackmore Drive.

Bloodworth, Dennis (1919–2005) Journalist and author. Born in London, Dennis Bloodworth was educated at Birchington House Preparatory School and Sevenoaks. He left school at the age of 17 and took up a variety of jobs, including pig-food analyst, press photographer, junior reporter and

Sir Robert Brown Black

Sophia Blackmore

Bishan: the new town development includes Bishan Park.

birds Singapore's geographical location, a tropical climate, a network of protected natural areas, and good governance have all helped to achieve a diversity of birdlife, despite high levels of urbanization.

There are 350 species of wild bird recorded in present-day Singapore, of which 165 are resident and can be spotted year-round. Another 152 species are found in Singapore only during the northern-hemisphere winter. Some rest for just a few days before moving south to Indonesia and Australia. These **passage migrants** come from northern countries, such as Russia, China and the Korean Peninsula. Examples are the curlew sandpiper (*Calidris ferruginea*) (*1*), Indian cuckoo (*Cuculus micropterus*) (*2*) and Asian paradise-flycatcher (*Terpsiphone paradisi*) (*3*). A large proportion of migrant birds stay on to exploit readily available food resources and are known as 'winter visitors'.

1

2

3

Of the remaining species, 16 are non-breeding visitors from neighbouring countries; and 17 are 'vagrants'—birds which become lost during migration due to bad weather.

The study of birds in Singapore began with the arrival of Sir STAMFORD RAFFLES in 1819. He started a collection of bird specimens with the establishment of the Raffles Museum. Zoologist and explorer Sir Alfred Russel Wallace—who developed the Theory of Evolution with Charles Darwin—also collected in Singapore in 1825. HENRY RIDLEY made a study of the birds of the Botanic Gardens in the late 1890s.

Since 1819, one-third of resident birds have become extinct, including the lesser adjutant (*Leptoptilos javanicus*) (*6*), a large stork which was found in marshy areas. The main cause is the depletion of forest cover—from 85 per cent of total land area in 1819 to less than 10 per cent in 1880—due mainly to agriculture and housing. Pollution of inshore waters has caused the decline of many waterbirds as well.

Still at risk of extinction are 53 species. The introduction of non-native birds poses a threat to indigenous birds. A naturalized species, the Javan myna (*Acridotheres javanicus*) (*4*), is now Singapore's most common bird. Competition from the more aggressive myna is believed to have led to the decline of the oriental magpie-robin (*Copsychus saularis*) (*5*). The house crow (*Corvus splendens*), which was introduced from India around 1940, has become a pest that has to be controlled by direct culling.

Another threat is poaching. Although the law protects virtually all wild birds, in remote areas poachers trap red junglefowls, straw-headed bulbuls and oriental magpie-robins. However, the biggest threat for some species is an unviable population level. The white-bellied woodpecker (*Dryocopus javensis*) is now reduced to just three birds, and there is only one beach thick-knee (*Burhinus giganteus*) which lives on the southern islands.

7

8

9

10

11

One main reason for the wealth of birdlife is Singapore's variety of habitats. **Rainforests** are home to species such as the changeable hawk-eagle (*Spizaetus cirrhatus*) (*7*), red-crowned barbet (*Megalaima rafflesi*) (*8*), and crimson sunbird (*Aethopyga siparaja*) (*9*). More than 170 species of birds have been found in BUKIT TIMAH NATURE RESERVE and the CENTRAL CATCHMENT NATURE RESERVE.

Birds such as the copper-throated sunbird (*Nectarinia calcostetha*) (*10*) and straw-headed bulbul (*Pycnonotus zeylanicus*) (*11*) can be found in **mangrove forests** such as SUNGEI BULOH WETLAND RESERVE, while the white-breasted waterhen (*Amaurornis phoenicurus*) (*12*) and white-bellied fish-eagle (*Haliaeetus leucogaster*) (*13*) inhabit **freshwater wetlands** such as Kranji Reservoir.

Similarly, **offshore islands** are rich in bird species. PULAU UBIN is home to over 180 bird species, including the long-tailed parakeet (*Psittacula longicauda*) (*14*) and two species not found elsewhere in Singapore—the oriental pied hornbill (*Anthracoceros albirostris*) (*15*) and the RED JUNGLEFOWL.

Grasslands and open areas play host to the paddyfield pipit (*Anthus rufulus*) (*16*), baya weaver (*Ploceus philippinus*) (*17*) and many others.

Singapore's parks also thrive with birdlife. For example, the SINGAPORE BOTANIC GARDENS has over 120 species, while Bishan Park has more than 100 species.

16

15

14

17

12

13

4

5

6

sub-editor. He served in World War II and joined *The Observer* as an assistant to the chief Paris correspondent in 1949. In 1954, he was posted to Saigon to cover the Indo-Chinese conflict and in 1956, he moved to Singapore as chief Far East correspondent of *The Observer*, a post he held until 1981.

Bloodworth wrote five books on the region: *The Chinese Looking Glass* (1967); *An Eye For the Dragon* (1970); *The Messiah and the Mandarins* (1982); *Reporter's Notebook* (1988); and *The Tiger and the Trojan Horse* (1986). He also co-wrote three books with his wife, Liang Ching Ping, herself a noted radio commentator and journalist: *Heirs Apparent* (1973); *The Chinese Machiavelli* (1976); and *I Married A Barbarian* (2000). Bloodworth was also responsible for editing the first volume of Lee Kuan Yew's memoirs, *The Singapore Story* (2000). He wrote five works of fiction, including *Any Number Can Play* (1972) and its sequel, *The Clients of Omega* (1975); *Have a Nice Day* (1992); and *Trapdoor* (1980).

Blundell, Sir Edmund (dates unknown) Colonial official. Prior to his appointment as governor of the Straits Settlements, Sir Edmund Augustus Blundell had served variously as commissioner of Tenasserim (1833–43), resident councillor of Malacca (1847–49) and resident councillor of Penang (1849–55). He had been expected to succeed SAMUEL GEORGE BONHAM as governor of the Straits Settlements in 1843 due to his familiarity with the local languages and customs as well as his keen interest in agriculture. However, the EAST INDIA COMPANY decided to appoint Colonel WILLIAM BUTTERWORTH instead.

Blundell succeeded Butterworth as governor in 1855. During his governorship he attempted to introduce port dues on shipping to increase revenue but the merchants opposed this decision as contrary to the principles on which the colony was established. In 1854, twelve consecutive days of violence, sparked by a dispute between the Hokkiens and Teochews, had seriously disrupted trade in Singapore. In view of the fragile security situation, Blundell decided to pass the Police Force Act of 1856 to vest full police powers upon the security forces then in existence, paving the way for uniforms to be introduced. However there were difficulties in enforcing the new Police Act which resulted in further riots. The press played up the negative publicity, and he was extremely unpopular by the end of his term.

Blythe, Wilfred Lawson (1896–1975) Colonial official. Wilfred Lawson Blythe was educated at the universities of Liverpool and Grenoble. He served in World War I and joined the Malayan Civil Service in 1921. From 1922 to 1924, he studied Chinese in Canton (present-day Guangdong). Between 1926 and 1936,

Blythe served as Protector of Chinese (*see* CHINESE PROTECTORATE.) in various parts of Malaya. Other important positions he held included deputy president, Penang Municipality (1936–37; 1939–40) and deputy controller of labour (Chinese) (1941–42). He served with the Army during World War II, and was interned during the Japanese Occupation (1942–45). After the war, Blythe was appointed secretary for Chinese affairs for the Federation of Malaya (1946–48). He returned to Singapore in 1948 to become president of the Municipal Commission. In 1950 he was appointed colonial secretary of Singapore, a post he held until his retirement in 1953. He wrote in that year *Historical Sketch of Chinese Labour in Malaya*, and in 1969 a classic study entitled *Secret Societies in Malaya*.

BNP Paribas Bank. The French bank BNP Paribas Singapore is one of a number of foreign banks licenced in Singapore as a Qualifying Full Bank, a status it acquired in October 1999 following the liberalization of the local BANKING sector. The banking group's presence in Singapore began in 1968 when BNP (Banque Nationale de Paris) established a representative bank. BNP acquired Paribas in 1999 and the merged group has since become the biggest bank in the Eurozone by market capitalization, employing some 140,000

people in over 85 countries as of 2006. The BNP Paribas operation in Singapore is its regional hub for corporate, investment and private banking, and oversees a team of more than 1,100 professionals in the region. It is located at Collyer Quay.

Board of Architects Statutory board. Under the MINISTRY OF NATIONAL DEVELOPMENT, the Board administers the Architects Act 1991, which sets out provisions for the registration of architects, the regulation of architectural qualifications, the practice of architecture by registered individuals and the supply of architectural services by corporations.

Board of Commissioners of Currency Singapore The Board of Commissioners of Currency Singapore (BCCS) was established in 1967 to continue with the 'currency board' system that had operated since colonial times. This is a regime where domestic notes and coins were fully convertible to a foreign currency at a fixed exchange rate, and also fully backed by foreign assets or gold. However, with the collapse of the Bretton–Woods system in 1973, the subsequent floating of the Singapore dollar and the repeal of the convertibility of domestic currency notes and coins into gold and other foreign currencies on demand in 1982, the role of

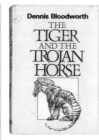

Dennis Bloodworth: The Tiger and the Trojan Horse *(1986) deals with the People's Action Party and the Communist United Front.*

Wilfred Lawson Blythe

Boat Quay Developed in the early 1820s as a public quay, the area was originally a swampy bank reclaimed with earth taken from a small hill at modern-day RAFFLES PLACE. Before the opening of New Harbour (Keppel Harbour) in the 1850s, Boat Quay and CLARKE QUAY, further up-river, were the main port areas on the banks of the SINGAPORE RIVER. The name Boat Quay originally referred to both banks of the Singapore River: North Boat Quay abutted River Valley Road, and South Boat Quay was closer to the old Ellenborough Market. GODOWNS, warehouses, and shophouses were built all along both North and South Boat Quay. Shophouses dominated the mid-river section along the two quays. The area was gazetted for conservation in 1989.

During the 1990s, the Urban Redevelopment Authority began transforming the area. Shophouses were sold, refurbished and adapted for reuse. Today, Boat Quay is the name of the southern quay. It is now a pedestrian-only strip bustling with restaurants, pubs, cafés, clubs, fast-food outlets and coffee shops.

Boat Quay: (clockwise from top left) coolies at work; working riverfront around 1900; still crowded with bumboats in the 1960s; a centre for restaurants and entertainment today.

George Edwin Bogaars: presenting certificates to Singapore Armed Forces trainees, 1969.

the BCCS was greatly reduced. Despite this, currency issue remained the responsibility of the BCCS until it was merged with the MONETARY AUTHORITY OF SINGAPORE on 1 October 2002.

Boat Quay *See* box.

Bogaars, George Edwin (1926–1992) Civil servant. George Edwin Bogaars was educated at St Patrick's School, St Joseph's Institution, Raffles College (where he was a Raffles College Scholar) and the University of Malaya. He graduated with a BA honours in history (1951) and was awarded a Shell Research Fellowship to complete his master of arts degree (1952).

Bogaars joined the ADMINISTRATIVE SERVICE after graduation, and was posted to the Ministry of Commerce and Industry (1952). He became director, SPECIAL BRANCH (1961–65); permanent secretary, Ministry of Interior and Defence (1965–70); head of the Civil Service (1968–75); and permanent secretary, finance-budget (1975–81). He has been described as the 'Archetypal Civil Servant'. He helped to set up the SINGAPORE ARMED FORCES and TEMASEK HOLDINGS, and re-organize the Special Branch.

After retirement in 1981, Bogaars became chairman of Keppel Shipyard (1981–84) and National Iron and Steel Mill (1981–85). After surviving a heart attack and several strokes, Bogaars died on 6 April 1992. For his contributions, Bogaars was awarded the MERITORIOUS SERVICE MEDAL (1962) and admitted to the DISTINGUISHED SERVICE ORDER (1967). He was also made an honorary doctor of letters by the University of Singapore (1972).

bomb shelters These reinforced enclosures are part of the government's plan for TOTAL DEFENCE. The long-term goal of the Civil Defence Shelter Programme, which is under the purview of the SINGAPORE CIVIL DEFENCE FORCE, is for every resident in Singapore to be protected by a purpose-built shelter berth, whether at work or at home.

When the programme was first mooted in 1983, nine underground MRT stations were identified as public shelters, or bomb shelters as they are often called. In 1987, the shelter programme took on a

larger scale, with public shelters at the foot of new HOUSING & DEVELOPMENT BOARD (HDB) residential blocks. Since then, public shelters have also been built in secondary schools, community centres and other public buildings.

The next phase came in 1994. Shelters were to be built inside all new HDB flats, no longer sited at the foot of HDB blocks. Essentially, the household shelter is a storeroom-cum-pantry with strengthened walls, floor and ceiling.

The Civil Defence Shelter Act 1997 made it compulsory for shelters to be included in all new residential developments. A six-month grace period was given before the Act came into operation on 1 May 1998.

Bongso, Ariff (1946–) Scientist. Professor Ariff Bongso was born in Sri Lanka and attended the Royal College in Colombo. He obtained an MSc and PhD with distinction from the Department of Biomedical Sciences of the University of Guelph in Canada in 1976.

Bongso has taught and carried out research at the National University of Singapore since the early 1980s, in the Department of Obstetrics & Gynaecology, and is scientific director of the In-Vitro Fertilisation (IVF) programme at the National University Hospital. His first major breakthrough came in 1991, when he developed co-culture, a means of growing human embryos in a laboratory dish. Co-culture was used by IVF programmes worldwide for a decade and it helped to double the pregnancy rate for childless couples going through IVF. In 1994, Professor Bongso was the first researcher to derive embryonic stem cells from five-day-old human embryos. In 2002, he achieved another first, deriving and growing human embryonic stem cells in an animal-free culture system, avoiding the risk of transmitting animal diseases to the human stem cells.

Professor Bongso earned a doctor of science degree from the National University of Singapore in 1995 for his work on human IVF. In 2002, he was awarded the National Science Award, 'for his pioneering work in human embryonic stem cell research which could lead to the potential treatment of a variety of incurable diseases'. In the same year, he was awarded the Asian Innovation Award (Gold) from the *Far Eastern Economic Review,* also for his work on stem cells. In 2003, he was given the Excellence for Singapore award and in 2005, was named ASEAN Outstanding Scientist by the ASEAN Society for Science and Technology. In September 2003, he was made a Fellow of the Royal College of Obstetricians and Gynaecologists (FRCOG ad eundem—a courtesy extended to people whose qualifications, obtained from another institution, are recognized as equivalent) of the United Kingdom for '30 years of contribution towards the well-

being of women' and in December 2005 received an honorary doctor of science degree from the University of Sri Lanka for his contributions to infertility services and research in Sri Lanka.

Bonham, Sir Samuel George (1803–1863) Colonial official. Appointed acting governor of the STRAITS SETTLEMENTS between 1833 and 1835, Samuel George Bonham was appointed substantive governor from 1836 to 1843. While in office, he earned a reputation for being approachable and gregarious. Bonham was one of the first Straits Settlements civil servants.

He was appointed by Sir Stamford Raffles in 1823 to handle the sale of land and collection of licence revenue in Singapore which had hitherto been performed haphazardly. He administered Singapore at a time when the EAST INDIA COMPANY (EIC) had lost its monopoly on the China trade, which resulted in an official policy of preventing financial deficit under any circumstance.

Bonham was one of a group of overworked and underpaid EIC officials on duty in the Straits Settlements and Singapore from 1830 to 1867. Due to the official policy of frugality, the number of senior officials in the Straits Settlements was reduced dramatically in 1830, from 19 to eight. In addition to his overwhelming administrative duties, Bonham also had to undertake the bulk of the judicial work with the resident councillor. Cases remained unheard for months because the RECORDER, whose job it was to deal with these cases, only paid periodic visits to Singapore.

During Bonham's term, piracy was a big problem for local merchants. In 1830 it had almost brought trade to a standstill in the Malay Peninsula. In 1835 Bonham complained to Calcutta that piracy was a threat to Asian trade. In response, a royal naval sloop, HMS *Wolf,* was despatched to the Straits Settlements to cooperate with the company's steamer, *Diana*, in combatting pirates, and for a few years they were effective. During Bonham's governorship, though the officials were under strain, the merchants enjoyed much prosperity.

Borneo Company McEwen and Co., the successor of Paterson and Co., registered the Borneo Company Limited in London in 1856. In 1857, an office was set up in Singapore with wharf operations in Telok Blangah. Its activities in the latter half of the century included the exporting of pepper and rice, rice-milling, saw-milling, steam-towing, passenger vessels, insurance agency and banking representation. It was also engaged in gambier, pepper, timber and rubber plantations. The company's administrative headquarters was in Singapore although it quickly extended its operations into Sarawak, Batavia (Jakarta), Calcutta, Hong Kong and Thailand.

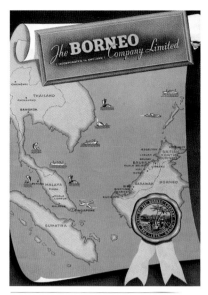

Borneo Company: advertising in the 1950s.

Before World War I, the company's most significant operations were centred in Sarawak and Thailand. Gold prospecting was the main activity in Sarawak between 1897 and 1923. In 1856, the company entered Thailand and opened up the export trade in rice. It also started to represent British banking and insurance companies. From the 1880s to the turn of the 20th century, the company was one of Thailand's largest teak firms.

The company took up brick-making in Singapore in 1899 and in 1928 established the Alexandra Brickworks Company. The 1920s were the company's most prosperous years. In 1925 it floated off Borneo Motors Limited which held franchises in Southeast Asia from the leading manufacturers (*see* BORNEO MOTORS). In 1967, the Borneo Company became a wholly owned Inchcape subsidiary. In 1975, Borneo Co Sdn Bhd was formed to take over business activities in Peninsular Malaysia. The company then became a wholly owned subsidiary of Kumpulan Inchcape Sdn Bhd. In 1993, the name of the company was changed to Inchcape Technical (M) Sdn Bhd and subsequently became a subsidiary of Inchcape Holdings Sdn Bhd. In 1999, Inchcape Technical (renamed Borneo Technical) was acquired by Li & Fung Distribution.

Borneo Motors One of the largest car distribution companies in Singapore. The distributor for Toyota, the most popular motor vehicle brand in Singapore, and of Lexus cars, Borneo Motors has a heritage which goes back to 1856.

The BORNEO COMPANY expanded into automobile sales in 1914. The automobile industry grew significantly and by 1925, it was spun off as a separate company, Borneo Motors. After World War II, the company distributed brands such as Austin, Riley, Vauxhall, Bedford, Chevrolet, Oldsmobile, Cadillac, Chrysler, Pontiac, Buick and Leyland; and marketed motoring-related products such as Goodyear tyres, Exide batteries and Castrol oil.

In 1967, the parent Borneo Company was merged with the Inchcape Group of Britain, and Borneo Motors' divisions in Singapore and Malaysia were set up as separate units. That same year, the group announced that it was dropping the Austin dealership in favour of Toyota. Within two years, the Singapore group had sold more than 3,000 Toyota commercial and passenger vehicles.

The mid-1980s saw the company doubling its training, workshop and warehouse space and expanding its showroom. In 1988, Borneo Motors Singapore was awarded the Triple Crown Award by the Toyota Motor Corporation for achieving the number one position in the saloon-car, commercial-vehicle and overall vehicle sales in Singapore. In 1992, the upmarket Lexus marque was launched.

Borneo Motors was the single biggest profit contributor to its London-listed parent in 2004, accounting for one-third of Inchcape's operating profit. It sells around 30,000 Toyota vehicles each year in Singapore and has 30 per cent market share for all cars sold. Its network of eight service centres supported by more than 400 staff is the largest locally.

Bose, Rash Behari (1886–1945) Indian political activist. Rash Behari Bose had wanted to join the British army but was twice rejected because he was deemed physically unfit. He subsequently became involved in revolutionary work. He was accused of being the organizing head in the 1912 Delhi-Lahore Conspiracy Case in which an attempt to assassinate the Viceroy Lord Hardinge failed. Bose fled to Dehra Dun (northern India) to evade arrest. With the arrest of fellow revolutionary V. G. Pingley in March 1915, Bose left India and eventually reached Japan in June 1915. He married a Japanese woman, became a Japanese citizen, and actively fostered the bond between Japan and India. In 1924, he founded the Indian Independence League (IIL) of Japan to mobilize support for India's liberation from British rule. When Japan declared the Greater East Asia War on 8 December 1941, Bose began organizing Indians in East Asia to fight for the freedom of the 'Motherland' (that is, India). He initiated the Tokyo Conference in March 1942 and invited prominent Indians from Singapore, Malaya, and Thailand.

Bose became the first president of the Council of Action of IIL at the Bangkok Conference of Indian delegates from East Asia held between 15 and 23 June 1942. Other council members included MOHAN SINGH of the Indian National Army (INA). Bose came to Singapore on 1 September and 18 November 1942 to meet other council members, chiefly about Japan's lack of response to accepting the Bangkok resolutions and recognizing the council as the supreme executive of the Indian independence movement. When Mohan Singh and three other members of the council resigned, Bose took command of the INA and IIL on 9 December 1942.

On 4 July 1943, at another conference held at the Cathay Building, he stepped down as president and appointed SUBHAS CHANDRA BOSE (no relation) as the leader of IIL who in turn made Rash Behari Bose the IIL's supreme advisor.

As his health was failing, Bose left for Japan in August 1943 to seek treatment and retired from political involvement. He died on 21 January 1945.

See also INDIAN NATIONAL ARMY AND MONUMENT.

Bose, Subhas Chandra (1897–1945) Indian political activist. Born in Calcutta, Subhas Chandra Bose was brought up in a wealthy family. He studied in the United Kingdom and took the examination for entry into the Indian Civil Service. Although successful, he refused to follow this career path. On his return to India, he immediately set about working for Indian independence. He believed in armed struggle, and saw the rise of National Socialism in Germany, and the ensuing conflict with the UK, as enhancing the possibility of overthrowing British rule in India. Believing that no political alignment was to be rejected if it helped to further his revolutionary goals, he also looked to Japan for support. In 1941, he founded the Indian National Army (INA), recruiting members from Indian prisoners-of-war in Germany and North Africa.

Bose arrived in Singapore on 2 July 1943. Two days later, he succeeded RASH BEHARI BOSE as president of the Indian Independence League (IIL). On 8 July 1943, he took command of the INA, declaring himself supreme commander. At a mass rally held the following day, the title 'Netaji' (leader) was conferred on him to

Subhas Chandra Bose: at Singapore airport during the Japanese Occupation.

Borneo Motors: advertisement from the 1940s (below); company premises in 1930.

great acclamation. Four days later, he was given a guard of honour comprising 40 women armed with fixed bayonets at a mass meeting of women in Singapore, marking the formation of the 'Rani of Jhansi Regiment' (RJR).

On 21 October 1943, he delivered an address at the Fifth Conference of the IIL, in which he explained the significance of the formation of the Provisional Government of Free India. As 'Head of State and Prime Minister of Free India', he swore to continue to fight for and preserve India's freedom. The following day, he inspected the guard of honour at the opening ceremony of the RJR Training Camp in Waterloo Street.

On 8 July 1945, Bose laid the foundation stone for a memorial to fallen INA soldiers on the Esplanade in front of the PADANG. The memorial was blown up by the British later that year. In 1995, the NATIONAL HERITAGE BOARD marked the site with a slab, on which the history of the INA is recorded.

Subhas Chandra Bose is believed to have died in a plane crash on his way to Tokyo on 18 August 1945.

See also INDIAN NATIONAL ARMY AND MONUMENT.

Boustead & Company Edward Boustead & Company was established in 1828 by Edward Boustead, British merchant and founding member of the SINGAPORE FREE PRESS which started publication in 1835. The firm's godown, built around 1832, was midway between Coleman and Elgin bridges, next to the Tan Kim Seng godown. In the 19th century, Boustead established itself with major interests in shipping and insurance, import and export. It traded in products such as banca tin, beer, rattan, silk and tea throughout Southeast Asia, China, Australia and Europe. The company also diversified into businesses such as estate management, marketing and mining.

Edward Boustead was the main benefactor of the Boustead Institute, built in Tanjong Pagar in 1892, which catered for the needs of transiting seamen.

Over the years, Boustead & Company expanded steadily and became synonymous with famous brand names such as Cadbury's, Johnny Walker, Hennessy and Thomas Cook. In the 1970s, the company underwent restructuring: three separate companies were publicly listed in Malaysia, Singapore and the UK under the Boustead name and focused largely on manufacturing and technical services. In 1996, the Singapore company acquired its current name, Boustead Singapore Limited, its core operations being engineering services and geo-spatial technology.

Boyanese Descendents of migrants from the Indonesian island of Bawean. The Boyanese (or Baweanese) constitute the

Boustead & Company: Boustead Institute, 1905.

third-largest immigrant population of Singapore's Malay community. The first Boyanese are thought to have come to Singapore in 1824 on a BUGIS ship. According to an 1849 census, there were 763 Boyanese, mostly men, in Singapore. The numbers increased gradually due to continuous immigration prior to World War II; however entry was more strictly controlled in the post-war period, especially after the implementation of the CITIZENSHIP ORDINANCE in 1957. The present Boyanese population is mostly made up of the descendants of these earlier immigrants.

According to the 2000 population CENSUS, there are 51,849 Boyanese in Singapore. A notable aspect of Boyanese culture is the tradition of *merantau*, the migration of men from the island in search of work. Historically, the Boyanese migrated to Singapore from Bawean Island in Indonesia in search of urban, waged work. From the onset, the Boyanese settled in Kampung Boyan, at the bank of the Rochor River between Jalan Besar and Syed Alwi Road. They organized themselves into *pondok* or *ponthuk* (communal lodging house) communities where they formed a social structure that ensured that their welfare was taken care of until they were economically secure to set up their

own houses. These houses usually catered for groups of migrants who came from the same district or village. Houses were also located in other parts of the city, including Pondok Adam at Ann Siang Hill, Pondok Teluk Dulam at Dixon Road and Pondok Dedawang at Sophia Road. The Boyanese were also among the early residents of Serangoon Road. Some of them established themselves in an area called Kampung Kapor, which was west of Kampung Boyan.

Typically, a *pondok* was a two- or three-storey house with shared facilities. The single residents, separated by gender, lived together in common rooms while couples and families lived in cubicles partitioned by curtains. The residents would share the rent. A *pondok* could house as many as 200 people and was often overcrowded. Each *pondok* was headed by a Pak Lurah (village head) usually an elderly man well respected by the residents. There were about 113 houses at one stage. Eventually, the houses came under an umbrella organization, Persatuan Bawean Singapura (Singapore Bawean Association), registered in the 1930s. The association is still in existence and active, organizing activities and events for the community. It has opened membership to non-Boyanese.

Over the years the houses were vacated, either because the residents moved to live in Housing & Development Board flats or because they were demolished for redevelopment. The last *pondok*, Pondok Peranakan Gelam Club or Pondok Gelam, at 64 Club Street, was designated as Singapore's 44th historic site by the National Heritage Board in 2000. It was restored to its original state, with a new tenant.

Many Boyanese were employed in the construction of the racecourse in the 1840s. Subsequently, many of them were employed as horse trainers. They were also employed as carriage and bullock-cart drivers, syces, and labourers, an occupational niche they secured as a group through the practice of mutual recommendation. This

Boyanese: group photograph, 1910.

Boys' Brigade: on parade in 1967.

niche continued through to the 20th century when they formed the majority of chauffeurs, syces or horse riders. The younger generation have taken on other jobs and professions.

Boys' Brigade Youth organization. The Boys' Brigade (BB) had its roots in Glasgow, Scotland, where it was founded by William Alexander Smith, on 4 October 1883. The first Singapore BB company was set up in 1930 at Prinsep Street Presbyterian Church, with the aim of providing purposeful and meaningful activities for youth. The organization is now endorsed by the Ministry of Education, and registered as a charity. By 2005, with more than 6,700 members, there were 110 BB companies in Singapore, each attached to a school or church. The BB teaches Christian moral and social values.

BP Singapore The history of BP's operations in Singapore dates back to 1964 with the purchase of one of the fledgling city-state's first oil refineries at Pasir Panjang Road. It later raised its refining capacity in 1979 by taking a one-third stake in a joint-venture refinery on Pulau Merlimau with partners, Caltex and the Singapore Petroleum Company, a move which helped to make Singapore one of the world's top three refining and trading hubs by the late 1970s and 1980s. At around the same time, BP chose Singapore as its base to develop its presence in Asia.

In 2004, BP Singapore sold its refining and retail network and liquefied petroleum gas (LPG) bottling assets. It is now the hub for the group's key businesses and functions in Asia including its legal, tax, information technology, audit, health, safety, security and environmental services.

BP Singapore's current activities include oil, gas and chemicals trading, shipping and lubricants. The oil, gas and chemicals trading business unit manages a global trading portfolio, and supports BP's regional marketing and business development

initiatives. BP Singapore also serves global markets and customers in the shipping and aviation sectors. Its marine division supplies bunker fuel and marine lubricants to ships, while the aviation unit markets fuel, lubricants and technical services to the aviation industry in the region.

In 2005, BP Singapore employed a staff force of some 600, with a turnover in excess of US$30 billion.

Braddell, Sir Roland (1880–1966) Lawyer and scholar. Roland St John Braddell was educated at Oxford (1900–04), and was called to the Middle Temple Bar (1905) and Singapore Bar (1906). He practised in BRADDELL BROTHERS, the firm founded by his father and uncle. He served as member of the Singapore Housing Commission, the Statute Law Review Commission and the Johor Executive Council and Council of State (1932–40). As legal adviser to the United Malays National Organisation (UMNO), Braddell played a vital role in the negotiations leading to the creation of the Federation of Malaya (1948), and continued as private legal adviser to the Conference of Rulers in the federation. He was knighted in 1948 and served on the Singapore Executive Council (1949–50). In 1949, he was appointed council chairman of the newly established University of Malaya. Braddell was also a scholar and historian, with numerous publications to his name, including the ground-breaking *Law of the Straits Settlements* (1915). After retiring in 1961, he moved to London, where he died in November 1966.

Braddell, Sir Thomas (1822–1891) Lawyer and colonial administrator. The young Thomas Braddell arrived in Penang in 1844 to be a manager of sugar estates. In due course he joined the EAST INDIA COMPANY (EIC) as deputy superintendent of police. Dissatisfied with his existing prospects in the EIC, he studied law and was called to the Bar at Gray's Inn on 10 June 1859. In 1862, he resigned from the EIC and moved to Singapore where he set up a legal practice with Abraham Logan under the name of Logan & Braddell. In 1864, he was appointed Crown counsel, and in 1867, became Singapore's first attorney-general, an office he held until the end of 1882. Braddell played a significant role in the negotiations leading to the Treaty of Pangkor in 1874. In 1875, Governor Sir ANDREW CLARKE appointed him colonial secretary and secretary for affairs relating to the Native States.

In addition to his legal career, Braddell also wrote extensively, and was recognized as a leading Malay scholar. He worked on the *Revised Edition of the Laws of the Straits Settlements*. Braddell married Anne Lee and had four children. Towards the end of 1882, he was injured in a carriage accident and was forced to retire. He died in London.

Braddell Brothers Law firm founded by Sir Thomas de Multon Lee Braddell and his brother, Robert Wallace Glen Lee Braddell, in 1883. Their father, Sir THOMAS BRADDELL, was Singapore's first attorney-general. The younger Thomas also distinguished himself in public service, serving as attorney-general and then chief judicial commissioner of the Federated Malay States, while his brother Robert was considered the finest criminal lawyer of his day. In the late 1880s and 1890s, the Braddells were joined in their practice by J.P. Joaquim and Sir John Bromhead Matthews (later chief justice of the Bahamas). The firm continues to operate today.

Sir Roland Braddell, 1951.

BreadTalk Bakery chain. BreadTalk, started by local entrepreneur George Quek, transformed the local bakery scene in mid-2000 when it introduced its chain of concept bakeries, with their signature glass panels that allowed customers to view the kitchen staff at work. Within a year, sales increased from $1.6 million to $16.7 million, and its presence grew from a single outlet at Parco Bugis Junction mall to more than 20 outlets island-wide selling breads, buns, cakes and pastries, earning the company a place among Singapore's top 50 local enterprises. BreadTalk's buns are a blend of East and West—Western buns filled with flavours or ingredients popular with Asians, as in its popular meat-floss buns. The bakery chain has branched out into Hong Kong, Indonesia, China, Malaysia, the Philippines, Taiwan and the Middle East, operating both owned and franchise outlets.

In 2003, BreadTalk diversified into the restaurant business by securing the rights to the Din Tai Fung restaurant, famous for its *xiao long bao* (steamed buns), and rated by *The New York Times* as one of the world's ten best restaurants in 1993. In October 2004, BreadTalk acquired Topwin Investment Holding, which owns and operates 13 food courts in China, for $11 million, to strengthen its foothold in that country. Listed on Sesdaq, the junior board of the Singapore Exchange, in June 2003, the group reported a net loss of $31,000 despite a 25 per cent rise in revenues to $50 million for the financial year 2004.

BreadTalk

Frank Brewer: designed by Frank Brewer, this building in Club Street now forms part of a condominium development.

Brewer, Frank (1886–1971) Architect. Born in Richmond, Surrey, Frank Wilhim Brewer was educated at King's College, London University, where he took a degree in architecture. After graduation, Brewer joined his father's architectural firm of Brewer, Smith & Brewer and continued practising there until the start of World War I, when he joined the Royal Engineers. He rose to the rank of captain by 1918 and when the war ended, he decided to head east. In 1919, he joined the firm of SWAN & MACLAREN in Singapore, becoming the first university-qualified architect to practise in Singapore. Brewer's design style was much influenced by the Edwardian architect C.F.A. Voysey, a proponent of the Arts and Crafts Movement. Among Brewer's most important buildings are the CATHAY BUILDING (1939), SINGAPORE SWIMMING CLUB (1936), KALLANG AIRPORT and several impressive BLACK-AND-WHITE HOUSES in Dalvey Estate and Cluny Road. Brewer left Swan & Maclaren in 1931 and joined the firm of H.R. Arbenz. In 1933, he established his own firm and was soon one of the most sought-after architects in Singapore.

During World War II, Brewer escaped by ship but the vessel was sunk off Pompong Island in the Riau archipelago by Japanese bombers. He landed in Sumatra and eventually made his way to Colombo, Ceylon (Sri Lanka) on another vessel. After the war, he returned to Singapore and re-established his practice. He retired in 1957 and died in Jersey in 1971.

Bright Vision Hospital The hospital was the brainchild of the Venerable Yen Pei, president of the Singapore Buddhist Welfare Services. Bright Vision is a 302-bed community hospital, nursing home and hospice offering holistic care to the needy, the sick and the elderly, regardless of race and religion. The hospital started operations in May 2002.

The hospital provides nursing care for the chronic sick and disabled, rehabilitation to help patients regain independence in their daily living activities as well as palliative care for terminally ill patients. Cases are referred to Bright Vision from government hospitals, the Singapore Cancer Society and hospices. Only vegetarian food is served in this hospital.

Britannia Club Recreational facility set up in 1951 by the British military. The clubhouse with a large swimming-pool was located in Beach Road, opposite Raffles Hotel, and was managed by the Navy, Army and Air Force Institutes and the Women's Voluntary Service. In 1971, the Singapore government acquired the club, allocating it to the Singapore Armed Forces (SAF). It became the SAF Non-Commissioned Officers Club. The club was renamed the SAF Warrant Officers and Specialists Club in 1994. After the clubhouse site was earmarked for land redevelopment, the club was relocated to new premises in Boon Lay, and was renamed The Chevrons.

British Council International organization which promotes cultural relations and education. The British Council was originally established in Britain in 1934 as the British Committee for Relations with Other Countries. It was renamed the British Council for Relations with Other Countries in 1935 and in 1936, it became the British Council. While the British Council established its first overseas representative offices in 1938, it was not until 1947 that it was established in Singapore with a temporary office in Empress Place. That year, it awarded its first British Council Scholarship to PAUL ABISHEGANADEN, who went to London to study music. The British Council office moved several times before settling down in Napier Road. Over the years, the British Council has gained a reputation for its English language courses, examinations and education counselling services. Other than its Napier Road premises, the British Council has branches at Marsiling, Tampines and Cecil Street.

British Malaya Broadcasting Corporation Private commercial radio broadcasting company. RADIO BROADCASTING in Malaya started as an experimental project in the 1920s. It was only in 1936 that Singapore launched its first radio station, with a regular service broadcast from Caldecott Hill by a private commercial company, the British Malaya Broadcasting Corporation, which had been set up in 1935.

The company was short-lived, with the British colonial authorities taking it over in 1940 and, in April 1941, transferring control to a quasi-government organization, the Malayan Broadcasting Corporation.

British Military Administration Interim military government during the period from the Japanese surrender to restoration of civilian rule on 1 April 1946. During World War II, Singapore fell to the Japanese on 15 February 1942. British plans for retaking Singapore and Malaya via a hard-fought amphibious military campaign had to be changed after Japan suddenly capitulated on 15 August 1945. The abrupt ending of the war brought special difficulties for

British Military Administration: with a police shortage, the military took on policing duties, including attempts to stamp out the black market.

Singapore, because the timetable for dealing with the post-war aftermath had to be accelerated considerably. Two days after Allied forces under the orders of Southeast Asia Command (SEAC) landed in Penang on 3 September 1945, the main reoccupation forces arrived in Singapore. Immediately, a military administration was proclaimed and Admiral Lord LOUIS MOUNTBATTEN, the Supreme Allied Commander, assumed full judicial, legislative, executive and administrative powers and responsibilities.

From 5 September 1945 to 31 March 1946, Singapore and Malaya were administered under the British Military Administration (BMA) headed by Major-General Sir Ralph Hone, chief civil affairs officer for Malaya. Brigadier P.A.B. McKerron as deputy chief civil affairs officer was responsible for Singapore and Brigadier H.C. Willan was his counterpart for the peninsula. This period of military administration, in which Singapore and the peninsula were to a degree administered separately, was followed by the MALAYAN UNION on the mainland. Singapore, on the other hand, reverted to Crown Colony status with Sir FRANKLIN GIMSON as governor.

The BMA faced pressing administrative and political priorities. One of its tasks was the disarming and removal of Japanese troops, liberating Allied prisoners-of-war and civilian internees, and the restoration of law and order. Some 12,000 surrendered Japanese military were eventually deployed as labourers on reconstruction work as they awaited repatriation to Japan. Those who had committed atrocities were interned to await trial. With the police force understaffed and in almost complete disarray, the BMA found itself increasingly forced to assume policing duties to maintain order, even as it began the process of recruiting and rebuilding the police force, a task it had accomplished by the end of the BMA period.

Britannia Club: recreation for the military, 1950s.

Though Singapore had been spared widespread destruction of operations because of the Japanese surrender, the dilapidation and neglect of its physical infrastructure was widespread and the task of rehabilitating public services proved particularly daunting. Nevertheless, the supply of water was restored by mid-October 1945, and production exceeded pre-war levels by about 13.6 million litres a day by the end of March 1946. Electricity supply also exceeded pre-war consumption. Fourteen Malay and 14 English schools were opened within three weeks, and by the end of 1945, 66 Chinese, 37 English, and 21 Malay schools were in operation. However, with much of the available accommodation requisitioned for military use, a housing shortage was inevitable and serious overcrowding forced thousands to become squatters. The shortage of supplies, particularly rice, had also caused great anxiety among the people. Available rice stocks had dwindled significantly as a consequence of the Allied wartime blockade and traditional rice-producing countries had no surplus to export. Food shortages resulted in soaring prices of essential commodities to seven or eight times the pre-war level, and made the task of distributing available supplies even more difficult. Price controls were impossible to enforce. The shortages led many officials to use the opportunity to profiteer, accounting for the counter-characterization of the BMA as 'Black Market Administration'.

On the political front, the BMA was faced with the difficult task of managing the nascent nationalism awakened by the war, and which was being organized by vocal and assertive left-wing groups opposed to the continuation of colonial rule. Tolerance was extended by Mountbatten to the previously outlawed MALAYAN COMMUNIST PARTY (MCP) and its military wing, the MALAYAN PEOPLE'S ANTI-JAPANESE ARMY (MPAJA). The party was allowed to operate openly, and their leaders awarded medals for their contributions to the Allied war effort. An uneasy truce, however, persisted, as the BMA was soon confronted by resurgent MCP-inspired labour activism and strikes, including one in January 1946 in which the Singapore General Labour Union, an MCP-front organization, mobilized some 173,000 people in a protest strike against the arrest of Soong Kwong, leader of the Selangor MPAJA, for threatening and extorting an alleged collaborator with the Japanese.

Mountbatten's liberal policy also led to the appearance of new political groups such as the the left-wing MALAYAN DEMOCRATIC UNION, a political party formed on 21 December 1945.

Across the Causeway, heightened communal tensions wrought by wartime antagonism resulted in outbreaks of racial violence between Malays and Chinese,

which required careful handling. Backed by their overwhelming military presence, British officials also conducted negotiations with the Malay rulers for the purpose of securing their acquiescence to far-reaching constitutional changes under the Malayan Union scheme that would require them to cede their sovereignty to the British Crown.

The BMA found itself conducting under great pressure an administration that was virtually civil in all but name. Its inability to deal with the high post-war expectations of the local population weakened its stature in the eyes of the people, who blamed it for the delay in a return to normality and for high prices. An expectation grew that, with the resumption of civil government, all that was undesirable about the BMA would be changed instantaneously.

British withdrawal from Singapore

In January 1968, the British government announced that it would pull out its troops in Singapore (and Malaysia) by spring 1971. This sudden and unexpected news shocked the Singapore government as it had been given to understand that the British would defend Singapore after its independence. Apart from security issues, the move would also affect the economy—at least 20 per cent of Singapore's economy then came from the presence of British military personnel. About 10 per cent of the working population depended on the troops for its livelihood. There were about 25,000 civilian workers in the bases. Thousands of women worked as domestic helpers and many shops depended on the patronage of British soldiers. British services spending in Singapore was as much as $550 million a year at the height of the CONFRONTATION in Malaysia. In short, Singapore was facing a major economic crisis in addition to physical insecurity.

During defence talks with British leaders in London, Prime Minister LEE KUAN YEW told reporters that he would forgo economic aid in return for security for Singapore and would have to hire mercenaries to defend Singapore if Britain pulled out its forces too quickly. The British agreed that the withdrawal of troops would be phased and completed only by the mid-1970s to facilitate major cuts in Britain's armed forces and overseas defence spending. However, the British later changed their mind and informed Singapore that the withdrawal was to be completed by November 1971.

To fill the vacuum that followed the ending of the Anglo-Malayan Defence Agreement (AMDA), the British proposed the FIVE-POWER DEFENCE ARRANGEMENTS (FPDA) made up of the United Kingdom, Australia, New Zealand, Malaysia and Singapore, that would be consultative, not a binding defence obligation. On 31 October 1971, AMDA was replaced by FPDA.

Bronco Singapore-built all-terrain, multi-purpose articulated tracked carrier (ATTC). The Bronco was Singapore's first ATTC, designed to augment the SINGAPORE ARMED FORCE'S mechanized force. Developed by ST Kinetics, the Bronco delivers a five-tonne payload to ensure that almost any combination of cargo—from troops and transport of military hardware to food and medical aid—is delivered safely through the toughest terrain. The Bronco's Active Articulation System is a unique design that allows any articulated platform to couple and decouple rapidly into two separate and smaller driven vehicles. It brings 'plug and play' convenience to articulated platforms through its quick insertion and swapping capabilities. The Bronco has been in service in the Singapore Armed Forces since 2001.

Brooke-Popham, Air Chief Marshal Sir Robert

(1878–1953) British military commander. Henry Robert Moore Brooke-Popham's military training at the Royal Military Academy, Sandhurst, was followed by combat in South Africa (1899–1900). Attachment to the Air Battalion followed in 1911, and he received Flying Certificate No 108 the same year. After service in World War I and in post-war Iraq, he held positions including air officer commanding fighting area (UK) and Middle East, before retiring to a governorship in Kenya (1937–39).

Brooke-Popham was called back into military service with the Royal Air Force (RAF) during World War II, and became commander-in-chief, British Far East Command, responsible for army and RAF (but not navy) coordination. He arrived in Singapore on 14 November 1940. His appointment ended disagreements between the army, who felt there were insufficient troops for a forward defence, and the RAF, who wanted air bases in northern Malaya protected. His coordinating role paved the way for the development of OPERATION MATADOR in 1941. On 5 December, Brooke-Popham was given discretion to launch Operation Matador, should a Japanese attack appear imminent. Japanese ships were spotted on 6 December, but by the time he was satisfied they were going to attack, it was too late to launch the operation. Brooke-Popham had already been told he would be replaced, and Lieutenant-General Sir Henry Pownall duly took over on 23 December 1941.

Air Chief Marshal Sir Robert Brooke-Popham

Bronco: all-terrain tracked carrier.

Brossard & Mopin: prayer hall of the Hajjah Fatimah Mosque, constructed by the firm.

Buddhism: Kong Meng San Phor Kark See.

Buddhism: statue of the Laughing Buddha, in Waterloo Street.

Buddha Tooth Relic Temple: artist's impression.

Brossard & Mopin French civil engineering firm. The French civil engineering firm of Brossard & Mopin established its presence in Singapore at the turn of the 20th century. It had its office in Battery Road and made a name as a specialist in tiles and reinforced concrete. Reinforced concrete was originally only used for casting bresummer beams, but was later used for roofs and floors as well. The first concrete structure ever built in Malaya was a concrete ferry built by Brossard & Mopin in 1912, and used to transport goods across the Johor Strait until the CAUSEWAY was built. Brossard & Mopin constructed the main prayer hall of HAJJAH FATIMAH MOSQUE and the TELOK AYER CHINESE METHODIST CHURCH.

Buddha Tooth Relic Temple According to Buddhist scriptures, Sakyamuni Buddha left behind four wisdom tooth relics and 40 tooth relics for future generations. One of these, temporarily housed at the GOLDEN PAGODA BUDDHIST TEMPLE in Tampines, will find a new home in the Buddha Tooth Relic Temple Singapore (BTRTS) in Sago Street when it is completed in 2007.

Relics are commonly used as instruments for spreading BUDDHISM as they help to establish new centres of religious significance. The construction cost of the BTRTS is estimated to be $53-million. It is to include a two-metre, all-gold stupa for the tooth relic. Within three months of the request for donations, more than 83 kg of gold, as well as $10 million, were collected. The effort was spearheaded by Venerable Fa Zhao, abbot of the Golden Pagoda Buddhist Temple.

The new BTRTS will be a six-storey structure comprising worship halls, museums, an exhibition centre and a basement performance theatre. The Sacred Buddha Tooth Chamber, which will have a gold canopy above the stupa, as well as gold-tiled floors, is located on the fourth level. The inner chamber is a restricted zone, and the public can venerate and observe the thrice-daily religious services only from the public viewing area, when the curtain shielding the 250-kg gold stupa is raised.

Buddhism During the period of the SRIVIJAYA EMPIRE, from the 7th to the 13th centuries, Buddhism flourished in the region. However, as ISLAM spread through Srivijaya in the 14th and 15th centuries, the influence of Buddhism was gradually displaced.

Elements of Buddhism were practised by early Chinese immigrants to Singapore. They built numerous temples and shrines in honour of deities such as Mazu (goddess of the sea) and Tua Peh Kong (see TAOISM). They included Buddhist worship as part of their religious expression.

The first Buddhist monastery, SIONG LIM TEMPLE (Twin Grove Temple), was built in 1903 at the initiation of a Buddhist master from Fujian, China. That year, an Irish monk started the first Buddhist organization, the Singapore Buddhist Missionary Society. The subsequent development of Chinese Buddhism in pre-Independence Singapore was entirely contingent upon the occasional visits by eminent monks from China, who were instrumental in building many Buddhist temples, including the historic KONG MENG SAN PHOR KARK SEE MONASTERY (Bright Hill Universal Enlightenment Temple) in 1920, as well as setting up numerous outreach organizations.

In 1925, Venerable Taixu helped establish the Chinese Buddhist Association, the first of its kind in Singapore. The eminent monk's missionary activities on the island in 1926 generated widespread interest in Buddhism among the Chinese population. It was no coincidence that the first Buddhist journal, *Juehua Weekly* (Flowers of Enlightenment), was published on the island in 1927. Numerous Buddhist publications sprang up in its wake as mainland Chinese monks continued to visit and give public homilies in Singapore. In 1940, before the Japanese invasion of Singapore, Master Cihang from China, while lecturing in sojourn, started a journal called *Zhongguo foxue*, which may be translated as 'China's Buddhist Studies' or 'Chinese Buddhist Studies'. The ambiguous title of the journal reflects the 'grafted on' nature of Chinese Buddhism in pre-war Singapore.

Chinese Buddhism in Singapore was an outgrowth of the religion in mainland China, in much the same way as literary works in Chinese by local writers of the same period primarily reflected the concerns and spirit of 20th-century Chinese literature. It was distinctly Mahayana and primarily Zen and Pure Land by sectarian affiliation.

Singapore's fall to the Japanese in February 1942 precipitated new developments in Chinese Buddhism. The Buddhist community instituted relief agencies and aid organizations to offer humanitarian assistance and disaster services to victims of the war. Refugee centres were set up in Buddhist temples. Buddhist-sponsored charitable organizations continued to proliferate after the Japanese Occupation. These include the Singapore Buddhist Free Clinic, the Singapore Buddhist Welfare Services, and REN CI HOSPITAL AND MEDICARE CENTRE.

Apart from humanitarian services, education—both Buddhist and non-Buddhist—became an overriding concern in the Buddhist social project in post-war Singapore. The first Buddhist primary school, Maha Bodhi School, was established in 1948. Other schools followed. In 1946, the Institute of Buddhist Studies was founded. However, it lasted only two years. In the 1960s, a Buddhist institute for girls, with Buddhism as the core of its curriculum, was established. The institute, however, was closed due to a change in the government's education policy. Still, Buddhist monks continued to give public sermons and conduct training classes unabated, often under the sponsorship of the SINGAPORE BUDDHIST LODGE and the Amitabha Buddhist Society of Singapore. More recently, the Buddhist College of Singapore offers specialized training for young Buddhist monks.

According to the Singapore census (2000) 42.5 per cent of the population professed to be Buddhist, compared to 31.2 and 27 per cent in the 1990 and 1980 censuses respectively. The majority of the Buddhists in Singapore belong to the Mahayana tradition and are ethnic Chinese, with the exception of a minority of Japanese expatriates, as well as an even smaller number of Caucasian and Eurasian converts.

The recent surge of interest in Buddhism may be attributed, in part, to the efforts of many modern-minded monks, nuns and lay practitioners who have differentiated Buddhism from ancestor worship and other Chinese folk religions (see CHINESE RELIGION), and many young people who are working to promote Buddhism. The Young Men's Buddhist Association, for instance, caters for the educational, social, recreational and spiritual needs of young Buddhists. It organizes weekly discussions for anyone interested in Buddhism and goes beyond the ritualistic worship activities that traditionally take place in a Buddhist temple. University Buddhist societies also provide channels for the promotion of Buddhism. In the Internet age, where information is easily accessible, knowledge of Buddhism is no longer dependent on the sporadic visits of foreign monks, nor is it confined to the missionary efforts of monks from China.

See also VESAK DAY.

Bugis The Bugis come from southwest Sulawesi (formerly known as Celebes). They were known for being skilled fighters and astute seafaring traders. They sailed as far as Australia, trading with Aboriginal tribes there. When Macassar—a thriving port in Celebes—came under Dutch influence in 1667, large groups of Bugis sailed away to found settlements in Borneo and the Malay Peninsula. The Bugis involved themselves in the political rivalries of the sultans in the peninsula, gaining influence in the Johor court. When Sultan Sulaiman of Johor was installed in 1721, he appointed Daing Merewah, a Bugis warrior, as Yam Tuan Muda (regent). The Bugis role in the Johor-Riau sultanate was documented in the *Tuhfat al-Nafis* (Precious Gift) written in 1866 by Raja Haji Ali, a relative of the first Yam Tuan Muda. In the early 1800s, Bugis traders dominated commerce in Riau. However, the imposition of Dutch control in Riau led to armed clashes, as a result of which 500 Bugis, led by Arong Bilawa, fled to Singapore in 1820. They established a settlement along the Kallang River.

Singapore was an important centre for Bugis trade. The Bugis trading fleet, which in the 1830s comprised about 200 ships (*prahu*), usually reached Singapore in September and left in November with the onset of the northwest monsoon. Their ships were anchored off KAMPONG GLAM and carried products such as coffee, tortoise shells and gold dust.

The Bugis population was at its peak with over 2,000 residents in the 1830s, but by 1931, the population had dropped to 792, and in 1980, it was 491. By the 2000 census, there was no longer a separate category for the Bugis as a Malay sub-group. Bugis Street commemorates the area where Bugis traders used to gather, while the road Kampong Bugis, off Kallang Road, marks the settlement that was once there.

See also TUHFAT AL-NAFIS.

Bugis Street Narrow street once famous for its food and transvestites. The original Bugis Street—named after the BUGIS or Buginese settlement in the area—connected North Bridge Road to Victoria Street. After World War II it became a prime tourist attraction when transvestites started appearing in large numbers. Flamboyantly and provocatively dressed, they sashayed up and down the street, weaving between the many food stalls patronized by Caucasian servicemen

and tourists. One of the most notorious spots on the street was the public toilet where transvestites and servicemen would dance on the flat roof. Some Americans referred to Bugis Street as Boogie Street; Singapore postcards depicted the sights and pleasures to be had there. In the mid-1970s, the government began a crackdown on the area, and within a decade the old Bugis Street was no more, obliterated by the Bugis Square development.

Bujang Lapok (1957) Film. *Bujang Lapok* (Confirmed Bachelor) was a popular comedy produced by the Shaw Brothers' MALAY FILM PRODUCTIONS studio. It was the first comedy feature directed by P. RAMLEE. His cast of Aziz Sattar and S. Shamsuddin along with himself as three poor but happy-go-lucky bachelors created a winning formula. The black-and-white movie blended the comic and romantic adventures of the characters Ramli, Aziz and Sudin, with incidents that reflected some of the social challenges faced by the working class in Singapore during the 1950s.

The film was a hit with audiences. It spawned three successful sequels: *Pendekar Bujang Lapok* (1959) (Confirmed Bachelor Warriors), *Ali Baba Bujang Lapok* (1961) (Ali Baba the Confirmed Bachelor) and *Seniman Bujang Lapok* (1961) (Confirmed Bachelor Actor). *Pendekar Bujang Lapok* was awarded Best Comedy trophy at the Asian Film Festival 1959 in Kuala Lumpur.

Bukit Batok Hill and town development. There are several versions of how the name for this hill (*bukit*) came about. One version was that it was the Javanese word for coconuts—'batok'—which grew in the area, while another is attributed to the corruption of the Malay word '*batu*', meaning 'stone' because the hill was of solid granite. The hill is one of the highest in Singapore and is today surrounded by Bukit Batok town, a housing estate developed by the HOUSING & DEVELOPMENT BOARD (HDB) in the early 1980s. The estate covers an area of 800 ha, but only about 36 per cent of it is built up. The rest of the estate is made up of a large nature reserve. A unique features is a picturesque former granite quarry with cliffs of great scenic beauty. It is called 'Little Guilin', a reference to a tourist attraction in the town of Guilin in southern China.

Two war memorials once stood at the top of Bukit Batok, one for the Allied forces and one for the Japanese (*see* SYONAN CHUREITO). The memorials were built by Allied prisoners-of-war under Japanese command. In 1945, towards the end of the occupation, the Japanese demolished both memorials. All that is left of the memorials are two pillars and a long flight of stairs leading to the top of the hill.

Bukit Batok town is bounded by the Pan-Island Expressway, Toh Tuck Road,

Upper Bukit Timah Road and Bukit Batok Road. In 2005, there were some 33,000 apartments in Bukit Batok, housing some 120,000 residents.

Bukit Brown Cemetery One of the oldest Chinese cemeteries in Singapore. It is located between Lornie Road and Mount Pleasant Road. Also known as Kopi Sua (Coffee Hill), it was named after its first owner, George Henry Brown, a shipowner with trading interests in China and Japan, who arrived in Singapore in the 1840s. In the early 20th century, municipal authorities came under pressure to provide a municipal cemetery for the Chinese communities in view of a shortage of burial space. A 86-ha site at Bukit Brown was acquired for this purpose, but it was not until the end of 1919 that the site passed into municipal hands. It was finally opened on 1 January 1922 and was managed as a public burial ground by a committee including community leaders See Tiong Wah and TAN KHEAM HOCK.

Initially unpopular with the Chinese because of its small plot size, Bukit Brown came to be more widely accepted after various improvements were made to its layout. By 1929, it accounted for about 40 per cent of all officially registered Chinese burials within municipal limits. The closed cemetery is now popular with nature-lovers as it is home to many bird species and other wildlife.

In the 1970s, the cemetery faced the possibility of being cleared for redevelopment, but has since enjoyed reprieve.

Bukit Chandu Hill at the southern end of Pasir Panjang Ridge, the World War II strategic defensive position where soldiers from the MALAY REGIMENT made an epic last stand against the Japanese in their invasion of Singapore. Bukit Chandu means 'Opium Hill' in Malay. It got its name from an OPIUM factory once located in Pepys Road, at the foot of the hill. The Telok Blangah Factory, as this facility was called, was in its heyday a major processing and packing centre supplying opium to most of British Malaya. It is unclear when it was first constructed, but it was operated privately until 1910, when control was taken over by the colonial government. In 1909, private enterprise in the preparation and

Bugis Street: the nightly gathering of transvestites helped make this a tourist destination into the 1970s.

Bujang Lapok *(1957)*

Bukit Batok: Little Guilin lake, a former granite quarry.

Bukit Brown Cemetery

Bukit Ho Swee fire

Bukit Larangan: map of 14th-century Fort Canning.

wholesale of opium was prohibited in British Malaya: the opium industry was converted into a government monopoly for the ostensible purpose of controlling opium consumption—in fact, as late as 1938, the factory produced almost 80 tons of consumable opium. It continued to operate during the Japanese Occupation—the Japanese, according to oral sources, encouraged the use of opium during the occupation period for reasons of profit. The Telok Blangah factory went on processing opium until an outright ban on the drug was imposed in the late 1940s.

Bukit Ho Swee fire Bounded by the Delta Canal to the north, Tiong Bahru Road to the south, Kim Seng/Outram Road to the east and Lower Delta Road to the west, Bukit Ho Swee was a densely populated area. There were once thousands of squatter homes here, built with combustible materials such as attap and wooden boards. Between 1934 and 1968, Bukit Ho Swee experienced three big fires. The second, which occurred on 25 May 1961, was the biggest fire in Singapore.

The fire broke out on a hillside squatter district in Kampong Tiong Bahru at around 3.30 p.m. during the Hari Raya Haji holiday. Although the cause remains a mystery, once ignited the fire spread quickly. Consuming combustible squatter huts, the fire was driven on by powerful winds; oil and petrol from several nearby godowns literally added fuel to the flames. The inferno zig-zagged its way, leaping across Tiong Bahru Road towards Beo Lane, before the winds swept the flames towards Havelock Road and thereafter towards the Delta area. Despite the presence of 22 fire engines, the conflagration was still at its height at 8.00 p.m. It was only after the last few huts were razed to the ground near Delta Circus that the fire was conquered.

The flames had devastated an area of around 250 acres. A school, a coffee mill, two oil mills, two junk shops, two tyre shops, three timber yards, three motor-workshops and four lives were lost. Around 2,800 houses were destroyed and nearly 16,000 people were left homeless.

The aftermath of the fire saw a conscious effort to help the victims. The victims' plight was publicized in *The Straits Times*; gifts poured in and a total of $584,202.17 was donated by the public. The government set up the Bukit Ho Swee Fire National Relief Fund Committee to raise funds for the victims. The Ministry of Education provided a free supply of exercise books and the free loan of textbooks until the end of school year. Some families were relocated to newly established HOUSING & DEVELOPMENT BOARD (HDB) flats in Queenstown and Tiong Bahru.

The Bukit Ho Swee fire of 1961 was the worst but not the last. It was however a spur to major efforts to redevelop squatter settlements and provide better housing and conditions for the population.

Bukit Larangan Meaning 'forbidden hill' in Malay, this was the name applied by Malays to the hill now known as FORT CANNING. According to the *Hikayat* (autobiography) of Munshi ABDULLAH ABDUL KADIR, the Temenggong told Colonel WILLIAM FARQUHAR that the name came about because the hill was once the site of a royal palace, and that nobody had been allowed to ascend the hill without permission. This prohibition was still respected 400 years after the last Malay king left Singapore. According to the SEJARAH MELAYU (Malay Annals), the first Malay ruler, SANG NILA UTAMA, and his chief minister, Demang Lebar Daun, were buried 'on a hill of Singapura', which is most likely Bukit Larangan.

Reluctance to climb the hill was only overcome after Farquhar imported labourers from Malacca to clear a path to the summit, up which a cannon was then hauled. Twelve rounds fired from the gun served to convince the population that the ghosts which were believed to inhabit the hill had been 'exorcised'.

The hill became known as GOVERNMENT HILL, after Sir STAMFORD RAFFLES built a house upon it. The first European cemetery in Singapore was also located on the hill, thus continuing the tradition of using the hill for burials.

Bukit Merah: modern high-rise apartments, 2006.

Bukit Merah New town. 'Bukit Merah' in Malay means 'red hill'. The name probably orginated due to the reddish-brown lateritic soils in the area but there is also a legend around its naming (*see* box). In the early 20th century, there were many villages here. The area that is now the site of the Bukit Merah bus interchange was once known as Beehoon Plain because villagers used to dry their rice vermicelli (*beehoon*) on the plain. The '*bukit*' or hill is now gone, bulldozed for development. In the late 1960s and early 1970s, the villages were cleared for housing development. Bukit Merah town covers some 860 ha with 36 per cent used for residential purposes. In 2005, the estate had some 50,000 apartments housing about 132,000 residents.

Bukit Panjang Hill and new town. Bukit Panjang literally means 'long hill' in Malay. The name derives from the low range of hills in the vicinity, ending in the south at Bukit Timah. Until the 1970s, Bukit Panjang was a small sleepy village. It has since been dramatically transformed into a major housing estate by the HOUSING & DEVELOPMENT BOARD (HDB). The estate occupies some 490 ha and is bounded by Bukit Timah Expressway, Kranji Expressway, Woodlands Road, Upper Bukit Timah Road, Cashew Road and Petir Road. Bukit Panjang estate is served by Singapore's first light rail train, which does a loop through seven stations from the Bukit Panjang MRT Station. Bukit Panjang is a relatively small housing estate, with

Legend of Bukit Merah Legend recorded in the SEJARAH MELAYU (Malay Annals). In one of the stories, the seas of present-day Singapore were plagued by garfish, which attacked the villagers by the sea with their long, spear-like snouts. The king, Rajah Paduka Sri Maharaja, ordered his soldiers to form a barrier with their legs to stop the fish. However, the garfish were too strong for them. A boy, who saw the incident, suggested making a barrier with banana tree trunks so that the garfish would impale themselves on the trunks when they attacked. The king agreed and the plan worked.

Fearing that this remarkably bright boy would one day be a threat to his throne, the king sent his soldiers to spy on the boy. Discovering that he lived on top of a hill near BUKIT LARANGAN (now Fort Canning Hill), he sent four men to kill the boy during the night. However, they were stopped by an old woman standing at the door of the boy's home. She discovered their plan and chanted some magic words. Blood then came flowing out from the house and flooded the hill and the surroundings. The soldiers fled and were not heard of, or seen again. Since then, the story goes, the colour of the soil on the hill has been blood red.

The hill became known as 'Bukit Merah' or 'Red Hill'.

Bukit Timah Nature Reserve

A 160-ha reserve consisting of primary and secondary forest. The Bukit Timah Nature Reserve is home to the largest contiguous remnant of forest that covered most of Singapore prior to its explosive development in the 19th century. The Bukit Timah forest is an example a 'coastal hill dipterocarp forest', characterized by a number of tree species most commonly found on mountain ridges or on coastal hills in the region.

Botanists have recorded over 840 species of flowering plants from Bukit Timah, over one-third of Singapore's documented plant diversity. In addition, over 100 fern species have been described from Bukit Timah, out of a total of 170 ferns known from Singapore. While a number of the original plant species have disappeared from Bukit Timah, there are the occasional surprises. A tree survey in 1993 turned up two enormous *Shorea ochrophloia* (*1*) trees, which were not only among the largest and most conspicuous trees of that part of the forest, but part of a species not

2

previously known to occur in Singapore.

There is an abundance of animal life in the reserve. However, the reserve is far too small to support large vertebrates. Today, the largest regularly sighted mammals at Bukit Timah—apart from humans—are the long-tailed macaques (*Macaca fascicularis*), a far cry from when tigers once roamed Bukit Timah and the adjacent forests.

Bukit Timah is also a refuge for smaller animals. Several species of frogs are known to occur in Singapore only at Bukit Timah, such as the St Andrew's cross toadlet (*Pelophryne brevipes*) (*2*), the black-spotted sticky frog (*Kalophyrnus pleurostigma*), and the spotted tree frog (*Nyctixalus pictus*). The yellow-banded caecilian (*Icthyophis paucisuicus*), a legless, snake-like amphibian, was twice recorded in Bukit Timah in the late

1

1980s and may still exist. A number of uncommon reptiles may also be spotted by the careful and fortunate reserve visitor, such as the spiny hill terrapin (*Heosemys spinosa*) (*3*), the earless agamid (*Aphaniotis fusca*) or the olive tree skink (*Dasia olivacea*). Of the three species of crab found only in Singapore, two can be found in Bukit Timah—Johnson's freshwater crab (*Irmengardia johnsoni*) and the aptly-named Singapore freshwater crab (*Johora singaporensis*) (*4*). Both are unfortunately endangered.

A history of Bukit Timah

Bukit Timah has been under some form of safeguarding since the mid-1800s, when its forest was retained for 'climatic purposes'. Formal protection for Bukit Timah, however, was not to occur till 1884, when Nathaniel Cantley, superintendent of the Singapore Botanic Gardens, recommended the establishment of a series of Forest Reserves scattered across the island. The Bukit Timah Forest Reserve had an original area of over 340 ha. The forested portion of the reserve was only about one-third of the total area, the remainder largely comprising grassland or resam fern (*Dicranopteris linearis*) (see FERNS.).

Over the years, the acreage under reserve status shrank until only 75 ha of Bukit Timah's core area of mature forest enjoyed protection by the 1950s. The year 1951 saw the redesignation of Bukit Timah as a Nature Reserve with the passing of the Nature Reserves Act, which was superseded by the National Parks Act of 1990. Since 1990, Bukit

3

Timah has been under the jurisdiction of the National Parks Board, which has steadily expanded the borders of the Reserve beginning with the addition of five hectares in 1990. Today, the Bukit Timah Nature Reserve covers more than twice its pre-1990 size, occupying over 160 ha.

Despite the increase in size, the reserve is bounded on all sides by some form of urban development. A forested link between Bukit Timah and the adjacent CENTRAL CATCHMENT NATURE RESERVE facilitating the movement of animals into and out of Bukit Timah, was severed in the mid-1980s by the construction of the Bukit Timah Expressway in the mid-1980s. Ecological theory predicts a gradual decay in species number unless active management of the forest is carried out to maintain current levels of species diversity.

4

30,000 units housing some 111,000 residents in 2005. During the 1980s, it was known as Zhenghua Town but the area has since reverted to its more historical name.

Bukit Timah Nature Reserve *See* box.

Burgess, Anthony (1917–1993) Novelist and critic. John Anthony Burgess Wilson (his real name) was born in Manchester, United Kingdom. The son of a bookkeeper and part-time pianist, he studied at Manchester University, became a soldier during World War II, then worked in education. As an education officer in Malaya in 1954, he wrote his first novels, *The Malayan Trilogy*. These three comic novels, *Time for a Tiger, The Enemy in the Blanket and Beds in the East,* chronicle the end of British rule in what is now Peninsular Malaysia. The main character, Victor Crabbe, arrives there as a teacher just before Independence. Amidst a group of British misfit expatriates, Crabbe gets caught up in a comedy of errors.

Diagnosed with a terminal illness in 1959, Burgess wrote prolifically to provide security for his wife. The diagnosis turned out to be wrong, and Burgess continued writing, publishing more than 50 books

under the names Anthony Burgess and Joseph Kell. His most controversial novel was *A Clockwork Orange* (1962), a story of teenage violence set in the future. He died in London in 1993.

Burmese Buddhist Temple With its characteristic architecture and stupa, this is the only Buddhist temple outside of Myanmar (Burma) constructed in the traditional Burmese style. Located at Tai Gin Road, it was built in 1990 by Venerable U Pannya Vamsa, replacing the smaller facility at Kinta Road. Enshrined within is the largest marble statue of the Buddha outside of Myanmar, standing at 3.4 m. Besides the major Buddhist festivals, the temple also observes traditional Burmese celebrations such as Thingyan (New Year).

buses The SINGAPORE TRACTION COMPANY (STC) first introduced bus services in 1925: trolley buses replaced the electric TRAMS that had operated in the city since 1905. Individual operators offered services in rural areas with seven-seater 'mosquito buses'. These formed the nucleus for the formation of 11 Chinese bus companies. By the mid-1950s, services provided by the

STC and the Chinese bus companies were plagued by operational difficulties, poor management and labour unrest. In 1971, following the publication of a White Paper on the reorganization of bus services, the Chinese bus companies were amalgamated, forming three large companies; the STC was the fourth company.

However, services failed to improve, and the government intervened. This resulted in the formation of a single company, Singapore Bus Services (SBS), in 1973. Trans Island Bus Service (TIBS) was formed in 1983 to provide competition. In 2001, when the need for the integrated operation of bus and train services became evident, SBS was renamed SBSTransit Ltd and SMRT Train Ltd acquired TIBS, which became SMRT Buses Ltd.

Today, there is a variety of bus services available in Singapore. Trunk bus services are provided on long and medium routes which run between bus interchanges and terminals. Feeder bus services are provided for short routes between bus interchanges and train stations. Premier bus services are semi-express, and special night services were introduced in 2000 in certain areas.

SBS Transit Ltd and SMRT Buses Ltd

Burmese Buddhist Temple

Buses: (clockwise from top left) trolley bus, 1930; mosquito bus, 1935; STC bus; SMRT articulated bus, introduced in 1996; SBS Transit double-decker (double-deckers were first introduced in 1985).

The Business Times

K.M. Byrne

operate 265 trunk and feeder services. The bus fleet consists of air-conditioned minibuses, single-deckers, double-deckers (introduced in 1985) and articulated buses (introduced in 1996).

Since 1985, almost all bus services have been operated by a single driver. Fares are paid either by tapping an EZ-LINK CARD on a card reader or by dropping change into a coin box.

Inter-city coach services operate from terminals in Singapore to various parts of Peninsular Malaysia.

Business Times, The English-language daily broadsheet. Launched by SINGAPORE PRESS HOLDINGS (SPH) in October 1976, *The Business Times* (BT) provides coverage of corporate, financial, economic and political news. Coverage centres on Singapore and Asia, although global developments are also monitored by the newspaper.

The paper's first editor was Tan Sai Siong, who was also the first local woman editor of a local English-language daily.

Butterworth, Colonel William (1801–1856) Colonel William John Butterworth of the Madras army succeeded Sir SAMUEL GEORGE BONHAM as governor of the Straits Settlements in 1843 and was to remain in office for 12 years. Regarded as stiff and pompous, he initially was an unpopular governor (irreverently referred to by some as 'the Great Butterpot'). He was able to win the good opinion of the population by the end of his term through his tireless efforts in promoting the trade interests of Singapore. This was much appreciated by the mercantile community. Trade rose from $24 million to $36 million during his tenure. He conscientiously supported education through the establishment of scholarships at the Singapore Institution in 1853, as well as the formation of the Singapore Library at the Institution in 1844. He supported the formation of the Singapore Volunteer Rifle Corps in 1854. Described as 'a perfect gentleman', Butterworth tried to introduce black as the colour of choice for social evening wear instead of the white of his day—probably trying to follow the

fashion for sombre colours in Victorian England. He also hoped to establish a museum in Singapore, but this had not been achieved by the end of his period of office.

Buttrose, Murray (1903–1987) Judge. Murray Buttrose was the last expatriate judge in the Supreme Court. He was educated at St Peter's College and Adelaide University, Australia. He was admitted and enrolled as barrister and solicitor of the Supreme Court of South Australia in August 1927. From 1940 to 1945, he served in the RAF Volunteer Rifles. In 1946, Buttrose joined Her Majesty's Colonial Legal Service; his first posting was as Crown counsel in Singapore. Three years later, he was promoted to senior Crown counsel. In 1955, he became Singapore's solicitor-general. That same year, he was admitted and enrolled as solicitor of the Supreme Court of Judicature in England. He was appointed PUISNE JUDGE in Singapore in 1956 and served till his retirement on 23 July 1968, when he went to live in Britain. He spent his last years in his native Adelaide, where he died in September 1987. Buttrose was known as a very tough prosecutor and a tough judge. He presided over two of the biggest trials in the 1960s: the SUNNY ANG trial and the Pulau Senang trial (*see* PULAU SENANG RIOTS).

Byrne, K.M. (1913–1990) Civil servant, politician and diplomat. Born in Singapore, the second son in a family of 11 boys, Kenneth Michael (generally known as 'K.M.') Byrne was educated at St Xavier's School in Penang, St Joseph's Institution and Raffles Institution. He proceeded to Raffles College in 1933 and graduated with a first class diploma in arts. In 1936, he joined the STRAITS SETTLEMENTS CIVIL SERVICE. In 1940, Byrne won the Queen's Fellowship which enabled him to pursue a degree in the United Kingdom. However, war intervened, and it was not until 1947 that he was able to leave for Oxford, where he read law. During World War II, Byrne served as a magistrate. From 1947 to 1950, Byrne studied law at Christ Church,

Oxford. He was called to the Bar at Middle Temple in 1950 and returned to Singapore shortly thereafter. While in the UK, Byrne, who had a lifelong disdain for British rule, became a member of the MALAYAN FORUM, though he was not active in this body. It was here that he met his colleague in the Colonial Administrative Service, GOH KENG SWEE. It was Byrne's friendship with Goh, and later with LEE KUAN YEW and his wife (who travelled back to Singapore aboard the same ship as Byrne), which led to his participation in politics.

On returning to Singapore, Byrne was appointed clerk of the Legislative Council and later became assistant secretary of the Establishments Division. In 1953, he was transferred to the Marine Department. He later became permanent secretary at the Ministry of Commerce and Industry.

Byrne and Goh were among the founders of the PEOPLE'S ACTION PARTY but their status as civil servants prevented them from taking too active or visible a role in the party. Two years earlier, Byrne and Goh acted in concert to protest discriminatory practices within the ADMINISTRATIVE SERVICE which favoured European staff. In 1958, Byrne retired from the service to contest the 1959 general election. He won a seat in Crawford constituency and was appointed Singapore's first minister for law and labour. He gave up the labour portfolio about six months into the job to concentrate on the law portfolio, and is credited as having had the landmark WOMEN'S CHARTER passed.

In 1963, he lost his seat in Crawford to S.T. BANI of the BARISAN SOSIALIS and retired from politics. He was appointed chairman of the Central Provident Fund and, later, chairman of the Singapore Tourist Promotion Board. He served as Singapore's high commissioner to New Zealand (1966–73) and India (1973–78). Thereafter, he retired and established his own law firm. Byrne practised intermittently until his death on 14 May 1990 from a heart attack.

Colonel William Butterworth

C

cable car Singapore's first cable-car service, which connected Mount Faber to Sentosa, was officially opened by then Deputy Prime Minister Goh Keng Swee on 15 February 1974. It cost $5.8 million and consisted of 43 cabins. The next day, more than 1,000 people rode the cable cars. In 1999, the world's first glass-bottomed cabins were installed. The cable-car service has a spotless safety record, save for one disaster in January 1983 (*see* CABLE CAR DISASTER).

cable car disaster Accident on the Mount Faber–Sentosa cable-car service. The disaster occurred in January 1983 and claimed the lives of seven people—Pritam Kaur and her son-in-law Mahinder Singh; engineer Fred Kunimoto; businessman Fred M. Kresser; and Dr Aileen Wong, her husband Dr John Sendrick and his nurse Pam Mitchel. At about 6 p.m. on 30 January 1983, a Port of Singapore Authority (PSA) tug began towing a drill ship, the *Eniwetok*, away from Keppel Wharf. Shortly afterwards, the vessel's gantry tower snagged one of the two cables above, pulling it out of place. Two cable cars were dislodged and flung more than 50 m into the water.

A major rescue operation was carried out to evacuate the remaining passengers trapped in four cars on the cables. An operations centre was established at PSA Tower under the control of Philip Yeo, then second permanent secretary (Defence). Eventually, helicopters rescued 13 people from the dangling cars. The grandson of victim Pritam Kaur, 22-month-old Taswinder Singh, survived the fall and was rescued from the water.

Cai Bixia (1972–) CHINESE OPERA actress, director and writer. Cai Bixia joined the CHINESE OPERA INSTITUTE in 1997 and has played roles in many of their productions, touring schools and overseas. After gradu-

Cable car disaster: wrecked cable car being hoisted from the water.

ating from the Fujian Opera School in 1989, she went to the Shantou Opera School to study TEOCHEW opera, and graduated with distinction in 1993. In the same year, she won the Bronze Medal at the First National Rising Star for TV and Drama Competition. Her first major success was *Huo Shao Lin Jiang Lou* (Fire at the Riverside Pavilion) at the Seoul International Theatre Festival, Korea (1999) and the Liverpool International Theatre Festival, Canada (2000). A versatile actress, she won acclaim in many productions in Singapore and internationally, including *Princess Sita* (Singapore and Thailand, 1999, 2002, 2005), *Green Snake* (Spain, 2000), *Nie Xiao Qian* (Singapore, Korea, 2002; Indonesia, 2005), *Diao Chan, The Beauty* (Singapore, 2003), *Mouse Daughter* (Singapore, 2004), *Ne Zha* (Singapore, Japan 2004; Indonesia, 2005) and *Goddess San Sheng Mu* (United States, 2006). She has taught at many schools in Singapore and has groomed numerous young actors. She is the author of *Teochew Opera in Singapore* (2002).

campaigns Nationwide drives to persuade Singaporeans to improve themselves, or to remind them of certain social goals or values, were first launched in the 1960s. Designed to effect social change and elevate the young nation's economic status, campaigns were the precursors to legislation, which was introduced when persuasion and cajoling failed. Since the late 1990s, campaigns have been less frequent. Themes covered by campaigns have included the need to consume wheat instead of rice (when a shortage of rice appeared imminent), public cleanliness, population control and language use.

The month-long Keep Singapore Clean campaign, launched in October 1968, was one of the earliest and most intensive campaigns. Its primary aim was to eradicate filth, as well as habits such as littering, in a bid to improve the country's image abroad at a time when the government was aiming to attract foreign investment. A National Campaign Committee, headed by the minister for Health, was formed to steer the programme. Members of Parliament, police officers and public health inspectors joined forces to visit constituencies, and advise and warn the public against littering. Penalties were imposed after the campaign had ended, and fines were handed down to persons who dirtied public places. The maximum penalty was $500. Offenders also suffered the ignominy of having their names published in the media.

The mid-1970s were dominated by two campaign themes: family planning and decadence. With the Stop at Two Campaign, the aim of limiting population growth was achieved (at the price of a population shortfall 20 years later),

Cable car: from Mount Faber to Sentosa.

although a policy change in the new millennium has led to pro-family campaigns. The campaign against decadence took the form of opposition to the hippie subculture, one measure being the barring of long-haired men from entering Singapore (although such men were allowed into the country if they agreed to have their hair cut by the authorities).

Launched originally in 1979, the National Courtesy Campaign has, since March 2001, been officially subsumed under the Singapore Kindness Movement. Other long-running annual campaigns include tree planting (initiated in 1963) and the Speak Mandarin Campaign. The latter, inaugurated in 1979, was designed to promote the learning and use of MANDARIN instead of dialects amongst the Chinese community.

In 1996, the government launched a two-month campaign to make Singapore a more 'gracious society'. As part of this campaign, people were encouraged to remember to flush public lavatories after use. Fines of $150 were introduced for the offence of failing to flush toilets, with fines of $500 for a second offence and $1,000 for subsequent offences. The law has rarely been enforced, however, as many public toilets have been fitted with automatic flushing systems.

Offshoots of the original cleanliness movement have included campaigns against spitting and—in the wake of the SARS epidemic—encouraging people to wash their hands. Indeed, the three-month SEVERE ACUTE RESPIRATORY SYNDROME (SARS) outbreak in 2003 led to a new form of campaign to promote a public-private sector partnership. With visitor arrivals down and Singapore residents shunning shops, food and entertainment outlets, the government launched a scheme to certify hotels, shopping centres and other establishments as SARS-free zones. These were marked with the word 'Cool'. The Step Out Campaign then invited people to resume normal daily activities once SARS had

Cai Bixia: as Princess Sita, left, in a Hokkien opera adaptation of the Indian epic, the Ramayana.

Campaigns: 1960s Save Water poster (above); courtesy campaign coasters in Singapore's four official languages.

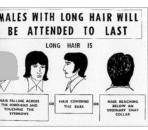

MALES WITH LONG HAIR WILL
BE ATTENDED TO LAST

LONG HAIR IS

| HAIR FALLING ACROSS THE FOREHEAD AND TOUCHING THE EYEBROWS | OR | HAIR COVERING THE EARS | OR | HAIR REACHING BELOW AN ORDINARY SHIRT COLLAR |

The more you have
The more they need

Two is enough

Family Planning/Sterilisation Information Service
telephone **538766** or go to your nearest Maternal and Child Health/Family Planning Clinic

Campaigns: anti-long hair poster as displayed in the 1960s and 1970s (top); family planning poster, 1978.

Cantonese: soya sauce manufacturing, c. 1950s.

been brought under control.

Health and safety-related themes promoted through campaigns have included the dangers of SMOKING; the dangers of drugs; road safety, and the dangers of drink-driving; awareness of AIDS and other sexually-transmitted diseases; crime prevention; fire prevention; workplace safety and—with a sudden surge in cases of DENGUE in 2005—the need to prevent Aedes mosquitoes from breeding by eliminating sources of stagnant water.

Besides banners, posters, flyers and other printed materials, government agencies have made use of the media, grassroots organizations and community centres to garner support for, and extend the reach of, campaigns.

caning A form of corporal punishment where a criminal's buttocks are whipped with a rattan cane (known as a *rotan*). Caning has been part of Singapore criminal law since 1824, and has generally been used against those convicted of begging; possessing, selling or dealing in pornography; treason; rape and other violent offences. In 1966, caning was made mandatory for those convicted of vandalism. This signalled a major departure from the traditional approach to caning that had hitherto been subject to judicial discretion. The government clearly considered caning an important deterrent in its fight against crime. By 1973, caning had become mandatory for about 30 crimes as a result of the enactment of three pieces of legislation: the MISUSE OF DRUGS ACT, the Dangerous Fireworks Act and the Vandalism Act. Today, caning is mandatory for over 40 different offences including rape, robbery, drug-trafficking, possession of offensive weapons, vandalism and illegal overstaying. Caning is discretionary for offences such as rioting, extortion, living off the immoral earnings of another, manslaughter, causing hurt, and certain road traffic offences.

The offender to be caned is stripped naked, tied down to a trestle in a right-angled position so that he is in a bent-over posture with his buttocks in the air. The caning is carried out by a specially trained

Dad pleads guilty, gets 8 years and cane

Jail, caning for stomping on pal who groped girlfriend

Caning: newspaper headlines.

officer who uses a rattan cane 1.2 m long and 1.3 cm thick. The cane is struck across the bare buttocks of the offender. The lower spine and kidney areas are protected by padding. The cane is soaked in water the night before to stop it from splitting or from shearing the skin, and is treated with antiseptic before being used. The caning is carried out privately, but a number of officers including a medical officer will be present. The medical officer may stop the caning if he believes the prisoner unfit to continue to be caned. If that happens, the matter is reported to the court, which can choose to remit the caning or sentence the offender to imprisonment in lieu of the strokes not carried out.

Only males aged between 16 and 50 can be caned. Foreigners are not spared. One of the mostly widely reported canings was that of American teenager, MICHAEL FAY, who was convicted of vandalism in 1994.

Cantonese The term 'Cantonese' refers to a dialect group as well as the language spoken by its members. According to the 2000 Census of Population, there were 385,630 Cantonese in Singapore, making up 15.4 per cent of Singapore's Chinese community. Domestic political unrest, overpopulation and competition for scarce farmland were among the factors that drove many Cantonese to leave China's Guangdong province. Many migrated to Southeast Asia, North America and Australia.

The first Cantonese immigrants to settle in Singapore did so within the section of CHINATOWN bordered by New Bridge Road, Keong Saik Road, South Bridge Road, Club Street and Cross Street. Early Cantonese immigrants brought Cantonese cuisine and culture to Singapore. Cantonese opera was a popular form of entertainment, and Lai Chun Yuen Theatre became a centre for this genre. As testimony to Cantonese opera's prominence, the Chinese names of the surrounding streets referred to the theatre: Hei Yuen Kai (Theatre Street), Hei Yuen How Kai (Theatre Back Street), and Hei Yuen Wang Kai (Theatre Side Street) were the Chinese names given to Smith Street, Temple Street and Trengganu Street, respectively.

In Singapore, Cantonese immigrants frequently worked as goldsmiths and tailors. They also opened restaurants and pawnshops, manufactured soya sauce, and founded CHINESE MEDICAL HALLS. One of these early medical halls—EU YAN SANG, which

was founded in 1879 by EU KONG, a native of Foshan in China's Pearl River Delta—has continued to operate. A prominent street in Chinatown (Eu Tong Sen Street) was named after Eu Kong's eldest son, EU TONG SEN, who was a successful businessman, banker and philanthropist.

Many Cantonese women migrated to Singapore to work as labourers and servants. The SAMSUI WOMEN (from the county of Sanshui in Guangdong province), often noted for their distinctive navy suits and red headdresses, worked as labourers on construction sites, particularly in the 1950s and 1960s; domestic workers—the amahs and *majies*—travelled to Singapore from the Shunde region of Guangdong.

As many Cantonese women worked for a living, the Cantonese were often seen as being more open or 'liberal' than other Chinese groups, although such perceptions may also be related to the longer period of exposure to 'the West' that the Cantonese had experienced in southern China.

In the colonial period, Cantonese women were often sold into PROSTITUTION. This led to the setting up of the Po Leung Kuk, a Chinese social organization aimed at protecting destitute young girls from vice within the Straits Settlements (*see* CHINESE PROTECTORATE).

In comparison with other dialect groups, a greater proportion of Cantonese speakers was born outside Singapore, even among younger age groups. There is also a high proportion of elderly people amongst the Cantonese community, as well as a sex imbalance (with more women than men) in the age group of 55 years and over. These figures may explain why this language community has succeeded in retaining its dialect, as Cantonese has continued to be spoken in the home.

The Cantonese community has founded organizations to provide for the welfare of its members. These include institutions such as the KWONG WAI SIEW PECK SAN THENG, which organizes funerals for Cantonese immigrants, and Yeung Ching School, founded in 1905 to provide primary education for Cantonese children living in Chinatown. In earlier periods, the community's Cantonese identity was reinforced by the cultivation of Cantonese opera and STORYTELLING. In more recent years, this has largely been replaced by Hong Kong-produced Cantonese entertainment in the form of movies, music, literature and television dramas—although restrictions in Singapore on the broadcasting of films and television programmes in dialects have also had an impact.

cantonments Military barracks. In 1819, Sir Stamford Raffles designated the site at what is now Cantonment Road for the barracks of the EAST INDIA COMPANY's sepoy troops (*see* SEPOYS). Troops were thus 'cantoned' in this area from 1824 to 1858. Because of the sepoy cantonments in this area, it became known as Sepoy Lines. Prior to 1853, what is now Outram Road was part of Cantonment Road. There were also cantonments for troops on Bras Basah Road.

capital markets In Singapore, the capital market has two components—domestic and international (for international or offshore, *see* ASIAN DOLLAR BOND MARKET). The domestic market is made up of securities traded on the SINGAPORE EXCHANGE (SGX), the Singapore Government Securities Market and the fund or asset management industry. The table shows the changes in this market over the last two decades.

The equity or share component of the capital market has a longer history than the debt component although during the last one-and-a-half decades, the latter has become more important. The corporate bond market is growing in both volume and sophistication as the SGX continues to attract foreign listings.

The Singapore government, through the MONETARY AUTHORITY OF SINGAPORE (MAS), issues marketable securities of varying maturities, ranging from three months (securities with maturities of one year and under are called Treasury Bills) to 15 years. Issued in denominations of $1,000, they are not listed on the SGX but traded through government securities dealers.

Government securities are typically issued to meet the state's budgetary needs as well as the statutory needs of banks and statutory bodies (especially the CENTRAL PROVIDENT FUND) for risk-free liquid assets. A liquid government securities or bond market also serves as a benchmark for corporate securities, and helps widen the range of financial services available in Singapore, enhancing the city's competitive position as a financial centre.

The fund or asset management industry is a relatively new addition to the financial scene in Singapore. Generally, these firms (which include the asset management arm of financial institutions) operate collective investment schemes dealing in unit trusts, money market funds, real estate investment trusts, property funds and hedge funds on behalf of clients.

The industry has grown rapidly since the mid-1990s. Like other facets of the financial sector's development, the fund management sector has received strong government support through tax incentives and other measures. Total assets managed at the end of 2004 amounted to $572.6 billion, making Singapore a leading regional centre for wealth and asset management in the Asia-Pacific region, with an annual average growth rate of 28 per cent between 1994 and 2004. Like other financial services, it is dominated by foreign asset management houses, attracted by both Singapore's strong fundamentals and by rapid economic growth in Asia.

capital punishment The judicially ordered execution of a prisoner as punishment, otherwise known as the death penalty. In Singapore, capital punishment means death by hanging. Like CANING, the death penalty has been part of Singapore's criminal law since the colonial period.

The death penalty is mandatory for a range of offences including drug trafficking, murder and firearm offences. The PENAL CODE stipulates the death sentence for at least ten different offences including murder, attempted murder, endangering a person's life during an act of piracy and 'offences against the President's person'.

Four other acts also provide for the imposition of the death penalty. The MISUSE OF DRUGS ACT provides for a mandatory death sentence for at least 20 different drug offences while the INTERNAL SECURITY ACT stipulates death for certain offences involving firearms, ammunition or explosives. The Arms Offences Act provides for a mandatory death sentence for anyone, including accomplices, using or attempting to use firearms or trafficking in arms. The Kidnapping Act provides for the death penalty for kidnapping for ransom. Under the Criminal Procedure Code, the death penalty may not be imposed on pregnant women or on offenders under 18 at the time of the offence.

In Singapore, prisoners who are sentenced to death are usually separated from other prisoners in a segregated part of the prison known unofficially as 'Death Row'. When the sentence is carried out, the prisoner is 'hanged by the neck until death' in a process known as 'drop-hanging'. The prisoner is led to a specially constructed elevated platform, or gallows, where a rope with a noose is placed around his neck. The floor-trap on the gallows on which the prisoner stands will then open and the 'long-drop' (a method developed by British hangman William Marwood) severs the spinal cord and dislocates the cervical vertebrae resulting in almost instantaneous death. Hanging is carried out in private and only in the presence of prison officials, usually in the early hours of the morning.

The High Court is the only court that can sentence a prisoner to death. The prisoner can appeal to the COURT OF APPEAL under Section 220 of the Criminal Procedure Code. If the prisoner chooses not to appeal, the judge who presided at the trial must forward to the minister of law a copy of the notes of evidence taken at the trial together with a written report stating whether the sentence of death should be carried out. If the prisoner chooses to appeal, the judge will forward to the Court of Appeal a copy of the notes of evidence taken at the trial and a written report on whether the sentence of death should be carried out. If the Court of Appeal dismisses the appeal, the chief justice or other presiding judge shall forward to the minister of law the notes of evidence, and report whether the Court of Appeal feels that the sentence of death should be carried out. Both these procedures are intended to give the Cabinet, and indirectly the president, the benefit of the judges' consideration on the matter before the prerogative of the presidential pardon is, or is not, exercised.

CapitaLand Property company. The CapitaLand Group—which was created from the merger of Pidemco Land and DBS Land in November 2000—is one of the largest listed property companies in Asia, with operations extending to 90 cities in 28 countries. Total assets were in excess of $27 billion in 2005, and the group recorded earnings of $750 million on a turnover of $3.8 billion.

The group's core businesses in residential, commercial and industrial property and property-related services, such as property funds and real-estate financial products, are concentrated in selected 'gateway' cities in China, Australia and the United Kingdom. Assets in China and Australia accounted for more than half of the group's profits in 2004.

The group's hospitality businesses, in hotels and serviced residences, cover more than 50 cities around the world. CapitaLand also uses its significant real-estate asset base and market knowledge to develop fee-based products and services in Singapore and the region.

The group is a majority stakeholder in The Ascott, which is the largest serviced residence provider in Asia-Pacific, and RAFFLES HOLDINGS, which sold its entire hotel business to US-based private equity firm Colony Capital in 2005 for $1.72 billion. Both The Ascott and Raffles Holdings are listed on the SINGAPORE EXCHANGE. Another majority-owned subsidiary, Australand Property Group, one of the largest developers in Australia, is listed on both the Australian and the Singapore exchanges.

CapitaLand marked an important milestone in the development of the Singapore capital market in July 2002, when it launched the CapitaMall Trust, the first listed real estate investment trust (REIT) on

CAPITAL MARKETS: NET FUNDS RAISED IN DOMESTIC CAPITAL MARKET				
	1983	1990	2000	2004
A Net funds raised by government	10,322	5,118	8,873	14,966
B New capital raised by private sector	1,068	3,037	5,515	5,987
C Issues of debt securities	190	1,632	14,532	1,699
Total	11,580	9,787	28,920	42,652

*Figures are in $ million.
Source: Monetary Authority of Singapore Annual Report (various)

CapitaLand: corporate headquarters in Capital Tower.

Capital punishment: the death penalty is mandatory for drug trafficking offences.

CAPITAL PUNISHMENT: NUMBER OF HANGINGS 2003–2005						
Year	Murder		Drug trafficking		Firearms		Total
	Local	Foreign	Local	Foreign	Local	Foreign	
2003	1	4	9	5	0	0	19
2004	2	2	3	0	1	0	8
2005	2	0	5	1	0	0	8
Total	5	6	17	6	1	0	35

Source: The Straits Times

Car ownership: the SPH CATS Classified Car-nival, held at Singapore Expo, July 2006.

Capitol Theatre: auditorium, 1930 (right); present-day street frontage.

the local exchange. This was followed by the listing of CapitaCommercial Trust REIT in May 2004. Both CapitaLand and CapitaMall Trust are component stocks in the benchmark Straits Times Index.

Capitol Theatre Located at the junction of North Bridge and Stamford Roads, Capitol Theatre was one of SHAW BROTHERS' leading movie theatres and events halls during the 1950s and 1960s. Originally owned by the Namazie family, this iconic building had been opened in 1929 by the firm of Keys & Dowdeswell. During the Japanese Occupation, it operated under the name Kyo-Ei Gekkyo until 1944, when it was damaged by a bomb.

The theatre was bought by the Shaw group in 1946. With a seating capacity of 1,688, it became a 'picture palace' for Hollywood movies and a venue for live entertainment. Malaya's first ice-skating show was performed there in 1951; in the 1960s, dance revues, beauty contests (such as the Miss Singapore pageant), and musical and variety shows by performers such as RITA CHAO, SAKURA and the QUESTS, and WANG SA and YE FENG were all held at the theatre.

Capitol Theatre was listed for preservation in August 1983 and was acquired by the Urban Redevelopment Authority (URA), with operations officially ceasing on 29 December 1998.

car ownership Owning and driving a car in Singapore is, by international standards, expensive. This is partly the consequence of various measures designed to restrain car ownership, promote the use of public trans-

port, and so ease traffic congestion, especially in the Central Business District.

After Separation in 1965, land-scarce Singapore needed a sound long-term plan to accommodate its growing economy. During the period 1967–71, the State and City Planning Study developed a concept plan for the physical development of the island. The study concluded that it would be environmentally unacceptable and physically impossible to build enough roads to meet the prevailing rate of growth in cars; and that buses alone would be unable to meet future public transport needs. From these findings has arisen an overall transportation strategy that attempts to maintain a desirable balance between the use of private and public transport. The emphasis is to improve public transport and encourage its use; and to restrain the widespread use of the private car by demand management. In addition, the transport strategy also calls for land-use planning to take transport into account and vice-versa, and for the construction of a modest road network complemented by good traffic management.

Demand management measures have mainly targeted private cars, which have always accounted for slightly more than half of the total vehicle population. The measures implemented since 1972 are restraint on vehicle usage and car ownership.

Vehicle usage restraint was introduced through an Area Licensing Scheme in 1975 (*see* AREA LICENSING SCHEME AND RESTRICTED ZONE), which was subsequently upgraded to ELECTRONIC ROAD PRICING (ERP) in 1998. Initially, usage restraint targeted only cars, but was later extended to include all classes of vehicles. Car ownership restraint began with measures that relied on high taxes and fees. These applied to import taxes, registration fees and Additional Registration Fees (ARF). The periodic tax and fee increases dampened the growth rate of car ownership from 1972 to 1989, but it became untenable to keep increasing taxes at regular intervals.

In August 1989, a Parliamentary Select

Committee reviewed the adequacy of existing policies on demand management and examined the need for additional measures. Amongst other things, the committee recommended a quota system as a long-term solution to manage the orderly growth in vehicle numbers. The vehicle quota system came into being in May 1990. The cost of a new car is the sum of its OPEN MARKET VALUE (OMV), registration fee, GOODS AND SERVICES TAX, the import tax, ARF, vehicle quota premium and the car dealer's mark-up.

The registration fee of $15 in 1968 was increased to $1,000 in 1980 and reduced to $140 in 1998, when the ERP was implemented. The GST, first introduced in 1994 at 3 per cent of OMV, was increased to 4 per cent in 2003 and 5 per cent in 2004.

The import tax of 30 per cent of OMV in 1968 was increased to 45 per cent in 1972, decreased to 31 per cent in 1998 (the year the ERP was introduced) and 20 per cent in 2002. The ARF, in existence since the 1950s at 10 per cent of OMV, was progressively increased from 1972 to 175 per cent in 1983, and then decreased since 1990 (the year the vehicle quota system was introduced) to 110 per cent in 2004.

Anyone registering a new car is required to hold a CERTIFICATE OF ENTITLEMENT (COE). This vehicle quota system, which started as a monthly closed bidding system in 1990, was replaced with a fortnightly open bidding system in 2004.

In 2004, the car-to-population ratio in Singapore was 1:10. Although this ratio is high compared with that of other Asian countries, it is much lower than the ratio of 1:2 found in most developed countries. Having paid large sums upfront, car owners tend to drive frequently. They clock an average travel distance of 20,100 km annually, which is high when compared with drivers from cities similar in size and affluence to that of Singapore.

Singapore has consistently used vehicle demand management measures since the mid-1970s to keep transport problems within tolerable levels.

Carpay, Frans (1940–) Scientist and businessman. Frans Carpay was born and educated in the Netherlands, earning his master's degree in physics and chemistry in 1964 and a PhD in chemistry in 1968 at Utrecht University. He went on to spend 40 years in research and development (R&D), starting with Philips.

From 1980 to 1988, Carpay was responsible for the development of optical discs, such as the VLP (video long-play), CD and CD-ROM, both within Philips and in joint ventures with Control Data Corporation (later Seagate) and later with DuPont. The first CDs were developed under his leadership.

In 1993, he was seconded to Singapore to serve as managing director of Gintic Institute of Manufacturing Technology

Cathay Building: facade after renovation, 2006.

(later the Singapore Institute of Manufacturing Technology). Gintic's mission was to establish R&D and to offer companies advice on how to move into computer-integrated manufacturing. Carpay was also involved in creating the National Science & Technology Plan for 1996, 2000 and beyond. He won the NATIONAL SCIENCE AND TECHNOLOGY MEDAL in 2001 for 'outstanding contributions in leading the Gintic Institute of Manufacturing Technology to the benefit of the industry in Singapore'. He relinquished his position as managing director of Gintic in April 2002.

carrot cake Popular hawker dish. Known locally as '*chye tow kueh*', carrot cake originates from southern China and is made from shredded radish mixed with a rice-flour batter. It is then steamed to create a firm paste which is cut into bite-sized chunks and fried with eggs, garlic, and *chai po* (pieces of dried pickled radish). There are 'black' and 'white' versions of carrot cake—'black' carrot cake is fried with sweet dark soy sauce. The Chinese regard the radish as a carrot and call it 'white carrot', hence the name of the dish.

casino ships Because GAMBLING is a strictly regulated activity in Singapore, casino players travel to nearby facilities in the Genting Highlands (in Malaysia) and BATAM to pursue their activities. They may also sign up for 'cruises to nowhere'—a term synonymous with casino cruises. Ferry operators such as Star Cruises open their onboard casinos once they leave Singapore waters, with the Friday-to-Sunday cruises typically packed with weekend gamblers. It is also common for casino players to make short, or day, trips to Batam's Nongsa, where they go onboard the casino ferries.

Cathay Building The flagship 1,300-seat Cathay cinema, belonging to Cathay Organisation (*see* CATHAY-KERIS FILMS), was housed in the Cathay Building on Handy Road. Both cinema and building were inaugurated on 3 October 1939 by LOKE WAN THO, with the screening of A. Korda's *The Four Feathers* (1939). The 17-storey building was 79.5 m high, making it the first skyscraper in Singapore and, at that

time, the tallest building in Southeast Asia. With luxury apartments and a restaurant, Cathay was also the first public building in Singapore to be air-conditioned.

The building, with its art deco facade, was designed by architect FRANK BREWER. At the start of the Japanese invasion, the BRITISH MALAYA BROADCASTING CORPORATION operated in the building, from which it transmitted updates on the progress of the war. The cinema screened its last movie prior to the British surrender on 15 February 1942. The building was then used temporarily as a RED CROSS casualty station and shelter.

During the JAPANESE OCCUPATION, the cinema was renamed Dai Toa Gekijo (Greater East Asian Theatre) and the building housed the Japanese Broadcasting and Military Propaganda departments and the Military Information Bureau. In the post-war period, it served as Admiral Lord Lous Mountbatten's headquarters.

Cathay was the first cinema to re-open after the war with the screening of *The Tunisian Victory* (1944) on 23 September 1945. The building was 'returned' to its Cathay owners in November 1946. Cathay Restaurant reopened in 1948, and the new Cathay Hotel was opened in 1954. The hotel was converted into office space in the early 1970s. In 1990, Singapore's first art-house cinema, the Picturehouse, was added to the complex and in 1991, the cinema was turned into a three-screen cineplex. The cinema screened its last movie in 2000.

In February 2003, the building was gazetted as a national monument. Extensive renovations under architect Paul Tange were completed in 2006 for the launch of the new Cathay Cineplex on the site.

Cathay-Keris Films Film studio. One of the two main movie studios active during the 'golden age' of Malay cinema, it was operational from 1953 to 1972. After its inception in the 1930s as Associated Theatres, Cathay Organisation, as it was known from 1959, largely focused on film distribution and screening. Following the example of his competitors, the SHAW BROTHERS, owner

Cathay-Keris Films: produced the **Pontianak** *series of films in the 1950s and 1960s.*

LOKE WAN THO decided to produce his own Malay movies. In 1953, he joined with HO AH LOKE to create Cathay-Keris Films, which soon had its own studios on East Coast Road. Its entry into the movie-making business brought the studio era into a new phase, which would end with the cessation of Cathay-Keris productions in 1972.

Loke Wan Tho took great pains with his new venture, visiting studios in India to study their working methods and inviting Hollywood professionals to coach his actors. In 20 years, the studio produced more than 120 movies, all of which were in Malay—the only exception being *Lion City* (1960), which was made in Mandarin. After the closure of Shaw's MALAY FILM PRODUCTIONS in 1967, Cathay-Keris Films was the only producer of Singapore-made Malay movies until 1972, producing 22 features under three directors in its final five years.

Cathedral of the Good Shepherd This Catholic church was built from 1843 to 1847 under the direction of Father JEAN-MARIE BEUREL, a French MEP—Société des Missions Etrangères de Paris, or the Paris Foreign Missions Society—missionary. The foundation stone was blessed and laid on 18 June 1843, and the building inaugurated on 6 June 1847. The church was dedicated to Christ the Good Shepherd in memory of Father Laurent Imbert—the first MEP priest to visit Singapore. According to Father Beurel, the total cost of the building was 18,355.22 Spanish dollars. Extended between 1887 and 1888 under Bishop Gasnier, the church was consecrated on 14 February 1897 by Gasnier's successor, Bishop René Fée.

The church's origins can be traced to a chapel that had originally been built in 1833 on land later occupied by ST JOSEPH'S INSTITUTION (later the SINGAPORE ART MUSEUM). As the Catholic community grew, a more extensive church became imperative, and a site on Bras Basah Road was chosen for the building of the new cathedral.

After completion, the Cathedral of the Good Shepherd became the principal

Cathay Building, photographed in 1958.

Carrot cake: white, foreground, and black versions of the dish.

Cathedral of the Good Shepherd

Catholicism: **Catholic News** *and special supplement.*

Catholicism: Cathedral of the Good Shepherd, interior.

church of the archdiocese, where the chair (known as the *cathedra*)—symbol of the archbishop's authority—was located. It served all members of the Catholic community in the town centre until other churches were built to accommodate different language communities.

See also CATHOLICISM.

Catholic High School Secondary school. Catholic High School (CHS) is an all-boys full school with secondary and primary sections. It is government-aided, and is one of ten SPECIAL ASSISTANCE PLAN SCHOOLS (schools at which students read both English and Chinese at the 'first-language' level). The secondary section is an AUTONOMOUS SCHOOL, which means it has additional flexibility in curriculum development and delivery; it also receives funding from the MINISTRY OF EDUCATION.

Founded in 1935 by French missionary Edward Becheras, CHS—previously known as the Sino-English Catholic High School—operated out of the Church of St Peter and St Paul on Queen Street. As a MISSION SCHOOL, it was favoured by many wealthy Chinese families—both Catholic and non-Catholic. The school moved to various locations to accommodate a rapidly rising number of students, before finding permanent premises on Bishan Street.

The school's alumni include LEE HSIEN LOONG. To date, the school has produced 19 President's Scholars (*see* PRESIDENT'S SCHOLARSHIP).

Catholicism The establishment of the Catholic Church in Singapore is closely linked with the development of the church in peninsular Malaya. It has its roots in the arrival of the Portuguese who, led by Alfonso d'Albuquerque, conquered Malacca in 1511. In 1558, the diocese of Malacca was established by the Portuguese

Catholicism: Church of St Teresa.

under the Padroado (patronage of the Portuguese monarch), but the practice of Catholicism was restricted by the Protestant Dutch, who captured Malacca from the Portuguese in 1641. The church later took its direction from the Société des Missions Etrangères de Paris (MEP)—the Paris Foreign Missions Society, which had been in Siam (present-day Thailand) since 1662, and was led by 'Apostolic Vicars' who were appointed by Rome to direct missionary activities and establish a local church.

In 1821, two years after Sir Stamford Raffles founded Singapore, Laurent Imbert, a missionary from France who had been teaching temporarily at the College General in Penang, was requested by Bishop Florens of Siam to search for Catholics as he stopped by Singapore on his way to China. Imbert reported finding a dozen Catholics living in wretched conditions on the island. In the following years, a Portuguese priest from Malacca, Father Jacob Joaquim Freire Brumber, came to Singapore to minister to the mostly Portuguese Eurasian Catholic community there.

In 1824, Catholics in Singapore wrote to Bishop Florens, requesting that he send priests to Singapore. The local apostolic vicar also wrote to Rome to establish who had jurisdiction over Singapore. The reply from Rome arrived in 1827, saying that Florens was in charge of Catholics in Singapore. Meanwhile, in 1825, Father Francisco da Silva Pinto e Maya arrived in Singapore from Macau, immediately claiming jurisdiction over the island on behalf of the Portuguese archdiocese of Goa. In 1830, Coadjutor Bishop Bruguière, who was an assistant of Bishop Florens, travelled to Singapore from Bangkok to show Father Maya the letter that had been sent from Rome, but Maya refused to recognize the document as being authentic.

In 1832, Father Pierre Clemenceau arrived in Singapore and took charge of the Catholic community. He was the first MEP missionary to reside on the island. Fathers Hilaire Courvezy and Etienne Albrand followed Clemenceau some years later. Father Courvezy started building a small chapel on a piece of land on Bras Basah Road which had been provided by the British government. This was completed under Father Albrand. Albrand also

started a mission for Chinese residents in Singapore. He was called to Siam in 1835, and Father John Chu from Siam was sent to replace him in 1838.

Throughout this period, the question of who had jurisdiction over the Catholic community in Singapore (i.e. the Portuguese priests or the missionaries from Siam), continued to cause conflict. In 1840, Pope Gregory XVI confirmed the earlier decree of 1827 giving the Apostolic Vicar of Siam jurisdiction over Singapore, Malacca and the region of Martaban in Burma. In 1841, a papal brief divided the Apostolic Vicariate of Siam into Eastern (Siam proper) and Western Siam, and the mission of Malacca, under Bishop Courvezy, became an independent vicariate with five districts: Singapore, Penang, Mergui (in present-day Myanmar), Tavay and Malacca.

That same year, FATHER JEAN-MARIE BEUREL, a young French missionary, was put in charge of the Catholic community in Singapore. He replaced the old chapel, which had become too small for the growing community, with a bigger church dedicated to Christ the Good Shepherd. This was officially opened on 6 June 1847. Beurel also brought in Religious Brothers and Sisters to run the first Catholic schools for boys (1852) and girls (1854).

While Father Chu and Father Beurel ministered to Catholics in town, Father Anatole Mauduit ministered to farmers and Chinese immigrants in the north of the island. In 1846, he built an *attap* chapel dedicated to St Joseph in Kranji and, later, the CHURCH OF ST JOSEPH in Bukit Timah.

In 1880, Rome chose Singapore as the venue for the first formal meeting of Apostolic Vicars in Southeast Asia. For three weeks, vicars discussed how best to develop guidelines for pastoral activity in the countries they represented, their main concern being the Portuguese Padroado and the problem of dual jurisdiction.

The conflict over jurisdiction was finally resolved by a concordat between Pope Leo XIII and King Dom Louis of Portugal on 23 June 1886. The Portuguese parishes in Singapore (St Joseph's Church on Victoria Street) and Malacca (St Peter's Church) were placed under the jurisdiction of the Bishop of Macau. This opened the way for the See of Malacca—which had been left vacant—being given a bishop under the direct authority of Rome. The Apostolic Vicar, Bishop Edward Gasnier, was thus made bishop of Malacca, with Malaya and Singapore forming one large diocese. The Church of the Good Shepherd in Singapore became a cathedral. The cathedral building itself was extended to its current size, and was consecrated in 1897 by Bishop René Fée. In 1925, the St Francis Xavier Minor Seminary was established to educate boys from Secondary Four up to the equivalent of the Higher School Certificate, preparing them to enter the major seminary with subjects like Latin and Bible study.

Under Bishop Adrien Devals (1934–45), more religious congregations were invited to Singapore to help see to the social and pastoral needs of local Catholics. These included the Redemptorists (Congregation of the Most Holy Redeemer) and the Carmelite Sisters, who arrived in 1935. The Brothers of St Gabriel—a teaching congregation—arrived in 1937 and opened a vocational school (Boys Town) in 1939. In 1939, the Little Sisters of the Poor arrived and opened a home for the elderly, while the Good Shepherd Sisters opened a centre for women and teenagers in crisis. The Canossian Daughters of Charity started a school for girls in 1894 on Victoria Street, then built a second school in Aljunied in 1941. In 1935, Bishop Devals also launched a weekly Catholic paper which was later named *Catholic News*. During the Japanese Occupation, some 300 Christians from Singapore were evacuated to BAHAU, a jungle settlement in Negeri Sembilan. Bishop Devals, who went with the Bahau settlers, contracted a disease there and died in 1945. His funeral was held in Singapore and was attended by Japanese officials.

In 1947, Monsignor Michael Olcomendy was named administrator of the Diocese of Malacca, and was appointed bishop of Malacca. More changes took place under Olcomendy's leadership. The Legion of Mary was introduced to Singapore in 1948. A radio programme, 'Catholic Hour', was broadcast three times a month, and the *Catholic News* resumed publication in 1950. Concern for social issues was expressed through the establishment of organizations such as the Society of St Vincent de Paul, Catholic Welfare Services, Young Christian Workers, Young Christian Students, and guilds for Catholic teachers, nurses and doctors. Many more Catholic schools were also opened. By the 1950s, there were 105,000 Catholics in the Malacca diocese.

It was also around this time that China expelled all missionaries. Some 60 priests and missionaries from China arrived in Singapore shortly thereafter. Bishop Carlos Van Melckebecke, one of these missionaries from China, together with a member of the Congregation of the Immaculate Heart of Mary, established the Chinese Catholic Central Bureau in 1954. The bureau opened a bookshop, and published the *Hai Sing Pao*—a correspondence course of catechism in Chinese, English and Bahasa Indonesia.

In February 1955, the diocese of Malacca was divided into three territories—the Archdiocese of Malacca-Singapore; the Diocese of Kuala Lumpur; and the Diocese of Penang. This was a clear sign that the MEP was fulfilling its goal of establishing a local church. Rome appointed two new bishops from the local clergy: Bishop Dominic Vendargon of Kuala Lumpur and Bishop Francis Chan of Penang. A further division completed the process: the diocese of Malacca-Johor was established in 1972; Kuala Lumpur became an archdiocese and the head of the ecclesiastical province; and Singapore remained an archdiocese directly attached to Rome. Following the Second Vatican Council (1962–65), the Conference of Catholic Bishops of the region was established to encourage coordination on common policies and issues and to strengthen relations with other conferences of bishops.

As new towns were built in Singapore, Catholics who used to live around the five churches in the city relocated to the suburbs. The Catholic Junior College was set up in 1974. On the retirement of Archbishop Olcomendy, Rome appointed Bishop Gregory Yong from the local clergy to succeed him.

In 1981, the Portuguese Mission ceased to operate in Singapore and Malacca. That same year, diplomatic relations between the government of Singapore and the Holy See were established, and the St Francis Xavier Major Seminary was opened, thus allowing young men from Singapore who had hitherto trained for the priesthood at the College General in Penang to train instead locally. When Archbishop Yong retired at the age of 75 in 2001, Father Nicholas Chia succeeded him, being officially ordained and installed on 7 October the following year.

By the turn of the 21st century, Catholics represented 7 per cent of the total population of Singapore. They consist mainly of Chinese, Tamils and Eurasians, with important communities of Filipino foreign workers and expatriates from Europe and Asia. Masses are held daily in 30 churches across the island. Weekend Masses are conducted regularly in English, Mandarin, Tamil, Tagalog, Bahasa Indonesia, French, German, Burmese and Korean.

Causeway The older of two fixed links between Singapore and the Malaysian state of Johor. In 1919, it was decided that such a link was needed. Over the next five years, $17 million was spent on constructing the Causeway, which is located in WOODLANDS and spans the STRAIT OF JOHOR. The cost was shared between the Federated Malay States, the Straits Settlements and the state of Johor. The contract was awarded to Messrs Topham, Jones and Railton and the Consulting Engineers were Messrs Coode, Fitzmaurice, Wilson and Mitchell. The granite bank, 1.056 km in length and 18 m in width, accommodated a double railway track, a road and a footway. Most of the granite used was quarried at Bukit Timah and PULAU UBIN. In September 1923 the Causeway was first opened to traffic in the form of goods trains. It was officially opened on 28 June 1924 by Governor Sir LAURENCE GUILLEMARD.

On 27 January 1942, to slow the Japanese military advance into Singapore, the Gordon Highlanders and Lim Bo Seng's Quarry Workers Union blasted a 20-m gap in the Causeway. It was mended a year later by the occupation forces and the Causeway has been in use ever since. In the last decade, there has been talk about replacing the Causeway with a bridge. In 1998, the TUAS SECOND LINK, a bridge linking Singapore to Malaysia, was built at Tuas. In 1996, then prime minister of Malaysia Mahathir Mohamad put forward a proposal to replace the Causeway with a new bridge, which was rejected by Prime Minister Abdullah Badawi in 2006.

Cavenagh, Colonel Orfeur (1821–1891) Colonial official. Colonel (later Major-General) Orfeur Cavenagh succeeded EDMUND BLUNDELL as governor of the STRAITS SETTLEMENTS in 1859, and served as the final governor prior to control of the Straits Settlements being transferred from the British authorities in India to the COLONIAL OFFICE in 1867.

Orfeur was a veteran of the 1857 Indian Mutiny, during which he had lost a leg. In Singapore, he was responsible for using Indian CONVICT LABOUR to build and improve public amenities, such as FORT CANNING, which was was built in 1860, and ST ANDREW'S CATHEDRAL, which was completed in 1862. Cavenagh Bridge, built in 1869, and the oldest bridge in Singapore, was named after him, as was Cavenagh Road.

Cavenagh was also successful in easing tensions between merchants and the gov-

Causeway

ernment by opposing attempts to impose prejudicial taxation such as income taxes and tonnage duties.

CDAC *See* CHINESE DEVELOPMENT ASSISTANCE COUNCIL.

cemeteries The diversity of cemeteries reflects the wide range of death rituals and burial customs prevalent among different ethnic and religious communities in Singapore. During the colonial period, the Malays preferred to bury their dead on sand ridges while the Chinese sought out round knolls and hillsides. The Hindu community practised cremation while the European and Eurasian Christian communities had a separate Christian cemetery on Fort Canning hill (later relocated to Bukit Timah Road).

The most numerous and extensive were the Chinese burial grounds. For the Chinese, burial grounds had to be accorded geomantically suitable locations as a means of propitiating their ancestors and ensuring the welfare of the deceased's descendants (*see* FENG SHUI). Burial grounds were important spaces where the dead received veneration, attention and offerings of food and joss paper.

By the late 19th century, the physical expansion of the city was increasingly restricted by the scarcity of suitable land for building purposes. Along with calls for sanitary reform, there was considerable pressure to clear Chinese burial grounds. In 1887, an attempt was made to bring Chinese burial grounds under control through a bill authorizing the licensing, regulation and inspection of burial grounds. Protests against the

Cemeteries: Chinese (top) and Malay graves at Choa Chu Kang Cemetery.

bill delayed the implementation of the Burials Ordinance. However, in 1896, the issue was again raised in relation to a bill to amend the Municipal Ordinance to license and inspect burial grounds; to close them if they proved dangerous to health; and to impose penalties for the disposal of corpses in unlicensed places.

The shortage of burial space was further exacerbated by the compulsory acquisition of several old grounds for the purpose of colonial urban development. The first of these to be cleared was the disused Cantonese public burial ground near CHINATOWN which was acquired in 1907–08 in order to provide landfill for the Telok Ayer Reclamation Scheme.

Conditions for the issue of new licences for private burial grounds were also made increasingly stringent. After 1 July 1906, the use of any place within municipal limits was prohibited by law. The Christian cemetery at Bukit Timah Road was closed at the end of 1907 and a new cemetery, the Bidadari Christian Cemetery, was consecrated and opened on 1 January 1908 (*see* BIDADARI CEMETERY). Apart from this cemetery, however, the authorities were extremely reluctant to commit themselves to a policy of providing municipal cemeteries for the various Asian communities. The Chinese community petitioned for a municipal cemetery and this eventually resulted in the establishment of the BUKIT BROWN CEMETERY.

In 1952, a Burials Committee was set up to consider the idea of encouraging cremation as an alternative means of disposal. With Separation in 1965, the government took primary responsibility for a number of 'cradle-to-grave' services, such as running schools, funeral parlours and cemeteries which had previously come under the purview of Chinese clan and welfare associations (*see* CLAN ASSOCIATIONS). In the context of national development, questions of hygiene and rational land use development also featured prominently in discussions on Chinese burial grounds. For example, the health threat that the Choa Chu Kang Cemetery posed, in spite of nationwide sanitary measures, was frequently raised in Parliament. The state also considered extensive burial grounds an extravagant form of land wastage, especially given the urgent national concern to build 'homes for the people'.

While only about 10 per cent of the Chinese dead were cremated in the closing years of colonial rule, the number of cremations began to climb steeply from the early 1970s. In 1996, there were 4,756 (32.2 per cent) burials and 10,477 (68.8 per cent) cremations for the Singapore population as a whole. Among those for whom burial is not required by religion, 10,451 (83 per cent) were cremated compared to 2,140 (17 per cent) buried in 1997. In part, the change from burial to

Cenotaph

cremation is a reflection of the weakening hold of 'traditional' ideas and beliefs concerning death and the afterlife. Specifically, the fear of retribution from the dead seems to hold much less sway than before. The clearance of cemeteries was also backed by the LAND ACQUISITION ACT which gave the government the right to compulsorily acquire land for public purposes.

The government offered burial space in a state-owned 318-ha public cemetery complex at Choa Chu Kang (first opened in 1947) while at the same time making it clear that it considered cremation as the only viable, long-term solution. The earliest government crematorium-cum-columbarium complex—MOUNT VERNON CREMATORIUM AND COLUMBARIUM—began operations in 1962. This was followed by the construction of several other crematoriums and columbariums at Mandai, Yishun and Choa Chu Kang. The state announced in 1998 that the burial period for all graves at the Choa Chu Kang Cemetery Complex would be limited to 15 years and that existing graves that were 15 years or older (some 17,000-18,000 graves each in two of the earliest cemetery blocks) would be exhumed.

Cenotaph This granite memorial was built to commemorate the British soldiers who had died during WORLD WAR I. It also bears a small plaque commemorating Vietnam-based French veterans of the same war. It was designed by Denis Santry of architectural firm SWAN & MACLAREN, while its foundation stone was laid in 1920, at what is now QUEEN ELIZABETH WALK, by Governor Sir LAURENCE GUILLEMARD. When completed two years later, the memorial was unveiled by the Prince of Wales (later King Edward VIII). After WORLD WAR II, the reverse side of the Cenotaph was inscribed with the names of persons who had died in that conflict.

Censorship Review Committee This national-level citizens' committee has been assembled approximately every ten years by the government ministry overseeing information and culture to review policies on regulating all types of media, which today include books, audio materials, films, videos, broadcasts, stage performances and the Internet.

The first panel of six members met in 1981 under the chairmanship of S. JAYAKUMAR, then minister of state for law and home affairs. A key recommendation of the panel was the establishment of more citizens' panels to advise the authorities and reflect shifting social mores. Another important point was to take a more contextual approach to allowing potentially objectionable materials. This laid the foundation for a gradual process of liberalization, as technology widened access to media and the public became more affluent.

A second committee, of 18 members, met in 1991–92 under then chairman of the NATIONAL ARTS COUNCIL (NAC), Tommy Koh. Among the key policy changes which resulted were the setting up of an appeals body for publications, refining the film and video classification system—including introduction of the Restricted (Artistic) and NC16 (no children under 16) categories—and a new scheme to exempt theatre groups with good track records from submitting scripts for vetting prior to staging. One of the decisions which reflected a move towards a more relaxed policy was the lifting of the ban on communist materials.

A third committee, with 22 members, met in 2002 and 2003 under then chairman of the NAC LIU THAI KER. Focus-group discussions were held with representatives from the general public, industry, academia and civil society. The panel recommended that greater community participation be encouraged; the appeals process to cover arts performances should be expanded; and focus on public education increased to reflect the rise of industry co-regulation and self-regulation. Landmark decisions included the lifting of a 20-year ban on the magazine *Cosmopolitan* as well as a ban on the television series *Sex and the City*. Film and video classification was further refined, with the introduction of new categories: R21 (restricted to persons 21 years and above) and M18 (for persons 18 years and above).

Public surveys conducted by the committee in 1991 and 2002 showed that tolerance towards allowing explicit materials had risen gradually over the years. However, one segment of society still held relatively conservative attitudes and wished, as they saw it, to protect 'family values' and the young.

See also UNDESIRABLE PUBLICATIONS ACT and OB MARKERS.

census The first census of Singapore's population was taken in 1871 as part of the Straits Settlement Census (although the first 'people count' was conducted in 1824). Since then, censuses have been taken regularly at ten-year intervals, with the exception of the Japanese Occupation period. The last prewar census was taken in 1931, and the first post-war census was taken in 1947.

The Statistical Bureau was renamed the Department of Statistics (DOS) in the 1950s, and was headed by the chief statisti-cian. In June 1957, the DOS was for the first time given responsibility for the taking of a census. Singapore's first post-SEPARATION Census of Population was conducted in 1970. This was taken in keeping with the United Nations' recommendation that years ending in '0' be designated as census years. Censuses have also been taken in 1980, 1990 and 2000.

The population censuses of 1970 and 1980 were conducted using traditional fieldwork methods. Houses were numbered to make sure nobody was left out, and thousands of interviewers made house-to-house visits to collect information using printed forms. In the mid-1980s, however, efforts were made to streamline the process. The People Hub database was set up using a Unique Identification Number for each Singapore citizen and permanent resident. For the 1990 census, information captured in People Hub was merged with other administrative databases. Information on each individual was thus first obtained from public agencies, and was then collated and printed onto census forms. Enumerators visited each household in order to check and edit the data contained on these forms.

The Household Registration Database (HRD) was set up in 1996 based on a one-time extraction of data from the Ministry of Home Affairs' People Hub as at end June 1995 and the 1990 Census Database, and is updated regularly with administrative data from various sources. That same year, the DOS database on dwellings was upgraded and renamed the National Database on Dwellings (NDD), and was later enhanced with more housing information. The NDD co-ordinates with the HRD to determine a physical location for each household in Singapore. Basic personal and demographic information on each household member is available from the HRD. For the 2000 census, a 'register-based census' was conducted, with all basic information needed taken from the HRD. In addition, only 20 per cent of the population was interviewed for additional data pertaining to socio-economic characteristics of the population. The number of field interviewers was cut, and data was gathered through a combination of Internet enumeration, telephone interviews and fieldwork.

Central Catchment Nature Reserve Home to much of Singapore's biodiversity, the Central Catchment Nature Reserve, which covers 25 sq km and includes four major reservoirs, is the country's principal 'green lung', and a popular destination for visitors. The reserve exemplifies all the major issues that surround nature conservation, recreational development, land-use planning and the protection of water resources.

The reserve covers the forested area surrounding Singapore's four central water RESERVOIRS—MacRitchie, Lower Peirce, Upper Peirce and Upper Seletar—and acts as

Central Catchment Nature Reserve

Central Catchment Nature Reserve: scaly anteater.

a repository of the country's natural heritage. It has been estimated that, of the roughly 190 ha of Singapore's remaining primary forest (forests left in their pristine state), about 80 per cent lies in the Central Catchment Nature Reserve. There is also about 15 sq km of secondary forest (forests that have re-established themselves on land previously cleared or disturbed) in the reserve.

The clearing of Singapore's jungles for settlements, timber and agriculture in the 19th century was so rapid that by 1890, less than 10 per cent of the island remained under forest cover. A few patches of forest, ranging from parcels smaller than a football field to some areas several hectares in size, managed to escape clearance. These remnants survive today in the reserve, some in almost pristine condition.

The unlogged forest blocks were originally left standing amidst cleared land, but the open spaces between them have since been colonized by fast-growing native trees which now form the secondary forests of the catchment area. The reserve is thus a mosaic of primary forests of various sizes surrounded by secondary forests in different stages of maturity and regeneration, giving some semblance of the original forest. These forests were protected under various guises through the first half of the 20th century as catchment areas for the island's expanding central reservoirs, beginning with the establishment of the Impounding Reservoir (today known as the MACRITCHIE RESERVOIR) in the late 1860s. The catchment forests were formally gazetted as a Nature Reserve in 1951 with the passing of the Nature Reserves Ordinance. Unlike Bukit Timah, the bulk of the Central Catchment Area was not formally protected, with the exception of the Chan Chu Kang Forest Reserve (in the vicinity of today's Upper Seletar Reservoir) and its surroundings.

No comprehensive survey of the reserve's flora and fauna was undertaken until the mid-1990s, over 100 years after the forest around MacRitchie Reservoir had been set aside as a catchment forest. The survey found that forests of the Central

Central Fire Station: built in neo-classical style (top); Fire Safety for Singapore—Yesterday, Today and Tomorrow, *sculpture erected 2001.*

Catchment are home to over 1,000 plant species and 200 bird species. Moreover, as a result of land clearances, the Central Catchment's rich wildlife is not randomly distributed, but is concentrated in a number of localities which correspond with the fragments of habitat left standing or little disturbed after the clearances of the 1800s. Chief among these is the NEE SOON SWAMP FOREST, a freshwater swamp forest sandwiched between the Upper Peirce and Upper Seletar Reservoirs, and a remnant of the Chan Chu Kang Forest Reserve.

Although this once-extensive freshwater swamp system is largely inaccessible to the public because of the Nee Soon Firing Range that occupies the greater part of the area, a portion adjacent to the driving range of the Executive Golf Course on Mandai Road has been made accessible. The Nee Soon Swamp Forest covers an estimated 87 ha, although the pristine portion of the swamp is much smaller. It is the last home for many species of Singapore's native fauna, particularly those dependent on fresh water. The rarest of Singapore's mammals—such as the banded leaf monkey (*Presbytis femoralis femoralis*), which is found nowhere else in the world—take refuge in the area.

Central Fire Station Throughout the 19th century, frequent serious fires caused massive destruction of property and many deaths. The Singapore Fire Brigade was established in 1888, and three stations were eventually built to serve the town area, including the Central Fire Station. In 1905, the municipal authorities employed Montague Pett as superintendent to reorganize the brigade. He recommended the construction of a modern central fire station, whose design included garage space for the first motorized fire engines, staff quarters, a host of time-saving devices and a watchtower.

The Central Fire Station opened in 1909 and the improved equipment and an increase in the staff led to a substantial decrease in the number and scale of fires in the crowded town area.

The building is distinguished by a facade of exposed red brick and white plaster bands, a style popular in the United Kingdom during the Edwardian period. Two extensions were added to the back of the building, in 1926 and 1954. The oldest

part of the building was later converted into the Civil Defence Gallery by the SINGAPORE CIVIL DEFENCE FORCE.

The station was gazetted as a national monument in December 1998, and has continued to provide fire fighting, ambulance and rescue coverage for the central district.

Central Limit Order Book Mechanism allowing over-the-counter trade in Singapore of Malaysian, Hong Kong and Philippine shares. Both Singapore and Malaysian stocks were listed on a joint stock exchange until 1973, when CURRENCY interchangeability between the two countries ended. Although both countries set up their own bourses, some 300 company counters remained co-listed on both the then Stock Exchange of Singapore (SES) and the Kuala Lumpur Stock Exchange (KLSE). Prices of such counters tended to move in tandem because of market arbitrage. In 1989, the KLSE delisted some 180 companies from SES, reducing market capitalization of the latter significantly. To counter this, the SES introduced Central Limit Order Book (CLOB) International to allow the continued trading of Malaysian shares. Equity counters from Hong Kong and the Philippines were also added to CLOB.

However, on 31 August 1998, the KLSE announced that all Malaysian securities had to be traded through the KLSE or through an exchange recognized by the KLSE. This was followed a day later by the announcement of capital exchange controls by the Malaysian government in a bid to shore up its currency in the wake of the 1997 ASIAN FINANCIAL CRISIS.

Such changes prompted the SES to decide on 3 September 1998 that trading of Malaysian shares on CLOB International was no longer viable. Trading in Malaysian shares came to a sudden halt, to the consternation of 172,000 Singapore investors. Their shares were frozen for 18 months, until a company called Effective Capital came up with a plan to unlock the shares in batches over 13 months. Investors could choose to go with the plan or alternatively wait until January 2003, when the shares would be released over nine months. About 93% of investors chose the Effective Capital option.

Central Narcotics Bureau Enforcement agency under the Ministry of Home Affairs. The Central Narcotics Bureau (CNB) directs the fight against drugs through the enforcement of Singapore's anti-drug laws and cooperation with local and foreign organizations on drug-related matters. It also promotes a drug-free lifestyle through education and community outreach programmes. Many CNB initiatives are targeted at students, and aim to help young people understand the negative impact of drug abuse. Drugs that are strictly controlled include heroin, cannabis, methamphetamine and ketamine.

Central Provident Fund Central pillar of Singapore's social security system. In 1955, when the Central Provident Fund (CPF) Scheme started under the British colonial government, it became mandatory for the employee and employer each to contribute 5 per cent of the employee's monthly gross salary to the CPF. By 1984, this level of contribution had reached 25 per cent each. Since then the rates have been periodically adjusted to cope with economic cycles as well as factors such as the age of employees. Contributions are credited into the Ordinary, Medisave and Special accounts. Cash savings in the Ordinary account are paid the average of deposit interest rates at local commercial banks. A minimum rate of 2.5 per cent is guaranteed by the CPF Act.

These compulsory savings can only be withdrawn at the age of 55, after setting aside a minimum sum for a retirement account; or in the event of permanent disability. Cash savings in the Special and Retirement accounts are paid 1.5 per cent above the normal CPF interest rate.

Since 1968, the use of CPF funds has been liberalized for approved purposes, of which housing finance has been the most important. Some 85 per cent of the population lives in owner-occupied housing, the bulk of which is financed by CPF funds.

The viability of the CPF scheme is based on the assumption of life-long continuous employment. However, globalization and corporate downsizing have not only raised concerns about job security, but have also led to non-standard employment arrangements. The challenge faced by the CPF is how to remain relevant in light of these changes.

Central Sikh Temple This was one of the earliest gurdwaras (Sikh temple) to be built in Singapore—the first being erected within the police compound at Pearl's Hill, which had served the spiritual needs of the Sikh police contingent. With the arrival of Sikh immigrants in other professions, the Sikh Temple at the police barracks became inadequate for the community's needs.

In 1912, a group of Sikhs, led by a Sindhi merchant called Wassiamull, acquired a bungalow at 175 Queen Street

Central Sikh Temple

and turned this into a gurdwara. This not only catered to the spiritual needs of Sikhs, but also became the focus of social activity for the Sikh community. Since it was the community's earliest attempt at self-organization, its membership cut across traditional regional and caste distinctions. It soon earned the title of Wadda Gurdwara (the Big Temple). The gurdwara was reconstructed in 1921.

In 1977, the government acquired the land on which the temple stood, and the temple was temporarily housed in the former Bukit Ho Swee Community Centre on Seng Poh Road. In November 1986, the new Central Sikh Temple building on Towner Road was officially opened.

Certificate of Entitlement A system aimed at limiting the growth of motor vehicles to an annual increase of 3 per cent. To register a vehicle, would-be owners bid in an open tendering exercise for the right to own a vehicle, called a Certificate of Entitlement (COE). The Government announces the quota in each of the five individual categories—namely small or medium cars and taxis; large cars; goods vehicles and buses; motorcycles; and 'open' (for any kind of vehicle)—and carries out two bidding exercises a month through an electronic tendering process. The bidder keys in a reserve price, which is the maximum amount he is willing to pay for a COE through Internet banking, phone banking or automatic teller machines. He will then have the opportunity to gain a COE until the current COE price exceeds the reserve price. He can revise his price upwards anytime before the bidding exercise closes. Successful bidders pay the quota premium for the COE, which is the highest unsuccessful bid price plus $1 for that category.

COEs are valid for eight years from the date of registration for taxis, and ten years for other vehicles. In mid 2006, COE prices were approximately $900 for motorcycles, $10,000 for small/medium cars and taxis, $11,000 for large cars, $6,000 for goods vehicles and buses and $11,000 for the open category. In the mid-1990s, the COE prices peaked at around $3,600 for motorcycles, $43,000 for small/medium cars, $66,500 for large cars, $36,000 for goods vehicles and $105,000 for the open category.

The vehicle quota premium to register a new car varies from bid to bid. The COE for a car is valid for ten years after first registration. If a car owner wishes to keep the vehicle after that, he has to pay the prevailing quota premium, which is the average of the quota premiums for cars in his category for the previous three months. This new COE revalidates his car for another ten years. He has an option of paying 50 per cent of the prevailing quota premium to revalidate for five years, but the five-year COE is not renewable. Initially, COEs for cars used to be transferable and this result-ed in their trading on the open market. To prevent speculation, new COEs are no longer transferable.

See also CAR OWNERSHIP.

Certificate of Honour National Day honour instituted in 1962. It is fourth in the hierarchy of awards, coming between the ORDER OF NILA UTAMA and the DISTINGUISHED SERVICE ORDER. The Certificate of Honour consists of a scroll bearing Singapore's Coat of Arms and the signature and seal of the president. Recipients are entitled to wear a silver badge known as the Badge of Honour. The Certificate has been awarded to only three people, all in 1962: LIM HAK TAI, the principal of the Nanyang Academy of Fine Arts; WONG PENG SOON, the badminton player and ZUBIR SAID, the composer. *See also* NATIONAL DAY HONOURS.

Ceylon Sports Club The Lanka Union was founded in 1920 by a group of students of Ceylonese (Sri Lankan) origin from the KING EDWARD VII COLLEGE OF MEDICINE, who believed in the need for a united Ceylonese body for the promotion of sport, in particular soccer and cricket. It originally held sporting events on the PADANG. But in 1922, the Lanka Union erected a small clubhouse on Balestier Plain. Six years later, it was registered as the Ceylon Sports Club (CSC). It was not until 1954 that permanent premises for the CSC were completed, these being officially opened by British Commissioner Sir MALCOLM MACDONALD. Since then, the CSC has continued to host sporting, recreational and social events.

Cham Tao Soon (1939–) Academic and engineer. Cham Tao Soon was educated at Raffles Institution and the University of Malaya, where he graduated with a bachelor of engineering in 1964. After graduation, he worked as a consulting engineer before joining the staff of Singapore Polytechnic as a lecturer. Two years later, he left for further studies at the University of London, and then went to Cambridge University where he obtained his PhD on a Commonwealth Scholarship.

Cham joined the University of Singapore in 1969 as a lecturer and became dean of the Engineering Faculty in 1978, a position he held until 1983. In 1981, he was appointed founding president of the NANYANG TECHNOLOGICAL UNIVERSITY (NTU). He was appointed professor in 1983 and Distinguished University Professor in 2003. During his tenure as NTU president, Cham was credited with building the university into an institution of high repute. In addition to his academic duties, Cham has been chairman of the Nanyang Academy of Fine Arts (2002–); Singapore Symphonia Company (1999–); NatSteel Ltd (1988–); and Wearnes Technology Pte Ltd (1986–99). He has served as director of Keppel Corporation (1982–2003), and became chairman of SIM

Kit Chan: in Forbidden City, 2002.

University's Board of Trustees (1997–), and deputy chairman of Singapore Press Holdings (2004–). Among his numerous awards, he received the Chevalier dans l'Ordre des Palmes Académiques (1979); was admitted into the DISTINGUISHED SERVICE ORDER (2003); and was presented the Royal Academy of Engineering Inaugural International Medal (2006).

Chan, Harry (1926–) Civil servant and diplomat. Harry Chan Keng Howe graduated from Raffles College with a diploma in arts (1949), and from the University of Malaya with a bachelor of arts with honours (1950). Upon graduation, he joined the ADMINISTRATIVE SERVICE as assistant secretary for economic affairs. In 1961 he became secretary of the PUBLIC SERVICE COMMISSION.

In 1968, Chan was made acting permanent secretary of the Ministry of Foreign Affairs. The following year, he was appointed Singapore's ambassador to Cambodia. Chan's diplomatic career included postings as high commissioner to New Zealand (1974–81); ambassador to Egypt with concurrent accreditation to Yugoslavia (1981–84); and high commissioner to India with concurrent accreditation to Sri Lanka, Bangladesh and the Maldives, and concurrent accreditation as ambassador to Iran and Nepal (1984–89). Upon retirement from the diplomatic service, he served briefly as secretary-general of the Singapore Federation of Chambers of Commerce and Industry.

Harry Chan

Chan, Kit (1972–) Singer. The album *Xin Tong* (Heartache) marked the entry of Kit Chan (sometimes known by her Chinese name, Chen Jieyi) into the Taiwanese popular music market in 1994. In 1997, she was chosen to play the lead role in Jacky Cheung's musical *Xue Lang Hu* (Snow Wolf Lake), which premiered in Hong Kong and toured overseas. Her performance in this musical led to roles in other productions such as *Manbu Rensheng Lu* (The Legend) (1998) in Hong Kong; *Forbidden City: Portrait of an Empress* (2002) in Singapore; and *Aiqing you Shenme Daoli?* (What's Love About?) (2003) in Taiwan. Kit was the first performer to be commissioned by the National Arts Council to perform for the National Day Parade in 1998, singing *Home* (*Jia*) in both Mandarin and English, and in 2001 became the first local singer to stage a concert at the SINGAPORE INDOOR STADIUM.

Chan Chee Seng
(Chan Thye Yat)

Michael Chan Chew Koon
(Baron Chan of Oxton)

Chan Chin Bock

Chan Heng Chee

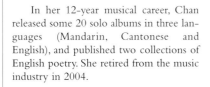

PATRICIA CHAN: SEAP GAMES MEDALS			
Year	Location	Medal	Time
1965	Kuala Lumpur	Gold	1:08.8
1967	Bangkok	Gold	1:07.1
1969	Rangoon	Gold	1:05.9
1971	Kuala Lumpur	Gold	1:04.74
1973	Singapore	Gold	1:03.47

Patricia Chan

In her 12-year musical career, Chan released some 20 solo albums in three languages (Mandarin, Cantonese and English), and published two collections of English poetry. She retired from the music industry in 2004.

Chan, Patricia (1954–) Sportswoman. Daughter of Dr Chan Ah Kow, Patricia Chan Li-Yin, popularly known as Pat Chan, dominated regional swimming from 1965 to 1973 using her father's revolutionary training techniques. Her two appearances at the Asian Games brought her eight medals, including three silver medals in 1970 in Bangkok. Her participation in five Southeast Asian Peninsular (SEAP) Games produced a total of 39 gold medals (*see* table). Her most consistent success was in the 100-m freestyle event at the SEAP Games. Each final yielded not only a gold medal but also a new SEAP Games record. She became an Olympian (Munich, 1972) and was inducted into the SINGAPORE SPORTS COUNCIL HALL OF FAME. She has been named Sportswoman of the Year on five occasions (1968, 1969, 1970, 1971 and 1972).

After her retirement from sport, Chan became a successful media and communications specialist, and even branched out into a career as a jazz singer.

Chan, Rose (1925–1987) Entertainer. Chan was born as Chan Wai Chang into a family of acrobats in Soochow (present-day Suzhou), China. She moved to Kuala Lumpur at the age of six, receiving virtually no formal education. In Malaya, she worked in various jobs, and was married off at the age of 16 as the fourth wife of a Singaporean harbour contractor. The couple split, however, after Chan's mother started making monetary demands on Chan's husband.

With her marriage in tatters, Chan worked as a cabaret dancer at the Happy World (later Gay World) Amusement Park in Geylang to support herself. She proved to be an accomplished dancer, and was runner-up in the All-Women's Ballroom Dancing Championships (1949) as well as the Miss Singapore Beauty Contest (1950). As a result of these successes, she became a highly popular dancer, sometimes performing in as many as five cabarets a night.

In 1952, while performing at the Majestic Theatre in Ipoh, Chan's brassiere snapped inadvertently; Chan won rapturous applause from the audience. From that night on, Chan changed her stage act and made a name for herself as the 'Queen of Striptease'.

Chan's daring acts and stunts (which included wrestling a python; bending iron rods stuck to the base of her throat; and having motorcycles ride over her) brought her fame, and she began to tour extensively. She would often dance in the nude, and some of her acts on stage were considered highly crude. Indeed, Chan was forced to stop performing for a time in Malaysia after the authorities revoked her licence on account of the lewdness and indecency of her performances.

Chan often donated part of her proceeds to charity. She retired in 1976, and died of breast cancer in May 1987.

Chan Chee Seng (Chan Thye Yat) (1932–) Politician. Chan Chee Seng was educated at St Andrew's School and Catholic High School. He was a founding member of the PEOPLE'S ACTION PARTY (PAP), and served as a member of Parliament (1959–84). From 1963 until his retirement from politics in 1984, he was PAP WHIP and senior Parliamentary secretary in various ministries, most notably the then Ministry of Social Affairs.

Chan became a committee member of the Jogging Association of Singapore in 1977. It was in that position that Chan and other joggers decided to start the Singapore Action Group of Elders (SAGE), a non-profit, non-religious and multi-ethnic voluntary welfare organization aimed at helping senior citizens. In 1981, Chan and his wife set up the International School of Singapore, which operates the American College and the Center for American Education. It also has a branch school in Beijing. He was awarded the MERITORIOUS SERVICE MEDAL in 1990.

Chan Chew Koon, Michael (Baron Chan of Oxton) (1940–2006) Doctor. Michael Chan Chew Koon was educated at Raffles Institution and studied medicine at Guy's Hospital Medical School in the United Kingdom. He then returned to work as a paediatrician in Singapore. In 1974, he won the Heinz Fellowship to study the bleeding disorder von Willebrand's disease (which has symptoms similar to haemophilia) at the Great Ormond Street Hospital for Children. In 1976, he was appointed senior lecturer at the Liverpool School of Tropical Medicine, where he taught until 1994. During that time, he helped the government of Orissa in India establish training of doctors and midwives. He was deeply involved in the welfare of the Chinese community in Britain and became chairman of the Chinese in Britain Forum (1997–2006). Among other important appointments, he was made commissioner, Commission for Racial Equality; director, National Health Service Ethnic Health Unit (1994–97); and chairman, Afiya Trust (1998–2006). He was co-editor of *Diseases of Children in the Tropics and Sub-Tropics*. In 2001, he was appointed a Peer in recognition of his work with medicine and ethnic communities, and became Baron of Oxton. He died after a sudden illness in January 2006.

Chan Chin Bock (1938–) Civil servant. Chan Chin Bock joined the ECONOMIC DEVELOPMENT BOARD (EDB) in April 1964 as a promotion and public relations officer. He was promoted to acting chief and chief of Investment Promotion Division in 1967. In 1968, he left for the EDB's New York office to attract American multinational corporations to Singapore. Chan was also asked to start up new EDB centres in Chicago, London, Stockholm, Frankfurt and Zurich. In July 1970, he was appointed director of the EDB, and in 1972 he returned to Singapore to become EDB's chairman. In 1974, Chan was asked to be alternate chairman of the EDB, based in New York. During this time, he oversaw the EDB's overseas network of 17 offices. He returned to Singapore in 1988, and retired from the civil service. However, the EDB requested Chan to continue in his duties as the chairman of its International Direct Investment Programme and as advisor to Corporate Development at EDB. In 1994, he became senior advisor to the EDB and deputy chairman of the EDB International Advisory Council (IAC). Chan officially retired at the end of 1995, but agreed to continue as the IAC's deputy chairman until 1999, and as chairman of the EDB Consulting Group. Chan also served for a period as a public relations manager at Ford Motor Company.

For his contributions, Chan was awarded the Public Administration Medal (Silver) (1969), Public Administration Medal (Gold) (1973) and the MERITORIOUS SERVICE MEDAL (1988).

Chan Heng Chee (1942–) Academic and diplomat. Chan Heng Chee was educated at Katong Convent and the University of Singapore where she obtained first class honours in political science. She later completed her master's degree in Southeast Asian studies at Cornell University and a

PhD in political science at the University of Singapore. After a brief career as a journalist, she joined the Department of Political Science of the University of Singapore as an assistant lecturer in 1967. She subsequently became a full professor in 1984. In the same year, she was appointed head of the Political Science Department, a position she held until 1987, when she was appointed founder-director of the Institute of Policy Studies. Her 1986 book, *A Sensation of Independence: A Political Biography of David Marshall*, was awarded the National Book Award, Non-Fiction Section.

In 1989, Chan was appointed Singapore's permanent representative to the United Nations and concurrently high commissioner to Canada and ambassador to Mexico. She then served as founding director of the Singapore International Foundation (1991–96) and as director of the Institute of Southeast Asian Studies (1993–96). In 1991, she was named Woman of the Year by *Her World* magazine. In 1996, she was appointed Singapore's ambassador to the United States, and in 2005, she was awarded the MERITORIOUS SERVICE MEDAL.

Chan Sek Keong (1937–) Judge. Chan Sek Keong was born in Ipoh, Perak, and received his early education at Anderson School, Ipoh. He read law at the University of Malaya in Singapore and graduated among the top three students in his class—the inaugural group of graduands from the Law Faculty in 1961. He was admitted to the Singapore Bar on 31 January 1962, and commenced practice at the firm of BRADDELL BROTHERS. In 1969, he joined the firm of SHOOK LIN & BOK, later becoming the firm's managing partner.

On 1 July 1986, Chan became Singapore's first judicial commissioner, and was appointed judge of the SUPREME COURT two years later. On 1 May 1992, Chan was appointed attorney-general of Singapore, and on 11 April 2006, he succeeded YONG PUNG HOW as CHIEF JUSTICE. Chan was the first graduate of the local law school to occupy both these positions.

In addition to his legal appointments, Chan has served as chairman of the Board of Legal Education; vice-president of the Singapore Academy of Law and a member of the PRESIDENTIAL COUNCIL FOR MINORITY RIGHTS and the Legal Service Commission. He was admitted into the DISTINGUISHED SERVICE ORDER in 1999.

Chan Soh Ha (1942–) Doctor. After obtaining his MBBS at Monash University, Australia, in 1966, and his PhD from Melbourne University in 1972, Chan Soh Ha returned to Singapore and began to research nose and throat cancer, the incidence of which was high among the Chinese, especially the Cantonese (Chan himself was the son of a Cantonese goldsmith). He discovered a Chinese genetic marker, the antigen HLA-B46, that is associated with the cancer.

Chan was awarded the 1992 NATIONAL SCIENCE AND TECHNOLOGY MEDAL for 'his discovery of new tissue type antigens and outstanding research in monoclonal antibodies'. He has also worked towards developing antibodies which fight specific diseases. He became a fellow of the Royal College of Pathologists of Australia in 1986, and a fellow of the Academy of Medicine, Singapore in 1989.

Chan Yoong Han (1974–) Musician. Chan Yoong Han studied in Australia and the United States. He has performed in music festivals worldwide, and as a solo violinist in concertos with the SINGAPORE SYMPHONY ORCHESTRA. A distinguished member of the orchestra's first violin section, he is also one of Singapore's most active practitioners of chamber music. In 1998–99, he curated, organized and performed in a series of eight solo chamber recitals entitled *Motifs and Murals*. Chan also won the YOUNG ARTIST AWARD (Music) in 1994.

Chandra Das, S. (1939–) Politician. S. Chandra Das was educated at Bartley Secondary School and the University of Singapore, where he graduated with an honours degree in economics (1965). He joined the Economic Development Board in 1965. He subsequently became managing director of Intraco Ltd (1977–86). In 1980, he entered politics on the People's Action Party ticket and was elected member of Parliament for Chong Boon.

From 1993 to 2005, Chandra Das served as chairman of the NTUC Fairprice Co-operative. He has also served as chairman, Nera Telecommunications; and director, NTUC Welcome Consumers Co-operative. In 2005, he was appointed chairman of the board of *Tamil Murasu*. For his services to the labour movement, Das was awarded the NTUC Friend of Labour Medal (1979), the NTUC Meritorious Service Award (1997), the Australian Business Council's President's Medal (2000) and the NTUC Distinguished Service (Star) (2005).

Changi The Changi area stretches from Kampong Kembangan to Telok Paku on the eastern extremity of Singapore island. Referred to as 'Tanjong Rusa' on the 1604 E.G. de Eredia map of Singapore, the area became known as Changi in the early 19th century (it was marked as 'Tanjong Changi' on an 1828 map of the island).

The origins of the name are unclear, although HENRY RIDLEY suggested that it was derived from the 'chengal' (also written and pronounced as 'chengai') tree (*Neobalanocarpus heimii*, also known as *Balanscorpus heimii* or *Balano scorpas*). Others have suggested that it may have been derived from the climbing shrub *Apama corymbosa* or '*changi ular*' (the Hopea Sangal),

Changi General Hospital: successor to the old Changi Hospital (left).

locally referred to as *chengal pasir* or *chengal mata kuching*. In the 19th century, the area was heavily forested and infested with tigers.

Changi Beach has become a popular recreational area. The district is also known for the historic CHANGI PRISON and CHANGI AIRPORT. Boats to PULAU UBIN and PULAU TEKONG depart from Changi.

Changi Airfield This military airfield was built by internees during the JAPANESE OCCUPATION on the site of what later became CHANGI AIRPORT, with work beginning in September 1943. The Japanese used prisoners-of-war to level the ground by carting soil from the hillsides at CHANGI to swampy areas near the sea. The first Japanese airplanes began to take off from the airfield's runway in late 1944.

In April 1946, the Royal Air Force (RAF) used Changi Airfield as a base for heavier planes, and switched the runway's operational direction from east–west to north–south. The airfield became the headquarters of the RAF in the Far East and was used for operations during the Malayan EMERGENCY and the Indonesian CONFRONTATION. After 1971, when the British military withdrew from Singapore, the airfield was turned over to the Singapore government, which transformed it and developed it for civilian use.

Changi Airport *See box.*

Changi General Hospital Changi General Hospital (CGH) was the result of a merger in March 1998 between Toa Payoh Hospital and the old Changi Hospital, located in what was originally a British military camp. Located on a site next to Simei housing estate and the Tampines new town, CGH has 23 wards with a total of 801 beds. It offers clinical specialities including neurosurgery,

Chan Sek Keong

Chan Yoong Han

Changi Airport The government decided in 1975 to build a new airport at Changi to replace the Paya Lebar Airport. A major land reclamation project ensured that the runways built could accommodate the needs of modern aviation, and that there would be sufficient land for the necessary facilities. The total area occupied by the airport is 1,300 ha. Of this area, 870 ha are reclaimed land. Changi Airport's Terminal One began operations in July 1981. The 80-metre-high control tower and the five-storey Terminal One building are located between two parallel runways. Terminal One has the capacity to handle 12 million passengers per year. By the mid-1980s, the number of passengers Terminal One handled was approaching capacity.

Terminal Two began operations in 1990, and essentially doubled the airport's capacity. In 1995, Terminal One was refurbished and its passenger

Departure display board in Terminal Two (above); the Changi Express *is a fortnightly publication of the Civil Aviation Authority of Singapore (right).*

capacity was increased to 16 million per year. By 2006, following further enhancements, the annual passenger capacity for Terminals One and Two were 21 million and 23 million respectively. In 2005, Changi Airport catered to over 32 million passengers in over 200,000 flights. With passenger arrivals expected to rise further, a third terminal is scheduled to begin operations in 2008. It costs $1.75 billion and will add a capacity of about 20 million passengers to Changi Airport, bringing the total capacity to over 60 million passengers a year. Another terminal, built specifically for the increasingly important low-cost carrier sector, the Budget Terminal, began operations in March 2006. It has a capacity of about 2.7 million passengers per year. Changi Airport is also a major airfreight centre. The Changi Airfreight Centre has nine terminals with the capacity to handle 3 million tons of freight. The centre is a free trade zone (FTZ).

Needs of passengers

Changi Airport caters to the varied needs of business travellers, tourists and transit passengers by providing a comprehensive range of facilities. It is known as one of the best airports for duty-free shopping, and has won

Branches of the Singapore Visitor Centre are located in Terminals One and Two. Managed by the Singapore Tourism Board, they offer information and assistance to travellers.

awards such as the Raven Fox Awards for Travel Retail in Asia/Pacific (eight times; 1998–2004, 2006). Passengers and visitors can transfer between terminals via the Skytrain. Transfers to and from the Budget Terminal are by bus. Changi Airport is linked to other parts of the island by two major expressways.

The East West line of the Mass Rapid Transit connects the airport (at Terminal Two) to the rail network.

Facilities for transit passengers
- Business centres, with services such as photocopying and faxing
- Internet kiosks
- Theme gardens
- Free two-hour bus tour of Singapore
- Shower facilities, fitness centres, swimming pool
- Movie theatres, video games
- Duty-free shopping

Response to change

Changi Airport has established itself as a major Asia-Pacific aviation hub. The two largest global airline alliances, Star Alliance and OneWorld, have chosen Changi as their Asian hub. Owned and operated by the Civil Aviation Authority of Singapore (CAAS), Changi consistently wins

international accolades. Changi Airport has won the Business Traveller 'Best Airport In The World' title 14 times in a row (1992–2005).

However, keen competition from regional airports such as Bangkok International Airport and the Kuala Lumpur International Airport have challenged Changi Airport's dominance

in the region. The introduction of ultra long-range aircraft, such as the Airbus A340-500, allowed airlines to fly non-stop from Singapore to North American destinations. However, these planes have also allowed airlines to bypass Singapore. CAAS is therefore upgrading existing facilities in Terminals One and Two in order for Changi Airport to remain competitive well into the future.

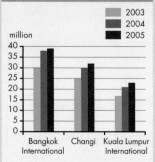

Changi Airport has upgraded its facilities to accommodate the large Airbus A380 double-decker plane.

PASSENGER MOVEMENT COMPARISON

	2003	2004	2005

(million)

40 35 30 25 20 15 10 5 0

Bangkok International — Changi — Kuala Lumpur International

Source: Airports Council International

Terminal One
In the mid-1970s, the first phase of construction began. It included the first terminal, control tower, runways and facilities such as hangars, workshops and catering kitchens. Terminal One became operational in July 1981.

Terminal Two
To cope with increased passenger movement, Terminal Two was opened in November 1990. The Skytrain was also constructed to transport passengers and visitors between terminals.

Budget Terminal
The no-frills Budget Terminal was opened in March 2006.

Terminal Three
Scheduled to open in 2008, the Terminal Three building will house a five-storey 'Green Wall' that features climbing plants and waterfalls. It will also have a uniquely designed roof with reflector panels that automatically adjust to allow optimal natural light in. When completed, the new terminal will boost the airport's annual passenger capacity to over 60 million.

Changi Prison: Dutch prisoners of war, 1945.

sports medicine, dermatology and rheumatology. The hospital provides outpatient obstetrics and gynaecology (O&G) services, with O&G specialists from SINGAPORE GENERAL HOSPITAL and KK WOMEN'S AND CHILDREN'S HOSPITAL running the clinic.

CGH runs support groups for asthma, breast cancer and diabetes patients. To help the poor and elderly, the hospital has set up HOPE (Holistic and Professional Eldercare), under which it helps to enhance community facilities and train volunteer carers. It has also started HomeCare Assist, a charity fund to help poor patients after their discharge from hospital.

Changi Prison A large area of the Changi district became a major prisoner-of-war (POW) settlement during WORLD WAR II. Approximately 50,000 British, Australian and other Allied military POWs and 3,500 civilians were imprisoned in Changi Prison (built as a civilian prison in 1936) and surrounding military buildings during the war. Not far from the prison was a boy scout camp (Purdy's Camp) which was requisitioned as a cemetery (informally known as Wing Loong Cemetery as it was located along Wing Loong Road). Inmates from the 18th Division Royal Engineers built a wooden lichgate at its entrance. Around 850 POWs died in Changi, but many more were shipped out as forced labour for the Japanese, and met their deaths working on such projects as the notorious Burma-Thailand railway.

After the Japanese surrender, the Commonwealth War Graves Commission sought to recover the remains of Allied soldiers buried in battle zones. The Changi graves were exhumed and the bodies reburied at Kranji War Cemetery in 1952 (*see* KRANJI WAR CEMETERY AND MEMORIAL). The lichgate was salvaged and relocated to ST GEORGE'S CHURCH at Tanglin. It remained at the Church grounds until 1971, when it was dismantled and shipped to the United Kingdom. A replica lichgate now stands outside the church.

During the war, a number of field chapels were set up within Changi. The most famous of these is the Changi Prison chapel, which became prominent after Chief Secretary Sir WILLIAM GOODE dedicated it in 1957. Soon afterwards, visiting ex-POWs and the relatives of Allied soldiers began the practice of placing plaques and cards at the chapel. Another notable chapel within Changi was St Luke's Chapel, at Block 151 Changi Camp, which contains the Changi Murals. In 1942, the chapel was founded on the ground floor of a building used as a POW hospital. One of the patients was STANLEY WARREN, a trained artist. During 1942–43, Stanley created five murals on the themes of The Nativity, Last Supper, Crucifixion, Ascension and St Luke in Prison. These murals survived the war and were later restored by the artist. Replicas of the Changi Chapel and Changi Murals can be viewed in the Changi Museum at Upper Changi Road North.

In post-war Singapore, Changi Prison was returned to its civilian role. However, for many Allied war veterans and their families, the prison was a landmark of the war in the Pacific and a symbolic link to the POWs who had been interned there.

In mid-2004 Changi Prison was demolished to make way for the new Changi Prison Complex (*see* PRISONS). Some items were sent to Australia and the United Kingdom for display in war museums. These included a cell door (with brass key and brass number plate), metal grilles, window frames and shutters from the prison clock tower, iron spikes from the top of the inner perimeter wall and 1-m pieces of the wall. A 180-m stretch of the wall, including the two turrets facing Upper Changi Road North, is to be preserved as part of the new prison complex, and the main prison entrance gate is to be relocated to this section of the wall. There are plans to have this surviving section of the old Changi Prison gazetted as a national monument.

Channel of Santa Barbara *See* NEW STRAIT.

Chao, Rita (1950–) Singer. Having performed with four-man group Super XX in 1965, Rita Chao signed to EMI in 1966. Her debut release was a Mandarin EP with the tracks 'Shake, Shake, Shake', 'I Know', 'Happy Happy Birthday Baby' and 'As Tears Go By' with instrumental backing from THE QUESTS. 'Pretty Flamingo', from her second EP, was also a hit. She began performing with SAKURA in 1967 as a double act, as both singers were doing well, and EMI felt that pairing them would give both their careers a boost. Chao continued recording until the early 1980s.

Chao Hick Tin (1942–) Lawyer and judge. The son of community leader Chao Yoke San, Chao Hick Tin was educated at Catholic High School and then at University College London, where he graduated with an LLB in 1965 and an LLM in 1966. He was called to the Bar at the Middle Temple in 1965, and was admitted to the Singapore Bar in 1971.

On Chao's return to Singapore, he joined the Legal Service as State Counsel (1967). In 1979, he was made Senior State Counsel and in 1982, head of Civil Division. In 1987, Chao was appointed judicial commissioner, and in 1990, judge of the SUPREME COURT. In 1989, he was made a judge of the COURT OF APPEAL. From 1993 to 1999, he served as president of the INDUSTRIAL ARBITRATION COURT. An expert in international law, Chao served as chairman of the ASEAN Law Association (Singapore) from 1987 to 1999. In 1999, he was appointed judge of appeal, and on 11 April 2006, he became attorney-general of Singapore. He was elected president of the ASEAN Law Association in 2003.

Chao Tzee Cheng (1934–2000) Forensic pathologist. Chao Tzee Cheng was born in Hong Kong, but his family later migrated to Singapore. He was educated at Catholic High School and Victoria School, but returned to Hong Kong to pursue a degree in medicine at Hong Kong University, where he obtained his MBBS in 1961. He then returned to Singapore. A serious road accident resulted in Chao's right arm being significantly weakened. However, determined to be a surgeon, Chao took up pathology.

During his career, Chao helped solve many criminal cases in Singapore. One involved a 58-year-old woman who had apparently drowned, and whose body was found in the sea off Pulau Ubin. Chao's autopsy revealed that the woman had been raped and killed, and that nine of her ribs had been broken, before her body was dumped into the water by the assailant, who was later brought to justice. Chao's forensic expertise was required after two disasters: the explosion of the SPYROS in 1978 at Jurong Shipyard; and the MI 185 SILKAIR CRASH in 1997. Chao was involved in the identification of victims who had been burned beyond recognition in both tragedies.

Chao came to be known as the 'Father of Forensic Pathology' in Singapore. He was also presented with three national awards, most notably the MERITORIOUS SERVICE MEDAL in 1995. He was the founding director of the Institute of Scientific and Forensic Medicine and continued to serve as special forensic adviser to that institute after his retirement. He also served as senior forensic pathologist with the Ministry of Health and clinical professor at the National University of Singapore. He served as master of the Academy of Medicine from 1992 to 1995.

Chao was a visiting professor at the Criminal Police College in Shenyang, China, and a fellow of the American College of Legal Medicine, as well as a fellow of the College of American Pathologists and a fellow of the Royal College of Pathologists in the United Kingdom. He was also a member of the American Board of Forensic Examiners.

On the academic front, Chao published no fewer than 140 papers in various medical

Changi Prison: Changi Chapel (top); security tower in the new Changi Prison Complex.

Chao Tzee Cheng

Rita Chao: her second EP included the hit 'Pretty Flamingo'.

Char kway teow

journals around the world. He co-authored a book, *Murder is My Business*, which featured some of the more interesting criminal cases with which he was associated. Professor Chao founded the Medico-Legal Society, which unified the medical and legal professions, and served as its president from 1985 until his death in February 2000. In 1995, he was awarded the MERITORIOUS SERVICE ORDER. He was posthumously made an Emeritus Consultant with Singapore General Hospital.

chap ji ki Form of gambling. The term *chap ji ki* literally means '12 units' in HOKKIEN. *Chap ji ki* is a type of lottery in which a gambler bets on a combination of two numbers from one to 12, in either a vertical or horizontal format. In the horizontal format, the gambler is paid providing that both numbers are picked (order is of no consequence). The payout for the vertical format, where one figure is placed above the other, is double—both figures, and their order of arrangement, must be correct. There is no limit to the size of the bet. Though the rules of *chap ji ki* changed over the years, winnings could be as high as 50 times the amount invested. For the vertical format, a bet of 50 cents could yield returns of up to $50.

Up until the 1960s, when gambling was banned in Singapore, *chap ji ki* was a popular game, especially amongst housewives. It was a well-organized operation in which specific runners would handle transactions according to their allocated areas. Bets, which were written on small pieces of paper, were rolled up and given to the runners. No names or phone numbers were necessary, as the parties knew each other by sight. The betting slip would typically contain such information as the 'chosen' numbers in the preferred format, and several noughts to denote monetary values. A big zero with a horizontal line through it would represent 50 cents, whilst a diagonal line signified $1. A smaller zero meant 10 cents.

Bets would be collected from around Singapore and brought to a central *chap ji ki* location, where the numbers would be drawn. The winning numbers would be publicized at noon each day, often written in coloured chalk on a wall. The syndicate's runners would present winners their money, minus a commission of 4 per cent.

Although *chap ji ki* has been banned in Singapore for over four decades, it has not been totally eradicated. The game continues to be played today, albeit covertly, with transactions taking place mostly in coffee shops and food centres. Commissions for runners have also risen to 5 per cent of winnings.

Leslie Charteris: The Saint Plays With Fire, 1952.

Chapman, Spencer (1907–1971) British military officer and teacher. Colonel Frederick ('Freddie') Spencer Chapman started out as an English teacher. He came under Kurt Hahn's influence while teaching at Gordonstoun School in Scotland.

Hahn, a German educator, was the founder not only of Gordonstoun, but also of the United World Colleges Movement, and the Outward Bound schools.

Chapman undertook expeditions to Antarctica (1930–32) and Tibet (1936–37), and soon gained a reputation for adventurousness. This led to his appointment as a special operations trainer in Scotland and Australia during WORLD WAR II. Later, he was appointed to 101 Special Training School (101 STS), located at the mouth of Singapore's Jurong River.

Arriving in Singapore in September 1941, Chapman was 101 STS' second- and then first-in-command. He helped train many of the men who joined DALFORCE, and many who formed the future MALAYAN PEOPLE'S ANTI-JAPANESE ARMY (MPAJA). Entering the jungle in January 1942, he remained there for the next three years. He made contact with the MPAJA, and helped train Chinese guerrillas. On Christmas Eve 1943, CHIN PENG reunited Chapman with Colonels John Davis and Richard Broome of FORCE 136. Chapman, alongside LIM BO SENG, Chin Peng and Lai Teck, was then party to the Bidor or Blantan Agreement of 31 December 1943–1 January 1944, which saw the MPAJA agree to assist the British in return for training and arms.

After the war Chapman, returned to teaching in South Africa and Germany. He was author of the book *The Jungle Is Neutral* (1948). Seemingly still afflicted by memories of the war, Chapman shot himself in 1971.

char kway teow Popular hawker dish. Singaporeans have a love-hate relationship with this dish—they love its taste, but worry about how unhealthy it is. Associated with the local TEOCHEWS, it is a platter of flat rice-flour noodles (*kway teow*), sometimes with yellow wheat noodles, wok-fried in savoury and sweet soya sauce—and traditionally, lard. Greens, bean sprouts, Chinese sausages and cockles are added. The dish has its roots in the Chaozhou region of China's Guangdong Province, and has evolved into different varieties, including Penang *char kway teow*.

Chartered Semiconductor Manufacturing
Largest wafer foundry in Singapore. Incorporated in 1987, the company is a key player in the local semiconductor industry, which accounted for 15 per cent of Singapore's manufacturing output and about 5,200 jobs in 2005. With one of the largest dedicated semiconductor foundries in the world and a 6.2 per cent market share in 2005, Chartered provides wafer manufacturing services and technologies to semiconductor suppliers and electronic systems manufacturers in the communications, computing and consumer markets. Its made-to-order chips are used in a wide range of applications including mobile phones, microprocessors, consumer elec-

Chartered Semiconductor Manufacturing

tronics, gaming devices and other telecom and networking equipment. To compete with the bigger foundries in Taiwan, Chartered entered into a joint development and reciprocal manufacturing agreement on advanced and next-generation nanotechnologies with IBM in November 2002. Since then, Infineon Technologies and Samsung Electronics have also joined the joint effort to build the industry's first Common Platform for nanotechnology. Chartered, IBM and Samsung are collaborating on the industry's first open platform aimed at providing customers early access to leading-edge semiconductor technologies and multi-sourcing flexibility to reduce risk. Through this collaboration, Chartered became the first foundry to have advanced silicon-in-insulator (SOI) technology in volume production, as part of a manufacturing agreement with IBM to produce microprocessors for Microsoft's Xbox 360 console.

Chartered operates a 300-mm fabrication facility and four 200-mm facilities in Singapore and has offices in nine locations around the world. The company, whose counter is a Straits Times Index component stock, was the first local company to be listed simultaneously on the Singapore Exchange and Nasdaq exchange in the United States (in 1999). It reported a $270.7 million net loss on a total turnover of $1.72 billion for financial year 2005. The group's biggest stakeholder is the investment arm of the Singapore government, TEMASEK HOLDINGS, who owns more than 60 per cent of the company's shares through its affiliates.

Charteris, Leslie (1907–1993) Author. Born Leslie Charles Bowyer-Yin at 5 Leonie Hill Road in Singapore's affluent District 9, Charteris was the son of a Chinese doctor, Yin Suat Chan, and his English wife, Lydia Bowyer. Charteris spent his formative years in Singapore, departing for the United Kingdom in 1919 at the age of 12.

Chateris was the creator of the fictitious character Simon Templar (a.k.a. The Saint). He documented the Saint's adventures in almost 100 books. These became the inspiration for 15 films, three television series, ten radio series and a comic strip that was syndicated around the world for more than a decade.

Singapore features only occasionally in

the Saint's many adventures. One notable example is a short story set in Malaya and Singapore in the 1950s, 'The Pluperfect Lady', from *The Saint Around the World* (1956). A wiser, older and more mature Saint seeks out a murdering wife, who finds poison useful in securing a swift divorce.

Chay Weng Yew (1928–2004) Sportsman. Chay Weng Yew was born in Kuala Lumpur, but moved to Singapore in the late 1940s. He ultimately chose weightlifting over his other passion—playing the piano—and was coached by the legendary Chua Tian Teck.

Chay was a national title-holder from 1948 to 1953 and a Champion of Champions in Singapore from 1950 to 1953. At the Helsinki Olympics (1952) he took sixth place—scoring a point—without the aid of a coach or an assistant. This achievement made him the fourth-best performer from Singapore at the Olympics, after TAN HOWE LIANG (silver, 1960), JING JUNHONG (fourth, 2000), and LI JIAWEI (fourth, 2004). His final total of 694 lbs enabled him to beat the national record held by Koh Eng Tong. The lift in the jerk was, in fact, the third-best in the competition. At the 1954 Asian Games in Manila, Chay claimed the bronze medal with 670 lbs. He retired in October 1955.

Cheang Hong Lim (1825–1893) Merchant and philanthropist. Cheang Hong Lim was the eldest of Cheang Sam Teo's four sons. He worked for his father's Chop Teang Wat shop on Telok Ayer Street before joining with two other major OPIUM farmers, TAN SENG POH and TAN YEOK NEE, in 1870 to form the Great Opium Syndicate. This would dominate Singapore's economy until its dissolution in 1880. Cheang was active in the HOKKIEN community and was appointed justice of the peace (1876). In the same year, he gave $3,000 to the colonial authorities to establish a green haven in the heart of Chinatown—now Hong Lim Green—and personally funded the building of the Singapore Chinese Recreation Club House there. (*See also* REVENUE FARMING).

Checkmates, The Popular music group. The Checkmates' initial line-up consisted of Reggie Verghese on lead guitar, Hans Hussein on rhythm guitar, Benny Chan on bass and Amir Samsoeddin on drums. Verghese left in early 1963 to join THE QUESTS as their lead guitarist, and was replaced by bassist Benny Chan. The band then recruited Lawrence Lee to play bass. The four debuted as a resident band at restaurant and nightclub The Cellar, which was located at Collyer Quay. The band then sought singers, and found one in Robert Song, known in his time as the 'Johnny Ray of Singapore'.

In late 1964, the Choy brothers, James and Siva, joined the group and provided

Chee Soon Juan: 2001 General Election rally.

back-up vocals as The Cyclones for Robert Song and the band. In 1965, the group moved on to play at the Golden Venus and approached Vernon Cornelius, previously from The Trailers and at that time singing with The Silver Strings, to front the band. Cornelius, however, was asked to join The Quests as their lead singer in April 1966, and The Checkmates found a replacement in Bryan Neale, a British serviceman who had his own band called The Easybeats. Signed to Philips in 1965, they released a total of four EPs, the first of which featured original instrumentals. Subsequent releases were originals of rhythm-and-blues, featuring vocals from The Cyclones and Bryan Neale. The band disbanded in 1968, and Siva Choy, guitar player Benny Chan and drummer Amir Samsoeddin continued their musical careers with other bands.

Chee Soon Juan (1962–) Politician. Chee Soo Juan was educated at the Anglo-Chinese School and at the University of Georgia in the United States where he obtained his master of science in physiological psychology and PhD in neurological psychology. In 1990, he returned to Singapore and joined the National University of Singapore (NUS) as a lecturer. In 1992, he joined the SINGAPORE DEMOCRATIC PARTY (SDP), contested and lost the by-election for Marine Parade group representation constituency. The following year, he was dismissed from NUS after accusations of improperly using research funds at his disposal. His refutation of the dismissal resulted in a defamation suit filed by his former head of department.

To protest against his dismissal, Chee went on a much-publicized hunger strike, which caused a falling out between him and then SDP secretary-general CHIAM SEE TONG, whom he ousted. Chee has been secretary-general of the SDP since 1993. In 1997, he stood again as SDP candidate in MacPherson constituency and lost. Together with J.B. JEYARETNAM, Chee founded the Open Singapore Centre in 2000 to push for greater openness and democracy in Singapore.

Chee's publications include *Dare to Change: An Alternative Vision for Singapore* (1994); *Singapore—My Home Too* (1995); *To Be Free: Stories from Asia's Struggle Against Oppression* (1998); *Your Future, My Faith,*

Our Freedom: A Democratic Blueprint for Singapore (2001); and *The Power of Courage: Effecting Political Change in Singapore Through Nonviolence* (2005).

Chee was jailed for eight days in March 2006 for contempt of court, after he implied, during a bankruptcy hearing, that the Singapore judiciary was not independent. He was not allowed to stand for the general election of 2006 because he was a bankrupt.

Chee Swee Lee (1955–) Sportswoman. The first Singaporean woman gold medallist in the Asian Games, Chee Swee Lee set a new track record by clocking 55.08 sec in the 400-m event at the seventh Asian Games in Tehran (1974). For this achievement she received the Sportswoman of the Year award from the Singapore National Olympic Council in the same year. She later entered the Singapore Sports Council Hall of Fame.

A protégé of coach Patrick Zehnder, she first raced at the age of ten. Within three years she was representing Singapore at the Southeast Asian Peninsular (SEAP) Games, winning a silver medal. She took an athletics scholarship at the University of Redlands in California, training with Vince Reel in February 1976. Focusing on the 800-metre event, she achieved an Olympic qualifying time of 2 min 7.4 sec—a national record. Shortly before the 1976 Olympics in Montreal, she sustained an injury to her Achilles tendon and was unable to complete her heat at the Olympic Stadium.

Surprising many, she returned to competition and continued her career for a further 14 years. In 1985, she set a college record for the women's 800-m event. The 'Golden Girl' finally retired from the track in 1990 at the age of 35.

Chek Jawa Inter-tidal zone on the northeastern tip of PULAU UBIN. Chek Jawa takes its name from a village that once existed in the area, and which was home to fishermen. In 1992, plans were announced to undertake a land reclamation project on Chek Jawa, and residents of the village were resettled in late 2000.

However, in December 2001, the Ministry of National Development decided

The Checkmates: EP recording with Bryan Neale.

Chee Swee Lee, 1973.

Chek Jawa: sponges exposed at low tide.

Chek Jawa: children with knobbly sea star (top); peacock anemone.

to defer the reclamation project for at least ten years after a campaign by local naturalists and scientists highlighted the ecological importance of the area. Staff of the RAFFLES MUSEUM OF BIODIVERSITY RESEARCH started providing guided walks on Chek Jawa for the public. The National Parks Board (NParks) was then given responsibility for managing visitors to Chek Jawa. In 2005, work began on developing boardwalks and other facilities for an increasing number of visitors.

Chek Jawa has multiple ecosystems: a natural coastal forest blankets the hill overlooking Chek Jawa; seagrass flourishes in the lagoon, providing shelter and food for snails, crabs and shrimps; the lagoon is ringed by natural sand bars; and further out to sea is a coral rubble area which is almost always submerged, except at extremely low tides.

chemicals sector The chemicals industry is the second-largest component of Singapore's MANUFACTURING SECTOR (the largest being eletronics). Output in 2004 amounted to $50.7 billion, a growth of 29 per cent on the 2003 figure. Of this, petroleum accounted for 60 per cent, followed by petrochemicals with 21 per cent and specialty industrial with 16 per cent.

During the late 1960s and early 1970s, three oil companies decided to set up facilities on scarcely populated islands off JURONG INDUSTRIAL ESTATE. Esso established a plant in Pulau Ayer Chawan; Singapore Refining Company was built on Pulau Merlimau; and Mobil Oil opted for Pulau Pesek. By 1980, petrochemicals had been identified by the government as a 'core cluster industry' that could provide significant economic growth. A regional petrochemical hub in Singapore was mooted, and in 1991, Jurong Town Corporation (JTC) was appointed as agent for the JURONG ISLAND project. Today, Jurong Island is home to companies such as ExxonMobil and DuPont.

Faced with competitive pressures in the refining segment, the government has sought to move to higher value-added activities in petrochemicals, specialty chemicals and pharmaceuticals. By 2010, the chemicals and life sciences are expected to contribute 35 per cent of Singapore's manufacturing output.

Louis H.Y. Chen

Chen, Bill (1936–) Scientist. Bill Chen was born in China, and received his undergraduate degree in electrical engineering at National Taiwan University in 1957. He then earned graduate degrees at the Georgia Institute of Technology (1960) and Stanford University (1965) in the United States. Chen worked with leading US research body Bell Labs from 1965 to 1991. In the 1980s, he served on the Technology Review Board in Taiwan, which played a major role in setting the direction for Taiwan's information-technology industry.

In 1991, Chen was seconded from

Georgette Chen: Self-Portrait *(1946).*

AT&T Bell Labs to Singapore's Institute of Microelectronics (IME)—a $30 million facility that concentrated on research in microelectronics systems, failure analysis and reliability, design of very large-scale integrated circuits and microelectronics processing technology—and was appointed that institute's first director. Chen retired from IME in 2000. He received the NATIONAL SCIENCE AND TECHNOLOGY MEDAL in 2001. From 2001 to 2004, Chen served as international consultant at the AGENCY FOR SCIENCE, TECHNOLOGY AND RESEARCH.

Chen, Georgette (1906–1993) Artist. Georgette Chen Liying was born in Paris, and was educated in Paris, New York and Shanghai. In 1930, she married Chinese foreign minister Eugene Chen, and travelled between Paris, Shanghai and Hong Kong, exhibiting her paintings at prestigious venues. House arrest by the Japanese in China ended in 1944 with the death of her husband, who had been her subject in a sustained portrait series (c.1932–44). Her seminal show at the Asia Institute in New York was sponsored by Nobel Prize laureate Pearl Buck. Chen relocated to Penang, then to Singapore in 1954, becoming a citizen in 1965. She took up teaching at the NANYANG ACADEMY OF FINE ARTS.

Chen was noted for applying post-Impressionist techniques to local still lifes, landscapes and portraits, in pursuit of a 'NANYANG STYLE'. She became known as '*Chendana*' (Malay for 'sandalwood') and 'Basket Chen' (due to her recurrent use of a basket motif in her work). In 1982, Chen became the first female CULTURAL MEDALLION recipient for ART.

Chen, Louis H.Y. (1940–) Academic. Louis Chen Hsiao Yun was educated at Catholic High School and St Joseph's Institution, and obtained a state scholarship to study mathematics at the University of Singapore, graduating with an honours degree in 1964. He then lectured in mathematics at

Singapore Polytechnic and the University of Singapore, while working towards his master's degree. In 1967, he was awarded a Fulbright-Hays Travel Grant and a Stanford assistantship, which allowed him to study at Stanford University. There, he studied probability theory under statistician Charles Stein. Chen received his PhD in 1971.

After a year of teaching in Canada, Chen returned to serve his undergraduate bond as a lecturer at the University of Singapore. He became professor in 1989, and head of the Department of Mathematics in 1996. In 2000, he became the founding director of the NATIONAL UNIVERSITY OF SINGAPORE's Institute for Mathematical Sciences. He also served for two years as head of the Department of Statistics and Applied Probability, from 2002.

Chen is known for having co-developed the 'Chen-Stein method of Poisson approximation'. This is a means of calculating probabilities of occurrences of 'dependent rare events'. The method has applications in computer science, molecular biology, statistical physics, epidemiology, reliability theory and game theory.

In 1989, Chen was elected fellow of the Institute of Mathematical Statistics. He was presented with the 1991 National Science and Technology Award. In 1997, he was the first Asian to be elected president of the Bernoulli Society for Mathematical Statistics and Probability. He was elected fellow of the Third World Academy of Sciences in 2000, and was awarded the title of Chevalier dans l'Ordre des Palmes Académiques by the French Government in 2005.

Chen Chong Swee: Village Scene *(1980).*

Chen Chong Swee (1910–1985) Artist and teacher. A graduate of Union High School in Swatow (present-day Shantou), China, and the Xinhua Arts Academy in Shanghai, Chen Chong Swee came to Singapore in 1931 and taught at Tuan Mong High School and Chung Cheng High School. In 1951, he was invited to head the Chinese Painting Department at the NANYANG ACADEMY OF FINE ARTS, remaining there until 1971. He also joined the historic Bali Field Trip of 1952 (*see* ART). A founder of both the Singapore Society of Chinese Artists (1935) and the Singapore Watercolour Society (1969), Chen was skilful in Chinese ink and watercolour. His paintings reflected the life and light of Southeast Asia, and he promoted the notion of a local style that was easily appreciated.

Chen is remembered as a teacher and avid watercolourist who was very much in touch with his students and his environment. His beliefs and principles inspired a key notion in the role of art in society, in Singapore. 'Art is a part of life and cannot exist independently from real life', Chen once said. 'Art is not just for self-gratification. Among the sane, there is neither literature written for oneself nor painting painted for oneself. We must bear in mind that the arts serve as a bridge of communication, in ideas and emotions, between people'.

Over the decades, Chen's art has captured the historical breadth of Singapore's changing environment, and has carried a mix of Chinese landscape painting and the Western ideal of draughtsmanship as a form of individual expression.

Chen Shucheng (1948–) Actor. Chen Shucheng appeared in his first Mandarin drama serial in 1971. He has since acted in more than 100 drama serials, playing roles ranging from a Teochew opera actor in *Xi Ban* (Painted Faces) (1987) to that of a retired forensic pathologist suffering from dementia in *Fayi X Dang'an* (Beyond The Axis of Truth) (2001). Chen has hosted variety and other programmes such as *Econ Nite* and *Ying Wanjing You Wanli Huanle Zhoumoye* (Weekend Delight) on Singapore television. He was honoured with the Special Achievement Award at MEDIACORP's Star Awards (2002).

Chen Su Lan (1885–1972) Doctor and philanthropist. Chen Su Lan was born in Foochow (present-day Fuzhou), China, and later moved to Singapore where he joined the first batch of students at the newly opened Government Medical College. A staunch Methodist, Chen is best remembered for campaigning against the use of opium. He opened the Anti-Opium Clinic in 1929 to treat poor, opium-addicted labourers. He also sat on the management committee of the Tan Tock Seng Hospital, the Central Midwives' Board and the Council of the King Edward VII College of

Chen Wen Hsi: Little Chicks in Autumn Grass.

Medicine. He founded the Alumni Association of that college, and was also made president of the Malayan Branch of the British Medical Association.

Chen was one of the founders—together with a group of leaders from the Methodist, Presbyterian and Anglican churches—of the Chinese Young Men's Christian Organisation in 1945. In 1947, Chen started the Chen Su Lan Trust which provided funding for Christian organizations such as the Scripture Union and for a children's home—the Chen Su Lan Methodist Children's Home.

Chen Wen Hsi (1906–1991) Artist and academic. Born in Baigong, Canton (present-day Guangdong), China, Chen Wen Hsi graduated from the Xinhua Academy of Fine Arts, Shanghai, in 1932. He taught at the South China College, Swatow (present-day Shantou) (1946–47). He then left China and travelled throughout Asia. He exhibited in Saigon (present-day Ho Chi Minh City), Bangkok and Malaya before settling in Singapore in the late 1940s.

Chen taught at Chinese High School (1949–68) and the NANYANG ACADEMY OF FINE ARTS (1951–59). A nature lover, he reared herons, ducks, gibbons and squirrels in order to closely observe these animals. He was sometimes referred to as the 'gibbon painter', and he was well known for his ink paintings of herons, in which he adapted cubist and abstract elements. He also incorporated cubistic principles into his oil paintings. Chen was one of the 'Big Four' artists (the others being LIU KANG, CHEN CHONG SWEE and CHEONG SOO PIENG), who made a trip to Bali in 1952 (*see* ART), and who were credited with catalysing the NANYANG STYLE of painting.

Chen exhibited extensively in Southeast Asia, Japan, the United Kingdom and Australia, and his works were collected by local museums as well as by the Oxford Museum in the UK, and the Cologne Museum in Germany. Chen was the recipient of the Public Service Star (1963) and was given an honorary doctorate by the National University of Singapore (1975). He also received a Gold Medal from the National Museum of History, Taipei (1980), and the first ASEAN Cultural and Communication Award in 1987, as well as,

posthumously, the MERITORIOUS SERVICE MEDAL in 1992. His former residence-cum-studio at 7 Kingsmead Road has been declared a heritage site.

Chen Zhicai, Edmund (1962–) Actor. Originally a graphic designer, Edmund Chen Zhicai made his first appearance on screen in 1986, playing the lead role in *Yuguo Qingtian* (Sunshine After The Rain). He went on to act in more than 40 television drama serials and telemovies. Chen has also hosted programmes ranging from documentaries (such as *Code Red* in 1997); variety shows (such as the President's Star Charity, 2001); and local coverage of the 1996 Atlanta Olympics.

Chen made his big-screen debut in *Yellow Wedding*, a Canadian art-house film that premiered at the Montreal World Film Festival in 1998. The following year saw Chen on the theatrical stage, with his debut in *Private Parts* (1999). He also appeared in *Xiang Zuozou, Xiang Youzou* (Turn Left, Turn Right) (2003), acting alongside Takeshi Kaneshiro and Gigi Leung. Chen has been consistently voted as one of the Top 10 Most Popular Male Artistes at MEDIACORP's Star Awards.

Cheng, Edmund (1953–) Businessman. Born in Hong Kong, Edmund Cheng Wai Wing was educated at Northwestern University, graduating with a bachelor degree in civil engineering, and Carnegie Mellon University where he gained a master's degree in architecture. He came to Singapore in 1979 to work for his family's WING TAI HOLDINGS. At that company, he rose to become deputy chairman and managing director. Cheng started the property arm of Wing Tai Holdings in 1987.

Cheng has served as chairman of The Arts House and the Singapore Tourism Board (1992–2001); DesignSingapore (2003–), National Arts Council (2005–), and The Esplanade Co Ltd. In 2002, he was presented with the Outstanding Contribution to Tourism Award.

Cheng, Vincent (1947–) Vincent Cheng Kim Chuan was a former theology student. In 1983, he became secretary of the Catholic Church's Justice and Peace Commission in Singapore. From June 1982 to June 1983, Cheng coordinated volunteers and their activities at a Catholic centre for foreign workers.

In 1987, Cheng and 21 other people were arrested under the INTERNAL SECURITY ACT for alleged involvement in a MARXIST CONSPIRACY to overthrow the Singapore government. The government issued a statement naming Cheng and former student leader, TAN WAH PIOW, as the masterminds and ringleaders of this plot.

Cheng was released in 1990, but was not allowed to issue public statements, publish or travel abroad without the INTERNAL

Chen Shucheng

Chen Su Lan

Edmund Chen Zhicai

Edmund Cheng

Cheng Tong Fatt

Colin Cheong: Tangerine *(1997).*

Chesed-El Synagogue

SECURITY DEPARTMENT's consent until July 1995, when all restrictions were removed.

Cheng Ho, Admiral *See* ZHENG HE, ADMIRAL.

Cheng Tong Fatt (1929–) Civil servant and diplomat. Cheng Tong Fatt was educated at the University of Glasgow, where he obtained a degree in veterinary medicine. He joined the Primary Production Department as senior primary production officer and in 1957, was promoted to veterinary surgeon. By 1967, he was director of the Primary Production Department. In 1970, he was promoted to deputy secretary of the Ministry of National Development, then acting permanent secretary in 1971 and permanent secretary in 1972. Cheng was awarded the MERITORIOUS SERVICE MEDAL IN 1970. He became permanent secretary of the Ministry of Culture in 1979. Cheng also served for a time as deputy chairman of the SINGAPORE BROADCASTING CORPORATION (SBC), and is credited with having started the SBC's Chinese Drama Division (*see* TELEVISION BROADCASTING).

In 1991, Cheng was appointed Singapore's first ambassador to China (after having served as ambassador to Japan), and ambassador-at-large in 1998.

Cheng Wai Keung (1950–) Businessman. Born in Hong Kong, Cheng Wai Keung was educated at Indiana University where he graduated with a bachelor of science degree (1971) and at the University of Chicago, where he obtained a master's degree in business administration (1973). Shortly thereafter, Cheng arrived in Singapore and was instructed by his father to look after the family's garment-manufacturing business, Wing Tai.

Under Cheng's younger brother Edmund Cheng, Wing Tai entered the property market in 1987 and has since become one of the strongest developers, with over 70 projects in the region. In the course of his career, Cheng has been active in public service, having served as chairman of Power Seraya (1995–2000), MediaCorp (1997–2002) and Media Corporation of Singapore Pte Ltd (1999–2002). He was appointed chairman and managing director of WING TAI HOLDINGS (1994–); chairman of Neptune Orient Lines (2002–) and Raffles Holdings (2001–); and vice-chairman of Singapore-Suzhou Township Development Pte Ltd. In recognition of his services, Cheng was awarded the Public Service Star (BBM) in 1987 and the Public Service Star (Bar) (BBM-Lintang) in 1997 by the government of Singapore. He was also appointed justice of the peace in 2000.

Cheong, Colin (1965–) Author. Colin Cheong Wye Mun majored in English literature and linguistics at the National University of Singapore. He worked as a journalist before becoming a junior college teacher. Cheong's partly autobiographical first novel, *The Stolen Child* (1989), which follows its protagonist from boyhood to adolescence, took eight years to write. Cheong's *Poets, Priests and Prostitutes: A Rock Fairytale* (1990) is divided into 24 'hourly' chapters. In Cheong's work, the youthful yearning for love and happiness is met with unrequited love or tragic death, and marriage denied as a possible source of happiness. His writing is characterized by an interest in form and technique, uncluttered prose and, despite occasional sentimentality, poetic resonance.

The 18 short stories in *Life Cycle of Homosapiens, Male* (1992) provide a narrative chronology of man's life. The novella *seventeen* (1996) uses a 'roll' of 36 plus two chapter frames to depict the tragedy of young love. *Tangerine* (1997), which won the 1996 Singapore Literature Prize for Fiction, is set in 1993 Vietnam. *The Man in the Cupboard* (1999), which won a Merit Award in the 1998 Singapore Literature Prize for Fiction, is the confessional monologue of Timid Tim who is planning to kill his wife. It was adapted for television in 2001. *Void Decks and Other Empty Places* (1996), Cheong's only work of poetry, secured a Commendation Award in the 1995 Singapore Literature Prize for Poetry.

Cheong Siew Keong (1925–) Engineer. Born in Malaya, Cheong Siew Keong was educated at the Anglo-Chinese School in Kuala Kubu Bahru; St Joseph's Institution in Kuala Lumpur; and the University of Hong Kong, where he graduated with a bachelor of science degree in civil engineering (1950). He later obtained a Higher National Certificate in electrical engineering from Stafford Technical College in the United Kingdom (1952).

From 1953 to 1968, Cheong worked in the London firm, English Electric Company, as technical representative to Southeast Asia. In 1969, he joined the General Electric Company of Malaysia Sdn Bhd as engineering director, and was concurrently engineering director of the General Electric Company of Singapore. There, Cheong became general manager (1973–82) and

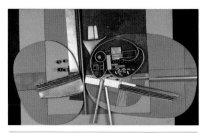

Cheong Soo Pieng: Metal Relief Triptych *(1969).*

deputy chairman (1982–83).

Cheong has been active in public service. He served as chairman of the National University of Singapore Council (1992–2000); member of the Council of Presidential Advisers (1991–); chairman of the Education Service Commission (1991–98); and member of the Land Transport Authority (1995–).

Cheong Soo Pieng (1917–1983) Born in Amoy (present-day Xiamen), China, and educated at the Amoy Academy of Art, and the Xinhua Academy of Fine Arts in Shanghai, Cheong Soo Pieng arrived in Singapore in 1946. He taught at the NANYANG ACADEMY OF FINE ARTS from 1947 until 1961. In 1952, he took part in the historic Bali Field Trip, which also involved artists such as LIU KANG, CHEN CHONG SWEE and CHEN WEN HSI (*see* ART).

In 1962, the Singapore government awarded Cheong the MERITORIOUS SERVICE MEDAL. Cheong then ventured to Europe, developing new avenues in his painting, and holding art exhibitions in London, Oxford and Munich. He returned to Singapore and opened his Zion Road Studio in 1964, but continued to exhibit in Asia and Australia.

Cheong began his practice using the traditional medium of Chinese ink, depicting scenes of life in Singapore and the surrounding region. For a time, he experimented with oil on canvas, creating a series of cubist and abstract works.

Cheong had a unique ability to register the tropical environment regardless of his subject matter. His art drew on local light and its visual registry. Within his oeuvre are clean, distinct works of Balinese women, indigenous communities, and Balinese and other Southeast Asian landscapes. Among some of his more famous oil paintings are abstract works of thick and tactile surfaces, geometric contemplations and spatial investigations.

Chesed-El Synagogue This synagogue was built in 1905 on Oxley Rise by Sir MANASSEH MEYER—one of the first Jewish businessmen to move to Singapore (*see* JEWS). By the late 1870s, Singapore's Jewish community, which had increased to more than 170 people, had established its own synagogue, MAGHAIN ABOTH SYNAGOGUE, on Waterloo Street. After a dispute with a fellow member of Maghain Aboth, Meyer decided to build his own private syna-

gogue, the Chesed-El, on the grounds of his palatial residence on Oxley Rise.

Designed by R.A.J. BIDWELL of the architectural firm SWAN & MACLAREN, the Chesed-El Synagogue was built in the Renaissance Palladian style, its simple white exterior contrasting with the surrounding tropical greenery. On the interior gallery deck, wrought iron railings incorporate the initials 'M M'—Manasseh Meyer. Chesed-El Synagogue was gazetted as a national monument in December 1998.

Cheshire Home Residential facility for the disabled. Leonard Cheshire—a decorated World War II Royal Air Force pilot and later Lord Cheshire of Woodhall—established the first Cheshire Home in 1948 when he turned over his family home in Hampshire, United Kingdom for the care of the disabled. He opened Singapore Cheshire Home in 1956. It provides care, rehabilitation and support services for its disabled adult residents.

Chettiars See NATTUKOTTAI CHETTIARS.

Chew, Andrew (1929–) Civil servant. Born in Sarawak, Andrew Chew Guan Khuan moved to Singapore in the 1930s and studied at St Andrew's School. Later, he entered the University of Malaya, where he graduated with an MBBS in 1955. He joined the MINISTRY OF HEALTH as a medical officer in 1957 and, two years later, was awarded a scholarship that enabled him to obtain his Membership of the Royal College of Physicians in London.

Within the Ministry of Health, Chew served as senior registrar (1962), senior consultant (1968), director of Medical Services (1977) and permanent secretary (1978). In 1985, he was appointed head of the Singapore Civil Service. He retired from the Administrative Service on 11 October 1994.

Chew was chairman of the Central Provident Fund (1994–98), the Public Service Commission (1998–); the Board of Governors of the Institute of Defence and Strategic Studies (1976–). He was also a member of the Presidential Council for Minority Rights (1994–) and the Legal Service Commission (1998–). For his public service, Chew was awarded the MERITORIOUS SERVICE MEDAL (1992) and was admitted into the DISTINGUISHED SERVICE ORDER (2002).

Chew, Elim (1965–) Businesswoman. Elim Chew was educated at Fairfield Methodist Girls' School before leaving school after Secondary 4, and studied hairdressing in London. With her sister Sulim, Elim founded 77th Street—a retail outlet specializing in street-wear for teenagers—in 1988 in Far East Plaza on Scotts Road. The company expanded to 15 outlets around Singapore and five joint-venture outlets in Malaysia. Chew's other ventures include 77th Street

Chew Chor Meng: as Mr Kiasu, centre.

Plaza, a 400,000 sq-ft shopping complex at Xidan Cultural Central in Beijing, which was established in 2004, and a spa and skincare centre in Shenzhen. Chew is also involved in various youth organizations in Singapore. She founded the Young Entrepreneur Mastery (TYEM), to encourage entrepreneurial activities among youths.

Chew's many accolades for entrepreneurship include Most Promising Woman Entrepreneur, awarded by the Association of Small & Medium Enterprises (2001); the Mont Blanc Businesswomen Award (2002); *Her World* magazine's Young Woman Achiever Award (2003); and the Leadership and Mentoring Award from Research Communications International (2003).

Chew Choo Keng (Khong Guan) (1916–2001) Merchant. Born in Fujian, China, Chew Choo Keng arrived in Singapore in 1937 and started working at TAN KAH KEE's biscuit factory. In 1947, he established the KHONG GUAN BISCUIT FACTORY, which became profitable almost immediately. Chew soon became known as the 'Biscuit King'. Chew also invested in businesses related to the production of biscuits, such as tin mining and flour milling. He was survived by 23 children from five wives.

Chew Chor Meng (1968–) Actor. Chew Chor Meng started his acting career after emerging first in the male category of the television programme *Star Search* in 1990, and played a swordsman in his first drama serial *Zuihou yige Daxia* (The Last Swordsman) (1991). He made his transition to comedy playing an opportunistic property agent—Lobang King—in the sitcom *Don't Worry, Be Happy* (1996).

Chew has consistently been voted as one of the Top 10 Most Popular Male Artistes since the list's inception in 1994. He was voted the Most Popular MEDIACORP Male Artiste in Malaysia in 2000. That same year, he won the Best Actor Award in MediaCorp's Star Awards 2000, for his performance in *Qiongyuan*

Kafei Xiang (Hainan Kopi Tales) (2000). Chew appeared in his first English sitcoms, *Mr Kiasu I and II*, in 2001 and 2002.

As well as acting, Chew has also hosted several variety programmes, including large-scale televised New Year events.

Chew Hock Leong (1897–1967) Banker. Chew Hock Leong was the son of Chew Boon Lay. He was educated at Raffles Institution, and joined the Chinese Commercial Bank in 1919. When the bank merged with Ho Hong Bank and Oversea-Chinese Bank to form the OVERSEA-CHINESE BANKING CORPORATION (OCBC), he became its Manager. He retired from banking in 1953. In 1956, Chew was appointed a member of the Public Service Commission and in the following year, its chairman. He stepped down from that position in 1959.

Chew Swee Kee (1918–1985) Politician. Born in Gopeng, Perak, Chew Swee Kee was educated at Chung Wah Chinese School and the Anglo-Chinese School, both in Kampar. He started working life in the Chinese Secretariat in Singapore and later worked as a Chinese interpreter in the Police Courts. After World War II, Chew became a businessman, practising as an accountant. He was elected to the Legislative Assembly in 1955 as assemblyman for Whampoa and was minister of education in the DAVID MARSHALL (and subsequently LIM YEW HOCK) governments. Chew was an important member of the LABOUR FRONT but was brought into disrepute when it was revealed in the Assembly in February 1959 that he had accepted a 'political donation' totalling $700,000. The money had been transferred from New York to his account and was meant as a political gift to the Labour Front for the fight against subversion and communism. He died of a heart attack in December 1985.

chewing gum A ban on chewing gum imports was first mooted in Cabinet in 1983 as the Ministry of National Development struggled to deal with van-

Andrew Chew

Elim Chew

Chewing gum: prices were slashed to clear stocks before the ban.

Steve Chia: after 2001 general election.

Chia Cheong Fook

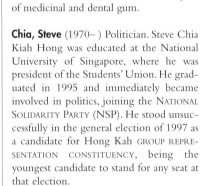

Chia Thye Poh: left, with Lim Chin Siong in 1962.

dals who disposed of spent gum in public areas. In 1987, when the multi-billion dollar Mass Rapid Transit (MRT) system began operations, vandals were reportedly sticking chewing gum on MRT train door sensors, thus preventing the door from functioning properly and causing disruption to train services. In January 1992, Prime Minister GOH CHOK TONG decided to impose a ban. The Control of Manufacture Act was amended to restrict the import of chewing gum into Singapore. As Singapore does not manufacture chewing gum, the sale of chewing gum came to a complete halt shortly after the ban. There is no ban on the chewing of gum, only on its import and sale. In 2004, as a result of the US–Singapore Free Trade Agreement, the rules were relaxed to allow for the import of medicinal and dental gum.

Chia, Steve (1970–) Politician. Steve Chia Kiah Hong was educated at the National University of Singapore, where he was president of the Students' Union. He graduated in 1995 and immediately became involved in politics, joining the NATIONAL SOLIDARITY PARTY (NSP). He stood unsuccessfully in the general election of 1997 as a candidate for Hong Kah GROUP REPRESENTATION CONSTITUENCY, being the youngest candidate to stand for any seat at that election.

During the 2001 general election, Chia stood against long-time People's Action Party incumbent Low Seow Chay in Choa Chu Kang constituency, and secured 34.6 per cent of the vote, making him the most successful of the unsuccessful candidates at that election. On this basis, he was appointed a NON-CONSTITUENCY MEMBER OF PARLIAMENT.

In December 2003, Chia resigned from his position in the NSP after reports appeared in the local media about his having photographed his maid scantily clad, and having had himself photographed in the nude. However, these allegations did not result in any criminal conviction, and in July 2005, Chia was re-elected to his former post as secretary-general of the NSP. In the general election of 2006, Chia again contested and lost Choa Chu Kang constituency, after which he kept to his pre-election promise of leaving politics in the event of his loss.

Chia Ann Siang (1832–1892) Merchant. Born in Malacca, the son of Chia Poh Eng, Chia Ann Siang joined the firm of BOUSTEAD & COMPANY at the age of 16. He was connected with the firm for 42 years, and built up a vast fortune. He was also a partner in Geok Teat & Co (established in 1863) alongside Tay Geok Teat, Tan Kim Tian and Tan Sam Chie. The firm dealt in warehousing and also acted as commission agents. Ann Siang Hill in CHINATOWN is named after him.

Chia Cheong Fook (1925–) Civil servant and diplomat. Chia Cheong Fook was educated at the Anglo-Chinese School and the University of Malaya where he graduated with a diploma in social studies. In 1954, he joined the Social Welfare Department where he served until 1962. He subsequently became: deputy secretary, Ministry of Labour; director of manpower, Ministry of Defence; permanent secretary, Ministry of Social Affairs; and permanent secretary, Ministry of Foreign Affairs. From 1987 to 1990, Chia was Singapore's high commissioner to New Zealand. He retired from the diplomatic service in 1990 and served as chairman of the Institute of Southeast Asian Studies until October 2002. Chia was awarded the Public Administration Medal (Silver) in 1971.

Chia Choo Suan (dates unknown) Actress and playwright. Chia Choo Suan was one of the most popular performers in Teochew radio plays broadcast by REDIFFUSION in the 1970s, and in Mandarin radio plays broadcast by Radio Television Singapura (later SINGAPORE BROADCASTING CORPORATION) during the 1980s. She has written more than 60 radio plays.

Since joining the I-Lien Drama Society in 1983, Chia has played the lead roles in that society's productions. She played Miranda in *The Tempest* (1983)—the first Shakespeare production in Mandarin. She played the title role in *Princess Jasmine* (1984)—a play which won the Best Production Award at the Drama Festival organized by the Ministry of Community Development. Other successes included Chia's performances in *Hu Fu* (Tiger Tally) (1985), *Yuan Ye* (Wilderness) (1986), *Wang Shao Jun* (Consort of Peace) (1987), *He Zhu Xin Pei* (The New Marriage of He Zhu) and *Qi Shi Er Jia Fang Ke* (The 72 Tenants) (1998). Chia also performed at the Masan International Theatre Festival in Korea in 2002 and 2004.

Chia Teck Leng (1959–) While employed as a finance manager at ASIA-PACIFIC BREWERIES, Chia Teck Leng embezzled $117 million from his company. According to the Commercial Affairs Department, this was largest sum ever misappropriated by an individual in Singapore. Chia was arrested in 2003 and sentenced to 42 years in prison.

Chia was an addicted gambler. At one time, he had apparently ranked second-highest on the list of the world's casino-goers, betting away some $62 million as a guest of casinos in the United Kingdom, Australia and elsewhere. He also forged documents that enabled him to secure loans from four European and Japanese banks—supposedly to his company—which he then used to finance his gambling habit.

In 2005, while still in prison, Chia wrote a paper analysing casino operations. This paper was made public by the authorities during a debate over Singapore's plan to open casinos at two new INTEGRATED RESORTS.

Chia Thye Poh (1933–) Politician. Chia Thye Poh was educated at the Chinese High School and Nanyang University where he graduated with a physics degree in 1961. At university, he served as vice-chairman of the student union and upon graduation, became a council member of the Guild of Graduates. He taught at Chung Cheng High School for a short time before returning to Nanyang University as a graduate assistant in the Physics Department. During this period, he was preparing to further his studies abroad. He joined the BARISAN SOSIALIS and stood as a candidate for Jurong constituency during the GENERAL ELECTION (1963), defeating Ong Soo Chuan (People's Action Party), Soh U Loh (United People's Party) and Wong Tuck Leong (Singapore Alliance Party).

In 1966, after the Barisan Sosialis decided to boycott Parliament, Chia resigned from Parliament. He was later detained under the INTERNAL SECURITY ACT for his alleged pro-communist activities. He was held for 23 years before being released onto Sentosa under a restriction order on 17 May 1989. He was unconditionally released in 1992, after which he decided to continue his studies for a PhD in the Netherlands. Chia Thye Poh was Singapore's longest-serving political detainee.

Chiam See Tong (1935–) Teacher and politician. Chiam See Tong was educated at the Anglo-Chinese School and then at Canterbury and Victoria Universities in

Chiam See Tong

New Zealand. Chiam first worked as a school teacher—first in Mahmud Secondary School in Pahang, and then at Cedar Girls' Secondary School—but subsequently studied for a law degree and was called to the Bar at the Inner Temple in 1974. From 1976 to 2002, he practised under the firm of Chiam & Co.

He came to national prominence during the general election of 1976 when he stood as an independent candidate against Cabinet minister LIM KIM SAN in Cairnhill constituency. In 1979, he stood again as an independent in Potong Pasir constituency, and lost to another cabinet minister, HOWE YOON CHONG. In 1980, he founded the SINGAPORE DEMOCRATIC PARTY (SDP) but lost to Howe again in the 1980 general election. Chiam scored the first of five successive election victories in the general election of 1984 in Potong Pasir, defeating MAH BOW TAN of the People's Action Party. In 1993, he was ousted from the leadership of the SDP. He eventually joined the SINGAPORE PEOPLE'S PARTY (SPP). In 1997, he was re-elected as Potong Pasir's MP on the SPP ticket. Chiam retained this seat with an increased majority at the 2006 general election.

Chiang Hai Ding (1938–) Academic, banker and diplomat. Born in Johor, Chiang Hai Ding came to Singapore as a 17-year old to study economics and Malay studies at the University of Malaya. He graduated with a first-cass honours degree in history (1959) instead, and won a scholarship to pursue a PhD at the Australian National University (1963). On his return from Australia, he joined the University of Singapore's Department of History and was introduced by Professor WONG LIN KEN to some PEOPLE'S ACTION PARTY (PAP) leaders, including LEE KUAN YEW and GOH KENG SWEE. After first declining to contest the 1968 general election, he changed his mind following the RACE RIOTS of 13 May 1969. Chiang won a seat in Ulu Pandan constituency on the PAP ticket in a by-election, and served as a member of Parliament until 1984.

In 1971, Chiang resigned from his position at the university to join the First National City Bank (later Citibank) as an economist. Soon afterwards he was appointed Singapore's high commissioner to Malaysia. He returned to Citibank as manager in 1973 after returning from Malaysia. From 1978 to 1982, he served as Singapore's ambassador to Germany. Thereafter, his diplomatic postings included the Vatican, the European Union, the Soviet Union and Egypt.

In 1994, Chiang retired from the diplomatic service and was appointed senior research fellow at the Institute of Southeast Asian Studies. He joined Neptune Orient Lines in 1995 as economic adviser to the chief executive officer,

Chicken rice

retiring in 2002. In 2001 he became part-time director of the Singapore Action Group of Elders Counselling Centre. In the same year, he obtained a graduate diploma in gerontology from Simon Fraser University, Canada. His younger brother is the playwright Michael Chiang.

chicken rice Popular hawker dish. Widely regarded as Singapore's national dish, chicken rice is found in virtually all HAWKER CENTRES and FOOD COURTS. It was made popular in the Beach Road area when the HAINANESE began setting up chicken rice stalls there in the early 1900s.

Chicken rice originated in Hainan, China, as a simple dish of boiled rice, topped with pieces of boiled chicken, gizzards, liver, intestines and slices of cucumber and tomato. But the local Hainanese have given it a uniquely Singaporean twist. They fry uncooked rice in flavoured oils and then cook it in chicken stock laced with garlic and *pandan* (pandanus). The whole chicken is boiled in stock and then dunked into cold water or ice. This gelatinizes the oils (while leaving the inside tenderly warm) and smoothes the skin. It is served with a tangy chilli sauce made of ground chilli, *calamansi* lime and garlic. Sometimes a dark soy and ground ginger dip accompany it. Another version of chicken rice commonly served today uses roasted—rather than boiled—chicken.

chief justice Highest judicial office in Singapore. The chief justice is appointed by the PRESIDENT on the advice of the PRIME MINISTER. He presides over the COURT OF APPEAL as its president, and is also responsible for the overall running of the judicial system. The chief justice also advises the prime minister on who should be appointed as judges to the SUPREME COURT. Beyond the courtroom, the chief justice is president of the Singapore Academy of Law, president of the Legal Service Commission and chairman of the PRESIDENTIAL COUNCIL FOR MINORITY RIGHTS.

The post of chief justice was first created in 1867, when the Court of Judicature of Prince of Wales' Island, Malacca and Singapore was transformed into the Straits Settlements Supreme Court. The first chief justice of the STRAITS

SETTLEMENTS was Sir PETER MAXWELL. When the Straits Settlements was abolished in 1946, Singapore was administered as a separate Crown Colony, and continued to have its own chief justice.

In 1963, Singapore became part of Malaysia, and within the federation, the top judicial post was that of Lord President. There were three chief justices, one each for Malaya, Singapore and Borneo. WEE CHONG JIN was Singapore's first chief justice following SEPARATION in 1965 (*see* table).

Chiang Hai Ding

chief of defence force Highest-ranking military officer and commander of the SINGAPORE ARMED FORCES (SAF). The chief of defence force (CDF) is also the senior military adviser to the minister of defence. The chief of army, chief of air force and chief of navy all answer directly to the chief of defence force (CDF), a lieutenant-general (three star general).

The CDF, assisted by the Joint Staff and service chiefs, plays a pivotal role in the integration of the different services for operations. He ensures that the SAF is adequately prepared to fulfill its peacetime and wartime duties.

The post of CDF was created to replace its predecessor—chief of the general staff (CGS)—after restructuring in 1990, due to the growth of the navy and air force. Singapore's first CDF is WINSTON CHOO.

CHIJMES The Convent of the Holy Infant Jesus (CHIJ) was founded in 1854 by Father JEAN-MARIE BEUREL who recruited the Infant Jesus Sisters of St Maur, an order of aristocratic, well-educated and socially conscious French nuns, to run it. The 'Town Convent' evolved from a lone bungalow (known as Caldwell House and designed by GEORGE D. COLEMAN) on Victoria Street into an entire city block, the high walls embracing several school buildings, an orphanage and an Anglo-French Gothic-style chapel, once considered Singapore's most beautiful religious building. The

CHIEF JUSTICES: STRAITS SETTLEMENTS AND SINGAPORE	
1866–71	Sir Peter Benson Maxwell
1872–86	Sir Thomas Sidgreaves
1886–89	Sir Theodore Ford
1890–92	Sir Edward Loughlin O'Malley
1893	Sir John Winfield Bonser
1893–1906	Sir William Henry Lionel Cox
1906–14	Sir William Hyndman Jones
1914–20	Sir John Alexander Strachey Bucknill
1921–25	Sir Walter Sydney Shaw
1925–33	Sir James William Murison
1933–36	Sir Walter Clarence Huggard
1936–46	Sir Percy Alexander McElwaine
1946–55	Sir Charles Murray Murray-Aynsley (first chief justice of the Colony of Singapore)
1955–58	Sir John Whyatt
1959–63	Sir Alan Rose (first chief justice of the State of Singapore)
1963–90	Wee Chong Jin (first chief justice of the Republic of Singapore)
1990–2006	Yong Pung How
2006–	Chan Sek Keong

CHIJMES: the entrance on Victoria Street.

Chilli (top) and black pepper crabs

Chin Peng: autobiography My Side of History (2003).

chapel and its flanking Gothic linkways were designed by Charles Benedict Nain and consecrated in 1904. Each of the 648 capitals on the columns in the ensemble was given a unique depiction of tropical birds and plants. The stained glass windows were produced in Bruges, Belgium; the wooden pews and other furniture came from France. In 1983 the school relocated to Toa Payoh and the block was divided into two, half becoming the headquarters of the Mass Rapid Transit Authority and the remaining buildings, including the chapel, revived as CHIJMES, a retail and restaurant complex. The chapel was restored with great attention to detail and renamed Chijmes Hall. In a nod to history, the doorway where abandoned babies were once left was commemorated as the Gate of Good Hope. The chapel and Caldwell House were gazetted as national monuments in October 1990. In 2002, UNESCO awarded CHIJMES the Asia-Pacific Heritage Award for Culture Heritage Conservation (Merit Award) for the restoration project.

See also CONVENT OF THE HOLY INFANT JESUS.

chilli and black pepper crabs Popular dish. In the past, crabs were simply boiled, steamed or grilled at the old row of seafood eateries along Upper East Coast Road. In the mid-1950s, the cooks at Palm Beach Restaurant tossed the steamed crabs in tomato and chilli sauce to produce the now famous chilli crab. Eggs, onions, lime and seafood stock have since found their way into more robust versions. Some time later, the cooks at Long Beach Seafood Restaurant created a counterpoint, pepper crab. This is made by tossing the steamed crabs in crushed black peppercorns, butter, stock, sugar and salt. Today, chilli and pepper crabs are served in practically all seafood restaurants in Singapore.

Chin Peng (1924–) Political activist. Born Ong Boon Hua in Sitiawan, Perak, Chin Peng studied at Hua Chiao Primary School or Sitiawan Overseas Chinese Primary School, then at at Nan Hwa School. He enrolled at the Anglo-Chinese School when he was 15 years old. He joined the MALAYAN COMMUNIST PARTY (MCP) in Perak in January 1940, and served as the liaison officer between the MCP, FORCE 136 and the Kuomintang (Chinese Nationalist Party). Chin Peng's organizational abilities caught the eye of LAI TECK, then leader of the MCP. Before long, Chin Peng found himself on the party's Central Standing Committee.

Chin Peng rose to prominence during the JAPANESE OCCUPATION, and is believed to have led the MALAYAN PEOPLE'S ANTI-JAPANESE ARMY (MPAJA). Chin Peng acted as liaison officer between the MPAJA and Lord LOUIS MOUNTBATTEN, leader of the British Southeast Asia Command (SEAC). After the war, he was awarded the Burma Star and the 1939–45 Star for his war efforts. In 1947, he was made an Officer of the Order of the British Empire (OBE).

In 1947, Chin Peng assumed the secretary-generalship of the MCP. A state of EMERGENCY was declared in 1948, and Chin Peng was exiled from Malaya. He led his troops deep into the jungles near the Thai-Malaya border. From there, the MCP carried on an armed insurrection, determined to overthrow the government of Malaya by armed force. By the early 1950s, Chin Peng was reputed to have more than 8,000 troops under his command.

In 1955, an attempt to end the conflict resulted in the Baling talks being held in Kedah. However, the talks broke down when Chin Peng demanded that the MCP be legitimized and allowed to contest elections.

On 2 December 1981, Chin Peng announced the dissolution of MCP's army, although the party itself remained in existence. He signed two memoranda—one with the Thai government and the other with the Malaysian government—agreeing to dissolve the MCP army. Chin Peng applied to be allowed to return to and live in Malaysia in 2005, but his application was rejected.

Chin Peng: with Lord Mountbatten, left, 1946.

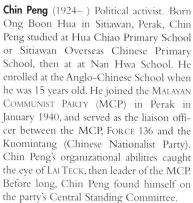
China Aviation Oil: creditors' meeting in 2005.

China Aviation Oil Company involved in a variety of oil-related businesses. Incorporated in Singapore in May 1993, China Aviation Oil Corporation was originally a shipping agency before becoming a wholly owned subsidiary of one of China's largest state-owned enterprises—China Aviation Oil Supply Corporation (CAOSC). It then diversified into jet fuel supply, international oil trading and other oil-related businesses, and was awarded Approved Oil Trader (AOT) status by the Singapore government in 1998, giving the company concessionary tax rates. In 2002, the company began to expand its reach outside China to markets in Asia, the Middle East, Europe and America. By then, its turnover had grown from $171 million in 1998 to $1.7 billion in 2002.

China Aviation Oil was listed on the Singapore Exchange in December 2001. It was named as the Most Transparent Company by the SECURITIES INVESTORS ASSOCIATION OF SINGAPORE and the 29th Most Transparent Company by THE BUSINESS TIMES. It was added to the Dow Jones Singapore Titans 30 Index in 2004.

In November 2004, however, trading of China Aviation Oil's shares was suspended after it was disclosed that the company was close to collapse, having sustained oil derivatives trading losses of US$550 million. A restructuring plan was announced in June 2005, with new capital amounting to US$130 million coming from CAOSC, BP Investments Asia and the Singapore government's investment arm, TEMASEK HOLDINGS. CAOSC was subsequently made to pay a civil penalty—the first such penalty imposed on a company in Singapore—for violating insider trading laws when it placed new shares in 2004, despite being aware of the company's losses. Five of the company's executives, including its chief executive officer—Chen Jiulin—were charged for their role in the affair. Chen was released on $2 million bail in June 2006 after being charged with breaching his duties as a director and making false and misleading statements relating to the company's options and trading losses.

China Aviation Oil reported a net loss of $864.9 million for the financial year 2004, compared to a net profit of $54.3 million in 2003, despite a 28 per cent increase in turnover. The company was relisted in March 2006.

China–Singapore relations China has long had trade and consular relations with countries in Southeast Asia. However, after the formation of the People's Republic in 1949, China's relations with Southeast Asia were negative, due largely to China's support for the communist insurgencies in the region. This gave rise to more than two decades of Cold War relations. It was not until the 1970s that individual Southeast Asian countries started to normalize relations with China. Singapore only formalized its diplomatic relations with China in October 1990, after Indonesia did.

Between 1949 and 1990, Singapore's relations with China had been guided by pragmatism. In separating trade from politics, pragmatism enabled Sino-Singapore relations to survive the Cold War. When China's trade with Indonesia, the Philippines and Thailand was either seriously disrupted or banned altogether, China's trade with Singapore continued uninterrupted. This is despite the absence of a formal diplomatic framework until 1990.

After 1979, China's approach to foreign relations was also characterized by pragmatism. This was when Deng Xiaoping began China's economic reform and open-door policy. This would lead to better relations between China and Southeast Asia in general, and between China and Singapore in particular. Economic ties were further boosted after Deng's tour of southern China (Nanxun) in early 1992, which heralded a further liberalization of China's economy. By 2005, Singapore, despite being a small country, had become China's seventh-largest trade partner with a total trade of US$33 billion, and China's sixth-largest investor with an accumulated total investment of US$28 billion. Two-way tourism has also thrived and Singapore has established itself as another gateway to China after Hong Kong.

On the political level, China and Singapore have continued to maintain a warm relationship, partly because of the congruence of interests and also because of the respect that Chinese leaders have for Minister Mentor LEE KUAN YEW. Following Deng Xiaoping's call to 'learn from Singapore' in early 1992, China organized numerous official 'observation groups' to come to Singapore to study Singapore's development experiences. This culminated in the joint development of the Suzhou Industrial Park which was started in 1994. The project faced initial hurdles but eventually took off successfully. Over the years, many top Chinese government and party leaders, including virtually all Politburo members, have visited Singapore. In return, most of Singapore's Cabinet ministers and senior civil servants have also regularly visited China to exchange views and strengthen ties.

Chinatown Name now given to a district that was allocated to the Chinese according to the 1822 town plan. The area is roughly triangular in shape: the base of the triangle is Telok Ayer Street, stretching from Anson Circus to the SINGAPORE RIVER; the Singapore River forms the second side, which stretches to Tan Kim Seng Bridge; the third side runs from Anson Circus to Outram Road. The area encompasses KRETA AYER, TANJONG PAGAR, and TELOK AYER.

The name 'Chinatown' did not achieve widespread usage until it was popularized by tourism authorities in the late 20th century. The name is perhaps ironic, given the size of Singapore's Chinese community. The Chinese themselves referred to parts of this area by various other names, such as Toa Por (Hokkien for 'big town') for the South Bridge Road area; and Gu Chia Chui (Hokkien for 'bullock cart water') for the Kreta Ayer area.

Chinatown Heritage Centre Three restored and connected CHINATOWN shophouses form this small museum, which presents the history of Singapore's Chinese community. The centre's three floors focus on different periods in Chinatown's history. The exhibits detail the harsh living conditions endured by early migrants to the area. The museum also details the practices of opium-smoking, PROSTITUTION (*see* AH KU), GAMBLING and SECRET SOCIETIES. Also documented here are the traditional festivals celebrated by other ethnic communities in Chinatown.

Chinese In 1824, the first census was taken in Singapore under the British administration, which counted the Chinese as making up 31 per cent of Singapore's total population of 10,683. By 1840, they made up half of the population. Since 1921, every census has shown that the Chinese comprise about three quarters of the population (76.8 per cent of a population of 3.3 million citizens and permanent residents in 2000). This makes Singapore the country with the

Chinatown Heritage Centre: replica of a shoe-seller's bunk.

Chinatown: Pagoda Street seen from Trengganu Street (above); one of Chinatown stamp series issued 1989 (below).

highest proportion of people of Chinese ancestry in any national population outside the People's Republic of China and Taiwan.

Given its multi-ethnic DEMOGRAPHY and its geographic location, however, Singapore should not be considered a 'Chinese society'. In particular, following Independence in 1965, the new nation-state had to demonstrate to the world that it was not a 'Third China'—that the Chinese majority in the citizenry and the government did not owe any political loyalty to China. The disavowal of political allegiance to China is not only a matter of geopolitics in light of neighbouring Malaysia and Indonesia. Historically, the Chinese who settled in Singapore did not constitute a homogeneous community with any singular Chinese identity or an unchanging 'Chineseness'.

Diverse forms of Chineseness may be discerned in relation to patterns of Chinese immigration. In the early decades of the 19th century, the island attracted increasing numbers of Chinese from neighbouring lands, especially pepper and gambier cultivators from Riau and traders from Malacca and Penang, the two other centres which made up the STRAITS SETTLEMENTS. Immigration from China increased steadily from the 1840s onwards with the absorption of unskilled Chinese labourers into the island, which was also a transit point, funnelling large numbers of coolies (*see* COOLIE TRADE) to places such as Deli in northeast Sumatra and elsewhere. The increase in Chinese immigration continued until the advent of World War II, especially with Japanese aggression against China in the late 1930s. Numbers fell after the establishment of the People's Republic of China in 1949, and during the decades immediately after Singapore's independence. From the late 1980s, however, the government sought to attract educated Chinese from Hong Kong and the People's Republic of China, especially those who had been trained in Western universities, to take up employment and permanent residence in Singapore.

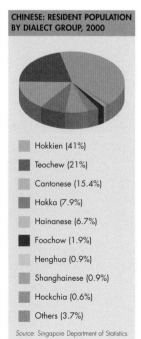

Chinese: coolies arriving in Singapore.

CHINESE: RESIDENT POPULATION BY DIALECT GROUP, 2000

- Hokkien (41%)
- Teochew (21%)
- Cantonese (15.4%)
- Hakka (7.9%)
- Hainanese (6.7%)
- Foochow (1.9%)
- Henghua (0.9%)
- Shanghainese (0.9%)
- Hockchia (0.6%)
- Others (3.7%)

Source: Singapore Department of Statistics

The early Chinese immigrants were familiar with local and colonial practices by virtue of generations of residence in the region. Given that few women migrated from China prior to the 20th century, inter-marriages between Chinese men and local women often took place. During the 19th century, there developed a distinction between the Straits or Straits-born Chinese and the China-born new arrivals (or SINKHEH in Hokkien). Also known as PERANAKANS or Babas, the Straits Chinese formed a culturally distinct group of Chinese, who retained Chinese customs in a modified form and who spoke Baba Malay, a combination of MALAY and HOKKIEN. Baba Malay also evolved as a written language based on Romanized Malay and played a role in keeping the Straits Chinese in touch with Chinese literary traditions. By the 1890s, Baba Malay translations of popular Chinese classics such as *Sam Kok* (The Romance of the Three Kingdoms)—known in Mandarin as *San Guo Yanyi*—and *Sang Kong* (The Water Margin)—known in Mandarin as *Shuihu Zhuan*—were published in Singapore.

Given their knowledge of local ways and their command of the ENGLISH language, the Babas mediated between different groups, especially Europeans, Malays and the *sinkheh*. Although they were a minority within the Chinese population, they thrived economically and socially because of their usefulness to the British in trading and administration. As a 'King's

Chinese', SONG ONG SIANG exemplified the highest achievement to which a Baba could aspire. Raised as a Christian, and a graduate of Cambridge University, Song practised law and served as a lay preacher and a civic leader, including as a member of the Legislative Council, and became a Knight Commander of the Order of the British Empire in 1936. He published *One Hundred Years' History of the Chinese in Singapore* in 1923, expressing the hope that Chinese descendants would 'get encouragement, incentive and stimulus to serve the Colony with equal public spirit, zeal and disinterestedness in their day and generation'.

Song paid little attention to China. Not so, however, his Baba contemporary LIM BOON KENG, a medical doctor who trained at the University of Edinburgh. He professed allegiance to the British and led the reform movement among the Straits Chinese. However, he also took an active interest in political developments in China, promoting the learning of MANDARIN and the revival of CONFUCIANISM. Lim was also close to some China-born leaders, in particular the industrialist and philanthropist TAN KAH KEE, who founded Amoy (Xiamen) University. Tan persuaded him to serve as the vice-chancellor of Amoy University from 1921 until 1937.

In the eyes of the Chinese authorities, all *huaqiao*—a term for 'Chinese sojourners' coined in the 1880s—were still subjects of China. For the most part, however, the Chinese in Singapore did not unite under a national banner but were divided into *bangs* or dialect-based groupings (such as HOKKIEN, TEOCHEW, CANTONESE, HAKKA and HAINANESE) which were subdivided according to place of origin in China. *Bang* identities were reinforced by the colonial urban policy of grouping Chinese from different provinces in different sections of the city centre that make up what is now called 'Chinatown'. When aligned with economic interests and backed by SECRET SOCIETIES, however, *bang* identities could come into open conflict. The clash of rival groups was dramatically seen in a

Chinese: Tan Si Chong Su Temple, built 1876.

riot which broke out between the Hokkiens and Teochews in 1854 (*see* SHORT DAGGERS REBELLION), which had deeper links to the struggle for the domination of gambier and pepper cultivation and OPIUM revenue farms (*see* REVENUE FARMING).

By the turn of the century, a wider *huaqiao* identity had been cultivated by the Chinese government, especially through the Chinese Consulate in Singapore. China was in the throes of political change. The modern ideas of the reformist KANG YOUWEI and the revolutionary SUN YAT SEN, both of whom spent time as political exiles in Singapore, were spread by the establishment of Chinese cultural societies, newspapers, schools and even a branch of the Kuomintang (Chinese Nationalist Party).

The ideological struggles that accompanied the rise of Chinese nationalism in the first half of the 20th century (marked by the establishment of the Republic of China in 1911; the May Fourth Movement in 1919; and the founding of the People's Republic of China in 1949) surfaced in Singapore among the China-born and those educated in the new Chinese schools (*see* CHINESE EDUCATION), which imported teachers and textbooks from China. For the *huaxiaosheng* (Chinese-educated), their identity as Chinese entailed taking sides on what was happening in China.

For both Kuomintang supporters such as LIM BO SENG and communist supporters such as TAN KAH KEE, nationalist sentiments led to involvement in the anti-Japanese movement of the late 1930s, including the boycott of Japanese goods and fund-raising activities for disaster relief in the mainland. Such activities among the Chinese in Singapore incurred the wrath of the Japanese when the British surrendered in February 1942 (*see* JAPANESE OCCUPATION). Thousands of Chinese men, especially the Chinese-educated, were rounded up, screened, and massacred, and many others were arrested and humiliated (*see* SOOK CHING). Tan, a wanted man, escaped to Sumatra before the Japanese invaded. Lim joined the anti-Japanese underground movement in Malaya, and was captured and tortured to death.

The question of Chineseness and political allegiance became more complex after the Japanese Occupation, and as Singapore made the transition to self-government and independence. Both the British-oriented Babas and the China-oriented *huaqiao* faced a radically new situation. The Baba community suffered a reversal of fortune during the era of decolonization. In light of the rise of the Chinese-speaking masses as a self-confident political force, the Babas were seen as culturally weak and isolated, if not also politically impotent and irrelevant.

Within the *huaqiao* community, the rift between Kuomintang and communist supporters deepened after the war. However, China-born immigrants, numbering about

380,000 in 1953, were regarded as 'aliens' in Singapore. Signalling a new sense of commitment to their adopted country, many campaigned for the extension of citizenship rights, which the majority eventually qualified for under the eight-year residential requirement of the 1957 CITIZENSHIP ORDINANCE. After the Bandung Conference of 1955, the People's Republic of China's position was that those who voluntarily adopted Singapore citizenship would not be considered citizens of China. In one stroke, therefore, Chinese identity and political allegiance to China were officially uncoupled.

In practical terms, many among the Chinese-educated continued to be influenced by ideological currents in China. 'Malayan' nationalism provided a larger platform for the multi-ethnic anticolonial movement, although this tended to be articulated by the English-educated elites (*see* ENGLISH EDUCATION), including the founders of the PEOPLE'S ACTION PARTY. As much as their predecessors were China-oriented, the Chinese-educated were in varying degrees also 'Malayanized'—as reflected in the growing body of literary works under the rubric of *mahua wenxue* (Malayan Chinese literature) (*see* CHINESE LITERATURE) and in the NANYANG STYLE of painting created by China-born artists in response to the local environment.

Apart from a strong sense of Chinese cultural inheritance, however, the predominantly working-class Chinese-educated were also socially and politically distanced from the English-educated. In the face of dire post-war social and economic conditions, and with limited job opportunities in a colonial occupational structure that favoured the English-educated, they were actively mobilized by the trade unions and the Chinese middle schools. Founding member of the People's Action Party and leader of the BARISAN SOSIALIS, LIM CHIN SIONG, was a prominent figure among the Chinese-educated.

It was at the height of such political activism in the mid-1950s that NANYANG UNIVERSITY was inaugurated, and it became a symbol of identity for the Chinese-educated. The economic disaffection of the Chinese-educated was ameliorated in the post-Independence decades. The civil service offered new job opportunities for the graduates of Chinese schools. Sustained economic growth also expanded employment in both the public and private sectors. From the late 1970s, Chinese-educated businesspeople also used their language skills and cultural knowledge to take advantage of the opportunities presented by the opening up of China.

By the early 1980s, however, enrolment in Chinese-medium schools had declined significantly. English was made the first language and main medium of instruction in all schools, although Mandarin was emphasized as a 'MOTHER TONGUE' for transmitting

traditional values. For practical reasons, Nanyang University adopted English as the medium of instruction in 1975 and was merged with SINGAPORE UNIVERSITY to form the NATIONAL UNIVERSITY OF SINGAPORE in 1980. This move, in effect, signalled the closure of the original Nanyang University, although its Jurong campus evolved into NANYANG TECHNOLOGICAL UNIVERSITY in 1991.

Against this background, many Chinese-educated felt marginalized vis-à-vis the English-educated. This sense, however, was more acute among the older generations of *huaxiaosheng* than those who had undergone bilingual education (*see* BILINGUALISM) from the 1980s. The latter include those who attended the SPECIAL ASSISTANCE PLAN SCHOOLS, a scheme started in 1978 as a way of retaining elements of the traditional Chinese-medium education; a number among them—for example, members of The Tangent, a civic group founded in 2002—have emphasized the need to engage with social and cultural issues in Chinese-language public discourse.

Chinese identity in Singapore has also been shaped by the Speak Mandarin Campaign (*see* CAMPAIGNS), launched in 1979 as a means of facilitating communication across dialect groups and reinforcing Mandarin as the official mother tongue. With the implementation of bilingual education and the promotion of Mandarin, patterns of language use have changed significantly over the decades. According to census data, the use of English among persons aged five years and above among the Chinese resident population increased from about 8 per cent in 1980 to about 24 per cent in 2000. In the same period, Mandarin speakers in the Chinese population increased from about ten per cent to about 45 per cent, while dialect speakers in the same population declined from about 80 to 31 percent.

With Mandarin replacing dialects as the most commonly used language at home, and with nearly a quarter of Chinese households predominantly English-speaking, the transmission of values from an older generation of dialect speakers has been impeded. Hence, for example, traditional Chinese clan or cultural associations have faced difficulties in attracting younger members. Dialect-based religious or food practices may also decline over time in an increasingly plural environment. With continued patterns of intermarriage across dialect lines, statistical data on dialect-group membership based on patrilineal descent have also become less meaningful as they do not indicate the actual use of the reported dialect or retention of dialect-based customs.

With the economic and political rise of China on the global stage from the 1990s, Chinese identity has again manifested in Singapore in different ways. For example, Mandarin (and, with it, Chinese cultural lit-

Chinese: early 20th-century painting, A Street in Chinatown.

eracy) is increasingly being promoted for its economic value. This has encouraged more people among the English-educated to take up the language. In the late 1990s, the government sought to ensure that there would be a new generation of 'Chinese-proficient elite' so that the Chinese community could maintain its roots. Within a few years, it emphasized the need for developing not just a 'bilingual elite' but also a 'bicultural élite' in order for Singapore to 'engage China' more deeply. At the same time, its 'FOREIGN TALENT' policy attracted Chinese nationals to study and work in Singapore with a view to eventually taking up permanent residence or citizenship. The wheel has come full circle: just as Chinese Singaporeans are encouraged to engage with a resurgent China by being 'culturally' and not 'politically' Chinese, new immigrants from China—in a sense, *xin huaqiao* (new Chinese sojourners)—continue to arrive and navigate their way through the varieties of Chineseness that have developed in the multiethnic and globalized context of Singapore.

Chinese: 'Speak Mandarin' campaign poster, 1983.

Chinese Advisory Board After abolishing SECRET SOCIETIES by means of the Societies Ordinance of 1889, Governor CECIL CLEMENTI SMITH created the Chinese Advisory Board (CAB) in 1890 to facilitate better liaison between the British authori-

Chinese: higher primary students at Chung Hwa Institution, 1950.

Chinese classical music

Chinese classical music in Singapore falls into genres corresponding to those found in China, where traditional folk instrumental ensembles (*sizhu*, *guchui* and *chuida*) exist alongside groups modelled on European orchestras, but in which Chinese instruments are used.

Instruments typically used in Chinese orchestras: (from top) the qing, sanxian, sheng and gehu.

The colonial era

During the colonial era, various Chinese dialect groups and clan associations organized musical events. The earliest known amateur organization was the Er Woo Amateur Musical and Dramatic Association, which was founded in 1912. Er Woo's Li Yeqi played a significant role in nurturing many outstanding students who later became leading figures in the Chinese orchestral movement during the 1950s.

Oral accounts also point to the important Tongluo Musical Society, which performed patriotic songs during the Sino-Japanese war (1937–1945).

Chinese clan association music group.

Chinese orchestras

Officially, the first Chinese orchestra to be formed in Singapore was the Singapore Middle School Arts Society. It was formed in 1953, and was composed mainly of students from secondary schools. Subsequent organizations were founded by school alumni associations, workers organizations and community arts groups. Founded in 1953 and 1954 respectively, Ai Tong Alumni and Kang Le Music Research Society were the largest and most active of these. But it was Tao Rong Musical Society which was perhaps the most significant. By 1959, Tao Rong featured a fully-fledged orchestra, made up of strings, wind instruments and percussion.

In 1960, the Central Cultural Board Chinese Orchestra was formed with government support. This was initiated by minister of state for culture Lee Khoon Choy, who was himself a player of the *guzheng* (Chinese zither).

Led by Li Yu Chuan, the orchestra played at many official functions, but became inactive in the 1970s, when most of its players were transferred to the National Theatre Chinese Orchestra.

National Theatre Chinese Orchestra.

After Separation

Following Independence in 1965, a National Theatre Trust was instituted to promote the arts with support from the Ministry of Culture. In May 1968, the National Theatre Arts Troupe was officially launched. It included a Chinese orchestra as one of its core divisions. The Chinese orchestra section of the troupe enjoyed immense success through a series of community concerts under its first musical director, Zheng Sishen.

On 16 March 1974, due to restructuring and policy changes, the National Theatre Trust announced that it would adopt a new sponsoring scheme for the performing arts, and would discontinue support for its current groups. In the same year, it was announced that the People's Association and the Singapore Broadcasting Corporation would each establish Chinese orchestras in September and October, respectively. The People's Association Chinese Orchestra was the first Chinese orchestra to engage musicians on a full-time basis. The orchestra started out with six full-time musicians, although this number would eventually grow to 32 in the following years. Its first director was Wu Dajiang, who had been trained in China and had established his career in Hong Kong. In 1992, this orchestra was renamed the Singapore Chinese Orchestra.

The Singapore Broadcasting Corporation Chinese Orchestra began as an amateur group. It expanded rapidly under the leadership of Zheng Chaoji. The orchestra was renamed the City Chinese Orchestra and came under the control of the Nanyang Academy of Fine Arts when the Singapore Broadcasting Corporation relinquished control over the orchestra in the 1990s.

Chinese orchestras in schools and community centres have also played a major role in the practice and development of Chinese classical music in Singapore. Dunman High School is known for its training, while Hwa Chong Institution is noted for playing new compositions. Among community centre orchestras, Keat Hong Community Centre Chinese Orchestra is one of the most accomplished in terms of professionalism and performance standards.

Chinese choirs

There is little material detailing Chinese choral music in the 19th century, but it may well have begun with the singing of Chinese hymns in churches. Songs performed by Tongluo Musical Society were inspired by patriotic songs popular in China during the Sino-Japanese war.

Few records concerning Chinese choral activities during the Japanese Occupation have survived, but the genre did grow in the 1950s and 1960s. The leading choirs in the post-war era included the Lee Howe Choral Society, founded in 1952; the Rediffusion Choir, founded in 1953 (and later renamed the Metro Philharmonic Society); and Herald's Choral Society, founded in 1961. These choirs mainly sang Chinese folk songs arranged for four-part choruses, or translations of Western choral works. Political songs from China also found their way into choral repertoires, but choirs were prohibited from performing these in public as it was feared they would promote 'pro-communist' sentiment.

Activity slowed in the 1980s due to educational reforms which required that vernacular schools switch to English as the main medium of instruction. The development of *xinyao* (see Chinese popular music) also saw students gravitating towards more popular genres of music.

By 2006, there were still some 30 choirs in Singapore, although these faced problems of membership renewal, as fewer young people have joined in recent times.

Poster for the People's Association Chinese Orchestra, 1979 (left); poster for the National Theatre Chinese Orchestra, 1978 (right).

From top: CD featuring Chinese choral works performed by various Singapore-based choirs; Singapore Chinese Orchestra.

ties and the Chinese community. The CAB was chaired by the Protector of the Chinese (later known as Secretary for Chinese Affairs) and comprised leaders from the HOKKIEN, CANTONESE, HAKKA, TEOCHEW and HAINANESE *bang* (dialect groups), which were represented proportionally. At its inaugural meeting in February 1890, the CAB's Hokkien representatives were Tan Jiak Kim, Tan Beng Wan, Lim Eng Keng and Lee Cheng Yan; Teochew representatives Seah Liang Seah, Tan Yong Siak and Low Cheang Yee; Cantonese representative Boey Ah Sam; and Hainanese representative Wang Joon Siang. The first FOOCHOW *bang* leader was appointed to the CAB in 1929.

For the local Chinese, the CAB was the only official forum in which they, their community leaders and the government could discuss matters of interest to the Chinese community as a whole. However, the CAB had little real power, since its main function was to advise and consult. Board members were selected on the basis of status, influence, age and moderation in outlook and ideology. The British used the CAB to co-opt the top Chinese community and *bang* leadership, and many of the CAB's members were handsomely rewarded, being appointed justices of the peace or presented with imperial or other orders. Prominent CAB members included LIM BOON KENG, TAN KAH KEE and LIM NEE SOON. The CAB's role was much reduced after World War II, and it was disbanded in 1959.

Chinese classical music *See* box.

Chinese Development Assistance Council This council is a joint development of the SINGAPORE FEDERATION OF CHINESE CLAN ASSOCIATIONS (SFCCA) and the SINGAPORE CHINESE CHAMBER OF COMMERCE & INDUSTRY (SCCCI). Set up on 22 May 1992, the Chinese Development Assistance Council (CDAC) was formally incorporated under the Companies Act and later granted the status of an 'Institution of Public Character' by the government. The mission of the CDAC is to nurture and develop the potential of the Chinese community in contributing to the success of a multiracial Singapore.

The CDAC set up the first Student Service Centres (SSC) in Singapore in November 1993. With ten centres around Singapore, total membership was about 23,000 students by May 2005. These centres offer enrichment programs, mentoring programs, exam preparation and motivational workshops, as well as IT-related courses, educational outings and camps. The ten centres organize more than 2,700 activities involving about 100,000 participants each year.

Chinese education The first account of Chinese schooling in Singapore was recorded by Rev G.H. Thomson in 1829, who noted that there was 'a CANTONESE

school at Kampong Glam of 12 boys, another at Pekin Street of eight boys, while there was a HOKKIEN school at Pekin Street of 22 boys'. It is probable that in these schools, boys were taught ideographic writing and the Chinese classics. Students were trained to help their fathers in business, and some were sent to China for further education. Chinese parents did not think it was worthwhile to give daughters an education since the girls would be leaving the family when they married, and their main task after marrying would be to raise a family.

Wealthy entrepreneurs such as TAN KAH KEE and TAN LARK SYE saw it as their moral duty to support education. Chinese schools went through a period of rapid expansion and modernization during the first two decades of the 20th century—a period of political and social upheaval in China. During this period, overseas Chinese education and politics in China became entwined. School curricula were identical to those used in China. A few schools were also established for girls. These included Chung Hwa (1911), Nanhua (1917) and the Singapore Nanyang Girls' School (1917) (*see* NANYANG GIRLS' HIGH SCHOOL). The first high school, CHINESE HIGH SCHOOL, was opened in 1918. Chinese schools were soon able to compete with English schools on an equal footing.

In 1919, responding to events in China, teachers and students of Chinese schools began to participate in organized anti-Japanese activities in Singapore. The British viewed such activities as a threat to their rule in Singapore, and passed the Schools Registration Ordinance in 1920. This ordinance required schools, teachers and managers of schools to be registered. In addition, the bill allowed the government to declare a school illegal when subject matter taught in the school was deemed to be 'revolutionary' in nature or conflicted with the 'interests of the colony'. In the years before World War II, Chinese education was treated by the authorities as subservient to English education, and policies were enacted to ensure that this status quo was maintained.

After the war, Chinese schools reestablished themselves more quickly than English-medium and other vernacular schools. In 1956, an All-Party Committee was set up to find solutions to the problems faced by Chinese schools. Most of the recommendations of this committee were adopted, and all schools in Singapore were made equal.

In 1953, a proposal for the establishment of a Chinese university in Singapore—NANYANG UNIVERSITY—was raised. This was enthusiastically supported by sections of the Chinese community. The university was sited in Jurong on land donated by the SINGAPORE HOKKIEN HUAY KUAN. But the university soon faced a host of problems over politicization and the

Chinese education: examination at Chung Hwa Institution, 1950.

quality of its education. Several negative reports—the Prescott Report (1959), the Gwee Ah Leng Report (1960) and the Nanyang University Curriculum Review Committee Report (1965)—further damaged the university's public profile. The university's degrees gained official recognition only in 1968, after more than ten years of protracted negotiations between the university and the government.

At around the same period, the Ngee Ann Kongsi, a Teochew organization, opened another post-secondary institution, the Ngee Ann College (*see* NGEE ANN POLYTECHNIC), where there was an emphasis on technical and commercial training. Thus, by the end of the 1970s, the Chinese community had developed a parallel system to compete with English-medium post-secondary institutions.

However, at around the same time, a decline in enrolment in Chinese schools prompted the CHINESE CHAMBER OF COMMERCE & INDUSTRY to study the situation. The chamber's ensuing report cited limited further education and job opportunities, government policies that favoured English education, and parents' ignorance of the value of Chinese education, as the major reasons for declining enrolment. What the report failed to mention was that Chinese schools were losing out to English schools in open competition. Increasingly, Chinese parents preferred to send their children to English-medium schools rather than Chinese ones to ensure better employment prospects. In response, the government converted some well-established Chinese schools into SPECIAL ASSISTANCE PLAN schools.

In 2004, the Ministry of Education announced refinements to its MOTHER TONGUE policy. Unlike the previous Chinese Language curriculum in Singapore, which gave equal emphasis to listening, speaking, reading and writing, the new curriculum was expected to give greater emphasis to character recognition and less to script writing in the lower primary years, thus facilitating the early acquisition of reading skills. It was envisaged that developing a proficiency in reading early would help students acquire proficiency in Chinese sooner.

Chinese Garden: lanterns displayed during Zhong Qiu Jie (mid-autumn festival).

Chinese Garden Also known as Yu Hwa Yuan, this 5,800-sq-m garden in Jurong was designed by Taiwanese architect Yuen-chen Yu, and was built in 1975. Over 2,000 tons of rocks, boulders and pebbles were used in its construction. The design of the garden followed the Imperial Song style, and included curved bridges, pagodas, fountains and courtyards reminiscent of the Beijing Summer Palace. In 1992, a Suzhou-style *penjing* (literally 'potted landscape') garden was added. The garden customarily hosts a lantern display during ZHONG QIU JIE.

Chinese Heritage Centre In May 1995 the Chinese Heritage Centre (CHC) was established by the SINGAPORE FEDERATION OF CHINESE CLAN ASSOCIATIONS. The CHC is governed by a Board of Governors, consisting of prominent ethnic Chinese from all over the world, and is managed by an Executive Committee. In 2006, this committee was headed by Professor Tommy Koh as chairman; Professor WANG GUNGWU (of the East Asian Institute) as deputy chairman; and Professor SU GUANING (of Nanyang Technological University) as treasurer. The CHC is housed in the former administration building of NANYANG UNIVERSITY, now located on the grounds of NANYANG TECHNOLOGICAL UNIVERSITY.

The objectives of the CHC are 'to promote knowledge and understanding of the people of Chinese descent outside China and their heritage through research, publications, conferences, public lectures and

Chinese Heritage Centre: The Encyclopedia of the Chinese Overseas (1998) (above); display gallery (below).

exhibitions'. It has a reference library, with a specialized focus on works relating to the Chinese overseas and their heritage.

The CHC has had four directors. The first, Lynn Pan, edited *The Encyclopedia of the Chinese Overseas*, which has appeared in several languages worldwide since its first publication by the CHC. The CHC's second director, Professor Kee Pookong, organized several international conferences and seminars on overseas Chinese genealogies, contemporary overseas Chinese clan associations, and works of ethnic Chinese movie directors during his tenure. Professor Ng Chin Keong, the CHC's third director, oversaw the publication of the *Journal of Chinese Overseas*, and the launch of a major exhibition entitled *The Chinese: More or Less*. Professor Leo Suryadinata, the fourth director, took office in January 2006.

Chinese High School, The Founded in 1919 by philanthropist TAN KAH KEE, The Chinese High School (CHS) was funded and supported by Tan until 1934. The school's clock tower, which was gazetted as a national monument in March 1999, was used by British forces during the defence of Singapore in World War II.

After the war, CHS continued to provide a predominantly CHINESE EDUCATION. In the 1950s and 1960s, the school and its alumni became known both for its academic rigour and political activism. Pro-communist sentiment, which had started during World War II and the years of the JAPANESE OCCUPATION, became synonymous with anti-colonialism in the postwar years. Moreover, pro-communist sympathies, already widespread among the Chinese community, were reinforced by events in mainland China. Students also agitated against the colonial government's refusal to accept Chinese educational qualifications as a basis for employment in the civil service; gave support to striking bus workers during the HOCK LEE BUS RIOTS; and protested against military conscription, which culminated in the CHINESE MIDDLE SCHOOL RIOTS in 1956. Levels of political activism in the school remained high throughout the 1950s and 1960s.

CHS has seen great academic and extra-curricular achievements in recent decades. Much of its success is attributable to the leadership of Tooh Fee San, principal from 1979 to 1999. In 1988, CHS was one of the first secondary schools to become independent. In 2005, it merged with Hwa Chong Junior College to form HWA CHONG INSTITUTION (HCI). HCI is a pioneer of the six-year INTEGRATED PROGRAMME, in which students bypass the traditional GCE 'O' levels and sit for 'A' levels at the end of six years of post-primary education.

Famous CHS alumni include President ONG TENG CHEONG; artist TAN SWIE HIAN and Kenny Yap, founder of ornamental fish exporter, Qian Hu Corporation.

The Chinese High School: statue of Tan Kah Kee.

Chinese ink painting and calligraphy The Nanyang Calligraphy and Painting Society (also referred to as United Artists Malaysia), formed in 1929 and based in Kuala Lumpur, is thought to have been the first association in Malaya dedicated to advancing ink and calligraphy practice. The Salon Art Society, formed in 1935 and renamed the Society of Chinese Artists (SCA) in 1936, was also pivotal in promoting ink and brush painting. The SCA's ink masters included CHEN CHONG SWEE, Wu Tsai Yen, Huang Pao Fang and Shi Xiangtuo, who were also influential educators. Many taught ink painting at the NANYANG ACADEMY OF FINE ARTS (NAFA).

Modern master painters Xu Beihong and Liu Haisu visited Singapore between 1925 and 1942 and held fundraising exhibitions for refugees of the Sino-Japanese War—giving inspiration to many local painters. The JAPANESE OCCUPATION immobilized most artistic practice in Singapore. But after the war the practice of Chinese art grew exponentially. Countless competitions, demonstrations and broadcasts on Radio Singapore (such as those delivered by Shi Xiangtuo from 1949 to the early 1980s) as well as patron–collectors such as Tan Tsze Chor, LEE KONG CHIAN and LOKE WAN THO did much, through their patronage and support, to promote ink appreciation and practice.

NAFA's founder, LIM HAK TAI, urged mindfulness of 'tropical settings', developing the notion of a Nanyang, or regional, style and sensibility. Ink painters such as Chen Chong Swee and Shi Xiangtuo incorporated motifs such as indigenous peoples, kampongs and tropical scenes into the scroll format. Others, such as CHEN WEN HSI, integrated Cubist expressions into Chinese ink works. The *xieyi,* or 'expressive style', exemplified in pioneer Fan Chang-Tien's work, shaped successive painters such as Nai Swee Leng, Tan Oe Pang, Chen KeZhan and CHUA EK KAY.

Notable ink societies include the Molan Art Association (founded in 1967), the Chinese Calligraphy Society of Singapore (founded in 1968), Siaw-Tao Chinese Seal-Carving, Calligraphy & Painting Society (founded in 1971), Hwa Hun Art Society (founded in 1973) and the San Yi Finger Painting Society (founded in 1978), which is believed to have been the first finger-painting society in the world.

The ink painter, calligrapher and seal-carver WEE BENG CHONG was the first recipient of the CULTURAL MEDALLION in 1979. Other ink artists who received the Cultural Medallion include PAN SHOU, LEE HOCK MOH, Tan Swie Hian, WANG SUI PICK, TAN KIAN POR, Chua Ek Kay, TAN SIAH KWEE and LIM TZE PENG. Contemporary ink painters such as Tan Swie Hian, Tan Oe Pang, Chen KeZhan and Hong Sek Chern (who received the President's Young Talent award in 2001) have participated in multi-disciplinary projects as well as overseas biennales such as those at Venice and Sao Paolo.

See also ART and NANYANG STYLE.

Chinese literature *See* box.

Chinese medical halls Places where TRADITIONAL CHINESE MEDICINE (TCM) is dispensed. There are over 600 Chinese medical halls in Singapore, most of them in the housing estate heartlands. They dispense over-the-counter Chinese proprietary medicine (CPM) and a myriad of herbal products as cures for common ailments such as coughs and diarrhoea, or to improve general health and boost immunity. Herbal products ranging from red dates, wolfberries and bird's nest to ginseng and cordyceps are commonly sold in medical halls for use in herbal brews or as ingredients in food.

One of the longest-established Chinese medical halls is EU YAN SANG, which was first opened in 1879 and has since expanded to 26 outlets all over Singapore. Some medical halls have their own in-house Chinese physician trained in traditional Chinese medicine, including Chinese massage and ACUPUNCTURE.

To safeguard the quality and safety of CPM, the Ministry of Health implemented new controls on its import, manufacture, sale and supply with effect from September 1999.

Chinese middle school riots On 24 September 1956, the LIM YEW HOCK government deregistered the SINGAPORE CHINESE MIDDLE SCHOOL STUDENTS' UNION following the disastrous HOCK LEE BUS RIOTS. In response, some 5,000 Chinese middle school students took control of their schools, threatening a sit-in until their union was reinstated. The minister for education, CHEW SWEE KEE, told the students to resume classes in an orderly fashion. Students subsequently left the school premises.

However, on 10 October 1956, Chew told the management committees of the CHINESE HIGH SCHOOL and CHUNG CHENG HIGH SCHOOL to expel 142 students on grounds of subversion. The students in both schools staged a strike, and Chew ordered the schools' closure. However, the schools remained occupied by thousands of defiant students who were supported by members of the SINGAPORE BUS WORKERS' UNION and other unions. Before long, the protest spread to nearby Yeok Eng High School, and received support from 2,000 female students who walked out of NAN CHIAU HIGH SCHOOL and Chung Hwa School.

On the evening of 24 October, the chief minister went on radio to announce that the students would have until 8.00 pm the following day to leave the school premises. Parents of the students were also warned to remove their children from the two schools. Political leader LIM CHIN SIONG urged his supporters to go to Chinese High School to 'save our brothers'.

At dusk, crowds gathered outside the Chinese High School and Chung Cheng High School. Outside the latter, a group of 400–500 people started rioting and clashing with the police. This spread to the Tanjong Katong Post Office and Geylang Police Station, both of which were attacked by the crowds. Meanwhile, at the Chinese High School, a crowd of 4,000 had gathered. Many people in this crowd had just attended an incendiary rally given by the PEOPLE'S ACTION PARTY. They turned into an angry mob, overturning three police vans and setting two others alight. The police charged at the crowd, using tear gas to disperse it.

At dawn on 26 October, army helicopters and armoured cars moved in, military roadblocks were set up and the riot squad knocked down barricades that had been set up at the two schools. In other parts of Singapore, rioting continued throughout the day and night as 7,000 bus workers and workers in other industries announced a sympathy strike. A day-long tussle finally brought the rioting to an end and union leaders—including Lim Chin Siong, FONG SWEE SUAN, C.V. DEVAN NAIR,

Chinese ink painting and calligraphy: from left, Calligraphy, Lim Tze Peng; Fun at Leisure, Wu Tsai Yen; Wayang Actor, Lim Tze Peng.

Chinese medical halls: weighing herbs with a daching.

Chinese middle school riots: banners outside the Chinese High School, 1956.

Chinese literature

The Chinese community in Malaya and Singapore before the late 19th century was an almost exclusively mercantile and agricultural one, and there was little interest in literary or cultural activities among its members. It was only during the second half of the 19th century that this began to change.

Chinese literary life in Malaya and Singapore was galvanized by the publication of Chinese newspapers. LAT PAU—the first Chinese daily to be published in Singapore—appeared in 1881, and was followed by *Xing Bao* in 1890 and several other newspapers in the following years. Teachers, journalists, legation staff, political refugees and visitors from China contributed to the literary supplements in these papers. Diplomat-poets of the period included Huang Zunxian and Zuo Binglong, who wrote miscellaneous essays, travelogues and poems in classical Chinese.

From left: Meng Tu *(Land of Dreams) (1967) by Liu Beian and* Sheng Ming Li Nan Yi Cheng Shou de Zhong *(Life's Heavy Burdens) (1992) by Xi Ni'er.*

From left: Bei Qi Yü *(Lamenting Her Fate) (1966) by Zhang Jinyan and* Zai Gandi Xiansheng Zuo You *(Next to Mr Gandhi) (1959) by Zeng Shengti.*

Nanyang Chinese literature

Under the influence of the Chinese literary revolution of 1917 and the May Fourth Movement of 1919, cultural circles in the Singapore Chinese community began to feel the need to incorporate vernacular Chinese and Western literary styles into their work. Around 1919, the *Xin Guomin Zazhi* (New Citizen Magazine), a literary supplement of *Xin Guomin Ribao* (New Citizen Daily), started publishing creative writing in vernacular Chinese. Many other Chinese newspapers followed suit, publishing new literary works in their supplements.

In 1927, interest in creating a local literature was roused among a group of editors. The first of these were the editors of *Huang Dao* (Deserted Island), the literary supplement of *New Citizen Daily*. They stated that it was their policy to 'introduce only works with

NANYANG colour into the literary world'. Among the new generation of writers who published their work in this supplement was locally born Zhang Jinyan. Zhang's stories, collected in *Bei Qi Yü* (Lamenting Her Fate), was characterized by the depiction of everyday situations which took place against a local background, and also included the use of Chinese dialects.

This stress on the 'NANYANG' elements of Chinese literature marked the first step towards developing an indigenous Singapore Chinese literature. Many writers, including Zhang Jinyan, Zeng Shengti and Chen Lianqing not only promoted the 'Nanyangization' of local literature, but they also wrote about local life.

Malayan Chinese literature

By the mid-1930s, writers had developed a stronger sense of identity, and they began to define the concept of 'Nanyang' as referring exclusively to the Malay Peninsula and Singapore. In the 1930s, 'Nanyang Chinese literature' became 'Malayan Chinese literature'. In 1934 Qiu Shizhen wrote an article in which he stated that he found the term 'Malayan Chinese literature' preferable to 'Nanyang Chinese literature'. He argued for the independence of Chinese literature in Singapore and Malaya from the overt influence of Chinese literature from China. He mentioned the names of 14 authors whom he claimed as 'Malayan Chinese local authors', due to their having been born in Malaya.

A new independence

After WORLD WAR II, more young, locally born Chinese writers emerged. Both local-born as well as writers who were born and educated in China—such as LIAN SHISHENG and LIU BEIAN—began developing the concept of a national identity in their works.

Most writers from this period not only included local themes in their work, but did so from a distinctly Singaporean angle. The poems of this period which depict local life and culture did not employ so-called 'Nanyang local colour' for merely aesthetic purposes. Works such as Zhou Can's *Qilou Di Xia* (At the Five-foot Way), which describes the life of an old sweet-seller, and Pao Di's 1961 poem 'Xie Ji Ge Shou Men Ren' (The Jagas), which describes the life of Indian watchmen ('*jagas*'), were portrayals of street life in the Singapore. Such works

were evidence of the growth of a so-called 'Singapore consciousness' in Chinese literature. Many representative works written during the period before Singapore's independence in 1965 have been included in FANG XIU's *Mahua Xin Wenxue Daxi* (A Comprehensive Anthology of Modern Malayan Chinese Literature) (2001).

The effects of the rapid urbanization which took place alongside the industrialization and commercialization of the country's economy after Independence has also been reflected in local Chinese literature.

Chinese literary organizations also contributed significantly to the growth of Chinese literature in Singapore. Important groups included the Mangrove Poetry Society of the former Nanyang University, which was in existence from 1973 to 1980, and May Poetry Society, under whose auspices many Chinese poets would not have had the chance to publish or develop their work. Active literary societies include the SINGAPORE ASSOCIATION OF WRITERS, the SINGAPORE LITERATURE SOCIETY and the Bukit Timah Literary Society.

Jin Se De Wei Xiao (A Golden Smile) (1991) by You Jin.

Significant developments

Chinese literature in Singapore over the past two decades has drawn from many diverse literary traditions. In the 1960s and 1970s, writers such as MENG YI, WANG RUNHUA, DAN YING and YING PEIAN experimented with symbolic realism and modernism. In the 1980s and 1990s, younger writers such as ZHANG HUI, XI NI'ER, LIANG WENFU and Cai Shenjiang have embraced movements and trends such as magic realism and post-modernism. Women writers such as Dan Ying, SOON AI LING, ZHANG XINA, Liu Peifang and many others have also challenged the male-dominated literary scene by exploring and interpreting women's experiences through fiction, essays and poetry. A number of works in English such as *Glimpses of the Past* (1981) by Wong Meng Voon (Meng Yi), *Beyond Symbols* (1984) by Wang Runhua and *Selected Verses* (2002) by XU FUJI have also been published.

Dan Ying (above); Fa Shang Sui Yue *(Time Passing Through my Hair) (1993).*

The audience for Chinese literature from Singapore has also expanded beyond local shores, extending to Taiwan, Hong Kong and China. You Jin's travel writings are very popular in China, while Dan Ying and Wang Runhua are well-known names in Taiwan.

From left: Author Meng Yi; Wang Runhua's Beyond Symbols *(1984);* Shou Shu Tai Shang *(On the Operating Table) (1968) by Ying Peian.*

A Singapore tradition

Singapore and Malayan (or Malaysian) Chinese literature were regarded as a single entity and categorized as *Mahua wenxue* (Malayan Chinese literature). Since 1965, however, Singapore Chinese literature has developed independently, and the term *Xin huawen wenxue* (Singapore Chinese literature), came into use soon after SEPARATION. The phrase '*Xin huawen wenxue*' is generally used to refer to works written in vernacular Chinese which make use of Western literary forms, and which are united by their attention to local subjects, themes and identities.

From left: Fang Xiu's Notes on the History of Malayan Chinese New Literature 1920–1942; Mahua Xin Wenxue Daxi *(A Comprehensive Anthology of Modern Malayan Chinese Literature) (2001).*

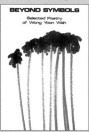

Chinese New Year: **Hongbao** *(top); Chinese sausages.*

Chinese New Year: street light-up, January 2004.

JAMES PUTHUCHEARY, SIDNEY WOODHULL and Chan Chiaw Thor—were detained. The riots left 13 people dead and 123 injured.

Chinese New Year The Chinese have celebrated this festival for thousands of years, with New Year's Day first being marked on the Chinese lunar calendar by Emperor Han Wu Di (1121–771 BCE). However, the origins of the festival are also linked to the story of the Nian—a mythical beast that is said to have once terrorized villages in China on New Year's Eve. In order to scare away the Nian, people would paste red-paper couplets on their doors, light torches and set off firecrackers, rejoicing when the Nian was kept away. Many of these practices are still part of New Year festivities today.

Preparations for Chinese New Year begin in the weeks leading up to the festival. Many families conduct a thorough 'spring clean', so that the household will be clean for the coming year, and because it is believed to be inauspicious to sweep during New Year itself (lest good luck be swept away). Moreover, shopping for traditional New Year products—'nianhuo' in Mandarin—is an important part of the preparations. Several streets in the CHINATOWN area are turned into bazaars, with stalls laden with *nianhuo*.

New Year's Eve is, for many people, the most important part of the festival. Families congregate for a traditional reunion dinner, and eat dishes with auspicious names, such as *facai* (a kind of algae, the Chinese name of which sounds similar to the phrase 'gaining wealth') and *niangao* (New Year's cake). Another popular New Year's dish in Singapore is YUSHENG—a raw fish salad. This is eaten throughout Chinese New Year.

Many families stay up all night on New Year's Eve. In the past, firecrackers were set off at midnight to welcome in the New Year, however, this practice was outlawed in the 1970s due to concerns over safety.

Taoists (*see* TAOISM) believe that Zao Shen (the kitchen god) returns to heaven to make an annual report on each household on New Year's Eve. Thus, sweet offerings are presented to this deity, and images of him (or, more precisely, his mouth) are smeared with honey or sugar so that his report will be favourable. Similarly, some people burn joss to welcome the Cai Shen (the god of wealth) at the start of the new year. Joss, flowers and other offerings are also made to ancestors.

Hongbao (red envelopes containing 'lucky money') are closely associated with this festival. These are given throughout the new year period, usually to the young. In keeping with the general focus on 'the new' during throughout this period, *hongbao* are filled with new banknotes. Another tradition is the giving of mandarin oranges. The word for this fruit in Cantonese ('gam') sounds similar to the word for gold, and it has thus come to symbolize wealth. People often present mandarin oranges when visiting friends and relatives, which is common throughout the New Year period.

In Singapore, the second and first days of Chinese New Year are PUBLIC HOLIDAYS. The festival comes to an end on the 15th day of the new year—Yuanxiao (Lantern Festival—when, once again, the family gathers for dinner.

Chinese opera *See* box.

Chinese Opera Institute Established in 1995, the Chinese Opera Institute (COI) is supported by the National Arts Council. It is a training and research centre responsible for the promotion of CHINESE OPERA. The COI's aim is to create original works and revive major classics, and cultivate audiences and performers for Chinese opera. It reaches out to schools in Singapore through its Arts Education Programme with workshops and productions. Its founding director Dr Chua Soo Pong, ethnomusicologist, dance scholar and playwright, set up COI's performing arm, the Singapore Chinese Opera Performing Ensemble (SCOPE), in 1997. The group has been acclaimed for its

productions in international theatre festivals throughout Asia, Europe and the United States. The COI also facilitates international programmes to give young talent the opportunity to perform overseas and work with artists around the world. The COI has also published books on Chinese opera in Singapore, among them *Teochew Opera in Singapore* (2003) by CAI BIXIA; *Beijing Opera in Singapore* (2004) by Wang Fang; and *Hokkien Opera in Singapore* (2005). The COI also conducts seminars and symposiums regularly to promote debate on, and discussion about, Chinese opera.

Chinese popular music *See* box.

Chinese Protectorate This department was established in 1877 to look after the needs of the Chinese community in the STRAITS SETTLEMENTS. The office was opened in Singapore on 1 June in a shophouse on North Canal Road. It was subsequently relocated to other addresses—Upper Macao Street (present-day Pickering Street), Boat Quay and, in 1886, Havelock Road (although the original building at this site was demolished in 1930).

WILLIAM PICKERING was the first protector of Chinese. Pickering was conversant in MANDARIN and various Chinese dialects when he first arrived in 1872, and continued to serve as protector until 1888. Pickering worked to establish a corps of European officers at the Chinese Protectorate who would be conversant in Chinese, and thus able to handle Chinese affairs. He conducted Chinese-language classes and held examinations for applicants. Subsequent protectors of Chinese included G.T. Hare, George Crofton Wray, Warren Barnes and C.J. Saunders.

The Chinese Protectorate had the broad role of overseeing all matters concerning the Chinese community. Its activities included the establishment of a group of civil servants conversant in Chinese; the management of newly arrived coolies (known as SINKHEH); the regulation of SECRET SOCIETIES; tackling the problem of the traffic in women and girls for PROSTI-

Chinese Opera Institute: **Lakeside Idyll,** *performed at Little Guilin, a former granite quarry in Bukit Batok, 1997.*

Chinese opera Also known by the Malay term *wayang* (performance). Chinese opera includes street opera as well as those performed in a more formal indoor setting. Street operas are acted out on temporary stages erected in an open space. Shows are usually patronized by Chinese temples. Such performances are often held to fulfil religious-communal functions. These include celebrations of deities' birthdays, appeasing the spirits of the dead and the celebration of festivals. It is also put on as entertainment for the local community during special social events. Historically, the religious context is the dominant one for staging Chinese opera, which dates back to at least the 12th century.

As reflected in *Lat Pau*, the first Chinese newspaper in Singapore, Thian Hock Keng and WAK HAI CHENG BIO temples were the principal sites for street operas performed by different dialect groups in the 19th century. Chinese opera was also often performed next to the SINGAPORE RIVER during this period. On 8 March 1889, the Chinese community celebrated the wedding and ascension to the throne of the Chinese emperor Guangxu. Musical and opera troupes of various genres were invited to perform at different locations along the Singapore River, from present-day Ellenborough Street to Upper Circular Road, then further east to Circular Road, Chulia Street, RAFFLES PLACE and Change Alley.

The Chinese Opera Institute giving a performance at Little Guilin in Bukit Batok.

From left: the dan *(female); and* sheng *(male) are the two main categories of roles; pamphlet for Er Woo Amateur Musical and Dramatic Association's 92nd anniversary show.*

Unlike a secular performance in a concert hall, street opera is performed as part of a religious event, and is characterized by its interaction with ritual. Before the main performance, the troupe traditionally performs a series of ritual playlets, such as *Ba Xian He Shou* (Birthday Celebrations of the Eight Immortals), *Jing Peng* (Purifying the Stage), *Jing Cheng Hui* (The Grand Reunion at the Capital), and *Liu Guo Feng Xiang* (The Joint Investiture of a Prime Minister by Six Warlords). They are performed to ask for blessings from the deities and bring good fortune to the community. The most well-known ritual opera in Singapore is *Mulian Jiu Mu* (Mulian Rescues his Mother from Hell). Usually put on by the HENGHUA community,

this play has been performed every ten years since 1944 in Kiew Lee Tong Temple.

In modern Singapore, the majority of Chinese operas are still staged outdoors for religious purposes, usually on vacant land or a parking lot outside a temple. As of 2006 there were about 30 professional groups, predominantly TEOCHEW and HOKKIEN troupes, which were performing. Over 90 per cent of these performances are for such ritual occasions. Kim Eng Teochew Opera troupe performs about 200 days per year. Before the 1997 Asian financial crisis led to a reduction in funds, major troupes, including SIN YONG HUA HENG TROUPE, Lao Sai Tao Yuan Teochew Wayang, Kim Eng Teochew Opera and SIN SAI HONG HOKKIEN WAYANG, performed

over 300 days in a year. The annual performance which is put on during the celebrations held in honour of the birthdays of the San Huang Wu Di (Three Kings and Five Lords) is an important event for the CANTONESE community.

Beyond the religious context, Chinese opera was also enjoyed as entertainment held in indoor theatres. Many of these were built in the late 19th and early 20th century in and around Chinatown, including LAI CHUN YUEN along Smith Street, Qing Sheng Ping, Qing Wei Xin and Tian Yan Dawutai along Wayang Street (Eu Tong Sen Street), Yi Yuan along Merchant Road and Zhe Yuan along New Market Road. Many of the opera theatres were owned by rich merchants who had prospered during this period of economic growth. There were also wealthy enthusiasts who formed amateur musical groups, several of which grew to become full-fledged amateur groups, such as ER WOO AMATEUR MUSICAL AND DRAMATIC ASSOCIATION, Ping Sheh (The Singapore Amateur Beijing Opera Society) and Siong Leng Musical Association.

The appeal of opera theatres decreased when AMUSEMENT PARKS such as NEW WORLD, GREAT WORLD and GAY WORLD emerged as alternative performance sites for Chinese opera and other forms of mass entertainment from the 1920s to the early 1960s.

Over the decades, with the construction of new performance theatres, Chinese opera has been staged at cultural venues such as the now-defunct NATIONAL THEATRE, Kreta Ayer People's Theatre, Victoria Theatre and ESPLANADE—THEATRES ON THE BAY.

From top: Performers' headgear are stored backstage; the orchestra practices before an open stage; Chinese operas are a dazzling spectacle of costume and colour.

Chinese Protectorate: new Chinese Protectorate Building, 1930s.

TUTION (*see also* AH KU); and the containment of venereal diseases.

The Protectorate worked to minimize the abuse suffered by *sinkheh* due to the workings of the COOLIE TRADE. Many *sinkheh* had arrived in Malaya under the credit-ticket system, and were treated like *zhu zai* ('piglets') for shipping as coolies to neighbouring regions. Upon arrival in Singapore, they would be herded into depots which were overcrowded and heavily guarded by thugs. Employment arrangements were handled by coolie brokers, who would hire secret societies to guard against *sinkheh* escaping.

The Protectorate thus laid out rules regarding the *sinkheh* and their administration upon arrival. An officer would board ships and distribute handbills to *sinkheh*, assuring government protection against any oppression. The *sinkheh* were told to seek help from the Protectorate instead of from secret societies. They were interviewed individually to ascertain their circumstances at arrival. When brought ashore, *sinkheh* would be accommodated in depots for more than a week until relatives collected them or agencies hired them. The Protectorate required employers to sign a contract with their *sinkheh*. The terms of the contract were explained to the *sinkheh* in his own dialect. These measures were refined in subsequent years as the coolie trade sought ways to circumvent them.

The task of registering secret societies also came under the purview of the Chinese Protectorate. The protector was made the Registrar of Societies, and was tasked with recording the societies' names and addresses, as well as details regarding office-bearers, members and subscriptions. Supervision of the societies, however, was the joint responsibility of the Chinese protector and the inspector-general of police.

During his tenure, Pickering also arbitrated in petty disputes amongst the Chinese, positioning himself as non-partisan with respect to the conflicting interests of the various Chinese community groups. Pickering thus presented the Chinese Protectorate as an alternative to the author-

ity of the secret societies.

In 1871, there were 46,104 Chinese males to 7,468 females in Singapore; in 1891, that ratio was 100,446 to 21,462. Given this imbalance, the government permitted prostitution, but only as long as women were not coerced into joining the profession. The Chinese Protectorate sought to protect Chinese women and girls who were cheated into working as prostitutes; free prostitutes from the control of brothels and secret societies; and check prostitutes for venereal diseases. It took on the responsibility of overseeing the implementation of the Contagious Disease Ordinance in 1881, to check the prevalence of venereal diseases among the British land and sea forces and to loosen secret society control of brothels. For this reason, the Protectorate screened newly arrived women and girls, especially those suspected to have been brought in for prostitution (but who were often passed off as cabin passengers or as wives, mothers or daughters).

The Protector was empowered to rescue any girl under 16 years of age from a brothel, and was also able to enter any premise where he had reason to suspect that any woman or girl obtained by fraud was being concealed. Agents of the Chinese Protectorate also visited female domestic servants to guard against inhumane conditions. All rescued women and girls were sent to a refuge set up by the Chinese Protectorate with the help of prominent Chinese in 1878. In 1886, the Po Leung Kuk Committee (Office for the Preservation of Virtue) was formed to expand the services of this refuge, with the Chinese Protector acting as its chairman. The Po Leung Kuk vetted applications from families interested in their female wards as adopted daughters, servants and wives. A committee of European ladies ran the home and taught the girls to cook, sew, do household chores and read and write Chinese. The home grew from a single room with fewer than a dozen residents to four large wards with a matron's house enclosed in a compound for 120 residents in 1896.

Thus, the Chinese Protectorate became

an intermediary between the Chinese and the government, not only on matters relating to immigration and emigration, but also on all matters affecting the Chinese community. The government relied on the Protectorate for the governance of the Chinese as it grew knowledgeable about the various sections of the Chinese community and their attitudes to proposed legislation.

Before World War II, as the British contemplated the formation of a Malayan nation-state, the notion of treating the Chinese as a separate community was done away with, and the Protectorate was disbanded. The office of the Secretary of Chinese Affairs, however, continued to advise the government on Chinese politics and the interests of the Chinese community.

Chinese Religion *See* box.

Chinese Swimming Club This club was originally founded as the Tanjong Katong Swimming Party by a small group of young men who used to gather for a weekly swim at East Coast Beach. In 1909, the group renamed itself the Chinese Swimming Club. The club was registered three years later. Most of the club's swimming took place in the sea, and was made safe by wooden piles that were driven into the water to ward off sharks. In 1921, the club started to search for a permanent home, and approached the philanthropist Lee Choon Guan for help. Lee offered the club use of Bungalow C, located in the grounds of his home, Mandalay House, for a nominal fee.

Bungalow C was sold to the club in 1925 by Lee's widow after his death. In 1939, work commenced on a 25-m swimming pool and a new clubhouse. These were opened in 1941. The club was then rebuilt ten years later, this time with an Olympic-size pool. The Chinese Swimming Club became not only an important social centre for the Chinese in colonial times, but also earned a reputation for producing swimming champions, such as PATRICIA CHAN.

The club built a new sports complex in 1979, and a new recreation complex in 1991. In 2002, the sports complex was replaced by a new building.

Chinese Swimming Club: opening ceremony, 1951.

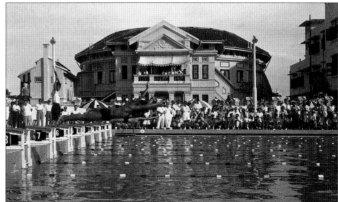

Chinese popular music

Chinese popular music in Singapore has its roots in the city's amusement parks: New World, Great World and Gay World. In the 1950s, New World even had its own getai (stage shows), while many amusement parks had cabarets. Singers of that era—including Huang Qing Yuan and Qin Huai, who were known for their ballads—often sang in Chinese dialects such as Cantonese and Hokkien, as well as in Mandarin.

Western popular music also had a considerable influence on Chinese singers. Henry Foo (Fu Su Yin) sang Mandarin renditions of Western popular songs with The Quests. Fu was also chairman of the Singapore Artists' Association in the 1950s and was the artist and repertoire manager for the Chinese section of EMI in Singapore.

Cathay Organisation, which owned the Odeon on North Bridge Road, produced the Early Bird Show, which ran on Sundays at 9 a.m. before the day's first movie screening at 11 a.m. The show provided a platform for singers such as Sakura, Rita Chao and Lara Tan, and backing bands such as The Trailers.

Clockwise from top: Eric Moo; Liang Wenfu; Ming Tian 21 (21 Tomorrow).

Clockwise from top: Great World Cabaret and New World Cabaret dance ticket; The Trailers; Rita Chao and Sakura.

The SBC singers

During the early 1980s, writers and producers from Hong Kong were hired by the Singapore Broadcasting Corporation (SBC) to work on Mandarin drama serials to be produced locally. These drama serials were highly successful, prompting SBC to initiate singing classes to develop the talent of actors who were especially popular. Singers who emerged during this period include Maggie Teng, who also acted in some television dramas. Another popular singer from this era was Jiang Hu. SBC also fostered several singers who performed regularly on Mandarin variety shows.

The rise of xinyao

The 1970s and early 1980s saw a rise in the composition of local popular songs in Mandarin. The year 1982 has been identified as the year in which xinyao emerged. The term xinyao is an abbreviation of the phrase 'Xin jia po

nianqing ren chuangzuo de geyao' (literally 'songs written by Singaporean youth'). Most xinyao songwriters and singers were students who came together informally to write and perform music.

Xinyao was initially influenced by Taiwanese xiaoyuan min'ge (campus folk music) and shiyue ('poetic music'): the former drew on American popular folk music of the 1960s and 1970s; the latter drew inspiration from the lieder of Brahms and Schubert, and from Chinese poetry. Largely performed by amateurs and consisting of simple melodies built around basic chord structures played on an acoustic guitar,

Maggie Teng

xinyao differed from other genres of Chinese popular music in terms of its simplicity. Singers who began recording in this genre include Eric Moo and Liang Wenfu.

The Speak Mandarin campaign, inaugurated in 1978, was also timely for xinyao songwriters, as it unified Chinese dialect communities and affirmed Mandarin as a medium of creative expression.

In May 1984, the xinyao album Ming Tian 21 (21 Tomorrow)—a compilation featuring several performers and produced by Billy Koh—was released. About 30,000 copies were sold. An annual xinyao festival, featuring xinyao performers and groups, began in 1985. The final festival was held in 1992.

The influence of xinyao

By the 1990s, the Chinese popular music industry in Singapore had begun to look to the larger markets of Hong Kong and Taiwan. Xinyao singers also tried to adapt lyrically and musically to these markets. The xinyao genre thus began to decline in popularity. However, xinyao underwent a revival in the early years of the 21st century. This started in 2002 at a sold-out two-night concert featuring xinyao performers, at the National University of Singapore's Cultural Centre. On 22 March 2003, the Xinyao Reunion Concert was held.

Xinyao's legacy can be seen in local labels such as Ocean Butterflies, at which singers such as Kit Chan, Tanya Chua and A-Do all started their careers. Regional star Stefanie Sun also started her career with the Li Wei Song School, run by Peter Li Sisong and Paul Li

From top: the Li Brothers; Tanya Chua, left, and Stefanie Sun; A-Do.

Weisong, both of whom were closely associated with xinyao. Xinyao performers such as Liang Wenfu, Tan Kah Beng and Loi Fei Huay have established themselves in Hong Kong and Taiwan as songwriters and lyricists for Wen Zhang, Tracy Huang, Alex To, Tony Leung Kar Fai and other singers.

Chinese Theatre Circle: Duel at Mount Cockerel, 2005.

Chinese theatre *See* box.

Chinese Theatre Circle Theatre group promoting Chinese opera, drama, dance and music. Established in 1981 by artistic director JOANNA WONG QUEE HENG and her husband, resident playwright Leslie Wong, the Chinese Theatre Circle has staged more than 2,000 performances in Singapore and 21 other countries, and has thus helped revive Chinese opera as an art form in Singapore. Its signature opera, *A Costly Impulse*, was recorded live in Beijing in 1993 and subsequently broadcast nationwide to a viewership of 700 million people. The group has helped non-Chinese-speakers appreciate Chinese opera by providing English subtitles at its productions. It was also the first to present Chinese opera productions in English and Malay. In 2001, its production of excerpts of *Madam White Snake* and *Picking The Jade Bracelet* incorporated elements of Malay dance and music. In 2005, it presented *Intrigues In The Qing Imperial Court*, the first full-length Chinese opera to be performed with English dialogue.

Chinese weddings Chinese marriages were traditionally determined by professional matchmakers, who were hired to match a couple's horoscopes, determine the *pinli*—comprising the *pinjin* (bride price) and *jiazhuang* (trousseau)—and other details pertaining to the wedding. These customs are no longer common practice, but the groom may still present his future in-laws with a *hongbao* (red packet containing money) in lieu of the bride price. An exchange of gifts (*nacai*) of food and money is also made, the specific items depending on the dialect groups to which the bride and groom belong.

In recent times, matchmaking is very rarely practised. A prospective groom will instead ask the parents of his wife-to-be for her hand. Families do their best to avoid holding weddings during the seventh month of the lunar calendar—ZHONG YUAN JIE (Hungry Ghost Festival)—which is believed to be an inauspicious time.

On the morning of the wedding day, the groom and his male friends and relatives make their way to the bride's house. They are barred from entering by the bride's female friends and relatives, who will only let them in upon being presented with a *hongbao* of an amount they have successfully haggled over. This traditionally Cantonese custom is now practised by most Chinese families regardless of dialect. Most couples dress in Western-style wedding attire, but some couples also choose to wear traditional Chinese wedding dress. The couple then make their way to the groom's house to perform the tea ceremony, which involves them serving cups of tea to elders in the family, and receiving *hongbao* or jewellery in return. The same ritual is repeated at the bride's house. Prior to the enactment of the WOMEN'S CHARTER, carrying out the ceremony marked the couple's entry into a common law marriage.

The festivities conclude with a wedding dinner, usually held in a hotel restaurant or ballroom. The dinner is typically a Chinese banquet of eight or nine courses. The groom was traditionally expected to pay for the wedding dinner, but nowadays both families may share the cost.

Chingay Street festival held during CHINESE NEW YEAR. The tradition of Chingay street processions began in the 19th century. A Chingay procession took place in Penang in the 1880s, and postcards depicting Singapore in the early years of the 20th century show scenes of Chingay processions. The meaning of the word 'Chingay' is unclear, but the word is probably a transliteration of a dialect phrase describing a stage borne on the shoulders of men.

The first 'official' Chingay procession was staged in Singapore in 1973 by the PEOPLE'S ASSOCIATION as an attempt to add colour to Chinese New Year festivities after a ban on FIRECRACKERS was introduced. The procession was such a success that it became an annual event, touring various housing estates. ORCHARD ROAD has, however,

Chng Seok Tin: Man and Environment, 1988.

Chinese weddings: bride and groom offer tea to parents in a traditional tea ceremony (top); tea set.

remained the most popular venue. Although Chingay was originally started as a Chinese street procession and carnival, Malay and Indian cultural items were added in 1977 and, in 1987, foreign groups began to take part. In 1990, Chingay made its evening debut, complete with lighted floats. Today, the Chingay Parade is a multi-ethnic, cosmopolitan street festival.

Ch'ng Jit Koon (1934–) Politician. Born in China, Ch'ng Jit Koon was educated at Chung Cheng High School and Beatty Secondary School in Singapore. In 1959, he graduated with a bachelor of arts in economics from Nanyang University. He entered politics in 1968 under the PEOPLE'S ACTION PARTY banner and won the seat of Tiong Bahru constituency. He held that seat until 1991 before switching to, and winning, the seat of Bukit Merah constituency. From 1982 to 1985, Ch'ng served as senior parliamentary secretary to the prime minister. Subsequently, he was minister of state for community development (1985–91) and senior minister of state for community development (1991–97). He retired from politics in 1997.

Ch'ng Jit Koon

Chng Seok Tin (1946–) Artist and author. A graduate of the NANYANG ACADEMY OF FINE ARTS, Chng Seok Tin proceeded to St Martin's School of Arts, London, and studied intaglio and engraving at Atelier 17, Paris. She received a master's degree in arts from New Mexico University (1983) and another in fine arts from the University of Iowa (1985). Chng's eyesight was impaired as a result of an accident in 1988, and her life and works thereafter could be said to be a triumph of will. She was named Distinguished Visiting Artist by San Jose State University, United States (1992), was made president of the Printmaking Society (1997); was conferred the Woman of the Year Award by *Her World* magazine (2001); and received the CULTURAL MEDALLION (2005). Chng is also credited with holding the first solo exhibition by a Singaporean at the United Nations Headquarters (2005).

Chingay

Chinese Religion Among Singaporeans of Chinese descent, some 53.6 per cent identify themselves as 'Buddhist', while 10.8 per cent identify themselves as 'Taoist', according to the 2000 Census of Population. The census lists the latter as 'Taoism/Chinese Traditional Beliefs'. However, as a worldview and belief system embedded in everyday life, Chinese Religion extends beyond this category, influencing the practices of those who identify themselves as 'Buddhist'.

The term 'Chinese Religion' as defined by Vivienne Wee denotes the symbolic logic that underlies the syncretic beliefs and practices of ethnic Chinese. Chinese Religion was brought to Singapore by migrants from China. Chinese Religion in Singapore thus contains elements derived from China's pre-history and history, including animistic beliefs that go back at least 10,000 years, as well as the numerous gods and goddesses in the pantheon. It also includes Hindu ideas of karma and nirvana, known in Chinese as *gongde* and *niepan*.

The syncretic nature of Chinese Religion means that although Chinese Religion arrived in Singapore as a fully formed belief system, it nevertheless took on local characteristics. Chinese Religion is marked by a number of basic principles. The entire universe, organic and inorganic, is animated by essence. When this essence animates human beings, it is called 'linghun' ('soul'). When it inhabits non-human matter, it is known as '*shen*' ('gods' or 'spirit/essence'). It is possible for human beings to communicate with all *shen*, during which they assume an

Joss sticks and food are placed before paper effigies of Chinese deities as offerings.

anthropomorphic form, represented by words, pictures, statues, or even possessed bodies.

When *linghun* or *shen* is dislocated from material embodiment, it becomes *gui*, generally translated as 'ghost'. To prevent the *linghun* of a deceased person from becoming *gui*, an alternative material embodiment is provided through a *shenzhupai* (spirit tablet) that becomes the focus of ancestor worship by descendants. Chinese Religionists thus say of a deceased person that he/she has become a *shen*. The part of the soul that becomes a *shen* retains the personality of the deceased, which is why Chinese Religionists often offer dead family members their favourite foods, remembering them as they were when alive. This form of ancestor worship converges with the principle of filial piety in Confucian orthodoxy (see CONFUCIANISM). The influence of Hindu/Buddhist ideas of rebirth have given rise to the belief that another part of the soul is reborn in another body, either animal or human. In a similar way, the *shen* of an object can be dislodged when its material

A priest presides over the recitation of prayers at an event organized by a Chinese temple.

embodiment is destroyed. Thus, prior to chopping down a tree, Chinese Religionists usually ask its *shen* to depart in peace and take up residence in another tree.

Ming ('fate') and *yun* ('luck')
In Chinese Religion, human lives are determined by *ming* ('fate') and *yun* ('luck'), in accordance with karmic laws of retribution, resulting in a *hao* ('good') or *ku* ('bad') fate, and one's fate is believed to be predestined. Human beings therefore can seek the help of supernatural powers through communication with *shen*, and alignment with supernatural forces in time and space through the practice of FENG SHUI (geomancy).

Human beings seeking to maximize good luck and minimize bad luck often

From top: the mirror, scissors and talisman are used to ward off evil; joss papers are burnt as offerings.

do so through communication with anthropomorphized *shen* in pictures or statues. This is achieved through *bai shen* (literally 'paying respects to *shen*'), a ritual action that can occur anywhere, from within the home to a temple, pavement or cemetery. Important components of ritual communication with *shen* include joss-sticks, gifts (such as joss paper, flowers, food, paper representations of gold ingots and robes), divining sticks and blocks. Other than communicating with *shen*, people can use feng shui to align themselves with auspicious supernatural forces. Feng shui (literally 'wind and water') is another expression of the idea of an animated universe. The aim is to maximize positive forces and minimize negative forces, so as to enhance one's luck. This is achieved by picking auspicious times and spaces for particular activities (for example moving house, weddings, funerals or starting a business).

The utilitarian focus of Chinese Religion militates against metaphysical enquiries about the ultimate meaning of good and evil. Rather, it presents an anthropocentric universe where human beings can draw on non-human sources of power for their own ends. Chinese Religionists invest tremendous effort and resources towards doing this. The

Communing with the gods
A more direct form of communication with the gods is spirit-mediumship. The local form of this practice derives from southern Fujian province, where the ancestors of most Chinese Singaporeans came from. Mediums are called *dangki* in the Minnan dialect of south Fujian, also known as HOKKIEN. This significantly translates as 'child medium', because mediums are believed to have short lives which are, however, lengthened through the intermittent suspensions of their souls during mediumship, thereby spacing out their limited amounts of *linghun* over a longer period of time. The underlying belief is that the medium's body becomes the physical embodiment of a *shen*, which unlike a picture or statue can move and speak.

Mediumship sessions enable devotees to seek the help of the possessing *shen*. After the medium has demonstrated possession by inflicting ritualized violence on him/herself, the devotees ask the same type of questions they would ask of the *shen* when embodied in an image, including questions about health, examinations, jobs, business, and relationships. The *shen*-in-the-medium gives advice in a divine tongue, which is interpreted by a ritual assistant. Apart from verbal advice, the *shen*-in-the-medium may give ritual prescriptions by writing unintelligible divine characters on red charm papers—some which are to be burnt, their ashes mixed with water and drunk, while others are to be posted on house doors to keep out evil spirits. The *shen*-in-the-medium may also provide treatment through magical gestures to cure or protect devotees present at the ritual.

practices involved indicate an optimism that practical needs and desires can be met with the help of supernatural forces, as well as a worldview that sees the human sphere as the fundamental reality from which all other 'realities' derive, including 'life' after death and the 'life' of gods and ghosts.

A hierarchy of deities

As in human society, gods are hierarchized according to their status within specific domains of influence. In the celestial hierarchy, the top three positions are occupied by Yü Huangdi (Jade Emperor), who is sometimes merged with the Hokkien deity Ti Gong (God of Heaven), Sakyamuni Gautama Buddha and Guanyin (Goddess of Mercy), an incarnation of the Mahayana bodhisattva Avalokitesvara. Yenluo Huang (Emperor Yenluo) is regarded as the highest god of the underworld. The gods who reside on earth can be classified into two categories: the attached *shen* of earthly objects such as mountains, seas, areas of land, trees and even man-made objects; and the earthly manifestations of the gods of heaven and the underworld as free *shen* made manifest in the material form of an image or *dangki* ('spirit medium').

Chinese Religionists tend to turn more often to free *shen* than to attached *shen* for help, because free *shen* are believed to be more compassionate. In the case of Guanyin, it is assumed that this free *shen* materializes in different ways through different images, as if each image contained its own specific bounded portion of the Guanyin essence as a whole. Thus, as Guanyin Dashi Ye (Most Powerful Grandfather Guanyin), the deity is represented as a male custodian of the ghosts who roam the earth during ZHONG YUAN JIE, when the gates of hell are believed to be open. In his/her more common female manifestations, Guanyin is venerated for her compassion.

Shifts and changes

Over the last two centuries in Singapore, Chinese Religionist places of worship have included tree shrines (usually at the foot of old trees), Malay shrines such as the KERAMAT KUSU on KUSU ISLAND, Hindu temples, *dangki* temples, Buddhist temples (both Theravada and Mahayana) and even the Roman Catholic NOVENA CHURCH. This highly syncretic approach to worship is on the one hand facilitated by the utilitarian and adaptive logic of Chinese Religion, and on the other by the multireligious nature of Singapore society.

However, societal changes since the 1950s have engendered significant transformations in Chinese Religion in Singapore. Massive re-urbanization has demolished many neighbourhood temples, especially smaller-scale *dangki* temples. In their place are new government-built temples that allocate altar space to each demolished temple that had been registered as such. Devotees of demolished temples which were not registered have to find their own alternative spaces, such as PUBLIC HOUSING apartments or other private residences. Despite such difficulties, many *dangki* groups still conduct elaborate annual festivals in large tents on open grounds, with CHINESE OPERA performances, feasts and marathon mediumship sessions which can extend over several days. The NINE EMPEROR GODS FESTIVAL is another spectacular ritual celebration which is carried out at certain temples.

The increase in the numbers of secondary- and tertiary-educated Chinese Singaporeans, many of whom have received an ENGLISH EDUCATION, has generated a demand for more text-based forms of religion, as well as those which address metaphysical questions in a more systematic fashion, and CHRISTIANITY and BUDDHISM have seen converts from Chinese Religion. The 2000 Census reported a shift from TAOISM to Buddhism among the Singapore Chinese population, but this shift, however, does not signal a clean break with Chinese Religion, by virtue of the centuries-old integration of Buddhist beliefs and practices within Chinese Religion.

From top: a statue of Guanyin; old trees are venerated, and shrines are built to shen *which are believed to reside within them.*

Datuk Gong worship

Chinese Religion is constitutively open to interpretation as it is not bound to a given scripture, but to the notion that wherever one is situated, there are always beneficial relationships to be sought between human and non-human forces. In Singapore, Malay animism is acknowledged and affirmed in Chinese Religion by the presence of Datuk Gong (Grandfather/Lord) shrines set up for the purpose of communicating with the indigenous spirit of a particular area. In deference to Islam, offerings made at such shrines would not include pork.

From top: giant joss sticks and oversized sheets of joss paper are burnt during special occasions such as festivals or deities' birthdays; an open altar to Tian Gong along the Singapore River; an altar table in a home, with joss sticks, incense and a sheaf of joss paper.

Artefacts for the dead

Veneration of the dead is an important part of Chinese Religion. Paper houses (right) are burnt during funerals in the belief that the spirit of the deceased will reside in the house. *Shenzhupai* (ancestral tablets) (above) are stored in temples, and bear the names of the deceased.

Chinese theatre

Modern Chinese theatre in Singapore dates back to the mid-1920s. The publication of a one-act play called *In the Coffee Shop* in 1925 in the literary supplement of Singapore's first Chinese newspaper *Lat Pau* inspired other writers to script new plays for the stage. Early plays like San San's *Prison of Conscience* and Huan Yu's *Crossroads* were primarily concerned with social injustice and the welfare of the poor. Such plays were presented by drama groups alongside other plays by playwrights from China as part of fund-raising activities for victims of natural disasters in China. Local dialects were also incorporated in these earlier works to reflect their origin, and were staged by old boys' associations of schools and amateur groups like Qing Nian Li Zhi She.

From left: The Chinese Industrial and Commercial Continuation School Alumni put up Yi Guan Qin Shou, *1954; and* Han Ye Qü, *1949.*

Veteran theatre practitioners formed the The Amateur Theatre Society (TATS) in 1937, which became the leading force in theatre and in turn encouraged the growth of smaller drama groups. That year, Japan invaded China and the war rapidly escalated. Chinese drama groups used their craft as a vehicle for anti-Japanese propaganda and as a means of collecting donations for fighters on the Chinese frontline. The society toured Malaya, visiting 81 towns and villages and staging a total of 145 performances in 1938. No less than 20 drama groups were formed in Malaya in the wake of this tour. In 1939, the Wuhan Choir from China performed in Singapore and presented anti-war sketches, songs and dances, leaving their mark on the local drama scene. With the advent of the Japanese Occupation in Singapore in 1942, however, many drama activities went underground.

The Chinese drama scene in the immediate post-war period drew their influences from the China Song, Dance and Drama Company, a prominent performing arts group which visited in 1947, and Tu Pian, Yeh Yeh and Zhao Lulin, who were well-known drama practitioners from China. These well-established companies and individuals imparted their knowledge of stagecraft and other details of the art to local groups. Zhao Lulin, who was formerly the principal of Canton Arts School, joined CHUNG CHENG HIGH SCHOOL after the war, and made a significant contribution by initiating drama activities there. Since 1947, the Chung Cheng Drama Society and the drama societies of THE CHINESE HIGH SCHOOL, NANYANG GIRLS' HIGH SCHOOL and Yu Ying High School have regularly presented Chinese drama.

In the mid-1950s, three groups formed by drama enthusiasts—KANG LE MUSIC RESEARCH SOCIETY (1954), the Singapore Amateur Players (1955) and the I-Lien Drama Society (1956)—were established. In their early days, these groups staged works written by established playwrights in China as well as translated plays by Western playwrights like Anton Chekhov and Henrik Ibsen. The Nanyang University Drama Society (1956) was also an active group from that period, staging plays, publishing drama magazines, organizing talks and encouraging the writing and production of plays which could capture the spirit of the age.

In the early 1960s, Chinese drama expanded its territory and gained popularity among the workers. Full-length plays such as *Night Song in the Coconut Plantation* by Sung Li Sang and LIN CHEN's *Tears and Blood at the Construction Site* were chosen by various workers' unions. There was a strong sense of community spirit among the Chinese drama groups as they were convinced that their work was part of a process they called the 'construction of new culture for the nation and the promotion of wholesome culture'.

By the mid-1960s the workers' unions, Kang Le, school drama groups and the Nanyang University Drama Group were dissolved by the government as they were suspected of engaging in leftist political activities. The vacuum was soon filled by the Children's Playhouse, which was formed by Tiah Mong Teck in 1965 and affiliated with Radio Television Singapore. It was later expanded to establish a Youth Play House in 1970 and became a professional theatre company. Initially set up to train child actors for radio plays, its scope of training expanded to include drama, dance, vocal and instrumental music, creative writing, painting and design, and became in effect a performing arts school which nurtured many young

talents. It was the most active theatre group throughout the 1970s until 1978, when dwindling audience numbers forced them to shut down.

Two other new groups active in the 1970s were the Singapore Performing Arts School (later renamed PRACTICE PERFORMING ARTS SCHOOL) founded by KUO PAO KUN and his wife GOH LAY KUAN in 1965, and the Rediffusion Chinese Drama Group set up by Chen Bohan in the same year. Kuo translated and staged Bertolt Brecht's *The Caucasian Chalk Circle* and Chen Bohan's *The Bursting of Life's Embankment*. Chen's biggest success was his own satirical play entitled *The Devils' World*, which was staged in 1971.

The influence of the Cultural Revolution in China was felt in Singapore Chinese theatre circles, and a number of theatre practitioners produced dramas which sought to depict the class struggle. The death of Mao Zedong in late 1976 and the subsequent abolition of the Cultural Revolution led to the demise of radical theatre in Singapore. The groups gradually changed their direction, and participated in the annual Drama Festival organized by the Ministry of Culture, which featured theatre groups performing in all four official languages (Malay, English, Mandarin and Tamil) in 1977. For many, that was the beginning of cross-cultural interaction in theatre. Throughout the 1980s, the audience saw many international classics adapted as Mandarin plays, and original plays written by veterans and newcomers to the scene alike. In the early 1980s, Chinese student drama activities saw a resurgence with the pioneering efforts of the Hwa Chong Junior College and Nanyang Junior College drama groups. The ETCeteras, a theatre group which produced original plays, was formed in

Titoudao by Toy Factory Theatre Ensemble.

the early 1990s by a group of alumni from Hwa Chong Junior College. Among the secondary schools, Nanyang Girls' High School was the most active in the 1980s.

In the 1990s, new Chinese theatre groups as well as older establishments were more diversified in their approach and focus. Older groups such as ARTS THEATRE OF SINGAPORE (ATS) (formerly known as Singapore Amateur Players) concentrated on children's theatre and audience development, while the Practice Theatre launched a multi-disciplinary training programme. Newer groups developed their own identity during this time. Toy Factory Theatre Ensemble, founded by GOH BOON TECK, evolved as a professional multi-disciplinary theatre company which focuses on staging new works and novel interpretations of established plays. DRAMA BOX, founded by Kok Heng Leun in 1990, reaches out beyond the usual theatre-going audience by bringing its performances to PUBLIC HOUSING estates where the majority of the population live, and its works seek to raise social awareness about current issues among a wider audience.

The new generation of Mandarin theatre practitioners is effectively bilingual, and is thus able to effectively draw their inspiration from both East and West. With a small group of young enthusiasts, new youth groups like the Young People's Theatre, founded by Ma Yeshen, and the Singapore Hokkien Huay Kuan Drama Group, with its large number of speech and drama classes for children, are likely to continue to cultivate a new pool of audiences and performers for Mandarin theatre in Singapore in the 21st century.

Forum theatre performance in the community (left); and Shithole *by Drama Box.*

Choa Chu Kang New town. Choa Chu Kang is bounded by Woodlands Road, Choa Chu Kang Way, Kranji Expressway and Choa Chu Kang Road. The estate occupies a land area of some 580 ha, 52 per cent of which is used for residential purposes. Some 100,000 residents live in the 35,000 housing units in Choa Chu Kang Town. The area also houses the largest remaining burial ground in Singapore—the Choa Chu Kang Cemetery.

Choa Chu Kang was named after the Choa family, who settled by the Kranji River. Villages along the river were typically named after the family controlling that part of the river; the headman of the village was known in Hokkien as the *kang chu*. It is unclear exactly when the Choa family settled there, but Chinese villages had grown up along several of Singapore's rivers by the 1840s. The original settlers of Choa Chu Kang Village were PEPPER and GAMBIER farmers. Many of them were TEOCHEW. Later, they were joined by pineapple, rubber and coconut planters, many of whom were HOKKIEN.

Choa Chu Kang Columbarium Located off Choa Chu Kang Road in northwest Singapore, this columbarium houses some 147,000 niches in 18 four-storey blocks. It was completed in 2001. The buildings are laid out in the shape of a Chinese fan. This design allows the buildings to achieve maximum natural cross-ventilation and natural light. The blocks of niches are named according to flowers, and the entire complex was designed to emulate a park.

Choe, Alan (1930–) Civil servant and architect. Alan Choe Fook Cheong studied at the University of Melbourne, where he received a bachelor's degree in architecture (1956) and a diploma in town and regional planning (1958). When he returned to Singapore in 1959, he worked at a local architectural firm before joining Singapore Polytechnic as a lecturer from 1960 to 1962. He then joined the Housing & Development Board as an architect and

planner. Between 1974 and 1978, he worked at the Urban Redevelopment Authority, where he formulated policies for the redevelopment of the central area of Singapore. He left for RSP Architects Planners & Engineers in 1978. In 1997, he formed his own consultancy, which he ran until his retirement from practice in 2001.

Choe joined the board of the Sentosa Development Corporation when it was launched in 1972, taking over as chairman in 1985. He is credited with introducing the monorail in 1982, developing the causeway link from Sentosa to Singapore island in 1992, the 12-storey replica Merlion and the new Siloso Beach. When he stepped down in 2001, he became chairman of Sentosa Cove Pte Ltd, a company formed to develop and manage the Sentosa Cove mixed-use project on Sentosa. Choe retired from the company in 2003.

Choe received the Meritorious Service Medal in 1990, and was admitted into the Distinguished Service Order in 2001.

cholera Disease caused by an infection of the intestine by the bacterium *Vibrio cholerae*. This infectious disease is most common in countries with poor sanitation and hygiene. Symptoms of cholera are severe diarrhoea, vomiting and, sometimes, abdominal pain and fever. Diarrhoea can lead to dehydration which may be life-threatening, especially for young children and the elderly. The disease is transmitted through the consumption of contaminated water or food, such as raw or poorly cooked seafood, peeled fruits and salads. Bacteria in the faeces of an infected person are a major source of contamination.

There were frequent outbreaks of cholera in 19th-century Singapore, and a cholera epidemic in 1873. This started in the Kandang Kerbau district, where the General Hospital (later SINGAPORE GENERAL HOSPITAL) and Lunatic Asylum were located. Patients from the General Hospital were quickly moved to the Sepoy Lines. After the epidemic was contained, the patients did not return to the General

Cholera: immunization, 1963.

Hospital as the Kandang Kerbau district was considered unhealthy.

With the improved sanitation, clean drinking water and better hygiene that came as Singapore modernized, cholera cases were reduced to a handful each year. The disease still occurs sporadically, with the source generally being the importation of contaminated seafood such as shellfish. There were eight cases of cholera recorded in 2001, and two each in 2002 and 2003.

Chong, Annabel (1973–) Born Grace Quek, Annabel Chong was educated at Raffles Girls' School and Hwa Chong Junior College, excelling academically in both schools. She then studied at the University of Southern California, where she adopted the persona of Annabel Chong. On 19 January 1995, Chong attempted to break the world record for having sexual intercourse with the greatest number of men in under ten hours. She filmed herself engaging in intercourse with 251 men. This footage was later released as a film entitled *The World's Greatest Gang Bang 1*. In 1999, first-time director Gough Lewis made a film about Chong's life entitled *Sex: the Annabel Chong Story*.

Chongay Organisation Film studio and distributor. Chongay produced a number of lesser-known movies in Singapore during the 1970s. Founded by Koh Tian Kit, it originally specialized in the distribution and screening of films from Taiwan, Hong Kong and China, catering to a local, Chinese audience.

Following the closure of SHAW BROTHERS and Cathay Organisation's studios, Chongay decided to move into the production of Chinese movies, and brought in technicians from Hong Kong. Its *Yi Jia Zhi Zhu* (Crime Does Not Pay) (1973) and *Huang Tang Shi Jia* (Hypocrite) (1973) were both directed by Hong Kong film-makers.

After understudying these Hong Kong film-makers, a local cast and crew made a third movie—Lim Ann's *Qiao De Liang An* (Two Sides of the Bridge) (1976)—the production of which was aided by foreign lighting and camera technicians. Production ceased after these three films due to rising costs, and Chongay closed down in the late 1970s.

Choo, Winston (1941–) Military officer and diplomat. Winston Choo Wee Leong was educated at the Anglo-Chinese School. He joined the SINGAPORE ARMED FORCES in 1959 and served as aide-de-camp to the president of Singapore. Choo later became director of general staff (1974), chief of general staff (1976) and CHIEF OF DEFENCE FORCE (1990–92). He was Singapore's first lieutenant-general and the first local-born chief of general staff.

After he retired from the military, Choo was appointed high commissioner to

Annabel Chong

Winston Choo

Choo Hoey

Chor Yeok Eng

Elizabeth Choy

Choo Hwee Lim

Australia and Fiji (1994-97); high commissioner to South Africa (2001–05); and ambassador to Israel (2005–). In 1996, he became chairman of the Singapore Red Cross Society. In 1990, Choo was awarded the Meritorious Service Medal (Military).

Choo Han Teck (1954–) Judge. Choo Han Teck was educated at the University of Singapore, where he obtained his bachelor's degree in law in 1979, and where he was an active student leader and sportsman. Upon graduation, he joined the firm of Murphy & Dunbar, where he practised for four years. In 1984, he joined the Faculty of Law of the National University of Singapore, where he taught constitutional law, evidence and procedure. Choo was awarded a scholarship to study for his master's degree in law, which he obtained at Cambridge University (1986).

Choo returned to Singapore to practise in 1988, joining the firm of ALLEN & GLEDHILL. In 1992, he left and became a founding partner of Helen Yeo & Partners, where he practised until 1995. He was appointed judicial commissioner on 1 April 1995, and in January 2003 was appointed judge of the Supreme Court.

Choo Hoey (1934–) Conductor. Born in Sumatra, Choo Hoey was educated in Singapore, the United Kingdom and Belgium. He was already enjoying an active conducting career in Europe, having served as the principal conductor of the Greek National Opera from 1968, when he returned to Singapore in the late 1970s—a move which marked a turning point in Singapore musical history. He was awarded the CULTURAL MEDALLION in 1980 and the Public Service Star in 1982.

Choo served as the founding conductor and music director of the SINGAPORE SYMPHONY ORCHESTRA (SSO) from 1979 to 1986. In that role, he was responsible for nurturing the orchestra; raising its performing standards; building a wide repertoire of works; taking the orchestra on several successful concert tours in Europe and Asia; and bringing the SSO international prominence. In 2001, he was appointed the orchestra's conductor emeritus.

Choo Hwee Lim (1931–) Singer and teacher. Choo Hwee Lim is a graduate of London's Royal College of Music, where

he majored in singing, conducting and teaching. Choo became active in musical theatre, and a pioneer and founding member of the SINGAPORE LYRIC OPERA, producing and directing several of its early operas. A former sportsman and teacher at the Anglo-Chinese Secondary School, Choo was also instrumental in developing its successful badminton training programme. He received the CULTURAL MEDALLION in 1992.

Chor Yeok Eng (1930–) Politician. Chor Yeok Eng attended Shuqun Primary School in Bukit Timah but left school to work at odd jobs. He joined the Malayan Democratic Youth Movement in 1946. He left that group when the colonial government banned it in 1948 following the EMERGENCY. By 1950, Chor had completed his secondary education at the former Chung Hwa Evening School. He joined the PEOPLE'S ACTION PARTY (PAP) in 1955, after attending the party's inauguration in November 1954. When the PAP set up a branch in Bukit Timah in 1955, he became its vice-chairman and treasurer. In 1959, he was elected legislative assemblyman for Jurong.

As parliamentary secretary in the Ministry of National Development in 1961, Chor was responsible for clearing squatters from TOA PAYOH so that the area could be developed into high-rise public housing. He would later do the same in Jurong, to make way for industrial development there.

Chor contested Bukit Timah constituency in the GENERAL ELECTION (1963), but lost to the BARISAN SOSIALIS. In 1966, he was elected MEMBER OF PARLIAMENT for Bukit Timah in a by-election, and became parliamentary secretary at the Ministry of Health. He was promoted to senior parliamentary secretary for the Ministry of the Environment in 1972. Chor retired from politics in 1990, and was awarded the Meritorious Service Medal in the same year.

Choy, Elizabeth (1910–2006) Teacher and war heroine. Born in North Borneo, Elizabeth Choy (née Yong) Su Moi came to Singapore in 1929 for an education, and was schooled at the Convent of the Holy Infant Jesus. She went on to become a teacher, first at St Margaret Girls' School, then at St Andrew's School. She married Choy Khun Heng in 1941.

During the JAPANESE OCCUPATION, she and her husband ran a canteen in Miyako Hospital (the Japanese name for Woodbridge Hospital), which was used as a 'postbox' through which Europeans held at CHANGI PRISON could communicate with persons outside. Some of these postings were alleged to detail radio parts, so that internees could build a radio set.

In October 1943, the KEMPEITAI (Japanese Military Police) apprehended her husband and took him to their notorious headquarters in the YMCA building on Stamford Road. Choy herself was arrested in November 1943 and was tortured by the Kempeitai to get her to 'confess' to her crimes. She was held for 200 days. When her husband was tried in a Japanese military court and sentenced to 12 years' imprisonment, she was released and no charges were filed against her. The Choys became the only married couple to be imprisoned by the Japanese in Singapore.

After the war, Choy's experiences at the hands of the Kempeitai made her famous. She and her husband were made Officers of the Order of the British Empire (OBE) in 1946. Choy became involved in politics in the 1950s, standing as an independent candidate in the first-ever LEGISLATIVE COUNCIL ELECTION (1951), in which she lost. She was a nominated member of the Legislative Assembly, the first woman to be nominated to the all-male assembly. She was persuaded to stand again for election in 1955, this time as a member of the SINGAPORE PROGRESSIVE PARTY, but lost again. She then gave up politics to concentrate on raising three adopted children, working with the blind and teaching fulltime at St Andrew's Junior School.

Choy was founding principal of the School for the Blind, where she worked until 1960. One of her pupils there was Theresa Chan Poh Lin, a deaf and blind child who grew up illiterate. Choy was instrumental in securing Chan a scholarship to the Perkins School for the Blind. In 2005, Chan played herself in the acclaimed ERIC KHOO film about her life, *Be with Me*.

Christianity The oldest extant church building in Singapore is the Armenian Apostolic Church of St Gregory the Illuminator (commonly referred to as the ARMENIAN CHURCH), consecrated in 1836.

Roman CATHOLICISM in Singapore has its roots in the Portuguese in Malacca. By 1830, there were approximately 300 Catholics in Singapore. The foundation stone for the first permanent Catholic church, the CATHEDRAL OF THE GOOD SHEPHERD, was laid in 1843.

Protestant Christianity was introduced into the region in 1807 by the London Missionary Society (LMS), which sent its first missionary in Asia, Robert Morrison, to Malacca. He started the Extra Ganges Mission at Malacca to coordinate all LMS work east of India. Sir STAMFORD RAFFLES granted permission to the society to establish a college in Singapore 'for the study of the Chinese language and the extension of Christianity'. The first LMS resident missionary to Singapore, Reverend Samuel Milton, arrived on 25 October 1819. Over the next nine years, the LMS started a total of four schools with 100 students. Raffles personally gave 150 Spanish dollars to support Milton's ministry on the condition that he conducted church services for the European community. The East India

Company leased 68,952 square feet of land at the junction of North Bridge Road and Bras Basah Road to the LMS, and a chapel was built here in 1824. For a decade, this was the only place of worship for Protestants in Singapore. The chapel no longer exists.

In 1834, the American Board of Commissioners for Foreign Missions (ABCFM) sent their first missionary, Reverend Ira Tracey, to Singapore. It started a printing press, which soon became the largest on the island. By 1837, there were 19 ABCFM missionaries in Singapore, Malacca and Penang. They unsuccessfully sought a grant of land to establish a colony in Singapore.

In fact, the primary concern of all these Protestant missions was China—Singapore and Malacca were seen chiefly as spring-boards into China. Neither LMS nor ABCFM established a local church in Singapore; indeed, with increased access to China after the 1842 Treaty of Nanking (present-day Nanjing), both the LMS and ABCFM shut down operations in Singapore and moved to Hong Kong and China. By this time, the established church of colonial Singapore was the Anglican Church, ST ANDREW'S CATHEDRAL having been consecrated in 1838. Presbyterianism was also established when an LMS mission-ary, BENJAMIN PEACH KEASBERRY, resigned from the LMS to remain in Singapore.

Education was an important concern of early Christians, who set up many MIS-SION SCHOOLS. The oldest girls' school is the Chinese Girls' School, started in 1842 (and later renamed ST MARGARET'S GIRLS' SCHOOL). Other mission schools still in exis-tence include ST JOSEPH'S INSTITUTION (1852), CONVENT OF THE HOLY INFANT JESUS (1854), ST ANDREW'S SCHOOL (1862) and St Anthony's Primary School (1879). By the

Christianity: St Andrew's Cathedral.

end of the 19th century, there were more students in mission schools than in govern-ment schools. Most of the early Methodist missionaries served in schools, and in 1900 the ANGLO-CHINESE SCHOOL was the largest school in Singapore. Because English was taught in Christian schools and with the presence of so many foreign missionaries, Christianity was seen as a 'western' religion. But the schools slowly changed the views of the Asian community.

Later arrivals included the Seventh-day Adventists (1908), the Assemblies of God (1933) and the SALVATION ARMY (1935). The YOUNG MEN'S CHRISTIAN ASSOCIATION came in 1902 and the first Baptist church, the Overseas Chinese (Swatow) Baptist Church, was built in 1937.

The shared hardship of World War II brought churches closer together and empowered local leaders. During the JAPANESE OCCUPATION all western mission-aries and pastors were interned at Changi Prison. For a while, locals took control over the church as the Japanese still allowed ser-vices to take place, although sermons had to be submitted to them for approval and read verbatim. In June 1942, the Anglican, Methodist, Presbyterian, Brethren and other churches formed the Federation of Christian Churches for support and relief work. This spirit of cooperation, as well as discussions in Changi prison among those interned, led to the setting up of the first theological college in Southeast Asia, Trinity Theological College in October 1948. The Singapore Bible College, set up by the Christian Nationals' Evangelism Commission to train Chinese Christian workers, followed in 1952.

The founding of the Malayan Christian Council (MCC) in January 1948—by the Methodist Church, the Presbyterian Church, the Anglican Diocese of Singapore, the Bible Society, the Young Men's Christian Association and the Young Women's Christian Association—continued the trend towards greater unity and cooperation. Later, it was joined by the Orthodox Syrian Church, the Mar Thoma Syrian Church, the Lutheran Church, the Salvation Army and Bethesda Katong Church.

The expulsion of foreign missionaries from communist China in 1951 redirected the attention of mission agencies to Southeast Asia. The Overseas Missionary Fellowship, the largest missionary organiza-tion in China, relocated its international head office to Singapore in 1951. The first missionaries of the Lutheran Church of America arrived in 1954, along with the Bible Presbyterians (1950) and the Evangelical Free Church (1959). International Christian youth organizations such as the Varsity Christian Fellowship (1952), Youth For Christ (1957) and the Fellowship of Evangelical Students (1959) were also established here.

Placing increased emphasis on vernac-

Christianity: Church of the Holy Trinity

ular languages, the Christian community grew steadily. In the years immediately after World War II, perhaps only 5 per cent of the population was Christian. This proportion doubled in 30 years. According to census data, the figure was 10.1 per cent in 1980, 12.7 per cent in 1990 and 14.6 per cent (364,000 people) in 2000.

With separation from Malaysia in 1965, churches and related organizations in Singapore were restructured and renamed: the Assemblies of God of Singapore (1967), the Anglican Diocese of Singapore (1970), the Presbyterian Church in Singapore (1975) and the Methodist Church in Singapore (1976). The Singapore arm of the the Malayan Christian Council was recon-stituted in July 1974 as the National Council of Churches of Singapore and membership included all main denomina-tions, established Christian organizations and individual churches.

In late 1972, a wave of spiritual renew-al started in the Anglo-Chinese School and in the Anglican Church. This 'charismatic' movement spread rapidly, although not all sections of the church welcomed it. In 1970, there were 147 Protestant congrega-tions with 29,511 members. By 1980, there were 244 congregations with 56,710 mem-bers. The Anglican Church was restructured in 1996 to form the Province of South East Asia and the Most Reverend Dr Moses Tay was its first Archbishop. The growth in the Catholic church led to the creation of the Archdiocese of Singapore with the Right Reverend Michael Olcomendy as the first Archbishop. In 1975, the Roman Catholic Archbishop Act was passed by Parliament, making him and his successors a body cor-porate with perpetual succession.

However, in May 1987, 22 people including Catholic church workers and social activists, were arrested and accused of participating in a MARXIST CONSPIRACY to overthrow the government. They were detained under the Internal Security Act but later released. In December, the Protestant Christian Conference of Asia was expelled from Singapore for providing 'covert support for radical activists'. The government noted both the 'heightened consciousness of religious differences and a new fervour in the propagation of religious beliefs'. It released a White Paper on the Maintenance of Religious Harmony in 1989, and the Maintenance of Religious Harmony Act came into effect in 1990.

Christianity: statue of St Peter at the Church of St Peter and St Paul, Queen Street.

Christianity: plaque in the Cathedral of the Good Shepherd in memory of a Chinese priest.

Christmas: annual light-up along Orchard Road.

Christians play significant roles in society and can be found in Parliament, in the Cabinet and in the judiciary. They have also been active in community service. For example, the St Andrew's Mission Hospital was started in 1913; between 1940 and 1958, it treated one out of every 13 Singaporeans under the age of 25. Free medical clinics were also offered. In the 1960s and 1970s, Professor Khoo Oon Teik, a Methodist, helped set up the National Kidney Foundation and the Christian Medical and Dental Fellowship. In addition to 14 homes for the elderly in 2001, Christian medical institutions include Mount Alvernia Hospital (1961), St Andrew's Community Hospital (1992), St Luke's Hospital for the Elderly (1996) and Bethany Methodist Nursing Home (2001).

Church welfare arms include the Singapore Anglican Welfare Council, the Methodist Welfare Services, the Presbyterian Community Services and the Catholic Welfare Services. Christian organizations such as TOUCH Community Services and Focus on the Family conduct Internet safety education and sex education in schools. There are more than 10 Christian-run rehabilitation and aftercare centres that help reform drug abusers, with encouraging results. Churches cooperate not only in ministries such as the Prison Fellowship Singapore and the Counselling and Care Centre (formerly the Churches' Counselling Service), but also in the annual Celebrate Christmas in Singapore event along Orchard Road.

According to the 2000 census, 16.5 per cent of Chinese, 12.1 per cent of Indians and 39.2 per cent of English-speakers were Christians. Christians were the largest religious category of university graduates, representing one out of every three (33.5 per cent). As at 2001, there were 64 denominations (including Catholics). The Catholics had 22 religious communities and orders. Christians worship in more than 450 Protestant and 30 Roman Catholic churches. Large independent megachurches such as City Harvest Church and New Creation Church have taken root, with rapidly expanding memberships.

In 2005, there were about 70 Protestant and Catholic mission schools, and over 143 kindergartens, childcare, and student-care centres. In addition, there were 22 theological and Bible colleges and seminaries, missions and leadership training centres. Until the Catholic St Francis Xavier Major Seminary was established in 1983, Catholic priests in training received only their initial instruction in Singapore at the minor seminary in Punggol before going abroad. Now Singapore trains clergy from other countries and is home to the headquarters of many international missionary organizations, including the World Evangelical Fellowship, the Overseas Missionary Fellowship, and the Asia Evangelistic Fellowship.

See also ANGLICANS, BAPTISTS CATHOLICISM, METHODISTS, LUTHERANS, PENTECOSTALS, PRESBYTERIANS and SYRIAN CHRISTIANS.

Christmas Festival marking the birth of Christ. Christians in Singapore celebrate by attending church services on Christmas Eve and Christmas Day (*see* CHRISTIANITY). Gifts are traditionally exchanged, and as in other countries, non-Christians have also adopted this practice. As a result, Christmas in Singapore has come to be associated with shopping. Every year in late November, colourful bunting is put up along ORCHARD ROAD, and the facades of hotels and shopping centres compete to provide the most extravagant lights and decorations. Christmas music is played in supermarkets and department stores from the beginning of November onwards. These festivities are part of the government's efforts to promote tourism. In 2002, the SINGAPORE TOURISM BOARD launched the celebrations under the theme of 'Christmas in the Tropics'.

In 2005, the world's tallest artificial Christmas tree, standing at 61 m high, was lit up on Singapore's highest point, MOUNT FABER. The tree's lights flickered to the accompaniment of music.

Christmas Day is one of 11 PUBLIC HOLIDAYS in Singapore.

Christmas Island Located in the eastern Indian Ocean at latitude 10°30' south, and longitude 105°40' east, Christmas Island is 19 km long and 14 km wide, with an area of 135,000 ha. The island was first discovered by Captain William Mynors, of the *Royal Mary*, who sighted it on Christmas Day in 1643. He was not able to land, however, and the island remained uninhabited until the latter part of 1888, when the first European settlement was established at Flying Fish Cove by George Clunies-Ross from the neighbouring Cocos-Keeling Islands, and Sir John Murray, a British naturalist. They were granted a joint land lease, covering all rights in the island. In the mid-19th century, the British government annexed the island as a result of presentations made by John Murray, who had examined the specimens of rock and soil taken from the island and found them to be composed of nearly pure phosphate of lime.

On 6 June 1888, Captain William May of the HMS *Imperieuse* landed at Flying Fish Cove and formally declared Christmas Island to be part of the British dominions, under the jurisdiction of the governor of the STRAITS SETTLEMENTS. Subsequently, on 9 January 1889, Letters Patent were passed appointing the governor of the Straits Settlements the governor of Christmas Island, and authorizing the island's annexation to the Straits Settlements. The Christmas Island Phosphate Company was formed in 1897 to work the island's rich deposits of phosphate.

A.R. Venning, treasurer of Selangor, who visited Christmas Island in 1893, described the island as rising 'precipitously from the sea in a series of cliffs which encircles it almost without a break, each cliff surmounted by a terrace overgrown with magnificent trees, the home of countless frigate birds, boobies, boatswain birds, terns and pigeons'. There were also huge crabs swarming all over the island, and these were of a 'bluish-yellow colour, with large claws and outstarting eyes, and most offensive to look at'.

Christmas Island was occupied by Japanese forces from March 1942 until the end of WORLD WAR II. With the dissolution of the Straits Settlements in 1946, Singapore was made a separate colony, and Christmas Island came under its jurisdiction. This association was based on administrative convenience.

In 1948, the governments of Australia and New Zealand, and the British Phosphate Commissioners, acquired the rights to the Christmas Island Phosphate Company. In 1957, the Australian government acquired Christmas Island from the Singapore government for £2.9 million, ex gratia compensation for loss of revenue. Christmas Island was administered as a CROWN COLONY until 1 October 1958, when, with the proclamation of the Christmas Island Act, it was transferred to the Commonwealth of Australia and became an Australian territory.

Chua, F.A. (1913–1994) Judge. Frederick Arthur ('F. A.') Chua was educated at St Joseph's Institution and later at Raffles Institution. In 1932, he left for the United Kingdom where he read law at Trinity Hall, Cambridge University. In 1937, Chua was called to the Bar at the Middle Temple. On his return to Singapore, he joined the Straits Settlements Legal Service. He was made assistant official assignee and assistant public trustee (1938). In 1940, he was transferred to Penang in the same capacity.

During WORLD WAR II, Chua was separated from his family and remained in Penang as a magistrate. He was appointed senior assistant registrar of the Supreme Court in Penang in 1947, and the following year, he was made district judge in Malacca. It was at this point that he was admitted into the colonial legal service.

In 1953, Chua returned to Singapore as district judge and magistrate. Two years later, he was made acting registrar of the Supreme Court when the incumbent, Tan Thoon Lip, was indisposed. In 1956, Chua was appointed district judge and first magistrate and, on 15 February 1957, was elevated to the Supreme Court. Chua was the second local person to be appointed to the Bench of the High Court, and served as PUISNE JUDGE until his retirement in 1992. In 1993, he was awarded the MERITORIOUS SERVICE MEDAL.

Chua, Jennie (1944–) Businesswoman. Jennie Chua Kheng Yeng is President and CEO of RAFFLES HOLDINGS and Chairman of RAFFLES HOTEL. Born in the Dutch East Indies (present-day Indonesia), Chua was educated at Singapore Chinese Girls' School and the School of Hotel Administration at Cornell University (1971). Upon her return to Singapore, she joined Mandarin Hotel as sales and public relations manager.

In 1988, she joined the Westin Stamford and Westin Plaza as director of sales and marketing and rose to become general manager of Raffles Hotel in 1990, a position she held until 2001, when she was made deputy CEO of marketing and operations at Raffles Holdings (2001-03). From 1995 to 1999, Chua was also executive vice-president of Raffles International; and from 1999 to 2003, president and chief operating officer of Raffles International.

Since 2003, Chua has also been active in public service, having served as deputy chairman of the National Training Awards Committee; chairman, Singapore Film Commission; and chairman of the Community Chest. Chua is the first Asian

Joi Chua

woman and Singaporean to win the Independent Hotelier of the World award from *HOTELS* magazine in 1997 and Hotelier of the Year from *Travel/Asia* magazine in 1999. She was the first woman to win the Pacific Area Travel Writers Association Hall of Fame Award in 2000. Chua received the Public Administration Medal (Silver) in 1984, and was appointed a justice of the peace in 2005.

Chua, Joi (1979–) Singer. Joi Chua (Cai Chunjia) made her first appearance on the music scene with her *Replugged* album in 1999. That same year, she also sang the theme song, 'Kanjian' (See), for DRAMA BOX's production *I Remember '99*. In 2000, her album *Cai Chunjia* (Joi Chua) proved commercially successful in Taiwan.

In 2004 Chua's album *Richu* (Sunrise) went double-platinum in Singapore. In 2005, she released the album *You Yi Tian Wo Hui* (One Day I Will). Chua was the bestselling female artiste in Singapore for two consecutive years (2004-05). In 2005, Chua was appointed ambassador for the Speak Mandarin Campaign (*see* CAMPAIGNS).

Chua, Simon (1970–) Sportsman. Simon Chua won his first gold medal in bodybuilding at the 1997 Southeast Asian (SEA) Games. He then won a gold medal in the welterweight category (75 kg) at the 2002 Asian Games in Busan, despite almost not participating in this competition due to a fever a week prior to his departure from Singapore. In 2005, he won a gold medal at the Manila SEA Games in the welterweight category. Chua has been inducted into the SINGAPORE SPORTS COUNCIL HALL OF FAME.

Chua, Tanya (1975–) Singer and songwriter. Tanya Chua (Cai Jianya) released her debut English album, *Bored* in 1997. It was one of the most critically acclaimed and fastest-selling albums in Singapore, and attracted the attention of recording labels in Taiwan. Her debut Mandarin album, *Huxi* (Breath), was released in 1998. By 2006, she had released three English solo albums and five Mandarin albums.

Chua has recorded and written music in a number of genres. Her songs have been recorded by regional artistes such as Faye Wong, Karen Mok, Nicholas Tse, STEFANIE SUN and Na Ying.

Chua Chong Long (1788–1838) Merchant and community leader. Chua Chong Long was born in Malacca, where his father had been KAPITAN CINA (Chinese community leader). Chua was a wealthy and influential man, so much so that a hill near TANJONG PAGAR was once named in his honour— Bukit Chong Long. In December 1836, Chua travelled to China, and then on to Macau, where he was murdered by thieves in 1838. One of his daughters married Kiong Kong Tuan, a Penang spirit farmer (*see* REVENUE FARMING).

Chua Ek Kay (1947–) Artist. Chua Ek Kay was born in Chenghai, Guangdong, but moved to Singapore during his youth. In Singapore, he studied under the master Chinese painter Fan Chang Tien for over a decade. Chua obtained an advanced diploma at LASALLE-SIA College of the Arts in 1989 followed by a bachelor of fine arts degree at the University of Tasmania, Australia, and a masters degree at the University of Western Australia.

Chua's work in calligraphy, painting, writing and seal-carving, shows a tapestry of complex influences. His art seeks a balance between the representational subject and the discipline of the Chinese brush. His landscapes in Chinese ink show a feeling for expressive form and the range of the monochromatic palette in black Chinese ink. This is evident in his street scenes of Singapore, China and Australia, for instance. His very abstract works, including those that denote the ubiquitous lotus flower and natural forms, such as rocks and plants, draw on the principles of positive and negative space between ink and paper.

Chua's work recreates the notion of the traditional *xieyi* (literally 'to write the meaning') style that captializes on the expressive range of the brushstroke as well as on scholarly reflection. While his practice is steeped in the traditions of TAOISM,

Simon Chua

Tanya Chua

Chua Ek Kay: the artist (below); Old Telok Ayer Street (1997) (left).

Chua Phung Kim

CONFUCIANISM and BUDDHISM, Chua has also sought to incorporate modernity and the contemporary. This is reflected in his purely abstract works, such as his 'Lotus' series, and large scale paintings, such as his 2004–05 'Water Village' series. Chua was awarded the CULTURAL MEDALLION in 1999.

Chua Kim Yeow (1926–) Civil servant. Chua Kim Yeow was educated at Gan Eng Seng School and Raffles Institution. In 1947, he took his London Matriculation and studied accountancy. In 1954, he became a fellow of the Association of Certified Accountants in the United Kingdom and returned to Singapore to join the Income Tax Service. Two years later, he joined the Accounting Service and rose within the service. In 1959, he was appointed deputy accountant-general and was appointed accountant-general in 1961. Chua was Singapore's first locally born accountant-general, and served in this capacity until 1979. After stepping down, Chua was appointed to various high-ranking positions: chairman, Security Industries Council (1981); president, Development Bank of Singapore (DBS) (1985); executive deputy chairman, DBS (1985); and executive chairman, POSBank (1986).

Chua retired as executive chairman of POSBank in 1993 to stand as a candidate against ONG TENG CHEONG for the inaugural presidential elections in 1993; Chua won 41.31 per cent of the votes.

Chua Nam Hai (1944–) Scientist. Chua Nam Hai obtained his basic degree in botany and biochemistry from the University of Singapore in 1965. He obtained his PhD at Harvard University. In 1969, he returned to Singapore to perform his national service, following which he lectured in the University of Singapore's medical school for two years. In 1988, he joined Rockefeller University and conducted research in cell biology, eventually becoming the Andrew Mellon professor

and head of the Laboratory of Plant Molecular Biology. In 1988, he became an elected fellow of the Royal Society.

Chua returned to Singapore periodically from 1995 onwards, and founded the Institute of Molecular Agrobiology (IMA), with the aim of doing genetic engineering research to produce hardier strains of plants and animals. The IMA merged with the Institute of Molecular and Cell Biology (IMCB) in 2002. Until 2000, Chua served as chairman of the IMCB, which aimed to develop Singapore's potential in biotechnology. In 2001, he helped Nanyang Technological University start up its School of Biological Sciences.

Chua was presented with the National Science and Technology Medal in 1998, and the Public Administration Medal (Gold) in 2002.

Chua Phung Kim (1939–1990) Sportsman. Chua Phung Kim took up weightlifting at the age of 21, training at the Evergreen Club. At the 1962 Commonwealth Games in Perth, he set a bantamweight record with a combined lift of 322 kg—a Commonwealth record by a margin of 22.5 kg. At the Tokyo Olympics (1964) he took 17th position. He was an Asian Games silver medallist in Bangkok (1966), and the following year, won a gold medal at the fourth Southeast Asian Peninsular Games. He competed at his second Olympics in Mexico (1968). At the 1970 Commonwealth Games in Edinburgh, he won a silver medal, losing the gold by a mere 2.5 kg.

In 1976, Chua became a coach with the Singapore Amateur Weightlifting Federation (SAWLSF). He continued serving at the SAWLF until his death from colon cancer. He was posthumously inducted into the SINGAPORE SPORTS COUNCIL HALL OF FAME in 2002.

Chua Sian Chin (1934–) Lawyer and politician. Chua Sian Chin was born in Malacca. He was educated at the High School in Malacca and the UNIVERSITY OF MALAYA where he graduated with a BA (1954). He became active in student politics and was a member of the Central Working Committee of the University Socialist Club (1953–54). Chua obtained a law degree

Chua Soo Bin

from the University of London in 1958 and was called to the Bar at the Inner Temple the following year. While in London, Chua became Secretary of the MALAYAN FORUM and editor of its newspaper, *Suara Merdeka*. He returned to Singapore in 1959 and joined the law firm of LEE & LEE.

Chua's first foray into politics was in 1964 when he stood as the PEOPLE'S ACTION PARTY's candidate for the Bandar Malacca seat (when Singapore was still part of Malaysia). He lost in that election, but was successful later in MacPherson constituency in Singapore in the general election of 1968. Chua served as minister for health (1968–75), home affairs (1972–84) and education (1975–79). He stepped down from the Cabinet in 1984, and was admitted into the ORDER OF NILA UTAMA (Second Class) in 1990. He set up his own law firm after retiring from politics in 1991.

Chua Soo Bin (1932–) Photographer and gallery owner. A graphic design graduate of the Nanyang Academy of Fine Arts in 1950, Chua Soo Bin was made an associate of the Royal Photographic Society (United Kingdom) in 1955. He established a reputation as an outstanding art director in advertising, and is often cited for the SINGAPORE GIRL images that clinched the Pacific Asia Travel Association Best Calendar Gold Award in 1985. That same year, Chua was invited to produce court portraits and the Queen Mother's birthday photographs for the Royal Thai Palace.

Chua's pioneering photography ventures include the 1989 landmark publication of black-and-white portraits of 14 of the world's top Chinese ink artists (including Le Keran, Liu Haisu, Chao Shao An, and Singapore's CHEN WEN HSI), entitled *Liuzhen: Portraits of Excellence*. This was relaunched in 2006. Chua founded Soo Bin Gallery in 1990. This became pivotal in cultivating contemporary art in Singapore, particularly avant-garde Chinese painting and photography. He also helped found the Art Galleries Association of Singapore, and played a key role in launching the Singapore Arts Festival. Chua received the CULTURAL MEDALLION in 1988.

Chulias Derived from 'Chola' (the name of a mediaeval south Indian dynasty) the term 'Chulia' is a generic label for Tamil-speaking Muslims of south Indian origin, and was commonly used in Southeast Asia from the 17th to the 19th centuries. The term was sometimes also used to refer to Hindus, and was used mainly by Europeans—it was largely unknown in India.

Chulias came to Singapore from towns in south India such as Porto Novo and Nagore, and from places in Southeast Asia such as Penang. Common occupations of Chulias during the colonial period included shipping as well as trading in cloth, precious stones and livestock. Intermarriage with Malays was common, as there were fewer Chulia women in Singapore than men. This gave rise to the community known as JAWI PERANAKAN. In practice, the terms 'Chulia' and 'Jawi Peranakan' overlap, although 'Chulia' tends to emphasize the Tamil, and 'Jawi Peranakan', the Malay aspects. Yet many religious and cultural practices are shared between Tamil and Malay Muslims, such as items of food and dress (for example, the sarong or lungi).

In the cultural field, Chulias contributed to the publication of Tamil literature and newspapers, and endowed mosques and shrines.

As the tendency to stress ethnicity over religion grew, most Chulias came to be simply identified as TAMILS or Malays. This coincided with the increase in Tamil Muslim labour that came to Singapore in the early 20th century. The term 'Chulia' had, by then, fallen into disuse, and was not extended to include these new arrivals. As a consequence, 'Chulia' is now understood to refer specifically to mercantile Tamil Muslim communities such as the Maraikkayar.

While the word 'Chulia' is rarely used today, it is still part of the historical memory of many Tamil Muslims, as well as the descendants of Chulias among the Malays, who can often be identified by typical Chulia surnames such as Merican (from Maraikkayan, the singular of Maraikkayar). Many contemporary Chulias are still active as cloth- and gem-traders and money changers. Chulia Street, near the Raffles Place commercial precinct, was assigned by Sir Stamford Raffles as an area for the Chulias in 1916.

See also INDIAN MUSLIMS.

Chung and Wong Architectural firm. The firm of Chung and Wong was founded in 1920. Little is known of its original founders. Among the more important designs for which it was responsible are JADE HOUSE on Nassim Road for Aw Boon Par; TAN KAH KEE's house in Cairnhill Road; the house of Dr S.C. Yin in Gilstead Road; and Happy World Stadium. The firm was also responsible for the restoration of what is now the SUN YAT SEN NANYANG MEMORIAL HALL and the reconstruction of

HAJJAH FATIMAH MOSQUE. The firm's principal partner and main designer was Chung Hong Woot. Chung's son, K.C. Chung, was also a partner. Another important architect in the firm's early years was Ho Kwong Yew, who worked there from 1926 to 1930.

Chung Cheng High School Established in 1939 and named in honour of Nationalist Chinese leader Chiang Kai-shek (Chung Cheng being a Mandarin version of Chiang's name), Chung Cheng High School has been associated with many Singapore personalities. LIM BO SENG was the first school supervisor, while AW BOON HAW was the founding chairman of the School Management Board. Between 2000 and 2004, UOB president WEE CHO YAW served as chairman of the board. Well-known alumni include CULTURAL MEDALLION winner KUO PAO KUN, and NANYANG UNIVERSITY vice-chancellor Chuang Chu Lin.

After World War II, the school started taking in female students for the first time. To accommodate the rapidly growing student population, the school opened a second campus on Goodman Road which it called Chung Cheng High School (Main). The school's original premises in Kim Yam was renamed Chung Cheng High School (Branch). The latter moved several times, and in late 2005, was re-established in new premises in Yishun as Chung Cheng High School (Yishun).

In the 1950s, when the government deregistered and banned pro-communist organizations such as the Singapore Women's Association and Chinese Musical Gong Society, and disallowed the political activities of the SINGAPORE CHINESE MIDDLE SCHOOL STUDENTS' UNION, pro-communist sympathizers protested by organizing sit-ins at schools such as Chung Cheng High School and THE CHINESE HIGH SCHOOL, staging demonstrations over a two-week period. These became known as the CHINESE MIDDLE SCHOOL RIOTS.

Chung Cheng High School has opened a heritage gallery showcasing its past achievements. Its array of artefacts, photographs and IT presentations make it

Chung Cheng High School (Main)

the largest gallery of its kind to be opened by a school in Singapore.

Church of Our Lady of Lourdes This church, gazetted as a national monument in January 2005, was the first Catholic church to serve Singapore's Indian community. Prior to 1870, Indian Catholics worshipped at the CATHEDRAL OF THE GOOD SHEPHERD. In 1870, Indian Catholics moved to worship together with Chinese Catholics at the CHURCH OF ST PETER AND ST PAUL.

In 1885, the STRAITS SETTLEMENTS government granted a site at Ophir Road for the construction of a Catholic church. In August of the following year, the foundation stone was laid and work began on the Church of Our Lady of Lourdes. This building was designed and built by architectural firm SWAN & MACLAREN in the neo-Gothic style, similar to the Basilica at Lourdes, France (which had been erected to commemorate the Apparition of Mary there). The church's pointed arches, spires, flying buttresses and 16 slender pillars were imported from France.

The Church of Our Lady of Lourdes was completed in 1888, together with a vicarage and a school. For approximately a century, the church was designated principally for use by Indian Catholics. In 1974, the Church became a 'territorial' church, catering to all Catholics regardless of

Church of Our Lady of Lourdes

Chung Cheng Drama Society Immediately after World War II, several newly formed groups created an enthusiasm for Chinese theatre. These groups were the Experimental Theatre, Ai Hua Music and Drama Society, Star Theatre, and Sea Gull Theatre. From 1945 to 1946, these groups staged ten full-length plays. The visit of the China Song, Music and Dance Troupe in 1947 further encouraged the development of Chinese theatre. Students from Chinese high schools formed several drama groups, with the Chung Cheng High School Drama Society becoming arguably the most important of these in terms of frequency and quality of productions.

From 1947 until it was dissolved in 1964, this drama society produced the classics of prominent Chinese playwrights such as Cao Yu, Chen Baichen, Tian Han and Wu Zuguang, as well as works by Singaporean writers. The society groomed many actors, designers, directors and theatre activists. Its alumni later formed two significant groups—Singapore Amateur Players, the Chinese theatre group with the longest history; and KANG LE MUSIC RESEARCH SOCIETY, an amateur group that played an important role in promoting Chinese dance, drama and music from 1954 to 1967 (see CHINESE THEATRE).

Church of St Joseph (left); Church of St Peter and St Paul.

ethnicity. However, it has retained a large Indian membership, and still offers a weekly Tamil mass.

Church of St Joseph This Catholic church has its origins in a plank-and-*attap* (thatched roof) chapel built in 1846 by Father Anatole Mauduit in Kranji. The chapel served a small Catholic community of immigrant farmers from China. However, the land these farmers worked was soon exhausted, and they moved further inland, to Bukit Timah.

In 1852–53, Father Mauduit built the Church of St Joseph in Upper Bukit Timah to replace the old Kranji chapel. The church was rebuilt in 1905. The majority of parishioners (about 300 people) were Catholic farmers from southern China. The number of parishioners declined in the late 1920s as farmlands in the area were exhausted and, looking for better prospects, the farmers moved to southern Johor.

The church was rebuilt again in 1965 by Father Joachim Teng. Following the development of the surrounding areas and Bukit Panjang Town, the congregation increased to several thousand people.

The Feast of St Joseph on the first Sunday of May is an annual celebration attracting crowds of 'pilgrims' from all over Singapore and beyond. Making use of its spacious grounds, the church has installed a life-size replica of the Stations of the Cross in Lourdes, France. This feature, unique in Singapore, attracts Catholics from all over the island for devotions during Holy Week.

Church of St Peter and St Paul The first Catholic chapel in Singapore was set up in 1832 on the future site of ST JOSEPH'S INSTITUTION, and was home to the French Catholic Mission, which included a Chinese Mission. During this period, there were some 200 Chinese Catholics in Singapore.

The first Catholic church, the Church of the Good Shepherd, was completed in 1846. The old chapel was converted into a parish school and Chinese missionary activities continued to be based there.

Owing to the expansion of the Catholic congregation at the Good Shepherd, a new church for Chinese and Indian Catholics was constructed in 1870 in Queen Street. This was the Church of St Peter and St Paul. Yet further expansion of the congregation saw Indian Catholics constructing their own CHURCH OF OUR LADY OF LOURDES in 1888. In 1910, the Cantonese and Hakka congregation of St Peter and St Paul constructed their own church at Tank Road, known as the Church of the Sacred Heart. The Hokkien Catholics of the Chinese Mission moved to their own CHURCH OF ST TERESA at Kampong Bahru in 1929.

In 2003, the Church of St Peter and St Paul was gazetted as a national monument.

Church of St Teresa Officially blessed and opened on 7 April 1929, this church was built by French missionary Emile Mariette and local priest Stephen Lee for Catholics living around the harbour, near the railway station and in Chinatown. It served Chinese, Indian and Eurasian congregations. With the development of the port around Keppel Harbour in the 1960s and 1970s, Catholic families living nearby were relocated to other towns. The boundaries of the parish were then extended to Clementi and Jurong. The Church of St Teresa maintains a club for Catholic seafarers—the Stella Maris Catholic Seamen's Mission.

Church of the Holy Trinity One of the largest Catholic churches in Singapore, the Church of the Holy Trinity was built in Tampines in 1988. Its parish includes Simei, Tampines and Pasir Ris towns. The church serves more than 13,700 Catholics, celebrating seven masses on Sundays to accommodate its congregation. The parish runs a kindergarten in the church building. It was one of the first Catholic churches in Singapore to build a columbarium for ashes of the deceased relatives of parishioners.

Church of St Teresa

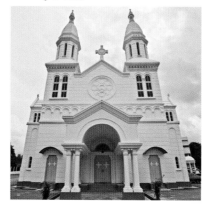

Church of the Nativity of the Blessed Virgin Mary

Church of the Nativity of the Blessed Virgin Mary The origins of this Catholic church can be traced to an *attap* (thatched roof) chapel that was built in 1853 on Upper Serangoon Road, its congregation comprising mainly Teochew farmers living in Serangoon and Punggol. Subsequently, a brick chapel was built in the area and named St Mary's Church. Father Jean Casimir Saleilles, parish priest from 1881 to 1911, was responsible for building the present church in 1901.

Father Saleilles also helped to spread the Catholic faith to Johor. He founded the Church of Our Lady of Lourdes (Johor), later renamed the Church of the Immaculate Conception and subsequently designated a cathedral. His good relationship with Sultan Ibrahim of Johor led the Sultan to present the Church in Johor, as well as the Church of the Nativity in Singapore, each with a statue of the Blessed Virgin Mary. The Church of the Nativity's statue still stands in front of the church building.

Architecturally, the Church of the Nativity was based on the Gothic designs of Father Charles Benedict Nain (who was also the architect of the Chapel of the Convent of the Holy Infant Jesus and the facade of ST JOSEPH'S INSTITUTION). The church was gazetted as a national monument in 2005.

The Church of Nativity founded many educational institutions in the region, including the Holy Innocents High School, Hai Seng Girls' High School, CONVENT OF THE HOLY INFANT JESUS Punggol, and Montfort School.

Church of the Sacred Heart This Catholic church was built in 1906 by Father Vincent Gazeau, on the site of an abandoned soya-sauce factory on Tank Road. It was built for the benefit of the CANTONESE- and HAKKA-speaking congregation living in and around the city. The original design of the church, French Baroque in style, was drawn up by Father L. Lambert.

The church's bells, with intricate carvings representing the stations of the cross, Sacred Heart of Jesus and two representations of the Blessed Virgin Mary, were directly imported from France in 1909. The

Church of the Sacred Heart

church and priests' house were blessed and consecrated on 11 September 1910. At that time there was no available shelter for orphaned boys, so Father Gazeau incorporated an orphanage for boys in the priests' residence.

The church today serves Catholics residing in the city centre, and holds regular masses in Mandarin and Cantonese.

Churchill, Sir Winston (1874–1965) British politician. As chancellor of the Exchequer from 1924 to 1929, Churchill reined in military expenditure, to the detriment of the Royal Navy and the facilities being constructed at Singapore's naval base. By contrast, from the late 1930s, Churchill adamantly supported accelerated rearmament, and was even more vehemently opposed to British appeasement of Adolf Hitler. In May 1940, some eight months after war was declared in Europe, Churchill became Britain's prime minister. He then took a major lead in formulating strategy, promising Australia that, should the Japanese attack, Singapore would be a higher priority for warships than the Middle East. But with the Royal Navy stretched by war against both Germany and Italy, in 1941 Churchill sent only a small naval force, FORCE Z, to Singapore. This comprised an aircraft carrier (which ran aground), the battleship HMS PRINCE OF WALES, the battle cruiser HMS REPULSE, and a destroyer escort. With insufficient air cover, Force Z's capital ships were sunk by Japanese aircraft on 10 December 1941.

Churchill was also heavily involved in the crucial decisions over OPERATION MATADOR. He endorsed the operation, which called for an air-land defence in northern Malaya and southern Thailand, in April 1941. But he later refused calls by his

chief of imperial and general staff, General John Dill, to send significant reinforcements of aircraft and tanks to Malaya. Churchill concentrated these on the Middle East and, after June 1941, the Soviet Union. He justified this as a concentration of resources in active theatres.

The contradictions Churchill embodied have made it difficult for historians to pass final judgement on his decisions. He was a Sandhurst-trained officer who often refused to accept military chiefs' recommendations. He was half-American on his mother's side and yet a die-hard imperialist, opposed to the 1935 Government of India Act. He was a nationalist who wrote about the 'English peoples', and yet a world statesman who supported greater European cooperation after the war. What is not clear, from a Singaporean viewpoint, is whether he was a strategic genius who correctly gambled that the United States would eventually blunt any Japanese attack and help win the war, or a chauvinist who over-estimated the Americans and British, and underestimated the Japanese.

Churchill survived Singapore's fall to cement his reputation as a great war leader. He lost the July 1945 election, but was prime minister again from 1951 to 1955, receiving a state funeral upon his death.

cicak Malay name for the common house gecko, or spiny-tailed house gecko (*Hemidactylus frenatus*). The *cicak* is one of the most common animal species associated with human habitation in both rural and urban areas. Active mainly at night and on overcast days, it hides under the eaves of buildings, behind cupboards, and in other indoor places on sunny days. A mottled dark to pale-brown colour, it feeds on small insects such as flies and mosquitoes.

cinema on wheels A mobile cinema consisting of a wooden box mounted on a tricycle. Cinemas on wheels were a frequent sight at AMUSEMENT PARKS and street corner shops until the late 1950s. A projector wired to a generator and battery was used to screen short cartoons and old movie reels in black-and-white without sound. Cinemas on wheels were popular with children who would pay the vendor a few cents to peep through one of 16 square slots on three sides of the wooden box, to view the short films. Prices ranged from 5 cents to watch a 50-ft (15.2-m) film reel, to 20 cents for a 200-ft (60.9-m) one.

Citigroup One of the largest financial services companies in the world, the history of Citigroup in Singapore dates back to 1 July 1902, when the International Banking Corporation (IBC) was the first American bank to set up a branch on the island. This was at Prince Street, between what is now Raffles Place and Finlayson Green. The bank was at the time involved primarily in

Cinema on wheels

the trade financing of Malayan commodity exports. As the economic landscape changed, so did the services offered by the bank. In 1918, IBC was acquired by National City Bank of New York, which, after other name changes, was named Citibank N. A. in 1976. Citibank's parent, Citicorp, merged with the Travelers Group in 1998 to become Citigroup.

After Prince Street, Citibank's main premises were in Ocean Building (from 1923), Denmark House (from 1958), Maritime Building (from 1969), and the UIC Building (from 1973). It now has office premises in Millenia Tower and several other locations.

Initially focussed on the business segment, it established a consumer division in 1982. Citibank was awarded the Qualifying Full Bank (QFB) Licence in 1999, which meant that it was able to expand its branch and ATM networks, and so compete on a more equal footing with local banks. With the signing of a US-Singapore Free Trade Agreement, which came into effect on 1 January 2004, Citibank also enjoyed privileges beyond those of a regular QFB. From 1 January 2006, all restrictions on the number of branch locations and ATMs were removed; other foreign QFB banks were capped at 25 ATMs and branch locations.

Citibank became the first foreign bank to incorporate a wholly owned subsidiary in Singapore, with a paid-up capital of $1.5 billion. This put it in a position to negotiate with local banks for access to their ATM network, giving it a

Citigroup: premises of the International Banking Corporation, Ocean Building, 1923 (left); the Citibank MacDonald House branch in 2006.

Citizenship Ordinance: Certificate of Registration.

competitive edge over other QFBs that are not allowed to join the ATM network. Citibank had 8 branches in Singapore by the end of 2005.

Citizens' Consultative Committee Umbrella body for grassroots organizations. To overcome the serious political, social, economic and communal problems Singapore faced in the 1950s and early 1960s, the PEOPLE'S ACTION PARTY government established the PEOPLE'S ASSOCIATION (PA) on 1 July 1960. The PA was formed to foster racial harmony and social cohesion as a basis for nation-building. This was to be done through the community centres. Some 28 centres were established to provide a meeting ground for various ethnic, language and religious groups. Community leaders served in the newly formed Community Centre Management Committees. The number of these active citizens increased with the establishment of the Citizens' Consultative Committees (CCCs) in 1965 and, later, the RESIDENTS' COMMITTEES and Neighbourhood Committees.

The CCC is responsible for planning and leading grassroots activities at the constituency level. It also oversees welfare programmes, and serves as a channel for communication between the people and the government. Under the People's Association Act, a CCC must be formed for each electoral constituency. The CCC's functions are to promote good citizenship among residents in the constituency; disseminate information and channel feedback on government policies and actions from residents; lead and coordinate projects and activities at the constituency and national levels; and recommend amenities and facilities for the constituency. One or more advisers to the CCC may be appointed by the chairman or deputy chairman of the Board of Management.

citizenship Citizenship determines a person's rights and responsibilities. Singapore's first citizenship law was the CITIZENSHIP ORDINANCE 1957.

Under the CONSTITUTION, one may acquire Singapore citizenship by birth, descent, registration, enrolment or naturalization. Citizenship is acquired at birth under the principle of *jus soli* (law of the soil), although there are some limitations to this. A person born in Singapore may not be a citizen if that person's father is either an envoy of a sovereign power or is an alien enemy. A person can become a citizen by descent (*jus sanguinis*) (law of blood) if one or both his parents are citizens. Any person above the age of 21 can apply for citizenship by registration. Persons likely to become citizens by registration are foreign-born spouses and children of citizens. This is subject to certain conditions and restrictions, such as residence, intention to reside in the country permanently, character and knowledge of the local language. Generally, a person will not be registered until he takes the Oath of Renunciation, Allegiance and Loyalty.

Citizenship carries privileges as well as obligations. For example, a citizen may not be banished from Singapore under Article 13 of the Constitution, and freedom-of-speech guarantees apply only to citizens. Citizenship may be lost in one of three ways: renunciation, cancellation or deprivation. It may be cancelled in cases of enrolment if it was obtained by fraud, false representation or concealment of any material fact, or if it was effected by a mistake. A citizen may also be deprived of his citizenship for, among other things, acquiring citizenship, or exercising the exclusive rights of a citizen, in a foreign country; or acquiring and travelling on a foreign passport; or being ordinarily resident outside Singapore for a continuous period of ten years.

Citizenship Ordinance This law gave Singapore CITIZENSHIP to all people born in Singapore on or before 1 March 1957. It also allowed British citizens or citizens of the Federation of Malaya to apply for Singapore citizenship after having resided in Singapore for two years. Citizenship by naturalization was also offered to those who had resided in Singapore for ten years (although this was later changed to eight years) and would swear loyalty to the government. The ordinance enfranchised many of the 220,000 China-born Singapore residents who hitherto had not been allowed to vote. Previously, voters had to be British subjects resident for one year, or British-protected persons born in the Federation of Malaya or the British-protected territories in Borneo.

City Council Local government authority overseeing the urban area. Previously known as the Municipal Commission, it was renamed the City Council when Singapore attained the status of a city (more than 1 million inhabitants) on 22 September 1951. The city area was administered by the City Council, while outlying areas came under the purview of Rural District Councils. The City Council was responsible for water supply, electricity, gas, roads and bridges and street lighting. Between 1951 and 1955, three commissions were appointed to study the local government system and make recommendations on it. In July 1957, following recommendations of the McNeice Commission, legislation was introduced to transform the City Council into a fully elected body comprising 32 members, one of whom would be mayor.

In December that year, Singapore's first CITY COUNCIL ELECTION was held, and the PEOPLE'S ACTION PARTY (PAP) won the most seats. ONG ENG GUAN, the PAP's treasurer, was elected mayor of the City Council. Ong's stance was anti-colonialist and populist, and his tenure as mayor was a tumultuous one. He removed the Mace of the City and dismissed civil servants at whim. In March 1959, the government took over part of the City Council's functions and absorbed the council into the central government, and Ong and his councillors resigned.

Until 1963, when the Public Utilities Board (*see* PUB) was established, the water, electricity and gas functions remained with the City Council, and it was the council that signed the 1961 and 1962 WATER AGREEMENTS with the government of the state of Johor.

City Council Election Singapore's first and only election for a wholly elected CITY COUNCIL. In 1957, the City Council became a wholly elected body of 32 members, of whom one would be the mayor. Candidates literate in any of the four official languages

City Council: People's Action Party rally in 1957, to 'sweep' the Liberal Socialists from the City Council.

were eligible for election. All adults automatically qualified as voters and were duly registered as such. For the first time, the vote was extended to half a million new voters who were non-British subjects.

Nomination day was 18 November 1957 and voting took place on 21 December 1957. Only 165,404 out of the 504,291 eligible voters cast their ballots, a turnout of only 32.8%. The Liberal Socialists, who dominated the old City Council, retained only seven seats. The PEOPLE'S ACTION PARTY (PAP) won 13 of the 14 seats it contested, making it the largest party in the new council. The PAP formed a coalition with the Singapore branch of the United Malays National Organisation (UMNO) to run the council. The PAP's ONG ENG GUAN, a Malacca-born, Australian-educated accountant, was elected the first mayor.

City Developments Limited Property and hotel company. City Developments Limited (CDL) was founded on 7 September 1963, with eight employees working from a rented office in Amber Mansions. Their job was to acquire, develop and sell property. The company completed its first housing project in Johor Baru in 1965. This was followed by its first condominium development in Singapore (Clementi Park) and the launch of its first high-rise development (City Towers) in 1966.

CDL was helmed by KWEK HONG PNG, the founder of the Hong Leong Group, who acquired a controlling interest in CDL in 1972. CDL then entered its first expansion phase by diversifying into commercial and industrial properties. It started with the launch of its first residential and shopping development, City Plaza, and soon acquired more investment properties, including The Arcade, Woh Hup Complex (now known as Golden Mile complex) and the Tanglin, Katong and Queensway shopping centres. CDL also forayed into the hotel business with the acquisition of King's Hotel and, soon after, the Orchid Inn. The next decade saw CDL launching 21 residential properties and completing 12 investment properties. CDL is now one of Singapore's largest commercial landlords, with over 400,000 sq m of office, industrial and retail space. It is also a leading residential property developer, having built more than 17,000 homes and 80 residential projects.

It was under chairman KWEK LENG BENG, who started the group's hotel arm in 1989, that CDL has made its biggest impact overseas, in particular the purchase of a stake in London-listed Millennium and Copthorne (M&C) Hotels in 1999. M&C's portfolio has since grown to more than 100 hotels in 17 countries.

CDL has operations in 21 countries spanning Asia, Europe, North America and Australasia. It has more than 250 subsidiaries and associated companies—six of which are listed on the stock exchanges of Singapore, London, Amsterdam, Hong Kong, New Zealand and the Philippines. The group, whose stock is a component of the Straits Times Index, has regularly chalked up annual turnover in excess of $2 billion between 1996 and 2005, while annual profits have ranged from $550 million in 1996 to $200 million in 2005.

City Hall This structure was designed by municipal architect F.D. Meadows. It was built from 1926 to 1929 as the Municipal Building, to bring together under one roof the departments of the Municipal Commission, which was responsible for services such as water, electricity, gas, roads and street-lighting. Its grand scale reflected the general economic prosperity that Singapore enjoyed, with minor interludes, from the late 19th century.

Meadows skilfully exploited the setting of St Andrew's Road facing Singapore's principal civic space, the PADANG, by designing a facade of grand proportions with 18 colossal Corinthian columns. The pre-cast concrete columns and the building's granolithic stone cladding were supplied by the Italian sculptor Cavalieri RODOLFO NOLLI. The building rests on a solid plinth. In plan, it is symmetrical and has two internal courtyards for light and ventilation. The generously proportioned stairway that leads to the main entrance conceals the porte cochère. The rear is, in contrast, bare and utilitarian. While architecturally pleasing, City Hall may seem less well-connected to its tropical setting than many of the older government buildings.

During the Japanese Occupation, the building was used as municipal headquarters by the Japanese. After Singapore acquired city status in 1951, the building was renamed City Hall. By 1963 the CITY COUNCIL was deemed obsolete and the Public Utilities Board (*see* PUB) was formed to administer water, gas and electricity. Post-Independence, the building continued to be known as City Hall, and housed the Prime Minister's Office, the Ministry of Foreign Affairs, the Ministry of Culture and the PUB.

In 1986, the Supreme Court assumed occupancy of City Hall in order to deal with the courts' increased case load; renovations allowed for a dozen courtrooms, the Supreme Court registry and the library. Other occupants included the Public Service Commission and the Industrial Arbitration Court. In 1992, City Hall was gazetted as a national monument. Shortly after the completion of the new Supreme Court building in 2005, plans were announced to transform both City Hall and the old Supreme Court into an arts facility.

City Hall—and in particular the spacious steps fronting it—is one of Singapore's most historic public spaces. It was there that in 1945, Admiral Lord Louis

City Harvest Church

MOUNTBATTEN formally accepted the Japanese surrender; in 1951, a Royal Proclamation from King George VI was read out, declaring Singapore a city; in 1959, LEE KUAN YEW proclaimed self-rule for Singapore. The steps have regularly played host to the president, the prime minister, Cabinet ministers and members of Parliament during the National Day Parade, and are a popular backdrop for wedding and graduation photographs.

City Harvest Church Independent church founded in Singapore in 1989 by Rev Kong Hee. With 18,500 people attending its services each weekend, City Harvest Church is one of three 'mega-churches' in Singapore (the others being Faith Community Baptist Church and the NEW CREATION CHURCH).

In early 2002, City Harvest moved into a $42.3 million titanium-clad building in Jurong. In that same year, Kong's wife, HO YEOW SUN, a worship leader, launched a career as a secular popular singer, performing mainly in Mandarin. In 2004, City Harvest Church became the first church in the world to attain ISO 9001 certification for total quality management. The webcast of its services reaches audiences of about 11,000 per weekend. Visitors to its website

City Hall

can also buy sermons via digital downloads.

The church continues to grow, and claims about 400 converts and rededications each week. It has nine branch churches in Malaysia, India and Indonesia. The church has moved its English services to one of the exhibition halls at Singapore Expo, while its Jurong premises are still used for Chinese and children's services.

Civil Aviation Authority of Singapore Statutory board. Set up in September 1984 under the purview of the Ministry of Transport, the Civil Aviation Authority of Singapore (CAAS) manages and develops the nation's civil aviation industry. It represents the government in the negotiation of air services agreements and advises on other civil aviation matters.

CAAS owns and operates CHANGI AIRPORT. It also provides consultancy services through its subsidiaries, Changi Airport Managers and Partners (CHAMPS) and Singapore Changi Airport Enterprise (SCAE), both of which are involved in investment. CHAMPS aims to become a major player in airport investment and management worldwide. It offers services across the entire spectrum of civil aviation, from airport consultancy, development and management, to investments in foreign airports. It has stakes in several airport projects around the world, including Juan Santamaria International Airport in Costa Rica, Jorge Chavez International Airport in Peru, Hato International Airport in Curacao, Netherlands Antilles and London's Luton airport. SCAE has invested in New Zealand's Auckland International Airport.

The training arm of CAAS is the Singapore Aviation Academy (SAA). Formed in 1958, this comprises three specialized schools which offer training in aviation management, air traffic services and airport emergency services. By 2005, the SAA had trained more than 31,700 people from over 188 countries.

CAAS also developed and manages Seletar Airport. Built in 1929, Seletar was the first airport in Singapore, but is now used mainly for charter flights.

civil defence *See* SINGAPORE CIVIL DEFENCE FORCE.

Civil Service College

Civilian War Memorial

Civil Service College Statutory Board. The Civil Service College (CSC), which comes under the Public Service Division of the PRIME MINISTER'S OFFICE, provides training for civil servants. It began operations in March 1971 as the Staff Training Institute. New officers in the Administrative Service received training in modern management concepts and techniques there. In 1974, training was broadened to include supervisory skills, and officers from other government services became eligible to undertake courses at the institute. A year later, it was renamed the Civil Service Staff Development Institute. This was shortened to Civil Service Institute (CSI) in May 1979. The CSI later became the Institute of Public Administration and Management (IPAM), providing public officers with skills in management, supervision and operations.

Another training unit, The Institute of Policy Development (IPD), was established in 1993 to provide more focus on developing public sector leadership. The IPD organized courses on governance, policy development and leadership development for senior public officers. In April 1996, the Civil Service College (CSC) was formed as a result of the consolidation of IPAM and the IPD. A consultancy unit, the Civil Service Consulting Group, was formed to offer professional advisory services on training matters. This was merged with the Personnel Guidance Unit to form CSC Consultants in 2001. In October 2001, the CSC became a statutory board.

Civilian War Memorial This structure was unveiled in 1967 by Prime Minister LEE KUAN YEW. It is 66.67 m (222 ft) high, and was built to commemorate civilians who lost their lives during the JAPANESE OCCUPATION in WORLD WAR II. The four identical pillars of which it is composed symbolize Singapore's four major ethnic groups: Chinese, Indians, Malays and 'Others'. The remains of unidentified war victims are buried beneath it. The shape of the memorial has given rise to it being popularly referred to as 'The Chopsticks'.

clan associations Organizations established by CHINESE immigrants to provide mutual help and welfare for new arrivals and fellow immigrants. They were known as *huiguan* in Mandarin or *huay kuan* in HOKKIEN. When the British founded modern Singapore in 1819, many Chinese were either drawn independently or recruited to the island to work, initially in construction and agriculture. Those who had already found their way to the Malay Peninsula came to Singapore from Penang and Malacca. Many others came directly from the Chinese provinces of Guangdong and Fujian, driven to leave by endemic poverty there.

These migrants felt the need to organize themselves for mutual assistance and protection, and formed associations based on dialect groups, common geographical origins, or shared surnames which indicated a common family origin '500 years ago'.

The first clan association to be formed is believed to have been Chao Kah Koon (Cao Clan Association), formed in 1819 by Cantonese migrants surnamed Cao. As the Chinese population grew, the number of clan associations increased. Over 300 clan associations have been registered in Singapore.

Clan associations can generally be grouped into two categories: locality clan associations; and kinship clan associations. The former can be further divided into provincial-level associations (for example, the SINGAPORE HOKKIEN HUAY KUAN, for people from, or whose ancestors originated in, Fujian province; and SINGAPORE KWANGTUNG HUI KUAN, for people from, or whose ancestors originated in, Guangdong province); and prefecture- or district-level associations (such as Tung Ann District Guild, Tung Ann being a district of Quanzhou prefecture in Fujian; and Foong Shoon Fui Kuan, Foong Shoon being a district of Chaozhou prefecture in Guangdong). A provincial-level association is basically a federation of prefecture- or district-level associations.

The structure of clan associations, however, is complicated. Some locality associations bring together members from several prefectures belonging to the same dialect group (such as the TEOCHEW POIT IP HUAY KUAN, which combines members from eight districts in the Chaozhou region —Chao'an, Chenghai, Chaoyang, Jieyang, Raoping, Puning, Huilai and Nan'ao); or a combination of a province and a prefecture in another province (such as Guangxi and Gaozhou Association, which includes people from Guangxi province and Gaozhou prefecture in Guangdong province).

Similarly, there are kinship clan associations which require all members to bear the same surname (for example, the Singapore Lee Clan General Association) while others require members to bear one of several surnames. For example, Singapore Liu Kwee Tang (Liu Gui Tang) is the clan association for those bearing the surnames of Hong, Jiang, Weng, Fang, Gong and Wang. Furthermore, some clan associations are for persons with a particular surname or surnames originating in a specific prefecture or province (for example, the Singapore Cantonese Wong Clan Association; and the Singapore Chuang & Ngiam Clansmen's Association, which is for members of the Zhuang and Yan clans of Hainan). For others, eligibility is by surname, regardless of locality (such as the Yang Clan General Association; and the Lam Soon Tang Chong Huay for clansmen bearing the surnames Rao, Yu, Chen, Hu, Tian, Yuan, Sun and Lu).

During the colonial period, clan associations played an important role in strengthening bonds among fellow Chinese from the same locality or clan. They offered practical help and moral support to fellow migrants 'from cradle (or at least from arrival in Singapore) to grave'. For instance, associations could arrange temporary shelters for new arrivals, assist them in finding jobs and provide healthcare, burial grounds and social welfare. The Kwong Wai Siew Peck Theng (Guang Hui Zhao Bishan Ting), for example, was the burial ground for clansmen of the 16 clan associations representing people from Guangdong.

Clan associations also established schools and temples. For example, the Hakkas' Ying Fo Fui Kun (Yinghe Huiguan) set up Ying Sin School in 1905; the Hokkien Huay Kuan set up Tao Nan

Clan associations: Kong Chow Wui Koon, based on the Xinhui district in Guangdong.

School in 1906; the Wak Hai Cheng Bio (Yuehai Qingmiao) was run by Teochew clanmen who later formed the Ngee Ann Kongsi and Teochew Poit Ip Huay Kuan.

Historically, a number of clan associations have had close ties with particular temples. As religious worship was an essential feature of Chinese immigrant life, temples were social and spiritual spaces where immigrants gathered to meet and worship. Some temples could also be considered predecessors to particular clan associations. For example, the THIAN HOCK KENG, established in 1839, was the most popular temple among migrants from Fujian province in the mid-19th century, and gradually grew to become the main meeting place for HOKKIENS from Fujian. When the Singapore Hokkien Huay Kuan was formed in 1860 under the leadership of TAN KIM CHING, son of Tan Tock Seng, its office was situated in the temple. The association moved to its own premises across the street from the temple in 1955.

Heads of clan associations were usually leaders of the Chinese community. This gave them authority to play a mediating role in conflicts between clans or groups within the Chinese community. Tan Kim Ching, TAN KAH KEE, LIM NEE SOON and TAN LARK SYE were all clan association heads as well as community leaders.

The role of clan associations has changed significantly since Independence. As many of their practical services were taken over by government agencies and COMMUNITY CENTRES AND CLUBS, clan associations lost their momentum and struggled for survival. A revival started in 1986 with the establishment of the SINGAPORE FEDERATION OF CHINESE CLAN ASSOCIATIONS. It counts about 200 members among its ranks, and assists clan associations in identifying their new role in society, which is focused on the promotion of Chinese language, culture and tradition, through classes and other activities.

The opening up of China since the early 1980s has given clan associations another role, which involves establishing business networks for their members in

Singapore and other countries, and exploring business opportunities in China. Clan associations have thus been able to retain their relevance.

clan schools With the support of clan leaders such as TAN KAH KEE, TAN LARK SYE and LEE KONG CHIAN, clan schools were set up by immigrant Chinese who believed that the British colonial authorities were providing insufficient support for their education. The schools were originally staffed by teachers from the particular clan, who used their own dialect as the medium of instruction. Modelled on schools in China, clan schools provided an education based on the classical curriculum, as well as letter-writing skills and the use of the abacus. Textbooks printed in China were used. Clan schools later used MANDARIN as the medium of instruction and, in some cases, English was also taught.

The Report of the All-Party Committee on Chinese Education in 1956 led to equal treatment for all schools, irrespective of the medium of instruction. The report committed the government to bilingualism based on the equality of the four official languages—Mandarin, Malay, Tamil and English. As a result, most clan schools became government-aided schools in 1957. However, some clan schools closed due to

Clan associations: literary award presentation at the Singapore Hokkien Huay Kuan (left); membership applications, 1948 (below); calligraphy lesson, one of the cultural classes conducted by the Singapore Hokkien Huay Kuan.

Clan schools: Yock Eng High School, established by the Singapore Hainan Hwee Kuan.

Clarke Quay

Sir Andrew Clarke

Sir Cecil Clementi

Sir Hugh Charles Clifford

declining enrolments, as parental demand for English-medium education increased. Others, such as Chung Hwa Girls' High School, became national schools accepting students of all races.

Some clan schools still in operation are THE CHINESE HIGH SCHOOL, NANYANG GIRLS' HIGH SCHOOL, TAO NAN SCHOOL, AI TONG SCHOOL, and the Kong Hwa, Nan Chiau and Chongfu schools.

Clarke, Sir Andrew (1824–1902) Colonial official. Clarke arrived in Singapore in 1873 to take office as the second governor of the STRAITS SETTLEMENTS to have been appointed under Colonial Office rule. He served in that role until 1875.

Clarke had travelled to Singapore with instructions from the secretary of state, Lord Kimberley, to investigate and report on conditions and the state of affairs in the west coast states of Malaya. Exceeding these instructions, he signed the Pangkor Engagement on 20 January 1874, paving the way for the eventual establishment of the Federated Malay States of Perak, Negeri Sembilan, Selangor and Pahang. Clarke's pivotal role in restoring peace and securing trade in the Malay States made him popular with merchants in Singapore. He was able to win their support in 1874 for the regulation of passenger ships, which in turn aided in the prevention of abuses in the COOLIE TRADE. In 1875, Clarke was transferred to India as head of the Public Works Department.

Clarke Quay Area upriver from north Boat Quay. Clarke Quay and Clarke Street are named after Sir ANDREW CLARKE, a governor of the Straits Settlements. Originally, the area was known simply as East Street and West Street. It was a busy trading district, with numerous warehouses and offices. Bumboats and lighters would bring produce and goods up the SINGAPORE RIVER for traders who kept warehouses in the vicinity. Goods would then be transported by road to various other parts of the island, making Clarke Quay a major distribution centre.

When the Singapore River was cleaned up in the 1980s, and port traffic moved to Tanjong Pagar and Keppel Harbour, the warehouses at Clarke Quay fell into disuse. Today, they have been restored and the area has been transformed into a centre for dining and entertainment.

classical music *See* box.

Clementi This town takes its name from Clementi Road, which connects Bukit Timah Road with Pasir Panjang Road. Clementi Road was, in turn, named after Sir CECIL CLEMENTI SMITH, governor of the Straits Settlements from 1887 to 1893.

The area around Clementi Road was originally occupied by military camps, barracks and squatter camps. In 1974, the HOUSING & DEVELOPMENT BOARD cleared the area for development. A new town with about 24,000 units and occupying some 400 ha was created. The town is bounded by Clementi Avenue 6, West Coast Highway, Clementi Road, and Sunset Way. Most of the units in this estate are three-room and four-room flats. These have proven popular with families whose children study at the nearby Singapore Polytechnic, Ngee Ann Polytechnic and National University of Singapore.

Clementi, Sir Cecil (1875–1947) Colonial official. Sir Cecil Clementi began his career in the Colonial Civil Service as a cadet in Hong Kong in 1899. He became proficient in both CANTONESE and MANDARIN, and was made governor of Hong Kong in 1925.

Clementi was appointed governor of the STRAITS SETTLEMENTS in 1930, and arrived in Singapore with a reputation as an able administrator and expert on China, qualities welcomed at a time of uncertainty due to the onset of the Great Depression. However, the harsh measures Clementi took to deal with economic distress and to counter political subversion made him unpopular. He censored the non-English press in an attempt to suppress anti-colonial propaganda and, in 1932, withdrew all grants-in-aid from Chinese- and Tamil-medium schools. He also imposed restrictions on immigration, and repatriated large numbers of Chinese and Indians. His departure in 1934 was greeted with relief by those alienated by his immigration and education policies.

Clementi Smith, Sir Cecil (1840-1916) Colonial official. Sir Cecil Clementi Smith succeeded Sir FREDERICK WELD as governor of the STRAITS SETTLEMENTS in 1887 (serving in that role until 1893), having briefly served in Ceylon (present-day Sri Lanka). A popular governor, Clementi Smith promoted education, with a particular focus on education for the Malays. He addressed the SECRET SOCIETIES problem by means of the Societies Ordinance of 1890 and, in the same year, created the CHINESE ADVISORY BOARD to provide a formal link between the colonial authorities and the Chinese community.

Clerk of Parliament Parliamentary office. The Clerk of Parliament is appointed by the PRESIDENT in consultation with the SPEAKER of Parliament and the PUBLIC SERVICE COMMISSION, and may only be removed by a two-thirds vote in PARLIAMENT.

The Clerk is responsible for the daily administration of the activities of Parliament and its secretariat. The secretariat's main duties are to assist the Speaker to regulate and conduct all matters connected with the business and proceedings of Parliament and its committees; process all notices of bills, motions, questions and other business handed in by MEMBERS OF PARLIAMENT; conduct research into parliamentary procedures, examine whether there are difficulties in the working of the standing orders, and build up memoranda to ensure uniformity of practice and procedure in Parliament; be responsible for the publication of the Votes and Proceedings and the Parliamentary Reports; and attend to matters of administration relating to Parliament, its members, staff, accounts and premises.

The Clerk's office demands great expertise in legislative procedure and parliamentary administration. He has custody of all votes and proceedings, records, bills and other documents presented to or laid before Parliament and advises the Speaker and members on matters of procedure. The Clerk also administers oaths, presides over the election of the Speaker, and is responsible for the printing and circulation of all bills and motions.

Clifford, Sir Hugh Charles (1866–1941) Colonial official. Sir Hugh Charles Clifford joined the Malayan Civil Service in 1883 and was made acting Resident of Pahang in 1887, and Assistant Resident in 1888 (*see* GOVERNORS). In 1900, he became governor of British North Borneo (present-day Sabah) for a short period, before assuming the office of Resident of Pahang in 1901. His next few appointments took him to Trinidad, Ceylon (present-day Sri Lanka) and the Gold Coast (present-day Ghana). Clifford returned as governor of the

Goh Soon Tioe, left, playing with the Singapore Musical Society Orchestra, 1953.

classical music The story of Western classical music in Singapore has been a progression from amateur pursuit to professionalism. Western classical music arrived in Singapore together with the city's British colonial founders during the early 19th century.

However, there was little by way of organized musical activity during the early colonial period, although well-to-do children would have taken music lessons. Interest in Western classical music was at that time the province of the educated and wealthy. Occasional recitals were given by visiting artists travelling en route to Australia or other ports in East Asia. The first major public concert venue in Singapore was the Victoria Memorial Hall (present-day VICTORIA CONCERT HALL), which was completed in 1905. However, it was not until after WORLD WAR II that classical music came to play a significant role in the cultural life of the island.

Growth and development
After World War II, the Entertainments National Service Association's (ENSA) Symphony Orchestra, led by Scottish conductor Erik Chisholm, became the first de facto 'Singapore Symphony Orchestra', but it lasted only a year. The Singapore Musical Society, led by Gordon van Hien; the Singapore Chamber Ensemble, under PAUL ABISHEGANADEN; and numerous choral societies were also active at that time.

Foreign-trained music teachers such as violinist GOH SOON TIOE and pianists VICTOR DOGGETT and Lucien Wang also made significant contributions, as did many of their students—including CHOO HOEY, Lee Pan Hon, SEOW YIT KIN, VIVIEN GOH, LYNNETTE SEAH and ONG LIP TAT—who went on to become important professional musicians.

With SEPARATION in 1965 and subsequent economic growth, there was a proliferation of new amateur musical groups, including the Singapore Youth Orchestra, Singapore Youth Choir, National Theatre Symphonic Band and the Chamber Players. The success of the short-lived Singapore Philharmonic Orchestra, led by Yoshinao Osawa, set the stage for the formation of Singapore's first professional orchestra, the SINGAPORE SYMPHONY ORCHESTRA (SSO).

New professionalism
The brainchild of former deputy prime minister GOH KENG SWEE, the SSO was inaugurated in 1979 with Singaporean conductor Choo Hoey as its first music director. It gradually built a reputation as the region's finest orchestra. Many Singaporean musicians, almost all foreign-trained under various musical scholarships, served with the SSO. These included members of the T'ANG QUARTET, Singapore's only professional chamber group, and conductors LIM YAU, Lim Soon Lee and Chan Tze Law.

This period also saw the emergence of Singaporean composers, among them LEONG YOON PIN, BERNARD TAN, PHOON YEW TIEN and Tsao Chieh. Their works blended elements of Asian music together with Western compositional techniques. Expatriate composers such as JOHN SHARPLEY and Robert Casteels also made their contributions. Renowned concert artists such as violinists VANESSA-MAE and KAM NING, and pianists MELVYN TAN and MARGARET LENG TAN were born in Singapore but are based overseas. Local composer of musicals, DICK LEE, has had a large following in Asia. Younger musicians, such as violinists LEE HUEI MIN (also known as Min Lee) and Tang Tee Khoon, as well as composer JOYCE KOH, are becoming known internationally. The establishment of the Singapore Lyric Theatre (present-day SINGAPORE LYRIC OPERA) also created room for the performance and development of Western opera.

Recent achievements
More recent developments in classical music in Singapore include the success of the Singapore Symphony Orchestra under music director LAN SHUI; the inauguration in 2002 of the Concert Hall at the ESPLANADE–THEATRES ON THE BAY as one of the best performance venues in Southeast Asia; the opening of the YONG SIEW TOH CONSERVATORY OF MUSIC in the NATIONAL UNIVERSITY OF SINGAPORE in 2003, the first tertiary music educational institution in Southeast Asia; and a revival of amateur music-making in the form of chamber, ensemble and choral groups.

From top: Leong Yoon Pin's Symphonic Works of Singapore (1993); Ong Lip Tat's Piano Solos (1993); Singapore Lyric Opera's Madama Butterfly.

STRAITS SETTLEMENTS, serving in that position from 1927 to 1929.

Clifford was a distinguished author who wrote much about Malaya and its peoples in short stories and other works. The best known of his stories were published in collections entitled *Bushwhacking* and *In Court and Kampung*. He authored a Malay dictionary jointly with Sir FRANK SWETTENHAM, and was responsible for translating the PENAL CODE into Malay.

Clifford Pier Built between 1927 and 1933 on the site of what used to be Johnston's Pier, this pier was named after Sir HUGH CHARLES CLIFFORD, governor of the STRAITS SETTLEMENTS from 1927 to 1929.

Johnston's Pier had been built in the 1850s and was the main landing point for seaborne passengers. By the 1920s, Johnston's Pier (named after popular 19th-century merchant ALEXANDER JOHNSTON) had fallen into disrepair and the Straits government decided to build a replacement. Clifford Pier was officially opened on 3 June 1933. However, the city's merchants boycotted the launch as they wanted Johnston's name reinstated.

A red beacon atop Clifford Pier was responsible for its colloquial Chinese name—Red Lantern Pier (*ang teng beh tau* in Hokkien; *hongdeng matou* in Mandarin). In April 2006, Clifford Pier was officially closed. The government has announced plans to sell the site, and to have the original building conserved while redeveloping it into a retail and lifestyle centre, as part of the wider development of MARINA BAY.

climate Singapore lies between the two main regions of the world which experience monsoons—the Indian subcontinent and northern Australia. Singapore therefore experiences two monsoonal seasons, broken by two periods of lower rainfall, every year. The northeast monsoon lasts from December to March. This season is marked by prevailing winds from the northeast, which bring periods of prolonged rain, particularly in the afternoons. During this period, an average of 623 mm of rain falls on the island. The inter-monsoon period between March and May is calmer and is typified by light evening showers. The average rainfall during this period is 432 mm. The southwest monsoon lasts from June to September, and is associated with hazy conditions, morning squalls and heavy rain during the late morning and early afternoon. The average rainfall for this period is 647 mm. The inter-monsoon period from October to December is characterized by light winds and occasional thunderstorms, with average rainfall of 574 mm.

High levels of rainfall during the monsoon seasons make Singapore prone to small-scale flash floods. The forests and other types of vegetation in the Central Catchment Area intercept a considerable amount of rainfall, and reservoirs help to

Clifford Pier: interior in 2006 (above); in full operation during the 1960s.

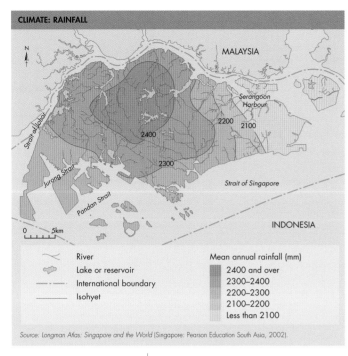

CLIMATE: RAINFALL

MALAYSIA

Serangoon Harbour

Strait of Johor

2200
2100
2400
2300

Jurong Strait

Pandan Strait

Strait of Singapore

INDONESIA

0   5km

River
Lake or reservoir
International boundary
Isohyet

Mean annual rainfall (mm)
2400 and over
2300–2400
2200–2300
2100–2200
Less than 2100

Source: Longman Atlas: Singapore and the World (Singapore: Pearson Education South Asia, 2002).

Cobras: king cobra.

counteract flooding. In urban areas, a network of storm drains, together with embankments on the lower courses of rivers, has helped prevent serious flooding.

As an island with a hilly interior, Singapore experiences the effects of 'relief rainfall'. However, most rainfall in Singapore is convectional, associated with high temperatures, high rates of evaporation and the formation of thick cumulonimbus clouds. Rainfall events are frequently intense but short-lived, and are accompanied by thunder and lightning. Average annual rainfall varies from 1,600 mm to 2,500 mm. Two areas in the island's interior experience over 2,400 mm of rain per year (*see* map). These are the area around Seletar Reservoir and the stretch of land between Jurong East and Tengah Reservoir. The driest part of the country is the EAST COAST, especially the area between the mouth of the KALLANG RIVER and CHANGI AIRPORT. There, less than 1,800 mm of rain falls per annum. This is partly due to a 'rain shadow' created by the hills of the interior.

As it is only one degree north of the equator, Singapore experiences very little variation in temperature. The average daily temperature range is low, with the average maximum between 31°C and 34°C and the average minimum between 23°C and 26°C. Extremes of temperature also fall within a narrow margin: the highest figure on record is 35.8°C whereas the lowest is 19.4°C. Temperatures generally peak at around 1 p.m. and reach their lowest just before dawn, at around 6 a.m. Heat is lost at night but the high level of cloud cover acts as a blanket and prevents too much radiation back into the atmosphere. In December and January, early morning temperatures tend to be 2–3°C lower than in July and August because of the much high-

er levels of night-time humidity associated with the northeast monsoon.

Cloutier, Frank (unknown–) Scientist. Frank Cloutier earned his bachelor's degree in physics at Northeast Louisiana University in 1973. He completed the Advanced Management Program at the University of Hawaii in 1991. During his 29-year career with Hewlett-Packard, he served as R&D manager at Hewlett-Packard Singapore's Asia Peripherals Division. Cloutier also served on boards and committees of the National Science and Technology Board and Gintic Institute of Manufacturing Technology. Cloutier was awarded the SCIENCE AND TECHNOLOGY MEDAL in 1992.

Club Street Located in Chinatown, Club Street's name is believed to have been derived from the various Chinese clubs and associations sited along the thoroughfare. However, the establishment of Chinese clubs in the area was gradual, and occurred over a long time, so this explanation seems unlikely. The name may have originated from one particular club in the area, perhaps the Chinese Weekly Entertainment Kee Lam Club (established in 1891), or the Chui Lan Teng Club (approximately the same vintage). Recently, a number of restaurants and bars have opened along the street, rejuvenating the area.

coal The Industrial Revolution made possible a number of technological advancements, and facilitated new systems of transport such as steamships and rail. In the late 19th and early 20th centuries, coal became essential to land and sea transport throughout the world. With the expansion of the British Empire across South and Southeast Asia, numerous new ports were established. The growing number of merchant ships berthing at these ports needed fuel, and with this came a need for coal depots or coaling stations. Colonial governments

Club Street

hired indigenous, in some cases slave, labour for the mining and transportation of coal.

Following Sir HENRY KEPPEL's recommendation in 1848, Singapore was developed into a major coaling station. Coolies, mainly from the HOKKIEN dialect group, were the chief source of labour; loading and unloading coal on the wharves. By 1881, it was estimated that up to 15,000 imperial tons of coal were loaded onto ships each month. Coal was an increasingly important commodity, and it was assumed at that time that any enemy attack would be to capture or destroy the massive coal stores in the harbour.

cobras There are two species of this venomous snake in Singapore. The black spitting cobra (*Naja sumatrana*) is common, and is often encountered in gardens, parks and even in houses. However, when threatened, an irritated cobra can spit venom into the eyes of an offender and cause temporary blindness. It generally feeds on small vertebrates.

The king cobra (*Ophiophagus hannah*)

Coal: coolies loading coal, c.1910.

Cockpit Hotel, 1970.

is the longest venomous snake in the world, often growing to a length of 3 m. It is not aggressive, but it can be dangerous when provoked. It is active in the daytime, and is usually found in forested or agricultural areas.

Cockpit Hotel With its distinctive windows and wrought-iron balconies, the Cockpit Hotel was built in 1972 by Indonesian businessman Hoo Liong Thing. The 13-storey building stood on the site of a colonial mansion that had also operated as a hotel. This hotel, which was known as the Hotel de l'Europe (not to be confused with the earlier HOTEL DE L'EUROPE, opened in 1857), had been established in 1947, and soon became the preferred accommodation for crew from and passengers of the Dutch airline KLM. It thus acquired the nickname 'the Cockpit'. This was made the hotel's official name in 1960.

The 230-room Cockpit Hotel was sold in 1980 to a Hong Kong jeweller, Kevin Hsu, for $45 million. It was then sold, three years later, to local hotelier Teo Lay Swee, for $63 million. Teo later purchased the nearby HOUSE OF TAN YEOK NEE for $20 million in 1991. By mid-1994, his hotel company, which was then listed on the stock exchange, had secured provisional permission to build an extension. This was to have comprised two blocks, a 390-room hotel and a serviced-apartment tower. However, the Teo family decided to sell the building and its adjoining land parcel to property developer, Wing Tai, in September 1996 for $360 million.

The Cockpit Hotel, which in its heyday was known for its nightclub and alfresco dining overlooking Orchard Road, was officially closed on March 1997.

coconuts In the 1830s, coconut plantations covered 264 ha in Singapore, with about 50,000 trees, chiefly at Tanjong Katong and Pulau Blakang Mati (Sentosa). The main coconut farmers included J.W. Angus (who held about 120 ha in Bedok) and Thomas R. Dunman (who held about 160 ha in Grove Estate, Katong). Coconut plantations were relatively productive in Singapore and

did not appear to suffer, like other crops, from unstable soil or disease. However, coconut was a low-value crop which gave a relatively low return on investment.

Coconuts were popular locally because of their extensive use in Asian cooking. The timber from the trunk of aged, sterile coconut trees could be used as building material; the fronds were sometimes used for roofing; and the fibres from coconut husks were used in a range of local crafts. During the early 19th century, coconut oil was even used for street lighting in Singapore.

When RUBBER became a substitute crop for coffee during the early years of the 20th century, the owner of the Trafalgar Coconut Plantation at Punggol grew rubber together with coconuts in 1907—thus making this coconut plantation the first place at which rubber was cultivated in Singapore.

Coffee Bean & Tea Leaf, The Since opening its first outlet at Scotts Shopping Centre in 1996, the Coffee Bean & Tea Leaf chain has grown into a multi-million dollar business with more than 40 outlets in Singapore, Malaysia and other countries. It is controlled by Sunvic, a company owned by VICTOR SASSOON, a Singapore-born businessman.

A chance meeting in 1995 between Sassoon and singer Paula Abdul in a Coffee Bean & Tea Leaf outlet in Los Angeles led to Sunvic obtaining the Singapore franchise from its founder, Herbert Hyman, who had started the business in California in 1963. The group is the oldest and largest privately-owned chain of speciality coffee and tea stores in the United States.

Coffee Club *See* HIANG KIE.

coffee shops A traditional, popular food and beverage outlet, the coffee shop, or *kopitiam*, is a familiar sight in Singapore. Many coffee shops are located in pre-war shophouses, and are owned and operated by the drink-stall owners. The selection of drinks is vast,

Coffee shops: Wah Heng Coffee Shop, 1981.

Coconuts: coconut workers.

and includes canned drinks, brewed coffee and tea, and beer. Other food stalls operate in the coffee shop as tenants of the owner.

The most successful coffee shops serve a variety of food. Most open early in the morning to cater for office-workers. Over the years, a distinctive fare has emerged—half-boiled eggs, served with soy sauce and pepper, toasted bread with *kaya* (coconut and egg jam), accompanied by coffee or tea. More recently, competition from food courts and Western coffee chains has forced coffee shops to serve a wider variety of food, and even create franchises, such as Ya Kun Kaya Toast and Killiney Kopi Tiam.

Cohen, Yahya (1920–2003) Doctor and academic. Yahya Cohen was born in Singapore to Sephardic Jewish parents from the Middle East. He studied at St Andrew's School and attended the King Edward VII College of Medicine in 1938. A recipient of the Queen's Scholarship, he undertook postgraduate studies in the United Kingdom. He returned to Singapore to serve as a surgeon, and progressed to become the clinical professor of surgery at the University of Singapore.

As well as being a founding member of the Academy of Medicine in Singapore, Cohen also served as president of the Singapore Medical Association (SMA) and of the Singapore Medical Council in the 1960s and 1970s. In 1965, he was visiting professor to the University of Tel Aviv, Israel, and head of the Surgical Unit in the Ichilov Hospital in Tel Aviv.

Cohen was an educator of and mentor to many doctors and surgeons in Singapore and Malaysia. He served as a member of the board of governors of St Andrew's School and the boards of trustees for Jewish Charities. In recognition of his achievements, the Chapter of Surgeons in Singapore named its annual lecture 'The Yahya Cohen Memorial Lecture'.

Cold Storage Supermarket chain. On 24 March 1905, a shipment of frozen cargo from Queensland, Australia—800 cattle, 4,800 sheep, 14 tons of poultry, 15 tons of butter and 25 cases of fresh milk—docked at KEPPEL HARBOUR, opening a new era in

Cockpit Hotel: **Twilight Zone,** *photograph by Tan Lip Seng, 1974.*

Cold Storage: Christmas, 1957 (above); 1958 advertisement.

For Aunt Emma...

THERE are umpteen fascinating things you'll want to buy in Singapore for all your family in the U.K. ... but don't forget a food parcel.

We arrange everything for you — you can send our 'made-up' parcels or choose your own items; we pack, post and insure.

COLD STORAGE

Singapore Cold Storage Co., Ltd.

(9)

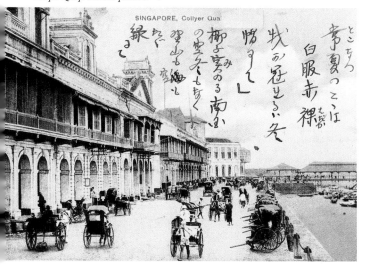

Collyer Quay: undated postcard.

the history of Singapore's food industry. For the first time, high-quality meat and dairy products were available, and were welcomed especially by the European community. The company that had made this possible by setting up a cold-store depot was called Cold Storage. It had been established on 8 June 1903. The depot business was farmed out to Yeo Swee Hee until 1909, when a new management team headed by Fred Heron took over. Heron played a major role in transforming the company into a profitable venture, and extending the business to Peninsular Malaya over the following two decades.

Cold Storage opened its first retail outlet in 1919, after it acquired a few shophouses adjacent to its existing premises on the corner of Orchard Road and Cuppage Road, near today's Centrepoint Shopping Centre. The business expanded into Malaya in 1923 after the Causeway was opened.

The year 1923 also saw the introduction of the first locally-made ice-cream from the company's Keppel Harbour plant, sold under the Bird of Paradise logo. The brand was renamed 'Magnolia' in 1937. Soon, the ice-cream vendor with his cart and pith helmet became a familiar sight on the streets of Singapore. Cold Storage's Magnolia MILK BARS, where ice-cream and other products were sold, also became popular when they were introduced during the 1950s.

Ice-cream in the 1920s was made from imported products. But Cold Storage soon turned to local dairy production. In 1929, it acquired a 24-ha plot of land in Bukit Timah (near the Dairy Farm Estate) and imported a herd of Friesian cattle from Europe. Soon, it was possible to buy hygienic, fresh milk locally. The company also bought the Chinese-run Royal Bakery in 1930, and hired skilled bakers from Scotland to produce bread in quantities for the local market. In 1959, Cold Storage switched from counter service to self-service, thus introducing the modern-day supermarket. In 1972, it also started the first self-service pharmacy at its Orchard Road outlet.

In 1982, Cold Storage Holdings was publicly listed. In 1988, FRASER & NEAVE (F&N) jointly acquired a controlling interest in Cold Storage Holdings with Goodman Fielders Watties. Auric Pacific Group Ltd was then incorporated to act as a holding company for the Cold Storage group. A restructuring of Cold Storage in 1990 ended the joint venture between F&N and Goodman Fielders Watties, and gave control of Cold Storage's dairy and property businesses to F&N. These came under the control of the publicly-listed (though later privatized) company, Centrepoint Properties. Cold Storage's retail business was sold in 1993 to Fitzpatrick Holdings, which was by that time part of the Dairy Farm group (*see* FITZPATRICKS).

The Cold Storage chain operates more than 70 stores in Singapore. These include 30 flagship Cold Storage supermarkets, seven Giant hypermarts, four Market Place premium food stores and 44 Shop N Save discount supermarkets. Cold Storage was also the first supermarket to offer its merchandise online in 1997. Cold Storage Causeway Point was the first supermarket to be awarded the halal certification in 1998.

Coleman, George D. (1794–1844) Architect and publisher. Born in County Louth, Ireland, Coleman first arrived in Singapore in 1822, but left the following year. He travelled again to Singapore in 1826, and commenced practice as an architect. In 1833, he was appointed Government Superintendent of Public Works. He built many Palladian-style houses that were adapted to suit the tropics, and set the fashion for Singapore's colonial architecture. He was also involved in LAND RECLAMATION and surveys of Singapore. His surveys of the island resulted in the printing of the first comprehensive map of the town and environs of Singapore in 1836. Coleman Street, where his house stood, as well as Coleman

George D. Coleman: his tombstone at Fort Canning.

Bridge, are named after him. The ARMENIAN CHURCH and Caldwell House are among the few remaining examples of buildings designed by Coleman. Examples of his work that no longer stand include RAFFLES INSTITUTION and the first ST ANDREW'S CATHEDRAL building.

Coleman was also a publisher. He teamed up with WILLIAM NAPIER and Edward Boustead to establish the newspaper, THE SINGAPORE FREE PRESS & *Mercantile Adviser*. The first issue of this newspaper appeared in October 1835. Coleman left Singapore, unwell, in 1841. He returned in 1843 and died in 1844.

College of Medicine *See* KING EDWARD VII COLLEGE OF MEDICINE.

Collyer, Captain George (1814–1897) Engineer. Captain (later Colonel) George Chancellor Collyer was a member of the Madras Engineers, a division of the Indian Army. He was appointed Chief Engineer of the Straits Settlements, and arrived in Singapore in 1858. At the behest of the Bengal Government, he drew up plans for the fortification of Singapore. These included, among other things, building coastal defences in the New Harbour with batteries at Tanjong Pagar, Pulau Blakang Mati and Mount Faber. However, his fortifications were of debatable value and were nicknamed Collyer's Folly.

Collyer is best remembered for having fortified GOVERNMENT HILL. While Pearl's Hill was deemed suitable for a fort, Collyer favoured Government Hill as the ideal site for defences against both internal and waterborne attacks. In an 1858 report, he outlined his ambitious plans for Government Hill. When finished, it was to be covered with a heavy defence system that included an arsenal, barracks, hospitals and magazines, at an estimated total of 1,747,525 Spanish dollars. Given the expense and the labour cost, and the fear that the island of Singapore would be turned into a military fortress, the colonial authorities were apprehensive about the project. However, work began on it in 1859, and despite changes to his original plans, Collyer was happy with the completed fortifications, considering the project 'a first-class field fortification'. Upon completion in 1860, it was named FORT CANNING, after Viscount Charles John Canning, the governor-general of India during the SEPOY MUTINY of 1857, and the first viceroy of India. Collyer left Singapore in 1862. COLLYER QUAY was named after him.

Collyer Quay The name Collyer Quay originally referred to the sea wall running from FORT FULLERTON to Telok Ayer Market. This sea wall was designed by Captain (later Colonel) GEORGE COLLYER in 1858. When the sea wall was completed, between 1864 and 1865, there was no road along it. Indeed, all the buildings abutted the sea with a connected verandah to allow workers to walk from office to office. Later, when a road was built to facilitate the movement of traffic, it was given the name that had originally been given to the sea wall—Collyer Quay. This was later transformed into one of the major arterial roads in Singapore's financial district.

Colombo Plan Officially known as the Colombo Plan for Cooperative Economic Development in Asia and the Pacific, the Colombo Plan came into operation in 1951 to strengthen the economic and social development of countries in South and Southeast Asia. The original members were Australia, Canada, Ceylon (present-day Sri Lanka), India, New Zealand, Pakistan and the United Kingdom. Malaya and British North Borneo (present-day Sabah) joined the plan in later years. Today Australia, Japan, New Zealand and the United States are the largest donors. The Colombo Plan offered aid in the form of educational and health aid, training programmes, loans, food supplies, equipment and technical aid. Intitially, the plan was to last only six years. However, it was extended several times until 1980, when it was extended indefinitely. The plan's headquarters are in Colombo, Sri Lanka.

Many students in Singapore were beneficiaries of the Colombo Plan, receiving scholarships to pursue their tertiary education. A total of 963 scholarships were awarded to students from Singapore in the 1962–88 period, with students pursuing studies in Australia (492), New Zealand (201), the United Kingdom (150), Canada (119) and Pakistan (1). The last Colombo Plan scholarship to be awarded to a Singaporean was in 1988.

Colonial Office This department of the British civil service was responsible for relations between the United Kingdom and its overseas territories (with the exception of India, which was administered by the East India Company and later by the India Office). The STRAITS SETTLEMENTS came under the juridiction of the Colonial Office from 1867.

The history of the Colonial Office goes back to the 19th century. In 1801, the office of Secretary of State for War and the Colonies was created. When the Crimean War broke out in 1854, the British government decided to separate colonial and military affairs, and the Colonial Office, which was headed by a secretary of state for colonies, was formed.

The governors of the respective colonies were responsible to the secretary of state for colonies at the Colonial Office for ensuring that the territories were properly governed; they received from the secretary the advice and decisions of the British government.

The Colonial Office was merged with the Commonwealth Relations Office to form the Commonwealth Office in 1966. This was later merged with the Foreign Office to the form the Foreign and Commonwealth Office.

comfort women This term was the Japanese euphemism for women who worked in Japanese military brothels known as 'comfort houses'. The system was started in 1938 after tens of thousands of women were raped during what came to be known as the Rape of Nanking. An estimated 100,000 women were forced to work in comfort houses. Top-level officers in the Japanese military were implicated in the setting up of these military brothels. Post-war Japanese Prime Minister, Nakasone Yasuhiro, admitted in his memoirs to organizing a comfort house for Japan's navy.

One of the rationales for the comfort women system was to prevent the spread of sexually transmitted diseases that would impair the ability of the Japanese soldier. The availability of recreational sex was also believed to improve his fighting ability and prevent attacks on civilian populations. Comfort women were subjected to regular health screening for venereal diseases, and condoms were issued to Japanese soldiers.

Comfort women were considered by the Japanese military to be supplies, and were listed as such in army manifests. They would sometimes arrive ahead of the ammunition, and were often exposed to the same battlefront risks as the soldiers they served. Although about 80 per cent of comfort women were Korean, others came from all Japanese-occupied territories. Many were as young as 12 years of age. Recruitment methods ranged from kidnapping to deception by civilian recruiting agents. For example, a group of Javanese women was brought to Singapore on the pretext of working as nurses. At a screening centre on Victoria Street, during SOOK CHING, some young women were separated from their families and kept locked-up, presumably for subsequent placement or sale into comfort houses. In some cases, girls were sold into slavery because of difficult family circumstances.

Among the most notorious comfort houses was the one on Cairnhill Road, near the Anglo-Chinese Primary School, and at the corner of Haig Road and Mountbatten Road.

This institutionalized sex slavery was never recognized as a war crime. After the war, there was just one case of prosecution in connection with 38 Dutch women who were made to work as comfort women in the Dutch East Indies (present-day Indonesia). It was only in the late 1980s that the comfort women system became better understood.

ComfortDelgro: Comfort taxi from 1970 (left).

ComfortDelGro Transport operator. Incorporated on 29 March 2003, the group was formed from the merger of what were already the two largest transport companies in Singapore—taxi operator Comfort and bus operator DelGro (formerly the Singapore Bus Services [SBS]). ComfortDelGro's businesses include taxi, bus and rail services; car rental and leasing; automotive engineering and maintenance; inspection, test and assessment services; driving instruction; insurance brokerage; and outdoor advertising.

The group was listed on 1 April 2003. It is a component STI stock and is the world's second-largest publicly-listed passenger land transport company with a fleet of more than 38,700 vehicles. ComfortDelGro runs more than 17,000 taxis. Net earnings for the financial year 2005 was $202 million on group revenues of $2.3 billion.

Two subsidiaries, SBS Transit and Vicom, have also been listed on the SINGAPORE EXCHANGE. SBS Transit was formed in 1973 through the merger of three private bus companies, and was listed in 1978 as Singapore Bus Service (1978) Limited. It was the first stock to be offered to all Singapore citizens at the time of its listing. It is Singapore's largest public bus-transport operator with a fleet of more than 2,400 buses, and is also the rail operator for the North East Line (NEL) and the Sengkang Light Rail Transit (LRT) line.

Vicom, which was established in 1981 and listed in 1995, provides testing and assessment services. Vicom has also been appointed by the General Insurance Association of Singapore to operate independent damage assessment centres (Idac).

ComfortDelGro has a significant overseas presence. The group's operations extend from the United Kingdom and Ireland to Vietnam and Malaysia, as well as 12 cities in China.

See also BUSES, MASS RAPID TRANSIT/LIGHT RAIL TRANSIT SYSTEM and TAXIS.

Commandos

Commandos Army special force. The SINGAPORE ARMED FORCES (SAF) Regular Battalion was formed in 1969, and renamed the 1st Commando Battalion in 1971. In 1975, the two Commando units were incorporated into the 7th Singapore Infantry Brigade (7 SIB). This brigade also had two GUARDS battalions, although these were transferred out some five years later. In 1981, its headquarters, the SIB's School of Commando Training, was founded and the winged bayonet emblem was adopted, along with the motto, 'For Honour & Glory'.

The red beret worn by the Commandos distinguishes them from other servicemen. They are trained to perform strike and reconnaisssance missions, and specialize in infiltrating enemy lines and using a wide range of weapons. Operations are extremely challenging, and Commandos are trained to withstand high levels of mental and physical stress. The Commandos also play a role in counter-terrorism and have been called on to safeguard national interests.

Commercial Affairs Department Agency investigating white-collar crime. Prior to 1984, when the Commercial Affairs Department (CAD) began operations within the Revenue Division of the MINISTRY OF FINANCE, Singapore did not have an enforcement agency with the expertise to handle complicated commercial offences.

To broaden its capabilities, in January 2000 the CAD merged with the Commercial Crime Division—which dealt with credit card frauds, financial scams and other forms of fraud—to form a unit within the SINGAPORE POLICE FORCE. The merger saw the creation of a single law-enforcement authority to deal with all kinds of commercial crime and fraud. These include securities and corporate offences, money laundering, terrorism financing and financial crimes. Increasingly, sophisticated technology and global cooperation have enhanced the CAD's ability to deal with more complex commercial crimes.

Commercial Square *See* RAFFLES PLACE.

Common Effective Preferential Tariff Scheme The Common Effective Preferential Tariff (CEPT) Scheme is a mechanism of the ASEAN FREE TRADE AREA (AFTA), by which tariffs on goods traded within the ASSOCIATION OF SOUTH EAST ASIAN NATIONS (ASEAN) region are reduced. The CEPT Scheme covers all manufactured and agricultural goods that meet the 40 per cent local content requirement, with the exception of products in the Highly Sensitive List (e.g. agricultural products such as rice) and a number of tariff lines in the General Exception (GE) List. Products in the GE List, representing about 1 per cent of all tariff lines in ASEAN, are permanently excluded for reasons of national security; protection of public morals; protection of human, animal or plant life and health; and protection of articles of artistic, historic and archaeological value.

By 2002, only 3.8 per cent of products in the CEPT Inclusion List (IL) of the original six ASEAN members (ASEAN-6) had tariffs of above 5 per cent. Since January 2003, tariffs on 64 per cent of the products in the IL of the ASEAN-6 have been completely eliminated. As of 2005, the average tariff for the ASEAN-6 under the CEPT Scheme was down to 1.51 per cent, from 12.76 per cent in 1993, when the tariff-cutting exercise commenced. ASEAN leaders agreed to eliminate all import duties by 2010 for the ASEAN-6, and 2015 for the four new members of ASEAN.

From January 2001, Singapore has accorded tariff-free access to all ASEAN goods under the CEPT Scheme. Thus, all of Singapore's tariff lines have been included in the CEPT Scheme. Reciprocally, Singapore companies may enjoy preferential tariffs on their exports to ASEAN under the CEPT Scheme.

Commonwealth Also known as the 'Commonwealth of Nations' or—until 1949—the 'British Commonwealth', the Commonwealth is an association of sovereign, independent states, most of which were once part of the British Empire. All members acknowledge the British monarch as the symbolic head of the association. Membership in the Commonwealth is expressed through cooperation, consultation, mutual assiststance and periodic conferences of national leaders, most notably the Commonwealth Heads of Government Meeting (CHOGM).

The origins of the Commonwealth can be traced to the Imperial Conferences of the 1920s, at which the independence of the self-governing colonies and dominions was recognized. At one of these conferences in 1926, the Balfour Declaration was issued. In this declaration, the United Kingdom and its dominions agreed that they were 'equal in status, in no way subordinate to one another in any aspect of their domestic or external affairs, though united by common allegiance to the Crown, and freely associated as members of the British Commonwealth of Nations'. This relationship was eventually formalized by the Statute of Westminster of 1931.

In 1950, the issue of republican status within the Commonwealth was resolved by the adoption of the London Declaration which provided for members to accept the British monarch as Head of the Commonwealth, regardless of their domestic constitutional arrangements.

The Commonwealth of Nations comprises 53 countries with 1.8 billion people. It has three intergovernmental organizations: the Commonwealth Secretariat, the Commonwealth Foundation and the Commonwealth of Learning. Singapore joined the Commonwealth in October 1965, shortly after Independence. In 1971, it hosted the first CHOGM held outside the United Kingdom. The Declaration of the Principles of the Commonwealth was adopted at that conference.

Commonwealth: 1971 Commonwealth Heads of Government Meeting, hosted by Singapore.

Singapore regularly participates in the biennial CHOGM, and contributes in areas such as the Commonwealth Private Investment Initiative, which promotes commercial investments in small- and medium-sized private enterprises in Commonwealth countries, and the Commonwealth Third Country Technical Cooperation Programme (TCTP) under the Singapore Cooperation Programme, which offers training courses to Commonwealth members.

community centres and clubs Venues for courses and recreational activities run by the PEOPLE'S ASSOCIATION (PA). During the early 1950s, the colonial government's Department of Social Welfare was assigned the task of setting up 28 community centres (CCs), which would serve as meeting places for the various ethnic, linguistic and religious groups. The PA, established in 1960, converted these CCs into semi-political organizations designed to foster racial harmony and social cohesion through mass participation in various activities.

Programmes organized by CCs are now open to all citizens, with many activities geared towards fostering community integration and national identity among the various ethnic and language groups. With Singapore's political stability and rapid socio-economic progress, CCs have evolved to fulfil the community's changing needs in educational and recreational activities.

Depending on population density and residents' needs, the PA has also set up community clubs with membership schemes, larger premises and better facilities. Some new community club buildings house both community clubs and residents' neighbourhood police centres. The PA runs 78 CCs and 37 community clubs. It also oversees RESIDENTS' COMMITTEES and CITIZENS' CONSULTATIVE COMMITTEES, to pool resources amongst the network of grassroots organizations.

Community Chest The NATIONAL COUNCIL OF SOCIAL SERVICES (NCSS) is the co-ordinating body for member Voluntary Welfare Organisations (VWOs) in Singapore. The Community Chest was founded in 1983 as the fund-raising arm of NCSS, to raise funds for programmes that help disadvantaged people. It serves as a single collection point for donations, which are then channelled to VWOs.

The SINGAPORE TOTALISATOR BOARD covers the operating costs of the Community Chest, so donations from individuals, corporations and other institutions go directly towards social service programmes. Organizations that receive funding from the Community Chest are not allowed to raise funds privately.

The Community Chest disburses funds to four basic categories of programmes. In the financial year 2004/05, 36 programmes nurturing children received $19.9 million,

or 46 per cent of the Community Chest budget, while 26 programmes for the elderly received $5 million (12 per cent). Another $9.9 million (23 per cent) went to 38 programmes for the disabled. The remaining 19 percent of funds, $8.2 million, was given to 31 programmes for the family.

In the interests of transparency, programmes funded by the Community Chest must implement a system which tracks their performances according to a set of defined standards. The Community Chest also publishes lists of the programmes to which it disburses funds.

Community Development Councils Local administrators of community and social services. The purpose of these grassroots organizations, first established in 1997, is to promote a cohesive, compassionate and self-reliant society. Since 2001, the delivery of some social services child, student and family care—has been devolved from the Ministry of Community Development, Youth and Sports to the Community Development Councils (CDCs).

Originally there were nine CDCs. However, these were streamlined to the current five: Central, Northeast, Northwest, Southeast and Southwest. Each CDC is headed by a full-time mayor, and assisted by a council of 12–80 members. The council is appointed by the chairman or deputy chairman of the PEOPLE'S ASSOCIATION. Each CDC is funded through an annual $1 grant from each resident living in the CDC's area, as well as from funds raised from the public, with a matching grant from the government (the government matches every dollar raised by the public with $3; to encourage longer-term donations, the government matches every dollar raised from local residents and businesses through electronic direct debit contributions with $4). The CDCs' cost of operations is met by the government.

competitiveness Maintaining international competitiveness is a fundamental tenet of the government's economic philosophy. Because Singapore has been able to achieve sustained high rates of growth in GROSS DOMESTIC PRODUCT (GDP) per capita, and has fared well in those factors on which

Community centres and clubs: distinctive architecture of the Marine Parade Community Club, designed by William Lim.

competitiveness indices are based, it has consistently been ranked highly amongst the world's most competitive nations.

The *World Competitiveness Yearbook 2006*, published by the International Institute for Management Development, ranks Singapore as the third-most competitive economy in the world. The competitiveness ranking is based on economic performance, government efficiency, business efficiency and infrastructure. The *Global Competitiveness Report 2005–2006*, published by the World Economic Forum, ranks Singapore sixth in its widely quoted Growth Competitiveness Index, which is based on indices of technology, public institutions and the macroeconomic environment; and fifth in the Business Competitiveness Index, which focuses on company operations and strategy and quality of the national business environment.

However, advancements in information and communication technologies, and the increasing extent of globalization and economic liberalization, have changed the rules of competition and the basis of wealth creation. A nation's competitive advantage is increasingly based on the application of knowledge; and competitiveness in a KNOWLEDGE-BASED ECONOMY (KBE) is predicated on intellectual capital, strong technological and innovation capability, and a strong entrepreneurial culture.

Concerted efforts are being made to transform Singapore into a KBE, especially as Singapore has lost some of its competitiveness in terms of land and labour. The specific recommendations of the Economic Review Committee (2003) to prepare Singapore for the transition to a KBE include the need to promote innovation, creativity and entrepreneurship; to further deregulate and liberalize the economy to allow enterprise to flourish; and the need to encourage self-reliance and minimal dependence on the state.

compradors The rise of compradors (*maiban* in MANDARIN) as an influential merchant group is attributable to the opening up of the treaty ports in China after the signing of the Treaty of Nanking (1842).

COMPETITIVENESS: 2006		
Rank	**Country**	**Score**
1 (1)	USA	100
2 (2)	Hong Kong	96.9
3 (3)	Singapore	91.0
4 (4)	Iceland	90.2
5 (7)	Denmark	86.0
6 (9)	Australia	82.5
7 (5)	Canada	81.7
8 (8)	Switzerland	81.5
9 (10)	Luxembourg	81.5
10 (6)	Finland	80.9

*Figures in brackets indicate 2005 rankings.
Source: IMD*

Compradors: home of Chia Keng Chin, comprador for Mercantile Bank in Singapore (above); International Banking Corporation's comprador Song Kim Pong, in 1907.

Concave Scream: Erratic *(1997).*

Francis Joseph de Conceicao

Babes Conde

'Comprador' was the term used to refer to Asian (and often locally-born) agents of foreign firms in China and other Asian countries. They acted as intermediaries in commercial transactions. The term was also used to refer to a Chinese head storekeeper of a foreign firm.

Compradors were deemed necessary for several reasons: first was the question of language; second, the complicated system of currency, weights and measures, and the circulation of money certificates and credit bills by traditional local banks—a system which proved too difficult for foreign traders to grasp. In short, the function of the comprador was to facilitate trade between foreign merchants and the Chinese.

The main responsibilities of the comprador included the employment and supervision of Chinese staff. The comprador was the treasurer and sometimes interpreter; provided market intelligence; took responsibility for native bank orders; and generally aided the foreign manager in transactions with the Chinese. He also handled the actual business transactions, acting as a commission agent. This involved the selling of western manufactured goods, mainly wool and cotton, and exporting tea and silk from China.

Most compradors were CANTONESE. This was due to the previous experience that the Cantonese had had in the Cohong (*gong hang*) system, whereby a group of merchants was officially authorized to handle China's early trade with Europeans. The role of compradors became more significant after the signing of the Treaty of Tientsin (1860), whereby more treaty ports were opened along the Yangtze River and the north China coast. As Cantonese merchants became more active in these trade centres, Cantonese compradors were brought to these regions by their foreign employers.

This practice was continued when China-based Western business firms expanded their activities overseas to areas such as the Straits Settlements. In Malacca and Singapore, they played an important role in trade and in dealing with Chinese labour.

As a result of the Great Depression, there were significant changes to Chinese business practices in Singapore, with many Chinese preferring to rely on more personal forms of trade involving regional organizations and family links. This contributed to the growth of the comprador system. However, the fortunes of the system began to decline as Chinese and foreign merchants became more acquainted with each other's practices and business patterns.

The comprador system ended altogether when the treaty system in China ended with World War II. Compradors continued to operate nominally for some years after the war. Some banks, for example, were still employing Chinese managers with the title of 'Comprador' in Malaysia in the 1970s.

compulsory education Singapore has achieved almost universal education at primary and secondary levels despite not having compulsory education for many years. In 2000, a mere 3 per cent of children were not enrolled in national schools. However, concerned that this group would be poorly equipped to become productive citizens in a KNOWLEDGE-BASED ECONOMY, the government introduced compulsory education in 2003.

Under the Compulsory Education Act, a child of compulsory school age (6–15 years old) born after 1 January 1996, and who is a citizen of, and residing in, Singapore, has to attend a national primary school regularly. The exemptions are children with special needs, children attending a 'designated school', or children receiving home-schooling. These designated schools are the six MADRASAHS currently offering full-time Islamic religious education for children of primary-school-going age and the San Yu Adventist School.

Parents who home-school their children have to furnish information on the curriculum and educational outcomes of the home-schooling programme and declare that their child will sit the Primary School Leaving Examination in four subjects (English, MOTHER TONGUE, Mathematics and Science) when the child is between 11 and 15 years old.

Comrade D (1930–) Political activist. Wong Meng Keong, known as Comrade D, was the head of the Student Movement and Workers' Movement Committees of the MALAYAN COMMUNIST PARTY (MCP) until 1954. Also known variously as Ng Meng Chiang, Chow Kong and Ah Kwang, he was the undercover communist agent tasked with unifying the student population in opposition to the British. In 1954, he escaped with EU CHOOI YIP and Chiam Chong Chian to the Riau Islands to avoid arrest, and continued to direct MCP operations from there. In 1957, Wong's role was taken over by FANG CHUANG PI ('The Plen') after his serial womanizing was

deemed inappropriate by the MCP hierarchy. Little was heard of him after he had escaped to Riau.

Concave Scream Popular music group. Dubbed 'promising' by ex-Sex Pistols manager Malcolm McLaren, Concave Scream started out as a two-piece group consisting of childhood friends Sean Lam and Lim Shu Pann, but soon expanded into a four-piece group. It released three albums— *Concave Scream* (1995), *Erratic* (1997) and *Three* (1999). After a hiatus which began in 2000, the band returned to the live music scene in 2004 with new members—drummer Dean Aziz and bassist Andy Yang—and released a fourth album, *Horizons*, in 2006. The group is closely associated with Lam's raw and emotional voice, and Lim's lead guitar work.

Conceicao, Francis Joseph de (1924–) Teacher, diplomat and politician. Francis Joseph de Conceicao was educated at St Patrick's School. He enrolled in Raffles College, but his education was interrupted by the Japanese Occupation.

In 1948, he began teaching at his alma mater. In 1955, he resumed his tertiary education at the University of Malaya, where he graduated with an Arts degree (1959), after which he returned to teaching at St Patrick's School. In 1965, Conceicao left to undertake a postgraduate diploma in adult education at Manchester University in the United Kingdom. When he returned to Singapore the following year, he joined the newly-formed Extra-Mural Studies Department of the University of Malaya as director.

Conceicao was persuaded to enter politics by GOH KENG SWEE of the People's Action Party and, in 1968, was elected member of Parliament for Katong. In 1977, Conceicao was appointed Singapore's ambassador to the Soviet Union, a post he held until 1981. He then served as ambassador to Indonesia (1981–86); high commissioner to Australia, and concurrently Fiji (1987–90); and, again, ambassador to the Soviet Union (and later Russia) (1990–94). He retired from politics in 1984, and from the diplomatic service in 1994.

Conde, Babes (1950–) Singer and musician. Born in the Philippines, Babes Conde made her debut as the music director and arranger of Filipino band The New Minstrels. In 1983 the group performed in Singapore at the International Jazz Festival. In 1985, the year she came to Singapore, she formed Street Smart, whose song 'Funny' became a local evergreen. In 1988, Conde ventured into theatre with THEATREWORKS' *Piaf* and *Beauty World*, serving as musical director and pianist for the former, and chorus mistress for the latter. She followed this up with a series of successful musicals and concerts. In 1996 Conde performed with the Shanghai

Condominiums: Eastpoint Green.

Philharmonic Orchestra at the SINGAPORE ARTS FESTIVAL. She became the first vocal coach for SINGAPORE IDOL when the series began in 2004 and in the following year, became the music director for *Broadway Christmas Carol*.

condominiums A form of private housing development. The term 'condominium', or 'condo' for short, was first used in North America. Typically, individual housing units are owned by tenants individually, while common areas and facilities—playgrounds, common walkways, swimming pools—are owned collectively. In countries such as the United Kingdom, Australia and Singapore, this form of land tenure is known as a 'strata' title. The term 'condominium' has been used more generally to denote a multi-unit dwelling (such as an apartment development) that is privately developed and owned, as opposed to state-subsidized housing built by the HOUSING & DEVELOPMENT BOARD. These condominiums also come complete with 'condo facilities' which typically include security guards and systems, pools, clubhouses, barbecue pits, and squash or tennis courts.

Singapore's first condominium development was Beverley Mai, which was built on Tomlinson Road in 1974. It was designed by Seow, Lee Heah and Partners, and was completed by Timothy Seow and Partners. It was the first apartment block to incorporate shared common facilities such as a swimming pool. The Beverley Mai consisted of 48 maisonettes, two deluxe apartments and two two-storey luxury penthouses. The site consists of two quite separate vehicular and pedestrian zones. This development was soon followed by Futura Apartments (1976), Ardmore Park Apartments (1978) and Pandan Valley Condominium (1979).

Confrontation Conflict between Indonesia and Malaysia lasting from 1963 to 1966. Confrontation, or *Konfrontasi* in Bahasa Indonesia and Malay, was Indonesian President Sukarno's response to the proposed merger of the FEDERATION OF MALAYA with Singapore and the Borneo territories of Sabah and Sarawak to form the Federation of Malaysia. Sukarno felt that the new Federation of Malaysia would be nothing more than a British puppet, and that the consolidation of the various territories would strengthen the British presence and power in the region. This would in turn threaten Indonesia's independence. At the same time, the Philippines laid claim to Sabah, arguing that it was historically linked to the Philippines through the Sulu Archipelago.

The first salvo was fired on 26 January 1963 by then Indonesian Foreign Minister, Dr Subandrio, who announced his country's policy of *Konfrontasi*. Less than three months later, Indonesian 'volunteers'—probably Indonesian military personnel—infiltrated Sabah and Sarawak, and engaged in raids and acts of sabotage. They also started spreading propaganda. On 27 July, President Sukarno declared that he would 'crush Malaysia'. Although the Philippines did not embark on a similar policy, it ended diplomatic relations with Malaysia on 16 September 1963.

The Federation of Malaysia was formed on 16 September 1963. On 18 September 1963, rioters burned the British embassy in Jakarta and ransacked the homes of Singaporean representatives and the Singapore trade office there. Indonesian troops and irregulars tried to occupy Sabah and Sarawak, but with little success. Meanwhile, Indonesian agents were captured in Malaysia, and crowds attacked the Indonesian embassy in Kuala Lumpur. The following year, Indonesian troops began raiding various areas in the Malay Peninsula. On 16 August 1964, Indonesian agents were captured in Johor. With the intensification of military activity, the United Kingdom deployed a number of warships, including aircraft carriers and aircraft squadrons, to help secure Malaysia's territorial integrity. Eighteen battalions of COMMONWEALTH ground forces, including a brigade of GURKHAS, three Malaysian battalions and two Royal Marines commando units, were committed to the conflict.

On 17 August 1964, Indonesian paratroopers landed on the southwest coast of Johor and attempted to start guerrilla groups there. This was followed by more paratrooper landings at Mersing on 2 September. On 29 October 1964, 52 Indonesian soldiers were captured in Pontian by New Zealand Army personnel.

Singapore was particularly hard hit by the Confrontation. Economically, it suffered from the cessation of its Indonesian barter trade. Indonesian commandos also raided Singaporean fishing boats. Indonesian terrorists bombed the Ambassador Hotel on 24 September 1964, beginning a year of

terrorism and propaganda aimed at creating communal unrest in Singapore. On 10 March 1965, a powerful bomb exploded on the mezzanine floor of MACDONALD HOUSE in Orchard Road. The explosion killed three people, injured 33, shattered all windows within a 100-m radius and damaged cars outside the building. The two Indonesian soldiers responsible for the bombing were arrested, charged with murder and hanged.

Towards the end of 1965, General Suharto came to power in Indonesia following a *coup d'état*. On 28 May 1966, at a conference in Bangkok, the Malaysian and Indonesian governments declared the conflict over. Violence ended in June that year. A peace treaty was signed on 11 August and ratified two days later.

Confucianism In Singapore, Confucianism is generally understood as a secular system of ethics rather than a religion. Although Confucius is worshipped in some of the Chinese temples in Singapore, Confucianism is not an institutionalized religion with a network of temples and clergy. A deified Confucius is venerated together with other deities in local Buddhist and Taoist temples. As Confucius is remem-

Confrontation (Konfrontasi): Indonesian guerrillas apprehended on Singapore's west coast, 1964.

Condominiums: advertising board for Kovan Melody show flats.

至聖先師

東安學校惠存

星洲書店敬贈

Confucianism: painting of Confucius.

Joseph Conrad

bered in history as a great scholar and an exemplary teacher, worshippers pray to Confucius for favours with regard to academic success. The most important festival for followers of the sage is the birthday of Confucius, which falls on the 27th day of the eighth lunar month (in September). This tradition of Confucian worship has probably been in existence since at least the late 19th century, when the local Chinese community had grown to a significant size. In recent years, the annual celebration of Confucius' birthday organized by Sanqing Gong, a local Taoist temple, has attracted over a thousand followers, according to press estimates.

Confucianism has been held by some to lie at the heart of the value system of the local Chinese community. Key Confucian moral precepts, such as humanity (*ren*), righteousness (*yi*), propriety (*li*), wisdom (*zhi*), trustworthiness (*xin*) and filial piety (*xiao*), are regarded as the foundations of an ethical system which sustains the ethnic and cultural identity of the community. Consequently, whenever there has been a perceived threat to the continuity of these cultural and ethnic traditions, Confucianism has often been used as a force for preservation of community heritage.

Two periods are particularly notable in the history of Confucianism in Singapore. Between 1899 and 1911, there was a movement to revive Confucianism in Singapore and Malaya. The movement had its roots in the 'Hundred Days Reform' (*Bairi Weixin*) in China launched by KANG YOUWEI. But the proponents of the movement in Singapore were mainly concerned with issues of social reform and cultural modernization. They perceived that there was, at the time, an increasing degree of Westernization and 'Babaization' among the younger generations of local Chinese, which they saw as possibly resulting from a lack of moral education, and so

they began a drive to establish Confucianism as a formal religion, setting up temples dedicated to Confucius, observing the sage's birthday, promulgating Confucianism through publications in the press (notably the *Tiannan Xinbao*, *Rixin Bao* and *Straits Chinese Magazine*) and writing simplified Confucian textbooks for students. Dr LIM BOON KENG and Khoo Seok Wan were the most prominent leaders of this movement.

Another campaign to promote Confucianism began in 1982 and lasted throughout the decade. This campaign was initiated and directed mainly by the government. After two decades of rapid industrialization, the government felt that social changes were leading to an erosion of values, and advocated the teaching of Confucianism in schools as part of a larger effort to deal with the problem. Confucian Ethics was offered alongside Bible Knowledge, Islamic Religious Knowledge, Buddhist Studies, Hindu Studies, Sikh Studies and Study of World Religions, which taken together constituted the Religious Knowledge (RK) curriculum, compulsory for Secondary 3 and 4 students. Textbooks on Confucian ethics were written by the Curriculum Development Institute of Singapore (CDIS) with the help of overseas and local Confucian scholars. The Institute of East Asian Philosophies was established by Dr GOH KENG SWEE in 1983 as an intellectual thinktank and aimed at connecting Singapore to the international network of Confucian scholars. It subsequently shifted its focus to the economy of China and was renamed the Institute of East Asian Political Economy in 1992. It was renamed the EAST ASIAN INSTITUTE in 1997, and now promotes research on China and other East Asian economies. Confucian Ethics, together with all the other RK subjects, was phased out as a required school course after 1990.

congkak This traditional board game has been played, especially by Malay women and girls (including those of the royal court), probably since the 18th century. The game was initially called '*jongka*', as the wooden board used in the game was shaped like a *jong* (boat). Over time, '*jongka*' evolved to become '*congkak*', possibly because the latter was easier to pronounce. The game is also known as '*dakon*' or '*sungka*'.

Congkak is usually played by two players. The board has two rows of holes. Each row typically has seven identical holes, with a larger hole at both ends—one for each player—which acts a store or 'home' for each player. The small holes are filled with seeds. Each player controls the seven holes on her side of the board, and the score is the number of seeds collected in her store—the large hole to her left. A player selects one hole under her control and removes all seeds from it, then distributes them in each

Congkak

hole, clockwise. The object of the game is to capture more seeds than the opposing player. The game requires strategy, mental agility and speed. The board may have five, seven or nine holes in each row.

Traditionally, the seeds used were those of rubber or sago trees. Objects such as marbles or small seashells are now used instead. A proper board may not even be necessary; in KAMPONGS, women and girls have been known to fashion boards by nailing plastic bowls on a plank. Holes can even be dug in the ground to play *congkak*.

Congkak was never particularly popular in urbanized settings, and is now only seen during cultural events or festivals. The cognitive element of the game was recognized when it was selected as one of ten 'thinking games' for the Mind Sports Olympiad held in Singapore in 2000—part of the first Singapore Learning Festival.

Conrad, Joseph (1857–1924) Author. Born Józef Teodor Konrad Korzeniowski in Ukraine on 3 December 1857, Conrad was of Polish descent, and his first contact with the English language took place when he was eight years old. He joined the French merchant marine in the 1870s, followed by a 16-year career in the British merchant navy. In 1884, he obtained British citizenship.

Over the following ten years, Conrad sailed between Singapore and Borneo, and to the Belgian Congo (present-day Democratic Republic of Congo). During Conrad's time in Asia, Singapore was his most frequent port of call, and he featured the port in some of his works. His novel *Lord Jim* (1900) was based on a true incident involving a ship, the *Jeddah*, which had Muslim pilgrims on board, and was abandoned by its British crew when it sprang a leak after leaving Singapore. A.P. Williams, the sailor who organized the desertion, is recorded as being buried in BIDADARI

Confucius' birthday The birthday of Confucius is celebrated as an expression of reverence for a historical figure who is remembered as an exemplary scholar and teacher. According to traditional sources, Confucius was born in the 21st year of the reign of Duke Xiang in the state of Lu, and on the 27th day of the 8th month of the Chinese agrarian calendar. The government of China had determined that, converted to the Gregorian calendar, the birthday of Confucius was on 28 September 551 BCE. Therefore in Taiwan and Hong Kong, people celebrate Confucius' birthday on 28 September. The day has been declared officially as Teachers' Day by both communities. However, in Singapore people choose to follow the date of Confucius' birthday according to the traditional Chinese calendar, which is the 27th day of the 8th month.

The celebration of Confucius' birthday in China, Taiwan and Hong Kong is marked by *bayi*, a ritual dance with eight rows of eight dancers. In Singapore, where the celebrations at Taoist temple Sanqing Gong draw the largest crowds, three students are chosen to represent the *zhuangyuan*, *bangyan*, *tanhua* (the Three Presented Scholars in the Chinese imperial civil examinations). Parents and students in Singapore make offerings and pray to Confucius for good results in school examinations.

conservation areas

Architectural conservation is overseen by the URBAN REDEVELOPMENT AUTHORITY (URA). Buildings are selected for conservation based on historical and architectural significance, rarity in terms of building types and styles, and contribution to the overall environment.

Renovation in progress, Bukit Pasoh.

Under the Preservation of Monuments Act, certain buildings are gazetted by the PRESERVATION OF MONUMENTS BOARD as national monuments. Their original character and architecture must be preserved, and original construction methods, architectural details and materials must be used.

Other buildings are conserved under the Planning Act, although the controls are somewhat less stringent. Conservation areas were first introduced in 1986, when the URA announced its Conservation Master Plan. The aim is to preserve and enhance the character or appearance of a conserved area. Adaptive changes are permitted to accommodate new uses more relevant to the present time. Contemporary construction techniques and new materials are allowed. Generally, the URA is guided by regard for the fundamental principles of conservation, and respect for the typology of the buildings concerned. Over 6,500 buildings have been gazetted for conservation.

Shown here are the main conservation areas. Any alteration to a preserved building requires URA clearance, but each group is subject to specific development regulations.

Residential historic districts include Emerald Hill, Cairnhill and Blair Plain. These mainly comprise terrace houses. There is greater freedom to extend the rear portion of the building, within limits.

From left: five-foot way and terrace houses at Emerald Hill.

Secondary settlements include Jalan Besar, Beach Road, River Valley, Geylang, JOO CHIAT and TIONG BAHRU. Here the main emphasis is on maintaining the streetscape. There is greater freedom to construct rear extensions, within limits.

Shophouses in Kampong Glam.

Balconies in Bukit Pasoh Road (above); shophouses in Temple Street (right).

Historic districts include BOAT QUAY, CHINATOWN (including Bukit Pasoh, Kreta Ayer, TANJONG PAGAR and Telok Ayer), KAMPONG GLAM and LITTLE INDIA. Here, the entire building is conserved. Commercial or residential use is allowed.

'Black-and-white' residence in bungalow area.

Bungalow areas include White House Park/Nassim Road, Chatsworth Park and Holland Park/Ridout Park and Mountbatten Road conservation areas. Here additional emphasis is placed on the wooded environment, though development to maximize the use of land is permitted within limits.

CEMETERY. Like the character Jim, Conrad was injured during a storm, and recovered at a Singapore hospital.

In 1894, Conrad retired from seafaring and began writing. His first novel, *Almayer's Folly*, was published in 1895 under the name Joseph Conrad. Works such as *An Outcast of the Islands* (1896), *Victory* (1915), and *The Rescue* (1920) are based on his adventures plying the Singapore–Borneo route. Besides *Lord Jim*, other important novels include *Nigger Of The Narcissus* (1897) and *Heart Of Darkness* (1902).

In February 2004, Polish President Aleksander Kwasniewski unveiled a plaque commemorating Conrad which had been erected outside the FULLERTON BUILDING by the National Heritage Board. Conrad used to collect his mail at the building when it served as Singapore's General Post Office.

conservation *See* NATURE CONSERVATION.

conservation areas *See* box.

constituencies For the purposes of parliamentary elections, Singapore is divided into electoral divisions or constituencies (*see* map). Under the CONSTITUTION, Parliament consists of the number of Members of Parliament required to be returned by the constituencies. The total number of constituencies is determined by PARLIAMENT under the Parliamentary Elections Act.

From 1948—when the first LEGISLATIVE COUNCIL ELECTION was held—to 1988, all constituencies in Singapore were single-member wards or single-member constituencies (SMCs). This meant that only one Member of Parliament could be elected for each constituency. In 1988, a constitutional amendment was passed to create a new type of constituency—the GROUP REPRESENTATION CONSTITUENCY (GRC). Under this system, between three and six members can stand for elections in a single ward, and are elected as a team instead of individually.

The number, size and nature of each constituency in Singapore is determined by the ELECTORAL BOUNDARIES REVIEW COMMITTEE. As of 2006, there are 23 constituencies in Singapore, comprising nine SMCs, nine five-member GRCs and five six-member GRCs.

Constitution Singapore has a written constitution that lays out the rules of government, such as the 'separation of powers' and the functions of its various branches. Article 4 of the Constitution declares the document to be the supreme law of the land, and further provides that any law that is inconsistent with the Constitution shall be deemed void.

Singapore's first constitution was granted

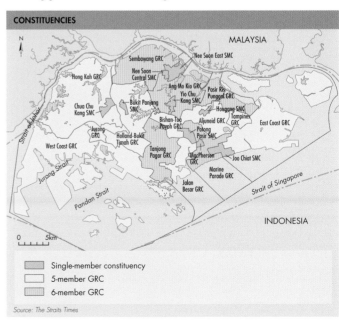

CONSTITUENCIES

Source: The Straits Times

by Letters Patent on 4 February 1867, when the STRAITS SETTLEMENTS was established. It was a colonial-style constitution, in which the governor ruled with the help of his Legislative Council (Legco) and Executive Council (Exco). Officials always outnumbered Unofficials (residents appointed by the governor) in both Legco and Exco. During the 1920s, the Constitution was amended to afford greater local representation by creating more seats for Unofficials than Officials.

During the JAPANESE OCCUPATION, British law continued to be administered through the courts established by the colonial government. In March 1946, the Straits Settlements was dissolved and Singapore became a Crown Colony. The governor then ruled with an Advisory Council, and nominated Unofficials until the Exco and Legco were restored in 1947. Under the Constitution, the governor retained control but six Legco members could be elected by popular vote. The first ELECTIONS were held on 20 March 1948, but turnout was very poor. The Progressive Party, led by English-educated lawyers, won all the seats.

In 1953, a Constitutional Commission under Sir George Rendel was established. The RENDEL COMMISSION recommended a new constitution with automatic voter registration, and a mainly elected Legislative Assembly of 32 members. This Constitution came into effect in 1955, followed by general elections, which saw the LABOUR FRONT sweep into power. DAVID MARSHALL, leader of the Labour Front, formed a coalition government and became Singapore's first chief minister. Marshall lobbied for constitutional talks, led an all-party delegation to London (1956), and resigned on his return after failing to secure full independence for Singapore. His successor, LIM YEW HOCK, led another all-party mission to London (March 1957). This time, the terms of self-government were agreed and in 1958, Singapore became a self-governing colony under a new Constitution. In the 1959 general elections, the PEOPLE'S ACTION PARTY (PAP), led by LEE KUAN YEW, swept to victory.

The Singapore (Constitution) Order-in-Council, enacted in 1958, abolished the post of Governor—the last vestige of a colonial-style constitution—and established the office of the Yang di-Pertuan Negara. Under the Constitution, the Yang di-Pertuan Negara 'is required to appoint as Prime Minister, the person most likely to command the authority of the Assembly. He also appoints ministers on the Prime Minister's advice'. Under Article 34 of the Constitution, the new Legislative Assembly comprised 51 elected members, while the judicial structure was left very much intact, the Chief Justice being appointed by the Yang di-Pertuan Negara on the advice of the Prime Minister.

The new constitution also formed the office of the British High Commissioner, who would act on royal instructions and be chairman of the new Internal Security Council. The high commissioner had considerable powers, including being entitled to see the agenda of cabinet meetings and all cabinet papers. Under Part VIII of the Constitution, responsibility for the external affairs of the State of Singapore was placed in the hands of the British Government.

The People's Action Party won 43 out of the 51 seats in the general elections of 1959. The outgoing Governor, Sir WILLIAM GOODE, brought into force, by Proclamation, the new Constitution on 3 June 1959. Goode then took his oath as the first Yang di-Pertuan Negara of the State of Singapore. LEE KUAN YEW became Singapore's first Prime Minister, and nine ministers were appointed.

On 16 September 1963, the new Federation of Malaysia—comprising the Federation of Malaya, Sabah, Sarawak and Singapore—was born. MERGER with the Federation was short-lived due to ethnic and economic disagreements, and on 9 August 1965, Singapore became independent (see SEPARATION). It retained its old state Constitution and augmented this with provisions from the Federation of Malaysia Constitution, as well as the Republic of Singapore Independence Act. In 1980, these documents were first consolidated into a Reprint of the Constitution of the Republic of Singapore; later revisions have been made and reissued as subsequent reprints.

construction sector This sector has provided infrastructural support for Singapore's rapid industrialization. In tandem with a high annual real growth in GROSS DOMESTIC PRODUCT (GDP) of 9.2 per cent between 1965 and 1985, value added by the construction industry increased by 10 per cent per year. Between 1986 and 1998, construction value growth was an average 8.4 per cent annually. The construction sector contributed 4.5 per cent of GDP in 2004, a sharp drop from its peak of 13 per cent in 1984. Causal factors for this decline includ-ed weak sentiment in the property market, high vacancy rates and an oversupply of building space.

Despite this sharp drop in demand, the number of construction firms did not correspondingly decline. Over-capacity led to price-cutting, with ramifications for professionalism, quality and safety. To raise professional standards, the government has announced that it is considering measures such as the licensing of contractors. It is also promoting exports to supplement low local demand.

Another challenge is the construction industry's reliance on foreign workers (see FOREIGN TALENT/WORKERS). While low-cost labour has kept construction costs down, labour productivity growth was negligible in the 1986–2004 period. To raise productivity, the government adopted a policy of moderating the number, and improving the quality, of foreign workers in the industry through a combination of higher levy and skills certification, while at the same time encouraging locals to join the sector.

Consumers Association of Singapore The abuse of trade practices and the rapid escalation of retail prices in the early 1970s, highlighted the need to regulate the trading environment. The Consumers Association of Singapore (CASE), a non-profit, non-political, independent organization, was established in 1971 to safeguard the interests of consumers.

CASE founded the Advertising Standards Authority of Singapore (ASAS) in 1973, which helps promote ethical advertising and serves as a self-regulatory body for the local advertising industry. CASE has also taken a proactive approach to consumer protection, working closely with the retail industry. This led to the implementation of the Casetrust Accreditation Scheme in 2001, which aims to reinforce and encourage fair and ethical trade practices for the benefit of the consumer and the retailer. The Consumer Protection (Fair Trading) Act became effective March 2004.

Contact Singapore Government agency. Contact Singapore is a network of international offices in Boston, London, Chennai, Shanghai and Singapore. It informs foreign talent about work opportunities in Singapore, and offers information on industry trends, and living, working and studying in Singapore. It also acts a bridge for Singaporeans living abroad, enabling them to keep in touch with developments and work opportunities in Singapore.

Contemplacion, Flor (1953–1995) A Filipina domestic worker, Flor Contemplacion was convicted in the Singapore High Court of killing another Filipina domestic worker, Delia Maga, and Nicholas Huang, the three year-old son of her Singaporean employer, on 4 May 1991.

Construction sector: the Cosmopolitan condominium (right); safety statistics displayed on a construction site.

think Safety ⊕ Work Safely

NCC WOH HUP · SHANGHAI TUNNEL ENGINEERING · NCC

CONTRACT : CIRCLE LINE STAGE 1 - C825   CONTRACT PERIOD : 07 AUG 01 - 30 JAN 06

ACCIDENTS STATISTICS DATED	24 01 06	
Accident-Free Hours Achieved :	1902421	Hrs.
Total of Man-hours worked :	16793116	Hrs.
Total of Loss-time Accident :	26	
Total No. of Fatal Accidents :	0	Frequency Rate : 1·55
Total No. of Crane Collapse :	0	Severity Rate : 47

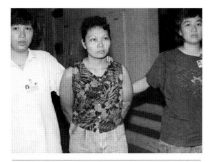

Flor Contemplacion

Contemplacion had originally confessed to the murders but later claimed that her confession had been extracted under duress, and that she had been of unsound mind when the crimes were committed.

The government of the Philippines requested a stay of execution (first through Solicitor-General Raul Goco, then through President Fidel Ramos personally) when a Filipina domestic worker, Emilia Frenilla, who worked for the brother of Wong Sing Keong—the father of Nicholas Huang and employer of Delia Maga—came forward to suggest that Nicholas Huang had drowned after an epileptic fit in the bathtub, and that Maga had been killed by Wong in a fit of rage afterwards. The Ministry of Home Affairs rejected the 'new evidence' as pure fabrication and President ONG TENG CHEONG rejected the appeals. Contemplacion was hanged on 17 March 1995 amidst unusually tight security. Police cars and motorcycles patrolled the streets in anticipation of protests by Filipinos working in Singapore. There were demonstrations outside the Philippine Embassy in Singapore. In the Philippines, widespread demonstrations and protests broke out on news of her execution, and the media denounced Singapore as a barbaric, tyrannical country with no respect for human rights.

Contemplacion's body was received by President Ramos' wife, Amelita in Manila. Thousands jammed the small town of San Pablo to pay their last respects, and more than 5,000 people tried to catch a glimpse of her coffin. President Ramos established a committee of inquiry which ordered the exhumation of Delia Maga's remains—which had been flown back to the Philippines for burial—to determine how she died. Experts from the Philippines, Singapore and the United States were brought in to determine the cause of death and if it was possible for a woman to have carried out the murder. The pathologists concluded that the conviction was correct. Ties between Singapore and the Philippines eventually returned to normal. In 1995, a Tagalog film, *The Flor Contemplacion Story*, directed by Joel Lamangan was released.

Convent of the Holy Infant Jesus Catholic school. The Infant Jesus Sisters is an order that was founded in France in 1666 by Father Nicolas Barré to reach out to the poor and disadvantaged in society, with a special focus on the education of girls. Nuns of the order arrived in Singapore in 1854, and opened their first school on the island, the Convent of the Holy Infant Jesus (CHIJ) on Victoria Street. Father JEAN-MARIE BEUREL, a priest from the Missions Etrangères de Paris (MEP), was already in Singapore setting up a Catholic boys' school (ST JOSEPH'S INSTITUTION) at the time, and was instrumental in funding the initial establishment of the CHIJ, although the Sisters soon became self-sufficient.

The convent took in both boarders and day pupils, and also ran an orphanage. Its premises originally occupied one building, Caldwell House, but gradually expanded to incorporate an entire block on Victoria Street delimited by Bras Basah Road on the east, Stamford Road on the west and North Bridge Road on the south. Eurasians and Europeans made up a large proportion of the school population, although all ethnic groups were represented. The Gothic chapel, which is still a landmark, was designed by MEP priest Father Benedict Nain, and was built in 1903.

For more than 70 years, the CHIJ on Victoria Street was the only school run by the Infant Jesus Sisters in Singapore. The school began its first expansion in the 1930s, venturing beyond the city to open Katong Convent in an eastern suburb, where a predominantly Eurasian and Straits Chinese population resided. In 1933, it opened a third school, St Theresa's Convent, in the poor, rural area of Kampong Bahru, populated mainly by Indian stevedores. The Sisters continued branching out with the setting up of St Joseph's Convent in Paya Lebar in 1938, to cater to the working-class TEOCHEW community in nearby Hougang and Serangoon.

The JAPANESE OCCUPATION halted the expansion of CHIJ schools. However, after the war, the Sisters continued to open more schools, starting with St Nicholas Girls' School, which was originally known as Victoria Girls' School, and was opened in 1933. This was a Chinese school, although it was run with the same ethos as the other CHIJ schools. The 1950s saw the establishment of Bukit Timah Convent in 1955, Our Lady of the Nativity in 1957 and Our Lady of Good Counsel in 1960.

CHIJ schools are particularly proficient in teaching the arts and humanities. CHIJ schools have modified and improved their facilities and programmes, and have followed the national curriculum while remaining true to their original mission of providing a Catholic education for girls.

Notable CHIJ alumni include CHAN HENG CHEE, diplomat; ELIZABETH CHOY, Legislative Counsellor and war heroine; and CONSTANCE SINGAM, social activist and author. The original convent premises which is located on Victoria Street is now known as CHIJMES.

Convent of the Holy Infant Jesus: music class in 1924.

convict labour During the late 18th and early 19th centuries, the use of convicts represented one response to the general shortage of labour in the emergent trading outposts of the British Empire, including Singapore. Most convicts sent to Singapore were Indians, although a small number of Chinese prisoners was also transported from Hong Kong. The first Indian convicts arrived in April 1825, being transferred to Singapore from BENCOOLEN, which had been ceded to the Dutch after the signing of the ANGLO-DUTCH TREATY. Records show that there were as many as 2,275 Indian convicts in Singapore by 1860. These convicts built roads, bridges and public buildings such as Government House (later the ISTANA); churches such as ST ANDREW'S CATHEDRAL; and Hindu temples including the SRI MARIAMMAN TEMPLE. Indeed, it has been argued that Indian convicts laid the foundation for Singapore's infrastructure.

The story of these convicts is vividly told in a book by colonial engineer J.F.A. MCNAIR, entitled *Prisoners Their Own Warders* (1899).

Disorderly behaviour amongst the convicts brought about numerous complaints to the authorities, and by 1845 the government of the STRAITS SETTLEMENTS

Convict labour: Indian labourers, photographed in 1870.

Punchardsheram ('Punch') Coomaraswamy

was beginning to have misgivings. When the Indian government began transporting to Singapore people who had taken part in the Indian Mutiny of 1856, there was an outcry. Newspapers on the island took up the matter and lodged several petitions opposed to transportation, as there was a fear amongst sections of colonial society that the mutiny of 1856 would be repeated in Singapore. The Grand Jury also made a number of representations on the 'inconvenience and danger of having such a large number of convicts staying in the heart of the town', and asked that a stop be put to transportation. This marked a major change from 1836, when the Indian government had contemplated removing convicts from the Straits Settlements—at that time, the governor had not only protested against this plan, but had asked for more convicts to be sent.

In 1860, the Supreme Government of India resolved that no more convicts would be sent to the Straits Settlements. The last group was shipped out on 8 May 1873. The last major project carried out by Indian convicts was Cavenagh Bridge. In that year, construction work fell under the jurisdiction of the Public Works Department. Most of the Indian convicts in Singapore were then transferred to Port Blair in the Andaman Islands (although some settled permanently in Singapore after serving out their sentences).

coolie trade The term 'coolie' refers to an indentured labourer imported for colonial enterprise in the 19th century. It is thought to be derived from the Hindi word '*quli*' (meaning 'hired labourer'), and is now considered derogatory, although it is still used in India to refer to railway porters.

During the 19th century, coolies were imported into various colonies in the Americas, Africa and Asia, including Singapore. A number of factors contributed to the expansion of the coolie trade during that period. Population growth; increased stress on agricultural lands; scarcity of food due to droughts and floods; and political upheavals—these were some of the reasons why people migrated from places such as

India and China to undertake manual labour abroad.

More importantly, the abolition of slavery meant that colonial governments were forced to search for cheap labour from other sources in order to satisfy the labour demands of mines, plantations, shipyards and construction sites. In order to facilitate a constant supply of workers, colonial merchants set up agents or brokerages to supply coolies for a commission. These included 'principal brokers' and 'subordinate brokers'. It was the latter, many of whom were connected with SECRET SOCIETIES, who became directly involved in recruiting coolies. Some of the key ports from which coolies were shipped abroad during the 19th and early 20th centuries were Amoy (present-day Xiamen) in the Chinese province of Fujian, the Portuguese colony of Macau and the south Indian port of Nagapattinam. Coolie houses, known as 'barracoons', were set up at these and other ports to collect workers and ship them overseas.

Through the coolie trade, recruiters profited from the poor and desperate. They exploited coolies by promising them better lives abroad, while often bonding them for life. Sometimes, people were even kidnapped and sold to barracoons. In Singapore, coolies who had arrived directly from China were often forced to work to pay off debts to the recruiters who had brought them to the island (*see* SINKHEH). While some merchants were keen on profiteering from the coolie trade, however, colonial officials attempted to regulate it.

During the 19th century, Singapore also experienced tremendous prosperity, and this attracted thousands of immigrants. The discovery of tin in the Malay states; the commercial development of rubber and other cash crops; several extensive building projects and land-reclamation schemes; and the building of major thoroughfares, housing and GODOWNS, were all a part of this new prosperity, and workers were needed.

Soon, in addition to the vast numbers of Chinese coolies, Indians and Malays also joined the stream of coolies to Singapore. Coolies pulled rickshaws, heaved coal in the dockyards, mined tin and worked on

rubber and other plantations where commercial crops were grown. The Tamil-speaking coolies from south India laid electric cables and tracks for trams; built and repaired roads; tapped rubber and participated in various construction projects.

Coomaraswamy, Punchardsheram ('Punch') (1925–1999) Judge and diplomat. Punchardsheram Coomaraswamy was born in Johor, was educated at the English College there and later read law at Nottingham University in the United Kingdom. On his return, he practised with BRADDELL BROTHERS in Singapore. In 1966, he was appointed deputy SPEAKER OF PARLIAMENT and became Speaker when A. P. RAJAH was appointed high commissioner to the United Kingdom. He served as Speaker until 1970, when he was appointed high commissioner to India. In 1980, he was awarded the MERITORIOUS SERVICE MEDAL. After several other diplomatic postings, including one as ambassador to the United States, he returned to Singapore in 1984 and was appointed to the Bench. He served as High Court Judge until his retirement in 1993.

Cooper, Alfred 'Duff' (1890–1954) British politician. Cooper was despatched to Singapore to report on 'Far Eastern affairs'. He arrived on 11 September 1941. His brief was to enquire into the civil administration of British territories in the region. He had been made chancellor of the Duchy of Lancaster prior to his arrival, thus giving him Cabinet rank. He arrived with his 49-year-old wife, Lady Diana Cooper, a film star in her youth, whom *Time* magazine described in August 1941 as 'the most beautiful woman in England', and who was famed for playing the Madonna in Max Reinhardt's play *The Miracle*.

Cooper, decorated in World War I, had been a Conservative member of Parliament since 1924, secretary of state for war (1935–37, and First Lord of the Admiralty in 1938. His resignation, in protest against the 'agreement' reached by British prime minister Neville Chamberlain with Adolf Hitler in Munich in September 1938, had aligned him with Winston Churchill as an anti-appeaser. When Churchill became prime minister in May 1940, he appointed Cooper minister of information.

Cooper set out for the Far East, via the United States, in August 1941. Once in Singapore, even he lacked the authority, time, vision and force of personality which would have been required to resolve differences between the military and civilian authorities. There was anyway little chance of anyone persuading Churchill to send much-needed aircraft and tanks.

In October, Cooper did not dissent from local assessments that Japan was still torn between the south and Russia, and unlikely to attack during the northeast

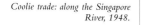
Coolie trade: along the Singapore River, 1948.

---

monsoon. His calls for the Governor and Commander in Chief to be replaced by one Commissioner-General for the Far East did not reach London until late November 1941.

After the Japanese attack, Cooper was formally appointed resident minister for Far Eastern Affairs, taking over chairmanship of the FAR EAST WAR COUNCIL from 10 December. However, Field Marshal Sir Archibald Wavell's arrival as the American-British Dutch-Australian Command (ABDA-COM) chief on 7 January 1942 rendered his position superfluous. Cooper flew out of Singapore on 13 January.

Cooper seems to have suffered little blame for Singapore's fall, becoming ambassador to France (1944–47). His writings include an autobiography, *Old Men Forget* (1953), *The Duff Cooper Diaries: 1915–1951* edited by his son, John Julius Norwich.

cooperative movement The cooperative concept was introduced into Singapore in 1924 with the passing of the Straits Settlement Cooperative Societies Ordinance. Forty-three thrift-and-loan societies were formed between 1925 and 1940. On 16 November 1933, the Singapore Urban Cooperative Union Ltd was established. This was renamed the Singapore Cooperative Union Ltd in July 1954, and became the Singapore National Cooperative Union Ltd in 1972. With the formation of the Singapore National Cooperative Federation (SNCF) in 1980, the union was renamed the Singapore Amalgamated Services' Cooperative Organization in 1982, and began to function as a secondary co-op focusing on welfare issues.

By 1960, there were 104 co-op societies in Singapore with a paid-up capital of $13.2 million. In 1969, the cooperative movement received a boost when the NATIONAL TRADES UNION CONGRESS (NTUC) recommended the setting up of trade union cooperatives, based on cooperation—instead of confrontation—with management. Within a decade, 13 such societies had been formed, some of which have become Singapore's largest and best-known cooperatives.

One cooperative, NTUC Welcome (later NTUC FAIRPRICE), was formed to sell essential commodities at low prices. This eliminated rampant profiteering. A taxi cooperative, NTUC Comfort (now COMFORTDELGRO), allowed taxi-drivers to become taxi-owners and to earn a decent living in an organized way. NTUC INCOME followed, covering low-income workers with insurance. Other cooperatives were set up in dental services, childcare and even private property.

The Cooperative Societies Act was revised in 1979, making provision for SNCF to be the body at the apex of the cooperative movement. In June 1985, SNCF aligned itself with the International Co-operative Alliance.

copyright For many years, British copyright law—the Imperial Copyright Act of 1911—applied in Singapore. Under this law, creative works received protection for the author's life plus another 50 years.

Singapore enacted its own law, the Copyright Act, in 1987. This was modelled primarily on Australian rather than British legislation. It provided protection for original literary, musical, artistic and dramatic works (collectively grouped as 'works'); sound recordings; cinematograph films; broadcasts; cable programmes; and publishers' rights in published editions of works (collectively grouped as 'subject matter other than works').

According to this act, copyright protection is automatically conferred on the author of an original work as soon as it is created and fixed in a material form. There is no need to file for registration, or use the symbol '©' to derive protection. Soon after the act came into force, Singapore entered into bilateral arrangements regarding copyright with the United States, the United Kingdom and Australia. Singapore also acceded to the convention establishing the WORLD INTELLECTUAL PROPERTY ORGANIZATION in 1990, the Agreement on Trade-Related Aspects of Intellectual Property Rights in 1995, and the Berne Convention for the Protection of Literary and Artistic Works in 1998.

In 2004, as part of Singapore's obligations under the US–Singapore Free Trade Agreement, the Intellectual Property (Miscellaneous Amendments) Act was brought into force, and major amendments were made to the original Copyright Act. One change was that the duration of the copyright monopoly over all work was increased to the author's life plus 70 years (an increase of 20 years on the original). Another change was that large-scale infringements, even those not involving any profit motive or distribution—such as the unauthorized uploading and downloading of copyright material on the Internet—became criminal offences. Those convicted of these offences could be fined up to $20,000 or imprisoned for up to six months, or both. Subsequent offences would make offenders liable to fines of up to $50,000, or jail terms of up to three years, or both.

coral reefs Singapore's reefs fringe the Southern Islands and consist of almost 200 species of hard coral. Dr JOHN CRAWFURD described the beauty of these islands in 1830: 'We made an excursion yesterday to some coral banks lying among the islands which form the western boundary of the harbour of Singapore. These banks exhibit the strangest and most fantastic forms of organic life that can be imagined, in the var-

ious shapes of corallines, madrepores (both corals), asteria (starfish) and sponges. In still deeper water, and off the southern extremity of the island, there are found those gigantic sponges, which are peculiar to the coast of Singapore, and which Europeans have called Neptunian Cups'.

From the 19th century, these reefs were exploited for building materials, based on the evidence of coral fragments retrieved from archaeological excavations. These were probably from reefs fringing the mainland between the Singapore River and Tuas. This early exploitation, and development until the 1960s, did not contribute heavily to reef degradation.

However, this changed from the 1970s, as development accelerated sharply. Land reclamation buried close to 60 per cent of Singapore's reefs, including those along the mainland coast. Reefs that escaped reclamation were subjected to the impact of heavy sedimentation resulting from reclamation, dredging of shipping channels and dumping of dredged spoils. Average underwater visibility was reduced from 10 m in the 1960s to 1 m in the early 21st century. Sedimentation retards coral growth by smothering and reducing sunlight penetration. Since the 1970s, sedimentation resulted in the loss of coral from below 6 m of the reef slope, and an average 34 per cent reduction in live coral cover from the upper slope.

Further pressure was added by the collection of reef animals for the aquarium trade, which started in the 1960s. Public concern was expressed in the media in the late 1970s when it became known that Korean construction workers were collecting large quantities of coral from the reefs and shipping them home, where the specimens fetched high prices. Harvesting of corals and reef animals decreased when Singapore ratified the Convention on International Trade of Endangered Species, but the damage was evident from the drop in the numbers of many reef species, particularly FISHES.

Reefs along Singapore's mainland coast have been totally eliminated, except for a small reef community at Labrador. There are some reef communities in the northeast islands of PULAU TEKONG and PULAU UBIN (*see* CHEK JAWA). However, most of Singapore's reefs fringe the Southern Islands. Although the abundance of many species has been depressed, species' elimina-

Coral reefs: (clockwise from left) reef enhancement unit being deployed; Acropora *corals were once abundant in Singapore waters;* Pocillopora *corals that have bleached in response to environmental stress;* Plerogyra, *commonly referred to as 'grape coral'.*

tion is not evident. Of the 200 species of hard coral recorded in these reefs, only two have been confirmed as lost. Other reef-associated animals, such as seashells, giant clams, sea cucumbers and sea stars, are also less common due to habitat loss, degradation and earlier unregulated exploitation.

Singapore's reefs have become dominated by foliose growth forms (flowery corals), which have a large surface area with which to capture the reduced sunlight energy. Branching *Acropora* coral, which dominates other reefs in the region, is now uncommon in Singapore. However, Singapore's reefs have been spared the coral-eating crown-of-thorns starfish. It is not known why this starfish has not established itself in Singapore, when outbreaks have occurred on reefs in nearby BINTAN and Tioman.

In September 1997, a collision between the *Eviokos* and the *Orapin Global*, two tankers, resulted in the spillage of 28,000 tons of crude oil. This threatened the marine environment, but had little impact on the reefs as containment measures diverted the slick. However, in early 1998, elevated sea temperature resulted in mass bleaching of Singapore's corals on a scale previously unknown. More than 90 per cent of all corals were bleached, and 20 per cent failed to recover after the sea temperature returned to normal.

Reef development and growth depends on successful spawning, and the availability of a suitable substrate for larval settlement and growth. Mass spawning, where many coral species release eggs and sperm or fertilized egg bundles, takes place over a few nights during the full moon in March or April. This major event is followed by a smaller one in September or October. These spawning events coincide with the inter-monsoon lull.

corporate taxes The corporate tax rate remained unchanged at 40 per cent between 1966 and 1986. Thereafter, to foster a competitive, pro-business environment, the nominal rate was reduced in steps to 20 per cent (on chargeable income), effective from 2005. The tax applies equally to resident and non-resident companies, and to both Singapore-incorporated subsidiaries as well as branches of foreign companies.

A one-tier corporate taxation system took effect on 1 January 2003. This replaced the imputation system of taxing dividends, where taxes paid by a company could be 'imputed', or passed on to shareholders. Under the new system, corporate income is taxed at the corporate level, and this is a final tax.

Since the 1960s, Singapore has used fiscal incentives not only to attract investment in manufacturing and services, but also to help facilitate a transition to newer industries. Following the 1997 ASIAN FINANCIAL CRISIS, a one-off 10 per cent tax rebate was also granted to sustain businesses. In 2002, to help the small and medium enterprise (SME) sector expand, the government introduced tax exemptions for small businesses. From 2002, a partial tax exemption was given on chargeable income of up to $100,000, which meant that the effective tax rate was between 5.5 and 11 per cent. Furthermore, with effect from 2005, full tax exemption could be granted on up to $100,000 of the normal chargeable income of a qualifying company.

Corridon, Richard Byrne (1908–1993) Police officer. Born in India, Richard Byrne Corridon served in the British Army in India before being posted to Kuala Lumpur in 1945 to work in the Malayan Security Service. For his efforts during the communist EMERGENCY in 1948, Corridon was awarded an MBE (Member of the Order of the British Empire) and the Colonial Police Medal.

From 1952 to 1955, Corridon served as deputy director, and later director, of the CORRUPT PRACTICES INVESTIGATION BUREAU (CPIB). In 1956, he was appointed superintendent of Police, SPECIAL BRANCH, a post he held until 1959. After retiring from the force, Corridon returned to the United Kingdom. It is perhaps in this capacity that Corridon is best known, for it was he who persuaded the colonial government to withdraw orders to detain LEE KUAN YEW, then in the opposition. In 1963, Corridon returned to Singapore, and headed the CPIB from 1964. He retired, for the second time, in 1968.

Corrupt Practices Investigation Bureau Independent body that investigates and prevents corruption. The Corrupt Practices Investigation Bureau (CPIB) was established in 1952, and is headed by a director, who reports directly to the prime minister. Prior to the CPIB's formation, corruption cases were investigated by the Anti-Corruption Branch, a unit within the SINGAPORE POLICE FORCE.

In the 1950s, the public was generally sceptical of the CPIB's investigative powers and wary of possible repercussions. The anti-corruption laws were also inadequate and obstructed the gathering of evidence. However, this changed in 1959 after the People's Action Party, which had taken a hard line against corruption, came to power. Anti-corruption laws were amended to give more powers to CPIB officers, and punishments for corruption offences were enhanced. The government's tough stance boosted confidence both in Singapore and abroad.

Over the years, the CPIB has uncovered graft involving well-known names in Singapore, such as national development minister Tan Kia Gan; minister of state for environment WEE TOON BOON; trade union leader PHEY YEW KOK; national development minister TEH CHEANG WAN; and commercial affairs director Glenn Knight.

Cosco Corporation (Singapore) This company was incorporated in October 1961 as the Singapore Fodder Company. It changed its name to Sun Corporation in May 1991, following its takeover by Unicentral Corporation. It then phased out its fodder-manufacturing operations and became an investment-holding and warehousing company. In 1993, it was acquired by China Ocean Shipping Group Companies, a state-owned enterprise that came under the jurisdiction of China's Ministry of Communications. It was listed the same year on the Singapore Exchange and soon diversified into shipping and shipping-related activities.

Cosco Corporation is the flagship investment-holding company for its Beijing-based parent and acts as a vehicle for raising funds in Southeast Asia. As part of the largest shipping conglomerate in China, Cosco Corporation conducts business in three distinct segments: shipping, shipping-related and onshore business. The company owns and operates a fleet of 14 dry-bulk carriers which serve major trading centres in Southeast Asia, the Pacific and the Atlantic seaboard. Its shipping-related segments provide support services such as ship agency services, marine engineering, ship repairs and container depots. The onshore division is engaged in property development and general trading.

The company's stock has been a component of both the Straits Times and the Financial Times indices since March 2004. In 2005, it acquired a 51 per cent share in the Cosco Shipyard Group. Cosco reported a net profit of $207 million on revenues of $873 million for the financial year 2005, a 300 and 750 per cent increase respectively from 2004.

Council of Presidential Advisers The council's fundamental role is to advise and make recommendations to the president on certain key issues. Its establishment was provided for in the Constitutional Amendment, 1991. When the inaugural Council of Presidential Advisers was introduced by then Prime Minister GOH CHOK TONG, he described the formation of the council as a case of the Government 'clipping its own wings'.

The president is obliged to consult the council under certain circumstances, such as before applying veto powers to the budgets of the government and key government-linked bodies (i.e. STATUTORY BOARDS and GOVERNMENT-LINKED COMPANIES listed in Schedule 5 of the Constitution), and before appointing key civil servants. The president's veto is considered final when he has the majority vote of the council supporting his decision. Otherwise, as long as the government can obtain a two-thirds vote in Parliament, the government may overturn the president's veto.

Appointment to the six-member council is made through a process of nomination and approval by top personnel from Singapore's legislative, executive and judiciary bodies. The president is entitled to appoint two members at his discretion; the prime minister nominates two; the chief justice is responsible for one nominee; and the chairman of the Public Service Commission the sixth. Members of the council are appointed for an initial six-year term, after which they are eligible for re-appointment for further four-year terms.

WEE KIM WEE was the first president who enjoyed the services of the council, albeit only for two years before he stepped down. ONG TENG CHEONG, Wee's successor and Singapore's first elected president, had more opportunities to work with the council throughout his term of office (1993–99).

The first chairman of the council was LIM KIM SAN, who served his first term of six years. He was subsequently re-appointed by the president for a second term, which ended on 1 January 2004. The chairman of the council is required to exercise the functions of the Office of the President in the absence of the president. If he is unavailable, this duty falls to the SPEAKER OF PARLIAMENT.

country clubs Clubs located outside the main commercial and residential districts. Country clubs offer recreational facilities that include social and leisure options, sports (particularly GOLF), dining and family activities. SINGAPORE ISLAND COUNTRY CLUB (established in 1891) is the oldest of these, and its membership fees the highest.

Once the preserve of the expatriate community, country clubs began admitting Asian guests only after much deliberation. In 1963, the government decreed that clubs should open their doors to all races. Today, country-club membership is included in the so-called 'five Cs'—alongside cash, credit card, car and condominium—to which some Singaporeans are believed to aspire.

Country clubs have made the most of relatively distant and expansive locations to develop golf courses and attractive buildings. For instance, a once swampy, crocodile-infested area was transformed into Jurong Country Club in 1975, as part of Jurong Town Corporation's plan to attract industrialists and senior-ranking executives to the western part of Singapore.

Another 'facilitated' development is Orchid Country Club. In August 1991, then secretary-general of the NATIONAL TRADES UNION CONGRESS, ONG TENG CHEONG mooted the idea of a golf and country club for workers who, he said, should have 'a fair share of the fruits of Singapore's economic progress', so that 'golf will no longer be a game for executives only'.

Other clubs established by government bodies include the Singapore Armed Forces Reservists' Association (SAFRA). The National Service (NS) Association also built a resort and country club, besides having five clubhouses to provide recreational facilities for NS men and their families. Similarly, the Civil Defence Reservists' Association (CDANS) Country Club in Bukit Batok, built in phases from 1998 to 2004, covers over 7 ha, and includes an adventure centre.

Court of Appeal Singapore's highest court. The Court of Appeal was originally established as the Straits Settlements Court of Appeal in 1873. Before that, all final appeals lay with the King-in-Council in the United Kingdom. At that time, the Straits Settlements Supreme Court comprised the CHIEF JUSTICE and a judge at Penang, as well as a senior and a junior PUISNE JUDGE. The SUPREME COURT had jurisdiction to sit also as a Court of Appeal. Three judges were required to make up a full Court of Appeal. At first, the Court of Appeal apparently sat only twice a year, but it subsequently came to be held 'at such time and places as the Chief Justice may appoint'.

In 1934, a separate Court of Criminal Appeal was created. The division of the Court of Appeal into civil and criminal divisions lasted until 1993 when, following a review by the Council of Judges, the Supreme Court of Judicature Act was amended to do away with the separate Court of Appeal and Court of Criminal Appeal. In their place, a permanent Court of Appeal was constituted for both civil and criminal appeals. The judges of appeal who were appointed to this permanent Court of Appeal were no longer required to engage in High Court work. The chief justice, when sitting, presides as the president of the Court of Appeal.

During the colonial period, Singapore's highest court of appeal was the Judicial Committee of the PRIVY COUNCIL, which ranked higher than the Court of Appeal. The Privy Council was retained as Singapore's highest court until 1994, when all appeals to the Privy Council were abolished.

crabs About 400 species of crab exist in and around Singapore. Crabs can be found in various ecosystems—on rocky beaches, among coral reefs, amidst the mud in mangrove swamps, and even among the leaf litter of BUKIT TIMAH NATURE RESERVE (this is where the *Johora singaporensis* is usually found). Of all these species, the orange mud crab (*Scylla olivacea*) is the crab with which most Singaporeans are familiar, as it is the main ingredient used in CHILLI AND BLACK PEPPER CRAB dishes. It lives in mangrove swamps.

Singapore is home to some unusual crab species. One of the smallest in the world is the Singapore pinhead crab (*Halicarcinus coralicola*), which is only about

Country clubs: Orchid Country Club.

2.5 mm in width. It is found on rocky shorelines. The strikingly coloured mosaic crab (*Lophozozymus pictor*), a reef crab found in Singapore waters, is the most poisonous crab known to man. Researchers have found that the toxins from one average-sized individual (about 50 mm in width) can kill up to 40,000 mice. As the toxins are heat-stable, the mosaic crab is deadly even after cooking and some people have died after eating it.

The 400 crab species include some only discovered in the last 20 years. Between 1985 and 1991, biologist Peter Ng discovered three freshwater species not found anywhere else in the world. They are the swamp crab (*Parathelphusa reticulata*), Johnson's crab (*Irmengardia johnsoni*) and Singapore crab (*Johora singaporensis*). Other recently discovered crabs include two new species of large-mouthed crabs (*Baruna mangromurphia* and *B. minuta*) found in 1991; a new genus and new species of Leucosiidae (*Praosia punctata*), found in 1993; two new species of large swimming crabs (*Thalamita cerasma* and *T. spinicarpa*), found in 1995; and a new genus and species of sesarmid crab (*Haberma nanum*), found in 2002.

In 2000, an undergraduate student, Koh Sok Koon, discovered that one of the most common crabs in Singapore's reefs, the so-called red-eyed reef crab, was actually new to science. Biologists had been calling this crab '*Eriphia smithi*' for decades, but Koh's research showed that the real *E. smithi* occurred only in Africa and the Indian Ocean. The Singapore crab previously known as *E. smithi* has yet to acquire a formal name.

As Singapore has so many species of crab, it is no surprise that over the years biologists here have been at the forefront of research. They include William Lanchester, Michael Tweedie, Raoul Serène and Desmond Johnson. Lanchester collected and reported on crabs in the early 1900s. He found and named a bizarre new genus and species, *Favus granulatus*, which has never been found elsewhere. Tweedie, of the old Raffles Museum (*see* NATIONAL MUSEUM OF SINGAPORE), discovered and named dozens of species; and along the way, was one of the first to study their complex behaviour and courtship habits. Serène, also

Crabs: Johnson's freshwater crab.

John Crawfurd

Creative Technology: MuVo digital audio player.

from the Raffles Museum, described hundreds of species from Singapore and nearby areas. Johnson, of the then University of Singapore, also described many species.

Crawfurd, John (1783–1868) Colonial official. In 1823, Dr John Crawfurd succeeded Colonel WILLIAM FARQUHAR as Resident of Singapore (*see* GOVERNORS). A Scotsman, Crawfurd had joined the EAST INDIA COMPANY's Medical Service in 1803 at the age of 20, and had been posted to Penang in 1808.

Crawfurd became famous as both an administrator and an author. His interests included languages, history and political administration. In 1820, he published *History of the Indian Archipelago*, which established him as an authority on the region. He also wrote papers on scientific subjects such as the geology of Singapore island, which in due course earned him praise from professional geologists.

As Resident, Crawfurd continued Sir STAMFORD RAFFLES' commercial policy; tightened and reformed judicial policy; promoted primary education; and licensed gambling, a move which invited criticism. His administration of Singapore resulted in a marked increase in population, trade and revenue. By 1826, Singapore's revenue had outstripped that of Penang.

While Raffles and Farquhar laid the basis for the founding of Singapore, it was Crawfurd who made Singapore a British possession. The 'paper-war' between the United Kingdom and the Netherlands was settled by means of the ANGLO-DUTCH TREATY of 1824—largely in favour of the former. The treaty saw the Dutch ceding Malacca to the British and withdrawing objections to the British occupying Singapore. In return, the British agreed not to interfere with Dutch involvement in the islands south of the Singapore Strait. To protect British interests in the face of imminent political upheavals within the Johor-Lingga empire, Crawfurd pressured the Malay chiefs in the same year into signing the Treaty of Friendship and Alliance, ceding Singapore and islands within 10 miles (16.09 km) of her shores perpetually to the East India Company and its heirs.

Some objects relating to Crawfurd remain in contemporary Singapore. An oil portrait of him is included in the collection of the NATIONAL MUSEUM OF SINGAPORE. There is also a little-known memorial to him in a stained-glass window in ST ANDREW'S CATHEDRAL; and Crawford Street—despite the difference in spelling—may have been named after him.

Crawfurd returned to the UK and spent his remaining years writing on matters relating to Southeast Asia. In the last year of his life, he became the first president of the Straits Settlements Association, which was formed in London to protect the settlements' interests.

Creative Technology Information technology (IT) company. Creative Technology was founded by SIM WONG HOO—a graduate of Ngee Ann Polytechnic who has twice been named *Business Times* Businessman of the Year—and was incorporated on 18 July 1983 as a designer, manufacturer and distributor of personal computer (PC) products. In 1984, it launched the Cubic 99, Singapore's first locally designed and produced PC. This was followed in 1986 by the Cubic CT, a multilingual, multimedia PC with voice and music functions.

However, it was the launch in 1989 of the Sound Blaster—a PC sound card that was to become the de facto audio standard for the personal computer—that saw the company make a name for itself in the global IT industry. Creative Technology became the first Singapore company to be listed on the United States Nasdaq stock exchange in August 1992. It made its debut on the Stock Exchange of Singapore on 15 June 1994. The counter is now a component Straits Times Index stock.

Despite a brief foray into the CD-ROM market in 1995, the group has emerged as a leading player in digital entertainment products for PCs and the Internet. Its range includes the Nomad MP3 players, Zen and MuVo lines of digital audio players, and web cameras. Its products are marketed through both original equipment manufacturers (OEM) and retail channels under a variety of trademarks, including the Blaster name. OEM partners include companies such as Acer America Corporation, Dell Computer, Digital Equipment Corporation, Gateway 2000, Microsoft, Intel, Micron and NEC.

Creative Technology's proprietary Environmental Audio Technology is regarded as the de facto industry standard for immersive 3D gaming, while products such as the Creative Prodikeys (the world's first music-and-PC dual keyboard), Zen Micro Photo and Zen Portable Media Centre, have consistently won awards at international consumer electronics shows.

The company employs more than 5,000 people worldwide, and besides regional headquarters in the US, Europe and Singapore, it also has two manufacturing facilities in Malaysia and China. The group posted a net income of US$588,000 for fiscal year 2005, down from US$134 million previously. Total sales amounted to US$1.22 billion—up 50 per cent on the 2004 figure of US$815 million.

Crescendos, The Popular music group. In 1963, The Crescendos became the first band in Singapore to be signed on by recording label Philips. The group started out as a trio with vocals in 1960, when guitarists John Chee, Leslie Chia and Raymond Ho came together to participate in Talentime—a local talent competition. When Susan Lim joined the band, the

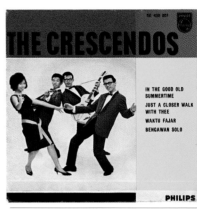

The Crescendos: one of the group's eight EPs.

definitive line-up of The Crescendos was formed. They released eight EPs in total. Their first release, 'Mr Twister', and their second, 'The Boy Next Door', were both hits. The Crescendos lasted until 1968 when Lim left to attend university. On 8 February 1970, while picnicking on the east coast of Malaysia, Lim disappeared, presumed drowned.

criminal law In the LEGAL SYSTEM, a distinction is made between civil law and criminal law. Crimes are offences against the state. Not all breaches of the law are crimes—only those acts which are harmful to society in general and which warrant the attention of the state. A breach of criminal law attracts prosecution by the state against the criminal on behalf of society at large.

In the early part of the 19th century, criminal law in Singapore was based on English common law. In 1871, the Straits Settlements PENAL CODE was passed into law. This was a virtual re-enactment of the Indian Penal Code drafted by Lord Thomas Macaulay. It came into operation on 16 September 1872. The bulk of Singapore's criminal law is dealt with in the Penal Code. However, there are many other crimes defined by other acts such as the MISUSE OF DRUGS ACT and the Road Traffic Act. Because of the seriousness of a crime, a very high standard of proof is needed in a trial. This standard is 'beyond a reasonable doubt'; whereas in civil cases, the standard can be 'on a balance of probabilities'.

When a crime is reported, the police or other relevant enforcement officers from customs, immigration or narcotics departments, carry out investigations. If a crime has indeed been committed, prosecution is generally instituted by the state through the ATTORNEY-GENERAL'S CHAMBERS. Individuals can also take out private summonses for certain minor offences or nuisances.

The attorney-general, who is also the public prosecutor, heads the Attorney-General's Department. He controls and directs prosecutions in Singapore with the assistance of several deputy public prosecutors and is appointed by the president on the advice of the prime minister from among persons qualified as SUPREME COURT judges.

The High Court has unlimited original jurisdiction in criminal cases. Generally, the High Court sits with one judge who is trier of both fact and law. In Singapore, TRIAL BY JURY was abolished in 1969.

The minimum age of criminal responsibility is seven. However, a child who is over the age of seven but under the age of twelve is not criminally responsible if he or she has not attained sufficient maturity of understanding to judge the nature and consequence of his or her action. Punishments prescribed under the Penal Code include death (*see* CAPITAL PUNISHMENT); imprisonment; forfeiture of property; fines; and CANING. Habitual offenders may be sentenced to corrective and reformative training or preventive detention.

Crocodile Clothing brand. Founded by a Malaysian, Dato' Dr Tan Hian Tsin, Crocodile started out in 1947 as a manufacturer of men's shirts. The company's first outlet in Singapore was opened that same year at 6 South Bridge Road, and a factory was set up soon after in the Geylang area. Within five years, the company had expanded into the production of men's undergarments, socks, handkerchiefs, slacks and sports shirts.

The company started to license the use of the Crocodile brand to other countries and areas including Malaya, Thailand and Indonesia in the 1950s. It ventured into Japan in 1961. In the 1970s, the company extended its range to neckties, wallets and footwear. Crocodile soon became one of the first Asian brands to outsell its Western competitors, with immigrants to Singapore and Malaysia from the Indian subcontinent often purchasing Crocodile products as gifts for relatives back home. This in turn gave the company a base for moving into India, Pakistan, Bangladesh and Sri Lanka.

China became a new market for Crocodile in the 1980s, and by the early 1990s, had became a manufacturing base for the company. Crocodile was named the top foreign brand in China from 1999 to 2004, while in India, it received the accolade of 'Most Admired Exclusive Brand Retail Chain' in 2002. It was named South Korea's 'Brand of the Year 2004' for its new line of women's clothing.

Crocodile distributes through more than 4,000 boutique outlets or counters worldwide, including 75 outlets in Singapore and more than 500 channels in Malaysia.

crocodiles The estuarine crocodile (*Crocodylus porosus*) is an endangered species, and is often hunted for its leather. Although they are known to have attacked humans, crocodiles generally feed on small animals such as fishes, birds and turtles. Found naturally in coastal habitats, croco-

diles can grow up to 9 m in length. Wild crocodiles are uncommon in Singapore, although some small specimens have been found in the SUNGEI BULOH WETLAND RESERVE and in RESERVOIRS. Crocodiles are also reared in specialized farms in Singapore to supply material for the leather market.

Crown Colony Territory over which the British Crown exercises absolute sovereignty, with local authority vested in a governor and his Council. The STRAITS SETTLEMENTS, which comprised Singapore, Malacca and Penang, became a Crown Colony on 1 April 1867. This ended administration of the Straits Settlements from British India, and brought them under the jurisdiction of the Colonial Office in London, and the ultimate legislative authority of the British Crown.

In 1826, the EAST INDIA COMPANY had united Singapore, Malacca and Penang to form the Presidency of the Straits Settlements. This presidency was abolished in 1830, and the Straits Settlements became a Residency dependent on the Presidency of Bengal, which came under the governor-general of India. In 1851, the Straits Settlements were separated from the Bengal Presidency and put under the direct charge of the governor-general. The East India Company was abolished in 1858 and the administration of India was transferred to the India Office, while the Straits Settlements continued to be ruled from Calcutta.

Indian administration had proven unsatisfactory for the Straits Settlements, which for several years had lobbied for transfer to the Colonial Office. In particular, merchants in the Straits Settlements felt that the government in Calcutta had failed to understand and respond rapidly to the needs of the people of the Straits Settlements.

In 1863, a commission was appointed to inquire into the advisability of transferring the Straits Settlements to the Colonial Office. Sir Hercules Robinson, the principal member of the commission, advocated the transfer in his report. The Colonial Office agreed with Robinson's conclusions, but negotiations ensued for some years before the India Office, War Office and Treasury all agreed to the transfer. The Treasury consented to the transfer, after the other departments, on 2 June 1866.

On 10 August 1866, an act was passed to transfer the Straits Settlements from the control of India to the Colonial Office. On 1 April 1867, the Indian government formally transferred the Straits Settlements to the Crown. The decision to place the Straits Settlements under the Colonial Office was influenced by the War Office's interest in making Singapore an alternative base for British forces that were stationed in Hong Kong at the time.

Additional areas were attached to the colony of the Straits Settlements over the years—the Dindings area of Perak formed part of the colony from 1874 to 1934; Labuan from 1906 to 1946; the Cocos-Keeling Islands from 1886 to 1955; and CHRISTMAS ISLAND from 1900 to 1958. Singapore was the centre of government, commerce and policy-making for the Straits Settlements. The colony was ruled by a governor, who was appointed by the Crown and who ruled with the help of the executive and a Legislative Council. The first colonial governor was Colonel Sir HARRY ORD (*see* GOVERNORS).

After World War II, Singapore and Malaya came under the BRITISH MILITARY ADMINISTRATION until April 1946, when Malacca, Penang and the Malay States on the peninsula were incorporated into a MALAYAN UNION (transformed into the FEDERATION OF MALAYA in 1948), thus bringing the Straits Settlements to an end. Singapore remained a separate Crown Colony. In 1958 the British Parliament passed the State of Singapore Act, which converted the colony into a state with control over all domestic affairs. The new CONSTITUTION was brought into force with the LEGISLATIVE ASSEMBLY ELECTION (1959).

crows In Singapore, the two main types of crow are the house crow (*Corvus splendens*) and the large-billed crow (*Corvus macrorhynchos*). The large-billed crow is usually found in coastal areas and forests. It generally lives and forages away from human dwellings. The house crow, however, is a scavenger that has adapted to living off leftovers and other food waste.

House crows are thought to have travelled to Singapore on ships from India and Sri Lanka. A colony was found at the Tanjong Pagar godowns in the 1940s. By the late 1960s, some 200–400 crows were roosting in the trees along the Tanjong Pagar dock gates. By 1968, the population had grown to about 2,000 birds island-wide. In 2001, the population was 120,000.

These crows, seen wherever waste food is readily available, represent a public health problem. The NATIONAL ENVIRONMENT AGENCY has developed a two-pronged strategy to tackle the crow problem: directly reducing the population of crows, and depriving them of food sources. Island-wide crow culling, along with the implementation of programmes to improve food waste disposal, has led to the crow population dropping to 10,000 by November 2005.

Crocodiles

Crystal Jade

Crystal Jade Restaurant chain. Established in 1990 by Alfred Leung and Ip Yiu Tung, the Crystal Jade group has grown to become one of the best known Chinese restaurant chains in Southeast Asia. Born in 1953, Leung arrived in Singapore from Hong Kong in 1981 to work at the Happy Valley Restaurant at the Singapore Shopping Centre. Later, he opened Wah Lok Restaurant in the Carlton Hotel, and in 1990, he started Crystal Jade Restaurant in the Cairnhill Hotel with Ip, his brother-in-law. A second, more casual, outlet opened about three years later, followed by the flagship Crystal Jade Palace restaurant at NGEE ANN CITY.

Leung's three brothers—Jimmy, Wilson and Vincent—were eventually brought in to help out, although they have since left the group. Jimmy and Vincent later started their own successful restaurant, My Choice. Leung and his wife Hera left the Crystal Jade group's management in June 2004, citing 'differences in philosophy' with Ip. They remain shareholders. The Crystal Jade group comprises over 30 outlets in Singapore, and over 50 in other Asia-Pacific countries including Indonesia, Vietnam, China and Japan.

Culan, Raja The first episode of the SEJARAH MELAYU (Malay Annals) mentions a king named Raja Shulan from Kalinga (an ancient kingdom on the east coast of India), descendant of Iskander Zulkarnain (a figure from Persian mythology) and his son, Raja Culan, who set out to conquer China. The Chinese, hearing of his plan, sent a ship to intercept him at TEMASEK, and, by a ruse common in Malay traditional literature, convinced Raja Culan that China was too distant to attack.

Cultural Medallion Arts award. The Cultural Medallion was inaugurated in 1979 to honour major contributions by artists in various fields to Singapore's cultural life. Managed by the NATIONAL ARTS COUNCIL and conferred by the MINISTRY OF INFORMATION, COMMUNICATIONS AND THE ARTS, this award was an initiative of President ONG TENG CHEONG. The Cultural Medallions are presented annually by the president at the Istana. They carry with them cash grants to enable winners to develop their talents.

From 1979 to 2005, 86 artists were awarded the Cultural Medallion for their contributions to Chinese opera; dance; literature; music; photography; theatre; and the visual arts. The award has recently begun to acknowledge the value of popular and mass culture. In 2005, film-maker JACK NEO and pop musician DICK LEE were honoured, as was performance artist LEE WEN.

currency *See* box.

curry murder This case ranks as one of the most bizarre in Singapore criminal history, because no body parts or weapons were found, and no one was convicted. Caretaker Ayakanno Marimuthu, 38, was reported missing by his wife, Naragatha Vally Ramiah, in December 1984. She said he had gone to Genting Highlands but did not return. In January 1987, police received information that three Indian men had murdered the hot-tempered and physically abusive Marimuthu, and that his body had been chopped into small pieces, cooked in a large pot of curry with rice, placed in garbage bags and dumped in roadside rubbish bins. The murder allegedly took place in the caretaker's quarters of Orchard Road Presbyterian Church on Penang Road.

On 23 March 1987, eight suspects were held for questioning; after two days, one corroborated the story. Naragatha and her three brothers (one a butcher and another a caretaker at the church) were arrested and charged with murder. Her mother and sister-in-law were accused of aiding and abetting them. However, owing to insufficient evidence, all were released on 6 June 1987, although not given a full acquittal. The men were detained under the Criminal Law (Temporary Provisions) Act and released four years later.

curry puff Popular snack. A curry puff is usually made of a rich buttered pastry or layered puff pastry wrapped around curried fillings, which is then fried or baked. While curried potatoes and chicken are the

Curry puff

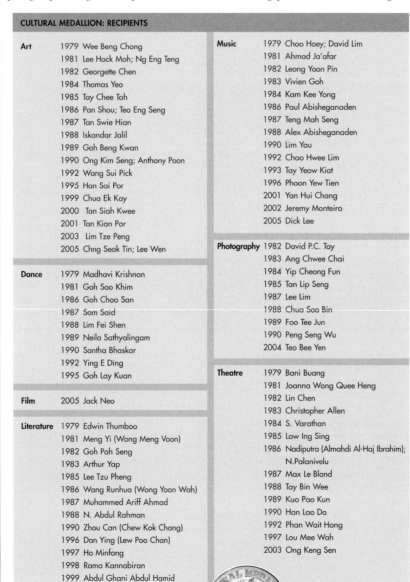

CULTURAL MEDALLION: RECIPIENTS

Art		Music	
1979	Wee Beng Chong	1979	Choo Hoey; David Lim
1981	Lee Hock Moh; Ng Eng Teng	1981	Ahmad Ja'afar
1982	Georgette Chen	1982	Leong Yoon Pin
1984	Thomas Yeo	1983	Vivien Goh
1985	Tay Chee Toh	1984	Kam Kee Yong
1986	Pan Shou; Teo Eng Seng	1986	Paul Abisheganaden
1987	Tan Swie Hian	1987	Teng Mah Seng
1988	Iskandar Jalil	1988	Alex Abisheganaden
1989	Goh Beng Kwan	1990	Lim Yau
1990	Ong Kim Seng; Anthony Poon	1992	Choo Hwee Lim
1992	Wang Sui Pick	1993	Tay Yeow Kiat
1995	Han Sai Por	1996	Phoon Yew Tien
1999	Chua Ek Kay	2001	Yan Hui Chang
2000	Tan Siah Kwee	2002	Jeremy Monteiro
2001	Tan Kian Por	2005	Dick Lee
2003	Lim Tze Peng		
2005	Chng Seok Tin; Lee Wen		
		Photography	
Dance		1982	David P.C. Tay
1979	Madhavi Krishnan	1983	Ang Chwee Chai
1981	Goh Soo Khim	1984	Yip Cheong Fun
1986	Goh Choo San	1985	Tan Lip Seng
1987	Som Said	1987	Lee Lim
1988	Lim Fei Shen	1988	Chua Soo Bin
1989	Neila Sathyalingam	1989	Foo Tee Jun
1990	Santha Bhaskar	1990	Peng Seng Wu
1992	Ying E Ding	2004	Teo Bee Yen
1995	Goh Lay Kuan		
		Theatre	
Film		1979	Bani Buang
2005	Jack Neo	1981	Joanna Wong Quee Heng
		1982	Lin Chen
Literature		1983	Christopher Allen
1979	Edwin Thumboo	1984	S. Varathan
1981	Meng Yi (Wong Meng Voon)	1985	Low Ing Sing
1982	Goh Poh Seng	1986	Nadiputra (Almahdi Al-Haj Ibrahim); N.Palanivelu
1983	Arthur Yap	1987	Max Le Blond
1985	Lee Tzu Pheng	1988	Tay Bin Wee
1986	Wang Runhua (Wong Yoon Wah)	1989	Kuo Pao Kun
1987	Muhammed Ariff Ahmad	1990	Han Lao Da
1988	N. Abdul Rahman	1992	Phan Wait Hong
1990	Zhou Can (Chew Kok Chang)	1997	Lou Mee Wah
1996	Dan Ying (Lew Poo Chan)	2003	Ong Keng Sen
1997	Ho Minfong		
1998	Rama Kannabiran		
1999	Abdul Ghani Abdul Hamid		
2003	Ying Peian		
2005	M. Elangkannan (M. Balakrishnan)		

Source: National Arts Council

currency The earliest conventionally shaped coin to be minted in the region around Singapore was the tin coin produced in Malacca by Sultan Muzaffar Shah in the mid-15th century. However, coins dating back to even earlier eras have been found at archaeological sites in Singapore. Chinese coins dating from the Northern Song Dynasty (960–1127) (right) were found during excavations at the site of Parliament House.

The 19th century
Following the Founding of Singapore in 1819, silver dollars of various type were widely used. These included the Mexican, Spanish (upper right) and, from 1895 to 1904, British trade dollars (lower right). Silver dollars were used by traders even after Singapore was governed directly from India, and the Indian rupee had been declared sole legal tender on the island.

From the 1850s, banks in Singapore, such as the Hongkong and Shanghai Banking Corporation (see HSBC), began to issue their own banknotes (below). In 1867, the Straits Settlements became a Crown Colony, and the silver dollar replaced the Indian rupee as legal tender in Singapore.

The early 20th century
In 1897, the Board of Commissioners of Currency was established. The board's new Straits dollar (below left) became the sole currency in 1904. In 1938, shared currency arrangements were established between Singapore and the Malay states, and the Malayan dollar (below right) replaced the Straits dollar. At times, some

organizations—such as the Singapore Harbour Board—also minted their own 'currencies' in response to metal shortages (above).

Occupation currency
During the Japanese Occupation, BANANA MONEY (right) became legal tender In Singapore. This currency was demonetized shortly after the war, and the Malayan dollar re-introduced.

A shared currency
The shared currency arrangements that had been established before the war were extended to include Sarawak, Brunei and British North Borneo (present-day Sabah) in 1950. The new Malaya and British Borneo dollar (right) continued to be used as legal tender in Singapore following Merger in 1963.

The Singapore dollar
It was only in 1967—two years after Singapore's separation from Malaysia—that individual currencies were introduced in Singapore, Malaysia and Brunei, although an agreement on

interchangeability for these currencies continued until 1973 (and between Singapore and Brunei until the present).

The Singapore dollar was first issued in 1967 (left). Polymer notes (above) were first introduced in 1990.

---

traditional filling, some curry puffs use sardines instead. OLD CHANG KEE and POLAR CAFÉ are among the well-known brand-names associated with curry puffs in Singapore.

Customs *See* IMMIGRATION AND CHECKPOINTS AUTHORITY.

CYC Singapore's oldest custom shirt-maker, CYC was founded in 1935 by Chinese immigrant Chiang Yick Ching and his wife Foo Ah Neok, who came from Ningbo (near Shanghai), China—hence the company's original name, the CYC Shanghai Shirt Company. The couple moved to Swatow (present-day Shantou) before heading to Singapore to seek their fortunes. The shirt-maker's reputation soon spread, and the brand became popular in Indonesia and

Malaya, prompting CYC to expand its product lines to include ready-made shirts.

In the 1960s, CYC began to open new retail outlets in Selegie and North Bridge Roads: these were among the first shops in Singapore to be air-conditioned. More shops in Tanglin, Katong, Thomson and High Streets were to follow in the 1970s. CYC continued to prosper until the 1983–84 recession, when it had to face the imposition of an exit tax on Indonesians, who made up a large part of its clientele. CYC also began to lose its market share to cheaper imports and an influx of new brands, and was forced to close some of its branches.

Chiang Loo Fern, the founder's eldest granddaughter who had started work on the shopfloor at the age of 12, took over management of CYC in 1992. She re-focused

the firm's business on custom-tailoring, rather than competing in the mass-market. Thereafter, the company set up a new division to make corporate uniforms. Corporate clients included the Conrad and Raffles group of hotels, retailers such as Takashimaya and John Little, and government bodies such as the Central Provident Fund Board, the Housing & Development Board and Singapore Armed Forces Reservists' Association. It also went into custom-made women's wear, and the manufacture of suits and T-shirts.

Its list of private clients is said to number up to 10,000, and to include local dignitaries such as Singapore's Senior Minister GOH CHOK TONG and Prime Minister LEE HSIEN LOONG. CYC currently operates two exclusive outlets at RAFFLES HOTEL and Republic Plaza II.

CYC: advertisement from 1970.

daching An instrument for measuring weight. Also spelt '*dacing*' in Malay. A typical *daching* consists of a wooden beam with a weighing pan on one end (sometimes a hook is used instead of a pan), which is suspended from the beam by a metal fixture containing a needle. A counterweight is moved along the opposite end of the beam until the needle is vertical. Different strings are suspended from the beam and act as balance points and the scale for each string is marked on the beam, which gives the weight of the object. The instrument is used symbolically in Peranakan weddings, signalling a 'balanced relationship'.

Daching

There are many different sizes of *daching* and in earlier days, before the metric system was in use, they were made in all the units of Chinese measurement. Since 1975, the *daching* has moved to the metric system except for weighing gold or medicinal herbs. The making of a *daching* is an ancient craft learned through apprenticing and now almost lost. It involved a fine knowledge of carpentry and metalwork. Some of the famous makers in Singapore include the Chye Soon Daching Company and the Lian Seng Weighing Company.

Dairy Farm Regional supermarket and retail store operator. In Singapore, its outlets operate under the COLD STORAGE, Shop N Save, Giant, Guardian and 7-Eleven brands.

The history of Dairy Farm dates to 1886 when a Scottish surgeon, Patrick Manson, joined with several partners and, with a working capital of 30,000 Hongkong dollars, embarked on a dairy business venture in Hong Kong. From such modest beginnings, Dairy Farm became a leading pan-Asian retailer. The group's businesses are still managed out of Hong Kong. Dairy Farm is a member of the Jardine Matheson group (*see* JARDINE, MATHESON & CO.).

The company's US-dollar-denominated stock has been listed on the local bourse since February 1991 and is part of the benchmark Straits Times Index (STI); it is listed also in Bermuda and London. It was not until 1993, however, that Dairy Farm began to establish a strong retail foothold in Singapore when it acquired the Cold Storage chain. This was followed by the takeover of eight Tops stores from Royal Ahold and the completion of its purchase of Guardian Singapore in 1999. In 2000, Guardian bought over 23 stores from Apex Pharmacy International, while the first Giant Hypermart was opened at the IMM

Building in Jurong East. In 2003 the group also acquired 35 Shop N Save outlets, bringing its number of supermarkets in Singapore to 75.

Dairy Farm employs 60,000 people in the region and had total sales of US$5.5 billion in 2005. Group net profit topped US$207 million on a gross turnover of almost US$4.7 billion.

Dalforce A Singapore Chinese volunteer battalion in WORLD WAR II. Some 1,250 Dalforce members (including at least 1,072 combatants) were sent to the front line in 1942, during the final two weeks of the battle for Singapore. With coloured bands on their heads, chests or arms in lieu of proper uniforms, and a varied assortment of weaponry, those sent to the front were deployed in eight companies, most of 150 men. Four of these companies saw action alongside British, Indian and Australian troops from 5 February until official disbandment on 13 February. Some continued the fight even after disbandment.

The name 'Dalforce' derives from Malayan Special Branch officer and force commander Lieutenant-Colonel John D. Dalley. Its deputy commander was Major Hu Tie Jun, and its Chinese names include Xinghua Yi Yong Jun (Singapore Overseas Chinese Anti-Japanese Volunteer Army) and Huaqiao Shou Bei Jun (Overseas Chinese Guard Force). These names reflect parts of Dalforce under communist and nationalist influences respectively.

Dalforce has been seen as an example of common *huaqiao* (overseas Chinese) patriotism espoused by various Kuomintang, communist and non-party members. These were recruited both through Dalley's contacts, and also under the umbrella of the Xingzhou Huaqiao Kangdi Dongyuan Zonghui (Singapore Overseas Chinese Anti-Enemy Mobilisation Council). The latter was established on 30 December 1941, following the governor's belated request for the Chinese to unite in Singapore's defence. The Mobilisation Council brought together the communist National Salvation Movement and the TAN KAH KEE-chaired Southseas China Relief Fund Union. Despite Tan Kah Kee's opposition, it formed a Popular Armed Force Department under communists Ng Yeh Lu and Lim Kang Sek.

Hence Dalforce fought as an auxiliary unit of MALAYA COMMAND, as a patriotic extension of the Sino-Japanese War, and because of related fears that *huaqiao* lives and property could suffer the fate of mainland Chinese cities. Dalforce became a synonym for bravery in the post-war Chinese community, particularly for actions fought at Tanjong Pagar godown, Lim Chu Kang, Jurong and Bukit Timah.

The 2nd Company took 50 per cent casualties while assisting the Australian 2/20th Battalion against the Japanese landings of 8 February, and in defending Lim

Chu Kang Road on 9 February. The 1st Company and remnants of the 2nd Company also made a significant contribution to the fight for Bukit Timah (*see* MALAYA CAMPAIGN). Except for another unit which fired on Japanese boats in the Causeway sector before retreat, most of the rest of Dalforce saw little or no action.

Acts of individual bravery were particularly notable given the hopelessness of the overall situation. British records confirm 134 dead for Dalforce. There were almost certainly more; but most survived, a significant number escaping both the fighting and the ensuing SOOK CHING to join British FORCE 136 or the MALAYAN PEOPLE'S ANTI-JAPANESE ARMY.

Dalhousie Obelisk Commemorative monument. In 1850, the Marquis of Dalhousie, governor-general of India, visited Singapore. To commemorate his visit, an obelisk was designed by the government surveyor, John Turnbull Thomson, who was thought to have derived his inspiration from Cleopatra's Needle in London. It was erected on what is now Connaught Drive. In the 1880s, it was moved because of land reclamation, and at the instigation of Sir CECIL CLEMENTI SMITH, governor of Singapore, re-erected at EMPRESS PLACE in front of the VICTORIA CONCERT HALL and Theatre.

D'Almeida, José (1784–1850) Doctor, businessman and agriculturalist. José d'Almeida was born in San Pedro do Sul in Portugal. He became a ship's doctor and travelled to Macau where he married. He moved with his family to Singapore in 1825, settling in Beach Road. He established a dispensary and went into business as a merchant. His firm soon became one of Singapore's most important businesses. D'Almeida was interested in agriculture and was a founding member of the Singapore Agricultural and Horticultural Society (1836). He owned a

Dalhousie Obelisk

large plantation called Bandula where he grew coffee, COCONUTS, cotton and NUTMEG, and co-discovered GUTTA PERCHA. D'Almeida served as consul-general of Portugal, and was knighted by the queen of Portugal as well as by the king of Spain. He died in 1850 and was buried at FORT CANNING. D'Almeida Street is named after him.

D'Almeida, Joaquim (c. 1805–1870) Businessman, agriculturalist and diplomat. Joaquim D'Almeida was the son of Dr JOSÉ D'ALMEIDA, and was born in Macau in 1805. He and his brother José managed their father's firm, D'Almeida & Sons, after the latter's death in 1850, but the firm folded during the economic slump of 1864. He had been made chairman of the Singapore Chamber of Commerce in 1853 and 1858.

Joaquim shared his father's interest in AGRICULTURE, and cultivated NUTMEG and SUGAR. He helped raise funds to build ST JOSEPH'S CHURCH, and was involved in Singapore's public affairs, including the movement to establish the Straits Settlements as a separate Crown Colony.

Dan Ying (1943–) Poet. Dan Ying is the pseudonym of Lew Poo Chan, who was born in Malaysia. Dan Yin taught Chinese language at the University of California at Santa Barbara before moving to Singapore in 1974; and at the NATIONAL UNIVERSITY OF SINGAPORE until her retirement in 2003. One of the best known feminist poets in the Chinese-speaking world, her work is widely published in Singapore, Taiwan, Hong Kong and China.

Mixing the lyrical tradition of classical Chinese poetry from the Tang and Song dynasties with the poetics of post-modernism, Dan Ying has created a new means of exploring subjectivism, turning from external reality to examine inner states of consciousness. Poems such as 'Inside and Outside the Umbrella' from the collection *Tai Ji Shi Pu* (Poems of Taiji) (1979) and 'Fa Shang Sui Yue' (Time Passing Through My Hair), from the collection of the same name, are on the surface simple lyrical poems; however they offer deep insights into the new sensibility and living conditions of the post-modern era.

Dan Ying's *Tai Ji Shi Pu* and *Time Passing Through My Hair* (1993) won the National Book Development Council of Singapore Book Award in 1980 and 1994 respectively. Dan Ying was also awarded the Southeast Asia Write Award (1995) and the CULTURAL MEDALLION (1996).

Danaraj, T.J. (1914–1996) Doctor and academic. Professor Thumboo John Danaraj was dean of the Faculty of Medicine, UNIVERSITY OF MALAYA in Singapore (1960–62). In 1963 he became founding dean of the university's Faculty of Medicine in Kuala Lumpur. For his research, mainly in the field of tropical eosinophilia (a respiratory disorder), he was

Dance: Four And A Half Rebels, *by Ecnad Project.*

awarded a master of medicine degree. His special fields of interest were neurology and cardiology. He did important work on primary arteritis of the aorta (Takayasu's disease) together with his wife.

In 1989, Danaraj was the first recipient of the joint medal of the Royal College of Physicians of London and the Academy of Medicine of Malaysia. The aim of this award is to encourage young doctors in Malaysia to pursue research in clinical medicine. He was also awarded the title 'Tan Sri'—the equivalent of a British knighthood—by the king of Malaysia, the Yang di-Pertuan Agung.

dance While dance fulfilled socio-cultural functions within Singapore's various ethnic communities in earlier years, it only began to grow as a theatrical art form after World War II. Chinese dance had a humble start in student presentations in schools, while Malay dance was initially a dance-hall activity. Indian dance was virtually unknown before dancer-choreographer Uday Shankar and his multi-national troupe visited the island in 1935.

Eventually, cultural establishments and global talent helped to raise ethnic-dance standards. Chinese dance benefited not only from the support of CLAN ASSOCIATIONS, but also from Taiwanese dancer LEE SHU FEN's extensive choreographic and teaching efforts. The popularity of Indian dance rose after the inception of the SINGAPORE INDIAN FINE ARTS SOCIETY and, later, Bhaskar's Academy of Dance. The presence of choreographers from Malaysia and Indonesia, invited by Malay cultural group SRIWANA, contributed to the growth of Malay dance.

During the anti-colonial and pro-Malaya campaigns of the 1950s, dance artists promoted greater interaction and understanding between Singapore's three main ethnic groups—Chinese, Malays and Indians. In the early 1960s, Chinese dance, Indian dance and Malay dance shared the stage in the many outdoor variety shows organized by the then Ministry of Culture; dancers were also keen to learn from one another. Dance thus served as an expression of racial diversity and of a common national identity, even before Singapore gained its

independence in 1965.

While dance would be established as a co-curricular activity in schools by the 1970s, the Ministry of Culture founded the part-time National Dance Company in 1970, which staged traditional dances for local and international audiences for 19 years. The People's Association Dance Company (*see* PEOPLE'S ASSOCIATION TALENTS)—a full-time outfit from 1971—reached out to the masses with island-wide performances and affordable classes from 1968 until the late 1990s. In 1982, the National Theatre Trust launched the first Singapore Festival of Dance, which showcased ballet alongside Chinese, Indian and Malay dance until 1991.

Ballet remained the domain of European expatriates until Maudrene Yap set up her own school in 1950, after returning from her dance studies with Phyllis Bedells in London. Britain's Royal Academy of Dancing (RAD) chose Yap's school, which soon drew over 200 students, to host the first RAD ballet examinations for Singaporean and Malayan students in 1953. In 1955, a well-received performance of classical excerpts by GOH SOO NEE, her brother Goh Choo Chiat, and Shanghai-born Blossom Shek, marked a new high point in ballet's rising appeal. More ballet schools sprang up, ballet productions became regular events, and local dancers looked overseas for performing and training opportunities; among those who found success abroad was GOH CHOO SAN.

At home, GOH SOO KHIM and ANTHONY THEN set up the SINGAPORE DANCE THEATRE in 1987, the country's first full-time ballet company. It remains the only troupe on the island that can afford to commission new works from local and foreign choreographers consistently, as well as acquire masterpieces of global repute—such as the 19th-century classic *Giselle* and the 'Rubies' section of George Balanchine's three-part *Jewels* (1967)—for its growing repertory. Apart from international acts on tour, it is Singapore's most constant source of professional ballet dancing on stage.

Contemporary dance took longer to take root in Singapore, but local audiences

José D'Almeida

Joaquim D'Almeida

Dan Ying

Dance: National Dance Company, c. 1980.

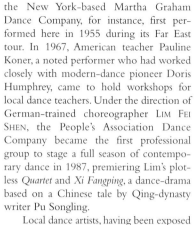

Dance Ensemble Singapore: Chamber, 2006.

Wilson David

DART (Disaster Assistance and Rescue Team): locating casualties using a search camera.

had seen some modern dance from abroad: the New York-based Martha Graham Dance Company, for instance, first performed here in 1955 during its Far East tour. In 1967, American teacher Pauline Koner, a noted performer who had worked closely with modern-dance pioneer Doris Humphrey, came to hold workshops for local dance teachers. Under the direction of German-trained choreographer LIM FEI SHEN, the People's Association Dance Company became the first professional group to stage a full season of contemporary dance in 1987, premiering Lim's plotless *Quartet* and *Xi Fangping*, a dance-drama based on a Chinese tale by Qing-dynasty writer Pu Songling.

Local dance artists, having been exposed to modern dance during their training, have since formed a handful of contemporary-dance groups—such as The ARTS FISSION COMPANY and ECNAD PROJECT—that make up Singapore's budding dance scene, which includes freelance dancers who present their choreography independently. Still, a significant part of the local dance calendar consists of imported acts.

Dance events have a firm place in the SINGAPORE ARTS FESTIVAL, which has commissioned new works from the Singapore Dance Theatre and other groups, as well as co-producing world premieres by London's Akram Khan Company in 2004 and Belgian troupe Ultima Vez in 2005. Dance also appears on the programmes of smaller festivals such as the M1 Singapore Fringe Festival, which The NECESSARY STAGE started in 2005, and those curated by ESPLANADE—THEATRES ON THE BAY.

Dance Ensemble Singapore Founded as the Yan Choong Lian Dance Troupe in 1988 by Yan Choong Lian, the company was renamed Dance Ensemble Singapore in 1993 and hosted the Singapore Chinese Dance Conference in 1996. Known for its Chinese traditional and contemporary dance, it draws on folk traditions and modern-dance techniques for its repertory, while its school offers classes in dance, music and martial arts. It debuted at the

SINGAPORE ARTS FESTIVAL in 1994 with a programme called *Rhythm of the Dance: Tea, Ink and Blooms*. In 1996, it staged a 30-minute version of David Henry Hwang's play *M. Butterfly*. It appeared again at the Singapore Arts Festival in 1999 with *Interweave*, featuring works by Yan, Sharon Low and Yap Guat Kim.

Danmaxi *See* TEMASEK.

DART (Disaster Assistance and Rescue Team) The SINGAPORE CIVIL DEFENCE FORCE formed the Disaster Assistance and Rescue Team (DART) in 1990 to carry out complex and difficult rescue operations, including tunnelling, MASS RAPID TRANSIT rescue and high-rise rescues. DART is equipped with robots, search cameras, fibre-optic scopes, thermal-imaging cameras and trapped-person locators, as well as rescue dogs. Beyond dealing with local emergencies, DART has also been deployed overseas in humanitarian and rescue operations, notably in the wake of the tsunami disaster in Aceh, Indonesia and Khao Lak, Thailand in December 2004, and the earthquakes which struck Pakistan in 2005 and central Java in 2006.

Darul Arqam Association for new converts to ISLAM. Originally known as Kumpulan Saudara Baru (New Converts' Group) in 1973, it was officially registered in 1979 as the Muslim Converts' Association of Singapore (MCAS), also known as Darul Arqam. Its main role is to provide religious guidance and support for converts, and it also organizes talks and seminars.

Das, Kay (1946–) Scientist. As research and development director of semi-conductor company STMicroelectronics Asia Pacific, Kay Das set up joint R&D programmes with Nanyang Technological University, Nanyang Polytechnic and other local research institutes, to enhance Singapore's edge in chip-making. He also initiated the DSP (Digital Signal Processing) R&D Centre in Singapore, which worked in the areas of audio, video and wireless. Das was a founding member of the Institute of Micro-

electronics (IME), where he helped initiate development activities in GSM (global system for mobile communication) and video systems. He was awarded the 2004 National Science and Technology Medal.

Datacraft Asia Datacraft Limited—the parent company of Datacraft Asia—was incorporated in Melbourne in 1974. It started out as a designer, manufacturer and distributor of data communications products such as modems. Datacraft Asia set up operations in Singapore in 1993 and grew into a leading information technology (IT) services and solutions company serving largely the Asia-Pacific region. Datacraft Asia is now a subsidiary of the South Africa-based and Johannesburg-listed Dimension Data Group, which had acquired Datacraft Limited in 1997.

Datacraft Asia has been listed on the main board of the Singapore Exchange since 1995 and its counter is a component of the Straits Times Index. Headquartered in Singapore, it has more than 1,200 employees in over 50 major cities and locations across 13 Asia-Pacific markets. In financial year 2005, Datacraft Asia reported a net profit of US$12.2 million on a turnover of US$456 million.

David, Wilson (1940–) Singer. Dubbed 'Singapore's Elvis Presley' and 'Singapore's King of Rock 'n' Roll' by show promoters and fans alike, Wilson David impersonated Elvis for over 30 years. Starting out in the late 1950s, he performed to capacity crowds at such venues as the Ocean Park Hotel, SEA VIEW HOTEL and the SINGAPORE BADMINTON HALL. David was at the peak of his career in the late 1950s and 1960s, hosting a major show at the NATIONAL THEATRE in 1964. He also opened for international artistes such as Freddie & the Dreamers, Helen Shapiro and The Honeycombs. David is the father of former television personality and host Darryl David.

Dawoodi Bohra A branch of SHI'A Muslims. The spiritual leader of the Bohra is the Da'i al-Mutlaq (the Absolute Caller). The Da'i is considered the vicegerent or representative of the Secluded Imam. Originally from Gujarat, India, Bohra traders started settling in Singapore as early as the 1820s. There are over a million adherents worldwide.

The Bohra community in Singapore is close-knit, with members seeking advice from the Da'i on important matters, both religious and otherwise. Bohra men wear white three-piece kurtas, comprising a pair of pants, a long shirt, and a light coat. White and gold caps (*topi*) complete the ensemble. Women don the *rida*, a colourful two-piece dress that usually has floral designs and lace trimmings.

The mosque for the Bohra community in Singapore is the Burhani Mosque located in Hill Street. The mosque was established in 1829. It has been rebuilt

twice—in the mid-1950s and in 2000—to accommodate the steadily growing community. The mosque is an 11-storey complex comprising prayer halls, function halls, residential quarters, MADRASAH (religious school), meeting rooms and offices.

The population of Bohras in Singapore is quite small, numbering fewer than 1,000 people in 2002.

DBS Bank Singapore's industrialization programme of the 1960s included the creation of an industrial finance institution or development bank. When the ECONOMIC DEVELOPMENT BOARD (EDB) restructured its operations in 1968, its industrial financing arm was spun off. This was to become the Development Bank of Singapore (DBS).

Incorporated under the Companies Act in 1968, DBS was also licensed as a commercial bank under the Banking Act. On account of its development bank status, it was initially exempted from certain provisions of the Banking Act. At the time of its incorporation, the government subscribed for 49 per cent of its equity, 25 per cent was offered to financial institutions and 26 per cent to the public. In 1987, the Public Sector Divestment Committee recommended that the government's share be reduced to around 30 per cent. In February 2006, government ownership through TEMASEK HOLDINGS and its subsidiaries was 28 per cent.

Initially, the operations of DBS focused on industrial financing through medium- and long-term loans, equity participation and guarantees, in line with the country's development plans, which included the development of a financial centre.

The growth of DBS mirrors the trajectory of the local economy. In the early 1970s, it began to expand its commercial banking activities, and in 1983, began calling itself the DBS Bank. It quickly became one of the Big Four (now Big Three) local banks, diversifying into commercial, international and merchant banking. DBS acquired POSBANK and its subsidiaries for $1.6 billion in November 1998, to become the largest retail bank in Singapore. With the merger of DBS Kwong On Bank with Dao Heng Bank and Overseas Trust Bank in 2003, DBS Bank (Hong Kong) Limited became the fourth-largest banking group in Hong Kong. For 2005, DBS reported a group net profit of $985 million, and group income before operating expenses was $4.64 billion.

D'Cotta, Denis (1911–1983) Judge. Born in Singapore, Denis Cosmas D'Cotta was educated at St Xavier's Institution in Penang and then at Raffles Institution, Singapore, before going to Britain for his law studies. He was called to the Bar at Inner Temple in January 1950 and then left to practise law in Brisbane, Australia. In 1952, he returned to Singapore and joined the Legal Service as

DBS Bank

assistant official assignee and First Magistrate. D'Cotta was elevated to the Bench as PUISNE JUDGE in 1970. He retired in 1981 at the age of 70.

de Barros, João (1496–1570) Historian. João de Barros was appointed official historian by King Manual of Portugal in 1523, serving in this position until 1567. He was also appointed treasurer (1523–28), and factor (1533–67) at the Casa da India (India House) at Lisbon.

The first part of his major work, the *Decadas da Asia*, contains a section on Malacca. This includes information on Singapore during the 15th and 16th centuries. It records that the father of Xaquem Darxa (ISKANDAR SHAH) had established a port-city at Malacca which competed directly with the Siamese-controlled port at Singapore.

During Xaquem Darxa's reign, the Malaccan navy forced merchant vessels to call at Malacca instead of Singapore, and Malacca thus flourished at the expense of Singapore. Subsequently, to appease the king of Siam (present-day Thailand), Xaquem Darxa proposed to pay Siam an annual tribute equivalent to the profits previously derived from Siam's operations in Singapore. The king agreed, and a sphere of influence of 90 leagues' radius was accorded to Malacca in return. Singapore marked the southern extremity of this sphere of influence. Consequently, many people left Singapore. After the MALACCA SULTANATE capitulated to the Portuguese in 1511, the *laksamana* (admiral) of Malacca settled in Singapore, taking the island as his fiefdom.

de Coutre, Jacques (1575–1640) Merchant-traveller allied to the Spanish Crown. Jacques de Coutre wrote a memorial in the early 1620s entitled *Enformación para se hazer algunos castillos o fortalecas en el estrecho de Sincapura* (Information Concerning the Construction of Some Citadels or Fortresses in the Straits of Singapore). The manuscripts were rediscovered in the early 1970s, and survive as one of the most important accounts of Singapore in the early 17th century.

In his memorial, de Coutre attempted to convince the Spanish Crown that its ailing fortunes in the East could be turned if several fortresses were established along the Straits of Singapore to protect Portuguese shipping. De Coutre proposed that one fortress be built on Ysla de Arenas (SENTOSA Island) and another on the eastern side of Singapore. He argued that five or six armed galleys could be permanently stationed off Singapore to support the two fortresses. Finally, De Coutre proposed that a port be established at the Estreito Viejo (VARELLA CHANNEL/OLD STRAIT), a body of water that separated the two fortresses. He suggested that a boom could be put across the strait to serve as a gate.

De Coutre's idea of a Spanish presence on Singapore has been seen by historians as a forerunner to Sir STAMFORD RAFFLES' vision of a port-settlement on the island.

de Cruz, Gerald (1920–1991) Journalist and politician. Born into a middle-class Eurasian family, Gerald de Cruz started work as a journalist with The *Straits Times* in 1940. At the end of World War II, he joined the MALAYAN COMMUNIST PARTY and was one of the earliest members of the pro-communist MALAYAN DEMOCRATIC UNION, Singapore's first political party. De Cruz became disillusioned with communism after the Soviet invasion of Hungary in 1956. In 1951, he took up a diploma course on teaching intellectually disabled children in London and then spent six years working in that field before returning to Singapore at the request of DAVID MARSHALL to be organizing secretary of the LABOUR FRONT government. He became a Muslim in 1968.

In the 1960s, de Cruz helped GEORGE G. THOMSON establish the government's Political Study Centre to educate civil servants on world affairs and local political changes. From 1975 to 1985, he was actively involved as a training consultant in the Sarawak Foundation, a government-sponsored body which provides scholarships for its people. He was also chairman of the

Gerald de Cruz

Dawoodi Bohra: at Tampines Stadium, 1998.

Deep Tunnel Sewerage System

Frederick Benjamin de Souza: winner (centre) of a friendly shooting competition with Thailand, 1964.

Deepavali: Serangoon Road in Little India.

Singapore Association for Retarded Children and an adviser to the NATIONAL TRADES UNION CONGRESS (NTUC). De Cruz received the Friend of Labour award from the NTUC.

De Cruz was diplomatic editor of the *New Nation* in the early 1970s, a columnist for *The Sarawak Tribune* and wrote *Rojak Rebel* (1993). He was the father of Justice JUDITH PRAKASH and diplomat Simon de Cruz. He died in Kuala Lumpur on 9 December 1991.

de Souza, Frederick Benjamin (1918–1964) Sportsman. Frederick Benjamin de Souza won the first Asian Games gold medal in shooting for Singapore in Jakarta in 1962, and was one of Singapore's most successful small-bore rifle shooters. In 1961, he won a gold medal at the second Southeast Asian Peninsular (SEAP) Games with a record score of 576. He achieved even greater success at the 1962 Asian Games with a score of 583. Entry into the SINGAPORE SPORTS COUNCIL HALL OF FAME followed shortly thereafter.

A lawyer by profession, de Souza was Chairman of the Singapore Rifle Association from 1962 to 1964. He died of a heart attack just before the 1964 Tokyo Olympics.

Deep Tunnel Sewerage System In 2000, PUB started building the Deep Tunnel Sewerage System (DTSS) to cater for Singapore's increasing population.

The DTSS is a cost-effective way to meet Singapore's long-term needs for used water collection, treatment and disposal. Phase One of the DTSS will comprise a 48-km North Tunnel stretching from Kranji to Changi, a water reclamation plant with a capacity of 176 million gallons (800,000 cu m) per day, a 5-km-long sea outfall at Changi, and some 60 km of link sewers.

When completed in 2008, used water will be conveyed through the deep tunnel using the natural force of gravity to the Changi Water Reclamation Plant, where it will be treated to international standards before being discharged into the sea through the deep-sea outfall. The DTSS will free up land currently used to site the six water reclamation plants and 130 pumping stations, as well as the buffer land surrounding the reclamation plants. The centralization of used water treatment at the Changi Water Reclamation Plant will be more cost effective.

Deepavali One of the most important Hindu festivals, celebrated by Hindus of all sects and linguistic groups. It is a PUBLIC HOLIDAY in Singapore. The word 'Deepavali' literally means 'row of lamps', and the festival is so called because of the illuminations that form part of the celebration. These symbolize the triumph of good over evil. The festival falls on the 14th day of the Tamil month of Aipasi (October–November).

The festival has a long history and there are many myths explaining its origins and significances. One account is that it is the day when King Vickramaditya of Ujjain, a historical capital of central India, was crowned. Another explanation is that it is the coronation day of Prince Rama (of the Ramayana epic), when he returned to Ayodhya after conquering Sri Lanka and vanquishing the demon king, Ravana. Most Hindus in Singapore know it as the day Lord Krishna annihilated Narakasura, the *asura* demon king who was oppressing the people.

In the week leading up to the festival, homes are painted, and upholstery changed. Living rooms are decorated with greeting cards and coloured light bulbs. On the morning of Deepavali, most Hindus rise early, have their heads anointed with oil and take a ritual bath at sunrise. This act symbolizes bathing in the River Ganges. A lamp is then lit for Lakshmi, the goddess of wealth. Offerings of oil, fruit, betel, nuts and sweetmeats are also presented to deities in the prayer room or altar. New clothes are worn and blessings are sought from the elders of the family. Gifts of food are exchanged with friends and neighbours during visits. In the evening, homes are lit with rows of tiny oil lamps while both young and old light sparklers and celebrate.

Deepavali: rangoli, floor decorations of coloured rice.

defamation Singapore's defamation laws are based on the common law and the Defamation Act. Three elements must be satisfied in any claim for defamation: the statement or words must be defamatory; the statement or remarks must identify or refer to the person claiming to have been defamed; and the defamatory words must be published, i.e. at least one other person must be exposed to the statement. A defamatory statement is one that affects the reputation of another and lowers that person in the estimation of right-thinking members of society. If, however, the maker of the statement can show that it is true, that is a complete defence.

Defamation may take the form of libel or slander. Historically, libel referred to defamation expressed in written form, while slander referred to defamation in verbal form. But this distinction has been complicated by technological advances; it is now best described in terms of whether the defamatory expression is permanent (libel) or transient (slander). Even so, the Defamation Act deems certain forms of modern communication to be libel, although they may appear to be transient—for example, a broadcast by means of telecommunication can be libel.

The only practical distinction between libel and slander is that slander is generally not actionable per se. To pursue an action, the claimant must show that he has suffered special damage, i.e. a financial loss or a loss that is estimable in money. There are, however, four exceptions to this requirement: imputing that the claimant has committed a crime for which the punishment is more than just a fine; imputing the suffering of a contagious disease; imputing that a girl or woman is unchaste; and imputing that a person is unfit or incompetent for his or her office, profession, calling, trade or business.

Politicians in Singapore, to guard their reputations, have used defamation actions on a number of occasions. In some countries, most notably the United States, the standard of proof required for defamation of public figures is higher than that in relation to the ordinary person. The public figure must show that the maker of the defamatory statement was malicious, or knew that the statement was false, or ought reasonably to have believed it was false. However, the Singapore courts have repeatedly held that there is no such 'public figure exception'. Therefore, someone accused of defamation cannot use as a defence the fact that their words were uttered or written in the heat of political debate, nor can they argue that a public figure should, as a matter of public policy, be expected to be more robust than other individuals in the face of adverse criticisms or defamatory statements. Damages awarded for the defamation of political figures in Singapore are very high, as the courts have ranked politicians' integrity and reputations much more highly than those of the ordinary person.

Defence Science and Technology Agency Statutory board. The agency was established under the MINISTRY OF DEFENCE (MINDEF) in March 2000, following the restruc turing of the Defence Technology Group (DTG). The agency's main functions include procuring and planning for defence materiel; developing and implementing defence technologies and infrastructure; and managing research for MINDEF. The Defence Science and Technology Agency (DSTA) also provides engineering support, including the routine management of maintenance operations, as well as the upgrading of IT, munitions and other systems for the SINGAPORE ARMED FORCES (SAF).

Collaborating with the SAF and key players in the defence industry, the DSTA has played a pivotal role in the development of technologies such as the SAR 21 rifle, the Armour Gunnery Tactical Simulator and the BIONIX Infantry Fighting Vehicle. The DSTA largely funds DSO NATIONAL LABORATORIES, an affiliated research and development organization.

Délifrance Bakery and patisserie. Délifrance was founded in 1983 as a wholesale and manufacturing business supplying bread and other pastries to hotels, clubs, supermarkets and airlines. In 1985, it opened its first café bakery at Clifford Centre, and the following year, opened its first bakery counter at Chancery Court.

In 1987, Délifrance commenced operations in Hong Kong and China and subsequently expanded into Australia (1989), Malaysia (1990), the Philippines (1995), Brunei (1996), Thailand (1997) and Sri Lanka (1999). In 1995, Délifrance was awarded Business Headquarters (BHQ) status in Singapore and established its regional headquarters here. In October the following year, it was listed on the Stock Exchange of Singapore (SES) as Délifrance Asia Ltd. The company was acquired by Prudential Asset Management Asia Limited in October 1999. Délifrance Asia's business is estimated to be worth over $150 million a year, with more than 200 retail outlets in nine countries.

Democratic Party Established by business groups with Chinese-educated members just before the 1955 general election, the Democratic Party (DP) comprised members of the Mandarin-speaking elite, many of them from the SINGAPORE CHINESE CHAMBER OF COMMERCE AND INDUSTRY. It was regarded as one of Singapore's two 'mainstream' political parties in the early 1950s, the other being the PROGRESSIVE PARTY (PP). The party's president at its inception was rubber tycoon Tan Eng Joo, while the headquarters were at the EE HOE HEAN CLUB (also known as the 'Millionaires' Club') in Bukit Pasoh Road. The DP fielded 20 candidates during the 1955 general election, but only two of its candidates won seats (C.K. Lim in Changi constituency and Ong Eng Lian in Rochore constituency). Just before the 1957 city council election, the DP merged with the PP to form the LIBERAL SOCIALIST PARTY.

demography In 2005, Singapore's total population was estimated to be 4.35 million people, 3.55 million of whom were residents (citizens and permanent residents). Singapore is a multi-racial country. The CHINESE are the largest group, making up 76.8 per cent of the population. The MALAYS who are the indigenous people of the country, constitute 13.9 per cent. The INDIANS are the third-largest ethnic group at 7.9 per cent. The rest of the population (categorized as 'Others' in the Census of Population) is made up of smaller ethnic groups such as EURASIANS, ARABS, JEWS, Thais and Japanese.

The composition of the population has changed over the years. In 2005, 18.3 per cent of the total population was non-resident; in 1970 the figure was 3 per cent. Reflecting a rapidly ageing population, the median age has risen from 19.5 in 1970 to 36 in 2005.

In 2005, 37,492 babies were born in Singapore. In the same year, there were 16,215 deaths. Singapore's crude death rate has declined over the years, reflecting an increase in life expectancy. The total fertility rate was at a historic low of 1.24 per female resident. Fertility rates had been below the replacement level of 2.1 per woman since 1976. This is one of the lowest birth rates in the world—far fewer than the 50,000 babies the population needs to replace itself annually. If the fertility rate

does not rise, Singapore's population will start to decline after 2020.

Over the years, numerous measures were implemented by the government to encourage and support parenthood. After the first Baby Bonus package in 1987, the total fertility rate (TFR) jumped to 1.96. This was partly because 1988 was a 'dragon' year, but the impact of the package was felt throughout the first half of the 1990s. (Chinese Singaporeans are predisposed to having babies in 'dragon years', as dragons are one of the auspicious animals in the Chinese zodiac, and it is believed that babies born in these years would grow up to be successful in life.) The effect seemed to have worn off over time, and the underlying trend of a falling TFR reasserted itself. By the next 'dragon year' in 2000, the TFR had declined to 1.60. The enhanced Baby Bonus scheme (2001) and further tax incentives introduced in 2000 have failed to reverse this trend. By 2005, more than $100 million has been disbursed under the Baby Bonus scheme, and over $200 million annually in tax reliefs and rebates. (*see* tables).

Dempsey Road Road leading into the former Tanglin Barracks from Holland Road. Tanglin Barracks was one of the earliest constructed in Singapore. Built in 1861, the barrack buildings were large, elevated wooden structures topped with *attap* (later zinc or asbestos) roofs. For more than 100 years, Tanglin Barracks was the home of the British military. From 1972 to 1989 it served as the headquarters of the MINISTRY OF DEFENCE, following the British withdrawal of troops. Today, some of the buildings have been leased out to shops and wine bars, offering ethnic furniture, carpets, antiques and exotic artefacts.

dengue Fever caused by the bites of Aedes mosquitoes. Dengue first appeared in

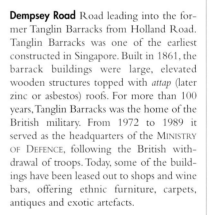
Democratic Party: logo.

Dempsey Road: carpets for sale outside a dealer's premises.

DEMOGRAPHY: KEY DEMOGRAPHIC INDICATORS

	1970	1980	1990	2000	2005
Total population ('000)	2,074.5	2,413.9	3,047.1	4,017.7	4,351.4
Residents ('000)	2,013.6	2,282.1	2,735.9	3,263.2	3,553.5
Sex ratio (males per 1,000 females)	1,049.0	1,032.0	1,027.0	998.0	987.0
Median age (years)	19.5	24.4	29.8	34.2	35.6
Total fertility rate (TFR) (per resident female)	3.07	1.82	1.83	1.60	1.24
Crude death rate (per 1,000 population)	5.2	4.9	4.7	4.5	4.3
Life expectancy at birth (years)	65.8	72.1	75.3	78.1	79.8

Source: Singapore Department of Statistics

DEMOGRAPHY: COMPARATIVE SELECTED SOCIAL INDICATORS, 2005

	Singapore	Australia	Canada	Hong Kong SAR	Japan	Korea	New Zealand	Taiwan	United Kingdom	United States
Population (million)	4.4	20	31	6.8	128	48	4	23	60	291
Life expectancy at birth (years)										
Males	77	77	77	79	78	73	77	73	76	75
Female	81	83	82	84	85	80	81	79	81	80
Infant mortality rate (per 1,000 live births)	2.5	4.8	5.3	2.3	3.0	5.0	4.9	4.9	5.3	7.0
Total fertility rate (TFR) (per female)	1.24	1.76	1.53	0.90	1.29	1.19	1.95	1.24	1.71	2.04
Doctors per 10,000 population	15	28	n.a.	16	20	17	22	16	n.a.	30
Home ownership (%)	93	70	66	53	61	54	68	85	70	68

Source: Singapore Department of Statistics

Dengue: public education campaign.

Singapore in 1960, with 70 hospitalized cases and one death. Since then, incidence of the disease has tended to reach serious levels at intervals of one to five years. In the late 1980s, there were only a few hundred dengue cases annually. However, this started to rise in the 1990s, reaching a high of 5,258 cases in 1998. Although the number was brought down to 673 in 2000, it started climbing again with a total of 9,459 cases in 2004. In October 2005, it reached a record high of 12,000 cases with 19 deaths.

An inter-ministerial committee was formed to tackle the dengue problem. One of the outcomes was the setting up of an inter-agency body headed by the NATIONAL ENVIRONMENT AGENCY. It launched its Mozzie Attack Campaign, entailing community-level activities, whereby residents clean up their estates and train household members and maids to detect and eliminate potential mosquito-breeding sites.

A few days after an infected Aedes mosquito bites a healthy person, the person develops a fever. This is infectious only in the sense that if an Aedes mosquito bites him, it will pick up the virus in the blood and pass it on when it bites another person. The fever does not spread directly from person to person.

Symptoms of dengue include a high fever lasting five to seven days, rashes, severe headache, muscle and joint pains, nausea, vomiting, fatigue and diarrhoea. Usually rashes appear as red dots on the skin on the limbs and are due to bleeding under the skin.

The dengue virus has four strains: serotypes 1, 2, 3 and 4. Getting infected with one serotype does not protect you against the others. In fact, getting a second dengue infection, particularly with serotype 2, can lead to an even worse illness such as Dengue Haemorrhagic Fever and Dengue Shock Syndrome, which can be fatal.

Desawarnana Javanese court poem. Previously known as the Nagarakretagama, the Desawarnana was written in 1365 by Mpu Prapanca, court poet of the kingdom of Majapahit. The poem identifies Temasek as a dependency of the MAJAPAHIT EMPIRE.

Prapanca refers to the Malay Peninsula as the 'island of Pahang'. It mentions the most important place there as Hujung Medini (probably the southern tip of Johor). Thereafter, he lists the names of other places in the region, including Lengkasuka (southern Thailand), Kelantan, Terengganu, Dungun, TEMASEK, Kelang, Kedah and Jere (Gunung Jerai, Kedah Peak) (*see also* PARARATON).

development status Singapore was re-classified by the World Bank as a 'high-income economy' in 1989. In 1992, the Organization for Economic Cooperation and Development removed Singapore from

S. Dhanabalan

Expert design & craftsmanship by . . .

DIETHELM'S

FURNITURE DEPARTMENT

Elegant furniture designed and produced locally are contributing to finer living in Malaya. Illustrated above is the Tungku Abdul Rahman Hall in Kuala Lumpur.

DIETHELM & CO., LTD.

(INCORPORATED IN SWITZERLAND) — 139A/149A MARKET STREET, SINGAPORE.

Diethelm: advertisement from 1958.

its list of aid recipients. In 1995, it, re-classified Singapore as a 'more advanced developing country'.

With a per capita gross national income of US$26,706 in 2005, Singapore has continued to be classified by the World Bank as a 'high-income economy', alongside developed countries such as the United States and Japan. However, the official position of the World Bank has been that Singapore is not yet a 'developed country', as the economy still lacks the depth and breadth of fully developed economies, especially in terms of technological capabilities. Recognizing this, the Singapore government set itself the goal of attaining 'developed country' status when it introduced the 1991 Strategic Economic Plan.

Another widely used yardstick of development status is the United Nations Human Development Index, a broader measure that takes into account the economic standard of living, literacy, education, life expectancy and childbirth statistics. According to figures issued in 2005, Singapore was placed in the 'High Human Development' category, ranking 25th overall out of a total of 177 countries surveyed (*see* table).

Dhanabalan, S. (1937–) Civil servant, politician and banker. Suppiah Dhanabalan was educated at Victoria School and the University of Malaya, where he obtained an honours degree in economics (1960). Upon graduation, he joined the civil service and was appointed assistant secretary at the Ministry of Finance. The following year, he was seconded to the ECONOMIC DEVELOPMENT BOARD as senior industrial economist. In 1968, he joined the Development Bank of Singapore (DBS) as vice president, later becoming the bank's executive vice president (1970–78).

In 1976, Dhanabalan stood for election under the People's Action Party banner and

became member of Parliament for Kallang. He served as senior minister for national development (1978–79); senior minister of state for foreign affairs (1979–80); minister for foreign affairs (1980–88); minister for national development (1987–92); and minister for trade and industry (1992–94). He retired from politics in 1997.

Other public offices Dhanabalan has held include chairman, Parameswara Holdings (since 1994); chairman, Singapore Airlines (1996–98); founding board member, Government of Singapore Investment Corporation (since 1981); chairman, Singapore Cultural Foundation Board of Trustees; president, Singapore Indian Development Association (1996–2002); permanent member, Presidential Council for Minority Rights; chairman, Temasek Holdings Ltd; chairman, DBS Group Holdings Ltd; and chairman, DBS Bank.

Dhoby Ghaut Area around present-day Stamford Canal, next to the Istana. Dhoby Ghaut is on what used to be the banks of Sungei (river) Bras Basah. The name is derived from two Indian words, '*dhoby*' meaning 'laundry' and '*ghaut*', meaning 'steps along the river bank'. The name came into popular use in the 1830s and 1840s largely because of the activities of Indian laundrymen (dhobis) who used to wash their clothes using the water from Sungei Bras Basah, and then drying them on the empty land which was later occupied by the Ladies Lawn Tennis Club (opposite Cathay Building). Today, Dhoby Ghaut is also the name of the Mass Rapid Transit station nearest to this location.

Diethelm Locally established multinational company. Wilhelm Heinrich Diethelm (1848–1932) arrived in Singapore in 1871 and began his career in Hooglandt and Co., where he was responsible for developing its textile business, rising to become a partner of the firm in 1877. When the last Hooglandt partner died in 1884, Diethelm took over the reins of the company. Under his direction, Hooglandt and Co. expanded its business activities from shipping, insurance, produce and banking to becoming involved in the import trade. In 1886, Diethelm went to Switzerland and opened an office in Zurich under his own name. From Zurich, he continued directing his Singapore enterprise through his partner W. Stiefel, and also acted as the company's buying agent.

In 1906, Wilhelm Diethelm founded Diethelm companies in Singapore, Zurich, Saigon and Bangkok. The Singapore firm, under J. van Lohuizen, took over the consumer and trading business of Hooglandt and Co. Until the 1920s, Diethelm and Co. traded mainly in imported goods. In 1928, it took over a Swiss firm that pioneered the aluminium business in Singapore. Diethelm died in 1932.

During World War II, Diethelm and Co., as a neutral Swiss concern, continued to operate. In 2000, it merged with another trading company, Ed. A Keller Holdings Ltd. Part of this new company then merged with SiberHegner in 2002 to create DKSH Ltd. The Diethelm group continues today as a diversified organization with interests including consumer goods, healthcare, chemicals and management services. It has branches in Switzerland, Malaysia, Indonesia, Vietnam, Thailand, the United States, Myanmar, Cambodia and Australia.

dikir barat Malay performance art form. *Dikir barat* was developed in Kelantan and is believed to have originated in Thailand, as the word '*barat*' (literally, 'west') to the people of Kelantan usually means 'from Thailand'. A *dikir barat* group comprises two lead singers, known as the *juara* and *tukang karut*, the *awok-awok* (chorus) and musicians. The group usually has between 15 and 30 members.

During a concert, the performers are seated on the floor in a semi circle or straight rows. The musicians are at the back, and the two lead singers are in front, facing the audience. The *juara*, who remains seated, starts at a slow pace, singing a quatrain, and the *awok-awok* repeats the verses. The *tukang karut*, who stands while singing, takes over with a more up-beat pace and sometimes makes up rhymes spontaneously. The singers sing verses that convey a common message based on themes such as education and cultural erosion. The *awok-awok* accompanies their singing with synchronized hand gestures and clapping. The singing is traditionally in the Kelantan MALAY dialect.

Dikir barat groups started performing around the late 1970s. The Gabungan Kumpulan Dikir Barat Singapura (Gabungan) (Singapore Dikir Barat Federation) was formed in 1992 as a coordinating body for *dikir barat* groups. It organizes Mega Perdana, the national *dikir barat*

Dikir barat

competition. In 2000, the final round of Mega Perdana was televised on Suria, the Malay television channel, and in 2006, the finals were held at the ESPLANADE— THEATRES ON THE BAY. *Dikir barat* has a large following among youth, who join school groups or the various *dikir* groups that have formed. One of the most well-known groups is Kelana Purba (Ancient Traveller), formed in 1990. It has won the Mega Perdana competition twice and its singers have also won individual awards in other competitions.

disk-drive sector The data-storage sector is an important segment of the electronics industry. In 2003, exports of disk drives accounted for approximately 15 per cent of non-oil domestic exports from Singapore. The disk-drive sector, worth $16 billion, contributed 26 per cent of the output of the electronics industry.

In 1981, Singapore entered a new phase of INDUSTRIALIZATION focused on developing high-technology industries. A year later, Seagate became the first disk drive manufacturer to set up a manufacturing facility in Singapore. Soon other disk-drive makers followed. Since then, Singapore has become the largest producer of hard-disk drives (HDD), accounting for about 30 per cent of total global output. It also hosts a concentration of major players such as Seagate, Maxtor and Matsushita-Kotobuki.

In the 1990s, Singapore's disk-drive sector faced intense competition from lower-cost markets such as Malaysia, Thailand and China. Some companies relocated their low-end production while others left Singapore altogether. In an effort to keep as many HDD producers in Singapore as possible, the government worked to move production up the value chain, funding collaborative R&D efforts, such as the Data Storage Institute, and providing direct financial incentives for firms to do their own R&D work in Singapore.

This strategy was successful, and Singapore continues to host high-end HDD operations, such as disk-media and optical-storage production, drive design and R&D activities. Singapore's niche in the high-end HDD segment was projected to grow by 25 per cent to 30 per cent by 2006, given strong demand from new digital consumer electronics applications.

See also ECONOMY.

Distinguished Service Order State decoration and honour. The Distinguished Service Order was instituted in 1968 and ranks, in precedence, below the Star of Temasek, the ORDER OF TEMASEK, the ORDER OF NILA UTAMA and the Certificate of Honour (*see* NATIONAL DAY HONOURS). A person admitted into the order has performed within Singapore (or in special circumstances outside Singapore) an act or series of acts constituting distinguished conduct.

DISTINGUISHED SERVICE ORDER: MEMBERS		
Name	Date	Appointment or profession
Phay Seng Whatt	3 Jun 1963	Chairman, Public Service Commission
Toh Puan Noor Aishah	3 Jun 1964	First Lady
Dr Albert Winsemius	9 Aug 1966	Economic adviser to Singapore
George Edwin Bogaars	9 Aug 1967	Permanent secretary, Ministry of the Interior and Defence
Hon Sui Sen	9 Aug 1967	Chairman, Economic Development Board
Howe Yoon Chong	9 Aug 1968	Permanent secretary, Ministry of Law and National Development (National Development Division) and chairman, Housing & Development Board
Tan Teck Khim	9 Aug 1971	Commissioner of police and former permanent secretary, Ministry of Health
Tang I-Fang	9 Aug 1972	Former chairman, Economic Development Board
Tan Boon Teik	9 Aug 1978	Attorney-general
Pang Tee Pow (posthumous)	9 Aug 1978	Former permanent secretary, Ministry of Defence
Tan Teck Chwee	9 Aug 1982	Chairman, Public Service Commission
Michael Fam	9 Aug 1983	Chairman-designate, Mass Rapid Transit Corporation and former chairman, Housing & Development Board
Ee Peng Liang	9 Aug 1985	Chairman, Singapore Council of Social Service
Lee Hee Seng	9 Aug 1989	Chairman, Public Service Commission
Yong Pung How	9 Aug 1989	Former chairman, Singapore Broadcasting Corporation
Chiang Hsiao-Wu	24 Apr 1990	Former trade representative, Taiwan
Lee Khoon Choy	9 Aug 1990	Special contributions to government, especially in the years 1961–63 and 1964–65
Rahim Ishak	9 Aug 1990	Special contributions to government, especially in the years 1961–63 and 1964–65
Ya'acob Mohamed (posthumous)	9 Aug 1990	Special contributions to government, especially in the years 1961–63 and 1964–65
Tommy Koh Thong Bee	9 Aug 1990	Ambassador-at-large
Sim Kee Boon	9 Aug 1991	Chairman, Civil Aviation Authority of Singapore
Wee Chong Jin	9 Aug 1991	Former chief justice
Tun Mohammed Hanif Omar	22 Jun 1993	Inspector-general of police, Malaysia
Ong Swee Law (posthumous)	9 Aug 1995	Late executive chairman, Singapore Zoological Gardens
Tan Sri Abdul Rahim Mohd Noor	25 Apr 1996	Inspector-general of police, Malaysia
Chan Sek Keong	9 Aug 1999	Attorney-general
Ngiam Tong Dow	9 Aug 1999	Permanent secretary, Ministry of Finance
Dato Paduka Seri Haji Ya'akub bin Pehin Orang Kaya Maharja Diraja Paduka Haji Zainal	23 Aug 1999	Commissioner of the Royal Brunei Police Force
Lee Ek Tieng	9 Aug 2000	Former head of civil service; group managing director, Government of Singapore Investment Corporation; chairman, Public Utilities Board; and deputy chairman, Monetary Authority of Singapore
Professor Lim Pin	9 Aug 2000	Former vice-chancellor, National University of Singapore and professor, Department of Medicine, National University of Singapore
Professor Lim Chong Yah	9 Aug 2000	Chairman, National Wages Council
Alan Choe	9 Aug 2001	Former chairman, Sentosa Development Corporation and chairman, Sentosa Cove
Lee Seng Wee	9 Aug 2001	Former member, Council of Presidential Advisers; former chairman, Singapore International Foundation; and member, Government of Singapore Investment Corporation
Yeo Ning Hong	9 Aug 2002	Chairman, PSA Corporation
Andrew Chew	9 Aug 2002	Chairman, Public Service Commission
Professor Cham Tao Soon	9 Aug 2003	University distinguished professor, Nanyang Technological University

Source: Prime Minister's Office

Victor Doggett

Donaldson & Burkinshaw: Alexander Leathes Donaldson (left) and John Burkinshaw.

The Badge of the Distinguished Service Order consists, on the obverse side, of a bronze enamelled circle depressed inwards on four opposite points with the words 'DARJAH UTAMA BAKTI CEMERLANG' ('Distinguished Service Order' in Malay) inscribed in gold letters. A green enamel wreath surrounds the circle. In the centre of the circle, on a white enamelled background, is a red shield bearing a crescent and five stars, with a scroll below carrying the inscription 'MAJULAH SINGAPURA' ('Onward Singapore' in Malay). The reverse side of the badge bears the STATE CREST. The Badge of the Distinguished Service Order is worn as a neck decoration suspended from a red-and-white striped ribbon.

District 10 Prime residential district. While Singapore now has a six-digit postal code system, many people still refer to the old postal district numbers. District 10 is one of Singapore's most sought-after residential districts. Located near ORCHARD ROAD (which is in District 9), and running along Holland Road, the area boasts the most exclusive and expensive properties in Singapore. Most of the properties in the district are either landed freehold property—including good class bungalows—or high-end condominiums and apartments. The district includes developments such as Queen Astrid Park,

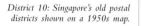

District 10: Singapore's old postal districts shown on a 1950s map.

Victoria Park, Nassim Road (Singapore's embassy row), Tanglin Hill, Oei Tiong Ham Park and Bin Tong Park.

Doggett, Victor (1919–2005) Music teacher. Victor Doggett was born in the United Kingdom, and was first trained in music by his father, Henry—a blind piano tuner. Doggett arrived in Singapore in 1945 as a member of the Royal Air Force, settling permanently on the island in 1947. He founded the Victor Doggett Music Studios in 1950. Prominent former students of his include SEOW YIT KIN, Lena Ching and Doggett's son Nicholas. Doggett also wrote for The *Straits Times* as a music critic. In recognition of his service to music, he was awarded a Fellowship by the Royal College of Music, London, in 1993.

Dollah Majid (1926–) Malaysian intellectual and politician. Born in Raub, Pahang, Dollah Majid, also known as Abdullah Majid, studied at Raffles College, precursor to the UNIVERSITY OF MALAYA. He was a contemporary of JAMES PUTHUCHEARY, and was an editor of *Malayan Undergrad*, which became a conduit for Malayan nationalist sentiment amongst students. Dollah was detained for his activities in the Anti-British League in January 1951, along with activists such as JOHN EBER, SAMAD ISMAIL, C.V. DEVAN NAIR and James Puthucheary. After a year and a half in detention, he was released, returning to the University of Malaya shortly thereafter to continue his studies. He then joined with Puthucheary to form the university's Socialist Club. He went back to Malaya in 1961 to work for the Socialist Front-controlled Georgetown City Council in Penang, and then later in the Dewan Bahasa dan Pustaka.

In 1966, Dollah became senior liaison officer at the Ministry of Information and Broadcasting, and in July 1968, assistant director for external information at the

Dong Zhi: family making tang yuan.

Ministry of Foreign Affairs. In 1970, Tun Razak appointed Dollah as his press secretary, and in 1974 Dollah contested and won the seat of Raub. He was then appointed deputy minister of labour. In 1976, he was detained under the INTERNAL SECURITY ACT for alleged 'pro-communist activities' and was released two years later. Dollah then worked for the Malaysian National Bureau of Language and Literature, and was reinstated as a member of the United Malay National Organisation (UMNO) in 1982. In later years, Dollah suffered a stroke and was bedridden.

Donaldson & Burkinshaw Singapore's oldest surviving law firm. It was originally established by Alexander Muirhead Aitken, Alexander Leathes Donaldson and John Burkinshaw in 1874 as Aitken, Donaldson & Burkinshaw. The firm gained its current name in 1879, when Aitken retired. All three original partners of the firm were active in public life in Singapore. When Singapore was part of Malaysia, the firm maintained offices in Singapore, Johor, Kuala Lumpur, Jesselton (present-day Kota Kinabalu) and Sandakan. After SEPARATION, the firm restricted its practice to Singapore.

dondang sayang Malay and Peranakan musical genre. The name means literally 'to sing with love'. It originated in Malacca in the 15th century and incorporates singing and the Malay *pantun* (rhyming quatrains). The singers, usually a male and female couple, exchange poems spontaneously, or what Malays call '*berbalas pantun*', during their singing. Usually, these ditties are words of advice and friendly sarcasm that provide comic relief to listeners. It is a challenging genre, because a good singer must be able to compose and sing *pantun*s on the spot. The *pantun*s are accompanied throughout by a violin, accordion, gong and *rebana* (drum). The tempo is slow and melancholic. There are different types of *dondang sayang*, such as *dondang sayang* Malacca and *dondang sayang* Baba Peranakan. These are differentiated by the way the *pantun*s are sung. PERANAKANS consider the *dondang sayang* to be a part of their culture.

In the early 1980s, *dondang sayang* was regularly featured on Malay television, in a programme called *Kelab Dondang Sayang* (Dondang Sayang Club). *Dondang sayang* is

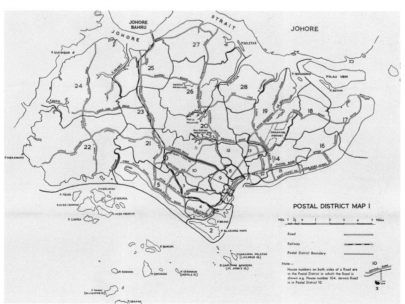

Dongxi Yangkao

kept alive in Malay cultural events and festivals. Traditional music groups such as Sri Mahligai perform *dondang sayang* and other traditional music genres at MALAY WEDDINGS and concerts.

Dong Zhi Literally 'arrival of winter', Dong Zhi is a Chinese festival celebrating the winter solstice. In ancient China, Dong Zhi was the second most important festival in the lunar calendar (after CHINESE NEW YEAR). Occurring on the 15th day of the 11th lunar month, it is the last festival on the lunar calendar.

Dong Zhi was originally the Chinese farmers' celebration of the year-end harvest. It falls on the longest night of the year for people living in the northern hemisphere, when the sun is at the tropic of Capricorn. According to the Chinese concept of *yin* and *yang*, the *yin* qualities of darkness and cold are at their peak on this day. Following this period will be the *yang* qualities of light and warmth, which represent new life and optimism. In fact, some Chinese emperors celebrated Chinese New Year on Dong Zhi.

Chinese families gather on Dong Zhi to give thanks for a good year, and celebrate it by eating *tang yuan*. These rice flour balls may have stuffings such as sesame seed or

red bean paste, and are served in a clear soup typically made of sugar and water, and seasoned with pandan leaves and ginger. Farming communities in China used to eat hot *tang yuan* because of the cold of winter. The word '*tang*' (meaning 'soup') sounds like '*tuan*' (meaning 'reunion'); '*yuan*' means 'round', and in the phrase '*yuan man*,' means 'complete'. *Tang yuan* thus signifies unity and prosperity for the family.

In Singapore, Dong Zhi is observed mainly by followers of CHINESE RELIGION, although a few Chinese restaurants promote the festival for commercial reasons.

Dongxi Yangkao Historical text detailing China's maritime relations with other countries. Written by Zhang Xie, and published in 1617 by the prefectural government of Zhangpu, Fujian, the *Dongxi Yangkao* (Treatise of the Eastern and Western Oceans) contains information accrued by the Chinese over the preceding three centuries, as well as during the Admiral ZHENG HE voyages. Chapter nine of the text, entitled 'The Ship Captain's Treatise', contains an entry on LONGYAMEN (Dragon's Tooth Strait/Keppel Straits). The entry notes that vessels sailing through the strait were often attacked by pirates from the immediate region. Zhang Xie acknowledged that this entry was adapted from the XINCHA SHENGLAN.

Double 10th incident The torture of civilian internees by Japanese military police. On 10 October 1943, the Japanese military police (KEMPEITAI) began taking civilian internees from CHANGI PRISON to the Kempeitai's headquarters in the old YMCA building on Orchard Road, and torturing them there. The Japanese mistakenly believed that the internees had been involved in providing intelligence to saboteurs in Malaya who the Japanese believed had sunk six Japanese cargo ships and an oil tanker in Singapore waters on 26 September 1943. At that time, the Japanese

Drama Box: performance of The Happy Prince, *2005.*

did not know that the sabotage had been the result of OPERATION JAYWICK—an operation launched independently from Australia. In the days and months that followed the first arrests, increasing numbers of civilian internees were taken to the YMCA building. A total of 57 internees were tortured. Of these, 15 men were tortured to death, while one was executed.

A war crimes trial of the perpetrators of the 'Double 10th incident'—as the episode came to be known due to the fact that it had commenced on the tenth day of the tenth month—was held from 18 March to 15 April 1946. Nineteen Kempeitai and two Chinese interpreters were accused. Eight were sentenced to death, seven received long jail sentences and six were acquitted. One of the convicted Chinese, Toh Swee Koon, was given the death sentence. However, on account of Toh's British citizenship, he was later tried by a civilian court and received a long jail sentence instead.

Dragon Boat Festival See DUAN WU JIE.

Drama Box Formed in 1990 by a group of National University of Singapore graduates, this is one of Singapore's most prominent Chinese-language contemporary theatre companies. In 1998, Drama Box became a full-time company, and moved from its original home at Telok Ayer Arts Centre to premises in Trengganu Street. In 2004, the company set up an education unit named NeNeMas (pronounced 'nanimous'), which stands for 'Never Neglect Mankind'.

Drama Box is under the artistic direction of KOK HENG LEUN. Its stage productions are often satirical and frequently abstract, including original works such as *Beautiful Day* and *Shithole*, and adaptations such as *The vaginaLOGUE* and *Cloud Nine*. The company is also known for its aim to heighten social awareness through community theatre. These short skits, which tour in housing estates, incorporate audience participation, and deal with issues of topical relevance. Past productions have dealt with domestic violence, AIDS, the plight of the elderly in Singapore, and others. Until 2004, this was a format discouraged through a lack of public funding. The lack of funds resulted in the group temporarily ceasing operations

Drama Box: poster for *Cloud Nine, 2003.*

Dondang sayang: *Peranakans enjoying* dondang sayang.

Duan Wu Jie: dragon-boat race (top); and zongzi, *rice dumpling eaten during the festival.*

in 2003. In 2005, Drama Box once again became a full-time theatre company.

Drama Centre Theatrical venue. The original Drama Centre was built in 1954 as the Cultural Centre in Fort Canning Park, and was officially opened by Chief Minister David Marshall in 1955. In 1980, it was renamed the Drama Centre.

Since its inception, the centre was a major venue for the performance of local productions, ranging from landmark Singapore plays such as *Lao Jiu* and *Army Daze,* to school drama productions. In 2002, the centre was closed and subsequently demolished to make way for the expansion of the Singapore History Museum. A new Drama Centre was officially opened at the new National Library building in November 2005.

Drew & Napier Law firm. It was established by Alfred Henry Drew and Sir Walter John Napier in 1889. Drew, who qualified as a solicitor in the United Kingdom in 1881, originally practised alongside Isaac Swinburne Bond until the latter retired in 1886. Drew then practised alone before being joined by Napier—a legal scholar, practitioner, Freemason, Unofficial member of the Legislative Council and attorney-general. Drew & Napier LLC is now one of Singapore's largest law firms, and has a joint law venture with international law firm Freshfields Bruckhaus Deringer.

DSO National Laboratories Military research and development body. Since its inception, DSO National Laboratories has focused on research and development in defence technologies, particularly electronic warfare systems. It has also embarked on projects relating to electronic surveillance, radio receivers, radar technology, encryption modules and combat simulations.

In 1971, defence minister GOH KENG SWEE founded the Electronic Warfare Study Group to undertake clandestine defence research. The three-man group in 1973 became the Electronics Test Centre, led by university lecturer TAY ENG SOON. In 1977, the group was merged with the System Integration and Management Team and was renamed the Defence Science Organisation (DSO). In 1979, PHILIP YEO took control of DSO and introduced a new expansion and recuitment plan.

The Gulf War in 1991 reinforced the Cabinet's awareness of the importance of defence R&D, and resulted in greater support to DSO. That year, DSO was granted Executive Agency status with greater autonomy. In 1997, DSO became DSO National Laboratories, a non-profit corporation.

Duan Wu Jie Festival. Celebrated on the fifth day of the fifth month in the lunar calendar, Duan Wu Jie (Fifth Moon Festival) is also known as the Dragon Boat Festival, and Dumpling Festival. It commemorates the death of Qu Yuan, an official in the kingdom of Chu during the Warring States (475 to 221 BCE). He was vilified by a corrupt prince, disgraced and dismissed. Heartbroken that the state was headed by corrupt leadership, Qu killed himself by jumping into the Mi Lo River (in today's Hunan province). Although many fishermen searched for his body, it was not found.

Every year, the people of Chu would throw rice into the river to feed his hungry ghost, until, one year, his spirit appeared and told them that the rice had been eaten by a river dragon. They were told to wrap the rice in silk and bind these dumplings with five different-coloured threads before tossing them into the water. One version of the tale has the dumplings thrown into the water to feed the marine creatures so that Qu's body would not become fish fodder. Another version has the fishermen thrashing the water with their paddles so that the sea animals would leave Qu's food, and body, alone.

During Duan Wu Jie, *zongzi* (Mandarin for dumpling) is eaten in remembrance of Qu. It is a leaf-wrapped glutinous rice pudding with ingredients such as beans, lotus seeds, chestnuts, pork fat and the yolk of a salted duck's egg. Each pyramid-shaped dumpling is wrapped with two bamboo leaves, bound with durable dried raffia made from leaves, and boiled in salt water for many hours, before it is ready for consumption. Modern-day Singapore offers a variety of stuffings ranging from black pepper chicken to peanut and vegetables, red bean paste and black-eyed peas.

The dragon-boat races represent the attempts to rescue and recover Qu's body. These races became popular in the Tang dynasty (618 to 907 CE) and spread rapidly to other Chinese-populated regions, including Singapore, where dragon-boat races have been organized for over 20 years.

The dragon is regarded as a symbol of power in Asia, and amongst the Chinese, it is believed to dominate the waters. A typical boat is between 15 and 30 m long, and painted in the bright colours of a dragon, complete with a specially constructed head and scaly tail. The two most basic rites for a boat involve its 'awakening' and its 'repose'.

Four days before the festival, the dragon boat is taken out of storage so that the head and tail can be attached. The elaborate ritual, which is believed to ward off evil and bless the boats, includes the burning of paper money, offerings, and prayers to the gods. When the ceremony is completed, the boat is rowed to sea and back, with the drummer beating the drum rhythmically. The procedure is carried out three times.

A new dragon boat is given 'life' at a ceremony performed by a Taoist priest a few days before the festival. With a bell and a sword piercing a paper bill, he chants and then proceeds to anoint the dragon head, tail and drum with the sword. The bill is burnt and the ashes sprinkled on the dragon head. The invited VIP guest, usually a community leader, will dot the eye in a symbolic gesture to 'awaken' the dragon. The eyes will be painted red later.

After the races, the dragon head, tail and drum are removed from the boat and stored. Incense is burnt to thank the gods, and the boat is returned to the storage-yard racks to 'repose' until the next use. In modern-day Singapore, these regatta-style races are held at the KALLANG RIVER, and are filled with colour, pageantry and noise.

Duclos, John Henry (1915–) Broadcaster and diplomat. John Henry Duclos was educated at the King Edward VII School in Taiping, Perak; the Anglo-Chinese School; St Andrew's School in Singapore; and Merton College, Oxford University. After graduating, Duclos joined the Advertising and Publicity Bureau in 1935. In 1938, he became a broadcaster. Duclos was made head of the Malay Service (Radio) in 1946, and remained in that post for ten years. In 1957, he was seconded to become head of Broadcasting in Brunei. In 1960, Duclos returned to Singapore to become controller of programmes in the Broadcasting Division of the Ministry of Culture. He also served as head of the Broadcasting Division and was later appointed Singapore's deputy high commissioner to Malaysia. He was awarded the MERITORIOUS SERVICE MEDAL in 1963.

Ducroux, Joseph (Serge Lefranc) (1904– unknown) Political activist. Born in Belleville-sur-Saone, Rhone, France, Joseph Ducroux was educated in the United Kingdom and France. At the age of 19, Ducroux became involved with the French Communist Party. Between 1926 and 1929, he acted as secretary to J.H. Dolsen of the Pan-Pacific Trade Union Secretariat (PPTUS), a Comintern organization responsible for directing communist activities in China and Southeast Asia. By this time, Ducroux had already become a Comintern agent.

In 1931, Ducroux travelled—under both his own name and the alias Serge Lefranc—to Asia. After a short stay in Shanghai, where he liaised with other Comintern agents, he arrived in Singapore on 27 April. His mission in Singapore was to conduct a survey of the Malayan communist movement; establish closer links between the MALAYAN COMMUNIST PARTY (MCP) and the PPTUS in Shanghai; and provide the MCP and its labour arm, the General Labour Union (GLU), with Comintern subsidies. Ducroux was also allocated resources to finance communist organizations in Malaya.

Ducroux was put under surveillance by the SPECIAL BRANCH, and was arrested on 1 June 1931 for possessing seditious literature. He was tried before the District Court in June 1931, and was sentenced to an 18-month prison term. However, the British were anxious to move Ducroux out of Singapore, and he was deported to Saigon (present-day Ho Chi Minh City) in August that year. Little is known of his movements thereafter.

durians Tropical fruit. Durian (*Durio zibenthinus*) is also known as the 'king of fruits'. It has a thick, thorny skin. Inside, the fleshy pulp of the seeds is edible.

In *The Malay Archipelago* (1869), the great naturalist Alfred Russel Wallace described the flavour of the fruit in these terms: 'A rich butter-like custard highly flavoured with almonds gives the best general idea of it, but intermingled with it comes wafts of flavour that call to mind cream-cheese, onion-sauce, brown sherry, and other incongruities. Then there is a rich glutinous smoothness in the pulp which nothing else possesses, but which adds to its delicacy. It is neither acid, nor sweet, nor juicy, yet one feels the want of none of these qualities, for it is perfect as it is. It produces no nausea, or other bad effect, and the more you eat of it, the less you feel inclined to stop. In fact, to eat durians is a new sensation, worth a voyage to the east to experience.'

Duxton Hill

Charles Dyce: The Old Bridge, Singapore *(1842).*

The durian is also noted for its strong, pungent odour, compared variously to that of an open sewer or rotten onions. The smell tends to put off people who have not grown up with it. As Wallace noted: 'When brought into a house the smell is often so offensive that some persons can never bear to taste it.' The durian is banned from the carriages of the Mass Rapid Transit (MRT) system and many other public places.

Wild durian species grow in Singapore's forests. One species is named *Durio singaporensis*—it is the size of a fist and has no edible flesh. Varieties of durian have been developed to suit different tastes, and devotees can buy durian cream puffs, durian ice-cream and even durian mooncakes.

Duxton Hill Conservation area on the fringe of Chinatown. The Duxton Hill area, which includes Duxton Park and Duxton Road, is a former nutmeg plantation. The plantation was owned by Dr J.W. Montgomerie (1797–1856) and covered an area of about 13 ha. Montgomerie had two houses on the plantation, one of which was named 'Duxton'. It was named after another house of the same name owned by Montgomerie's good friend, Dr JOSÉ D'ALMEIDA.

When Montgomerie died in 1856, the property was sold and the site developed. Even so, it continued to be called Duxton Hill. The Rev Dickenson built a children's home in the vicinity (now the Kreta Ayer Community Centre), and the hill came to be known as Dickenson Hill or Bukit Padre. SHOPHOUSES lined Duxton Road and Duxton Hill, although the two streets were populated by rather different groups of people: Duxton Road was the home of brothels, opium and gambling dens while the ornate houses along Duxton Hill were home to many wealthy Straits Chinese families. Today, Duxton Hill is an important CONSERVATION AREA and most of its build-

ings have been adapted for re-use as shops, offices and restaurants.

Dyce, Charles (1816–1853) Scottish trader and amateur watercolourist. Born in Aberdeen, Scotland, Charles Andrew Dyce was educated at Marischal College, where he graduated with a master of arts degree in 1833. Dyce left for Calcutta, arriving in 1836, and worked for the agency house of Fergusson, Brothers & Co. until 1842. On 13 March 1842, Dyce arrived in Singapore to join his family's trading firm.

A good amateur watercolourist, Dyce painted Singapore's rapidly developing urban scene, and rural landscapes and seascapes in Malacca, Penang, Java and Singapore. He also produced an embellished manuscript, which was intended to accompany paintings presented to Governor WILLIAM BUTTERWORTH.

Dyce is remembered mainly for the collection of 35 watercolour paintings and a 22-page manuscript illuminating his travels in the region, now in the MUSEUM, NUS CENTRE FOR THE ARTS. He left Singapore around the end of 1847 and died in Calcutta.

Durians

E

Early Founders' Memorial Stone

East India Company: coin minted by the company in 1804 (top); the company crest.

East Coast Park: recreational use of reclaimed land.

Early Founders' Memorial Stone This memorial was commissioned by Alumni International Singapore in 1969 to commemorate the 150th anniversary of the FOUNDING OF SINGAPORE and early migrants of all races. It consists of a four-sided granite block mounted on a brick pedestal. The four faces of the stone are inscribed in Singapore's four official languages. It was laid on 18 January 1970 by President Yusof Ishak at Collyer Quay, facing the Fullerton Building. It was moved across the road in 1994; and to its present position outside the National Archives of Singapore at 1 Canning Rise in 1998.

East Asia Summit The origins of the East Asia Summit (EAS) can be traced to Malaysian Prime Minister Mahathir Mohamed's proposal for an East Asian Economic Grouping (EAEG), which was mooted in the early 1990s in response to the rise of the European Union's single market and the North American Free Trade Area.

However, opposition from the United States, and hesitation on the part of Japan and other countries, ensured that the idea did not develop. The ASIAN FINANCIAL CRISIS of 1997 gave the concept a new lease of life as it created a new and urgent rationale for regional financial cooperation to prevent future economic crises. The idea of East Asian regionalism also gained momentum with the failure of ASIA-PACIFIC ECONOMIC COOPERATION (APEC) to deal with the 1997 crisis and the growing economic links amongst East Asian nations, partly induced by the economic dynamism of China. Intra-Asian trade and investment has boomed and globalization has led to the evolution of an East Asian manufacturing platform.

The report of the East Asian Vision Group, set up at the behest of former South Korean President Kim Dae Jung, and released in 2001, offered a blueprint for an East Asian regional grouping based on economic interdependence, shared political outlook and a desire for a common identity. The momentum led to the formation of an annual summit meeting—consisting of the ten members of the ASSOCIATION OF SOUTH EAST ASIAN NATIONS (ASEAN) together with China, Japan and South Korea—known as ASEAN+3.

The inaugural East Asian Summit was held in Kuala Lumpur on 14 December 2005. It was attended by the leaders of the ten members of ASEAN, plus those of South Korea, China, Japan, India, Australia and New Zealand. This ASEAN+3+3 formula was the result of a compromise between those who wanted to keep the summit an exclusively 'East Asian' affair, and those—including Singapore—who wished to see a regional forum that would be more open and inclusive. The EAS is seen by many to be the first step towards the realization of an East Asian Community.

East Asian Institute Research Institute. The East Asian Institute (EAI) was established in April 1997 under a statute of the National University of Singapore, succeeding the former Institute of East Asian Political Economy (IEAPE), which had been established by Goh Keng Swee in 1983 for the study of CONFUCIANISM. The EAI is devoted to the study of developments in East Asia, focusing on contemporary China, with plans to expand its coverage to Japan and Korea. The EAI's long-term vision is to become the region's foremost research institution specializing in East Asian development. Its founding director is Professor WANG GUNGWU, former professor of Far Eastern history at the Australian National University and vice-chancellor of the University of Hong Kong. The institute has a staff of research fellows and a specialist library with collections of English and Chinese materials on China and East Asia. Its main collections cover the fields of economics, politics, sociology, law, culture, foreign relations as well as trade and investment in China.

East Coast Name generally used for the residential area on Singapore's eastern coastline. The old East Coast was associated with large weekend homes on the seafront, east of the Kallang River. After extensive land reclamation, the name is now applied to the stretch of East Coast and Upper East Coast roads stretching from Mountbatten Road to Bedok. The East Coast Parkway is a highway leading all the way to Changi Airport on Singapore's eastern tip, and East Coast Park (built on reclaimed land) is one of Singapore's most popular recreational destinations, with holiday chalets, bicycle rentals, rollerblade tracks and artificial beaches.

East India Company Trading company that built the British empire in India and

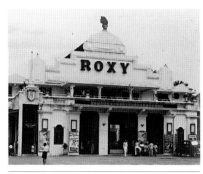

East Coast: Roxy Theatre, East Coast Road.

Southeast Asia; also known as the British East India Company. When it was first granted a monopoly charter by Queen Elizabeth I on 31 December 1600, it was known as the Governor and the Company of Merchants of London, Trading into the East Indies. It later became the United Company of Merchants of England Trading to the East Indies after merging with a younger rival in 1702. It was also known as the 'Honourable East India Company' or, simply, 'John Company'.

The maiden voyage of the company in 1601 was successful, with the fleet returning safely in 1603 laden with peppercorns after freebooting and trading through India, Aceh and Java. It established a trading post at Bantam, Java, which operated until 1683, when the Dutch persuaded the local ruler to evict the company. The outpost was moved to BENCOOLEN (Fort Marlborough), Sumatra, where it became a collecting centre for pepper.

However, it was in India that the company's future really lay: Indian cotton cloth, along with pepper, became an important trade item in both Southeast Asia and Europe. The company's first foothold was in Madras in 1640, followed by Bombay in 1668 and Calcutta in 1690. With the decline of the Mughal Empire in the 18th century, the company was able to expand significantly, pushing out the French, and eventually ruling the whole subcontinent.

At the end of the 17th century, the company had a presence in Bencoolen and Penang. Sir STAMFORD RAFFLES was an agent of the company, and in 1818 was made lieutenant-governor of Bencoolen. In 1819, Raffles sailed to Singapore and signed an agreement with Temenggong ABDUL RAHMAN to set up a trading post. In 1824, the *temenggong* and the sultan ceded all of Singapore to the East India Company, and its heirs, in perpetuity.

Singapore would continue to be held by the company, until it was dissolved in 1858. Thereafter, Singapore was administered by the British government's India Office, though out of Calcutta.

Eastern Orthodox Church The term 'orthodox' is applied to a number of Christian churches whose origins lie in a split during the 9th–11th centuries between Christians in the West, who came to be known as 'Catholic', and those in the East, who came to be known as 'Orthodox'. The Eastern Orthodox Church in Singapore falls under the Orthodox Metropolitanate of Hong Kong and Southeast Asia of the Ecumenical Patriarchate of Constantinople (the other patriarchates being Alexandria, Antioch and Jerusalem).

The history of this church in Singapore is relatively short. Early efforts to organize worshippers began in the early 1970s, when a deacon of the Eastern Orthodox Church, Father Peter Danilchick, was posted to Singapore as an executive for a petrochemical firm. He organized prayer and Bible study sessions in his home. During his second posting to Singapore in the early 1990s, he arranged for a priest to come from Bangkok once a month to conduct communion. Space at the ARMENIAN CHURCH was rented for the services.

During this time, Singapore was nominally under the diocese of New Zealand. However, in 1997, the Orthodox Metropolitanate of Hong Kong and Southeast Asia was formed, and Singapore was re-grouped under this new diocese. In October 2000, the church was registered as a charity in Singapore. In November 2002, the Holy Resurrection Orthodox Church moved to River Valley Road. It joined the National Council of Churches in 2003.

The regular congregation has grown from about eight in the 1990s to about 40 in 2005. It contains over 18 nationalities, with Singaporeans now the largest group.

The Eastern Orthodox Church should not be confused with the Armenian Apostolic Church or the community of SYRIAN CHRISTIANS.

Eastern Sun English-language broadsheet daily newspaper, launched in July 1966 by Dato Aw Kow, the eldest son of businessman and newspaper magnate AW BOON HAW. The *Eastern Sun* faced problems from its inception. It began its short but influential life just after Singapore's separation from Malaysia in 1965. Malaysian authorities required newspapers published in Singapore to set up a Malaysian edition if they wanted to continue circulation in Malaysia. Refusing to comply, the *Eastern Sun* withdrew from the Malaysian market—its primary advertising base—in 1968, creating huge financial problems for the company.

With limited resources, it could not compete with the more established papers. Compounding the newspaper's financial problems were allegations of its alleged involvement in covert activities financed and organized by foreign elements outside Singapore, suspicions that were exacerbated by the communist insurgency in Malaya (see EMERGENCY). The *Eastern Sun* continued to record heavy losses until it closed down in 1971 after a government disclosure that it

Ecnad Project: performance at Suntec City, 1997.

had received nearly HK$8 million from an alleged communist source in Hong Kong,

Eastern Telegraph Company John Pender, a trader in cotton in Glasgow and Manchester, invested in the Anglo-Irish Magnetic Telegraph Company in 1852 before becoming a director of the Atlantic Telegraph Company in 1856. He invested further in telegraphy, initiating the construction of submarine cables internationally and founding a number of telegraph companies.

As Singapore was an important trading centre, cables were laid to link Singapore with Penang and Madras. In 1869, Pender formed the China Submarine Telegraph Company to link Singapore and Hong Kong with a cable which was completed in 1871. In 1872, cables were also laid to connect Singapore with Batavia (present-day Jakarta) in Java, and Australia. The company was merged with other, smaller firms to form the Eastern Telegraph Company that same year.

By 1900, the Eastern and its associated companies held a virtual monopoly on telegraph communications throughout the British Empire, which remained unchallenged until the emergence of long-distance wireless radio communication in the 1920s. Telegraph lines were extended to South America by smaller companies which were taken over by the Eastern, which was renamed the Eastern and Associated Companies. This group suffered the impact of short-wave radio transmissions which were cheaper and could handle speech. The cable and the wireless resources of the British Empire were merged in 1929, operating under the name Imperial and International Communications. This was changed to Cable & Wireless in 1934.

Eating Air (1999) Film co-directed by KELVIN TONG and Jasmine Ng. Lauded as a refreshing look at Chinese working-class youth culture, the film was an innovative mélange of styles—equally acknowledging kung fu and biker movies—which capitalized on the portrayal of local archetypes. Telling the tale of hoodlum Ah Boy, his friends and his girlfriend, Ah Lian, drifting

through the city on their motorbikes, the film was noted for its strong art direction and aesthetic qualities, and successfully avoided falling into the trap of teen movie clichés. It won the Young Cinema Award at the 2000 SINGAPORE INTERNATIONAL FILM FESTIVAL and the FIPRESCI Prize at the 2000 Stockholm International Film Festival.

Eber, John (1916–) Lawyer and political activist. John Francis St John Eber was born in Singapore and was educated at Harrow School and Cambridge University. After World War II, Eber became involved in nationalist activities and, in his capacity as a lawyer, defended workers and left-wing union leaders. From 1946 to 1947, he served on the Executive Committee of the MALAYAN DEMOCRATIC UNION (MDU) and rose to become its vice-chairman. When in London, he was an active spokesman for PUTERA-AMCJA (Pusat Tenaga Ra'ayat [Centre for People's Power]-All Malaya Council for Joint Action). In 1951, the colonial authorities detained Eber—along with C.V. DEVAN NAIR, then secretary of the SINGAPORE TEACHERS' UNION and SAMAD ISMAIL, then chief sub-editor of UTUSAN MELAYU—for involvement in subversive activities. Upon release in February 1953, Eber left for London where he remained for many years. Together with his brother-in-law Wan Hamid and intellectual LIM HONG BEE, he captured the leadership of the London-based discussion group the MALAYAN FORUM, becoming its secretary. In February 1956, Eber and his committee were ousted from the group on a motion of no-confidence led by GOH KENG SWEE.

Ecnad Project Dance company. Founded as Dance Dimension Project in 1996 by Lim Chin Huat and Tan How Choon, it is known for its outreach efforts in outdoor venues and visually affective dance theatre. It debuted at THE SUBSTATION with *Ecnad—Dance from the E Point* (1996). In 1999, it launched Fresh From The Oven, the first talent development workshop for budding dance artists in Singapore. A one-time Seed Grant from the National Arts Council spurred its transition to Ecnad ('dance' spelled backwards) Project in 2001. That year, it became the first Singaporean arts group to perform at the Belgrade International Theatre Festival, where it presented *a-the-bird* (2000) and *Floating Mirror* (2001). In 2002, Ecnad staged *Missing in Tall Pillars*—a Singapore Arts Festival commission—at the Asian Civilisations Museum in Empress Place.

Economic Development Board Statutory board. The Economic Development Board (EDB) was established in 1961 to attract foreign investment and spearhead Singapore's INDUSTRIALIZATION programme. Singapore's early industrial base consisted largely of low-skilled, labour-intensive gar-

Eastern Sun: Final issue, 14 May 1971.

Eating Air (1999)

ECONOMY: MAJOR ECONOMIC INDICATORS, 2005	
GDP (at current market prices)	$194.4 b
Per capita GDP	$44,666
Per capita GNP (at current market prices)	$44,455
Annual inflation rate	0.5 %
Total trade	$715.7 b
Exports	$382.5 b
Domestic exports	$207.4 b
Imports	$333.2 b
Current account balance	$55.4 b
Capital and financial account balance	$33.7 b
Overall balance of payment	$20.4 b
Foreign direct investment (2004)	$272.6 b
Singapore's direct investment abroad (2004)	$172.2 b
Official foreign reserves at year-end	$193.6 b
Money supply (M1)	$46.1 b
Labour force	2.37 m
Employed persons	2.27 m
Unemployment rate at year-end (seasonally adjusted)	3.4 %
Labour force participation (population aged 15 years and over)	67.4 %
Visitor arrivals (excluding Malaysian arrivals by land)	8.9 m
Sea cargo volume	423.2 m freight tons
Air cargo volume	1.84 m tons

Source: Singapore Department of Statistics

Economy: Schering Plough's second major pharma-ceuticals manufacturing facility in Singapore, opened 1999.

$194.4 billion, which placed it amongst the largest 40 economies in the world. Having grown by 5.7 per cent per year on average since Independence in 1965, its per capita GROSS NATIONAL PRODUCT (GNP), calculated in purchasing power parity terms, was $44,455 in 2005, making Singapore one of the richest countries in the world.

Singapore's economic rise can be traced to its colonial role as the ENTREPÔT of Southeast Asia, importing primary commodities from the regional hinterland and re-exporting them to the rest of the world. This entrepôt trade gave rise to supporting service industries and commercial activities such as shipping, bunkering, transportation, logistics, warehousing, wholesale trading, banking and insurance, all of which continue to be important. During the last three decades of the 20th century, Singapore developed into an international financial and business centre, offering stockbroking, foreign-exchange trading, fund management, real estate and advertising services. The financial and business services sector currently contributes slightly less than a quarter of real GDP and one in six jobs. In addition, ship repairing, aircraft servicing and oil-rig construction are important industries in modern Singapore.

When the process of INDUSTRIALIZATION started in the mid-1960s, the small size of Singapore's market of about 2 million people compelled the country to export the bulk of what was produced. A lack of natural resources, despite an excellent geographical location at the crossroads of international shipping routes, also meant that Singapore could not afford any form of protectionism. The overwhelming dependence on exports was matched by a similarly heavy reliance on imports of intermediate inputs and final consumption goods from the industrial economies. Today, import duties are essentially confined to a select few consumer items such as cars, perfume, liquor and tobacco. By 2005, total foreign trade amounted to more than three times the size of overall output, suggesting that external demand plays a very important role as an engine of growth.

Singapore's economic performance can partly be attributed to a buoyant world demand for Singapore-made products. In the early days, these comprised labour-intensive goods such as transistor radios, clothing and leather products. Since then,

there has been a continuous expansion of production capacity driven by FOREIGN DIRECT INVESTMENT (FDI) and companies which have been given incentives by the ECONOMIC DEVELOPMENT BOARD (EDB) to establish facilities in JURONG and other INDUSTRIAL ESTATES scattered across the island. Net investment commitments in manufacturing reached $8.52 billion in 2005, most of it destined for plant and machinery spending. The bulk of commitments came from foreign investors in the United States, Europe and Japan.

Multinational corporations (MNCs) play an important role in the Singapore economy. In 2003, foreign firms (wholly and majority foreign-owned) accounted for 71 per cent of net fixed assets in the manufacturing sector, 73 per cent of value-added and 44 per cent of employment. This extreme dependence on MNCs could well have stemmed inadvertently from the dearth of local entrepreneurs at the onset of the industrialization drive in the 1960s, but it also is the consequence of a deliberate government policy of cultivating foreign enterprise with a wide range of tax incentives and export benefits. In terms of output, the average foreign company produces 12 times the amount of the average local firm—typically a small or medium-sized enterprise (SME)—and is also more profitable. The domestic corporate sector, by contrast, has been perceived to be fragile and inefficient in spite of a slew of government assistance schemes.

If the heights of the economy are occupied by the MNCs, then standing on their shoulders are the hundreds of GOVERNMENT-LINKED COMPANIES (GLCs) mainly owned by TEMASEK HOLDINGS. These are, *inter alia*, corporatized or privatized public enterprises and statutory boards which provide utilities, banking, property, telecommunications, port, shipping and airline services (Power Supply, DBS BANK, CAPITALAND, SINGTEL, PSA INTERNATIONAL, NEPTUNE ORIENT LINES and SINGAPORE AIRLINES, respectively). In recent years, GLCs have expanded overseas in line with the government's exhortation to 'grow a second wing'. They and Temasek are in the

ment and textile factories. With the loss of the Malaysian hinterland after Singapore's independence in 1965, the EDB embarked on an export-led industrialization strategy. Through co-investments with the private sector, the EDB helped launch several capital-intensive projects in the OIL-REFINING SECTOR, as well as in ship-building and repair.

This was followed by investments in the ELECTRONICS SECTOR in the 1970s, while the 1980s saw an upsurge of investments in more capital-intensive industries and the establishment of wafer fabrication plants. With the emphasis on knowledge-intensive activities in the 1980s, the EDB began to promote cluster development in the electronics, petrochemical and engineering sectors, as well as launching an aggressive plan to develop Singapore into a biomedical hub for the region. In 1999, Technopreneurship 21 was started to provide a conducive environment for technological entrepreneurs. Further schemes and initiatives, such as Start-up EnterprisE Development Scheme (SEEDS), aim to make funds accessible to investors and encourage the venture capital industry.

economy Singapore has a land area of just 699 sq km and a labour force of 2.37 million workers, yet its real GROSS DOMESTIC PRODUCT (GDP) in 2005 amounted to

ECONOMY: SELECTED ECONOMIC INDICATORS, 2003										
	Singapore	Australia	Canada	Hong Kong SAR	Japan	Korea	New Zealand	Taiwan	United Kingdom	United States
Real growth in GDP (%)	2.9	3.8	1.7	3.1	-0.1	3.1	4.7	3.3	2.5	3.0
Per capita GNP (US$)	21,524	21,960	24,470	25,110	34,190	12,720	15,530	13,139	28,320	37,995
Unemployment rate (%)	3.7	5.8	7.6	7.9	5.3	3.6	4.6	5.0	5.0	6.0
Labour force participation rate (%)										
Males	76	72	73	72	74	75	73	68	71	74
Females	54	56	62	52	48	49	59	47	56	60
Inflation rate (%)	0.5	2.	2.8	-2.6	-0.3	3.6	1.5	-0.3	1.4	2.3

Source: Singapore Department of Statistics

Economy: Singapore's Keppel Corporation is a major builder of oil rigs.

Economy: stamp celebrating economic achievements since the Founding of Singapore.

vanguard of Singapore's outward investments across the globe, both direct and portfolio, which amounted to $294 billion by end-2003.

Manufacturing will continue to be a leading sector in Singapore, especially in view of the government's plan to double its output by 2018. Unlike in Hong Kong, there appears to be no imminent danger of a 'hollowing-out' taking place, despite the fact that a number of companies are outsourcing their operations to lower-cost countries. As at 2005, industrial output accounts for 26 per cent of GDP and 21 per cent of total employment. The major pillars of the manufacturing sector are electronics, refined oil, petrochemicals, pharmaceuticals and biomedical products. Within manufacturing, the electronics industry is dominant. It attracts more than half of inward FDI and generates about half of Singapore's non-oil exports. Furthermore, these statistics underestimate the true importance of the industry. The health of supporting industries in precision engineering, for example, is affected by the electronics industry, while the vibrancy of the seaport and airport is directly dependent on the cargo volumes generated by Singapore-made exports as well as re-exports of electronic components and parts.

Not surprisingly then, swings in the global demand for electronic products are a potent cause of domestic business cycles.

Economy: circuit-board manufacture, Venture Corp.

When the information technology (IT) industry suffered a massive downturn in 2000–01, Singapore's economic growth rate swung wildly from 10 per cent in one year to -2 per cent in the next, plunging the country into its worst recession on record (see RECESSIONS). At the same time, shipments of non-electronic goods hinge critically on general economic conditions in Singapore's biggest markets, namely Malaysia, the European Union, the United States, Indonesia, Hong Kong, China and Japan—in that order of importance. In keeping with its economic philosophy, Singapore has signed a number of regional or bilateral FREE TRADE AGREEMENTS (FTAs) with its major trading partners, including some of the countries listed above.

Singapore's small and open economy has been instrumental in shaping the *modus operandi* of macroeconomic policies. The most obvious instance of this influence is in the conduct of monetary policy. Due to the large import content of domestic consumption and production, the MONETARY AUTHORITY OF SINGAPORE (MAS), has chosen to fight imported inflation by strengthening the external value of the Singapore dollar against a weighted basket of currencies of Singapore's trade partners and competitors rather than by increasing local interest rates. Domestic interest rates tend to be quoted at a discount to US rates because market participants expect the Singapore dollar to appreciate most of the time. However, a currency that is too strong would have adverse effects on export competitiveness and, hence, economic growth. The MAS, therefore, has had to steer a delicate course to avoid both inflation and recession.

Due to the high propensity to import, fiscal policy is relatively ineffective in Singapore. The beneficial effects on the economy of an increase in government spending are limited. Consequently, the Singapore government has used public construction projects which add to the national capital stock rather than bonuses for civil servants to stimulate economic activity during recessions. A substantial proportion of the state's developmental and recurrent expenditures—constituting one-fifth of GDP in an average year—are spent on 'merit goods' such as education and healthcare, now also receiving attention as promising service export industries.

In terms of revenue, the government derives slightly over 40 per cent of its receipts from personal income and corporate taxes and the remainder from indirect sales taxes, such as the GOODS AND SERVICES TAX (GST), and fees and charges on public services rendered (see TAXATION). Overall, fiscal policy is extremely prudent, as a result of which, the government routinely accumulates budget surpluses in non-recessionary years. This is reflected in the large current account surpluses on the BALANCE OF PAYMENTS, which have overrun 20 per cent of GDP. At the same time, the country's official foreign reserves have steadily risen to US$116.6 billion by the end of 2005, providing more than 100 per cent backing for the local currency and underwriting the central bank's strong dollar policy.

One of the most enduring economic institutions in Singapore is the CENTRAL PROVIDENT FUND (CPF), a fully funded pension scheme into which employers and employees are each required to contribute a proportion of monthly salary. The CPF scheme has been successful in helping Singaporeans own their homes, though as a result, many elderly Singaporeans retire with homes, but inadequate savings. This is in spite of Singapore having one of the highest national savings rates in the world of over 40 per cent. In the past, domestic savings provided a cheap source of finance for public fixed capital formation in infrastructure and housing. But as the share of national income devoted to investment declined from a peak of 49 per cent in 1982 to 19 per cent in 2005, it meant that Singapore had become a net lender to the world. Through

Economy: container terminal.

the GOVERNMENT OF SINGAPORE INVESTMENT CORPORATION (GIC), most of the excess savings have been used to buy equities, bonds and real estate overseas, earning a rate of return which exceeds that of domestic assets and is certainly much higher than the interest paid on CPF balances. Such income from abroad has been more than sufficient to offset the repatriation of profits and wages by foreigners in Singapore back to their home countries.

Singapore has a liberal immigration policy. The long-term goal is to augment the stock of the working-age population—a total population of 5.5 million is targeted by the year 2040—to ensure that the supply of labour keeps pace with demand. Concurrently, the influx of migrant workers into the country is allowed on a short-term basis to alleviate labour shortages in specific industries. FOREIGN WORKERS currently account for nearly 30 per cent of the labour force and they not only serve as a buffer to the domestic workforce during bad times when workers have to be retrenched, but also help to sharpen Singapore's international competitiveness by holding wages down.

A unique feature of Singapore's political economy is the harmonious state of LABOUR RELATIONS. The symbiotic cooperation between workers, employers and the government is institutionalized in the NATIONAL WAGES COUNCIL (NWC), a tripartite body of employers, trade unions and officials formed in 1972 that collectively sets wage guidelines in the light of macro-economic conditions.

The near-term forecast for Singapore's economy is bright. The unemployment rate has fallen, incomes have rebounded and property prices are trending up. This suggests that the government's efforts to liberalize and restructure the economy have

Education: classroom scene, 1920s.

been successful. Coupled with reductions in rentals and business costs, Singapore is poised to compete with its regional rivals and benefit from the economic dynamism that is being released by China and India. Servicing the needs of these economies may add a percentage point or two to Singapore's projected economic growth rate of 3–5 per cent per annum. The decision to build two INTEGRATED RESORTS and the implementation of a five-day working week for civil servants have also had an impact. These measures are expected to revive consumer spending by residents and visitors alike, boost GDP by nearly 2 per cent and create more than 30,000 new jobs.

Yet challenges remain. Apart from the problems associated with an ageing population, structural unemployment in the form of a mismatch of skills between workers and jobs is on the rise due to technological change. For those in employment, there has been a widening of the gap between rich and poor, an official survey showing that the household incomes of the lowest 20 per cent of wage-earners stagnated between 1998 and 2003. This is the dilemma Singapore faces—how to remain relevant to the world without having to suffer the undesirable effects of globalization.

education The earliest efforts to provide educational facilities in Singapore were dogged by two problems: controversy over the medium of instruction and lack of adequate financial support. Although there was support in principle for vernacular education, only Malay qualified, and the financial policy at that time forbade any expansion of facilities. For much of the 19th century, the provision of educational facilities in English continued to be largely the responsibility of missionary bodies.

The period from 1900 to the outbreak of World War II saw an increasing compartmentalization of education: education in Christian MISSION SCHOOLS; community and estate-run Chinese and Tamil schools; education through the media of English, Chinese, Malay and Tamil; differences in

financial assistance, control and supervision and types of management; and differences in types of curricula, quality of teaching staff and teaching methods. If any pattern existed at all, it was one of confusion.

The main feature of the system was the existence of four categories of school: those divided according to medium of instruction; government schools; government-aided schools; and private schools. The latter three were almost exclusively Chinese- and English-medium, while Malay-medium education had government support. Additionally, there was a growing sense of hostility between the private Chinese schools and the government. The introduction of the Education Ordinance Bill in 1920 was significant as the first major attempt by the British government to control Chinese schools. The ordinance was politically motivated and designed to weed out what the government felt to be undesirable political ideologies spread in these schools.

In April 1946, an advisory council was set up. The council recognized the importance of giving priority to educational policy, and unveiled the Ten Years Programme, which was adopted in 1947. This was an attempt to relate educational policies to clearly defined goals. It adopted a broad integrative approach to the problem of vernacular education, and emphasized the development of civic loyalty and responsibility to Singapore by means of education and equal educational opportunity through support for MOTHER TONGUE education.

The Report of the All-Party Committee on Chinese Education in 1956 established the principle of equality of treatment for all schools, whether English-medium or vernacular. It committed the government to bilingualism based on the equality of the four languages—Mandarin, Malay, Tamil and English. The Chan Chieu Kiat Report (1961) and the Lim Tay Boh Report (1964) proposed refinements to the initial recommendations. The former laid the foundation for a diversification of school structure by recommending technical and

EDUCATION: FULL-TIME ENROLMENT, 2004

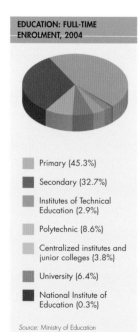

- Primary (45.3%)
- Secondary (32.7%)
- Institutes of Technical Education (2.9%)
- Polytechnic (8.6%)
- Centralized institutes and junior colleges (3.8%)
- University (6.4%)
- National Institute of Education (0.3%)

Source: Ministry of Education

Education: art class at Nanyang Girls' School (top); and science class at Ai Tong School.

vocational education; and the latter recommended changes in curriculum, teacher education and extra-curricular activities.

The government adopted English and three local languages (Chinese, Malay and Tamil) as official languages in 1956 and started compulsory bilingual education in 1966 at primary and in 1969 at secondary level. The bilingual policy requires students to learn two languages: English plus a mother tongue, which may be Malay, Chinese or Tamil. English is the working language in Singapore and the medium of instruction in schools. The policy is based on the premise that English is the language of international business, science and technology, and a high level of proficiency in it will give students access to opportunities globally. At the same time, the government asserts that it is important for students to learn their mother tongue for as long, and to as high a level, as possible, to give them access to their cultural heritage and help them retain their cultural identity and roots.

By the end of the 1970s, it was clear that the bilingual requirements were making excessive demands on students, many of whom were failing the Primary 6 examinations and leaving school prematurely. Many who went on to graduate from secondary school were not adequately bilingual. At that time, less than 40 per cent of the student population had the minimum competency level in two languages. Another problem was the low literacy rate. The Report on the Ministry of Education (Goh Report, 1978) proposed the introduction of ability-based streaming after three or four years of primary education, and the introduction of an ability-differentiated curriculum and extensions to the

length of schooling for weaker pupils. In practice, students were initially streamed after they had completed their Primary 3 year. In addition, students were streamed at the secondary level. This report heralded the 'efficiency-driven' phase in Singapore's educational development. This system was further tweaked by the postponement of streaming in primary school by one year (from Primary 3 to Primary 4), the Primary School Leaving Examination evolving into a placement examination and paving the way for all students to go on to secondary schools to complete an additional four to five years of secondary education.

The 'Thinking Schools, Learning Nation' initiative of 1997 was a mandate to overhaul the Singapore education system extensively, from pre-school to university admission criteria and curriculum. It highlighted the need for more emphasis on experimention, so as to produce pupils with critical and creative thinking skills, able to apply knowledge in solving problems, and to show initiative and enterprise. This led to a reduction of content of up to 30 per cent, introduction of project work, teaching of thinking skills and greater use of information technology.

In October 2002, the Committee on the Review of Junior College (JC)/Upper Secondary Education recommended a broader and more flexible JC curriculum and a more diverse JC/Upper Secondary landscape. The committee also recommended the introduction of the Integrated Programme to provide for a seamless upper secondary and JC education, and specialized schools to cater to exceptional talent in sports, mathematics and science.

In four decades, a divided, underresourced system has been transformed.

Ee Hoe Hean Club (now demolished).

Literacy rates are high. Singapore students have won international recognition for achievements in mathematics and science. Schools are well resourced and teachers have opportunities for professional development. The education system has been moving in recent years towards more flexibility and diversity, with the aim of giving students a greater degree of choice in learning.

Edusave Shortly after taking office as prime minister in December 1990, Goh Chok Tong announced a $5 billion scheme whereby Edusave accounts would be set up for all children between six and 16 years of age. The Edusave Endowment Fund was established in 1993 to maximize opportunities for Singaporean children. The government contributed an initial capital sum of $1 billion to the fund, which reached the target of $5 billion in August 1997. The scheme rewards students who perform well or who make good progress in their academic and non-academic work, and provides students and schools with funds for enrichment programmes or additional resources. The Edusave Awards are designed to encourage academic excellence. The Edusave Merit Bursary scheme aims to motivate students from lower-middle and low-income homes to do better academically.

To be eligible, pupils must be within the top 25 per cent of each level and stream (*see* STREAMING) and their household income must be below $3,000 per month. In most schools, Edusave provides a means for students to benefit from 'non-standard' activities such as overseas and field trips, and specialized enrichment courses.

Ee Hoe Hean Club Founded in 1895, the Ee Hoe Hean Club was originally located at Duxton Hill before moving to Club Street in 1910. In the 1920s, it moved to a new location on Bukit Pasoh Road. It was established mainly as a social club for HOKKIEN businessmen, who would gather there to relax, socialize and play mahjong. Only men were admitted. In 1923, the chairman of the

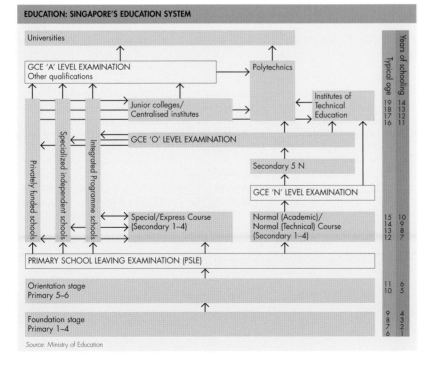

EDUCATION: SINGAPORE'S EDUCATION SYSTEM

Source: Ministry of Education

Eid-ul-Adha: distribution of meat.

Eid-ul-Fitr:
duit raya.

Ee Peng Liang

Elangovan

club was the wealthy businessman and philanthropist TAN KAH KEE. It was from here that Tan operated the headquarters of the Singapore China Relief Fund Committee and the Southseas China Relief Fund Union in Southeast Asia between 1937 and 1942 to raise funds for China in its struggle against the Japanese.

To remind its wealthy members of their humble origins, the club developed a tradition of serving a free lunch at 1.15 p.m. sharp every day, except for Mondays. The fare is Spartan—sweet potato porridge, with simple side dishes such as fried fish, *char siew* (roast pork) and stir-fried vegetables. Today, the club admits women as associate members, but it is essentially a male preserve. Members have included GAN ENG SENG, TAN JIAK KIM and LIM BOON KENG.

Ee Peng Liang (1913–1994) Businessman and philanthropist. Ee Peng Liang was educated at St Joseph's Institution and later qualified as a chartered accountant. He founded his own accounting firm, Ee Peng Liang and Company, which merged with Ernst and Whinney (later Ernst & Young) in 1986. Ee is best known for his life-long dedication to charitable causes and organizations. Among the numerous organizations which he headed were the National Council of Social Service (1958–92); the Marymount Vocational Centre; Boys' Town; Catholic Welfare Services; Mount Alvernia Hospital; the Singapore Scout Association; and the Community Chest of Singapore (1983–92).

For his efforts to help the less fortunate, Ee was nicknamed the 'Father of Charity', 'Mister Charity' and the 'Professional Beggar'. He also won numerous accolades for his humanitarian work, including the Public Service Star (1964); the MERITORIOUS SERVICE MEDAL (1967); the Distinguished Service Award, Singapore Scout Association (1970); the Meritorious Service Medal, Singapore Red Cross (1977); an honorary doctorate of letters, University of Singapore (1976); the DISTINGUISHED SERVICE ORDER (1985); the ORDER OF NILA UTAMA (Second Class) (1991); Bronze Wolf, World Scout Bureau (1991); and the ASEAN Achievement Award for Charity (1994). He was also made an Officer of the Order of St John's Ambulance (1971); and a Knight Commander of the Order of St Gregory the Great (1974).

Eid-ul-Adha Muslim festival. The 'Feast of Sacrifice' is celebrated on 10 Dhulhijjah, the 12th month of the Islamic calendar. It commemorates the sacrifice made by the prophet Ibrahim (Abraham) for the sake of Allah (God). The prophet was commanded to offer his son, Ismail (Ishmael), for sacrifice, and, though grieved, he agreed. However, God stopped him before the sacrifice was made and revealed that the command was a trial. Ismail's life was spared, and a ram was sacrificed in his place. Thus, on the day of Eid-ul-Adha, Muslims sacrifice animals such as sheep and cattle to commemorate the act, and distribute the meat among their neighbours, relatives and the needy. This festival also marks the end of the HAJ, the annual pilgrimage to Mecca, which is one of the five tenets of Islam.

Eid-ul-Adha is a public holiday in Singapore, known as Hari Raya Haji. In the morning, Muslims perform a special prayer, similar to the one for EID-UL-FITR. The rest of the day is spent visiting friends and relatives. Live sheep, usually shipped in from Australia, are sacrificed, generally in mosque compounds. People, especially those who have paid for their sheep to be sacrificed, can witness the ritual and the distribution of meat. It is not uncommon for Singaporean Muslims to have sheep sacrificed in other countries, such as China or Indonesia.

Eid-ul-Fitr Muslim festival. This celebration is held on the first day of Syawal, the tenth month of the Islamic calendar, marking the end of the Ramadan fast. It is one of the two Eid festivals in the Islamic year. Eid-ul-Fitr is a public holiday. Also known as Hari Raya Puasa in Singapore, it is celebrated on a larger scale than EID-UL-ADHA.

Fasting during the month of Ramadan is one of the five tenets of Islam and is compulsory for all Muslims who are fit. The fast requires abstinence from food and drink, and other conditions such as restricting sexual activity. In addition, every Muslim with the means to do so must give *zakat-ul-fitr* (alms), approximately 2 kg of basic foodstuffs—or the cash equivalent. The *zakat-ul-fitr* is usually collected at mosques and distributed to needy Muslims. Special prayers, called *tarawih*, are performed each night during Ramadan, and Muslims are encouraged to perform them in congregation. The last ten days of Ramadan are believed to be particularly blessed. Many stay awake during the nights of these ten days in order to receive the blessings of *Lailatul Qadr* (The Night of Power). It is believed that angels descend and shower blessings on this night.

Preparations to celebrate Eid-ul-Fitr take place during Ramadan. Many Muslims usually go to GEYLANG SERAI, the centre of Singapore's ethnic Malay community, to shop for new clothes or materials to deco-

Eid-ul-Fitr: seeking forgiveness for wrongdoings.

rate their homes. Temporary stalls are set up during Ramadan for businessmen to ply their trade. They sell a large range of items including food (for breaking the fast), clothes, shoes, curtains and carpets. These stalls do brisk business, especially in the last two weeks of Ramadan. The 'Hari Raya Bazaar' has become a regular feature in public housing estates, next to MRT stations and in the void decks of HDB blocks. These bazaars are popular with both Muslim and non-Muslim residents. Generally, a week prior to Eid-ul-Fitr, Muslim homes are spring-cleaned and decorated.

On Eid-ul-Fitr, Muslims dress in their best clothes and attend a special Eid prayer performed in congregation. Before the prayer, the congregation recites the *takbir*, which expresses the superlative qualities of Allah (God). The prayer is followed by a *khutbah*, or sermon, and concludes with a supplication for forgiveness and mercy. It is thereafter customary for Muslims to clasp the hands of the persons sitting next to them. They also do so when they visit their relatives—particularly elders—and friends. A custom practised by Singapore Muslims (and those of neighbouring countries such as Malaysia and Brunei) is asking forgiveness for past wrongdoings. During these visits, children and the elderly are usually given gifts of money, known as *duit raya*. These are given in small decorated envelopes—an adaptation of the Chinese *hongbao* given during CHINESE NEW YEAR. Festive food such as *lontong* (rice cakes with coconut milk gravy), *ketupat* (rice cakes wrapped in coconut leaves), *serunding* (dessicated coconut fried with chilli), *rendang* (beef cooked with spices and coconut milk), curry chicken and many types of cakes and biscuits are served. Celebrations typically last for the first two weeks of Syawal, although it is not uncommon for Muslims to visit friends and family throughout the month. During Eid, visits are also made to cemeteries where deceased loved ones are remembered and supplications are made to Allah.

Elangkannan, M. (1938–) Author. Born M. Balakrishnan in 1938, M. Elangkannan distinguished himself as a short-story writer and novelist while working at the Ministry of Culture (present-day Ministry of Information, Communication and the Arts). A CULTURAL MEDALLION recipient in 2005, he has written hundreds of short stories and several novels, and was the first Tamil writer to receive the Southeast Asia Write Award (1982).

Elangkannan's writings centre around the local Tamil community, documenting the lives of Tamils from different social strata as well as the experience of the larger Indian community. He has published seven books, four of which are short story collections—*Vazhi Piranthathu* (Path is Born) (1975), *Kungkuma Kannathil* (On Rosy

Cheeks) (1977), *Kodugal Oviyangal Agindrana* (Lines Are Becoming Art) (1998), *Thoondil Meen* (Fish On the Hook) (2001); and three novels, *Alaigal* (Waves) (1976), *Vaikarai Pookkal* (Flowers of Dawn) (1990) and *Ninaivugalin Kolangal* (Drawings of Memories) (1993). He won the Tamizhavel Award (2000) from the Association of Singapore Tamil Writers and the Singapore Literature Prize (2004) for *Thoondil Meen*.

Elangovan (1957–) Playwright, theatre director and poet. Regarded as a pioneer of modern Tamil poetry and Tamil experimental theatre, Elangovan is best-known in his capacity as artistic director of theatre company AGNI KOOTTHU, and his plays have been staged both in Singapore and overseas. Elangovan has published eight collections of plays and three volumes of poetry. Among his most controversial plays are *Oodadi* (Medium) (1992) and *Talaq* (Divorce) (1998). *Oodadi* dealt with the power relations between lower- and upper-caste Indians, while *Talaq* was about marital abuse in the Indian Muslim community. Elangovan received the Singapore Internationale Award from the Singapore International Foundation in 2002, 2003 and 2005 for his play collections *Flush* (2002), *Oodadi* (Medium) (2003) and *1915* (2005). The Southeast Asia Write Award was given to him in 1997 for his bilingual (Tamil and English) contribution to literature and theatre in Singapore. He has adapted plays by KUO PAO KUN and HAN LAO DA into Tamil, among them Kuo Pao Kun's *The Coffin is Too Big for the Hole* (1984), staged as *Kuzhi* (Hole) (1991), and *Annian* (Alien) (1992).

See also TAMIL THEATRE.

eldercare Healthcare services for the elderly. They are run mostly by voluntary welfare organizations (VWOs). An ElderCare Fund was set up in April 2000 to finance subsidies for the operational costs of elderly care facilities and services run by these VWOs.

To address concerns about the increasing health needs of a rapidly ageing population, the Inter-Ministerial Committee on Health Care for the Elderly (IMC) was set up in 1997 to put in place appropriate policies and strategies, and to ensure that long-term care for the elderly is affordable at individual, family, community and national levels.

As at 2006, Singapore has four public acute-care hospitals with geriatric departments; five community hospitals; four chronic sick hospitals; 53 nursing homes; 27 day rehabilitation centres; ten VWOs with home medical services; and 13 VWOs with home nursing services. Additionally, there are a number of private establishments catering to the elderly sick.

Community hospitals provide step-down care for patients who are discharged from hospitals and require some form of rehabilitation before they can go home. The chronic sick hospitals cater to patients who need long-term medical and nursing care. Those who need nursing care, such as tube feeding, can be admitted to any of the nursing homes.

Integrated Care Services coordinates and facilitates the placement of elderly patients to step-down care facilities such as nursing homes, based on applications through medical social workers at hospitals, polyclinics and other healthcare centres for admission, treatment and aftercare.

ElderShield Disability insurance scheme providing coverage to elderly Singaporeans who need long-term care. Linked to the CENTRAL PROVIDENT FUND (CPF), ElderShield helps to defray out-of-pocket expenses in the event of severe disabilities. Policyholders of ElderShield pay a small regular premium until the age of 65, or a one-off single premium, after which they will be covered for the rest of their lives.

The scheme was launched in September 2002. Two private insurers, Great Eastern Life Assurance Company Limited and NTUC Income Insurance Co-operative Limited, won the tender to administer ElderShield.

Singaporeans and permanent residents who are CPF members are automatically covered under ElderShield when they reach the age of 40—unless they choose to opt out of the scheme. The premium payable depends on the age of the insured. There is a difference in premiums between males and females, as women have higher claims risk due to their longer life expectancy. Premiums are kept low to insure as many people as possible. The government raised the interest rate of contributions from CPF members with healthy Medisave balances, the higher interest earned is to pay for the ElderShield premiums.

For ElderShield policyholders who choose to pay the Regular Premium Plan, where premiums are paid annually, the premiums are based on the age at which the policyholder joins the scheme. For example, a male who signed up for ElderShield in 2006 at age 40 pays $148.84 every year until he turns 65. By then, he would have paid a total of $3,869.84 in premiums, for which he would receive a total cash payout of $18,000.

ElderShield pays out $300 cash each month for up to five years if the insured becomes severely disabled for any reason such as old age or illness. The money can be used for any expenses—such as domestic help, medical bills and household expenses—to ease the financial burden on the family of someone who is old, disabled and not working, and who has no income.

elected presidency See PRESIDENCY.

elections General elections, those by which parliamentary representatives are chosen, must be held every five years. A by-election may also be called if a seat becomes vacant between general elections, though this is not obligatory. Parliamentary elections in Singapore are governed by the Parliamentary Elections Act.

Before elections can be called, the president must dissolve Parliament and issue a Writ of Election. Singapore's electoral system is based on the single plurality or 'first-past-the-post system' of voting in which the candidate with the highest number of votes wins. Until 1988, each electoral division or constituency was allowed to elect just one representative. These were known as Single Member Constituencies (SMCs). In 1988, the Constitution was amended to create GROUP REPRESENTATION CONSTITUENCIES (GRCs) in which groups of candidates are elected as a team, rather than as individuals (see CONSTITUENCIES).

The Writ of Election specifies when the nomination of candidates is to take place (between five days and one month from the date of the writ) and the place of nomination. On Nomination Day, candidates must present their nomination papers, statutory declarations and Political Donation Certificate personally at the nomination centre. At the close of the nomination period, if there is only one candidate (in the case of an SMC), or one group of candidates (in the case of a GRC) for the ward, the assistant returning officer

Elections: PAP election rally (top) and campaign brochures, 2006.

ELECTIONS: OVERALL ELECTION RESULTS

Year	Type of election	Party returned	Seats won by returning party	Uncontested seats	% of valid votes cast in favour of returning party
1955	Legislative Assembly	No clear majority*	10/25	0	27.06
1959	Legislative Assembly	PAP	43/51	0	53.68
1963	Legislative Assembly	PAP	37/51	0	46.93
1968	Parliamentary	PAP	58/58	51	86.72
1972	Parliamentary	PAP	65/65	8	70.17
1976	Parliamentary	PAP	69/69	16	72.40
1980	Parliamentary	PAP	75/75	37	77.66
1984	Parliamentary	PAP	77/79	30	64.95
1988	Parliamentary	PAP	80/81	11	63.36
1991	Parliamentary	PAP	77/81	41	60.97
1997	Parliamentary	PAP	81/83	47	64.98
2001	Parliamentary	PAP	82/84	55	75.30
2006	Parliamentary	PAP	82/84	37	66.60

*Labour Front forms coalition
Source: Elections Department Singapore

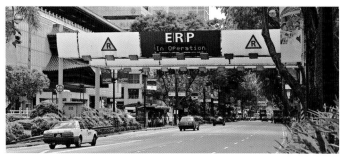

Electronic Road Pricing: overhead gantry (top); in-vehicle cashcard unit.

will declare that the candidate or the group of candidates have been returned as MEMBERS OF PARLIAMENT. If there is more than one candidate (SMC) or one group of candidates (GRC), the returning officer will adjourn the decision to Polling Day, which is between nine days and eight weeks after Nomination Day.

Candidates can commence campaigning after nominations close, and continue until the eve of Polling Day. The Parliamentary Elections Act restricts the amount any candidate can spend on electioneering.

The minimum voting age in Singapore is 21. Voting is compulsory and must be done in person at the assigned polling station. Polling takes place between 8 a.m. and 8 p.m. and ballots are counted at the end of the voting period. The results are officially published in the *Government Gazette*.

Singapore held its first official election, the LEGISLATIVE COUNCIL ELECTION (1948), on 20 March 1948. In that election, only six of the nine seats were contested, with the other three allotted to the various chambers of commerce. As only those born in Singapore were eligible to vote, and voting was not compulsory, voter turnout was disappointing. The first parliamentary general election took place in 1968, after Singapore separated from Malaysia. Close to 78,000 people—or 92 per cent of total voters—turned out to cast votes on 13 April. According to records, this was the general election that had the longest campaigning period but the least number of contested seats in Singapore's political history. The main party—the People's Action Party (PAP)—won all the seats, thus forming a single-party Parliament.

Another kind of popular vote is a national referendum. The only one held in Singapore since self-government took place on 1 September 1962 when Singaporeans had to decide on the country's relationship with the Federation of Malaysia. Although calls for a national referendum have been made since—a recent issue being that of setting up INTEGRATED RESORTS (IR) in Singapore—referenda have been rejected as unsuitable for such debates.

See also ELECTIONS DEPARTMENT *and* ELECTORAL BOUNDARIES REVIEW COMMITTEE.

Elections Department Reporting to the Prime Minister's Office, the Elections Department has the mandate to plan, pre-

pare for, and manage the conduct of presidential and parliamentary ELECTIONS, and any national referendum, in Singapore. Between elections, it has to ensure the currency and accuracy of the registers of electors, so that relevant information is up-to-date when an election is called.

Via the Registry of Political Donations, the Elections Department administers the Political Donations Act, which aims to prevent foreign interference in the domestic politics of Singapore through funding. The department also develops and implements programmes to promote public understanding and awareness of the electoral system and voting processes.

Electoral Boundaries Review Committee Government committee determining the geographical division of electoral constituencies. The Electoral Boundaries Review Committee (EBRC) has no constitutional standing and there is no law that mandates its creation. Typically, the prime minister appoints the committee just before a general election to review the electoral division boundaries and recommend changes. The five-member committee comprises a number of senior public servants as well as the head of the ELECTIONS DEPARTMENT. It considers factors such as population growth and population shifts arising from housing developments since the last boundary delineation exercise before issuing its report. Once the government accepts the EBRC's report, changes to the number of constituencies and their corresponding boundaries are effected by publication in the *Government Gazette*.

Electrico Popular music group. Regarded as having given the local independent music scene a jolt, the band is made up of singer-guitarist David Tan, guitarist Daniel Sassoon, bassist Desmond Goh, keyboardist Amanda Ling and drummer William Lim Jr. Originally formed in 1996 as Electric Co., the band soon faded from the scene. In 2003, with a new lineup and new songs, the band recorded a debut album entitled *So Much More Inside*. This was released the following year to rave reviews. Their sound is best described as rock and roll with some slower, more melancholic songs. In September 2004, the band toured Australia, performing in six cities alongside Australian indie-rock band Screamfeeder.

Electronic Road Pricing Automation of the Area Licensing Scheme (ALS) implemented in 1998 (*see* AREA LICENSING SCHEME AND RESTRICTED ZONES). Overhead gantry signs demarcate the Electronic Road Pricing (ERP)-control points. Based on the pay-per-use principle, the system tracks all vehicles passing through the gantry and deducts from each one a levy from a stored-value card (CashCard), inserted into a small in-vehicle (IV) unit installed on the dashboard,

or in the case of motorcycles/scooters, on the handlebar. To smooth traffic flow, the levy may vary at half-hour intervals. Licence plates of vehicles that violate the rule are automatically captured by the system for follow-up enforcement.

electronics sector The electronics industry is a key economic engine for Singapore, accounting for 43 per cent of domestic EXPORTS and 40 per cent of total manufacturing output in 2003.

The electronics sector emerged in the 1960s, with foreign companies setting up assembly plants for products such as transistors and low-end consumer electronics. From the early 1980s to the early 1990s, Singapore was a key manufacturing base for original equipment manufacturers (OEMs); by the mid-1990s, electronics was contributing to over half of the economy's manufacturing output, rising from 10.7 per cent in 1975 and 23.6 per cent in 1985.

The sector's relative importance as a source of exports has declined since 1998. In 2001, Singapore went through a severe recession as a result of the slowdown in the United States' economy and a decline in the global electronics industry. The economy contracted by 2 per cent and suffered the consequences of overdependence on electronics as a key export. By 2003, electronics exports accounted for only 43 per cent of domestic exports and 52 per cent of non-oil domestic exports (NODX), compared with 60 per cent of domestic exports and 69 per cent of NODX in 1998.

Since the mid-1990s, the government has made huge efforts to reinforce Singapore's attractiveness as a centre for value-added manufacturing, research and development (R&D) and product design. Today, Singapore remains a critical node in the regional electronics supply chain, focussed on producing more capital intensive products such as semiconductors and advanced disk-drives, as well as computer peripherals and infocommunications and consumer electronics.

Eleuterio, Herbert (c. 1928–) American scientist and academic. Professor Herbert Eleuterio obtained a doctorate in physical organic chemistry from Michigan State University, and worked at DuPont for 39 years. He won an American Institute of Chemists award in 1987. As a visiting professor at the National University of Singapore (NUS), he helped that university's Faculty of Engineering design a one-year course on creativity. The faculty also invited Eleuterio to teach innovation in technology management. Besides straddling chemistry and engineering, he has helped forge links and exchange programmes with overseas organizations. His efforts in planning Singapore's direction in science and technology have helped the country keep up with advances in environmental technolo-

Electrico

gy, materials technology and electric vehicles technology. In 1995, Eleuterio was awarded the NATIONAL SCIENCE AND TECHNOLOGY MEDAL.

Elias, Harry (1937–) Lawyer. Born in Singapore, Harry Elias attended St Andrew's School and the Teachers Training College. He earned a law degree from the University of London (1963); and was admitted to the Bar at Middle Temple (1963), to the Malaysian Bar (1965) and the Singapore Bar (1969). Elias was the key counsel in many high profile commercial, criminal and defamation cases, and successfully represented then Prime Minister Goh Chok Tong in a defamation suit against the *International Herald Tribune* in 1995 (*see* PRESS FREEDOM). He was president of the Law Society from 1984 to 1986. He played a key role in establishing and organizing the Criminal Legal Aid Scheme to give free legal assistance to the poor, and from 1985 to 1991, he was chairman of this scheme. In 1988 he set up his own law firm, Harry Elias Partnership, which became one of the leading law firms in Singapore. In January 1997, Elias was among the first batch of lawyers to be appointed SENIOR COUNSEL.

Ellenborough Market Ellenborough Market was erected in 1845 in response to the growing needs of the population after TELOK AYER MARKET (Lau Pa Sat) was built in 1822. The first building, built by Captain Charles E. Faber, stood next to the Ellenborough Building at BOAT QUAY. It was also known as Pasar Bahru, or New Market, distinguishing it from Lau Pa Sat (meaning 'old market' in Hokkien). A second Ellenborough Market was built near Read Bridge in 1891. It was extended eight years later in 1899, when a pavilion from the Edinburgh Exhibition of 1897 was shipped to Singapore and re-assembled. The market was gutted by fire in 1968, and demolished in 1970.

Emergency Sustained effort by the MALAYAN COMMUNIST PARTY (MCP) to overthrow the government of Malaya during the period between 18 June 1948 and 31 July 1960. Though initially outlawed by the colonial authorities, the MCP had emerged after World War II as an ally of the British, owing to its role as an anti-Japanese resistance movement during the Japanese

Emergency: terrorist incident on Malay Peninsula.

Occupation. Permitted to operate openly during the period of the BRITISH MILITARY ADMINISTRATION (BMA), the MCP started to subvert law and order through its control of trade union activism, and gained support by exploiting popular grievances against the BMA, which had been blamed for, among other things, food shortages, high prices, and the failure to restore normality after the war.

With the resumption of civil government on 1 April 1946, the MCP continued its agitation against the constitutional changes wrought by the inauguration of the controversial MALAYAN UNION scheme, the constitution of Singapore as a separate British colony, and the formation of the FEDERATION OF MALAYA as the union's replacement.

By February 1948, the MCP was having difficulty pursuing a policy of peaceful constitutional struggle and decided that armed struggle was inevitable. Four months after failing to prevent the establishment of the Federation of Malaya in February 1948, the MCP launched an armed insurgency. After its secretary-general, LAI TECK, who had favoured constitutional struggle, was exposed as a Japanese and British double agent in March 1947, his 'peaceful' strategy was discredited and the leadership of the party passed to CHIN PENG, who pursued a more militant strategy.

MCP-inspired trials of strength through the staging of strikes and mass rallies were met by robust British counteractions and arrests of union leaders. The MCP's control over the trade unions was further curtailed by the tightening of labour laws that disallowed convicted persons from holding office in labour unions and allowed union membership only to those with more than three years of experience in a particular trade, effectively excluding the majority of MCP members from holding such offices.

To neutralize the strength of the MCP-controlled SINGAPORE FEDERATION OF TRADE UNIONS, laws were passed disallowing labour unions from different economic sectors from coming under a larger umbrella federation. By May 1948, fearing further crackdowns by the British, the majority of communists left Singapore for Malaya and commenced preparations for armed struggle in the jungle.

Acts of violence increased from May onwards and, on 18 June 1948, two days after three European planters had been killed by armed MCP elements in Sungei Siput, Perak, the colonial authorities declared a 'state of emergency' in Malaya. This was followed by a similar declaration in Singapore a week later. Although the British were unprepared for an insurrection, the MCP appeared also less than fully ready for armed struggle in June, and had been caught off-guard by the British declaration. But backed by its support network

Ellenborough Market, 1953.

in the Minh Yuen (People's Organization) among Chinese squatters living at the jungle periphery, the communist Malayan Races' Liberation Army (MRLA) rapidly gained ground in its terror campaign of assassinations and economic disruption.

In Malaya, the communists' armed campaign reached a high point when MCP agents ambushed and killed the British high commissioner, Sir Henry Gurney, on 6 October 1951. Thereafter, their campaign stalled as their terror tactics had alienated many and they were unable to establish 'liberated' areas. Under the forceful leadership of General Sir Gerald Templer as both high commissioner and director of operations, government forces regained the initiative. By 1955, the communists had all but lost the jungle war, and Chin Peng made an unsuccessful attempt to negotiate with Tunku ABDUL RAHMAN and DAVID MARSHALL—the Malayan and Singaporean chief ministers respectively—for an end to the insurgency in talks in Baling, Kedah, on 28 and 29 December that year.

The failure of the jungle war in Malaya had revived some interest in urban subversion in Singapore, which had been spared most of the violence (except in 1950–51, when the MCP carried out a campaign of

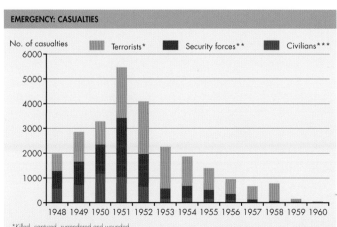

EMERGENCY: CASUALTIES

No. of casualties — Terrorists* — Security forces** — Civilians***

*Killed, captured, surrendered and wounded
**Regular police, special constables, auxiliary police and military forces, killed and wounded
***Killed, wounded and missing
Source: Mohd Azzam Mohd Hanif Ghows, *The Malayan Emergency, 1948–1960* (Kuala Lumpur: AMR Holding and Petaling Jaya: Yayasan Pelajaran Islam, 2006).

arson and murders, including an attempted assassination of the governor, Sir FRANKLIN GIMSON). The crackdown on left-wing activism after June 1948, however, had created an environment inimical to a communist uprising in Singapore. In January 1951, for instance, the police had broken up a section of the clandestine Singapore Anti-British League, an MCP-front organization. From 1955, as liberal conditions returned prior to the holding of elections, the MCP revived its 'united front' strategy—trying to subvert labour, student and political bodies, including political parties such as the People's Action Party. It continued to take advantage of anti-colonial nationalism. Its efforts failed finally when Singapore achieved independence from the British through MERGER with Malaysia in September 1963, three years after the official end of the Emergency in Malaya, which had cost some 11,000 lives.

employment In the 1960s, the Singapore government embarked on an INDUSTRIALIZATION plan to create employment opportunities for the growing population. At the time, unemployment stood at a high of 13 per cent. Due to this export-orientated strategy, coupled with success in attracting FOREIGN DIRECT INVESTMENT (FDI), Singapore experienced average annual gross domestic product growth of 10–13 per cent from 1966 to 1973. The employment situation improved significantly and unemployment rates fell to less than 3 per cent from 1973 onwards. The economy weathered its first recession in 1985 with unemployment hitting a high of 6.9 per cent. Through a combination of cost-cutting and other stimulatory measures, the economy rebounded by 1988 with unemployment down to 3.3 per cent.

In 2005, Singapore had a population of 4.4 million and a labour force of 2.4 million. Total employment was 2.3 million and the unemployment rate 3.4 per cent. Of those employed, 26.5 per cent were in professional and technical jobs, 21.4 per cent in manufacturing, and 15.8 per cent in the business and financial services sectors; the

Eng Wah: Jubilee Theatre, 1966 (top); Hong Kong actors with Goh Eng Wah, second from right.

Endau: settlers undertaking agricultural work.

remaining 10.8 per cent worked in administrative and managerial jobs. The labour force participation rate was 67.4 per cent, with 78.2 per cent male participation and 56.6 per cent female participation. While the participation rates of men have remained fairly constant over time, female labour-force participation has increased dramatically from 28.2 per cent in 1970.

Singapore is faced with a serious and intensifying problem of structural unemployment. Structural unemployment occurs when there is a mismatch between the existing skills of the workforce and the needs and requirements of evolving industries. This issue plagues modern economies and is a consequence of economic progression, as industries move to the higher end of the value chain. The WORKFORCE DEVELOPMENT AGENCY (WDA) was established in September 2003 to give a boost to workforce training programmes. In 2005, a national budget of $100 million was set aside to upgrade skills and help workers meet the demands of the new KNOWLEDGE-BASED ECONOMY.

To help low-skilled and less-educated Singaporeans cope with restructuring, the government continues to emphasize life-long learning, training and upgrading. The government has also indicated that it would not shut out FOREIGN WORKERS as a means of protecting jobs for locals. It would, however, put a cap on the proportion of foreign workers to locals that a company can hire. In this way, employment opportunities for locals are created alongside jobs for foreigners.

Empress Place Reputed to be the first pedestrian area in Singapore, Empress Place is located at the mouth of the Singapore River and spans the area occupied by Government Offices (present-day Empress Place Building, which houses the ASIAN CIVILISATIONS MUSEUM), Victoria Memorial Hall (present-day Victoria Concert Hall) and Town Hall (present-day Victoria Theatre). It was named Empress Place by the Municipal Council in 1907 to commemorate Queen Victoria's reign as Empress of India. It was colonial Singapore's first civic district, and Government Offices housed the Secretariat, Audit Office, Registration of Deeds Office, Land Office

and Offices of the Colonial Engineer, the Official Assignee, the Inspector General of Police and the Legislative Chamber. It also operated as the Registry of Births and Deaths, the Citizenship Registry and the Immigration Department. The Empress Place Building was used as a government office until the late 1980s, when plans were made to renovate and restore the building. The Empress Place Museum opened in 1989 before closing in 1997, after which it was renovated and renamed the Asian Civilisations Museum.

Endau Located on the eastern coast of Johor, near the border with Pahang, Endau was chosen as the site for a resettlement scheme for the Chinese in Singapore during the JAPANESE OCCUPATION. The scheme was organized by the Japanese-sponsored Overseas Chinese Association with the help of welfare officer SHINOZAKI MAMORU, in order to alleviate wartime food shortages in Singapore. The first settlers went in the third quarter of 1943. The settlement, known as New SYONAN, was a success, and settler numbers were reported as being 10,000 by the newspaper *Syonan Shimbun*. After 1945, some settlers from Singapore chose to remain in Endau. *See also* BAHAU.

energy Deregulation of Singapore's energy sector started in 1995 when the Public Utilities Board (later PUB) was corporatized and its responsibilities vested in seven successor companies, namely: three power generation companies (Tuas Power, PowerSenoko and PowerSeraya); one transmission and distribution company (PowerGrid); one electricity retail company (SP Services); one gas supply company (PowerGas); and one holding company (SINGAPORE POWER). PUB became the regulator of both the electricity and gas industries. In 1998, the Singapore Electricity Pool (SEP) was established to oversee wholesale electricity trading, with PowerGrid as the pool administrator.

In 2001, the Energy Market Authority (EMA) was formed to take over as the regulator of the energy sector. To enhance competition, the generation companies were separated from the transmission and distribution company at the ownership level. A new company (Energy Market Company) was formed to replace PowerGrid as the wholesale market administrator. In 2003, the new National Energy Market of Singapore commenced operations, replacing the SEP. Generation companies bid to sell electricity in the new wholesale electricity market. Electricity retailers buy electricity in bulk to sell to consumers. The retail electricity market has been progressively liberalized since 2001, starting with 'contestable' consumers with the highest electricity consumption. 'Non-contestable' consumers continue to buy electricity at regulated tariffs.

With increased demand for liquefied natural gas (LNG) as a fuel for electricity generation, there are plans for the gas industry to also be liberalized. The gas transportation business—a monopoly—is being separated from gas import, trading and retailing, the competitive parts of the industry, at the ownership level. Three pipelines serve the LNG system in Singapore: the northern pipeline from Malaysia; another from Indonesia's West Natuna gas fields; and a third from south Sumatra. The EMA is exploring the best way for Singapore to import and store LNG.

Eng Wah Cinema operator, film exhibitor and distributor. The Eng Wah Organisation was founded by GOH ENG WAH in the 1940s. It operated the Happy Theatre and the open-air Victory Theatre at Happy World Amusement Park (*see* GAY WORLD). It screened Chinese movies from Hong Kong and Taiwan, and later introduced screening theatres to public housing estates—the 'heartlands'—pioneering the conversion to digital screens. In late 2005, Eng Wah also brought the Crazy Horse Paris dance troupe—a nude cabaret show—to Singapore. Eng Wah was listed on the Singapore Stock Exchange in 1994.

English Several labels have been applied to the varieties of English used in Singapore. The usual cover term for all of these is 'Singapore English' or 'Singaporean English'. Singaporeans who are comfortable with English may use a relatively standard form of the language in formal or polite situations—Standard Singapore(an) English (SSE). When talking with friends in informal situations, however, they may switch to a more colloquial version of English, usually referred to as SINGLISH. The term 'Singlish' was popularized in (Sylvia) Toh Paik Choo's books *Eh, Goondu!* (1983) and *Lagi Goondu!* (1986). Some people use the same term to refer to the kind of English produced by non-fluent speakers who are uncomfortable with English. Therefore, some linguists differentiate this 'Learner English' from the slang variety, called 'Colloquial Singapore(an) English'. In this entry, the term Singlish refers to the slang variety rather than the learner variety. Learner English varies from speaker to speaker, although the structure tends to follow that of the speaker's first language. Here

is one sentence as it might be spoken in these different varieties of English:

SSE: Although Mr Lim lives in a big bungalow, he still frequents the neighbourhood coffee shop and has his *char kway teow* there weekly.

Singlish: Mr Lim stay in big big bungalow hor, but he still like to go to the coffee shop in his neighbourhood, wah, and some more he order *char kway teow* from there every week.

Learner English: Mr Lim live big big bungalow, also like go his place coffee shop, one week buy *char kway teow* one time.

Although Singaporean English—in particular Singlish—has been labelled a pidgin or creole, it developed in a rather different way from other pidgins and creoles, many of which arose in communities where no common language existed, but where there was a need to communicate for a limited purpose, such as trade. Singaporean English arose in the playgrounds of English-medium schools during the 19th and early 20th centuries. As Singapore (and the Straits Settlements in general) was administered by the East India Company (until its transfer to the Colonial Office in 1867), teachers in these schools were often EURASIANS, and many came from the Indian subcontinent. The pupils' model of English was therefore varied, and included local, Indian and Ceylonese (Sri Lankan) characteristics. During this period, the lingua franca in Singapore was a form of MALAY known as bazaar Malay; everyone was assumed to have some acquaintance with this language, and it was thus also used for explanations in the classroom. Ethnic Chinese pupils began to enrol in English-medium schools in significant numbers in the early years of the 20th century; the majority came from homes in which Hokkien was used. In such a context, it is not surprising that the major influences on Singlish were Malay (in particular bazaar Malay) and Hokkien.

Because of the partial shared history with the Indian subcontinent and Malaya, Singaporean English shares many characteristics with Indian English and Malaysian English. Examples include some vocabulary items and the use of the '-ing' form in constructions such as 'I am having a headache'.

When Singapore became independent in 1965, English was declared one of the country's official languages, alongside Mandarin, Malay and Tamil. English became the main working language. Schools that provided instruction through languages other than English began to be phased out in the 1980s, so that today, all Singaporean schools and universities are English-medium. In 2004, according to the Ministry of Education, 50 per cent of ethnic Chinese pupils entering primary school

came from homes in which English was the dominant language, compared with 10 per cent in 1980. English therefore appears to have made inroads into all spheres of life in Singapore.

Linguists are not able to give a precise date for the emergence of a relatively stable form of Singlish. Because Singlish is a spoken form of English, there is no record of its use in the early days of its development. However, the linguist Anthea F. Gupta notes that from the 1930s, a Singaporean variety of English would have begun to be passed on from parents to children as the first Chinese and Indians who received an English-medium education began to have children of their own.

In 1999, then Senior Minister Lee Kuan Yew voiced his concern that Singlish was becoming a 'handicap' to international intelligibility. The perception was that Singlish was beginning to gain acceptability, and was encroaching on situations in which a more standard variety should be the norm. The fear was that the increased use of Singlish on television and other media might become a stumbling block for Singaporeans wishing to acquire a more 'internationally acceptable' variety of English. Although many speakers could switch between Singlish and SSE, some did so less successfully. The variety of English employed in the popular television situation comedy PHUA CHU KANG was singled out for mention. The subject was hotly debated in Parliament and by the public. Eventually, the character Phua Chu Kang went for English classes and emerged speaking English with fewer Singlish characteristics.

In 2000, the Speak Good English Movement was launched. Since then, it has

English: cartoon satirizing Singlish, as spoken by the television character Phua Chu Kang.

English: abbreviations One trait of Singapore English is the widespread use of abbreviations and acronyms. They are used as substitutes for the full names of government agencies, companies, schools and expressways. Some abbreviations have eventually become names. Below are some examples:

Government agencies
CPF Board: Central Provident Fund Board
EDB: Economic Development Board
HDB: Housing & Development Board
URA: Urban Redevelopment Authority

Companies
SIA: Singapore Airlines
SMRT Corporation: Singapore Mass Rapid Transit Corporation
UOL: United Overseas Land

Schools and universities
ACS: Anglo-Chinese School
CHIJ: Convent of the Holy Infant Jesus
NJC: National Junior College
NTU: Nanyang Technological University
NUS: National University of Singapore
SJI: St Joseph's Institution

Road names
ECP: East Coast Parkway
PIE: Pan-Island Expressway
TPE: Tampines Expressway

Abbreviations that have become names
DBS Bank (formerly Development Bank of Singapore)
JTC Corporation (formerly Jurong Town Corporation)
PSA International (formerly Port of Singapore Authority)

Acronyms
A*STAR: Agency for Science, Technology and Research
NETS (Network for Electronic Transfers)
SAFTI Military Institute (formerly Singapore Armed Forces Training Institute)
SPRING Singapore: Standards, Productivity and Innovation Board

English literature

When Singapore gained full independence in 1965, the first generation of writers in English were already well established. However, a younger generation felt the need for its own voice, and began to undermine and even subvert accepted parameters of style and content. The work by the pioneer writers, including those who had been writing sporadically before WORLD WAR II, contained both personal and nationalistic themes, but they did not fully break out of colonial literary frameworks. The power of colonial education to impress itself upon the local imagination should not be underestimated; having been taught that the best writers in the English language came from the United Kingdom, it was inevitable that early writers tried their best to imitate the canon. Developments in America, let alone Africa, India and the West Indies, were left largely unnoticed.

From left: Down the Line *by Arthur Yap (1980);* Raffles Place Ragtime *(1988) by Philip Jeyaratnam; and* Stand Alone *(1990) by Simon Tay.*

EDWIN THUMBOO was among the local writers who sought his own personal voice, but the profound impact of poets such as W.B. Yeats, T.S. Eliot and W.H. Auden is evident throughout his work. It was his exploration of post-colonial literatures, however, which led him to assert that Singaporeans should consider the idea of 'literatures in English', as opposed to 'English literature'.

This concept opened up a realm of possibilities for local writing, as Singaporean authors realized that writing in English did not necessarily

Edwin Thumboo

mean that one had to imitate the canon of English literary works. The pioneer generation of authors such as Lim Thean Soo, GOH POH SENG, Goh Sin Tub and Nalla Tan, in addition to Thumboo himself, paved the way for a burst of creative energy from the following generation. Writers such as ROBERT YEO, ARTHUR YAP, LEE TZU PHENG, Chandran Nair, Mervin Mirapuri, CATHERINE LIM, Sng Boh Khim, Yeo Bock Cheng, Ho Poh Fun, HO MIN FONG, SUCHEN CHRISTINE LIM, Tan Mei Ching, PHILIP JEYARETNAM, Simon Tay, Kirpal Singh, Chiung Yee Chong, Boey Kim Cheng, Lim Li, Rosaly Puthucheary, Tan Jwee Song, Geraldine Heng and Heng Siok Tian, among others, were freer in their quest for new modes of creative expression, especially in the use of 'SINGLISH' (the Singaporean version of spoken English), as well as their directness when it came to documenting their personal perspectives. The variety of this group's output is remarkable, as they struggled to define a Singaporean identity which is constantly in flux.

In multicultural Singapore it has not been easy for writers in English to gain general acceptance. National awards are one sign of approval; others are community recognition, and also regional and international exposure. A younger generation of writers, which includes Felix Cheong, Paul Tan, TAN HWEE HWEE, Alvin Pang, Daren Shiau, Cyril Wong, Aaron Lee, Madeline Lee, Yong Shu Hoong, Koh Buck Song, Grace Chia and ALFIAN SA'AT, have each developed their distinct strengths and styles. A stronger, if still fluid, sense of identity informs their work, giving it greater depth. These younger writers attempt to give voice to their views of Singapore from both within and without.

Prejudices are still hard to overcome, and despite efforts to introduce local writing into the literature syllabus in schools, it is still true that for most Singaporeans, 'English writers' come from abroad. However, outreach programmes and other activities such as writing residencies, reading clubs and literary festivals are helping to create a wider awareness of Singaporean writing in English. In 1990, the Creative Arts Programme was jointly established by the Gifted Education Branch of the Ministry of Education and the Centre for the Arts at the National University of Singapore to give secondary school and junior college students greater exposure to the arts, and also to offer selected participants a mentorship programme through which students can hone their literary skills under the guidance of an established local writer. More research into local literature is also being undertaken, and an increasingly sophisticated body of literary criticism is finding its rightful position within the larger arena of Singaporean literature.

Cyril Wong, right, at a reading.

become an annual event with activities such as quizzes and competitions. In 2001, a new English language curriculum was launched in schools; this involved, among other things, explicit teaching of grammar.

Although SSE is not distinct grammatically, it has distinct features in terms of vocabulary. As English is used for domestic purposes also, SSE has developed to describe items relevant to Singaporeans. Vocabulary items found in SSE tend to be nouns. These pertain to food (e.g. '*nasi lemak*', 'chicken rice', 'steamboat', '*kachang puteh*', 'brinjal'); architecture (e.g. 'void deck', 'shophouse', 'air-well', 'bungalow', 'hawker centre'); institutions (e.g. 'neighbourhood school', 'independent school'); flora (e.g. 'lalang', 'money plant'); culture (e.g. Deepavali, 'filial piety'); and even general objects (e.g. 'handphone'). Some other examples include 'molest' as a noun (rather than 'molestation'); 'retrenchment' (rather than 'redundancy'); and 'heaty' and 'cooling' (referring to food items).

Verbs are sometimes omitted, such as in the case of 'on the light' and 'off the light', rather than 'switch on/off the light'; 'go straight' as an instruction to continue moving straight ahead; and 'last time' for 'in the past'. The conditional 'would' is often used

where it would not be in other contexts, as is the pluperfect. Thus, 'I had worked in a bank' would be used, rather than 'I have worked in a bank' or 'I worked in a bank'.

Furthermore, some vocabulary commonly used in conversation would be considered archaic in other contexts, where such items only appear in formal notices. Examples include 'purchase' for 'buy', and 'alight' for 'get off'.

Singaporean speech, whether SSE or Singlish, is marked by a Singaporean accent, of which there can be a range. In general, there is less distinction between stressed and unstressed syllables, so that a word such as 'inspector' will be pronounced with three fairly even syllables, with the middle syllable being only slightly more prominent. In most British and American accents, one syllable is much more prominent, and the other syllables are very light: 'inSPECtor' and 'PURchase', for example. Some vowel sounds which are distinct in other accents become merged in the Singaporean accent; most speakers distinguish between 'live' and 'leave', but many speakers will not distinguish between 'cup' and 'carp'; 'cot' and 'caught'; 'sat' and 'set'; and 'pull' and 'pool'. The 'th' sound, as

in 'this' and 'thin', is often substituted with other sounds, such as the 't' sound (for 'thin'), the 'f' sound (for 'bath') and the 'd' sound (for 'this'). As in accents spoken in parts of the United Kingdom and Australia, the Singaporean accent is generally non-rhotic—i.e. the 'r' is not sounded in words like 'word' or 'lawyers'. There are often complaints about the accents used by disc jockeys on radio. When a local disc jockey uses, for example, an Americanized accent, he is said, disparagingly, to be 'slanging'.

With the Speak Good English Movement and the government's apparent disapproval of Singlish, some have concluded that the death knell of Singlish has been sounded. However, cockney, as spoken in parts of London, as well as the Bronx slang of New York, have co-existed with more standard forms of English for centuries. This suggests a social need for a variety that allows individuals to 'let their hair down' and have something they can call their own. Given this social need, Singaporeans might not be willing to have Singlish completely extirpated.

English education

During the colonial era, education in various languages developed separately, led mainly by Christian missions and various local communities. The colonial government did establish schools for 'natives'—Malay schools, mainly in what is now Malaysia. However, because the economy during the pre-independence period was mainly based on the ENTREPÔT trade, English education was designed primarily to produce personnel for clerical and lower administrative positions in the colonial government, and in commerce.

Two institutions of higher learning were established during the colonial period—the KING EDWARD VII COLLEGE OF MEDICINE in 1905, and RAFFLES COLLEGE, for the study of arts and social sciences, in 1929. These were amalgamated to form the UNIVERSITY OF MALAYA in 1949. The University of Malaya was, in turn, renamed the University of Singapore in 1962.

The landmark document that shaped education in Singapore was the 1956 Report of the All-Party Committee of the Singapore Legislative Assembly on Chinese Education. The recommendations of this report were implemented in 1959. The key policy recommendation was parity of treatment for all official-language streams. The main language of instruction in schools could be in any of the four official languages (namely Chinese, English, Malay and Tamil), although schools that used Chinese, Malay or Tamil as the main language of instruction had to teach English as a second language. Similarly, schools that used English as the main language of instruction had to provide for the learning of a MOTHER TONGUE as a second language.

The popularity of English-medium schools has continued to grow since the mid-1960s. Though it is impossible to pinpoint the exact cause of this popularity, two contributory factors can be identified. The first has been the pragmatism of parents, who recognize that there are more employment opportunities for workers proficient in English. The second has been the decision to use English, rather than Chinese or Malay, as the language of business and administration.

All schools now use English as the medium of instruction. While this has undoubtedly contributed to Singapore's economic growth and social cohesion, there have also been some unintended consequences. Learning English remains a challenge for many students who come from families in which English is not the main language used. English is the most frequently used language for only 23 per cent of the population. Furthermore, the use of English correlates with the educational level and socio-economic status of families.

Since proficiency in English affects a student's performance in other subjects, the Ministry of Education has worked to improve the teaching and learning of English in all schools.

English education: McNair Road School, c. 1950.

English literature *See* box.

English popular music *See* box.

English theatre *See* box.

Enright, D.J. (1920–2002) British poet, novelist and academic. Born in Royal Leamington Spa, Warwickshire, Dennis Joseph Enright was educated at Leamington College and then at Downing College, Cambridge University, where he was a student of F.R. Leavis. In 1947, he began his academic career with a teaching post at the University of Alexandria in Egypt. In 1959, he became Johor Professor of English at the University of Malaya in Singapore. He angered the newly elected People's Action Party (PAP) government in his inaugural lecture when he attacked the government's plans to curb so-called 'yellow culture' by banning jukeboxes and pornography. He quoted W.B. Yeats, arguing that culture grew from 'the foul rag and bone shop of the heart', and warned that Singapore should not be allowed to degenerate into a Sunday-school class. PAP leaders were incensed and branded Enright a 'beatnik mendicant professor'. He almost lost his work permit; but a conciliatory letter to Lee Kuan Yew and mediation resolved the controversy, and Enright remained in Singapore until 1970.

Enright wrote of his experiences in Singapore in his *Memoirs of a Mendicant Professor* (1969) which was banned in Singapore. In 1970, he returned to the United Kingdom to work as an editor (1970–72) and director (1974–82) of Chatto and Windus, a publishing house. He also accepted an honorary professorship at Warwick University. His other published works include *The Laughing Hyena and Other Poems* (1953); *Poets of the 1950s* (1955); *Academic Year* (1955); *The Joke Shop* (1976); *Wild Ghost Chase* (1978); and *Beyond Land's End* (1979). Enright died of cancer on 31 December 2002.

entrepôt Singapore's foreign trade in the 19th century can be divided into three categories. Firstly, there was international trade which involved the import of commodities for local consumption (such as rice and cotton piece goods) and the export of domestic produce (such as gambier and sugar). Secondly, there was the transshipment trade which included the transfer of goods from one ship to another while in transit. Thirdly, and most importantly, was entrepôt trade, the international distribution of imported manufactures, foodstuffs and 'Straits produce'—the name given collectively to the produce of the Malay archipelago. These imports were subsequently re-exported after processing, grading, packaging, other services and profit mark-up. Thus, the export value of these commodities was always greater than their import value due to the value-added services performed in the colony. Since Singapore had no significant agriculture or industrial exports of its own, it had to finance its consumption of imported goods through the profits made from entrepôt trade.

There were several reasons why Singapore was popular as an entrepôt. One was the free-port status that had been offered in Singapore since the settlement was founded in 1819. Ships were exempted from the payment of import and export duties, tonnage and port dues, wharfage and anchorage dues, port clearance fees and stamp duties. This proved attractive to Chinese merchants, who had been paying high duties in Dutch-controlled ports. In fact, this status was fiercely guarded by the merchant community, as evidenced by the failure of the Calcutta government in the 1850s to impose port charges in Singapore to subsidize the cost of new shipping facilities. Although some have argued that the trade of the colony was not completely 'free' because taxes were still levied on goods such as opium, toddy and petroleum, taxes were only imposed on consumption and not re-export, thus keeping the entrepôt free. In this way, both Western and Asian goods could be collected and exchanged without taxes being paid.

Another reason for Singapore's success as an entrepôt was its strategic location. Situated at the southern end of the Malay Peninsula, the port attracted traders from Southeast Asia, China, India and Europe. Singapore was also easily accessible to small boats from Siam (present-day Thailand), the Dutch East Indies (present-day Indonesia) and elsewhere in the region. With the advent of steamships and the opening of the SUEZ CANAL in 1869, Singapore became the port of call for both sailing ships and steamships.

The seasonal trade winds brought traders from various countries to the settlement and then back again, particularly during two main trading periods—the junk season and the BUGIS season. The junk season, which brought junks from China, Cochin China (now northern Vietnam) and Siam, was regulated by the northeast mon-

D.J. Enright

English popular music Popular music in Singapore was given a boost by a Cliff Richard and The Shadows concert in November 1961, which introduced the concept of an instrumental band playing electric guitars. Prior to their arrival, the scene in Singapore had been mainly an acoustic one, and the use of electric guitars had been limited to professional musicians playing in nightclubs. There was a rise in the use of electric guitars in popular music bands, who played mostly instrumental covers of hit songs.

The rise of the Beatles a few years later had a considerable impact, prompting bands to include vocalists in their line-ups and write original songs. However, as audiences dictated that bands play covers of international hits, bands played a mix of originals and covers. A few distinct trends at this time can be seen: there were instrumental bands influenced by The Shadows and The Ventures; those with vocalists who drew their inspiration from the Beatles; and yet another group of bands who played what was then termed rhythm-and-blues, as exemplified by the Rolling Stones, The Yardbirds and The Animals. The dominance of instrumental bands meant that local bands such as The Silver Strings, The Checkmates and The Trailers started out as instrumental bands featuring singers, but their vocalists were ancillary to the band.

From left: X-Periment were popular in the 1970s, playing a mix of soul and rhythm-and-blues; poster featuring the mid-1980s line-up of Heritage.

From left: Cliff Richard and The Shadows performing at the Singapore Badminton Hall in 1961; advertisement for a tea dance at The Baron.

Audiences were exposed to popular music on television, where bands were featured on shows such as Pop Inn, which began airing in June 1964, talent competitions and concerts. WILSON DAVID was one of the first musicians to headline his own show when he hosted the Wilson David Show at the NATIONAL THEATRE on 24 December 1964, which featured a host of other supporting acts. TEA DANCES on weekend afternoons were put on at venues such as Golden Venus, a nightclub in Orchard Hotel, Flamingo Night Club at GREAT WORLD amusement park, and Princes at Prince Hotel Garni in Orchard Road, among others. Variety shows featuring bands, dancers, comedians and magicians were put on in theatres owned by film companies SHAW BROTHERS and CATHAY ORGANISATION.

All this activity drew the interest of international record labels such as Philips and EMI. Local independent labels such as Eagle Records, Hi Fi Records, Cosdel (later RCA), Magpie Records and Panda Records also featured in the music scene. THE CRESCENDOS joined the Philips stable in 1963, and were the first local band to be signed with an international label. EMI also signed THE QUESTS in 1964, who grew to become the most popular local band of the 1960s. The advent of soul and psychedelic music saw the rise of bands like X-PERIMENT, The Surfers, Straydogs, Pests Infested, and the Bee Jays.

In the 1970s, the English music scene was largely made up of bands playing covers of Jimi Hendrix, Led Zeppelin and Deep Purple, with the occasional original thrown in. Groups such as Pests Infested, Heritage, Flybaits and Sweet Charity played at the National Theatre at FORT CANNING to near-full-capacity crowds of about 3,000 people each week. A tax on live music led many nightclubs and similar music venues to stop hiring bands. The government's opposition to what it saw as 'yellow culture' meant that long hair and rock music were frowned upon by the authorities as being commonly associated with drug use.

The 1980s saw a revival in the music scene, particularly with acts like Zircon Lounge (which featured X'HO, then known as Chris Ho), DICK LEE and Tokyo Square in the earlier part of the decade, and THE ODDFELLOWS, Opposition Party and Corporate Toil in the late 1980s. Tokyo Square topped local and regional charts with 'Within You'll Remain'. Support from the media came in the form of BIGO (Before I Get Old), a magazine started in 1985 by brothers Philip and Michael Cheah, which introduced independent rock groups such as THE PADRES, The Shades, Stompin' Ground, The Black Sun and The Watchmen to the local audience.

From 1991 to 1998, Pony Canyon, a Singapore-based Japanese record label and its subsidiary Springroll Music released more than 30 English popular music albums from musicians such as Chris Ho, The Black Sun, Zul, Najip Ali, The Lizard's Convention and Douglas Oliveiro. It released Humpback Oak's critically acclaimed 1994 debut *Pain-Stained Morning*. However, the label ceased its Singapore operations in 1999 due to poor reception of its releases. Odyssey Music released albums by The Pagans, The Watchmen and Ordinary People, while BMG marketed AWOL and The Oddfellows. In 1998, radio airplay of bands such as CONCAVE SCREAM, Livonia, Sugarflies, TANYA CHUA and the Stoned Revivals was seen as an encouraging sign as radio stations generally gave minimal support to local bands, and the availability of THE SUBSTATION as a venue for rock performances provided musicians with a space in which to perform.

By 2003, however, local English albums were experiencing sluggish sales. On average, independent bands were selling only between 1,000 to 2,000 copies of their albums, and could not compete with Mandarin popular music performers such as STEFANIE SUN or TANYA CHUA—who had switched from English to Mandarin—who could easily sell more than 100,000 copies in Taiwan and 8,000 copies in Singapore (see CHINESE POPULAR MUSIC).

In the following years, musicians themselves began organizing events, with Music For Good, Rockstar Collective, Wallwork Records—run by members of Astreal, Awakening Productions, Aging Youth Productions and Double Yellow Line among the more prominent organizers. The opening of ESPLANADE–THEATRES ON THE BAY also provided bands with another performance venue, and is the location of Baybeats, an annual three-day music festival. New developments took place with bands such as THE OBSERVATORY and Aspidistra Fly, both of whom took on a more experimental musical direction.

In 2004, the inaugural SINGAPORE IDOL competition was held and viewed by a live television audience. Winner TAUFIK BATISAH sold over 30,000 copies of his debut album *Blessings*, making it a double-platinum release by local standards and signalling a new interest in mainstream local popular music.

Clockwise from left: Flyer for Baybeats 2006; Stoned Revivals' demo tape Soul Detergent *(1995); Humpback Oak's* Pain-Stained Morning *(1994); Astreal's* Fragments of the Same Dead Star *(2006); Aspidistra Fly's EP* The Ghost of Things *(2004); and Livonia's* Zerofeel *(1999).*

soon in November. With the help of the southwest monsoon in April, these traders departed for home. The Bugis season saw the entrance of traders from the Celebes, Bali, southern Borneo and other ports south of the equator. They normally reached Singapore in September or October, leaving again in November with the onset of the northeast monsoon. Thus, Singapore became a market place in which goods from all over the world could be exchanged.

Singapore's position as an entrepôt was further enhanced by the additional services it provided to traders. In May 1848, New Harbour (present-day KEPPEL HARBOUR) was established to cope with congested marine traffic at BOAT QUAY. Located west of the Singapore River, this new harbour had deep water close to the shore, and provided safe anchorage to large vessels, square riggers and steamers which were becoming a frequent sight in Singapore, especially after the 1840s. After congested marine traffic was diverted away from Boat Quay, the smaller coasting vessels, dominated by the Chinese, could continue to use roads and the river for intra-Asia trade. In addition, docking facilities sprang up with the opening of New Harbour. Wharves and COAL sheds were built. Ship-repairing facilities were provided by companies such as the Tanjong Pagar Dock Company (1864). With the opening of the Suez Canal in 1869, Singapore became a coal depot, for the new route could only be navigated by steamships; and so the island acquired a new strategic and economic significance in the trade between Europe and the Pacific.

Singapore also ensured that it set up a network of communications that could access trading information all over the world. In December 1870, the Singapore–Madras submarine cable was laid, placing the colony in direct communication with India, Europe and North America. From Singapore, the line branched off to Java, Australia and China.

Another attraction of Singapore was the creation of special services to meet the new demands of trade. In conjunction with the development of TIN as the most important single commodity in the colony's entrepôt trade, smelting facilities were offered by the STRAITS TRADING COMPANY (1887) on Pulau Brani, off Singapore. As a result, Singapore became the largest centre of tin smelting in the world.

The success of Singapore as an entrepôt can be attributed to many factors. However, only one—a strategic location—was permanent, while others were government policies and initiatives taken by private companies.

The first container terminal was built by the Port of Singapore Authority in 1966. This signalled the beginning of the growth of the container industry in Singapore. By the 1980s, Singapore had become the world's third-largest petroleum-refining centre as well as the third-largest oil-trading centre,

serving the needs of oil-rich Indonesia and Malaysia. By 1988, it had overtaken Rotterdam to become the world's busiest port in terms of tonnage.

In 2000, however, Singapore faced new challenges posed by the opening of the Port of Tanjung Pelepas in the Malaysian state of Johor. This new port became a strong contender for Singapore's entrepôt trade and the patronage of international shipping lines, offering modern port facilities, information technology infrastructure and a free-port status.

Singapore's role as an entrepôt has continued to drive economic growth. Singapore re-exports approximately half of what it imports. In 2004, imports were more than $293 billion while re-exports totalled $144.4 billion. Although oil continues to be an important re-export product, its contribution at $3.4 billion is significantly smaller than the re-export of non-oil goods such as machinery, transport equipment and electrical and electronic products, which contributed $276.8 billion.

entrepreneurship The education system has been criticized for being too focused on producing skilled labour for multinational corporations (MNCs) and GOVERNMENT-LINKED COMPANIES (GLCs). One consequence of this has arguably been the erosion of entrepreneurial instincts in post-Independence Singapore, in contrast to the entrepreneurial spirit which flourished in Singapore during the colonial period.

In 1985 the Economic Committee on Singapore's Future Growth identified local SMALL- AND MEDIUM-SIZED ENTERPRISES (SMEs) as being key to Singapore's development. The first SME Master Plan was launched in 1989. However, despite a plethora of SME assistance schemes, local firms continued to lag behind non-SMEs in productivity. Another master plan, SME 21, was crafted in 2000 to take Singapore SMEs into the future. This new ten-year plan was intended to transform the SME sector into a source of innovation and entrepreneurship and thus enhance Singapore's economic COMPETITIVENESS.

The Action Community for Entrepreneurship (ACE)—a collaborative effort between the private and government sectors—was set up in May 2003. Such moves were seen as necessary not only to cultivate a more vibrant SME sector, but also to speed Singapore's transformation into a KNOWLEDGE-BASED ECONOMY. A new Cabinet portfolio was created—minister in charge of entrepreneurship—whose job was to cultivate a more conducive environment for entrepreneurial activities by creating, for instance, a more level playing field for new start-ups and SMEs vis-à-vis MNCs and GLCs. Singapore has a Competition Act (2004) that aims to enhance market efficiency and strengthen the competitiveness of the economy. The

state has also adopted a 'Yellow Pages' rule for starting new businesses, so that it does not get involved in industries in which there is already a private sector presence.

Equator Art Society Society of artists associated with social realism. The Equator Art Society was established in 1956 and dissolved in 1974. It held studio classes, and its exhibitions and publications featured sculpture, and works in watercolour, graphite and oils including still lifes, portraits and landscapes. However, it is best known for its 'social realist' subjects—embodied in images of labourers and the working class, often depicted in conditions of austerity. Artists affiliated with the society included Chua Mia Tee, Lee Boon Wang, Lim Yew Kuan and Koeh Sia Yong.

Er Kwong Wah (1946–) Civil servant. Er Kwong Wah was educated at Griffiths Primary School, Raffles Institution and the University of Toronto where he obtained a first class honours degree in electrical engineering (1970). He subsequently completed an MBA at the Manchester Business School (1978). Er joined the Ministry of Defence in 1970 and began his career in the Administrative Service, serving variously as permanent secretary, Ministry of Education (1987–94), permanent secretary, Ministry of Community Development (1994–97) and secretary to both the Legal Service and Public Service Commissions. He was appointed chairman and chief executive officer of Cathay ACEL in 1999; chairman, Centre for Cleaning Technology in 2002; chairman, Unidux Electronics, also in 2002; and executive director of ITM Capital.

Er Woo Amateur Musical and Dramatic Association Formed in 1912 by a group of TEOCHEW businessmen, the Er Woo Amateur Musical and Dramatic Association set out to promote Han opera and music. These art forms originated in Hubei province in the 16th century. By the 19th century, they had spread to Guangdong

Entrepôt: cartoon showing water-born traffic congestion around Singapore, 1927 (top); promotion of Singapore as an entrepôt, 1938.

English theatre

English theatre English theatre in Singapore has its roots in the military bases and expatriate clubs of colonial Singapore, with the spouses of British officers staging drawing-room comedies—such as those of Oscar Wilde and Noel Coward—until the withdrawal of British forces in the 1970s. Such were the origins of the Stage Club, founded shortly after World War II and continuing into the 21st century.

Local groups were a later development, although some did attain prominence by the 1960s. These included the University of Singapore Drama Society, the Experimental Theatre Club (ETC), Centre 65 and the Theatre World Association. This last group was established by Gracia Tay-Chee who was one of the first Singaporeans to receive drama training in the United Kingdom.

The Stage Club has averaged five productions per year since its foundation in 1945. In 1956 it staged Jane (left) at the Victoria Memorial Hall (now the Victoria Concert Hall). The Sword Has Two Edges (far left) was presented in 1990 as part of a retrospective festival of Singapore plays.

Postcolonialism—1960s and 1970s

The ETC and Centre 65 were particularly significant in promoting early Singaporean plays, the former staging the first two full-length plays written by Lim Chor Pee, namely *Mimi Fan* (1962) and *A White Rose at Midnight* (1964); the latter producing two full-length plays by GOH POH SENG— *When Smiles Are Done* and *The Elder Brother*. Goh's maiden effort, *The Moon is Less Bright*, was staged by the Lotus Club of King Edward Hall at the University of Singapore. These plays dealt with issues such as cultural identity in the post-Separation era. However, while postcolonial in agenda, many critics felt that neither playwright had successfully captured the Singapore vernacular.

Not until the first part of ROBERT YEO's political trilogy *Are You There, Singapore?* (1974) did another full-length play endeavour to capture both Singaporean concerns and the country's characteristic use of English. The ETC continued to promote Singapore plays, staging both Li Lien Fung's quasi-historical epic *The Sword Has Two Edges* and STELLA KON's *Emily of Emerald Hill* in the following decade. Kon's play was the first Singapore production to play at the Edinburgh Festival Fringe.

Lao Jiu *(The Ninth Born) was first staged in English in 1993.*

Although the SINGAPORE ARTS FESTIVAL, which began in 1959, was revived in 1977, it involved more adaptations of foreign works and did not succeed in creating a playwriting tradition in the country. However, as a result of the Youth Festival, drama did begin to flourish in Singapore's schools.

Professionalism—1980s and 1990s

The 1980s were a pivotal decade in the history of Singapore English-language theatre, despite events such as the detaining of members of Third Stage in 1987 (*see* MARXIST CONSPIRACY).

In 1984, American-Chinese director Tzi Ma was invited to head a production of original Singapore short plays. Ma encouraged aspiring playwrights such as Michael Chiang, who went on to write successful comedies and musicals such as *Army Daze, Beauty World, Mixed Signals* and *Private Parts*. Ma also encouraged veteran playwright KUO PAO KUN to work in English. Kuo had previously made a name for himself in Mandarin-language theatre. He would go on to establish himself as the doyen of Singapore theatre, with such seminal works as the monologues *No Parking on Odd Days* and *The Coffin is Too Big For the Hole* and the polyglottal *Mama Looking for Her Cat* and *Lao Jiu*.

The first local theatre group to turn professional was the children's drama outfit Act 3. This was followed by THEATREWORKS. Many significant groups arose in the late 1980s, most comprising writers who had first collaborated within the milieu of the university campus. Such groups included The NECESSARY STAGE (TNS) and ACTION Theatre. Kuo Pao Kun also led several directorial workshops that spawned many of the second generation of young theatre practitioners, such as ONG KENG SEN, Ekachai Uekrongtham, ALVIN TAN and HARESH SHARMA.

Meanwhile, the setting up of the Singapore Cultural Foundation provided impetus and opportunities for funding and training, as well as awards such as the CULTURAL MEDALLION. Initiatives such as the Ministry of Culture's Playwriting Competition ensured a renewed effort in generating Singaporean works. The National University of Singapore (NUS)-Shell Short-play Competition was especially instrumental in discovering a new generation of young Singapore playwrights, such as Desmond Sim, ELEANOR WONG, OVIDIA YU, Chua Tze Wei and Theresa Tan.

From 1991, theatre companies benefited from the setting up of the NATIONAL ARTS COUNCIL. This organization spearheaded the promotion of the arts through the annual Singapore Arts Festival, an improved funding model, and infrastructural support. Grassroots initiatives also resulted in the conversion of an old electrical substation into an arts venue—The SUBSTATION—where experimental works were promoted, and theatre groups such as Theatre Ox and InSource Theatre were provided with a permanent home.

A recognizable Singapore identity

Various platforms for discovering and nurturing local playwriting talent were established in the next 15 years: TheatreWorks' Singapore Young Dramatist Awards, the 24-Hour Playwriting Competition and the Writers Laboratory, which unveiled the talents of TAN TARN HOW, Ng Yi Sheng and Chong Tze Chien; TNS' Playwright's Cove; and ACTION Theatre's Hewlett Packard Ten-Minute Play Contest and its Playwriting Spa/Theatre Idols series.

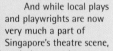

GLIDE DOWN. HOLD TIGHT. SPICE UP.

AUTUMN TOMYAM
A spicy new play for all adventurous taste buds

Although censorship caused such plays as ELANGOVAN's *Talaq* (Divorce) (which explored the issue of wife-abuse in the Indian Muslim community) to be banned, and DRAMA BOX's *VaginaLOGUE* to be denied funding, most playwrights veiled political critiques with satire, allegory and other metaphoric devices. Despite the claim that playwrights in Singapore circumvented government control by experimenting with form rather than content, many landmark plays extended the perimeters of permissible discourse: Eleanor Wong's lesbian trilogy *Invitation to Treat*; Tan Tarn How's *The Lady of Soul and the Ultimate S Machine, Undercover* and *The Emperor's Last Days*; Haresh Sharma's drama about racial tensions *This Chord and Others* and *Off Centre*; and Desmond Sim's *Autumn Tomyam*, which explored homosexual themes. By the beginning of the new millennium, even Forum theatre and performance art, which had previously suffered de facto bans because they involved unscripted

performances, had been reinstated in the artistic repertory.

Internationalism

The number of educational institutions providing training in theatre grew in the 1990s with the inception of the NUS Theatre Studies Programme by K.K. Seet in 1992 and the Theatre Training and Research Programme by Kuo Pao Kun towards the end of that decade. Both LASALLE-SIA COLLEGE OF THE ARTS and the NANYANG ACADEMY OF FINE ARTS also helped to meet the demand for trained personnel in the field.

Others were trained at institutions such as the Royal Scottish Academy of Music and Drama in Glasgow, where a number of people went on scholarship. These include actors IVAN HENG and NEO SWEE LIN. Other well-known professional actors include Glen Goei, who starred opposite Sir Anthony Hopkins in the London production of *M. Butterfly*, and Adrian Pang, who trained at the Royal Academy of Dramatic Art in London.

And while local plays and playwrights are now very much a part of Singapore's theatre scene, international works have not been ignored. SINGAPORE REPERTORY THEATRE, W!LD RICE, Luna-Id, and Toy Factory are local companies that are known for performing international plays. David Mamet's *Oleanna*, Harold Pinter's *Dumb Waiter*, John Pielmeier's *Agnes of God*, Martin Sherman's *Bent*, John Guare's *Six Degrees of Separation* and Friedrich Durrenmatt's *The Visit* have all been performed in Singapore since 2000.

The ESPLANADE—THEATRES ON THE BAY opened in 2002, becoming Singapore's premier venue for the performing arts.

David Mamet's
Oleanna
18 Aug-2 Sep

Bent *(below) was staged by the Toy Factory Theatre Ensemble in 2003.*

province, and were well received by the HAKKA and Teochew communities, proving especially popular with Teochew businessmen in the Chinese city of Swatow (present-day Shantou).

In the 1950s, opera movies produced in Hong Kong, such as *Chen San Wu Niang* (Chen San and Fifth Madam) (1954); *Huo Shao Lin Jiang Lou* (Fire at the Riverside Pavilion) (1959); and *Su Liu Niang* (1960) had sparked off a new interest in Teochew opera, and Er Woo began to stage Teochew opera performances. Its first success, *Bao Lian Deng* (Magic Lotus Lantern), was staged in 1963. Thereafter, Er Woo became one of the foremost amateur Teochew opera troupes in Singapore.

Placing great importance on training, Er Woo was the first group to engage trainers from China. Courses conducted by Er Woo since 1985 have helped many young talented Teochew opera artistes develop their skills. Er Woo has represented Singapore at international theatre festivals in China, France, Japan, Korea and Malaysia. Its well-known productions include *Hu Die Meng* (Dream of the Butterfly), *Pan Hun Ji* (Judging the Marriage) and *Princess Turandot*.

Esplanade–Theatres on the Bay *See* box.

Eu, Richard (1923–) Banker. Born the seventh son of EU TONG SEN, Richard Eu Keng Mun was educated in Singapore and then at Princeton University, where he graduated with a degree in economics. He joined Lee Wah Bank on his return to Singapore in 1948 and soon rose to be managing director. When the bank merged with UNITED OVERSEAS BANK (UOB) in 1973, he became a member of UOB's board and remained Lee Wah's managing director until 1980. He retired as vice-chairman of UOB in 1989.

Eu was active in the community, serving as council member of the University of Singapore (1963–68); and chairman of the Singapore Cancer Society (1964–71), the Singapore Institute of Management Governing Council (1964–96), and the Community Chest (1992–2000). He has also been awarded the Public Service Medal (1995) and the Public Service Star (2000).

Eu, Richard ('Dick') (1947–) Businessman and sportsman. Born in Hong Kong, Richard ('Dick') Eu Yee Ming is the eldest child of RICHARD EU, and has been resident in Singapore since 1949. He was educated at the Anglo-Chinese School and then at Kent College, Canterbury, and the University of London, where he graduated with a law degree. He started out as a merchant banker for the Haw Par Group before becoming a stockbroker and then managing director of a computer company.

In 1989, he joined the family business as group general manager. In 1993, he masterminded the buyback of the family's EU

YAN SANG business from Lum Chang Holdings for $21 million, and became its group chief executive officer. Active in sport, Eu represented Singapore in water-skiing at the 1983 Southeast Asian (SEA) Games, winning a bronze medal.

Eu Chooi Yip (1918–1995) Political activist. Eu Chooi Yip was born in Kuantan, Pahang. Little is known of his early life. In 1937, he arrived in Singapore to study at Raffles College, where he graduated with first class honours in economics. Upon graduation, Eu joined the civil service but later resigned to become a reporter with *The Straits Times* and, later, with *Nan Chiau Jit Poh*. In 1945, he joined the MALAYAN DEMOCRATIC UNION, rising to become its highly-influential secretary-general. Eu soon became embroiled in communist activities as a member of the MALAYAN COMMUNIST PARTY (MCP), and emerged as one of the MCP's most important leaders. By 1951, the colonial authorities were offering $5,000 as a reward for his arrest in connection with the distribution of communist propaganda.

Eu's health had never been robust, and he suffered from tuberculosis. When fleeing the colonial authorities, he sought refuge in various places, including the houses of S. RAJARATNAM and PHAY SENG WHATT. In 1953, Eu and FANG CHUANG PI ('the Plen') fled to the Riau Islands, where Eu managed MCP operations. While in Indonesia, he ran the outlawed communist organ, *Freedom News*, and maintained direct lines with communist chiefs in Malaya. When his tuberculosis worsened, Eu returned to Singapore for treatment, staying at the home of S. Rajaratnam in Chancery Lane. Fang Chuang Pi operated a motorized sampan, bringing Eu across the Riau archipelago before escorting him on foot to Rajaratnam's house. After treatment, Eu returned to Indonesia to head the Malayan National Liberation League in Jakarta. He was arrested by the Indonesian authorities in 1965 and deported to Hanoi.

In 1966, the Singapore government banned Eu and eight other communists from entering Singapore. The following year, North Vietnam granted him political asylum. He later left Hanoi for Beijing where he held a senior research post before becoming an English-language teacher at the Changsha Railway Institute in Hunan.

He retired as a teacher in 1990. In the same year, he wrote to an old friend, Goh Keng Swee, seeking Goh's help to lift the ban on his entry into Singapore, where he hoped to be reunited with his two daughters, Jing Lin and Hong Nian. Goh forwarded his request to the Ministry for Home Affairs, stating that he believed Eu had renounced communism. In January 1991, the ministry revoked the prohibition order upon an undertaking that Eu would not engage in any political activity. Goh

offered Eu a post at the Institute of East Asian Philosophies (predecessor of the EAST ASIAN INSTITUTE) as a consultant specializing in China affairs. Eu died of a lung infection in October 1995.

Eu Kong (c. 1852–1890) Merchant. Born in Canton (present-day Guangzhou), China, Eu Kong—also known as Eu Kwong Pai—left for Penang to seek his fortune in 1879. He first worked as a shop assistant and then as a miner. Using his savings, he started a provisions shop, Chop Yan Sang, in Gopeng, Perak. Eu saw that the miners were turning to opium to sooth their pains. He thus decided to found a Chinese medical hall (see CHINESE MEDICAL HALLS), EU YAN SANG, which prospered, as his herbal prescriptions proved popular amongst the mining community.

Eu died suddenly in 1890, aged only 38, possibly murdered by a jealous husband. By this time, he was well-known throughout Singapore's business world. He left most of his estate to his only son, EU TONG SEN, who was then only 13 years old.

Eu Tong Sen (1877–1941) Businessman. Born in Penang, the only son of EU KONG, Eu Tong Sen grew up in Kampar and Gopeng in Perak, but was educated in China.

He returned to Ipoh aged 15, two years after his father's death. When he turned 21, he took over his father's Chinese medical hall, EU YAN SANG, and expanded it. He became one of the wealthiest men in the region by the time he was 30, with a fortune that was derived mainly from TIN (he was known as the 'King of Tin'), rubber, palm oil, real estate, pharmaceutical products and banking.

Eu was also a major figure in Singapore's film industry, converting his Chinese opera theatre Tien Yien Moh Toi (built in 1927) into the Majestic Cinema (*see* MAJESTIC THEATRE). He opened the first Eu Yan Sang store in Singapore on South Bridge Road in 1910. This is still the company's flagship store today. In 1920, he founded Lee Wah Bank with Ng Sing Phang and Yow Ngan Pan.

Er Woo Amateur Musical and Dramatic Association: poster for 2005 production of Pan Hun Ji *(Judging the Marriage).*

Eu Kong

Eu Tong Sen

Eu Tong Sen Street.

Esplanade—Theatres on the Bay

Esplanade—Theatres on the Bay Performing Arts Centre. The centre, constructed at a cost of over $600 million, was opened with a 3-week gala festival that started on 12 October 2002. The idea of creating a centre for the performing arts in Singapore was mooted in the 1970s, but it was not until 1989, when the Advisory Council on Culture and the Arts, chaired by then Deputy Prime Minister ONG TENG CHEONG, that details for the centre began to take shape.

Architects Michael Wilford and Partners (based in London), and DP Architects (based in Singapore), designed the Esplanade. The overall design comprises the theatre, concert hall, and outer building. The theatre and concert hall are encased under two superstructures made of double-glazed laminated glass and aluminium sunshades. The triangular aluminium sunshades on the cladding have prompted Singaporeans to affectionately dub the Esplanade 'Durians'.

The two main venues, the theatre and concert hall, are accessed via the concourse. The venues, as well as the concourse, are acoustically isolated from each other. The venues sit on pads made of rubber and steel. The rubber pads are also placed under the cladding structures. These pads help minimize vibration and external noise from the car park below and from inclement weather above.

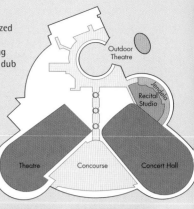

Aerial view of the Esplanade.

Theatre

The seats in the theatre are arranged in a horseshoe, in the style of traditional Italian opera houses. This ensures that everyone in the audience has a good view of the stage. The theatre has three stages. A sprung floor, designed to prevent injuries to performers, may be deployed during dance performances. The theatre also has a fly tower that contains bars that facilitate the suspension of scenery, lighting, and even performers. The theater has seen locally produced performances such as *Forbidden City: Portrait of an Empress* (Singapore Repertory Theatre Company) and international productions such as *West Side Story* (Sundance Productions).

Key facts
- Seating capacity: 1,923
- Floor area: 23,721 sq m
- Speakers: Meyer Sound
- Three stages: main, side and rear stages
- Stage floor: jarrah (a species of *Eucalyptus*) and fibreboard

Acoustic canopy of the Concert Hall (top); SSO performs Mahler's Symphony of a Thousand *with choirs from Singapore, Latvia and China, 2004.*

Concert Hall

The acoustics in the hall was designed by Russell Johnson of Artec Consultants Inc, USA. The acoustic characteristics in the hall can be adjusted to accommodate a range of musical performances from classical solo recitals to rock concerts. The reverberation chamber spans three floors and encircles the hall. Computer-controlled doors open or seal parts of the chamber to vary the reverberation quality. The ceiling has an acoustic canopy that allows musicians to hear themselves perform. The centrepiece of the hall is the pipe organ built by Johannes Klais Orgelbau of Germany. The Singapore Symphony Orchestra (SSO) regularly performs in the hall.

Key facts
- Seating capacity: 1,811
- Floor area: 26,490 sq m
- Speakers: d&b Audiotechnik
- Reverberation chamber: 9,500 cu m volume, with 84 concrete doors
- Acoustic canopy: 3 acoustic reflectors, 17 tonnes each
- Orchestral platform: 24 m x 12 m, accommodates 120 musicians
- Pipe organ: 25 tonnes, with 4,740 pipes
- Stage floor: Tasmanian oak

The Outdoor Theatre is used as a venue for free events.

Other venues
- Recital Studio, 245 seats
- Theatre Studio, 220 seats
- Outdoor venues:
  - Outdoor Theatre
  - Stage@Powerhouse

Facilities
- Jendela ('window' in Malay), exhibition space for visual art
- library@esplanade, with Arts-related material, both print and multimedia
- Esplanade Mall, three levels of shops and restaurants

Eu was also active in politics as the Chinese representative on Malaya's Federal Council from 1891 to 1920 and was vice-president of the Anti-Opium Society. He contributed generously to education, most notably to Raffles College and the University of Hong Kong.

Because of the number of Eu's female companions, it is not known exactly how large his family was, though he is known to have had six registered wives who bore him 13 sons and 11 daughters. Eu was found dead in the bedroom of his Hong Kong villa, Sirmio, in May 1941 on the eve of his departure to Australia, where the family hoped to seek refuge from the impending Japanese invasion. Eu Tong Sen Street in Singapore, upon which stands the Majestic, is named after him.

Eu Villa Family home of EU TONG SEN, of the EU YAN SANG Chinese medical halls. Built in Mount Sophia in 1914 in the Edwardian Baroque style, Eu Villa was once one of the largest residences in Singapore. Designed by the firm of SWAN & MACLAREN, it was a five-storey building with a dome over the double-storey entrance, and a sub-basement which accommodated a kitchen and cellar. The main living areas were in the front of the building. These afforded magnificent views of the town and harbour, while the bedrooms (numbering more than ten) were located in the rear. The house, which cost $1 million to build, was one of the first buildings in Singapore to be partially constructed in reinforced concrete with steel bars. It was used as the residence of the extensive Eu family (Eu Tong Sen had six registered wives and numerous other 'companions') until 1973, when it was sold. It was demolished in the early 1980s to develop a condominium project.

Eu Yan Sang Chinese medical hall. While family-run or sole-proprietor CHINESE MEDICAL HALLS are a common sight in Singapore's housing estates, one name stands out—Eu Yan Sang. 'Eu' is the surname of the company's founder, EU KONG, and 'yan sang' means 'caring for mankind' in Cantonese.

The Eu Yan Sang Group has more than 80 retail outlets in Singapore, Malaysia and Hong Kong. It sells more than 250 products under its Eu Yan Sang brand name, as well as 1,000 different Chinese herbs and medicinal items through more than 6,000 wholesalers, medical halls, supermarkets, spas, health clubs and pharmacy chains.

The group has also expanded its reach to new overseas markets such as North America and Western Europe. It has an e-shop for online purchases; best-sellers include birds' nest, Bak Foong pills for women and Bo Ying infant compound.

Eu Yan Sang also operates a dozen clinics in Singapore and Malaysia, and in Australia, a number of East-West fusion

medicine centres that combine the best practices of conventional medicine, TRADITIONAL CHINESE MEDICINE (TCM) and other natural therapies.

The group was listed on the Singapore Exchange in 2000. Turnover has grown from $72 million in 2000 to $166 million for the financial year 2005. Net profit for 2005 was $12.4 million.

Eurasian Association Few records detailing the early history of this association still exist, but it appears that it was formed in 1919 from the Eurasian Literary Association, which had been set up a year earlier. Its primary objectives were to promote the political, economic, social, moral, physical and intellectual advancement of all Eurasian subjects in the British Empire; to promote among its members an active interest in the affairs of Malaya; and generally to look after the interests of all EURASIANS in the empire. After separation from Malaysia, the objectives of the association began to reflect the importance of Singapore, rather than the United Kingdom, to Eurasians.

Education has always been accorded a high priority by the association, and many of its efforts have gone into helping the less fortunate. Tuition classes in Mandarin were instigated in 1994 with assistance from the Chinese Development Assistance Council (CDAC). Malay classes were started in 1997.

The association's welfare programmes are aimed at five different groups: the elderly; female-headed households; families in which a member is physically or mentally disabled or ill; children of school age who are not in school; and individuals who have health problems.

Eurasians The term 'Eurasian' is applied to people who claim both European and Asian descent. In 2005, there were estimated to be about 15,000 Eurasians living in Singapore. Some of the more common

Eu Yan Sang: South Bridge Road, 1980s

Eu Villa

Eurasian surnames include de Souza, Hendricks and Clarke.

The earliest Eurasian communities in Asia were formed in Ceylon (present-day Sri Lanka); Goa, in India; Malacca; and Macau, mainly through the union of Portuguese traders or military personnel and local women. During the early colonial period, Eurasians were generally known as 'Kristang', 'Mestizos' or 'Luzos'. Other groups of Eurasians were formed when the Dutch and British colonized Asia. Dutch Eurasians were known as 'burghers' while British Eurasians were known as 'Anglo-Indians'. In Malacca, which was ruled in turn by Dutch and British colonial administrations, there were also inter-Eurasian marriages. Due to the numerical dominance of the Portuguese group and their willingness to inter-marry, many Dutch and British Eurasians became Catholics during the colonial period. There are many Protestant Eurasians, but in Southeast Asia they are fewer in number than Catholic Eurasians.

Throughout much of the colonial period, Europeans were socially close to Eurasians. This was partially because of their shared religious affiliation, CHRISTIANITY, but also because the two communities were culturally similar. In many colonial cities, Eurasians were schooled and trained by Europeans to fill various posts in the colonial civil service. This has been interpreted as a colonial strategy to reduce costs (by not having to ship Europeans to Asia for these jobs) but also to consolidate a community that would remain loyal to colonial administrators. The British in India, as well as in Hong Kong and the Straits Settlements, employed this system. Thus, in many colonial cities across Asia, Eurasians were often a relatively privileged class, ranking in status and power slightly below Europeans, but above local and migrant Asian communities.

When Singapore was founded in 1819, many Eurasians, mostly from Malacca but some also from Goa and Macau, moved to the island to earn a living. Between 1819 and 1869, Europeans generally treated Eurasians in Singapore as peers. There are records of many marriages taking place between Europeans and Eurasians during

Eurasians: Eunice Olsen (top) and Lionel Lewis.

Eurasian cuisine

Devil's curry

This dish may have its origins in Goa, but it is well-loved fare in Singapore, and is often reserved for Christmas. Its main ingredients are various forms of meat, vegetables and potatoes. Although there are several recipes for devil's curry, the practice is to utilize all leftover meat from Christmas Eve dinner, which might include turkey, beef, chicken or sausages. As might be expected from its name, Devil's curry is a hot, spicy dish.

Smore

A meat stew, where beef or pork is used along with a generous inclusion of vinegar.

Sugee cake

Although the Peranakan and Malay communities also claim sugee cake as their own, using ingredients such as almonds, semolina, butter and eggs, the Eurasian version is distinct because of its generous use of brandy. The cake is also often reserved for special occasions, such as weddings and christenings, when the cake is coated with thick sugar icing.

Devil's curry (top); sugee cake.

the period. Even though there were separate sporting clubs for each community—the SINGAPORE CRICKET CLUB for Europeans and the SINGAPORE RECREATION CLUB for Eurasians—the two communities met in friendly competition to play cricket, hockey, tennis and rugby.

However, after the opening of the SUEZ CANAL in 1869, Europeans began to socially marginalize Eurasians. The Suez Canal halved the travelling time from Europe to Asia. Thus, many more Europeans—particularly European women—came to Asia. With more Europeans in Singapore, Europeans began to close ranks as a community to protect their privileged social status. Marriages between Europeans and Eurasians declined significantly, as European men either chose to marry European women who were already in Singapore, or took advantage of the relative ease of travel by returning to Europe to find a spouse.

As Eurasians were not close to other Asian communities in Singapore at the time, they were compelled to build a community from within. Many recollections of this period speak of a strong sense of pride

in being Eurasian. The main source of Eurasian identity during this time was CATHOLICISM. There were two churches in colonial Singapore that served the Eurasian community: ST JOSEPH'S CHURCH in the city centre, which was the Portuguese Mission and first Roman Catholic Church to have been established in Singapore in 1825; and the Church of the Holy Family, which was established in Katong in 1902, after several Eurasian families moved into the area.

Other important indicators of Eurasian identity during colonial times included food and popular culture (particularly music and dance). Many Eurasians used Kristang—a Malacca creole that combined Portuguese and Malay—within their own community during this period. Economically, Eurasians retained positions in the colonial administration. However, many felt frustrated by the lack of advancement in the colonial administration, and blamed Europeans for having created a 'glass ceiling' for their own protection.

In 1919, the EURASIAN ASSOCIATION (EA) was formed to promote the interests of Eurasians. It also served as the community's third social hub after the Singapore Recreation Club and the churches with predominantly Eurasian congregations.

The onset of World War II in Singapore in 1942 marked the darkest years for the Eurasian community. Eurasians were generally regarded as British sympathizers during the JAPANESE OCCUPATION because they were partly European. Many were kept under house arrest in Singapore, while several families were voluntarily moved to a special autonomous settlement in BAHAU in Negri Sembilan. Eurasians remember Bahau as a 'concentration camp without the executions'.

Due to political uncertainty surrounding Malaya and Singapore, a large proportion of Eurasians emigrated to other locations within the Commonwealth (especially Perth in Australia), taking advantage of their British subject status. Most of those who remained in Singapore aligned themselves with the People's Action Party's (PAP) vision of a 'Malaysian Malaysia', with its emphasis on non-racial politics, as the political destiny of the whole of Malaya was being shaped. Ultimately, when Singapore was eventually expelled from Malaysia, most Eurasians were firmly behind the newly independent Singapore government's policy of MULTIRACIALISM. One prominent Eurasian was E. W. BARKER, a founding member of the PAP and minister of law, who drafted Singapore's CONSTITUTION.

However, the immediate post-Independence period saw ethnic politics take a new turn, as Singapore's multiracialism served to intensify personal ethnic identification. For example, the Singapore government stressed that all students in Singapore had to learn their MOTHER

TONGUE as part of their education. Kristang was not officially recognized as a 'mother tongue'. As a consequence, many Eurasian schoolchildren not only had to learn either Mandarin or Malay as their second language, but also had to pass examinations in these languages in order to enter tertiary education. It was also around this time that Eurasian families stopped transmitting Kristang to the young, since the language was not considered to be useful in modern Singapore. Furthermore, Singapore's multiracial policy seemed to imply that society was constituted solely on the Chinese, Malay, Indian and Other (CMIO) model. Many Eurasians disliked being classified as 'Other,' as opposed to 'Eurasian', on their identity cards.

For these reasons, between 1965 and 1980, the Eurasian community became an 'invisible' community. Eurasians, apparently, had 'no culture'—at least not in the multiracial-CMIO sense. Although the community seemed to be searching for its own identity at the time, it was ironic that the head of state at that time was a Eurasian: the president of Singapore between 1971 and 1981 was BENJAMIN SHEARES, a prominent obstetrician and academic.

After 1980, there was a strong resurgence of interest on the part of Eurasians in their community identity. This led to the revival of the EA, which saw its paid membership rise from a low of 96 in 1986 to over 1,000 by the 1990s.

In the late 1990s, when the Singapore government was promoting ethnic-based self-help welfare groups such as the Chinese Development Assistance Council, Mendaki and the Singapore Indian Development Association, the EA stepped forward to act on behalf of Eurasians. It was also around this time that the EA began broadening its own definition of the word 'Eurasian'. Although never explicit, the EA was once hesitant about including 'new' Eurasians (first generation Eurasian children who had one Caucasian and one Asian parent). Since 1995, the EA has openly accepted anyone who has both European and Asian ancestry. That is why there are Eurasians today, with traditionally Eurasian names, as well as some with entirely Chinese, Malay or Indian names, but who might have a Eurasian or Caucasian mother.

expatriates Foreign nationals—historically 'white' (Caucasian)—who live and work in Singapore. Sir STAMFORD RAFFLES and Colonel WILLIAM FARQUHAR might loosely

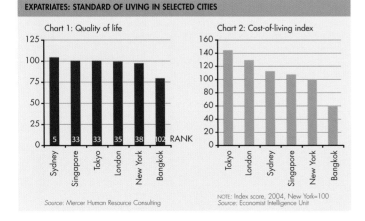

EXPATRIATES: STANDARD OF LIVING IN SELECTED CITIES

Chart 1: Quality of life

						RANK
Sydney	Singapore	Tokyo	London	New York	Bangkok	
5	33	33	35	38	102	

Source: Mercer Human Resource Consulting

Chart 2: Cost-of-living index

Tokyo, London, Sydney, Singapore, New York, Bangkok

NOTE: Index score, 2004, New York=100
Source: Economist Intelligence Unit

be considered to be the first expatriates in Singapore. Singapore's rapid growth brought an influx of British and European arrivals in the mid-19th century. For more than a century, 'expats' (the abbreviated term which is used locally to describe foreign white-collar workers) lived in upmarket enclaves, enjoying handsome privileges.

From the late 20th century onwards, multinational corporations which had set up offices in Singapore posted staff to the country, and technical specialists also joined these professionals, managers and businessmen as the government sought to attract urgently-needed FOREIGN TALENT—highly skilled, qualified and experienced people who were believed to be able to boost economic growth—as part of an ongoing policy.

Quality of life and cost of living (see table) have been important factors in drawing expatriates to Singapore. Present-day expatriates include Europeans, North Americans, Australians and professionals from India, China and the Philippines. Asian expatriates, however, are to be distinguished from 'FOREIGN WORKERS' or 'foreign labour', who are not Singapore citizens and are employed at salaries not exceeding $1,500 a month (or any sum stipulated by legislation). This latter group includes MAIDS and construction workers, who together make up the largest proportion of the group, and other foreigners working in blue-collar professions.

Expat and *Expat Living Singapore* magazines both cater to expatriates, providing them with information on recreational pursuits, social life and housing.

exports Total exports are made up of both domestic exports—oil and non-oil commodities—re-exports, and service exports. Exports of commodities increased from $3 billion in 1965 by an average of 12.6 per cent per year to $303.5 billion in 2004. Between 1965 and 1973, in order to lower unemployment rates, the Singapore government focused on labour-intensive export-oriented manufacturing such as crude materials, textiles and transistors. Exports grew rapidly by an average of 19 per cent annually during the 1965–74 period. After 1974, the electronics industry began a calculated transition away from labour-intensive products towards goods with higher technological content and worker skills. Despite the 1979 oil crisis, Singapore's total exports, driven by the newer electrical and electronics industries, continued to grow at an average of 5.5 per cent per year during 1981–84.

In the second half of the 1980s, refined oil accounted for almost half of Singapore's domestic exports, while about one-third came from the ELECTRONICS SECTOR. With rapid expansion in the production and export of disk drives and personal computers in the early 1990s, the electronics share of exports grew signifi-

Expatriates: lifestyle magazines catering to the expatriate community.

cantly during the 1991–95 period. The late 1990s saw higher value-added semiconductors gaining importance as several wafer fabrication plants came into operation. However, due to increasing competition, intense efforts have since been made to diversify into the biomedical sector and the PETROCHEMICALS SECTOR.

In 2005, Malaysia was Singapore's largest export partner (13.2 per cent), followed by Europe (12.7 per cent), the United States (10.2 per cent) and Hong Kong (9.3 per cent).

Singapore's world ranking as an exporter of services such as food, beverage and accommodation; transport and communications; and finance and real estate, increased from 18th position in 1986 to 12th in 1996 before sliding back to 18th in 2003. Key exportable services experienced rapid growth in the early 1990s, but between 1996 and 2001, exports of commercial services fell by an average of 2.3 per cent per annum, due in part to the Asian financial crisis. However, this bounced back to register 3 per cent growth in 2002.

expressways An expressway network of 150 km links Singapore's major activity centres: the central area, the new towns, industrial estates, the port and Changi Airport. The first expressway, the East Coast Parkway (ECP), was opened in 1981. The others are the Pan-Island Expressway (PIE), Ayer Rajah Expressway (AYE), Central Expressway (CTE) (with two tunnels through the city), Bukit Timah Expressway (BKE), Kranji Expressway (KJE), Seletar Expressway (SLE) and Tampines Expressway (TPE). The Kallang-Paya Lebar Expressway, to be completed in 2008, will have 9 km of tunnel.

ExxonMobil Petrochemical company. The company's presence in Singapore dates back to 1893, with the establishment of the Vacuum Oil Company, which sold lubricants under the Mobiloil brand name. It became part of Standard Oil Company of New York in 1931, and was renamed Standard-Vacuum Oil Company. This lasted

until 1962, when the company was dissolved, leading to the formation of two new companies, Esso (which took its name from the first two letters of Standard Oil) and Mobil.

Both Esso and Mobil started to build their own refineries in Singapore from the 1960s. By the early 1970s, Singapore had become the third largest refining centre in the world after Houston and Rotterdam. New investments were added in the 1980s and 1990s as both Mobil and Esso upgraded their refining capacities and added more downstream petrochemicals and lubricant plants to their Singapore operations. In 1999, Exxon Corporation and Mobil Corporation merged.

A single new state-of-the-art US$2 billion petrochemical plant on JURONG ISLAND was commissioned in 2001. With that investment, ExxonMobil became the largest single foreign investor in Singapore, having invested more than US$6.5 billion in Singapore since the early 1960s. After the merger, ExxonMobil could also boast Singapore's largest petrol station network, with over 70 outlets.

EZ-Link card Contactless card used on buses and the MASS RAPID TRANSIT/LIGHT RAIL TRANSIT SYSTEM. Passengers tap the card against a card reader on entry and exit at the fare gates of train stations or at the doors of buses. The correct fare is deducted on a distance-related basis. Fare rebates are provided for multiple rides when passengers transfer between buses or between bus and train within stipulated periods. Personalized cards permit concession travel for senior citizens, students and national servicemen. Prior to the introduction of EZ-Link in 2002, fare cards were magnetic-strip stored-value cards. In 2005, there were 7 million EZ-Link cards in use.

EXPORTS: AVERAGE ANNUAL NOMINAL GROWTH IN TOTAL EXPORTS	
Year	%
1965–69	12.1
1970–74	31.3
1975–79	24.8
1980–84	5.5
1985–89	14.8
1990–94	11.5
1995–99	3.8
2000–04	6.3

Source: International Monetary Fund

EZ-Link card

Expressways: Pan-Island Expressway (PIE).

Michael Fam

Fang Chuang Pi

Fandi Ahmad

Faber House bombings Series of bomb attacks which took place in the mid-1980s at Faber House, an office block at the junction of Cairnhill and Orchard Roads. The largest occurred on Sunday 17 March 1985. No one was injured but damage to the building, owned by UNITED OVERSEAS LAND, was estimated at $50,000.

It was suspected that the bomb was intended for the Israeli Embassy, which had its offices in the building, although the embassy itself denied receiving any bomb threats. The police and the Internal Security Department were unable to find the perpetrators.

Fajar trial Trial of University of Malaya students in the 1950s. In February 1953, JAMES PUTHUCHEARY persuaded the University of Malaya authorities to allow students to establish a socialist club. The club produced a newsletter, *Fajar* (meaning 'dawn' in Malay), a radical leftist publication popular with students and English-educated intellectuals. The seventh issue of *Fajar*, published in May 1954, was memorable for an editorial entitled 'Aggression in Asia', which the British government considered seditious. Three days after it appeared, Chinese middle school students clashed with the police. The editorial board was arrested two weeks later and charged with sedition. Among them were Puthucheary and author EDWIN THUMBOO.

LEE KUAN YEW, legal advisor to the club and a *Fajar* subscriber, arranged for Queen's Counsel D.N. PRITT to travel from the United Kingdom to defend the students. Lee acted as Pritt's junior counsel. The students were tried before District Judge F.A. CHUA, and were acquitted.

Falck, Anton (1777–1843) Dutch politician and diplomat. Born in Utrecht, Anton Reinhard Falck entered the Dutch diplomatic service after studying at the University of Leiden. He was a key figure in the Dutch revolt of 1813 against French domination in the Netherlands, and emerged as a major player in the political restructuring of Netherlands after the Congress of Vienna in 1815.

As foreign minister of the Kingdom of the Netherlands, Falck played a decisive role in negotiating, and was one of those who signed, the ANGLO-DUTCH TREATY (1824). It was through this treaty that Singapore was formally assigned to the British sphere of influence in the region.

Fall of Singapore *See* MALAYA CAMPAIGN and WORLD WAR II.

Fam, Michael (1927–) Businessman. Born in Sandakan, British North Borneo (present-day Sabah), Michael Fam Yue Onn was educated at St Andrew's School in Singapore, and then at the University of Western Australia, where he graduated with a first class honours degree in civil engineering.

Fam has served as chairman of Haw Par Brothers International Ltd (1975–77); Carnaud Metal Box Asia Ltd (1993–96); Singapore Airlines (1998–2001); the Housing & Development Board (1975–83); Nanyang Technological University Council (1982–93); Mass Rapid Transit Corporation (1983–91); the Public Transport Council (1987–1989); Fraser & Neave (1983–); Asia-Pacific Breweries (1990–); and Centrepoint Properties Ltd. Fam was appointed to the Council of Presidential Advisers in 1991. He was awarded the MERITORIOUS SERVICE MEDAL in 1976, and was admitted into the DISTINGUISHED SERVICE ORDER in 1983 and the ORDER OF NILA UTAMA (First Class) in 1990.

Family Court Part of the SUBORDINATE COURTS, the Family Court was established on 1 March 1995 to provide a specialized forum for the legal resolution of family disputes. A Family Court judge—whose rank is equivalent to that of a district judge—presides over the court.

Originally, the court dealt only with applications for maintenance, protection orders and adoption. Its jurisdiction was later expanded to cover matrimonial cases, custody applications and the division of matrimonial assets. All proceedings are filed and heard in the first instance at the court, with appeals going to the High Court. As well as hearing cases, the Family Court provides mediation and counselling services, and houses a Family and Justice Centre.

Fandi Ahmad (1962–) Sportsman. Fandi joined Singapore's national football squad at the age of 16—the youngest player to have done so at the time of writing. He scored the winning goal in Singapore's 2–1 Malaysia Cup victory over Selangor in 1980. In 1981, he became a professional footballer, his career thereafter including periods· with the Dutch teams Ajax Amsterdam and FC Groningen, as well as with Indonesia's Niac Mitra and the Kuala Lumpur Football Club.

Fandi represented Singapore at the Southeast Asian (SEA) Games in 1983, 1985 and 1989; the team won a silver medal on each occasion. In 1994, he played for Singapore in the Malaysia Cup final against Pahang, with Singapore winning 4–0. Fandi was captain of the national team (1993–97), and received a Public Service Medal (PBM) in 1994.

Fajar trial: defence lawyer D.N. Pritt, far right.

As coach of the Singapore Armed Forces Football Club, he took the team to an S-League and cup double in 1997. In 2001, at the age of 38, he became the youngest former international football player to be appointed a council member of the Football Association of Singapore. Fandi is married to South African-born model, Wendy Jacobs.

See also SOCCER.

Fang Chuang Pi (1924–2004) Political activist. Also known as Fong Chong Pek and 'The Plen', Fang Chuang Pi was born in Canton (present-day Guangdong), China, and arrived in Singapore at the age of six. He was educated at Chinese High School, but also spent a year at St Andrew's School. Fang's political proclivities while at school attracted the attention of EU CHOOI YIP who introduced him into the MALAYAN COMMUNIST PARTY (MCP).

After graduating, Fang joined the *Nan Chiao Jit Poh* newspaper as a reporter, while editing the underground *Freedom News* in the evenings. He soon rose to third-in-command in the MCP's Singapore branch. In 1950, he escaped a raid by SPECIAL BRANCH on the *Nan Chiao Jit Poh*'s Cross Street premises. He then fled Singapore, as the police also closed in on the Lorong Tai Seng works where *Freedom News* was printed. A $2,000 reward was offered by the authorities for his arrest.

Fang is mainly remembered for the secret meetings he had with Lee Kuan Yew. Fang first approached Lee in March 1958, and they met in the Select Committee Room of the Legislative Assembly Building (present-day Old Parliament House). Fang informed Lee that he represented the MCP in Singapore, and that he wanted to establish cooperation between the communists and non-communists in the People's Action Party (PAP) so that a united front could be formed to head the next government. Lee asked Fang for proof of his authority over communist and pro-communist cadres in the PAP, and told Fang to instruct the WORKERS' PARTY's Chang Yuen Tong—who had won the City Council seat for Kallang—to resign from both the Workers' Party and the City Council. As Fang did not reveal his true identity to Lee at this meeting, the latter referred to him as 'the Plen' (short for 'plenipotentiary').

Chang resigned from both the Worker's Party and the City Council within eight weeks. Lee met 'the Plen' several more times, with Fang asking for concessions, including the abolition of the Internal Security Council, to give the communists more space for united front activities. When Lee refused these requests, Fang began to cause unrest within the PAP. After the GENERAL ELECTION (1963), Lee publicly told Fang to leave Singapore, as internal security was in the hands of the Federation of Malaysia's central government, and Lee had to reveal Fang's identity to them.

Little is known of Fang's activities in the following years, although he may have resided in southern Thailand. He appeared publicly again in 1989 when the MCP signed a peace agreement with the Malaysian and Thai governments. Fang later met Lee several times in China and sought permission to return to Singapore. In 1995, he was granted a one-week pass to return to Singapore on a social visit, an offer he subsequently declined because of a disagreement over conditions. He died of cancer at the age of 79 in Hat Yai, Thailand.

Fang Xiu (1922–) Editor and author. Fang Xiu is the pseudonym of Wu Zhiguang. Wu is one of the few remaining members of the China-born generation of writers who had worked as editors of literary supplements in early Chinese-language newspapers in Singapore. These supplements were a significant force in the growth of the Chinese literary scene in Singapore. Fang was the editor of the literary supplement of SIN CHEW JIT POH until he retired in 1979. Fang Xiu's best known works are anthologies, and several books about the history of CHINESE LITERATURE in Singapore and Malaysia, including *Ma Hua Xin Wen Xue Da Xi* (A Comprehensive Anthology of Malayan Chinese New Literature) (10 volumes, 1971–72); *Ma Hua Xin Wen Xue Shi Gao* (Draft History of Malayan Chinese New Literature) (3 volumes, 1962–65); and *Zhan Hou Ma Hua Wen Xue Shi Chu Gao* (A Tentative History of Malaysian Chinese Literature of the Post-War Period) (1978).

Fann Wong (1971–) Actress and singer. Born Fann Woon Fong, Fann Wong won a beauty contest organized by HER WORLD at age 16. She soon became a successful model in Singapore and Taiwan. This led to her discovery by a television producer, and an invitation to act in a Singapore drama serial, *Mei Meng Cheng Zhen* (Dreams Come True) in 1994. In her first year as an actress, she won both the Most Popular Newcomer and Best Actress awards at the Star Awards (1995).

In 1996, Fann released her first album, *Fanntasy*. Her second album, *Yi Ge Ren Sheng Huo* (I Live Alone) (1997), sold more than half a million copies. She became the

first Singaporean singer to hold a solo concert at the SINGAPORE INDOOR STADIUM.

Fann made her big screen debut with *Zhen Xin Hua* (*The Truth About Jane & Sam*) (1999), a film by Hong Kong director Derek Yee. The role earned her a nomination for Best Newcomer at the Hong Kong Film Awards 2000. In 2003, she appeared alongside international stars Jackie Chan and Owen Wilson in her first Hollywood production, *Shanghai Knights*.

Far East Command Singapore has twice come under the direction of a Far East Command. The first period was from October 1940 to January 1942; the second was from 1963 to 1971. During the first period, the command was headed by Air Chief Marshal Sir ROBERT BROOKE-POPHAM, and then by Lieutenant-General Sir Henry Pownall, as commander in chief (CIC) Far East. The command was responsible to the chiefs of staff for the higher defence planning and operational control of British land and air forces in Malaya, Burma and Hong Kong. Naval forces were excluded.

Administrative and financial responsibilities, as well as day-to-day functions, remained under the command of the general and air officers commanding the respective areas. The CIC was served by a small staff, with intelligence coming from the admiralty-controlled and Hong Kong-based Far East Combined Intelligence Bureau. It was Brooke-Popham, as CIC Far East Command, who was responsible for OPERATION MATADOR.

Far East Command was superseded by American British Dutch Australian Command, which was headed by Sir ARCHIBALD WAVELL. After World War II, military coordination was maintained by a British Defence Coordinating Committee (Far East), chaired by the governor general for Southeast Asia.

When Singapore merged with Malaya and the Borneo territories to form Malaysia in 1963, a new Far East Command was established. This was responsible for coordinating activities relating to China, Hong Kong and Singapore. This was an inter-service command, comprising Far East land forces, the Australian army, and air and naval elements. Following the British decision to scale down forces in the region (*see* BRITISH WITHDRAWAL FROM SINGAPORE), Far East Command was discontinued in 1971, and was superseded by a token ANZUK Force which left the region in May 1976.

Far East Organization Property development company. Founded in the 1960s by NG TENG FONG, Far East Organization (FEO) had become Singapore's largest private property developer by 2006.

FEO has developed more than 700 properties in Singapore, ranging from condominiums, hotels and offices, to industrial

and commercial real estate. Some of its best-known residential developments have included The Bayshore, River Place and Tanglin View, as well as developments such as The Icon and Water Place. FEO has also carried out award-winning conservation projects which include FAR EAST SQUARE as well as the FULLERTON BUILDING (The Fullerton Hotel Singapore). It also developed the Novena Medical Centre.

FEO is the largest owner-operator of serviced apartments in prime locations, such as the Orchard Parksuites, Regency House and Riverside View. It own and operates Orchard Parade Hotel, The Elizabeth Hotel, Albert Court Hotel, Golden Landmark Hotel, Changi Village Hotel and The Fullerton Hotel Singapore.

Besides its two listed arms—Orchard Parade Holdings Limited and the food and beverage company YEO HIAP SENG—FEO owns more than 180 privately-held development and investment companies. Its sister company, the Sino Group, is the one of the largest foreign-owned developers in Hong Kong. Ng Teng Fong's sons, Philip and Robert, head FEO and Sino respectively.

Far East Square Development incorporating 61 restored two- and three-storey SHOPHOUSES of various architectural styles. It includes the FUK TAK CHI TEMPLE, which has been converted into a museum, and the Chui Eng Free School, which was established by TAN KIM SENG. Originally separate units, the shophouses have been linked together by connecting spaces to create a larger commercial floor area. The shophouse facades, the air wells and the walls separating each unit were left intact to retain architectural character. The development received the Urban Redevelopment Authority Architectural Heritage Award in 1999.

Far East War Council 'War Cabinet' designed to coordinate civil and military authorities and the defence of British territories in East Asia during WORLD WAR II. Originally, the Defence Committee (pre-September 1939) and War Committee (1939–41) were both chaired by Sir

Fann Wong

Fang Xiu: 1970–71 volume of **Mahua Xin Wenxue Daxi** *(A Comprehensive Anthology of Modern Malayan Chinese Literature).*

Far East Square

SHENTON THOMAS, as governor of the Straits Settlements and high commissioner to the Federated Malay States. However, a new council, with a similar composition, was formed in Singapore two days after Japanese troops attacked Malaya and Thailand on 10 December 1941.

The main difference between the old committee and the new 'war Cabinet' was that the latter's chairman, ALFRED DUFF COOPER—Cabinet representative in the Far East—had authority to coordinate and deal with diplomatic matters, although he did not hold executive authority. Other council members included the governor (Sir Shenton Thomas); the commander-in-chief Far East; the commander-in-chief Eastern Fleet; the general officer commanding Malaya; the air officer commanding Far East; and, later, Sir George Sansom, who was responsible for propaganda and press control. Its first secretary was Major Lindsay Robertson—Argyll and Sutherland Highlander, and staff officer to Alfred Duff Cooper. Lieutenant-General GORDON BENNETT, commander of the Australian 8th Division, also sat on the council when matters affecting Australia were discussed.

The council met on an almost daily basis at Malaya Command's Sime Road operational headquarters, each meeting lasting about two hours. Brigadier IVAN SIMSON joined from 30 December 1941, upon becoming director general of civil defence. After Duff Cooper's departure in January, the governor took over as chairman. The council's final meeting was held on 9 February 1942.

See also MALAYA CAMPAIGN.

Colonel William Farquhar

Farquhar, Colonel William (1774–1839)

Colonial official. Colonel William Farquhar was born in Newhall, Scotland. He was appointed on a cadetship to the Indian branch of the British EAST INDIA COMPANY (EIC) at the age of 17. Arriving at Fort St George in Madras, he was posted to the Corps of Engineers. In 1795, he was involved in the military expedition against Dutch-held Malacca. British forces occupied the settlement, leaving the Dutch government to administer the settlement under British supervision. For the next 23 years, Farquhar was largely based in Malacca. He was promoted to commandant of Malacca in 1803.

One of his administration's achievements was that he was able to persuade the East India Company to reverse their decision to destroy the fortifications and other buildings in Malacca. Unfortunately, the fortress, A Famosa, had been blown up by that time, but the Christ Church, the Stadthuys and other public buildings were spared.

It was while in Malacca that Farquhar indulged his interest in natural history and wildife, sending men to collect plant and animal specimens, which he then commissioned artists to paint. Some of these speci-

mens are held at the Wallich Herbarium at the Royal Botanic Gardens at Kew, in the United Kingdom. The collection of watercolours ended up with the Royal Asiatic Society, which auctioned them at Sotheby's in 1995. Stockbroker and philanthropist GOH GEOK KHIM purchased the collection in its entirety and donated it to the NATIONAL MUSEUM OF SINGAPORE in April 1996.

Farquhar was Resident and commandant of Malacca when it was handed over to the Dutch authorities on 21 September 1818. He then left Malacca for Penang, where he was instructed by Sir STAMFORD RAFFLES—at that time lieutenant-general of BENCOOLEN—to accompany Raffles on a mission to explore the islands of Riau, Karimun and Singapore, with the intention of establishing a British trading post in the area. On 29 January 1819, Raffles and Farquhar landed at Singapore and obtained permission from Temenggong ABDUL RAHMAN of Johor to establish a trading post. Farquhar was then sent to Riau to pacify the Bugis ruler, Raja Jafar, and to secure his approval for a British settlement. Farquhar returned to Singapore on 3 February. Three days later, Sultan HUSAIN SHAH of Johor, who was newly recognized by the British, and the *temenggong*, signed a treaty with Raffles, which granted the EIC permission to establish a trading factory at Singapore in return for annual payments of $5,000 and $3,000 to the sultan and *temenggong* respectively.

Farquhar was appointed Resident and commandant of the settlement, a position he held for four years. By the end of 1820, Singapore's trade had already exceeded that of Malacca during its most prosperous period. The population had increased dramatically to 6,000 by 1821.

The greatest problem that Farquhar faced was a lack of revenue. He could not collect taxes or duties, so he decided to impose port charges to cover the expenses of the Master Attendant's Department and introduce REVENUE FARMING for the sale of opium, arrack and gaming. The farming system gained the reluctant approval of Raffles, but the gaming licence was disapproved on the grounds that it encouraged

William Farquhar: the Chinese community presented this epergne to Farquhar before his departure.

vice (*see* GAMBLING). Farquhar had problems persuading the senior officers at Calcutta of the need for investment in public works, and consequently he had to pay for a number of expenses from his own funds.

There was also a long delay in the exchange of letters between Singapore and West Sumatra, where Raffles was stationed. As a result, Farquhar had no assistance in dealing with urgent matters, and his increasing frustration at having to act under Raffles' immediate supervision and what he perceived as Raffles' lack of understanding of the actual situation resulted in a breakdown in relations between the two. On 28 April 1823, Raffles summarily dismissed Farquhar as Resident with effect from 1 May. Three weeks later, Farquhar was also removed as commandant. He remained in Singapore until the end of 1823. At a farewell dinner on the eve of Farquhar's departure, the Chinese inhabitants of Singapore arranged with London silversmiths Rundle, Bridge & Rundle to have a large silver epergne made as a mark of their regard for him. The epergne is currently in the possession of the National Museum of Singapore.

Farquhar retired to Scotland, bitter about his dismissal. In 1824, he wrote to the directors of the EIC claiming he had founded Singapore, complaining about his unfair dismissal and requesting a reinstatement.

William Farquhar: images from the Farquhar collection of natural history drawings (1803–18).

The request for reinstatement was unsuccessful, but Farquhar never gave up his claim to have been at least partly responsible for the founding of Singapore. An inscription on his tomb would note: 'During 20 years of his valuable life he was appointed to offices of high responsibility under the civil government of India having in addition to his military duties served as Resident in Malacca and afterwards at Singapore which later settlement he founded'.

Farrer Park Originally a swampy piece of land, this area was the site of the Singapore Sporting Club, formed in 1842. Singapore's first race meeting was held there in 1843, shortly after the land had been drained. In 1891, Singapore's first organized game of GOLF was played on a nine-hole golf course in the middle of the racecourse. The area was also used for cattle grazing, and as a rifle range.

In 1911, the park became the first place in Singapore from which an aeroplane took off. The plane was piloted by a Frenchman, Joseph Christiaens, who had shipped the aircraft to Singapore. In 1919, the first aeroplane to land in Singapore—a Vickers Vimy piloted by the brothers Captain Ross Smith and Lieutenant Keith Smith, who were undertaking a flight from the United Kingdom to Australia—also did so on the racecourse. In the same year, celebrations marking the centenary of the Founding of Singapore were held there. In 1924, the Singapore Sporting Club was renamed the SINGAPORE TURF CLUB (the club moved to Bukit Timah in 1933).

The area was renamed Farrer Park in 1935, in honour of Municipal Councillor R.G. Farrer, who ran the Singapore Improvement Trust in the 1930s. During the Japanese Occupation, the park was an assembly point for Malay and Indian prisoners-of-war. After the war, Farrer Park became the scene of many People's Action Party rallies, and was used as a sporting venue. Farrer Park later became the site of a housing development.

Fatimah, Hajjah (dates unknown) Businesswoman and philanthropist. Little is known of the life of Hajjah Fatimah. It has, however, been recorded that she was born

Michael Fay

in Malacca to a wealthy Malay family, and that she married a Bugis prince from Sulawesi (Celebes). Widowed at a young age, she carried on a large, lucrative business and owned many sea-going vessels. Hajjah Fatimah's house on Java Road in Kampong Glam was torched by robbers on two occasions and she decided not to rebuild the house after the second incident. Instead, she financed the building of a mosque, now known as the HAJJAH FATIMAH MOSQUE. Hajjah Fatimah's daughter, Raja Siti, married Syed Ahmad Abdul Rahman Alsagoff, a wealthy trader who owned several sailing vessels and steamers (*see* ALSAGOFF FAMILY). Hajjah Fatimah passed away at the age of 98. Her tombstone and that of her daughter's were placed side by side in a special chamber within the Hajjah Fatimah Mosque, while that of Syed Ahmad Abdul Rahman Alsagoff can be found at the rear of the mosque.

Fay, Michael (1975–) American teenager caned for vandalism. On 3 March 1994, Michael Peter Fay, an American teenager living in Singapore, was sentenced to four months' jail and six strokes of the cane, and was fined $3,500, after pleading guilty to vandalizing a number of cars. Fay faced 53 charges in all. He and a number of accomplices had damaged 18 vehicles over ten days. Fay pleaded guilty to two vandalism charges, two counts of mischief and one charge of possessing stolen property.

The story received widespread media coverage, especially in the United States, where President Bill Clinton declared that the punishment of CANING was 'excessive', and urged the Singapore government to waive the caning. On 4 May 1994, the government announced that Cabinet had recommended to President Ong Teng Cheong that Fay's punishment be reduced to four strokes of the cane as a gesture of respect to President Clinton. Fay was caned the next day.

After his release a few weeks later, Fay returned to the United States. In September that year, he was admitted into a rehabilitation centre for his butane addiction. Four years later, he was arrested on a minor drugs charge.

The caning affected UNITED STATES-SINGAPORE RELATIONS, but bilateral relations returned to normal within a few years.

Federal Election (1964) Malaysia's only federal election to involve Singapore politicians. When Singapore joined the Federation of Malaysia in 1963, the leadership of the ruling People's Action Party (PAP) pledged not to participate in the federal election of 1964, assuming that the party could work with the United Malays National Organisation (UMNO) to forge a common political front. However, Kuala Lumpur had actively supported Singapore UMNO and the Malayan Chinese

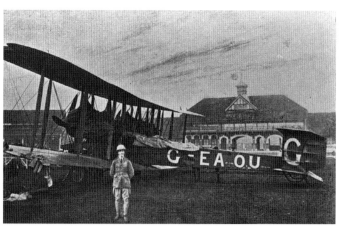

Farrer Park: Captain Ross Smith with his three-engined plane, 1919.

Association (MCA), and UMNO candidates had contested Singapore's general election in September 1963 (failing to win any seats). The PAP therefore decided to contest the federal election in April 1964.

In March 1964, PAP chairman and deputy prime minister, TOH CHIN CHYE, announced the PAP's intention to field a token team to demonstrate that the party would be a 'force to be reckoned with in five years'. PAP leaders feared that if they did not try to win support amongst centrist sections of the electorate, radical sections of the urban Chinese population would abandon the MCA and support the BARISAN SOSIALIS.

However, the PAP was seen as having attempted to drive a wedge between the MCA and UMNO. Both these parties saw the PAP's appeal to urban voters in peninsular Malaysia as a cause for concern. Moreover, leaders in Kuala Lumpur considered the PAP's decision to put up candidates in the 1964 election as a breach of faith. Even though the PAP was competing against the MCA, the party was viewed by many sections of the Malay population as representing a threat to their dominance. Tunku ABDUL RAHMAN rebuffed the PAP's suggestions to form an alliance with UMNO, and Malay politicians attacked the PAP.

The PAP had no branches in peninsular Malaysia and no organizational structure there. It fielded 11 candidates for the parliamentary elections, and 15 candidates in state elections. Only one candidate—C.V. DEVAN NAIR—was successful, winning a seat in Bangsar constituency in Kuala Lumpur. The PAP's excursion into federal politics is believed by some to have been a contributory factor in bringing about SEPARATION.

Federation of Indian Muslims Umbrella organization of Indian Muslim social organizations. It coordinates and facilitates policies and activities—promoted by organizations such as the Islamic Religious Council of Singapore, Mendaki and the Singapore Indian Development Association (SINDA)—which relate to the Indian Muslim community.

ferns Ferns are classified as non-flowering plants, together with algae and mosses. Worldwide, there are over 12,000 species of fern. Of these, about 85 per cent are found in the tropics. Singapore once had about 170 species. However, with widespread deforestation, this number declined to about 100 in the 1960s. No detailed survey has been conducted since that time.

Ferns do not develop flowers and thus have no fruit or seeds. When in a reproductive state, the underside of a frond will be covered with a thick layer of dark sporangia (*1*) containing tiny spores. As the sporangia mature, they burst during dry weather to eject these spores. Fern spores are light and can travel long distances to colonize new areas. If a spore lands on a moist surface, it will germinate, giving out a germ tube that gradually expands into a single-celled prothallus. This delicate prothallus bears rhizoids, the equivalent of roots in

flowering plants, and male and female sex organs. The fertilization of an egg by a sperm results in an embryo, and the embryo eventually gives rise to a young fern plant.

Ferns grow in a wide variety of habitats. However, Bukit Timah Nature Reserve is the last remaining refuge for most fern species. Its Fern Valley is particularly rich in ferns. However, through the decades, the environment within the forest has deteriorated, and many species have disappeared. For example, Ridley's staghorn fern

(*Platycerium ridleyi*) (*2*) has been extinct since the 1940s. Many other species that were once found in Fern Valley no longer grow there.

Forest ferns
The elephant fern (*Angiopteris evecta*) (*3*) and Singapore fern (*Tectaria singaporeana*) (*4*) grow on the forest floor. In the upper branches of tall trees are bird's-nest ferns (*Asplenium nidus*) (*5*). These epiphytes—plants that grow on other plants—have fronds to trap falling leaves and twigs from surrounding trees. The compost that develops from this rotting organic material helps to store moisture, and provides nutrients for the epiphytic ferns.

The dragon's-scale fern (*Pyrrosia piloselloides*) is often found close by on tree trunks. It has two distinct types of fronds—oval fronds which are sterile, and elongated fronds which are fertile.

Freshwater ferns
In freshwater ponds and reservoirs, two species thrive—the mosquito fern (*Azolla pinnata*) and the water spangle (*Salvinia molesta*) (*6*). Both of these are non-native species, also known as exotics, and grow on the surface of the water.

Mangrove ferns
Ferns can also be found in mangrove areas—the most prominent being swamp ferns (*Acrostichum aureum*) (*7*), which form pure stands in areas that have been cleared of mangrove trees. Swamp ferns are easily recognized by their upright fronds bearing a thick layer of almost-black sporangia on the underside.

Urban ferns
Ferns are common even in the urban environment. Many wayside trees have bird's-nest and staghorn ferns (*Platycerium coronarium*) (*8*) growing on them, while the ladder fern (*Nephrolepis biserrata*) clambers up walls of old buildings.

The federation was formed in 1992 by nine social organizations serving Indian Muslims. In 2005, seven more associations joined. It is headed by a president, who is elected every two years from among the federation's member associations.

Federation of Malaya *See* MALAYA, FEDERATION OF.

Feedback Unit Government agency. The Feedback Unit was established on 15 April 1985 as a mechanism through which people could voice their concerns regarding government policy. The unit's role has since been expanded to that of a forum in which citizens can ask questions, debate policies, contribute suggestions and participate in decision making. Government ministries and statutory boards also use the unit to obtain public views on policy.

Initially, the unit would send staff into the streets to solicit feedback from ordinary people. However, it now accrues information through dialogue sessions, straw polls, public forums, focus groups, telephone calls, e-mail messages, internet relay chats and short-message-service (SMS) messages.

feng shui Chinese geomancy. Literally meaning 'wind' (*feng*) and 'water' (*shui*), feng shui holds that all things have to be placed in harmony with the environment.

Feng shui influences many Chinese Singaporeans in their choice of site and design for residences and workplaces, as well as their arrangement of furniture, and the dates and times chosen for auspicious occasions. The eight-sided *ba gua* (with a mirror in the centre) is often placed above the main doorway leading into the house to ward off evil spirits and bad luck.

Feng shui: Suntec City—laid out according to feng shui principles.

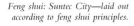

Feng shui principles are also evident in the orientation and design of several residential and commercial buildings in Singapore, including SUNTEC CITY and its Fountain of Wealth. Inspired by the *mandala* (an ancient philosophical representation of the universe), the fountain was designed to symbolize a ring in the palm of the hand, with the five office towers of Suntec City representing a thumb and four fingers.

festivals *See* box.

FH 2000 Locally-produced 52-calibre 155-mm field howitzer. The gun weighs 13.5 tons, and has a maximum range of 40 km, a firing rate of three rounds in 20 seconds (burst rate), and six rounds per minute (maximum rate). Officially commissioned on 27 May 1995, it first went into service with the 23rd Battalion of the Singapore Artillery. The FH 2000 was jointly developed by the Ordnance Development and Engineering Company of the Singapore Technologies Group, Singapore Artillery, SAP's Maintenance and Engineering Support Agency and Defence Material Organisation.

15 *(2003)*

15 (2003) Film directed by ROYSTON TAN. This started as a short film and was extended to a full-length feature. It was shot entirely with amateur actors, on whose lives the script was loosely based. It focused on five marginalized teenagers and their relationships.

Produced by ERIC KHOO, *15* was the first Singaporean film to be selected for the Venice International Film Festival. It was released with major cuts in Singapore, because of references to local youth gangs and SECRET SOCIETIES.

film The business of exhibiting films was first brought to Singapore—mainly by the British and the French—at the beginning of the 20th century. It expanded steadily until the mid-1920s. However, with the advent of talking movies, two companies were set up which would dominate the cinema business in Singapore until the beginning of the 21st century: the Shaw Organisation (started in 1927), and the Cathay Organisation (1935). Shaw opened Singapore's first cinema in 1927—the Empire in Tanjong Pagar. Both companies eventually came to run cinema chains in Singapore and throughout the wider region.

In 1933, local film production began with the first Malay movie, *Laila Majnun*, directed by India-born B.S. RAJHANS and produced by Motilal Chemical Company of Bombay (present-day Mumbai). After the

Film: Homerun *(2003).*

end of the Japanese Occupation, the local film industry was revived. Singapore witnessed a 'golden age' of cinema from 1947 to 1972. In 1947, SHAW BROTHERS reopened their own film studio at Jalan Ampas. This was called MALAY FILM PRODUCTIONS. This studio was responsible for more than 160 feature films before it closed in 1967. Its films were in Malay and were made for a local and regional Malay-speaking audience. Shaw initially hired Indian directors such as B.S. Rajhans, L. KRISHNAN and B.N. RAO, capitalizing on their skills and their knowledge in the bustling Indian film industry, and then took on Malay directors such as Jamil Sulong, Omar Rojik and P. RAMLEE. P. Ramlee became Shaw's most celebrated director.

In the 1940s, Shaw initially had a virtual monopoly over film production in Singapore. Competition came only from a few small independent production houses such as NUSANTARA FILM and Keris Film. Serious competition began only when LOKE WAN THO of Cathay Organisation and HO AH LOKE of Keris Film founded CATHAY-KERIS FILMS in 1953. That year, they released Singapore's first colour movie, *Buloh Perundu* (Bamboo Grove, also known as *The Magic Flute*), directed by B.S. Rajhans. Although Ho Ah Loke left at the end of the 1950s and Loke Wan Tho died in an air accident in 1964, Cathay-Keris remained active until 1972. It produced close to 120 feature films in Malay, with the exception of *Shi Zi Cheng* (Lion City) (1960) in Mandarin.

With a total of over 300 films produced over 25 years, the golden age of Singapore cinema represents the bulk of local film history. Unfortunately, possibly because none of them attracted international acclaim, most films from this period have sunk into obscurity.

With the closing of their studios, Shaw and Cathay focused on their highly profitable film screening businesses. As for local film production, the 1970s saw a handful of movies made by independent parties. Where all but six of the Malay movies of the golden age were black-and-white affairs, the 1970s films were in colour and were very different from the Malay films of earlier years. Examples include RING OF FURY (1973) in Mandarin, and three action films in English produced towards the end of the decade: BIONIC BOY (1977), THEY CALL HER...CLEOPATRA WONG (1978) and *Dynamite Johnson* (also known as *The Return of Bionic Boy*) (1978). All three were co-productions by Singapore, Malaysia and the Philippines, and were aimed at an international market.

Despite attempts in the 1970s to widen the appeal of Singapore films by producing them in English, the 1980s saw the collapse of local film production as local cinema halls thrived with movie releases from Hollywood, Bollywood and Hong Kong.

FH 2000: locally produced field howitzer.

The first signs of a possible revival came in 1991 with the introduction of the Silver Screen Awards for local and regional films at the SINGAPORE INTERNATIONAL FILM FESTIVAL, and the release of *Medium Rare* (1991), a feature film shot entirely in Singapore. Based on the notorious case of murderer ADRIAN LIM, it had a largely foreign cast. Four years later, ERIC KHOO's *Mee Pok Man* (1995) was released to local critical acclaim. In 1997, Singapore cinema found an international audience with another Eric Khoo film, 12 STOREYS; it was selected as part of the 'Un Certain Regard' category at the Cannes Film Festival. The films that heralded the beginning of the revival in the mid-1990s included *Army Daze* (1996) by ONG KENG SEN; *God or Dog* (1997) by Hugo Ng—a re-telling of the

FESTIVALS	
Chinese New Year*	January–February
Thaipusam	January–February
Ponggal	January–February
Good Friday*	March–April
Panguni Uthiram	March–April
Holi	March–April
Qing Ming	April
Tamil New Year	April
Vesak Day*	May
Duan Wu Jie (Dragonboat Festival)	June
Qi Qiao Jie	July–August
Onam	August–September
Zhong Yuan Jie (Hungry Ghost Festival)	August–September
Zhong Qiu Jie (Mid-Autumn Festival)	September
Navarathiri	September–October
Theemidhi	October
Deepavali*	October–November
Nine Emperor Gods festival	October–November
Christmas*	25 December
Dong Zhi (Winter Solstice)	December
Eid-ul-Fitr (Hari Raya Puasa)*	1st day of 10th month of the Islamic calendar
Eid-ul-Adha (Hari Raya Haji)*	10th day of 12th month of the Islamic calendar
Prophet Muhammad's Birthday	12th day of 3rd month of the Islamic calendar
*Public holidays	

film: Singapore through a foreign lens

Hollywood and other 'foreign' film studios were, as early as the 1920s, using Singapore as an exotic or somewhat mystical locale in film (and later, television) productions. In the silent film *Across to Singapore* (1928; director, William Nigh), starring Joan Crawford and Ramon Navarro, the plot involves a voyage to Singapore, where one of the protagonists is stranded, and where a search for him ensues. Like many foreign films of this period that make reference to the 'East', there is less concern with fidelity to historical or geographic detail than with suggesting Singapore as a fertile setting for passionate intrigues.

Similarly, the casual imperialist and racist overtones of early 'talkies' such as Paramount's *The Letter* (1929; director, Jean de Limur), set in colonial Singapore and based on Somerset Maugham's 1927 play, could make for unsettling viewing in contemporary contexts—as would its more famous remake in 1940, directed by William Wyler and starring Bette Davis. The 1940 version features one of the most celebrated film noir opening sequences, in which the camera pans over a tropical rubber plantation (including a sign that reads: L Rubber Co., Singapore, Plantation No.1) before a gunshot devastates the composure of the night.

The farthest point on the map

The notion of the tropical heat insidiously altering the good sense of the movie protagonists is suggested in the romance *The Road to Singapore* (1931; director, Alfred E. Green). A similarly titled, but far more popular movie, *Road to Singapore* (1940; director, P. Schertzinger), is an instance of Hollywood films adopting a kind of free licence in referencing the 'Far East' or 'tropics', paying scant attention to geographical accuracies or mapping. The first of the immensely successful '*Road*' movies with Bing Crosby and Bob Hope, *Road to Singapore* (originally called *Road to Mandalay*—a title dropped in favour of the more romantic 'Singapore') was among the highest-grossing movies of that year. In the film, Singapore, the avowed destination of the two playboy protagonists, is declared 'the farthest point on the map'. The film never quite made it to Singapore as the two ended up in the fictional tropical island of 'Kaigoon', apparently somewhere in Southeast Asia. Notable movies shot or produced in Singapore during this time include the American movie *Samarang* (1933; director, Ward Wing), released in the same year as the first locally-made feature film, *Leila Majnun* (1933; director, B.S. RAJHANS).

The mysterious East

The idea of Singapore as an exotic locale is difficult to dislodge, as is evident in *Singapore* (1947; director, J. Brahm), an action-romance set in Singapore with Fred MacMurray and Ava Gardner as the leads. The ease with which exotic locations are interchangeable is demonstrated by the fact that the film was later re-adapted and remade as *Istanbul* (1957) with Errol Flynn. In the spy-adventure *World for Ransom* (1954; director, Robert Aldrich), the protagonist is a private eye working in Singapore, dealing with spies threatening nuclear annihilation. One particular scene, with the hero clad in white and walking past the cheap bars and neon-lit streets of Singapore, has been interpreted by cultural theorists as signifying the heroic individualism of this character in triumph over the dark, somewhat tawdry, side of the mysterious 'East'. The film is often cited as one of the 'cheapies' of its day—shot in ten days, on a budget of US$90,000 and using second-hand sets from a related television series.

Oriental stereotypes

Recent films, such as *Rogue Trader* (1998; director, James Deardon) with Ewan McGregor (based on the true account of Nick Leeson and the Barings bank saga in 1995), construct another version of Singapore: as a centre of aggressive capitalism, characterized by a dominant culture of credit and commodities. There have been criticisms of the film replaying stereotypes—from its script to music score, with 'pseudo-oriental' music to denote Asian locations—and failing to engage any Asian character or setting satisfactorily. Similar assessments have been made of an earlier film—one of the more notorious films to feature Singapore—*Saint Jack* (1979; director, Peter Bogdanovich), adapted from the equally infamous novel by PAUL THEROUX. Moving away from the more obvious clichés of romantic fantasy and the limitations of inherited sets, *Saint Jack* was shot entirely on location. Financed by *Playboy*'s Hugh Hefner, the film captures the 'sleazier' facets of Singapore, the protagonist (played by Ben Gazzara) being an American hustler who operates a high-end prostitution ring in town.

Cinematographer Robert Muller and the directorial vision invest the film with a degree of visual realism and authenticity in representing the city that had not been attempted previously. However, its emphasis on the more tawdry and steamy side of Singapore has been criticized as yet another instance in which a 'foreign' film has failed to engage local (or Asian) characters or locale effectively or with any depth.

Peter Bogdanovich's Saint Jack—*starring Ben Gazzara as Jack Flowers (above, at right) and filmed in Singapore in 1978—was banned from commercial release in Singapore until March 2006.*

The Singapore Tourism Board launched the 'Film in Singapore! Scheme' in 2004, to attract filmmakers and television producers to Singapore. Director Rakesh Roshan was one of the first beneficiaries of the scheme, filming the Indian action movie Krrish *(2006).*

Adrian Lim case with a local cast; and *The Road Less Travelled* (1997) by Lim Suat Yen.

The watershed year for the local film industry was 1998. That year saw the inception of the SINGAPORE FILM COMMISSION, the creation of MEDIACORP RAINTREE PICTURES and the success of JACK NEO's MONEY NO ENOUGH (1998), the first blockbuster Singapore could call its own.

In the years that followed, the local film industry produced some four to five feature films a year. There was consistent output from director Jack Neo, mostly by Raintree Pictures. These included *Liang Po Po—The Movie* (1999), *I NOT STUPID* (2002), *Homerun* (2003), *The Best Bet* (2004), *I Do I Do* (2005) and *One More Chance* (2005). All were box-office earners.

There was also growth in the number of short-film producers, credited in part to the Singapore Film Commission. A few young short-film directors ventured into art house feature films. One is Djinn, who made *Return to Pontianak* (2001), a tribute to the Malay horror genre (released as *Voodoo Nightmare* in the United States) and *Perth* (2005); and ROYSTON TAN's controversial 15 (2003).

Among local documentary film-makers are Tan Pin Pin with *Moving House* (2001), which traced a family's experience of the exhumation and cremation of a dead relative's remains, and Martyn See with *Singapore Rebel* (2005), a film about opposition politician CHEE SOON JUAN. These directors represent a new generation of filmmakers who are engaging audiences with Singaporean issues.

financial services sector The contribution of the financial services sector to nominal GROSS DOMESTIC PRODUCT (GDP) was 10.8 per cent in 2005. This is higher than the average of between 4 and 8 per cent of GDP sustained by most economies. Since the government's efforts to develop the sector began in the 1970s, the sector has grown rapidly and is currently an important

Firecrackers: part of village celebration, 1963.

Film: They Call Her...Cleopatra Wong *(1978).*

contributor to skilled employment and foreign-exchange earnings.

Broadly speaking, financial services are provided by the financial system, comprising financial institutions and markets. These transfer funds from lenders to borrowers in two ways: directly, through the sale of securities by borrowers, in the form of shares and bonds; or indirectly, through financial intermediaries such as banks.

The table shows the number of financial institutions in Singapore between 1975 and 2005. Although commercial banks remain the predominant financial institutions, capital market activity has grown significantly. This has contributed to breadth and depth in the financial services sector.

fine city Pun used to refer to the practice of using fines to control behaviour. Social behaviour in Singapore is regulated largely through a series of policies buttressed by punitive measures, the most common of which is the fine. The imposition of fines for what might elsewhere be perceived as minor social infractions—such as LITTERING, failure to flush the toilet, JAYWALKING and failure to remove mosquito larvae from water receptacles—has become so prevalent that locals and tourists alike have capitalized on this pun. Indeed, some of the most popular tourist souvenirs found in Singapore are T-shirts emblazoned with the words 'Singapore is a fine city' and mock signposts indicating acts which can incur fines.

Finlayson, G.A. (dates unknown) Pathologist. Although pathology was practised in the first 86 years of Singapore's medical history, there was no official pathologist. In 1905, concerned about the high death rate in Singapore, the governor consulted the principal civil medical officer, who advised that the most effective way to reduce it was to start a Department of Pathology headed by a full-time specialist pathologist who would conduct postmortems to ascertain causes of death, and thus the major public health issues. Dr G. A.

Finlayson was appointed the first government pathologist. He was responsible for all hospitals in Singapore. He was also a lecturer in pathology at the Medical School, then known as the Straits Settlements and Federated Malay States Government Medical School (later the King Edward VII College of Medicine).

firecrackers Traditionally, firecrackers have been set off to celebrate CHINESE NEW YEAR and to scare away evil spirits. In 1971, restrictions were placed on firecrackers, as their use had resulted in six deaths, 68 injuries and damage to property worth $361,200 in 1970. Nine people were injured during the Chinese New Year period in 1971, and the following year, two unarmed police officers were attacked when they attempted to stop the unlawful use of firecrackers.

In June 1972, a total ban on firecrackers was imposed with the introduction of the Dangerous Fireworks Act. After several instances of firecrackers being discharged in 1988, stiffer penalties were imposed on the importation and discharge of firecrackers, including fines and imprisonment, as well as CANING for importers and traffickers.

However, official approval was given for the limited use of firecrackers in 2004. Long strings of firecrackers were set off before a crowd of 100,000 in Chinatown to mark the commencement of Chinese New Year celebrations, and again on New Year's Eve, that year. In 2005, firecrackers were featured in the annual CHINGAY procession on Orchard Road. Thus, although the public ban on firecrackers has remained in force, permits have been granted to allow

Fine city: T-shirt satirizing the imposition of fines for a variety of misdemeanours.

FINANCIAL SERVICES SECTOR: FINANCIAL INSTITUTIONS IN SINGAPORE					
	1975	1980	1990	2000	2005
Banks	70	91	141	140	111
Local	13	13	13	8	5
Foreign	57	78	128	132	106
Full licence	24	23	22	23	24
Wholesale	12	13	14	16	35
Offshore	21	42	92	93	47
Asia Currency Units*	66	108	199	195	153
Finance companies	36	34	28	14	3
Merchant banks	21	36	68	63	48
Discount houses	4	4	—	—	—
Insurance companies	69	71	124	153	140
Insurance brokers	—	—	—	—	61
Representative offices*	38	47	45	66	45
International money brokers	5	7	8	9	10
Licensed financial advisors	—	—	—	—	56
Capital market services licensees**					
Dealing in securities	—	—	—	77	65
Trading in futures contracts	—	—	—	45	34
Advising on corporate finance	—	—	—	—	30
Fund management	—	—	—	154	91
Leveraged foreign exchange trading	—	—	—	—	11
Securities financing	—	—	—	—	15
Providing custodial services for securities	—	—	—	—	27

NOTE: *of banks and merchant banks
** Data for earlier years are unavailable/unreported due to changes in classification, etc.
Source: Monetary Authority of Singapore

Fitzpatrick's: advertisement dating from the 1950s (above); the Orchard Road store, 1958 (right).

fish-head beehoon

fish-head curry

for firecrackers to be used at certain public events, providing that prior police approval has been granted and safety precautions put in place.

fiscal policy The stated aim of Singapore's fiscal policy is to promote sustained, non-inflationary economic growth by ensuring a balanced budget over the medium term, creating a fiscal environment that supports investment, entrepreneurship and job creation. Notwithstanding this, the fiscal system has traditionally exhibited a bias towards persistent and large budget surpluses. This provides the resources to deal with the challenges of an uncertain security environment, economic restructuring and an ageing population. However, the budget was in deficit in the recession years of 2001 and 2003.

In 2005, total government expenditure was $28.8 billion. Education, economic infrastructure, basic healthcare and national security continued to be the key priorities. As in previous years, a large part of the operating expenditure was allocated to social development (30 per cent) and security and external relations (36.7 per cent). Economic development and government administration accounted for another 4.5

and 3.7 per cent, respectively, of operating expenditure. Development expenditure was 28.2 percent. In the fiscal year 2005, the government registered another budget surplus of $430 million, which was about 0.2 per cent of Singapore's GROSS DOMESTIC PRODUCT for that year.

fishes *See* box.

fish-head *beehoon* Popular local dish. This dish consists of the head of the toman fish (also known as 'snake head') which is stewed in a broth with ginger until the broth turns milky in colour. Thick *beehoon* (rice vermicelli) is then cooked in the broth as it absorbs the flavour of the soup. The dish is served with fresh greens like *kai lan* or *choy sum*. Some cooks add a hint of brandy to enhance the sweetness of the dish—a version known as XO fish-head *beehoon*.

fish-head curry Popular local dish. This dish is believed to have been created in a curry restaurant in Singapore. The original Singapore-style fish-head curry has a spicy and sour tang to it. The curry is laced with tamarind for a piquant flavour. As for the heads, most chefs prefer those of the giant snapper fish.

While originally an Indian dish, today, Chinese and Peranakan versions exist. The Chinese version uses a lighter masala curry mix and adds dried tofu (*taupok*), brinjal and pineapple to the concoction. The Peranakans lace the curry with coconut milk for a thicker and more robust curry.

Fitzpatrick's Supermarket. In 1946, W.F. Fitzpatrick founded a ship chandler and army tender business in a small office in Raffles Place. In 1947, he was joined by George Holt, and the pair expanded into the retail food industry. Both men had worked as butchers with COLD STORAGE.

Holt took over the company after Fitzpatrick died in an air crash in Malacca in 1951. In August 1958, he opened a supermarket on Orchard Road (on the current site of The Paragon). Fitzpatrick's became popular with the expatriate com-

munity due to its range of imported produce. The supermarket also had its own shopping arcade with tenants such as Glamourette, stockist of imported ladies' apparel, and Hilda's, where textiles and made-to-measure ladies wear was sold.

Holt retired in 1967, selling his stake in the business to the Australian company Woolworths. Ownership was later transferred to Malayan Credit before the company was sold in 1973 to Hongkong Land, who subsequently transferred the company's shares to the DAIRY FARM Group in July 1985. Fitzpatrick's thereafter became part of the Cold Storage chain. The acquisition of Fitzpatrick's for $21 million—which included the company's leased warehouses in Jurong, regarded as the best food distribution centre in Singapore at the time—helped secure a dominant retail presence for Cold Storage (and hence Dairy Farm) in Singapore.

five-foot way Covered pedestrian arcade commonly, but not exclusively, found in front of SHOPHOUSES. It was modern Singapore's founder, Sir Stamford Raffles, who decreed that all buildings in Singapore should include a five-foot walkway in front of the shop, abutting the street. This meant that the second storey of each shophouse overhung its front entrance, shading it.

This 'five-foot way' ('*kaki lima*' in Malay) created a continuous covered walkway in front of the shophouse block, providing shelter against the elements. The floors of many five-foot ways featured aesthetic finishes including mosaic, terracotta and clay tiles. Tile patterns on the five-foot way would sometimes be repeated on the front wall of the shophouse.

By the 1870s, settlers began to ply simple businesses along the five-foot way, and it developed a lifestyle and social culture of its own.

five-foot way

FISCAL POLICY: GOVERNMENT EXPENDITURE		
	2000	**2005**
Operating expenditure	18,896.9	20,674.6
Security and external relations	9,043.7	10,443.4
Social development	6,180.0	8,548.0
Education	3,901.9	4,980.7
Health	990.2	1,670.7
Community development, youth and sports	386.4	817.7
Information, communications and the arts	225.9	274.5
Environment and water resources	357.2	442.7
National development	318.3	361.8
Economic development	2,920.3	924.2
Communications and information technology	2,427.8	—
Transport	—	285.1
Trade and industry	391.3	443.7
Manpower	101.2	165.2
Info-communications technology	—	30.2
Government administration	752.9	759.0
Development expenditure	9,077.6	8,106.8

NOTE: Figures are in $m.
Source: Singapore Department of Statistics

fishes

In Singapore, the majority of fishes are found in coastal waters. Only about 12 per cent are confined to freshwater. Half of the freshwater species are non-native. They were introduced for aquaculture, angling or mosquito-control, or are abandoned ornamental fishes—many of which prey voraciously on native species. With the loss of forests and streams, most native freshwater fishes are now endangered. The first comprehensive study of Singapore's freshwater fishes was published in 1966. Updated in 1996, it listed 104 species, 39 of which are presumed to be locally extinct. The two major groups of fishes found in Singapore are cartilaginous fishes and bony fishes.

Bony fishes

Bony fishes are far more numerous than cartilaginous fishes in Singapore. Bony fishes include:

Perciformes

The order Perciformes is the largest and most diverse component of Singapore's fish fauna. They are generally recognizable by their two dorsal fins, one of which is supported by stiff spines, as well as their scale-covered bodies. Many members of this order are encountered in the market, such as the barramundi (*Lates calcarifer*), orange-spotted grouper (*Epinephelus coioides*), mangrove red snapper (*Lutjanus argentimaculatus*) and threadfin breams (*Nemipterus* spp.).

1

2

Damselfishes are common around coral reefs. An example is the clown anemonefish (*Amphiprion ocellaris*) (**1**), which lives in symbiotic association with large sea anemones. Also found around corals is the copperband butterflyfish (*Chelmon rostratus*) (**2**).

In freshwater, the most conspicuous perciform is the tilapia (*Oreochromis mossambicus*). It was apparently imported from Africa for aquaculture during the JAPANESE OCCUPATION. Another popular table fish is the marbled goby or SOON HOCK (*Oxyeleotris marmorata*). Also a freshwater perciform, it is the largest of over 100 species of gobies found in Singapore.

Some freshwater perciforms are able to survive for periods outside water. The climbing perch (*Anabas testudineus*) breathes atmospheric air and can crawl over land between bodies of water, aided by its strong, serrated gill covers. Other air-breathers include mudskippers (family Gobiidae) and snakeheads (*Channa* spp.).

Clupeiformes

This order includes sardines and herrings—some of the most abundant fishes in Singapore waters. Anchovies (*Stolephorus* spp.) are sold—fresh or dried—for food, while tamban (*Sardinella* spp.) are used for animal feed. Anchovies and tamban occur in large schools and feed on plankton.

Beloniformes

Halfbeaks and garfishes belong to this order and have extremely long jaws. Garfishes, such as the spot-tailed garfish (*Strongylura strongylura*), are carnivorous. Their jaws are of about equal length, lined with numerous sharp teeth. Halfbeaks tend to be insectivorous, their lower jaw much longer than the upper. Examples are the stripe-nosed halfbeak (*Zenarchopterus buffonis*) and the forest halfbeak (*Hemirhamphodon pogonognathus*).

Gasterosteiformes

Belonging to this order are seahorses and pipefishes. Clad in leathery armour plating, they have tubular mouths with a small gape, and can only eat small organisms like zooplankton. They occur mainly in coastal waters where they are well-camouflaged amongst seagrass and coral. The estuarine seahorse (*Hippocampus kuda*) (**3**), blue-speckled pipefish (*Hippichthys cyanospilos*) and slender seamoth (*Pegasus volitans*) are all examples. The seahorse is a protected animal in Singapore.

3

Cartilaginous fishes

These include rays and sharks. Sharks are found in Singapore waters, although large man-eating varieties are rare. In 1967, a locally-caught tiger shark (*Galeocerdo cuvier*) was found to have human remains in its stomach. Most sharks found locally are relatively small and harmless.

Rays are dorso-ventrally depressed sharks with eyes on their backs, and gill-slits and mouth located on their undersides. Some rays can generate electricity to stun their prey or predators, while some look like sharks. Yet others have venomous spines on the tail.

*Spotted eagle ray (*Aetobatus narinari*) (left); brown-banded catshark (*Chilosyllium punctatum*).*

Tetraodontiformes

Known as puffer-fish (**4**), these fishes can inflate their bodies by inhaling air or water when threatened. Some relatives of puffer-fishes have box-shaped bodies with hardened rigid skin, and are unable to puff themselves up. The short-nosed boxfish (*Rhynostracion nasus*) (**5**) is a common example. Besides its body armour, it can also protect itself by exuding a poisonous mucous.

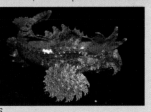

4

5

Scorpaeniformes

Scorpionfishes belong to this order. They have venomous spines on their dorsal fins. A handful of species are found in Singapore's coastal waters. They tend to resemble rocks and corals. The little longspine scorpionfish (*Paracentropogon longispinis*) (**6**) is common, but it is the larger estuarine stonefish (*Synanceja horrida*) that is much feared. People have died from being stung by it. However, it is not poisonous to eat.

fish rearing as a hobby

Rearing ornamental fishes is a popular pastime in Singapore. The most popular are guppies, which are hardy, cheap and easy to breed. First brought into Singapore in the early 20th century to help control the mosquito population, wild guppies from Brazil—often referred to as *longkang* (Malay for 'drain') fish, as they populated drains and canals—gained popularity

in the 1940s due to their vibrant colours. Interest in guppies (**7**) waned in the 1970s, but has since been revived with the development of new strains of attractive and disease-resistant guppy.

From the early 1960s to the 1980s, schoolchildren often reared fighting fish (**8**) for sport. Fighting fish were relatively expensive, and children would often try to find them in drains and canals, rather than purchase them.

Many businesspeople rear fish that are believed to be auspicious, for example the AROWANA and the flowerhorn (*luohan*). There have even

been unsubstantiated claims of people winning lotteries after staring at flowerhorns for protracted periods. Also considered lucky are koi, which are the most common ornamental fish in ponds at residential and business premises.

Singapore is the world's top exporter of ornamental fishes, holding a quarter of the industry's global trade. In 2004, this amounted to $86 million. Over 1,000 varieties are bred in Singapore and exported to some 50 countries by companies such as Qian Hu Corporation Limited.

7

8

6

Fock Siew Wah

Five Power Defence Arrangements

Collective defence arrangement. In April 1971, shortly after the BRITISH WITHDRAWAL FROM SINGAPORE, the United Kingdom, Australia, New Zealand, Malaysia and Singapore established the Five Power Defence Arrangements (FPDA). Under the FPDA, the five signatories agreed to consult with each another—either jointly or separately—in the event of any external aggression or threat of attack against Malaysia or Singapore.

Under the FPDA, the Integrated Air Defence System (IADS) for Malaysia and Singapore was established. The IADS is led by an air defence council, consisting of one senior representative from each party to the agreement, and is based at the Royal Malaysian Air Force (RMAF) base in Butterworth, PENANG. The IADS is under the command of a Royal Australian Air Force air vice-marshal. In 2001, the IADS was renamed the Integrated Area Defence System. Since 2004, exercises have been expanded to include counter-terrorism drills.

FJ Benjamin This company was founded by FRANK BENJAMIN in 1959 as a sole-proprietorship store on Middle Road, trading in paper, consumer novelties and photographic equipment. In the mid-1960s, it began to venture into the fashion business, and in the 1970s, introduced the single-brand boutique and 'shop-within-a-shop' concepts to Singapore. By the 1980s, it had become known for marketing foreign brands such as Guess? in Asia, and had secured exclusive rights to distribute retail designer goods from labels such as Lanvin, Gucci and Fendi.

In June 1973, it became a private limited company under the name FJ Benjamin & Son. This name was changed to FJ Benjamin Holdings in June 1993, reflecting the company's status as a holding company for its subsidiaries. FJ Benjamin Holdings Ltd was publicly listed in November 1996.

The group operates more than 100 regional retail outlets and is an exclusive distributor of brands such as Valentino, Inez, Guess?, Guess Kids, La Senza, Lalique and Sheridan. In 2006, it signed a franchise agreement with US clothing retailer Gap,

Fong Sip Chee: constituency tour, 1964.

FJ Benjamin: Raoul outlet, Ngee Ann City.

and its offshoot Banana Republic, to open the only Gap stores in Asia outside Japan. FJ Benjamin has also developed its own shirt label, Raoul. The first Raoul store was opened in September 2002, and since then the company has opened more than a dozen outlets in Singapore, Malaysia, Indonesia and the Middle East.

In the timepiece market, FJ Benjamin represents brands such as Girard-Perregaux, Jean Richard, Victorinox Swiss Army, Guess?, Nautica and Nike. It also operates the retail franchise for the Manchester United Football Club in Singapore, and is a partner in the Reds Café chain of food and beverage outlets throughout the Asia-Pacific region. The group is part of a consortium which is transforming the former St James Power Station into an entertainment centre.

The group reported an after-tax profit of $4.3 million on sales of $146 million for the financial year 2005.

flag *See* NATIONAL FLAG.

flag of convenience Flag flown by a ship which is different from that of the ship's country of ownership. Low registration fees, tax breaks and less stringent labour laws are some of the reasons why a ship-owner might choose to fly the flag of another country.

In the late 1960s, Singapore opened its ship registry to any person or company, regardless of nationality, in order to increase merchant maritime tonnage. This was done to save on foreign exchange, create jobs and better control foreign trade. The open registry incorporated many rules common for flags of convenience (FoCs). The fees charged under Singapore's FoC were lower than those charged by Liberia and Panama—the main countries under which FoCs had been registered.

However, by the late 1970s, the use of FoCs was being increasingly criticized. Ships flying FoCs had been responsible for a large proportion of tonnage losses and maritime casualties. Singapore therefore tightened its FoC requirements in 1979. It put in place policies to increase transparency of vessel ownership, so as to identify firms with a bad record. It also imposed age

restrictions to ensure that Singapore-registered vessels would be kept young.

Flint, Captain William Lawrence (1781–1828) Colonial official. William Lawrence Flint was born in Scotland. He was married (as second husband) to Mary Anne Raffles, the favourite sister of Sir STAMFORD RAFFLES, in Malacca.

Flint arrived in Singapore on 23 April 1820. He took over as master attendant—a position Raffles had specifically reserved for him—from Francis James Bernard, whom Raffles had appointed acting master attendant (Bernard was the son-in-law of incumbent Resident Colonel WILLIAM FARQUHAR).

In 1826, Flint's title was changed to first assistant master attendant. The East India Company had decided to rate the Straits Settlements of Penang, Singapore and Malacca as a single unit; there was therefore to be a master attendant stationed at Penang, as well as a deputy master attendant and two assistant master attendants appointed to the Straits Settlements as a whole.

As master attendant, Flint received anchorage and port-clearance fees from vessels, and gained monopolies in the supply of wood, water and ballast to ships. He also profited from hiring out boats. His fortunes changed, however, when JOHN CRAWFURD, third Resident of Singapore, introduced regulations in 1823 abolishing port charges, and forbidding the master attendant from engaging in commercial transactions.

Flint also had intermittent differences with the first Resident, Farquhar. However, Flint had the advantage of a close relationship with Raffles, to the point of his being able to stay with the latter in his bungalow after it was finished in January 1823. Before the bungalow was built, Raffles had stayed at Flint's residence. Crawfurd had some difficulty in evicting Flint from the bungalow after Raffles returned to Bencoolen in June 1823. On 20 September 1828, Flint took long leave, and set sail for Macau with his wife. He died at sea 13 days later.

Fock Siew Wah (1940–) Banker. Fock Siew Wah attended Pearl's Hill Primary School and Outram Secondary School. His plans for university were abandoned after his father died. He started work as a junior clerk in the Oversea-Chinese Banking Corporation (OCBC) at the age of 19, studying on his own to earn a banking diploma from the Institute of Bankers in the United Kingdom. Eight years later, he became acting secretary of OCBC's Bank of Singapore. Fock then headed the commercial banking division of the Development Bank of Singapore (DBS Bank), and was seconded to run a joint-venture merchant bank set up by DBS, New York's Morgan Guaranty Trust (MGT) (now JP Morgan) and National Discount Co. Ltd.

In 1976, Fock became the first Asian treasurer of MGT's Singapore offshore banking branch. Posted to its New York head office in 1978, he became JP Morgan's senior vice-president and regional treasurer of its Asia-Pacific operations. In 1988, he became president and chief executive officer of Overseas Union Bank.

The Singapore government enlisted Fock as a special economic adviser for investment opportunities in Hong Kong and China in 1991–94. He later became the first chairman of Singapore MRT (now SMRT Corporation) (1987–1995); chairman of the Land Transport Authority (1995–2002), during which he oversaw the drafting of a white paper on a fully integrated public land transport system; and chairman of PSA International (2005–). He was awarded the MERITORIOUS SERVICE MEDAL.

Fong Sip Chee (1938–1992) Politician. Fong studied at Catholic High School and Beatty Secondary School. He started his political career in 1963 as parliamentary secretary to the minister for culture. He wrote *The PAP Story: The Pioneering Years* (1980).

In 1982, during his tenure as minister of state for culture (1981–85), Fong announced that he wished to be known as 'Major Fong', becoming one of the first public servants to use his military rank before his name. In 1984, he led 400 people, including some members of Parliament, in a swim across the SINGAPORE RIVER to demonstrate that the river was clean enough for water sports.

After leaving the government in 1985, Fong was appointed adviser to the Tianjin Economic and Technological Development Zone in China. In 1986, he became managing director of C & E Holidays. He retired from politics in 1988, and was awarded a MERITORIOUS SERVICE MEDAL in 1990. He died of lung cancer in 1992.

Fong Swee Suan (1931–) Trade unionist and politician. Fong was educated at The Chinese High School. He was a member of the students' Anti-British League and barely escaped arrest in 1951 for his role in organizing a boycott of classes. Fong and a fellow schoolmate, LIM CHIN SIONG, found employment with a bus company—Fong as a bus conductor and Lim as a clerk. They both joined the SINGAPORE BUS WORKERS UNION (SBWU), and Fong became general secretary of the union in 1954.

Fong and Lim also became leaders of what was then the largest and most organized trade union on the island—the Chinese Middle School Students' Union. Their leadership of this union, coupled with Fong's leadership of the SBWU and Lim's leadership of the SINGAPORE FACTORY AND SHOP WORKERS' UNION, made them the most powerful trade unionists in Singapore. They were supported by other union leaders such as ST BANI, JAMES PUTHUCHEARY,

C.V. DEVAN NAIR, SIDNEY WOODHULL, JAMIT SINGH and TAN WEE KENG.

Fong was instrumental in initiating the strike that resulted in the HOCK LEE BUS RIOTS of May 1955. Following the riots, he was arrested, along with four other union leaders, and jailed for 45 days. The following year, he was jailed again when more riots involving Chinese middle school students and bus companies broke out (*see* CHINESE MIDDLE SCHOOL RIOTS).

Fong was released in 1959 when the PEOPLE'S ACTION PARTY (PAP) came to power. In 1960, he was appointed political secretary to the Ministry of Labour and Law. However, he began to openly criticize government policies and continued to foment labour unrest. By March 1960, both Fong and Lim were in effective charge of the Singapore General Employees' Union (SGEU). Two months later, the SGEU merged with 11 other trade unions to form the Federation of Factory and Workshop Employees' Unions, with over 23,000 workers. A month later, Fong was transferred from the Ministry of Labour and Law to the Deputy Prime Minister's Office.

In 1961, Fong and others broke away from the PAP to form the BARISAN SOSIALIS. Fong was elected to that party's central executive committee. Following Merger, Fong was detained a third time under OPERATION COLD STORE. At the time of his arrest, he was a committee member of the SINGAPORE ASSOCIATION OF TRADE UNIONS. While in detention in peninsular Malaysia, Fong was barred from entering Singapore because of his subversive activities. Fong was released from prison in 1967. He later started his own business in Johor.

Foo Tee Jun (1935–) Photographer. More than 500 of Foo Tee Jun's images have been exhibited in international and local salons. Foo was made an associate of the Royal Photographic Society in 1973, and received the Excellence Distinction from La

Fédération Internationale de l'Art Photographique in 1975. He also received the Gold Medal from the Photographic Society of America in 1988 for best entry in Singapore's International Salon. In 1989, he was a recipient of the CULTURAL MEDALLION.

Foochow The term 'Foochow' (sometimes given as 'Hockchew' or 'Fuzhou') refers to the Chinese dialect group as well as the dialect spoken by its members. The group originates in China's Fujian province (specifically in the region from Fuan in northeastern Fujian to Fuzhou in east-central Fujian). According to the 2000 Census of Population, there were some 46,894 Foochows in Singapore, representing about 2 per cent of the total Chinese population.

The first waves of Foochow migrants arrived in Singapore at the turn of the century. The Foochows are traditionally associated in Singapore with COFFEE SHOPS—a trade which was also dominated by the HAINANESE. Early Foochow coffee shops were located in the vicinity of Jalan Besar,

Fong Swee Suan: addressing Barisan Sosialis rally, 1962.

Foo Tee Jun: **Huan Ying** *(Water fantasy) (1980).*

Foo Tee Jun

Force 136: Richard Broome, far left, and John Davis, second from left.

Food: cooking, hawker-style.

Queen Street and on the outskirts of Chinatown. The Foochows subsequently expanded their reach to other areas as they became more firmly established. The Singapore Foochow Coffee Restaurant and Bar Merchants' Association was set up in 1920, with links to the Singapore Foochow Association. The Foochow dominance of this trade can be attributed to the sale of coffee shops to Foochows by Hainanese who were either returning to China or moving into other areas of business.

A major Chinese deity worshipped by the Foochow community is Mazu—the Goddess of the Sea (also known as Tianhou, or 'the Empress of Heaven'). An altar to Mazu is located on the seventh floor of the Singapore Foochow Association building. The Reverend Ling Chin Mee founded the Foochow Methodist Church in 1897. This is the second-oldest Chinese Methodist church in Singapore (after the Telok Ayer Methodist Church). Prominet Foochows include doctor CHEN SU LAN.

food Thanks to Singapore's multi-ethnic community, a wide range of inexpensive local food can be found at COFFEE SHOPS, HAWKER CENTRES and FOOD COURTS around the island. Many dishes originated outside Singapore, but distinctively Singaporean versions have since evolved. CHICKEN RICE, for example, is a dish originally from Hainan, China, but the Singapore version is

Food courts: Food Republic, Wisma Atria.

now quite different from the Hainanese original. Chicken rice is one of Singapore's most popular hawker foods and can be found in almost all hawker centres.

ROTI PRATA is another dish whose origins lie outside Singapore but which has developed Singapore variants. *Roti prata* was originally an Indian dish, but some establishments in Singapore sell versions of *roti prata* that include non-traditional elements such as sliced bananas, melted cheese and sliced tomatoes.

As befitting a country surrounded by the sea, seafood is very popular in Singapore. Many seafood restaurants serve uniquely Singaporean dishes such as CHILLI AND BLACK PEPPER CRABS. Other popular seafood dishes include FISH-HEAD CURRY and BARBECUED STINGRAY.

Singapore's favourite foods also include dishes with a Malay or Indonesian origin. These include NASI LEMAK, a favourite breakfast item, and SATAY, which is usually eaten in the evening. Malay influence, by way of ingredients, can also be found in dishes like LAKSA. Another interesting characteric of Singapore food is the extensive use of chilli. Chilli paste is used when frying dishes like CHAR KWAY TEOW. Chicken rice comes with a dip made of a mixture of garlic and chilli. Dishes such as BAK CHOR MEE come with a dip of sliced chillies in soya sauce while HOKKIEN MEE is served with a dollop of chilli paste, known as *sambal*, on the side.

Given the sheer availability and variety of food in Singapore, it is not surprising that Singapore is marketed as a 'food paradise'.

food courts Indoor dining establishments featuring multiple stalls selling a variety of food. The food court is an indoor version of the hawker centre (*see* HAWKER CENTRES) and an extension of the traditional coffee shop or *kopi tiam* (*see* COFFEE SHOPS). Singapore's first food court was Scotts Picnic Food Court, which opened in 1987. This was located in Scotts Shopping Centre. Typically, food courts feature vendors selling a wide variety of what might be termed 'hawker food', such as CHICKEN RICE, CHAR KWAY TEOW, drinks and local desserts. These days, food courts also have stalls selling Japanese and Korean food.

football *See* SOCCER.

Force 136 Intelligence-gathering and subversion unit active during the JAPANESE OCCUPATION. The unit was first codenamed Oriental Mission. In 1941, Oriental Mission officers from the Special Operations Executive (SOE)—British covert operations service—were sent to Malaya to develop underground resistance in the event of a Japanese invasion. They trained locals—Chinese, Malays and Indians—in sabotage, espionage, small arms and intelligence gathering. The locals were

also trained to spread anti-Japanese propaganda and assist anti-Japanese operatives from other countries.

In July 1941, Oriental Mission opened the 101 Special Training School (101 STS) at Tanjung Balai, near the mouth of the Jurong River, to conduct training. The 101 STS intensified its efforts when the Japanese invasion began (*see* MALAYA CAMPAIGN).

When Singapore fell, the officers of Oriental Mission and the staff of 101 STS merged to form what was later known as Force 136. Their mission was to disrupt Japanese rule in Malaya. Force 136's first operation to insert British officers and Chinese agents into Malaya by submarine began in May 1943 and was codenamed Gustavus I. It was led by former police officer John Davis. Gustavus II was launched a month later, and was led by Richard Broome. LIM BO SENG, who was also a Kuomintang (Chinese Nationalist Party) leader, led Gustavus V in October 1943. Lim, together with Davis and Broome, were later escorted by CHIN PENG to the Blantan Camp where the Blantan Agreement, outlining British cooperation with the MALAYAN PEOPLE'S ANTI-JAPANESE ARMY (MPAJA), was signed.

More Force 136 agents were secretly parachuted into Malaya between late 1944 and 1945. Their mission was to aid the planned Allied invasion. When the Japanese surrendered in August 1945, Force 136 agents came out of hiding to help contain some of the turmoil that had erupted in the hunt for Japanese collaborators. The SOE, including Force 136, was disbanded in 1946.

Force Z British naval force that sailed from Singapore up the east coast of Malaya to engage the Japanese on 8 December 1941. The force comprised two battleships, the newly built HMS PRINCE OF WALES and the World War I-vintage HMS REPULSE. They also had an escort of four destroyers, *Electra*, *Express*, *Tenedos* and *Vampire*. Force Z sailed without its intended aircraft carrier, *Indomitable* (which had a complement of 45 aircraft), which had run aground off Jamaica in November. As a result, Force Z did not have adequate air cover. It turned back when detected by Japanese aircraft but delayed its return to investigate what turned out to be false reports of landings at Kuantan. On 10 December 1941, Japanese bombers torpedoed HMS *Repulse* and HMS *Prince of Wales*, sinking both off the coast of Kuantan. Admiral Sir TOM PHILIPS, commander in chief of the Eastern Fleet, was among those killed.

See also MALAYA CAMPAIGN.

foreign direct investment Attracting foreign investment can be said to be the government's key economic strategy since Separation in 1965. Through foreign direct investment (FDI), Singapore has prospered

Ford Motor Factory The Ford Motor Company of Malaya Limited was incorporated in Singapore on 9 November 1926. It began operations in a rented shophouse on Enggor Street, off Anson Road. The company was originally formed to supervise the supply and distribution of Ford products, including Lincoln automobiles and Fordson tractors, in Malaya, Burma, the Dutch East Indies (present-day Indonesia) and Thailand. Four years later, the company moved into a warehouse on Prince Edward Road, where imported units were assembled.

The high demand for Ford's vehicles in the years prior to World War II led Ford Malaya to move to a new assembly plant at 351 Upper Bukit Timah Road in October 1941. This was the first car assembly plant to be built in Southeast Asia. Before World War II the principal supplier to the plant was Ford's affiliate in Canada.

The Japanese invaded Singapore only months after the plant's opening, and it was in the boardroom that the British formally surrendered Singapore to the Japanese on 15 February 1942. Lieutenant-General YAMASHITA TOMOYUKI made the building his headquarters in the latter stages of his conquest of Singapore (see MALAYA CAMPAIGN).

During the JAPANESE OCCUPATION, the factory was used to produce Nissan trucks rather than Ford vehicles. Part of the plant was also used as a servicing depot for Japanese army vehicles.

From 1945 to 1947, the plant was used for the repair of British military vehicles, while civilian motor vehicles were produced there in later decades. The plant ceased operations in June 1980.

On 16 February 2006, the factory was re-opened as Memories at Old Ford Factory, and was made a national monument. The gallery is home to a permanent exhibition detailing the Japanese Occupation. The exhibition features many archival photographs; sound recordings of oral history interviews; maps; and artefacts owned by the National Archives of Singapore. There is a small audio-visual theatre on the mezzanine floor screening documentaries about World War II and the Japanese Occupation. The garden behind the old main wing has been planted with crops that were commonly grown as subsistence foods during the Occupation, including sugarcane, tapioca, oil palm and rice.

British surrender at the Ford Factory, 1942 (top); locally assembled Ford Cortinas, early 1960s.

and evolved into a base for multinational corporations to engage in manufacturing and product development, and coordinate regional procurement, production, marketing and distribution.

FDI inflows have risen from an average of $13.2 billion annually in the 1990s to $21.7 billion annually between 2000 and 2003. FDI inflows have consistently been in excess of $10 billion in each year since 1994.

In 2003, the total stock of FDI in Singapore was $245.5 billion. Since 1997, Europe has overtaken Asia as the largest source of FDI, accounting for 42.6 per cent of all FDI by the end of 2003. The United Kingdom is Singapore's largest foreign direct investor, with investment from that country accounting for 16.2 per cent of FDI in Singapore, followed by the United States and Japan at 15.4 per cent and 13.5 per cent, respectively. The bulk of FDI has been in manufacturing (37 per cent) and financial and insurance services (34 per cent).

foreign exchange reserves Due to Singapore's high domestic savings rate (about 45 per cent), the country has one of the highest per capita foreign exchange (forex) reserves in the world.

In 2005, Singapore's official foreign reserves amounted to $193.6 billion, 99.6 per cent of Gross Domestic Product. The GOVERNMENT OF SINGAPORE INVESTMENT CORPORATION (GIC) manages Singapore's foreign reserves. GIC invests in international equities and money market instruments,

real estate and other special investments such as venture capital and leveraged buyouts. Ultimately, the Ministry of Finance, which the GIC reports to, is responsible for ensuring a suitable rate of return on Singapore's reserves.

The MONETARY AUTHORITY OF SINGAPORE (MAS) also holds reserves in order to back the Singapore dollar. The Reserve and Monetary Management Department in MAS is responsible for keeping the Singapore dollar within a certain band, as well as for investing the short-term reserves prudently.

foreign missions Singapore maintains diplomatic relations with over 160 countries. In 2005, Singapore's resident missions abroad included seven high commissions, 17 embassies, two permanent missions to the UNITED NATIONS and 14 consulates-general or consulates. There are also more than 20 non-resident high commissioners or ambassadors based in Singapore. In addition, Singapore has appointed 24 honorary consuls-general and consuls abroad.

There are 55 resident foreign embassies and high commissions, as well as 39 foreign consular posts, in Singapore. More than 60 non-resident foreign ambassadors are accredited to Singapore. Non-resident ambassadors, while representing their country's interests in Singapore, are based outside Singapore, sometimes in a third country. For example, the Embassy of the Republic of Albania to Singapore is based in Beijing.

foreign policy The challenge for Singapore's foreign policy has always been to maximize political and economic space. This Singapore has done successfully despite limited resources. In the early post-Separation years, Singapore faced three challenges which required foreign policy actions to resolve. First, Singapore had no defence force. As a result, it accepted an offer from Israel, which was the only country to offer assistance to set up the Singapore Armed Forces. Secondly, after Singapore had separated from Malaysia, there was no longer a natural hinterland or large domestic market for the island. Singapore thus sought substitutes, such as

Force Z: Japanese war artist's impression of Force Z under attack.

Foreign policy: APEC Summit, Busan, 2005 (top); Goh Chok Tong, left, with PRC leader Deng Xiaoping, 1987.

Forever Fever (1998)

through the ASSOCIATION OF SOUTH EAST ASIAN NATIONS (ASEAN). This was finally achieved with the signing and coming into operation of the ASEAN FREE TRADE AREA. The third challenge was a lack of a domestic manufacturing and industrial sector, as hitherto Singapore had been a trading hub. The solution was to court multinational corporations (MNCs), which brought not just foreign capital and technology and jobs, but also trading networks and distribution and logistics systems.

After Separation in August 1965, the government's main aim was to ensure the survival and prosperity of the new, weak and vulnerable state of Singapore. To do so, it had to ensure and obtain foreign investment and markets; partners (such as MNCs); allies in defence (such as through the FIVE POWER DEFENCE ARRANGEMENTS and, later, the United States); and peace in the immediate region.

After this initial phase, Singapore began to expand its political and economic space. In the 1980s, it sought to transcend the limitations of being air- and sea-locked by its closest neighbours—all of which were beginning to catch up economically and develop their own infrastructure.

Singapore's foreign policy is driven by factors such as trade, security and economics (including market access, foreign investment, oil and gas supplies, water, civil aviation and maritime access). As a small state, it behoves Singapore to be friendly to all, but to pay special attention to the United States and other major powers, such as the permanent members of the United Nations Security Council. Singapore's interests in trade, communications, markets and international peace and stability dictate an active role in international organizations such as the UNITED NATIONS; in specialized international organizations such as the INTERNATIONAL CIVIL AVIATION ORGANIZATION (ICAO), the INTERNATIONAL MARITIME ORGANISATION (IMO), the WORLD TRADE ORGANIZATION (WTO), the International Monetary Fund and the World Bank; and in regional organizations such as ASEAN, the EAST ASIA SUMMIT and

ASIA PACIFIC ECONOMIC COOPERATION (APEC). Singapore has also sought to engage rising powers, particularly China and India.

Singapore has a high international profile, thanks to issues such as Cambodia (following the 1978 invasion of that country by Vietnam); the Law of the Sea (UN Conference on Law of the Sea, or UNCLOS); and the Earth Summit (UN Conference on Environment and Development, or UNCED). All of these issues impinged on Singapore's vital national interests. During the 2003 Cancún WTO negotiations, Singapore's minister for trade and industry, George Yeo, was elected chairman of the sensitive Agriculture Committee. Successful initiatives by Singapore, such as the Asean Regional Forum (ARF), the Asia-Europe Meeting (ASEM) and the Asia-Middle East Dialogue (AMED) also demonstrated that the country could contribute to the success of international systems, and that it was a responsible stakeholder.

With its immediate neighbours, Malaysia and Indonesia, Singapore has maintained good relations. Singapore has provided assistance to these countries during crises, such as after the December 2004 tsunami and during the SEVERE ACUTE RESPIRATORY SYNDROME (SARS) epidemic.

One main characteristic of Singapore's foreign policy is adaptability. During the Cold War, the government adopted the 'balance of power approach', and was a member of the Non-Aligned Movement and G77. In the post-Cold War period, the government understood that Singapore had become less useful to the great powers. It compensated by joining the US-led coalitions in the first Gulf War (1990–91), as well as the second Gulf War (2003).

Foreign policy formulation is marked by planning and anticipation. Much use is made of scenario planning and crisis simulation and practice. Within the MINISTRY OF FOREIGN AFFAIRS, attention is paid to identifying the drivers of change and the centres of new growth and ideas.

Among the most difficult foreign policy issues that Singapore will have to face in the future are those posed by the rise of China and India. Another issue will be globalization, which has the potential to further sharpen competition for markets, talent, resources and technology. Singapore does not have the political weight of larger countries, and its growing success may provoke the imposition of non-tariff barriers on its goods and services. Singapore's response has been to seek assured access to developed markets via FREE TRADE AGREEMENTS. Another effect of globalization may be the spread of religious extremism; Singapore's response has been to improve social cohesion and engage with those countries in which moderate teachings are promoted.

Having achieved some measure of development, Singapore will need to adapt to the foreign policy of a developed country (i.e. one with a different agenda and focus from the foreign policy adopted by developing countries). It will also need to address global issues such as climate change, global governance, competition for resources and threats to international security—such as terrorism—that impact on Singapore's interests.

See also CHINA–SINGAPORE RELATIONS; INDIA–SINGAPORE RELATIONS; JAPAN-SINGAPORE RELATIONS; MALAYSIA–SINGAPORE RELATIONS; INDONESIA–SINGAPORE RELATIONS; and UNITED STATES–SINGAPORE RELATIONS.

foreign talent Term describing non-citizens who work in highly-skilled jobs in Singapore. Foreign talent are distinguished from 'FOREIGN WORKERS' on the basis of salary (foreign talent being persons who earn more than $2,500 a month) and the nature of their employment. They hold an employment pass instead of a work permit. As employment pass holders, they do not face the same restrictions on marrying Singaporeans that foreign workers do. To qualify for an employment pass, foreign nationals need to have acceptable degrees, professional qualifications, skills and experience. Employment pass holders also have the option of applying for permanent residency, which allows them greater flexibility in terms of working and living in Singapore.

Singapore relies on attracting foreign talent to increase its talent pool and thus increase its economic capability. An organization called CONTACT SINGAPORE has also been established with the aim of attracting foreign talent to work in Singapore. Apart from an internet presence, Contact Singapore has offices in China, India, the United Kingdom and the United States.

foreign workers Term describing non-citizens who work in low-skilled jobs or manual labour, and who earn less than $2,500 a month. Foreign workers are distinguished from 'FOREIGN TALENT', who are non-citizens who earn more than $2,500 a month in skilled employment. Instead of an employment pass, foreign workers are given a work permit, which has more restrictions than the employment pass.

Most foreign workers are employed in the CONSTRUCTION SECTOR or work as domestic helpers (see MAIDS). However, they can also be found in the manufacturing and service industries. They include the thousands of daily commuters from the neighbouring Malaysian state of Johor. Traditional sources of foreign workers are Malaysia and Indonesia, but over the past 20 years, foreign workers have come increasingly from the Philippines, Thailand, Bangladesh, India and China. According to the Ministry of Manpower, there were 671,000 foreigners working in Singapore in

2005 (which includes those on employment passes). Foreign nationals make up about 29 per cent of Singapore's total work force. The government controls the number and distribution of foreign workers through quotas and levies.

Forever Fever (1998) Film directed by GLEN GOEI. In a time when local film production was dominated by ERIC KHOO's social dramas and JACK NEO's comedies, *Forever Fever* stood out. It tells the story of Hock, a grocery clerk who longs to own a motorbike. He lives with his parents and sister, who idolize Hock's younger brother, Beng, a medical student. Inspired by the film *Saturday Night Fever* (1977), Hock enrols for dance lessons with his friend Mei, in the hope of winning a contest and buying a bike.

This loose remake of John Badham's original *Saturday Night Fever* is, like *Bugis Street* (1995) and *Homerun* (2003), a movie from the 1990s revival of Singapore filmmaking, which revisits the 1970s—the latter stage of Singapore cinema's 'golden age'.

Forever Fever was the first Southeast Asian film to be selected for the Sundance Film Festival (1999), and the first local film to be acquired by Miramax International for distribution in the United States, for which it was re-titled *That's the Way I Like It*.

Fort Canning and Park Formerly known as BUKIT LARANGAN (meaning 'Forbidden Hill' in Malay), it was renamed GOVERNMENT HILL in 1819. In 1822, Sir STAMFORD RAFFLES had a wooden house built on the hill as his private residence. Raffles also established Singapore's first experimental botanic gardens on the hill, although these failed and were abandoned in 1829. During the same period, a Christian cemetery was established on the hill, and this continued to be used until 1865.

Raffles' bungalow was used as the residence of the British governor until the late 1850s. In 1859, it was demolished to make way for a military fort, named Fort Canning in honour of Viscount Charles John Canning, the first Viceroy of India. Constructed as part of a strategy to fortify Singapore against possible attacks by the French, this structure did more to overawe the locals than to protect against seaborne assaults. It was constructed by CONVICT LABOUR and at great expense. Construction began in 1859. By May that year, the site had seven 68-pounder guns mounted at its south end, facing the sea.

However, by the late 1870s, the fort was found wanting. With its 17 guns standing 200 ft (61 m) high on the hill and a quarter-mile (400 m) from the shore, it could not prevent an attack on the harbour because its guns could not reach the entire roadstead. In addition, the fort was undermanned, and its wells were dry and useless in an attack. In 1891, Fort Canning was considered unsuitable for defence.

The fort did, however, serve as a base for the Royal Artillery in 1892. When the division left in 1907, the fort became the British army's headquarters until World War II. Between 1923 and 1927, the top of Fort Canning Hill was converted into a municipal reservoir. In 1929, the fort was demolished to make way for British army headquarters, as well as an elaborate underground network comprising an operations centre, ammunition bunkers and meeting rooms. This command centre, now called the BATTLE BOX, was completed in 1939, and was used as MALAYA COMMAND's headquarters until the British surrender to the Japanese in February 1942 (*see* MALAYA CAMPAIGN). After World War II, Fort Canning continued to be used by the British military, and later by the Singapore Armed Forces until the 1970s.

Originally named King George V Park, Fort Canning Park has become a popular venue for outdoor concerts. The ASEAN SCULPTURE GARDEN is located there. The former military buildings house Fort Canning Centre (which houses performing arts groups, including the SINGAPORE DANCE THEATRE); and a country club. Nearby is a spice garden, as well as remnants of the old cemetery with its Gothic gates, built in 1846. Fort Canning has also been the site of important archaeological work (*see* ARCHAEOLOGICAL SITES).

Fort Connaught Fort Connaught was built in 1878 on the eastern end of Pulau Blakang Mati (present-day SENTOSA). Along with FORT SILOSO and FORT SERAPONG, on the same island, Connaught was a major part of the colony's line of defence against attacks on the docks, and shipping and coal stores. All these forts were equipped and functional until the Fall of Singapore to the Japanese during World War II.

Known initially as Fort Blakang Mati East, it was renamed Fort Connaught after a visit by the Duke and Duchess of Connaught in 1890. In 1892, the fort was manned by a Royal Artillery gunner strength of 44 men. In February 1942, during the Japanese invasion, the guns at Fort Connaught fired on Japanese troops at Tengah Airfield. When the British surrendered on 15 February 1942, they spiked all the guns (*see* MALAYA CAMPAIGN).

After the government decided to redevelop Sentosa as a tourist attraction, Fort Connaught was destroyed to make way for the Coralarium (present-day Underwater World, a tropical oceanarium) and a golf course.

Fort Fullerton In 1827, Captain Edward Lake of the Bengal Engineers was asked to report on the island's defences. Lake made a number of recommendations for the protection of Singapore from seaborne attacks. One result was the construction of a battery at the entrance of the Singapore River. Called Battery Point, it was later renamed Fort Fullerton after the first governor of the Straits Settlements, ROBERT FULLERTON. Battery Road was named after it.

Situated on the beach where the FULLERTON BUILDING now stands, the fort was built in 1829. It was enlarged to three times its original size in 1861, and extended from the river to JOHNSTON'S PIER. The

Fort Canning: military building now converted into Fort Canning Centre (left); the former Fort Canning lighthouse, c. 1900 (right).

Foreign workers: sign posted outside construction site.

NOTICE TO ALL FOREIGN WORKERS

ALL FOREIGN WORKERS ARE TO PRODUCE THEIR ORIGINAL WORK PERMITS WITHOUT DEMAND. FOREIGN WORKERS WITHOUT PERMITS ARE NOT ALLOWED ON THIS SITE.

所有外地劳工必须随时出示工作准证
没持有工作准证的外地工人不准进入及逗留在工地内

SEMUA PEKERJA LUAR NEGERI HENDAKLAH MENUNJUKKAN PERMIT ASLI TANPA DIMINTA. PEKERJA LUAR NEGERI TANPA PERMIT TIDAK DIBENARKAN.

அனைத்து வெளிநாட்டு உழியர்களும், தாங்களின் வேலை அனுமதி பத்திரத்தை தாங்களாகவே கொடிக்கவும் வேலை அனுமதியில்லாத வெளிநாட்டு உழியர்கள் இந்த பகுதியில் அனுமதியில்லை

คนงานชาวต่างชาติทุกคนต้องยื่นใบอนุญาติทำงานปราศจากคำยื่นร้อง
คนงานชาวต่างชาติที่ไม่มีใบอนุญาติทำงานไม่อนุญาติให้อยู่ในบริเวณที่ทำงานนี้

fort consisted of a commander's quarters, barracks and ten guns. It was demolished in 1873 partly because it was felt that its proximity to the city centre could endanger the town in the event of an attack.

Fort Palmer Constructed between 1859 and 1862 on Mount Palmer near TELOK AYER, Fort Palmer overlooked the eastern entrance of New Harbour (present-day KEPPEL HARBOUR). It was named after John Palmer, a respected member of the local merchant community.

Two guns from Fort Canning were brought to the fort for practice in 1866. Fort Palmer was provided in 1892 with 26 Royal Artillerymen and four breech-loading cannon, the first in Singapore to be fired by electricity.

Between 1905 and 1915, the fort was dismantled as soil from Mount Palmer was used to reclaim the Telok Ayer area.

Fort Serapong Along with FORT SILOSO and FORT CONNAUGHT, Fort Serapong was part of Singapore's coastal defences. It was situated on Mount Serapong at the eastern end of Pulau Blakang Mati (present-day Sentosa), overlooking Pulau Brani. It was operational by 1892 and had two 9.2-inch breech loading guns. Stationed at Serapong were 36 members of the Royal Artillery. Like FORT PALMER, Serapong was self-contained and functional until the Fall of Singapore during World War II. A paved road now leads to its ruins.

Fort Siloso Constructed in the 1880s, Fort Siloso was one of three main coastal fortifications intended by the British to protect Singapore against attacks from the south, and to protect KEPPEL HARBOUR. It was built at the western tip of Pulau Blakang Mati (present-day SENTOSA). In 1907, it became the headquarters of the Royal Artillery. During the 1930s, the fort was upgraded with new guns and searchlights. An underground tunnel complex, with stores for fuel and ammunition, was also built. When the Japanese invaded Singapore from the north in 1942, the fort's guns were turned around and fired towards the invad-

Fort Siloso

ing forces, but with limited effect. During the JAPANESE OCCUPATION, the fort was used as a prisoner-of-war camp. It was returned to the British after the Japanese surrender. Following the BRITISH WITHDRAWAL FROM SINGAPORE, the fort was taken over by the Singapore Armed Forces. In 1969, the government decided to develop Sentosa into a recreational island and the fort was restored. It was opened to the public in 1975. Fort Siloso is Singapore's last remaining near-intact pre-World War II fort.

Fort Tanjong Katong Merchant demands that the eastern side of the island be protected resulted in the building of Fort Tanjong Katong in 1879. The fort stood at what is now Fort Road and Meyer Road, surrounded by a moat of sea water. Along with four other forts at Pasir Panjang, Blakang Mati East (FORT CONNAUGHT), FORT SILOSO and FORT SERAPONG, Fort Tanjong Katong was part of Singapore's line of defence against seaborne attacks. It received two 8-inch Armstrong guns in 1888. In 1888–91, the Singapore Volunteer Artillery Corps used the fort and the area around it for training. In 1892, 30 Royal Artillery gunners were stationed there.

However, as the fort stood on sandy, low-lying land, it had poor foundations. It was unable to support a high tower erected later for firing practice. Dubbed the 'Wash-Out Fort', it was abandoned in the early 19th century. Rather than being demolished, it was buried by the British, then largely forgotten, though a nearby road carried the name Fort Road. However, in 2001, a local resident came across parts of the structure in the ground in Katong Park, sparking a project to uncover the fort. The project began in 2004, and for ten months, volunteers and archeologists slowly cleared the soil. They uncovered the entire perimeter wall, two infantry bastions, and signs of a drawbridge. The fort was then reburied to protect it from the elements while the authorities decided on what to do with the site.

See also TANJONG KATONG.

Fort Teregah This fort was the only defence on the island of PULAU BRANI in KEPPEL HARBOUR. Pulau Brani was believed to be a good site for fortification as early as 1843, although no fort was built on it until 1861.

Fort Teregah had a separate platform with gun emplacements overlooking the entrance of the harbour. It was not a fort in the usual sense because living quarters were some distance away from the platform, and there was no established perimeter encompassing both sites. The bunkers, which housed both soldiers and ammunition, were located underground, and were insufficiently ventilated. The fort was later abandoned and its remains obliterated as part of the 1973 Pulau Brani reclamation project.

Fortis Private Banking This private bank has been active in Singapore since 1988. Then known as MeesPierson Asia, it conducted mainly private bank and trust operations as well as commodity banking and specialized finance. MeesPierson started out as a merchant bank in Singapore, but entered the trade and commodity finance business in Singapore in 1994 as part of its expansion into Asia. MeesPierson, which was founded in 1720 in Rotterdam, the Netherlands, was acquired by Fortis in 1997. The Singapore office serves as the regional private banking centre for Fortis Private Bank in Asia.

Fortress of the East Phrase used to describe the city prior to the Fall of Singapore. Popular in the British press, the phrase suggested that Singapore's defences were virtually impregnable. In British military terminology, however, the term 'fortress' also had other specific meanings relating to Singapore. Firstly, Singapore Fortress was the name given to a sub-district of MALAYA COMMAND, which in 1941 included Singapore, the surrounding islands and part of the south Johor coast at Pengerang.

Secondly, 'fortress' was a term used to refer to an integrated system of weapons and supporting equipment which, in Singapore's case, included 29 coastal guns in two fire commands (Changi and Faber), as well as numerous smaller close-defence guns and associated equipment.

founding of Singapore Singapore's founding is usually traced back to 6 February 1819, the day on which Sir STAMFORD RAFFLES, an EAST INDIA COMPANY official, concluded a treaty with Sultan HUSAIN SHAH and Temenggong ABDUL RAHMAN, the Malay rulers of Singapore island.

In 1819, Raffles established a British 'factory' or trading settlement on a narrow coastal strip of Singapore, the existence of which had been established long before in maps of the region. There was no transfer of sovereignty. A further treaty of 25 June 1819 defined the boundaries of the lands under British control, but involved no cession of sovereignty or even transfer of property. It stipulated that matters of common concern should come before a council comprising the Resident, the sultan and the *temenggong*. The convention of 17 June 1823 extended

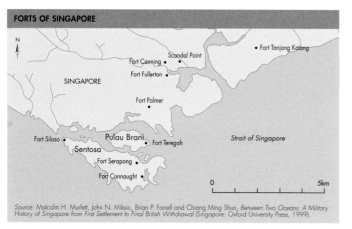

FORTS OF SINGAPORE

N

SINGAPORE

Fort Canning • Scandal Point • Fort Tanjong Katong
Fort Fullerton •
Fort Palmer •
Fort Siloso • Pulau Brani
Sentosa Fort Teregah • Strait of Singapore
Fort Serapong •
Fort Connaught •

0 ⊢ ⊣ ⊢ ⊣ 5km

Source: Malcolm H. Murfett, John N. Miksic, Brian P. Farrell and Chiang Ming Shun, *Between Two Oceans: A Military History of Singapore from First Settlement to Final British Withdrawal* (Singapore: Oxford University Press, 1999).

British control over the entire island, apart from the sultan's and *temenggong*'s reserves, and compensated both for loss of revenue. Though British rule was becoming more direct, this convention still stopped short of ceding sovereignty to the British.

Raffles had come to Singapore because he had been searching for a British base at the southern end of the Strait of Malacca. He obtained authorization to do so in November 1818 from the governor-general of India, Lord Hastings. Raffles made the final selection of Singapore at the suggestion of Captain Daniel Ross and with the support of Colonel WILLIAM FARQUHAR, though the latter preferred the Karimun islands as the site for a base.

Raffles clearly appreciated the historical antecedents and geopolitical situation of Singapore, and sensed its potential economic and strategic significance. He appointed Farquhar, former Resident and commandant of Malacca (which had been returned to the Dutch) as Resident and commandant of Singapore, and gave him the initial instructions on dealings with the Dutch and their Malay protectorates, and other groups who might come to Singapore for trade or for protection.

It was the second Resident, JOHN CRAWFURD, who made Singapore a British colonial possession in 1824. Crawfurd received the necessary authorization from British India in early March 1824. His task was facilitated by the ANGLO-DUTCH TREATY (1824) which, among other things, involved Dutch recognition of the British position in Singapore. Crawfurd's treaty with the Malay rajas was finalized on 2 August 1824, and secured the cession of Singapore 'in full sovereignty and property to the East India Company, its heirs and successors'.

While Raffles is usually cited as the founder of Singapore, credit should also go to early and enterprising co-founders and pioneers, namely the first two British Residents, Farquhar (1819-23) and Crawfurd (1823-26); the Malay, Arab, Bugis, Chinese, Indian, European and Armenian notables (mostly traders); and the numerous unnamed, pioneering settlers.

It was Farquhar, with his knowledge of the Malay world and connections with Malacca, who worked alongside the Malay rulers for the next four years to secure the survival and growth of the settlement. Raffles himself supervised Farquhar's administration fitfully from his backwater post of Fort Marlborough, BENCOOLEN, in west Sumatra. He visited Singapore thrice: for ten days in January–February 1819; about four weeks in May–June that year; and—after more than three years' absence—for eight months from October 1822 to June 1823.

Other early settlers were Syed Mohammed Harun Aljunied and his nephew SYED OMAR ALI ALJUNIED, who came from Palembang in Sumatra, and who settled near KAMPONG GLAM. The BUGIS, led by Arong Bilawa, also took refuge from the Dutch in Singapore.

While most of the Indians in Singapore at that time were SEPOYS and camp-followers in CANTONMENTS, there were also Indian merchants, the most famous of whom was NARAYANA PILLAY, who came from Penang with Raffles on his second visit in May 1819.

Most of the Chinese pioneers came from the immediate vicinity of the settlement, from the Malay Peninsula and archipelago. The most prominent early leaders were TAN CHE SANG, who built the first warehouse and was agent for the early Chinese junks; TAN TOCK SENG, who established a hospital; and CHUA CHONG LONG, son of the KAPITAN CINA of Malacca.

In the social heirarchy, the most influential traders were the Europeans, and the most prominent among them were the Scots. They included ALEXANDER JOHNSTON, a former ship's owner and captain, who

Fraser & Neave: beverage advertisement featuring Maria Menado, 1950s.

founded the firm which bore his name, and ALEXANDER GUTHRIE, who gave his name to a company which still survives (*see* GUTHRIE & CO.). Most of the magistrates appointed by Raffles were Scottish merchants. Another early arrival was the Armenian trader, Aristarchus Sarkies (*see* MOSES, CATCHICK).

In January 1819, it was estimated that Singapore had around 1,000 inhabitants. Through the exertions of its founders and pioneers, the population had risen to nearly 11,000 by January 1824.

Fraser & Neave Food and beverage conglomerate. The firm was founded in 1883 by John Fraser and David Neave, to produce carbonated soft drinks. Originally known as the Singapore and Straits Aerated Water Company, the company was renamed Fraser & Neave (F&N) in 1898.

In 1931, F&N expanded into the beer-brewing business by entering into a joint venture with Heineken to form Malayan Breweries (present-day ASIA PACIFIC BREWERIES). It launched its flagship brand, TIGER BEER, a year later. The Coca-Cola franchise for Singapore and Malaya was secured by F&N in 1936.

F&N ventured into dairy products in 1959 when it set-up a joint venture with Beatrice Foods of Chicago to build a condensed milk plant in Malaya. Its dairy operations in Singapore commenced in 1968. F&N subsequently extended its dairy operations into Vietnam and Thailand, selling dairy products under the Magnolia, Daisy and Farmhouse brands.

In beverages, F&N has diversified by producing traditional Asian drinks such as chrysanthemum tea and barley water under its Seasons brand; fruit juices under the Fruit Tree brand; and isotonic drinks under the 100Plus brand. It has also continued to produce carbonated beverages, such as its signature orange squash, sarsaparilla and ice-cream soda.

Founding of Singapore: watercolour by H.E. Edgell depicting Singapore in the 1820s.

Peter Fu

In 1988, F&N, together with Goodman Fielders Watties, aquired a controlling stake in COLD STORAGE. Two years later, the joint venture was dissolved and F&N aquired the property arm of the company, Centrepoint Properties. F&N entered the publishing and printing business in 2000 with the acquisition of Times Publishing.

The F&N Group maintains operations in more than 20 countries and employs more than 11,000 employees worldwide; its total assets exceed $7 billion. In 2005, the group registered an after-tax profit of $300 million and group revenues of $4.3 billion.

free trade agreements Contractual arrangements between two or more countries with the aim of enhancing trade and investment flows. Under a free trade agreement (FTA), member countries accord each other preferential market access by lowering or eliminating tariffs and other restrictions on trade and investment with each other, but retain autonomy in determining their external tariffs and restrictions with non-members.

As a major trading nation and a beneficiary of free trade, Singapore is a vocal advocate and supporter of the multilateral trading framework embodied by the WORLD TRADE ORGANIZATION. However, the Singapore government also strongly believes that regional and bilateral FTAs not only enable the country to secure economic ties with its strategic trading partners and access to their markets, but also provide the impetus to accelerate the process of multilateral trade liberalization.

Freemasons: Masonic emblem, the compass and set-square (below); Freemasons' Hall, Coleman Street.

As at 2005, Singapore has concluded ten FTAs. It has a regional agreement with the ASEAN FREE TRADE AREA and a joint agreement with Brunei Darussalam, Chile and New Zealand known as the 'Trans-Pacific SEP'. The remaining eight agreements are bilateral FTAs with New Zealand, the European Free Trade

Frontier Danceland: performance at Singapore Botanic Gardens, 2003.

Association, Japan, Australia, the United States, Jordan, India and South Korea. The United States-Singapore FTA is expected to spur other ASEAN-wide trade liberalization initiatives.

Freemasons International society for mutual help and fellowship. The Freemasons have been in Singapore since the time of Sir STAMFORD RAFFLES, who is said to have been a Freemason. Several lodges were established in Singapore in the 19th century, including Lodge Zetland No. 748, established in 1845, and Masonic Hall Esplanade, established in 1856. On 14 April 1879, the foundation stone of the Masonic hall on Coleman Street was laid. The building was consecrated as Freemasons' Hall on 27 December 1879. The Masonic Club, Singapore, was inaugurated on 2 July 1888.

Among the many other Freemasons in Singapore during the 19th century were officials and public figures such as WILLIAM NAPIER, W.H. Read, Colonel Samuel Dunlop and Sir HENRY KEPPEL. Read and Dunlop were district grand masters.

Freemasonry in Singapore survived the two world wars, with Lodge Zetland in the East (formerly Lodge Zetland No. 748) celebrating its centenary in December 1945. Meetings are still held at Freemason's Hall.

Frisby, Alfred (1898–1973) Teacher and civil servant. After graduating from Oxford University, Alfred William Frisby joined the colonial education service and was posted to Malaya. He taught at the Penang Free School and Victoria Institution (Kuala Lumpur) and was subsequently promoted to director of education. After he retired from the education service, Frisby was appointed chairman of the Public Service Commission (1952–56). The University of Malaya awarded him an honorary doctorate of laws (1955). In June 1956, he retired and returned to the United Kingdom.

Frontier Danceland Non-profit dance company. Founded in 1991 by LOW MEI YOKE and Tan Chong Poh, its focus is on finding a brand of cross-cultural contemporary dance unique to Singapore. It debuted with a mixed bill entitled *Asking Dance* in 1991,

featuring five of Low's works and two creations by guest choreographers from Hong Kong and Malaysia. Its repertory, such as Low's *Retrospect* (1991) and *Cloud* (1998), draws on Asian and Western sources, and includes collaborations such as its *New Dance Lab* series (1998–2000) and *Soulless Souls* (2001) with Malaysian group Dua Space Dance Theatre.

Frontier Danceland has represented Singapore at oveseas dance festivals, such as 2000 Feet: A Celebration of World Dance (United States, 1999) and the Tari 2000 Dance Festival (Malaysia, 2000). The company also conducts an Arts Education Programme for schools.

Fu, Peter (1923–2005) Businessman. Peter Fu Yun Siak's company Kuo International began trading in timber, wax and tin, but later ventured into oil trading after Fu became closely acquainted with leading executives from the Indonesian oil company Pertamina. Fu subsequently built Kuo International into the world's largest oil-trading company with an annual turnover of over US$1 billion.

In 1980, Fu expanded into the hotel industry when he purchased the Hilton Hotel, thereby founding HOTEL PROPERTIES LIMITED, which was publicly listed in 1982. Together with his son-in-law, ONG BENG SENG, Fu has built the company into one of the most prominent local hotel groups, managing interests in 18 hotels across nine countries.

Fujii Tatsuki (dates unknown) Journalist. Fujii Tatsuki grew up in the United States, but returned to Japan, where he became a journalist. In 1940, he was sent to work with the *Singapore Herald*, a Japanese-owned English-language newspaper set up in Singapore to counter the British-run media. He was interned when the Japanese invasion began in December 1941 and, together with other internees, was sent to India. As part of a prisoner-exchange programme, Fuji was released in exchange for British internees in East Asia. He returned to Singapore in 1943, joining the *Syonan Shimbun* newspaper. He authored a book about pre-war Singapore entitled *Nippon Assignment*, which was published in 1943.

Alfred Frisby: opening of Catholic High School, 1951.

Fullerton Building: under construction (left) and during the 1920s (centre); river frontage of The Fullerton Hotel Singapore (right).

Fullerton Building Commissioned in 1919 as part of the colony's centennial celebrations, the Fullerton Building was designed by the Shanghai-based architectural firm of Keys & Dowdeswell, and completed in 1928. Sited on the waterfront, the building is one of the best examples of neoclassical architecture in Singapore; perhaps only two other buildings of the period, CITY HALL and the Supreme Court building, are of similar grandeur.

An interesting feature of the Fullerton Building was the lighthouse that was built on top of the building.

Called Fullerton Light, it was a revolving beacon of 540,000 candlepower that could be seen 29 km away.

The Fullerton Building was named in honour of Governer ROBERT FULLERTON, and was used as Singapore's general post office for many years. A tunnel under Fullerton Road connected the post office to the pier, thus facilitating the delivery of mail between ships and the building. Its premises also housed, at different stages, the local stock exchange, the Chamber of Commerce, the Singapore Club and various government ministries and

departments, such as the Inland Revenue Authority and the Ministry of Finance. During the JAPANESE OCCUPATION, it was used by the Japanese military administration department.

The building was refurbished and reopened in 2001 as The Fullerton Hotel Singapore. Both the hotel and One Fullerton—a nearby waterfront commercial development comprising offices and restaurants—are majority-owned by FAR EAST ORGANIZATION and its Hong Kong-based sister company, Sino Group.

Fujimura Masuzo, Lieutenant-General (dates unknown) Japanese military official. Fujimura Masuzo replaced WATANABE WATARU in March 1943 as chief of the Malaya Military Administration during teh JAPANESE OCCUPATION. Fujimura adopted a more conciliatory style than his predecessor, and encouraged co-operation with different ethnic groups in Singapore, particularly the Chinese. He ended Watanabe's repressive policies towards the Chinese and attempted to include members of the Chinese community in the administration's bureaucracy. When the economy began to suffer, Fujimura tried to curtail the activities of Japanese profiteers and encourage the Chinese business sector.

Fuk Tak Chi Temple One of the oldest Chinese temples in Singapore, Fuk Tak Chi was built by early immigrants to give thanks for their safe sea passage from China. Apparently, Chinese fishermen found a body which they then buried under a tree at the temple site on Telok Ayer Street at the end of the 18th century. They prayed to the spirit of the dead person. When their prayers were answered, Hakka and Cantonese devotees constructed a shrine in 1824. Over the years, the building expanded to include a neighbouring site and developed into a temple thanks to donations from immigrants who had made their fortunes.

Fuk Tak Chi has several important signboards and calligraphic displays of historic value, including an 1822 signboard given by the Cantonese, and an 1856 one presented by the Cantonese and Hakkas. There are also calligraphic poems given by the Teochews. Architecturally, the temple is typically Chinese in style, with a beam-based structural framework, trusses and posts. It has an elegant half-gable roof and ornate decorations.

The patron deity of Fuk Tak Chi is Tua Peh Kong, and an inscription on one of the wooden pillars of the temple extols this deity's ability to bring peace on land and at sea. He is worshipped amongst Chinese dialect groups from southern China, who brought the deity to Singapore (*see* TAOISM).

Fuk Tak Chi is no longer a temple, and is now known as the Fuk Tak Chi Museum.

Fullerton, Robert (1773-1831) Colonial official. In 1826, Penang, Malacca and Singapore were incorporated by the East India Company as a single entity, the Straits Settlements, under the government of Penang. Robert Fullerton was the first governor of the Straits Settlements, and resident councillors were appointed for Singapore and Malacca. Fullerton was governor from 1826 to 1827 (*see* GOVERNORS).

The new governor faced an immediate challenge regarding land. Lands cleared and occupied were estimated at some 13,800 acres (5600 ha), and were often held without title. Fullerton helped to reorganize the land titles system, forming the basis for the Singapore Land Regulation of 1830.

Fullerton is also remembered for introducing schemes for the payment of tuition fees and bonuses to officials proficient in Malay, Chinese or Siamese (Thai). These were abolished at the end of his term.

He was replaced in 1827 because the governor-general was unhappy with the increasing expenditure and decreasing revenue in the Straits Settlements. Fullerton was replaced by ROBERT IBBETSON, resident councillor of Penang.

Funan Digitalife Mall Shopping centre housing a large concentration of digital electronic product retailers. It was built in 1984 and was originally known as Funan Centre, a name it is still known by. 'Funan'

is the Mandarin pronunciation of the Hokkien 'Hock Lam'. The seven-storey shopping centre was one of the URBAN REDEVELOPMENT AUTHORITY's largest resettlement projects. Four rows of old shophouses on Hock Lam Street and Chin Nam Street were demolished for the construction of the mall.

Future Systems Directorate Coming under the purview of the MINISTRY OF DEFENCE, the Future Systems Directorate (FSD) was established in February 2003. Its main role is to conduct experiments and develop new concepts in warfare. It is affiliated with the Singapore Armed Forces (SAF) Centre for Military Experimentation.

FSD is headed by the future systems architect (FSA) who reports directly to the permanent secretary (defence) and the CHIEF OF DEFENCE FORCE. FSD personnel are recruited from the armed services, as well as from the DEFENCE SCIENCE AND TECHNOLOGY AGENCY and DSO NATIONAL LABORATORIES. FSD also collaborates with local and foreign industry partners.

Fuk Tak Chi Temple

G

gambier *See* PEPPER AND GAMBIER.

gambling In the years shortly after the arrival of Sir Stamford Raffles in Singapore, gambling dens and cockpits were being established on the island, even though Raffles' plan for the colony was the elimination of vice. Resident Colonel William Farquhar permitted licensed gambling on the island, but Raffles was swift to reverse this by confiscating buildings used for gambling and having their owners and patrons flogged. In August 1823, however, Singapore's second Resident, John Crawfurd, went against Raffles' wishes and licensed ten gaming houses in the town area and a cockpit in Kampong Bugis, supporting what he felt was a practical action, as gambling amongst the Chinese, Malays and Bugis could not be eradicated. Gambling provided a considerable source of revenue for the colony through the gambling tax farm, which had been banned by Raffles but was revived by Crawfurd in 1823. In 1825, almost half of all revenue from tax farms came from gambling.

The effects of gambling were considered debilitating, however, and in 1829 gambling was banned. Despite this, it still remained popular. The SINKHEH, who had no families and few pastimes, indulged frequently in gambling. Popular games included *ho lan pai*, fan-tan and CHAP JI KI. Gambling dens were run by syndicates which sprang from SECRET SOCIETIES. Under secret societies, gambling became a highly organized activity, and police were frequently bribed to keep silent about gambling dens.

During the Japanese Occupation, two amusement parks were reopened, mostly to

Gan Eng Seng

Gambling: Chinese gambling establishment, 1800s.

Gambling: Singapore Sweep tickets.

serve gamblers. The Japanese initiated Singapore's first lottery in August 1943, and at the end of that year, gambling was legalized for the first time since 1829.

Gambling dens flourished well after the end of World War II in Singapore, and when the People's Action Party assumed power in June 1959, it closed down gambling dens and brothels, suppressing the secret societies that had run such establishments. The SINGAPORE TURF CLUB, however, which had been formed in 1842, was allowed to continue operations.

The government decided to regulate gambling through the establishment of SINGAPORE POOLS in 1968. Besides acting as the official channel for betting, the surplus earnings of Singapore Pools are now donated to community causes. The SINGAPORE TOTALISATOR BOARD owns Singapore Pools. Singapore Pools provides four lotteries: Toto, 4-Digit Numbers (popularly known as 4D), Singapore Sweep and ScratchIt!. SCORE and Strike! are football betting games for local and international games respectively. According to a survey run by the Ministry of Community Development, Youth and Sports in 2004–05, 4D, Toto and Singapore Sweep have become the most popular games. Gamblers also travel to the Genting Highlands in Malaysia or Batam in Indonesia to visit casinos there. Casino cruises are also popular, with CASINO SHIPS taking passengers out of Singapore waters and providing gaming facilities on board.

In early 2004, the idea of introducing INTEGRATED RESORTS with casino facilities was mooted by the government. Subsequent discussions on the subject roused political and public debate. On 18 April 2005, the decision was taken to build two integrated resorts, one at Marina Bayfront and the other on Sentosa, to be opened in 2009. In the wake of this decision, the government resolved to take preventive measures to curb the rise in problem gambling, and is expected to set aside up to $40 million a year for this purpose. The National Council on Problem Gambling was also established in August 2005 to address problem gambling at the national level.

Gan Eng Seng (1844–1899) Merchant and philanthropist. Gan Eng Seng was the oldest in a family of five children. His parents had emigrated to Malacca from Fujian, China, where he was born. He received a rudimentary education in which he picked up English and accounting. When his father died, the 17-year-old Gan came to Singapore and entered the nutmeg business. He joined GUTHRIE & CO. as an apprentice, and rose through the company's ranks.

Gan donated large sums of money to various local hospitals. In 1867, with other prominent Chinese leaders such as Khoo Cheng Tiong and Choo Yam Lam, Gan set up the Thong Chai Medical Institution (*see*

Gan Eng Seng School

OLD THONG CHAI MEDICAL INSTITUTION). This became an important meeting place for Chinese immigrants and the local Chinese community generally in early Singapore. The restored building is now a national monument. In 1885 he also founded the Anglo-Chinese Free School, which was renamed GAN ENG SENG SCHOOL in 1923.

Gan died at the age of 55, and was survived by five wives, seven sons, five daughters and four grandsons.

Gan Eng Seng School Only local school established by a private citizen, GAN ENG SENG. In 1885, Gan founded the Anglo-Chinese Free School (not to be confused with Anglo-Chinese School). It operated out of a row of shophouses on Telok Ayer Street, giving free education to poor children living in the area. In 1893, a new school building was officially opened by the governor, Sir Cecil Clementi Smith. The school's name was changed to Gan Eng Seng School (GESS) in 1923.

GESS is the only school founded by the Chinese to provide boys with a bilingual education. It was also the first to form a parent-teacher association. It was an aided school until 1938, when it became a government school. In 1961, it took in its first female pre-university students for GCE 'A' levels. Younger girls were accepted for secondary school from 1987. The school moved several times, settling into new premises on Henderson Road in 2002.

The school's alumni have included businessman TAN KEONG SAIK, doctor LIM BOON KENG (who sat on the Board of Trustees) and politician YEO NING HONG.

Garden City During the 19th century, the jungle was cleared in Singapore, first to make way for agriculture, and later to make room for urban growth. The colonial government introduced street plantings and civic spaces, attempting to preserve the remaining natural vegetation and ameliorate the loss of greenery. This was, however, interrupted by the onset of World War II and the Japanese Occupation.

In 1963, Lee Kuan Yew identified a 'Green Singapore' as a key competitive factor in attracting foreign investment and contributing to the quality of life of Singaporeans. Resources were directed towards building up Singapore's natural environment through the active planting of trees and shrubs along roads, on vacant plots and on new development sites. The Parks and Recreation Department (PRD) was formed in 1976 for this purpose. As most of Singapore's streets were devoid of greenery, the key task of the PRD was to increase the amount of plants and vegetation in public spaces. Fast-growing indigenous trees such as the angsana, rain tree, yellow flame and ketapang were introduced.

The next phase of the Garden City programme saw the cultivation of free-flowering trees and shrubs like frangipani and bougainvillea, which added colour to the landscape. In addition, paved areas, such as car parks, were planted with trees to attenuate the build-up of heat over asphalt surfaces. Concrete structures, such as fly-overs, were also planted with creepers, such as the climbing fig.

By the 1980s, Singapore had tree-lined roads interspersed with parks filled with flowering plants and greenery. 'Green lungs' had been created in commercial areas such as the Marina City Park, while developers of residential areas were required to plant roadside trees and set aside land for open space. Parks competed with residential, commercial and industrial developments for land use, and park plannners had to consider factors such as the location of population centres and accessibility.

In 1990, the NATIONAL PARKS BOARD (NParks) was formed, comprising the SINGAPORE BOTANIC GARDENS and research divisions of the PRD. NParks also undertook a major programme to rejuvenate the Singapore Botanic Gardens. Fort Canning Park found new life as a performance venue. Singapore's nature reserves were also given new resources for conservation.

On 1 July 1996, the PRD as a whole merged with NParks. NParks instituted community outreach and education programmes such as the 'Adopt-a-Park' scheme, through which schools and other organizations were encouraged to help tend their own special garden plots with an aim to cultivating a sense of ownership of the natural environment.

Gasing

As the Garden City took shape, NParks introduced the HERITAGE TREES concept in 2002 to preserve and maintain prime specimens of old trees, while the HERITAGE ROADS scheme (also launched in 2002) sought to preserve distinctive roadside landscapes.

NParks now manages a hierarchy of parks and open spaces, including nature reserves, roadside greenery and vacant state land. The Park Connector Network, a comprehensive network of park corridors, links major parks and nature areas. To sustain the development of the Garden City, NParks has completed its islandwide Streetscape Greenery Master Plan, which is aimed at creating distinctive landmarks out of future roadside greenery. Skyrise and rooftop greenery is also encouraged as part of the aim to optimize land use. Such features include rooftop gardens, landscaped bridges, terraces, decks and balconies. Other forms of skyrise greenery are plants on flyovers and pedestrian overhead bridges, as well as landscaped gardens above basement carparks.

See also NATURE CONSERVATION.

gas The Energy Market Authority of Singapore (EMA), a statutory board under the Ministry of Trade and Industry (MTI), is responsible for the economic, technical and competition-related regulations governing Singapore's gas industry. Created on 1 April 2001, EMA replaced SINGAPORE POWER, which had earlier replaced the Electricity and Gas Undertakings of State Monopoly under PUB (Public Utilities Board) in October 1995.

EMA differentiates between manufactured gas (manufactured from naphtha)—also known as 'town gas'—and natural gas. Town gas is distributed by a pipeline network to about 450,000 customers, who use it primarily for cooking and heating water. Few industries use town gas for specialist purposes. EMA plans to progressively convert the existing town gas system to natural gas.

Malaysia and Indonesia export natural gas to Singapore. The Senoko Power generating plant is connected to the Malaysian gas import pipeline. Another pipeline serving power stations and large industrial consumers in the Jurong and Tuas areas transports gas from the West Natuna Basin (near the Riau Islands). Singapore consumed an estimated 2.5 billion cu m of natural gas imported from Malaysia and Indonesia in 2001. In 2002, the government aimed to have 60 per cent of the country's electricity generated from natural gas by 2012. The goal was met in 2003.

Tokyo Gas Engineering has been appointed to study the feasibility of a liquefied natural gas (LNG) import terminal. If this project goes ahead, the terminal could be ready by 2012, opening up the possibility of the establishment of a futures markets in which gas and LNG contracts could be traded.

Garden City: park planned from the outset as a part of Toa Payoh new town.

gasing *Gasing*—literally meaning 'spinning top' in Malay—is a popular form of recreation amongst rural Malay men. The sport was brought to Singapore by players from Malacca, Johor and Negri Sembilan. The *gasing* itself is made of tough wood such as *bakau* (mangrove), *assam jawa* (tamarind) and teak. A length of rope, which is wound around the *gasing*, unwinds quickly as the top is thrown. A *gasing* is usually 35–46 cm wide and is 8–12 cm tall. It has an axis of about 9 cm in the centre and a 'head' of 3 cm. The player coils the rope around this 'head'.

Gasing is usually played by teams of four. There are two main types of *gasing* and *gasing* games—*gasing uri* and *gasing pangkah*. The outcome of a game of *gasing uri* is decided on the basis of how long the *gasing* spins. After a *gasing* is released, it is quickly scooped off the ground with a thin wooden bat and transferred onto a metal receptacle on a short wooden post. The *gasing* of expert players can spin for hours. In *gasing pangkah,* players try to strike and stop the spinning *gasing* of opposing teams. The team that makes most strikes is declared the winner.

The *gasing* association, Fedegasi (Persekutuan Gasing Singapura), which was formed in 1981, managed to secure plots of land to build *gasing* courts within public housing estates. In the 1980s, Fedegasi organized regular local and regional competitions. However, interest in the game gradually declined due to factors such as a lack of materials for *gasing*-making and the limited number of *gasing* craftsmen.

Gay World Amusement park. Originally named Happy World, this park was opened in 1937 by George Lee on a plot of land between Geylang and Mountbatten Roads. It catered to families with children, and offered a festive, carnival atmosphere. It was best known for its sporting events. The covered Happy World Stadium, which could accommodate 7,000 spectators, hosted boxing, wrestling, basketball, table tennis and badminton competitions. It was the venue for the 1952 THOMAS CUP badminton tournament, in which the Malayan team defended and won the title. Singapore's

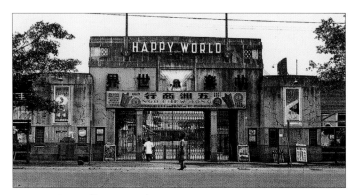

Gay World: entrance to Happy World Amusement Park (as Gay World was originally known), 1940s.

fourth president, WEE KIM WEE, then a *Straits Times* sports reporter, often visited Gay World on his 'sports beat'. ENG WAH opened its first cinemas there—Happy Theatre and the open-air Victory Theatre.

Gay World, together with NEW WORLD and GREAT WORLD, went into decline from the 1950s. From the early 1970s onwards, no further shows were held at Gay World, although the park continued to exist as a collection of individual shops until 2000, when the Land Office served notice to the remaining 150 tenants to vacate the site. The Geylang Indoor Stadium—formerly Happy World Stadium—was allowed to stay on for some time longer, as was the New Happy Cinema. However, all structures on the site were demolished in 2001.

Gemini Chit Fund Landmark fraud case. The Gemini Chit Fund Corporation Ltd was incorporated by Abdul Gaffar Mohamed Ibrahim in 1964 as a private limited company. The chit fund scheme originated in India. Usually practiced in rural societies, it is both a lending and saving scheme in which investors are also borrowers. Members make contributions to a common pool at periodic intervals. At the end of each period, the pooled funds are auctioned and the person with the lowest bid wins. Rural chit fund schemes usually involve ten people.

The Gemini Chit Fund attracted between 40,000 and 50,000 members, and promised high returns on investment. In 1973, Abdul Gaffar was charged with three counts of criminal breach of trust amounting to $3.2 million. The loss resulting from his crimes was estimated at $50 million. In sentencing Gaffar to life imprisonment, trial judge Choor Singh dubbed the case 'the swindle of the century'.

Gemini Chit Fund: Claimants outside People's Park office.

General Election (1963) Election held five days after Singapore became part of Malaysia. The PEOPLE'S ACTION PARTY (PAP) held a 'snap election' on 21 September 1963. The election was crucial for the PAP as the party could not count on the support of radical left-wing elements that had split from it to form the BARISAN SOSIALIS (BS) in July 1961. Given only nine days for campaigning, opposition parties denounced the election, and DAVID MARSHALL made an

abortive attempt to challenge the legality of the schedule in court.

Only four parties put up sufficient candidates to be in the running for control of the state. The PAP fielded a full slate of 51 candidates, while the BS contested 46 constituencies. The UNITED PEOPLE'S PARTY (UPP), led by former PAP minister ONG ENG GUAN, put up 46 candidates, while the LIM YEW HOCK-led SINGAPORE ALLIANCE PARTY (SAP) fought in 42 constituencies. Lim himself was not a candidate. Four other parties fielded token candidates—the United Democratic Party (UDP), Partai Rakyat Singapura, the Pan-Malayan Islamic Party (PMIP), and the WORKERS' PARTY (WP), putting up one, three, two and three candidates respectively. There were also 16 independents, including David Marshall who was fighting to retain his Anson seat.

On polling day, 587,487 (a record 93 per cent) of an electorate of 617,640 went to the polls; the PAP won 37 of the 51 available seats. The UPP and SAP were virtually eliminated—only Ong was elected—while the BS captured 13 seats. This reflected the absence of that party's top leadership (most had been detained under OPERATION COLD STORE seven months earlier), and the split in the opposition vote. The defeat of the SAP, and in particular the loss of its three former Singapore United Malays National Organization (UMNO)-held constituencies—Geylang Serai, Kampong Kembangan and the Southern Islands (*See* OFFSHORE ISLANDS)— to the PAP were to adversely affect future relations between the PAP and the Malaysian government.

General Labour Union Short-lived radical left-wing union active in the immediate post-war period. Before World War II, unions in Singapore were small. During the Japanese Occupation, a trade union federation was formed under the auspices of the MALAYAN COMMUNIST PARTY (MCP) to organize labour. This underground federation claimed a membership of 70 unions. After the war, most of the old unions, which had gone underground during the Occupation, reappeared and reformed themselves with the lead taken by the General Labour Union (GLU).

The GLU's main power bases were the rubber estates and tin mines. The British regarded GLU leaders with suspicion, and sought to reduce the group's influence, as many GLU leaders were MCP militants who used the labour movement as a front for a wider anti-colonial struggle. The colonial authorities brought in trade union advisers from the United Kingdom to help organize moderate unions and leadership to counter those thought to be pro-communist.

At its inception, the GLU comprised some 60 unions and 200,000 members. The GLU organized numerous strikes in 1945

General Election (1963): PAP rally, Fullerton Square.

and early 1946, including a two-day general strike in January, involving some 173,000 workers, which brought transport to a standstill. One of the GLU's first successful actions was a port workers' strike called in October 1945 to demand higher wages. This was followed by strikes by other groups of workers. In February 1946, after the formation of the Pan-Malayan Federation of Trade Unions (PMFTU), which claimed 450,000 members from 289 unions in Singapore and peninsular Malaya, the British Military Administration arrested 27 leading communists and banished ten of them without trial. Following the proclamation of the EMERGENCY in June 1948, some PMFTU leaders were detained or executed, while others fled into the jungle or were forced underground.

In Singapore, the GLU unions were reorganized under the SINGAPORE FEDERATION OF TRADE UNIONS, which had been registered on 18 June 1947.

Genome Institute of Singapore Research institute. Operating under the direction of the AGENCY FOR SCIENCE AND TECHNOLOGY RESEARCH (A★STAR), this institute was originally called the Singapore Genomics Programme when it started in 2000 in Biopolis—a 180-ha biomedical centre within ONE-NORTH. It was renamed the Genome Institute of Singapore (GIS) in 2001 to reflect its role as a research institute.

In that year, Professor Edison T. Liu, former director of the Clinical Sciences Division of the National Cancer Institute (USA), became its first executive director. GIS recruits biomedical scientists, clinical investigators and computer scientists from around the world.

In 2002, GIS, A★STAR's Biomedical Research Council and the Ministry of Health started the Singapore Tissue Network, a repository for human tissue and DNA. In 2003, GIS scientists worked with Roche Diagnostics to develop a sensitive and accurate SEVERE ACUTE RESPIRATORY SYNDROME (SARS) detection kit. Two years later, GIS researchers created an avian influenza test kit, which detects BIRD FLU in poultry in under four hours. In 2005, researchers at the institute discovered a 'genetic fingerprint' from a

Genome Institute of Singapore

set of 32 human genes that can predict the survival prospects of cancer patients.

geology For its size, Singapore is geologically complex. A mixture of igneous and sedimentary rocks forms the basic structure of the main island and the offshore islands. The western part of the main island is dominated by sedimentary rocks known as the Jurong Formation, which dates from the Triassic Period (about 200 million years ago). The central part of the island is formed from Bukit Timah granite—igneous rocks which pushed up in molten form into the sedimentary layers and then solidified deep underground. Subsequent erosion removed some of the sedimentary layers and exposed the more resistant granite, bringing it to the surface.

Today, Bukit Timah granite forms Singapore's highest point at 162 m. Neighbouring Bukit Gombak (133 m) is located on top of a small eroded dome of norite—a coarse-grained igneous rock which is formed in much the same way as granite, but which is more alkaline in its chemical composition. Bukit Timah granite also appears on the surface in the east of Singapore, at Changi, where it forms the Changi Hills; and on Pulau Ubin, where GRANITE QUARRIES operated until the 1990s. The eastern part of Singapore island is dominated by older deposits of alluvium (sedimentary material deposited by flowing water), which sit within a basin formed by Bukit Timah granite. Newer alluvial deposits are found near coastal areas and along the lower courses of some of Singapore's longer rivers.

Geology and drainage determine the quality of Singapore's soil. Those types of soil which occur on the granite are the poorest, as they are thin, acidic and easily eroded. Those formed on the new alluvial deposits are potentially the richest, but are easily

waterlogged. The types of soil that have developed on the sedimentary formations and older alluvial deposits are of a medium quality, but are generally better drained.

GES International Original design manufacturer (ODM). Founded in 1975, GES International started out as Goh Electronics Services, a small hobbyist shop selling electronic components, before becoming a manufacturer of its own Datamini brand of personal computers (PCs) in 1986.

Renamed GES in 1988, the group switched its focus to electronics product design after PC prices and margins plunged in the early 1990s. It has since transformed itself into an original design manufacturer (ODM) as well as a service provider for original equipment manufacturers (OEMs) such as IBM, NCR and NEC, with clients in China, Singapore, Malaysia and the United States. The group is a leading ODM in Point-of-Sales (POS) terminals (cash registers used in supermarkets and retail stores). It has also expanded its ODM reach to include utility metering, industrial control and medical instrumentation products.

The company was listed on the Singapore Exchange in 1999, but was split into two separate listed entities in March 2002—GES, whose focus was on product design and manufacturing, and Digiland International, a wholesale distributor of IT products such as PCs, notebooks and printers for vendors such as Apple, Compaq, Epson, Fujitsu, Hewlett-Packard and Sharp. Digiland was originally set up as the distribution arm of GES' Datamini computers.

GES exited from the PC-making business in 2004. The group reported net earnings of $45.3 million on a turnover of $624.3 million in the financial year 2005.

getai Variety entertainment shows held on open stages. The term '*getai*' is derived from the Chinese words '*ge*', meaning 'song', and '*tai*', meaning 'stage'. The term refers both to the stage as well as the performance. *Getai* shows are most often associated with the Chinese festival known as ZHONG YUAN JIE, but they also take place during other important dates in the Chinese religious calendar.

The stages are makeshift, temporary structures which are typically set up in suburban parts of Singapore, usually in an empty field or in a carpark. The performances are boisterous and, to the onlooker, rather at odds with the solemn mood of Zhong Yuan. The tradition of these performances goes back to the days when street opera, or *wayang,* performances were held to entertain ghosts and, coincidentally, guests who attended prayers and auctions during Zhong Yuan. Over the last 30 years, CHINESE OPERA performances have diminished in number and have been replaced by pop performances featuring singers, usually performing in Chinese dialects or Mandarin. The shows are anchored by hosts who supply entertainment and banter with the artistes throughout the performances.

Geylang Serai Historic district. The Geylang Serai area is bounded by Paya Lebar Way, Aljunied Road, Guillemard Road, Dunman Road and Joo Chiat Road.

Getai: performer on makeshift stage in Toa Payoh.

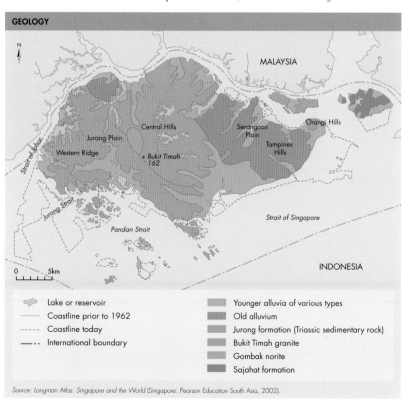

GEOLOGY

MALAYSIA

Central Hills

Jurong Plain

Serangoon Plain

Changi Hills

Western Ridge

Tampines Hills

+ Bukit Timah 162

Strait of Johor

Jurong Strait

Strait of Singapore

Pandan Strait

INDONESIA

0 5km

☁ Lake or reservoir
— Coastline prior to 1962
----- Coastline today
– – – International boundary

▨ Younger alluvia of various types
▨ Old alluvium
▨ Jurong formation (Triassic sedimentary rock)
▨ Bukit Timah granite
▨ Gombak norite
▨ Sajahat formation

Source: Longman Atlas: Singapore and the World (Singapore: Pearson Education South Asia, 2002).

Geology: granite cliff at Bukit Batok.

One of the earliest Malay settlements in Singapore, it was first occupied in the 1840s after the British dispersed the Malay village that existed at the mouth of the Singapore River. At that time, wealthy Arab families bought large tracts of land in the area.

A large section of Geylang Serai formed part of the Perseverance Estate, owned by the ALSAGOFF FAMILY. The settlement was originally called Geylang Kelapa ('kelapa' means 'coconut' in Malay) because of the coconut plantations there. The name 'geylang' is believed to be a corruption of the word 'kilang' which is the Malay word for 'mill' or 'factory' (there were mills on the coconut plantations, where oil was produced from copra). The area's name was changed to Geylang Serai when the coconut plantations were replaced by plantations of citronella (lemongrass, or 'serai' in Malay). Lemongrass was processed commercially to produce oil for the manufacture of soaps and perfumes. The area changed during the Japanese Occupation, when tapioca replaced the lemongrass plantations.

Geylang Serai was home to many Malay KAMPONGS. However, these were eventually torn down to make way for development. By 1980, the last of Geylang's kampong dwellers had moved into flats.

In the run-up to EID-UL-FITR (Hari Raya Puasa), various streets in Geylang Serai are lit up with festive lights. A month-long bazaar is set up around the GEYLANG SERAI MARKET, and the entire area becomes extremely busy as Muslims do their shopping in preparation for the festival.

Abdul Wahab Mohamed Ghows

Geylang Serai Market The Geylang Serai area has been a major Malay enclave since the 1920s. When squatters there were resettled in the 1960s in flats built by the Housing & Development Board (HDB), a large market developed around Blocks 1–5 of Jalan Pasar and Geylang Serai. This became one of the most popular markets in Singapore, especially for the Malays. The market was made up of two main sections: a wet market and a hawker centre. It also contained stalls selling traditional Malay clothing, textiles and household goods. The market had a rustic ambience that many Singaporeans and tourists enjoyed and was particularly busy during EID-UL-FITR.

In February 2003, the HDB announced plans to replace the market with

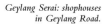

Geylang Serai: shophouses in Geylang Road.

Geylang Serai, c. 1960.

a \$17-million landmark 'regional market' with modern facilities. Residents and stall holders were consulted on the design of the new two-storey structure, which was reminiscent of rural Malay architecture. The hawkers were moved to a temporary market near the Singapore Post Centre in March 2006. The new market is expected to be completed by 2008.

ghazal Traditional Malay musical genre that involves poetry. *Ghazal* was probably introduced into the Malay world by Arab and Persian traders. It was played in the royal courts of the JOHOR SULTANATE. The lyrics are in the form of SYAIR (a genre of Malay poem). There are two kinds of *ghazal* music: one originated in Persia and is known as *ghazal Parsi*; the other originated in India, and is called *ghazal Urdu*. The royal courts, particularly in Johor, developed the Persian-inspired *ghazal* music. Originally slow and melancholic, this form of *ghazal* became popular as court musicians added new musical instruments and lyrics, and increased the tempo.

Ghazal is played with the harmonium, tabla, violin, *gambus* (a stringed instrument), guitar, tambourine and maracas. The lyrics touch on themes such as the beauty of nature or love. Emphasis is placed on the harmonization of the music with the singer's voice. *Ghazal*, like other traditional musical genres, is not regularly featured on television or radio in Singapore; it still has a following, however, as *ghazal* songs are performed by popular recording artistes in Malaysia. In Singapore, there are traditional music groups made up of musicians who play *ghazal* music. *Ghazal* can be heard at weddings and during cultural festivals and concerts.

Ghows, Abdul Wahab Mohamed (1921–) Judge. Born in Ipoh, Perak, Abdul Wahab Mohamed Ghows was educated at Outram School, Raffles Institution and then at Raffles College, where he graduated with a diploma in arts (1941). He then joined the Far East Bureau of the British Ministry of Information in Singapore.

When World War II came to Asia, Ghows left Singapore on a cattle boat bound for Batavia (present-day Jakarta) with other officers of the ministry. In 1942, he was evacuated to India, where he worked in the Far Eastern Bureau of the British Ministry of Information in Delhi until 1944. He joined FORCE 136 as a 2nd Lieutenant and trained in Akyab, Burma. In February 1945, he was recalled to Calcutta, promoted to lieutenant and sent for training in preparation for the liberation of Malaya. Ghows continued in his work with the Ministry of Information until he was demobilized in 1946. He was then offered a contract to work for the Department of Information.

When his contract ended in 1949, Ghows left for the United Kingdom to study law. He was called to the Bar at the Middle Temple in 1952. On his return to Singapore, he joined the government service. He went on to hold appointments as district judge and magistrate; assistant official assignee and public trustee; Crown Counsel; district judge; senior district judge; acting solicitor-general (1971–74) and solicitor-general (1974–80). In December 1980, Ghows was elevated to the Bench as puisne judge. He retired in 1986 and moved to Canada.

Gibson-Hill, Carl (1911–1963) Curator, naturalist and photographer. Dr Carl Alexander Gibson-Hill was appointed curator of the Raffles Museum (*see* NATIONAL MUSEUM OF SINGAPORE) in 1947, and was its last expatriate director (1957–63). Interested in Malayan history and archaeology, he was a key figure in expeditions throughout Southeast Asia and was instrumental in developing the bird collection at the Raffles Museum. He archived data and published guides on bird species, often accompanied by his own photographs and illustrations.

Gibson-Hill was a founding member of Singapore's first 'multicultural' art society, the Singapore Art Society, in 1949. He was also the society's first president. A supporter of the Singapore Camera Club (founded in 1950; now the PHOTOGRAPHIC SOCIETY OF SINGAPORE), he launched Singapore's first salon of photography at the Camera Club in 1950 with LOKE WAN THO. Gibson-Hill was a skilled photographer who exhibited and published his work. Believed to be burdened by many personal problems, he committed suicide a few days before his official retirement.

Gifted Education Programme Implemented in 1984, the Gifted Education Programme (GEP) is an enrichment programme aimed at 'intellectually gifted' children. For admission into the GEP, Primary 3 pupils sit for a screening test. About 3,000 pupils are short-listed after the screening test to sit for a selection test. The selection of pupils to join the GEP at Primary 4 is based on their performance in three areas: English language, mathematics and general ability.

The programme is offered in nine primary schools and seven secondary schools. All primary GEP students are required to take the Primary School Leaving Examination (PSLE). The secondary programme is a four-year programme, which is an extension of the Primary GEP, and leads to the Singapore-Cambridge General Certificate of Education (GCE) 'Ordinary' (O)-Level Examination. Both the PSLE and GCE 'O'-Level examinations are also taken by students who are not in the GEP.

The Gifted Education curriculum is intended to build upon and supplement the content covered in the regular curriculum. In addition, the Gifted Education Branch at the Ministry of Education (MOE) organizes enrichment activities, camps and out-of-class activities that complement the GEP-enriched curriculum.

Programmes which are part of the GEP, such as the Music Elective Programme (MEP) and the Art Elective Programme (AEP), are meant to foster musically and artistically gifted students.

Although the GEP has been characterized as 'elitist', the MOE's view is that it develops outstanding talent essential to the country's interests. With the introduction of the Integrated Programme (IP), secondary schools offering the IP have replaced the GEP with School-Based Gifted Education, a six-year programme for GEP students which culminates in the GCE 'A'-level examinations and the International Baccalauréate (for Anglo-Chinese School [Independent]).

See also STREAMING.

Gilfillan, Wood and Co. Trading firm. Gilfillan, Wood and Co. was founded by three former managers of BORNEO COMPANY: Samuel Gilfillan, Henry Wood and William Adamson. The Singapore branch of the company was called Gilfillan, Wood and Co., while the London branch was called Adamson, Gilfillan and Co. It prospered in handling Asian produce and textiles. In 1904, the London and Singapore companies merged to become Adamson, Gilfillan and Co., with Gilfillan as its first chairman. It became Harper, Gilfillan and Co. when it later merged with A.C. Harper and Co. between 1930 and 1935.

Gimson, Sir Franklin (1890–1975) Colonial official. Sir Franklin Charles Gimson was Singapore's first post-war governor following the transformation of Singapore into a CROWN COLONY. During his tenure (1946–52), the colonial authorities began to work gradually towards self-government for Singapore.

Gimson set up an advisory council consisting of seven officials and ten unofficials. He exercised his right to force measures through on only one occasion. This was in 1947, when he sought to enact the Income Tax Ordinance. Attempts by earlier governors to impose an INCOME TAX (in 1860, 1910 and 1921) had been strongly resisted. Although the only support Gimson had was from the Malayan Democratic Union, he believed the economic state of the colony justified introduction of this tax. The Income Tax Ordinance was enacted in November 1947.

The 1947 census showed that a large proportion of the population was born in Singapore. This strengthened the argument for the development of political responsibility and self-government. Gimson, in consultation with his superiors, decided that a transfer of power from the British colonial administration to self-rule could best be achieved in stages. The first step was the creation of a new CONSTITUTION, which was implemented after the LEGISLATIVE COUNCIL ELECTION (1948). This allowed for an executive council and a legislative council, and the right of the governor to veto the Legislative Council's proceedings.

Gimson considered social welfare and education as important issues for a self-governing society. The Social Welfare Department was established in 1946 to deal with post-war hardship, and a ten-year programme was launched in 1947 to provide six years of primary education in any of the four main languages. In 1948, the government increased loans to the SINGAPORE IMPROVEMENT TRUST and launched an interim plan to house 36,000 homeless people. The expansion of education and other social services was financed by revenue from income tax as well as the economic boom Singapore experienced as a result of the Korean War (1950–53).

In 1951, Gimson presented the Royal Charter, granted by King George VI, conferring the status of city upon the municipality of Singapore. Gimson was succeeded by Sir JOHN NICOLL as governor the following year.

Girl Guides Singapore The Girl Guides in Singapore began as a district of the Malayan Girl Guides Association, and was first registered at St Mary's Home (present-day site of

Sir Franklin Gimson, right, c. 1950.

Girl Guides Singapore: Remembrance Day, 2005.

the University of Chicago Graduate School of Business). The earliest units were registered in 1917 at Raffles Girls' School (RGS), Singapore Chinese Girls' School (SCGS) and the Church of England Zenana Missionary Society School (present-day St Margaret's Girls' School), all of which were English-medium schools during the colonial period.

The first district commissioner was Jessie Kilgour (1928–34), and the Guides' first headquarters—known as 'The Hut'—were located on Buyong Road. With the increase in Guide numbers, the organization was divided into four districts: central, east, north and west. In 1953, the Singapore Girl Guides Association separated from the Malayan Girl Guides Association and became a branch of the Girl Guides Association of Great Britain.

Patrons of the Association since Independence have been First Ladies. Girls can participate in Brownies (a junior version of the Girl Guides for primary school girls) and Girl Guides as co-curricular activities (CCAs) in 245 schools in Singapore.

Girls' Brigade One of the oldest uniformed organizations for girls in Singapore, the Girls' Brigade was started in Singapore as the Girls' Life Brigade by Elsie Lynn—a young officer with the 1st Gateshead Company in Durham, United Kingdom. In 1927, Lynn came to Singapore to teach at the METHODIST GIRLS' SCHOOL, and started the Girl's Life Brigade movement at that school in the same year. The brigade spread to three other Methodist schools over the next decade.

After World War II, the movement continued to expand through churches and schools of various denominations. In 1964, two related organizations—the Girls' Brigade and the Girls' Guildry—merged with the Girls' Life Brigade to form the Girls' Brigade.

The Girls' Brigade continues to serve as an interdenominational fellowship which is concerned with the spiritual, physical, educational and social development of members. It now has more than 70 companies in Singapore, with most based in primary and secondary schools.

Girls' Brigade: badge displayed outside the GB Centre, Upper Serangoon Road.

Gifted Education Programme

PRIMARY SCHOOLS OFFERING GEP IN 2006
Anglo-Chinese School (Primary)
Catholic High School (Primary)
Henry Park Primary School
Nan Hua Primary School
Nanyang Primary School
Raffles Girls' Primary School
Rosyth School
St Hilda's School
Tao Nan School

SECONDARY SCHOOLS OFFERING GEP IN 2006
Anglo-Chinese School (Independent)
Dunman High School

Source: Ministry of Eduation

Godowns: agency warehouse, 1890s.

GloFish

Glen Goei

Sam Goh

Gleneagles Hospital Gleneagles Hospital was founded in 1957 as a 45-bed nursing home. From the outset, Gleneagles, located in the prestigious Napier Road area, was regarded as a 'top-end' private nursing home, partly on account of its location and clientele, and partly due to the reputation of its doctors. By 1979, the nursing home had expanded to become a 126-bed hospital offering a complete range of services and facilities. The hospital, which had hitherto been in private hands, was purchased by PARKWAY HOLDINGS in 1987. By 1993, it had become a tertiary heathcare hospital with a ten-storey hospital building. The following year, the Gleneagles Medical Centre, housing 150 medical specialists, was opened. Gleneagles Hospital is home to numerous 'firsts'. It was the first hospital in Southeast Asia to perform living donor liver transplants for children; it was also the first hospital in Southeast Asia at which sextuplets were delivered.

GloFish Genetically modified variety of fish that glows. Normal zebra fishes have silver or black stripes. However, the 2.5 cm long GloFish is bright red, green, orange or yellow. Genes from jellyfish and anemone are inserted into zebra fish embryos. The GloFishes that develop from this procedure have the ability to absorb and re-emit light. When lit by ultraviolet or infrared light (which is invisible to the human eye), the fishes re-emit a visible glow.

GloFishes were developed by Associate Professor Gong Zhiyuan of the Department of Biological Sciences at the National University of Singapore (NUS). The fishes were genetically engineered to detect water pollution, in research that sought to make them glow in specific colours depending on the pollutant present. Fishes that do not glow indicate clean water. The production of fishes that glow all the time is an intermediate step to achieving this goal. NUS has a patent on the GloFish.

godowns The term 'godown', commonly used in India and East Asia, refers to a warehouse that is located on the docks. Typically, godowns were built next to harbours or rivers. In Singapore, the oldest godowns date to the 1820s and were built along the SINGAPORE RIVER. It was on the docks of the Singapore River that the most famous traders and trading houses such as Kim Seng & Co. (see TAN KIM SENG), GUTHRIE & CO. and BOUSTEAD & COMPANY built their godowns. Some of these godowns were situated in the area along Upper Circular Road. Others, such as Patterson, Simmon & Co., Industrial and Commercial Bank and TAN YEOK NEE, built their godowns at CLARKE QUAY and along Magazine Road.

The initial impetus to build godowns near the river can be traced to the start of colonial trade in Singapore. Sir Stamford Raffles envisioned a free-trade environment, and also planned to settle different ethnic groups in enclaves along the Singapore River. Accordingly, reclamation work was carried out on the south bank of the river. As a result, land became available on which to build godowns and conduct commerce. Given that the river was narrow and had limited water volume, ships had to anchor in the bay, while smaller craft would transport cargo from ships upriver and unload it into godowns. Cargo to be exported would then be loaded onto these vessels and sent to waiting ships.

The architecture used in the design of godowns was functional. Godowns were spacious and dry, and provided convenient access. The design of the facades of godowns had a Palladian symmetry and were usually a blend of double-storied Doric columns, round arches, tall windows, entablatures and Chinese jack roofs.

In the 1970s, many godowns were demolished to make way for redevelopment. While Yeo Kim Swee's godown, one of the oldest (built in 1842–43), was destroyed in 1981, Tan Yeok Nee's godown, originally built in 1891, was restored in 1989. It is now part of the Clarke Quay Festival Village buildings, at the junction of North Boat Quay and Read Street.

Goei, Glen (1963–) Actor and director. Glen Goei was educated at Anglo-Chinese School, Cambridge University (where he graduated with a degree in history) and Mountview Theatre School in London (1988). He made a name for himself in the London theatre scene, co-starring with Anthony Hopkins in the West End production of David Henry Hwang's *M Butterfly,* and receiving a nomination for the Laurence Olivier Award for Best Newcomer (1990). Goei has also directed *Madame Mao's Memories*; *Porcelain* (which received the London Fringe Awards for Best Play and Best Production); *The Magic Fundoshi* (*Times* Award for Best Comedy,

1993); *Three Japanese Women*; and *Suzy Wrong: Human Cannon.*

In Singapore, his works included *Into the Woods* (1994); *Kampong Amber* (Singapore Arts Festival, 1994); and *Land of a Thousand Dreams* (1995). Goei also directed and produced the feature film FOREVER FEVER (1994).

In 1991–98, Goei founded and ran Mu-Lan Arts in London, after which he became associate artistic director of the theatre company W!LD RICE. Besides acting and directing, Goei is also a major events choreographer. He was the creative director of the NATIONAL DAY parades from 2003–05.

Goethe-Institut German cultural institution. Founded in 1925 as the Deutsche Akademie, this non-profit organization is named after Johann Wolfgang von Goethe, one of Germany's greatest poets. The Goethe-Institut is dedicated to promoting German language and culture outside German-speaking countries, with a focus on the teaching of German as a second language. It is financed by the government of Germany and currently has 16 branch institutes in Germany and 128 branch institutes in 77 countries with headquarters in Munich.

The Goethe-Institut was established in Singapore in 1978. It holds German lessons; provides space for local and international artists to exhibit their works; and organizes film screenings. It is also the venue for the free programme of the annual SINGAPORE INTERNATIONAL FILM FESTIVAL.

Goh, Sam (1958–) Sportsman. Bowler Sam Goh Heng Soon and teammate Patrick Wee won the silver medal in the World Duos event at the 11th FIQ World Tenpin Bowling Championships in Helsinki in 1986. The pair beat 113 teams from 44 countries. Goh also came seventh in the men's Masters, even though this was his first world competition. For their achievement,

Theresa Goh: at the Athens Paralympics, 2004.

Goh Chok Tong: with Tony Blair, right, 1996.

both Goh and Wee were inducted into the Singapore Sports Council's Hall of Fame.

Goh, Theresa (1987–) Sportswoman. One of Singapore's most successful swimmers, Theresa Goh Rui Si recorded two fifth places and two seventh places in the 2004 Paralympics in Athens. She achieved nine personal bests in ten swims. She was coached by ANG PENG SIONG, a national coach, former swimming champion and Olympian.

Goh was born with spina bifida and is paralysed from the waist down. She competed in the S5 category in the Paralympic Games. In May 2005, she won a silver medal in the 100 m breaststroke at the Visa Paralympic World Cup in Manchester, United Kingdom, and was presented with a Singapore Youth Award in June 2005.

At the third Association of Southeast Asian Nations (ASEAN) Para Games in Manila in December 2005, Goh won three gold medals. She clocked 1 min 34 sec in the 100-m freestyle, which was an improvement on her Paralympic time. In the 100-m butterfly, she recorded 2 min 8 sec; in the 50-m butterfly, she clocked 58 sec.

Goh, Vivien (1948–) Musician and conductor. Daughter of violinist GOH SOON TIOE, Vivien Goh took violin lessons from her father, and continued her musical education in the United States and Europe. She was conductor of the Goh Soon Tioe String Orchestra (1975–83), and music director and resident conductor of the Singapore Youth Orchestra (1980–90). She regularly performs in the Chamber Players, and also plays the piano and organ. Her biography of her father, *Goh Soon Tioe: One Great Symphony*, was published in 1992.

Goh, Zechariah (1970–) Composer. Zechariah Goh Toh Chai studied piano performance and composition at the University of Kansas, where he was awarded the Anthony B. Cius Music Composition Award in 2000 and 2001. His works, which include choral, chamber and orchestral pieces, have been performed in Singapore, Korea, the United States, Australia, Europe and Brazil. He teaches at the Nanyang Academy of Fine Arts. In

2003, he was given the Young Artist Award by the National Arts Council.

Goh Beng Kwan (1937–) Artist. Born in the Dutch East Indies (present-day Indonesia), Goh Beng Kwan began his art education with the Art Students' League of New York (1962–65). He eventually based his practice in Singapore, exhibiting in numerous shows. Goh received the Salon des Artistes Français silver medal in 1985 and the CULTURAL MEDALLION in 1989. He also won the United Overseas Bank Painting of the Year competition in 1982. Goh's works have ranged from abstract oil paintings to ink-on-paper and mixed media, incorporating found materials.

Goh Boon Teck (1971–) Theatre director. After graduating from the Nanyang Academy of Fine Arts with a diploma in visual art in 1990, Goh Boon Teck founded Toy Factory Theatre Ensemble, a bilingual theatre company. His directorial debut in *Liang Shan Bo Yu Zhu Ying Tai* (The Butterfly Lovers) generated great interest in the theatre community as a new interpretation of a Chinese classic. Goh directs, writes scripts, acts and designs sets.

Since its inception, Toy Factory has staged over 60 productions. These include classics of both eastern and western theatre such as *Thunderstorm*, *Guys and Dolls*, *A Mid-Summer Night's Dream*, as well as Goh's own plays such as *Mee Pok Man*, *Spirits* and his most successful script, *Ti Tou dao* (The Shaving Knife), which is based on the experiences of his mother who was a Hokkien opera actress. *Ti Tou Dao* premiered in 1994 and won five awards at the inaugural LIFE! Theater Awards in 2001 when it was re-staged that year. In 1994, Goh obtained his master's degree in theatre directing from the University of Wales. He won the National Arts Council's Young Artist Award in 2001 and the Singapore Youth Award by the National Youth Council in 2005.

Goh Chew Chua (c. 1895–1971) Politician. Known as the 'Grand Old Man of the PEOPLE'S ACTION PARTY (PAP)', Goh Chew Chua was born in Kuala Lumpur but came to Singapore with his parents at an early age. He was educated at Anglo-Chinese School and worked as a clerk for the Singapore Municipality for over 20 years before he started his own contracting business. Goh was a founding member of the PAP and was also a champion of farmers, fishermen and the rural community in which he lived. In the 1955 legislative election, he won a seat in the Tampines-Ponggol constituency. Goh was re-elected in the 1959, this time for the Tampines division of his former constituency. He was appointed parliamentary secretary to the deputy prime minister and vice-chairman of the PAP's Central Executive Committee.

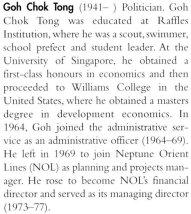

Goh Beng Kwan

He failed to win re-election in 1963, and retired from politics. In 1969, he was awarded the Public Service Star.

Goh Chok Tong (1941–) Politician. Goh Chok Tong was educated at Raffles Institution, where he was a scout, swimmer, school prefect and student leader. At the University of Singapore, he obtained a first-class honours in economics and then proceeded to Williams College in the United States, where he obtained a masters degree in development economics. In 1964, Goh joined the administrative service as an administrative officer (1964–69). He left in 1969 to join Neptune Orient Lines (NOL) as planning and projects manager. He rose to become NOL's financial director and served as its managing director (1973–77).

In 1976, Goh entered politics on the People's Action Party (PAP) ticket and was elected member of Parliament for Marine Parade, a constituency he has continued to represent ever since. In 1979, he was appointed senior minister of state for finance and was elected to the PAP's Central Executive Committee. He then served as minister for trade and industry, health and defence (1979–90). In 1985, he was appointed first deputy prime minister

Goh Chew Chua

Vivien Goh

Goh Chok Tong: visiting Tampines, 1996.

Goh Choo San

Goh Eng Wah

Goh Hak Su

Goh Keng Swee

and minister for defence and, on 28 November 1990, became Singapore's second prime minister. Goh continued to hold his defence portfolio until 1991.

In August 2004, Goh Chok Tong stepped down as prime minister and was succeeded by LEE HSIEN LOONG. Goh then assumed the posts of SENIOR MINISTER in the Prime Minister's Office and chairman of the Monetary Authority of Singapore. Within the PAP, he served as second assistant secretary-general (1979–84); assistant secretary-general (1984–89); first assistant secretary-general (1989–92); and secretary general (1992–2004).

During Goh's tenure as prime minister, significant changes took place in the structure of government and in the economy. Constitutional changes included the introduction of non-constituency members of Parliament (*see* NON-CONSTITUENCY MEMBER OF PARLIAMENT) (1984); group representation constituencies (*see* GROUP REPRESENTATION CONSTITUENCY) (1988) and the creation of the office of elected president (1991). Goh was also responsible for introducing MEDISAVE and EDUSAVE. Goh argued for the need to make government responsive. He promoted the idea of a 'kinder and gentler Singapore', and initiated Singapore 21, so that more Singaporeans would put forward their own ideas regarding the future development of the country. Goh is married to lawyer Tan Choo Leng. They have two children.

Goh Choo San (1948–1987) Dancer and choreographer. Goh Choo San began training at the Singapore Ballet Academy at the age of ten and joined the Dutch National Ballet as a dancer in 1970. From 1976 to 1986, he served as resident choreographer and assistant artistic director of the Washington Ballet, where he developed his neoclassical style. He received choreographic commissions from other companies, including the American Ballet Theatre and the Joffrey Ballet.

Some of Goh's best-known works are *Fives* (1978) and *Birds of Paradise* (1979). Goh was a CULTURAL MEDALLION recipient in 1986. He died in New York at the of age of 39. In 1991, Goh's estate co-founded the Choo-San Goh & H. Robert Magee Foundation, which awards grants for choreographers' fees. He was the brother of GOH SOO KHIM and Goh Soo Nee.

Goh Eng Wah (1923–) Businessman. Born in Muar, Johor, Goh Eng Wah was the elder of two sons of a rubber trader. His secondary education was interrupted by the Japanese Occupation, when he was forced to flee to Singapore, where his sister was living. After World War II, he started distributing films. His first cinema was the Victory Theatre, which came into operation in the Happy World (later renamed GAY WORLD) Amusement Park in 1945. Goh also managed the neighbouring Happy and Silver Theatres. In the 1950s and 1960s, he faced a movie market dominated by SHAW BROTHERS, which screened its own productions exclusively.

During the 1960s, he befriended HO AH LOKE. Ho screened Goh's films in his Metropole Cinema, and when Ho joined forces with LOKE WAN THO, Goh was able to gain a foothold in Cathay Organization's circuit. In 1966, Goh bought Jubilee Theatre, and in the following year he acquired King's Theatre in GREAT WORLD.

Over the next decade, Goh opened theatres in Toa Payoh, Kallang Bahru, Clementi, Ang Mo Kio and Marina. Goh focused on Taiwanese films and imported sentimental movies featuring celebrities such as Lin Ching-hsia, Lin Feng-jiao and Chin Han, which were more popular than Hong Kong-made movies in the 1980s. Goh's business is currently run by his four children: Min Yen, Cynthia, James and Bob.

Goh Geok Khim (1932–) Businessman. Goh Geok Khim is the second son of Goh Seng Choo, a rubber miller and real estate developer. He was educated at Raffles Institution and took a degree in civil engineering. Goh started working in his father's rubber business. At the age of 36, he set up the firm of E.G. Tan with his brother-in-law. He decided to go into business on his own in 1979 and established G.K. Goh Stockbrokers. In 1990, the firm was incorporated as G.K. Goh Holdings, with offices in Hong Kong, Jakarta and the Philippines. It was listed in the Singapore Stock Exchange in the same year.

In 1996 Goh purchased the famous Farquhar Collection (*see* FARQUHAR, WILLIAM), consisting of paintings from the Royal Asiatic Society, and donated it to the Singapore History Museum (*see* NATIONAL MUSEUM OF SINGAPORE). The collection of 477 drawings and paintings of flora and fauna of the Malay Peninsula is valued at $3 million and was displayed at the Goh Seng Choo Gallery.

Goh also served for many years on the Board of the Singapore Symphony Orchestra. In 1996, Goh was named distinguished patron of the arts by the National Arts Council.

Goh Hak Su (1948–) Doctor and researcher. The Malaya-born Goh Hak Su attended London University, where he held the Arthur Pike Charity Trust Scholarship and Fellowship. He undertook his surgical training in the United Kingdom before coming to Singapore in 1981.

As a lecturer at the National University of Singapore in the 1980s, Goh became interested in colorectal cancer. He spent a year as a research fellow at the Imperial Cancer Research Fund in London in 1985. In 1989, he established the Department of Colorectal Surgery at Singapore General Hospital. Working with technology from IBM, he set up a comprehensive colorectal cancer database as well as a hereditary cancer registry, both essential for clinical and laboratory-based research.

With a grant from the Lee Foundation, he created the Colorectal Cancer Molecular Genetics Laboratory, dedicated to the study of molecular changes and their clinical applications in colorectal cancer. The laboratory also helps other research bodies study molecular biology, and trains surgeons and technicians. After six years as head of Colorectal Cancer Surgery, Dr Goh went into private practice in 1995. That year, he was awarded the NATIONAL SCIENCE AND TECHNOLOGY MEDAL.

Goh Joon Seng (1935–) Judge. Goh Joon Seng was born in China and was educated at the University of Singapore. He graduated with a bachelor of laws in 1962. He was called to the Singapore Bar the following year. By the time he was appointed judicial commissioner in October 1990, Goh was senior partner of the firm of Goh, Poh and Partners. Just a month after his appointment, he was made judge of the Supreme Court. He retired in 2000 at the age of 65.

Since retiring, Goh has served as consultant to the firm of Lee & Lee (2000–); chairman of the Consumer Mediation Unit (2003–); chairman, Singapore International Arbitration Centre (2004–); and chairman, Insurance Disputes Resolution Organisation (2003–). An expert in commercial law, Goh chaired the committee that reviewed the Moneylenders Act, Hire Purchase Act and Pawnbrokers Act. He also served as chairman of the Singapore Mediation Centre (1997–2003).

Goh Keng Swee (1918–) Civil servant and politician. Goh Keng Swee was born in Malacca to Straits-born Chinese parents. He arrived in Singapore at the age of two and was educated at Anglo-Chinese School. Goh later graduated from Raffles College with a diploma in arts.

After World War II, Goh left to study at the London School of Economics (LSE), obtaining a first class honours degree in economics there. He visited Hungary in 1949 and was a delegate at the World Federation of Democratic Youth Meeting in Budapest. He won the William Farr Prize for his performance at LSE and was awarded a University of London postgraduate scholarship in 1951. Goh obtained a doctorate in economics from the University of London in 1956.

Goh had joined the colonial civil service Social Welfare Department before he left for the United Kingdom. On his return, he worked as assistant to Dr Frederic Benham, economic advisor to then-Chief Minister LIM YEW HOCK. Goh became a member of the People's Action Party (PAP) and resigned from the colonial

civil service. In 1959, he became party vice-chairman. The secretary-general of the PAP was Lee Kuan Yew, whom Goh had met while studying in London. Goh was elected in May 1959 to the Singapore Legislative Assembly from the Kreta Ayer electoral division, and was appointed minister of finance. He was returned unopposed in four subsequent general elections and remained the representative of this constituency. He oversaw the building of the Kreta Ayer Peoples' Theatre. The Cantonese operas which were subsequently staged there were highly popular with the mainly Cantonese-speaking constituents.

Goh was responsible for initiating Singapore's INDUSTRIALIZATION plan and the establishment of the ECONOMIC DEVELOPMENT BOARD (EDB), the Development Bank of Singapore (see DBS BANK) and JURONG INDUSTRIAL ESTATE. Goh's priority was to embark on an industrialization programme that would create jobs quickly, and he worked towards a common market with Malaya. This resulted in Singapore becoming part of the newly created Malaysia in 1963.

However, common market negotiations floundered. Amidst racial and political tensions, Goh played an important part in negotiating the separation of Singapore from the federation. When independence was declared on 9 August 1965, Goh was appointed minister for interior and defence. In seeking to lay the foundations for the country's defence, he sought help from the Israeli Defence Force.

Appointed deputy prime minister in 1973, Goh focused on turning Singapore into a financial centre, aided by the introduction of the Asian dollar market. Goh gave up the defence portfolio when he was appointed minister for education in

Goh Keng Swee: at Shell refinery, right, 1964.

Goh Lay Kuan, foreground right.

February 1979. As education minister, he introduced STREAMING, religious education in schools and the GIFTED EDUCATION PROGRAMME, which were discussed in the Goh Report of 1979.

Ill health led to Goh's retirement from ministerial and parliamentary work in 1984. Nevertheless, he accepted appointment as deputy chairman of the Monetary Authority of Singapore (MAS) in 1985, relinquishing the post in 1992. He was also deputy chairman of the Government of Singapore Investment Corporation (GIC) from 1981 to 1994.

In his later years, Goh turned his attention to more academic pursuits and was the chairman of the Board of Governors of the Institute of East Asian Philosophies (1983–92) (present-day EAST ASIAN INSTITUTE). In 1985, he was appointed economic advisor to the State Council of the People's Republic of China on coastal development, and advisor on tourism at the invitation of State Counsellor Gu Mu. Goh studied Mandarin as an adult and delivered a speech in Mandarin in China at the age of 79. He wrote *Economics of Modernization and Other Essays* (1972), *The Practice of Economic Growth, Singapore* (1977) and *Wealth of East Asian Nations, Speeches and Writings* (1995).

Outside of economics, Goh is credited with initiating numerous projects, including the JURONG BIRDPARK and the SINGAPORE ZOO. Goh also became patron of the Singapore Symphony Orchestra (SSO) in 1979. He wrote and delivered speeches on subjects ranging from economic development to sociology and psychology, not only with regard to the Asia-Pacific region but also concerning Latin America, in which he had an academic interest. Goh was admitted into the Order of Temasek (First Class) in 1985.

Goh Lay Kuan (1939–) Dancer and choreographer. Goh Lay Kuan was born in the Dutch East Indies (present-day Indonesia) and came to Singapore when

she was only five weeks old. She began studying ballet at the age of 17, training at the Victorian Ballet Guild in Melbourne, Australia, and dancing with the Victorian Ballet Company.

She married playwright-director KUO PAO KUN in 1965 after returning to Singapore. Goh was detained under the INTERNAL SECURITY ACT with Kuo for four months in 1976 for alleged communist activities.

In the 1980s, she studied at the Martha Graham School of Contemporary Dance in New York. Her best-known work is the full-evening contemporary-dance production, *Nu Wa: Mender of Heavens* (1988), a Singapore Festival of Arts commission involving some 200 dancers. She teaches t'ai chi and meditation at the Theatre Training and Research Programme. A 1995 CULTURAL MEDALLION recipient, she is co-founder and executive advisor of the PRACTICE PERFORMING ARTS SCHOOL.

Goh Poh Seng (1936–) Author. Regarded as a pioneer of Singapore literature in English, Goh Poh Seng was born and educated in Malaya, and graduated in medicine from University College, Dublin. He returned in 1961 to Singapore, where he practised for 25 years. Goh set up Island Press, founded the literary magazine *Tumasek*, and formed Centre 65 to promote the arts. Goh chaired the National Theatre Trust and was vice-chairman of the Arts Council from 1967 to 1973.

Goh's first play, *The Moon Is Less Bright* (1964), is set in rural Singapore just before and during the Japanese Occupation, and is strongly nationalistic and anti-Japanese in sentiment. His sympathies for the working class and the common man are also evident in *When Smiles Are Done* (1965; subsequently retitled *Room with Paper Flowers*) and *The Elder Brother* (1966). Whereas *Moon* has local characters incongruously speaking the 'Queen's English', Goh's subsequent plays were among the earliest attempts to use Singlish in drama.

Goh has published four novels. *If We Dream Too Long* (1972), one of the first two Singaporean novels in English (Kirpal Singh's *China Affair* was the other), which won the inaugural National Book Development Council of Singapore (NBDCS) Award for Fiction in 1976; *The Immolation* (1977), *A Dance of Moths* (1995), and *Dance with White Clouds: A Fable for Grown-ups* (2001). While self-actualization and fulfilment are presiding themes in Goh's fiction, his poetry focuses on the lyrical and personal. Goh has authored five volumes of poetry: *Eyewitness* (1976), *Lines from Batu Ferringhi* (1978), *Bird with One Wing* (1982), *The Girl from Ermita and Selected Poems, 1961-1988* (1988) and *As Though the Gods Love Us* (2000).

Goh received the CULTURAL MEDALLION for Literature in 1982. He emi-

Goh Poh Seng: the author and If We Dream Too Long *(1972) (top).*

Goh Soo Khim: giving a ballet class.

grated to Canada in 1986 and continued to practise medicine until 1995, when Parkinson's disease forced him to retire. He lives in Vancouver with his wife and family, and is working on his autobiography.

Goh Soo Khim (1944–) Dancer and choreographer. Goh Soo Khim was the first Asian student to study at the Australian Ballet School, doing so in 1964. On her return to Singapore, she taught at her alma mater, the Singapore Ballet Academy. She later led the National Dance Company's Ballet Group with ANTHONY THEN. Her first work was *Temple Tone Poem* (1978). In 1981, she was awarded the CULTURAL MEDALLION. She was commissioned to create *Dilemma* and *Five Emotions* for the Singapore Festival of Arts in 1982. In 1987, she and Then formed the SINGAPORE DANCE THEATRE, sharing directorship until Then's death in 1995. Goh was the first Asian jury member for the prestigious Prix Benois de la Danse (Moscow, 2003). She is the sister of GOH CHOO SAN.

Goh Soon Tioe (1911–1982) Musician. Born in Sumatra, Goh Soon Tioe studied music in Switzerland, Spain and Belgium, where the legendary guitarist Andrés Segovia was one of his teachers. Goh founded the Goh Soon Tioe Music Studio and Goh Soon Tioe String Orchestra, and was conductor of the Singapore Youth Symphony Orchestra from 1971 to 1975. His students included CHOO HOEY, Lee Pan Hon, KAM KEE YONG, VIVIEN GOH, LYNNETTE SEAH and DICK LEE. Goh was awarded the MERITORIOUS SERVICE MEDAL in 1962.

Goho, S.C. (1891–1948) Community leader. S.C. Goho arrived in Malaya in 1919 after studying law in the United Kingdom. From 1941 to 1942, he was vice-president of the Central Indian Association of Malaya (CIAM), he was at the same time president of CIAM's Singapore branch, the Singapore Indian Association.

During the JAPANESE OCCUPATION, Goho, like other CIAM branch leaders, was

Goh Soon Tioe

made a branch president of the Indian Independence League (IIL) at the request of Japanese officer Major Iwaichi Fujiwara, commander of Japanese intelligence unit F Kikan. Goho had not been pro-Japanese at the start of the war, although the British had suspected him of being so. His motivation to join the IIL seems to have been to protect his own community, as he was aware of the Japanese massacre of Chinese in February 1942 known as the SOOK CHING. He was one of the Indian leaders who attended the Tokyo meeting in March 1942 at which exiled Indian nationalist leader RASH BEHARI BOSE was elected overall president of the revitalized league. Rash Behari Bose was replaced by SUBHAS CHANDRA BOSE in July 1943.

In October 1945, Goho was arrested with other branch presidents in Malaya and accused by the British of collaboration. The charges were eventually dropped. Goho resumed his legal career and was elected to the Singapore Legislative Council in March 1948 as an independent candidate.

gold bar murders This murder case of the early 1970s involved three victims and nine accused. The dead were Ngo Cheng Poh, a non-resident gold buyer, and his close friends, Leong Chin Woo and Ang Boon Chai. Ngo had been involved in a gold-smuggling racket involving Andrew Chou Hock Guan, who worked for Air Vietnam as a ground operations supervisor. Ngo bought gold bars and delivered them to Chou's home the evening before an Air Vietnam flight would depart with the gold for Saigon (present-day Ho Chi Minh City). On the evening of 29 December 1971, Ngo, Leong and Ang left Ngo's house to deliver 120 gold bars to Chou. They never returned. Their bodies were found the next day. They had been brutally assaulted and strangled.

Police investigations led to the arrest of Chou, his brother David and seven accomplices: Peter Lim Swee Guan, Alex Yau Hean Thye, Ringo Lee Chiew Chwee, Richard James, Stephen Francis, Konesekaram Nagalingam and Stephen Lee Hock Khoon. They were charged and convicted for murder. All were sentenced to death, except for two—Ringo Lee and Stephen Lee—who were under the age of

18 at the time of the offence, and were detained 'at the president's pleasure'.

Golden Mile Complex This unique, terraced building was originally known as Woh Hup Complex. It was conceived by the Design Partnership (then comprising architects William Lim, Tay Kheng Soon and Koh Seow Chuan). Built in 1973 on a site occupied by squatters and small marine industries, the 16-storey building, now known as Golden Mile Complex, comprises shops, offices, residences, eateries and a large underground parking lot.

It was the first building to use stepped terracing to reduce road noise (from the nearby Nicoll Highway). At the same time, the terraces gave its homes and offices an unobstructed view of the sea. The building was intended to set an urban pattern for the 'golden mile' of Beach Road, with all the buildings connected by a continuous pedestrian walkway, but this did not materialize. Many of the shops, bars and restaurants in the building now cater to Thais working in Singapore.

Golden Pagoda Buddhist Temple Located in Tampines, the Golden Pagoda Buddhist Temple was founded by the Venerable Shi Fazhao in May 1989, who became abbot of the temple in 1992. The temple was built to venerate the Medicine Buddha, and a statue of the Medicine Buddha is located in the temple's central hall. Also referred to as the Teacher of Medicine, he is revered for his powers of healing. The temple presently houses a tooth relic of the Buddha, which will be moved to the Buddha Sacred Tooth Relic Temple, which is due for completion in 2007. Venerable Shi established the Metta Welfare Association in 1992 and was appointed its president. In December 1996, the title of Chaokun Phra Vithethamanusith (Chief of Chinese Monks) was conferred upon him by King Bumibol Adulyadej of Thailand for his contributions to the development of Buddhism in Myanmar and Thailand. Later in May 1997, he also received a Golden Dharma Chakra Award from the Princess of Thailand, given in recognition of his contributions to the advancement of Buddhism.

Golden Village Multiplex operator. Golden Village is a joint venture between film company Golden Harvest of Hong Kong and publicly-listed Village Roadshow of Australia. Golden Village launched Singapore's first multiplex on 28 May 1992 with the opening of the Yishun 10 Multiplex. As of 2005, the company has eight multiplexes and cineplexes in Singapore, including GV Grand at Great World City, which opened in 1999.

golf The first game of golf was played in Singapore in 1891 at the race course in Farrer Park. An avid golfer, Justice Goldney,

Golf: Orchid Country Club.

had persuaded like-minded members of the Sporting Club to join him in setting up a golf club. Goldney drove the first ball at the opening of the Singapore Golf Club on 17 June 1891. At the time, the entrance fee to the club was $2, and the annual subscription was $6.

In 1924, the Singapore Golf Club moved to Bukit Timah. It changed its name to the Royal Singapore Golf Club in 1938. However, there were members of the Turf Club (formerly the Sporting Club) who refused to move out. They stayed behind and formed the Turf Club Golf Club, which opened its doors to Chinese, Indian and Eurasian members. However, this club also moved to another location, and became known as the Island Club. The two clubs eventually merged to become the Singapore Island Country Club in 1963. There are now more than ten golf clubs in Singapore. Keppel's nine-hole course has the distinction of being Singapore's oldest existing golf course, dating back to 1902.

Golf in Singapore is usually seen as an elite sport because of high membership prices. At its peak, membership to the Singapore Island Country Club was sold for $200,000. However, a number of public golf courses have now opened, including the 18-hole Marina Bay Golf Course, which allows Singaporeans to play on the links for $30 per nine-holes.

Golf is a popular activity for buinessmen and politicians who use the informality of a golf game to maintain ties and make deals. The genesis of Singapore's free trade agreement with the United States can be traced to

Good Friday: candlelight service, St Jospeh's Church.

a midnight game of golf between then Prime Minister Goh Chok Tong and US President Bill Clinton in November 2000.

Golf is also taken seriously as a sport in Singapore. It is taught at the SINGAPORE SPORTS SCHOOL. In 2006, Mardan Mamat became the first Singaporean to win a European tour event, the Singapore Masters.

See also COUNTRY CLUBS.

Good Friday Good Friday is a public holiday in Singapore. Most Christians consider Good Friday the most important day of the year, as it is the day on which, it is believed, Jesus redeemed the world by his death. Good Friday usually falls in March or April, on the friday before Easter Sunday. Easter Sunday is the first Sunday after the first full moon following the northern spring equinox. *See also* CHRISTIANITY.

Goode, Sir William (1907–1986) Colonial official. Sir William Allmond Codrington Goode joined the Malayan Civil Service in 1931 and studied law in his spare time. He was admitted to the Bar at Gray's Inn in 1936. From 1936 to 1939, he served as district officer at Raub, in Pahang, Malaya. In 1940, he was appointed assistant commissioner for civil defence, Singapore. During the Japanese Occupation, Goode was taken prisoner and sent to work on the Burma–Siam railway.

Goode remained in Malaya after the war, and in 1948, became deputy economic secretary to the Federation of Malaya. In 1949, he was posted to Aden (in present-day Yemen) as chief secretary and acting governor (1950–51). Goode returned to Singapore as chief secretary in 1953. On 9 December 1957, he was appointed governor, the last in Singapore's history. On 2 June 1959, he assumed the office of Yang di-Pertuan Negara (head of state) under the new State of Singapore Constitution. This was an interim position which Goode held for six months before being succeeded by YUSOF ISHAK. From 1960 to 1963, Goode was governor and commander-in-chief of North Borneo (which thereafter became part of Malaysia). He retired in 1963.

Goods and Services Tax Tax on domestic consumption. The Goods and Services Tax (GST) was introduced in Singapore on 1 April 1994 at 3 per cent; it was increased to 4 per cent in 2003, and subsequently to 5 per cent in 2004. It is a 'multi-stage' tax, collected at every stage of the production and distribution chain. The tax is paid when money is spent on goods or services, including imports. However, the sale and lease of residential land, financial services and exports are exempted.

The introduction of GST was part of a reform intended to shift the tax system from being income-based to being consumption-based, so as to boost Singapore's international competitiveness. The addi-

tional revenue from GST allowed reductions in individual and corporate income tax rates as well as in property tax rates. A further advantage is that a consumption-based tax system creates a more resilient tax base as the population ages.

The GST rate is applied across-the-board even on basic goods and services. To mitigate the cost impact, several rebates on user charges (such as conservancy fees for public housing) and lump-sum payout (economic restructuring shares) were provided. A limited refund scheme exists for tourists.

Goodwood Park Hotel Located on Scotts Road, the building was opened on 21 September 1900 as the TEUTONIA CLUB, a gathering place for the German community. Built by R.A.J. BIDWELL of SWAN & MACLAREN after he had completed work on Raffles Hotel, the club was taken over by the British Custodian of Enemy Property in August 1914 after the outbreak of World War I.

In 1918, the Manasseh brothers (Ellis, Morris and Ezekiel) purchased the building at a public auction and renamed it Goodwood Hall, after a famous racecourse in the United Kingdom. It was used as a public concert and dance hall before a restaurant-café licence was obtained in 1922. In April 1929, the name 'Park' was added when it was converted into a fully fledged hotel. During the Japanese Occupation, it was used by the Japanese army. The hotel grounds also served as war crimes court at the end of World War II.

Goodwood Park was handed back to the surviving Manasseh brothers—Ezekiel had died in Changi Prison—and Ezekiel's stepson, Vivian Bath, who then paid his stepuncles $600,000 and became the sole owner. Incorporated as a publicly-listed company in September 1947, it was opened for business again with the distinction of being the first hotel in Singapore to have a swimming pool. During the 1950s, the hotel operated without its landmark tower, which was to reappear in 1959. In that year, the hotel became the first to hire female chambermaids, and to feature an air-condi-

Golden Village: automated ticket-dispensing kiosk.

Sir William Goode (top) and memorial plaque in St George's Church.

Goodwood Park Hotel

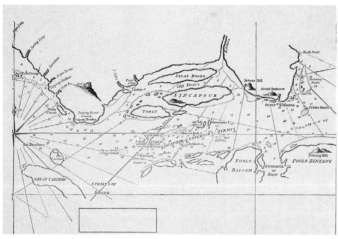

Governor's Strait: navigational chart, 1604.

GOVERNORS OF THE STRAITS SETTLEMENTS AND SINGAPORE
1819–23 Col William Farquhar*
1823–26 Dr John Crawfurd*
1826–30 Robert Fullerton
1830–33 Robert Ibbetson
1833–37 Kenneth Murchison
1837–43 Sir Samuel Bonham
1843–55 Col William Butterworth
1855–59 Sir Edmund Blundell
1859–67 Col Orfeur Cavenagh
1867–73 Col Harry Ord
1873–75 Sir Andrew Clarke
1875–77 Sir William Jervois
1877–78 Sir William Robinson
1880–87 Sir Frederick Weld
1887–93 Sir Cecil Clementi Smith
1894–99 Sir Charles Mitchell
1901–03 Sir Frank Swettenham
1904–11 Sir John Anderson
1911–20 Sir Arthur Young
1920–27 Sir Laurence Guillemard
1927–30 Sir Hugh Clifford
1930–34 Sir Cecil Clementi
1934–42 Sir Shenton Thomas
1945–46 Sir Shenton Thomas
1946–52 Sir Franklin Gimson
1952–55 Sir John Nicoll
1955–57 Sir Robert Black
1957–59 Sir William Goode

*Residents
NOTE: Acting governors not included.

tioned wine cellar and air-conditioned hotel taxis. Over the coming decades, it was to play host to a number of celebrity guests such as Hollywood actors John Wayne and Shirley MacLaine; singers Cliff Richard, Shirley Bassey, Frankie Avalon, Eartha Kitt, Kitaro and Cilla Black; sports personalities Muhammad Ali and Bobby Moore; and dignitaries such as the Sultan of Brunei, Queen Beatrix of the Netherlands and former British prime minister Edward Heath.

In 1963, the hotel was bought over by the Malayan Banking Group, but ownership was soon passed in 1968 to the family of the late hotel and banking tycoon KHOO TECK PUAT, who was also the founder of the bank. After Khoo's death in 2004, the hotel company, along with two other of his listed vehicles Hotel Malaysia and Central Properties were delisted from the Singapore Exchange. Goodwood Park Hotel was gazetted as a national monument in 1989.

Government Hill The landmark renamed Fort Canning Hill in 1860, and still known as such today, was known in the early 19th century as Government Hill or Residency Hill. It was also known as BUKIT LARANGAN (Forbidden Hill). When the British arrived in Singapore, they found a spring of water on the slope of the hill. Munshi ABDULLAH ABDUL KADIR had heard that it was called Pancur Larangan (Forbidden Spring) by the locals because the princesses of ancient Singapore had bathed there. During the early colonial period, the spring was used to supply fresh water for ships, until it dried up. Singapore, like the other early Malay capitals of Palembang and Malacca, had a particular topographical feature: a hill overlooking a river. In each case the hill probably represented the celestial Mount Meru, and the ruler's residence symbolized the palace of the gods. Thus, the name Forbidden Hill denoted a sacred place that was dangerous for ordinary mortals to approach without permission.

Sir STAMFORD RAFFLES had a bungalow designed by GEORGE D. COLEMAN built on the hill—it was completed in January 1823. When Raffles left, JOHN CRAWFURD (the

third Resident of Singapore) moved into the house and enlarged it. The house became the official residence of Singapore's chief authority, hence the name Government Hill. The house was later reconstructed; it stood until 1859, when a fort, later named after Viscount George Canning, first governor-general and later first viceroy of India, was built on the site.

See also FORT CANNING AND PARK.

Government of Singapore Investment Corporation State-owned investment company. The Government of Singapore Investment Corporation (originally GSIC, now GIC) was incorporated on 22 May 1981. It is wholly owned by the government of Singapore. The rationale for its incorporation lay in the fact that a high national savings rate and repeated budget surpluses had led to the build-up of huge foreign reserves. It was decided that the bulk of Singapore's reserves should be invested in longer term, high-yielding assets to be managed by a corporation acting as a fund manager. This arrangement allows the government of Singapore to oversee the management of the country's reserves while allowing the company to respond quickly to market forces without the need to obtain parliamentary approval for all its actions.

GIC invests in more than 30 markets worldwide, in equities, fixed income, money market, real estate and other investments. It has six overseas offices in key financial capitals around the world. GIC manages over US$100 billion in assets, making it one of the world's largest fund management companies. On the occasion of its 25th anniversary, its chairman, Minister Mentor Lee Kuan Yew, revealed that GIC had earned an annual return of 9.5 per cent over the past 25 years.

government-linked companies This term is used to describe companies in which the Singapore government has an indirect interest. In the 1960s, the government took stakes in a number of firms in strategic sectors, which initially were held by

the Ministry of Finance. Government stakes are held by two main investment arms, TEMASEK HOLDINGS and the GOVERNMENT OF SINGAPORE INVESTMENT CORPORATION (GIC).

Pioneer government-linked companies (GLCs) include the Keppel, Sembawang, and Jurong Shipyards, DBS BANK, and NEPTUNE ORIENT LINES (NOL). Chartered Industries and Allied Ordnance is a GLC in the defence industry.

With rapid economic growth in the 1980s and early 1990s, the GLCs expanded, diversified and internationalized their operations. A number of statutory boards were converted into GLCs and a number of GLCs—such as SINGAPORE AIRLINES (SIA), DBS Bank and SINGTEL—were divested through limited initial public offerings. While the overall policy direction is to divest or dilute the government's shareholdings in GLCs that are no longer relevant to the government's objectives, the government will still retain its majority or significant stakes for activities that are strategic to Singapore.

GLCs are important players in the Singapore economy, contributing 12.9 per cent of GROSS DOMESTIC PRODUCT (GDP) in 1998.

governors Singapore's rule by British Residents and governors began with the establishment of a British EAST INDIA COMPANY (EIC) base on the island in 1819. The system ended with Singapore's political independence in 1965.

This system of governance began with the appointment of Residents who functioned as administrators for each trading base. When Singapore came under the control of the Colonial Office in London, it severed its links with the EIC in 1867, and the post of Resident was replaced with that of governor. The governor held executive powers and was assisted by a legislative and executive council.

The system was interrupted by the Japanese Occupation. When the Japanese surrendered, a British military administration briefly took control of the island.

Government Hill: painting by Charles Dyce, 1844.

Singapore then became a separate CROWN COLONY and colonial rule resumed in 1946. Singapore's post-war governors, however, faced growing anti-colonial sentiment in the years leading to self-rule.

The appointment of YUSOF ISHAK as the first local yang di-pertuan negara (head of state) in 1959 marked the end of 146 years of British Residents and governors in Singapore (*see* table).

Governor's Strait Governor's Strait—also called the Phillips Channel and the Strait of John de Silva—is known today as the Main Strait. The passage was discovered in 1616 by a Spanish fleet from Manila under the command of Juan de Silva, governor of the Philippines (1609–16). It runs south of Pulau Satumu (where RAFFLES LIGHTHOUSE is located). It is the main passage by which ships reach the Indian Ocean from the South China Sea.

Govindasamy, Naa. (1947–99) Author. Naa. Govindasamy founded the Ilakkiya Kalam (Literary Critics' Circle) in 1977. Among his published works are *Velvi* (Religious Fire) (1990), a novel; and *Thedi* (Search) (1991), a collection of short stories. His works focus on social problems and the importance of leaders in the Indian community.

Govindasamy is also credited for having put the Tamil language on the Internet. He developed a 16-bit Unicode system which uses the TamilNet and Tamilfix fonts, and which enables a user to input Tamil on Windows, Macintosh and Unix platforms. He launched the first internet page in Tamil, and also played an instrumental role in the upload (in 1995) of *Journey: Words, Home and Nation: Anthology of Singapore Poetry* (1984–95) onto the internet, a collection of poems in the four official languages of Malay, English, Mandarin and Tamil.

G.R. Lambert & Co. Photographic studio. G.R. Lambert arrived in Singapore from Dresden, Germany, and established a photo-

graphic studio at No. 1 High Street in 1867. Subsequent studios were set up in Orchard Road and Gresham House in Battery Road, and were managed by Alexander Koch and later H.T. Jensen. The firm also had offices in Sumatra, Kuala Lumpur and Bangkok. They were the official photographers for key political and social events in the region. The firm was appointed the official photographers of the king and court of Siam (present-day Thailand), and the sultan of Johor.

G.R. Lambert & Co. was the publisher of the most extensive collection of photographic records of Southeast Asia during the late 19th and early 20th centuries. The firm was engaged in the postcard trade during the 1890s, offering over 250 views. It had a turnover of some 250,000 cards annually. The firm eventually wound up in 1918.

Graduate Mothers' Scheme Incentive scheme to encourage graduate women to have more babies. In the 1960s, Singapore's population growth rate was among the highest in the world. Family planning policies were therefore formulated to lower the birth rate from 30 to 17 per 1,000. The Singapore Family Planning and Population Board was established for this purpose in 1966. Abortion and sterilization were legalized in 1970. Children of sterilized parents were given priority in primary school registration, and preference for better schools.

In August 1983, the government noted that few female graduates were getting married, and those who married were having only one or two children. It set about to reverse this trend with the Graduate Mothers' Scheme. Enhanced Child Relief had been introduced earlier to encourage highly qualified married women to continue working: this was increased for better-educated women, with up to three children, subject to a maximum of $10,000 total relief for each child. Priority in school registration was also given to children whose mothers had acceptable university degrees or approved professional qualifications.

Granite quarries: Pulau Ubin.

The Graduate Mother's Scheme was a policy based on the theory that the offspring of educated mothers would be intellectually superior to those of less educated mothers. It gave rise to some controversy, and was soon abandoned as couples continued to have children for reasons other than financial incentives.

granite quarries About 25 per cent of Singapore's land area has granite exposed at the surface. Known as Bukit Timah granite, these main outcrops are found in the Central Hills, in the Changi Hills and on PULAU UBIN. A hard but versatile stone, granite has been used for a wide variety of purposes, from road foundations and ballast on railway lines to ornamental buildings. In the first half of the 20th century, small quarries were located throughout those areas where the rock was exposed; extraction was carried out in a variety of places according to local needs.

Granite quarrying in Singapore reached its peak in the mid-1970s, when there were 21 major quarries employing 1,230 workers. From the early 1960s, however, there were problems with quarry workers suffering from silicosis (a lung disease caused by breathing in silica dust). A survey of quarry workers in 1971 showed that 15 per cent of workers were suffering from this disease. The government imposed dust control regulations and also stopped renewing quarry licences. By 1995, there were only three operational quarries left. These have since closed down. The main ornamental stone companies in Singapore, such as Central Granite Industries, have thus taken to importing raw materials from neighbouring countries.

In the 1990s, quarries in Pulau Ubin supplied between 30–40 per cent of the country's needs. Some of Ubin's disused quarries have since been flooded, are overgrown with vegetation, and have become scenic attractions.

See also GEOLOGY.

Great Eastern Holdings Insurance group. Established in 1908, Great Eastern has $40 billion in assets and 2.6 million policyhold-

Naa. Govindasamy: **Thedi** *(1991).*

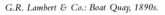

G.R. Lambert & Co.: Boat Quay, 1890s.

G.R. Lambert & Co.: newspaper advertisement, 1920s.

Great World, 1930s.

Joseph Grimberg

Great World: children riding on 'motor boats', 1960.

ers in Singapore and Malaysia. It is the only life insurance company to be listed on the Singapore Exchange, and is the largest insurance company in Southeast Asia in terms of assets and market capitalization. The company has 20,000 agents, and covers life, personal accident and health insurance, and annuity plans to individuals. It also provides loans, investment management and other related services. Its subsidiary, Lion Capital Management, is one of the largest asset management companies in Southeast Asia, with assets under managment of $30 billion.

Headquartered in Singapore, Great Eastern has 24 branches in Malaysia, with subsidiary companies and representative offices in China, Indonesia, Brunei, Hanoi and Ho Chi Minh City. In August 2005, Great Eastern and Chongqing Land Properties Group set up a joint-venture life insurance company named Great Eastern Life Assurance (China) Co. Ltd, to lead the group's expansion plans into the rest of China. Great Eastern is a subsidiary of OCBC Bank. Great Eastern Holdings reported a net profit of $373 million in the financial year 2005.

Great World Amusement park. Located on Kim Seng Road, Great World was founded by Lee Choon Seng in the 1920s,

shortly after the opening of NEW WORLD. It was later bought over by SHAW BROTHERS and New World's Ong Peng Hock. Subsequently, it was owned solely by Shaw Brothers.

Great World was one of a trio of popular amusement parks, the other two being GAY WORLD and New World. It was best known for its TEA DANCES, during which men could choose *ronggeng* (a Malay dance), *joget* (a folk dance) or cha cha at 20 cents a dance. Great World was also known for its *bangsawan* or Malay opera performances. Other attactions included the Flamingo Night Club and four cinema halls: Canton, Atlantic, Sky and Globe. The park's activities ceased in 1964. However, cinema operations continued until 1978. The site is now occupied by Great World City.

Greater East Asia Co-Prosperity Sphere Known in Japanese as '*Dai Toa Kyoeiken*', the Greater East Asia Co-Prosperity Sphere was a Japanese concept associated with the idea of liberating colonies in Asia from the rule of the United Kingdom, France, the Netherlands and the United States, and making these liberated territories part of a Japanese empire. The concept included Singapore, Malaya, the Dutch East Indies (present-day Indonesia), Burma and the Philippines. It did not, however, include the Japanese colonies of Korea or Taiwan; Japanese territories in Micronesia; or the puppet state of Manchukuo (in present-day China). The concept was one rationale for Japan's war in Southeast Asia.

JAPANESE OCCUPATION policies in the Greater East Asia Co-Prosperity Sphere concentrated on the exploitation of resources for Japan's war efforts. Much effort was put into the 'Japanization' of populations by teaching the Japanese language and promoting cultural practices, such as emperor worship and bowing as a sign of respect.

Grimberg, Joseph (1933–) Lawyer. A prominent member of the local Jewish community, Joseph Grimberg was educated in the United Kingdom, and returned to Singapore to practise as an advocate and solicitor. He was a senior partner at Drew & Napier for 20 years before being appointed judicial commissioner of the Supreme Court in 1987. Grimberg served for two years before returning to private practice. He was the first lawyer in Singapore to be appointed SENIOR COUNSEL (in January 1997).

Grimberg's professional experience includes representing two prime ministers, Lee Kuan Yew and Goh Chok Tong, in defamation cases involving opposition politician J.B. JEYARETNAM. He also represented ONG TENG CHEONG in a constitutional case relating to presidential powers. Grimberg has also arbitrated in local and international arbitration cases.

gross domestic product Measure of the market value of newly produced final goods and services produced within the domestic boundaries of a country or area in a given period. 'Gross' indicates that it is measured before an estimate of depreciation has been taken into account.

Singapore's gross domestic product (GDP) has grown considerably since 1965. In 2005, Singapore's GDP was $194.4 billion, compared with $39.0 billion in 1985 and $3.0 billion in 1965. Likewise, Singapore's per capita GDP has also grown. In 2005, it was $44,666, compared to $14,267 in 1985 and $1,567 in 1965. Despite this growth, the Singapore economy is relatively small. In 2004, Singapore's total GDP was 1 per cent that of the United States and 52 per cent that of Hong Kong—an economy often compared to Singapore. In per capita terms, these ratios were 69 per cent and 81 per cent respectively.

Singapore's GDP can be classified into two broad categories—goods-producing industries ($62.2 billion in 2005) and service industries ($121.9 billion in 2005). The main components of the goods-producing industries are manufacturing ($52.1 billion); construction ($7.0 billion); utilities ($2.8 billion); and other goods industries ($0.2 billion). The service industries include wholesale and retail trade ($28.8 billion); hotels and restaurants ($3.6 billion); transport and communications ($23.1 billion); financial services ($20.9 billion); business services ($24.6 billion); and other service industries ($20.8 billion).

As the domestic economy is small, many industries export their goods. Exports totalled $382.5 billion in 2005. Domestic goods that are exported fall into the categories of oil ($57.4 billion) and non-oil ($325.1 billion). Non-oil exports consist mainly of electronics (more than 50 per cent of exports); agriculture and raw materials; manufactured goods; and chemicals. Besides domestic goods, Singapore also re-exports many of its imports. These amounted to about $175.1 billion in 2005.

Singapore is also an oil-refining hub, even though it does not have any domestic oil reserves. Petroleum is an important component of the chemicals sector, which is Singapore's second largest industry in manufacturing after the electronics sector. In 2004, petroleum output was valued at $27.8 billion; the figure for petrochemicals was $17.1 billion.

Expenditure estimates show a very low level of personal consumption at about 40 per cent of GDP, with government consumption at about 10 per cent and a gross savings rate of 50 per cent on average. The personal consumption share is one of the lowest in the world and is far removed from the two-thirds of GDP typical of developed economies.

gross national product Measure of the value of newly produced final output, and incomes earned, by a country's factors of production, both within its domestic boundaries and in other countries. Gross national product (GNP) is also referred to as 'gross national income' (GNI). 'Gross' means no allowance for depreciation has been made.

GNP is a relatively better measure of income than GROSS DOMESTIC PRODUCT (GDP) because it takes into consideration the net income from abroad (i.e. all earnings remitted from abroad back to Singapore minus earnings, dividends and interest remitted out of Singapore from foreign workers and foreign companies).

Singapore's GNP has been rising steadily since Independence. In 2005, Singapore's GNP was $193.4 billion, compared to $40.3 billion in 1985 and $3.1 billion in 1965. Likewise, Singapore's per capita GNP has risen. In 2005, it was $44,455, compared to $14,717 in 1985 and $1,618 in 1965.

As Singapore has a large number of foreign workers and foreign companies that remit profits, there has always been a large outflow of income. However, the government has followed a policy of building a 'second wing' for the economy by encouraging Singapore firms to establish themselves abroad—particularly, but not exclusively, in China and India, with the intention of generating a larger positive inflow of earnings.

group representation constituency Constituency in which a team of three to six candidates is elected as a group. The group representation constituency (GRC) concept was introduced just before the general election in 1988 because the government noted 'a voting trend which showed young voters preferring candidates who were best suited to their own needs without sufficiently being aware of the need to return a racially balanced party slate of candidates'. The Constitution was amended accordingly, so that 'at least one of the three candidates in every group shall be a person belonging to the Malay, or Indian, or other minority communities'.

Since 1988, the GRC scheme has been expanded twice: in 1991 and 1996, just before general elections. In both instances, the number of GRCs was increased, and more significantly, the number of members within each GRC team also increased. The trend appears to be to increase the number of seats in GRCs to bring larger segments of Singapore's voting population under the GRCs. During the 1988 general election, there were 13 GRCs with a total of 39 seats. In 1991, there were 15 GRCs with 60 seats; and in 1997, the total number of GRCs was kept at 15, but accounted for a total of 74 seats, with only nine seats being single-member

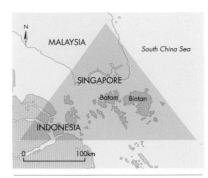

Growth Triangle: Singapore, Johor and Riau.

constituencies. In both 2001 and 2006, there were 14 GRCs—all consisting of either five or six members—accounting for 75 (out of the 84) seats.

See also ELECTIONS and TOWN COUNCILS.

Growth Triangle Tripartite arrangement between Singapore, Johor (in Malaysia) and Riau (in Indonesia) that seeks to exploit the competitive strengths of the three areas, and make the sub-region more attractive to regional and international investors.

The Singapore-Johor-Riau (SI-JO-RI) Growth Triangle (SIJORI) was officially announced on 20 December 1989 by then Deputy Prime Minister Goh Chok Tong. Formalized in 1994, it links the logistics, transportation and financial facilities of Singapore with the natural and labour resources of Johor

and Riau. The development of SIJORI is largely led by the private sector, with governments facilitating the flow of goods, services, investment and people.

The Singapore-Riau link has since emerged as the strongest leg of the growth triangle, with collaborative efforts leading to several new industrial parks, and resorts being established on the islands of Batam, Bintan and Karimun. Both Bintan and Batam have become manufacturing bases for multinational corporations as well as Singapore firms looking to reduce costs.

While trade and industrial links between Singapore and Johor are also well established, the Johor-Riau link has not been as active owing to the lack of complementarity between the two areas.

Guards The SINGAPORE ARMED FORCES Guards Unit (SAFGU) was first introduced on 1 July 1976 under the 7th Singapore Infantry Brigade (7 SIB), adding to the 7th and 8th Singapore Infantry Regiments (SIR). In 1977, SAFGU was renamed 1st Battalion Singapore Guards (1 Guards), and in 1978, 8 SIR was renamed 2nd Battalion Guards (2 Guards).

On 1 April 1978, 7 SIB was given elite status, and its units included the following: 1 Guards, 2 Guards, School of Commando Training, and the Commando Battalions (*see* COMMANDOS). In 1980, the commando sub-

GDP: BREAKDOWN BY INDUSTRY, 2005

- Manufacturing (27.3%)
- Wholesale and retail trade (15.1%)
- Business services (12.9%)
- Other services industries (10.9%)
- Financial services (11.9%)
- Transport and communications (12.1%)
- Construction (3.7%)
- Owner-occupied dwellings (3.6%)
- Hotels and restaurants (1.9%)
- Utilities (1.5%)

Source: Singapore Department of Statistics

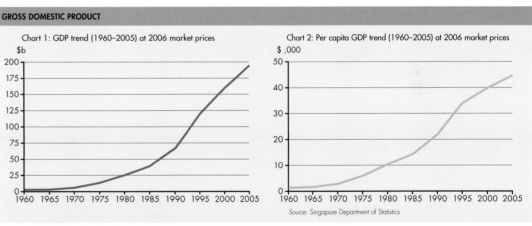

GROSS DOMESTIC PRODUCT

Chart 1: GDP trend (1960–2005) at 2006 market prices

Chart 2: Per capita GDP trend (1960–2005) at 2006 market prices

Source: Singapore Department of Statistics

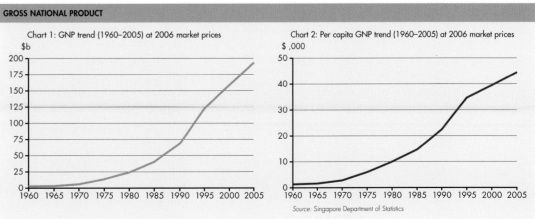

GROSS NATIONAL PRODUCT

Chart 1: GNP trend (1960–2005) at 2006 market prices

Chart 2: Per capita GNP trend (1960–2005) at 2006 market prices

Source: Singapore Department of Statistics

Guards: elite infantrymen demonstrating rappelling, a specialized skill

Sir Laurence Guillemard

Alexander Guthrie

units broke off from 7 SIB, and 7 SIR, which had been transferred to 3 SIB earlier, was reabsorbed to 7 SIB and renamed 3 Guards.

Guardsmen are identified by a shoulder tab and khaki beret. They are trained to engage in rapid deployment operations. Their emplaning and deplaning skill set includes hover-jumps, heli-rappelling and fast-rope down in full battle order. Their training also includes watermanship and and survival training.

Guillemard, Sir Laurence (1862-1951) Colonial official. Sir Laurence Nunns Guillemard was made governor of the Straits Settlements in 1919. When taking up the post, Guillemard realized that the Constitution had essentially not changed since 1867. According to the Constitution, the governor only needed to consult with the upper strata of European unofficial members and a few wealthy, English-speaking Asians when making administrative decisions. He decided that it was time to reform the constitution and to increase participation.

In 1921, Guillemard started allowing certain organizations to nominate municipal commissioners. The Singapore branch of the Straits Settlements Association nominated three; the Singapore and Chinese Chambers of Commerce nominated two each; and the Straits Chinese British Association, Eurasian Association, Muslim Advisory Board and Hindu Advisory Board nominated one each. In 1924, the Legislative Council was enlarged and comprised equal numbers of officials and unofficials.

Guillemard, who had worked for the British Treasury, also introduced the Straits Settlements Income Tax Ordinance in 1921, although this was was subsequently withdrawn due to strong opposition. Guillemard completed his term as governor in 1927.

Gujaratis Group within the Indian community whose origins lie in the state of Gujarat in northwest India. They speak Gujarati, and may be Hindus, Muslims or Jains. In 2000, according to census figures, there were some 3,260 Gujaratis in Singapore.

The first wave of Gujaratis is thought to have come to Malaya and Singapore in the late 19th century. In Singapore, they settled in areas such as Market Street, Chulia Street, High Street and Arab Street. The Hindu Paropkari Fund (Hindu Benevolent Fund), founded around 1912, was probably the earliest Gujarati organization to be established in Singapore. It looked after needy Gujaratis and provided free accommodation to Gujarati travellers in transit to Australia and Fiji. In the years before World War II, three Gujarati businessmen—Keshavjee Jivram Joshee, Ratilal Sukhlal Narechania and RAJABALI JUMABHOY—were made justices of the peace in the Straits Settlements.

On 2 October 1947, the Singapore Gujarati School was opened on Waterloo Street. This school is still in operation, although it has been relocated to Goodman Road.

In the past, Gujarati life was generally traditional. The male acted as the head of the household and sole breadwinner. The wife was entrusted with household chores and looking after the children. These days, however, many Gujarati women work.

Many Gujaratis are now businesspeople, entrepreneurs, civil servants and IT professionals. The community has two leading representative organizations—the Singapore Gujarati Society and the Singapore Jain Religious Society. Religious talks and seminars are organized by these bodies to maintain the community's cultural heritage. Gujaratis celebrate festivals such as NAVARATHIRI, Diwali (also known as DEEPAVALI) and HOLI.

Gurkhas Part of the SINGAPORE POLICE FORCE (SPF), the Gurkha Contingent, headquartered at Mount Vernon Camp, is made up of soldiers from Gorkha (western Nepal). The Gurkha Contingent was established in April 1949, after the demise of the

Gurkhas

Sikh Contingent following World War II. The contingent guards key installations such as the Istana and prisons, and functions as a riot squad.

There are currently six Gurkha Guard companies led by Nepalese chief inspectors. There is a Gurkha Band Contingent for parades. Since its inception, the contingent's senior officers have been British army personnel on contract or loan service.

The Gurkhas are descendants of the North Indian Rajput tribes who seized Gorkha in the early 16th century, and are considered by many to be formidable and fiercely loyal warriors. They are recruited from predominantly Hindu and Buddhist rice- and wheat-growing villages, the youngest recruits being 18 years of age. They undergo rigorous training and are schooled in martial arts. They generally work in Singapore for 15–20 years before returning to Nepal.

The Gurkhas played a role in quelling the MARIA HERTOGH RIOTS in 1950, which sparked off tensions between the Malay and European communities. In 1955 and 1956, they were called in to suppress the HOCK LEE BUS RIOTS and CHINESE MIDDLE SCHOOL RIOTS respectively.

Gurkha officers made up a portion of the SPF contingent that was sent to Iraq in 2003 to train local police officers in that country. On 18 March 2004, when a trio of armed robbers fled Johor and arrived at Pulau Tekong on a motorized sampan, a search party of 700 SPF and SAF personnel was mobilized. It was the Gurkhas who found and apprehended two of the three fugitives. The Gurkhas' tracking skills have also been put to use during raids on illegal immigrant hideouts in forested enclaves and mangrove areas.

Guthrie, Alexander (1796–1865) Merchant. Alexander Guthrie was born in Scotland, and was the fifth and youngest son of a farmer. He began his mercantile career in 1816 by joining the firm of Harrington & Co. in Cape Town. He arrived in Singapore on 27 January 1821 and opened a branch of Harrington & Co. The name was changed to GUTHRIE & CO. in 1833.

Guthrie helped establish the SINGAPORE CHAMBER OF COMMERCE (1837), and later chaired the chamber (1846–47). He was also interested in education and chaired a meeting to reorganize Singapore Institution (present-day Raffles Institution) in 1835. He became a trustee of that institution in 1836 and, together with his nephew, James Guthrie, helped establish scholarship funds for Hokkien, Teochew and Malay language classes for students training to be court interpreters.

Guthrie left Singapore in 1847 after turning his firm over to his nephew. While living in the United Kingdom, he supported the transfer of the Straits Settlements to the Colonial Office but died in London before the transfer was effected. Guthrie Lane (expunged), Guthrie House and Guthrie Bridge (demolished) were named in his honour.

Guthrie, James (1813–1900) Trader. James Guthrie arrived in Singapore in 1829 from Scotland to join his uncle ALEXANDER GUTHRIE, who founded the agency house GUTHRIE & CO in 1821. When the latter died in 1865, Guthrie took over the firm's management and remained in Singapore until he retired in 1876. He was sheriff of the Incorporated Settlement in 1851 and served as deputy chairman of the Straits Settlements Association. Guthrie died in Tunbridge Wells, Kent, in the United Kingdom.

Guthrie & Co. Agency house. Guthrie & Co. was established by ALEXANDER GUTHRIE in 1821 as Harrington & Co. In 1833, the company was renamed Guthrie & Co. after a change in partnership. Guthrie's nephew, James Guthrie, became a partner in 1837 and headed the Singapore office from 1847 when Alexander returned to London. The firm prospered through its import and export trade and the renting and selling of property in the Tanjong Pagar and Orchard Road areas.

In 1903, Guthrie & Co. merged with Scott & Company to become Guthrie & Co. Ltd, with its own London office. Businessman Sir JOHN ANDERSON (not to be confused with the governor of the same name) became the governing director of the company and launched many of its planting and mining business interests. He also shaped Guthrie's policies for the first quarter of the 20th century.

By 1910, Guthrie had established itself as one of the largest import and export AGENCY HOUSES for trade between Europe and Southeast Asia. Besides being a general trader, Guthrie acted as an agent for banks, insurance companies, shipping companies, and the Singapore Electric Tramways Company. It was also an agent for various products such as tin, tobacco, sugar, whisky, beer, wine, spirits, Jeyes' Fluid and Lipton products. It also became one of the largest rubber-producing businesses, acquiring new plantation companies with estates in Malaya, Borneo and Sumatra.

The business ceased operations when the head office in Singapore was bombed during World War II. During the Japanese Occupation, many employees were sent to Japanese internment camps.

The company's head office was transferred to London after the war, and Guthrie & Co. became a world-wide network of interests which included Guthries' of Singapore and Malaysia (later merged with an offshoot of Jardine, Matheson & Co. to become Guthrie Waugh); Guthries' of Rhodesia (present-day Zimbabwe); and other subsidiaries in various countries.

Gutta percha: late 19th-century photograph of gutta percha tree.

Guthrie Berhad became a publicly-listed company in Singapore in 1974. In 1988, the company was acquired by the Masagung family of Indonesia and was renamed Guthrie GTS. Guthrie GTS owns Guthrie Engineering (Singapore), and is involved in projects for airports; commercial, industrial and residential buildings; hospitals; and power stations.

gutta percha Gum-like resin obtained from the sap of the gutta percha tree (*Isonandra gutta*). The resin was first used in the manufacture of riding whips. In 1843, British surgeon Dr William Montgomerie suggested that it could be used for surgical instruments.

By 1847, the tree had disappeared from Singapore. Thereafter, the resin was harvested and collected in Malaya, and sent to Singapore for packing and export.

Gutta percha became a valuable commodity for the *temenggong* Malays: their annual trade was recorded as running at 10,000–12,000 piculs, worth between $150,000 and $200,000 in 1847.

Gwee Ah Leng (1920–2006) Doctor. Gwee Ah Leng was educated partly in China (where he lived for 13 years) and partly at Raffles Institution in Singapore. He graduated from the King Edward VII College of Medicine in 1949, and joined the medical services as a house doctor in Unit 1 of the Outram Road Hospital (later Singapore General Hospital).

Gwee read for his MRCP on a Queen's Scholarship. When he returned to Singapore, he continued work at the General Hospital. In 1961, Gwee became the first Singaporean master of the Academy of Medicine (AM) (1961–64).

Gwee was a pioneer of renal dialysis, introducing the procedure in 1961 while working in Medical Unit II with KHOO OON TEIK, Lim Cheng Hong and Lee Yong Kiat. Later, the attics above two wards in the Bowyer Block at Outram Road Hospital became the Renal Dialysis Unit. In 1965, Gwee was made head of a new unit—Unit III (also known as the 'Government Unit').

Gwee retired from the medical service in 1971 at the age of 50. He then established his own consultancy. Among his many public service appointments have been deputy president for the Society for the Aged Sick (1968); chairman, Nanyang University Review Committee (1960); and chairman, Raffles Institution Advisory Board. He was awarded the MERITORIOUS SERVICE MEDAL in 1963. He was made a justice of the peace and a Commander of the Most Venerable Order of St John in 1980.

Guthrie & Co.: crest indicating the company's range of activities and principal locations.

H

Habib Noh (1788–1866) Habib Noh Mohamed Alhabshi is regarded as a saint. The title 'Habib' means that he was a descendant of the Prophet Muhammad. He was also an Arab with ancestors in Yemen. Habib Noh was born in Kedah and lived in Penang before coming to Singapore in 1819. He was a pious man and preached Islam in Singapore and the region. He was also known as a great healer, and for his accurate premonitions. He was remembered for his affection for children, who would gather around him to listen to his stories and religious parables. He was known to go into shops and help himself to handfuls of sweets and money to distribute to needy children. Shop-owners welcomed Habib Noh and allowed him to take whatever he wanted as, it was said, business usually increased whenever he came. He died on Friday, 27 July 1866, and was buried on a hill at Palmer Road. His tomb became a KERAMAT and is known as Keramat Habib Noh.

The chamber surrounding the tomb was built by Syed Mohamad Ahmad Alsagoff in 1890. In 1903, the Haji Mohd Salleh Mosque was built at the foot of the hill. The *keramat*, along with the mosque, was renovated in 1987. People from Singapore and the region regularly visit the *keramat*, especially during the *haul* (death anniversary) of Habib Noh. The *haul* in 2005 was attended by over 3,000 people.

Hainanese Chinese dialect group. The term 'Hainanese' refers to the members of this group, as well as the language they speak. According to the 2000 Census of Population, there were over 160,000 Hainanese in Singapore, making up almost 7 per cent of the Chinese population. Originating on Hainan Island, China, Hainanese immigrants arrived in Singapore only after HOKKIEN, TEOCHEW and

Han Lao Da: the playwright and his work, Lao Da Ju Zuo *(1986) (top).*

Hainanese: baking, an occupation traditionally associated with the dialect group.

CANTONESE immigrants had settled there, and found that the more lucrative trades were already dominated by the larger dialect groups. The predominance of the Hainanese in the coffee shop trade and the service sector can be traced to these historical factors. The Hainanese owned the vast majority of COFFEE SHOPS in Singapore. Many also worked as cooks, waiters and butlers. Many Hainanese-owned coffee shops were located in the vicinity of Beach Road, Purvis Street and Seah Street.

After the end of the Japanese Occupation, the Hainanese began moving into other lines of business and either sold or rented their coffee shops to members of the FOOCHOW community. Many Hainanese then ventured into the hotel and restaurant trade. One well-known Hainanese-owned restaurant chain is Jack's Place, a steakhouse which serves Western-style dishes. CHICKEN RICE—an extremely popular dish in Singapore—is also a Hainanese dish.

The Singapore Hainan Hwee Kuan on Beach Road was established in 1854 as the Kiung Chow Hwee Kuan. The Tin Hou Kong temple shares premises with the clan association. Devotees pray to Mazu (the Goddess of the Sea) and other deities at this temple (*see* TAOISM). Prominent Hainanese include academic Wu Teh Yao, politician MAH BOW TAN, judge CHAO HICK TIN and civil servant NGIAM TONG DOW.

haj Pilgrimage to Mecca. The haj is one of the five pillars of ISLAM. Every able-bodied Muslim who can afford to do so is obliged to perform it at least once in his life. During the month of the haj, Mecca receives approximately 4 million pilgrims from around the world. Entrance to Mecca is forbidden to non-Muslims, as the entire city is considered a holy site. Upon their return, pilgrims are usually addressed as 'haji' (in the case of men) and 'hajjah' (in the case of women).

While all Muslims are required to perform the haj, it was the arrival of steamships that made the journey easier. In the 19th century, the pilgrimage from Singapore was controlled by *sheykh haji* (haj brokers) who were mostly Arabs. These *sheykh haji* would liaise with brokers in Mecca and make the necessary arrangements for pilgrims.

From the middle of the 19th century, Singapore had become the centre for haj departures for Muslims in British Malaya as well as the Dutch East Indies. Indonesian pilgrims were restricted by the Dutch government in performing the haj, but managed to overcome this by travelling to Singapore first. Many would come to Singapore to earn enough money to finance their trip. Some never went on to Mecca, staying in Singapore permanently. These people were referred to as 'Haji Singapura'.

The British colonial government eventually regulated the administration of the

Hajjah Fatimah Mosque

haj to manage the health and social problems that pilgrims faced. Living conditions on the ships were unsanitary, and the threat of smallpox and cholera epidemics were a cause for concern. Many pilgrims were forced to work for long hours for low wages as indentured labour for the haj brokers to pay off their passage. From 1889, passports were required to control the haj traffic. In 1905, an ordinance was passed which required haj brokers to be licensed.

Since 1975, MAJLIS UGAMA ISLAM SINGAPURA (MUIS), has been handling issues relating to the haj. Initially, MUIS only licenced brokers. However, the use of brokers was discontinued in 1990, after 200 people were left stranded. From 1991, people planning to go on the haj had to register with MUIS, and had to use travel agencies that were endorsed by the Singapore Tourist Promotion Board (later SINGAPORE TOURISM BOARD).

Saudi Arabia has set up a quota system for the haj, and each country may send only 0.1 per cent of its population each year. Singapore was originally allocated 3,000 visas, but this was increased to 4,000 in 1997 and to 4,500 in 1999. The quota is not always used up each year. The numbers fluctuate depending on factors such as the timing of the haj season and the health of the economy. Between 1992 and 2000, over 4,000 pilgrims went for the haj each year. The peak was in 1992 when there were 5,216 pilgrims. In 2005, 2,550 Muslims went on the pilgrimage. MUIS also sends volunteer medical staff, as well as its own officers, to monitor the welfare of pilgrims.

Hajjah Fatimah Mosque This mosque on Beach Road was built in 1846 by a wealthy businesswoman, HAJJAH FATIMAH, on the site of her residence. Her house had been burgled several times and set on fire, and she decided to build a mosque in gratitude for having escaped unharmed.

The mosque has a main prayer hall, an ablution area, gardens and other buildings

Hakka: pawnbroking, a traditional Hakka business.

enclosed by the high walls of the compound. There is also a garden cemetery, where flat, square headstones mark the graves of women, and round ones the graves of men. Hajjah Fatimah is buried in a private room to the side of the main prayer hall, along with her daughter and son-in-law, Syed Ahmed Abdul Rahman Alsagoff.

Designed by architect J.T. Thomson, the building shows traces of Moorish, Chinese and European architectural styles, but the overall design is British. The minaret in the front is purportedly a copy of the original spire of St Andrew's Cathedral. It leans a little to one side and has a sacred heart motif carved on the outside. The mosque was gazetted as a national monument on 6 July 1973.

Hakka The term 'Hakka' refers to the Chinese dialect group and the language spoken by its members, and literally means 'guest people'. Also known as 'Kheks', the Hakka originated in the provinces of Henan and Shanxi in northern China, migrating to southern China during the Yuan (1279–1368) and Ming (1368–1644) Dynasties. According to the 2000 Census of Population, there are some 198,435 Hakka in Singapore, forming 7.9 per cent of the total Chinese population.

In Singapore, the Hakka have tended to work in certain trades, such as pawnbroking, tailoring and the Chinese herb and medicine trade. Hakka from the Dapu district had a virtual monopoly in the pawnbroking trade. Members of the community's business elite also enjoyed good relations with the colonial goverment, and a number were appointed Kapitan Cina.

The first Hakka association to be founded in Singapore was the Ying Fo Fui Kun, which was established in 1822, three years after the landing of Sir Stamford Raffles. It was formed by Hakka from Jiayingzhou in Guangdong, China. Its clan house on Telok Ayer Street, gazetted as a national monument in 1988, also housed the Ying Sin School from 1905 to 1971. Fuk Tak Chi Temple, one of the oldest temples in Singapore, was established by Hakka and Cantonese immigrants as a shrine in 1824.

The Singapore Hakka Methodist Church was started in 1911. In 1929, Hakka businessman Aw Boon Haw established an umbrella body for Hakka clan associations named the Nanyang Khek Community Guild. Locally well-known Hakka dishes include yong tau foo and *lei cha fan*, which is rice served with a herbal soup. Prominent Hakkas in Singapore include merchant Tan Che Sang, first prime minister Lee Kuan Yew and judge Yong Pung How.

Hall of Fame *See* Singapore Sports Council Hall of Fame.

Hamidah Hassan (1927–1990) Journalist. Born in Penang, Hamidah Hassan started her working life as a schoolteacher in Hutton Lane, Penang. During the Japanese Occupation of Malaya, she became active in a Japanese-sponsored youth movement. In 1945, Hamidah left Penang to work as a reporter in Singapore at *Berita Malai* (a war-time amalgamation of Utusan Melayu and Warta Melayu newspapers). She was one of the first women to work as a journalist in Singapore.

Hamida ceased work after marrying Samad Ismail, a journalist from the newspaper *Utusan Melayu*. When Samad was detained for undertaking anti-colonial activities in 1951, Hamidah took his place at *Utusan Melayu*. She was also active in politics, joining the United Malays National Organization (UMNO) in the early 1950s, and later becoming the head of Wanita UMNO in Singapore.

Hamidah later worked as a journalist for Berita Harian where she was well known for her advice columns under the pen names 'Kak Timah' and 'Sri Siantan'.

Hamilton, Captain Alexander (unknown–c. 1732) Scottish sailor. Alexander Hamilton

Han Sai Por

was apparently a good friend of Abdul Jalil, the sultan of Johor. During one of his voyages, Hamilton called on the sultan, who offered him Singapore island as a gift. Hamilton turned down the offer, writing in his report that 'it could be of no use to a private person though a proper place for a company to settle a colony on, lying at the centre of trade…'.

Hamilton's voyages in the East Indies were documented in a two-volume work, *A New Account Of The East-Indies: Being The Observations And Remarks Of Captain Alexander Hamilton From The Year 1688 to 1723.*

Han Kee Juan (1958–) Dancer. After his first lessons with Scottish teacher Florrie Sinclair at age ten, Han trained at the Singapore Ballet Academy before entering the Australian Ballet School as a scholarship student. Upon graduation, he pursued a performing career abroad; besides dancing with the Sydney Dance Company and the Indianapolis Ballet Theater, he was a noted soloist with the Boston Ballet. In 1991, he returned briefly to Singapore to stage Goh Choo San's *Ballade* (1986) for the Singapore Dance Theatre.

Han was director of the Arizona Ballet School from 1992 to 2003. He joined the Dance Faculty of the North Carolina School for the Arts in 2003 and became co-director of the American Ballet Competition a year later.

Han Lao Da (1947–) Playwright and theatre director. Han received training at the Practice Performing Arts School in the late 1960s. His first major work, *Zou Chu Lao Fang De Ren* (Walking Out of Prison: Ah Seng's Story*),* premiered in 1972. He coordinated and directed his first 'devised' play, *Five Libras,* for the Singapore Drama Festival in 1986 and 1991. Another fulllength play, *Tan Kah Kee Story*, was devised with a cast of Chinese High School students. Han also co-founded Sin Feng Cross-Talk Society. He has written over 40 pieces of cross-talk in two books, using Tan Tian as his pen name. He was awarded the Cultural Medallion in 1990.

Han Sai Por (1943–) Sculptor. A graduate of the Nanyang Academy of Fine Arts (1977) and subsequently the Art Colleges of East Ham (1979) and Wolverhampton (1983) in the United Kingdom, Han Sia Por has produced work ranging from the subtle, sensuous marble pieces in the Singapore Art Museum collection to monumental public sculptures in Singapore and overseas, including the United Kingdom, China, New Zealand and Malaysia.

Han's work has been described as 'organic modernism', typified by abstraction inspired by nature—strong, purified forms combined with integrity of material. Her *Seeds* series earned an award at the

Hakka: traditional Hakka dishes, including suan panzi ('abacus balls') (in foreground) and yong tau foo.

Han Kee Juan

Hang Chang Chieh, left.

Harun Abdul Ghani

Harun Aminurrashid

Hang Tuah (1956)

Indian Triennale 2005. She was awarded the CULTURAL MEDALLION in 1995.

Hanafi School Islamic school of jurisprudence with adherents in Singapore mainly from the Indian Muslim community. Named after Abu Hanifa al-Nu'man Thabit (699–765 CE), more commonly known simply as Imam Abu Hanifa, this school is also prevalent in India and countries formerly under Ottoman rule.

Although the majority of Muslims in Singapore adhere to the SHAFI'I SCHOOL, the Hanafi School is recognized by the Fatwa Council of MAJLIS UGAMA ISLAM SINGAPURA (MUIS) as a source of legal opinion. Like other Islamic schools, the Hanafi School covers almost all aspects of life, from eating and conducting business, to marriage and divorce.

Hang Chang Chieh (1948–) Scientist and academic. Hang graduated with a first class honours degree in electrical engineering at the University of Singapore in 1970. He earned his PhD in control engineering from the University of Warwick, United Kingdom, in 1973. He worked as a computer and systems technologist for Shell Eastern Petroleum Company (in Singapore and the Netherlands) between 1974 and 1977.

Hang has been with the NATIONAL UNIVERSITY OF SINGAPORE since 1977, his posts including vice-dean of the Faculty of Engineering, head of the Department of Electrical Engineering and deputy vice-chancellor. In 1994, he was also appointed director of research, Vice-Chancellor's Office. He was appointed by the Ministry of Education to be founding director of the Singapore-MIT Alliance in 1998. Hang was awarded the Public Administration Gold Medal in 1998, and the NATIONAL SCIENCE AND TECHNOLOGY MEDAL in 2000.

Hang Jebat (1961) Film. *Hang Jebat* was directed by HUSSAIN HANIFF and produced by CATHAY-KERIS FILMS at their studios on East Coast Road. The film was Haniff's first as director, and starred Nordin Ahmad and M. Amin. It was based on a play by Ali Aziz entitled *Hang Jebat Menderhaka* (The Rebellion of Hang Jebat) (1959). Rather than focusing on the character of Hang Tuah (the hero of the play), the movie showed Hang Jebat as the hero. This was considered highly innovative for the time.

Hang Tuah (1956) Film. Directed by Phani Majumdar, *Hang Tuah* was the first film about a historical Malay warrior to be made in Malaya. It was shot in Eastman colour and was produced for $300,000—a substantial sum for the time. It was produced by SHAW BROTHERS' MALAY FILM PRODUCTIONS studio on Jalan Ampas off Balestier Road, and starred P. RAMLEE in the title role.

The film depicted the MALACCA SULTANATE at the height of its power. Its screen-

Hang Jebat (1961)

play was adapted from M.C. Sheppard's *The Adventures of Hang Tuah* (1949). In the film, a female character, Melor, played by former child actress Sa'adiah, was introduced as Hang Tuah's love interest.

The film was awarded the Best Music Award at the Third Asian Film Festival in Hong Kong in 1956 for its soundtrack—composed by P. Ramlee and featuring lyrics by Jamil Sulong—while one of the film's actresses, Zaiton, won the Best Supporting Actress Award.

Hari Raya Haji See EID-UL-ADHA.

Hari Raya Puasa See EID-UL-FITR.

Harry's Bar This bar was opened in a restored shophouse at Boat Quay in 1992. It soon emerged as a popular venue for live jazz. The success of Harry's Bar at its original site prompted the opening of six more outlets around the island.

Harun Abdul Ghani (1939–2005) Politician. Harun Abdul Ghani was a former teacher at Sang Nila Utama Secondary School and at Tun Seri Lanang Secondary School. He became member of Parliament for Hong Kah group representation constituency, being elected in 1991 and again in 1996, before retiring from politics in 2002. Harun was also political secretary with the Ministry of Home Affairs (1989–2001), where he was involved in setting up rehabilitation centres. He also played a big part in campaigning against the drug problem in the Malay community. He died of complications arising from lung cancer at the age of 66. Harun was awarded the MERITORIOUS SERVICE MEDAL posthumously in 2005 for 'significant contributions to Singapore's effective campaign against drug abuse'.

Harun Aminurrashid (1907–1986) Teacher, author and journalist. Harun Aminurrashid was the pen name used by Harun Mohd Amin. Harun studied at the Sultan Idris Training College, Perak. He then worked in education and was, among other roles, superintendent of education in Brunei. He

was a pioneer of the historical novel in Malay. His first novel, *Melur Kuala Lumpur* (Kuala Lumpur Jasmine), was published in 1930. Nationalism and anti-colonialism were common themes in his work. In *Wan Derus*, for example, a local hero fights against the colonial government. *Panglima Awang* (Awang the Warrior) (1959) is a historical novel with strongly nationalist undertones. Many of his essays and poems called on the Malays to unite and take advantage of economic opportunities to avoid being marginalized.

Harun was one of the most prolific writers of his time. For his contribution to MALAY LITERATURE, language and culture, the Tun Seri Lanang Award was conferred on him posthumously by the Malay Language Council of Singapore in 1995.

Haw Par Corporation This company began operations during the early years of the 20th century as a manufacturer and distributor of pharmaceutical products. Its best known product was TIGER BALM, an ointment that was developed in the late 1800s—based on an ancient formula—by a Chinese physician from Burma, Aw Chu Kin. Aw had passed the formula for the balm down to his sons AW BOON HAW and Aw Boon Par.

In 1926, Aw Boon Haw relocated from Rangoon to Singapore, and opened a factory on Neil Road. He repackaged and trademarked the balm under his own name, 'Haw' (the Hokkien word for 'tiger'). More factories and distributorships were then established in Malaya, Hong Kong, Indonesia, Thailand and China before the brothers diversified into other areas such as publishing and banking. The Chung Khiaw Bank in Singapore, for instance, was founded by Aw Boon Haw in 1950.

Aw Boon Haw died in 1954, and control of the company was passed to his nephew, Aw Cheng Chye. In 1969, the business was dual-listed on the stock exchanges of Singapore and Malaysia as Haw Par Brothers International. In 1976, it became the fifth largest company on the Singapore Stock Exchange after a series of corporate manoeuvres by the UK investment group Slater Walker Securities.

However, the company later became embroiled in a financial scandal relating to non-disclosure of profits. This almost led to its collapse, and resulted in a three-way battle for control involving major shareholders: the Hong Leong Group, Jack-Chia Limited and UNITED OVERSEAS BANK (UOB). UOB, headed by WEE CHO YAW, eventually won control, and rebuilt the company by divesting many of its non-core interests in textiles, engineering, commodities trading and computers.

The group was renamed Haw Par Corporation in December 1997. Thereafter, its activities were focused on areas such as healthcare and leisure products. It also opened recreational centres such as bowling centres, and two Underwater World oceanariums—one on Sentosa and a second in Pattaya, Thailand. The group's other interests included investment properties and the management of securities investments, these accounting for more than half of the company's core assets. Its flagship healthcare products have continued to be manufactured and marketed under the Tiger, Kwan Loong and Drug Houses of Australia brands.

The company reported a net profit of $80 million on a turnover of $120 million for the financial year 2005.

Haw Par Villa Formerly called Tiger Balm Gardens, the villa was constructed on Pasir Panjang Road in 1937 by AW BOON HAW as a residence for his younger brother, Aw Boon Par, who had helped the former establish TIGER BALM as a popular product throughout the region. Aw Boon Haw built an entertainment and educational park on the site, including statues and tableaux depicting anecdotes from Chinese folklore and legend.

The Hua Song Museum opened in a new wing of the villa in early 2006. Meaning 'In Praise of the Chinese Community', Hua Song tells the stories of overseas Chinese in the 18th and 19th centuries.

hawker centres Buildings housing a number of low-cost food-stalls. Hawker centres were established from the 1960s as a result of government efforts to remove itinerant food hawkers from streets and public spaces. Before the establishment of hawker centres, hawkers would often obstruct traffic, and their stalls were not subject to effective hygiene regulations.

Hawker centres are purpose-built, and are a feature of most housing estates. There are over 100 centres islandwide. Stall operators are required to be licensed, and their stalls are checked regularly by public health officials. In 1997 a grading system was introduced for food stalls based on standards of cleanliness and hygiene: A is excellent, B good, C average and D below average. By 2004, 43% of stalls were A grade, and 48% B grade. Hawker centres and markets are progressively being renovated and upgraded under the Hawker Centre Upgrading Programme, launched in 2001.

haze The haze occasionally experienced in Singapore is a form of smog (a compound word for smoke and fog). Atmospheric pollution creates solid hygroscopic particles which absorb moisture; this leads to condensation and the formation of a type of dirty, low-lying cloud. Haze is produced by the combination of a hot, humid climate and pollution from motor traffic and industry as well as the burning of vegetation in neighbouring countries. Haze is monitored by the NATIONAL ENVIRONMENT

AGENCY. A POLLUTANT STANDARDS INDEX (PSI) is used to inform the public of haze pollution levels.

Haze is at its worst when El Niño occurs (every five to ten years)—the ocean currents in the Pacific reverse and Southeast Asia experiences drier than usual weather. During such periods, agricultural and forest fires in Indonesia and Malaysia can burn out of control. The most severe occurrence was in 1997, when forest fires raged on both Sumatra and Borneo. The PSI became dangerously high in Singapore and visibility was less than 2 km for 12 consecutive days.

Health Promotion Board Statutory board. Set up in 2001, the Health Promotion Board (HPB) spearheads programmes such as the National Healthy Lifestyle Programme, which encourages healthy eating and regular exercise (see OBESITY); the National Smoking Control Programme, to curb smoking through public education, legislation and taxation (see SMOKING); and the National Myopia Prevention Programme, to address MYOPIA in children.

The HPB also provides health screening for cervical and breast cancer. It maintains a number of telephone hotlines, such as HealthLine, offering pre-recorded messages on health matters, and the QuitLine, for those who wish to give up smoking.

Health Sciences Authority Statutory board. Formed in 2001, the Health Sciences Authority (HSA) brings together five former agencies: the Centre for Drug Evaluation, the Institute of Science and Forensic Medicine, the Product Regulation Department, the National Pharmaceutical Administration and the Singapore Blood Transfusion Service.

The HSA is responsible for the quality, safety and efficacy of medicines, medical devices, radiation equipment, blood and its products, and all health-related products available in Singapore. It also provides scientific, investigative and analytical support for governmental functions, such as foren-

Haze: city skyline dimly seen from Benjamin Sheares Bridge, September 1997.

sic expertise for the courts, drug and criminal investigations, and the regulation of food safety and industrial and environmental health.

healthcare Healthcare services are provided by both the government and the private sector. Currently, the government provides 80 per cent of hospital care by admissions and 20 per cent of PRIMARY HEALTHCARE.

The state of health in Singapore has improved over the years and is comparable to other developed countries. In 2005, the infant mortality rate stood at 2.1 per 1,000 live births; average life expectancy was 79.7 years (77.9 years for men and 81.6 years for women). In 2004 there were 6,492 doctors (15 per 10,000 population); 1,227 dentists (3 per 10,000 population); and 18,964 nurses (45 per 10,000 population).

The pattern of ill-health has changed with improvements in the standard of living and health services. In the early years, the main causes of death were infectious conditions, but by 2005, cancer, heart disease and stroke together accounted for close to 60 per cent of deaths.

In 2003, Singapore spent about $6.3 billion, or 3.8 per cent of gross domestic product, on healthcare. Of that, government expenditure on health services was $2 billion. Healthcare is kept affordable through heavy government subsidies, supplemented

Haw Par Villa

Hawker centres: Maxwell Hawker Centre (left); hawker centre hygiene certification (below).

Mavis Hee

Ivan Heng

by MEDISAVE, MEDISHIELD and MEDIFUND. By 2030, senior citizens are forecast to make up 20 per cent of Singapore's population. This is expected to pose a major challenge for the healthcare system.

heartlanders Term coined by then Prime Minister GOH CHOK TONG and popularized by the media. Goh first used the term in a National Day speech in 1999, juxtaposing 'heartlanders' with 'cosmopolitans'. Goh described the latter as international in outlook; English-speaking; employed in high-skilled and high-income sectors; highly mobile; and able to adapt to other countries easily.

Heartlanders, on the other hand, were more likely to speak SINGLISH; live in public housing estates; be employed locally; and be less mobile than cosmopolitans.

Heath, Lieutenant-General Sir Lewis (1885–1954) British military officer. Lieutenant-General Sir Lewis Macclesfield Heath was born in India, and joined the army in 1906. He served in Afghanistan, Persia (present-day Iran), the Northwest Frontier, India and North Africa. He was eventually given command of the Indian III Corps which, from 1941 to 1942, was

HEALTHCARE

Demographic indicators, 2005

Crude birth rate (per 1,000 population)	10.0
Crude death rate (per 1,000 population)	4.3
Infant mortality rate (per 1,000 live births)	2.1
Life expectancy at birth (years)	79.7
Male	77.9
Female	81.6

Source: Singapore Department of Statistics

Health facilities and manpower, 2005

No. of hospitals/speciality centres	29
Public sector	13
Private sector	16
Total number of hospital beds	11,830
Public sector hospital beds	8,159
Private sector hospital beds	3,671
Total number of doctors	6,748
Doctor to population ratio	1:648
Total number of dentists	1,277
Dentist to population ratio	1:3,410
Total number of nurses/midwives	20,167
Nurse to population ratio	1:220
Total number of pharmacists	1,330
Pharmacist to population ratio	1:3,270

Source: Ministry of Health

Main causes of death, 2005

Total number of deaths	16,217
Cancer	26.4%
Ischaemic heart disease	18.1%
Pneumonia	14.9%
Cerebrovascular disease (including stroke)	9.9%
Accidents, poisoning and violence	4.9%
Other heart diseases	4.0%
Chronic obstructive lung disease	3.5%
Diabetes mellitus	3.1%
Nephritis, nephrotic syndrome and nephrosis	2.0%
Septicaemia	1.6%

Source: Ministry of Health

tasked with OPERATION MATADOR and the defence of northern Malaya.

The Indian III Corps was decimated at Jitra and the disastrous Battle of Slim River. Its remnants were then deployed in February 1942 to defend Singapore's northern coast. In mid-December 1942, Heath suggested that British forces be more concentrated on a narrow front, perhaps on a defence of Johor, but Lieutenant-General ARTHUR PERCIVAL insisted that a tactic of maximum delay be implemented instead (*see* MALAYA CAMPAIGN).

Following the British surrender, Heath was captured by the Japanese and spent the remainder of the war as a prisoner of war in Singapore, Formosa (present-day Taiwan) and Manchukuo (Manchuria; in present-day China). He retired in 1946.

Hee, Mavis (1974–) Singer. Mavis Hee (Xu Meijing) responded to a newspaper advertisement 'in Search of a Star' in 1993 and subsequently recorded a duet, 'Shao Nian De Wo' (Young Me), for a Chinese New Year album *Chun Tian Li* (Spring Lane).

Hee released her debut album *Ming Zhi Dao* (Knowingly) in August 1994. Her second album, *Yi Han* (Unfortunate) (1996), sold 200,000 copies in Taiwan within a month. The album was popular in Singapore for its local television serial themes. That same year, Mavis won 'Best Local Singer' and 'Media Most-Recommended' titles at the Singapore Hits Awards.

Hee's foray into Hong Kong's pop market was also a success. She was crowned 'All-Round Winner Pop Diva of Hong Kong' in 1997. That year, director Ang Lee chose her song 'Man Yan' (Extending) as the Chinese theme for his movie *The Ice Storm* (1997).

Hee went on to make a movie, *Away With Words,* in 1999. However, soon after releasing *Jing Dian* (Classic Hits) (2000), she vanished from the music scene.

Heng, Ivan (1964–) Theatre practitioner. Ivan Heng Ai Jin graduated with a law degree from the National University of Singapore in 1988, but left in 1990 for the Royal Scottish Academy of Music and Drama in Glasgow to pursue a Diploma in Dramatic Arts. Heng won prizes in performance and for outstanding studentship.

He won the Scotsman Fringe First Award and the Scottish Daily Express New Names of 1993 Award for his production of Ovidia Yu's *The Woman in a Tree on the Hill* at the Edinburgh Festival Fringe.

In London, he founded the Tripitaka Theatre Company, which staged *Journey West* and *An Occasional Orchid.* The former won Heng, its co-author and sole actor, the Spirit of the Fringe Award at the 1995 Edinburgh Festival; the latter, also co-authored by him, was voted 'Best of the Hong Kong Fringe' in 1997.

Between 1997, when Heng returned to Singapore, and 2000, when he founded

Heartlanders: a game of chequers.

W!LD RICE Theatre Company, he acted in Manuel Puig's *Kiss of the Spider Woman* and directed several productions including Ovidia Yu's *Breast Issues* (1997) and *Ah Kong's Birthday Party* (1997)—co-authored by Heng and Dick Lee—the longest-running play in Singapore. He also directed Lee's *Phua Chu Kang—The Musical* (2000) for the President's Star Charity. Heng was the NATIONAL ARTS COUNCIL's Young Artist Award for Theatre in 1996.

Heng played Emily Gan (the first time a male actor had taken her on) to critical acclaim in W!LD RICE's inaugural production of Stella Kon's *Emily of Emerald Hill*. *Animal Farm* won Heng the Best Director Award in the 2002 Life! Theatre Awards. He has directed more than 30 productions in Singapore, Malaysia and Europe. He has acted in film, on television, and has taught theatre in Singapore and abroad.

Heng is a member of the Tokyo Setagaya Public Theatre's Lohan Journey—an international collective of 16 leading theatre artists from seven Asian cities. Heng was artistic director of the Singapore Theatre Festival in August 2006.

Henghua The term 'Henghua' refers to the Chinese dialect group and the language spoken by its members. According to the 2000 Census of Population, the Henghua make up approximately 1 per cent of the Chinese population in Singapore.

Henghua migration to Singapore began in the late 19th century. They settled mostly along Rochor Canal Road, Sungei Road, Arab Street and Queen Street. As most other trades were already monopolized by other dialect groups, the Henghua predominantly earned a living as rickshaw pullers in the early days (*see* RICKSHAWS). The Henghua came to dominate the transport sector, but also branched out into other areas of business in the 1950s.

Henghua places of worship include the Hinghwa Methodist Church, which was founded in 1911 and is the oldest Henghua organization in Singapore; and Hin Ann Tian Hou Temple, which was founded in 1921. The grandest Henghua temple is Kiew Lee Tong Temple on Thomson Road.

Prominent Henghua include Chen Yau Ru, founder of Far East Bank and Hin Ann Huay Kuan, and property magnate NG

TENG FONG of FAR EAST ORGANIZATION. Hong Wen School, founded by Hin Ann Huay Kuan, is also one of the few surviving clan association schools in Singapore.

Her World Magazine. *Her World* was first published in July 1960. With fashion spreads, beauty tips, 'how-to' articles, entertainment news and human relationship columns, it soon became the best-selling and most widely read women's magazine in Singapore.

Her World has been responsible for fostering many new models and actresses, such as FANN WONG, who won the *Her World* cover contest in 1988. The magazine has also helped shape the careers of local designers such as Tan Yoong and Thomas Wee.

By the 45th anniversary of the founding of *Her World*, the magazine had a circulation of 75,000.

Heritage Conservation Centre A purpose-built facility, the Heritage Conservation Centre (HCC) stores and conserves all artefacts under the care of the NATIONAL HERITAGE BOARD (NHB). Before the completion of the HCC, most nationally administered historical artefacts and artworks were stored at the National Museum building on Stamford Road. As the collection grew, however, the need for more specialized storage facilities increased.

The construction of the HCC was made possible through a government grant of $22.5 million. The centre's new building, located at Jurong Port Road in western Singapore, was completed in 1997, and officially opened in 2000. The building includes concrete, re-inforced and aluminium-clad walls to ensure maximum security and insulation; large steel doors to allow for the moving of large artefacts; and epoxy floors to minimize dust.

heritage roads Thoroughfares listed as part of Singapore's national heritage. The NATIONAL PARKS BOARD (NParks) has encouraged developers to retain and conserve roads along which plantlife has become so well established and distinctive that it is deemed worthy of conservation under the Parks and Trees Act 2005. Thoroughfares thus listed include Arcadia Road, Lim Chu Kang Road, Mandai Road, Mount Pleasant Road and South Buona Vista Road.

heritage trees The Heritage Trees Scheme was announced by the NATIONAL PARKS BOARD (NParks) in 2001. The idea of listing particular trees as 'heritage trees' was a response to concerns about increasing levels of commercial, industrial and residential development.

The process started with a call for public nominations of particular trees. More than 400 public nominations were received. A panel of arborists, botanists, academics, urban planners, nature enthusiasts and community representatives then assessed the worthiness of these nominated trees for conservation. Particular trees were assessed and selected according to their age, size (height and girth), prominence, historical significance, rarity and heritage value. More than 160 trees on public and privately owned land were eventually listed as heritage trees.

One of the trees to be chosen was the tembusu (*Fagraea fragrans*) tree on Lawn E in the SINGAPORE BOTANIC GARDENS. This tree is more than 100 years old, and has a long, low branch upon which visitors often rest. The tree has become so well known that it has been pictured on the Singapore five-dollar note.

A 60-year-old angsana (*Pterocarpus indicus*) tree on Upper Serangoon Road, near Woodleigh Park, was saved from being cleared for redevelopment when drainage channels under the local road were realigned.

Hertogh, Maria (1937–) Huberdina Maria Hertogh was born to a Catholic couple that lived near Bandung in Java. Maria's Dutch father, Adrianus Petrus Hertogh, was a sergeant in the Royal Netherlands East Indies Army. He was interned by the Japanese in 1942. Though accounts of what actually transpired differ on material points, Maria came into Aminah Mohamed's care in 1942 when she was five. Aminah, a Malay Muslim, was a friend of Maria's mother, Adeline.

In 1947, Aminah and Maria left Java to settle in Kemaman in Terengganu. Raised as a Muslim, Maria, like Malay girls her age, spoke Malay, wore Malay clothes, practised Islam and had a Muslim name—Nadra Maarof.

After the war, Adrianus and Adeline Hertogh relocated to the Netherlands, but asked the Dutch authorities in Java and Singapore to help determine Maria's

Heritage trees: in Singapore Botanic Gardens.

whereabouts for them. Arthur Locke, a local British official, discovered Maria in September 1949. This led to a custody battle in Singapore. While in Singapore, Maria married Mansoor Adabi—according to Muslim rites. Mansoor was, at that time, a trainee teacher at Bukit Panjang Government School. The court ruled in favour of Adeline, and also ruled the marriage invalid. The judgement of the court, along with the media's handling of the whole episode, sparked off what became known as the MARIA HERTOGH RIOTS.

In December 1950, Adeline and Maria left for the Netherlands. Maria got married in 1956 to Johan Wolkenfeld and had ten children. Her marriage broke down in the late 1970s after she was accused of planning to murder her husband. She was last reported to be living in the United States.

Hertogh, Maria riots *See* MARIA HERTOGH RIOTS.

Herzog, Chaim The visit to Singapore of the Israeli president Chaim Herzog in November 1986 at the invitation of the Singapore government resulted in anti-Singapore demonstrations in Brunei, Indonesia and Malaysia. Malaysia accused Singapore of being insensitive to its Muslim citizens and neighbours, and recalled its high commissioner to Singapore for the duration of the visit. Bilateral military exercises between the two countries were cancelled. Protestors called for Singapore's expulsion from the ASSOCIATION OF SOUTH EAST ASIAN NATIONS, as well as a review of WATER AGREEMENTS and MALAYSIA–SINGAPORE RELATIONS in general. The Singapore government took the position that, as a sovereign nation, it had the right to conduct its own FOREIGN POLICY.

Hiang Kie Coffee company. Hiang Kie—meaning 'fragrance' in Hokkien—was first established in 1936 by ONG WEI SOEIJ, a merchant from Palembang in Sumatra. It began as a re-exporter of Indonesian coffee beans and other products.

In the 1950s, the company built a warehouse complex in the MacPherson area. In 1961, it became the first company to introduce electronic coffee-sorting equipment. It later became a trader on the New York, London and Singapore commodity exchanges.

However, Hiang Kie's revenues declined from about $150 million in the mid-1980s to $70 million in 1990 due to falling coffee prices. The company therefore diversified into industrial property, as well as specialty café and restaurant businesses, to reduce its dependence on coffee trading. It set up Singapore's first gourmet coffee outlet at Boat Quay, as well as the first Singapore specialist coffee chain with the opening of a Coffee Club outlet in Holland Village in 1991. The group then added

Maria Hertogh, centre.

Chaim Herzog: during his visit to Singapore, 1986.

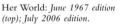

Her World: June 1967 edition (top); July 2006 edition.

Hiang Kie: Coffee Club outlet.

smaller self-service Coffee Club Xpress cafés to its chain in 1996. It introduced its own Kaffa Kaldi brand of coffee, produced at a plant in Singapore.

At its height, the group operated more than 20 Coffee Club, Coffee Club Xpress and Kaldi's Kafé outlets in Singapore, Hong Kong, Malaysia, China and the Middle East. Hiang Kie was seeking to penetrate further into the China market when, in 2004, it was wound up after defaulting in 2002 on debts totalling $150 million. The Coffee Club and Kaffa Kaldi businesses were sold to Hong Kong-based Sumipac Hospitality for $7 million in December 2002.

hills and ridges A cross-section through Singapore from west to east reveals a sequence of four separate areas of ridges and hills. The western ridges are formed from the Triassic sedimentary rocks of the Jurong formation, which rise to a series of low peaks (50–90 m) in the Choa Chu Kang area. The central hills, which represent the highest points in the country and culminate in Bukit Timah (162 m), were formed from the igneous intrusions of granite and norite which erosion subsequently exposed. The east of the island has two smaller ranges which rise to less than

30 m—the Tampines Hills, composed of folded old alluvial deposits, and the Changi Hills, which are an outlying exposure of the Bukit Timah granite system.

The only place which varies significantly from this general pattern is in the south, where a branch of the Jurong formation rises up to create the ridges of Pasir Panjang and MOUNT FABER.

Hindi Society Organization operating centres for the teaching of Hindi. Prior to the 1990s, a sizeable number of non-Tamil-speaking Indian students in Singapore did not have the option of studying Hindi as a second language at school. The majority of these students studied Malay as their second language.

The SINGAPORE NORTH INDIAN HINDU ASSOCIATION, representing the North Indian community, believed that a lack of opportunities to learn Hindi was proving detrimental to the Hindi-speaking community. In 1988, it thus formed the Hindi Pro-Tem Committee, which comprised representatives from the SHREE LAKSHMINARAYAN TEMPLE and ARYA SAMAJ. In 1989, members of other north Indian associations such as the Singapore Gujarati Society and Sindhi Merchants Association were invited to join.

Hindu Endowments Board: detail of Sri Srinivasa Perumal, a temple managed by the board.

The Hindi Pro-Tem Committee studied the issue and made representations to the Ministry of Education.

In October 1989, the government announced that Indian students could choose to study Hindi, Bengali, Punjabi, Gujarati or Urdu as a second language. In 1990, the committee then began Hindi classes, with 90 students taking these classes at Bengwan Primary School. The Hindi Society was registered in the same year. It has opened centres in several schools, and has also started Hindi classes for adults.

Hindu Advisory Board Statutory board. This government-affiliated board was set up in 1915 to counsel the colonial government on matters pertaining to HINDUISM in Singapore. It has continued to advise the government on all matters connected with Hindu practices and worship.

Hindu Endowments Board Statutory board. The Hindu Endowments Board was set up in 1969 as one of the two bodies to replace the MOHAMMEDAN AND HINDU ENDOWMENTS BOARD. It was given the task of administering the affairs and activities of four Hindu temples—the SRI MARIAMMAN TEMPLE, SRI SRINIVASA PERUMAL TEMPLE, SRI SIVAN TEMPLE and SRI VAIRAVIMADA KALIAMMAN TEMPLE—and ensuring the proper enactment in Singapore of two Hindu festivals, THAIPUSAM and THEEMIDHI.

The board has 12–16 members, all of whom are Singaporean Hindus. Each member is appointed for a three-year term by the Ministry for Community Development, Youth and Sports. The board includes professionals, civil servants and representatives from the private sector. Only the board's secretary is required by law to be from the civil service.

The board has often been consulted informally by government departments on matters such as the registration of new religious groups and temples; the granting of work permits to foreign temple staff; and the securing of permits for religious processions.

Hindu weddings Hindu marriages have traditionally been 'arranged'. In modern

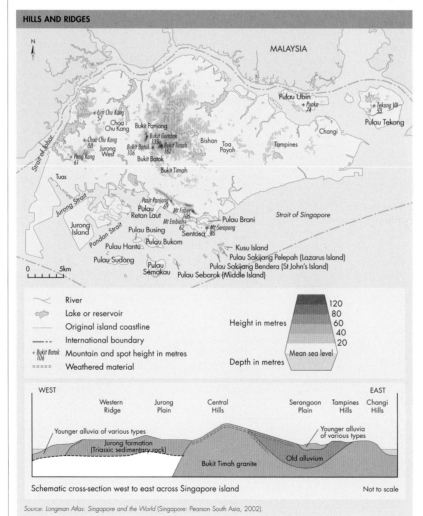

HILLS AND RIDGES

MALAYSIA

Pulau Ubin
Pulau Tekong
+ Tekong VII 53
+ Punai 74

+ Lim Chu Kang 57
Choa Chu Kang
Bukit Panjang
+ Choa Chu Kang 88
Jurong West
+ Bukit Gombak 139
+ Bukit Batok 106
+ Bukit Timah 162
Bukit Batok
Bishan
Toa Payoh
Changi
Tampines
+ Peng Kang 61

Strait of Johor

Bukit Timah

Tuas

Pasir Panjang
Pulau Retan Laut
Mt Faber 105
Mt Embiah 67
Pulau Brani
Strait of Singapore
Jurong Island
Pandan Strait
Pulau Busing
Mt Serapong 62
Sentosa 85
Jurong Strait
Pulau Hantu
Pulau Bukom
Kusu Island
Pulau Sakijang Pelepah (Lazarus Island)
Pulau Sudong
Pulau Semakau
Pulau Sakijang Bendera (St John's Island)
Pulau Sebarok (Middle Island)

0   5km

≈ River
⬮ Lake or reservoir
— Original island coastline
-- International boundary
+ Bukit Batok 106 Mountain and spot height in metres
===== Weathered material

Height in metres
120
80
60
40
20
Mean sea level
Depth in metres

WEST   EAST
Western Ridge | Jurong Plain | Central Hills | Serangoon Plain | Tampines Hills | Changi Hills

Younger alluvia of various types
Jurong formation (Triassic sedimentary rock)
Younger alluvia of various types
Bukit Timah granite
Old alluvium

Schematic cross-section west to east across Singapore island   Not to scale

Source: *Longman Atlas: Singapore and the World* (Singapore: Pearson South Asia, 2002).

Hindu weddings: joining hands in front of the **agni** *(fire).*

Singapore, there is still a strong preference for arranged marriages, although love marriages (i.e. non-arranged marriages) are on the increase. Today, arranged marriages are very different from those of earlier times. Previously, it was common for the couple not to set eyes on each other until the final wedding ritual. Now, when couples enter into an arranged marriage, they are given the time and opportunity to get to know their potential spouse beforehand.

Preparations for a Hindu wedding can start as early as a year before the wedding itself. An auspicious date has to be found, wedding invitations are usually delivered personally, and the parents of the bride have to make gold jewellery for their daughter. Weddings are usually held in temples. Dowries are uncommon, especially when both the bride and groom are Singaporeans.

A day before the wedding, the palms and feet of the bride are decorated with henna-like drawings called Mehndi. A canopy or *mandapa* decorated with flowers is erected where the wedding is to take place. On the wedding morning, various ablutionary rituals are performed on both the bride and the groom in their own homes. Their bodies are anointed with turmeric, sandalwood paste and oils, which cleanse the body, softening the skin, and making it aromatic.

The Hindu marriage ceremony is an elaborate process lasting one to two hours. The rites are highly symbolic, but vary from community to community. However, the

Hinduism: Sri Srinivasa Perumal Temple (detail).

thali (marriage pendant)-tying rite is an essential part of these religious ceremonies, during which the bridegroom ties the *thali* around the bride's neck with three knots. It is imperative that all Hindu women, once married, wear their marriage pendants. By accepting the *thali*, the bride promises that she will henceforth serve God, her husband and her parents-in-law (symbolized by the three knots). This act confirms the marriage. A female relative of the groom actually helps in tying the third knot. This is essentially because of the importance given to the final nature of the marriage.

Another important rite is the donning of two rings, symbolizing faithfulness, by both the bride and groom.

Hinduism Hindus make up about 4 per cent of the total population. This figure has remained stable over the past four to five decades, with only slight fluctuations due to migration and conversion.

However, this numerically small group is also diverse. Indeed, although TAMILS have historically been the dominant group within Singapore's Hindu community, other regional and linguistic groups of Hindus have also been present in Singapore since the early years of the 20th century. The interests of most of these groups are protected by officially registered institutions. In more recent years, the increasing number of Indian nationals living and working in Singapore has also had an impact on the local Hindu community, in terms of both numbers and practice.

Twenty-four Hindu temples—a majority of which are built in south Indian architectural styles—have been registered in Singapore. They have all been constructed and consecrated in strict accordance with prescriptions set down in the Agamas—the scriptures of the three major theological traditions in Hinduism (Vaishnavism, Shaivism and Shaktism). The temples are staffed by trained ritual specialists, most of whom are from Tamil Nadu in India. A large number of these temples are dedicat-

ed to Siva—one of the three principal deities in the Hindu pantheon (the other two being Vishnu and Brahma)—and to mother goddesses.

Regional festivals, fasts and rituals from both south and north India, as well as 'festival Hinduism'—the colourful celebrations of THAIPUSAM, THEEMIDHI and DEEPAVALI—are all prominent in Singapore.

'Home-grown' Hindu groups—those which have formulated their own specific versions of Hinduism—have also developed. Some examples are Krishna Our Guide (registered in 1970); the Hindu Centre (registered in 1978); and Sri Samayapuram Mariamman Pillaigal (registered in 2005).

Hindustanis Term used to describe the north Indian community. At various times, it has included people known as 'Bengalis', 'Baboos', 'Upwallahs', 'Bhojpuris' and 'Biharis'. Up until the late 20th century, many Hindustanis worked as dairy farmers (*doodhwallahs*), washer-men (dhobis), watchmen (chowkidars), tea-shop owners (*chaiwallahs*) and Indian sweet-meat sellers (*mithai-wallahs*).

The only north Indian Hindu temple in Singapore, the SHREE LAKSHMINARAYAN TEMPLE, is run by the Hindustani community. Hindustanis are also prominent in other organizations such as the SINGAPORE NORTH INDIAN HINDU ASSOCIATION and ARYA SAMAJ. Hindustanis have been instrumental in promoting the teaching of Hindi in Singapore's school (*see* HINDI SOCIETY).

HIV/AIDS Human Immunodeficiency Virus/Acquired Immune Deficiency Syndrome. The first case in Singapore was reported in 1985. By October 2005, 2,584 Singaporeans were known to have been infected with HIV, including 25 children. Of these, 999 were asymptomatic carriers, 631 had full-blown AIDS, and 954 had died.

About 96 per cent of cases were sexually transmitted—66 per cent among heterosexuals, mostly through casual sex with prostitutes, and 30 per cent in homosexuals and bisexuals. Only a small number were transmitted through intravenous drug use and mother-to-child transmission.

HIV/AIDS: Action for AIDS poster advertising candlelight memorial, 16 May 2004.

Hinduism: India-derived reform movements Hinduism in Singapore includes a range of 'India-derived movements' (also described as 'neo-Hindu movements', 'Hindu reform movements' and 'new religious movements'). Some prominent examples are the Ramakrishna Mission (left), Radha Soami Satsang, the Brahma Kumari Raja Yoga Centre, the Sai Baba Movement, the Sri Aurobindo Society, Amma's Society, Eckankar Satsang and the Sree Narayana Mission.

Twenty-five of these movements have been established, the earliest registered in 1948 and the most recent in July 2005. Some of the more recently founded are closely integrated with 'mainstream' Hinduism, and draw on standard Hindu rituals, belief structures and sacred texts. Many focus on specific aspects of the religion, such as yoga, meditation and self-development.

Ho Ah Loke

Ho Ching

Ho Kwon Ping

Jesmine Ho

The majority of cases were males (93 per cent), with 57 per cent in the 30–49 age group. However, women and children are considered a vulnerable group, leading the Ministry of Health to set up the HIV Women and Children's Fund, for HIV-positive women and their children.

In 2004, HIV-testing was made a standard of care during pregnancy, with the aim of preventing mother-to-child transmission. Since then, 11 women have been found to be HIV-positive. From July 2005, the government has also made it compulsory for people to be informed if their spouse is HIV postive, so as to encourage early testing and the taking of necessary precautions. Since then, 41 women have been told of their husbands' infection.

One in 25 gay men in Singapore is HIV-positive (*see* HOMOSEXUALITY). Following discussions with gay activists, the government has launched a pilot project to make HIV self-test kits more widely available. The objective is to encourage early detection and treatment, and the prevention of transmission. The kits can detect HIV from saliva in 20 minutes.

See also ACTION FOR AIDS.

Ho, Jesmine (1966–) Sportswoman. Jesmine Ho Yen Wah won the World Masters tenpin bowling title when she defeated Denmark's Iben Tchu at the inaugural World Masters Championship in Abu Dhabi in 1991. She withdrew from the sport after the Asian FIQ Championships in 1992.

Ho returned to bowling three years later, partnering Katherine Lee to win the doubles silver medal at the World FIQ Championships in Reno, United States. The pair became the first Singaporean women to win medals in that competition.

Ho won both bronze and silver medals at the Asian Games in 1998. She was also winner of the Singapore Masters Cup and the Singapore Open title. In 1999, her achievements included winning the ATBC Championship; silver and bronze medals at the Southeast Asian Games; and the Cathay Super Bowl Classic title. She also won the Malaysian Open; the Malaysia Masters Cup; and the First Tournament of Champions the following year. Ho was later inducted into the SINGAPORE SPORTS COUNCIL HALL OF FAME.

Ho Ah Loke (1901–1982) Businessman and film producer. Born in British Guiana (present-day Guyana), Ho Ah Loke studied in Edinburgh and Hong Kong. He later settled in Penang, where he started out screening films in 1925, developing his business in northern Malaya and southern Thailand. In order to extend his reach, he began a partnership with SHAW BROTHERS, and by the start of World War II, Ho was recognized as Malaya's 'movie tycoon'. In 1948, he approached LOKE WAN THO. Together, they formed a company called Associated, International and Loke Theatres, of which Ho became director.

Eager to explore film production, Ho moved to Singapore and started his own production house, Keris Film, in 1951. This became CATHAY-KERIS FILMS in 1953. Ho's confidence in local talent gave the industry a considerable boost and raised levels of creativity. Among his accomplishments was the production of *Buloh Perundu* (Bamboo Grove) (1953), believed to be the first local movie in colour, and PONTIANAK (1957), the first film in the series of the same name.

In 1960, Ho moved back to Kuala Lumpur, where he co-founded Merdeka Studio. Ho was the younger brother of PHILIP HOALIM SR.

Ho Chee Kong (1963–) Composer. Ho Chee Kong completed his musical studies at the University of Cincinnati in Ohio, and began teaching composition at the YONG SIEW TOH CONSERVATORY OF MUSIC. He became associate director of that institution in 2002.

Ho's compositions include orchestral, chamber, choral, piano and electro-acoustic works, which have been performed throughout Asia, Europe and North America. He has been composer-in-residence of the Philharmonic Chamber Choir and music advisor to the Huqin Quartet, and chaired the International Computer Music Conference in Singapore in 2003. He is also active on committees within the Ministry of Education and the National Arts Council.

Ho Ching (1953–) Businesswoman. Ho Ching was educated at the University of Singapore where she graduated with a first class honours degree in electrical and electronics engineering. She later obtained a master of science from Stanford University in 1982. Ho started out as an engineer with the Ministry of Defence. In 1987, she joined the Singapore Technologies Group as deputy director of engineering, and became its president and chief executive officer before retiring in 2001. She became executive director and chief executive officer of TEMASEK HOLDINGS in May 2002.

Ho Kah Leong: Speak Mandarin campaign, 1992.

Under her leadership, Temasek Holdings has become more transparent, and has a strategy to invest in Asia and other emerging markets, and to grow Singapore's gross national product. In 1985, Ho Ching married LEE HSIEN LOONG (who became prime minister in 2004). In 2005, *Fortune* magazine ranked her 11th among the world's most powerful women in business outside the United States.

Ho Kah Leong (1937–) Teacher, politician and artist. Ho Kah Leong was educated at Chung Cheng High School, the Nanyang Academy of Fine Arts (NAFA) and Nanyang University, where he obtained a degree in physics (1963). He began his career as a teacher at Nan Chiau High School (1965–70) before moving to Chung Hwa Girls' School (1970–75).

Ho was elected member of Parliament for Jurong in 1966 on the People's Action Party ticket, and rose to become senior parliamentary secretary at the Ministry of Education; the Ministry of Communications, Information and the Arts; and the Ministry of the Environment.

From 1968 to 1981, Ho served as president of the Singapore Chinese Teachers' Union. From 1975 to 1981, he also served as general manager of the Educational Publications Bureau.

Ho also became known as a painter, and held his first solo exhibition in 1990. When he retired from politics in 1996, he was appointed principal of NAFA, remaining in that office until 2004.

Ho Kwon Ping (1952–) Businessman, activist and journalist. Born in Hong Kong, Ho Kwon Ping was the eldest son of HO RIH HWA and Li Lienfung. He grew up in Thailand, attending an American school, but later travelled to Taiwan, where he studied Chinese at Tunghai University. He then went to Stanford University in the United States, becoming involved in student politics and journalism there. He was suspended from Stanford due to his involvement in radical activities.

Ho then returned to Singapore. He studied at the University of Singapore, graduating with a degree in political science and economics. He then worked as a journalist, writing for the *Far Eastern Economic Review*. However in 1979, Ho was detained for several months under the INTERNAL SECURITY ACT for obtaining and using classified information for his articles.

After his release, Ho went to Hong Kong to continue his work for the *Far Eastern Economic Review*, but later returned to Singapore to join his father's family business, after the latter suffered a stroke. Ho and his wife, Claire, expanded the family's Wah Chang and Thai Wah Groups, and established BANYAN TREE Hotels and Resorts.

Ho has served as chairman of MediaCorp (2004–), the Singapore

Herman Hochstadt, left.

Management University Board (2000–), Singapore Power (1994–2000), the Singapore Environment Council and the Speak Mandarin campaign; and main board director of Standard Chartered Bank.

Ho Minfong (1951–) Author. Born in Rangoon, Ho Minfong grew up in Thailand and Singapore. She attended Tunghai University in Taiwan and Cornell University and has worked as a lecturer, journalist and relief worker in Singapore, Thailand and along the Thai-Cambodian border.

Ho's 'Tanjong Rhu' won first prize in the 1982 Singapore Short Story Competition and first prize in the 1983 Asiaweek (Hong Kong) Short Story Competition. 'Sing to the Dawn' was a 1975 prize-winning story which Ho developed into a novel (1984) which was then turned into a musical. Ho's second novel, *Rice without Rain* (1986), won the 1988 National Book Development Council of Singapore Award for Fiction, and was runner-up in the 1987 Commonwealth Book Awards. Together with *The Clay Marble* (1992) and *The Stone Goddess* (2003), these novels for young adults feature young and strong female protagonists from villages in Thailand or Cambodia. Her books for younger children include *Hush! A Thai Lullaby* (1996), which won the Caldecott Honor Award in 1997. Ho received the Southeast Asia Write Award in 1996, and the CULTURAL MEDALLION for Literature in 1997. Ho is the daughter of writer Li Lienfung and the late HO RIH HWA, and sister of HO KWON PING. She lives in Ithaca, New York state, with her American husband and their three children.

Ho Rih Hwa (1917–1999) Businessman and diplomat. Ho Rih Hwa was educated at Yeung Ching Chinese School; Lingnam High School; Nanking University in China (1942); and Cornell University in the United States (1944). In 1946, he married Li Lienfung, daughter of K.C. Li (head of Wah Chang Trading Corporation) and began working in his father-in-law's firm. In 1948, Ho was sent to Bangkok to work in Wah Chang's Thai branch, known as Thai Wah. He turned this into one of Thailand's largest producers of and traders in tapioca. Ho became chairman of the Wah Chang Group in Singapore and the Thai Wah

Group in Thailand, retaining these positions until his death.

In 1967, he was appointed Singapore's ambassador to Thailand, and later Singapore's representative to the European Economic Community. He also served as Singapore's ambassador to Belgium and West Germany, and representative to the United Nations in Geneva (1972–74).

Over the period 1974–81, he built Wah Chang International into a multinational group, but in 1981 he suffered a mild stroke and transferred most of his business responsibilities to his eldest son, HO KWON PING.

Ho was awarded the Public Service Star (BBM) (1969) and the MERITORIOUS SERVICE MEDAL (1972). He was also admitted into the most Noble Order of the Crown of Thailand (1966) and was made Chevalier de la Légion d'Honneur (France, 1978).

Ho Yeow Sun (1972–) Singer. Popularly known as Sun, Ho Yeow Sun released her debut album, *Sun With Love,* in 2002. Since then, her three Mandarin albums have reached multiple platinum status. In 2003, she embarked on an 80-concert Asian tour. Her homecoming concert in January 2004 at the SINGAPORE INDOOR STADIUM was the first time a local singer drew an audience of over 11,000.

In recognition of Ho's contributions to volunteer and community work, the Junior Chamber of Singapore awarded her the *Outstanding Young Person 2002* Award. In November 2003, she won the *Outstanding Young Person of the World* Award under the auspices of Junior Chamber International.

Ho is married to Kong Hee, the founder of CITY HARVEST CHURCH. The singer and church were at the centre of a controversy in 2002 when allegations were made that the church had promoted Ho's singing career.

Hoalim, Philip, Sr (1895–1980) Lawyer and politician. Born in British Guiana (present-day Guyana), Philip Hoalim Sr was educated in Guyana and London. His younger brother was film producer HO AH LOKE. Hoalim was called to the Bar at Middle Temple but was subsequently persuaded to settle in Singapore by SONG ONG SIANG. Hoalim initially worked with Song but later established his own firm.

In 1945, Hoalim's nephew LIM KEAN CHYE, and LIM HONG BEE, asked him to set up a political party. The MALAYAN DEMOCRATIC UNION was formed shortly thereafter, Hoalim becoming the party's chairman.

Hochstadt, Herman (1933–) Civil servant and diplomat. Herman Ronald Hochstadt was educated at St Andrew's School and at the University of Malaya in Singapore, where he graduated in 1957 with an honours degree. He joined the Administrative Service as assistant secretary at the Ministry

of Finance (1959–62), and became permanent secretary for the Ministry of Communications in 1972 and for the Ministry of Finance in 1981.

Hochstadt has served as Singapore's high commissioner to Mauritius, Tanzania, South Africa, Botswana, Swaziland and Namibia. He was appointed group chairman of ECICS Holdings Ltd, and has served on the boards of numerous organizations, including the Civil Service College, the Singapore International Foundation, the Presidential Council for Minority Rights and the Presidential Elections Committee. In 1995, he was appointed pro-chancellor of Nanyang Technological University.

Hochstadt was awarded the Public Administration Medal (Gold) (1978) and the Public Service Star (1998).

Hock Lee bus riots Workers at the small Hock Lee Amalgamated Bus Company belonged to two rival unions—the left-wing SINGAPORE BUS WORKERS' UNION (SBWU), led by FONG SWEE SUAN; and the Hock Lee Employees' Union, backed by company management.

In 1955, Hock Lee Bus workers affiliated with the SBWU decided to launch a strike in order to seek higher wages and better working conditions. Although a settlement with the company at first appeared likely, pro-communist elements within the union exploited the dispute as a means of forcing a confrontation with the government.

Fong Swee Suan declared that Hock Lee workers were to strike on 23 April 1955, and urged workers from other bus companies to strike as well if the dispute was not resolved. Events escalated when the Hock Lee Bus Company dismissed 229 employees belonging to the SBWU. These employees then started a hunger strike and picketed the company's depot.

Students from Chinese middle schools joined the pickets. However, the bus company stood by its decision to dismiss the employees, and managed nevertheless to have 40 of its 70 buses provide transport services.

On 27 April 1955, police tried to break up the picket. Fifteen strikers were injured.

Ho Minfong

Ho Rih Hwa

Ho Yeow Sun

Hock Lee bus riots: driver's company badge (below); picketers sheltering from water cannons.

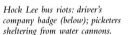

Hock Teck See Temple: temple doors (top); Cai Shen—the God of Wealth.

The strikers and students were thus able to gain greater public support. The situation became so volatile that police advised the company to cease bus operations.

On 30 April, the company offered to reinstate the dismissed workers. However, this did not satisfy the picketers. On 8 May, riot police were despatched to disperse them. Three days later, the SBWU declared a two-day strike in protest against the police use of force. All bus services in Singapore came to a halt.

The following day, police again moved in to disperse picketers, using fire hoses and tear gas. One student, Chong Loon Chuan, was shot and wounded. Instead of sending Chong to a nearby hospital for treatment, student protesters paraded him for more than two hours in an effort to garner public support. By the time Chong was sent to hospital, he was dead.

By dawn on 13 May the riot was finally over. Four persons had been killed and 31 injured.

See also CHINESE MIDDLE SCHOOL RIOTS.

Hock Teck See Temple Also known as Palmer Road Fuk Tak Chi in Cantonese (not to be confused with FUK TAK CHI TEMPLE on Telok Ayer Street), this small single-storey temple on Palmer Road is one of the oldest in Singapore. Established as a joss house in 1819 by HAKKA immigrants from Guangdong, the original temple building was constructed in 1844. It is dedicated to Tua Peh Kong—a tutelary deity believed to watch over an area (*see* TAOISM). Also enshrined in the temple are Guan Di (the God of War) and Guanyin (the Goddess of Mercy).

In terms of its physical attributes, the temple is well-known for its 69-cm high copper bell dating from the late Qing dynasty. Today, the bell is rung during festivals or when a devotee makes a donation to the temple.

Hockchia The term 'Hockchia' refers to both the Chinese dialect group and the language spoken by its members. According to

the 2000 Census of Population, there were only 15,468 Hockchia, forming 0.6 per cent of the total Chinese population.

The Hockchia first arrived in Singapore in the late 19th century. As lucrative trades were already dominated by other dialect groups which had arrived earlier, the Hockchia had to earn their living as rickshaw pullers (*see* RICKSHAWS) and manual labourers. In the early days, their residences were clustered around Victoria Street, Queen Street and Ophir Road. Singapore Futsing Association was founded in 1910 to cater to the community.

Transport is one major trade run by the Hockchia. The automotive parts industry also became a trade dominated by the Hockchia. Two major bus companies, Hock Lee Amalgamated Bus Company and Green Bus Company, were founded and managed by the Hockchia.

Established in the early 20th century, the Church of the True Light and Hock Ching Kong Kien Poh Toh, founded in 1927, are significant places of worship for the Hockchia. Prominent Hockchia include Ong Ban Guan, founder of automotive components distributor Tye Soon Limited and Goi Seng Hui, 'Popiah King' and chairman of food manufacturing company TEE YIH JIA.

Hoffman, Leslie C. (1915–1987) Journalist and editor. Born in Penang, Leslie C. Hoffman was educated at St Xavier's School. On leaving school, he joined the MALAYA TRIBUNE, and by 1941, he was editorial chairman of the *Morning Tribune*—a tabloid owned by the Tribune Group.

During the Japanese Occupation, Hoffman was detained by the Japanese. While in detention, he met Robert Burns, a fellow inmate and chairman of THE STRAITS TIMES. Burns offered to give Hoffman a position at that newspaper once the war ended. Hoffman joined *The Straits Times* in September 1945 as a sub-editor. In April 1956, he was appointed editor-in-chief, making him the first Asian to head the newspaper.

Hoffman retired from journalism in 1970 and emigrated to Australia. There, he lectured at the Royal Melbourne Institute of Technology's School of Journalism, eventually becoming dean. He retired from that post in 1985.

Hokkien Chinese dialect group. The term 'Hokkien' refers to the members belonging to the community as well as the dialect they speak. Originating in China's Fujian (Hokkien) province, primarily Xiamen and Quanzhou, Hokkiens make up the largest Chinese dialect group in Singapore, with the TEOCHEW and CANTONESE forming the next largest groups. According to the 2000 Census of Population, Hokkiens number more than a million and thus make up 41 per cent of Singapore's Chinese community.

During the 19th and 20th centuries, many Hokkiens migrated to Southeast Asia due to social and political unrest, overpopulation and scarce farmland in China. The first major wave of Hokkien immigrants arrived in Singapore around 1821, shortly after the founding of the free port by the British East India Company. One of the early structures set up by these immigrants was a small shrine in Telok Ayer dedicated to Mazu (the Goddess of the Sea). By 1842, this was replaced by the THIAN HOCK KENG TEMPLE, which was built by the then thriving Hokkien community and operated as the headquarters for the Hokkien Huay Kuan (present-day SINGAPORE HOKKIEN HUAY KUAN) from 1850 to 1954.

Early Hokkien immigrants engaged in trading spices, coffee, rubber and rice, but were also involved in banking, finance and shipping. The *chap he tiam* (literally 'mixed goods shop' or 'provisions shop') trade, in which canned goods originating in Fujian and household items were sold, was dominated by the Hokkiens. Many such shops grew to become modern 'minimarts', but even these are now struggling in the face of competition from larger supermarket chains.

The Telok Ayer and Amoy Street areas of Chinatown were dominated by Hokkiens. Like other communities, they set up mutual aid associations—such as the Singapore Hokkien Huay Kuan on Telok Ayer Street— to represent their interests in dealing with the British colonial administration and other Chinese dialect groups. Other organizations soon followed. The size and dominance of the Hokkien community was such that many influential Chinese could be counted among its ranks. These included merchants TAN TOCK SENG and CHEANG HONG LIM, and businessmen LEE KONG CHIAN and TAN LARK SYE. Contemporary members of the community who have made their mark include banker WEE CHO YAW.

Under the auspices of the Singapore Hokkien Huay Kuan, the community also provided for the education of Hokkien children by setting up a number of schools. Established in 1849, Chong Wen Ge (now defunct) was Singapore's earliest recorded public educational institution. Among the

Hokkien: provisions shop, Bukit Panjang, 1986.

other schools founded by the community were AI TONG SCHOOL, Chong Fu School and Kong Hwa School. The land on which NANYANG UNIVERSITY was built was donated by Tan Lark Sye in 1853.

Hokkien cuisine is not as popular as Teochew or Cantonese cuisine. Hokkien dishes which have gained a wider popularity include HOKKIEN MEE and oyster omelette (known as 'or lua' in Hokkien).

While the number of Hokkien speakers has decreased over the years due to changes in educational policies, the Speak Mandarin campaign and intermarriage between Chinese dialect groups, Hokkien has had a significant influence on SINGLISH, with many Hokkien terms and phrases having made their way into Singapore's local patois.

Hokkien mee It is believed that Hokkien migrant workers, who toiled in the local noodle (mee) factories, invented this dish in Singapore. They would gather around Rochor Road at the end of the day with bags of extra noodles from the factory and fry them at night. Within a short period of time, 'copycat' hawkers had set up stalls in the vicinity. Many older Singaporeans still call this dish 'Rochor mee'. Hokkien mee consists essentially of yellow wheat noodles fried with rice vermicelli. It is flavoured with prawn stock and topped with prawns, squid rings and thin slices of pork. The ingredients used for the stock are often a trade secret but might include a mix of pork bones, clams, fried and dried flat fish (tee po), sugar cane and, of course, prawns. The trick is to smother the noodles in the stock and fry its flavour into the noodles until almost dry.

Holi Also known as the 'festival of colours' or 'festival of spring', Holi falls in the month of Chaitra (March–April). Holi originated in the Uttar Pradesh and Bihar regions of India, and took its name from a story about Holika—the daughter of an evil king who was sent by her father to burn her brother, a devotee of Vishnu. Holika was herself burnt—as her brother was protected by Vishnu—and sought repentance. The religious component of the festival involves the lighting of bonfires to destroy evil. The cultural side of Holi is displayed in the practice of people spraying coloured water and powder at each other. These colours signify spring.

In Singapore, Holi has been celebrated on a large scale only since the 1990s, with Hindi schools, and groups such as the Bhojpuri Society, organizing events. In 2006, Holi celebrations, organized jointly by community groups and temples, including the SHREE LAKSHMINARAYAN TEMPLE, attracted 3,000 people. Holi celebrations commence in the evening in Singapore, rather than in the morning, as is the case in India. Locally, Holi has emerged as one of the most popular Indian festivals. Its recent

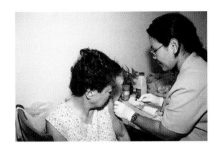

Home Nursing Foundation

popularity has been attributed, to some extent, to Holi's inclusion in many Bollywood films.

Holland Village Small commercial enclave at the junction of Holland Road and Holland Avenue. Holland Village and Holland Road are believed to be named after an early resident, Hugh Holland, who was an architect. In the 1950s and 1960s, the 'Village', with its shops and places to eat and drink, was a regular haunt for British servicemen from the nearby Portsdown area. After the BRITISH WITHDRAWAL FROM SINGAPORE in 1971, the village attracted local residents from the Buona Vista Housing Estate (built in 1972) as well as EXPATRIATES employed in the education and commercial sectors, who stayed on in the district. Today, it is a fashionable hangout for both Singaporeans and expatriates, drawn mainly by its restaurants, specialist shops and relaxed atmosphere.

Hollandse Club This club was formed in 1908 by Dutch businessmen for social and family activities. It's first clubhouse was located on Cairnhill Road. After World War II a plot of land was acquired at Camden Park on which a new clubhouse was constructed. The pre-war grounds and facilities were sold to Char Yong Association. Throughout the years the club increased its range of facilities, with spas, swimming pools, tennis and squash courts, a bowling alley, gymnasium and several food and beverage outlets. As of 2006, membership stood at 1,700, which was made up of members of over 40 nationalities.

Home Nursing Foundation Voluntary welfare organization founded in December 1976 by Dr TOH CHIN CHYE. The Home Nursing Foundation (HNF) offers home nursing care for the elderly sick who cannot afford private nursing care. During its early years, the HNF nurses in their distinctive white uniforms travelled all over Singapore to kampongs and new housing estates.

Between 1986 and 1996, the HNF underwent a reorganization on the advice of the National Advisory Council for the Aged. Full-time home nursing, rehabilitative and day-care services were started. Seven Senior Citizens' Health Care Centres were also opened to provide day-care, rehabilitation, health education and health-

screening programmes for the elderly sick.

The HNF, which subsidizes needy patients, now runs 12 home nursing centres. Patients pay between $15 and $35 per visit, compared to between $60 and $120 charged by private home nursing agencies. Fees are waived for those who cannot afford them.

homosexuality Sexual acts between men are illegal in Singapore. The legal prohibition of homosexuality originated in Victorian anti-sodomy statutes that were handed down through the Penal Code. Most men who have been convicted of having sex with another man have been tried under 'Outrages on Decency' (Section 377A of the code) and 'Outraging Modesty' (Section 354) charges.

Arrests of men for homosexuality peaked in the 1980s, when police decoys were often deployed to apprehend men who sought sex with other men. Punishment ranged from jail terms and fines to CANING, as well as media exposure. However, from the mid-1990s, these tactics were discouraged, and the authorities confined their activities to raids on discotheques on grounds such as checking for drugs and minors.

In Singapore it is a crime to engage in what section 377 of the Penal Code defines as 'carnal intercourse against the order of nature with any man, woman or animal'. Offenders can be punished with imprisonment for life, or with imprisonment for up to ten years, and are also liable to a fine.

Section 377A of the code further provides that 'any male person who, in public or private, commits, or abets the commission by any male person, of any act of gross indecency with another male person, shall be punished with imprisonment for a term which may extend to two years'.

Sex between two or more consenting males is thus illegal, although the law does not forbid sex between two or more consenting females. The Singapore courts have also ruled that oral sex (both fellatio and cunnilingus) constitutes a crime unless followed by penile-vaginal sex.

Holi: revellers splashed with coloured water and powder.

Hokkien mee

Holland Village: al fresco dining.

Hon Sui Sen

Hoo Ah Kay

Honey wagon: final collection of night soil by the traditional method, January 1987.

Continued legal prohibition and police pressure eventually led to the birth of PEOPLE LIKE US (PLU)—an informal group which sought to have homosexuality decriminalized, and which advocated equality and fairness.

The 'Asian values' discourse was invoked to justify an official non-acceptance of homosexuality. Films dealing with gay and lesbian issues were either banned or restricted to single screenings at the SINGAPORE INTERNATIONAL FILM FESTIVAL. For example, Taiwanese film *Formula 17* (2004), was banned in Singapore because its plot, involving gay characters, was said by the censors to 'create an illusion of a homosexual utopia'.

Even though gay parades continued to be prohibited and homosexual acts were still considered illegal, there was a brief period of seemingly greater official tolerance of homosexuality in 2003, after Prime Minister GOH CHOK TONG announced in an interview with *TIME* that gays could hold positions in government in Singapore.

Gay theatre also flourished in 2003-04. Local plays with a gay theme, such as *Asian Boys*, *Top or Bottom* and *Mardi Gras*, and musicals such as *The Wedding Banquet* and *M Butterfly*, were also well-received. Bars and discos catering to a gay clientele began to open in greater numbers.

However, the atmosphere of tolerance was affected by the spread of HIV/AIDS. There was public concern over a slight increase in HIV infection rates among gay men recorded in 2004. This concern was occasionally expressed in an irrational manner. For example, in April 2005, a private school spent $40,000 to replace toilet bowls, chairs and fixtures after a teacher was discovered to be gay. Health authorities alleged that events such as 'Nation'—an annual party which had been organized by gay entrepreneurs on National Day since 2001—were linked to the rise in AIDS cases. Such events were no longer granted official approval, some being relocated to neighbouring countries such as Thailand.

There is relatively little reference to lesbians in public debates about AIDS in Singapore. The lesbian community has managed to transcend official censure by operating on the internet. PLU has started an online news service and discussion group called SIGNEL. A website, Yawning Bread, has archived information relating to gay and lesbian issues in Singapore. ADLUS and MenAfterWork were established as recreational groups. Lesbian websites include RedQuEEn, Looking Glass and Herstory.

Hon Sui Sen (1916–1983) Civil servant and politician. Born in Balik Pulau, Penang, Benedict Hon Sui Sen was educated at St Xavier's Institution.

In 1935, Hon moved to Singapore to study at Raffles College, where he graduated with a first class diploma in science (1938).

He was appointed a cadet in the Straits Settlements Civil Service where he was made a magistrate, and then deputy collector of land revenue. Hon specialized in Land Office work, and was subsequently transferred to the Administrative Service.

In 1957, he was appointed commissioner of lands and permanent secretary to the Ministry of Local Government Lands and Housing (1957–59). Later, he was made permanent secretary in the Prime Minister's Office (1959–61). In 1961, under the first Five-Year Development Plan, the ECONOMIC DEVELOPMENT BOARD (EDB) was established and Hon was appointed its first chairman.

Hon retired from the Administrative Service in 1965, but continued to serve as chairman of the EDB. In 1968, he was appointed first chairman and president of the Development Bank of Singapore (DBS BANK).

For his services, Hon was awarded the MERITORIOUS SERVICE MEDAL (1962); the Malaysia Medal (1964); the DISTINGUISHED SERVICE ORDER (1967); and an honorary doctorate by the University of Singapore (1969). He also served as chairman of Jurong Shipyard Ltd; National Iron and Steel Mills Ltd; Keppel Shipyard; Sembawang Shipyard; Jurong Shipbuilders Ltd; Neptune Orient Lines; and the Insurance Corporation of Singapore.

In 1970, Hon contested the seat of Havelock constituency on the People's Action Party ticket. He won this seat, and was appointed minister for finance, a post he held until his death from a heart attack on 14 October 1983. Hon was admitted into the ORDER OF TEMASEK (First Class) posthumously in 1984. The Hon Sui Sen Memorial Library at the National University of Singapore was named in his honour.

honey wagon Popular term for the truck that was used to carry night soil, or human waste. The honey wagon was a familiar sight on Singapore roads before the advent of modern sanitation. It carried three tiers of night-soil buckets. Filled buckets were collected from shops and homes every morning and replaced by empty ones. Rural dwellers had to provide their own buckets, and collection was of waste was made once in every two or three days. Immediately after World War II, this unpleasant task was performed by Japanese prisoners-of-war. With the introduction of modern sanitation across the island, the collection of night soil was eventually phased out, and finally ceased in 1987.

Hong Leong Foundation This foundation was established in 1980 by the Hong Leong Group. It has made major contributions to charities and cultural organizations, including the NATIONAL KIDNEY FOUNDATION and the NATIONAL ARTS COUNCIL. Major donations have included a $2.8 million gift to the ASIAN CIVILSATIONS MUSEUM, which

named a gallery in honour of Hong Leong's founder, KWEK HONG PNG. In 2005, the foundation was named a Friend of the Arts.

Hong San See Chinese temple. The original Hong San See (literally meaning 'Phoenix Hill Temple' in Hokkien) was erected in 1829 on Tras Street by immigrants from the Lam Ann district of Fujian province, China. It was built in honour of the deity Guangze Zunwang. When the land the temple occupied was acquired by the government in 1907, the temple trustees used their $50,000 compensation to rebuild the temple on MOHAMED SULTAN ROAD. As with many Chinese temples, Hong San See's premises were also used as a school, catering to children from nearby villages such as Bukit Ho Swee Nan Ming School, as it was called, had to close in 1925 due to financial problems.

The 1907 temple reconstruction was headed by main contractor Lim Loh, the father of LIM BO SENG. The temple was completed in 1913 at a cost of $56,000. Carved brackets, frames and columns support the roof, which is held together without nails. Typical of beam-frame construction, the rounded timber rafters are a showcase of complex trusses using vertical and horizontal struts. Colourful *chien nien* ornamentation and plaster reliefs provide the decorative elements (*chien nien* being a traditional southern Chinese technique which uses small porcelain pieces to create shapes such as leaves, flowers and birds).

The temple's main hall, which is raised on a 9-m podium to reflect its importance, houses the altar to patron deity Guangze Zunwang, and secondary altars to Chenghuang (the City God), Xuantian Shangdi and Guanyin (the Goddess of Mercy). On the back columns of the main hall are verses penned by the late poet and calligrapher PAN SHOU. Hong San See was gazetted as a national monument in November 1978.

Hoo Ah Kay (Whampoa) (1816–1880) Businessman and community leader. Born in Whampoa (present-day Huangpu) in Canton (present-day Guangzhou), China, Hoo Ah Kay came to Singapore in 1830 to assist in his father's ship-chandling business—Whampoa and Co. Hoo's nickname, 'Whampoa', was derived from his place of birth as well as the name of his family's business.

Whampoa and Co. had offices on the corner of Bonham Street and BOAT QUAY. It supplied ships and local residents with meat, bread and vegetables. Later, the business moved to Telok Ayer Street.

Hoo took over the business when his father died, and from 1840 he became the exclusive provisioner and ship chandler to the British Royal Navy. His ability to speak English, as well as his close connections with naval officials, helped Hoo emerge as one of the most successful businessmen of his time.

In 1854, Hoo opened Whampoa Bakery on Havelock Road, which soon became the largest bakery in Singapore. At one point, Whampoa and Co. supplied all of Singapore's bread.

Hoo had wide-ranging business interests. He was named director of the Tanjong Pagar Dock Co. Ltd, and was elected provisional director of the Singapore Railway Co. Ltd (1871). He also owned numerous properties, including a plot of land in Tanglin that he donated to the colonial authorities for use as part of the SINGAPORE BOTANIC GARDENS in exchange for some land on the banks of the Singapore River. It was here that Whampoa opened Singapore's first ice house in a godown at CLARKE QUAY.

Hoo was the first Asian to be appointed a member of the Legislative Council (1869); was appointed Singapore consul for China in 1877; and later became the only ethnic Chinese ever to become an extraordinary member of the Executive Council. He sat on the committee to establish a public library and museum in Singapore, and on the boards of Raffles Institution, Raffles Girls' School and Tan Tock Seng Hospital.

The gardens of Hoo's homes were famous. These were named Nansheng Gardens, and were planted on a neglected piece of land on Serangoon Road that Hoo had bought in 1840. The 17-acre (6.8 ha) gardens were famous for their aquariums, dwarf bamboo and topiaries.

After Hoo's death, his remains were taken to China and interred near his place of birth. The property on which the gardens were located was sold to SEAH LIANG SEAH, another prominent Chinese businessman. The government named the Whampoa district and the WHAMPOA RIVER after Hoo.

Horsburgh, James (1762–1836) British hydrographer. Captain James Horsburgh of the British EAST INDIA COMPANY was one of the most knowledgeable Europeans of the early 19th century as regards maritime routes between China, Southeast Asia and India. He wrote two important books— *Directions for Sailing To and From the East Indies, China, etc.* (1811) and *Memoir of a Chart Educidating the Navigation of the Straits of Malacca and Sincapour* (1805).

Memoir included a map featuring Singapore and its adjacent islands, as well as the depth-soundings of the surrounding waters. The chart recorded three passageways past Singapore—GOVERNOR'S STRAIT, NEW STRAIT and the VARELLA CHANNEL/OLD STRAIT.

In 1823, Horsburgh's 1805 chart was updated and republished with more detailed depth soundings of the waters around Singapore. In the chart, however, the Keppel Strait remained unidentified, and the Johor Strait was incorrectly labelled as the Old Strait.

See also HORSBURGH LIGHTHOUSE.

Horsburgh Lighthouse Lighthouse built on the island of PEDRA BRANCA. In 1836, a group of merchants in Canton (present-day Guangzhou), led by W. Jardine of JARDINE, MATHESON & CO., decided to raise funds to construct the lighthouse as a memorial to Captain JAMES HORSBURGH, a hydrographer with the British EAST INDIA COMPANY whose intimate knowledge of the seas surrounding India and China, together with improved charts based on his surveys, had greatly contributed to safer navigation. Pedra Branca was a treacherous reef and a hazard to shipping.

Funds amounting to $4,191 were collected, and in 1842 the trustees of the fund informed the government of the Straits Settlements that they were ready to pass the money over for the project to proceed. In 1849, John Turnbull Thomson, the surveyor in Singapore, was instructed to go ahead with the project. He designed a tower 29 m high with a light visible to a distance of 15 nautical miles. The entire lighthouse was to be made of granite to withstand the rough seas and pirate attacks. The light-keeper's quarters were located at the top.

The project took two years to complete. Work on the site was limited to seven months in the year due to heavy seas during the northeast monsoon. Pirates were a constant source of trouble. Granite was quarried at PULAU UBIN and transported 40 km. The lighthouse was completed in 1851 at a total cost of $23,665. While the merchant community had initiated the project and contributed some of the money, the East India Company provided most of the funds on behalf of the Crown. Horsburgh Lighthouse, described as the 'First Pharos of the Eastern Seas', was lighted on 15 October 1851 and still stands.

hospice care Care for patients with life-limiting illnesses. It takes three main forms: inpatient care, day care and home care.

Hospice care in Singapore started in 1985 when the St Joseph's Home set aside 16 beds for terminally ill patients. Over the years, other hospices, such as the Assisi Home and Hospice and the Dover Park Hospice, were established for inpatients. An inpatient hospice provides short-term respite care (to give caregivers a break), and terminal care for patients in the final stages of their illnesses.

Hospice day care involves social and rehabilitative programmes to enhance patients' quality of life. The major portion of the care is home care. Doctors and nurses make regular visits to provide counselling and education, medical and nursing care and pain management services. Patients can also rent equipment such as wheelchairs, oxygen concentrators, special mattresses and commodes.

The Hospice Care Association, a voluntary welfare organization, is the biggest provider of home hospice care. Its teams make more than 26,000 visits a year.

hospitals In 2006, Singapore had 13 public and 16 private hospitals. These include acute-care hospitals (such as NATIONAL UNIVERSITY HOSPITAL and MOUNT ELIZABETH HOSPITAL), community hospitals (such as ANG MO KIO–THYE HUA KWAN HOSPITAL and REN CI HOSPITAL AND MEDICARE CENTRE) and speciality centres (such as the National Cancer Centre). The acute-care hospitals run 24-hour accident-and-emergency units. Community hospitals, nursing homes and hospices, mostly run by voluntary welfare organizations, provide step-down care—for patients who no longer need high-end acute medical care but are not well enough to return home.

Public hospitals account for 80 per cent of hospital care by admissions. They offer medical care at varying service levels depending on the ward chosen. These range from single-bed Class A wards to B1 (four-bed) and B2 wards (six-bed to 12-bed) to open wards in C class. These hospitals take in both private and subsidized patients.

Since 1985, the government has restructured five of its hospitals and six speciality institutes to run as private companies wholly owned by the government.

Hotel de l'Europe Opened in 1857, the Europe—as the hotel was originally known—occupied two GEORGE D. COLEMAN-designed bungalows facing the PADANG.

In the early 1900s, a syndicate was formed to finance the rebuilding of the hotel. Refurbishment was completed in 1907, and the 120-room hotel was renamed the Grand Hotel de l'Europe. When Alfred Viscount Northcliffe visited Singapore in 1921, he observed that 'there are two great rival hotels, the Raffles—which always figures in Far Eastern novels—and the Europe which is said to be the quieter'.

In 1932, the hotel was closed down due to a decline in business and an obligation under the terms of the lease to rebuild.

Horsburgh Lighthouse

Hong San See

Hotel de l'Europe: before demolition to make way for the Supreme Court building.

Initial plans for the hotel's revival were abandoned when the government acquired the land upon which the hotel stood for the SUPREME COURT BUILDINGS in 1934.

See also COCKPIT HOTEL.

Hotel New World collapse On 15 March 1986, at approximately 11.30 a.m., the six-storey Lian Yak Building at 305 Serangoon Road collapsed without warning. In less than a minute, the whole building was reduced to a pile of rubble, burying all those inside. While the building was generally referred to as the Hotel New World, the hotel in fact only occupied the third to sixth floors; on the ground floor was a branch office of the Industrial & Commercial Bank, and on the floor above was a nightclub.

Over the next few days, 17 survivors were dug out from the rubble. The Singapore Civil Defence Force, the Singapore Armed Forces, the Police Task Force and civil engineers involved in tunnelling works for the Mass Rapid Transit system were involved in the rescue work, which was done in several phases. First, beams and debris were removed from the top and the side to give access to the people trapped just below the top layer of rubble. In the second, harder phase, tunnels were made at the side to reach those buried deeper. Rescuers had to use life detection devices to find survivors. The tunnelling had to be done very carefully to avoid triggering a further collapse. By the fourth day, no more survivors were detected. The final death toll was 33.

Hotel New World collapse

Singaporeans from all walks of life contributed to the rescue effort. Companies offered food, drinks and life-saving equipment to the rescue team. People queued to donate blood. Doctors were on standby in all government hospitals to provide immediate medical assistance to survivors.

President Wee Kim Wee appointed Justice L.P. THEAN to head a commission of inquiry to investigate the cause, and recommend measures to prevent a recurrence. The panel found that 'there had not been any triggering act or incident that brought the entire building to the ground'. The panel was of the opinion that 'the root and main cause of the collapse lies in the structural design of the building [which] was so grossly inadequate that it was a matter of time before the building would collapse unless a major and comprehensive effort was made to save it'.

Hotel Properties Limited Property development company. First incorporated in 1980 when it acquired the Hilton Hotel on Orchard Road from the Far Eastern Hotels Group, Hotel Properties Limited (HPL) was founded by PETER FU, and was listed on the Stock Exchange of Singapore in 1982. ONG BENG SENG (Fu's son-in-law) was appointed managing director.

In the following decades, the range of HPL's business activities was extended to include hospitality, food and beverages, and retail and investment holdings. It acquired the franchises for Hard Rock hotels and cafés in a number of Asian countries, and opened a Planet Hollywood in Singapore.

The group has acquired or maintained interests in hotels in many countries, such as the Four Seasons Hotel, Le Meridien and the Hilton in Singapore; and the Concorde Hotels in Kuala Lumpur and the Gold Coast, Australia. It also operates Four Seasons resort-hotels in Bali, the Maldives and London, as well as a number of resorts in Bhutan, Myanmar and Vanuatu.

HPL is also known for residential developments in Singapore, such as Four Seasons Park, Cuscaden Residences, Nassim Jade and Scotts 28, and has maintained a stake in various retail and commercial properties, such as the Forum and Le Meridien Shopping Centre.

The group acquired the franchise to sell and distribute Häagen-Dazs ice-cream in Singapore and Malaysia, and expanded into the manufacture and distribution of sporting goods. HPL's group revenue for 2005 totalled $304 million, with net earnings of $38.3 million.

hotels and restaurants sector The establishment of the SINGAPORE TOURISM BOARD in 1964 marked the beginning of government efforts to promote Singapore as a tourist destination. Between 1970 and 2004, visitor arrivals increased by 8.5 per cent average per annum; over the same period the annu-

House of Tan Yeok Nee, 1910.

al revenue generated by the hotel and restaurant sector, which is heavily dependent on tourism, rose from $200.5 million to $3.5 billion.

In 2003, there were 4,300 food and beverage (F&B) outlets in the country. These generated revenue of $1.5 billion. Restaurants formed the largest group in this category (25.6 per cent of establishments), employing 22,500 people (36.8 per cent of the F&B workforce). In 2005, 37,200 gazetted (as tourist hotels) and non-gazetted hotel rooms, with an average occupancy rate of 84 per cent, generated $1.2 billion in revenue.

The hotel and restaurant sector is particularly vulnerable to global trends. Events such as the ASIAN FINANCIAL CRISIS; the 9/11 terrorist attacks; and the outbreak of SEVERE ACUTE RESPIRATORY SYNDROME (SARS) in 2003, all slowed growth in the industry.

Hougang New town. The name Hougang is the Hanyu Pinyin version of the name Au Kang (literally meaning 'end of the river' in both Hokkien and Teochew). Before its transformation into a public housing estate in the mid-1980s, Au Kang was a rural area stretching from the junction of Yio Chu Kang Road and Serangoon Road, up to the confluence of Tampines Road and Upper Serangoon Road. There were pig farms, vegetable farms and orchards here. The last pig farm was cleared in the mid-1990s. Today, Hougang New Town is a major housing estate with more than 40,000 units. Many Chinese residents of Hougang are TEOCHEW, who were originally from Kampong Ponggol and neighbouring areas.

House of Tan Yeok Nee TAN YEOK NEE was a Teochew businessman who served as Major China (head of the Chinese community) in Johor.

Tan had a house built on high ground near Orchard Road in 1882. The house was designed on a central axis of two main courtyards but also included two adjacent axes with linear courtyards. Craftsmen were brought to Singapore from China to build the house.

After Tan died, the house was acquired by the government for the station master of Tank Road Station, on Singapore's first railway line, which had been opened in 1902.

The house was then leased to various charitable organizations, including the Anglican Church to establish St Mary's Home and School for Eurasian girls in 1912. The Salvation Army bought the property in 1938. The building was gazetted as a national monument in July 1973.

The Salvation Army used the house until 1991. The property was then sold to the adjacent COCKPIT HOTEL. Five years later, both the house and the Cockpit Hotel were purchased by a consortium led by WING TAI HOLDINGS, and were offered to the UNIVERSITY OF CHICAGO GRADUATE SCHOOL OF BUSINESS as the site of the school's Asian campus.

The house was then restored, the project involving research on a larger traditional courtyard-style house that Tan had built in his home town in China in around 1870. Chinese craftsmen were hired to restore the building's many decorative elements. The house was re-opened as the business school campus in September 2000, the only traditional courtyard house remaining in Singapore.

household income In 2005, the average monthly household income in Singapore was $5,400, as compared with $2,127 in 1988—an average annual increase of 5.6 per cent (see table). Between 1988 and 1993, while real gross domestic product (GDP) growth averaged 8.8 per cent per annum, household income grew at 10.2 per cent per annum. Thereafter, income growth slowed to 6.9 per cent per annum during 1993–98, and further still to 2.3 per cent in the period 1998–2005.

Historically, lower-income households have generally experienced slower income growth, in percentage terms, than households with higher incomes.

Despite the RECESSIONS of 1998 and 2001, household income growth resumed in 1998–2005 for the majority of households; however, the incomes of households in the lowest quintile actually declined, mainly due to a fall in household size and the average number of working persons within households, as well as a corresponding rise in the number of households that generated no employment income.

In the same period, the ratio between the average income of the highest 20 per cent of households and that of the lowest 20 per cent showed an increasing disparity.

See also INCOME DISTRIBUTION.

Housing & Development Board Statutory board responsible for the provision of PUBLIC HOUSING in Singapore. The Housing & Development Board (HDB) reports to the minister of national development.

The HDB was established on 1 Feburary 1960, at a time when housing was in short supply. It was tasked with fixing the problem quickly. At the same time, the HDB also resettled people from urban slums and rural areas being cleared for redevelopment. In 1964, the government introduced the Home Ownership for the People Scheme to give citizens an asset in the country, a means of financial security and to hedge against inflation; and in 1968, it allowed the use of the CENTRAL PROVIDENT FUND (CPF) to aid housing payments.

The HDB oversees planning and development as well as the rental and sale of public housing units. With 83 per cent of the population living in publicly built housing in 2005, the HDB is not only one of the largest property developers in Singapore but is also one of the largest property owners.

The HDB managed all the estates it had developed until TOWN COUNCILS were introduced in 1990 to take over the day-to-day operations.

Apart from housing, the HDB also does agency work for the government such as coastal reclamation works, and the building of factories, COMMUNITY CENTRES AND CLUBS, recreational facilities and religious buildings. The HDB has developed more than 20 new towns and close to a million units of property.

Housing & Urban Development Company Set up to provide housing for middle-income households, the Housing & Urban Development Company (HUDC) was incorporated in February 1974. Middle-income families did not qualify for HOUSING & DEVELOPMENT BOARD (HDB) units. However, with the rise in prices in the private property market in the early 1970s, these families were also unable to buy private homes. HUDC housing was designed as an alternative.

Other groups that were unable to buy HDB units, such as single people, were also allowed to purchase HUDC homes. The HUDC units were largely high-rise, but were larger than HDB units. They were usually in good locations.

In 1980, HUDC estates were integrated into the overall planning and development of the HDB, partly to achieve a better social mix. In 1982, the HDB absorbed the functions of the HUDC and has been managing the estates since. Since 1995, some HUDC estates have been privatized, a process which requires the agreement of over 75% of owners.

Howe Yoon Chong (1923–) Civil servant and politician. Born in China, Howe Yoon Chong was educated first at St Francis' Institution in Malacca and then at Raffles College and the University of Malaya in Singapore, where he obtained an honours degree in economics. He began his working life as a teacher, subsequently becoming a broadcaster and police magistrate.

In 1960, Howe was appointed the first chief executive officer of the HOUSING & DEVELOPMENT BOARD. He was awarded the MERITORIOUS SERVICE MEDAL in 1963. He rose through the ranks of the Administrative Service and became chairman and president of the Development Bank of Singapore (DBS Bank) and, concurrently, chairman of the Port of Singapore Authority (1970–79). He also served as deputy chairman of the Economic Development Board and permanent secretary at the Ministry of Finance, the Ministry of National Development and the Prime Minister's Office. At the time of his retirement from the Administrative Service in 1979, he was head of the Singapore Civil Service.

That same year, Howe won a seat in Potong Pasir constituency on the People's Action Party ticket. He was appointed minister for defence (1979–82) and then minister for health (1982–84). He retired from politics in 1984 to become chairman and chief executive officer of DBS Bank (1985–90). Howe was executive chairman for Great Eastern Life Assurance (1992–2000). In 1999 he was appointed chairman of the Straits Trading Company.

HSBC An agency of the Hongkong and Shanghai Banking Corporation was first set up in Singapore in 1871; a branch office was opened in December 1877 (on Battery Road), although it did not achieve full branch status with the right to issue CURRENCY notes until 1881. It was often called simply the 'Hongkong Bank'. After acquiring the premises of A.L. Johnston and Co. (see JOHNSTON, ALEXANDER) at Fullerton Square in 1890, the bank completed a new building on the site in 1892, the first of three successive buildings in that location. The bank continued to acquire adjacent properties, and a new building was put up in 1925. This in turn was demolished in

Housing & Urban Development Company: Pine Grove HUDC flats, 1994, subsequently privatized.

Howe Yoon Chong

HOUSEHOLD INCOME: AVERAGE NOMINAL MONTHLY HOUSEHOLD INCOME ($)					
	1988	1993	1998	2003	2005
All households	2,127	3,458	4,608	4,867	5,400
Lowest 20%	615	887	933	795	590
Second quintile	1,072	1,645	2,118	2,059	2,590
Third quintile	1,566	2,487	3,374	3,379	4,345
Fourth quintile	2,328	3,799	5,162	5,309	6,575
Highest 20%	5,055	8,469	11,450	12,792	12,890
Ratio of highest 20% to lowest 20% income	8.2	9.5	12.3	16.1	21.8

Source: Singapore Department of Statistics

Hsu Tse-Kwang

Huang Wenyong

Richard Hu: during the general election vote count, 1988.

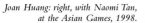

Joan Huang: right, with Naomi Tan, at the Asian Games, 1998.

1979 and replaced by a 21-storey building—the Hongkong Bank Building, completed in 1982. All three buildings were designed by SWAN & MACLAREN.

Other important buildings put up by the bank include the bank's former house at Mount Echo, designed on a grand scale to replace an earlier house in 1912 (which was later demolished); and MACDONALD HOUSE, which accommodated the Orchard Road branch for many years.

The bank has played an important role in financing Singapore's business community for more than a century, its focus reflecting the broader evolution of Singapore's economy as a whole, with, for example, tin and rubber playing important roles in earlier years. In 1959, two big names in Singapore's banking scene came together, when the Hongkong Bank acquired the MERCANTILE BANK, with its prominent premises in Raffles Place.

A qualifying full bank (QFB) since 2001, HSBC has maintained a large network of offices in Singapore (QFBs are non-Singaporean banks licensed by the Monetary Authority of Singapore). It has been approved as a primary dealer in Singapore government securities, and listed as an approved bond intermediary (ABI). In 2005, the HSBC Group's profit before tax was US$61,704 million, with a net operating income of US$20,966 million.

HSBC TreeTop Walk Situated in the MacRitchie forest, this canopy walk is made from a suspension bridge anchored to two steel structures. Beginning at Bukit Pierce—the second highest point in the CENTRAL CATCHMENT NATURE RESERVE—it allows visitors to walk along a 200-m-long steel walkway to Bukit Kalang. At its highest point, the TreeTop Walk stands at about 28 m above the ground.

Sponsored by HSBC and costing $1.6 million to build, the walk was constructed with minimum impact on the forest, as the NATIONAL PARKS BOARD (NParks) had put in place stringent measures to ensure that the flora and fauna in the area were left undisturbed. Work on the bridge commenced in August 2002, and was finished in July 2004.

The TreeTop Walk has helped facilitate scientific studies and plant identification work. Prior to its construction, little was known about the wildlife that dwells in the canopy of Singapore's forests.

Hsu Tse-Kwang (1929–1999) Civil servant and diplomat. Hsu Tse-Kwang was educated at the University of Malaya, where he graduated with an honours degree in economics (1954). He then joined the Inland Revenue Department as an income tax service officer.

In 1962, at the request of the National Trades Union Congress (NTUC), Hsu was seconded to the trade union movement to help set up the Labour Research Unit. He was appointed chairman of the governing board of the NTUC-Research Unit, and served as director of this Unit (1962–63; 1966–67). He served as permanent secretary of the Ministry of Culture (1968–70) and commissioner of Inland Revenue (1970–91). In 1973, he was presented with the MERITORIOUS SERVICE MEDAL.

Hsu retired from the civil service in 1991 and was appointed executive chairman of the Sembawang Group of Companies (1991–94); president, Football Association of Singapore (1991–94); and consultant to the Sembawang Group (1994–99). Hsu also served as ambassador to Poland (1991–99) and the Czech Republic (1997–99).

Hu, Richard (1926–) Academic, businessman and politician. Richard Hu Tsu Tau was educated at the Anglo-Chinese School and then at the University of California, Berkeley, where he took a degree in chemistry (1952). He pursued postgraduate studies at the University of Birmingham in the United Kingdom, and earned a doctorate in chemical engineering (1957). He then taught chemical engineering at the University of Manchester (1957–60).

In 1960, he joined the oil company Shell. He was appointed director of marketing and general manager, Malaysia (1970); chief executive for Malaysia (1974); chairman and chief executive officer for Singapore (1977); and chairman, Shell Singapore (1982).

From 1983 to 1984, Hu served as managing director of the Government of Singapore Investment Corporation (GIC). In 1984, he won a seat in the Kreta Ayer constituency on the People's Action Party ticket. He then served as chairman of the Monetary Authority of Singapore

HSBC: main Singapore office, Collyer Quay.

HSBC TreeTop Walk

(1985–97). In 1985, he was appointed minister for finance and minister for trade and industry. He later dropped the latter portfolio and became minister for health (1985–87), then minister for national development (1992–93), while retaining the finance portfolio. From 1985 to 2001, he was also chairman of the Inland Revenue Authority of Singapore and the Board of Commissioners of Currency. Hu retired from politics in 2001. In 2002 he was appointed chancellor of Singapore Management University.

Huang, Joan (1982–) Sportswoman. Joan Huang, together with her teacher, Naomi Tan, won a gold medal for sailing in the International 420 Class at the 1998 Asian Games in Thailand. She was only 16 years of age at the time. To prepare for the games, Huang had to postpone sitting for her GCE 'O'-level examinations by a year while Tan had to take unpaid leave. They were inducted into the SINGAPORE SPORTS COUNCIL HALL OF FAME.

Huang Wenyong (1953–) Actor. Malaya-born Huang Wenyong was part of the first batch of graduates from the Drama Training Class run by the TV Drama Division of the Singapore Broadcasting Corporation. His acting career began in 1981 with the drama serial *Xiang Ru Fei Fei* (Fantastic Idea). However, he is better remembered for his role as a humble, honest and courageous rubber-tapper in the period drama serial *Wu Suo Nanyang* (The Awakening) in 1984.

Huang has acted in more than 80 serials since his debut, often playing the 'good guy', but also adapting to other roles, such as an adulterous manager in *Zui Jia Pei Ou* (Marry Me) (1990); a hen-pecked miser in *Bao Yu Kuang Hua* (Angel of Vengeance) (1993); and a scheming businessman in *Jin Zhen Tou* (Golden Pillow) (1996). He also made the transition to comic roles in the sitcom *Gan Gan Zuo Ge Kai Xin Ren* (Don't Worry, Be Happy) (1996–97, 1999–2002), playing a wacky but stingy taxi-driver. That role also won him the title of Best Comedy Performer at the Star Awards in 2000.

Huber, Werner Ernst (1924–) Swiss businessman. Werner Ernst 'Jim' Huber was born in Zurich, Switzerland. He worked first as a commodity trader in Switzerland, coming to Singapore in 1946. Huber returned to Switzerland in 1953, but came back to Singapore in 1955 to start his own company—the Anglo-Swiss Trading Company.

In 1960, Huber began trading in coffee, experimenting with different varieties to develop his own blend. In 1962, he established Boncafé International with a factory in Jurong. The company grew into a multi-million-dollar firm, selling roasted and ground coffee and beverage-dispensing equipment, with branches in Australia, Cambodia, Malaysia, Thailand, Hong Kong and Switzerland.

Hungry Ghost Festival *See* ZHONG YUAN JIE.

Husain Shah, Sultan (1776–1835) Malay royal. Sultan Husain Shah was the rightful claimant to the throne of the Johor-Riau kingdom after the death of his father, SULTAN MAHMUD. However, as Husain was away in Pahang for his marriage to the daughter of the Pahang *bendahara* (treasurer), he was bypassed in the succession, due to the efforts of the powerful Bugis Yang di-Pertuan Muda Raja Jafar, who arranged for Husain's younger brother ABDUL RAHMAN to ascend the throne. The *bendahara* tried to intervene in support of his son-in-law Husain, but was unsuccessful.

Husain was left in the political wilderness, awaiting a suitable opportunity to press his claim. This came about when Colonel WILLIAM FARQUHAR, the EAST INDIA COMPANY'S (EIC) commandant of Malacca, met him in Riau in 1818. Husain met Farquhar together with Sir STAMFORD RAFFLES in Singapore in February 1819, a meeting which led to a treaty that gave Husain a new kingdom in Singapore, and the EIC a foothold on the island.

Husain relocated to Singapore from Riau with his family and followers. In the tradition of maritime Malay sultans, he collected taxes and received tributes from the *nakhoda* (captains) of Asian trading vessels calling at the new ENTREPÔT of Singapore. This was not consistent with Raffles' vision of the entrepôt as a free port. Before leaving Singapore in 1823, Raffles tried to moderate Husain's claims. JOHN CRAWFURD, as the incoming EIC Resident in Singapore, continued Raffles' efforts, blocking Husain's customary claims to slaves and debt-bondage. Husain submitted his grievances to the EIC governor-general in Calcutta but found no support. Instead, the

EIC in Calcutta gave Crawfurd a mandate to work towards full cession of sovereignty over Singapore to the EIC. Crawfurd negotiated with Husain and achieved the desired outcome by means of a treaty signed in August 1824. From that time on, Husain's fortunes declined. He tried to press his claims to the Karimun Islands and Johor but was unsuccessful and left for Malacca, where he died in 1835.

See also FOUNDING OF SINGAPORE.

Hussain Haniff (1934–1966) Film director and actor. After working as a film editor for CATHAY-KERIS FILMS in the late 1950s, Hussain Haniff made his directorial debut in 1961 with HANG JEBAT, an ambitious work known for its cinematic qualities and the way it revisited Malay classical history. Its success immediately positioned him as a top film-maker.

In the five years that followed, Hussain directed 12 more movies spanning a variety of genres. They included period dramas such as *Dang Anom* (1962) and *Dua Pendekar* (Two Warriors) (1964), and contemporary social dramas such as *Chinta Kaseh Sayang* (Love Love Love) (1965) and *Jiran Sekampong* (Village Neighbours) (1965). Hussain died of liver cancer at the age of 32.

Hwa Chong Institution Independent educational institution established in 2005 through the merger of the Chinese High School and Hwa Chong Junior College. Hwa Chong Institution (HCI) offers an integrated programme where students bypass the traditional GCE 'O' levels, and sit for the GCE 'A' level examinations after six years of post-primary education. The curriculum in the first two years is designed to stimulate the students' curiosity and interest. Students are encouraged to pursue and expand on their interests over the next two years. Knowledge gleaned is then consolidated in readiness for the national examinations at the end of the sixth year.

HCI offers four Ministry of Education special programmes spanning language and humanities, and remains the leading Oxford-entry centre in the world outside the United Kingdom. HCI was also one of the pioneers of the Bicultural Studies Programme, which aims to nurture a bicultural-bilingual elite.

The year 2005 also saw the launch of the privately-funded Hwa Chong International School, for students not only from Singapore but also from other countries in the region.

Hwang Peng Yuan (1936–) Civil servant and diplomat. Hwang was educated at Raffles Institution and later at Queen's College, Cambridge University, where he obtained a degree in the natural sciences (1958). He joined the Economic Development Board in 1964, and became

its chairman (1982–85). He also served as Singapore's ambassador to Belgium (1972–82); vice-chairman of the Community Chest of Singapore (1993–) and deputy chairman of Temasek Holdings (1986–96). Hwang has been awarded the NTUC Friend of Labour Medal, the Public Administration Medal and the Public Service Medal.

Hyflux Company specializing in water treatment. It began in 1989 as Hydrochem (S) Pte Ltd, a three-person outfit selling water treatment and filtration systems. In little more than a decade, Hyflux became one of Asia's leading water- and fluids-treatment firms, with both industrial and municipal clients in Asia and the Middle East. The group's technology has found applications in electronics, pharmaceuticals and biotechnology. Hyflux made a foray into the consumer market in 2003 with its Aquosos system, essentially a water cooler able to produce potable water by extracting moisture from the air.

Forbes magazine named Hyflux one of the Best 200 Small Companies globally in 2002. This was followed by the *Business Times*/DHL Enterprise Award 2003. A year later, Hyflux founder OLIVIA LUM became the first woman in the 20-year history of the Singapore Business Awards to collect the top honour—Businesswoman of the Year Award. By the end of 2005, Lum was running a $1.4 billion company, which employed some 680 people and had won the contract to build Singapore's first desalination plant.

Within a five-year period, Hyflux listed on the junior board of the Singapore Exchange (2001), was promoted to the main board (2003) and designated a Straits Times Index stock (March 2005). The group registered a net profit of $49.2 million in 2005 on the back of revenue of $131.5 million.

Hussain Haniff

Hyflux: water treatment plant.

I Not Stupid (2002) Film. A comedy and social satire directed by JACK NEO, the film focuses on three 12-year-old schoolboys who have been relegated to the EM3 stream in school, which groups together students with poor academic results. Through the travails of the boys and their families, Neo explores a range of issues touching on the education system, the economy, class and race. The film drew both critical and commercial acclaim. Its popularity generated a spin-off Mandarin television series in which cast members reprised their roles, an album of Chinese New Year songs, a Mandarin comic book, and a sequel. At the time of its release, *I Not Stupid* was the second-highest grossing local film, after *Money No Enough* (1998) (which Neo wrote and acted in).

Iau, Robert (1935–2005) Civil servant and impresario. Robert Iau Kuo Kwong was educated at the Anglo-Chinese School and the University of Malaya. In the 1960s, he worked on the planning, programming and installation of the first computer system for the CENTRAL PROVIDENT FUND (CPF) Board, of which he was general manager (1973–80). His leadership in information technology led to his induction into the Singapore Computer Society's IT Hall of Fame in 2000.

An accomplished pianist, Iau was active in the arts scene and served as executive chairman of the Singapore Arts Centre Company, which oversaw the development of the ESPLANADE–THEATRES ON THE BAY. He also served on the steering committee of the Singapore Arts Festival and the National Arts Council.

Ibbetson, Robert (1789–1879) Colonial official. Robert Ibbetson was appointed governor of the Straits Settlements by Lord William Bentinck, the governor-general of India in 1830, and served in that position until 1833. He succeeded ROBERT FULLERTON, the first governor. Ibbetson had previously served as Resident Councillor of Penang, and is credited with being the first governor to initiate cultivation on a large scale in Penang.

During his governorship, there was considerable friction between the executive and the judiciary. In September 1831, a meeting of the mercantile community was held to draw up a petition to Parliament on the subject of the Court of Justice. For 15 months, the Court of Justice had not been operating in any of the three states of the Straits Settlements. A copy of this petition to the House of Commons was also published in the *Singapore Chronicle and Commercial Register* of 13 October. In response to this petition, the Privy Council in London held a meeting to hear the appeal from Sir John Claridge, against his removal from the office of RECORDER of the Straits. The main complaint hinged on his refusal to do a circuit of all the three states within the Straits due to a dispute with Fullerton over certain court expenses. As a result of the investigation, Claridge was relieved of his duties. Until the arrival of the new recorder in 1833, Ibbetson himself held the Courts in Singapore. He also conducted the criminal Assizes.

When Ibbetson's term ended on 7 December 1833, Kenneth Murchison was sworn in as Governor of the Straits Settlements. Ibbetson returned to the United Kingdom in 1869.

Ibrahim, Temenggong (1810–1862) Malay royal. Ibrahim was the younger son of TEMENGGONG ABDUL RAHMAN. After his father's death in 1825, Ibrahim (or Daing Ibrahim) was left with only his father's pension and his kampong at Telok Blangah. Many of his father's followers, the ORANG LAUT (sea nomads), drifted into piracy to find an alternative source of income. Joining them in piracy were groups from the Riau region of the politically-split Johor-Riau kingdom and other areas as well. They posed a dangerous threat to Singapore's growing trade.

As Ibrahim came of age in the 1830s and rallied his *orang laut* followers, Governor GEORGE BONHAM of the Straits Settlements turned to him as the only influential Malay chief capable of offering help in efforts to stamp out piracy. Ibrahim's position strengthened as a result, and he became the most important Malay

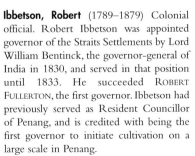

I Not Stupid

ally of the EAST INDIA COMPANY (EIC) government in Singapore and the principal negotiator between the EIC and the peninsula's Malay rulers. As the anti-pirate actions took effect, other *orang laut* pirates in Riau sought refuge with Ibrahim, further boosting his position. He directed his *orang laut* followers to a new, profitable and legitimate occupation, the GUTTA PERCHA trade, when gutta percha was discovered in the forests of Johor in the 1840s and became an overnight commercial success. Ibrahim quickly declared a monopoly over the trade and controlled its price and distribution in the Singapore market. On his road to power and recognition, Ibrahim was formally installed as Temenggong Sri Maharaja by Bonham in 1841. During the 1850s, Ibrahim was involved in a struggle with Ali, successor of the late Sultan Hussein of Singapore, over Johor. The two came to an agreement through a treaty in 1855 when Ali gave up his claim to Johor.

In the next phase, Ibrahim encouraged Chinese gambier and pepper planters to move to Johor where he was laying the foundations of a new kingdom when he died in 1862. His son Abu Bakar would later become the Sultan of Johor.

ice kachang Popular dessert. *Ice kachang* consists of a mound of finely-shaved ice over red beans (*kachang*), sweetcorn, grass jelly, agar-agar cubes and *attap chee* (palm seed). More imaginative versions might include crushed peanuts, fruit cocktail, soursop or durian. Multi-coloured syrups including *gula melaka* (palm sugar) syrup and evaporated milk are drizzled over the shaved ice, which is topped with creamed corn.

identity card All Singaporeans and permanent residents are given an identity card (IC)—a credit card-sized plastic card which contains the owner's name, address, date of birth, country of birth, ethnic group and photograph. Each card carries an image of the holder's right thumbprint as well as a unique seven-digit number, known as an NRIC (National Registration Identity Card) number. This number is also rendered as a bar code to make it machine-readable. The identity card number is identical to the birth certificate number.

Singapore citizens carry a pink IC while 'permanent residents' carry a blue version. All Singaporeans, upon reaching the age of 15, must apply for an IC. The cards are issued by the National Registration Department, which is part of the IMMIGRATION AND CHECKPOINTS AUTHORITY.

The use of ICs in Singapore can be traced back to 1938. It was in that year that the Registration of Births and Deaths Ordinance made birth and death registration mandatory. In 1948, paper identity cards were introduced to identify people who were born in Singapore. A year after

Robert Iau

Ice kachang

Identity cards

SEPARATION, the National Registration Act (1966) was passed requiring all Singaporeans to register, or re-register, themselves in order to obtain new ICs. These were laminated pieces of paper which had improved security features, such as a photograph that was difficult to substitute.

In 1991, new, credit-card-sized ICs were introduced. These plastic cards introduced the bar code, and carried a photograph and thumbprint, which made them even harder to alter.

Immigration and Checkpoints Authority

Border control agency. The Immigration & Checkpoints Authority (ICA) is a government agency under the Ministry of Home Affairs. It was formed on 1 April 2003 through the merger of the former Singapore Immigration & Registration and Customs & Excise Departments.

The ICA's main responsibility is to protect Singapore's borders from the illegal entry of undesirable goods and persons through its five major immigration checkpoints. It began to use computers to screen travellers at these checkpoints in June 1981. The ICA is also the key issuer of passports, travel documents and identity cards to Singapore citizens. To maintain an accurate database of the Singapore population, the ICA also oversees the registration of births and deaths.

For foreigners, the ICA works with other relevant government agencies, such as the MINISTRY OF MANPOWER and the ECONOMIC DEVELOPMENT BOARD, to issue immigration passes and work permits.

imports

Having very few natural resources of its own, Singapore has always been economically dependent on imports, including imports of food and water

Singapore's main imports are machinery and equipment, electronic components, telecommunication equipment, personal computers and parts, diodes and transistors, mineral fuels for refining purposes, chemicals and foodstuffs. In 2005, Singapore's main import partners were Malaysia (13.7 per cent), Europe (13.6 per cent), China (12.3 per cent), the United States (11.6 per cent), Japan (9.6 per cent), Taiwan (5.9 per cent), Indonesia (5.2 per cent), Saudi Arabia (4.5 per cent), South Korea (4.3 per cent) and Thailand (3.8 per cent). Total imports were valued at $333 billion.

Singapore Customs is responsible for enforcing rules on imports of certain product categories such as liquors, tobacco, and motor vehicles, which are subject to taxes. Licences are also required for imports of meat products, fruits and vegetables, and other items, such as irradiated foods and genetically modified foods.

income distribution

Over three-and-a-half decades, Singapore has been able to reduce poverty and raise living standards. Real per capita income (i.e. earnings) grew at an average annual 6.5 per cent in the 1965–2000 period.

In 2003, Singapore had an average monthly per capita income of $1,457 (about $17,500 per annum). This amounted to an overall 2.3 per cent increase per annum in the 1998–2003 period; however the lowest quintile experienced negative growth in per capita monthly income of 1.6 per cent per annum in the same period (see Table 1). This was mainly attributable to the downturn brought about by the ASIAN FINANCIAL CRISIS and the subsequent recession caused by a sharp fall in global electronics demand. However, if government financial assistance for the lower-income bracket is taken into account, all quintile groups—including the lowest 20 per cent—experienced positive income growth over that period.

While it is true that no one in Singapore lives in absolute poverty by World Bank standards, Singapore's income divide is getting wider. In 1998, Singapore's wealthiest 20 per cent were about 12.3 times richer than the poorest 20 per cent. In 2003, this figure had risen to 16.1 times (see Table 2). One cause of this trend has been the steady inflow of cheap workers from other developing countries. The effect of their entry into Singapore has been to depress wage levels for local lowly-paid workers. Another factor is global technological change which favours higher-skilled workers.

To tackle this problem, the government has launched retraining programmes and other measures, rather than offering direct handouts. Only in exceptional cases does it provide a basic subsistence grant of $115 a month.

income tax

Income tax was first introduced in Singapore in 1948 by the British colonial government, and is levied on incomes derived or received in Singapore by individuals and corporations. There is a one-year lag in income tax payments, as the tax liability in a given year is based on the previous year's income.

The nominal rates for resident individual income tax have been decreasing since the 1980s. In 2005, the rates ranged between 0 per cent and 22 per cent. To help attract and retain highly skilled individuals, the top marginal income tax rate is due to be further reduced to 21 per cent in year of assessment (YA) 2006 and then to 20 per cent in YA2007.

From YA2003, non-residents have enjoyed a lower flat tax of 15 per cent on their gross income (which do not enjoy deductions for tax relief), or resident rates, whichever are higher. To keep pace with other countries which have lowered their corporate tax rates—such as Australia, Ireland and the Netherlands—the corporate income tax was also lowered, from 24.5 per cent in YA2002 to 20 per cent in YA2005. To meet various socio-economic objectives, a wide range of deductions and tax incentives are also available.

Since 2005, the taxable annual income threshold for salaried employees has been $22,000. More than two-thirds of working adults in Singapore do not pay any income tax. To bridge the resultant shortfall in government revenue, the GOODS AND SERVICES TAX (GST) was increased from 4 to 5 per cent on 1 January 2004.

Independence *See* SEPARATION.

independent schools

This category of school was introduced in 1987 to give principals of government secondary schools more autonomy in setting fees, student admission, implementation of school programmes, and administration. However they are subject to the overall national education guidelines and policies, such as the BILINGUALISM POLICY and the teaching of civics and moral education.

An over-centralization of authority at the MINISTRY OF EDUCATION (MOE) had led to a general disinclination of schools to introduce new educational programmes or activities. A climate had been created in which schools waited for directives from the Ministry before taking

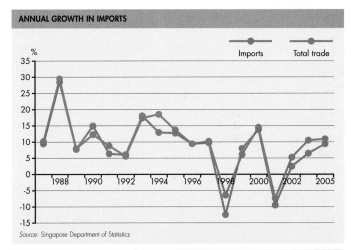

ANNUAL GROWTH IN IMPORTS

Source: Singapore Department of Statistics

TABLE 1 AVERAGE NOMINAL MONTHLY HOUSEHOLD INCOME GROWTH

	1988–1993	1993–1998	1998–2003	2003
All households	10.2	5.9	1.1	5.7
Lowest 20%	7.6	1.0	-3.2	1.7
Second quintile	8.9	5.2	-0.6	4.4
Third quintile	9.7	6.3	0.0	5.3
Fourth quintile	10.3	6.3	0.6	5.6
Highest 20%	10.9	6.2	2.2	6.4

NOTE: All amounts are in %.

TABLE 2 CHANGES IN AVERAGE MONTHLY HOUSEHOLD INCOME BY QUINTILE

Household income group	1998 ($)	2003 ($)	% change	% change per annum
All households	4,608	4,867	5.6	1.1
Lowest 20%	933	795	-14.8	-3.2
Second quintile	2,118	2,059	-2.8	-0.6
Third quintile	3,374	3,379	0.1	0.0
Fourth quintile	5,162	5,309	2.8	0.6
Highest 20%	11,450	12,792	11.7	2.2

Source: Singapore Department of Statistics

action. In addition, the MOE found it difficult to introduce innovative measures because when new schemes were introduced, they had to be implemented across the board, in all schools.

Independent schools, therefore, were a first step in introducing flexibility to the system. The Ministry sought to use them as places for trying out new ideas that could then be disseminated throughout the system.

As of 2005, there were 11 independent schools in Singapore, each run by their own board of governors. They have started to develop their own identities and modes of operation. The 11 are: Anglo-Chinese (Independent), METHODIST GIRLS' SCHOOL (Secondary), NANYANG GIRLS' HIGH, NATIONAL UNIVERSITY OF SINGAPORE HIGH SCHOOL OF MATHEMATICS AND SCIENCE, RAFFLES GIRLS' SCHOOL, RAFFLES INSTITUTION, SINGAPORE CHINESE GIRLS' SCHOOL, SINGAPORE SPORTS SCHOOL, ST JOSEPH'S INSTITUTION, the CHINESE HIGH SCHOOL (renamed Hwa Chong Institution) and Raffles Junior College.

India–Singapore relations Relations between Singapore and India have deep historical roots. There is evidence that Indian merchants were trading in and around the island of Singapore as early as the 9th century CE. In the early 19th century, Singapore became part of the British Indian empire when the East India Company established a trading settlement on the island. For the first 50 years of its colonial history, Singapore was governed from the Indian city of Calcutta, and although Singapore became a separate Crown Colony in 1867, the ties with British India remained strong, underpinned by colonial trading networks as well as the movement of Indian workers and traders to Singapore. Indeed, much of the legal and administrative structures that were established in Singapore in the 19th and early 20th century were derived from British India.

In the 1960s, a newly-independent Singapore looked to India as a model of

Indian Muslims: group photograph, c. 1900

multiracial and multicultural tolerance, and admired its foreign policy of non-alignment. Singapore was keen to develop bilateral relations with India, and the 1960s and early 1970s witnessed a series of high-level exchange visits by leaders of both countries.

With the impending withdrawal of British forces east of Suez, Singapore felt that it was important to have greater Indian involvement in the security arrangements as well as economic development of Southeast Asia. India, preoccupied with its own domestic developments and more concerned about stability in the South Asian region was, however, reluctant to promote any specific security scheme other than to signal a commitment to 'positive, creative and mutually profitable' regional organizations.

From the early 1970s, India began isolating itself from the non-communist countries of Southeast Asia by developing close relations with the Soviet Union. Indian relations with Southeast Asia reached a nadir when Prime Minister Indira Gandhi, after returning to power, chose to recognize the Vietnamese-backed Heng Samrin regime in Cambodia, much to the consternation of Singapore and the rest of the ASSOCIATION OF SOUTHEAST ASIAN NATIONS (ASEAN). India's position on Cambodia was essentially motivated by its strategic concern to keep China at bay in Southeast Asia (by supporting China's rival—Vietnam), but the result was a gulf between Singapore and India.

Political and economic relations between India and Singapore during the period of the Cold War remained cordial but did not develop in any significant manner. Singapore continued to trade with India, but there were no significant bilateral economic gains in real terms in the 1970s and 1980s. For Singapore and other ASEAN countries, concerns lingered about India's intentions in the region, especially in the wake of India's naval build-up and its actions in Sri Lanka and Maldives.

From the early 1990s, the radically altered geopolitical realities and circumstances following the end of the Cold War forced a re-thinking of India's overall posture, particularly towards its eastern neighbours. This re-orientation brought about a 'renaissance' in relations between India and Southeast Asia, and with Singapore in particular. India's renewed engagement with Southeast Asia was driven by Prime Minister Narashima Rao's radical economic liberalization programme in India and his 'Look East' policy. This led to a flurry of diplomatic activities—including missions personally led by Rao to Thailand, Vietnam and Singapore.

Singapore played a major role in bringing India's engagement with Southeast Asia by ensuring India's inclusion in the ASEAN network, first as a sectoral dialogue partner (Singapore, 1992) and then as a full dia-

logue partner (Bangkok, 1995). This, in turn, ensured India's membership in the ASEAN REGIONAL FORUM. Singapore also sponsored the ASEAN-India Summit and fought for India's inclusion in the inaugural EAST ASIA SUMMIT. Bilateral ties warmed, and this led to a series of joint naval exercises between the two countries in the mid-1990s as well as co-operation in defence technology. Singapore and India also sought to cement ties in cultural terms. A memorandum of understanding concerning the arts, heritage and the archives was signed between the two countries in February 1993.

In the 1990s, trade between the two countries increased dramatically as India's 'Look East' policy, as well as its economic liberalization efforts, coincided with Singapore's regionalization strategy of investing in emerging economies. At the turn of the century, Singapore was India's 14th largest trading partner. Singapore was also one of the largest foreign investors in India. In June 2005, the two countries signed a Comprehensive Economic Co-operation Agreement (CECA) that included agreements on trade in goods and services, investment, e-commerce, intellectual property, technology, educational exchanges and dispute settlement. The CECA was a milestone for both countries. It was Singapore's first with a South Asian country and India's first bilateral comprehensive economic trade pact with an ASEAN country. The CECA has anchored India to the ASEAN region through its presence in Singapore.

Indian classical music *See* box.

Indian Muslims Indian Muslim traders have been active in Southeast Asia since the 15th century and settled in Singapore soon after it was founded. In the mid-19th century, Muslims formed the majority of the Indian population in Singapore. About a quarter of all INDIANS in Singapore are Muslims.

As with Indians of other religions, there is regional and linguistic variety among Indian Muslims. While TAMIL is the most prominent language among Indian Muslims, other languages, such as Bengali, Gujarati, Malayalam and Urdu, are also spoken, as well as English and Malay. The partition of British India into India, Pakistan, and later Bangladesh, has also left its mark on Indian Muslims. Each regional group has followed different trajectories in migrating to and settling in Singapore, with trade, the British army and labour migration being the most common factors.

Muslims from southern and western India have a long history as traders and shop-owners in Singapore. Some affluent businessmen have come from among their ranks, especially from the GUJARATIS from west India and the Tamils from the south (CHULIAS). Food-stalls and restaurants run

Indian classical music

Indian classical music Although people from all the major ethno-linguistic groups in India are represented in Singapore, the Tamil community (*see* TAMILS) constitutes approximately 75 per cent of Singapore's Indian population; the Punjabi community makes up about 51 per cent among those considered 'northern Indians', a group which also includes BENGALIS, GUJARATIS, Marathis and SINDHIS. Indian classical music in Singapore is therefore predominantly South Indian, usually linked to the Hindu tradition, and has often been performed in temples as part of religious rituals from the early 19th century.

Well into the 1920s, Indian dances, dramas and folk performing arts could be seen around Selegie, offered free of charge in public spaces by actors and directors from India. The length of the performance varied with the crowd; the bigger the crowd, the longer the performance would be.

Among the crowd favourites was *silambu*, a martial arts dance with a long bamboo pole, which would be featured in *kalai nigalchi*, which roughly translates as 'arts programmes'. When the chariot, considered the vehicle of the gods, was carried from the temple during THAIPUSAM, the *silambu* troupe would follow sometimes with the horse and tiger dances—folk dances then popular among Tamils and featuring two animals significant in Hindu mythology. Stories such as the Ramayana were also enacted, and audience members came from as far as Johor Bahru and Kuantan. At one point, however, the government banned these street performances as they were considered too rowdy.

Drama and music

Some of the earliest drama troupes are said to have arrived in Singapore in the 1930s. Epic dramas were staged at Alexandra Hall while *kathakali* drama, which originated in Kerala, was staged at Sembawang. Publicity consisted of posters on horse coaches and newspaper advertisements. TANJONG PAGAR, Potong Pasir and SERANGOON ROAD were the main sites for such events. Bands provided musical accompaniment; they were essentially musical ensembles which were attached to drama troupes, and sometimes broke off to become independent groups. Names associated with such ensembles in the 1950s and 1960s included M.P. Gurusamy and Pundit Ramalingam, both of whom were identified with the South Indian classical tradition as well as a semi-classical tradition. The latter is sometimes defined by its degree of conformity or deviation of the music to the raga and south Indian film music.

NEW WORLD, the amusement park at Serangoon Road, was a site where various Indian dramatic productions were performed. The Singapore Indian Artistes Association put up plays in Tamil from the late 1940s till the 1960s. One of the pioneers of Indian classical music in Singapore was Edmund Appau who, together with tabla player V. Sinniah, founded the New Indian Amateur Orchestra in 1948. The first Indian musical group in Singapore, it was a classical ensemble which performed music in the Carnatic tradition. Appau later became the leader of the most enduring ensemble in the field, the Singapore Indians Music Party (SIMP).

Movie music

After World War II, the gramophone and radio broadcasts played an important part in disseminating music. Songs by Thiagaraja Bhagavathar and T.R. Mahalingam, who were from the Carnatic and semi-classical traditions, proved very popular. Movies with mythological themes ran to full houses. Songs, especially those by Thiagaraja, A. Kittapa and K. Ramasamy from films which told stories of Hindu gods and goddesses, were also well-received. The role of cinema went beyond

Performers at the Sri Thendayuthapani Temple use a mix of traditional and modern instruments.

entertainment, serving to provide an education in Hinduism and classical Indian music. Hindu temples played a major role in promoting music and dance, and organized performances where Carnatic vocal and instrumental music would dominate the first half of the evening, while the second half consisted of dance routines from popular films.

Music organizations

Indian classical music continues to be played and transmitted in Singapore mainly through the efforts of private schools, temples, community clubs and individuals. There is a regular flow of artistes and teachers from India. Contemporary groups teaching and performing Indian classical music in Singapore include the SINGAPORE INDIAN FINE ARTS SOCIETY, Alaapana, Sri Sabari Fine Arts, Indian Classical Music Centre, Prenavam KalaSadhana, NRITYALAYA AESTHETICS SOCIETY, KALAMANDHIR TEMPLE OF FINE ARTS, APSARAS ARTS and the Kolam Ayer Youth Orchestra.

Carnatic and Hindustani are the main categories of Indian classical music which can be found in Singapore, but this division aside, the sitar and tabla have become popular musical instruments among local Indians, and the fusion of both styles, known as *jugalbandhi*, has become a regular feature of performances.

Dance-drama music

In South Indian classical music, a symbiotic relationship between dance and music is evident in the highly structured forms of *bharatanatyam*, *kathakali*, *odissi* and *katak*. The teaching and performance of these dance forms have become a staple of private Indian music schools here. Recent trends have moved towards more contemporary forms. Despite attempts to fuse the skills and efforts of dancers, choreographers, musicians, composers, set designers, mural painters, lighting designers and scriptwriters since the early 1990s, instrumentation for musical accompaniment tends to be orchestral and influenced by theatre musicals. As Indian classical musicians rely heavily on improvisation, it is not unusual to find pre-recorded music used in dance-dramas—a practical solution to the problem of rehearsing episodes with detailed dance choreography.

Singapore Indian Orchestra and Choir

Efforts have been made to create more original forms of Indian music identifiable with a post-Independence Singapore. The idea to establish an ensemble of Indian instruments was realized in 1985 when the Singapore Indian Orchestra was established under the PEOPLE'S ASSOCIATION. A choir was added in 1990, and the name became Singapore Indian Orchestra and Choir. This group has given more than 100 performances, with a number of composers writing music for it. The Indian orchestra plays two types of music—Indian classical and what can be termed 'experimental' music. Instruments used include the *veena*, sitar, violin, flute, clarinet and percussion instruments consisting of the *mrdangam*, tabla, *ghatam*,

ganjira and other small percussion instruments. Occasionally, other musical instruments from the Western, Chinese or Malay traditions are employed when working with repertoires which contain works from outside the Indian classical tradition. Syncretism is also evident in the orchestra's use of multi-layered melodic lines and ideas from popular music and instruments from Chinese

and Malay traditions. At the SINGAPORE ARTS FESTIVAL in 2002, the Indian Orchestra and Choir joined with the People's Association Youth Chinese Orchestra, Orkestra Melayu Singapura (Singapore Malay Orchestra), Singapore Wind Symphony, The Vocal Consort and Singapore National Youth Orchestra to perform Wolfgang Amadeus Mozart's *Symphony No. 40 in G minor*, Antonio

Vivaldi's *Double Violin Concerto* and even some jazz numbers.

The performance of devotional songs played by Western-style ensembles highlights contradictions between the sacred and the secular. While Indian classical music continues to play its traditional role as a main component of Hindu worship and ritual, non-Indians now have the opportunity to engage with Indian classical music and dance. An ensemble such as the Singapore Indian Orchestra and Choir takes advantage of local cultures and traditions by performing Indian classical music with instruments which are not conventionally associated with the form, thereby attempting to broaden its repertoire and thus expanding the parameters for Indian classical music in Singapore.

by south Indians have added popular items such as ROTI PRATA, *biryani* and *murtabak* to Singapore's culinary landscape.

Indian Muslims in Singapore have founded their own social organizations which conduct religious functions, provide religious education in Indian languages, and offer social services. Many date back to the early 20th century, when organizations such as the Indian Muslim Society (established around 1907) were set up to provide religious education. The organizations cater to particular ethnic groups, such as the MALABAR MUSLIM JAMA-ATH; religious groups or communities, as did the now-defunct Singapore DAWOODI BOHRA Muslim Association; or people from a common hometown in India, such as the towns of Tenkasi, Kadayanallur and Thiruvithancode.

With Singapore's Independence, many became actively involved in nation-building. The formation of the FEDERATION OF INDIAN MUSLIMS in 1992 provided a forum for Indian Muslims to address a common agenda.

While many Indian Muslims maintain their cultural identity, some—due to inter-marriage, for example—are taking on the cultural attributes, speech and dress of the Malay community.

Indian National Army and Monument The Indian National Army (INA) was an army raised for the liberation of India. It was formed, mainly, from British Indian soldiers and officers in Southeast Asia who had surrendered to the Japanese. Influenced by the independence movement in India, it was set up in 1942.

The INA's first commander was MOHAN SINGH. Mohan Singh had been persuaded by Pritam Singh of the Indian Independence League to cooperate with the Japanese in order to fight against the British. However, Mohan Singh was arrested by the Japanese in December 1942 on the charge of being too independent of the Japanese military.

The INA declined after Singh's arrest. However, the army witnessed a dramatic revival in July 1943 when former Indian

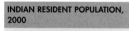

INDIAN RESIDENT POPULATION, 2000

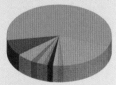

Tamil (58.3%)

Malayalee (8.4%)

Sikh (5.1%)

Hindustani (2%)

Punjabi (1.8%)

Sindhi (1.6%)

Hindi (1.5%)

Gujarati (1.3%)

Urdu (1.2%)

Sinhalese (0.9%)

Others (17.9%)

Source: Singapore Department of Statistics

Indian National Army Monument

Indian National Army: Subhas Chandra Bose reviews 'Rani of Jhansi' regiment at Waterloo Street, 1943.

Congress Party President SUBHAS CHANDRA BOSE arrived in Singapore. The Provisional Government of independent India was declared by the INA, under Bose's leadership, in Singapore in October 1943.

Bose's high profile in the Indian independence struggle attracted many Indian soldiers and members of the Indian community in Malaya and Singapore. They believed that once the INA crossed the India-Burma border with Japanese troops, the Indian public would rise against the British and rally to the INA.

In 1944, the INA took part in the Burma campaign to take the town of Imphal on Indian soil near the India-Burma border. However, the INA failed in its objective and suffered many casualties.

At the end of the war, INA leaders decided to erect a memorial to the army's soldiers who had died in battle from 1942 to 1945. On 8 July 1945, Bose laid the foundation stone of the memorial at Singapore's PADANG, near Connaught Drive. The memorial was completed and unveiled on 23 August 1945. The words inscribed on the monument in Urdu were *Itteaq* (unity), *Itmad* (faith) and *Kurbani* (sacrifice). This was also the motto adopted at the first major meeting of the Indian Independence League, held in Bangkok in June 1942.

In September 1945, when the British returned to Singapore, they had the INA memorial destroyed. However, Indians continued to visit the site to pay their respects to the INA war dead. In 1995, the NATIONAL HERITAGE BOARD of Singapore marked the site with a large slab which included an inscription detailing the history of the army and the monument.

Indians The term 'Indian' in Singapore's context has been used since the 1950s to include all people originating from the Indian subcontinent, which today consists of India, Pakistan, Bangladesh, Sri Lanka, Nepal, Bhutan and the Maldives. In the

past, many terms were used to describe some of the prominent groups: CHULIA, SIKHS, Pathan, Bengalee (BENGALIS) and Ceylonese (SINHALESE).

Indians have been in Singapore from the first day of its founding as a British trading post by Sir STAMFORD RAFFLES in January 1819. In addition to 120 SEPOYS and lascars (sailors from the East Indies), and possibly assistants and domestic servants, Raffles' entourage on his second visit included NARAYANA PILLAY, a Hindu trader from Penang. Two years later, there were 132 Indians—apart from the garrison and camp followers—out of a total Singapore population of 4,727. With the arrival of labourers and traders—in response to Raffles' liberal policies and expanding opportunities for employment—the Indian population rapidly increased, and by 1871, had reached 11,580.

As the British Empire abolished slavery in 1833, the STRAITS SETTLEMENTS, of which Singapore was a part, looked to British India for labour. As Singapore was also declared a convict station, Indian CONVICT LABOUR was transported to build the city's infrastructure of roads, buildings and canals. Indian convicts provided much of the labour for erecting ST. ANDREW'S CATHEDRAL, GOVERNMENT HOUSE (now the ISTANA), CITY HALL and other public buildings; constructing roads such as North Bridge Road, South Bridge Road, Serangoon Road and Thomson Road. One of the oldest Hindu temples in Singapore, SRI MARIAMMAN TEMPLE, had its initial structures built by Indian convicts in 1828.

The convicts were trained as bricklayers, blacksmiths and carpenters. When the administration of the Straits Settlements was transferred to the Colonial Office in 1867, many Indian convicts were pardoned, and settled in Singapore.

The expansion of the Malayan economy, and the consequent development of

Singapore, resulted in the arrival of more Indians. Indian labour proved indispensable to the success of many projects aimed at the transformation of Singapore, such as the CAUSEWAY, the Sembawang Dockyards and KALLANG AIRPORT.

Educated Indians were recruited to operate the British administrative machinery, becoming clerks, interpreters, overseers, lawyers and draughtsman, and staffing the education and police departments. In the early days, both mission and government schools were staffed largely by Indians. The police constabulary was practically dominated by SIKHS and TAMILS.

A third group of Indians, the traders and businessmen—SINDHIS, NATTUKOTAI CHETTIARS, Mudaliars and Muslims from Tamil Nadu, Kerala and Surat (near Mumbai)—came to Singapore to establish trading and finance houses. Urban Indians also arrived to work as doormen and security personnel for commercial banks, offices and large stores in the commercial area, and carried out manual work in private residences within the European residential areas.

The earliest Indian settlements, consisting mainly of Tamil groups, were aggregated along the western fringe of the business zone, west of the SINGAPORE RIVER. They had been allocated a river frontage of about half a kilometre, but spread close to the mercantile establishments near present-day Chulia Street.

By the early 20th century, the Indian population, located around the commercial core of the island, had expanded and spread along SERANGOON ROAD where many of them became small shopkeepers. Later, government housing for labourers employed by the PUBLIC WORKS DEPARTMENT—mainly Tamils—was also established in this vicinity.

After 1920, the British, in anticipation of Japanese military expansion, developed

Indians: detail of Hindu temple gopuram.

the northern part of the island as a naval base, building a military base in Sembawang and an airbase in CHANGI. Civilian workers were needed for the construction and maintenance of such bases, and this led to an inflow of Indians into these areas. By 1962, the number of Indians living in Chong Pang, Jalan Kayu, Nee Soon and Yew Tee villages far outnumbered the Malay population there.

In the 1960s, when Singapore experienced many political, social and economic changes, the settlement pattern of Singapore Indians changed. With urban renewal and resettlement of the population into the government-managed Housing and Development Board housing estates, Indians tended to buy apartments in estates close to their earlier residential areas. Thus, new townships at Ang Mo Kio, Toa Payoh, Queenstown, MacPherson and Woodlands became focal points for Indian families. The Indian population in earlier settlement areas—Chulia Street, Market Street, High Street, around docks, railways and military establishments—decreased. While the Serangoon Road area, referred to as 'Little India', and the Arab Street locality, retained their Indian business character, the Indian proportion of their populations declined. At the end of the 20th century, urban redevelopment and the rising cost of housing near the city caused further shifts to outlying towns such as Yishun, Hougang, Tampines and Jurong. As of 2005, Indians made up approximately 9 per cent of the population, or about 309,300.

While Tamil is the predominant language among Indians in Singapore, other languages—Gujarati, Hindi, Malayalam, Punjabi, Sindhi, Telugu and Urdu—are also spoken. Each Indian linguistic group has a voluntary association in Singapore to promote its specific language and culture.

Indians in Singapore have embraced all the major religions. HINDUISM has the largest number of adherents, accounting for slightly more than 50 per cent of the Indian population. While THAIPUSAM (a festival dedicated to Lord Murugan) and THEEMIDHI (fire-walking festival) are Hindu festivals widely known to other Singaporeans and tourists, many other festivals are celebrated throughout the year.

ISLAM, CHRISTIANITY and Sikhism are the other major religions among Indians in Singapore. Many mosques provide sermons in Tamil, Urdu, Bengali and Gujarati to accommodate the different linguistic groups. Some of Singapore's oldest mosques, such as AL-ABRAR MOSQUE, JAMAE MOSQUE and ABDUL GAFFOOR MOSQUE, owe their origins to INDIAN MUSLIMS.

There are Indians in most Christian denominations, with Catholicism having the largest number of adherents. Indian Christians have long been involved with the activities of the various churches in Singapore. Some, such as the MAR THOMA SYRIAN CHURCH, Syrian Orthodox Church, Lady of Lourdes Church and Christ Church, have a long history of predominantly Indian congregations, services conducted by Indian pastors and hymns sung in Tamil or Malayalam.

A small number of Indians are Buddhist, this group increasing as more Sri Lankans come to work in Singapore as domestic helpers and businessmen. Sikhism has a large following among Punjabi speakers, with nearly 20,000 followers (*see* SIKHS). Jainism has about 500 adherents (*see* JAINS).

In 2005 there were about 172 voluntary organizations catering for the needs of Indians. The SINGAPORE INDIAN DEVELOPMENT ASSOCIATION (SINDA), is a major umbrella organization.

Two Indians have served as President of Singapore: C.V. DEVAN NAIR and S.R. NATHAN. Among Indians who have played prominent roles in Singapore's Cabinet are S. RAJARATNAM, S. DHANABALAN, S. JAYAKUMAR—all three having served as Minister of Foreign Affairs—and Education Minister THARMAN SHANMUGARATNAM.

Indonesia–Singapore relations

Indonesia is the biggest country in Southeast Asia. It is the world's third largest democracy and it has the world's largest Muslim population – more than Iran, Iraq, Egypt and Saudi Arabia combined. It is rich in natural resources and some of the world's most important sealanes pass through its archipelagic waters and territorial sea.

Relations between independent Singapore and Indonesia got off to a rocky start. In 1965, Indonesia was in the middle of its CONFRONTATION (Konfrontasi) campaign against Malaysia and Singapore. The hanging of the two Indonesian marines involved in the bombing of MACDONALD HOUSE in Singapore during Confrontation, and Singapore's rebuff of Suharto's personal appeal for clemency in 1968 worsened ties. Relations only began to improve in 1973 after then-Prime Minister Lee Kuan Yew scattered flowers on the graves of the two marines during a visit to Jakarta.

The gesture by Lee ushered in an era of stability and built a lasting relationship between the two leaders. It was during this period that economic and defence links were entrenched. In August 1990, for instance, Singapore and Indonesia signed two economic agreements on "The Promotion and Protection of Investments" and "Economic Cooperation in the Framework of the Development of the Riau Province". The armed forces of both countries have held regular military exercises since the 1990s. Singapore also worked closely with Indonesia to strengthen the ASSOCIATION OF SOUTHEAST ASIAN NATIONS (ASEAN), which provides the foundations for regional peace and stability

Indians: weekend relaxation in Little India.

that contributed to a sustained period of economic growth in the region.

However, the fall of Suharto exposed fissures in the relationship. This animosity peaked in 1998 when then-President B.J. Habibie dismissed Singapore as a "little red dot" in a sea of green, the green representing the extensive territory of Indonesia, and criticized Singapore for being an unhelpful neighbour during the Asian financial crisis. This was in spite of the fact that Singapore joined other countries to contribute to a multi-billion dollar International Monetary Fund bailout package for Indonesia in November 1997. Relations during the presidency of Abdurrahman Wahid (Gus Dur) were generally on an even keel notwithstanding his unhappiness with Singapore when it did not support his proposal for Timor-Leste and Papua New Guinea to join Asean in November 2000. Relations improved following Gus Dur's impeachment in July 2001. Megawati Sukarnoputri, his successor, enjoyed close personal ties with Singapore leaders. Then-Prime Minister Goh Chok Tong met her several times and various attempts were made to resolve difficult outstanding issues against the backdrop of a vibrant, democratic and nationalistic environment in Indonesia.

Under President Susilo Bambang Yudhoyono, bilateral relations have found a new equilibrium, helped by the personal rapport between Prime Minister Lee Hsien Loong and President Yudhoyono, both of whom represent a new generation of leaders. Outstanding problems, such as the delimitation of maritime boundaries, are being negotiated. Singapore and Indonesia worked closely on various Asean issues and on the formation of a new regional forum in the EAST ASIA SUMMIT in 2005. Both countries have also enhanced counter-terrorism cooperation.

Singapore was among the first countries to send help to Aceh following the earthquake and tsunami in 2004. Singapore's disaster relief efforts in Indonesia focused on the remote town of Meulaboh, whose communication and transportation links to other parts of Aceh had been completely cut off. The tsunami also saw an unprecedented number of private Singaporeans and non-governmental organisations volunteer to take part in the post-tsunami rehabilitation efforts.

Economically, links between both countries are strong. Singapore has consistently been one of Indonesia's major investors. In 2005, Singapore was Indonesia's top investor. Singapore's investments in Indonesia totaled US$3.9 billion, constituting nearly a third of all investments into the country. Indonesia supplies natural gas for use in Singapore's power stations and in return, Singapore will pay Indonesia US$17 billion over 22 years. The rise of China and India is providing an impetus to enhance this economic partnership. Both sides signed an Investment Guarantee Agreement in February 2005 to promote greater investment flows. Singapore is also helping Indonesia to establish Special Economic Zones in neighbouring Riau Islands province as another means of enhancing bilateral economic ties.

Industrial Arbitration Court Created in October 1960 with the passage of the Industrial Relations Act, the Industrial Arbitration Court (IAC) was set up to deal with matters concerning employer-employee relations and the settlement of trade disputes. Due to the high number of industrial disputes in the early 1960s, a second IAC was constituted in 1962, although it ceased to function in 1970 when industrial peace was restored through tripartite cooperation between employers, labour and the government.

The court makes awards, certifies and registers collective agreements, resolves disputes through a referee, interprets an award, sets aside or varies an award, mediates, and provides an advisory service on industrial relations matters. For example, the IAC ruled in 1969 that the management of a company (in this case Metal Box (Malaysia) Ltd) had the right to introduce shift duties and regulate working hours since such concerns were no longer a matter for collective bargaining. One of the IAC's most celebrated cases was heard in 1966 when it ordered the Port of Singapore Authority (PSA) to award $4 million in back-pay to its 11,500 employees under a new collective agreement. The first President of the IAC was Professor Charles Gamba.

See also LABOUR RELATIONS.

industrial estates The first industrial zone to be established in Singapore was the JURONG INDUSTRIAL ESTATE. It was the idea

Industrial estates: Jurong Industrial Estate, 1964.

of GOH KENG SWEE and represents the first step in Singapore's INDUSTRIALIZATION plan in the 1960s. The government was successful in attracting foreign investors to set up their factories in Jurong, creating employment opportunities and paving the way for Singapore's economic success in the MANUFACTURING sector.

Jurong Town Corporation (JTC) was established in 1968 with the primary responsibility of acquiring, developing and managing industrial sites in Singapore. The corporation provides manufacturers with a choice of industrial land sites on which to build their own factories or ready-built factories for the immediate start-up of manufacturing operations.

By 2005, JTC was managing 38 industrial and specialized parks in Singapore. In 2005, it also announced plans to restructure itself, so as to focus on more strategic projects such as specialized industrial parks.

Industrial estates are grouped in industry clusters such as chemicals, wafer fabrication, biomedical products, food and logistics. JURONG ISLAND predominantly houses chemical industries, while wafer fabrication parks are located in Tampines, Pasir Ris and Woodlands. JTC also caters for evolving business trends, with the branding of some industrial zones as Technopreneur Centre, Business Park and iPark.

Industrial estates focused on light manufacturing can also be found near Housing and Development Board (HDB) estates such as TANGLIN HALT. They are set up to facilitate the relocation of cottage industries to free up land for public housing, and to provide jobs easily accessible to HDB residents.

industrial relations *See* LABOUR RELATIONS.

industrialization In 1959, when Singapore became self-governing, the immediate economic tasks facing the government were the restructuring of the economy so as to reduce its dependence on entrepôt trade, and the alleviation of unemployment. Following advice from a team of United Nations experts led by Dutch economist ALBERT WINSEMIUS, the government launched a four-year development plan in 1961. The ECONOMIC DEVELOPMENT BOARD was established in 1961 to address the task.

Industrial strategy in the initial years was based on import substitution. A system

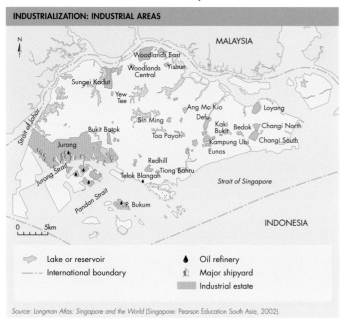

INDUSTRIALIZATION: INDUSTRIAL AREAS

MALAYSIA

Woodlands East
Woodlands Central
Yishun
Sungei Kadut
Yew Tee
Ang Mo Kio
Sin Ming
Defu
Loyang
Bukit Batok
Kaki Bukit
Bedok
Changi North
Jurong
Toa Payoh
Kampung Ubi
Changi South
Eunos
Redhill
Tiong Bahru
Telok Blangah
P. Bukum

Strait of Johor
Jurong Strait
Pandan Strait
Strait of Singapore
INDONESIA

0   5km

◁▷ Lake or reservoir
--- International boundary
♦ Oil refinery
⚓ Major shipyard
▦ Industrial estate

Source: Longman Atlas: Singapore and the World (Singapore: Pearson Education South Asia, 2002).

of import quotas was introduced for a limited number of goods, with controls on how many enterprises could enter a particular field. When Singapore achieved independence in 1965, the industrial sector was still small, with MANUFACTURING accounting for only 11 per cent of GROSS DOMESTIC PRODUCT and commerce accounting for 32 per cent.

In 1967, the British announced their intention to withdraw from their Singapore military bases—which accounted for 40,000 jobs—by the end of 1971. Import substitution was succeeded by a strategy of export-oriented, labour-intensive industrialization—such as textile manufacturing—to assuage the anticipated unemployment situation. The ECONOMIC DEVELOPMENT BOARD, as the government's agent, became the spearhead for the industrialization drive. The plan was also supported by the introduction of tax and other incentives and further enhanced by the 1968 Employment Act, and the Industrial Relations (Amendment) Act aimed at promoting industrial peace among workers. The JURONG INDUSTRIAL ESTATE had been established in 1961 to provide the necessary physical infrastructure for industrialization. The government also created public enterprises in areas where the private sector lacked capital or expertise, for example, SINGAPORE AIRLINES, NEPTUNE ORIENT LINES, Development Bank of Singapore (now DBS BANK) and Sembawang Shipyard.

Capitalizing on a buoyant world economy that absorbed Singapore's manufactured exports, full employment was effectively reached by 1970. The resulting labour shortage eventually led to an escalation of wage costs. With increased competition from lower-cost countries in the region and the threat of protectionism rising, industrial restructuring had become necessary. By 1979, efforts to upgrade the overall industrial structure and to accelerate the trend toward skill- and technology-intensive, higher value-added economic activities were intensified. Fiscal incentives were introduced to encourage automation and mechanization, productivity was encour-

Industrial estates: HDB flatted factory, Delta Road.

aged, and new technology-intensive industries such as the manufacture of computer peripherals and machinery were identified and aggressively promoted. At the same time, a 'high wage policy' was introduced for three years starting from 1979.

The 1980s saw Singapore experiencing a 'second industrial revolution', which placed emphasis on knowledge-intensive activities such as research and development (R&D), engineering design, and computer software services. The Science Park was set up next to the National University of Singapore to stimulate R&D activities by the private sector. During the decade, almost all the large electronics multinational companies found their way to Singapore and the production of disk drives and computers became important. PETROCHEMICALS also became a leading industry. By the late 1980s, Singapore was the world's third-largest oil-trading centre and also the third-largest centre for petroleum refining.

The 1985 recession exposed structural strains in the economy, which had been masked by strong economic growth. An Economic Committee, led by then Minister for Trade and Industry, LEE HSIEN LOONG, looked at ways to restore Singapore's competitiveness. Cluster development became part of the industrial strategy in order to maximize synergies at both company and industry levels. Mutually supporting industries were identified, e.g. electronics, petrochemicals and engineering. To build a broader base for the economy, the SERVICES SECTOR was promoted together with manufacturing as twin pillars of the economy. The government encouraged regionalization to overcome local resource and market constraints.

Infocomm Development Authority of Singapore Statutory board. Infocommunications (infocomm) can be defined as the convergence of INFORMATION TECHNOLOGY and telecommunications. A regulatory and promotional body formed in 1999 from the merger of the National Computer Board and the Telecommunication Authority of Singapore, the Infocomm Development Authority of Singapore (IDA) aims to establish Singapore as a leading infocommunications hub in Asia. As the regulator of the industry, IDA formulates policies to ensure a competitive environment in the fully liberalized telecommunications market. In 2000, it unveiled Infocomm 21, a strategic plan to develop Singapore into a 'global infocomm capital with a thriving and prosperous e-Economy, and a pervasive and infocomm-savvy e-Society'. This was followed up in 2003 by Connected Singapore, which further developed the strategy.

By 2005, Singapore had high penetration rates of telecommunications, personal computer and Internet usage, and pervasive use of IT by government, businesses and

the public. Broadband accessibility was near-universal. Future key growth areas are wireless broadband and e-commerce. The aim is to grow Singapore into a trusted global e-business hub in the Asia Pacific for both business-to-business and business-to-consumer activities.

The 5th Infocomm Technology Roadmap Symposium in 2005 identified the possibilities created by the confluence of info-, nano- and bio-technologies. The Roadmap guides IDA's national effort to craft Intelligent Nation 2015 (iN2015), a new master plan to take Singapore to 2015.

Industrialization: Dr Goh Keng Swee, minister for finance, at the opening of United Paints' factory in Bendemeer Industrial Estate, in 1965 (top); worker in modern automated factory.

information technology In the late 1970s, government policy began to be developed around the harnessing of information technology (IT) to shift the economy towards higher value-added activities. A key policy initiative was the computerization of the public sector, which began in earnest in 1981. This marked the beginning of the development of a national IT policy. The National Computer Board was established as the lead coordinating agency.

The National IT Report was formulated in 1986. The period 1986 to 1991 saw the integration of computer and communications technologies to permit electronic data interchange across government departments and industry. TradeNet was implemented in 1989 and was followed by LawNet and MediNet.

In 1992, the IT2000 Plan was unveiled to develop Singapore into an 'intelligent island'. In 1997, a nationwide broadband infrastructure known as Singapore ONE (One Network for Everyone) was launched, linking businesses, educational establishments and homes.

By 1999, computing, TELECOMMUNICATIONS and broadcasting technologies were converging rapidly. To meet the challenges and opportunities posed by this convergence, the INFOCOMM DEVELOPMENT AUTHORITY OF SINGAPORE (IDA) was formed.

ink painting *See* CHINESE INK PAINTING AND CALLIGRAPHY.

insects Animals with three pairs of legs, two pairs of wings and an external skeleton, insects are members of the Arthropoda phylum. More than one million species of insects have been identified, but there may be 10–30 million species altogether. The Smithsonian Institution estimates that at any given time, some 10 quintillion (10,000,000,000,000,000,000) of these creatures live on the planet.

Forest insects

Singapore is home to a wide variety of insects. It is estimated that there are over 10,000 species of beetles, 200 of ants and 200 of cockroaches in BUKIT TIMAH NATURE RESERVE alone. After the naturalist Alfred Russel Wallace walked into Bukit Timah forest in 1860, he wrote: 'In about two months I obtained no less than 700 species of beetles...Almost all these were collected in one patch of jungle, not more than a square mile in extent, and in all my subsequent travels in the East I rarely if ever met with so productive a spot.'

Some of the loudest sounds heard in the forest are the calls of cicadas (*Purana* spp.). They produce buzzing, whining or trumpeting sounds, each unique to a species. The male makes these sounds by using its muscles to rapidly vibrate two drum-like membranes at the base of its abdomen. Also easily heard is the black-horned locust (*Valanga nigricornis*). Males 'sing' to females, by rubbing parts of their bodies together, a process called stridulation.

The praying mantis (family Mantidae) (*1*) is a close relative of the cockroach and grows up to 15 cm long. It is the only insect with the ability to turn its head 180 degrees.

It whips out powerful forelegs to grab its victims—usually insects, although the adult mantis has been known to catch and kill frogs and small birds.

Playing an important role in the forest are termites (*2*). Belonging to the order Isoptera, they consume large quantities of dead plant material. To help them break down wood for their food, termites use their droppings as compost to grow fungus in their nests.

The forest is also home to some rare denizens. Two species of the trilobite larvae (*Duliticola* spp.) (*3*) are found in Singapore, and both are new to science. These strange creatures belong to the family of net-winged beetles. The females remain in larval form throughout their lives and mature sexually while still in that form. In contrast, the males look like typical beetles and are less than half a centimetre in length. Little else is known about these insects.

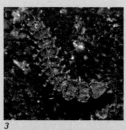

3

1

2

Ants

There are more than 200 ant species in Singapore but the one frequently found in homes is the black crazy ant (*Paratrechina longicornis*), which is attracted to food around the house. A common sight in the garden, weaver ants (*Oecophylla smaragdina*) (*4*) weave leaves together with larval silk.

4

They grow up to 8 mm in length. The worker ants are orange or red while their queens are black.

In the forest, the giant forest ant (*Camponotus gigas*), one of the largest ant species in Singapore, grows to about 2.5 mm in length. It is a non-aggressive ant, usually seen alone.

The giant jumping ant (*Harpegnathos venator*) was recorded only once in Singapore, in a patch of secondary forest at Sime Road. It has elongated curving mandibles which are flicked on the ground when the ant is leaping into the air. It is said to catch flies in mid-air. It is not known if this ant still exists in Singapore.

5   **6**

7

Beetles

Beetles are the largest and most diverse group of living organisms on earth; they form the largest insect order, with

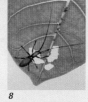

8

more than 400,000 species described worldwide. Dominant families include the ground beetles (Carabidae) (*5*), scarab beetles (Scarabaeidae) (*6*), leaf beetles (Chrysomelidae) (*7*), jewel beetles (Buprestidae), weevils (Curculonidae) and longhorn beetles (Cerambycidae) (*8*), the last so named because of their long antennae.

Many species of beetles are aquatic as well. Diving beetles (family Dytiscidae) swim with their hind legs, using them like oars on a rowboat. They can stay under water for a long time, as the air they carry under their wings or hairs allows them to breathe.

Camouflage and deception

Many insects employ camouflage and other forms of deception to protect themselves. Leaf insects (*13*) and stick insects (*14*) belong to the order Phasmida. Leaf insects blend extraordinarily well with the surrounding foliage, while stick insects rely on their stillness and twig-like bodies for concealment.

13

14

Butterflies

Singapore has about 1,000 species of butterflies. Common butterflies include the lime butterfly (*Papilio demoleus*), whose caterpillars resemble bird droppings and feed on the leaves of citrus plants. The painted Jezebel (*Delias hyparete*) (*9*) is a weak flyer, but its bright colours warn predators of its unpleasant taste.

Some butterflies live primarily in the forest. One of the most beautiful forest dwellers is the Malay lacewing (*Cethosia hypsia*) (*10*). The common birdwing (*Troides helena*) (*11*) flies high in the forest canopy. It is often sought by collectors and traders because of its size and striking looks. The common tree nymph (*Idea stolli*) (*12*) also frequents the canopy, but its slow, fluid flight gives it the appearance of being carried by the wind.

9   **10**

11

12

Butterflies usually have bright colours and eye spots to frighten away predators. The female of the common mormon (*Papilio polytes*) (*15*) looks like the poisonous common rose (*Pachliopta aristolochiae*) (*16*), thus deterring would-be predators. Many insect nymphs have bright warning colours and may cluster together on the underside of leaves for greater effect.

Other insects make mobile shelters in which to hide. Caterpillars and females of bagworm moths (belonging to the family Psychidae) build a 'bag' of tiny twigs, leaves or pebbles and live in it. To walk, they stick out their head and front legs.

15   **16**

Inland Revenue Authority of Singapore The Inland Revenue Authority of Singapore (IRAS) was established by legislation as a statutory board under the MINISTRY OF FINANCE in 1992. It took over functions previously performed by the Inland Revenue Department which, in turn, superseded the Singapore Income Tax Department in 1960.

As Singapore's tax authority, IRAS is responsible for administering the Income Tax Act, the Property Tax Act, the Estate Duty Act, the Stamp Duties Act, and the GOODS AND SERVICES TAX Act amongst other duties. IRAS achieves close to 90 per cent voluntary compliance, with tax collection for 2003/4 amounting to $16.5 billion. The tax processes are highly automated: tax-related transactions can be performed through an Internet portal. In 2000, the World Bank cited IRAS as a model tax administration body. The IRAS Act was amended in September 2004 so that the minister for finance no longer needed to be the chairman of IRAS (as had been the case since 1992).

INSEAD Business school. Founded in 1957 in Fontainebleau, France, as the European Institute for Business Administration, over the years it became known as INSEAD. It provides MBA, PhD and executive programmes. The Asia campus in Singapore was officially opened in 2000. INSEAD also has a strategic alliance with the Wharton School of the University of Pennsylvannia. An INSEAD MBA student can study at any of the three campuses.

insects *See* box.

Institute of Bioengineering and Nanotechnology Biomedical research institute. Established in 2003, the Institute of Bioengineering and Nanotechnology (IBN) is one of several research institutes under the AGENCY FOR SCIENCE AND TECHNOLOGY RESEARCH (A★STAR), and occupies over 8,900 sq m of laboratory space in Biopolis—a 180-ha biomedical city within the Buona Vista Science Hub (*see* ONE-NORTH). IBN's founding director is Professor Jackie Ying, previously with the Massachusetts Institute of Technology.

IBN conducts research in six main

Institute of Contemporary Art Singapore

areas: nanobiotechnology; delivery of drugs, proteins and genes; cell and tissue engineering; artificial organs and implants; medical and biological devices; and biological and biomedical imaging. In 2005, a team of IBN researchers created nano-sized drug delivery vehicles to transport cancer drugs to where they are needed. The scientists developed 'smart' nanocarriers with shells that protect enclosed drugs from degradation and digestive fluids. These nanocarriers reduce the side effects of chemotherapy.

Institute of Contemporary Art Singapore Established in 2004 by the LASALLE-SIA COLLEGE OF THE ARTS, the Institute of Contemporary Art focuses on the promotion and research of international and contemporary Asian art. Its permanent collection comprises over 900 works of Asian art. The Institute also oversees the Earl Lu Gallery (*see* LU MING TEH, EARL).

Institute of Defence and Strategic Studies Established in 1996 as an autonomous teaching and research institute within NANYANG TECHNOLOGICAL UNIVERSITY, the Institute of Defence and Strategic Studies (IDSS) focuses on security, strategic and international issues. It also provides general and graduate education in strategic studies, international relations, defence management and defence technology. The institute provides educational opportunities at an advanced level through its graduate programmes, culminating in the award of Master of Science in Strategic Studies, International Relations or International Political Economy degrees. It offers a doctoral programme for research in these fields. In addition to these graduate programmes, the Institute teaches various modules in courses conducted by the SAFTI Military Institute, SAF Warrant Officers' School, Civil Defence Academy and the Defence and Home Affairs Ministries.

Constituents of the IDSS include the International Centre for Political Violence and Terrorism Research, the Centre of Excellence for National Security and the Asian Programme for Negotiation and Conflict Management. The IDSS's motto is 'Ponder the Improbable'. The founding director of the institute was President S.R. Nathan.

Institute of Mental Health/Woodbridge Hospital Psychiatric hospital. The first mental institution in Singapore was the Insane Hospital, opened in 1841. It became the Mental Hospital in 1928 before being renamed Woodbridge Hospital in 1951. In 1993, the name Institute of Mental Health (IMH) was added, to reflect added emphasis on research, training and mental health education. Institute of Mental Health/Woodbridge Hospital, which has

2,425 beds, is located in the 30-ha Buangkok Green Medical Park.

IMH manages psychiatric patients with a combination of drugs and other forms of therapy such as psychotherapy, which provides a more holistic care covering patients' personal and social problems outside the hospital. This multidisciplinary approach is supported by the nursing, clinical psychology, occupational therapy and medical social work departments.

In addition to its seven clinical departments—general psychiatry, child and adolescent psychiatry, community psychiatry, geriatric psychiatry, forensic psychiatry, early psychosis intervention and addiction medicine—IMH has three specialized clinics treating specific disorders, namely anxiety and mood, sleep disorders and sexual dysfunction. It also runs four satellite clinics, three day centres and does home visits.

Aside from treatment, IMH organizes mental health programmes for the public, including programmes tailored to help corporations promote the mental wellbeing of staff. The institute also oversees the research and training of clinicians in psychiatry.

Institute of Molecular and Cell Biology This research institute was established in 1987 at the NATIONAL UNIVERSITY OF SINGAPORE. The Institute of Molecular and Cell Biology (IMCB) later became an autonomous research institute under the AGENCY FOR SCIENCE, TECHNOLOGY AND RESEARCH (A★STAR), funded mainly by A★STAR's Biomedical Research Council. IMCB's mission is to foster a research culture for the biomedical sciences, and to help train PhD students for the biotechnology and pharmaceutical industries that Singapore is promoting.

Located at Biopolis in the Buona Vista Science Hub (*see* ONE-NORTH), IMCB operates 35 research labs and has more than 500 research scientists. Its research focuses

Institute of Bioengineering and Nanotechnology: microscopic images of 4T1 mouse breast cancer cells taking up an anti-cancer drug.

Institue of Molecular and Cell Biology

on six main areas: cell biology, developmental biology, structural biology, infectious diseases, cancer biology and translational research.

IMCB's achievements include a breakthrough in cancer research: its researchers discovered in 2005 that a naturally-occurring cell in the body, once thought to induce the death of cancer cells, actually maintains their malignant state. An IMCB team also found that a major suppressor of tumours also checks the development of bone. The institute led an international consortium that successfully sequenced the entire pufferfish genome, after identifying it as an important model for analysing the human genome sequence. The principal investigator in that programme was Nobel Laureate (Medicine) Sydney Brenner.

Institute of Policy Studies Think-tank. Established in 1988, the Institute of Policy Studies (IPS) is one of Singapore's oldest think-tanks. It analyses issues of concern to Singapore, and communicates its research findings to a wider community, while seeking to generate greater awareness of policy issues. Its core areas of research are arts and culture; demography and family; economics; environmental and urban studies; information society; international relations and international law; multiculturalism and identities; and politics and governance. The IPS' first Director was Professor CHAN HENG CHEE.

Institute of Southeast Asian Studies Think-tank. The Institute of Southeast Asian Studies (ISEAS) specializes in the study of socio-political, security and economic trends and developments in Southeast Asia. It was the brainchild of then Deputy Prime Minister GOH KENG SWEE, who, in 1966, began considering the establishment of a research institute in Singapore which would focus specifically on Southeast Asian matters. This coincided with growing concern in Cabinet that, although Singapore occupied a key strategic location in the region, Singaporean policy makers and scholars had limited knowledge of Southeast Asia. As a result of Goh's efforts, Parliament passed the Institute of Southeast Asian Studies Act in June 1968 to establish ISEAS as an independent regional research organization. Its first director was Harry J. Benda.

ISEAS conducts a range of research programmes; holds conferences, workshops, lectures and seminars; publishes research journals and books; and provides a range of research support facilities, including a large library collection.

Institute of Technical Education Operating under the MINISTRY OF EDUCATION, the ITE provides pre-employment training for secondary school leavers, and continuing education and training for working adults. It accepts students who have completed the

Institute of Southeast Asian Studies: publication of scholarly papers and journals.

Institute of Technical Education: hands-on education for students.

Singapore-Cambridge General Certificate of Education Ordinary or Normal Level Examinations, and offers them a range of one- to two-year technical or vocational courses. Students who do well are able to proceed to POLYTECHNICS for diploma programmes and subsequently apply for university admission.

Although officially established on 1 April 1992, the ITE is an upgraded version of its predecessor, the Vocational and Industrial Training Board. It provides a multidisciplinary curriculum that ranges from engineering to technical, business and service skills courses.

The ITE has three colleges: ITE College East, ITE College Central and ITE College West. Total enrolment in 2005 was a record high of 23,029.

The ITE also provides Continuing Education and Training programmes for workers. Its part-time courses are designed to meet the specific needs of adult learners, and are offered at various skill and academic levels. The ITE is the biggest provider of continuing education programmes in Singapore, with 34,000 students enrolled, and a further 20,000 on ITE-accredited courses conducted by industry training partners.

Integrated Programme The Integrated Programme (IP) was introduced in 2004 as an alternative model for upper secondary and junior college education. Three IP models are offered: the six-year IP model, starting at Secondary 1 (the terminal qualification for which is the International Baccalaureate Diploma or the 'A' Level Examination); the Secondary 1 to Junior College model (the terminal qualification of which is the GCE 'A' Level Examination); and the four-year high school model (the terminal qualification of which is the GCE 'A' Level Examination).

The IP is designed to cater to the top 10 per cent of each cohort, who are expected to enter university. Compared to the usual school curricula, the syllabi for IP are broader-based and more multidisciplinary.

In-depth research, project work, independent study, industrial attachments and overseas tie-ups complement traditional teaching methods. This approach is not meant for the general student populace, who continue in the highly structured education programme leading to GCE 'O' levels, followed by two years in junior college or three years at a polytechnic.

Currently offered at seven schools, the IP has a fallout rate of less than 10 per cent. Each school runs its own tailored IP, and independent schools have full discretionary admission rights; selection procedures include interviews and aptitude tests. The IP schools charge fees of $200–$450 per month.

integrated resort The term 'integrated resort' (IR) first came into public use in December 2004 when the Singapore government called for concept proposals to develop two plots of land at MARINA BAY and SENTOSA. The IRs, targeted for completion in 2009, were to offer amenities such as hotels, restaurants, shopping and convention centres, theatres, museums and theme parks. However, it was the inclusion of Singapore's first casinos in the IRs which caused great controversy in 2004 and 2005.

Integrated resorts: much debate before decision.

MM Lee on casino: Can Singapore afford to say no?

His remarks are the strongest hint yet that Govt will give casino the go-ahead

By SUE-ANN CHIA & LESLIE KOH

The casino proposal had arisen in 1985 but had been rejected by then First Deputy Prime Minister Goh Chok Tong. In 2002, when Singapore faced a recession, the idea resurfaced as a possible means of boosting the economy. Although a number of groups expressed concern about the negative impact of gambling, the government proceeded with the IR plans, seeing them as essential to Singapore's development.

The IRs are expected to bring substantial economic spin-offs. More than 35,000 jobs are expected to be created, tourist numbers have been forecast to double to 17 million a year, and tourist spending is estimated to grow three-fold, to $18 billion.

To address public concerns about gambling, the government announced that it would put in place several social safeguards. These include implementing a membership scheme for Singapore residents; guidelines on casino advertisements; limiting casino signage within the IRs; self-exclusion programmes; the setting of voluntary loss limits; and guidelines on extending credit.

Las Vegas Sands was awarded the contract for the first IR at Marina Bay.

Intellectual Property Office of Singapore Statutory board. In September 1999, the Registry of Trade Marks and Patents, which was established in 1937, was restructured as the Intellectual Property Office of Singapore (IPOS) to oversee the entire range of intellectual property laws in Singapore. It was converted into a statutory board under the Ministry of Law in April 2001.

IPOS is the leading government agency that formulates and administers intellectual property (IP) laws, promotes IP awareness and provides the infrastructure to facilitate the greater development of IP in Singapore. Its core functions include the provision of a sound legal and administrative framework for the promotion and protection of intellectual property; formulating and reviewing IP rights' policies and legislation; maintaining and disseminating IP information and documents; representing the Singapore government internationally on IP matters; training and nurturing IP agents; collaborating with other organisations and IP offices on IP programmes; and promoting the awareness, respect and the effective use of intellectual property rights.

See also WORLD INTELLECTUAL PROPERTY ORGANISATION.

interest rates Until mid-1975, interest rates in Singapore were determined by the Association of Banks in Singapore in consultation with the MONETARY AUTHORITY OF SINGAPORE, the de facto central bank. Since then, commercial banks and finance companies have been free to quote their own rates (*see* table).

Internal Security Act Preventive detention was one of the measures available to the British colonial authorities in Malaya before World War II—it was first introduced into the Federated States of Malaya by the Emergency Enactment 1930. The early legislation was used mainly to deal with the subversive activities of the South Seas (Nanyang) Communist Party in Singapore and the MALAYAN COMMUNIST PARTY (MCP) in Malaya, who were committed to the overthrow of the British government by force. The British battle against communism, and the MCP in particular, resumed in 1948, when a state of EMERGENCY was proclaimed and the MCP outlawed. Regulations were passed to deal with the communists, but these had to be reviewed and re-issued every few months, as the Emergency was meant to be a temporary state of affairs.

The first attempt to put preventive detention laws on a more permanent footing occurred in Singapore when the Legislative Council passed the Preservation of Public Security Ordinance (PPSO) on 21 October 1955. The PPSO was based on Indian, Pakistani and Burmese precedents. A person could be detained for up to two years to prevent them from acting in a manner which was prejudicial to the security of Malaya, the maintenance of public order, or the maintenance of essential services. The PPSO gave the final decision on whether a person should be detained to a panel of three judges. The Internal Security Act was enacted by the Federation of Malaya government on 22 June 1960, to make possible the cessation of the 1948 Emergency on 31 July 1960.

The Malayan Internal Security Act (ISA) of 1960 was subsequently imported into Singapore when Singapore became part of the Federation of Malaysia on 16 September 1963. With several amendments to the Malayan ISA and to the Singaporean PPSO, the legislation in both states became practically the same. The ISA continued to apply to Singapore when it left the Federation in August 1965.

Public order and safety continue to be the primary justifications for detention under the ISA. A person may be detained without trial and without recourse to the judicial system, without the need for the executive to produce substantial evidence against the detainee. Typically, a person may be detained for up to two years at a time. This period may be extended by a renewal of the detention order.

The longest anyone has been detained under the ISA is almost 23 years; the detainee in this case was CHIA THYE POH, who was arrested in 1966, and only released—under strict conditions—in 1989. In 1979, the Internal Security Deparment neutralised a local network of the Liberation Tigers of Tamil Ealam headed by Sri Lankans working in Singapore. In 1987, the government detained four Malays for spreading rumours of impending racial clashes and making active preparations for communal disturbances. In May/June 1987, the government arrested 22 people in connection with a Marxist conspiracy. In 1988, FRANCIS SEOW was detained following alleged foreign interference in Singapore's internal affairs. Since late 2001, the government has invoked its preventive detention powers with regard to members of the JEMAAH ISLAMIAH for planning a series of bombings and terrorist acts.

Internal Security Department An agency under the MINISTRY OF HOME AFFAIRS (MHA), the Internal Security Department is responsible for collecting intelligence, investigating and countering threats to the internal security of Singapore. It protects the country from—among other threats—subversion, racial and religious extremism, terrorism and espionage.

The ISD began as the Criminal Intelligence Department in 1916 and it was renamed SPECIAL BRANCH (SB) in 1933. It was subsumed by the Malayan Security Service after World War II. In 1948, the Special Branch was established as a department of the SINGAPORE POLICE FORCE. Following MERGER in 1963, SB became part of its Malaysian counterpart. Two years later, after Singapore's separation from Malaysia, SB came under the aegis of the Ministry of the Interior and Defence. In 1966, SB became known as the Internal Security Department. In 1970, when Home Affairs and Defence became separate ministries, the ISD was placed as a department under the MHA.

One of the ISD's main tasks has been to keep watch over racial and religious harmony in Singapore. For instance, during the MARIA HERTOGH RIOTS of 1950 and the RACE RIOTS of 1964, the ISD worked in conjunction with the police and armed forces to contain the turmoil.

The ISD's history is also closely related to the communist presence in the region. In 1948, the British colonial authorities introduced the Emergency Regulations (*see* EMERGENCY); these were the precursor to the 1963 INTERNAL SECURITY ACT (ISA). Operations were carried out in the 1950s and 1960s to enervate the communist front. Among the most notable, in 1963, was OPERATION COLD STORE.

INTEREST RATES					
	Banks' PLR	Banks' 3-mth FD	Banks' savings deposit	Banks' 3-mth Dom	Banks' 3-mth US$ SIBOR
1975	7.25	4.31	3.50	4.81	5.88
1980	13.60	11.22	9.52	13.05	17.75
1985	7.20	4.58	5.18	5.38	8.00
1990	7.73	5.05	3.83	4.85	7.63
1995	6.37	3.50	2.81	2.59	6.01
2000	6.83	1.71	1.30	2.57	6.53
2005	5.30	0.56	0.30	3.25	4.54

NOTE: PLR—prime lending rate; FD—fixed deposit; Dom—domestic Inter-bank Offered rate, sometimes known as DIBOR; SIBOR—Singapore Inter-bank Offered rate in US$.
Source: Monetary Authority of Singapore Monthly Statistical Bulletin (various)

International schools: art class under way at the Canadian International School.

In December 2001, the ISD came under the spotlight again when a plot for a series of truck-bomb attacks on American and other Western targets in Singapore was uncovered. Thirteen members of the terrorist network JEMAAH ISLAMIAH (JI) were detained under the ISA. In August 2002, the ISD detained another 18 Singaporeans for alleged terrorist activities. Several more have been detained by the ISD since.

International Civil Aviation Organization A specialized agency of the United Nations that is tasked with developing the principles and techniques of international air navigation, and fostering the development of international civil air transport. The constitutional document of the International Civil Aviation Organization (ICAO) is the Convention on International Civil Aviation, which was drawn up at a conference in Chicago in 1944. There are currently 189 ICAO contracting states. Headquartered in Montreal, Canada, the ICAO is made up of an assembly of all contracting states; a governing council, made up of 36 states elected by the assembly for three-year terms; and a secretariat. The chief officers of ICAO are the president of the council and the secretary general, who heads the secretariat.

As the governing body of ICAO, the council oversees the bulk of the ICAO's work. In particular, the council adopts the standards and recommended practices (SARPs), which govern much of international civil air transport. SARPs are adopted as annexes to the Convention on International Civil Aviation, and regulate technical matters relating to the safety, security and facilitation of civil aviation. The council is assisted in its work by several bodies such as the air navigation commission (dealing with technical matters), the air transport committee (economic matters) and the committee on unlawful interference (on aviation security). The council's work is facilitated by the staff of the secretariat, which is divided into five main divisions: the air navigation bureau, the air transport bureau, the technical co-opera-

tion bureau, the legal bureau and the bureau of administration and services.

The work of ICAO is extremely important to Singapore. Singapore's role as a leading air transport hub has also seen it participate in ICAO bodies and meetings, as well as in ICAO technical co-operation programmes. Singapore is currently a member of the ICAO's governing council, and has a representative on the air navigation commission.

International Enterprise Singapore Statutory board. The Singapore Trade Development Board (TDB) was formed in 1983 by merging the Department of Trade with the Timber Industry Board. The TDB was renamed International Enterprise Singapore (IE Singapore) on 1 April 2002, with the objective of developing the capabilities, connections and access to capital of Singapore-based enterprises—both local and foreign-owned—to facilitate their internationalization. IE Singapore also took over from SPRING the responsibility of helping Singapore's SMALL AND MEDIUM-SIZED ENTERPRISES (SMEs) expand overseas.

IE Singapore works to position Singapore as a base for foreign businesses to regionalize in partnership with SMEs. These new functions go beyond the former TDB's traditional role of trade promotion. However, as trading is the first step towards internationalization, IE Singapore continues to promote and develop the trade sector.

International Maritime Organization The International Maritime Organization (IMO) is the United Nations' specialized agency responsible for improving maritime safety and security, preventing pollution from ships and handling maritime-related liability and compensation issues. Key to the IMO's mission is the International Convention for the Safety of Life at Sea (SOLAS) (1974); the International Convention for the Prevention of Pollution from Ships or MARPOL (1973/78); and the International Shipping and Port Facility Security Code (ISPS Code) (2004). The IMO consists of an assembly, a council and four main committees—the maritime safety committee; the marine environment protection committee; the legal committee; and the technical co-operation committee. By 2006, the IMO assembly had 166 member states. The IMO council—of which Singapore is a member—comprises 40 member states in total, and is elected by the assembly on a two-year term to supervise the work of the organization.

Since 1966, Singapore has been an IMO member and has participated actively in IMO meetings. Singapore has served on the IMO council since 1993. It also served as chairman of the IMO council from 2001 to 2003. Through the IMO, Singapore has contributed in the area of capacity-building through programmes such as the integrated

technical co-operation programme (ITCP). To this end, Singapore signed a memorandum of understanding on the third country training programme with the IMO in 1998 to provide technical assistance to developing IMO member states.

As a major port, and with the fourth largest ship registry in the world, Singapore is strongly supportive of the work of IMO. Singapore has continued to implement major IMO conventions, and has encouraged other IMO member states to do the same.

international schools There are about 40 international schools registered with the Ministry of Education. Many of them are affiliated to school systems outside Singapore and cater to non-Singaporeans who want their children to continue their education using the curriculum of their home country. These schools include the Australian International School, the Hollandse School, the Japanese School, the Lycée Français de Singapour, Sekolah Indonesia, the Singapore American School, the Singapore Korean School and the Swiss School Singapore.

There are also schools that offer a curriculum based on the International Baccalaureate. Such schools include the United World College of South East Asia and the ISS International School Singapore. Some schools, such as Bhavan's Indian International School, offer both the International Baccalaureate as well as a home-country curriculum.

There are schools outside Singapore that offer the Singapore curriculum. These include the Shanghai Singapore International School, the Singapore International School in Hong Kong, the Suzhou-Singapore International School, the Singapore International School (Jakarta) and the Singapore International School of Bangkok.

Internet Singapore's first Internet service provider (ISP) was Technet, formed in 1991. At that time Internet access was offered only to institutions of higher learning. Technet was based at the NATIONAL UNIVERSITY OF SINGAPORE. In 1994, SINGTEL launched SingNet, a commercial ISP.

In 1995, Technet became Pacific Internet (PacNet), and shed its academic roots to become a commercial ISP. A third ISP, Cyberway, was launched in 1996. It was later purchased by Singapore's other telecommunications operator, STARHUB, and renamed StarHub Internet. In 2006 SingNet, Pacific Internet and StarHub were the three major ISPs in Singapore.

SingNet was the first to launch a broadband multimedia service (Magix) in 1997, while PacNet was the first to offer unlimited broadband Internet access and wireless broadband services in 2001. In 2002, StarHub and Singapore Cable Vision merged and PacNet was the first to sign a wholesale agreement with StarHub to offer cable broadband services in 2003.

Also in 2003, PacNet launched VoIP (Voice-over-Internet-Protocol/Internet telephony) services and was subsequently able to offer fixed phone numbers for calls over the Internet. The industry is also set to offer Multimedia-over-Internet-Protocol (MoIP) services. In 2005, six operators (including the three ISPs) secured the wireless spectrum for providing a nationwide wireless broadband access network.

With such a spread of Internet services, the proportion of households owning computers had increased to 74 per cent by 2004, while the household Internet penetration rate had risen to 65 per cent.

Inter-Racial Confidence Circles This state-initiated structure was formed in 2002, in response to a heightened fear of religious tensions following the 9/11 terrorist attacks and the arrests of local members of JEMAAH ISLAMIAH. The terrorists had made foiled attempts to bomb several key installations and sites in Singapore in December 2001.

Singapore society is commonly represented as comprising four groups: the Chinese, Malays, Indians and others. The IRCCs' basic function is to 'to formulate strategies and initiatives to promote greater knowledge and understanding among the different races and religions'.

While the formation of these groups was announced soon after the 9/11 attacks, the idea for an organization to handle race relations long preceded that of the IRCCs. 'Goodwill Committees' were formed to address communal tensions in the wake of the 1964 RACE RIOTS. These eventually evolved into the CITIZENS' CONSULTATIVE COMMITTEES. However, the IRCCs are better equipped for managing racial-religious relations. They receive broad guidance from the National Steering Committee (chaired by the minister of community development, youth and sports) comprising representatives from various religious and social organizations. Their agenda is further reinforced by Inter-Racial Harmony Circles organized in schools, work places and youth organizations.

By early 2004, total IRCC membership was 962, of which the Chinese constituted 58 per cent, Malays 23 per cent, Indians 17 per cent, and others 2 per cent.

Beyond the main focus on community bonding, the groups have been involved in youth engagement, problem identification and tension resolution. Notably, collaborations between IRCCs and organizations representing the Malay/Muslim community, such as mosques, have been particularly significant since 2002.

investment banks Investment, or merchant, banks are non-depository financial institu-tions specializing in various aspects of corporate finance. Their activities include corporate finance, mergers and acquisitions, money-market operations, investment management, international financing, and corporate secretarial services. In contrast to commercial banks, their activities are fee-based, not interest-based, and they are often described as wholesalers, since they are involved in raising large sums of money.

Investment banks have been present in Singapore since 1970 when offshore banking licenses were first introduced. Their expanded role in Singapore today is due in part to the rapid growth of Southeast Asia and East Asia, keen competition in the developed financial centres of Europe and the United States, as well as state initiatives to develop offshore financial activities in Singapore.

Iqbal, K.T.M. (1940–) Poet. Born in India, K.T.M. Iqbal came to Singapore at an early age, and began writing poems in 1958. He wrote short stories in the earlier part of his career, but later concentrated on poetry. His poems cover a wide range of subjects, and his writing makes use of both traditional and modern styles.

Among his accolades are the Mont Blanc Literature Prize (1996), the Tamizhavel Award from the Association of Singapore Tamil Writers (2000) and the Southeast Asian Write Award (2001). His poem 'Thanneer' (Water) was the first Tamil poem to be part of 'Poems on the Move' in 1995, where local poems were selected to be displayed in Mass Rapid Transit trains. The same poem was also chosen by the Goethe Institute to be displayed in multiple languages at the Hanover Expo in Germany. Iqbal has published seven volumes of poetry, the most recent of which is *Vaanavarkal Mannil Irukkirarkal* (Angels are on the Earth) (2005).

Isham, Ashley (1976–) Fashion designer. Eshamuddin Ismail—better-known as Ashley Isham—left Singapore in 1996 to pursue a pattern-cutting course at the London College of Fashion, and was later accepted into the prestigious Central St Martin's College. After graduating from Middlesex University in 2000, he established his own label, Ashley Isham. The following year, he opened a boutique, aQuaint, in the Seven Dials area of Covent Garden, London, hoping to 'promote fashion talent and support other young designers'.

The boutique proved to be a success, and Isham went on to stock brands such as Lanvin, Roland, Mouret, Tracy Boyd and Emma Cook, alongside his own collection. He also gained an international reputation after showing his Autumn/Winter 2003 collection during the London Fashion Week. Following this success, he opened his flagship boutique, Ashley, in 2005. He was the official womenswear

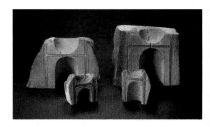

designer for the Orange British Academy Film Awards in 2004.

Iskandar Jalil: (left) **Vessel 101** *(2000); the sculptor (above).*

Iskandar Jalil (1939–) Artist and teacher. Master potter Iskandar Jalil has played a major role in Singapore's modern ceramics history. He studied ceramics engineering in Nagoya, the centre of pottery in Japan, under a COLOMBO PLAN Scholarship in the 1970s, and embraced Japanese aesthetics and traditions. Combining these with Southeast Asian and Islamic influences and motifs, his works encapsulate an individual yet quintessential Asian identity. His signature 'Iskandar Blue', rich tactile surfaces and incorporation of twigs, are characteristics of his work. Iskandar was a 1988 recipient of the CULTURAL MEDALLION and was awarded the Pingkat Apad by the Singapore Malay Arts Society (1998) and the BERITA HARIAN Achiever of the Year Award (2002). His work can be viewed at serveral venues, including CHANGI AIRPORT and Tanjong Pagar MRT Station.

Iskandar Shah The SEJARAH MELAYU (Malay Annals) records that the last Temasek (now Singapore) ruler—who also established Malacca—was named Iskandar Shah. According to Tomé Pires, who wrote the Suma Oriental (1512–15), the last ruler of Temasek was an usurper from Palembang, Sumatra named Parameswara.

The name Parameswara means 'supreme lord'. It is used as a synonym for the Hindu god Siva. The title was popular for rulers on the Southeast Asian mainland.

Parameswara may have been either the name or the title of a Malay prince of Palembang who attempted to throw off Javanese domination of the Malays of Sumatra after the king of MAJAPAHIT, Haya Wuruk, died in 1389. Javanese forces attacked Parameswara, and he was forced to flee, taking refuge in Temasek. This suggests that Temasek was sufficiently prosperous at that time to be a candidate for a new Malay capital.

Parameswara assassinated the local ruler—who was married to a daughter of the king of AYUTTHAYA—and took power. Around 1396, Temasek was attacked by forces from Ayutthaya, seeking to punish

Ashley Isham

DISCREPANCIES BETWEEN THE MALAY ANNALS AND SUMA ORIENTAL		
	Malay Annals	**Suma Oriental**
Founder of Malacca	Iskandar Shah	Parameswara (also Ming Dynasty Records)
First kingdom	Singapore	Palembang
Ruler expelled from Singapore	Iskandar	Parameswara
Singapore's attacker	Javanese	Siamese

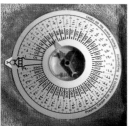

Islam: at prayer at the Sultan Mosque (top); prayer rug with built-in compass showing direction of Mecca.

Parameswara for killing the Siamese king's son-in-law. Parameswara, however, escaped again and fled to Muar, then to Bertam, Malacca. The half-Portuguese, half-BUGIS cartographer Manuel Godinho d'Eredia wrote in 1613 that the ruins of Parameswara's tomb, made of blocks of stone, were still to be seen at Tanjung Tuan, north of Malacca. A lighthouse now occupies the site.

Parameswara had a son, Iskandar Shah, born in Singapore. According to the Sejarah Melayu, when Iskandar Shah was on a hunting expedition, a mousedeer attacked one of his hunting dogs. Impressed by this incident, Iskandar Shah decided to found a city in the area, and named it 'Malacca' after the tree under which he was standing. Parameswara may well have lived at Bertam, and his son at Malacca—this internship, or junior kingship, system was widespread in early Southeast Asia.

The Sejarah Melayu refers to Iskandar Shah as both the last ruler of Singapore and the founder of Malacca. The Ming Shilu (Ming Dynasty Records) states that Parameswara was the founder of Malacca, that he visited CHINA in the early 15th century, and that his death was reported by his successor, Iskandar Shah, in 1414. British historian Sir Richard Winstedt, who preferred to rely on Malay sources, believed that Parameswara died in 1424; and that he changed his name from Parameswara to Iskandar Shah upon his conversion to Islam.

There are numerous discrepancies between the Sejarah Melayu, the Suma Oriental and other texts, and many issues remain unresolved. In Singapore, the KERAMAT ISKANDAR SHAH is located at the foot of Fort Canning. It is locally believed to be the burial site of the last ruler of Temasek from the 14th century.

Islam As early as the 7th and 8th centuries, Arab Muslim traders set up small colonies in several coastal areas of the Malay Archipelago. In the early 13th century, merchants and Sufi missionaries from Hadramaut (Yemen) and the southern parts of India also came to this area.

By 1819, there was already a community of Muslims in Singapore. Singapore's success as a leading trading port in the region, along with the presence of a Muslim community, attracted many more traders from the Malay Archipelago, almost all of them Muslim.

As the community grew, Muslim traders collectively funded the building of the first mosque in Singapore, in 1823, known as the OMAR KAMPONG MALACCA MOSQUE, near the banks of the SINGAPORE RIVER. The mosque still exists today at Havelock Road. Other Muslim traders, especially ARAB Muslims, arrived and were concentrated in the KAMPONG GLAM area. In 1826, a large mosque was built there, known to this day as the SULTAN MOSQUE. Indian Muslim communities were clustered further to the west in areas near South Bridge Road. Some INDIAN MUSLIM mosques, such as the JAMAE MOSQUE (1827) and the AL-ABRAR MOSQUE (c. 1850) were built in the area.

According to the census of 1901, Muslims in Singapore comprised 23,060 MALAYS, 12,335 various ethnicities from the Malay Archipelago, 1,508 Arabs and about 600 JAWI PERANAKANS. Arabs enjoy a certain prestige among Muslims as they hail from the 'cradle of Islam'. They were successful merchants who were also pious. Many dedicated their wealth as WAKAF, helping to build mosques and schools. Some Arabs provided HAJ services.

The haj further strengthened the link between local Muslims and those in the Middle East. Many Indonesian Muslims had to travel to the haj via Singapore because of the repressive measures against Muslims by the Dutch. As economic conditions and transportation improved, more Muslims went for the haj. Some pilgrims did not return immediately after the haj, preferring to spend a few years in Mecca or Medina (both in present-day Saudi Arabia) to study the religion. A growing number of Muslims were also going to institutions in the Middle East such as the Al-Azhar University in Cairo to study. They returned to the region as respected religious scholars and teachers.

Singapore became a centre for Islamic activities for Malays in the region with the establishment of MADRASAHS; the efforts of those who had studied in Mecca and Cairo; and in the publishing of periodicals and books. The first Malay newspaper in Singapore was the JAWI PERANAKAN (1876). In 1906, SYED SHEIKH AL-HADI launched a journal, AL-IMAM. It called for social change and religious renewal among Malay/Muslims, and set the tone for other Islamic journals championing moral reform.

After Independence, the ADMINISTRATION OF MUSLIM LAW ACT (AMLA) was passed. It led to the appointment of the MUFTI, and the formation of the MAJLIS UGAMA ISLAM SINGAPURA (MUIS), SYARIAH COURT and REGISTRY OF MUSLIM MARRIAGES.

According to the census of 2000, Muslims make up about 16 per cent of the population in Singapore. The majority are Malays; the rest are INDIANS, Pakistanis and Arabs. Muslims in Singapore, like other Muslims in the region, are mainly Sunni and adhere to the SHAFI'I SCHOOL.

islands There are more than 60 scattered islands, most of them very small, in Singapore's territorial waters. The northern group is dominated by the two large islands of Pulau Tekong and Pulau Ubin. Both have cores of hard, resistant rock: Pulau Tekong has metamorphic rock of the Sajahat formation; Pulau Ubin was formed from Bukit Timah granite, hence its irregular, hilly interior.

The western island group has been transformed drastically through land reclamation. Seven small islands and numerous

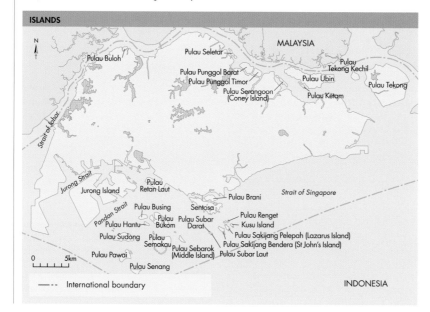

ISLANDS

N

MALAYSIA

Pulau Buloh

Pulau Seletar

Pulau Punggol Barat
Pulau Punggol Timor

Pulau Tekong Kechil

Pulau Ubin

Pulau Tekong

Pulau Serangoon
(Coney Island)

Pulau Ketam

Strait of Johor

Jurong Strait

Jurong Island

Pulau Retan Laut

Pulau Brani

Strait of Singapore

Pandan Strait

Pulau Busing

Sentosa

Pulau Renget

Pulau Hantu

Pulau Bukom

Pulau Subar Darat

Kusu Island

Pulau Sudong

Pulau Semakau

Pulau Sakijang Pelepah (Lazarus Island)

Pulau Sakijang Bendera (St John's Island)

Pulau Pawai

Pulau Sebarok
(Middle Island)

Pulau Subar Laut

0   5km

Pulau Senang

- - - International boundary

INDONESIA

islets have been consolidated into the much larger Jurong Island, a focal point for heavy industry and electricity generation.

The Southern Islands are the most numerous and varied group. They include the much altered and extended resort island of Sentosa; the landfill island of Pulau Semakau, where most of Singapore's solid waste is currently being dumped; the pilgrimage and beach island of Kusu; and the complex of PULAU SAKIJANG BENDERA (also known as St John's Island, PULAU SAKIJANG PELEPAH (also known as Lazarus Island) and Pulau Renget, earmarked for a land reclamation scheme, and transformation into a single island with tourist, recreational and nature conservation appeal.

The island of PEDRA BRANCA is another of Singapore's islands. The site of HORSBURGH LIGHTHOUSE, this island is the subject of a territorial dispute with Malaysia.

Ismail Marjan (1921–1991) Sportsman. Ismail Marjan formed an almost invincible badminton doubles partnership with ONG POH LIM, another ex-national champion, winning several major honours in Asia and Europe. He was a household name in Singapore and Malaya in the 1950s.

Ismail was a member of the Dapat Badminton Party (BP) and later the Devonshire BP and Rose BP. He became the second-best singles player in Singapore after WONG PENG SOON. Until his death at the age of 70, Ismail served as an advisor to the F&N (FRASER & NEAVE) Badminton Training Scheme.

Istana and Sri Temasek The Istana is the official residence of the president. Sri Temasek is a 19th-century bungalow located within the Istana's compound, and which used to be assigned to the Colonial Secretary. Before Independance, what is now the Istana was known as Government House (an earlier building bearing that name was built by SIR STAMFORD RAFFLES on FORT CANNING in 1822, and was demolished to make way for fortifications). It was commissioned by SIR HARRY ORD, the first governor of Singapore, and was ready for occupation in October 1869.

In architectural terms the Istana is something of a hybrid. In its picturesque landscaped setting, it resembles a British country house in the manner of Anglo-Indian architecture, while its symmetrical and cross-shaped plan echoes the form of a traditional Malay *istana* (palace). Its Renaissance Revival façade reflects the mid-19th century British fascination with the architecture of the Italian Renaissance.

The building was renamed the Istana in 1959 and became the official residence of the President. Its grounds are open to visitors on select public holidays. In the mid-1990s it underwent a major restoration and rejuvenation. It has continued to be used for state and ceremonial occasions. The Istana and Sri Temasek were gazetted as national monuments in February 1992.

Istana Kampong Gelam Official residence of SULTAN HUSAIN, the first Sultan of Singapore. Istana Kampong Gelam literally means 'Kampong Gelam Palace'. The Sultan built the Istana, which was made of wood, in the area to the east of Beach Road. When completed in 1820, it occupied an area twice the size of the present compound, which was reduced in 1824 for the construction of North Bridge Road.

The present building was built on the site of the original between 1836 and 1843 by SULTAN ALI Iskandar Shah, the son of Sultan Husain. The two-storey building is believed to have been designed by GEORGE D. COLEMAN. Its design is a combination of traditional Malay motifs with the Palladian style popular in the United Kingdom at the time. Some of its architectural features are similar to those of other buildings Coleman designed, such as the Old Parliament House and the Armenian Church.

The extensive compound of the Istana is enclosed by a perimeter wall. Small kampong-style houses were built around this perimeter for the Sultan's kin, servants and artisans. Another building near the entrance of the Istana is known as Gedung Kuning (Yellow Mansion). It was built around the middle of the 19th century for one of Sultan Husain's grandsons, Tengku Mahmoud. It was sold to

Istana Kampong Gelam

Malay businessman Haji Yusoff Haji Mohamed Noor in 1912 and became a private residence.

In 1896, there was a succession dispute in Sultan Husain's family over rights to the Kampong Glam estate, and the matter went to court. In 1897, the court ruled that no one could rightfully claim to be the successor of the Sultan and that the estate belonged to the Crown. (The estate became state land when Singapore gained independence.) In 1904, the Sultan Hussein Ordinance was enacted to provide the descendants of Sultan Husain with income derived from the Kampong Glam estate. The amount was capped at $250,000 in 1991, revised by the government in 1999. Under the new scheme, the beneficiaries could opt either for a share of $350,000 a year for 30 years or for a lump-sum payment. Residents still living in the Istana were resettled, as the building was to undergo conservation works. Until that time, the Istana had been the private residence for the Sultan's descendants.

The Istana Kampong Gelam has been restored. In June 2005, it became the home of the MALAY HERITAGE CENTRE. The Gedung Kuning is part of the centre and houses a restaurant serving Malay food.

Ismail Marjan: holding trophies, next to Ong Poh Lim, 1951.

Itagaki Seishiro

Itagaki Seishiro, General (1885–1948) Japanese military officer. Itagaki Seishiro was Commander of the 7th Area Army based in Singapore. He was one of the signatories of the actual surrender instrument signed on 4 September 1945. At the official surrender of the Japanese on 12 September 1945, Itagaki signed and sealed 11 copies of the Instrument of Surrender on behalf of Field Marshal Count Terauchi Hisaichi—Supreme Commander, Japanese Expeditionary Forces, Southern Regions—who had suffered a stroke.

As an officer in the Manchuria-based Kwangtung Army, Itagaki had been involved in the Mukden Incident (1931) that led to the Japanese seizure of Manchuria. He was tried and convicted at the Tokyo War Crimes Trials in 1946, and was hanged in 1948.

Istana: official residence of the president of Singapore.

Jade House Businessman Aw Boon Haw, Singapore's 'Tiger Balm King', began a jade collection in 1932. He housed it in his second residence, on Nassim Road, which became known as the Jade House. The collection comprised over 300 carvings in jade, jasper, aventurine, cornelian, rose quartz, agate, crystal and lapis lazuli. They were largely decorative carvings from the Qing Dynasty (1644–1911). Aw initially opened the house to the public every Chinese New Year, but later on a daily basis.

During World War II, the jade items were packed in crates and hidden in the basement. After the war they were found, mysteriously, in a warehouse near the harbour. The collection was largely intact, with only a few large items lost or broken.

In 1979, the Aw family donated part of the jade collection to the National Museum. The Jade House was torn down in 1990 and a new one was built in Haw Par Villa in 2004. There, some 150 pieces from the collection were exhibited, on a two-year loan from the National Museum. The pieces have since been returned to the museum.

Jainism The presence of Jains in Singapore has been recorded since the beginning of the 20th century. Early religious activities, mainly the observation of traditional Jain festivals, were organized on an ad-hoc basis at Waterloo Street from the early 1900s.

Modern Jainism can be traced to about 2,600 years ago with the birth of Lord Mahavir in 599 BCE. In Jain philosophy, the ultimate aim is to be a Jina, that is, someone who has conquered worldly passions such as desire, hatred, anger, greed and pride. Jains are strict vegetarians, and abstain from the use of animal products.

The community celebrates five major events each year: Mahavir Jayanti (March/April), a celebration of the birth of Lord Mahavir; Ayambil Oli (March/April), when Jains practise nine days of partial abstinence and food restrictions; Paryushan

Jainism: Singapore Jain Religious Society.

Jade House, 1964

(August/September), an eight-day period of fasting and introspection and one of the most important Jain festivals; Samu-Parna, a joint breaking of fasts, held on the ninth day after Paryushan; and Bestu-Varas prayers, held the day after Deepavali to celebrate Lord Mahavir's attainment of nirvana.

The Singapore Jain Religious Society was officially registered as a religious society and charitable trust in 1972. The society currently has 800 members, the majority of whom originate from Gujarat, with the rest from Marwad and Punjab. A large percentage of its members are born in Singapore.

Jamae Mosque The initial construction of this mosque, on South Bridge Road, was begun by a group of Chulia merchants around 1827, and was completed in 1835. The front entrance is flanked by two octagonal minarets. Each minaret bears the double-*mihrab* (curved prayer niche) motif, also found in mosques in south India. Inside, the architecture is European Neoclassical in style. The oldest part of the mosque is possibly the memorial dedicated to Muhammad Salih Valiullah, an early local Muslim preacher. The mosque was gazetted as a national monument in 1974.

Jamiyah Muslim welfare organization. Jamiyah was formed in 1932 by Maulana Abdul Aleem Siddique (*see* Abdul Aleem Siddique, Maulana), together with other religious leaders in Singapore and Malaya. At the time, it had branches in Malaysia. After Separation, the organization renamed itself Jamiyah Singapore, but is still popularly referred to simply as Jamiyah. It continues to maintain cordial ties with its former branches in Malaysia.

Jamiyah provides a range of welfare services. It operates a free medical clinic and offers legal advice and counselling services. It also distributes provisions to the poor and needy, and runs a 'meals-on-wheels' programme to bring food to elderly and destitute people who live alone. Jamiyah runs Darul Ma'wa Children's Home, Darul Takrim Home for the Aged and Darul Syifa Nursing Home.

Japan-Singapore relations Japan and Singapore have transcended the unhappy experience of Japan's military occupation of Singapore between 1942 and 1945 and the two countries enjoy close political, economic and cultural ties. In 1966, the newly independent city-state accepted token reparations from Tokyo which were used to build a cenotaph and a Japanese institute to train Singaporeans in electronics. Symbolizing the excellent bilateral relations between the two countries, Emperor Akihito and Empress Michiko made a state visit to Singapore in June 2006 to mark the 40th anniversary of the establishment of diplomatic relations between Japan and Singapore.

Jamae Mosque

Japan is Singapore's third largest trading partner. There are more than 2,200 Japanese companies based in Singapore and they have a cumulative investment of $3.76 billion. Singapore seeks to learn from Japan in many areas and a number of Japanese innovations have been introduced into Singapore. This includes the neighborhood police post system (Koban), WITs (Work Improvement Teams) to increase productivity, and the promotion of house unions to enhance the loyalty of workers to their companies. The Department of Japanese Studies was also established at the National University of Singapore in 1981 to promote greater knowledge and understanding of Japan. It is now one of the largest departments devoted to Japanese studies in the Asia-Pacific region.

To Japan, Singapore is a very important littoral state with a key strategic location at the entrance to the Strait of Malacca, an economic artery for Japan. Significantly, Japan picked Singapore as the first country in the world to sign a Free Trade Agreement with. Known as the Japan-Singapore Economic Partnership Agreement, it came into force on 30 November 2002.

The strong relations between Singapore and Japan were evident during the Asian financial crisis which led to the end of the Suharto regime in Indonesia. In 1998, Tokyo asked if a few military transport planes could be temporarily stationed in Singapore in case Japan needed to evacuate its nationals from Jakarta. The Singapore government promptly granted permission.

Singapore was the only country in the Association of Southeast Asian Nations (ASEAN) to publicly support Japan's bid for a permanent seat in the United Nations Security Council. Both countries also share the common aim of anchoring the United States in the region, and plan to build an East Asian Community with other countries in the region. However, on issues such as the

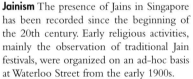

accounts of WORLD WAR II in Japanese history textbooks and visits to the Yasukuni Shrine, Singapore has always held the view that Japan should emulate Germany and come to terms with its wartime past in order to close that chapter of Japan's history.

On the people-to-people level, relations have also blossomed. J-Pop (Japanese popular music), manga (comics), anime (cartoons), cultural icons (like Hello Kitty) and fashion from Japan appeal to many Singaporean youths. Japanese food has become very popular among Singaporeans and Japanese restaurants can be found in most local shopping centres. Singapore is also a popular destination for Japanese tourists, with almost half a million visiting in 2005.

Japanese Cemetery Park Located at Chuan Hoe Avenue in Yio Chu Kang, the Japanese Cemetery was established in 1891 by Futaki Tagajiro, a Japanese owner of brothels and rubber-plantations. He wanted to provide a proper burial ground for the large number of KARAYUKI-SAN (Japanese prostitutes) then working in Singapore. Many *karayuki-san* were subsequently buried here. A large portion of its space is devoted to commemorating the Japanese war dead from WORLD WAR II, although it was not designated a war cemetery. Several tombstones from the war period are prominent, including 21 plank-shaped stone markers closely aligned in a row. The most impressive tombstone from the war is a large, austere, stone-lantern-styled monument to Ueyama Kano, who died in 1942 when his plane crashed at Sembawang Airbase. The cemetery also houses a small Shinto shrine.

Japanese Occupation *See* box.

Jardine Cycle & Carriage Motor vehicle distributor. The origins of Jardine Cycle & Carriage (C&C) can be traced back to 1899, when the Chua brothers established the Federal Stores in Kuala Lumpur, sellers of sundry products. The company was renamed Cycle & Carriage that same year and started selling bicycles, motorcycles and cars. It moved to Singapore in 1926, and was awarded the local Mercedes-Benz franchise in 1951. In 1969, Cycle & Carriage was listed on the Stock Exchange of Malaysia and Singapore.

The company also began expanding into property interests with the acquisition of Malayan Credit Limited in 1992. The real estate developer had begun as a provider of hire-purchase services but ventured into property development from 1969. Over the years, it came to own and develop hotels, commercial buildings and residential properties in Singapore and parts of Malaysia. In 1997 it was renamed MCL Land. In 2006, C&C divested its interest in MCL Land through a distribution of MCL Land shares to shareholders.

Japanese Cemetery Park

C&C was acquired by long-term shareholder, Jardine Strategic Holdings, in 2002, and became a subsidiary of the Jardine Matheson Group. The Employees Provident Fund of Malaysia also acquired an 8 per cent stake in the company, which was renamed Jardine Cycle & Carriage on 1 January 2004.

In 2000, the company acquired an interest in PT Astra International—an Indonesian conglomerate with business interests in motor vehicle distribution, retail, property investment and development. Since then, Jardine C&C has steadily increased its stake, and PT Astra is now a subsidiary.

In Singapore, Jardine C&C has become most widely associated with its exclusive Mercedes-Benz dealership, and with its local Mitsubishi and Kia distributorships. It reported net earnings of US$282 million on sales of US$3.8 billion in 2005. The company's stock is a component of the Straits Times Index.

Jardine, Matheson & Co. Trading company. Founded in China in 1832 by Scottish businessmen William Jardine and James Matheson, the company played a central role in the founding and development of Hong Kong and was among the first European companies to establish itself in Shanghai and Japan. The firm expanded from agency house to managing agent to investment house between 1832 and 1885. It built *Jardine*, the first steam-powered merchant ship in China in 1835, which became one of the first regular vessels to be used for trade with Singapore. In the 19th century, the company specialized in the tea trade. It also became the agent for several RUBBER plantations and tin mines in Malaya.

The Jardine Matheson group has diversified enormously since, becoming a large conglomerate with operations in several Southeast Asian countries and the United Kingdom. In the mid-1990s, the group moved its main Asian share trading from Hong Kong to Singapore. The company's business interests include Dairy Farm, which owns supermarket chain COLD STORAGE, and JARDINE CYCLE & CARRIAGE.

Javanese The second largest subgroup of Singapore's Malay population. There was a gradual increase in the island's Javanese population from the mid-19th century to around 1945. Immigration was more controlled in the post-war period. There were 3,240 Javanese in 1871, growing to 16,063 in the 1931 census and 48,266 in 1970. In 1980, the census records that about 6 per cent (42,460) of the Malay population identified themselves as Javanese. They came as free migrants or as indentured labour. Many were attracted both by urban wages and by freedom from the constraints of their native villages, where they often occupied the lower reaches of the economic and social order.

They came to Singapore in several waves. During the first wave in the mid-19th century, there were Javanese craftsmen and merchants who established a trading centre in Kampong Java. Their crafts included metal and leatherwork; they traded in religious texts, spices, cloth and other goods. They slowly spread out and formed largely Javanese settlements including Kampong Tempei, Kampong Pachitan, and Kampong Bukit Chermin (since demolished).

Pilgrim brokers were also in this mercantile group and played a crucial role in promoting Javanese migration. Dutch restrictions on the pilgrimage to Mecca led many of them to make their pilgrimage via Singapore. They worked in Singapore for several years before or after their pilgrimage to pay off their debts to the pilgrim brokers. In fact, many stayed permanently in Singapore without fulfilling their original haj plans. Until the 1920s, pilgrim brokers also recruited bonded labourers (*orang tebusan*) who worked to clear land for settlement in Johor. Between 1886 and 1890, an estimated 21,000 Javanese labourers signed contracts with the Singapore CHINESE PROTECTORATE and were sent out to areas of labour demand, such as rubber estates. Many stayed on after their contracts expired and opened up land to settle there.

The second wave, not so well documented, took place during World War II, when the Japanese brought into Singapore some 10,000 Javanese as conscript labour.

Javanese: early-20th-century image of Javanese family in Singapore.

Jardine Cycle & Carriage: car dealership, Alexandra Road.

Japanese Occupation

Japanese Occupation The Occupation lasted from 16 February 1942, the day after the British surrender (*see* MALAYA CAMPAIGN), to 4 September 1945. During this era, Singapore was known as SYONAN, meaning 'Light of the South' in Japanese.

Administration

- **February 1942:**
  Japan's 25th Army takes control of Singapore. This army's Military Administration Department is nominally answerable to Japan's Southern Army in Saigon (present-day Ho Chi Minh City), which in turn answers to Imperial Army Headquarters in Tokyo. Singapore is made part of Japan's 'Special Defence Area', which also includes Malaya and Sumatra; administration of the area is run from the FULLERTON BUILDING.
- **April 1943:**
  Singapore and Malaya are separated from Sumatra when the Southern Army relocate from Saigon to Singapore and take control of the island.
- **January 1944:**
  Japan's Southern Army gives up direct administration of Singapore and Malaya; the newly created 29th Army, which is based in Taiping, Perak, runs a decentralized administration of Malaya and Singapore, scattering its various departments in Taiping, Kuala Lumpur and Singapore.

- **May 1944:**
  Japan's 7th Area Army is created to take command of the 29th Army, and military administration is again centralized in Singapore under the former.
- **12 September 1945:**
  The Japanese sign the Instrument of Surrender; the Occupation comes to an end.

Throughout these changes, a Japanese civilian municipal administration was also maintained in Singapore. A mayor, together with other civilian appointees, was assisted by Asian civil servants who had worked in the pre-war colonial Civil Service. The civilian administration operated out of the Municipal Building (present-day CITY HALL).

Clockwise from top: Japanese troops marching through Singapore; propaganda poster promoting pan-Asian unity; Indian National Army recruits; Japanese street signs; Japanese soldiers at Kallang Airport.

Society

Despite Japanese propaganda that portrayed the Occupation as an era of racial harmony, the Japanese themselves implemented racially divisive policies in Singapore. They generally regarded the Chinese as anti-Japanese. This was due to the community's pre-war boycott of Japan, and the fund-raising efforts that many Singaporean Chinese had undertaken since 1937 to support China's war effort against Japan. At the beginning of the Occupation, the Chinese community was subjected to a mass screening exercise that resulted in the deaths of thousands of Chinese in an atrocity known as the SOOK CHING.

In occupied Malaya, the local police force—which was largely staffed by Malays—was used by the Japanese in the hunt for anti-Japanese elements, who were mainly Chinese. A Japanese intelligence unit called Fujiwara Kikan (also known as F Kikan), also subverted Indian loyalty, particularly that of British Indian Army soldiers who made up more than half of British Empire troops who had been engaged in the Malaya Campaign. Many members of Singapore's pre-war Indian community thought of themselves as Indian nationals rather than as Malayans or Singaporeans. And the support of this community for the Indian independence movement

made it easy for F Kikan to hold out the false promise of Japanese help in this struggle, and to convince many British Indian troops to support the Japanese. F Kikan channelled Indian nationalist sentiment into the formation of the Indian National Army (*see* INDIAN NATIONAL ARMY AND MONUMENT). Differences in Japanese treatment of Singapore's various ethnic communities meant that some Indians and Malays were able to protect Chinese and Eurasian friends and neighbours.

Surviving under Occupation

Before the war, rationing had been unknown in Singapore. The Occupation, however, led to a freeze in international trade, including the important tin and rubber industries. Consequently, Singapore experienced severe food shortages, as well as shortages in medicine, textiles and other essentials. At the start of the Occupation, all residents were made to register for identity certificates (*ankyosho*). These needed to be produced by anyone seeking to obtain rations.

The Japanese military administration was expected to be self-sufficient in the supply of food. Thus, a Grow More Food campaign was promoted from early in the Occupation, encouraging people in Singapore (including prisoners-of-war) to grow their own crops. The keeping of livestock and breeding of poultry were encouraged, and vegetable seeds were distributed. All unused land, including that found by the side of roads, and gardens and schools, was transformed into vegetable plots. Rubber trees were cut down to clear land for food crops. Tapioca—a common substitute for rice—was even cultivated on the PADANG. Agricultural exhibitions were organized and farming communities established outside Singapore. The two best known

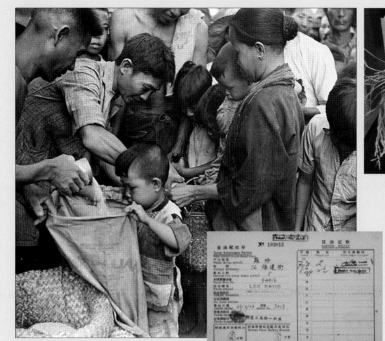

Clockwise from top: rice grown in Endau; tools used by Endau settlers; ration card; food rationing.

of these were ENDAU in the state of Johor, and BAHAU in the state of Negri Sembilan. Due to food shortages, starvation was common, especially in the latter years of the Occupation as the Japanese military hoarded food supplies in anticipation of a long defence of Singapore against an expected Allied re-invasion.

A monopolistic distribution system and severe shortages of essentials resulted in the growth of the black market. This became an essential feature of the Occupation economy, and was seen by many as a lifeline, despite the corruption it involved. Petty theft also became common. In the early years of the Occupation, the Japanese had implemented a policy of decapitating looters and displaying their heads in public spaces. However, this did not put a stop to increases in blackmail, theft and other crimes over the course of the Occupation.

Japanese-language school diploma (left); students at a Japanese school.

'Japanization'

The Japanese military administration also attempted to 'Japanize' Singapore society during the Occupation. The official time was moved forward one and a half hours to Tokyo time. The calendar was also changed, with the years of the Gregorian calendar being replaced by the reign years of the Japanese emperor. Thus 1942 became 'Showa 17'—the seventeenth year of the Showa Emperor (i.e. Hirohito). In other instances, the date was calculated from the birth of Jimmu Tenno—the legendary first emperor of the Japanese imperial household. In this system, 1942 was listed as the year 2602.

The Japanese attempted to change people's behaviour. Japanese sentries positioned all over the island expected people to bow to them as a sign of respect. Bowing to sentries;

facing northeast to bow in the direction of the emperor; and observing a moment of silence for the Japanese war dead at public functions all formed part of a new system of social etiquette. Slapping and senseless punishment for non-compliance became the norm. Enduring such humiliation and accepting the divinity of Japan's emperor were considered to be tantamount to acquiring the 'Japanese spirit'.

Japanese-language schools were opened all over the island, and primary school teachers returned to school so that they could learn and teach Japanese as a compulsory subject in schools. The KING EDWARD VII COLLEGE OF MEDICINE was re-opened as the Syonan Medical College, although the main subject taught there was Japanese, rather than medicine.

Legacy

The Japanese Occupation lasted only three years and eight months, but it was brutal and trying. Occupation policies bred corruption. Opium smoking and gambling emerged as major social problems. Juvenile delinquency and teenage prostitution were rife. Singapore's infrastructure fell into ruin, and the economy became moribund. Moreover, the Fall of Singapore, and the failure of the British to protect their colonial subjects, gravely damaged the standing of the British in the eyes of the local population.

Japanese soldiers in Singapore, shortly after the Japanese surrender (top); celebrations marking the Japanese surrender.

S. Jayakumar

Jawi Peranakan: issue of 24 January 1887.

Jawi Peranakan family, 1930s.

The third wave of Javanese came to Singapore via Malaya, and later Malaysia. The 1970 statistics reveal that about 21,000 Malaya-born Malays moved to Singapore from 1946 to 1955 and approximately 29,000 between 1956 and 1970. A substantial number were young men or families of Javanese descent leaving the insecurities of Johor smallholdings in search of work in the city. However, most were uneducated and unskilled and constituted a large section of the lower economic levels of Singapore's post-war Malay society.

The 2000 census of population recorded 80,062 Javanese out of a total Malay resident population of 453,633. There is a Javanese association, Persatuan Jawa Al-Masakin, founded in 1905. It suffered from dwindling membership and was closed in 2002, but was revived in 2005.

Jawi Peranakan Malay term for the locally born descendants of marriages between Indian Muslim men and Malay women. The term was replaced by 'Jawi Pekan' or 'town Muslim' especially in Penang, where the majority of this community is found. One of the earliest uses of the term can be found in the *Hikayat Abdullah* by Munshi Abdullah (*see* ABDULLAH ABDUL KADIR, MUNSHI).

Indian Muslim migrants were influential in the economic development of Singapore and peninsula Malaya, primarily as intermediaries between foreign merchants and Malay rulers. As one of several minority migrant groups in Singapore, male Indian Muslims far outnumbered the females—few Indian women migrated to Singapore, particularly before the 1860s. Therefore, the men often came into contact with the indigenous Malays, and marriages with local women were not uncommon. This led to a fusion between the culture of Indian Muslims and that of the indigenous Malays. Intermarriage, facilitated by shared religious belief, produced children raised with the language and domestic *adat* (customs) of their Malay mothers, and in the commercial world of their Indian Muslim fathers. As a result of continued intermarriage over generations, the Jawi Peranakans have evolved their own cultural traditions including their own dialect and manner of speaking.

By 1901, there were about 600 Jawi Peranakans in Singapore. They had established themselves as a significant ethnic subgroup within the Malay community. They were mostly English-educated and familiar with the British colonial administration. Also, their ability to converse and write both in English and Malay helped them enter commerce. They flourished as clerks, interpreters, schoolteachers, shopkeepers and journalists. They established the JAWI PERANAKAN, the first Malay-language newspaper in Malaya.

Like the Arabs, the Jawi Peranakans began to adopt the Chinese and European practice of forming clubs and associations, notably the Persekutuan Islam Singapura founded in 1900. Also like the Arabs, the Jawi Peranakans, being prosperous and educated, assumed a leadership role in the Malay-Muslim community until the 1920s. At that time a group of English-educated Malays began to challenge this right, with the appointment of the first Malay member of the Legislative Council and the formation of the Kesatuan Melayu Singapura (Singapore Malay Union).

Jawi Peranakans have since been assimilated and integrated into Singapore's Malay community, much like other Malay-Muslim dialect groups; there is no Jawi Peranakan subdivision in the census of population. However, some people still identify themselves as Jawi Peranakan and retain parts of the culture, such as dialect and dress.

Jawi Peranakan (1876–1895) Newspaper. The *Jawi Peranakan* was established in 1876 by Singapore Indian Muslims. Its first editor was Munshi Muhammad Said Dada Mohyddin. The paper's news was largely drawn from the local English media, as well as from the Egyptian and other Arab press, although much of the paper was devoted to commercial information and advice columns.

The *Jawi Peranakan* had an initial circulation of 250. Published every Monday, it was distributed throughout Singapore and Malaya, as well as in Riau and West Sumatra.

Written in Jawi (a modified Arabic script for writing the Malay language), the newspaper promoted the Malay language. As there was a dearth of Malay language textbooks in the 19th century, the newspaper was used in Malay schools as teaching material. The *Jawi Peranakan* played a significant role in the history of Malay journalism and Malay intellectual life.

The newspaper ceased publication in April 1895.

Jayakumar, S. (1939–) Academic, diplomat and politician. Born on 12 August 1939, Shanmugam Jayakumar was educated at Raffles Institution and the University of Singapore, where he graduated with LLB Honours in 1963. He was called to the Singapore Bar the following year. Two years later, he obtained his LLM from Yale Law School. He taught at the University of Singapore's Law Faculty (1964-71), before he was seconded to the MINISTRY OF FOREIGN AFFAIRS in 1971 to serve as Singapore's permanent representative to the UNITED NATIONS (UN) and high commissioner to Canada. He served in this capacity until 1974, when he returned to the Law Faculty and became dean. From 1974 to 1979, he continued to be active in diplomatic work as a member of Singapore's delegation to the UN Conference on the Law of the Sea.

Jayakumar was made a full professor in 1978. In 1980, he stepped down as dean to enter politics, and was elected MEMBER OF PARLIAMENT for Bedok constituency. He was appointed minister of state for law and minister of state for home affairs (1981–84), then minister for labour (1984–85), second minister for home affairs (1984–85) and second minister for law (1984–88). He also became minister for home affairs (1985–94) and subsequently minister for law (1988–) and minister for foreign affairs (1994–2004).

Since 12 August 2004, Jayakumar has served as deputy prime minister, while retaining the law portfolio. In addition to these duties, he was made co-ordinating minister for national security on 1 September 2005. In 1980, he was awarded the Public Service Star.

Jayamani, K. (1956–) Sportswoman. A middle- and long-distance runner, Kandasamy Jayamani made her name as a race-walking champion, competing in walking competitions in her teenage years.

She was identified as a potential middle- and long-distance runner by the Singapore Amateur Athletic Association. She was a double gold medallist in both the 1,500-m and the 3,000-m events at the 1977 and 1979 Southeast Asian Games. In 1983, Jayamani also took the bronze medal in the 3,000-m event.

She was named Sportswoman of the Year in 1976 after winning three silver medals at the Indonesian Open and two gold medals at the Malaysian Athletic Union meet, a title she won again in 1981. While she is believed to have attained Olympian standard at her peak, she did not take part in the Olympics because Singapore joined the US-led boycott of the 1980 Moscow Games.

jaywalking Under the Road Traffic Act, 'jaywalking' includes the act of crossing a street when a traffic signal forbids pedestrians from doing so; walking on a road where there is no traffic light or pedestrian crossing; and walking across bus bays and bus interchanges. Persons caught jaywalking may be fined up to $500 for their first offence. Repeat offenders can be fined up to $2,000, or imprisoned for six months.

Jehovah's Witnesses Fundamentalist Christian sect, originating in the United States in 1872 that denies many traditional Christian doctrines, including the divinity of Christ. The government deregistered the movement and banned their activities in Singapore in 1972 on the grounds that the group's members refused to perform NATIONAL SERVICE, salute the national flag and swear allegiance to the state. All materials published by the Jehovah's Witnesses, the International Bible Students Association and the Watch Tower Bible and Tract Society are also banned.

Jek Yeun Thong (1930–) Politician. Jek Yeun Thong was educated at the Chinese High School, which he entered at the age of 17. He became a student union leader and the editor of a wall newspaper. In 1950, he was expelled from the school for anti-colonial activities. He was monitored by the Special Branch and, as he had been 'black-listed' by the British, was unable to continue his studies anywhere in Singapore. Jek later joined the left-wing Chinese newspaper, *Sin Pao*.

When the PEOPLE'S ACTION PARTY (PAP) was inaugurated in 1954, Jek became a member. In the lead-up to the general election of 1955, he played an active role in the PAP's campaign, writing speeches and pamphlets in Chinese. Indeed, it was Jek who wrote LEE KUAN YEW's first Chinese speech for a rally at Bandar Street Square in 1955.

In 1957, Jek was arrested by the LIM YEW HOCK government under the Preservation of Public Security Ordinance on the charge of attempted sedition. He was unconditionally released in April 1958.

In January 1959, Jek was appointed secretary to Mayor ONG ENG GUAN, but resigned from this position in May of the same year to help the PAP contest the general election of 1959. After the PAP's victory in that election, Jek was appointed political secretary to the prime minister, a post he held until 1963.

In 1961, Jek stood against Ong Eng Guan in the Hong Lim by-election and lost. It was only in 1963 that he won the seat for Queenstown constituency and was appointed minister for labour.

In 1968, he became minister for culture, a post he held until 1978. From 1976 to 1980, Jek also served as minister for science and technology. He was deputy chairman of the People's Association (1971–77), and was a member of the team of Chinese-educated MEMBERS OF PARLIAMENT—also including ONG PANG BOON and LEE KHOON CHOY—assigned to decide on the future of NANYANG UNIVERSITY. Jek was critical of what he saw as declining standards in Chinese education.

Jek stepped down from the Cabinet in 1980 and left politics in 1988. He was admitted into the ORDER OF NILA UTAMA (Second Class) in 1990.

Jek Yeun Thong: at the opening of New Town Secondary School, 1966.

Jemaah Islamiah Southeast Asian terrorist network. The origins of the Jemaah Islamiah (JI), also known as Al Jama'ah Al-Islamiyyah (or 'Islamic Group'), lie in the Darul Islam (or 'House of Islam') rebellion in Indonesia. This began with the proclamation of a Muslim state of Negara Islam Indonesia in 1948, in opposition to the secular nationalist government of President Sukarno. Darul Islam's campaign of civil violence ended only in 1962, and resulted in the loss of 25,000 lives. The JI was formed in 1993 by Indonesian religious teachers who saw themselves as inheritors of the Dural Islam tradition, and many JI leaders came from families involved in the Darul Islam movement.

The JI is a loose network of individuals and autonomous cells united by extremist religious principles. It has four main operational networks: Mantiqi 1, which covers Thailand, Malaysia and Singapore; Mantiqi 2, which covers Indonesia; Mantiqi 3, which covers the Philippines; and Mantiqi 4, which covers Australia. JI's objective is to establish a pan-Islamic caliphate covering much of this area (including northern Australia, southern Thailand and the Philippines) ruled under sharia (Islamic law).

In late 2001, a series of JI bomb plots were uncovered in Singapore. In conjunction with al-Qaeda, the JI had planned to launch a series of terrorist attacks in Singapore, targeting the embassies of the United States and Israel; the British and Australian High Commissions; the offices of several US companies; US naval ships at Changi Naval Base; US military personnel who used the Mass Rapid Transit system to travel to work; local Singaporean military facilities; and pipelines carrying water into Singapore from Malaysia. The operation was to involve the use of seven truck bombs and 21 tons of ammonium nitrate. The size and scope of the operation suggested that Singapore was seen as a key target by the JI.

During US military operations in Afghanistan in late 2001, a surveillance videotape was discovered, showing the intended targets of a JI attack in Singapore. A copy of the same tape was found in Singapore. These discoveries led to the arrest of over 400 alleged JI activists throughout the region, including 39 in Singapore.

The JI was blamed for a series of bombings in Indonesia and the Philippines in late 2000. It was also responsible for the terrorist attack on Kuta Beach in Bali, Indonesia, on 12 October 2002, that resulted in 202 deaths. The Bali attack was followed by a suicide bombing at the Marriott Hotel in Jakarta on 5 August 2003. On 1 October 2005, another attack took place in Bali, at Kuta Beach and Jimbaran Bay, killing more than 20 people. Singapore reacted to these and other developments by establishing a new homeland security structure. This was announced to the public in August 2004 in the form of the National Security Strategy.

Jenkins, Roger (1953–) Theatre practitioner, author, and artistic director of Dramaplus Arts. Born in Singapore, where his father was stationed with the British forces, Roger Vaughan Jenkins grew up and worked in Britain before returning to Singapore in 1978 as a drama teacher at United World College of Southeast Asia.

Jenkins was associated for ten years with Hi! Theatre which came into being in 1986 as a result of his collaboration with a group of hearing-impaired performers. He received the Singapore Association for the Deaf's Friend of the Deaf Award in 1990. Jenkins was a founder-member in 1991 of the Madhatters Comedy Company, a professional improvisational comedy group. In 1992, he became a Singaporean and founded the theatre company Dramaplus Arts. In 1995, he turned it into a non-profit company, providing arts and drama education to schools and organizations, and staging public performances. Jenkins won the 1995 Singapore Literature Prize for Poetry in English for *From the Belly of the Carp: Singapore River Voices*. Since 1997, he has written five award-winning plays—four of which he directed—for the biennial Singapore Youth Festival Drama Competition for schools.

Roger Jenkins

Jervois, Sir William (1821–1897) Colonial official. Born on the Isle of Wight, Sir William Francis Drummond Jervois entered the Royal Military Academy at Woolwich (1837) and attended the School of Military Engineering at Chatham (1839-41). His term as governor of the STRAITS SETTLEMENTS (1875–77) was a difficult one due to the aftermath of the Pangkor Treaty, which required Malay sultans to be advised by British Residents on all matters except those relating to religion and customs.

Instead of strictly following the treaty requirements, Jervois proposed that Residents be made 'Queen's Commissioners' and rule the states directly on behalf of the sultans. While carrying out Jervois' plan, Perak Resident James Wheeler Woodford Birch was murdered by locals acting on orders from the Perak royalty, and Jervois

K. Jayamani: picture taken 1991.

265

Jews: Menorah.

launched a series of attacks to capture the perpetrators. Although his actions ushered in the era of British control over the Malay States, Jervois was reprimanded by the Colonial Office for attempting to replace the Residential System with direct rule, and was removed from his post.

See also GOVERNORS AND RESIDENTS.

Jewish Welfare Board Founded shortly after the end of World War II, the board, an elected committee of volunteers, provides information concerning the Jewish community, as well its institutions and culture. With encouragement from Singapore's most famous Jew—DAVID MARSHALL who, in 1955, became the first chief minister of Singapore—it has undertaken many initiatives, such as developing a Jewish educational infrastructure in Singapore, administering a home for the elderly, and providing medical aid and scholarships for the needy.

Jews Jewish immigrants first arrived in Singapore in the 1820s. Many were Sephardic Jews fleeing persecution and discrimination in the Middle East, and worked as merchants and traders in Singapore. This pioneer community spoke Arabic, and a significant number could speak English and Bazaar Malay.

The 1846 census stated that six out of 43 merchant houses in Singapore were owned by Jewish people. The Jewish population in Singapore increased gradually over the decades. The 1830 population census noted that there were nine Jewish traders. According to the 1841 census, there were 18 Jewish men and four Jewish women in Singapore. In 1841, the small but expanding Jewish community managed to rent a piece of land from the British colonial government to set up their first synagogue, in present-day Synagogue Street, near Boat Quay, and obtained land for the Orchard Road Cemetery.

One of the first recorded leaders of this migrant community was Abraham Solomon. Born in Baghdad, Solomon later went to Calcutta to engage in trade for five years before establishing his home and successful trading business in Singapore in 1836. Another significant figure was Sir MANASSEH MEYER. In the third quarter of the 19th century, Meyer played a vital role

Jews: dedication of Sefer Torah, 2006.

in building the MAGHAIN ABOTH SYNAGOGUE on Waterloo Street, which replaced the one on Synagogue Street. Maghain Aboth was open for services in April 1878. Many Jews lived within walking distance of the synagogue, and their homes could be found in Waterloo Street, Prinsep Street, Selegie Road, Sophia Road and Adis Road.

By the turn of the 20th century, there were more than 460 Jewish people in Singapore. Faced with the issues of an increasing population and overcrowding in Maghain Aboth, Meyer built a second synagogue next to his home in Oxley Rise. The year 1905 saw the completion of the CHESED-EL SYNAGOGUE, designed by ALFRED JOHN BIDWELL of architectural firm SWAN AND MACLAREN. Meyer also funded the development of the Talmud Torah (Hebrew School) in Singapore. Today, religious classes are still conducted at the Hebrew School in Oxley Rise.

The community seriously decreased in size during and after WORLD WAR II. A significant proportion of Jewish residents in Singapore fled for India before the JAPANESE OCCUPATION. Those who remained were interned, some at first in CHANGI PRISON. The whole Jewish community was eventually interned in Sime Road Camp. In the post-war era, many Jewish people left Singapore for Australia, the US, Israel and Europe for more opportunities. The population declined substantially from more than 1,500 in the pre-war period to less than 300 as of 2006.

Despite the small size of the Jewish community, its members have contributed significantly to Singapore's history. They include former Chief Minister DAVID MARSHALL, doctor YAHYA COHEN and Senior Counsels JOSEPH GRIMBERG and HARRY ELIAS. Companies led and managed by Singaporean Jews include fashion and watch distributor FJ BENJAMIN and THE COFFEE BEAN & TEA LEAF.

A number of streets and buildings are reminders of the legacy of the Jewish community. In the Katong area, Amber Road, Elias Road, Penhas Road and Meyer Road bear the names of Jews who have made their mark in their respective fields. In the central area, Nassim Road and Nathan Road bear the names of wealthy Jewish immigrants, as does the David Elias building along Selegie Road.

Today, the Jewish community uses the MAGHAIN ABOTH SYNAGOGUE in Waterloo Street and CHESED-EL SYNAGOGUE in Oxley Rise. These are Orthodox synagogues where the services are conducted according to the Sephardic tradition. The Chesed-El Synagogue is used for services on Monday morning and during the High Holidays. The Maghain Aboth Synagogue is used during the High Holidays and for all other services during the week, except for Monday morning.

The community meets for the Shabbat lunch in the Maghain Aboth Synagogue on Saturday afternoon. There is also a weekly Monday morning breakfast held in Chesed-El Synagogue after the service. The major Jewish holidays celebrated in Singapore are Rosh Hashanah, Yom Kippur, Passover, Sukkot, Shavuot and Hanukkah.

Jeyaretnam, J.B. (1926–) Lawyer and politician. Born in Sri Lanka, Joshua Benjamin Jeyaretnam received his early education at the English School in Muar and then the English College in Johor Baru. He moved to Singapore to study at St Andrew's School, before leaving for University College, London, in 1948. He graduated with an LLB (Hons) in June 1951. He also read law at Gray's Inn, and was called to the Bar in 1951.

Jeyaretnam returned to Singapore in 1952. He joined the legal service and served in a variety of posts, including magistrate, district judge, crown counsel, deputy public prosecutor, member of the Income Tax Board of Review, chairman of the Valuation Review Board and senior district judge. He also tutored in criminology and legal philosophy at the University of Malaya in Singapore's Faculty of Law.

In 1969, he resigned from the legal service to enter private practice. In 1971, he was elected secretary-general of the WORKERS' PARTY. Ten years later, he won the Anson constituency by-election, becoming the first non-PAP MEMBER OF PARLIAMENT in over 13 years. He was re-elected to the Anson seat in 1984.

In the same year, he was charged for financial impropriety relating to the collection of party funds. He was acquitted by the district court but was found guilty on appeal, and was sentenced to three months' imprisonment. The high court later reduced this sentence, imposing a $5,000 fine which automatically disqualified Jeyaretnam from holding a seat in Parliament. The conviction also led to him being disbarred by the LAW SOCIETY, but he was reinstated after a successful appeal to the PRIVY COUNCIL against the disbarment. It was not until 1997 that he returned to parliament as a Non-Constituency Member.

Jeyaretnam has been the target of several high-profile defamation suits brought by members of the ruling PAP, all of which he has lost. He has been found liable for over $1 million in damages. In 2001, he was declared bankrupt and disqualified from contesting the general election. He resigned as leader of the WORKERS' PARTY in October 2001. His son is lawyer and author PHILIP JEYARETNAM.

Jeyaretnam, Philip (1964–) Lawyer and author. The younger son of J.B. JEYARETNAM and the late Margaret Walker, Philip Anthony Jeyaretnam secured a double first in law at Corpus Christi College,

J.B. Jeyaretnam: with garland, after 1981 victory.

Cambridge University in 1986. He won second and first prizes in the 1983 and 1985 National Short Story Writing Competitions for 'Campfire' and 'Evening Under Frangipanni' respectively. His first book, *First Loves* (1987), a collection of nine linked stories, stayed on *The Straits Times*' bestseller list for 18 months. Jeyaretnam has published two novels—*Raffles Place Ragtime* (1988), and *Abraham's Promise* (1995) which was 'Highly Commended' in the 1996 National Book Development Council of Singapore Awards. *Tigers in Paradise* (2004) collects all the above works and includes two essays on the state of Singaporean literature in English.

Jeyaretnam received the NATIONAL ARTS COUNCIL's Young Artist Award for Literature in 1993, and the Southeast Asia Write Award in 2003. A senior counsel in private legal practice, Jeyaretnam was elected president of the Law Society in 2004, and re-elected in 2006. He is also adjunct professor at the Department of Building, National University of Singapore.

Jiang Hu (dates unknown) Singer. Jiang Hu became the first celebrity from the *xinyao* scene (*see* CHINESE POPULAR MUSIC), after releasing his debut album *Bu Shi Bu Yuan Yi* (Not That I Don't Want To) (1984). His biggest hit was 'Lian Zhi Qi' (Love's Refuge), which stayed on local radio charts for 29 weeks in 1986. He is also well-known for his rendition of the theme song to the Mandarin television series *Bian Yuan Shao Nian* (On the Fringe) (1988). Since leaving the music scene in the early 1990s, Jiang Hu has been concentrating on his work as a graphic designer.

Jing Junhong (1968–) Sportswoman. Jing Junhong was born in Jiangsu, China, and became a Singapore citizen in April 1994. Jing won gold medals in table tennis at every Southeast Asian Games between 1995 and 2003. At the Atlanta Olympics in 1996, she reached the final round of 16. The following year, she won the individual gold, as well as the doubles gold with Li Jiawei at the 13th Commonwealth Championships in Glasgow, Scotland. At

the Sydney Olympics in 2000, she lost to Jing Chen of Taiwan in the bronze medal play-off match.

Jing was a member of the successful national team that won an Asian Games bronze medal in Busan (2002). In the same year, she won a gold medal at the Manchester Commonwealth Games.

Even after her subsequent retirement from international competition, Jing retained a high place in the table tennis world rankings. She is a member of the SINGAPORE SPORTS COUNCIL HALL OF FAME and was named the Singapore National Olympic Committee's Sportswoman of the Year in 1997, 1998 and 2001.

Jinricksha Station Prominently located at the junction of Tanjong Pagar Road and Neil Road, the Jinricksha Station was built in 1903–04. It was the main station for rickshaw services, once ubiquitous on Singapore's streets. The first rickshaws—small, lightweight, two-wheeled carts drawn by rickshaw-pullers—were imported into Singapore from Shanghai in 1880; and by 1888, a Jinricksha Department was established to register, license and control the Singapore rickshaw population. By 1919, there were some 9,000 rickshaws manned by over 20,000 pullers working in shifts. After World War II, rickshaws were phased out and trishaws replaced them for short-distance transportation.

The building was designed by Samuel Tomlinson (municipal engineer 1896–1902) and D.M. Craik (municipal architect). The triangular site makes it an eye-catching landmark. The building's brickwork, originally exposed, has been painted over. It has been gazetted for conservation, and is currently leased out as shops and restaurants.

joget moden Dance form. Meaning 'modern dance', it is derived from *joget* (dance), a Malay folk dance believed to have originated in Malacca. *Joget* music has lively

beats and a fast tempo with repeated rhythmic patterns. Traditionally, *joget* music is played by a small group. The music is led by the violin and accordion and accompanied by the *rebana* (a type of drum) and gong. Along with the music, an exchange of PANTUN (traditional Malay poetry) between male and female singers takes place. The *pantun* may also be sung solo. This culminates in the *tandak* (another Malay dance form), which serves as an exit. *Joget moden* developed during the 1930s, and was popular in Singapore during the 1950s in dance halls and cabarets.

John Little Department store. The firm was originally founded in 1845 by three brothers from Scotland. The best known was Dr Robert Little, who ran a medical practice and managed the Singapore Dispensary in Raffles Place (known then as Commercial Square). As well as being the island's first coroner, Little was also a justice of peace, twice elected municipal commissioner, and at one time a Legislative Council member.

John M. Little, a cousin of Robert Little, started out as an employee of the company, but later took over the firm with a partner. The firm—which was renamed Little, Cursetejee and Company—was involved in several activities: besides being a property and land auctioneer, it also conducted general trading; ran a motor garage; manufactured furniture; and operated a café, beauty salon and general store which catered to the needs of the growing European community.

The partnership was dissolved in 1853. It was then revived under the name John Little and Company, after Martin Little—a brother of Robert Little—joined the business. It became a limited company in 1900. The company commissioned the building of a new store in 1907.

By the early years of the 20th century, John Little and Company had become one of Singapore's two main department stores—the other being Robinson's (now

Jing Junhong

Philip Jeyaretnam

Joget moden: partygoers at New World in 1949.

Jinricksha Station: junction of Tanjong Pagar and Neil Roads, 1905.

John Little: frontage of store at Raffles Place, 1955.

ROBINSONS). John Little expanded into Malaya, opening stores in Kuala Lumpur (1914), Penang (1926) and Ipoh (1929). With the onset of the Depression, John Little began to promote itself as a place of 'moderate prices' and 'affordability'.

Like many other businesses that had been owned or managed by Europeans, the store was closed during the JAPANESE OCCUPATION, at which time the store's premises became known as the Daimaru Building. Although it opened again in June 1946, the store was acquired by Robinsons in 1955.

A replica of the facade of the original John Little storefront was included in the design of entrances to the Mass Rapid Transit station at Raffles Place. However, the original building that housed John Little on Battery Road was demolished in 1982 (the Singapore Land Tower was built on the site).

In more recent years, John Little has continued to trade from a number of different stores in the traditional shopping area of Orchard Road and in suburban shopping malls.

Johns Hopkins Singapore International Medical Centre A private medical centre that opened in October 2000, the centre was originally called Johns Hopkins-National University Hospital Medical Centre and located at the NATIONAL UNIVERSITY HOSPITAL. It was established to provide oncology services and as part of the government's drive to develop Singapore into a medical hub.

To facilitate its growth, the centre was relocated to TAN TOCK SENG HOSPITAL in 2005 and renamed Johns Hopkins Singapore International Medical Centre.

It is the clinical arm of Johns Hopkins Singapore, the Southeast Asian base of the well-known Johns Hopkins University.

Johnston, Alexander (unknown–1850) Businessman. A native of Dumfrieshire, Scotland, Alexander Laurie Johnston joined the merchant navy as a young man and came to Singapore some time in 1819–20. In 1823, he helped found the Singapore

Alexander Johnston: sculpture at Boat Quay.

Institution, and was appointed magistrate by SIR STAMFORD RAFFLES. He was also one of the town planners hand-picked by Raffles, and was responsible for the decision to create FIVE-FOOT WAYS. In 1837, Johnston became the first chairman of the Singapore Chamber of Commerce. Johnston left Singapore in 1841, and died in Scotland in 1850, but his firm—A.L. Johnston & Co.—continued to operate until 1892. JOHNSTON'S PIER was named after him.

Johnston's Pier Built in 1855, Johnston's Pier was named after Alexander Laurie Johnston, one of early Singapore's most important businessmen. The red beacon placed above it led many local Chinese of Hokkien origin to name it '*ang teng beh tau*' (literally 'red lantern harbour' or 'red lantern landing place'). By the 1920s, the pier had fallen into disrepair. In 1933, Johnston's Pier was demolished and replaced by CLIFFORD PIER. Many European residents were unhappy about the decision to name the new pier after Sir Hugh Clifford and wanted Johnston's name restored. Their protests fell on deaf ears.

Johor Baru Also spelled as 'Johore Bahru' and popularly known as 'JB', the city is the capital of the Malaysian state Johor. It is located at the southernmost tip of the Malay peninsula, and is Malaysia's second largest city. It was founded in 1855 by TEMENGGONG IBRAHIM, whose son, Sultan Abu Bakar, moved the seat of the Johor government from Singapore to Johor Baru. Abu Bakar built the modern capital to prove to the British that Johor was not just another 'wild native state'. Its link to Singapore via the Causeway has made tourism a major income earner for the state. Many Singaporeans make use of the favourable exchange rate to shop and dine there.

Johor sultanate Formed by members of the Malacca elite after the fall of Malacca to the Portuguese in 1511, the Johor sultanate was attacked a number of times throughout the 16th century by the Portuguese and Acehnese (*see* ACEH). This made it difficult

for the sultanate's rulers to firmly establish power, and the sultanate was forced to continue to shift its capital, first from eastern Sumatra to the Riau archipelago, and then to the area near the Johor River.

Eventually, the leaders of the Johor sultanate reached an agreement with the Dutch VEREENIGDE OOSTINDISCHE COMPAGNIE (VOC) whereby Johor would help Dutch representatives defeat the Portuguese in Malacca, which they did in 1641. With its new powerful allies, Johor gained access to military supplies and trade, and was able to use these to control maritime traffic and maintain power in the Strait of Malacca for the remainder of the 17th century.

However, following the death of SULTAN MAHMUD in 1699, Johor's power began to wane. A chief official (*bendahara*) assumed leadership of the sultanate, but the chaos and uncertainty that ensued allowed other states that had come under Johor's domination to rebel against it.

Ultimately, these groups united under a leader named Raja Kecik, who claimed to be Minangkabau (an ethnic group from Sumatra) and a Malay prince. Raja Kecik and his followers captured Johor in 1718, executed the *bendahara* sultan the following year, moved to eastern Sumatra and founded the Siak sultanate.

Ibrahim, the son of the *bendahara* sultan of Johor, gained control over Johor in the early 1720s after establishing an alliance with Bugis mercenaries. But for the remainder of the 18th century, there were numerous conflicts between Johor, Siak and the VOC in Malacca as these groups battled for trade, cultural and political hegemony in the Strait of Malacca. These battles eventually exhausted all sides, and by the early 19th century, Johor had become a shadow of its former self.

The Malay ruler of Johor, Sultan Mahmud died in 1812, and a dispute arose over who should be the next sultan. In 1819, Sir STAMFORD RAFFLES was able to exploit this dispute: he appointed one of Sultan Mahmud's sons—Tengku Long (later SULTAN HUSAIN SHAH)—Sultan of

Johnston's Pier, 1890.

Singapore, and signed treaties with him allowing for the establishment of a British trading base on the island. The other claimant to the throne, Tengku Abdul Rahman, was based in Riau. He was installed as sultan in 1823 by the Dutch.

With the Anglo-Dutch treaty of 1824, the Johor sultanate was split between the English and the Dutch spheres of influence. As a result, Abdul Rahman lost Johor and Pahang, and the Johor sultanate became split between the Riau-Lingga sultanate under Abdul Rahman, and the Johor sultanate under Husain Shah. The Riau-Lingga sultanate was eventually abolished by the Dutch in the first decade of the 20th century. Over in Singapore, the line of Sultan Husain Shah lost the sultanate when the British refused to recognise Husain's son. In 1880, the British crowned Abu Bakar, the son of the TEMENGGONG IBRAHIM, as Sultan of Johor instead. The ruling family of the modern state of Johor traces its lineage to Sultan Abu Bakar.

Joo Chiat Area in the eastern part of the island, first developed in the 1820s when European and Chinese merchants began establishing coconut plantations there. At the time, it was considered part of Katong.

In the late 19th century, a Chinese trader named Chew Joo Chiat arrived in Singapore and began to acquire land from plantation owners. By the 1920s, he had amassed a considerable acreage. A dirt road that ran through Chew's estate was paved by the government in the 1920s and was named Joo Chiat Road, and the name 'Joo Chiat' was later applied to the area.

Joo Chiat wasn't just plantation land though. It also had seaside bungalows and villages. In the years prior to World War II, more roads were built, and plantations were converted into homes, businesses, schools and places of worship. The population of the area, which to this day includes a large number of EURASIANS and PERANAKANS, increased dramatically.

Development ceased during the Japanese Occupation, but began again in the decades following World War II. In the process, much of old Joo Chiat was lost. Ongoing land reclamation schemes also saw Joo Chiat increasingly distanced from the coast. In the 1990s, however, conservation became seen as a major priority, and buildings of heritage value found in Joo Chiat were gazetted. Landmarks that were saved included the Katong Confectionery and Bakery, and shophouses on several key streets, such as Koon Seng Road, Joo Chiat Place and Everitt Road. Like many other historic neighbourhoods of Singapore, Joo Chiat offers an attractive mix of the old and the new.

While the architectural heritage of Joo Chiat was being conserved in the 1990s, the commercial and social character of the suburb was also changing. Old cottage businesses closed down and were replaced by nightlife venues and, for a time, massage parlours. Many residents felt that vice threatened to affect the identity of the suburb. They sought assistance from the authorities, and by the the end of 2005, the area had been largely cleaned up.

Joseph, Professor V.T. (1940–) Paediatric surgeon. Professor Vijeyakaran Thuraisingam Joseph established paediatric surgery as a separate speciality when he was at the SINGAPORE GENERAL HOSPITAL (SGH). He later practised at KK WOMEN'S AND CHILDREN'S HOSPITAL (KKWCH) when the paediatric department at SGH moved over to KKWCH in 1997. He was chairman of the Division of Paediatric Surgery until 2002.

Joseph has a special interest in hepatobiliary (pertaining to the liver and bile ducts) and hypospadias (a condition relating to the penis) surgery involving children and has spoken extensively on these subjects internationally. He was secretary-general and president of the Asian Association of Paediatric Surgeons and a member of the Pacific Association of Paediatric Surgeons.

JTC Corporation Statutory board. JTC Corporation was originally known as the Jurong Town Corporation (JTC). Its brief was to develop and run Singapore's first industrial estate at Jurong (see JURONG INDUSTRIAL ESTATE). From 1961, 1,600 ha of swamp and wasteland in Jurong was transformed into an industrial estate. The first phase of Jurong's development was completed in 1967, and the JTC came into being on 1 June 1968. The JTC expanded its operations to building the Singapore Science Park, Singapore's first petrochemical complex on Jurong Island, the International Business Park, Singapore's first wafer fabrication plant in Woodlands, and ONE-NORTH at North Buona Vista Road.

Jubilee Hall Located in RAFFLES HOTEL, this theatre was named after the old Jubilee Theatre on North Bridge Road that had been removed to make way for the redevelopment of RAFFLES HOTEL. The 388-seat hall was completed on the third floor of the hotel in 1991. It was designed by Charles Cosler and adorned with fresco murals of Southeast Asian scenes by Carlo Marchioni. It is used for plays, concerts and seminars.

judicial commissioner Judicial office of THE SUPREME COURT. The post of judicial commissioner was created in 1979 as a means of attracting senior practising lawyers to take on temporary judicial appointments. Unlike that of judges, the term of office of a judicial commissioner is fixed, but may be renewed.

From 1979 to 1986, no legal practitioners were induced to take up this position.

Joo Chiat

Singapore's first judicial commissioner was CHAN SEK KEONG, who was appointed on 1 May 1986. Following Chan's appointment, several other practitioners—including Michael Hwang, C.R. Rajah and JOSEPH GRIMBERG—have accepted the appointment.

Judicial commissioners have typically been appointed for one to three years, but have also been appointed to attend to single cases. When the office was first created, it was felt that its temporary nature would allow leading practitioners the option of returning to legal practice once their tenure had been completed.

An appointment to the post of judicial commissioner has often been seen as a prelude to full appointment to the bench as a PUISNE JUDGE. Like puisne judges, judicial commissioners may also preside over the COURT OF APPEAL.

judiciary The judiciary is the chief guardian of Singapore's CONSTITUTION, which it safeguards through the process of judicial review. Judicial power is vested in the SUPREME COURT, and in such subordinate courts as may be provided for by any written law for the time being in force.

The Constitution establishes two levels of courts: the Supreme Court and the SUBORDINATE COURTS. The Supreme Court consists of the High Court and the COURT OF APPEAL. The High Court is presided over by PUISNE JUDGES, led by the CHIEF JUSTICE. All Supreme Court judges are appointed by the PRESIDENT, who acts on advice from the PRIME MINISTER. In order to ensure judicial independence, Supreme Court judges enjoy constitutional protection. This is provided for through guarantees on tenure and remuneration, so that judges cannot be arbitrarily removed, their offices abolished or their salaries reduced. Judges have security of tenure up to the age of 65.

Judges appointed to the Court of Appeal are known as judges of appeal. In addition to puisne judges and judges of appeal, there are JUDICIAL COMMISSIONERS, who hold the same rights and privileges as puisne judges, but do not enjoy the same security of tenure or remuneration.

Judiciary: figure of 'Justice' by Rodolfo Nolli on the facade of the old Supreme Court building.

Jurong BirdPark: flamingos.

JUNIOR COLLEGES
Independent
Hwa Chong Institution
Raffles Junior College
Government-aided
Anglo-Chinese Junior College
St Andrew's Junior College
Catholic Junior College
Nanyang Junior College
Government
Anderson Junior College
Innova Junior College
Jurong Junior College
Meridian Junior College
National Junior College
Pioneer Junior College
Serangoon Junior College
Tampines Junior College
Temasek Junior College
Victoria Junior College
Yishun Junior College
Source: Ministry of Education

The Subordinate Courts include the District Courts, the Magistrates' Courts, the FAMILY COURT, the SYARIAH COURT and the Small Claims Tribunal. Judges, registrars and assistant registrars in the Subordinate Courts are members of the legal service, and do not enjoy security of tenure or remuneration. Typically, they are rotated between various courts, the Attorney-General's Chambers and government ministries. The Subordinate Courts are headed by the senior district judge, who works with the Legal Service Commission to determine the placement of junior judges.

Jumabhoy, Rajabali (1898–1998) Businessman. Rajabali Jumabhoy was born in India, the youngest of 12 children. After completing his matriculation at the Bharda High School in Bombay (now Mumbai), Rajabali left for Singapore, arriving on the island in June 1916 to join his brother as a partner in the family business— R Jumabhoy. This firm traded in coffee, black pepper and sago flour. In 1921, the partnership was dissolved following a dispute between the brothers, but Rajabali stayed on, concentrating on the export of coffee and other regional produce.

The business was devastated by the stock-market crash of 1929. Jumabhoy then diversified by moving into other areas of business such as insurance, and was appointed chief agent for Bombay Life Assurance Co. Ltd. However, World War II disrupted his activities, and Jumabhoy returned to India in 1942, travelling back to Singapore in October 1945 to rebuild the business.

Jumabhoy purchased land on Scotts Road and built a residence there. In 1946, his company was renamed R Jumabhoy & Sons (Pte) Ltd, as his son, Ameerali, joined the firm's management.

In 1952, Jumabhoy retired from active business, but remained chairman of the company. The group continued to prosper, eventually changing its name to Scotts Holdings, and being publicly listed. By the late 1980s, its business interests included hospitality, retail and food and beverage. However, in 1995, a family dispute over the running of the business resulted in members of the Jumabhoy family being removed from the management of Scotts Holdings.

Jumabhoy was a prominent member of the GUJARATI community. He was a founder member of the Singapore Gujarati School Committee, the Gandhi Memorial and the Singapore Anti-Tuberculosis Association. He also held positions as president of the Indian Merchant Association (1929-39) and of the Indian Chamber of Commerce (for a total of nine years in the period 1935-55); justice of the peace (1930); municipal commissioner (1938); and legislative councillor (1948-55). When a partially-elected Legislative Assembly replaced the Legislative Council in 1955, Jumabhoy won an assembly seat as an independent candidate. He retired from politics in 1959.

junior colleges The apex of Singapore's pre-university school system. Junior colleges (JCs) offer two years of academic curriculum intended to prepare students for university education. The first JC, National Junior College, was established in 1969. In 2005, there were 17 JCs (*see* table).

Students who do well in their Singapore-Cambridge General Certificate of Education Ordinary (GCE 'O') level examination, can apply for entry to a JC. Admission is based on a points system computed from the aggregate of the student's 'O' level results. At the end of the JC course, students sit for the Singapore-Cambridge General Certificate of Education Advanced (GCE 'A') level examination. Alternatively, students can apply to a centralized institute, the MILLENNIA INSTITUTE, formed by the merger of the Jurong and Outram institutes.

Jurong Industrial area in western Singapore. The name Jurong is probably a derivative of the Malay word '*jerung*', meaning 'voracious shark'. Jurong Road was constructed between 1852 and 1853, when gambier plantations (*see* PEPPER AND GAMBIER) sprang up in the area. Many Chinese residents referred to the area as '*peng kang*' (Hokkien for 'gambier'). The gambier plantations were later replaced by RUBBER plantations.

Other than these plantations, the swampy, forested area remained generally undeveloped until the early 1960s, when the government decided to establish a new industrial town there. This necessitated clearing and developing almost 7,000 ha of land, of which about 1,600 ha was designated for the JURONG INDUSTRIAL ESTATE. The brainchild of then Finance Minister GOH KENG SWEE, the idea was to create a new industrial estate and persuade foreign businesses to invest and establish factories. Jurong was selected for several reasons: it was a large tract of undeveloped and mostly state-owned land; the deep coastal waters were suitable for a port; and Jurong was close to the existing commercial port of Singapore.

The infrastructural costs were enormous, and many initially called the reclaimed swampland 'Goh's Folly'. Reclamation began in 1962. Eleven hills in the area were levelled to provide earth to fill in the swamps and the Jurong River. The hard work and persistence paid off and by the 1970s, Jurong was teeming with activity. The Jurong Town Corporation, responsible for Jurong's development, built flats to accommodate people working in Jurong, and to provide recreational facilities for all Singaporeans (*see* JTC CORPORATION, JURONG BIRDPARK and CHINESE GARDEN). Jurong is still Singapore's main industrial area today.

Jurong BirdPark During a World Bank Meeting in Rio de Janeiro in 1968, DR GOH KENG SWEE, then Singapore's minister for finance, visited a zoo and was impressed by its free-flight aviary. This inspired the idea for Jurong BirdPark, which Dr Goh envisaged would be a place for Singaporeans to enjoy nature, even in an industrial area like Jurong.

The park was constructed on the western slope of Jurong Hill, at a cost of $3.5 million. During its construction, ambassadors and foreign dignitaries to Singapore were invited to contribute birds, and when the park opened on 3 January 1971, contributions had been received from 12 countries, seven zoos and 40 private donors.

The BirdPark's collection has since grown to over 9,000 birds from 600 species, making it one of the most extensive in the world. It specializes in birds from Southeast Asia, with about 260 Southeast Asian species in its collection. Occupying 20.2 ha, the BirdPark is the largest park of its kind in the Asia Pacific. Of its four aviaries, one is the world's largest. In it is the world's tallest man-made waterfall, which serves as a dramatic backdrop for free-flying birds from South America and Africa. Like the Singapore Zoological Gardens, exhibits and enclosures at the BirdPark are designed to closely resemble natural habitats. Complementing this are the landscaping and exotic flowering plants lining the pathways and open spaces throughout the park.

The BirdPark also engages in research and conservation. Launched in 1988, its

Jurong BirdPark

breeding and research centre includes 110 breeding aviaries for individual pairs of birds, as well as supporting facilities like an incubator room, nursery and laboratory. Successes to date include the world's largest breeding colonies of Humboldt penguins, and the world's first 12-wired bird of paradise to be bred in captivity.

Jurong BirdPark belongs to the same parent company as the SINGAPORE ZOO and NIGHT SAFARI—namely, Wildlife Reserves Singapore, a TEMASEK HOLDINGS subsidiary.

Jurong Drive-In Cinema Opening on 14 July 1971 with the film *Doctor in Trouble* (1970), Jurong Drive-In Cinema was the largest drive-in in Asia at the time. It was owned and managed by CATHAY ORGANISATION on land leased from the Jurong Town Corporation. The drive-in covered 55,602 sq m and could take up to 900 vehicles. It had two nightly screenings, at 7.30 p.m. and 9.30 p.m., with midnight screenings on Saturdays. It employed a 14-m by 33-m screen elevated 7.6 m above the ground and tilted at 6.5 degrees. It also had a sheltered gallery that could hold some 300 viewers. Films played to packed audiences, but by the 1980s, the drive-in suffered from waning attendance due to the influx of videos and growth of video piracy; audience numbers slipped to an average of only 200 a night. The cinema finally closed on 30 September 1985.

Jurong East and Jurong West New towns. In the late 1960s, JURONG was developed as an industrial estate, and housing estates were planned for its growing population. Jurong East covers an area of about 380 ha, of which 43 per cent is used for residential occupancy. In all, there are some 22,600 housing units in Jurong East accommodating some 80,000 residents.

Jurong West Town lies at the opposite side of Jurong East and is a much larger housing estate. It covers some 990 ha, of which 56 per cent is used for residential purposes. Jurong West Town is bounded by the Pan Island Expressway, Upper Jurong Road, Boon Lay Way and Jurong Lake. Together with Jurong East, Jurong West is one of four proposed regional centres under Singapore's Concept Plan (*see* URBAN PLANNING). Jurong West has about 55,800 units housing some 183,000 residents.

Jurong Fisheries Port The port began operations in 1969 on 5.1 ha of land at the mouth of the Jurong River. It was designed to cater to foreign fishing vessels operating in the Pacific and Indian Oceans. A 400 m long wharf, a wholesale fish market and shops have also been built on the site.

Jurong Fisheries Port serves as a marketing and distribution centre for more than 100 seafood species, including fish imported from Malaysia and other countries.

Jurong Industrial Estate The estate originated as part of plans drawn up by the ECONOMIC DEVELOPMENT BOARD (EDB) to transform Singapore into a MANUFACTURING centre—a strategy based on the recommendations of a United Nations Industrial Survey Team headed by DR ALBERT WINSEMIUS. Once a swamp, the EDB set about building factories, roads and utilities in the JURONG area in the early 1960s. It also identified potential investors, persuading them to set up factories through industrial financing and incentive packages. The first such investor was the National Iron and Steel Mill (NATSTEEL), which established itself at Jurong in August 1963.

The first phase of Jurong's development as an industrial estate was completed in 1967. By then, total investment in fixed assets amounted to $178 million, and some 6,500 workers were employed on the estate. Many of the businesses that opened in Jurong were joint ventures between local entrepreneurs and overseas industrialists.

In 1968, Jurong Town Corporation (*see* JTC CORPORATION) was formed to oversee the industrialization and management of the estate. Jurong Industrial Estate eventually came to house more than 300 factories, making it Southeast Asia's largest industrial estate by the start of the 21st century.

Jurong Island Largely man-made, Jurong Island was created by LAND RECLAMATION and the merging of seven smaller islands (Pulau Pesak, Pulau Pesak Kecil, Pulau Ayer Chawan, Pulau Ayer Merbau, Pulau Sakra, Pulau Seraya and Pulau Merlimau) and a number of islets, with the objective of housing Singapore's petrochemical industries. The original island group, off the southwest coast of Singapore, was less than 10 sq km in area. The individual islands were palm-fringed and dotted with traditional Malay *kampung laut*—fishing villages on stilts. With reclamation and the merging of islands, the land area was more than tripled to 32 sq km. Jurong Island was extended and given new deep-water port facilities. A large number of oil and chemical companies have installations on the island. They include Chevron, ExxonMobil,

Jurong East: view across Jurong Lake.

Celanese, Mitsui and Sumitomo. By concentrating these heavy industries, as well as power-generating stations, offshore, Singapore has managed to locate these potentially pollutive industries well away from the city and residential areas. In 1999, a 2.3-km causeway was opened linking Jurong Island to the mainland. As most of the coral reefs were to be lost in the reclamation process, a translocation project was carried out in 1995 by the NATURE SOCIETY (SINGAPORE), which large quantities of living coral being moved to SENTOSA.

Jurong Technologies Established in 1986 to provide electronics contract manufacturing services for original equipment manufacturers (OEM), both in Singapore and overseas, Jurong Technologies Industrial Corporation has production facilities in Singapore, Malaysia, China, Indonesia, Thailand and Brazil, as well as sales and marketing offices in Singapore and the United States.

The company's main areas of business include printed circuit board assemblies; hard-disk drives and semiconductor manufacture and assembly; the design, manufacturing and testing of products; procurement of materials; and the provision of turnkey supply-chain management for manufacturers.

Jurong Technologies was listed on the Singapore Exchange in April 2000. The company reported a net profit of $66.4 million on a turnover of $1.93 billion for the 2005 financial year.

Jurong Island: ExxonMobil's chemical plant.

Kalamandhir Temple of Fine Arts Indian society. A non-profit organization, the Temple of Fine Arts (TFA) was founded in 1981 by a group of dance teachers inspired by their religious guru, Swami Shantanand Saraswathi. With centres in Australia, Malaysia, India and Sri Lanka, the TFA provides courses in classical and folk dance, and in vocal and instrumental music. The institution is known for its shows that bring together professional foreign-based artistes and local talent. Funds collected through its affiliate organizations (Lavanya, a visual arts centre and Annalakshmi, a vegetarian restaurant) contribute towards the cost of such performances.

Kallang Airport Singapore's first civilian airport was designed by Public Works Department (PWD) Chief Architect Frank Dorrington Ward. Construction took place in the 1930s with the reclamation of the Kallang Basin. The airport, with its seaplane wharves, hangars, workshops and terminal building, was officially opened in 1937.

The Japanese used the airport during the JAPANESE OCCUPATION, and transformed its original grass runway into concrete.

In the post-war years, MALAYAN AIRLINES provided services from Kallang to cities as far afield as Bangkok, Saigon (present-day Ho Chi Minh City) and Hong Kong. British Overseas Airways Corporation (BOAC) and Qantas flights also stopped at Kallang. By 1954, more than 143,000 passengers and 11,000 aircraft were passing through Kallang Airport annually.

However, with the increasing use of larger aircraft, Kallang Airport was soon unable to meet the demands of the aviation industry, and a much larger airport was constructed at Paya Lebar (see PAYA LEBAR AIRPORT). Kallang's final years were also marked by a tragic accident—in 1954, a BOAC Lockheed Constellation jet, the *Belfast*, crashed on landing at the airport, killing 33 people on board.

Kallang Airport was decommissioned in 1955. The terminal building and control tower were converted into offices and other facilities for the People's Association (PA).

Kallang River Approximately 2 km northeast of the SINGAPORE RIVER basin, the Kallang River has long been the site of a satellite of the island's main settlement on the north bank of the SINGAPORE RIVER. As early as the 14th century, a settlement of ORANG LAUT, or sea nomads, existed on the

Kallang Airport: Qantas passenger plane, 1938.

Kam Kee Yong: Cicada *(2002) (top); left, with daughter Kam Ning.*

Kallang River, 1975.

river's banks. In the early 1960s and 1970s, several large Chinese blue-and-white porcelain sherds dating from the Ming Wanli period (1573–1620) were dredged up from the river basin during the cleaning of the river, indicating that habitation and trade had occurred in the area in the late 16th and early 17th centuries.

Between 1819 and 1824, in accordance with the initial agreement allowing the United Kingdom an economic and strategic presence in Singapore, SULTAN HUSAIN was allowed to establish his own port on this river. Insular Southeast Asian shipping arriving at Singapore had to call here rather than at the Singapore River. Consequently, a MALAY and BUGIS settlement emerged in the area between the Sultan's residence at KAMPONG GLAM and the southwest bank of the Kallang Basin.

After 1824, Sultan Husain gave up his rights to maintaining a port at the river. The riverbank continued to be the site of a large *orang laut* settlement until the river underwent cleaning in the 1950s and the *orang laut* were resettled. Up until the 1970s, however, Kallang River remained heavily polluted with sewage from kampongs, and pollution from poultry and pig farms and small factories. The government embarked on a successful ten-year programme (1977–87) to clean up the Singapore River and Kallang Basin. Since then, the river has been a water sports centre and home to the Singapore Coast Guards.

In 2005, plans were announced to put a barrage across MARINA BAY in order to create a large freshwater 'Reservoir in the

Kallang/Whampoa: new housing, 1980s

City'; the Kallang River will be one of the main sources of water for this reservoir.
See also MARINA BARRAGE.

Kallang Theatre One of the largest cinemas in the 1970s, the Kallang Theatre was converted into a performance and concert venue, and re-opened in 1986. It is situated near the National Stadium and Singapore Indoor Stadium. It is managed by the NATIONAL ARTS COUNCIL, and its auditorium has a seating capacity of 1,744. It has hosted conferences, university convocations, and ballet, concert and musical theatre performances, including productions of Broadway musicals *Les Misérables, Cats* and *Miss Saigon*. The theatre also houses four music studios, a dance studio and an orchestral room.

Kallang/Whampoa New town. Kallang/ Whampoa new town (formerly known as Jalan Besar town) is located south of Toa Payoh and west of Geylang. The word 'Kallang' is a Malay reference to the ORANG LAUT who were known as '*orang biduanda kallang*'. The word 'Whampoa' is the nickname of WHAMPOA HOO AH KAY, a wealthy Chinese merchant who lived in the Kallang vicinity. Formerly, the area was sparsely populated. Most of its inhabitants made a living by fishing and, in later years, preparing nipah leaves for cigarette wrappers. The area was first cleared for development when Kallang Airport was built in the 1930s. Today, the Kallang/Whampoa new town covers an area of 800 ha, of which only 22 per cent is used for residential purposes. Most of the 34,300 residential units are in the Kallang Basin area. Some 111,000 people live in this estate.

Kam Kee Yong (1938–) Composer and musician. Penang-born Kam Kee Yong has has played an active part in Singapore cultural life as a violinist, composer, conductor, teacher and painter. He studied in Singapore and London, including composition under Alan Bush, and his works have been performed in the United Kingdom, Asia, the United States and Australia. In 2002, he released *Cicada*, an album of works inspired by Tang poetry, which featured his daughter KAM NING on violin. Kam resides in Canada.

Kam Ning (1975–) Musician. A recipient of the NATIONAL ARTS COUNCIL's YOUNG ARTIST AWARD in 2000, Kam Ning is the daughter of composer KAM KEE YONG. She started playing the violin at the age of six. In 2001, she won second prize in the prestigious Queen Elisabeth International Music Competition in Brussels. A former student of the Menuhin School (United Kingdom) and Curtis Institute (United States), she performed with Sarah Chang and the SINGAPORE SYMPHONY ORCHESTRA at the Inauguration Concert of the Concert Hall at ESPLANADE—THEATRES ON THE BAY in 2002. She has also made several recordings, which include *Transatlantic* (2001) and her father's compositions.

Kampong Glam Historic district. Located east of the Singapore River, the area was demarcated under Sir STAMFORD RAFFLES' Town Plan of 1822 as belonging to the Sultan of Singapore, his household and the Malay, Bugis and Arab communities. The name of the area comes from the Malay word 'KAMPONG' (or *kampung*—Malay for village), and '*glam*' (or '*gelam*')—a white-barked tree (*Melaleuca leucadendron*) known for its medicinal properties and the strength of its timber.

The area has been demarcated as a Heritage Conservation Area, with the ISTANA KAMPONG GLAM restored and transformed into the MALAY HERITAGE CENTRE. Most of the shophouses in the area have been retrofitted and let out to various businesses.

Kampong Lorong Buangkok Located off Lorong Buangkok in Yio Chu Kang, this is the last remaining kampong (village) in Singapore (as at 2006), with 28 households and a population of about 200. Occupying an area of less than 2.5 ha, the low-lying land was reclaimed from a swamp and is extremely flood-prone, hence the name Kampong Selak Kain (literally 'Pull-Up-Your-Sarong Village'). Few developers have

Kampong Lorong Buangkok

been keen to venture into the area due to its constant flooding and this was probably what kept the kampong intact for so many years. It has a provisions shop dating back to the 1970s and a small mosque.

In March 2004, the area was badly affected by flash floods, and the local community united to help the kampong residents through a *gotong royong* (self-help) project. Grassroots leaders from Jalan Kayu and Member of Parliament, Wee Siew Kim; 20 students from NGEE ANN POLYTECHNIC; and officials from the NATIONAL ENVIRONMENT AGENCY and PUBLIC UTILITIES BOARD helped about a dozen villagers to repair damage caused by the flooding. They also helped build a picket fence along a stream running through the village to prevent people from falling into the water. A 2-m footbridge was also built over the stream to replace the old one that had become unsafe.

kampongs The word 'kampong' is an English variation of the Malay word *kampung*, meaning 'village'. While a majority of the people who used to live in kampongs were Malay, there were many non-Malay kampongs in Singapore. In fact, the population of each village settlement often included both Malays and non-Malays.

Kampongs were part of the rural development of Singapore. Beginning in the 1840s and 1850s, Chinese agricultural settlements developed along many of the newly constructed roads leading out from the town. Cultivation of pepper and gambier led to the clearance of forest, the conversion of land into plantations and the creation of 'interior' villages such as those at Ang Mo Kio, Yio Chu Kang and Serangoon. In the early 20th century, RUBBER plantations led to the establishment of further villages. Many of these originated as service or collection centres for neighbouring rubber estates. These villages tended to be located near major roads. A number, such as Jurong, Ama Keng, Sungei Mandai and Lokyang, were small-scale vegetable production centres serving the urban population. Rural settlements grew up at the junctions of trunk roads.

By the 1960s, the population of rural settlements was shrinking due to new household formations, the attraction of modern homes in public housing estates, and resettlement by state agencies aiming to free land for new-town and other public-sector developments. There was little regular employment to be found in kampongs, many of which were later integrated into new towns or public housing developments (*see also* MALAY SETTLEMENTS).

Kan Ting Chiu (1946–) Judge. Kan Ting Chiu was educated at Raffles Institution and the University of Singapore where he graduated with an LLB in 1970, whereupon he joined the legal service. While in

Kampong Glam

the service, Kan held appointments as state counsel, magistrate and senior magistrate. He was called to the Singapore Bar in 1973. In 1976, he resigned and joined the firm of Hilborne and Co., where he was made a partner. In 1985, he left for R.C.H. Lim and Co. where he practised till 1988, when he joined Low Yeap and Co. That same year, he obtained his LLM from the National University of Singapore. Kan was active in legal circles, serving as Council Member in the Law Society between 1983 and 1984. In 1991, he was appointed judicial commissioner; and in 1994 he was appointed a puisne judge of the Supreme Court.

Kang Le Music Research Society Established in 1954 by a group led by Huang Weiyong, Ke Chaoping, Liang Wenchen, Lin Qidong and Liu Jiechen, Kang Le Music Research Society comprised a choir, a Chinese orchestra, a Chinese dance group, a drama group and a poetry recitation ensemble. Kang Le attracted many talented artists and performers from amongst the alumni of Chinese schools of the era.

The society conducted workshops and training courses for performing arts enthusiasts and advocated local writing and creation of music and dance. It produced dance, drama and music productions, featuring one-act and full-length plays written by Singaporean writers, and dances choreographed by local artistes. It also staged works by well-known dramatists from China, such as Guo Moruo's *Kongque Dan* (The Peacock's Gallbladder) and Mao Dun's

Kampongs: Toa Payoh before redevelopment, 1962.

Rama Kannabiran

Rama Kannabiran: Vaadai Kaatu (Chill Wind) (1981).

Qing Ming Qian Hou (Clear and Bright; Front and Rear). In the 1960s it also popularized poetry recitation with musical accompaniment. In 1967, Kang Le's permit was revoked by the Registrar of Societies, as key members were suspected of being involved in leftist activities.

See also CHINESE THEATRE.

Kang Youwei (1858–1927) Chinese scholar and political activist. The leader of the reform movement in China supporting the establishment of a constitutional monarchy in that country, Kang Youwei was born in Guangdong, China, and lived in exile for 16 years after his failed attempt to reform the Chinese political system in 1898. He visited Singapore seven times between 1900 and 1911.

After Kang's attempts at reform failed, China's Empress Dowager Cixi issued an order to arrest Kang, who had by then arrived in Singapore for the first time on 2 February 1900. Kang's passage was paid for by Khoo Teck Him (also known as Khoo Seok Wan), a Singapore merchant who had heard of Kang's reform efforts. Khoo also made significant contributions to Kang's Society to Save the Emperor (also known as the China Reform Association).

In Singapore, Kang kept company with people such as Khoo Seok Wan and LIM BOON KENG. In May 1900, Kang made a public appearance at an observance of the birth of the Qing emperor in Singapore's Chinatown. Learning of an assasination attempt, Kang hid on a small island (probably Tanjung Butun, one of a series of islands across the Sembilan Strait), from 26 July to 9 August 1900. After that, he was personally taken to Penang by JAMES SWETTENHAM, the governor.

Kang's subsequent visits to Singapore were brief. During his last visit in January 1911, Kang faced another assassination attempt when his driver responded to a knock at the door, only to have an axe thrown at his forehead by an assassin. Kang left Singapore for Japan on 8 May 1911.

Kannabiran, Rama (1943–) Author. Born in India, Rama Kannabiran was educated at Raffles Institution. He began his career as an English-language teacher in Rosyth Primary School until 1985 before teaching Tamil at the same school until his retirement in 2003.

Best-known as a short-story writer, he has written numerous short stories, novels, poems, plays and essays. He has published four short story collections and one novella. His short stories have been translated into English and Malay, and his most well-known works are *Irupathainthu Aandugal* (25 Years) (1980), which won the National Book Development Council of Singapore Award for Tamil fiction in 1982.

His other achievements include representing Singapore at the Iowa International

Literary Forum in 1988. He was also appointed honorary writing fellow by the University of Iowa, where he had completed the first draft of his novella *Beedam* (Seat of Power) (1992) over a period of three months. He is also the recipient of the Southeast Asian Write Award (1990), the Mont Blanc Award for Literature (1998) and the CULTURAL MEDALLION (1999).

kapitan cina Chinese headman appointed by colonial authorities to mediate between the Chinese population and the authorities. The *kapitan cina* (or 'kapitan china') was responsible for looking after the general welfare of the Chinese population, helping the colonial authorities enforce law and order and collecting revenue on the authorities' behalf. Most *kapitans cina* were prominent Chinese merchants or revenue farmers (*see* REVENUE FARMING).

The *kapitan cina* system was first adopted in Malacca in the 16th century by the Portuguese, and later by the Dutch. The British extended the system to Penang in the late 18th and early 19th century. However, as more and more Chinese immigrants flocked to the STRAITS SETTLEMENTS, the British feared that the various *kapitans cina* were becoming too powerful, and therefore sought to replace the system with administrative institutions such as the CHINESE ADVISORY BOARD.

In Singapore, the *kapitan cina* system was employed only during the first few years of British settlement. When the 2nd Charter of Justice of 1826 was introduced in 1827, the system was supplanted, and while the British continued enlisting the help of prominent Chinese merchants to help govern the Chinese population, they were not given any official titles. In the early 1870s, when riots involving SECRET SOCIETIES were rampant and abuse in the COOLIE TRADE was endemic, prominent Chinese businessmen such as WHAMPOA HOO AH KAY and TAN CHE SANG suggested reverting to the *kapitan cina* system. This suggestion was not taken up, however, and in 1877, the British created the CHINESE PROTECTORATE.

karayuki-san This Japanese term (literally meaning 'one who goes to China') was originally used in reference to Japanese seasonal labourers (specifically those from Kyushu) who went abroad to work during the Meiji and Taisho periods (1868–1926). It was only after World War II that the term was applied to Japanese women who had lived and worked abroad as prostitutes in the pre-war years. Due to poverty, many girls, some as young as six or seven years old, were sold into a life of prostitution overseas (mainly Southeast Asia), to help support their families and boost foreign exchange for the fledgling Japanese industrial economy during the late 19th century.

Between 1900 and 1910, the average price for a Japanese woman sold at dockside

Karayuki-san: early 1900s.

in Singapore was 500–600 yen. Demand for prostitutes rose sharply with the surge in the number of immigrant labourers in Singapore and the region. A one-hour session with a Japanese prostitute cost about two yen; if the client stayed the night, the fee was ten yen. She retained 60 per cent of the fee; her Japanese keeper took the remainder. The rates for a night with a Japanese prostitute were less than what Chinese clients would pay an AH KU (a Cantonese term to describe local Chinese prostitutes) in the same district. Unlike the *ah ku*, who exclusively catered to their own countrymen, Japanese prostitutes accepted clients irrespective of nationality. They also learned Malay and even adopted local dress to gain greater acceptance.

The Japanese brothels operated from the 1870s to the 1920s around the Bugis Street area. By 1921, the number of Japanese prostitutes had begun to decline as a result of a Japanese imperial decree which prohibited prostitution overseas and recalled women to Japan. Some ignored the decree, and many of those who stayed behind continued to work in the Malay Street and Banda Street areas.

Karthigesu, M. (1923–1999) Judge. Born in Johor Baru, Mootatamby Karthigesu was educated at St Thomas College in Ceylon and originally intended to study medicine. His education was interrupted by World War II, during which he joined the Royal Navy Volunteers. However, the war ended just as he had completed his training. Karthigesu then read law at the University of London, graduating in 1950. He was called to the Bar at the Inner Temple (1951) and the Singapore Bar (1952). After a stint in the legal service he went into private practice.

In 1957, Karthigesu joined ALLEN & GLEDHILL. After six months, he became the first Asian partner in the large European law firm. In 1977, he struck out on his own to establish Karthigesu and Arul. He later practised at Cooma Lau & Loh (1984–88) and Tan Rajah & Cheah (1988–90).

Kati: coupons used for trading of dry rubber.

In 1990, he was appointed a JUDICIAL COMMISSIONER and then judge of the High Court. In 1993, Karthigesu was appointed one of the first two judges of appeal, the other being L.P. THEAN. Karthigesu served in that capacity until his death from stomach cancer.

kati Measure of weight. During the colonial era, the *kati* was known as a *gin* in Singapore and Malaya, and was used virtually everywhere in East Asia. In China, it was referred to as a *catty*, in Korea a *chin*, in Hong Kong a *kan* and in Japan a *kin*. One *kati* was equivalent in weight to 16 *taels*, or TAHILS, equivalent to 1.33 pounds or 600 grams. A hundred *kati* equalled one *picul* or about 133.33 pounds. The *kati* has largely been replaced by the metric system, although it is still occasionally used in WET MARKETS.

Katong Residential area. The name 'Katong' is a variation of the Malay word '*katung*'—the name for the Leatherback Sea Turtle (*Dermochelys coriacea*) which used to be seen off Singapore's shores. The area was slow to develop, and up to the 1920s, was mainly occupied by coconut plantations. In the 1920s and 1930s, the area became popular as a weekend retreat and wealthy town dwellers built seaside homes in Katong. The Katong district stretches from Katong Park at Fort Road and Meyer Road, up to the junction of Siglap Road and East Coast Road and is often associated with its large EURASIAN and PERANAKAN communities. Today, the area is popular for its restaurants and food, especially Katong LAKSA, believed to have been created in the 1950s.

Katz Brothers Trading firm. Herman Katz arrived in Singapore from Europe in 1864 and was joined by his brother, Aaron, the following year. Together, they founded the firm of Katz Brothers Ltd in 1865. Starting out as retailers, the Katzes became wholesale and commission agents. The firm flourished when they secured a contract to supply the Dutch army for three years. In 1878, Aaron Katz retired, leaving Herman as sole proprietor in the business.

Katz Brothers built up a thriving general import business supplying PEPPER, and started several ice plants in Singapore. As the agents of Benz and Cie, Katz Brothers imported the first automobile into Singapore in 1896. Branches of the firm were established in London and Frankfurt as well. In 1897, the firm was turned into a limited company, and by 1929, it had become Henry Waugh and Co.

Kawamura Saburo, Lieutenant-General (1895–1947) Japanese military officer. Lieutenant-General Kawamura Saburo was the commander of the Singapore garrison immediately after the fall of Singapore (see MALAYA CAMPAIGN and JAPANESE OCCUPATION), and oversaw the SOOK CHING operation. He joined the Japanese Army in 1915 as a cadet at Japan's Military Academy and served as a 2nd lieutenant in Siberia in 1918. He was a colonel in Peking (present-day Beijing), Shanghai, and central and northern China from 1938 to 1941. On 18 February 1942 in Singapore, he was given two battalions of the 5th Division and No. 2 Field KEMPEITAI. The Sook Ching massacre occurred when he received an order from General TOMOYUKI YAMASHITA'S headquarters to screen and eliminate anti-Japanese elements in the Chinese community.

After the campaign in Singapore and MALAYA, he returned to the Southern Army's headquarters in Saigon, and then in 1945 went back to the Ministry of War in Tokyo.

In the WAR CRIMES trial held from 10 March to 2 April 1947, Kawamura was found guilty as the highest officer in charge of the Sook Ching operation. He was hanged, along with his subordinate MASAYUKI OISHI, at CHANGI PRISON on 26 June 1947; the occasion was witnessed by representatives of the Chinese community and relatives of the massacre victims.

kaya toast Popular breakfast or snack item. It consists of thinly sliced, toasted bread with butter and *kaya* spread on it. *Kaya* (meaning 'rich' in Malay), is a jam made from eggs, sugar, coconut cream and *pandan* (pandanus) leaves. It is vigorously stirred over a low fire to create the thick, creamy consistency. While *kaya* is associated with PERANAKANS, it was the Hainanese who popularized this dish in COFFEE SHOPS all over Singapore. At breakfast, *kaya* toast is often accompanied by soft-boiled eggs. At least two popular franchises have built their reputation on *kaya* toast—Ya Kun Kaya Toast and Killiney Kopitiam.

Keasberry, Benjamin Peach (1811-1875) Missionary, teacher and printer. Born in 1811 in Hyderabad, India, Keasberry was the youngest son of a British colonel. He was educated in Mauritius and Madras, and opened a shop in Singapore as a young man, before moving to Batavia (present-day Jakarta) to work for a British firm. In Batavia, Keasberry met the London Missionary Society's Dr Medhurst, from whom he learned the art of printing and bookbinding. It was also during his time in Batavia that Keasberry decided to become a missionary.

After studying in the United States for three years, Keasberry set sail for Singapore as a missionary in 1837 under the auspices of the American Board of Commissioners for Foreign Missions. In Singapore, Keasberry studied Malay, and in 1839, he opened a small school for Malay boys. He left the American Board in that same year and joined the London Missionary Society. In 1843, Keasberry founded the Malay Chapel (Greja Keasberry) in Prinsep Street (now PRINSEP STREET PRESBYTERIAN CHURCH).

In 1847, Keasberry left the London Missionary Society after that group ordered all its missionaries to relocate to China. Thereafter, Keasberry remained in Singapore as an independent, self-supporting missionary, opening a school for Malay girls on River Valley Road, and relying on a printing press—the Mission Press—that he had established for funds.

He died while preaching on 6 September 1875, and was buried at Bukit Timah Cemetery. (His remains were subsequently exhumed and reinterred in Bidadari Cemetery in 1967.) Keasberry's printing press—which, in addition to printing the Bible in Malay, was much used by merchants of the day—was later purchased by John Fraser and David Neave *See also* PRESBYTERIANS.

Kempeitai Military police responsible for containing anti-Japanese resistance and for maintaining civilian law and order during the JAPANESE OCCUPATION. Although 'Kempeitai' has usually been translated as 'military police force', the unit was also responsible for civilian police duties, intelligence-gathering and subversion and surveillance of civilians. In Japanese-occupied territories, including Singapore, the local police force came under the command of the Kempeitai.

Katong: terraced houses with elegantly ornamented facades.

Kaya toast

Benjamin Peach Keasberry

Kempeitai: group photograph, 1942.

Sir Henry Keppel

Formed in 1881 as a semi-autonomous unit attached to the Imperial Japanese Army but reporting directly to the War Minister, the Kempeitai was a law unto itself. Its officers were trained in special schools to conduct espionage, break codes, run spy networks, and use explosives and arms. A Kempeitai school was set up in Singapore in 1942.

The uniform of a Kempeitai officer could be the standard Japanese Army uniform, coupled with an armband on which were written the Japanese characters for 'Kempeitai', or a white uniform with an armband. They could also be plain-clothed. Officers carried a sword and a stick, and non-commissioned officers were armed with a bamboo stick with which they struck captives.

The Kempeitai were responsible for many war-time atrocities in Singapore. Suspects arrested by this unit were often tortured mercilessly. An unknown number of people in Singapore died as a result. Among the most notorious Kempeitai buildings was the original YMCA building (later demolished) on Stamford Road (site of the present-day YMCA building). Others were the Central Police Station building (demolished) in South Bridge Road, a private residence in Smith Street, and a mansion on Oxley Road whose garage was turned into detention cells.

Infamous Kempeitai incidents include the DOUBLE 10TH INCIDENT and the torture of those suspected of taking part in OPERATION JAYWICK. Civilians in Singapore who were arrested by the Kempeitai included ELIZABETH CHOY and her husband Choy Khun Heng; Bishop John Leonard Wilson of the Anglican Church; and J. Francis, the driver of the Changi Prison Camp commandant.

Kent Ridge Canopy Walk A 280-m long boardwalk that links Kent Ridge Park to the REFLECTIONS AT BUKIT CHANDU museum. The boardwalk opened in November 2003. Costing $1.3 million to construct, it allows access to wheelchairs and perambulators, and signs provide information on plants which can be viewed along the boardwalk. Various species of birds, lizards and other fauna resident in Kent Ridge Park can be viewed at treetop level.

Keppel, Sir Henry (1809–1904) British military officer. Keppel was born into an aristocratic family with close ties to British royalty. Also known as 'Harry', he was nicknamed 'the Little Admiral' because of his small physical stature. He joined the navy at the age of 13, along with his brother Tom, and quickly rose through the ranks, despite a rebellious streak.

Keppel had traversed the West Indies with the *Galatea* before he visited the East Indies with the *Magicienne* between 1831 and 1833, when he first passed through

Singapore. On 1 November 1847, he was in command of the *Meander*, the ship carrying James Brooke from Singapore to Labuan to assume his governorship. On arrival in Singapore, Keppel reported on 30 March 1848 that he was surprised by Singapore's deep waters, and strongly recommended—to both the Board of Admiralty in the British Navy and The Peninsular and Oriental Steam Navigation Company (P&O)—Singapore's development as a coaling station and harbour.

Keppel was the senior naval officer of the STRAITS SETTLEMENTS when James Brooke sent for him to help suppress pirates around Borneo. He went on to take part in other major conflicts, including the Crimean War (1853–56) and the second Opium War (1856–60). In 1869, Keppel was promoted to Admiral. He remained in active service for another six years, and was knighted on 20 May 1871. He relinquished his naval post in 1876, and was given the honorary appointment of Principal Naval Aide-de-Camp to the Queen in March 1878. At the age of 90, Keppel took to sea in 1900, this time as a passenger on a P&O mail steamer. This was probably his last journey through Singapore. Governor SIR FRANK SWETTENHAM marked the occasion by renaming Singapore's harbour in his honour.

Keppel Corporation The Keppel Group was incorporated on 3 August 1968 under the name of Keppel Shipyard. The group was renamed Keppel Corporation in 1986 and operates core businesses in offshore and marine, property and infrastructure. Its commercial interests and activities span 30 countries in the Americas, Asia, Europe, and the Middle East.

Keppel Offshore and Marine (Keppel

Kent Ridge Canopy Walk

O&M) operates 17 shipyards and occupies a key global position in the design and production of jack-up rigs, as well as the design, construction, conversion, upgrading and repair of offshore structures and vessels. It is a leader in the conversion of Floating Production Storage and Offloading (FPSO) vessels and Floating Storage and Offloading (FSO) vessels, and also repairs, converts and builds a diverse range and capacity of vessels.

Keppel Land, which is the property arm of the group, is an established developer of premier residential and office properties in Asia.

The group's infrastructure business includes environmental engineering, power generation and network engineering. One of the units, Keppel Energy, is an independent power supplier in Singapore licensed to provide electricity and steam. It also operates power generation plants in Nicaragua. Keppel provides total solutions in environmental engineering from the designing and building of plants and equipment to their operation and maintenance.

Listed in 1980, the Keppel Corporation counter is a component stock of the Straits Times Index. The group posted record net earnings of $564 million on a group turnover of $5.7 billion in financial year 2005. Keppel Corporation's bottom-line was boosted by higher offshore and marine earnings, and its 44 per cent stake in its oil and gas, SINGAPORE PETROLEUM COMPANY, which reported a net profit of $403.6 million for the same period.

Keppel Harbour Natural deep harbour in the southern part of Singapore. The existence of a fine, large and sheltered deep-water harbour was brought to Major William Farquhar's attention in July 1819, but Raffles vetoed Farquhar's suggestion to develop the harbour, especially since established firms were reluctant to move from Boat Quay. This stretch of water, originally known as New Harbour, lies between mainland Singapore and the southern islands of Pulau Brani and Pulau Blakang Mati (now SENTOSA). New Harbour was only developed in the 1850s with the advent of steamers, and the Peninsular and Oriental Steam Navigation Company (P&O) was the first to establish itself there in 1852. Strategically, New Harbour was significant and the British planned an ambitious scheme to protect it from potential invaders.

In 1848, Captain (later Admiral) HENRY KEPPEL surveyed New Harbour and reported its advantages to the Admiralty. However the authorities decided to situate its Far East naval headquarters in Hong Kong. The harbour was renamed in Keppel's honour. Today, it houses the Tanjong Pagar Port, one of the world's busiest ports, and an important revenue earner for Singapore.

Keppel Railway Station Located on Keppel Road, which is in close proximity to KEPPEL

HARBOUR, this railway station was designed by D.S. Petrovitch of SWAN AND MACLAREN. Petrovitch, who was Serbian, was trained at the Architectural Association School of Architecture in London. The building was completed in 1932 on reclaimed land in TANJONG PAGAR, replacing the old station at Tank Road. The upper walls of the central waiting area are decorated with ceramic tiles depicting colourful scenes of Malayan life. The arcaded façade of the station has four sculptures depicting Commerce, Agriculture, Industry and Transport. The sculptures are attributed to the Singapore-based Italian sculptor, CAVALIERI RODOLFO NOLLI, who also created the sculptures on the pediment of the SUPREME COURT.

keramat A *keramat* is usually a grave of an early Muslim missionary, holy man, village founder or other prominent individual. In Singapore, there are approximately 80 such sites. They vary in size and grandeur, and can range from a simple grave to a mausoleum. Among the better-known are KERAMAT HABIB NOH in Palmer Road, KERAMAT RADIN MAS in Telok Blangah and KERAMAT ISKANDAR SHAH on Fort Canning Hill. Keramat Habib Noh and Keramat Radin Mas have been restored with the permission of MUIS (MAJLIS UGAMA ISLAM SINGAPURA, or the Islamic Religious Council of Singapore).

People would normally visit a *keramat* to seek intercession. Some spend the night there, continuously reciting verses from the Qur'an. *Kemenyan* (incense) and food offerings such as *pulut kuning* (yellow glutinous rice), *bunga telur* (red-dyed eggs), fruit and flowers are presented. Within the *keramat*, the grave is usually marked by two *batu nisan* or gravestones—one marking the head and the other the feet—and are covered with yellow or green cloth. *Keramat* visits have become less popular over the years.

Keramat Iskandar Shah This KERAMAT takes its name from ISKANDAR SHAH—the last ruler of 14th century TEMASEK—although Iskandar Shah himself is believed to have been buried elsewhere. The remains of the

Keramat: Keramat Habib Noh.

Keppel Railway Station

keramat, located at the foot of what is now Fort Canning Hill, were recorded by Resident JOHN CRAWFURD when he was transiting Singapore on his way to Siam (present-day Thailand) in February 1822. During his exploration of the hill, Crawfurd saw foundations of 'baked brick of good quality' covering 'the greatest part' of the surface on the north and east sides of the hill. Between the foundations, Crawfurd observed that the ground was strewn with fragments of Chinese and local pottery 'in great abundance' as well as Chinese copper coins which date back hundreds of years.

The most interesting ruins were situated on a terrace of about 12 sq m, near the summit. There were remains of a structure, which may have been either a sanctuary or a roofed hall with wooden pillars and open sides. Crawfurd mentioned 14 square sandstone blocks (which have disappeared) analogous to pillar bases found in Sumatra, Java, Bali, and Kedah. The structure lay approximately where a microwave station was later built.

Crawfurd had been told that another large terrace was the gravesite of 'a ruler'. Sir STAMFORD RAFFLES' letter of 21 January 1823 refers to 'the tombs of the Malay Kings' near his bungalow on Fort Canning Hill. Neither Raffles nor Crawfurd recorded any details about the ruins on this spot. 'A rude structure' was quickly built on the site, which soon became known as the Keramat Iskandar Shah. G.P. Rouffaer states that in 1909, a domed structure there was described as resembling Islamic tombs in south Sulawesi, which probably date from the 17th century.

Further evidence of Keramat Iskandar Shah can be found in an 1892 guidebook, which states that '... crossing part of the old moat [the remains of the PARIT SINGAPURA, part of 14th-century Singapore's defences] ...the visitor enters the said place [i.e. the *keramat*]'. A picture of Fort Canning, taken about 1900, shows a rather large structure on the site of the *keramat*, enclosed by an earthen wall. Maps of the period label this 'the fakir's redan' (a military term denoting a fortification wall). A photograph taken in

the early 20th century captioned 'the tomb of Iskandar Shah, Singapore' shows a wooden bridge over a trench, and a set of pillars at the entrance to a compound with a low-roofed structure. Other photographs from the 1950s, 1970s and 1980s each depict a very different building on the site.

Nothing now remains of the probable 14th-century structure which once occupied this site. Excavations carried out in the 1990s for the construction of a new roof and other improvements to the site revealed that all traces of earlier buildings had disappeared.

Keramat Kusu This KERAMAT was built in 1917 to commemorate a man called Syed Abdul Rahman as-Saqaf, as well as his mother Nenek Ghalib, and sister Puteri Fatimah. Situated on the top of a hill at the end of Kusu Island, the site has three graves. Chinese devotees pray there and offer joss sticks during the ninth month of the Chinese lunar calendar (which usually falls between mid-October and mid-November).

Keramat Panjang Three people were buried at this KERAMAT—two men and one woman. One of the men was Maulana Abdul Rahman, known as a Muslim saint, who passed away in 1822. The land upon which the *keramat* was located—on Ringwood Road, in the Mountbatten area—was conveyed to the MOHAMEDAN AND HINDU ENDOWMENT BOARD by its owners, a Jewish family. It was frequently visited by villagers from nearby Kampong Amber. The *keramat* was said miraculously to have grown longer over the years ('*panjang*' means 'long' in Malay). In the 1950s, it was estimated to be about 5 m long; other reports have it at 14 m in length. During the late 1950s, the *keramat* was restored by a private benefactor. At that time, there was a small adjoining hut inhabited by a woman, who tended the large *keramat*. The *keramat* has since been exhumed.

Keramat Radin Mas This KERAMAT, located at the foot of Mount Faber, was built for RADIN MAS, who is believed to have been buried there. It is located along the road access to Mount Faber, off Kampong Bahru Road. In the early 21st century, it was renovated by a private benefactor.

Kesatuan Guru-Guru Melayu Singapura Singapore Malay Teachers' Union, registered as a trade union on 13 June 1947. The Malay name is abbreviated as KGMS. It has its origins as a welfare organization known as the Majlis Perhimpunan Guru-Guru Melayu Singapura (Council of Singapore Malay Teachers) in 1926. The organization has three important roles: to improve the conditions of service of Malay teachers, to develop the Malay language and culture, and to be the representative for issues on Malay education.

Keramat Kusu

Khaw Boon Wan

Eric Khoo

Khong Guan Biscuit Factory: company founders Chew Choo Keng (top) and Chew Choo Han.

The political influence of KGMS was felt when it sought to protect Malay education by opposing the Re-orientation Plan for Malay schools in 1951, which would have expanded the use of the English language. In 1955, KGMS, with other leading Malay organizations, formed the Majlis Pelajaran Melayu (MPM) or Malay Education Council, which championed the restoration of traditional Malay schools and the development of Malay education at secondary and tertiary level. In 1961, these efforts resulted in the setting up of SANG NILA UTAMA SECONDARY SCHOOL, the first Malay secondary school. The first Malay-medium pre-university classes began in Sang Nila Utama in 1964.

However, with Separation, Malay-language education began to decline and KGMS had to re-evaluate its role. In 1970, it proposed a National System of Education, a proposal that now seems ahead of its time. Its recommendations were that the main medium of instruction would be English, the National Language (Malay) would be taught to non-Malay pupils, and all pupils would learn their own mother tongue. The proposal was presented and endorsed by the MPM in 1971. However, it was not taken up. KGMS continues to represent the interests of Malay teachers.

Khan, Ahmad (1912–) Police officer. Ahmad Khan joined the police force in the Punjab as a junior officer in 1930. He worked there until 1934, when he resigned and came to Singapore to look for a job. At the end of 1934, he secured a part-time job at SPECIAL BRANCH as an Arabic translator. On 1 February 1937, a Security Sub-Branch of Special Branch was established, and Khan and four other officers were absorbed into it.

From 1937 to the outbreak of WORLD WAR II, Khan was responsible for overseeing the activities of enemy nationals—Germans, Italians and Japanese. After passing his law examinations in 1937, Khan was promoted to the rank of Inspector and was made a permanent member of the force. During the war, he was arrested by the Japanese and sentenced to death but was rescued through the intervention of Zainal Abideen—a jeweller from Ceylon (present-day Sri Lanka)—and his Japanese wife. Khan was then drafted into the Japanese Special Branch as a typist.

When the British returned to Singapore, Khan rejoined Special Branch and rose to the rank of superintendent of Police. He was known for his intelligence-gathering abilities and his interrogation strategy. He wanted to retire in 1958, but was persuaded to stay on. In 1960, he again indicated his desire to retire but was persuaded by then-Prime Minister LEE KUAN YEW to stay for a further year to help train local Special Branch Officers.

Khong Guan Biscuit Factory: advertisement, 1958.

Khan was awarded the Meritorious Service Medal in 1963. He returned to Pakistan in 1964 after his father died, and spent the remainder of his days farming his father's land.

KhattarWong Law firm. KhattarWong was founded in 1974 by Sat Pal Khattar, a former senior legal officer in the Inland Revenue Department, and David S.Y. Wong, a former academic. The firm soon grew to become one of the largest law firms in Singapore. In June 2003, it opened a branch office in Shanghai. It has also established an exclusive strategic alliance with Eversheds LLP, one of the world's biggest law firms.

Khaw Boon Wan (1952–) Civil servant and politician. Born in Penang, Khaw was educated at the University of Newcastle, Australia, on a Colombo Plan Scholarship. He graduated with a bachelor of engineering (honours) and a bachelor of commerce, and was a University Gold Medallist (1977).

Khaw returned to work in the Ministry of Health and rose to become the chief executive officer of the NATIONAL UNIVERSITY HOSPITAL, the Kandang Kerbau Hospital (present-day KK WOMEN'S AND CHILDREN'S HOSPITAL) and the SINGAPORE GENERAL HOSPITAL consecutively. In 1992, he became then Prime Minister GOH CHOK TONG's principal private secretary. He became permanent secretary of the Ministry of Trade and Industry in 1995 and remained there until 2001, when he resigned to enter politics.

At the 2001 general election, Khaw was elected member of Parliament for Moulmein (Tanjong Pagar GRC) on the People's Action Party ticket, and was immediately appointed senior minister of state for transport and information, and communications and the arts. In 2003, he was appoint-

ed acting minister for health and senior minister of state for finance, and was part of the team which handled the SEVERE ACUTE RESPIRATORY SYNDROME (SARS) crisis. In 2004, he was appointed minister of health.

Khaw was re-elected as a member of Parliament in the Sembawang Group Representation Constituency in the 2006 general election.

Khong Guan Biscuit Factory First established in 1947, Khong Guan Biscuit Factory was set up in Singapore by two brothers—Chew Choo Keng and Chew Choo Han—who came from Fujian in China. From its first factory in Paya Lebar, the business expanded to peninsular Malaya in the late 1950s, Indonesia and Thailand in the 1970s, and the Philippines in the 1980s. Khong Guan first ventured into China in 1981 and has since expanded its manufacturing base to cities such as Shekou, Shanghai, Tianjin, Chengdu and Zhengzhou.

In an effort to break into the American and Japanese markets, the company sought the help of Singapore's Trade Development Board (present-day INTERNATIONAL ENTREPRISE SINGAPORE) in 1987 and came up with new packaging designs and a product brand name—Miss Kate—to cater to the American market. In Japan, the biscuits were packaged under the name Handy Pack. The company's regional presence is manifested in factories and associate companies in the Philippines, Malaysia, Indonesia, Thailand, Hong Kong and China, while its products are sold in more than 40 countries. In the United States, it operates a subsidiary company, myAsianStore.com, which distributes food products, including Brand's Essence of Chicken, Owl instant beverages, Isabelle and Emperor cookies, and its own Khong Guan products.

Khoo, Eric (1965–) Film director and producer. Eric Khoo Kim Hai is credited by many with spearheading the renaissance of Singapore cinema that began in the 1990s. He has gained considerable recognition on the international art-house circuit. His 1990 short film *Barbie Digs Joe* won five prizes at the Singapore Video Competition. From 1991 to 1994, he directed more short films, including *August* (1991), *Carcass* (1992) and *Symphony 92.4* (1993). *Pain* (1994), the graphic portrait of a sado-masochistic young man, won him Best Director and Special Achievement awards at the SINGAPORE INTERNATIONAL FILM FESTIVAL.

In 1995, Khoo made his first feature film, *Mee Pok Man*, which revolved around a *mee pok* (noodle) seller and a prostitute. This was followed in 1997 by *12 Storeys*, a drama with satirical overtones which became the first Singaporean film to screen at the Cannes Film Festival. The multi-layered nature of the script was to become his trademark, and he took the same approach in *Be With Me* (2005), which opened the Directors' Fortnight at the Cannes Festival in the same year and raised the international profile of Singapore cinema. With his company Zhao Wei Films, Khoo has produced his own movies as well as works from independent film-makers such as ROYSTON TAN. Khoo is the youngest son of businessman KHOO TECK PUAT.

Khoo, T.S. (1922–2004) Journalist. Khoo Teng Soon was educated at Anglo-Chinese School. While waiting for his examination results, he joined Cold Storage as a clerk (1939). He left ten days later, after being offered a position to report for the MALAYA TRIBUNE. He rose within the *Tribune*, becoming acting editor of the *Tribune's* Sunday paper.

The JAPANESE OCCUPATION brought an abrupt halt to Khoo's career at the *Tribune*. He worked briefly for the Domei News Agency, but when the agency closed in 1945 after the Japanese surrender, Khoo was jobless. He approached lawyer T.W. Ong and secured funds to revive the *Tribune*, which he worked to restore to its pre-war position.

In 1948, Khoo left the *Tribune* to join *The Straits Times*. In 1953, he was promoted to chief sub-editor and to managing editor in 1956. He served at the paper's Kuala Lumpur office until late 1970, when he returned to Singapore as deputy chief editor. In 1972, he was appointed group chief editor. He retired in 1981 but continued to be active in newspaper publishing. In 1986, Khoo launched one of Singapore's first free tabloids, *WeekendEast*. He was also responsible for launching the Singapore Press Club (1971) and served as President for 19 years.

Khoo, widely acknowledged as one of the finest journalists Singapore ever produced, was nicknamed 'The Fastest Pen in the East'. He died of throat cancer.

Khoo, Warren (1934–) Judge. Born in Penang, Warren L. H. Khoo was educated at Chung Ling High School, Penang; Wesleyan University, Connecticut; Antioch College, Ohio, where he graduated with a bachelors degree in political science (1958); and the London School of Economics, where he graduated with a law degree (1961).

Khoo was subsequently called to the Bar at Lincoln's Inn (1963), West Malaysia Bar (1966) and Singapore Bar (1970). From 1958 to 1960, Khoo worked in the Town Planning Department in the London County Council. From 1960 to 1964, he was senior planning assistant in the Middlesex County Council. On his return to Penang, he joined the firm of Lim Kean Siew and Co., where he worked as a legal assistant (1966–70). He came to Singapore in 1970 and joined the legal service as state counsel (1970–73). He rose quickly through the ranks to become deputy senior state counsel (1973–77), senior state counsel (1977–82) and head, civil section (1975–82).

In 1982, Khoo left the service to commence practice under the name of Warren Khoo and Co. In 1991, he was appointed judge of the SUPREME COURT. Khoo retired in 1999. Since then, he has been active in arbitration work and served as chairman of the Singapore International Arbitration Centre from 1999 to 2004.

Khoo Boon Hui (1954–) Military officer and police officer. Khoo Boon Hui won the Singapore Armed Forces (SAF) Overseas Scholarship in 1973 and obtained a Bachelor of Arts degree in engineering and economics from Oxford University in 1976. After graduation, he joined the SAF, then moved to the SINGAPORE POLICE FORCE (SPF) in 1977. He worked his way up, being appointed to positions such as director, strategic planning (1987), police chief of staff (1990) and director of the Criminal Investigation Department (1991). He was made deputy commisioner of Police in 1995, and became commissioner of the SPF in 1997. He was presented with the Public Administration Medal (Silver) in 1992 and the Meritorious Service Medal in 2003.

Khoo Foundation In 1981, businessman KHOO TECK PUAT established the Khoo Foundation with a fund of $20 million. Run by Khoo's daughter, Mavis Oei, the foundation provides financial assistance for social welfare and education. In 1981, it endowed the Distinguished and Senior Fellowships in International Economics and Finance at Singapore's Institute of Southeast Asian Studies. The foundation was honoured with the Arts Supporter Award by the National Arts Council in 2001.

Khoo Oon Teik (1921–) Doctor specializing in dermatology and nephrology. Born in Penang, he went to Anglo Chinese School there, and was admitted to the King Edward VII College of Medicine in 1937. During the Battle of Singapore, he was responsible for deploying senior medical students at operating theatres at the General Hospital. After the surrender, he worked in Penang as a medical officer and was later sent to the infamous Burma-Siam railway. During the British Military Administration, he worked as a nutritional officer.

He obtained his LMS from the medical college in 1947. He later obtained his Masters from the University of Malaya in 1952. He was admitted as a Member of the Royal College of Physicians (Edinburgh) in 1952, the Royal Faculty of Physicians and Surgeons (Glasgow) in 1953 and the Fellowship of the Royal College of Physicians (Edinburgh) in 1966, among other qualifications.

He joined the medical college in 1947 and worked there, and at its successor institutions, the University of Malaya, then the University of Singapore, until his retirement in 1979.

By 1965, Khoo had risen to become professor of clinical medicine at Medical Unit II, which was based at the General Hospital. In 1971, he became professor of medicine and head of Medical Unit II and was made chairman, Department of Medicine at the University of Singapore. He started the Skin and Leprosy Clinic at the General Hospital in 1948, and was the first director of the Renal Unit in 1961. He helped set up the National Kidney Foundation in 1969. He also set up the first Drug Dependence Clinic in 1971.

Khoo was a founder member of the Academy of Medicine and was its Master from 1964 to 1966. He was also a founder member of the Association of Physicians of Malaya as well as the Singapore Dermatological Society. He was president of the latter from 1960 to 1975. A devout Methodist, he served as chairman, and later president, of the International Congress of Christian Physicians.

Khoo Swee Chiow (1964–) Best-known for his mountaineering exploits, Khoo Swee Chiow scaled Himalayan peak Cho Oyu, the sixth highest mountain in the world, in 1997; and the highest, Mount Everest, in 1998. He trekked 1,100 km to the South Pole in 1999 and 800 km to the North Pole in 2002. In 2000, Khoo climbed all 'Seven Summits'—the highest peaks in seven continents. A year later, he climbed to the top of Shishapangma (8,027 m) in Tibet without oxygen.

In 2003, Khoo cycled 8,200 km to Beijing in 73 days, covering 150 km a day in his journey through Malaysia, Thailand, Laos and Vietnam. In 2004, he attempted to climb Mount Everest without bottled oxygen but was unsuccessful. In the same year he swam 40 km across the Strait of Malacca. In December 2005, he broke the Guinness World Record for the longest scuba dive, staying underwater for a total of 220 hours. And in May 2006, he completed his second ascent of Mount Everest.

Khoo also gives motivational talks to schools and organizations, drawing on his own experiences for material.

T.S. Khoo

Khoo Oon Teik: picture taken 1956.

Khoo Swee Chiow: on Shishapangma, Tibet, 2001.

King Edward VII College of Medicine: college building, shortly after its completion in 1911.

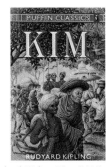

Rudyard Kipling: Kim *(1901).*

Khoo Teck Puat

Killer litter: the tragic consequences.

Khoo Teck Puat (1917–2004) Banker and hotelier. Khoo Teck Puat was the son of Khoo Yang Thin, a trader and landowner who owned stakes in several banks that later merged to become the OVERSEA-CHINESE BANKING CORPORATION (OCBC). Educated at St Joseph's Institution, the younger Khoo joined OCBC as an apprentice clerk at the age of 16. He eventually rose to become deputy general manager. In 1959, he resigned and the next year, founded the Malayan Banking Corporation (later Malayan Banking Berhad or MAYBANK) in Malaya. Among the subsidiaries Maybank acquired were GOODWOOD PARK HOTEL and Cathay Hotels.

In 1965, Khoo left Maybank and set up the Goodwood Group, the base for his business empire. He repurchased all his major Singapore investments from Maybank and then went on to add other hotels in Singapore such as the York Hotel, Holiday Inn Singapore, the Ladyhill Hotel, Hotel Malaysia (later Omni Marco Polo) and the Ming Court Hotel (now Orchard Parade Hotel). Between 1981 and 1988, he also owned Southern Pacific Hotel Corp, Australia's largest chain of hotels.

In 1986, he was one of three financiers who rescued Standard Chartered from a hostile takeover bid by Lloyds Bank in the United Kingdom. Khoo would eventually end up owning 11.55 per cent of STANDARD CHARTERED BANK, making him the bank's single largest shareholder. He was listed as Singapore's richest man by *Forbes* magazine in 2003.

A philanthropist, he set up the KHOO FOUNDATION in 1981 with a $20 million grant. In 1990, Khoo and the fund donated $10 million to a charity fund to help children, the elderly and the disabled.

Khoo died of a heart attack at the age of 87 and was survived by 14 children, the youngest of whom is film director ERIC KHOO. Upon his death, Khoo's family sold his stake in Standard Chartered to Dover Investments, a wholly-owned subsidiary of TEMASEK HOLDINGS, for an estimated $6.5 billion.

Kidney Dialysis Foundation A charitable organization, the Kidney Dialysis Foundation (KDF) was established in February 1996. With the support of the Ministry of Health, it provides subsidized haemodialysis treatment and the services of volunteer kidney specialists to needy patients. KDF subcontracts its dialysis services to a third party, paying the subcontractor a fixed fee to handle all dialysis treatment, nursing and ancillary staff and the maintenance of equipment.

killer litter Objects thrown from an upper-storey flat, endangering the lives of those below. Those caught and found guilty of throwing killer litter are typically charged under Section 336 of the Penal Code, which provides that anyone who 'does any act so rashly or negligently as to endanger human life or the personal safety of others, shall be punished with imprisonment for a term which may extend to three months, or with fine which may extend to $250, or with both'. To further deter would-be offenders, the Housing and Development (Amendment) Act was passed in 1986 to empower the HOUSING & DEVELOPMENT BOARD (HDB) to compulsorily acquire a flat or recover a rental flat if the lessee, tenant or authorized occupier is convicted of a killer litter offence. Owners whose apartments are confiscated will be refunded the amount they originally paid for them and they will be barred from buying or renting government housing for five years.

King Edward VII College of Medicine First known as the Straits Settlements and Federated Malay States Government Medical School, this institution was established in 1905 in the grounds of SINGAPORE GENERAL HOSPITAL. It started with 23 students, and was the first institution of higher learning in Singapore. The college's first permanent building—the two-storey Tan Teck Guan Building on College Road—was built in 1911. This was named in honour of the father of Tan Chay Yen—the successful rubber planter who had funded the building's construction. In 1912, the medical school received about $120,000 from the King Edward VII Memorial Fund, which had been started by Dr Lim Boon Keng. The next year, the name of the school was changed to King Edward VII Medical School, in recognition of this donation and to reflect the fact that the school had been established during the reign of Edward VII. It was renamed King Edward VII College of Medicine in 1921.

A new college building—designed by Major P.H. Keys—was unveiled on 15 February 1926. The facade of this neo-classical-style building was characterized by tall columns and bas reliefs, the latter designed by sculptor CAVALIERI RUDOLFO NOLLI.

During the war, the the college was closed, and the building used by the Japanese as a serological institute. It reopened in 1946, and about 200 students returned to continue their education.

In 1949, the medical college was amalgamated with RAFFLES COLLEGE to become the University of Malaya, and continued to

King Edward VII College of Medicine: relief over main entrance

operate as that university's Faculty of Medicine. The faculty moved in 1986 when the new National University of Singapore campus at Kent Ridge was completed.

The college's alumni include Singapore President BENJAMIN SHEARES and Prime Minister Mahathir Mohamad of Malaysia. The college building was gazetted as a national monument in December 2002.

Kipling, Rudyard (1865–1936) Author. Born in Bombay, Rudyard Kipling was educated in the United Kingdom before he moved back to India, where he worked as a journalist for seven years. He started writing poetry and stories when he was 21 years old. In 1889, he became a roving correspondent, visiting Burma, Hong Kong, China, Japan and the United States before returning to the United Kingdom. During his travels, he also stopped in Singapore. He wrote of his stay at RAFFLES HOTEL, '… where the food is as excellent as the rooms are bad. Let the traveller take note, feed at Raffles and sleep at the HOTEL DE L'EUROPE'.

A Nobel Prize winner for literature (1907), and known to many as the author of *The Jungle Book* (1894), Kipling portrayed British imperialism in stories such as *Kim* (1901), which concerned British soldiers in India. He also wrote stories for children such as the *Just So Stories for Little Children* (1902). Singapore is mentioned in several of his poems, among them 'The English Flag', 'The Song of The Cities' and 'The Mother-Lodge'.

KK Women's and Children's Hospital The KK Women's and Children's Hospital is Singapore's largest maternity and paediatric hospital. It is also a major tertiary referral centre for high-risk pregnancies, gynaecological cancer treatment, urogynaecological problems, neonatology and paediatrics.

Its original name was Kandang Kerbau Hospital. 'Kandang Kerbau' means 'buffalo enclosure' in Malay, as buffaloes were kept nearby. The hospital was known to the Hokkiens and Teochews as *Tek Kah* (Bamboo Corner) because it was situated below hillocks where clumps of bamboo grew. Called 'KK' for short, the name became synonymous with the hospital, and it was retained when the hospital was renamed 'KK Women's and Children's Hospital' following the move in 1997 to a new location on Bukit Timah Road.

In 1966, a record 39,835 babies were delivered at the hospital. KK Hospital was listed in the *Guinness Book of Records* for the highest number of births in a single maternity facility that year—a record it held for ten years. In 2005, it delivered one-third of all babies born in Singapore. The hospital's infant mortality rate is one of the lowest in the world.

The services for patients at the women's hospital include general obstetrics and gynaecology, fertility medicine and aesthetic and reconstructive surgery. The children's hospital sees patients from babies to 16-year-olds. The paediatric sub-specialty services range from cardiology and neurology to oncology. The hospital has the capability to carry out bone-marrow transplants and open-heart surgery in children.

KK Hospital operates a 24-hour children's emergency service and has the largest neonatal intensive care unit with 24 beds. As a tertiary paediatric referral centre, KK Hospital provides the Children's Hospital Emergency Transport Service (CHETS) for children who are critically ill.

knowledge-based economy

Singapore's transition from a manufacturing to a knowledge-based economy, in which the production, distribution and use of knowledge are the main drivers of growth, wealth creation and employment, can be viewed as occurring in three distinct phases.

The 'acquisition' phase (1965–78) began when Singapore first adopted an export-oriented INDUSTRIALIZATION strategy. Its openness to trade and FOREIGN DIRECT INVESTMENT (FDI) allowed Singapore to acquire capital, technological knowledge and management expertise from foreign multinational corporations (MNCs) as well as access to world markets. This phase was supported by investment in the technical and educational infrastructure.

Knowledge acquisition continued into the 'diffusion' phase (1979–98) and coincided with the economic restructuring and diversification phases of Singapore's development. Higher value-added FDI was encouraged, and knowledge diffusion from foreign MNCs to local companies intensified with the enhancement of the technical knowledge base of the workforce. Diffusion took the form of joint MNC-government training institutes to train workers in the supporting industries. The ECONOMIC DEVELOPMENT BOARD's (EDB) local industry upgrading programme and the defence establishment's transfer of proprietary knowledge to the private sector created a cohort of competent engineering professionals and technologists who, in turn, provided the human capital for technology-based businesses.

Since the 1990s, Singapore has been aiming to improve and build up its knowledge infrastructure, undertaking technology investment in order to strengthen its economic COMPETITIVENESS. This period also saw the EDB encouraging innovative projects and the establishment of research and development (R&D) institutes in order to build indigenous capabilities.

From 1999, efforts have been made to move to the 'knowledge-creation' phase. Technopreneurship 21 was launched to foster a climate of innovation and harness the growth potential of technological entrepreneurship. ONE-NORTH at Buona Vista is being developed in phases as a focal point for R&D and technological activities. It comprises a biomedical hub (Biopolis), an infocommunications and media hub (Fusionpolis) and a business hub.

Ko Teck Kin (1906–1966) Businessman, diplomat and philanthropist. Ko was born in Fujian, China, but emigrated to Palembang, Sumatra, at the age of ten, where his father started an import and export business. At the age of 20, Ko began helping his father in the business and travelled regularly between Singapore and the Dutch East Indies (present-day Indonesia). In the late 1940s, he fled to Singapore in the wake of anti-Chinese riots in Palembang, and established his own firm— Ho Chiang Shipping Company. He made a fortune trading in RUBBER. He was active in many civic organizations and best known for his role in helping fund NANYANG UNIVERSITY, whose council he chaired.

Ko was also President of the SINGAPORE CHINESE CHAMBER OF COMMERCE (1954–56 and 1958–65), and was awarded the Meritorious Service Medal in 1963. In 1963, he became one of only two Singapore senators to serve in the Dewan Negara (Upper House) of the Malaysian Parliament. He was appointed Singapore's first High Commissioner to Malaysia in 1965. The following year, Ko travelled to Hong Kong to seek medical treatment for cancer, but died shortly thereafter.

Koek, Edwin (1897–1948) Lawyer. Born into one of the oldest legal families in Malaya, Edwin Rowland Koek was educated at Raffles Institution and was later called to the Bar at Middle Temple in 1918. He returned to Singapore, practising in his father's firm and then in partnership with Reynold Eber. He was active at the Bar and served on numerous committees. Koek was also president of the Singapore Football Association and the Singapore Boxing Association. Shortly before he died, he proposed the establishment of the SINGAPORE PROGRESSIVE PARTY.

Koh, Billy (1963–) Songwriter and record producer. Billy Koh Whuan Liang (Xu Huanling) began writing songs at the age of 18, and started the group Shui Cao San Chong Chang (The Straws) with Huang

Yuancheng and Xu Nansheng. Koh was a key figure in the local Mandarin popular music scene. In 1984, Koh produced the first album in the *xinyao* genre—*Ming Tian 21* (21 Tomorrow)—which sold 30,000 copies (*see* CHINESE POPULAR MUSIC).

In 1986, Koh and a group of friends established Ocean Butterflies, Singapore's first music production company. The company expanded to include Halo Music (Malaysia) in 1997, Ocean Butterflies Music (Taiwan) in 2001 and Ocean Butterflies Music (Beijing) in 2003.

Koh is also credited with having discovered and groomed local performers, such as KIT CHAN and J.J. LIN. Throughout his career, he has produced more than 100 albums. In 2006, he became director of Ocean Butterflies Music and regional artiste & repertoire director of Ocean Butterflies Music Holdings.

Koh, Edmund (1960–) Banker. Edmund Koh Kian Chew was educated at the University of Toronto. He joined the Hongkong and Shanghai Banking Corporation and rose to become its group head of marketing in Singapore. He has worked in numerous financial institutions, including Prudential Assurance Company, Singapore, where he was chief executive officer (1999–2000). In 2001, he joined DBS BANK as its head of consumer banking.

Koh has served on various public bodies, including the Singapore Totalisator Board, the Housing and Development Board, the Singapore Symphonia Company and the National Youth Achievement Award Council.

Koh, Joyce (1968–) Composer. Joyce Koh Bee Tuan studied at King's College London and the University of York, and in France, where she spent two years at IRCAM (Institut de Recherche et de Coordination Acoustique/Musique). She was mentored by leading modern composers such as Henri Dutilleux, Tristan Murail and conductors Peter Eötvös and Diego Masson. Her works have been performed at the Sir Henry Wood Pre-Promenade Concerts, and by other groups such as the Nash Ensemble, BBC Symphony Orchestra, SINGAPORE SYMPHONY ORCHESTRA, Malaysian Philharmonic

Ko Teck Kin

KK Women's and Children's Hospital: ward in the old premises, 1950.

Kok Heng Leun

Stella Kon

Orchestra, and Magnetic Band. Her work, *Tai,* premiered at the Singapore Arts Festival in 1998.

Koh Beng Seng (1950–) Civil servant and banker. Koh Beng Seng was educated at Nanyang University, where he graduated with first-class honours in commerce (1973), and Columbia University, where he obtained an MBA (1979). He joined the MONETARY AUTHORITY OF SINGAPORE (MAS), where he rose to become deputy managing director (1988–98). In 1987, he was awarded the Meritorious Service Medal. In 2000, he joined the OVERSEAS UNION BANK (OUB) as deputy president and managing director of the Far Eastern Bank. When OUB merged with the UNITED OVERSEAS BANK (UOB) Group, he became UOB's deputy president and joined UOB's board. He resigned from UOB in January 2005. He then became chief executive officer of Octagon Advisors, a business and management consulting company.

Koh Boon Hwee (1952–) Businessman. Koh Boon Hwee was educated at St Andrew's School before going on to Imperial College London (where he graduated with first-class honours in mechanical engineering in 1972), and Harvard University (where he obtained an MBA with distinction in 1976). He joined Hewlett-Packard Singapore and rose to become its first non-American managing director (1985–90). In 1991, he joined Wuthelam Group as executive chairman (1991–2000), but later left to join SINGAPORE AIRLINES (SIA) in 2001 as its chairman, a position he held until he stepped down on 31 December 2005. From 1986 to 2001, he was also chairman of SINGTEL (and its predecessor institutions). In January 2006, he was appointed chairman of DBS BANK and DBS Group Holdings. Koh is also a well-known venture capital investor.

In addition to his corporate duties, Koh has served on the boards of the Singapore International Foundation, Securities Industry Council, Institute of Policy Studies, Singapore-US Business Council and Singapore Business Federation. In 1991, he

won the Outstanding Chief Executive Award given by *The Business Times* and DHL. In 1995, he received the Meritorious Service Medal.

Koh Eng Kian (1956–) Sportsman. Koh dominated the heavyweight judo class at the National Schools Championships, Pesta Sukan and throughout the army and People's Association competitions during the 1970s. He became an Olympian at the age of 19, and carried the national flag at the Opening Ceremony of the 1976 Olympics in Montreal. His hopes were dashed in the second round of the competition after being defeated by Panamanian Jorge Comrie in 6 minutes. The winning throw injured his elbow so badly that he could not compete in the consolation rounds.

In 1975, Koh won a gold medal at the Bangkok Southeast Asian Peninsular (SEAP) Games in the open weight category. Six years later, he won a silver medal at the Southeast Asian (SEA) Games in Manila. He was banned from competing for three years in 1982 after speaking out against the Singapore Judo Federation. When his own career in competitive judo ended, Koh—popularly known as 'Rocky'—became managing director of his own security company in Singapore, and focused on training judo practitioners.

Koh Yong Guan (1946–) Civil servant. Koh Yong Guan was educated at Siglap Secondary School and Raffles Institution, where he won a Colombo Plan Scholarship to study at the University of Toronto. He graduated with first-class honours in mechanical engineering and a master's degree in applied science in mechanical engineering and biomedical engineering. He also holds an MBA from the Catholic University of Leuven (1981) in Belgium.

Koh joined the MINISTRY OF HEALTH as a biomedical engineer in 1972, was absorbed into the administrative service in 1979 and was made second permanent secretary at the MINISTRY OF DEFENCE in 1989. From 1991 to 1997, Koh served as commissioner of Inland Revenue. In 1998, he was appointed managing director of the MONETARY AUTHORITY OF SINGAPORE (MAS), a position he held until his retirement on 1 June 2005, whereupon he became chairman of the CENTRAL PROVIDENT FUND. Koh was awarded the Meritorious Service Medal in 1995.

Kok Heng Leun (1966–) Theatre director. Kok was educated at the National University of Singapore. After graduation, he joined THE SUBSTATION as a programme executive and then THE NECESSARY STAGE as artistic director of its Theatre For Youth Branch (1994-98). He was also in charge of M1 Youth Connection 1998, a theatre festival for youth, and organized community cultural events such as Tampines Cultural Day.

Joyce Koh

In 1990, Kok and a group of friends founded MANDARIN theatre group DRAMA BOX. Kok also established a name for himself as a set and lighting designer, with his creations being seen in Austria, Taiwan, Australia and the United Kingdom. In 2000, he received the YOUNG ARTIST AWARD from the NATIONAL ARTS COUNCIL (NAC), and in 2003, the Culture Award from the Japanese Chamber of Commerce and Industry.

kompang Malay musical instrument. The *kompang* is a small, round, shallow-frame hand drum. It is believed to have been introduced into Java in the 13th century by Arab traders who used it to attract the attention of buyers to their wares.

To make a *kompang*, goat hide or cowhide is stretched and nailed to one side of the wooden frame known as the *baluh*. A velvet ribbon is used to cover the sides of the skin and is then nailed down using brass nails. The skin is stretched using rattan that is tucked underneath the skin, inside the drum. The *kompang* comes in different sizes, 6–12 cm in height, and 20–38 cm in diameter. It is held with one hand and beaten with the other.

The *kompang* is played in ensembles that produce overlapping rhythmic patterns to accompany choral singing. The songs are sung in either Arabic or Malay. The *kompang* is used during social occasions such as celebrating PROPHET MUHAMMAD'S BIRTHDAY. In Singapore, it is most popularly used in MALAY WEDDINGS: a *kompang* ensemble escorts the groom when he visits the bride or when the couple returns to the groom's residence. The ensemble consists of about 15–20 members. A *kompang* ensemble may also perform to open official functions or ceremonies. The Persatuan Hadrah dan Kompang Singapura (PEHAKS, Singapore Association for Kompang Ensembles) was formed in 1978 to preserve and promote this traditional art form, but membership declined from about 100 ensembles in the 1980s, to less than 10 in the early 21st century. Occasionally, community clubs or PEHAKS organize *kompang* competitions.

Kon, Stella (1944–) Playwright and author. Stella Kon Sing Po was born in Edinburgh to parents from established Peranakan fam-

Kompang: students of the instrument.

ilies. Her mother, Kheng Lim, was a noted actress in Singapore in the 1950s.

Kon read philosophy at the University of Malaya in Singapore, graduating in 1966. She was awarded the first prize in the National Playwriting Competition on the three occasions when it was run by the Ministry of Culture. The awards went for *The Bridge* (1977), *Trial* (1982) and *Emily of Emerald Hill* (1984).

A monodrama based on Kon's grandmother and revolving around the protagonist's rise from waif to Peranakan matriarch, *Emily* was invited to the 1985 Commonwealth Arts Festival in Edinburgh, and was the first English-language theatre production from Singapore to be featured at the 1986 Edinburgh Festival Fringe.

Kon's shorter plays are collected in *The Immigrant and Other Plays* (1975), and *Emporium and Other Plays* (1977). Her later plays include *The Towkay's Daughter* (1989), for STARS, the forerunner of Singapore Repertory Theatre, *Butterflies Don't Cry* (1989), and *Human Heart Fruit* (2002). Despite the range of Kon's works, none has matched *Emily*—arguably the most frequently produced and widely travelled Singaporean play—in stature, fame and popularity.

Less well known for her fiction, Kon has published short stories in various anthologies, and has written two novels, *The Scholar and the Dragon* (1986) and *Eston* (1995), which won the Merit Award in the 1994 Singapore Literature Prize for Fiction.

Kong Meng San Phor Kark See Monastery

Also known as Guang Ming Shan Pu Jue Chan Si (Bright Hill Temple) in Mandarin, this complex is one of the most important Buddhist temples in Singapore.

The monastery is also the largest religious establishment in Singapore, comprising several prayer halls, monks' quarters, a retirement home, a library, a crematorium, a columbarium and other buildings on its 12-ha grounds. Most of the buildings follow traditional Chinese architectural precepts, and are laid out according to principles of geomancy (*see* FENG SHUI).

Kong Meng San was founded in 1921 by Venerable Zhuan Dao as Singapore's first 'forest tradition' monastery. The forest tradition emphasizes meditational practice, rather than ceremonial or scholarly activities.

Leadership of the monastery was passed in 1947 to Venerable Hong Choon, who served as abbot for 43 years, during which time he greatly expanded the temple and its religious following.

Though primarily of the Chinese Mahayana school of BUDDHISM, Kong Meng San monastery officially welcomes other expressions of Buddhist faith. It is committed to educational outreach and public awareness among Buddhists and non-

Buddhists alike, with a regular schedule of talks, classes and other activities, as well as a publication department that distributes free educational materials.

Besides its regular prayer recitations and meditation retreats, Bright Hill Temple is well known for its 'Three Steps, One Bow' ritual, a popular expression of repentance among devout believers performed on the eve of Vesak Day.

koro panic *Koro* is a term for shrinkage of the penis and its retraction into the body, accompanied by pain and death. The term itself is believed to have been derived from the Malay word for the head of a turtle.

Koro panic is not a real condition, but a delusion produced by a psychological disorder amongst men, and is associated with the belief that unhealthy or abnormal sexual acts (such as sexual intercourse with prostitutes, masturbation or even nocturnal emissions) upset the equilibrium achieved when a husband has sex with his wife during 'normal intercourse'.

In 1967, there was a panic in Singapore after reports appeared in the press that *koro* was caused by the consumption of pork from pigs that had been inoculated against swine fever. This caused demand for pork to plummet, and hundreds of *koro* cases were reported. Steps were taken by the Singapore Medical Association and Ministry of Health to quell the panic.

koyan Liquid and dry measure of volume and weight. One *koyan* is equivalent to 800 *gantang*, or approximately 3,634.7 l (a *gantang* being a dry measure, which is equivalent to approximately 4.54 l). By weight, one *koyan* is equivalent to 2,419.16 kg and 4,000 *gin* or KATI.

The *koyan* was used in the STRAITS SETTLEMENTS and British North Borneo (present-day Sabah) during the colonial period, and has continued to be used in Malaysia in more recent times. It is used primarily to measure seeds and grains, such as rice.

Kranji–Jurong Line This defensive line used by British forces during WORLD WAR II stretched along the Kranji and Jurong Rivers, and across the gap between them. It was one of two 'switchback' positions—the other being Serangoon-Kallang in the east—that were to be used in the event of a Japanese penetration of Singapore's coastal defences. However, little work had been done on fortifying the line prior to the Japanese attack, with LIEUTENANT-GENERAL GORDON BENNETT even rejecting plans to fortify the line properly.

After unleashing a massive bombardment on defensive positions, the Japanese started landing on Singapore's northwest coast on the night of 8 February 1942, engaging in close-quarter fighting with

Kong Meng San Phor Kark See Monastery

the defending Australian troops. After suffering heavy losses, the Australians, led by BRIGADIER HAROLD TAYLOR, retreated to the Kranji-Jurong Line on the afternoon of 9 February, finding little by way of defences there.

On learning of the successful Japanese landing in the northwest, LIEUTENANT-GENERAL ARTHUR PERCIVAL decided that the Kranji-Jurong Line would become the place from which a defensive stand against the Japanese would be conducted. However, on 10 February, Taylor misread an order from Percival, and ordered the remnants of his troops to retreat to peripheral positions, thus leaving a huge gap in the Kranji-Jurong Line, and opening the way for further Japanese advances (*see also* MALAYA CAMPAIGN).

Kranji War Cemetery and Singapore Memorial

Constructed and maintained by the Commonwealth War Graves Commission, the Kranji War Cemetery and Singapore Memorial is the largest military commemorative structure in Singapore.

The cemetery contains the marked graves of some 4,458 Allied servicemen and women, and was officially opened by governor SIR ROBERT BROWN BLACK in 1957.

The main memorial, the Singapore Memorial, commemorates 24,000 Allied military casualties with no known graves. Its design reflects the three arms of the British military in WORLD WAR II—the British Army, Royal Navy and Royal Air Force. The names of the casualties are inscribed on these columns.

Kranji Cemetery also houses military graves of soldiers killed during World War I and whose graves were relocated from BIDADARI CEMETERY.

In 1975, the War Graves Commission allowed the relocation to Kranji of non-World War I or World War II graves. Owing to the closure of the military cemeteries at Pasir Panjang and Ulu Pandan, the remains of British and GURKHA soldiers and their families were exhumed and relocated to Kranji, and two small Gardens of Remembrance were created. There are also several other smaller memorials in the cemetery.

Koro panic: Eastern Sun *news story, 5 November 1967.*

No relation between Koro and pork-eating —SMA

L. Krishnan

Kumar

C. Kunalan: picture taken 1973.

At the northern end of the War Cemetery is the STATE CEMETERY, which holds the graves of presidents YUSOF ISHAK and BENJAMIN SHEARES.

Kreta Ayer Area bound by Kreta Ayer Road, Neil Road, South Bridge Road and North Canal Road. 'Kreta' is derived from the Malay word *kereta* (cart); *ayer* is Malay for water. Thus, Kreta Ayer literally means 'water cart', and takes its name from the bullock carts that were once used to haul water drawn from a well near Ann Siang Hill for distribution in the area. The Cantonese, who used to dominate the area, called it '*ngau chair sui*' or 'bullock cart water'. In the 1880s, this was a red-light district filled with brothels, restaurants and theatres. By the 1920s, bullock carts had given way to piped water, but the name remains today, given by the Municipal Commission to Kreta Ayer Road in 1922.

Krishnan, L. (1922–) Film director. Born in India, Lakshmanan Krishnan is the most prolific film-maker in the history of Singapore cinema, having directed 30 feature films despite the fact that he only lived on the island from 1950 to 1960. His first trip to Singapore was in 1940, when he worked at the Singapore Cricket Club and Raffles Hotel before being repatriated.

After the success of his first feature film, a Sinhalese movie called *Amma*, in the late 1940s, Krishnan was brought to Singapore by the SHAW BROTHERS. He broke his three-year contract with them in 1952 and teamed up with HO AH LOKE, subsequently following him to CATHAY-KERIS FILMS. Reputed for his keen eye for talent, he gave P. RAMLEE his first lead role in *Bakti* (Faithfulness) (1950) and Maria Menado her first role in *Penghidupan* (Life) (1950). He also initiated a new horror genre with his 1958 film *Orang Minyak* (Oily Man).

After moving to Kuala Lumpur in 1960, Krishnan became the first film-maker in the new Merdeka Studio, where he pursued his directing career until 1963, when he launched his own company, Gaya Film Berhad, to produce commercials.

Krishnan, P. (1932–) Author, poet and playwright. Born in Johor, P. Krishnan writes under the pseudonym Puthumaithasan. He studied in Johor Baru and Singapore. After getting his Senior Cambridge certificate, he joined Radio Singapore as an announcer. He rose to become senior executive producer-presenter, retiring from his post in 1992 at the end of a 31-year career.

Krishnan has written over 500 short stories, poems, essays and plays for the stage, radio and television. He has also dramatized ancient Tamil literary texts and translated works by Shakespeare, Byron, Keats and George Orwell into Tamil. His radio dramas enjoyed a large following, in particular

Adukku Veettu Annasamy (*Annasamy of the Multi-Storey Flats*), a social comedy which depicted the problems and issues faced by HDB flat-dwellers. His works are marked by a simple, humorous style, documenting the trials and tribulations experienced by the Indian community in adjusting to social changes. Krishnan was awarded the Tamizhavel Award by the Association of Singapore Tamil Writers in 1998 and the Southeast Asian Write Award in 2005.

Kulasekaram, T. (1919–1988) Judge. Born in Ipoh, Perak, Thilliamapalam Kulasekaram was educated at Victoria Institution in Kuala Lumpur. In 1939, he joined University College, Colombo, and obtained an honours degree in mathematics in 1943. From 1943 to 1947, he read law at the Ceylon Law College, Colombo. He was called to the Ceylon Bar in 1948; and later to the Bar at Middle Temple.

In 1950, he came to Singapore and joined the legal service as assistant official assignee and assistant public trustee. He moved quickly through the ranks, serving as district judge and magistrate of Singapore (1952–55); deputy registrar and sheriff, SUPREME COURT (1955–56); acting registrar, Supreme Court (1956); and registrar, Supreme Court (1957–63). In 1963, he was elevated to the Bench as a PUISNE JUDGE. He retired in 1984.

Kumar (1968–) Actor. Born Kumar Chinnadurai, he was educated at Monk's Hill School. After leaving school, Kumar worked as a cashier at a 7-Eleven store before joining a nightclub called the Boom Boom Room in 1992 to perform as a female impersonator and singer. He became known for his witty and risqué humour, and his skimpily-attired male 'Solid Gold' dancers. Kumar has since established a name for himself on television, starring in variety shows and the sit-com *Oh Carol*. The Boom Boom Room closed in 2005, and Kumar opened Gold Dust at Orchard Towers with Gwen Khoo, where he also performs. Gold Dust was closed in 2006.

Kunalan, C. (1942–) Sportsman. Canagasabai Kunalan made his name based on his sprint performances and role as a

sports educator. He was inducted into the SINGAPORE SPORTS COUNCIL'S HALL OF FAME as a double Olympian (Tokyo, 1964; Mexico, 1968), an Asian Games silver medallist (Bangkok, 1966) and Asian Games bronze medallist (Bangkok, 1966; Bangkok, 1970; Tehran, 1974). He was twice Sportsman of the Year (1968 and 1969). Barely a year after he switched from soccer to athletics, he found himself competing in the 1964 Olympics in Tokyo.

Kunalan's most publicized moment was the 100-m photofinish at the 1966 Asian Games in Bangkok, when he lost the gold to Malaysia's Mani Jegathesan by 0.01 seconds. His national 100-m record of 10.38 seconds was set at the 1968 Olympics in Mexico, a record which was only broken by U.K. Shyam's time of 10.37 seconds in 2001). The following year, Kunalan experienced his most successful series of wins at the Southeast Asian Peninsular (SEAP) Games. He won the 100 m in 10.5 seconds; the 200 m in 21.3 seconds; and he anchored the 4x400-m relay team to win in a time of 3 minutes 15.4 seconds.

Injury and self-imposed retirement at the end of 1970 brought him into coaching. He re-entered competition and stayed on until 1979, after which he concentrated on nurturing young athletes. In 2005, he was appointed president of the Singapore Olympian Association.

The 4x400-m national relay record of 3 minutes 10.55 seconds set in Tehran at the 1974 Asian Games (held by Kunalan, Ong Yeok Phee, Cheah Kim Teck and Godfrey Jalleh) was still standing in 2005.

Kuo Pao Kun (1939–2002) Playwright. Born in Hebei, China, Kuo arrived in Singapore in 1949. He was educated in both Chinese and English, and was exposed to modern CHINESE DRAMA. He left for Melbourne in 1959 to work as a translator for Radio Australia, and then studied at the National Institute of Dramatic Art in Sydney.

Returning to Singapore in 1965, Kuo married dancer and choreographer GOH LAY KUAN. They co-founded the Practice Performing Arts School, which has trained young talents in dance, drama and music for more than four decades, interrupted only when Kuo was detained without trial

Kranji War Cemetery and Singapore Memorial: the architect was Colin St Clair Oakes

under the INTERNAL SECURITY ACT from March 1976 to October 1980 and had his Singapore citizenship withdrawn.

Kuo's oeuvre includes social-realist plays in Chinese such as *The Struggle* (1969), critical and humorous plays in English such as *The Coffin is Too Big for the Hole* (1984), multilingual Singaporean plays such as *Mama Looking for her Cat* (1988), experimental plays like *0Zero01* (1991), and allegorical plays such as *Descendants of the Eunuch Admiral* (1995) and *The Spirits Play* (1998). As a dramatist, Kuo translated and directed plays such as Bertolt Brecht's *The Caucasian Chalk Circle* (1966), Athol Fugard's *The Island* (1985) and the Malay play *Atap Genting Atap Rumbia* (1982). As a teacher, he nurtured many theatre practitioners and artists. He founded THE SUBSTATION as a conducive 'home for the arts' (opened 1990) and co-founded (with T. Sasitharan in 2000) the Theatre Training and Research Programme based on in-depth immersion in classical Asian and contemporary theatre.

Kuo's plays and essays address universal humanistic concerns. But they are also rooted in the multicultural environment of Singapore, which led him to interact with and bring together individuals from diverse ethnic, linguistic and national backgrounds. His works have been translated into Malay, Tamil, Hindi, Japanese and German, and have been performed in many countries.

In 1990, Kuo was awarded the CULTURAL MEDALLION, but it was only in 1992 that his citizenship was reinstated. Kuo's other awards include the ASEAN Award for the Performing Arts (1993) and the Excellence for Singapore Award (2002). He was appointed Chevalier de l'Ordre des Arts et des Lettres (Knight of the Order of Arts and Letters) by the French government in 1996.

Kuok Khoon Ean (1955–) Businessman. Born in Malaya and educated at the University of Nottingham, Kuok Khoon Ean is the second son of businessman Robert Kuok. He joined the family business in 1978, coming onto the Board of the *South China Morning Post* in October 1993, and was appointed chairman in January 1998. He is also director of Kerry Media, Kerry Holdings, Kerry Group and several other listed companies in Singapore, Malaysia and Hong Kong. Kuok currently manages the diverse interests of his family business in Singapore, including trading, property, hotels and retailing.

Kusu Island With an area of just 8.5 ha, Kusu is one of the smallest islands in the group of Southern Islands. It was previously known as Goa Island, then Peak Island, and also as Pulau Tembakau.

Kusu takes its name from a legend that a giant turtle rescued two fisherman, one Chinese, the other, Malay. The two men were in a boat that was in danger of capsizing in a storm. The turtle saved them by turning itself into an island. They were so grateful that they later revisited the island as a form of pilgrimage and founded shrines. Today, there are both Chinese and Malay places of pilgrimage which attract thousands of visitors. The large Chinese Tua Pek Kong temple, built in 1923, attracts thousands of pilgrims during the ninth lunar month, which usually falls in October. The pilgrims pray for prosperity and fertility. The precincts of the temple have a turtle lake and large stone turtle statues.

On the wooded hill above the temple are perched three small KERAMAT, built to commemorate Syed Abdul Rahman, his mother and his sister. The faithful climb up to the shrines to pray for wealth, good health and fertility. The island itself is said to have resembled the shape of a turtle, but reclamation works have made this less obvious. Today, it has two well-sheltered lagoons, beaches and a huge diversity of marine life around its fringing reefs of hard and soft corals.

Kwa Soon Bee (1930–) Doctor and civil servant. Kwa Soon Bee was educated at the Anglo-Chinese School and at the University of Malaya, where he graduated with a degree in medicine, winning the Brunel Hawes Gold Medal for Clinical Medicine and the Lim Boon Keng Medal for Medicine.

In 1962, Kwa joined the medical service as a medical officer and within a year became consultant haematologist. Kwa rose quickly through the ranks, holding positions of senior consultant haematologist (1971); medical superintendent, Kandang Kerbau Hospital (1968); superintendent, SINGAPORE GENERAL HOSPITAL (1972–84); director of medical services (1984–96); and founding chairman, Health Corporation of Singapore (1987–96).

During the restructuring of government hospitals in Singapore (1985–90), Kwa also served as chairman of SINGAPORE GENERAL HOSPITAL, the National Skin Centre, the National Eye Centre, Toa Payoh Hospital, Kandang Kerbau Hospital and TAN TOCK SENG HOSPITAL. From 1984 to 1996, Kwa also served as permanent secretary at the MINISTRY OF HEALTH.

Kwa has been appointed managing director of the Jurong Bird Park (1977–89) and chairman of the Singapore Zoological Gardens (1995–2003). He also holds directorships in a number of companies. He retired from the civil service in 1996.

Kwa was awarded the Public Administration Medal (Gold) in 1969 and the Meritorious Service Medal in 1992. He is the brother of Kwa Geok Choo, who is the wife of Minister Mentor LEE KUAN YEW.

Kusu Island: visitors touching turtle statues in hope of longevity.

Kwan, Robert (1950–) Businessman. Robert Kwan, son of KWAN SAI KHEONG, left school at the age of 18 to set up Mei's Bookshop at Collyer Quay with $20,000. He then became a wholesaler of toys. In 1975, he saw a McDonald's restaurant in Las Vegas and decided to pursue the franchise. In 1978, he signed a joint-venture agreement with the hamburger chain and opened the first McDonald's outlet in Singapore at Liat Towers on 27 October 1979. As of 2005, there were 125 outlets in Singapore. He stepped down as managing director of McDonald's in 2002 to become chairman of the company. He became executive chairman of Wildlife Reserves Singapore in 2004. Kwan also has three Southeast Asian Games gold medals in waterpolo.

Kwan Im Thong Hood Cho Known in Mandarin as Guanyin Tang Fo Zu Miao, or more popularly as Si Ma Lu Guanyin Tang, this is one of Singapore's most important Chinese temples. Located in Waterloo Street, it is dedicated to Guanyin, the Goddess of Mercy, but other deities are also enshrined there, such as Hua Tuo, the patron saint of Chinese physicians.

The temple is busy throughout the year, but it becomes especially crowded during Chinese New Year, when thousands of worshippers vie for the privilege of offering the first joss stick of the year. On the first and fifteenth days of the Chinese lunar month, it is filled with devotees. Part of its popularity may be attributed to the widespread belief in the accuracy of divinations sought at the temple and the efficacy of blessings granted by its deities.

The temple is well-known for its involvement in social welfare and charitable causes. During the JAPANESE OCCUPATION, it provided refuge for the wounded, sick and homeless. It has also made sizeable donations to educational and healthcare organizations.

The temple was originally constructed in 1884. It was rebuilt in 1984, with many features of its original 19th-century architecture being preserved, but with additional elements such as a new façade. To prevent the interior being blackened by smoke from incense, the incense urn was moved outside.

Many Chinese devotees, after completing their devotions at the Kwan Im

Kuo Pao Kun

Kwa Soon Bee

Robert Kwan

...end

Kwan Im Thong Hood Cho: Chinese New Year.

Kwan Sai Kheong

Kwek Leng Beng

Kwek Leng Joo

Thong Hood Cho temple, stop at the SRI KRISHNAN TEMPLE (a Hindu temple located next to Kwan Im Thong) to offer up incense and a short prayer—an indication of the pragmatic approach to religion taken by these devotees.

Kwan Sai Kheong (1920–1981) Teacher, musician, civil servant and diplomat. Born in Malacca, Kwan Sai Kheong studied at a Chinese-medium school and Raffles Institution. He went to Raffles College on a scholarship and obtained an arts diploma, then won another scholarship to study painting at the Royal College of Art in London. He obtained a bachelor of arts in classical Chinese from the University of London.

In 1946, Kwan returned to Raffles Institution as a teacher, and took up residence in a wooden shack in Changi. He played the violin and the saxophone at nightclubs to make ends meet while continuing to work as a teacher during the day. Kwan also founded the Young Musicians Society in 1968.

Kwan became vice principal of the Teachers' Training College, and, later, permanent secretary at the Ministry of Education (1964–75). From 1975 to 1980, he was the vice chancellor of the UNIVERSITY OF SINGAPORE. He was responsible for designing the MERLION.

Kwan served as ambassador to the Philippines (1980–81). He was awarded an honorary Doctorate of Letters by the University of Singapore in 1973. Kwan also received the Public Administration Medal (Gold) in 1963 and the Meritorious Service Medal in 1968. His son is entrepreneur ROBERT KWAN.

Kwek Hong Png (1913-1994) Businessman. Born in Fujian, China, Kwek Hong Png was the second child of a poor farmer. He came to Singapore at the age of 16 and found a job as an apprentice in a hardware store. While working there, he attended night classes to learn English and Mandarin. He stayed with the store for 12 years and eventually became its general manager.

In 1941, Kwek started Hong Leong Company to deal in ropes, paint, ship supplies and rubber-estate supplies. He invited his three brothers, Hong Khai, Hong Lye

and Hong Leong, to join him. He was forced to close down the business for six months during the JAPANESE OCCUPATION but was later able to resume trading. It was during this time that Kwek made his first property investments.

The post-war years proved highly profitable for Kwek, and in 1948, Hong Leong Company became Hong Leong Company Private Limited, with a paid-up capital of $300,000. In the late 1940s, Kwek bought rubber plantations in Malaya. His investments reaped spectacular profits in the early 1950s, when the Korean War broke out and prices rose sharply. Kwek achieved particualr success in the fields of finance (Hong Leong Finance) and property (City Developments Limited). Kwek retired from the chairmanship of Hong Leong Finance and Singapore Finance in 1984, passing it on to his elder son, Kwek Leng Beng.

The elder Kwek also contributed significantly to charity and established the Hong Leong Foundation in 1980.

Kwek Leng Beng (1941–) Businessman. The eldest son of HONG LEONG FINANCE founder KWEK HONG PNG, Kwek Leng Beng trained as a lawyer. He entered the family business as general manager and director of Hong Leong Finance in 1967. He engineered the takeover of CITY DEVELOPMENTS in 1971 and launched the takeover of Singapore Finance in 1979. In 1995, Kwek made headlines when he and Saudi Prince Alwaleed Talal Alsaud bought the Plaza Hotel in New York from Donald Trump. The following year, he was named Businessman of the Year by *The Business Times*. In 1990, Kwek succeeded his father as chairman of the Hong Leong Group of companies, which includes CDL Hotels and the London-based Millenium & Copthorne Group. *Forbes* has listed Kwek as one of Singapore's wealthiest men.

Kwek Leng Joo (1953–) Businessman. Kwek Leng Joo is the second son of HONG LEONG GROUP founder KWEK HONG PNG. He was educated at Maris Stella High School and holds diplomas in economics and hotel management from New York University and Takushoku University, Japan. He is the managing director of CITY DEVELOPMENTS and an executive director of Hong Leong Group Singapore. He was the president of the SINGAPORE CHINESE CHAMBER OF COMMERCE AND INDUSTRY (SCCI) (1993–97). He was that organization's youngest-ever president when he was elected at the age of 39. He is an avid photographer, and his work has been showcased at a number of public exhibitions.

Kwong Wai Shiu Hospital This hospital and nursing home is located at Serangoon Road. It is dependent on public donations, and provides free and heavily-subsidized medical care to the elderly and indigent. It was founded in 1910 by leaders of the

CANTONESE communities from three prefectures in China's Guangdong province—Kwong Chou (present-day Guangzhou), Wai Chou (present-day Huizhou) and Shiu Heng (also known as Siew Heng; present-day Zhaoqing)—which lent their names to the hospital.

Among Kwong Wai Shiu Hospital's founders was the influential immigrant businessman Wong Ah Fook, who served as the hospital's first president, and who signed the Kwong Wai Shiu Free Hospital Ordinance in 1911. Under the ordinance, land from the old TAN TOCK SENG HOSPITAL grounds was granted to Kwong Wai Shiu Hospital on a lease of 99 years. The hospital originally served the Chinese immigrant community, but was opened to patients from all ethnic groups in 1974 after its constitution was revised. It caters, in particular, to patients who suffer from severe disabilities or terminal illnesses and who cannot afford adequate care at other institutions.

The hospital provides a range of in-patient and out-patient services, including Western and TRADITIONAL CHINESE MEDICINE, a day rehabilitation centre for the elderly, physiotherapy and occcupational therapy, dietary and pharmaceutical services, ambulances for non-acute cases, and medical social workers. Residents of the nursing home are also provided with social activities.

Kwong Wai Siew Peck San Theng Charitable organization. Kwong Wai Siew Peck San Theng was established in 1870 by immigrants largely from the three prefectures of Kwong Chou (present-day Guangzhou), Wai Chou (present-day Huizhou) and Siew Heng (also known as Shiu Heng; present-day Zhaoqing) in Guangdong, China. It has continued to cater mainly to Singapore's CANTONESE community. In 1870, it founded a cemetery which, within a century, was expanded to hold 100,000 graves.

In the 1970s, many graves were exhumed to make way for the construction of Bishan New Town ('Bishan' being the Mandarin pronunciation of 'Peck San', meaning 'green hill'). The organization's Peck San Theng Memorial Hall and Columbarium continues to provide funeral services for the local Cantonese population.

Kwong Wai Siew Peck San Theng: cremation urns.

Labour Front Political party founded by DAVID MARSHALL and LIM YEW HOCK just before the LEGISLATIVE ASSSEMBLY ELECTION (1955). The centre-left grouping won the most votes, securing ten of the 25 seats and forming a coalition government with three members of the SINGAPORE ALLIANCE PARTY. The Labour Front's (LF) leader, David Marshall, became Singapore's first chief minister.

Between 1955 and 1956, the LF government led two all-party delegations to London for talks with the British on self-government for Singapore. In 1955, negotiations broke down and Marshall resigned as chief minister. His deputy, Lim Yew Hock, took over as chief minister. The following year, Lim led a second all-party delegation to London and succeeded in securing self-government (*see* MERDEKA). In preparation for the next general elections, the LF merged with the LIBERAL SOCIALIST PARTY (LSP)—itself a merger of the Progressive and Democratic Parties—to form the Singapore People's Alliance (SPA).

At the LEGISLATIVE ASSSEMBLY ELECTION (1959), the SPA won only four seats. It fared worse in the GENERAL ELECTION (1963), failing to win any seats. The party was dissolved after Singapore gained independence in 1965.

labour relations In the early days of migrant labour in Singapore, poor working conditions resulted in frequent industrial unrest. In 1914, the contract system for the Chinese and the indentured system of recruitment for Indians were abolished. However, the colonial government, fearing labour militancy, did not permit the formal organization of labour. Associations providing trade union functions were allowed to exist only as clubs and guild houses under the Singapore Societies Ordinance of 1909.

To manage industrial unrest, the British government passed three items of legislation: The Trade Unions Bill (1940), the Industrial Courts Bill (1940) and the Trade Disputes Ordinance (1941). With a more conducive legal environment, the significance of trade unions rose. But their development was disrupted by the Japanese Occupation, which diverted the unions from their socio-economic goals to fighting the Japanese. Trade union development was revived after the war. Both the GENERAL LABOUR UNION (GLU) and its local chapter, the SINGAPORE FEDERATION OF TRADE UNIONS, set up in 1945, were affiliated with the MALAYAN COMMUNIST PARTY. They controlled most of the trade unions in the private sector.

The GLU played an active role in the post-war struggle for independence. The British government imposed many restrictions and suppressed trade union activities. Workers were discouraged from joining the labour movement. This, along with other factors, contributed to the collapse of the trade union movement. In 1948, there were ten registered unions in Singapore with a membership of 74,000. By 1949, union membership had dropped drastically to 47,000.

The colonial government took this opportunity to form the SINGAPORE TRADES UNION CONGRESS (STUC), a body to guide unions formerly under the Singapore Federation of Trade Unions. It held its first congress in 1951 but made little impact as it represented only 28 of the 107 registered unions.

When the PEOPLE'S ACTION PARTY split over the issue of Merger, this led to the dissolution of the STUC. In its place, the SINGAPORE ASSOCIATION OF TRADE UNIONS was set up under the BARISAN SOSIALIS, and the NATIONAL TRADES UNION CONGRESS (NTUC) under the PAP in 1961.

The period 1963-71 saw the NTUC working closely with the PAP government and employers to develop the Singapore economy and create a climate conducive to foreign investment. In 1968, the Employment Act and Industrial Relations (Amendment) Act were enacted to foster harmonious labour relations. This was a period of transition, with labour becoming more focused on broader deveopment issues. To regulate wages, the NATIONAL WAGES COUNCIL (NWC) was set up in 1972, with equal representation from trade unions, employers and the government.

Today, labour relations in Singapore are based on tripartism. Tripartism refers to the national-level interaction between representatives of labour, management and government to form policy. Most collective agreements are arrived at through direct negotiation, with disagreements largely resolved through conciliation. Only a limited number of disputes are referred for arbitration to the Industrial Arbitration Court.

The last strike in Singapore was in 1986. This strike in the shipping industry was sanctioned by ONG TENG CHEONG and lasted two days, after which all issues were settled.

Labrador Battery

Labour Front: Lim Yew Hock of the Labour Front greeting visiting members of the British Labour Party in 1963.

Labrador Battery Situated on the southern coast of Singapore, Labrador's strategic value was recognized by the British as early as 1843, when plans were made to protect the entrance of New Harbour (present-day KEPPEL HARBOUR). However, it was only in 1878 that a fortification (named Fort Pasir Panjang) was constructed at the site. Although the location was recorded in some records as a point opposite the island of St George (Pulau Blakang Mati; present-day Sentosa), it is clear from extant relics that Labrador was the actual site of the fort. The fort was upgraded in 1892 from its original two-gun emplacements to a six-gun defence battery together with underground accommodation and ammunition storerooms.

Before WORLD WAR II, when it was believed that there could be an attack on Singapore by Japanese battleships, an extensive network of coastal defences was deemed necessary, and the fortification was upgraded. Labrador Battery, built in 1939, was armed with two 6-inch cannons of 1900-18 manufacture. All the battery guns were directed southwards, in anticipation of an attack from the sea. Towards the end of the MALAYA CAMPAIGN, the Japanese came from the north, marching across the Causeway from peninsular Malaya. However, contrary to a popular belief that the coastal guns were useless as they faced the wrong direction, they did see action. During the BATTLE OF PASIR PANJANG in 1942, the MALAY REGIMENT swung the guns around to fire at the advancing Japanese troops, causing significant casualties.

Relics and ruins of a command post, machine-gun posts, large gun positions and ammunition storage compartments can still be seen at Labrador. Four underground complexes beneath the gun positions have been explored, and two tunnels were opened to the public in 2005 (*see* ABINGDON TUNNELS). They have been preserved, by and large, in their original state. The ammunition store in the tunnels is the only place in Singapore where the destruction from World War II is still visible. An intact 6-inch cannon (identical to the Labrador cannons) was excavated in 2001 at a former military camp on Beach Road. It was restored and now stands at the original Labrador battery site. The cannon and tunnels are now part of a heritage trail.

See also LABRADOR NATURE RESERVE.

Labrador Nature Reserve This is a nature reserve on the southern coast of Singapore Island. It is located on Labrador Villa Road, off Pasir Panjang Road.

Labrador was originally designated a nature reserve in 1951 when the Nature Reserve Ordinance was enacted. The original 4 ha of cliffside vegetation at Labrador were set aside for conservation, to protect the habitat of the primitive fern *Dipteris conjugata*. Once growing wild in parts of Singapore's coastal areas, this endangered species was confined to Labrador in the 1950s. However, by the late 1970s, the population had dwindled, and was thought, at one point, to be extinct. That may have been one reason for the downgrading of Labrador's status to that of a nature park in the 1970s. In 2002, however, Labrador was again gazetted as a 10-ha nature reserve.

Labrador's natural vegetation consists of a wide variety of shrubs and trees, essentially of coastal forest species. Of special interest is a large, 12-m tall tree *Dracaena maingayi*,

1   2

estimated to be more than 80 years old. This species is the largest monocotyledonous tree in Singapore. The forest canopy consists mainly of tall sea apple trees (*Eugenia grandis*), and some sea almond trees (*Terminalia catappa*).

Examples of resident fauna are crickets, cicadas, white-crested laughing thrushes, yellow-vented bulbuls and white-bellied sea eagles.

However, Labrador's natural history significance centres on its narrow, 300-m stretch of rocky shore, the last remaining rocky beach and coral reef on Singapore's main island. Representative species of nearly all the major phyla of marine animals and plants of the Indo-Pacific region are found here. These include the green seaweed Caulerpa (*2*), which resembles grapes, and Singapore's smallest crab species, *Halicarcinus* (*4*), which measures only 2.5 mm across the carapace. In the 1990s, four new species of crustaceans were discovered at Labrador.

Crabs that have been seen on the rocky shore of Labrador include the moon crab (*Matuta lunaris*) (*3*), the

leaf porter crab (*Neodorippe callida*) (*1*) and the common hairy crab (*Pilumnus vespertilio*) (*5*). The coastal horseshoe crab (*Tachypleus gigas*) can also be found at Labrador, though it is not a crab and is more closely related to spiders and scorpions.

Some of Labrador's marine creatures are of special value to human life. For example, the simple sponges house bacteria with antibiotic properties, while the fish-eating cone snails can release a toxin to paralyse prey instantly. This same toxin (conotoxin) can be extracted and converted into non-addictive painkillers up to ten thousand times more potent than morphine.

In 1990, the Port of Singapore Authority (PSA) announced plans to construct new port facilities in the vicinity. These would have involved land reclamation at Labrador Beach. However, scientists and lay citizens alike successfully argued for the conservation of Labrador.

Abutting the southeast edge of Labrador is the 6.8-ha Labrador Park, which was created in 1978 on land reclaimed from the sea. The park was formerly known as Tanjong Berlayar Park, apparently named for Batu Berlayar, or Lot's Wife as the early Europeans knew it (*see* LONGYAMEN). This was a mass of rocks sited at the entrance of New Harbour present-day KEPPEL HARBOUR).

See also LABRADOR BATTERY.

4   5

Male horseshoe crab clinging on to the back of a female horseshoe crab.

3

Lai Chun Yuen Cantonese opera hall at the junction of Trengganu Street and Smith Street. Although its official year of completion was 1887, the theatre is believed to have been in existence earlier. Lai Chun Yuen was the most impressive opera house built in Singapore during the late 19th century. After renovation in 1918, it could accommodate 834 people on its two floors.

Cantonese opera was performed at Lai Chun Yuen twice a day to capacity crowds until the late 1920s, when the introduction of movies practically destroyed the opera industry. In the 1910s and 1920s, it hosted such famous CHINESE OPERA stars as Leng Yuen Hung, Ma Si Chang and Hung Sin Nui.

During World War II, bombing destroyed much of the original building. It was later rebuilt and used as a merchandise shop, then as a warehouse. In the early 1990s, a Taiwanese businessman bought the building for $50 million and restored it to its former grandeur. He later donated it to the Taiwan-based Tzu Chi Foundation, a Buddhist charity group. In November 2001, the CHINESE THEATRE CIRCLE staged a Cantonese opera performance as a fund-raiser for the SUN YAT SEN NANYANG MEMORIAL HALL.

Lai Kew Chai (1941–2006) Judge. Born in Slim River, Perak, Lai Kew Chai was educated at St Andrew's School in Singapore and then at the University of Singapore, where he obtained his law degree in 1966. After being called to the Bar, Lai joined the firm of LEE & LEE, where he established a strong reputation as a shipping law expert. In 1971, he was made a partner of the firm. Between 1979 and 1981, Lai served as

vice-president of the LAW SOCIETY OF SINGAPORE.

In 1981, he was appointed to the bench as puisne judge, the youngest judge ever to be appointed to the High Court. His other appointments include: member, Military Court of Appeal; member, Singapore Broadcasting Corporation; registrar, Diocese of Singapore Anglican Church; chairman, Singapore Cheshire Home; and chairman, Singapore Dance Theatre.

Lai retired from the High Court in February 2006 and died of cancer barely three weeks later.

Lai Siu Chiu (1948–) Judge. Born in Malacca, Lai Siu Chiu graduated from the University of Singapore with an honours degree in law in 1972. She was called to the Bar the following year and joined the firm of Allen & Gledhill, where she was made a partner in 1980. While in practice, she obtained a master's degree in law from the University of London (1977). In 1991, she became the first woman to be appointed JUDICIAL COMMISSIONER, and in 1994, the first woman to be appointed a High Court judge.

Lai Chun Yuen

Lai Teck (dates unknown) Political activist. Lai Teck, whose real name was Hoang A Nhac, was a Chinese-speaking Vietnamese. He first appeared as an informer for the French in Indochina in the 1930s, and came to Malaya at the end of 1934. The French introduced him to the British authorities in 1936 with a view to having him infiltrate the MALAYAN COMMUNIST PARTY (MCP). By this time, he went by several different aliases, including Wong Kim Geok, Comrade Wright, Loi Tek, Lai Tek and Huang Shaodong.

In 1936, he became a central committee member of the MCP and quickly rose to be its deputy secretary. Three years later, he became the party's secretary-general. During the Japanese Occupation, he led MCP guerrillas into the jungles of Johor. In March 1942, he was arrested by the Japanese KEMPEITAI (secret police), who persuaded him to be an informant for the Japanese as well. Lai informed on the MCP to both the British and the Japanese, informed on the Japanese to the British and informed on the British to the Japanese. His betrayal of his own comrades—especially during the Japanese Occupation, when many of them were ambushed, killed or arrested—went undetected until after the war.

In December 1946, Lai returned from a visit to Hong Kong and issued a directive to his MCP colleagues in Kuala Lumpur to refrain from armed insurrection, rely on 'united front' tactics and limit demands for self-government, so long as the British Labour Party was in office. Although these moderate policies were at odds with the MCP's revolutionary stance, the central committee of the party endorsed the directive, as well as Lai's appointment as secretary-general. However, these endorsements were a ruse to bring Lai to the surface. The central committee had heard from a Vietnamese waiter that Lai had been seen during the war as a table guest of Japanese officials. An investigation was undertaken, and in March 1947, charges of treachery were brought against Lai. He went into hiding—but not without first misappropriating all of the MCP's funds.

Lai apparently fled to Bangkok, where he was probably assassinated by MCP operatives or members of the Thai Communist Party. He was replaced as the MCP's secretary-general by CHIN PENG.

Laju hijacking In January 1974, four terrorists armed with machine guns and explosives attacked the Shell Oil Refinery on Pulau Bukom Besar, bombing petroleum tanks. Two of the terrorists were Japanese (members of the Japanese Red Army) and the other two were members of the Popular Front For the Liberation of Palestine (PFLP). The former wanted to overthrow the 'imperialist' government of Japan, while the latter aimed to retaliate against 'imperialist countries that were

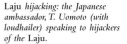

Laju *hijacking: the Japanese ambassador, T. Uomoto (with loudhailer) speaking to hijackers of the* Laju.

oppressing the Arab masses'.

Their plan was to disrupt oil supplies from Singapore to South Vietnam. However, the attack did not go smoothly. Their boat ran aground on a coral reef and they had to have another craft tow them to the island. The raid was abortive, but in their attempt to escape, the terrorists hijacked a passenger ferry, *Laju*, taking five Singaporean crew members hostage. At the Eastern Anchorage, they were intercepted and surrounded by marine police boats and three Singapore Maritime Command gunboats. Two of the hostages escaped.

After several days of negotiations, the terrorists agreed to release the remaining hostages in exchange for a party of guarantors which included four Singapore Armed Forces COMMANDOS and eight other government officials—led by S.R. NATHAN, then director of security and intelligence for the Ministry of Defence.

The hijackers also negotiated safe passage to South Yemen after their comrades seized the Japanese Embassy in Kuwait. On 7 February 1974, the terrorists were transferred by boat and taken to the airport. At the airport, they surrendered all their arms to the police and released the three hostages. On 8 February, the four terrorists—and the Singaporean officials—flew to Kuwait aboard a special Japan Airlines flight. The Singaporean officials later returned safely to a heroes' welcome.

lakawood Scented heartwood and root wood of a thick liana, *Dalbergia parviflora*. One of the consistently sought-after aromatics of the Malay Peninsula, lakawood may have been introduced to China at the beginning of the 10th century. Known to the Chinese as 'truth descending incense' (*jiangzhen xiang*) or 'purple vine incense' (*ziteng xiang*), lakawood was a familiar product in China, and on account of its low price, was being used by both rich and poor in South China by the 13th century.

All ports in the Malay Peninsula made lakawood available for export. Chinese traders overtook those from Southeast Asia

as the key shippers of this product to China, and graded the quality of lakawood available from the respective ports. TEMASEK (Singapore) was known to have exported the second-highest quality lakawood in Southeast Asia.

Lakawood's popularity in China in the 14th century led to a rise in its status. From being a low-value product during the 10–13th centuries, it became sufficiently valuable to be presented by Sukhothai (present-day Thailand) and Lambri (present-day Aceh) as tribute to China's Ming court.

Lakawood continues to be imported by China for the making of incense or joss sticks.

laksa Popular hawker dish. The name of this dish may have come from the Sanskrit word '*laksha*', meaning 'many'. Laksa consists of thick *beehoon* (rice noodles) served in a spicy soup. Two main types of laksa exist: curry laksa (also known as laksa *lemak*); and *assam* (tamarind) laksa, which uses a sour, fish-based soup—an example being Penang laksa. Curry laksa, which originates from the PERANAKANS, is more common in Singapore. It uses a base of coconut milk and various other ingredients, including lemongrass, shallots, candlenut, garlic, chilli, turmeric and cockles. The soup is poured over the noodles just before serving, and topped with prawns, bean sprouts, dried or fried beancurd, fishcake slices and sometimes a hard-boiled egg. This is then garnished with finely chopped laksa leaves (*Polygonium minus*). In Katong laksa, which

Lai Teck

Laksa

Lan Shui

is a variant curry laksa, the noodles are cut into short pieces before serving, so that the dish can be eaten with only a spoon.

Lan Shui (1957–) Conductor. China-born Lan Shui was appointed the second music director of the SINGAPORE SYMPHONY ORCHESTRA (SSO) in 1997. He had previously served as conductor of the Beijing Symphony Orchestra, and associate conductor at the Baltimore and Detroit Symphony Orchestras. His tenure at the SSO saw the orchestra perform to critical acclaim in Europe, North America and China, and numerous commercial recordings on the Swedish BIS label. Lan Shui is known for championing Asian composers, and has conducted the SSO in recordings of Chen Yi's *Momentum* (2003) and Zhou Long's *Rhymes* (2004).

Land Acquisition Act Legislation introduced in 1966 to enable the government to redevelop land. At the time, most land was privately owned, and much of it was fragmented. Land acquisition allowed the state to put together substantial parcels for public use, such as PUBLIC HOUSING and road construction. The resulting transfer of land from private to state ownership has made the state the largest landowner in Singapore.

When a piece of land is to be acquired, the Act requires the landowner to be notified, an inquiry to be conducted, and reasonable compensation to be made to the landowner.

Appeals from landowners are heard by the Appeals Board, which comprises a commissioner (or a deputy) and a panel of assessors from relevant fields. The decision of the Appeals Board is final, and landowners are allowed no further appeals unless the matter concerns a question of law and the award determined by the board is more than $5,000.

land reclamation With a population of 4.3 million (2005) and a land area of 660 sq km, Singapore is one of the most densely populated countries in the world. Before the early 1970s, most new land for housing and industry came from former farmland and forests, but since then, land reclamation has been carried out in coastal areas to create new land.

The practice of land reclamation goes back to the early 19th century. The first schemes took place close to the present city centre and the banks of the SINGAPORE RIVER. Beach Road, as the name suggests, was originally on the sea front and the RAFFLES HOTEL, as shown in old photographs, overlooked the sea. What is now BOAT QUAY used to be a swamp that was filled with earth from a levelled hill in the 1820s. In the 1930s, the TELOK AYER Basin was reclaimed to form what is now SHENTON WAY.

Between 1960 and 1990, land reclamation added 7.6 per cent to Singapore's land area, an increase of 44 sq km. The Concept Plan of 1991 estimated that the total amount of reclaimed land would reach 25 per cent when all schemes were complete. The Concept Plan of 2001 stated that future reclamation can increase land area by 15 per cent.

The earliest phases of land reclamation took place in seas up to 5 m deep, and the method used was the infilling of marshes and shallow sea areas through the dredging and dumping of locally available sand. Over time, it became necessary to move into deeper waters. Current technology enables reclamation in water up to 15 m deep. In the near future, this will be extended into water 20 m deep. As reclamation has moved into deeper waters, the costs have escalated. The 20 sq km of reclaimed land at CHANGI AIRPORT used 272 million tons of sand at a cost of $1.9 billion in raw materials alone.

Easily dredged sand supplies are no longer plentiful in Singapore, and although solid waste has become a source of landfill, sand is imported for reclamation projects from Indonesia and Malaysia.

Reclamation has been a point of disagreement between Singapore and Malaysia. Malaysia has protested that land reclamation has encroached into Malaysian waters in the Strait of Johor. Malaysia took the issue to the International Tribunal for the Law of the Sea but subsequently settled the issue with Singapore through negotiation.

Within Singapore, land reclamation activities have been concentrated in different parts of the country to meet different land use needs. Close to the central business district, extensions such as the MARINA BAY area have added to commercial and residential space. At JURONG and on JURONG ISLAND, reclamation has provided new industrial land.

See also URBAN PLANNING.

Land Transport Authority Statutory board. Formed in 1995, the Land Transport Authority (LTA) seeks to maximize the use of the road network, improve public transport, and develop and implement policies to guide commuters to use the most appropriate transportation mode.

LTA designs and supervises the construction and maintenance of roads and operates the traffic control systems. It also designs and supervises the construction of the MASS RAPID TRANSIT/LIGHT RAIL TRANSIT SYSTEM, and appoints companies to operate these. In addition, the LTA administers the regulations on vehicle parking and on the construction and use of vehicles.

landed property Landed properties can be defined in broad terms as detached, semi-detached or terrace houses. In Singapore, where most of the population live in high-rise blocks of flats, a distinction is made between these homes built at ground level and 'strata-title' apartments or flats. Naturally, owners of landed property pay a premium for the luxury of living on the ground, perhaps with a garden, and in a low-density setting.

Most landed properties are estates in perpetuity (freehold) or on 999-year leases. Strata-title apartments, on the other hand are typically held on 99-year leases. Since 1973, restrictions on foreign ownership of landed properties have been imposed. Exceptions are made for high-net-worth foreigners who want to live permanently in Singapore.

Land reclamation: to the east of the Singapore River.

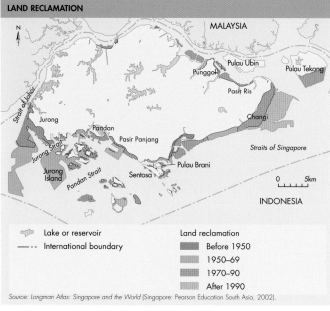

LAND RECLAMATION

Lake or reservoir
International boundary

Land reclamation
Before 1950
1950–69
1970–90
After 1990

Source: Longman Atlas: Singapore and the World (Singapore: Pearson Education South Asia, 2002).

Landed property

Landed properties are to be found throughout Singapore. The more expensive properties are located in areas such as Nassim, TANGLIN and Holland where zoning laws prevent these areas from being too heavily built up. The lowest-density, highest-premium landed properties in Singapore are found in 'good class bungalow' areas—this is a planning term employed by the URBAN REDEVELOPMENT AUTHORITY (URA). In 'good class bungalow areas', each property is at least 1,400 sq m in size and no more than two storeys in height.

Landing Ship Tank Sea-going vessel that can carry troops, tanks and cargo. The Endurance-class Landing Ship Tank (LST) is the largest class of naval vessel to be designed and built locally. It is the result of a collaboration between the DEFENCE SCIENCE AND TECHNOLOGY AGENCY, Singapore Technologies Electronics and Singapore Technologies Marine. The LST was designed to meet the Republic of Singapore Navy's requirements. The first vessel was launched in 1998 and so far, four vessels have been put into operation. They are used by 191 Squadron, based at the Changi Naval Base.

The LST measures 141 m by 21 m, displaces 6,000 tons, and has a top speed of 20 knots. The LST is 40 per cent larger than the County-class LST it replaced but requires a crew of only 65, due to its extensive array of advanced systems and technologies. The vessel, which has a helipad, is capable of carrying 350 troops or 18 main battle tanks. Alternatively, the LST can carry 2,500 tons of cargo. In 2000, an Endurance-class vessel called the RSS *Endurance* completed a circumnavigation of the globe. Three LSTs also played a pivotal role in Singapore's relief mission to Banda Aceh following the December 2004 tsunami.

LASALLE-SIA College of the Arts Brother JOSEPH MCNALLY, an educator and sculptor, established the St Patrick's Arts Centre in 1984. The school initially conducted courses on painting, ceramics, music and sculpture. Drama classes were added in its second year when it moved to its second campus at Telok Kurau. As a general awareness about

arts education began to grow in Singapore, there was need for greater space. Therefore, the college moved to larger premises at the former Tun Sri Lanang School on Goodman Road in 1992.

A year later, the college formed an alliance with SINGAPORE AIRLINES (SIA), receiving a contribution of $15 million for the construction of a new building, and was renamed LASALLE-SIA College of the Arts. It received accredited institution status from the Open University in the United Kingdom in March 2004. It introduced a comprehensive range of creative programmes at the diploma, bachelor's and master's levels in fine arts, design, drama, music and art management. The college has also spearheaded other areas of art research.

Lat Pau Newspaper. *Lat Pau* was the first Chinese-language daily newspaper to be published in Singapore. It was started in December 1881, and was published by See Ewe Lay, scion of a wealthy Peranakan family. Profit appears not to have been a motive in the newspaper's founding, as *Lat Pau*'s circulation never exceeded 550; nevertheless it was well-respected. *Lat Pau* survived until 1932 when, with no competent writer to take over after the death of its leading journalist, Yeh Chi-Yun, it ceased publication.

Law Society of Singapore Main body regulating Singapore's LEGAL PROFESSION. Regulation of Singapore's lawyers began in 1873 with the passage of the Courts Ordinance. The statute restricted the admission of lawyers in Singapore to those admitted as barristers or solicitors in England, Scotland and Ireland, or those who passed a local examination. To this end, a Bar council in each of the three Straits Settlements was established. The first honorary secretary of Singapore's Bar Council was Alan Donaldson (of the firm DONALDSON & BURKINSHAW).

Following Singapore's independence from Malaysia in 1965, the Legal Profession Act was passed, creating both the Singapore Advocates and Solicitors Society and the Board of Legal Education. In 1970, the Advocates and Solicitors Society was renamed the Law Society. Among its roles are maintaining and improving the standards of conduct and learning of the profession; representing, protecting and assisting members of the profession; protecting and assisting members of the public on all matters relating to the law; and operating a legal aid scheme.

The society is managed by a council, comprising 15 elected members and three members nominated by the minister for law. It is the job of the council to make rules regulating the practice and conduct of lawyers, manage the society and its funds, and deal with complaints of misconduct.

Laycock, John (1887–1960) Politician. Born in the United Kingdom, John Laycock graduated from the University of London, and was admitted as a solicitor in 1907. After a distinguished military career, in the course of which he was awarded the Military Cross, he came to Singapore in 1920, where he had a successful law practice and established himself as one of the leaders of the Singapore Bar.

Laycock served as a municipal commissioner between 1926 and 1948. During World War II, he relocated to Bombay where, together with Joe Elias, Tunku Abu Bakar and H. Fancott, he founded the Malayan Association, a social club for expatriates and an organization for taking care of refugees. Returning to Singapore after the war, he was instrumental in founding the SINGAPORE PROGRESSIVE PARTY (SPP)

In 1950, he offered to take in LEE KUAN YEW as a pupil in his law firm, Laycock & On. Lee later served as Laycock's election agent during the LEGISLATIVE COUNCIL ELECTION (1951). Laycock was elected to the Legislative Council in 1948 as an SPP candidate. He was re-elected in the 1951, but was defeated in the 1955 elections.

After resigning from the SPP, he formed the LIBERAL SOCIALIST PARTY with C.C. TAN and N.A. MALLAL, but subsequently retired from politics.

Lazarus Island *See* PULAU SAKIJANG PELEPAH.

Le Blond, Max (1950–) Theatre director and practitioner. An early advocate of local theatre, Francois Maxmillian Gerard Le Blond drew attention to the potential in Singaporean speech and materials for the development of an indigenous ENGLISH THEATRE. He introduced relatively unknown plays by Athol Fugard, STELLA KON and ELEANOR WONG to Singaporean audiences, and took Singaporean plays abroad. He also adapted well-known plays to local contexts.

Le Blond directed ROBERT YEO's politically provocative *One Year Back Home* (1980) and turned Peter Nichols' *The National Health* into *General Hospital, or, Nurse Angamuthu's Romance* for the 1981 National Drama Festival. In 1982, his adaptation of Brecht's *The Threepenny Opera* became *The Samseng and the Chettiar's Daughter* a Festival of Arts commission. He

Lat Pau: 1887 issue.

John Laycock

Max Le Blond: scene from David Henry Hwang's F.O.B., directed by Le Blond in 1982.

Dick Lee

Gloria Lee

Lee Boon Yang

Lee Cheng Yam

headed the Singapore production team and co-directed *F.O.B.*—another 1982 Festival of Arts commission—with its American playwright, David Henry Hwang. Le Blond also directed Stella Kon's *Emily of Emerald Hill* (1985; 1993), the first English-language theatre production to be invited to the 1986 Edinburgh Festival Fringe.

Le Blond received the CULTURAL MEDALLION for Theatre in 1987. He was an academic at the National University of Singapore and Nanyang Technological University for almost two decades. He left Singapore in 1997 to read for the juris doctor degree at the University of Washington School of Law. He now lives in Sydney with his wife and their two daughters.

Le Cain, John (1912–1993) Police officer and civil servant. Born in Bangkok, John Le Cain came to Singapore at the age of two. He was educated at St Andrew's School and Raffles Institution. He joined the police force as a probationary inspector in October 1939, after spending eight years as an articled clerk in a law firm. Le Cain's first posting was at Tanjong Pagar Police Station.

In 1940, he was transferred to SPECIAL BRANCH, staying there until the onset of the Japanese Occupation. He was interned at Changi Prison during the Occupation, and returned to Special Branch in 1945. In 1947, he became senior investigating officer of F Division and then assistant officer-in-charge.

In January 1948, Le Cain was one of only four Asian officers promoted to the rank of assistant superintendent. Among the important posts he held were commandant, Police Training School, and director, Corrupt Practices Investigation Bureau. In 1962, he was appointed deputy commissioner, only the second Asian to hold this post, the first being Song Kok Hoo. In 1963, Le Cain succeeded A.E.G. Blades as commissioner of police.

Le Cain retired in 1967 and became chairman of Singapore Pools. In 1969, he was appointed counsellor with the Singapore High Commission in London. Among his many decorations were: Colonial Police Medal for Meritorious Service (1957), Public Administration Medal (Gold) (1963) and the MERITORIOUS SERVICE MEDAL (1967).

Leader of the House Senior member of Parliament responsible for making representations to the Speaker on urgent matters of public interest that may require sittings. The office originated in British parliamentary practice in the days when prime ministers were also peers of the realm. They often had to be present in the House of Lords and thus, were absent from the House of Commons. To represent them, they appointed a leading minister as Leader of the House.

The Leader of the House also advises the Speaker on the seating arrangements within the House. In the prime minister's absence, the Leader expresses the sense of the House on formal occasions, such as in moving motions of thanks or congratulation. The Leader is also responsible for arranging government business and the legislative programme in the House (in consultation with the government WHIP), advising the House on any difficulty which may arise, and moving procedural motions relating to the business of the House on formal occasions.

Lee, Dick (1956–) Singer and songwriter. Also known as the 'Mad Chinaman', Dick Lee Peng Boon has spent over 30 years in the music industry. He has written and staged musicals such as *Life Story* (1974), *Beauty World* (1988) and *Fried Rice Paradise* (1991). As of 2006, he has recorded 19 pop albums, including *Life Story* (1974) and *The Mad Chinaman* (1989). He has won the award for Top Local Composer of the Year at the Composers and Authors Society of Singapore (COMPASS) Awards six times since 1995. He has also been appointed associate artistic director of the Singapore Repertory Theatre (1996–).

In 1992, Lee married singer JACINTHA ABISHEGANADEN. They were divorced in 1997. That year brought Lee success in Hong Kong, with the Jacky Cheung-led Cantonese musical *Snow.Wolf.Lake*, for which he wrote most of the music. Lee has also written music for Hong Kong artistes such as Sandy Lam and Aaron Kwok.

Lee's fame spread to Japan in the 1990s, and he received the prestigious Fukuoka Arts and Cultural Prize in 2003. Lee was the creative director of TV Station TV Works, which later became SPH MediaWorks. He received the CULTURAL MEDALLION in 2005.

Lee, Gloria (unknown–) Stockbroker. Gloria Lee Sau Yin was the first woman stockbroker in Singapore. She is also the founder of Kim Eng Securities. Born in Hong Kong, she came to Singapore in 1958, and married Lee Kim Yew (the brother of LEE KUAN YEW) in 1969. She started stockbroking in the early 1970s in the now-defunct Robert Wee & Co. In 1972, she put together $700,000 in personal savings and bank loans to buy the 21st seat on the stock exchange, which at that time was part of the Malaysian bourse. She ran Kim Eng Securities for over 30 years, before handing over the day-to-day operations of the company to her two sons from a previous marriage, Douglas and Ronald Ooi.

Lee & Lee Law firm. Lee & Lee was founded by LEE KUAN YEW, his wife Kwa Geok Choo, and his brother Lee Kim Yew on 1 September 1955. Lee Kuan Yew resigned from the firm in 1959 to contest the election that year, and went on to become Singapore's first prime minister. The practice began in a small office at 10B Malacca Street but grew quickly to become one of Singapore's largest firms.

Lee Boon Yang (1947–) Politician. Lee Boon Yang was educated at Montfort School and the University of Queensland, from which he graduated with a degree in veterinary science. He joined the Primary Production Department as a research and development officer in 1972, and rose to become senior manager of the Primary Industries Enterprise Pte Ltd (1982–84).

Lee entered politics in 1984, and won a seat in Jalan Besar constituency on the People's Action Party (PAP) ticket. The following year, he was appointed parliamentary secretary for the Ministries of the Environment, and Communications and Information. He was promoted to minister of state for trade and industry and for home affairs (1986); and senior minister of state for home affairs (1988), national development (1988) and defence (1990). In 1991, he became minister in the Prime Minister's Office. Since then, he has overseen the Ministries of Defence, Labour (later Manpower), and Information, Communications and the Arts. In 1988, he was appointed government whip. In 2001, he was presented with the NTUC May Day Medal of Honour. In 2006, he was re-elected to his seat in Jalan Besar group representation constituency.

Lee Cheng Yam (1841–1911) Merchant and philanthropist. Born in Malacca, Lee Cheng Yam, also known as Lee Cheng Yan, came to Singapore in 1858, and started a general trading and commission agency firm, Lee Cheng Yan & Co., on Telok Ayer Street. Within ten years, the firm, trading under the name and style of Chop Chin Joo, became one of the principal Chinese trading houses dealing with Europeans. In 1890, Lee helped found the STRAITS STEAMSHIP COMPANY. When Lee retired from active business to spend more time in community service, his son, Lee Choon Guan, took over the business.

Lee served on the Chinese Advisory Board (1889–1910) and the committees of Tan Tock Seng Hospital and the Po Leung Kuk (a charitable organization under the Chinese Protectorate). He founded two clan associations—the Eng Choon Hway Kuan and the Long Say Lee See Kong So—as well as Hong Joo Chinese Free School on Serangoon Road. He was among the original trustees of the Anglo-Chinese Free School (later Gan Eng Seng School), and a board member of Toh Lam Chinese School (later Tao Nan School).

Lee Chiaw Meng (1937–2001) Politician. Lee Chiaw Meng was educated at Catholic High School, Chung Cheng High School and the University of Malaya, where he graduated with a degree in engineering. After obtaining a PhD in civil engineering from Imperial College London (1965), Lee became a lecturer in the Department of Civil Engineering at Singapore Polytechnic (1965–68).

In 1968, Lee entered politics and won the Farrer Park constituency seat on the People's Action Party (PAP) ticket. He was immediately appointed parliamentary secretary for the Ministry of Education (1968–70), minister of state for education (1970–72) and minister for education (1972–75). In 1977, he was appointed minister for science and technology. He retired from politics in 1988 and practised as principal partner in his own civil engineering firm, Dr Lee Chiaw Meng and Associates. He died in 2001, after a two-year battle with cancer.

Lee Ek Tieng (1933–) Civil servant. Born in Perak, Lee Ek Tieng was educated at the Anglo-Chinese School and the University of Malaya, where he graduated with a degree in engineering. He later obtained a diploma in public health engineering from the University of Newcastle-Upon-Tyne on a Colombo Plan Scholarship.

Lee joined the City Council as an engineer in 1958, and became head of the Anti-Pollution Unit in 1970. In 1971, he was appointed permanent secretary to the Ministry of Health and, subsequently, to the Ministry of the Environment, Ministry of Finance, and the Prime Minister's Office. From 1994 to his retirement in 1999, he was head of the Civil Service.

Lee was chairman of Temasek Holdings (1987–96) and also served at the Monetary Authority of Singapore (MAS) as managing director (1989–97) and deputy chairman (1998–2000). In 1999, he was appointed group managing director of the Government of Singapore Investment Corporation. Lee has also been a director of Fraser & Neave, chairman of the Public Utilities Board (1978–2000), a member of the Lee Kuan Yew Exchange Fellowship, and a director of the Lee Kuan Yew Scholarship Fund.

Lee has been awarded the MERITORIOUS SERVICE MEDAL (1984) and admitted into the DISTINGUISHED SERVICE ORDER (2000).

Lee Foundation Charitable foundation established by businessman LEE KONG CHIAN. The foundation was established in 1952 with an initial capital sum of $3.5 million. Its objectives include the advancement of education, medicine and cultural activities; helping the poor; and assisting victims of fire, flood and famine. When he died in 1967, Lee Kong Chian left half of his shares in the LEE RUBBER COMPANY to the foundation. Income earned from these assets continues to finance the Lee Foundation. The Lee Foundation is Singapore's largest foundation. Over the years, it has contributed to Singapore's society, education, welfare, research and the arts. LEE SENG GEE was made chairman of the foundation in 1967.

Lee Hock Moh: Couple *(undated).*

Lee Hee Seng (1927–) Banker. Lee Hee Seng was educated at Raffles Institution and the Administrative Staff College in the United Kingdom. He started working life in the Commonwealth Development Corporation, the British government's instrument for investment in the private sector of developing countries. He joined the Malaysia Building Society Berhad (MBSB) in 1950. He then became managing director of the Singapore Building Society, formed to take over the Singapore operations of the MBSB after 1965.

In 1972, Lee joined OVERSEAS UNION BANK (OUB) as a director. He became LIEN YING CHOW's deputy, taking over as chairman of OUB in 1995, when Lien retired. Lee also took over Lien's chairmanship of various companies in the OUB group, such as the International Bank of Singapore, Overseas Union Trust, Overseas Union Holdings and Overseas Union Bank Trustees.

When OUB was acquired by UNITED OVERSEAS BANK (UOB) in 2001, Lee joined the UOB board as senior deputy chairman. He retired in May 2003.

Lee was also chairman of the Public Service Commission (1988–98), and sat on the board of Singapore Press Holdings (1984–2003). In 1993, he was appointed chairman of the Presidential Elections Committee. He was awarded the MERITORIOUS SERVICE MEDAL in 1976, and was admitted into the DISTINGUISHED SERVICE ORDER in 1989.

Lee Hock Moh (1947–) Artist. Shortly after graduating from the Nanyang Academy of Fine Arts (1970), Lee Hock Moh co-founded the Siaw Tao Chinese Seal-Carving, Calligraphy & Painting Society (1971) and was active in leading arts societies. While his formative influences included pioneer ink master Shi Xiangtuo, Lee evolved his own unique mode of expression, and a repertoire that included lush, romantic landscapes, demonstrating his command of the medium. For his artistic accomplishments, Lee received the Special Award in 1975, 1976 and 1983 from the then Ministry of Culture. He received the CULTURAL MEDALLION in 1981.

Lee is popularly known as the 'Orchid Artist' for his sustained, distinctive treatment of Singapore's national flower. He was the first local artist to interpret orchids in the Chinese ink *gongbi* style—typified by extreme clarity, conscientious delineation of form, meticulous detail and refined colours.

Lee Hsien Loong (1952–) Politician. Lee Hsien Loong was born on 10 February, the the eldest son of Singapore's first prime minister, LEE KUAN YEW, and Kwa Geok Choo. The younger Lee was educated at Catholic High School and National Junior College. In addition to English and Mandarin, Lee studied Malay and Russian. He won a President's Scholarship and a Singapore Armed Forces (SAF) Scholarship to study mathematics at Trinity College, Cambridge University, graduating with first class honours in mathematics, and a diploma in computer science (with distinction). He later obtained a master of public administration degree from Harvard University's John F. Kennedy School of Government.

Lee joined the SAF as an artillery officer after graduation, becoming brigadier-general at the age of 32. Trained at the US Army Command and General Staff College at Fort Leavenworth, Kansas, Lee was made the SAF's director of the Joint Operations

Lee Chiaw Meng

Lee Hock Moh

Lee Hsien Loong: during the 2006 General Election.

Lee Hsien Loong

Lee Hsien Yang

Lee Huei Min

Lee Khoon Choy

Lee Kong Chian

and Plans Directorate and, later, chief of staff (general staff).

On 29 January 1983, an oil rig, *Eniwetok*, struck the cable of the Sentosa Cable Car and caused two cable cars to plunge into the sea (*see* CABLE CAR DISASTER). Lee, then a senior colonel, directed the rescue operation involving all three services of the SAF.

The following year, Lee resigned from the SAF and entered politics under the PEOPLE'S ACTION PARTY (PAP) banner. He was voted in as member of Parliament (MP) for Teck Ghee constituency during the 1984 general election. He was immediately appointed minister of state for trade and industry, and defence. During the recession of 1985, he chaired an economic committee that proposed changes to Singapore's economy. The changes helped pull Singapore out of the recession. In 1986, he was promoted to acting minister for trade and industry and second minister for defence. Lee was confirmed as minister for trade and industry in 1987, a post he held until 1992.

In 1990, Lee was appointed deputy prime minister with responsibilities for economic and civil matters. Lee became chairman of the Monetary Authority of Singapore (1998) and minister for finance (2001). In August 2004, he succeeded GOH CHOK TONG as prime minister, while retaining his portfolio in finance. Within the PAP, Lee was elected to the Central Executive Committee in 1986. He rose to become second assistant secretary-general (1989), first assistant secretary-general (1992) and secretary-general (December 2004). In 2006, Lee was returned as MP for Ang Mo Kio group representation constituency.

In 1978, Lee married Wong Ming Yang. Wong passed away in 1982. In 1985, Lee married HO CHING. He has one daughter and one son from his first marriage, and two sons from his second marriage. In 1992, Lee was diagnosed with lymphoma, which went into remission after chemotherapy.

Lee Hsien Yang (1957–) Military officer and businessman. The second son of LEE KUAN YEW, Lee Hsien Yang was educated at Catholic High School. He won the President's and Singapore Armed Forces Overseas Merit Scholarships to read engineering at Cambridge University, where he graduated with a double-first. He later obtained a master's degree in management science from Stanford University. A career soldier, Lee attained the rank of brigadier-general before resigning from the army in 1994 at the age of 37. He joined SINGTEL as executive vice-president (local services) in 1994, and in May 1995 was appointed president and chief executive officer of the company. He also holds appointments as chief executive, Seasami Inc; chairman, Republic Polytechnic Board of Governors;

and chairman, Singapore Science Centre Board. In 1996, he was named one of the Top 100 Global Leaders of Tomorrow at the World Economic Forum. Under his leadership, SingTel has been privatized and has pursued the goal of becoming the best telecommunications company in the Asia Pacific. In July 2006, Lee announced his intention to step down as chief executive officer of SingTel.

Lee Huei Min (1982–) Musician. Recording under the name Min Lee, Lee Huei Min has been described as Singapore's 'poster girl' of classical music. Lee gave her first violin concert at the age of five, and was admitted at 14 to the master's programme at Yale University, where she studied with Erick Friedman. She has performed concertos with the Royal Philharmonic, Philharmonia, NHK Symphony and Russian National orchestras under conductors such as Charles Dutoit, Vladimir Ashkenazy, Mikhail Pletnev and Matthias Bamert. Lee released a recording of violin concertos by Tchaikovsky and Prokofiev on Universal with Ashkenazy in 2004.

Lee Khoon Choy (1924–) Journalist, politician and diplomat. Born in Penang, Lee Khoon Choy was educated at Yeok Keow Chinese School and Chung Ling High School, graduating in 1941. He joined the Chinese-language daily *Sin Min Jit Poh* as a journalist (1946). The following year, he was transferred to its sister paper in Singapore, *Sin Chew Jit Poh*.

In 1949, Lee left for London's Regent Street Polytechnic, graduating with a diploma in journalism in 1950. He then returned to Singapore and joined the English daily, *The Singapore Standard*. From 1950 to 1959, Lee worked for the *Nanyang Siang Pau* and *The Straits Times*. As a journalist, he covered several important international conferences, including the Bandung Afro-Asian Conference in 1955 and the 1957 talks on Merdeka for Malaya in London.

In 1959, Lee entered politics on the People's Action Party (PAP) ticket, winning the seat of Bukit Panjang constituency. From 1959 to 1963, Lee was the government whip. He was also parliamentary secretary, first to the Ministry of Culture (1959–61) and then the Ministry of Education (1961–63). Lee lost his seat during the 1963 election; thereafter, until 1965, he served as political secretary to the prime minister and editor of *Petir*, the PAP's official organ. In 1965, he re-entered Parliament by winning the by-election at Hong Lim constituency. He was appointed minister of state for culture (1965) and minister of state, Prime Minister's Office (1968–70).

Lee's diplomatic career began as ambassador to Egypt. He handled discussions with the Egyptian government over Singapore's intention to recognize Israel.

He was concurrently accredited to Pakistan, Yugoslavia, Ethiopia and Lebanon (1968–70). He was appointed ambassador to Indonesia (1970–74) at a time when INDONESIA-SINGAPORE RELATIONS were strained in the aftermath of the 1968 sacking of the Singapore embassy and the 1968 hanging of two Indonesian marines involved in the MACDONALD HOUSE bombing. Lee's diplomacy paved the way for the first official visit of then Prime Minister Lee Kuan Yew to Indonesia in 1973.

Lee served concurrently as senior minister of state for foreign affairs (1972–79). In 1975, he was part of the first official Singapore delegation to visit the People's Republic of China. He was then appointed ambassador to Japan (1984–88) and was also accredited to Korea. Upon completion of the posting, he retired from public life. He was admitted into the DISTINGUISHED SERVICE ORDER in 1990.

Lee Khoon Choy was one of the first politicians to write about his life in politics in the autobiographical *On the Beat to the Hustings* (1988). His diplomatic experiences and observations are recounted in *Diplomacy of a Tiny State* (1993). He is also the author of *Indonesia: Between Myth and Reality* (1976); *A Fragile Nation: The Indonesia Crisis* (1999); and *Japan: Between Myth and Reality* (1995).

Lee Kong Chian (1894–1967) Businessman and philanthropist. Born in Fujian, the son of Lee Kuo Chuan, a tailor, Lee Kong Chian came to Singapore at the age of eight. He was educated at the Anglo-Tamil School on Serangoon Road and at St Joseph's Institution. In 1908, he won a scholarship from the Manchu Qing government in China to study at Chi Nan School, Nanjing. He was forced to return to Singapore in 1912 with the cancellation of the scholarship following the 1911 Republican revolution in China. He worked as municipal surveyor and translator before joining Tiong Hwa Chinese Goods Company as assistant manager. In this role he was noticed by the rubber millionaire, TAN KAH KEE, who offered him the opportunity to work in his rubber company, Khiam Aik (1918). Lee rose to the position of manager, and married Tan's eldest daughter, Ai Lay (1920).

In the 1920s, Lee started his own business. In 1927, he set up a rubber smoking house (later LEE RUBBER COMPANY) in Johor, and diversified into PINEAPPLES. When Tan Kah Kee's company went into liquidation, Lee acquired Tan's assets and became known as the 'Rubber and Pineapple King'. He then invested in Oversea-Chinese Banking Corporation (OCBC) (1932), later becoming chairman.

In 1941, Lee and his family left for Washington D.C. to attend a rubber conference. When the Japanese Occupation began in Singapore, they remained in the United

States. In 1945, Lee returned to Singapore to resurrect his business. The Korean War (1950–53) had led to a rubber shortage, and as a result, Lee was able to rebuild his business to even greater levels of success. When he retired in 1954, his sons—Seng Gee, Seng Tee and Seng Wee—took over the Lee business empire.

Lee then devoted himself to public service, especially in education. He was chairman of Chinese High School (1931–56) and chancellor of the University of Singapore (1962–65). He encouraged the education of girls by donating to a number of girls' schools. He also donated generously to the University of Malaya and Nanyang University.

Through the LEE FOUNDATION, he gave millions of dollars to a wide range of charities. In 1966, the Yang di-Pertuan Agong of Malaysia bestowed on Lee the title of *Tan Sri*. Lee was also honoured by the University of Malaya (1958) and the University of Singapore (1965) with honorary doctorates in law. He died in June 1967.

Lee Kuan Yew (1923–) Lee Kuan Yew was the first prime minister of the Republic of Singapore, serving from June 1959 to November 1990. During his tenure, Singapore was transformed from a struggling third-world country into a first-world state, a leading player in the world economy and a thriving Asian metropolis, of which Lee has often been described as the main architect. Well-respected in Singapore, Lee is a world statesman whose views, insights, perspectives and analyses are often sought.

Born on 16 September 1923 in Singapore, Lee received his secondary education from 1936 to 1939 at Raffles Institution. Emerging from the Senior Cambridge Examinations as the top student in Singapore and Malaya, he was offered a scholarship to study at Raffles College but his studies were interrupted by the outbreak of WORLD WAR II in the Pacific and the JAPANESE OCCUPATION. During the war, Lee worked as a clerk and later as a cable editor in a Japanese propaganda agency. Later, he was to attribute his subsequent political awakening to the experience of the Occupation years.

Lee Kuan Yew: with wife Kwa Geok Choo, 1950.

In September 1946, Lee left for the United Kingdom to study law at the London School of Economics, but transferred to Fitzwilliam House, Cambridge University, in January 1947. Graduating with a first class honours degree and awarded a star for distinction in 1949, Lee joined Middle Temple in London to qualify as a barrister. In London he became involved with the MALAYAN FORUM, a discussion group comprising students from Malaya and Singapore whose objective was to awaken political consciousness and press for an independent Malaya, inclusive of Singapore. During his time in the United Kingdom, he was drawn to Fabian socialism and befriended political leaders in the British Labour Party in the hope that they would be sympathetic to his desire for early independence for Malaya (inclusive of Singapore). In February 1950, he campaigned on behalf of one of his Cambridge friends, a Labour Party candidate. His growing political involvement while in the United Kingdom, however, had drawn the attention of Singapore's SPECIAL BRANCH, which kept Lee on its watch list.

After he was called to the Bar at Middle Temple in June 1950, Lee returned to Singapore in August 1950, and joined the law firm Laycock & Ong. During the LEGISLATIVE COUNCIL ELECTION (1951), he campaigned for his employer, JOHN LAYCOCK, a SINGAPORE PROGRESSIVE PARTY leader.

After completing his pupillage in August 1951, Lee was called to the Singapore Bar. He soon became increasingly involved in left-wing and labour causes, taking on a number of high-profile cases that helped to raise his professional standing and brought him into the public eye. Lee became legal adviser to a number of trade unions and CLAN ASSOCIATIONS, which he was happy to pull together as potential political supporters. After arranging for the admission of British Queen's Counsel D.N. PRITT and assisting him in the successful defence of a group of English-educated University of Malaya students charged with sedition for an article published in *Fajar*, an undergraduate magazine, in August 1954 (*see* FAJAR TRIAL), Lee was asked to represent another group of Chinese-educated middle school students in their appeal against a conviction for rioting against the National Service Ordinance in May 1954. He again enlisted the help of Pritt.

Though the appeal was dismissed, Lee's willingness to take up these causes and stand up to the government helped win him support from student groups who looked to him as their legal adviser. To Lee, however, it was also an introduction to the Chinese-educated world, and a political opportunity.

Lee's growing interest in politics led him to be one of the founding members of a new democratic-socialist political party,

Lee Kuan Yew: walkabout in Nee Soon constituency, 1966.

the PEOPLE'S ACTION PARTY (PAP), which initially sought support mainly from labour unions and Chinese-educated students, and included pro-communist activists within its ranks. As secretary-general of the party, Lee contested the LEGISLATIVE ASSEMBLY ELECTION (1955) and won his first parliamentary seat in Tanjong Pagar, a constituency he continued to represent as of 2006. As one of three successful PAP candidates in the 1955 election, he became de facto opposition leader in the Legislative Assembly. For the next few years, Lee used his position in the assembly to establish the PAP as a left-wing and anti-colonial party, committed to the swift ending of British rule through non-violent constitutional struggle. Meanwhile, he deployed his considerable political skills to fend off efforts by the pro-communist faction to control the PAP. During the LEGISLATIVE ASSEMBLY ELECTION (1959), his party won spectacularly, sweeping the polls with 43 of the 51 seats. Lee became the first prime minister of a self-governing Singapore.

Lee's efforts to persuade the Malayan premier and leader of the Alliance Party, Tunku ABDUL RAHMAN, to include Singapore in a wider political merger bore fruit in May 1961 when the latter publicly floated the possibility of bringing Malaya, Singapore and the Borneo territories closer together in a speech given in Singapore. This later became known as the 'Malaysia plan'. However, this initiative resulted in the pro-communist faction splitting from the PAP and moving into opposition as the BARISAN SOSIALIS in July 1961.

Five days after the formation of Malaysia on 16 September 1963, Lee led his party to another electoral victory in Singapore. He subsequently became one of 15 Singapore parliamentarians appointed to the Malaysian Parliament. But Singapore remained in Malaysia for only 23 months, during which time relations between the two sides—marked by political competition and sharp public exchanges between their leaders, and the outbreak of RACE RIOTS in Singapore in July and September 1964— deteriorated over political and economic differences that touched on Singapore's position and role in Malaysia. The heightened

Lee Kuan Yew

Lee Seng Gee

Lee Lim: the photographer (above); **Into a New Horizon** *(below)*

political antagonism and racial tension that ensued led the *tunku* to decide that only with Singapore's separation—which took place in August 1965—could the potentially explosive situation be contained. At a press conference in Singapore announcing SEPARATION, Lee Kuan Yew wept in anguish at the shattering of his goal of a united Malaya inclusive of Singapore, and the abandonment of his Malayan and Bornean political allies.

Faced with the formidable task of survival, Lee galvanized support for pragmatic economic and social programmes, built a strong government team backed by a highly competent and virtually corruption-free civil service, created a credible defence force from scratch, and masterminded

Singapore's external relations. He led the PAP to six more electoral victories before stepping down as prime minister in November 1990 in favour of GOH CHOK TONG, after preparing an entire tier of second-generation leaders to take over. By then, he was the longest serving prime minister in the world and one of the longest-serving heads of government in Asia.

Lee, however, remained influential as SENIOR MINISTER in the Goh Cabinet, although he resigned as secretary-general of the PAP in November 1992.

Under Lee Kuan Yew's leadership, Singapore had been transformed into one of the most stable, safe, cosmopolitan, and economically successful countries in Asia; a major international and regional shipping, aviation and financial hub which enjoys a role and influence out of proportion to its size.

After resigning as prime minister, Lee found time to research, reflect and write his memoirs. A strong advocate of 'Asian values', Lee held firm to his belief that Western liberal democracy has to be adapted to the special circumstances of Singapore. In August 2004 he was appointed by Prime Minister LEE HSIEN LOONG, his son, to the new Cabinet position of MINISTER MENTOR.

Lee Kuan Yew School of Public Policy
Autonomous school within the National University of Singapore (NUS). NUS first established a public policy programme (PPP) in 1992 which it developed in partnership with the John F. Kennedy School of Government at Harvard University. In 1998, during a review of the NUS PPP, the Harvard team concluded that a new school of public affairs should be established. The team recommended steps to strengthen the existing master in public policy programme and establish the Lee Kuan Yew fellows programme, offering the master in public management. On the occasion of then Senior Minister LEE KUAN YEW's 80th birthday, funds were raised for the new school. In 2004, the school was established as an autonomous body within NUS, with KISHORE MAHBUBANI as dean. The school offers master's degrees in public policy, public administration and public management, as well as a diverse range of executive programmes.

Lee Lim (1931–1989) Photographer. Lee Lim was noted for his darkroom techniques, such as printing with multiple negatives for a single image. He also adopted the format of scroll paintings in his photographs, adding colophons and Chinese seals in his depictions of kampongs and tropical life. He received a Royal Photographic Society (UK) Fellowship (1959), Artist Distinction (AFIAP) by the International Federation of Photographic Art (1977), and the CULTURAL MEDALLION (1987). The Photographic Society of

Lee Rubber Company: the Nee Soon factory, 1953

Singapore also conferred an honorary fellowship on Lee, and named a memorial award after him.

Lee Rubber Company This company was founded by LEE KONG CHIAN, son-in-law of prominent businessman TAN KAH KEE. In 1927, Lee set up a rubber smoking house in Muar, Johor, called Nam Aik Rubber Company. The name was changed to Lee Rubber Company in 1929. The company was involved in planting, processing and manufacture of RUBBER; the planting of PINEAPPLES; and food canning. It soon expanded to other parts of Southeast Asia. The family-owned rubber company went on to become the largest rubber house in the world, with factories in Malaysia and Indonesia. It is a leading producer and exporter of standard rubber and natural latex for the manufacture of tyres and gloves.

Lee Seng Gee (1921–) Businessman and philanthropist. The eldest son of LEE KONG CHIAN, Lee Seng Gee was educated in Singapore and then in the United States, graduating with a bachelor of economics degree from the University of Pennsylvania and an MBA from the Wharton Business School.

Lee was about to begin his PhD studies when World War II ended, but was asked to return to Singapore to help re-establish the family's Lee Rubber Group of companies (*see* LEE RUBBER COMPANY). The group owned rubber, oil palm and pineapple plantations in Malaya. In 1947, Lee went to Indonesia to rebuild the family business there. By 1949, all the Lee factories were turning profits. In 1955, he took over the management of the Lee Group's Indonesian companies, and in 1965, became chairman and chief executive officer of the entire Lee Group in Singapore. He became chairman of the LEE FOUNDATION in 1967.

Lee Seng Tee (1924–) Businessman and philanthropist. The son of LEE KONG CHIAN, Lee Seng Tee was educated in Singapore and North America, graduating from the Wharton School of Business in 1950. Like his brothers (*see* LEE SENG GEE and LEE SENG WEE), he quickly became involved in the family business, becoming a director of the

Lee Group of companies and eventually chairman of Lee Pineapple Company.

Lee's record of philanthropy and support for scholarship includes benefactions to Wolfson College, Cambridge University; Oriel College and Bodleian Library, Oxford University; the British Academy; Victoria University, New Zealand; Harvard University; the American Academy of Arts and Sciences; London University; the National University of Singapore; and Singapore Management University. He is a fellow of Wolfson College, Cambridge University; honorary fellow of the British Academy and of Oriel College, Oxford University; and foreign honorary member of the American Academy of Arts and Sciences. Named in his honour are the Lee Seng Tee Reading Rooms at Cambridge and Oxford Universities; the S.T. Lee Lounge at the Library of the University of Pennsylvania; and the Lee Seng Tee Research Library at Addenbrooke's Hospital in Cambridge.

Lee Seng Wee (1930–) Banker. The youngest son of LEE KONG CHIAN, Lee Seng Wee was educated in Singapore and then Canada, where he studied engineering. He later earned an MBA at the University of Western Ontario. He joined LEE RUBBER COMPANY in 1951, eventually becoming vice-chairman. In 1995, he took over as chairman of Oversea-Chinese Banking Corporation, a position he held until 2003. He has also served as chairman of the Singapore International Foundation and on the board of the Government of Singapore Investment Corporation, the Board of Commissioners of Currency and the Council of Presidential Advisors. Lee was admitted into the DISTINGUISHED SERVICE ORDER in 2001. He was listed as the third richest man in Singapore according to the *Forbes* 2006 Billionaires List

Lee Shu Fen (1925–) Dancer and choreographer. Born Shi Yuxiu in Taiwan, Lee Shufen learnt her first dance steps from her mother before training in ballet and folk dancing in Tokyo. A prominent dancer, choreographer and teacher in Taiwan, she settled in Singapore in the 1960s and choreographed extensively for the National Dance Company, the People's Association Dance Company and other groups.

Lee's best known works include cross-cultural works such as *Unity in Rhythm* (1980)—a joint effort with choreographers SOM SAID and MADHAVI KRISHNAN—and adaptations of Chinese mythology and literature, such as *Dream of the Red Chamber* (1989). In 1991, former students founded the Lee Shu Fen & Dancers Society.

Lee Siew Choh (1917–2002) Politician. Lee Siew Choh was born in Kuala Lumpur, the son of a Chinese schoolteacher. He was educated at Victoria Institution in Kuala Lumpur, where he was Treacher Scholar (1933) and Rodger Scholar (1934), and then at the King Edward VII College of Medicine in Singapore where he captained the rugby team for seven years. He was a top student and passed his licentiate in medicine and surgery with distinction in medicine in 1942. He started out as a physician at Kandang Kerbau Hospital but later set up the Rakyat Clinic on Rochor Road.

Lee was recruited as a member of the People's Action Party (PAP) by GOH KENG SWEE, and won the Queenstown constituency seat in the 1959 elections. In 1960, he was appointed parliamentary secretary to the Ministry of Home Affairs.

In 1961, he and 13 other members of Parliament resigned from the PAP and formed the BARISAN SOSIALIS (BS). The BS objected to merger with Malaysia, and Lee gave the longest speech ever delivered in Singapore's Legislative Assembly—over seven hours' long—on the topic. Lee was a fiery orator who could switch between several languages easily. His election speeches were always well-attended. As party chairman, he led the BS to win 13 of 51 seats contested during the GENERAL ELECTION (1963). However, Lee himself lost to TOH CHIN CHYE in Rochor constituency by a mere 89 votes. He retired from politics in 1966.

When the BS merged with the WORKERS' PARTY in 1988, Lee stood as a Workers' Party candidate in the Eunos group representation constituency in the general election of 1988. He lost, but was appointed the first NON-CONSTITUENCY MEMBER OF PARLIAMENT. He retired from politics for a second time in 1993.

Lee Seiu Kin (1954–) Judge. Born in Seremban, Lee Seiu Kin was educated at St Paul's Institution in Seremban before coming to Singapore to study at National Junior College as an ASEAN Scholar. He won a Colombo Plan Scholarship to study engineering at the University of Adelaide and joined the Public Works Department (PWD) as an engineer. He obtained a masters degree in construction engineering from the National University of Singapore (NUS) in 1982, and in 1984 was inducted into the inaugural advanced graduate programme at the NUS Faculty of Law. He then obtained his master's degree in law at Cambridge University in 1987 and joined the legal service as deputy public prosecutor. From 1997 to 2002, he served as judicial commissioner, and from 2002 to 2006, as second solicitor-general. He was elevated to the Bench as puisne judge in 2006.

Lee Tiah Khee (1965–) Photographer. Lee Tiah Khee received the YOUNG ARTIST AWARD (Photography) in 1993, and became an associate of the Royal Photographic Society in the United Kingdom. He has won many photography prizes, including

Lee Tiah Khee

the Distinguished Photographer Award in the 25th Anniversary National Photo Competition (1990), and first prize (open section) in the Singapore Red Cross Photographic Competition (2004). In 2004, he was appointed chief photographer at LIANHE ZAOBAO.

Lee Tzu Pheng (1946–) Poet. Lee Tzu Pheng graduated from the University of Malaya (Singapore) and taught at the university from 1969 until her retirement in 2001. Many of the poems in her first volume, *Prospect of a Drowning* (1980), including Lee's most anthologized poem, 'My Country and My People', were written during her undergraduate years. 'My Country and My People' was banned in the early 1970s from being read over the air, presumably because it was deemed unpatriotic.

Lee Siew Choh

Against the Next Wave (1988) signalled Lee's return to poetry after a long silence, the product of a troubled period in her personal life. Lee's poetic reawakening may be attributed to the spiritual awakening that led to her conversion to Roman Catholicism in 1989. The religious quest for personal salvation and fulfilment in *The Brink of an Amen* (1991) and *Lambada by Galilee and Other Surprises* (1997) is further confirmed by poems which commemorate Lee's pilgrimages to Europe (1990) and the Middle East (1992). Among the several satirical poems in *Lambada by Galilee*, 'The Merlion to Ulysses' was the first poetic critique of EDWIN THUMBOO's iconic 'Ulysses By the Merlion'.

Lee won the National Book Development Council of Singapore Award for Poetry in 1982 for *Prospect of a Drowning*, and in 1992 for both *Against the Next Wave* and *The Brink of an Amen*. She received the CULTURAL MEDALLION for Literature in 1985 and the Southeast Asia Write Award in 1987. In 1996, she received both the Gabriela Mistral Award from the government of Chile for her poetry and promotion of children's reading—Lee wrote *Growing Readers* (1987), a children's reading guide—and the Montblanc-NUS Centre for the Arts Literary Award for services to literature.

Lee Wen (1957–) Artist. Lee Wen studied at LASALLE-SIA College of the Arts and the City of London Polytechnic. He is best

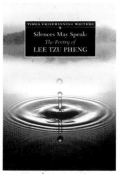

Lee Tzu Pheng: Silences May Speak (1999) (below); the author.

Lee Wen: Yellow Man.

Lee Yong Leng

known for his performance art spectacle, *Yellow Man*, which addresses the politics of post-colonial, ethnic and urban identities. His *Yellow Man* persona is Lee stripped bare, except for briefs, and coated in yellow paint.

Lee's *A Waking Dream* features his drawings and poems—signalling the surrealist-influenced, quirky dramas of later performances. His activities have extended to giving lectures, writing critiques and curating art programmes. He participated in the 4th Asian Art Show, Fukuoka (1994), the Kwang Ju Biennial (1995), Sexta Bienal de La Habana (1997), 3rd Asia-Pacific Triennial (1999), Busan Biennale (2004), and National Review of Live Art (Scotland, 2004–05).

Lee Wen was the artistic director of Future of Imagination (2003), a performance art initiative. A recipient of the CULTURAL MEDALLION in 2005, Lee has been appointed associate artist (visual art) at THE SUBSTATION. He is based in Tokyo and Singapore.

Lee Yock Suan (1946–) Politician. Lee Yock Suan was educated at Queenstown Secondary School and Raffles Institution. He won a President's Scholarship to study at Imperial College London, graduating with first class honours in chemical engineering (1969). He then joined the Economic Development Board and rose to become divisional director of projects. In 1981, he joined Petrochemical Corporation of Singapore (Pte) Ltd as deputy managing director.

Lee entered politics in 1980, winning a seat in Cheng San constituency on the People's Action Party (PAP) ticket. He served as minister of state for national development (1981–83) and finance (1983–84); acting minister for labour (1985–86); minister for labour (1987–91), minister for education (1992–97), minister for trade and industry (1997–98); second minister for finance (1997–98); minister for trade and industry (1998–99); minister for information and the arts (1999–2001), and minister for the environment (1999–2001).

At the time of his retirement in 2005, he was minister in the Prime Minister's Office and second minister for foreign affairs.

Lee Yong Leng (1930–) Academic and diplomat. Lee Yong Leng graduated from the University of Malaya with an honours degree in arts. He obtained a master's degree at Oxford University, and a PhD in geography at the University of Singapore (1969), specializing in population and settlement in Sarawak. In 1956, Lee joined the University of Malaya as a lecturer, eventually rising to the rank of full professor. From 1971 to 1975, he served as Singapore's high commissioner to the United Kingdom.

Leeson, Nick (1967–) Futures trader who caused the collapse of the United Kingdom's oldest merchant bank, Barings, in 1995. Arriving in Singapore in 1992, after Barings had acquired a seat on the Singapore International Monetary Exchange (Simex), Nick Leeson began as the derivatives operations manager of Barings Futures. He became general manager the following year, and started dealing in Japanese government bonds, then dabbling in Nikkei 225 futures and options.

Holding the positions of both chief trader and head of settlements, Leeson was able to conceal his losses and unauthorized trades in an error account with the designation 88888. Ironically, Leeson's superiors in London had sanctioned the setting-up of this account, which was used initially to track bona fide trading mistakes and minor accounting discrepancies.

By December 1994, with undetected losses mounting to US$512 million, Leeson bet heavily against the Nikkei index falling below the 19,000 mark. The Japanese economy was stable at the time, so this move was quite reasonable. However, the Nikkei plunged after an earthquake hit the Japanese city of Kobe on 17 January 1995. In a futile bid to claw back escalating losses, Leeson continued to raise the stakes. By the time Barings discovered the deficit in mid-February 1995, it amounted to US$1.3 billion, exceeding the bank's capital and reserves.

Leeson fled to Malaysia, before catching a flight to London, but was arrested en route in Frankfurt. He was sentenced in

Nick Leeson: at Changi Airport, 1995.

1995 to six-and-a-half years in prison in Singapore, but was released in 1999 for good behaviour.

The Futures Trading Act was tightened after the Barings debacle. However, investigations revealed that much of the blame lay in the bank management's failure to implement strong internal controls in audit and compliance matters. The absence of such safeguards eventually allowed a single employee—one who had failed his final mathematics exams in school—to bring down a 233-year-old financial institution.

In March 1995, Barings was sold for a token £1 to the Dutch ING Group, which agreed to take over the bank's debt. Many of Barings top executives resigned or were dismissed, including its chief executive officer, Peter Norris, and chairman, Peter Baring. The Nick Leeson story made newspaper headlines around the world, inspiring books and a film, *Rogue Trader* (1999), starring Ewan McGregor.

legal education Prior to the establishment of the Department of Law at the University of Malaya in 1956, no formal legal education was available in Singapore. Anyone wishing to study law had to travel to the United Kingdom to study either at a British university or at one of the four Inns of Court. Some law was formally taught at Raffles College before World War II, to the Malayan Administrative Service probationers, but this was sporadic at best.

The first public suggestion that a local law faculty should be set up came from Professor C. Northcote Parkinson in an article entitled 'University Hopes of Tomorrow', published in *The Straits Times* on 3 March 1953. Three months later, the University of Malaya's vice-chancellor, Sir Sydney Caine, intimated that he would like to see an independent faculty of law at the university 'in the fairly near future'. A chair of law was created in December 1953, as part of the Social Studies Faculty, with a view to creating a distinct faculty by 1957.

Meanwhile, the University of Malaya commissioned Professor R.G.D. Allen, a professor of statistics at the University of London, and Sir Roland Braddell, one of the most senior and respected members of the local Bar, to conduct a study into the organization of courses in social studies and law. The Allen-Braddell Report recommended that separate faculties of social studies and law be established.

On 10 March 1956, Caine announced that the long-awaited Department of Law would be established at the university, and as a first step, some law teaching would begin in October 1957. Dr Lionel Astor Sheridan, a 29-year-old barrister-at-law (Lincoln's Inn), was appointed to the Chair in law, becoming the first professor of law and head of the Law Department. The Law Department became a full faculty of law in 1959. By the 1980s, the Law Faculty of the

National University of Singapore was the main provider of legal education in Singapore.

legal profession Singapore's legal profession developed in parallel with the city's economic growth. In the early years of British administration, the Second Charter of Justice provided for five types of law representatives: advocates, solicitors, attorneys, proctors and agents. The first regulation of lawyers came in the 1830s when licences were granted to law agents to practise. Law agents were mainly merchants who also undertook legal work. The first of these was WILLIAM NAPIER, who was admitted as law agent in 1833. There was little regulation for many years, and it was only in 1862 that Sir William Jefcott was able to impose special qualifications and examinations for lawyers. When the Straits Settlements was established in 1867, provisions were made for the admission of advocates and attorneys.

An important statute governing the legal profession was the Courts Ordinance of 1873. Admission was restricted to those admitted as barristers or solicitors in England, Scotland or Ireland, or those who passed a local examination. A yearly fee was also imposed. At the same time, any person who was not enrolled but practised litigation was made guilty of contempt of court, and subject to a fine of up to $250. Thus the law became the province of professionals only. The Bar Council was also formally instituted; its first honorary secretary was Alan Donaldson. The first lawyers admitted to the Bar were former law agents, the first being James S. Atchison, who was admitted in 1859. In 1893, SONG ONG SIANG, became the first Asian to be called to the Bar. Song had studied law at Cambridge University on a Queen's Scholarship.

In 1878, further changes were introduced. Instead of advocates and attorneys, lawyers were styled advocates and solicitors, a designation that remains to this day. Furthermore, local qualifications were recognized for the first time. In 1907, provisions were made for articled clerks (formerly law clerks) to be examined for qualification as lawyers. Women lawyers were admitted for the first time under an amendment to the law in 1927. According to the rolls of the Supreme Court, the first woman to be admitted to the Singapore Bar was Lim Beng Hong, on 4 July 1927.

Lawyers in each of the Straits Settlements formed themselves into associations known as Bar committees. The Bar committee was elected by a meeting of advocates and solicitors in that settlement, and presided over by the senior advocate and solicitor. It had two main functions: to make representations as to the character of persons seeking admission; and to investigate complaints against advocates and solicitors. Following Singapore's independence in 1965, the Singapore Advocates and

Solicitors Society, together with the Board of Legal Education, was established under the Legal Profession Act. The former replaced the Bar Committee while the latter regulated professional education for local graduates. In 1970, the Advocates and Solicitors Society was renamed the LAW SOCIETY.

Qualification for legal practice has become more complicated over the years. Before the Faculty of Law was established in Singapore, qualification was either by article clerkship or qualification and a call to the Bar in the United Kingdom. Since 1961, local degrees have been recognized, alongside British qualifications. Later, recognition was accorded to Malaysian practitioners. Today, the Legal Profession Act recognizes law degrees from designated law schools in the United Kingdom, Australia, New Zealand and the United States for the purposes of admission to the Bar. However, foreign graduands must have done reasonably well in order to qualify for practice. The local law school provides the bulk of each cohort.

All lawyers who have been called to the Bar are advocates and solicitors of the Supreme Court of Singapore. There is no distinction between solicitors and barristers.

In 1996, a new class of lawyers was created, that of SENIOR COUNSEL. Lawyers who have more than ten years of legal experience may apply to be made Senior Counsel. The concept of Senior Counsel is akin to that of QUEEN'S COUNSEL in the United Kingdom.

legal system The main sources of Singapore law are the CONSTITUTION, common law, equity, statutes and customary law. The English common law system was formally imported into Singapore through the grant of Letters Patent known as the Second Charter of Justice. From that date (27 November 1826), all of the English common law, equity and English statutes became part of Singapore law.

Singapore has a unicameral legislature; there is a single chamber elected during general elections. Bills are usually introduced by the government through the relevant minister, although there have been a few private member's Bills. Under section 3 of the Interpretation Act, every Act shall be a public Act affecting the whole community. Each Bill goes through three readings before being passed into law as an Act (also known as a statute). All statutes must be published in the *Government Gazette*. Although Singapore now passes the bulk of its own statutes, some English statutes are still made applicable to Singapore through the Application of English Law Act.

The executive branch of government comprises the president, the prime minister and his Cabinet. The prime minister and Cabinet are drawn from among the members of Parliament and the member who

commands the confidence of the majority of the House is appointed prime minister.

Up until 1991, the president was nominated and elected by Parliament. The president's office was essentially a ceremonial one. This changed in 1991, with the creation of the elected presidency. The President is now popularly elected, and has limited powers to veto legislation that would draw down Singapore's foreign reserves, and appointments to key posts in the civil service. The president's veto has never been used.

Under Article 93 of the Constitution, judicial power is vested in the Supreme Court and in the SUBORDINATE COURTS. The independence of the judiciary is constitutionally safeguarded through provisions guaranteeing security of remuneration to all judges, and security of tenure (up to age 65) for Supreme Court judges.

There are two main tiers of courts: the Supreme Court and the Subordinate Courts. The Supreme Court comprises both the Court of Appeal and the High Court. Since 1994, the Court of Appeal has been Singapore's final appellate court. Its decisions are final and there can be no appeal against them. The CHIEF JUSTICE, who is the president of the court and justices of appeal, heads the Court of Appeal. The chief justice also heads the High Court on which sit PUISNE JUDGES and JUDICIAL COMMISSIONERS. The High Court has unlimited original jurisdiction in civil and criminal cases and has the sole jurisdiction to try all criminal cases involving CAPITAL PUNISHMENT.

As Singapore's justice system is based on the common law model, litigation is an adversarial process where lawyers for contending parties argue their case in court, with minimal intervention by the judge. (This is in contrast to the civil law system where judges play a more inquisitorial role.) In recent years, Singapore's judicial system has been recast to discourage litigation. Parties are encouraged to resolve their disputes through mediation and negotiation instead.

Legislative Assembly Election (1955) First election under the Rendel Constitution, which provided for the replacement of the Legislative Council with the Legislative Assembly. Of the 32 members on the Legislative Assembly, 25 would be elected

Legislative Assembly Election (1955): David Marshall, left, with Lee Kuan Yew; campaign poster (right).

Legislative Council Election (1948): group photo of members of the Legislative Council.

by the people. A total of 79 candidates contested the 25 seats; 158,424 out of the 298,042 eligible voters cast ballots. Nomination Day was 28 February 1955, and a month-long campaign period was assigned. Voting took place on 2 April 1955.

The front-runners for the election were the SINGAPORE PROGRESSIVE PARTY (SPP), which had dominated all elections since 1948, and the newly formed DEMOCRATIC PARTY (DP), a party funded by the Chinese Chamber of Commerce. However, the LABOUR FRONT, led by DAVID MARSHALL, won ten of the 25 seats. The remaining seats were won by the SPP (four), the DP (two), the PEOPLE'S ACTION PARTY (PAP) (three), the SINGAPORE ALLIANCE PARTY (SAP) (three) and independents (three). David Marshall forged a coalition government with the SAP and became Singapore's first chief minister.

Legislative Assembly Election (1959)

First election for a fully elected legislative body. Changes wrought by the 1958 Constitution of the State of Singapore, provided for a fully elected, 51-seat legislative assembly. It also introduced automatic voter registration and made voting compulsory. Nomination Day was 25 April 1959 and Polling Day was 30 May 1959, giving the parties a lengthy 35-day campaign period. A total of 194 candidates contested the election—34 independents and the rest representing 12 political parties.

Legislative Assembly Election (1959): PAP celebrating success.

The PEOPLE'S ACTION PARTY (PAP), led by LEE KUAN YEW, secured 53.4 per cent of votes cast and won 43 seats. The Singapore People's Alliance, led by LIM YEW HOCK, former chief minister, won four seats. The only independent to win a seat was Lee Choon Eng, who did so in Bukit Merah constituency. Following the elections, the PAP formed government and Lee Kuan Yew became Singapore's first prime minister.

Legislative Council Election (1948)

First post-war election. Soon after the re-establishment of civil government in Singapore on 1 April 1946, a reconstitution committee was appointed by the governor, Sir FRANKLIN GIMSON, to make recommendations for developing existing executive and legislative bodies, and widening representation. The CONSTITUTION that was subsequently proposed made provisions for a 22-seat legislative council, comprising nine officials and 13 unofficials, of whom four would be nominated by the governor, three elected by the Chinese and Indian chambers of commerce (to reflect the importance of trade to the colony's future prosperity), and the remaining six by popular ballot. Only registered adult voters who had been British subjects for at least a year prior to the election were eligible to vote.

Though the franchise was limited, the recommendation of an unofficial majority was a step forward, and was far in advance of the constitutions of the MALAYAN UNION and its successor, the FEDERATION OF MALAYA, where no provisions for elected legislative councillors had been made. But public response to the registration exercise from August to September 1947 was muted. Only 22,395 out of an estimated 200,000 eligible voters registered, with the majority (45 per cent) being Indian British subjects. A mere 25 per cent of those who registered to vote were Chinese British subjects.

After the MALAYAN DEMOCRATIC UNION boycotted the election on the grounds that the process was not sufficiently democratic, only one other party, the SINGAPORE PROGRESSIVE PARTY (SPP), took part. It fielded five candidates against ten

independents for the six seats. On polling day (20 March 1948), three SPP candidates were elected, and the remaining three seats went to independents. Despite the Chinese-majority population, only one of the six elected councillors was Chinese (C.C. TAN of the SPP). Three were Indian, one was British and one was Malay.

Legislative Council Election (1951)

Second post-war election, held on 10 April 1951. British plans for post-war Singapore's political advancement through the electoral experiment continued after the lacklustre LEGISLATIVE COUNCIL ELECTION (1948). Faced with a full-blown communist insurgency from June 1948, the British were, however, not keen to accelerate constitutional change. Rather, they deferred to their traditional doctrine of tutelage, that would see the country take small steps to self-government through gradual reform. While the number of seats in the new 1951 legislature increased from 22 to 25, only nine seats would be popularly elected.

The CONSTITUTION, however, would permit the Legislative Council to elect two of their members to serve on the Executive Council, where there would be the same number of officials and non-officials for the first time. However, the British would remain in charge, with the governor retaining powers over reserved matters, including veto powers over the proceedings of the Legislative Council.

As before, the British-subject franchise was retained, although it was enlarged to include British-protected persons born in the federation, Sarawak, British North Borneo (present-day Sabah) and Brunei. To curb unwarranted alien influence in the elections, however, certain safeguards were introduced, such as extending the residential qualification for voters from one to three years.

Again, there was no automatic registration of eligible voters, and electoral interest was consequently weak. Only 48,155 people registered to vote, of which only 52 per cent voted on polling day, despite a 32-day campaign. This poor turnout may have reflected the after-effects of the MARIA HERTOGH RIOTS in 1950.

Only two political parties contested the election. The SINGAPORE PROGRESSIVE PARTY (SPP) contested eight seats and won six. Its chief rival, the SINGAPORE LABOUR PARTY, newly formed in 1948, captured two of the seven seats it contested. The remaining seat went to one of seven independent candidates.

Lembaga Biasiswa Kenangan Maulud

Prophet Muhammad's Birthday Memorial Scholarship Fund Board, originally known as the Prophet Muhammad's Birthday Memorial Donation Committee. It was formed on 23 June 1963 at a meeting of Muslim organizations to discuss celebra-

Legislative Council Election (1951): ballot boxes.

tions to commemorate the PROPHET MUHAMMAD'S BIRTHDAY. A prominent Arab businessman, Syed Ali Redha Alsagoff, mooted the idea of holding a flag day to collect donations. Instead of having large-scale celebrations, part of the proceeds could be put into a fund for needy students. A total of $3,600 was raised on flag day that year.

The Prophet Muhammad's Memorial Scholarship Fund Board was set up formally on 22 August 1965. The board provides bursaries to students, and financial grants for research projects of an educational, cultural, economic, social or religious nature. By its 40th year, it had disbursed more than $6 million worth of bursaries and study grants to more than 9,000 students.

Lennox-Boyd, Alan (1904–1983) British politician and colonial official. Alan Tindal Lennox-Boyd was educated at Sherborne School in Dorset, United Kingdom, and then at Christ Church, Oxford University, where he read law. From 1931 to 1960, he was Conservative member of Parliament for Mid-Bedfordshire. He was admitted to the Bar (Inner Temple) in 1941 and became privy councillor in 1951.

From 1954 to 1959, Lennox-Boyd was secretary of state for the colonies, and handled the delicate negotiations preceding Singapore's self-government. Most notably, he presided over the constitutional talks of 1956 and 1957, and negotiations concerning Singapore's CONSTITUTION in 1958.

Alan Lennox-Boyd

After stepping down from government, he became managing director of Arthur Guinness & Sons (1959–67).

Leong Yoon Pin (1931–) Composer. Leong Yoon Pin was a student of Nadia Boulanger in Paris during the 1960s. His music, including two symphonies, combines Asian melodic spontaneity and strong harmonic foundations with European traditions and contemporary devices. His opera *Bunga Mawar* (Rose Flower) (1997), based on Peranakan culture, was probably the first Western-style opera to be written by a Singaporean. He was made the SINGAPORE SYMPHONY ORCHESTRA'S (SSO) first composer-in-residence in 2001, and his most famous work, *Dayung Sampan* (Rowing the Boat)*,* was recorded by the SSO for its tenth anniversary CD. Leong was awarded the CULTURAL MEDALLION in 1982.

Leow Siak Fah (1939–) Businessman and singer. Born in Malaysia and trained in law, Leow Siak Fah was active in singing, opera production and direction before he became founding chairman of the Singapore Lyric Opera (SLO) in 1990. An amateur singer, he has studied with Vera Rozsa (Dame Kiri Te Kanawa's voice teacher), and has sung lead tenor roles in SLO productions of *Carmen, Tosca, The Merry Widow, Fiddler on the Roof* and *Bunga Mawar* (Rose Flower). He has also been active in introducing Western opera to Malaysia, Thailand and the Philippines.

Les Amis Gourmet French restaurant and restaurant group. The flagship Les Amis ('Friends') was opened on 15 March 1994. The restaurant serves fine French cuisine. In 1998, Les Amis opened its second restaurant, Au Jardin, and two weeks after that, Café Les Amis. Both these outlets are located in the Singapore Botanic Gardens, with Au Jardin in a restored colonial black-and-white house. In 2003 and 2004, The Les Amis Group opened more outlets: the high-end Japanese restaurant Aoki, The Canteen and Lazy Gourmet Deli (all at Shaw Centre); Canelé Pâtisserie—Chocolaterie (at Robertson Walk); and Sebastien's Bistrot, Coq & Bull Rotisserie & Grill, and L'estaminet Peperoni Pizzaria (all at Greenwood Avenue). In 2004, long-time executive chef Justin Quek left the group to start up his own business. In 2006, The Canteen was replaced with La Strada, an Italian restaurant, while the Lazy Gourmet Deli was replaced with La Strada Pizzeria. The Coq & Bull Rotisserie & Grill was renamed The Grill On Hillcrest in 2006.

Li Jiawei (1981–) Sportswoman. China-born Li Jiawei first represented Singapore in table tennis after emigrating to Singapore at age 15. By 2000, she was ranked 18th in the world, moving up to fourth place in the rankings within the following five years.

Les Amis

The four-time Sportswoman of the Year (2002, 2003, 2004, 2005) won three of the four gold medals at stake at the 14th Commonwealth Championships in 2001. She is a Commonwealth Games gold medallist (Manchester, 2002), and an Asian Games bronze medallist (Busan, 2002).

Li also represented Singapore at the Sydney (2000) and Athens (2004) Olympic Games. Her semi-final match against North Korea's Kim Hyang Mi at the Athens Olympics was one of Singapore's most dramatic televised sporting events; Li was two points away from victory before succumbing. Li has been inducted into the SINGAPORE SPORTS COUNCIL HALL OF FAME.

Li Li (1983–) Sportswoman. China-born Li Li joined the national badminton squad after arriving in Singapore at age 14. In 2002, she became Singapore's first Commonwealth women's singles champion, when she defeated Tracey Hallam for the gold medal in Manchester. This led to her entry into the SINGAPORE SPORTS COUNCIL HALL OF FAME.

One year later, she was part of the Singapore team that won the Southeast Asian Games gold medal in Vietnam. In 2004, she won both the Croatia International and the Iran Fajr International, and represented Singapore at the Olympic Games in Athens. In 2005, she defeated Xie Xingfang of China (ranked second in the world at the time) in the first round of the Proton Malaysia Tournament, and climbed to 20th in the world rankings.

Li Nanxing (1964–) Actor. Nicknamed 'Singapore's Chow Yun Fatt', Li Nanxing started his acting career with the Singapore Broadcasting Corporation in 1986. He is best remembered by audiences in Singapore, Malaysia and China for his role in the trilogy *Shuang Tian Zhi Zun I, II and III* (The Unbeatables I, II and III) (1993, 1996, 2002).

In 1995, he won the first Best Actor Award (Star Awards) for his performance in the telemovie *Shang Cheng Ji* (Wounded

Leong Yoon Pin

Leow Siak Fah

Li Jiawei: at the Asian Games in Busan, 2002.

Li Li: after her Commonwealth win in Manchester, 2002.

Li Nanxing

Lian Shisheng: Qiu Shui Ji *(1974)*.

Liang Wenfu

Lianhe Wanbao

Lianhe Zaobao

Liberal Socialist Party: logo

Tracks) (1994). He was also the first MediaCorp artiste to cross over to film, acting alongside Hong Kong star Andy Lau in the movie *Qi Yi Lu Cheng (What a Wonderful World)* (1995). At the Star Awards, he was voted Best Male Actor in Malaysia (2003), one of the Top 5 Most Popular Male Artistes (1994–96) and since 1997, one of the Top 10 Most Popular Male Artistes

After 18 years of acting, Li took part-time directing and scriptwriting classes at New York University in 2003. The following year, he signed a five-year contract with American artist management company LNX Global, and was introduced to English-speaking audiences as Jonathan Li.

Li Sisong, Peter and Li Weisong, Paul (both 1966–) Singers and songwriters. Twin brothers Peter Li Sisong and Paul Li Weisong made their mark composing the theme songs for many local Mandarin television serials and dramas. Their careers were launched when Paul participated in and won Singapore Broadcasting Corporation's *Talentime*. They released five albums between 1987 and 1992 before moving on to writing songs for Hong Kong artistes such as Sandy Lam, Aaron Kwok and Andy Lau, among others. They are also linked to the *xinyao* movement of the 1980s and 1990s (*see* CHINESE POPULAR MUSIC).

In 1995, Paul founded the Lee Wei Song School of Music to train and groom singers and musicians, while Peter moved on to songwriting and set up Tofu Street, a music production company. Paul is credited with having discovered STEFANIE SUN, who was a student at the Lee Wei Song School from 1997 and 2000. The two brothers were awarded the Special Achievement Award at MediaCorp's 2001 Star Awards.

Li Xueling (1938–1989) Musician and conductor. One of the most important and influential figures in CHINESE CLASSICAL MUSIC to be born and trained in Singapore, Li Xueling was known for his skill on the *yangqin* (Chinese dulcimer), and was sought after as a conductor of Chinese orchestras. Many of the current generation of Chinese orchestral musicians were nurtured by him.

Li was the assistant principal leader of the National Theatre Chinese Orchestra when it was formed in May 1968. Four

Peter Li Sisong, left, and Paul Li Weisong

years later, he was appointed music director. During his tenure, he expanded the orchestra in every department. He also mentored many young musicians who later became professional musicians, arrangers and composers. Li applied this training and development approach to all the orchestras he conducted or guest conducted, including the National Theatre and the Ministry of Education Youth Chinese Orchestras, the People's Association Chinese Orchestra and the Singapore Armed Forces Reservists Association Chinese Orchestra.

Li devoted much effort to designing training programmes at the National Theatre and the Ministry of Education. During his career, he initiated many musical exchanges, and conducted and performed concerts in Singapore, Australia, Hong Kong, Malaysia, the Philippines and Switzerland.

Lian Shisheng (1907–1973) Editor and author. As chief commentator and editor-in-chief with NANYANG SIANG PAU from 1948 to 1971, Lian Shisheng was influential and respected as an intellectual and writer. He published 24 volumes of travel writing, essays, letters and biographies. His best known book is *Hai Bin Ji Jian* (Seaside Letters) (6 volumes, 1963–74). These essays, in the form of letters, were first serialized in the literary supplements of *Nanyang Siang Pau*. By sharing his experiences as a social and cultural leader and drawing from traditional Chinese ideas, Lian sought to inspire young people. His life and works have continued to provoke and inspire readers since his death.

Liang Wenfu (unknown–) Singer, songwriter and poet. In a 2003 COMPASS poll, Liang Wenfu was voted the person 'most representative of the *xinyao* spirit' (*see* CHINESE POPULAR MUSIC). The same poll placed seven of his songs among 'the ten greatest *xinyao* songs', with 'Liu Shui Ci' (Song of Flowing Water) (sung by Liang) in top position.

Liang's ability to combine local flavour with literary flair, adding a learned elegance to popular music, gave him the image of a singer-scholar. From 1986 to 1992, he released five albums. Among these, *Men* (Door) (1986) was the first local Mandarin album to be completely composed and written by the same artiste. 'Yi Bu Yi Bu Lai' (One Step at a Time) (1987) sat for six weeks at the top of the charts, while 'Lian Zhi Qi' (Love's Refuge)(1986) was at the top for 29 weeks, an unbroken record for a local pop song (*see* JIANG HU)

Liang is also a writer and poet, the first recipient of the National Art Council's YOUNG ARTIST AWARD (1992). His works, such as the essay collection, *Zui Hou De Niu Che Shui* (The Last Years of Kreta Ayer) (1988); poetry collection *Qi Shi Wo Shi Zai He Shi Guang Lian Ai* (In Fact I am in Love

with Time) (1989); and short-story collection entitled *Liang Wenfu De 21 Ge Meng* (The 21 Dreams of Liang Wenfu) (1992) showed a new direction for Singapore Chinese literature. They recorded the changes in modes of feeling and expression brought about by the pressure and complexity of life in a post-modern society.

In the mid-1990s, Liang turned to teaching and research but continued to compose works for a new generation of local and overseas singers. He wrote Singapore's first Mandarin musical, *Yu Ji* (December Rains) in 1997.

Lianhe Wanbao Newspaper. This Chinese-language broadsheet is published by SINGAPORE PRESS HOLDINGS. It was established on 16 March 1983, following the merger of NANYANG SIANG PAU and SIN CHEW JIT POH. It is a tabloid-style newspaper which focuses on human-interest stories and the latest news. It is written in simpler Chinese than its sister paper LIANHE ZAOBAO.

Lianhe Zaobao Newspaper. Published by Singapore Press Holdings, *Lianhe Zaobao* is the highest circulating Chinese daily in Singapore. It has a daily readership of about 600,000. It is also circulated in Indonesia, Brunei, Hong Kong, Vietnam and major cities of China including Beijing and Shanghai. It was established in 1983 with the merger of NANYANG SIANG PAU and SIN CHEW JIT POH. The internet edition, Zaobao.com, has an estimated 8 million page views a day, accounted for mainly by readers from China.

Liberal Socialist Party The Liberal Socialist Party (LSP) was a centrist conservative political party formed by the merger of the SINGAPORE PROGRESSIVE PARTY and the DEMOCRATIC PARTY (DP), just before the LEGISLATIVE ASSEMBLY ELECTION (1959), in which the LSP did not win any seats.

libraries See PUBLIC LIBRARIES.

Lido Theatre Owned by the Shaw Organisation (*see* SHAW BROTHERS), Lido Theatre was developed on Orchard Road within the same ten-level complex as Shaw House. The theatre obtained its certificate of fitness on 4 February 1959 and was inaugurated by Sir Robert Scott, then commissioner-general for Southeast Asia. The MGM film *Torpedo Run* (1958) was screened for the opening's charity premiere, the first of many charity film screenings there. Lido, as the widest single-screen theatre, soon outstripped Shaw's CAPITOL THEATRE as the most popular 'picture palace' for blockbusters such as *Ben Hur* (1959) and *Lawrence of Arabia* (1962), as well as most of the James Bond movies. Lido was also the red-carpet venue for 'glamour visits' by stars like Greta Garbo and, more recently, Michelle Yeoh and Tom Cruise. Renovations in 1993 and 1997 extended the building into a 22-storey complex for offices, shops and restaurants, as well as a cineplex.

Lien, Margaret (1942–) Businesswoman. Wife of the late LIEN YING CHOW, Margaret Lien Wen Hsien holds an honours degree in law from the London School of Economics. Her appointments include governor of the LIEN FOUNDATION, and director of Lien Ying Chow Pte Ltd, Wah Hin & Co. Ltd, United Overseas Bank and Overseas Union Enterprise. She has served as president of the Singapore Girl Guides Association, a member of the Ladies' League of the Singapore Symphony Orchestra, and a member of the National Parks Board.

Lien Foundation Charitable foundation established by the banker LIEN YING CHOW in 1980. It awards scholarships, such as the Lien Foundation-National Council of Social Services scholarships, and donates to charitable and humanitarian causes.

Lien Ying Chow (1906–2004) Banker, diplomat and community leader. George Lien Ying Chow was born in Dapu, Canton province (present-day Guangdong). He received his early education at home. At the age of ten, he went to Hong Kong, and four years later, arrived in Singapore. He found his first job through a friend who was a ship chandler. In 1928, he established Wah Hin & Co. on Robinson Road and was its general manager. The company supplied hotels in Singapore with imported food and agricultural products from Australia.

At age 34, Lien became the youngest ever president of the Singapore Chinese Chamber of Commerce and Industry. When World War II broke out, he returned to China. Back in Singapore after the war, Lien gathered a number of Malayan-Chinese business leaders to raise the capital required to establish the Overseas Chinese Union Bank Limited. This later became OVERSEAS UNION BANK (OUB). Lien also diversified his business empire and became owner of the Mandarin Hotel.

Lien Ying Chow: greeted by Wee Kim Wee, 1993.

Lien supported education, and was one of the most prominent businessmen involved in setting up NANYANG UNIVERSITY. He also donated generously to the University of Malaya and sat on many school boards. He later established the LIEN FOUNDATION.

In 1963, Lien was awarded the MERITORIOUS SERVICE MEDAL. In 1966, he was appointed high commissioner to Malaysia, being a close friend of the Malaysian prime minister Tunku ABDUL RAHMAN. He served without salary, and played a crucial role in bridging differences between the two countries. Lien retired from active management of business at the age of 89. In 2001, OUB merged with the UNITED OVERSEAS BANK. Lien died in 2004 and was survived by his wife, MARGARET LIEN, as well as four sons and four daughters from three previous marriages.

Lim, Adrian (1942–1988) Adrian Lim, his wife Catherine Tan Mui Choo, and his mistress Hoe Kah Hong, were convicted in 1986 of murdering two children, Agnes Ng Siew Heok and Ghazali Marzuki (aged nine and ten, respectively) in 1981. Lim and Tan were also charged with the murder of Hoe's husband, Loh Ngak Hua.

Lim—a wireman working for Rediffusion—and his conspirators were members of a cult that worshipped the Hindu goddess, Kali. They believed that the sacrifice of children would bring them good luck. The two children were drowned in a bath-tub after being repeatedly tortured, sexually abused and electrocuted. The trio then drunk the children's blood.

Lim's descent began in 1973 when he began practising as a medium. He exploited dance hostesses and prostitutes for his own sexual purposes and for financial gain. Lim's wife, Lilian Tan, divorced him. Lim then married Catherine Tan and the couple took to the stage as a performing duo, with Tan as a stripper. Lim told the court that he had killed the two children as an act of revenge against the police who were 'giving him trouble' with their investigations into Loh's death.

The case, with its elements of gore, sex and black magic, horrified the nation. Tan and Hoe appealed against their convictions and sentences on the grounds of diminished responsibility. Lim chose not to appeal. All three were hanged.

Lim, Arthur (1934–) Doctor and philanthropist. Born in Hong Kong, Arthur Lim Siew Ming was educated at St Andrew's School and the University of Singapore. He was an enthusiastic sportsman, becoming national junior tennis champion in 1950 and captaining the University of Singapore's tennis team. After graduation, Lim proceeded to London to specialize in ophthalmology, and was the first Singaporean to obtain the fellowship of the Royal College of Surgeons of

London (1962). He went into private practice and soon made a name for himself internationally as an ophthalmologist.

Lim has written over 350 scientific papers and 24 books—including *The Colour Atlas of Ophthalmology*, which has been translated into eight languages. In 1986, he was instrumental in setting up departments of ophthalmology at the National University of Singapore (NUS) and at National University Hospital. In 1990, he became founding medical director of the Singapore National Eye Centre, a post he held until 1999.

Lim is an active fund-raiser, art collector and artist. He helped raise over $162 million for the NUS Endowment Fund (of which he is chairman). He has also donated artworks from his personal collection to NUS.

In his younger days, Lim was politically active, becoming the assistant to the secretary-general of the LABOUR FRONT (1958). His father, Richard Lim Chuan Hoe, was a prominent lawyer and leader of the front. It was the younger Lim who exposed CHEW SWEE KEE's acceptance of US$1 million from the US Central Intelligence Agency.

Lim, Catherine (1942–) Author. Catherine Lim Poh Imm was born in Kulim, Kedah. After graduating with a degree in English literature from the University of Malaya (Kuala Lumpur) in 1965, she became a teacher, and continued teaching after moving to Singapore in 1969. Lim, who has a doctorate in applied linguistics, retired from teaching in 1992 to write fulltime. She is Singapore's most prolific writer of English fiction.

Little Ironies: Stories of Singapore (1978) and *Or Else, the Lightning God and Other Stories* (1980), draw from traditional settings in Singapore and Malaysia. Lim's supernatural tales are collected in *They Do Return* (1983) and *Tales of the Dead and their Return* (1999). Love provides the themes for *Love Stories of Singapore* (1987), *Deadline for Love and Other Stories* (1992) and the novella *A Leap of Love* (2003). *Love's Lonely Impulses* (1992) is Lim's only collection of poems.

Lido Theatre: 1963 photograph and ticket from the same period.

Margaret Lien

Arthur Lim

Catherine Lim

Sir Han Hoe Lim: at the University of Malaya convocation cerremony in 1954.

Peter Lim

Suchen Christine Lim

William Lim

Novels such as *The Serpent's Tooth* (1982), *The Bondmaid* (1995) and *The Teardrop Story Woman* (1998) merge the discrete themes in Lim's short fiction—cultural mindsets, cross-cultural tensions and forbidden love. *O Singapore! Stories in Celebration* (1989) describes the quirks of Singapore society. Lim has also written two non-fictive works: *The Woman's Book of Superlatives* (1993) and *Unhurried Thoughts at My Funeral* (2005).

In 1995, Lim authored a *Straits Times* article entitled 'The Great Affective Divide' in which she discussed 'an arrogant, high-handed and authoritarian government'. Responding, Prime Minister GOH CHOK TONG said that he would not allow his authority to be undermined by 'writers at the fringe' and invited Lim to enter the political arena. Nevertheless, in 2000, Lim wrote a less unflattering, still critical, sequel—'PAP and the People: A Return of Disaffection?' (*see* OB MARKERS).

Lim received the Southeast Asia Write Award in 1999. She was awarded an honorary Doctor of Letters by Murdoch University, Australia (2000), and made a Chevalier dans l'Ordre des Arts et des Lettres (France, 2003). In 2005, she was appointed ambassador for the Hans Christian Andersen Foundation.

Lim, David (1933–) Conductor. David Lim Kim San has directed the SYC Ensemble Singers (formerly the Singapore Youth Choir) since 1964. He was also the organizing secretary of the first Singapore Festival of Arts, and general manager of the Singapore Symphony Orchestra (1981–85). Lim was awarded the CULTURAL MEDALLION in 1979.

Lim, David (1956–) Politician. David Lim Tik En studied at the Anglo-Chinese School. Awarded the President's Scholarship and the Colombo Plan Scholarship, he graduated from the University of Melbourne in 1977 with a first class honours degree in engineering (also obtaining an MBA at the National University of Singapore in 1989). Lim worked for various statutory boards, as well as in the private sector. He was deputy director of the National Computer Board from 1983 to 1986, when he joined the Economic Development Board, the North American operations of which he headed. In 1992, he became chief executive officer (CEO) of Jurong Town Corporation. He was also chief executive officer of PSA and the Suzhou Industrial Park.

In 1997, Lim was elected member of Parliament for Aljunied group representation constituency. He was appointed minister of state for defence (1998) and information and the arts (1999), and acting minister for information, communications and the arts. He was also chairman of the National Youth Council (1998). He retired from politics in 2003 and became chief executive officer of Neptune Orient Lines (2003–06).

Lim, Sir Han Hoe (1894–1983) Doctor and politician. Han Hoe Lim was educated at St Andrew's School, Raffles Institution and the King Edward VII College of Medicine. He then left for Scotland and graduated with a MBChB (1918). Lim practised at St Andrew's Hospital in Scotland and later at North Devon General Hospital (1919). He was active in public service, serving as: secretary, Straits Chinese British Association (1920–22); president, Straits Chinese Football Association (1924); vice-president, Singapore Football Association (1925); member of the Legislative Council; and pro-chancellor, University of Malaya (1949–60).

Lim, Peter (1953–) Businessman. Peter Lim Eng Hock spent many years in the securities industry, most notably at Morgan Grenfell Asia and Partners Securities (1988–90) and Kay Hian Securities (1990–95). It was at Kay Hian that he became widely known for his deal-making abilities, and earned the nickname 'King of the Remisiers'. In 1995, Lim went through a much-publicized divorce and resigned from Kay Hian. In 1996, Lim and his friends Lawrence Ang, WILLIAM TAN and Dennis Foo, founded Raffles Town Club.

Lim, Raymond (1959–) Politician. Raymond Lim Siang Kiat was educated at Raffles Institution and studied economics at Adelaide University on a Colombo Plan Scholarship. He subsequently won a Rhodes Scholarship to read law at Oxford University, where he obtained a bachelor's degree, and then at Cambridge University, where he obtained his master's degree. He joined the Faculty of Law of the National University of Singapore as a lecturer, but left after a few years to join *The Straits Times* as a journalist. He then became chief economist for Asia for ABN AMRO Asia Securities; managing director for DBS Securities; and managing director for strategic overview of business at Temasek Holdings.

In 2001, Lim entered politics on the People's Action Party ticket, winning a seat in East Coast group representation constituency (GRC). He was then appointed minister of state for foreign affairs and for trade and industry. In 2005, he was appointed minister in the Prime Minister's Office, second minister for finance and second minister for foreign affairs. In 2006, he became minister for transport, continuing to serve concurrently as second minister for foreign affairs. In 2006, Lim was re-elected to his seat in East Coast GRC.

Lim, Suchen Christine (1948–) Author. Born in Ipoh, Malaysia, Suchen Christine Lim moved to Singapore with her family when she was 15 years old. She graduated from the National University of Singapore in 1983. Lim was a teacher and curriculum

specialist at the Ministry of Education for 28 years. The death of a victim of SEVERE ACUTE RESPIRATORY SYNDROME (SARS) triggered her resignation in 2003 to write fulltime.

Lim has written a number of uncollected stories for adults and for children. 'Valley of Golden Showers' won a Merit Prize in the 1980 Writing for Children Competition organized by the Ministries of Education and Culture. *The Amah: A Portrait in Black and White*, which Lim co-wrote with Ophelia Ooi, won a Merit Prize in the 1986 NUS-Shell Short Play Competition.

Her four novels are characterized by an awareness of historical, political and cultural contexts in Singapore and Malaysia. Set in the latter part of the 1960s, shortly after Singapore's separation from Malaysia, *Rice Bowl* (1984) explores student involvement in politics. *Gift from the Gods* (1990) treads the area between Chinese tradition and a Western-influenced modernity, while *Fistful of Colours* (1993), winner of the inaugural 1992 Singapore Literature Prize, addresses individual identity framed by personal and familial relationships, and the constraints of gender, religion, race, history and politics. *A Bit of Earth* (2001) deals with the lives of immigrant Chinese in the tin mines of Perak in the 19th and early 20th centuries. Lim recently completed a fifth novel.

Lim, William (1932–) Architect. William Lim Siew Wai is a graduate of the Architectural Association (London) and Harvard University. In 1960, Lim set up Malayan Architects Co-Partnership with LIM CHONG KEAT and Chen Voon Fee, and they won a competition for the National Trades Union Congress Conference Hall (1961). The practice was dissolved in 1967. Subsequently, Lim set up Design Partnership with TAY KHENG SOON and Koh Seow Chuan. The partnership leapt to prominence with its proposal for the Peoples Park Complex. Lim resigned from Design Partnership in 1981 and formed William Lim Associates. His other work includes Tampines North Community Centre, Reuters House, Marine Parade Community Centre and the Gallery Hotel. In 2002, Lim retired from practice to concentrate on writing about the culture of Asian cities in the context of post-modernity. He is an adjunct professor at RMIT University in Melbourne, and a guest professor at Tianjin University, China.

Lim Bo Seng (1909–1944) Businessman, community leader and war hero. Born in Nan-Ann, Fujian, Lim Bo Seng was the 11th child and first son of Lim Chee Gee. At the age of 16, he moved from Malaya to Singapore, studying at Raffles Institution. He then attended the University of Hong Kong. Upon his father's death, he returned to Singapore in January 1930, to head the

Lim Bo Seng Memorial

family's Hock Ann biscuit and brick manufacturing businesses. He also became a Singapore Chinese Chamber of Commerce board member. In 1931, he married Gan Choo Neo, a St Margaret's School teacher. The couple had four sons and three daughters.

As a leader of the Kuomintang (Chinese Nationalist Party) in Singapore, Lim played a leading role in the Nanyang Chinese National Salvation Movement after the start of the Sino-Japanese War in 1937. Together with Chuang Hui Tsuan, he led the movement's labour corps, recruiting volunteers for China. In February 1938, they also persuaded Chinese workers at the Japanese-owned Dungun iron-ore mines to quit. When the Chinese Anti-Japanese Mobilization Council was set up on 30 December 1941, Lim took charge of the Labour Service Department, providing 2,000–3,000 labourers daily.

After the Japanese invaded Singapore, Lim escaped on 12 February 1942, travelling by sea via Sumatra and Ceylon (present-day Sir Lanka) to India, leaving behind his family. On 6 April 1942, he continued on to Chungking (present-day Chongqing) in China, where the Chinese Nationalists made him a colonel and asked him to organize Chinese seamen. In India, a Malayan Country Section of FORCE 136 had been set up, headed by Captain Basil Goodfellow. Goodfellow asked Lim to help organize infiltration into Malaya. Lim secured Nationalist Chinese agreement that he should recruit Chinese agents needed by Force 136.

Lim—at this point using the alias Tan Choon Lim—was made head of the Malayan Chinese section of Force 136. Its officers infiltrated Malaya by submarine from May 1943, and Lim himself arrived on 2 November 1943, transferring to a Chinese junk near Pangkor Island, Perak. He was escorted to a MALAYAN PEOPLE'S ANTI-JAPANESE ARMY (MPAJA) camp at Blantan by CHIN PENG, and took part in negotiations on the Bidor Agreement of 1 January 1944.

This agreement secured MPAJA cooperation with British operations.

Lim's initial plan was to collect intelligence and return, but he stayed instead. He moved to Ipoh in March 1944 to establish his own intelligence network and raise funds, and was arrested at a Japanese checkpoint on 27 March 1944. After torture by the KEMPEITAI, he died in Batu Gajah Prison on 29 June 1944, of illnesses that included dysentery.

When the war ended, the Nationalist Chinese government made Lim a major-general posthumously; the British adopted him as a symbol of Force 136 heroism; and the local Chinese embraced him as both a Chinese and Malayan patriot. His remains, buried outside Batu Gajah Prison near Ipoh, were disinterred. On 3 December 1945, they were placed in a coffin draped in the Chinese flag, and displayed in Ipoh and Kuala Lumpur. The body was then returned to Singapore for memorial services at CITY HALL and the Singapore headquarters of the Kuomintang. Finally, on 13 January 1946, it was carried with a British military escort to a burial site overlooking MacRitchie Reservoir. A white pagoda, 3.5 m in height, was erected in his memory at Esplanade Park on Connaught Drive. Called the Lim Bo Seng Memorial, it was unveiled in June 1954.

Lim Boon Heng (1947–) Politician. Lim Boon Heng was educated at Montfort School and won a Colombo Plan Scholarship to study naval architecture at the University of Newcastle-Upon-Tyne. He joined Neptune Orient Lines as a naval architect after graduation in 1970, and rose to become manager for corporate planning.

In 1980, he entered politics, winning a seat in Kebun Baru constituency on the People's Action Party ticket. The following year, he joined the National Trades Union Congress. He became its deputy secretary-general in 1987 and secretary-general in 1993. Lim was appointed deputy Speaker of Parliament (1989–91) and served as senior minister of state for trade and industry (1991–93); second minister for trade and industry (1993); minister without portfolio (1993–2001); and minister in the Prime Minister's Office (1993, 2001–). In 2006, he was returned unopposed as a member of Parliament for Jurong group representation constituency.

Lim Boon Keng (1869–1957) Doctor and philanthropist. Lim Boon Keng was born a third-generation Peranakan in Penang. He was first educated in the Confucian classics at a Hokkien clan temple, before starting his English education at the Government Cross Street School. He then proceeded to Raffles Institution. The principal of that institution personally persuaded Lim's mother to let Lim continue with his studies after his father died unexpectedly and he was expected to

leave school to earn a living.

Although he was the first recipient of the QUEEN'S SCHOLARSHIP, Lim faced many difficulties when studying at the University of Edinburgh, from which he graduated with a first class honours degree in medicine in 1892. He faced discrimination from fellow students from China because he was unable to speak Mandarin or read Chinese. This had a profound impact on Lim. He took up Mandarin and Cantonese upon his return to Singapore in 1893, and immersed himself in the study of the Chinese classics. He attained such proficiency in Mandarin that he began teaching the language in 1899. He was also an ardent supporter of education for girls, and was one of the founders of Singapore Chinese Girls' School.

Lim also came into contact with diverse segments of Singapore society through his roles in public service. He was a justice of the peace, a legislative councillor, a municipal commissioner and a member of the Chinese Advisory Board. As one of the doctors responsible for certifying the deaths of prostitutes who had died from infectious diseases, Lim visited brothels to treat prostitutes. He also headed a commission of enquiry in 1896 which uncovered the terrible living conditions of the majority of people in Singapore, and recommended sanitary improvements. As an anti-opium activist, he ran an experimental rehabilitation centre funded by a group of PERANAKANS under the auspices of the Singapore Anti-Opium Society, which was established by the Chinese Consulate in 1906.

Lim's public-spiritedness and loyalty to the British Crown were further cemented by his enlistment as a private in the Straits Chinese company of the Singapore Volunteer Infantry, in which he served for four years.

Despite adhering to his Peranakan roots, Lim was also progressive. He was highly critical of many traditions in the Straits Chinese community which he saw as restrictive. He co-founded *The Straits Chinese Magazine* in 1897 to serve as an 'organ of progressive Straits-born Chinese opinion'. Due to financial problems and a lack of support from its target audience, the magazine ceased publication in 1907.

Within the mostly Malay- and dialect-speaking Straits Chinese community, Lim was something of an anomaly, as he could speak Mandarin well and was acquainted with many China-born individuals such as TAN KAH KEE. He had even been married twice to China-born wives. Lim led the Straits Chinese Reform Movement, which campaigned for an end to the wearing of the queue as a protest against the rule of the Manchu Qing dynasty in China, but such social activism estranged him from the Straits Chinese community.

Lim was disappointed with the limited opportunities which were available—even

Lim Bo Seng

Lim Boon Heng

Lim Boon Keng

Lim Chee Onn

Lim Chin Siong

Lim Chong Keat

for an accomplished Straits-born Chinese such as himself—to participate in the administration of the Straits Settlements. It was his disappointment that may have led to his decision to leave Singapore for China in 1921. A year before his departure, he rose objections to the ban on hiring locals in the Malayan Civil Service, but his request that some departments of the service be open to natives of the colony was rejected.

At the behest of Tan Kah Kee, Lim assumed the vice-chancellorship of Amoy University (set up by Tan) in China, at the expense of his medical and business interests in Singapore. He only returned to Singapore in 1937 at the outbreak of the Sino-Japanese War.

During the JAPANESE OCCUPATION, Lim was forcibly made president of the Overseas Chinese Association, and tasked to raise a 'donation' of $50 million to Japan from the Chinese community in Malaya. This was regarded by the Japanese as a 'gift of atonement' for Overseas Chinese opposition to the Japanese military incursion into China. After the war, Lim led a reclusive life as an ordinary citizen until his death. At the time of his death, *The Straits Times* referred to Lim as the 'Grand Old Man'. Boon Keng Road is named after him.

Lim Chee Onn (1944–) Trade unionist, politician and businessman. Lim Chee Onn was educated at St Anthony's Boys' School and St Joseph's Institution, before attending the University of Glasgow on a Colombo Plan Scholarship. He graduated with first class honours in naval architecture (1967) and joined the Liverpool firm of Ocean Fleets Ltd as an assistant naval architect. He returned to Singapore in 1968 and joined the Marine Department as ship surveyor and naval architect. In 1975, he joined the Civil Service.

Lim became deputy director of the National Trades Union Congress Research Unit in 1977, and its secretary-general in 1979. He entered politics in 1977, winning the by-election for Bukit Merah constituency on the People's Action Party ticket. He was appointed political secretary to the Ministry of Science and Technology (1978–80), and minister without portfolio in the Prime Minister's Office (1980–83).

Lim resigned from his Cabinet post in 1983 but remained a member of Parliament until his exit from politics in 1991. He joined Keppel Land as chairman and managing director in 1993. In 2000, he became executive chairman of Keppel Corporation.

Lim Chin Siong (1933–1996) Trade unionist and politician. Lim Chin Siong was the son of a shopkeeper. His family moved to Kampong Rambah in Johor during the Great Depression. After World War II, he returned to Singapore to attend Catholic High School and Chinese High School.

Lim was by far the single most influen-tial left-wing politician and trade union leader in Singapore during the 1950s and 1960s. In 1951, he was involved in organizing a boycott of school examinations, and was detained by SPECIAL BRANCH for a week. After his release, he was expelled from Chinese High School in 1952. Thereafter, he worked as a part-time teacher, before joining the SINGAPORE BUS WORKERS UNION (SBWU) as a paid secretary in 1954. When Lim took over at the union, membership stood at 375. By the end of 1955, it had risen to 30,000. Shortly thereafter, he became general secretary of the SINGAPORE FACTORY AND SHOP WORKERS' UNION.

On 21 November 1954, Lim became a founding member of the PEOPLE'S ACTION PARTY (PAP). Chinese-educated Lim was introduced to LEE KUAN YEW and the English-educated faction of the PAP by ROBERT SOON, then president of the SINGAPORE CHINESE MIDDLE SCHOOL STUDENTS UNION.

Lim's dedication to the workers' cause, his self-sacrificing lifestyle and self-effacing manners made him popular among the working class, and he soon became the leader of 16 unions. He was a charismatic orator, adept at public speaking in his own dialect, Hokkien. He later learned to speak in Mandarin and English. At many junctures in the history of the PAP, Lim was seen as an alternative leader to Lee Kuan Yew. However, the English-educated moderates in the PAP saw Lim's popularity and left-wing nationalism as a threat.

In 1955, Lim stood for election in Bukit Timah constituency under the PAP banner and was elected to the Legislative Assembly. At 22, he was the youngest assemblyman in Singapore's history. However, his stint in the assembly was short-lived. That year, he and FONG SWEE SUAN instigated a labour strike that resulted in the HOCK LEE BUS RIOTS. In 1956, he led students of the Chinese middle schools in clashes with the police that led to his arrest and detention under the Preservation of Public Security Ordinance (*see* CHINESE MIDDLE SCHOOL RIOTS). He was only released on 4 June 1959, after the PAP had won the general election.

After his release, Lim was appointed political secretary to the Ministry of Finance. However, he spent little time at the ministry and was not even allocated his own office, as the minister, Goh Keng Swee, felt that the job was 'of no consequence'. In fact, Lim spent most of his time at the MIDDLE ROAD UNIONS.

During the campaign for MERGER, the tensions that had been growing within the PAP led to a rupture. JAMES PUTHUCHEARY had led a group of PAP assemblymen—including Lim—to a meeting with LORD SELKIRK at Eden Hall, to gauge the probable British response to a split within the PAP and the formation of a new party. They also wanted to know if the British would countenance a left-wing party winning power. The meeting became known as the 'Eden Hall Tea Party'. Lee Kuan Yew criticized the British, and criticized the left-wingers for cavorting with the 'British lion'. In July 1961, 13 PAP assemblymen, including Lim, were expelled from the party.

These members went on to form the BARISAN SOSIALIS (BS), with Lim as secretary-general. On 2 September 1963, Lim and several others were rounded up and detained under the INTERNAL SECURITY ACT in OPERATION COLD STORE. Lim was not released until July 1969 when he resigned from the BS and publicly announced his intention to give up politics. In the same year, he went into exile in London.

Lim returned to Singapore in 1979 and kept a low profile. He died on 5 February 1996. Some 700 people, including his former comrades in the PAP and BS, attended his funeral. Some 500 people also attended a memorial service in Kuala Lumpur.

Lim Chong Keat (1930–) Architect. The nephew of Sir HAN HOE LIM, Lim Chong Keat was born in Penang and attended Penang Free School. He graduated in 1955 with first class honours in architecture from the University of Manchester. In 1956, he was awarded the Commonwealth Fund (Harkness) Fellowship. He received his master's degree in architecture at the Massachusetts Institute of Technology the following year. He moved to Singapore in 1958, and helped set up the School of Building and Architecture at Singapore Polytechnic (the precursor of the Department of Architecture at the National University of Singapore). He later started the firm Malayan Architects Co-Partnership, which was succeeded by Architects Team Three. He worked on buildings such as the SINGAPORE CONFERENCE HALL, and Jurong Town Hall (both won by competition), the original SIA Building on Robinson Road, the earlier UOB Building in Raffles Place and the DBS Building. He was deeply influenced by his friendship with inventor and philosopher Buckminster Fuller. The geodesic dome, which Fuller invented, is featured in buildings designed by Lim, such as Komtar in Penang and the Geodesic Pavilion at Suan Luang Rama IX Royal Park in Bangkok.

Lim helped to set up the Singapore Institute of Architects, and was its president from 1966 to 1969. He was founder chairman of the Architects Regional Council Asia, and chairman of the Board of Architectural Education of the Commonwealth Association of Architects. His publications include *Penang Views, 1770–1860* (1986) and *Frank Swettenham & George Giles: Watercolours & Sketches of Malaya*, 1880–1894 (1988).

From 1995–2004, he served as visiting

professor at the University of Manchester and was Quatercentenary Visiting Fellow at Emmanuel College, Cambridge University, in 1995. The University of Manchester awarded him an honorary doctorate of laws in 1998. Lim was awarded Singapore's Public Service Star in 1965. In 1979, the Penang State Government awarded him the DSPN (Darjah Setia Pangkuan Negeri), giving him the title of Datuk. In 2002, he received the DGPN (Darjah Gemilang Pangkuan Negeri), which carries the title of Datuk Seri. He was awarded a Gold Medal by the Malaysian Institute of Architects in 1997.

Lim retired from professional practice in 1995 and is now based in Penang as chairman of Hotel Bellevue. He has been active in botanical conservation and research into native palms and gingers of Malaysia. Since 2000, he has been the publisher of a botanical journal *Folia Malaysiana*. His older brother is Lim Chong Eu, former chief minister of Penang.

Lim Chong Yah (1932–) Economist and academic. Born in Malacca, Lim Chong Yah earned an honours degree in economics from the University of Malaya, Singapore, in 1955. After four years in the Administrative Service, he joined the University of Malaya, Kuala Lumpur, working his way up to head the Division of Applied Economics. In 1962, he won a British Commonwealth Scholarship to Oxford University, where he studied under the Nobel laureate John Hicks. He completed his doctorate in just two years, before returning to Kuala Lumpur. In 1969, he joined the University of Singapore as a reader in economics and acting head of the Department of Economics and Statistics. He became dean of the Faculty of Arts and Social Sciences in 1971.

Lim was chairman of the National Wages Council from its inception in 1972 until 2001. He also served as chairman of the Skills Development Fund Advisory Council from 1979 to 1982. He retired from NUS in 1992 and became emeritus professor.

Among Lim's many books and publications are *Economic Development of Modern Malaya* (1967), *Development and Underdevelopment* (1991) and *Southeast Asia: The Long Road Ahead* (2001). He is most widely known for his textbook *Elements of Economic Theory* (1971).

Lim received the Public Service Star in 1976 and the MERITORIOUS SERVICE MEDAL in 1983, and was admitted into the DISTINGUISHED SERVICE ORDER in 2000.

Lim Chuan Poh, Lieutenant-General (1961–) Military officer and civil servant. A recipient of a Singapore Armed Forces Overseas Scholarship in 1980, Lim Chuan Poh graduated with an honours degree in mathematics from Cambridge University (1983) and, later, a master's degree in mathematics

from the same university under an SAF Postgraduate Scholarship. He later obtained his MBA at Cornell University (1993).

Lim joined the Administrative Service in 1995 but remained in the SAF, where he became chief of army. In 2000, he was appointed CHIEF OF DEFENCE FORCE, a position which he held until 2003. In 2001, he was made lieutenant-general, the youngest chief of defence force in the history of the SAF to attain this rank.

In 2003, Lim retired from the military and was appointed second permanent secretary of the Ministry of Education. He received the Public Administration Medal in 1997, the Public Administration Medal – Military (Gold) in 1999, and the MERITORIOUS SERVICE MEDAL (Military) in 2003.

Lim Fei Shen (1945–) Dancer and choreographer. A 1988 CULTURAL MEDALLION winner, Lim Fei Shen is a pioneer of contemporary dance in Singapore. Having trained at the Folkwang Hochschule for Music, Theatre and Dance in Germany, she performed on stage and television during the 1970s and 1980s after returning to Singapore. She directed the People's Association Dance Company from 1985 to 1991, and earned a master's degree in dance at New York University in 1992.

Lim has been a frequent collaborator with composer John Sharpley. Her interest in exploring dance's creative possibilities has spawned cross-disciplinary projects, such as *Homecoming: A Journey into the Space Within* (1994) and *Earth and Matter* (1999), joint efforts with visual artists TAN SWIE HIAN and Baet Yeok Kuan respectively. In 2002, Lim joined the dance department at the Nanyang Academy of Fine Arts as head of studies (curriculum development and projects).

Lim Hak Tai (1893–1963) Artist. Born in Amoy (present-day Xiamen), Lim Hak Tai was a graduate of the Provincial Art Teachers' Training College in Foochow (present-day Fuzhou) in 1916, where he

Lim Fei Shen

specialized in Western painting. He subsequently took up posts at the Amoy Academy of Fine Arts and Chip Bee Secondary School in China. He was trained in both Western and Chinese art.

Lim moved to Singapore in 1937 and became founding principal of the Nanyang Academy of Fine Arts the following year. At the academy, Lim taught both WATER-COLOUR and oil painting. He was also an early promoter of the NANYANG STYLE. Lim felt that artistic endeavour should reflect the needs of the local masses, and show the tropical environment of the region.

In 1941, he became president of the newly-formed Singapore Art Association. In 1942, during suspended operations of the academy under the Japanese Occupation, he pressed on to work at the Chin Kiang Clan Association, gathering information and encouraging communities to unite and render mutual support in the face of adversity during the Occupation. For his contribution to the development of art in Singapore, Lim was awarded the Sijil Kemuliaan (Certificate of Honour) in 1962 by President Yusof Ishak.

Lim Hng Kiang (1954–) Politician. Lim Hng Kiang was educated at Raffles Institution and Cambridge University where he obtained first class honours with distinction in engineering on a President's Scholarship. Upon graduation in 1976, he joined the Singapore Armed Forces, rising to the rank of lieutenant-colonel as head of air plans. From 1987 to 1991, he was deputy secretary in the Ministry of National Development.

Lim entered politics in 1991, winning a seat in the Tanjong Pagar group representation constituency (GRC) under the People's Action Party banner. He was immediately appointed minister of state for national development. In 1994, he was promoted to acting minister for national development and senior minister of state for foreign affairs. He has served as minister for national development (1995–99); second minister for foreign affairs (1995–98) and health (1999–2003); second minister for finance (1998–2004); minister for the Prime Minister's Office (2003–04); and minister for trade and industry (2004–). In 2006, he was returned unopposed as member of Parliament for West Coast GRC.

Lim Hock Koon (dates unknown) Political activist. Lim Hock Koon was the son of a fishmonger and a student of Chinese High School. He was the brother of LIM HOCK SIEW. He mobilized students at Chung Cheng High School and formed an action committee, which decided that he should play an open role as agitator. His role was short-lived, however, as he was forced to go into hiding after some 500 students from Chinese High School and Chung Cheng High School rioted on 13 May 1954.

Lim Chong Yah

Lim Hng Kiang

Lim Kay Siu

Lim Kay Tong

*Lim Kim San:
picture taken 1963*

Lim hid in Singapore before being evacuated to Indonesia in 1962. In 1969, he travelled to Malaysia and slipped back into Singapore, where he was arrested in 1971 under the INTERNAL SECURITY ACT. In June 1972, he staged a hunger strike to protest a 'confession' allegedly made by him, which the government had placed in several newspapers without his consent.

In May 1978, he suffered a stroke, resulting in partial paralysis. He was transferred to Changi Prison Hospital and subsequently released in 1979. He later left for Sydney, Australia.

Lim Hock Siew (dates unknown) Politician and doctor. Unlike his younger brother, LIM HOCK KOON, Lim Hock Siew was educated in English. As a student at the University of Malaya, he served on the editorial board of *Fajar* and was president of the Socialist Club during the 1956 riots.

Lim joined the PEOPLE'S ACTION PARTY (PAP) after graduation but defected to the BARISAN SOSIALIS (BS) in 1962, serving as a member of its central executive committee. He also ran the English-language organ of the BS, *Plebeian*. In 1963, he was detained under OPERATION COLD STORE because of his involvement in the activities of the Communist United Front. He was released in 1978, but was confined to PULAU TEKONG. He was allowed to reside—with some restrictions—on Singapore island in 1982. He went on to be a general practitioner with Rakyat Clinic, the medical practice started by LEE SIEW CHOH.

Lim Hong Bee (1917–) Political activist. Born in Kuala Lumpur, Lim Hong Bee was educated there at Pudu English School and Victoria Institution. He then left for Singapore, studying at Outram School and Raffles Institution. In 1937, he won the Queen's Scholarship to read law at Cambridge University. Active in the British communist movement, he failed to complete his legal studies, and returned to Singapore.

During the Japanese Occupation, Lim worked on a farm in Johor and met Wu Tian Wang. Wu was a communist guerrilla leader in the MALAYAN PEOPLE'S ANTI-JAPANESE ARMY, and the MALAYAN COMMUNIST PARTY's official representative in Singapore. Lim, Wu and Lim's friend, LIM KEAN CHYE, then approached PHILIP HOALIM SR to establish a new political party—the MALAYAN DEMOCRATIC UNION (MDU). Lim was the MDU's first secretary and, with JOHN EBER's help, established MDU branches throughout Malaya.

In 1947, Lim returned to London to continue legal studies, but abandoned those after becoming embroiled in further Marxist and Malayan nationalist activities. He represented PUTERA-AMCJA—a coalition of Malayan political parties and mass organizations opposed to the MALAYAN UNION plan—and acted as MDU's spokesman in London. In 1948, the EMERGENCY was proclaimed in Malaya, and Lim became a hunted man.

In 1957, the Federation of Malaya government imposed a lifetime ban on Lim's re-entering the territory. The Singapore government followed with a similar ban.

Lim Kay Siu (1956–) Actor and theatre director. Lim Kay Siu was educated in Singapore and London. His brother is LIM KAY TONG. Lim Kay Siu has acted in more than 40 plays in Singapore and London, including *Wayang Tempest* (as Prospero) and *The Letter* with Joanna Lumley and Tim Piggot Smith at the Lyric Hammersmith. On television, he played the lovable rogue, Frankie Foo, in the local sitcom PHUA CHU KANG. In film, he acted alongside his wife, NEO SWEE LIN, in *Anna and the King* (1999), as Prince Chowfa, the king's brother.

In 1995, Lim took a year off acting to study directing at the Central School of Speech and Drama in London. He wrote and directed *Ballroom Dancing* for TheatreWorks; directed the world premiere of *Half-Lives* by Chay Yew, which won *The Straits Times* Award for Best Play (1997); *The Journey West* (written and performed by Ivan Heng); and *The Crucible* and *Club Tempest* for 3.14 Company. He was also assistant director to Krishen Jit for *Nagraland*, which played in Japan, Hong Kong and Singapore.

Lim Kay Tong (1954–) Actor and author. The son of two doctors, Lim Kay Tong was educated at the Anglo-Chinese School and then at the University of Hull, where he obtained a degree in English and drama. Thereafter, he studied at the Webber-Douglas Academy of Dramatic Art in London.

Lim worked as a journalist for the *New Nation* before becoming a professional actor. He co-founded local company THEATREWORKS. Among Singaporean actors, he has had one of the most prolific careers on stage, film and television, including appearances in British and Hollywood productions. Plays in which he has starred include *Oleander*, *Beauty World* and *The Coffin Is Too Big for the Hole*. His film credits include *The Last Emperor* (1987), *Dragon: The Bruce Lee Story* (1993), *One Leg Kicking* (2001) and *Perth* (2004).

However, Lim is best remembered by local television audiences for his role as the father, Charlie Tay, in MediaCorp's longest-running English-language serial, *Growing Up*. His book, *Cathay: 55 Years of Cinema* (1991), was commended by the National Book Development Council. His brother is fellow actor LIM KAY SIU.

Lim Kean Chye (1917–) Lawyer and political activist. Born in Penang, Lim Kean Chye was educated at the Penang Free School and Christ's Church College, Cambridge University, where he read law. At Cambridge, he was a prominent member of the communist movement, as well as the Council of Action in Aid of China, and was chairman of the Chinese Students Committee.

In 1941, Lim returned to work in his father's law firm in Penang until the start of the Japanese Occupation. In January 1946, he became an important member of the MALAYAN COMMUNIST PARTY. It was Lim Kean Chye who took LIM HONG BEE and Wu Tian Wang to see his uncle, PHILIP HOALIM SR, with a view to forming the MALAYAN DEMOCRATIC UNION (MDU). In August 1946, he was instrumental in forming the Singapore Co-operative Stores Society, of which he became first manager. The following year, he became secretary of the MDU, as well as its treasurer.

After being called to the Bar in London in August 1949, Lim returned to Penang. By then, the MDU had been dissolved. Lim sought refuge in Beijing, remaining there until July 1957. He was permitted to enter Singapore in September 1958, but was then detained for three months. Upon his release, Lim returned to Penang and began practising law in earnest.

Lim Kim San (1916–2006) Businessman and politician. Lim Kim San was educated at the Anglo-Chinese School and then at Raffles College, graduating with a diploma of arts from the Department of Economics (1939). Shortly thereafter, he married Pang Gek Kim, daughter of pawnbroker turned banker, Pang Cheng Yean. The couple had six children.

Lim started work as a pump attendant at his father's petrol kiosk. During the Japanese Occupation, he was twice detained and tortured by the KEMPEITAI. After the Occupation, he helped his father run the family businesses in rubber, commodities, salt, sago and gasoline. He revolutionized the sago business by inventing a machine to produce sago pearl cheaply and efficiently, and made his first million by the age of 34. Lim also took over the management of his father-in-law's business, becoming director of United Chinese Bank and managing director of Batu Pahat Bank (1951).

In 1959, Lim was appointed a member—and later, deputy chairman—of the Public Service Commission. In 1960, he accepted the honorary position of chairman of the HOUSING & DEVELOPMENT BOARD (HDB). Within the first two years of his chairmanship, the HDB built 26,168 apartments, about as many as its predecessor, the Singapore Improvement Trust, had built in its 32 years.

Lim entered politics in 1963 and was elected member of Parliament for Cairnhill constituency, under the People's Action Party (PAP) banner. He was appointed minister for national development (1963–65,

1978–79). Lim was also minister for: finance (1965–67), interior and defence (1967–70), education (1970–72), environment (1972–75, 1979–81); national development and communications (1975–78); and national development (1978–79). He was also chairman of the Public Utilities Board (1971–78).

In 1980, Lim retired from politics, but continued to serve in other public appointments. He was chairman of the Port of Singapore Authority (1979–94); deputy managing director of the Monetary Authority of Singapore (1981–82); chairman of the Council of Presidential Advisers (1991–2004); and executive chairman of Singapore Press Holdings (1988-2002). Lim was admitted into the ORDER OF TEMASEK (1962); he also received the NTUC Medal of Honour (1977) and the PAP Distinguished Service Medal (1990). In 1965 he was a recipient of the Ramon Magsaysay Award for community leadership.

Lim Kwee Eng (1858–unknown) Businessman. Born in Amoy (present-day Xiamen), Lim Kwee Eng, also known as Lim Tong Kok, came to Singapore at the age of 18 and worked as a book-keeper in CHEANG HONG LIM's firm, Chop Wan Seng. In 1879, he married Cheang's eldest daughter, Cheang Cheow Lian Neo. He was a partner in the opium and spirit farm and invested his fortune in pineapple preservation under the name of Choo Lam & Co. He was one of the promoters of the Chinese Chamber of Commerce and served as that organization's secretary (1909–18). He also served as first superintendent of the Toh Lam (Hokkien) Chinese School.

Lim Leong Geok (1932–2004) Civil servant. The son of LIM BO SENG, Lim Leong Geok was educated at St Andrew's School and at the University of Adelaide, where he studied civil engineering on a Colonial Development and Welfare Fund Scholarship, graduating in 1958. On his return, he joined the Public Works Department (PWD) as an engineer and rose to become deputy director. He also obtained a master's degree in engineering with a specialization in transportation from Imperial College London on a Colombo Plan Scholarship.

In his 24-year career at the PWD, Lim held various posts, including chief planner (1978–79) and executive director (1979–82). He was subsequently appointed executive director of the newly-formed Mass Rapid Transit Corporation (1983–94) (*see* MASS RAPID TRANSIT/LIGHT RAIL TRANSIT SYSTEM). His main task there was to oversee the construction of the MRT system. In 1987, a new company—Singapore MRT Ltd—was established to manage the MRT. Lim became its managing director (1987–96), and later deputy chairman (1996–99). Lim was awarded the Public

Administration Medal (Silver) (1971), the Public Administration Medal (Gold) (1976) and the MERITORIOUS SERVICE MEDAL (1988).

Lim Nee Soon (1879–1936) Businessman and political activist. The son of a Teochew trader, Lim Nee Soon was orphaned at eight years of age and was brought up by his maternal grandparents. He studied at a private school and then at St Joseph's Institution and the Anglo-Chinese School. He began his career in a cloth shop owned by his uncle, Teo Eng Hock. He went on to work for a timber merchant, Tan Tye, and his son, Tan Chor Nam.

Like Teo, Tan Chor Nam was a strong supporter of SUN YAT SEN's Republican revolution in China. Influenced by Teo and Tan, Lim too became a supporter, later donating hundreds of thousands of dollars to Sun's cause. He also escorted Sun on his eight visits to Singapore, and acted as courier for Sun.

In 1905, Lim became the first Chinese manager of a RUBBER estate in Singapore when Tan appointed him to run his estates. Lim set up Thong Aik Rubber Factory and later Lim Nee Soon & Co. at 5 Beach Road (1911). He then teamed up with LIM BOON KENG, Lee Choon Guan and Yap Geok Song to found Bulim Plantations in Chua Chu Kang (1913). The following year, he set up Han Yang Plantations in Johor. The rubber boom of the 1910s made Lim a millionaire.

Lim also planted PINEAPPLES among his rubber trees, and became a major supplier of this fruit. He made a fortune during the 'pineapple boom' and was referred to as the 'Pineapple King'.

By 1918, Lim owned the Marsiling Estates, Yunnan Estates and Eho Yuan Estates, and was director of the Chinese Commercial Bank, Eastern United Assurance Co. Ltd, Ulu Pandan Rubber Estates Ltd, United Sawmills Ltd, Hanyang Plantations Ltd and Bulim Plantations Ltd. He also had interests in property and banking, serving as vice-chairman of the Chinese Commercial Bank (1924), and setting up the Overseas Chinese Bank (1919) with some friends. He was also a co-founder of the Chinese High School (1919).

Lim was appointed a member of the Welfare Board (1917) and a justice of the peace (1918). He served as president of the Singapore Chinese Chamber of Commerce (1921–22; 1925–26), and founded and chaired the Teochew Poit Ip Huay Kwan (1928). Lim died in Shanghai and was given a state funeral by China's Nationalist government.

Lim Pin (1936–) Doctor and academic. Born in Penang, Lim Pin studied medicine at Cambridge University. He graduated in 1963 and received his master's degree a year

later. He was admitted as a member of the Royal College of Physicians in London in 1965 and was registrar at the Diabetic Department at King's College Hospital.

Returning to Singapore as a specialist in internal medicine, particularly endocrinology and metabolism, Lim became a lecturer at the University of Singapore in 1966. He received his doctorate from Cambridge University in 1970, became senior lecturer in 1971, then associate professor in 1974, and full professor and head of the Department of Medicine in 1978. At the age of 45, Lim became the youngest ever vice-chancellor of the National University of Singapore. He stepped down in 2000 to return to full-time academic pursuits, and was appointed the first university professor (the institution's highest academic position).

Lim sits on the board of many biotech companies, and is on the National Wages Council and the National Bioethics Advisory Council. He was made honorary fellow, College of General Practitioners, Singapore (1982); honorary fellow, Royal Australian College of Obstetricians & Gynaecologists (1992); honorary fellow, Royal College of Physicians and Surgeons of Glasgow (1997); and honorary fellow, Royal College of Surgeons of Edinburgh (1997). Lim was presented with the MERITORIOUS SERVICE MEDAL in 1990 and was admitted into the DISTINGUISHED SERVICE ORDER in 2000.

Lim Siong Guan (1947–) Civil servant. Lim Siong Guan was educated at the Anglo-Chinese School and the University of Adelaide, graduating with first class honours in engineering. A Colombo Plan scholar, he started out as an engineer in the Public Works Department (1970–75). Thereafter, he served as permanent secretary at the Ministry of Defence (1981–94), Prime Minister's Office (1994–98), Ministry of Education (1997–99) and Ministry of Finance (1998–). He was head of the Civil Service (2000-05) and has also served as chairman of the Inland Revenue Authority of Singapore and deputy chairman of Temasek Holdings. In 1991, Lim received the MERITORIOUS SERVICE MEDAL.

Lim Swee Say (1954–) Politician. Lim Swee Say was educated at Catholic High School and National Junior College. He then studied electronics, computer and systems engineering in the United Kingdom at the Loughborough University of Technology on a Singapore Armed Forces Scholarship, graduating with first class honours (1976).

He started out as an assistant director in the Ministry of Defence (1976–84) and later became general manager of the National Computer Board (1986–91). Lim moved to the Economic Development Board in 1991 and rose to the position of

Lim Nee Soon

Lim Pin

Lim Siong Guan

Lim Swee Say

Lim Tze Peng

Lim Yau

Lim Yew Hock

managing director (1994–96). He entered politics in 1996 and won a seat in the Tanjong Pagar group representation constituency (GRC) on the People's Action Party (PAP) ticket. Since then, he has served as: deputy secretary of the National Trades Union Congress (1997–99); minister of state for communications and information technology (1999–2001); minister of state for trade and industry (1999–2000); acting minister for the environment (2000–01); minister for the environment (2001–04); second minister for national development (2004–05); and minister for the Prime Minister's Office (2004–). In 2006, he was returned unopposed as a member of Parliament for Holland-Bukit Timah GRC.

Lim Tze Peng (1923–) Artist. Lim Tze Peng's full-time career as an artist took off in the 1970s. His works in oil, Chinese ink and calligraphy are notable for their vitality and rich detail, most evident in his monumental calligraphic strokes and his depictions of old trees. He has painted the varied terrains of Southeast Asia, China and Europe, but is best known for over 400 works featuring CHINATOWN and the SINGAPORE RIVER. He was awarded the CULTURAL MEDALLION in 2003.

Lim Yau (1952–) Conductor. Lim Yau has been resident conductor of the SINGAPORE SYMPHONY ORCHESTRA and music director of the Singapore Symphony Chorus since 2001, although his association with both goes back to 1981. He also founded the Philharmonic Chamber Chorus and the Philharmonic Chamber Orchestra. He was also a founding member of the Singapore Lyric Opera and New Music Forum.

Lim has made several recordings of choral and orchestral music, and has conducted in Asia and Europe. He has also directed many first performances of foreign works in Singapore, and of works by Singaporean composers at home and overseas. He was awarded the CULTURAL MEDALLION in 1990.

Lim Yew Hock (1914–1984) Politician. Lim Yew Hock completed his secondary education at Raffles Institution, where he received a scholarship for four years, and graduated in 1931. His father's death that year interrupted his studies and, after remaining unemployed during the Great Depression, he started work as a junior clerk at the Singapore Cold Storage Company (1933). Through self-study, he worked up to the position of confidential stenographer. During the Japanese Occupation, he sold charcoal for a living.

After the war, Lim rejoined COLD STORAGE but became interested in the trade union movement. He resigned from his job to become the first full-time general secretary of the Singapore Clerical and Administrative Workers' Union (SCAWU). His involvement with the trade unions soon carried him into the political arena and led him to join the SINGAPORE PROGRESSIVE PARTY (SPP) in 1947.

When the new Singapore Legislative Council was established in April 1948, Lim served as one of its nominated members, together with three SPP colleagues who had been popularly elected. In July 1949, he resigned from the SPP after he was persuaded by M.P.D. NAIR, a founder-member of the SINGAPORE LABOUR PARTY (SLP), to transfer his allegiance in view of his close links with the labour movement. In June 1950 he was elected president of the SLP and, in July, he was also re-elected president of the SCAWU.

With labour support, he contested one of the nine seats in the April 1951 polls. As the SLP candidate for Keppel, he defeated the SPP's A.P. RAJAH by winning 68 per cent of votes cast. A month after the election, on 20 May 1951, together with SLP leader V.K. Nair, Lim established the SINGAPORE TRADES UNION CONGRESS (STUC), with some 24 affiliates and an estimated membership of 25,000. He was its president until 1955. But an internal power struggle over nomination of candidates for the 1952 city council elections soon engulfed the SLP and the STUC, with Lim succeeding in capturing the latter while control of the party was wrested by its secretary-general, PETER WILLIAMS. After an abortive attempt in August 1952 to form an opposing Singapore Council of Workers' Union, Williams succeeded in constituting the Singapore Workers' Union with a membership of 3,000 workers. In December 1952, Williams expelled Lim from the SLP.

The United Kingdom's wish to invigorate the political process precipitated Lim's appointment in 1953 to the RENDEL COMMISSION and his decision in 1954 to form, with FRANCIS THOMAS and DAVID MARSHALL, a new political party—the LABOUR FRONT (LF)—in preparation for the April 1955 polls. Standing for the seat of Havelock in the election, he received, with labour backing, the biggest majority of votes cast for any candidate and was appointed a minister (labour and welfare) in the new coalition government headed by David Marshall.

When Marshall resigned in June 1956, Lim succeeded him as chief minister. The British colonial secretary advised Lim to show firmness in his dealings with the communists as a prerequisite to any further constitutional advance. Lim subsequently cracked down hard on pro-communist student and labour activism in September–October 1956 and August 1957 respectively. He held a series of meetings with the British in December 1956, April 1957, and May-June 1958, and secured their agreement to grant self-government but not independence. However, his security purges of Chinese middle school students alienated a large portion of the Chinese-speaking electorate.

The opposition PEOPLE'S ACTION PARTY (PAP) capitalized on this, branding Lim's party—now named the Singapore People's Alliance (SPA)—a 'colonial stooge'. During the historic LEGISLATIVE ASSEMBLY ELECTION (1959), Lim won the Cairnhill seat, one of only four taken by the SPA, against the PAP's 43.

Lim supported Singapore's merger with Malaysia in 1963 and maintained close ties with the Malaysian premier, Tunku ABDUL RAHMAN. He declined to contest the GENERAL ELECTION (1963). His party—by then part of a wider coalition known as the SINGAPORE ALLIANCE PARTY and backed by the Malaysia Alliance Party—failed to win any seat.

With the support of the *tunku*, Lim subsequently served as Malaysia's high commissioner to Australia. He took Malaysian citizenship in 1965, when Singapore separated from Malaysia. In mid-1966, while still serving as Malaysia's high commissioner in Canberra, Lim caused a public stir when he mysteriously went missing for nine days. He returned to the foreign service but resigned in August 1968. He then converted to Islam, took the name Haji Omar Lim, and moved to Saudi Arabia as an official of the Islamic Conference. He died in that country in November 1984.

Lin, JJ Singer and songwriter. Formerly known as Wayne Lim Junjie, JJ Lin was talent-spotted in 1998 by BILLY KOH of Ocean Butterflies Music. He started his career as a songwriter-producer. By 2006, Lin had released four albums. He won Best Newcomer at Taiwan's 15th Golden Melody Awards (2003) with his debut album *Yue Xing Zhe* (Music Voyager). In 2006, Lin's fourth album *Cao Cao* sold 30,000 copies in Singapore and 500,000 in Asia within one week of its release. Lin has also written for various Taiwanese artistes including Zhang Huimei, Harlem Yu, Elva Hsiao, Energy and S.H.E. Within the first three years of his career, Lin had won more than 25 awards in Singapore, Taiwan and China.

Lin Chen (1917–2004) Writer and theatre director. A major figure in Singapore's CHINESE THEATRE scene, Lin Chen wrote essays, commentaries and short stories for newspapers and magazines under the pseudonyms Bai Meng, Ai Meng, Bai Dan and Bai Ni in the late 1930s. He was also well-known for his woodcuts and cartoons. He was actively involved in the Amateur Stage Play Society (ASPS) formed by people who saw drama as a means of heightening resistance to the Japanese during World War II. Lin toured extensively in peninsular Malaya with ASPS, staging many plays with an anti-war theme.

After the formation of Singapore Amateur Players in 1955, Lin directed most of that company's productions until the early 1990s. These included classics from China such as *Lei Yu* (Thunderstorm), *Beijing Ren* (Peking Man) and *Jia* (Family). He also led the creative team of *Di Er Ci Ben* (The Second Run), a landmark work collectively created in 1973 in the style of the 'model dramas' which had prevailed during the Cultural Revolution in China. In addition, Lin was a strong advocator of local playwriting. He directed *Yan Fei* (The Flying Sparrows) and *Zhen Xiang* (The Truth)—major works by LIN MINGZHOU. From 1981 to 1990, Lin served as instructor and director of the People's Association's Drama Group.

Lin Mingzhou (1937–) Playwright and author. A member of the Chung Cheng High School Drama Society in the 1950s (*see* CHUNG CHENG HIGH SCHOOL (MAIN)), Lin Mingzhou was also active in the KANG LE MUSIC RESEARCH SOCIETY. All the plays he wrote in the late 1950s and early 1960s were staged by Kang Le. These included *Gen Zhe Da Huo'er Zou* (Follow the Masses), *We Must Act*, *Zhen Zheng De Ai Ren* (The True Lover), *Root of Crime*, *The Destroyed Youth* and *Rhythm of Life*.

In the 1980s, Lin wrote two more full-length plays—*Yan Fei* (The Flying Sparrows) and *Zhen Xiang* (The Truth)—as well as a one act play entitled *Two Sides of the Door*. Lin has also written essays, commentaries and short stories, and was a member of the Singapore Association of Writers, Singapore Literature Society and Tropical Arts Club. He has also written and directed a Mandarin film, *Qiao De Liang An* (Two Sides of the Bridge) (1976), and has published a novel, *Zhui Xing* (Chasing the Stars) (1985).

Lin Zhujun (dates unknown) Singer. Lin Zhujun won Singapore's first-ever *Talentime* organized by Radio Television Singapore (RTS) in 1969. After signing a contract with RTS, Lin released her first album, *Chun Lai Ren Bu Lai* (Spring Has Come, But No One Is Here).

One of her most significant albums was *Ai Mu* (Admiration) (1981). Weng Qingxi, the renowned Taiwanese songwriter, wrote many songs specially for that album, and the Singapore Broadcasting Corporation also produced a special television feature about it. Lin went on to record many more television themes, such as 'E Yu Lei' (Crocodile Tears), 'Jia Bian' (Changes at Home) and 'Tie Hu Die' (Iron Butterfly). She retired in the late 1980s.

lion dance Traditional Chinese ceremonial and celebratory dance performed by one or two people using a mock lion head and cape or costume. There are two main types of lion—the northern or 'Beijing lion' (which is hairy and has a long mane) and the southern lion (which has a stylized head and a decorated cape). The southern lion is more popular than the northern lion in Singapore.

The lion dance is usually performed during festive or auspicious occasions, such as CHINESE NEW YEAR or the opening of new business premises. Skilled 'lion dancers' are capable of extraordinary feats of dexterity and athleticism, such as dancing on fragile earthen pots or scaling perches as high as a three-storey building to snatch *hongbao* (red envelopes containing money).

In January 2005, the SINGAPORE TOURISM BOARD unveiled the 'new lion'. This lion featured a locally-inspired version of the traditional lion head. The 'new lion' was designed as a Singapore icon, and it was hoped that it would become established in lion dances abroad.

literature See ENGLISH LITERATURE, CHINESE LITERATURE, MALAY LITERATURE and TAMIL LITERATURE.

littering October 1968 saw the launch of a month-long Keep Singapore Clean campaign. The poor environmental conditions at the time were the result of years of indiscriminate littering, waste dumping and improper disposal of refuse. The campaign was Singapore's first large-scale public education exercise (*see* CAMPAIGNS). For the first time, fines of up to $500 were imposed on those who dirtied public areas.

In November 1992, the Corrective Work Order (CWO) scheme was implemented to shame and deter litterbugs. Under the scheme, litterbugs serve up to 12 hours of community service, which usually involves the clearing of litter while wearing

Littering: offenders in Corrective Work Order scheme.

a vest that marks the person as an offender. Repeat offenders face a maximum fine of $5,000.

See also KILLER LITTER.

Little India The Little India core conservation area is bounded by Sungei Road, Jalan Besar, Rowell Road, Serangoon Road, Belilios Road (and Lane), Kerbau Road, Chander Road, Rotan Lane, Race Course Road and Buffalo Road. In the 1840s European families were among the first to set up residences in the area. Streets such as Dunlop Street and Clive Street reflect the names of the families that once lived there. The most historically significant trade in the area was cattle trading. In the 1840s cattle traders, such as Calcutta-born I.R. Belilios, almost exclusively hired Indian workers. By the 1880s INDIANS made up most of the population, with new immigrants from India being attracted to the area. By the 1900s, other commercial activities that catered specifically to Indians began to develop.

Little India remains important for the Indian community, especially during DEEPAVALI when there are bazaars and street decorations in the area. Historical sites in the area include the Sri Veeramakaliamman Temple (built in 1855) and the TEKKA MARKET.

JJ Lin: Cao Cao (2006).

Lin Chen

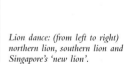
Lin Zhujun

Lion dance: (from left to right) northern lion, southern lion and Singapore's 'new lion'.

Liu Kang: the artist (right);
Life by the River (1975) (above).

Liu Beian: Wu Se De Hong (The Colourless Rainbow) (1978).

Liu Thai Ker

adaptations from Beijing opera.

In 1947, Liu's troupe was re-named the New Unicorn, with Chen Jin Ying, another well-known actor, becoming the troupe's new star. In 1992, Liu took over the troupe and re-named it the Little Unicorn. The troupe still performs regularly in Singapore and Malaysia.

Liu Kang (1911–2004) Artist and academic. Born in Fujian, Liu Kang lived in Muar until 1926. He then went to study at the Shanghai College of Fine Arts and, later, the Xinhua Academy of Fine Arts in Shanghai. He travelled to Paris to study at the Académie de la Grande Chaumière (1929–33), and his works were exhibited in France. He became professor of Western art at the Shanghai College of Fine Arts (1933–37). When the Sino-Japanese War broke out in 1937, he resettled in Malaya.

During the JAPANESE OCCUPATION, Liu opened a hotel and café in Muar and worked in a film distribution company. Following the Japanese surrender, he launched Morrow Studio at Dhoby Ghaut in Singapore, taking on advertising work and cinema billboards, while resuming his teaching in local schools until his retirement in 1971. He produced political cartoons on the Occupation, publishing these in 1946. He was the first post-war president of the influential Society of Chinese Artists (formed in 1935), a position he held for 12 years. Liu was a founding member of the Singapore Art Society and its president (1968–79).

Liu is known as one of the pioneers of the NANYANG STYLE. In 1952, Liu, together with CHEN WEN HSI, CHEONG SOO PIENG and CHEN CHONG SWEE went on a historic field trip to Bali. They went in search of Southeast Asian visual expression, and Bali provided the visual material and inspiration for Liu and his fellow artists to develop the Nanyang Style. Mentored by Chinese artist Liu Haisu and influenced by the French post-Impressionists, Liu developed a mature style characterized by simplicity, and boldness of form, colour and line.

Major retrospectives of Liu's work have been undertaken, including one at the Singapore Art Museum (1997). His work has also been exhibited in touring exhibitions to the United States (2000) and to Beijing and Shanghai (2000–01).

Liu was the recipient of the Public Service Star (1970) and the MERITORIOUS SERVICE MEDAL (1996). A gallery in the Singapore Art Museum was also named after him following his donation of over a thousand paintings and sketches to the museum in 2003.

Liu Thai Ker (1938–) Architect. The eldest son of LIU KANG, Liu Thai Ker was educated at the University of New South Wales, and Yale University. He worked in the practice of IMPei & Partners in New York

before returning to Singapore to join the HOUSING & DEVELOPMENT BOARD (HDB). He eventually rose to become chief executive officer of the HDB (1979). In 1989, he left to become chief executive officer and chief planner at the URBAN REDEVELOPMENT AUTHORITY (URA), working there until 1992. Liu then left to become a director of the firm of RSP Architect Planners & Engineers.

At the HDB, Liu oversaw at various levels the designs of most of the new towns and housing environments, adapting them to the distinctive style and conditions of Singapore. Under his stewardship, the high-rise, high-density housing typology became a working norm, and the notion of public housing moved from the provision of shelter to the development of self-sufficient communities.

As chief planner at URA, Liu was behind the vision of an infrastructure of public urban spaces, linkages and networks of parks. He was largely responsible for the 1991 revised Concept Plan (see URBAN PLANNING). He also championed the conservation and preservation of Singapore's built heritage by establishing guidelines and best practices.

Liu has received the MERITORIOUS SERVICE MEDAL (1985), the Singapore Institute of Architects Gold Medal (2001), the Second ASEAN Achievement Award for Outstanding Contributions to Architecture (1998) and the Medal of the City of Paris (2004). Liu was chairman of the National Arts Council from 1995 to 2005.

Loh, Robert (1925–) Doctor. Robert Loh Choo Kiat was educated at St Andrew's School, and graduated from the University of Bombay with a degree in medicine in 1949. In 1959, he was made a fellow of the Royal College of Surgeons (Edinburgh). He entered the fellowship of the Royal Australian College of Ophthalmologists in 1973, and was admitted to the fellowship of the Royal Australasian College of Surgeons a year later. From 1976 to 1979, he was elected to the Mastership of the Academy of Medicine of Singapore.

Loh worked in Singapore General Hospital's Eye Department as senior consultant ophthalmologist until 1969, when he became honorary consultant ophthalmologist at Singapore General Hospital and the Ministry of Health until 1992. He was given an honorary fellowship by the Royal College of Physicians and Surgeons of Glasgow in 1978. He was founding president of the Ophthalmological Society of Singapore (1963–76).

Loh has served as president of the Young Men's Christian Association of Singapore (1971–93) and has worked with the Singapore Council of Social Service, where he was vice-president between 1984 and 1992, serving as president of the

Liu Beian (1905–1995) Poet. Liu Beian is the pseudonym of Chua Boon Hean, who was among the last group of writers born and raised in China who were able to integrate themselves into Singapore society after their arrival in Singapore prior to World War II. Liu's works marked a period of maturity in Chinese poetry. His travel poems about places such as Karachi and Kinkakuji Temple in Kyoto are distinguished by the musicality of their tone. He published half a dozen collections of poems including *Shi Er Cheng Zhi Lü* (A Journey to 12 Cities) (1963) and *Meng Tu* (The Land of Dreams) (1967). In 1978, he published *Wu Se De Hong* (The Colourless Rainbow), which won the National Book Development Council of Singapore Book Award. He was awarded the Southeast Asia Write Award in 1988.

Liu Huchen (1928–) Actor. Born in Shanghai, Liu Huchen became an actor in his parents' CHINESE OPERA troupe at the age of eight. Adopted as a son and disciple by Zhang Helou, Liu came to Singapore with the Shanghai Combined Beijing Opera Troupes. When the Japanese Occupation began, Liu found himself unemployed, as all opera troupes were disbanded.

After the war, as key members of the Shanghai Combined Beijing Opera Troupes had dispersed, Liu joined a Hokkien opera group—the Jade Unicorn Troupe—and began his second career as a Hokkien opera actor. With his martial arts skills, Liu became arguably the most popular Hokkien opera actor in Singapore, enriching the Hokkien repertoire with

National Council of Social Service (1992–2002). Loh was awarded the Public Service Medal in 1982 and the Public Service Star in 1996.

Loke Wan Tho (1915–1964) Businessman and philanthropist. Loke Wan Tho was born in Kuala Lumpur, one of three children of LOKE YEW's fourth wife.

Loke was educated at Victoria Institution, Kuala Lumpur, and later at Chillon College in Montreux, Switzerland (1929–33), where he was the 1932 Swiss Vaud Canton Champion in the long jump. In 1933, Loke went to read English literature and history at King's College, Cambridge University. He graduated in 1936 and spent a brief period at the London School of Economics, where he won London University's badminton championship in 1937 and 1938.

On 18 July 1935, Mrs Loke Yew, Max Baker, Khoo Teik Ee and Loke Wan Tho incorporated the company Associated Theatres Limited in Kuala Lumpur. The company opened two cinemas—one in Kuala Lumpur on 5 August 1936, and the other, Cathay Cinema, in Singapore on 3 October 1939. After his studies, Loke returned home in 1939 to oversee this new business and to expand the movie industry in Singapore. He spent two years in the film business, but progress was interrupted by the arrival of the Japanese in 1942. Loke escaped to India. There, he developed a passion for ornithology which led him to become one of the world's finest bird photographers.

In 1947, Loke returned to Singapore and embarked on an ambitious plan to rebuild the local film industry. Under his leadership, Cathay Organisation—comprising Associated Theatres, International Theatres, Loke Theatres and International Film Distribution Agency—became one of the most dominant film producers and distributors in Southeast Asia.

Loke also volunteered his services in the public and private sectors. Among other things, he was pro-chancellor of the University of Malaya; and chairman of the Singapore Telephone Board, Malaysian Airlines, Malayan Banking and the National Library Board.

Loke was made an Officer of the Royal Order of Cambodia, and received honorary first class membership of the Most Honourable Order of the Life of the Crown of Kelantan, and Darjah Setia Pangkuan Negeri.

Loke and his third wife, Mavis Chew, died in an air crash on 20 June 1964 while returning from the 11th Asian Film Festival in Taipei. Loke was awarded the MERITORIOUS SERVICE MEDAL posthumously in 1965.

Loke Yew (1846–1917) Businessman and philanthropist. Loke Yew was born in Canton province (present-day Guangdong),

China. He spent his early childhood in China before leaving for Singapore at the age of 11, where he worked as an assistant in a shop on Market Street. With his savings, Loke later set up his own shop, Heng Loong, on New Market Street.

In 1872, Loke left his shop in the care of a manager and went to Perak, where he tried his luck at tin mining. His initial successes in that industry were threatened by the Larut Civil Wars (battles for the control of tin mines along the Larut River in Perak which lasted from 1861–74), but at the end of the 1870s, Loke won the right to the general revenue farm at Kamunting, Perak (*see* REVENUE FARMING). By the 1890s, Loke was running a number of revenue farms throughout Kuala Lumpur and the Klang Valley. With the resultant profits, Loke returned to tin mining and soon became one of the wealthiest men in Kuala Lumpur.

Loke was also involved in agriculture, growing pepper, gambier and rubber in Ulu Selangor. By the turn of the century, his business interests included tin mining, rubber plantations, coconut plantations, oil mills and a cement factory. He also held shares in numerous major companies in Malaya. He became an important leader of the Chinese community in Kuala Lumpur. He continued running Hing Loong in Singapore, although his Singapore interests were managed by his fourth son, LOKE WAN THO.

Longyamen Term used by the Chinese in the 13–14th centuries to refer to part of the island now known as Singapore, as well as to various nearby straits. It literally means 'Dragon's Tooth Gate' in Chinese.

In 1225, Zhao Rugua, in his description of Sanfoqi (the Chinese name for the SRIVIJAYA EMPIRE), commented that 'in the winter, with the monsoon, you sail a little more than a month and then come to Lingyamon, where one-third of the passing merchants [put in] before entering this country [of Sanfoqi]'. Lingyamon was a convenient harbour for ships coming from the west. During this period, Lingyamon may have been Berhala Strait, south of Lingga Island.

However, about a century later, the name Longyamen was being applied to a strait closer to Singapore. This reference appears in a text known as the *Dao Yi Zhi Lüe* (Description of the Barbarians of the Isles). The text is dated 1349, but was probably based on experiences accumulated around 1330 by WANG DAYUAN, who visited many of the places described in the text.

Like other Chinese of his time, Wang Dayuan believed that the world had two oceans, eastern and western. Song Dynasty (960–1279) authors considered the Sunda Strait to be the dividing line between the two oceans. Wang, however, believed that the two seas met at Longyamen; thus, he

placed Singapore at a highly symbolic centre point between east and west.

Wang described Longyamen as being a particularly dangerous pirate lair. He said that the strait lay between two hills belonging to the people of TEMASEK. Ships going west were not attacked, but those returning to China had to be prepared to defend themselves against attacks by men in dugout canoes shooting poisoned darts from blowguns who murdered ships' crews and stole their goods. On the other hand, Wang's account states that some Chinese lived there. Wang described the people of the area as wearing their hair in buns, and wearing short shirts of coarse cotton of a dark blue-green colour. Interestingly, Wang recorded that the Chinese traded with these pirates, obtaining LAKAWOOD and tin in exchange for gold, silk, cotton, ceramics and metal objects.

It has been suggested by some scholars that Longyamen in fact referred to what is now KEPPEL HARBOUR. Another theory links Longyamen with Singapore Main Strait, on the other side of what is now SENTOSA. In any case, the main route for travel between the Indian Ocean and the South China Sea seems to have run through the strait designated by the name Longyamen. It is not known why or when this alteration in navigational practice took place. But by 1350 several sources suggest that Singapore had become a settlement of some importance as a result of this change in sailing routes.

Longyamen also appears in some Yuan Dynasty (1279–1368) records dating from around 1320, in which it is mentioned as a place to which a Mongol mission was sent to procure tame elephants. Perhaps as a result of this contact, Longyamen is recorded as having sent a diplomatic and commercial mission to China in 1325.

Look Yan Kit (1849–unknown) Dentist. Born in Canton (present-day Guangzhou), Look Yan Kit studied dentistry in Hong Kong before coming to Singapore in 1877. He established a surgery on South Bridge Road and quickly earned a reputation for his skill. The raja of Solo and Sultan ABU BAKAR of Johor were among his clients. Look invested his earnings and savings in property, acquiring more than 70 houses and two rubber plantations. He was involved in the founding of the Kwong Wai Shiu Free Hospital in 1910, and served on its committee for many years. Yat Kit Road and the Yan Kit Swimming Pool (closed in 2001) were named after him.

Lou Mee Wah (1951–) Actress. Lou Mee Wah was discovered by JOANNA WONG QUEE HENG when she joined Kong Chow Wui Koon, one of the oldest CANTONESE clan associations in Singapore, in the 1970s. She was soon coached to play the lead male role in Cantonese operas, and learned mar-

Loke Wan Tho

Loke Yew

Lou Mee Wah

Low Ing Sing

Low Kim Pong

Loy Keng Foo

Low-cost carriers: Jetstar Asia, Valuair and Tiger Airways (wtih stripes on tail).

tial arts from Yam Tai Fen, a renowned opera instructor from Hong Kong. Lou became a versatile performer, playing the roles of gentle, young scholars as well as those of warriors. She and Wong formed a highly regarded team on stage in the 1980s and 1990s. Her most memorable role was that of the assassin Jing Ke, immortalized in the Cantonese opera classic *Yi Shui Song Jing Ke* (Seeing Jing Ke Off at the Yi River).

Lou received the National Youth Award in 1980 and the CULTURAL MEDALLION in 1997. She has since turned to teaching and has served as an instructor at the Tanjong Pagar Community Club Cantonese Opera Group.

Low Ing Sing (1924–2002) Actor. Born in Sibu, Sarawak, Low Ing Sing joined the Children's Drama Troupe in Sibu when he was 15 years old and played leading roles in many anti-war dramas. He moved to Singapore in 1941.

In 1946, Low was one of the leading actors in the newly founded Experimental Theatre. While studying at CHUNG CHENG HIGH SCHOOL soon after the war, he co-founded the school's drama society, which became an important groups in the CHINESE THEATRE scene. After graduating in 1947, he continued to be actively involved in the society, and directed eight full-length plays. These included adaptations of Western classics such as Anton Chekhov's *The Proposal* and *The Boor* and Henrik Ibsen's *The Doll House*, and Chinese works such as Wu Zuguang's *The Cowherd and The Fairy*.

Low co-founded Singapore Amateur Players in 1955. His full-length plays included: *The Educator* (1966) (co-written with Chan Kwee Meng), which pays tribute to the pioneers of Chinese schools in the 1950s; *The Gold Fish Bowl* (1983), which deals with the craze in buying stocks; and *Spring of Kopi Tiam* (1985), with a multiracial cast from various drama groups. Low was also a key player in two productions collectively presented by all the Mandarin drama groups in Singapore: *The Little Sailing Boat* and *Oola World*. He was awarded the CULTURAL MEDALLION in 1985.

Low Kim Pong (1837–1909) Merchant. Born in Amoy (present-day Xiamen), Low Kim Pong came to Singapore in 1858. He commenced business as a general trader under chop Ban San, which later included a Chinese druggist's store. He served on the committees of the Chinese Advisory Board, the Po Leung Kuk (a charitable organization under the Chinese Protectorate) and the Chinese Chamber of Commerce, and was a member of the Royal Society of Arts. Together with Yeo Poon Seng, he founded the Shuanglin Buddhist Temple (SIONG LIM TEMPLE) on Jalan Toa Payoh, which opened in 1902. Low was also a major property owner. Kim Pong Road was named after him.

Low Teck Seng (1955–) Academic and scientist. Low Teck Seng studied at the University of Southampton, United Kingdom, where he was awarded a first class honours degree in electrical engineering in 1978, and earned his PhD in engineering in 1982. He joined the National University of Singapore (NUS) in 1983.

In 1992, he founded the Magnetics Technology Centre, and in due course transformed this from a 20-strong team into the Data Storage Institute (DSI)—a national research institute focusing on technologies in magnetics and optics relevant to data storage—with a staff of 250.

Low served as dean of engineering at NUS (1998–2000), promoting ties between universities, research institutes and industry with joint appointments of faculty members and research staff. Low left NUS to become the founding principal and, in 2003, chief executive officer of Republic Polytechnic. He was presented with the NATIONAL SCIENCE AND TECHNOLOGY MEDAL in 2004.

Low Thia Kiang (1956–) Politician. Low Thia Kiang was educated at Lik Teck Primary School, Chung Cheng High School and Nanyang University. He graduated with a bachelor of arts degree, majoring in Chinese language and literature, and government and public administration (1980). He later earned an honours degree in Chinese studies from the National University of Singapore, after Nanyang University had

Low Thia Kiang: 1997 general election.

been merged with the University of Singapore. After graduation, he enrolled at the National Institute of Education to train as a teacher and taught for several years thereafter, before venturing into business.

In 1982, Low joined the WORKERS' PARTY and was subsequently appointed its organizing secretary. In 1984 he served as J.B. JEYARETNAM's election agent for the Anson constituency. In 1988, he stood as candidate for Tiong Bahru group representation constituency alongside Gopalan Nair and Lim Lye Soon. They lost by less than 7 per cent of votes cast. At the 1991 general election, Low defeated the People's Action Party's Tang Guan Seng to become member of Parliament for Hougang constituency. He was re-elected to the same seat in 1997, 2001 and 2006. Low became secretary-general of the Workers' Party in 2001.

low-cost carriers Airlines that offer low airfares but eliminate most frills, such as free meals and inflight entertainment, offered by traditional, 'full service' airlines.

The cheaper fares of low-cost carriers (LCCs; also known as 'budget airlines') tend to encourage more people to fly. To capitalize on the low-cost carrier boom, Singapore has encouraged the formation of such carriers and has constructed the Budget Terminal for them at CHANGI AIRPORT.

Singapore's first LCC, Valuair, was launched in May 2004, prompting SINGAPORE AIRLINES to invest in Tiger Airways. In response, Qantas Airways started Singapore-based Jetstar Asia Airways in December 2004. Though they continue to operate under their own brands, Jetstar Asia and Valuair merged in July 2005 to form Orange Star.

Loy Keng Foo (1936–) Academic and diplomat. Loy Keng Foo was educated at Nanyang University and Tokyo University, where he obtained a master's degree and doctorate in human geography. He joined the teaching staff of Nanyang University's Geography Department and eventually became its chairman. As an academic, Loy was concerned with land use in small countries. In 1971, he was appointed Singapore's ambassador to Japan. After retirement, he taught Japanese at Nanyang University.

Lu, Earl (1925–2005) Doctor, artist and philanthropist. Born in Hong Kong, Earl Lu Ming Teh was a medical graduate of the University of Sydney. He settled in Singapore in 1958, and was mentored by pioneer painter CHEN WEN HSI. He later emerged as a premier authority on Chen's works. Lu has been eulogized as a romantic 'painter of roses', for his expressive works in Chinese ink. He was also an accomplished figurative and landscape artist who attended life drawing classes and travel expeditions led by fellow art advocate, Majorie Chu.

Lu served in the Singapore Armed Forces' Field Hospital, and was reputedly the first surgeon to have operated on acute appendicitis in the field in 1974. He was awarded the Commendation Medal (Military Gold) (1985), made a justice of the peace (1990) and awarded the Public Service Star (1995). He lectured at University of Malaya and the Royal College of Surgeons of Australia. He was also examiner in anatomy and physiology at the National University of Singapore, and started a private surgery practice in partnership with Dr Yeoh Ghim Seng.

Coming from a family of art-collectors, Lu developed an extensive knowledge of Asian art and ceramics, and was president of the Southeast Asian Ceramics Society and Society of Chinese Artists. He was founding chairman of the Singapore Art Museum (1992–2000), and also chaired the Lee Kong Chian Museum's Acquisitions Committee and the Istana Art Advisory Committee (2000–05). He was also a member of the National Heritage Board and United Overseas Bank Art Committee.

Lu's philanthropic efforts included the donation of his Southeast Asian ceramics collection to the Asian Civilisations Museum, and a collection of paintings by Chen Wen Hsi to the Singapore Art Museum. The Earl Lu Gallery (opened in 1986) was named after him, following his donation of art works to the Lasalle-SIA College of the Arts.

Lucky Plaza Shopping centre in Orchard Road. Built in 1981 by FAR EAST ORGANIZATION, Lucky Plaza was designed by BEP Akitek. Like earlier mixed-use

Lucky Plaza

developments, it has a podium block which houses shops set around an open atrium, and a high-rise office and residential block.

From the early days, Lucky Plaza has been a popular destination for tourists because of the large number of specialist shops catering to their needs, especially for jewellery, luggage and electronic and camera equipment. Today, it remains a popular haunt, not least for Filipino migrant workers, because of the large number of remittance agencies located there.

Lui Pao Chuen (1942–) Scientist. Lui Pao Chuen graduated from the University of Singapore in 1965 with a physics degree, and became a scientific officer in the United Kingdom Radio and Space Research Station in Singapore. The following year, he joined the Ministry of Defence (MINDEF) where he started as officer-in-charge of the Tests, Evaluation and Acceptance Section. He later built up the Technical Department in the Logistics Division and in 1970 established the Science and Management Group. The following year, he won the inaugural MINDEF fellowship for postgraduate education and went to the United States Naval Postgraduate School in Monterey, California, graduating with a master's degree in operations research and systems analysis (1973).

Lui became chief defence scientist in 1986. One of his innovations was the creation of the underground ammunition facility in Mandai. In 2002, he received the NATIONAL SCIENCE AND TECHNOLOGY MEDAL.

Lum, Olivia (1962–) Businesswoman. Born in Kampar, Perak, Olivia Lum Ooi Lin was educated at Tiong Bahru Secondary School, Hwa Chong Junior College and the National University of Singapore, where she graduated with an honours degree in science (1986). She joined Glaxo Pharmaceuticals as a chemist and worked there until founding her own company, Hydrochem (S) Pte Ltd, in 1989. Hydrochem sold water treatment systems in Singapore, Malaysia, Indonesia and China. The company went public as HYFLUX.

Lum was the first woman to be named Businesswoman of the Year (2004) at the Singapore Business Awards, and won the Global Female Invent and Innovate (GWIN) Award (2004). She was awarded *Asiamoney*'s Corporate Executive of the Year in Singapore (2005). From 2002 to 2004, Lum served as a nominated member of Parliament.

Lutherans There have been Lutherans in Singapore since the early 1900s. The earliest local Lutherans were Tamils from India and Bataks from Indonesia. The first Lutheran missionaries were from the United Lutheran Church of America group (1953)

Lutherans: Lutheran Church, Bedok.

who worked in the 'New Villages' in Malaya, among those relocated away from areas of communist concentration during the Emergency. They worked their way to urban areas, and eventually to Singapore.

Among them was an American couple, John Robert Nelson and his wife, Elizabeth Louis Wood. Elizabeth, a fifth generation missionary, was born in India. She often wore saris to church in her later years. She and Nelson arrived in Malaya in 1955 and studied Cantonese. They were then assigned to Petaling Jaya, and Elizabeth helped to set up a clinic in Balakong, a village in Selangor.

In 1960, the first Lutheran church was set up in Singapore—the Lutheran Church of Our Redeemer (LCOR). The following year, Nelson was assigned as its pastor. The LCOR at 30 Duke's Road brought together different language groups under one roof—Bataks, Tamils, Americans and Chinese. It stood on land that was flood-prone and occupied by squatters and plantations, presenting fertile ground for missionary work.

The Nelson's were aided by Yang Tao Tung, a China-born Buddhist monk who had converted to Christianity. Yang was trained at the Lutheran Seminary in Hong Kong, and joined the Nelsons at the LCOR in 1961. Three years later, he became the first Chinese pastor to be ordained by the Lutheran Mission. The Nelsons started other churches in Queenstown and Bedok before John Nelson's retirement in 1995.

The Lutheran Church in Singapore (LCS) separated from the Lutheran Church in Malaysia in 1997. Rev John Tan Yok Han was elected the LCS' first bishop. There are six congregations—the LCOR, Queenstown, Jurong Christian Church, Bedok, Yishun Christian Church and Mas Kuning Lutheran Church. Services are held in English, Mandarin, Tamil and Chinese dialects. By 2004, membership had increased to 4,256.

An elected bishop governs the congregations with the help of an executive council, comprising a secretary, treasurer, two laypersons and two clerics. There is also a ministerium—made up of all the ordained pastors—which guards the doctrine of the church. Every congregation has a locally elected church council to assist the LCS-assigned pastor.

Olivia Lum

M1 Brand name of telecommunications company MobileOne, which was formed in August 1994. Its founding shareholders included Keppel Telecoms and SPH Multimedia. The firm started offering cellular telephone and radio paging services in 1997 following liberalization of the Singapore telecommunications market.

M1 was listed on the Singapore Exchange on 4 December 2002. As of 9 February 2006, SunShare Investments, a joint venture between Telekom Malaysia and Khazanah Nasional, owned 25.17 per cent of the company. In financial year 2005, M1 posted an after-tax profit of $161 million on total sales of $774 million.

MacDonald, Sir Malcolm (1901–1981) British politician and colonial official. The son of Britain's first socialist prime minister Ramsay MacDonald, Sir Malcom John MacDonald was first elected to the British Parliament in 1929. When Ramsay MacDonald retired in 1935, the new prime minister, Stanley Baldwin, appointed Malcolm Macdonald secretary of state for the Dominions. He was subsequently appointed to numerous posts, including governor general of Southeast Asia (1946–48); commissioner-general in Southeast Asia (1948–55); and high commissioner to India (1955–60).

In Southeast Asia, MacDonald tried to bridge the divide between Europeans and local peoples by adopting a non-formal approach to government. He became known for eschewing protocol, and for his egalitarian approach to the treatment of non-Europeans. For instance, he made it publicly known that he did not require local residents of Singapore to bow in his presence, and invited local, non-European guests to Singapore's exclusive TANGLIN CLUB.

During his 14 years in Asia, MacDonald helped prepare Malaya's various racial groups for independence and improved strained

Sir Malcolm MacDonald

relations between India and Britain following the Suez crisis of 1956.

MacDonald House Designed by architectural firm PALMER & TURNER for the Hongkong and Shanghai Banking Corporation (*see* HSBC), MacDonald House was built in 1949 in a neo-Georgian style, with a reinforced concrete framed structure clad in red brickwork. It was named after Governor General MALCOLM MACDONALD. The building housed the bank's Orchard Road branch, as well as the offices of British, US and Australian organizations. It was also the location of the EMI studios, where THE QUESTS recorded their first album in 1966.

At 3.07 p.m. on 10 March 1965, a bomb went off in the building, killing three people—Elizabeth Suzie Choo Kway Hoi and Juliet Goh Hwee Kuang (both bank employees); and Yasin Kesit (a driver employed by the Malaya Borneo Building Society)—and injuring some 33 others. Every window within 100 m of the blast was shattered, and almost every vehicle immediately outside the building was damaged. This event became known as the 'MacDonald House Bombing'.

The bomb went off at the height of Indonesia's policy of CONFRONTATION, whereby the Indonesian government opposed the formation of the Federation of Malaysia in 1963, labelling it a 'neo-colonialist plot'.

Within four days, police had arrested two Indonesian commandos—Harun Said and Osman Haji Mohamed Ali. They were both later convicted of planting the bomb, and were executed. The refusal by the Singapore government to advise the President of Singapore to exercise the prerogative of mercy in respect of the two saboteurs, despite an appeal from President Suharto—who had just come to power in Indonesia—led to a diplomatic chill between the two countries which lasted until 1973 (*see* INDONESIA-SINGAPORE RELATIONS).

MacDonald House survived the bombing and was gazetted as a national monument in 2003.

Mace of Parliament Ceremonial baton. The Mace of Parliament was inherited from the first Legislative Assembly. It symbolizes the authority of Singapore's PARLIAMENT and the SPEAKER. Without it, the House cannot be constituted and no proceedings can take place.

The mace was created in 1954 in the United Kingdom by silversmith Leslie Durbin, in collaboration with the famous American-born sculptor Sir Jacob Epstein. Durbin, who was London's most celebrated silversmith in the 1950s and 1960s, had been responsible for the creation of many other ceremonial maces used in other parliaments around the world.

MacDonald House

The design of the mace is in three parts: the upper section, which is crowned by a winged lion carrying a trident; the middle section, which is decorated with embossed lion heads and Chinese junks; and the base, which is encircled by a ring of fishes. During ceremonies, such as the Opening of Parliament, the mace is carried by the SERJEANT-AT-ARMS.

MacRitchie, James (1848–1895) Civil engineer. Born in Scotland, James MacRitchie studied engineering at the Universities of Edinburgh and Glasgow. Prior to his arrival in Singapore as Municipal Engineer in 1883, he held various appointments in India, Japan and Latin America.

Major engineering projects in Singapore finished under his supervision include bridges across the SINGAPORE RIVER; the city's water supply and drainage systems; the construction of market buildings; and the introduction of Welsbach gas burners for street lighting. MACRITCHIE RESERVOIR was named in his honour.

MacRitchie Reservoir In 1823, British Resident JOHN CRAWFURD proposed the building of a reservoir and waterworks in Singapore, as water supplies were inadequate for the island's increasing needs. However, nothing came of Crawfurd's plans. It was only in 1857, when Chinese businessman TAN KIM SENG donated $13,000 for the improvement of the town's water supply, that plans were drawn up for a reservoir in the Thomson area. However, the projected total cost of the reservoir came to more than $100,000, and colonial authorities in Calcutta refused to contribute the balance required.

In 1868, an impounding reservoir was finally built in the Thomson area. The

M1: branch at Paragon Shopping Centre.

Mace of Parliament

pumps and distribution network, however, were not completed until 1877, with the waterworks being opened a year later. In 1891, the dam was enlarged under the supervision of Municipal Engineer JAMES MACRITCHIE. It was then further enlarged in the years leading up to 1907. Although it was originally called the Thomson Road Reservoir, the reservoir was renamed the MacRitchie Reservoir in 1922.

In more recent decades, the reservoir—besides serving its primary purpose—has become a popular site for nature enthusiasts. There are extensive boardwalks along the water's edge, giving good views of secondary forest and freshwater wildlife. Within walking distance is the HSBC TREETOP WALK, where a free-standing suspension bridge connects the two highest points (Bukit Peirce and Bukit Kalang) in MacRitchie and offers a bird's eye view of the community of plants and animals that live in the forest canopy.

Madhavi Krishnan (1941–) Dancer. During the 1950s, Madhavi Krishnan studied the classical dance traditions of *bharatanatyam* and *kathakali* in India, becoming a film actress in that country in the 1960s. After returning to Singapore, she became a founding member of the National Dance Company (1970), serving as a lead dancer and choreographer. The company premièred her *Thaipusam* (1971) at the Adelaide Arts Festival, and performed it again in Moscow two years later. For the ASEAN Dance Festival in 1990, she created *Savitri*, an English opera based on the Hindu epic, the Mahabharata, and danced in the title role. Madhavi was awarded the first CULTURAL MEDALLION for Dance in 1979.

madrasahs Islamic religious schools. Historically, madrasahs began as schools for the learning of Islamic subjects. Classes were conducted in the halls and annexes of mosques to educate Muslims about Islam. They served an important role during the colonial period as they offered affordable education. Many of the full-time madrasahs that exist today were established by philanthropists. Part-time madrasahs are usually attached to mosques and organizations, and provide religious education for students who attend mainstream schools.

MacRitchie Reservoir

Madrasahs: reading programme at Aljunied.

Like other private schools, madrasahs are regulated by the Education Act. While the ADMINISTRATION OF MUSLIM LAW ACT (AMLA) makes provisions for MAJLIS UGAMA ISLAM SINGAPURA (MUIS) to administer the madrasahs, in practice, many of the madrasahs are managed by their respective boards of trustees.

All full-time madrasahs offer primary- and secondary-level education, while three (Al-Maarif, Aljunied and Wak Tanjong) offer education up to the pre-university level. All full-time madrasahs teach Islamic subjects, as well as secular subjects including English, Mathematics and Malay. While each madrasah determines its own curriculum, all provide secular curricula similar to those in schools run by the government. For the religious subjects, students are required to sit for common examinations administered by MUIS, such as the Sijil Thanawi Empat taken at Secondary Four. Students in part-time madrasahs also sit for common examinations administered by MUIS.

Madrasahs are privately funded. Some receive donations from the public or from WAKAF (endowment) properties, while others undertake their own fund-raising initiatives. The Ministry of Education provides a grant to some madrasahs on a quarterly basis. This amounts to $10 per student per year. MUIS also provides grants to madrasahs on an annual basis. Furthermore, to generate a more consistent flow of funding, MUIS, with the cooperation of the six full-time madrasahs, MENDAKI and PERGAS, launched the Madrasah Fund in 1994.

Enrolment in madrasahs has fluctuated over the years. In the 1970s, the number of madrasahs declined due to the expansion of the public education system and the resettlement of villagers to housing estates in new towns. In the early 1980s, some people even viewed madrasahs as a 'last resort' for children who could not secure a place in other schools. In the late 1980s, however, madrasahs underwent a revival. Many Muslim parents saw them as providing a balanced education. Throughout the 1980s and 1990s, there has been a steady increase in enrolment.

In 1998, preliminary discussions regarding COMPULSORY EDUCATION sparked a debate as to whether enrolment in madrasahs at the primary level fulfilled the requirements of compulsory education. The government has since allowed madrasahs to provide education at the primary level, subject to qualifying standards. At the same time, annual enrolment at madrasahs at the primary level is kept under 400.

Maghain Aboth Synagogue Singapore's first synagogue was built in the 1840s in the Boat Quay area by the island's Jewish community—most of whom were Indian JEWS of Baghdad origin, Jews from Iran and Iraq. Synagogue Street was named after it, although the synagogue there was later removed.

In 1873, the government granted Singapore's Jewish community a site on Waterloo Street for a new synagogue—the orthodox Maghain Aboth Synagogue ('Shield of Our Fathers' in Hebrew). The two-storey neo-classical building was consecrated in 1878. It is the oldest extant synagogue in Southeast Asia.

Not long after Maghain Aboth was built, a number of alterations were made. For example, a gallery for women was installed, funded by MANASSEH MEYER, a leading Jewish businessman. During the Japanese Occupation, the synagogue became an important meeting place, as well

Madhavi Krishnan

Full-time madrasahs

Al-Arabiah Al-Islamiah
This madrasah at Jalan Selamat traces its origins to the 1930s, when it was operating at Masjid Haji Mohammad Yusuf located on Hillside Drive. In the 1980s, management of the madrasah was taken over by MUHAMMADIYAH.

Al-Irsyad Al-Islamiah
Founded in 1946 at Kampung Kuari on Hindhede Road, the madrasah was almost closed in the 1990s due to redevelopment in the area. It has since been temporarily relocated to Winstedt Road. Al-Irsyad will form part of the Islamic complex that will be completed in 2009 at Braddell Road.

Aljunied Al-Islamiah
Set up by Syed Abdul Rahman Aljunied in 1927, this madrasah is the second-oldest surviving madrasah in Singapore. Before World War II, it was regarded as the premier Islamic school in Southeast Asia. Alumni include Syed Isa Semait, Mufti of Singapore, and Pehin Dato Seri Utama Dr Haji Mohamad Zain Haji Serudin, the Bruneian Minister for Religious Affairs.

Al-Maarif Al-Islamiah
Founded in 1936 by Syeikh Muhammad Fadhlullah Suhaimi, this madrasah was the first in Singapore to admit both female and male students. After World War II, it was turned into an all-female madrasah. It is located at Ipoh Lane on a piece of land donated by Syeikh Omar Bamadhaj.

Alsagoff Al-Arabiah
In 1912, Syed Mohamed Ahmad Abdul Rahman Alsagoff established this madrasah at Jalan Sultan. It started out as an boys' school but was converted to a girls' school in 1967. It is Singapore's oldest surviving madrasah (right).

Wak Tanjong Al-Islamiah
Located at Sims Avenue, this madrasah was established in 1955 by Mohamed Noor Taib. It was rebuilt in 1997.

Mah Bow Tan

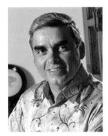

Kishore Mahbubani

Mah Li Lian

as a place for disseminating information and collecting funds for the needy. The synagogue was gazetted as a national monument in 1998.

Mah Bow Tan (1948–) Civil servant and politician. Mah Bow Tan was educated at St Joseph's Institution, and then at the University of New South Wales, Australia, where he graduated with first class honours in industrial engineering (1971) on the President's and Colombo Plan Scholarships.

Mah joined the Administrative Service in 1973. He was seconded to the Singapore Bus Services (1974–83) and then to Singapore News and Publications Ltd as group general manager and chief executive officer of the SINGAPORE MONITOR. He also served as group general manager (coordination) of SINGAPORE PRESS HOLDINGS Ltd (1985–88).

Mah first entered politics in 1984 on the People's Action Party ticket, contesting the seat of Potong Pasir constituency. He lost to the incumbent, CHIAM SEE TONG, but was elected as a member for the Tampines group representation constituency in 1988.

He was appointed minister of state for trade and industry and was promoted to full minister in 1991. He has served as minister for the environment (1993–95); minister for communications (1991–99); and minister for national development (1999–). Mah has also been adviser, Football Association of Singapore (FAS) Council (1991–99; 2004–); president, FAS (1999–2004); chairman, National Youth Achievement Award Advisory Board (1994–); patron/adviser, Samaritans of Singapore (1994–); and chairman of the Singapore Labour Foundation (2001–).

Mah Li Lian (1968–) Sportswoman. In squash, Mah Li Lian was a six-time Asian Champion (1988-94); an Asian Games bronze medallist (Bangkok, 1998); and a triple Southeast Asian Games gold medallist (Manila, 1991; Singapore, 1993; Chiangmai, 1995). In 1987, she was named Sportsgirl of the Year by the Singapore National Olympic Council. She was also named Sportswoman of the Year in 1989 and 1991. She was a recipient of the Public Service Medal.

Mahbubani, Kishore (1948–) Diplomat and academic. Kishore Mahbubani was educated at Tanjong Katong Secondary School, St Andrew's School and the University of Singapore, where he graduated with first class honours in philosophy (1971). He won a President's Scholarship and obtained a masters in political philosophy at Dalhousie University, Canada.

In 1971, he joined the Ministry of Foreign Affairs. He was made Singapore's permanent representative to the UNITED NATIONS in 1984, serving in this capacity over two periods (1984–89; 1998–2003). He also served as permanent secretary to the Ministry of Foreign Affairs (1989-91).

Maghain Aboth Synagogue

In August 2004, Mahbubani was appointed inaugural dean of the LEE KUAN YEW SCHOOL OF PUBLIC POLICY at the National University of Singapore. He is the author of *Can Asians Think?* (1998) and *Beyond the Age of Innocence: Rebuilding Trust Between America and the World* (2005).

Mahmud, Sultan (1760–1812) Malay royal. Mahmud was installed as Sultan of the Johor-Riau Kingdom by the Bugis Yang di-Pertuan Raja Muda (Prince) Daeng Kemboja, who managed the affairs of state. During Mahmud's reign, his kingdom became a centre of regional trade with China and India. His accession to the throne was not fully accepted by the Malay nobles of the court, who were unhappy with the dominant role played in the court by the BUGIS. This conflict was fought out in Singapore between the Malay factions and the Bugis nobles, and it was Mahmud who reconciled the two sides. During Mahmud's reign, the Dutch attacked his kingdom, and demanded the expulsion of the Bugis. After his defeat, Mahmud signed a treaty with the Dutch in 1784, giving them exclusive trading rights and a measure of control over the kingdom.

Following his death, a succession dispute between his two sons, Tengku ABDUL RAHMAN and Tengku HUSAIN SHAH, resulted in the kingdom being split, with one portion in Riau and the other in Singapore, and both brothers becoming sultans.

See also MALAY ROYALTY.

Mahmud Ahmad (1906–1976) Teacher and author. Born in Riau, Mahmud Ahmad was educated in Singapore after his family migrated here. He studied in Malay schools at Telok Kurau and Kampong Glam, before continuing his studies at Sultan Idris Training College, Perak. He wrote a number of essays and he was instrumental in organizing several regional Malay language congresses held in Singapore in the 1950s. Mahmud was an active member of the literary organization Sahabat Pena (Pen Pal) and a founder member of the Malay Language Institute (Lembaga Bahasa Melayu). His novels include *Kosong* (Empty) (1966) and *Doktor Tan* (1969). His short stories were published as a compilation in 7 *Cherpen Kenangan* (Seven Memorable Short Stories) (1963). He also

published essays on culture and language, as well as textbooks. For his contribution to Malay literature and language, he was posthumously granted the Anumerta Tun Seri Lanang award in 1998.

maids During the colonial era, the employment of maids was not only a practical measure, but also a sign of a family's status. European civilians customarily employed servants (as they would have at home) to undertake specific household duties. Wealthy Chinese families took on *mui tsai*—girls sold by poor parents—who often faced a lifetime of unpaid and arduous domestic labour. In the early years of the 20th century, *majie*—organized domestic workers from Kwangtung (present-day Guangdong), China, who were also known as 'black-and-whites' on account of their habit of wearing black trousers and white samfus—came to Singapore.

The government of post-SEPARATION Singapore initially opposed the importation of foreign domestic workers, and the demand for domestic labour was met by local women, who generally worked for agreed hours but did not live in their employers' homes. However, rapid economic development led to a change of policy, and as an increasing proportion of married women entered the workforce, the demand for domestic help intensified.

In 1978, the government began to issue work permits to women from Thailand, Sri Lanka and the Philippines. Employing a foreign domestic worker (commonly referred to as a 'maid'), soon became common practice for middle-class families as well as the wealthy. By 2005, there were some 150,000 foreign domestic workers employed in Singapore, with one in every seven households employing a maid. The majority of these workers were from the Philippines, Indonesia and Sri Lanka and others came from Thailand, India and Myanmar—all of which were government-approved sources.

Most domestic workers are recruited and placed through 'maid agencies'. They work in Singapore to pay for the education of younger relatives; to help their families buy land at home; or simply to make a living. They are amongst the lowest-paid workers in Singapore. Since 2006, maid employment contracts have been standardized. All contracts now specify job scope, rest hours, leave and salary. Advocacy and support groups for domestic workers include the Archdiocesan Commission for the Pastoral Care of Migrants and Itinerant People, Humanitarian Organisation for Migration Economics (H.O.M.E.) and Transient Workers Count Too (TWC2).

See also FOREIGN WORKERS.

Maintenance of Parents Act The Maintenance of Parents Bill was first moved by nominated member of Parliament Walter

Woon in 1994. It was the first private member's Bill (i.e. legislation emanating from the backbenches) to be introduced since 1965. Through this measure, Woon proposed that children should be legally required to take care of their elderly parents.

The Bill was passed into law on 2 November 1995, coming into operation on 1 June 1996. A Tribunal for the Maintenance of Parents was established. This three-person tribunal is chaired by a president, and is empowered to make and review maintenance orders. Its first president was former judicial commissioner, K.S. Rajah.

Under the Act, parents above the age of 60 who are unable to support themselves have the right to claim maintenance from their children. Any person disregarding or disobeying an order by the tribunal may be fined up to $5,000 and/or jailed for up to six months. In the first three years after the Act came into force, more than 400 elderly Singaporeans sought aid from the tribunal.

Maintenance of Religious Harmony Act

Enacted in 1990, the Maintenance of Religious Harmony Act is intended to prevent religious groups from acting in ways that would incur 'ill-will among different groups', and to guard against political activities disguised as religion. It was introduced in response to a number of specific developments and events—including growing religiosity amongst Christians and Muslims from the 1970s onwards; the MARXIST CONSPIRACY of 1987; and what was perceived as overly aggressive proselytizing on the part of certain Christian groups.

Among other things, the Act empowers the government to ban anyone who threatens religious harmony from preaching; it allows measures to be taken to ensure that 'common spaces' remain religiously neutral (e.g. by banning religious preaching and gatherings in schools); it empowers the Minister of Home Affairs to restrain any person who causes ill-feeling amongst religious groups, or who promotes a political cause under the guise of religion; and it allows for the setting-up of a PRESIDENTIAL COUNCIL FOR RELIGIOUS HARMONY.

Three religious groups have been banned under the Act: the JEHOVAH'S WITNESSES, the UNIFICATION CHURCH and the Divine Light Mission.

Ma'it

The Arab accounts, *Al-Masalik wal Mamalik* (Roads and Kingdoms, c. 850) and the *Ajaib al-Hind* (Marvels of India, c. 1000), mention a settlement called Ma'it, and locate it between Zabaj (Srivijaya, present-day Palembang), Qmar (Khmer, or Cambodia) and the southern end of Tioman Island. Ma'it was likely to have been at the end of the Malay Peninsula or on the northern islands of the Riau archipelago. It may also have been a settlement on Singapore or adjacent islands.

These Arab accounts note that gold, cotton and bees' wax were produced at Ma'it—goods similar to those mentioned in the 14th-century Chinese accounts by WANG DAYUAN in connection with the TEMASEK settlements of LONGYAMEN and Banzu on Singapore.

Majapahit Empire

The kingdom of Majapahit was founded in eastern Java in 1294. It grew to become the greatest empire in what is now Indonesia. The PARARATON, a Javanese text written in the early 16th century, reports that Majapahit's prime minister, Gajah Mada, swore in 1336 to conquer TEMASEK (Singapore), as well as other islands and settlements in the region. The DESAWARNANA, a Majapahit poem written in 1365, includes Temasek in its list of Majapahit's dependencies. It is likely that Temasek paid tribute to Majapahit for much of the 14th century.

Majestic Theatre

Located in Chinatown, the Majestic Theatre was designed and built in 1927 by the architectural firm of SWAN & MACLAREN. It was later acquired by Cathay Organisation's Datuk LOKE WAN THO for the screening of Chinese movies. The single-hall cinema closed in 1998. After major renovations costing some $8 million were undertaken, the building was converted into a shopping mall. The Majestic, as the mall was named, was opened to the public in 2003.

Majid, M.A.

(dates unknown) Political activist. Born Mirza Abdul Majid in India, Majid served as president of the Singapore Seamen's Union and president of the Muslim Welfare Association. In the LEGISLATIVE COUNCIL election of March 1948, he contested the South-west constituency, where two seats were at stake, but lost to the two founding members of the SINGAPORE PROGRESSIVE PARTY—C.C. TAN and N.A. MALLAL.

It was after that failed bid that Majid began discussing with his supporters the idea of forming a new political party. He sought to break the MALAYAN COMMUNIST PARTY's dominance over the labour movement, and was inspired by the success of the 'welfare state' experiment in the United Kingdom. He therefore decided to found a new party—the SINGAPORE LABOUR PARTY—on the model of the British Labour Party, as this would also ensure that the party's socialist platform would not invite proscription under the EMERGENCY regulations. On 1 September 1948, the Singapore Labour Party was inaugurated, with Majid as president. However, it soon split into two groups, and Majid lost his position as head of the party to Francis Thomas in 1949.

In the 1951 Legislative Council election, Majid contested the City constituency, but lost with only 4 per cent of the vote. He was defeated again in the Cairnhill by-election of

29 June 1957, which had been precipitated by DAVID MARSHALL's resignation. Majid got only 91 votes, or 1.6 per cent of votes cast.

Majlis Pusat

Established on 12 April 1969 with the aim of preserving, promoting and developing Malay culture and values, Majlis Pusat is an umbrella organization with 37 affiliated member bodies. It coordinates Malay education, sports activities and the advancement of the religious, cultural, social and economic welfare of Singapore's Malays.

Majestic Theatre: building (top); detail of façade.

Majlis Pusat works closely with government agencies such as the Ministry of Community Development, Youth and Sports, Ministry of Information, Communications and the Arts, Ministry of Defence and Singapore Tourism Board. It provides these agencies with feedback and suggestions on various issues important to the Malay community. It also offers other services, such as assisting Malay youths in education and job-seeking, and organizing forums, lectures and discussion groups.

Majlis Ugama Islam Singapura

Statutory board. Also known as the Islamic Religious Council of Singapore, Majlis Ugama Islam Singapura (MUIS) was established in 1968 following the introduction of the ADMINISTRATION OF MUSLIM LAW ACT. Under the Act, MUIS advises the President of Singapore on all matters relating to Islam. It is administered under the MINISTRY OF COMMUNITY DEVELOPMENT, YOUTH AND SPORTS but reports to the Minister-in-charge of Muslim Affairs. MUIS also aims to deepen the Muslim community's understanding and practice of Islam.

MUIS is responsible for the promotion of religious, social, educational, economic and cultural activities in accordance with the principles and traditions of Islam. Its other main functions include the administration of *zakat* (donations) and WAKAF; HAJ affairs; halal certification; *da'wah* (promotion of Islamic values) activities; the construction and administration of MOSQUES and MADRASAHS; the issuance of fatwas (religious rulings); and the provision of financial relief to needy members of the Muslim community.

Walter Makepeace

Malay: textbook for Higher Malay in secondary schools.

Makepeace, Walter (1859–1941) Journalist and author. Born in Coventry, United Kingdom, Walter Makepeace was educated at the Birmingham & Midland Institute, and then at Saltry College. He arrived in Singapore in 1884 to join the Straits Education Department, but taught for only three years.

He joined the *Singapore Free Press* as an assistant in July 1887 and remained there until 1926. From 1916, he was editor and manager.

Makepeace was also active in other areas. He was a FREEMASON, and was made Master of Lodge Zetland in 1894. He was one of the first recruits of the Singapore Volunteer Artillery (1888), retiring as captain and honorary major (1914), and remaining on the reserve list until 1920 (earning a Long Service Medal). During the SEPOY MUTINY (1915), Makepeace commanded 200 special constables. Other public offices he held included secretary and treasurer of the Singapore Merchant Guild Association and Justice of the Peace.

Makepeace was also, for 20 years, Reuters' correspondent in Singapore and correspondent for the Paris edition of the *New York Herald*. He was the Malaya Delegate to the Imperial Press Conference at Ottawa (1920). However, he is best remembered for having co-authored *One Hundred Years of Singapore* (1921) with Dr Gilbert E. Brooke and Sir ROLAND ST JOHN BRADDELL.

Malabar Mosque The foundation stone for the Malabar Mosque, which is also known as the Golden Dome Mosque, was laid in 1956 on a site at the corner of Victoria Street and Jalan Sultan, where there was a Malabar Muslim cemetery dating back to 1819. However, due to a lack of funds, construction of the mosque was delayed, and the building was not opened until 1963. The mosque was built to cater to the Malabar Muslim community—originating in the south Indian state of Kerala—and its construction was made possible through the efforts of the MALABAR MUSLIM JAMA-ATH.

The mosque was designed in a traditional style, surrounded on three sides by verandahs. An octagonal tower is surmounted by a golden dome, topped by a crescent moon and star. After completion of the structure, the surrounding area underwent rapid urbanization. For ease of maintenance, the paintwork finish of the building's exterior was replaced with green and blue tiles. The mosque's management committee then decided to tile the interior as well; this was completed in 1995.

Malabar Muslim Jama-ath Association catering to Malayalam-speaking Muslims. First registered in 1929, it was originally based in Changi Road. It was this association that planned the building of the MALABAR MOSQUE—to where the Malabar

Malabar Mosque

Muslim Jama-ath later moved its headquarters. It was a founding member of the FEDERATION OF INDIAN MUSLIMS.

Malacca sultanate Historical Malay state. According to local accounts, the founder of the Malacca sultanate was ISKANDAR SHAH, the former ruler of TEMASEK who had fled around 1400 from what is now Singapore island, due to a threat from either Siam or Java.

The port of Malacca prospered due to its access to trade and its important geographic position on the Strait of Malacca. The sultanate also sought recognition from the Ming Emperor of China. Its ruler, and most of his followers, also converted to Islam.

At its peak in the late 15th century, Malacca was one of the busiest ports in the world. The sultanate's power thus grew, and it gained control over neighbouring Malay states. However, in 1511, Alfonso d'Albuquerque captured Malacca for the Portuguese. The sultanate's ruling elite then fled to the south, where they eventually founded the JOHOR SULTANATE.

The influence of the Malacca sultanate on the Malay world was strongest in terms of Islam, trade and political heritage. Following the conversion of Parameswara to Islam in around 1414, Malacca became an important Islamic regional centre. Every person in Malacca was subject to the *Undang-undang Melaka* (Laws of Malacca), which was a combination of local traditions and Islamic jurisprudence. After the fall of Malacca in 1511, Islam spread from Malacca to other ports throughout Southeast Asia.

The port of Malacca was cosmopolitan—a tradition that had begun with the SRIVIJAYA EMPIRE. Because of its trade in spices (cloves, nutmeg and mace) from Maluku, and other produce from around Southeast Asia, the port attracted merchants from all over Asia.

The Malacca sultanate came to be glorified as an ideal state in Malay court literature, much of which was sponsored by the rulers of Johor. The sultanate and its rulers were romanticized in texts such as *Hikayat Hang Tuah* and the SEJARAH MELAYU (Malay Annals). Many tenets of Malay political culture and ethics were encoded in these works. These tales also include accounts of the Malay rulers of Temasek.

malaria In 1911, malaria was the cause of 20 deaths a day in Singapore. By the 1970s, however, it had been largely eliminated here, and in 1982, the World Health Organization declared Singapore malaria-free. However, in 2000, some 266 cases of malaria were reported in Singapore. Of these, it was determined that in 264 cases the disease had been contracted overseas.

In 2004, researchers from the National University of Singapore invented an automated system using a computer programme to check the percentage of infected red blood cells, thus allowing doctors to determine a patient's condition quickly and accurately.

Malay Malay is an indigenous language of Singapore and the surrounding region that includes Peninsular Malaysia, southern Thailand, the central eastern parts of Sumatra, and the western coasts of Borneo. The type of Malay spoken in Singapore belongs to the widely distributed Johor-Riau dialect group that encompasses the Malaysian states of Malacca, Pahang, Johor, the central eastern parts of Sumatra, and the Riau Islands. These were territories held by the Johor sultanate in the 17th to 19th centuries.

Historically, while there existed several dialect groups in the Malay peninsula, it was the Johor-Riau dialect that formed the basis for the standard language in Malaysia and Singapore. This was due in part to the fact that Singapore was the centre of cultural, political and socio-economic activities in colonial times. It was in Singapore that Malaya saw its first Malay press in the late 19th century—the JAWI PERANAKAN. Naturally, the local Johor-Riau dialect became the model for the language of printed materials. The radio service also had its start in Singapore in the 1920's. As the announcers and news readers were mostly from the southern parts of the peninsula, the Johor-Riau pronunciation became the norm. This continued when Kuala Lumpur and Penang opened their own radio services. The media thus played a significant role in familiarizing the rest of Malaya with the Johor-Riau dialect.

The norms established for writing, spelling, grammar, vocabulary and pronunciation thus spread to schools and government offices throughout the peninsula. The formation of the Federation of Malaya in 1948 merely provided a formal passage for the rise of this supraregional standard language, later renamed Bahasa Malaysia.

After SEPARATION, Singapore inherited this standard type of Malay, in both print and spoken form. It was, and still is, one of two major social dialects of Malay spoken here. The other is colloquial Malay of the Johor-Riau variety. While standard Malay (or formal Malay) has evolved into a primarily written variant and is used in schools, the media, and on formal occasions, colloquial Malay is a largely unwritten form of Malay, used at home and in informal situations. Standard Malay is characterized by a complex system of affixation—the addition of prefixes and suffixes to a root word (e.g. '*mengajak*' from '*ajak*', 'invite')—a feature largely absent in colloquial Malay. Discourse markers and some lexical items also differ between the dialects. In colloquial Malay, frequently used function words appear in a shortened form (e.g. '*tidak*' (no) as '*tak*' and '*hendak*' ('want') as '*nak*').

The non-uniformity of standard Malay across the Malay-speaking countries has prompted a move to standardize the language on a regional basis. The Majlis Bahasa Brunei Darussalam Indonesia-Malaysia (Brunei Darussalam-Indonesia-Malaysia Language Council), a regional body entrusted with standardizing the language, recommended the adoption of *bahasa baku* (uniform language). While the standardization of spelling has made significant progress, the standardization of other aspects has not been as successful, including pronunciation. The proposed model, *sebutan baku* (uniform pronunciation), requires speakers to pronounce words according to the way they are spelt. Thus for the word '*luar*', the last consonant 'r' is to be heard, and in '*lupa*', the vowel 'a' is to be pronounced much like the English vowel sound in 'hut'. While this is consistent with standard Indonesian Malay, it deviates from the standard prevailing in the Malay peninsula, which keeps 'r' in final syllable position silent, and pronounces 'a' in final open syllables much like the first vowel sound in the English word 'about'. Asking a Malay speaker from Malaysia and Singapore to substitute his pronunciation of '*luar*' and '*lupa*' with *sebutan baku* is akin to asking a British English speaker to give up his pronunciation of 'car' and 'ask' in favour of the American pronunciation. Malaysia adopted *sebutan baku* in 1988 but dropped it ten years later. Singapore, under the guidance of Majlis Bahasa Melayu Singapura (Malay Language Council Singapore) (MBMS), a committee in the MINISTRY OF INFORMATION, COMMUNICATION AND THE ARTS, has implemented *sebutan baku* in both the media and the schools in stages since 1993. This policy has remained.

Native speakers of Malay in Singapore number around 500,000, about 15 per cent of the Singapore population. This comprises mostly indigenous Malays and second, third and fourth generation JAVANESE, BOYANESE and other Indonesian islanders whose forefathers settled here over the last few centuries and who have since identified themselves as Malays. Muslims of Indian and Arab origin who adopted the Malay language and culture also form a noticeable minority. In the past when Malay was still the lingua franca in Singapore, members of all ethnic groups could speak at least the pidgin variant of the language, or bazaar Malay. Some features of bazaar Malay include a reduced vocabulary and a simplified grammar sometimes derived from the Chinese dialects or Tamil.

While Malay is officially the national language of Singapore, English has become the language of administration, education and commerce as well as the language of wider communication. Today the use of Malay in Singapore is limited to native speakers and the older generation of non-native Malay speakers. The pervasive use of English is also reshaping the dynamics of language use within the Malay community. Today's primary school students are more likely to come from bilingual homes. The BILINGUALISM policy has at least ensured that Malay continues to be taught in schools. But from the late 1990s, concerns arose about the decline in the standard of spoken Malay among students. The government thus formed a committee in 2004 to review the teaching of Malay in schools. On a positive note, non-Malays are renewing an interest in acquiring Malay as a third language in school through the Malay Special Programme (MSP) and through conversational Malay language lessons.

Other than MBMS, the MINISTRY OF EDUCATION, BERITA HARIAN (a Malay daily), Suria and Warna (the Malay broadcasting stations), as well as grassroots and non-governmental organizations such as Angkatan Sasterawan 50 (*see* ASAS 50) and Persatuan Persuratan Pemuda Pemudi Melayu (Malay Youth Literary Association) are active in supporting and promoting the use of Malay in Singapore. Together with them, MBMS organizes the Malay Language and Culture Month campaign and the Literary Award, two major events that alternate over the years.

See also MALAY LITERATURE.

Malay Annals *See* SEJARAH MELAYU.

KENDI 26

berkendaraan menggunakan kendaraan (seperti berbasikal, berkereta dan lain-lain).
kendi sejenis bekas air yang bermuncung dan bertangkai (biasanya dibuat daripada tembikar atau tin).
kendong (kéndong); **mengendong** membawa barang dengan membungkus dalam kain sarung dan lain-lain.
kendur 1 tidak tegang (berkenaan tali,

Malay: part of a page from a Malay dictionary.

Malay Bureau Division of the PEOPLE'S ACTION PARTY. The bureau was established in 1954 under the direction of OTHMAN WOK as a forum for Malay affairs. It is headed by the most senior Malay minister from the party. Its main responsibility is to recruit capable Malay members into the party.

Malay education In the early 1800s, the education of MALAYS was largely informal. A Malay child's education was largely centred upon learning a trade such as farming, fishing and craft-making from elders. Formal education was closely associated with the learning of religion taught by religious teachers in essentially three types of schools. The first, and most common type was the home-based schools of village religious teachers. The second type was the *surau*-based schools (a *surau* is a place for congregational prayer that is smaller than a mosque). The third type was residential schools in which children were sent to live with a teacher and received religious instruction while assisting on the teacher's farm.

European involvement in Malay education began in the mid-1800s. The British colonial government set up a number of Malay vernacular schools that were funded by grants. However, these schools were poorly managed and attended. Management of and funding of these schools received greater attention with the appointment of various commissions tasked to look into the problems and direction of Malay education.

In 1876, the government adopted a dual education policy system providing Malay vernacular and English education.

Malay education: Sang Nila Utama Secondary School, Singapore's first Malay secondary school, 1968.

Malay literature

Malay literature Historically, Singapore was important in Malay court histories and literature. The island was referred to several times in old texts such as the Malay Annals (SEJARAH MELAYU), Hikayat Hang Tuah (Life of Hang Tuah) and the 19th-century historical work TUHFAT AL-NAFIS (Precious Gift). Modern Malay literary activity in Singapore began in the early decades

Typewriter used by Suratman Markasan.

of the 19th century. Amongst the earliest works that were published and circulated here were MUNSHI ABDULLAH ABDUL KADIR's *Syair Kampong Gelam Terbakar* (Poem of the Burning of Kampong Glam)(1830), *Kisah Pelayaran Abdullah* (Travels of Abdullah) (1843) and *Hikayat Abdullah* (Life of Abdullah) (1849). Other early works include *Syair Potong Gaji* (Poem of the Pay-cut), *Syair Dagang Berjual Beli* (Poem of Commerce) and *Syair Tenku Perabu* (Poem of Tenku Perabu) which were banned from circulation by the colonial authorities. What is significant is that these works departed very much from traditional, *istana* (palace)-centric literature. They were works of realism that captured the concerns, interests, anxieties and hopes of the ordinary Malay people in Singapore. This would be a central feature of Malay literature in years to come.

Literary centre

The introduction of the printing press in 19th-century Singapore had a great

impact on Malay literary development. By the mid-19th century, Singapore was the leading centre for Malay literature, housing several Malay newspapers and publishing companies. This led to Singapore becoming a major centre for Malay intelligentsia, especially at the beginning of the 20th century. Many leading Malay journalists and literary figures worked here, such as Abdul Rahim Kajai, a prolific writer of the modern Malay short story, who worked at UTUSAN MELAYU in the 1930s. Keris Mas (pen name of Kamaluddin Muhammad), famous for his short stories and reflective essays, also worked in Singapore and was active in the Singapore-based Angkatan Sasterawan 50 (Writers' Movement) (ASAS 50), alongside Usman Awang and A. Samad Said.

The formation of ASAS 50 provided the impetus for the development of Malay literature in Singapore. It also created competition amongst language and literary activists. Soon after its formation, Lembaga

Diary of Harun Aminurrashid, 1965.

Bahasa Melayu (Malay Language Board) was set up to provide an alternative. In 1954, journalist and writer Hamzah Hussin led an association, the Persatuan Angkatan Persuratan Melayu Baru (Union of The New Malay Literary Movement), which opposed ASAS 50's arts-for-society philosophy for being propagandistic.

The separation of Singapore from Malaysia in 1965 saw the shift of the Malay literary centre from Singapore to Kuala Lumpur. Prominent Malay writers

Malay Literature Timeline

1800s

The Hikayat Abdullah *was written in 1849.*

1930s

Abdul Rahim Kajai was the editor of Utusan Melayu *and is remembered as the 'Father of the Malay Short Story'.*

1950s

Literary activists founded ASAS 50, a movement that remains active, and influential. Masuri S.N. is seated second from the left.

During the period between 1872-1882, the number of Malay schools in the colony rose from 16 to 85. In 1882, the Malay school at Telok Blangah was converted into a training college for Malay teachers. Problems in the administration and standards of Malay schools persisted and in the 1890s all were closed pursuant to the recommendations of a Commission set up in 1893. In 1924, Richard Winstedt, a Malay language scholar, was made Director of Education. He tailored the curriculum of Malay vernacular schools to focus on skills such as fishing, gardening and basket-weaving.

After World War II, virtually no provisions were made for Malay education. In 1951, policies relating to Malay education were revised. The revisions proposed that Malay be made the medium of instruction for the first three years of schooling, with English as a separate subject. English would then become the medium of instruction for most subjects from the fourth to the seventh year. Students who excelled would qualify for the 'Special Malay Class' in an English-medium school at Standard 5.

Malay education thrived when the PEOPLE'S ACTION PARTY (PAP) came into power in 1959 and campaigned for MERGER. The teaching of Malay at the secondary and

the pre-university level in Singapore became an important political point in the PAP's pro-Malaysia campaign. Malay was declared the NATIONAL LANGUAGE and opportunities were made available both in schools and through adult-education classes to learn the language. Malay-medium secondary schools were also opened. In the years that followed, enrolment in Malay-stream schools rose.

The emphasis on industrialization, especially in the 1960s, led many Malay parents to send their children to English medium schools. By the 1980s, Malay medium schools had all closed down.

More recently, concerns have been raised within the community about the dwindling usage of the Malay language. In view of this, the Ministry of Education set up the Malay Language Review Steering Committee in 1999. The objective was to have every Malay Singaporean study the Malay language for as long as possible, and to as high a level as possible.

A Malay Language Advisory Committee was set up to solicit feedback from the community. The committee's proposals included a four-year enrichment programme for secondary school students who took Higher Malay from 2001, as well as a Malay Language Elective Programme

for university students who had taken Higher Malay at 'A' level. Students who took this option would also be eligible for the Malay Language Elective Scholarship. In addition, a new syllabus—the 'ML B'—was introduced at the secondary level for students who faced exceptional difficulties in learning the language. Students who pass the ML B would be deemed to have met the threshold requirement for entry into junior college or university.

Malay Film Productions Film studio. The SHAW BROTHERS opened Malay Film Productions (MFP) in 1947 at Jalan Ampas, off Balestier Road, to produce movies in Malay.

The studio produced over 160 movies before closing in 1967, making it the most prolific in the history of Singapore cinema. This high rate of productivity was due to the Shaw Brothers' adoption of the successful Hollywood model, in which production was integrated, and producers were granted final control over all films made.

MFP signed up many actors and directors, including Kasma Booty, S. Roomai Noor, B.S. RAJHANS, L. Krishnan, Siput Sarawak and P. RAMLEE—all of whom were leading names in Malay cinema. The first film produced by the studio was *Singapura*

Malay Film Productions: screen logo (above); studio gate passes (below).

and literary activists, such as Keris Mas, migrated to Kuala Lumpur. Those who remained in Singapore were mostly Malay teachers. The late 1960s and 1970s was a gloomy phase of Malay literary development in Singapore. With the exception of Harun Aminurrashid's *Simpang Perinang* (Junction) (1966), most works of the period were pessimistic. However, this was also the period when Singapore Malay literature evolved an identity of its own. Themes like nationalism and patriotism, which once dominated the pre-Independence period, receded. Religion began to dominate, especially in the context of the religious revivalism that started in the 1970s.

The new wave
In the mid-1980s, English-educated Malays were beginning to make their presence felt. Amongst them are Isa Kamari, Ahmad Muhammad Tahir and Khalid Lani. Significantly also, graduates of the Malay Studies department of the University of

Singapore, such as Rasiah Halil, Hadijah Rahmat, Saeda Buang, Sharifah Maznah, and Mohd Raman Daud began making an impact, providing literary commentaries and criticism, and also producing creative works themselves.

The challenge of promoting and developing a literary culture has been taken up consistently by various organizations and individuals. ASAS 50 continues to exist, though it is no longer as influential as it was in the 1950s and 1960s. The Malay Language Council of Singapore (MLCS), the NATIONAL ARTS COUNCIL and NATIONAL LIBRARY BOARD all actively promote Malay literature.

The MLCS gives out the Tun Seri Lanang Award to outstanding Malay literary figures of Singapore who have made significant contributions to the Malay literary world. Recipients include MUHAMMAD ARIF AHMAD, MASURI S.N., ABDUL GHANI ABDUL HAMID, SURATMAN MARKASAN, ALIMAN HASSAN, HARUN AMINURRASHID, NOOR S.I., MAHMUD AHMAD, and SURADI PARJO.

Today, a new generation of writers, who are mostly bilingual, dominate the scene, experimenting with new literary styles and themes. It includes writers like Rafaat Hamzah, Muhammad Rafi Abu Bakar, Noridah Kamari and Noor Hasnah Adam. However, as in the past, Malay literary culture still has a strong didactic slant and it still documents the community's experience of adjustment, despair, anxiety, hope and determination. The Malay press continues to become an important platform for Malay

literature. BERITA HARIAN regularly publishes literary pieces. It is also proactive in setting up Kelab Coretan Remaja (Youth Writing Club) with the aim of promoting literary activities amongst Malay youths.

Malay literature in Singapore today reflects a literature of a developing community that has to make sense of the changes and expectations of living in a multi-racial, modern Singapore.

1960s

Literary figures such as Usman Awang migrated to Malaysia after the 1965 Separation, shifting the Malay literary centre to Kuala Lumpur.

1980s

Malay writers that are English-educated, such as Hadijah Rahmat, began to make an impact with their research publications as well as creative writing.

Present

Berita Harian's Kelab Coretan Remaja encourages Malay youth to write by featuring their short stories and poems. Over 3,200 works from 1,600 writers have been published since the 1960s.

Di Waktu Malam (Singapore At Night) (1947). It was from 1952 onwards, however, that MFP was most active, with household names like P. Ramlee directing films such as *Bujang Lapok* (Confirmed Bachelor) (1957), *Musang Berjanggut* (The Bearded Fox) (1959), *Antara Dua Darjat* (Between Two Social Classes) (1960), *Labu dan Labi* (Labu and Labi) (1962) and *Ibu Mertuaku* (My Mother-in-Law) (1962).

In the light of growing competition from Merdeka Studio in Kuala Lumpur, and following Singapore's SEPARATION from Malaysia, the Shaw Brothers decided to limit production of Malay movies in Singapore. The company eventually decided to close MFP after the film *Raja Bersiong* (The King With Fangs) (1967) failed at the box office.

Malay Heritage Centre This institution was opened in July 2005 to showcase Malay culture, traditions and heritage. It occupies the former ISTANA KAMPONG GELAM. The centre regularly hosts activities and courses in crafts such as pottery-making and BATIK painting. The centre is supported by the Ministry of Information, Communication and the Arts.

Malay literature *See* box.

Malay Mail, The Newspaper. Founded by John Henney Matthews Robson in Kuala Lumpur in 1896, *The Malay Mail* catered to the European community with news and advertisements. With the onset of the Japanese Occupation, the paper was renamed *Malai Sinpo* and used as a propaganda channel by the Japanese.

In 1952, the paper was taken over by the Straits Times Press and merged with the SINGAPORE FREE PRESS. Kuala Lumpur and Singapore editions were published. In 1972, *The Malay Mail* became part of The New Straits Times Press. The following year, the paper became a tabloid, with a focus on human interest topics.

Malay Regiment Approval to establish a regiment of Malay soldiers was first granted by the Colonial and War Offices in 1932.

An 'Experimental Company' was established on 1 March 1933 in Port Dickson, Negri Sembilan, and a sum of $75,000 was put aside to acquire land for training grounds for the new company. The recruitment of an initial batch of 25 men began in February 1933. The Experimental Company was officially re-designated the Malay Regiment on 1 January 1935.

Under the command of Major G. McI. S. Bruce, the Malay Regiment grew. By

Bruce's retirement in 1938, it had reached a strength of 800 men. The Malay regiment was viewed by the British as an economical alternative to Indian troops and the Burma Rifles, and the Legislative Council recommended further expansion of the regiment in the lead-up to the outbreak of WORLD WAR II. A second battalion was raised in 1941, just days before the landing of Japanese forces in northern Malaya.

The Malay Regiment fought alongside British forces during the Japanese invasion of Malaya and Singapore. The most important moment for the regiment came at the BATTLE OF PASIR PANJANG, where Lieutenant ADNAN SAIDI led the regiment in trying to stave off the advancing Japanese troops. Heavily outnumbered, the regiment fought bravely but

The Malay Mail

Malay Heritage Centre

Malay royalty According to the SEJARAH MELAYU (Malay Annals), a Malay dynasty ruled Singapore—or Temasek as it was then known—during the 14th century. After the reign of five kings, the Temasek kingdom came to an abrupt end as a result of an invasion. From then onwards, no Malay dynasty ruled in Singapore until the early 19th century, when Sultan HUSAIN SHAH was installed as Sultan of Singapore by Sir STAMFORD RAFFLES in February 1819. Thus began a new line of Malay royalty in Singapore. Sultan Husain was descended from a ruling line of the Riau-Lingga royalty. He settled with his family and followers in KAMPONG GLAM, where an *istana* (palace) was built.

However, Sultan Husain's stay in Singapore was brief, as he was forced to cede power over the new settlement of Singapore to the EAST INDIA COMPANY (EIC) in 1824. He died in Malacca in 1835, leaving amongst other descendants, his eldest son, Tengku Ali. Ali was not recognised as sultan by the EIC at the time of his father's death. But in 1840, he was recognised by the EIC as holding the same powers as Sultan Husain had. Ali was also acknowledged as sultan by Temenggong Daing IBRAHIM after a period of rivalry between the two over the territory of Johor came to an end— the two signed a treaty with each other in 1855. In this treaty, Ali ceded his contested right over the territory of Johor—with the exception of a small area in Muar—to the temenggong.

Sultan Ali continued his possession of the ISTANA KAMPONG GELAM, and later moved to Malacca, where he died in 1877. His eldest son, Tengku Alam (who became Sultan Alaudin Alamshah),

resided in the Istana Kampong Gelam until his death in 1891. Shortly thereafter, an internal dispute broke out between members of the royal family over the Istana Kampong Gelam. Tengku Alam's eldest son was Tengku Ali. Tengku Ali's right to the *istana* was disputed by Tengku Mahmoud (half-brother of Tengku Alam and son of Sultan Ali by his third wife). The dispute was eventually referred to the Singapore Supreme Court, which decided in 1897 that the Istana

Kampong Gelam was no longer subject to the treaties that had been signed with Sultan Husain, and that the building was to be considered Crown property. The descendants of Sultan Husain continued to reside in the Istana Kampong Gelam until the property was transformed into the MALAY HERITAGE CENTRE.

Even after the Kampong Glam royalty faded into obscurity, relatives of the family living in Riau-Lingga continued to maintain close links with

Singapore, despite the division of the Riau-Lingga kingdom into British and Dutch spheres of influence following the signing of the ANGLO-DUTCH TREATY of 1824. For example, Sultan Mahmud of Lingga made frequent visits to Singapore and entered his boats in an annual regatta in Singapore. After the abolition of the sultanate by the Dutch in the first decade of the 20th century, the last Sultan of the Riau-Lingga kingdom relocated to Singapore, where he later died.

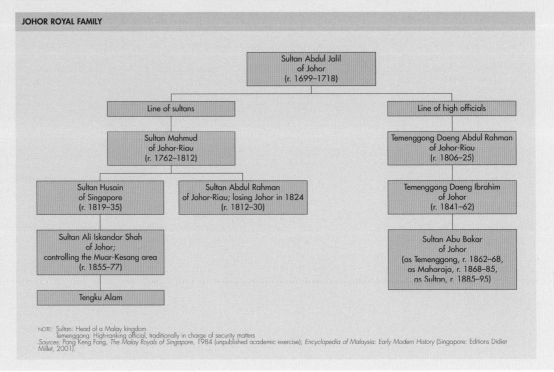

JOHOR ROYAL FAMILY

Sultan Abdul Jalil of Johor (r. 1699–1718)
- Line of sultans
  - Sultan Mahmud of Johor-Riau (r. 1762–1812)
    - Sultan Husain of Singapore (r. 1819–35)
      - Sultan Ali Iskandar Shah of Johor; controlling the Muar-Kesang area (r. 1855–77)
        - Tengku Alam
    - Sultan Abdul Rahman of Johor-Riau; losing Johor in 1824 (r. 1812–30)
- Line of high officials
  - Temenggong Daeng Abdul Rahman of Johor-Riau (r. 1806–25)
    - Temenggong Daeng Ibrahim of Johor (r. 1841–62)
      - Sultan Abu Bakar of Johor (as Temenggong, r. 1862–68, as Maharaja, r. 1868–85, as Sultan, r. 1885–95)

NOTE: Sultan: Head of a Malay kingdom
Temenggong: High-ranking official, traditionally in charge of security matters
Sources: Pang Keng Fong, *The Malay Royals of Singapore*, 1984 (unpublished academic exercise); *Encyclopedia of Malaysia: Early Modern History* (Singapore: Editions Didier Millet, 2001).

was decimated. Their bravery is commemorated at REFLECTIONS AT BUKIT CHANDU.

Malay settlements The earliest references to Malay settlements in Singapore appear in the SEJARAH MELAYU (Malay Annals), which mentions seven settlements in 13th-century Singapore: Telok Belanga, Tanjung Ru, Tanah Merah, Padang Temasik, Bukit Singapura, Kallang and Seletar.

In 1819, there were several settlements ruled by Temenggong ABDUL RAHMAN. He

Malay Regiment: men in 'Walking Out' dress, 1942.

and his followers lived in a KAMPONG at the mouth of the SINGAPORE RIVER known as Kampung Temenggung. This was the main Malay settlement at that time. With the arrival of the British, two Malay settlements grew around the centres of Malay royalty— Kampung Temenggung and KAMPONG GLAM. Kampung Temenggung was moved to Telok Blanga in 1823. The first Malay school and the Malay Teachers' Training College were built here.

Another early settlement was Kampung Melaka. Colonel WILLIAM FARQUHAR, the first Resident of Singapore, invited immigrants from Malacca to settle in Singapore. These immigrants settled in the area around what is now Havelock Road. The first mosque in Singapore, OMAR KAMPONG MELAKA MOSQUE, was built there in 1820.

In 1820, Arong Bilawa, a BUGIS chieftain, together with 500 followers (including women and children) come to Singapore from Riau seeking political asylum from the Dutch. Farquhar granted the Bugis asylum and they built their settlement, Kampung Bugis, on the banks of the Kallang River.

Flourishing trade attracted more immigrants from the region. By 1849, settlements such as Kampung Boyan, Tanah

Merah Besar, Kampung Tanjong Katong and Kampung Telok Kurau were established to house the growing population.

Kampung Boyan was built on the banks of the Rochor River by BOYANESE immigrants from Bawean Island during the late 19th century. The Boyanese also lived in communal lodging houses (*pondok*) in areas such as Ann Siang Hill (Pondok Adam) and Sophia Road (Pondok Dedawang).

The JAVANESE established Kampung Java near ARAB STREET. Settlers from BENCOOLEN (now Benkulu), Sumatra, established Kampung Bencoolen, located in the area around Bencoolen Street and Waterloo Street. The Sumbawanese (from the Lesser Sunda Islands) founded Kampung Sumbawa. It was located in the area near the Rochor River.

Settlements also developed near plantations. These plantations grew coconut, banana, tapioca and other crops. Examples of these settlements include Kampung Ubi ('*ubi*' means 'tapioca' in Malay) in GEYLANG SERAI, Kampung Pisang ('*pisang*' means 'banana' in Malay) at Tanjong Pagar, and Kampung Wak Hassan in Sembawang. There were also fishing villages such as Kampung Tanjung Changi,

Padang Terbakar, and Kampung Ponggol. Offshore islands such as Pulau Brani, Pulau Tekong, and Pulau Merlimau also had Malay settlements.

Several kampongs were located in the Geylang Serai area ('*serai*' means 'lemongrass' in Malay). The Malays who worked in the lemongrass plantations there settled in nearby kampongs such as Kampung Lorong Ungku Aman, and Kampung Jalan Betik.

The British gazetted four settlements for Malays under the Malay Settlements Programme. These were Kampung Melayu Jalan Eunos, Kampung Ayer Gemuroh, Kampung Melayu West Coast and Kampung Tengah. These settlements were built on government-owned land and were allotted on temporary occupation licences under the Crown Land Ordinance. Unlike other kampongs, these settlements were restricted to Malay residents. Kampung Melayu Jalan Eunos, the first gazetted settlement, was established in 1928 on 240 ha of land at Jalan Eunos. Kampung Melayu West Coast was gazetted in 1957. It was made up of 40 families that were resettled due to the construction of KALLANG AIRPORT. Kampung Ayer Gemuroh, a fishing village near Changi, was set up to house Malay fishermen affected by the construction of CHANGI AIRFIELD. In 1959, this land was gazetted as a Malay settlement. The last area gazetted was Kampung Tengah in Sembawang. It was set up when the British relocated Malay workers from a naval base to a new location in the 1960s.

Following the 1966 LAND ACQUISITION ACT, landowners and dwellers of Malay settlements—gazetted or otherwise—gradually resettled in public housing estates. The last kampong on an offshore island was Kampung Melayu on Pulau Ubin, while the last kampong on the main island was KAMPUNG LORONG BUANGKOK at Yio Chu Kang Road.

Malay theatre *See* box.

Malay weddings Normally held on a weekend, a Malay wedding is a regal affair, with the bride and groom treated as king and queen for the day. Before the wedding, there is a meeting between the couple's parents to discuss the bride's *hantaran* (gifts), the *mas kahwin* or *mahr* (dowry), and the date of the *akad nikah* (solemnization). The latter is usually conducted a few hours (sometimes weeks or months) before the *walima* (wedding feast). The *akad nikah* is presided over by a *kadhi*, a religious official appointed by the SYARIAH COURT. The ceremony may be held in the bride's home, at the REGISTRY OF MUSLIM MARRIAGES, in a mosque or in a function hall.

The *akad nikah* is a verbal contract between the groom and the bride's father, or his representative—in most cases, the *kadhi*. The *mas kahwin* can be cash, or gold or silver items. Gifts are usually exchanged at this time also.

On the wedding day, the families of the groom and the bride host separate wedding feasts. The groom arrives at the bride's place first. His arrival is heralded by a *hadrah* troupe, who beat the *kompang* (hand-held drums) and sing traditional songs. The groom is often flanked by people carrying *bunga manggar* (palm blossoms, usually artificial), relatives and friends. The *mak andam* (wedding beautician) and members of the bride's family waylay the groom in jest, and ask for an 'entrance fee' before he can see his bride.

The couple wear elaborate wedding outfits. They sit on a decorated wedding dais and have their photographs taken with family members, friends and guests. During the *bersanding* (sitting on a dais) ceremony, relatives and guests may sprinkle petals and rice—traditional Malay symbols of fertility—on the couple. The groom then brings the bride to the wedding feast held by his family, and the *bersanding* ceremony is repeated there.

The wedding feast lasts the whole day; invited guests may attend at any time between 11 a.m. and 5 p.m. The feast, usually held in a void deck or community hall, is often a lively and informal affair, with lots of food and music. The parents, or guardians, of the bride and groom are the hosts of the feast; guests, before they leave, extend their congratulations to the parents and present them with a token cash gift. Each guest is then presented with a *bunga telur* (literally, flower-egg), a wedding souvenir in the form of a hard-boiled egg. In recent years, chocolates, jelly or even soap have been given as wedding souvenirs.

Malaya, Federation of The introduction of the MALAYAN UNION on 1 April 1946 provoked widespread Malay opposition, threatening the stability of British rule in Malaya. British officials, together with representatives of Malay rulers and the United Malays National Organization (UMNO), met in July 1946 for confidential discussions on establishing a legal framework for an alternative centralized form of government and common citizenship that would provide the basis for a future 'Malay' nation-state in which Malays would be given preferential rights.

By December 1946, a working committee had agreed in principle to create a Federation of Malaya. This federation would include the same territorial units that were part of the former Malayan Union (comprising the nine Malay states) together with the settlements of Penang and Malacca. The sovereignty of Malay rulers was to be restored, as was Malay primacy, and a high commissioner was to replace the British governor. The sole feature of the Malayan Union which would remain was the exclusion of Singapore. UMNO's leaders supported this, as the Chinese population would otherwise out-

Malay settlements: early-20th-century view of a coastal Malay kampong.

number the Malays. UMNO endorsed the proposals in mid-January 1947. After further consultations with non-Malay groups, the final form of the scheme was published for public discussion in mid-1947.

From December 1946, however, many non-Malay leaders—including non-UMNO Malay leaders and communists—fearing that their interests might be compromised, formed a Council of Joint Action in Singapore to protest against their exclusion from the Anglo-Malay discussions. The council was expanded to become the PAN-MALAYAN COUNCIL OF JOINT ACTION (renamed the All Malaya Council of Joint Action in August 1947). However, despite drawing up a series of counter-proposals and successfully executing a nationwide strike in October 1947, the council was unable to prevent the formation of the Federation of Malaya on 1 February 1948.

By returning political primacy to the Malays, the Federation of Malaya established the framework for the future political development of Malaysia. It allowed Malays to set the pattern and agenda for the creation of a future 'Malayan' nation-state. However, the twofold purpose of the Malayan Union policy—creation of a strong central government and common citizenship—was retained in the new federal structure. Significantly, for non-Malays, this meant that Malaya no longer belonged

Malay weddings: feast (left); bersanding *ceremony.*

Malay theatre

BANGSAWAN, believed to have appeared in the late 1800s, could be considered the first form of Malay theatre to be staged in Singapore. It narrated fantastical, mythical stories interspersed by music and rhymed poetry. It was a very popular form of entertainment from the 1900s to the 1930s. *Bangsawan* was also known as 'opera' especially when European theatrical styles and themes were incorporated. *Bangsawan* performances were basically commercial ventures that were financed by Malays and non-Malays. *Bangsawan* enthusiasts of all races were known to congregate in Singapore to watch performances here, while some troupes travelled in the region to stage their repertoires. *Bangsawan* had significant influence on the development of modern Malay theatre and the Malay film industry in Singapore.

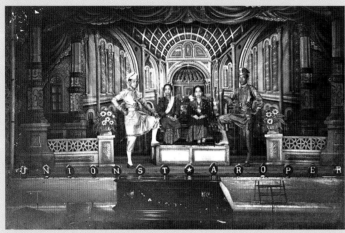

Bangsawan *opera troupe on an elaborate stage.*

By the 1930s, another theatrical genre, the *sandiwara*, was brought into Singapore by Indonesian drama troupes. The *sandiwara* was distinct from the *bangsawan* in that it employed elements of modern stage directing and script-writing. *Sandiwara* also moved away from fantasy and depicted real-life situations. It ushered in modern Malay theatre.

Modern theatre

It is difficult to identify the first modern Malay theatre ever staged. One possibility is BANI BUANG's amateur staging of *Helang Hitam* (Black Eagle) in the 1940s. Another possibility is Syed Alwi al-Hady's *Tarek ben Ziad Pahlawan Islam* (Tarek ben Ziad, Warrior of Islam) and *Hang Tuah, Pahlawan Melayu* (Hang Tuah the Malay Warrior) performances at the Victoria Theatre during the Japanese Occupation. By the 1950s, more *sandiwara* groups were formed, boosted by the surge of literary activities led by ASAS 50. Renowned playwright Kalam Hamidy was actively involved in Persatuan Persuratan Pemuda Pemudi Melayu (Malay Youth Literary Association) and contributed significantly to the exposure of local Malay theatre to realism as a theatre style. *Qalam* (Pen), which was a local magazine, even featured articles on script-writing techniques and published drama scripts.

The socio-political milieu of newly independent Singapore led to the exploration of new themes and forms. Though *sandiwara* eclipsed *bangsawan*, the latter did not completely disappear. By this time, *bangsawan* troupes used modern script-writing and stage direction methods. The 1970s saw E.F. Kamaruddin and NADIPUTRA making significant impacts on the theatre scene. E.F. Kamaruddin's works showcased social protests and religious issues, while Nadiputra adhered to more conventional themes such as good versus evil. The 1970s also saw a new generation of amateur playwrights, namely Sapiee Ahmad Razali, who experimented with poetical imageries, and Raman Daud who dealt with the notion of the hero and other human predicaments. In the 1980s, comedy theatre, including comedy *bangsawan*, became popular, with M. Safri A. Manaf and Yusoff Maruwi making significant contributions.

The 1980s also saw a new generation of Malay theatre activists emerging, such as Sabri Buang and Khairul Anwar Salleh who later inspired the younger groups to come to the fore. By now, more theatre activists, including Sabri and Khairul, received formal training in theatre studies. Their daring thematic explorations, styles and techniques created a new enthusiasm in local Malay theatre. By the 1990s, professional Malay theatre companies such as Teater Artistik, Teater Kami, and Teater Ekamatra were set up, following government funding for the arts, a burgeoning young audience, and corporate sponsorships. The younger theatre activists, who were primarily bilingual, experimented with Malay-English combinations in their theatre repertoire, and even co-staged with non-Malay theatre groups. They also went beyond conventional themes to highlight issues considered taboo, such as marginalization, ethnicity, religion and gender inequality. Theatre exponents such as Rafaat Hamzah, Aidli 'Alin' Mosbit, ALFIAN SA'AT and Nor Effendi Ibrahim, continued to push the boundaries and articulated their views and observations through satires, parodies and tragic comedies. The groups considered to be more traditional, such as SRIWANA and Persatuan Kemuning, however, still showcased *sandiwara* and *bangsawan* repertoires. Theatre festivals and workshops such as Teater Ekamatra's *Pesta Peti Putih* (White Box Festival) initiative, which started in 1999, encourage youths to participate in and to support theatre.

Cerita–cerita Asia *(Asian Stories) 2002 Programme by Teater Ekamatra and Mendaki.*

Leading playwrights and directors such as Bani Buang and Nadiputra have received Cultural Medallions for their contributions to Malay theatre. The Malay Language Council also recognizes Malay theatre and drama in its biannual Literary Awards. From the period of 1993–2001 works by Hamed Ismail (*Anjing Untuk Diplomat* [Dog For a Diplomat] and *Singkap* [Push]), Aidli 'Alin' Mosbit (*Kosovo*), Hadijah Rahmat (*Munsyi*), Alfian Sa'at (*Causeway*) and M. Safri A. Manaf (*Terminal Akhir* [Last Terminal]) were recognized for their respective contributions.

Clockwise, from top left: Minah Monyet *(Monkey Girl), 2003, directed by Alfian Sa'at;* Anak Bulan di Kampung Wak Hassan *(New Moon Over Kampong Wak Hassan), 2001, directed by Gene Sharudyn;* Causeway, *Singapore Arts Festival 2002, directed by Aidli 'Alin' Mosbit;* Dhavusya, *1997, directed by Khairuddin Hori.*

only to indigenous Malays, but also to non-Malays who qualified for citizenship.

The Federation of Malaya was superseded by the Federation of Malaysia in 1963.

Malaya *See* MALAYA, FEDERATION OF and MALAYAN UNION.

Malaya Campaign *See* box.

Malaya Command From 1929 to 1957, overall control of British land forces in Malaya and Singapore came under Malaya Command or (for a brief post-war period) Malaya District. Malaya Command was headed by a General Officer Commanding, this being Lieutenant-General ARTHUR PERCIVAL for the period between May 1941 and February 1942.

Malaya Command was divided into sub-districts. Singapore was one of these sub-districts, being referred to as 'Singapore Fortress' (*see* FORTRESS OF THE EAST) up until WORLD WAR II, and Singapore Base District thereafter.

Malaya Tribune, The English-language newspaper started in 1914 to serve the EURASIAN community. In 1919, the paper only had a circulation of 1,200. But in later years, it challenged even THE STRAITS TIMES in popularity. During the Japanese Occupation, most of the newspaper's assets were either stolen or destroyed. The paper eventually folded in 1951.

Malayalees Indian cultural-linguistic group. The Malayalees were originally from Kerala, a state on the southwestern coast of India. The majority of Malayalees in Singapore are Hindu, with Catholicism and Islam also practised by a significant proportion. A smaller number are SYRIAN CHRISTIANS. However, regardless of these religious differences, members of this community share a common language—Malayalam—which has its own script.

The first Malayalees to come to Singapore did so in the late 19th century, many gaining clerical employment in the colonial administration.

On 29 September 1917, the 1,500-strong Malayalee community formed its first social and cultural organization—the Keraleeya Mahajena Sangham (Association of the People from Kerala). This was renamed the Singapore Kerala Samajam (Singapore Kerala Association) in 1952. The other major organization to have been closely associated with this community is the Naval Base Kerala Library. Located in the north of the island, the library caters to the largest concentration of Malayalees in Singapore—a legacy of the British Naval Base which once provided employment for many members of the community.

The British military departure from Singapore in the 1970s saw many Malayalees emigrate to India and the United Kingdom. The size of the community remained around 16,000 until the 1990s, when a new wave of Malayalees began arriving from India in search of professional and high-skilled employment in the information technology and financial sectors. In 2004, there were 21,736 Malayalees, representing 8.43 per cent of the total ethnic Indian population.

Well-known Malayalees include President C.V. DEVAN NAIR, politicians JAMES PUTHUCHEARY and DOMINIC PUTHUCHEARY, diplomat Vanu Gopala Menon, lawyer Subhas Anandan and former president of AWARE, CONSTANCE SINGHAM.

Malayan Airlines This airline began operations on 1 May 1947. Its inaugural service was from KALLANG AIRPORT to Kuala Lumpur, Ipoh and Penang, three times a week. The airline's single British-made Airspeed Consul had space for only five passengers and no cabin crew, on-board refreshments being limited to a flask of iced water per passenger.

By 1955, the carrier had acquired a fleet of Douglas DC-3s. Operations were extended to Jakarta, Medan, Palembang, Saigon, Bangkok, Sabah, Sarawak, Rangoon and Brunei. In 1962, it began using larger Comet jets on international routes. Malayan Airlines was renamed Malaysian Airways after MERGER in 1963. In 1966, after SEPARATION, the carrier was renamed Malaysia-Singapore Airlines (MSA).

In 1967, MSA expanded its network beyond Southeast Asia. It bought three Boeing 707s. It also introduced the *sarong kebaya* uniform (designed by Pierre Balmain) for its flight attendants.

Disagreements between Singapore and Malaysia as to how the airline should be operated caused MSA to cease operations in 1972. In its place, two new airlines were formed: SINGAPORE AIRLINES and Malaysia Airlines.

Malayan Auxiliary Air Force This air force unit was formed in 1950 to train Malayans and Singaporeans to fly military aircraft.

MAAF had three squadrons (one each in Singapore, Kuala Lumpur and Penang). Training was undertaken in de Havilland Tiger Moth biplanes, although these were phased out in 1957, replaced by de Havilland Chipmunk planes. In 1960, the MAAF was disbanded due to planned reductions in British military expenditure in the region.

Over the ten years of its existence, 900 men served in the MAAF's Singapore Squadron No. 224, which came under the command of Air Vice-Marshal Ramsay Rae, and produced 20 pilots and 200 ground staff. Other prominent members of the MAAF included Wing Commander Tan Kay Hai—who was decorated for his services as a bomber and reconnaissance pilot

Federation of Malaya: first Rulers' Conference of the Federation, 15 February 1948.

over Italy and France during World War II—and Flight-Lieutenant Jimmy Chew.

Malayan Communist Party Communism first came to Malaya in the early 1920s as a result of the Comintern's (international communist organization) efforts to spread communism in Indochina and the rest of Southeast Asia. In March 1924, Alimin, a Moscow-trained leader of the Indonesian Communist Party, declared that he had established agents operating in Singapore. In May 1925, an agent of the Chinese Communist Party (CCP), Fu Ta Ching, arrived in Singapore from Shanghai to establish a communist movement here and use the island as a staging post for communist insurrection in Indonesia. Nothing appears to have come off these plans.

Between November 1927 and January 1928, five CCP representatives travelled to Singapore to establish the Nanyang Communist Party, also without tangible success. In late 1929, it was decided that the Third Representatives' Conference of the Nanyang Communist Party would be held in Singapore in March 1930. At that conference, the old Nanyang Communist Party and the Nanyang General Labour Union were dissolved, with the Malayan Communist Party (MCP) being established in their place. The MCP (also known as the Communist Party of Malaya, or CPM) came under the direct control of the Comintern's Far Eastern Bureau.

At the 1935 World Conference of the Comintern, delegates declared their intention to fight fascism and imperialism alongside non-communist organizations that shared these objectives. This was the concept of a 'United Front'. In the context of Malaya, this meant a united labour front to organize communist labour unions and use labour

The Malaya Tribune

Malayan Auxiliary Air Force: Tiger Moth plane at Tengah Air Base, 1950.

Malayan Airlines: logo of Malaysian Airways (top); the twin-engined Airspeed Consul.

Malaya Campaign

The Malaya Campaign refers to the Japanese conquest of Malaya, including Singapore, between 8 December 1941 and 15 February 1942. Throughout this campaign, the 5th, 18th and Imperial Guards Divisions of the Imperial Japanese Army were collectively referred to as the 25th Army, and were commanded by Lieutenant-General YAMASHITA TOMOYUKI.

The Japanese occupied Singapore 30 days earlier than they had projected. Each day, they advanced an average of 20 km. They managed to overcome some 130,000 troops of the British Army, the Indian Army and the Australian Imperial Force and eventually take Singapore.

Japanese troops enter Kuala Lumpur.

Europeans evacuated from Penang.

Japanese artist's impression of the landing at Kota Baru.

Japanese artist's impression of the sinking of HMS Prince of Wales.

Japanese troops enter Johor Baru.

Australian troops defend at Muar.

Timeline

1941

2 December: FORCE Z (comprising HMS PRINCE OF WALES, HMS REPULSE and four destroyers) arrives in Singapore.

4 December: Japanese invasion force sets sail from Hainan, China.

7/8 December
- 0045, 8 December (Singapore time): landing of Japanese troops on the beaches off Kota Baru
- 0200, 8 December (Singapore time): bombing of Pearl Harbor
- 0230, 8 December (Singapore time): landing of troops at Singora (present-day Songkhla) and Patani
- 0300, 8 December (Singapore time): Japanese bomb Singapore.

8 December: Japanese launch attacks on the Philippines, Guam, Hong Kong and Wake Island. Force Z heads up the east coast for Kota Baru without

Streets in Singapore littered with debris from Japanese bombing.

air cover. Japanese cross the Thai-Malaya border; there is a skirmish, during which a map showing British positions at Jitra is captured.

9 December: British troops fall back from Jitra to Alor Star (present-day Alor Setar).

10 December: Japanese planes sink HMS *Prince of Wales* and HMS *Repulse* off the east coast.

13 December: Alor Star captured.

14–15 December: Action in Gurun.

16 December: Evacuation of European civilians from Penang.

17 December: British withdraw southwards to the line of the Perak River.

19 December: Japanese enter Penang with no loss of Japanese lives; two thousand Penang civilians die during Japanese bombardment.

26 December: Japanese break through Perak River defences and move towards Ipoh.

31 December: The Japanese take

Kuantan. British defend Kampar in a fierce three-day action.

1942

2 January: British pull back from Kampar to the Slim River.

7–8 January: Japanese break through the Slim River defences, and the British lose 3,200 men during the Battle of Slim River.

9–15 January: The Australians, under the command of Lieutenant-General GORDON BENNETT, try the Japanese tactic of outflanking the enemy, at first successfully. Nonetheless, the Japanese break through defensive lines and win the Battle of Gemas. The British withdraw to Batu Pahat.

11 January: The Japanese enter Kuala Lumpur. Imperial Guards Division goes west towards Malacca, and plans are made for the remainder of 18th Division to land at Singora and to travel south by road.

14 January: Malacca captured.

20 January: Sir ARCHIBALD WAVELL arrives in Singapore to find that little has been done about Singapore's northern defences.

Rubber plantations destroyed by the British as they retreat towards Singapore.

21 January: Collapse of the Batu Pahat-Yong Peng line. British withdraw towards Singapore.

22 January: Labis captured.

22–24 January: Some 40–50,000 British reinforcements—mainly new recruits—arrive in Singapore.

25 January: Kluang taken by Japanese 5th Division; the British withdraw to the Johor River line. Kluang becomes the assembly point for 25th Army before moving on to Singapore.

26 January: Endau and Mersing taken by a detachment of Japanese 18th Division sweeping down east coast.

28 January: Lieutenant-General ARTHUR

Ford Motor Factory: site of the British surrender.

Poster for Japanese propaganda film.

Propaganda leaflet dropped in Singapore by the Japanese.

British reinforcements arriving in Singapore.

The Malay Regiment made its last stand at Bukit Chandu.

Many of the Japanese soldiers who died during the campaign were buried at Singapore's Japanese Cemetery Park.

PERCIVAL orders British troops to withdraw from Malaya into Singapore by 31 January.

29 January: Main body of British 18th Division arrive in Singapore.

30 January: Rear-Admiral E.J. Spooner orders the evacuation of Sembawang Naval Base without informing Percival. Seamen are evacuated, and only a small force is left behind to demolish the base. The demolition is inadequately completed, leaving stores and supplies to be looted.

31 January: The last British troops cross over into Singapore by 0530, and the CAUSEWAY is dynamited. The Japanese begin repairing the breach, forcing Johor Baru civilians to help their engineers in the process. Yamashita congratulates his commanders on their rapid progress.

1 February: In Johor, Yamashita gives out the battle orders for the capture of Singapore. He drinks a toast with wine that has been sent from the Japanese royal family.

1–4 February: Yamashita orders the reconnaissance of the north coast of Singapore; Japanese artillery begins shelling Singapore.

6 February: Yamashita moves his headquarters to the highest building in Johor Baru facing Singapore—the sultan of Johor's palace—for a commanding view across the strait.

7–8 February: A detachment of the Imperial Guards Division slips across to Pulau Ubin, occupies it with little resistance and installs artillery amongst the rubber trees. The guns begin firing on Changi on the morning of 8 February. The Japanese are accompanied by a company of Indian National Army soldiers.

8 February: At about 2300, the main Japanese force, made up of the 5th and 18th Divisions, begins moving out from the river estuaries of Johor for the short crossing to Singapore. They land on the north-west coast in Sarimbun. A decoy group also goes to the north-east in Sembawang.

9/10 February: Japanese tanks begin crossing the repaired Causeway in the evening. The Imperial Guards cross into Singapore during the next two days. Yamashita reaches Singapore on the evening of 9 February.

10 February: Wavell visits Singapore to assess the situation, exhorts Percival to keep fighting, and cables WINSTON CHURCHILL to inform him that the situation is dire. There is fierce fighting along Bukit Timah Road, with the British withdrawing further and further towards the city centre.

11 February: The Japanese capture Bukit Timah. This coincides with the Japanese celebration of Kigensetsu—a holiday celebrating the ascension to the throne of Jimmu Tenno, the first emperor of Japan. Yamashita drops his surrender offer in a communications tube behind enemy lines.

12 February: Japanese 5th Division attacks the reservoir sector.

12–14 February: Battle of Pasir Panjang, between MALAY REGIMENT and men of the 18th Division.

13 February: Yamashita moves his headquarters to the FORD MOTOR FACTORY at Bukit Timah. Percival confers with his commanders, most of whom report their troops to be exhausted and demoralized.

14 February: Percival cables Wavell, informing him that Singapore cannot resist the Japanese for more than a day, and requesting that he be given the discretion to surrender if necessary. Wavell orders Percival to keep fighting. Civil authorities report that the water supply may be shut down due to breaks in the water mains and pipelines. Winston Churchill gives Percival the discretion to surrender if necessary. The Malay Regiment's last stand is fought at the Battle of BUKIT CHANDU.

15 February: Percival surrenders some 130,000 men to Yamashita.

16 February: The JAPANESE OCCUPATION begins.

British surrender party arrives at the Ford Motor Factory.

Malayan People's Anti-Japanese Army: the Chinese characters on the flag mean 'Malayan People's Anti-Japanese Army— First Independent Regiment'.

strikes as a weapon to paralyse industry and overthrow the British; a united racial front that included all races and aimed to expel the British through a struggle for self-determination; and an anti-Japanese front of Chinese in Malaya. Within the MCP hierarchy, Singapore was placed under the South Malaya command.

The MCP's first major activities came in the field of labour. It organized major strikes in Selangor, and sympathy strikes in Penang, Malacca, Johor and Singapore. In Singapore, these strikes closed down stone quarries and building sites. However, in September 1940, the CCP instructed the MCP to halt all anti-British activity and concentrate on resistance against the Japanese instead. Strikes in Singapore thus ended. By this time, the MCP had some 5,000 members and over 100,000 sympathizers.

With the outbreak of World War II, the MCP, led by LAI TECK, organized its military arm—the Malayan People's Liberation Army—into an anti-Japanese fighting force known as the MALAYAN PEOPLE'S ANTI-JAPANESE ARMY (MPAJA).

After the war, attempts by the British to dismantle the MPAJA failed, and the MCP launched an armed insurrection to overthrow British rule. In 1948, the British authorities declared a state of EMERGENCY and outlawed the MCP. By this time, the leadership of the party was in the hands of the new secretary-general, CHIN PENG, who succeeded Lai Teck after the latter had been exposed as a double agent. Chin Peng and the MCP—which by this time had several regiments, including the all-Malay 10th regiment—went 'underground'.

By the 1950s, the MCP adopted a different strategy. The party found that it could no longer describe itself as a champion of the Malays. CPM leaders felt that it was necessary to legitimize the party in a new way. Peace talks at Baling in December 1955 between CHIN PENG, Tunku ABDUL RAHMAN (chief minister of Malaya), TAN CHENG LOCK (president of the Malayan Chinese Association) and DAVID MARSHALL (Singapore's chief minister) ended in failure when the Tunku refused to grant MCP members a blanket amnesty. Chin Peng viewed the Tunku's conditions as a call to surrender, and vowed that the MCP would continue to fight. In 1960, the Malayan government ended the Emergency.

With Merger in 1963, and the Tunku's apparent willingness to use the Internal Security Act against communists and pro-

communists, life for the MCP and its guerrillas became increasingly difficult. Many retreated to areas on the border between Malaysia and Thailand. The party also underwent several internal purges. By the mid-1970s, it no longer represented a significant political force.

The normalization of diplomatic relations between China and Malaysia (1974) and between China and Thailand (1976) meant that China substantially reduced support for the MCP. A series of peace initiatives were undertaken by the Thai and Malaysian governments in an effort to end the MCP's armed insurrection. On 2 December 1989, the MCP signed peace treaties with the Thai and Malaysian governments at Hatyai, Thailand, thus formally ending all hostilities.

Malayan Democratic Union The Malayan Democratic Union (MDU) was formed on 21 December 1945 to work towards the objective of an independent and united Malaya, inclusive of Singapore. Its leadership, drawn largely from English-educated intellectuals, included JOHN EBER, LIM KEAN CHYE, LIM HONG BEE, GERALD DE CRUZ, PHILIP HOALIM and Wu Tian Wang—a member of the Malayan Communist Party (MCP).

Despite the presence of an MCP member in its leadership ranks, the MDU's platform was based on anti-colonialism and socialism, rather than communism. The party has even been described as a precursor to the PEOPLE'S ACTION PARTY (PAP) in terms of its multiracial and largely English-educated leadership. Like the PAP, the MDU sought to attract support from the Chinese-educated population. Its willingness to co-operate with the MCP in fulfilling its anti-colonial aims was based, in part, on its belief in the MCP's pervasive influence over Chinese-educated sections of the population.

Initially, the MDU adopted a moderate stance with regard to British proposals for Malaya and Singapore. It did not reject outright the MALAYAN UNION scheme introduced by the British in April 1946. Indeed, the MDU announced that it was willing to support this scheme provided that Singapore was not separated from the union.

However, the British responded to Malay opposition to the scheme by negotiating with Malay rulers and representatives from the United Malays National Organization (UMNO) on the replacement of the Malayan Union by a federation (*see* MALAYA, FEDERATION OF). In response, a coalition of groups opposed to the federation scheme was formed, the PAN-MALAYAN COUNCIL OF JOINT ACTION, of which the MDU was part. The MDU helped draft the alternative People's Constitution and organize a strike in response to the rejection of this constitution by the British. It also boycotted the March 1948 elections.

After its failure to halt the establishment of the Federation of Malaya in February 1948, the MDU grew increasingly radical in its stance, and sought to develop itself into a mass movement. However, with the EMERGENCY in 1948, the MDU's political activities were curtailed by the British. As a result, the MDU voluntarily dissolved itself on 24 June 1948.

Malayan Forum Political discussion group. The Malayan Forum was established in London by a group of Malayan students concerned about the political fate of their country. It was formed in 1947, and its first chairman was GOH KENG SWEE, at that time studying economics at the London School of Economics. Mohamed Sopie, a Malayan, was its first secretary. Other key members were MAURICE BAKER (later Professor of English at the University of Malaya), and Lee Kip Lin (later an architect). Other active members were PHILIP HOALIM (and his fiancée Miki Goh), Eu Cheow Chye, Abdul Razak and Mohammed Nur.

At its peak, the forum had 50–60 members, although meetings were also attended by non-members, including students studying at Cambridge University (such as LEE KUAN YEW and Kwa Geok Choo) and Oxford University (such as K. M. BYRNE). Many of the group's early meetings were held in students' rooms and at pubs. Activities consisted mainly of inviting guest speakers from the United Kingdom, or from other British colonies. The main topic of discussion was how Singapore and Malaya could achieve independence, and what problems an independent Malaya would face. When the Singapore and Malayan governments established a Students' Centre at Bryanston Square near Marble Arch, this became the forum's meeting place.

In 1951, Goh Keng Swee returned to Singapore, and TOH CHIN CHYE became the forum's chairman. In October 1953, control of the group fell into the hands of the leftist JOHN EBER and his brother-in-law, Wan Hamid. Goh Keng Swee travelled again to London in 1954 to embark on doctoral studies. By 1955, he was ready to reclaim the forum from Eber and the other leftists, and did so with the help of CHUA SIAN CHIN, Hedwig Anuar and J.Y. PILLAY.

The Malayan Forum continued to function until 1962, when it had become clear that Singapore would be merged with Malaysia.

Malayan Motors Established in November 1926, Malayan Motors started as a franchise car dealer for Morris cars. It operated out of an office on Orchard Road. Two years later, it was awarded the Rolls-Royce franchise. The company continued to grow in the decades preceding World War II, acquiring the Wolseley and Riley brand names, and establishing the MG sports label. Malayan

Motors introduced the famous Morris Minor and the Morris Oxford diesel taxi to Singapore in 1948.

During a downturn in the automobile market in the mid-1970s, Malayan Motors' operations were merged with those of Federated Motors and Progress Motors—which also held the Austin and Leyland truck and bus franchises.

In August 1989, Malayan Motors added the Volvo truck franchise to its list of agencies. By the beginning of the 21st century, it had developed into a multi-agency car dealership, distributing and servicing Bentley, Jaguar, Chevrolet, Volvo, Mazda and Ford cars, as well as Volvo trucks. Malayan Motors is a subsidiary of Singapore-listed conglomerate Wearnes International.

Malayan People's Anti-Japanese Army

Guerrilla army organized by the MALAYAN COMMUNIST PARTY (MCP) to fight the Japanese. In 1941, when the Japanese invaded Thailand and northern Malaya, the governor of Singapore, Sir SHENTON THOMAS, agreed to release MCP political prisoners and provide guerrilla training for them at the British 101 Special Training School at Tanjong Balai (near the mouth of the Jurong River) so that they could participate in the defence of Malaya and Singapore. In January 1942, a number of men who had trained at Tanjong Balai were sent to Malaya with instructions to remain behind enemy lines as the Japanese advanced. These men formed the nucleus of the group that was officially named the MALAYAN PEOPLE'S ANTI-JAPANESE ARMY (MPAJA) in March 1942.

Many of the MPAJA's early operations were poorly planned, and ended disastrously. However, the Japanese acknowledged that the MPAJA represented a threat, and became particularly brutal in their treatment of the Chinese civilian population in efforts to destroy the MPAJA. This in turn forced the MPAJA to retreat into the jungle. The MPAJA itself would also later be accused of brutality in its treatment of persons which it perceived to be traitors.

In the course of the war, the MPAJA claimed to have launched 340 operations against the Japanese, to have killed 5,500 Japanese soldiers and to have eliminated 2,500 'traitors'. Japanese figures suggest that the Japanese lost 600 troops, and 2,000 local police and volunteers, to the MPAJA, while inflicting 2,900 MPAJA casualties.

The MPAJA contacted officers of Britain's FORCE 136 in May 1943. From 31 December 1943 to 1 January 1944, it agreed to support British preparations for a re-invasion of Malaya. The MPAJA received weapons and training in return, but kept part of their army secret.

When the war ended, the MPAJA confiscated a large cache of Japanese weapons, and gained effective control over most of Malaya within days. The MPAJA claimed a strength of 10,000 men, although British estimates put MPAJA strength at between 3,000 and 4,000 men at the time of the Japanese surrender, and between 6,000 and 7,000 men when it disbanded in 1946.

In 1948, the MPAJA was re-formed as the Malayan People's Anti-British Army (MPABA), and later, the Malayan Races Liberation Army (MRLA).

See also EMERGENCY.

Malayan Union

Post–World War II British plan to create a peninsular union out of the nine Malay states and the British settlements of Penang and Malacca. Under this plan, Singapore would be excluded because of concerns that the addition of its Chinese majority would make the scheme unacceptable to Malays. The plan also involved a common citizenship for all who regarded Malaya as their home, a proposal that would be advantageous to the large number of Chinese and Indian residents of migrant origin who did not enjoy political rights under Malay rule.

For the Malayan Union to be realized, fresh treaties had to be negotiated with autonomous Malay rulers, whereby they would be asked to surrender their sovereignty to the British Crown, which would thereupon be legally empowered to legislate and bring about the desired scheme. However, the coercive manner pursued to relieve the rulers of their sovereign status by Sir Harold MacMichael—who had been dispatched after the war as a special representative to Malaya to negotiate the new treaties—confirmed for the Malays that their political position was under threat.

The constitutional controversy that ensued threatened to undermine the very basis of British rule in Malaya. Malays closed ranks behind the newly formed United Malays National Organization (UMNO) to oppose the Malayan Union when it was inaugurated on 1 April 1946. UMNO dissuaded its representatives from attending the ceremony marking the installation Sir Edward Gent as governor of the Malayan Union. Mass rallies and demonstrations were also organized to protest against the scheme.

Faced with the prospect of violence, the British decided to discard their experiment barely three months later. A negotiated settlement resulted in the founding of the FEDERATION OF MALAYA in February 1948.

Malays

Malays were living in Singapore prior to the arrival of Sir Stamford Raffles in 1819. The Malays of Singapore today are a heterogeneous community in terms of historical origins and cultural background. The majority are descendants of people from the Malay Peninsula and the Indonesian archipelago; smaller numbers are of mixed parentage as a result of inter-marriage between local Malay women and Arab or

Malayan Motors: advertisement for a range of car marques familiar in Singapore up to the 1960s.

Indian Muslim men, who had been drawn to the economic opportunities available in Singapore in the 19th and 20th centuries.

The ORANG LAUT are one of the ethnic groups which make up the Malay community, and their presence has been reported as dating back to the 16th century. They have played a significant role in the power structure of the Malay courts since the rule of the Malacca sultanate in the 15th century. Studies of Orang Laut descendants in Singapore document accounts of their close ties with the Johor royal family.

Malays from the Peninsula mostly arrived in the late 19th century as followers of chiefs or notables who had come to Singapore to ask for aid, meet their legal advisers and government officials, or to make business deals. They came mostly from Johor, Malacca or Penang, and to a lesser extent from the east coast states of Pahang, Terengganu and Kelantan. Others came in search of work, and found employment as policemen, watchmen, office boys and house servants. Some made a living from petty trading, and a few became religious teachers or mosque officials. A large number of Peninsular Malays lived in KAMPONG GLAM, an area which fronted the

Malayan Union: formal signature of the Malayan Union agreement at King's House in Kuala Lumpur, 1946.

MALAYS: RESIDENT POPULATION, 2000

- Malay (68.3%)
- Javanese (17.6%)
- Boyanese (11.4%)
- Other Malays (2.6%)

Source: Census of Population, 2000

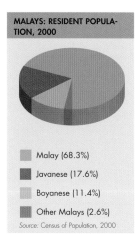

Malays: shopkeeper selling perfume.

Singapore River and in which was located SULTAN MOSQUE and ISTANA KAMPONG GLAM. Those who had ties with the Temenggong of Johor lived in Telok Blangah on land allocated to Temenggong ABDUL RAHMAN and his followers by Raffles in 1823.

Some Malays in Singapore can trace their origins to the Malay Archipelago. A number of Temenggong Abdul Rahman's followers were BUGIS from Celebes (present-day Sulawesi) and Malays from Riau. Some came initially as traders and adventurers, such as the BOYANESE, from the island of Bawean off the north coast of Java, and the JAVANESE. In the last quarter of the 19th century, large numbers of Javanese came to Malaya to work as either indentured or free labour, while the Bugis and Minangkabau from western Sumatra came to Singapore to trade.

The government in the Dutch Indies imposed strict regulations on HAJ pilgrims in the 19th century, so many travelled to Mecca by way of Singapore as British requirements were less stringent. Would-be pilgrims often lived in Singapore for several years before they earned sufficient money to continue their journey. Others worked on their return from Mecca to pay off debts incurred. Those who failed to earn their passage, or pay their debts, remained permanently in Singapore.

Arab links with the Malay world go back to the 9th century, when Arab traders, explorers and religious scholars travelled to the Malay Archipelago. In the 19th century Arab migrants to the Malay archipelago came from Hadramaut, in present-day Yemen. They were best known as traders and merchants dealing with a wide range of products including batik and other cloth, spices and tobacco. Inter-marriage with local Malay women was common, and the Arab community in Singapore today is mostly locally born.

Another group, the JAWI PERANAKAN, is made up of locally born INDIAN MUSLIMS descended from marriages between Malay women and South Indian Muslim merchants.

All these different groups have assimilated, to various degrees, into the Malay community in Singapore, and Islam and the

Malays: group photo, 1900s.

Malays: family celebrating Eid.

Malay language have been unifying factors for the community as a whole. According to the 2000 Census of Population, ethnic Malays form about 68.3 per cent of Malays (which includes the Orang Laut). Javanese form 17.6 per cent of the Malay population, Boyanese 11.4 per cent and other groups from the archipelago, such as the Minangkabau, Balinese and Bugis, 2.6 per cent. Overall, Malays make up 14 per cent of Singapore's total population.

Historical factors have given rise to a number of social issues with respect to the Malay community in Singapore. Since the 1880s, Malays received vernacular education, while English education was confined largely to Malay royalty. The shift of emphasis away from vernacular education after Independence, and the dominance of English-medium national schools by the 1980s, caused difficulties for Malay-educated workers (*see* MALAY EDUCATION). Malays were over-represented at the lower end of the spectrum of educational qualifications and income levels. This has been a concern of the government as well as of Malay political and community leaders since the 1960s. However, progress has been evident, and according to various censuses of population, increasing numbers of Malays are forming part of Singapore's middle class, with rises in educational and occupational levels and average monthly household incomes.

Malays, Peninsular The origins of this group—also known as 'indigenous Malays'—can be traced to Yunnan, China, through the Proto-Malays and Deutero-Malays, both of whom belonged to the broader Malayo-Polynesian group of peoples. These early aboriginal groups first reached the peninsula in around 2000 BCE. Since then, the culture of the Peninsular Malays has been shaped and reshaped by many different influences, including the cultures of Java, Sumatra, the Indian subcontinent, China, the Middle East and Europe. Peninsular Malays speak MALAY—a language now written in the Roman alphabet and, less frequently, in Jawi (an alphabet derived from Arabic).

When Sir Stamford Raffles first arrived in 1819, there were only about 150 people living on Singapore, 120 of whom were Malays (the remainder being Chinese). Subsequent migrants from Malaya were of

indigenous Malay origins (as opposed to other subgroups such as the JAVANESE, BUGIS and BOYANESE). Indeed, hundreds of indigenous Malays migrated to Singapore from Malacca within the first few months of the FOUNDING OF SINGAPORE, in response to an appeal for settlers made by Colonel WILLIAM FARQUHAR. Over subsequent years, economic opportunities in Singapore attracted more migrants from Penang, Malacca and Johor, most settling in urban areas.

The 1931 census recorded that there were about 11,200 indigenous Malay males in 'gainful employment' in Singapore. Some 30 per cent worked as fishermen and farmers. Another portion of the Malay population was made up of young men from Malaya recruited into the British armed forces. By 1957, there were more than 10,000 Peninsular Malays in the armed forces (the British tended not to recruit Malays of Javanese or other Indonesian origins). However, most of these servicemen returned to peninsular Malaya after retiring, and thus did not form a large proportion of Singapore's permanent Malay population. In fact, according to the 1970 census, about 25,000 peninsula-born Malays had returned to live in peninsular Malaya/Malaysia in the 1957–70 period.

In the 2000 population census, the total Malay resident population (defined as 'persons of Malay or Indonesian origins, such as Javanese, Boyanese, Bugis, etc') was recorded as 453,633. Historically, the Malays and Indonesian subgroups in Singapore have mixed and inter-married freely, and the population is now collectively known simply as 'Malay'.

Malaysia Cup The HMS Malaya Cup—as this SOCCER competition was originally called—was inaugurated on 1 October 1921, when the captain of a British battleship, HMS *Malaya*, presented two trophies to commemorate rugby and soccer matches played during the battleship's stay in Malayan waters in 1920.

Singapore was a founder member of this tournament, as were Selangor, Perak, Negri Sembilan, Malacca and Johor. Singapore played in each cup final from 1921 to 1941. It won the cup on 12 occasions, lost seven times and drew twice.

Between 1948 and 1966, Singapore played in 11 finals (winning 7 and losing 4). After 1967, when the competition was renamed the Malaysia Cup, Singapore played in ten finals (winning three and losing seven). Singapore withdrew from the competition after winning the 1994 final, as it was felt that the time had come to establish a professional league in Singapore. However, this withdrawal is widely seen as having caused a decline in spectator interest in local soccer.

Malaysia-Singapore relations On 16 September 1963, four years after gaining self-government, Singapore joined the FEDERATION OF MALAYA and the British protectorates of Sabah and Sarawak to form the Federation of Malaysia. This political configuration lasted just two years. On 9 August 1965, Singapore and Malaysia went their separate ways.

Since SEPARATION, relations between the two countries have waxed and waned, though they have been fundamentally sound. Relations reached their lowest point in November 1986 when Israeli President CHAIM HERZOG paid an official visit to Singapore. Initially, Malaysia chose to ignore the matter as Singapore's internal affair. However, domestic pressure exerted especially by the ruling party's youth wing in the state of Kedah forced Kuala Lumpur to make a formal protest and to withdraw its High Commissioner temporarily. Singapore considered these acts an attempt by Malaysia to dictate Singapore's foreign policy. The issue of loyalty among Singapore's Malays added to the distrust between the two countries.

A symbolic reconciliation was effected when the King of Malaysia visited Singapore in July 1988. There was also a tacit agreement by Singapore to avoid openly discussing subjects that were sensitive to Malaysia. After this, relations improved.

Between 1997 and 2002 though, relations worsened because of disagreement over several bilateral issues. These included the return of Central Provident Fund (CPF) contributions to West Malaysian workers previously employed in Singapore; railway land leased to Malaysia for 999 years that runs from north to south through the island of Singapore and ends at Tanjong Pagar railway station; the pricing of WATER from Johor state to Singapore; the use of Malaysian air space by the Singapore air force; dispute over the ownership of the island of PEDRA BRANCA; Singapore's LAND RECLAMATION works close to the Malaysian border; and the bridge that Malaysia planned to build to replace the CAUSEWAY.

Failure to reach a settlement on these issues led to an impasse, which ended when Datuk Seri Abdullah Badawi became Malaysia's prime minister in October 2003. This led to a more conducive atmosphere for bilateral relations. He had, in fact, visited Singapore in February 2001 as deputy prime minister, and had held talks with Singapore leaders on the thorny issues that plagued bilateral relations. He had also expressed the wish 'to resolve whatever remains to be resolved'.

In the meantime, certain international developments have altered the landscape. Religious extremism, in connection with international terrorism, provided a common enemy that had to be contained through bilateral security cooperation. Epidemics also threatened in the form of outbreaks of SEVERE ACUTE RESPIRATORY SYNDROME (SARS) and BIRD FLU. Facing

these common threats have brought the two countries closer.

Both sides have been motivated to settle their differences because of globalization and the rise of India and China. To meet these challenges, both countries believe that a common Southeast Asian market would be in a better position to compete against China and India. This would require members of the ASSOCIATION OF SOUTHEAST ASIAN NATIONS (ASEAN) to increase the speed, depth and breadth of regional economic integration. Economic ties between Malaysia and Singapore would be an important supporting pillar for such a project as both are stable and growing economies with close ties. Malaysia is Singapore's top trading partner, while Singapore is Malaysia's chief source of foreign direct investments.

Other developments have also helped to significantly change the bilateral situation. Water, once a major source of contention, has been relegated to the background largely because of Singapore's success in increasing local supply through desalination, increasing reservoir capacity and producing usable NEWATER from waste water.

The issue of whether Singapore's land reclamation works had encroached into Malaysian waters in the Strait of Johor was taken by Malaysia to the International Tribunal for the Law of the Sea. However, the matter was eventually settled through negotiations and the settlement agreement was signed in Singapore on 26 April 2005.

The dispute over Pedra Branca (known in Malaysia as Pulau Batu Puteh), will be settled by the International Court of Justice in The Hague. Both sides have agreed to abide by the Court's decision.

Seen broadly, bilateral relations have become much warmer since Abdullah Badawi became prime minister. Official visits have increased and economic links have improved greatly as well, both in the private and public sectors. Major companies from both sides have made huge investments across the Causeway. Educational and sporting events have also been encouraged at all levels. Ties between the people of Singapore and Malaysia also continue to remain close.

Malaysian Solidarity Convention United front of Malaysian opposition parties led by the PEOPLE'S ACTION PARTY (PAP). The convention was first discussed by the PAP in November 1964, when examining the viability of forming a united opposition front with political groups in Sabah, Sarawak and Malaya.

In the aftermath of the RACE RIOTS that occurred in Singapore in July and September 1964, the ruling PAP had come under strong internal pressure to reassess its policy of cooperation with the United Malays National Organization (UMNO),

MALAYSIA CUP: VICTORIES			
1921	vs	Selangor	2-1
1923	vs	Perak	2-1
1924	vs	Selangor	1-0
1925	vs	Selangor	2-1
1928	drew with	Selangor	2-2
1929	drew with	Selangor	2-2
1930	vs	Selangor	3-0
1932	vs	Selangor	5-3
1933	vs	Selangor	8-2
1934	vs	Penang	2-1
1937	vs	Selangor	2-1
1939	vs	Selangor	3-1
1940	vs	Kedah	2-0
1941	vs	Penang	3-1
1942–47 no competition			
1950	vs	Penang	2-0
1951	vs	Perak	6-0
1952	vs	Penang	3-2
1955	vs	Kelantan	3-1
1960	vs	Perak	2-0
1964	vs	Perak	3-2
1965	vs	Selangor	3-1
1967	renamed Malaysia Cup		
1977	vs	Penang	3-2
1980	vs	Selangor	2-1
1994	vs	Pahang	4-0

Malaysia Cup: Coach Jita Singh, with arm in the air, celebrates the 1980 victory.

the dominant Malay partner in the governing Alliance Party of Malaysia. Radical UMNO activists had been believed to be involved in the riots in Singapore.

UMNO had also announced in October 1964 its intention to overhaul the Alliance Party in order to end PAP rule in Singapore by 1967. As a PAP-Alliance coalition had failed, and as UMNO appeared determined to unseat the PAP in Singapore, the PAP announced in November 1964 that it would assume the role of an opposition party on a non-communal and socialist platform, and seek to unite all like-minded political groups in Malaysia for the purpose of winning national power.

The PAP began to seek political allies on the peninsula, in Sabah and in Sarawak, not only to overcome containment by Kuala Lumpur, but also as a means of putting pressure on the Alliance Party. Although PAP leaders had been in contact with leaders of parties in Sabah and Sarawak prior to Malaysia's formation, and had considered the idea of forming a unit-

Malaysian Solidarity Convention: rally held at Singapore's National Theatre, 1965.

ed front with these groups during the final stages of discussions leading to MERGER, they had not broached the subject of a common front for fear of rupturing ties with the ruling Alliance government.

In February 1965, however, PAP leaders met representatives of the United Pasok-Momogun Kadazan Organization (UPKO), the Sarawak United People's Party (SUPP), the United Democratic Party (UDP) and the People's Progressive Party (PPP) in Singapore to consider a draft statement for the formation of a Malaysian Solidarity Convention (MSC) of non-communal opposition political parties to fight for a 'Malaysian Malaysia'. At a meeting held in March in Kuala Lumpur, a decision to launch the coalition was taken.

On 9 May, leading members of the five opposition parties from the states of Singapore, Malaya and Sarawak—the PAP, UDP, PPP, SUPP and Machinda Party— met in Singapore to launch the MSC formally. Only UPKO decided to remain outside the convention, as it was still undecided about leaving the Sabah Alliance.

The declaration of the convention's founding called for the establishment of a Malaysia 'that is not identified with the supremacy, well-being and the interests of any one particular community or race' and urged all Malaysians to unite to 'fight for the ideal' of a 'Malaysian Malaysia'. A mass rally was staged at the National Theatre in Singapore on 6 June 1965 to set in motion a series of rallies that would spread to other cities in Malaysia. PAP chairman, TOH CHIN CHYE, declared that the MSC had embarked on a 'crusade to preach interracial unity, to propagate the basic rights of all races which go to form our multiracial society'.

The launch of the MSC and its mass rally in Singapore set the PAP at odds with the Alliance Party. The PAP was accused of seeking to remove Malay rulers. Alliance leaders warned of interracial strife, and urged the central government to either detain PAP leaders or banish Singapore from Malaysia.

At its first council meeting, 17–18 July

1965, the MSC announced that it would hold rallies throughout Malaysia to bring the message of a 'Malaysian Malaysia' to all parts of the country. The first such rally was planned to be held in Penang on 14 August. However, the Malaysian premier, Tunku ABDUL RAHMAN, had decided to expel Singapore. The outcome, on 9 August 1965, was SEPARATION.

Mallal, Bashir A. (1898–1972) Author, editor and publisher. Bashir Ahmad Mallal moved to Singapore from present-day Pakistan in his teens. In 1918, he joined the firm of Battenberg and Silva as a law clerk. Mallal did not hold a university degree, nor was he ever called to the Bar in any country. Yet he was the first non-European in Singapore to author a book on Malayan law, when he wrote *Criminal Procedure* (1931). He then wrote *Money-Lenders' Ordinance* (1936); *Straits Settlement Practice* (1937); *Malayan Cases* (1939); *Digest of Malayan Law* (1940); and *The Double-Tenth Trial* (1947).

As well as writing legal treatises and digests, Mallal was perhaps best known for founding the *Malayan Law Journal* in 1932. The 'MLJ'—as most lawyers called it—has remained the most important law report in Malaysia and Singapore, and is the only law report to have been published continuously from its inception through into the 21st century (save for the interregnum of World War II).

When plans were drawn up for the establishment of a law faculty at the University of Singapore, Mallal donated the bulk of his personal library as the basis for a law library. He was awarded an honorary doctorate of laws by the university in 1962.

Mallal, N.A. (1903–1974) Lawyer and politician. Born Nazir Ahmad Mallal in what is now Pakistan, Mallal was educated at Raffles Institution. After graduating from the University of London, he was called to the Bar in January 1928, and was admitted as an advocate and solicitor of the Straits Settlements in October 1928.

As well as being a member of the advisory editorial board of *The Malayan Law Journal*, Mallal was active in public service, serving as a Municipal Commissioner from 1936 to 1941.

He successfully contested the 1948 and 1951 elections as a member of the SINGAPORE PROGRESSIVE PARTY (SPP)—a party he had helped found. Elected to the Legislative Council in 1948, he served until his defeat in the 1955 election, after which he retired from politics.

Among his contributions was a motion he initiated in the Legislative Council for the establishment of the PUBLIC SERVICE COMMISSION to deal with appointments and promotions in the public services. He was also appointed a member of the select committee to consider the report of Sir Alexander Carr-Saunders on the establishment of the UNIVERSITY OF MALAYA in Singapore.

mammals *See* box.

Manaki Takanobu, Lieutenant-General (dates unknown) Japanese military official. Manaki Takanobu served as Lieutenant-General YAMASHITA TOMOYUKI's vice-Chief of Staff until becoming Chief in February 1942. According to SHINOZAKI MAMORU, during the SOOK CHING massacre, it was Manaki who persuaded Yamashita to stop the round-up of Chinese. Manaki was transferred out of Malaya because he was believed by the Japanese military authorities to be too sympathetic to the Chinese.

Manaki served briefly as Mayor of Syonan-to (Singapore) before moving, in April 1942, to become Chief of Staff of the North Borneo Garrison 37th Army. He remained there until the end of the war.

Mandai Crematorium and Columbarium In July 2004, the brand new Mandai Crematorium and Columbarium Complex (MCC) replaced Mount Vernon Crematorium as Singapore's main crematorium complex. Located off remote Mandai Road, the MCC is equipped with 10 cremators and four halls for funeral services. The complex also includes six blocks of columbaria, which can house 77,320 niches.

Mandarin Mandarin is one of Singapore's official languages (the other three are MALAY, ENGLISH and TAMIL). The 1990 Census showed that the percentage of households speaking Mandarin had more than doubled from 10 per cent in 1980 to 26 per cent in 1990, while the percentage of households in which Chinese dialects were predominantly used (such as HOKKIEN, CANTONESE, TEOCHEW, HAINANESE and HAKKA) had declined from 60 per cent in 1980 to 37 per cent in 1990.

The 2000 Census showed that the proportion of households speaking Mandarin had increased from 30 per cent to 45 per cent, while households in which Chinese dialects were predominant had declined from 50 per cent to 31 per cent.

This increase in the use of Mandarin has largely been the result of education and promotional campaigns.

Mandarin was made the medium of instruction in Singapore's Chinese public schools shortly after it became the national language of the Republic of China in

Mandai Crematorium and Columbarium

mammals Singapore's wild mammals number about 60 species. The first comprehensive documentation of local wild mammal diversity was published in 1924. By the time this was updated in 1990, at least eight species were confirmed as being locally extinct—including the tiger (*Panthera tigris*), which was considered a common menace until it was hunted to extinction in the 1930s. It is believed, though, that the extirpation of most of these species was caused not so much by excessive hunting, but by decades of industrial and urban development. Despite massive deforestation, however, five resident mammal species new to Singapore have been recorded since 1990. These include the brown spiny rat (*Maxomys rajah*), the hollow-faced bat (*Nycteris tragata*) and the glossy horseshoe bat (*Rhinolophus lepidus*).

Bats

About one-third of Singapore's mammal fauna consists of bats—the only mammals capable of true flight. There are two groups of these nocturnal creatures. The common fruit bat (*Cynopterus brachyotis*) is an example from the fruit and nectar feeding group, whose members generally have dog-like heads and large eyes with excellent night vision. One other member, the large flying fox (*Pteropus vampyrus*) (**1**), is the largest of all living bats. It is probably not resident in Singapore, but visits when trees are fruiting. The yellow house bat (*Scotophilus kuhlii*) and the pouched bat (*Saccolaimus*

1

saccolaimus) belong to the group that feeds mainly on insects. They have small eyes and use echolocation to navigate in the darkness and to hunt.

2

3

Squirrels

The plantain squirrel (*Callosciurus notatus*) occurs commonly in parks and gardens. It has distinct black and white stripes on its sides and a reddish-brown belly. The cream-coloured giant squirrel (*Ratufa affinis*) (**2**) is the size of a small cat, and has a tail twice as long as its body. First discovered in Singapore, it was named by Sir STAMFORD RAFFLES. As it has not been seen since the turn of the new millennium, it may be locally extinct.

While most squirrels are active in the day, some are strictly nocturnal. One example is the Horsfield's flying squirrel (*Iomys horsfieldii*) (**3**), which can glide from tree to tree with the help of large skin flaps.

4

Carnivores

Of the wild carnivores, the common palm civet (*Paradoxurus hermaphroditus*) (**4**) is often found in suburban gardens. This nocturnal animal sometimes sleeps in the roof spaces of houses. Despite being classified as a carnivore, it is actually omnivorous, feeding on fruit as well as small animals.

A true carnivore is the leopard cat (*Prionailurus bengalensis*) (**5**). Secretive and nocturnal, it occurs in forest and scrubland. Resembling a stray domestic cat, it can be distinguished by its beautiful marbled coat and rounded ears.

5

Rats and shrews

Rats and mice are considered household pests—the brown rat (*Rattus norvegicus*) being a common example. The Singapore rat (*Rattus annandalei*) (**6**), however, lives only in forests and scrubland.

Although shrews resemble rats, they belong to the order insectivora, whose members have small, sharp and pointed teeth, instead of

6   7

enlarged incisors characteristic of rats and squirrels. The house shrew (*Suncus murinus*) (**7**) is common in housing estates. It subsists on table scraps and cockroaches.

8

Primates

Of the three extant species of non-human primates in Singapore, the long-tailed macaque (*Macaca fascicularis*) (**8**) is the commonest.

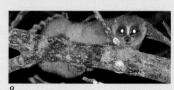
9

It lives in groups, and is omnivorous. The banded leaf monkey (*Presbytis femoralis*), on the other hand, is largely herbivorous. It is slightly larger than the macaque and is black with a white stripe on its chest, belly and the inside of its thighs. Unlike MONKEYS, the slow loris (*Nycticebus coucang*) (**9**) is active only at night, and tends to live alone, feeding on fruits and insects.

Marine mammals

At least four species of marine mammals are known to frequent Singapore waters. The Indo-Pacific humpback dolphin (*Sousa chinensis*) (**10**) has been occasionally seen around the Southern Islands. Its broadly triangular dorsal fin, long snout and grey, sometimes pink colour are all distinctive. Much less conspicuous is the dugong (*Dugong dugon*) (**11**), which feeds on seagrass and is known as the 'sea cow'.

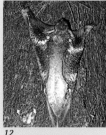

10   11

Rare mammals

The Malayan colugo or flying lemur (*Cynopterus variegatus*) (**12**) is a nocturnal leaf-eater. Like the flying squirrels, it is capable of gliding from tree to tree. In the day, it clings to the trunks of large forest trees, pretending to be a patch of lichen.

The Sunda pangolin (*Manis javanica*) (**13**) is a strange denizen of the forests and scrubland. Covered in an armour of scales, which are in fact modified hairs, it uses its long, sticky tongue to collect termites for food.

Another rare mammal is the wild pig (*Sus scrofa*), the largest resident land mammal. Supposedly extinct locally in the 1950s, it has re-colonized Singapore by swimming from Johor. It now inhabits PULAU UBIN and PULAU TEKONG, and the northern shores of Singapore island.

In 1990, three Asian elephants (*Elephas maximus*) also swam from Malaysia and stayed briefly on Pulau Ubin and Pulau Tekong, until they were captured and repatriated. Not long before, a Malayan tapir (*Tapirus indicus*) had been found dead on Pulau Ubin. It appeared to have strayed over

from Johor as well. These were the first recorded occurrences of wild elephants and tapirs in Singapore.

12

13

1917. Before that, the language used in these schools had been the various dialects spoken in the immigrant Chinese communities.

In 1966, the government implemented the Mother Tongue Policy, introducing BILINGUALISM into schools. This policy meant that monolingual Mandarin schools were transformed into bilingual 'Mandarin-stream schools'. In 1979, students were required to obtain a minimum pass in Mother Tongue to gain admission to pre-university and junior college.

Singapore Mandarin

The majority of older Singaporean Mandarin-speakers learnt the language informally. The different Chinese dialects originally spoken by these people contributed to the development of a variety of dialectal accents. Thus, although people who were educated after 1979 are likely to speak Mandarin with a more 'standard' accent, their Mandarin is still likely to include features of various other dialects.

One phonological feature of Singapore Mandarin is its lack of the initial retroflex featured in standard Mandarin. For example, the word 'shi' (meaning 'poetry') would be pronounced 'si'. Another feature is the lack of differentiation between the nasals 'n' and 'ng'. For example 'xin'—the word for 'heart'—is often indistinguishable from 'xing' (meaning 'star').

A feature of the syntax of Singapore Mandarin is the tendency to place the word 'you' ('have') before the main verb. An example would be the question 'Did you go?' which would be rendered 'Ni you qu ma?' in Singapore, rather than as 'Ni qu le ma?'. Another feature is the placing of the adverb at the end of the phrase, instead of at the beginning. One example would be the phrase 'to eat first', which would be rendered as 'chi fan xian' rather than 'xian chi fan' (in standard Mandarin).

Lexically, non-standard features include the dropping of the 'zi' suffix from words such as 'qunzi' (skirt) or 'kuzi' (pants), reducing them to 'qun' and 'ku'. This feature clearly originates from Cantonese, Hakka and Hainanese, in which no suffix is used. Another non-standard feature is the replacement of disyllabic forms by monosyllabic forms such as 'ming' for 'mingzi' ('name'); 'se' for 'yanse' ('colour'); and 'gong' for 'gongzuo' ('work'), as these occur in monosyllabic form in many southern Chinese dialects. In addition, the meaning of some words may be extended. For instance, 'dong' carries not only the meaning 'to understand', but is also used to infer 'to know' (whereas in standard Mandarin, the word 'zhidao' would be used).

Lexical items are often borrowed from Malay and English. Terms such as 'basha' (from the Malay for 'market'); 'bashi' (from the English for 'bus'); and 'baxian' (from the English 'per cent') are all common.

However, the most unique feature of Singapore Mandarin is characterised by code-switching. This means that the Mandarin spoken in Singapore is often mixed with English, sometimes with other Chinese dialects and even with Malay. One example might be: 'Wo zai MRT deng ni' ('I will wait for you at the MRT station') and 'Wo chi fan then qu zuogong' ('I will eat, then go to work'). In these examples, 'MRT' and 'then' are borrowed from English.

One group of borrowings is the discourse markers (such as the English words 'OK' or 'then'), as well as English toponyms. The second group of borrowings consists of single words and phrases borrowed from Hokkien, Malay or English.

In 1999, the Ministry of Education introduced the use of Hanyu Pinyin—a system of Mandarin Romanization first devised in China—in all schools.

On 7 September 1979, then Prime Minister LEE KUAN YEW inaugurated the 'Speak Mandarin' Campaign. At the launch of this campaign, Lee delivered his address, entitled 'Mandarin or Dialect?' in Mandarin, Hokkien and English, stressing the challenge faced by Chinese school children in having to learn two languages at school (English and Mandarin), as well as a dialect at home.

The initial objective of the campaign was to make Mandarin the lingua franca of the various Chinese dialect communities. In subsequent years, the campaign focused on specific social groups, such as white-collar workers and executives.

Since 1991, increasing emphasis has been placed on the promotion of Mandarin amongst English-educated Chinese. In 2005, the campaign began to focus on transforming Mandarin into a language of everyday life in Singapore.

mangroves This group of plants used to cover most of Singapore's coastline. But with LAND RECLAMATION, less than 0.5 per cent of original coastal forests have been left intact. Mangrove forests have only survived in small fragments in parts of northern Singapore, where the only protected area is the SUNGEI BULOH WETLAND RESERVE. Mangroves are also found on offshore islands, namely PULAU TEKONG, PULAU UBIN and PULAU SEMAKAU.

However, Singapore has one of the richest mangrove ecosystems in the world, with 62 species of mangrove plants having been recorded. Mangroves live in saline water. To cope with salinity, many mangrove species partially exude salt at the roots, and have specialized glands that excrete salt through leaves. In the mornings, droplets of water can be seen on the leaf surfaces of plants like the sea holly (*Acanthus spp.*) and *Avicennia*. These droplets become crystals of salt when the water evaporates, and are removed by wind and rain. Others accumulate salt in their leaves, which eventually drop off.

Mangroves have adapted to the soft, oxygen-poor mud by developing aerial roots, or pneumatophores, that stick out of the mud. The pencil roots of the *api api* (*Avicennia spp.*) are arranged on long cable roots that radiate out for metres from the tree's main trunk, and provide stability in the soft mud.

The *bakau* (*Rhizophora spp.*) has distinctive prop and stilt roots, making the tree appear as if it is upside down. The roots support the tree in soft mud. The long, smooth seedlings hang from the parent tree; when they drop into the water, they float and are dispersed away from the parent tree.

The *bakau putih* (*Bruguiera cylindrical*) is one of the most common mangroves in

Mandarin: Huayu Cool promotional poster, 2006.

Singapore, and can grow on stiff clay unsuitable for other mangroves. Its pneumatophores, resembling bent knees, help aerate the plant's root system. Like the previous group of mangroves, the *Bruguiera* has fruits that germinate on the parent tree.

The rare *nyireh bunga* (*Xylocarpus granatum*) is a distinctive tree with plank buttress roots. Its bark is smooth and light brown in colour, and regularly flakes off. The fruit is a grapefruit-sized large capsule. When ripe, it breaks into several fragments, dispersing the seeds into the water.

Towards the landward side of the mangrove forest is a tree called *buta-buta* (*Excoecaria agallocha*). Also known as 'blind-your-eyes', the *buta-buta*'s milky sap can cause temporary blindness if it comes in contact with the eyes. During certain times of the year, the leaves of this species change colour before dropping, giving one the impression of being in the midst of autumn.

One palm found only in the mud is the *nipah* (*Nypa fruticans*), which looks like a small coconut palm, but has no tall, vertical stem.

The mature leaves of the *nipah* are used traditionally as roofing material, while young leaves are used as cigarette wrappers. The seeds, known as *attap chee*, are eaten in local desserts. The fruit of the *bakau putih* are also edible, while the tree is often used for firewood and timber.

Various creatures are part of the mangrove ecosystem. Mounds of mud found at the back of mangrove forests are built by the mud lobster (*Thalassina anomala*). This lobster excavates and feeds on organic matter in the mud. Its mounds provide microhabitats for ants, tree-climbing crabs and shrimps, and plants such as the mangrove fern (*Acrostichum spp.*) and sea holly (*Acanthus spp.*).

An isolated stand of *berembang* (*Sonneratia caseolaris*) was discovered in the upper reaches of Sungei Seletar in 1998. Prior to this, only a single tree of this species was known to have existed in Singapore. The *berembang* is the only tree species where synchronous flashing fireflies have been found.

Huge clusters of tiny red insects on the underside of mangrove leaves are the larvae of the cotton stainer bug (*Dysdercus decussates*) and shield bug (*Calliphara nobilis*). Their colour serves as a warning to would-be predators.

The larvae of the mangrove longhorn beetle (*Aeolesthes holosericeus*) bore into the trunks of dead or sick trees, usually the *buta-buta*, causing characteristic cut-out discs of between 3 and 5 cm in diameter.

Other examples of mangrove insects are ants, pond skaters (*Xenobates sp.*) and mangrove moths.

The tree-climbing crab (*Episesarma spp.*), otherwise known as the 'vinegar crab', burrows at the base of trees and mud-lobster mounds. It eats mainly leaves, and young mangrove propagules, although it also scavenges for meat. During high tide, it climbs up trees, just high enough to rest above the water level, remaining motionless on tree trunks, roots and man-made structures, thus avoiding predators. The TEOCHEW prize the tree-climbing crab as a delicacy, pickling and eating it with porridge.

Snails are common in mangrove areas. The common nerite (*Nerita lineata*) grazes on algae at night during low tide. Its hard shell and ability to stay above the water during high tide means that it can avoid being eaten by predators. Mangrove periwinkles (*Littoraria spp.*) are common snails that live on mangrove trees, spending most of their time out of water.

Mangrove areas act as nurseries for many fish species, the most conspicuous being mudskippers. These include the giant mudskipper (*Periophthalmodon schlosseri*), which is the largest mudskipper in Singapore and measures up to 27 cm in length.

Bats are important pollinators of mangrove trees. Smooth otters (*Lutrogale perspicillata*) also reside in SUNGEI BULOH WETLAND RESERVE. Their smaller relative, the small-clawed otter (*Amblonyx cinereus*), can be found in Pulau Ubin and Pulau Tekong.

Mangrove forests not only represent an important habitat, but are also known to filter heavy metals and bind soil particles, thus preventing soil erosion.

manufacturing sector In the late 1960s, the government pursued an industrialization strategy, of which attracting foreign investors to produce manufactured goods for export was an important component. Consequently, the contribution of the manufacturing sector to GROSS DOMESTIC PRODUCT rose from 11 per cent in 1960 to 29 per cent in the period 1980–90, before dipping to 28 per cent in 2005. Only 21 per cent of the workforce were employed in manufacturing—lower than the 29 per cent in 1990 and 26 per cent in 1975.

Over the decades, Singapore has shifted from low-value, labour-intensive manufacturing, such as in food and beverages, furniture and garments, to higher value-added industries such as petrochemicals and pharmaceuticals. In 2002, the government identified four key areas—electronics, chemicals, biomedical sciences and transport engineering—which would be the nuclei of new 'manufacturing clusters'.

The electronics sector has developed from assembly and contract manufacturing to cover the entire production process. Chemicals—especially petroleum, petrochemicals and speciality chemicals—have come to contribute about 31 per cent of total manufacturing output. Biomedical sciences and transport engineering accounted for 8.6 per cent and 7.4 per cent of manufacturing output, respectively, in 2005. The government has stressed that its objective in the near term is to keep manufacturing at least 25 per cent of GDP and 20 per cent of total employment.

Mardan Mamat (1967–) Sportsman. In March 2006, Mardan Mamat became the first Singaporean golfer to win a European Tour event. Competing at the Laguna National Golf and Country Club, he led from the first round with a 65, followed by rounds of 70, 70 and 71 to win the OSIM Singapore Masters by a single shot. This European Tour victory assured Mardan a place in the circuit until the end of 2008.

Mardan began his association with GOLF at age nine. While studying at Boon Lay Primary School, he worked as a part-time caddy. At age 13, he dropped out of school to caddy full-time at the Jurong Country Club. Fifth in a family of eight children, the $8 he earned from each four-hour round helped with the family finances. The job also gave him the opportunity to practise. As a caddy, he was only allowed to play on the green on Mondays but sneaked in every night after hours. His first complete set of clubs was a used set a club member gave him when he was 15.

Mardan's first major win was a Southeast Asian Games team silver medal in 1993. Later that year, he won the individual title at the Putra Cup and the team title with Dino Kwek, Lam Chih Bing and Mohammed Said. In 1994, he finished joint-eighth at the Asian Games and turned professional. In 1997, he became the first Singaporean to qualify for the British Open but did not make the cut. He then became the first Singaporean to win an Asian Tour event when he won the Indian Open in 2004. Since turning professional, Mardan has earned about $1.5 million in total winnings.

Maria Hertogh riots In 1942, MARIA HERTOGH, a five-year old girl of Dutch parentage, was placed under the care of Aminah Mohamed. According to Adeline Hertogh (Maria's biological mother), Maria was to have stayed with Aminah for only three days. When Aminah failed to return Maria, Adeline tried to find her daughter, but was arrested by the Japanese for travelling without a pass. From her internment camp, Adeline wrote to her

Mangroves: (clockwise from left) bakau tree; mud lobster; tree-climbing crab.

mother, Nor Louise, requesting that her children be sent to her. Louise arranged to collect Maria from Aminah, but Aminah and Maria were not present when Louise visited their house. After her release, Adeline could not locate Aminah or Maria. Aminah, however, claimed that Adeline had suggested that Aminah, being childless, adopt Maria as her own daughter, and that she had agreed to this with the understanding that she would raise Maria as a Muslim. Disputing Adeline's claim of internment, Aminah said that she had continued to meet Adeline frequently after the adoption, ceasing to do so only after Adeline travelled to Surabaya (in Java) to seek employment in late 1943 or early 1944.

After World War II, the Hertoghs asked the Dutch authorities in Java and Singapore to locate Maria. She was eventually discovered in Kemaman, Terengganu in September 1949 by Arthur Locke, a local British official. Locke alerted the Dutch consul-general in Singapore of his discovery and began negotiations with Aminah, persuading her to travel to Singapore with Maria, ostensibly to formalize Maria's adoption papers, but also to speak to Dutch consular officials regarding the Hertoghs' request to see their daughter. Dutch officials, who met Aminah and Maria on three occasions shortly after their arrival in Singapore in April 1950, offered Aminah $500 as compensation for having taken care of Maria for eight years. Aminah rejected this offer.

In order to prevent Aminah from taking Maria back to Kemaman, the Dutch consul-general applied successfully on 22 April for a High Court order to deliver Maria into the custody of the Social Welfare Department. The department then placed Maria in a girls' home pending a further court hearing. With assistance from M.A. MAJID, president of the Muslim Welfare Association, Aminah initiated legal action against the Dutch consul-general's application. On 19 May, after a short hearing, the chief justice ruled that Maria be placed in the custody of the Dutch consul prior to being returned to her parents. Upon hearing the verdict, the crowd, which had formed outside the court, started a commotion.

On 22 May, a day before Maria's scheduled departure, Aminah's lawyers obtained a stay of execution pending appeal against the chief justice's order. On 28 July 1950, the court ruled in favour of Aminah's

Maria Hertogh riots: coverage in the *Singapore Standard*, 5 December 1950.

Mardan Mamat: winning the OSIM Singapore Open, 2006.

Marina Barrage: artist's impression.

appeal on a technicality, and Maria was returned to Aminah.

Four days later, on 1 August 1950, Maria entered into a marriage with Mansoor Adabi, a 22-year-old trainee teacher. The Dutch consul-general, on behalf of the Hertoghs, challenged the legality of the marriage through an application to the courts on 26 August 1950.

Court hearings began on 20 November, and on 2 December it was found that the marriage was void, as Maria had not reached the age of consent under Dutch law. The court also ordered that custody of Maria should be restored to her father, Adrianus Hertogh, who had not been consulted when Aminah first took the girl.

Maria was billeted temporarily in a Catholic convent. Journalists and photographers entered the convent premises; newspapers subsequently reproduced photographs of Maria in the convent. On 5 December, the *Singapore Standard* published, in its front page, a photograph of Maria holding hands with the Reverend Mother. On page two of the same newspaper, the words 'Bertha Knelt Before Virgin Mary Statue' was printed in large type (Maria was also known as 'Bertha'). The reports deeply distressed the Muslim community, who knew Maria to be Muslim at that time. Radicals also seized the opportunity to undermine the position of the colonial authorities.

An application for a stay of execution of the order pending appeal was refused, but the judge allowed a further application to appeal against this decision to be heard on 11 December 1950. On that day, a restive crowd of over two thousand people gathered outside the court. The judge, however, rejected the appeal within a few minutes. A riot ensued, and for three days, rioters vented their fury on any European or Eurasian in sight. Eighteen people were killed and 173 injured. Maria and her mother were swiftly sent to the Netherlands.

Marina Bay: perspective of planned new high-rise district.

The post-SEPARATION Singapore government attributed these riots to the colonial authorities' failure to exercise sensitivity in their management of racial and religious differences. The incident has also been cited as an example of the media whipping up religious sentiments and causing widespread outrage.

Marina Barrage In 2005, the government announced plans to build an artificial barrier across the mouth of the Marina Channel, between reclaimed land at Marina East and Marina South. This $226 million project was designed to turn Marina Bay and Kallang Basin into Singapore's 15th freshwater reservoir, adding 10,000 ha of catchment area. The reservoir, which will be known as Marina Reservoir, will also assist in flood control, and serve as a venue for water-based events and competitions.

The Marina Barrage will be fitted with nine hydraulic steel gates (each 26.8 m long). This will allow for water levels to be raised for navigational purposes, or lowered in the event of flooding. The barrage is expected to be completed in 2007.

Marina Bay Artificial bay, into which the SINGAPORE RIVER flows. The bay was created by three phases of land reclamation over a period from the 1970s to the 1990s. Marina Bay is also the name for the surrounding area, which is destined to be a 360-ha extension of the downtown area.

Marina Bay will include commercial, residential and recreational developments. By 2005, several of these developments had been completed, including One Marina Boulevard, The Fullerton Singapore, the Merlion Pier and the ESPLANADE—THEATRES ON THE BAY. Other projects slated for completion by 2009 include the Sail@Marina Bay (a 70-storey condominium development), the Business and Financial Centre, the INTEGRATED RESORT, the Singapore Flyer (a 178-m high observation wheel), and a 280-m bridge. Right in the heart of the city, there will be three waterfront gardens with some of the best displays of foliage in the world.

A holistic approach is being taken for the development of Marina Bay, with the appointment of the URBAN REDEVELOPMENT AUTHORITY as the development agency. The authority is tasked to market and promote the development opportunities in the area, implement key infrastructure, co-ordinate and organize events, and place-manage the area.

See also MARINA BARRAGE.

Marine Parade Public housing estate. Marine Parade was originally a seaside promenade stretching from what is now Parkway Parade Shopping Centre to Martia Road. When land was reclaimed along the East Coast in the 1970s, this promenade was extended from Amber Road to Bedok South Road, and became the major road serving the Marine Parade public housing estate.

Compared to other public housing estates in Singapore, Marine Parade is relatively small, with only 58 blocks of flats. Most of the 7,866 flats were built in 1972–73, with those in Marine Drive being built in 1973–75. Units in Marine Parade have been highly sought-after due to the estate's proximity to the coast and the views of the sea afforded by high-rise units.

Maritime and Port Authority of Singapore Statutory board. The Maritime and Port Authority of Singapore (MPA) was formed on 2 February 1996 after the Marine Department, the National Maritime Board and the regulatory departments of the Port of Singapore Authority were merged.

In addition to regulating and licensing port and marine services and facilities, the MPA manages marine traffic and controls Singapore's merchant fleet. The MPA is also responsible for navigational safety, and port and maritime security, and for ensuring a clean marine environment. It advises the government on all matters relating to sea transport.

The MPA promotes the use and development of the port, and formulates strategies to improve the business environment for maritime industries.

Marshall, David (1908–1995) Lawyer, politician and diplomat. The son of merchant Saul Nassim Marshall, David Saul Marshall was educated at St Joseph's Institution, St Andrew's School and Raffles Institution. In preparing to sit for a Queen's Scholarship examination, Marshall worked himself to exhaustion and had to be sent to Switzerland to recuperate. It was not until September 1934 that he travelled to the United Kingdom to pursue studies in law. In 1937, he was called to the Bar at the Middle Temple and, in 1938, to the Singapore Bar.

After returning to Singapore in 1938, Marshall joined the firm of Aitken and Ong Siang. In the period leading up to World War II, he concentrated on his legal career, eventually resigning from Aitken and Ong Siang to join ALLEN & GLEDHILL. He also joined the Singapore Volunteer Corps. During the Japanese Occupation, Marshall was detained as a civilian internee.

Marine Parade: one of Singapore's smaller estates.

After the war, Marshall resumed practice at Allen & Gledhill, becoming its first Asian partner in 1949. In 1950, he resigned from Allen and Gledhill to pursue studies in medicine. He later discontinued his medical studies and returned to legal practice with the firm of Battenberg and Talma.

Marshall dedicated much of his time during this period serving the Jewish community. He served as president of the JEWISH WELFARE BOARD from 1946 to 1951.

In June 1947, he was elected a committee member of the Singapore Association, of which Sir ROLAND ST JOHN BRADDELL was president. Later, in November 1949, Marshall joined the SINGAPORE PROGRESSIVE PARTY (SPP). In March 1950, he was elected to the party's committee. Earlier that year, JOHN LAYCOCK had suggested to Marshall that he stand for the office of Municipal Commissioner.

As a prominent lawyer and social figure, Marshall was much sought after by various political groups and parties following the convening of the RENDEL COMMISSION. Marshall began to move away from the SPP, and began associating with LIM YEW HOCK and Francis Thomas, the founders of the SINGAPORE SOCIALIST PARTY (SSP). Marshall was in fact offered the presidency of the SSP, although he decided to accept this position only after the SSP merged with the SINGAPORE LABOUR PARTY to form the LABOUR FRONT.

When the Labour Front unexpectedly won a majority of seats at the 1955 general election, Marshall became Singapore's first chief minister. His tenure was brief, however. In his 14 months as chief minister, he called for an end to colonial rule, and independence for Singapore. He adopted an anti-colonial stance, and took every opportunity to either challenge British authority or to embarrass British officials. His difficult relationship with the colonial authorities was exacerbated by Governor JOHN NICOLL's view of Marshall as a junior minister.

On the day of his assumption of office as chief minister, Marshall arrived to find that no office had been allocated to him in Assembly House. It was only after Marshall threatened to set up an office 'under the old apple tree' in the building's grounds that Colonial Secretary Sir WILLIAM GOODE made arrangements for a small room under a flight of stairs to be allocated to Marshall.

Frequent confrontations between Marshall and the governor, especially in relation to Marshall's right to appoint four assistant ministers, precipitated the first round of all-party constitutional talks in London in 1956 (see MERDEKA). Marshall had promised to deliver independence to Singapore at these talks, but negotiations faltered over issues of internal security, and Marshall returned to Singapore unsuccessful, resigning as chief minister on 7 June 1956. Less than a year later, he resigned

from the Labour Front and started the WORKERS' PARTY. LIM YEW HOCK succeeded him as chief minister.

In 1961, Marshall stood as a WORKERS' PARTY candidate for the Anson by-election, winning by a small margin. However, when he stood at the 1963 general election as an independent candidate, he lost his seat. Thereafter, he retired from politics.

Marshall continued his legal practice. In 1978, he was appointed Singapore's ambassador to France. He retired from this post in 1990; in that same year, he was awarded the MERITORIOUS SERVICE MEDAL. In December 1994, the National University of Singapore awarded him an honorary doctorate of laws.

Martens, Melanie (1960–) Sportswoman. Born into a family of hockey and cricket players, Melanie Martens began her international hockey career in 1974. She went on to make over 100 appearances for Singapore over 25 years.

Martens participated in seven Southeast Asian (SEA) Games, winning medals in six of these. She won a gold medal at the 1993 SEA Games in Singapore; was voted an 'All-Star' after the 1994 Asian Games in Hiroshima—a tournament in which she scored the only goal for Singapore; was voted the Players' Player of the Year in 1995; and was top scorer and Player of the Tournament at the 1997 Asia Cup qualifying rounds in Singapore.

She retired from international hockey after the SEA Games in 1999, and was awarded a Public Service Medal in 2000. In 2005, she became vice principal of St Theresa's Convent.

Marxist conspiracy On 21 May 1987, 16 persons were arrested under Singapore's INTERNAL SECURITY ACT on the grounds that they were members of a clandestine communist network. The Ministry of Home Affairs alleged that the group had planned to 'subvert the existing social and political system in Singapore through communist united front tactics to establish a communist state'. On 20 June 1987, another six persons were detained.

The alleged architect of the conspiracy was TAN WAH PIOW, a former student activist who had fled Singapore after being convicted of unlawful assembly and rioting in 1976. Tan was accused of having established a network of communist infiltrators in Singapore. The head of the group was said to be Vincent Cheng, a Catholic lay worker.

Cheng was supposedly coordinating a number of Catholic groups—including the Student Christian Movement of Singapore, the Young Christian Workers' Movement, the National University of Singapore Catholic Students' Society, Singapore Polytechnic Catholic Students' Society, the Justice and Peace Commission of the Catholic Church and the Catholic Welfare

Centre—to subvert the state. Other groups that the government claimed were part of Cheng's network included the WORKERS' PARTY and a theatre group called Third Stage.

By the end of 1987, all but one of the detainees had been released, subject to restrictions on their freedom of movement and association. In April 1988, eight were re-arrested following their publication of a signed public statement denying the accusations against them and alleging mistreatment in detention. Among those detained were lawyers Teo Soh Lung and Tang Fong Har, law graduate Kevin De Souza, lecturer Chng Suan Tze, businessman Chew Kheng Chuan, and Wong Souk Yee, who was active in the theatre. All the detainees were released by 1990.

Mass Rapid Transit/Light Rail Transit system *See* box.

Masuri S.N. (1927–2005) Poet and author. Known for his mastery of SAJAK, Masuri Salikun is a founding member of ASAS 50. He attended Telok Kurau Malay School and Sultan Idris Training College, Perak, before joining the education service (1949-82). He began writing at 17, and his poems, 'Ros Kupunya' (My Rose) and 'Bunga Sakura' (Sakura Flower) appeared in the newspaper *Berita Malai* in 1944. He has written more than 1,000 poems, which can be found in anthologies such as *Awan Putih* (White Cloud) (1958), *Puisi Melayu Baru* (New Malay Poetry) (1961), *Selagi Hayat Dikandung Badan* (As Long As I Still Live) (1970), *Dalam Makna* (Meaning) (1984) and *Suasana Senja* (Evening Ambience) (2003). His poetry addresses tradition, social justice and spirituality in a modern setting. He has also published a collection of essays, *Kreativiti dan Kemanusian* (Creativity and Humanity) (1998).

Masuri was awarded the Southeast Asia Write Award (1980) and the Tun Seri Lanang Award (1995) from the Malay Language Council of Singapore. In 2000, he was awarded the MERITORIOUS SERVICE MEDAL. He received an honorary doctorate from his alma mater in 2002.

MATADOR 'Man-portable Anti-Tank, Anti-DOoR' weapon system. The SINGAPORE ARMED FORCES, together with DEFENCE SCIENCE & TECHNOLOGY AGENCY (DSTA) and Dynamic Nobel of Germany, developed a Short Range Anti-Armour Weapon

David Marshall

Melanie Martens

Masuri S.N.

MATADOR

Mass Rapid Transit / Light Rail Transit

The first railway line in Singapore was the Singapore–Kranji Railway, built in 1903, running northwards from the town to the shores of the Strait of Johor. The line served mainly the rural population, and was not an urban mass transit system. Passenger operations ceased during the 1930s, although parts of the route were incorporated into the main rail link between Singapore and Peninsular Malaya.

The basis for the current Mass Rapid Transit (MRT) system was the State and City Planning Study of 1967–71. This study indicated that buses would not sufficiently meet future public transport demands. Further studies recommended the laying of two rail lines—one running east to west, the other running north to south. Since the construction of the MRT would involve substantial investment, another study was conducted in 1981 to examine the feasibility of a rail system versus an all-bus system. The study concluded that an all-bus system was untenable given road-traffic congestion, and that an MRT system would be necessary. Planning of the MRT network and its stations has since been an important factor in URBAN PLANNING.

Growth of the MRT network

Work on the MRT line started in 1983. The first trains started running in 1987 on the North South Line. By 1990, the 67-km, 42-station MRT system was completed. The LAND TRANSPORT AUTHORITY (LTA) owns the rail infrastructure and leases the rail system to operators. Operators are responsible for the cost of running and maintaining the trains and stations. SMRT Trains Limited was appointed to run the North South and East West Lines which were designed to run underground within the city, and on overhead viaducts elsewhere. The Changi Airport Extension, completed in 2002, added two stations to the East West line—Expo Station and Changi Airport Station. By 2002, the North South and East West Lines had a total track length of 90 km, with 51 stations.

SBS Transit Ltd was appointed to run the fully underground, driverless North East Line (NEL), with 20 km of track and 16 stations. In 2003, 14 stations on the NEL were opened. SBS Transit initially planned to open Buangkok station only after the housing projects in these areas are

Construction of Raffles Place station, 1980s.

completed and populations there are large enough to ensure that the stations do not operate at a loss. However, in response to public pressure, Buangkok Station was opened in 2006.

The EZ-Link card, which supercedes the stored-value card (above), makes the transfer between trains and buses seamless.

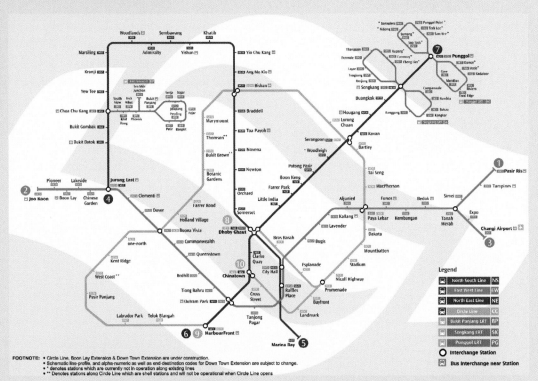

FOOTNOTE: • Circle Line, Boon Lay Extension & Down Town Extension are under construction.
• Schematic line-profile, and alpha-numeric as well as end-destination codes for Down Town Extension are subject to change.
• * denotes stations which are currently not in operation along existing lines
• ** Denotes stations along Circle Line which are shell stations and will not be operational when Circle Line opens

MRT Key Facts
- 3 lines
  - East West Line: from Pasir Ris to Boon Lay, with the Changi Airport Extension
  - North South Line: from Marina Bay to Jurong East
  - North East Line: from Punggol to HarbourFront

- 2 operators
  - SMRT runs the East West Line and North South Line, with 1.1 million trips daily
  - SBS Transit runs the North East Line, with 200,000 trips daily
- 60 stations, including 9 interchanges

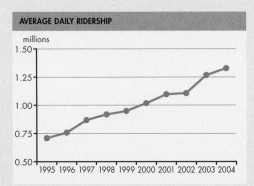

AVERAGE DAILY RIDERSHIP

Future developments

A further development is the Circle Line. This line was designed to cover 34 km of track and have 29 stations. Like the NEL, the trains will be driverless. It is set to be the world's longest fully automatic underground rail system. Sections are scheduled to be operational by 2008, with full operations slated for 2010.

Other projects include the Downtown Extension. The 3.4-km line will run from the Circle Line's Promenade Station at Temasek Avenue, into the Marina Bay Area (servicing INTEGRATED RESORT), until the NEL's Chinatown Station. Another project in the pipeline is the Boon Lay extension. It is to add two more above-ground stations west of Boon Lay on the East West Line.

The Light Rail Transit

The Light Rail Transit (LRT) systems are feeder services to the MRT. Three driverless systems, all of which run on overhead viaducts with one or two carriages per train, began servicing the new towns of Bukit Panjang in 1999, and Sengkang and Punggol in 2004. The Bukit Panjang LRT is run by Singapore LRT, a wholly owned subsidiary of SMRT. The Sengkang and Punggol systems are run by SBS Transit. The LRT systems have a total of 43 stations.

As LRT trains run close to HDB (Housing & Development Board) flats, there has been some concern about preserving the privacy of residents. To solve this problem, the Bukit Panjang LRT trains have been installed with specially-designed window panes that automatically become opaque when the trains pass near flats and become clear again as the trains move away.

Specially-designed panes ensure privacy.

LRT Key Facts
- 2 operators
  - SMRT runs the Bukit Panjang service
  - SBS Transit runs the Sengkang and Punggol services
- 3 services
  - Bukit Panjang from Choa Chu Kang Station
  - Sengkang: east and west loops from Sengkang Station
  - Punggol: east and west loops from Punggol Station
- 43 stations

Dhoby Ghaut Interchange

Dhoby Ghaut Interchange is the largest—and most complex—station on the MRT network. One of the technical difficulties in building the interchange was ensuring that service on the North South Line and traffic on Orchard Road were not disrupted. Engineers also had to deal with the Stamford Canal, which now passes above the fare gates for the North East Line. The interchange costs $268 million and is 28 m deep. It connects the North South Line, North East Line, and the Circle Line. Commuters can crossover between lines without going through the fare gates. Commuters may also exit the station and go to Plaza Singapura, the Atrium@orchard, or the Istana Park via pedestrian links. The station includes a large Civil Defence shelter.

Clockwise from top: view of station interior; cross-sectional diagram; entrance to the station.

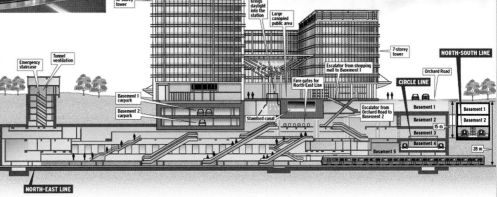

Matthew and The Mandarins: **II**, *1970.*

W. Somerset Maugham: **The Casuarina Tree**, *an edition published in Singapore.*

Sir William Maxwell

in 1999. The new weapon, known as 'MATADOR', replaced the ARMBRUST light anti-tank weapon, which had been in service since the 1980s.

MATADOR was developed as the first weapon in the world to have both anti-armour and anti-brickwall capabilities. It weighs 8.9 kg, is 1 m in length and has a 90-mm calibre. It can produce a 45-cm-wide hole in a double brick wall, thus providing soldiers engaged in built-up areas with a non-conventional point of entry. It has a range beyond that of small arms.

Matthew and The Mandarins Popular music group. Founded by Matthew Tan in 1965, the group also recorded with ANITA SARAWAK on her first EP with EMI in 1969.

The band developed its signature country-and-western sound in the 1970s, when this genre of music began to gain popularity in Singapore. Guitarist Neil Alexander was held by many to be Singapore's best country-and-western guitarist.

The band included Derrick Danker on lead guitar; Michael Png on lead guitar and pedal steel guitar; Richard Danker on bass guitar; and Philip Monteiro on drums. However, the group underwent several personnel changes, with Matthew Tan its only permanent member.

The group released four LPs, the first on Life and the subsequent three on EMI. Matthew Tan recorded a solo LP, *Singapore Cowboy*, in the late 1970s.

Maugham, W. Somerset (1874–1965) Author. Born in Paris, William Somerset Maugham was orphaned at the age of ten and brought up by an uncle. He qualified as a medical doctor in 1897. However, he gave up medicine in the same year with the release of his first novel, *Liza of Lambeth*.

Maugham's travels to British colonies in Asia inspired his *Far Eastern Tales*. In 1921, he visited RAFFLES HOTEL for the first time. He would return to that establishment in 1926 and again in 1959, describing it as the symbol for 'all the fables of the Exotic East'. He is said to have written each morning under a frangipani tree in the hotel's Palm Court.

Many of Maugham's stories described persons he had met on his travels—and he was sued for writing some of these stories.

His short stories about colonial life in Singapore include 'The Outstation', 'Yellow Streak' and 'The Casuarina Tree'. His play, *The Letter* (1927), was based on the true story of a rubber planter's wife who murdered her lover. His more famous novels include *Of Human Bondage* (1915) and *The Razor's Edge* (1944).

Maxwell, Brigadier Duncan (1892–1969) Australian military official. Duncan Struan Maxwell was decorated for his service in World War I, seeing action at Gallipoli and in France. After the war, he studied medicine and became a doctor in Tasmania, Australia.

In 1940, during World War II, Maxwell was appointed by Lieutenant-General GORDON BENNETT to command the 27th Brigade of the Australian 8th Division in Malaya. On the night of 9 February 1942, when the Japanese Imperial Guards attacked his brigade, Maxwell decided that the battle was lost, and gave up the Causeway linking Singapore to Johor. His premature withdrawal was in defiance of standing orders. Maxwell was captured, and his ordeal as a prisoner of war adversely affected his health for the rest of his life.

Maxwell, Sir Peter (1816–1893) Judge. Sir Peter Benson Maxwell was educated first in France, and later at Trinity College, Dublin. He was called to the Bar at the Inner Temple, and practised as a barrister in London.

Maxwell became RECORDER of Penang on 20 March 1856, and in 1866, he succeeded Sir Richard McCausland as Recorder of Singapore. A year later, he became the first chief justice of the newly constituted Straits Settlements of Singapore, Malacca and Penang.

In 1866, Maxwell published *The Duties of Straits Magistrates* through the Government Printing Office. This was prescribed for all civil service examinations. The fifth chapter of the book, entiled 'The Construction of Statutes', formed the core of the textbook *Maxwell on Statutes*, published in London in 1875.

On 26 July 1871, Maxwell retired. In 1883, he travelled to Egypt to organize the court system after the British occupation of that country. In August 1885, he resigned his appointment in Egypt and retired to London.

Maxwell died from pneumonia and was buried in Grasse, France. In 1925, Maxwell Road was named after Sir Peter's family, including his son Sir WILLIAM MAXWELL.

Maxwell, Sir William (1846–1897) Colonial official. The second son of Sir PETER MAXWELL (the first chief justice of the Straits Settlements), William Edward Maxwell had a varied career. As the commissioner of Lands of the Straits Settlements, he instituted various ordinances to put in place an efficient land-

management system. He was appointed colonial secretary of the Straits Settlements in March 1892 and was briefly acting governor in Singapore, before being named governor of the Gold Coast (present-day Ghana) in 1894.

Maxwell is believed to have hoped to return to Singapore as governor. However, he died while still in Africa, having contracted a severe case of blackwater fever in December 1897. He was buried at sea, off the Canary Islands.

May 13 incident (5-1-3) Student riots which took place on 13 May 1954 following the colonial government's passage of the National Service Ordinance. The ordinance required all males between the ages of 18 and 20 to register for conscription, or face jail or fine. The ordinance was highly unpopular amongst Chinese-educated students, and there was widespread resistance to its introduction.

Communist elements also saw this as an ideal opportunity to stage a mass-resistance movement against the colonial authorities. As the final day for registration (12 May 1954) approached, students from CHUNG CHENG HIGH SCHOOL sent a petition to the governor asking for an 'exemption' from registration. This was turned down, and the students decided to stage a demonstration outside Government House the following day. Police withheld permission for this demonstration.

The Chung Cheng students then joined forces with students from CATHOLIC HIGH SCHOOL and the CHINESE HIGH SCHOOL. Together, they enlisted the support of Chinese female students who hired lorries to take male students to King George V Park (present-day Fort Canning Park) where they were joined by more students from Chung Hwa Girls' School and NANYANG GIRLS' SCHOOL.

Protestors then marched on Government House. When the police warned protestors to disperse, the students linked arms and started singing Chinese revolutionary anthems.

Some 500 students then fought police in the streets, pelting them with stones and jeering. Another 1,000 students barricaded themselves inside Chung Cheng High School. Over 20 were injured; 48 were arrested. As a result of the May 13 incident, the Singapore Chinese Middle School Students' Union was formed.

Maybank Malayan Banking Berhad (popularly known as Maybank) was founded by KHOO TECK PUAT, and started operations in Singapore in 1960 out of a single branch on South Bridge Road. It soon established another 21 branches throughout the city, eventually becoming one of the largest banks in ASEAN.

In 1962, Maybank acquired a site for its Singapore headquarters overlooking the

Singapore River. The original building was demolished in 1998, and the 32-storey Maybank Tower was erected in its place.

By 2005, Maybank had amassed total assets worth more than $11 billion in Singapore, and was employing some 1,000 people.

mayors The first two mayors of independent Singapore, OW CHIN HOCK and Eugene Yap, were appointed on 29 March 1997 as heads of pilot Community Development Councils (CDCs)—Tanjong Pagar and Marine Parade, respectively. Following the success of these pilots, the number of CDCs increased. By 2005, there were five mayors for five CDCs.

Prior to SEPARATION, Singapore's only mayor was ONG ENG GUAN. Ong was a founding member of the PEOPLE'S ACTION PARTY (PAP). After the PAP won 13 of the 32 seats at the CITY COUNCIL election of 1957, Ong was elected mayor. Ong and other PAP councillors resigned from the City Council in 1959 after the LIM YEW HOCK government took over part of the City Council's functions.

McCormac, Charles (1915–1985) Charles E. McCormac was a Royal Air Force serviceman who was a prisoner of war in Singapore. During the JAPANESE OCCUPATION, escape from the prison camps was virtually impossible. However, in April 1942, McCormac, along with 16 other inmates, escaped from a Pasir Panjang work camp. All but four of the escape party were killed before they reached Sumatra.

McCormac and another survivor, an Australian named R.G. Donaldson, trekked through the East Indies (present-day Indonesia) for five months, during which they were assisted by friendly villagers and anti-Japanese guerrillas. In later years, McCormac acknowledged that without this help, he would have died. In 1955, he published *You'll Die in Singapore*, an account of his escape.

McNair, J.F.A. (1828–1910) Civil engineer, architect and colonial official. Little is known about John Frederick Adolphus McNair's early life. He joined the Madras Artillery in 1845 and was posted to Malacca in 1853. In 1856, he was sent to Singapore to act as adjutant to the Artillery in the Straits. Between 1857 and 1873, McNair served as comptroller of Indian Convicts in the Straits Settlements; and from 1867 to 1881, he served as colonial engineer at the Public Works Department.

John McNair was arguably the most important architect and builder in Singapore during the latter half of the 19th century. He was responsible for building Government House (now the ISTANA) (1867–69); ST ANDREW'S CATHEDRAL (1856–61); and the New Court House or Secretariat (now the ASIAN CIVILISATIONS MUSEUM) (1864–67). He was also responsible for completing Singapore's waterworks.

McNair later served as chief commissioner in Perak (1875) and lieutenant-governor of Penang (1880–84). In 1861, McNair took up photography while on home leave in the United Kingdom. On his return to Southeast Asia, he began photographing the convicts who were in his charge and who were used as labour in many of the public works projects that McNair was involved in. He wrote two books: *Perak and the Malays: Sarong and Kris* (1878); and *Prisoners Their Own Warders* (1899). He retired in 1884.

McNally, Brother Joseph (1923–2002) Sculptor, missionary and teacher. McNally was born in Ballintubber, Ireland, but became a Singapore citizen in 1985. A member of the De La Salle order, he came to Singapore in 1946, teaching at St Joseph's Institution. In 1963, he became principal of St Patrick's School, retiring in 1982. Two years later, he founded the St Patrick's Arts Centre, which was later renamed the LASALLE-SIA COLLEGE OF THE ARTS. McNally was president of the college until 1997 and helped the Ministry of Education to draw up the Art Elective Programme for schools. For his contribution to the arts, McNally was awarded the Public Service Medal in 1990 and the MERITORIOUS SERVICE MEDAL in 1997.

McNally saw a deep spirituality in art and was known for his sculptures in bronze, oak and bogwood. He held seven solo exhibitions in Singapore and the USA, including a major retrospective at the SINGAPORE ART MUSEUM in 1998. His sculptures are found in public places like the Singapore General Hospital, schools and government buildings, as well as private collections.

McNally died on 27 August 2002, while visiting his hometown in County Mayo, Ireland. In 2003, a posthumous exhibition of his works was held in Dublin. The Singapore government presented a bronze, scaled-up cast of McNally's sculpture *Counsellor II* to Ireland in 2004. The work was installed at the National Museum of Country Life, near McNally's hometown.

Media Development Authority Statutory board. The Media Development Authority (MDA) was created on 1 January 2003 with the passage of the Media Development Authority Act. Three existing media regulators—the Singapore Broadcasting Authority, the Films and Publications Department and the SINGAPORE FILM COMMISSION—were merged to form the board. It was set up in response to the convergence of various media.

MDA's mission is two-pronged: to develop the local media industry; and to regulate content so as to safeguard 'core values' and consumers' interests. Under its blueprint Media 21, launched in July 2003, MDA aims to increase the media industry's contribution to GROSS DOMESTIC PRODUCT from 1.56 per cent to 3 per cent within 10 years.

MediaCorp MediaCorp Pte Ltd has a history of radio broadcasting that goes back to June 1936, and it has been in television broadcasting since February 1963. It was previously known as Radio Television Singapore and SINGAPORE BROADCASTING CORPORATION. The state-owned company currently has a monopoly on free-to-air broadcasting.

In 2000, MediaCorp ventured into newspaper publishing. It was given the licence to publish TODAY while SINGAPORE PRESS HOLDINGS (SPH) was, in turn, given the licence to run two new television channels—Channel U and Channel-i—in 2001, to compete with MediaCorp's Channel 8 and Channel 5, respectively. SPH also obtained the licence to launch a freesheet, *Streats*, to compete with *Today*. In 2004, MediaCorp and SPH merged their television operations under a new company—MediaCorp TV Holdings. MediaCorp came to own 80 per cent of this new vehicle.

MediaCorp Raintree Pictures This production branch of MEDIACORP was set up in

Brother Joseph McNally and (below) his sculpture Self-portrait.

MediaCorp Raintree Pictures: movie posters.

1998 under the direction of Daniel Yun to produce commercial films. Unlike the major studios that rose to prominence in earlier decades, such as MALAY FILM PRODUCTIONS and CATHAY-KERIS FILMS, this new organization was not supported by its own theatre chain. Its first movie was *Liang Po Po—The Movie*, a Mandarin comedy that centred on a character first played by JACK NEO in a local variety show called *Comedy Nite*. The film was co-produced with ERIC KHOO's Zhao Wei Films.

Raintree has released five more films by Jack Neo: *I NOT STUPID* (2002), *Homerun* (2003), *The Best Bet* (2004), *I Do I Do* (2005) and *I Not Stupid Too* (2006). KELVIN TONG's *The Maid* (2005) was a local horror movie which took its inspiration from Japanese and Korean films of the same genre.

Raintree has attempted to produce and release local 'art-house' films, such as CheeK's *Chicken Rice War* (2000), in which the story of *Romeo and Juliet* was adapted to a Singaporean context. It has also collaborated with regional partners, mainly from Hong Kong. Co-productions have included *The Truth About Jane And Sam* (1999) starring FANN WONG; horror movie *The Eye* (2002); *Turn Left Turn Right* (2003); and *Infernal Affairs II* (2003)—a prequel to the 2002 Hong Kong production *Infernal Affairs*.

Medifund The government established Medifund in 1993 as a way of helping needy and underprivileged Singaporeans pay for medical care. The scheme was initially set up with an amount of $200 million, but with plans to increase this amount by $100 million per year, depending on economic growth.

Originally, only patients receiving in-patient treatment in Class B2 or C wards, or subsidized outpatient treatment in public hospitals, were eligible to apply for financial assistance through Medifund. The scheme was later extended to cover step-down care facilities, such as community hospitals run by voluntary welfare organizations (VWOs). By September 2004, 23 VWOs had been accredited by Medifund.

Applications for Medifund are made through medical social workers at hospitals. The amount of aid provided through Medifund depends on the individual circumstances of the patient, as well as the patient's financial situation.

In 2002, 178,209 applications for Medifund were lodged. Of these, 177,949 were approved. The amount of Medifund assistance provided amounted to $26.4 million. Of this sum, 57.7 per cent was given to assist Class B2 and C in-patients; 37.3 per cent was used to assist subsidized outpatients; and 5 per cent was used by VWOs.

Medisave This scheme, which allows part of CENTRAL PROVIDENT FUND (CPF) savings to be used for hospitalization expens-

Mee goreng

es, was introduced in 1984. Under it, every working individual contributes between 6 and 8 per cent (depending on age) of his monthly income to a personal Medisave account. The money accumulated in this account can then be used to pay for hospitalization expenses incurred by that individual or by members of that person's immediate family.

A total-sum ceiling has been set for contributions to Medisave accounts. Any excess contribution beyond the maximum amount is diverted into what is referred to as an Ordinary Account, which members can use for housing instalments, investment and education expenses. In 2005, the contribution ceiling was set at $32,500. When a member reaches the age of 55, he must retain a minimum of $27,500, or the actual Medisave account balance, whichever is lower. He is then able to withdraw the amount in excess of the minimum sum.

Medisave can be used to pay for hospitalization, subject to withdrawal limits based on Class B2 and C wards, although some Singaporeans who are still working and earning higher incomes may have more funds in their Medisave accounts and may opt to go to Class A, B1 and private wards. Medisave can also be used for out-patient treatment, such as hepatitis-B vaccinations; assisted conception procedures; renal dialysis treatment; radiotherapy and chemotherapy for cancer patients; HIV anti-retroviral drugs; and immuno-suppressant drugs. In 2006, use of Medisave was further liberalized to cover outpatient treatment of four chronic diseases: stroke, diabetes, high blood pressure and high cholesterol levels.

MediShield This medical insurance scheme was introduced in 1990 to cover Singaporean citizens and Permanent Residents, as well as their dependents (up to the age of 80). It allows for premiums to be paid from the CENTRAL PROVIDENT FUND (CPF). Premiums range from $30 per year for those aged 30 or over; to $705 for those aged 84–85.

Reimbursement from MediShield is calculated as three elements: the claimable limit, 'deductibles' and co-insurance. The claimable limit is the portion of the patient's bill that is eligible for reimbursement. The deductible is the 'claim amount', below which no reimbursement can be sought from MediShield. 'Deductibles' are small claims that can be paid using

MEDISAVE and/or cash. Co-insurance is a system in which MediShield covers 80–90 per cent of the claimed amount in excess of deductibles. The remaining 10 per cent of the cost is paid by the patient.

As MediShield is intended for patients in Class B2 and C wards, MediShield claims for patients in higher-level wards or private hospitals are calculated based on a percentage of the hospital bill. MediShield Plus Plan A and Plan B were introduced on 1 July 1994 to provide greater coverage for members who prefer to stay in Class A or B1 wards.

mee goreng Popular hawker dish. It consists of yellow wheat noodles fried in a wok with minced mutton, green peas, shredded cabbage, and tomatoes. While primarily an Indian Muslim dish, Malay and Chinese versions exist also. The Indian Muslim version uses a tomato-based sauce that colours the dish red. The Malay version uses the same ingredients but omits the tomato sauce. The Chinese version uses prawns, squid and fish as ingredients.

members of Parliament Members of PARLIAMENT (MPs) can be classified into three categories.

The first category comprises members directly elected by their CONSTITUENCIES, including those who are elected in GROUP REPRESENTATION CONSTITUENCIES (GRCs) and those elected in single-member constituencies.

The second category comprises NON-CONSTITUENCY MEMBERS OF PARLIAMENT (NCMPs). NCMPs are not directly elected, but are awarded a seat in parliament on the basis of their having gained the highest percentage of votes among the candidates who were not elected. The total number of NCMPs cannot exceed six. The inclusion of NCMPs ensures representation of opposition parties.

The third category of MPs—NOMINATED MEMBERS OF PARLIAMENT (NMP)—was created in 1989. NMPs are non-partisan, and are appointed without election.

To qualify as a candidate for a parliamentary election, a person must be a Singapore citizen; over the age of 21; resident in Singapore at the date of nomination; able to take an active part in parliamentary proceedings; and—unless blind—able to read and write one of the official languages. Any potential candidate must be a registered voter.

A person may be disqualified from standing for election as an MP if he is of unsound mind; is bankrupt; is a full-time civil servant; fails to lodge 'any return of election expenses'; or has voluntarily exercised or acquired citizenship of a foreign country. A person can also be disqualified for standing if they have been convicted of an offence entailing a term of imprisonment or a fine exceeding $2,000, or have been convicted of an offence under any law relating to parliamentary elections.

No person can be an MP for more than one constituency at the same time. An MP's seat becomes vacant upon dissolution of parliament. A vacancy can also occur if a member ceases to be a citizen of Singapore; ceases to be a member or is expelled from his political party; resigns his seat; absents himself for 'two consecutive months in each of which sittings of parliament…are held'; or is expelled from parliament.

Menado, Maria (1933–) Actress and producer. Born Libeth Dotulong in Sulawesi, Indonesia, Maria Menado adopted her screen name after moving to Singapore and winning a beauty contest. Her acting career began with L. Krishnan's *Penghidupan* (Life) (1950). This was followed by roles in S. Ramanathan's *Pulau Mutiara* (Mutiara Island) (1951) and B.S. RAJHANS' *Gadis Peladang* (The Farmer Girl) (1952).

However, it was with the role of the *pontianak*—a female vampire from Malay folklore—that Menado became most closely associated. Menado played this role in *Pontianak* (1957), *Dendam Pontianak* (Revenge of the Vampire) (1957) and *Sumpah Pontianak* (Curse of the Vampire) (1958), which were made by B.N. RAO.

In 1959, Menado established Maria Menado Productions to produce, in association with CATHAY-KERIS FILMS, *Korban Fitnah* (Victim of Slander), a social drama in which she also acted. She then starred in an Indian film, Shakti Samanta's *Singapore* (1960). While continuing with her acting career, Menado co-produced B.N. Rao's *Siti Zubaidah* (1961) with Cathay-Keris Films, K.M. Basker's *Raja Bersiong* (The King with Fangs), and Ramon Estella's *Darahku* (My Blood), the last two in 1963. She also acted in a belated instalment of the *pontianak* genre, 1963's *Pontianak Kembali*

Maria Menado

(Return of the Pontianak).

In the mid-1960s, Menado retired from acting and moved to Kuala Lumpur. The second of her three marriages was to the then Sultan of Pahang in 1963.

Mendaki Malay/Muslim community association. Mendaki, officially launched on 10 October 1981 as Yayasan Mendaki, seeks to improve the level of education amongst Malay Muslim children. The name 'Mendaki' is an abbreviation of the organization's first official title—Majlis Pendidikan Anak-anak Islam (Council on the Education of Muslim Children). Funding for the organization was provided by the government and from 1984, by a compulsory CENTRAL PROVIDENT FUND deduction from every Malay/Muslim worker (*see* MOSQUE BUILDING FUND).

In 1989 Mendaki was reconstituted with an expanded role and objectives to promote the educational, social and economic development of the Malay community. Mendaki was set up as a company limited by guarantee and since then, it was also known as the Council for the Development of the Singapore Muslim Community. It provided social services such as family service centres and began its foray into business with such ventures as the Amanah Saham Mendaki (Mendaki Growth Fund).

Mendaki underwent a restructuring in 2002 and has refocused its energies on education and aiding lower-income families. It is no longer actively involved in business projects. One of its strategic goals is to have at least 90 per cent of Malay Muslim students obtain post-secondary education by 2008. It has introduced financial aid programmes and various educational programmes for students and families.

The Mendaki Tuition Scheme (MTS), Mendaki's longest-running and most popular programme, provides low-cost group tuition to primary and secondary school students. The classes are conducted by volunteer tutors. Since the scheme began in 1982, more than 100,000 students have enroled. There are more than 6,000 primary and secondary school students in the scheme, attending classes in 46 tuition centres all over Singapore. Since its restructuring, Mendaki has also adopted a more holistic approach, addressing factors detrimental to education such as low family income and delinquency. The Education Trust Fund, launched in 2003, provides financial assistance to low-income families. Funds are raised through public donations. Another initiative is the Youth-In-Action programme. It aims to motivate those aged between 10 and 14 years—particularly 'at risk' youths—to stay in school, and to develop character and competency.

Meng Yi (1937-) Author. Meng Yi is the pseudonym of Huang Mengwen (Wong Meng Voon). He was born in Malaya. In his first collection of stories, *Zai Jian Huilan De Shi Hou* (When I See Huilan Again) (1968), Meng Yi returns as a native to the land where he is disillusioned by the country life he so admired before. The title story captures the symbolic scenery of a rubber plantation in Malaya and the struggle of the author's childhood girlfriend against destiny.

Meng Yi went on to publish *Wo Yao Huo Xia Qu* (I Want to Live) (1970), *An Le Wo* (The Happy Nest) (1991), and other works of symbolic realism. He is also best-known among Chinese readers for a new genre, the mini-story, which he started writing in the late 1980s. A mini-story is about 500 to 1000 Chinese characters in length, dealing with a suspenseful episode and leaving the meaning to the imagination. The publication of *Xue Fu Xia Dong* (Stories of a School: A Collection of Wong Meng Voon's Mini-Stories) (1994), established Meng Yi as a prominent writer of the genre.

Mercantile Bank The Mercantile Bank of India, London and China was founded in 1853. It received its charter in 1858, but was forced to give this up in 1893 when it underwent financial reconstruction. The Singapore branch was opened in 1856, and by the 1890s its customers included not only many of the major AGENCY HOUSES, such as Boustead and Guthrie, but significant local business, conducted with the aid of its COMPRADOR, and in many instances through chettiars.

The Mercantile began to issue currency notes in Singapore in 1861. Although this right was later withdrawn, in 1903, the bank still had $100,000 (Straits Dollars) in currency still in circulation. The bank's Singapore office also helped finance businesses in the neighbouring ports of Bangkok and Saigon (present-day Ho Chi Minh City), where its agents were Windsor and Co. and Banque de l'Indo-Chine, respectively. The main Singapore premises were in Raffles Place, where it purchased a lease on a building in 1916, to be replaced in 1930 by a more imposing structure with classical facade designed by Swan and Maclaren (this landmark was demolished when the Raffles Place MRT station was built). The Mercantile Bank was taken over by its long-time competitor, the Hongkong

Mercantile Bank: specimen note printed for the Chartered Mercantile Bank of India, London and China in 1864.

Meng Yi: Zai Jian Huilan De Shi Hou (When I See Huilan Again) (front); Zhao Yang Cong Wo Shen Bian Lüe Guo (The Morning Sun Shines Past Me) (back).

Merdeka: signature campaign, 12 March 1956.

Merdeka celebrations

and Shanghai Bank, in 1959, although it was a number of years before the two were operationally fully integrated. The Mercantile brand, familiar not only in Singapore but across much of Malaysia, was phased out at the beginning of 1974.

Merdeka 'Independence' in Malay. In the immediate aftermath of World War II, the British Colonial Office drew up a scheme for the constitutional unification of the Straits Settlements, the Federated Malay States and the Unfederated Malay States. Under this plan, Singapore was to be left out of a new Malayan Union because the British believed that Malay rulers would prefer that the island's large Chinese population not be absorbed into Malaya. At the time, Singapore's inclusion in the Malayan Union would have meant that the Union's ethnic Chinese community would have outnumbered the Malays.

Thus, when the Straits Settlements were dissolved in 1946, control of Singapore was transferred to the Colonial Office. Singapore was then administered as a separate colony, while Penang and Malacca—the other two Straits Settlements territories—were united with the rest of the Malay states to form the Malayan Union.

Between 1946 and 1953, the immediate priority was to rebuild Singapore's economy. The only major political groups to be formed in this period were the MALAYAN DEMOCRATIC UNION (1946) and the PROGRESSIVE PARTY (1947). Neither of these parties lobbied for self-government for Singapore. Indeed, progress was so slow on the question of self-government that Governor JOHN NICOLL appointed a commission to review Singapore's constitutional and political structure 'to enable Singapore to develop as a self-contained and autonomous unit in any larger organization with which it may ultimately become associated'.

The commission (*see* RENDEL COMMISSION), headed by Sir GEORGE RENDEL, recommended partial internal self-government for Singapore, with the United Kingdom retaining control over internal security, finance, defence and foreign affairs. It also proposed a single-chamber legislative assembly of 32 members, of which 25 would be elected and the rest either provided by the constitution or nominated by the governor. The commission also proposed a nine-member Council of Ministers that would act as a Cabinet while the governor would retain his veto power over legislation, and his right to suspend the constitution.

The constitution came into effect in February 1954, and elections for the Legislative Assembly were held in 1955. Unlike the 1948 elections, voters were automatically registered (i.e. they were not required to complete a registration form before they could vote) and for the first time had the opportunity to vote for representatives.

The LABOUR FRONT, founded by prominent lawyer DAVID MARSHALL, LIM YEW HOCK and teacher FRANCIS THOMAS, won 10 of the 25 seats and formed a government through a coalition with the UMNO-MCA (United Malays National Organization; Malayan Chinese Association) Alliance Party. Marshall thus became Singapore's first chief minister.

In order to avert a crisis and ensure that the government did not fall to communism, the British agreed to hold constitutional talks with an all-party delegation from Singapore in April 1956. Marshall, who had to face labour unrest in Singapore and factional struggles within his own party, undertook to secure independence for the island. He led the 13-man delegation, which included members of all political parties represented in the Assembly, including the PEOPLE'S ACTION PARTY's (PAP's) LEE KUAN YEW and LIM CHIN SIONG. The subsequent negotiations became known as the 'Merdeka Talks'.

At the talks held between 23 April and 15 May 1956, Marshall demanded full internal self-government by 1 April 1957, with foreign policy and defence left in British hands, but with Singapore allowed a veto on defence, and the right of consultation on foreign affairs.

Merdeka: David Marshall in London, 1956.

This proposal was rejected by the British who instead agreed to a fully elected assembly and the removal of ex-officio members. Under these terms, Singapore residents would have their own citizenship and complete control over trade and commerce. The major demand of the Colonial Office concerned the proposed Defence Council, on which Britain and Singapore should have equal representation. The Colonial Office argued that the casting vote be in the hands of the British High Commissioner, who would only use this in the event of an emergency. Marshall refused to concede on this point, and talks faltered.

Unable to fulfil his pledge to secure independence, Marshall resigned upon returning to Singapore in June 1956. Lim Yew Hock succeeded him as chief minister. In March 1957, Lim led a second all-party delegation to London to renew discussions on self-government. These negotiations progressed as the FEDERATION OF MALAYA was about to gain independence. However, the terms offered by the British were almost identical to those offered to Marshall's delegation the year before, with the exception that, with regard to internal security, a new arrangement was proposed. Under this scheme, a seven-member Internal Security Council would be established, with Britain and Singapore having three representatives each, the seventh member being appointed by the Federation of Malaya.

Lim's delegation accepted these terms. The subsequent report, which was presented to the Legislative Assembly, was accepted by the majority of its members. And a third all-party delegation left for London in 1958 to settle the final terms for the new constitution.

On 1 August 1958, the British Parliament passed the State of Singapore Act, which effectively converted the colony into a self-governing state. Under the Singapore Constitution Order-in-Council, 1958, one of the last vestiges of a colonial-style constitution—the post of governor—was abolished, and the office of the Yang di-Pertuan Negara established in its place. Under Part VIII of the constitution, however, responsibility for Singapore's external affairs were to be placed in the hands of the British government.

Elections for the 51-seat fully-elected Legislative Assembly were scheduled for May 1959. For the first time, voting was compulsory. Ten parties contested the elections, and the PAP, under Lee Kuan Yew emerged victorious. It won 43 of the 51 seats, forming Singapore's first self-governing administration. The outgoing governor, WILLIAM GOODE, brought the new constitution into force on 3 June 1959. Goode was then inaugurated as the first Yang di-Pertuan Negara of the State of Singapore. Lee Kuan Yew became Singapore's first prime minister, and a total of nine ministers were appointed.

Thus Singapore's Merdeka was achieved in 1959, albeit only as a prelude to a short-lived MERGER with Malaysia in 1963 before SEPARATION in 1965.

Merdeka Bridge This bridge across the Kallang River is part of Nicoll Highway and was completed in 1956 by the Public Works Department. The bridge was named to mark the birth of the FEDERATION OF MALAYA in 1957. Spanning 610 m, the bridge provided a link between the city centre and the East Coast, that was being rapidly developed at the time. It was designed to have three lanes, with two lanes open to traffic moving into the city centre in the mornings, and the flow reversed during the evening peak hour.

The bridge features three spanned arches. When it was first opened, it was adorned with two stone lions sculpted by the Italian artist RODOLFO NOLLI. When the bridge was widened in the 1960s, the lions were moved to a nearby park, and moved again in 1988 to the SAFTI Military Institute.

On 20 April 2004, a section of Nicoll Highway collapsed during the construction of a new MRT line, resulting in the closure of Merdeka Bridge for nearly eight months (see NICOLL HIGHWAY COLLAPSE).

Merger On 27 May 1961, Malayan Premier Tunku ABDUL RAHMAN announced that he was willing to consider a merger between Singapore and Malaya in the context of a

wider association involving British colonial territories on Borneo.

The Tunku had previously opposed any merger with Singapore because of a fear that unification would lead to political domination by the Chinese population. Singapore's inclusion in the federation would have resulted in a combined Chinese population of 3.6 million as opposed to a total Malay population of 3.4 million. The Tunku was also alarmed about the growing influence of communists in Singapore politics. And as long as the British continued to rule Singapore, it was unlikely that communists would come to power there.

However, the Tunku was willing to consider the inclusion of Singapore within a larger grouping. Privately, he had broached this subject with the British on at least two occasions—once in December 1958, when he told MALCOLM MACDONALD that he would readily agree to merger with Singapore if the three British territories on Borneo were included in the federation at the same time; and again, in June 1960, when he made the same proposal to the Colonial Office's Minister of State Lord Perth.

The Tunku may have also been concerned that either the Philippines or Indonesia might make a bid for one or more of these territories on Borneo. He also believed that most of the people in the Borneo territories would be glad to join with Malaya. The non-Chinese populations in those territories could also serve as a counterweight to the Singapore Chinese, tipping the racial balance against the Chinese in a newly-formed confederation.

Singapore's status came up for constitutional review in 1963, with independence appearing to be the next stage in the process. Thus the issue of merger could not be postponed. The danger of radical, pro-communist groups winning power from the PEOPLE'S ACTION PARTY (PAP) in upcoming polls in Singapore would expose Malaya to possible security risks. The Tunku believed that a Singapore outside the federation would prove more dangerous than a Singapore within it.

The Tunku's initiative was welcomed

by the British, who had long held the prospect of a 'grand design' to bring about a 'British dominion of Southeast Asia' comprising their five dependencies in the region: Malaya, Singapore, Sarawak, North Borneo (present-day Sabah) and Brunei.

The origins of this scheme for regional consolidation can be traced to British planning for the post-war region during World War II. But momentum for the proposed confederation was lost in the immediate aftermath of the war and subsequent events.

By the first quarter of 1961, however, the deteriorating position of the ruling PAP government in Singapore refocused attention on the British 'grand design'. A power struggle within the party had threatened to split the PAP. A by-election in Hong Lim towards the end of April 1961 resulted in defeat for the PAP candidate. Without gaining support for its declared policy of 'independence through merger', the PAP found its position increasingly vulnerable in Singapore. British officials feared that, unless some move was made towards a 'grand design', growing calls for a separate independence for Singapore might become unmanageable, and could lead to the fall of the PAP government.

The PAP also welcomed the Tunku's initiative. The party took the position that a Singapore-Federation merger would not only afford a larger common market and sustain Singapore's industrialization efforts, but would also neutralize the PAP's radical leftist opponents in a Malaya ruled by the anti-communist Alliance Party.

On 9 May 1961, LEE KUAN YEW

Merger: proclamation ceremony, 1963 (top); information booklet for the general public, 1962.

Merdeka Bridge: official opening, 1956.

MERITORIOUS SERVICE MEDAL RECIPIENTS

1962

Ahmad Mohamed Ibrahim	State Advocate-General
K.P. Bhaskar	Principal, Bhaskar Academy of Dancing
George Edwin Bogaars	Director, Special Branch
Cheong Soo Pieng	Artist
Goh Soon Tioe	Violinist
Gwee Ah Leng	Former chairman, Nanyang University Review Committee and Chairman, Joint Government and University of Malaya, Singapore Division Committee
Hon Sui Sen	Chairman, Economic Development Board
Lien Shih Sheng	Author and journalist
Lim Choon Seng	Former Inspector of Police
Lim Chuan Kim	Assistant secretary, Prime Minister's Office
S.T. Stewart	Permanent secretary, Prime Minister's Office and permanent secretary, Ministry of Home Affairs
Tai Chen Hwa	Chairman, Teachers' Training College Advisory Board; chairman, Syllabuses and Textbooks Committee; member, Educational Advisory Council
Tan Howe Liang	Sportsman
Tan Siak Kew	Deputy chairman, Singapore Telephone Board and member, Singapore Harbour Board
Tham Ah Kow	Consultant, Primary Production Department, Ministry of National Development
Leslie Woodford	Chief commissioner for Boy Scouts for the State of Singapore
Woon Wah Siang	Chief administrative officer, City Council and Director of Social Welfare
Yoong Siew Wah	Deputy superintendent of Police

1963

Abu Bakar Pawanchee	Senior Trade and Cultural Representative for Singapore in Indonesia
D.T. Assomull	President, Indian Chamber of Commerce
Richard Byrne Corridon	Superintendent of Police
John Henry Duclos	Head, Broadcasting Division, Ministry of Culture
Howe Yoon Chong	Permanent Secretary, Ministry of Finance
Major P.L. James	Director of Prisons
Ahmad Khan	Superintendent of Police
Ko Teck Kin	President, Chinese Chamber of Commerce
Lien Ying Chow	Banker
P.S. Raman	Deputy head, Broadcasting Division, Ministry of Culture
Sim Kee Boon	Acting permanent secretary, Ministry of National Development
Dato Teo Hang Sam	Merchant
Wong Chooi Sen	Secretary to the Cabinet

1964

K.M. Abdul Razak	President, Indian Chamber of Commerce
Rev Brother Albert	Former director, Boys' Town Singapore
Foo Chee Fong	Former president, Kheng Chew Huay Kuan

1965

Lim Ho Hup	Acting director, Economic Development Board
Loke Wan Tho (posthumous)	Late chairman, Malaysian Airways
Sergeant C.R. Clifton	No. 2 Detachment, Ammunition Inspectorate, Federation Armed Forces Ammunition Depot
Lieutenant-Colonel Lamb	Former commanding officer, 2nd T.B.M. Battalion, Singapore Infantry Regiment

1966

Aramvally Gopalan	Deputy superintendent of Police

1967

Ee Peng Liang	Social and community worker
John Le Cain	Commissioner of Police
Gordon Arthur Ransome	Professor of Medicine, University of Singapore and consultant physician, General Hospital, Singapore
Tan Teck Khim	Permanent secretary (Special Duties), Ministry of Health
Tay Seow Huah	Director, Security and Intelligence, Ministry of Interior and Defence
George Gray Thomson	Director, Political Study Centre
Lieutenant-Colonel Kirpa Ram Vij	Director, Singapore Armed Forces Training Institute

1968

Kwan Sai Kheong	Permanent secretary, Ministry of Education
Ernest Monteiro	Ambassador to Cambodia
Ong Kah Kok	Principal assistant secretary, Ministry of the Interior and Defence
Ong Swee Law	Chairman, Public Utilities Board

1969

P.H. Meadows	Former Chairman, Singapore Tourist Promotion Board
Wan King Cheong	Former head, Research Department, Ministry of the Interior and Defence

1970

Cheng Tong Fatt	Director of Primary Production Department
Pang Tee Pow	Permanent secretary, Home Affairs Division, Ministry of the Interior and Defence

1972

K.R. Chandra	Permanent secretary, Ministry of Law and Commissioner, Bases Economic Conversion Department
Ho Rih Hwa	Ambassador to Belgium and former Ambassador to Thailand
Low Guan Onn	Social and Community Worker
J.D. Van Oenan	Vice president, International Financial Centre, Bank of America, London

1973

Hsu Tse-Kwang	Commissioner of Inland Revenue

1974

S.R. Nathan	Director, Security and Intelligence Division, Ministry of Defence

1975

Seah Cheng Siang	Deputy director, School of Post-Graduate Medical Studies, University of Singapore
Wong Hock Boon	Director, School of Post-Graduate Medical Studies, University of Singapore

1976

Michael Fam	Chairman, Haw Par Brothers International Limited
J.J. Gerzon	Industrialist and Member, Port of Singapore Authority
Lee Hee Seng	Former chairman, Housing & Development Board
Teh Cheang Wan	Chief executive officer, Housing & Development Board

1977

Chi Owyang	Ambassador to Thailand
Runme Shaw	Former chairman, Singapore Tourist Promotion Board

1978

Ngiam Tong Dow	Permanent secretary, Ministry of Finance (Development Division)
J.Y.M. Pillay	Permanent secretary, Ministry of Finance (Revenue Division)
Wee Mon Cheng	Ambassador to Japan

1979

Tommy Koh Thong Bee	Permanent representative to the United Nations
Wee Kim Wee	High commissioner to Malaysia

1980

Haji Buang Haji Siraj	Former president, Majlis Ugama Islam Singapura
Punchardsheram Coomaraswamy	Ambassador to the United States of America

1982

Goh Keng Chew	Deputy director of Public Works (Airport)

1983

Lim Chong Yah	Professor in Economics & Statistics, National University of Singapore and Chairman, National Wages Council
Tan I Tong	Chairman, Singapore Tourist Promotion Board and Chairman, Sentosa Development Corporation

1984

Goh Seng Kim	General manager, Telecoms
Lee Ek Tieng	Permanent secretary, Ministry of the Environment and Chairman, Public Utilities Board

1985

Liu Thai Ker	Chief executive officer, Housing & Development Board
Yeo Tiam Siew	Contributions to social and community service

1987

Maurice Baker	High commissioner to Malaysia
Koh Beng Seng	Director Banking and Financial Institution Department, Monetary Authority of Singapore

1988

Chan Chin Bock	Alternate chairman, Economic Development Board
Lim Leong Geok	Executive director, Mass Rapid Transit Corporation

1989

Wong Heck Sing	Deputy chairman, Public Service Commission

1990

Fong Sip Chee	Special contributions to government, especially in the years 1961–63, 1964–65
Sia Kah Hui	Special contributions to government, especially in the years 1961–63, 1964–65
Chan Chee Seng	Special contributions to government, especially in the years 1961–63, 1964–65
Chor Yeok Eng	Special contributions to government, especially in the years 1961–63, 1964–65
Alan Choe	Chairman, Sentosa Development Corporation
Professor Lim Pin	Vice-chancellor, National University of Singapore
David Marshall	Ambassador to France

1991

Lim Siong Guan	Acting chairman of the Executive Group, first permanent secretary, Ministry of Defence and Chairman, CPF Board
Philip Yeo	Chairman, Economic Development Board
Tan Eng Liang	Chairman, Singapore Sports Council
John Yip	Director of Education, Ministry of Education

1992

Kwa Soon Bee	Permanent secretary, Ministry of Health
Wong Hung Khim	President and chief executive officer, Singapore Telecom
Chen Wen Hsi	Artist

1993

F.A. Chua	Former Judge of the Supreme Court
Hsuan Owyang	Chairman, Housing & Development Board

1994

Andrew Chew	Senior administrative officer, Prime Minister's Office
Pan Shou	Artist and poet

1995

Chao Tzee Cheng	Director, Institute of Science and Forensic Medicine
Koh Boon Hwee	Chairman, Singapore Telecom
Koh Yong Guan	Commissioner of Inland Revenue

1996

Liu Kang	Artist

1997

Fock Siew Wah	Chairman, Land Transport Authority of Singapore
Brother Joseph McNally	Director, LaSalle Foundation Pte Ltd
Eddie Teo	Permanent secretary, Ministry of Defence
Police General Bibyo Widodo	Chief of Indonesian National Police

1998

Tee Tua Ba	High commissioner to Brunei

2000

BG (NS) Choi Shing Kwok	Director, Security & Intelligence Division, Ministry of Defence
Masuri Salikun	Arts adviser, National Arts Council

2001

Tan Gee Paw	Former permanent secretary, Ministry of the Environment and Chairman, Public Utilities Board

2002

Robert Loh	Former president, National Council of Social Service
Koh Cher Siang	Commissioner of Inland Revenue and CEO, Inland Revenue Authority of Singapore

2003

Khoo Boon Hui	Commissioner of Police
Tan Swie Hian	Artist

2004

Wee Heng Tin	Former director-general of Education, Ministry of Education

2005

Chan Heng Chee	Ambassador to the United States of America
Tan Chin Tiong	Ambassador to Japan
M.P.H. Rubin	Former Judge of the Supreme Court
Harun Abdul Ghani (posthumous)	Significant contributions to Singapore's effective campaign against drug abuse

Source: Prime Minister's Office

Merger: Tunku Abdul Rahman (in dark suit) and Lee Kuan Yew board a plane for Kuala Lumpur.

submitted a statement to the Tunku reiterating the view that, without merger by 1963, the PAP would not be able to hold its position in Singapore. It also proposed the introduction of safeguards to address concerns about the loss of Malay primacy in an enlarged federation. Eighteen days later, at a lunch of the Foreign Correspondents' Association of Southeast Asia in Singapore, the Tunku made his historic speech, which suggested that merger should be considered.

In Singapore, the Tunku's speech triggered a political crisis, resulting in yet another by-election defeat for the PAP in Anson in mid-July, and culminating in the formation of BARISAN SOSIALIS by PAP dissidents later that month. To seek popular endorsement for merger, a referendum was held in September 1962. Seventy-one per cent of the electorate supported the PAP's proposals for merger.

In the Borneo territories, there was public opposition to absorption into the federation as concerns over Malayan 'colonialism' resurfaced. This prompted the British, in consultation with Malaya, to set up a joint Anglo-Malayan Commission of Enquiry in mid-January 1962 to assess opinion in Sarawak and North Borneo. The commission found that while there was support for the formation of Malaysia, there were also apprehensions, particularly at the prospect of Malayan rule in Borneo. Brunei subsequently opted not to join Malaysia.

Conflicting claims by the Philippines and Indonesia over Malaysia's formation further delayed the formation of the new federation. Inauguration was set for 31 August 1963, thus allowing enough time for a fact-finding mission from the United Nations to ascertain opinion in Borneo. London played host, and indigenous leaders reconciled contradictory objectives and brokered compromises that eventually

resulted in an agreement on the nature of the new federation.

As a result, on 16 September 1963, Singapore was united with Malaya through the formation of Malaysia, thus achieving freedom from British rule.

See also SEPARATION.

Meritorious Service Medal This award was instituted in 1962. It is presented to any person who has performed, within Singapore, 'service of conspicuous merit characterized by resource and devotion to duty, including long service marked by exceptional ability, merit and exemplary conduct'. In exceptional circumstances, the medal can also be awarded to persons whose service has been outside Singapore.

Merlion Sculpture. The merlion—a mythical creature with the body of a fish and the head of a lion—occurs in a number of different artistic traditions. Lions with fishtails can be found on Indian murals at Ajanta and Mathura, and on Etruscan coins of the Hellenistic period. Merlions, or 'heraldic sea-lions', are an established element of Western heraldry, and have been used on the coat of arms of the city of Great Yarmouth in the United Kingdom; the City of Manila; and the East India Company.

Singapore's Merlion sculpture was created in 1972 by sculptor Lim Nang Seng (1907–1987). It was based on a concept of artist and educator KWAN SAI KHEONG. The original idea of using a merlion to represent Singapore can be traced back to 1964, however, when the newly established Singapore Tourist Promotion Board (STPB)—precursor to the SINGAPORE TOURISM BOARD—unveiled a logo that included a merlion floating above stylized waves, over a motto carrying the words 'lion city'.

The board credited the design of this

logo to Frank Brunner, a curator at the VAN KLEEF AQUARIUM and a member of the Souvenirs Committee at the STPB. At the time, the logo was said to have been derived from the literal meaning of the toponym Singapore (i.e., 'lion city').

The sculpture was commissioned at a cost of $165,000, in the hope of establishing a specific landmark that would come to be associated with Singapore. It was constructed of concrete around a steel frame, and designed to spout water into the harbour. The 8.6-m high, 70-tonne sculpture was sited in Merlion Park, at the mouth of the SINGAPORE RIVER. The then Prime Minister LEE KUAN YEW opened the park on 15 September 1972.

A 37-metre-high Merlion Tower was unveiled as a tourist attraction on SENTOSA in 1996.

In 2002, the original Merlion was moved to a new Merlion Park built on reclaimed land on the MARINA BAY side of the Esplanade Bridge—a structure that had cut off the former site from the sea. The move cost some $7.5 million, but the new park proved to be popular with tourists. The Merlion was set upon a new base, and the original pump, which drove the Merlion's spout, was replaced by two more powerful pumps.

The Merlion has been commonly featured in Singapore literature. Examples include poet EDWIN THUMBOO's *Ulysses by the Merlion* (1977); LEE TZU PHENG's *The Merlion to Ulysses* (1997); ALFIAN SAAT's *The Merlion* (1998); and Alvin Pang's *Merlign* (1998).

Meteorological Services Division The division traces its beginnings to 1927, when a Meteorological Service was set up as a branch under the Malayan Survey Department. It is now a division within the NATIONAL ENVIRONMENT AGENCY.

The Meteorological Services Division operates six manned weather observation stations around Singapore that have rain gauges and thermometers to measure rainfall and temperature. It also has radar stations, satellite stations, lightning detectors,

Merlion: at the mouth of the Singapore river.

Methodism: Methodist Girls' School, c. 1915.

Methodism: **Methodist Message** *newsletter, 2006.*

unmanned rainfall gauges and seismic stations around Singapore.

It produces weather predictions based on data obtained from various sources such as weather radar, which monitors the distribution and intensity of rainfall over Singapore, cloud pictures from weather satellites and from computer modelling.

The division is now developing an early warning system for tsunamis. It has upgraded its central processing system to exchange real-time earthquake data with seismic networks operated by countries in the region. It will eventually add three more seismic sensors to the existing four. The national tsunami early warning system will be part of the regional Indian Ocean Tsunami Warning System.

Methodism Missionaries from the American Methodist Episcopal Church had begun missionary work in India in the mid-1850s. From there, the first team of Methodist missionaries, led by James Mills Thoburn, travelled to Singapore in February 1885.

Thoburn returned to India after establishing a small Quarterly Conference of Methodists in Singapore. This was left in the charge of the Reverend WILLIAM OLDHAM, another member of the mission team from India, after Thoburn's departure. It was from that original congregation, which met at the MIDDLE ROAD CHURCH (then known as the 'English Church') that the first Methodist church in Singapore grew.

A number of early Methodist missionaries, including Oldham himself, spoke various local dialects and languages; recruited and worked closely with local evangelists; and helped to establish a number of Methodist churches for different language communities in Singapore. For instance, Methodist missionaries began working amongst Tamils in the Serangoon Road area almost as soon as the Singapore mission was established. And by 1885, regular Tamil services were being offered. When C.W. Underwood, a Tamil preacher, arrived in 1887, a Tamil Methodist church was established on the site of the present-day TEKKA MARKET; this later became the Short Street

Tamil Methodist Church.

In 1889, the first Chinese Methodist church was established in Singapore. It catered to the Hokkien-speaking Chinese who originated in China's Fujian province, where Methodist missionaries had been active since 1847. This church later became known as the TELOK AYER CHINESE METHODIST CHURCH.

More churches catering to various Chinese dialect groups were then established. These included the Foochow Methodist Church (1897), the Hinghwa Methodist Church (1911), the Hakka Methodist Church (1913) and the Cantonese Kum Yan Methodist Church (1918).

Methodist missionaries were also active in other ethnic communities. In 1888, a Malay-speaking gathering was established with the assistance by WILLIAM SHELLABEAR, a Malay-speaking former Royal Artillery Officer. And in 1894, a Methodist church ministering to PERANAKANS was established in Middle Road (*see* MIDDLE ROAD CHURCH). This later became the Kampong Kapor Methodist Church.

The Methodists were also active in publishing. They established their own press in Selegie Road in 1890. They produced a variety of printed materials in English, as well as in Malay, Chinese, Tamil and Tagalog. In October 1890, the Methodist monthly periodical, *The Malaysia Message,* was launched. This periodical was renamed *The Methodist Message* in 1952.

The Methodist church in Malaysia and Singapore was originally administered together as the Malaysia Mission, then as the Malaysia Annual Conference. In 1924, this became the Malaya Annual Conference. The early decades of the 20th century saw a period of rapid expansion and growth, and this led to significant re-organization. From 1932 onwards, Chinese- and Tamil-speaking Methodists began mooting the possibility of starting their own separate annual conferences. In 1936, the Chinese Mission Annual Conference was established. In 1942, this became the Chinese Annual Conference. Similarly, the Tamil Provisional Annual Conference was formed in 1968 after the Singapore and Malaysia Annual Conferences gained autonomy as the Methodist Church in Malaysia and Singapore. In 1976, the Methodist Churches of Singapore and Malaysia became two separate churches.

The Methodist Church in Singapore later came to be organized under three Annual Conferences: the Chinese Annual Conference, governing the churches providing services in Mandarin and dialects; the Trinity Annual Conference, consisting of the churches where services are provided in English; and the Emmanuel Tamil Annual Conference for Tamil churches.

While the Methodists arrived in Singapore relatively late (compared to other

Methodism: Wesley Methodist Church.

denominations such as the Anglicans and Presbyterians), Methodism grew to become one of the largest protestant denominations in Singapore. Indeed, by 2005, the church could claim more than 31,000 members in 41 local churches and 'seven preaching points'.

Much of the church's success has been based on its work in education. The first Methodist school—the ANGLO-CHINESE SCHOOL—was established in March 1886. The METHODIST GIRLS' SCHOOL was established in 1887 by Australian Methodist missionary SOPHIA BLACKMORE. In 1888, Blackmore started another school catering to girls from Peranakan families; in 1912, with the aid of contributions from an American donor, this school built new premises on Neil Road, and was renamed the Fairfield Girls' School (and later the Fairfield Methodist Primary and Secondary Schools). In 1948, the Methodist Church became one of the co-founders of the Trinity Theological College, the campus of which was built on a free lease of Methodist land in Mount Sophia.

By 2005, there were some 14 Methodist schools in operation, including a junior college (Anglo-Chinese Junior College), and private schools such as St. Francis Methodist School and Anglo-Chinese School International, as well as the Methodist School of Music.

Methodist Girls' School This school was founded in 1887 by SOPHIA BLACKMORE with the support of the Women's Foreign Missionary Society of the Methodist

Metro Holdings: department store at Paragon Shopping Centre.

Episcopal Church of America. Classes were first held in a shop house on Short Street. In 1925, the school moved to Mount Sophia, remaining there until 1992, when it moved again to Blackmore Drive.

Alumni of the school include Kwa Geok Choo, wife of LEE KUAN YEW; lawyer and playwright ELEANOR WONG; playwright OVIDIA YU; and sportswomen PATRICIA CHAN and JOSCELIN YEO.

Metro Holdings Retail and property investment company. Metro Holdings was founded in 1957 by ONG TJOE KIM, a businessman from Indonesia. It was listed on the Singapore Stock Exchange in 1973. The business started as a textile store operating out of a two-storey shop house at 72 High Street. A film enthusiast, Ong named the store after the Hollywood studio Metro-Goldwyn-Mayer (MGM).

In 1965, Metro became one of the first retailers to open a department store on Orchard Road. Initially called Metrotex, the store became Metro Orchard after it was relocated to the Holiday Inn Shopping Complex on Scotts Road in 1973. By that time, the store had become widely associated with its ubiquitous 'M' logo and uniformed sales staff .

At one stage, Metro operated five outlets along Orchard Road, including Far East Plaza and Lucky Plaza. The Metro Grand store at Lucky Plaza, which opened in 1978, was Singapore's first 'high-end' department store to adopt a 'brand boutique' concept. The 1970s saw Metro introducing luxury European fashion and accessories such as Cartier, Charles Jourdan and Givenchy.

In 1974, the group took a stake in the development of a vacant site on Orchard Road. This was later to become NGEE ANN CITY. In 1979, Metro co-founded the luxury watch retailer chain, The Hour Glass, which was subsequently sold in 1987. The group also introduced US retailer Toys 'R' Us to Singapore in 1986.

In the mid- to late-1990s Metro branched into leisure and travel, with the building of an $85 million hotel in Cairns, Australia, and expansion into the regional cruise market with the launch of Sun Cruises in 1997. The latter ceased operations in 2000 in the wake of the ASIAN FINANCIAL CRISIS. An attempt to introduce US store K-mart to Singapore in 1994 was short-lived.

In the mid-1990s, Metro began to invest in commercial and retail properties in China and Indonesia. New suburban stores were also opened at Century Square, Tampines in 1996; Metro Woodlands at Causeway Point in 1998; and Metro Sengkang at Compass Point in 2002.

Since then, property and retail have been Metro's core areas of business, and its geographical focus has remained Singapore, and key cities in Malaysia, Indonesia, China

and Australia. Metro posted net profits of $31 million on a turnover of $204 million in the financial year 2005. Its 27 per cent stake in Ngee Ann City was eventually parlayed into a real estate investment trust (REIT) and sold to Prime REIT, which was subsequently floated on the Singapore Exchange in September 2005.

Metropolitan Young Men's Christian Association Non-profit organization. The Young Men's Christian Association (YMCA) is a non-sectarian movement that originated in London in 1844, which aims to develop character through a range of activities for adults and children. The Metropolitan YMCA started out as the Chinese YMCA in 1946 to complement the 'European YMCA' (*see* YOUNG MEN'S CHRISTIAN ASSOCIATION OF SINGAPORE) by providing programmes for Chinese-speaking youth. In 1971, the name of the organization was changed to the Metropolitan YMCA. It now offers programmes for all races. It is located on Stevens Road.

Meyer, Sir Manasseh (1846–1930) Businessman and community leader. A Sephardic Jew born in Baghdad, Meyer spent his early years in Calcutta, moving to Singapore in 1861. He studied at St Joseph's Institution for three years before moving back to Calcutta to work in his uncle's business. He settled in Singapore permanently in 1873, setting up Meyer Brothers, an import and export business which became one of the largest local companies involved in trade with India.

During the mid-1880s, Meyer expanded into real estate, and soon became one of Singapore's most prominent landowners. His properties ranged from shophouses in the city and suburban areas such as Tanjong Katong, to hotels and commercial buildings, among them the Adelphi Hotel, the SEA VIEW HOTEL, the TEUTONIA CLUB, and Meyer Chambers in RAFFLES PLACE. He built Crescent Flats in the Katong area in 1928. These were some of the first modern apartments to be constructed in Singapore.

Meyer was instrumental in the building of the MAGHAIN ABOTH and CHESED-EL Synagogues. He played a leading role in Singapore's public life, giving financially to many charitable causes. One of his most significant contributions was a donation of $150,000 to RAFFLES COLLEGE. In recognition of his generosity, a building on the college's Bukit Timah campus was named the Manasseh Meyer Building.

Meyer served as municipal commissioner and board member of the Straits Committee on Currency. In recognition of his contributions and achievements, he was knighted in 1929. Meyer was buried in the Jewish cemetery at the junction of Thomson and Newton Roads (the site upon which Novena MRT Station was later built) (*see also* JEWS).

Methodist Girls' School: knitting class, 1950.

MI 185 SilkAir crash On 19 December 1997, a SILKAIR Boeing 737-300 en route from Jakarta to Singapore crashed near Palembang, Sumatra. All 97 passengers on board, the five cabin crew, Captain Tsu Way Ming and co-pilot Duncan Ward died in the crash.

Flight MI 185 had taken off from Jakarta at 3.37 p.m., climbing to a normal cruising altitude of 35,000 ft. At some time after 4 p.m., radar readings revealed that the aircraft had dropped some 400 ft below cruising altitude, and had entered into a rapid descent. The plane then disappeared from radar screens, and crashed into the Musi River.

There was a general outpouring of public grief in Singapore following the crash, and a memorial service was held at the Singapore Indoor Stadium.

Three years later, the Indonesian National Transport Safety Committee reported that it was unable to establish why the aircraft had strayed from its normal cruising level. At one stage, there was speculation that pilot suicide was the cause, but no conclusive evidence was produced to confirm this theory. In August 1999, the Singapore Police Force initiated its own investigation. However, after careful examination and analysis of all available materials, the police announced in December 2000 that there was no evidence of any wrongdoing.

Sir Manasseh Meyer

MI 185 SilkAir crash: Indonesian coastguards, assisted by villagers, transporting parts of the wreckage on Musi River, 1997.

MICA Building: what was formerly the Hill Street Police Station in a new guise.

Middle Road Church

Although most families accepted the US$200,000 compensation per victim offered by SilkAir, several other relatives initiated lawsuits against the airline, Boeing and equipment manufacturer, Parker Hannifin Corp. On 8 July 2004, a Los Angeles Superior Court jury found that a malfunctioning component in the Boeing 737's rudder control system had caused the accident, and ordered Parker Hannifin to pay US$43.6 million to the relatives of three victims. The manufacturer is appealing against the ruling.

MICA Building This architectural landmark on the corner of Hill Street and River Valley Road has been known by many names and has housed many different organizations since it first opened as the Hill Street Police Station and Barracks in 1934. The building was designed in a Classical Renaissance style. When it was opened, it was the largest government building in Singapore and was at the time considered—at six storeys high—a 'skyscraper'. It housed charge rooms, offices, garages, and living quarters for the staff of the police department. It remained a police station during the Japanese Occupation and a police post up to 1980.

The building was renamed Hill Street Building in 1983 and served as offices for the National Archives of Singapore, the Official Assignee and Public Trustees and the Board of Film Censors till 1997. It was gazetted as a national monument in 1998 and underwent extensive redevelopment, including the colourful painting of its 911 window frames and shutters, now a distinct feature of the building. The building reopened in 2000 and is now the home of various organizations, including the Ministry of Information, Communications and the Arts, the Media Development Authority, National Arts Council, National Heritage Board and the Singapore Kindness Movement. The central courtyard, renamed the ARTrium, is now a popular venue for arts events, and is surrounded by an array of art galleries.

Mid-Autumn Festival *See* ZHONG QIU JIE.

Middle Road Church Built in 1875 at the corner of Middle Road and Waterloo Street, in an area now known as SCULPTURE SQUARE, this building was first used by the Christian Institute.

The institute's founder was Charles Phillips, a British army officer, who believed that there was a need for a non-denominational space in which people could learn about Christianity without necessarily being affiliated to any particular church.

Although it was not a formal church, services were conducted in the building by Phillips himself. These services attracted a large number of EURASIANS from various Christian denominations.

When Methodist missionaries arrived in Singapore in 1885, they were given free use of the institute (*see* METHODISM). It was then renamed the 'English Church', and was used temporarily by the Methodists until they built a church of their own. In 1891, the Methodists returned to the building, and in 1894 it was officially inaugurated as the Baba Church, becoming the first Chinese Methodist church in Singapore.

The Tamil Girls' School, initiated by SOPHIA BLACKMORE, used the church until 1900. The Baba Church left the building in 1929 when it was felt that the premises were too small.

From the 1930s onwards, the old church was used for a variety of purposes, including, for one period, as a garage. It was later restored as an exhibition hall.

Middle Road unions Group of trade unions with headquarters on Middle Road. The Middle Road unions were active in the 1950s. The most important was the SINGAPORE FACTORY AND SHOP WORKERS UNION (SFSWU), led by LIM CHIN SIONG. Also active in the group were figures such as FONG SWEE SUAN (leader of the Singapore Bus Workers' Union); C.V. DEVAN NAIR (Singapore Teachers' Union); JAMES PUTHUCHEARY; SIDNEY WOODHULL; and S.T.

BANI. In time, this group (with the exception of Nair), together with JAMIT SINGH, would come to be known collectively as the 'Big Six'.

It was estimated that hundreds of communists and communist sympathizers were also members of the Middle Road unions. This network of trade unions controlled the largest and most organized labour force in colonial Singapore at the time.

milk bars Western-style eateries serving dairy products. In the 1960s, COLD STORAGE opened a number of Magnolia Snack Bars in Taiping, Kuala Lumpur, Malacca, Penang, Kuantan and Singapore to promote dairy products sold under its Magnolia brand.

Two outlets were opened in Singapore—one at CAPITOL THEATRE; the other next to the Cold Storage Supermarket on Orchard Road. These milk bars proved to be popular with families, and became closely associated with Magnolia ice cream.

The milk bar at Orchard Road was demolished in the 1970s to make way for the development of the Centrepoint Shopping Centre, while the Capitol Theatre outlet was shut down in the 1980s. In 2002, an attempt was made to capitalize on nostalgia for the original Magnolia bars with the opening of a new milk bar in TIMES THE BOOKSHOP. However, this outlet, operated by FRASER AND NEAVE, was short-lived.

Millennia Institute This institution was established in January 2004 following the merger of two Centralised Institutes (CIs)—Jurong Institute and Outram Institute. It inherited the existing premises of the two CIs at Bartley and Toh Tuck. A move to new premises on Bukit Batok West has been scheduled for 2007. The institute offers a three-year programme to help students prepare for the Singapore-Cambridge GCE 'A'-level examination.

Milk bars: opening of Tong Lee Milk Bar & Confectionery on Orchard Road, 1960.

Minister Mentor Senior Cabinet post. The office of Minister Mentor was created in 2004 as part of a major leadership reshuffle. The post is not mandated in the CONSTITUTION, and is thus administrative rather than legal in nature. Singapore's first minister mentor was LEE KUAN YEW, who took office on 12 August 2004. Because of his institutional knowledge and experience, the Minister Mentor is expected to advise and consult with the Cabinet on a wide range of matters.

Ministry of Community Development, Youth and Sports When the Social Welfare Department was first formed in June 1946 under the Ministry of Labour and Welfare, it was intended to cater to the needs of the community in the immediate post-war years. It comprised five main sections—Food, Settlements, Relief, Youth Welfare, and Women and Girls. A Social Research Section was added in 1947.

In 1963, the Department was transferred from the Ministry of Labour to the new Ministry of Social Affairs. This later merged with the Ministry of Culture, to form the Ministry of Culture and Social Affairs on 24 September 1965 but split again into two ministries shortly after.

Almost two decades later, on 2 January 1985, the Ministry of Social Affairs was expanded with several portfolios to become the Ministry of Community Development (MCD), integrating most of the functions of the former Ministry of Social Affairs, the Cultural Affairs Division and some other departments. On 1 April 2000, to place more emphasis on sports development, the ministry was renamed the Ministry of Community Development and Sports (MCDS), with the role of providing policies and directions for sports. When LEE HSIEN LOONG took over as Singapore's prime minister in 2004, he emphasized the government's commitment to seek the views of young Singaporeans, and to cultivate a stronger sense of belonging. With this objective MCDS was renamed Ministry of Community Development, Youth and Sports (MCYS).

MCYS also organizes social activities and matchmaking programmes through its SOCIAL DEVELOPMENT UNIT, set up in 1984.

Ministry of Defence The main divisions of the Ministry of Defence (MINDEF) are: the Future Systems Directorate; the Defence Policy Group; the Joint Operations and Planning Directorate; the Defence Management Group; the Defence Technology and Resource Office; and the DEFENCE SCIENCE AND TECHNOLOGY AGENCY.

In August 1965, following Singapore's separation from Malaysia, the Ministry of Interior and Defence (MID) was set up in response to Singapore's need for security forces. Dr GOH KENG SWEE was the first defence minister. Goh and his staff worked

out of offices borrowed from the Ministry of Culture and Social Affairs at Empress Place. In November, the MID moved to the former police headquarters at Pearl's Hill. At this time, the ministry was responsible for both the SAF and the Police Force.

On 11 August 1970, to cater to the rapid expansion of the military, the MID was divided into MINDEF and the MINISTRY OF HOME AFFAIRS. Two years later, MINDEF moved to the Tanglin Complex on Napier Road. In April 1989, the ministry moved its headquarters to Bukit Gombak.

See also SINGAPORE ARMED FORCES.

Ministry of Education Ministry that directs the formulation and implementation of Singapore's education policies. It controls the development and administration of all government and government-aided schools, junior colleges, and a centralized institute. It also registers private schools and oversees pre-school education.

The MOE slogan, 'Moulding the Future of Our Nation', encapsulates its twin goals of developing the individual and educating the citizen from an early age. MOE has succeeded in propelling Singapore's education system into world-class standards within a space of 40 years. The system has produced students that have been recognized internationally for their levels of achievement, especially in mathematics and the sciences.

See also EDUCATION SYSTEM.

Ministry of the Environment and Water Resources Set up in 1972 as the Ministry of the Environment, the ministry now has a wider role. Originally, its main mission was to provide Singaporeans with a good living environment, a high standard of public health and protection against the spread of communicable diseases. In this context, the ministry works closely with the Ministry of Health.

Over the years, as problems of ensuring a reliable and sustainable source of potable water became an increasing concern, the ministry has become more involved in the management of natural resources. Together with its two statutory boards, the National Environment Agency and the PUB, the ministry now manages Singapore's limited resources in partnership with the public and private sector. Its mission is to 'deliver and sustain a clean and healthy environment and water resources for all in Singapore'. The Ministry of the Environment was officially renamed the Ministry of the Environment and Water Resources on 1 September 2004.

Ministry of Finance The primary aims of the Ministry of Finance (MOF) are to steward and to invest public funds; maintain a balanced budget by ensuring that the government operates within its means; and create a financial environment con-

ducive to business.

The MOF reviews all rules relating to finance and banking in Singapore. It also ensures that the country's regulatory regime is comparable with international standards and best practice in areas such as company law, accounting standards and corporate governance principles. The main regulatory statutes administered by the MOF are the Companies Act, Business Registration Act, Currency Act and Accountants Act.

Ministry of Foreign Affairs The Ministry of Foreign Affairs (MFA) was established in CITY HALL in the hours following SEPARATION on 9 August 1965. Former journalist and Minister of Culture S. RAJARATNAM was appointed the first foreign minister, and Penang-born, Cambridge-educated ABU BAKAR PAWANCHEE was the ministry's first permanent secretary.

Singapore's first diplomatic mission was established in Kuala Lumpur on 6 September 1965, with businessman KO TECK KIN appointed high commissioner to Malaysia. A second mission was opened in New York following Singapore's admission to the UNITED NATIONS (UN) on 21 September 1965. Between 1966 and 1969, missions were opened in London, Phnom Penh, Canberra, Wellington, Bangkok, Washington D.C., Cairo, New Delhi, Jakarta, Tokyo and Manila.

As Singapore was lacking in trained diplomats, the government initially appointed businessmen, lawyers, academics and parliamentarians as envoys. The MFA's pioneer staff included civil servants seconded from other ministries. In 1972, a Foreign Service Scheme was introduced to facilitate recruitment and enable the ministry to grow in a more orderly manner. Gradually, a professional service emerged. Notable appointments included SEE CHAK MUN, who became the first career officer to serve as head of mission when he was appointed high commissioner to Australia in 1976; and PETER CHAN, who in 1983 was the first career officer to be appointed permanent secretary.

Singapore's establishment of diplomatic relations with China in October 1990; the establishment in 1992 of the Singapore Cooperation Programme (a scheme administered by the MFA and designed as a means of sharing development expertise); the securing of a seat for Singapore on the UN Security Council in 2001; and the increasing mobility of Singaporeans have all influenced the work of the MFA and mandated the need for a larger ministry. The MFA has thus continued to expand, moving into new premises in the Tanglin area in May 2001.

See also FOREIGN MISSIONS.

Ministry of Health This ministry formulates national health policies, co-ordinates the development and planning of the private and public health sectors, and regulates health standards. It oversees the two public

Ministry of Community Development, Youth and Sports

Ministry of Defence

Ministry of Education

Ministry of the Environment and Water Resources

MINISTRY OF FINANCE
Ministry of Finance

MINISTRY OF FOREIGN AFFAIRS
Ministry of Foreign Affairs

Ministry of Health

Ministry of Home Affairs

Ministry of Information, Communications and the Arts

SINGAPORE
Ministry of Law

Ministry of Manpower

Ministry of National Development

Ministry of Transport

healthcare clusters, SINGHEALTH and the NATIONAL HEALTHCARE GROUP. All public hospitals and speciality clinics belong to one of these two clusters. The ministry also has six statutory boards under its wing: the Health Promotion Board, Health Sciences Authority, Singapore Dental Council, Singapore Medical Council, Singapore Nursing Board and the Traditional Chinese Medicine Practitioners Board.

Ministry of Home Affairs Shortly after Singapore's independence, a new Ministry of the Interior and Defence (MID) was created with Dr GOH KENG SWEE as minister. Because its responsibilities were both external and internal security, it controlled both the Armed Forces and the Police. On 11 August 1970, MID was split into two ministries: the MINISTRY OF DEFENCE; and the Ministry of Home Affairs (MHA). The MHA oversees the internal security of Singapore. The SINGAPORE POLICE FORCE, INTERNAL SECURITY DEPARTMENT, SINGAPORE CIVIL DEFENCE FORCE, Singapore Prisons Service, IMMIGRATION & CHECKPOINTS AUTHORITY, CENTRAL NARCOTICS BUREAU, Home Team Academy and the Singapore Corporation of Rehabilitative Enterprises come under MHA's purview.

Ministry of Information, Communications and the Arts Successor of the Ministry of Culture set up in 1959, headed by Culture Minister S. RAJARATNAM. When the Ministry of Culture was dissolved in 1985, its functions were split between two other ministries; then in 1990, they were reunited to form the new Ministry of Information and the Arts (MITA) with GEORGE YEO as acting minister and subsequently minister. In 2001, the communication technology function, previously under the Ministry of Communications and Information Technology, came under MITA. The expanded ministry was renamed the Ministry of Information, Communications and the Arts but retained the acronym MITA until 2004, when it became MICA. Its headquarters are housed in the MICA BUILDING.

MICA has a number of statutory boards under its charge: the INFOCOMM DEVELOPMENT AUTHORITY OF SINGAPORE; the MEDIA DEVELOPMENT AUTHORITY; the NATIONAL ARTS COUNCIL; the NATIONAL HERITAGE BOARD; the National Library Board (*see* PUBLIC LIBRARIES); and the PRESERVATION OF MONUMENTS BOARD.

Ministry of Labour Building *See* OLD MINISTRY OF LABOUR BUILDING.

Ministry of Law The Ministry of Law (also known as Minlaw) was established in 1959 as the Ministry of Law and Labour, with K.M. BYRNE as its first minister. In 1963, separate ministries were created for Law and Labour. Since its inception, a lawyer has

always headed the ministry: K.M. Byrne (1959–63); E.W. BARKER (1963–88); and S. JAYAKUMAR (1988–).

The ministry's primary responsibility is the formulation and implementation of the broad legal policies of the government. (This role is different from that of the attorney-general, who is the government's legal adviser and public prosecutor.) MinLaw aims to ensure that Singapore's legal infrastructure is efficient, transparent and well-adapted to the changing demands put on the system. Areas managed by MinLaw include constitutional and trustee matters, legal policies on civil and criminal justice, alternative dispute resolution and community mediation, the administration of intellectual property rights, as well as the administration of land titles and the management of state properties.

Ministry of Manpower The former Ministry of Labour was renamed the Ministry of Manpower (MOM) on 1 April 1998. It administers the Employment Act, draws up policies to develop the competitiveness of Singapore's workforce, and promotes workers' welfare and occupational health and safety. Under its purview are two statutory boards: the CENTRAL PROVIDENT FUND Board and the WORKFORCE DEVELOPMENT AGENCY.

The ministry oversees efforts to reduce unemployment and facilitates the resolution of labour disputes. It works closely with the NATIONAL TRADES UNION CONGRESS and the Singapore National Employers' Federation. This tripartite system of LABOUR RELATIONS, involving the government, employers and trade unions, has its origins in the labour riots of the 1950s and 1960s.

MOM also plays a role in attracting FOREIGN TALENT and sets guidelines on the employment of FOREIGN WORKERS.

Ministry of National Development This ministry's portfolio covers land use planning; urban redevelopment; building conservation; public housing; the construction industry; parks; and food safety. It has a number of statutory boards under its charge, namely the HOUSING & DEVELOPMENT BOARD; the Building and Construction Authority; the Board of Architects; the Professional Engineers Board; the URBAN REDEVELOPMENT AUTHORITY; the NATIONAL PARKS BOARD; and the Agri-Food & Veterinary Authority.

Ministry of Trade and Industry Formed in March 1979, the origins of the Ministry of Trade and Industry (MTI) can be traced to the former Development Division of the MINISTRY OF FINANCE. MTI oversees ten statutory boards whose responsibilities range from raising the level of science and technology, to regulating the energy market and promoting Singapore as a tourist destination.

Domestically, MTI studies and identifies key sectors and clusters; assesses the impact of policy initiatives implemented by other government agencies; and produces periodic research and analyses of the Singapore and global economies. In addition, it develops policies for the use of industrial land so as to achieve competitiveness in land costs. It also decides on policies relating to energy security and the liberalization of the electricity and gas markets.

Internationally, MTI is responsible for establishing and maintaining bilateral economic relations and strengthening Singapore's role in the ASSOCIATION OF SOUTHEAST ASIAN NATIONS (ASEAN) and Asia Pacific Economic Cooperation (APEC).

Ministry of Transport Ministry responsible for policies regarding roads, cars and other vehicles, all forms of public transport, the port and the airports. Its statutory boards, namely, the CIVIL AVIATION AUTHORITY OF SINGAPORE, the LAND TRANSPORT AUTHORITY, the MARITIME AND PORT AUTHORITY OF SINGAPORE, and the PUBLIC TRANSPORT COUNCIL, carry out the operations and regulatory work. The ministry also oversees the operations of the Air Accident Investigation Bureau of Singapore.

Mirror Magazine. Originally known as the *Malaysian Mirror*, this weekly news magazine was started in March 1965 by the Ministry of Culture, and was published in the four official languages. The main objective was to help explain government policies and programmes.

After SEPARATION in 1965, the magazine was renamed *The Mirror*. From 1968, it was published only in English. For the next 11 years, *The Mirror* was distributed free of charge to schools and government departments every week. It contained policy statements, extracts of press reports on Singapore from foreign media sources, and news on community projects. In 1979, *The Mirror* was made into a fortnightly publication; fewer articles were reprinted from foreign sources, with original articles being commissioned instead. A further change in editorial policy came in 1986, when the magazine was renamed *Mirror*, and remodelled as a 16-page current affairs magazine. It carried feature articles on the economy, education, housing and other issues.

In 1991, the Ministry of Information and the Arts—which had taken over control of the magazine from the former Ministry of Culture—announced that, given alternative sources of information, the *Mirror* was no longer necessary, and it ceased publication.

mission schools Schools established by missionary groups. The first such school to be established was St Joseph's Institution—an English-medium school on Bras Basah Road. This was founded in 1852, and was run by the Christian Brothers (a Catholic group). The following year, Methodist missionary Sophia Cooke founded an English-medium school for girls. This was known initially as the Chinese Girls' School, but was later renamed St Margaret's Girls' School. The Anglican Church opened St Andrew's School in 1862; in 1886, Cooke, with the support of the local Chinese, opened the Anglo-Chinese School.

Unlike vernacular schools, mission schools accepted students of all races and religions. They provided education with a Christian orientation, but also followed a policy of non-interference in the religious tenets of non-Christian students.

Mission schools came to share a number of features. For instance, they favoured a full school system, in which primary and secondary education were offered at the same institution. This differentiated mission schools from government schools, where primary and secondary levels of education were divided between different institutions. Mission schools also encouraged the growth of student alumni groups and parent support groups.

Although mission schools receive government financial support, and follow the national curriculum, many have developed distinct identities.

Misuse of Drugs Act In 1973, the Misuse of Drugs Act was introduced to replace previous legislation controlling the use of illicit drugs. The Act not only gives the state power to enforce bans on drugs that had first been introduced in 1946, but also prescribes compulsory treatment for drug users. Since 1975, the death penalty has been employed as a sentence for drug traffickers. In addition, CANING has been prescribed as punishment for certain drug-related offences.

Under the Act, arrested drug addicts are required to undergo compulsory treatment at government-run Drug Rehabilitation Centres (DRC). Since July 1998, long-term imprisonment has also been imposed on convicted drug users who fail to overcome addiction after receiving treatment.

The Act classifies illicit drugs into three categories—Class A, Class B and Class C. The severity of punishment imposed depends on the category of the drug used. The Act further entails a presumption of trafficking for anyone possessing certain threshold amounts of different drugs. For heroin, this amount is 15 g; for morphine, 30 g; and for cannabis, 500 g. Any person found to be in possession of these amounts, is assumed to be engaged in trafficking, and for this offence, the death penalty is mandatory.

Under the Act, any person possessesing keys to premises in which drugs are stored is presumed to possess those drugs. The Act allows law-enforcement officers to search premises and individuals without a search warrant if a narcotics officer 'reasonably suspects that there is to be found a controlled drug or article liable to seizure'. Section 31 allows officers to demand a urinalysis of suspected drug offenders.

In July 1998, a new provision was included in the Act whereby the consumption of drugs outside Singapore by a citizen or permanent resident of Singapore is viewed as an offence that has taken place in Singapore.

Singapore is a signatory to all three United Nations conventions relating to illicit drugs. As a result, it has legislated to control the movement of precursor substances used in the manufacture of illicit drugs.

Mitchell, Lieutenant-Colonel Sir Charles (1832–1899) Colonial official. Charles Bullen Hugh Mitchell was an officer in the Royal Marines and a veteran of the Crimean War. He had also served in the colonies of British Honduras (present-day Belize), Fiji, Natal and Zululand (the last two in present-day South Africa).

Mitchell was appointed governor of Singapore in 1894, at a time when the island found itself in difficult financial circumstances due to decreasing trade. By the end of his term, however, Singapore was experiencing an economic recovery.

Mitchell is best remembered for his role in the issue of military contributions demanded by the British government. In 1890, the secretary of state for colonies, Lord Ripon, had announced that a military contribution of £100,000 per annum would be demanded of Singapore. This demand led to a wave of protests. In 1894, a deputation of the Straits Settlements Association requested that Mitchell refuse to pay this amount to London. Lord Ripon eventually accepted Mitchell's offer of a reduced contribution.

From 1896, the governor of the Straits Settlements also became high commissioner for the Federated Malay States (FMS), thus making Mitchell the first high commissioner for the FMS.

mobile phones SINGTEL introduced Singapore's first cellular mobile radio system in 1988, and the country's first digital cellular system in 1994. SingTel launched Singapore's first short message service (SMS) in 1995. In 1998, SingTel Mobile became the first mobile operator in Asia to offer a dual band service.

In 1995, MOBILEONE (M1) won the licence to operate Singapore's second cellular-telephone service, and a radio-paging service. Both services were launched in 1997, when SingTel's monopoly ended.

STARHUB was awarded a licence to operate a cellular-telephone service in 1998. This company was the first to intro-

Mobile phones: campaign advertisement on a double-decker bus, promoting courteous phone use.

duce per-second billing and free incoming calls when its service was launched in 2000. In 2003, StarHub also launched the BlackBerry—a wireless e-mail platform—and by 2005, all three telecommunication companies (telcos) were offering this service. In 2005, the three operators launched commercial third-generation (3G) mobile data services. In more recent years, the three telcos have started examining the prospect of introducing technologies that will bring media content to mobile phones.

Mobile phones in Singapore operate on GSM (Global System for Mobile Communications) technology on both the 900 and 1800 MHz frequency.

In Singapore and Malaysia, mobile phones are popularly known as 'handphones'.

MobileOne *See* M1.

mobilization After studying the Swedish and Swiss approaches, the SINGAPORE ARMED FORCES (SAF) devised two systems of mobilization for Operationally Ready National Servicemen (NSmen): silent mobilization and open mobilization (*see* NATIONAL SERVICE).

Until the mid-1980s, the SAF had a silent mobilization system. Notices were served by discreet methods, mainly through telephone and pager calls, as well as physical dispatch by couriers. It took 24 hours to recall NSmen and 6 more to equip them.

The open mobilization system was launched by the then second minister of defence, Dr YEO NING HONG, on 9 March 1985. Codenames of units and any accompanying messages were broadcast over mass-media channels: radio, television and cinemas. This system took six hours to recall NSmen, followed by six hours to prepare them for combat. The first publicly announced open-mobilization exercise attained an 84 per cent response within the first three-and-a-half hours, and 97 per cent in five hours. By 1989, the mandatory response time had been reduced from 12 to 6 hours. With the opening of the Mass Rapid Transit (MRT) system in 1989, and improvements in telecommunications technology in the 1990s and 2000s, recall times

Lt-Col. Sir Charles Mitchell

Mohamed Sultan Road: a busy nightlife area.

Mohamed Latiff Mohamad

Mohammad Eunos Abdullah

have become shorter still, even for large mobilization exercises involving over 10,000 men. From 1994, the Ministry of Defence, to save time in distributing equipment during recalls, allowed NSmen to keep their uniforms and equipment at home.

Modern Art Society Registered in June 1964 by seven artists (Ho Ho Ying, Wee Beng Chong, Tay Chee Toh, Johnda Goh, Tay Chee Toh, Tan Yee Hong and Tong Siang Eng), this society was first headed by Ng Yat Chuan. Its objective was to embrace 'the art of its time', encompassing forms such as abstraction and action painting. Impetus for the founding of the society had come from an exhibition of modern art by the society's founders at the National Library in 1963.

The society has facilitated numerous overseas exhibitions and exchanges since its inception, involving artists from Japan, Malaysia, Taiwan, the Philippines and China. It established a Creative Award and Contribution Award in October 1979 to encourage creativity in art. Ho Ho Ying, Wee Beng Chong, Chieu Shuey Fook, Thang Kiang How, Thomas Yeo, Jeremy Ramsey, Lim Leong Seng and Baet Yeok Kuan have served as presidents of the society.

Mohamed Latiff Mohamed (1950–) Poet and author. Mohamed Latiff Mohamed was educated at Guillemard Malay School and the Tun Seri Lanang and Kaki Bukit

Mohamed Mustafa & Samsuddin: Mustaq Ahmad.

Secondary Schools. Upon graduating from Teachers' Training College, he worked in the teaching service (1968-2000). His major works include *Kota Air Mata* (City of Tears) (1977), *Keimanan* (Faith) (1982), *Dalam Keasingan* (In Alienation) (1989), *Batas Langit* (Limit of the Sky), (1996), *Ziarah Cinta* (Visit of Love) (1998), *Bagiku Sepilah Sudah* (2002) and *Nostalgia Yang Hilang* (Lost Nostalgia) (2004). Protest and dissent are hallmarks of his poetry. Mohamed Latiff received the Southeast Asia Write Award in 2002. The following year, he received the Tun Seri Lanang Award from the Malay Language Council of Singapore.

Mohamed Mustafa, Haji (1916–2001) Businessman. Born in India, Haji Mohamed Mustafa moved to Muar, Johor, in 1950, where he made a living peddling dumplings in local villages. In 1952, he moved to Singapore, and started travelling about the island with his second son, Mustaq Ahmad, selling food from a make-shift cart. Together, they later ventured into the sale of clothes and garments, before establishing a small outlet in Campbell Lane with a relative named Samsuddin. Over subsequent years, this partnership—MOHAMED MUSTAFA & SAMSUDDIN—would transform into a highly successful retail business. Mohamed died in India.

Mohamed Mustafa & Samsuddin Retail company. The company is headed by Indian-born Mustaq Ahmad who, in 1971, started the business with his father and another relative in a small shop on Campbell Lane. The company started out by selling ready-made garments. A second shop, at which electronic goods were sold, was opened two years later. In 1985, the business expanded, moving into a 3,700-square-metre department store in Serangoon Plaza.

The six-storey Mustafa Centre was opened in 1995 after the family acquired and redeveloped a row of shophouses along Syed Alwi Road. The company eventually came to employ some 600 people, and had

an annual turnover of about $360 million in 2005.

Besides department stores, the company has also opened a supermarket, jewellery store, pharmacy, hotel and travel agency, as well as an 'on-line' store. In 2003, it began 24-hour trading.

In later years, Mohamed Mustafa & Samsuddin started to expand into overseas markets. It opened a jewellery shop in Chennai, India, with plans to open more outlets on the Indian subcontinent, and in Sri Lanka.

Mohamed Sultan Road In the 1980s, this road was lined with derelict GODOWNS. However, in 1991, a pub called Front Page was opened here. This was followed in 1994 by another pub called Wong San's. The opening of these two pubs inspired interest in the area amongst bar and nightclub operators, and various establishments began to open along the road, including Dbl O, The Liquid Room and Soundbar.

Many of these establishments were opened in shophouses that had been gazetted for conservation, with the façades preserved, and interiors renovated and structurally reinforced. Since the mid-1990s, most of the road's godowns have also been restored.

Mohammad Eunos Abdullah (1876–1934) Civil servant and community leader. Educated at the Kampung Glam Malay School and Raffles Institution, Mohammad Eunos Abdullah went on to serve in various positions in the civil service, starting as Master Attendant of Singapore Harbour, and eventually becoming Harbour Master in Muar, Johor. He also served as justice of the peace, municipal commissioner, and in 1924, became the first Malay Unofficial member of the Legislative Council. Eunos served as a member of the Muslim Advisory Board after World War I. Later, he became a co-founder and first president of the Singapore Malay Union (Kesatuan Melayu Singapura or KMS)—the first organized movement of Malays in the peninsula. KMS sought to represent Malays in government; secure higher and technical education for Malays; and provide a vehicle through which Malays could become more involved in civic life. Eunos, often described by historians as a 'British loyalist', regularly argued with members of the Legislative Council, particularly the director of education, Richard Winstedt, over MALAY EDUCATION.

Eunos was a pioneer in the newspaper industry, working as an editor at two leading Malay newspapers. In 1907, he was invited by WILLIAM MAKEPEACE to edit the Malay edition of the English-language newspaper, THE SINGAPORE FREE PRESS, the UTUSAN MELAYU. Under the editorship of Eunos, it became the leading Malay newspaper of its day. In 1914, Eunos left *Utusan*

Melayu to become editor of *Lembaga Melayu*—the Malay edition of THE MALAYA TRIBUNE which, from 1922 to 1931, was the only Malay daily in existence.

However, Eunos is perhaps best remembered for securing from the British 670,000 sq m of land on which a large Malay settlement was built—the area was later named Eunos (*see* MALAY SETTLEMENTS).

Mohammedan and Hindu Endowments Board The Mohammedan and Hindu Endowments Board (MHEB) was established in 1905 by the British colonial authorities in response to complaints from the local Hindu and Muslim communities concerning the mismanagement of funds. It was given responsibility for administering endowments and charities in the name of these two communities. To this end, the MHEB appointed a *panchayat* (council) to oversee the financial affairs of temples and mosques.

The board was discontinued in 1969 and replaced by the MAJLIS UGAMA ISLAM SINGAPURA and the HINDU ENDOWMENTS BOARD.

Monetary Authority of Singapore Statutory board. The establishment of the Monetary Authority of Singapore (MAS) in 1971 brought together, under one authority, various central-banking functions that had previously been performed by different government departments. The only exception was CURRENCY issue which, until October 2002, was performed by the BOARD OF COMMISSIONERS OF CURRENCY.

Like central banks in other countries, MAS formulates and implements monetary policies, and acts as the regulatory body for the financial sector. It is also the banker to and financial agent of the Singapore government, as well as a banker to commercial banks and financial companies.

Besides using MONETARY POLICY to promote non-inflationary growth, MAS is responsible for pursuing policies to develop and upgrade financial infrastructure.

monetary policy Singapore introduced a managed-float exchange rate regime in 1973. This provided the MONETARY AUTHORITY OF SINGAPORE (MAS) with some control over the exchange rate. In order to promote medium-term sustained non-inflationary growth, the MAS switched to an exchange rate-centred monetary policy in 1981. Since then, the Singapore dollar has been managed against the currencies of the country's major trading partners and competitors with the main intention of countering imported inflation. The trade-weighted exchange rate has been allowed to fluctuate within an undisclosed policy band. The MAS has intervened whenever market forces have threatened to push the rate out of this band, by either buying or selling Singapore dollars against foreign currencies. The policy band

Monitor lizard

has been reviewed from time to time to accommodate prevailing economic conditions as well as short-term volatility in financial markets, as was the case during the ASIAN FINANCIAL CRISIS of 1997.

Money No Enough (1999) Film Written by JACK NEO and directed by Tay Teck Lock, this 1999 comedy probed the aftermath of the 1997 ASIAN FINANCIAL CRISIS, and the nature of Singapore society. It was also the first local film made in the 1990s to include dialogue in HOKKIEN. The movie was very successful, and became the highest-grossing local film to date.

monitor lizard Also known as the Malayan water monitor, the monitor lizard (*Varanus salvator*) is a large reptile that can both swim and climb well. It is usually found in or near water, and is often mistaken for a crocodile. It feeds on water birds, fishes and carrion. It is traditionally hunted for its hide and meat. Although it can grow up to 2.5 metres in length, it is not aggressive. Indeed, it is harmless to humans, and will usually run away when approached. It is commonly seen in the SUNGEI BULOH WETLAND RESERVE.

monkeys The most common monkey in Singapore is the long-tailed macaque (*Macaca fascicularis*). It is especially common in Singapore's nature reserves. Each troop of long-tailed macaques consists of an alpha male, several females and several young adults.

Due to a lack of predators, Singapore's long-tailed macaque population has grown rapidly over the years. Because of their constant contact with humans, these monkeys have lost their fear of people. Indeed, instead of foraging for food in the forest, they can be found at the edges of forests, where they wait for handouts from humans, or raid rubbish bins for food. Macaques have become such a nuisance that campaigns have been launched to educate the

public not to feed them.

Unlike the long-tailed macaque, the banded leaf monkey (*Presbytis femoralis*) is extremely timid. Its numbers have dwindled to less than 20 over recent years, and the population has been listed as highly endangered. The genetic makeup of this population is considered unique, as it is only found in Singapore. The monkey usually stays at the top of tall trees, feeding on fruits and young leaves. Banded leaf monkeys are occasionally seen in the Central Catchment forests.

Monteiro, Ernest (1904–1989) Doctor, academic and diplomat. Ernest Steven Monteiro was educated at St Anthony's Boys' School, Raffles Institution and King Edward VII College of Medicine, where he graduated in 1929. He then joined the Singapore Medical Service.

In 1939, Monteiro became the first local appointed to the Malayan Medical Service as a medical officer. From 1946 to 1948, Monteiro, (or 'Monty' as he came to be known), completed several examinations which earned him membership of the Royal College of Physicians of London and fellowship of the Royal Faculty of Physicians and Surgeons of Glasgow.

On his return to Singapore from Britain in 1948, he was offered the Chair of Clinical Medicine at the University of Malaya. At that university, he became the first local graduate to be appointed professor. From 1955 to 1960, Monteiro served as dean of medicine. In 1960, he became deputy principal of the University of Malaya. When he retired from teaching in 1965, he was made emeritus professor of medicine and pro-chancellor of the University of Singapore.

In the course of his career, Monteiro pioneered research in preventive medicine. He was the first doctor to introduce the oral Sabin vaccine to prevent children from contracting poliomyelitis. He discovered the link between beri-beri and vitamin B1 found in rice husk. He was the first to eliminate diphtheria in children by using toxoid, and the first to use the antibiotic chloramphenicol to treat typhoid fever.

Monteiro was appointed a Commander of the British Empire (CBE) in 1957. He was also awarded the MERITORIOUS SERVICE MEDAL (1968) and fellowship of the Royal Society for the Promotion of Health (1972).

In 1965, Monteiro began his career as a diplomat. He served as Singapore's ambassador to Cambodia (1966–68), and later as ambassador to the United States and Brazil (1969–77). He later resumed medical prac-

Ernest Monteiro

MONETARY POLICY: AVERAGES OF THE SINGAPORE DOLLAR							
Period average	1970	1975	1980	1990	1997	2000	2005
US$	3.09	2.34	2.14	1.81	1.48	1.72	1.66
100 Japanese yen	0.86	0.79	0.95	1.28	1.22	1.60	1.51
Euro	–	–	–	–	–	1.59	2.07
Pound sterling	7.41	5.25	4.97	2.84	2.43	2.61	3.03
Malaysian ringgit	1.00	0.98	0.98	0.67	0.53	0.45	0.44

Source: Monetary Authority of Singapore and Singapore Department of Statistics

Jeremy Monteiro

Eric Moo

tice, starting his own specialist clinic after his return from the United States. Monteiro remained active in medicine until just before his death from liver failure.

Monteiro, Jeremy (1960–) Musician. Jeremy Monteiro was born in Singapore, but spent his early childhood in Brunei. He later returned to Singapore to study at St Joseph's Institution. He left school after passing his GCE 'O' levels and, against the wishes of his father—a guitarist—pursued a career in music.

Monteiro had been trained in classical music on the piano but later switched to jazz in order to overcome what he saw as the 'restrictions' of the classical idiom. He started working professionally as a musician immediately after leaving school, leading a group that performed at Club 392 on Orchard Road. He later began undertaking session recordings with singers such as ANITA SARAWAK and Tracy Huang. He released his first jazz album, *Back to Basics*, in 1986.

In 1988, Monteiro became the first Southeast Asian musician to perform on the main stage at the Montreux Jazz Festival. He also began writing music, completing over 700 songs, theme songs and jingles. In 2001, he was appointed artistic director of the Singapore Jazz Festival. The following year, he became the first jazz musician to be awarded the CULTURAL MEDALLION.

Moo, Eric (1963–) Singer and actor. Eric Moo (Wu Qixian) was born in Malaysia but made his name in Singapore's Chinese pop scene (*see* CHINESE POPULAR MUSIC). Moo's vocal group, *Dixia Tie* (Subway), which he formed with some friends from school, became one of the most influential groups of the *xinyao* movement.

His first solo album was *Xin Qing* (Feelings) (1984). Moo won the Best Performance Award and Highest Honour Award at the inaugural Xin Yue awards in Singapore in 1987. In 1986, Moo signed up with Taiwanese record label Fei Ying, on which he released the album *Ni Shi Wo De Wei Yi* (You are My Only One) (1988), which was a hit in Taiwan. Moo began acting in 1995, and won the Best Newcomer Award at the 1996 Hong Kong Film Awards for his role in *Xin Shi San Tai Bao* (Those Were The Days). Moo did not perform live in Singapore until 2003. He later moved on to hosting variety shows in Taiwan.

Mooncake Festival *See* ZHONG QIU JIE.

Moses, Catchick (1812–1892) Businessman and community leader. Catchick Moses came to Singapore from Calcutta in 1828. He started work as an apprentice at BOUSTEAD AND COMPANY, and later began trading on his own. In 1840, he joined his uncle, Aristarchus Sarkies, to form the firm

of Sarkies and Moses. When Sarkies died in 1841, Moses took over the firm.

On 15 July 1845, Moses started THE STRAITS TIMES and the *Singapore Journal of Commerce* with ROBERT CARR WOODS. *The Straits Times* struggled in its first year, and in September 1846, Moses tried to sell the newspaper. As he was unable to find any willing buyers, Moses handed ownership of the newspaper to Woods. Despite the financial losses that Moses suffered through his ownership of *The Straits Times*, his trading firm thrived.

Moses emerged as a leader of Singapore's ARMENIANS. He died at his house on Oxley Hill, and was buried in the compound of the ARMENIAN CHURCH.

Mosque Building Fund This fund for the building of MOSQUES catering to Muslim residents of public housing estates was first established in 1975. Through the fund, optional deductions of fixed amounts are collected from the monthly salaries of Muslims through the CENTRAL PROVIDENT FUND.

When the Mosque Building Fund was first introduced, the minimum optional deduction rate was 50 cents. This was raised to $1 in July 1977, and later to between $3 and $5, depending on income. The fund became the Mosque Building and Mendaki Fund in 1984 when the contribution schemes for both were combined (*see* MENDAKI). In July 2005, rates were again increased to between $4 and $11 a month.

The fund is not only used for the construction of mosques, but also for the purchase of land upon which mosques are built. It is managed by MAJLIS UGAMA ISLAM SINGAPURA.

mosques The mosque (derived from the Arabic '*masjid*' meaning 'a place of prostrations') is the house of worship for Muslims. All mosques have an open, uncluttered space, which allows worshippers to stand in rows during congregational prayer. There is a *mihrab* (niche) to indicate the direction of the Kaaba in Mecca, which Muslims face during prayer, and a *mimbar* (pulpit), where the imam delivers the Friday *khutbah* (sermon).

In Singapore, mosques were built through endowment funds (WAKAF) from wealthy families and merchant communities. Funds were also raised through individual contributions and ad hoc fund raising activities. In 1975, the MOSQUE BUILDING FUND was introduced to systematically raise funds to build mosques. Since 1975, the fund has financed the construction of 22 mosques (as of 2006). The government has also facilitated mosque building by allocating suitable sites within major housing estates.

The oldest mosque is the OMAR KAMPUNG MELAKA MOSQUE built in 1820. The early mosques were built by the Arab

and Indian Muslim communities, and this is reflected in their designs; AL-ABRAR MOSQUE and ABDUL GAFFOOR MOSQUE, for example, resemble mosques in India. British influences can also be seen in mosques built during the colonial period, such as the HAJJAH FATIMAH MOSQUE. As of 2006, there were 69 mosques in Singapore. Modern mosques completed after 2000 include Assyafaah Mosque (2004) in Sembawang and An-Nahdhah Mosque (2006) in Bishan. The largest mosque in Singapore is Assyakirin Mosque (2002) in Jurong. It can accommodate 6,000 worshippers. Some historic mosques such as the SULTAN MOSQUE and the HAJJAH FATIMAH MOSQUE have been gazetted as national monuments.

With the enactment of the ADMINISTRATION OF MUSLIM LAW ACT, MAJLIS UGAMA ISLAM SINGAPURA (MUIS) administers all mosques. Each mosque is managed by a mosque management committee, which comprises officials appointed by MUIS. The committee is assisted by staff or volunteers who help run the mosque. In 2005, the Mosque Convention was held to outline a unified direction for Singapore's mosques. The four main goals were to redevelop Islamic religious education, revise the social development role of the mosque, restructure mosque leadership, and reorganise mosque management. Among its major strategies are to reach out to the youth, to enhance relations with the wider community, and to promote a new Islamic curriculum for children and the youth.

mother tongue BILINGUALISM is a cornerstone of Singapore's education system, and since 1966, the learning of 'mother tongues' has been compulsory for Singaporean students. For economic reasons, and because of the country's multiracial character, Singaporeans have accepted English as the lingua franca, and as the working language of government and business. However, to ensure that they remain connected to their ancestral cultures and values, students are required to study one of three mother tongues—MANDARIN, MALAY or TAMIL. Ethic Indian students have a choice of studying Bengali, Gujarati, Hindi, Punjabi or Urdu, instead of Tamil. Every Singaporean is encouraged to study his or her mother tongue in school for as long as possible and to as high a level as possible. Admission to local universities is dependent upon successful completion of this requirement. The policy has transformed the linguistic profile of Singapore society since the mid-1960s, one consequence being the near-elimination of Chinese dialects within the Chinese community.

The MINISTRY OF EDUCATION completed a major review of the curriculum for the teaching of mother tongues in 2005, and has announced plans to implement the recommendations of this review in phases. These recommendations include helping students develop a love for their mother tongue by encouraging them to actually use it, rather than just learn it for examinations.

motoring The first motorcar in Singapore was imported in 1896 by Herman Katz of Katz Brothers, for a B. Frost of the Eastern Extension Telegraph Company. This 1894 single-cylinder belt-driven 5-horsepower Benz was later purchased by Charles Burton Buckley, lawyer and author of *An Anecdotal History of Old Times in Singapore, 1819–1867*. Thanks to the way it rattled and shook, it acquired the nickname 'Coffee Machine'. The local Chinese called automobiles 'devil wind carriages'.

The first recorded garage in Singapore was Federated Engineering Company, a branch of two Singapore firms, Riley, Hargreaves & Co. and Howarth Erskine. In 1900, Federated began offering a repair and renovating service at Merbau Road, the first such service in the Far East.

As people became convinced of the functionality of motorcars, accidents involving errant drivers with no licences constantly made newspaper headlines. During this period, the tin and rubber boom had enveloped Malaya. SYME & CO. advertised benzene for motorcars at 75 cents per imperial gallon, and offered a Rover 6-horsepower two-seater complete with hood and lamps for $1,600.

In 1906, William Kennedy of Federated registered his 10-horsepower, one-cylinder, two-seater Adams-Hewitt with 84-inch wheels and was allocated the license plate S1. Thereafter referred to as 'Ichiban', it was eventually passed on to one Mrs. Dare (later Mrs. G.P. Owen), Singapore's first woman motorist. Buckley's Benz was issued with number plate S6.

The Singapore Automobile Club was formed on 22 March 1907, with Governor Sir John Anderson as president. On 16 June 1907, the club staged its inaugural meet, with major importers represented—The Borneo Company Ltd, Syme & Co., C.F.F. Wearnes & Co., Riley & Hargreaves, Central Engine Works, and Cycle & Carriage (*see* JARDINE CYCLE & CARRIAGE).

By 1913, Singapore with a population of 330,000 boasted about 700 motor vehicles. Wearnes even had a very modest assembly operation for Canadian-made Ford cars in Singapore in 1916. By 1922, a trunk road connected Johor with Butterworth; a year later, the Causeway linking Singapore to Johor was completed. From 1926, Ford began assembling cars at its plant in Bukit Timah.

During the late 1920s, there was a good mix of American and European makes. The established importers were Federated Motors (previously Federated Engineering) with the Durant agency; Eastern Auto with Nash and Bayliss-Thomas; Lyons Motors with Dodge;

Guthrie with Buick; Imperial Motors with Erskine; General Motors Export Company with Chevrolet, Oldsmobile, Oakland and British Vauxhall; and Borneo Motors with Austin and La Salle.

The Great Depression caused a consolidation of the motor industry. After business picked up again, Wearnes dominated the Malayan market, with 60 per cent market share by the 1930s. Other major players were BORNEO MOTORS, with agencies for Austin, Plymouth, Chrysler, Riley, Chevrolet, La Salle and Bedford (trucks); and Cycle & Carriage, with Willys-Knight, Renault, Singer, Hudson and Talbot. In 1935, there were over 27,000 registered vehicles in Malaya; 28 per cent were in Singapore. About 65 per cent of cars in Malaya were British-made.

With the arrival of World War II, most importers followed Wearnes' scorched earth policy, destroying all plant machinery and spares. After the war, Europe frantically rebuilt factories and designed engines with austerity in mind. The post-war recovery meant strong demand for all vehicles. In 1965, Ford's Bukit Timah plant was making 16 models, including the Anglia and the Cortina (though production capacity was a mere 13 units a day, or 18 with overtime).

In the 1960s, the British car was still king of the road. Borneo Motors' and Wearnes' joint distributorships of Austin cars accounted for a quarter of sales in the country. But the removal of preferential tariffs for vehicles of Commonwealth origin, and the withdrawal of British troops, caused a decline. Borneo Motors dropped the Austin franchise in favour of Toyota in 1967, marking the start of Japanese automobiles' reign over Singapore roads.

By 2005, Japanese makes accounted for over two-thirds of the 438,000 cars in Singapore (Toyota cars alone made up more than a quarter of the car population). Despite the high price of CAR OWNERSHIP and the well-developed public transportation networks, cars are popular for their convenience, as a status symbol, and for trips to Malaysia. The latter activity continues to be a popular option for family vacations and, in recent years, for self-drive excursions by motoring clubs.

Mount Alvernia Hospital Mount Alvernia Hospital opened as a 60-bed hospital in 1961. It was funded by public donations and the Congregation of Catholic Sisters of the Franciscan Missionaries of the Divine Motherhood (FMDM), who were employed as nurses and trainers in colonial government hospitals. It is the only privately owned, not-for-profit hospital in Singapore founded by nursing professionals.

The hospital occupies a seven-acre parcel of land on Thomson Road, purchased by the congregation in 1956. Upon opening, it set new standards of in-patient care and soon became a leader in maternity care.

Motoring: dealer advertising from the 1930s (top left) and 1950s (top right) promoting makes once familiar in Singapore; the diminutive Austin Seven, c. 1932 (left), designed for the popular market.

Extensions and new services were rapidly added to meet demand. In 1984, it became the only hospital to have its own blood bank. Local recruits to the congregation were sent for professional training and work experience in the global network of FMDM institutions. The hospital was entirely managed by the nuns until 1987, when the first lay administrator was appointed. In 1989, work began on a medical centre to house specialist clinics.

New services introduced over the years include health screening, day surgery, rehabilitative care and sports medicine. In addition to technological capabilities, high intensity nursing care is a special focus for the hospital, which also offers specialist clinical pastoral care.

The Assisi Home and Hospice, located within its grounds, was set up by the congregation in 1969 as a residential facil-

Mount Alvernia Hospital

Mount Vernon Crematorium and Columbarium.

ity for chronically ill patients in financial need and continues to be supported by the hospital.

Mount Elizabeth Hospital The Mount Elizabeth Hospital and Medical Centre was a joint venture between Singaporean and Indonesian businessmen. Construction commenced in 1976, and the hospital was opened in December 1979. The hospital, then the most modern and up-to-date in Singapore, became known for the quality of its services. The first private cancer centre in Southeast Asia was established at Mount Elizabeth. Besides local patients, the hospital is popular with Indonesians and other nationalities coming to Singapore to seek medical treatment.

A new wing was added to the medical centre in 1992. The following year, the Brunei royal family built the Royal Suite for their private use; this suite is now open to other patients as well.

Ownership of the hotel has changed hands since its opening. In 1985, it was sold to National Medical Enterprises Incorporated, America's largest healthcare company, and then acquired in 1994 by PARKWAY HOLDINGS Ltd, currently Singapore's largest private healthcare company.

Mount Faber Reaching 105 m above sea level, Mount Faber is the fourth highest point in Singapore. Geologically, it is an extension of the Jurong Triassic sedimenta-

Mount Faber: view from the top.

ry rock system, which also extends to Sentosa and the Southern Islands (*see* GEOLOGY). Mount Faber's original Malay name was Telok Blangah—meaning 'cooking pot bay' in Malay, because of the shape of the bay. The site was renamed Mount Faber in 1845 when Captain Charles Edward Faber established a signal station at the summit. Mount Faber was originally covered in primary rainforest. It was later turned into a 56-ha park. Parts have been regenerated as secondary rainforest, while other sections have been transformed into gardens. The highest point in the park, Faber Point, affords view of the harbour, Sentosa and other islands. Mount Faber is the terminus of the cable-car link with Sentosa.

Mount Vernon Crematorium and Columbarium Built in 1962, Mount Vernon Crematorium was the first crematorium in Singapore. It was later expanded to include a columbarium. When it was officially closed on 30 June 2004, cremations were held at the MANDAI CREMATORIUM AND COLUMBARIUM COMPLEX. Some members of the public feared that the closure of the crematorium at Mount Vernon was a prelude to the relocation of the site's columbarium. However, the columbarium has remained open. The government has indicated 2007 as a possible date for a decision on the columbarium's fate.

Mountbatten, Lord Louis (1900–1979) British military official. Born Louis Francis Albert Victor Nicholas Battenberg, Mountbatten's family changed their surname when World War I broke out due to anti-German sentiment. His mother was a granddaughter of Queen Victoria, and his father was German aristocrat Prince Louis of Battenberg. Mountbatten joined the Royal Navy at age 13 and attended the Royal Navy Colleges at Osborne and Dartmouth. In 1941, Prime Minister WINSTON CHURCHILL appointed him as head of the Combined Operations Command. He oversaw the Dieppe Raid in 1942, where large numbers of the 5,000 Allied troops involved perished.

In 1943, Mountbatten was put in charge of the South East Asia Command, and his presence and morale-boosting policies encouraged the troops, driving them to victories in Burma (present-day Myanmar). On 12th September 1945, he received the surrender of 680,879 officers and men from the Japanese Imperial Army in the Council Chamber of the Municipal Building (present-day CITY HALL). Mountbatten also presented CHIN PENG and other leaders of the MALAYAN PEOPLE'S ANTI-JAPANESE ARMY with medals for their wartime efforts against the Japanese. After the war, he presided over the transition from military to civilian administration in South East Asia.

Prime Minister Clement Attlee appointed Mountbatten viceroy of India in 1947, a position he occupied from March

Mountbatten: reading order of the day for the surrender at the Municipal Building, 1945.

to August of the same year, after which he became governor-general of a newly independent India until June 1948. Mountbatten was killed by an Irish Republican Army bomb when sailing in the Donegal Bay, Ireland.

MPH Bookstores The history of Singapore's oldest book retailer can be traced back to 1815, when William Milne, a Methodist missionary, founded a mission press in Malacca. This publishing house moved to Singapore in 1890. The company was known as Amelia Bishop Press and subsequently, the American Mission Press. In 1906, it was renamed the Methodist Publishing House (MPH). Initially, the company printed bibles and textbooks for use in schools throughout Singapore and Malaya.

In 1908, MPH moved into premises on Stamford Road, that eventually became the company's landmark building. The company was renamed Malaya Publishing House in 1927, and Malaysia Publishing House following MERGER in 1963.

In 1972, MPH was acquired by the Singapore-based Thai businessman Jack Chiarapurk (Jack Chia), who added it to his portfolio of firms involved in pharmaceuticals, food, consumer products, real estate and engineering. Under the name of Jack Chia-MPH (JC-MPH), the company was transformed into a conglomerate, and was used by Chia in acquisitions of listed companies in Singapore, Hong Kong, Thailand, Australia and the United Kingdom.

By the early 1990s, the bulk of the group's revenues and profits came from Chia's property business in Australia.

MPH Bookstores: flagship branch at Stamford Road, closed in 2003.

However, JC-MPH also established a magazine publishing arm, which published titles such as *Female* magazine.

Jack Chia died in 1996. Four years later, the Chiarapurk family sold its 39 per cent stake in the company to local businessman Simon Cheong. Cheong then sold the group's interests in the book retail and distribution business for $42 million to Malaysian businessman Syed Mokhtar Al-Bukhary in 2002.

Two years later, MPH's magazine publishing division was sold to SINGAPORE PRESS HOLDINGS for $33 million. Under its new Malaysian owner, the book chain opened five MPH Bookstores in Singapore and 26 in Malaysia. Its Malaysian subsidiary also started Bookmark—a secondary chain of bookstores.

Mufti Highest-ranking official within Sunni Islam responsible for religious rulings and opinions. It is an appointment provided by the ADMINISTRATION OF MUSLIM LAW ACT. The office of the mufti is a division within MAJLIS UGAMA ISLAM SINGAPURA and its main role is to coordinate the Fatwa Council, which is headed by the mufti himself. Fatwas are religious rulings and are passed on matters of religious significance. The Fatwa Council deliberates on Islamic issues or problems faced by the Muslim community. Singapore's first mufti was Mohamed Sanusi Mahmood, who served from 1967 to 1972. He was succeeded by SYED ISA SEMAIT.

Muhammadiyah Non-profit Islamic welfare organization. Muhammadiyah was formed in 1958 to conduct religious classes, and offer financial assistance to poor families, orphans and other needy sections of the community. It also provides burial services, and has established a welfare home for young people and a day-care centre for the elderly. The organisation runs Madrasah Al-Arabiah Al-Islamiah (*see* MADRASAHS) and Muhammadiyah Welfare Home.

Muhammed Ariff Ahmad (1924–) Author. Muhammed Ariff Ahmad uses 'MAS' as his pen name. After graduating from Sultan Idris Training College, Perak (1949), he joined the teaching service until his retirement. A founding member of ASAS 50, he has written numerous short stories, novels, poems, plays and essays, and produced several reference books and books for children. Amongst his noted works are two novels *Mail Mau Kawin* (Mail Wants To Marry) (1976) and *Syarifah* (1998), while his many poems are published in several anthologies such as *Puisi Melayu Baru* (New Malay Poems) (1961) and *Tiga Warna Bertemu* (Meeting of Three Colours) (1987). His works have a strong didactic slant.

Muhammed Ariff has been active in local Malay/Muslim organizations such as the Singapore Malay Teachers Union and MAJLIS UGAMA ISLAM SINGAPURA. He received the CULTURAL MEDALLION in 1987. In 1993, he was given the Southeast Asia Write Award and the Tun Seri Lanang Award.

Muharam First month of the Islamic calendar. The first day of Muharam is celebrated as the Muslim New Year. The Hijrah—the migration of the Prophet Muhammad from Mecca to Medina in 622 CE—is also commemorated during Muharam.

The first day of Muharam is not a public holiday in Singapore. Public celebrations of Muharam are generally subdued, and include activities such as public lectures in mosques and public halls. In order for Muslims to appreciate the Hijrah better, MAJLIS UGAMA ISLAM SINGAPURA and other organizations have held night walks to commemorate the Prophet's journey. In recent years, people from other communities have also participated in these night walks.

MUIS *See* MAJLIS UGAMA ISLAM SINGAPURA.

multiracialism As at end June 2005, 76 per cent of Singapore's population was ethnically Chinese, 14 per cent Malay, 9 per cent Indian and a small percentage 'Other' ethnic groups. Race has long been an issue of political significance in Singapore—a demographically Chinese-predominant city-state in the Malay world of archipelagic Southeast Asia.

Singapore's policy of multiracialism is based on the concept of racial equality, which is reflected in the text of the NATIONAL PLEDGE. Under the Constitution, it is the government's responsibility to care for the interests of the racial and religious minorities in Singapore. In 1970, the PRESIDENTIAL COUNCIL FOR MINORITY RIGHTS was set up as a safeguard against any legislation that might discriminate against any ethnic or religious community.

This concept of equality is applied in various spheres of public life. Although MALAY is officially the NATIONAL LANGUAGE of Singapore, MANDARIN, TAMIL and ENGLISH have the status of 'official languages'. The distinction between 'national' and 'official' languages is now largely symbolic. Major holidays observed by different ethnic groups are celebrated as PUBLIC HOLIDAYS, and ethnic or religious festivals are supported directly or indirectly by the state through the allocation of funding, space and other administrative resources. Government officials also make it a point to attend events organized by different racial groups, and policies have been formulated with the express objective of integrating different ethnic communities. A prominent example of this is the ethnic quota for public housing, a policy introduced in 1989 to prevent racial enclaves from developing.

The government has often referred to the RACE RIOTS and MARIA HERTOGH RIOTS,

Muharam: Mufti Syed Isa Semait leads the New Year supplication at Darul Ghufran Mosque. Yaacob Ibrahim, in red shirt, is seated in the front row, 2005.

and has warned that racial harmony is 'tenuous'. A number of events—including the TUDUNG ISSUE of 2002, and the uncovering of a plot involving 15 alleged members of JEMAAH ISLAMIAH in the same year—have led to public doubts about multiracialism. In response, non-governmental organizations, schools and other institutions have been asked by the government to organize INTER-RACIAL CONFIDENCE CIRCLES to try to eliminate racial barriers.

The government takes a stern view of public grievances expressed in racial terms. Individuals responsible for such expressions have been publicly criticized as 'racial chauvinists'. Inflammatory racist remarks are punishable by law. In 2005, three persons were convicted under the Sedition Act for making racist comments on their blogs; two were jailed, the first persons to be jailed under the Act since 1966.

Municipal Commission Early body responsible for local government. The Municipal Commission was created by the Municipal Ordinance of 1887. The local governance of Singapore was divided between the municipal or city area, and the rural districts. A full-time salaried Municipal President was appointed by the governor while the body was made up of elected members. The municipality's finances were also separated from general revenue.

The creation of the Commission made a great difference to local government. It created a professional fire brigade (1888); took over waterworks and created the Thomson Road Reservoir (now MACRITCHIE RESERVOIR) and constructed filter beds (1889); completed the Kallang Extension River Scheme (now Peirce Reservoir) (1911); renovated the Town Hall (now VICTORIA THEATRE) (1909); built the VICTORIA MEMORIAL HALL (1905); took over the Gas Company (1900); and provided electric lighting (1906).

In 1913, the Municipal Commission was reorganized and municipal elections were abolished while the municipality's finances were placed in the hands of the governor. After World War II, the Municipal Commission's authority was expanded to

Municipal Election: first Municipal Commission, 1949.

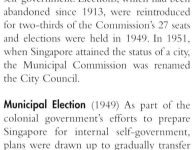

Lt-Gen. Mutaguchi Renya

Museum, NUS Centre for the Arts: exhibits in the Ng Eng Teng Gallery.

make it more democratic as a training for self-government. Elections, which had been abandoned since 1913, were reintroduced for two-thirds of the Commission's 27 seats and elections were held in 1949. In 1951, when Singapore attained the status of a city, the Municipal Commission was renamed the City Council.

Municipal Election (1949) As part of the colonial government's efforts to prepare Singapore for internal self-government, plans were drawn up to gradually transfer power to Singaporeans. These included holding the LEGISLATIVE COUNCIL ELECTION (1948), and reinstituting elections for the MUNICIPAL COMMISSION. This was held in 1949.

Nomination day for the Municipal Election—the first since 1913—was 7 March 1949, with polling on 2 April 1949. Eighteen seats were contested, with three seats in each of six wards—City, North, South, East, West and Rochor. Members of the remaining nine seats on the commission were nominated by the colonial government.

Voter turnout was poor, however, with only 10 per cent of the 8,688 eligible voters lodging ballots. The PROGRESSIVE PARTY, led by C.C. TAN, won 13 of the 18 elected seats.

Murchison, Kenneth (1794–1854) Colonial official. Born in Scotland, Kenneth Murchison was the third governor of the STRAITS SETTLEMENTS (1833–37). He began his career in the Straits Settlements when he was appointed Resident Councillor of Penang on 29 November 1827. The following year, he became Resident Councillor of Singapore, and also presided over courts on the island until the arrival of a RECORDER. He sat with Governor Robert Fullerton to hold the first Assizes (a court of law that judged cases of a serious or sensitive nature) on 22 May 1828 in the absence of Recorder Sir John Thomas Claridge, who had refused to come to Singapore.

In 1830, the Straits Settlements were reduced to the status of a residency dependent on the Presidency of Bengal. Before leaving for the United Kingdom, Governor Fullerton dismissed the judicial establishment of the Settlements by closing the courts. Murchison opened a temporary court at the request of local merchants, but had to close it after receiving an official reprimand. The courts reopened in 1832, and in order to support judicial authority, the offices of Governor and Resident Councillors were revived, but without their former status, rendering Murchison a governor in name but a resident in practice (*see* GOVERNORS).

Murugadiyan (1944–) Poet. Born V. Palani in India, Murugadiyan wrote under the pseudonym 'Murugathasan' before adopting 'Murugadiyan' as his pseudonym in 2005. At the age of 16 he came to Singapore, where he began work as an electrician, a job he held until he retired. He has written short stories, essays and plays, but is best noted for his poetry, which encompasses themes of community, nation and nature, and also includes religion; all written in a traditional style. Murugadiyan's awards include the Mont Blanc Award for Literature (1998) and the Tamizhavel Award (2003) from the Association of Singapore Tamil Writers.

Museum, NUS Centre for the Arts Established in 1997, this institution brings three distinct collections under one roof. The Lee Kong Chian Art Museum covers Chinese art from the late Neolithic period to the 20th century; the Ng Eng Teng Gallery is named after and features the work of the late Singaporean sculptor NG ENG TENG (1934–2001); and the South and Southeast Asian Gallery houses ceramics, textiles and classical sculpture from South and Southeast Asia (including a collection of stone sculpture from India), along with modern Singapore paintings. Temporary exhibitions are shown in the Visiting Exhibition Gallery.

Mutaguchi Renya, Lieutenant-General (1888–1966) Japanese military official. Mutaguchi Renya was one of the most experienced commanders in the Japanese Army. He had been involved in the 1937 Marco Polo Bridge Incident which marked the beginning of the Sino-Japanese War. During WORLD WAR II, he commanded the 18th Division in the MALAYA CAMPAIGN.

Known for his drinking, Mutaguchi is said to have sworn at the start of the Malaya Campaign in December 1941 that his 'next drink would be in Singapore'. He was wounded during the Japanese assault on Singapore in February 1942 but recovered. In 1944, Mutaguchi was despatched to Burma, where he organized the ill-fated 'March on India' (the Battle for Imphal) led by the INDIAN NATIONAL ARMY.

myopia Singapore has one of the highest rates of myopia (nearsightedness) in the world. Surveys have shown that myopia afflicts 25 per cent of seven-year-olds; 33 per cent of nine-year-olds; 50 per cent of 12-year-olds; and more than 80 per cent of 18-year-old males in Singapore.

Myopia usually develops in children of school-going age and continues to worsen through to the early 20s, after which the condition stabilizes. The earlier a child develops myopia, the higher the possibility that the individual will suffer from severe myopia later in life.

The HEALTH PROMOTION BOARD launched the National Myopia Prevention Programme in August 2001. The programme's slogan—'Fight Myopia. Give Your Eyes A Break'—acknowledged the fact that modern lifestyles and working environments may contribute to the problem of nearsightedness. Studies have also indicated that there are genetic factors which make certain people (and ethnic groups) more susceptible to myopia. People of Chinese descent are believed to be more prone to myopia, and the risk of developing myopia is higher if one or both of a child's parents are also myopic.

As with people in other countries, most Singaporeans resort to wearing eyeglasses or contact lenses to deal with myopia, an increasing minority opting instead for surgery.

Myopia: poster by the Health Promotion Board.

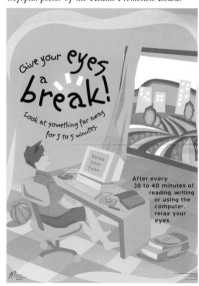

N

Nadiputra (1946–) Theatre practitioner. Nadiputra is the pseudonym of Almahdi Al-Haj Ibrahim. His first acting experience was his involvement in school plays. He later joined the Malay Youth Literary Association and SRIWANA, a leading Malay theatre group in Singapore. He went on to lead Sriwana from 1978 to 1990. He has written and directed more than 200 plays. They include *Kutukan* (Critique) (1982), *Malaikat* (Angel) (1983), *Awang Kerambit* (1980), *Puncak* (Peak) (1983), and *Alang-alang* (1986). In 1985, Nadiputra together with another playwright Sabri Buang, formed Teater Nadi, which staged several plays such as *Encong, Masjid Bersalib* (Crossed Mosque), and *Bahtera* (Ship). He joined state broadcaster SINGAPORE BROADCASTING CORPORATION in 1983. Since then he has been writing and directing drama productions for television and radio. He was awarded the CULTURAL MEDALLION in 1986. *See also* MALAY THEATRE.

Nagore Durgha This building was built between 1828–30 on Telok Ayer Street. It was previously known as Shahul Hamid Durgha after Syed Shahul Hamid Qadir of Nagore in South India. He lived in the 15th century and is regarded as a saint by INDIAN MUSLIMS.

The building's architectural features include an elaborate balustrade linking the four corners. Each corner is marked by a 14-level square minaret topped by an onion-shaped dome and a finial. The levels are marked off by moulding and niches.

Nagore Durgha

Nagore Durgha was gazetted a national monument in 1974. A \$1.8 million restoration project will restore it as a heritage centre of Indian Muslim history that will display artefacts.

Nair, C.V. Devan (1923–2005) Trade unionist, politician and head of state. Born in Malacca, Chengara Veetil Devan Nair moved with his family to Singapore at the age of ten. He was educated at Rangoon Road Primary School and Victoria School. He began his career as a teacher at St Joseph's Institution in 1945, later moving to St Andrew's School. Nair was active in the Singapore Teachers' Union (STU), becoming the union's general secretary in 1949. In 1951, he was detained by the British authorities on charges of being involved in anti-colonial activities, and was not released until April 1953, whereupon he became secretary of the SINGAPORE FACTORY AND SHOPWORKERS' UNION.

In 1954, Nair was one of the conveners of the PEOPLE'S ACTION PARTY (PAP) and was elected to the PAP's Central Executive Committee (CEC). He was detained again in 1956 on charges of being involved in pro-communist activities and remained in custody until the PAP government released him following the 1959 general election. On his release, he was appointed political secretary to the minister for education. However, he resigned from this post in 1960 and returned to teaching. That year, he was appointed chairman of the Prisons Inquiry Commission and launched the Adult Education Board, becoming its first chairman (1960–64).

In 1961, Nair helped to found the NATIONAL TRADES UNION CONGRESS (NTUC), and was elected as the NTUC's first secretary-general. In 1964, he stood for election to the Malaysian Parliament and won a seat in the Bangsar constituency. He served the full five-year term in Parliament, founding the Democratic Action Party of Malaysia, and in the process serving as that party's first secretary-general.

He returned to Singapore in 1969 to resume his post as secretary-general of the NTUC. He served in that capacity until 1979 when he became the NTUC's president. From 1969 to 1979, he transformed the trade union movement, bringing government and unions into a close symbiotic relationship that would later evolve into tripartism, an alliance of the NTUC, the government and employers. He initiated the establishment of the NTUC insurance cooperative INCOME, the taxi co-operative COMFORT and the WELCOME chain of cooperative supermarkets (which would later become NTUC FAIRPRICE).

In the Anson constituency by-election of 1979, Nair was elected to Parliament on the PAP ticket. He retained his seat at the 1980 general election but resigned in October 1981 when Parliament elected

him the third president of the Republic of Singapore. In recognition of Nair's contributions to the labour movement, he was awarded the Public Service Star (1963), and was also awarded an honorary doctorate by the University of Singapore (1976).

On 28 March 1985, Nair resigned as President, after serving just over three years. Prime Minister LEE KUAN YEW said in Parliament that Nair had resigned to seek treatment for alcoholism—a charge that Nair subsequently denied.

Nair was married to Avadai Dhanam, also a PAP activist and member of Parliament. She died in 2005.

Nair died on 7 December 2005 in Canada at the age of 82. On his death, Lee said in a condolence letter to Nair's son: 'Devan Nair played a significant part in the building of modern Singapore. He stood up to be counted when the communists attacked the PAP in the 1960s, and he initiated the modernisation of the labour movement that made the NTUC an important partner in the development of our economy.'

In January 2006, the NTUC held a memorial service which was attended by the prime minister and other cabinet ministers, members of Parliament, labour leaders and old friends.

Nair, M.P.D. (1920–1989) Politician. Founding member of the SINGAPORE LABOUR PARTY. Born Madai Puthan Damodaran Nair in India, he was a clerk in the Army Civil Service Union. Inspired by the success of the United Kingdom's welfare state, he was initiated into Labour Party politics by journalist and politician GERALD DE CRUZ, and elected as a member of the Singapore City Council from 1950 to 1953. Elected to the Legislative Council in 1955, Nair served as assistant minister to the chief secretary (1956–59) and briefly as minister for communications and works (1959).

After losing his seat in the 1959 elections, Nair left to undertake a law degree in the United Kingdom. He returned in 1963 and began a legal practice. That same year, he returned to politics. Running on the Singapore Alliance ticket, he was unsuccessful in his bid for a seat in the Jalan Kayu constituency. Contesting as an independent, he failed in his bids for the constituencies of Bukit Merah in 1966, Thomson in 1967, and Farrer Park in 1968, all against People's Action Party candidates. In 1972, he joined the WORKERS' PARTY, under whose banner he unsuccessfully contested the general elections of 1972, 1976, 1980 and 1984. He was then offered a non-constituency seat in Parliament in 1984. His party turned the seat down, holding to its pre-election stand of opposing the scheme.

Naito Kanichi (dates unknown) Japanese mayor. Naito was formerly the governor of Ibaragi Prefecture in Japan, and had been

Nadiputra

C.V. Devan Nair

M.P.D. Nair

Naito Kanichi

Nan Chiau High School: Nan Chiau Girls' High School, Kim Yam Road premises, 1950 (top); the co-educational school in Sengkang, 2006.

director of Industries in the Malaya Military Administration, before being appointed mayor of SYONAN-to (Singapore) Municipality in July 1943. He held this position until the end of the JAPANESE OCCUPATION. His arrival in Singapore, together with the departure of WATANABE WATARU in March 1943, ended the feuding and rivalry that had existed between the Japanese army's Malaya Military Administration and the Syonan-to Municipality.

Namazie, Mohamed Javad (1907–1993) Lawyer, politician and community leader. Namazie was born into a family of Persian origin in Madras, India. He moved to Singapore at the age of six, and was later educated at Raffles Institution. He studied at Queen's College, Oxford University, and graduated with a Bachelor of Arts (Honours) and a Bachelor of Civil Law.

He returned to Singapore in 1930 and, after working in different law firms, founded his own firm, Mallal & Namazie, in 1933. He left for India before the Japanese invasion of Singapore, returning to the city as part of the civil section of the BRITISH MILITARY ADMINISTRATION after the end of the war.

Namazie was instrumental in framing the constitution for the first, partially elected, Legislative Council. He contested a seat during the LEGISLATIVE COUNCIL ELECTION of 1948, winning by 1,050 votes. Thereafter, he sat on the boards of numerous organizations, including the SINGAPORE POLYTECHNIC, the War Damage Commission, the Singapore

Mohamed Javad Namazie

Telephone Board and the SINGAPORE IMPROVEMENT TRUST.

Throughout his life, Namazie was involved in the affairs of the Muslim community. From 1947, he sat on the Muslim Advisory Board that advised the British on religious and social matters relating to Muslims in Singapore. He was closely involved in the development of the ADMINISTRATION OF THE MUSLIM LAW ACT (AMLA) of 1966; and he was the longest serving member of MAJLIS UGAMA ISLAM SINGAPURA (MUIS), serving on this body from 1968 until 1986.

Namazie was president of the Muslim Trust Fund Association (MTFA) for 34 years. During his tenure there, the first and only orphanage for Muslim girls—the Darul Ihsan Lilbanat—was opened in 1980. Another of Namazie's contributions to the Muslim community was the building of the Moulana Mohamed Ali Mosque (originally on Market Street, later relocated to the basement of UOB Plaza in Raffles Place) for the benefit of Muslims working in the area. For his services to the community, Namazie was made a Commander of the Order of the British Empire (CBE) and was awarded the Pingat Bakti Masyarakat (Public Service Medal).

Nan Chiau High School Founded in 1941 by TAN KAH KEE, as the Nan Chiau Teachers' Training College, the school was built on land donated by LEE KONG CHIAN. In 1947, it was renamed Nan Chiau Girls' High School. An ancillary primary school provided basic education for the children of Chinese immigrants.

On 8 March 1969, the secondary school moved to larger premises on Guillemard Road. The implementation of a new education system saw the medium of instruction change from Chinese to English in 1980. It enrolled its first male students in 1987, after its name was changed to Nan Chiau High School. It moved to Sengkang in 2001 and began operating as two separate schools—Nan Chiau High School and Nan Chiau Primary School. The school is managed by the SINGAPORE HOKKIEN HUAY KUAN.

Nanking cargo The Nanking cargo is the name given to Chinese blue-and-white porcelain retrieved from an 18th-century wreck, the Dutch East Indiaman *Geldermalsen*. The ship was en route to Dutch East Indies from China with a cargo of Chinese gold bars, 240,000 pieces of blue-and-white porcelain, and a large quantity of tea used as packing material between the ceramics.

The *Geldermalsen* struck the Admiral Stellingwerf reef on 3 January 1752 and foundered off the south coast of Singapore. The wreck was identified by several pieces of evidence. Two Dutch cannons bearing the initials 'V.O.C.', which are the initials

for the Dutch East India company (VERENIGDE OOST-INDISCHE COMPAGNIE), were found. The ship's bell was dated 1747, the year the vessel was completed and several medicine bottles bore the initials of the ship's surgeon.

The cargo was retrieved by marine salvage operator Michael Hatcher between 1983 and 1985. He recovered 170,000 pieces of blue-and-white porcelain and a large number of gold bars. The Nanking cargo was eventually put on auction by Christie's of London in 1986. It raised a total of £10 million.

Nanyang Term used by the Chinese to refer to Southeast Asia. Initially, it was closely associated with the Chinese in Singapore and Malaya rather than Chinese in other parts of Southeast Asia. Many early Chinese writers who migrated from China to Malaya and Singapore used Nanyang to refer to these two areas.

Nanyang, meaning 'southern ocean', was first used in the Qing Dynasty (1644–1911), with reference to the southern coastal provinces of China: Jiangsu, Zhejiang, Fujian, Guangdong and Guangxi. The term 'Nanhai' (south seas) was more commonly used in Chinese historical records to refer to Southeast Asia. Hsu Yunt'siao, an associate professor of History at Nanyang University, argued that Nanhai was the ancient Chinese term for Nanyang in his book, *Nanyang Shi*.

Li Changfu, a pre-World War II Chinese historian, maintained that there were two concepts of Nanyang: the broader concept included the Indo-Chinese Peninsula, Malay Peninsula, Malay Archipelago, Australia and the South Pacific, while the narrower concept referred only to the Malay Peninsula and Archipelago, that is present-day Southeast Asia.

The narrower concept became accepted among the overseas Chinese and Chinese-educated in Southeast Asia. In 1908, Chinese students in Tokyo published the *Nanyang Qun Dao Shang Ye Yanjiuhui Zazhi* (Magazine of the Research Association for Commerce in the Nanyang Archipelago). That same year, China's *Zhongguo Tongmenghui Nanyang Youbu* (Tongmenghui Nanyang Branch) was set up in Singapore.

Nanyang became a very popular word among the Chinese-speaking population, especially those who lived in Singapore and Malaya/Malaysia after World War II. The first Chinese-medium university in Singapore was named NANYANG UNIVERSITY.

Nanyang Academy of Fine Arts Formerly the Nanyang Fine Arts College, the Nanyang Academy of Fine Arts (NAFA) was founded by artist LIM HAK TAI and businessman Tan See Siang in 1938. Early staff members were art teachers who followed Lim from China to Singapore after the out-

Nanyang Girls' High School: Linden Drive campus.

Nanyang Academy of Fine Arts: NAFA Campus 2 building (left); class in session.

break of the Sino-Japanese war in 1937. Closed during the Japanese occupation, it reopened in 1946. It became known as NAFA in 1982 although the name was adopted officially only in 1990.

In January 1994, the original aims and aspirations of founder Lim Hak Tai were revisited. These loosely translated into integrating the cultures of East and West to create a unique NANYANG identity in the arts, and the use of multidisciplinary means to nurture artistic talent, in order to 'augment the scientific spirit and thoughts of societies'.

In 1996, NAFA's various departments were grouped into three schools—the School of Visual Arts, School of Performing Arts and School of Fashion Studies. That same year, the academy moved into the premises of an old mission school in Middle Road.

The government upgraded its status to a tertiary institution in April 1999. NAFA began operating from a brand-new $115 million campus along Bencoolen Street in July 2004.

Nanyang Girls' High School Independent girls' secondary school. Founded in 1917, it was originally known as the Singapore Nanyang Girls' School, where lessons were taught in Chinese.

When the school moved from Dhoby Ghaut to King's Road in 1930, its name was changed to Singapore Nanyang Girls' High School. The current campus at Linden Drive includes boarding facilities for girls.

The school was the first to implement an elective art programme for artistically proficient students in 1984. In 2004, the school joined HWA CHONG INSTITUTION to offer the INTEGRATED PROGRAMME. Famous alumna include Ling Siew May, wife of former president ONG TENG CHEONG.

Nanyang Khek Community Guild Initated in 1923, the Nanyang Khek Community Guild is the umbrella organization of all HAKKA associations in the NANYANG region. Construction of a building for the guild's use was started in 1926. It was completed at the end of 1928 and the guild was officially launched on 23 August 1929. Well-known philanthropist 'Tiger Balm King' AW BOON HAW was elected as president.

Aw used the guild to generate community support for the Chinese Nationalist campaign. It raised $300,000 Chinese National Dollars, the single largest donation by Chinese organizations in British Malaya. This success allowed Aw to challenge TAN KAH KEE's leadership of the Chinese community in Singapore. Aw remained a dominant force in the guild until his death in 1954. Like many other self-help community groups, the guild established a school, set up a library and boarding house, and awarded scholarships. Its clubhouse is in Peck Seah Street.

Nanyang Polytechnic Located in Ang Mo Kio, Nanyang Polytechnic was established in 1992. Its founding principal and chief executive officer is Lin Cheng Ton. It admitted its first batch of students to its School of Health Sciences and School of Business Management in July. In 1993, it established its Schools of Engineering and Information Technology. In February that year, the Economic Development Board transferred the French-Singapore Institute, German-Singapore Institute and the Japan-Singapore Institute to the polytechnic. It is best known for its Information Technology and Digital Media programmes.

Nanyang Siang Pau Chinese-language newspaper. It was launched in 1923 by multi-millionaire TAN KAH KEE but was shut down by the colonial government in October that year. The government claimed that it 'was involved in party politics'. It resumed publication on 1 February 1924.

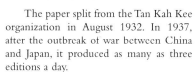

The paper split from the Tan Kah Kee organization in August 1932. In 1937, after the outbreak of war between China and Japan, it produced as many as three editions a day.

Publication stopped on 15 February 1942, along with that of all other newspapers in Singapore, when the island fell to the invading Japanese army. Its presses were used to print the *Shonan Daily*, a Japanese propaganda newspaper. *Nanyang Siang Pau* resumed publication after Japan surrendered on 8 September 1945.

On 2 May 1971, three of its senior executives were arrested under the INTERNAL SECURITY ACT as the paper was accused of stirring up Chinese racial sentiments. The paper survived the crisis and became a public company on 15 February 1975, in accordance with the Newspaper and Printing Presses Act.

In 1982, *Nanyang Siang Pau* teamed up with rival SIN CHEW JIT POH, leading to the formation of Singapore News and Publications Limited (SNPL). Under the new parent company, both newspapers were restructured and became LIANHE ZAOBAO and LIANHE WANBAO in March 1983. These two new Chinese-language papers became part of SINGAPORE PRESS HOLDINGS when SNPL merged with the Straits Times Press and Times Publishing Bhd on 4 August 1984. *Nanyang Siang Pau* continues to be published in Malaysia.

Nanyang Style A school of painting which consciously attempted to visually represent the lifestyle, landscape, people, and flora and fauna of Southeast Asia, a region known to the Chinese as NANYANG. Although termed 'style', the Nanyang works represent a broad stylistic spectrum from Chinese ink on scroll to Post-Impressionist easel paintings, along with experiments in fusion of eastern and western stylistic elements. LIM HAK TAI, founder of the NANYANG ACADEMY OF FINE ARTS, is regarded as the first proponent of the Nanyang Style in his call for a Southeast Asian identity in art. Artists who were pioneers of the Nanyang Style include

Nanyang Siang Pau

Nanyang Khek Community Guild: 35th anniversary celebrations.

Nanyang Style: Chen Chong Swee's Grooming Hair *(1952) (left); Liu Kang's* My Young Wife *(1944).*

LIU KANG, CHEN CHONG SWEE, CHEN WEN HSI and CHEONG SOO PIENG. Chen Chong Swee, for example, rendered beaches, coconut trees and attap huts of Southeast Asia, in the Chinese ink painting format.

See also ART.

Nanyang Technological University In 1980, NANYANG UNIVERSITY merged with the UNIVERSITY OF SINGAPORE (founded in 1905) to form the NATIONAL UNIVERSITY OF SINGAPORE on a shared campus at Kent Ridge. The Nanyang University campus at Jurong became the Nanyang Technological Institute in 1981, established with government funding. It contained three schools of engineering.

The institute's emphasis on technology was aimed at meeting the manpower needs of a growing economy anchored in manufacturing. In 1987, a school of accountancy and business was formed. A school of applied science followed the next year.

The name Nanyang Technological University (NTU) was adopted in 1991 with the absorption of the NATIONAL INSTITUTE OF EDUCATION. In 1992 the

Nanyang Technological University: freshmen orientation.

School of Communication Studies was established. Nanyang University's alumni rolls were taken over by NTU in 1996.

Diversification of the university's research-intensive disciplines continued into the 21st century, particularly in areas such as biological sciences and various branches of engineering.

Another phase began in 2004 with the setting up of the School of Humanities and Social Sciences. This embraced subjects such as economics, Chinese, English, psychology and sociology. In the following year, art, design and media, and physical and mathematical sciences were added. The engineering schools also expanded into new fields, such as chemical and biomolecular engineering, aerospace engineering and maritime studies. NTU has collaborated with overseas universities such as Cornell in the United States, Shanghai Jiaotong in China and IIT Bombay in India.

NTU had an enrollment of just under 18,000 undergraduates and about 8,000 post-graduates in 2005.

Nanyang University Privately funded, Chinese-medium institution established in Singapore in 1955. It was the only Chinese-language university outside China then, created under unusual historical circumstances. It was popularly known as 'Nantah', which is a contraction of 'Nanyang Daxue', its full Mandarin name.

The founding of Nanyang University was highly significant for the Singapore Chinese community. It united the Chinese from all walks of life in their support of it, and it had an impact on Chinese education in the region and beyond.

The British colonial government in Malaya and Singapore did not support Chinese-language education. This forced the Chinese community to rely on itself to meet its educational needs. The years after World War II saw rapid growth in Chinese-language schools in the region, producing highly talented graduates. However, when the government in China changed in 1949, these graduates were denied an opportunity for higher education there. This resulted in a severe shortage of qualified high-school teachers. The establishment of a Chinese-language university to train high-school teachers then became a priority for the Chinese community.

Nanyang University owes its origin primarily to TAN LARK SYE. In January 1953, at a meeting of the Singapore Hokkien community, he articulated the need for a Chinese-language university. The Chinese in Singapore, Malaya and other parts of Southeast Asia responded enthusiastically. In the following month, representatives of 215 Chinese associations and the Singapore CHINESE CHAMBER OF COMMERCE & INDUSTRY came together, decided on the name 'Nanyang University', and registered it officially in May 1953.

Nanyang University: gateway arch, 1956 (top); Tan Lark Sye hoists a flag, opening ceremony, 1956.

Generous cash donations came from the Chinese community from all levels of society. Tan offered up to $5 million towards the building of Nanyang University. The SINGAPORE HOKKIEN HUAY KUAN donated 523 acres of its land at Upper Jurong Road for the campus. Work on Nanyang University started in July 1953 and the first lessons were held on 30 March 1956—this became the university's anniversary. The university was officially opened in March 1958 by Sir WILLIAM GOODE, then governor of Singapore.

However, Nantah was soon beset by a series of controversies. In 1956, the government declared it would not recognize degrees awarded by Nantah because of unsatisfactory academic standards. It took another 12 years before the government finally recognized degrees conferred by the university. In addition, several review reports—the Prescott Report (1959), the Gwee Ah Leng Report (1960) and the Nanyang University Curriculum Review Committee Report (1965)—damaged the university's public profile.

As part of the process of Singapore's Merger with Malaysia and, later, Separation, Nantah was told by the Education Review Council to 'meet the needs of modern Singapore'. This ostensibly meant that Nantah should have a multi-ethnic representation in their student body and provide education in languages other than Chinese.

At that time, graduates of Nanyang University were facing difficulties in getting employment. Graduates who found employment were paid a lower salary than graduates from the English-medium University of Malaya in Singapore (later known as UNIVERSITY OF SINGAPORE).

The People's Action Party (PAP) government's efforts to reform the university, and the release of the the report by the Nanyang University Curriculum Review Committee were the main causes of the student demonstrations of October and November 1965. Riots occurred again in 1966. A wave of arrests eventually helped to suppress these violent demonstrations.

In 1978, the government announced that Nantah would change its teaching medium to English, to be on par with the University of Singapore and to produce bilingual graduates. That year, students of Nanyang University began their semester at the joint campus in Bukit Timah.

A new inquiry in 1979, chaired by Sir Frederik Dainton, chancellor of Sheffield University, suggested that Nanyang University should merge with the University of Singapore to form a 'single and strong university'. The 21st and final convocation of Nanyang University was held in August 1980.

In the same month, the National University of Singapore Act came into effect for the merger of the University of Singapore and Nanyang University in 1980, which created the National University of Singapore. The next year, the Nanyang Technological Institute was founded on the old campus of Nanyang University. The institute was renamed Nanyang Technological University in 1991. The alumni roll of Nanyang University was transferred to Nanyang Technological University in 1996. In 2004, there were some moves to rename the university 'Nanyang University', but university authorities decided against it.

The library and administration building of the old Nanyang University was a four-storey building constructed like a fortress but with elegant Chinese architectural features. Since 1995 it has been the home of the Chinese Heritage Centre.

The Nanyang Gateway Arch, with its roof of glazed green Chinese tiles, was originally located at the entrance of Nanyang University. It has been preserved in a community park in Jurong West, near the Yunnan Gardens housing estate.

The library and administration building, and the gateway arch were gazetted as national monuments in 1998.

Naomi & The Boys Popular music group. Signed to recording label Philips, it was led by Naomi Suriya on vocals, her brother Robert Suriya on lead guitar, Moses Tay on rhythm guitar, Peter Richards on keyboards, Henry Richards on bass and Joe Ahmad on drums. This 1960s band was noted for its lead singer's detached vocal style, and Robert Suriya's prowess on the guitar.

Naomi & The Boys released their first EP in June 1965. It consisted of three originals and a cover of 'Tennessee Waltz'. One original, 'It's All Over', made 'No. 1' on the Malaysian charts.

Three members of the original band— Peter Richards, Henry Richards and Joe Ahmad—left, but were replaced by Peter Thomas on rhythm guitar, Alphonso Soosay on drums, and Moses Tay, who had switched from guitar to keyboards and bass. With this line-up, Naomi & The Boys released its second EP, *Happy Happy Birthday Baby*, in October 1965. The title track went to the top of the local charts and was voted Song of the Year.

The band went on to produce many hits over the next four years. Although predominantly a popular music band, it also included country and rhythm-and-blues covers in its repertoire. In late 1967, it switched to record label Decca, releasing one EP on the label in January 1968. The band toured Malaysia regularly, building up a loyal fan base before disbanding in 1969. Naomi Suriya moved on to a solo career with Polydor in 1971.

Napier, William (dates unknown) Law agent. Formerly a merchant, Napier was admitted as a law agent in 1833. He was known for his talent as an actor, and for his wit. In 1835, together with Edward Boustead and George Coleman, he founded the Singapore Free Press and served as its editor until 1846. In 1848, he was made lieutenant-governor of Labuan and became legal adviser to the temenggong of Johor. Napier was the first Freemason initiated in Singapore. Napier Road, named after him, led to his house, which he built in 1854. *See also* Legal profession.

nasi lemak Popular hawker dish. Rice (in Malay, *nasi*) is steamed with coconut milk for a rich (*lemak*) taste. It is traditionally served with fried *ikan kuning* (yellow-striped scad) or *ikan bilis* (anchovies), cucumber slices, boiled or fried egg and the all-important *sambal* (chilli paste). It is then wrapped in a banana leaf into a distinctive pyramid-like shape before being sold.

nasyid Musical genre. *Nasyid* was originally sung in Arabic with or without musical accompaniment. It later developed to incorporate mainly percussive instruments, and was sung in harmony to the accompaniment of frame drums played in interlocking rhythms. The lyrics of the songs often carry moral or religious messages. Modern forms of the genre include *nasyid kontemporary* (contemporary *nasyid*).

In Singapore, *nasyid* underwent a revival in the late 1970s and 1980s. In the late 1970s, an all-female *nasyid* group, Al-Mizan (led by Faridah M. Amin), signed a recording contract with record label WEA. The group's first album, *Tangan Kuhulur Maaf Kupohon* (I Extend My Hand in Asking for Forgiveness), featuring contemporary *nasyid* music, was released in 1978. The album made Al-Mizan and their *nasyid* music so famous that they were featured in a Malaysian-produced film, *Kau Sumber Ilhamku* (You Are My Inspiration).

The success of Al-Mizan encouraged the formation of two more all-female *nasyid* groups in Singapore: Hidayah, which recorded with EMI and was led by singer Rohaya Mohd Taib; and Al-Jawaher, which recorded with Polygram and was led by singer Habibah Osman. All three groups recorded several albums, and many of their songs have continued to be played on Singapore radio well into the 21st century.

Nasyid's popularity spread within the Muslim community; numerous *nasyid* competitions were held and *nasyid* groups formed in mosques and workplaces. However, the commercial success of the genre could not be sustained, with the move from vinyl to cassettes, the high cost of record production and increasing levels of piracy.

In the mid-1990s, *nasyid* underwent another revival in Malaysia. The Malaysian all-male *nasyid* group Raihan was formed (by a Singapore-born manager) in that period. Raihan was then followed by groups such as Rabbani, Brothers and Hijjaz. In more recent years, some *nasyid* groups have collaborated with rap groups.

In Singapore, no *nasyid* group has achieved success comparable with the three all-female groups formed in the 1980s, although the genre has remained popular. Local groups such as Shoutul Jundil Muslim (from Madrasah Aljunied), Kafilah and Nur Mutiara have all recorded albums, although these have not been widely promoted.

Nathan, S.R. (1924–) Head of state. Sellappan Ramanathan was educated at Anglo-Chinese Primary and Middle Schools, Rangoon Road Afternoon School and Victoria School. His education was interrupted by World War II. After the war, Nathan finished his secondary education through self-study and won a place at the University of Malaya in Singapore, graduating with a diploma in social studies (distinction) in 1954.

He joined the Singapore Civil Service as a medical social worker (1955) and was appointed seamen's welfare officer the following year. In 1962, he was seconded to the Labour Research Unit of the Labour

S.R. Nathan

Naomi & The Boys: Happy Happy Birthday Baby! EP, 1965.

Nasi lemak

Nasyid: Hadratul Islam performing, 1980.

367

S.R. Nathan: open house at the Istana, 2005.

Movement as assistant director, and later director, serving with the unit until January 1966. He continued as a member of its board of trustees until April 1988.

In February 1966, Nathan was transferred to the Ministry of Foreign Affairs as assistant secretary. He was made acting permanent secretary of the Ministry of Home Affairs in January 1971. By August, he was moved to the Ministry of Defence as director of the Security and Intelligence Division. It was in this capacity that he was involved as a negotiator in the LAJU HIJACKING in 1974.

In 1979, he returned to the Ministry of Foreign Affairs to become its first permanent secretary.

He left the post in February 1982 to become executive chairman of the Straits Times Press until 1988. Between 1982 and 1999, he also held directorships in several

national anthem
MAJULAH SINGAPURA
Mari kita rakyat Singapura
sama-sama menuju bahagia
Cita-cita kita yang mulia
Berjaya Singapura!
Mari-lah kita bersatu
Dengan semangat yang baru
Semua kita berseru
Majulah Singapura!
Majulah Singapura!

ONWARD SINGAPORE
We, the people of Singapore
Together march towards happiness
Our noble aspiration
To make Singapore a success
Let us all unite in a new spirit
Together we proclaim
Onward Singapore!
Onward Singapore!

companies, including the Singapore Mint Pte Ltd, Singapore Press Holdings Ltd, and Singapore International Media Pte Ltd. He was also chairman of Mitsubishi Singapore Heavy Industries from 1973 to 1986.

Nathan is active in the Indian community. He was chairman of the HINDU ENDOWMENTS BOARD from 1983 to 1988 and a founding member of the SINGAPORE INDIAN DEVELOPMENT ASSOCIATION (SINDA).

Nathan began a second career in April 1988, when he was appointed Singapore's high commissioner to Malaysia (1988–90). He was subsequently made ambassador to the United States (1990–96), and ambassador-at-large concurrently with being director of the Institute of Defence and Strategic Studies at the Nanyang Technological University (1996–99). He resigned from both these posts to contest the 1999 presidential elections.

As he was the only qualified candidate, Nathan was declared elected President of the Republic of Singapore on 18 August 1999. Six years later, he won a second term as president. Once again, he was the only qualified candidate. He was sworn in on 1 September 2005.

S.R. Nathan was awarded the Public Service Star (1964), the Public Administration Medal (Silver) (1967) and the MERITORIOUS SERVICE MEDAL (1974).

national anthem Before self-government in 1959, Singapore's national anthem was that of the British—*God Save the Queen*. The song that would become its national anthem, *Majulah Singapura*, was originally commissioned as a patriotic song by the City Council to commemorate the re-opening of the Victoria Theatre after its 1958 renovations. ZUBIR SAID, the prolific Sumatra-born composer and songwriter for Cathay Keris studio, was asked to compose it in 1956.

Although the City Council was dissolved in 1959, the song was not forgotten. When Singapore became a self-governing colony, deputy prime minister TOH CHIN CHYE led a high-level government committee set up to establish state symbols such as the NATIONAL FLAG, a national coat-of-arms and a national anthem. Toh was reminded about the City Council song, which he felt might be adaptable for the purpose. A number of musicians and orchestras, including the Radio Singapore Orchestra, the Military Forces Band and the visiting Berlin Chamber Orchestra, helped to shape the anthem.

The anthem, flag and coat-of-arms were unveiled to Singaporeans at the launch of Loyalty Week on 3 December 1959, after the installation of the Yang di-Pertuan Negara (head of state), YUSOF ISHAK.

When Singapore separated from the Federation of Malaysia in August 1965, *Majulah Singapura* was adopted as the new republic's national anthem.

National Archives of Singapore Statutory board. Established in 1968, the National Archives of Singapore (NAS) was initially known as the National Archives and Records Centre (NARC). In 1993, it came under the management of the National Heritage Board (NHB).

Most of the archives' collections are records created by the government. These include documents, films, sound recordings, maps, photographs and building plans. The NAS has also been tasked with collecting and preserving private archival records. The collections of the NAS are stored in two locations, one at Canning Rise and the other at the former FORD MOTOR FACTORY site. The holdings of the NAS are essential primary-source material for researchers seeking to understand the political, economic and social history of Singapore. The NAS also promotes public interest in Singapore's heritage through educational programmes and exhibitions.

National Arts Council Statutory board. The National Arts Council (NAC) was formed in October 1991 by the merging of the Singapore Cultural Foundation, the Cultural Division of the Ministry of Community Development, the Festival of Arts Secretariat and the National Theatre Trust. It administers policies on arts and culture—mainly theatre, music, dance, literature, photography and visual arts—under the MINISTRY OF INFORMATION, COMMUNICATIONS AND THE ARTS.

The NAC gives annual and project grants to artists and arts groups, commissions artworks, and manages arts facilities and venues such as the VICTORIA CONCERT HALL and KALLANG THEATRE. Under the Arts Housing Scheme, the council also identifies and converts heritage buildings suitable for use by artists and arts groups in Waterloo Street, Little India and Chinatown. It establishes collaborative agreements with foreign governments including France (2000) and Mexico (2002). NAC's flagship event is the annual SINGAPORE ARTS FESTIVAL, featuring performances from around the world. Other initiatives have included the revival of busking to 'enliven the cityscape', arts education programmes to nurture the young, and overseas scholarships in the arts and arts administration.

The NAC gives recognition for artistic achievement through national awards, especially the annual CULTURAL MEDALLION and YOUNG ARTIST AWARD. Citizen involvement in the NAC's work has been broad, through numerous advisory and resource panels.

National Council of Social Service The National Council of Social Service (NCSS) grew out of the Singapore Council of Social Service, an umbrella body formed in 1958 to cover all community services and social welfare activities. In 1983, fundraising was centralized by setting up

COMMUNITY CHEST. This freed voluntary welfare organizations (VWOs) to concentrate on providing better care and services without being overwhelmed by efforts to raise funds. The Singapore Council of Social Service was restructured in 1992 and NCSS formed. In 1994, NCSS was appointed by the Ministry of Community Development to be the national co-ordinator of Family Service Centres. NCSS launched the 'Volunteer a Day' programme in 1996 and its 'Vision of Social Services in the 21st Century' in 1999, to encourage volunteerism and guide the development of social services respectively.

National Day Singapore became an independent sovereign nation on 9 August 1965. To commemorate the first anniversary of this momentous event, a parade was held at the PADANG on 9 August 1966. It began with the arrival of President YUSOF ISHAK on the steps of CITY HALL. He was met by defence minister and colonel of the Artillery, GOH KENG SWEE. The Cabinet was also present. The march-past that followed took 90 minutes and consisted of 23,000 men, women and children. Many Cabinet members and members of Parliament wore uniforms and joined the parade, which marched through Chinatown to Tanjong Pagar, and was televised live. The National Day Parade has since become a major highlight of the national holiday.

In addition to the parade, dinners, speeches and many other events are held throughout the island at both local and national levels to celebrate independence. Of particular note are the National Day Message, and the National Day Rally Speech in which the prime minister gives an overview of the government's performance and the challenges confronting Singapore. The speech is often an occasion for revealing new directions and changes in state policy.

National Day honours Honours are presented on NATIONAL DAY in recognition of various forms of merit, and of the service that individuals have performed for Singapore. These honours are usually pre-

National dress: S. Dhanabalan, left, and Ong Teng Cheong, right, wearing shirts with orchid motifs.

sented by the President of the Republic personally at the ISTANA or some other public venue. The highest honour is the Star of Temasek, which may be awarded to a member of the Singapore Armed Forces, the Singapore Police Force or the Singapore Civil Defence Force for an act of exceptional courage. The highest civilian honour is the ORDER OF TEMASEK.

See table.

national dress As a multi-ethnic society, Singapore does not have one national dress or costume, but a variety. Efforts to create a national dress have often been attempts at fusing elements and characteristics of traditional costumes of the island's main ethnic groups (CHINESE, MALAY, INDIAN and others). These efforts have not caught on.

One major push was the National Trades Union Congress' attempt to create an 'orchid shirt'—a long-sleeved shirt with orchid motifs worn untucked.

Because Singapore's NATIONAL LANGUAGE is Malay, and because of its historical ties with the Malay Peninsula, the term 'national dress' also sometimes refers to the *sarong kebaya* for women and long-sleeved batik shirt for men.

Today, it is considered appropriate to respond to an invitation specifying 'national dress' by wearing ethnic clothing from any of the country's major ethnic groups.

National Education Initiated in 1996 by the MINISTRY OF EDUCATION to foster national cohesion and instill a sense of national identity. It develops an understanding of Singapore's particular challenges and vulnerabilities. National Education emphasizes the core values of meritocratic, multiracial and multi-religious harmony. It is not taught as a subject but infused throughout the curriculum. Examples are the daily flag-raising and oath of allegiance, and visits to key state institutions.

National Education also includes core annual events such as Total Defence Day and Racial Harmony Day. Total Defence Day marks Singapore's fall to the Japanese in 1942 and is held on 15 February. School activities are designed to remind pupils that Singapore can be defended and is worth defending, and that Singaporeans themselves must defend Singapore. Racial Harmony Day is 21 July. On this day in 1964, RACE RIOTS broke out in Singapore. Racial Harmony Day reminds students that social division weakens society, and that race and religion will always be potential fault-lines in Singapore's society. It is a day for students to reflect on and celebrate the nation's success as a harmonious society, built on cultural diversity.

National Environment Agency Statutory Board. The National Environment Agency (NEA) oversees the implementation of environmental policies. It was

National Day: celebrations at Yishun Central, 2005 (above); parade in front of City Hall, 1966.

formed by the MINISTRY OF THE ENVIRONMENT AND WATER RESOURCES (MEWR) in July 2002. The NEA has three divisions—Environmental Protection, Environmental Public Health, and METEOROLOGICAL SERVICES.

The Environmental Protection division operates the four waste incineration plants. It also promotes efforts to minimize waste and pollution, and to recycle. The Environmental Public Health division works to raise public health standards by conducting disease surveillance, improving food handling hygiene, researching disease vectors such as mosquitoes, and encouraging environmental cleanliness. The Meteorological Services department provides weather information.

NATIONAL DAY HONOURS	
1	Star of Temasek
2	Order of Temasek
3	Order of Nila Utama
4	Certificate of Honour
5	Distinguished Service Order
6	Medal of Honour
7	Conspicuous Gallantry Medal
8	Meritorious Service Medal
9	Public Service Star
10	Public Administration Medal (Gold)

NOTE: Honours are listed in order of precedence.
Source: Prime Minister's Office

National Day: celebrations at the Padang, 2000.

national flag Prior to 1959, the Union Jack—the national flag of the United Kingdom—was used to represent Singapore. With the passage of the 1958 CONSTITUTION, Singapore achieved self-governing status (*see* MERDEKA). The new state flag was unveiled and raised on 3 December 1959 during the launch of Loyalty Week, after the installation of the Yang di-Pertuan Negara (Head of State), YUSOF ISHAK.

In terms of design, the flag is divided horizontally in two: red over white, with a crescent moon and five stars in a circle, all in white. Red symbolizes brotherhood and the equality of men, while white symbolizes purity and virtue. The crescent moon represents Singapore's youth as a country, while the five stars represent democracy, peace, progress, justice and equality.

On 30 November 1959, the Singapore State Arms and Flag and National Anthem Ordinance was passed to regulate their use. When Singapore was part of the Federation of Malaysia (1963–65), the flag of the federation was used to represent Singapore at international events and functions.

national flower *See* VANDA MISS JOAQUIM.

National Healthcare Group This is one of two healthcare clusters in Singapore, the other being SINGHEALTH. The National Healthcare Group (NHG) comprises four public hospitals (Alexandra Hospital, National University Hospital, Tan Tock Seng Hospital and the Institute of Mental Health/Woodbridge Hospital); one national centre (the National Skin Centre); three specialty centres (The Cancer Institute, The Eye Institute and The Heart Institute); and nine polyclinics. The Ministry of Health divided Singapore's public hospitals into two clusters in 1999. The rationale was to bring down organizational barriers between the hospitals within each cluster, increase collaboration and foster the integration of medical services.

National Heritage Board Statutory board. The National Heritage Board (NHB), under the MINISTRY OF INFORMATION, COMMUNICATION AND THE ARTS, organizes exhibitions, festivals and educational programmes that aim to make heritage accessible and relevant to Singaporeans and international visitors. The NHB has its roots in the 1887 inception of the Raffles Museum and Library on Stamford Road. In 1960, the library relocated to a new building next door (*see* NATIONAL LIBRARY BUILDING), and the museum retained its title as Raffles Museum. After separation, the museum was renamed the National Museum.

The NHB was formally established in August 1993 as a statutory board which would take responsibility for the National Museum, the NATIONAL ARCHIVES OF SINGAPORE and the Oral History Department of the then Ministry of Information and the Arts. The board has since come to operate eight heritage institutions. These include four national museums: the ASIAN CIVILISATIONS MUSEUM; the SINGAPORE ART MUSEUM; and the NATIONAL MUSEUM OF SINGAPORE (formerly the Singapore History Museum). In addition, it administers the SINGAPORE PHILATELIC MUSEUM; the NATIONAL ARCHIVES OF SINGAPORE; the HERITAGE CONSERVATION CENTRE; REFLECTIONS AT BUKIT CHANDU; and Memories at Old Ford Factory (*see* FORD MOTOR FACTORY).

By 2005, with the national museums developing their own independent identities, the NHB decided to review its focus. Gaps were identified in the heritage and cultural sectors, a lack of public awareness and resources being identified as key issues. The NHB's role was thus expanded to include a focus on building a strong museum-going culture in Singapore. This

National flag

prompted greater levels of collaboration with public and private organizations that shared an interest in heritage and culture.

One key strategy employed by the NHB was the Museum Roundtable (MR). The MR brings together over 30 leading public and private museums, heritage centres and galleries, and promotes museum-going.

National Institute of Education The predecessors of the National Institute of Education (NIE) were the Teachers' Training College and the Institute of Education (IE), established in 1950 and 1973 respectively.

The Teachers' Training College gave certificate courses in education for non-graduates; the Institute of Education offered certificates and diplomas in Education for non-graduates and graduates. The institutes also gave part-time teaching cadetships to those who wished to study and teach in schools at the same time. In 1980, the teaching cadetship scheme was replaced by a full-time teacher-in-training scheme.

Shortly thereafter, IE moved from its Paterson Road grounds to Bukit Timah. The College of Physical Education (CPE) was set up there in July 1984 to train teachers specializing in physical education. The IE functioned as an autonomous college and conducted a two-year diploma programme in physical education .

In 1990, in preparation for creating NIE, the certificate and diploma programmes at IE and CPE were upgraded to diploma and post-graduate diploma levels for non-graduates and graduates respectively. For the first time, training of graduates to teach in primary schools was introduced through a one-year Post-graduate Diploma in Education (Primary).

IE and CPE formally merged to form NIE in July 1991, which was established as an institute of the NANYANG TECHNOLOGICAL UNIVERSITY. As part of the University, NIE offered two four-year degree courses. When NIE shifted to its present Yunnan Campus in 2000, the two courses were restructured to become the current Bachelor of Arts (Education) and Bachelor of Science (Education).

NIE opened with schools of Arts, Science, Education and Physical Education. In 2000, NIE adopted a matrix structure with three offices—the Foundation

National Institute of Education: tutorial (right); Teachers' Training College, 1954.

Programmes Office, the Graduate Programmes and Research Office, and the Dean (Academic)'s Office. Since then, three research centres have been formed. They are the Centre for Research in Pedagogy and Practice (the largest educational research centre in the Asia-Pacific region), the Learning Sciences Laboratory and DNA Centre. As of January 2006, NIE enrolment was 5,438 full-time equivalent students, of which 70 per cent were female and 30 per cent male.

National Junior College Established in 1969, the National Junior College (NJC) was the first junior college established in Singapore. Originally located on Linden Drive, it is currently located on Hillcrest Road. NJC offers two educational routes— the four-year INTEGRATED PROGRAMME and the two-year Junior College Programme. It offers the Arts Elective Programme and the Language Elective Programme (German). NJC's alumni includes Prime Minister LEE HSIEN LOONG, and ministers LIM SWEE SAY and VIVIAN BALAKRISHNAN.

National Kidney Foundation Dr Khoo Oon Teik, a nephrologist whose brother had died of kidney disease in the early 1960s, was one of a group of people who established Singapore's first dialysis unit in 1969. The unit initially operated in the attic of the SINGAPORE GENERAL HOSPITAL. The inauguration of the National Kidney Foundation (NKF) followed on 7 April that year, officiated by the first President of the Republic of Singapore and patron of the foundation, Encik YUSOF ISHAK.

The cost of dialysis at that time was prohibitive—$4,000 a month. Kidney transplants were rare, and death from kidney failure was inevitable. Singapore's first renal transplant took place in 1970. It was performed on a female patient who survived another 20 years. History was made in 1983 when, with the help of SINGAPORE AIRLINES, NKF flew in a kidney from the United States. This was the first time in Singapore that a kidney, kept in cold storage for 48 hours, was transplanted.

Since opening its first Dialysis Centre with ten dialysis machines in 1982, NKF has gone on to become the world's largest not-for-profit dialysis provider. Besides its dialysis programme, its other services and programmes include preventive healthcare, organ donation advocacy, research and development in renal medicine, nursing education and research.

In 1994, the NKF invited donations by means of a television show, featuring performances by international and local stars. More than $3.9 million were collected for kidney patients. Donations from television and other shows, and regular contributions by Singaporeans from all walks of life made NKF the nation's biggest charity, with accumulated reserves of $262 million.

However there was public disquiet in July 2005 following disclosures of inappropriate spending and poor management. Amidst growing outcry, chief executive officer T.T. Durai and the entire NKF board of directors resigned. They were replaced by a new chairman and board comprising eminent professionals and administrators, hand-picked by Singapore's Health Minister to refocus NKF on patients' needs. In 2006, the NKF sued Durai and three former NKF officers for an estimated $12 million in an effort to recover money allegedly improperly paid or used by them. Durai and the other three officers also faced criminal charges.

national language Singapore's national language is MALAY. ENGLISH, MANDARIN, Malay and TAMIL are official languages.

Under DAVID MARSHALL'S government, journalist SAMAD ISMAIL suggested to Hamid Jumat, then minister for local government, lands, and housing, that a provision should be inserted into the CONSTITUTION making Malay the national language.

Marshall included a clause in his memorandum to the colonial government which, among other things, committed the government of Singapore to 'at all times protect the political, economic, social and cultural interests of the Malays, EURASIANS and other minorities domiciled in Singapore' and to 'recognise the special position of the Malays, who are the indigenous people of the Island and … to support, foster and promote their political, economic, social and cultural interests, and the Malay language'. These words were affirmed by the British government and encapsulated in the Preamble to the 1958 Constitution.

When Singapore achieved independence in 1965, PARLIAMENT passed the Republic of Singapore Independence Act, Section 7(2), subject to the provision that the national language 'shall be the Malay language and shall be in the Roman script'. This provision was incorporated into the Constitution as Article 153A(2).

National Library Board See PUBLIC LIBRARIES.

National Library Building This modern-style building faced with red brick housed the first branch, the main reference library and the

National Junior College

administrative headquarters of the National Library. It was located in Stamford Road, next to the National Museum.

It was one of the first national buildings in newly self-governing Singapore and was officially opened in 1960 by then Yang di-Pertuan Negara YUSOF ISHAK. Funds for construction were raised from the public. Local philanthropist LEE KONG CHIAN donated $375,000. At the time it was opened, it was criticized for being 'forbidding', 'intimidating' and 'monumental but clumsy'. However, by the time its doors closed 44 years later, it had become such a landmark that its demolition, on account of road works necessitated by the building of the SINGAPORE MANAGEMENT UNIVERSITY campus, was mourned. The building was closed on 31 March 2004.

In July 2005, a new National Library building was opened. The new premises, located on Victoria Street, were designed by Malaysian architect Ken Yeang to include the Lee Kong Chian Reference Library, a lending library, a drama centre and other spaces.

National Museum of Singapore See box.

National Parks Board Also known as NParks, the National Parks Board is a statutory board within the Ministry of National Development. NParks manages 1,763 ha of parks, playgrounds, park connectors and open spaces, 3,326 ha of nature reserves and 4,200 ha of roadside greenery and vacant state land. It owns the SINGAPORE BOTANIC

National Library Building: former building on Stamford Road (left); new building on Victoria Street.

National Museum of Singapore

National Museum of Singapore This institution was originally founded in 1887 as the Raffles Library and Museum. It was built on Stamford Road by the Colonial Office of the Straits Settlements, with Governor FREDERICK WELD taking an active role. The establishment of a public repository of knowledge for the Malayan world in the form of a school, a museum and a library was something that Sir Stamford Raffles had called for as early as 1823.

Well known for its Southeast Asian zoological and ethnographic collections acquired prior to World War II, the Raffles Museum became an important centre for research. Successive directors and curators of the museum included zoologists R. Hanitsch, John C. Moulton, Cecil Boden Kloss and other scholars such as H.D. Collings and CARL GIBSON-HILL. The museum edited the *Journal of the Malayan Branch of the Royal Asiatic Society*, and was frequently visited by scholars conducting fieldwork in Southeast Asia. Significant collections deposited at the museum included a selection of northern Nias objects collected during the field trips of A. Modigliani, as well as basketwork from west Borneo and the Malay Peninsula gifted by Dr William L. Abbott from the United States National Museum (later renamed the Smithsonian). During the Japanese Occupation, the museum's extensive collections were spared by the Japanese.

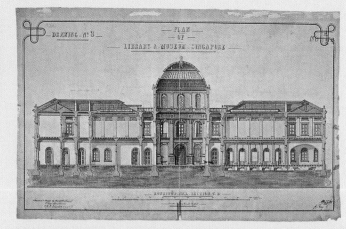

Drawing of the Raffles Library and Museum from 1892 (above). An iconic artefact of the pre-1969 period was the skeleton of a blue whale (left) which had been washed ashore at Port Dickson, Malacca, in 1893, and displayed in the museum for many years.

The Raffles Museum was renamed the National Museum in 1969 and its focus was altered to reflect the policies of the post-Separation government. Zoological collections were deposited at the Biological Department of the University of Malaya (later forming the basis of the THE RAFFLES MUSEUM OF BIODIVERSITY RESEARCH), or repatriated to national museums in former British colonies such as India and Malaysia.

The new National Museum functioned with the remaining archaeological, ethnographic and art collections. The National Museum Art Gallery was opened in 1976 to accommodate the exhibition needs of a growing community of artists working in Singapore. The History of Singapore Gallery was formally established in 1984 after the museum underwent a major refurbishment.

In 1987, the Ministry of Community Development compiled a long-term development plan which called for the establishment of a museum precinct comprising a number of themed museums. This became the blueprint for the establishment of the

NATIONAL HERITAGE BOARD (NHB) in 1993. The NHB was tasked with developing colonial-era public buildings into a series of new museums at which the core collections of the National Museum could be displayed. The art collection went to the SINGAPORE ART MUSEUM (January 1996); the ethnological and smaller collections went to the ASIAN CIVILISATIONS MUSEUM

(1997) and the history collection stayed with the National Museum in Stamford Road, which was renamed Singapore History Museum.

The building closed and underwent major renovations, including the building of a second extension, between 2003 and 2006. It was scheduled to reopen in 2006 as the National Museum of Singapore, with an additional 10,000 sq m of floor space, including a permanent gallery dedicated to the history of Singapore.

A new glass rotunda (left) and the restored original dome (below left) are architectural highlights of the newly renovated National Museum of Singapore.

*Three treasures from the **Singapore History Gallery:** embroidered silk coffin cover (above left); portrait of Sir Frank Swettenham, governor of the Straits Settlements (above) and gold ornament from Fort Canning (below).*

*Four new **Living Galleries** showcase the creative side of Singapore culture, featuring food, fashion, photography and film. Puppet stage (right) from the Film and Wayang gallery, and comic book (left).*

Galleries and collections
- largest museum in Singapore, with total gallery space exceeding 18,000 sq m
- features a 15-m-high, 24-m-wide glass rotunda
- Singapore History Gallery (2,800 sq m) tells the story of Singapore from the 14th century to modern times
- column-free 1,300 sq m gallery for travelling exhibitions
- four Living Galleries for lifestyle displays: Food, Fashion, Film and Photography
- Gallery Theatre with seating for 250

GARDENS and Fort Canning Park (*see* FORT CANNING AND PARK), and is the trustee for the various nature reserves. As Singapore's scientific authority on nature conservation, it monitors and coordinates measures to ensure the health of designated nature areas.

The history of NParks can be traced to 1967 when the Parks and Trees Unit was formed within the Public Works Department. The emphasis then was to plant roadside trees and to build parks. In 1976, it became the Parks and Recreation Department and was tasked with implementing the Garden City Campaign. In 1990, management of the Botanic Gardens, Fort Canning Park and the nature reserves were removed from the department and given over to the newly-formed National Parks Board. The board's mission was to develop, manage and promote these parks and spaces as resources for recreation, conservation, research and education. In July 1996, the Parks and Recreation Department merged with National Parks Board.

national pledge *See* box.

National Science and Technology Medal

Originally known as the National Science and Technology Award, the medal is given to individuals who have made a significant contribution to Singapore through the promotion and management of research and development. The award is conferred by the AGENCY FOR SCIENCE, TECHNOLOGY AND RESEARCH (A★STAR). Recipients of the National Science and Technology Medal receive a specially designed gold medal and a citation. In 1991, Professor Louis Chen of the Department of Mathematics at the National University of Singapore was the first recipient, being rewarded for his research on probability and statistics. A★STAR also gives out the National Science Award to reward basic research leading to the discovery of new knowledge or the development of scientific methods; and the National Technology Award which recognises research that leads to industrial application.

NATIONAL SCIENCE AND TECHNOLOGY MEDAL: RECIPIENTS	
1991	Louis H.Y. Chen
1992	Chan Soh Ha
1992	Frank Cloutier
1993	Christopher Y.H. Tan
1995	Goh Hak Su
1995	Herbert Eleuterio
1997	Sim Wong Hoo
1998	Chua Nam Hai
1999	Leo Tan
2000	Hang Chang Chieh
2001	Frans Carpay
2001	Bill Chen
2002	Lui Pao Chuen
2003	Su Guaning
2004	Low Teck Seng
2004	Kay Das

Source: Agency for Science, Technology and Research

National Service After SEPARATION from Malaysia in 1965, Singapore needed to build up its own defence force. It decided on the model of a citizen army similar to Israel, Finland and Switzerland. Singapore attempted to get assistance from India and Egypt to build up its armed forces, but was unsuccessful. In the end, Singapore accepted Israel's offer of assistance. On 14 March 1967, the National Service (Amendment) Act was passed and four months later, the first batch of 900 National Servicemen reported for duty.

Apart from a defensive role, national service (NS) is also seen as a nation-building tool, fostering ties between young men of diverse backgrounds. Enlistees are usually conscripted at age 18, but a fraction of draftees (mainly those who leave school early) are enlisted at 16 or 17. Some are exempted for medical reasons.

Operationally fit enlistees go through a Basic Military Training (BMT) phase which includes drill, physical, weapons and fieldcraft, training. BMT ranges from 9 to 26 weeks, depending on an individual's physical fitness. Enlistees who are not operationally fit take on modified training schemes that match their medical status.

After BMT, recruits are posted to combat, technical or service vocations based on their performance and aptitude. Those with leadership potential are selected for officer or specialist training. Some full-time national servicemen get posted to the Air Force or Navy, while about 15 per cent of them are placed in the Police or Civil Defence Force.

Under the NS (Amendment) Act of 1967, officers had to serve three years of NS while non-officers had to serve two years. The Enlistment Act of 1970 provided for 30 months of NS liability for those ranked corporal or above while all other servicemen continued to serve for two years. Since 2004, all full-time National Servicemen (NSF) serve two years of NS, regardless of rank. This reduction was due to the move towards a technologically advanced third-generation force.

On completion of mandatory full-time military service, NSF become Operationally Ready National Servicemen (NSmen). They were previously known as 'reservists', but the name was officially changed to emphasize their front-line status. After completing full-time service of two years, they serve in the reserves for a maximum of 40 days per year until the age of 40. Officers serve until the age of 50.

NSmen form the bulk of Singapore's military might. Their mobilization boosts the total strength of the SINGAPORE ARMED FORCES (SAF) to 350,000 men; the strength of the full-time ARMY is 50,000. Active units and reserve NS units are integrated within the same divisions.

From 1983, the NSmen training cycle was 13 years. The cycle includes 'high key'

national pledge Pledge of loyalty, written in 1966 by S. RAJARATNAM, Singapore's then minister for foreign affairs. Rajaratnam was a strong believer in multiracialism. With the 1964 race riots fresh in his mind, he included in the pledge the words, 'one united people, regardless of race, language or religion'. The texts below are in English and Malay.

The pledge
We, the citizens of Singapore,
pledge ourselves as one united people,
regardless of race, language or religion,
to build a democratic society
based on justice and equality
so as to achieve happiness, prosperity and progress for our nation.

Ikrar Kita
Kami, warganegara Singapura,
Sebagai rakyat yang bersatu padu,
Tidak kira apa bangsa, bahasa, atau ugama,
Berikrar untuk membina suatu masyarakat yang demokratik,
Berdasarkan kepada keadilan dan persamaan untuk mencapai kebahagian,
Kemakmuran dan kemajuan bagi negara kami.

in-camp trainings (ICT), each at least a week long, and 'low key' ICTs, lasting no more than six days. Those who complete their training cycle are put on the MINDEF (Ministry of Defence) Reserve List. In 2006, the training cycle was reduced to ten years.

In order to keep NSmen fit, MINDEF

National Service: NSmen training.

National Stadium: National Day celebrations, 1988.

National Solidarity Party: Yip Yew Weng, then secretary general, speaking at a rally in Chua Chu Kang, 1996.

National Trades Union Congress: One Marina Boulevard, building in which NTUC Centre is located.

started providing reservists with exercise facilities in 1979. In the following year, the Individual Physical Proficiency Test (IPPT) was introduced. NSmen have to take the IPPT annually. Those who fail undergo Remedial Training (RT). In 2006, the IPPT Preparatory Training (IPT) programme was introduced. It complements RT, providing differentiated training packages for NSmen to improve their physical fitness.

National Solidarity Party Established on 6 March 1987, the National Solidarity Party (NSP) has contested each general election since 1988 but has yet to win a seat.

In 1988, the party fielded eight candidates and polled an average of 35 per cent of votes. In the 1991 general election, its teams contesting the Cheng San and Tampines group representation constituencies (GRC) returned with an average of 38 per cent. In 1992, it contested the by-election at the Marine Parade GRC, but its team gathered only 1.4 per cent of the vote.

The party's first secretary-general, Tan Chee Kien, was later succeeded by Steve Chia, who became a non-constituency member of Parliament in the 2001 general elections. The party failed to win any seats at the 2006 General Election.

National Stadium This 50,000-seat sports stadium at Kallang Park was opened in July 1973 by then Prime Minister LEE KUAN YEW. Funded mainly from lottery proceeds, it was completed in time to stage the 7th Southeast Asian Peninsular Games in September 1973. The stadium has since been the venue for many local and international events, including the Southeast Asian Games in 1983 and 1993, and the 1996 inaugural Tiger Cup football series. SOCCER has always figured prominently in the schedule of regular sporting events at the stadium. Before the local league was formed, MALAYSIA CUP matches were played there. Football games held in the stadium are renowned for the Kallang Roar—a guttural cry from the fans intended to spur on the local team and intimidate visiting ones.

NATIONAL DAY parades are frequently held at the stadium. Pop concerts and cul-

tural programmes have also been held there.

Adjacent to the stadium are 8,000 sq m of training facilities, shops and restaurants. There is also a sports museum devoted to local sports heroes. It has displays of traditional and indigenous games and pastimes.

The stadium will be demolished by 2007 and replaced by a multi-purpose sports hub by 2010.

national symbols *See* NATIONAL ANTHEM, NATIONAL FLAG, NATIONAL PLEDGE and STATE CREST.

National Theatre This theatre was built at the corner of Clemenceau Avenue and River Valley Road in 1963. Dubbed the 'Peoples' Theatre', funds for its construction were collected by public subscription. Set into the slopes of Fort Canning and designed by ALFRED WONG, it featured a cantilevered roof, with an open-air auditorium. With a capacity of 3,420, it served as the venue for many important events and performances, including National Day Rallies (held there between 1966 and 1982) and university convocations. Maintenance problems, decreasing use (the auditorium lacked air-conditioning and padded seats) and the impending construction of a tunnel for part of the Central Expressway tunnel nearby led to the demolition of the National Theatre in 1986.

National Trades Union Congress A confederation of trade unions, associations, cooperatives and related organisations that protects and promotes workers' rights and interests. The National Trade Union Congress (NTUC) was formed in 1961 following a split in the ruling PEOPLE'S ACTION PARTY (PAP), with its left-wing dissidents forming the BARISAN SOSIALIS party. The ideological differences that split the PAP caused a corresponding split in the labour movement, the Singapore Trades Union Congress. Union supporters of the PAP, led by C.V. DEVAN NAIR, founded the NTUC while the other faction formed the SINGAPORE ASSOCIATION OF TRADE UNIONS (SATU) to back the Barisan Sosialis.

SATU then led strikes in a bid to undermine the ruling PAP government's authority. Barisan Sosialis subsequently lost electoral support and its political fortunes

National Theatre: an icon of its time.

waned. Some unions under SATU crossed over to join the NTUC. In 1963, SATU and its other unions were deregistered.

After Singapore's Independence in 1965, there was high unemployment and workers often took their grievances to the streets. The NTUC though, focused on negotiating collective agreements and fighting cases in the Industrial Arbitration Court. The NTUC's first major challenge came in 1968 when the British decided to pull-out its military forces from Singapore (*see* BRITISH WITHDRAWAL FROM SINGAPORE). Many people were anxious as the military pull-out would affect many jobs. To help save jobs, the NTUC supported the government's decision to transform the military bases for civilian use.

To stimulate the economy, the government set about attracting foreign investment, including revamping the employment legislation in 1968 to create a favorable investment climate. Unions, at first concerned with the legislative changes as their scope for negotiations were reduced, later gave their endorsement after the government promised that employers would not be allowed to take advantage of workers. These changes helped Singapore attract substantial foreign investment and enabled Singapore to be transformed from a trading economy into one with a large manufacturing component.

However, changes in the labour legislation and situation had an unsettling effect on workers in the unionized sectors. Morale dipped and union membership dropped to low levels. NTUC organized the Modernisation Seminar in 1969 to set new directions for the labour movement, which moved NTUC's policy towards employers from confrontation to cooperation. The principle of tripartism—an alliance between the NTUC, government and employers—was also put into practice at the NATIONAL WAGES COUNCIL.

Following the Modernisation Seminar, the NTUC formed cooperatives in the 1970s to keep essential goods and services affordable for union members and Singaporeans. NTUC first established NTUC Welcome (predecessor of NTUC FAIRPRICE) to combat rampant profiteering by selling essential commodities at low prices. NTUC Comfort was formed to help unlicensed taxi drivers become taxi owners. NTUC Income brought low premium insurance coverage to low-income workers.

The early 1980s saw the NTUC restructuring its unions. Omnibus unions were transformed into industry-wide unions. Later, house unions were formed to bring about better rapport between labour and management.

The NTUC Club was started to look into workers' social and recreational needs by providing amenities not normally available to them. In 1990, the Singapore Institute of Labour Studies (SILS) (now

known as the Ong Teng Cheong Institute of Labour Studies) was formed to strengthen the labour movement's leadership. More cooperatives in areas like healthcare, child and elder care, and thrift and loan were also formed.

There are strong links between the PAP and the NTUC, which can be traced to PAP's labour roots. When the PAP held its inaugural meeting at the Victoria Memorial Hall in November 1954, 90 per cent of those present were trade unionists. In addition, more than half of the first PAP Central Executive Committee were unionists. The 'symbiotic relationship' between the PAP and the NTUC was formally endorsed in 1980 at the NTUC Ordinary Delegates Conference. To further strengthen this relationship, some PAP members of Parliament work fulltime for the NTUC while others are appointed as advisors to various unions. This enables the PAP MPs to articulate the interests of the unions in Parliament. The secretary-general of the NTUC is a minister-without-portfolio in the Prime Minister's Office.

National University Hospital This 928-bed hospital was opened in 1985 as Singapore's only university hospital. Its in-patient facilities include 26 wards, 19 operating theatres, six intensive care units, 22 clinical departments, three dental departments, six paramedical departments, four medical institutes and a wide spectrum of specialist out-patient clinics. Most National University Hospital (NUH) clinicians also teach at the Yong Loo Lin School of Medicine, NATIONAL UNIVERSITY OF SINGAPORE.

Among the specialist services available at the National University Hospital are cardiac, thoracic and vascular surgery; hand and reconstructive microsurgery; obstetrics, gynaecology and paediatrics. The hospital also has four medical institutes: the Children's Medical Institute, the Eye Institute, the Cancer Institute and the Heart Institute. The Children's Medical Institute provides holistic care and treatment for young patients; it also runs the Children's Emergency Section. Specialist doctors within the NATIONAL HEALTHCARE GROUP provide care to eye, heart and cancer patients through the Eye Institute, Cancer Institute and Heart Institute, respectively.

In 1990, the hospital started its Liver Transplant Programme when it carried out the first liver transplant in Singapore. In 2005, the hospital conducted the first kidney-cum-bone marrow transplant in Asia.

National University of Singapore The National University of Singapore (NUS) is Singapore's oldest university. It can be traced back to 1905, with the founding of The Straits Settlements and Federated Malay States Government Medical School, the first institution of higher learning in Singapore. This was renamed the King Edward VII Medical School in 1913, and renamed again as KING EDWARD VII COLLEGE OF MEDICINE in 1921.

In 1949, the College of Medicine and RAFFLES COLLEGE were merged to form the UNIVERSITY OF MALAYA, which had full degree-granting powers. Ten years later, autonomous divisions of the university were set up in Singapore and Kuala Lumpur. The two governments then decided to have separate national universities. This led to the establishment of the University of Singapore in 1962, based mainly in the Bukit Timah campus. The university moved to a much larger site at Kent Ridge in 1969, but the transfer of all faculties and departments was only completed in 1986.

NUS came into existence with the merger of the University of Singapore and NANYANG UNIVERSITY in 1980. Then President BENJAMIN SHEARES was its first Chancellor. His successors included Presidents C.V. DEVAN NAIR (1981), WEE KIM WEE (1985), ONG TENG CHEONG (1993) and S.R. NATHAN (1999).

From the mid-1990s, NUS began incorporating features of American universities, such as a semester-based modular system (1992) and Scholastic Aptitude Test for admissions (2003).

NUS is listed as a Class One research university under the Carnegie Classification System and was first among the region's tertiary institutions to have two-way video-conferencing lectures (1992).

NUS collaborates with many foreign universities, including Johns Hopkins University and Georgia Institute of Technology. Student exchange programmes have been run with institutions such as Stanford University. Joint degrees are offered with foreign universities from China, Germany and other countries. In 2004, NUS was listed 18th in a global ranking of universities published by *The Times* of London.

NUS hosts 14 affiliated research institutes and more than 50 other research centres. It is also home to the LEE KUAN YEW SCHOOL OF PUBLIC POLICY, which makes Singapore's experience in public policy formation and implementation available to governments in the region. In 2005, NUS had 13 faculties, over 23,000 undergraduates and over 8,000 postgraduates.

National Volunteer & Philanthropy Centre Set up in July 1999, the National Volunteer & Philanthropy Centre (NVPC) serves as the national coordinating body for the promotion of volunteerism and philanthropy at all levels of society. Expanded in August 2003, the NVPC functions as a non-profit, non-government organization. Operational funding comes from the MINISTRY OF COMMUNITY DEVELOPMENT, YOUTH AND SPORTS. While NVPC promotes and develops philanthropy, it does not raise funds for, or donate to, charity.

National Wages Council The National Wages Council (NWC) was set up in 1972 to ensure that labour is rewarded for its contribution to production without undermining Singapore's competitiveness. The NWC is responsible for setting wage and benefits guidelines based on key macroeconomic developments. These include gross domestic product growth, labour market changes, productivity improvements and inflation. Its recommendations are made to the government. The basic principle is to ensure that real wage increases do not exceed productivity gains. Although the council's recommendations are subject to the government's approval and are not mandatory, they are widely followed.

The NWC is a common platform for three important economic groups—the government, employers and trade unions/workers. It has been able to help employers and workers negotiate wages and labour issues amicably, ensuring economic progress by maintaining harmony in the workplace.

NatSteel NatSteel was incorporated on 12 August 1961 as the National Iron and Steel Mills with a start-up capital of $24 million. A joint venture between the Singapore government and a group of local investors, it became the backbone of Singapore's growing industrial programme.

National University of Singapore: panoramic view of the campus (top); flags of the university, with the national flag in the centre.

National University Hospital: press coverage of liver transplant programme, 1990.

National University Hospital

nature conservation

nature conservation Since 1819, Singapore's natural history has suffered considerable loss, with the extinction of 38 per cent of butterfly species, 43 per cent of freshwater fish species, 70 per cent of forest bird species, and 40 per cent of mammal species.

Other species are at risk. The cream-coloured giant squirrel (*Ratufa affinis*), a rodent which was discovered and named by Sir Stamford Raffles, is now so rare that its extinction seems almost assured. Yet in his time, Raffles commented that it was common in the orchard. The banded leaf monkey (*Presbytis femoralis*), discovered and named by a German scientist over 150 years ago, has a population so low that experts believe it is doomed.

What biodiversity is left is still impressive though. Singapore has over 2,000 species of flora, 340 species of birds, 250 species of butterflies, 110 species of reptiles, 70 species of mammals, 29 species of amphibians, 200 species of hard corals covering 55 genera, and 111 reef fish species in 30 families.

Rare sighting of banded leaf monkey.

Although over 95 per cent of Singapore's original vegetation cover has been cleared because of urbanization, there are still some 200 ha of (mostly secondary) rainforest left, as well as stretches of MANGROVES. And despite sedimentation and land reclamation, there are also many areas with healthy seagrass beds, reefs and intertidal habitats—CHEK JAWA on Pulau Ubin being the best-known.

Biologists still regularly rediscover rare and extinct flora and fauna, and uncover species completely new to science. In 2005, a Belgian entomologist discovered over 100 species of forest flies in Singapore over just one year of study.

Cream-coloured giant squirrel (stuffed).

In recent years, the 'green movement' has resulted in a change of heart towards conservation. The NATIONAL PARKS BOARD (NParks), schools and non-governmental organizations are spreading the conservation message. Areas under protection are studied and properly managed; new green areas are being identified while damaged areas are recovered.

NParks has been designated the Scientific Authority on Nature Conservation. One of its projects is to reduce the rate of biodiversity loss in the fragmented natural areas of Singapore. It focuses on the propagation of endangered and rare species of plants found in the wild and planting them in natural habitats similar to their source of origin.

The gazetted forests—BUKIT TIMAH NATURE RESERVE, CENTRAL CATCHMENT NATURE RESERVE, LABRADOR NATURE RESERVE and SUNGEI BULOH WETLAND RESERVE—represent the major ecosystems in Singapore. The forests are protected from commercial logging, and are conserved for recreation, education, scientific research and the maintenance of ecological processes and services.

In addition to nature reserves, several sites have been designated nature areas which, while not legally protected, 'will be kept for as long as possible'. These are areas where diverse species of natural flora and fauna are still relatively undisturbed. Chek Jawa is an example of a nature area.

Developments near nature areas or nature reserves are subject to NParks' assessment of their potential impact on the ecosystem.

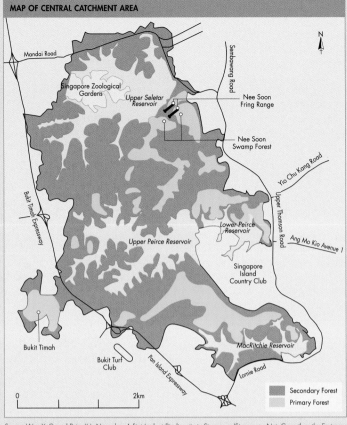

MAP OF CENTRAL CATCHMENT AREA

Mandai Road
Singapore Zoological Gardens
Upper Seletar Reservoir
Sembawang Road
Nee Soon Fring Range
Nee Soon Swamp Forest
Yio Chu Kang Road
Upper Thomson Road
Ang Mo Kio Avenue 1
Lower Peirce Reservoir
Upper Peirce Reservoir
Bukit Timah Expressway
Singapore Island Country Club
Bukit Timah
Bukit Turf Club
Pan Island Expressway
MacRitchie Reservoir
Lornie Road

0   2km

Secondary Forest
Primary Forest

Source: Wee Y. C. and Peter K.L. Ng, eds., *A First Look at Biodiversity in Singapore* (Singapore: Nat. Council on the Environment, 1994)

Animals endemic to Singapore
- Dragonfly (*Drepanosticta quadrata*), endemic to Singapore & southern Johor
- Singapore toadfish (*Allenbatrachus reticulatus*)
- Common iora (*Aegithina tiphia singaporensis*), endemic to Singapore & southern Johor
- Singapore freshwater crab (*Johora singaporensis*)
- Johnson's crab (*Irmengardia johnsoni*)
- Swamp forest crab (*Parathelphusa reticulata*)

Animals and plants named after Singapore
- Singapore durian (*Durio singaporensis*)
- Monitor lizard fern (*Tectaria singaporeana*)
- Singapore adenia (*Adenia macrophylla* var, *singaporeana*)
- Singapore vinegar crab (*Episesarma singaporense*)

- Kerinting (*Rhopaloblaste singaporensis*)
- Common iora (*Aegithina tiphia singaporensis*)
- Singapore freshwater crab (*Johara singaporensis*)
- Temasek shrimp (*Caridina temasek*)
- Singapore black caecilian (*Ichthyophis singaporensis*)
- Singapore toadfish (*Allenbatrachus reticulatus*)
- Plantain squirrel (*Callosciurus notatus singapurensis*)
- Singapore kopsia (*Kopsia singapurensis*)
- Singapore psechrus (*Psechrus singaporensis*)
- Keyhole limpets (*Diodora singaporensis*)
- Singapore mole cricket (*Gryllotalpa fulvipes*)
- Singapore fishing spider (*Thalassius* sp.)
- Singapore roundleaf horseshoe bat (*Hipposideros ridleyi*)
- Singapore whiskered bat (*Myotis oreias*)

VEGETATION IN SINGAPORE, 1819

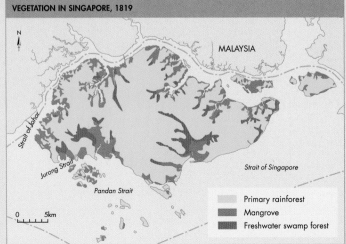

MALAYSIA
Strait of Johor
Jurong Strait
Pandan Strait
Strait of Singapore

0   5km

Primary rainforest
Mangrove
Freshwater swamp forest

VEGETATION IN SINGAPORE TODAY

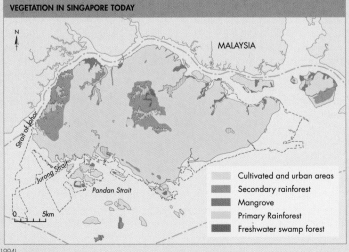

MALAYSIA
Strait of Johor
Jurong Strait
Pandan Strait

0   5km

Cultivated and urban areas
Secondary rainforest
Mangrove
Primary Rainforest
Freshwater swamp forest

Source: Wee Y. C. and Peter K.L. Ng, eds., *A First Look at Biodiversity in Singapore* (Singapore: Nat. Council on the Environment, 1994)

The company began to diversify into steel fabrication and construction-related products and services in the 1980s. It was renamed NatSteel in 1990 and expanded into the electronics business shortly after. It set up NatSteel Electronics and acquired NatSteel Broadway. Both were listed on the Singapore Exchange but were sold in December 2000 and September 2002 respectively. NatSteel Electronics was the world's sixth largest contract manufacturer, with clients such as Apple and Intel, when it was acquired by US-based Solectron for US$2.4 billion. NatSteel Broadway was sold to US electronics components maker Flextronics for US$363 million.

Laden with cash-rich assets but burdened with loss-making steel operations, in late 2002 the group became the target of an eight-month tussle between its own management buyout team, businessman OEI HONG LEONG, and a group led by hotelier ONG BENG SENG, and backed by TEMASEK HOLDINGS. The consortium led by Ong prevailed after garnering more than 51 per cent of the company's stock in early 2003.

To enhance shareholder value, the group sold its steel businesses—under NatSteel Asia—to India's Tata Steel for $486.4 million. The acquisition was completed in 2005. All its steel assets in Singapore, Malaysia, Thailand, Vietnam, the Philippines, Australia and China were consolidated under the Tata group.

NatSteel has since focused on strengthening its sizeable operations in construction products, chemicals and engineering in ten countries. These include plans to expand its businesses in China and the Middle East.

NatSteel's construction products division is the Singapore market leader in cement, concrete, pre-cast concrete, premix mortar and related building products. NatSteel generated net profits for 2005 of $69.9 million on a turnover of $303.6 million.

Nattukottai Chettiars The Tamil term 'Nattukottai Chettiar' means 'people with palatial houses in the countryside'. They hail from Chettinad in Tamilnadu, South India, and are one of the earliest Indian merchant communities in Singapore. They are also known as the Nagarathars, meaning city dwellers, traders and temple-based people. They are grouped by social definition (such as marriage and adoption) according to nine Siva temples in Chettinad. Their association with the temples and the prefix Nattukottai differentiate the group from other Chettiar communities.

According to A. Ramanathan Chettiar, who compiled the group's history in 1953, the Chettiars first sailed to Penang and Singapore in 1824. They established their businesses, especially money-lending and banking, at Market Street in Singapore.

Besides money-lending, the Chettiars invested heavily in property—some Singapore roads are named after prominent members of the community. These include Arnasalam Chetty Road, Narayanan Chetty Road, Muthuraman Chetty Road and Meyyappa Chettiar Road.

The group's commercial interests were looked after by the Chettiar Chamber of Commerce, established on 18 January 1931, but it could not stop the Chettiars' commercial activities from declining as a result of various factors: laws against money-lending passed between 1930 and 1940; the Japanese Occupation; the introduction of stricter immigration controls; post-1965 independence employment policies; the development of banks and other financial institutions; and the lack of interest on the part of the younger generation in taking up the money-lending business.

Nevertheless, the community is responsible for several important temples in Singapore. One of these is the temple on Tank Road, the Sri Thendayuthapani Temple, dedicated to Lord Murugan. Another is the Sri Layan Sithi Vinayagar Temple at Keong Saik Road. THAIPUSAM is the most important annual festival celebrated at the Tank Road temple. It attracts thousands of devotees and tourists.

At present, there are more than 500 Chettiar families living in Singapore. Only a few Chettiars are involved in the money-lending trade. Others work as professionals in fields such as education, engineering, law, business and medicine. The group continues to contribute significantly to Singapore's economic, cultural and religious development.

nature conservation *See* box.

Nature Society (Singapore) Non-government, non-profit organization. The Nature Society (Singapore) (NSS) is dedicated to the appreciation, conservation and study of the natural heritage of Singapore and the surrounding region. It has a membership of more than 2,000, making it one of Singapore's largest non-government organisations.

Formerly part of the Malayan Nature Society, the Singapore branch was formed in 1954. It became independent in 1991. Run by volunteers, NSS depends financially on contributions from its members, as well as companies, institutions and individuals.

The NSS has 10 sub-groups specializing in birds, butterflies, education, conservation, marine conservation, plant and vertebrate studies. The society organizes nature appreciation activities on a regular basis—including walks, talks and overseas eco-trips for members. It collaborates with many schools and community groups to promote an appreciation of nature.

The society also works closely with government bodies to find a balance between protection of natural habitats and urban development. It has persuaded the government to set aside Sungei Buloh as a

NatSteel: electric arc furnace operated by what is now NatSteel Asia.

mangrove and bird sanctuary. Sungei Buloh is now gazetted as a wetland reserve (*see* SUNGEI BULOH WETLAND RESERVE). Together with other organizations and individuals, the NSS has persuaded the government to delay, for the time being, the reclamation of CHEK JAWA, a unique marine habitat in Pulau Ubin.

See also NATURE CONSERVATION.

Naval Diving Unit Elite team of divers of the REPUBLIC OF SINGAPORE NAVY. Naval Divers specialize in maritime security operations, search and rescue, explosive ordnance disposal and underwater diving operations including mine clearance and salvage. The Naval Diving Unit (NDU) has four arms: the Diving School, the Clearance Diving Group, the Underwater Demolition Group and Combat Divers.

In addition to basic dive training, naval divers undergo a range of courses to hone their specialist skills. The NDU's holistic training programme aims to imbue physical and mental toughness. The unit's training facilities include a deep diving pool, a fully equipped gym, a multi-purpose Confidence Tower and a Hyperbaric Medical Facility. NDU divers also participate in overseas training stints with elite forces such as the US Navy SEALs.

In 1990, the divers cleared 21 World War II bombs in the waters off Pulau Brani. They were also called in to salvage the

Nattukottai Chettiars: moneylenders on Chulia Street, 1987.

Naval Diving Unit

Nee Soon Swamp Forest: swamp forest crab.

wreckage of SilkAir flight MI 185 (*see* MI 185 SILKAIR CRASH) at the Musi River, Sumatra in December 1997. The divers have also contributed their expertise to recent humanitarian and disaster relief programmes such as the tsunami reflief operations in 2005. NDU continues to contribute to the humanitarian relief efforts, and search and boarding security operations in the North Arabian Gulf.

Navarathri Hindu festival. Navarathri stands for 'nine nights' and is dedicated to the Hindu goddess Devi who occurs in three major forms: Durga (representing the destructive aspect), Saraswathi (representing learning and creative arts) and Lakshmi (representing wealth and prosperity). The nine-day festival is observed between mid-September and mid-October in accordance with the Tamil lunar calendar.

The significance of the festival lies in the intricate rituals conducted at a grand scale on all nine days in most Hindu temples in Singapore. The nine days are segmented into groups of three days, each dedicated respectively to Durga, Lakshmi, and Saraswathi. The festival proper actually includes a tenth day known as Vijaya Dasami (Victory Star). This day symbolizes the day when the goddesses gained victory over the demons. The Sri Thendayuthapani Temple on Tank Road, as well as the vari-

Navarathri: presenting offerings at Sri Thendayuthapani Temple on Tank Road, 1991.

ous temples dedicated to the goddess Sri Mariamman, celebrate this festival on a grand scale. While the level of intricacy of rites and rituals may differ according to the different temples, one common ritual occurs on the tenth day, where there is the shooting of arrows from the bow that has been part of the Saraswathi ritual.

Necessary Stage, The Arts company. The Necessary Stage (TNS) was officially identified as one of four major arts companies by virtue of a two-year grant from the NATIONAL ARTS COUNCIL starting in 2000. It was founded in 1987 by director ALVIN TAN and playwright HARESH SHARMA to produce indigenous, original, socially engaged theatre. They developed a process of research and improvisation as the basis for script and direction, resulting in finely-nuanced multi-lingual plays in which pathos, comedy and alienation are deployed in rapid succession. Staging tended to be minimal.

In 1994, a *Straits Times* article attributed a political agenda to TNS, citing Tan's and Sharma's participation in the Brecht Forum workshops in New York. Tan and Sharma responded to the article by stating that they attend many workshops with the aim of improving as theatre practitioners and have no political motivations.

TNS has toured extensively and has presented work by foreign companies, culminating in the annual multi-disciplinary Fringe Festival. It has presented over 60 original works in under twenty years, including *Lanterns Never Go Out* (1989), in which a teenage girl grapples with roles and expectations; *Off Centre* (1993), which studies the friendship of two former mental patients; and *godeatgod* (2002), a response to the attacks of 9/11.

Nee Soon Swamp Forest Singapore's last permanently flooded freshwater swamp forest. The swamp is protected as a Nature Reserve and is managed by the Nature Reserves Board. Part of the reserve has been declared a Protected Area by the military for training purposes. Public access is restricted due to its proximity to a military live-firing range.

The swamp forms part of the catchment area for the public reservoir system in the centre of the island. It is fed by rainfall and drainage from nearby hills. Much of the five square kilometres of swamp forest catchment area is secondary scrub, hills and non-swamp forests. The actual swamp and pristine aquatic habitat occupy less than 0.5 square kilometres, making it a very vulnerable habitat.

Trees of the swamp forest usually have unmistakable stilt roots growing from the trunk. Stilt roots are also common among species of palm and ginger. Many other trees typical of swamp forests have cylindrical boles without buttresses or stilts, such as most of the soursop (*Annonaceae*), cinnamon (*Lauraceae*), and mangosteen (*Calophyllum*)

families. Some species may feature buttresses and air-breathing roots. However, most of the vegetation here is secondary forest, and typical sun-loving trees of this forest type, like the *petai* (*Parkia speciosa*) and *terentang* (*Campnosperma auriculata*), can be seen. Highly endangered plants can be found too, such as the herbaceous, water-loving Griffiths cryptocoryne (*Cryptocoryne griffithii*), which only grows in slow forest streams in Nee Soon and Bukit Timah.

Nee Soon Swamp's distinctive vegetation is particularly valuable because it has the highest concentration of native freshwater flora and fauna in Singapore, especially fish and crustaceans. Native freshwater fish such as the endangered jewel-like pygmy rasbora (*Rasbora maculata*) live in the swamp's mildly acidic water. Another fish, the Harlequin rasbora (*Rasbora heteromorpha*), is a favourite of the aquarium trade. The fish now lives only in some streams in Nee Soon and the Central Catchment forest. Another attractive resident is the six-banded tiger barb (*Puntius johorensis*). Unfortuntely, it is threatened by poachers. Scientists discovered the spotted coolie loach (*Pangio muraeniformis*) in Nee Soon Swamp Forest in 1933. The forest halfbeak (*Hemirhamphodon pogonognathus*), a colourful fish with a fleshy appendage at the end of its lower jaw, and the dwarf snakehead (*Channa gachua*), the smallest and prettiest of all snakeheads, are endangered species here.

Nee Soon Swamp Forest is also refuge to the last of Singapore's giant squirrels (*Ratufa affinis*), one of the largest squirrels in the world. These squirrels live in the canopies of tall trees, feeding mainly on fruit, and seldom come to the ground. First discovered by Sir STAMFORD RAFFLES in 1819, it was seen at BUKIT TIMAH NATURE RESERVE and the Central Catchment forests until 1987. Fewer than ten of these squirrels survive today, with rare sightings reported in Nee Soon Swamp Forest over the last 20 years.

The last remaining population of fewer than 20 banded leaf monkeys (*Presbytis femoralis*) also lives in this small forest. This population is a distinct sub-species, *P. f. femoralis*, known only in Singapore.

Although small, this forested area continues to surprise. A new species of freshwater crab was described by local zoologist Dr Peter K.L. Ng in 1990. The swamp forest crab (*Parathelphusa reticulata*) is found only

The Necessary Stage: **Boxing Day, The Tsunami Project, 2005.**

in a small part of the forest. There is evidence that water is draining from Nee Soon Swamp Forest faster than previously realized, which could threaten the flora and fauna there.

Neo, Jack (1960–) Comedian, actor and film director. Jack Neo Chee Keong first became a household name in Singapore after playing the character of *Liang Po Po* (Grandmother Liang) on the television variety show *Gao Xiao Xing Dong* (Comedy Nite). His first film appearance was in ERIC KHOO's *12 Storeys*. He then wrote and starred in the film MONEY NO ENOUGH (1998) before bringing the character of Grandmother Liang back to life in *Liang Po Po, The Movie* (1999).

Neo's directorial debut came with *That One No Enough* (1999), which dealt with love, sex and marriage. This was followed by I NOT STUPID (2002), arguably Neo's most popular film. Subsequent films included *Homerun* (2003)—a remake of the 1997 Iranian film *Children of Heaven*—which was banned by the Malaysian government due to its allusions to Singapore-Malaysia relations; *The Best Bet* (2004), which concerned gambling; and *One More Chance* (2005), a film about ex-convicts trying to find their place in society. Many of Neo's films have been praised as timely critiques of Singapore society, with scripts rich in local colloquialisms and Chinese dialects.

Neo was awarded the Public Service Medal in 2004 and the CULTURAL MEDALLION in 2005.

Neo Chwee Kok (1931–1986) Sportsman. This star swimmer, also known as 'Flying Fish' and 'Boy Marvel', was the fifth child in a family of eight. He learned to swim competitively at the age of 18 at the Chinese Swimming Club in 1949 under coaches Koay Teck Choo and Kee Soon Bee.

At the inaugural Asian Games in New Delhi in 1951, Neo won four gold medals. These were in the 400 m (5:13.8), 800 m (11:02.2), 1500 m (21:43.6) and the 4x100 m relay (4:19.8) with Lionel Chee, Wiebe Wolters, and Barry Mitchell. Three of these wins set new records.

His triumphs in New Delhi led to proposals to reward him with a new watch, but this caused consternation among traditionalists in Singapore, who supported strict amateur principles.

Neo was the first Singapore swimmer to compete in the Olympics, and was considered one of Singapore's best bets for an Olympic medal—his 58.8 second best for the 100-metre freestyle event being close to the Olympic record of 58.7. However, he failed to win a medal at the 1952 Olympics in Helsinki.

At the 1954 Asian Games, he claimed a bronze in the 100-m freestyle with a time of 58.2 seconds. His most memorable event was a narrow defeat at the hands of world champion, Jon Henricks of Australia. In this battle, Neo established a new national record.

Neo turned professional unintentionally: he was working as a pool superintendent and was deemed to have lost the amateur status that would have allowed him to compete in the Melbourne Olympics. He turned to coaching younger generations of swimmers. Neo has been inducted into the SINGAPORE SPORTS COUNCIL HALL OF FAME.

Neo Swee Lin (1962–) Actress. Neo Swee Lin graduated with a law degree from the National University of Singapore in 1986, but eschewed legal practice for a career in acting. In 1990, she won a British American Tobacco (BAT) Arts Scholarship to study at the Royal Scottish Academy of Music and Drama.

Neo has taken on more than 40 theatre, film and television roles in Singapore, Malaysia, India, the United Kingdom, Croatia and the United States. Among her noted international appearances have been roles in the film *Anna and the King* and the musical *Chang and Eng*.

Neo became well known locally as Ah Ma—a character she played in the local sitcom PHUA CHU KANG. She won Best Actress at the Asian Television Awards (1999) for her performance in this role. She is married to fellow actor LIM KAY SIU.

Neptune Orient Lines Global transportation company. The Neptune Orient Lines (NOL) Group started as Singapore's national shipping line in December 1968. It operated out of a small office in the Fullerton Building with a fledging fleet of just five vessels.

By the 1970s, an era marked by the move to containerized cargo, NOL's fleet had grown to 20. It started earning its first profits in 1972 under managing director GOH CHOK TONG. NOL was the first company to offer a containerized service from Asia to Australia in 1975. The company entered the Asia-Europe trade in 1976 as part of the ACE liner consortium with partners Orient Overseas Container Line and K Line. In 1978, it launched its trans-Pacific service. Intra-Asia feeder routes were added in the 1980s.

NOL became the first wholly owned government company to be publicly listed on the Singapore stock exchange in 1981. It moved into its current global headquarters, the NOL Building, in 1983. It diversified into the lightering business with oil and petroleum product tankers in the early 1990s.

In November 1997, it acquired America's oldest shipping company, American President Lines (APL), for US$825 million. This gave it the critical mass needed to expand and compete globally—APL was nearly twice the size of NOL and had a 149-year history. The deal, the largest in Singapore history then, created one of the world's top five global liner groups with revenues exceeding US$4 billion. The acquisi-

tion also brought with it key terminal hubs in Asia and North America, along with a valuable inter-modal transport network in the United States that included ocean, rail and terminal operations.

The capability of the company's supply chain management became an area of increasing focus, and APL Logistics was established as a separate business unit in 2001. In 2003, the product tankering business was divested, allowing NOL to concentrate on core liner and logistics services.

The group has emerged as one of the world's largest container shipping conglomerates, employing about 11,000 staff globally. Its core divisions, APL and APL Logistics, are leaders in the global container transportation industry.

The group posted a net profit of $1.3 billion on a turnover of $12 billion in financial year 2005. As of 2005, NOL operated a fleet of more than 100 vessels with services to more than 140 countries in Asia, Europe, the Middle East, and North and South America.

NOL stock is a component of the Straits Times Index. The Singapore government investment arm, TEMASEK HOLDINGS, holds the largest share of the company at 69 per cent.

Neptune Theatre Restaurant The two-storey club, with capacity for 1,500 diners, is one of two nightclubs in Singapore licensed to feature topless revues. It started with its own Neptune Dance Revue, the only local troupe then. Topless shows came in 1987 to address falling patronage. Two nightly shows by foreign troupes entertain both diners and non-diners.

The size of the club makes it popular for events such as dance competitions, formal dinners, beauty pageants and concerts. It is located in Collyer Quay.

NETS Abbreviation of Network for Electronic Transfers. Leading electronic payments provider. Consumers have been able to make cashless payments at retail outlets in Singapore with ATM cards since January 1986 through NETS. It operates

Jack Neo

Neo Chwee Kok

Neo Swee Lin: 'Ah Ma' persona in Phua Chu Kang.

Neptune Theatre Restaurant performance, 1976.

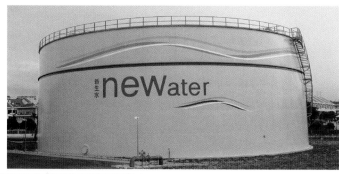

NEWater: the Seletar plant.

The New Nation

The New Paper

the main Electronic Funds Transfer at Point of Sale system and is accepted at over 12,000 retail outlets throughout the island.

Additionally, the NETS cashcard—a multi-purpose stored-value card most commonly used for Electronic Road Pricing payments and car park fees—can be used virtually island-wide for a variety of minor transactions. Over six million cashcards have been issued.

New Creation Church This independent 'charismatic' church is one of the three biggest churches in Singapore. It was registered in 1984 when it had an average attendance of 25. The church grew slowly in its early years, reaching 150 members in 1990. That year, the church appointed Joseph Prince as senior pastor.

Church membership has since grown tremendously. By 2005, it had 12,000 members and 84 full-time staff. In the first months of 2005, it averaged a weekly attendance of 11,844 at its various Sunday services. After years of holding Sunday services in small auditoriums, it now holds them at the Rock Auditorium at Suntec City.

There was some controvesy when the church bought the 21,000 sq m East Coast Recreational Centre for $10 million through its business unit, Rock Productions. After permission to build a church there was denied, a resort-style family attraction called Marine Cove, open to the public, was developed. The church regards it as an investment towards its future premises.

New Nation, The English-language newspaper. *The New Nation* began its life as an daily afternoon broadsheet on 18 January 1971, under the joint ownership of the Straits Times Press and the *Melbourne Herald* of Australia. It was set up to compete with the SINGAPORE HERALD, which appeared for a short time in the early 1970s.

Designed originally as a quality paper, stressing news features rather than news articles, it had greater intellectual appeal than THE STRAITS TIMES. Although popular for a while, it soon became clear that the reading public was not ready for serious reading of this kind. The paper became a tabloid and swung to the other extreme: it went 'soccer-mad', cashing in on Singaporeans' craze for coverage of the Malaysia Cup matches in the 1970s.

It later tried to strike a better balance in its strategy to increase readership, and was succeeding—until management decided to fold it in 1982 to make way for THE SINGAPORE MONITOR.

This was an unusual move involving the then two rival newspaper groups, Singapore News and Publications Ltd (SNPL) and the Straits Times Press group. The *New Nation* masthead was handed over to SNPL to help it launch its newspaper, *The Singapore Monitor. The Singapore Monitor* existed initially as *The New Nation* before assuming its own name.

New Paper, The English-language afternoon tabloid owned by SINGAPORE PRESS HOLDINGS (SPH). *The New Paper* (TNP) was launched on 26 July 1988 to fill a market vacuum created by the exit of *The Singapore Monitor* in 1985, which failed even after being helped by the closure of the NEW NATION.

Recognizing the keen competition coming from the Internet, cable television and elsewhere, TNP adopted the 'soundbite' approach—complete with colourful graphics—to meet the needs of a young, busy readership. It presents complex issues in a simplified, easy-to-read manner, along with lively sports and entertainment sections.

The tabloid is also well-known for organizing *The New Paper* Big Walk, a sponsored annual mass-fitness event which won a place in the 2000 *Guinness Book of Records* as the largest of its kind in the world.

New Strait In 1585, the Sultan of Johor sank a number of junks in the VARELLA CHANNEL to prevent Portuguese ships from using it. The Portuguese en route to Malacca from the South China Sea then discovered another passage in 1586—the New Strait.

Also called the Channel of Santa Barbara, it runs from Sisters Fairway, south of present-day Sentosa Island, and turns north of St John's Island onto the East Keppel Fairway. It was wider and deeper than the Varella Channel, and therefore an easier passage around Singapore.

New World Amusement park. The first of three 'worlds', the New World Amusement Park at Kitchener Road was opened in 1923 by prominent Peranakan merchant Ong Boon Tat and his younger brother Ong Peng Hock. It soon established a reputation for a vibrant carnival atmosphere, boxing and wrestling matches, and the best opera in Malaya—New World's City Opera. A year after opening, New World started showing Singapore's first open-air talking shows with first-run films.

After opening its first public cabaret in 1929, New World maintained its status for having the youngest cabaret girls, both local and foreign. It was also famous for ROSE CHAN, who would become known as the

'Queen of Striptease'. Among her dance routines was one involving a python entwined around her lithe frame.

New World, together with the other two 'worlds'—GREAT WORLD and Happy World (later renamed GAY WORLD)—went into slow decline from the 1950s. New World closed in the mid-1980s.

NEWater NEWater is used water that has been treated and purified through advanced dual-membrane and ultraviolet technologies.

In 1998, the Public Utilities Board (PUB) and the Ministry of the Environment and Water Resources initiated the Singapore Water Reclamation Study (NEWater Study), to determine the viability of NEWater as a source of raw water to enhance Singapore's water supply. NEWater can be mixed and blended with reservoir water, and treated conventionally to produce drinking water. NEWater can also be used to produce non-potable water to supplement water for manufacturing processes and industries.

NEWater factories at the Bedok and Kranji Water Reclamation Plants have been in commission since late 2002. PUB has been mixing and blending NEWater with raw water in RESERVOIRS since September 2002. Almost 14,000 cubic m (3 million gallons) of NEWater goes into Singapore's raw water reservoirs daily. This is about 1 per cent of water used daily. The amount will be increased to about 2.5 per cent of total daily water consumption by 2011.

Since February 2003, NEWater has also been supplied to wafer fabrication plants at Woodlands and Tampines/Pasir Ris, and other industries for non-potable use.

New World: Jalan Besar entrance, c. 1950 (top); Kitchener Road entrance, c. 1950.

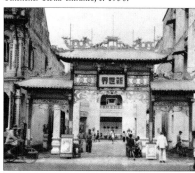

In January 2004, a third NEWater factory at the Seletar Water Reclamation Plant began supplying NEWater to the wafer fabrication plants at Ang Mo Kio.

Together, the three NEWater factories produce 92,000 cubic m or 20 million gallons of water per day.

newspapers Newspapers have been published in Singapore since 1824, when the English-language SINGAPORE CHRONICLE was launched as a medium for official notices and information on trade and shipping. The history of Singapore's newspapers reflects the country's linguistic diversity and also the growing use of English.

Singapore's leading newspaper is the English-language daily, THE STRAITS TIMES (and its Sunday edition *The Sunday Times*). It had an average daily circulation of more than 386,000 (and more than 392,000 for *The Sunday Times*) in 2005. The other English papers are THE NEW PAPER, THE BUSINESS TIMES and TODAY. English-language papers accounted for 64 per cent of Singapore newspapers circulated daily in 2003.

Chinese newspaper publishing started with LAT PAU in 1881. This newspaper lasted 52 years. The main Chinese daily today is LIANHE ZAOBAO, averaging a daily circulation of 181,000 (and over 193,000 for its Sunday edition) in 2005. LIANHE WANBAO and SHIN MIN DAILY NEWS are the other local Chinese papers.

The Malay-language BERITA HARIAN (and its Sunday paper *Berita Minggu*), sold around 60,000 copies a day in 2004. The Tamil-language TAMIL MURASU had weekday sales of almost 9,000, with Sunday circulation exceeding 15,000. Together, Malay and Tamil newspapers account for four per cent of total newspaper circulation.

The publicly listed SINGAPORE PRESS HOLDINGS (SPH) publishes all of Singapore's daily newspaper titles, except *Today*. *Today* is a free newspaper published by MEDIACORP Press, a government-owned company in which SPH has a 40 per cent stake.

Newspapers' editorial direction and social roles have changed over the decades, affected by both global media trends and socio-political shifts within Singapore. From the start, Singapore newspapers imported publishing conventions, as well as editors and journalists, from Britain, India and elsewhere. This gave them a physical appearance and mix of content similar to other newspapers around the world.

Newspapers in recent decades have become less explicitly ideological and more commercially driven than they were before independent Singapore. Then, it was not uncommon for a newspaper to be published at a financial loss in the service of the publisher's political cause.

The main shift in Singapore's press history has been the alignment of newspapers with the nation-building mission of the People's Action Party (PAP). Before PAP rule, newspapers were disparate in their loyalties, reflecting Singapore's status as an immigrant settlement with no vision of a united, independent nationhood.

Chinese-language newspapers, for example, were more caught up with the politics of China than the fate of Singapore. *The Straits Times* had just begun to localize its editorial leadership and remained tied to British-dominated commercial interests. Newspapers addressed their respective communities without much concern for multicultural understanding. The most cited example of this in Singapore's press history is probably the MARIA HERTOGH RIOTS of 1950, in which ethnic rioting was catalyzed partly by insensitive reporting of a controversial custody battle.

After independence in 1965, the PAP focused the press on creating a sense of nationhood among Singaporeans. The government also intervened to ensure representation for Singapore's official languages. When declining readership threatened the viability of Chinese newspapers, the government engineered their merger with the highly-profitable *Straits Times* group, resulting in the creation of SPH. SPH later took over the ailing *Tamil Murasu*.

The PAP believes that the press should not undermine an elected government's ability to set the national agenda. Local newspapers are licensed, and this has resulted in charges from some quarters that local newspapers fail to reflect the full range of political debate (*see* PRESS FREEDOM).

While not averse to using laws to influence the editorial direction of the press, the state has not nationalized newspapers either. The editors of mainstream newspapers maintain that they are primarily pro-Singapore, and that they support the PAP government only to the extent that it serves Singapore's interests. However, their uniform closeness to government remains controversial. Newspapers in Singapore are generally well-managed, priding themselves on offering accurate and comprehensive coverage, attractive design, and good printing.

In addition to the local press, several foreign and regional newspapers are easily available in Singapore. Around 30 such newspapers and news periodicals are printed in the country, including *The Asian Wall Street Journal*, *Financial Times* and *International Herald Tribune*. Media companies also use Singapore as a hub for their news-gathering operations.

While most cities have a wide range of non-mainstream publications, Singapore's alternative press is relatively limited, due partly to laws that require every publication—including newsletters released at irregular intervals—to obtain a government licence.

The longest-running opposition party paper is *The Hammer*, published three times

Newspapers: vendor outside Bedok MRT station.

a year by the WORKERS' PARTY. Campus newspapers include Nanyang Technological University's *Nanyang Chronicle* and Ngee Ann Polytechnic's *Tribune*. An independent current affairs newspaper for children, *What's Up*, has been published monthly since 2003.

Newer media and communication technologies have changed the reach and role of newspapers. Radio and television are now frequently the people's first source of news, prompting newspapers to provide more interpretation, analysis and opinion. The Internet has enabled the exchange of more diverse opinion, bypassing newspaper editors who act as gatekeepers to the public sphere. However, early predictions of newspapers' demise have proven to be off the mark.

While television and online audiences are highly fragmented, newspapers' continued ability to reach a mass audience makes them a key medium for advertisers. The resulting revenues support resources for operations on a scale that other media cannot match. Newspapers, therefore, continue to employ the bulk of full-time journalists in Singapore, and remain highly influential as political and cultural media.

In 2005, there were nine Singapore newspapers, publishing at least five days a week. Total daily newspaper circulation, as a percentage of the total population, rose from 31.1 per cent in 1993 to 40.8 per cent in 2003, when it averaged 1.7 million copies.

Newton Food Centre Hawker centres were built when the government decided, in the early 1970s, to relocate itinerant street food hawkers around the island and re-site them in a fixed location. Called hawker centres, they were basically huge roofed sheds housing small individual stalls provided with clean water, electricity and sanitation. Built in the early 1970s, Newton Hawker Centre shot to fame when the legendary Orchard Gluttons Square push-cart hawkers on Orchard Road had to make way for urban redevelopment in 1979. Some of the hawkers were relocated to Newton.

Located next to the Newton MRT

Newton Food Centre: reopened after upgrading, 2006

Ng Eng Hen

Ng Teng Fong

Vincent Ng

Ng Liang Chiang

train station, it is a collection of about 80 hawkers selling all sorts of Indian, Malay and Chinese hawker food in an environment shaded by giant angsana trees. Grilled seafood is especially popular at Newton. It underwent a $4.8 million facelift in 2005 and re-opened in July 2006 to much fanfare.

Ng, Vincent (1975–) Sportsman and actor. Vincent Ng Cheng Hye is a *wushu* champion who won his first South East Asian Games gold medal in Singapore in 1993 when he was 18 years old. In that same year, he won the silver in cudgel and a bronze in swordplay at the biennial World Championships.

In 1995, Ng gave a gold-winning performance in broadsword at the World Championships, picking up a bronze in the cudgel as well. He also won the Coca Cola/The Sunday Times Sports Annual Award that year. In 1997, he won two more SEA Games gold medals in Jakarta and a silver medal in *changquan,* a form of shadow boxing, at the World Championships in Rome. It was his first medal in *changquan.*

After winning another gold medal in broadsword that year, Ng gave up *wushu* for acting. He emerged as a finalist in a TELEVISION CORPORATION OF SINGAPORE Star Search competition in 1997. Now a MEDIACORP actor, he is also a promoter of Chinese culture.

Ng Eng Hen (1958–) Politician. Ng Eng Hen was educated at Anglo-Chinese School, the National Junior College and obtained his medical degrees from the National University of Singapore. He trained at the MD Anderson Cancer Centre, University of Texas (surgical oncology fellow) and the New York Hospital–Cornell Medical Center (research fellow). He is a fellow of the Royal College of Surgeons of Edinburgh and the American Societies of Surgical and Clinical Oncology.

Ng entered politics on the People's Action Party ticket in 2001 and won a seat in the Bishan-Toa Payoh group representation constituency, a seat to which he was returned unopposed in 2006. In 2002, he was appointed minister of state for education (2002–04) and manpower (2002–03).

Ng subsequently became acting minister for manpower (2003–04) and was promoted to full minister for manpower (2004–), second education minister (2004–05) and second defence minister (2005–).

Ng Eng Teng (1934–2001) Sculptor. Ng Eng Teng studied at the Nanyang Academy of Fine Arts in the late 1950s. He continued his education at the North Staffordshire College of Technology and Farnham School of Art in the United Kingdom.

Ng is known for his inventive human forms and sensitive public art installations. At his peak, Ng worked in clay, *ciment fondu,* pigments, bronze casting and steel forging. Ng's sculptures, such as the *Mother & Child* opposite Liat Towers, as well as *Balance* for the ASEAN SCULPTURE GARDEN in Fort Canning, reveal his fascination with basic geometric forms and their symbolic values. He was awarded the CULTURAL MEDALLION in 1981.

Ng Jui Ping, Lieutenant-General (1948–) Military officer. Ng Jui Ping studied at Tanjong Rhu Boys' School, Charlton School and Raffles Institution. He was among the first recruits to join the School of Artillery's Basic Artillery Officers Course in 1967. Ng later travelled to the United States to study at Duke University, where he obtained a master's degree in history.

On returning to Singapore, Ng rose through the ranks of the SINGAPORE ARMED FORCES (SAF) to become chief of army from 1990 to 1992. Ng became chief of defence in 1992, after Lieutenant-General Winston Choo stepped down from that position.

In 1995, Ng retired from the military. He was appointed deputy chairman of the CENTRAL PROVIDENT FUND Board and chairman of Chartered Industries of Singapore. He also served in the Singapore Technologies Group. He was awarded the Public Administration Medal (Gold) (Military) in 1991 and the MERITORIOUS SERVICE MEDAL (Military) in 1995.

Ng Liang Chiang (1921–1992) Sportsman. Ng Liang Chiang's first international success in hurdling came when he broke the All-China Record for the

Ng Eng Teng: **Sitting Pretty,** *1990.*

110-m and 400-m hurdles at the 7th Annual China National Athletics Meet in Shanghai in 1948. He had in fact planned to represent Nationalist China at the 1948 Olympics in London, but failed to record a competitive time during the heats after suffering from an infected tooth. Two years later, Ng represented Singapore at the British Empire Games (what later became the Commonwealth Games) in Auckland, where he was again unplaced. In 1951, Ng won Singapore's first Asian Games gold medal when he won the 110-m hurdles at New Delhi. Ng retired from competitive hurdling in 1954, and turned to coaching. He died of lung cancer at the age of 71.

Ng Teng Fong (1928–) Businessman. The China-born real-estate tycoon and founder of FAR EAST ORGANIZATION came to Singapore as a young child. Ng's first foray into business was the opening of a provision store, which failed to do well. In 1962, he ventured into the property market and succeeded spectacularly.

By the 1980s, Ng, with Far East Organization, had become the largest private landowner and developer in Singapore. Through Lucky Realty, the nucleus of Far East Organization, he owned and developed one-fifth of all private property projects in Singapore. Overseas, he began making his mark in the Hong Kong property market in the 1970s, with his Sino Group of Companies.

Since the 1990s, Ng's eldest son, Robert, has been in charge of the family's interests in Hong Kong. His youngest son, Philip, runs his Singapore ventures. Ng was named Singapore's richest man—with assets of US$3.8 billion—in *Forbes'* 2006 Billionaires List.

Ngee Ann City Shopping centre and office complex. Ngee Ann City was opened as the largest shopping mall in the Orchard Road area on 21 September 1993 by then Prime Minister GOH CHOK TONG. The complex was built on an area originally known as Tai Shan Ting, bounded by Orchard, Paterson and Grange Roads. Tai Shan Ting had originally been one of several burial grounds managed by the Ngee Ann Kongsi—a TEOCHEW association. The cemetery was cleared in 1957, and parts of the site were leased to the Mandarin Hotel, Cathay Cineleisure Orchard and Wisma Atria. Where Ngee Ann City now stands, the ten-storey Ngee Ann Building stood for many years.

Ngee Ann City was built at a cost of $520 million as a joint project between Ngee Ann Development and Orchard Square Development Corporation. Ngee Ann Development had been formed in 1988 through a joint venture between the Ngee Ann Kongsi and the Takashimaya Company of Japan. Takashimaya department store became the main tenant at Ngee Ann City.

At completion, Ngee Ann City covered 110,450 sq m of retail space, with some 130 specialty shops and 30 restaurants. The project also included two office towers.

Ngee Ann Kongsi *See* TEOCHEW POIT IP HUAY KUAN.

Ngee Ann Polytechnic Set up by Ngee Ann Kongsi as Ngee Ann College on 25 May 1963, it was located at Teochew Building on Tank Road. The college offered four-year courses in three main areas: language, commerce and technology. It later changed its name to Ngee Ann Technical College, before taking on its current name in 1982. The tertiary institution has 14 academic departments and more than 20 fields of study. Some 14,300 full-time and 5,400 part-time students attend classes at the 36-ha campus in Clementi.

Ngee Ann Primary First Chinese girls' school in Singapore, now a government-aided primary school for girls and boys. It was founded as the Ngee Ann Girls School in 1940 and subsidized by Ngee Ann Kongsi, a TEOCHEW organization.

The school was set up in a bungalow owned by a member of the Ngee Ann Kongsi in River Valley Road. This is now the headquarters of the Teochew Clan Association. In 1967, the school began accepting male students. In 1980, it took on its current name. Two years later, the school moved to Marine Parade.

Ngiam Tong Dow (1937–) Civil servant. Ngiam Tong Dow was educated at St Andrew's School and the University of Malaya in Singapore, where he obtained first class honours in economics (1959). In 1964, he attended Harvard University's Master in Public Administration course.

Ngiam joined the Administrative Service in 1959 and became permanent secretary of the Ministry of Communications by the age of 33. He then

Ngee Ann City

went on to serve as permanent secretary at the Ministries of Finance (1972–79 and 1987–99); Trade and Industry (1979–86); National Development (1987–89); and at the Prime Minister's Office (1979–94).

Ngiam was also chairman of the Singapore Telephone Board, the Economic Development Board, Telecommunications Authority of Singapore, Sentosa Development Corporation, Singapore Technologies Holdings Pte Ltd, DBS, and the Housing & Development Board.

Ngiam was awarded the MERITORIOUS SERVICE MEDAL (1978) and was admitted into the DISTINGUISHED SERVICE ORDER (1999). He retired from the civil service in 1999. In recent years, Ngiam has often articulated alternative views, including criticism of the civil service, through the local media. These views have been published in a collection entitled *A Mandarin and the Making of Public Policy* (2006).

Nicoll, Sir John (1899–1981) Colonial official. John Fearns Nicoll succeeded Sir FRANKLIN GIMSON as governor of Singapore in 1952. Nicholl was governor until 1955.

In 1953, the PROGRESSIVE PARTY (PP) announced that it would seek to achieve self-government for Singapore within ten years. Nicoll favoured the PP, as he believed that it represented the possibility of stable transition to self-government without disturbance to the economy. Recognizing that the CONSTITUTION of 1948 did not satisfy the Chinese community, Nicoll believed that more challenging opportunities needed to be provided in central and local government in order to encourage people to support the idea of self-government.

In 1953, the RENDEL COMMISSION was formed to decide what form self-government would take. However, Nicoll was succeeded as governor by Sir ROBERT BROWN BLACK in 1954, before the new constitution drawn up by the commission could be implemented.

Nicoll can be credited with promoting restoration work on many of Singapore's public buildings in the post-war period. Nicoll Highway was named after him.

Nicoll Highway collapse At about 3.30 p.m. on 20 April 2004, a section of a MASS RAPID TRANSIT (MRT) tunnel being built underneath Nicoll Highway collapsed. The tunnel formed part of the Circle Line project. The cave-in resulted in a hole 150 metres in width, 100 metres in length and 30 metres in depth, cutting across six lanes of the Nicoll Highway.

The collapse claimed the lives of four persons: Vadivil Nadeson, a crane operator; Liu Rong Quan, a construction worker; John Tan Lock Yong, a Land Transport Authority (LTA) engineer; and Heng Yeow Peow, a foreman. Three others were also injured. Repairs to the tunnel and the highway took eight months.

Nicoll Highway collapse

Investigations revealed that the probable cause of the collapse was the failure of a retaining wall built to hold up the tunnel. An inquiry found the main contractor, Nishimatsu Construction Co., and its officers, as well as several LTA officers, responsible for the collapse. Nishimatsu was fined $200,000 for failing to ensure that the worksite was safe, while Ng Seng Yoong, a former project director of the MRT's Circle Line, was fined $8,000 for negligence. Three senior executives of Nishimatsu were also given fines ranging from $120,000 to $160,000.

Night Safari Tourist attraction. Ninety per cent of tropical animals are nocturnal and are most active after dark. The Night Safari at Mandai Lake Road exhibits the nocturnal behaviour of over 1,000 animals of 130 species, many of which are endangered. The animals live in surroundings that closely simulate their natural habitats, and where mostly natural barriers separate them from human visitors.

Contained in a 40-ha site of lush secondary jungle next to the SINGAPORE ZOO, the Night Safari has become one of Singapore's most successful attractions since its opening in 1994, drawing around 1 million visitors each year.

Nine Emperor Gods festival This Chinese religious festival is celebrated by followers of TAOISM and CHINESE RELIGION in honour of the Nine Emperor Gods, who are believed to descend to earth for nine days, beginning on the first day of the ninth

Sir John Nicoll

Night Safari

Nine Emperor Gods festival: devotees from Leong Nam Temple carrying sedan chair.

lunar month, to cure ailments and to bestow good fortune, spiritual guidance and assistance to their devotees.

The festivities were traditionally held in temple compounds, but increasingly, in order to accommodate the large numbers of worshippers, the celebrations are also held in large open spaces in housing estates. TOU MU KUNG Temple at Upper Serangoon Road is one of the more well-known venues for the celebration of the festival.

On the night before the festival, temple priests and mediums as well as devotees gather to receive the Nine Emperor Gods at a river or the seaside as the gods are believed to travel along waterways. The spirits of the gods are then escorted to the temple by the *lor chu*, or incense urn bearer, and the attendants in a grand procession.

During the celebration itself, priests chant prayers and mediums write charms in blood, Hokkien opera is performed for the gods and vegetarian offerings are presented. Devotees burn incense, candles and joss paper. Those who approach the altars observe strictures such as a white attire, vegetarian diet and abstention from alcohol, sexual intercourse and profanity. At the climax of the festival, the gods are paraded on sedan chairs and a grand dinner is thrown, during which devotees bid for auspicious items at an auction. The violent rockings of the sedan chairs are believed to be doings of the gods which have possessed the chairs and their carriers. Fire-walking was also once practised on the last day of the festival. On the ninth night, the gods are escorted back to the waterway.

Nishimura Takuma, Lieutenant-General

(1899–1951) Japanese military officer. Nishimura was the commander of the Imperial Guards Division, one of three Japanese divisions that captured Singapore in 1942. He was tried in Singapore in 1947 for the division's role in the SOOK CHING massacre and sentenced to life imprisonment. In 1951, he was ordered to be sent to Australia to stand trial for the beheading of some 200 Australian and Indian Army prisoners captured in Muar in 1942. He was convicted and hanged in 1951.

Nolli, Cavalieri Rodolfo

(1888–1963) Sculptor. Cavalieri Rodolfo Nolli was born into a family of artists in Milan in 1888. He trained as an apprentice sculptor. In 1913,

Nolli followed his uncle, his cousin and a group of Italian artists to Bangkok, where they had been commissioned to decorate the new Throne Hall for the King of Siam (present-day Thailand). After completing his commission, Nolli remained in Bangkok to lecture at Chulalongkorn University.

In 1921, Nolli moved to Singapore, where he was appointed to produce external ornamental stonework for the new Mansfield Building. Nolli soon found himself to be in high demand, and opened a home studio at 47 Scotts Road. He specialized in stone-like claddings and pre-cast concrete columns, and for the following 15 years was responsible for most of the faux stonework adorning many of public buildings. The most important building was the SUPREME COURT BUILDING. Others included the Fullerton Building, City Hall, the Bank of China, the College of Medicine building and the Tanjong Pagar Railway Station. One of his most famous works was the 13-tonne panel resting atop the pediment of the old Supreme Court building.

During World War II, Nolli was interned as an enemy alien in Australia. However, he returned to Singapore to resume his work after the war.

nominated member of Parliament

A non-elected member appointed by the President to provide a wider representation of independent and non-partisan views in the House. The nominated member of Parliament (NMP) scheme is seen as a 'logical progression' of the NON-CONSTITUENCY MEMBER OF PARLIAMENT scheme. It is meant to fulfil the PEOPLE'S ACTION PARTY'S (PAP) 1984 election promise to 'systematically create more opportunities for Singaporeans to participate actively in shaping their future'. In moving the bill, then First Deputy Prime Minister GOH CHOK TONG argued that opposition members did not 'adequately express significant alternative views' held outside Parliament. He lamented the fact that the PAP was unable to attract a greater number of talented individuals into politics, and pointed out that the new scheme would allow the appointment of such individuals.

The Bill was passed in spite of strong opposition from a number of PAP backbenchers. As a compromise, a 'sunset clause' was included in the legislation. Each new Parliament may decide whether or not any NMP would be appointed. In 1990, even though up to six NMPs would have been allowed under the new constitutional provisions, Parliament decided to nominate just two NMPs: businessman Leong Chee Whye, and cardiologist Maurice Choo. They were appointed NMPs in December 1990. Parliament dissolved within a year and a half of their appointment.

Following the PAP's victory in the 1997 general election, Prime Minister Goh Chok Tong stated that he wanted to 'build

up' the NMP scheme in order to ensure a high quality of parliamentary debate in the House. Later that year, the CONSTITUTION was amended to increase the total number of NMPs from six to nine.

Section 3(2) of the new Fourth Schedule of the Constitution gives a Special Select Committee the responsibility of selecting nominees who 'shall be persons who have rendered distinguished public service, or who have brought honour to the Republic, or who have distinguished themselves in the field of arts and letters, culture and sciences, business, industry, the professions, social or community service or the labour movement; and in making any nomination, the Special Select Committee shall have regard to the need for nominated members to reflect as wide a range of independent and non-partisan views as possible'.

non-constituency member of Parliament

The non-constituency member of Parliament (NCMP) scheme was introduced just before the 1984 general election to ensure that there would always be a number of opposition MEMBERS OF PARLIAMENT. If there are less than three elected opposition members, the highest-scoring opposition candidates among those who have lost in the general election will be declared NCMPs, thus bringing the total number of opposition members in Parliament to three.

An NCMP holds his seat for the term of Parliament, but does not represent any constituency. He is entitled to vote on all matters except supply Bills, money Bills, constitutional amendments, motions of no confidence in the government and motions to remove the President from office.

Following the 1984 general election, two opposition candidates—J.B. JEYARETNAM and CHIAM SEE TONG—won their seats outright, creating one NCMP post to be filled. The government first offered it to M.P.D. NAIR of the WORKERS' PARTY, who declined. It was then sent to Tan Chee Kien of the Singapore United Front, who also declined. The government did not make further offers thereafter. The

Rodolfo Nolli: statuary on façade of Keppel Railway Station. 'FMSR' stands for Federated Malay States Railway.

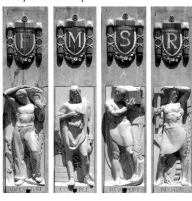

Novena Church

first NCMP was veteran Barisan Sosialis leader, Lee Siew Choh, who was sworn in following the 1988 general election.

Noor Aishah, Toh Puan (1933–) First Lady. Born in Kuala Lumpur, Noor Aishah married Yusof Ishak in 1955, when he was serving as managing director of Utusan Melayu. The couple had three children: Orkid Kamariah, Imran and Zuriana.

In 1959, Yusof became self-governing Singapore's Yang di-Pertuan Negara ('Head of State'). As the wife of the head of state, Noor Aishah was entitled to the use of the title 'Toh Puan' (First Lady). One of Noor Aishah's first tasks as First Lady was to present the Istana at its best, and she had the building decorated with local orchids. She developed menus for state banquets. At the Istana, Noor Aishah employed a household manageress, Jean Leembruggen, to assist her. She engaged an English tutor to improve her English to a level whereby she could converse easily with foreign dignitaries.

Noor Aishah undertook her first official state visit when she accompanied Yusof to Cambodia and Ceylon (present-day Sri Lanka) in April 1963. She was active in charity work, and served as a patron to numerous organizations, including the Red Cross, Girl Guides Singapore, the Association for the Deaf, the Young Muslims Association and the Trained Nurses Association. She was admitted into the Distinguished Service Order (1964), and was awarded an honorary doctorate by the University of Singapore (1971). After Yusof died in 1970, Noor Aishah left the Istana and dedicated herself to bringing up her three children while continuing to be active in charitable work.

Noor Mohamed Hashim Mohamed Dali, Captain (1880–1944) Military officer and civil servant. A Jawi Peranakan born in Penang, Noor Mohamed Hashim joined the colonial civil service. He was posted to Singapore in 1898 as a Malay interpreter of the Singapore Police Court.

In February 1910, Hashim and E.E. Coleman, both office-bearers of the Malayan Football Association, were asked to urgently raise a company of volunteer Malay soldiers to serve in the Singapore Volunteer Corps. This experimental company, recruited from the association's 42 football clubs, marked the first-ever involvement of Malays in the modern military history of Singapore and Malaysia.

The Malay company had expanded from 61 to 120 soldiers by 1911. It served beside the Chinese company of the Singapore Volunteer Corps and replaced the Eurasian company. On 19 September 1912, Colour Sergeant Hashim was commissioned 2nd Lieutenant of the Malay Company, the first Malay Muslim to be commissioned a military officer in Singapore's military history.

Hashim was mobilized together with a mixed British military contingent to restore order at Pasir Puteh, Kelantan, following an uprising in that state on 29 April 1915. In the second Kelantan expedition, he served as company commander beside Captain R.J. Farrer as an intelligence officer to the Kelantan British Adviser.

Hashim was promoted to captain of the Malay Company in February 1916. The colonial government transferred him to the Mohammedan Advisory Board as assistant secretary. In 1919, Hashim was appointed district officer, assistant district judge and magistrate in Penang. During 1924–35, he served in the Co-Operatives Societies of the Federated Malay States as an assistant registrar.

After retirement, Hashim returned to Singapore. He was appointed the Unofficial Malay member of the Straits Settlements Legislative Council 1936. Hashim was the third and last member of this council.

During the Japanese Occupation, Hashim was imprisoned and tortured by his captors at Outram Jail. His health deteriorated after his release. He died aged 64, and was buried in the Muslim section of Bidadari Cemetery. In 2004, his gravestone was among the few selected for transfer to the Bidadari Memorial.

Noor S.I. (1933–1990) Poet. Noor S.I. was the pen name of Ismail bin Haji Omar. He was born in Singapore and received his early education in Malay, Arabic and English schools. He worked in the Civil Service before joining a local publishing house, Pustaka Nasional, as an editor. As early as the 1950s, Noor experimented with expression and style in his poetry, which was highly lyrical but notoriously difficult to understand. He wrote plays, short stories and essays. Some of his published works are collections of poems in *Setanggi Waja* (1960), *Rakaman Roh* (Records of the Spirit) (1963), *Sajak-sajak Padang Pahlawan* (Poems of Field Warriors) (1985) and *Dewi Alam dan Burung Senja* (Earth Angel and Evening Bird) (1986). Some of his other poems are published in several anthologies of *Sajak-sajak Melayu Baru* (New Malay Poems) (1963). Noor was an active member of the literary organization ASAS 50. In 1985 he was awarded the Southeast Asia Write Award.

Novena Church Also known as the Church of St Alphonsus, Novena is a Catholic church where Mass and other forms of prayer are held although no other normal parish activities, such as baptisms and weddings are conducted there. It is run by the Congregation of the Most Holy Redeemer, which arrived from Australia in 1935. The church at Thomson Road began as a small chapel in the house of the Redemptorist Fathers. It was expanded to accommodate a rapidly increasing number of devotees.

The church has become known for its Saturday Novena, a nine-day prayer series. Highlights of the 30-minute sessions are the letters asking for the help of the Blessed Virgin Mary and letters thanking her for favours received.

Starting with 81 Catholics in January 1949, the Saturday Novena now attracts some 20,000 people, including non-Christians, from Singapore and Malaysia. The annual procession on the first Sunday of September brings together 20,000–50,000 participants.

Nrityalaya Aesthetics Society This Indian classical dance society was originally established as the Bhaskar's Academy of Dance in 1952. It concentrated on teaching *bharatanatyam* (a form of classical Indian dance), with founder K.P. Bhaskar and his wife Santha Bhaskar as its principal teachers. It was renamed Nrityalaya Aesthetics Society in 1987.

The society has undertaken cross-cultural performances in Singapore and Malaysia, and offers a number of cultural courses in North and South Indian dance and music. It has become involved in the National Arts Council's Art Education Programme, and established a professional performing wing, Bhaskar's Arts Academy, in 1999.

NTUC *See* National Trades Union Congress.

NTUC FairPrice Supermarket chain. Its origins date back to the early 1970s, when the

Toh Puan Noor Aishah, 1960.

Nrityalaya Aesthetics Society: Vinayaka, 2005.

NTUC FairPrice: supermarket entrance.

oil crisis and inflation led to rapidly increasing prices. To check profiteering, the two largest labour unions—the Singapore Industrial Labour Organisation and Pioneer Industries Employees' Union—came together in 1973 to set up the NTUC Welcome Co-operative Limited to run its own supermarkets.

The first Welcome outlet was opened in Toa Payoh in July 1973 by then Prime Minister LEE KUAN YEW. In 1976, the chain had seven supermarkets and had started keeping a stockpile of a minimum 900 tons of rice. It sold rice 10–17 per cent cheaper than other providers, and profiteers were forced to lower their prices. By then, it was clear that Welcome supermarkets were beginning to have an effect on prices in general. Food prices fell 6.4 per cent that year, as compared to the almost 50 per cent rise between 1972 and 1973.

Further mergers, including one between Welcome and the Singapore Employees' Co-operative Limited in 1983, led to the creation of the NTUC Fairprice Co-operative and the next growth phase for the supermarket chain.

NTUC FairPrice launched no-frills house-brand products in 1985. In 1992, barcoding was introduced, leading to shorter customer waiting times and higher productivity.

By the late 1990s, FairPrice had started to venture into new formats and service concepts. One example is The Pasar store, a fusion of the traditional wet market with the modern-day convenience of a supermarket. The concept of a country themed store-within-a-store under the Liberty Market brand was launched in 1998. It offered imported foodstuffs from the United States. Since then, the Australian Pavilion and country-theme corners from Japan, South Korea and Thailand have also been added. Other new store formats have included the 24-hour Cheers convenience store, targeted at the younger generation, the Baker's Corner and Homemart.

FairPrice also caters to increasingly popular niche markets. These include halal deli items for Muslim shoppers, more

Nurhisham Adam with national squad team-mate, Eddie Abdul Kadir, right.

choice products and nutrition programmes for health-conscious shoppers, and online shopping for the Internet-savvy.

In 1998, NTUC FairPrice took full ownership of its central warehouse and distribution company, and renamed it Grocery Logistics of Singapore. It has since invested in a new warehouse management system to improve efficiency. In January 2003, it opened its own fresh food distribution centre to centralize the distribution of temperature-sensitive fresh and chilled products to its outlets. It is the first supermarket retailer to build, own and operate such a refrigerated distribution facility in Singapore.

NTUC Fairprice is now a retail network of more than 130 stores islandwide. It serves more than a million customers daily and rings up average annual sales of $1 billion. Run as a co-operative, it employs more than 5,000 staff. They serve more than 450,000 members who receive rebates for their purchases and enjoy annual dividends.

NTUC Income Insurance provider. NTUC Income was set up in 1970 by the NATIONAL TRADES UNION CONGRESS (NTUC) to protect the financial security of workers. From an initial capital of $1.2 million, it grew to become the local market leader in life, motor, annuity and health insurance, with total assets of $16 billion and more than 1.8 million policy-holders—almost half of Singapore's population. In 1994, NTUC Income became the only insurer willing to provide a catastrophic medical insurance plan as an alternative to the coverage operated by the CENTRAL PROVIDENT FUND. In 1999, it was given an AA rating by Standard & Poor's. In 2005, the cooperative had about 2,700 insurance advisers, 1,500 office staff and a network of 11 branches island-wide.

Nurhisham Adam (1969–) Sportsman. SEPAK TAKRAW player known as 'The Killer' and acknowledged as one of the finest 'tekongs', or servers, in the game. Nurhisham made his international debut at the 1989 Southeast Asia Games, and is one of the few sportsmen to win medals at four consecutive Asian Games (two in Beijing, 1990; one in Hiroshima, 1994; one in Bangkok, 1998; and one in Busan, 2002).

In 1990, Nurhisham starred in the match that saw Singapore defeat the defending world champions, Thailand, 2–1. The team ultimately finished behind Malaysia and Thailand, winning the bronze by defeating Indonesia in the play-off for third spot.

A near free-for-all in a national league match in 1997 caused him to be suspended from the national team, but he was invited to mentor players preparing for the SEA Games in Jakarta. He returned to the national team after the controversy died down and won two more medals at the Asian Games.

NUS High School of Mathematics and Science Specialized independent school. It is developed and managed by the NATIONAL UNIVERSITY OF SINGAPORE (NUS). It takes in students with exceptional talent in science and mathematics. The curriculum emphasizes critical thinking, independent learning, problem solving, formal writing, and research and development. Students have access to NUS resources and facilities while lecturers from the university provide coaching and guidance. The school took in its first cohort in January 2005. These students will graduate with an NUS High School Diploma at the end of six years.

Nusantara Film Film studio. Established in 1950 by Hsu Chiu Meng and Ong Keng Huat, this independent film production house operated for only four years. It introduced diversity and variety into local cinema through the directors and actors it hired. Unlike MALAY FILM PRODUCTIONS (MFP), which hired film-makers exclusively from India, Nusantara drew its talent from the immediate region, employing Indonesian and Malayan directors.

Nusantara's first two films, *Pelangi* (Rainbow) and *Sesal Tak Sudah* (Regrets Are Not Over)—both made in 1950—were directed by Indonesians Naz Achnas and A.R. Tompel, respectively. Others films produced by Nusantara included *Dian* (Candle) (1952) and *Pacar Putih* (White Lover) (1952) by Naz Achnas; and *Norma* (1952) by A.R. Tompel. Although these two directors' careers in Singapore were short, they are credited with having paved the way for Malay film-makers such as P. RAMLEE and S. Roomai Noor, both of whom went on to work at MFP and Cathay-Keris.

nutmeg Cash crop. Manufactured from the fruit of the *Myristica fragrans* tree, nutmeg was a popular commodity in the 19th century. Nutmeg seeds first arrived in Singapore at the instigation of Sir STAMFORD RAFFLES. While in Bencoolen, Sumatra, in 1819, Raffles sent some nutmeg to Colonel WILLIAM FARQUHAR to be planted near GOVERNMENT HILL.

The number of nutmeg trees in Singapore grew to around 7,000 by 1848. Private gardens were cleared to make way for nutmeg plantations across the island. However, due to the relatively poor quality of soil on most plantations, a full crop could be harvested only once every three years. Dr. THOMAS OXLEY, who owned Oxley Estate, also owned one of the better nutmeg plantations in Singapore, due to his diligence in fertilizing and conditioning the soil to ensure prime conditions for growth.

The nutmeg is now the logo of the ORCHARD ROAD district although nutmeg farming faded out after disease swept through the plantations in 1850.

NUS High School of Mathematics and Science

OB markers In Singapore's political discourse, the term 'out-of-bounds (OB) markers' (a golf term) indicates the limits of acceptable political and artistic expression. The original use of the term in a political sense is attributed to Cabinet minister GEORGE YEO in 1991, in the context of the government's pledge of greater openness and consultation. The government has said that OB markers will always exist, but that the area within bounds will widen steadily as Singapore matures politically.

One of the best-known OB marker cases occurred in 1994, when writer CATHERINE LIM wrote about 'an arrogant, high-handed and authoritarian government'. The prime minister's press secretary responded sharply to this criticism, and Lim responded by saying that she had never intended to question the prime minister's fitness to govern. In the words of LEE HSIEN LOONG, 'a boundary had been probed, and an out-of-bounds (OB) marker firmly planted'.

OB markers can be distinguished from laws and regulations associated with criminal prosecution. They are a largely political construct, a breach of which attracts a political response. However, artists accused of crossing OB markers have occasionally faced legal action, as when performance-artist Josef Ng was fined, in 1994, for committing an obscene act—cutting his pubic hair in public. The government has claimed that clear OB markers enhance the freedom of those who operate within them although some commentators have viewed OB markers as excessively vague.

See also PRESS FREEDOM.

obesity Studies have shown that Asians, including Singaporeans, have higher percentages of body fat than Caucasians of the same age, gender and Body Mass Index (BMI). These studies have also shown that Asians have a higher risk of cardiovascular diseases and diabetes mellitus even at a relatively low BMI. In Singapore, about half of all adult Singaporeans with a BMI of 22–24 kg/m^2 have at least one cardiovascular risk factor (such as smoking). Accordingly, the World Health Organisation recommends considering Asians with a BMI of 23 kg/m^2 or higher as overweight, and those with a BMI of 27.5 kg/m^2 or higher as obese.

Using this criteria, it was calculated that the proportion of obese adults aged 18–69 was 6.9 per cent in 2004. There were more obese females (7.3 per cent) than obese males (6.4 per cent). Malays had the highest proportion of obese adults (19.1 per cent) followed by Indians (13.4 per cent) and Chinese (4.2 per cent). Of note is the almost doubling of obese Malay males from 8.8 per cent in 1998 to 16.9 per cent in 2004.

Obesity is due to both genetic and dietary factors. To encourage healthy living and combat obesity, programmes such as the Trim and Fit Programme for school-children and the Workplace Health Promotion Programme for adults, were initiated by the HEALTH PROMOTION BOARD in 1992 and 2000 respectively.

obscenity laws Most of the provisions in Singapore's criminal law regarding obscenity can be found in the PENAL CODE, the UNDESIRABLE PUBLICATIONS ACT and the Miscellaneous Offences Act. Obscenity is defined by the 19th-century English case of *R. v Hicklin,* as the tendency 'to deprave and corrupt those whose minds are open to such immoral influences and into whose hands a publication of this sort may fall'. Whether an act is obscene depends on the nature of the act and the community that is meant to be protected. Generally speaking, obscene acts are those involving simulated or actual sexual intercourse, exposure of the genitals, and acts of HOMOSEXUALITY. The law is primarily concerned with acts performed or conducted in public.

A slightly different approach is adopted for the same acts if they are included as part of a theatrical or artistic performance or movie. Singapore's film and theatre classification system allows otherwise obscene acts to be depicted provided they enhance the artistic value of the performance. Strict adherence to rating rules and restrictions on young audiences have mitigated the constraints of Singapore's obscenity laws.

Observatory, The Popular music group. The Observatory uses electronic gadgets and classical instrumentations to produce a unique sound. Since the release of its 2004 debut album, *Time Of Rebirth*, The Observatory has been labelled 'the best kept secret' of the local indie music scene. It is made up of singer-songwriter-guitarist Leslie Low (formerly of Humpback Oak); keyboardist-singer Vivian Wang (ex-TV presenter); electric guitarist Dharma (who also plays in Throb); programmer-keyboardist Evan Tan (formerly of THE PADRES); and guitarist-bassist Victor Low (formerly of CONCAVE SCREAM). In late 2004, the band took in drummer Adam Shah and subsequently released *Blank Walls* in 2005. Wang, Tan and Low also have a side-project called Snake Blood Union, which plays improvisational music.

October Cherries Popular music group. One of the most recorded bands in Singapore, the October Cherries were originally known as The Surfers, and signed with EMI in 1968. The line-up included Jay Shotam on vocals, bass and organ; Peter Diaz on lead guitar; Benny Siow on rhythm guitar; and Richard Khan on drums. Eager for international exposure, the group found a way out of its contract with EMI by changing its name to October Cherries in October 1969 and establishing its own label, Baal Records. The band's first release was a cover of Humble Pie's 'Natural Born Bugie'. The band also had hits in Europe and South America. 'Butterfly' was a big hit in Singapore in 1972. The band also released records under other names, but with the same line-up. They performed extensively in Europe and Asia, finally disbanding in the mid-1970s after a final performance in New Delhi.

Odate Shigeo (dates unknown) Japanese war-time official. Odate Shigeo, who held the honorary rank of full general, succeeded MANAKI TAKANOBU as mayor of SYONAN (Singapore) in March 1942, during the JAPANESE OCCUPATION. He was able, by means of influence, to negate the frequently harsh edicts of the Malaya Military Administration's director, Colonel WATANABE WATARU. He was promoted to governor-general of Tokyo in June 1943. Odate's connections seemed to have been powerful. According to the official SHINOZAKI MAMORU, Odate had been sent to Singapore by Prime Minister Hideki Tojo to check the latter's arch rival, Lieutenant-General YAMASHITA TOMOYUKI.

Oddfellows, The Popular music group. The Oddfellows was formed in early 1988 by drummer Soo Wai Cheong and singer-guitarist Patrick Chng. Bassist Stephen Tan joined soon thereafter. In 1991, the band saw a change in line-up with the introduction of guitarist Kelvin Tan and bassist Vincent Lee; a new drummer, Johnny Ong, joined in 1993.

The group's 1991 debut album, *Teenage Head*, yielded 'So Happy', which went to the top of the charts on local radio station Perfect 10 (98.7 FM). For five consecutive years from 1988 to 1992, and again in 1995, The Oddfellows were voted 'Favourite Local Band' by readers of music magazine BIGO. The band released an EP, *Seven Year Itch,* in 1995, and a compilation of rare tracks, lesser-known singles and live recordings entitled *Bugs And Hisses* in 2001. Singer Patrick Chng also plays in Typewriter.

Odeon Theatre. Built in 1953 on North Bridge Road, the Odeon was one of the earliest air-conditioned cinemas in Singapore, along with the CAPITOL THEATRE, the Cathay (*see* CATHAY BUILDING), the Pavilion, the ALHAMBRA and REX CINEMA. It was a popular venue for movies, baby shows and charity premieres. In 1965, during CONFRONTATION, a Morris car was blown up in the Odeon's ground-

Odate Shigeo

October Cherries: record album distributed in Europe by EMI, 1970.

The Oddfellows: Bugs and Hisses *(2001).*

The Observatory: pages from the booklet accompanying the Time of Rebirth *CD (2004).*

Odeon: cinema building in 1963 (above); ticket stubs.

floor car park, damaging four other vehicles. The Odeon belonged to the Cathay Organization until it was sold in the 1980s. Its closure was a consequence of a slump in cinema attendance due to video piracy, and losses incurred by the Cathay film division. The cinema was replaced by an office building, Odeon Towers.

Sir George Oehlers

Odyssey Dance Theatre Dance company. Founded in 1999 by artistic director Danny Tan, the Odyssey Dance Theatre seeks to explore the forms, dynamics and cross-cultural traits of contemporary dance, especially through regular exchanges with foreign dance artists. It debuted with Tan's evening-length *Odyssey to the Sublime* (2000) in Singapore and Taiwan. The company has since danced abroad, showcased new works and organized several initiatives, including the biennial *Xposition 'O' Contemporary Dance Fiesta*, which began in 2001; and the eight-week-long *DanzINC—International Dancers & Choreographers Residency Festival* in 2004. In 2001, it premiered Tan's *The White Sensation*, a full-evening production commissioned by Seagate Technology as part of its year-long sponsorship programme; three years later, aromatherapy firm Bel'Air became its main sponsor. With *Synesthesia* (2005), a joint effort between Tan and Korean choreographer Seo Dong Hyun, it became one of the few dance companies to stage a performance at the SINGAPORE INDOOR STADIUM.

Oei Hong Leong

Oehlers, Sir George (1908–1968) Lawyer, community leader and first Speaker of the Legislative Assembly. Nicknamed 'Geno', Sir George Edward Noel Oehlers was educated

OG Department Store: Orchard Point branch.

at St Andrew's School and Raffles Institution before reading law in the United Kingdom. He was called to the Bar in 1931, and thereafter returned to Singapore and commenced legal practice. Oehlers was a sportsman and represented Singapore and the Straits Settlements in hockey. He was also active in community work, serving as Municipal Councillor, City Councillor and president of the Eurasian Association.

Oehlers was made an Officer of the Order of the British Empire (OBE) for his community work (1953); appointed first Speaker of Singapore's Legislative Assembly (1955); and was the first Singaporean Eurasian to be knighted (1958). He served two terms as speaker (1955–1963) before stepping down to become Speaker for the Sabah Legislative Assembly. Oehlers later became chairman of the Public Utilities Board and president of the Industrial Court in Kuala Lumpur.

Oei Hong Leong (1948–) Businessman. Born in Indonesia, Oei Hong Leong spent part of his childhood in China, where he also received his early education. His father, Eka Tjipta Widjaja, was the founder of the Sinar Mas conglomerate. Oei became chairman of China Strategic Holdings, which has invested in a wide range of industries, including beverages and paper. He is best known in Singapore for using United Industral Corporation (UIC), which he controlled, to launch a $2.6 billion hostile takeover of property firm Singapore Land in 1990, as well as his 2004 attempt to take over NATSTEEL.

Oei Tiong Ham (1866–1924) Businessman. Oei Tiong Ham was born in Semarang in the Dutch East Indies (present-day Indonesia), the eldest son of Ong Tjie Sien, founder of the firm Kian Gwan. In 1890, he took over his father's business and began trading in sugar. He made large profits by cornering the Java sugar market, and became known as the 'Sugar King'. He acquired five sugar factories and modernized their operations with the help of foreign scientists and experts. He also acquired opium farms in Semarang, Yogyakarta, Surakarta and Surabaya, and made huge profits from their operations. These farms were taken over by the Dutch colonial authorities in 1904.

In 1910, Oei set up an office in London to sell sugar, and in 1914, he opened a branch of Kian Gwan in Singapore to sell sugar and other East Indies produce. Oei moved to Singapore in 1921 to escape Dutch taxes, and to avoid Dutch succession laws.

Oei contributed substantially to education in Singapore. He donated $150,000 to RAFFLES COLLEGE. The institution's Oei Tiong Ham Hall, at the original Bukit Timah campus, was named after him. He also donated land to TAO NAN SCHOOL.

Oei died of a heart attack in Singapore in 1924. His wealth was estimated at 200 million guilders, making him one of the region's wealthiest men. He was survived by 8 wives, 13 sons and 13 daughters. His business empire—the Oei Tiong Ham Concern—ended abruptly on 10 July 1961, when the Sukarno-led Indonesian government confiscated its Indonesian assets.

Off-peak Car Scheme Designed to reduce traffic congestion, this scheme allows specially-licensed cars to be driven during off-peak hours. These cars bear red number plates with white letters, and may be driven only between 7 p.m. and 7 a.m. on weekdays, after 3 p.m. on Saturdays and all day on Sundays and public holidays. In consideration of this restricted usage, owners enjoy upfront tax rebates on the first registration and a discount on annual road tax. To drive outside the stipulated hours, the driver must buy and display a $20 special licence, which is valid for a day. These cars are commonly known as 'weekend cars' because the scheme started originally as the Weekend Car Scheme in May 1991 before being replaced by the Off-peak Car Scheme in 1994.

OG Department Store Best known for its women's wear, the family-owned OG Department Store started out as Ocean Garments, with the setting up of a factory in Redhill in September 1962. The company was founded by China-born Tay Tee Peng, who had arrived in Singapore in 1958 after living in Indonesia for 25 years.

Two OG stores were soon opened at Coleman Street and North Bridge Road before the company bought a plot of land on Upper Cross Street in Chinatown and opened the landmark OG Building store in 1972. At that time, OG was one of the biggest department stores in Singapore, and among the first to have a section of its store—the toys and stationery departments—on an overhead bridge. The opening of OG Elite at Plaza Singapura followed in the mid-1970s. OG Orchard opened in 1983. In late 1999, OG bought over Albert Complex (renamed OG Albert Complex in June 2005), opening a store there in June 2000 when the Chinatown store was torn down for redevelopment. OG People's Park re-opened its doors in December 2002 in the refurbished OG Building. OG also owns the Orchard Point Mall.

OG carries not only international brands, but the Nina label, a house brand. Besides its factory in Singapore, OG has also maintained a production facility in Shanghai since the mid-1990s.

oil-refining sector Singapore is the world's third largest oil-trading centre after London and New York, as well as a leading refining centre. In 2005, the oil refining sector accounted for about $57.4 billion—8 per cent of the country's total exports, or 29.6 per cent of the country's GROSS DOMESTIC PRODUCT (GDP). Ranked fifth in Asia, Singapore has a total crude oil refining capacity of about 1.4 million barrels per day (bpd) from its three main refineries: these are operated by ExxonMobil (580,000 bpd), Shell (500,000 bpd) and Singapore Refining Company (SRC) (285,000 bpd). The three facilities are capable of processing some 40 different types of crude from the Middle East, Southeast Asia and China. For much of the 1980s, Singapore was the world's third-largest oil-refining centre, after Rotterdam and Houston. Although it has been overtaken in recent years by China, India, Japan and South Korea, which have been developing their refining capacities to meet domestic consumption, Singapore remains an important 'swing' producer that balances oil demand and supply in the region.

Singapore's oil refining industry started with a 20,000 bpd refinery in 1961. It was set up by the Royal Dutch/Shell Group on Pulau Bukom. This was soon followed by Mobil's 19,000 bpd facility on Pulau Pesek (now part of JURONG ISLAND, an amalgamation of seven smaller islands) in 1963. In 1969, Esso built a 90,000 bpd refinery on Pulau Ayer Chawan (now part of Jurong Island); while a fourth 65,000 bpd refinery was set up in July 1973 on Pulau Merlimau (now part of Jurong Island) by SRC, an oil consortium that included the Singapore Petroleum Company and, later, Caltex. The facilities of Esso and Mobil have been integrated following the merger that formed ExxonMobil in 1999.

Besides the presence of these refineries, Singapore is also a key oil-storage facility with a capacity for 100 million barrels. Storage of refined oil accounts for 88 million barrels. The remaining capacity is used by independent storage operators such as Vopak, Oiltanking and Tankstore. In anticipation of rising demand within Asia, especially China, this storage capacity is expected to double by 2008 with an estimated US$1 billion investment by Horizon Terminals, Vopak, Oiltanking, Chemoil and Singapore's Hin Leong Trading. The government has announced plans to build a $760 million underground cavern complex at Jurong Island for the stockpiling of petroleum products: this will enhance Singapore's position as a leading oil logistics, storage and trading hub.

Singapore's oil industry has benefitted from the country's strategic location at the crossroads of global shipping routes, and from the government's policy of allowing market forces to determine the direction of development. There are no laws favouring local refiners or homegrown trading houses over other companies. Government interventions, when they do occur, often come in the form of infrastructural support such as land reclamation for new facilities (Jurong Island), or commercial incentives such as the

Global Trader Scheme (formerly known as the Approved Oil Trader Scheme) introduced in 1989 to entice global companies and trading houses to set up here.

Singapore is the world's top bunkering port and is a key offshore support base for exploration companies in the region. It is also home to the biggest oil-rig builder in the world, Keppel FELS (part of KEPPEL CORPORATION).

Oishi Masayuki, Lieutenant-Colonel (1895–1947) Japanese military officer. Oishi Masayuki's military career began in 1916 when he was admitted to Japan's Military Academy. After graduating, he served in Manchuria in 1918 as a second lieutenant in the 25th Infantry Brigade. Oishi joined the KEMPEITAI (Japanese military police) in Korea in 1925, becoming a full lieutenant. After a brief stint in Manchuria in 1941, Oishi arrived in Singapore in 1942, during the JAPANESE OCCUPATION, as commander of the No. 2 Field Kempeitai.

On 18 February 1942, Oishi, with Lieutenant-General KAWAMURA SABURO, received instructions from Lieutenant-General YAMASHITA TOMOYUKI's headquarters to screen the Chinese population for anti-Japanese elements, and to eliminate them. It was Oishi's subordinates who conducted the screening and sent many Chinese to their deaths. This became known as the SOOK CHING massacre.

After the war, Oishi was put on trial for his role in the massacre, together with six other Japanese officers, and was found guilty. He was sentenced to death and hanged on 26 June 1947 at CHANGI PRISON.

Old Admiralty House National monument. Located at Old Nelson Road, this two-storey brick bungalow was constructed in 1939. It was one of the largest houses to be built within the Sembawang naval base. During World War II, it served as the strategic planning headquarters of the British armed forces. Except for the period during the Japanese Occupation, the house was the official residence of the Royal Navy Commander-in-Chief, Far East Station, until the withdrawal of the British military from Singapore.

The naval base—including Old Admiralty House—was then transferred to the Singapore government. The late-Victorian-style building is now part of the Karimun Admiralty Country Club. It was gazetted as a national monument in 2002.

Old Chang Kee This company built its reputation on its signature handmade CURRY PUFFS—a popular local snack. This was the only item sold when the business started in 1956 in a coffee shop near REX CINEMA on MacKenzie Road. The Old Chang Kee name was coined to distinguish it from nearby stalls that were imitating the puffs.

The business expanded in 1986, after

Oil-refining sector: Shell's facility at Pulau Bukom, 1996.

Han Kee Juan bought the Old Chang Kee company. By 1992, Han had expanded it to eight outlets. While these outlets were located in coffee shops in the mid-1990s, Han began to set up stand-alone kiosks at MRT stations and other strategic locations. In January 2005, Old Chang Kee expanded into Malaysia, after obtaining its halal certification (fit for Muslim consumption).

In 2005, Old Chang Kee produced 20,000 curry puffs a day for its 40 outlets in Singapore, compared to the 300 it sold daily when the company was first set up. The extended menu now includes more than 20 hot snacks.

Old Kallang Airport building See KALLANG AIRPORT.

Old Lines Remains of a defensive wall and moat. On 3 February 1822, the second Resident of Singapore, JOHN CRAWFURD, traced the course of a stream then known as the Freshwater Stream (present-day Stamford Canal). A map from the same year depicts this stream and a feature labelled 'Old Lines of Singapore'. G. A. FINLAYSON described the Old Lines as a 'mud wall, probably the remains of an ancient fortification'. Sir STAMFORD RAFFLES, in a letter dated 31 January 1819, mentioned 'the lines of the old city and its defenses'. Crawfurd described the wall as the northern boundary of 'the ancient town of Singapore'. It was 4.5 m wide at the base and around 2.5 m high.

At the foot of Fort Canning Hill, the stream turned toward its source on Mt Sophia, while the wall turned in the opposite direction, up the side of the hill, where a dry ditch flanked its outer edge. This stream corresponds to the *Parit Singapura* (moat, or ditch, of Singapore) mentioned in the SEJARAH MELAYU (Malay Annals). It is said that Sang Rajuna Tapa—Sultan ISKANDAR SHAH's treasury officer—and his wife, were turned to stone in the moat as punishment for betraying TEMASEK (Singapore) to the invading Majapahit.

WANG DAYUAN mentions that the city of Temasek 'shut up its gates' and held off attacks by the Siamese for a month. Although the rampart has no gates, there may have been wooden palisades, either on

Old Chang Kee: first stall near Rex Cinema, c. 1960 (top); Far East Plaza branch.

Old Ministry of Labour Building: photographed in 1986.

Douglas Oliveiro

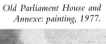

Old Parliament House and Annexe: painting, 1977.

top of it or around the foot of Fort Canning Hill (*see* FORT CANNING HILL AND PARK).

Old Ministry of Labour Building National monument. This neoclassical building at Havelock Road was constructed in 1928. It was first used in 1930 to house the head-quarters of the CHINESE PROTECTORATE, staffed by British colonial officials who were proficient in Chinese dialects. The protectorate operated until World War II. The Immigration Department, set up in 1933 to administer the Aliens Act, had its head office in this same building.

Following the Japanese surrender in 1945, the building was used by Australian officials as a venue for war crimes trials. Afterwards, it was renovated for use by the Ministry of Labour and Welfare (as it was then known), which occupied the building from 1956 to 1990. The Small Claims Tribunal used the building from 1990 to 1994. In 1998, the building was gazetted as a national monument, and in 1999, repair and restoration works were started to retro-fit it as the Family and Juvenile Court of Singapore (*see* FAMILY COURTS).

Old Nanyang University Library, Administration Building, Memorial and Gateway Arch See NANYANG UNIVERSITY.

Old Parliament House and Annexe National monument. Though much renovated, this edifice lays claim to being Singapore's oldest structure. Commissioned by the merchant John Argyle Maxwell as a private mansion, it

was designed by GEORGE D. COLEMAN and completed in 1827. Maxwell never used it; he leased, and later sold the building, to the government for $15,600. The building was Singapore's first courthouse. A series of major alterations and enlargements (1874–75, 1901 and 1909) eventually oblit-erated Coleman's design and the original neoclassical character was progressively replaced by an eclectic style. With the com-pletion of the new SUPREME COURT in 1939, the judiciary relinquished it. The building then served as a storehouse and was used by the Social Welfare Department. It then sat derelict until it was renovated (1953–54) to become the Assembly House, with a cham-ber to accommodate 48 members.

Following SEPARATION in 1965, the building was rechristened Parliament House. By the time it was gazetted a national monument in February 1992, the number of members of Parliament had increased beyond the capacity of the cham-ber, and plans for a new Parliament house were drawn up. When this opened on 6 September 1999, the old building was restored as THE ARTS HOUSE, and reopened in March 2004. Gracing its exterior is a bronze elephant statue—a gift from King Chulalongkorn of Siam (present-day Thailand) in 1871. The annexe was built in 1912 as a district court and today forms part of the Arts House.

Old Thong Chai Medical Institution Opened in 1867 on Upper Pickering Street as the Thong Chai Yee Say (literally meaning 'Benefit All Medical Association' in Cantonese), this organization was sup-ported by donations from wealthy Chinese businesses and clan leaders. Although it was established by members of the Chinese community, it provided medical care to the poor and needy regardless of race or reli-gion.

In 1886, the colonial government granted the Thong Chai Yee Say a plot of land on which permanent premises could be built. The building that was subsequent-ly constructed there was officially opened as the Thong Chai Medical Institution on 14 November 1892.

The institution's building—an excep-tionally long shophouse—consisted of four halls arranged along a central axis with two courtyards and a smaller airwell. In 1960, the institution's management announced plans to rebuild it. However, the hall was declared a national monument in July 1973. It has thus survived as a rare example of southern Chinese secular architecture. Since 1975, the institution itself has offered medical care from a new site, while the original building has been leased to other tenants, including architect Chan Seng Kee and various restaurants.

Oldham, William (1854–1937) Cleric. William Fitzjames Oldham was the first

Methodist pastor appointed to Singapore, and the founder of the ANGLO-CHINESE SCHOOL (ACS). An Irishman, Oldham was born into a Roman Catholic family in India. Oldham and his wife were sent to Singapore as missionaries, together with Dr James Thoburn, leader of the Methodist group in India. They were met in Singapore by Presbyterian elder Charles Phillips, who claimed to have seen, the previous night, a vision of people sailing into port—he had turned up at the pier to find the SS *Khandalla*, with Oldham's party on board.

Oldham secured a site at Coleman Street for a boarding house (now Oldham Hall); a school (now ACS); and the first Methodist Episcopal Church (later WESLEY METHODIST CHURCH), which he designed, and dedicated on 15 December 1886—coincidentally his birthday.

The non-Christian Chinese donated liberally to his work, and together they broached the idea of starting a university college—the aborted Anglo-Chinese College. Fifty years later, TAN CHENG LOCK, founding president of the Malayan Chinese Association and one of the most prominent Chinese in Malaya, claimed that RAFFLES COLLEGE had its genesis in this initiative.

Oldham spearheaded efforts to reach out to all races, and preached in English and Tamil. Ill health forced him to leave Singapore in 1889, but he returned in 1904 as a bishop for the region. He was also appointed to a government OPIUM commis-sion. At the Golden Jubilee of METHODISM in 1935, the colonial secretary, Sir Andrew Caldecott, lauded Oldham for introducing CHRISTIANITY into Malaya.

Oliveiro, Douglas (1958–) Singer. Douglas Oliveiro was the singer for Energy, a cover band which played at the now-defunct Fire Disco, at Orchard Plaza. His career started in 1977, and he began performing in bands such as 9Lives, Krosmode, Culture Shock and Rhythm 2. He has spent much of his career providing live entertainment in clubs in Singapore, such as Sparks and Bar None, as well as in Bali, Beijing and other places throughout Asia.

Oliveiro was voted 'Singapore's sexiest man' by *The New Paper* in 1994; co-hosted a TV show called *Rollin' Good Times* from 1994

Old Thong Chai Medical Institution, c. 1950.

to 1996; and was a judge on the inaugural SINGAPORE IDOL television show in 2004.

Olympic Games Singapore's earliest involvement with the Olympic Games was in 1936. Chua Boon Lay, who owned a chicken stall at Telok Ayer Market, was selected to be part of the football team representing China at the 1936 Berlin Olympics. The first Singaporean to represent the colony before independence was LLOYD VALBERG. He was a high-jumper who reached the finals of the event in London (1948). The first Singaporean woman to reach the finals in athletics was Tang Pui Wah in Helsinki (1952).

TAN HOWE LIANG is, thus far, Singapore's only Olympic medallist. He won a silver medal for weightlifting in Rome (1960). There have been other notable performances in weightlifting. CHAY WENG YEW came closest to a medal, finishing sixth in the final of the featherweight competition in 1952. TAN SER CHER finished seventh in the same weight category in Melbourne (1956). Lon bin Mohamed Nor (1952) and Wong Kay Poh (1956) also finished in the top ten of their respective events.

In more recent times, Singaporean women have taken centre stage. In 2000, JING JUN HONG came one match short of securing a medal in table tennis in Sydney. In 2004, LI JIA WEI repeated the experience in Athens, narrowly missing a medal for table tennis. Her younger teammate, Zhang Xueling, also reached the final eight in the singles event. Also in Athens (2004), RONALD SUSILO, a badminton player, toppled the highly-rated Chinese player Lin Dan but could not advance beyond the top eight.

Two notable atheletes have been denied Olympian status: JUNIE SNG (swimming) and K. JAYAMANI (track). They missed out on the Moscow games (1980) because Singapore joined the Olympic boycott that year.

Omar Kampung Melaka Mosque Located at Keng Cheow Street, this was the first mosque in Singapore (*see* MOSQUES). It was originally built in 1820 and then rebuilt in 1855, and again in 1982. It can hold 1,000 people. In 1985, a tall minaret capped with a small dome was added to its entrance. The mosque was named after its founder, Syed OMAR ALI ALJUNIED, an Arab merchant from Palembang. It was listed as an historic site by the National Heritage Board on 11 November 2001.

On Shaw Ming (1978–) Sportsman. SINGAPORE ARMED FORCES serviceman On Shaw Ming took the gold medal in the 25 m Centre Fire Pistol event at the 18th Commonwealth Games in Melbourne, Australia, in March 2006. This was an unexpected win, as On was the least experienced member of the Singapore squad. He scored 289 in both the precision rounds and the

rapid rounds for a total of 578. This was enough to assure him a place in a three-way shoot-off against Samaresh Jung, the Indian shooter who had already won five gold medals at the Commonwealth Games, and Australian Greg Yelavich. During the first round of the shoot-off, Jung was eliminated, being unable to match On's and Yelavich's score of 48 out of 50. In the next round, both shooters scored 48, with On coming close to losing when he only managed an eight on his fifth shot. In the final round, Yelavich faltered, scoring 47, leaving On the winner with 49 and a total of 144 against Yelavich's 142.

Onam Indian festival. Onam is the foremost festival of the MALAYALEES, who originate from the Indian state of Kerala. Often referred to as the 'harvest festival', it falls in the month of Chingam in the Malayalam calendar—in August or September. In Kerala, Onam is a ten-day celebration—of singing, dancing, river-boat racing and other sports—culminating in a vegetarian lunch on the day of Thiruonam.

In Singapore, the celebration is simpler. The highlight is still the vegetarian lunch, or Ona Sadhya (Onam Meal), on Thiruonam. Friends and colleagues of all races and cultures are invited to the meal which is served on banana leaf. Family members dress in traditional new clothes (*Vasta*), and the floor at the entrance of the home is decorated with a multi-coloured flower arrangement, called *Onapookkalam*.

one-north Research and development (R&D) complex. Covering an area of almost 200 ha around Portsdown Road and Buona Vista Road, one-north is an integrated facility with residential and commercial units, tertiary and research institutions, sports facilities and gardens. The site, managed by JTC CORPORATION, is being developed in three phases, with completion of the final phase scheduled for 2020. Located near the National University of Singapore and the Singapore Science Park, it is intended to act as a focal point for research and development as well as for technopreneurial activities. The park is designed to attract biomedical, info-communications and media companies. It is home to Biopolis—a centre for research in biomedical science.

Ong, Christina (unknown–) Businesswoman. Daughter of oil trader PETER FU and wife of ONG BENG SENG, Christina Ong is the chief executive officer of Club 21, which she started in 1972. Ong had originally wanted to open an English-style tailoring shop in Singapore but the enterprise failed to take off when the tailor emigrated to Canada. Confronted by an empty shop in Tanglin Shopping Centre, Christina decided to market and sell top fashion brands, introducing to Singapore

Remy Ong

leading labels such as Giorgio Armani, Donna Karan and Prada. Her flagship Club 21 Boutique handles over 40 fashion labels, and has 72 boutiques in Singapore, the United Kingdom and elsewhere. She has been dubbed the 'Queen of Fashion'.

Ong, Remy (1978–) Sportsman. A tenpin bowling champion and multiple Southeast Asian (SEA) Games gold-medallist, Remy Ong Lei Ming was ranked Asia's 'No. 1' by the Asian Bowling Federation in 2002. He won the Sportsman of the Year title in the same year.

Ong was introduced to competitive bowling at the age of ten, and had become a national bowler by the time he was 16. He achieved his first perfect game in 1998.

At the Busan Asian Games in 2002, he became only the second male multiple-gold medallist from Singapore in the 51-year history of the games. He won three gold medals, one each in the singles, trios and masters events. He later won other titles, including the Qatar Open and the Guam Open, both in 2004. He has been inducted into the SINGAPORE SPORTS COUNCIL HALL OF FAME.

Ong Beng Seng (1946–) Businessman. Ong Beng Seng was born in Teluk Anson (present-day Teluk Intan), Perak. His family arrived in Singapore when he was four, and he was educated at the Anglo-Chinese School—where he was a champion sprinter and long jumper—before furthering his studies in the United Kingdom. On his return, he joined Motor & General

Christina Ong

On Shaw Ming

Ong Beng Seng

Olympic Games: Zhang Xueling in Athens, 2004.

	Name	Sport	Medal/Postiton	Year
1	Tan Howe Liang	Weightlifting	Silver	1960
2	Jing Jun Hong	Table tennis	Fourth	2000
2	Li Jia Wei	Table tennis	Fourth	2004
4	Chay Weng Yew	Weightlifting	Sixth	1952
5	Tan Ser Cher	Weightlifting	Seventh	1956
6	Ronald Susilo	Badminton	Last eight	2004
7	Zhang Xueling	Table tennis	Last eight	2004
8	Lon Mohamed Noor	Weightlifting	Eighth	1952
8	Team	Hockey	Eighth	1956
10	Wong Kay Poh	Weightlifting	Ninth	1956
10	Ang Peng Siong	Swimming	Ninth	1984

OLYMPIC GAMES: SINGAPORE'S TOP RESULTS

Source: Nicholas Aplin, David Waters and Leong May Lai, Singapore Olympians (Singapore: SNP International, 2005), 24.

Ong Eng Guan: first day of one-week campaign to spring clean the city, 1959.

Ong Keng Sen

Ong Pang Boon

Ong Kim Seng: Emerald Hill Entrance (2005).

Underwriters Investments Holdings Ltd. He later moved to Kuo International, the firm of his father-in-law PETER FU, where he became managing director.

Kuo International, a large oil-trading operation, ventured into hotels with the purchase of Hilton Hotel and the establishment of HOTEL PROPERTIES LIMITED (HPL) in 1980. HPL diversified into various other businesses, including stockbroking (J. Ballas & Co.), film-making (*Pumping Iron II: The Women*), lifestyle franchises (Tower Records and Häagen-Dazs), cars (Komoco Auto, agent for Hyundai cars) and property development (Nassim Jade). Ong was named Businessman of the Year in 1991 by *The Business Times*.

Ong Eng Guan (1925–) Politician. Born in Malacca, Ong Eng Guan went to the University of Melbourne to study accountancy. He graduated with a degree in commerce and a diploma in public administration. Ong was active in student politics and was elected president of the Australian Overseas Club. He was also the founder president of the Asian Students Federation, which united Asian students in the fight against Western imperialism.

Ong returned to Singapore to work as an accountant. He became treasurer of the People's Action Party (PAP) when it was formed in November 1954. He was also secretary of the editorial board for *Petir* (the party magazine), chairman of the PAP Funds Committee and a member of the PAP Local Government Committee. In 1957, Ong stood as a PAP candidate for Hong Lim for the first fully-elected city council elections. The PAP won 13 seats out of 32 contested. Ong Eng Guan was elected Singapore's first mayor.

The inaugural meeting of the City Council was chaotic. There were riots outside the Town Hall and Ong was arrested. The inaugural council meeting had to be postponed until the following day. Ong's antics in the council made front-page news. He ordered the removal of the City Council mace from the chambers as well as portraits of four British former presidents of the Municipal Council. Ong encouraged the

public to attend council meetings, and City Hall became packed with onlookers. Meetings were described as 'bedlam' and 'pandemonium'. Ong was re-elected as mayor in December 1958. However, by early 1959, the City Council could no longer function properly and the minister for local government stripped it of its powers.

Ong resigned in April 1959 to contest the general election on the PAP ticket. His HOKKIEN-speaking prowess stood him in good stead in the mainly Hokkien-speaking Hong Lim constituency, and he won his seat with the largest margin of any candidate. Following the election, Ong was appointed minister for national development and also had a seat on the Internal Security Council. He was later forced to resign from the party for 'arbitrary and unprincipled acts without consultation or discussion with colleagues'. In April 1961, he contested the Hong Lim by-election (the 'Ong-Lim' by-election as it was jokingly called), and defeated the PAP candidate JEK YEUN THONG. He then set up the UNITED PEOPLE'S PARTY. In July 1965, he resigned from his seat in parliament and left politics.

Ong Keng Sen (1963–) Interdisciplinary theatre practitioner and curator. A lawyer by training (he graduated from the National University of Singapore in 1987), Ong Keng Sen made his directorial debut with the Michael Chiang and Dick Lee musical, *Beauty World* (1988). In 1992, Ong spent a year studying intercultural performance at the Tisch School of Arts, New York University, on a Fulbright scholarship.

Internationally, Ong is arguably the best known of Singapore's directors and practitioners. His productions have toured cities in Asia, Australia and Europe. He mooted the Flying Circus Project in 1994, to bring together traditional and contemporary Asian artists from different artistic fields. It expanded in 2004 to include European, Arab and African artists.

Ong's Singaporean productions include the site performance at Fort Canning of *Broken Birds: An Epic Longing* (1995), about pre-war Japanese prostitution in Singapore, which he co-authored with Robin Loon; and Kuo Pao Kun's *Descendants of the Eunuch Admiral* (1995). He directed Dick Lee's musical, *Fried Rice Paradise* (1997) and turned the Asian version of Kuo's play about the Pacific War, *The Spirits Play* (2000), into a site performance at the Battle Box, Fort Canning.

Ong's Asian Shakespeare Trilogy—*Lear* (1997), *Desdemona* (2000), and *Search: Hamlet* (2002)—fused different theatrical traditions while reinventing the classics. In *The Continuum: Beyond the Killing Fields* (2001) and *The Myths of Memory* (2003), Ong dealt with the subject of genocide in Cambodia and the former Yugoslavia. *Sandakan Threnody* (2004), a collaboration on the multicultural dimensions of the

Pacific War between composers and artists from Australia, Japan and Singapore, was performed at the 2004 Singapore Arts Festival and Melbourne International Festival. In 2006, Ong presented *Geisha* at the Singapore Arts Festival, the Spoleto Festival in Charleston, United States, and the Lincoln Center Festival in New York.

Ong has curated exhibitions and festivals in Berlin, London and Singapore. He became the artistic director of THEATREWORKS in 1988. Ong is the first Singaporean to have received both the NATIONAL ARTS COUNCIL's Young Artist Award for Theatre (1992) and the CULTURAL MEDALLION for Theatre (2003).

Ong Kim Seng (1945–) Artist. Ong Kim Seng is a watercolourist and art journal editor. Ong's dedication to *plein air* painting (painting in the open air) is rooted in his formative years painting outdoors with pioneer watercolourists such as Lim Cheng Hoe. He became known as the 'Nepal Painter' because of his paintings of the Himalayas. Ong has produced paper-pulp works and prints in collaboration with the SINGAPORE TYLER PRINT INSTITUTE. He was awarded the Dolphin Fellowship in 2000 by the American Watercolour Society. He is honorary president of the Singapore Watercolour Society, having served as its president between 1991 and 2001. He is a life fellow of the Centre of the Arts at the National University of Singapore. He was awarded the CULTURAL MEDALLION in 1991. His works were exhibited at the United Nations' 60th anniversary celebrations in Geneva, and have been featured on Singapore stamps.

Ong Lip Tat (1956–) Musician. A pianist with a reputation for formidable virtuosity, Ong Lip Tat began performing at the age of 6. He later studied under Lucien Wang, who was taught by Alfred Cortot. Ong received further musical training at the Royal Academy of Music in London and the Hochschule fur Musik und Theater in Hamburg.

In 1979, he was invited by the SINGAPORE SYMPHONY ORCHESTRA to perform Beethoven's *Emperor Concerto* at its inaugural concert. Although he has become much better known as a teacher, he occasionally performs publicly in collaboration with other musicians, including accompanying singers. He released *Piano Solos* in 1993. In 2005 he made his concerto debut with the SINGAPORE CHINESE ORCHESTRA.

Ong Pang Boon (1929–) Politician. Born in Kuala Lumpur, Ong Pang Boon was educated at Min Chung Public School, Confucian Middle School and Methodist Boys' School in Kuala Lumpur. Later, he obtained an honours degree in geography at the University of Malaya in Singapore (1954). Ong's introduction to politics came when he was treasurer of the University of

Malaya Socialist Club (1952–54). He was outraged by the sedition charges in the FAJAR trial and became active in raising funds to pay for the defence of the accused.

It was during the trial that Ong first met LEE KUAN YEW. After graduation, Ong went back to Kuala Lumpur but could not find work. He returned to Singapore in February 1955 and worked at the Federal and Colonial Building Society. He also joined the newly formed People's Action Party (PAP) that year and was appointed Lee's election agent in Tanjong Pagar constituency. Ong's organizational skills were much valued by the party, and he set up branches in all the constituencies that the PAP contested. He was also secretary for the Tanjong Pagar branch. In early 1956, his employers transferred him to Kuala Lumpur and he remained there for eight months.

Lee Kuan Yew approached Ong to become the PAP's full-time organizing secretary. Ong accepted, returned to Singapore, organized the party and published both the English and Chinese editions of *Petir*—the party organ. During this time he met his future wife, Chan Choy Siong, who was to become a member of Parliament. In the general election of 1959, Ong won a seat in the Telok Ayer constituency and was appointed minister for home affairs (1959–63). He later served as minister for education (1963–70); labour (1971–81); the environment (1981–84); and communications (1983). Ong also served as the PAP's assistant secretary-general (1963); city councillor and deputy mayor (1957–59); and first vice-chairman of the PAP (1981–83). For much of his early political career, Ong acted as a bridge between the Chinese-educated populace and the English-educated leaders within the PAP, especially Lee Kuan Yew. He is most known for, among other things, his recommendation that Mandarin be made a compulsory subject in schools.

Ong retired from politics in 1984 and joined Hong Leong Finance as a director, a post he held until his retirement in 2001. In 1990, he was admitted to the ORDER OF NILA UTAMA (First Class).

Ong Poh Lim (1920–2003) Sportsman. Ong Poh Lim partnered ISMAIL MARJAN to form the best-known badminton duo in Southeast Asia after World War II. He won a series of titles, including the All-Ireland, All-Malayan, All-Singapore, All-England and World Invitational in both the singles and doubles events. He became widely known for his unique 'crocodile serve'.

The partnership he formed with Ismail Marjan helped Malaya retain the THOMAS CUP in the 1950s. In 1951, they made their debut at the All-England Championships and emerged doubles runners-up. They then swept the Singapore Open doubles titles for four consecutive years (1952–55). Ong received the Meritorious Service Award in 1997 from the International Badminton Federation (IBF).

Ong Siong Kai (1944–) Businessman. Ong Siong Kai is the son of 'Coffee King' ONG WEI SOEIJ. He studied at the Anglo-Chinese School and then at the Bible Institute of Malaysia. He worked in a church for a year before joining the family business at the age of 21.

In 1981, Ong took over his father's firm, HIANG KIE. He made headlines by introducing Singapore to gourmet coffee culture with the opening of the first Coffee Club outlet (at Holland Village, in 1991). He was also president of the Singapore Yachting Association (1993–99), and once sailed a yacht named *Kopi-O*—the local term for black coffee.

Ong Swee Law (1930–1995) Civil servant. Ong Swee Law was chairman of the Public Utilities Board (PUB) from 1966 to 1970. The PUB was in charge of water supply, including the forested catchment areas adjoining the country's reservoirs. Ong came up with the idea of a zoo next to Upper Seletar Reservoir, and set aside 88 ha of land around the reservoir for the construction of the SINGAPORE ZOO. He was executive chairman of the Singapore Zoo from its inception in 1971 until his death from cancer in 1995. He supervised the development of both the zoo, which opened in 1973, and the NIGHT SAFARI, which opened in 1994.

Ong was also on the PRESIDENTIAL COUNCIL FOR MINORITY RIGHTS from its formation in 1970 until 1994. In 1968, he was presented with the MERITORIOUS SERVICE MEDAL. In 1995, he was posthumously admitted to the DISTINGUISHED SERVICE ORDER.

Ong Teng Cheong (1936–2002) Architect, politician and head of state. Ong Teng Cheong was the fifth president of the Republic of Singapore. Born on 22 January 1936, Ong was the second-eldest of five children. He entered school late because of the Japanese Occupation. After completing his secondary education at the Chinese High School in 1955, he left for Australia to study at the University of Adelaide. He graduated with a bachelor of architecture in 1961 and worked in Adelaide before returning to Singapore in 1964. A year later, he took up a Colombo Plan scholarship to complete his master of civic design (town planning) degree at the University of Liverpool.

Ong joined the Planning Department of the Ministry of National Development in 1967 as an architect planner. He subsequently left the civil service in 1971 to set up his own practice with fellow architect, Ling Siew May, whom he married.

In 1972, he entered politics and was elected on the People's Action Party (PAP)

Ong Poh Lim

in Kim Keat constituency. After three years on the backbench, he joined Cabinet as senior minister of state for communications (1975) and was later acting culture minister (1977) and communications minister (1978). He served as labour minister (1981) before becoming minister without portfolio and secretary general of the NATIONAL TRADES UNION CONGRESS (NTUC) (1983). He was appointed deputy prime minister in 1985. At the party level, Ong became chairman of the PAP in 1981.

He resigned all posts to contest the presidential election, defeating former civil servant Chua Kim Yeow in 1993 to become the country's fifth, and first ever elected, president.

Ong was often described as a bridge between the English-educated national leadership and the majority Chinese population. He pushed strongly for a rail-based mass transport system for over ten years before the go-ahead finally came (*see* MASS RAPID TRANSIT/LIGHT RAIL TRANSIT). And he oversaw the construction of CHANGI AIRPORT, the development of telecommunications systems and the expansion of Singapore's port. As secretary-general of NTUC, he revitalized the trade union movement by focusing on membership benefits outside wage negotiations, and by establishing the Institute of Labour Studies. An avid pianist, he championed major arts development strategies and lobbied for the construction of the ESPLANADE—THEATRES ON THE BAY.

Ong Teng Cheong: with his wife, Ong Siew May, during Istana open house, 1994.

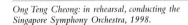

Ong Teng Cheong: in rehearsal, conducting the Singapore Symphony Orchestra, 1998.

As president, Ong supervised extensive renovations to the Istana (*see* ISTANA AND SRI TEMASEK), initiated a series of charity events and attempted to institutionalize new presidential powers as a guardian of national reserves. This latter effort ran into some resistance as there were disagreements over the process of institutionalizing presidential powers. Ong continued to serve as president despite being diagnosed with low grade lymphoma in 1992. In 1999, he officiated his final National Day Parade, despite the death of his wife from colon cancer on 30 July that same year.

Ong returned to private practice on 30 August with his sons, Tze Guan and Tze Boon. Ong died on 8 February 2002. His funeral was attended by thousands of mourners. In 2005, a team of Singaporean climbers named a mountain in Kazakhstan after the late Ong Teng Cheong.

Ong Tjoe Kim

Ong Tjoe Kim (1910–) Businessman. founder and chairman of METRO HOLDINGS Ltd. Ong Tjoe Kim was born in Fujian, China. He left for the Dutch East Indies (present-day Indonesia) as a teenager and worked for a retail company in Batavia (present-day Jakarta) for 25 years, eventually becoming a director.

Faced with anti-Chinese sentiment in Jakarta, Ong came to Singapore and opened his first Metro store at 72 High Street in 1957, naming it after Hollywood production house Metro-Goldwyn-Mayer (MGM). Ong broke new ground in retailing, being the first in Singapore to invite stars to open his new stores; introduce store promotions; have shop-floor staff dress in uniforms; and have customers served with welcome drinks.

Ong Wei Soeij (unknown–) Businessman. Ong Wei Soeij hailed from the Dutch East Indies (present-day Indonesia), where he

Operation Jaywick: commandos en route to Singapore, 1943 (top); HMAS Krait.

and his father started a coffee-trading business in the late 1920s. By the mid-1930s he was a dominant figure in the coffee trade in the Dutch East Indies. In 1936, he came to Singapore and opened a coffee- and spice-trading company. His Singapore business flourished but was disrupted by the Japanese Occupation. After World War II, Ong quickly rebuilt his business and by the 1950s, he was known as Singapore's 'Coffee King'. His son, ONG SIONG KAI, took over the business in 1981.

open market value This is the price of a vehicle bought directly from the factory, together with other charges associated with its sale and delivery to Singapore, such as shipping and insurance. The method of valuation is based on the customs valuation code endorsed by the World Trade Organization. The import tax, goods and services tax, and the additional registration fee (ARF)—which together with the open market vaue (OMV) determine the car's sale price—are computed as a percentage of its OMV.

Operation Cold Store Codename for the police raid on, and mass arrest of, suspected communist politicians and trade unionists in February 1963. Operation Cold Store was planned as the authorities were becoming increasingly anxious about left-wing activism in Singapore. In December 1962, 50 people had been already rounded up by the Malayan Special Branch in Peninsular Malaya for suspected communist activities.

The first raid was undertaken in the early hours of 2 February 1963, when 107 suspects were arrested. A few days before the operation, plain-clothed Special Branch officers had begun checking the sleeping patterns of their intended targets. On the night of the raid, some 500 police officers formed into 100 teams and assembled in Johor to avoid attention. They then returned to Singapore in private cars during the night, and hauled their targets out of bed. By the end of February, 116 persons had been arrested, including left-wing politicians and trade unionists. Among the detainees were LIM CHIN SIONG, SIDNEY WOODHULL, Said Zahari, JAMES PUTHUCHEARY, DOMINIC PUTHUCHEARY, LIM HOCK SIEW, Poh Soo Kai and JAMIT SINGH. Many of them were detained for several years, while those originally from the Federation of Malaya were sent back there. Despite the secrecy, news of the raid leaked out and a number of persons escaped capture, including FANG CHUANG PI.

The operation had been planned by the Singapore and Malayan Special Branches and representatives from the Singapore and Kuala Lumpur British High Commissions. The code name is thought to have been suggested by Maurice Williams, the British security liaison officer (MI5) in the British High Commissioner's Office in Kuala Lumpur.

With Operation Cold Store, the

Operation Matador: RAF planes at Tengah Airbase, 1941.

Malayan government smashed the entire left-wing political network and decimated the BARISAN SOSIALIS (although this party was allowed to continued to operate). Operation Pechah was mounted a few months later to sweep up those who had escaped arrest during the first operation.

See also INTERNAL SECURITY DEPARTMENT.

Operation Jaywick This WORLD WAR II operation, which took place on the night of 26 September 1943, resulted in the sinking of six Japanese cargo vessels and an oil tanker. Allied commandos of the Special Operations Executive left northern Australia on 2 September 1943 aboard the HMAS *Krait* (formerly a Japanese fishing boat named *Kofuku Maru*). They arrived at Subar Island near Singapore undetected, then used canoes during the night to plant limpet mines on the ships. They returned to Australia safely aboard the *Krait* on 19 October 1943.

Operation Matador Codename for the WORLD WAR II British plan to deny Japanese forces a base in southern Thailand from which they might prepare an attack on Singapore.

From 1937, British military planners assumed any Japanese attack on Singapore would begin with the seizure of ports and airfields in southern Thailand and northeastern Malaya. They did not believe that a major army presence was justified: a relieving fleet could be sent—arriving within 42 days—to isolate any invading force. The outbreak of war in September 1939 and the fall of France in 1940 changed all this, making it difficult to predict when a British fleet might in fact be sent.

In early 1941, local planners began to draft their own operation—Matador. This required 48 hours' notice, and called for

Operation Rimau: submersible canoes, like the two being transported here, were used, 1945.

British forces to advance from northwestern Malaya and seize the southern Thai port of Singora (present-day Songkhla). A second force, Krohcol, would advance from the northern Malayan town of Kroh to seize a good defensive position known as the Ledge, about 60 km into Thailand, on the Patani–Kroh Road. A third force would hold the beaches in Kelantan, in northeastern Malaya. Meanwhile, the air force would attack the invaders at sea.

The plans to launch Operation Matador were compromised on several fronts. Insufficient aircraft were provided—around 158 to Japan's 600—and no tanks were sent. British commanders were also unwilling to launch the operation until it was certain that Japanese ships were heading for Thai beaches. The ships were first spotted around midday on 6 December 1941, but by the time their direction was confirmed it was too late for troops to reach their destination and dig in. Air Chief Marshal Sir ROBERT BROOKE-POPHAM had been cautious, lest he be tricked into invading Thailand, thus undermining American support. Consequently, the Japanese landed in southern Thailand, virtually unopposed, early on the morning of 8 December.

Debate continues about whether Sir WINSTON CHURCHILL—who endorsed planning in April 1941 but refused to send extra aircraft or tanks—should have sent the additional resources required. It is also debatable whether forward defences would have maximized enemy casualties and blocked the Japanese, or whether it would merely have been outflanked by Japanese landings either side of Singora, and crushed by their tanks and aerial superiority. Either way, the late cancellation of Operation Matador, on 8 December 1941, was crushing for troop morale, and it meant that the fallback defence position at Jitra in Kedah, was less prepared than it could have been.

See also MALAYA CAMPAIGN.

Operation Rimau This was a disastrous attempt in October 1944 to repeat the success of OPERATION JAYWICK the previous year in sinking Japanese ships in Singapore. 'Rimau' is the Malay word for 'tiger'.

Five British and 17 Australian commandos left Fremantle, Australia, on 11 September 1944 on board the submarine HMS *Porpoise*. Dropped off near the coast of Borneo, they captured a sailing boat, which they used to approach Singapore. However, 20 km south of Singapore, they were spotted by the water police, exchanging fire with them.

The operation's leader, Lieutenant Colonel Ivan Lyon, decided to abort the mission, and use the canoes to escape and wait for their appointed rendezvous with a submarine that was to pick them up. Lyon still managed to make a much scaled-down

sabotage attack on Singapore Harbour, sinking three ships.

However, the Japanese methodically combed all the islands south of Singapore and, on 16 October, killed Lyon and three of his men. Eventually, the Japanese either killed or captured all the remaining Operation Rimau men. Those taken prisoner were held in Singapore and beheaded on 7 July 1945.

Operation Tide-Race Codename for Admiral Lord LOUIS MOUNTBATTEN's Southeast Asia Command (SEAC) plan—drawn up on 4–8 August 1945—to occupy Singapore as soon as possible after the capitulation of the Japanese. In order to do this, the British needed to recapture Penang.

When SEAC learned on 4 August 1945 that the war was about to end, new plans had to be drawn up to spearhead the recapture of Southeast Asia. Should the Japanese put up any resistance in Singapore, the British planned to abandon operation Tide-Race, and wait for the implementation of OPERATION ZIPPER—the previously planned invasion to recapture Malaya.

SEAC wanted to reach key cities earlier than in the original plan, so as to re-establish a commanding position and avoid a possibly dangerous power vacuum. In Operation Tide-Race, a small naval force would depart from Burma and Ceylon (present-day Sri Lanka). It would head for Penang first. Having secured Penang's harbour and all-weather airfield, it would then send a naval detachment to arrive off Singapore 14 days later. The Japanese would come onboard a Royal Navy warship to sign 'Instructions' to Japanese forces. The objectives of the operation were to show the flag, assume control of Japanese forces, and deal with prisoners-of-war and internees in Singapore.

The Japanese emperor announced Japan's surrender on 15 August 1945. A Japanese delegation signed an effective surrender for the SEAC area in Rangoon on 23 August. British ships arrived off Penang by 28 August, and on 4 September—two days after General Douglas Macarthur had accepted the main Japanese surrender aboard USS *Missouri* off Tokyo—Vice Admiral Fukudome Shigeru signed 'Instructions' to the Japanese Forces 'to pre-

Operation Tide-Race: Japanese surrender at Rangoon, Burma, 1945.

Operation Zipper: men of the Royal Air Force Regiment aboard a landing raft off Penang, 1945.

pare for the acceptance of the surrender of the Japanese forces in the Singapore area'.

Operation Zipper This plan to recapture Malaya from the Japanese was drawn up on orders issued in May 1945 by Lord LOUIS MOUNTBATTEN, head of Southeast Asia Command (SEAC). After Operation Zipper, scheduled to begin on 9 September 1945, Singapore was to be recaptured in Operation Mailfist. Over seven army divisions were initially allocated.

Operation Zipper was to include an amphibious assault on the Malayan coastline between Port Swettenham and Port Dickson. However, with Japan about to surrender in August 1945, it was decided to proceed with Operation Zipper as a re-occupation exercise, as much of the shipping and transportation was already in place.

On 2 September 1945, the British reoccupied Penang. On 9 September, British forces assembled off the Swettenham–Dickson coastline, and landed unopposed. However, the first landings at Morib Beach by the 25th British Indian Army Division went astray as landing craft and vehicles became bogged in the outgoing tide. Many amphibious landing craft could only be refloated when the tide came back in 12 hours later, although the tide also claimed most of the trucks that had been stuck in the mud. Even ashore, many vehicles found the inland areas inaccessible. The defending Japanese 29th Army had already moved inland to urban areas to await the arrival of the British forces. By the afternoon of 9 September, Port Swettenham was reoccupied; on 10 September, the 23rd British Indian Army Division was in Port Dickson; and by 13 September, the British were in Kuala Lumpur.

opium The history of opium in Singapore goes as far back as Singapore's founding as a British settlement. In November 1819, WILLIAM FARQUHAR, the island's first Resident, recommended that Sir STAMFORD RAFFLES impose restrictions on the sale of opium. Subsequently, in 1820, taxes were imposed on the commodity by Farquhar, despite Raffles' objections to such measures.

Opium: den, c. 1900 (top); customs officers with sacks of seized opium, c. 1960.

Orchard Cinema: building, 1994 (above); ticket stubs.

Orang Laut: family group in the Johor Strait, 1950.

Throughout the 19th century, the opium trade brought profitable returns for Singapore; it contributed substantially to the settlement's revenues. The government earned most of its revenue through franchising the opium trade to well-to-do and reputable Chinese businessmen. These individuals became part of what was known as the 'Great Syndicate', a term coined by Singapore merchant W.G. Gulland.

The migrant Chinese community in Singapore, particularly coolies, were a lucrative market (*see* COOLIE TRADE). Historian James F. Warren, in his book *Rickshaw Coolie*, notes that the 'lack of family comforts, the strenuous nature of their occupation, and the total absence of any healthy form of rest and recreation pre-disposed rickshawmen to smoke opium'. In 1910, the colonial government took over the production of opium to control the drug's quality. The opium was produced in a factory in Pepys Road at the foot of Bukit Chandu, or Opium Hill. As the number of addicts rose, individuals and groups came forward to speak up against the habit, and opium was eventually banned completely in the late 1940s.

Orang Laut The Orang Laut (meaning 'people of the sea' in Malay) were nomadic sea people. They were organized into *suku*, or divisions, including the Suku Tambus, Suku Mantang and Suku Galang. Each *suku* was assigned a role by the Malay overlords, and greater prestige was accorded to the *suku* that was deemed to provide a more important service. Hence, the Suku Galang,

who were organized into pirate armadas and led Malay war-boats, were ranked highest among all *suku*. In contrast, the Suku Tambus were ranked lowest of all because they were in charge of the hunting dogs—a task considered lowly.

The Orang Laut were among the earliest inhabitants of Singapore. There were at least four sub-groups in Singapore—the Orang Selat, Orang Seletar, Orang Kallang and Orang Gelam.

The Orang Selat are also known as the Celates, Saletes or 'Straits People'. The name applies to the people of the Straits of Singapore and Batam. 'Celates' (sometimes spelt 'Cellates') is the Portuguese plural form of 'Orang Selat'. The presence of the Orang Selat plying the waters around the southern coast of Singapore and inhabiting the coastal niches of the island was reported as early as the 16th century. The Orang Selat were also to be found along the Tebrau Strait on the southern coast of Johor. They were a predominantly sea-faring people who sometimes traded fish and fruit with passing ships, or lay in wait to pillage vessels that ran aground in the sandbanks and shallows.

The Orang Seletar traversed the northern creeks along the present Johor Strait. They roamed the mangrove creeks and islets around the island of Singapore, particularly along the shores of the Old Strait to the north of the island and the mouth of the SELETAR RIVER. They have been described as river nomads rather than sea nomads. They collected crustaceans and shellfish along tidal flats and gathered wild jungle plants. Their lifestyle and economy differed so greatly from most other Orang Laut, to whom they are assumed to be related, that local Malays referred to them as 'Orang Utan Seletar' (People of the Seletar Forest).

The Orang Kallang lived only along rivers, particularly the KALLANG RIVER. They avoided the sea and would always proceed upstream before sundown. Subdivisions of the Orang Kallang included the Kallang Roko, Kallang Laut, Kallang Pasir and Kallang Darat. Although they were nomadic, they fixed temporary fishing stakes near the mouth of the river to obtain food. Their economic specializations included the processing of nipah leaves to make wrappers for *rokok daun* (palm-leaf cigarettes), *menambang* (water transportation) and gathering firewood.

The Orang Gelam had a settlement of boats and huts near the mouth of the SINGAPORE RIVER from as early as 1807. They were one of the *suku* or divisions from the Batam Archipelago, most likely from the southern part of Bulan Island. The Suku Gelam were assigned the role of building boats. They were also the warriors on the Sultan's ships and were the temenggong's boatmen, supplying him with fish.

Most of the Orang Selat who had previously lived in the waters around the

southern coast of Johor moved to the northern coast of Singapore in about 1948. This was because the imposition of a curfew in Johor during the EMERGENCY made it impossible for them to carry out their night-time fishing activities. The majority of them requested permission from the headman of Punggol (on the northern coast of Singapore) to allow them to move to Singapore. Others moved to the Southern Islands. After the Emergency, those in possession of land in Johor returned there, while others opted to remain along the northern coast of Singapore. In the 1930s, the Orang Kallang were moved out of the Kallang area to make way for the construction of KALLANG AIRPORT. Most were resettled in the Jalan Eunos area. Others who wanted to maintain their way of life moved to the offshore islands to the south, or to the northern coast of Singapore. Therefore, up until the 1980s, the Orang Selat, Orang Kallang and Orang Seletar could still be found on the northern coast of Singapore in Kampung Tanjong Irau (located in the Sembawang area) and Kampung Wak Sumang in Punggol (located to the east of the Causeway). However, due to development projects, these villages no longer exist today.

Up until the time their settlements were demolished, the Orang Laut lived chiefly by spearing fish. The *tenggiri* (Spanish mackerel), *parang-parang* (dorab) and mussels collected from the shore constituted their chief sources of food. They occasionally supplemented their diet by gathering produce from the jungle. Pandan leaves were also gathered to make *kajang* (a plaited mesh of pandan leaves) mats.

With the obliteration of their villages in Singapore, the Orang Selat, Orang Kallang and Orang Seletar were assimilated into Malay culture, and with their conversion to Islam, they became ethnically identified as Malay. They were relocated to flats in various places including Kampung Melayu Jalan Eunos (Jalan Eunos Malay Settlement). Some Orang Seletar moved to Johor.

Orchard Cinema Cinema. Orchard Cinema was first opened on Grange Road in January 1965 and was closed in 1995. It was the first cinema in Singapore to have an escalator. The building that housed the cinema also included a 24-lane bowling alley, Jackie's Bowl (later renamed Orchard Bowl). The building was torn down and replaced by a mall-cum-cineplex called Cathay Cineleisure Orchard in 1997.

Orchard Road In the 1830s, the area around Orchard Road contained numerous gambier and pepper plantations. Later, other crops such as nutmegs and fruit dominated the area, and it was these orchards that gave the road its name.

In the 1840s, a number of cemeteries were established along Orchard Road. The

Orchard Road: rickshaws, c. 1900 (left); aerial view of the Orchard-Cairnhill junction, 2005.

Teochews had a large burial ground at the current site of NGEE ANN CITY and the Meritus Mandarin Hotel, while Sumatrans from Bencoolen had a burial ground at present-day Kramat Lane, stretching right into what is now the Istana's grounds. A Jewish cemetery was also established at the site of the present-day Orchard MRT station. By the 1860s, people began settling in the area. King Chulalongkorn of Siam (present-day Thailand) acquired Hurricane House (on the site of the present-day Royal Thai Embassy).

Largely because of the cemeteries, which many businessmen considered inauspicious, it was not until the 1930s that Orchard Road became a commercial area. Today, its shopping centres, hotels and office buildings make it the premier shopping district of Singapore.

Orchard Towers Office and shopping blocks at the junction of Orchard Road and Claymore Road. Built in 1975 and designed by Chng Heng Tat and Associates, Orchard Towers comprises two buildings—linked by a bridge—each with its own podium and tower block. Shops and entertainment facilities occupy the first six floors of the block nearer Orchard Road and the first two floors of the other block. Illegal sex workers have been known to operate in the area.

orchids *See* box.

Ord, Colonel Sir Harry (1819–1885) Colonial official. A member of the Royal Engineers, Harry St George Ord had served in the West Indies, and had been governor of Bermuda immediately prior to his appointment, in 1867, as governor of the STRAITS SETTLEMENTS. He was the first person to serve in that office following the transformation of the Straits Settlements into a CROWN COLONY. In accordance with the Crown colony constitution, an executive and a legislative council were set up to assist him.

Ord was lauded as a capable administrator by the British authorities due to his ability to balance the colony's finances, something that had never been achieved previously. However, he did not have the authority to ensure the safety of the merchants who dealt in tin in the Malay states,

or to tackle the problems created by Chinese SECRET SOCIETIES.

Ord was responsible for the building of Government House on Orchard Road, which later became the Istana (*see* ISTANA AND SRI TEMASEK). He retired from his post as governor in 1873. Ord Bridge was named after him.

See also GOVERNORS.

Order of Nila Utama One of the NATIONAL DAY HONOURS, the Order of Nila Utama was instituted in 1975. Persons who have performed outstanding and distinguished service to the nation are admitted into this order. It has three grades: First Class, consisting of the Badge (worn on a sash) and the Star of the Order; Second Class, consisting of the Badge (worn around the neck) and the Star of the Order; and Third Class, consisting of the Badge of the Order (worn around the neck). *See* table.

Order of Temasek One of the NATIONAL DAY HONOURS, the Order of Temasek was instituted in 1962 with three grades: First Class, consisting of the Badge (worn on a sash) and the Star of the Order; Second Class, consisting of the Badge (worn around the neck) and the Star of the Order; and Third Class, consisting of the Badge of the Order (worn around the neck). Only Singapore citizens can be admitted into this order. Non-citizens may, in special cases, be admitted in an honorary capacity. *See* table.

Oriental Telephone and Electric Company Registered in London in 1881, the Oriental Telephone and Electric Company (OTEC) was set up to develop the telephone system in many countries, territories and colonies east of Malta. Within the following two years, it had opened telephone exchanges in various places including Alexandria, Cairo, Bombay, Calcutta, Madras, Hong Kong and Singapore.

In Singapore, OTEC bought over the Private Telephone Exchange—which was started in 1879 by Bennet Pell—and officially opened its Singapore branch on 1 July 1882. Bennet Pell was appointed its first general manager. The telephone lines were owned by four entitities—the Imperial

government, the colonial authorities, the Municipality and OTEC, which controlled most of the lines. In 1916, the government-owned telephone lines were handed to OTEC, which continued to expand the telephone system.

After the end of the Japanese Occupation, OTEC was given the task of restoring the war-damaged telephone system. By 1950, there were 18,860 telephone lines—1.6 telephones per 100 persons—but there was still a large, unmet demand. The government terminated OTEC's licence and took over the network. The assets of OTEC were acquired on 1 January 1955 and the newly-formed Singapore Telephone Board (*see* SINGTEL) became responsible for providing telephone services and developing Singapore's telephone infrastructure.

Colonel Sir Harry Ord

Order of Nila Utama: Badge and Star

Order of Temasek

ORDER OF NILA UTAMA

Member	Date awarded	Grade
Prince Jefri Bolkiah	12 Feb 1990	First Class
Toh Chin Chye	9 Aug 1990	First Class
Ong Pang Boon	9 Aug 1990	First Class
E.W. Barker	9 Aug 1990	First Class
Yong Nyuk Lin	9 Aug 1990	Second Class
Jek Yeun Thong	9 Aug 1990	Second Class
Othman Wok	9 Aug 1990	Second Class
Chua Sian Chin	9 Aug 1990	Second Class
Michael Fam	9 Aug 1990	First Class
Ee Peng Liang	9 Aug 1990	Second Class

Source: Prime Minister's Office

ORDER OF TEMASEK

Member	Date awarded	Grade
Lim Kim San	3 Jun 1962	—
Ahmed Ben Bella	11 Jul 1963	—
Lieutenant-Colonel Gamal Abdul Nasser	20 Jan 1964	—
Eisaku Satu	25 Sep 1967	—
Prince Norodom Sihanouk	Dec 1967	—
Queen Elizabeth II	18 Feb 1972	—
Prince Philip	18 Feb 1972	—
Ferdinand Marcos	16 Jan 1974	—
Suharto	29 Aug 1974	—
Hon Sui Sen	9 Aug 1984	Awarded posthumously
Goh Keng Swee	9 Aug 1985	First Class
Sultan Haji Hassanal Bolkiah Mu'izzaddin Waddaulah	12 Feb 1990	First Class
S. Rajaratnam	9 Aug 1990	First Class
Wee Kim Wee	3 Nov 1993	First Class
Yong Pung How	9 Aug 1999	First Class

Source: Prime Minister's Office

orchids Singapore is an important centre of orchid cultivation. Around 2,000 hybrids have originated on the island, and the variety known as VANDA MISS JOAQUIM is Singapore's national flower. The first major orchid collector in Singapore was HOO AH KAY (also known as 'Whampoa'), a prominent mid-19th century Chinese merchant. He kept his prized orchids in a 12-acre manicured garden, and in 1857 he sold 60 acres of choice land at Tanglin to the government for the construction of the Botanic Gardens (present-day SINGAPORE BOTANIC GARDENS), which would eventually include an important orchid house. The Gardens then embarked on an active orchid exchange programme with other botanical institutions around the world. Among the various species of orchids it received was an enormous tiger orchid (*Grammatophyllum speciosum*) that weighed over a ton. The tiger orchid is the world's second-largest orchid, bearing numerous sprays over a metre long, with thousands of flowers the size of a person's palm (*1*). A record of orchid thefts from the Gardens reflects the interest in orchids at that time. Former director of the Botanic Gardens HENRY RIDLEY, who is best known for his contribution to the RUBBER industry, was another important collector.

1961. The visits of Prince Norodom Sihanouk, Queen Elizabeth II, Prince Akihito and Princess Michiko, Margaret Thatcher, Zhu Rongji and other famous personalities were also commemorated in similar fashion.

Famous Singapore hybrids
The list of renowned Singapore hybrids includes *Vanda* Miss Joaquim, which features in the parentage of over 450 later hybrids; *Aranthera* James Storie, the first successful cut-flower red spider orchid, which brought together two genera of orchids and was bred by the Botanic Gardens in 1939; *Arachnis* Maggie Oei, the first orchid to succeed as an export cut flower and the parent of numerous hybrids, bred by John Laycock in 1941; *Aranda* Deborah, the first, and an extremely prolific, *Aranda* which was bred by Eric Holttum in 1945; *Arachnopsis* Eric Holttum, not striking by itself but a parent of many beautiful hybrids, bred by the Botanic Gardens in 1950; and the *Vanda* Tan Chay Yan (*3*), the first orchid flower from Singapore to earn a First Class Certificate from the Royal Horticultural

Society (RHS), which was bred by Tan Hoon Siang in 1952.

For export as cut flowers, good colour and durability of vase life, the spider orchids (those with *Arachnis* in their parentage) and the *Dendrobiums* (*4*) excel. Three hybrids have earned the First Class Certificate, highest horticultural honours: *Vanda* Miss Joaquim from the RHS in 1897; *Vanda* Tan Chay Yan from the RHS in 1954; and *Mokara* Zaleha Alsagoff from the OSSEA in 1997.

1   2

The cultivators
One of the earliest hybrids was the *Vanda* Miss Joaquim, which was locally cultivated by an Armenian, Agnes Joaquim, and registered in 1893 (*2*). It was a cross between *Vanda hookeriana*, a swamp-growing species from the tin-rich Kinta Valley in Perak, and *Vanda teres* from the foothills of the Himalayas.

In 1928, Eric Holttum, director of the Botanic Gardens, succeeded in raising orchid seedlings from seed. Together with his friend John Laycock, a prominent lawyer, he took up the challenge of producing free-flowering orchid plants suited to the tropics by breeding orchid species from tropical

lowlands. Holttum, Laycock and horticulturist Émile Galistan founded the Malayan Orchid Society that same year, which was the first society of its kind in Southeast Asia. In 1965, this became the Orchid Society of Southeast Asia (OSSEA). With the support of the Botanic Gardens, Holttum and Laycock experimented with many hybrids.

In 1957, the Botanic Gardens began a tradition of naming orchids after important visitors to the Gardens, first naming *Aranthera* Anne Black after Governor Sir ROBERT BROWN BLACK's wife. *Dendrobium* Noor Aishah was named for the wife of the first president of Singapore, YUSOF ISHAK, in

Native orchids
In Singapore, about 200 native orchid species have been recorded. In 1894, Ridley alone recorded 147 species. Nearly all are locally extinct, due to the loss of habitat. Some tens of species still survive in small pockets of natural habitat. Common wild orchids include the pigeon orchid (*Dendrobium crumenatum*) (*5*), which grows on tree trunks in clumps. The bamboo orchid (*Arundina graminifolia*) (*6*) has slender stems and can grow up to two metres tall. It is becoming rarer, but can sometimes be found growing among *lalang* (wasteland grasses) and secondary scrubland.

6

5

OSIM International: iSymphonic massage chair.

OSIM International Distributor of lifestyle and healthcare products. OSIM International started out in 1980 as a sole proprietorship, R. Sim Trading, which sold kitchen appliances and household goods at the People's Park Complex in Chinatown. The company was named after its founder Ron Sim Chye Hock. In 1987, Sim began to switch his focus to home healthcare products and branched out into regional markets such as Hong Kong, Taiwan, Indonesia, Thailand and Malaysia. By 1994, the company had opened more than 60 outlets and had an annual growth rate of 30 per cent. Two years later, the company was rebranded as 'OSIM' and focused on developing its own product brand in the health, hygiene, nutrition and fitness business.

OSIM was listed on the main board of the SINGAPORE EXCHANGE in July 2000, and had by then transformed itself into a region-

al marketer, distributor and franchise owner of a range of healthcare and lifestyle products, including its signature massage-sofa chairs.

OSIM's network has since grown to more than 500 outlets in more than 20 countries worldwide, including markets outside the Asia–Pacific region such as Canada, the United Kingdom, Ireland, Kuwait, Saudi Arabia, South Africa, Ukraine, the United Arab Emirates and the United States. Most of its production needs are outsourced to contract manufacturers in Japan, Taiwan, Spain, Italy, the United States, Australia and Korea. For the financial year 2005, OSIM reported a net profit of $31.7 million on revenues of $332 million.

Othman Wok (1924–) Journalist, politician and diplomat. Othman Wok was the son of Wok Ahmad, a school principal, and Embon Mohamad, who was a descendant

of one of the ORANG LAUT who were living in Singapore when Sir Stamford Raffles arrived in 1819. He was educated at Radin Mas School and Raffles Institution, and later obtained a diploma in journalism from the London School of Journalism (London Polytechnic) on a Colonial Development Scholarship.

Othman Wok: touring Redhill constituency, 1964.

Othman started working life as a radio technician in 1946, but shortly thereafter became a reporter with the Malay newspaper, UTUSAN MELAYU. He rose quickly in the organization to become news editor (1951–57) and then deputy editor (1957–63). While at *Utusan Melayu*, Othman became involved in local politics and he joined the PEOPLE'S ACTION PARTY (PAP) when it was inaugurated in 1954. Othman had met LEE KUAN YEW, the PAP's secretary-general, the year before while he was secretary of the Singapore Printing Employees Union, and Lee was the union's legal adviser.

Othman entered politics in the general election of 1959, during which he contested the Kampong Kembangan seat. Some members of the Malay community accused him of being a traitor, and he lost by fewer than 250 votes. In 1963, Othman stepped down from his position as deputy editor of *Utusan Melayu* to contest Pasir Panjang constituency. This time, he won comfortably against Tay Cheng Kang of the BARISAN SOSIALIS. After the election, Othman was appointed minister for social affairs and, concurrently, director of the MALAY BUREAU, a post he held until 1977 when he became ambassador to Indonesia.

Othman retired from politics in 1980 and became a director of several companies and statutory boards, including the Singapore Tourist Promotion Board (1981–94) and the Sentosa Development Corporation (1981–97). In 1980, he was awarded the Jasa Utama Star by the Indonesian government for his role in forging closer INDONESIA-SINGAPORE RELATIONS. In 1990, he was admitted into the ORDER OF NILA UTAMA (Second Class). In 2001, he wrote an autobiography entitled *Never in My Wildest Dreams*.

Otokichi Yamamoto (1817–1867) Born in Mihama, Japan, Otokichi Yamamoto set off in November 1832 as an apprentice sailor on a routine trade journey between Mihama and Edo (present-day Tokyo). A storm set his ship adrift in the Pacific Ocean. The vessel drifted for 14 months before touching land at Cape Alava, in what is now Washington State, with only Otokichi and two shipmates surviving the journey. After landfall, the three were enslaved by a native American tribe.

In 1834, they were rescued by John McLoughlin of the Hudson Bay Company, who placed them on a brig called the *Eagle*, for a circuitous journey home. McLoughlin hoped to establish trade with the Japanese shogunate through these Japanese men, and believed the *Eagle's* stopover in the United Kingdom would help garner British support for his endeavours. Otokichi and his friends may have been among the first Japanese to visit the United Kingdom.

Travelling under the British flag, the Japanese voyagers stopped at Macau in December 1835, where they met Karl

Friedrich August Gutzlaff, a German missionary. They taught Gutzlaff Japanese, and Otokichi assisted in the Japanese translation of the Gospel of John. Finally, they embarked for Japan in July 1836. Unfortunately, however, the *sakoku*, or 'closed-door' policy, of the Japanese government, made the Japanese authorities suspicious of the foreign ship, and the voyagers were turned back by gunfire.

Otokichi turned to Christianity thereafter, adopting the name John Matthew Ottoson. Working for various British companies, he travelled between Macau, Shanghai and Singapore, helping to repatriate shipwrecked Japanese to Japan. Otokichi returned twice to Japan. On the second occasion, he accompanied Admiral James Stirling when, on 14 October 1854, the admiral negotiated the first limited treaty between the United Kingdom and Japan. For this service, Otokichi was awarded British citizenship and a sum of money, which was believed to have paid for the purchase of his large estate in Singapore.

Otokichi is believed to have moved to Singapore around 1862, and records show he had been naturalized by 1864. He was known to have a residence off Killiney Road in the 1860s and another at Siglap, which he had rented from Robert Little (*see* JOHN LITTLE). It was at Siglap that he finally succumbed to tuberculosis on 17 January 1867. His remains were interred in the Bukit Timah Christian cemetery before they were moved to the Japanese Cemetery off Yio Chu Kang Road. In February 2005, following the trail of their forefather around the globe, some of Otokichi's descendents and townsmen visited Singapore. They took a portion of Otokichi's ashes from Singapore and returned them to Mihama.

Ottoson, John Matthew *See* OTOKICHI YAMAMOTO.

Outram Prison Singapore's first purpose-built prison. In 1847, the prison was built at Outram Road based on plans prepared by John Turnbull Thomson. The foundation stone were laid in February 1847. In 1879, the prison was extended according to designs prepared by Major J.F.A. MCNAIR, colonial engineer and superintendent of convicts (*see* CONVICT LABOUR). McNair was a keen photographer, and photographed the convicts for identification. It became popular for wealthy people to visit the prison to have their own photographs taken.

The perpetrators of the SEPOY MUTINY of 1915 were executed by firing squad in the grounds outside the prison.

The prison was rebuilt in 1929 by Captain Edward Lake and remained in use until 1968, when it was demolished to make way for the Outram Park housing project. The blocks of flats in that project were, in turn, torn down in 2004 for urban redevelopment.

Outward Bound Singapore: OBS Centre, 1997.

Outward Bound Singapore Non-governmental organization. Outward Bound Singapore is the Singapore chapter of an international educational movement originating in the United Kingdom in 1941, and founded on the belief that values learned in the classroom can only be made meaningful through experience. With programmes attended by 20,000 children, youths and adults each year, Outward Bound Singapore (OBS) is the largest Outward Bound operation in the world.

The Outward Bound School of Singapore (OBSS) was created in 1967 by the PEOPLE'S ASSOCIATION, with the mission to 'provide education, leadership and character training; developing the physical, mental and spiritual faculties of boys, girls, young men and women of all races of Singapore'.

From 1970, the OBSS was managed by the Ministry of Defence, which used it to prepare boys for NATIONAL SERVICE. The school was renamed Outward Bound Singapore in 1991, when it was returned to the People's Association. The philosophy of experiential learning was re-established when, in 1997, a 257-ha OBS centre was opened on PULAU UBIN, with special training facilities. In 1999, the OBS Leadership Development Centre was set up to run corporate and professional courses on personnel development and leadership skills.

Outram Prison: the main gate, 1961.

Ouzo Racehorse. Bred and reared at Trelawney Stud, New Zealand, Ouzo was trained by Malcolm Thwaites, and was named Singapore Horse of the Year in 1999 and 2000. He won 13 races from 28 starts, including top local feature races such as the Singapore Derby and Queen Elizabeth II Cup. His greatest achievement was capturing the inaugural $3 million 2,000-m Singapore Airlines International Cup in 2000, against champion thoroughbreds from the United States, the United Kingdom, Argentina, New Zealand, Ireland and Hong Kong. In a career that spanned just five years, Ouzo amassed winnings amounting to $4.5 million. He was retired in 2002.

Ouzo: Saimee Jumaat rides Ouzo to victory in the Singapore Airlines International Cup, 2000.

Oversea-Chinese Banking Corporation: plasterwork logo on former branch, South Bridge Road (left); former building at Chulia Street, c. 1950 (above).

Oversea-Chinese Banking Corporation

The oldest local bank in Singapore, Oversea-Chinese Banking Corporation (OCBC) has a history dating back indirectly to 1912. It was formed in 1932, during the Great Depression, out of the merger of three banks—the Chinese Commercial Bank (established in 1912), Ho Hong Bank (1917) and Oversea-Chinese Bank United (1919). Under the leadership of LEE KONG CHIAN (1938–64) and his successors such as TAN CHIN TUAN (1966–83) and Lee Choon Seng (acting chairman during the Japanese Occupation), it grew to become one of the largest banks in Singapore and the region. OCBC was the only foreign bank to have branches operating in China during the 1950s. By 1970, OCBC had become the banking organization with the largest deposit base in Singapore, with total resources exceeding $1 billion.

OCBC has introduced many innovations to the local banking sector, such as the night-safe system in 1948, which allowed customers to deposit cash and valuables after office hours. In 1958, the mobile bank was created, targeting customers living in suburban areas. It was also one of the pioneers in the Asian dollar market in the 1980s. In August 2001, OCBC Bank acquired the Keppel Capital group and by February 2002, both OCBC and Keppel TatLee banks were operationally and legally integrated.

With assets totalling more than $131 billion as of end-2005, OCBC operated one of the most extensive regional banking networks with more than 110 branches and representative offices in 13 countries, including Malaysia, China, Hong Kong, Japan, Australia, the United Kingdom and the United States. Group earnings crossed the billion-dollar mark for the first time in 2004 after the bank raised its stake in the insurer Great Eastern Holdings from 49 per cent to 81 per cent. In 2005, OCBC posted a net profit of $1.4 billion on a group total income of $2.89 billion. OCBC is a component of the benchmark Straits Times Index.

Overseas Union Bank

Overseas Union Bank (OUB) was first set up in China in 1943 by its founder, LIEN YING CHOW, who had fled to Chungking (present-day Chongqing) during World War II. The bank relocated to Singapore in 1949 with a paid-up capital of $2 million.

OUB expanded outside Singapore to Malaya, Hong Kong, Tokyo and London in 1959; and by 1968 had also extended its network in Singapore to 32 branches. It was the first Singapore bank to open a branch in New York, doing so in 1973. In 1974, together with DBS BANK, OVERSEA-CHINESE BANKING CORPORATION (OCBC) and UNITED OVERSEAS BANK (UOB), it set up the International Bank of Singapore (IBS) to spearhead the global expansion of Singapore banks. UOB subsequently acquired the IBS in 1983, giving it the largest overseas network of Singapore banks.

As a measure of OUB's expansion and diversification after 50 years in operation, around 30 per cent of its earnings were derived from overseas operations. In Singapore, however, OUB remained the smallest of the 'Big Four' local banks, as it had followed a path of organic growth rather than growth through mergers and acquisitions, as was the case with OCBC and UOB. Although known for its innovative approach to banking—it was the first local bank to offer the credit card in 1976, and one of the first to computerize its operations—its smaller size relative to the other 'Big Four' banks made it vulnerable to a takeover. OUB was finally acquired by UOB in 2002.

Ow Chin Hock (1943–) Academic and politician. Ow Chin Hock was educated at the Catholic High School and then at the University of Singapore where he graduated with an honours degree in economics before proceeding to Vanderbilt University in the United States to obtain his masters (1968) and PhD (1972) in economics. He joined the Department of Economics at the University of Singapore as a lecturer on his return in 1972.

Ow entered politics in 1976 on the People's Action Party ticket, winning the seat of Leng Kee constituency. Over the next two decades, he served as parliamentary secretary, Ministry of Culture (1977–80) and Education (1981); minister of state for foreign affairs (1997–2001); and chairman of the FEEDBACK UNIT (1991–96). He was also the first chairman of the Speak Mandarin Campaign (see MANDARIN and CAMPAIGNS). Ow retired from politics in 2001 and was appointed ambassador-at-large.

Owyang, Chi (1897–1988) Banker and diplomat. Born in China, Chi Owyang was educated at a private Chinese-medium school in Bangkok before returning to China where he studied at the Anglo-Chinese College and Fudan University in Shanghai, graduating with a degree in commerce and banking (1921).

Owyang joined the Wuhan branch of the Industrial and Commercial Bank, and in 1923 became assistant manager of its Canton (present-day Guangzhou) branch. In 1930, he joined the China State Bank. After Canton fell to the Japanese in 1938, he relocated first to Hong Kong, then to Manila to join the Philippine Bank of Communication. In 1943, he accepted an offer from the Overseas Chinese Union Bank to establish a branch in Liuchow (present-day Liuzhou), and became the bank's manager in Chungking (present-day Chongqing). He came to Singapore in 1947 to help in the relocation of the OVERSEAS UNION BANK (OUB). The bank officially opened in February 1949, and Owyang subsequently became its first general manager. He retired from OUB in December 1968 and became an adviser on commercial banking to the Development Bank of Singapore (see DBS BANK). In 1971, Owyang was appointed Singapore's ambassador to Thailand, and later, concurrently, the country's first ambassador to Burma (present-day Myanmar).

Owyang received the MERITORIOUS SERVICE MEDAL (1977) and an honorary doctorate of law from the National University of Singapore (1983). In 1983, the King of Thailand conferred on Owyang the Knight Grand Cross of the Most Exalted Order of the White Elephant, Thailand's highest honour, for his role in fostering ties between Singapore and Thailand. In February 1988, Owyang retired as Singapore's envoy to Thailand and died in Bangkok the same year.

Owyang, Hsuan (1929–) Banker. Born in China, Hsuan Owyang is the eldest son of CHI OWYANG. He graduated at the University of Dubuque, Iowa, with a bachelor of science in business administration. He received an MBA from Harvard University in 1952. He then worked as an investment advisor on Wall Street for 12 years with companies such as Thomas & McKinnon.

Owyang came to Singapore in 1965 and was made director and general manager of OVERSEAS UNION BANK, serving in that position until 1983, when he was appointed executive deputy chairman of POSBANK. He was also chairman of the HOUSING & DEVELOPMENT BOARD (1983–98).

Owyang was chairman of the Film Appeal Committee from 1985 to 1998. He has also served as chairman emeritus of the Institute of Policy Studies; and chairman of the East Asian Institute, NM Rothschild & Sons (Singapore) Limited and Ayala International Holdings Limited. He is a director of MOBILEONE. He was awarded the Distinguished Alumni Award of the Harvard Club of Singapore in 1987 and the MERITORIOUS SERVICE MEDAL in 1993. His autobiography, *From Wall Street to Bukit Merah*, was published in 1998.

Overseas Union Bank advertisement, c. 1970.

Ow Chin Hock

Chi Owyang

Hsuan Owyang

P

p-10 Independent art-curatorial team with project space at Perumal Road in LITTLE INDIA. p-10 was established in 2004 by five artists: Lee Sze-Chin, Charles Lim, Lim Kok Boon, Jennifer Teo and Woon Tien Wei. Their experience spans the fields of art practice, art education and art curation. The team works mainly with contemporary visual arts, focusing on dialogue and development, organizing talks, residency programmes and exhibitions. Many of the shophouses in the same row as p-10's premises are set aside for artists' studios.

P&O The Peninsular and Oriental Steam Navigation Company (P&O) was originally a partnership formed in 1822 between former navy clerk Arthur Anderson and London shipbroker Brodie McGhie Wilcox. Anderson and Wilcox had a small fleet of sailing ships plying between Britain and the Iberian Peninsula (Spain and Portugal). By 1836, they were offering regular steamer services under the name Peninsular Steam Navigation Company.

In 1845, P&O's regular steamer service was extended to Malaya, Singapore and China, hence the addition of the word 'Oriental' to the Company's name. In 1852, a bi-monthly service between Singapore and Australia was inaugurated. The following year, P&O operated journeys from Southampton to Capetown and Australia. The opening of the SUEZ CANAL in 1869 shortened this journey considerably.

In the 1920s, P&O was at its peak of ship ownership, with some 500 ships. Post-World War II, the company entered the leisure industry, becoming one of the largest cruise operators in the world.

In 1974, P&O acquired US-based Princess Cruises and Sitmar Cruises in 1988. The P&O group later diversified to include investments in properties, hotels, exhibition centres, shopping centres, oil-drilling equipment, road vehicles and aircraft livery. However, the company has concentrated on maritime and transport interests since 1999.

By 2005 P&O was a major port operator, and Singapore's PSA INTERNATIONAL and Dubai Ports World began a bidding war to take it over. Dubai Ports World succeeded in its bid in February 2006.

Pacific Economic Cooperation Council
Regional forum for cooperation and policy coordination to promote economic development in the Asia-Pacific region. Formed in 1980, it is a tripartite body with representatives from government, business and academia. Its international secretariat is located in Singapore.

Singapore is represented in the Pacific Economic Cooperation Council (PECC) through the Singapore National Committee for Pacific Economic Cooperation (SINCPEC). SINCPEC is made up of representatives from all the universities in Singapore as well as research institutes including the INSTITUTE OF SOUTHEAST ASIAN STUDIES, the EAST ASIAN INSTITUTE and the Lien Foundation Centre for Social Innovation. Business is represented by the Singapore Manufacturers' Federation, the Singapore Human Resource Institute, and businessmen. Officials from the MINISTRY OF FOREIGN AFFAIRS, which sponsors SINCPEC's activities, are key government representatives.

SINCPEC played a significant role in the discussions that led to the formation of the ASIA-PACIFIC ECONOMIC COOPERATION (APEC). APEC was formed following the PECC meetings from 1989 to 1991 when Singapore chaired the Standing Committee.

The PECC has influence in APEC as it is the only non-governmental official observer of APEC. PECC provides support to APEC ministerial and working level meetings, and contributes through research and the production of policy position papers. It also channels and facilitates private sector participation in the APEC process. Some of SINCPEC's contributions have been in the areas of economic structures, economic policy options, free trade and FREE TRADE AGREEMENTS.

Padang Open space in the heart of the civic district. The Padang ('flat field', in Malay) was formerly known as Raffles Plain until around 1906. The centrepiece of colonial life, it fronted the sea and was the place to promenade and exercise horses. It was here that Sir STAMFORD RAFFLES' statue was unveiled on 27 June 1887 to mark Queen Victoria's Golden Jubilee. The statue was moved in 1919 to its present

Padang: bullock-drawn turf-roller, 1946.

location in front of the VICTORIA THEATRE.

By then, the Padang had become associated with sports, especially cricket. The SINGAPORE CRICKET CLUB, initially a European preserve, was formed in 1852. Its progressively grander clubhouse became a landmark at one end of the field. In 1884, the Eurasian community was granted the opposite end, and the SINGAPORE RECREATION CLUB pavilion was opened in 1885. The Padang's park-like quality was considerably enhanced by LAND RECLAMATION in the 1890s, when Connaught Drive and the Esplanade were created, and large angsana trees were planted.

On the first morning of the JAPANESE OCCUPATION, thousands of European prisoners-of-war commenced the march from the Padang to CHANGI PRISON; at the end of the war, the Japanese climbed the steps of CITY HALL overlooking the Padang to surrender. LEE KUAN YEW declared Singapore's independence from the same location on 9 August 1965. The Padang's civic importance is underlined whenever it is used as a venue for NATIONAL DAY celebrations.

It is still a popular recreational space for concerts, rallies and sporting events. Cricket and rugby continue to be played there, and various races begin or end at the Padang.

Padres, The Rock group. The Padres initially consisted of singer Joe Ng, guitarist Nigel Hogan, bassist Evan Tan and drummer Dean Aziz. Drummer Ren Ren replaced Dean at the end of 1995. The members were originally from other bands such as The Mother, Opposition Party and Silent Sorrow. The Padres signed a three-album contract with Rock Records, and it was the recording company's first contract with a Singapore English-language band (*see* ENGLISH POPULAR MUSIC).

During the group's career, The Padres released the single 'Radio Station' (1993); mini-album *What's Your Story* (1994) and a debut album *Night* (1997). It was the first Singaporean band to have its music aired on the BBC World Service radio programme, *The John Peel Show*. John Peel played the songs 'Teenage Story' and 'Mary Said', calling them 'spankingly good tunes'. The Padres broke up in 1998. Evan Tan plays in THE OBSERVATORY, and Joe Ng formed Localbarboy, which plays cover versions of Singapore songs.

Paglar, C.J. (1894–1954) Doctor and politician. Born in Perak to a British father and Indian mother, Charles Joseph Pemberton was orphaned and later adopted by the Eurasian Catholic Paglar family from Malacca. Paglar studied at the KING EDWARD VII COLLEGE OF MEDICINE in Singapore, and served as a medic in the Singapore Volunteer Corps during World War I.

Paglar graduated with a diploma in medicine in 1918 and worked at the SINGAPORE GENERAL HOSPITAL. In 1926, he

The Padres

C.J. Paglar

N. Palanivelu: Kathal
Kiliyum Thiyaga Kuyilum
*(Loving Parrot and Quail of
Sacrifice) (1976).*

went to Edinburgh to further his medical studies. On his return to Singapore, he continued his medical career in private practice. He set up the Paglar Pharmacy at North Bridge Road and the Paglar Maternity and Nursing Home (present-day East Shore Hospital) at Joo Chiat Place. In 1930, he became personal physician to Sultan Ibrahim of Johor.

Shortly before the JAPANESE OCCUPATION, Paglar joined the Medical Auxiliary Services as a volunteer surgeon, and provided medical services until the Fall of Singapore. During the war, he was coerced by the Japanese to serve as president of the Eurasian Welfare Association, which was involved in preparing BAHAU as a resettlement scheme for Eurasians and Catholics. Following the Japanese surrender, the British charged Paglar with treason and collaboration with the Japanese in a BRITISH MILITARY ADMINISTRATION court, but he was not convicted.

Paglar returned to his medical practice at Paglar Maternity and Nursing Home, and rebuilt his medical career. In the LEGISLATIVE COUNCIL ELECTIONS (1951), he was elected to the Changi constituency seat on the SINGAPORE PROGRESSIVE PARTY ticket. His first term in the Legislative Council ended prematurely in December 1954 when he passed away after a short illness.

Palanivelu, N. (1908–2000) Playwright and poet. Born in India, N. Palanivelu arrived in Singapore in 1930. He worked as a clerk in the SINGAPORE TRACTION COMPANY for 19 years before joining Radio Malaya in 1948. He retired from his job in 1968.

Palanivelu wrote hundreds of poems, short stories, serial stories, stage plays and radio, television and poetry dramas. He was a progressive thinker who worked for reform, advocating women's rights and highlighting the inequalities of the caste system in his writing. His more well-known plays are *Suguna Sundaram* (1936)—which documented the atrocities of the caste system—and *Gowri Shankar* (1937), which was about the injustice of arranged marriages between young girls and old men. His books include *Kavithai Malargal* (Poems in Blossom) (1947), which was reprinted in 1975; *Kathal Kiliyum Thiyaga Kuyilum* (Loving Parrot and Quail of Sacrifice) (1976), a short story collection; poetry drama *Kaliyin Nalivu* (Deterioration of Current Times) (1981); and *Pappa Padalgal* (Songs for Children) (1990), a collection of his lyrics to children's songs.

He was awarded the CULTURAL MEDALLION in 1986, and also won the Muthamizh Vithakar (A Person with Extraordinary Skill in Tamil) Award (1980) from the Association of Singapore Tamil Writers. He also received the Kala Ratna Award (1987) for drama from the India Fine Arts Society and the Tamizhavel Award for Literature (1997) from the Association of Singapore Tamil Writers. After his death his son published a two-volume collection of his father's works, *Poet N Palanivelu Padaippu Kalanjiam* (Collective Works of Poet N. Palanivelu), in 1997 and 1999.

Palmer and Turner Civil engineering and architecture firm. Palmer and Turner was one of the leading architectural practices in British colonial Asia. Its Singapore office opened in 1937. The firm's roots can be traced back to London-born architect William Salway, who practised in Hong Kong for 11 years (1865–76). Salway persuaded Hong Kong Surveyor-General Wilberforce Wilson to join the firm, and they made a mark on the island with commissions such as the German Club (1872), the St Peter's Seamen's Church (1872) and the Chartered Bank (1878). After Salway left for Australia, Godfrey Bird, another architect from the Surveyor-General's office, joined the firm.

In 1883, Clement Palmer joined the firm and became the dominant force in the partnership over the next 20 years. Prestigious commissions during this time were the Hongkong and Shanghai Bank (HSBC) (1886), Hong Kong Club (1897) and P&O Building (1887).

Arthur Turner, a structural engineer, joined the firm in 1884 and was made a partner in 1891. Under the new name Palmer and Turner, it expanded to Shanghai, where it was responsible for most of the buildings on the Bund (including the spectacular former Hongkong and Shanghai Bank building). It made its mark too in Malaya and Singapore. Notable commissions in Singapore include the REDIFFUSION building (1948–49), MACDONALD HOUSE (1949) (originally HSBC's Orchard Road branch), and the BANK OF CHINA building (1952–54). Among the prominent architects in Palmer and Turner's Singapore office were P.O.G. Wakeman and James Ferrie.

Pan-El crisis The shares of Pan-Electric Industries Limited (Pan-El) were listed on both the Singapore and the Kuala Lumpur stock exchanges. Its business ranged from marine engineering to hotels and real

Palmer and Turner: Rediffusion building.

estate. It had a market capitalization of $230 million, but was mired in debt and forward trading contracts. By 1985, it owed $450 million to 600 individual and corporate creditors. Its 5,500 shareholders found their shares to be worthless, and both the Singapore and Kuala Lumpur exchanges were closed when the company went into receivership in December 1985.

The Pan-El crisis led to the three-day closure of the Stock Exchange of Singapore (SES) (now the SINGAPORE EXCHANGE) for the first and only time in its history. This crisis extended to Malaysia, leading to the closure of the Malaysian Stock Exchange, which was twinned with the SES. Two Pan-El directors, including Tan Koon Swan, were jailed for breach of trust and forgery of share certificates.

The Pan-El crisis was a systemic threat to the survival of the whole stockbroking industry, and led to widespread loss in public confidence; this was evidenced by plummeting prices on the SES. The MONETARY AUTHORITY OF SINGAPORE (MAS) adopted two main measures: closure of the SES and the setting up of a lifeboat fund, a line of emergency credit for stockbroking firms, underwritten by Singapore's four largest local banks. The crisis also highlighted to the MAS the importance of developing a public communications strategy.

Before the Pan-El crisis, the stockbroking community, along with the companies listed on the SES, was basically unregulated. The new Singapore Securities Industries Act came into effect in 1986 soon after the crisis. This ended self-regulation by members of the SES and introduced direct supervision of securities trading by the MAS. The MAS immediately imposed new limits on the permissible degree of broker exposure to individual clients, and introduced more stringent broker capital-adequacy requirements.

Pan-Malayan Council of Joint Action In September 1946, a disparate group of political organizations and parties joined to oppose British proposals to establish the MALAYAN UNION. In December 1946, the group adopted the name Pan-Malayan Council of Joint Action (PMCJA). It consisted of representatives from the Malay Nationalist Party, the MALAYAN DEMOCRATIC UNION, SINGAPORE FEDERATION OF TRADE UNIONS (the Singapore branch of the General Trade Union), Singapore Clerical Union, Straits Chinese British Association, Malayan Indian Congress, Indian Chamber of Commerce and Singapore Tamils Association. The Chairman of the PMCJA was Sir TAN CHENG LOCK.

The PMCJA was renamed the All-Malaya Council of Joint Action (AMCJA) in August 1947. The dominant force behind the AMCJA was the MALAYAN COMMUNIST PARTY (MCP) who acted through a number of front organizations, especially the Malayan People's Anti-Japanese Ex-Service Comrades' Association. The AMCJA joined forces with the Pusat Tenaga Ra'ayat (People's United Front or PUTERA). PUTERA was formed by the left-wing Malay Nationalist Party (which had earlier left the PMCJA), the Peasants' Union, the Angkatan Wanita Sedara (Awakened Women's Union) and the Angkatan Pemuda Insaf (Union of Aware Youth).

The British did not recognize the PMCJA as representing domiciled non-Malay opinion, accusing it of being a communist-dominated organization with a partisan agenda. By February 1948, the PUTERA-AMCJA was in tatters as the British plan to establish the Malayan Union had the support of the United Malays National Organisation (UMNO). Its secretary-general GERALD DE CRUZ resigned, citing a shortage of funds. When TAN CHENG LOCK's son TAN SIEW SIN accepted nomination as a member of the Federal Legislative Council under the Malayan Union plan, PUTERA-AMCJA collapsed.

Pan Shou (1911–1999) Artist and poet. Born in Fujian, China, Pan Shou (also known as Pan Guoqu) arrived in Singapore in 1930 and became an editor of LAT PAU, Singapore's earliest Chinese newspaper. He later became the principal of TAO NAN SCHOOL. He was the secretary-general of NANYANG UNIVERSITY from 1955 to 1960. Over 600 of his poems have been published, including a four-volume collection , *Pavilion Beyond the Ocean* (1970). His Chinese calligraphic work can be found in the SINGAPORE ART MUSEUM and on stelae of the Confucian Temple in Shandong, China. A prolific artist, Pan Shou produced around 2,000 calligraphic scrolls and poems during his lifetime.

Awards he has received include the Public Service Star (1970), the CULTURAL MEDALLION (1986), the MERITORIOUS SERVICE MEDAL (1994) and the ASEAN Award (1997).

Pang Tee Pow (1928–1977) Civil servant. Pang Tee Pow was educated at Raffles Institution and then at the University of Malaya, graduating with an honours degree in arts. He joined the civil service as a laboratory assistant in 1949, and was promoted to labour inspector in the labour service a year later. In 1955, he was absorbed into the Administrative Service, where he became permanent secretary to the minister of labour (1969). Later that year, he was also appointed permanent secretary of the Ministry of Interior and Defence, and was placed in charge of its Home Affairs Division and the Central Manpower Base.

When the Ministry of Interior and Defence was split into the Ministry of Home Affairs and the Ministry of Defence, Pang remained in the latter. He was award-ed the Meritorious Service Medal in 1970, and was admitted posthumously to the Distinguished Service Order in 1978.

Panguni Uthiram Hindu festival which takes place on the day of the full moon in the Tamil month of Panguni (March–April). It is considered an auspicious day for worship. It commemorates celestial marriages and, in astronomical terms, is held on the day on which the planet Mars is closest to the earth.

There are several legends that explain the origins of this festival. One legend says that it marks the day of the marriage of Lord Subramaniam (younger son of Lord Shiva) to Theivanai—this is the story accepted by most Hindus in Singapore as the reason for the festival. According to the legend, Indra, King of the Gods, gave Subramaniam his adopted daughter Theivanai in marriage as a symbol of gratitude for his role as commander-in-chief of the gods in their victory over the demon Soorapathman.

In all temples for Subramaniam, devotees carry *kavadi* (semi-circular steel frames, decorated with flowers and peacock feathers) and milk pots to fulfil their vows to Subramaniam. This festival is celebrated on a grand scale at the Murugun Hill Temple and the Holy Tree Balasubramaniam Temple. Although it is a popular local festival, Panguni Uthiram is observed on a smaller scale than THAIPUSAM.

pantun Form of Malay poetry. Richard Winstedt, president of RAFFLES COLLEGE in the early 1930s who studied Malay literature extensively, once remarked that Malay culture cannot be fully appreciated by someone who does not know the *pantun*. A typical *pantun* comprises four rhyming lines with the 'A-B, A-B' rhyme scheme, where the first line rhymes with the third and the second with the fourth. Less common forms have two, six or eight lines. A *pantun* is made up of two parts. The first two lines make up the *pembayang* (shadow), which serves as a metaphor. The next pair of lines carries the *maksud* (meaning).

The *pantun* can be recited by a single person, but is more often thrown back and forth between two or more people in spontaneous exchanges known as *berbalas pantun* (literally 'exchanging poems'). The exchange starts when someone recites a *pantun*. This usually sets the theme for the *berbalas pantun*. An adversary will respond by reciting another *pantun*. The exchange is almost always light-hearted, but the themes explored can be quite serious. In Singapore, callers to Malay radio stations frequently participate in *berbalas pantun*. *Berbalas pantun* is also used as an icebreaker during formal events such as marriage proposals.

See also SAJAK.

Parameswara *See* ISKANDAR SHAH.

Paranan (1944–2005) Poet. Born C.Velu in Johor, Paranan received his primary education in Kerala, India, and his secondary education in Singapore. He worked briefly as a sub-editor at Tamil daily *Tamil Malar*, and wrote over 3,000 poems. He also wrote novels and essays. His poems are traditional in form, dealing mostly with the themes of the Tamil language, nationhood, nature and community. He published four poetry collections—*Thoni* (Boat), *Mazhai* (Rain), *Thendral* (Breeze) and *Ethiroli* (Echo). His poems were also published in two anthologies, *Singapore Kavithaigal* (Singapore Poems) and *Malaysia Kavithai Kalanjiam* (Malaysian Poetry Journal). Paranan won the Southeast Asia Write Award in 1986.

Pararaton Sixteenth-century manuscript presenting a view of events connected with the foundation and expansion of MAJAPAHIT in the 14th century. The Pararaton (Book of Kings in Javanese) also describes how Majapahit coveted TEMASEK, among other territories, during that period.

The Pararaton describes an oath taken in 1336 by Majapahit's *patih,* or chief minister, Gajah Mada, not to enjoy '*palapa*' until he has conquered the Nusantara (signifying the Indonesian archipelago and the MALAY PENINSULA). What *palapa* meant is unknown. However, the Sumpah Palapa (Palapa Oath) has become an important metaphor in modern Indonesia for national unity. (The name Palapa was given to Indonesia's communications satellites to reflect their role in binding the far-flung islands of the nation together.)

The oath lists numerous territories outside Java. One of these, listed together with other toponyms known to have been located in the region of Sumatra and the Malay Peninsula, is Temasek. The DESAWARNANA, written 29 years after the Sumpah Palapa is supposed to have taken place, lists Temasek as a vassal of Majapahit, thus suggesting that Gajah Mada had, at least partly, succeeded.

The historical authenticity of the Sumpah Palapa is uncertain; like much else in the Pararaton, it may have been created later for dramatic effect. The Pararaton also presents a different point of view from the account of the Desawarnana. However, several sources do confirm the fact that 14th-century Singapore was coveted by Java and probably came under its sway for some time during that period.

parit Singapura *See* OLD LINES.

Parkinson, C. Northcote (1909–1993) Academic. Born in Durham, United Kingdom, C. Northcote Parkinson read history at Cambridge, and obtained his PhD from King's College, London.

In 1950, he became Raffles Professor of History at the UNIVERSITY OF MALAYA in Singapore, where he remained until 1958.

Pan Shou: the artist and Lion *(1994) (top).*

parks The NATIONAL PARKS BOARD (NParks) manages a hierarchy of regional parks, neighbourhood parks and park connectors, with both natural and man-made elements.

Neighbourhood parks located within walking distance of residential areas and PUBLIC HOUSING estates provide greenery and open spaces for residents. Shade trees, exercise equipment, shelters and benches are standard provisions.

Regional parks such as Bishan Park, however, are designed to attract visitors from larger areas. Accessibility by private car and public transport is optimized, and seamlessness with the surrounding residential areas is also key when they are nearby.

The appeal of regional parks lies in the wide variety of experiences they provide. Beach parks such as Marina South (*1* and *2*), East Coast Park (*3*), Pasir Ris Park (*4*) and Changi Beach Park offer activities such as sea sports, picnicking, camping, fishing and cycling. Ridge parks such as Telok Blangah Hill Park, Kent Ridge Park and Mount Faber Park offer panoramic views. Historic parks such as FORT CANNING Park and Labrador Park (see LABRADOR NATURE RESERVE) are the sites of relics and ruins. Many parks also have restaurants on their grounds.

Parks have also become popular venues for the arts. The SINGAPORE BOTANIC GARDENS and Fort Canning Park play host to regular events such as concerts, SINGAPORE DANCE THEATRE'S Ballet Under the Stars, and World of Music and Dance (WOMAD).

While not strictly parks, the four nature reserves—BUKIT TIMAH NATURE RESERVE, CENTRAL CATCHMENT NATURE RESERVE, SUNGEI BULOH WETLAND RESERVE and Labrador Nature Reserve—are also managed by NParks.

C. Northcote Parkinson: this collection, The Law (1979), contains the text of 'Parkinson's Law' and other writings.

In 1955, he published his famous Parkinson's Law in *The Economist*: work expands so as to fill the time available for its completion. He developed his ideas in books such as *Parkinson's Law, or The Pursuit of Progress* (1958) and *The Law and The Profits* (1960).

parks *See* box.

Parkway Holdings Regional HEALTHCARE provider. Parkway Holdings started out as Singapore Glass, which was incorporated in Singapore in February 1974 as an investment holding company. After hiving off its non-profitable glass business to ACI Asia for $15.42 million, the company was acquired by Eady Investment and subsequently renamed Parkway Holdings in 1985. It dealt in property investment and development.

The group ventured into the private healthcare sector when it bought and expanded the Gleneagles Hospital and Medical Centre in 1991. In 1995, it acquired Tenet Healthcare Corporation's Singapore operations, which included the Mount Elizabeth and East Shore hospitals.

Parkway has since developed the most extensive network of private hospitals and healthcare services in Asia. Besides the three hospitals in Singapore, the group also operates the Gleneagles chain of hospitals in Jakarta, Surabaya, Medan, Kuala Lumpur, Penang, Brunei, Kolkata and Colombo. It also has a specialist heart hospital in London.

The group's other healthcare network includes Parkway Shenton, one of Singapore's biggest general practices (acquired in 1995); radiology service provider Medi-Rad Associates; and Parkway Laboratory Services. In all, the group has some 1,400 accredited specialists who deliver advanced treatments across 40 specialities. The group provides contract research services through its subsidiary, Gleneagles Clinical Research Centre. It has offices in China, Bangkok, Bangladesh, Hong Kong, Indonesia, Myanmar, the Philippines, Russia and Sri Lanka.

Parkway, which is a Straits Times Index stock, has been listed on the SINGAPORE EXCHANGE since April 1975. It posted net earnings of $62 million on group revenues of $549 million in 2005. Its biggest shareholder is Newbridge Capital, a San Francisco-based private equity firm.

Newbridge secured 26 per cent of Parkway from the founding Tan and Ang families for $312 million in June 2005.

Parliament In colonial times, the legislature was a branch of government. However, it originally took the form of the Legislative Council, which came into being in 1867 with the creation of the STRAITS SETTLEMENTS. In 1955, as Singapore took the first tentative steps towards self-government, a mainly elected Legislative Assembly came into being. In 1965, when Singapore became independent, the assembly was renamed Parliament; it sat as such for the first time on 8 December 1965. Throughout its history, Singapore's legislature has always been unicameral, i.e. consisting of one chamber only.

Its composition and powers have not always been the same. During the period of colonial administration, the Legislative Council was not an elected body but one in which members were nominated from among various groups, most notably the business community. During this period, Officials (who were part of the colonial administrative service) always outnumbered Unofficials (members appointed from

Parliament: one of the early sessions (top); the new Parliament House.

among the local notables).

Singapore adopted a Westminster-style parliamentary system of government in which the executive branch of government is drawn from the legislative branch. The government, comprising the prime minister and Cabinet, is drawn from among the membership of Parliament instead of being elected or appointed independently. Parliament comprises the PRESIDENT and the MEMBERS OF PARLIAMENT (MPs) and, for the most part, is presided over by the SPEAKER. The president's role in Parliament is limited to the delivery of the Presidential Address at the opening of Parliament when he sets out the government's policies. MPs must be: Singapore citizens aged 21 or older; listed on the current register of electors; able to communicate in one of the four official languages (English, Malay, Mandarin, or Tamil); and of sound mind.

The life of each Parliament is five years. Thereafter, Parliament must be dissolved and general elections have to be called. Parliament may, however, be dissolved any time before its five-year lifespan is up. A general election must be held within three months of Parliament being dissolved. Parliament convenes at least once a year, scheduling its meetings after the president summons the first session. At the end of each Parliamentary session, Parliament is prorogued.

Parliamentary procedure is based on the British parliamentary model. Bills are deliberated in three readings with a committee stage between the second and third readings. A simple majority passes all Bills, except for constitutional amendments, which require a two-thirds majority of elected MPs. Only the government may introduce money bills. Once passed, a Bill becomes an Act (i.e. law) after the president gives his assent and the law is published in the Government Gazette. Before the president gives his assent to the Bill, all laws passed by Parliament must be sent to the PRESIDENTIAL COUNCIL FOR MINORITY RIGHTS for its scrutiny. If the Council gives an adverse opinion on any bill, it will not be passed into law, unless it is either modified or passed by a two-thirds majority in Parliament. Since its inception, the Council has never issued an adverse report.

MPs enjoy certain immunities and privileges in their conduct of parliamentary business. This is to ensure that members can debate freely. In addition to MPs who are elected into office, there are two other types of parliamentarians: NON-CON-STITUENCY MPs and NOMINATED MPs. Both these types of MP have the same rights and privileges as regular MPs but they are not allowed to vote on money bills, constitutional amendments, or motions of no confidence against the government.

See also ELECTIONS and POLITICAL SYSTEM.

Parsis Followers of the Zoroastrian faith, who fled from Persia (present-day Iran) in the 8th century, and settled on the west coast of India. Parsis began arriving in Singapore in the 19th century.

The first Parsi to live in Singapore was a convict named Muncherjee. When Muncherjee fell ill in 1829, an Armenian merchant persuaded Parsis living in China to purchase land for a Parsi cemetery in Singapore. Land in what is now Parsi Road was acquired for this purpose. In 1848, land adjacent to the cemetery was also acquired for a Parsi Lodge where Zoroastrian ceremonies could be held. In 1889, the Parsi Lodge Charity was started, and income from this trust was used for the upkeep of the burial ground.

The Parsi Association was established in 1954, and took over the running of the Parsi Lodge Charity. In the late 20th century, the religious needs of the community were served by Behram Vakil, a Zoroastrian priest, who died in the 1990s. Religious ceremonies such as initiations into the faith (*navjot*) were thereafter conducted by part-time priests, as well as by ordained Parsis who also held regular jobs.

One of the first Parsis to make a name for himself in Singapore was entrepreneur Cursetjee Framjee who, in 1845, was one of the founders of Little Cursetjee & Co., which eventually became the JOHN LITTLE department store. Another well-known Parsi was Navroji Mistri who came to Singapore in 1912 as an engineer to work on the building of Keppel Wharf. He stayed on after the project and eventually started the Phoenix Aerated Water Company. He also ran the well-known G.H. Café on Battery Road. In the 1950s, Mistri donated $1 million to the paediatric wing of SINGAPORE GENERAL HOSPITAL. The wing was later named after him. Many other Parsis have contributed to Singapore's civic life and to charity, an example being orthopaedic surgeon Dr Jimmy Daruwalla, who was the founder president of the Dyslexia Association of Singapore.

Over the years, the Parsi community has grown due to the arrival of those who have moved to Singapore to work. By the early years of the 21st century, there were some 200 Parsis in Singapore.

pasar malam Malay for 'night market'. The *pasar malam* is a cluster of itinerant stalls offering food, drinks and other inexpensive products. Until the 1970s, the *pasar malam* were largely makeshift. Vendors would get together and set up shop in the evenings along a roadside, usually in the more populous PUBLIC HOUSING estates. Few of the

Parsis: priest performing the navjot, *1979.*

Pasar malam: *searching for bargains.*

stalls were sheltered and lighting was supplied by either pressure lamps or small generators. When the government started to ban itinerant stall-holders in the 1970s and ordered all vendors to move into HAWKER CENTRES, the *pasar malam* started to decline. In the 2000s, *pasar malam* are organized by authorities such as TOWN COUNCILS. These modern *pasar malam* have covered stalls supplied with electric power and lighting.

Pasir Ris PUBLIC HOUSING estate. The name Pasir Ris was first used in an 1852 map, in the form 'Passier Reis Village'. Geographers have suggested that it could be a contraction of the Malay *pasir iris* (meaning 'shredded sand'), in reference to the fine white sand found on local beaches. Pasir Ris was later transformed into a major public housing estate, close to holiday beach resorts and chalets. Pasir Ris is bounded by Loyang Avenue, Pasir Ris Drive 3, Pasir Ris Drive 12 and the Tampines Expressway. There are some 27,400 residential units in the estate, and its 7,500 executive-type units are the largest in any public housing estate.

patents For many years, patent protection could be obtained in Singapore only if one registered a patent in the United Kingdom, and then, within three years, re-registered it locally under the Registration of UK Patents Act. A re-registered patent of this sort would be conferred the same 'privileges and rights' in Singapore to those it had been accorded in the UK. Thus, there were essentially no local laws regarding the patentability of inventions, or the validity of and infringements on patents.

On 23 February 1995, a local Patents

Pasir Ris Beach at Pasir Ris Park.

Act (modelled largely on its UK namesake) came into force in Singapore. Almost immediately, the popularity of patenting surged. In 1994, before the promulgation of the Patents Act, only 1,818 re-registration applications had been filed; in 1995, the number of applications more than doubled to 4,741 (2,329 re-registrations and 2,412 direct national filings).

Since 1995, patents have been filed with the Registry of Patents of the Intellectual Property Office of Singapore (IPOS), which examines and grants patents. Singapore's patent laws are largely compliant with international standards prescribed in the Agreement on Trade-Related Aspects of Intellectual Property Rights—a treaty which sets minimum standards for the protection of intellectual property in signatory countries. On 23 November 1994, Singapore also acceded to the Patent Cooperation Treaty (PCT), administered by the WORLD INTELLECTUAL PROPERTY ORGANIZATION. This means that patent protection in Singapore can be obtained not only through a domestic application with IPOS, but also through an international application which has been filed in a PCT-acceding country.

A patent in Singapore generally lasts for a period of 20 years from the filing of the application. However, amendments to the act, which came into force on 1 July 2004, introduced for the first time the possibility of extending the term by up to five years. An extension can be granted if there was any unreasonable delay on the part of IPOS in granting the patent; or where the patent includes a substance which is an active ingredient of a pharmaceutical product, and obtaining market approval for the product causes an unreasonable curtailment of the opportunity to exploit the patent.

Paterson, Simons & Co. Trading firm. William Paterson came from Lerwick, United Kingdom, to Singapore in 1842 to join Ker, Rawson and Co. as an assistant. He was made partner of the firm in 1853 along with Henry Minchin Simons. The firm was later renamed Ker, Rawson, Paterson and Simons. In 1859, when the senior partners retired, it became Paterson, Simons and Co. The firm's main business was trade, and it pioneered the export of GUTTA PERCHA. Other exported goods included RUBBER, gambier, copra (dried coconut kernel), tapioca, sago flour and PINEAPPLE. After Paterson's death in 1898 and Simons' death in 1901, Paterson's son, Graham Paterson, continued to run the family business till his own retirement in 1920. No longer based in Singapore, the firm has its main offices in Hong Kong and South Africa.

Paya Lebar Airport Until 1955, Singapore's aviation needs were served by KALLANG AIRPORT (built in 1937) and SELETAR AIRBASE (1929). The phenomenal growth of

aviation led to a government decision in 1951 to build a new civilian airport at PAYA LEBAR, just eight kilometres from the city centre. The airport was opened on 20 August 1955 and could handle up to 300,000 passengers a year. Within 15 years, the number of passenger arrivals had hit 1.7 million and Paya Lebar was bursting at the seams. One of the most memorable planes to take off and land regularly at Paya Lebar was the now defunct supersonic passenger airliner, the Concorde.

CHANGI AIRPORT replaced Paya Lebar Airport as Singapore's main civilian airport in 1981. Paya Lebar was handed over to the Air Force and renamed Paya Lebar Air Base. Its Air Movement Centre handles passengers and cargo arriving on REPUBLIC OF SINGAPORE AIR FORCE flights, MINISTRY OF DEFENCE charter flights and foreign military aircraft. Paya Lebar Airport currently houses the C130 Hercules and F5 Tiger IIs. The flying units based there are 122, 144, 141 and 149 Squadrons.

peacekeeping Since 1948, the United Nations (UN), through the Department of Peacekeeping Operations (DPKO), has conducted peacekeeping missions all over the world. As a member of the global community, Singapore recognizes this stabilizing role of the UN and has actively participated in missions since 1989. More than 1,200 Singapore troops have been involved in 13 operations taking place in over 11 countries.

In 1989, the first SINGAPORE ARMED FORCES (SAF) Peacekeepers were deployed to Namibia as part of UNTAG (UN Transitional Authority Group). Fourteen SAF officers, 48 police officers and 20 civil servants acted as election supervisors after South Africa agreed to end its administration of Namibia. When the Allied Forces carried out Operation Desert Storm during the 1991 Gulf crisis, a 30-man medical team from Singapore was sent to Saudi Arabia for three months to give medical support under the mission name Ops Nightingale. In April that same year, SAF officers were sent to Kuwait on the UN Iraq–Kuwait Observation Mission (UNIKOM) as military observers. As of 2005, UNIKOM was still active and SAF officers continued to render their services.

During the 1993 UN-sponsored elections in Cambodia, election monitors and

Peacekeeping: Singapore troops on peace mission.

helicopter support were supplied by Singapore for the UNTAC (UN Transitional Authority in Cambodia) operation.

From November 1995 to February 1999, SAF officers were seconded to the DPKO at UN Headquarters. In 2001 and 2002, Singapore posted mission planning officers to the DPKO.

Singapore peacekeepers have also taken part in INTERFET (UN-sanctioned International Force in East Timor), UNTAET (UN Transitional Administration in East Timor) and UNMISET (UN Mission of Support in East Timor). Cumulatively, 373 Singaporean medical and logistics personnel were involved with INTERFET from 1999 to 2000. During 2000–02, when UNTAET was in operation, Singapore sent armed peacekeepers, military observers and medical support. After East Timor gained independence from Indonesia, UNTAET was replaced by UNMISET.

Pearl, James (dates unknown) Merchant. James Pearl was the owner and captain of the ship *Indiana*, which accompanied Sir STAMFORD RAFFLES on his voyages to Java and Sumatra, and was one of the six that first sailed to Singapore in 1819. Pearl's extensive trade in the region made him a wealthy man. He later decided to invest in property and a plantation in Singapore. He chose a hill in the Outram area, naming it Mount Stamford in honour of Raffles. However, Raffles was unhappy with Pearl's acquisition, and tried to persuade him to surrender the property. Pearl fought to keep his hill, and Raffles relented—but after the unpleasant encounter, Pearl decided to rename the property Pearl's Hill. Pearl sold the hill to the government after his retirement.

Pedra Branca The island of Pedra Branca is a rocky island at the eastern end of the Singapore Straits. It was named Pedra Branca ('White Rock') by the Portuguese because of the accumulation of white droppings from the numerous black-naped terns which used it as a resting place during their search for fish near the reef in certain months of the year. It was a hazard to shipping not just because of the reef, but also because the surrounding waters were, at one time, infested by pirates. The British acquired the island and constructed the HORSBURGH LIGHTHOUSE on it between 1847 and 1851.

Ownership of the island is disputed by Singapore and Malaysia. As recently as 1974, a Malaysian government map still marked the island as belonging to Singapore. This changed in 1979 when a new Malaysian government map designated Pulau Batu Puteh ('White Rock Island'), as it is known in Malay, as part of Malaysian territory. Singapore immediately protested against this claim. In 1989, Singapore

Pegasus being lowered by a helicopter.

proposed bringing the case to the International Court of Justice at The Hague, to which Malaysia agreed in 1994. The two governments submitted a Special Agreement to the International Court of Justice on 24 July 2003. By mid-2006, the two sides had completed the exchange of written pleadings and were waiting for the oral hearing.

Pegasus Artillery weapon. This lightweight howitzer was developed by the SINGAPORE ARMED FORCES in 2005. It is a 155-mm, 39-calibre artillery gun capable of self-propulsion. Weighing 4.8 tons, it was specially designed to be deployed by helicopter. The Pegasus is the fifth 155 mm artillery gun to be developed by either Singapore Technologies Kinetics (ST Kinetics) or Chartered Industries of Singapore.

See also PRIMUS.

Penal Code Statutory code of law creating criminal offences and providing for their punishment. The Singapore Penal Code was adopted from the Indian Penal Code, which was drafted by Lord Thomas Macaulay, and passed into law in 1860. For most of the 19th century, Singapore's CRIMINAL LAW was based on English COMMON LAW in so far as local circumstances permitted. In 1872, the Straits Settlements Penal Code was passed to apply the Indian Penal Code to PENANG, MALACCA and Singapore. It was practically a re-enactment of the Indian Penal Code, which sought to consolidate the law relating to all criminal offences.

Since then, the Code has been amended several times. It is not exhaustive; PARLIAMENT has enacted many other statutes to supplement it, setting out the law relating to certain types of offences. However, the Penal Code is still the main piece of criminal legislation in Singapore.

Penang Island off the northwest coast of the Malay Peninsula, also known as Pulau Pinang (Malay for 'Betel Nut Tree Island'). Originally part of the Kedah sultanate, Penang was ceded by Sultan Abdullah of Kedah to the EAST INDIA COMPANY in 1786 in exchange for military protection from Siamese and Burmese armies. On 11 August 1786, Captain Francis Light of the East India Company landed on the island, which had a largely Chinese population, and renamed it Prince of Wales Island. Penang's location at the opening of the Strait of Malacca proved attractive to the British settlers, and its deep natural harbour provided ideal anchorage for trading ships.

In 1826, Penang, Malacca and Singapore collectively became the STRAITS SETTLEMENTS, which was administered from India. Because the British had settled in Penang far earlier than it had in the other two territories, Penang was the capital of the Settlements, with Penang's governor, Robert Fullerton as the first governor of the Settlements. However, as Singapore grew in importance, it, rather than Penang, became the administrative capital of the Straits Settlements in 1832. In 1867, the Straits Settlements ceased to be run from India, and became a CROWN COLONY administered directly by the Colonial Office in London. In 1946, the Straits Settlements ceased to exist. Penang and Malacca became part of the MALAYAN UNION, while Singapore continued to be administered as a separate colony.

Penarek Becha (1955) First movie directed by P. RAMLEE. *Penarek Becha* was produced by Shaw Brothers' MALAY FILM PRODUCTIONS in their Jalan Ampang studio off Balestier Road. Set in Singapore, *Penarek Becha* tells the story of a poor trishaw rider played by P. Ramlee, who helps and subsequently falls in love with a rich young woman, played by Sa'adiah. It was voted Best Picture by readers of *Utusan Filem dan Sport* magazine in 1956. The readers also voted its theme song 'Inang Baru' Best Song. 'Inang Baru' was composed by director P. Ramlee with lyrics by S. Sudarmadji. The dance sequence which accompanied the song in the film became an overnight craze.

Penarek Becha (1955)

Penang: Burmah Road in the Chinese Quarter, 1911.

The film broke new ground with its tackling of social issues in contemporary Malay society (see MALAYS) at the time. It also set the tone for P. Ramlee's subsequent films, which highlighted the economic and social divisions present in the Malay community. These social issues were part of the agenda of ASAS 50, an important Malay literary activist organization.

Pennefather, Percy (1923–1975) Sportsman. Percy Pennefather was a student at St Joseph's Institution and member of one of Singapore's most illustrious sporting families. He played cricket, badminton and tennis, but it was in hockey that he made his name. Pennefather made his debut on the national hockey team at right-half in 1947. Nine years later, he moved permanently to centre-forward. Pennefather played in the 1956 Olympic Games, where Singapore finished eighth.

Pennefather scored 290 goals in his 110 international caps for Singapore. He retired at age 38, but continued with club hockey, and eventually became a coach and administrator. He was the national coach for the pre-Olympic tournament in 1967. In 1972, he became president of the Singapore Hockey Association.

Pentecostals The Pentecostal movement stresses the experience of speaking in tongues as a sign of being 'filled with the Spirit'. Another distinctive feature is the exercise of 'supernatural' gifts such as prayer for divine healing and exorcism.

The movement began in the United States at the beginning of the 20th century, and spread rapidly to other parts of the world. It consists of numerous independent churches and denominations, of which the largest is the Assemblies of God (AOG).

The first AOG missionaries, Cecil and Edith Jackson, came to Singapore in 1928. Other missionaries who joined them soon afterwards were Carrie Anderson, Esther Johnson and Katherine Clause. Women have always played a crucial role in the spread of the Pentecostal movement. Their efforts were concentrated in the SERANGOON ROAD area and resulted in the establishment of Elim Church in 1940.

Besides the AOG, there were smaller Pentecostal groups such as the Finnish Free Foreign Mission, whose missionaries came to Singapore when forced to cease work in China after 1949. Salem Chapel, Glad Tidings and Praise Evangelical Church were part of a loose network of Finnish Pentecostal Churches, but have since become, for all practical purposes, independent churches.

Other independent Pentecostal churches were often the result of splits when a group within a traditional church embraced Pentecostal beliefs and practices. The Church of Singapore in Marine Parade was one such church. About a hundred members were forced out of a Brethren church after they came under the influence of itinerant evangelist Madam Kong Mui Yee, a converted film actress from Hong Kong. Until the early 1960s, foreign missionaries played a key role in founding new churches. However, since the 1980s, most new churches have been the result of local initiatives.

In Singapore, as well as worldwide, the growth of Pentecostal churches has been dramatic. Membership of the AOG, for example, grew from 640 in 1972 to more than 25,000 in 2004. As with most Pentecostal churches elsewhere, attendees usually outnumber registered members.

The AOG is a loose fraternity of autonomous congregations. The clergy and lay delegates of the various churches elect an executive committee of nine headed by the general superintendent in an annual session known as the General Council. The executive committee issues credentials to the clergy and oversees such joint efforts as seminary training and community programmes. The General Council runs a uniformed group for youths called Royal Rangers, and various community projects, such as services to senior citizens and before-and-after-school care. It runs a highly successful drug and alcohol recovery centre, a hostel for young delinquents, and a halfway house under the umbrella of Teen Challenge.

In the 1970s and 1980s, Pentecostal-like revivals occurred in many churches in the West, and these have found their way into their respective affiliates in Singapore. The result has been a proliferation of independent Charismatic (*charisma* meaning 'gift' in Greek) churches, such as CITY HARVEST CHURCH and NEW CREATION CHURCH, as well as Charismatic groups within older denominations, including the Roman Catholic Church. Those involved in the newer revivalist movements prefer to call themselves Charismatics rather than Pentecostals.

See also CATHOLICISM and CHRISTIANITY.

People Like Us Singapore's first gay and lesbian organization, People Like Us (PLU) has evolved from an informal network into a virtual community. In 1993, members met at THE SUBSTATION to discuss strategies for coping with homophobia (in situations such as 'coming out' to family, finding accommodation, or dealing with the law). To operate as a civil society organization, PLU filed for legal status in 1996 and again in 2004, but it was denied on both occasions. The group now exists as an internet discussion group, SiGNeL, with over a thousand subscribers.

See also HOMOSEXUALITY.

People's Action Party Political party. The People's Action Party (PAP) was established by a group of English-educated middle-class professionals and intellectuals, and a group of working-class, Chinese-educated trade unionists. They were united by their opposition to British imperialism and their ambition to build a more equal society. The PAP was inaugurated at the Victoria Memorial Hall (present-day VICTORIA CONCERT HALL) on 21 November 1954 before a gathering of 1,500 people. Among those present were Malayan political leaders Tunku ABDUL RAHMAN, president of the United Malays National Organisation (UMNO) and TAN CHENG LOCK, president of the Malayan Chinese Association (MCA).

From its inception, the PAP had two main factions: the moderates, led by a young lawyer, LEE KUAN YEW, who was its secretary-general; and the radicals, led by Chinese-educated LIM CHIN SIONG. While the PAP positioned itself as a leftist socialist party, some of its members were clearly either communists or pro-communists, who believed in the use of united front tactics to topple the British colonial government. The party contested its first LEGISLATIVE ASSEMBLY ELECTIONS (1955). It fielded only four candidates, three of whom were elected, including Lee.

The PAP faced its toughest years between 1955 and 1963, with internecine struggles and conflicts within the party. The alliance between the moderates and the radicals within the PAP was tenuous at best. Lim, a highly popular figure, was viewed as an equal to Lee, who dominated the party from its inception. When Lim was elected to the 3rd Central Executive Committee (CEC) in July 1956, he garnered more votes than Lee, who had no alternative but to appoint Lim assistant secretary-general of the Party.

In August 1957, half of the 12-member CEC were members of Lim's group. Claiming that Lim had rigged the elections, Lee and party chairman TOH CHIN CHYE refused to take office, and were temporarily replaced by T.T. Rajah and Tan Chong Kim respectively. The matter was later resolved when the LIM YEW HOCK government

People's Action Party: badge (top); Legislative Assembly Election in front of City Hall, 1959.

People's Action Party: the 2006 election campaign.

detained all the radical PAP CEC members (except T.T. Rajah) under the Preservation of Public Security Ordinance.

The battle for supremacy within the PAP impacted events at the national level, particularly after the party's landslide victory in the 1959 general election. Things came to a head in the battle for MERGER. The Lim faction supported independence and opposed merger while the Lee faction supported merger with Malaysia. This led to a split within the Party. Lim and his faction were expelled, and formed a new party, the BARISAN SOSIALIS, in 1961.

With the departure of the party's radical faction and by means of preventive detention under OPERATION COLD STORE, the PAP was purged of its pro-communist elements. When the Barisan Sosialis decided not to contest the 1968 general elections, the PAP became Singapore's dominant political party. The PAP won every single seat in the 1968, 1972, 1976 and 1980 general elections. Only in 1981 did a single opposition politician, J.B. JEYARETNAM, succeed in breaking the PAP's complete hold on Parliament. Since then, opposition parties have made little headway in breaking the PAP's dominance.

In the PAP, members of the CEC are elected by cadres, who are themselves appointed by the CEC. Lee Kuan Yew led the party as secretary-general from 1954 to November 1992 when GOH CHOK TONG succeeded him in the post. Goh, who succeeded Lee as Singapore's prime minister in 1990, handed the premiership to LEE HSIEN LOONG, Lee Kuan Yew's elder son, on 12 August 2004. Lee took over as the PAP's secretary-general in December 2004. He led the PAP into the 2006 general election in which the party obtained 66.6 per cent of the popular vote.

See also POLITICAL SYSTEM and table.

People's Association Statutory body. In order to counter racial and political tensions that had developed in Singapore during the 1950s and 1960s, and to foster closer ties between different ethnic groups, the government established the People's Association (PA) through an act of Parliament in 1960. The PA came into

being on 1 July 1960, its mission being firstly to organize and promote group participation in social, cultural, educational and athletic activities so that people realized they belonged to a multiracial society; and secondly to establish institutions for the training of leaders, and instil in those leaders a sense of national identity and a spirit of dedicated service to a multiracial community. In 1960, the PA established 28 community centres throughout the island at which ethnic, linguistic and religious groups could meet. Community leaders were invited to serve on the PA's subsequently established Community Centre Management Committees (1965), CITIZENS' CONSULTATIVE COMMITTEES, RESIDENTS' COMMITTEES and Neighbourhood Committees (late 1990s).

The prime minister serves as chairman of the PA Board of Management, while the deputy chairman is typically a senior member of Cabinet. The PA also runs Outward Bound Singapore, the National Community Leadership Institute, the National Youth Council, the Social Development Service, and a number of water sports clubs.

People's Association building *See* KALLANG AIRPORT.

People's Association Talents Formed in 1968 as a full-time cultural unit of the PEOPLE'S ASSOCIATION (PA) under the name People's Association Dance Company, the company began by presenting traditional Chinese, Malay and Indian dances at roadshows, community events and local and overseas festivals, including CHINGAY AND the NATIONAL DAY Parade. It turned professional in 1971. During the mid-1980s modern dance and jazz were added to its repertoire. It staged its first contemporary dance programme in 1987 with the title *Next Step*, featuring Christine Chin's *Riverbank Haze*, and LIM FEI SHEN'S *Quartet* and *Xi Fangping*. In 1988, the company was invited to perform in Paris to celebrate France's Year of Dance. By the late 1990s the company had dissolved, though several dance groups continue performing under PA Talents.

People's Defence Force The People's Defence Force (PDF) places emphasis on interior defence, urban combat, guarding key installations, coastal defence and route protection.

The PDF's history can be traced to the Singapore Volunteer Corps. Formed in 1854, the corps played a supporting role to the local constabulary when dealing with threats to national security. European residents made up the first Singapore Volunteer Rifle Corps, which suppressed the SEPOY MUTINY in 1915, retaking ALEXANDRA BARRACKS from Indian Army mutineers. During WORLD WAR II, the volunteers

fought the Japanese and lost over 2,000 officers and men. Again between 1963 and 1967, the corps was called upon to defend important sites such as waterworks and oil installations in southern Johor and Singapore at the height of the Indonesian CONFRONTATION, while some volunteers were deployed to fight the communists in Sarawak and PENANG.

In 1965, the People's Defence Force Act was passed, and the volunteers came under the PDF. The government had plans to raise the force to about 10,000 men. Five training depots were announced—1 PDF at Beach Road Camp, 2 PDF at Kallang Camp, 3 PDF at Pearl's Hill, 4 PDF at Shenton Way and 5 PDF at Haig Road. By March the following year, 3,200 volunteers had stepped forward. However, the PDF still remained small as soldiering was looked upon unfavourably by the CHINESE community; moreover, Singapore had hitherto depended on the British for its defence, and the local population had no background of soldiering and seafaring. The economy was doing well and the employment rate was rising; the result was a dearth of volunteers.

After 1968, the PDF was restructured to include regular personnel, volunteers and Operationally Ready National Servicemen. By March 1984, the main volunteer corps, 101 PDF, became defunct. The next year, the PDF split into 1 PDF Command at Maju Camp and 2 PDF Command at Beach Road Camp. 2 PDF Command moved to Clementi Camp in 2000. As part of the Army's transformation efforts since 2005, 1 PDF Command had been drawn down, and their PDF brigades transferred to enhance the operational capability of the Combined Arms Divisions.

pepper and gambier Cash crops important in the 19th century. Gambier, which was used primarily for tanning and dyeing, was one of the earliest cash crops grown in Singapore. When Sir STAMFORD RAFFLES arrived in 1819, the CHINESE were already cultivating it in the hills. Pepper and gambier were often grown together. The pepper plant was trained to grow up the gambier trees, 1.2 ha of pepper usually planted for

PEOPLE'S ACTION PARTY: ELECTION RESULTS				
Year	Type of election	Seats won	Uncontested seats	% of valid votes cast
1955	Legislative Assembly	3/25	0	8.72
1959	Legislative Assembly	43/51	0	53.68
1963	Legislative Assembly	37/51	0	46.93
1968	Parliamentary	58/58	51	86.72
1972	Parliamentary	65/65	8	70.17
1976	Parliamentary	69/69	16	72.40
1980	Parliamentary	75/75	37	77.66
1984	Parliamentary	77/79	30	64.95
1988	Parliamentary	80/81	11	63.36
1991	Parliamentary	77/81	41	60.97
1997	Parliamentary	81/83	47	64.98
2001	Parliamentary	82/84	55	75.30
2006	Parliamentary	82/84	37	66.60

Source: Elections Department Singapore

People's Association

Pepper (above) and gambier (below).

Peranakans: wedding couple in traditional dress (top), 1927; embroidered slippers (above); Peranakan men often wore Western-style attire (below).

every 12 ha of gambier. Dead gambier leaves were used to fertilize the soil and promote pepper growth. Gambier and pepper plantations were at their peak in the 1840s. However, the aggressive cultivation of gambier resulted in soil exhaustion and gambier planters eventually moved out of Singapore. One of the best-known gambier planters was SEAH EU CHIN, whose estate is thought to have spanned 16 km.

Peranakans General term for Straits Chinese. Males are known as Babas and females as Nyonyas. Peranakans have their own distinctive culture, which is a combination of Malay, Chinese as well as other influences.

The Peranakans are known for their adaptability. They would claim, when the occasion arose, to be 'more Chinese than the Chinese', 'more English than the English' and 'more Malay than the Malays'. The Peranakans followed many Chinese traditional customs which were practised less elaborately among other Chinese; the Babas dressed like Englishmen, engaged in English sports and were, at times, fervent 'British-born' patriots; and the community even published the first newspaper in romanized Malay and developed the art of DONDANG SAYANG, where a group of participants banter with one another. In modern Singapore, Peranakan culture is associated with the *sarong kebaya* (an embroidered blouse worn together with a sarong), its cuisine (*see* box) and styles of architecture, furniture, porcelain and jewellery.

The roots of the Singapore Peranakans can be traced to Chinese settlements in MALACCA and the Dutch East Indies from at least the 17th century onwards, when intermarriages took place between male Chinese migrants and local non-Chinese women. Peranakan identity has undergone many changes since then, and can be traced through four phases.

The first phase occured in the 19th century, when Peranakan identity was asso-

ciated with the legal status of a 'British-born subject', wealth, political allegiance to the British and the intention of permanent residence in Singapore. The Peranakans were often perceived as a 'better class of Chinese in Singapore', an elite, and different from the China-born (SINKHEH) population. Whereas the *sinkheh* were mostly men who had left their families back in China or remained unmarried, the Peranakan community had an occasional surplus of women. The Peranakans further differentiated themselves through their linguistic abilities (speaking a variant of Malay and some English) and the adoption of Malayanized and later English cultural markers. At the same time, the Peranakans placed much emphasis on traditional Chinese wedding, funeral and ancestral rites, thus becoming somewhat paradoxical custodians of Chinese culture.

The second phase spans the years between 1894 and 1942, which constituted the coming of age of the Peranakans' political stake in the CROWN COLONY: English-educated and politically moderate Baba leaders played key roles in the administrative councils and commissions. However, 'Peranakan identity' during this period has often been defined as cultural. Interestingly, the Baba Reform Movement (led by LIM BOON KENG and SONG ONG SIANG) fought against many aspects of 'Peranakan culture' such as the pigtail, divination, matchmaking and other aspects of the 12-day wedding. The definition of 'Peranakan culture' tend-

ed to differ with gender. The Nyonyas adhered to Malay cultural influences and were usually more comfortable speaking 'Baba Malay'; the Babas were more anglicized, conversing in English and adopting Western attire and leisure pursuits.

The third phase is usually thought to have begun with the JAPANESE OCCUPATION and to mark the decline of Peranakan culture. The Peranakans lost much of their material culture and their many ceremonies, which were cumbersome and costly, had to be simplified or even discarded. During the twilight years of British rule in Singapore between 1945 and 1959, the British openly viewed the 'King's or Queen's Chinese' as the 'natural leaders' of 'the Chinese of Singapore'. However, with the vast majority of Chinese-educated Chinese being vehemently anti-colonial, the status of the Peranakans became increasingly ambiguous. Eventually, with the waning of British influence and the rapid rise of the PEOPLE'S ACTION PARTY (PAP), which led to self-rule in 1959, the Peranakans reached a second crucial turning point.

The fourth phase began after Singapore achieved self-governance in 1959, and the Peranakans as a group were openly belittled as 'deculturalised', although leading members of the PAP such as LEE KUAN YEW and GOH KENG SWEE were publicly described as English-educated Babas. As a politically, legally and economically defined 'group', the Peranakans became rel-

Peranakan cuisine A blend of Chinese, Malay and Indian culinary influences distinguishes the food of the PERANAKAN community. For example, *mee char* (fried noodles), a weekend lunch favourite in Peranakan homes, is Chinese-inspired, but the inclusion of *sambal nanas* (pineapple condiment) as an accompaniment renders the dish distinctively Peranakan. Steamed duck soup, another dish with Chinese origins, is garnished with crushed green chillis and lime juice to cater to Peranakan tastebuds. The popular *ayam buah keluak* (chicken with *Pangium edule* nut) utilizes ingredients common in Malay cooking such as chillis, *bawang merah* (shallots), *belacan* (shrimp paste), *buah keras* (candlenut), *serai* (lemon grass) and *lengkuas* (galangal). While the modern preference is to use chicken in this dish, pork ribs were customarily the meat of choice, and still are for those who prefer to keep to tradition. Curry dishes also feature in Peranakan cuisine, but are less spicy than the Indian originals.

Peranakan cakes (Nyonya *kueh*) are also based on the Chinese and Malay cuisines but with a Peranakan touch. The *kueh chang* (glutinous rice dumpling) is traditionally Chinese but with the addition of *ketumbar* (coriander), *bawang merah* (shallots), pepper and *tangkua* (sweetened dried melon) to the filling. Similarly, *kueh ku* (glutinous rice cake with green bean paste) differs from the Chinese version because of the added ingredient of coconut milk. *Kueh dada* (coconut pancake roll) is common to the Malays and Peranakans, but the latter serve it with a dip of coconut cream.

Peranakans are known for exacting standards in food preparation and presentation. When preparing basic condiments, many Nyonyas forsake the electric blender for the time-

and energy-consuming mortar and pestle in their quest for a finer end-product. When making *kueh belanda* (wafer rolls, popularly known as 'love-letters'), they endure the heat from live charcoals to manually bake the batter in a hand-held mould. They eschew the electric mould, whose rapid high heat would cause the coconut oil to separate from the batter, and thus render the resulting wafers less rich to the taste.

atively unimportant, and drastic cultural changes occurred as well. Traditional courtship, marriage, ancestral and funeral rites were largely abandoned. Many Peranakans deserted Chinese ancestral worship and embraced CHRISTIANITY, particularly CATHOLICISM. In many cases, Malay language standards among Peranakans deteriorated, and the *sarong kebaya* was seen less often in public.

Generally, the younger generation has become less distinguishable from non-Peranakan Chinese. The government's equation of Mandarin with the 'Chinese' language was an important move towards developing a single 'Chinese identity' in Singapore. While the public focus until the PAP's electoral victory in 1959 was clearly on 'Peranakan politics', the late 1960s began to witness a public emphasis on 'Peranakan culture'. This switch of emphases is reflected in the changing role of the Straits Chinese British Association. It had once considered becoming a political party, but later adopted a largely cultural role and was renamed the Peranakan Association. Ironically, the change occurred at a time when aspects of Peranakan culture not only began to disappear, but were commercialized and used to promote tourism. Peranakan restaurants, antique shops, Peranakan festivals and plays are examples of a continued commercial interest in things Straits Chinese. The ASIAN CIVILISATIONS MUSEUM in Armenian Street will become a Peranakan museum when it reopens in 2008.

Percival, Lieutenant-General Arthur

(1887–1966) British military officer. Born into a middle-class Victorian family in Hertfordshire, United Kingdom, Arthur Ernest Percival had an upbringing which was conventional for his time and social class. He was educated at Rugby public school, and joined a trading firm in the City of London in 1906. When World War I broke out, Percival enlisted immediately in August 1914, rising to Acting Brigadier. He won the Military Cross on the notorious first day of the Battle of the Somme (1916), the Croix de Guerre, and was admitted to the Distinguished Service Order (1918).

He remained active just after the war, serving in the ill-fated Allied intervention in the Russian Civil War (1919) and fighting the Irish Republican Army (1920–22). However, Percival spent most of the rest of the inter-war years in staff appointments, holding five such appointments. During this time, he came to the notice of John Dill, commandant-general of the Royal Naval College, who became his mentor. In 1930, Percival spent a year studying in the College and was appointed an instructor at the Staff College.

Serving in Singapore as the chief staff officer of MALAYA COMMAND (1936–37), Percival developed a plan for defending the island. From 1938, the British high command agreed that in order to hold the naval base, the British had to defend the entire Malay Peninsula. When war broke out again in Europe, Percival was promoted, becoming assistant chief of the Imperial General Staff in May 1940. There, he renewed his connection with Dill, now chief of the Imperial General Staff, and the only member of the British high command who felt Singapore should be higher in strategic priority than the Mediterranean and the Middle East. Dill could not persuade Prime Minister Winston Churchill to agree, but was impressed by Percival's grasp of the Malayan situation and his analytical skill. In 1941, Dill pulled Percival from his post as General Officer Commanding 44th Division, appointing him over the heads of more senior officers to take charge as General Officer Commanding Malaya Command.

The Japanese invaded on 8 December 1941, just where Percival expected them to, but advanced so ferociously that they drove his army onto Singapore island by the end of January 1942 (*see* JAPANESE OCCUPATION and WORLD WAR II). Percival was forced to capitulate on 15 February 1942; Churchill never forgave him for walking to the FORD MOTOR FACTORY carrying a Union Jack next to a white flag of surrender in front of newsreel cameras.

Percival tried to help his troops cope with captivity but was soon transferred to a senior officers' camp in Taiwan. After being liberated in 1945, he enjoyed sympathetic treatment from General Douglas MacArthur, who brought him to Manila to witness YAMASHITA TOMOYUKI's surrender to the Americans, and to Tokyo Bay to watch Japan's unconditional surrender. Percival also regained some affection from his army, whose survivors made him the first president of the National Federation of Far East Prisoners of War. But apart from a brief sympathetic audience with the king, the British political and military establishment made Percival a scapegoat for the Fall of Singapore and Malaya. Percival never saw active service again, and fought a lonely battle with official historians to prevent blame being attached to his army for the collapse of Malaya. In his own published account, *The War in Malaya* (1949), he did not dwell on his superiors' refusal to let him fight as he saw fit, maintaining the dignified stance that the British government had had no choice but to take risks in the Far East.

Pergas

Association of Islamic teachers and scholars. Pergas is an acronym for Persatuan Ulama dan Guru-guru Agama Islam Singapura (Singapore Islamic Scholars and Religious Teachers Association). Pergas was formed in 1957 initially to provide a forum for the welfare and professional development of members. Its objectives have since been expanded to include nurturing Islamic scholars. It conducts diploma courses on Islam and co-manages degree programmes in Islamic subjects with the International Islamic University of Malaysia.

Lieutenant-General Arthur Percival

personal income tax

The statute governing personal income tax is the INCOME TAX Act. Singapore taxes on a territorial basis. Only income derived in Singapore, or income derived overseas but received in Singapore, is subject to tax. Foreign income received in Singapore by non-residents is not subject to taxation. Benefits attached to employment, such as cost-of-living allowance, housing and stock options, are all taxable. Besides employment income, income from sources such as rent, dividends, royalties and directors' fees are also taxable (*see also* TAXATION).

The tax year is known as the year of assessment (YA) and runs from 1 January to 31 December. Tax is imposed on a preceding year basis, that is, income earned in calendar year 2004 is taxed in YA2005. Individuals are required to file their tax returns by 15 April of the YA. Individual income is taxed progressively. The top marginal tax rate is 22 per cent (YA2005), due to be reduced to 21 per cent in YA2006 and then to 20 per cent in YA2007, with all other rates reduced correspondingly. With introduction of the GOODS AND SERVICES TAX in 1994, which allowed for reductions in personal income tax rates, over two-thirds of working adults do not pay income tax.

Pertapis

Non-profit welfare organization. Pertapis is an acronym for Persatuan Taman Pengajian Islam Singapura (Islamic Theological Association of Singapore). The association traces its origins to the efforts of Haji Mohamed Ali who provided religious education to the youth in the Geylang area in the early 1960s. Pertapis was founded in 1971 as Pancaran Bahru Taman Pengajian (New Ray Islamic Theological Association), and its name was changed to the current one soon after. The association runs welfare programmes for needy families, troubled youth and recovering drug abusers, as well as the Pertapis Children's Home, Pertapis Centre For Women and Girls, and the Pertapis Halfway House. The Pertapis Halfway House's drug rehabilitation programme is based on the Therapeutic Community model that helps abusers reintegrate with society through counselling, religious education and vocational training. The halfway house is one of the largest drug rehabilitation centres in Singapore and has helped over 1,200 abusers.

Pertubuhan Kebangsaan Melayu Singapura

Political party. Pertubuhan Kebangsaan Melayu Singapura (PKMS or Singapore Malay National Organisation) was originally a branch of the United Malays National Organisation (UMNO). UMNO Singapore was registered on

Phey Yew Kok

20 February 1961, after operating as the Singapore division of UMNO since 1954. The party did well in elections between 1955 and 1957, winning the Malay-dominated wards of Southern Islands, Ulu Bedok, Tanglin, Telok Blangah, Geylang Serai and Kampong Kembangan. The PKMS split from UMNO when Singapore achieved independence and left the Federation of Malaysia in 1965, and it took on its present name on 5 May 1967.

Between 1968 and 1991, PKMS took part in every general election but failed to win a single seat. Since 2001, it has been a member of the SINGAPORE DEMOCRATIC ALLIANCE. The party owns a building in Geylang called the PKMS Building and has its headquarters there.

petrochemicals sector The petrochemicals sector accounted for about 1.75 per cent of total national exports in 2005 (about $12.5 billion) and contributed 6.4 per cent of GROSS DOMESTIC PRODUCT (GDP). Petrochemical plants produce feedstock such as ethylene, propylene and benzene, as well as materials needed by other chemical plants to produce products such as synthetic fibres for clothes and furniture, paint, insulating materials and plastic cases used in personal computers and telephones. The sector grew out of a need to create an integrated petrochemical industry (*see* OIL-REFINING SECTOR).

Construction work on the first phase of the Singapore Petrochemical Complex, costing $2 billion, began in 1980 on Pulau Ayer Merbau. Four years later, commercial production began. The second phase, which cost $3.4 billion, started in 1994 and was completed in 1997. The complex now included more petrochemical plants on Pulau Ayer Merbau and nearby Pulau Seraya and Pulau Sakra. These small islands were later merged with others to form JURONG ISLAND. The complex has since doubled in area to about 160 hectares. More than a dozen companies have set up plants there. In 2002, ExxonMobil's petrochemical complex, built at a cost of US$2 billion, became operational. Other companies that set up plants there include Chevron Texaco, BASF

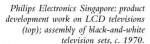

Philips Electronics Singapore: product development work on LCD televisions (top); assembly of black-and-white television sets, c. 1970.

Phan Wait Hong: onstage in Women Warriors of the Yang Family, *performed in 1982.*

and Mitsui Chemicals. In 2005, ExxonMobil and Shell announced plans to add new plants that will produce feedstock for chemical plants supplying plastics manufacturers.

Phan Wait Hong (1912–) Actress. Born in Shanghai, Phan Wait Hong attended private opera classes from the age of eight. She had no formal education and is said to have been illiterate. In 1926, aged 14, she joined a CHINESE OPERA troupe that moved to Singapore. She performed at a tea house in CHINATOWN and NEW WORLD. In the late 1930s, she became lead actress. In the mid-1950s, she travelled with a Beijing opera troupe to towns in Java, Indonesia, where she performed for several months.

Specializing in *laosheng* (old male roles), Phan performed in many classical Beijing operas. She stopped performing professionally in the late 1950s, but remained active in amateur groups until the early 1990s. She was an instructor at Hua Nan Amateur Opera Troupe, Ping Sheh, National Theatre Club and Tien Yun. In 2002, the CHINESE OPERA INSTITUTE organized a gala in honour of her contributions to the development of Beijing opera in Singapore. She received the CULTURAL MEDALLION in 1993.

Phang, Andrew (1957–) Academic and judge. Andrew Phang was educated at the Anglo-Chinese School and then at the National University of Singapore (NUS) where he graduated with first-class honours in law in 1982. From 1982 to 2000, Phang taught at the NUS Faculty of Law, specializing in contract law, the Singapore legal system and jurisprudence. In 2001, he resigned and joined the SINGAPORE MANAGEMENT UNIVERSITY as head of the law department in the university's School of Business. Phang is the author of numerous articles and books in his fields.

In 2004, he was appointed SENIOR COUNSEL and elevated to the Bench as judi-

cial commissioner on 3 January 2005. On 8 December 2005, he was appointed a judge. On 28 February 2006, Phang was made judge of appeal.

Phay Seng Whatt (1921–) Doctor and civil servant. Phay Seng Whatt was educated at Raffles Institution, where he won a scholarship to the King Edward VII College of Medicine in 1939. His medical education was interrupted by the JAPANESE OCCUPATION. Upon graduation (1949), he was immediately recruited into the Municipal Health Department. In 1952, he left the Municipal Service and started his own practice, which he ran for the next decade.

In 1962, Phay was appointed chairman of the PUBLIC SERVICE COMMISSION and gave up his medical practice. Phay held the position for 13 years, and was responsible for revising the regulations for State Scholarships, so that they were 'awarded to the cream of each school-leaving year', on the basis of school results, not on what or where the students preferred to study. This scholarship was later to become the prestigious PRESIDENT'S SCHOLARSHIP. In 1975, the University of Singapore made him an honorary doctor of letters.

Phey Yew Kok (dates unknown) Trade unionist and politician. On 11 December 1979, Phey Yew Kok, then Chairman of the NATIONAL TRADE UNIONS CONGRESS (NTUC), general secretary of three unions and a PEOPLE'S ACTION PARTY (PAP) member of Parliament, was charged with four counts of criminal breach of trust between February 1975 and May 1976, involving a total sum of $82,520. He also faced two charges under the Trade Unions Act for using $17,145 of union funds to purchase shares in a private supermarket in September 1978.

Out on $100,000 bail, Phey failed to appear in court on 7 January 1980, and a warrant of arrest was issued. His disappearance was apparently a mystery to family and friends; his wife said he had not returned home since 31 December 1979.

Phey had resigned from the three unions while under investigation. The NTUC had held back from taking action, but immediately dismissed Phey when he absconded. Despite rumours and speculation about Phey's disappearance, no further evidence surfaced. He has not returned to Singapore nor have his exact whereabouts been established, although some reports have put him in Taiwan, others in Thailand.

Philips Electronics Singapore Philips started out in Singapore as a four-man company in 1951 dealing mainly in lighting products. In the early 1960s, it took over the distributorship of other electrical and electronic products such as radios and gramophones. In 1968, Philips set up its own black-and-white television assembly line in a rented flatted factory. It later expanded its assembly lines to make transistor radios and telephone equipment. In 1969, it helped to set up and manage Singapore Electronics and Engineering Pte Ltd (SEEL), which was involved in the maintenance and repairs of electronics and weapons for the navy.

Philips moved to its own Toa Payoh factory site in 1972, which assembles radios, televisions and cassette recorders for the Asian and global markets. One of the early products designed by the local team was a mono radio recorder. The Singapore unit eventually shipped more than 10 million units of this radio worldwide. By 1984, the division in Singapore became the Dutch multinational's largest colour TV manufacturing centre outside of Europe. Philips was also involved in the Electronic Road Pricing (ERP) system used for managing traffic flow in the city-state, as well as the lighting system for the NIGHT SAFARI.

In 1996, Singapore became the Asia-Pacific headquarters for Philips. As of 2005, it employed more than 5,200 people and had a sales turnover of more than $1.1 billion. Its staff include more than 1,300 development engineers and industrial designers housed under one roof at the Philips Innovation Campus (PIC) who have been responsible for generating more than US$5 billion in sales for Philips globally. Approximately 1,000 new products are developed by the PIC each year. The centre was responsible for 176 inventions, which resulted in 1,418 patents filed by Philips worldwide in the last five years. Several of Philips' regional competence and test bedding facilities are also located in Singapore, including its lighting, semiconductor and medical systems divisions.

Phillips, Admiral Sir Tom (1888–1941) British naval officer. Tom Spencer Vaughan Phillips was vice-chief of Naval Staff and acting admiral and commander-in-chief of the Eastern Fleet. On 8 December 1941, he sailed FORCE Z—the PRINCE OF WALES, REPULSE and four destroyer escorts—from Singapore in an attempt to intercept Japanese transport ships landing an invasion on the coast of Malaya. His force was sunk by the Japanese on 10 December, and Admiral Phillips went down with the *Prince of Wales*.

Phoon Yew Tien (1952–) Composer. Singapore's most-recorded classical music composer, Phoon Yew Tien attended the Queensland Conservatorium of Music and has had numerous works performed and recorded in Singapore, Australasia, Europe and North America. His music combines Chinese idioms with contemporary compositional techniques and styles. In 2001, his arrangement of the NATIONAL ANTHEM was adopted as the official version. His largest-scale work, *Confucius—A Secular Cantata*,

was commissioned for the SINGAPORE ARTS FESTIVAL in 2002.

Phoon has collaborated with prominent Singapore artists, playwrights and choreographers, and was head of music at NANYANG ACADEMY OF FINE ARTS (1993–96), where he also lectured (1984–99). He was awarded the CULTURAL MEDALLION in 1996.

Photographic Society of Singapore The society's roots go back to 1950, when it was formed as the Singapore Camera Club. It took on its current name in 1956. Its first photography competition in 1950 became an annual event. In 1957, it took over organization of the International Photographic Exhibition (present-day Singapore International Salon of Photography) from the Singapore Art Society.

The Photographic Society actively participates in international salons and became affiliated with international bodies such as the Royal Photographic Society (United Kingdom), the Photographic Society of America and the International Federation of Photographic Art, adopting their systems of recognition and accreditation. The society conducts workshops, field trips, overseas exchanges, exhibitions and photographic programmes. It had a membership of more than 1,200 in 2001 and is located at Selegie Arts Centre.

photography *See* box.

Phua Chu Kang Popular locally produced sitcom. The character, Phua Chu Kang—a fast-talking, irreverent and boastful contractor, complete with permed hair, large mole, long pinkie fingernail and yellow boots—made his first appearance in the second season of *Gurmit's World* (1996), a comedy in which local comedian and host Gurmit Singh portrayed his 'relatives' in a series of skits. The series features Phua and his family—wife Rosie; brother and architect Chu Beng and his wife, his son Aloysius; and his mother—and his two lazy workers, King Kong and Ah Goon. The show's eighth and final season began filming in March 2006. The highly successful series also spawned a musical which debuted in 2005.

Pickering, William (1840–1907) Colonial official. William Alexander Pickering was of humble origins and received little education. Having worked at the Imperial Maritime Customs in Foochow in Fujian province, China and Taiwan, he was said to have been proficient in written and spoken Mandarin, and spoke the Chinese dialects of FOOCHOW, TEOCHEW, HOKKIEN, HAKKA and CANTONESE.

William Pickering came to the notice of Sir HARRY ST GEORGE ORD, Governor of the STRAITS SETTLEMENTS (1867–73), then on leave in London, who offered him a position in the public service as Chinese

Phua Chu Kang and family as played by Gurmit Singh, left.

Interpreter to the Straits Government. As he was possibly the first European Straits officer to be able to speak Chinese, Pickering's political star ascended as the issue of control over the immigrant Chinese community began to preoccupy the Straits Government. A series of events—riots in Singapore in 1872, unrest in Penang in 1873 due to clashes between rival SECRET SOCIETIES, and the subsequent Post Office Riots of 1876 in Singapore—made the colonial government aware of the pressing need for a system to check unrest stemming from the Chinese population, and to ensure that British trade interests were not compromised.

Pickering was appointed Protector of Chinese on 3 May 1877 under the Chinese Immigrants Ordinance, the purpose of which was to check on the legality of employment contracts of the new immigrants; and the Crimping Ordinance, which aimed to prevent any illegal recruitment of emigrants for service outside Singapore. His appointment at the age of 37 was unusual, most civil servants attaining a similar rank only after many years in the civil service.

Upon setting up office at North Canal Road, Pickering was faced with the immediate task of dealing with the immigration problem. He arranged for the licensing of all recruiters of emigrants and of the depots of the main recruiting agencies. He also set about the supervision of disembarking and dispersal of all immigrants arriving from China. By the end of the year, he had successfully put in place a system of safeguards against the main dangers to which the Chinese labourers were most vulnerable at the points of immigration and emigration.

In 1877, he was also made a Registrar of Societies, jointly with Major S. Dunlop, Inspector-General of Police. He viewed these additional duties as part of his existing portfolio.

Pickering believed the task of 'governing the Chinese' to be the most pressing problem confronting the government. He recognized that to control the Chinese population, he had to control the SECRET

Admiral Sir Tom Phillips

Phoon Yew Tien

William Pickering

photography The earliest daguerreotypes (pioneering photographic process invented by Louis-Jacques-Mandé Daguerre in 1839) of Singapore were thought to have been made in the early 1840s. A detailed account of how daguerreotype images of Singapore town were produced can be found in the memoirs of Sir Stamford Raffles' interpreter Munshi Abdullah Abdul Kadir, the *Hikayat Abdullah*. Other early daguerreotypists who immortalized old Singapore include Jules Itier of the French Customs Service, whose work is now featured in collections and exhibitions put on by international museums. In 1844, Itier visited Singapore while on a trade mission and took quarter-plate (8.3 x 10.5 cm) daguerreotypes of the town, including the Thian Hock Keng Temple and Singapore River, as seen from Government Hill. The earliest advertisement for commercial daguerreotype portraits is thought to have been placed by Frenchman Gaston Dutronquoy, who had settled in Singapore in 1839, in an 1843 issue of the Singapore Free Press. Other daguerreotypists included Saurman, H. Husband, C. Duban and J. Newman.

The view from Mount Faber as photographed by G.R. Lambert and Co., c. 1890s.

The rise of studios and amateur photographers

Daguerreotyping was superseded by the wet-collodion process, which was made commercially available in Singapore by Edward A. Edgerton in the late 1850s. Similar services were offered by photographers such as Thomas Hermitage from London and O. Regnier from France, who set up studios in Queen Street and Oxley Road respectively. The illustrious 19th-century Edinburgh photographer John Thomson visited Singapore in 1861 and established his studio, Thomson Brothers, on Beach Road. Thomson was hailed for his outstanding images of Singapore and the region, as well as his expertise in practising photography in tropical conditions.

Photography from this era consisted largely of portraiture (individual or group), the *carte de visite* panoramic landscapes, and, later, postcard images. Firms such as Sachtler and Co. (formed in the early 1860s) and Carter & Co., as well as photographers Henry Schuren & G.A. Schleesselmann, formed part of the photographic scene. G.R. Lambert & Co. is the best known of these early studios. The firm produced the most comprehensive and significant pictorial records of Singapore and Southeast Asia in the late 19th and early 20th century. With offices in Thailand, Indonesia and Malaya, the firm was assigned to capture major political, diplomatic and social events, and was the official photographer for the king and court of Siam. Other photographers of the era included George S. Michael with The Original American Lighting Gem Photographic Studio and The Celestial Studio. Chinese studios such as Lee Brothers Studios emerged at the turn of the century, with a focus on commissioned portraits. The Cantonese photographer Lee Yuk advertised photography services as early as 1861, and the earliest known Chinese photographic manual to be published in Singapore appeared in 1873.

Amateur photographers such as E.W. Newell emerged in the 1900s. The first amateur photographic association was established in 1887. This signalled the early enthusiasm of photographers who would later adopt specific areas of interest such as nature, ornithological and/or salon photography. Amateur photography also laid the ground for

the rise of later photographic patrons such as businessman and philanthropist Loke Wan Tho.

World War II and after

The Japanese Occupation put a halt to photographic activity. Photographic war reportage was the beginning of modern photo-journalism, and countless clandestine snapshots of Japanese atrocities were taken during the period.

The idea of photography as a fine art form began to take shape in the post-war period. Founded in 1949, the Singapore Art Society was the first multicultural art association to be established in Singapore. It also mounted photographic art exhibitions with the support of the Singapore Camera Club. Later, the responsibility for organizing dedicated photographic displays and activities was taken over by the Photographic Society of Singapore.

Advertisement for George S. Michael's photographic studio.

In the 1950s, local photographers established affiliations with the Royal Photographic Society (RPS) in the United Kingdom and were given fellowships or recognition by the RPS. The rise of glamour and celebrity photography also took shape during the 1950s and 1960s, which has been called the 'golden age' of Singapore cinema (*see* FILM). Autographed shots of movie stars, some taken against the backdrop of elaborate sets, were immensely popular. This genre, which also extended to include fashion and advertising photography, is one of the most prominent forms of photography in Singapore as epitomized by Willy Tang, Chua Soo Bin, Russel Wong, Geoff Ang, Leslie Kee and Kirby Koh.

Jackie Chan (2000) by Russel Wong

Junction of Stamford Road and Armenian Street by photo studio Wilson and Co., c. 1903.

Daguerreotype of palanquin and drivers by Frenchman Jules Itier, 1843.

Photography as art

By the 1970s, photography had gained respectability as an art form. The National Museum Art Gallery launched an exhibition of Henri Cartier-Bresson's photographs in 1976, the same year that the museum was formally opened to the public. The programming of photographic exhibitions has continued into the present, with the Singapore Art Museum holding exhibitions which featured international photographers such as Arthur Tress, Sugimoto and Pierre and Gilles. Photographic techniques have also had a considerable impact on painters such as Chua Mia Tee and Lai

The Lee Brothers Studio was originally located in Chinatown.

Kui Fang, some of whose works are in the photorealist style. The subsequent relationship between photo-journalism and art photography was to become much more complex from the 1990s, as seen from the work of photo-journalists Tay Kay Chin and Jerome Ming.

Into the 21st century

As of 2006, some 300 businesses offer studio services, equipment, aerial views,

Rhythm of the Rain *by David P.C. Tay*

Drum *(1999) by Jerome Ming*

processing, photo restoration, stock images and a host of other photography-related services and products. Photo galleries emerged, and the first CULTURAL MEDALLION for photography was awarded to DAVID P.C. TAY in 1982. Since then, nine other photographers have received the Medallion, including ANG CHWEE CHAI, FOO TEE JUN, LEE LIM, TAN LIP SENG, WU PENG SENG and YIP CHEONG FUN. The YOUNG ARTIST AWARD, which is instituted by the National Arts Council (NAC), has also been granted to three photographers. Photography has also been used by contemporary artists such as Amanda Heng, TANG DA WU and LEE WEN. Artist Francis Ng's winning entry in 2002 for the Philip Morris ASEAN Art Awards marked the first time in the history of the competition in which a photograph had won the Grand Prize. The 2005 Research and Development grant by the NAC to a photographic project also indicated its commitment to recognizing photography as a major art form in Singapore. Numerous photographic clubs, societies, photo galleries and photographic schools, many operating in community centres and schools, have also been established.

SOCIETIES. He worked through them, converting their headmen into government agents, and acting as the mediator for disputes between them. Any headman who refused to cooperate was banished by Pickering from Singapore. He also educated the SINKHEH about the work of the CHINESE PROTECTORATE and encouraged them to settle their disputes through the Protectorate. Gradually, the Protectorate supplanted the societies in settling financial and domestic disputes for the Chinese population.

Pickering's unwelcome interference in the affairs of the secret societies resulted in his being attacked by a Teochew carpenter on 18 July 1887. In response, the government forbade the Chinese community the use of public spaces until the mastermind of the attack was found. This eventually led to the Verandah Riots in 1888, which pitted the government against the local population. The newly appointed governor, Sir CECIL CLEMENTI SMITH, decided to suppress the secret societies by force, much to the dismay of Pickering, who felt that this approach was unwarranted and unrealistic.

Pickering never fully recovered from the attack. After repeated extensions of leave and seeing no improvement in his health, he retired in 1888.

picul Unit of weight invented for customs and tax requirements and used in parts of Asia mainly from the mid-19th century to the early 20th century. The term itself is derived from a Malay or Javanese expression, which means 'the load that can be carried by one man'. One *picul*, or 100 *kati*, is equal to 60.4788 kg. In some Asian countries the *picul* continues to be used as a metric measure equal to 50 kg or 60 kg.

Pillay, J.Y. (1934–) Civil servant and diplomat. Born in Malaya, Joseph Yuvaraj M. Pillay graduated from Imperial College London with first class honours in science (1956). He joined the ADMINISTRATIVE SERVICE in 1961 and rose to become permanent secretary in 1972. Pillay is well known for his role in building SINGAPORE AIRLINES, of which he was chairman (1972–96). From 1985 to 1989, he was managing director of the MONETARY AUTHORITY OF SINGAPORE and the GOVERNMENT OF SINGAPORE INVESTMENT CORPORATION. Pillay was also the chairman of TEMASEK HOLDINGS (1974–86), Development Bank of Singapore (DBS BANK) (1979–84), and also SINGAPORE TECHNOLOGIES HOLDINGS (1991–94). When he retired from the Administrative Service in 1995, he was appointed Singapore's High Commissioner to the United Kingdom and Ireland (1996–99). He became the chairman of the Singapore Exchange on his return from Britain in 1999. He has been chairman of the COUNCIL OF PRESIDENTIAL ADVISORS since 2005.

Picul: coupon used for the export of rubber, 1941.

Pillay, Narayana (dates unknown) Merchant and community leader. Narayana Pillay arrived from Penang in mid-1819 with Sir STAMFORD RAFFLES on the *Indiana* during Raffles' second visit to Singapore. Pillay set up the island's first brick kiln just outside town, soon establishing himself as one of the first building contractors in Singapore. He also started a shop in Cross Street selling cotton piece goods, but it subsequently burnt down. With help from Raffles, Pillay rebuilt his business. A leader of the TAMIL community, he was responsible for founding and building SRI MARIAMMAN TEMPLE in South Bridge Road.

pineapples Pineapples were one of the few crops to flourish in Singapore. Their cultivation was originally dominated by the Bugis. There were plantations on many of the islands around Singapore, including Pulau Blakang Mati (present-day SENTOSA). The fruit was sold cheaply for local consumption, but it was the Chinese who turned it into a profitable industry from the 1850s. Fibre extracted from pineapple leaves was made into fishing lines, sewing thread and piña cloth, which was exported to China. When the canning process was pioneered in the 1880s, tinned pineapple was produced for export (*see* TIN). TEOCHEWS were leaders in the pineapple canning industry (*see* LIM NEE SOON). However, one of the most prominent growers of pineapples in the early 20th century was a HOKKIEN, TAN KAH KEE, who by 1915 owned eight canneries.

Pires, Tomé (c. 1468–1540) Portuguese diplomat and scholar. While supervising the Portuguese spice trade in MALACCA between 1512 and 1515, Tomé Pires collected information on local traditions and data from local Malays and merchants

J.Y. Pillay

Pineapples: transporting the harvest, 1900.

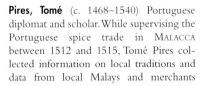

Pitcher plant

Plastique Kinetic Worms: director Vincent Leow, left, and manager Yvonne Lee, 2002.

Poh Kong Chye: last day of business on 5 February 2005.

calling at Malacca. He focused mainly on the history and socio-economic conditions of Malacca and neighbouring areas, including the people, products and geography. These enquiries culminated in his text *Suma Oriental*. When it was presented to the Portuguese crown, readership was highly restricted, and only in 1944 was a full copy of the work found and published. The 1944 edition is based on the so-called Paris Manuscript. The far shorter but older Lisbon Manuscript was first published as a separate text in 1996. The differences between the two manuscripts have raised important questions about textual evolution, transmission and authenticity.

The *Suma Oriental* contains several references to the island now called Singapore, including its ORANG LAUT population, known to the Portuguese as the Celates ('people of the Straits') and its ruler Iskandar Shah. The text also mentions that the island was an important source of blackwood (a generic European trade term for Asian rosewood). This timber was regularly shipped from the island to Malacca, where it was then sold to CHINESE traders who maintained a high demand for it. They purchased and shipped it in great quantities to China for the construction of expensive furniture.

pitcher plants 'Carnivorous' plants (*Nepenthes* spp.) which have leaves with tips shaped like a 'pitcher' containing a protein-digestive enzyme. Insects attracted to the nectar on the underside of the slippery lid fall into the pitcher; the drowned insects provide nutrients for the plant, which is found in nitrogen-poor soils on open, sunny ridges, slopes and stunted forests. The plants have slender stems and climb by means of tendrils. There are three species of *Nepenthes* in Singapore—*N. gracilis*, *N. ampullaris* and *N. rafflesiana*. Another species, *N. trichocarpa*, is a hybrid between *N. gracilis* and *N. ampullarias*. It is endangered and under threat of being overgrown and overshadowed by other species.

Plastique Kinetic Worms Artists' cooperative. Plastique Kinetic Worms (PKW) was established as a non-profit organization in 1998 by a group of artists, curators, professionals and volunteers to create an alternative space for contemporary and experimental art. Among the founders were members of THE ARTISTS VILLAGE. PKW organizes events and exhibitions for young and established artists, both foreign and local. Some of its more notable events include the annual Worms Festival showcasing a wide selection of artists who participate in a thematic visual art exhibition. It also publishes a quarterly arts journal, *Vehicle*. PKW was first located in a shophouse on Pagoda Street, but later moved to Kerbau Road.

Poh Kong Chye Now-defunct goldsmith shop. Poh Kong Chye ('House of Glitter' in the TEOCHEW dialect) was established in 1897 by Ng Siak Khuan, an immigrant from China. It was later sold to Lim Teck Long, a former apprentice who was also a Teochew immigrant from Swatow (present-day Shantou), China. Lim made his fortune trading gold in Penang during the Korean War in the 1950s. He bought Poh Kong Chye for $100,000, retired in the 1990s and handed the business to his three sons.

However, Poh Kong Chye, whose business relied on the sales of gold bullion, gold bars and accessories, failed to keep up with the times. It resisted offering white gold jewellery, which had become popular with younger customers in the 1990s, sticking with the traditional view that white gold symbolized bad luck. Poh Kong Chye also neglected design, which was important to the new generation of buyers who bought gold not for investment but for fashion purposes. Poor marketing also meant that Poh Kong Chye fared badly against competitors who offered year-round promotions and discount schemes. Poh Kong Chye kept to its premises in Chinatown and older PUBLIC HOUSING estates such as BUKIT MERAH while new entrants set up brightly lit, modern outlets in suburban shopping centres.

Despite efforts to rejuvenate the brand, including endorsements by actress ZOE TAY in 1995 and the launch of the Valentine Butterfly white gold series in 2004, Poh Kong Chye finally went into receivership in December 2004. Ironically, it had planned at the time to build a museum in Chinatown near its shop at South Bridge Road for visitors to learn about Singapore's gold trading history. Instead, Singapore's oldest goldsmith faded into the annals of local history after 107 years of existence.

Polar Café Best known for its CURRY PUFFS, Polar Café was founded in 1926 by Chan Hinky, who arrived from Hong Kong in the 1920s with only 90 cents in his pocket. With dreams of starting a café, he saved enough to open Polar Puffs at 51 High

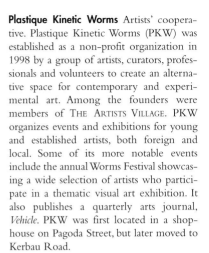

Polar Café

Street. Located near the Supreme Court and Parliament House, the café became popular with lawyers, judges and politicians who frequented the area. By the early 1950s, it was turning out some 600 of the famous puffs each day. It was one of the few places that remained in business during the JAPANESE OCCUPATION. In 1986, the government acquired 51 High Street to make way for a new Parliament House. This paved the way for the company's expansion, with Polar's first takeaway outlet at RAFFLES PLACE and larger production facilities at Leng Kee Road (since relocated to WOODLANDS).

Polar has more than 20 outlets, and its curry puffs, chicken pies and assorted pastries and cakes are also sold at Esso and Mobil petrol stations islandwide. The pastries are prepared in the Woodlands central kitchens and baked fresh at each outlet. The original café concept was revived when Polar opened a sit-in café at Suntec City in 2001.

political parties In Singapore, political parties must be registered under the Societies Act. Most operate under a constitution similar to that of the PEOPLE'S ACTION PARTY (PAP). One feature of these constitutions is a cadre system, which tends to ensure that an inner group will elect their chosen candidates onto the party's central executive committee.

The first registered political party in Singapore was a branch of the China-based Kuomintang. It was registered in 1912 but banned by the British in 1914. Arguably, the first local political party in Malaya was the Kesatuan Melayu Singapura (KMS) (Singapore Malay Association), established in 1926 to express dissatisfaction with the plight of Singapore MALAYS. Leaders of the KMS were English-educated Malays such as MOHAMMED EUNOS ABDULLAH, Tengku Kadir and Dr ABDUL SAMAD. The party succeeded in attracting the attention of the British who helped improve the lot of Malays. It was the activism of KMS and other similar groups on the Malay Peninsula that led to the formation of the United Malays National Organization (UMNO).

The first post-war political party was the MALAYAN DEMOCRATIC UNION, formed on 21 December 1945 and voluntarily dissolved in 1948. The most important party in

the immediate post-war period was the Progressive Party, formed on 25 August 1947. Other important parties that emerged during this period included the SINGAPORE LABOUR PARTY (1948), LABOUR FRONT (1954), PAP (1954), WORKERS' PARTY (1957) and BARISAN SOSIALIS (1961). The 'golden era' for multiparty politics in Singapore lasted from 1955 to 1961; voters were offered a staggering choice of candidates and political platforms during the 1955 and 1959 general ELECTIONS. By 1961, the PAP had emerged as Singapore's dominant political party.

The split within the PAP that led to the formation of the Barisan Sosialis marked the end of this era. The Barisan's decision to abandon parliamentary politics and take the struggle to the streets in 1965 allowed the PAP to dominate Singapore's political landscape from then on.

Since 1980, a number of new political parties have been formed. Among them are the SINGAPORE DEMOCRATIC PARTY (SDP) (1980); the NATIONAL SOLIDARITY PARTY (1987); and the SINGAPORE PEOPLE'S PARTY (1994). Most of Singapore's active political parties are essentially political vehicles for individual politicians. The SDP is dominated by CHEE SOON JUAN, the Singapore People's Party by CHIAM SEE TONG, and the National Solidarity Party by Tan Chee Kien and formerly STEVE CHIA. One notable exception is the Workers' Party, which was founded in 1957 by DAVID MARSHALL. In the 1970s, the Party was revived by lawyer J.B. JEYARETNAM, who became the first opposition politician to break the PAP's hold on Singapore parliamentary politics when he won the ANSON BY-ELECTION (1981). Unlike many other parties, the Workers' Party has succeeded in recruiting new blood and managing a successful transition in its top echelon. Although dominated by secretary-general LOW THIA KIANG, it brought in prominent local activists such as James Gomez and Sylvia Lim, who took over chairmanship of the party in 2004.

political system Singapore is a democratic republic, operating under a Westminster-style constitution inherited from the British. As in most other states with a parliamentary system of government, there is little separation of powers between the executive and parliamentary arms of government. The head of state is the PRESIDENT, who has very limited veto powers under the CONSTITUTION. The head of government is the prime minister who is chosen from among the MEMBERS OF PARLIAMENT (MPs). Typically, the prime minister is the leader of the party with the largest majority in PARLIAMENT.

General ELECTIONS are held at least once every five years. Successful candidates will then take office as MPs. The primary responsibility of legislators is to deliberate policy and pass laws. The main power lies in the hands of the executive branch compris-

ing the prime minister and his Cabinet, collectively referred to as the government. The government of the day is responsible for setting state policy and ensuring that the will of Parliament is carried out.

MPs acting collectively have influence in Singapore because party discipline is enforced strictly. Occasionally, the WHIP is lifted, allowing MPs to vote according to conscience rather than being required to toe the party line. No government bill has ever been defeated since Singapore became independent in 1965. The judicial branch of government comprises the judges of the SUPREME COURT and the SUBORDINATE COURTS (*see* LEGAL SYSTEM.)

The government is assisted by civil servants responsible for the day-to-day administration and functioning of the various ministries. Singapore's civil servants, government ministers and judges are among the best paid in the world. The PAP government believes that paying them well is a key weapon against the temptation of corruption.

Pollutant Standards Index The NATIONAL ENVIRONMENT AGENCY (NEA) monitors air quality throughout the day, and provides regularly updated statistics and maps relating to pollution levels and HAZE. Monitoring is carried out at five locations, with levels of sulphur dioxide, particulates, ozone and carbon monoxide all measured. These are converted into an overall Pollutant Standards Index (PSI).

When the PSI reaches levels in the range of 51–100, the situation is regarded by the NEA as 'moderate'; when it reaches 101–200, the situation is registered as 'unhealthy'; levels of 201–300 are 'very unhealthy'. The range 301–400 is deemed 'hazardous', and a PSI in excess of 400 is 'very hazardous'. Conditions in Singapore have rarely surpassed PSI 200, although during the Indonesian forest-fire crisis of 1997, the PSI was at 'unhealthy' levels for over a week.

polytechnics Educational institutes that offer practice-orientated tertiary education to teach students specific skills for the workplace. Upon graduation, these diploma-holders fill mid-level professional positions, or go on to university to obtain undergraduate degrees. Subjects offered range widely from engineering and business to new media and biomedical sciences. Polytechnics also provide continuing education and post-employment professional development programmes. In 2006, there were five polytechnics in Singapore: NANYANG POLYTECHNIC, NGEE ANN POLYTECHNIC, REPUBLIC POLYTECHNIC, SINGAPORE POLYTECHNIC and TEMASEK POLYTECHNIC (*see also* EDUCATION SYSTEM).

Ponggal Hindu festival. A celebration held during the harvest season, Ponggal does not have the same significance in Singapore as

Ponggal: priest preparing ponggal.

in India, and is marked by prayers in homes and temples.

The festival is observed for four days in the month of Thai (January–February) in India. In Singapore, though, it may not be celebrated for this entire period. Ponggal is celebrated in honour of the sun god Surya. On the first day, celebrants begin by paying homage to Indra, the leader of the gods and controller of the clouds, who is believed to have the power to grant or deny rain. Some people mark the occasion by throwing out old household items. Decorative patterns, known as *kolam,* are drawn at the entrances of homes. Stalks of sugarcane are tied to each side of front doors.

The day begins with a bath and the wearing of new or newly washed clothes. As this is a festival of thanksgiving for the new harvest, a special dish known as *ponggal,* which consists of newly harvested rice boiled in milk and water, is prepared. The cooked rice is offered to Surya. Camphor is lit and the deities are invoked, after which the family eats the rice. Later in the evening, people visit temples where special *pooja* (worship rituals) are carried out. Singaporeans generally do not observe the practices commonly carried out in India on the third day, when homage is paid to cattle.

Pontianak (1957) First of a series of Malay horror films. Starring MARIA MENADO, *Pontianak* was directed by B.N. RAO and produced by CATHAY-KERIS FILMS at their studio in East Coast Road. The film was a

Pontianak: mobile advertising for Pontianak Gua Musang *(The Vampire of the Cave) (1964), last film in the Pontianak series.*

Anthony Poon: works in various media.

S.K. Poon

Popiah

box-office turning point for Cathay-Keris and helped consolidate its fortunes. It also sparked an increase in the production of Malay horror films.

In the film, Maria Menado plays a hag who discovers a spell which will change her into a beauty. However, she turns into a vampire (*pontianak*) on tasting human blood, has to be exorcized and reverts to her original state. The popularity of the film resulted in its run being extended from the scheduled two days during HARI RAYA PUASA to two months. Its screening at Cathay cinema (present-day CATHAY BUILDING) was testament to its success, as the venue was normally reserved for Hollywood films.

Pontianak's appeal spread well beyond the Malay community; in 1958, it was the first Malay film to be dubbed in Cantonese and screened in Hong Kong. Maria Menado became a household name, and acted in the first three of four sequels: *Dendam Pontianak* (Revenge of the Vampire) (1957), *Sumpah Pontianak* (Curse of the Vampire) (1958), *Pontianak Kembali* (Return of the Vampire) (1963) and *Pontianak Gua Musang* (The Vampire of the Cave) (1964).

A homage to the Pontianak genre, *Return to Pontianak*, directed by Djinn and produced by Juan Foo, was released in 2001.

Poon, Anthony (1945–2006) Artist. Anthony Poon was educated at the NANYANG ACADEMY OF FINE ARTS and subsequently in the United Kingdom at the Regional College of Art, Bradford, and the Byam Shaw School of Art, London. Poon was one of Singapore's earliest abstract artists, and later worked in three dimensions, breaking the plane with three-dimensional works on canvas. In the early 1990s he began practising formalist sculpture in polished or coloured metal. Many of Poon's sculptures are displayed in public areas. He was awarded the CULTURAL MEDALLION in 1990.

Poon, S.K. (1936–) Singer. S.K. Poon (Pan Xiuqiong) was born in Macau, spent her childhood in Kuala Lumpur, and came to Singapore at the age of 15. Pan started her professional career at the age of 12. In 1952,

Pan was the first singer from Malaya to sign a contract with EMI in Hong Kong. Her hits include 'Qing Ren de Yan Lei' (A Lover's Tears), 'Wo Shi Yi Zhi Hua Mei Niao' (I Am a Thrush) and 'Ni Shi Chun Ri Feng' (You Are the Spring Breeze). Pan's distinctive low voice earned her the nickname 'Di Yin Ge Hou' (Bassy Diva).

After singing professionally for more than 20 years, Pan stopped recording and performing in the 1970s. She appeared as a judge in the 1980s show *Dou Ge Jing Yi* (Talentime). She then became a voice coach for the Singapore Broadcasting Corporation's singing classes, and began recording again. After recovering from a brain tumour operation, she volunteered her performances at various charity organizations. In 2002, she celebrated her 50th anniversary in show business with three concerts at the ESPLANADE—THEATRES ON THE BAY.

pop ye ye This Malay music genre was popular in Malaysia, Singapore and Brunei in the 1960s and 1970s. It was greatly influenced by The Beatles; particularly by the hit 'She Loves You' with its infectious 'yeah, yeah, yeah' refrain. The first local *pop ye ye* song, 'Suzanna', was produced by M. Osman in 1964. At the peak of the *pop ye ye* era, songs were performed by music groups known as *kumpulan gitar rancak* (literally 'band with upbeat guitar'), usually abbreviated as '*kugiran*'. The groups emulated The Beatles in their looks, presentation and style. Normally, these groups comprised four members: vocalist, electric guitarist, bassist and drummer. Many recording companies in Singapore and Malaysia were created in the 1960s to cater to demand for this type of music.

Among the more popular singers were A. RAMLI, Jeffridin (from the SIGLAP FIVE), Adnan Othman, J. Kamish, Ahmad Jais, M. Osman, Hussein Ismail, A. Halim, S. Jibeng and P. RAMLEE. The popularity of *pop ye ye* eventually waned in the 1970s.

popiah Popular hawker dish. *Popiah*, meaning 'thin pastry' in HOKKIEN, consists of a *popiah* skin made of dough which is filled with shredded turnip, carrot, minced garlic, lettuce, crushed peanuts, sweet soy sauce and chilli paste. It might also contain other ingredients such as prawns, omelette strips and bean sprouts. This is a Hokkien dish popular not only at hawker centres but also at home. Some people organize *popiah* parties where those attending make their own. The secret in making it at home is not to overstuff the *popiah*. An overstuffed *popiah* is hard to fold and collapses after the first bite. Fried *popiah* is also available, though not from *popiah* stalls. In Malay, the fried version is called *popiah goreng* ('*goreng*' means 'fried'), while the other version is called *popiah basah* (wet *popiah*). Local company TEE YIH JIA is the world's biggest manufacturer of *popiah* skins.

Popular Holdings: bookshop in Bras Basah Complex.

Popular Holdings Founded by Chou Sing Chu, father of current chairman Chou Cheng Ngok, Popular Holdings began in 1924 as a sole-proprietor firm, Cheng Hing Company, located at Tanjong Pagar. The firm was an importer of Chinese-language books and magazines. A second venture, World Book Company, was set up in 1934 in South Bridge Road, and subsequently took over the distribution of books from Cheng Hing. The first Popular Bookstore opened in 1936 in North Bridge Road. Through the latter part of the 1930s, Popular expanded its reach to Selangor, Penang and Ipoh in Malaysia, as well as to Jakarta and Surabaya in Indonesia.

The group started a publishing arm, World Publishing Company, in Hong Kong in 1949, after the establishment of the People's Republic of China led to a halt in the supply of Chinese-language books and lifestyle magazines from the mainland to Southeast Asia. The group's activities soon extended to textbook publishing in 1952 for Singapore and Malaysian schools. This was followed by a similar move in Hong Kong, where Popular became a major player in the market for pre-school and elementary educational books. By the 1980s, Popular began re-positioning itself as a bilingual book and stationery supplies retailer. The next two decades saw rapid growth and Popular was listed on the Singapore Exchange in 1997.

Popular also acts as agent and distributor for other publishers through its network of 104 Popular Bookstores in Singapore, Malaysia and Hong Kong, and nearly 300 Popular-managed bookshops across Taiwan. In 2000 the group entered the e-learning business.

The group has more than 40 subsidiaries and operations in Singapore, Malaysia, Hong Kong, Macau, Taiwan, China, Britain and Canada. It recorded $360 million in revenue and a net profit of $10.6 million for the financial year 2004/05.

popular music *See* CHINESE POPULAR MUSIC, ENGLISH POPULAR MUSIC and POP YE YE.

Portsdown Road Portsdown Road links Ayer Rajah Expressway to Buona Vista Road, and is a long, winding two-lane road running through the estates of Wessex Estate and Nepal Park, which were built for British

POSBank advertisement from 1976.

servicemen in the 1930s. Today, the area is one of the main parts of the ONE-NORTH development. The road is lined in sections with old BLACK-AND-WHITE HOUSES and quarters, and is home to the Temasek Club, Tanglin Trust School and Singapore Judo Association. The rustic Colbar eatery (short for Colonial Bar), which opened in 1953, was moved a short distance from its old site to make way for a road and reopened next to the Temasek Club in early 2004.

POSBank The Post Office Savings Bank (POSB) of Singapore was the largest financial institution in Singapore before it was acquired by DBS BANK. As a community bank, it played an important role in encouraging national savings. Some 95 per cent of Singaporeans had at least one POSB account each. The history of the bank dates back to 1 January 1877, when the British colonial government established the Post Office Savings Bank in the General Post Office Building at Raffles Place.

In 1951, the number of depositors reached 100,000, growing to a peak in 1955 and languishing thereafter. In the mid-1960s, the Post Office Savings Bank was revived by then-minister for finance GOH KENG SWEE. He saw the potential in tapping national savings for the development of Singapore's infrastructure. On 1 January 1972, the bank was made a statutory board, under the care of the Ministry of Communications. Its principal functions under the Post Office Savings Bank Act of 1971 were to carry on the general business of a savings bank and to promote saving and encourage thrift, as well as mobilize domestic savings for the purpose of public development.

In 1974, responsibility for the bank was transferred to the Ministry of Finance. In the same year, the bank set up a subsidiary, Credit POSB, to tap into the housing market. In 1976, the number of accounts hit

one million, while deposits exceeded $1 billion. In 1981, its first Cash-On-Line ATM machine opened at Newton Branch, and 1984 saw the introduction of a current account facility. By 1986, deposits had reached $10 billion. After a corporate makeover, the name of the bank was changed to POSBank in March 1990. In 1998, DBS Bank acquired the bank and its subsidiaries for $1.6 billion, to become the largest retail bank in Singapore.

postal services From 1819 to 1822, the British military administered a lone mail office. Located at the former Parliament House, it had a staff of three, who collected and delivered a small number of letters. In 1823, the Post Office—no longer under the military—became a branch of the Indian Post Office under the authority of the director-general at Calcutta, local responsibility being given to the master attendant (harbour master).

As Singapore's port flourished, so the volume of mail grew. The Post Office became a department separate from the Marine Office in October 1858. In 1873, the General Post Office (GPO) building was constructed near the mouth of the SINGAPORE RIVER. Author JOSEPH CONRAD, who visited Singapore as a sailor, described the GPO as 'the most important post office in the east'. The GPO building was later demolished and replaced by the Fullerton Building, constructed between 1925 and 1928. The GPO was housed in the basement and two lower floors of the FULLERTON BUILDING. The waterfront along COLLYER QUAY was used to transfer the mail onto ships. The tunnel under Fullerton Road that was used to load mail onto waiting ships still exists.

From 1949, the Singapore Postal Department was linked with the Postal Department of the Federation of Malaya. Both territories had a joint administrative headquarters in Kuala Lumpur, under the central administration of the postmaster general of Malaya. The government of each territory retained revenue collected in its region.

After Independence in 1965, Singapore took over its own postal functions by stages. On 8 January 1966, the Post Office gained

POSBank automated teller machines outside bank.

admission to the Universal Postal Union, an organization that supervises international postal efficiency. On 1 January 1967, the Singapore Postal Services Department obtained full autonomy.

In 1982, the Postal Services Department merged with the Telecommunication Authority of Singapore, or Telecoms. In 1992, the authority split into three, forming the restructured Telecommunication Authority of Singapore (now under the INFOCOMM DEVELOPMENT AUTHORITY), Singapore Telecommunications Private Limited (now SINGTEL) and Singapore Post Private Limited, a subsidiary of SingTel. In May 2003, Singapore Post Limited, or SINGPOST, launched its $684 million initial public offering.

Postal service: delivery workers setting off on their rounds, 1956 (top); SingPost's Self-Service Automated Machine (S.A.M.).

postgraduate education Singapore universities have been urged to develop a wide range of research-based postgraduate programmes. The aim is to rapidly increase the number of post-graduate students, to cater to a maturing economy and more complex socio-economic challenges.

Postgraduate education and research at the two major local universities, the NATIONAL UNIVERSITY OF SINGAPORE (NUS) and NANYANG TECHNOLOGICAL UNIVERSITY (NTU), have been expanded through collaborative research projects, joint postgraduate and professional courses, and student-exchange programmes with established overseas institutions such as Imperial College London; Massachusetts Institute of Technology; and Harvard, Cornell, Cambridge, Stanford and Tokyo Universities. NUS and NTU have also substantially increased the number of collaborative projects with multinational companies, governmental bodies and SMALL- AND MEDIUM-SIZED ENTERPRISES. More inter-disciplinary research projects are also being adopted, such as the Biomedical Engineering Research Programme, a joint project between NTU and four major hospitals.

Other local institutions offering postgraduate education are the Management

Development Institute of Singapore, SINGAPORE INSTITUTE OF MANAGEMENT, SINGAPORE MANAGEMENT UNIVERSITY and Wealth Management Institute. There are also several reputable overseas institutions of learning offering master's and doctoral-level courses in Singapore. They include the UNIVERSITY OF CHICAGO GRADUATE SCHOOL OF BUSINESS, Johns Hopkins University School of Medicine and INSEAD. All three have their own campuses in Singapore. The University of New South Wales (UNSW Asia) is scheduled to set up a Singapore campus in 2007 offering postgraduate and undergraduate courses. The ECONOMIC DEVELOPMENT BOARD is in continual discussion with reputable universities overseas, to encourage them to establish branch campuses in Singapore.

Practice Performing Arts School Bilingual dance and theatre institution. Practice Performing Arts School (PPAS) was founded in 1965 by dramatist KUO PAO KUN and his dancer-choreographer wife GOH LAY KUAN. Since its inception, PPAS has been at the forefront of innovation in the arts scene. It introduced multilingual and multicultural theatre practice and founded THE SUBSTATION, Singapore's first arts centre, as well as THE THEATRE PRACTICE, a major theatre company. The operating philosophy of PPAS is that arts education forms an integral part of an individual's total development. In 2000, PPAS launched its Theatre Training & Research Programme (TTRP), a practice-oriented training programme that equips its graduates with the ability to work across cultural, aesthetic and linguistic boundaries.

Prakash, Judith (1951–) Judge. Judith Evelyn Jyothi Prakash was born the daughter of politician GERALD DE CRUZ in the United Kingdom. She was educated at Raffles Girls' School and then at the law faculty at the University of Singapore, where she graduated with a first class honours degree.

She was called to the Singapore Bar the following year. She practised at the firm of Chor Pee & Hin Hiong before moving to DREW & NAPIER, where she was made a partner in 1978. Between 1974 and 1978, she tutored in family law at the NATIONAL UNIVERSITY OF SINGAPORE's law faculty. On 1 April 1992, she was appointed Judicial Commissioner, and on 1 April 1995, she was elevated to the Bench as judge of the Supreme Court—the second woman to be appointed to that office. Prakash was awarded the Public Service Medal in 2005.

Preferential Additional Registration Fee An incentive to keep the car population young, the Preferential Additional Registration Fee (PARF) was introduced in December 1975. If a car is scrapped or exported before its tenth year, the owner is granted a PARF benefit, which increases its scrap value. Until 2002, the PARF benefit was a percentage of the OPEN MARKET VALUE (OMV) ranging from 80 per cent to 130 per cent, depending on the age of the deregistered car. For cars registered from May 2002 onwards, the PARF benefit is a percentage of its Additional Registration Fee (ARF) (*see* CARS AND CAR OWNERSHIP) ranging from 50 per cent to 75 per cent of ARF, depending again on the age of the deregistered car.

pre-modern history In 1891, HENRY RIDLEY reported the discovery of a stone tool (an 'edge-ground round-axe of dark brown stone') on the beach at Tanjong Karang, southwest Singapore. In the 1930s archaeological research was carried out at the nearby site of Tanjong Bunga, on the south coast of Johor. Various kinds of stone tools were found, including rectangular ground Neolithic axes, round axes, and microliths, which were first found in Malaya. P.D.R. Williams-Hunt found round axes and flakes on PULAU UBIN, but a test excavation yielded no further artefacts. These discoveries prove that Singapore was occupied several thousand years ago. However, no archaeologists have explored Singapore for prehistoric remains since the 1930s.

Sources for the pre-modern history of Singapore are ambiguous, and until recently lacked archaeological confirmation, which led some historians to question whether they referred to Singapore at all. The ambiguity arises from the fact that the name Singapore does not seem to have been used for this island until the late 14th century. Before that, several other names were used for various places around and on Singapore. These include LONGYAMEN (DRAGON'S TOOTH or Keppel Strait), TEMASEK and Banzu (Pancur).

Archaeological corroboration that Singapore existed as a port of trade by the early 14th century lends much greater credence to the conclusion that all these names do refer to Singapore (*see* ARCHAEOLOGICAL SITES). One complication is that the name Longyamen also appears in Zhao Rukuo's Zhufanzhi (Survey of Foreign Countries) of 1225. This is about 75 years older than any other evidence for historic-period life in Singapore. It is possible that the name originally referred to another location.

Pre-modern history: 14th-century Javanese-style statue excavated at Empress Place.

Another complication arises from the Vietnamese Royal Chronicle, Dai Viet Su Ky Toan Thu, for the year 1330. It says that a prince named Nhat Duat was able to translate when an ambassador from Sach Ma Tich (Vietnamese transliteration of Temasek) arrived at the royal court in the reign of Nhan Tong (1279–93). This implies that Temasek existed as early as 1293.

Singapore's history in the conventional sense, began in 1320 when the name Longyamen appeared in Yuan Dynasty records of diplomatic activity in the Yuan Shih, the official dynastic history. In 1325, Longyamen sent a mission to China with a memorial and tribute. The Yuan court must have known of Longyamen before 1320, since such missions were planned in advance.

The only surviving eyewitness account of Singapore by any ancient writer is Daoyi Zhilue (Description of the Barbarians of the Isles) written by Wang Dayuan in 1349. In it, he describes what seems to be an account of a much earlier settlement in the same area: 'In ancient times, when digging the ground, a chief came upon a jewelled head-dress.' The story of the jewelled head-dress is reminiscent of a tale in the SEJARAH MELAYU (Malay Annals), which says that SANG NILA UTAMA had to throw his crown into the sea before he could reach Temasek.

Other sources suggest that Temasek was under Javanese control during this period. These include the Javanese texts DESAWARNANA, a 14th-century court poem, and the 16th-century PARARATON (Book of Kings). A further indication that the port was under the control of another country—probably Java—is that there are no Chinese records of missions from Temasek after 1325.

The period 1380–1400 is not well-documented in the Ming Annals due to turmoil in China. The second Ming emperor was overthrown by his uncle, and his reign was written out of existence in official records. This rewriting may have extended back into the 14th century, obscuring the history of the Singapore region.

Around 1391, Parameswara (*see* ISKANDAR SHAH), the chief of Palembang, decided to evacuate the ancient port and shift the capital of the Malay realm to Singapore. He must have thought it possessed the best combination of attributes to be a potential successor to Palembang, and was possibly easier to defend against Javanese attacks. It was probably he who changed Temasek's name to Singapore. The ruler of Temasek at the time bore the title Sang Aji; he was killed by Parameswara's men. In retaliation, Singapore was attacked by Sang Aji's in-laws, who probably lived in the Patani region of southern Thailand. Parameswara was forced to flee around 1396. He founded a new settlement at MALACCA, survived threats from the Javanese and the Siamese, and succeeded in

Presbyterians: Orchard Road Presbyterian Church.

forming a new port, which drew much of Singapore's population away.

Further evidence of this period of Temasek's history comes from the Sejarah Melayu. It tells of how the first Malay ruler Sang Nila Utama journeyed to Singapore, where he founded a settlement which became a flourishing trading port. After a century of prosperity, Singapore was destroyed by an attack from Java, but the ruler, Iskandar Shah, escaped and founded Malacca.

Between the 15th and the 19th centuries, the island of Singapore was of little political or commercial importance. With the rise of Malacca, trade bypassed Singapore. This would change only with the arrival of Sir STAMFORD RAFFLES.

Presbyterians The first Presbyterian church in Singapore was the Malay Chapel, which was set up in Prinsep Street in 1843. It was founded by BENJAMIN PEACH KEASBERRY of the London Missionary Society. He had stayed behind in Singapore while other missionaries from the society were sent to China from Singapore and Malaya after China signed the Treaty of Nanking in 1842. The Malay Chapel would later become the PRINSEP STREET PRESBYTERIAN CHURCH. In 1862, Keasberry started a church service in Bukit Timah with the help of Tan See Boo, which became Glory Presbyterian Church in 1881. This was the first Chinese Presbyterian church in Singapore.

The Synod in Singapore was formed in 1881 when the Presbyterian Church in England sent J.A.B. Cook to Singapore. Cook first went to Swatow (present day Shantou) to learn TEOCHEW. With the assistance of the Scottish Church in Singapore (present-day ORCHARD ROAD PRESBYTERIAN CHURCH), Cook joined the church ministry in Bukit Timah. In 1897, the first Chinese pastor, Tay Sek Tin, was employed to specially serve the HOKKIEN-speaking congregation. This led to a church being set up in Tanjong Pagar that would become the

Jubilee Presbyterian Church. Subsequently, preaching centres were set up in other places around Singapore, and also in Johor Bahru and Muar. The Malay Chapel started by Keasberry was also assimilated into the Synod.

In 1901, Cook held the first general meeting of the Synod, and the assembly was named The Singapore Presbyterian Synod. Four years later, it was renamed The Singapore and Johor Presbyterian Synod due to the development of other churches in Johor. In 1948, the Synod joined the General Assembly of the Church of Christ in China and changed its name to Singapore-Malaya Synod of the Church of Christ in 1949. In 1966, it joined the World Alliance of Reformed Churches, becoming the 101st member of the Alliance. Two years later, the Synod became known as The Presbyterian Church in Singapore and Malaysia and in the same year, instituted a common constitution for regulations and practices for the churches to follow. In 1971, the Orchard Road Presbyterian Church joined the Synod.

Due to SEPARATION and geographical and administrative concerns, separate synods were formed for Singapore and Malaysia. The first annual general meeting of the Synod of the Presbyterian Church in Singapore was convened in 1975 and Stephen Tan Chin Kwang was elected to be the first Synod Moderator. In 1993, Chinese and English Presbyteries were set up because of the increasing number of

churches with English-speaking congregations. To date, the Synod and its English and Chinese Presbyteries have 40 member churches with a combined congregation of 16,000. There are four schools affiliated with the synod. They are Presbyterian High School, Kuo Chuan PresbyterianSecondary School, Kuo Chuan Presbyterian Primary School and Pei Hua Prebyterian Primary School. To provide social services, the Presbyterian Community Service arm was formed in 1974.

Preservation of Monuments Board
Statutory board. The Preservation of Monuments Board (PMB) was founded in 1971 with the enactment of the Preservation of Monuments Act. The Board is responsible for safeguarding monuments as historical landmarks that provide a link to Singapore's past. It identifies buildings and structures of historical, cultural, archaeological, architectural or artistic interest, and recommends them for preservation as national monuments (*see* table).

National monuments can be religious, civic, cultural or commercial buildings. Among the 55 gazetted national monuments are the SUPREME COURT BUILDING, ISTANA, THIAN HOCK KENG TEMPLE, SULTAN MOSQUE, SRI SRINIVASA PERUMAL TEMPLE, ARMENIAN CHURCH, CHESED-EL SYNAGOGUE and GOODWOOD PARK HOTEL.

The Thian Hock Keng Temple and CHIJMES (chapel and Caldwell House of the former CONVENT OF THE HOLY INFANT

PRESERVATION OF MONUMENTS BOARD: NATIONAL MONUMENTS			
Old Thong Chai Medical Institution	6 Jul 1973	National Museum of Singapore	14 Feb 1992
Armenian Church	6 Jul 1973	Former St Joseph's Institution	14 Feb 1992
St Andrew's Cathedral	6 Jul 1973	(Singapore Art Museum)	3 Jul 1992
Telok Ayer Market (Lau Pa Sat)	6 Jul 1973	Old Attorney-General's Chambers	14 Feb 1992
Thian Hock Keng Temple	6 Jul 1973	Sun Yat Sen Nanyang Memorial Hall	28 Oct 1994
Sri Mariamman Temple	6 Jul 1973	Wak Hai Cheng Bio	28 Jun 1996
Hajjah Fatimah Mosque	6 Jul 1973	Maghain Aboth Synagogue	27 Feb 1998
Cathedral of the Good Shepherd	6 Jul 1973	Old Ministry of Labour Building	27 Feb 1998
Nagore Durgha	6 Jul 1973	Old Tao Nan School	27 Feb 1998
Al-Abrar Mosque	29 Nov 1974	Chesed-El Synagogue	18 Dec 1998
House of Tan Yeok Nee	29 Nov 1974	MICA Building (Hill Street Police Station)	18 Dec 1998
Tan Si Chong Su Temple	29 Nov 1974	Ying Fo Fui Kun	18 Dec 1998
Jamae Mosque	29 Nov 1974	Central Fire Station	18 Dec 1998
Sultan Mosque	14 Mar 1975	Old Nanyang University Library &	18 Dec 1998
St George's Church	10 Nov 1978	Administration Buiding, Memorial and Arch	
Hong San See	10 Nov 1978	The Chinese High School Clock Tower	19 Mar 1999
Sri Perumal Temple	10 Nov 1978	Building	
Abdul Gaffoor Mosque	10 Nov 1979	Prinsep Street Presbyterian Church	12 Jan 2000
Siong Lim Temple	17 Oct 1980	Tan Teck Guan Building	2 Dec 2002
Raffles Hotel	6 Mar 1987	College of Medicine building	2 Dec 2002
	3 Jun 1995	Old Admiralty House	2 Dec 2002
Telok Ayer Chinese Methodist Church	23 Mar 1989	Cathay Building	10 Feb 2003
Goodwood Park Hotel	23 Mar 1989	Church of St Peter and St Paul	10 Feb 2003
Old Convent of the Holy Infant Jesus	26 Oct 1990	MacDonald House	10 Feb 2003
(CHIJMES)		Church of St Joseph	14 Jan 2005
Istana and Sri Temasek	14 Feb 1992	Church of Our Lady of Lourdes	14 Jan 2005
City Hall	14 Feb 1992	Church of the Nativity of the Blessed	14 Jan 2005
Victoria Theatre and Concert Hall	14 Feb 1992	Virgin Mary	
Parliament House and Annexe Building	14 Feb 1992	Tou Mu Kung	14 Jan 2005
	3 Jul 1992	Old Ford Motor Factory	5 Feb 2006
Supreme Court	14 Feb 1992	NOTE: Dates refer to day on which building was gazetted.	
Empress Place Building	14 Feb 1992	Source: Preservation of Monuments Board	

Preservation of Monuments Board: Thian Hock Keng Temple detail.

President S.R. Nathan at a performance by D'Artistes, a performance group for intellectually disabled children and teenagers, on Vesak Day, 2005.

JESUS) won the Asia-Pacific Heritage Conservation Award of the United Nations Educational, Scientific and Cultural Organization (UNESCO) in 2001 and 2002 respectively

In the period 1971–97, PMB was a statutory board within the Ministry of National Development. On 1 April 1997, it was transferred to the Ministry of Information and the Arts (later known as the MINISTRY OF INFORMATION, COMMUNICATION AND THE ARTS). The Minister appoints 16 board members to serve two-year terms.

president As a republic with a parliamentary system based on the United Kingdom's Westminster model, Singapore has a president as head of state.

The first president of Singapore was YUSOF ISHAK. He was Yang di-Pertuan Negara ('head of state') from December 1959, when Singapore obtained self-government from the British. He was appointed president in 1965, when Singapore achieved independence from Malaysia.

Until 1991, Singapore's non-executive president was nominated and elected by PARLIAMENT. At the NATIONAL DAY RALLY in 1988, Prime Minister LEE KUAN YEW mooted the idea of transforming the office of president into an elected one. In 1991, the CONSTITUTION was amended to provide for a popularly elected head of state. Among the reasons given were the need to institutionally safeguard Singapore's massive foreign reserves and protect the integrity of its civil service from a profligate and populist government. Under the scheme, the popularly elected president would hold the 'second key' to the reserves, and have veto power on the appointment of top civil servants. At the same time, the amendments gave the elected president veto powers over the continued preventive detention of prisoners and the issuing of prohibition orders against extremist religious proselytes.

There are several notable features of the new presidency. First, constitutional provisions relating to the elected presidency cannot be amended without the president's concurrence unless a two-thirds majority in

a national referendum supports the change. Second, the qualifications for candidacy are extremely stringent—for example, candidates are required to have been a former minister, judge, permanent secretary or head of a company with $100 million in paid-up capital; a three-man Presidential Elections Committee determines who is or is not eligible. Third, any candidate wishing to run for office has to be non-partisan in that he or she cannot be a member of any political party; and fourth, the Presidential Elections Act provided that if there is only one candidate for the election, there is no need for a formal election and that candidate would be deemed elected as president.

When the Constitution was amended in 1991 to incorporate provisions relating to the elected presidency, the incumbent, President Wee Kim Wee, was deemed to be Singapore's first elected president even though he was not elected. President Wee was thus the first person to wield the presidency's enhanced powers. The first presidential election was held on 29 August 1993. ONG TENG CHEONG, a former deputy prime minister, chairman of the PEOPLE'S ACTION PARTY and long-time trade union leader and politician, defeated retired banker and former accountant-general CHUA KIM YEOW to become Singapore's first elected president. When Ong's term came to an end in 1999, the sole candidate, S.R. NATHAN, was declared Singapore's elected president. In 2005, S.R. Nathan again returned uncontested when the Presidential Elections Committee decided that there were no suitable candidates among those who had applied to run for office.

See also COUNCIL OF PRESIDENTIAL ADVISORS and POLITICAL SYSTEM.

Presidential Council for Minority Rights The Council was set up in 1970, after recommendations by a Constitutional Commission chaired by then Chief Justice WEE CHONG JIN.

The commission was created by PARLIAMENT in 1965, the year Singapore became a nation state, to propose ways to safeguard the rights of racial, linguistic and religious minorities in the CONSTITUTION. It was to ensure that such minorities would not be discriminated against in legislation or by any government body.

The commission received and considered representations on how the rights of these minorities could be upheld. It also recommended provisions barring discrimination along racial, linguistic or religious lines, as well as putting forth a machinery of redress in cases of alleged discriminatory treatment.

The commission proposed that the Constitution be amended to allow for the formation of the Presidential Council. This was renamed the Presidential Council for Minority Rights in 1973.

As the Constitution now stands, Article

152 states that: 'It shall be the responsibility of the government to constantly care for the interests of the racial and religious minorities in Singapore.' Under Article 69 of the Constitution, the council comprises a chairman who presides for three years, ten permanent members appointed for life, and not more than ten other members appointed for a period of three years.

In 2005, Chief Justice YONG PUNG HOW was the chairman. Permanent members include Senior Minister GOH CHOK TONG, Minister Mentor LEE KUAN YEW, and Deputy Prime Minister and Minister for Law S. JAYAKUMAR. The other members were prominent individuals from the SINGAPORE CIVIL SERVICE, private sector and social organizations.

The group's duties include considering and reporting on matters affecting persons of any racial or religious community referred to it by Parliament or the government. It is also required to draw attention to any Bill or legislation that has been given a final reading and passed by Parliament, which it considers disadvantageous to persons of any racial or religious community.

Most Bills that come before Parliament are given to the council for vetting. However, it has no formal powers to veto Bills, and it has to date presented no adverse findings.

Presidential Council for Religious Harmony Advisory body to the government. The Presidential Council for Religious Harmony (PCRH) was created under the MAINTENANCE OF RELIGIOUS HARMONY ACT in 1990. The Act was passed in response to what the government viewed as actions threatening religious harmony in Singapore, including 'insensitive proselytizing' and the 'mixing of religion and politics'. The Council—which comprises between 6 and 15 members—reports to the minister of home affairs and is empowered to issue restraining orders against leaders and members of religious groups to prevent them from carrying out political activities that excite disaffection against the government, create ill-will between religious groups, or carry out subversive activities. These orders place individuals on notice that they should not repeat such acts. Contravention of a restraining order may attract fines up to $10,000 or imprisonment of up to two years for a first offence. The Council also reports to the minister for home affairs on matters affecting the maintenance of religious harmony that are referred to the council by the minister or by Parliament.

President's Scholarship Singapore's most prestigious scholarship, awarded annually to students who have demonstrated, beyond academic ability and excellence in co-curricular activities, a strong commitment to public service; who possess an unwavering dedication to improving the lives of

PRESIDENT: PRESIDENTS OF SINGAPORE	
1965–70	Yusof Ishak
1971–81	Benjamin Sheares
1981–85	Devan Nair
1985–93	Wee Kim Wee
1993–99	Ong Teng Cheong
1999–	S.R. Nathan

Source: The Istana

Singaporeans; and who have shown soundness of character and the potential to lead.

The President's Scholarship has its roots in the QUEEN'S SCHOLARSHIP, which was founded in 1885. Initiated by Sir CECIL CLEMENTI SMITH, the Queen's Scholarship was awarded to the best student of the year by a board comprising six members and headed by the CHIEF JUSTICE.

Candidates shortlisted for the President's Scholarship are interviewed by a selection committee headed by the chairman of the PUBLIC SERVICE COMMISSION (PSC). Other members of the Selection Committee include PSC members, as well as representatives from local universities. There is fierce competition for the award. Each President's Scholarship is generally awarded concurrently with a PSC Scholarship. President's Scholars may study any course leading to a first degree tenable at local or overseas universities except for medicine, which is tenable only at the NATIONAL UNIVERSITY OF SINGAPORE. The first recipients included LEE YOCK SUAN, who became minister of the PRIME MINISTER'S OFFICE and second minister for foreign affairs; Barry Desker, who became director of the INSTITUTE OF DEFENCE AND STRATEGIC STUDIES; and KOH CHER SIANG, who became commissioner of the INLAND REVENUE AUTHORITY OF SINGAPORE. Many President's Scholars have gone on to become Cabinet ministers, the most prominent being Prime Minister LEE HSIEN LOONG.

press freedom While freedom of speech is enshrined as a fundamental liberty in Article 14 of the CONSTITUTION, this right is subject to any restriction that Parliament 'considers necessary or expedient' in the interests of security, public order or morality, and to protect against contempt of Parliament, contempt of court, defamation or incitement to any offence. The press is not free to act as the fourth estate. The position of the PEOPLE'S ACTION PARTY (PAP) on press freedom was clearly stated by LEE KUAN YEW in 1971: 'Freedom of the press, freedom of the news media, must be subordinated to the overriding needs of Singapore, and to the primacy of purpose of an elected government.'

The Newspaper and Printing Presses Act (NPPA) of 1974, the cornerstone of which is a discretionary licensing system, governs the press. A legacy of colonial rule, licensing laws require would-be newspaper publishers to apply for an annual permit which can be withdrawn at any time. Applications must state the nature of the publication and the kinds of content it will carry. Critics say licensing partly accounts for Singapore's lack of a vibrant alternative press—small independent publications representing non-mainstream political and cultural communities. Large publications have also felt the brunt of licensing laws. In 1971, the government used this mechanism

to close down the ten-month-old *Singapore Herald* after accusing it of 'black operations' against the republic's security. However, the controversy surrounding this and other crackdowns prompted a rethink of the largely inherited tools—the Printing Presses Act of 1920, and the earlier Gagging Act—for managing the press. The 1974 Act introduced deeper and subtler controls.

In addition to a new ban on foreign ownership, the NPPA made it mandatory for newspaper companies to be publicly listed, and to create management shares to be held by government nominees. Public listing—with ordinary shareholders limited to a 3 per cent stake after a 1977 amendment to the act—meant that newspapers would have to answer to anonymous business interests, rather than to individual owners who might have idiosyncratic ideological motivations for bankrolling a newspaper. Management shares provided a mechanism for the government to influence a newspaper's workings without interfering with ownership, which could be left to the stock market. They were allocated to banks and other establishment individuals. Management shares have 200 times the voting rights of ordinary shares, giving them effective control of the board and top editorial positions. This system has enabled the PAP to achieve near-watertight supervision of the press without either nationalizing ownership of the media or brutalizing journalists. Newspapers have been allowed enough independence to make handsome profits and create rewarding careers for professional journalists. There is no mechanism of censorship or vetting of articles by officials prior to publication. However, editors are sensitized to political limits through their long experience and close on-going discussions with government leaders.

The NPPA includes special provisions for foreign-based newspapers circulating in Singapore. Such periodicals, which include weekly news magazines, can be declared to be 'engaging in the domestic politics of Singapore' and subjected to quotas. The stated rationale is not to deny Singaporeans free access to information and ideas, but to prevent offending publishers from commercially exploiting the relatively lucrative Singapore market. In practice, publications are deemed to be interfering in domestic politics if they deny the Singapore government the right to an unedited reply to any offending article. Many foreign publications circulating in Singapore—including *TIME,* the *Asian Wall Street Journal* and *The Economist*—have fallen foul of this requirement and been gazetted at some time. At the World Congress of Newspaper Publishers in 1987, Lee Hsien Loong said: 'The Singapore Government is not against the free flow of information. But it will not allow the foreign press full license to mis-

President's Scholarship: recipients with President and Mrs S.R. Nathan, third and fourth from left.

inform, subvert, or campaign in Singapore.'

Publishers and journalists are subject to numerous other laws. The INTERNAL SECURITY ACT, which allows arrest without warrant and detention without trial, was used against four executives of NANYANG SIANG PAU who were accused of inciting Chinese racial sentiments in 1971. The act has not been used against the press in recent decades. Contempt of court legislation has been used against allegations that the Singapore JUDICIARY is not independent. The Official Secrets Act, which makes it a crime to receive or publish government information without proper authorization, has been levelled at THE BUSINESS TIMES, whose editor and a correspondent were fined. Singapore's defamation laws do not follow the American tradition, in which plaintiffs who are public officials must show 'actual malice' on the defendant's part. Courts in Singapore have ruled against defendants in most libel actions brought by politicians of the ruling party. However, the main targets of such litigation have been opposition politicians rather than the mainstream press. In 1998, for example, Singapore courts awarded plaintiffs $265,000 for a libellous article published in *The Hammer*, the newsletter of the WORKERS' PARTY.

All broadcast media in Singapore are state-owned, and satellite television is largely banned. The Internet is the only medium not subject to discretionary licensing. However, Internet communication is subject to DEFAMATION and other laws applying offline. In 2005, for example, three people were charged under the Sedition Act for making racist comments online. Regulations require Internet service providers to route all Internet traffic through proxy servers that allow filtering. In practice, however, the filtering is aimed at blocking pornographic sites. Political and news sites have not been blocked.

While the government has pledged greater openness and transparency, there has been no move towards reforming press laws and regulations. Gradual liberalization has instead taken the form of greater tolerance of alternative viewpoints. Comments and questions that would not have surfaced a decade earlier are now aired openly in the mainstream media.

HMS Prince of Wales

See also NEWSPAPERS, RADIO BROADCAST-ING, TELEVISION BROADCASTING and UNDESIRABLE PUBLICATIONS.

primary education In 1979, minister for education Dr GOH KENG SWEE published a report that addressed problems associated with primary education at the time—the high dropout rate, and poor literacy and numeracy. One of the key recommendations was to stream primary students according to their learning ability, particularly with respect to language learning. After 1979, the emphasis of the first three years of the six years of primary education was on language learning. Less emphasis was given to the mastery of content. At Primary Four, students were placed into three streams: Normal, Extended and Monolingual. Exceptionally bright students were enrolled in the GIFTED EDUCATION PROGRAMME. The students in the Normal Stream learned English and Mother Tongue. They sat for the Primary School Leaving Examination (PSLE) at the end of Primary Six. Students in the Extended Stream also learned two languages, but took two years longer. They sat for the PSLE at Primary Eight. Students in the Monolingual stream learned only one language and did not sit for the PSLE.

Primary education: Malay and English textbooks for primary school children.

The streaming policy was modified in 1992. Students were now streamed at Primary Five into three streams: EM1, EM2 and EM3. The students in EM1

Primus

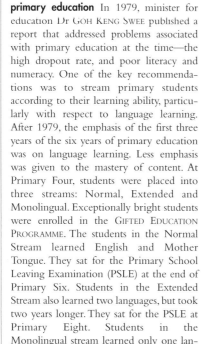

learned English and Mother Tongue as first languages. In EM2, students learned Mother Tongue as a second language. Students in EM3 learned Foundation English and Basic Mother Tongue (as well as Foundation Mathematics). EM1 and EM2 students sat for the PSLE at the end of their sixth year.

The streaming policy was revised again in 2004. Primary education today is divided into two stages. The first four years make up the Foundation Stage and the final two years make up the Orientation Stage. The Foundation Stage is designed to provide all students with a sound grasp of language and mathematics. At the end of Primary Four, students are streamed according to their ability before entering the Orientation Phase in Primary Five. The EM1 and EM2 streams have been merged, while the EM3 stream remains distinct.

See also COMPULSORY EDUCATION and EDUCATION SYSTEM.

primary healthcare The private sector provides 80 per cent of primary care in Singapore. The other 20 per cent is provided by the state through polyclinics. There are about 1,800 general practitioners in private practice, and their clinics can be found in almost all major private and public housing estates. Many of the clinics are run independently by the doctors themselves, though companies such as Raffles Medical and Parkway Shenton run their own network. Patients from private clinics are referred as necessary to specialists in government and private hospitals. State-run polyclinics offer subsidized outpatient medical care for minor and chronic illnesses, maternal and child HEALTHCARE services, health screening, family planning and immunization. The two public healthcare clusters—NATIONAL HEALTHCARE GROUP (NHG) and the Singapore Health Services (SINGHEALTH)—have a network of 18 polyclinics located in all the major public housing estates, with subsidized charges for consultation.

Prime Minister's Office Located at the ISTANA, the Prime Minister's Office (PMO) comprises the PMO headquarters (PMO HQ), Public Service Division, CORRUPT PRACTICES INVESTIGATION BUREAU (CPIB), and ELECTIONS DEPARTMENT.

PMO HQ is used to designate the department which provides advice to the prime minister, and logistics and administrative support for the private offices of the prime minister, SENIOR MINISTER and MINISTER MENTOR. The term 'PMO HQ' came into use after the Public Service Division of the MINISTRY OF FINANCE was transferred to PMO on 1 June 1994. It was previously known simply as 'PMO'.

PMO HQ handles the following: policy matters pertaining to political office-holders; the administration of rules applying

to the Singapore STATE CREST, NATIONAL FLAG and NATIONAL ANTHEM; matters pertaining to NATIONAL DAY HONOURS and awards; the processing of petitions to the prime minister, senior minister and minister mentor; the organization of state functions such as the National Day celebrations; the use of state cars by ministers on official functions and foreign dignitaries visiting Singapore; and the overseeing of the CPIB and ELECTIONS DEPARTMENT.

Primus Singapore-designed field artillery unit. The Singapore Self-Propelled Howitzer 1 (SSPH 1) Primus is a self-propelled artillery unit mounted with a 155-mm, 39-calibre howitzer. At 28.3 tons, and with a tracked chassis mounted on seven road wheels on each side, the Primus is, for an artillery unit, light and mobile. With an automatic loading and targeting system based on the Global Positioning System and Datalink, the Primus operates with a crew of four. It can deliver all NATO-compliant ammunition at a maximum range of 30 km.

The Primus was developed jointly by the SINGAPORE ARMED FORCES (SAF), the DEFENCE SCIENCE AND TECHNOLOGY AGENCY and Singapore Technologies Kinetics (ST Kinetics) with the aim of providing better fire support to the armour brigades in the Combined Arms Divisions.

Development began in May 1996. The first working prototype was created in April 2000 and underwent two years of testing. Specifications include mobility on paved roads and soft terrain, which are common in Singapore, as well as the capability of rapid deployment. The Primus was certified in 2002, and was introduced to the Republic of Singapore Artillery in 2004.

Prince of Wales, HMS King George V class Royal Navy battleship featuring ten 14-inch guns, capable of a speed of 28.5 knots, and the flagship of FORCE Z. HMS *Prince of Wales,* along with the rest of Force Z, was caught off Kuantan at 11.15 a.m. on 10 December 1941 by a force of 34 Japanese high-level bombers and 51 torpedo-carrying bombers. In three waves of attacks, six 'Long Lance' torpedoes and one bomb hit the *Prince of Wales,* the first crippling its steering. The ship went down at 1.18 p.m., 327 of its crew perishing, including acting admiral Sir TOM PHILLIPS.

The *Prince of Wales* was the first battleship sunk entirely by aircraft while under way. The general shock felt was compounded by the ship's illustrious and very public past. Commissioned only in January 1941, the ship had engaged the German battleship *Bismarck* in May, carried Winston Churchill to Newfoundland in August for the Atlantic Conference with Franklin Roosevelt, and been shown off to foreign correspondents in Singapore in December as the very latest in battleship technology.

Prinsep Street Presbyterian Church

Prinsep Street Presbyterian Church Soon after the founding of Singapore, Christian missionaries began to arrive, many under the auspices of the London Missionary Society, including BENJAMIN PEACH KEASBERRY. He arrived in 1839 and founded a school for Malay boys. In 1843, the school moved to a newly completed church building in Prinsep Street named The Malay Chapel. The land on which it stood was leased from the EAST INDIA COMPANY for 99 years at a rental of $3 per annum. In 1885, the Presbyterian community bought the building and renamed it Prinsep Street Church. This church was attended by various congregations, including the PERANAKANS.

In 1901, plans were made for a new church, but the building was not constructed until 1931. The Romanesque-style church was most notable for its deep-red bricks and the raised brickwork on its tower and belfry. Since the church was now affiliated to the English Presbytery, it was renamed The Straits Chinese Presbyterian Church. In 1953, the first full-time pastor was appointed. Subsequently, owing to a decline in the Straits Chinese congregation, it was renamed Prinsep Street Presbyterian Church in 1956. In the 1980s, a growing congregation gave rise to the addition of a four-storey building.

The church has also had a long association with the BOYS' BRIGADE of Singapore, which was founded there in 1930. The chuch building was gazetted as a national monument in January 2000.

printing Shortly after Sir STAMFORD RAFFLES arrived in 1819, the London Missionary Society sent Samuel Milton to start up a mission in Singapore. In 1822, Claudius Henry Thomsen joined Milton, bringing with him a small press. Thomsen became the pioneer of printing and publishing in Singapore. In January 1823, he obtained the first printing permit and established the Mission Press at a private residence where RAFFLES HOTEL now stands. There is no record of printing presses existing in Singapore before that.

The Mission Press printed and bound books, and was soon printing public documents for the Straits Settlements government in both ENGLISH and MALAY. It was later bought by the Singapore Institution (later RAFFLES INSTITUTION) and many early books carried the imprint of the Institution Press as well as the Mission Press. The first scholarly book published in Singapore was John Anderson's description of British commerce in his *Political and Commercial Considerations Relative to the Malayan Peninsula and the British Settlements in the Straits of Malacca* (1824). Other important books printed by the Mission Press were the *Journal of the Indian Archipelago and Eastern Asia* and a steady stream of religious publications. It also printed two of Singapore's early newspapers, *Tifang Jih Pao* (1845) and *Jit Sheng* (1858). When BENJAMIN PEACH KEASBERRY, who refused to leave Singapore when other London Missionary Society members left for China, died in 1875, the press was bought by John Fraser and D.C. Neave (*see* Fraser & Neave) and renamed Printers Ltd. It survived until 1942. Its most enduring publication is Charles Burton Buckley's *An Anecdotal History of Old Times in Singapore* (1902).

Singapore's first Indian press was Denothaya Venthira Press run by S.K. Makadoom Saiboo. Located at 1 Mohammed Ali Lane, it published two periodicals and four literary works in Tamil. It also printed works in English, Malay and Arabic. The first Japanese press was the Japanese Commerce Museum in Middle Road. It published translations of laws, surveys and studies prepared by the museum's scholars. Malay presses began to emerge during the 1920s and the early ones included Bintang Press, Geliga Limited, Qalam and the Melayu Raya Press.

Singapore has since developed into a major international printing centre, with over 500 companies offering printing services. In 2003, the printing industry's exports amounted to more than $670 million a year.

prisons Prisons in Singapore were first established as a result of colonial policy. The British confined Indian convicts in a penal colony established in Burma (present-day Myanmar), and from there convicts were transported to other colonies in the region, especially peninsular Malaya, to provide labour. The first group, around 80, were transferred from Bencoolen (present-day Bengkulu) to Singapore on 18 April 1825. A week later another 122 convicts were resettled here.

These first two groups of convicts were housed in the penal settlements which were improvised wooden sheds where EMPRESS PLACE later stood, and they were placed under four native Indian petty officers. As the numbers grew they were

Prisons: Outram Prison, 1963 (now demolished) (top); Queenstown Remand Prison, 2006 (below).

moved to a temporary site currently bordered by Victoria Street, Bras Basah Road and Stamford Road up to Dhoby Ghaut. More convicts followed, including several groups from Penang. From 1838 to 1841 some 1,100–2,000 convicts were housed there before a permanent building was erected in 1841 on Bras Basah Road, just below Fort Canning.

The prison at Fort Canning started as a single brick structure built with convict labour. Later, staff quarters, a workyard, hospital, dormitory wards and a store area were added. By 1857, this first proper prison headed by a superintendent had 2,139 convicts. After the construction of this jail, the British were to build three more over the next 100 years.

A civil jail was built at Outram Park at the base of Pearl's Hill in 1847 and called Her Majesty's Prison. The convicts were allocated to many construction projects on the island, filling swamps, reclaiming marshlands, constructing drainage works, laying roads and building bridges (*see* CONVICT LABOUR). In the 1870s a Commission of Enquiry recommended the building of cellular structures modelled on British prison designs of the time. A new facility was constructed beside Her Majesty's Prison in 1882 and the complex became known as Outram Prison. Prisoners from Bras Basah were transferred there and the Bras Basah jail was abandoned; what remained was the chief warden's quarters, where the YOUNG MEN'S CHRISTIAN ASSOCIATION stands today.

A section for young offenders, a block for female offenders as well as a gallows were subsequently added to Outram Prison. This remained the only facility until 1936.

By the beginning of the 20th century the prison had a population of 900, but

Printing: book production at Tien Wah Press today, a highly automated process.

crime rates were still on the rise due to SECRET SOCIETIES. Another prison was needed and this led to the construction of a new jail at Changi. Built to accommodate about 600 inmates, and complete with four cellular blocks, the prison walls stood 7.3 m high and were 915 m long. CHANGI PRISON was occupied on 4 January 1937, but within five years, it came under the control of the Japanese and was used as a prisoner-of-war camp. After WORLD WAR II, the prison reverted to British supervision and several of the Japanese officers who were convicted of war crimes were executed in Changi Prison.

Until Independence in 1965 there was a gradual expansion of prison facilities in Singapore. The Reformative Training Centre for selected offenders aged 16 to 21 years moved to new premises in Bedok, while the area round Changi Prison Complex was developed to include a medium-security prison with perimeter fencing, and a women's prison.

In 1960, a bold experiment to set up a penal settlement on Pulau Senang ended in disaster when a riot in July 1963 led to the death of the prison superintendent and two staff (see PULAU SENANG RIOTS). Eighteen of the culprits were convicted for murder and executed. The settlement was closed down.

Outram Prison was demolished in 1968 to make way for redevelopment, and a commemorative plaque now marks the site. The inmates were shifted to Changi Prison and Queenstown Remand Prison, which was built in 1966.

After Independence, two significant prison reforms were introduced: the setting up of the Singapore Corporation of Rehabilitative Enterprises (SCORE) in 1974 to provide work and vocational training programmes for prison inmates; and the development of drug-rehabilitation centres (DRCs) to eliminate heroin addiction, a problem that had arisen in the 1970s. SCORE helped private firms set up workshops in the prisons and DRCs to equip inmates with skills, and boosted after-care efforts through links with halfway-houses and other help groups in the community. SCORE continues to help inmates being discharged from prisons, providing a job-bank and in-prison learning opportunities.

Sustained anti-drug efforts over 30 years have led to a dwindling addict-inmate population in the DRCs. In 1995, the average number of inmates in the DRCs was about 7,400; by 2004 this had dropped to 241.

A plan to centralize all the jails in a single complex at Changi, able to accommodate more than 20,000 inmates, led to the demolition of the historic Changi Prison, save for a conserved section of the perimeter wall. The first cluster of five new jails in the new Changi Prison Complex opened in April 2004, housing some 4,500 inmates in a modern, high-tech security system. The pilot Internet Home Tele-visits scheme for inmates and their families, the first of its kind in the world, enables families to connect with inmates through a PC and video-conferencing system. Two more clusters are to be completed by 2012, after which work will begin on a fourth cluster.

The 15 prisons and DRCs island-wide are administered by the Singapore Prison Service; in December 2005 there were some 14,500 inmates, including 1,800 women. The new millennium saw a push for more community-based reform programmes such as the Home Detention Scheme, introduced in May 2000, which enabled suitably assessed inmates to serve the end of their sentences at home under an electronic-tagging system. The Yellow Ribbon Project, a multi-agency drive to raise community awareness of the rehabilitation needs of ex-offenders, was launched in October 2004.

Pritt, D.N. (1887–1972) British lawyer and politician. Born in London and educated at Winchester College and the University of London, Denis Nowell Pritt was a strong supporter of Britain's military alliance with the Soviet Union and was expelled from the Labour Party in 1940. In 1949, Pritt and four other expelled Labour members of Parliament formed the Labour Independent Group. After his defeat in the 1950 British general election, Pritt concentrated on his legal practice. He was the Queen's Counsel engaged by LEE KUAN YEW to come to Singapore to defend the students involved in the FAJAR TRIAL in 1954. He later became professor of law at the University of Ghana (1965–66), chairman of the Howard League for Penal Reform and a member of the World Peace Council.

private housing The term 'private housing' is used to refer to housing developments that are not subsidized by the state. Private housing projects are undertaken by private sector developers on land purchased from the state or by private treaty with individual owners. As the cost of acquiring land and construction is not subsidized by the state, private residential units typically cost more than PUBLIC HOUSING units.

In recent years, the line between private and public housing estates has become increasingly blurred. The HOUSING & DEVELOPMENT BOARD oversees purchasers' eligibility for executive condominiums, which are developed and sold by private developers. Private housing estates are managed by their own management corporations. The estates are not managed by TOWN COUNCILS, as are PUBLIC HOUSING estates. Among the major local developers of private housing are CITY DEVELOPMENTS LIMITED, FAR EAST ORGANIZATION, MCL Land, Lippo Land, Wheelock Properties, CAPITALAND, HOTEL PROPERTIES LIMITED and KEPPEL LAND.

See also LANDED PROPERTY.

privatization Since Independence, the state has invested directly in strategic sectors of the economy such as shipyards, defence industries, aviation and BANKING through GOVERNMENT-LINKED COMPANIES (GLCs). Many of these GLCs are held by TEMASEK HOLDINGS, the government's investment arm.

Starting in 1985, Temasek has completely or partially privatized many operations and continues to do so. These divestments were done to exit from non-core businesses and small operations, and were also intended to create more investment opportunities for the public (such as the sale of SINGTEL shares), or to restructure an industrial sector such as the ENERGY sector.

Temasek companies that have been completely or partially privatized include NATSTEEL, Jurong Shipyard, Semac, DBS BANK, SEMBCORP, KEPPEL CORPORATION, SINGAPORE AIRLINES and NEPTUNE ORIENT LINES.

In 2003, the Economic Review Committee recommended that the government adopt a 'yellow pages rule' and stop supplying services already provided by the private sector. It advised that the government regularly review its stable of GLCs and keep only those that serve strategic purposes, while divesting non-strategic companies in an orderly fashion.

Privy Council Singapore's highest court until 1994. The Judicial Committee of the Privy Council, or Privy Council for short, is the court of final appeal for the United Kingdom's overseas territories and Crown dependencies, and also for those Commonwealth countries that have retained the appeal to the Privy Council. It sits in the Privy Council Chamber in Downing Street, London and is presided over by the highest-ranking judges in the UK and the Commonwealth.

So far as Singapore is concerned, appeals to the Privy Council were abolished in May 1989, except for criminal cases involving CAPITAL PUNISHMENT and civil cases in which the parties had agreed in writing to such an appeal at the outset. By the late 1980s, the number of appeals had diminished due to the time and expense involved. The government therefore decided to restrict the type of appeals to the Privy Council. It abolished all appeals to the Privy Council in 1994, and the Court of Appeal became the highest court in Singapore.

Prophet Muhammad's Birthday Also known as Maulud Nabi, the Prophet Muhammad's Birthday is observed on 12 Rabiulawal, the third month of the Islamic calendar. It is not a public holiday in Singapore. The occasion is celebrated by remembering the life of the Prophet and the love he had for his *ummah* (community of Muslims). In the past, Muslims in Singapore held large processions on public roads for this event, but since the RACE

Prophet Muhammad's Birthday: celebrations at the National Stadium, 1982.

RIOTS in 1964—involving one such procession—the practice has been banned. Maulud ceremonies are still carried out in homes and mosques throughout Singapore. These feature the recitation of *qasida* (poetry) in praise of the Prophet, followed by a feast. Commemorations may also be in the form of public lectures on related themes.

prostitution It is not known when the first prostitutes arrived, but in the late 18th and early 19th centuries prostitution thrived in Singapore, which was a male-dominated immigrant port city. Chinese gangs are reported to have fought one another in the 1860s and 1870s over consignments of prostitutes from China. Chinese prostitutes were known as AH KU.

The existence of KARAYUKI-SAN (Japanese term for Japanese prostitutes in Singapore) dates back at least to 1877 when two Japanese-owned brothels on Malay Street operated with a total of 14 prostitutes. An area comprising Malabar Street, Hylam Street and BUGIS STREET eventually became a major red-light district. According to Japanese records, there were 633 Japanese women operating in 109 brothels in Singapore in 1905. The British authorities tolerated prostitution in designated brothels and large numbers of Chinese and Japanese women were brought here. In 1920, Japanese brothels were banned by the Japanese consulate in Singapore. Many *karayuki-san* were then forcefully repatriated to Japan.

Apart from Chinese and Japanese prostitutes, there were also prostitutes from Europe. The demand for these came almost exclusively from the British and other Europeans residing in Singapore, who rarely brought their families to the colony

Today, prostitution is legal while soliciting is not. The areas said to be red-light districts include the vicinities of GEYLANG, Desker Road and ORCHARD TOWERS. Many of the prostitutes are foreign nationals.

See also COMFORT WOMEN.

PSA International The history of PSA began with the Tanjong Pagar Dock Company, which was formed in 1866. Within three decades, it had gained virtual control over the entire shipping business in Singapore. Besides operating five dry docks, it owned over 2 km of wharf frontage, and warehouses for 200,000 tons of cargo and 250,000 tons of coal, while its properties covered over 375 acres. The company was taken over by the government in 1905, and its facilities were handed over to the Singapore Harbour Board in 1912. The Board was replaced by the Port of Singapore Authority (PSA) in 1964. PSA took the pioneering step of building a container port in Singapore in the 1970s. It received its first container ship in 1972, and by 1981, the number of containers handled had crossed the one-million mark.

In 1996, PSA's regulatory functions were handed over to the Maritime and Port Authority of Singapore (MPA). PSA Corporation Ltd was formed in 1997 to manage and operate the terminals and related businesses. PSA has since invested overseas in Belgium, Brunei, China, India, Italy, Japan, the Netherlands, Portugal, South Korea and Thailand. In Singapore, it operates the world's largest transshipment hub, providing shippers a choice of 200 shipping lines with connections to 600 ports in 123 countries. Its flow-through gate system processes one truck every 25 seconds.

In December 2003, PSA became PSA International. In 2005, PSA handled some 41 million containers at all its ports around the world, including 22.3 million in Singapore. PSA chalked up net profits of $1.06 billion on a gross turnover of $3.68 billion in 2005. It is a wholly owned subsidiary of TEMASEK HOLDINGS.

In 2006, PSA was finally outbid by Dubai Ports World in a battle for control of another major ports operator, P&O.

PUB Statutory board. When the first local parliament was elected in 1955, many of the functions previously handled by the City Council were transferred to various ministries, leaving the water, gas and electricity departments to be absorbed into the newly established Public Utilities Board (PUB), which remained a part of the City Council. When the City Council was abolished in 1959, the PUB became an independent statutory board. It was originally housed in City Hall but moved to its own building on Somerset Road in the 1970s.

In April 2001, PUB was restructured and the newly formed Energy Market Authority (*see* ENERGY) took over the electricity and gas regulation functions.

PUB is responsible for managing Singapore's RESERVOIRS, waterworks, rivers, drainage system, water reclamation plants and sewerage system in an integrated manner, and to optimize Singapore's limited WATER resources. Its mission is to secure an adequate and affordable supply of water for Singaporeans. It has produced NEWATER and desalinated water as alternative sources.

See also WATER AGREEMENTS.

public holidays Singapore observes 11 public holidays a year. Three are secular: New Year's Day (1 January), Labour Day (1 May) and NATIONAL DAY (9 August). The rest cater to the major groups in Singapore's multiracial, multireligious population. Of these, only the Christian holiday of CHRISTMAS is celebrated on the same date each year on the Gregorian calendar (25 December). The other Christian holiday, GOOD FRIDAY, comes in either March or April, with the date varying according to a complex formula. The Chinese have two days for the CHINESE NEW YEAR holiday, which falls in either January or February. The date is determined by the the Chinese lunar calendar. VESAK DAY, which marks Buddha's birth, enlightenment and death, can occur from April to June. DEEPAVALI, the Hindu festival of lights, is celebrated on the last day of the Asvina month of the Hindu calendar, between 15 October and 15 November. The two Muslim holidays are EID-UL-FITR, marking the end of Ramadan, and EID-UL-ADHA, which marks the conclusion of the annual HAJ or pilgrimage to Mecca. The Islamic lunar calendar is about 11 days shorter than the Gregorian year. As a result, Islamic holidays move forward by 11 days each year according to the Gregorian calendar.

See also FESTIVALS.

PUB campaign poster promoting water conservation featuring mascot Water Wally.

Prostitution: a residential property used as a brothel.

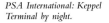
PSA International: Keppel Terminal by night.

public housing During the colonial period, some residential accommodation was provided by the SINGAPORE IMPROVEMENT TRUST (SIT), which launched a public-housing programme in the 1930s. The SIT developed about 23,000 homes. One of its early projects was the TIONG BAHRU estate, much of which still stands and was built in the 1930s. The estate has been designated as a conservation area for its architectural interest. The SIT's efforts to address the housing shortage were brought to a halt by WORLD WAR II. After the war, accommodation was short and rents soared. The Control of Rent Act was introduced in 1947, but not enacted for some years, and landlords saw little gain in building new homes for letting. However, 1947/48 brought the Housing Commission Report and a $5 million government grant, which meant that the SIT could begin to address the post-war housing shortage more effectively.

At the time of Independence, living space was still in short supply, particularly for low-income families. Much of the population lived in SHOPHOUSES, where the lower level of the building was used for business and commerce. The upper levels were often partitioned into small living quarters. Many people lived in desperately overcrowded conditions. Adequate sanitation was not often available, and residents often shared common kitchen and toilet facilities.

Clockwise from top left: SIT housing in Tiong Bahru, 1930s; Upper Pickering Street, early 1950s; and Forfar House, completed in 1956.

Early HDB developments Selegie House (1963) (top); and MacPherson Estate (1970s).

Dealing with the housing shortage was identified by the government as one of two top priorities, the other being jobs. The public housing programme began as a strategy to provide affordable homes; however, it evolved into a social development process that saw the relocation and resettlement of the majority of the island's population.

As the SIT's efforts had been concentrated in and around the central urban area, a land shortage had developed there. Hence, some of the HOUSING & DEVELOPMENT BOARD's (HDB) early efforts were on the outskirts of the central area. After the BUKIT HO SWEE FIRE, affected families were quickly re-housed in high-density HDB blocks. In the wake of the fire, the need for proper public housing and the role the HDB would play became all the more apparent.

In large part, the early success achieved by HDB's public housing programme was due to the fact that homes were still located not far from the central urban area. This meant firstly that the relocation of residents was less difficult, and secondly, that in the early days of Independence when

public resources were limited, estates could still manage without a large range of facilities for everyday goods and services. Residents were also still living close to their workplaces, schools, shops, restaurants and leisure facilities.

A major attraction of the new public housing was the provision of modern sanitation, electricity and drinking water. For families previously living a cramped existence in small cubicles in shophouses, the HDB flats were comparatively luxurious.

At the heart of government housing policy since Independence has been the idea that home ownership reinforces stability by giving people a vested interest in social, economic and political order. The HDB began to market 99-year leasehold ownership in 1964. After buyers were allowed to use money from the CENTRAL PROVIDENT FUND for monthly mortgage payments in 1968, applications to purchase flats grew, which encouraged the HDB to expand supply. The pursuit of '100 per cent homeownership' became national policy, aimed at transforming Singapore into a 'home-owning democracy'. Rental flats are the smallest units available, and the income ceiling for eligibility to rent is set very low.

Public housing has also played a key role in the integration of the main ethnic and cultural communities that make up Singapore's population. In an effort to maintain a racial balance within all neighbourhoods, quotas for HDB estates were introduced in 1989.

By the early 1990s, 85 per cent of the total population was living in public-housing flats, with 90 per cent of those households owning a 99-year lease. Since then, the number has not changed greatly. The HDB became, in effect, a monopoly supplier of housing for all but the small minority who live in PRIVATE HOUSING. Demand for new public housing is at a lower level than

Chinatown Complex, 1981 (top) and extension to MacPherson estate, 1980.

in past decades, and is forecast to remain so, relative to the rapid development from 1960 to 1990. Factors include lower marriage rates, reductions in family size and demographic change.

Over some 25 years, the housing problem was essentially solved. Singapore's public housing success was internationally recognized when Tampines New Town won the United Nations World Habitat Award in 1993.

From top: Proposals for upgrading: Bukit Ho Swee; and Kim Keat, both mid-1990s. Since the 1990s, upgrading programmes have been implemented to bring ageing estates up to modern standards.

Flatted factories at Kampong Ubi, 1984.

New towns

One of the earliest HDB developments was QUEENSTOWN, which had been initiated by the SIT. However, the first new town to be built completely by the HDB was TOA PAYOH New Town. It was developed some 6 to 8 km outside the central urban area. The flats were three-room units, comprising two bedrooms and a living-cum-dining room. These units were larger than the first homes built, which were one-room and two-room units. The two-room unit has one bedroom and living room while the one-room unit is essentially a bedsitting room—a bedroom-cum-living room with washing facilities. Today, the norm is the four-room unit with three bedrooms. Both larger and smaller units are also available. Over the years, the HDB went on to build five-room flats and also two-storey maisonettes.

New towns have the full range of education facilities, ranging from kindergartens to junior colleges. Some also have polytechnics and Institutes of Technical Education. Places of worship such as churches, mosques and temples can also be found in new towns. Most estates and new towns are located near major expressways as well as MASS

1

2

3

4

5

6

7

8

9

ESTIMATED RESIDENT POPULATION* BY TOWN AS OF 31 MARCH 2005	
HDB town	Population
Ang Mo Kio	149,200
Bedok	187,300
Bishan	67,300
Bukit Batok	119,900
Bukit Merah	132,200
Bukit Panjang	110,700
Choa Chu Kang	148,300
Clementi	72,600
Geylang	97,800
Hougang	173,500
Jurong East	79,800
Jurong West	223,800
Kallang/Whampoa	97,400
Pasir Ris	110,100
Punggol	51,600
Queenstown	79,400
Sembawang	62,900
Sengkang	138,300
Serangoon	74,200
Tampines	226,000
Toa Payoh	105,400
Woodlands	216,000
Yishun	157,600
Other estates	
Central Area	27,800
Bukit Timah	8,500
Marine Parade	21,400
Total	2,939,000

*Refers to Singaporeans and Permanent Residents only. Figures are rounded off to the nearest '00.

Source: HDB Annual Report 2004/2005.

RAPID TRANSIT (MRT) routes, ensuring easy access to the rest of the island. New towns further away from the city centre have a wider range of facilities, such as bus interchanges, shopping centres, parks and sports complexes.

In the 1980s, the HDB sub-divided new towns into smaller neighbourhoods in an effort to engender a stronger sense of place and identity among residents. Each precinct, with its population of 4,000 to 6,000 residents, has a neighbourhood centre with commercial as well as recreational and sports facilities. These centres have HAWKER CENTRES as well as WET MARKETS.

1. *Queenstown, 1962*
2. *Toa Payoh, 1970s*
3. *Tampines Way, 1978*
4. *Bukit Batok, 1986*
5. *Ang Mo Kio, buildings for local industry in foreground, 1980*
6. *Sembawang*
7. *Jurong East*
8. *Woodlands Mosque, 1980*
9. *Chinese opera stage, 1980s*

POPULATION LIVING IN HDB FLATS

%
100 — — — 81% — — — 83%
80 — — 67% 87% 86%
60 — 47%
40 — 35%
20 — 23%
9%
0
1960 1965 1970 1975 1980 1985 1990 1995 2000 2005 (Mar)

Source: Housing & Development Board

Public libraries: mobile library at Tanjong Pagar Community Centre, 1964.

public housing *See* box.

public libraries Singapore's public libraries trace their history to Sir STAMFORD RAFFLES' third objective for the Singapore Institution (later known as RAFFLES INSTITUTION) 'to collect the scattered literature…of the country'. Although the foundation stone was laid in 1823, the Singapore Institution was not completed until 1836, due to a lack of funds and leadership issues. The library was first mentioned in the 1837 annual report of the Singapore Free School. Although primarily a school library, the public was given free admission with borrowing privileges for a monthly fee of 25 cents.

In 1844, a meeting at the office of Thomas O. Crane, a Singapore Institution trustee, saw the formal establishment of the Singapore Library. It was set up as a proprietary institution with shareholders paying up to $50 each, while subscribers paid $2.50 monthly to borrow materials. Opened on 22 January 1845, the library moved from the Singapore Institution to TOWN HALL in 1862. Fourteen years later it moved back to the Institution.

In 1874, the library, including a growing collection of artefacts, was acquired by the government. It reopened on 14 September 1874 as the Raffles Library and Museum. Besides receiving the STRAITS SETTLEMENTS' records and publications, the library also collected Malay publications following the Book Registration

Public libraries: the Lee Kong Chian Reference Library in the new National Library building.

Ordinance of 1886, which legislated that copies of local publications be deposited in colonial libraries. To reflect the library's new standing as a public institution, a neoclassical building along Stamford Road was completed in 1887 to house the collections. Karl Richard Hanitsch, who headed the institution between 1895 and 1919, also raised the status of librarian-curator to that of director. Hanitsch was instrumental in enhancing the professional standing of library staff and in improving the preservation of the collections.

In 1920, James Johnston, the first qualified librarian, was brought in to head the Library. In applying the Dewey Decimal Cataloguing System and the Browne System of charging for book loans, Johnston helped professionalize library operations. During his term, the Junior Library, which was the first Malayan public library for children, was opened in 1923. The JAPANESE OCCUPATION resulted in the loss and destruction of many library collections across Malaya. However, the Raffles Library and Museum—renamed Syonan Tosyokan and Syonan Hakubutsukan—was kept almost intact. Although most of the British staff was interned, the British staff of the Botanic Gardens, along with local Chinese clerks, worked with Japanese naturalists to preserve the collections, both sides braving accusations of collaboration.

After the war, the Malayan push toward nationhood also shaped the identity of the Raffles Library and Museum. In 1953, LEE KONG CHIAN offered to donate $375,000 for a free public library. His donation required the library to collect books in the vernacular. In 1955, the gradual separation of the museum from the library began, culminating in the opening of the NATIONAL LIBRARY BUILDING next door on 12 November 1960.

As a national library, a key responsibility was the Legal Deposit, which included housing, preserving and making accessible titles deposited by local publishers. The Singapore National Bibliography, which is a listing of the titles deposited, was first published in 1969.

Headed by the first Singaporean director, Hedwig Anuar, the new National Library gained standing with researchers particularly through its Southeast Asian collections. The Southeast Asian Room—opened on 28 August 1964—held Malayan resources which had been collected since the last century, and included the collections of noteworthy scholars such as Tan Yeok Seong and CARL GIBSON-HILL.

Unlike most national libraries, Singapore's national library had dual functions, serving as a public library as well. Besides the lending library services at Stamford Road, the public library services were initially delivered through mobile libraries and part-time branch libraries. The first part-time branch library was opened as

early as 1953. By 1960, the mobile library service had been set up with two vans funded by the United Nations Educational, Scientific and Cultural Organization (UNESCO). The first full-time branch opened at Queenstown on 2 May 1970. By 1988, nine full-time libraries, including the one at Stamford Road, were in existence. The mobile library service ended in 1991.

The NATIONAL LIBRARY BOARD (NLB) was formed following the *Library 2000 Report*. With a budget of $1 billion for the next eight years, new buildings and services followed, prompting Harvard Business School to use NLB as an innovation case study.

The report recommended a three-tier public library system. Dense residential areas in outlying Singapore were identified locations for Regional Libraries. These were to serve both the residential and industrial population of the area; the first regional library was built in TAMPINES in 1994. Community Libraries were situated in HOUSING & DEVELOPMENT BOARD estates to meet the reading needs of their residents. The third tier would consist of Children's Libraries, initially set up by the PEOPLE'S ASSOCIATION with support from NLB. As the three-tier library service evolved, niche libraries such as library@esplanade, with a collection focused on the performing arts; and library@orchard, which was set up especially for young working professionals, were established. These niche libraries sought to attract adult users with a range of specific interests.

The opening of libraries in SHOPPING centres also marked their evolution into places for leisure outings. The first such library was Jurong West Community Library in March 1996.

On 12 November 2005, exactly 45 years after the first National Library building was opened, President S.R. NATHAN officially opened the new National Library building at Victoria Street. It houses the Lee Kong Chian Reference Library, the Central Lending Library and NLB's corporate headquarters. The reference library includes the Singapore and Southeast Asian Collections—the result of more than a century of collecting works from the region.

Public Service Commission Body responsible for safeguarding the integrity, impartiality and meritocracy of the civil service. The colonial government introduced the principle of meritocracy to Singapore in January 1951 when it established the Public Service Commission (PSC). This was adapted from the United Kingdom's own Civil Service Commission (CSC), which had been formed in May 1855 on the recommendation of the 1854 Northcote-Trevelyan report on the organization of the permanent civil service in Britain. In 1946, Whitehall issued a White Paper, Command Paper No. 197, recommending that PSCs should be set up in the colonies to ensure that qualified local candidates would be recruited into the public services. Accordingly, the 1947 Trusted Commission, appointed to review the salaries and conditions of the public services in the Malayan Union and Singapore, recommended creating a PSC in Singapore and Malaya.

The PSC was formed with two aims: to insulate the SINGAPORE CIVIL SERVICE from politics, by ensuring recruitment and promotion based on merit and not patronage; and to increase the pace of localization in the service. The latter ceased to be important after self-government was attained in 1959. However, the primary aim remains relevant: the purpose of the PSC's programme, as stated in the national budget, is 'to meet the staffing requirements of the government in accordance with the merit principle'.

From 1951 to 1982, the PSC's major function was recruitment and selection of candidates for Divisions I and II appointments. This function was transferred to the Public Service Division in 1983 (now part of the PRIME MINISTER'S OFFICE), and largely devolved to personnel boards in 1995. However, the PSC continues to appoint officers to the elite ADMINISTRATIVE SERVICE and highest levels of management in the civil service.

Since 1961, the PSC has been responsible for the disciplinary control of all civil servants, and for selecting candidates for government scholarships. The aim of the scholarships is to attract the 'best and brightest' Singaporeans to work in the civil service.

Public Transport Council Independent body safeguarding the interests of commuters by ensuring adequate public transport services and affordable fares and the interests of operators by ensuring their long-term financial viability. Formed in 1987 under the Public Transport Council Act, the Public Transport Council (PTC) approves new bus services, regulates bus service standards and approves bus and train fares. The government appoints PTC members from a cross-section of society, so that a wide range of views are represented, and to ensure that the PTC's decisions are acceptable to the public. The operating companies have to apply to the PTC for any bus and train fare increases. These are only allowed in small steps and are tied to changes in the consumer price index and wage index.

The forerunners of the PTC were the Omnibus Services Licensing Authority set up in 1956, and the Bus Services Licensing Authority formed in 1971. They regulated bus services but not fares, which was a matter for the government at that time.

public transport system Providing reliable, affordable and good-quality public transport is a pillar of Singapore's transportation strategy. There is a two-pronged approach: the 'pull' factor (making public transport attractive), and the 'push' factor (restraining the widespread use of private transport by demand management). This has resulted in a marked shift towards the use of public transport, with three out of five daily trips being made by this means.

Public transport in Singapore consists of MASS RAPID TRANSIT (MRT) trains, light rail transit (LRT) trains, buses and taxis. The trains and buses are run by two publicly listed operating companies, SMRT Corporation Ltd and SBSTransit Ltd. Transit Link Pte Ltd, a company jointly owned by these two companies, provides integrated ticketing via the EZ-LINK CARD, which permits passengers to use a single fare card on both buses and trains.

The companies run the train and bus services on a commercial basis within the maximum fares approved by the PUBLIC TRANSPORT COUNCIL with no direct operating subsidies from the government. Fare and advertisement revenues are used to cover operating and maintenance expenditure and depreciation.

However, the government funds the capital cost of public transport infrastructure. For trains, the construction of MRT and LRT lines and the purchase of the first set of operating assets such as trains are fully funded. For purchasing the second set of operating assets at the end of the useful life of the first set, the companies need only meet the original cost, with government financing the balance. Public buses are exempt from CERTIFICATE OF ENTITLEMENT payments. The construction of bus interchanges, bus shelters and bus priority measures such as bus lanes and bus signals are fully funded. The LAND TRANSPORT AUTHORITY is responsible for these public transport infrastructure developments.

In addition, a few private and school transport bus operators are licensed to run supplementary bus services along designated routes during peak hours, and shuttle services between developments and major transport nodes. TAXIS are operated by seven taxi companies and individual driver-owners.

Public Works Department The Public Works Department had its genesis in 1833 with the appointment of GEORGE D. COLEMAN as superintendent of public works and convicts. Over the next century, the Public Works Department built roads, schools, amenities and many of Singapore's early iconic buildings, such as the Supreme Court and the Victoria Memorial Hall (present-day VICTORIA CONCERT HALL). In 1999, the Department was corporatized as PWD Corporation under TEMASEK HOLDINGS, and in 2002 renamed CPG Corporation. The latter was acquired by the Downer EDI Group of Australia in 2003.

puisne judge Pronounced 'puny' and literally, 'younger-born' or junior judges, from the French puisné. In England, there are four inferior judges of the Court of Queen's Bench, and the four inferior judges of the Court of Common Pleas. These judges are known as puisne judges. In Singapore, the term refers to judges who are appointed to sit in the High Court or at an equivalent level such as the Court of Judicature between 1826 and 1867

Pulai River See SUNGAI PULAI.

Pulau Blakang Mati See SENTOSA.

Pulau Brani Island located between the main island and SENTOSA, with an area of 122 ha. Its name means 'Island of the Brave' in Malay. There were several Malay KAMPONGS on the island, such as Kampung Selat Sengkir, Kampung Kopit, and Kampung Telok Saga. Most of the villagers were either employed by the master attendant (harbour master) or were involved in other maritime activities. In 1890, the STRAITS TRADING COMPANY built a tin-smelting operation on Pulau Brani. TIN ore used to be brought all the way from the Kinta Valley in Perak to Pulau Brani to be smelted. In the 1900s, tin was used extensively in the pineapple canning industry.

By the end of the 1960s, the kampongs and smelting facility had moved off the island to make way for the Brani Naval Base. Construction began in August 1972, and in January 1974, the republic's first naval base was opened officially by LEE KUAN YEW. In 1991 the four-lane Brani causeway linking Pulau Brani to Singapore was opened, forming part of the Keppel-Brani-Sentosa road link and paving the way for Singapore's second container terminal to be located at Pulau Brani. The Brani Container Terminal was opened by GOH CHOK TONG in 1992.

With the annually increasing volume of containers handled at the terminal and the expanding naval fleet at the Brani Naval Base, Pulau Brani was getting significantly overcrowded. By October 2002, the naval base was closed and the fleet

Pulau Brani: kampung *life, 1957.*

Pulau Bukom: site of a major oil refinery owned by Shell.

redeployed at Tuas Naval Base and Changi Naval Base. In 2006, the Police Coast Guard Headquarters relocated from the Kallang Basin to the southern part of Pulau Brani.

Pulau Bukom Island south of Singapore. It was formerly two islands, Pulau Bukom Besar and the smaller Pulau Bukom Kechil, which are now joined. In the 19th century, Pulau Bukom was a source of fresh water for passing ships. It now hosts the third-largest Shell oil refinery in the world, with a capacity of 500,000 barrels per day. Shell first used the island in 1891 for storing kerosene.

See also LAJU HIJACKING and PETROCHEM-ICALS SECTOR.

Pulau Merlimau fire Major petrochemical fire. On 25 October 1988 at 1.27 p.m., a naphtha tank belonging to Singapore Refining Company situated on Pulau Merlimau—south of Singapore, off Jurong—caught fire. At its most intense, the blaze affected three floating-roof naphtha storage tanks, each approximately 40 m in diameter and containing 294,500 barrels of product. The resultant property loss was estimated at over $10 million. The fire threatened to involve adjacent tanks containing kerosene, reformate, motor gasoline and diesel products. As the refinery was located off-shore, fire-fighting equipment and manpower had to be ferried to the site. It took the combined efforts of the SINGAPORE ARMED FORCES, the SINGAPORE CIVIL DEFENCE FORCE, the SINGAPORE POLICE FORCE, the Port of Singapore Authority Fire Service, the Airport Fire Service and other oil refineries four days to

Pulau Merlimau fire

control the fire. More than 250,000 litres of foam compound was used to fight the fire.

Pulau Panjang Malay name, literally 'Long Island', used by Malay and Dutch mariners to denote the island of Singapore from the 17th century to 1819. Most Dutch maps, notably the chart by A.E. van Braam Houckgeest, refer to it as *Lange Eiland*.

Pulau Sakijang Bendera Also known as St John's Island, Pulau Sakijang Bendera is one of the Southern Islands lies 6.5 km due south of Singapore island. Only 41 ha in area and geologically an outcrop of the Triassic rocks which form the Jurong formation on the main island, Pulau Sakijang Bendara is hilly and has a varied coastline with cliffs, lagoons, mangrove swamps and fine white beaches. There are coral reefs offshore with both hard and soft corals. Besides being a tourist destination, Pulau Sakijang Bendera houses an important Aquaculture Centre. In the past, the island had a quarantine hospital for lepers, housed political prisoners, and was later a prison where gangsters were incarcerated. In 2004 the government introduced a strategy to link the Southern Islands, including Pulau Sakijang Bendera, by bridge or boat to Sentosa as part of a plan for a new resort.

See also ISLANDS.

Pulau Sakijang Pelepah Also known as Lazarus Island, Pulau Sakijang Pelepah is one of the Southern Islands group, 4 km south of Sentosa. With an area of 47 ha, it is largely hilly and jungle-clad and is fringed with small beaches and CORAL REEFS. Pulau Sakijang Pelepah has become the pivotal part of the Southern Islands Development Group Plan for a new resort in the area, achieved by linking it to neighbouring PULAU SAKIJANG BENDERA with a new bridge and to Pulau Seringat by way of a reclamation project which includes a broad, semi-circular protected sandy beach and new boat moorings. These islands were linked in order to create a resort area of a viable size. The main areas of low-rise housing and hotels, as well as harbours, have

Pulau Sakijang Bendera: outside a quarantine station.

been deliberately located on newly reclaimed areas to protect the natural environments of Pulau Sakijang Pelepah.

It is estimated that at least 80 per cent of the terrestrial habitats will remain unaffected by the developments. The marine habitats have been further protected by the creation of a Marine Conservation Area around the whole island group, to preserve the diversity of life in the fringing reefs of both hard and soft corals.

See also NATURE CONSERVATION.

Pulau Semakau One of the Southern Islands, it serves as Singapore's only landfill. Pulau Semakau is managed by the NATIONAL ENVIRONMENT AGENCY (NEA). It covers a total area of 350 ha and has a capacity of 63 million cu m. To create the required landfill, a 7-km perimeter rock bund was built to enclose part of the sea off Pulau Semakau and Pulau Sakeng. It is estimated that the landfill operation, which began in 1999, will last until 2040.

There was a small village on Pulau Semakau until the landfill operations required the inhabitants to be relocated to the mainland. The western part of the island still has the original mangrove habitat. New MANGROVES exist on the northern and southern tips of the island. In total, the mangroves occupy 13.6 ha. Pulau Semakau has become a recreational destination; the open landfill, surrounded by water, coexisting with mangrove, grassland and shoreline habitats, is open to the public for activities such as fishing, bird-watching and intertidal nature walks.

Pulau Semakau

Pulau Senang riots

Pulau Senang riots Riots at Singapore's first penal settlement. Pulau Senang, southwest of Singapore, was a penal experiment where prisoners were allowed to roam freely on the island. The concept behind this experiment was that detainees could be reformed through their own labour. The settlement started on 18 May 1960 with the arrival of 50 detainees and Superintendent Daniel Dutton. Over the next three years, the number of detainees rose to 320, and they transformed the island into an attractive settlement.

Dutton believed that through hard work, the detainees could be reformed and he did away with the bearing of arms by the guards. However, on 12 July 1963, a group of some 70 to 90 detainees rioted and burned down most of the buildings. They hacked Dutton to death and killed two other officers. Fifty-eight people were accused of rioting and murdering Dutton and officers Arumugam Veerasingham and Tan Kok Hian.

Because of the large number of accused, a special dock had to be constructed for them. The case went to trial on 18 November 1963 and lasted an unprecedented 64 days. On 12 March 1964, the seven-member jury found 18 of the accused guilty of murder, 18 guilty of rioting with deadly weapons and 11 guilty of rioting. The remaining 11 accused were acquitted. Those found guilty of murder were sentenced to death, while those found guilty of rioting with deadly weapons were sentenced to three years' imprisonment; the rest of the rioters were sentenced to two years' imprisonment. Most of those involved in the rioting were members of SECRET SOCIETIES who were detained without trial and had no hope of leaving the island. As a result of the riots, the penal experiment came to an abrupt end.

Pulau Tekong With an area of 2,365 ha, Pulau Tekong is the largest of Singapore's offshore islands. It is the only part of Singapore extensively made of metamorphic rock known as the 'Sajahat formation'. The interior is hilly, rising to 53 m in one place. LAND RECLAMATION schemes have been proposed which would double the size of the island, although studies of the potential effects on currents, patterns of erosion, marine life and shipping in the STRAIT OF JOHOR have yet to be completed. Pulau Tekong is designated for use exclusively by the military, and has a resident armed-services population of around 5,000. It is off-limits to civilian visitors.

Pulau Ubin Covering an area of 1,020 ha, Pulau Ubin was Singapore's second largest offshore island prior to the reclamation projects which created JURONG ISLAND. Also known as Granite Island, Pulau Ubin was itself the amalgamation of five smaller islands joined by bunds constructed to develop prawn-farming. It is a long, narrow island with hilly eastern and western regions where granite is exposed. By contrast, the island's centre is low-lying, and was formed from newer sedimentary rock. It is here that aquacultural and agricultural activities such as prawn-farming and the cultivation of orchids are carried out. *Kelongs* (Malay for 'palisade traps', but also used to refer to the stilt houses above the traps) were built to catch fish and house the *kelong* operators. Granite quarrying was the most important industry on the island for much of the 20th century. It reached a peak in 1980, employing some 1,200 people. The workforce declined to 400 in 1995, and the GRANITE QUARRIES were eventually abandoned.

Ubin was earmarked for housing, industrial and infrastructural development in the URBAN RENEWAL AUTHORITY's Revised Concept Plan of 1991. Since then, however, its role has been reassessed, and the island has emerged as a recreational area where the rural character of 'old' Singapore can still be found. Pulau Ubin attracts more than 300,000 visitors annually.

Puluozhong Kang Tai, the Chinese envoy of the state of Wu, was dispatched in the mid-third century CE to Funan (present day Oc-Eo, Vietnam). In his account of his travels, Kang Tai mentions several places on the Malay Peninsula he claimed he had either visited or had heard of while at Funan. Amongst these was Puluozhong, a place inhabited by savages. Philologists have argued that 'Puluozhong' may be a transliteration of 'Pulau Ujong', Malay for 'Island at the End'. It is possible that this is the earliest Chinese reference to Singapore.

Punggol What is now known as 'Punggol Point' or 'Tanjong Punggol' was first marked as Tanjong Rangon on Franklin and Jackson's 1828 map of Singapore. At that time, the area was rural, populated primarily by smallholders who planted vegetables and reared livestock. Punggol Point was a favourite spot for watersports and the consumption of seafood. The area's farms had all been cleared by 1990, when the government announced plans to transform

Pulau Ubin: **Kelongs,** *palisade fish traps (above); village houses on the island (left).*

the area into a new town under the Punggol 21 Initiative. New public housing estates have since been built in the area as part of SENGKANG New Town and Punggol New Town. The name has sometimes been spelled 'Ponggol'. By 2005 there were some 15,000 units of PUBLIC HOUSING in Punggol and 38,000 in Sengkang, accommodating about 190,000 residents.

Punggol River The Punggol River (Sungei Punggol) rises in the Central Catchment Area near ANG MO KIO New Town, and flows into the Jurong Strait. Although fairly short, it has a long, broad estuary which gives the watercourse a total length of 9 km. Until the late 1990s, the shores of the estuary were noted for their large, open fields, which served as an important

Punggol: public housing apartments.

Pusara Aman and Pusara Abadi: visiting graves during Eid-ul-Fitr.

Dominic Puthucheary, 1960.

Pythons: members of a local volunteer force and their quarry, 1930.

recreational space. The building of SENGKANG New Town has changed the local environment substantially, and the Punggol River divides the new town in two. A considerable amount of greenery has been preserved along the banks of the river, and serves as the main artery of the extensive network of urban PARKS in Sengkang.

Purvis, John (1799–1872) Merchant. Scotsman John Purvis arrived in Singapore and established his firm John Purvis & Co. in 1822. The following year, he was appointed one of Singapore's first magistrates. He managed his firm for 40 years, retiring in 1862. The business folded two years later. Purvis was noted for his generosity and support for the building funds of ST ANDREW'S CATHEDRAL, the CATHEDRAL OF THE GOOD SHEPHERD and the Singapore library. Purvis Wharf (now defunct) and Purvis Street were named after him. He died in London.

Pusara Aman and Pusara Abadi Muslim CEMETERIES located along Jalan Bahar and Lim Chu Kang Road respectively. These two cemeteries, not far from one another, together represent the largest burial area reserved for the Muslim community.

Pusara Aman is the older cemetery. At its edge is a mosque, built in 1975, where congregational prayers for the deceased are carried out just before burial. The newer cemetery, Pusara Abadi, is the final resting place of Muslims who were exhumed from the BIDADARI CEMETERY. Muslims usually visit the graves of deceased family members at least once a year during EID-UL-FITR. The graves are customarily cleared of debris and weeds before then.

Puthucheary, Dominic (1934–) Trade unionist and lawyer. Dominic Puthucheary was born in Kerala, India, the fifth son of schoolteachers. The family, including Dominic's older brother JAMES PUTHUCHEARY, who also became a trade unionist and politician, emigrated to Malaya in the late 1930s. In 1956, Puthucheary quit training as a teacher and joined the civil service, but left barely a year later to champion workers' rights. He rose to prominence as a fiery trade union activist and adviser, soon catching the eye of PEOPLE'S ACTION PARTY (PAP) leader LEE KUAN YEW, who handpicked him to be the PAP's assistant organizing secretary in 1960.

Personal differences led Puthucheary to leave the PAP in 1961. He and others formed the BARISAN SOSIALIS, of which he was a committee member. In 1963, he was detained under OPERATION COLD STORE for alleged communist activities. When he was released, he left to read law at the University of Belfast (1964–71).

When he returned to Malaysia, he commenced legal practice with Skrine and Company, remaining there for many years. In the late 1990s, he established his own law firm Puthucheary, Firoz and Mai.

Puthucheary, James (1924–2000) Trade unionist and lawyer. James Puthucheary, the older brother of DOMINIC PUTHUCHEARY, was born in Kerala, India. His family emigrated to Malaya in the late 1930s. He grew up in Ayer Molek, Johor and completed his secondary education there. In 1943, he joined the INDIAN NATIONAL ARMY (Azad Guerrilla Regiment) and spent two years in the Burmese jungles. Between 1947 and 1948, he went to India and studied at Santiniketan, the university founded by Rabindranath Tagore. He came to Singapore in 1948, studying economics, English and history at RAFFLES COLLEGE. Active in student politics, Puthucheary was elected to the Executive Committee of Raffles College Union and later became first secretary-general of the UNIVERSITY OF MALAYA Students' Union.

James Puthucheary was detained first for his activities as a student leader in January 1951, together with other activists including JOHN EBER, SAMAD ISMAIL, C.V. DEVAN NAIR, and DOLLAH MAJID. He was released after a year and a half, and rejoined the University of Malaya to complete his degree. In February 1953, he persuaded the university authorities to allow students to form the Socialist Club. The official organ and publication of the Club was *Fajar* (Dawn), which became popular with students and intellectuals.

In 1954, the editorial board of *Fajar*, including Puthucheary, was arrested and charged with sedition. The FAJAR TRIAL created a sensation. The accused were represented by LEE KUAN YEW, who brought in QUEEN'S COUNSEL D.N. PRITT to lead the defence. They were acquitted.

In 1954, Puthucheary helped Lee Kuan Yew form the PEOPLE'S ACTION PARTY (PAP). The following year, he was appointed one of the secretaries of the SINGAPORE FACTORY AND SHOP WORKERS' UNION. In 1956, he was elected assistant secretary-general of the union. That same year, he was arrested and detained by the LIM YEW HOCK government along with LIM CHIN SIONG and FONG SWEE SUAN for his involvement in the CHINESE MIDDLE SCHOOL RIOTS.

While in custody, Puthucheary wrote *Ownership and Control in the Malayan Economy*, a socialist economic analysis. He was released only when the PAP came to power in 1959. For a brief period, he was general manager of the Industrial Promotions Board, chairman of the CENTRAL PROVIDENT FUND and chairman of the Tariff Advisory Committee.

In 1961, Puthucheary resigned all his appointments and went to the University of Singapore to read law. Like his younger brother Dominic, he was also one of the committee members in the BARISAN SOSIALIS. He was arrested a third time under OPERATION COLD STORE in February 1963 and banished from Singapore. After his release, Puthucheary practised law in Kuala Lumpur, becoming a partner in the prominent law firm Skrine and Co. He also became an advisor to Malaysia's second prime minister Tun Abdul Razak. Puthucheary died of a stroke.

Pyramid Club Club established in the mid-1960s by the government to act as an informal mechanism of coordination between government, the business community and the intelligentsia. The Club has around 300 members, including senior civil servants, businessmen and professionals. Its clubhouse is a colonial black-and-white house on Goodwood Hill with dining, social and sports facilities. The Club has two tiers defined by age: the Junior Pyramid Club and Senior Pyramid Club.

pythons One of the world's largest snakes, the reticulated python (*Python reticulatus*) can grow up to a length of 10 m. Although large specimens can be dangerous, they are usually shy and avoid human contact. Pythons are fairly common in Singapore, and can be foundfound in all terrestrial habitats, from forests and MANGROVES to urban areas. They are mainly nocturnal, feeding on birds and small mammals. A python kills by wrapping its body around the victim, suffocating it before swallowing it whole.

Q

Qi Qiao Jie This Chinese festival is celebrated on the seventh day of the seventh lunar month of the Chinese calendar. Also known as the Festival of the Cowherd and Weaving Maiden, or Double-Seventh Day, it is the Chinese equivalent of Valentine's Day, though it is not celebrated as widely.

There are two versions of the legend, one of which depicts Niulang (literally 'cowherd') and Zhinü (literally 'weaving maiden') as two fairies in love with each other who lived on opposite sides of the Milky Way and could not meet. Taking pity on them, Tiandi (god of heaven) arranged for them to wed. However, the two fairies neglected their duties, which led Tiandi to declare that they could only meet on the seventh night of the seventh lunar month.

A second version states that Zhinü was the immortal seventh daughter of Tiandi. She fell in love with and married the mortal Niulang. On hearing of the marriage, Zhinü's mother Wangmu Niang Niang (the goddess of heaven) forbade her to meet Niulang. Wangmu Niang Niang subsequently took pity on them and allowed them to meet once a year on the seventh night of the seventh lunar month.

Qi Qiao is not celebrated by many observers of CHINESE RELIGION. In the 1950s and 1960s, however, lights were put up all over Chinatown on the evening of the festival by Qi Jie Hui (Seven Sisters' Associations), which were formed by young, single women. These associations would set up paper shrines with offerings of fruits, cosmetics and flowers. Miniature articles of clothing and embroidery were also made for the occasion.

Qing Ming Chinese festival. Literally meaning 'clear and bright', this festival is observed on the third month of the lunar calendar, 106 days after DONG ZHI (the win-

Qi Qiao Jie: altar dedicated to Niulang and Zhinü.

ter solstice). It is a time to honour the dead and to show respect for deceased family members and ancestors.

During Qing Ming, families tidy the graves of their ancestors, make offerings of food and wine, and burn incense and candles. Some people bring bland food as an offering, as it is believed it will not be plundered by wandering spirits. By contrast, food offered at altars in homes typically comprises a huge feast with roasted poultry, meat, eggs and other food believed to be favoured by the deceased. It is also believed that the burning of incense expedites the transfer of food to the 'other world'.

Because cremation of the dead is far more prevalent than burial these days, it is common to see families paying their respects at temples and columbaria—where the ashes of the deceased are kept—rather than at cemeteries. Temples such as the Kong Meng San Phor Kark See Monastery see devotees arriving at dawn to offer prayers and incense in memory of their deceased forebears.

Qing Ming is believed to have originated in Shanxi province, China, in 600 BCE. A man named Jie Zhitui was said to have saved a starving nobleman's life when he served him meat taken from his own leg. When the nobleman became the ruler of a principality, he invited Jie to join him, but Jie preferred to remain in the mountains with his mother. The nobleman tried to force Jie out by setting the forest on fire, but killed him instead. To commemorate Jie, the nobleman ordered all fires to be extinguished on the anniversary of Jie's death. As home fires could not be lit, only cold food would be eaten on this day. This 'cold food' ritual is observed on the eve of Qing Ming and is considered part of the festival.

Queen Elizabeth Walk An esplanade and seafront promenade were constructed in the 1880s adjacent to the mouth of the Singapore River. (The area, with its European houses, was regarded as a prime residential neighbourhood at the time.) Major LAND RECLAMATION in the 1890s extended the promenade and enlarged the area, turning it into a popular place for evening strolls, sports and other social activities. In 1943, Esplanade Park was constructed. In 1953, to commemorate the accession of Queen Elizabeth II to the throne, the promenade alongside the park was renamed Queen Elizabeth Walk. People flocked there to enjoy the sea breeze, view ships and, in the evenings, dine at the nearby Satay Club—a collection of hawker stalls selling SATAY. The park was further developed in 1991, and the Satay Club relocated to Clarke Quay in 1995.

Queen Elizabeth Walk leads to a number of notable memorials, including the CENOTAPH, the TAN KIM SENG FOUNTAIN, the LIM BO SENG Memorial and the Indian National Army Monument Plaque. Many

Queen Elizabeth Walk: shown in a painting, 1900s.

people still stroll along Queen Elizabeth Walk, although views of the sea are now obscured by the Esplanade Bridge and the ESPLANADE—THEATRES ON THE BAY.

Queen's Counsel Also known colloquially as 'Silks' on account of their silk gowns, Queen's Counsels, or QCs (King's Counsels, or KCs, if the monarch reigning at the time is male) are barristers—or, in the case of Scotland, advocates—appointed by Letters Patent to be one of 'Her Majesty's Counsel learned in the law'. QCs are a separate order or degree of lawyers with enhanced status and privileges. For example, they may sit within the Bar of court, and wear silk gowns of a special design.

Qing Ming: prayers and offerings on temple grounds (left), and at a graveside (below).

Queen's Scholarship: group of scholars, 1860

QCs are typically drawn from among senior barristers, since their appointment is to conduct court work on the Crown's behalf. Taking silk not only enhances the standing of a lawyer, it also means higher fees for courtroom work. QCs used to be granted ad hoc admissions to the Singapore Bar as a matter of course to argue cases, but in recent years, their admission is allowed only where they have special expertise or if a case is overly difficult or complicated. Singapore has developed a local equivalent, known as the SENIOR COUNSEL.

Queen's Scholarship Named in honour of Queen Victoria, and inaugurated in 1885 by

Queenstown: flats under construction in 1962 (right); in the 1970s (below).

Sir CECIL CLEMENTI SMITH, governor of the Straits Settlements, the scholarship was awarded to the best student of the year by a special selection board comprising six members under the chairmanship of the chief justice.

The two objectives of the scholarship were 'to allow promising boys an opportunity of completing their studies in England', and 'to encourage a number of boys to remain in school and acquire a really useful education' (although the scholarship was later offered to female students as well). These were important aims at a time when many families had no way of financing their children's education, still less to send them to the United Kingdom.

Among the recipients of the Queen's Scholarship were E.W. BARKER, who was later the minister for law; Professor LIM PIN, who became vice-chancellor of the National University of Singapore; and Kwa Geok Choo, lawyer and wife of minister mentor LEE KUAN YEW.

The scholarship was superseded by the Singapore State Scholarship in 1959, when self-government was granted to Singapore.

Queenstown Housing estate. The first satellite town in Singapore, Queenstown was initially developed by the SINGAPORE IMPROVEMENT TRUST (SIT) in the 1950s as a low-cost estate; development was intensified with the formation of the HOUSING & DEVELOPMENT BOARD in 1960.

The estate was named after Queen Elizabeth II to mark her coronation in 1953. A number of roads in the Queenstown area also bear the names of British royalty, such as Prince Charles Crescent, Prince Philip Avenue and Margaret Drive. The main arterial road, Queensway, was officially named in 1955.

In 2000, Queenstown had an area of approximately 2,200 ha with about 29,700 units and some 100,000 residents. The main neighbourhoods are TANGLIN HALT, Forfar Heights, Commonwealth Green, Mei Ling Heights, Stirling View, Strathmore Road and Rumah Tinggi.

Quests, The Popular music group. Coming together in 1960, The Quests became the most successful local band of their time, with hits in Singapore, Malaysia and Hong Kong. Guitarist Jap Chong Chow Pin and his friend Raymond Leong played alongside bassist Henry Chua and drummer Lim Wee Guan. Leong's departure to further his studies saw Reggie Verghese from THE CHECKMATES joining the band.

The Quests began as an instrumental backing band. After taking part in a talent competition organized by Radio Singapore, they were signed by EMI. The Quests' debut single featured the original instrumental 'Shanty', which became the band's signature tune, displacing 'I Should Have Known Better' by The Beatles from

the top of the charts. In 1966, Vernon Cornelius, late of The Trailers, took over vocal duties from Keith Locke.

In 1966, The Quests released their first album Questing—the first local album to be recorded in stereo—at EMI's MACDONALD HOUSE studio. Their second LP, 33rd Revolution, was released in December 1967.

On New Year's Day 1968, The Quests began a 10-month stint at the Mocambo in Hong Kong, during which singer Cornelius announced that he would be leaving the band. Verghese and Chong then stepped in to take on vocal duties, and in January 1969, they returned to the Mocambo. They released seven more EPs after their return to Singapore in July, one of which was an ANITA SARAWAK EP featuring 'Rain', 'Happy Heart', 'Come into my Arms' and 'I'm Gonna Make You Love Me'.

The band split up in 1970, and EMI released The Sound of The Quests, a compilation of tracks from the later part of their career. In 2001, Call It Shanty! by Henry Chua, an account of his time in the band, was published, and a musical of the same name was staged in 2002. The following year, EMI released a compilation, Recollecting The Quests. A second volume was released in 2004.

The Quests: record cover (top); the band featured in a 1960s issue of Fanfare magazine.

race riots On 21 July 1964, an estimated 20,000 Muslims—some from organizations including political parties and Muslim associations—gathered at the PADANG to celebrate PROPHET MUHAMMAD'S BIRTHDAY. The crowd headed in a procession towards a dispersal point in Geylang. During the procession, rioting broke out, which turned out to be a clash between the Malays and the Chinese. As news of the clashes spread, further incidents occurred, and rioting spread to other parts of the island.

The scale and nature of the violence severely taxed police resources, and military reinforcements had to be deployed. An islandwide curfew, from 9.30 p.m. to 6.00 a.m. the following day, brought temporary relief. However, as soon as the curfew was lifted, violence re-erupted. As a result, the curfew was imposed again for 11 days, during which it was lifted only for brief periods to let people purchase daily necessities.

Singapore was still part of the Federation of Malaysia at this time. A racially mixed team of federal ministers led by Tun Abdul Razak, who was deputy premier and (in the absence of Tunku ABDUL RAHMAN, who was abroad) the acting prime minister of Malaysia, arrived in Singapore on the second day of the riots. They toured the city and appealed for calm. 'Goodwill committees'—mixed teams of Malay and Chinese community leaders—also visited neighbourhoods to try to restore calm.

By the fourth day, the violence had subsided. But by the time the curfew was lifted on 2 August, 23 people had died and 454 had been injured. Of 3,568 persons arrested, 715 were charged in court and another 945 placed in preventive detention.

Different explanations have been offered for the origins of the July riots. In one version, supported by Tun Razak, the outbreak of violence was spontaneous, probably sparked off by a Chinese individual who threw a bottle at the procession. Angered by the provocation, some Malays assaulted the Chinese person. A Chinese constable who tried to intervene was also set upon. Some Malays then ran towards Geylang Road, overturning stalls in the process.

Although Tun Razak and other Alliance Party leaders did not discount the possibility of Indonesian and communist provocateurs having instigated the riots, they felt that it was the PEOPLE'S ACTION PARTY (PAP) government's mistreatment of the Malay minority in Singapore that was ultimately to blame.

However, a different version put forward by the Singapore government was that the riots had been deliberately provoked for political reasons. The attack on the constable, PAP leaders charged, had been carefully orchestrated to occur near the PAP contingent in the procession, so that the PAP could subsequently be blamed. The PAP also noted that racially charged leaflets had been distributed to the crowd at the Padang, and that Malay opposition leaders at the religious rally had made racially inflammatory speeches.

Three months earlier, shortly after the PAP's ill-fated intervention in the FEDERAL ELECTION (1964), United Malays National Organisation (UMNO) activists, led by their secretary-general, SYED JA'AFAR HASSAN ALBAR, had launched a campaign in an effort to regain support amongst the Malay electorate, using Malay newspapers and provocative speeches to accuse the PAP of oppressing Malays in Singapore. For instance, in a rousing speech to representatives of some 123 Malay and Muslim bodies on 12 July at the New Star Cinema, Syed Ja'afar had launched a pointed attack on the PAP government and its premier, LEE KUAN YEW, for allegedly mistreating Malays. His strategy had been to incite Malays—so as to defuse the PAP's political challenge; put the PAP on the defensive in Singapore; and discredit the PAP's multiracial platform amongst Malay voters.

In the wake of the riots, Singapore leaders called for a commission of inquiry, confident that this would exonerate the government of the charge of mistreating Malays in Singapore. But the Malaysian government declined to hold an inquiry.

On 2 September 1964, three days before the UMNO General Assembly, race riots broke out again. A 57-year-old Malay trishaw-rider was killed in Geylang Serai. This provoked Malays to retaliate, resulting in isolated cases of assaults and stabbings. By the morning of 4 September, these incidents had escalated into communal clashes.

An islandwide curfew was imposed from 2.00 p.m. on 4 September, and again the military were called into action. By the time the curfew was lifted at 4.00 p.m. on 11 September, 13 lives had been lost and 106 people injured. Of 1,439 people arrested, 268 were detained and 154 charged in court.

Although racial tensions had continued to simmer after the July riots, both the Malaysian and Singapore governments have attributed the September riots to Indonesian provocateurs who set out to weaken Malaysia under Indonesia's CONFRONTATION policy at the time.

After this second outbreak of racial violence, the Malaysian Cabinet, on 3 September, agreed to the formation of a commission of inquiry to investigate the causes of the riots. However, hearings started only on 20 April 1965, some seven months later. The proceedings were closed to the public and the press.

The race riots of 1964 deeply influenced the PAP's relationship with UMNO. Before the riots, the PAP had entertained hopes of working with UMNO. After the riots, it could no longer do so, especially as senior UMNO leaders seemed willing to condone the openly communal campaign being waged against the PAP by radical UMNO activists in Singapore. Dismayed by the turn of events, and conscious of its own vulnerability in Singapore, the PAP announced in November 1964 that it would assume the role of an opposition party in Malaysia, and intensify efforts to expand in the peninsula and in Borneo, in an attempt to form the MALAYSIAN SOLIDARITY CONVENTION. Singapore and Malaysia eventually separated in August 1965 (*see* SEPARATION).

Race riots: riot police (far left); and the aftermath.

Radio broadcasting: studio in 1967 (top); Larry Lai hosting radio programme, 1975.

Since 1997, 21 July, the date on which the first race riots began in 1964, has been commemorated in Singapore schools as Racial Harmony Day.

See also MULTIRACIALISM.

Radin Mas Story recorded in the SEJARAH MELAYU (Malay Annals). The legend of Radin Mas begins in Java, when Pangeran Adipati Agung, the brother of a sultan, leaves his kingdom for Singapore with his daughter, Radin Mas Ayu, after his wife is killed by the sultan.

While in Singapore, the Pangeran helps defend the island from pirates. His exploits make him a local hero, and he is married off to the daughter of a local sultan. His wife, the princess, bears him a son named Tengku Chik. However, the princess soon becomes jealous of her husband's love for his daughter, Radin Mas.

The princess engages the help of her nephew, Tengku Bagus, who tricks the Pangeran into a well, and leaves him there to die. The princess then coerces Radin Mas into marrying Tengku Bagus, whom Radin Mas detests. However, during the wedding ceremony, Radin Mas is asked if she has sought her father's permission to

marry. Fearing for her father's life, she lies by saying he is dead. Her half-brother, Tengku Chik, then reveals the Pangeran's whereabouts. With the plot uncovered, the Pangeran is rescued from the well. Out of desperation, Tengku Bagus tries to stab the Pangeran; in the scuffle, Radin Mas is instead stabbed and dies in her father's arms. The princess, fearing retribution, tries to flee, but is struck dead by lightning.

Radin Mas is believed by some to be buried at the foot of MOUNT FABER. A shrine built in her honour, KERAMAT RADIN MAS, can still be found there.

radio broadcasting While a number of amateur radio enthusiasts did broadcast out of Singapore in the period immediately following World War I, it was only in 1920 that the first commercial radio broadcasts commenced. These soon ceased, however, due to a lack of public support.

In 1924, the Amateur Wireless Society of Singapore experimented with radio transmissions from the Dutch East Indies (present-day Indonesia). In 1926, in response to this increasing amateur radio activity, the Malayan government established regulations for radio broadcasting, including licensing rules and specifications on radio content.

In 1930, the Singapore Port Authority commenced a fortnightly short-wave radio broadcast. And in 1937, Governor SHENTON THOMAS officially opened the studios of the Broadcasting Corporation of Malaya (BCM), together with a transmitter on Caldecott Hill. By 1941, the BCM had come under the control of the British Information Ministry, and had been renamed the Malayan Broadcasting Corporation (MBC). Senior staff for the MBC were recruited from the British Broadcasting Corporation (BBC).

During the JAPANESE OCCUPATION, the MBC was managed by the Japanese authorities, and was renamed Syonan Hoso Kyoku (Light of the South Broadcasting Corporation). Programming included Japanese music, language and military propaganda. The Japanese set up other stations in Penang, Malacca, Kuala Lumpur and Seremban, and so improved the region's radio broadcasting infrastructure.

After the war, radio broadcasting in Singapore once again came under the control of the British. In 1946, the radio service was reorganized as Radio Malaya, with headquarters in Singapore. The outbreak of the EMERGENCY also prompted an expansion of radio services, Radio Malaya playing an important role in response to MALAYAN COMMUNIST PARTY (MCP) propaganda and relaying messages from the government to communist rebels.

In 1949, a wire radio service called REDIFFUSION began to broadcast to British military personnel based in Singapore. During the 1950s, radio also came to be

used for educational purposes, with schools receiving educational broadcasts.

When the Federation of Malaya gained independence from the United Kingdom in 1957, its radio headquarters was shifted from Caldecott Hill in Singapore to Kuala Lumpur. Radio Malaya was split into two entities: Radio Malaya and Radio Singapore. Advertising on Radio Singapore started in 1960. When the Federation of Malaysia was formed on 16 September 1963, the two stations were recombined to form Radio Malaysia.

Radio Malaysia reorganized its Singapore broadcasting arm, providing services in Chinese dialects such as Cantonese, Teochew and Hokkien, as well as in English, Malay and Tamil.

Television broadcasts commenced in Singapore in 1963, and in the same year, Radio Singapore merged with the government-run television broadcaster to become RadioTelevision Singapore (RTS).

In August 1965, following Singapore's separation from Malaysia, RTS became wholly government-owned. In 1967, FM transmissions were introduced, as the number of high-rise buildings being built around the island was adversely affecting the reception of AM broadcasts. By the 1970s, four FM radio stations had been established. In 1975, the BBC established a relay station in Singapore from which to broadcast its World Service.

The SINGAPORE BROADCASTING CORPORATION (SBC) was established in 1980. It was corporatized five years later, following an amendment to the 1979 Broadcasting Act.

In the late 1980s, local radio broadcasting began to face competition from a number of independent stations transmitting out of Batam, Indonesia. In 1988, ZOO FM Batam began broadcasting on 101.6 MHz, as did Coast 100 Batam on 100.7 MHz in 1989. Both stations could be received in Singapore. SBC responded to this challenge in the 1990s by incorporating its radio stations under Radio Corporation of Singapore (RCS). Radio programming was revamped, and market demographic studies were conducted. In order to foster competition, RCS increased its range of broadcasting to ten stations.

In 1990, the NATIONAL TRADES UNION CONGRESS commenced broadcasting on 91.3 and 100.3 MHz in 1991. Singapore Armed Forces Radio established stations during the same period. Both organizations targeted the English and Mandarin markets. With this increase in the number of new channels, radio's popularity peaked during the 1990s, with a 100 per cent take-up of RCS advertising slots. Passion 99.5 FM, Singapore's first radio station dedicated to the arts, was launched in December 1997. Funded by the National Arts Council of Singapore, the station continued to broadcast until December 2003, by which time it

Radio broadcasting: some of Singapore's radio stations.

Lady Sophia Raffles

was no longer seen to be commercially viable. In 2005, MEDIACORP Radio (RCS' successor) and Temasek Polytechnic jointly launched a radio station on the same frequency, called Lush.

In 1999, Singapore launched the first commercial digital radio service in Southeast Asia, SMART Radio, operated by MediaCorp Radio. The station operated six digital audio services, and one existing FM transmitter. The following year, the MEDIA DEVELOPMENT AUTHORITY issued a five-year license to Rediffusion to operate its own digital audio broadcasting multiplex. Rediffusion has continued to broadcast both English and Chinese programmes, distributing these via cable. Simultaneous broadcasting via the Internet has also gained in popularity, with most radio stations hosting their own websites.

The radio-listening habits of Singaporeans have changed markedly since 9/11, the Iraq War and the SARS epidemic, with an increase in listeners for Newsradio 93.8 FM. The combined audience share of the five local Mandarin stations has remained the highest among the different language categories. Approximately 95 per cent of Singaporeans aged 15 and above listen to the radio, with the average Singaporean tuning in for nearly three hours a day.

MediaCorp Radio operates Singapore's largest radio network with more than 2.6 million regular listeners. Its 11 local stations and three international stations include the Chinese language stations Y.E.S. 93.3 FM, Capital 95.8 FM and Love 97.2 FM; the Malay language stations Ria 89.7 FM and Warna 94.2 FM; and the Tamil station Oli 96.8 FM. SAF Radio continues to operate two radio stations, Power 98 and Dong-Li 88.3 FM. Radio 91.3 FM and Radio 100.3 FM are now operated by SPH Unionworks, a subsidiary of Singapore Press Holdings. The BBC World Service remains the only foreign broadcaster.

Raffles, Lady Sophia (1786–1858) Lady

Sophia Raffles was born Sophia Hull, daughter of a retired British East India Company (EIC) official. She met the widowed STAMFORD RAFFLES in 1816 when the latter was 'taking the waters' in the spa town of Cheltenham, United Kingdom. Sophia was 30 years old, and Raffles had returned to the United Kingdom after serving in Java as lieutenant-governor. The couple married in February 1817 before Raffles' book *The History of Java* was published.

In October 1817, Sophia accompanied her new husband to the EIC settlement of BENCOOLEN (present-day Bengkulu) on Sumatra, where he had been appointed lieutenant-governor. While in Bencoolen, Sophia undertook pioneering journeys with her husband into central Sumatra, which created a sensation in London society. In September 1818, she accompanied Raffles to EIC headquarters in Calcutta,

where he obtained authority for his mission to Singapore in January 1819. She visited Singapore with Raffles in June 1819, and again from October 1822 to June 1823. By this time, three of Sophia's four children to Raffles had died from illness in Bencoolen; her surviving daughter Ella was sent to the United Kingdom. Broken in spirit, Sophia left Asia for good with Raffles in 1823.

After Raffles' death in 1826, Sophia arranged for the publication of the *Memoir of the Life and Public Services of Sir Thomas Stamford Raffles* (1830), and commissioned a life-sized marble statue of Raffles, which was later placed in Westminster Abbey.

Raffles, Sir Stamford (1781–1826) Founder

of colonial Singapore. Thomas Stamford Bingley Raffles was born at sea in the West Indies on 5 July (or 6 July, according to some sources) 1781, the son of Captain Benjamin Raffles and his wife Anne. Most of his career, however, was to be spent in the East Indies, where he was to serve as lieutenant-governor of Java and, later, BENCOOLEN. It was in the latter capacity that Raffles was responsible for founding the British EAST INDIA COMPANY's settlement on Singapore island in February 1819, the achievement for which he is best remembered.

In 1795, at the age of 14, Raffles joined the East India Company's service in London as a temporary clerk. Straitened family circumstances had cut short his formal education. He studied on his own, and in 1805 was promoted and posted to PENANG, as assistant secretary to the government. In 1810, his proficiency in the Malay language and other skills led the governor-general Lord Minto to appoint him as

Sir Stamford Raffles: statue beside Singapore River.

agent with the Malay States, and in the following year as lieutenant-governor of Java, which the British had occupied to prevent it from falling under the control of Napoleonic France.

Raffles' administration of Java involved a number of controversial decisions and reformist measures, and had ambivalent outcomes. His first wife Olivia died there in 1814, and Java was returned to the Dutch at the end of the Napoleonic Wars.

On his return to England, Raffles wrote the monumental *History of Java*. Its publication, along with his achievements, earned him a knighthood in 1817. In that year he married Sophia Hull, with whom he sailed east to assume his appointment as lieutenant-governor of Bencoolen (present-day Bangkulu) in west Sumatra in 1818.

Reportedly concerned with the monopolistic tendencies of the Dutch authorities in maritime Southeast Asia, Raffles sought permission from Lord Hastings, governor-general of India, to conclude treaties with Malay rulers in the region, and particularly to establish a British base at the southern end of the Strait of Malacca. Accordingly, on 6 February 1819, Raffles concluded a treaty with Tengku Long (whom he recognized as Sultan HUSAIN SHAH) and Temenggong ABDUL RAHMAN of the Riau-Johor empire. He thereby established a 'factory', a settlement and free-trade port on the island of Singapura (meaning 'Lion City' in Malay), which was administered jointly by the Malay and British authorities until 1824.

Before this event, Singapore had played only a marginal role in the Malay Archipelago; henceforth, through the efforts of Raffles, together with those of the first British Residents, WILLIAM FARQUHAR and JOHN CRAWFURD, and pioneers of different races, the settlement grew into a modern emporium and port city. Raffles regarded the settlement as 'a Child of my own' and 'my new Colony', but he was an absentee father for more than three years. His first visit lasted for ten days (29 January to 7 February 1819), his second was for four weeks (May–June 1819), and he returned only in October 1822 for his third and final visit, which lasted until June 1823. While he gave instructions—including a town plan—to Farquhar, the first British Resident, he only supervised the settlement from Bencoolen.

In April 1823, during his final visit, Raffles laid the foundations of the Singapore Institution, conceived as a centre for study and research into the arts and sciences of the region. It was later renamed the RAFFLES INSTITUTION and operated as a boys' school. The original vision was realized only with the establishment in 1928 of RAFFLES COLLEGE.

In June 1823, after replacing Farquhar with Crawfurd as Resident, Raffles returned to Bencoolen. When he and his wife departed in February 1824 for Britain, their ship, *Fame*, caught fire and sank with practically all their possessions. They were rescued, and in April 1824, left Bencoolen on another ship, *Mariner*.

By then, as dictated by the ANGLO-DUTCH TREATY of 17 March 1824, the British government had ceded Bencoolen to the Dutch in return for Malacca, and the Dutch government recognized Singapore as being part of the British sphere of political influence. This paved the way for a treaty concluded by Crawfurd with the Malay rulers on 2 August 1824, by which Singapore became a British possession.

Raffles also had a great interest in zoology and botany, and is also remembered as the founder and first president of the Zoological Society of London. It was fitting that the first Raffles Museum was a natural history museum, and part of its collections has been preserved in the RAFFLES MUSEUM OF BIODIVERSITY RESEARCH in the National University of Singapore.

Raffles died of a fall (possibly brought on by a brain tumour) at his home, High Wood, in London on 5 July 1826. He was buried in Hendon Parish Church cemetery. His widow, Lady SOPHIA RAFFLES, helped to ensure his historical reputation with her biography of Raffles, *Memoir of the Life and Public Services of Sir Thomas Stamford Raffles* (1830), and with a commissioned monument to his memory in Westminster Abbey. None of their children survived into adulthood.

Lady Sophia's *Memoir* helped to develop a British hagiographic tradition, which celebrated Raffles as a pioneer and hero of the empire, and a social reformer connected with William Wilberforce, who was a neighbour of Raffles during the last year of his life. In contrast, several Dutch writers

Raffles Girls' School: during the Queen Street days (below); at Anderson Road (right).

drew attention to certain episodes of Raffles' governorship of Java, during which they claimed atrocities were committed, or at least an abuse of power. This hostile tradition has also been reflected in a few recent writings, but has not dispelled the generally favourable impression of Raffles as a visionary reformer who laid the foundations of modern Singapore. The name of Raffles has proliferated in the names of streets and institutions in the republic.

Raffles College This establishment was the result of a proposal by Sir STAMFORD RAFFLES to set up an institute of higher learning for education and research. Built by funds raised by public subscription, Raffles College was established in 1928 and officially opened in 1929 at Bukit Timah. Due to the Great Depression, it did not do well in the early 1930s. Between 1934 and 1935, it registered only 80 students. The development of higher education came to an abrupt halt during the JAPANESE OCCUPATION. The buildings of Raffles College were used as the Japanese military headquarters during the war years. In 1945, after a brief occupation by the British military, Raffles College resumed operations as an educational institute.

In October 1949, the University of Malaya was formed with the merger of Raffles College and the KING EDWARD VII COLLEGE OF MEDICINE. Expanding rapidly, the university operated two campuses of equal status—one in Singapore and the other in Kuala Lumpur. In 1962, the NATIONAL UNIVERSITY OF SINGAPORE was established when the campuses became autonomous national universities.

Raffles College was attended by various prominent leaders, the most famous of whom is LEE KUAN YEW. Having topped the senior Cambridge examinations in Singapore and Malaya in 1939, he attended Raffles College on the Anderson Scholarship from 1940 to 1942. He enrolled as an arts student, majoring in English, economics and mathematics, before his studies were interrupted by the Japanese Occupation. TOH CHIN CHYE was a science student a year ahead of Lee, while GOH KENG SWEE was Lee's economics tutor.

Raffles Girls' School Secondary school which began as the girls' section of RAFFLES INSTITUTION in 1844. At its inception, it had 11 girls, and classes were limited to sewing and cookery. But by 1879, Raffles Girls' School (RGS) was functioning as an independent entity. It moved to its own premises on the grounds of Raffles Institution on Bras Basah Road in 1883. The school had a largely English-speaking intake, with Latin taught as a second language for those expecting to study law and medicine.

RGS began operating as a combined primary and secondary school in 1903. The school relocated to a new building on

Raffles College: aerial view, 1937.

Queen Street in 1928. During the JAPANESE OCCUPATION, the school building was used as barracks, a prison and as headquarters for the KEMPEITAI (Japanese military police). Classrooms were converted into torture chambers and cells.

In 1959, RGS' secondary classes moved to Anderson Road, where it has remained. Primary classes remained at Queen Street and became a separate school—Raffles Girls' Primary School.

Alumni of RGS include Supreme Court Justice JUDITH PRAKASH; singers STEFANIE SUN and KIT CHAN; violinist SIOW LEE CHIN; and businesswoman OLIVIA LUM.

Raffles Holdings Hospitality company. Raffles Holdings Limited was incorporated in Singapore on 26 August 1995, as the hotel arm and investment holding company of DBS Land (later CAPITALAND). In addition to its flagship property, the RAFFLES HOTEL, it took over the management of the former Westin Stamford and Westin Plaza in 2002. These hotels were renamed Raffles The Plaza and Swissotel The Stamford, after Raffles Holdings acquired the Swissotel Group for $420 million in 2001. With the acquisition, the company doubled its inventory to over 13,000 rooms, and expanded its activities to 17 countries.

In 1999, Raffles Holdings took over management of the Merchant Court hotels in Bangkok, Berlin, Sydney and Singapore. Two Raffles resorts were opened that same year in Mallorca and Bali. In 2000, Raffles acquired its first North American hotel— the Raffles L'Ermitage Beverly Hills in Los Angeles. In 2006, the group had a portfolio of 41 hotels in 21 countries.

Raffles Holdings was listed on the Singapore stock exchange in December 1999. In September 2005, the company divested its entire hotel business to Colony Capital, an international investment firm, for $1.72 billion. Raffles Holdings recorded earnings of $678.3 million on a turnover of $417.9 million in 2005.

Raffles Hotel The hotel first opened on 1 December 1887 in an old bungalow. Its subsequent expansion was guided by Tigran Sarkies, of the SARKIES BROTHERS, and culminated in the opening of the main building—designed by R.A.J. Bidwell of SWAN & MACLAREN—in November 1899. This building's three-storey edifice included classical architectural features and modern innovations such as electric lighting supplied by the hotel's own generator.

After completion of the main building, the hotel let rooms to long-term 'residents' such as the Russian, French, Belgian and American consuls, as well as to royalty, businesspeople and international travellers. During the 1920s, film stars such as Charlie Chaplin, and writers such as Noel Coward and W. SOMERSET MAUGHAM, frequented the hotel. During this era, Raffles Hotel also came to be associated with the SINGAPORE SLING—a cocktail invented by a barman at the hotel's Long Bar.

In 1931, the firm of Sarkies Brothers was declared bankrupt, and the hotel's future was in doubt. After two years of negotiations, a new company, Raffles Hotel Limited, was incorporated for the specific purpose of acquiring the hotel. By then, Raffles Hotel was already being referred to as 'the historic hotel of Singapore'.

During the Japanese Occupation, the Japanese renamed the hotel Syonan Ryokan (Light of the South Hotel), and shifted its entrance to the east side of the main building. After the war, the hotel was refurbished, with modern interiors and air-conditioning. Singapore's elite enjoyed 'Race Dinners' and New Year's Eve parties at the hotel. Film stars such as Elizabeth Taylor, Mike Todd, Ava Gardner and Rita Hayworth all stayed at the hotel during this period, as did political leaders such as Indian prime minister Jawaharlal Nehru and his daughter Indira Gandhi. When W. Somerset Maugham paid his final visit to the hotel in 1960, he described it as 'standing for all the fables of the exotic East'.

Over later years, the hotel's business declined as ORCHARD ROAD developed into the main district for shopping and hospital-

Raffles Hotel

Raffles Lighthouse in 1954.

ity. But a renewed emphasis on heritage sparked a revival of Raffles Hotel's fortunes in the 1980s. It was gazetted as a national monument in 1987. In March 1989, Raffles Hotel closed temporarily for restoration. Architectural redevelopment was undertaken based on the hotel's 1915 blueprint. On 16 September 1991, a larger and reinvigorated Raffles Hotel was reopened.

Raffles Institution Secondary school for boys. Founded as SINGAPORE INSTITUTION in 1823, the school was renamed Raffles Institution (RI) in 1868 in honour of Sir STAMFORD RAFFLES.

The first government secondary school to be established in Singapore, RI's original site was on Bras Basah Road (it was later demolished to make way for Raffles City). The school relocated to Grange Road in 1973, and in 1990 it moved to a site at Bishan, where boarding facilities were provided on campus. RI became the first secondary school in Singapore to have a street named after it—Raffles Institution Lane.

RI offers students the six-year Raffles Programme—a broad-based curriculum also offered at RAFFLES GIRLS' SCHOOL. This programme allows students to skip the Singapore-Cambridge GCE Ordinary Level examinations and continue directly on to Raffles Junior College. It also offers a GIFTED EDUCATION PROGRAMME.

RI's alumni include prime ministers LEE KUAN YEW and GOH CHOK TONG; and presidents YUSOF ISHAK, BENJAMIN SHEARES and WEE KIM WEE.

Raffles Lighthouse The rocky outcrops and coral reefs known as Pulau Satumu ('One Tree Island' in Malay) mark the southernmost area of land within Singapore's territorial waters. Raffles Lighthouse was built on this spot in 1854, as Pulau Satumu was a hazard to ships during bad weather. Granite from PULAU UBIN was shipped to Pulau Satumu for its construction. Despite the lighthouse, the surrounding seas still present

problems for shipping. In 2003, for instance, the 10,000-tonne container ship MV *Milena* ran aground near the lighthouse.

The zone around Pulau Satumu is protected as a marine reserve; its clear waters and biodiversity make it popular with divers.

Raffles Medical Group The Raffles Medical Group was founded in 1976 to care for patients requiring general medical services, as well as those requiring specialist treatment or surgery. The group operates a network of 60 general practice clinics in Singapore serving both corporate clients and individuals. It also runs a tertiary care hospital—Raffles Hospital in North Bridge Road—with 380 beds and 12 specialist clinics covering a range of specialties, including paediatrics, obstetrics, cardiology, oncology and orthopaedics. The Raffles International Patients Centre provides a personalized service to international patients and their family members. To cater to the Japanese community, the Raffles Japanese Clinic is located in the hospital.

In 2002, the hospital featured in the headlines when it carried out extremely difficult surgery to separate conjoined 28-year-old Iranian twins Ladan and Laleh Bijani, who unfortunately did not survive the operation.

Raffles Institution: former premises at Bras Basah.

Raffles Institution, Singapore.

Raffles Place: (from top) looking eastwards,1920s, showing the premises occupied by the Mercantile Bank from 1916; looking west about the same time towards the Chartered Bank building; looking eastwards in the 1960s, showing the later Mercantile Bank, built 1930, and the Asia Insurance building in the background; looking westwards in the 1960s (John Little on the right, Robinsons on the left); the same view westwards today.

The group has expanded regionally with four clinics in Hong Kong and representative offices in the region. Its subsidiary Raffles Health develops and markets healthcare products, such as over-the-counter medication, dietary supplements, and surgical supplies. In 2005, the group's profit after tax was $12 million on a turnover of almost $113 million.

Raffles Museum of Biodiversity Research, The Situated within the Faculty of Science at the NATIONAL UNIVERSITY OF SINGAPORE, the Raffles Museum of Biodiversity Research (RMBR) was officially opened on 1 October 1998. The RMBR's animal collection—the Zoological Reference Collection—is the successor to the famous Raffles Collection. It contains items formerly held at at the Raffles Museum, which Sir STAMFORD RAFFLES established in 1849. It is the largest single collection of Southeast Asian fauna in the region, containing at least 400,000 catalogued specimens. The RMBR also inherited the *Raffles Bulletin of Zoology*—an academic journal first published in 1928.

As well as curating the museum's collections, RMBR staff and students engage in ecological and taxonomic research, covering the terrestrial, freshwater and marine environments. They also conduct surveys, expeditions and collaborative work throughout the Asia-Pacific region. The RMBR plays an active role in public education. Besides featuring a public gallery, the museum offers ecological and nature education programmes for schools.

Raffles Place Commercial precinct. Sir STAMFORD RAFFLES envisioned Singapore's first commercial centre in his 1822 town plan. He planned to site it on the south side of the SINGAPORE RIVER, even though the terrain was entirely unsuitable to such a project. A hillock between the chosen area and Battery Road had to be removed, and swamps in the vicinity drained.

Commercial Square was developed and laid out between 1823 and 1824, with trees and flower beds planted in its centre. It was renamed Raffles Place in 1858. Raffles Place soon became the premier business address on the island. From 1857 to 1865, the land on the south side of Raffles Place was reclaimed for commercial use, and was named Collyer Quay.

The second half of the 19th century also saw the setting up in Raffles Place of two department stores—ROBINSONS and JOHN LITTLE. As Singapore's economy grew, more buildings were constructed around the square to accommodate shops, banks and merchants' offices. Older, low-rise buildings in the area were demolished to make way for skyscrapers, such as the headquarters of the OVERSEAS UNION BANK and the UNITED OVERSEAS BANK, two of Singapore's tallest buildings.

Raffles Quay Stretch of road running from Finlayson Green to Boon Tat Street. It was originally built as a reinforced bank along Singapore's shoreline, where ships docking in the nearby Telok Ayer Basin could unload cargo. The quay was named in honour of Sir STAMFORD RAFFLES when it was first created in 1910 with the second phase of LAND RECLAMATION in the Telok Ayer Basin. The third phase, carried out in 1930, created the financial district of SHENTON WAY, of which Raffles Quay is a part.

Rahim Ishak (1925–2001) Politician and diplomat. Rahim Ishak was educated at Raffles Institution and then at King Edward VII School in Taiping, Malaya (his family having relocated to Taiping in anticipation of World War II). After the war, Rahim and his family moved back to Singapore where he commenced—but did not complete—studies at Raffles College.

In 1947, Rahim joined the Malay-language newspaper, UTUSAN MELAYU (founded by his brother YUSOF ISHAK), as a reporter. He also completed his training as a teacher at the Teachers' Training College, and returned to Perak to teach at his alma mater, the King Edward VII School in Taiping, in 1950.

He returned to Singapore as associate editor of *Utusan Melayu* in 1955, and continued working at the newspaper until 1959, when he was appointed political secretary to the Ministry of Culture. He contested the 1959 general election as a PEOPLE'S ACTION PARTY candidate, and was elected MEMBER OF PARLIAMENT for Siglap constituency. He was then appointed parliamentary secretary for the Ministry of Education (1963–65). In the ensuing years, he served as minister of state for education (1965–68) and senior minister of state for foreign affairs (1972–81). Rahim was a strong believer in MULTIRACIALISM and an opponent of affirmative action. Many of his speeches were aimed at reassuring Singapore's Malays that their lot was better than that of Malays in Malaysia.

From 1974 to 1977, Rahim served as ambassador to Indonesia. He was also president of the Singapore Athletics Association (1966–75) and chairman of the Film Censor's Appeal Committee (1960–65). In 1984, he retired from politics. He was admitted into the Distinguished Service Order in 1990.

Rahimah Rahim (1956–) Singer. Rahimah Rahim is the daughter of singer Rahim Hamid—known as 'Singapore's Nat King Cole'—and actress Mariam Baharom. Her hits include 'Doa' (Prayer) and 'Gadis dan Bunga' (Girls and Flowers). After recording 11 albums, she left the entertainment industry in 1989, but returned to acting and singing in the 1990s. She appeared in television drama serials such as *Anak Metropolitan* (Metropolitan Child), *Permintaan Aishah*

Rahim Ishak: greeting Yusof Ishak, left.

(Aishah's Request), and *Anak Pak Awang Temberang* (Child of Pak Awang the Storyteller). She has produced a greatest-hits album, *Suatu Memori* (A Memory).

railways Plans for the construction of a railway line in Singapore were introduced in 1865, when docking and wharfing companies at the New Harbour (Keppel Harbour) applied for the right to lay a railway track from there to Telok Ayer, so that goods could be transported from the harbour to town. Although these plans were approved by the colonial government, the line was never built.

In 1871, the Tanjong Pagar Dock Company applied for permission to build a railway line between the company's wharves and the town. The company faced competition from the Singapore and New Harbour Railway Company, which had proposed the construction of a longer line. The Legislative Council and the Secretary of State of the Colonies would only agree to the construction of the longer line if a company representing the interests of the public could be formed. As a result, all companies withdrew from the process, and the railway line was never built.

It was not until 1899 that the Legislative Council approved the building of a proposed railway from Singapore to the the shores of the Johor Strait. This project was undertaken by a special railway engineer, working under instructions from consulting engineers based in the United Kingdom. Indian labourers and other groups were employed for the job. The line ran from Tank Road, along Cuppage Road; behind Orchard Road; across Monk's Hill Road to Newton Circus; onwards to Bukit Timah; and then towards Woodlands. It was completed in 1903, with the first section as far as Bukit Timah opening on 1 January of that year. The remaining part opened in April. Thus, the Singapore Railway was born. Tank Road Station served as the main passenger terminus.

In 1913, properties and land belonging to the Singapore Railway were sold to the Federated Malay States for $4,136,000 and incorporated as the Federated Malay States Railway. In 1923, the completion of the

Singapore-Johor Causeway saw Singapore connected to Bangkok by rail.

The Straits Settlements Legislative Council approved the plan for a new railway line and station site in January 1929. The colonial government commited $2,638,320 to a new railway deviation line from Bukit Timah to Tanjong Pagar. In 1930, the Federated Malay States Railways acquired the land and began construction of a new station at Tanjong Pagar docks. On the day the KEPPEL RAILWAY STATION opened, the Tank Road Station ceased operation, and tracks to it were dismantled.

When Singapore left the Federation of Malaysia, the Federated Malay State Railways retained its railway possessions, pursuant to the 1965 SEPARATION Agreement. Rail services continued to run to Keppel Railway Station, with an immigration and customs checkpoint there. In subsequent years, negotiations have taken place between the governments of Singapore and Malaysia over several issues concerning railway land. In 1990, a Points of Agreement was concluded between the two governments; it has yet to be implemented, and negotiations are still in progress. On 18 July 1995, Singapore moved its Customs, Immigration and Quarantine Checkpoint to Woodlands.

Rajah, A.P. (1911–1999) Politician, diplomat and judge. Born in Port Dickson, Malaysia, Arumugam Ponnu Rajah studied at Raffles Institution and Oxford University. On his return from the United Kingdom, he practised at RODYK & DAVIDSON. He then established the firm of Tan, Rajah & Cheah with C.C. Tan and H.S. Cheah. Tan was the leader of the SINGAPORE PROGRESSIVE PARTY, and Rajah became the party's secretary.

In 1959, Rajah was elected to the Legislative Assembly as an independent, but lost his seat in the general election of 1963. In 1964, he was appointed SPEAKER OF PARLIAMENT. Two years later, he became Singapore's first high commissioner to the United Kingdom.

Following another diplomatic posting to Australia, Rajah returned to Singapore to resume legal practice, and was elevated to

Rahimah Rahim

Rajah & Tann: Tann Wee Tiong, centre.

the High Court in 1976. He retired from the Bench in 1990, and returned to Tan, Rajah & Cheah as a consultant, remaining with the firm until his death.

Rajah, V.K. (1957–) Judge. Vijaya Kumar Rajah is the son of lawyer and politician T.T. Rajah. V.K. Rajah was educated at the Anglo-Chinese School and then at the Faculty of Law at the National University of Singapore (NUS), where he graduated near the top of his class in 1982. He then joined his father's firm, RAJAH & TANN. In 1986, he obtained a master's degree in law at Cambridge University. He returned to Singapore, continued legal practice, and taught banking law part-time at NUS. Within a few years, he became managing partner of Rajah & Tann.

In 1997, Rajah was among the first batch of lawyers to be appointed SENIOR COUNSEL. He was appointed JUDICIAL COMMISSIONER on 2 January 2004, and on 1 November the same year, he was elevated to become a judge of the SUPREME COURT.

Rajah & Tann Law firm. Rajah & Tann was founded in the 1950s by Thampore T. Rajah and Tann Wee Tiong, two founding members of the PEOPLE'S ACTION PARTY. The firm achieved its greatest expansion—in size and scope—under the management of V.K. RAJAH, Thampore's son. Although based in Singapore, the firm has opened an office in Shanghai, and has established a strategic alliance with the American law firm Weil, Gotshal & Manges LLP.

Rajaratnam, S. (1915–2006) Journalist and politician. Sinnathamby Rajaratnam was born in Ceylon (present-day Sri Lanka), and was raised in colonial Malaya, the elder of two sons of a Tamil plantation owner from Jaffna. He spent his early years on the outskirts of Seremban and was educated in nearby mission schools. He was later admitted to Raffles Institution in Singapore, and completed his Senior Cambridge in 1934 at Victoria Institution in Kuala Lumpur.

In 1936, Rajaratnam left for London to enrol at King's College as a law student. He developed an anti-imperialist and anti-British stance during his time in London,

A.P. Rajah

The Raffles Museum of Biodiversity Research

joining the Left Book Club and establishing relationships with Indian nationalists, socialists, and other left-wing thinkers.

When the JAPANESE OCCUPATION of Malaya made it impossible for his family to transfer funds to him in the United Kingdom, Rajaratnam turned to journalism for a living. In 1941, he married a young Hungarian woman, Piroska Feher.

In 1947, the couple settled in Singapore. Rajaratnam joined the staff of the pro-British THE MALAYA TRIBUNE. In 1950 he was appointed associate editor of the *Singapore Standard*. However, his editorial views were anti-British, and occasionally incurred rebuke from the colonial establishment. At one point, Rajaratnam's column— 'I write as I please'—attracted such attention that he was summoned by Sir Gerald Templer, then governor of Malaya.

Rajaratnam joined THE STRAITS TIMES in 1954 and was a founder member of the Singapore Union of Journalists.

In 1954, Rajaratnam became a founding member of the PEOPLE'S ACTION PARTY (PAP) and one of its leaders. He assumed the role of party theoretician and ideologue. He resigned from *The Straits Times* in 1959 to take a more active role in politics, running for the Legislative Assembly seat of Kampong Glam. When the PAP came to power that year, he was named minister for culture. In that role, he expressed a strong belief in the policy of MULTIRACIALISM.

Following SEPARATION in 1965, Rajaratnam was appointed Singapore's foreign minister, and was tasked with heading the newly created MINISTRY OF FOREIGN AFFAIRS. In that role, he became one of the founding fathers of the ASSOCIATION OF SOUTH EAST ASIAN NATIONS (ASEAN).

Rajaratnam continued to serve as member of Parliament for Kampong Glam until his retirement from public life in 1988. He held several other ministerial positions, including minister for labour

P. Ramlee: the actor (below); poster for the Malay movie Anak-ku Sazali, *1956 (right).*

(1968–71); second deputy prime minister (foreign affairs) (1980–85); and senior minister in the Prime Minister's Office (1985–88). Upon his retirement, he was appointed senior distinguished fellow at the Institute of Southeast Asian Studies. He was admitted into the prestigious Order of Temasek (First Class) in 1990, and he received the ASEAN Heads of Government Citation Award in 1997.

At his state funeral on 25 February 2006—the first for a government minister— mourners recited the NATIONAL PLEDGE, which Rajaratnam had written in 1966.

Rajendran, S. (1938–) Judge. Born in Malaysia, S. Rajendran graduated with a law degree from the University of Singapore in 1962; he was called to the Singapore and Malaysian Bars in 1965 and 1966 respectively. Upon graduation, he joined the Singapore Legal Service where he was appointed deputy public prosecutor and then magistrate. In 1965, he became the first local graduate to be appointed district judge. Three years later, he was made Senior State Counsel in the ATTORNEY-GENERAL'S CHAMBERS, a post he held till he resigned from the service in 1977 to become a partner in the firm Khattar Wong and Partners (*see* KHATTARWONG). On 1 September 1990, he was appointed JUDICIAL COMMISSIONER and just three months later, on 1 January 1991, he was elevated to the Bench as PUISNE JUDGE. He retired in October 2003 on turning 65. During his career, Rajendran was a council member of the Law Society (1979) and a member of the Inquiry Panel of the LAW SOCIETY OF SINGAPORE (1980–90). As of 2006, he was also chairman of the HINDU ENDOWMENTS BOARD.

Rajhans, B.S. (unknown–1957) Film director. B.S. Rajhans was the first Indian filmmaker brought to Singapore, and is regarded as the founding father of Malay cinema. Having started shooting movies in India in 1930, he came here on a commission to direct *Laila Majnun* in 1933; it was an instant success. He returned in 1942 to shoot *Menantu Derhaka* (The Rebellious Daughter-in-Law). In 1946, he was responsible for *Seruan Merdeka* (The Call for Freedom), independently produced by Malayan Arts Production.

When the SHAW BROTHERS started their Malay studio in 1947, Rajhans became their first director, and made 20 movies for them up to 1953. Actors such as P. RAMLEE, Siput Sarawak, and S. Roomai Noor began their careers under his direction. In 1953, he joined the newly created CATHAY-KERIS FILMS, for which he made five films.

Raman, P.S. (1920–1976) Civil servant and diplomat. Born and educated in INDIA, Papanasam Setlur Raman came to Singapore in 1947. He joined the Department of Broadcasting in 1954,

S. Rajaratnam: campaigning in Malaysia, 1964.

becoming acting director in 1965. When Prime Minister LEE KUAN YEW broke down during a press conference on 9 August 1965 (*see* SEPARATION), Raman advised against cutting footage of the now-famous scene.

Raman subsequently joined the foreign service and was appointed Singapore's first ambassador to Indonesia in 1968. Shortly after his appointment, mobs sacked the Singapore embassy in Jakarta to protest the hanging of two Indonesian commandos for the MACDONALD HOUSE bombing. Raman also served as Singapore's first ambassador to the Soviet Union (1971–76). Following in his footsteps, his son, Bilahari Kim Hee P.S. Kausikan, became ambassador to Russia in 1994.

Ramlee, P. (1929–1973) Director, actor, musician, singer and composer. Also known as Ramlee Puteh, he was born Teuku Zakaria Teuku Nyak Puteh in Penang, and had a natural gift for music as a child. During his career he acted in 65 movies and directed 34 feature films, 16 of which were shot in Singapore, where he worked between 1955 and 1964. His other 18 films were shot in Kuala Lumpur from 1964 to 1973. He also composed the music and lyrics for more than 250 songs.

P. Ramlee was first spotted during one of his live performances by B.S. RAJHANS, who then brought him to Singapore to work for the SHAW BROTHERS. He began his acting career in Rajhans's film *Chinta* (Love) (1948). His first lead role came in L. Krishnan's *Bakti* (Service) (1950), followed by lead roles in *Penghidupan* (Life) (1950) and *Takdir Ilahi* (God's Will) (1950) by the same director. His directorial debut, PENAREK BECHA (Trishaw Man) (1955), was a resoundingly successful social drama. His 1956 film *Semerah Padi* showed a range of influences, from the Italian neo-realism of Giuseppe de Santis's *Riso Amaro* (Bitter Rice) (1949), to post-war Japanese movies such as Akira Kurosawa's *Shichinin no Samurai* (Seven Samurai) (1954). Unlike some of his peers who crossed over to CATHAY-KERIS FILMS, he stayed on with Shaw, making numerous films.

P. Ramlee's crowning moment as an actor came when he was presented with the Best Actor Award at the 1957 Asian Film Festival, Tokyo, for his dual roles in *Anak-ku Sazali* (My Son Sazali) (1956), a drama directed by Phani Majumdar. With the comedy *Bujang Lapok* (Confirmed Bachelor), he inaugurated a series of movies: *Pendekar Bujang Lapok* (The Warrior Bachelor) (1959), for which he won the Best Comedy Award at the 1959 Asian Film Festival in Kuala Lumpur; *Ali Baba Bujang Lapok* (Ali Baba, Confirmed Bachelor) and *Seniman Bujang Lapok* (The Bachelor Actors), both in 1961. In 1963, he received the award of Asia's Most Versatile Talent for his performance in *Ibu Mertuaku* (My Mother-in-Law) (1962), the story of a struggling musician, based on his own life.

He had an extraordinary range of talents, above all a gift for composing and singing songs, such as 'Azizah' and 'Getaran Jiwa' (The Stirring of My Soul).

In 1964, P. Ramlee left Singapore for Kuala Lumpur, where he joined Merdeka Film Productions.

Ramli, A. (1948–) Singer. Born Ramlee Ahmad, he was one of the POP YE YE singers in the 1960s. He recorded 20 albums and won the Anugerah Penyanyi Popular Singapura (Award for the Most Popular Singer in Singapore). Among his hits were 'Oh Fatimah', 'Ku Nanti Kau Pulang' (I Await Your Return) and 'Kenangan Mengusik Jiwa' (Memories Stir My Soul). He was diagnosed with Parkinson's disease in 1992.

Ramli Sarip (1952–) Singer. Also known as 'Papa Rock', Ramli Sarip was a member of the group Sweet Charity in the late 1970s. After releasing nine albums with Sweet Charity, including *Pelarian* (Escapee) and *Live Reunion*, he started a solo career in 1989. He has produced eight solo albums and two duet albums. His repertoire includes rock songs, ballads and Malay folk songs. In 1998, he was given the Excellence Award by the Composers and Authors Society of Singapore (COMPASS).

Ransome, Sir Gordon (1910–1978) Doctor. Sir Gordon Arthur Ransome may be considered the founder of modern medicine in Singapore. Born in England, he earned a licence to practise medicine from the Royal College of Surgeons and Physicians of London in 1933. In six years of postgraduate studies, he earned the Membership of the Royal College of Physicians in 1935 and passed part one of both the Graduate Diploma Programme in Tropical Medicine and Hygiene and the Fellowship of the Royal College of Surgeons. In 1938, he arrived in Singapore as associate professor of medicine, KING EDWARD VII COLLEGE OF MEDICINE.

During the war, Ransome served in India and Burma (now Myanmar), and established a method of feeding patients unconscious from cerebral malaria—by feeding them with a tube to the stomach. He replaced Brunel Hawes as professor of medicine in 1948, and held the title until his retirement, when he was made emeritus professor. Together with BENJAMIN SHEARES and YEOH GHIM SENG, Ransome was a founder-member of the Singapore Academy of Medicine, and its first master in 1957. Besides teaching, he was also a clinician, and headed a unit at the Singapore General Hospital from the 1950s to 1969. When he retired in 1971, after 33 years in the region, the Gordon Arthur Ransome Oration was inaugurated in his honour. It is given every two years during the Singapore-Malaysia Congress of Medicine, organized by the Academy of Medicine, Singapore.

Ransome was made a Commander of the Order of the British Empire (CBE) in 1962. In 1967, he was given the Meritorious Service Medal. He received the Datoship of the Sultan of Kelantan in 1969, the year in which he was awarded an Honorary Doctorate of Medicine. He also received an Honorary Fellowship of the College of General Practitioners, Singapore, in 1973.

Rao, B.N. (1908–unknown) Film director. B.N. Rao began his career in India in 1935. He became one of several Indian directors brought in by local studios to make Malay films. Between 1953 and 1956, he made nine movies for the SHAW BROTHERS, including *Hujan Panas* (Hot Rain) (1953). He later joined CATHAY-KERIS FILMS, where he directed 14 movies between 1956 and 1964, including *Mahsuri* (The Maid of Langkawi) (1958) and the *Pontianak* (Vampire) series, comprising PONTIANAK (1957), *Dendam Pontianak* (Revenge of the Vampire) (1957), *Sumpah Pontianak* (Curse of the Vampire) (1958) and *Pontianak Gua Musang* (The Vampire of the Cave) (1964), his last Singapore-made film. Rao returned to India, where he was filming Indian movies until 1974.

Ratnam, S.S. (1928–2001) Doctor. Born in Sri Lanka, Shanmugaratnam Sittampalam, also known as S. Shan Ratnam or S.S. Ratnam, graduated with an MBBS from Sri Lanka in 1957. In 1964, he obtained his MRCOG, FRCSE (Obstetrics and Gynaecology), FRCSGlas and FRCS, followed by the FRCOG in 1972.

Ratnam joined the University of Singapore and was stationed at Kandang Kerbau Hospital in 1963. In 1970, he was appointed professor and head of the Department of Obstetrics and Gynaecology, a post he held until 1995. He continued to serve as professorial fellow in the department until 2001. He was also the

director of the Postgraduate School of Medicine until 1999.

S.S. Ratnam performed the first sex change (male to female) operation in Asia at the Kandang Kerbau Hospital in July 1971. It was the culmination of his research interest on sex reassignment surgery for transsexuals, which was his forte for nearly three decades. Twenty years later a Gender Identity Clinic and Gender Reassignment Surgery Clinic were set up at the National University Hospital, headed by Ratnam until his retirement in 1995. He led the team to produce Asia's first in-vitro fertilization baby in May 1983, Asia's first frozen embryo babies in 1987, and the world's first microinjection baby in 1989.

Ratnam became the first president of the Obstetrical & Gynaecological Society of Singapore in 1972. He collaborated with the World Health Organization (WHO) on numerous research projects and was director of the WHO Collaborating Centre for Research in Human Reproduction, and of the WHO Collaborating Centre for Maternal & Child Health. He was president-elect of the International Federation of Gynaecology and Obstetrics (1982–85) and its president (1985–88). Ratnam was posthumously made an honorary fellow of the College of Family Physicians.

recessions After merger with Malaysia, Singapore's activities as an entrepôt were badly affected by Indonesia's policy of CONFRONTATION (1963–64). In 1964, Singapore suffered a recession, with the economy contracting by 3.8 per cent.

Following Independence in 1965, the government pursued an export-led INDUSTRIALIZATION strategy. Singapore experienced the fastest growth in its economic history in this immediate post-Separation period. Yet it was brought to an abrupt halt by the first international oil crisis of 1973. Growth slowed to 6.1 per cent in 1974, and 4.1 per cent in 1975.

While most oil-importing countries were badly affected by the second international oil shock of 1979, Singapore had already become an important oil-refining and exporting centre, and hence economic growth was not so adversely affected by the crisis. Singapore then implemented a three-year wage-adjustment policy to restructure the economy towards higher value-added industries. The consequent domestic cost pressures and a sharp weakening of the external environment led to a severe recession in 1985, when the economy shrank by 1.4 per cent. The implementation of several cost-cutting measures by the government, coupled with wage restraint on the part of workers, enabled the economy to rebound the following year.

As a result of the ASIAN FINANCIAL CRISIS (1997–98), Singapore's economy contracted by 1.4 per cent in 1998. It recovered strongly in the following two years, grow-

P.S. Raman

Sir Gordon Ransome

S.S. Ratnam

Ramli Sarip

Rediffusion: newspaper advertisement, 1950s; record of finalists of Rediffusion Mandarin singing contest, 1967.

Red junglefowl

Red House Bakery

ing by 7.2 per cent in 1999 and 10.0 per cent in 2000. But with the bursting of the 'dot.com bubble' in 2000, followed by the 9/11 terrorist attacks, the economy shrank by 2.3 per cent in 2001. A package of off-budget measures implemented by the government in October 2001 spurred economic recovery, with a growth rate of 4 per cent in 2002. And despite the outbreak of Severe Acute Respiratory Syndrome in 2003, the economy managed to grow by 2.9 per cent that year. Real recovery came only in 2004, with growth of 8.7 per cent.

reclamation *See* LAND RECLAMATION.

Recorder The office of Recorder was created with the issue of the Second Charter of Justice in 1826. Originally, Recorders were part-time judges who sat on courts in towns or boroughs in the United Kingdom. In Singapore's early colonial history, it was considered a small outpost, and its court the equivalent of that servicing a British town or borough. Nevertheless, 'Recorders of the Court of Judicature' were men of high legal standing: all were knighted, and many went on to become chief justices in other colonies and British possessions. However, the first Recorder of the STRAITS SETTLEMENTS, Sir John Claridge, was recalled to face charges of insubordination, and administration of the courts fell to ROBERT FULLERTON, the Resident. Meanwhile, budget cuts prevented the appointment of a new Recorder until 1833.

The office of Recorder was abolished when the Straits Settlements Supreme Court was created in 1867.

Red Cross In 1859, Swiss businessman Henry Dunant proposed the creation of national relief societies comprising volunteers who could be trained in peacetime to provide neutral and impartial help to people in times of war. The founding charter of the Red Cross was drawn up in 1863.

The British Red Cross Society began its work in Singapore on 30 September 1949. The Singapore Red Cross was incorporated by an act of Parliament on 6 April 1973.

Rediffusion: Ong Toh on the air in 1978.

Red House Bakery This shophouse in Katong, with its bright red facade, was built initially as a private residence with a sea view, but in 1925 one Jim Baker opened a bakery on its premises. In 1931, Baker sold the business to Tan Siang Fuan, a Hainanese seaman, for $600. Tan's son, Tan See Fang, later took over operations of the Katong Bakery & Confectionery Company.

The bakery was famous for making the first three-tier wedding cake in the 1920s. It was also known for its fresh Swiss rolls, *char siew* (barbecued pork) and pork *pau* (buns), cakes and curry puffs. The bakery closed in 2003.

The shophouse itself is a WAKAF property managed by MAJLIS UGAMA ISLAM SINGAPURA since the 1990s. The property was put in trust by Sheriffa Zain Alsharoff Syed Mohamed Alsagoff (a descendant of Hajjah FATIMAH). She stipulated that earnings from the shophouse should be channelled towards providing free medicine to people regardless of race or religion.

The renovated Red House—which will keep its signature colour—is scheduled to open in 2006 as a multi-tenant food and beverage complex with a halal food court.

red junglefowl (*Gallus gallus*) The ancestor of all domestic chickens, the red junglefowl is native to Asia and was first domesticated in India about 5,200 years ago. The bird lives in thickly wooded areas, and feeds on seeds, buds, fruits and insects. The male is 'polygamous' and takes no part in nest-building or rearing of the young.

The red junglefowl was not recorded in Singapore until a small breeding population was discovered in 1985 on PULAU UBIN.

Rediffusion Cable radio service. Rediffusion started as British Electric Traction—a company which provided power cables for trams in the United Kingdom in the late 19th century and early 20th century. When RADIO BROADCASTING began in the United Kingdom in 1922, the company decided to capitalize on its existing network of cables by running additional 'cable radio wires' through them. These wires carried radio signals using an alternating current (AC) through the same cables that carried direct-current (DC) power to trams. Thus, Rediffusion (literally 'broadcasting again') was founded in March 1928.

Rediffusion was first introduced to Singapore in 1949, marking the company's

first foray into broadcasting in Asia. The combination of affordable subscriptions ($5 a month) and local programming made the service extremely popular, and the ubiquitous Rediffusion box was soon found in almost every home, shop and office.

Many well-known names from Singapore's entertainment industry were first featured on Rediffusion. Cantonese storyteller Lee Dai-Soh and his Hokkien counterpart, Ong Toh, all began their careers on Rediffusion.

In the 1970s, Rediffusion, like radio itself, lost some of its popularity due to the rise of television. However, it has continued to broadcast to its customers (for a monthly charge) and, since 2000, it has ventured into digital audio broadcasting.

Reflections at Bukit Chandu WORLD WAR II 'interpretative centre', developed and managed by the NATIONAL ARCHIVES OF SINGAPORE. Located at 31-K Pepys Road, off Pasir Panjang Road, the restored Tudor-style colonial bungalow is the last remaining of three buildings which originally stood on Bukit Chandu (also known as Opium Hill). It was the site of one of the fiercest encounters in the BATTLE OF PASIR PANJANG in February 1942.

The centre commemorates the bravery of the men of the MALAY REGIMENT and also tells the tales of other survivors of the JAPANESE OCCUPATION.

Regional Language Centre The Regional Language Centre (RELC) was formerly known as the Regional English Language Centre and was introduced by the Southeast Asian Ministers of Education Organization (SEAMEO) in July 1968. Its headquarters were in Singapore.

The main goals of the RELC have been to train 'key personnel' in language education, and organize seminars on various issues of linguistic, psycholinguistic, sociolinguistic and educational interest to the region, as well as to disseminate information. Another stated aim of the RELC is to promote international cooperation among language professionals and provide consultancy and advisory services.

Originally located at Watten Estate, the RELC relocated to premises on Orange Grove Road in May 1972. In 1977, the centre became known as the Regional Language Centre, reflecting its expanded role in language-teacher education in the

RECORDERS OF THE STRAITS SETTLEMENTS	
1827–29	Sir John Thomas Claridge
1829–33	Vacant
1833–35	Sir Benjamin Malkin
1835–36	Sir Edward Gambier
1836–47	Sir William Norris
1847–50	Sir Christoper Rawlinson
1850–55	Sir William Jeffcott
1856–66	Sir Richard Bolton McCausland
1856–66	Sir Peter Benson Maxwell

Ren Ci Hospital and Medicare Centre

region. However, it continues to be known by the abbreviation 'RELC'.

The centre is an autonomous international institution administered by a director, under the overall policy direction of a governing board. The board is composed of one representative from each member country appointed by the SEAMEO Council on the recommendation of each country's minister of education.

The centre publishes the *RELC Journal*, *Journal of Southeast Asian Education* and several anthologies. It conducts courses in languages from outside the region. The RELC also holds conferences and seminars, such as the RELC International Seminar, which is held in April each year.

Registry of Marriages Even though marriage records in Singapore can be traced back to 1875, it was not till 15 September 1961 that the Registry of Marriages (ROM) was established. In 1961, the first batch of 160 couples was married under the WOMEN'S CHARTER. The following year, 4,900 marriages were registered; by the time civil marriage was fully legislated in 1967, 10,500 couples were married. In recent years, the ROM has solemnized about 21,000 marriages a year.

Although most marriages in Singapore are solemnized and registered at the ROM, couples may opt to be married in church by priests or in civil ceremonies by justices of the peace. In the early days, the ROM was housed at a bungalow at Fort Canning. In 1983, it was relocated to Canning Rise.

Registry of Muslim Marriages Provisions in the ADMINISTRATION OF MUSLIM LAW ACT, passed in 1966, regulate the registration of Muslim marriages and divorces. Since 1978, the registration of Muslim marriages and divorces have been separated, with marriages handled by the newly formed Registry of Muslim Marriages (ROMM) and divorces handled by the Syariah Court.

The main function of the ROMM is the registration and solemnization of Muslim marriages. Marriages are solemnized by a *kadi* (senior official), of whom there were more than 30 in 2006. The reg-

istry, in conjunction with other organizations, also runs family life and marriage education programmes for couples. Marriage guidance courses are compulsory, and there are courses specially for young couples aged 16–20.

The ROMM solemnizes marriages of Muslim couples only; mixed-religion marriages are referred to the REGISTRY OF MARRIAGES. In the case of polygynous marriages, the prospective couple, as well as the existing wife or wives, must be interviewed separately before the marriage can be registered and solemnized.

The ROMM was initially located in a bungalow at Fort Canning Park. It moved to Canning Rise in 1983.

Ren Ci Hospital and Medicare Centre Welfare organization. Established in 1994 by the Foo Hai Ch'an (Buddhist) Monastery, the centre provides medical, nursing and rehabilitative care for people suffering from severe physical disabilities or long-term illnesses. Most of its patients are underprivileged. The centre has two facilities, one in Hougang and one in Moulmein.

The hospital raises funds to subsidize the cost of care. The hospital's chief executive officer, Venerable SHI MING YI, has taken part in fund-raising shows on television.

The new Ren Ci Hospital, scheduled for completion in 2008, will have 277 beds, outpatient clinics, laboratories and a Traditional Chinese Medicine clinic. It will be located at Irrawaddy Road.

Rendel Commission In 1953, the British government established the Rendel Commission in an attempt to speed up progress towards self-government in Singapore through increased public participation in political affairs. The commission, asked to conduct a comprehensive review of the CONSTITUTION, was headed by Sir George Rendel. Other members of the commission were E.J. Davies, T.P.F. McNeice, TAN CHIN TUAN, LIM YEW HOCK, N.A. MALLAL, C.C. TAN, AHMAD MOHAMED IBRAHIM, C.F. Smith and John D. Higham (Secretary).

The Rendel Commission recommended automatic registration of voters (i.e. voters were not required to complete a registration form before they could vote) and a new Legislative Council of 32 members, 25 of whom would be elected Unofficial members, three of whom would be ex-officio Official members, and four of whom would be nominated Unofficial members.

The commission also recommended the creation of a Council of Ministers comprising three ex-officio Official members and six elected members appointed by the governor on the recommendation of the LEADER OF THE HOUSE, who would be the leader of the largest party in the assembly or of a coalition of parties assured of majority

Rendel Commission

support. These recommendations were implemented under the 1955 constitution, and 79 candidates contested the 25 seats at the general election that followed.

One major problem with the Rendel constitution was that ministers' powers, especially those of the chief minister, were not well-defined. Furthermore, the retention of the portfolios of finance, administration and internal security and law by the British proved to be a major impediment to the development of self-government. Difficulties emerged in the working relationship between the British and the newly elected chief minister DAVID MARSHALL, and the Rendel Constitution was later superseded by the State of Singapore Constitution.

Rent Control Act The colonial government introduced the Rent Control Act in 1947, in an attempt to deal with spiralling rents and the severe housing shortage of the immediate post-war era.

The aim of the act was to protect tenants. However, landowners were discouraged from building new homes because of the necessity to comply with rent controls that the act entailed. At the same time, an inability on the part of landowners to raise rents resulted in the condition of many properties deteriorating. The act thus failed to ease housing shortages; furthermore, it prompted prospective or desperate tenants to start offering 'tea money' (bribes) to

Reflections at Bukit Chandu: sculpture depicting men of the Malay Regiment.

reptiles and amphibians

Singapore has a high diversity of reptiles and amphibians (collectively known as herpetofauna), with about 150 recorded species of reptile (over 90 of which are snakes) and 27 species of amphibian. The first accounts of snake and lizard diversity in Singapore were published in the 1920s. Since that time, at least 14 species of reptile and one species of amphibian—the endemic caecilian (*Ichthyophis singaporensis*)—appear to have become locally extinct.

1

2

3   4

Many commercially valuable herpetofauna are prone to human exploitation. Crocodiles and marine turtles in Singapore's immediate region have suffered significant population declines due to a long history of excessive hunting and the collection of their eggs by humans. However, the biggest threat to herpetofauna is habitat destruction. Large tracts of natural habitat in Singapore have been cleared to make room for housing and industrial development.

Nonetheless, some large reptiles can still be found in Singapore. The world's largest living reptile, the salt-water crocodile (*Crocodylus porosus*) is extremely rare, but has been occasionally seen along the coast and in estuaries. The water monitor lizard (*Varanus salvator*), sometimes mistaken for the crocodile, is common. It can often be seen sunning itself or prowling along the edges of canals, even in built-up areas with heavy human traffic.

In addition, since 1989, five species of amphibian and ten species of reptile have been recorded in Singapore for the first time. These include the four-ridged toad (*Bufo quadriporcatus*) (**1**), the Bornean chorus frog (*Microhyla borneensis*) (**2**), the five-banded flying dragon (*Draco quinquefasciatus*) (**3**), the blue bronzeback (*Dendrelaphis cyanochloris*) (**5**), the brown tree skink (*Dasia grisea*) and Kuhl's gliding gecko (*Ptychozoon kuhli*) (**4**).

5

Rainforests

The rainforest habitats found in the Bukit Timah Nature Reserve and Central Catchment Nature Reserve are home to many reptiles and amphibians. The banded bent-toed gecko (*Cyrtodactylus consubrinus*) is a lizard that dwells in trees and on large boulders. The Wagler's pit-viper (*Tropidolaemus wagleri*) (**6**) is a venomous snake that sits coiled and motionless in shrubs, waiting for birds and lizards to approach within striking range.

The spotted keelback (*Xenochrophis maculatus*) hunts for frogs in the leaf litter. Forest streams are home to the forest softshell turtle (*Dogania subplana*) (**7**), a nocturnal animal that spends the day buried in mud. The Sumatran banded caecilian (*Ichthyophis paucisulcus*) is a rarely seen burrowing amphibian; it resembles a large worm with eyes.

The world's longest living snake can also be found in Singapore. Known to grow to almost 10 m in length, the reticulated python (*Python reticulatus*) (**8**) is not only found in Singapore's forests and amongst mangroves, but also in the city's sewers.

6

7

8

Mangroves

The mangrove forests that fringe the northern coast of Singapore are the natural habitat of the mangrove pit-viper (*Cryptelytrops purpureomaculatus*) (**9**), a venomous tree-dwelling snake that sits motionless on branches in the day, and becomes active at night. The mildly venomous and aquatic dog-faced water snake (*Cerberus rynchops*) (**11**) is common in mangrove streams, where it can be seen hunting for fishes at night. The crab-eating frog (*Fejervarya cancrivora*) (**10**) eats small crabs, as well as insects, and is one of the few amphibians able to tolerate salt water.

9

10

11

Urban areas, parks and open grassland

Many species of reptile and amphibian have adapted to living in Singapore's urban environment. The most conspicuous are probably the geckos (*Hemidactylus frenatus*, *Cosymbotus platyurus*, and *Gehyra mutilata*) that scamper over walls and ceilings in many homes. In gardens, the changeable lizard (*Calotes versicolor*) (**14**) clings to fences. While very common now, this species is not native to Singapore. They occur naturally in northern peninsular Malaysia and have only been noted in Singapore from the early 1980s. In garden hedges, the pencil-thin and emerald green oriental whip snake (*Ahaetulla prasina*) (**12**) tries to escape detection by hiding in the bushes, swaying its body along with the foliage when the wind blows. Gliders such as the paradise tree snake (*Chrysopelea paradisi*) and the Sumatran flying dragon (*Draco sumatranus*) (**13**) can be found in many urban parks. To maintain buoyancy in the air, the former flattens its body such that a cushion of air is trapped underneath it, while the latter has a pair of broad skin flaps on its side, supported by ribs extending beyond its body.

In roadside drains and puddles, the loud bellow of the painted bullfrog (*Kaloula pulchra*) (**15**) can be heard on rainy nights. In open grassy spaces, the black spitting cobra (*Naja sumatrana*) can sometimes be seen. It greets human trespassers by rearing up, flattening its neck and emitting a loud hissing sound. The king cobra (*Ophiophagus hannah*) (**16**), the world's largest venomous snake, and one of the most most dangerous snakes in the world, has been sighted on Singapore's golf courses and farmland.

12

13

15

14   16

property owners, in return for which premises would be made available to them.

In 1970, the Controlled Premises (Special Provisions) Act was introduced. It allowed landlords to repossess properties for redevelopment, by compensating tenants for vacating the premises. Rent control was finally abolished in 2001.

reptiles and amphibians *See* box.

Republic of Singapore Air Force The ancestry of Singapore's air force can be traced to the Singapore Volunteer Air Force, which was established during World War II. After SEPARATION in 1965, Singapore inherited air bases from the departing British, and set up the Republic of Singapore Air Force (RSAF) with refurbished second-hand aircraft such as Hunters and A4 Skyhawks, and Bloodhound anti-aircraft missiles.

By the late 1980s, investment in air defence had transformed the RSAF into one of the region's most modern air forces. The RSAF acquired four E2C Hawkeye airborne early warning aircraft and eight F-16A/B jetfighters. These modern aircraft complemented the RSAF's existing Skyhawks (which had been re-engined and equipped with advanced avionics), Hunters and F-5E Tiger fighter-bombers.

In the early 1990s, the RSAF's F-5E fleet was upgraded. And in 1994, Singapore began to procure large numbers of F-16C/D jetfighters. These provided the air force with new all-weather fighter-bomber capabilities.

By 2005, the RSAF's fleet of combat aircraft included F-16C/Ds, F-5Es and A4-SU Super Skyhawks. The RSAF also procured air-to-air refuelling tankers, as well as Fokker 50 aircraft, an assortment of transport aircraft, medium and heavy helicopters (such as Super Pumas and Chinooks) and a fleet of S211 training aircraft. In 2006, the RSAF decided to acquire the US-made F-15SG Strike Eagle.

The air force also operates Searcher UAVs (Unmanned Airborne Vehicles). Its ground-based air defence capability consists of Improved Hawk, RBS-70, Rapier, Mistral and SA-18 Igla missiles and 35-mm Oerlikon guns.

The RSAF operates out of four airbases: Tengah, Paya Lebar, Sembawang and Changi. It can also operate from prepared

HMS Repulse

roadways should the airbases be rendered inoperative in the event of attack. Due to a lack of available space in Singapore, the RSAF maintains overseas training facilities in Australia, France and the United States.

See also SINGAPORE ARMED FORCES.

Republic of Singapore Navy The forerunner of the Republic of Singapore Navy was the Straits Settlements Royal Navy Volunteer Reserve, which was established in 1934. After SEPARATION, the Singapore Naval Volunteer Force was established on 1 January 1966. It was subsequently renamed the People's Defence (Sea), Sea Defence Command (1967) and then the Maritime Command (1968). On 1 April 1975, when the SINGAPORE ARMED FORCES made its three component forces into distinct services, the Republic of Singapore Navy (RSN) came into being.

The RSN remained little more than a coastal patrol and army support force for many years. By the early 1980s, however, it had acquired six Vosper Thornycroft large patrol boats; six Lurssen TNC-45 missile gun boats; 12 coastal patrol craft; five ex-US Navy County-class landing ship tanks (LSTs); and two ex-US Navy minesweepers. In 1983, the RSN announced that it had decided to acquire the capability to patrol Singapore's sea lanes of communications. This led to the purchase of six 62-m missile corvettes.

In the 1990s a major expansion of the navy was undertaken, involving the upgrading of existing missile craft and the acquisition of new vessels. Harpoon anti-ship missiles equipped the RSN's existing missile gunboats and corvettes. Barak anti-missile defences were fitted onto the RSN corvettes in 1996.

Other new deliveries included four Landsort mine counter-measure vessels from Sweden and twelve 500-ton Fearless-class patrol vessels. Four ex-Swedish Sjoormen-class submarines were acquired and refurbished. To replace its ageing LSTs, the navy also acquired four new 6,000-ton, 141-m Endurance-class LSTs. It also placed orders in 2000 for six 3,200-ton Lafayette frigates from France.

The RSN operates out of two bases: one at Tuas; the second at Changi. The Changi Naval Base often plays host to vis-

iting foreign warships and can accommodate visiting US Navy aircraft carriers.

Republic Polytechnic Founded in August 2002, Singapore's newest polytechnic started operations in the premises of the Data Storage Institute at the National University of Singapore, before moving to its Tanglin Campus (the former Ministry of Education Building at Kay Siang Road). Republic Polytechnic took in its first cohort of 800 students in July 2003. In March 2006, it moved to a permanent home in Woodlands.

It is the first polytechnic to have a School of Sports, Health and Leisure. The polytechnic's four other schools include: Applied Science; Engineering; Information and Communications Technology; and Technology for the Arts. It has five centres: Culture and Communication; Educational Development; Innovation and Enterprise; Science and Mathematics; and Professional Development. It is the first educational institution in Singapore to fully adopt the problem-based learning approach. The school's founding principal and chief executive offcer is Professor Low Teck Seng.

Repulse, HMS This British battlecruiser, built in 1916, formed part of the ill-fated

Republic of Singapore Navy

Republic of Singapore Air Force

Restroom Association (Singapore)

FORCE Z, which arrived in Singapore on 2 December 1941, only to be defeated by Japanese aircraft off the coast of Malaya on 10 December. The vessel was hit by torpedoes and sank at 12.35 p.m. on 10 December, only an hour before the sinking of HMS PRINCE OF WALES.

reservoirs Construction of the first major waterworks in Singapore started in 1868, when municipal commissioners decided to build an impounding reservoir to provide piped water to the town. The reservoir was completed in 1877, and was named the Impounding Reservoir.

This reservoir was enlarged twice (in 1894 and 1904) by municipal engineer JAMES MACRITCHIE. The reservoir was renamed Thomson Road Reservoir in 1907, and then MACRITCHIE RESERVOIR in 1922, in recognition of MacRitchie's work.

Singapore's second impounding reservoir was the Kallang River Reservoir. This was created when a dam was built in 1910 across the lower reaches of the KALLANG RIVER. In 1922, the reservoir was renamed Peirce Reservoir in honour of the work of Robert Peirce, the municipal engineer who had planned it. In 1975, Peirce Reservoir was enlarged and divided when a dam was constructed in its upper reaches, forming Upper and Lower Peirce Reservoirs.

Over the years, many reservoirs have been built by damming rivers, most of them named after the rivers concerned. These include Jurong Lake Kranji Reservoir; Tengah Reservoir; Upper and Lower Seletar Reservoirs; Pandan Reservoir; Murai Reservoir; Poyan Reservoir; and Sarimbun Reservoir.

Singapore also has a number of service or covered reservoirs where treated water is stored for distribution during peak periods; these are located on high ground, so that the cost of pumping can be reduced. The first of these was Fort Canning Reservoir,

built in 1822 to supply water to ships in the harbour. It was expanded in 1928.

Other service reservoirs include Pearl's Hill Service Reservoir; Murnane Service Reservoir; Jalan Eunos Service Reservoir; Bukit Panjang Service Reservoir; Central Service Reservoir; Changi Creek Service Reservoir; and Yishun Service Reservoir. Plans have also been introduced for new reservoirs, such as Marina Reservoir (*see* MARINA BARRAGE), Punggol Reservoir and Serangoon Reservoir.

Residents' Committees Organizations introduced in public housing estates in 1978, to promote neighbourliness and harmony. Residents' Committees (RCs) organize activities for residents and work with government agencies to improve the living environment in their neighbourhoods. Like CITIZENS' CONSULTATIVE COMMITTEES, RCs initially came under the Prime Minister's Office and, later, the Ministry of Community Development. Since 1993, RCs have come under the purview of the PEOPLE'S ASSOCIATION. As of 2006, there were over 550 RCs.

Restroom Association (Singapore) Non-profit organization. Established in 1998, the Restroom Association (Singapore) (RAS) aims 'to promote the development, research, usage and attitudes, aesthetics and functionality in the design of public toilets in Singapore'. Working closely with Community Development Councils, schools and grassroots organizations, the RAS promotes clean toilets and encourages productivity in the cleaning industry. The RAS is the founding member of the World Toilet Organisation.

revenue farming In the 18th and 19th centuries, revenue farming was common in Southeast Asia as a means of collecting revenue for the state. The state gave a pri-

vate contractor exclusive rights, for a specific period, to collect taxes or provide goods and services. In return, the private contractor paid the state a fixed rent and enjoyed certain rights. The Chinese and the Dutch together developed a model of tax farming, in which the revenue farm was auctioned to the highest bidder. This mode of revenue farming was also adopted by the British.

Revenue farming was introduced to Singapore in 1820 by WILLIAM FARQUHAR, against Sir STAMFORD RAFFLES' wishes. Farquhar auctioned monopoly rights for the operation of gambling dens and the sale of arrack (spirits) and OPIUM. Between 1823 and 1825, revenue from such tax-farms nearly tripled, from under $26,000 to over $75,000. This revenue would continue to rise, in part due to the increase in trade and production.

With the exception of the Indian-held toddy farm, it was the Chinese, with their numerical strength and organizational network, who dominated revenue farming. Chinese merchants like CHEANG HONG LIM, TAN YEOK NEE and TAN KHEAM HOCK made their fortunes from revenue farms.

In the 1860s and again in 1907, there were proposals to replace revenue farming with income tax. However, these met with little support, and revenue farming continued. Until the early 20th century, opium-farming accounted for more than half of government revenue. However, a series of crises in the commodity markets to which Singapore exported, coupled with a rise in the international anti-opium movement, led to the eventual demise of the revenue farming institution in Singapore.

Rex Cinema A SHAW BROTHERS cinema, the Rex opened in 1946 with the inaugural screening of *The Jungle Book* (1942). It ceased operations in 1983, having screened its last film, *Jaws 3-D* (1983). The Rex was located on MacKenzie Road, conveniently next to the bus depot of the Singapore Traction Company.

rickshaws Human-powered two-wheeled wooden vehicles used mainly in Asia. The first rickshaws appeared in Japan around 1869, during the Meiji era. The word 'rickshaw' originates from the Japanese term '*jin-rikisha*' ('*jin*' means 'human', '*riki*' means 'force', and '*sha*' means 'vehicle').

The rickshaw was introduced into Singapore in 1880. It not only provided a new way of getting around, but also gave rise to a new type of employment for the less-educated. Until the clampdown on SECRET SOCIETIES in 1890, most rickshaw coolies (*see* COOLIE TRADE) were HOKKIEN and CANTONESE. The HOCKCHEW and HENGHUA then gradually took over. By 1888, it was estimated that there were over 5,000 rickshaw coolies, a number which quadrupled by the early 1900s.

Rex Cinema as it was in the 1950s.

Rickshaw pulling was a physically demanding occupation, and the age of rickshaw coolies ranged from 21 to 50. Most were unmarried and lived in crowded tenement housing. They plied their trade within the confines of the area they lived in due to ethnic rivalries and restrictions imposed by the secret societies.

A ride on a rickshaw cost 6 cents per mile (1.6 km) in the 1890s, and in 1893, a coolie could earn a daily gross amount of 40 cents. Rickshaws were let out on two shifts. The day puller went out at 6 a.m. and returned between 2 and 3 p.m., while the night puller had a choice between two shifts: 2 p.m. to midnight, or 5 p.m. to 3 a.m. Owners preferred daytime pullers who were non-smokers of OPIUM. The Opium Commission of 1908 estimated that the number of rickshaw coolies who were smokers was 30–40 per cent, although it was thought to be as high as 80 per cent if those who used opium intermittently were included. Advancement from coolie to owner status was possible during the early years, although less than 5 per cent of total owners had more than 50 rickshaws. Most owners possessed fewer than 20 rickshaws.

The colonial government created the Rickshaw Department in 1892 to register rickshaws and to regulate vehicle cleanliness. Unclean rickshaws were impounded by the Malay peons acting under the strictures of the Rickshaw Ordinance. The need to ensure cleanliness meant that the owners received less profit. This led to the Rickshaw Strike of 1897. Owners refused to allow their rickshaws to ply for hire until the department relaxed the rules. The strike lasted four days and crippled the transportation system. Over 15,000 rickshaw coolies were left idle, with owners losing about $3,000 a day in earnings.

In 1904, the Rickshaw Department opened a Jinricksha Station at the junction of Neil Road and Tanjong Pagar Road. The station was adjacent to the thoroughfare leading from the nearby Tanjong Pagar Docks to the town area, making it an ideal location to pick up passengers.

By 1924, there were about 28,000 rickshaws on the roads. The number started to decline by the mid-1930s. They were eventually replaced by trishaws and other modes

Ring of Fury *(1973)*

of transport. The Jinricksha Station, however, has been conserved and still stands.

Ridley, Henry (1855–1956) Colonial official and scientist. Born in Norfolk, United Kingdom, Henry Nicholas Ridley attended Haileybury School where he became an active member of the school's natural history society. He later attended Exeter College at Oxford University, obtaining a second-class honours degree in science in 1877.

Ridley was then offered a position at the British Museum's Botany Department. In 1886, he joined an expedition to Fernando de Noronha—an island off the coast of Brazil—that had been sponsored by the Royal Society, and completed reports on the botany, zoology and geology of that island. Ridley first came to Singapore in 1888, when he was appointed director of the Botanic Gardens (*see* SINGAPORE BOTANIC GARDENS). In Singapore, he became known as 'Mad Ridley' or 'Rubber Ridley' due to his obsession with RUBBER trees. Ridley worked in the gardens for over 20 years, propagating Brazilian rubber plants that had been shipped to Singapore from London's Kew Gardens; experimenting with seeds; and developing a new method of tapping—a technique that came to be widely used in the rubber industry.

From 1896, most of the early rubber estates in Malaya grew rubber trees from seeds provided by the Botanic Gardens. Ridley sent seeds to other parts of the world after devising a method of packing that ensured the survival of a high proportion of seeds on long journeys.

Ridley also explored the region's forests and islands, identifying and collecting plant species. For instance, he identified 73 new species of the ginger family in

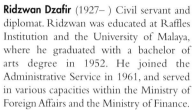

Henry Ridley, left, with rubber tree.

Malaya—in the three decades following his retirement, only 30 more were discovered.

After retiring from his Singapore post in 1912, Ridley began work on his monumental *Flora of the Malay Peninsula* at Kew, where he resided for the rest of his life. The first of its five volumes was published in 1922. Later, Ridley completed another major work, *The Dispersal of Plants throughout the World*. This 740-page book first appeared in 1930. Ridley remained keenly interested in botany, and spent the rest of his long life increasing his knowledge of tropical plants.

Ridzwan Dzafir (1927–) Civil servant and diplomat. Ridzwan was educated at Raffles Institution and the University of Malaya, where he graduated with a bachelor of arts degree in 1952. He joined the Administrative Service in 1961, and served in various capacities within the Ministry of Foreign Affairs and the Ministry of Finance.

In 1983, Ridzwan was appointed director-general of the Trade Development Board, a post he occupied until 1998. In 1986, he was appointed non-resident ambassador to Argentina, Brazil, Chile and Panama. He has also served as high commissioner to Bangladesh (1997–99); pro-chancellor of the National University of Singapore (1993–); member of the Council of Presidential Advisers (1991–); and member of the Presidential Council for Minority Rights (2005–).

Ring of Fury (1973) Film. Directed by Tony Yeow and James Sebastian, *Ring of Fury* was one of a host of kung fu movies produced in the wake of Bruce Lee's success. It starred local karate master Peter Chong, in the role of a hawker who, resisting extortion by gangsters, is forced to learn martial arts for self-defence. A controversial rape scene in the jungle was cut from the movie. The film was banned for its depiction of gangsters and Chinese SECRET SOCIETIES. It was not officially premiered in Singapore until 2005, 32 years after it was made.

Ridzwan Dzafir

Rickshaws

Sir William Robinson

Ritz-Carlton, Millenia Singapore, The This hotel was designed by American architect Kevin Roche, and was built at a cost of $470 million. It opened in January 1996 with 608 rooms and 32 storeys.

The Ritz-Carlton, Millenia Singapore is jointly owned by the property investment and development company Pontiac Marina and SINGAPORE AIRLINES, the latter with a 20 per cent stake. Pontiac Marina is a subsidiary of the family-owned Pontiac Land group. Pontiac Land purchased the 7-ha site for the hotel in 1989 from Indonesian businessman Hendra Rahardja, who had planned to build three hotels there in the 1980s.

The Ritz-Carlton, Millenia Singapore holds a 4,200-piece art collection. This contains lithographs, paintings and sculptures, and 350 pieces that were specially commissioned by the hotel. The collection includes works by David Hockney, Andy Warhol and Frank Stella.

rivers As an island with high rainfall and mainly made up of impermeable rocks, Singapore has a high-density drainage pattern. Although much of this network has been altered by the building of canals, storm drains and RESERVOIRS, some of the upper reaches of the rivers remain in a natural or semi-natural state in the interior. The overall pattern of drainage takes a radial form, with all the main rivers arising in the interior and radiating out to the low-lying lands, towards the sea. As the upper courses of many of the rivers have been dammed to create reservoirs, their 'sources' are now reservoir outflows rather than springs or saturated boggy ground.

Most of Singapore's rivers have been greatly modified, either by the construction of reservoirs in their upper courses or by the building of flood-prevention embankments in their lower courses. The KALLANG RIVER, with a total course of 16 km is Singapore's longest river, and the highly modified SELETAR RIVER, which now has reservoirs on its upper and lower courses, would have had a total length of about 11 km in its natural state. The SINGAPORE RIVER is just 6 km long. Other rivers include the Jurong River, PUNGGOL RIVER, SERANGOON RIVER and WHAMPOA RIVER.

road tax A vehicle-owner pays an annual tax, broadly reflecting the vehicle's use of road space, the road wear it causes, and the need for social equity. Specifically, for cars and motorcycles, the tax is based on engine capacity; for goods vehicles and buses, it is based on the maximum laden weight and number of axles. For vehicles more than ten years old, the tax increases at the rate of 10 per cent (of the basic road tax payable) per annum from the 11th year to a maximum of 50 per cent in the 15th year.

roads In 2005, Singapore had some 3,225 km of road. The roads are classified into five categories.

Expressways have three or more lanes running in each direction, separated by wide central medians. The speed limit is 70, 80 or 90 km per hour.

On roads of the second category—semi-expressways—the speed limit is 70 km per hour. Semi-expressways have traffic-light-controlled junctions.

The third category, major arterial roads, are either one-way with 4–5 lanes; or two-way with 2–4 lanes in each direction and usually with a central divider. The speed limit is 50, 60 or 70 km per hour.

The Ritz-Carlton, Millenia Singapore

The fourth category, collectors or distributors, are roads with 1–2 lanes running in each direction. These usually have no central divider and the speed limit on them is 50 km per hour.

The fifth category, local access roads, have one lane running in each direction and no central divider. The speed limit is 40 or 50 km per hour. Access to individual properties is given by these local access roads and collector/distributor roads, which feed traffic into and out of major arterial roads and expressways.

Robinson, Sir William (1834–1897) Colonial official. Sir William Cleaver Francis Robinson entered the service of the Colonial Office in 1858 as a private secretary to his elder brother, Hercules Robinson, who was then lieutenant-governor of St Kitts. When his brother was appointed governor of Hong Kong, William followed him in his capacity as secretary. His first major appointment was in 1862 when he returned to Montserrat as administrator for three years. In 1873 he was appointed governor for the Province of Prince Edward Island in Canada. He oversaw the union of the island with the rest of Britain's North American colonies.

In 1874, Robinson was posted to Western Australia as governor, after which in 1877 he was appointed governor of the STRAITS SETTLEMENTS, where he replaced Sir WILLIAM JERVOIS. Robinson had never visited the Malay States, but believed that the role of a Resident was solely to advise and not to rule. His term ended in 1878, and he was succeeded by acting governor Edward Anson before Sir FREDERICK WELD assumed the position definitively in 1880, the year that Robinson returned to Western Australia for a second term as governor. Robinson retired from active service in 1895.

Robinsons Department store. The firm began as Spicer & Robinson in February 1858, when Philip Robinson, who had come to

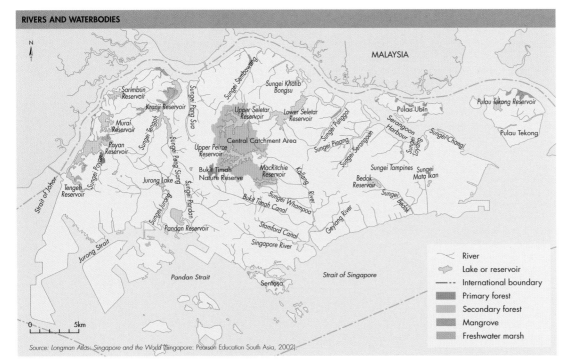

RIVERS AND WATERBODIES

MALAYSIA

Sarimbun Reservoir
Kranji Reservoir
Murai Reservoir
Poyan Reservoir
Sungei Sembawang
Sungei Khatib Bongsu
Upper Seletar Reservoir
Lower Seletar Reservoir
Sungei Pang Sua
Sungei Tengah
Sungei Peng Siang
Central Catchment Area
Upper Peirce Reservoir
Sungei Punggol
Sungei Pinang
Serangoon Harbour
Sungei Serangoon
Sungei Changi
Pulau Ubin
Pulau Tekong Reservoir
Pulau Tekong
Bukit Timah Nature Reserve
MacRitchie Reservoir
Jurong Lake
Tengeh Reservoir
Sungei Poyan
Strait of Johor
Sungei Jurong
Sungei Pandan
Bukit Timah Canal
Sungei Whampoa
Kallang River
Sungei Tampines
Sungei Mata Ikan
Bedok Reservoir
Sungei Bedok
Pandan Reservoir
Stamford Canal
Geylang River
Singapore River
Jurong Strait
Pandan Strait
Sentosa
Strait of Singapore

〜 River
Lake or reservoir
‒ ‒ ‒ International boundary
Primary forest
Secondary forest
Mangrove
Freshwater marsh

N

0   5km

Source: Longman Atlas: Singapore and the World (Singapore: Pearson Education South Asia, 2002).

Rojak

Singapore from Australia, joined James Spicer to set up a general merchandise shop catering to the local European community. Despite the success of the shop, the partnership was dissolved a year later, and Robinson moved his operations—Robinson & Co.— to premises on the corner of Coleman Street and North Bridge Road.

What distinguished Robinson & Co. from its competitors was the company's preference for hiring travelling salesmen to canvass Malaya and Borneo, rather than setting up permanent stores in the region. As a result of this strategy, the store's clientele soon included Malay and Siamese (Thai) royalty.

Philip Robinson died in 1886, and ownership of the business was transferred to his son, Stamford Raffles Robinson. The business moved to RAFFLES PLACE in 1891, and became a limited company in 1920. In 1940, the department store opened an air-conditioned café and hair salon. It kept its doors open during the Japanese attack on Singapore, despite twice being hit by bombs.

The store was looted and closed during the JAPANESE OCCUPATION, but resumed operations in April 1946, recording record profits over the following years. In 1955, it acquired rival department store JOHN LITTLE, and became the first store in Asia to be fully air-conditioned.

In November 1972, a fire at Robinsons landmark Raffles Place store claimed nine lives and destroyed the building. Robinsons subsequently moved to Specialists' Shopping Centre in Orchard Road. It moved again to Centrepoint in June 1983. A second flagship store at Raffles City opened in March 2001. The company then expanded its

reach to suburban malls throughout Singapore, operating 14 John Little and Marks & Spencer outlets.

In September 2003, a disagreement between Robinsons and OVERSEA-CHINESE BANKING CORPORATION—one of the company's substantial stakeholders—led to an attempt by Robinsons to sell off its retail business. This was met with public protests from customers and shoppers, some of whom signed petitions against divestment plans. As a result, Robinsons announced in January 2004 that it had called off the planned sale. In 2006, the Lippo Group acquired a controlling stake in Robinsons.

The group recorded net profits of nearly $37 million on revenues of $350 million in 2005.

Rodyk & Davidson Law firm. First established in 1861 as Woods & Davidson, the firm was founded by ROBERT CARR WOODS—the first editor of *The Straits Times*, who later became attorney-general—and rubber magnate James Guthrie Davidson. The firm became Rodyk & Davidson in 1877, when Bernard Rodyk joined the firm. On 1 November 2002, Rodyk & Davidson merged with Helen Yeo & Partners (a firm established in 1992). It has since established offices in Shanghai and Hong Kong.

rojak Popular hawker dish. *Rojak* is typically a tossed salad of various ingredients. Different ethnic groups have different versions of the dish. The Chinese cut up pineapple, cucumbers, turnips, bean sprouts and *youtiao* (dough fritters), and toss them with a sauce made of chilli, tamarind, lime and lime peel, and a prawn paste. The mixture is then topped with crushed roasted peanuts. The Malay version is similar except that it contains *tempeh* (a patty made from cooked, fermented soya beans) and *tahu goreng* (fried bean curd). With Indian *rojak*, customers choose which specific ingredients they would like in their dish; these might include boiled diced potatoes, hard-boiled eggs, fried bean curd, *vadai* (fried dough with a chilli or prawn embedded in it) and fried squid, all served with a sweet

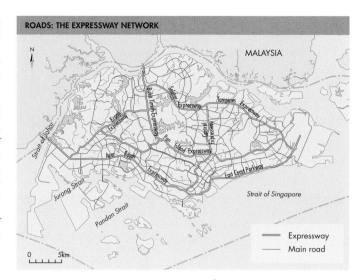

ROADS: THE EXPRESSWAY NETWORK

MALAYSIA

Strait of Singapore

Expressway
Main road

chilli sauce.

Rojak has its origins in Indonesia where it is called 'rujak'. A popular dish in east Java is *rujak cingur* which is similar to the Malay version of Singapore rojak except that it has a distinctive ingredient, cartilage from the nose of an ox (*cingur*).

The word 'rojak' has entered Singapore English to mean 'mix'.

roti john Popular hawker dish. Literally meaning 'John's bread', this Malay dish was first created in the 1970s by a stall-owner at the now-defunct Taman Serasi food centre outside the Singapore Botanic Gardens. Originally, it consisted of half a French loaf, sliced lengthwise and pan fried with a spread made of beaten eggs and onions, flavoured with salt and spices. These days, minced chicken or beef, and even cheese, is added to the spread. A tomato and chilli sauce accompanies this dish.

There are differing explanations for the name of the dish. One account has it that 'John' was the name of the first customer to order the dish. According to another version, the sandwich-like *roti john* was designed to appeal to Caucasian visitors, whom locals referred to generically by the name 'John'.

roti prata Popular hawker dish. This is essentially a pancake or bread served with a

Roti john

Robinsons fire On 21 November 1972, the Robinsons department store building at Raffles Place caught fire. Nine people, including a pregnant woman, were killed in the blaze, that caused damage worth $21 million. The fire, traced to an electrical fault, led to a review of fire safety laws and to the passage of the first Fire Code in 1974. The store was never rebuilt. The land was compulsorily acquired by the government and later sold. Robinsons moved to the Specialists' Centre in ORCHARD ROAD (built in 1974) and later across the street to the Centrepoint shopping centre.

Robinsons: the premises at Raffles Place, c. 1960.

Rubber: mural on the interior wall of Keppel Railway Station depicting rubber-tapping (above); workers in rubber factory, 1953 (right).

chicken or mutton curry. To make this dish, the cook takes a piece of dough, and stretches, flips and folds it. The flipping stretches the dough and the folding traps air pockets inside it. An egg is sometimes added before the dough is fried. The result is a pancake that is crispy on the outside and fluffy on the inside. Modern variations of *roti prata* have fillings like sliced bananas, cheese, garlic, chocolate and even durian.

Roti prata has is origins in Chennai, India, where it is called *roti parota* or *parata*. In Malaysia, the same dish is known as *roti canai* (Chennai).

Roundtable, The Political discussion group. The Roundtable was established in September 1993 by a group of ten intellectuals led by RAYMOND LIM and Tan Kim Song. When Lim and Tan first applied to the Registrar of Societies to have The Roundtable registered as a non-partisan political discussion group, their application was unprecedented, as no such group had been formed in Singapore previously. It took the Registrar of Societies more than nine months to approve the application.

The group's constitution, approved by the registrar, restricted the activities of The Roundtable to the group's members. Three members—Zulkifli Baharudin, Simon Tay and Chandra Mohan—became NOMINATED MEMBERS OF PARLIAMENT, while two others—Raymond Lim and James Gomez—left to join political parties.

Throughout the 1990s, the group's commentaries were regularly published in Singapore's English-language press.

However, at The Roundtable's tenth annual general meeting in April 2004, members of the group—which never numbered more than 17—decided that The Roundtable would be discontinued.

rubber In 1877, 22 rubber plants (*Hevea brasiliensis*) were sent from Ceylon to Singapore. Nine were planted in Kuala Kangsar, Perak while 11 seedlings were planted successfully in Singapore, at the Botanic Gardens (*see* SINGAPORE BOTANIC GARDENS). However, rubber did not at that time gain favour with planters; they were more interested in the profitable sugar and coffee plantations. Besides, little was known of rubber planting, and they were reluctant to take the risk of planting a crop that would require seven years to mature. From the mid-1870s to the 1890s, experiments were carried out to find ways of making rubber planting commercially viable.

It was in Singapore that several breakthroughs in rubber planting were achieved. This was due mainly to the efforts of HENRY RIDLEY, a botanist appointed to be director of the Singapore Botanic Gardens. One of Ridley's important achievements was the invention of the herringbone method of tapping. Unlike the traditional method of incision which often resulted in over-tapping and killed the tree, this new method allowed for just a section of the bark to be removed. Carefully executed cuts then gave a controlled flow of latex. Ridley's method involved the use of a special knife, so that the planter could avoid tapping too deeply. He also discovered that the bark would renew itself after some time, making re-tapping possible.

Ridley also researched the most suitable places for planting, the ideal density per acre, the best method of raising seedlings, the most effective processing techniques, and the best means of packing and shipping. His findings (published from 1891 to the 1910s), provided useful and important guidelines which enabled planters to cultivate rubber very profitably.

Throughout the late 1880s and 1890s, Ridley set out on a personal mission to

convince existing coffee growers to switch to rubber. In 1907, the owner of the Trafalgar Coconut Plantation in PUNGGOL decided to grow rubber alongside his coconuts. Around the same time came an explosive growth in world demand for rubber due to the burgeoning automobile industry—aided by the invention of the pneumatic tyre by Dunlop in 1888. Coincidentally, this was also the period when coffee plantations in Malaya were destroyed by diseases. Consequently, more and more planters started growing rubber.

The establishment of the Singapore Rubber Association in 1911 was an important milestone in that instead of being sent from Singapore to London for sale, the rubber could be sold locally. By 1920, Malaya was producing 50 per cent of the world's rubber, and Singapore was the rubber capital of the world. Rubber continued to be the main cash crop grown in Singapore till the 1950s. Cultivation, harvesting and trading in rubber was responsible for the creation of many local millionaires like TAN KAH KEE, TAN LARK SYE, LEE KONG CHIAN, LIM NEE SOON and Ng Quee Lam. However, the volatility of world rubber prices also meant that traders could be wiped out completely, as in the case of Tan Kah Kee.

The last rubber price boom was in the 1950s and 1960s, brought on by the increased demand during the Korean War and its immediate aftermath. By then, increased demands on land in Singapore made it inefficient and costly to grow rubber on its previous scale.

Rubin, M.P.H. (1940–) Judge. Mohideen M.P. Haja Rubin was educated at the University of Singapore, where he obtained a bachelor's degree in law in 1966. Instead of going into legal practice, he joined the Straits Times Press group as a management executive and worked there until 1973. He then left to join the law firm of DAVID MARSHALL. Rubin was called to the Singapore Bar in 1974 and went on to head David Marshall's civil litigation and conveyancing department. When Marshall closed his practice to become ambassador to France in 1978, Rubin and the remaining partners commenced practice as Amarjit, Rubin and Partners.

From 1987 to 1991, Rubin served as chairman of the Syariah Court of Appeal Board (*see* SYARIAH COURT). He was appointed a JUDICIAL COMMISSIONER in March 1991 and was elevated to the Bench as PUISNE JUDGE in March 1994. Rubin retired from the Bench in February 2005 upon reaching the age of 65.

On 18 April 2005, Rubin joined the firm of RAJAH & TANN as consultant, with the primary task of mentoring the litigation lawyers of the firm. In August 2005, he was awarded the MERITORIOUS SERVICE MEDAL; and in October that year, he was appointed high commissioner to South Africa.

Roti prata: *served with curry (below); flipping and frying the dough.*

Sabana The Greek astronomer Claudius Ptolemaeus (Ptolemy) lived in Alexandria, Egypt, around 100 CE. He compiled astronomical co-ordinates for places in the Indian Ocean, which he was able to obtain from Graeco-Roman traders who voyaged to south India. His original text was lost and the only knowledge of his work that has survived is based on medieval copies. His geographical work mentions several places in the vicinity of the Golden Khersonese, probably the Malay Peninsula. One of these, Sabana, lay at or near the southern tip of the peninsula. It was designated a trading port, implying that international traders knew of such a site somewhere in the vicinity of Singapore 2,000 years ago.

SAF Centre for Military Experimentation
The SINGAPORE ARMED FORCES (SAF) and the DEFENCE SCIENCE AND TECHNOLOGY AGENCY started planning for the SAF Centre for Military Experimentation (SCME) in 2002, recognizing the need to incorporate new war-fighting concepts and technologies into the SAF. Minister for defence, Rear Admiral (NS) Teo Chee Hean officially launched the SCME on 5 November 2003. The centre operates under the FUTURE SYSTEMS DIRECTORATE.

Located in Stagmont Camp, the SCME houses three laboratories: the Command Post of the Future (CPoF) Lab; the Battle Lab; and the Command, Control, Communications, Computers and Intelligence Lab. These laboratories create an environment for experimenting with and demonstrating concepts and technological capabilities for the SAF. For instance, within the CPoF Lab, multi-level command posts can be simulated and reconfigured to explore command and control concepts, and to develop ways to improve the decision-making processes.

SAFTI MI Established on 14 February 1966 to train officers and non-commissioned officers for the nascent SINGAPORE ARMED FORCES (SAF), the Singapore Armed Forces Training Institute (SAFTI) was first planned in late 1965, with the Jurong Primary School chosen as its first premises—leading many people to refer informally to SAFTI as the 'Jurong Military School'.

Some months later, construction of a permanent home at Pasir Laba began. By 1 June 1966, SAFTI was ready for its first batch of officer cadets. The institute was officially opened on 18 June 1966 by the defence minister GOH KENG SWEE. SAFTI

had two main facilities: the Officer Cadet School and the School for Infantry Section Leader Training. Over the following two decades, the SAF expanded, and SAFTI's facilities at Pasir Laba became stretched. Plans were drawn up for a new institute, to be named SAFTI Military Institute (SAFTI MI). A ground-breaking ceremony for this was held on 9 June 1990 at an 88-ha site at Upper Jurong Road.

SAFTI MI was offically opened on 25 August 1995. A prominent landmark on its grounds is a 60-m-high, three-sided tower symbolizing the three armed forces. Training of officers is conducted at three levels by the Officer Cadet School, SAF Advanced Schools, and the Singapore Command and Staff College.

Said Zahari (1928–) Journalist, poet, author and politician. Said Zahari was educated at Tanglin Tinggi Malay School. In 1951, he joined UTUSAN MELAYU as a journalist. By 1956 he was its chief editor, a post he held until 1961. During his tenure, the United Malays National Organisation (UMNO) attempted to dictate the editorial policy of *Utusan*, and Said led the journalists on a 91-day strike. After the strike, Said was banned from the Federation of Malaya. He returned to Singapore, joining *Utusan*'s Singapore office.

On 2 February 1963, just a few hours after Said was elected president of the Partai Rakyat Singapura (People's Party of Singapore), he was arrested under the INTERNAL SECURITY ACT as part of OPERATION COLD STORE. No specific reasons for his arrest were given, other than that he was a threat to national security. He remained in detention for 17 years and was released only in 1979. Since 1992, he has lived in Kuala Lumpur where he is an academic. In 2001, Said published his autobiography, *Dark Clouds At Dawn: A Political Memoir*. He was also the subject of a documentary film, *Zahari's 17 Years* (2006), by director Martyn See.

Saiedah Said (1985–) Sportswoman. Saiedah Said hails from a family of *silat* (a Malay martial art) practitioners; her uncle, Hidayat Hosni, is a *silat* coach. Saiedah first competed in *silat* at the age of 14, gaining a place in the national squad selection trials the following year.

Sajak: 'Bertanya' (Ask) by S.N. Masuri.

Sakura

At 18, Saiedah won a bronze medal in *silat* at the 2003 Southeast Asian Games in Vietnam. She won the 2004 World Championship in Singapore, after defeating competitors from Vietnam, Indonesia and Malaysia. She has also won gold medals at the Swiss Open, Belgian Open, World Open in France and the Sijori Pencak Silat Championships. In 2005, she was named Sportsgirl of the Year by the Singapore National Olympic Council.

sajak Modern form of Malay poetry. The *sajak* is less structured than the SYAIR (a traditional form made up of rhyming quatrains). The *sajak* tends to cover themes such as personal struggle, love, patriotism, religion and social issues. One of the most famous *sajak* writers is S.N. MASURI.

Sakura (1948–) Singer. Sakura was born Teng Ying Hua—'Ying Hua' meaning 'cherry blossom' in Mandarin. She became a household name in the 1970s along with RITA CHAO, with whom she released records and performed as a duo. Born in Muar, Johor, Sakura was a protégée of Henry Foo (Fu Su Yin), the artist and repertoire manager of EMI's Chinese section (*see* CHINESE POPULAR MUSIC). She began her career singing in the NEW WORLD Cabaret. Signed to EMI in 1966, she released her first EP in Mandarin, which featured 'Like I Do', 'My Bonnie', 'Sad Movies' and 'Listen People'. She was backed on this release by THE QUESTS, who were credited as Sounds Anonymous. The EP sold well, and Sakura entered a busy period in her career, performing nightly at The Mandarin Room.

Sakura's vocal 'trademark' was her yodelling—she came to be known as the 'Yodelling Singer'. Along with Rita Chao, she popularized the 'a-go-go' style of music and fashion. They were both known as 'A-Go-Go Queens of the Sixties'. Sakura and Chao toured Singapore, Malaysia, Taiwan, Hong Kong and Japan, building a fan base at each port of call. Chao played the part of the impish naif, and Sakura was the more mature half of the duo. They split up in the mid-1970s, but are fondly remembered in Japan.

SAF Centre for Military Experimentation

Saiedah Said: shown far right, at 2004 World Championship.

Sakya Muni Buddha Gaya Temple

Sakya Muni Buddha Gaya Temple
Buddhist temple on Race Course Road, also known as the 'Temple of a Thousand Lights'. It is closely associated with its 15-m-tall statue of Sakya Muni Buddha (the largest indoor seated Buddha statue in Singapore), which is lit on special occasions each year by a halo of 989 lights.

The temple was founded by a Thai monk, the Reverend Vutthisasara, who arrived in Singapore in 1927 and spent the rest of his life at the temple, meditating and conducting rites. Much of the temple's iconography reflects its Thai origins.

During the JAPANESE OCCUPATION, the temple was left alone by the Japanese—ties between Thailand and Japan were close at the time. It therefore became a place of refuge for many, and assisted British prisoners of war in passing messages secretly to their families in the United Kingdom.

Beneath the temple's central statue of Sakya Muni Buddha is an Indian-style diorama depicting the major events in the Buddha's life. The inner sanctum houses a reclining Buddha statue. Also enshrined in the temple are the Laughing Buddha, the Four-Faced Brahma and Ganesha. The temple holds a piece of bark from the Bodhi Tree (the tree under which, it is said, the Buddha was sitting when he attained enlightenment), brought to Singapore by the Reverend Vutthisasara.

Sali, J.M. (1940–) Author. Born in Tamil Nadu, Jamaludeen Mohamed Sali began his writing career at the age of 15. He arrived in Singapore in 1964, and worked as a sub-editor at TAMIL MURASU (1964–71), then returned to Tamil Nadu to work for popular Tamil weekly *Ananda Vikatan* (Happy Jester) and youth magazine *Mayan*. In 1983 he returned to Singapore to work at *Tamil Murasu* again, and later joined the SINGAPORE BROADCASTING CORPORATION

(present-day MEDIACORP). He retired in 2000 but continued to contribute to MediaCorp television and radio news as a part-time news editor.

A prolific Tamil writer, Sali has written over 400 short stories, 80 plays, 30 novels and 200 essays, as well as published more than 45 books in various languages. Some of his stories have been translated into English, Hindi, Urdu and Sinhala, and a number of his books have been adopted as texts by colleges in Tamil Nadu. His writings are observations on the intricacies of family and inter-personal relations. His novel *Vellai Kodukal* (White Lines) (1994) documents the problems faced by a widow. His stories for children include *Iru Kankal* (Two Eyes) (1961) and *Thanga Kilikal* (Golden Parrots) (1975).

Among the awards Sali has received for his works are the Tamizhavel Award (2001) from the Association of Singapore Tamil Writers. His novel *Kana Kanden Thozhi* (I Had a Dream, Girlfriend) (1978) was awarded a prize by the State Government of Tamil Nadu.

Salvation Army Voluntary organization whose charitable activities in Singapore include provision of nursing homes and daycare for the elderly, childcare and homes for neglected children, counselling and family services.

Founded in 1865 by Methodist minister William Booth in the United Kingdom, the Salvation Army was established in Singapore in 1935 by Brigadier Herbert Lord. Its first headquarters were on Killiney Road. A home for women was opened two years later, on Paterson Road. It catered to women who were destitute, lost or had been forced into prostitution. They were taught English and skills such as tailoring. The home developed into the Women's Industrial Home which later relocated to River Valley Road.

As the Salvation Army's work in Singapore expanded, its headquarters moved to the HOUSE OF TAN YEOK NEE on Tank Road (later known as Clemenceau Avenue) in January 1938. The house, today a national monument, had belonged to a Teochew businessman. After 50 years there, the Salvation Army shifted its headquarters again, eventually settling into purpose-built premises in BISHAN.

Sam Kiang Huay Kwan Clan association. The term 'sam kiang' (or 'san jiang' in Mandarin)—literally meaning 'three rivers'—refers to the Chinese provinces of Jiangsu, Zhejiang and Jiangxi, all of which have the word 'jiang' ('river') in their names. Originally established as the Singapore Sam Kiang Office in 1906 by Chinese immigrants from these three provinces, the name 'Sam Kiang Huay Kwan' was adopted by the association in 1927. Initally located at Jalan Ampas in Balestier, it moved to

Cuppage Road as most members lived in the surrounding areas of Tanglin and Orchard Road.

Around 1937, the association founded Sam Kiang Public School. Both the school and association ceased to function during the Japanese Occupation. After the war, the association moved to new premises at St Thomas Walk. However, Sam Kiang Public School closed in the 1970s due to the decline in the enrolment of schools offering vernacular education.

Various initiatives undertaken by the association included establishing the Sam Kiang Charity Medical Centre in 1974 to provide free medical care to all races, a home for the aged in 1975, and the Sam Kiang Ancestral Hall in 1989, where the ashes of members' forebears could be stored. In 1996, the association moved to new premises on Wilkie Road. It has over 500 members. In 2004, the Sam Kiang Public School reopened. Also known as the Shanghai Institute of Chinese, it offers courses in Mandarin and Chinese culture for children and adults.

Samad Ismail (1925–) Journalist, author and political activist. Abdul Samad Ismail was educated at Rochore School and Victoria School. In 1941, he joined UTUSAN MELAYU as a reporter, and helped YUSOF ISHAK revive the paper after WORLD WAR II.

Samad became politically active, and was a founding member of the Malayan Nationalist Party. Following the MARIA HERTOGH RIOTS, he was arrested in January 1951 by the British and identified as 'one of the leaders of the communist party of Malaya'. Among those who campaigned for his release was LEE KUAN YEW.

In 1953, Samad returned to the helm of *Utusan Melayu*, and in 1954, was one of the original convenors of the PEOPLE'S ACTION PARTY (PAP). He helped draft the party's constitution and manifesto, and recruited influential Malays as members.

Samad left the PAP in 1957 and travelled to Indonesia, where he became *Utusan Melayu*'s Indonesia correspondent. After eight months, he returned to Singapore, and after another 12 years with *Utusan*, he accepted an offer to write for THE STRAITS TIMES. He subsequently became *de facto* editor of the *Berita Harian* in Kuala Lumpur, turning it into a leading Malay daily, while continuing to write editorials and features in English for *The Straits Times*. Samad had close ties to Tun Abdul Razak.

Between 1967 and 1970, Samad wrote nine novels on themes such as Malay language and culture, nationalism, journalism, writing and the everyday lives of ordinary Malays. In February 1976, he was honoured with Malaysia's highest literary award for his role in promoting Malay as a national language. Just five weeks later, however, he was implicated in an alleged communist plot to undermine the governments of Singapore and Malaysia, and was arrested under the Internal Security Act. He was only released in 1981, when Mahathir Mohamad became Malaysia's prime minister.

After his release, Samad returned to journalism, becoming a consultant to the *Star* newspaper group and editorial adviser to the *New Straits Times* Group. He remained with these Malaysian newspapers until his retirement in 1987. In 1992, Samad was awarded the title of Tan Sri. In 1994, he received the Ramon Magsaysay Award for Journalism, Literature and Creative Communication Arts.

Samaritans of Singapore Conceived in London in 1953, Samaritans has grown into a global organization. The Samaritans of Singapore (aptly, 'SOS' for short) began in December 1969 as a telephone hotline service. They provide help to the despairing and suicidal. Relationship difficulties are the main reasons for calls, most callers simply needing to talk to someone. The service, free and available 24 hours a day, is manned by trained volunteers.

***samsui* women** Women labourers hailing from the upper Samsui or Sanshui (literally 'three rivers') districts of Guangdong province, China. In the early 20th century, some 2,000 *samsui* women came to Singapore to find work alongside men on construction sites. They wore distinctive red or blue cloth caps with blue or grey samfus (long-sleeved blouses and trousers). They were accustomed to hard physical labour, carrying bags of cement, bricks and other building material.

Most *samsui* women left China to help support their families as economic conditions in their hometowns were dire, although some came to Singapore to gain greater independence—freedom from arranged marriages and foot-binding. The majority, who on arrival were in their teens or early twenties, chose to remain single and never married or started families. They shared accommodation in 'coolie houses'.

There are fewer than 100 *samsui* women left in Singapore. Most of these women, who played an important part in building Singapore, have returned to China or passed away. A sculpture by Liu Jilin of three *samsui* women stands outside the URA Centre to mark their contributions.

Sang Nila Utama (Sri Tri Buana) The SEJARAH MELAYU (Malay Annals) tells the story of an Indian prince, Raja Culan. He married a fairy princess who lived beneath the sea. Three young princes born of this union later appeared on the summit of a hill in Palembang. The Raja of Palembang, Demang Lebar Daun (Chief Broad Leaf) abdicated so that one of the three, Sang Nila Utama, could become king. Then a man called Bath magically appeared from the mouth of a cow and saluted Sang Nila

Utama as Sri Maharaja, ruler of Suvarna-bhumi (the ancient Sanskrit name for the Malay Peninsula) and gave him the title 'Sri Tri Buana'. The term, meaning 'Lord of the Three Worlds' in Sanskrit, was sometimes used as a title by early Southeast Asian kings; it referred to the belief that the universe was divided into a world of gods, a world of humans and an underworld.

Sri Tri Buana and Demang Lebar Daun agreed that the Malays would always be faithful to Sri Tri Buana's descendants, who would in turn never oppress their subjects. Eventually, Sri Tri Buana went to Bintan Island, which was ruled by Queen Sakidar Shah. One day from the top of a rock at Tanjong Bemian, he saw another island with a beach of sand so white that it looked like a sheet of cloth. This, he was told, was TEMASEK. (Archaeological research has shown that Singapore's south shore in the early 14th century was in fact a bright, almost blindingly white beach of fine white sand.) Sri Tri Buana sailed toward the island, but a storm struck and his ship began to founder. As they drifted helplessly toward Telok Blangah, Sri Tri Buana threw his crown overboard, and the weather immediately calmed.

Hunting on open ground at Kuala Temasek (the mouth of the Temasek River, the open ground being the present-day PADANG near the SINGAPORE RIVER), Sri Tri Buana and his party saw a strange animal. One man said that in ancient times lions were reported to have such an appearance. Sri Tri Buana then decided to establish a city at Temasek and call it 'Singapura' (Lion City).

It has been noted many times that lions are not found in Southeast Asia. The animal described in the Sejarah Melayu is clearly not a lion. The text describes it as very active, dignified and powerful in bearing, with a red body, black head and white breast, slightly bigger than a he-goat. These colours do not accord with normal lion fur. However, in 1011, according to Chinese sources, a lion was shipped from India to China via Sumatra. No doubt the story of the lion's passage was much discussed at the time; it is equally probable that Malay sailors who had been to India, and Indian visitors to Sumatra, would have recounted their experiences with lions in India.

According to the Sejarah Melayu, Sri Tri Buana died 48 years later and was buried 'on the hill of Singapura'. This helps to explain why the inhabitants of Singapore in 1819 were in awe of the hill called BUKIT LARANGAN.

Sang Nila Utama Secondary School Established in 1961, Sang Nila Utama Secondary School was the first Malay-medium secondary school. It was located in Upper Aljunied Road. It was co-educational, and could accommodate about 1,500 pupils in two sessions. It was the third

secondary school built by the PEOPLE'S ACTION PARTY government. Its opening was a historic occasion.

The Malay Education Council, with support from the Government, aimed to preserve the MALAY EDUCATION system and to provide post-secondary education. The school started pre-university classes in 1965 but ceased intake at this level in 1975. The school was closed in 1987. Former students include members of Parliament Mohamad Maidin Packer Mohd and Yatiman Yusof.

Samsui *women: sculpture by Liu Jilin (top);* samsui *women at work.*

***Santa Catarina* incident** In February 1603, the Dutch admiral Jakob van Heemskerk, with the help of the Sultan of Johor, captured the Portuguese carrack *Santa Catarina* at the mouth of the Johor River, off present-day CHANGI Point. The *Santa Catarina's* cargo was sent to Holland and auctioned off for a total of 3.5 million florins. It included raw Chinese silk, dyed damask, atlas tafetta and silk, spun gold, cloth woven with gold thread, robes and canopies, porcelains, sugar, a variety of spices, gum, musk and furniture.

The cargo was representative of goods carried by most ships on their way from the South China Sea to the Malacca Strait. Most of the cargo would have normally been traded within Asia, a minimal remainder being shipped to Europe. The wholesale shipment of the *Santa Catarina* cargo to

Sang Nila Utama Secondary School

Sarabat *stalls*: 'Milo Godzilla', a concoction of Milo, ice-cream and whipped cream.

Govindasamy Sarangapany

Sarkasi Said: the artist with world's longest batik painting.

Holland would therefore have seemed spectacular to the European audience.

The *Santa Catarina* incident led the Dutch to regard the area off Changi Point as a place where they could accost, and pillage the cargo of, Portuguese vessels arriving from China and heading for Malacca. Several such incidents occurred in the 17th century. For the Portuguese, this came to be regarded as a treacherous part of the Strait of Singapore. Naval squadrons were regularly dispatched to escort Portuguese vessels from Pulau Tioman to Malacca. This led, as early as October 1603, to naval standoffs between the Portuguese and the Dutch. It also led to Portuguese proposals, such as the one by Jacques de Coutre, to build a number of forts on or around Singapore Island.

The incident was to have a major impact on international law. In defence of Dutch actions in taking the *Santa Catarina*, the VERENIGDE OOST-INDISCHE COMPAGNIE (VOC) asked the noted Dutch jurist Hugo Grotius to draft an official legal opinion on the matter. In Chapter 12 of the treatise *De Jure Praedae* (On the Law of Prize and Booty, 1604–06), Grotius argued—against the policies of Spain and Portugal—that the high seas could not be appropriated by any single person or nation, and that oceanic waters should be freely navigable to all. The chapter was published as *Mare Liberum* in 1609. The thinking behind the United Nations Convention on the Law of the Sea can be traced back to Grotius and his work.

Santry, Denis (1879–1960) Architect. Born in Cork, Ireland, Santry was educated at the Cork School of Art and then at the Royal College of Art in London. He was then apprenticed to J.F. McMullen, an architect and civil engineer. Santry emigrated to Cape Town, South Africa, in 1903 because of ill health. There, he worked as a cartoonist. Santry and his wife Madeleine became major figures in the Arts and Crafts Movement in South Africa, being adept at metalwork, oriental art, enamelling, and jewellery. In 1910, he moved to

Sarabat *stalls*: preparing teh tarik.

Johannesburg and worked as a cartoonist, becoming an influential cultural figure and a pioneer in animated film. He left for the United States during World War I, and arrived in Singapore in 1918.

By 1924, Santry was a partner in the firm of SWAN & MACLAREN. One of his most important buildings in Singapore is the SULTAN MOSQUE in Muscat Street. He was commissioned to design the new building in 1925. He adopted designs from the Taj Mahal, the Dome of the Rock and a mix of Persian, Moorish, Turkish and classical styles to form an Islamic Saracenic style. Santry also designed the CENOTAPH (1922). He retired in 1935 and returned to South Africa, where he died.

SAR 21 Developed jointly by the Singapore ARMY, the Defence Technology Group and the Chartered Industries of Singapore (now called Singapore Technologies Kinetics), the SAR 21 was developed as a new-generation rifle to replace the American-developed M-16. Built from a tough, high-impact polymer, the SAR 21 is 20 per cent shorter than the M-16. This makes it easier for soldiers to manoeuvre in dense vegetation and tunnels, and inside armoured vehicles and helicopters. It has a built-in laser-aiming device and a 1.5X optical scope, which improves aim in low light. The SAR 21 is reliable, and has low recoil, allowing soldiers better control. It can fire at 450–650 rounds per minute and has a range of 460 m. It incorporates various features, such as a Kevlar cheek plate that protects the user in the unlikely event of a chamber explosion. The weapon was launched on 11 September 1999.

sarabat **stalls** Makeshift coffee and tea stalls. The term *sarabat* is a corruption of the Malay word 'serbat', meaning 'ginger juice'.

It was the beverage known as '*teh serbat*' (hot tea with condensed milk and ginger juice, now popularly known as '*teh halia*') that gave *sarabat* stalls their name. The stalls also sold coffee, tea, Milo, Ovaltine, Horlicks and soft drinks, as well as light snacks.

Sarabat stalls often comprised little more than a few tables and stools crowded around the vendor's pushcart. Unlike COFFEE SHOPS, they were seldom set up in permanent premises. Until the late 1980s, they could be seen operating on street corners or in busy alleyways.

In recent years, the number of genuine *sarabat* stalls in Singapore has dwindled, as modern versions have opened in FOOD COURTS and shopping malls. Besides old favourites like *teh halia* and TEH TARIK, many of these permanent stalls have invented new beverages with names like 'Milo Dinosaur' and 'Milo Godzilla', which are variations on the chocolate drink Milo.

Sarangapany, Govindasamy (1903–1974) Editor and social activist. Born in Tamil Nadu, Govindasamy Sarangapany—popularly known as Thamizhavel—was educated in India. At the age of 21, he left for Singapore to seek his fortune. Soon after he arrived, he was given a clerical job in a shop in Market Street and rose to become its manager. Soon, fired by revolutionary zeal, he tried to awaken the Tamil-speaking masses in Singapore and Malaya through the power of the pen. In 1929, he founded and edited two Tamil news bulletins, *Munnetram* (Progress), a weekly, and *Seerthirutham* (Reformation), a monthly. In 1930, he and two friends formed the Tamil Reformist Club, which led to the formation in 1932 of the TAMILS REFORM ASSOCIATION. It was this association that launched the Tamil weekly, TAMIL MURASU (Tamil Drum), on 6 July 1935. Initially, the paper sold only 200 copies at one cent each. Sarangapany peddled it from house to house and gave away unsold copies to poor Tamils. By May 1936, circulation exceeded 5,000.

In 1954, when the colonial government allowed immigrants from Commonwealth countries to obtain Singapore citizenship by registration, Sarangapany persuaded 20,000 Tamils to register. In 1960, *Tamil Murasu* collected $16,000 for the setting up of Umar Pulavar Tamil Secondary School. Sarangapany was also instrumental in getting more than 50 organizations—representing various sectional interests of the Tamil-speaking community—to work together through the Tamil Representative Council and the annual Tamil Festival.

SAR 21

Sarangapany remained at the helm of *Tamil Murasu* until his death. In 1998, the paper was sold to publishing group SINGAPORE PRESS HOLDINGS.

Sarawak, Anita (1952–) Singer. Anita Sarawak is the daughter of Malay actress Siput Sarawak and actor-director Roomai Noor. Born Ithnaini Mohammad Taib. She started singing professionally at the age of 16, and soon became known for her stage presence and ability to fuse different musical genres. She recorded albums in both English and Malay, including *Love Me* and *Dunia Oh Dunia* (Oh World). She has also performed at Caesar's Palace in Las Vegas.

Sarawak owns a boutique, Poise, and has written a cookbook, *Cooking with Love*. She has hosted variety and talk shows on television in both Singapore and Malaysia.

Sarkasi Said (1940–) Artist. Known as the 'Baron of Batik', Sarkasi Said has dedicated his life to BATIK painting. He has held solo and group exhibitions in Singapore, Malaysia, Thailand, New Zealand, the United States, Japan and France. His works are found in many distinguished public and private collections. His many awards include the Pingat APAD (an award from the Angkatan Pelukis Aneka Daya or Association of Artists of Various Resources) in 1974, and Best Foreign Entry (Sarasota Art Exhibition, United States) in 1981.

Over five days in 2003, Sarkasi created the world's longest batik painting, measuring 103.9 m by 0.55 m—a Guinness world record. He has contributed to numerous charitable events and volunteered his services on various national councils. In 2005, he received a Special Recognition Award from the Ministry of Information, Communication and the Arts.

Sarkasi has a studio in the MALAY HERITAGE CENTRE (the refurbished ISTANA KAMPONG GLAM), where he conducts workshops on batik painting.

Sarkies Brothers Hoteliers. The four Sarkies brothers—Martin, Tigran, Aviet and Arshak—were born in Persia (present-day Iran) but travelled east as part of the ARMENIAN diaspora. Martin, the eldest, settled in Penang in the late 1860s and worked initially as an engineer. By the 1880s, he was listed as a hotelier. Together with Tigran, Martin opened two hotels in Penang—the Eastern Hotel (1884) and the Oriental Hotel (1885). These were later merged to form the famous Eastern & Oriental (E&O) Hotel. In 1884, Aviet joined their hotel business, by now known as Sarkies Brothers, and went to Rangoon (present-day Yangon) to establish the Strand Hotel. Martin Sarkies retired from the business around this time and his place was taken by Arshak, the youngest brother. The Sarkies Brothers' first hotel in Singapore was RAFFLES HOTEL, which opened in 1887.

Sarkies Brothers: Tigran, second from left, and Martin, seated, with staff, 1906.

Arshak was an extravagant individual who borrowed heavily to expand his business. By the time he died in 1931, the firm of Sarkies Brothers was bankrupt.

Sassoon, Victor (1957–) Businessman. Victor Sassoon was born into a Sephardic Jewish family in Singapore in 1957. After completing his studies at St Joseph's Institution, he travelled to Indonesia to work in his family's watch-manufacturing and wholesale business. Under his management, the business became the agent for Rolex, Cartier and other luxury watch brands in Indonesia.

In 1979, Sassoon returned to Singapore. Four years later, he married Michelle Elias, also a Sephardic Jew. Subsequently, the couple set up Sunvic Productions, an entertainment company. In the 1990s, Sunvic brought performers such as Paula Abdul and Michael Jackson to the region for concert performances.

In 1995, Sassoon met singer Paula Abdul at a COFFEE BEAN AND TEA LEAF outlet in Los Angeles, and Abdul suggested that Sassoon purchase the company. In November 1996, he established the first overseas Coffee Bean outlet in Singapore. Its success enabled Sassoon and his partners to acquire The Coffee Bean & Tea Leaf from its founders in 1998.

In 2000, the SINGAPORE TOURISM BOARD awarded Sassoon the Tourism Entrepreneur of the Year Award. In addition to managing his business, Sassoon has been an active member of Singapore's Jewish community (*see* JEWS).

satay Popular hawker dish. Satay is believed to have originated in Indonesia. The Singapore version consists of skewered meat—usually chicken, beef or mutton—grilled over charcoal. It is usually served with cucumber and onion slices and *ketupat* (rice cakes), accompanied by a spicy peanut dip. The Chinese in Singapore have a pork version of satay and sometimes add pineapple sauce to the peanut dip.

Satay was originally sold by peddlers, who would carry two baskets strung on a pole across their shoulders. One basket contained the charcoal grill and the other the raw satay, sticks and sauces. A popular place for satay in the 1950s and 1960s was the Beach Road area, from which the sellers were relocated to the Satay Club near the Esplanade. This in turn made way for redevelopment in 1995. A popular place for satay today is Boon Tat Street next to Lau Pa Sat (*see* TELOK AYER MARKET). On weekdays, the road is closed to traffic after 7 p.m. and tables are laid out. Another popular place for satay is the open space outside Sembawang Shopping Centre.

satellite television Reception of direct-to-home satellite broadcasts is prohibited in Singapore. However, international broadcasters, such as ESPN, HBO and Disney, use satellite facilities extensively in Singapore to uplink their signals to satellites across the region. StarHub Cable TV also uses communication satellites to receive programming from major broadcasters, which is then monitored before distribution via the cable network.

Satellites are also used by MEDIACORP's Channel NewsAsia to receive international news and special events, and to uplink its programming across the region. In 1997, Television Corporation of Singapore International launched its first Mandarin satellite channel, Xin Shi, to cable television in Taiwan.

Since May 1991, organizations that need to access time-sensitive information for business purposes have been able to apply for a TV Receive-Only System. In 2003, these licences were extended to hotel, tourist and entertainment venues.

Sathyalingam, Neila (1938–) Dancer, choreographer and teacher. Born Neila Balendra in Sri Lanka, Neila Sathyalingam trained in Indian classical dance from the age of five, later furthering her dance studies at the Kalakshetra College of Fine Arts in Chennai. In 1974, she moved to Singapore with her husband. Three years later, she set up Apsaras Arts, an Indian dance group and school.

Anita Sarawak

Victor Sassoon

Satay: served with dip (below), and being grilled.

Neila Sathyalingam.

*Scouts: chief Scout,
President S.R. Nathan, right.*

Besides producing dance-dramas such as *Kannagi* (1998) and *Aarupadai* (2002), Sathyalingam has also experimented with cross-cultural productions while choreographing for the PEOPLE'S ASSOCIATION. She was awarded the CULTURAL MEDALLION in 1989. In 1996, she worked with choreographers SOM SAID and Yan Choong Lian on *Singapore Surprise*, a multicultural dance programme presented in Chennai. Sathyalingam became a Singapore citizen in 1994.

savings Singapore's high level of savings is an outcome of mandatory contributions to the CENTRAL PROVIDENT FUND, voluntary savings and government surpluses. It has allowed the economy to grow without the accumulation of external debt.

Singapore's gross savings as a percentage of GROSS DOMESTIC PRODUCT averaged 48 per cent between 1994 and 2004, higher than any other country in Southeast Asia. Gross national savings reached $80 billion in 2004, up 24 per cent, having grown 9 per cent in 2003.

National savings are more than sufficient to finance gross fixed-capital formation, as shown by the large current account surplus of $55 billion in 2005. Excess savings are invested.

SBS *See* COMFORTDELGRO.

Scandal Point This was the name of a place where people gathered to gossip while enjoying the sea breeze. It is believed to have been where the SINGAPORE RECREATION CLUB was later built, at the northeast corner of the PADANG.

Scandal Point was the first and only place to have been fortified in response to Sir STAMFORD RAFFLES' instructions to establish a series of defences in the area. After convincing the British authorities in India of the importance of Singapore to British interests, Raffles had suggested that the island be fortified—although no action was taken at first because of objections from the Dutch.

In 1819, however, a large blockhouse was built on BUKIT LARANGAN, and a small

battery was mounted on Scandal Point—although at the time, the site was known as the Saluting Battery as its guns were used only for salutes. In 1851, in response to continuing British military concerns about the lack of defences on the island, four eight-inch guns were mounted at the site. Scandal Point itself was levelled in 1851, to make way for the construction of a sea wall.

Scouts Although calls to establish Scout troops, or the Baden-Powell Corps, were made as early as 1908, Scouting officially started in Singapore only on 2 July 1910, with the establishment of the Boy Scouts Association. At a meeting chaired by Major Ernest Stephenson, a committee, comprising T.C. Hay, T.R. Hill, Percy C. Fenwick, Brother Stephen (principal of St Joseph's Institution), O.A. Morris and Percy Gold, elected Major Stephenson president of the local association. The first Scout troop had, in fact, been established about two years earlier by surveyor K.M. Mauleffinch, who was assisted by T.C. Hay.

Scouting took off after August 1910 with the arrival of Nottingham scoutmaster Frank Cooper Sands. Universally acknowledged as the 'Father of Malayan Scouting', Sands soon had two troops—the First and Second Singapore Troops—up and running under the sponsorship of the YOUNG MEN'S CHRISTIAN ASSOCIATION OF SINGAPORE. Milestones in the movement were the establishment of the Wolf Cubs for younger boys (1916); the first Malay Troop (1919); school-based Scout Troops (1922); Rover Scouting (1927); and Sea Scouts (1938).

Scouts have a track record of serving society in times of crisis. During the SEPOY MUTINY, Scouts took over from the army and police the duties of dispatch riders, telephone operators and clerks from the army and police. During World War II, Scouts served as air-raid wardens, fire watchers, first aid men and police officers, until their units were disbanded with the Fall of Singapore. During the Japanese Occupation, Scouts met clandestinely to keep the movement alive.

In 1966, Singapore was admitted as a full member of the World Organization of Scout Movements. Originally confined to boys, the Singapore Scout Association now admits girls to its Venture (16-18 years old) and Rover (18-25 years old) sections. The highest award for Scouts—the President's Scout Award—is personally presented by the head of state, who is traditionally also the chief Scout.

The Scout Headquarters has moved many times over the years. It now has a permanent home in Bishan, the EE PENG LIANG Building, which was named for the long-time president (1973–94) of the Singapore Scouts Association.

scrap value If a motor vehicle is de-registered during the validity period of the CER-

Scouts: Singapore troop in the 1950s.

TIFICATE OF ENTITLEMENT (COE), there is a rebate for the unused portion of the COE. This is the scrap value for vehicles other than cars. For cars, the owner may also be eligible for a PREFERENTIAL ADDITIONAL REGISTRATION FEE benefit, in which case the scrap value is the sum of this and the unused COE rebate. There is no cash refund for the scrap value, but it can be used to offset upfront taxes in the registration of a new vehicle.

Sculpture Square Art space focusing on the dynamics of contemporary three-dimensional practice. Created from the shell of a 19th-century Peranakan church, Sculpture Square was set up in 1999 as part of the government's arts housing scheme aimed at providing affordable spaces to art groups and artists. Many prominent artists such as Milenko Pravcki, HAN SAI POR and Sun Yu-Li, have exhibited at Sculpture Square. Besides exhibitions, symposiums, workshops and classes are held there.

Sea View Hotel The original Sea View Hotel opened in 1906 in a coconut grove in the Katong area. Boasting an unobstructed view of the sea, it comprised 40 guestrooms, tennis courts, a beer garden and a swimming enclosure. Ownership was passed on to the Armenian SARKIES BROTHERS—who also owned RAFFLES HOTEL—and MANASSEH MEYER.

The original buildings were demolished in the 1960s and replaced by an 18-storey, 454-room hotel built at a cost of $15 million. When it reopened in 1969, the Sea View Hotel was one of the biggest hotels in Singapore, and one of the few on the city outskirts. As it was located near PAYA LEBAR AIRPORT, it was popular with airlines whenever passengers were stranded in Singapore due to cancelled or delayed flights, earning it the nickname 'Delayed Flight Hotel'. In 1973, the Sea View was designated the Games Village for the Southeast Asian Games. At the time, the hotel was owned by a private company, Kong Hoa Realty Company, which changed its name to Sea View Hotel Ltd when it was listed in 1968.

The hotel finally ceased operations on October 2003, two months after the site was sold to listed developer Wheelock Properties for $255 million. The site has

Sculpture Square: Oasis by Han Sai Por, 2006.

since been developed into a 546-unit condominium project, The Sea View.

Seah, Lynnette (1957–) Musician. Violinist Lynnette Seah became the Acting Leader and Associate Concertmaster of the SINGAPORE SYMPHONY ORCHESTRA (SSO) at its inauguration in 1979, and in 2006 was its longest-serving member. She was taught by her mother, Lau Biau Chin, GOH SOON TIOE and Alphonso Anthony, and received further musical training in Europe and the United States. Besides performing with the SSO, Seah has been active in chamber music and is the leader of the Jade Quartet. In January 2006, she performed the world premiere of BERNARD TAN's *Violin Concerto*, a work dedicated to her.

Seah Eu Chin (1805–1883) Merchant. Born in Swatow (present-day Shantou), Seah Eu Chin worked as a clerk on board a Chinese junk and arrived in Singapore in 1823, where he was attached as a clerk on several trading vessels. Over the next five years, he traded and bartered locally. In 1830, he established himself as a commission agent supplying junks trading between Singapore, Riau, Sumatra and ports in the Malay Peninsula. Seah's business flourished and he invested his profits in property. Possibly the first person to start PEPPER AND GAMBIER planting on a large scale in Singapore, he was known as the 'Gambier King'. He also traded in tea and cotton.

Seah was also the main figure behind the establishment of the Ngee Ann Kongsi (*see* TEOCHEW POIT IP HUAY KUAN) in 1845. When riots broke out between the Hokkiens and Teochews in 1854, Seah was asked to mediate between the two groups, in recognition of his role as a Teochew community leader. He was also one of the first Chinese to be appointed justice of the peace (1872). He retired from active business in 1864 and spent his remaining years studying Chinese literature. Eu Chin Street in Tiong Bahru is named after him.

Seah Liang Seah (1850–1925) Merchant. The second son of SEAH EU CHIN, Seah Liang Seah was educated at St Joseph's Institution and studied Chinese under a private tutor. In the late 1880s, Seah and some friends started a pineapple cannery under the chop 'Chin Choon'. Located on Thomson Road, it produced tinned pineapple marketed under the Lion brand and soon dominated the tinned pineapple business.

Seah was active in public life, serving as an Unofficial member of the Legislative Council (1883–90), member of the Municipal Council (1883–90), justice of the peace (1885), member of the first Chinese Advisory Board (1889) and trustee of Raffles Institution (1889–1902). He was instrumental in founding the SINGAPORE CHINESE CHAMBER OF COMMERCE & INDUSTRY as well

as the Straits Chinese British Association.

In 1894, Seah bought HOO AH KAY's (WHAMPOA) residence in Serangoon and renamed it BENDEMEER HOUSE. In the 1920s, he and his brothers were involved in the development of Emerald Hill. Liang Seah Street in the Bugis area is named after him.

second wing policy Singapore is heavily reliant on trade and FOREIGN DIRECT INVESTMENT (FDI), mostly from developed nations, to maintain economic growth. The government has recognised that the small domestic market and relatively high cost of labour and land put Singapore at a competitive disadvantage. Therefore, while FDI remains vital, Singapore's outward investment in other countries is the 'second wing' of the economy, providing an extra source of income from repatriated earnings.

In line with the second wing policy, Singapore embarked in the late 1980s on a strategy of regional economic cooperation with its neighbours. The ASSOCIATION OF SOUTHEAST ASIAN NATIONS (ASEAN) has been the main vehicle for progress in this area. This has helped Singapore to diversify from dependence on developed countries. Singapore is now a major investor in other ASEAN nations, as well as in Australia, China and India. Direct investment overseas has risen from $22 billion to over $150 billion in the period 1992–2004.

In 1998, after the ASIAN FINANCIAL CRISIS, Singapore strove to develop its 'second wing' further by shifting from regionalization to globalization. A major part of this plan is to build world-class companies able to withstand future crises. To this end, INTERNATIONAL ENTERPRISE SINGAPORE was established in 2002.

secondary education Based on their results in the national Primary School Leaving Examinations (PSLE), pupils move on to one of the four secondary school courses: Special, Express, Normal (Academic), or Normal (Technical). These are designed to match learning abilities and interests.

The Special course (for the top 10 per cent of the PSLE cohort) and Express course (for the next 20 per cent of the cohort) are four years in duration, concluding with the Singapore-Cambridge General Certificate of Education Ordinary (GCE 'O') Level Examination. The range of subjects in both courses is similar, but all Special course students learn Higher MOTHER TONGUE Language, while only some Express course students do (*see* SPECIAL ASSISTANCE PLAN SCHOOLS).

The Normal (Academic) and Normal (Technical) courses also take four years. Students sit for the Singapore-Cambridge General Certificate of Education Normal (GCE 'N') Level Examination at the end of the fourth year. Those who do well proceed to a fifth year of secondary education and sit for the GCE 'O' Level Examination.

Those who do not qualify to enter the fifth year have the opportunity to take up technical-vocational education and training at the INSTITUTE OF TECHNICAL EDUCATION.

In an effort to inject more flexibility into the education system, a number of elective subjects have been introduced over the years. The secondary school landscape has also become more varied and now includes government and government-aided schools offering mainstream education; AUTONOMOUS SCHOOLS; INDEPENDENT SCHOOLS; and privately funded schools. In addition, Specialised Independent Schools—such as the SINGAPORE SPORTS SCHOOL and the NUS HIGH SCHOOL OF MATHEMATICS AND SCIENCE—cater to students with talents in specific fields.

secret societies General term for gangs whose origins can be traced back to China. The notion of 'brotherhood' or fictive kinship employed by Chinese organizations as a unifying force for their members dates back to the period of the Warring States (475–221 BCE). Chinese migrants who arrived in Singapore in the early 19th century brought with them this practice of forming brotherhoods, which provided them with a social structure, livelihood, protection and possibly some measure of spiritual fulfillment.

Ghee Hin Kongsi (literally 'The Rise of Righteousness Association') was the first secret society in Singapore. An offshoot of the Heaven and Earth Society in Fujian, it was formed in 1820 as a self-help organization for Chinese immigrants. By 1830, it had emerged as the strongest secret society with an estimated membership of nearly 3,000.

Membership in a secret society was for life. The punishment for trying to leave was death. To become members, individuals had to participate in an initiation ceremony held at night in a secret location. The elaborate and dramatic ceremony was rich in Chinese symbolism and mysticism. It caused deep emotional and psychological effects on initiates who would pledge their lifelong allegiance. Initiation was complete only with the taking of the blood oath. For this purpose, a cockerel was decapitated and its blood mixed in a bowl with sugar and

Lynnette Seah

Seah Eu Chin

Seah Liang Seah

Sea View Hotel: advertisement, 1970s (below); postcard, 1920.

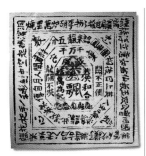

Secret societies: Ghee Hin Kongsi membership certificate.

Seet Ai Mee: celebrating her election win, 1988.

Ken Seet

Chinese wine. Initiates pricked their middle fingers, letting their blood collect in the bowl. Drinking from the bowl, they were sworn into the brotherhood. They then took turns to rest a knife or wooden stick over the dead cockerel whilst reciting the vow of secrecy. They paid their membership fees wrapped in red paper, and received a membership certificate. Their names were added to the society's membership scroll, and only then were the hierarchy, rules and codes (such as hand signals and body gestures) of the society made known to them, under a strict code of silence.

The decades after the 1830s saw a proliferation of secret societies as Chinese immigrants poured into Singapore. Conflict within the Ghee Hin over competition for REVENUE FARMING rights and the interests of the various dialect groups led to the formation of four sub-lodges, namely the HOKKIEN, TEOCHEW, CANTONESE and HAKKA Ghee Hin lodges. New secret societies also emerged, such as the Hokkien Ghee Hok and Hok Hin, the Teochew Ghee Sin, and the Teochew-Hakka society Ghee Kee.

Secret societies obtained revenue from farming OPIUM, PEPPER AND GAMBIER, running brothels and gambling dens, and the COOLIE TRADE. They also engaged in robbery, extortion, kidnap and murder. A 15-minute walk around Chinatown in the 1880s showed up 70 gambling houses, almost all of which belonged to the Ghee Hok. Secret society clashes were frequent and created social unrest, such as the Post Office Riots in 1876.

Policing the secret societies was difficult, as the police force was small, with a ratio of 133 police to 32,132 members of the Chinese community in 1843. Furthermore, with European officers and Indians forming its rank and file, the police knew too little of Chinese ways to counter the secret societies. The establishment of a CHINESE PROTECTORATE in 1877 and increased legislative powers all failed to bring secret society activities under control.

In 1889, a Societies Ordinance was passed to abolish all secret societies in the STRAITS SETTLEMENTS. There were then 10 secret societies registered: Hokkien Ghee Hin, Hok Hin, Tsung Peh Society, Kwong Wai Shiu, Kwang Hok (or Ghee Kee), Ghee Hok, Hong Ghee Thong, Lee Seng Hong, Yuet Tong Kun and Heng Sun. In total, they had 1,321 office-bearers and 68,316 registered members. Secret societies responded to suppression by going underground, re-forming as smaller groups registered as 'recreational' societies. There were 37 such organizations in 1890, and this number doubled by the following year.

Secret societies in the 20th century, especially in the post-war years, were unlike their predecessors. They were smaller groups loosely banded together, and had little regard for hierarchy, ritual and customs. They were common gangs. In the post-

Independence years, penal measures allowing for arrest and detention without trial (deemed effective as witnesses had always feared testifying in open court), together with reformative programmes, kept gang activities in check.

Securities Investors Association of Singapore

Non-profit organization founded in June 1999 initially to champion the CENTRAL LIMIT ORDER BOOK issue. The association promotes investor education, corporate transparency and good corporate governance, and is a watchdog for investor rights. It is the largest organized investor lobby group in Asia, with almost 61,000 retail investors as members. It is run by volunteer professionals.

See Chak Mun

(1941–) Diplomat. See Chak Mun graduated from the University of Singapore with an honours degree in economics (1966). He joined the Ministry of Foreign Affairs and has served as high commissioner to Australia (1976–79), ambassador to Germany (1982–86), permanent representative to the United Nations in Geneva and concurrently ambassador to Turkey, Italy and Austria (1986–91), commissioner to Hong Kong (1994–97), and representative to the International Atomic Energy Agency (1997). In 2002, he was appointed high commissioner to India.

Seet, Ken

(1973–) Photographer. After graduating from Temasek Polytechnic in 1993, Ken Seet Thiam Wui worked as a graphic designer whilst teaching photography. He established his own photographic studio in 1996. Seet gained critical appraisal for atmospheric black-and-white images (often of unorthodox subjects), and for his travel landscape photography.

In 2002, Seet collaborated on a multidisciplinary project entitled *Abhinaya: My Journey of Return*, which featured dance, video and photography. He was also

Secret societies: initiation ceremony.

involved in a photographic exhibition showcasing the SINGAPORE ARMED FORCE's peacekeeping mission to East Timor in 2003. Seet's photography was featured in a SINGAPORE ART MUSEUM-organized exhibition in Hong Kong in 1998, and an exhibition at the inauguration of THE ARTS HOUSE in 2004. He received the National Arts Council's YOUNG ARTIST AWARD (Photography) in 2003.

Seet Ai Mee

(1943–) Scientist and politician. Born in Malacca, Seet Ai Mee was educated at the Methodist Girls' School in Malacca. She then attended the University of Adelaide on a Colombo Plan Scholarship, earning first class honours in biochemistry (1965). She joined the Department of Biochemistry at the University of Malaya as a tutor (1965–66), but later moved to Singapore to join the Ministry of Health as a biochemist in its Department of Pathology (1966–73). In 1969, she obtained a PhD in clinical biochemistry at the University of Singapore. From 1973 to 1977, Seet was principal research fellow at the Singapore Institute of Standards and Industrial Research, and then managing director of AML Sci-Ed Consultants Pte Ltd.

Seet entered politics on the PEOPLE'S ACTION PARTY ticket in 1988, winning a seat in Bukit Gombak constituency. That year, she was appointed minister of state for community development and education. In 1991, she was made acting minister for community development, the first woman to be appointed to the Cabinet. She was, however, unsuccessful in the 1991 general election, and retired from politics to concentrate on community service. Seet became the founder chairman of the Dover Park Hospice and first chairman of the Singapore Hospice Council.

Sejarah Melayu

Malay Annals. Early Southeast Asian kingdoms placed significant emphasis on royal genealogies. Southeast Asian kinship patterns lack strong lineage organizations, but most societies believed that rulership required the possession of inherited qualities. Malay societies were no exception. No Malay texts written in Malacca survive, but one of them may have formed the inspiration for a work known as *Sulalat Us-Salatin* in Arabic (*Penurunan Segala Raja* in Malay, or Story of the Origin and Descent of the Malay Rajas). The book is commonly referred to as the Sejarah Melayu (History of the Malays), but this implies, wrongly, that the work was written as a history in the modern sense of the term. Its function was rather to gain support for the ruling line of Malacca and to inculcate certain ideas of the proper relations between rulers and subjects within society.

Different versions of the Sejarah Melayu were written in different periods, both shaping and reflecting changes in Malay identity. The first version may have been written as early as 1436, when Islam was becoming increasingly influential among the Malay ruling class in Malacca as ancient concepts of political legitimacy based on Buddhism were losing vigour. The nobility needed new means of legitimizing their position; the Sejarah Melayu reinterprets the origins of Malay royalty, retaining ideas of the importance of continuous descent, stripped of all but the faintest traces of earlier Buddhist beliefs.

The oldest surviving copy of *Sulalat Us-Salatin* is known as Raffles MS 18 because it was acquired by Sir STAMFORD RAFFLES. A comparison of Raffles MS 18, which was probably edited around 1612, with another well-known version, written in Riau around 1750 and known as the Shellabear Recension (after WILLIAM SHELLABEAR, who had it printed in Singapore), demonstrates how the text evolved in accordance with its historical context. One of the heroes of Malacca, Hang Tuah, in the Shellabear Recension, is depicted as being of BUGIS rather than Malay ancestry. In 1750, the Riau kingdom was dominated by people of Bugis origin. This kind of rewriting occurred frequently during the evolution of the Sejarah Melayu.

In the Raffles MS 18, Malay court writers portrayed Singapore as the site of the first great port in their history. No scholar would argue that the Sejarah Melayu is a reliable guide to dates or events, but historians can use it to try to solve other problems. Although we may never know the names of Singapore's rulers before ISKANDAR SHAH, we may be able to accept some of the Sejarah Melayu's description of Singapore's appearance and importance during the 14th century.

The first episode of the Sejarah Melayu mentions a meeting between an Indian king named RAJA CULAN and the Chinese at TEMASEK, the old name for Singapore. Thus, Singapore appears at the very beginning of Malay history as a place where Indians and Chinese interacted.

According to the Sejarah Melayu, Raja Culan fathered Sri Tri Buana (SANG NILA UTAMA), who was responsible for renaming Temasek 'Singapura'. When the Raja of Palembang abdicated in favour of Sri Tri Buana, it was agreed that the Malays would be perpetually faithful to Sri Tri Buana's descendants, who would never oppress their subjects. Sri Tri Buana was succeeded by his son, Paduka Sri Pikrama Wira. Then 'Singapura became a great city, to which foreigners resorted in great numbers so that the fame of the city and its greatness spread throughout the world'. During Pikrama Wira's 15-year reign, the Raja (Batara) of MAJAPAHIT in Java heard that Singapura was a great city. First using diplomacy, then violence, he attempted to make Singapura his vassal. He sent his fleet to capture

Singapura, but was defeated. Pikrama Wira's reign was also famous for the appearance of a Herculean strongman, BADANG, who is associated with a boom or moveable barrier which guarded the entrance to the SINGAPORE RIVER. Raffles MS 18 remarks that the boom still existed when the chronicle was compiled. This is one of several such marginal notes on Singapore landmarks said to have been extant when the text was written. Another story about Badang says that in a contest of strength, he threw a large stone from a hill—which must have been Fort Canning—to a projecting point at the mouth of the Singapore River. This corresponds precisely to the spot where the SINGAPORE STONE and other large rocks were found in the 19th century.

Pikrama Wira's son, Sri Rama Wikrama, succeeded him and ruled for 13 years until his death. He was succeeded by his son, who became Paduka Sri Maharaja. The reign of Maharaja is when the contract between ruler and ruled in Singapura was breached. A man from Pasai unwisely tried to impress his queen by making a betel palm growing in front of the palace change by magic into two trees. Maharaja saw this and executed him. After this, Singapura was attacked by *ikan todak* (garfish). A young boy saved the city by suggesting that a barrier of banana tree trunks should be made to block the fish. The garfish impaled themselves on the trunks, and Maharaja, fearing that such an intelligent boy might become a threat, had him killed. This story also became known as the legend of BUKIT MERAH. These two incidents are examples of unjust acts which set the stage for the ruler of Singapura eventually to receive divine retribution by losing his kingdom to a Javanese attack.

After twelve-and-a-half years, Maharaja died and his son, Sri Sultan ISKANDAR SHAH, succeeded him. Islam was introduced in Malacca during his reign. He too committed a crime, unjustly shaming one of his wives by exposing her in the market. Her father, Sang Rajuna Tapa, took revenge by opening the gates for another invasion sent by Batara Majapahit. Iskandar Shah fled to Saletar and then Muar before settling in Malacca. There, he laid the foundations for its greatness, ruling for 20 years.

When the capital moved to Malacca, Singapura became the domain of the son of Sri Bija Diraja. Sri Bija Diraja held an important office: that of *laksamana*, the commander of the sultanate's maritime forces. During the reign of Sultan Mansur Shah, Singapura possessed 40 cruisers, each with three masts, making Singapura the main naval base of Malacca. Eventually Hang Tuah became *laksamana*. Thus, the greatest hero in the Sejarah Melayu is directly associated with Singapore.

In the tenth chapter of the Sejarah Melayu, during Mansur Shah's reign, the toponym 'Ujung Tanah' ('Land's

Selarang Barracks, 1942

End'), appears. It includes Malacca and all its domains as far south as Bintan. The name 'Singapura' then disappears from the narrative.

Historian W. Linehan has worked out a possible chronology of Singapura's history based on the Sejarah Melayu. This could be done because Iskandar Shah was a historical personage, whose existence is independently confirmed by the Ming Annals. By adding up the regnal periods of the five kings (totalling 114 years) Sri Tri Buana hypothetically arrived in Singapore in 1299, and the Javanese conquest would have taken place in 1375–76.

Selarang Barracks Built in 1936–38 to house the 2nd Gordon Highlanders Battalion, the barracks were located at the British Army military base at Changi. They were arranged in a square around a parade ground, and the seven blocks could accommodate about 800 men. In September 1942, however, the Japanese interned more than 15,400 Australian prisoners of war (POWs), alongside POWs of other nationalities, at Selarang Barracks in extremely poor conditions. There were only two water taps, and holes dug into the square served as latrines. The Japanese demanded that the POWs sign pledges not to escape. To put pressure on the officers, the Japanese executed, on 2 September 1942 at Changi beach, four men who had attempted to escape several months earlier. After holding out for three days, the Australian officers, fearing an outbreak of disease, ordered their men to sign the pledges.

After the war, the British army used Selarang Barracks until 1971, when the camp was handed over to the Singapore Armed Forces. In the early 1980s, most of the original buildings were demolished; a small museum was created in one of the remaining structures.

Select Bookstore Independent book retailer. Located in Tanglin Shopping Centre, the store was founded in 1976 by former librarian Lena Lim, her architect husband WILLIAM LIM, and two other partners. Initially intended to fill a void in the market for books on Southeast Asia, the business expanded its range to include more titles on the rest of Asia, particularly China, after coming under new management in August 2004. More than half of its sales come from overseas, as Select Books has become a valuable resource centre for libraries and academics worldwide. Aside from its retail business, Select Books is a distributor for international publishing houses, as well as a publisher with its own imprint.

Seletar Airbase Plans to establish an airfield, flying-boat base and naval base in Singapore were formulated by the Royal Air Force (RAF) in 1921. A site at Seletar was chosen for the purpose. RAF Seletar was completed in 1928, and the first plane landed on the airstrip on 7 November of that year. The base was also used for civilian traffic until the opening of Singapore's first civilian airport at Kallang on 12 June 1937, after which Seletar continued to be used as a military airport. Seletar Airport was managed by the British until 1968, when it was handed over to the Department of Civil Aviation (DCA) before passing into the hands of the Civil Aviation Authority of Singapore when the DCA became a statutory board. Seletar Airport housed the Singapore Aviation Academy in 1972 (presently located in Changi), and is used for chartered flights. The airport and its surrounding area, which hosts about 30 aerospace companies, are to become part of Seletar Aerospace Park.

Seletar River The Seletar River has a highly controlled flow pattern due to the two RESERVOIRS which were constructed along its course. The headwaters were dammed in the 1920s to create the Upper Seletar Reservoir, which provides Singapore with up to 10 per cent of its water supply. In 1986, a dam was constructed across the estuary of the river to create the Lower Seletar Reservoir. In contrast with the Upper reservoir, which is mainly surrounded by secondary forest, parts of the Lower reservoir and its shoreline have been developed to provide sporting and leisure facilities.

Selkirk, Lord (1906–1994) British politician and diplomat. Sir George Nigel Douglas-Hamilton, tenth Earl of Selkirk, was educat-

Sembawang: ships moored at Sembawang Wharves.

Seletar Airbase

ed at Eton College, Edinburgh University (where he obtained an LLB) and Oxford University (where he obtained an MA). He fought in WORLD WAR II, and was appointed an Officer of the Order of the British Empire (OBE) in 1941. In January 1960, he was appointed high commissioner to Singapore, a post he held until 1963. During this period, he was also commander-general of Southeast Asia and the United Kingdom's representative to SEATO.

Selkirk is best known for his deft handling of the difficult negotiations between the Federation of Malaya government and the political factions within Singapore leading up to MERGER. His meeting with left-wing politicians including LIM CHIN SIONG, SIDNEY WOODHULL and JAMES PUTHUCHEARY at Eden Hall, his official residence, on 18 July 1961, became known as the 'Eden Hall Tea Party'. At this meeting, Selkirk was asked if the British were prepared to accept a left-wing elected government, to which he replied that the British would abide by the Constitution and the people's wishes. This faction then broke away and established the BARISAN SOSIALIS. The PEOPLE'S ACTION PARTY lambasted the British over this 'conspiracy'.

After his stint as high commissioner, Selkirk was invested as a Knight Grand Cross of the Order of the British Empire (GBE) in 1963.

Selvam, G.P. (1936–) Judge. Govinda Pannir Selvam was educated in Singapore and started work as a teacher. In 1965, he decided to study law. He graduated at the top of his class at the University of Singapore (1968) and was called to the Singapore Bar in 1969. He joined the firm of DREW & NAPIER and practised there for the next 22 years, rising to the position of senior partner, and earning a reputation as a shipping and insurance lawyer.

In 1991, Selvam was appointed JUDICIAL COMMISSIONER. He was elevated to the Bench as a Supreme Court judge in 1994. He retired from the Supreme Court in 2001. In August of the same year, he was appointed C.J. Koh Professor of Law at the National University of Singapore where, as editor-in-chief, he worked on *Singapore Civil Procedure* and lectured. He later resumed practice as a founding partner of the firm Haq and Selvam.

Sembawang The first reference to Sembawang can be found in Franklin and Jackson's 1830 Plan of Singapore, which refers to the River Tambuwang. It is believed that the area (in the north of the island) was named after the *sembawang* tree (*Kayae ferruginea*). In the 19th century, it was fairly rural with a few isolated villages. At the turn of the century, Sembawang became known for its numerous rubber estates, one of the most prominent being the Nee Soon Rubber Plantation. In the 1920s and 1930s, the area was developed to provide housing for British armed forces and navy personnel working in the Sembawang Air Base and Sembawang Naval Base. Sembawang has one of the last two natural beaches in Singapore and one of the largest concentrations of colonial BLACK-AND-WHITE HOUSES. Sembawang is also the site of a public-housing estate, and covers the areas of Sembawang, Woodlands, Admiralty, Chong Pang, Nee Soon Central and Nee Soon East. As of 2005, Sembawang's population stood at 62,900.

SembCorp Industries One of Singapore's largest GOVERNMENT-LINKED COMPANIES. SembCorp Industries Ltd was incorporated on 20 May 1998, following the merger of two Singapore Exchange-listed companies, Singapore Technologies Industries Corp and Sembawang Corp. As of 2006, SembCorp Industries had assets exceeding $7 billion in five core business areas: utilities, engineering and construction, environmental engineering, logistics and marine engineering. It is the largest engineering and construction company in Asia outside Japan and South Korea, and runs the largest ship repair and conversion operation in East Asia. The company has more than 12,000 employees.

SembCorp Industries is among the largest 20 companies in Singapore by market capitalization, and its listed counter is a component of the Straits Times Index, FTSE/Hang Seng Asian Sector Indexes and several MSCI indices. It posted net earnings of $303.3 million on a turnover of $7.4 billion for financial year 2005. One of its units, SembCorp Marine, is also listed on the Singapore stock exchange. TEMASEK HOLDINGS owns more than 50 per cent of shares in the group. In March 2006, SembCorp sold its 60 per cent share in another unit, SembCorp Logistics, to Australia's Toll Holdings for $749.2 million.

Seng Ong Bio This temple, dedicated to Cheng Huang Ye—the City God—was built on Peck Seah Street in 1904 by Reverend Swee Oi from Fujian province and a scholar named Khoo Sok Guan. In the early 1900s, it served not only as a place of worship, but also as a place where immigrant workers from China could gather and socialize. Indeed, its founders had conceived of the temple as a haven for poor immi-

Seng Ong Bio

grants living in the TELOK AYER area. The stature and importance of the temple grew, and in 1907, it was presented with a scroll of calligraphy written by the Chinese ambassador, Zuo Bing Long, on behalf of the Chinese Emperor.

Seng Ong Bio is perhaps the best known of several temples dedicated to the City God. The Chinese have traditionally believed that each urban district has its own city god responsible for monitoring the behaviour of the residents of that district, and who therefore has a say in a person's fate in the afterlife. Also worshipped at Seng Ong Bio are Hu Shen (tiger god), Confucius, Tai Sui (god of yearly duty) and several other deities.

Seng Ong Bio is the only temple in Singapore to have continued the practice of 'ghost weddings', in which the souls of two deceased persons are wed in the afterlife. Another popular adjunct to prayers to Hu Shen at this temple is the practice of *da xiaoren* (literally 'beating the lesser person'), in which devotees ask for assistance in circumventing obstructions caused by difficult persons at their places of work or study.

Sengkang The name 'Sengkang' is derived from Lorong Sengkang, a road off Lorong Buangkok. In Chinese, 'Sengkang' ('Shen-gang' in Pinyin) means 'prosperous harbour'. Development of Sengkang into a public housing estate has been a recent phenomenon as this area, in northern Singapore, was formerly one of fishing villages and rubber and pepper plantations. In 2005, the estate had over 38,000 residential units, but up to 95,000 units are planned. A Light Rail Transit line connects the estate to the North-East Mass Rapid Transit line.

Senior Counsel Rank accorded to senior legal practitioners in recognition of their expertise and distinction in the profession. The Senior Counsel is the equivalent of a QUEEN'S COUNSEL in the United Kingdom. The rank was introduced in 1996, with the passage of the LEGAL PROFESSION (Amendment) Act. Under the new section 30, a selection committee comprising the chief justice, the attorney-general and the judges of appeal is constituted for the purpose of selecting Senior Counsels. Under the act, all persons who, immediately preceding 21 April 1989, hold the office of

attorney-general and SOLICITOR-GENERAL, are deemed to have been appointed as Senior Counsel.

Selection is based on applications received from persons who have for at least ten years been advocates and solicitors or legal service officers, or both. The committee may appoint a member of the Bar a Senior Counsel if they are of the opinion that, by virtue of the person's ability, standing at the Bar or special knowledge or experience in law, the person deserves such distinction.

In 1996, the first batch of 12 Senior Counsels were appointed. They were: JOSEPH GRIMBERG, K.S. Rajah, Michael Sydney Hwang, HARRY ELIAS, Giam Chin Toon, Michael Khoo, Tan Kok Quan, Wong Meng Meng, WOO BIH LI, V.K. RAJAH, Davinder Singh and Kenneth Michael Tan.

senior minister Cabinet post. The post of senior minister, unlike that of the prime minister, is not constitutionally mandated. It was created in 1984 and is part of the establishment of the PRIME MINISTER'S OFFICE. Singapore's first senior minister was S. RAJARATNAM, Singapore's long-serving foreign minister and second deputy prime minister.

When LEE KUAN YEW retired as prime minister in 1990, his successor GOH CHOK TONG appointed him senior minister in his Cabinet. Lee held this position until 2004, when he assumed the newly created post of MINISTER MENTOR. Goh himself was appointed senior minister in August 2004 following his retirement as prime minister.

Senoko Power Wholly owned by the investment arm of the Singapore government, TEMASEK HOLDINGS, Senoko Power is the largest power generation company in Singapore, providing over 30 per cent of the nation's electricity needs.

Senoko Power was the first in the country to import clean natural gas for power generation in 1992. Around two-thirds of the electricity used in Singapore is produced from natural gas, which is sourced from Indonesia and Malaysia.

Senoko Power has a combined installed capacity of 3,390 megawatt (MW), comprising 1,250 MW of thermal plants, 1,930 MW of combined cycle plants and 210 MW of fast-start gas turbines. Senoko Power owns and operates two facilities in Singapore—the Senoko Power Station and Pasir Panjang Gas Turbine Station. It has been awarded ISO 9001 certification for its operations, and it also operates its own water desalination plant.

Sentosa Island 500 m south of Singapore's main island. Prior to 1972, Sentosa was previously called Pulau Blakang Mati meaning in Malay 'behind (it) death', possibly referring to early pirate activities. It was the site of a fishing village until the 1880s, when

the British began using it as a military base. Three artillery forts were built on the island (FORT SERAPONG, FORT CONNAUGHT and FORT SILOSO), to protect the shipping lanes to the south of Singapore.

After World War II, the British handed over the base to the Singapore government. In 1967, the Singapore Naval Volunteer Force (*see* REPUBLIC OF SINGAPORE NAVY), the School of Maritime Training and the first Naval Medical Centre were relocated to the island. In 1970, it was decided to transform it into a recreational island, and the public was invited to give it a new name. 'Sentosa' ('peace and tranquility' in Malay) was chosen in 1972.

The island, 3 km long and 1 km wide, was converted into a holiday resort, complete with hotels, golf courses, and other attractions. It has a 3.2-km stretch of white sandy beach. One of the original forts, Fort Siloso, is now a popular tourist attraction. The island can be reached from the mainland by cable car or by road over a bridge.

Seow, Francis (1928–) Lawyer and politician. Francis Seow Tiang-Siew was educated at ST JOSEPH'S INSTITUTION and then at King's College London where he obtained his LLB. He was called to the English Bar in 1955 at Middle Temple, and admitted to the Singapore Bar and the Federation Bar in 1956. After completing his pupillage at Tan Rajah & Cheah, he joined the legal service on 3 July 1956 as Crown Counsel and deputy public prosecutor. Seow became SOLICITOR-GENERAL in 1968.

In 1970, Seow left the service for private practice. In 1973 and 1984, he was suspended from practice for professional misconduct and an offence involving a false declaration. In October 1986, he was elected into the Council of the Law Society by 223 of the 332 votes cast in the senior section, and became president of the society.

Seow felt that the society should play a more critical role in legislation—this led to several highly publicized confrontations with the government, the most notable of which involved the Legal Profession (Amendment) Act. The act, which passed into law on 27 October 1986, disqualified persons who had been disbarred for professional misconduct from serving in the Council of the Law Society, forcing Seow to vacate his presidency.

Sentosa: dolphin show at Underwater World (top); beach volleyball.

Francis Seow

In May 1988, Seow was arrested under the INTERNAL SECURITY ACT for being a 'willing partner to acts of interference in Singapore's internal affairs by representatives of a foreign power'. Soon after Seow's arrest, Mason 'Hank' Hendrickson, first secretary of the US Embassy in Singapore, was expelled from the island for 'meddling in Singapore politics'. Seow was detained for 72 days and released in July 1988.

In August 1988, Seow joined the WORKERS' PARTY and contested the general election, standing as a candidate for Eunos Group Representation Constituency (GRC) alongside LEE SIEW CHOH and Mohd Khalit Mohd Baboo. It was one of the most closely contested GRCs in Singapore's history: the PEOPLE'S ACTION PARTY team of TAY ENG SOON, ZULKIFLI MOHAMMED and Chew Heng Ching beat the Workers' Party team by a mere 1,279 votes, a 1.8 per cent majority.

Lee and Seow were each offered a seat as a NON-CONSTITUENCY MEMBER OF PARLIAMENT, but Seow never took his seat, fleeing Singapore over charges of tax evasion. He became a fellow at Harvard University where he wrote *To Catch A Tartar: A Dissident in Lee Kuan Yew's Prison*.

Seow Yit Kin (1955–) Musician. Seow Yit Kin studied with VICTOR DOGGETT and GOH SOON TIOE in Singapore before entering the Yehudi Menuhin School, where he was mentored by Menuhin, Nadia Boulanger and Vlado Perlemuter, among others. At 19, he won the BBC Piano Competition and soon made his debut at the Henry Wood Promenade Concerts in London. He also won a medal at the 1977 Arthur Rubinstein Piano Competition in Israel, where he received high praise from Rubinstein himself. Seow has performed widely at music festivals around the world and has made several recordings, among them Erik Satie's *Piano Music* (2000). He currently resides in London.

sepak takraw Traditional Malay sport, originating in the 15th century. A match is played between two teams comprising

Sepak takraw

Seow Yit Kin

three players each. They compete by spiking a ball—made of cane or rattan—into the opponent's court. Each team has three opportunities to kick, knee, shoulder or head the ball back into the opposing team's court. There are also passes, sets and spikes, but the ball cannot be hit with hands or arms. The sport was formerly known as *takraw* in Thailand, *sipak* in the Philippines and *sepak raga* in Malaysia and Singapore. A naming consensus was reached in 1965 when it was proposed as a medal sport for the Southeast Asian Peninsular Games (precursor of the Southeast Asian Games). The name *sepak takraw* is a combination of the Thai and Malay names.

In Singapore, the sport is played mostly by Malays. The Singapore Sepak Takraw Federation (Persekutuan Sepak Takraw Singapura, or Perses) has been in existence since 1958 and is part of the Asian and international *sepak takraw* federations. Perses organizes league tournaments for youths and adults. *Sepak takraw* is classified as a merit sport by the Singapore Sports Council, and receives up to $2 million a year for development.

Sepak takraw has been played at the Asian Games since 1990, and the international *sepak takraw* body is seeking the sport's acceptance as a world and Olympic sport. The Singapore team won the bronze medal at the 2002 Asian Games in Busan.

Separation After MERGER in 1963, there were divergent opinions on what the new Malaysia should represent. Federation leaders, particularly the Malay leaders of the UNITED MALAYS NATIONAL ORGANISATION (UMNO), saw Malaysia as an extension of the 'Old Malaya' in which political power was vested in the communally aligned Alliance government, and in which Malays would be given special privileges.

Singapore was admitted on the understanding that it would have to adjust to this conception of Malaysia. But LEE KUAN YEW and the PEOPLE'S ACTION PARTY (PAP) saw Malaysia not as an extension of the 'old Malaya' but as a 'qualitatively different country' altogether—one which would be a 'Malaysian Malaysia' rather than a 'Malay Malaysia'.

Moreover, an intense political rivalry developed between the PAP and the Alliance Party. The PAP's left-wing and non-communal stance—albeit supported

by a largely Chinese base—contrasted with the Alliance's right-wing, communal orientation, and pro-Malay bias. Suspicious of the political ambitions of the socialist PAP, Malaysia's premier, Tunku ABDUL RAHMAN, had sought to insulate the federation from the influence of the PAP by granting Singapore only restricted representation in Malaysia's federal parliament, thereby excluding Singapore's ministers from his Cabinet. He also barred Singapore citizens from contesting peninsular elections, and peninsular politicians from taking part in Singapore elections.

The Tunku viewed Singapore as the commercial centre of the federation—the 'New York of Malaysia'—but had never been reconciled with the idea of a Singapore ruled by the socialist PAP. Consequently, he had sought to undermine the PAP's influence through the SINGAPORE ALLIANCE PARTY (SA). In the September 1963 election in Singapore, for instance, federal ministers, including the Tunku, expressed support for the SA in Singapore in an effort to unseat the PAP. However, the SA failed to win a single seat, and despite the Tunku's personal intervention, the Singapore United Malays National Organisation (Singapore UMNO), one of the partners within the SA, lost each of the three seats it had previously controlled in predominantly Malay constituencies to PAP Malay candidates.

The federation's attempts to contain and dominate Singapore politically were met by the PAP's equally determined efforts to avoid containment and political demise. So long as the PAP remained a Singapore-bound party, it would have no effective counter to the Alliance government, which had the ability to bring federal power to bear on the island.

A token PAP team subsequently contested the FEDERAL ELECTION (1964). The PAP was hopeful that it would be able to win some seats, establish itself as a 'Malaysian' party and persuade UMNO to invite it to join government, allowing the PAP to play a wider national role and avoid confrontation with UMNO. The PAP deliberately avoided opposing UMNO candidates and only contested constituencies in which Malayan Chinese Association (MCA) candidates stood. But the Tunku stood by his MCA partner in the Alliance Party, and the PAP won only one seat.

After the election, PAP-Alliance rivalry intensified as UMNO activists began a campaign to undermine the multiracial basis of the PAP's support in Singapore. UMNO accused the PAP of mistreating Singapore's Malay population. The tense atmosphere that resulted from this three-month campaign is believed to have contributed to two RACE RIOTS in Singapore, in July and September 1964.

In October 1964, UMNO announced its intention to reinvigorate the SA with a

Separation: announced by Lee Kuan Yew, far right.

Proclamation of Singapore

WHEREAS it is the inalienable right of a people to be free and independent;

AND WHEREAS Malaysia was established on the 16th day of September, 1963, by a federation of existing states of the Federation of Malaya and the States of Sabah, Sarawak and Singapore into one independent and sovereign nation;

AND WHEREAS by an Agreement made on the seventh day of August in the year one thousand nine hundred and sixty-five between the Government of Malaysia of the one part and the Government of Singapore of the other part it was agreed that Singapore should cease to be a state of Malaysia and should thereupon become an independent and sovereign state and nation separate from and independent of Malaysia;

AND WHEREAS it was also agreed by the parties to the said Agreement that, upon the separation of Singapore from Malaysia, the Government of Malaysia shall relinquish its sovereignty and jurisdiction in respect of Singapore so that the said sovereignty and jurisdiction shall on such relinquishment vest in the Government of Singapore;

AND WHEREAS by a Proclamation dated the ninth day of August in the year one thousand nine hundred and sixty-five the Prime Minister of Malaysia Tunku Abdul Rahman Putra Al-Haj Ibni Almarhum Sultan Abdul Hamid Halim Shah did proclaim and declare that Singapore shall on the ninth day of August in the year one thousand nine hundred and sixty-five cease to be a state of Malaysia and shall become an independent and sovereign state and nation separate from and independent of Malaysia and recognised as such by the Government of Malaysia.

Now I LEE KUAN YEW Prime Minister of Singapore, DO HEREBY PROCLAIM AND DECLARE on behalf of the people and the Government of Singapore that as from today the ninth day of August in the year one thousand nine hundred and sixty-five Singapore shall be forever a sovereign democratic and independent nation, founded upon the principles of liberty and justice and ever seeking the welfare and happiness of her people in a more just and equal society.

Lee Kuan Yew
Prime Minister, Singapore

Dated the 9th day of August, 1965.

view to ending PAP rule by the next election. In November, the PAP announced its readiness to assume the role of an opposition party in Malaysia, and to seek national power. After unsuccessful negotiations between both sides between December 1964 and February 1965, the PAP intensified efforts to expand on the peninsula and in Borneo, and to build a united front of like-minded opposition parties from Malaya and Sarawak. In May 1965, this was formally established as the MALAYSIAN SOLIDARITY CONVENTION.

To avoid racial conflict, the Tunku decided that Singapore should separate from Malaysia. Separation took place on 9 August 1965, which is now marked as NATIONAL DAY in Singapore.

Sepoy Mutiny The origins of this mutiny, by Indian troops in Singapore on 15 February 1915, lay in a three-tiered problem: British forces East of Suez had been reduced to a minimal level; Ottoman Turkey had declared war against the United Kingdom in November 1914; and the German cruiser *Emden*'s raids had undermined British prestige.

The first problem arose when the 1st King's Own Yorkshire Light Infantry was sent to the front in France in late 1914. This left the Bengal 5th Light Infantry—a mixture of Rajputs and Pathans—as the only regular infantry battalion in Singapore. It was supplemented by the paramilitary Malay State Guides, who were largely SIKHS. The Malay State Guides were normally based in Taiping, Perak, where some were involved in small-scale businesses.

The Turkish declaration of war posed a problem because the Turkish Sultan claimed the title of Khalifatul-Islam (Caliph of Islam) or notional spiritual leader of the Muslim community. Muslim troops were disgruntled by the United Kingdom's war against a Muslim power, and anxious lest they be deployed against their fellow believers. By early 1915, some feared an impending move might not be to Hong Kong but to France or Turkey.

In December 1914, the Malay States Guides, agitated by Gujarati merchant Kassim Ismail Mansur, refused to embark for East Africa, on the grounds that their terms of recruitment only specified service in Malaya. Kassim even hoped that Turkey might send warships. But the impetus to revolt was provided by the German cruiser *Emden* (*see* WORLD WAR I). By her daring Indian Ocean escapades—setting oil storage at Madras alight, raiding PENANG, and capturing merchant ships—the *Emden* undermined British prestige. Worse still, when her crew surrendered, they were sent to Singapore and imprisoned under sepoy guard. The prisoners may not have directly agitated their sepoy guards to revolt (the Germans' own escape tunnel being almost complete), but the guards believed that the Germans might help them.

On the afternoon of Monday, 15 February, about half the 818 Indian officers and men of the 5th Light Infantry at Alexandra Barracks, and most of the 97 Indians of the Malay States Guides' Mountain Battery, mutinied. They tried to free about 309 German sailors and civilian internees from Tanglin Barracks. Only 17 of the prisoners escaped, of which most escaped by boat to the Dutch East Indies. One of three sections of the mutineers attacked their commander's bungalow. Elsewhere, mutineers indulged in sporadic killings at Keppel Harbour and Pasir Panjang, killing civilian men and women as well as military personnel. This led the government to send European women and children to the safety of boats offshore.

Marines and crew from HMS *Cadmus* were brought ashore, and helped halt a rebel advance on the city from Alexandra Road. Assistance was sought from India and nearby warships. By Wednesday, the French cruiser *Montcalm* and a Russian and two Japanese warships had sent men ashore. The mutineers scattered, some fleeing for Johor, where the sultan's forces rounded them up. On Saturday, 20 February, six companies of the 1/4th Shropshire Light Infantry arrived from Rangoon (present-day Yangon) to find the mutiny over, bar mopping up. Courts-martial began on 23 February.

The Gujarati merchant, Kassim, was hanged. Some 41 mutineers were sentenced to be shot, the Singapore Volunteers doing the job in public, outside Outram Prison. Another 126 mutineers were sentenced to jail. The remainder of the 5th Light Infantry was sent to fight German forces in Cameroon, and the Malay States Guides were dispatched to Aden.

The bulk of the fighting had been done by the Singapore Volunteer Corps (*see* STRAITS SETTLEMENTS VOLUNTEER FORCE), Malay States Volunteer Rifles, Johor Military Forces, marines, sailors, engineers and artillery totalling around 500, and about 400 specially enlisted constables, 190 of the latter being Japanese. Deaths included 56 mutineers, three Chinese and two Malay civilians, and more than 40 Europeans, of whom 18 were civilians.

The mutiny cemented the case for the Singapore Volunteer Rifles. The 1915 Civil Guard Ordinance made registration of male British subjects of European descent between the ages of 18 and 45 for military training compulsory. Post-war, it led to the dissolution of the Malay States Guides in 1922 and helped spur the Malay sultans into demanding a regular local force. Initiated in 1933, this local force became the MALAY REGIMENT by 1941. The mutiny also prompted the establishment in 1918 of a Police Criminal Intelligence Department (that is, SPECIAL BRANCH) in the Straits Settlements, with help from India, so that

Prime Minister, Singapore

Dated the 9th day of August, 1965

Separation: Proclamation of Singapore.

the government would not be caught unawares a second time. The 1/4th Shropshire Light Infantry remained on the island for the duration of WORLD WAR II.

sepoys Indian troops raised by the EAST INDIA COMPANY and British Indian Army. Sepoys were the mainstay of British power in the East until India's independence in 1947. They first arrived in Singapore from the East India Company settlement of PENANG in January 1819, on board the troop ships *Mercury* and *Nearchus*, part of Sir STAMFORD RAFFLES' and WILLIAM FARQUHAR'S fleet of eight vessels. By March 1819, Farquhar, the first Resident, had just 150 sepoys, and 30 Europeans and their guns from the Bengal Light Artillery. Some 485 Bengal Native Infantry arrived from Bencoolen in April, the reinforcements helping to ease fears that the Dutch might attack. By 1824, the Royal Navy was unchallenged at sea, and the Dutch had recognized British control in signing the Treaty of London (17 March 1824) (*see* ANGLO-DUTCH TREATY).

Free trade meant that the settlement generated only limited funds for defence. As a result, Singapore's local defence force continued to be limited to a small number of sepoys, together with British officers, artillery and engineers. The sepoys built their first barracks at the foot of Bukit Larangan (Fort Canning), eventually moving to new quarters near Outram Road.

The Indian Mutiny of 1857–58, a period of armed rebellion against East India Company rule in India, led to the military regulation that there should be one European unit for every three Indian units. The mutiny caused the government and merchants also to favour European troops. In 1872, the sepoys of the Madras Regiment were replaced by a European regiment, the STRAITS SETTLEMENTS administration contributing towards defence costs. In practice, this meant 600–900 infantry (a portion stationed in Penang) and 200 gunners at any one time—clearly not enough to defend the six forts and 34 coastal defence guns, let alone repel a land-

ing or defeat an insurrection. At root, the East India Company, and subsequently London, insisted external defence rest mainly with the Royal Navy, with troops existing to counter surprise attacks and local unrest. Sepoys were, however, also used to expand and protect Singapore's hinterland in the Malay States, notably in the Perak War of 1874–75.

Indian infantry returned to Singapore when the European Regiment was deployed to the Boer War, leaving one sepoy battalion and one European battalion. After WORLD WAR I broke out, the British battalion of 1st King's Own Yorkshire Light Infantry was withdrawn (1914). In February 1915, however, the sepoys of the Indian 5th Bengal Light Infantry mutinied (*see* SEPOY MUTINY).

The reluctance to rely on Indian troops led to the post-war raising of an experimental Malay Force from 1933, which evolved into the MALAY REGIMENT. But despite the Malay Regiment's expansion to two battalions in December 1941, the Indian military presence did not come to an end. Instead, Japan's forward movement in East Asia forced the British to rely on unprecedented numbers of Indian troops in order to swell the garrison to over 86,000 men by 1941. Roughly half were from India; only the tiniest fraction were locally recruited regulars. Even after Singapore's fall, LORD LOUIS MOUNTBATTEN's 250,000 troops in the Southeast Asia Command (1942–46) were largely Indian. They underpinned the re-occupation of Southeast Asia, as well as British attempts to manage the post-war decolonization process.

After Indian independence, in 1947, the British kept eight Gurkha battalions, deploying most to Malaya and Singapore, Brunei and Hong Kong. Even after the BRITISH WITHDRAWAL FROM SINGAPORE between 1971 and 1975, some GURKHAS remained as the Gurkha Contingent of the SINGAPORE POLICE FORCE.

Serangoon Although SERANGOON ROAD has existed since about 1821, the development of the area with a public housing estate and new town has been a fairly recent phenomenon. Serangoon Town is located in central Singapore, and covers 740 ha, of which 21 per cent is earmarked for residential use. By 2005, Serangoon town had 21,500 units housing about 78,000 residents.

Serangoon River The Serangoon River takes its name from a species of stork that once inhabited its waters (*see* SERANGOON ROAD). The river's source is in the low hills of Paya Lebar and it flows out into Serangoon harbour, opposite PULAU UBIN and the islet known as Coney Island. The lower course of the river is much less urbanized than many of Singapore's other rivers; it still retains a natural aspect with tree-lined banks, thickets of tropical forest

and mangrove swamps in its estuary. Relatively unpolluted, its waters can however be very muddy after heavy rainfall. The Serangoon River is host to a wide range of fish and mollusc species.

Serangoon Road What is today Serangoon Road was first marked on a map in 1821 as a bridle path that reached as far as the vicinity of what is now Woodsville Close. By 1827, it had been transformed into a road that reached as far as the SERANGOON RIVER.

The origins of the name Serangoon are unclear. It was probably derived from '*ranggung*', the Javanese name for the painted stork (*Mycteria leucocephala*). An 1828 map contained three names that included variant spellings of the term *ranggung*: Tanjong Rangung, Rangung River and Pulau Rangung. On an 1836 map by GEORGE D. COLEMAN, these names were spelt as 'Tanjong Rangon' and 'the Rangon River'. The 'Se' prefix is believed to be an abbreviation of the Malay word '*satu*', meaning 'one' or 'single', thus possibly signifying that this was a single road linked to a swamp area inhabited by storks.

During the 19th century, the area around Serangoon Road was occupied largely by the Indian community. Many brick kilns and cattle sheds were built in the area, and so it came to be known as Kandang Kerbau (Malay for 'buffalo enclosure'). Today, 'Serangoon Road' generally means the area between the Bukit Timah Road junction and the Balestier Road junction, and includes LITTLE INDIA. Prominent buildings along it include the Sri Veeramakaliamman Temple, Mustafa Centre (*see* MOHAMED MUSTAFA & SAMSUDDIN), Little India Arcade and TEKKA MARKET. The first traffic lights in Singapore were installed at the junction of Serangoon Road and Bukit Timah Road in 1948.

Serjeant-at-Arms Officer appointed by PARLIAMENT to keep order during meetings, and, if necessary, forcibly remove any members who are overly rowdy or disruptive. He is also the custodian of the MACE OF PARLIAMENT and performs a ceremonial function as bearer of the mace during the ceremony for the opening of Parliament.

services sector This sector of the economy encompasses a wide range of activities, including wholesale and retail trade; finance and insurance; food, beverage and accommodation; transport and communications; and real estate. Of these, finance and insurance services have registered the highest profitability ratios—72.9 per cent in 2003.

In 2004, the services sector contributed about 63 per cent of total GROSS DOMESTIC PRODUCT and 68.9 per cent of total employment in Singapore. The services sector is important to the continued growth of the economy, as Singapore lacks physical

Sepoys

Severe Acute Respiratory Syndrome: precautions taken at Tan Tock Seng Hospital during outbreak.

resources and has a small domestic market. SPRING SINGAPORE, the national standards body and supporter of small businesses, has been actively working to set national standards for the services sector.

Severe Acute Respiratory Syndrome This highly infectious disease was brought into Singapore in March 2003 by three Singaporeans who had contracted it in Hong Kong. One of them was later identified as the 'index case', as others, including relatives and the healthcare workers who attended to her, soon caught the virus as well. Severe Acute Respiratory Syndrome (SARS) soon became a national emergency as more cases were detected in the country.

SARS was identified as a new type of atypical pneumonia that infects the lungs, and that spreads through droplets when an infected person coughs or sneezes. Most cases of SARS were acquired through close, person-to-person contact. Those who cared for, lived with, or had had direct contact with SARS patients were most at risk.

TAN TOCK SENG HOSPITAL was designated as the institution for the treatment of SARS cases. Doctors and nurses were often torn between the call of duty and the fear of catching SARS or of infecting members of their own families. Healthcare workers, including even administrative staff working in other hospitals and clinics, also found themselves shunned by people who feared catching the virus.

To control the spread of SARS and facilitate the monitoring of people who had been in contact with SARS patients, the Ministry of Health invoked the Infectious Diseases Act to impose home quarantine orders. People placed under home quarantine (who did not necessarily have SARS but who had been in touch with SARS patients) were confined to their homes as a precaution. To prevent new SARS cases from entering Singapore, all visitors were required to undergo temperature screening at border checkpoints.

By the time Singapore was declared free of SARS by the World Health Organization on 31 May 2003, 33 people had died from the disease locally. In total, there were 239 reported cases of SARS in Singapore, with 97 of these being health care workers. Globally, SARS infected more than 8,000 people, the majority of cases being in China, Hong Kong, Taiwan and Singapore.

Singapore has developed a number of strategies that can be employed should SARS recur. Researchers at Temasek Life Sciences Laboratory have worked with Tan Tock Seng Hospital, SINGAPORE GENERAL HOSPITAL and the NATIONAL ENVIRONMENT AGENCY to develop an accurate series of diagnostic tests for the disease.

sewerage The first plan for the disposal of sewage was prepared in 1890 by municipal engineer JAMES MACRITCHIE, who proposed collecting night soil and dumping it in the sea. However, this was not feasible because of unfavourable currents and tidal conditions. In 1893, MacRitchie proposed disposal by a processing plant, and the first experimental plant was established in 1898. The plant was coal-fired, boiling off the liquid portion of the night soil; the solids were reduced to powder (poudrette) for use as fertilizer. The plant was discontinued in 1904 as it was expensive, and farmers did not like poudrette and its pungent smell.

In 1907, W.J.R. Simpson, a health officer from Fremantle, presented the findings of the First Survey of the Sanitary Conditions of Singapore and recommended the introduction of a two-bucket system of removing night soil until a water carriage sewerage system could be implemented. There was strong resistance to the bucket system initially—it was only in 1913 that it became widely used. By 1940, nearly 20,000 households or 35 per cent of the population were participating in the bucket system. On 24 January 1987, the last bucket latrine was replaced by on-site sanitation, and removal of night soil came to an end.

In 1911, the new municipal engineer, R. Peirce, proposed dividing the city into three areas, each served by a trunk sewer that drained into a pumping station. Sewage would be sent to a new Sewage Disposal Works at Alexandra Road where it would be treated by trickling filters and humus tanks, before being discharged into the SINGAPORE RIVER. The scheme was completed in 1917. Later, the night-soil was collected and pumped to a new activated sludge plant at the Kim Chuan Treatment Works where it was mixed and digested with sludge. The digested sludge was sent to the Serangoon Sludge Treatment Works.

After World War II, Singapore's population grew rapidly and the Alexandra Sewage Disposal Works became overloaded. In 1961, the Ulu Pandan Sewage Treatment Works, located away from the city, was completed; the Alexandra Sewage Disposal Works was decommissioned. Following the growth of satellite towns such as Queenstown and Toa Payoh, new sewage treatment works were built in Bedok, Kranji, Seletar and Jurong.

On 1 April 2001, the six treatment works were renamed Bedok, Jurong, Kim Chuan, Kranji, Seletar and Ulu Pandan Water Reclamation Plants, to emphasize their new role: treating used water not only for disposal but also for re-use (*see* NEWATER). To meet future needs, a DEEP TUNNEL SEWERAGE SYSTEM is being built.

Shafi'i School Principal school of Islamic jurisprudence (in Arabic, *madhhab*) in Singapore, and the region. Named after Muhammad ibn Idris al-Shafi'i (767–820), better known as Imam Shafi'i, this school is also prevalent in Central Asia, Yemen, and the Malabar Coast of India. It is believed that merchants and preachers arriving from Yemen and the Malabar Coast were responsible for the establishment of this school in the region. Born in Palestine and raised in Mecca, Imam al-Shafi'i was the architect of systematic Islamic law, setting out the principles of jurisprudence based on the Qur'an, *Hadith*, deductive analogy and scholastic consensus. His methodology was universally adopted by the other schools.

The other large school in Singapore is the HANAFI SCHOOL. Its adherents are mainly the INDIAN MUSLIMS. The other two schools of Sunni Islam worldwide are the Maliki and Hanbali. Among Sunni Muslims, each school regards the other as valid. The two prominent Shi'ite schools are the Ja'fari and Zaydi (*see* SHI'A). These schools of jurisprudence cover almost all aspects of life, from eating, to doing business, to marriage and divorce.

Shahbandar Persian title (also spelled *xabandaría* in Portuguese) adopted by Malay rulers of port-states along the Malacca Strait to denote the post of harbour master, who had jurisdiction over foreign traders calling or residing at the ports.

References to a Shahbandar on the island of Singapore are found in some 17th-century maps. The *Descripçao*

Serangoon Road: Sunday shopping (below); Sri Vadapathira Kaliamman Temple.

Shangguan Liu Yun: left, in the 1950s film Wealth of Jiang Family.

Chorographica dos Estreitos de Sincapura e Sabbam Ano 1604 (Chorographic Description of the Straits of Sincapura and Sabbam) by Manuel Godinho de Erédia notes that the *xabandaría* was located along the southern coast of the island, between what is now Tanjong Rhu and PULAU BRANI, possibly at the KALLANG RIVER or the SINGAPORE RIVER.

Another chart by the Portuguese cartographer André Pereira dos Reis, dating from around 1650, also features the *xabandaría* on the island of Singapore. Of the two surviving copies of this chart, only the one owned by the Maritime Museum of Rotterdam features the entry.

Accounts by Cornelis Matelieff de Jonge and François Valentijn both mention that the Sultan of Johor had, in 1606, dispatched Singapore's Shahbandar to Malacca to confirm news that the Dutch were planning an attack on Portuguese Malacca. These documents also suggest that foreign traders were calling at Singapore to conduct trade up until the 17th century.

Shangguan Liu Yun (1922–2002) Songwriter. Shangguan Liu Yun had no formal education as a child, as he came from an impoverished family. He later joined a Hokkien opera troupe and remained with it for several years, playing the lead male role in many of its productions.

As a teenager, Shangguan began writing songs, and enjoyed his first success in 1941 with the song 'Wu Ye Xiang Wen' (Sweet Kisses at Midnight). Another of his songs, 'Hang Fai Fak La!' (Walk Faster) (1965)—in which Shangguan set Cantonese lyrics to the Beatles song 'Can't Buy Me Love'—was highly successful in Hong Kong. Shangguan acted in a number of Hokkien films, including the film *Ma Lai Ya Zhi Lian* (Love of Malaya) (1959), produced by the local studio ENG WAH. He also wrote songs for Hong Kong-produced films in the 1950s. In 1996, Shangguan published a book about his life in the entertainment industry, *Wu Ye Xiang Wen* (Sweet Kisses at Midnight), giving it the same title as his most successful song.

Shanghainese The term 'Shanghainese' as used in Singapore refers to immigrants from the three provinces of Zhejiang, Jiangsu and Jiangxi. Those from Wenzhou or Ningbo who owned furniture shops had signboards advertising 'Shanghainese carpentry', and their owners claimed to be Shanghainese as they had inherited the intricate craftsmanship of the Shanghainese carpenters. The colonial government knew little about areas outside Guangdong and Fujian provinces, and labelled people who departed from Shanghai for Singapore as Shanghainese, regardless of their province of origin. Of these so-called Shanghainese immigrants, the Wenzhou people made up the largest numbers, followed by the Ningbo people.

According to the 2000 Census of Population, only 21,550, or less than 1 per cent of Singapore's total Chinese population, are Shanghainese. The Shanghainese in Singapore form a closely-knit community, and they established the SAM KIANG HUAY KWAN in 1906. 'Sam Kiang' refers to the three provinces of Zhejiang, Jiangsu and Jiangxi, which is why Shanghainese also used to be known as Sam Kiang people.

Before World War II, besides the few who earned a living working in trades such as bookstores, leather and tailoring, Shanghainese dominated the local carpentry trade and virtually monopolized the dry-cleaning trade. They settled downstream of Kallang River and Rochor River in the early days, congregating around Sumbawa Road (now expunged), Syed Alwi Road and Geylang Road.

With increased mechanization, those who worked in craft-based or manual jobs were forced to make occupational switches from the 1960s onwards. They turned to the teak, fibre board, construction and food and beverage industries, as well as the retail of pianos, spectacles, electrical goods and handicrafts. Nonetheless, the Shanghainese from Wenzhou continue to lead the furniture business today. The birthday of Lu Ban, patron deity of carpentry and construction, falls on the 13th day of the sixth lunar month, and has always been one of the community's most grandly celebrated occasions.

The Shanghainese founded Sam Kiang Public School and Chiao Nam School, and established Sam Kiang Charity Medical Clinic and Sam Kiang Ancestral Hall. Prominent Shanghainese personalities include film and media magnate RUNME SHAW; Chen Yoh Shoo, founder of Shanghai Book Co.; historian Professor Hsu Yun T'siao and philanthropist Chwee Meng Chong.

Shangri-La Hotel Luxury hotel. Built in 1971, the name 'Shangri-la' was inspired by James Hilton's novel *Lost Horizon*. The hotel's landscaped grounds cover 6 ha and contain over 130,000 plant varieties, reflecting Singapore's 'Garden City' identity. The hotel has hosted numerous visiting heads of state and government, international conferences and society weddings.

From this first property, Shangri-La Hotels and Resorts has grown into the largest Asian-based deluxe hotel group, with properties in many other Asian and Middle Eastern locations. The founder of the group is Malaysian entrepreneur, Robert Kuok.

Shanks, Ernest (1911–) Colonial official. Ernest P. Shanks was educated at Downing College, Cambridge. He was called to the Bar at the Inner Temple in 1936, and went into private practice thereafter. In 1939, he joined the army and stayed on till 1946, when he joined the colonial legal service as a district judge in Terengganu. In 1947, he

was appointed district judge and first magistrate. In 1950, Shanks was appointed Crown Counsel. In 1956, he became SOLICITOR-GENERAL, and within a year, attorney-general. Shanks was the last expatriate attorney-general. He retired in 1959.

Shanmugam, S.V. (1933–2001) Author and playwright. Born in India, S.V. Shanmugam came to Singapore in 1951. He worked for Singapore Port (Keppel) and retired in 1991, storekeeper being his last-held post. Shanmugam began his literary career in 1949, and wrote hundreds of short stories, essays and plays for the stage, radio and television. He has also dramatized ancient Tamil literary texts such as the Tamil epic *Kundalakesi*, as well as works by Shakespeare, Charles Dickens and Robert Louis Stevenson in Tamil for Radio Singapore (present-day MediaCorp Radio).

Among his works are prize-winning short stories 'Thirai Azhagi' (Screen Beauty), 'Meenda Vazhvu' (Resurrected Life) and 'Singapore Kulanthaikal' (Singapore Children). 'Chan Lai Seng' and 'Paatty' (Grandmother) were awarded the second prize by the Ministry of Community Development; 'Matrondru' (Another) won the first prize in a competition held by the Tamil Language and Cultural Society in 1988; and 'Puthiya Savithri' (Modern Savithri) received first prize in a competition jointly organized by the National Arts Council and Singapore Press Holdings in 1995.

The main themes in Shanmugam's work are racial and religious harmony, as exemplified in 'Singapore Kulanthaikal', 'Chan Lai Seng' and 'Paatty'.

Shanmugam was presented with the Tamizhavel Award by the Association of Singapore Tamil Writers in 1996.

shared values In 1988, first deputy prime minister GOH CHOK TONG identified certain key tenets and attitudes which he believed had been essential to the nation's survival and sense of identity. Incorporating elements of Confucian beliefs (commonly

Shangri-La Hotel

referred to as 'Asian values') and Singapore's cultural norms, these shared values are: nation before community and society before self; family as the basic unit of society; community support and respect for the individual; consensus, not conflict; and racial and religious harmony.

The concept of shared values has been extended by the government to other domains, such as family life—where it should be manifested as love, care, concern, mutual respect, filial responsibility, commitment and communication.

Sharma, Haresh (1965–) Playwright. A graduate of the National University of Singapore, Haresh Sharma obtained a master's degree in playwriting at the University of Birmingham (1996). He enjoys a long-standing working partnership with ALVIN TAN, founder and artistic director of THE NECESSARY STAGE. Sharma has been its resident playwright since 1990.

Sharma has written more than 50 plays, some in collaboration with others. *Rigor Mortis* won a Merit Prize in the 1988 Shell-NUS Short Play Competition. *Still Building*, comprising three plays (*Lanterns Never Go Out*, *Still Building*, and *More*), secured a Merit Prize (Drama) in the 1993 Singapore Literature Prize awards. The published version (1994) won a Commendation Award from the National Book Development Council of Singapore in 1996. His published work appears in *This Chord and Others* (1999) and *Off Centre* (2000). He received the NATIONAL ARTS COUNCIL's Young Artist Award for Theatre in 1997.

Lanterns Never Go Out was part of the 1990 SINGAPORE ARTS FESTIVAL. *Superfriends at the Hall of Justice* was written for the 1998 Festival, and *One Hundred Years in Waiting* co-written with Kuo Pao Kun and Chong Tze Chien for the 2001 Festival. *Revelations*, co-written with Chong Tze Chien, was commissioned for the 2003 festival. Sharma devised *Completely With/Out Character* (1999) with the late Paddy Chew, an AIDS sufferer who played himself, and Alvin Tan, who directed it. *Separation 40* (2005) was co-written with Malaysian playwright Jit Murad to commemorate the 40th anniversary of Singapore's separation from Malaysia. Sharma's collaboration with Japan's Setagaya Public Theatre resulted in *Hotel Grand Asia* (2005). He was the head writer for *Mobile*, a regional collaborative project about migrant workers which was staged at the 2006 Singapore Arts Festival.

Sharma, P.V. (unknown–1994) Trade unionist and political activist. P.V. Sharma (also spelt 'Sarma') was born in Kerala, India, and trained as a school teacher. By the late 1940s, he had become active in politics and in trade unions. He was a member of the MALAYAN DEMOCRATIC UNION and was the General Secretary and later president of the SINGAPORE TEACHERS' UNION.

Sharma was reputedly a ranking MALAYAN COMMUNIST PARTY member who succeeded in converting C.V. DEVAN NAIR to communism and 'supervised' SAMAD ISMAIL, giving him the code-name 'Zainal'.

In 1952, Sharma was banished from Singapore. He travelled to India and then China, where he worked for 32 years as a Tamil broadcaster for Beijing radio. He was allowed to re-enter Singapore in 1991.

Shaw, Run Run (1907–) Businessman. Born in China, Run Run Shaw received his education at Western-run schools in Shanghai. In 1926, he moved to Singapore to join his elder brother, RUNME SHAW. They built Singapore's first and largest cinema empire, venturing into film screening, distribution and production (*see* SHAW BROTHERS).

In the 1930s, Run Run took charge of the family's operations in southern Malaya (including Singapore), while his brother took charge of activities in northern Malaya. In the late 1940s and early 1950s, Run Run became involved in the production of Malay movies. In 1953, he expressed support for the establishment of the Asian Film Producers Federation. The following year, this federation held the inaugural Asian Film Festival in Tokyo.

In 1957, Run Run left Singapore and moved to Hong Kong, where other members of his family had settled in the 1930s. There, he reorganized the family business; created Shaw Brothers (HK) Ltd; and opened the new Shaw Studio (also known as Shaw Movie Town) in 1961, which went on to produce hundreds of films until its closure in 1985.

In the 1970s, Shaw began to turn his attention to television, investing in Television Broadcasts Ltd (commonly known as TVB), a Hong Kong broadcaster founded in 1967. He became chairman of TVB in 1980, and turned the company into the largest producer of Chinese-language television programmes in the world.

A known philanthropist, Shaw set up the SHAW FOUNDATION with his brother, Runme. He made contributions to many schools, and established an international award, the Shaw Prize for Academic and Scientific Research, which was first given in 2004. He was made a Commander of the Order of the British Empire (CBE) in 1974, and was knighted in 1977.

Shaw, Runme (1901–1985) Businessman. Runme Shaw was born the third of eight children in China, and moved to Singapore in 1924. He was followed some years later by his younger brother RUN RUN SHAW. Together, they built the successful film and cinema company, SHAW BROTHERS.

Shaw was responsible for the establishment of ALLIANCE FRANÇAISE in Singapore in 1949, and also co-founded the SHAW FOUNDATION in 1957. He was awarded the MERITORIOUS SERVICE MEDAL in 1977.

Shaw Brothers Film studio. Shaw Brothers was founded by RUNME SHAW and RUN RUN SHAW in the 1930s. They were sons of businessman Shaw Yuh Hsuen, who came from Zhejiang, China. The Shaw family had started out in the film industry in Shanghai in 1924, forming a company called Tian Yi Film Co. (also known as Unique Films Company), which produced silent movies. Looking for opportunities for expansion, Runme and Run Run were sent to Singapore in the mid-1920s, where they started the Hai Seng Company, initially in a rented shophouse on Robinson Road. This company was renamed Shaw Brothers Pte Ltd in 1938, when the two brothers ventured into the production of Malay movies.

From the mid-1930s onwards, the Shaws expanded their business beyond movies, with the development of amusement parks such as GREAT WORLD on Kim Seng Road, and NEW WORLD at Jalan Besar. These were highly profitable, and the Shaws opened a string of other parks throughout Malaya, including Jubilee Park in Ipoh.

After Singapore fell in 1942, all the Shaw cinemas were seized by the Japanese propaganda unit. Cinemas had their names changed to Japanese ones, an example being the renaming of Cathay Cinema as Dai Toa Gekijo (Greater East Asian Theatre). They were only allowed to show Japanese propaganda films and a few Indian films. In the early months of the JAPANESE OCCUPATION, Hollywood films were still shown, but these were banned by November 1943.

After WORLD WAR II, the Shaw Brothers resumed their business activities; their Malayan Theatres Limited was responsible for screening films, and their MALAY FILM PRODUCTIONS (MFP) was responsible for the production of such films. Shaw and Shaw, incorporated in 1949, was formed as a group holding company.

In 1957, Run Run Shaw decided to leave Singapore for Hong Kong in order to take over the Shaw family business there. Another branch of the family had moved to Hong Kong after the Japanese invasion of China, and had opened Nanyang Studio there in the late 1930s, as well as Shaw and Sons in 1950. In 1958, Run Run Shaw founded Shaw Brothers (HK) Ltd in Hong Kong. This grew into Hong Kong's most successful film studio.

By 1965, Shaw Brothers owned 35 companies; 130 cinemas in Southeast Asia (including 19 in Singapore); nine amusement parks; and three production studios (MFP in Singapore, Shaw Studio in Hong Kong, and Merdeka Film Productions in Kuala Lumpur). The Shaws also owned Shaw Printing Works, through which they published magazines such as *Movie News* (which ran from 1948 to the late 1980s in Singapore); *Movie News Hong Kong*; *Majallah Filem*; and *Indian Movie News*.

In 1967, Shaw Brothers began to slow film production. The group ceased to pro-

Haresh Sharma

Ernest Shanks

Run Run Shaw

Shaw Vee Meng

Benjamin Sheares

Sheik Alauddin

William Shellabear

Shaw Brothers: advertisements from the 1950s.

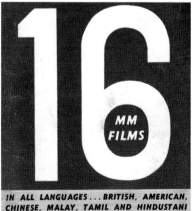

duce films altogether when MFP studio at Jalan Ampas was closed. In 1988, the business was reorganized under the umbrella of Shaw Organisation Pte Ltd.

Shaw Foundation Since it was established by RUNME and RUN RUN SHAW in 1957, the Shaw Foundation has become one of Singapore's leading philanthropic organizations, having donated over US$150 million to education, welfare, medicine, arts and heritage and various other fields. Funding comes from investments as well as various properties donated by the Shaws to the foundation, including the land housing Shaw Centre at Scotts Road. Since the late 1970s, all revenue collected from the 25-storey office block has been donated to various charities. The Hongkong Shaw Foundation was established in 1973.

Shaw Vee Meng (1933–) Businessman and philanthropist. The son of RUN RUN SHAW, Shaw Vee Meng was educated at the Anglo-Chinese School and then at St Catherine's College, Oxford University, where he read law. He was called to the Bar at Gray's Inn. On returning to Singapore in 1957, he joined the family business, taking over the Shaw Organisation in the early 1980s. In addition to his duties as chairman of the Shaw Organisation and the SHAW FOUNDATION, he is director of the Great Eastern Assurance Co. Ltd, Overseas Assurance Corporation and Great Eastern Holdings. He serves on the boards of numerous other organizations, including the ALLIANCE FRANÇAISE. In 1992, the French government appointed him to the Légion d'Honneur (Legion of Honour), with the rank of Chevalier (Knight).

Sheares, Benjamin (1907–1981) Head of state. Benjamin Henry Sheares was the son of a former Public Works Department technical supervisor. He attended St Andrew's School and Raffles Institution. In 1923, he enrolled in the King Edward VII College of

Medicine, where he graduated with an LMS in 1929. He served the next two years as assistant medical officer at the Sepoy Lines General Hospital (now SINGAPORE GENERAL HOSPITAL) before specializing in obstetrics and gynaecology. In 1940, he was awarded the Queen's Fellowship to pursue two years' post-graduate study in Britain. But he was unable to do so, due to the outbreak of World War II.

During the Japanese Occupation, Sheares was head of the Department of Obstetrics and Gynaecology at Kandang Kerbau Hospital, and medical superintendent for the local patients' section of the hospital. In 1945, he became the first Singapore-born doctor to be appointed acting professor of obstetrics and gynaecology at the King Edward VII College of Medicine. In May 1947, Sheares went to London for post-graduate study, and in January 1948, became the first Singapore obstetrician to qualify as a Member of the Royal College of Obstetricians and Gynaecologists of England. In March 1948, while studying for the degree of Fellow of the Royal College of Surgeons in Edinburgh, he was recalled to Singapore to act as professor of obstetrics and gynaecology. In 1951, Sheares spent the remainder of his Queen's Fellowship at several leading universities in the United States and concentrated on teaching and research in post-graduate obstetrics and gynaecology.

Sheares was professor of obstetrics and gynaecology at the University of Malaya in Singapore from 1950 until 1960, when he retired and went into private practice. He also became honorary consultant at the Kandang Kerbau Hospital (present-day KK WOMEN'S AND CHILDREN'S HOSPITAL), and continued teaching both undergraduate and postgraduate students.

On 2 January 1971, Sheares was sworn in as the second PRESIDENT of Singapore; he was the first Eurasian to hold the nation's highest office. He died in office on 12 May 1981, and was buried in the STATE CEMETERY at Kranji. The Benjamin Sheares Bridge—the first bridge in Singapore to be named after a president—was officially opened in 1982.

Sheik Alauddin (1967–) Sportsman. At 18, Sheik Alauddin became the national *silat* (a Malay martial art) champion. He held the title a record 13 consecutive times. He won the world title at the 1990 World Silat Championships in the Netherlands. In 1991, he won his first Southeast Asian (SEA) Games gold, and won gold in the following two SEA Games. In 1994, Sheik won the Men's Open title at the World Silat Championships—every bout saw a unanimous 5-0 decision in his favour.

Appointed national coach in 1998, Sheik retired from competition a year later to concentrate on coaching. He is a member of the SINGAPORE SPORTS COUNCIL HALL

OF FAME, and was voted Coach of the Year three times (2000, 2002 and 2003).

Shellabear, William (1862–1948) Missionary. A graduate of Woolwich Royal Academy, which trained officers for the British army, William Girdelstone Shellabear arrived in Singapore in 1887. He was appointed commanding officer of a Malay army company.

Shellabear resigned his commission in 1890 to join the Methodist Mission in Singapore and set up what became the largest publishing house in Southeast Asia: the Methodist Publishing House, which later became the Malaya Publishing House (*see* MPH BOOKSTORES). He started the first Malay Methodist mission; gatherings were initially held at Arab Street and Kampong Glam, in the streets. Eventually, they included the Straits Chinese (PERANAKANS) and the group would meet at the METHODIST GIRLS' SCHOOL. This church is now the Kampong Kapor Methodist Church.

Passionate about the Malay language, Shellabear wrote Malay textbooks and produced new editions of classic Malay works such as the SEJARAH MELAYU (Malay Annals, 1924) and *Hikayat Hang Tuah* (Life of Hang Tuah, 1908). He also prepared a Malay Methodist hymnal and book of worship.

After retiring in 1920, Shellabear went on to become professor of Muhammedan studies at the Kennedy School of Missions at Hartford Seminary in the United States. His final project was the translation of parts of the Qur'an into Malay.

Shelley, Rex (1930–) Author. Rex Anthony Shelley grew up in Singapore and Malaya. After graduating from the University of Malaya (Singapore), he read engineering and economics at Cambridge. Shelley's literary significance lies in what is informally referred to as his 'Eurasian quartet'—four novels about his community. Between them, *The Shrimp People* (1991), winner of the 1992 National Book Development Council of Singapore (NBDCS) Award (Fiction); *People of the Pear Tree* (1993), winner of the 1994 NBDCS Award (Fiction); *Island in the Centre* (1995), which was Highly Commended by the NBDCS in 1996; and *A River of Roses* (1998), winner of the 2000 Dymocks Singapore Literature Prize—cover a century of Eurasian social history, woven into robust and interlinked narratives of love, friendship, espionage and conflict such as the JAPANESE OCCUPATION. Until the publication of these novels, Eurasians had made only sporadic appearances in Singaporean fiction.

Shelley has worked in the public and private sectors, and runs his own business. He was one of the founders of the Singapore Science Centre. He has served for 27 years on the Board of the PUBLIC SERVICE COMMISSION, and was awarded the Public Service Star in 1978.

Shenton Way Road and district. Shenton Way was built on land reclaimed in 1932 from the TELOK AYER Basin. The original 27-m-wide road was designed by chief municipal engineer D. Wexton.

At first, the road was named Raffles Way, but in 1951, considering that there was already a surfeit of places named in honour of Sir Stamford Raffles, the municipality renamed the street Shenton Way in honour of Sir SHENTON THOMAS, who had been governor from 1934 to 1946.

In 1951, land along Shenton Way was opened up for redevelopment to ease traffic congestion around RAFFLES PLACE. Soon, banks and other commercial firms began to move into the large new buildings being built along this stretch of road. By the 1970s, Shenton Way had become the main financial district, earning the epithet 'the Wall Street of Singapore'.

Shi Ming Yi (1962–) Cleric. Venerable Shi Ming Yi was educated at Raffles Institution, the University of Wales (where he earned a master's degree in healthcare management) and Mannin University, United Kingdom (PhD in philosophy). He entered the Foo Hai Ch'an Monastery in 1983 and became its abbot in 1991. In 1992, he established Ren Ci Buddhist Institute and the Yuhua Benevolence Society. In 1994, the monastery took over the management of the 174-bed Chronic Sick Unit of Woodbridge Hospital, turning it into Singapore's first Buddhist-run hospital, the REN CI HOSPITAL AND MEDICARE CENTRE.

Shi is a familiar face in the local media, and famous for his death-defying stunts, which he performs to raise money for the hospital. In 2003, he abseiled down one of the towers at Suntec City, drawing pledges totalling $750,000.

See also BUDDHISM.

Shi'a Second-largest branch of Islam. Shi'a form about 10 per cent of all Muslims (about 90 per cent of Muslims are Sunni). The largest division of the Shi'a is the 12-Imam Shi'a, known as Shi'a Ithna Asheri, so called because they hold that there are 12 Imams. The Imams are supreme leaders who form a line of succession that begins with the foremost Imam, Ali ibn Abu Talib—the son-in-law of the Prophet Muhammed. The Shi'a have schools of jurisprudence. The 12-Imam school is known as the Ja'afari, after Imam Ja'afar al-Sadiq (*see* SHAFI'I SCHOOL and HANAFI SCHOOL). For Sunni Muslims, belief in the Imams and leadership through succession is not integral to doctrine. In practice, differences between Shi'a and Sunni are slight; ritual practices are very similar. Despite a history of sectarian conflict, the moderate view, as defined by the 2005 Declaration by the International Islamic Conference in Jordan, is that all Sunni and Shi'a are Muslims with common basic beliefs and practices.

In Singapore, the history of the Shi'a Ithna Asheri began approximately around the time of World War I, with the immigration of the Khoja community from India. They initiated the holding of large ceremonies in the Islamic month of MUHARAM to commemorate the martyrdom of Imam Hussain and his followers at Karbala in 680. The Khoja are a prominent community in Singapore. RAJABALI JUMABHOY, a Khoja businessman, bought a shophouse at Lim Ah Woo Road for the activities of the growing Shi'a community in the 1970s. This centre is known as Imam Bargah.

During the mid-1980s, Malays (numbering over 400) from the Muslim Youth Assembly (Himpunan Belia Islam), joined the Shi'a community. A new centre at Guillemard Road, known as Hussainiyah Azzahra, was later established, housing a large collection of Malay and English books on Islam. AMEERALI JUMABHOY spearheaded the founding of the Ja'afari Muslim Association Singapore. It was registered in 1998, and represents the Shi'a Ithna Asheri in Singapore, of whom there are less than 1,000. In Singapore, the other large group of Shi'a Muslims is the DAWOODI BOHRA.

Shin Min Daily News Chinese-language evening daily, started by Louis Cha of Hong Kong and Singaporean Leung Yun Chee on 18 March 1967. The paper, whose ownership eventually passed into the hands of SINGAPORE PRESS HOLDINGS, focused on covering entertainment and social news, sometimes highlighting them on its front page.

Shin Min Daily News was revamped in 2004, with full-colour content on all its new pages and more special feature

---
Shi Ming Yi: Abseiling down Suntec City, 2003.

columns. Its daily average circulation in 2005 was 123,526 on weekdays and 124,363 on weekends.

Shinozaki Mamoru (1908–1991) Japanese wartime official. A Japanese embassy press attaché, Shinozaki Mamoru was convicted by the British for spying and jailed in CHANGI PRISON in 1940. He was released at the start of the JAPANESE OCCUPATION in 1942 and became adviser to the Japanese military administrator. In this position, he was able to save thousands of Chinese during the SOOK CHING, by issuing them good citizen passes in February to March 1942.

As press attaché, Shinozaki had cultivated good relations with leading personalities in the different communities. To help the Eurasian and Chinese communities obtain official protection, Shinozaki was instrumental in the formation of welfare associations, the two most significant being the Overseas Chinese Welfare Association under LIM BOON KENG and the Eurasian Welfare Association under C.J. PAGLAR.

Shinozaki was also education officer and welfare officer in the war-time Japanese civilian administration, and thus had access to valuable food supplies. He was able to help many people such as the Little Sisters of the Poor and the settlers in ENDAU and BAHAU. He once explained that his family name, Shinozaki, meant 'cape of China' and Mamoru meant 'protector of people'.

ship-building and repair Singapore is among the busiest ports in the world, and its largest bunkering hub. Ship-building and ship-repair, therefore constitute an important part of the marine industry.

In 2005, total revenue for Singapore's marine industry was $7.4 billion. Ship-repair and conversion accounted for 51 per cent ($3.79 billion) of the industry's total turnover. Revenue from ship-building amounted to $1.26 billion in 2005. A total of 97 vessels with an aggregate of 149,855 gross tons were launched in 2004.

Singapore has over 200 companies dealing in ship-building and repair, which has led major equipment suppliers and service companies to set up offices or station representatives here. Major companies in the industry include Keppel Offshore and Marine (*see* KEPPEL CORPORATION) and SEMBCORP INDUSTRIES.

Shook Lin & Bok Law firm. Shook Lin & Bok was founded in 1918 by Yong Shook Lin and Tan Teow Bok in Kuala Lumpur. Yong (whose son YONG PUNG HOW would become chief justice) was the first Chinese to be called to the Bar in the Federated Malay States. The Singapore firm was established in 1964, and within 20 years, grew to become one of the largest law practices here. In September 2000, the firm entered into a joint law venture with international firm Allen & Overy LLP.

Rex Shelley

Shinozaki Mamoru

Shin Min Daily News

Shi Ming Yi

shophouses Built mostly between 1840 and 1960, shophouses are an important part of Singapore's architectural heritage. They traditionally contained business premises on the ground floor and residences on the upper floors. The term 'shophouse' is a literal translation from Chinese ('*tiam chu*' in Hokkien; '*dian wu*' in Mandarin). Shophouses have narrow frontages and 2–3 storeys, and are built in contiguous blocks. Sir STAMFORD RAFFLES, through the Town Planning Committee of 1822, prescribed a prototype: 'All houses constructed of brick or tile should have a uniform type of front, each having a verandah of a certain depth, open to all sides as a continuous and open passage on each side of the street.' Hence the FIVE-FOOT WAY.

Among the colonial architects who designed shophouses were GEORGE D. COLEMAN, J.T. Thomson and R.A.J. BIDWELL. They were followed by local 'shophouse architects' such as Wee Teck Moh and Mohamad Kassim.

First Transitional Style: Telok Ayer St.

Mythical beast, Thomson Road.

Shophouses can be roughly categorized into six architectural styles. Buildings in the **Early Shophouse Style**, are low (two storeys) and squat, with minimal ornamentation, usually of an ethnic nature. They typically feature only one (at most two) windows, on the upper floor.

Early Style: an old shophouse on North Bridge Road, and a slightly later corner unit.

The **First Transitional Shophouse Style** is more vertically proportioned than its predecessor, and almost without exception features two windows on the upper floor. A trademark of First Transitional shophouses is their elegant simplicity and relatively restrained ornamentation.

By the time the sixth style— the **Modern Shophouse Style**— emerged in the 1950s and 1960s, some of the earlier elements began to be omitted. The five-foot way and party walls remained, but modern materials such as concrete were used. Modern shophouses are more functional and austere. Their facades feature thin concrete fins that double as air vents and as simple decoration, features also of some Art Deco shophouses.

While details of shophouses may vary, key common elements include party walls, which normally project above the roof; tiled pitched roofs; five-foot way with over-hanging upper floor; and timber windows. Internally, many elements of older shophouses are of timber. Air-wells opening to the sky between roof sections provide ventilation and natural light. By the beginning of the 20th century, air-wells—and back lanes for waste collection—were health and sanitary requirements.

The influence of buildings elsewhere in the region is evident. In Batavia, for instance, godowns of the Dutch East India Company had a continuous verandah, Chinese attap shophouses had air-wells, and there were fire walls protruding above the roofline of terrace houses. Conversely, Singapore shophouse architecture was brought to southern China and Bangkok by traders and King Rama V respectively.

In 1989, the URBAN REDEVELOPMENT AUTHORITY initiated a programme which protects over 5,000 shophouses in Conservation Areas. Besides use as shops and residences, conserved shophouses have been put to new uses, for example as restaurants, spas, offices and hotels. Shophouses have become fashionable and, consequently, valuable real estate.

In recent decades, the term 'HDB shophouse' has come into use, applied to buildings constructed by the HOUSING & DEVELOPMENT BOARD (HDB); units at ground level are used as shops, and units on upper storeys are residential. They are similar in spirit, if not strictly in form, to the traditional shophouse.

In contrast, the **Late Shophouse Style** displays the most striking, varied and eclectic ornamentation, such as decorative wall tiles; even the actual wall space is reduced by the presence of windows, pilasters and other decoration. After the Late Style, there was a move towards simpler ornamentation and more streamlined design, that culminated in the Art Deco Style.

Late Style (clockwise from above): decorative tilework, Geylang; shophouse terrace, Serangoon Road; townhouses, Petain Road; ornamented upper storey, Geylang.

Bridging the Late and Art Deco styles is the **Second Transitional Shophouse Style** (left), which mixes some Late Style decorative elements, such as wall tiles, with Art Deco motifs, such as geometric designs.

The **Art Deco Shophouse Style** (right) is distinguished by its stream-lined motifs and seldom utilizes decorative wall tiles. Many Art Deco shophouses have date plates. Often, this style of shophouse emphasizes proportion and the composition of an entire grouping of similar buildings, with special focus on the street corners.

Second Transitional: Stanley Street.

Art Deco: Ann Siang Road.

Style chronology
- Early
- First Transitional
- Late
- Second Transitional
- Art Deco
- Modern

shophouses *See* box.

shopping It has been said that life for Singaporeans is not complete without shopping. Many people associate shopping with ORCHARD ROAD. However, before the 1970s, there were three main shopping areas: RAFFLES PLACE, North Bridge Road and High Street and People's Park.

Throughout the 1950s and 1960s, Raffles Place was the upscale shopping centre, and ROBINSONS (located where the UNITED OVERSEAS BANK now stands) was its premier store. Facing Robinsons was The Arcade, Singapore's only European-style shopping arcade with steel girders and a glass roof, which was built by the wealthy ALKAFF FAMILY. Beside this was JOHN LITTLE. Another European department store was Whiteaways, run by WHITEAWAY, LAIDLAW AND CO. Surrounding these European enterprises were upscale but smaller establishments: G.C. de Silva for fine jewellery, Gian Singh for Indian saris, Vanity and Elsie Mary for clothes, Michelle Beauty Parlour, and Mrs. Tommy Thompson's for formal wear and woollens. One floor below Mrs Thompson's was a popular rendezvous—the G.H. Cafe. The only 'downmarket' shopping space in Raffles Place was Change Alley, where Indian money changers plied.

Raffles Place, as a shopping area, had a tragic end when, on 21 November 1972, Robinsons was gutted by fire. Robinsons re-opened for business just before Christmas of the same year at Orchard Road, which was rapidly transforming into a shopping strip.

Wealthier Asians shopped at the North Bridge Road and High Street area. On the ST. ANDREW'S CATHEDRAL side of North Bridge Road was a string of small, Indian-owned retail establishments that sold imported European shoes and US-made men's shirts. Where North Bridge Road meets High Street were two department stores, Peking Store and the Aurora. Across the road was the main outlet of Bata Shoes.

On High Street was B.P. de Silva, a jewellery and silverware shop; the well-stocked Ensign Bookstore, a rarity when bookstores were scarce; and Chotirmall, a small department store. At the corner of South Bridge Road and High Street was The Miscellaneous Agency, a shop selling musical instruments. Sandwiched between it and Chotirmall was the POLAR CAFÉ. Across North Bridge Road was an entire row of mostly Chinese-owned wholesale fabric shops. Among the retail shops in this section of High Street was Metro, then a small clothing shop.

The Chinese masses shopped in what is now known as CHINATOWN. Its focal point was People's Park, one part of which was dedicated to FOOD, and the other to fabric stalls. Eating out was not common, so to eat at People's Park was something to talk about. Those who could not sew engaged

Shopping: promoting the Great Singapore Sale.

the services of seamstresses there. People's Park was razed in the late 1960s to make way for People's Park Complex, where fabric stalls can still be found.

Orchard Road was a sleepy shopping street catering to the wealthy, until the rise of five-star hotels in the early 1970s served to catalyse the development of shopping facilities. With hotel bars, restaurants, dance clubs and shopping complexes, Orchard Road quickly became the entertainment strip for increasingly affluent Singaporeans.

Since the 1990s, alternative shopping centres have developed in new towns such as Yishun, Bishan, Woodlands and Tampines. Well-known department stores have opened branches in these suburbs. However, none of these suburban centres can displace the primacy of Orchard Road in terms of the sheer variety it offers.

Short Daggers Rebellion In 1853, members of the Short Daggers Society—so named for the short dagger each member carried—seized control of Amoy (present-day Xiamen) and nearby counties in southern China for almost half a year.

Much of the funding and leadership for the rebellion had been provided by Singapore Hokkiens. When the rebellion failed, thousands of Hokkien and Teochew rebels fled to Singapore. This upset the delicate balance between the two groups and their respective SECRET SOCIETIES. The Hokkien-Teochew riots of 1854, which had been sparked off by a quarrel between

a Hokkien and Teochew merchant over the weight of rice being traded, also involved the Teochew Ghee Hin Society and Hokkien Ghee Hock Society. The riot lasted ten days, during which an estimated 600 Chinese were killed and a larger number wounded. Some 300 houses were burned or pillaged. Thereafter, about 500 men were arrested, of whom half were committed for trial. The sessions lasted 17 days—6 men were sentenced to death, but only 2 were executed; 64 were sentenced to hard labour; and 8 were sent to Bombay (present-day Mumbai) for 14 years.

Shree Lakshminarayan Temple Only Hindu temple in Singapore where activities are conducted in Hindi. The need for a temple where religious ceremonies could be conducted in Hindi concerned the Hindi-speaking Indian community for several years. The issue was addressed by the SINGAPORE NORTH INDIAN HINDU ASSOCIATION and a decision to build such a temple was made in 1955. The association purchased the land at Chander Road and G. Uttamram, a prominent member of the community and businessman, laid the foundation stone in 1960. The temple was officially opened in 1969 by the Speaker of Parliament, Punch Coomaraswamy.

The temple has attracted an increasing number of members to its weekly *satsang* (congregation) and regular ladies' *satsang*. Scholars are invited to give talks. It is also a popular venue for marriages, Satya Narayan Puja (worship of one of Lord Vishnu's forms) and social activities. The temple celebrates DEEPAVALI, HOLI and Krishna Jan. One thing that sets it apart from other temples is that its office-bearers are elected from various Hindi sub-groups—SINDHIS, Punjabis and Biharis.

Shui Lan *See* LAN SHUI.

Sia Kah Hui (1923–) Politician. Sia Kah Hui became MEMBER OF PARLIAMENT (MP) for Upper Serangoon at the GENERAL ELECTION (1963), standing under the PEOPLE'S ACTION PARTY banner. He represented that ward until 1980, when he

Shree Lakshminarayan Temple

Sia Kah Hui

Siew Shaw Her

became MP for Paya Lebar. He stepped down before the 1984 general election.

Sia served as parliamentary secretary to the Ministry of Health (1964–66) and the Ministry of Labour (1967–70), before becoming minister of state for labour (1970–81). In 1973, he called for a ban on tipping in hotels and restaurants, recommending that a fixed service charge be levied instead. The 'no tipping policy', which Sia argued would eliminate discrimination in terms of the quality of service provided to Singaporeans and foreigners, was implemented in 1979. In 1990, Sia received the MERITORIOUS SERVICE MEDAL.

Siemens Founded by Werner von Siemens in Germany in 1847, Siemens is a global supplier of products, systems and solutions in the fields of electrical engineering and electronics. Sales for Siemens in Singapore amounted to approximately 660 million euros for the fiscal year 2005. The company has some 2,200 employees in Singapore, engaged in a wide range of activities, including engineering, design, software development, marketing, maintenance and manufacturing. Siemens delivers solutions and technologies in the fields of information and communications, automation and control, power generation, transportation, healthcare, lighting and home appliances. Siemens was presented the Distinguished Partner in Progress Award by the ECONOMIC DEVELOPMENT BOARD, the highest corporate award given by the government.

Siew Shaw Her (1957–) Sportsman. A member of the SINGAPORE SPORTS COUNCIL HALL OF FAME, and the Singapore National Olympic Council's Sportsman of the Year (1999), sailor Siew Shaw Her has amassed 20 national titles, six SEA Games gold medals, and Asian Games silver (1994) and gold (1998) medals. He has also won the Asian Championship (1996) and the Sail-the-Gulf International Regatta (1996).

Siew first represented Singapore at the Olympics in Seoul (1988), with Joe Chan as his crew. During the race, Chan was thrown into the sea amid high waves. Another competitor, Canadian Lawrence Lemieux, risked his life—and sacrificed his own medal chances—to rescue Chan, and was awarded the Pierre de Courbetin Medal for Sportsmanship. Siew subsequently participated in two more Olympics (Barcelona, 1992, and Atlanta, 1996).

Siglap Five, The Popular music group. The Siglap Five was started in 1965. The initial line-up consisted of Hamid on vocals, Abdul Karim on guitar, Mohamed bin Ali on bass, Hamidon Abdullah on organ and Mohamed Ariff bin Taib on drums. They were signed by Philips, after which Jeffridin from the Rhythm Boys came on board to replace Hamid. Under the name Jeffridin and The Siglap Five (despite the fact that

The Siglap Five

there were now four members), the group's first self-titled album yielded two hits, 'Seruling Anak Gembal' (The Fat Boy's Flute) and 'Berjanji' (Promise).

The Siglap Five's biggest hit, 'Peristiwa di Awang Awang' (Mystical Event), rose to number one in Singapore and Malaysia. In 1967, rhythm guitarist Kamsin joined the line-up, and drummer Ariff was replaced by Jaffar Kupe. The group disbanded in 1968 when its members were called up for National Service, but re-formed and signed with EMI in 1970. Jeffridin moved to Malaysia in the 1970s, and became a household name there.

Sikh Advisory Board Established in 1915 to advise the colonial government on 'matters regarding the Sikh religion and customs', the Sikh Advisory Board (SAB) continues to function as a consultative body for the government on all matters relating to SIKHS in Singapore. The various regional and caste groups that exist within the community are represented on the SAB committee.

Sikh Welfare Council Established in 1995 out of rising concerns for the welfare of SIKHS, the Sikh Welfare Council seeks to build a strong and valued Sikh community. Its objectives include counseling youths against drug addiction, and assisting the needy. Its various committees offer assistance to rehabilitated drug addicts, hospital patients, the bereaved, and prisoners.

Sikhs Sikhs trace their roots to the state of Punjab in India. They have been in Singapore since the 19th century, some of them arriving as convicts of the colonial authorities. The most prominent were the political prisoners Nihal Singh (popularly known as the Sikh holy man, Bhai Maharaj Singh, whose shrine is revered at the SILAT ROAD SIKH TEMPLE) and his attendant, Kharak Singh. They were brought to Singapore in July 1850 and interned at the Outram Road Jail.

In the second half of the 19th century, Sikhs were actively recruited as policemen, watchmen and caretakers. They had acquired the reputation of being a 'Martial

Class' and were seen by the British as suitable for paramilitary and policing duties. Their fierce appearance was found to be effective in quelling clashes amongst the Chinese SECRET SOCIETIES. On 26 March 1881, the British recruited 54 Sikhs from the Punjab to form the nucleus of the Sikh Police Contingent whose numbers grew to 165 by November of the same year. The contingent was stationed at the Pearl's Hill Barracks.

Sikhs who came as fare-paying passengers to Singapore established themselves in entrepreneurial pursuits, becoming moneylenders, shopkeepers and textile merchants. They conducted their businesses in the High Street area. As the Sikh population grew, they began to build their places of worship, known as gurdwaras. There are seven gurdwaras in Singapore. The first was built by the British for the Sikh Police Contingent at the Pearl's Hill Barracks to fulfil their spiritual needs and for the contingent's ceremonies. The Central Sikh Temple was established in Queen Street in 1912.

Due to factional rivalry according to regional, caste and class affiliations, several other gurdwaras were set up. Gurdwara Sahib Sri Guru Singh Sabha at Wilkie Road, established in 1918, attracted Sikhs from the Manjha region in the Punjab. Gurdwara Khalsa Dharmak Sabha at Niven Road drew a congregation of Sikhs from the Malwa region. In 1927, 50 Sikhs from the Doaba region set up the Gurdwara Pardesi Khalsa Dharmak Diwan. Later, the Sikh police decided to invest in larger premises for a gurdwara and for a halfway house for Sikh sojourners, as they found it difficult to house relatives and friends at the barracks. In 1924, they built the Silat Road Sikh Temple. In 1953, Sikhs of the business community initiated the Gurdwara SRI GURU NANAK SATSANG SABHA, now at Katong. The gurdwara at Yishun is an amalgamation of two earlier gurdwaras: one at Sembawang, dating back to 1925, which is associated with the Sikh police and employees of the Naval Base; and one at Jalan Kayu, established in the 1930s by Sikh employees at the SELETAR AIRBASE.

Besides religious institutions, Sikhs also set up other organizations. The Singapore Sikh Cricket Club, founded by English-educated Sikhs, was a precursor to the

Sikhs

SINGAPORE KHALSA ASSOCIATION, which was established in 1931. In 1989, the Sikh Education Foundation was started to monitor Punjabi language education, while the SIKH WELFARE COUNCIL was formed in 1995 to cater to the needy in the community.

The Sikh religion evolved as a result of the devotion of a community of Punjabis to the teachings of the Ten Gurus. The first, Guru Nanak, initiated a pacifist movement preaching the need to reform religious practices of the Punjab during his time. It was the tenth Guru, Gobind Singh, who ordained a brotherhood of the Sikhs known as the Khalsa (pure) and encouraged the Sikhs to don five symbols: a dagger, drawers, a comb, unshorn hair and a steel bangle. This was the genesis of the unique Sikh physical appearance. The day when Guru Gobind Singh ordained the Khalsa in April 1699 coincides with the beginning of the harvest in the Punjab known as Besakhi, and has come to be the main festival—apart from the birthdays of the Gurus—celebrated by the Sikhs.

Silat Road Sikh Temple This temple was built in 1924, and was the first Sikh temple (gurdwara) in Singapore to feature domes and arches as part of its architectural design. Its origins can be traced to the worship requirements of SIKHS who served in the police contingent based at Pearls Hill. The Sikh community had outgrown its existing temple at Pearl's Hill. Land was thus leased from the Singapore Harbour Board for the building of a new two-storey temple on Silat Road. The temple is administered by the Central Sikh Gurdwara Board, and was declared a historic site by the National Heritage Board.

SilkAir SilkAir has its origins in Tradewinds, the travel and tour arm of national carrier SINGAPORE AIRLINES (SIA). Started in 1975, Tradewinds was formed primarily to develop and sell wholesale holiday tours. It became so successful that by the early 1980s, it was one of the top wholesalers of holiday packages. The company then branched out into air charters. Soon, it became apparent that Tradewinds had outgrown its initial purpose. On 21 February 1989, Tradewinds the airline was born.

When the airline first took to the skies as the regional wing of SIA, its focus was on serving several secondary, regional holiday destinations (many of which were still relatively untouched by mass tourism), such as Pattaya, Phuket, Hatyai, Kuantan and Tioman, with Singapore as the transit hub. Soon regional business destinations such as Jakarta, Phnom Penh and Yangon were added to its network.

In April 1992, the airline was renamed SilkAir, while the company's travel arm became a wholly owned subsidiary, Tradewinds Tours and Travel Pte Ltd. Like SIA, SilkAir operates one of the youngest

SilkAir

fleets in the region. As of December 2005, it had a fleet of 12 aircraft, comprising seven Airbus A320-200 and five Airbus A319-100 aircraft, with an average age of less than four years. SilkAir flies to 26 cities in the region, and operates charter services to selected destinations.

See also MI 185 SILKAIR CRASH.

Sim Kee Boon (1929–) Civil servant. Sim Kee Boon was educated at the Anglo-Chinese School and then at the University of Malaya in Singapore, graduating with an honours degree in economics (1953). He joined the ADMINISTRATIVE SERVICE in 1953 and worked as an administrative officer in the Ministry of Commerce and Industry (1953–62). At age 33, he was appointed acting permanent secretary of the Ministry of National Development (1962) and then of the Ministry of, Finance. He was promoted to permanent secretary (1966–74) and subsequently served as permanent secretary of the Ministries of Communications (1975–84) and Finance again (1983–84). From 1979 to 1984, Sim was head of the Singapore Civil Service.

Upon his retirement, Sim joined KEPPEL CORPORATION as Executive Chairman (1984–99). Other positions he has held include: chairman, Insurance Corporation of Singapore (1968–82); chairman, National Grain Elevator Ltd (1968–87); chairman, Straits Steamship Land Ltd (1984–96) and chairman, COUNCIL OF PRESIDENTIAL ADVISORS (2004–05). Sim was awarded the MERITORIOUS SERVICE MEDAL (1963), and was admitted into the DISTINGUISHED SERVICE ORDER (1991).

Sim Lim Square Located at the junction of Rochor Canal Road and Bencoolen Street, Sim Lim Square was developed by cement and construction dealer and property developer, Soon Peng Yam. Soon's Sim Lim Company was publicly listed in 1976, and moved into property development soon thereafter. In the early 1980s, Sim Lim Investments acquired two plots of land in Rochor Road and Bencoolen Street on which to build Sim Lim Tower and Sim Lim Square. Built as a 99-year leasehold property, Sim Lim Square opened in 1983 with 500 shop units on six levels of commercial space, and soon became one of Singapore's two main retail centres for electronics and computers, the other being FUNAN DIGITALIFE MALL.

Sim Wong Hoo (1954–) Businessman and philanthropist. The tenth of 12 children, Sim Wong Hoo was educated at Bukit Panjang Government High School and then at Ngee Ann Polytechnic, where he obtained a diploma in electrical and electronic engineering. In 1981, he founded CREATIVE TECHNOLOGY with only $10,000. The company is one of the world's largest producers of sound cards and MP3 players, and was the first Singapore enterprise to list on NASDAQ. Sim is also known for donating generously to charities.

Sime Darby Trading firm founded by Major William Middleton Sime (1873–1943). Sime arrived in Singapore to work for SYME AND CO as a mercantile assistant. In 1906, he moved to Malacca to cultivate RUBBER, acquiring the Radella Rubber Estate, which he renamed Bukit Lintang Rubber Estate Ltd. In 1910, he joined with banker Henry Darby to form a rubber estate management firm called Sime Darby and Co. Ltd. It prospered, and as an increasing number of rubber estates owned by European interests came under the firm's management, Sime Darby expanded into other industries.

In 1915, Sime Darby opened an office in Singapore, and soon became one of the

Sim Kee Boon

Sim Wong Hoo

Silat Road Sikh Temple

leading AGENCY HOUSES on the island, representing various firms and supplying a wide range of consumer products. In 1936, it opened an office in London to market rubber, and the head office was moved to Singapore.

In the late 1970s, the Malaysian government became the major shareholder in the company. By 1985, Sime Darby had become one of the largest multinational companies in Singapore and Malaysia. Its core business continues to be plantation ownership and management, but it has also diversified into manufacturing, insurance, property development, engineering, vehicle distribution and travel, with operations in Hong Kong, Macau, Japan, Australia, the United Kingdom and the United States. Its head office is in Kuala Lumpur.

Sin Chew Jit Poh

Sime Road Pillbox World War II landmark near the Sime Road entrance to the Singapore Island Country Club. Built prior to 1941, this squat concrete pillbox—a small fortification—formed part of a network of pillboxes built to defend Flagstaff House at 64 Sime Road. Flagstaff House was the Combined Operations Headquarters of the British Army and Air Force, where Lieutenant-General ARTHUR PERCIVAL ran the Malaya campaign against the Japanese until moving to Fort Canning four days before the surrender.

One of the last battles of the war in Singapore was fought nearby. The 1st Battalion of the Cambridgeshire Regiment tried to stem the Japanese advance in the Bukit Timah area on 12 February 1942 and held on until their surrender three days later. The regiment's headquarters at 7 Adam Park is now the clubhouse for the National University of Singapore Society. The Sime Road Pillbox was designated a historic site in 1999.

Simmons, Major-General Keith (1888–1952) British military officer. Simmons was appointed Singapore Fortress Commander in 1941. This made him responsible for the garrison forces, reporting to Lieutenant-General ARTHUR PERCIVAL'S MALAYA COMMAND. In February 1942, with Air Chief Marshal ROBERT BROOKE-POPHAM and Percival in Singapore, and all remaining British forces in Malaya concentrated on the island, Simmons and his 1st and 2nd Malayan Brigades were given responsibility for Southern Area. He was a prisoner of war from 1942 to 1945.

Sindhis: prominent member of the Sindhi community, Ashok Kumar Mirpuri.

Simson, Brigadier Ivan (1890–1971) British military officer. Simson arrived from Scotland Command in August 1941 to revamp local defences. Finding only uncompleted defences at Jitra in north Malaya and on Singapore's south coast, he gave MALAYA COMMAND an in-depth plan for fixed defences in October 1941. These were to include anti-tank obstacles and

machine-gun positions, minefields, and bridges pre-prepared for demolition. Northern Johor and northern Singapore were to be included.

Malaya Command allowed Simson to work, but because he had arrived without written orders, he could do little to overcome the lukewarm response in the field. Despite real difficulties raising labour—priority being given to rubber and tin production, and restricted funds available for hiring civilian labour—Simson's frustrations reflected a real poverty in preparation. On 1 January 1942, he was made director-general of Civil Defence, but maintained an uneasy relationship with Governor SIR SHENTON THOMAS while in that position. He was a prisoner of war from 1942 to 1945.

Sin Chew Jit Poh Chinese-language newspaper. The *Sin Chew Jit Poh* was founded in 1929 by brothers AW BOON HAW and Boon Par. Within months, circulation reached 7,000 copies, eventually reaching 120,000 in 1979. It was the first Chinese newspaper to produce a Sunday edition, and the first to introduce both morning and evening editions. Its 54-year history ended when, in 1982, the paper merged with long-time rival NANYANG SIANG PAU, the two eventually becoming the LIANHE ZAOBAO and LIANHE WANBAO.

Sin Sai Hong Hokkien Wayang One of the most well-known and oldest family-owned Hokkien opera troupes in Singapore, Sin Sai Hong Hokkien Wayang was founded in Johor by Chinese immigrant Wei Wenyu in 1910. The troupe performed *gaojiaxi*, an operatic genre in the Minnan dialect, which is popular in the southern region of China's Fujian province. Following the arrival and popularity of the Taiwanese genre *gezaixi* in Malaya in the 1930s, Sin Sai Hong converted to performing this genre in 1936. The versatility and astute management of the troupe ensured and sustained its popularity. Prior to World War II, the troupe performed across Malaya at religious events as well as in AMUSEMENT PARKS owned by SHAW BROTHERS. After the Japanese Occupation, Sin Sai Hong moved its base to Singapore in 1953 in search of better prospects. Over the decades, a number of family members left to establish troupes of their own, including Xiao Feng Minju Tuan in 1957 and Xin Yan Ling Geju Tuan in 1978. By 2005, Sin Sai Hong was under the management of the fourth generation of the Wei family.

Sin Yong Hua Heng Troupe This troupe was one of the most well-known and oldest Teochew opera troupes in Singapore. Founded in 1827, it originated in Swatow (present-day Shantou) in southern China. At its peak, Sin Yong Hua Heng comprised as many as 60 cast and crew members, and performed on television during the late

1950s and early 1960s. In the 1980s, the troupe suffered from mismanagement and was taken over by Tan Khar Luang, a veteran actress and daughter of a musician from the troupe. Sin Yong Hua Heng remained active until 2001. It staged *Wan Gu Liu Fang* (An Everlasting Legacy) as its final performance on 15 Jan 2001 at Block 111, YISHUN Ring Road. Following its closure, Tan donated over 600 items belonging to the troupe to the NATIONAL MUSEUM OF SINGAPORE.

SINDA *See* SINGAPORE INDIAN DEVELOPMENT ASSOCIATION.

Sindhis Sindhis are an Indian community who originated in Sind, in what is now Pakistan. In Singapore, they have long been associated with the textile trade. Hindu Sindhis who were merchants and traders (Baibands), not professionals (Amils), began coming to Singapore from the city of Hyderabad Sind in the late 1800s. At first they sold Indian handicraft items, but eventually focused their businesses on the import and sale of textiles.

The first Sindhi business in Singapore, T. Chanrai, was started in the 1860s. By the 1890s, K.A.J. Chotirmall & Co. and Wassiamull, Assomull & Co. were also well-established. Their textile shops on High Street, in what was then the heart of the retail district, sold fashionable silks and cottons from Japan, China, Europe and India. Many of the shop proprietors brought their families to Singapore, but their Sindhi employees—young men who came to Singapore at the age of 17 or 18, and lived in quarters above the shop—did not.

By 1940, Singapore had about 20 Sindhi-owned companies. The Sindhi Merchants Association had been established in 1921. The majority of the 200-strong Sindhi population were textile salesmen and shopkeepers whose families had remained in Sind. The Sindhi merchants' versatility helped them survive the Japanese Occupation. Unable to import textiles, they instead sold locally made items and necessities such as razor blades. The Sindhi community had to endure the same oppression and hardship as other residents during the occupation, but the Japanese did not single Indians out for maltreatment. Some Sindhis supported Subhas Chandra Bose's INDIAN NATIONAL ARMY, and its civilian counterpart, the Indian Independence League. The league gave the Sindhis, like others in the Indian community, a channel of appeal to the Japanese authorities, for example, to seek permission to import goods for sale.

The partition of India and Pakistan in 1947 led to the exodus of the Hindu community from Sind. The Sindhi salesmen and textile shopkeepers in Singapore moved their families here. The community's growth accelerated after 1949, when it became known that the British had plans to restrict immigration from the Indian sub-continent to Malaya and Singapore. By the time the restrictions took effect in 1953, the Sindhi community in Singapore had grown to over 3,000 people.

The post-Independence generation of Sindhis, like other Singaporeans, took advantage of the wider educational and economic opportunities available to them. Some of the traditional Sindhi textile firms branched out into other businesses such as electronics, high fashion and property development. Young Sindhi Singaporeans became doctors, lawyers, civil servants, diplomats and designers.

From the late 1800s through the 1960s, the heart of the community was High Street, where most of the Sindhi textile shops were located. Every year the Sindhis' DEEPAVALI festivities were centered there. Apart from being a religious festival, Deepavali also marked the end of the financial year for Sindhi firms. The textile shops were decorated, refreshments were laid out, and Sindhi families went from shop to shop, celebrating. In the 1970s, however, Singapore's SHOPPING activity started to shift from areas like High Street, to Orchard Road. Government buildings began to take the place of textile shops on High Street, and the Sindhi community moved on.

According to the 2000 Census, out of 257,791 Indians in Singapore, there were 4,017 Sindhis. Well-known Sindhis in Singapore include B.H. Melwani, chairman of fashion retailer MB Melwani; Singapore's high commissioner to Malaysia, Ashok Kumar Mirpuri; and former diplomat KISHORE MAHBUBANI.

Singai Mukilan (1922–1992) Poet. Born N. Abdul Rahman in Tamil Nadu, Singai Mukilan was the pseudonym of one of the most respected Tamil poets in Singapore. A prolific writer, he produced nine volumes of poetry and a collection of parables as well as short stories. At age 16, he left India for Malaya in search of better prospects. He began writing while working in Malacca. His first poem was published by renowned Indian Tamil social reformist E.V. Ramasamy, popularly known as Periyar.

Mukilan's first two books of poetry, the two-volume *Tamil Oli Geetham* (Tamil Oli Dance), were published in 1939. His other works include *Thudikkum Ullam* (Throbbing Heart) (1954) and *Uruvaga Kathaigal* (Parables) (1976).

Mukilan was a socially conscious writer whose literary work and engage-ment with political reform were closely linked. His politically charged poems championed the underprivileged and advo-cated social change in the immigrant Tamil community, and are noted for their simplic-ity of style and the universality of their themes, while reflecting the contemporary concerns of Tamil society in Singapore.

Singam, Constance (1936–) The eldest of seven sisters and one brother, Singam is a feminist, writer and teacher. Her key achievements include groundbreaking research and advocacy on family violence, as president of the ASSOCIATION OF WOMEN FOR ACTION AND RESEARCH (AWARE, 1987–89 and 1994–96) and of the Singapore Council of Women's Organis-ations (1990–93). Also notable is her lead-ership of The Working Committee (TWC, 1998–99) to raise awareness of civil society activism; and lobbying for MAIDS' rights as a founding member of TWC2 (Transient Workers Count Too) in 2003.

Singapore Airlines One of Singapore's most recognized brands, Singapore Airlines (SIA) is one of the most admired and profitable airlines in the world. It chalked up record net profits of $1.2 billion on group revenues of $13.3 billion for the financial year 2005/06. With an operating fleet of more than 90 aircraft and at least another 30 on its order books at the end of 2005, SIA flies to over 90 destinations in 39 countries.

The airline's history can be traced back to a thrice-weekly schedule that started on 1 May 1947, when an Airspeed Consul touched down at KALLANG AIRPORT under the banner of Malayan Airways. Over the next two decades, it expanded its flights and its fleet, with the addition of Douglas DC-4 Skymaster, Vickers Viscount, Lockheed Super Constellation, De Havilland Comet and Fokker aircraft. In 1966, a year after Singapore gained independence, the com-pany was renamed Malaysia-Singapore Airlines (MSA), and saw revenues cross the $100 million mark in 1968. The first transcontinental flight between Singapore and London was launched in 1971, but the following year, MSA became two separate entities: Malaysia Airline System (now Malaysia Airlines) and Singapore Airlines.

With the change came SIA's first Boeing aircraft, the B707. The form-fitting *sarong kebaya* uniform of the SINGAPORE GIRL was designed by Pierre Balmain. SIA soon began to build a reputation for its in-flight service, with its motto 'A Great Way To Fly'. It was the first airline to offer free drinks and complimentary headsets. The following decade saw the build-up of its fleet, reputed to be one of the youngest in the world, with the addition of the A300 Superbus, A310-200, B757, B747-300 Big Top and the B747-400 Megatop.

In the 1990s, SIA revolutionized in-flight communications through the KrisFone, the first global sky telephone ser-vice. In 2000, SIA placed a US$8.6 billion order for 25 units of the world's largest commercial plane, the A380, and will be the first airline to fly it. Other firsts have included the world's longest non-stop commercial flight—between Singapore and New York in 2004, on an Airbus 340-500. This broke the previous record, also held by

Singapore Airlines

SIA, for its non-stop flights between Singapore and Los Angeles, launched earli-er that same year.

SIA also operates regional airline SILKAIR, has a 49 per cent stake in the bud-get carrier Tiger Airways (*see* LOW-COST CARRIERS), and owns 49 per cent of Virgin Atlantic Airways. Its other subsidiaries include: publicly listed SIA Engineering, which handles aircraft maintenance for more than 80 international air carriers; SIA Cargo, which serves more than 68 global destinations; and the publicly listed SATS, which provides ground handling, baggage and airline catering services. Another sub-sidiary, Tradewinds Tours and Travel, offers travel packages to regional destinations. SIA also has a 20 per cent stake in THE RITZ-CARLTON, MILLENIA SINGAPORE.

Singapore Alliance Party

Singapore Alliance Party Coalition of political parties that contested several elec-tions in Singapore, notably the LEGISLATIVE ASSEMBLY ELECTION (1955) and GENERAL ELECTION (1963). Sometimes known simply as the Singapore Alliance, it was heavily backed by the local chapter of the United Malays National Organisation (UMNO) and included the Singapore Malay Union, a local chapter of the Malayan Chinese Association and the Singapore Malayan Indian Congress. In the 1963 election, its campaign strategy was similar to that of UMNO in the Federation of Malaysia. It alleged that the ruling PEOPLE'S ACTION PARTY (PAP) mistreated the Malays, and that the alliance would redress the problem if elected. Its participation in the 1963 elec-tion contributed to the feud between UMNO and the PAP, as they had implicit-ly agreed that neither would participate in the other's elections until the Federation of Malaysia was more mature. The Singapore Alliance expected to retain its seats in the Malay-dominated areas of Geylang Serai, Kampong Kembangan and the Southern Islands, but did not. It was dissolved some time after the 1963 election.

Singai Mukilan: Nalla Mudivu (Good Decision) (1989).

Singapore Anti-Tuberculosis Association: mobile X-ray unit, 1956.

Singapore Anti-Tuberculosis Association

Non-governmental organization. The Singapore Anti-Tuberculosis Association (SATA) was registered on 23 August 1947 by a group of expatriate doctors and local and expatriate businessmen. It provides the public with affordable health screening, including chest X-rays to check for tuberculosis, at its four clinics. Through its mobile X-ray unit, SATA offers screening of employees to any company, thus promoting health in the workplace. It also attends to community projects for the aged. SATA is run on a voluntary, non-profit basis.

Singapore Armed Forces

The Singapore ARMY, REPUBLIC OF SINGAPORE NAVY and REPUBLIC OF SINGAPORE AIR FORCE are considered the most modern armed forces in Southeast Asia. The system of NATIONAL SERVICE followed by reservist duties has meant that there is a military presence in most sectors of society.

SEPARATION in August 1965, CONFRONTATION with Indonesia, and the

Singapore Armed Forces

SINGAPORE ARMED FORCES IN 2006	
Army	40,600 active troops, with 280,000 NSmen
	Armoured vehicles: 2,024 (M113, Commando, AMX10P, AMX-10 PAC90, IFV 40/50, IFV 25 and AMX13)
	155 mm howitzers: 187 (38 Soltam M-71S, 16 M114A1, 45 M68, 52 FH88, 18 FH2000 and 18 SSPH-1 Primus)
	Other artillery: LG1 105 mm, 120 mm and 160 mm mortars
	Anti-tank missiles: Milan, Armbrust and Spike
Navy	Missile-equipped naval vessels: 23 (6 Victory-class missile corvettes, 6 Sea Wolf-class missile boats, 11 Fearless-class patrol vessels and ASW patrol vessels)
	Submarines: 4 Challenger class (Sjoormen class)
	Mine countermeasure vessels: 4 Bedok class
	Others: 4 Endurance-class landing ship tanks
	On order: 6 Formidable-class frigates
Air Force	Fighter aircraft: 125 (A4-SU, F5, F16 C/D and F16D Block 52+)
	Transport/cargo helicopters: 47 (AS-332M, AS-532UL and CH-47D/SD)
	Transport aircraft: 14 KC130B, C-130H, KC-130H and F50
	4 Hawkeye E2C AEW
	1 maritime reconnaissance squadron with 5 Fokker 50
	Training aircraft: 25 S-211
	Helicopters: 10 AS-550 training helicopters and 20 AH-64D Apache helicopters
	1 UAV squadron with Searcher and Chukar III RPV
	SAM: Hawk, Rapier, Mistral, RBS70 and Igla
	On order: 6 Sikorsky S-70B naval helicopters and 12 F15 SG
Source: Ministry of Defence	

impending BRITISH WITHDRAWAL FROM SINGAPORE in 1971, were the impetus for Singapore to set up its own armed forces. After failing to enlist the assistance of Switzerland, India and Egypt, an agreement was reached for Israel to help train and advise the fledgling Singapore Armed Forces (SAF). National Service was first introduced in 1967, and has been developed and refined since then.

The SAF's focus has been on deterring and, if necessary, defeating external threats. The defensive strategy of 'Poison Shrimp', necessitated by the small size of Singapore's military capabilities in the 1970s, gradually gave way to a more confident, pre-emptive Forward Defence by the 1980s. Although it began by inheriting British installations, the SAF soon built new infrastructure, including a large naval base at Changi able to accommodate visiting US Navy aircraft carriers. Due to a lack of space, much training is carried out overseas, in countries such as Brunei, Australia and France. In 2006, the SAF had 55,000 active troops and 300,000 active reservists which it could mobilize in six hours using a system of open or 'silent' MOBILIZATION. As with Switzerland and Israel, the bulk of the SAF's fighting capability lies with its reservist formations, which undergo regular training.

The SAF has pushed strongly for a transformation of its military capabilities, modelled after the so-called Revolution in Military Affairs that is taking place in the United States under its IKC2 (Integrated Knowledge-based Command and Control) doctrine of network-centric combined arms warfare.

The SAF is headed by a CHIEF OF DEFENCE FORCE (CDF), who reports to the elected political leadership at the MINISTRY OF DEFENCE. Within the SAF, the chiefs of Army, Air Force and Navy report to the CDF. Two directorates—the FUTURE SYSTEMS DIRECTORATE and the Joint Operations and Planning Directorate—report to both the CDF and the permanent secretary for defence.

The SAF has benefited from Singapore's rapid economic growth, which has

provided the funds for sustained development. Since the 1960s, defence expenditure has kept within 6 per cent of gross domestic product. The DSO NATIONAL LABORATORIES and the DEFENCE SCIENCE AND TECHNOLOGY AGENCY manage research and development, procurement and integration of military technologies. The government has established a number of key military enterprises under the holding company Sheng-Li Holdings (renamed Singapore Technologies Holdings in 1989), such as Singapore Aerospace, Singapore Technologies Marine, Singapore Technologies Kinetics and Singapore Technologies Electronics.

Singapore Army *See* Army.

Singapore Art Museum *See* box.

Singapore Arts Festival

The first Singapore Arts Festival was organized by the Young Musicians' Society and the Ministry of Education, with financial support from Mobil Oil Singapore. The opening on 24 April 1977 at the Victoria Theatre featured the Pembroke Girls' Choir from Australia and the Singapore Youth Orchestra. The festival showcased local talent, and awards were given to successful entrants such as the Phoenix Dance Troupe, the Rose Eberwein Dancers and Les Petites Fleurs. There were also performances by the Maris Stella High School Orchestra and Singapore American School Concert Band.

Since then, the festival has become a multi-million dollar event organized by the NATIONAL ARTS COUNCIL. Originally staged biennially, it is now held annually, and has built a reputation for showcasing contemporary performing arts, particularly from Asia. Besides the main productions, the festival includes an outreach programme of largely free performances. In 2006, the festival presented 1,758 artists from 26 countries and regions.

Singapore Association of the Visually Handicapped

Voluntary welfare organization formerly known as the Singapore Association for the Blind. Founded in 1951, the association is open to Singapore citizens and permanent residents who are certified blind or of low vision. Its primary purpose

Singapore Arts Festival: performance, 2005.

Singapore Art Museum

Singapore Art Museum Founded in 1996 as the third arm of the old National Museum (see NATIONAL MUSEUM OF SINGAPORE), the Singapore Art Museum (SAM) showcases modern and contemporary art. It is housed in the converted 19th-century ST JOSEPH'S INSTITUTION building, in the heart of the city's museum district.

The building was gazetted as a national monument in 1992. Many of the original features—the shuttered windows, airy inner quadrangle and ceramic floor tiles—and the early 20th-century additions—a central dome and sweeping arcade verandahs—were preserved in the 1990s conversion. A dramatic glass hall was incorporated, which is flanked by courtyards with sculpture displays.

The museum was originally established to house the national collection of Singapore art and to assemble works by 20th-century Southeast Asian masters. Much of the art exhibited has been acquired since 1996. Since 2001, the museum has been targeting the whole of Asia for its collections.

Detail from Zaw Zaw Aung's Girl and Boy *(left), from* Beneath the Pavement: Discovering the City *(far left), an* **educational exhibition** *held in 2006 on the ever-changing nature of cities.*

The facade and dome of the Singapore Art Museum—previously St Joseph's Institution—was inspired by the colonnade in front of St Peter's Basilica in Rome. The former school chapel is now the museum's auditorium.

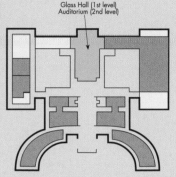

Glass Hall (1st level)
Auditorium (2nd level)

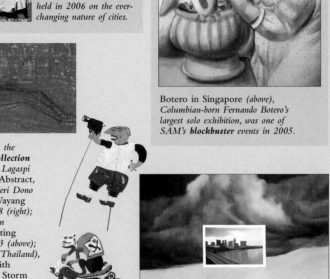

Botero in Singapore (above), Columbian-born Fernando Botero's largest solo exhibition, was one of SAM's **blockbuster** *events in 2005.*

Artworks from the **permanent collection** *include: Cesar Lagaspi (Philippines),* Abstract, *1976 (left); Heri Dono (Indonesia),* Wayang Puppets, *1988 (right); Tran Trung Tin (Vietnam),* Sitting Woman, *1973 (above); Natee Utarit (Thailand),* Landscape with Approaching Storm After Rembrandt (Petchaburi) No. 3, *2001 (far right).*

Galleries and collections

- more than 6,500 works
- the largest public collection of 20th-century Southeast Asian art in the world
- 10,000 sq m total floor space
- 14 galleries
- international and local loan exhibitions; semi-permanent displays from SAM's permanent holdings; major travelling loan exhibitions; cyber art, much of it interactive; art education for children

---

is to help and train the visually handicapped to fend for themselves. It also works as a lobby group for the abolition of any barrier to the integration and equal treatment of the visually handicapped.

Singapore Association of Trade Unions

Left-wing conglomeration of trade unions. After sweeping to power in 1959, the PEOPLE'S ACTION PARTY (PAP) amended the Trade Union Ordinance, giving the registrar powers to deregister unions deemed to be acting against workers' interests. To bring the unions under its control, the government deregistered many anti-government unions and affiliated them with the moderate Singapore Trades Union Congress.

Conflict within the PAP between the moderates and the left-wing faction led to the establishment of the BARISAN SOSIALIS. It also split the Singapore Trades Union Congress into the pro-PAP NATIONAL TRADES UNION CONGRESS (NTUC), led by C.V. DEVAN NAIR, and the Singapore Association of Trade Unions (SATU).

The NTUC quickly became the leading trade union organization, largely because of its effectiveness and government support. However, SATU had the support of the Singapore General Employees' Union led by LIM CHIN SIONG, the SINGAPORE BUS WORKERS' UNION led by FONG SWEE SUAN, and the Singapore Business Houses Employees' Union led by S.T. BANI. The government accused SATU of instigating 77 strikes between August and December 1961, and maintained a close watch on SATU.

On 25 August 1963, SATU and the Singapore Chinese Chamber of Commerce organized a mass rally to press the Japanese for compensation for wartime atrocities. The registrar of trade unions asked seven SATU unions why their registration should not be cancelled for displaying anti-Malaysian banners and placards at the rally—activities that were deemed communist united front activities. In October 1963, these unions were deregistered, and 50 branches of deregistered SATU unions left to join the NTUC.

Singapore Association of Writers

Established in 1970, this association has contributed to the development of Chinese literature in Singapore. Its biannual journal *Xin Hua Wenxue* (Singapore Chinese

Singapore Arts Festival

Singapore Botanic Gardens

Singapore Botanic Gardens Situated at the junction of Cluny Road and Napier Road, the Botanic Gardens is also a community park and tourist destination. In 1822, Sir Stamford Raffles, himself a keen naturalist, planted a Botanical Garden on Government Hill. He planned to introduce economic crops such as cocoa and nutmeg. However, lacking funding and a full-time salaried director, the garden was closed in 1829. It was re-established at its present site in 1859 on land still infested with tigers, as a pleasure park for members only.

Detail from gate.

In 1875, the Botanic Gardens was taken over by the government as one in a chain of British colonial gardens that circled the globe. Its mission was botanical exploration, documentation, experimentation and research, particularly in the economic potential of tropical plants. Expert staff were recruited from the Royal Botanic Gardens in Kew. The founding of a technical journal in 1891 supported experimentation and research. It continues today as *The Gardens' Bulletin, Singapore*, a publication on tropical botany.

Postcard, c. 1910.

The first director of the gardens, HENRY NICHOLAS RIDLEY, tirelessly experimented with, and persuaded landowners to grow, para rubber (*Hevea brasiliensis*) instead of other tropical crops. By 1917, the gardens had distributed over 7 million rubber seeds, which were a major source of income.

Since then, the gardens have had a succession of directors and key staff who were eminent botanists. Their publications and achievements form the backbone of regional botany. At the heart of research efforts is the herbarium, a scientific archive of around 650,000 preserved plant specimens from the region. The orchid-breeding programme initiated in 1928 has also continued. A unique feature of the programme is the naming of selected new hybrids after visiting dignitaries.

In 1967, the 'Garden City' campaign was launched, and this redirected the focus of the gardens from mainly research, to spearheading the national 'greening' effort. A School of Ornamental Horticulture was established in the gardens in 1972 to train the workers needed to implement and maintain the Garden City.

In 1995, the National Orchid Garden—the world's largest exposition of tropical orchids—opened, and a symphony stage for performances was built. A new visitor centre was completed in 1998, to serve the more than 3 million visitors a year. In 2003, a ginger garden was opened; and a unique cool house simulating a tropical montane forest and featuring tropical upland plants in 2004. Two years later, the Evolution Garden, telling the story of plant life through geological time, was added. 2006 also saw the completion of the Jacob Ballas Children's Garden.

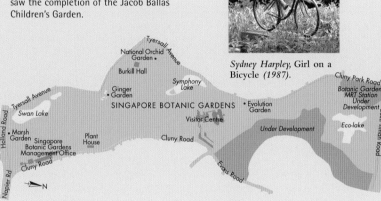

Sydney Harpley, **Girl on a Bicycle** *(1987).*

Literature) publishes translations, as well as creative and critical works.

Most of the active members and leaders of the Singapore Association of Writers (such as MENG YI, WANG RUNHUA, ZHANG HUI, DAN YING, XI NI'ER and XU FUJI) are avant-garde writers who work in some area of modernist literature. The association promotes new movements in literature, and encourages experimentation with new literary techniques and forms, such as symbolism, imagism and magic realism.

Singapore Ballet Academy

The association's members are bilingual writers, and activities are largely multiracial and multilingual in nature. The association promotes creative writing and literary criticism and organizes poetry readings. It has conducted exchange visits to China and has participated in the publication of anthologies, activities which have involved authors writing in the four official languages—English, Mandarin, Malay and Tamil.

Singapore Badminton Hall Historic site. In 1949, the Malayan badminton team won the Thomas Cup, an international competition held in the United Kingdom, and thus were entitled to host the next tournament. As Malaya did not have a suitable stadium, plans were made to construct a badminton hall in Singapore. In 1951, a site was chosen on Guillemard Road. But the new hall could not be completed in time for the staging of the 1952 Thomas Cup that year. The tournament was therefore held at Happy World Stadium instead, and the Malayan team won the Cup.

The Singapore Badminton Hall was finally opened in June 1952 by Governor Sir John Nicoll, and hosted the 1955 and 1958 Thomas Cup in 1955 (when the Malayan team won for a third consecutive year) and 1958 (when the Malayan team lost to the Indonesians in the final).

The hall was used for other purposes as well. It was where the People's Action Party celebrated its election victory in 1959, and it was the vote counting centre in 1962 for a referendum on Singapore's merger with Malaysia, Sabah and Sarawak. The hall hosted entertainment events, including a concert by the popular Malay actor P. RAMLEE in 1959, and a performance by the Rolling Stones in 1965. In the 1970s, it reverted to its original function as a sports venue. In 1978, the Singapore Sports Council took over its management, holding the Southeast Asian (SEA) Games in 1983 and 1993 at the hall. In 1999, the Singapore Badminton Hall was designated a historic site.

Singapore Ballet Academy This school was formed in 1958 following the merger of the Malaya School of Ballet, founded in 1956 by Goh Soo Nee, and a school managed by Frances Poh and Vernon Martinus, which they had taken over from Maudrene Yap. It was initially housed in a colonial-era bungalow on Lloyd Road, but moved to Cox Terrace at Fort Canning in 1995

Singapore Biennale

The academy has introduced ballet classes based on the syllabus used by the Royal Academy of Dance in the United Kingdom. Former students include GOH CHOO SAN, GOH SOO KHIM (who became its principal in 1971), LIM FEI SHEN and ANTHONY THEN. Besides staging classical productions, the academy has offered scholarships to promising students, many of whom have since joined the SINGAPORE DANCE THEATRE.

Singapore Biennale Visual arts event organized by the NATIONAL ARTS COUNCIL in partnership with the NATIONAL HERITAGE BOARD. The inaugural Singapore Biennale held in 2006 was led by Artistic Director Nanjo Fumio (Japan), while its curatorial team comprised Roger McDonald (Japan), Sharmini Pereira (Sri Lanka/United Kingdom), Eugene Tan (Singapore), and Ahmad Mashadi (Singapore). The biennale will showcase a range of international artists, with about half from Asia. The theme of the 2006 event was 'Belief', and a number of public institutions and spaces such as the NATIONAL MUSEUM OF SINGAPORE, the PADANG, and religious buildings such as the ARMENIAN CHURCH and Buddhist temple KWAN IM THONG HOOD CHO.

Singapore Botanic Gardens *See* box.

Singapore Broadcasting Corporation On 1 February 1980, Radio and Television Singapore (RTS) was restructured as the Singapore Broadcasting Corporation (SBC), under the 1979 Singapore Broadcasting Act. RTS had been a government department under the Ministry of Culture, but SBC became a statutory board, allowing it greater financial autonomy. The requirement for public service broadcasting was also reduced, resulting in progamming changes designed to raise SBC's advertising revenue. In 1984, SBC introduced a third free-to-air channel, TV12, which featured arts, cultural, educational and information programming. Under the SBC broadcasting structure, the advertising market expanded rapidly for both television and radio. In 1994, SBC was corporatized as three entities: the TELEVISION CORPORATION OF SINGAPORE, Radio Corporation of Singapore and Television 12. These were subsequently reorganized as MEDIACORP.

Singapore Buddhist Federation Established in 1948 as the Xing Zhou Buddhist Federation, the mission of the Singapore Buddhist Federation is to unite the various Buddhist organizations and devotees in Singapore and to carry out work relating to Buddhist education, culture, charity and welfare for the benefit of the society. The federation established the Maha Bodhi School in 1948 and the Manjusri Secondary School in 1981. It offers various Buddhist studies classes for adults, and has founded the Buddhist College of Singapore. It has been publishing *Nanyang Buddhism*, a monthly magazine, since 1969, and organized the International Buddhist Academic Symposium in 2004 and 2005 respectively. The federation also has two counsellors' groups, one dealing with drug issues and the other extending help to prisoners and soldiers in detention, along with various charity organizations.

See also BUDDHISM.

Singapore Buddhist Lodge Originally known as the Distribution Point of Buddhist Sutras in Singapore in 1933, the Singapore Buddhist Lodge was officially established in 1934. The SBL's mission is 'furthering the Dharma, guarding Buddhism, helping the world with compassion, cultivating blessings and wisdom, and working towards universal enlightenment without inequality', which it seeks to fulfil though promoting Buddhist teachings, practicing compassionate acts, medical care, education, culture. The SBL maintains an Education Fund, publishes the periodical *Shi Cheng Chao Yin* (Sound of Waves in the Lion City), and conducts courses in Chinese culture.

Singapore Bus Workers' Union Left-wing trade union. The Singapore Bus Workers' Union (SBWU) was registered on 20 December 1948, drawing its membership mainly from workers of the Green Bus Company. Originally headquartered in Queen Street, it moved to Bukit Timah Road. The union was established to cater to employees of Chinese bus companies. In 1953, the infiltration of left-wing elements led to a radicalization of the union's thinking and modus operandi. Many of its office-bearers had been radical students, including FONG SWEE SUAN, a student leader from THE CHINESE HIGH SCHOOL. He became the SBWU's general secretary in 1954.

The union disrupted bus services in 1955 when it organized a strike at the Paya Lebar Bus Company and then another in April that year at the Hock Lee Amalgamated Bus Company. The latter was precipitated by the company's sacking of 229 employees, all of whom were SBWU members. On 12 May 1955, the strikers clashed with police and a riot ensued. This came to be known as the HOCK LEE BUS RIOTS. On 13 May 1955, all bus workers went on a sympathy strike, and the public transport system came to a standstill.

Singapore Business Federation In 1998, Prime Minister GOH CHOK TONG urged the Singapore Federation of Chambers of Commerce and Industry (SFCCI) to consider restructuring itself, so as to enhance its effectiveness in serving its members and promoting national interests.

The SFCCI proposed the formation of the Singapore Business Federation (SBF). In February 2001, a pro-tem Committee was put together. In response to its recommendations, the Singapore Business Federation Act was passed into law on 5 October 2001.

The SBF was formed on 1 April 2002. All companies with a paid-up capital of at least $500,000 are eligible for membership. The SBF is managed by a council, with a government-appointed board of trustees to protect the SBF's assets and to ensure that it does not deviate from its mission.

Singapore cat Also known as the Kucinta (a combination of the Malay '*kucing*', meaning 'cat', and '*cinta*', meaning 'love'), Singapura cat, Singapore drain cat or Singapore River cat. The cat has been described as having a rounded head with a broad, straight blunt nose and well-defined chin. Its ears are large, deeply cupped, set at a slight angle and taper from a wide base to a slightly pointed tip. The cat's large, almond-shaped eyes may be hazel, green or yellow. The Singapore cat weighs 2–4 kg, enjoys a life span of 9–15 years, and typically has litters of about five kittens.

In 1991, the cat was adopted by the SINGAPORE TOURISM BOARD as a tourism icon. It was initially believed to be indigenous to Singapore, and thought to inhabit the drains and alleys in the vicinity of the Singapore River. However, a controversy arose when *The Straits Times* reported that the cat had first been brought to Singapore from the United States by Tommy Meadow in 1974, who claimed that she had bred the cats in Singapore from three indigenous stray cats. She later revealed that the cats had been smuggled into the US from Singapore by her husband and bred before she arrived in Singapore. Other sources have alleged that the cat is a cross between Burmese and Abyssinian breeds. A sculpture of a family of Singapore cats is located on the banks of the Singapore River, near Cavenagh Bridge.

Singapore cat

Singapore Chinese Chamber of Commerce & Industry: entrance dooway.

Singapore Chinese Chamber of Commerce & Industry

Founded in 1906 by a group of Chinese businessman, the Singapore Chinese Chamber of Commerce & Industry (SCCCI) was originally known as the General Chinese Trade Affairs Association. Its first president was Goh Siew Tin. In 1921, it was renamed the Singapore Chinese Chamber of Commerce, and in 1977, it adopted its current name. The SCCCI has a membership network of some 120 trade associations and 4,000 corporate entities. It plays a key role in representing the interests of its members, and in promoting economic development and international trade for Singapore. The SCCCI founded the biennial World Chinese Entrepreneurs Convention and the World Chinese Business Network, a global online business information portal.

Singapore Chinese Girls' School

Consisting today of a primary school and an independent secondary school, Singapore Chinese Girls' School (SCGS) was originally founded in 1899 by a group of PERANAKANS, including Sir SONG ONG SIANG and Dr LIM BOON KENG. The school began with an enrolment of seven girls who were taught subjects such as romanized Malay and sewing, to equip them for their future roles as wives and mothers. Though it was pri-

Singapore Chinese Girls' School: students at play (below); premises at Dunearn Road (right).

marily a girls' school, boys aged seven to ten years were admitted between 1905 and 1936. Over the years, the school had several locations, including the site on Hill Street where the CENTRAL FIRE STATION now stands. In 1923, the school moved to a new building on Emerald Hill, where it stayed for the next 70 years, before moving to its present premises at Dunearn Road.

Identifiable by her blue, sleeveless sundress-style uniform, the SCGS girl is known as '*kim gek*'—a Hokkien term meaning 'gold and jade'. In Chinese tradition, this connotes a Chinese girl brought up and educated in the best manner. Today, SCGS is open to girls regardless of race.

Singapore Chinese Middle School Students' Union

Collective term for Singapore's highly politicized Chinese-medium secondary school students of the 1950s. Under the traditional Chinese school system, middle school accommodated students aged 13 to 18. Among Singapore's leading Chinese middle schools were THE CHINESE HIGH SCHOOL, Catholic High School, CHUNG CHENG HIGH SCHOOL, NANYANG GIRLS' SCHOOL and NAN CHIAU HIGH SCHOOL.

During the early to mid-1950s, procommunist politicians fomented rebellion through Chinese middle school students. This was possible because such schools were outside British colonial control. Furthermore, many students educated in Chinese-medium schools were unhappy with the British government because of unequal opportunities for university admissions. Their job prospects were also bleaker due to their language handicap.

One of the first and most significant public protests by the Chinese middle school students was the riot of 13 May 1954 (*see* MAY 13 INCIDENT), when more than 500 students gathered at King George V Park (now Fort Canning Park) for a demonstration march to Government House. The students were protesting against the unpopular NATIONAL SERVICE Ordinance. The army and police had to be

brought in. The Chinese students were also involved in the notorious HOCK LEE BUS RIOTS that same year.

When the government closed down the Singapore Chinese Middle School Students' Union in October 1956, the Chinese school students were provoked once again. The arrest of four Chinese school students and expulsion of students who were involved in communist activities made things worse and the students started a riot. Several thousand students from Chinese middle schools staged a sit-in to protest changes in the school system in October 1956 (*see* CHINESE MIDDLE SCHOOL RIOTS).

Student activism in the Chinese middle schools eased somewhat with the establishment of the Chinese-medium NANYANG UNIVERSITY in 1955 and the detention of many pro-communist leaders under laws such as the INTERNAL SECURITY ACT.

Singapore Chinese Orchestra

The history of this orchestra can be traced back to 1968. It was originally one of the amateur performing groups within the PEOPLE'S ASSOCIATION Cultural Troupe. In September 1974, it was decided that it should turn professional and engage full-time musicians. Initially, the effort was modest, as financial constraints meant that only six paid positions could be afforded. However, this number was gradually increased to 32 over subsequent years. This was the first time that Chinese orchestra musicians were recognized as professionals.

Under musical director Wu Dajiang and his three successors—Lin Zheyuan, Gu Limin and Qu Chunquan—the troupe developed into a fully fledged orchestra, collaborating with well-known musicians and conductors, including Liu Dehai, Min Huifen, Takako Nishizaki, Peng Xiuwen and Yan Huichang.

In 1992, the troupe was officially named the Singapore Chinese Orchestra (SCO). Three years later, it was upgraded to an 'orchestra of national standing'. On 8 May 1996, the Singapore Chinese Orchestra Company Limited was set up to provide professional management support. Five years later, the orchestra gained a permanent rehearsal and performance space in the refurbished SINGAPORE CONFERENCE HALL, moving into these premises in 2001.

Under the guidance of directors such as Hu Bingxu, Qu Chunquan, Xia Feiyun and Ye Cong, the SCO has established a reputation for innovative programmes and for premiering new contemporary Chinese orchestral compositions, one of which was a 2005 musical production based on the story of Admiral ZHENG HE. As well as regular concerts, it has initiated a series of community concerts in the public housing estates; education programmes in schools; and performances in public places such as parks. For the 2000 Millennium Concert, it organized an event showcasing more than 1,400 musicians from various Chinese orchestras across Singapore. In 2004, it staged a NATIONAL DAY concert featuring over 2,300 performers.

Other initiatives undertaken by the SCO include the Arranger-in-Residence Programme, the Assistant Conductor Programme and the Singapore Youth Chinese Orchestra, which it took over from the Ministry of Education. The SCO has toured in China, Taiwan and Europe.

Singapore Chinese Teachers' Union
Established in 1953, the Singapore Chinese Teachers' Union (SCTU) was set up to provide Chinese-language teachers with opportunities for training. In more recent years, the SCTU has cooperated with the Ministry of Education on changes to the teaching of the Chinese language. It has also worked with universities in China to develop jointly a degree course on Chinese-language teaching and Chinese literature. In 2005, the SCTU set up a Learning Hub on its premises. The hub conducts training classes on new teaching methods, as well as work-related and self-improvement courses for Chinese-language teachers.

Singapore Chronicle, The First newspaper to be published in Singapore. Founded by a former superintendent of police, it was also known as the *Commercial Register*. The application to publish it was sponsored by JOHN CRAWFURD, Resident of Singapore. Crawfurd was also its principal contributor. Started on 1 January 1824 as a single-sheet, two-page fortnightly, *The Singapore Chronicle* grew to four pages in 1831. It was closed down in 1837, perhaps due to competition from the SINGAPORE FREE PRESS.

Singapore City Gallery *See* box.

Singapore Civil Defence Force Provider of emergency services, under the purview of

Singapore Chinese Orchestra

the Ministry of Home Affairs. The origins of the Singapore Civil Defence Force can be traced to 1888, when the municipal commission formed Singapore's first professional fire brigade. In 1980, the Singapore Fire Brigade was renamed the Singapore Fire Service.

In 1981, the Civil Defence Command was formed, under the authority of the SINGAPORE POLICE FORCE. The year 1982 saw the launch of the National Civil Defence Plan, modelled on the successful Swiss concept of 'total defence'.

The following year, 1983, the Civil Defence Command was renamed the Singapore Civil Defence Force (SCDF). In 1986, it became an independent organization under the MINISTRY OF HOME AFFAIRS. Three years later, on 15 April 1989, the SCDF was integrated with the Singapore Fire Service, providing emergency ambulance and firefighting services, as well as other rescue capabilities.

The service has had an eventful history. It functioned throughout World War II. It tackled the BUKIT HO SWEE FIRE in 1961, as well as the ROBINSONS FIRE in 1972. The HOTEL NEW WORLD COLLAPSE required a coordinated response by the civil defence and fire services, and led indirectly to their formal integration.

The SCDF is equipped for disaster rescue and assistance. At home, it trains for eventualities including terrorist or other incidents that may involve chemical or biological agents. Overseas, it has assisted in rescue missions, including those after the 1999 earthquake in Tai Chung County, Taiwan, and the 2004 Boxing Day tsunami in Phuket, Thailand.

Singapore Civil Service The origins of the Singapore Civil Service (SCS) can be traced to the nucleus of the civil service set up by Sir STAMFORD RAFFLES, who appointed his deputy Major WILLIAM FARQUHAR as Resident, to be assisted by six officials. During the Crown Colony period (1867–1942), senior positions were restricted to expatriate officers from the United Kingdom; qualified local candidates were

recruited only for junior positions at lower salaries. The discontented local civil servants opposed such discrimination during the post-war period. The establishment of the PUBLIC SERVICE COMMISSION (PSC) in January 1951 by the colonial government removed such discrimination and speeded the localization of the SCS. The PSC's role was also to insulate the SCS from politics by ensuring that recruitment and promotion were based on merit.

In June 1959, when the PEOPLE'S ACTION PARTY government assumed office, there were 28,253 civil servants employed in nine ministries. By 2004, the SCS had more than doubled in size, to 61,516 employees in the Prime Minister's Office and 14 ministries: Community Development, Youth and Sports; Defence; Education; the Environment; Finance; Foreign Affairs; Health; Home Affairs; Information, Communications and the Arts; Law; Manpower; National Development; Trade and Industry; and Transport.

There have been five major changes concerning the SCS since the post-war period. First the profile of the SCS has changed significantly. In 1947, the Trusted Commission recommended that the SCS be divided into four divisions according to the duties and salaries of its members. Secondly, the government created STATUTORY BOARDS to share the SCS's workload and to allow for greater autonomy and flexibility. The HOUSING & DEVELOPMENT BOARD was the first statutory board formed in February 1960 to provide low-cost public housing for the population. The ECONOMIC DEVELOPMENT BOARD was created in August 1961, to promote economic development in Singapore through foreign investment. The success of both these statutory boards has led to the proliferation of such agencies.

Thirdly, the government strengthened anti-corruption measures. The CORRUPT PRACTICES INVESTIGATION BUREAU was set up by the British colonial government in 1952, but lacked the necessary powers to perform its functions effectively. The enactment of the Prevention of Corruption Act in 1960 gave officials more power.

The Singapore Chronicle

Singapore Civil Defence Force: firefighters.

Singapore City Gallery Located in the URA Centre at Maxwell Road, the gallery demonstrates the work of the URBAN REDEVELOPMENT AUTHORITY (URA), the body with overall responsibility for URBAN PLANNING and conservation. The gallery is a visual account of both the evolution of Singapore and plans for future development. Among the many exhibits are scale models which show in miniature both the central city area and the entire island. The gallery is divided into thematic sections.

Scale models The central area model (below) focuses on an area of some 16 sq km, almost half of which is reclaimed land; the island-wide model (right) shows the main island of Singapore.

History This section traces the story of Singapore's development, from its founding in 1819, through the age of rural townships, to the busy city of today. Interactive displays help to present history in an engaging manner.

Conservation Despite massive redevelopment in the decades of economic growth following Independence, many of Singapore's historic buildings have been saved for posterity. This section shows the importance of thorough research and careful regulation in conserving built heritage. There are also exhibits devoted to two important local building types: the Singapore shophouse and the bungalow.

Planning This section is devoted to the URA's primary role. Interactive exhibits show the dilemmas faced by planners in land-scarce Singapore, and how creative solutions have been developed to create a quality environment for live, work and play.

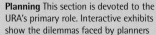

Young visitors learning to read maps and plans.

Singapore Conference Hall: May Day rally, 1983.

Fourthly, salaries were further increased in 1973, 1979, 1982, 1989 and 1994, to reduce the wage gap between the public and private sectors. In October 1994, a White Paper was presented in Parliament, benchmarking the salaries of ministers and senior civil servants to the average salaries of the top earners in six private sector professions, with the aim of minimizing corription and attracting talent.

Finally, in 1985, the FEEDBACK UNIT was formed to enable Singaporeans to provide their feedback on public policies. In April 1991, the Service Improvement Unit was created to reduce bureaucracy and improve service in the SCS. In May 1995, PS21 (Public Service for the 21st Century) was introduced to further improve the quality of service in the SCS, and to prepare civil servants for change.

In recent decades, the civil service has trimmed its staff strength from 69, 630 in 1985 to 62,792 in 2005. There was a notable shift in the educational profile of civil servants during this period: the number of staff in Division I (where the minimum entry requirement is a university degree) had more than tripled, while the number of staff in Divisions II–IV had reduced significantly. The ADMINISTRATIVE SERVICE, which was established in 1950, is the elite section of the civil service.

Singapore Club Colonial social club founded in 1862. The Singapore Club was originally situated at Beach Road. Its first officials were all well-known inhabitants of Singapore: W.H. Read (Chairman); R.B. Read (Secretary); A. Bauer; Sir THOMAS BRADDELL, C.H. Harrison, Captain Protheroe, Captain Tireman and A.

Shrieder. In 1869, the club moved to premises in De Souza Street and then later Raffles Square. It moved several times more, on the last occasion to the FULLERTON BUILDING. The club has been dormant since World War II.

Singapore Conference Hall In the 1930s, a major land reclamation exercise took place in the area where SHENTON WAY is today. The reclaimed site stood empty for nearly 30 years until several new buildings were constructed. In 1961, Malayan Architects Co-Partnership (MAC) won a national competition to design the Conference Hall, as it was then known. The design inspired a new architectural trend whereby buildings were given a distinctly Malayan character. It was completed in 1965 at a cost of $4 million and opened officially in October by Prime Minister Lee Kuan Yew.

The hall served as the headquarters of the NATIONAL TRADES UNION CONGRESS for many years, and was thus also known as the Trade Union House. For its time, it was equipped with the most modern facilities needed for staging a major conference, including multilingual translation equipment. The Commonwealth Heads of Government Meeting was held there in 1971; it was the first such conference to be held outside London.

The Singapore Conference Hall has been surpassed both in size and facilities by other newer venues, but it remains a symbol of an era in Singapore's development. With its excellent acoustics, the hall is now home to the SINGAPORE CHINESE ORCHESTRA.

Singapore Cricket Club Cricket has been played on the PADANG—the large green field in front of what is now the Singapore Cricket Club (SCC)—since 1837. The SCC, established in 1852, is the second-oldest club in Singapore, after the SINGAPORE TURF CLUB. The first 28 members of SCC were men from the British business and mercantile community, mostly clerks or 'junior assistants'. By the 1880s, membership had grown to almost 400 and was regarded as a social honour not only by businessmen but also high-ranking government officials.

Among the early SCC presidents were Sir CECIL CLEMENTI SMITH (1883); Sir FRANK SWETTENHAM (1902–03) and Sir ARTHUR YOUNG (1909–10)—all governors of the Straits Settlements.

With legislation in 1963 leading to the liberalization of private club membership policies, some of the elitism wore off. However, SCC admitted women as full members only in 1996. In 2006, women were still excluded from the Men's Bar.

Singapore Customs Department responsible for collecting and protecting customs revenue and the GOODS AND SERVICES TAX, as well as facilitating trade and travel. The department was formed on 1 April 2003 under the Ministry of Finance.

Singapore Customs had been part of the Customs and Excise Department, which was established in 1910 and subsequently underwent several name changes. It is one of the oldest tax-collecting agencies in Singapore. The first duties were imposed on hard liquor and OPIUM.

On 1 April 2003, another part of the Customs and Excise Department merged with Singapore Immigration & Registration to form the IMMIGRATION & CHECKPOINTS AUTHORITY, which is responsible for protecting Singapore's land, air and sea borders against undesirable entry.

Singapore Dance Theatre Founded in 1987 by GOH SOO KHIM and ANTHONY THEN, the Singapore Dance Theatre was Singapore's first professional ballet company. It made its debut at the Singapore Festival of Arts in 1988 with only seven dancers, but has since grown to employ more than 20.

While the company has excelled mainly in contemporary pieces, with an interest in acquiring the works of choreographer GOH CHOO SAN, its repertory has also included classical ballets such as *Coppélia* and *Giselle*. Ballet Under the Stars—a series of outdoor performances at Fort Canning initiated in 1995—has become one of the company's most popular offerings. Besides having toured to Australia, Mexico and France, the Singapore Dance Theatre made its London premiere in 2005, as part of the NATIONAL ARTS COUNCIL-funded Singapore Season.

Singapore Democratic Alliance Formed a few months prior to the 2001 general election, the Singapore Democratic Alliance's purpose was to form a common front in opposition to the ruling People's Action Party. The constituent members are: National Solidarity Party; Singapore Malay National Organisation, also known as Pertubuhan Kebangsaan Melayu Singapura (*see* PKMS); SINGAPORE PEOPLE'S PARTY (SPP); and Singapore Justice Party (which was absorbed into the SPP after 2001).

Following the 2001 general elections, the SPP's leader, veteran opposition leader CHIAM SEE TONG, retained his seat in

Potong Pasir constituency, while the National Solidarity Party's STEVE CHIA was appointed a NON-CONSTITUENCY MEMBER OF PARLIAMENT. On 18 January 2006, the Singapore Democratic Alliance announced that it would contest three group representation constituencies (Tampines, Jalan Besar and Pasir Ris-Punggol) and five single member constituencies (Potong Pasir, Choa Chu Kang, Bukit Timah, Ayer Rajah and MacPherson) in the 2006 elections. Chiam See Tong won in Potong Pasir.

Singapore Democratic Party Political party. The Singapore Democratic Party (SDP) was founded in 1980 by CHIAM SEE TONG. Chiam had previously contested several elections and by-elections as an independent but decided to establish a party base for the 1980 general election, where he lost to the PEOPLE'S ACTION PARTY (PAP) candidate, HOWE YOON CHONG, in Potong Pasir. The SDP then made a conscious decision—in the name of opposition solidarity—not to contest the ANSON BY-ELECTION (1981), which was won by J.B. JEYARETNAM of the WORKERS' PARTY.

Chiam was elected MEMBER OF PARLIAMENT for Potong Pasir during the 1984 election and retained the seat in 1988. The SDP's strongest showing was in the 1991 election. Three of its candidates—Chiam, Cheo Chai Chen and Ling How Doong—won seats in Potong Pasir, Nee Soon Central and Bukit Gombak respectively. This made the SDP the leading opposition party in Parliament. In 1992, the SDP contested the by-election for Marine Parade GROUP REPRESENTATION CONSTITUENCY with their new recruit,

Singapore Cricket Club: postcard dated 1911 (top); a game on the Padang in 2006.

Singapore Dance Theatre

Singapore Democratic Party

CHEE SOON JUAN, a university lecturer. They won 24.5 per cent of the votes. In 1993, following Chee's hunger strike, a split occurred in the party, which led to Chiam's resigning and joining the SINGAPORE PEOPLE'S PARTY. Chee took over as secretary-general of the SDP. The SDP lost all its seats during the 1997 general election and failed to win any seats in the 2001 and 2006 general elections.

Singapore Department of Statistics Even before self-government in 1959, data and statistics were being collected, collated, analysed and published. This was made possible by the enactment of the Statistics Ordinance in 1921, which also provided for the establishment of the Statistical Bureau, which later became the Singapore Department of Statistics (DOS).

Today, DOS is the national statistical authority responsible for developing, coordinating and managing the national statistical information system. Using statistical data, DOS is able to analyse and monitor national trends. It provides professional advice on utilization and interpretation of statistics and undertakes special statistical projects on topics of current interest as inputs for government planning. As the custodian of Singapore's official statistics, DOS is also responsible for collating and disseminating official statistical information to the general public.

Prior to 1959, DOS was virtually the sole compiler of all statistical series. Emphasis was placed largely on data related to external trade, shipping and cargo, as well as basic demographic information. In the 1960s, the mandate of DOS was expanded to include statistics on manufacturing, commerce and the service industry.

In 1973, a decentralized statistical system was introduced which saw various government ministries and statutory boards collecting and compiling statistics on areas under their own purview. DOS, however, maintained its authority as Singapore's central coordinator of statistics.

Although DOS originated in the 1920s, the history of statistics collection dates back to 1871 when the first population CENSUS was taken. Such censuses are compiled every ten years, except for a brief disruption during World War II. The latest census was conducted in 2000.

Singapore ear An ear infection known to the medical profession as *Otitis externa*, which occurs frequently in hot and humid climates such as that of Singapore. An inflammation of the inside of the external ear around the auditory canal, it is caused by excessive moisture that carries bacteria into the ear. Swimmers are particularly prone to the condition. The main symptom is a burning sensation or itchiness in the ear. The infection can easily be treated.

Singapore Exchange The growth of the rubber and tin industries in Malaya provided the impetus for the issue of shares from the early years of the 20th century, and for the subsequent establishment of the Malayan Stock Exchange in 1960, with trading rooms in Kuala Lumpur and Singapore. This joint arrangement came to an end in 1973 when the currency interchangeability agreement between Singapore and Malaysia was terminated, leading to the formation of the Stock Exchange of Singapore Limited (SES) in the same year.

SES was renamed the Singapore Exchange (SGX) on 1 December 1999, after it became an integrated securities and derivatives exchange, following the merger of its operations with the SINGAPORE INTERNATIONAL MONETARY EXCHANGE.

SGX comprises two divisions: the SGX-Securities Trading Division (SGX-ST), for trading of shares and bonds; and the SGX-Derivatives Trading Division (SGX-DT), for trading of derivative products. SGX-ST operates a fully electronic and floor-less exchange. As with other exchanges, it allows firms to raise capital via stock listings on either the main or the junior board (Sesdaq), and allows investors to trade in a variety of assets ranging from shares and bonds, to futures and other derivative instruments.

On 23 November 2000, SGX itself was listed as a counter on its own main board. This demutualisation turned the exchange into a profit-making entity.

See also CENTRAL LIMIT ORDER BOOK.

Singapore Expo Largest exhibition centre in Southeast Asia. Singapore Expo in Simei was built as an alternative to the ageing World Trade Centre in Telok Blangah. The complex was designed by Australian architectural firm Cox Richardson and was built at a cost of more than $220 million. The centre sits on a 25-ha site and offers 10 halls with 100,000 sq m of indoor, column-free, exhibition space. There is a further 25,000 sq m of outdoor exhibition space with 19 conference halls and meeting rooms. Singapore Expo opened its doors on 4 March 1999. It is managed by Singex Venues Pte Ltd, a wholly owned subsidiary of TEMASEK HOLDINGS.

Singapore Factory and Shop Workers' Union In May 1954, the Singapore Factory and Shop Workers' Union (SFSWU) was registered with the government. Its general secretary was LIM CHIN SIONG. Both FONG SWEE SUAN (general secretary of the SINGAPORE BUS WORKERS' UNION) and C.V. DEVAN NAIR (of the SINGAPORE TEACHERS' UNION) were also members of SFSWU's executive board. The charismatic Lim led several well-organized small strikes that succeeded in bettering conditions for the union's workers and in attracting thousands of recruits. By 1955, the SFSWU included 30 industrial unions with a membership of almost 30,000. The SFSWU worked closely with the Singapore Bus Workers' Union, and was instrumental in precipitating the HOCK LEE BUS RIOTS of 1955.

Singapore Federation of Chinese Clan Associations The idea of setting up this umbrella organization for CLAN ASSOCIATIONS was first floated at a seminar in December 1984 entitled 'The Role of the Chinese Clan Association in the New Era'. The Singapore Federation of Chinese Clan Associations (SFCCA) was registered a year later, and officially started operations on 27 January 1986. From an initial membership of 70, it has grown to represent some 191 member associations.

Initially, the SFCCA was involved in activities such as organizing sporting tournaments. However, it soon expanded its scope to include the provision of educational bursaries for students; the organization of the annual Singapore River Hongbao (a festival held during CHINESE NEW YEAR); the founding of the CHINESE HERITAGE CENTRE at NANYANG TECHNOLOGICAL UNIVERSITY; and the promotion of the Speak Mandarin Campaign. The SFCCA has also sought to encourage the participation of young Chinese Singaporeans in clan activities.

Singapore Federation of Trade Unions When the British Military Administration proscribed the GENERAL LABOUR UNION for its left-wing activities and militancy, its

Singapore Federation of Chinese Clan Associations: publications by the Federation.

members formed the Pan-Malayan Federation of Trade Unions in February 1946, with two constituent parts, one in peninsular Malaya, and the other registered as the SINGAPORE FEDERATION OF TRADE UNIONS (SFTU) in Singapore. Both divisions were dominated by MALAYAN COMMUNIST PARTY elements.

By mid 1947, the SFTU claimed control of two-thirds of Singapore's trade unions, with a membership of over 51,000 workers. In 1948, the SFTU planned a massive strike on May Day with an estimated 100,000 workers to take part. However, the government banned the procession and the strike was called off. Shortly thereafter, the majority of leading Malayan Communist Party members within the SFTU left for Malaya to join the communist armed struggle, and a state of EMERGENCY was declared. The SFTU disbanded on the eve of the communist insurrection.

Singapore Film Commission Government agency set up in 1998 to provide financial support and training for local film-makers, while also seeking to raise public awareness of Singapore FILM. It was merged in 2003 with the Singapore Broadcasting Authority and the Films and Publications Department to form a new statutory board, the MEDIA DEVELOPMENT AUTHORITY.

Two of the commission's earliest schemes were the Short Film Grant and the Feature Film Investment Programme. From 1998 to 2005, more than 200 short films received support from the commission. Feature films which received support include *Chicken Rice War* (2000), *One Leg Kicking* (2001), *15* (2001) and *Perth* (2005).

Singapore Film Society Non-profit organization. The Singapore Film Society (SFS) was officially registered by a nine-member committee in 1958 to promote FILM appreciation. It was initially based at the UNIVERSITY OF MALAYA, but later moved to Golden Village Marina after entering into a 1996 agreement with GOLDEN VILLAGE that allowed the SFS to hold high-quality film screenings on a regular basis.

Throughout its history, the Singapore Film Society has organized regular screenings for its members, and has collaborated with foreign diplomatic missions and cultural institutions such as the Malaysian Art Film Club, as well as local film distributors. SFS film festivals have featured movies from many different countries.

Singapore flap Surgical procedure. The Singapore flap refers to a piece of tissue from the thigh—comprising muscle, nerve and blood vessels—used in vaginal reconstruction. This procedure, pioneered by plastic surgeon Julian Wee and paediatric surgeon V.T. JOSEPH, was first performed at the SINGAPORE GENERAL HOSPITAL in 1992. It is carried out to create a vagina for

patients who have been born without one, or who suffer from vaginal defects such as recurrent pelvic malignancy.

Singapore Foochow Association Clan association. Established in 1909, the Singapore Foochow Association was first located at Club Street. The association was committed to various welfare causes, notably in the aftermath of the Marco Polo Bridge Incident of 1937 in China, when members raised funds to provide relief for child refugees in Foochow (present-day Fuzhou). In 1946, the association re-established San Shan Primary School, which had run from 1925–27 but had closed down due to the poor economic situation and decline in student numbers at the time. In 1982, the school finally closed down due to changes in education policies which led to decreased enrolment in vernacular schools.

In 1977, the Foochow Building was built at Tyrwhitt Road, near Jalan Besar, and has since housed the association. In an effort to renew its membership, the association set up a Chinese orchestra and dance troupe under its Youth Section, which was established in 1982. It also regularly holds events promoting Foochow and Chinese culture. It has around 900 members.

Singapore foot This skin condition, known to doctors as *Tinea pedis*, is also commonly known as athlete's foot. Usually occurring between the toes, it is caused by a fungus. Symptoms include dry skin, itchiness, scaling, inflammation and blisters. In Singapore's hot and damp climate, shoes create a warm, dark and humid environment which encourages fungal growth. Antifungal medications are used to treat the condition.

Singapore Free Press English-language newspaper. Singapore Free Press was started by WILLIAM NAPIER to mark the abolition of the Gagging Act in 1835, which required newspapers to be submitted to the colonial government before publication. The *Singapore Free Press* started off as a four-page weekly, carrying a page of commercial and shipping news catering to the colony's burgeoning commercial enterprise. With the demise of THE SINGAPORE CHRONICLE, the *Singapore Free Press* was unrivalled for ten years until THE STRAITS TIMES was started in 1845. In 1869, the *Singapore Free Press* folded, but was revived in 1884 by Charles Burton Buckley, who had bought over the old plant. In 1887, the weekly became a daily. The *Singapore Free Press* was bought over by its competitor, *The Straits Times*, in 1933, and was eventually merged with THE MALAY MAIL (also owned by *The Straits Times*) in 1952.

Singapore General Hospital Established in 1821 as the General Hospital, this institution was first located within a British mili-

Singapore Expo

tary base near the Singapore River. It was relocated to Pearl's Bank, then to the vicinity of Kandang Kerbau before moving permanently to the Sepoy Lines, Outram Road, in 1882. In 1926, it was renamed the Singapore General Hospital (SGH) with the opening of the Bowyer, Stanley and Norris Blocks, providing a total of 800 beds. Only the Bowyer Block has survived into the 21st century—although it is commonly known today as the 'Clock Tower', and is used as the hospital's museum.

SGH has four specialist centres: the Singapore National Eye Centre; the National Heart Centre; the National Cancer Centre, Singapore; and the National Dental Centre. The hospital also serves as the national referral centre for plastic surgery and burns; renal medicine; nuclear medicine; and pathology and haematology. There are more than 30 clinical specialities covered, including gastroenterology, dermatology, geriatrics, neonatal and developmental medicine, nuclear medicine and obstetrics and gynaecology.

SGH's Nuclear Medicine Centre is one of the region's largest, providing a range of clinical services in radio-isotope imaging and therapy for oncology, cardiac, orthopaedic and neurology patients. The Department of Neonatal and Developmental Medicine provides pre-conception and prenatal counselling, as well

Singapore Free Press

Singapore General Hospital

Singapore Herald: *final issue.*

as care for high-risk pregnancies and prematurely born babies.

The hospital's Burns Centre is a 52-bed unit that provides acute medical care to burn-injury victims in Singapore and the region. The centre also researches new modes of treatment for burns patients.

Singapore Girl The SINGAPORE AIRLINES (SIA) flight stewardess, popularly referred to as the 'Singapore Girl', has become synonymous with the carrier. Clad in a *sarong kebaya* uniform designed by Pierre Balmain, the Singapore Girl has become Singapore's most recognizable ambassador. Conceived in 1972 when SIA split from Malaysia-Singapore Airlines, the Singapore Girl has since become an iconic figure, personifying warmth, hospitality and grace. With the airline's global expansion, the Singapore Girl is not necessarily a Singaporean, but could be a Malaysian, Japanese, Indian or other national.

Singapore Grand Prix Between 1961 and 1973, Singapore played host to an international Grand Prix competition on a street circuit at Upper Thomson Road. Initially known as the Orient Year Grand Prix, it was renamed the Malaysian Grand Prix in 1962. From 1966, it was known as the Singapore Grand Prix.

The Grand Prix would eventually become a major event that attracted both sponsorship as well as quality drivers. At the first Grand Prix, the main event was for sports and racing cars and had an entry list of 30 cars ranging from a motorcycle-engined Cooper-Norton of 500 cc capacity to a Ferrari Monza and an Aston Martin DB3S. There were nine different races for cars and motorcycles. Prize money for a win was $1,000, plus a gold cup. The two-day event attracted an estimated 100,000 spectators. The winner of the first Grand Prix was Ian Barnwell, a Pahang-based planter from the United Kingdom driving the Aston Martin DB3S.

The course was three miles long (4.8 km) and began on Upper Thomson Road and covered the old Sembawang Circus, backtracking up Old Upper Thomson Road and past Upper Peirce Reservoir Road (known as Devil's Bend) and back

Singapore Grand Prix: programme (below); route map.

down to the main road. This circuit would remain for the most part unchanged throughout its 13-year run.

Between 1961 and 1970, the main event was a Formula Libre one (free engine format) with single-seaters mixing with sports and saloon cars. Rules were at a minimum and strategy was limited to reliability and a large petrol tank or two to run the 60-lap event (changed to a 20-lap preliminary followed by a 40-lap main race in 1970). Up to 1967, the winners had largely been Singaporeans, but by 1968, this changed when Australian racing car builder Garrie Cooper won in his Elfin 600 prototype.

From 1971, Australian AF2 Formula rules applied to the main event, turning it into a single-seater race, with the engine restricted to 1600-cc capacity. Sponsorship became big and backers included the old Malaysia-Singapore Airlines, Cathay Pacific, Air New Zealand and Rothmans.

April 1973 was the last time that the event was held. Factors such as the oil crisis were cited as reasons for Singapore dropping the race. Safety was another possible reason for ending the competition. On average there would be one recorded death a year from the event, generally because of the lack of safety features on cars—and also due to the inherent nature of the Thomson Road circuit, which had monsoon drains and bus stops along the course.

Singapore Hainan Hwee Kuan First established in 1854 as the Kiung Chow Hwee Kuan to provide social support for newly arrived immigrants, this clan association shared its premises with the Tin Hou Gong (Queen of Heaven) temple. In 1878, it moved to its current location at 47 Beach Road. The association organized activities and was in charge of handling external affairs, while the temple oversaw financial matters and fund-raising. This arrangement lasted from 1880 to 1932. In 1910, Yock Eng High School was founded and run with funds raised by the temple. During the Japanese Occupation, the association ceased operations, resuming in 1945. The subsequent growth of its membership led to reconstruction of the premises, and the current building was completed in 1962.

The association has been actively involved with the HAINANESE and wider Chinese community, working with the Federation of Hainan Associations Malaysia in 1954 to establish scholarships, and making education bursaries available to children of association members. In 1976, the Hwee Kuan also upgraded the facilities of the Loke Tin Kee medical centre, which it had set up in 1902. Since 1986, it has promoted Hainanese culture by organizing lectures and through the establishment of an arts section. It is also one of six major CLAN ASSOCIATIONS which form the SINGAPORE FEDERATION OF CHINESE CLAN ASSOCIATIONS.

Singapore Girl, centre, with Pierre Balmain, right.

In 1994, the association changed its name to Singapore Hainan Hwee Kuan to reflect Hainan's new status as a province of China. It also engaged in a successful membership drive in the mid-1990s, and has over 4,000 members.

Singapore Herald Originally a Japanese-owned English-language newspaper published before the outbreak of WORLD WAR II, the *Singapore Herald* was re-launched in July 1970 as a lively challenge to *The Straits Times*, which had, many felt, grown complacent due to a lack of competition in post-Independence days. On 28 May 1971, the government withdrew the licence of the *Singapore Herald*, stating that the paper was a front for foreign interests; the newspaper's senior expatriate staff were expelled from Singapore.

Singapore Heritage Society Non-governmental organization. The Singapore Heritage Society was founded in 1986 by a group of intellectuals and professionals led by architect WILLIAM LIM, who became its founder-president. The society promotes interest in the cultural life and history of Singapore through research, evaluation, documentation, publication, collection, display, preservation and restoration of skills and items of historical interest. It publishes books, organizes talks and forums, and conducts heritage tours for members and the general public.

SINGAPORE GRAND PRIX: WINNERS		
Date	**Driver**	**Constructor**
Sep 1961	Ian Barnwell	Aston Martin DB3S
Apr 1962	Yong Nam Kee	Jaguar E-Type
Apr 1963	Albert Poon	Lotus 23
Mar 1964	race cancelled due to rain	
Apr 1965	Albert Poon	Lotus 23B
Apr 1966	Lee Han Seng	Lotus 22
Mar 1967	Rodney Seow	Merlyn Mk 10 Lotus-Ford
Apr 1968	Garrie Cooper	Elfin 600 prototype Ford Twin Cam
Apr 1969	Graeme Lawrence	McLaren M4A Cosworth
Mar 1970	Graeme Lawrence	Ferrari 246T
Apr 1971	Graeme Lawrence	Brabham BT29
Apr 1972	Max Stewart	Mildren-Waggott
Apr 1973	Vern Schuppan	March 722

Singapore Hainan Hwee Kuan

Singapore Hokkien Huay Kuan This CLAN ASSOCIATION was founded in 1840 to promote education, social welfare and Chinese language and culture, particularly within the HOKKIEN community. Membership was open to all people of Hokkien origin who traced their roots back to the regions of Fujian province where the Minnan dialect was spoken. In the decades following its foundation, the association helped many immigrants who had recently arrived from Fujian to find housing and employment. At one time, it served also as the registrar of marriages for many immigrants from Fujian.

The association has long looked after the religious needs of Singapore's Hokkien community by building temples. In 1839, businessman and philanthropist TAN TOCK SENG, together with other prominent members of the community, built the THIAN HOCK KENG TEMPLE on Telok Ayer Street. This temple, together with Chong Wen Ge (a school run by the association) served as the association's offices until permanent premises were found on Telok Ayer Street in 1919.

The association has also promoted the development of education. Chong Wen Ge was its first school. The Singapore Hokkien Huay Kuan later founded other schools, including Cui Ying Institution (1854); TAO NAN SCHOOL (1906); AI TONG SCHOOL (1912); Chongfu Primary School (1915); NAN CHIAU HIGH SCHOOL and Primary School (1947); and Kong Hwa School (1953). The association also donated 212 ha of land towards the founding of NANYANG UNIVERSITY in 1953.

The Singapore Hokkien Huay Kuan continues to promote education by providing scholarships, bursaries and training awards for needy and deserving students. In addition, financial donations have been made to educational and research institutions such as the CHINESE HERITAGE CENTRE at NANYANG TECHNOLOGICAL UNIVERSITY, the NUS Biological Research Fund, the Tan Lark Sye Professorship and the Mendaki Education Trust Fund.

Singapore Idol Singing talent competition. The first Singapore Idol contest was held in 2004, and was based on the same formula as American Idol, where audiences called in to vote for their favourite contestants. The Singapore Idol series started on 9 August 2004 and it attracted over 3 million viewers, and making it the highest-rated production in the history of MEDIACORP's Channel 5. In all, 3 million votes were cast throughout the six months it was aired.

The finals were held at the Singapore Indoor Stadium on 1 December 2004. A record 1.8 million viewers tuned in to the live broadcast. Taufik Batisah was pronounced the first Singapore Idol. The second season began airing in May 2006.

Singapore Improvement Trust Formed in 1927 'to provide for the Improvement of the Town and Island of Singapore', the Singapore Improvement Trust (SIT) is commonly thought to be the predecessor of the HOUSING & DEVELOPMENT BOARD, although its original intention was not to build housing on a large scale. It was only later, when the housing shortage became acute, that the SIT began to build housing, mostly for the poorer sections of society.

Singapore Improvement Trust: flats at Tiong Bahru.

In 1926, the government earmarked a sum of $10 million for the clearance of slum areas and acquiring land for rehousing and for the construction of houses. The first houses erected by the SIT in 1932 were at Lorong Limau. In 1936, the SIT undertook its own building work with the construction and development of public housing at TIONG BAHRU estate.

During the JAPANESE OCCUPATION, the work of the SIT came to a stop. After the war, the SIT's priority was to place its tenancies on a satisfactory basis as most of the Trust buildings were dirty and badly in need of repair. Furthermore, some of the buildings in the city centre had been occupied by the Japanese and within a day or two of the liberation, by various clubs and political societies.

In 1947, a Singapore Housing Committee was formed under the chairmanship of C.W.A. Sennett, the commissioner of lands. It recommended that the matter of PUBLIC HOUSING should come under a public building authority, which would operate at a very small profit or even, if necessary, at a loss.

In 1948, the SIT undertook another major initiative. The government granted the SIT a loan of $5 million, which enabled the SIT to build its own housing instead of depending on private developers to meet the demand for housing. Three years later, a Singapore Improvement Bill was introduced, encompassing the legislation necessary for the SIT's three main tasks—improvement and slum clearance, town and country planning, and public housing.

In 1959, the Housing and Development Ordinance and the Planning Ordinance were enacted. The SIT was then dissolved and the Housing & Development Board was formed. Some of the flats built by the SIT still stand, the best-known ones being those beside Tiong Bahru Road, and those at Short Street and Prinsep Street.

Singapore Idol: Taufik Batisah, winner in 2004.

Singapore Indian Association Association formed in 1923 by a group of Indians—including, among others, RAJABALI JUMABHOY and BASHIR MALLAL—with the purpose of promoting the welfare of Indians and providing the community with opportunities

Singapore Hokkien Huay Kuan: members of its Arts & Cultural Troupe before Thian Hock Keng Temple.

Singapore Indian Development Association

Singapore International Film Festival

for leisure pursuits. Its first premises were on Short Street, although the association also acquired land on Balestier Plain for sporting fixtures. The Balestier grounds later became the site of permanent premises, with Prime Minister Jawaharlal Nehru of India laying the foundation stone for these premises in 1950.

In addition to its social activities, the association has long played a role in promoting sports. In 1999, it acquired S.LEAGUE team Krida Arsenal, and it has continued to field teams in national hockey and cricket competitions.

Singapore Indian Chamber of Commerce and Industry This organization traces its roots to the Indian Merchants' Association. It was formed in 1924 out of the SINGAPORE INDIAN ASSOCIATION. In its first decade, it acted as a social club for merchants from Bombay (present-day Mumbai).

By 1935, it was felt that a single organization was needed, to represent Indian business interests, and so the Indian Chamber of Commerce was founded, with RAJABALI JUMABHOY as its first president. In 1970, the organization was renamed the Singapore Indian Chamber of Commerce and Industry.

Singapore Indian Development Association The Singapore Indian Development Association (SINDA) was established in August 1991 to address the pressing educational and socio-economic issues facing Singapore's Indian community. In July 1991, the Action Committee on Indian Education presented a report, *At The Crossroads*, to the government. The report highlighted the educational under-performance of Indian students and recommended wide-ranging remedial measures.

SINDA's declared mission is to 'build a well-educated, resilient and confident community of Indians that stands together with other communities in contributing to the progress of multi-racial Singapore'. To this end, SINDA has focused its efforts on raising the educational performance of Indian students, promoting family unity and helping foster the social and economic development of Singapore's Indians.

SINDA's first president was J.Y.M. PILLAY and its first chief executive officer was S. Iswaran.

Singapore Indoor Stadium

Singapore Indian Fine Arts Society: at a rehearsal for the Chingay street procession, 1980.

Singapore Indian Fine Arts Society Indian classical music and dance society. Started in 1949, Singapore Indian Fine Arts Society (SIFAS) is a non-profit Indian organization which provides training in dance, vocal and instrumental music, with an emphasis on syllabus-based education. Dependent on staff mainly from India, SIFAS is involved in an exchange of ideas with Indian artistes and organizes shows and seminars presented by Indian performers. An active participant in the SINGAPORE ARTS FESTIVAL, SIFAS also has a Performing Arts Company and Visual Arts School.

Singapore Indoor Stadium After the NATIONAL STADIUM opened in 1973, there were ongoing discussions on building an indoor stadium complete with a velodrome. However, this idea was put on hold while Singapore was recovering from the oil crisis. Construction on the new indoor stadium—without velodrome—began in early 1988 and was completed by December 1989. On 31 December 1989, the stadium was declared open by Prime Minister Lee Kuan Yew.

The stadium was designed by Japanese architect Kenzo Tange and features a Shinto-inspired, concave cone-shaped roof. Built at a cost of $90 million by Guan Ho Construction & Ssangyong Engineering, the stadium is Singapore's largest covered arena and has a seating capacity of 12,000. Its flexible stage configurations make it the prime venue for many large-scale events, such as rock concerts, major stage productions and indoor spectator sports such as ice-skating.

Singapore Institute of Management Founded by the ECONOMIC DEVELOPMENT BOARD in 1964, the Singapore Institute of Management (SIM) is an independent, non-profit professional membership organization. SIM boasts a strong network of about 19,000 individual and corporate members, including all its students.

In its early years, SIM offered crash courses in management disciplines for senior managers and for supervisory per-

sonnel. After the launch of the Diploma in Management Studies programme in 1973, the institute's portfolio grew to incorporate a wide range of diploma, bachelor's, master's and doctoral programmes in partnership with more than ten established international universities. By 2000, it was offering two doctoral, nine master's, 37 bachelor's and over 20 diploma and certificate programmes. In 2004, SIM's enrolment in these programmes exceeded 15,500, with 5,400 graduates for that year.

With its experience in running continuing education programmes for working adults, SIM was selected by the Ministry of Education in 1992 to run the Open University Degree Programme in Singapore. In 2002, the programme was renamed SIM Open University Centre, when SIM was granted accreditation by The Open University of the United Kingdom. It has enabled some 2,000 working adults to obtain tertiary qualifications since 1994. In January 2005, the Ministry of Education granted SIM approval to form Singapore's fourth university, SIM University. SIM University was formally registered in April 2005 and its first student intake was in January 2006.

Singapore International Chamber of Commerce Founded in 1837, the Singapore International Chamber of Commerce (SICC) is not only the oldest commercial organization in Singapore; it is also the oldest chamber of commerce in Asia. It is accepted by the government as representing the business interests of the chamber's membership, which encompasses both multinational corporations with operations in Singapore and locally owned businesses. The SICC constantly monitors and, where appropriate, speaks up on issues or developments of concern to its members. Virtually all GOVERNMENT-LINKED COMPANIES are members of the SICC.

Singapore International Film Festival This festival showcasing international and local 'art-house' films, was first held in 1987. The Singapore International Film Festival (SIFF) was initially planned as a biennial event, but was made into an annual festival in April 1989. The SIFF has always placed a strong emphasis on Asian film, and has promoted new talent from China, Taiwan, the Philippines, Thailand, Indonesia and Malaysia. In 1991, the SIFF inaugurated the Silver Screen Awards for local and regional movies. Local director ERIC KHOO won the first Silver Screen Award for his short film *August* (1991).

Singapore International Foundation Non-profit organization. The Singapore International Foundation (SIF) actively aims to engage Singaporeans in international volunteerism. The SIF was established on 1 August 1991 to help promote

Singapore's globalization efforts. It was incorporated as a public company limited by guarantee. Its mission is to 'build a corps of active global citizens for Singapore'. Its programmes include the Singapore Volunteers Overseas programme and the Singapore Executive Expeditions, while programmes focusing on international networking are the Friends of Singapore programme and the Overseas Singaporeans programme. Its first executive director was Professor CHAN HENG CHEE, who served from 1991 to 1996.

Singapore International Monetary Exchange To capture a slice of the growing market in global futures, the Singapore International Monetary Exchange (SIMEX) was established in 1984 to replace the Gold Exchange of Singapore, which traded only in gold futures. A special characteristic of SIMEX was its link-up with the Chicago Mercantile Exchange in the United States and the system of mutual offset: positions in one exchange could be liquidated against the other, thus enhancing liquidity while lowering trading risks and transaction costs under a round-the-clock trading arrangement.

SIMEX was caught up in the Barings Bank crisis of 1995, when the Singapore-based trader, NICK LEESON, incurred US$1.4 billion in losses on Nikkei 225 futures contracts and Japanese bonds. SIMEX continued to perform strongly without external financial assistance, but the crisis precipitated a review of its rules, audit, surveillance and clearing practices.

SIMEX was merged with the Stock Exchange of Singapore in 1999. Now it operates as the SGX Derivatives Trading Division of the SINGAPORE EXCHANGE, offering a wide range of global futures contracts. In 2005, to boost Singapore's position as a regional commodities trading centre, SGX signed a Memorandum of Understanding with the Chicago Board of Trade to set up jointly a derivatives exchange to trade in Asian commodities.

Singapore Island Country Club The club is the product of the merger of the Royal Singapore Golf Club and the Royal Island Club. The Royal Singapore Golf Club was originally founded in 1891 as the Singapore Golf Club, focusing primarily on providing GOLF facilities. It had two 18-hole courses and a clubhouse at Sime Road. The Royal Island Club was set up in 1927 as The Island Club. It was a country clubhouse with amenities for golf, swimming, tennis and other forms of recreation. Its multiracial membership enjoyed an 18-hole golf course as well as social activities.

In the early 1960s, members of the Royal Singapore Golf Club initiated the merger. At a conference of delegates from both clubs on 21 June 1963, the two clubs became one, the Singapore Island Country Club. This accounts for the club's two adjacent sites—the Bukit and Island locations. There are four 18-hole golf courses. Of these, the Bukit Course, opened in 1924, is a championship course with more than 3,000 fully grown trees.

Singapore Khalsa Association Association founded in May 1931 by a group of students from Raffles Institution who sought to establish a sports club for Singapore's Sikh community. In the 1960s, it also began to provide cultural and social activities. In 1992, it opened the Khalsa Kindergarten.

The association's original premises were built next to playing fields in Whampoa that had been acquired in 1932. In 1969, the association built a new and permanent clubhouse on the corner of Balestier and Tessensohn Roads (near Balestier Plain) after the Whampoa land had been requisitioned by the Government.

Singapore Khalsa Association's original focus on sport has seen it foster teams in hockey, badminton, cricket and other sports; in soccer, it has maintained an affiliation with S.LEAGUE club Balestier Khalsa.

Singapore Kwangtung Hui Kuan Clan association. The Singapore Kwangtung Hui Kuan was founded in 1937 by 76 men representing the CANTONESE, HAKKA, TEOCHEW and HAINANESE peoples from Kwangtung (present-day Guangdong) province, to provide assistance and welfare to Chinese in Singapore who could trace their roots to the province. The first president was Lee Wee Nam, a prominent Teochew businessman and chairman of the TEOCHEW POIT IP HUAY KUAN.

During the first 20 years of the association's existence, it was based at the Teochew Building on Tank Road. Since 1957, the association has been housed in various localities, including the premises of a temple, the Wak Hai Cheng Bio. Based at

Singapore International Monetary Exchange

Manhattan House on Chin Swee Road since 1995, the association primarily focuses on cultural and welfare activities and providing community service. Prominent past presidents of the association include Dr LIEN YING CHOW.

After Hainan Island became a separate autonomous Chinese province in 1988, the association stopped accepting Hainanese members. The Singapore Kwangtung Hui Kuan is a founding member of the SINGAPORE FEDERATION OF CHINESE CLAN ASSOCIATIONS.

Singapore Labour Foundation Founded in 1977, the Singapore Labour Foundation (SLF) was set up to promote the welfare of trade union members and further the development of the trade union movement in Singapore. With initial funding from trade unions, labour cooperatives and employers, SLF started off by providing bursaries and scholarships to children of members of trade unions as well as educational funds for workers to pursue further studies or undergo skills training. It also launched welfare schemes to provide financial assistance to victims of industrial accidents and their families.

In the mid-1980s, the SLF embarked on the development of large-scale holiday resorts and country clubs for workers. In 1996, SLF introduced a group insurance scheme to cover all union members, up to the age of 65 against death and permanent total disabilities from accidents or natural causes. As of 2006, SLF's membership comprised 76 institutional members including nine co-operatives and 67 unions and associations. SLF is funded mainly by contributions from unions and co-operatives, and returns from investments.

Singapore Labour Foundation

Singapore Island Country Club

Singapore Labour Party Political party. The idea of forming the Singapore Labour Party (SLP) was mooted by M.A. MAJID, president of the Singapore Seamen's Union and a defeated candidate in the 1948 elections. Majid wanted to capture the large number of eligible Indian voters. Though its leadership comprised other English-educated Indians such as PETER WILLIAMS and M.P.D. NAIR, two clerical workers from the Army Civil Service Union representing workers from the military civil service, the party also included FRANCIS THOMAS, an English schoolteacher and admirer of Fabian socialism. Thomas attended the public meeting of the party's founding on 1 September 1948, and was surprised to find himself elected to the leadership. The party also succeeded in winning over LIM YEW HOCK from the SINGAPORE PROGRESSIVE PARTY. Lim was named its president in 1950.

Modelled after the British Labour Party, and drawing its support from labour unions, the SLP was a non-communal and multiracial party with the goal of an independent, socialist Malaya, inclusive of Singapore. It called for full self-government by 1954 through constitutional means, independence through merger with Malaya, nationalization of the TIN and RUBBER industries, social welfare for workers, and the participation of unions in politics. With support mainly from Indians working in the British military service, the party contested seven of the nine seats in the 1951 general election, winning two. In the city council election a few months later, it captured three out of the six constituencies, mainly through its association with the Army Civil Service Union (the SLP having little support from other unions, particularly those with Chinese-speaking workers).

Lacking strong organization and ideological convictions, the SLP suffered from internal dissent following the city council election in 1951. In December 1952, a split over personalities and over control of the party occurred—between the English-educated, white-collar, Indian leaders under Peter Williams, and the business-professional leaders under Francis Thomas and Lim Yew Hock. Lim and Thomas left the party. The SLP never recovered from the split, and did not become a significant force in Singapore politics.

Singapore Literature Society This society was established in 1981 to promote all manner of cultural and literary activities, such as international conferences and seminars on creative writing. Its official journal, *Xinjiapo Wenyi* (Singapore Literature), is the longest-running literary journal in the country. Another achievement of the society has been the publication of a series of literary works and studies of Singapore writers, including the 'Singapore Literature Series', the 'Young Writers Series' and the

Singapore Management University

'Women Writers Series'. The society has established two annual literature awards.

Following a traditional Chinese concept of literature, the society considers authors of all types of work—from news reports to travelogues—as writers, and so lists some 594 writers in its *Directory of Singapore Chinese Writers* (2005).

Singapore Lyric Opera Singapore's only Western opera company was formed in 1990, by a group of opera aficionados who had previously produced operas under the banner of the NATIONAL UNIVERSITY OF SINGAPORE Society. Since its inaugural production in 1991, it has presented an annual season of full-length works as well as concert versions. Some notable productions have included Benjamin Britten's *A Midsummer Night's Dream* (1997), Verdi's *Macbeth* (2001), Puccini's *Madama Butterfly* (2005) and the Singapore premiere of Mozart's *The Marriage of Figaro* (2006).

The Singapore Lyric Opera has an active choral, youth, education and outreach programme, which aims to bring the vocal arts to schools and to the grassroots.

Singapore Malay Chamber of Commerce and Industry Organization formed by a group of Malay businessmen with the aim of mutual assistance and co-operation, and the exchange of information. Incorporated on 28 July 1956, it plays a role similar to the Chinese CLAN ASSOCIATIONS by building on communal and business networks. It was originally known as Dewan Perniagaan Melayu Singapura (Singapore Malay Chamber of Commerce).

The organization's influence was minimal in its early decades as membership was low. Membership gradually expanded when it was opened to non-Malay Muslim businesses. It became more prominent in the 1980s with the increasing awareness and involvement of Malays in business. A major achievement in the 1990s was its organizing of the International Muslim Food and Technology Expo, which was held every two years from 1990 to 2001.

One of the organization's aims is to become a one-stop centre for business information and training for Malays. In 1995, its name was changed to Dewan Perniagaan dan Perusahaan Melayu Singapura, or the Singapore Malay Chamber of Commerce and Industry (SMCCI). A rejuvenated SMCCI was inaugurated in 2004, with the mission to nurture a successful entrepreneurial culture.

Singapore Malay National Organisation *See* PERTUBUHAN KEBANGSAAN MELAYU SINGAPURA.

Singapore Management University Singapore's third university. Officially incorporated in January 2000, the Singapore Management University (SMU) models its system on the Wharton Business School of the University of Pennsylvania, geared towards preparing graduates mainly for business and entrepreneurship. The main subject areas include business, accountancy, economics and social sciences; as well as information systems, in which the university has a partnership with Carnegie Mellon University. Newer subjects include leadership and community service.

SMU sets out to differentiate itself from the two older universities—NATIONAL UNIVERSITY OF SINGAPORE and NANYANG TECHNOLOGICAL UNIVERSITY—by engaging the business community to a greater extent, and so adding a practical aspect to the curriculum.

SMU occupied temporary premises at Bukit Timah (formerly the campus of the NATIONAL INSTITUTE OF EDUCATION) before moving in July 2005 to its permanent campus in the city centre. The location was controversial initially, as it involved, among other things, demolishing the original NATIONAL LIBRARY BUILDING. The move was aimed at injecting vibrancy into the civic district, and facilitating even closer engagement with working professionals.

Singapore Medical Association Formed in 1959, the Singapore Medical Association (SMA) is a national organization representing the majority of medical practitioners in Singapore. All doctors have a duty to maintain good medical practice, while patients must be protected from poor practice. The SMA thus embraces a strategy of strengthening the culture of medical professionalism while promoting continuing medical education and personal professional development throughout a doctor's career.

Members are expected to develop and promote medical ethics and medical practice, and their application for the betterment of patient care and public health. To this end, the SMA publishes papers, journals and other materials; it voices its opinion so as to acquaint the government and other relevant bodies with the policies and attitudes of the profession.

In 1963, the SMA made a grant to the Faculty of Medicine at the NATIONAL UNIVERSITY OF SINGAPORE, to establish an annual lecture on medical ethics and related topics. SMA Lecturers are appointed at the invitation of the SMA Council.

Singapore Mint Established in 1968 as a department of the Chartered Industries of Singapore, the mint has evolved from a basic minting facility into an integrated business operation, and is now a business unit of SEMBCORP INDUSTRIES. It provides customized minting services, producing circulation coins for the Monetary Authority of Singapore and numismatic gifts and collectibles for overseas customers. The mint also houses a Coin Gallery with displays on the history and evolution of coinage. *See also* CURRENCY.

Singapore Monitor, The English-language afternoon tabloid launched by Singapore News and Publications Ltd (SNPL) to compete with THE STRAITS TIMES. SNPL was the holding company of the Chinese newspapers SIN CHEW JIT POH and NANYANG SIANG PAU. The government gave its blessing to *The Singapore Monitor* as a means for the publisher to support the Chinese newspapers.

The paper was first published on 1 May 1982, initially under the NEW NATION title, before being renamed *The Singapore Monitor* on 16 November 1982. Unable to maintain circulation, having depleted its $20 million capital and owing another $6 million to SNPL, the last issue of the paper went out on Sunday, 15 July 1985.

Singapore National Employers' Federation Starting in 1948 as the Federation of Industrialists and Traders in Singapore, this organization began as a 'trade union' of 23 employers. They named it the Singapore Employers' Federation in August 1953. Through amalgamation with the National Employers' Council—another group founded in 1965—the Singapore National Employers Federation was established on 1 July 1980. With a membership of 1,800 employers in 2005, its mission is to preserve industrial harmony (*see* LABOUR RELATIONS).

Singapore North Indian Hindu Association Popularly known as Bharty Bhavan, the Singapore North Indian Hindu Association is one of the oldest associations in Singapore to still be in existence. In 1921, prominent members of the Hindi-speaking Indian community met at a shophouse on Dunlop Street, to form an organization to help Hindu destitutes. As a result, the North Indian Funeral Association was established in 1921 and housed at 47 Cuff Road. At the time, many Hindus were single, with few friends and relatives. When death occurred, many of them could not be accorded the final Hindu rites.

Singapore Mint

The association's name was eventually changed to the Singapore North Indian Hindu Association. Besides helping the Hindu community, it also provides an avenue for cultural activities among Hindi-speaking Indians. In fact, it was this association which mooted the idea of a Hindu temple for North Indians, and purchased the land on Chander Road where the SHREE LAKSHMINARAYAN TEMPLE now stands.

The association, together with the temple, formed a Hindi Protem Committee to ask the government to offer Hindi as a second language. Together with Shree Lakshminarayan Temple, the association donated $5,000 to start Hindi classes at Beng Wan Primary School.

Singapore People's Anti-British League Front organization and recruiting apparatus for the MALAYAN COMMUNIST PARTY (MCP). Formed in September 1948, in the wake of the Communist-inspired insurgency in June, and directed by the underground Singapore Town Committee of the MCP, the Singapore People's Anti-British League (SPABL) aimed to provide a nationalist front that would draw within its fold anti-colonial elements committed to the revolutionary task of ending British rule—from people unwilling to join the MCP to those who could be groomed as recruits to the party. Mirroring the MCP's cellular organization and clandestine activities, it was made up of Chinese-speaking and English-speaking cells.

The latter succeeded in attracting a group of English-educated intellectuals and activists, many of them leaders from the defunct MALAYAN DEMOCRATIC UNION, who were involved in the UNIVERSITY OF MALAYA, the Singapore Co-operative Society, and the SINGAPORE TEACHERS' UNION. One such activist was JOHN EBER, who edited the SPABL's English-language organ, *Freedom News*. Through reliance on propaganda, publishing literature focusing on specific issues, and portraying the insur-

gency as a national liberation movement, they hoped to stir up anti-British sentiments and induce people to support the communist cause. Their sharp analysis and well-written leaflets led SPECIAL BRANCH to surmise that a group of English-educated intellectuals, probably university graduates, was behind the MCP propaganda machine.

In January 1951, Special Branch broke up the English-educated section of the SPABL by arresting 34 of its leaders, including Eber, P.V. SHARMA, SAMAD ISMAIL, JAMES PUTHUCHEARY and C.V. DEVAN NAIR. But others such as FANG CHUANG PI, EU CHOOI YIP and LIM KEAN CHYE managed a narrow escape.

After their release from detention in 1952, Samad, Puthucheary and Devan Nair helped found a new left-wing political party, the PEOPLE'S ACTION PARTY. The SPABL's Chinese-speaking wing, however, established close links with labour unions, the Kuomintang (Chinese Nationalists) and SECRET SOCIETIES. In 1949, a third wing of the SPABL was formed—the Singapore Students' Anti British League (SSABL). It targeted students and teachers in Chinese schools, where there was a strong upsurge of pride in communist China's rise as a world power. The SSABL recruited many bright Chinese students to work towards forming a pro-communist student-labour movement. Those with potential were absorbed into the MCP.

Singapore People's Party Political party founded in 1994 by Sin Kek Tong, who led the pro-CHIAM SEE TONG faction when it split from the SINGAPORE DEMOCRATIC PARTY. From 1994 to 1996, Sin was temporarily secretary-general of the Singapore People's Party (SPP). Chiam became secretary-general of the party in 1996 and retained his Potong Pasir seat under the SPP banner in the 1997 general election, as well as in 2001. In 2001, the SPP became a member of the SINGAPORE DEMOCRATIC ALLIANCE; the SPP later absorbed the Singapore Justice Party.

Singapore Petroleum Company Established in 1969, the Singapore Petroleum Company (SPC) started refining oil in the 1970s. It built its first refinery on PULAU MERLIMAU in 1973. SPC continued to expand its refin-

The Singapore Monitor

Singapore People's Party: button with logo (top); founder Sin Kek Tong at election rally, 2006.

Singapore Petroleum Company: petrol station.

Singapore Philatelic Museum

million on a turnover of $7.5 billion. Its largest shareholder is KEPPEL CORPORATION.

Singapore Philatelic Museum Located at the foot of Fort Canning Rise, the Singapore Philatelic Museum is housed in a colonial-era building formerly part of the ANGLO-CHINESE SCHOOL. The museum was set up in 1995 by the Telecommunication Authority of Singapore. Comprising seven galleries, the museum exhibits postage STAMPS from the Straits Settlements period to those of more recent eras, and some rare specimens from private collectors.

Singapore Police Force Colloquially referred to by Singaporeans as 'mata mata' (Malay for 'eyes'), the police started in 1819 as a force of 11 men—one sergeant, eight constables, one jailer and a Malay writer (it is said that there was also a tailor among their ranks). Since then it has grown into a law enforcement team of 13,300.

In the early years of the force and even as recently as the 1960s, the main source of lawlessness and violence was organised gangs. These had roots in the SECRET SOCIETIES, which ran brothels, gambling dens and smuggling rings and engaged in all manner of criminal activity. They were at first tolerated by the colonial-run police force, which saw them as a controlling force over the Chinese masses. But when these gangs fought each other in bloody turf wars, some involving thousands of gang members, the police force had to be expanded to deal with them.

The foundation for a professional outfit was laid when Thomas Dunman became the first commissioner of police in 1857. He set up police posts and initiated mobile patrols. By 1861, the force had swelled to 410. A milestone was reached in the professional upgrading of the police force in 1903, when the Detective Branch was formed. This was the forerunner of the CRIMINAL INVESTIGATION DEPARTMENT. In the same year, in a move that revolutionised crime control, the fingerprinting system was implemented.

The lawlessness in early Singapore was tamed when a series of legislative measures equipped the police to act against the secret societies. The Societies Ordinance of 1890 helped the authorities to suppress the secret societies. The triads were driven underground and fragmented into smaller, more controllable gangs, and eventually became a spent force.

From the 1920s to the post-World War II period, the development and agenda of the police force was shaped by communalism and Communism. The political foment in China spilled over into Singapore, and the Criminal Intelligence Branch was set up in 1916 to deal with political subversion. It later evolved into the INTERNAL SECURITY DEPARTMENT. The brief interregnum in the post-war period following the defeat and

withdrawal of Japanese forces saw the start of a destabilizing campaign by the Communists to wrest power. Tough security laws were enacted to deal with the EMERGENCY. These included the Emergency Regulations, which allowed for detention without trial and the deportation of aliens. In February 1963, the Singapore and Malaysian police forces launched OPERATION COLD STORE to crack down on the communists.

The MARIA HERTOGH RIOTS of 1950 broke out when attacks on Eurasians, Europeans and other Christians by Malay-Muslims outside the Supreme Court were not sufficiently prevented by the Malay policemen standing guard at the scene. This incident had a profound impact on the police force and led to its radical and far-ranging reorganisation. The force comprised 90 per cent Malay during the riots which claimed 18 lives. Later, large numbers of Europeans, Chinese and Indians were recruited to redress this disproportionate racial mix.

Another change was the establishment of a riot-control team called the Riot Squad and the modernization of police command and communications channels. A new radio patrol system with a 24-hour Central Command Room and 40 patrol cars with police lieutenants as car crew commanders was introduced. A police secretary was appointed to liaise closely with the public and media. The reforms strengthened the capabilities of the police in dealing with violent demonstrations.

In 1963, Singapore appointed its first Asian commissioner of police, JOHN LE CAIN. Since then, the force has continued to evolve to meet the challenges of modern-day policing. In 1991, the police force introduced a national criminal identification system, the Automated Fingerprint Identification System, which matches not only fingerprints but palm prints as well. The Criminal Investigations Department has also begun building a DNA database to enhance the force's investigative capabilities. In 2000, the Singapore Police Force set up two dedicated groups to address crimes arising from a knowledge-based economy: the Computer Forensics Branch counters high-tech crimes, and the Intellectual Property Rights Branch tackles violations of intellectual property rights.

ing capabilities and capacity in the 1980s. Through partnerships with international oil firms such as BP and Caltex, the Singapore Refining Company was formed in 1979. Over the course of the 1980s and 1990s, it became a supplier of liquefied petroleum gas (LPG), chemical naphtha, motor gasoline, aviation fuel, diesel, fuel oil, asphalt and sulphur, as well as a storage and terminal operator. It has operations on Pulau Sebarok in Singapore and at various sites in southern China.

As well as establishing a reputation as a supplier of refined petroleum products, SPC ventured into oil and gas exploration and production in Indonesia, Vietnam and Cambodia in the 2000s.

In 1990, SPC was listed on the SINGAPORE EXCHANGE. In 2004, it purchased half of BP's refining capacity in the Singapore Refining Company, as well as BP's 28 stations and retail marketing business in Singapore, for US$140 million. This move gave SPC control over the third-largest retail fuel network in the country and doubled its share of the local LPG market.

In 2005, SPC recorded a 50.3 per cent rise in group revenues, with profits of $404

Singapore Police Force: John Le Cain, centre, at his farewell parade, 1967 (left).

Singapore Police Force: officers with patrol car.

Singapore Pools: betting outlet.

Singapore Polytechnic First polytechnic in Singapore. Singapore Polytechnic was established in 1954 to train manpower for the industrial sector. The polytechnic's first building was opened at Prince Edward Road in February 1959 by Prince Philip, Duke of Edinburgh. By the mid-1970s, the polytechnic grew to occupy an annex across the road, at Shenton Way, as well as two feeder campuses at Ayer Rajah and Dover Road. It finally settled into a permanent campus at Dover Road in 1978. In 2005, Singapore Polytechnic had 16,500 full-time and part-time students pursuing 53 diploma and post-diploma courses in 12 different fields of study.

Singapore Pools Lottery operator. Singapore Pools (Private) Limited was incorporated by the government on 23 May 1968 to provide a legal avenue for betting in Singapore, and help reduce illegal gambling. Besides acting as the official channel for betting, surplus earnings of Singapore Pools are donated to community causes. Singapore Pools is wholly owned by the SINGAPORE TOTALISATOR BOARD.

Neighbourhood Police Posts In

1983, the Singapore Police Force (SPF) introduced the Neighbourhood Police Post (NPP) System. Under this system, police functions were decentralized into local police posts. This was an attempt to replicate a successful Japanese model of community policing known as Koban. The main objective was to improve police-community relations, and prevent and suppress crimes by means of public cooperation.

Changes in population distribution—especially the establishment of HOUSING & DEVELOPMENT BOARD (HDB) housing—facilitated the adoption of the NPP system. New living arrangements, in high-rise HDB flats forced the police to adopt a method known as 'vertical policing', which involved the movement of patrol officers from floor to floor.

Accompanying this shift was what the government saw as a need to rejuvenate neighbourhood cohesion and informal social control mechanisms that had once been associated with the traditional KAMPONG way of life.

The first public lottery offered was a simple, manual version of Toto (*see* TOTO AND 4-D), launched on 9 June 1968. This was followed by the Singapore Sweep on 28 February 1969, with tickets sold from small stand-alone booths all over the island. Punters had a chance to win up to $400,000 (first prize) for the price of a $1 ticket. The top prize has increased progressively over the years, passing the $1 million mark in 1983, and the $2 million mark in February 2004. On 26 May 1986, 4-Digit numbers betting, or 4-D, was introduced alongside the company's move from a manual to a computerized gaming system. On 30 March 1999, Singapore Pools launched the first legal football betting game, Score, to heighten interest in local soccer.

There are over 300 Singapore Pools betting outlets located on the island. In December 2000, Singapore Pools and the Singapore Turf Club decided to combine and streamline their operations. Singapore Pools' lottery and sports betting games are now sold by both organizations.

Singapore Power Incorporated in October 1995 to take over the electricity and gas businesses from the Public Utilities Board (*see* PUB), Singapore Power transferred the ownership of the generation companies Senoko Power and PowerSeraya to TEMASEK HOLDINGS, and the energy management unit of PowerGrid to the Energy Market Authority (EMA) on 1 April 2001. The EMA also took over as the regulator of the electricity and gas industry.

Since then, Singapore Power has grown into one of the leading energy utility companies in the Asia-Pacific region. It was rated AA by Standard & Poor's and Aa1 by Moody's Investor Service.

Singapore Power owns four utility business units, including a utility market support services unit in the domestic market. They are: SP PowerAssets, SP PowerGrid, PowerGas and SP Services. SP PowerAssets owns the electricity transmission and distribution assets, which are in turn managed and operated by SP PowerGrid. PowerGas owns, manages and operates gas transmission and distribution assets. SP Services provides market support services, which include meter reading, integrated billing and data management, to electricity, gas and water customers.

In Asia, Singapore Power owns and operates an industrial co-generation and water treatment plant in South Korea, and has an investment in an electricity generation business in Taiwan. In Australia, a wholly owned subsidiary of Singapore Power, Singapore Power International Pte Ltd owns a 51 per cent interest in SP AusNet. On 14 December 2005, SP AusNet was publicly listed on the Australian Stock Exchange and the Singapore Exchange. Along with the gas distribution assets, SP AusNet's electricity transmission

Singapore Polytechnic

and distribution networks will enable it to deliver a full range of energy-related products and services to industrial and domestic customers.

For the financial year 2005, Singapore Power and its subsidiaries reported total revenues of $5.5 billion, a net profit of $861 million and total assets worth $20.1 billion. Currently, the group employs more than 3,400 people in the Asia-Pacific region.

Singapore Press Holdings Singapore Press Holdings (SPH) Limited was incorporated on 4 August 1984 as a new holding company to effect the merger of Times Publishing Berhad, Straits Times Press (1975) Limited and Singapore News and Publications Limited, all of which became wholly owned subsidiaries of the newly formed SPH. In 1988, Times Publishing Limited became a separate company, and was acquired by the FRASER & NEAVE group.

SPH has over 1,000 journalists and correspondents in Singapore and 16 overseas bureaux. It publishes 14 newspapers—including major dailies THE STRAITS TIMES and LIANHE ZAOBAO—in English, Chinese and Tamil, giving it a virtual monopoly over newspaper publishing in Singapore.

In addition to its stable of newspapers, the company has a portfolio of some 80 periodicals, including magazines HER WORLD, *Citta Bella*, *Men's Health*, *Maxim* and *Seventeen*. In addition, the company also holds a 40 per cent stake in MediaCorp Press Pte Ltd, which publishes the freesheet TODAY. SPH also owns a 20 per cent share

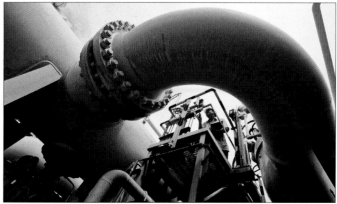

Singapore Power: natural gas plant.

Singapore Sling

in MediaCorp TV Holdings Pte Ltd, which operates Channels 5, 8, U and TV Mobile. Through a joint venture with NTUC Media, the group operates two radio stations—Chinese station Radio 100.3 FM and English station Radio 91.3 FM (*see* RADIO BROADCASTING). Aside from the media industry, SPH's interests include stakes in the listed telecommunications companies MOBILEONE and STARHUB, and ownership of the Paragon shopping mall on Orchard Road.

SPH's Print Centre, on an 11-ha lot in Jurong, delivers more than 1 million copies of SPH newspapers each day, and is also responsible for the regional editions of international newspapers such as *Asahi Shimbun*, *Nihon Keizai Shimbun*, *The Asian Wall Street Journal*, the *Financial Times* and the *International Herald Tribune*.

SPH reported net earnings of $495 million on a turnover of $1 billion for the financial year 2005.

Singapore Prison Service *See* PRISONS.

Singapore Progressive Party Formed on 25 August 1947 by English-educated lawyers C.C. TAN, JOHN LAYCOCK and N.A. MALLAL, the Singapore Progressive Party (SPP) participated in the LEGISLATIVE COUNCIL ELECTION (1948), winning three of six seats. The party also performed well in the LEGISLATIVE COUNCIL ELECTION (1951), winning six of nine seats contested.

The party's willingness to accept gradual independence for Singapore meant that it was favoured by the British, who groomed it for office. The SPP introduced reforms, including the establishment of the PUBLIC SERVICE COMMISSION in 1951, the recruitment of locals to the civil service and the initiation of the CENTRAL PROVIDENT FUND.

However, from 1954, the fortunes of the party began to decline. The SPP won only four of the 22 seats it contested during the LEGISLATIVE ASSEMBLY ELECTION (1955). Its decline has been attributed to the automatic registration of voters—this removal of the requirement to register before voting enlarged the electorate by including non-English-speaking Chinese voters. As a party of the English-educated professional elite, the SPP was unable to gain support from the Chinese voters or the working class.

Singapore Recreation Club

Singapore Sevens

The party never recovered from its 1955 defeat. In February 1956, it merged with the DEMOCRATIC PARTY to form the LIBERAL SOCIALIST PARTY.

Singapore Recreation Club In 1883, the Singapore Recreation Club (SRC) was founded by some 30 members of the EURASIAN community. The SRC then had a clubhouse on Waterloo Street, and used a pavilion on the PADANG. In 1904, a new clubhouse was built at the Padang site.

Membership of the SRC was limited to men. However, in contrast to the 'all-white' Singapore Cricket Club at the other end of the Padang, the SRC was a 'non-white' (i.e. Eurasian) club. It became a focal point for Eurasian men, who met for sporting and social events. Over the decades, the SRC nurtured many of Singapore's better known sportsmen, including Lloyd Valberg (in athletics), Douglas Nonis (in hockey) and Natahar Bava (in athletics and rugby).

In 1948, Sir GEORGE OEHLERS proposed that membership of the SRC be open to non-Eurasians. Although not immediately accepted, this proposal eventually gained support, and in 1955, a category of 'subscribing membership'—open to persons of all communities—was introduced. A year later, membership was opened to women for the first time.

In 1994, transferable memberships were introduced, and the additional revenue generated from these has enabled the SRC to redevelop its clubhouse.

Singapore Repertory Theatre A professional theatre company, Singapore Repertory Theatre (SRT) was established in 1993 by artistic director Tony Petito. It had its roots in an amateur theatre company called STARS which drew from the American community in Singapore.

In 2001, SRT opened its own 400-seat theatre in Merbau Road. It now also has a children's theatre arm called The Little Company. SRT employs more than 15 full-time staff for its five divisions.

SRT has brought a number of well-known actors to the Singapore stage. They include Lea Salonga, Shabana Azmi, Ming-Na Wen, Nancy Kwan and Pat Morita.

Its previous productions include *Rent* (2001), Harold Pinter's *Betrayal* (2005),

Neil Simon's *The Odd Couple* (2004), David Mamet's *Oleanna* (2000) and Manuel Puig's *Kiss of the Spiderwoman* (1998). In 1998, SRT was a co-producer of a Broadway production, David Henry Hwang's *Golden Child*.

Singapore River A statue of Sir STAMFORD RAFFLES marks the spot on the north bank of the Singapore River where Raffles first landed in 1819. The settlement that subsequently developed there continued to expand around the river, and the river's marshy banks were transformed.

The north bank, known as North Boat Quay, was set aside for government use, while the south bank, or South Boat Quay, was designated a commercial area. Merchants built their godowns here, and goods were ferried by lighters (flat-bottomed boats) from ships to stores. Further upriver, godowns and small businesses were established in the areas known as CLARKE QUAY and Robertson Quay.

For more than 150 years, the river was a busy waterway and the centre of commercial activity on the island. When large shipping gradually moved to new port facilities away from the river, the Singapore River became a base for regional trade. Such heavy use brought with it the problem of pollution, as garbage and sewage were dumped, together with industrial by-products, directly into the river.

In 1977, Prime Minister LEE KUAN YEW, at the opening of Upper Peirce Reservoir, emphasized the need to keep Singapore's waters clean. He set a target of ten years for the Ministry of the Environment to clean up the Singapore River and Kallang Basin. What followed was a large-scale, concerted effort by various government agencies, which included resettling squatters and moving pollutive uses away from the river; introducing modern sanitation to all households; improving the riverbanks and dredging the river. The last lighter departed in August 1983. Since

Singapore River

Singapore Sports School

then, many of the shophouses and godowns along the river bank have been granted conservation status (*see* CONSERVATION AREAS) and have been converted into cafés, restaurants and arts venues.

Singapore Sevens This is the Singapore leg of the IRB Sevens World Series, a rugby competition organised by the International Rugby Board (IRB). As the name implies, this is rugby played with seven rather than 15 players on each side. The IRB Sevens World Series is an annual series consisting of eight tournaments, each played in a different city. For the 2005/2006 season, tournaments were played in Dubai, South Africa, Wellington, Los Angeles, Hong Kong, Singapore, Paris and London.

Singapore has played host to the series since 2002, with a break in 2003 because of the outbreak of Severe Acute Respiratory Syndrome. New Zealand won the inaugural Singapore Sevens, beating Argentina 21–17 in the final. Since 2004, the tournament here has been called the Standard Chartered Sevens Singapore. In 2006, the two-day tournament at the NATIONAL STADIUM drew 16 teams and a crowd of 16,000 spectators.

In July 2006, however, the IRB announced that Singapore had failed in its bid to continue hosting the tournament; the 2006/2007 season would see Adelaide taking the place of Singapore to host a leg of the IRB Sevens World Series.

Singapore Sling In the early 1900s, Ngiam Tong Boon, a Hainanese bartender at the RAFFLES HOTEL, concocted this pink cocktail. The Singapore Sling quickly achieved widespread popularity. The recipe is as follows:

30 ml gin
15 ml cherry brandy
120 ml pineapple juice
15 ml lime juice
7.5 ml Cointreau

SINGAPORE SEVENS WINNERS		
2002	New Zealand v Argentina	21–17
2003	cancelled	
2004	South Africa v Argentina	24–19
2005	New Zealand v England	26–5
2006	Fiji v England	40–19

7.5 ml Dom Benedictine
10 ml grenadine
A dash of Angostura bitters
Garnish with a slice of pineapple and cherry.

The cocktail is still served at the Raffles Hotel's Long Bar, and the hotel's museum claims to house the safe in which the recipe was stored by its inventor.

Singapore Soka Association Buddhist organization. The association, which promotes a general understanding of BUDDHISM, is based on the practice of Nichiren Buddhism—a school of Buddhism founded in 13th-century Japan. The term *soka* means 'value creation' in Japanese. The association began as a small community of believers at a time when Nichiren Buddhism was largely unheard of in Singapore. The growth of the Nichiren community was mainly due to Koh Kian Boon, who assumed spiritual leadership as the group's first general director. Koh and other pioneer leaders facilitated the organization's legal registration under the name of the Singapore Nichiren Shoshu Buddhist Association in 1972.

In 1991, the Nichiren clergy became mired in controversy after declaring that lay believers who did not subordinate themselves to the authority of the priesthood would be excommunicated. The organization changed its name to Singapore Soka Association (SSA) in 1992, in part to dissociate itself from the controversy.

In 1992, Ong Bon Chai became the second general director. Under Ong's leadership, the SSA expanded its membership to about 28,000 people; established eight Soka activity centres islandwide; and established itself as a civic organization engaged in community services, cultural activities and educational work. Events in which the SSA has been involved include NATIONAL DAY parades and CHINGAY performances. It has also established the Soka Wind Ensemble, the Soka Chorus and Junior Choir, the Sunflower Dance Troupe and the Soka Kindergarten.

Singapore Sports Council Hall of Fame This gallery in the SPORTS MUSEUM was inaugurated in 1985 by the Singapore Sports Council. Among the first to be inducted were badminton player WONG PENG SOON, swimmer NEO CHWEE KOK and weightlifter TAN HOWE LIANG. Since then, more than 30 individuals and groups have been honoured. Inductees are presented with a medal in the shape of a laurel wreath as a mark of their achievements in a given sport or their contribution to sport more generally.

Both individuals and teams can be inducted into the Hall of Fame. To qualify, they must be Olympic medallists; or be Asian Games or Commonwealth Games gold medallists; or have won a gold medal

Singapore Repertory Theatre

or championship in certain international competitions; or have made an outstanding contribution to sport in general.

Singapore Sports School Opened in April 2004, the Singapore Sports School (SSS) develops talented young sportsmen and sportswomen in Singapore at its $75 million campus in Woodlands. SSS offers four- or five-year academic courses to prepare students for the Singapore-Cambridge General Certificate of Education Ordinary Level Examination. Enrolment is competitive, requiring applicants to take part in selection trials and interviews. The school specializes in nine sports: BADMINTON, ten-pin bowling, SOCCER, netball, sailing, swimming, table tennis, GOLF, and track and field.

SINGAPORE SPORTS COUNCIL HALL OF FAME	
Individuals and duos	**Sport**
Abdul Halim Haron	Bodybuilding
Ang Peng Siong	Swimming
Azman Abdullah	Bodybuilding
Patricia Chan	Swimming
Chee Swee Lee	Athletics
Chua Phung Kim	Weightlifting
Fred B. de Souza	Shooting
Fandi Ahmad	Soccer
Sam Goh and Patrick Wee	Bowling
Jesmine Ho	Bowling
Joan Huang and Naomi Tan	Sailing
Canagasabai Kunalan	Athletics
Li Jiawei and Duan Yong Jun	Table Tennis
Li Li	Badminton
Neo Chwee Kok	Swimming
Ng Liang Chiang	Athletics
Ong Poh Lim and Ismail Marjan	Badminton
Remy Ong	Bowling
Sheik Alauddin	Silat
Siew Shaw Her and Colin Ng	Sailing
Simon Chua	Bodybuilding
Junie Sng	Swimming
Tan Howe Liang	Weightlifting
Tan Ser Cher	Weightlifting
Henry Tan	Bowling
Benedict Tan	Sailing
Jennifer Tan	Bowling
Adelene Wee	Bowling
Wong Peng Soon	Badminton
Source: Singapore Sports Council	

Singapore River bridges

Alkaff Bridge
Built in 1997, the design of this bridge resembles a tongkang (large flat-bottom barge). It was named after the ALKAFF FAMILY. In 2004, the Filipina artist Pacita Abad covered this pedestrian bridge in 900 litres of paint in 52 different colours.

Ord Bridge
Built in 1886, the bridge was named after Colonel Sir HARRY ORD, the first governor of Singapore. It was also known as 'Toddy Bridge', due to its proximity to toddy shops then. It also marked the landing point for weapons and ammunition which were stored at Magazine Road.

Coleman Bridge
Built in 1840, the original bridge was designed by GEORGE D. COLEMAN. It was replaced in 1865 and 1886. The 1886 cast-iron bridge was once considered the most elegant bridge in Singapore. Due to roadworks, the bridge was rebuilt in 1989.

Cavenagh Bridge
Built in 1869, this is the oldest existing bridge. The cast iron used in this bridge was imported from Glasgow. The bridge was named after ORFEUR CAVENAGH, governor of the Straits Settlements (1859–67). It was later reserved for pedestrian only.

Pulau Saigon Bridge
The original bridge, built in 1890, was demolished in 1986 during the construction of the Central Expressway. It was named after a small island in the river that no longer exists. The bridge was rebuilt in 1997.

Clemenceau Bridge
Named after visiting French statesman George Clemenceau, this large concrete bridge was built in 1920.

Kim Seng Bridge
Named after the philanthropist Tan Kim Seng, it was built in 1862, and rebuilt in 1951.

Read Bridge
This bridge was built in 1889 to replace Merchant Bridge, which was too low for boats to pass under. It was named after Willam Henry McLeod Read, a merchant who successfully petitioned for the Straits Settlements to be ruled directly from London as a Crown Colony. It became known as 'Storytellers' Bridge' as Teochew storytellers used to entertain labourers here.

Elgin Bridge
In the 1819 agreement between Sir STAMFORD RAFFLES and Sultan HUSAIN SHAH, a wooden bridge was mentioned as a landmark. This bridge was rebuilt by Lieutenant Phillip Jackson in 1822 and was known as Presentment Bridge. In 1845, it was replaced by Thomson's Bridge, built by John Turnbull Thomson. In 1862, the iron Elgin Bridge was built, named after Lord Elgin, governor-general of India (1862–63). In 1929, a concrete bridge replaced it. RODOLPHO NOLLI made the cast iron lamps on the bridge as well as the plaques depicting a lion and a tree.

Anderson Bridge
Located at the mouth of the river, this bridge was built in 1910 and named after JOHN ANDERSON, governor of the Straits Settlements (1904–11). During the Japanese Occupation, the severed heads of criminals were hung on this bridge as a warning to would-be criminals.

Singapore stone

It is the only school in the country to have a sports science academy with its own team of sports scientists.

Singapore stone A sandstone boulder bearing inscriptions was discovered at the mouth of the SINGAPORE RIVER in June 1819. The stone's inscription has never been deciphered. The SEJARAH MELAYU contains a possible reference to the stone in the story of Badang, who is said to have thrown a large stone from Fort Canning to the mouth of the river.

According to JOHN CRAWFURD, second Resident of Singapore, the inscription had been carved on one face of a boulder which had been split in two. He claimed that the rock was originally 3 m high and 3 m wide, with 50 or 52 lines of script on an area 2.1 m in width and 1.5 m in height. J. Prinsep, a scholar based in Calcutta, noted that 40 lines of script were discernible, but about 12 lines at the beginning of the inscription were not distinct.

Before it could be studied further, the stone was blown up in 1843 to clear the Singapore River for ships to pass. Three fragments were salvaged and sent to Calcutta; one of these pieces was returned to Singapore in 1918. Dutch scholar Hendrik Kern deciphered a few words, including *safiga/a/asayanara*, *yaamanavana*, *kesarabhara/a*, and *yoda/ama* (meaning unknown) and argued that the inscription dated from the early 13th century, even though he was unable to identify the language used. Another scholar, J.G. de Casparis, believed that the script dated from the 10th or 11th century, and that the language was Old Javanese. Other scholars speculated that the script was closer to Sumatran than Javanese, and that the language was Sanskrit—in which case the inscription could have been carved as recently as the 14th century.

Singapore Swimming Club Located on Singapore's east coast, the Singapore Swimming Club (SSC) opened in February 1894. Its original members—all Europeans—rented an *attap* (thatched roof) hut to encourage swimming in the sea. A new clubhouse which opened in 1904 included dressing rooms. A bathing enclosure and a diving platform were later added, and the club's first swimming pool was installed in 1931.

Despite the opposition of some members, the club began admitting women as 'honorary members' in 1923. But it was only from 1937 that women were allowed to use the club's facilities without restriction. Club membership was opened to all races only in 1963, when a government decree ordered that private clubs end racially discriminatory membership policies.

Singapore Symphony Orchestra The idea of establishing a professional symphony orchestra in Singapore was envisaged by Dr GOH KENG SWEE during his term as deputy prime minister. Under his patronage, the Singapore Symphony Orchestra (SSO) was inaugurated in 1979 with 41 musicians, performing its first concerts at the SINGAPORE CONFERENCE HALL.

Under the leadership of conductor CHOO HOEY, the SSO built up a large performing repertoire, with a strong emphasis on 20th-century music. In 1980, the Singapore Symphony Chorus was established to perform symphonic choral music with the orchestra. From 1980 to 2002, the SSO made its home at Victoria Concert Hall.

The orchestra toured regularly and established itself as one of Asia's leading orchestras. In 1994, the SSO performed at the Salle Pleyel in Paris and was hailed as one of the 'top twenty orchestras in the world'. In 1995, renowned Finnish conductor Okko Kamu was appointed principal guest conductor of the SSO.

China-born conductor LAN SHUI was appointed the SSO's second music director in 1997. The orchestra continued to tour extensively in Asia, Europe and North America, and signed a recording contract with Scandinavian label BIS. Its performances and recordings of music by contemporary Asian composers have garnered the orchestra a worldwide reputation for music linking the musical cultures of the East and the West.

The SSO has a comprehensive outreach programme, regularly performing its very popular Familiar Favourites and Open Air Concerts under the direction of resident conductor LIM YAU. In 2002, the SSO performed at the inaugural concert of the Concert Hall at the ESPLANADE—THEATRES ON THE BAY, which has become the orchestra's new performing home.

Singapore Teachers' Union The largest teachers' organization in Singapore, the Singapore Teachers' Union (STU) was founded in 1947 principally to protect the interests of teachers in English-medium schools. From the 1970s, the STU has implemented the concept of the 'school community', and most of its activities have been aimed at bringing together teachers, principals and educational administrators.

One of the STU's main achievements was the successful completion, in 1971, of salary negotiations which brought greater monetary benefits and promotional opportunities to teachers. In the same year, the STU set up a Professional Wing through which it emphasized the importance of professional competence as the basis for recognition and rewards.

The STU's Teachers' Centre was officially opened in July 1976 by Deputy Prime Minister GOH KENG SWEE. In 1981, the union set up a Special Tutorial and Enrichment Programme for members' children, this later being extended to members of the general public.

Singapore Tiger Standard, The Newspaper. Established in 1950 by AW BOON HAW— proprietor of the SIN CHEW JIT POH—*The Singapore Tiger Standard* competed directly with THE STRAITS TIMES for the English-reading market. It built up a circulation of 46,000. S. RAJARATNAM was one of its most prominent writers. Poor management led to the paper's demise in 1959.

Singapore Totalisator Board Statutory board. The Singapore Totalisator Board (also known as the Tote Board) was established on 1 January 1988. It has the exclusive right to operate horse-racing and totalizator operations through its proprietary club, the SINGAPORE TURF CLUB; and Singapore Sweep, football betting, TOTO AND 4-D through its wholly owned subsidiary, SINGAPORE POOLS. The Singapore Totalisator Board also manages all surplus funds generated from the operations of the Singapore Turf Club and Singapore Pools. Its stated mission is to 'ensure that horse racing and all forms of betting and gaming operated by the two entities are conducted with honesty and integrity; and to donate funds for activities that will make for a stronger nation and a better people'. *See also* GAMBLING and INTEGRATED RESORTS.

Singapore Tourism Board Statutory board. The Singapore Tourist Promotion Board (STPB) was established in 1964 with a staff of 25. Throughout the 1960s and 1970s, the board encouraged investment in the development of infrastructure (such as hotels, shopping centres and tourist attractions), and marketed Singapore as a convention and events venue.

In the 1980s, as a result of the introduction of the $1 billion Tourist Product Development Plan, the STPB focused on conserving historic districts (*see* CONSERVATION AREAS), such as KAMPONG GLAM, LITTLE INDIA and CHINATOWN, under threat of redevelopment and destruction.

On 19 November 1997, the STPB was renamed the Singapore Tourism Board (STB) with the opening of its new headquarters on Cuscaden Road. On 11 January 2005, minister for trade and industry Lim Hng Kiang announced the creation of a $2 billion Tourism Development

Singapore Symphony Orchestra

Fund to help the board achieve its target of tripling tourism revenue to $30 billion, doubling visitor arrivals to 17 million, and creating 100,000 more jobs in the services sector by 2015.

The STB has a network of 20 regional offices and two marketing representatives in eight regions around the world.

Singapore Traction Company Public transport provider. The Singapore Traction Company (STC) was formed in 1925. Its trolley-bus service commenced on 14 August 1926 on a route between Geylang and TANJONG PAGAR. By 1929, the STC had 90 trolley buses serving a total distance of 30.5 km, as well as motor BUSES.

During the JAPANESE OCCUPATION, the facilities of the STC and other bus companies were combined in the establishment of a single, island-wide bus operator. In 1945, after the Japanese surrender, the STC found less than half of its pre-war fleet serviceable. Only 29 of its trolley buses and 22 of its motor buses were put into service, and orders had to be placed for more vehicles. Moreover, while services resumed, operations were affected by employee strikes in the 1945–56 period, and the STC began to face competition from smaller bus companies that mainly served outlying districts. The trolley bus system ceased operations in December 1962. By the 1960s, the STC was running at a loss.

Control of the STC—originally registered in the United Kingdom—was transferred into local hands in 1964. In January of that year, the company's directors resigned and were succeeded by appointees resident in Singapore and Kuala Lumpur. A new company, which went under the same name as the original STC, was incorporated in Singapore in September 1964, and entered into an agreement with the old STC to acquire all of its undertakings, property and assets. The new STC began operations on 1 October 1964, its first obligations being to discharge all of the outstanding obligations of the old STC.

In the 1960s, the new STC unsuccessfully sought to acquire or merge with other bus companies. In April 1971, other bus

The Singapore Tiger Standard

Singapore Tourism Board: promotional brochure.

Singapore Swimming Club, 1950.

Singapore Traction Company: No. 17 bus, 1956 (top); tickets of the same period.

operators in Singapore were amalgamated into three large companies, and the country's bus services were restructured. Each company, including the STC, was given a particular sector of the city in which to operate services. The STC, which had already been incurring debt, found its revenue further reduced by this reorganization, incurring losses of as much as $15,000 a day. In 1971, it closed down.

With the intercession of the government, the other three bus companies agreed to purchase the STC's 407 buses for $2.75 million and take over the STC's 33 routes. The STC's buses were transferred on 4 December 1971.

Singapore Trades Union Congress In the years immediately following the 1948 prohibition of the Singapore Federation of Trade Unions and the Pan-Malayan Federation of Trade Unions, most trade unions operating in Singapore were apolitical and moderate in nature. One of these, the Singapore Trades Union Congress (STUC), founded in May 1951 by V.K. Nair and LIM YEW HOCK, became closely affiliated with the LABOUR FRONT, one of its largest affiliates being the 40,000-strong Federation of Services Unions.

In 1955, the left-wing Singapore General Employees' Union held secret talks with the STUC with hopes of establishing a united trade union front. This led to a further affiliation with 29 radical unions associated with the 'Big Six'—LIM CHIN SIONG, FONG SWEE SUAN, JAMES PUTHUCHEARY, SIDNEY WOODHULL, JAMIT SINGH and S.T. BANI—and the MIDDLE ROAD UNIONS. In merging with these groups, the STUC became the largest conglomerate of unions in Singapore.

In 1961, the STUC was outlawed by the government and deregistered. The congress then splintered into the SINGAPORE ASSOCIATION OF TRADE UNIONS (which supported the BARISAN SOSIALIS) and the NATIONAL TRADES UNION CONGRESS (which supported the People's Action Party).

Singapore Turf Club The Singapore Turf Club has its roots in the Singapore Sporting Club, established in 1842 by a group of racing enthusiasts. The first horse race took place on 23 February 1843 and the prize-money was $150. Races took place on a regular basis at the old racecourse in what is now FARRER PARK. In 1896, official racing rules were introduced with the formation of the Straits Racing Association (now known as the Malayan Racing Association). The Singapore Sporting Club changed its name to Singapore Turf Club in 1924. In 1933, the club moved its premises to a new facility at Bukit Timah.

In 1988, the government established the SINGAPORE TOTALISATOR BOARD, and appointed the Bukit Turf Club—a new entity—the Board's agent to take over racing and 4-D operations (*see* TOTO AND 4-D). The old Singapore Turf Club was subsequently deregistered, and the Bukit Turf Club assumed its name in 1994. This new Singapore Turf Club subsequently moved to Kranji, and the new Singapore Racecourse was declared open on 4 March 2000 by President S.R. Nathan.

Singapore Tyler Print Institute Founded in 2002 with the assistance of New York-based printmaker Ken Tyler, the Singapore Tyler Print Institute maintains a Visiting Artists Programme which brings together local and international artists. Its premises at Robertson Quay house a workshop, gallery and paper-mill equipped with paper pulp beaters, lithography presses and etching presses.

Singapore University *See* UNIVERSITY OF MALAYA.

Singapore Youth Choir Ensemble Singers The Singapore Youth Choir (SYC) was formed in 1964 as a combined schools choir under the Ministry of Education. Its first director was Benjamin Khoo. David Lim Kim San succeeded him in 1967, when the choir became the flagship ensemble of the Young Musician's Society. Under his leadership, the SYC was the first Singapore choir to win first prize in the Youth Choir section at the International Eisteddfod in Llangollen, Wales (1974).

Singapore Turf Club

Lim was succeeded by Young Artist Award recipient Jennifer Tham in 1986. The SYC repeated its Youth Choir win in 1989. It has since received worldwide recognition for performing contemporary a cappella choral music, specializing in the works of Singaporean and other Asian composers.

On its 40th anniversary in 2004, the choir was renamed the Singapore Youth Choir Ensemble Singers.

Singapore Zoo *See* box.

Singh, Choor (1911–) Judge. Choor Singh Sindhu was born in the Punjab region of northwestern India. At the age of six, he left his village to join his father in Malaya under the charge of his mother and uncle. Singh studied at Pearl's Hill School, Outram Road School and Raffles Institution. Singh was an outstanding athlete, playing cricket for his school and the Singapore Indian Association. His father had relocated to Singapore to work as a night watchman at a godown in Havelock Road. After leaving school, Singh could not get a job and resorted to giving private tuition. In 1934, he found a job in the General Clerical Service. He later worked as a solicitor's clerk and saved to go to the United Kingdom to further his education at the University of London. Singh was called to the Bar at Gray's Inn in 1949. He returned to Singapore and was appointed magistrate, the first Indian to hold such a position in Malaya. In 1963, he was appointed PUISNE JUDGE of the Supreme Court and served till his retirement in 1980.

Singh, Harbans (1926–2004) Lawyer and politician. Harbans Singh started life as a schoolteacher but later switched to law. He first stood as a UNITED PEOPLE'S PARTY candidate in Kampong Glam constituency during the GENERAL ELECTION (1963). In 1972, he stood as a BARISAN SOSIALIS candidate. Two years later, he left the Barisan to form the United People's Front. Between 1963 and 1988, Singh stood against PEOPLE'S ACTION PARTY leaders—including LEE KUAN YEW, S. RAJARATNAM, HON SUI SEN, TONY TAN and LIM BOON HENG—losing on every occasion. Singh was best known for his oratorical skills, and for establishing a 'Shadow Cabinet' in 1975 in which he listed himself as 'Shadow Prime Minister', and his legal secretary, Ang Bee Lian, as 'Shadow Defence Minister'.

Singh, Jamit (1929–1994) Trade unionist. The son of a railway station-master in Ipoh, Perak, Jamit Singh moved to Singapore to study at the UNIVERSITY OF MALAYA in the early 1950s. There, he became involved in campus politics and was one of the founding members of the University's Socialist Club, but failed to complete his education.

It was LEE KUAN YEW who, wanting the support of the trade union movement, had

Singapore Zoo The idea to set up a zoo at the Upper Seletar Reservoir Catchment Forest was mooted by Dr ONG SWEE LAW in 1968. In 1970, Lyn de Alwis, Director of the Dehiwala Zoo—an 'open-concept zoo'—in Sri Lanka, was seconded as a consultant to design the Singapore zoo. With an initial development cost of $9 million provided by the government, the zoo was opened on 27 June 1973 by Dr GOH KENG SWEE. The zoo houses over 300 species of animals, 20 per cent of which are endangered. Perhaps the most famous animal in the zoo is Ah Meng, the orang utan.

The zoo is designed as an 'open zoo'. Animals are kept in spacious, landscaped enclosures which resemble their natural habitats, and are separated from other enclosures and from visitors by visually unobtrusive barriers such as moats. Particularly dangerous and agile animals, such as leopards and jaguars, are housed in specially landscaped glass-fronted enclosures.

The zoo has become known for its breeding and conservation programmes, especially of endangered species. In 1998, it became the first zoo in the world to breed proboscis monkeys in captivity. It has also bred the largest number of orang utans in

captivity, the first of which was born in 1975. The zoo is also a 'learning zoo' with educational initiatives such as the *Zoo-Ed Magazine* (started in 1979) for primary school students, and the secondment of teachers from the Ministry of Education to conduct talks and organize activities for children. In August 2000, the zoo, NIGHT SAFARI and JURONG BIRDPARK were organizationally integrated under Wildlife Reserves Singapore, a subsidiary of TEMASEK HOLDINGS.

SINGAPORE ZOO

Exhibits
- Australian Outback
- Cat Country
- Children's World Animal Land
- Children's World Playland
- Elephants of Asia
- Fragile Forest Biodome
- Free-ranging Orang Utans
- Hamadrayas Baboons
- Komodo Dragons
- Polar Bears
- Primate Kingdom
- Reptile Garden
- Treetops Trail

Clockwise from top left: the orang utan, Ah Meng; elephant; douc langurs; cheetah; zebras.

Singh appointed secretary of the Singapore Harbour Board Staff Association (SHBSA). At a time when many were lobbying to have low wage rates reviewed, Singh proved popular with many SHBSA members. When negotiations on these issues collapsed in 1955, the SHBSA voted to go on strike in tandem with May Day rallies that year. Subsequent negotiations undertaken by Singh won the harbour workers significant concessions.

Singh's oratory and leadership helped unite various waterfront trade unions that

Jamit Singh, far right, outside courthouse, 1963.

had previously been divided along ethnic and occupational lines. By 1956, he succeeded in uniting the various unions among the SHBSA's 10,000 workers, making it one of the most powerful unions in Singapore. Singh, LIM CHIN SIONG, FONG SWEE SUAN, JAMES PUTHUCHEARY, SIDNEY WOODHULL and S.T. BANI were known collectively as the 'Big Six' trade union leaders.

Although Singh did not stand as a PEOPLE'S ACTION PARTY (PAP) candidate in the LEGISLATIVE ASSEMBLY ELECTION (1959), he supported the PAP's harbour-district candidates, including Lee Kuan Yew. However, when the PAP split in 1961, Singh joined the BARISAN SOSIALIS.

In 1962, Singh was charged with unauthorized withdrawal of union funds and sentenced to 18 months' imprisonment. The sentence was reduced to a fine upon appeal. The following year, he was arrested under OPERATION COLD STORE. He then served a year in Malaysian prisons under the Preservation of Public Security Ordinance, and was barred from returning to Singapore. After his release in March 1964, Singh returned to Ipoh and taught at the Anglo-Chinese School there, later becoming principal of the Methodist School.

Singh, Mohan (1909–unknown) Indian military officer. Born in Punjab, Mohan Singh joined the British Army at the age of 17. After training and serving in various parts of British India, he was appointed Captain of Unit 1/14 Punjab, which was subsequently stationed in Malaya in 1941. The unit was defeated by the Japanese at Jitra.

On 15 December 1941, Mohan Singh was persuaded by PRITAM SINGH, founder of the Indian Independence League Movement, to join the F Kikan, a subver-

Harbans Singh: centre, with United People's Front candidates, 1988.

SingTel: Pickering Operations Centre, near Boat Quay.

sive group set up by the Japanese and headed by Fujiwara Iwachi, to fight the British. He began organizing Indians taken as prisoners of war (POWs) by the Japanese, to set up the INDIAN NATIONAL ARMY (INA).

For this purpose, Singh travelled to Singapore. On 17 February 1942, he addressed a crowd of POWs at FARRER PARK, encouraging them to 'volunteer for the freedom of India' and to join the INA. On 1 September 1942, the 1st Division of the INA was formed, with its headquarters at Mount Pleasant. Singh—who had by this time been appointed a general in the INA—led the army's first military review, on 10 September at the PADANG.

However, by the end of 1942, Singh had fallen out with the Japanese because he believed that the Japanese did not intend to make the INA a real army, but to keep it as a puppet force. The Japanese arrested him on 29 December 1942 for wilful insubordination and spreading discontent among INA members. In April 1943, he was moved to PULAU UBIN. He was released in Sumatra on 26 August 1945 after 32 months of confinement.

Singh, Pritam (1910–1942) Political activist. Pritam Singh served as Secretary of the Indian Independence League (IIL) during the JAPANESE OCCUPATION, after having served as secretary-general of the IIL's Bangkok branch before the outbreak of WORLD WAR II.

Singh established contact with Japanese intelligence officers in Singapore who promised support for the IIL. Major Fujiwara Iwaichi was assigned the task of using Singh and other IIL leaders to persuade Indian soldiers who had been serving the British to align themselves with the Japanese. One of the first to do so was Captain MOHAN SINGH. He, Pritam Singh and Fujiwara helped establish the INDIAN

NATIONAL ARMY, as well as IIL branches throughout Malaya and Singapore.

Pritam Singh died in March 1942 in a plane crash en route to Tokyo to attend a key meeting of IIL branch delegates.

SingHealth Singapore decided to divide its public hospitals into two clusters in 1999. The rationale was to bring down organizational barriers between hospitals within each cluster, increase collaboration and foster integration of medical services. The two clusters are Singapore Health Services (SingHealth) and the NATIONAL HEALTHCARE GROUP.

SingHealth comprises: three hospitals—Changi General Hospital, KK Women's and Children's Hospital and Singapore General Hospital; five national speciality centres—the National Heart Centre, Singapore National Eye Centre, National Dental Centre, National Cancer Centre and National Neuroscience Institute; and nine polyclinics.

Singlish There are three varieties of ENGLISH that stand out in Singapore. Singaporeans fluent in English use Standard Singaporean English in formal or polite situations. In casual situations, a more colloquial version of English called 'Singlish' is used. Singlish is different from English spoken by non-English speaking people learning the language, which some linguists refer to as Learner English.

Singlish has sometimes been termed pidgin, but it did not come from a need for communication among communities with no common language. It evolved as people of many cultures and languages constantly met and interacted in a variety of daily situations. Influences come from a casual form of MALAY known as Bazaar Malay or Melayu Pasar, the lingua franca of the 19th and 20th centuries; Hokkien, Teochew and

Cantonese from the migrant Chinese; TAMIL and Indian-English from the time when Singapore was administered from India; and a smattering of other languages that represent the past and present diversity of Singapore's population.

Singlish combines English with words and inflections from these languages and dialects. Sentences are loosely constructed with grammar borrowed from these languages. Complex phrases are avoided, verbs can be left out, and indications of plurality and tenses are optional. Diction is also peculiar. For all its inelegance and idiosyncracies, or perhaps because of these qualities, Singlish is also seen by many as witty, inventive and colourful.

The Singlish label and manner of speaking was popularized by humourist Toh Paik Choo's books *Eh, Goondu!* (1983) and *Lagi Goondu!* (1986). A more recent influence in the new millennium has been talkingcock.com, a popular, satirical website (*see* TALKINGCOCK).

The widespread use of Singlish prompted the government to start the Speak Good English Movement in 2000 and a new English Language curriculum for schools in 2001, to ensure that English as spoken by Singaporeans would be universally understood and, in particular, that it would be intelligible when used in international business encounters.

SingPost Singapore Post has a heritage dating back to the founding of Singapore in 1819 (*see* POSTAL SERVICES). In 1982, the Postal Services Department merged with the Telecommunication Authority of Singapore (TAS). This arrangement lasted until 1992, when the government announced plans to separately privatize the telecommunications and postal services.

Incorporated on 28 March 1992, SingPost operates more than 60 post offices

Singlish: a sampler

ah beng: a young street-smart Chinese male (Hokkien and Teochew: *'beng'*, 'clever')

alamak: oh dear! (Malay: *'alah'*, exclamation of regret; *'mak'*, 'mother')

ang moh: a Caucasian (Hokkien: *'ang'*, 'red', *'moh'*, 'hair')

bo chap: couldn't care less (Hokkien: *'bo'*, negative; *'chap'*, 'care')

botak: bald (Malay)

buaya: playboy or ladies' man (shortened from Malay *'buaya darat'*, literally 'land crocodile')

fierce: daring or strong

don't play-play: a warning not to fool with things (literal translation from Hokkien). Often deliberately mispronounced '*donch pray-pray*'.

goondu: fool (Tamil: literally 'fat')

kachau: to annoy (Malay)

kaypoh: busybody (Hokkien)

kena: to be adversely affected (Malay: literally 'cause to be')

kiasu: afraid to lose (Hokkien: *'kia'*, 'afraid'; *'su'*, 'lose')

koyak: lousy (literally 'tear' in Malay)

lauyah: lousy (Hokkien)

powderful: deliberate mispronunciation of 'powerful'.

sian: tiring, tiresome (Hokkien)

some more: furthermore

suay: jinxed (Hokkien)

talk cock: spouting nonsense

wah!: wow!

where got?: expression of disbelief

For emphasis, the particles *'lah'*, *'ah'*, *'hah'*, *'leh'*, *'meh'* and *'ma'*, which are derived from Malay and Chinese dialects, are often tagged on at the end of a word, phrase or sentence, as is the English word 'man'. An outsider unable to make sense of Singlish could be said by amused Singaporeans to 'catch no ball *lah*!'—derived literally from the Hokkien phrase '*liak bo kiew*'. If one did not catch that, one could be described as 'blur like *sotong*' (clueless as a squid) (Malay: *'sotong'*, 'squid').

Sinhalese: reclining Buddha statue some 15 m long at Sri Lankaramaya Buddhist Temple.

and manages about 80 authorized postal agencies, 660 stamp vendors and close to 200 self-service automated machines islandwide. Mail is collected from more than 800 post boxes and sent to the Singapore Post Centre, which processed more than 2.4 million local and overseas items per day, or about 830 million items in total, in 2005. The installation of an automated system in 1998, following the introduction of a six-digit postal code in 1995, enabled more than 80 per cent of the mail to be sorted mechanically. This is an increase from the 30 per cent rate when mechanization was first introduced in 1985.

In addition to mail and parcels, SingPost also offers the full range of logistics services including warehousing, fulfilment and distribution. Companies have also outsourced their mailroom, messenger and administrative procurement operations to SingPost. The company has established a presence in Malaysia and the Philippines.

SingPost offices are one-stop centres for non-postal services such as the payment of certain bills, fines, taxes and licence renewals. SingPost also offers pick-up and drop-off services at selected locations where people can receive bulk online purchases, purchase air tickets, drop off films and collect photos, and even return library books. Customers can use SingPost's internet portal to pay their bills or shop online. Other innovations include the offering of financial, remittance and pawnshop services since 2004; and the introduction of MyStamp, which allows customers to personalize their stamps.

Listed on the Singapore Exchange since May 2003, SingPost is a component stock of several benchmark indices, including the Straits Times Index, Morgan Stanley Capital Index and several FTSE indices. In 2005, the company posted a net profit of $110.5 million on a turnover of $375 million.

SingTel Info-communications company. Telecommunications in Singapore goes back to 1879, when Singapore became one of the first cities in Asia to get a telephone service just three years after Alexander Graham Bell patented his invention. Bennet Pell started a private telephone exchange in Singapore with some 50 lines. In 1907, the

first local central telephone exchange was opened at Hill Street.

Until the mid-1950s, telephone services were managed by the British. In 1955, the Singapore Telephone Board (STB) was incorporated as a statutory board. This was followed in 1974 by the merger of STB and the Telecommunications Authority of Singapore (TAS). Until that time, the STB had been responsible for local services, while the TAS had provided international services. Overseas expansion began with the formation of a subsidiary, Singapore Telecom International, in 1988.

Singapore Telecommunications (SingTel) was incorporated on 1 April 1992 and listed a year later. It was the biggest public listing in Singapore and all citizens were given free SingTel shares through TEMASEK HOLDINGS, which has remained SingTel's largest stakeholder. To focus on its core telecommunications services business, SingTel then sold 69 per cent of its existing stake in Singapore Post (SINGPOST). In the same year, it divested its stake in Yellow Pages, its directory business, for $220 million. SingTel's revenues exceeded $10 billion for the first time in 2003.

SingTel operates out of two major centres, Singapore and Australia, where it has a wholly owned, listed subsidiary called SingTel Optus. In addition, SingTel has become the second-largest satellite operator in the Asia-Pacific, and has invested in numerous submarine-cable and satellite systems. The group has made profitable investments in the Philippines, India, Indonesia, Thailand and Bangladesh.

SingTel employs more than 19,000 people worldwide. In May 2005, its market capitalization was $43 billion. Its net profit after tax for the year ended 31 March 2006 was $4.16 billion on a turnover of $13.14 billion.

Sinhalese The first Sinhalese (or Sinhala) to arrive in Singapore from Ceylon (present-day Sri Lanka) did so in the 1860s. In the late 1920s, the Sinhalese established a community organization—the Singapore Sinhala Association (SSA)—in a shophouse at the junction of Orchard Road and Tank Road opposite the grounds of Government House (the present-day Istana). As well as serving as a place at which members of the community could gather, the SSA's original premises were used as a boarding house for Sinhalese immigrants. The community also acquired premises in 1920 for the building of the Sri Lankaramaya Buddhist Temple. Since then, this temple has operated out of various locations, in Short Street, Race Course Road, Dhoby Ghaut, Niven Road, Wilkie Road and Outram Road. Today, it is located in permanent premises on St Michael's Road, where it caters to the religious needs of the community.

Up until the late 1930s, most members of the Sinhalese community lived in

SingPost: Singapore Post Centre (top); local post office.

'enclaves' around Jansen Road and Upper Serangoon Road; Middle Road and Wilkie Road; and Sophia Road. The Sinhalese were active in a wide range of professions. Many brought with them arts and crafts skills, while others worked in the jewellery and gem trade. Others found work in the colonial civil service, while Sinhalese labourers worked on the wharves near Keppel Road. In the 20th century came Sinhala doctors, lawyers, accountants, academics and engineers. Two Sinhalese were elected to the Legislative Council and the Municipal Council.

After World War II, a substantial number of enlisted Sinhalese men came to Singapore with the British army. They were followed in 1946–47 by Sinhalese members of the Ceylon Pioneer Corps, some of whom stayed on in Singapore after being demobilized.

The SSA has continued to act as an important channel of exchange for the Sinhalese community. In 1991, it established an educational foundation that has continued to provide scholarships for Sinhalese students.

sinkheh 'Sinkheh' is Hokkien for 'new arrival'. The word 'kheh' literally means 'guest' and is used to describe CHINESE immigrants arriving in Singapore in the early 19th century because they never expected to settle permanently on the island. The practice of sojourning abroad to find work was an extension of a Chinese rural tradition, whereby young men would venture to other cities for work. Such men would return to their hometowns after making their fortunes.

SingTel: Sentosa Satellite Earth Station.

Siong Lim Temple: main prayer hall (top); Laughing Buddha.

Siow Lee Chin

Some immigrants made good and went back to China to help recruit more immigrant labour. Those who returned to Singapore were known as '*ku kheh*' ('old guests'), while those arriving for the first time were known as '*sinkheh*'. Most *sinkheh* came from the southern Chinese coastal provinces of Fujian, Guangdong and Hainan.

Sinnathuray, T.S. (1930–) Judge. Thirugnana Sampanthar Sinnathuray (popularly known as 'Sam' Sinnathuray) was the son of a school principal. He was educated at Pearl's Hill School and Outram School. After World War II, he studied at Raffles Institution, completing his Senior Cambridge examinations there in 1948. He then left to study law at University College, London. He graduated in 1953 and was called to the Bar at Lincoln's Inn.

Upon his return to Singapore, Sinnathuray went into practice with the firm of Oehlers and Choa. He later joined the legal service as a magistrate (1956–59). Other positions he held included: deputy registrar, Supreme Court, and sheriff (1959–60); registrar, Supreme Court (1963–66); Crown Counsel and deputy public prosecutor (1960–63); Senior State Counsel (1966–67); first district judge (1967–70); and senior district judge (1971–78).

In 1978, Sinnathuray was elevated to the Bench and served as PUISNE JUDGE until his retirement in 1997. After his retirement, he established with P.C. Cheung the auction house of Mavin International, a firm dealing in rare coins and banknotes.

Sintercom Website. Founded in 1994 by Tan Chong Kee (a graduate student at Stanford University), this website was originally a collection of messages from an online discussion group, soc.culture.Singapore. As Tan began putting these messages together, he received offers of help from Singaporean students in other foreign institutions, particularly Oxford and Yale Universities. This community evolved into Sintercom, short for 'the Singapore Internet Community'.

In 1996, Tan was persuaded to host the Sintercom website in Singapore. He maintained Sintercom with the help of volunteers until August 2001, when he announced his decision to close it. Tan told the media that his reasons for closing Sintercom were purely personal. However, Tan's announcement came in the wake of the introduction of new laws designed to control political websites. The Singapore Broadcasting Authority had given Tan 14 days to sign an undertaking that he would be responsible for all of Sintercom's content, and to register Sintercom as a political website.

Before Tan discontinued the website, it was getting an average of 7,000 'hits' a day. A 'New Sintercom' was established shortly after the demise of the original, and has continued to be maintained by volunteers.

Siong Lim Temple Established in 1898, Siong Lim temple, also known in Mandarin as Lian Shan Shuang Lin Shi (Twin Groves of the Lotus Mountain Monastery) in Mandarin, was built to commemorate the birth and death of Buddha. Located in Toa Payoh, the temple took 11 years to complete. It is considered an architectural masterpiece of the 19th century, for its exquisite decorations and its combination of three distinct Chinese regional styles. Drawing on resources and expert artisans from the Fuzhou, Quanzhou and Zhangzhou provinces in China, the temple reflects the influences of the major dialect groups which funded its construction.

The monastery is modelled after Xi Chang Shi, a famous temple in Fuzhou. It is a rare example of a *conglin* (layers of forest) temple—a type of monastery where an orderly way of life is manifested in the layout and the monks' highly regulated routine. The daily schedule would be marked by the use of ritual instruments such as the drum and bell.

There are three main sections to the monastery—the entrance, the towers and three main halls. The entrance features two magnificent 9.1-m gates with stone pillars and wooden roof structures. The two pillars are inscribed with calligraphy. Occupying a central position within the first courtyard is the Maitreya Buddha, more commonly known as the Laughing Buddha. Flanking the main courtyard are Gu Lou (Drum Tower) and Zhong Lou (Bell Tower). The Dragon Light Pagoda is a seven-storey octagonal structure adorned with carvings.

Of the three halls, Da Xiong Pao Dian (Mahavira Hall) is the main prayer hall. Housing the main altar, it was built for the worship of the 18 Lohan, Sakyamuni Buddha and other Bodhisattvas. It is spectacular both inside and out, with colourful beams, carvings of lotuses and writhing dragons. The doors feature carved latticed patterns of flowers, birds and Chinese symbols denoting longevity; the exterior walls are finished with tortoise-shell design.

Tian Wang Dian (Hall of Celestial Kings) has a simple roof with elegant timber trusses. Its granite walls and panels depict scenes of Chinese culture and history. The Dharma Hall—the temple's oldest building—was built in 1903 and had to be replaced in 1978 as its timber had deteriorated beyond repair. The hall now houses the figurines of Guan Yin and is used to store ash urns.

In 1980, Siong Lim Temple was gazetted as a national monument. A decade-long restoration began in 1991, involving some 80 craftsmen from China using traditional methods to preserve as much of the original architectural style as possible. Many Singapore kung fu associations have their origins at the monastery. In the years immediately after the end of World War II, many Toa Payoh residents learned martial arts from the abbot Cao Cen, to fend off constant threats from gangsters.

Siow Lee Chin (1966–) Musician. An alumnus of Curtis Institute, Mannes College and Oberlin Conservatory, Siow Lee Chin made her New York debut at Carnegie Hall's Weill Recital Hall in the Young Artists Winner Series. She won first prize at the 1994 Henryk Szeryng International Violin Competition in Mexico City and the Louise D. McMahon International Competition for Strings. Siow was made assistant professor of violin and director of strings at the College of Charleston, South Carolina. In 1996, she won the National Arts Council's YOUNG ARTIST AWARD. Her live performances have been broadcast on Voice of America and the television programme *CBS Sunday Morning*.

Sisters' Islands The two Sisters' Islands are part of the Southern Islands. Subar Laut (Big Sister, covering 3.9 ha) is exposed to the open sea; Subar Darat (Little Sister, 1.7 ha) is sheltered, as it faces the Singapore mainland. The islands are fringed by reefs of hard and soft corals, with a great diversity of marine life such as giant clams, octopus and seahorses. Subar Laut also has long-tailed macaques (*see* MONKEYS).

The origin of the islands' name comes from a legend. Two sisters, Minah and Lina, were devoted to each other and inseparable. One day, the chief of the ORANG LAUT (sea people) spotted Lina and fell in love with her. Despite protests from both sisters, Lina was taken against her will in the chief's sampan. The sea suddenly turned black and a large wave dragged Minah into the water. Lina struggled with her captor, managed to free herself and jumped into the sea to join her sister. The next day, the Orang Laut of the area were shocked to find two new islands at the spot where the sisters had drowned.

As of 2006, the Sisters' Islands were not part of any major development plan. However, the sandy beaches on Subar Laut were extended by LAND RECLAMATION in the late 1990s.

Smoking: poster publicizing ban.

slavery Sir STAMFORD RAFFLES called for the abolition of slavery in Singapore in 1823. His 'Regulation for the Prevention of the Slave Trade at Singapore' decreed that all individuals enslaved since 26 February 1819 'are entitled to claim their freedom'.

The regulation also extended to the indenture of Chinese immigrants who were forced to offer their labour in lieu of payment of passage. Under the regulation, the maximum amount that creditor-employers could demand of such labourers was set at $20—and this amount had to be paid in the form of labour within two years. However, the regulation was not strictly enforced for several decades. While blatant human trafficking was eradicated, less obvious forms of slavery continued. In the case of Chinese contract labour, the regulation was not enforced effectively until the creation of the CHINESE PROTECTORATE in 1877.

S.League The Football Association of Singapore withdrew from the MALAYSIA CUP series in 1995. A year later, a new professional SOCCER league was initiated— the S.League. KWEK LENG JOO was appointed chairman, and Douglas Moore chief executive officer. The S.League was officially launched by Prime Minister Goh Chok Tong at the NATIONAL STADIUM in 1996. The eight teams that participated in the league then were Balestier Central FC, Geylang United FC, Police FC, Tampines Rovers FC, Sembawang Rangers FC, Singapore Armed Forces FC (SAFFC), Tiong Bahru United FC, and Woodlands Wellington FC.

The teams competed in a two-series format—the Tiger Beer Series and the Pioneer Series. Geylang emerged champions in the S.League's first year. The following year, the two-series format was replaced by a single series. The Singapore League Cup (Singapore Cup since 1998) was also introduced in 1997. Two new teams—Jurong FC and Landmark Marine Castle—drew up plans to join the league, although Landmark withdrew at the last minute after claiming to be 'not fully prepared'. SAFFC, with FANDI AHMAD, won the league in its second year.

small- and medium-sized enterprises In Singapore, a small- or medium-sized enterprise (SME) is defined as a manufacturing business with a fixed asset investment not exceeding $15 million, or a services sector business employing not more than 200 workers. SMEs made up over 90 per cent of all enterprises in Singapore in 2004, employed more than half of the workforce, and contributed 40 per cent of GDP.

The non-profit ASSOCIATION OF SMALL & MEDIUM ENTERPRISES works with the ECONOMIC DEVELOPMENT BOARD and SPRING SINGAPORE to help local firms with all aspects of their businesses.

In 2000, the SME 21 Plan was formulated. This ten-year plan seeks to increase the capabilities of SMEs by creating a knowledge-based, pro-enterprise economy; developing productive SME sectors; and supporting innovative, high-growth SMEs.

smoking The government first introduced laws restricting smoking in public places and prohibiting cigarette advertisements with the Smoking Act of 1970. Under this act, smoking was banned in cinemas and on buses. The ban was later extended to apply to all government buildings, sports facilities, public transport, schools, hospitals, shopping centres, convention halls, underground pedestrian walkways and public queues, as well as offices, factories and restaurants. Since July 2006, smoking has only been permitted in designated areas in HAWKER CENTRES and COFFEE SHOPS. Plans have also been announced to restrict smoking to particular sections within pubs and karaoke lounges from July 2007.

In 1986, the MINISTRY OF HEALTH launched the National Smoking Control Programme (NSCP) with the slogan 'Towards a Nation of Non-Smokers'. The aims of the NSCP are to reduce the prevalence of smoking in Singapore by discouraging young people from taking it up; educating, motivating and assisting smokers to give it up; promoting environments in which non-smokers are not subject to 'second-hand smoke'; and establishing non-smoking as a social norm. The programme includes public education, legislation, taxation of tobacco products and the provision of services to assist people to stop smoking.

The Committee on Smoking Control (CSC) was formed in 1996 to review the NSCP and recommend new directions for the programme. The objectives of the CSC are to increase community involvement and support for the NSCP, and to turn the pro-

S.League

motion of a smoke-free environment into a civic movement. In 2001, the HEALTH PROMOTION BOARD was formed to oversee and coordinate health promotion programmes, including the NSCP.

The NSCP has had some impact. For instance, between 1980 and 2000, there was a 28 per cent reduction in the incidence of lung cancer in males and 25 per cent in females. Yet there has also been an increase in the rate of smoking in females aged 18–24, from 2.8 per cent in 1992 to 8.2 per cent in 2001. Moreover, a survey conducted in 2000 found that one in ten secondary school students smoked at least one day a month, and that one in four students had tried smoking—20.5 per cent having done so before the age of ten.

SMRT Corporation Public transport company. Incorporated originally as Singapore MRT Ltd in 1987 and publicly listed in 2000, SMRT Corporation Ltd (SMRT) was formed to build and operate the Mass Rapid Transit (MRT) system (*see* MASS RAPID TRANSIT/LIGHT RAIL TRANSIT SYSTEM). It operates the two main MRT arteries—the North-South and East-West lines.

SMRT has since diversified into other areas of transport. It has operated Singapore's Light Rail Transit system since 1997. In December 2001, it acquired TIBS, Singapore's second licensed public bus operator, which has a fleet of over 800 buses and nearly 3,000 taxis. SMRT also took over the City Shuttle Service and Bus-Plus Services.

In addition, the group offers automotive maintenance and repair, as well as

S.LEAGUE: WINNERS		
Year	S.League	Singapore League/ Singapore Cup
1996	Geylang United	Not held
1997	SAFFC	SAFFC
1998	SAFFC	Tanjong Pagar United
1999	Home United	SAFFC
2000	SAFFC	Home United
2001	Geylang United	Home United
2002	SAFFC	Tampines Rovers
2003	Home United	Home United
2004	Tampines Rovers	Tampines Rovers
2005	Tampines Rovers	Home United

S.LEAGUE: MILESTONES	
1998	Marine Castle United and Gombak United boost the number of teams to 11.
1999	The S.League revises the policy on foreign player quotas. From five per team, the number is reduced to four.
2000	Geylang goalkeeper Lutz Pfannenstiel and Jurong's Mirko Jurilj are convicted of match-fixing and banned.
2001	The number of teams is increased to 12.
2003	A number of changes are made in the league roster. Sinchi FC from China becomes the first foreign club to joins the S.League. In addition, the Singapore national Under-23 team (Young Lions) joins the league. Balestier Central and Clementi Khalsa amalgamate to form Balestier Khalsa.
2004	Japanese club Albirex Niigata joins the league.
2005	Paya Lebar Punggol becomes the tenth team in the S.League after Tanjong Pagar United withdraws.

Junie Sng

turnkey consultancy and project management services in railway systems. SMRT also receives non-fare revenues from the commercial lease of some 20,400 sq m of space at its 51 stations, as well as from media advertising in its trains, buses and taxis.

In 2000, SMRT formed a joint venture with MEDIACORP to publish the newspaper TODAY. Launched in November the same year, the paper is distributed free at MRT stations daily. SMRT sold its 14.6 per cent stake in the newspaper in August 2004 for $3.5 million. For the financial year ending March 2006, SMRT reported a profit of $103.6 million on a turnover of $711.7 million.

Sng, Junie (1964–) Sportswoman. Junie Sng Poh Leng was a swimming prodigy who made her international debut at the eighth Southeast Asian Peninsular (SEAP) Games in 1975 when she was only eleven years old; she won a gold and a silver medal. Two years later at the Southeast Asian Games (successor to the SEAP Games), Sng won five gold medals and broke six SEAP and two Asian Games records. She even broke the Singapore Open men's 800 m record the same year. She had the rare distinction of being made the Singapore National Olympic Council's Sportsgirl of the Year and Sportswoman of the Year simultaneously (1978, 1979, 1980).

Sng was the first Singaporean to win a gold medal in a women's event at the Asian Games in 1978. Indeed, at the age of 14, she was also the first and the youngest to win two gold medals—first in the 400 m freestyle when she beat the record by more than four seconds, and then in her pet event, the 800 m freestyle. That same year, she made it to the finals of the 800 m freestyle at the Commonwealth Games in Canada.

Sng missed the 1976 Olympic Games in Montreal because Singapore swimmers had been banned for competing against China, which was not a member of the International Olympic Committee. Four years later, Singapore boycotted the Moscow Olympic Games in support of the

United States. Sng retired from swimming after winning 10 gold medals at the 1983 Southeast Asian Games in Singapore. Although she never became an Olympian, she is remembered as one of Singapore's most successful swimmers. She won a total of 26 individual and 12 team gold medals during her eight-year career, and is honoured in the SINGAPORE SPORTS COUNCIL HALL OF FAME.

soccer Commonly referred to as 'football', soccer was introduced by British military units in the late 19th century. The first recorded game took place in 1889, when teams of engineers played on a field in Tank Road. Within two years of that first game, the Chinese National Football Association was founded. From 1892, the Association Challenge Cup was the main fixture on the calendar. The competition was dominated by military teams and it was not until 1901 that the Singapore Cricket Club would claim the title for the first time.

In the period leading up to World War I, there was considerable inter-state rivalry between Singapore and Selangor. Singapore defeated its rival six times between 1901 and 1913. Selangor only managed one win and three draws.

There was a strong non-European element to the game and soccer soon became Malaya's national game. Writing in 1926 in the periodical *Malaya*, W.A. Wilson, reported that 'gatherings of 10,000 people have been approached, if not attained'. During the inter-war years, the Chinese and Malay football teams became increasingly competitive, often ousting the expatriate teams. A major stimulus to the game came with the introduction of the Malaya Cup in 1921, the forerunner of the MALAYSIA CUP. Singapore and Selangor continued to dominate this competition until World War II.

Singapore had the use of a stadium by 1922—or at least an enclosed ground with two stands—near the dock area and close to Chinatown. The Anson Road Stadium was built for the Malaya-Borneo Exhibition and preserved after its conclusion. All the most important soccer matches and other sporting fixtures took place there until the Jalan Besar stadium was built in 1930.

The most eagerly awaited games in the inter-war period were not just the Malaya Cup games, but also games arranged against touring teams from China. In 1929, spectators were treated to a visit from the Hong Kong Chinese team. The visitors defeated the Singapore Chinese, Perak Chinese and Singapore Europeans, drew with the Malacca and Selangor Chinese, and were only beaten narrowly by the combined Malayan Chinese side. In May 1936, the All-China team drew crowds in excess of 20,000 for their matches against local Chinese and European teams. Nationalist feelings ran very high as the All-China team defeated both opponents.

After World War II, football remained at centre stage. The Singapore Amateur Football Association became affiliated to the Federation Internationale Football Association (FIFA) in 1952. At the time, there were over 80 active clubs in Singapore, with 1,300 registered players and 50 registered referees. In 1955, there was a landmark event when Singapore defeated Kelantan in the final of the Malaya Cup at Jalan Besar stadium. It was the only time that the Cup final was played at Jalan Besar.

The Football Association of Singapore (FAS) was formed in January 1966. After a number of internal problems, administration of the association was transferred to the Ministry of Social Affairs in 1971. The period 1975 to 1981 represented a return to the glory days of the 1950s for the national team. By this time, the 55,000-seat NATIONAL STADIUM had been built, and was the venue of many matches, including the Malaysia Cup. The 'Kallang Roar'—the cheers of football fans—resounded from the stands on such occasions.

Singapore won the Malaysia Cup in 1977 and 1980; in 1994, its last year as a participating team, Singapore again took top honours. In 1996, Singapore set up the S.LEAGUE as the major soccer competition in Singapore. The S.League was supposed to replace the Malaysia Cup as the centerpiece of local football, but the intense passion generated by the Malaysia Cup was never replicated. However, the 'Kallang Roar' was heard once more when Singapore won the Tiger Cup in a 2–1 victory over Indonesia in 2005. It was the first time that the national team had won a major tournament at the National Stadium.

Soccer has consolidated its place as the national game, with more than a century's history and several homegrown players regarded as soccer legends (*see* box).

Social Development Service Following the establishment of the SOCIAL DEVELOPMENT UNIT, a similar initiative was introduced for non-graduates. The Social Development Service (SDS) was formed by the PEOPLE'S ASSOCIATION in November 1985.

Social Development Unit In August 1983, the government noted that few female graduates were getting married. The Social Development Unit (SDU) was therefore set up in 1984 with two aims: to promote marriage among the growing number of single graduates, and to arrest the falling birth rate among them. It emphasizes the importance of marriage and family, and organizes events for singles to meet and interact. Matchmaking services are available for those seeking to marry. Despite nicknames such as 'Single, Desperate and Ugly', the SDU is seen by some graduates as a useful additional platform for socializing, thanks to a range of subsidized activities such as cruises and overseas tours.

social welfare Apart from medical and public health contributions, government efforts at social welfare up until World War II were a patchwork of damage-control measures, such as attempts to protect child bond servants in the 1930s. For the most part, social welfare was left to CLAN ASSOCIATIONS, religious organizations and charities. By the late 19th century, various clan associations were financing schools and refuge homes for the old and sick. Mosques and Hindu temples also engaged in welfare work, mainly dispensing food and cash relief to the poor. Efforts by Christian missions—such as the SALVATION ARMY, which arrived in the 1930s—included the care of abandoned or needy children, and education.

The emergence of the British welfare state in the 1940s led the colonial government to set up a Social Welfare Department in Singapore in 1946. However, in the immediate post war period, coping with destitution and rampant malnutrition took priority, and the department's focus remained remedial.

Since Independence, social welfare has continued to be the province mainly of voluntary welfare organizations (VWOs), but for deliberate and entirely different reasons. The government has repeatedly stated its position against creating a welfare state, on the basis that this would erode the work ethic on which Singapore's economic success depends. Instead, the government has extolled self-reliance and encouraged the growth of VWOs, and public policy has been tailored accordingly.

The number of VWOs has burgeoned since the 1950s, aided by increased public interest in volunteerism, generous tax exemptions for charitable donations, and the coordination efforts of the NATIONAL COUNCIL OF SOCIAL SERVICE, a statutory board under the Ministry of Community Development, Youth and Sports.

The government has also encouraged the establishment of community-based self-help groups such as MENDAKI, the SINGAPORE INDIAN DEVELOPMENT ASSOCIATION and the CHINESE DEVELOPMENT ASSISTANCE COUNCIL.

Public expenditure on social welfare has been relatively small and is generally restricted to subsidizing VWOs and helping the very neediest members of society. A range of modest public assistance schemes is available, including subsidies for childcare, utilities and healthcare (*see* MEDIFUND). All such assistance is subject to stringent means-testing. For the general population, government subsidies are available for basic needs such as housing, education and healthcare, but the citizen is expected to make co-payment through the CENTRAL PROVIDENT FUND (CPF) and related schemes such as MEDISAVE and MEDISHIELD, or personal savings. Similarly, the aged are expected to use their CPF and savings to finance their retirement years. And while public grants for skills re-training and assistance with job placement are available for the unemployed, there are no unemployment benefits per se.

Economic and demographic changes, such as increasing employment uncertainty and the rapidly ageing population, pose a challenge to current policies on social welfare. For example, the Medishield insurance scheme does not provide lifelong cover, although healthcare needs tend to increase with age. And citizens' withdrawal of CPF funds for pre-retirement expenditure, particularly housing, means that less is left for retirement—unless housing wealth can be converted effectively into retirement income flow.

Society for the Prevention of Cruelty to Animals The existence of the Society for the Prevention of Cruelty to Animals (SPCA) was noted in the 19th century, in a report in THE STRAITS TIMES dated 3 October 1878, commenting on the number of cases brought before it. There were no other records until 1947 when it was revived as the Royal Society for the Prevention of Cruelty to Animals (RSPCA) by Lucia Bach, an English-woman. She ran a boarding house and sheltered stray animals. The RSPCA was formally set up in 1954 on Orchard Road. In 1959, it was renamed the SPCA. In 1984, the SPCA moved to 31 Mount Vernon Road. The SPCA takes in more than 12,000 animals a year. Animals for which suitable homes cannot be provided, may be euthanized by lethal injection. The SPCA promotes respect for animals through educational publications and talks.

Soin, Kanwaljit (1942–) Doctor and social activist. One of very few female surgery students of her generation, Kanwaljit Soin was a triple-medal winner in the medical school final examinations at the National University of Singapore in 1966.

Soin was the first woman NOMINATED MP (1992-96). Her Private Member's Bill on Family Violence 1995 was defeated but later incorporated in amendments to the WOMEN'S CHARTER. She led AWARE (ASSOCIATION OF WOMEN FOR ACTION AND RESEARCH), the United Nations Development Fund for Women (Singapore), and the International Women's Forum (Singapore) in promoting gender and human equality. Through the global network HelpAge International, Soin also seeks to address the concerns of ageing populations.

Kanwaljit Soin

solicitor-general Unlike the office of the attorney-general, the solicitor-general's office is not constitutionally prescribed. In England, Australia and some other Commonwealth countries, the solicitor-general is the government's chief legal adviser and the attorney-general acts as the minister for law. In Singapore, however, the attorney-general is the government's chief legal adviser and it is the job of the solicitor-general to assist him in the work of providing advice to the government.

Under section 336(2) of the Criminal Procedure Code, the solicitor-general also has the powers of a deputy public prosecutor, and he may act as the public prosecutor in the absence of the attorney-general.

Som Said (1951–) Dancer, choreographer and teacher. Som Said is a former member of SRIWANA and the National Dance Company. Her choreographic ventures in traditional and contemporary Malay dance have ranged from *Sekapur Sirih* (Welcome Dance) to the 1998 dance opera *Dendam Berahi* (A Revenge of Passion). For the 2004 SINGAPORE ARTS FESTIVAL, she served as artistic director for the Malay musical *Gentarasa 2004: Langit Bukan Batasan* (The Sky is Not the Limit). She was founder and artistic director of SRI WARISAN SOM SAID PERFORMING ARTS, Singapore's first fully professional Malay dance company. In 1979, Som Said was awarded the National Youth Service Award for her outreach efforts with children. She was a recipient of the CULTURAL MEDALLION IN 1987.

Som Said

Society for the Prevention of Cruelty to Animals

509

Quah Kim Song, right, playing for Singapore at the National Stadium, 1980.

soccer legends

1920s

L.M. Pennefather (1894–1982) Pennefather's ferocious defence as fullback earned him the nickname 'Son of the Devil', but he was a staunch advocate of sportsmanship. He played for Singapore in six Malaya Cup finals, helping Singapore to win thrice, in 1923, 1924 and 1925.

Lim Yong Liang (dates unknown) A dominant centre forward, Lim was known as 'Pop' and 'Mr Elegant'. He represented Singapore in the Malaya Cup (1920–30) and was on the winning side in 1923 and 1924. In 1925, the finals were played at the Anson Road Stadium in Singapore for the first time, and Lim scored the winning goal. He became a successful national coach from 1935 to 1941.

1930s

Mat Noor (1913–) Singapore's most celebrated Malaya Cup player, Mat Noor was called the 'Wizard of Nod' because of his heading ability. Although only

Majid Ariff

1.52 m tall, he out-jumped taller European players by training in the sea. He represented Singapore Malays when he was 14. He played inside-right in the Malaya Cup final every year from 1928 to 1938. Mat Noor was a member of the team that recorded Singapore's most one-sided Malaya Cup victory (8–2 against Selangor in 1933).

Dolfatah (dates unknown) Famous for his dribbling skills, Dolfatah was the attacking inside-left in the replayed Malaya Cup final at Anson Road Stadium in 1930, which Singapore won 3–0. In Kuala Lumpur (1931) and in Singapore (1932), he was also on the winning side. On all three occasions, Singapore defeated arch-rival Selangor.

Chia Keng Hock (1913–) A fearsome centre forward known as 'the Bull' because of his robust play, Chia was favourably compared to China's greatest player of the time, Lee Wai Tong. Chia was a six-time Malaya Cup finalist, and a winner in 1932, 1933 (when he scored a hat-trick in the 8–2 victory), and 1934. He survived the Japanese Occupation and was still a redoubtable opponent for the Singapore Chinese Football Association when he played in Hong Kong in 1947.

Choo Seng Quee (1914–1983) Choo represented Singapore as a halfback. He was rewarded with a Cup-winner's medal in 1937, when Singapore defeated Selangor 2–1. He later became one of the most respected coaches of the national team.

1940s

Chia Boon Leong (1925–) Known as 'Twinkletoes', Chia was one of only three Olympians to represent football from Malaya. He played for China in the 1948 Olympic Games in London. As inside-forward, he inspired Malaya Cup wins in 1950, 1951 and 1952. He trained briefly with Arsenal in England before retiring in 1955.

1950s

Awang Bakar (1936–1964) A deadly striker dubbed 'Golden Boy', Awang was an unorthodox player, known for volleying corner-kicks and goalkeepers' clearances straight into the goal—as he did in the 1950 Malaya Cup final. He scored a hat-trick in the 1951 final, when Singapore beat Perak 6–0. He died unexpectedly at the age of 37, while playing a friendly game.

Rahim Omar (1930–1990) Rahim's national career lasted from 1952 to 1966. He was a Malaya Cup winner for Singapore in 1952—scoring the winning goal—and in 1960, 1964 and 1965. He took over the striker's mantle from Awang Bakar in the 1960s. Rahim was also known as the first 'banana-kick' specialist in Singapore, able to make the ball curve through the air instead of travelling straight.

Dollah Kassim carrying the Malaysia Cup, 1977.

1960s

Quah Kim Swee (1936–) Quah played for Malaysia during the period of Merger (1963–65) but moved to play for Singapore after Separation. As team captain in 1965, he led the new republic to fourth place in the 1966 Asian Games in Bangkok—Singapore's best showing in that competition to date. With his heading ability, confidence and calm temperament, he was one of the few players to get offers to play professionally in England.

Majid Ariff (1938–) One of Singapore's finest midfield players in the 1960s, Majid's strength was in his fast and deceptive ball control. He represented Singapore at the 1958 Asian Games and was a Malaya Cup winner in 1964 and 1965. He was the only Singaporean selected for the Asian All-Stars team during the 1960s.

Lee Kok Seng (1933–) Lee captained Singapore to the Malaya Cup final a total of seven times, leading the team to victory in 1960, 1964 and 1965. He was reputed to be the ultimate centre-half, so much so that he was 'never known to have a bad game'. His nickname 'Horse' was a tribute to his speed, strength and grace on the field.

1970s

Quah Kim Song (1951–) A speedy and deceptive forward, Quah was on the Singapore side that lost the Malaysia Cup final in 1975 and 1976.

He came back in 1977 to score the winning goal against Penang in a thrilling 3–2 victory. He also played in the 1978 and 1981 finals.

Dollah Kassim (dates unknown) The 'Gelek King' was a skilled dribbler, who represented Singapore in five consecutive Malaysia Cup finals (1975–79). However, Dollah was on the winning team only once, when Singapore defeated Penang 3–2 in 1977. He was one of the stars of Geylang International (now Geylang United Football Club), and scored Singapore's only goal against Arsenal in a 5–1 defeat in 1977.

1980s

Fandi Ahmad (1962–) Singapore's most famous footballer, FANDI AHMAD scored the winning goal in Singapore's 2–1 Malaysia Cup victory in 1980. He went on to play professionally in the Netherlands and Asia. He was again on Singapore's winning team in the 1994 Malaysia Cup final.

V. Sundramoorthy (1965–) Known as the 'Dazzler' for his fancy footwork, Sundram's first national cap was in 1983, when Singapore reached the Southeast Asian Games final for the first time. In his Malaysia Cup debut in 1986, he was the tournament's top scorer, with a total of 18 goals. He later joined Kedah and helped them to a 3–1 win in the 1990 final against Singapore. Playing for Singapore again, he scored with a memorable bicycle kick against Brunei during the 1993 Malaysia Cup tournament.

Fandi Ahmad, right, playing for Dutch club FC Groningen, 1983.

Song, Wykidd (1964–) Fashion designer. Wykidd Song studied fashion at Kingston Polytechnic in the United Kingdom. In 1993, he met and formed a partnership with British graphic artist Ann Kelly.

When Song returned to Singapore in 1995 with Kelly, they established Song + Kelly, a clothing design and manufacturing company that attracted international attention. Its customers included Harrods of London and Nieman Marcus of the United States. Although the couple eventually broke up, the company survived. In 2000, Song and Kelly sold a majority stake in the company to Club 21, the luxury lifestyle company owned by Christina Ong. The company was renamed Song + Kelly21.

Song Koon Poh (1954–) Sportsman. Song Koon Poh made his national rugby debut at the age of 18. Five years later, he captained the state squad at the Southeast Asian Games. The team won the silver medal in Kuala Lumpur, losing only to Thailand in the last game contested at that level. His team recorded their greatest triumphs in 1978—finishing third behind Japan and South Korea in the Asian Championships, and also reaching the quarter-finals of the Hong Kong Sevens. Song was named Sportsman of the Year by the Singapore National Olympic Council in 1979, the only rugby player to have received this honour.

Song's faced controversy when a life ban was imposed on him in 1982 for playing in apartheid South Africa. The ban was lifted two years later, enabling Song to become player-coach of the national team. He retired in 1990.

Song Ong Siang (1871–1941) Lawyer. First Chinese to be admitted to the local Bar. Song was educated at Raffles Institution where he won the Queen's Scholarship to study at Downing College, Cambridge University. He won prizes in Constitutional Law, International Law, Jurisprudence and Roman Law. Song was called to the Bar on 14 June 1893. With schoolmate James Aitken he formed the law firm of Aitken and Ong Siang. He is best remembered for his monumental *One Hundred Years' History of the Chinese in Singapore* (1902). He was knighted in 1936.

Sook Ching Chinese term meaning 'purification through cleansing'. In Singapore, it has particular reference to the JAPANESE OCCUPATION, specifically the military operations whereby suspected anti-Japanese elements among the Chinese community were identified and eliminated.

On 18 February 1942, the Sook Ching directive was issued by the 25th Army, which was under the command of Lieutenant-General YAMASHITA TOMOYUKI. The directive specified a search for former members of volunteer forces, communists,

Wykidd Song: left, with Ann Kelly.

looters, people posessing weapons, and anyone obstructing Japanese operations or threatening law and order.

At the top of the list were Chinese community leaders such as TAN KAH KEE, his family members and others who had been supporting China in the 1937 Sino-Japanese War. Also sought were the mostly Chinese communists who had organized effective pre war Japanese trade boycotts, and those in DALFORCE, a hastily trained group of Chinese—of Kuomintang (Chinese Nationalist Party) and communist persuasion—who had earned the enmity of the Japanese during the battle for Singapore. Besides them, there were the Chinese Volunteers in the STRAITS SETTLEMENTS VOLUNTEER FORCE as well volunteers of the various civil defence groups organized by the British, such as the Medical Auxiliary Corps and the Air Raid Precaution Wardens.

Although only men between the ages of 18 and 50 were called up, whole families came because of confusing instructions.

The screening of the 600,000-strong Chinese community was conducted by the 2nd Field Unit KEMPEITAI (Japanese military police). It was augmented by about a thousand soldiers from the 18th, 5th and Imperial Guards Divisions. Local police and people were also pressed to assist the Kempeitai. The screening process was arbitrary. At the Jalan Besar centre, men who wore glasses were considered educated and, therefore, guilty of anti-Japanese activities. At another, soft hands were evidence of education. At the Telok Kurau School centre, people were picked according to whether they were businessmen, civil servants and so on.

Those selected were summarily executed. There was little attempt to conceal these killings. People living nearby and prisoners of war were ordered out to dispose of the bodies. The Japanese estimate that there were between 5,000 and 6,000 executions, while the local Chinese put it between 40,000 and 50,000 (which may have included those killed by shelling and bombardment during the MALAYA CAMPAIGN). The true numbers are unlikely ever to be known.

The EURASIANS were also screened. They were made to identify themselves as enemy aliens with badges. While the Malay community was not screened in general, a

group of nearly 100 Malays who were Volunteers or had worked for the British were executed.

According to SHINOZAKI MAMORU, the welfare officer in the Japanese civilian administration, official screening was over in three days. However, the rounding up of anti-Japanese elements continued because the Kempeitai had uncovered lists of anti-Japanese supporters during their search of clan association buildings and offices.

After the war, in 1947, seven Kempeitai and Imperial Japanese Army officers were tried for the Sook Ching atrocities. Only two were sentenced to death: Lieutenant-General KAWAMURA SABURO, commander of the Syonan Defence Garrison and Lieutenant-Colonel OISHI MASAYUKI, commander of 2nd Field Kempeitai. The others—Lieutenant-General NISHIMURA TAKUMA, Lieutenant-Colonel Yokota Yoshitaka, Major Jyo Tomotatsu, Major Onishi Satoru, and Captain Hisamatsu Haruji—were sentenced to life imprisonmen, as was Captain Mizuno Keiji who was tried a year later. All except one were repatriated to Japan when the American occupation of Japan ended in 1952. In 1951, Nishimura was sent to Australia to face trial and execution for another war crime. The Japanese government subsequently decriminalized the convicted men, including those executed for war crimes.

The officer widely accepted in Japanese military circles as responsible for the Sook Ching massacres was the directive's supervising officer Colonel TSUJI MASANOBU. He was never brought to justice. He went into hiding at the end of the war and re-surfaced in Japan in 1948.

In the 1960s, the remains of those executed during Sook Ching were recovered from mass graves all over Singapore and interred at the foot of the CIVILIAN WAR MEMORIAL on Beach Road.

Soon, Robert (1934–) Political activist. Robert Soon Loh Boon attended a Chinese primary school but had to stop because his family was poor. He started work and found himself hampered by his poor English. Philanthropist LEE KONG

Song Koon Poh, right

Song Ong Siang

Sook Ching

Special Operations Command

*Soon Ai Ling: Lü Lü
Yang Liu Feng (1988).*

CHIAN came to Soon's rescue by putting him through THE CHINESE HIGH SCHOOL.

Soon read voraciously and was much influenced by communist literature. In the 1950s, the MALAYAN COMMUNIST PARTY had penetrated the Chinese Middle Schools through the SINGAPORE PEOPLE'S ANTI-BRITISH LEAGUE. Student agitation was commonplace. In October 1954, the students formed the SINGAPORE CHINESE MIDDLE SCHOOLS STUDENTS' UNION. Registered in October 1955, its chairman was Soon. The union had almost 10,000 members. Following the HOCK LEE BUS RIOTS, the authorities ordered the union to be dissolved in September 1956. This led 5,000 students to stage a sit-in at six schools. Soon was arrested about a week later, under the Preservation of Public Security Ordinance, and was detained until 1964.

See also CHINESE MIDDLE SCHOOL RIOTS.

Soon Ai Ling (1949–) Author. Many of Soon Ai Ling's short stories concern women and the arts (including crafts and traditions such as Chinese tea culture, CHINESE OPERA and BATIK painting). Her two most successful short-story collections have been *Lü Lü Yang Liu Feng* (Wind in the Green Willows) (1988) and *Bi Luo Shi Li Xiang* (The Fragrance of 'Bi Luo' Tea) (1988). Soon won the National Short Story Writing Competition (1979), the Golden Lion Literary Award (1982, 1985), and the Southeast Asia Write Award (2004).

soon hock (*Oxyeleotris marmorata*) The *soon hock* or marbled goby is a fish that superficially resembles a grouper, but lives and breeds in fresh and brackish water. It grows to over 50 cm in length and is an expensive delicacy in Singapore. Wild populations can be found in the island's reservoirs. They tend to lurk camouflaged and motionless on the muddy beds of their habitat to ambush prey such as small fish and prawns. *See also* FISHES.

Speaker of Parliament The role of the Speaker is to preside over PARLIAMENT and to regulate the conduct of debate. He also rules on matters of procedure and order,

and tries to ensure that the voice of the minority is heard. The Speaker is empowered to mete out punishments to errant members. In the Speaker's absence, the Deputy Speaker takes on his duties.

Parliament elects a Speaker after a general election. Traditionally, the Speaker is also a MEMBER OF PARLIAMENT, but this is not always necessarily the case. Singapore's first Speaker, Sir George Oehlers, was not one when he was elected Speaker, nor were A.P. RAJAH and PUNCHARDSHERAM 'PUNCH' COOMARASWAMY.

Speakers' Corner Established at Hong Lim Park on 1 September 2000, Speakers' Corner is a place where citizens may speak their minds to the public without applying for permits, which would otherwise be required by the Public Entertainments and Meetings Act.

The need to liberalize the rules on public speaking was raised by opposition politician CHEE SOON JUAN, who challenged the law by speaking in public without a permit in 1998 and 1999. Commentators asked whether Singapore should have its own version of London's Speakers' Corner in Hyde Park. The government initially resisted the idea, but later decided to introduce Singapore's own Speakers' Corner.

Under the Public Entertainments and Meetings (Speakers' Corner) (Exemption) Order, speakers using the site are free from discretionary licensing, but must register at a police station. Speakers must be Singapore citizens. Religious matters are off-limits. Also not allowed are sound-amplification devices, banners and placards. Speakers receive no immunity from other laws limiting free speech, such as those relating to DEFAMATION and contempt of court.

Although used occasionally by individuals and organizations—notably the political reform group, THINK CENTRE—Speakers' Corner has had little impact on political debate.

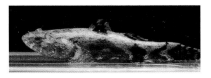

Soon hock

Special Assistance Plan schools Commonly known as SAP schools, these allow students to learn MANDARIN as a first language. The aim is to enable pupils to be effectively bilingual in both English and Chinese and also inculcate in them traditional values in a Chinese-school environment.

SAP schools were established in 1979 by the Ministry of Education to preserve the unique culture and traditional values taught in old Chinese schools. Many SAP schools are historically associated with the Chinese community in Singapore.

See also BILINGUALISM.

Special Branch A branch of the state police that deals with national security matters. A Special Branch was established in 1916 to deal with subversion in Singapore. However, it was understaffed and did not become a major security force until the EMERGENCY was declared in 1948.

In 1963, when Singapore became part of Malaysia, the department became part of the Malaysian Special Branch. After SEPARATION in 1965, the Special Branch became part of the Ministry of the Interior and Defence until 17 February 1966, when it was established as the INTERNAL SECURITY DEPARTMENT.

Special Operations Command Front line unit of the SINGAPORE POLICE FORCE. The predecessor of the Special Operations Command (SOC) was the anti-riot squad formed in 1952, in the wake of the MARIA HERTOGH RIOTS. This squad eventually became the Police Tactical Unit. On 10 September 1992, the SOC was created to place under one command the Police Task

Speakers' Corner: speaker and audience on launch day, 2000.

Force, the Police Tactical Team (replaced by the Special Tactics and Rescue Unit in 1993) and the Police Dog Unit.

In response to changing urban security demands, the Police MRT Unit was formed in 2005 to provide security within and around Mass Rapid Transit stations and trains (*see* MASS RAPID TRANSIT/LIGHT RAIL TRANSIT SYSTEM). It was the first SOC unit to be formed with regular front-line policing from its inception. The SOC also provides secretariat support for the United Nations Peace Keeping Force.

Special Operations Force Counter-terrorism force. The Special Operations Force (SOF) is an independent unit within the ARMY's elite Commandos. SOF troops train rigorously with the US Delta Force, US Navy SEALs and other foreign special services. It takes about four years and many overseas stints before a soldier qualifies as a full-fledged SOF trooper.

The SOF was founded in 1984, but its existence was not publicized until 13 years later. Much about it is still secret. The number of troopers is not made known and identities of active personnel are classified.

The force was instrumental in the rescue of the passengers of Singapore Airlines Flight 117 on 27 March 1991 (*see* SQ 117 HIJACKING). For their courage, the commandos involved in the rescue were awarded the Medal of Valour.

Special Tactics and Rescue Unit Elite unit of the SINGAPORE POLICE FORCE, formed to provide 24-hour tactical armed-response capability. The Special Tactics and Rescue Unit (STAR) is equipped to respond to any incident involving armed criminals, hijacking or hostage situations.

STAR began as a part-time outfit, the Police Tactical Team. It was re-designated STAR under the SPECIAL OPERATIONS COMMAND in 1993. All officers undergo a gruelling nine-month selection and training programme. Before 11 September 2001, STAR's primary role was to neutralize armed and dangerous criminals, to resolve urban sieges involving hostages or firearms, to protect VIPs, and to escort particularly dangerous prisoners. After 9/11, the unit undertook anti-terrorism duties.

Sports Museum

In 2005, STAR acquired maritime assault capability to augment the Police Coast Guard and the REPUBLIC OF SINGAPORE NAVY in dealing with seaborne threats.

SPH MediaWorks Television station. Set up by SINGAPORE PRESS HOLDINGS (SPH) in May 2001, SPH MediaWorks Ltd was granted two free-to-air television licences following the liberalization of Singapore's media industry in June 2000. It launched the Mandarin Channel U and the English-language channel TVWorks in May 2001. Channel U proved to be a strong competitor in the Chinese television market.

However, TVWorks failed to attract large audiences and incurred substantial losses. The station found it difficult to compete with rival MEDIACORP's Channel 5, which had existing syndication deals for popular British and American programming. By mid-2001, SPH MediaWorks had re-packaged TVWorks as Channel i.

From 2002, MediaWorks and MediaCorp's channels competed for ratings. Discounted advertising rates, economic recession, the outbreak of Severe Acute Respiratory Syndrome in 2003 and the increasing popularity of cable television affected MediaWorks adversely.

On 17 September 2004, SPH MediaWorks announced a joint agreement with MediaCorp, to merge the television broadcast operations of the two companies under a new company, MediaCorp TV Holdings Pte Ltd. On 1 January 2005, Channel i ceased transmission, while Channel U continued to operate under the banner of MediaCorp TV.

See also TELEVISION BROADCASTING.

spiders *See* box.

Sports Museum Showcase for Singapore's sporting heritage. Located at the National Stadium, the Sports Museum was opened in May 1983 to coincide with the 12th Southeast Asian Games which Singapore hosted. The museum is a repository for sports objects of historical, aesthetic and scientific value, including the only Olympic medal won by a Singaporean (TAN HOWE LIANG). It also honours Singapore's most distinguished sportsmen and women in the SINGAPORE SPORTS COUNCIL HALL OF FAME.

Other displays include indigenous games and pastimes, and Singapore's sporting milestones.

SPRING Singapore Statutory board. SPRING (Standards, Productivity, and Innovation for Growth) Singapore was orginally the National Productivity Board (NPB), which was set up in 1972. In 1996, the merger of the NPB with the Singapore Institute of Standards and Industrial Research led to the formation of the Productivity and Standards Board. In 2002,

Spyros

this was renamed SPRING Singapore. Its overall mission is to enhance the competitiveness of enterprises. This involves promoting productivity, industry development, market access, enterprise capabilities and service excellence.

In addition, as the national standards authority, SPRING Singapore coordinates product standards, codes of practice and management system standards. It also regulates weights and measures.

SPUR The Singapore Planning and Urban Research Group (SPUR) was formed in 1964 to discuss issues related to the physical planning and development of Singapore at that time. It was de-registered as a society in 1973. By then, it had contributed much to the debate over the planning of modern Singapore.

SPUR was made up mainly of young architects and planners from Singapore's private and public sectors, idealistic and passionate about the effort to modernize Singapore. Among them were TAY KHENG SOON and WILLIAM LIM. Their alternative ideas and strategies were discussed at workshops, seminars, lectures and exhibitions, and in magazines they published. The group was one of the most energetic non-governmental organizations in its time.

Spyros Tanker involved in an industrial accident. At about 2.15 p.m. on 12 October 1978, a Greek tanker, *Spyros*, exploded at Jurong Shipyard while undergoing repairs. Some 76 persons were killed and another 69 injured, making this Singapore's worst-ever industrial accident. The explosion occurred just after about 150 workers had returned to the engine- and boiler-rooms of the vessel to start repairs and cleaning. The powerful blast threw debris 100 m from the 35,600-ton *Spyros*, while the resulting fire prevented dockside workers from rescuing those trapped in the vessel.

Eight fire engines and ambulances were called to the scene, but rescue workers were not able to board the ship to rescue the injured and remove the bodies of those killed in the blast until the fire had been brought under control. Casualties were evacuated by ambulance and helicopter. A commission of inquiry later discovered that many safety practices and pro-

spiders

Spiders are part of the arthropod family. Arthropods are animals with jointed legs and an outer skeleton. They include crustaceans (crabs, prawns), INSECTS, centipedes, millipedes and arachnids (spiders, mites, harvestmen and scorpions). Spiders are distinguished from other arthropods by having four pairs of legs, with no wings or antennae. They are equipped with spinnerets at the end of their abdomen for producing silk.

It is suspected that, out of over 40,000 spider species in the world, Singapore has hundreds. Spiders are little studied here but, with few exceptions, all spiders are venomous, equipped with poison fangs for overpowering prey and defending themselves.

It used to be a popular pastime among local children to catch fighting spiders (*Thiania bhamoensis*) and put them together to watch them fight. The fighting spider has no need for a web. It catches prey by pouncing on them.

In homes
Many spiders can be found inside homes. The housefly catcher (*Plexippus* spp.) is very common, often spotted on walls or on tree trunks, in sheltered corners or crevices. The common house jumper (*Menemerus bivittatus*) is a 'domestic' spider associated with man-made structures. Its eggs are laid in a white silken sac hidden in a crevice and guarded by the mother until they hatch.

Tiny house dwellers (family Oecobiidae) live in the walls of car porches, balconies and verandas. These fast-running spiders make small flat webs over wall crevices and indentations. Tent spiders (*Cyrtophora* spp.) (*1*) build huge, irregular three-dimensional webs. In neglected building corners, loose tangled webs of long-legged spiders can be found. Commonly known as daddy-long-legs (Pholcidae) (*2*), they hang upside down in their webs and vibrate vigorously when disturbed, becoming a blur to the intruder.

1

2

In forests
The St Andrew's cross spider (*Argiope* spp.) (*5*) lives in forests and mangroves. It builds a distinctive web 1–2 m from the ground, recognizable by the X-shaped, zig-zag bands of white silk in the centre of the web. The brilliantly coloured spider sits head down in the centre of the web, holding its legs in pairs in such a way that they are aligned along the four arms of the 'X'.

The leaf-dwelling daddy-long-legs (*Uthina atrigularis*) is found only in Singapore, in the primary forest of

In gardens and parks
One of the larger, more common spiders of forest, wasteland and garden is the golden web spider (*Nephila maculata*) (*3*). It spins golden silk. A similar but less common species, the batik golden web spider (*Nephila antipodiana*) is named for the intricate batik-like pattern on its abdomen. Squatting in the webs of these spiders are silver spiders (*Argyrodes* spp.). Many of them have long, thin legs and silvery spots on their bodies. They help themselves to insects trapped in the web of the host.

Jumping spiders (Salticidae) can be found in gardens, mangrove

Bukit Timah.

Wolf spiders (Lycosidae) (*6*) are ground creatures. The females are protective mothers. They carry their eggs in an egg-sac attached to their spinnerets. When the spiderlings emerge, they are carried on their mother's back, living off the remains of their yolk.

Vegetation above mangrove swamps and jungle streams is home to the Singapore fishing spider (*Thalassius* spp.) (*7*). The female is only 16 mm in length but capable of attacking small fish by diving into the water and dragging them ashore for feeding.

Crab spiders (Thomisidae) look and move like crabs. They wait stationary on flowers to ambush their prey. One species of crab spiders lives inside the

3

4

swamps, wasteland, forest and urban areas. They do not spin webs, preferring to spring on their prey and away from danger.

The fighting spider (*Thiania bhamoensis*) is a type of jumping spider. Some jumping spiders look like ants. By mimicking ants, the spiders protect themselves from predators who avoid ants.

The hairy Singapore tarantula (*Phlogiellus inermis*) (*4*) is a nocturnal creature that hides in silk-lined spaces among leaf litter in wasteland and gardens.

pitchers of common PITCHER PLANTS (*Nepenthes gracilis*).

In the forest, spiny spiders (family Araneidae) can easily be recognized; they have a hard, flat body armed with spines on the edge of the abdomen. The curved spiny spider (*Gasteracantha arcuata*) can be found among tree branches in BUKIT TIMAH NATURE RESERVE.

5

6

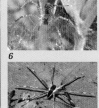

7

---

cedures had been ignored while the *Spyros* was undergoing repairs.

SQ 006 crash On 31 October 2000, SINGAPORE AIRLINES flight SQ 006 crashed at Chiang Kai Shek International Airport in Taipei, Taiwan. Of the 179 passengers on board the flight, 83 perished. The airplane had been preparing to take off in bad weather during Typhoon Xangsane, and had taxied down a runway that was closed for repairs. As the plane attempted to take off, it smashed into concrete barriers and heavy construction machinery on the runway, and exploded.

An 18-month inquiry undertaken by Taiwan's Aviation Safety Council found that poor weather and pilot error were the 'probable causes' of the tragedy. Singapore's Ministry of Communications and Information Technology concluded, however, that the accident was due to 'a failure of the aviation system' rather than any single factor.

SQ 117 hijacking On 26 March 1991, SINGAPORE AIRLINES shuttle flight SQ 117 took off at 9.15 p.m. from Kuala Lumpur with 118 passengers and a crew of 11. A few minutes later, four Pakistani men, armed with explosives and knives, hijacked the plane. When it landed at CHANGI AIRPORT at 10.15 p.m., the hijackers identified themselves as members of the Pakistan People's Party (PPP). They demanded the release of 11 PPP leaders from prisons in Pakistan. They also wanted to speak with the Pakistani ambassador, and with PPP leader Benazir Bhutto, the former prime minister of Pakistan. In addition, the hijackers demanded that the plane be refuelled to take them to Australia.

They threw two crew members off the plane and issued an ultimatum at 6.45 a.m., threatening to kill one passenger every ten minutes if their demands were not met, starting five minutes after their announcement. Three minutes into the countdown, a team of 20 commandos from the SPECIAL OPERATIONS FORCE stormed the plane. All the hijackers were shot dead. The rescue was completed in 30 seconds. None of the 129 hostages on board were injured.

SQ 006 crash: wreckage on runway at Chiang Kai Shek International Airport.

Sri Mariamman Temple

Sri Srinivasa Perumal Temple

Sri Sivan Temple

Sree Narayana Mission Charitable organization. The mission was registered in Singapore in 1948 and named after the Indian saint-philosopher and social reformer, Sree Narayana Guru. Engaging mostly volunteers, it provides social and community services such as family and legal counselling, daycare, scholarships and bursaries for the needy. It also runs homes for the destitute, regardless of race, religion or language.

Sreenivasan, B.R. (1909–1977) Doctor. At the age of 15, Baratham Ramaswamy Sreenivasan won a scholarship to study at the King Edward VII College of Medicine. He graduated at the age of 21 and joined the Colonial Medical Service as an assistant doctor. During the JAPANESE OCCUPATION, it was local doctors, including Sreenivasan, who took over the running of the medical service from the British.

Sreenivasan resigned from the government service in 1947 and set up his own general medical practice on Serangoon Road. He saved enough funds in this period to be able to travel to the United Kingdom to obtain his MRCP. Upon his return to Singapore, Sreenivasan taught at the General Hospital (later Singapore General Hospital) twice a week while continuing to run his own general practice.

Together with other physicians, Sreenivasan formed the SINGAPORE

Sri Krishnan Temple

MEDICAL ASSOCIATION in 1959 to represent all doctors in Singapore, becoming the founding president of this association. He was also founding president of the College of General Practitioners in Singapore (1971). In this and other positions, he lobbied for the recognition of general practice as a distinct discipline of medicine in Singapore. Sreenivasan was appointed principal of the University of Malaya in Singapore (1961–62) and was the first Asian vice-chancellor of the University of Singapore (1962-63).

Sri Guru Nanak Satsang Sabha This temple was founded in 1953. Its early members were SIKHS from Western Punjab—a region incorporated into Pakistan as a result of the partition of India in 1947. Many Sikh immigrants settled in Singapore following Partition.

The Sri Guru Nanak Satsang Sabha was originally based in an old KATONG bungalow on Wilkinson Road. As the local congregation grew, an adjoining bungalow was also acquired. In 1969, a new two-storey temple was constructed on the site at a cost of $600,000.

Sri Krishnan Temple Located at Waterloo Street, the Sri Krishnan Temple originated as a shrine built in the 1870s by a Gujarati, Hanuman Bheem Singh. Though the temple began with the worship of Lords Vinayaka and Hanuman, Lord Krishna is now its primary deity. It is famous for its DEEPAVALI and Krishna Jayanthi celebrations. Many worshippers from the KUAN IM THONG HOOD CHO temple next door light incense sticks in front of the Sri Krishnan Temple as well.

Sri Mariamman Temple Singapore's first Hindu temple was established in 1827 on South Bridge Road, in the heart of Chinatown. It was built for believers in the goddess Sri Mariamman, most of whom came from South India. A statue of the

deity was consecrated at the time and still stands in the main sanctum.

Credit for establishing the temple goes to NARAYANA PILLAY, a clerk with the East India Company in Penang who arrived in Singapore with Sir Stamford Raffles in 1819. The temple was also known as Sithi Vinayagar and Gothanda Ramaswamy Mariamman Temple, or the Kling Chapel. In its early days, the temple served as the Registry of Marriages, Registry of Deaths and mediation centre for Hindus. Since the 1980s, free medical services have been available at its premises. The temple has been renovated several times. It remains the site of the annual THEEMIDHI (fire-walking ceremony). The temple was gazetted as a national monument in 1973.

Sri Sivan Temple Hindu temple. The temple was originally built in 1821 and rebuilt in the 1850s on Orchard Road. It was gazetted under the MOHAMMEDAN AND HINDU ENDOWMENTS BOARD in 1915. When it encountered financial difficulties, funds from the Chettiar community helped in the maintenance of the temple, especially in its early years. Since its beginnings, the temple has undergone at least four consecration ceremonies—in 1905, 1943, 1964 and 1993. In the 1980s, the temple faced a change in location due to construction of the Mass Rapid Transit line, moving from Orchard Road to a temporary site at Serangoon Road. In 1993, it shifted to a permanent site at Geylang East Avenue 2.

The structure of the present temple is unique, as it blends both north and south Indian architectural elements. The main idols enshrined in the temple, Vishwanathar and Vishalakshi, are god-forms venerated in Benaras, India. Visited frequently by North and South Indian devotees, the temple is particularly known for celebrating Shivarathiri, a festival associated with Shiva.

Sri Srinivasa Perumal Temple Singapore's first temple for worshippers of Lord Vishnu (also known as Perumal). The temple was established in Serangoon Road in 1855, on

Sri Guru Nanak Satsang Sabha

Sri Thendayuthapani Temple

land bought from the East India Company. The building has been renovated several times since, but one feature remains: a well dug in the early 1900s.

The temple caters to the spiritual, social and cultural needs of Vishnu worshippers, and also to the larger Indian community. It has played a significant role as a starting point for the *kavadi*-carriers in the THAIPUSAM festival. The temple was gazetted as a national monument in 1978.

Sri Thendayuthapani Temple The oldest Hindu temple in Singapore devoted to Lord Murugan, second son of Lord Shiva. The Sri Thendayuthapani Temple was built in Tank Road in 1859 by the NATTUKOTTAI CHETTIARS. It is also known as the Subramaniam (one of Murugan's many names) Temple and the Chettiar's Temple.

The temple began as a small shrine under a bodhi tree. Over the next 140 years, it developed because of its importance to the growing number of Hindu Tamils in Singapore. It was renovated and restored in 1936 and 1955, and rebuilt in its present form in 1983. At THAIPUSAM, the temple is the finishing point for the 4-km procession from SRI SRINIVASA PERUMAL TEMPLE in Serangoon Road.

Srivijaya Empire: Buddha image from c. 8th century CE.

Sri Vairavimada Kaliamman Temple One of the oldest Hindu temples in Singapore dedicated to the goddess Kali. The Sri Vairavimada Kaliamman Temple, built in the mid-19th century, originally stood at Killiney Road, where it served workers and residents living in and around the orchards there. It moved three times before settling in Toa Payoh.

The new temple was consecrated in March 1986. When additional sanctums and facilities were added in 2001, another consecration ceremony was held. It is one of four temples administered by the HINDU ENDOWMENTS BOARD, and was the first Hindu temple to have a kindergarten on its premises.

Sri Warisan Som Said Performing Arts Performing arts company founded by SOM SAID in 1997 to promote Malay culture, particularly dance and music, through stage shows and arts-education programmes. Besides offering regular showcases of new works in traditional and contemporary Malay dance, it has performed on television and has represented Singapore at festivals abroad, such as the first Manila International Folk Dance Festival in 2003 and the World Festival of Folklore in Belgium in 2005. It has also participated in cross-cultural projects such as *Africa Meets Asia* (2002), in which it worked with musicians from Ghana, Senegal and Zimbabwe as part of the World of Music, Arts and Dance Festival in Singapore.

Srivijaya Empire Kingdom formed in Palembang, south Sumatra, in the 7th century CE. It is first mentioned in the year 672 CE, when a Chinese pilgrim named Yijing, on his way to India, sailed in ships belonging to the ruler of Srivijaya. Yijing stayed in Srivijaya for six months, and recorded it having a large Buddhist monastery. Returning from India after 17 years, he stopped and spent three more years in Srivijaya before finally reaching China in 695 CE.

In the late 7th century Srivijaya expanded its control to encompass the major ports of Malayu (Jambi) and Kedah at the north end of the Strait of Malacca. Its main goal may have been to monopolize trade with China. For the next 350 years, until around 1025, Srivijaya seems to have been China's main link with India and the Persian Gulf and Red Sea. Internally, Srivijaya's rule probably extended from Jambi to Lampung and the offshore island of Bangka, corresponding to the distribution of early inscriptions containing oaths of loyalty to the Srivijayan ruler.

Srivijaya's ruling clan were Buddhist. Their history is not well known, but in the mid-9th century, Balaputra, a Javanese prince of the Sailendra clan, was expelled from Java; according to an inscription found in India, he became Srivijaya's ruler. It is believed that Srivijaya had some previous relationship with the Sailendras. Chinese sources record frequent conflicts between Srivijaya and Java, in which Srivijaya was often the winner.

Archaeological excavations at Palembang have yielded remnants of temples, sculptures, inscriptions, and foreign goods such as ceramics and glass, all evidence of Srivijaya's extensive trading network. Chinese sources of the Tang Dynasty depict Srivijaya as one of the wealthiest kingdoms in the world.

In the early 11th century an important Buddhist scholar from India, best known as Atisha, moved to Srivijaya where he remained for several years. He was then invited to move to Tibet and reform Buddhism there. This and other information suggest that Srivijaya was an active centre of Buddhist thought and teaching for over 300 years.

Srivijaya's downfall occurred in 1025, when the Chola kingdom in Tamilnadu sent a fleet which conquered Palembang, Kedah, and Srivijaya's other important vassals. Palembang remained an important port, but its political grip over the Strait of Malacca was irretrievably lost. Malayu became the central node of Malay culture for the next 250 years, until it in turn came under Javanese influence around 1275. Thereafter, Chinese sources refer to Sanfoqi (Three Vijayas), rather than Shili Foshi (Srivijaya). Nevertheless, Palembang retained its lustre in Malay folklore. In the SEJARAH MELAYU (the Malay Annals), the first Malay ruler, Sri Tri Buana (SANG NILA UTAMA), appears on Bukit Seguntang, a hill in Palembang, and resides there for some time before moving to BINTAN, then to Singapore. The name Srivijaya does not appear in the Malay Annals, but traces of Srivijayan culture—

Sri Vairavimada Kaliamman Temple

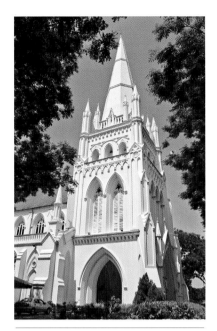

St Andrew's Cathedral: consecrated in 1862.

such as the title Sri Maharaja used by Srivijaya's rulers—indicate Srivijaya's long history as the focus of Malay identity.

Sriwana Cultural group. Sriwana was established in 1955 as a traditional orchestra for Malay wedding parties and fund-raising events. Led by dramatist and choreographer Nongchik Ghani, it was one of the earliest organizations to promote and develop Malay arts and culture.

Sriwana established its own dance troupe in 1957. The group presented its first dance-drama, *Puteri Gunung Ledang* (Princess of Mount Ophir), in 1962. Under the leadership of SOM SAID from the early 1970s until 1999, Sriwana's dance troupe performed regularly both locally and abroad, and held special workshops for children and young people. Sriwana has also established groups for drama, music and DIKIR BARAT (a type of choral singing). For the SINGAPORE ARTS FESTIVAL in 1999, Sriwana staged Sabri Buang's *Laluan* (Passage)—the first Malay play to have a pre-performance tour.

St Andrew's Cathedral Named after St Andrew, patron saint of Scotland, this church was constructed with funds from Scottish merchants. The site at the junction of North Bridge Road and Stamford Road was specially reserved for a church by Sir STAMFORD RAFFLES in 1823, when Church of England worshippers still depended on chaplains of EAST INDIA COMPANY ships and missionaries of other denominations.

What is seen today is not the first church built on the site. The first church was designed by GEORGE D. COLEMAN, in the neoclassical style. Its foundation stone was laid in 1834 and construction was completed in 1835. A steeple was later added. However, after being struck twice by light-

ning, the building was declared unsafe and closed in 1852. The foundation stone of the present building was laid on 4 March 1856 by Bishop Daniel Wilson of Calcutta. The architect was Lieutenant-Colonel Ronald MacPherson, and construction was carried out by Indian convicts. The church was consecrated on 25 January 1862, by Bishop G.E. Cotton of Calcutta, and was elevated to cathedral status in 1869.

St Andrew's Cathedral is one of the few examples of English Gothic architecture left in Singapore; MacPherson chose this style for its simplicity, which the convict labourers would be capable of executing. Despite its obvious resemblance to English churches, the cathedral includes some adaptations to the tropical climate, such as the porte cochère which allows passengers to alight from a vehicle under shelter, and generously proportioned windows that cool and ventilate the building

In 1973, St Andrew's Cathedral was gazetted as a national monument.

St Andrew's Community Hospital This was the first community hospital to be established in Singapore for non-chronic patients. It was opened by the St Andrew's Medical Mission in February 1992. The St Andrew's Medical Mission was founded in 1913 by Dr Charlotte Ferguson-Davie—wife of the first Anglican Bishop of Singapore—to provide medical care for the destitute, with a particular focus on women and children. Over the years, the mission provided a range of health care services. It opened dispensaries in 1913; became the St Andrew's Mission Hospital in 1923, then the St Andrew's Orthopaedic Hospital for Children in 1938; and finally a community hospital in 1992.

Being a voluntary welfare organization, the hospital is funded by government grants, subsidies and public donations. Some 90 per cent of its beds are subsidized. It provides in-patient services, including rehabilitative care, continuing medical care, sub-acute care, respite care, physiotherapy, occupational therapy and speech therapy. The hospital runs a Day Rehabilitation Centre for discharged patients as well as for others who have been referred for regular therapy sessions. The hospital is located next to Changi General Hospital.

St Andrew's School One of Singapore's oldest boy's schools, it comprises St Andrew's Junior and Secondary Schools. It was founded on 8 September 1862, as St Andrew's (Church of England) Mission School. The school later moved to Upper Hokkien Street, then to Victoria Street and then to Stamford Road in 1875, where it remained for the next 65 years. In July 1940, it moved to a pink, two-storey building with fish-scale markings at Woodsville.

In January 2006, St Andrew's three separate schools—St Andrew's Junior and

St Andrew's School

Secondary Schools, and St Andrew's Junior College—came together at St Andrew's Village in Potong Pasir.

Popularly referred to as the 'Saints', St Andrew's students are known for their rugby-playing prowess. Diplomat KISHORE MAHBUBANI, and academic and social critic Cherian George are alumni.

ST Engineering Singapore Technologies Engineering (ST Engineering) is an engineering group active in the aerospace, electronics, marine and land industries. Created in December 1997, it is an amalgamation of four listed companies: ST Aerospace, ST Electronics, ST Kinetics and ST Marine.

ST Aerospace is the world's largest company operating in third-party independent aviation maintenance, repair and overhaul. It supports a range of aircraft, engines and related components through its international network of aviation hubs. ST Electronics specializes in the design and delivery of proprietary electronics system solutions. ST Kinetics is a supplier of specialty vehicles and defence products and services. ST Marine provides shipbuilding, repair and conversion services for vessels.

ST Engineering is a major player in the defence and military sectors. Outside Singapore, its clientele includes the various armed forces of the Philippines, the United States, Botswana, New Zealand, Sweden, India, Thailand and Kuwait.

The group has about 16,000 staff in more than 100 subsidiary and joint-venture

Sri Warisan Som Said Performing Arts

St Joseph's Church

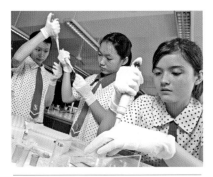

St Margaret's Girls' School

companies, in 29 cities over 17 countries. It posted net profits of $396 million on revenues of $3.34 billion in 2005. ST Engineering is a government-linked company; its largest shareholder is TEMASEK HOLDINGS, which holds a 55 per cent stake.

St George's Church Standing on a small hill once known as Mount Harriet, St George's Church was built for British troops at the nearby Tanglin Barracks. Designed by colonial architect William Henry Stanbury, it cost £2,000 to construct with materials imported from England.

The Romanesque-style church of 1910 has a distinctive tropical feature: it is open on both sides. Before the Japanese invasion, the garrison chaplain had the stained glass windows removed for safekeeping. As he did not survive the JAPANESE OCCUPATION, no one knows where the glass went. The replacement windows commemorate the British troops involved in defending Malaya and Singapore during the MALAYA CAMPAIGN. The Japanese used the church as an ammunition dump between 1942 and 1945.

The church lychgate was built in 1942 by interned soldiers of the British 18th Division for the Changi Camp cemetery. The gate was relocated to the church in 1952 when the graves were moved to KRANJI WAR CEMETERY AND MEMORIAL. When British troops withdrew from Singapore in 1971, the gate was dismantled and taken to Britain, and a replica installed at the church. St George's Church was gazetted as a national monument in 1978.

St John's Island *See* PULAU SAKIJANG BENDERA.

St Joseph's Church Shortly after the founding of modern Singapore in 1819, the first Catholics arrived in 1821. They were Portuguese. The first Catholic priest to be permanently based in Singapore was Father

Francisco de Silva Pinto Maia, who arrived from Macau on 7 April 1825. He started a small chapel on Victoria Street. He was succeeded by Father Vincente de Santo Catharina in 1850, who completed the building. This was consecrated as St Joseph's Church and used by the Portuguese and Eurasian Catholics for five decades.

Between 1906 and 1912, the congregation had a new church built. They commissioned the architectural firm of SWAN & MACLAREN. Officially opened on 30 June 1912, the new church took the form of a Latin cross, which was 65 m long and could accommodate a congregation of 1,500. The church has five altars. The main altar is dedicated to the Sacred Heart of Jesus. Saint Joseph's Church was gazetted as a national monument in 2005.

St Joseph's Institution Boys' secondary school. St Joseph's Institution (SJI) was founded in 1852 by six members of the De La Salle Brothers, a French Catholic order. Formerly known as St John's, the school started in an old chapel before moving to an *attap* (thatched roof) hut, and subsequently to the building at Bras Basah Road occupied by the present-day SINGAPORE ART MUSEUM.

During WORLD WAR II, the school served as a Red Cross Hospital and housed the Air Raid Precautionary Group. During the Japanese Occupation, SJI was renamed Bras Basah Road Boys' School and run along military lines, but it was returned to the De La Salle Brothers after the war. By 1988, the school had outgrown its premises and moved to a bigger site at Malcolm Road.

Well-known SJI alumni include politicians TONY TAN and GEORGE YEO, and PHILIP YEO, chairman of the Economic Development Board.

St Luke's Hospital This community hospital for the elderly was originally named St Luke's Hospital for the Elderly, and was

opened on St Luke's Day (18 October) 1997. Initially, most of the patients were elderly people who had suffered strokes and so experienced varying degrees of physical disability. In recent years, however, the hospital has served stroke patients from 40 years of age—a fact that prompted the hospital to change its name to St Luke's Hospital in 2004. The hospital also specializes in wound management and stoma care.

As a voluntary welfare organization, St Luke's Hospital is supported by funds from the Ministry of Health, as well as from Christian organizations and public donations. The total cost of building the hospital was $12.5 million, $8.7 million of which was provided by the government.

St Margaret's Girls' School St Margaret's Girls' School was the first girls' school in Singapore. A government-aided primary and secondary school, it was founded in 1842 by Mrs Maria Dyer, a missionary of the London Missionary Society. Moved by the sight of young girls being sold into slavery, Mrs Dyer started a home for homeless girls of all races in a tiny shophouse on North Bridge Road. The girls were taught English, sewing, cooking and Christianity.

The school relocated several times, finally settling in Sophia Road in 1861, where it was renamed the Chinese Girls' School. In 1900, it was taken over by the Church of England Zenanah Missionary

St George's Church

State crest

Society, and called the CEZMS School. The Bishop of Singapore gave the school its present name after World War II: it commemorates the 11th-century Scottish Queen Margaret, later St Margaret.

The school expanded academically and in enrolment. In 1960, the secondary school separated from the primary school and moved to its own premises on Farrer Road. The primary school remained at the original site on Wilkie Road, but in a new and larger building.

stamps *See* box.

Standard Chartered Bank The history of the London-based Standard Chartered Bank in Singapore goes back to 1859, when it established a banking agency to conduct exchange, deposit and remittances in connection with its other establishments. The bank's arrival was welcomed by the SINGAPORE FREE PRESS—it was observed that some of the most respected Singapore merchants had joined the Court of Directors. A high degree of local confidence and support was predicted.

In 1861, a supplemental charter allowed the agency to become a branch and engage in competitive exchange operations with China. Over the decades that followed, the bank maintained a close connection with the rapidly developing tin and rubber industries in Malaya, while playing an active part in financing a variety of other commercial ventures. Like its rivals the Hongkong and Mercantile banks, it was authorized to issue bank notes, a privilege it was to exercise until the end of the 19th century.

With the Japanese invasion of Singapore in 1942, normal operations were disrupted: officers were interned, and the premises were taken over by the occupation authorities. The bank came under Japanese administration. When Singapore was liberated, the bank's premises were found to be intact, although equipment and furniture had been removed.

In modern times, the bank has played an important part in establishing Singapore as a key financial centre. In 2006, Standard Chartered Bank had 3,200 employees and 19 branches in Singapore, including a Priority Banking Centre in Suntec City.

On 20 October 1999 it was among the first four foreign banks to be awarded qualifying full bank status, which allows banks to have additional branches and/or off-premise automated teller machines (ATMs), as well as to share ATMs.

The bank's premises have always been in the heart of the business district. After starting out in Prince Street (close to the Ocean Building) the bank moved to Battery Road; and then to a second site in Battery Road, at the end of RAFFLES PLACE, where SWAN & MACLAREN designed impressive premises in the classical style, completed in 1904. These were demolished in 1981 to make way for the present 44-storey structure now officially called Six Battery Road, but still known to many as the 'Stanchart Building'.

StarHub Info-communications company. StarHub was incorporated in 1998 as a provider of services over fixed, cable, mobile and Internet platforms. It was listed on the Singapore Exchange in October 2004. The stock is a component of the Straits Times Index as well as the FTSE ASEAN Index. The group's major shareholders include ST Telemedia, NTT Communications and MediaCorp.

With over 700,000 households subscribing to at least one of the group's services by 2005, and a network reaching over 99 per cent of homes, StarHub has become the second-largest telecommunications company in Singapore after SINGTEL.

StarHub is Singapore's sole licensed cable television provider. The group launched a digital cable television service in May 2004, and Singapore's first video-on-demand television service in June 2005.

In 2005, StarHub recorded profits of $221.4 million on a turnover of almost $1.6 billion.

State Cemetery The State Cemetery is located in Kranji, just next to the Kranji War Memorial. Spread over 2 ha, it is reserved for the burial of persons who have made a significant contribution to Singapore. President YUSOF ISHAK was buried there on 25 November 1970, and President BENJAMIN SHEARES on 15 May 1981. These are the only two graves at the cemetery. In 2005, the government also offered to bury former president WEE KIM WEE at the cemetery, but respected his wish to be cremated instead. The State Cemetery is maintained by the National Environment Agency.

state crest Singapore's present coat of arms was introduced on 3 December 1959, together with the national FLAG and NATIONAL ANTHEM, and was unveiled at the installation of the Yang di-Pertuan Negara (head of state), YUSOF ISHAK, on the steps of CITY HALL. This symbolized the attainment of statehood for Singapore. Prior to this, the coat of arms that had been used to represent Singapore was the British Royal Coat of Arms, featuring the lion and unicorn.

The state crest was designed by a committee headed by Deputy Prime Minister TOH CHIN CHYE. The crest consists of a shield emblazoned with a white crescent moon and five white stars against a red background. The red symbolizes universal brotherhood and equality, while the white signifies purity and virtue. The five stars represent five ideals: democracy, peace, progress, justice and equality. Supporting the shield are a lion on the left and a tiger on the right. Below the shield is a banner inscribed with the Republic's motto: 'Majulah Singapura' ('Onward Singapore'). The lion represents Singapore while the tiger represents Singapore's historical links with the Malay Peninsula. The state crest cannot be used for any advertisement or other commercial purpose. Only government bodies may display the crest within their premises.

STATS ChipPAC Known originally as ST Assembly Test Services, the company was set up in 1994 to complement its sister company, CHARTERED SEMICONDUCTOR MANUFACTURING, by providing chip assembly and testing support services.

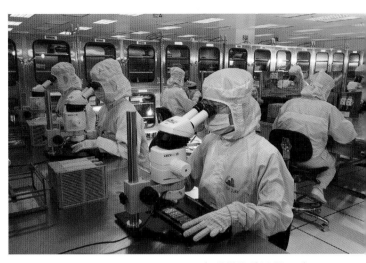

STATS ChipPAC: workers assembling chips.

Standard Chartered Bank: premises of the Chartered Bank in 1900 (left); advertisement from the 1960s.

In 2000, it was listed on both the Singapore and Nasdaq stock exchanges, and has since become a component of the Straits Times and Morgan Stanley Capital International benchmark stock indices.

ST Assembly Test Services acquired United States rival ChipPAC for US$1.2 billion in 2004 to emerge as the world's third-largest chip-testing and packaging firm. It leads in mixed signal testing and advanced packaging technology for semiconductors. The company has manufacturing facilities in Singapore, China, Malaysia, Taiwan and the United States, and a clientele of leading semiconductor companies in Asia, Europe and the United States.

In 2005, Stats ChipPac recorded a loss of $44 million on a turnover of $1.9 billion.

statutory boards Semi-independent government organizations with autonomy over operational functions. Each statutory board usually reports to a specific ministry, carrying out the plans and policies of that ministry. There are over 60 statutory boards looking after all aspects of Singapore life, including housing, education, defence, energy and health.

Along with joint-venture companies and state-owned companies, statutory boards came into existence after 1959 when Singapore attained self-government. They were established to implement the government's post-independence development strategies, such as promoting exports, attracting foreign investment, creating employment and diversifying the economy.

The first statutory board was the HOUSING & DEVELOPMENT BOARD, formed in 1960 to provide affordable housing for Singapore's rapidly growing population. In 1961, a second statutory board, the ECONOMIC DEVELOPMENT BOARD, was established to spearhead Singapore's industrialization.

As the term suggests, statutory boards are established by special acts of Parliament, which specify their functions, duties and powers, and their relationship to the responsible ministers. The boards may recruit, promote and remove their own staff, supervised by the responsible ministry. The Ministry of Finance may also issue overall government guidelines with which the boards are expected to comply.

See also SINGAPORE CIVIL SERVICE.

Stewart, S.T. (1910–1992) Civil servant and diplomat. Born in Penang, Stanley Toft Stewart was educated at St Xavier's Institution in Penang and then at Raffles College, Singapore, where he graduated with a first class diploma in arts (1933).

After graduation, Stewart joined the STRAITS SETTLEMENTS CIVIL SERVICE and served as assistant district officer in Province Wellesley and Penang. After World War II, he joined the Colonial Administrative Service and became district officer in Balik Pulau and Butterworth,

Stikfas: ball-jointed action figure.

Barbecued stingray

Penang. In 1952, he moved to Singapore to take up his appointment as deputy chairman of the Singapore Rural Board. He became chairman two years later.

In 1955, Stewart was appointed deputy secretary of the Ministry of Local Government, Lands and Housing. Subsequently, he became deputy chief secretary (1957), acting chief secretary (1958), permanent secretary of home affairs (1959–61), permanent secretary, Prime Minister's Office (1962–65) and head of the civil service (1962–65). In 1962, he was awarded the Meritorious Service Medal.

When Stewart left the Administrative Service in 1966, he was appointed Singapore's high commissioner to Australia (1966–69). He returned to become permanent secretary to the Ministry of Foreign Affairs. He retired in 1973; his last appointment was as chief executive director of the Singapore Sports Council.

Stikfas Company manufacturing model assembly figures. Founded by toy enthusiast Ban Yinh Jheow in December 2001, the name 'Stikfas' is short for 'stick and fasten'. This aptly describes the small, highly articulated action figures made up mostly of ball joints. In 2002, Ban landed a prestigious co-branding contract with computer games giant Electronic Arts when the latter bundled the action figure with the game *Emperor: Battle for Dune*. Consumers bought the game just for the action figures and the first lot of 200,000 pieces sold out. Stikfas was given the Best Original Concept award by *Toyfare*, an influential American toys magazine.

From 2002 to 2004, Stikfas was licensed to international toy company Hasbro Inc and saw a significant increase in Stikfas' product range, distribution network and market recognition. In mid-2004, Stikfas decided to regain control of its core line and manage it from Singapore.

stingray, barbecued A popular hawker dish. Stingray is a relatively recent addition to the Singapore food scene, having appeared only in the last 20 years. Grilled stingray is served with a spicy sambal sauce on a banana leaf.

stockbroking During the late 19th century, share-broking, or stockbroking, was carried out merely as an adjunct to the activities of plantation management and ENTREPÔT trad-

ing. Share-brokers provided financial services to support the buying and selling of shares by British corporations operating in Singapore. Typically, stockbroking firms would buy and sell shares on the London market through the intermediary of London brokers.

By the 1910s, share-broking had become a lucrative business in its own right, especially with the boom in RUBBER. As no local stock exchange existed during this era, trading was dominated by a single company, Fraser and Co. (founded in 1873), part of the FRASER & NEAVE Group. Fraser and Co. was so successful that it came to play the role of an unofficial stock exchange.

In 1930, the Singapore Stockbrokers' Association was formed, and trading was conducted on a more formal basis. In 1937, brokers from the Malay Peninsula were admitted, and the body was renamed the Malayan Stockbrokers Association.

In 1960, a number of brokers combined to form the Malayan Stock Exchange. The trading room was located in Kuala Lumpur. The following year, another room was opened in Singapore. In 1961, a board system was established with trading rooms in both Singapore and Kuala Lumpur. The two trading rooms were linked by direct telephone lines, thus forming a single market with the same shares listed at a single set of prices on both boards.

In 1964, the Stock Exchange of Malaysia was established. Following Singapore's separation from Malaysia in 1965, it was renamed the Stock Exchange of Malaysia and Singapore. In 1973, currency interchangeability between Malaysia and Singapore ceased, and the Stock Exchange of Malaysia and Singapore was divided into the Kuala Lumpur Stock Exchange Berhad and the Stock Exchange of Singapore (*see* SINGAPORE EXCHANGE).

storytelling Vernacular Chinese oral tradition, known in Mandarin as '*jianggu*' ('*gonggu*' in CANTONESE) or '*shuoshu*'. It was brought to Singapore by immigrants from China, and was a popular form of street entertainment until the 1960s.

Originally, itinerant storytellers performed on the streets to an impromptu audience often of coolies and day labourers.

Storytelling: performing to an audience in 1950.

stamps On average, Singapore Post produces over a million stamps—and nine new stamp issues—every year.

Singapore's first stamps
The first mail was sent from Singapore in 1826—the same year in which the EAST INDIA COMPANY established jurisdiction over the island. However, from 1826 to 1853, letters from Singapore were stampless. Stamps issued in India were used in Singapore from 1854 until September 1867, when Indian stamps (*1*) were issued for use in the newly-formed Straits Settlements.

The Straits Settlements
In December 1867, the Straits Settlements' first definitive stamps were issued (*2*). Straits Settlements stamps used portraits of reigning British monarchs (*3*)—a practice that would continue into the 20th century.

The Occupation
During the Japanese Occupation, pre-war Straits Settlements and Malaya stamps were overprinted for use in 'SYONAN'.

Since Independence
Since 1965, Singapore has issued definitive stamps every few years. In 1969, the 150th anniversary of Singapore's founding was commemorated by the issue of six stamps (*9*). In 2004, a set of four stamps was issued to mark the 150th anniversary of the first stamp to be used in Singapore (*10*).

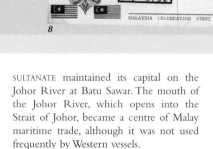

The post-war years
In 1946, Singapore became a separate Crown Colony, and overprinted pre-war Straits Settlements stamps were used. The first stamps featuring the word 'Singapore' were issued in 1948 (*4*). A $1 stamp featuring an image of the statue of Sir Stamford Raffles (*5*) was printed in 1955. Further stamps were issued following the achievement of self-government in 1959 (*6–7*). Following merger with Malaysia in 1963, Malaysian stamps (*8*) were used in Singapore.

Before beginning, the storyteller would light a joss stick. As he told his story, the joss stick would burn. When it burned out, he would stop, and leave the audience in suspense. At this point, a can would be proffered and the audience invited to put in money in order to hear the rest of the tale.

The stories told were usually folktales or excerpts from Chinese classics. These performances eventually disappeared along with the Chinese day labourer. However, storytelling enjoyed widespread popularity in the 1970s and early 1980s on the REDIFFUSION radio station. One of its most famous Cantonese exponents was Lee Fook Hong, better known to listeners as Lee Dai Soh (Big Fool). A famous Hokkien storyteller was Ong Toh, and a famous Teochew counterpart, Ng Shia Keng.

In the 1990s, Beijing actor Ren Baoxian held storytelling sessions at THE SUBSTATION Garden. The Storytelling Association, which was registered in 2006, was established to revive the tradition and bring it to a wider audience.

Strait of Johor The Strait of Johor separates Singapore from the Malay Peninsula. From the 16th to the 18th century, the JOHOR SULTANATE maintained its capital on the Johor River at Batu Sawar. The mouth of the Johor River, which opens into the Strait of Johor, became a centre of Malay maritime trade, although it was not used frequently by Western vessels.

Maritime use of the Strait of Johor declined markedly after the capital of the Johor sultanate was moved to the Riau Islands in the 18th century. The Strait of Johor regained importance only during the second half of the 19th century, when Chinese PEPPER AND GAMBIER plantation operators, having opened up the central and northern parts of Singapore between the 1820s and 1840s, began to shift their operations to Johor in the face of soil exhaustion and a decreasing supply of arable land in Singapore. At the peak of these plantation operations in Johor, as many as 50 junks plied between the SINGAPORE RIVER and Johor, carrying supplies across the Strait of Johor.

See also CAUSEWAY.

Straits of Malacca and Singapore The Malacca and Singapore Straits have been part of the main trade route between Europe and China for centuries. Singapore's growth as an ENTREPÔT in the 19th century can be partly attributed to its location astride this important sea lane. The straits continue to be vital today. About 63,000 ships pass through the Strait of Malacca each year, carrying half of the world's oil and a third of the world's trade. About 26 tankers, carrying a total of 10 million barrels of crude oil, pass through the straits each day.

The Straits of Malacca and Singapore also carry a significant amount of container traffic. In fact, three of the top 20 container ports in the world—the Port of Singapore, Port Klang and the Port of Tanjung Pelepas—are located along these waterways. In 2005, Singapore, the top container port in the world, handled 23.2 million TEUs (Twenty-foot Equivalent Units) while Port Klang (ranked 14th) handled 5.5 million TEUs. The Port of Tanjung Pelepas (ranked 19th) handled 4.2 million TEUs.

The straits are vital to Singapore's economic health. To safeguard these sea lanes, Singapore has adopted a multi-pronged strategy. Equipped with its stealth frigates, the REPUBLIC OF SINGAPORE NAVY plays an important role in keeping the lanes open. Singapore also works with Malaysia and

Indonesia to conduct joint sea and air patrols to combat threats like piracy and maritime terrorism. Indonesia, Malaysia and Singapore are parties to the United Nations Convention on the Law of the Sea (UNCLOS), which gives the right of transit passage to ships navigating through the straits. UNCLOS recognizes that the Malacca and Singapore Straits are straits used for international navigation. The three littoral states cooperate to maintain the safety of navigation and to prevent marine pollution through a Tripartite Technical Experts Group and by working with the International Maritime Organization.

In 2005, the foreign ministers of Indonesia, Malaysia and Singapore jointly issued the Batam Statement which reaffirms the sovereignty and sovereign rights of the littoral states in and over the Straits of Malacca and Singapore; upholds their primary responsibility over the safety of navigation, environmental protection and maritime security in the straits; acknowledges the interest of user states and relevant international organizations and the role they play in the straits; and welcomes closer collaboration with, and the assistance of, the user states, relevant international organizations and the shipping community in the areas of capacity-building, training and technology transfer.

Straits Settlements In 1826, the EAST INDIA COMPANY united the settlements of Singapore, Malacca and Penang to form the Presidency of the Straits Settlements. This presidency was abolished in 1830, and the Straits Settlements became a residency. It was dependent on the Presidency of Bengal, under the governor-general of India. In 1851, the Straits Settlements were removed from the Bengal presidency and brought directly under the governor-general. When the East India Company was abolished in 1858, the administration of India was transferred to the British Crown. The Straits Settlements continued to be ruled from Calcutta. However, the Indian government there was too far away from and unfamiliar with conditions in the settlements. It failed to understand and respond quickly to the needs of the local population. The Straits Settlements agitated for a transfer to the Colonial Office.

In 1863, a commission was appointed to investigate the matter. Sir Hercules Robinson, the principal member of the commission, advocated the transfer. Negotiations went on until 2 June 1866, before the India Office, War Office and Treasury all agreed to it.

On 1 April 1867, the Straits Settlements became a British Crown Colony, making the settlements directly answerable to the Colonial Office in London instead of the Calcutta government in India. Earlier, on 4 February, a 'Letters Patent' had granted the settlements a colonial constitution. This allocated much power to the settlements' governor (*see* GOVERNORS).

Additional territories became part of the Straits Settlements colony over the years—the Dindings area of Perak (1874–1934), Labuan (1906–46), the Cocos Keeling islands (1886–1955), and Christmas Island (1900–58). Singapore was the centre of government, commerce and policy-making. The first colonial governor appointed by the Crown was Colonel Sir HARRY ORD. He ruled with an Executive and a Legislative Council.

World War II brought the Straits Settlements to an end. After the end of the JAPANESE OCCUPATION, Singapore and Malaya came under British Military Administration. This lasted until April 1946, when Malacca, Penang and the peninsular Malay States were incorporated into a MALAYAN UNION that became the Federation of Malaya in 1948. Singapore remained a separate colony.

Straits Settlements Civil Service The emergence of a distinct civil service for the STRAITS SETTLEMENTS can be traced to 1805 when Penang was made a presidency under the EAST INDIA COMPANY (EIC). Prior to this, Penang had been administered as a residency under the Bengal presidency, and had been governed by the Bengal Civil Service.

When Penang was constituted as the Eastern Presidency in 1805, the EIC decided to establish a Straits Civil Service that would be separate from the civil service in India, composed of men specifically trained for local conditions. Civil servants destined for the Straits received preliminary training in the form of a general education at the EIC's Haileybury College in the United Kingdom. They were also to receive specific training at the destinations of their service. However, there were no institutions in the Straits at which civil servants could be trained in local languages and customs. Many civil servants thus became acquainted with local customs in the course of their work and learnt local languages on their own initiative. It was only in 1826 that measures and funding were introduced to encourage civil servants to learn local languages.

Singapore and Malacca were combined with Penang to form a single presidency with a centralized civil establishment in 1826. The EIC had introduced this centralized system in order to economize on expenditure. However, the presidency incurred heavy deficits, and the EIC reduced it to the rank of residency under the control of the Bengal government in 1830. This brought to an end regulations encouraging the learning of local languages, and reduced the number of positions that each official could hold. For example, the three civil servants stationed in Singapore divided between them the duties of superintendent of lands; chief of police; superintendent of convicts, magistrate and commissioner of the Court of Requests; superintendent of public works; and various other responsibilities. The number and distribution of civil servants remained largely unchanged between 1830 and 1867.

The Straits Settlements Civil Service took its most distinct form after 1867, when control of the settlements was transferred to the Colonial Office. The Colonial Office saw the necessity to provide the Strait Settlements with a civil service which would, from the beginning, be acquainted with the languages and customs of the local population, rather than a collection of officials who had experience in India. After 1867, cadets were recruited specifically for service in the Straits Settlements.

Initially, cadets were nominated by the secretary of state for the Colonies, and took a non-competitive examination designed to ensure that they possessed a certain level of general intelligence and writing skills. In 1869, examinations were made competitive. In 1882, recruitment was made open to public competition, and the practice of nomination by the secretary of state was abandoned. In 1896, the civil service of the Straits Settlements was joined by that of the recently formed Federated Malay States of Perak, Selangor, Negri Sembilan and Pahang. The two were viewed as different branches of a single service, and officers could be transferred from one service to the other. In 1920, the name Malayan Civil Service was approved for the Straits Settlements and Federated Malay States. From 1921, the service became widely known in official parlance by its abbreviation—the MCS.

See also SINGAPORE CIVIL SERVICE.

Straits Settlements Volunteer Force The first volunteer corps was formed in Singapore in 1854 after the recurrence of riots between the Hokkiens and Teochews in Singapore. Formed to protect internal security, it was called the Singapore Volunteer Rifle Corps

STRAITS SETTLEMENTS

N

Penang

Malacca

Strait of Malacca

0   100 km

Singapore

Straits Settlements Volunteer Force

The Straits Times: *1869 issue (top); contemporary issue of the paper.*

and supported by the governor, Colonel WILLIAM BUTTERWORTH. A second corps was formed in 1857 and was officially recognized by the Indian government after the Indian Mutiny broke out. After this corps was disbanded, the Singapore Volunteer Artillery Corps was formed in 1888. This was succeeded by the Singapore Volunteer Corps in 1901, which was itself absorbed into the Straits Settlements Volunteer Force formed in 1921.

The force was deployed during the Malaya Campaign—including the Battle for Singapore in 1942. Following the JAPANESE OCCUPATION, some Eurasian Volunteers were interned as prisoners of war with their British officers. Malay Volunteers were released while some 200 out of 300 Chinese Volunteers were massacred during mopping-up operations by the Japanese (*see* SOOK CHING). The Straits Settlements Volunteer Force was disbanded in 1954, and the Singapore Volunteer Corps was absorbed into the Singapore Military Forces without a change of name.

One of the best-known Volunteers was Dr GOH KENG SWEE, who later became Singapore's first defence minister. Several other Volunteers became pioneer officers of the SINGAPORE ARMED FORCES.

Straits Steamship Company This company was founded in 1890 by Dutch trader T.C. Bogaardt, as a partnership with Chinese businessmen in Malacca and Singapore, including TAN JIAK KIM, LEE CHENG YAM and TAN KEONG SAIK. The company began with five ships, of which three were contributed by the Tans' family business. Set up to serve ports along the coast of the Malay Peninsula, the Straits Steamship Company transported immigrant labour and supplies to the tin mines in the area, returning with tin ore for Singapore's PULAU BRANI smelter. Later, it offered passenger services.

Over the years, the company diversified, moving into areas such as property,

warehousing and distribution. In 1983, it was acquired by KEPPEL CORPORATION. In 1997, Straits Steamship was renamed Keppel Land, becoming the property arm of the Keppel Group.

Straits Times, The Singapore's most widely circulated and oldest surviving newspaper, its use of English, the main business language, allows it to reach a culturally diverse audience, unlike newspapers published in Malay, Chinese or Tamil. The paper started as *The Straits Times and Singapore Journal of Commerce* on 15 July 1845. Its founder-proprietor was Armenian businessman CATCHICK MOSES, and its first editor, ROBERT CARR WOODS, was a 29-year-old English journalist.

Although not Singapore's first newspaper, *The Straits Times* overtook its predecessors and fended off competitors to enjoy long periods of dominance. Publication was interrupted during the JAPANESE OCCUPATION of 1942–1945, when its premises were used by the *Syonan Times*, the English-language newspaper of the occupation administration.

Originally identified with major British-owned businesses, after the war *The Straits Times* began consciously to localize itself, in response to the rising tide of

nationalism. As Singapore framed its post-colonial future as part of Malaya, *The Straits Times* branded itself as 'Malaya's national newspaper' and moved its headquarters to Kuala Lumpur in 1959.

After Singapore separated from MALAYSIA in 1965, the newspaper continued to serve the two markets until the Malaysian government nationalized its Malaysian operations in 1973 and created the *New Straits Times*.

The Straits Times is the flagship of Singapore's largest newspaper group, SINGAPORE PRESS HOLDINGS. Selling more than 386,000 copies a day in 2005, *The Straits Times* is Singapore's most profitable media entity. It has unmatched news-gathering capacity, and is seen as Singapore's newspaper of record.

In view of competition from alternative news sources such as the Internet, *The Straits Times* launched an online edition, *The Straits Times Interactive*, in 1995. In 2006, it also launched an interactive forum STOMP (an acronym for Straits Times Online Mobile Print).

Straits Trading Company The Straits Trading Company Limited was incorporated in 1887, when founders Herman Muhlinghaus and James Sword decided to establish a business for the smelting of TIN. In 1890, the company opened its first smelting plant at PULAU BRANI, Singapore, and in 1902, it built eight more furnaces in Butterworth, Malaya. By 1912, it had become the largest tin-smelting company in the world, handling a third of the world's supply of tin.

The company subsequently diversified into hotel investment and management, property and financial investments. It is listed on the Singapore Exchange.

streaming Separation of students into various groups learning at different paces, based on academic performance in national standardized testing. The Report on the Ministry of Education 1978 proposed the introduction of ability-based streaming at the end of Primary 3, an ability-differentiated curriculum, and extensions to the length of schooling for weaker pupils. In

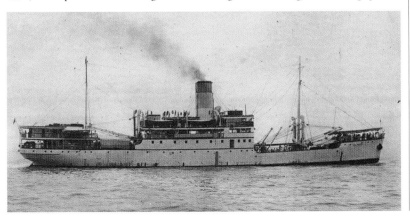

Straits Steamship Company: SS Darvel, *c. 1930.*

Su Guaning

addition, students were to be tracked at the secondary level. Over the years, there have been modifications to the programme, most notably postponing streaming to the end of Primary 4. In 2004, the ministry further relaxed the streaming system, giving schools the flexibility to develop their own Primary 4 year-end examinations. However, the streaming of pupils based on examination performance remains a major feature of the system.

Pupils who are academically less inclined are posted to the EM3 stream which focuses on foundational knowledge, while pupils who do well in the examinations may be offered the choice of studying Higher MOTHER TONGUE Language.

study mamas Popular term for mothers from China who accompany and support their children enrolled in Singapore schools. Known in Mandarin as '*peidu mama*', these women stay in Singapore on long-term social-visit passes. Few speak English, and most take on menial jobs to help make ends meet.

Stylers, The Popular music group. The instrumental band was formed in 1961 with Stewart Chen on vocals, John Teo on lead guitar, Randy Lee on rhythm guitar, Frankie Affendi on bass and Othman Neek on drums. This line-up came in runner-up in the 1962 Shadows Contest.

In early 1967, singer Ronnie See and drummer Elvin Wong joined the band. See brought a rhythm-and-blues sound to the group. Its unflagging performances at TEA DANCES gave it wide exposure. The Stylers were much sought after as a backing group for singers such as Robert Song, Lisa, Simon Junior, and Wong Ching Yen.

Guitarist Teo was considered one of the top five guitar players of the decade. He popularized the 'party LP' (a long-playing record including instrumental medleys of top hits). The band continued playing into the 1970s and 1980s. By the time they split up in the early 1980s, they were the most-

The Substation: promotional materials (below); building at Armenian Street.

The Stylers

recorded group in Singapore, with hundreds of releases on many different labels.

Su Guaning (1950–) Scientist, engineer and academic. Born in Taiwan, Su Guaning moved to Singapore when he was seven years old. He studied at Catholic High and Raffles Institution, and won a PRESIDENT'S SCHOLARSHIP. In 1967, he was awarded a COLOMBO PLAN Scholarship. He studied electrical engineering at the University of Alberta, Canada, and went on to earn a master's degree from the California Institute of Technology, and a PhD from Stanford University.

From 1986 to 1997, Su was Director of the Defence Science Organisation, corporatizing it as DSO NATIONAL LABORATORIES in 1997. He left in 1997 to head the Defence Technology Group at the Ministry of Defence. In 2000, he became the first chief executive of the Defence Science and Technology Agency. He has also played a prominent role in national science and technology policy since 1988, helping to establish the National Science and Technology Board, and serving on it from 1991 to 2001.

Su was awarded the Public Administration Medal (Gold) in 1998 and received the National Science and Technology Medal in 2003. He was awarded the Chevalier of the Legion of Honour by the president of France in 2005. He became president of NANYANG TECHNOLOGICAL UNIVERSITY in 2003.

Subordinate Courts Courts established under the Subordinate Courts Act. These include the District Courts, Magistrates' Courts, Coroners' Court, Juvenile Court, FAMILY COURT and Small Claims Tribunal. Some District and Magistrates' Courts—such as the Civil, Commercial, Criminal, Family and Traffic Courts—are specialized courts.

The senior district judge is the most important administrative and judicial officer in the Subordinate Courts. He presides over district judges, magistrates, coroners, registrars, deputy registrars and referees of the Small Claims Tribunal. He is appointed by the PRESIDENT of Singapore, on the recommendation of the CHIEF JUSTICE.

The civil jurisdiction of the District Court for all tort or contract matters is $250,000. In equity matters, the limit is $3 million. In criminal matters, it can mete out imprisonments of not more than seven years, impose fines not exceeding $10,000, or order up to 12 strokes of the cane.

The civil jurisdiction of the Magistrates' Courts is $60,000. Its criminal jurisdiction extends to imprisonment not exceeding two years; fines not exceeding $2,000; or a maximum six strokes of the cane.

Substation, The First independent contemporary arts centre, founded by the late playwright KUO PAU KUN in 1990. Formerly a PUB substation, its facilities include a visual arts gallery, a 120-seat theatre, and a café-cum-courtyard popular for musical performances. The Substation promotes local arts and culture in many ways, from film screenings and performances to poetry readings and forums. Its best-known events are *Moving Images*, a year-round film programme, and *Sept Fest*, an annual festival of various art forms.

Suez Canal This 193-km-long canal was conceived by French engineer Ferdinand de Lesseps, who also supervised its construction (1859–69). It opened to traffic on 17 November 1869. The canal reduced travelling time between Europe and Asia by one-third, and had a major impact on the growth of trade in Singapore during the late 19th and early 20th centuries.

The opening of the Suez Canal precipitated the replacement of sail by steam propulsion in the trans-oceanic trade, as the Red Sea could be successfully navigated only by steamships. This increase in steamship traffic in turn made necessary the establishment of coal depots along shipping routes between Europe and East Asia. As a result, the Strait of Malacca replaced the Sunda Strait as a preferred route for shipping, and Singapore became a coal depot. This solidified the island's position as the main port of call in the ENTREPÔT trade between Europe and Southeast Asia.

Singapore's imports and exports grew tremendously after the opening of the Suez Canal. There was a greater rate of growth in trade in Singapore in the period 1869–1914 than in the first 50 years after its founding.

sugar Europeans in Singapore developed an interest in the cultivation of sugar from the late 1830s onwards, after noting the success of Teochew planters in Penang and Province Wellesley. The first sugar estate on the island was established in 1836. WILLIAM MONTGOMERIE and JOSEPH BALESTIER founded sugar estates (known as the Kallangdale and Balestier estates, respectively) on the banks of Sungai Kallang. JOSE D'ALMEIDA also founded a smaller estate at Paya Lebar. However, all three of these estates failed, as Singapore had been excluded from the Sugar Act of 1835, which accorded preferential duties to various British overseas possessions by removing discriminatory tariffs that had favoured West Indian sugar imports to the United Kingdom. Moreover, there was inadequate land for large-scale sugar plantations in Singapore.

By the 1860s, European planters had overtaken the Chinese in terms of sugar cultivation in the Straits Settlements, although both groups maintained a symbiotic relation. The former provided processing technology and capital, while the latter provided labour. This relationship lasted until the end of the 19th century, when RUBBER overtook sugar as the most important crop.

Sultan Mosque Regarded as Singapore's principal mosque, it began as a simple structure with a three-tier tiled roof on North Bridge Road. This was built in 1826, in accordance with the 1824 treaty ceding Singapore to the British, which also promised a sum of money for rebuilding an old mosque in the Sultan's enclave.

The mosque has since been rebuilt on land added by the Sultan's descendants. In 1925, DENIS SANTRY of SWAN & MACLAREN was commissioned to design the present structure, paid for by grants from the royal family and contributions from the Muslim community. This included donations of green glass bottles from the poor, which have been incorporated into the base of the dome. After its completion, a constitution was drafted stipulating that the trustees of the mosque must comprise MALAYS, JAVANESE, BUGIS, ARABS, TAMILS and North Indian Muslims, to represent the multiracial nature of Singapore's Muslim community.

The mosque was gazetted as a national monument in 1975. In 1993, an annex was added for an auditorium and a multi-pur-

Suez Canal: in use in the 1870s.

pose hall. Sultan Mosque remains one of the largest MOSQUES in Singapore. Its prayer hall can accommodate 5,000 worshippers.

Sumida Haruzo, Lieutenant-Colonel (1902–46) Japanese military officer. Sumida joined the Japanese army in 1925. In 1935, he was trained as a KEMPEITAI (Japanese military police) officer. He was posted to China, and in May 1943 to Singapore, where he was appointed commanding officer of Kempeitai Section Number 3. In this position, Sumida came under pressure from his superiors to apprehend guerrillas responsible for acts of sabotage against Japanese interests. He became obsessed with finding evidence relating to the sinking of ships in Singapore harbour during OPERATION JAYWICK, and came to believe that the sabotage had been directed by civilian internees in Singapore using wireless communications. These suspicions led to the torture of civilian internees during the DOUBLE 10TH INCIDENT. In 1946, Sumida was tried for his role in authorizing the incident. He was found guilty and hanged.

Sun, Stefanie (1978–) Singer. Stefanie Sun Yanzi obtained a degree in sales and marketing from Nanyang Technological University. She released her first album, *Yan Zi*, in May 2000. One of the songs from this album—'Tian Hei Hei' (Cloudy Day*)*—soon became the most-requested song on Singapore radio, while the album itself sold 300,000 copies in Taiwan; 200,000 copies in China; 12,000 copies in both Hong Kong and Malaysia; and 17,000 copies in Singapore, making Sun the first Singaporean to sell more than 10,000 copies of an album locally.

Sun released her second album, *Wo Yao De Xing Fu* (My Desired Happiness), in 2000. More than 350,000 copies were sold worldwide, while a million copies of her

third album, *Feng Zheng* (Kite), released in 2001, were sold worldwide.

Sun won many popular music awards in the early years of her career, including Taiwan's Golden Melody Award in 2001. She was named Best Local Female Artiste at the Singapore Hits Awards several times, and was highly sought-after as a spokesperson and commercial star, especially in Taiwan. After taking a year's break from the music industry in 2003, Sun released her ninth album, *Wan Mei De Yi Tian* (A Perfect Day), in January 2005.

Sun Thian Keng Temple An inscribed tablet found at the original Malabar Street site of this Hokkien Taoist temple in 1981 suggests the temple was built between 1796 and 1821, making it one of the earliest temples to be built in Singapore. It was rebuilt and enlarged in the 1840s, and redecorated in 1903. Due to redevelopment of the area, the temple was temporarily located at Albert Street in 1986, before being moved to a permanent site at Geylang Lorong 29.

Sun Yat Sen (1866–1925) Chinese political activist and head of state. Born in present-day Guangdong, Sun was educated in Hawaii and Hong Kong. He worked mainly outside China to raise funds and support for a revolution to topple China's Qing Dynasty. His revolutionary alliance, known as the Tongmeng Hui, was founded in Japan in 1905.

Sun visited Singapore eight times between 1900 and 1911. He established the Singapore branch of the Tongmeng Hui on 6 April 1906 at a villa owned by a local supporter (*see* SUN YAT SEN NANYANG MEMORIAL HALL). In Singapore and the wider region, Sun and his supporters mobilized Chinese support for the revolutionary cause, and propagated an ideology known as the 'Three Principles of the

Sultan Mosque

Stefanie Sun

People'—nationalism, populism and 'the people's livelihood'.

Following an uprising in China in October 1911, the Qing Dynasty collapsed. The Republic of China was founded in 1912, and Sun was made president. In August of that year, the Kuomintang (Nationalist Party) was formed. In 1913, however, Sun was driven into exile by China's new president, Yuan Shikai. Sun returned to China in 1916, and by 1923, had become head of the Kuomintang government which ruled from the city of Canton (present-day Guangzhou), but which exerted little authority over many other parts of China. Sun died of liver cancer in Peking (present-day Beijing) shortly thereafter.

Sun Yat Sen Nanyang Memorial Hall Built in 1900 by businessman Boey Chuan Poh, this two-storey villa was later bought by Teo Eng Hock, a rubber magnate and supporter of the Chinese revolutionary movement led by SUN YAT SEN. Teo had originally acquired the property for his mother, and had named it Wan Qing Yuan (meaning 'a haven of peace in one's latter years'). He offered Sun Yat Sen use of the villa as a base when Sun visited Singapore in February 1906 to establish a branch of his alliance, the Tongmeng Hui. Sun visited the villa on subsequent trips to Singapore when undertaking fund-raising activities in the years before the Chinese revolution of 1911.

In 1937, the building was purchased by six of Sun's former comrades, who offered it to the Chinese Nanjing Republican Government. The villa was subsequently placed under the care of the Singapore Chinese Chamber of Commerce, so that it could be preserved as a historical site. During the JAPANESE OCCUPATION, the building was used by the Japanese as a communications centre and KEMPEITAI branch offices. After the war, it was used as the office of the Singapore Branch of the Kuomintang (Chinese Nationalist Party). It was handed back to the Chamber of Commerce in 1951. From 1964 to 1965, the the villa was refurbished to commemorate Sun and his revolutionary movement; it then became known as Dr Sun Yat Sen Villa. In 1966, a museum was opened at the villa to commemorate the 100th anniversary of Sun's birth.

The villa was gazetted as a national monument in 1994, and the Chinese Chamber of Commerce and Industry purchased additional land behind the villa to enlarge the building's exhibition space. After four years of restoration and the construction of an annex, the Sun Yat Sen Nanyang Memorial Hall was officially opened in November 2001, complete with a bronze statue of Sun in the gardens.

Sunfeng Xiangsong The *Sunfeng Xiangsong* is a Chinese rutter (navigator's diary), containing a vast collection of detailed sailing routes. It was written during the Ming dynasty. LONGYAMEN (Dragon Tooth Strait) is mentioned in eight different sets of sailing directions. Depth readings at both entrances into the strait are given, as well as the part flanked by present-day SENTOSA Island. The text instructed navigators not to sail through the strait at night—but gave no reason.

Sungai Pulai Major river system in Johor. Since 1964, Singapore's Public Utilities Board (PUB) has operated three water-treatment plants in Sungai Pulai, Sungai Skudai and Sungai Tebrau. Under the 1961 WATER AGREEMENT, Singapore is entitled to draw 86 million gallons of raw water per day from the Sungai Pulai (Gunung Pulai Reservoir) and Sungai Tebrau (Pontian Reservoir) water catchment areas until August 2011. Construction of these two reservoirs began in 1924. In 2002, Johor

Suntec City: inside the shopping mall.

announced that the three plants would be taken over by the state in 2011 when the water agreement ends. The Pulai River is also one of the few areas in the region with a natural deep harbour that can accommodate large ships. It was thus selected for the construction of the Port of Tanjung Pelepas.

Sungei Api Api Literally meaning 'Avicennia River' in Malay ('sungei' means 'river' and 'api api' refers to *Avicennia*, a MANGROVE plant species), Sungei Api Api is located in Pasir Ris. From the 1950s, large sections of the mangrove swamps along the coast of river were cleared. This led to the erosion of the beaches, which the mangroves had previously protected from the force of the waves. In the mid-1980s, the NATIONAL PARKS BOARD re-established mangrove swamps and extended the shoreline at the mouths of Sungei Api Api and Sungei Tampines. Park connectors (greenery-lined passages) were also built along their banks to link Pasir Ris and Tampines. About 10,000 seedlings of the fast-growing *Avicennia alba* mangrove were planted, enabling 2 km of shoreline to be extended 100 m into the sea.

Sungei Buloh Wetland Reserve *See* box.

Suntec City Singapore's largest office, convention and shopping complex. Built by a group of 11 Hong Kong businessmen, including Tan Sri Frank Tsao, Dr Li Ka Shing, Sir RUN RUN SHAW, Dr Li Dak Sum and Dr Cheng Yu Ting, Suntec City was officially opened on 20 August 1995.

The complex was master-planned by American architects I.M. Pei with Tsao & McKown, who worked with local firm DP Architects. The enormous complex, which includes one convention podium block and four office towers, offers 650,000 sq m of office, retail, exhibition and convention facilities. It also boasts Asia's largest column-

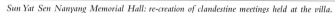

Sun Yat Sen Nanyang Memorial Hall: re-creation of clandestine meetings held at the villa.

Sun Yat Sen

1

Sungei Buloh Wetland Reserve

Nature reserve in northwest Singapore. One of the first gazetted nature reserves in independent Singapore, Sungei Buloh Wetland Reserve (SBWR) is a 131-ha wetland.

Shorebirds from Siberia make an annual journey to escape the harsh winter by flying south to Australia and New Zealand. One of the routes they take is the East Asian Flyway. Sungei Buloh lies on this route, and is one of the places that the BIRDS stop to rest, feed and prepare themselves for the next leg southward.

A significant number of migratory birds are recorded during the migratory season between September and April annually. Some of these birds spend the winter here. More than 1,000 Pacific golden plovers (*Pluvialis fulva*) and 200 whimbrels (*Numenius phaeopus*) were recorded during this period in 2001. The pacific golden plover, lesser sand plover (*Charadrius mongolus*) (*1*), the grey heron (*Ardea cinera*) (*3*), curlew sandpiper (*Calidris ferruginea*), little egret (*Egretta garzetta*) (*2*), whimbrel and common greenshank (*Tringa nebularia*) all winter at SBWR.

2

SBWR was officially opened on 6 December 1993 by then Prime Minister Goh Chok Tong, and gazetted and given legal protection in January 2002. Since 2002, the reserve has been part the East Asian Australasian Shorebird Network. It shares and exchanges information and expertise with an international community of more than 30 sites for the conservation of shorebirds.

MANGROVES, brackish ponds, freshwater ponds/marshes, mudflats and grassland are the five natural habitats SBWR protects. More than 200 bird species have been recorded, which is 61 per cent of the total bird species found in Singapore. SBWR's 60 ha of mangroves abut those at Kranji Dam, and together represent the largest stretch of intact mangrove forest left on mainland Singapore. This forest is a remnant of the extensive mangrove systems that used to fringe the Singapore coast.

The mangroves and mudflats of SBWR lie in the inter-tidal zone along the coast and the three main rivers, Sungei Buloh Besar, Sungei Bilabong Buloh and Sungei Buloh Kechil, that flow through the reserve. Relatively undisturbed mangroves are found at Pulau Buloh, a 9.5-ha island north of the reserve. Most trees here are more than 55 years old. These mature mangroves form a dense, closed canopy forest. Over the years, ongoing conservation and tree-planting programmes have added 10 more species of mangroves to SBWR.

The 53 species here are about 85 per cent of the total mangrove species in Singapore. Within the mangroves are good specimens of *Rhizophora* spp, *Bruguiera* spp, and *Sonneratia* spp. Ephiphytes and climbers such as *Dischidia* spp, *Finlaysonia obovata* and *Cymbidium bicolor* are also present.

As for animal life, visitors usually get to see the water monitor lizard (*Varanus salvator*). These 1- to 3-metre-long reptiles are often seen along the trails, swimming in the ponds or sunning themselves. Two 1.5-metre-long estuarine crocodiles (*Crocodylus porosus*) have been reported basking in the mudflat in Sungei Buloh Besar and next to the main bridge. A family of six smooth otters (*Lutra perspicillata*) and the palm civet cat (*Paradoxurus hermaphroditus*) have been regularly sighted. The long-tongued nectar bat (*Macroglossus minimus*) and the cave fruit bat (*Eonycteris spelaea*) are also common.

SBWR is one of Singapore's best places for spotting coastal fishes. It has about 100 species of marine fishes, or 25 per cent of the total fish species in the country.

Common fishes at SBWR are the giant mudskipper (*Periophthalmodon schlosseri*) (*4*), common tilapia (*Oreochromis mossambicus*), green

3

chromide (*Etroplus suratensis*), banded archerfish (*Toxotes jaculatrix*) and the spotted archerfish (*Toxotes chatareus*).

SBWR also serves as a popular outdoor classroom, providing innovative educational programmes and activities with the help of volunteers, corporate sponsors, schools and the local community. On average, the reserve gets 90,000 visitors annually. In 2003, Sungei Buloh was recognized as an ASEAN Heritage Park.

4

Mangroves.

---

free meeting area, covering 12,000 sq m. There is a multi-purpose ballroom, a gallery, 31 meeting rooms and a 596-seat theatre. Another notable feature of Suntec City is its 13.8-m-high Fountain of Wealth, which was listed by the *Guiness Book of Records* in 1998 as the world's largest fountain. The mall and office towers are owned by Suntec Real Estate Investment Trust (REIT), which is traded on the Singapore Exchange. The convention centre, which is not part of the REIT, is known as the Suntec City International Convention and Exhibition Centre. It has 100,000 sq m of exhibition space on six levels.

sup tulang Popular hawker dish. '*Sup tulang*' literally means 'bone soup'. This Indian Muslim dish consists of mutton leg and shin bones cooked in a spicy chilli sauce with a rich mutton soup base. The cartilage and marrow are eaten.

Supreme Court Highest court of the land. The Supreme Court comprises the High Court and the COURT OF APPEAL. The Court of Appeal has the following judges: the CHIEF JUSTICE as president of the court; vice-presidents; judges of appeal (other than vice-presidents); and other PUISNE JUDGES of the High Court.

The Court of Appeal has only appellate jurisdiction (the power to hear appeals and review court decisions), over all civil and criminal matters. It sits as a bench of at least three judges, or as many as seven, and hears appeals on points of law only, not fact. As such, it will not re-examine witnesses,

documents or other materials tendered at trial. The Court of Appeal's decision is final and binding on all courts in the judicial hierarchy except the Court of Appeal itself.

The High Court consists of puisne judges and JUDICIAL COMMISSIONERS. It has both original and appellate jurisdictions. In its appellate jurisdiction, it hears appeals

Sup tulang

Suratman Markasan

from the SUBORDINATE COURTS. In its original jurisdiction, it hears cases which are beyond the authority of the Subordinate Courts. Certain types of cases (e.g. murder) can only be tried at High Court. Likewise, cases where damages amount to more than $250,000 must be heard at the High Court.

The High Court also exercises supervisory and revisionary jurisdictions. In its supervisory jurisdiction, it ensures that all lesser courts and tribunals act within their given limits. The revisionary jurisdiction of the High Court empowers it to call for and examine proceedings of Subordinate Courts to satisfy itself of the correctness and legality of these decisions.

The High Court has no jurisdiction over certain family matters under Muslim law, such as marriage and divorces, but does have concurrent jurisdiction with the SYARIAH COURT over civil proceedings relating to maintenance of wife and child, custody and disposition, and division of property on divorce in the case of Muslim marriages.

Supreme Court buildings From 1939 to 2005, the Supreme Court was housed in the last great classical building commissioned in the colonial era. The site was bought by the government in 1934. Frank Dorrington Ward, Public Works Department chief architect (1930–39), was put in charge of the project and had to make the building fit in visually with its neighbour, the Municipal Offices building (*see* CITY HALL). The building's most striking features are its Ionic and Corinthian columns, and the 13-ton frieze—an allegory of justice, all produced by Milan-born sculptor RODOLFO NOLLI at a workshop in Scotts Road.

The building was gazetted as a national monument in 1992. In 2005, however, the Supreme Court moved to new premises along Supreme Court Lane (formerly Colombo Court). There are plans to convert the old Supreme Court building and City Hall into an art museum.

The new Supreme Court building's structure is made of glass and marble, and is distinguished by a futuristic disc at the top, that contains the nation's highest court, the Court of Appeal. The layout of the nine-storey building is meant to be user-friendly and has features that meet the demands of a modern legal system. The courts have real-time electronic transcription systems and electronic queue management systems, and are equipped to allow the presentation of a variety of digital media. For security, prisoners are shuttled to and from court in corridors separate from those used by lawyers and the public. Judges have private corridors as well. The new building cost $208 million and was designed by British architect, Lord Norman Foster.

Suradi Parjo (1926–96) Teacher and author. Suradi Parjo started writing when he was a student at the Sultan Idris Training College, Perak. He was active in the Singapore Malay Teachers Union (KESATUAN GURU-GURU MELAYU SINGAPURA) and the literary organization ASAS 50. His published works include novels, short stories and essays. Examples are *Keris Sempena Riau* (Riau Dagger) (1958), *Sang Rajuna Tapa* (1959), *Telatah* (Behaviour) (1985), *Jejak Bara* (Stepping On Ember) (1988) and *Mendung* (Overcast) (1992). He also produced textbooks and reference books. His compilation of Malay proverbs, *Peribahasa Warisan* (Traditional Proverbs), was published in 1990. He received a posthumous Tun Seri Lanang Award in 2001 from the Malay Language Council, Singapore.

Suratman Markasan (1930–) Author. After completing his studies at Sultan Idris Training College, Perak, in 1950, Suratman Markasan joined the teaching service. In 1968, he enrolled in Nanyang University in Singapore and graduated in Malay and Indonesian studies. He lectured at the Institute of Education and was also assistant director for Malay and Tamil studies at the Ministry of Education.

Suratman was active in several Malay organizations, occupying important positions in the Singapore Malay Teachers

Supreme Court buildings: old building, left (with dome), and new building, right (with disc).

Ronald Susilo

Union (KESATUAN GURU-GURU MELAYU SINGAPURA), the literary organization ASAS 50, and the Central Council of Malay Cultural Organisations (Majlis Pusat). He has written a number of novels, short stories, poems and essays. Novels he has written include *Tak Ada Jalan Keluar* (No Way Out) (1962), *Subuh Hilang Senja* (Dawn, Lost Evening) (1990), *Tiga Lelaki* (Three Men) (1994), *Di Bumi Mana* (Which Earth) (1996) and *Penghulu yang Hilang Segala-galanya* (Leader Who Lost Everything) (1998). His short stories are published in several anthologies. His book *Bangsa Melayu Singapura Dalam Transformasi Budayanya* (Transformation of the Culture of Singapore Malays) (2005) is a collection of essays on the cultural, intellectual and religious life of the Malays. He was awarded the Southeast Asia Write Award in 1989 and the Montblanc-NUS Centre for the Arts Literary Award in 1997. In 1999, he was given the Tun Seri Lanang award by the Malay Language Council, Singapore.

Susilo, Ronald (1979–) Sportsman. Ronald Susilo is a badminton player whose major international successes came after the age of 21. In 2001, he defeated top seed Hendrawan from Indonesia in the first round of the China Open. Later that year, he triumphed over Ong Ewe Hock of Malaysia and Lin Dan of China.

In 2002, Susilo was runner-up in the Singapore Open, defeating Wong Choong Hann (ranked world number one); world champion Hendrawan; 2001 All-England champion P. Gopichand of India; and world number seven, Shon Seung Mo of Korea. Playing singles and doubles, Susilo helped the team obtain a silver medal.

Susilo's first international title came at the Thailand Open 2003, when he beat Thailand's Boonsak Ponsana, ranked tenth, in the final. In the 2004 All-England Championships, Susilo reached the semifinals. He then clinched the Japan Open title with a victory over China's Bao Chunlai, raising his ranking to ninth in the world. At the opening singles match of the Athens Olympics that year, he defeated the world number one, Lin Dan of China, 15–12, 15–10. Unfortunately, he lost to Boonsak Ponsana in the quarter-finals.

Susilo was named the Singapore National Olympic Council's Sportsman of the Year in 2005.

Swallows, The Popular music group. Serving as back-up band on actor Ahmad Daud's 'Dendang Pontianak' (Song of the Vampire) in the 1960s, The Swallows caught the attention of EMI, which signed the group in 1966. It featured Kassim Selamat on vocals, Yahya on lead guitar, Yussof on rhythm guitar, Hamid on bass and Affendi on drums. The group was noted for blending rhythm-and-blues with Boyanese music and lyrics, and their first release was 'Angkok Angkok Bilis', with 'La Obe' on the flip side.

'La Obe' was a hit in Singapore and West Germany. It stayed on a radio station's Top 10 chart for three weeks, making the Swallows the only Singapore band to have had a hit in Europe. The group released a total of five EPs and two singles before they disbanded in 1968.

Swan & Maclaren Architectural firm. The company started out as Swan & Lermit (1887–92), a firm of civil engineers. In 1892, it became Swan & Maclaren, after James Waddell Boyd Maclaren joined as partner. In 1897, R.A.J. BIDWELL joined the firm, after leaving the Public Works Department of the Federated Malay States. Because of his talent and reputation, Swan & Maclaren soon became the dominant architectural firm in Singapore, winning the most prestigious commissions, including RAFFLES HOTEL (1899), TEUTONIA CLUB (now GOODWOOD PARK HOTEL) (1901) and VICTORIA MEMORIAL HALL (1905).

By 1904, Swan & Maclaren was the largest architectural firm in Singapore. Bidwell dominated its work between 1897 and 1914. In the inter-war years, it continued to lead the local market with

The Swallows

Swan & Maclaren: the old Ocean Building.

commissions such as the SULTAN MOSQUE (1925–28), Ocean Building (1923), Hong-kong and Shanghai Bank (1922) and the Singapore Turf Club (1934).

The firm remained important but lost some of its dominance after World War II, due to increased competition.

Swettenham, Sir Frank (1850–1946) Colonial official. Governor of the STRAITS SETTLEMENTS from 1901 to 1904, Frank Athelstone Swettenham was the only governor who spent his entire career in the Straits Civil Service. He arrived in Singapore as a civil service cadet in 1871. He was one of the commissioners appointed by then governor ANDREW CLARKE to settle the Chinese dispute in the Malay States, which led to the signing of the Pangkor Treaty in 1874. The event was the beginning of British intervention in the affairs of the Malay States.

In 1901, Swettenham was appointed governor. He had an extensive knowledge of the history and language of the native population of the Straits Settlements. A keen writer, his books *The Real Malay* and *Malay Sketches* introduced Malaya to the larger world. His *British Malaya* is often referred to for its details on the history of Malaya and the Federated Malay States.

To commemorate Swettenham's long service to the Straits Settlements, the Straits Association commissioned a portrait of him by leading Edwardian painter, John Singer Sargent. This prized painting now belongs to the NATIONAL MUSEUM OF SINGAPORE.

See also GOVERNORS.

Swiss Club The club started in 1871 as the Swiss Rifle Shooting Club of Singapore. Its rifle range was located in a secluded valley near Balestier Road. The Swiss shot for sport here as they did in their homeland.

Some 30 years later, it was realized that the land belonged to Chinese businessman HOO AH KAY (WHAMPOA). He protested that stray bullets not only missed their target but also shredded the orchids in his garden. So, in 1902, the club bought and moved to a piece land off Dunearn Road. In 1909, however, the clubhouse and shooting range burned down. A new clubhouse was opened a year later. In 1925, the name was shortened to Swiss Club and, in 1927, H. R. Arbenz built a new clubhouse.

To preserve its 20 ha of land, the club leased parcels to the Swiss embassy and other foreign communities. The shooting range was closed in 1982. In 1986, the clubhouse was again rebuilt and extended.

Swissôtel The Stamford and Raffles The Plaza Formerly known as The Westin Stamford and Westin Plaza, these hotels were renamed when Raffles International Hotels & Resorts assumed management in 2002. At one time the tallest hotel in the world, the 73-storey Swissotel The Stamford has been the venue for the annual vertical marathon since the mid-1980s. In 2005, the top runner completed the 1,336-step race in 7 min and 18.2 sec. Offering some 2,000 rooms, the two hotels are among the biggest hotel properties in Singapore.

syair A form of Malay poetry. A *syair*, unlike a PANTUN, is usually long and narrates a story or a complex concept. Influenced by Arab and Persian poetry, the *syair* comprises quatrains with the 'A-A-A-A' rhyme scheme. The *syair* is sung, with or without musical accompaniment, while the *pantun* is usually recited. It is believed that the pioneer of *syair* in the Malay world is the 17th-century mystic, Hamzah Fansuri. One of the earliest *syair* written in Singapore was penned by the scholar and writer Munshi

Sir Frank Swettenham

Syed Abdul Kadir

Syed Isa Mohamad Semait

Syed Ja'afar Hassan Albar: at Singapore UMNO rally, 1963.

ABDULLAH ABDUL KADIR. He wrote *Syair Kampong Glam Terbakar* (The Poem On the Great Fire of Kampong Glam) in 1830.

Syariah Court The Syariah Court was established with the introduction of the Muslim Ordinance of 1957, and came into operation on 25 November 1958. The 1957 ordinance was amended in 1960, and in 1966, the ADMINISTRATION OF MUSLIM LAW ACT (AMLA) was introduced. This act allowed the Syariah Court to 'hear and determine all actions and proceedings in which all the parties are Muslims or where the parties were married under the provisions of the Muslim law and which involve disputes relating to marriage, divorces, betrothals, disposition or division of property on divorce, and the payment of *mas kahwin* [dowry], maintenance and *muta'ah* [compensation upon divorce]'.

The Syariah Court performs the role of an arbitration court for matrimonial disputes. The court also declares rights of inheritance of properties belonging to Muslims under the Islamic Law of Inheritance (*fara'id*). The court has no jurisdiction over marriages where only one person is a Muslim (that is, a marriage solemnized under the WOMEN'S CHARTER).

Muslims may refer to the SUBORDINATE COURTS for disputes about financial support (maintenance). They may also refer to the Subordinate Courts for ancillary matters pertaining to divorce such as the division of matrimonial property and custody.

Appeals against decisions of the Syariah Court may be heard by the Appeal Board. The board is made up of three people, formed from a panel of at least seven Muslims. Members of the panel are nominated by the president of Singapore, on the advice of MAJLIS UGAMA ISLAM SINGAPURA. The decision of the Appeal Board is final.

Generally, the the Court adheres to the methods and rulings of the SHAFI'I SCHOOL, although rulings from other schools of Islamic jurisprudence are also used when necessary. The administration of the Syariah Court falls under the MINISTRY OF COMMUNITY DEVELOPMENT, YOUTH AND SPORTS, unlike other courts that are administered under the MINISTRY OF LAW.

See also REGISTRY OF MUSLIM MARRIAGES.

Syed Abdul Kadir (1948–) Sportsman. Syed Abdul Kadir started boxing at St Andrew's Primary School. By age 18, he was competing in the light flyweight division. He represented Singapore at the SEAP Games from 1969 to 1979, winning one gold and two silver medals. His greatest fight was in 1971 SEAP Games when he defeated Burma's Vanlal Dowla, then the best boxer in Asia, in the final.

Syed also competed in the Asian Games in 1970 and 1974 and at the 1972 OLYMPIC GAMES. At the Olympics, he won

Syed Sheik Alhadi, far right, at the Jelutong Press (where **Al-Ikhwan** *was printed), Penang, 1920s.*

the first bout, but the second was stopped because of a cut on his eyebrow. In 1974 he gave Singapore its first Commonwealth Games boxing medal, in New Zealand. Syed was the most prolific of Singapore's boxers from 1968 to 1976. He was named Singapore National Olympic Council's Sportsman of the Year in 1974. He became the national coach after retiring from competition and was Coach of the Year in 1986. He set up Kadir's Boxing School, continuing his 40-year association with the sport.

Syed Isa Mohamad Semait (1936–) MUFTI of Singapore. Syed Isa Mohamad Semait was appointed by the president of Singapore in 1969, under the ADMINISTRATION OF MUSLIM LAW ACT, and is regarded as the island's highest Islamic authority. Educated at the Al-Azhar University in Egypt, he also acts as chairman or member of numerous religious and legal committees in MAJLIS UGAMA ISLAM SINGAPURA and has been involved in many inter-religious dialogues and collaborations.

Syed Ja'afar Hassan Albar (1914–1977) Malaysian politician. Born in Tondano, Sulawesi, Syed Ja'afar Hassan Albar was educated in Malay and Arabic schools in Johor and Singapore. He started working life as a businessman, and later became a religious teacher and journalist. His political career began in the 1940s when he became editor of *Suara Umno*, forerunner of *Merdeka*, an organ of the United Malays National Organisation (UMNO).

In 1949, Syed Ja'afar became UMNO's chief publicity officer. An outspoken and extremely frank person, he was at the forefront of many a political controversy. His penchant for calling things as he saw them earned him the soubriquet Singa Umno (Lion of Umno). He was an impressive speaker and in the years leading up to MERDEKA (1957), he travelled extensively throughout the Malay Peninsula speaking at every available platform to rally support for

TUNKU ABDUL RAHMAN and UMNO. In 1955, he was appointed second secretary at the Malayan High Commission in London. He returned to Malaya to fight the 1959 elections but was returned unopposed in the Johor-Trengganu constituency and became deputy minister for Information and Broadcasting (1959–61).

Syed Ja'afar resigned two years later, citing health reasons. In 1963, he returned to active politics and was made UMNO secretary-general, and it was in this capacity that he became best known in Singapore. After the smarting defeat of all UMNO candidates in the Singapore GENERAL ELECTION (1963), the Malaysian conglomerate of political parties led by UMNO dispatched Syed Ja'afar to rebuild Singapore UMNO.

To regain Malay support, Syed Ja'afar began playing the ethnic card, accusing the PEOPLE'S ACTION PARTY (PAP) of being a 'Chinese party' hostile to Malay interests. He began a campaign to demand special rights and privileges for Malays in Singapore along the same lines as those enjoyed by Malays in mainland Malaysia. This action heightened racial tensions in Singapore and erupted into a full-scale anti-Chinese campaign. When the PAP invited 114 Malay organizations to meet with OTHMAN WOK, minister for social affairs, to discuss programmes to assist Singapore Malays, militant UMNO agitators called for a boycott, organized a mass protest rally of some 12,000 Malays, and formed an action committee to press for Malay demands. Those who cooperated with the PAP were labelled 'traitors'. Syed Ja'afar became increasingly personal in his attacks. He called LEE KUAN YEW 'an enemy of Malaysia and an agent of Indonesia' and an 'agent of the communists'. Lee sued him for libel but the case was later settled out of court. When rioting broke out at the PROPHET MUHAMMAD'S BIRTHDAY procession in July 1964 (*see* RACE RIOTS), Lee blamed Syed Ja'afar and his 'Ultras' for fomenting racial discord.

In August 1965, Syed Ja'afar resigned as secretary general of UMNO, citing differences with the Tunku over Singapore's separation from Malaysia. In 1976, Syed Ja'afar returned to active politics as the head of UMNO Youth. However, he served in this capacity for only six months before he died of a stroke in Johor.

Syed Sheik Alhadi (1867–1934) An Islamic reformist and publisher, Syed Sheik Ahmad Alhadi was born in Malacca. He studied Islam in Riau, Egypt and Mecca, and was regarded as one of the leaders of the Islamic reformist movement.

In 1901, Syed Sheik worked as a manager in the Singapore office of Batam Brickworks, a company started by his adoptive father, Raja Ali Kelana. While in Singapore, he became an active member of the Arab Club in Serangoon Road. There he expounded his ideas and gathered likeminded men. In 1906, he and several others started the AL-IMAM magazine. When the Batam Brickworks failed, he moved to Malacca, and later Penang. There, he tried writing novels—mainly adaptations of modern Arab works—such as *Hikayat Faridah Hanum* (The Life of Faridah Hanum). He was very successful and spent the rest of his life writing and publishing. In 1926 he started the *Al-Ikhwan* (Brotherhood) magazine and in 1928 he began producing *Saudara* (Brother), a weekly newspaper.

Syed Sheik lived at a time of political awakening among the Malays. He devoted his energies to questioning the authority of political and religious leaders while urging the Malays to be more proactive in solving the problems they were facing.

Syme & Co. Company established in 1823 by Hugh Syme, a prominent merchant in Singapore who also served as commissioner of the peace in 1826. The company played an important role in the early development of the mineral oil trade in Southeast Asia. In 1891, Syme & Co, together with the London firm of M. Samuel & Co—pioneers of the bulk oil trade in Asia and, later, founders of the Shell Transport and Trading Co.—established a petroleum tank depot at PULAU BUKOM, the first of its kind in Asia.

Syonan The Japanese name for Singapore during the JAPANESE OCCUPATION from 1942 and 1945. '*Nan*' means 'south', while '*syo*' means 'light' and comes from Emperor Hirohito's reigning title: Syowa Tenno. Syonan therefore means Light of the South, or Brilliant South. It was sometimes written as 'Shonan' or 'Syonan-to' ('*to*' meaning 'island' in Japanese).

Syonan Chureito Shinto shrine and war memorial. This was built at BUKIT BATOK in 1942 by 500 Allied prisoners of war, as a memorial to Japanese soldiers killed in the

invasion of Singapore. Behind a 12-m-high wooden pylon topped with a brass cone, a small hut housed the ashes of those killed in the BATTLE OF BUKIT TIMAH. Behind this, the prisoners were allowed to erect another monument to their own dead, a 3-m-high wooden cross. Before the return of the Allied Forces in 1945, the Japanese destroyed both monuments, moving the ashes of their compatriots to a tomb in the JAPANESE CEMETERY PARK. A broadcast tower now stands at the former location of Syonan Chureito. *See also* SYONAN JINJA.

Syonan Jinja Shinto shrine. Located at the western end of MACRITCHIE RESERVOIR, near Sime Road, this memorial was one of two—the other being SYONAN CHUREITO—that commemorated Japanese soldiers killed in the battle for Singapore. It was erected in 1942 by Allied prisoners of war from the Sime Road Camp. The shrine was raised on a stone platform. There was also a large granite ceremonial fountain. Many religious and cultural ceremonies were held here. The Japanese destroyed the shrine just before their surrender in 1945.

Syrian Christians The first wave of Syrian Christians—all MALAYALEES—arrived in Singapore at the end of World War I. The first documented Syrian Christian immigrant to arrive was Isaac Benjamin, who came to Singapore in 1911 after encountering problems with the colonial authorities in Kerala. The early immigrants worked in the civil service as teachers, lawyers, policemen, and at the British Naval Base. A second wave of immigrants—mostly tertiary-educated—arrived in the early 1950s. With their strong command of the English language, most found white-collar jobs. While the majority became Singapore citizens, many families returned to India in 1971 following the BRITISH WITHDRAWAL FROM SINGAPORE.

The Syrian Christian community probably numbered no more than 250 fam-

Syonan Chureito

Syonan Jinja

ilies until the mid-1990s, when a third wave of Indian expatriates came, attracted by job opportunities in the computer and healthcare industries.

Syrian Christians believe that in 52 CE, St Thomas, one of Jesus Christ's 12 apostles, brought Christianity from Palestine to the Hindu and Jewish communities near the port of Cochin, Kerala. In 1653, the Syrian Christians broke away from Roman Catholic leadership. Around 1889, one branch aligned itself with the Protestant reformation movement, forming the Mar Thoma Church. The original group remained part of the Oriental Orthodox faith and is known as the Orthodox Syrian Church. The Syrian Christian community in Singapore is made up of these two branches.

In the 1950s, the two churches in Singapore established their respective places of worship off Serangoon Road. The churches have since undergone redevelopment and their members now worship in their churches off Upper Thomson Road and Old Yio Chu Kang Road. The descendents of the pioneer members of both churches have inter-married and share a common cultural heritage. Syrian Christians can be recognized by their surnames, the more common ones being Abraham, Cherian, George, Jacob, Joseph, Matthew, Philip and Varghese.

The community faces several challenges. Knowledge and use of the mother tongue, Malayalam, is in danger of being lost, as most Syrian Christian children speak only English. The two churches have attempted to bridge the language gap by holding more services in English. Few from the local community join the clergy, resulting in the need to bring priests from India. Moreover, many young Syrian Christians are marrying non-Indians and therefore may not pass on the traditions to the next generation. In 2006, the population of Syrian Christians in Singapore was about 1,500.

T

Taha Suhaimi

Sheik Tahir Jalaluddin

Taha Suhaimi (1916–1999) Scholar. Muhammad Taha Muhammad Fadhlallah as-Suhaimi was educated at RAFFLES INSTITUTION and Al-Azhar University, Egypt. He was appointed as a lecturer at Ngee Ann College and was the first president of the SYARIAH COURT (1968). He was instrumental in sustaining Madrasah Al-Ma'arif Al-Islamiah financially through a travel company he set up (*see* MADRASAHS). He was also the chairman of Madrasah Al-Ma'arif from 1990 until the end of his life. He prepared scripts for religious programmes on local radio, taught religious classes, and also published books in both English and Malay, among them *Hakikat Syirik* (The True Meaning of Heresy) and *Muhammad Foretold in Earlier Scriptures.*

tahil Unit of weight. Originally introduced into Asia by Spanish and Portuguese traders, the *tahil* was used for customs and taxes all over Asia during the colonial era, and was commonly known as the 'Chinese tael'. The word '*tahil*' was also used for a silver coin of the same weight. One *tahil* was equivalent to 37.8 g, and 16 *tahils* made up one KATI (or *catty*).

Tahir Jalaluddin, Sheik (1869–1956) Scholar. Born in West Sumatra, Indonesia, Muhammad Tahir Sheikh Muhammad Ahmad Jalaluddin studied in Mecca and Al-Azhar University, Egypt. In Egypt, he was introduced to the teachings of Muhammad Abduh, a leading promoter of the reformist movement in ISLAM. In 1899, he returned to Southeast Asia, travelling throughout the region teaching Islam and arguing for the eradication of pre-Islamic Malay practices. In 1901, he settled in Perak.

Tahir often expressed concern about the plight of the MALAYS, whom he believed were victims of colonialism and traditionalism. He expounded a reformist agenda through AL-IMAM magazine and *Saudara*, a newspaper he founded in Penang in 1928. He spent most of his career teaching in MADRASAHS in Malaya and Singapore, including Madrasah Aljunied Al-Arabiah. While in the Dutch East Indies (present-day Indonesia) in 1926, Tahir was charged with inciting an armed uprising against the Dutch and jailed for six months.

Takase Toru (unknown–1964) Japanese military officer. Takase Toru was deputy to WATARU WATANABE, chief of the Malaya Military Administration during the JAPANESE OCCUPATION. He had been a special service agent in Japanese-occupied China, and had studied the Chinese of Southeast Asia in some depth. Watanabe believed that Takase was quarrelsome, arrogant and aggressive, but believed that these characteristics made him the right person to carry out Watanabe's own harsh policies. Takase was instrumental in coercing a $50 million 'gift' from the Chinese community for the Japanese war effort.

Takase's abrasive style antagonized many Japanese bureaucrats in Malaya and Singapore, and he returned to Japan in September 1942. In 1947, he was elected as a member of Parliament in Japan.

TalkingCock Website. TalkingCock was started in August 2000 by lawyer-turned-cartoonist Colin Goh. The phrase 'talking cock' is SINGLISH for 'talking nonsense' or 'shooting the breeze'. The site began as a forum where friends shared jokes with a strong local flavour.

The objectives of TalkingCock are 'preserving and advancing the authentic voice of Singaporeans'. Goh and a group of regular contributors often use Singlish in their parodies of local personalities, policies and current events. In 2002, Goh published the best-selling *Coxford Singlish Dictionary*. Goh and his wife, Joycelyn Woo, produced and directed *TalkingCock The Movie,* which premiered on 19 April 2002 at the SINGAPORE INTERNATIONAL FILM FESTIVAL.

Tamil Tamil has been one of the four official languages of Singapore—alongside ENGLISH, MANDARIN and MALAY—since 1956. It is spoken by roughly 65 per cent of the country's Indian population. Tamil may be used in Parliament, with a simultaneous interpretation facility provided to members of Parliament, and the word 'Singapore' is inscribed in Tamil on CURRENCY notes. Most government announcements are published in Tamil alongside the other official languages. On 2 February 1996, President ONG TENG CHEONG officially launched Singapore's first Tamil website.

The use of Tamil in Singapore dates back to the time of Hindu trader NARAINA PILLAY and the group of SEPOYS, assistants and domestic servants who were brought to the island by Sir STAMFORD RAFFLES from Penang during his second visit in May 1819. Raffles' liberal policies also attracted many Tamil immigrants from the coastal region of Cholamandalam in south India. These people were referred to as CHULIAS.

The earliest record of the Tamil language in Singapore can be found in an inscription at SRI MARIAMMAN TEMPLE on South Bridge Road recording the donation of the holy feet of Sri Rama by Seshalam Pillai of Cuddalore in 1828. The earliest Tamil literary works produced in Singapore and Malaya are believed to have been written by Yazhpanam Vannai Nagar C. N.

TalkingCock: website (above); **Coxford Singlish Dictionary** *(2002) (right).*

Sathasiva Pandithar in 1887. *Kuthirai Pandhaya Laavani* (Ode to Race Course) was written by Rangasami Dasan in 1893 (*see* TAMIL LITERATURE).

Over the decades, a common standard spoken Tamil has developed in Singapore which incorporates non-Tamil words for modern gadgets and concepts, and several regional, caste and professional dialects. The Tamil Language and Culture Division of the NATIONAL INSTITUTE OF EDUCATION, which is part of NANYANG TECHNOLOGICAL UNIVERSITY, trains Tamil teachers and oversees research in Tamil language, literature and culture. Tamil language and Tamil studies have been offered as electives to non-Tamil and Tamil students of undergraduate programmes at the National University of Singapore (NUS) since 1999.

In the late 1990s, a group consisting of prominent Tamils, the Valar Thamizh Iyyakam (Tamil Language Council), was formed under the advisorship of Indian members of Parliament with the aim of promoting the use of Tamil in Singapore. Despite the efforts of such groups, however, the percentage of Singapore households in which Tamil is used has decreased over recent years. In 1980, 52.2 per cent of Indian households used Tamil. This figure had decreased to 42.9 per cent by 2000.

Nevertheless, radio and television have been instrumental in continuing to encourage the use of Tamil in Singapore. Radio station Oli 96.8 broadcasts Tamil programmes 24 hours a day. Newspapers such as TAMIL MURASU, TAMIL MALAR, *Malaya Nanban, Tamil Nesan,* and *Sinai Nissan* have also played a significant role. Similarly, the National Book Development Council, established to promote local writers, presents awards biennially for the best books in all official languages, including Tamil.

Tamil education An opportunity to learn through the medium of Tamil was first provided at the SINGAPORE FREE SCHOOL, which opened in 1834. The class had a promising start—18 students attended the first Tamil class. At the same time, there were 12 students in each of the Chinese and Malay classes and 32 pupils in the

Tamil: primary school Tamil textbook.

English class. A year later, the Tamil class was discontinued, owing in part to the lack of suitable textbooks. Several other attempts to set up Tamil classes failed. Reasons included the unsuitability of the teachers, the low level of cooperation from Indian students and their parents, the difficulty in securing a European superintendent for Tamil education, and the government's negative attitude towards Tamil and CHINESE EDUCATION. The British government was more interested in supporting those schools providing English (see ENGLISH EDUCATION) or MALAY EDUCATION, which were available to students of any race or religion.

It was only 30 years later that Tamil education was revived in Singapore. The demand for Tamil interpreters and English-speaking Indian clerks grew in tandem with the growth of Singapore as a major trading centre in the region. This resulted in the establishment of two Anglo-Tamil schools in 1873 and 1876. These two schools provided, for the first time, the means to learn English through the medium of Tamil. Until then, English in Singapore was only taught to Asians through the Malay medium.

The two Anglo-Tamil schools had an additional role—that of acting as branch English schools to RAFFLES INSTITUTION, which absorbed successful pupils from the two schools. The two schools gradually reduced their use of Tamil and were converted into Preparatory English Schools. Around the turn of the 20th century, Tamil-language education became non-existent.

Part-time Tamil-language classes in some English-medium secondary schools were started in 1955, and offered in many English-medium primary schools only in the late 1950s. Tamil language was given a boost in 1966 when MOTHER TONGUE was made compulsory for Indian pupils taking the Primary School Leaving Examination (PSLE). By 1970, more than 13,000 pupils were studying Tamil as a second language in some 100 English-medium schools.

However, as more Indian parents chose to place their children in English-medium schools, enrolment in the vernacular schools fell. This led to the closure of all Tamil-medium primary schools by the late 1970s. The last Tamil-medium school, Umar Pulavar Tamil High School, was closed in 1983 (see UMAR PULAVAR TAMIL SCHOOL). Not long after, in 1986, students whose PSLE scores came within the top 10 per cent of the cohort could take Tamil at the Higher Tamil level. Later, this option became available to students who made up the top 30 per cent. BILINGUALISM within an English-medium school system has kept the learning of the Tamil language sustainable. From about 2000 to 2006, over 50 per cent of Indian students, most of whom are of Tamil origin, study Tamil in primary and secondary schools.

In 2005, critical changes were made to Tamil language syllabi. The emphasis shifted to creating more listening and speaking opportunities. One key revision was the use of the 'bilingual' approach in teaching mother tongue to students from English-speaking homes, which was a turnaround from the earlier days of teaching English through Tamil.

Tamil literature *See* box.

Tamil Malar Newspaper. This TAMIL-language newspaper, published in Singapore from 1964 to 1980, was one of two main Tamil-language publications. It was owned by a Malaysian, N.T.S. Arumugam Pillai. In 1978, legal battles erupted over finance, content and publishing rights between its management (in Singapore) and the owner (in Malaysia), leading, at one time, to the publication of two separate versions. Owing to legal problems, the Singapore edition closed down in 1980.

Tamil Murasu Newspaper. This TAMIL-language broadsheet was founded in 1935, following a series of short-lived Indian newspapers dating back to 1876. It soon became one of the better-known Tamil publications. *Tamil Murasu* (Tamil Drum) began as a substitute for the TAMILS' REFORM ASSOCIATION's weekly news bulletin, *Munnetram* (Progress). It was Singapore's first Tamil daily, and was founded by GOVINDASAMY SARANGAPANY. In the early years, the newspaper was at the vanguard of the social reform movement which was taking place among Indians in Singapore. Taken over by SINGAPORE PRESS HOLDINGS (SPH) in 1995, the paper had, as of June 2006, daily sales of 10,000 on weekdays and 17,000 on weekends. Its coverage covers current affairs, including local and overseas developments. Particular attention is given to news from the Indian community and the sub-continent.

Tamil New Year This festival falls in mid-April, on the day the sun enters the zodiac house of Mesham (Aries). Mesham is the first sign of the zodiac, and according to Hindu cosmology, is the ultimate cause of everything in the universe. The Tamil almanac begins its calculations from the New Year. It records, in detail, the positions of the planets and stars on this day, and gives a reading of the significance of these signs. The almanac is used to predict, in a general way, what will happen in that year. It also indicates auspicious times for holding New Year celebrations and the times at which various ceremonial duties must be performed. As it is not a public holiday, Tamil New Year is not celebrated on a large scale.

Tamil theatre *See* box.

Tamils Tamils in Singapore refer to people who came originally from Tamil-speaking areas of India, including the Coromandel coast and northern Sri Lanka. They form the majority—about 64 per cent—of the 293,100 Indians (according to 2004 figures) in Singapore.

Being largely rural migrants brought into a wage-labour colonial economy, the early Tamils formed a highly cohesive community. As early migration was essentially the import of Tamil labour, Tamils formed the largest Indian community in Singapore by the end of World War II. Tamils were predominantly employed in the construction of public works, roads and ports. In the early 20th century, there was increased migration of educated Tamils, who came to occupy positions in Singapore's growing governmental and commercial sectors. Tamils from the commercial and trading castes were also attracted to Singapore.

The closely knit community of NATTUKOTTAI CHETTIARS, Mudaliyars, Tamil Muslim traders (see INDIAN MUSLIMS) and others came to Singapore to expand their businesses. They engaged in merchandising, from peddling, hawking and vending of edibles in small kiosks to the running of grocery shops, textile shops and other retail businesses; jewellery making; pawnbroking; moneylending; and incipient banking.

Tamils come from a caste-based society. Social and political movements in pre-war south India—including the Dravidian social reform movement and the Indian independence movement—were closely followed by Tamil migrants in Singapore. The Dravidian movement called for the removal of caste hierarchy, women's freedom and the abolition of superstitious beliefs. The movement used the Tamil language to propagate its ideas. It appealed to Tamil business groups and labour. The Indian independence movement attracted a large section of English-educated Indians as well as educated Tamils. During World War II, thousands of Tamils served in the INDIAN NATIONAL ARMY, which was constituted in Singapore to liberate India from British rule.

In the 30 years following Singapore's independence, the former concentrations of Tamils in government labour quarters and British military bases, as well as on

Tamil Malar

Tamil Murasu

Tamil education: Methodist Mission Anglo-Tamil School, late 19th century.

Tamil literature The history of Tamil literature in Singapore can be traced to the 1870s, when Tamil printing presses were first established. Tamil dailies and magazines proliferated and went on to play a vital role in the cultivation of Tamil literary talents. Publications such as Tamil Malar, *Malaya Nanban*, *Tamil Nesan*, Tamil Murasu, *Singai Nesan* and *Singapore Express* provided a forum for aspiring writers.

Most, if not all, of the early works were anthologies of poems, reflecting the higher status traditionally accorded to the genre. The very first volume of verse was written by Yazhpanam Vannai Nagar C.N. Sathasiva Pandit. In subsequent years, other writers contributed to the growth of Tamil literature in Singapore, notably N.V. Rangasamy Dasan with *Kuthirai Pandhaya Laavani* (Ode to Race Course) (1893), Ponnusamy Pillai with *Sallaba Laavani* (Amorous Ode) (1893), K. Velupillai with *Singai Murugesar Pathigam* (Devotional Poems for Singai Murugesar) (1893), and Mohamed Abdul Kader with *Kirthanai Thirattu* (Anthology of Devotional Songs) (1896). These volumes reflected the challenges faced by a migrant society.

The first few decades of the 20th century saw a slump in output. One reason was the lack of outlets for writers; the weekly publication *Singai Nesan*, which was first published in 1887 and had served as a showcase for aspiring poets and writers, ceased publication in 1890. The dominant theme of the few works published during this time was religion.

Growth and the Japanese Occupation
Tamil literature received a boost in the 1930s. The independence movement in India encouraged a greater social consciousness, and focus moved away from religious themes to narratives which were concerned with ideas of reform and progress. The Tamils Reform Association launched the monthly *Seerthirutham* (Reformation) in the 1930s. Writers such as N. Palanivelu and Singai Mukilan spread radical reformist ideas through prose and poetry. The period saw the growth of genres such as short stories, novels and plays, many of which appeared in *Tamil Murasu*. Its editor Govindasamy Sarangapany, popularly known as Thamizhavel, encouraged the development of Tamil literature through the paper.

During the Japanese Occupation, Singapore Tamil literature languished again, and *Tamil Murasu* ceased publication. The interim Azad Hind government, established by Subhas Chandra Bose with the help of the Indian National Army, which propounded an anti-imperialist ideology, whipped up political zeal in Singaporean writers like Fakrudin Sahib, S.I. Durai, R. Sreenivasan, Sarangapany and Mugilan, who contributed articles to local publications such as *Independent India*, *Yuvabaratham* and *Suthanthira Uthayam*. The primary theme of literary works written in this epoch was anti-colonialism, particularly with relation to Indian independence.

Rama Kannabiran's Chozhan Bommai *(Chola Doll) (1981).*

Changing themes
After 1945, there was a gradual but consistent growth in poetic output. Poetry of the 1950s was dominated by patriotic verses dedicated to the independence movement in India and also to Singaporean independence. From the 1960s, there were several poets writing 'nature poems' and poems written in praise of the Singaporean state and its leaders. A number of didactic verses were also written with a view to encouraging social reform.

In the latter half of the 1960s, education was a prominent theme. There were many Tamil dailies such as *Malaya Nanban*, and several dedicated scholars led by Sarangapany were instrumental in ensuring the growth of Tamil literature. Among the prominent figures involved were sub-editors of *Tamil Murasu* such as N. Devarajan, Murugadiyan, V.T. Arasu, Re Sreenivasan, M. Chidambaram, T. Selvaganapathy and Murugu Subramaniam. As a result of their efforts, many writers and poets were given a platform. These writers include P. Krishnan, who wrote and published under the pseudonym Puthumaithasan, R. Vetrivelu, R. Nagaiyan, P. Shanmugam, M.K. Thuraisingam and Jegadeesan.

From left: Thudikkum Ullam *(Throbbing Heart) (1954), a volume of verse by Singai Mukilan; a flyer announcing the launch of a weekly newsletter 'Thendral' (Breeze) by the poet.*

Since 1965, there has been steady progress in the development of Tamil prose, with several short story compilations and plays being written and launched every year. Writers such as Naa. Govindasamy, Rama Kannabiran, M. Elangkannan, J.M. Sali, Nara Puthumaipittan, Tamilselvam and Pon Sundararaju have put Singapore on the international Tamil literary map.

Developments post-Independence
Poetry has also developed significantly since Independence in 1965, with notable contributions from poets such as N. Palanivelu. Other poets who have made a mark include Murugadiyan, Samsudin, K. Perumal, M. Elamaran, V. Ikkuvanam, Peri Neela Palanivelan, P. Thiruvengadam, A Palani, A.P. Shanmugam, M.A. Masoothu, Parvathy Poobalan, Sugumaran and Narana Puthumai Piththan, Amallathasan and Naa. Aandeappan.

In the last few decades, *marabukkavithai* (traditional verse) has been surpassed in popularity by *puthukkavithai* (new poetry). Whereas *marabukkavithai* follows the rules of versification known as *yappillakanam*, *puthukkavithai* scorns such strictures. Practitioners of *puthukkavithai* believe that poetry should not be constrained or contained by rules of metre and versification. Poets writing in the traditional style such as K.T.M. Iqbal have switched over largely to new poetry. His anthology *Mugavarigal* (Addresses) contains poetry written in both styles. Iqbal is one of the few

Tamil poets whose works have been translated into English, thereby giving a wider readership beyond the Tamil community access to his works.

Another notable pioneer of *puthukkavithai* is Elangovan, who is best known as a playwright and director working with Agni Koolthu (see also Tamil drama). His poetry collections *Vizhi Sannalkalin Pinaallirunthu* (Behind Windows of Eyes) (1979) and *Maunavatham* (Silent Annihilation) (1984) and the bilingual *Transcreations* (1988) are grim, sardonic critiques of local politics and social ills.

A younger generation of poets and writers is now contributing to the growth of Tamil literature, and it includes Amaruddin, Tajuddin, Muhamed Ali, Azhagiya Pandian, Latha, Shahul Hameed and Malarthamizh. Some, such as Pichinikkaadu Ilango and M. Anbazhagan, choose to write in both verse and prose. A new diversity of themes which includes gender, globalization and issues specific to the Indian community, such as the problems of the caste system, have also begun to make their way into Tamil literature written in Singapore.

From left: Sithira Seiyul *(Illustrative Verses) (2000) by V. Ikkuvanam;* Puthiya Minalgal *(New Awakenings) (1999) by M.A. Masoothu;* Pullangkuzhal *(Flute) (2003) and* Tamizhar Thalaivar Thamizhavel *(Thamizhavel, Leader of the Tamils) (2005) by Amallathasan;* Ippadikku Naan *(Yours Sincerely) (2003) by M. Anbazhagan.*

SERANGOON ROAD, were dispersed across the island in PUBLIC HOUSING estates.

Government-sponsored organizations which cater to the needs of Tamils include COMMUNITY CENTRES, the SINGAPORE INDIAN DEVELOPMENT ASSOCIATION, the HINDU ADVISORY BOARD and the HINDU ENDOWMENTS BOARD.

Of the 172 Indian voluntary organizations, almost 70 per cent are Tamil. These cater to the linguistic, religious, cultural and social needs of the community. Four of the 23 Tamil Hindu temples in Singapore are administered by the Hindu Endowments Board, while the others are run by volunteers. Similarly, Tamil cultural events are promoted by voluntary organizations.

While a large majority are Hindu, Tamils in Singapore are united more by linguistic affinity than religious affiliation. There is greater interaction amongst Tamils of different religious affiliation than between Indians from different linguistic groups which share the same religion. Religious affinity between Tamil Muslims and Malays has been a factor in inter-racial marriages. Most Tamils still marry within their religious groups, with caste being a criterion although this is not an issue which is publicly discussed. There are caste groups among Tamils which emphasize intra-caste marriages, while for most Tamils in Singapore, marriage across a range of mid-status castes is the norm. For Tamils who have close connections with their places of origin in Tamil Nadu, caste is a determining factor when deciding on a spouse.

In 2005, there were eight Tamils among the ten Indians serving as members of Parliament. All of them were members of the ruling PEOPLE'S ACTION PARTY, and some, like THARMAN SHANMUGARATNAM and S. JAYAKUMAR, held key Cabinet positions. Another prominent Tamil is President S.R. NATHAN.

Tamils Reform Association This association was set up in June 1932 by a group of reform-minded Tamils who sought to raise the social and economic status of the local Tamil community. The group was inspired by the Dravidian movement of south India.

The association's achievements include educating the Tamil community through the newspaper *Tamil Murasu*, which had its origins in the association's weekly news bulletin *Munnetram* (Progress). The association was renamed in 2001 due to a lack of strong central leadership, limited funds and ineffective publicity.

Tampines New town. The name 'Tampenus' first appeared in Franklin and Jackson's 1828 map of Singapore. It was probably derived from the name of the tampinis tree (*Streblus elongatus*), which was much in demand on account of its strong, durable ironwood timber. The name was later changed to 'Tampines', the closest romanized equivalent of the tree's original name.

Originally, this area in eastern Singapore was inhabited mainly by farmers and rubber planters. In the late 1980s, the HOUSING & DEVELOPMENT BOARD began transforming the rural area into a new town. Tampines is one of the four regional centres to be developed in Singapore. The town is demarcated by Upper Changi Road East, Tampines Expressway, Tampines Avenue 9, Tampines Avenue 10, Tampines Avenue 5 and Simei Avenue. In 1991, Tampines Town won the United Nations World Habitat Award for its innovative design and construction. By 2005, some 61,000 PUBLIC HOUSING units in Tampines accommodated about 226,000 residents.

Tan, Alvin (1963–) Theatre director. Alvin Tan Cheong Kheng was educated at the National University of Singapore, the Institute of Education and the University of Birmingham in the United Kingdom. In 1997, he studied for three months at New York University on a Fulbright Scholarship.

Tan is artistic director of THE NECESSARY STAGE, which he co-founded with HARESH SHARMA. Experimentation with form has taken Tan from minimalist-style 'poor theatre' to musicals and multimedia work. Among the plays he has directed are *godeatgod* (2002) and *Separation 40* (2005). Tan received the National Arts Council's YOUNG ARTIST AWARD in 1998.

Tan, Benedict (1967–) Sportsman. Benedict Tan studied at the National University of Singapore and the Australian Institute of Sport. He won gold medals in sailing in four consecutive Southeast Asian (SEA) Games (Kuala Lumpur, 1989; Manila, 1991; Singapore 1993; and Chiang Mai, 1995), and was Sportsman of the Year three times (1992, 1995 and 1996). An Asian Games gold medallist (Hiroshima, 1994), Tan attained a world top-50 ranking in 1995, and competed in the Atlanta Olympics in 1996.

Tan received the Singapore Youth Award (1995), Public Service Star (1995) and Public Service Medal (1993). He later became head sports physician at Changi Hospital's Changi Sports Medicine Centre and has served as a member of the

Benedict Tan

Tampines

Singapore National Olympic Council. He has been inducted into the SINGAPORE SPORTS COUNCIL HALL OF FAME.

Tan, Bernard (1943–) Scientist and composer. A professor of physics at the NATIONAL UNIVERSITY OF SINGAPORE since 2002, Bernard Tan Tiong Gie was a former acting head of the university's music department. He was instrumental in the formation of the SINGAPORE SYMPHONY ORCHESTRA (SSO), and is the longest-serving member of its board of directors. A largely self-taught composer, his compositions have received popular and critical acclaim. His *A Classical Overture, Piano Concerto* and *First Symphony* have been recorded by the SSO and released on CD.

Tan, C.C. (1911–1991) Lawyer and politician. Born Tan Chye Cheng and educated at St Joseph's Institution, Tan studied law in London. He was admitted to the Middle Temple in 1928 and called to the Bar in 1933. He was active in Singapore's political, legal and sporting circles.

Tan was a founding member and first president of the SINGAPORE PROGRESSIVE PARTY (SPP). He was elected to the Legislative Assembly in 1948 and re-elected in 1951, but was beaten by DAVID MARSHALL in the 1955 election. Resigning from his party, he formed the LIBERAL SOCIALIST PARTY with the DEMOCRATIC PARTY but retired from politics after his defeat in the 1959 election. As a member of the 1954 RENDEL COMMISSION, he helped to redraft a new CONSTITUTION for Singapore.

A former president of the Law Society of Singapore, Tan was a senior partner with the legal firm of Tan Rajah & Cheah at the time of his death at age 80. He held various chairmanships and directorships, including chairmanship of THE STRAITS TIMES Press from 1974 to 1982. He was also president of the Singapore Olympic and Sports Council from 1951 to 1962.

Tan, Christopher Y.H. (1941–) Scientist. Christopher Tan Yin Hwee was born in Singapore but spent his childhood in the hill station of Kalimpong in India, to which his

Alvin Tan

C.C. Tan

Bernard Tan

Tamil theatre

Tamil theatre The earliest Tamil theatre productions in the 1920s and 1930s were based on simple moralistic tales relating to the *Puranas*—ancient Sanskrit texts. These were performed by groups from India, and were supported by individual patrons such as Thambaiyah Pillai, Murthi Aiyar, Azhagappa Chettiyaar, Sokkalingam Chettiyaar and Mathanavel Pillai. These groups included Moideen Sahib Company, Devi Gana Sabha, the Madurai Boys Company, the Puliyampatti Boys Company, the Manamogana Arangasamy Naidu Drama Troupe, Murali Ghana Sabha, the P.S. Govindan Drama Troupe and C.V.V. Banthaloo's Drama Troupe.

S. Varathan (left) and N. Palanivelu (right): Cultural Medallion recipients for their contributions to Tamil theatre.

Progressive undertones

Between 1935 and 1942, E.V. Ramasamy began introducing realistic social plays as part of his social progressive movement in India. Thamizhar Seerthirutha Sangam and M.K. Radha also began producing plays with progressive undertones. Tamil theatre in Singapore was highly influenced by such trends. In 1935, *Jani Aalam*, a play written and produced solely by Tamils from Singapore, was performed, with N. PALANIVELU writing the dialogue and songs.

From the late 1940s to the 1960s, numerous new Tamil organizations were founded. Many of these attempted to use theatre and drama to galvanize the Tamil community socially and politically. Groups such as Vennilaa Kalai Arangam, Paari Naadaga Mandram, Pagutharivu Naadaga Mandram, Sembawang Kalai Mandram, Kalaivaanar Arts and Kalaivaani Nadaga Kuzhu, staged various social dramas in this period. Writers and directors such as P. Govindarajoo, S.S. Sarma, CULTURAL MEDALLION-recipient S. VARATHAN, M.K.

Narayanan, P. KRISHNAN, M. Thangaraasan and S.V. Nathan added local content and acting abilities.

Promotion of Tamil theatre

In the 1970s and 1980s, the Singapore Indian Artistes Association (SIAA), spearheaded by S. Varathan, tried to bring together those involved in various performance arts under one umbrella organization. However, the main achievement of this body was the promotion of Tamil theatre in Singapore. The SIAA has staged numerous plays and has also promoted theatre and drama via publications and exhibitions, and by rewarding theatre practitioners for their contributions to Singaporean theatre.

Other groups that were active during this period were Vennila Kalai Arangam, the Tamils Representative Council, Indian Kalai Mandram and the Singapore Tamil Radio Station now

known as Oli 96.8. Writers and directors such as P. Krishnan, Re Somasundaram, Re Shanmugam, M.K. Narayanan and S.S. Sarma made important contributions to the Tamil theatre scene through these groups.

Bilingualism

The late 1980s saw the birth of a new bilingual (i.e. Tamil-English) theatre group, Ravindran Drama Group (RDG), run completely by young people. This group received a Youth Achievement Award in 1997 from the Indian Activity Group of Boon Lay Community Centre. RDG provided a platform for new theatre practitioners and also allowed for experimentation in content and craft. Prominent theatre practitioners who have worked in RDG include G. Selvanathan, V. Ravi and Vadi PVSS. RDG, which opened its own theatre education arm, also began promoting Tamil theatre in schools. The group has worked closely with community groups such as the SINGAPORE INDIAN DEVELOPMENT ASSOCIATION.

Another bilingual group that came to the fore in the early 1990s was AGNI KOOTTHU. By producing plays that explored the harsh socio-political realities of the Tamil minority community in Singapore,

Ravindran Drama Group staged **Kuraloviyam** *(above and left) in 2004: nine plays based on the sayings of a Tamil poet. Ali Baba (below left), staged in 2005, was the group's first children's production. The Miror Theatre's Shanmugam,* **The Kalinga Trilogy Part 1** *(below centre) was staged in 2005 and was nominated for the Life! Theatre awards.* **Talaq** *(below right), a play about an abusive marriage staged by Agni Kootthu, confronted racial and religious sensibilities.*

Agni Kootthu added another dimension to the Tamil theatre scene. In fact, a play by its resident playwright, ELANGOVAN, entitled *Talaq* (Divorce), caused controversy within the Indian Muslim community as it touched on a number of sensitive religious issues.

In 2005, T.T. Dhavamanni and Vadi PVSS formed a bilingual group called Miror Theatre. This group's maiden effort in Singapore, *Shanmugam, The Kalinga Trilogy Part 1*—an English play about Tamil immigrants—was well received.

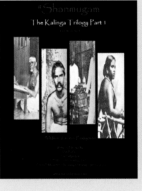

---

family had been evacuated during World War II. After the war, he returned to Singapore and was educated at Raffles Institution. He completed his honours degree in biochemistry at the University of Singapore and was awarded a scholarship to undertake his PhD in biochemistry at the University of Manitoba. He subsequently worked at the National Institute of Aging (Baltimore), Johns Hopkins University, and the University of Calgary Health Science Center. In 1987, he founded the INSTITUTE OF MOLECULAR AND CELL BIOLOGY. Tan retired in 2002.

Tan undertook important research on the protein interferon. In 1969, while conducting postdoctoral research in the United States, he discovered a method to produce interferon in larger quantities than

was previously possible, and in so doing, he helped to prove its existence. Today, interferon is used in treating viral hepatitis, herpes, hairy-cell leukaemia and multiple sclerosis. More recently, it was used in combination with steroids to treat SEVERE ACUTE RESPIRATORY SYNDROME (SARS) In 1973, he was the first to assign genes to human chromosome 21, which helped scientists in understanding Down's Syndrome. In 1979, he reported the chemical make-up of a sub-type of interferon called beta-interferon.

Tan was awarded the NATIONAL SCIENCE AND TECHNOLOGY MEDAL in 1993. He was awarded the Public Administration Medal (Gold) in 2001, and in the same year was awarded the Centre of Excellence Professorship at the University of Tokyo.

Tan, Henry (1943–) Sportsman. Henry Tan Yoke See began tenpin bowling in 1964, and began his competitive career in 1968. The following year, he made his international debut at the Asia Invitational in Hong Kong, where he won a silver medal. Tan won an individual silver medal at the World Games in Copenhagen in 1970. He achieved the highest single game total of 298 out of a possible 300. He also won the silver medal (duo) at the 1975 World FIQ Championship in London

At the Southeast Asian (SEA) Games (Kuala Lumpur, 1977) he won gold in the team of eight. Six years later, when the games were held in Singapore (1983), he was both coach and competitor, and helped the men's threes and the men's fives win gold medals. The team dominated the

Leo Tan

event, taking seven of the nine gold medals. He continued to coach the national team for the next ten years. Tan was voted Sportsman of the Year (1971, 1976) and Coach of the Year (1984). He has been inducted into the SINGAPORE SPORTS COUNCIL HALL OF FAME.

Tan, Jennifer (1978–) Sportswoman. Jennifer Tan took up tenpin bowling at the age of 17, and joined the national squad in 1999. Her first win was in the Taiwan Open that same year. In 2001 she was Champion of Champions and Thailand Open champion.

In 2002, Jennifer Tan became the second Singaporean to be crowned World Masters Women's champion in Denmark. On the way to victory, she defeated 23 bowlers from Asia, the United States and Europe, and faced defending champion and compatriot JESMINE HO in the final. She defeated her team-mate (205-172, 223-200) to become the world's top woman bowler.

Tan, Kelvin (1964–) Musican and author. Kelvin Tan started playing with independent rock band THE ODDFELLOWS in 1991. However, in 1995, he formed an experimental trio called Stigmata with bassist Ian Woo and saxophonist Guoh Siew Terh. It broke up in 2000. A year before, Tan had formed another experimental/avant garde outfit called Path Integral, together with Woo. Tan joined with fellow Oddfellow member Patrick Chng and DJ Rajesh Hardwani to form fusion band Prana vs r-H in 2004. Path Integral and Prana vs r-H perform occasionally. Tan is also a writer, having published *All Broken Up and Dancing* (1992) and *The Nethe(r); R* (2001). Tan is most noted for his solo efforts, having released over 20 albums since 1996.

Tan, Kenneth (1967–) Sportsman. Kenneth Tan began cycle racing at the age of 16. His first international competition was the Tour of Indonesia (1985) and his first Southeast Asia (SEA) Games medal was a bronze in 1987 in the 4-km individual pursuit. Tan competed in five SEA Games from 1987 to 1995, winning six medals.

One of the top cyclists in Asia in his prime, he outraced everybody except Korean Park Min Su at the Asian Cycling

Championships in New Delhi in 1989 to seize the silver medal, which was his greatest sporting achievement. He also participated in the Asian Games in Beijing (1990) (fourth, individual pursuit) and Hiroshima (1994). He retired in 1997.

Tan, Leo (1944–) Academic. Leo Tan Wee Hin graduated from the University of Singapore with an honours degree in zoology (1969) and a doctorate in marine biology (1974). He lectured at the university from 1973 until 1986. He gained public attention as director of the Singapore Science Centre (SSC), which he joined in 1981, holding the post alongside his senior lectureship at the university. In 1986, he worked full-time at the SSC. When the NATIONAL INSTITUTE OF EDUCATION was formed, Tan joined in 1991 as founding dean of science, and was appointed professor, then director of the National Institute of Education in 1994. Awards he has received include the Public Administration Gold Medal in 1988, the Public Service Medal in 1995, the Public Service Star (2001), the Green Leaf Environmental Award (1997), the National Order of Merit from the French government in 2002, an honorary doctorate of science from Loughborough University (2003) and the Singapore Green Plan 2012 Award (2005). He was awarded the 1999 NATIONAL SCIENCE AND TECHNOLOGY MEDAL for 'his outstanding contribution to the promotion of science and technology in education, and to the young, in Singapore'.

Tan, Margaret Leng (1953–) Musician. Margaret Leng Tan has been described as the 'diva of avant-garde pianism'. Her repertoire includes contemporary classical music and pieces for prepared piano and toy piano. The first woman to receive a doctorate of musical arts from Juilliard School, New York, she was a close associate of John Cage, and has championed his piano music in performances and recordings, most famously his piece '4'33'''. In 2003, she gave the world premiere of Aaron Jay Kernis' *Toy Piano Concerto* with the SINGAPORE SYMPHONY ORCHESTRA in the Concert Hall at ESPLANADE–THEATRES ON

Margaret Leng Tan

THE BAY. Tan has also released *The Art of the Toy Piano* (1997) and John Cage's *The Seasons* (2000). She is based in New York.

Tan, Melvyn (1956–) Musician. Melvyn Tan studied at the Yehudi Menuhin School and London's Royal College of Music. He specialized in the harpsichord and fortepiano, becoming one of the world's pre-eminent fortepianists and an authority on period performance practice. Based in London, he has recorded much music on fortepiano, including Beethoven's complete piano concertos with the London Classical Players on EMI Classics, and has toured Europe with Beethoven's historic Broadwood piano.

His proposed piano recital in 2005 was to be his first in Singapore in 30 years, but was cancelled because of a public outcry over his earlier evasion of NATIONAL SERVICE, for which he was fined $3,000.

Tan, Royston (1976–) Film director. One of the most controversial of the new generation of film-makers, Royston Tan established himself with the critically acclaimed short films *Sons* (2000), *Mother* (2001), *24 Hours* (2001), *Hock Hiap Leong* (2002) and *15* (2002). The feature-length version of *15* was released in 2003 and screened at the Venice Film Festival that year, which was a first for a local director and brought Tan international acclaim. However, scenes portraying youth gangs and SECRET SOCIETIES were cut for the film's local release. Tan's response was *Cut* (2004), a musical satire about censors and the state of censorship in Singapore. In 2005, he directed the feature film *4:30*.

Tan, Tony (1940–) Banker and politician. Tony Tan Keng Yam was educated at St Patrick's School and St Joseph's Institution. He later attended the University of Singapore on a State Scholarship. He obtained a first-class honours degree in physics (1962), after which he obtained an MSc in operations research from MIT. He undertook postgraduate work at the University of Adelaide, Australia on a research scholarship, obtaining a PhD in

Kelvin Tan: the performer (left); his debut solo album, the bluest silence (1998).

Royston Tan

Kenneth Tan

Tony Tan

Tan Boon Teik

William Tan

Tony Tan: Boon Lay constituency tour, 1983.

applied mathematics (1967). Thereafter, he taught at the University of Singapore. Two years later, he left for the OVERSEA-CHINESE BANKING CORPORATION (OCBC), where he was appointed manager in 1978.

Tan entered politics on the PEOPLE'S ACTION PARTY ticket. He contested and won the by-election for the Sembawang constituency and was immediately appointed senior minister of state for education. In 1980, he was made minister for education and concurrently vice-chancellor of the National University of Singapore (NUS) (1980–81). While in Cabinet, Tan served as minister for trade and industry (1981–83), minister-in-charge of NUS and Nanyang Technological Institute (1981–83), minister for finance, trade and industry (1983–85) and minister for education (1985–91).

In 1992, Tan returned to the private sector, becoming OCBC's chief executive officer. However, in 1995, when both deputy prime ministers—LEE HSIEN LOONG and ONG TENG CHEONG—were diagnosed with cancer, Prime Minister GOH CHOK TONG asked Tan to rejoin the Cabinet. He served as minister for defence (1995–2003) and deputy prime minister (1995–2005). In 2003, Tan was appointed co-ordinating minister for security and defence (2003–05). He retired from politics in August 2005. In December 2005, he succeeded Lim Chin Beng as non-executive chairman of the Singapore Press Holdings Group.

Tan, William (1957–) Sportsman and scientist. William Tan Kian Meng lost the use of both of his legs to polio at the age of two. His family was unable to afford a wheelchair during Tan's childhood, and it was not until Tan was a teenager that he first used a wheelchair.

Tan was educated at Raffles Institution, and the National University of Singapore, where he graduated with a bachelor of science degree (1980). He went on to earn a master of science degree at Oxford University as a Raffles Scholar; a PhD at Auckland University, New Zealand; and a master of occupational health degree at Harvard University on a Fulbright Scholarship. He has also undertaken post-doctoral research at Mayo Clinic in the United States.

Tan represented Singapore at the Seoul Paralympics (1988). He was winner of the inaugural President's Social Service Award (2001). In 2005, Tan became the first para-

plegic to complete ten marathons on seven continents over a period of 70 days. Two months later, he secured another entry in the record books when he covered the greatest distance in a wheelchair in 24 hours. He completed 607 laps (243 km) of the Raffles Institution running track, in order to raise $100,000 for the Women's and Children's Healthcare Foundation (WCHF). In total, Tan has helped raise some $14 million for charitable causes around the world.

Tan Ah Tah (1906–1976) Judge. Born in Kuala Lumpur and educated in Penang, Tan Ah Tah won the Queen's Scholarship in 1925 to read law at Cambridge University, United Kingdom. He was called to the Bar in 1930 and spent the next ten years working in a Penang law firm. In 1946, he became the first Asian to be appointed Commissioner of Estate, Duties and Stamps. In 1947, he was one of the first two Chinese to be promoted to the Colonial Legal Service, and in 1948 he was made a judge of the Singapore District Court.

In 1955, Tan Ah Tah became the first Asian to be appointed to the High Court in Singapore. On reaching the age of 65 in 1971, he retired from the Bench. The constitution was then amended to allow his service to be extended, and Tan continued until his second retirement in 1975.

Tan Beng Swee (1828–1884) Merchant. The elder son of TAN KIM SENG, Tan Beng Swee joined the family firm, Kim Seng & Co., in 1852, and took over the company when his father died in 1864. Under Tan, Kim Seng & Co. became a pioneer in the steamship business, starting a ferry service that operated in the Strait of Malacca. The vessels used on this service later formed part of the fleet of the STRAITS STEAMSHIP COMPANY.

Tan Beng Swee was active in public affairs, and was a member of the Grand Jury (1864) and justice of the peace (1867). He was offered a seat on the LEGISLATIVE COUNCIL in 1882, which he declined. He supported many educational institutions, including Chui Eng Free School and Raffles Institution, and founded the Kim Seng Free School in Malacca in memory of his father. He actively ran the TAN TOCK SENG HOSPITAL and donated generously to it.

Together with TAN KIM CHING, he founded the TAN SI CHONG SU TEMPLE in Magazine Road as an ancestral temple for the Tan clan in 1876. He died in Singapore at his house in River Valley Road, and was buried in Malacca.

Tan Boon Teik (1929–) Lawyer and diplomat. Tan Boon Teik was born in Penang. He was educated at Penang Free School and read law at University College London. He graduated with an honours degree in law in 1951, was called to the Bar at the Middle

Temple in 1952 and obtained his LLM at the University of London in 1953. After his return to Penang, Tan practised privately for two years before joining the legal service.

In 1955, Tan was appointed magistrate in Singapore and rose through the ranks, holding appointments as Deputy Registrar and Sheriff of the Supreme Court, and Senior Crown Counsel. In 1959, he was appointed director of the Legal Aid Bureau, and in 1963, he became solicitor-general of Singapore. In 1967, Tan served as acting attorney-general after AHMAD MOHAMED IBRAHIM retired, and was formally appointed attorney-general on 1 January 1969. He served in this capacity until 30 April 1992. For his contributions, he was admitted into the DISTINGUISHED SERVICE ORDER in 1978.

After he retired from the legal service, Tan was appointed Singapore's non-resident ambassador to Hungary (1992–99), Austria (1994–99) and the Slovak Republic (1995–99).

Tan Chan Boon (1965–) Composer. Tan Chan Boon has the distinction of being the Singaporean composer who has written the most number of symphonies. By the age of 40, he had completed four full-length symphonies. He studied composition with LEONG YOON PIN and completed his musical studies in Paris. Tan is the founder-president of the Gustav Mahler and Anton Bruckner Societies in Singapore. In 2000, he conducted and recorded his Symphony No. 2 'Genèse' with the Moravian Philharmonic Orchestra. Movements from the hour-long symphony have also been performed by the SINGAPORE SYMPHONY ORCHESTRA. *See also* CLASSICAL MUSIC.

Tan Che Sang (1763–1836) Merchant. Tan Che Sang was born into a HAKKA family in Canton (present-day Guangzhou). In 1778 he left for the Riau Islands, then Penang

Tan Beng Swee

(1800) and Malacca (1810). He arrived in Singapore in 1816. By this time, he was already a famous and wealthy merchant, trading in goods and spices. Tan was reputedly the wealthiest Chinese merchant of his day and an incorrigible gambler. He encouraged Chinese immigration to Singapore. After Tan died, his funeral was attended by thousands of mourners.

Tan Cheng Bock (1940–) Doctor and politician. Tan Cheng Bock was educated at Radin Mas Primary School, Raffles Institution and the University of Singapore, where he obtained an MBBS. He started medical practice when he opened Ama Keng Clinic in the farming village of Ama Keng.

In 1980, Tan entered politics on the PEOPLE'S ACTION PARTY ticket and won a seat in Ayer Rajah constituency. He served as chairman of the FEEDBACK UNIT and chairman of the Government Parliamentary Committees for Education (1987–90), National Development (1991–95) and the Environment (1996–97). In 1991, Tan became chairman of listed firm Chuan Hup Holdings. Tan stepped down from politics in 2006.

Tan Cheng Lock, Tun Sir (1883–1960) Businessman and politician. Born in Malacca, Tan Cheng Lock was educated at Malacca High School and then at Raffles Institution (RI) in Singapore. On leaving school, Tan joined RI as a teacher of English language and literature (1902–08). He then returned to Malacca and joined his cousin Lee Choon Guan's Bukit Kajang Rubber Estates as assistant manager before starting two rubber companies on his own. His business interests were wide-ranging, and he held directorships in some of the top companies in Malaya, including OVERSEA-CHINESE BANKING CORPORATION (OCBC), SIME DARBY and the STRAITS STEAMSHIP COMPANY.

Beyond business, Tan led an active public life. In 1912, he was appointed commissioner for the Municipality of the Town and Fort of Malacca and justice of the peace. He was also made an unofficial member of the Straits Settlements LEGISLATIVE COUNCIL (1923–35), the Straits Settlements Executive Council (1933–35) and member of the Straits Settlements Trade Commission (1934–35). His earlier connection with education in Singapore continued with his appointment in 1918 to the Anglo-Chinese College Council, which led to the founding of RAFFLES COLLEGE. During WORLD WAR II, his family evacuated to Bangalore, India where he founded the Oversea-Chinese Association for Malayan Chinese in exile. After the war, he took an active part in political activities to prepare Malaya for self-government. In 1949, he founded the MALAYAN CHINESE ASSOCIATION and became its first president (1949–58).

On 21 November 1954, he addressed the Inaugural Meeting of the PEOPLE'S ACTION PARTY (PAP), the formation of which was in line with his dream of a multiracial political platform.

Tan received numerous honours for active public service; he was made Commander of the Order of the British Empire (CBE) (1933); Knight Commander of the Order of the British Empire (KBE) (1952); Paduka Mahkota Johor (DPMJ) by the Sultan of Johor; and Seri Maharaja Mangku Negara (SMN), the highest civilian award presented by the Yang di-Pertuan Agung of Malaya (1958). Tan died in Malacca and was given a state funeral. Heeren Street in Malacca, where his ancestral home is located, was renamed Jalan Tun Tan Cheng Lock in his honour.

Tan Chin Tuan (1908–2005) Banker and philanthropist. Tan Chin Tuan was educated at Anglo-Chinese School. He was the heir to his father's rubber estates and the debts it incurred, which he was able to discharge by 1925. In that year, he joined the Chinese Commercial Bank (CCB). When the CCB merged with the Overseas Chinese Bank and Ho Hong Bank to form the OVERSEA-CHINESE BANKING CORPORATION (OCBC) in 1932, Tan was made manager of Eastern Realty Company, the bank's property arm. In 1933, he became the company's managing director.

On 4 February 1942, Tan was sent by the OCBC directors to re-establish the bank in an area out of enemy control and in the British empire. He was to have proceeded to Rangoon but ended up in India, where he temporarily registered OCBC's headquarters.

When WORLD WAR II ended, Tan returned to Singapore, relocating OCBC's headquarters here. He took over as the bank's managing director. When civilian rule was re-established in 1946, he continued to play an active role in public affairs following his appointments to the governor's Advisory Council, the Legislative Council and the RENDEL COMMISSION. In 1951, he was appointed Deputy President of the Legislative Council, the highest position then available for a Singapore national. That same year, he was appointed Commander of the Order of the British Empire (CBE). He withdrew from public office to concentrate on his commercial responsibilities in 1955.

Tan is credited with building OCBC. The bank started in 1932 with an issued capital of $10 million. OCBC saw its shareholders' funds rise from about $15 million in 1945 to $70 million when Tan assumed the chairmanship in 1966. By the time he retired in 1983, the funds exceeded $1.1 billion. The bank's market capitalization stood at a record $5.3 billion.

For his contributions to banking and finance, Tan was made the first Asian fellow of the Australian Institute of Management, and of the Institute of Bankers in London. In 1991, the NATIONAL UNIVERSITY OF SINGAPORE (NUS) conferred on Tan an honorary doctorate of laws. Tan founded the TAN CHIN TUAN FOUNDATION which supports charitable and educational causes.

Tan Chin Tuan Foundation, The Founded by TAN CHIN TUAN in 1976 and previously known as the Tan Foundation, this foundation provides assistance to the aged, poor, needy and sick, and to various charitable and educational causes. In recent years, sizeable donations have included $500,000 to the 2003 Courage Fund (for SARS) and $29 million to the NATIONAL UNIVERSITY OF SINGAPORE (NUS) to establish four Tan Chin Tuan Centennial Professorships and one Visiting Professorship (2005).

Tan Eng Liang (1937–) Academic, sportsman and politician. Tan Eng Liang was educated at Raffles Institution where he was a top student and sportsman, representing Singapore in swimming and water polo. He graduated from the University of Malaya in Singapore with an honours degree in chemistry in 1961 and won the prestigious Rhodes Scholarship to pursue his postgraduate studies at Oxford University, United Kingdom. Tan was the first Singaporean to be awarded the Rhodes Scholarship.

Tan was a keen water polo player, and represented Singapore in that sport at the Olympic Games in Melbourne (1956), the Asian Games in Tokyo (1958) and the Asian Games in Bangkok (1966). In 1964, he obtained his PhD in chemistry and taught organic chemistry at the University of Singapore (1964–66). In 1966, he left academia for the private sector and became chief chemist and director of research at ZUELLIG GROUP (1966–75).

In 1972, Tan entered politics on the PEOPLE'S ACTION PARTY ticket and became MEMBER OF PARLIAMENT for River Valley constituency. He served as senior minister of state for national development (1975–78) and senior minister of state for finance (1979–80). He has since held a number of management positions in listed companies.

Tan has also served on many sport-related committees, including the Singapore National Olympic Council and the Singapore Amateur Swimming Association. He was the Singapore contingent's chef de mission to the 1984 Olympic Games in Los Angeles and the Southeast Asian Games in 1993 and 1995. He was awarded the MERITORIOUS SERVICE MEDAL in 1991.

Tan Eng Yoon (1928–) Sportsman. Tan Eng Yoon became a champion athlete in Singapore and Malaya in 1950. He successfully competed in both track and field

Tan Cheng Bock

Tun Sir Tan Cheng Lock

Tan Chin Tuan

Tan Eng Liang

Tan Eng Yoon

events, setting national records for the 100-yard sprint (9.8 seconds) and triple jump (15.13 m). His most memorable personal sporting moment came in Singapore in 1955 when he defeated Fijian champion Thomas Naidole in the long jump.

Tan participated in the Melbourne Olympics in 1956, but did not qualify due to injury. He competed with distinction at the Commonwealth Games in Cardiff in 1958, and in 1959 took the first gold medal for Singapore in the Southeast Asian Peninsular (SEAP) Games in Bangkok.

Tan also enjoyed an illustrious career as a teacher, coach and administrator. After obtaining a diploma at the Singapore Teachers' Training College, he won a scholarship in 1955 to study physical education at Loughborough College in the United Kingdom. He went again to that country to sit for the British AAA examinations for coaching and track and field judging, and was awarded the Honorary Senior British Coach badge.

In Singapore he was appointed honorary national coach, a position he held until 1970, after which he spent time in administration, most notably in the cycling association and as secretary of the Football Association of Singapore (FAS). He was Coach of the Year in 1970. In 2005, Tan was awarded an honorary doctorate by Loughborough University for his contribution to sport.

Tan Gee Paw (1944–) Civil servant. Tan Gee Paw studied at the UNIVERSITY OF SINGAPORE, and then joined the civil service in 1967. He worked in the Public Works Department and the PUB (Public Utilities Board), and was principal of Ngee Ann Polytechnic (1989–95). As permanent secretary at the Ministry of the Environment from 1995 to 2001, Tan promoted the NEWATER project to recycle wastewater. Upon retiring from the Administrative Service in 2001, he became chairman and chief executive of PUB. He was awarded the MERITORIOUS SERVICE MEDAL in 2001.

Tan Howe Liang (1933–) Sportsman. Born in Swatow (present-day Shantou), China, Tan Howe Liang settled in Singapore after World War II. In 1952, he joined a weightlifting club, and within two years participated in the Asian Games in Manila,

taking fourth place. Tan's bid for a medal in the 1956 Olympic Games in Melbourne was unsuccessful, but at the Commonwealth Games in Cardiff two years later, he not only won a gold medal, but also established a world record in the jerk with a lift of 347 lbs. That year, he also won gold at the third Asian Games in Tokyo.

Tan was a triple Olympian. Besides the 1956 Olympics in Melbourne, he also participated in Rome (1960) and Tokyo (1964). He is Singapore's sole Olympic medallist. In September 1960, the 27-year-old lifted 380 kg in the lightweight (under 67.5 kg) category to take the silver. For this remarkable achievement, Tan received the MERITORIOUS SERVICE MEDAL in 1962.

Tan is the only Singaporean to have won a medal in all the major international games: Olympic, Commonwealth, Asian, and Southeast Asian Peninsular (SEAP) Games (silver at the Olympics; all others gold). He was the first weightlifter in the world to be awarded the International Weightlifting Federation Gold Award in 1984. He was also awarded the International Olympic Committee (IOC) Silver Pin in 1988 for his medal-winning performance at the 1960 Rome Olympic Games. He was inducted into the Singapore Sports Council Hall of Fame in 1985.

Tan Hwee Hock (1929–) Sportsman. Tan Hwee Hock was a key player in the national WATER POLO team which won an Asian Games silver medal in New Delhi in 1951 and a gold medal in Manila in 1954, which was Singapore's only gold for a team sport at the Asian Games. Tan graduated from the Teachers' Training College (TTC) and later from Loughborough College in the United Kingdom, and became a pioneer physical education teacher and aquatics coach. He was the swimming coach for the Malaysian team at the 1964 Olympic Games in Tokyo.

Tan is associated with the progress of the swimming association and the water polo team which dominated regional com-

Tan Howe Liang

Tan Hwee Hock, centre.

petition throughout the history of the SEAP/SEA Games from 1965 to 2003. He became a College of Physical Education lecturer when the institution opened in 1984. Tan was Coach of the Year (1987) and was later inducted into the Singapore Olympic Academy (2003).

Tan Hwee Hwee (1974–) Author. Tan Hwee Hwee left Singapore at 15 to live for three years in the Netherlands where her father had been posted. She graduated from the University of East Anglia, United Kingdom. Tan's debut novel, *Foreign Bodies* (1997), was published while she was pursuing a master's degree in English studies at Oxford. A New York Times Foundation Fellowship (1997–2000) enabled Tan to secure a Master of Fine Arts in Creative Writing from New York University. *Mammon Inc.* (2001), which was written in New York and inspired by Tan's own nomadic, cross-cultural life, won the 2004 Singapore Literature Prize for Fiction in English. It was adapted for the stage for the 2002 SINGAPORE ARTS FESTIVAL. Tan received the NATIONAL ARTS COUNCIL's Young Artist Award for Literature in 2003.

Tan I Tong (1921–) Businessman. Tan I Tong, was born in Medan, Dutch East Indies (present-day Indonesia). He was educated at the Su Tong Middle School in Medan (1936); the Chip Bee Commercial College, Amoy (present-day Xiamen), China (1936–37); and Khalsa English School (1938–42). Tan became known in Singapore as one of the first directors of the National Iron and Steels Mill (later NATSTEEL) (1961–2003). Subsequently, he held directorships in a number of companies, including Hong Leong Finance (1979–2004) and CITY DEVELOPMENTS LIMITED (1973–2004). He was a member of the Jurong Town Corporation (1968–71), vice-chairman of the Basketball Association of Singapore and director of the National Productivity Board. In 1976, Tan was appointed chairman of the Singapore Tourist Promotion Board (STPB). In 1984, Tan stepped down as chairman of STPB but remained chairman of the Sentosa Development Corporation until 1985, when he was succeeded by ALAN CHOE. Tan received the MERITORIOUS SERVICE MEDAL in 1983.

Tan Hwee Hwee

Tan Jiak Kim (1859–1917) Businessman and philanthropist. Tan Jiak Kim was the eldest son of merchant TAN BENG SWEE. He was educated at home, and in 1877 joined the family business of Kim Seng & Co. as an apprentice. In 1884, following the death of his father, he was taken into partnership by his uncle Tan Beng Gum.

In 1890, Tan Jiak Kim and five other businessmen established the STRAITS STEAMSHIP COMPANY. He invested in property and was one of the first of his generation to be interested in RUBBER cultivation. Tan was later to become director of the United Rubber Estate Company in Singapore and several other rubber estates in Malacca. He also grew PEPPER AND GAMBIER on a smaller scale. In 1915, he formed Kim Seng Land Co., which managed Pasir Panjang Rubber Estate.

Tan was the longest-serving Chinese member of the Legislative Council (1890–93; 1903–15), and was also a member of the MUNICIPAL COMMISSION (1888–92; 1894–97). He served as the Hokkien representative on the government's CHINESE ADVISORY BOARD (1890–1906); a committee member of the Po Leung Kuk (Office for the Preservation of Virtue) (1890–1906) (*see* CHINESE PROTECTORATE); justice of the peace (1891–1917); member of the TAN TOCK SENG HOSPITAL Committee (1896–1916); and member of the Opium Commission (1908). He was a staunch supporter of education, donating generously to Chui Eng Free School, RAFFLES INSTITUTION and the ANGLO-CHINESE SCHOOL. In 1912, he was made a Companion of the Order of St Michael and St George.

Tan is remembered for having spearheaded efforts to establish a medical college in the Straits Settlements. In 1905, the Straits Settlements and Federated Malay States Government Medical School (renamed the King Edward VII Medical School in 1913) commenced operations with $87,077 raised by Tan. He personally contributed $12,000 to the institution. Just before his death, he contributed two medical travelling scholarships worth $1,500, enabling students to pursue specialist studies abroad. He died of heart failure at his seaside home in Pasir Panjang.

Tan Kah Kee (1874–1961) Businessman, community leader and philanthropist. Born in Chip Bee (Jimei) village in Fujian province, China, on 21 October 1874, Tan Kah Kee arrived in Singapore at the age of 17 to work in his father Tan Kee Peck's rice store. When the business collapsed in 1904, Tan managed to raise enough money to start a small pineapple-canning business. From the pineapple business, Tan ventured into RUBBER and made his fortune. Aside from rubber, his business empire included rubber plantations and manufacturing, sawmills, canneries, real estate, import and

Tan Jiak Kim

export brokerage, ocean transport and rice trading. He amassed a huge fortune, and became known as the 'Henry Ford of Malaya'.

After the 1911 revolution in China, Tan resolved to contribute to nation-building efforts in that country. He delegated control of his business empire to his brother and junior partner, Keng Hean. In 1925, Tan Kah Kee & Company registered a net profit of $7.8 million, and the company had 32,000 staff on its payroll.

After 1925, the fortunes of Tan Kah Kee & Company began to decline due to depressed world rubber prices, competitive manufactured goods from Japan, competition from other rubber traders and heavy bank borrowings. In 1934, Tan's empire collapsed and he focused his energies on public education. Tan founded a number of educational institutions in his native Chip Bee and Singapore. Locally, these included TAO NAN SCHOOL (1906), AI TONG SCHOOL (1912), Chung Hock Girls' School (present-day Chongfu Primary School) (1915), THE CHINESE HIGH SCHOOL (1919), Nanyang Chinese Normal School (1941) and Nan Chiau Girls' High Full School (present-day NAN CHIAU HIGH SCHOOL) (1947).

In 1921 he set up Amoy University (present-day Xiamen University) in China, where LIM BOON KENG was first vice-chancellor, and maintained it for 16 years even after his financial collapse before the Chinese government took over the university in 1937. In Singapore, Tan supported Chinese schools and made contributions to the ANGLO-CHINESE SCHOOL and RAFFLES COLLEGE. He was active in campaigning for educational and social reforms in the 1920s and 1930s.

Tan was highly regarded as a community leader in Singapore. He was twice chairman of the Chinese Chamber of

Commerce and helped reorganize the SINGAPORE HOKKIEN HUAY KUAN. In 1923, when he was general manager of the EE HOE HEAN CLUB, the so-called 'Millionaires' Club' of Singapore, he launched the Chinese newspaper NANYANG SIANG PAU. During the years of China's struggle against the Japanese invasion, he provided leadership in organizing relief funds. Tan's role in Singapore's Legislative Council is less well known. In fact, Tan was an accomplished debater in the Council and consistently spoke out on community affairs. During World War II, the British authorities asked Tan, who was leader of the Singapore Chinese Mobilization Council, to help in the civil defence of the island, and to help sell war bonds for the war effort.

When the Japanese finally invaded Singapore, Tan fled to the Riau Islands. He spent much of the war in Malang, Java, and returned to Singapore in October 1945. He remained in Singapore until 1950, after which he returned permanently to China. Tan was anxious to help rebuild China, and his relationship with the British was becoming increasingly strained because of his open support for the communists. In China, he held several important posts, including vice-chairman of the People's Political Consultative Conference (1954–61), executive member of the Central People's National Congress (1954–61), chairman of the All-China Returned Overseas Chinese Association, and member of the People's Government and the Overseas Chinese Affairs Commission (1949–61).

Tan had four wives and 17 children. He died in Beijing at the age of 87, and was honoured with a state funeral.

Tan Kah Kee Foundation This charitable foundation was set up in memory of businessman and philanthropist TAN KAH KEE, who died in China in 1961. Initially, donations collected at his memorial service were used to establish the Tan Kah Kee Scholarship Fund (1961). In April 1968, the Tan Kah Kee Scholarship Trust Fund was established. In February 1982, the Tan Kah Kee Foundation was founded and granted Institution of Public Character status. It was empowered to raise an endowment fund of $8 million. Its mission is to carry on charitable works and foster the spirit of entrepreneurship and dedication to education promoted by Tan Kah Kee.

Tan Keong Saik (1850–1909) Businessman. Born in Malacca, Tan Keong Saik was sent to Penang for his education before moving to Singapore. He worked in Lim Kong Wan & Sons as a shipping clerk before becoming a storekeeper at the BORNEO COMPANY. For many years, Tan served as manager in the firm Chop Sin Heng Tye. His father and his uncles, Tan Choon Bock and TAN BENG SWEE, started a ferry service in the Strait of

Tan Kah Kee

Tan Kheam Hock: with family.

Tan Keong Saik

Tan Kian Por: the artist (below); Wisdom (2001).

Malacca. The vessels used on this service would later be acquired by the STRAITS STEAMSHIP COMPANY—a company upon whose board Tan Keong Saik served as a founding director. In 1890, Tan also became director of the Singapore Slipway Co. and Tanjong Pagar Dock Co.

Tan was one among five municipal commissioners in 1886 and one of the first members of the CHINESE ADVISORY BOARD and Po Leung Kuk, a welfare association. He was also made a justice of the peace. Keong Saik Road is named after him.

Tan Kheam Hock (1862–1922) Businessman. Born in Penang, the son of well-known Penang merchant Tan Teng Pong, Tan Kheam Hock was educated at Penang Free School. Later, he joined the Chartered Mercantile Bank of India. In 1887, he went to Calcutta and opened a general produce business there. He then moved to Singapore in 1889, and worked for the Great Opium Syndicate (see OPIUM) until 1906, except for the period 1898–1900.

In December 1901, Tan obtained a lucrative contract to supply labourers for the Tanjong Pagar Dock Co., which employed 2,500 labourers. He became chairman of Eastern United Assurance Corporation and director of numerous other rubber, tin and industrial companies.

Tan served as municipal commissioner and with the Straits Chinese British Association, CHINESE ADVISORY BOARD, welfare association Po Leung Kuk (see CHINESE PROTECTORATE), Council of the King Edward VII Medical School and Prince of Wales' Relief Fund, and was made a justice of the peace in 1912. Kheam Hock Road is named after him.

Tan Kian Por (1949–) Artist. Tan Kian Por graduated in 1970 from the Nanyang Academy of Fine Arts (NAFA), and was mentored by CHEN CHONG SWEE and Shi Xiangtuo. A lecturer at NAFA since 1980, Tan has been art advisor for numerous committees, including those for the CULTURAL MEDALLION and YOUNG ARTIST AWARD in Singapore, and the Chinese Canadian Arts Council.

Tan has been president of the Siaw-Tao Chinese Seal Carving, Calligraphy and Painting Society since its inception in 1971. He is a life member of the Korea Chinese Seal-Carving Society (Seoul) and the first Singaporean to be appointed an honorary member of the Xiling Seal-Carving and Calligraphy Society (Hangzhou, China).

Tan is known for his *Lotus* series—rendered in his signature blue wash—and use of tropical motifs such as angel-fish. An accomplished Chinese ink portraitist, he is also known for his unique fluid calligraphy and seal-carving skills. He received the Cultural Medallion in 2001.

Tan Kim Ching (1829–1892) Businessman, community leader and philanthropist. Tan Kim Ching was the eldest son of TAN TOCK SENG. Educated in both Chinese and English, he was fluent in several languages. He joined the family business Chop Chin Seng, and inherited the company upon his father's death in 1850. Tan was then among the richest men in Singapore, playing an influential role in business, local politics and Chinese community activities throughout the Malay Peninsula. Tan was also actively involved in international affairs, serving as Siamese consul in Malaya, and acting on behalf of the Japanese and Russian governments in Singapore.

Tan Kim Ching was the first president of the SINGAPORE HOKKIEN HUAY KUAN when it was established in 1860. In 1876, he and TAN BENG SWEE founded the TAN SI CHONG SU TEMPLE in Magazine Road. He was also appointed member of the Grand Jury (1864), justice of the peace (1865) and member of the MUNICIPAL COMMISSION (1888). He was much honoured and decorated for his public service and philanthropy.

After Tan's death, his body was buried in CHANGI.

Tan Kim Seng (1805–1864) Merchant and philanthropist. Born in Malacca, Tan Kim Seng embarked on a career as a trader on his arrival in Singapore around 1819, and amassed a large fortune. He was the founder of Kim Seng & Co. In 1850, he was appointed a justice of the peace.

Tan was a major public benefactor, building Kim Seng Bridge in Malacca; building and endowing the Chui Eng Free School on Amoy Street; and dedicating Kim Seng Road to the public. He was president of the Cheng Hoon Teng Temple in Malacca and leader of the Chinese communities in Singapore and Malacca, as well as a supporter of the TAN TOCK SENG HOSPITAL. On 18 November 1857 he offered the Straits government $13,000 to bring a better supply of fresh water into the town. Unfortunately, the first waterworks were established in 1878, 14 years after his death.

Tan Kim Seng died in Malacca. He was survived by his two sons, Tan Beng Gum and TAN BENG SWEE. The TAN KIM SENG FOUNTAIN is named in his honour.

Tan Kim Seng Fountain Originally erected in Fullerton Square in 1882, this Victorian-style fountain bears a resemblance to the Eros statue in London's Piccadilly Circus. It was commissioned to honour the memory of businessman and philanthropist TAN KIM SENG, whose donation was originally meant for the construction of a freshwater supply line from Bukit Timah to the town centre, but which was instead used for the impounding of a reservoir. The fountain was moved to QUEEN ELIZABETH WALK in 1925 to make way for the FULLERTON BUILDING.

Tan Lark Sye (1897–1972) Businessman and philanthropist. Born in Chip Bee (present-day Jimei), Fujian, China, Tan Lark Sye was the sixth in a family of seven brothers. He was educated at Chip Bee Primary School in his hometown, but did not pursue any further education. At the age of 18, he came to Singapore to work for TAN KAH KEE, who had come from the same village in China as Tan and was Chip Bee Primary School's main benefactor.

By the late 1920s, Tan was regarded as one of the leading figures in Malaya's RUBBER trade. In 1924, he founded Aik Hoe Rubber with his third brother Boon Khak, and the venture proved extremely profitable. Aik Hoe became the largest rubber exporter in Malaya and Singapore.

Tan was elected President of the Chinese Rubber Merchants' and the Rubber Packers' Associations. His business grew, but was devastated by the JAPANESE OCCUPATION. After the war, Tan worked to rebuild his empire and soon became one of Singapore's wealthiest men.

Outside the rubber business, Tan was chairman of the Board of Directors of the NANYANG SIANG PAU Press Ltd, and a director of the OVERSEAS UNION BANK Ltd (OUB) and OVERSEA-CHINESE BANKING CORPORATION (OCBC). He was also vice-president and president of the Singapore Chinese Chamber of Commerce (1941–45 and 1950 respectively), and president of the SINGAPORE HOKKIEN HUAY KUAN.

Tan donated substantial sums of money to his alma mater, Chip Bee School, in China, and led the Singapore Hokkien Huay Kuan to establish an educational trust fund for needy students. In his time, he was also the largest donor to the UNIVERSITY OF MALAYA, contributing some $300,000. However, it is his role in the establishment of NANYANG UNIVERSITY for which he is best remembered. Tan performed the ground-breaking ceremony for the university on 26 July 1953, and chaired its executive committee (1953–63). However, in 1963, Tan's Singapore citizenship was revoked by the PEOPLE'S ACTION PARTY government due to his overt support for Nanyang graduates running in the general election that year.

Tan continued to live in Singapore after having his citizenship revoked but travelled regularly to Ipoh, Perak, where he became chairman of Tasek Corporation—a cement producer. He also invested in paper milling in peninsular Malaysia, and continued to serve as chairman of Chiyu Banking Corporation, a Hong Kong-based bank he had joined in the 1940s.

In 1965, Tan was made honorary chairman of the Tung Ann District Guild. And in the following year, he took over as chairman of the insurance company Asia Life (*see* ASIA INSURANCE) after the death of his brother, Tan Boon Khak, who had previously served in that position. Tan retired in 1969, passing away in 1972. His funeral was attended by some 7,000 people, with thousands of others lining the streets.

Tan Lee Meng (1948–) Academic and judge. Born in Selangor, Malaya, Tan was educated at Victoria Institution in Kuala Lumpur, and then the University of

Tan Lark Sye: left, with Tan Kah Kee, 1949.

Tan Kim Seng Fountain

Singapore, where he graduated at the top of his law class with first class honours. Upon graduation, he joined the law faculty as a lecturer. After obtaining an LLM with distinction at University College London (1974), he returned to lecturing in Singapore. He later became associate professor (1982–88) and then professor of law (1988) at the National University of Singapore. From 1987 to 1992, he was also dean of the law faculty there.

Tan, whose particular expertise was in shipping and insurance law, authored two key treatises on these subjects. On 1 February 1997, he became the first academic to be appointed judicial commissioner and the first academic lawyer to be made a judge of the Supreme Court in 1997.

Tan Lip Seng (1942–) Photographer. Tan Lip Seng first got involved with photography at the age of 12. He is now ranked among the world's top photographers working in colour. He was the first Singaporean to be awarded a fellowship by the Royal Photographic Society (FRPS) of the United Kingdom for his colour slides in 1970. Tan is the honorary president of the Nusantara Photo Club of Indonesia and honorary advisor to numerous societies and art committees, including the Overseas Chinese Photography Society, Beijing, and the National Arts Council. Tan received the CULTURAL MEDALLION in 1985. That year, he was the first Asian to receive Diamond Galaxy rating from the Photographic Society of America, which was followed by a second Diamond rating in 1996. In 1998, he was awarded the Fenton Medal by the Royal Photographic Society, and was enrolled as an honorary life member.

Tan Seng Poh (1830–1879) Merchant and community leader. Tan Seng Poh was born in Perak, Malaya, the son of Tan Ah Hun, Perak's wealthy KAPITAN CINA. In 1837, his sister married SEAH EU CHIN and he came to Singapore for her wedding. He remained in Singapore to pursue an education, and later managed his father's OPIUM farms in

Singapore and Johor. Tan was also active in Seah Eu Chin's PEPPER AND GAMBIER business, and was Seah's assistant until the latter retired from active business around 1864. Tan then managed the business with Seah's two older sons until he retired in 1876.

By the 1860s, Tan was a major opium trader, and rivalry grew between him and CHEANG HONG LIM. The rivalry turned to partnership when Tan, Cheang and TAN YEOK NEE of Johor merged their opium and spirit farms to form the Great Opium Syndicate in November 1870. The Syndicate dominated Singapore's local economy and Chinese society from 1871 to 1879. Between 1874 and 1876, Tan was also manager of the largest pepper and gambier concern in Singapore. His other businesses at the time included the Alexandra Gunpowder Fireworks Factory at Tanah Merah.

Tan was active in public life, having been appointed municipal commissioner (three terms from 1870), justice of the peace (1871) and magistrate (1871). Tan retired in 1875. He died in 1879 and the Great Opium Syndicate died with him. Seng Poh Road and Seng Poh Lane were named after him.

Tan Kim Ching

Tan Kim Seng

Tan Ser Cher (1933–) Sportsman. Tan Ser Cher joined the Evergreen Club in Sophia Road and began training at the age of 16. He won the 1954 'Champion of Champions' title in the featherweight category at a local weightlifting competition when he was 21. Two years later, he represented Singapore at the 1956 Melbourne Olympics—his first international competition—and was placed seventh.

At the third Asian Games in Tokyo in 1958, he finished fourth. Two months later, he won the gold medal at the Commonwealth Games in Cardiff, lifting a total of 685 lbs in the featherweight division. He then retired. However, he was recalled to represent Singapore at the inaugural Southeast Asian Peninsular (SEAP) Games in Bangkok in 1959, where he won a bronze medal.

Tan is one of only three Singaporean athletes to have won a Commonwealth Games gold medal (the others being TAN

Tan Lip Seng: the photographer and his work (below).

Tan Siak Kew

HOWE LIANG and CHUA PHUNG KIM). He has been inducted into the SINGAPORE SPORTS COUNCIL HALL OF FAME.

Tan Si Chong Su Temple Chinese temple. Built in 1876, Tan Si Chong Su is the ancestral temple of the Tan clan in Singapore. It was originally sited on the banks of the SINGAPORE RIVER, close to a small islet known as Pulau Saigon. Today, the temple sits away from the river on Magazine Road, as part of the river has been reclaimed and the islet removed. In 1889, a school was established on its premises, and the school's name (Po Chiak Keng) became synonymous with the temple's. The school closed in 1949.

Construction of the temple was funded by two men from prominent Tan families: Tan Kim Ching, the eldest son of TAN TOCK SENG, and TAN BENG SWEE, the son of TAN KIM SENG. Other prominent Tans associated with the temple were TAN SIEW SIN and his father TAN CHENG LOCK.

The temple is elaborately decorated. The entrance hall is closed on three sides by double-leafed solid timber doors secured by a timber crossbar. 'Door gods'—Shen Tu and Yu Lei, dressed as guards and armed with bows, arrows and swords—have been painted on the temple's doors to ward off evil spirits.

Two timber plaques bearing the name of the temple are hung above the central bay in front of the prayer hall (Po Chiak Keng hall). As is typical of Chinese temple architecture, the hall is elevated about 35 cm above the level of the entrance hall. This hall is where the temple's major patron deities—Chen Sheng Wang and Da Bo Gong, statues of whom have been placed in niches behind an antique altar table—are worshipped. Other deities such as Guanyin are also worshipped in this chamber.

Chen Shengwang, known as Chen Yuanguang in life, was a general who led an army to conquer seven provinces during the Tang dynasty (618–907 CE). Da Bo Gong (also known as Tua Peh Kong), who protects devotees from illness and danger, is variously portrayed as a smiling old man with a long white beard; a red-cheeked old man with a white beard and white eye-

Tan Si Chong Su Temple

Tan Ser Cher

brows; and a bald old man with a staff in his right hand, and a gold ingot in the left.

The ancestral hall is hidden behind the prayer hall, a layout which reflects the Chinese concept of *li* (the humbling of oneself in respect of others). The ancestral tablets of illustrious members of the Tan clan, including the founders and past trustees of the temple, are stored in this hall. Newly inscribed tablets which chronicle the history of the Tan clan and the temple are also found here.

Tan Si Chong Su Temple was designed in the traditional style of southern Chinese temples, with features such as a curved roof, dancing dragons at the end of the roof ridges, and generous use of symbols such as phoenixes, flowers, dragons and lions. At the back of the prayer hall, on each side of the main altar, are two granite columns featuring a phoenix. These are said to be the only ones of their kind in local Chinese temples.

The history of the temple can be read from its signboards and plaques. There are five signboards made in 1880, and three more in 1898. They contain messages such as 'help the world and the people', to remind devotees to hold fast to virtue. The plaques record significant events and people such as the temple renovations in 1898 and 1926, as well as names of its benefactors. Tan Si Chong Su was gazetted as a national monument in November 1974.

Tan Siah Kwee (1948–) Calligrapher and teacher. Also known as 'Youzi', Tan Siah Kwee came to Singapore from China in 1955. He established the Chinese Calligraphic Society of Singapore in 1968. He has also taught calligraphy at the NANYANG ACADEMY OF FINE ARTS (1974–86) and NANYANG TECHNOLOGICAL UNIVERSITY (1995–). Tan has been an adviser to calligraphy societies in Hong Kong, the Philippines and Malaysia, and more than 30 calligraphy organizations in China, including the famous Guangzhou Poetry Society. His efforts have been recognized in the granting of the Long Service Award (1987), Public Service Medal (1991), ASEAN Achievement Award (1992), and Montblanc

Art Patronage Award (2002). In 2000, Tan was awarded the CULTURAL MEDALLION.

Tan Siak Kew (1903–1977) Banker, community leader and diplomat. Born in Guangdong, China, Tan Siak Kew came to Singapore at the age of seven. He was educated at St Anthony's School and Raffles Institution. In 1921, he undertook further studies in China and returned to Singapore after graduation. Tan then worked as a clerk at the Chartered Bank. At the age of 22, he married the daughter of well-known Teochew merchant Liau (Leow) Chia Heng, and joined his father-in-law's business. In 1931, he established Ban Lee Seng to deal in produce and spices—pepper, copra, fish maw and coffee. His business flourished, but he had to cease operations during the JAPANESE OCCUPATION.

After the war, Tan revived Ban Lee Seng and profited from the post-war shortage of all commodities. In the 1950s, he invested in the Sze Hai Tong Bank (Four Seas Communications Bank) and soon owned a controlling stake. In 1964, he took over as chairman and managing director of the bank (1964–78). He sponsored many educational institutions, including the University of Singapore and Nanyang University. He was appointed to the Singapore Chinese Chamber of Commerce, the TEOCHEW POIT IP HUAY KUAN and the Ngee Ann Kongsi.

Tan was also active in public service. In 1958, Tan was one of two nominated members of the Legislative Assembly. He was appointed Singapore's first ambassador to Thailand in 1966. In 1962, Tan received the MERITORIOUS SERVICE MEDAL. Siak Kew Avenue is named after him.

Tan Siew Sin, Tun (1916–1988) Malaysian politician. Tan Siew Sin was born in Malacca, and was the only son of TAN CHENG LOCK, founder of the MALAYAN CHINESE ASSOCIATION (MCA). He started his political career as division secretary of Malacca MCA in 1949. In 1955, he was elected member of Parliament for Malacca. He became Malaya's finance minister in 1959, a post he held for 15 years. He took over the helm of the MCA in 1961 and led the party until his retirement in 1974.

As finance minister of the Malaysian Federation, Tan believed that his ministry in Kuala Lumpur was responsible for controlling the machinery for tax collection in Singapore. He argued that the federation had struck a bad bargain with Singapore over a proposed development loan which Singapore was to give the federation. He also opposed proposals for a common market for Singapore and Malaysia. As head of the MCA, Tan was concerned by the impact the PEOPLE'S ACTION PARTY (PAP) was making on his Chinese constituents on the Peninsula, and campaigned vigorously against the PAP in the FEDERAL ELECTION

Tan Siah Kwee

(1964). Negotiations between Tan and his Singapore counterpart, finance minister GOH KENG SWEE (who was Tan's cousin) proved difficult.

Tan Soo Khoon (1949–) Businessman and politician. Tan Soo Khoon was educated at the Anglo-Chinese School and the University of Singapore. He was elected member of Parliament for Alexandra constituency at the age of 27, and became noted for his outspoken views expressed from the backbench. Tan has also been a successful businessman, running his own company, Crystal Time, since 1978. He was appointed deputy Speaker in 1985, then Speaker (1989–2002). He presided over Parliament's move to the new Parliament House in 1999.

Tan Swie Hian (1943–) Artist, sculptor, poet and calligrapher. Born in the Dutch East Indies (present-day Indonesia), Tan Swie Hian settled in Singapore and graduated with a degree in modern languages and literature from NANYANG UNIVERSITY in 1968. His poetry collection, *The Giant*, was published that same year—the first of some 40 publications. The quadrilingual Tan has translated works by Samuel Beckett, Henri Michaux, Latiff Mohidin and Marin Sorescu. He was chief editor of *Chao Foon*, a monthly literary review.

Tan has described his work as 'trying to combine the spirit of ancient Chinese philosophy, Western philosophy, Indian philosophy, particularly Buddhism, and the feelings and thoughts of a Chinese Singaporean'. His numerous honours have included three French accolades: Chevalier de l'Ordre des Arts et des Lettres (1978); Gold Medal, Salon des Artistes Français (1985); and Chevalier de l'Ordre Nationale du Mérite (1989). Tan was the first Southeast Asian correspondent-member admitted into l'Académie des Beaux-arts of the Institut de France (1987). That same year, he received the Pingkat Apad from the Angkatan Pelukis Aneka Daya (Association of Artists of Various Resources), as well as the CULTURAL MEDALLION.

Tan is the only living artist to have had a private museum in Singapore dedicated to him (Tan Swie Hian Museum, opened in 1993). The Tan Swie Hian Collection at the National Library was so named following

Tan's donation in 2003 of over 6,000 publications and artefacts from his collection.

Tan won the Chinese Literature Prize (in Singapore) in 1988, and the Marin Sorescu International Poetry Prize (in Romania) the following year. In 2003, he was awarded an honorary doctorate of letters by NANYANG TECHNOLOGICAL UNIVERSITY; represented Singapore at the 50th Venice Biennale; and was awarded the MERITORIOUS SERVICE MEDAL. The SINGAPORE ART MUSEUM held a major exhibition of Tan's works in 2004.

Tan Tarn How (1960–) Playwright. Tan Tarn How was educated at Cambridge University, United Kingdom on a government scholarship. He served part of his teaching bond before joining THE STRAITS TIMES in 1987 where he worked, off and on, for 16 years. Tan was head scriptwriter for English-language drama at MEDIACORP (1996–99) (*see* TELEVISION BROADCASTING) and associate artistic director of THEATREWORKS (2002–04).

Tan's *In Praise of the Dentist*, co-written with Cheam Li Chang, won a Merit Prize in the 1986 NUS-Shell Short Play Competition. His *Two Men, Three Struggles* won a Merit Prize in the 1987 competition. Under TheatreWorks' Writers' Laboratory programme, Tan wrote *Home* (1992), *Undercover* (1992), and *The Lady of Soul and Her Ultimate 'S' Machine* (1992), plays characterised by wit, farce, social comment and criticism. The satirical *Lady of Soul* went through a year of negotiations before a performance licence was secured. The imprisonment of Michael Fay inspired *Six of the Best* (1996). Other plays include *First Emperor's Last Days*, a 1998 Festival of Arts commission, and *Machine* (2002). Tan is currently a senior research fellow at the INSTITUTE OF POLICY STUDIES.

Tan Teck Chwee (1917–1988) Teacher, businessman and civil servant. Born in Amoy (present-day Xiamen), China, Tan Teck Chwee came to Singapore at a young age and was educated at Gan Eng Seng School and Raffles Institution. He then read engineering at the University of Hong Kong, but had to discontinue his studies and return to Singapore due to a change in his family's fortunes. Tan was awarded a Raffles College Scholarship, which enabled him to study science at Raffles College (1936). After graduation, he obtained his diploma in education and commenced teaching at St Andrew's School (1940). After World War II, Tan taught at Raffles Institution until 1957 when he moved into business, running Johore Granite Quarries.

Thereafter, Tan became involved in numerous businesses associated with building and construction. He was also active in public service, serving on the Boards of the Public Service Commission, PUB (Public Utilities Board) and the Singapore Institute

of Standards and Industrial Research (SISIR). In 1971, Tan became chairman of Jurong Shipyard and Jurong Engineering. He retired from these two appointments in 1988 because of ill health. In 1975, he was appointed chairman of the Public Service Commission and was credited with improving the system of scholarship awards, and the recruitment and promotion of public officers. For his contributions, Tan was admitted into the DISTINGUISHED SERVICE ORDER in 1982.

Tan Teck Khim (1925–2003) Police officer and civil servant. Tan Teck Khim was educated at St Andrew's School. In 1945, he joined the police force as a constable and was promoted to the rank of inspector the following year, just ten months after joining. Between 1958 and 1960, Tan was commandant of the Police Training School, and later superintendent in charge of Area 2. In September 1969, at the age of 38, he was appointed assistant commissioner of police.

From 1965 to 1968, Tan was seconded to the Ministry of Defence to become director of general staff, and became involved in defence planning and the introduction of NATIONAL SERVICE. In 1968, he was seconded to the Ministry of Health as acting permanent secretary. After overseeing the Keep Singapore Clean campaign, Tan returned to the police force as commissioner of police. In 1978 at 46 years of age, he was the youngest man to have held that post. He retired in 1978.

Tan Teck Khim's numerous awards included the MERITORIOUS SERVICE MEDAL (1967), and he was admitted to the DISTINGUISHED SERVICE ORDER (1971). When he retired, the Malaysian government conferred on him the title of Tan Sri

Tun Tan Siew Sin

Tan Soo Khoon

Tan Swie Hian: the artist/calligrapher (below); **The Six Indriyas** *(1996) (left).*

Tan Tarn How

Tan Tock Seng Hospital

when he was awarded the Panglima Setia Mahkota. He became chairman of Hotel Negara and a director of the United Motor Works and the OVERSEAS UNION BANK. Tan died of a heart attack in June 2003.

Tan Tian Boon (1927–) Civil servant. Tan Tian Boon graduated from the University of Malaya with a bachelor of science in 1952, and started his career with the SINGAPORE IMPROVEMENT TRUST (SIT). He later joined SIT's successor, the HOUSING & DEVELOPMENT BOARD (HDB). In 1956, he went to London and qualified as a professional member of the Royal Institution of Chartered Surveyors (RICS). On his return, he was involved in the valuing of land acquired for PUBLIC HOUSING and the resettlement of farmers. He also gave the urban renewal programme impetus by helping to launch the first sales of urban renewal sites for private development. In 1978, he left to become general manager of Jurong Town Corporation, which he led until 1981. He received the silver Public Administration Medal in 1963, and the gold medal in 1979. He was awarded the National Trades Union Congress' Friend of Labour medal in 1980.

Tan Tiong Boon (1966–) Sportsman. Tan Tiong Boon began playing billiards and snooker at the age of nine, often skipping school in order to play with his friends. He did not remain in school for long, and worked in billiards and snooker saloons to earn a living.

Tan won medals at six consecutive Southeast Asian (SEA) Games (*see* table). As

Tan Tiong Boon

TAN TIONG BOON: MEDALS WON

Year	Event (location)	Medal
1991	SEA Games (Manila)	Silver
1993	SEA Games (Singapore)	Silver
1995	SEA Games (Chiang Mai)	Bronze
1997	SEA Games (Jakarta)	Silver
1998	Asian Games (Bangkok)	Silver
1999	SEA Games (Brunei)	Silver, bronze
2001	SEA Games (Kuala Lumpur)	Bronze

Source: Singapore Sports Council

a 32-year-old, he won Singapore's first silver medal of the 1998 Asian Games in Kuala Lumpur—in eight-ball—after succumbing 6-13 in the final to the Taiwanese former world champion Chao Fong Pang. Tan specialized in the nine-ball, and attempted eight-ball just months before winning this medal. In 1999, he won a silver medal in nine-ball doubles with Ricky Chong at the SEA Games in Brunei, and a bronze in 15-ball doubles with his partner Ang Boon Lay.

Tan Tock Seng (1798–1850) Merchant, community leader and philanthropist. Born in Malacca, Tan Tock Seng arrived in Singapore in 1819. He began selling vegetables, fruits, betel nut and poultry. He opened a shop at Boat Quay and went into partnership with an English merchant, J. Horrocks Whitehead, of Shaw, Whitehead and Company, to trade in wholesale local produce in 1823. They exported tropical produce such as PEPPER AND GAMBIER, and imported construction materials. During their 20-year partnership, Tan and Whitehead became leaders in the commercial field. The business also made Tan his fortune.

In 1844, Tan became the first Asian justice of the peace in the Straits Settlements, and was often involved in dispute settlement for the CHINESE community. His status within the Chinese community was reflected by the fact that he also acted as KAPITAN CINA.

Tan's enduring legacy in Singapore is found in the TAN TOCK SENG HOSPITAL, which was originally a pauper's hospital. From 1843 until his death in 1850, Tan paid for the burial of all Chinese paupers who died on the streets. His son, TAN KIM CHING, continued this tradition after his death. Tan offered to build a pauper's hospital at Pearl's Hill for $5,000, provided the government undertook its maintenance. The hospital was opened in 1849. Tan was survived by his wife, Lee Seo Neo, a wealthy landowner and his three sons: Kim Ching, Teck Guan and Swee Lim.

Tan Tock Seng Hospital Built with $5,000 donated in 1844 by its founder, philanthropist TAN TOCK SENG, this institution started as a pauper's hospital at Pearl's Hill. The colonial government undertook the hospital's maintenance when it was opened in 1849. This site was expropriated by the government in 1856. Thereafter, patients were housed in temporary buildings until 1860, when a hospital building was completed at the corner of Balestier and Serangoon Roads. In 1909, the hospital moved again to Moulmein Road when the previous site was given to the Cantonese community to build Kwong Wai Shiu Free Hospital (*see* KWONG WAI SHIU HOSPITAL). Its premises at Jalan Tan Tock Seng were completed in 1999.

One of Singapore's largest hospitals, Tan Tock Seng Hospital (TTSH) has 1,400 beds and provides a range of healthcare services through the main hospital, the Rehabilitation Centre and the Communicable Disease Centre. It is an acute-care general hospital with 23 clinical disciplines and a full range of sub-specialities. TTSH's particular strengths are in infectious diseases, geriatric medicine, rehabilitation medicine, respiratory medicine and rheumatology.

The Communicable Disease Centre provides services for such infectious diseases as community-acquired infections and HIV infection, outbreak disease management, infection control, tropical medicine and travel-related illnesses. It also conducts research and clinical trials for infectious diseases. In March 2003, when SEVERE ACUTE RESPIRATORY SYNDROME (SARS) struck Singapore, TTSH was the designated screening and treatment centre.

TTSH also runs Yew Tee Specialists Clinic in Choa Chu Kang. Specialists in ENT (ear, nose and throat), eye and urological problems are sent there. TTSH also has a Foot Care and Limb Design Centre for the design, fabrication and fitting of braces, splints and prosthetic limbs.

Tan Wah Piow (1952–) Political activist. Tan Wah Piow rose to prominence in his third year of architectural studies at the University of Singapore, when he was president of the students' union. In 1974, he was charged with rioting inside the offices of the Pioneer Industries Employees' Union (PIEU), and was jailed. After his release, Tan fled to the United Kingdom in 1976. He continues to live in London, where he is a partner in a law firm. Tan's Singapore citizenship was revoked in 1987.

Tan Yeok Nee (1827–1902) Merchant. Tan Yeok Nee, also known as Tan Hiok Nee and Tan Hock Nee, left China for Singapore at a young age. He started work-

Tan Tock Seng

Tan Tock Seng Hospital: the old building at Pearl's Hill.

Tanah Kubor Temenggong

ing as a coolie, later peddling cloth woven by his wife. During his daily visits to Telok Blangah, he struck up a friendship with ABU BAKAR, who would later become Sultan of Johor. In the 1850s, Tan went to Johor, where he partnered Tan Ban Tye and obtained a *surat sungai* (Malay for 'river letter'), which allowed its holder to open plantations, collect taxes, manage local government and control agriculture on the river. Through his friendship with Abu Bakar, he managed to obtain several other *surat sungai* and eventually became the biggest Chinese tycoon in Johor.

Tan's businesses flourished through the farming of OPIUM, PEPPER AND GAMBIER. By 1866, he established himself in Singapore under the trading name of Kwang Hong. In 1870, he was named 'Major China of Johor'—the only person ever to be granted this title—and was one of only two Chinese to serve in the 24-member council of Abu Bakar's government.

In the same year, three opium tycoons, TAN SENG POH, CHEANG HONG LIM and Tan Yeok Nee, joined together to form the Great Opium Syndicate, merging the opium and spirit farms of Singapore, Johor, Riau and Malacca under one company. Tan resigned from the syndicate at the end of 1875 when he retired to Singapore. He is remembered today for his mansion on Clemenceau Avenue, which was built in 1885 and houses the Singapore campus of the UNIVERSITY OF CHICAGO GRADUATE SCHOOL OF BUSINESS (*see* HOUSE OF TAN YEOK NEE). The mansion was a replica of one in his home village, Sa Lin, in China. Tan returned to Sa Lin in his final years, and died there.

Tanah Kubor Raja Muslim cemetery. The Tanah Kubor Raja is thought to have been established in the early 19th century. It is owned by the Sultan of Johor, and is located at Bukit Purmei, off Kampong Bahru Road. It is also believed to house the KERAMAT of Tengku Ali. The cemetery has been largely neglected over the years, and is not accessible to the public. The mosque next to the cemetery was originally a pavilion of the former Istana, which was located further up the slope.

Tanah Kubor Temenggong This Malay cemetery is located off Telok Blangah Road, next to the TEMENGGONG DAENG IBRAHIM MOSQUE. It is maintained by the

Sultan of Johor. The cemetery is believed to have been built in the early 19th century. There is also a mausoleum housing the tombstones of Sultan Daeng Ibrahim and his father, TEMENGGONG ABDUL RAHMAN. It is visited annually by the Sultan of Johor.

Tanah Merah Country Club This club is located near CHANGI AIRPORT, and has two 18-hole golf courses straddling the EAST COAST Parkway. The club has hosted a number of international tournaments. Although membership was originally open only to civil servants, membership soon became prestigious and exclusive.

The club's Garden Course (which was first conceived in 1981 and took four years to complete) is a caddie/walking course; its Tampines Course is a buggy course which is set around a lake. Preliminary concept designs for the Tampines Course were prepared in late 1982; the course was not completed until February 1988, and was renovated in 1999.

Tang, Kelly (1961–) Musician. Educated in Canada and the United States, Kelly Tang Yap Ming has been described as a 'musical all-rounder'. Although rooted in Western CLASSICAL MUSIC, his compositional style springs from a confluence of diverse sources including jazz, rock, pop, film and world music. Besides a formal musical education, he also studied south Indian drumming under legendary *mrdangam* virtuoso Trichy Sankaran. He lectures at the NATIONAL INSTITUTE OF EDUCATION (NIE), where he is also founder and director of the NIE Composers' Ensemble, which was commissioned in 2001 to produce five new works for ESPLANADE—THEATRES ON THE BAY.

Tang Choon Keng (Tang Un Tien) (1901–2000) Businessman. Tang Choon Keng was born in Swatow (present-day

Tanah Kubor Raja

Shantou), China, the son of a Presbyterian minister. He arrived in Singapore in 1922 with two trunks—one containing his personal effects and the other filled with $2,000 worth of lace and handmade embroidery work. He made a living by peddling this linen from door to door with the aid of a hired rickshaw. Tang returned to China briefly in 1930 to marry, later bringing his new wife, Sok Kiar, and his mother, to Singapore.

In 1932, Tang set up a shop at 231 River Valley Road to cater for a growing clientele. This was the forerunner to the department store TANGS. Tang's business floundered during the JAPANESE OCCUPATION. However, as he began to record profits again in the postwar years, Tang decided to sell his entire stock to raise capital for the acquisition of land on Orchard Road for a new building for his C.K. Tang Department Store, erecting the new building in 1958. Tang was kidnapped in 1960, but was released unharmed after his family reportedly paid a substantial ransom. When Tang died in September 2000, his sons, Wee Sung and Wee Kit, took over the day-to-day operations of TANGS.

Tan Wah Piow

Tang Da Wu (1943–) Artist. In 1974, Tang Da Wu obtained first-class honours in fine art (sculpture) at Birmingham Polytechnic in the United Kingdom. Following advanced courses at St Martin's School of Art, he obtained a masters of art from Goldsmiths College, University of London (1985). His return to Singapore in 1979 gave a boost to the alternative art scene; he shaped a generation of contemporary artists, especially through THE ARTISTS VILLAGE, which he founded.

Tang began engaging in performance art in 1979, participating in international performance festivals from the early 1980s. Employing simple, powerful motifs and the poetics of myths and narratives (such as the *Jantung Pisang* series), his performances and signature graphite drawings address topical, environmental and social issues—for example the consumption of endangered animal parts in *Tiger's Whip* (1991); and national and cultural identities in *I Was Born Japanese* (1995). His belief in the potential of the individual and the collective to effect social change underlie his community and public art projects and performances, such as *One Hand Prayer Project* (1996). In 1999 Tang was the recipient of the 10th Fukuoka Asian Culture Prize (Arts & Culture), Japan.

Tan Yeok Nee

Tang I-Fang (1924–) Businessman. Tang I-Fang was born in Anhui, China, and was educated at the National 8th Middle School there. He took a bachelor of science degree in mechanical engineering at the National Central University in China (1945), and an MBA at Harvard University (1948).

After launching an engineering business in the United States, Tang became

Tang Choon Keng

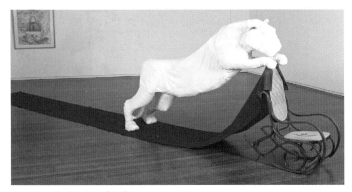

Tang Da Wu: Tiger's Whip *(1991).*

Tang Liang Hong

involved in development issues at the United Nations. He came to Singapore as a United Nations official in 1959. With Dutch economist ALBERT WINSEMIUS, he helped chart an industrial plan for Singapore. He was the first chairman of the ECONOMIC DEVELOPMENT BOARD (EDB) (1968–1972), and was admitted into the DISTINGUISHED SERVICE ORDER in 1972. He was subsequently chairman of the EDB Executive Committee (1975–1986), as well as Jurong Town Corporation (1979–1986), persuading many companies to invest in the industrial area of Jurong.

Tang was also chairman of the Sub-Committee on the Service Sector of the Singapore Economic Committee in 1985. He led automotive firm WBL Corporation Ltd (Wearnes) from 1978, and was named Singapore Businessman of the Year in 1989. He has also held directorships at Oversea-Chinese Banking Corporation, Times Publishing and Singapore Press Holdings.

Tang Liang Hong (1935–) Lawyer, community leader and political activist. Tang Liang Hong was one of eight children born into a family of farmers in Singapore. He only commenced studies at the age of 13, when he entered Yeung Ching Primary School. After graduating from high school, he taught in a village school for five years before entering NANYANG UNIVERSITY. He then enrolled at the UNIVERSITY OF SINGAPORE, graduating with a law degree in 1967 and taking his place at the Singapore Bar the following year.

Tang became active in the CHINESE community, serving in leadership positions in many community organizations. He later joined the WORKERS' PARTY and campaigned in the 1997 general election for a seat in the Cheng San Group Representation Constituency. PEOPLE'S ACTION PARTY leaders labelled Tang a 'Chinese chauvinist', and a series of defamation suits were filed against him. He was also accused of tax evasion. Shortly after the election, Tang fled to Malaysia and then to Australia to avoid arrest, and his assets were frozen.

T'ang Quartet This chamber group was formed in 1992 by violinists Ng Yu Ying and Ang Chek Meng, violist Lionel Tan and

cellist Leslie Tan. In 1999 it was awarded a Special Jury Prize for contemporary music at the Joseph Joachim Chamber Music Competition in Weimar, Germany. It has performed at numerous international music festivals around the world. The Quartet made its London debut at the Wigmore Hall in 2005 as part of the Singapore Season. The quartet released its first CD recording, *The Art of War*, in 2005.

Tanglin Residential district. The term 'Tanglin' is derived from the name of WILLIAM NAPIER's house—'Tang Leng' (later renamed TYERSALL)—which was built in 1854. The name 'Tang Leng' is believed to have been derived from the TEOCHEW term for the area—*twa tang leng*, meaning 'Great Eastern Peaks'. The Teochews were the first to venture into what was a TIGER–infested area in the years following the founding of Singapore. They were followed by European merchants, who built villas and plantations there.

The Tanglin area now stretches from the junction of Tanglin Road and Commonwealth Avenue to the junction of Orange Grove Road and ORCHARD ROAD. Several embassies and the Ministry of Foreign Affairs are located in Tanglin.

Tanglin Club The Tanglin Club was founded in 1865 when '40 good men and true' met for the purpose of establishing 'a club for the English in Singapore'. In 1866, the club's committee purchased a property which was then part of the Claymore Estate, and developed a clubhouse 'together with bowling alleys and carriage house'.

In March 1981, a new clubhouse was opened on the site of the original Claymore Estate property. Plans for a new sports complex were then drawn up. Protracted debates delayed major structural work until September 2005, however, when a special groundbreaking ceremony launched the first phase of development for the new complex. Although the club originally only admitted Europeans as members, it was later opened to people of all races. By 2005, the club could claim 5,500 members from 70 different countries.

Tanglin Halt Light industrial and residential area. The area was named after the now-

T'ang Quartet

defunct Tanglin Railway Station in the vicinity. Trains plying the route between TANJONG PAGAR and Johor would stop at the station to pick up passengers—hence the name 'Halt'. *See also* RAILWAYS.

Tangs Department store. The history of Tangs can be traced back to 1932, when businessman TANG CHOON KENG set up a shop on River Valley Road. He later took over six adjacent shops across the street, and built a three-storey building in 1940. This was the first C.K. Tang department store. It stocked embroidery, antique furniture, curios and Chinese art and crafts.

In 1958, the C.K. Tang Department Store moved to a landmark building on ORCHARD ROAD. The new building, with ornate Chinese decor, red pillars and a curved tiled roof, was built at a cost of $200,000, and was opened under the name of C.K. Tang. The new store was closed briefly in 1960 following differences between Tang Choon Keng and trade unions. It opened its doors again in 1961, and continued to expand.

In 1975, Tang Choon Keng decided to tear down the old building and construct a 33-storey hotel and shopping complex on the same site. The new building was opened in June 1982. It was topped by an octagonal, tiled pagoda roof. Besides the store, it also housed the Dynasty Hotel, which was sold to Marriott and renamed Marriott Hotel Singapore in 1995.

The store was exceptional in that it did not open on Sundays, a family tradition in deference to Tang, who was the son of a Presbyterian minister. This tradition was preserved until July 1994. As of 2006, C.K. Tang operates one flagship store—now known simply as Tangs—in Singapore, and a number of niche boutiques and speciality businesses in Singapore and Malaysia. It is also engaged in the wholesale and retail of merchandise as well as food-catering. Listed on the Singapore Exchange in December 1975, the group reported a net profit of $1.1 million on a turnover of $170 million for the financial year 2005.

Tanjong Katong Before land reclamation drove the sea back by more than a kilometre, Tanjong Katong was a pier at the end of what is now Amber Road. Until the 1950s, the name Tanjong Katong more broadly meant the seaside area where the old SEA VIEW HOTEL was situated. Today, it is the area stretching from Dunman Road, along Tanjong Katong Road, up to Amber Road. '*Tanjong*' means 'cape' in Malay, while 'Katong' is a variation of the Malay word *katung*, meaning 'leatherback sea turtle'.

Tanjong Pagar Tanjong Pagar Road was built in 1823. Its name, Malay for 'Cape of Stakes', may refer to the area's origin as a fishing village where there were *kelongs* (palisade traps).

In the 1830s, many European planters established NUTMEG plantations in the area. When the nutmeg market collapsed in the 1860s, the area reverted to secondary forest. However, a number of developments took place along the shoreline. Between 1850 and 1885, a number of wharves and docks were built. In 1852, P&O moved into the area and built a wharf there. Other major companies followed. When Tanjong Pagar Dock Co. was incorporated in 1864, it was decided that Victoria Dock should be built at Tanjong Pagar. In 1869, the dock was ready to handle all kinds of steamer traffic.

Tanjong Pagar remains a dock area, lending its name to the whole of PSA's complex parallel to Keppel Road. Tanjong Pagar is also the name of an electoral constituency, which was for many years under Minister Mentor LEE KUAN YEW, who is still part of the team representing the Tanjong Pagar GROUP REPRESENTATION CONSTITUENCY in Parliament.

Tao Nan School This was the first modern HOKKIEN school to be founded in the STRAITS SETTLEMENTS, and one of six modern Chinese schools set up in Singapore under the influence of educational reforms in China at the end of the 19th century (*see* CHINESE EDUCATION). The school was officially established on 18 November 1906 under the auspices of the SINGAPORE HOKKIEN HUAY KUAN, although classes did not commence until 1907, and even then were held in rooms in Siam House—the residence of TAN KIM CHING—on North Bridge Road.

Prominent benefactors of the school included Tan Boon Liat, Lee Cheng Yen, LOW KIM PONG, TAN KAH KEE and OEI TIONG HAM, who donated land for a building in Armenian Street. This new three-storey school building, which was completed in 1912, was designed in the Eclectic Classical style with a central air-well and decorative facade. The opening of the school's new premises coincided with the overthrow of the Qing dynasty in China.

Tao Nan School became the first Chinese-medium school to admit students from other dialect groups, rather than only HOKKIEN pupils. The school began to use MANDARIN as a medium of instruction in 1916, and it counts LEE KONG CHIAN among its graduates.

Although the Armenian Street building was extensively damaged during the JAPANESE OCCUPATION, it was repaired in 1945. The school continued to operate there until 1982, when it moved to a new building in Marine Parade. The original building was re-opened as the ASIAN CIVILISATIONS MUSEUM in 1997. It was gazetted as a national monument in February 1998.

Taoism The name 'Taoism' is derived from the concept of the *tao* (or *dao*)—'the Way'. The *tao* is conceived as a metaphysical reality, the origin of heaven and earth, and the beginning of all things. In the 5,000-character Daode Jing (Classic of the Way and Virtue)—the earliest and most important work on Taoism—is the statement: 'The Tao gave birth to the One. The One gave birth to the Two. The Two gave birth to the Three. And the Three gave birth to the myriad creatures.' This process of creation, as suggested by Taoists, can also be understood as a process of differentiation from unity to multiplicity.

As an organized religion, Taoism started during the Eastern Han dynasty (25–220 CE) in China. Zhang Ling, a native of Jiangsu province, established the first Taoist group in Sichuan, China. By means of sacred incantations, talismans and purification rites, he sought to restore the spiritual and physical health of his followers.

It is difficult to say exactly when Taoism was first introduced into Singapore. According to the TAOIST FEDERATION

Tanjong Pagar: conserved shop-houses in Tanjong Pagar Road.

(SINGAPORE), Taoism in Singapore can be traced back to 1821, when THIAN HOCK KENG TEMPLE was established. However, according to one early Chinese gazetteer, when the Chinese maritime explorer ADMIRAL ZHENG HE undertook his expeditions in the early 15th century, the deity worshipped by the crew on board his ships was Mazu, the patron deity of mariners, and one of the most popular deities in Singapore. During this time, the cult of Mazu grew significantly, with many new temples established all along the southeastern coast of China. It seems reasonable then to trace the beginning of Mazu worship in Southeast Asia to at least the 15th century, when the Chinese fleet brought not only goods for trade but also new forms of worship into the region.

The first Taoist temple in Singapore was probably the Shuntian Gong (Temple in Submission to Heaven), which was dedicated to Tua Peh Kong. It is believed to have been first built in 1796 at Malabar Street (which is now part of Bugis Junction shopping centre), and moved several times until it settled in its present premises in Geylang Lorong 29.

From the beginning of the 19th century, the number of Taoist temples in Singapore rose with the rapid influx of Chinese immigrants. Taoism gradually became the main religion in Singapore with the largest number of declared adherents. According to the 1980 census, among the Chinese population, 38.2 per cent were Taoists, while Buddhism, Christianity, and 'no religion' claimed 34.3 per cent, 10.6 per cent, and 16.7 per cent respectively. However, with the ageing of the old and the lack of young followers, the number of Taoists has dropped significantly. The 2000 Census of Population indicates that 10.7 per cent of the Chinese population still claim adherence to Taoism/CHINESE RELIGION. It should be noted, however, that due to the syncretic nature of Chinese Religion, many Chinese, particularly the less educated, do not make a clear distinction between Taoism and Buddhism. Many who claim to be Buddhists are actually Taoists or practitioners of folk religions, which include ancestor worship.

Tangs: the Orchard Road store.

Tao Nan School: staff and students, 1940.

Tanjong Katong: postcard, early 1900s.

Taoism: Taoist priest conducting a rite.

Taoism is the only indigenous religious tradition in China. Shaped and formed by native religious beliefs, it embodies a synthesis of traditional Chinese culture. It incorporated ancient astronomy, medicine, mathematics, alchemy and other religious arts into its understanding of 'the Way', and has developed various forms of divination such as astrology and geomancy. All these activities were and are still intimately related to the everyday life of the Chinese, including those in Singapore.

Taoist Federation (Singapore) Taoism in Singapore did not have a strong central organization in the past. It was not until 1979 that the Sanqing Taoist Association led a drive to set up an umbrella Taoist group. The result was the Taoist Federation (Singapore), which officially came into being in February 1990. With an elected central committee, the federation outlines its main objectives in its mission statement: promoting and strengthening Taoism in Singapore; enhancing a closer relationship and facilitating greater understanding and cooperation between the various Taoist organizations and the community of believers at large; promoting, organizing and supporting various educational, cultur-

al and social activities so as to bring Taoism closer to the people; and organizing, participating in, and supporting social and community services. Today, it has a membership of 166 temples.

Taoist Mission (Singapore) Taoist Mission (Singapore) was founded on 16 February 1996 with the aim of promoting Taoism and preserving Chinese traditions and values in Singapore. It states that its objectives are to promote Taoism and the Taoist spirit; to undertake research related to traditional Taoist culture; and to preserve Chinese values, traditions and heritage.

Since its inception, the Taoist Mission has realized the importance of communication and exchanges between different religious faiths, and has extended its educational and cultural programmes not only to devotees but also to the larger community. Themed exhibitions, such as 'Knowing Taoism', 'Taoist Identity' and 'Living in Harmony with Chinese Festivals and Celebrations', have been held annually together with Taoist Day, which falls on the fifteen day of the second lunar month and marks the birth of Lao Zi, the founder of Taoism (*see* box). The group has also conducted talks and seminars for government ministries and public organizations.

In 1996, the Taoist Mission was the first Taoist body admitted into the Inter-religious Organisation, Singapore (IRO). The president of the Taoist Mission Master Lee Zhiwang, was elected president of the IRO in 1999. Earlier this year, the Taoist Mission announced the establishment of the Tao Theology and Culture Centre to promote educational programmes and to conduct Taoist classes and related activities for the general public.

taxation The colonial authorities first introduced INCOME TAX in Singapore in 1948. The present government's declared strategy is 'to pursue low taxes and tight expenditures'. Rates for PERSONAL INCOME TAX and corporate income tax have thus been progressively reduced since the 1980s. In the year of assessment 2006, the maximum personal income tax rate was 21 per cent and

slated to drop to 20 per cent the following year, while the corporate income tax rate stood at 20 per cent (*see* CORPORATE TAXES).

In 2005, a total of $25.2 billion was collected in taxes. Besides personal and corporate income taxes, other taxes include GOODS AND SERVICES TAX (GST), property tax, betting taxes, customs and excise duties, and taxes on motor vehicles. Singapore has no capital gains tax. The GST was introduced in April 1994 as part of a strategy to move away from taxes on income and profits. The GST rate was increased from an initial 3 per cent to 4 per cent in 2003, and subsequently to 5 per cent in 2004.

Property tax was introduced in 1960. Since the early 1990s, the tax rate for owner-occupied residential property has remained at 4 per cent of the annual value of the property, while the tax rate for other properties has dropped from 16 per cent to 10 per cent.

As in many other countries, taxation has also been used in line with state policies. In order to encourage mechanization and automation, for example, the government has allowed accelerated capital allowance for most assets used for business purposes. Betting taxes and duties on liquour and tobacco are aimed at deterring behaviour that is deemed to incur a social cost, and in order to boost the fertility rate, tax rebates are given to families on the birth of the first to fourth child.

In May 1990, the CERTIFICATE OF ENTITLEMENT was introduced for motor vehicles (*see* CARS AND CAR OWNERSHIP). Since then, there has been a gradual shift from ownership taxes to usage taxes on motor vehicles, including fuel taxes, congestion tolls and the ELECTRONIC ROAD PRICING scheme. These taxes are aimed at minimizing traffic congestion and pollution. Since 2000, taxes on motor vehicles have represented close to 7 per cent of total operating tax revenue.

taxis The first motorized taxis appeared in Singapore in the late 1940s. Taxi meters were first installed in 1953, but many private cars continued to operate as 'pirate taxis' throughout the 1950s and 1960s,

Taoism: (from left) Chinese deities Mazu (Goddess of the Sea); Tua Peh Kong; Cai Shen (God of Wealth).

Lao Zi's birthday Lao Zi, the founder of the Taoist philosophy, is believed to have been born in China on the 15th day of the second month of the lunar calendar in 1301 BCE. His name means 'the old one' in Chinese, a reference to his extraordinary appearance at birth (he is said to have had a boy-like, youthful face and white hair). One finger on his left hand was purportedly pointed at the heavens, whilst a finger on his right hand was pointed to earth. Lao Zi is believed to have been a historian and custodian of the Imperial Archives of the Zhou dynasty. Later, he left for Han Ku Kuan, a frontier pass in western China. Lao Zi is said to have completed the 5,000-word Daode Jing before leaving the frontier pass. It is this book which teaches the attainment of *tao*, or 'the Way'.

Taoist scriptures teach that Lao Zi was the incarnation of Shen Pao Jun, through the incarnation of Yuanshi Tian Huang, or the Celestial Lord of the Ancient Beginning. He was deified as Taishang Lao Jun (Venerable Lord), and recognized as the patriarch of Taoism—the highest deity in the Taoist echelon. On Lao Zi's birthday, Taoist temples, such as San Qing Taoist Temple, and the Taoist Federation and Taoist Mission, hold celebrations ranging from cultural exhibitions; dinners; blessings for harmony, longevity and good health; and chanting of the Daode Jing. This day is celebrated annually by Taoists around the world as 'Taoist Day'.

Taxis: some company liveries (clockwise from lower left) Yellow-Top Cabs; Premier Taxis; ComfortDelGro; CityCab; TransCab Services; Smart; SMRT Taxis.

taking passengers to popular destinations for fixed fares. In 1970, there were an estimated 8,000 pirate taxi operators. However, most of these left the business during the 1970s with the formation of COMFORT (a transport co-operative established by the NATIONAL TRADES UNION CONGRESS), increases in diesel taxes, and more stringent regulation of the industry. In the late 1960s, non-transferable taxi licences were issued to individuals. However, new licences have been issued only to taxi companies since the 1970s.

A number of new companies were formed during the 1990s. By 2005, there were seven companies running a fleet of 21,800 air-conditioned, metered taxis in Singapore. The largest operator is ComfortDelGro, which had a fleet of more than 11,700 taxis in 2005. Others include SMRT Taxis, CityCab, Premier Taxis, Smart Automobile, TransCab Services and Yellow-Top Cabs.

Since September 1998, taxi fares have been deregulated, allowing operators to set fare rates according to market conditions. All taxis employ a standard flag-down rate, which covers the first kilometre of a journey. Thereafter, a meter is used to determine the fare according to distance travelled and time accrued. Additional surcharges apply during peak periods; between midnight and 6 a.m.; and for journeys from CHANGI AIRPORT. The LAND TRANSPORT AUTHORITY conducts periodic monitoring of the quality of service standards.

Almost all taxis are diesel-powered and carry a maximum of four passengers. Taxis can be hailed by the side of the road, except in the central business district, where they can pick up or drop passengers off only at designated taxi stands.

Tay, David P.C. (1945–) Photographer and publisher. In 1982, David Tay Poey Cher became the first recipient of the CULTURAL MEDALLION for photography. He is known for his composition and unusual perspectives. He earned the Honorary Excellence Distinction from the International Federation of Photographic Art in 1981. The Royal Photographic Society, United Kingdom, awarded him a fellowship in 1987 and the Fenton Medal in 1999.

Tay has been president of the PHOTOGRAPHIC SOCIETY OF SINGAPORE since 1990 and was instrumental in relocating the society to its Selegie Arts Centre premises in 1995. He has been a member of the National Arts Council Arts Advisory Panel since 1992. Awarded the Public Service Medal in 1999, Tay is also the former chief executive officer of the Singapore Press Holdings Magazines group.

Tay, Zoe (1968-) Actress. Brought up on a pig farm in Lim Chu Kang, Zoe Tay (Zheng Huiyu) was educated at Yuan Ching Secondary School. She was a successful model before she was crowned champion in the inaugural Star Search talent competition in 1988. She then went into acting full-time. Her first appearance in a drama serial was in *Miaotiao Shu Nü* (My Fair Ladies) (1988). In 1990, she became the first local celebrity to be featured in Lux commercials. In the following year, she played a materialistic and malicious woman, Bobo, in *San Mian Xia Wa* (Pretty Faces). The role demonstrated her versatility, and the media labelled her 'the woman of a thousand faces'.

In 1999, Tay ventured onto the big screen, starring as herself in *Liang Po Po Chong Chu Jiang Hu* (Liang Po Po The Movie). She was lead actress in her second movie, *Haizi Shu* (The Tree) (2001).

Tay has consistently been voted one of the Top 10 Most Popular Female Artistes at the MEDIACORP Star Awards. She clinched Best Actress Award in 1996 for her role in *Jin Zhentou* (Golden Pillow) (1995) and was nominated Best Actress at the 2000 Asian Television Awards. She was named LIANHE ZAOBAO's Favourite Asian Idol in 2003.

Tay Bin Wee (1926–2000) Theatre director. One of the founders of CHINESE THEATRE group Singapore Amateur Players (SAP), which later became ARTS THEATRE OF SINGAPORE. Tay Bin Wee co-directed Cao Yu's adaptation of Bai Jin's classic *Jia* (Family) for Chung Cheng High School Drama Society in 1954 and Xia Yan's *Fang Cao Tian Ya* (Fragrant Grass in Faraway Places) for the SAP in 1958. When he performed in the 1950s and early 1960s, he was well-known for portraying the antagonist. He acted in SAP's inaugural production, Cao Yu's *Ri Chu* (Sunrise) (1955) and SAP's production of Cao Yu's *Beijing Ren* (Peking Man) (1966). He also directed SAP's production of Henrik Ibsen's *The Doll House*.

In the 1980s, Tay was active in combined productions of Chinese drama groups staged for the SINGAPORE ARTS FESTIVAL, including *Xiao Bai Chuan* (The Little White Sailing Boat) (1982), *Wula Shijie* (Oola World) (1984), *Kafei Dian* (Kopitiam) (1986) and *Kabai Kabai* (1988). Tay was awarded the CULTURAL MEDALLION in 1988.

Tay Buan Guan Supermarket. This store was established in 1948 by entrepreneur Tay Leck Teck, who had already established a successful sundries business in JOO CHIAT before World War II. It was located in a cul-de-sac off Joo Chiat Road.

Tay Buan Guan was the first modern supermarket in the Joo Chiat area. It sold a range of imported goods, which drew the Peranakan, Eurasian and English-educated Chinese residents living in the area. The Tay Buan Guan Milk Bar on the same premises became well-known for its pastries.

Tay Buan Guan began to face competition in the 1970s and 1980s from larger shopping centres nearby such as Katong Shopping Centre and Parkway Parade, and was forced to close down. In early 2000, Tay Buan Guan's original building was demolished, and a condominium built in its place.

Tay Chee Toh (1941–) Artist. Painter and sculptor Tay Chee Toh was born in Johor and attended the NANYANG ACADEMY OF FINE ARTS in 1958–60. He was one of the founding members of the MODERN ART SOCIETY in 1964. Tay's early work was in batik, frequently using Dayak images from his 1965 visit to Sarawak. In the early 1980s he began working with three-dimensional forms: sculpture, mobiles and sculptural murals. He was one of the early winners of the UOB Painting of the Year Award, which was started in 1982.

In conjunction with his 2001 exhibition, *Body Lines*, Tay launched the Tay Chee

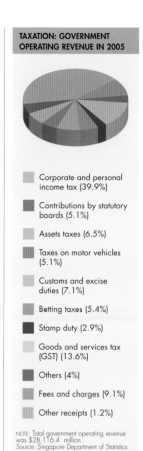

TAXATION: GOVERNMENT OPERATING REVENUE IN 2005

- Corporate and personal income tax (39.9%)
- Contributions by statutory boards (5.1%)
- Assets taxes (6.5%)
- Taxes on motor vehicles (5.1%)
- Customs and excise duties (7.1%)
- Betting taxes (5.4%)
- Stamp duty (2.9%)
- Goods and services tax (GST) (13.6%)
- Others (4%)
- Fees and charges (9.1%)
- Other receipts (1.2%)

NOTE: Total government operating revenue was $28,116.4 million.
Source: Singapore Department of Statistics

Zoe Tay

Tay Chee Toh: Red Aqua Magnum, *1975 (top);* Nude 2, *2000.*

Toh Visual Arts Fund to promote exchange programmes for local artists. Tay was awarded the CULTURAL MEDALLION in 1985.

Tay Chong Hai (1932–) Doctor. In 1969, Tay Chong Hai discovered a hereditary disease, trichothiodystrophy, now better known as Tay Syndrome. He was the first doctor in Southeast Asia to have a disease named after him.

Tay Syndrome is characterized by brittle hair, photosensitivity, abnormal fingernails and toenails, a prematurely aged-looking face, mental retardation and short stature. Often, patients have recurrent infections; bone and teeth abnormalities may also occur. Tay Syndrome is now well-documented in major dermatology and genetics textbooks.

Tay Chong Hai

Tay also identified the first outbreak of childhood hand, foot and mouth disease in Singapore (1972). He established the National Arthritis Foundation in 1984, and was chairman for 14 years.

Tay Eng Soon (1940–1993) Academic and politician. Tay Eng Soon was educated at the ANGLO-CHINESE SCHOOL, and then at the University of Bristol in the United Kingdom where he graduated with a first-class honours degree in electrical engineering. From 1963 to 1966, he pursued his PhD at University College London. Upon graduation, Tay worked as a research associate at Culham Laboratory in the United Kingdom.

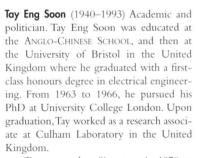

Tay Eng Soon

Tay returned to Singapore in 1970 to join the University of Singapore's Engineering Faculty, where he remained until 1978. He then left academia to become director of the DEFENCE SCIENCE ORGANISATION. During this time, Tay became a familiar face on television, hosting the popular Science and Industry Quiz for Schools.

Tay Kheng Soon

In 1980, Tay entered politics on the PEOPLE'S ACTION PARTY (PAP) ticket and was elected member of Parliament for River Valley constituency. The following year, he was appointed minister of state for education, and senior minister of state. He took part in the 1988 general election as a member of the PAP team that beat the WORKERS' PARTY team of FRANCIS SEOW, LEE SIEW CHOH and Mohd Khalit Mohd Baboo in a closely fought contest for the GROUP REPRESENTATION CONSTITUENCY of Eunos. Tay is best remembered for his advo-

cacy of polytechnic and technical education and the Open University programme. Tay died from heart failure. He was the older brother of architect TAY KHENG SOON.

Tay Kay Chin (1965–) Photographer. A graduate in photojournalism from the University of Missouri-Columbia, Tay Kay Chin was picture editor of THE STRAITS TIMES in 1999. His signature 'panoramic shots' are collected by the European House of Photography, Paris. His works were featured in the Month of Photography (2002, 2003, 2004) in Singapore; at Esplanade—Theatres on the Bay in 2003; and at the inauguration of The Arts House at Old Parliament House in 2004.

In 2001, Tay was presentation editor of *The Sun* newspaper in Bremerton, Washington. His front-page coverage of the 9/11 terrorist attacks was named one of the top ten cover designs in the world by the Poynter Institute, a centre for journalism in the United States. Tay was designated 'Hasselblad Master' in 2003.

An instructor at photographic school Objectifs and Nanyang Technological University, Tay sits on the selection panel for the CULTURAL MEDALLION.

Tay Kheng Soon (1940–) Architect. A 1959 graduate of SINGAPORE POLYTECHNIC, Tay Kheng Soon was a founding partner of Design Partnership, but left the practice in 1973. He returned in 1976 to form Akitek Tenggara. Tay was also a member of urban planning group SPUR. He argued that the climatic and cultural suitability of imported architectural models be reassessed. Parkway Builders Centre (1985) was his riposte to the ubiquitous enclosed atrium, and the Institute of Technical Education at Bishan (1986) questioned the general reliance on air-conditioning. In the Kampong Bugis Development Guide Plan (1990), he raised fundamental questions about the planning of megacities in the tropics. Subsequently with KK WOMEN'S AND CHILDREN'S HOSPITAL (1997), Tay developed a modern tropical architectural language of 'Line, Edge, Mesh and Shade' to a high level of sophistication. In 2000, Tay took up the post of adjunct professor of architecture at the National University of Singapore, but continued to practice. He is known for his strong views on architectural production in Singapore and for his spirited attacks on 'the lack of self-regard that drives always towards Western solutions'. He is the younger brother of politician TAY ENG SOON.

Tay Koh Yat (1880–1949) Businessman and community leader. Born in Fujian, China, Tay Koh Yat was orphaned at the age of eight. He moved to Singapore in 1902 to join Chop Guan Seng Hin, where he became a managing partner within ten years. He established his own firm, Guan Soon Company, in 1912. Its success allowed Tay to establish two other firms—

Aik Seng Hin and Chin Joo Seng. In 1937, Tay started the Tay Koh Yat Bus Company, which had the largest fleet of buses in pre-war Singapore.

When the Sino-Japanese war broke out in 1937, Tay helped raise $500,000 in war bonds to support China's war effort. He also contributed to Singapore's civil defence by rallying more than 10,000 Chinese as part of the Defence Corps. Due to his involvement in anti-Japanese activities, Tay was forced to flee to the Dutch East Indies (present-day Indonesia) during the JAPANESE OCCUPATION. However, he returned to Singapore after the JAPANESE OCCUPATION, and quickly re-established his bus company.

Tay was active in public life, serving as chairman of the Kim Mui Hoey Kuan clan association and president of the Thong Chai Medical Institution (*see* OLD THONG CHAI MEDICAL INSTITUTION), and founding the Appeal Committee for Singapore Chinese Massacred by the Japanese (*see* SOOK CHING). He advocated that the 10,000 civil defence personnel who had been killed by the Japanese should be honoured with proper burials. He spent considerable time and money obtaining information on the victims of Japanese attrocities in Singapore, and locating mass graves. Such work continued for more than a decade after Tay's death in 1949. For his services to the community, the British government made Tay an Officer of the Order of the British Empire (OBE).

Tay Seow Huah (1933–1980) Civil servant. Tay Seow Huah was educated at the University of Malaya, where he graduated with an honours degree in history in 1956 and joined the Administrative Service the same year. Tay became assistant secretary at the Ministry of Commerce and Industry (1958–61). He then moved to the Port of Singapore Authority (now PSA INTERNATIONAL) as staff manager (1961–65). In 1965, after the government announced that Tay would be made director of Special Branch (1965–66), the 11,000-strong Port Workers Union appealed to Prime Minister Lee Kuan Yew to allow him to stay on at the PSA.

In 1967, Tay was awarded the MERITORIOUS SERVICE MEDAL. He subsequently served as permanent secretary for

Tay Buan Guan Supermarket, 1967.

the Ministry of Home Affairs (1970–74) and the Ministry of Defence (1974–76). In 1974, Tay headed the government team which dealt with the *Laju* hijacking. That same year, he underwent open-heart surgery in the United States. Ill health forced him to retire from the civil service in 1977. In 1978, he joined the Singapore Manufacturers' Association (SMA) as executive director. He also began teaching in the University of Singapore's history department. In 1980, Tay travelled to London to have a brain tumour removed and died shortly thereafter.

Tay Teow Kiat (1947–) Conductor. Tay Teow Kiat (Zheng Caoji) started studying under Yang Haoran in the 1960s. In 1980, he studied conducting and music theory with Li Yi of the Shanghai Conservatory of Music and conductor Cao Peng.

Currently the music director of East Zone Schools Chinese Orchestra Development Centre and president of the Singapore Chinese Instrumental Music Association, Tay is also Resident Conductor of Dunman High School Chinese Orchestra and music director of the NANYANG ACADEMY OF FINE ARTS City Chinese Orchestra. Since 1982, he has taken both orchestras on concert tours to Thailand, Hong Kong, Taiwan, Malaysia, Brunei and major cities in China.

Tay is known for mentoring young musical talents and improving the standards of CHINESE CLASSICAL MUSIC in Singapore. He was awarded the National Day Efficiency Medal (1989), the Ministry of Education Commendation Plaque (1991), and the CULTURAL MEDALLION (1993).

Since 1985, Tay has guest-conducted professional Chinese orchestras in Shanghai, Tianjin, Shanxi and Shandong, adjudicated in international Chinese music conferences and competitions in Chicago, China, Taiwan and Hong Kong, and served as honorary committee member or advisor to music organizations including the China Chinese Music Society, the Tianjin Musicians' Association, and the China Broadcasting Orchestra. He has also been a guest lecturer at Shanxi Arts Academy.

Tay Yong Kwang (1956–) Judge. Tay Yong Kwang graduated from the law faculty of the NATIONAL UNIVERSITY OF SINGAPORE in 1981. He joined the legal service after graduation and was called to the Singapore Bar in 1984. In 1986, he obtained his master of law degree at Cambridge University with first class honours. His posts within the legal service included legal officer, official assignee and Public Trustee's Office; assistant registrar, Supreme Court; deputy registrar, Supreme Court (1988–89); and district judge (1991–97). On 15 October 1997, Tay was appointed JUDICIAL COMMISSIONER, and on 2 January 2003, he became a judge of the SUPREME COURT.

Taylor, Brigadier Harold (1890–1966) Australian military officer. Harold Burfield Taylor was born in Sydney and was trained as a chemist. He was decorated during World War I. During WORLD WAR II, he was given command of the 22nd Brigade of the Australian Imperial Forces. When the Japanese attacked Singapore on 8 February 1942, Taylor's soldiers bore the brunt of the attack (*see* KRANJI-JURONG LINE).

Taylor was relieved of his command on 12 February 1942. He was later held as a prisoner-of-war at CHANGI PRISON. While imprisoned, Taylor helped set up educational classes for other inmates—an effort which earned him the nickname 'the Chancellor of Changi'.

See also MALAYA CAMPAIGN and WORLD WAR II.

tea dances A British tradition imported into Singapore of literary readings being held in the afternoons and accompanied by high tea. In the 1920s, RAFFLES HOTEL and GOODWOOD PARK HOTEL hosted such events. With the advent of rock-and-roll in the early 1960s, tea dances were held on Saturday or Sunday afternoons. Patrons could watch bands play and dance to their music. Venues such as the Cellar in Collyer Quay, Golden Venus in Orchard Hotel, Princes in Prince Hotel Garni, Katong Palace, Fishing Pond, and Celestial Ballroom hosted bands throughout the 1960s. Notable bands of the time, such as THE QUESTS, The Trailers, THE CHECKMATES, The Cyclones, The Dukes, THE THUNDERBIRDS, THE STYLERS, The Mysterians, and The Vigilantes performed at these venues before rising to mainstream popularity (*see* ENGLISH POPULAR MUSIC).

The trend slowed in the 1970s, but evolved in the 1980s when tea dances were held at venues such as Fire Disco and Warehouse. A ban in 1997 against under-16s entering venues where alcohol was served put an end to tea dances. Starting from around 2000, however, tea dances have become events for a more middle-aged clientele who engage in ballroom and Latin dancing.

Tee Tua Ba (1942–) Police officer and civil servant. Tee Tua Ba was educated at Serangoon English School, Raffles Institution and Victoria School. He obtained his law degree at the University of Singapore in 1966, and joined the SINGAPORE POLICE FORCE as assistant superintendent in 1967. He spent the next 30 years in various appointments at the Ministry of Home Affairs, including director of the CENTRAL NARCOTICS BUREAU, director of the Criminal Investigation Department and director of PRISONS.

Tee was commissioner of police from 1992 until his retirement from the police force in 1997. He was then appointed high commissioner to Brunei. In 2002, he was

appointed Singapore's ambassador to Egypt with concurrent accreditation to Jordan, the United Arab Emirates and Cyprus.

In 1974, Tee was awarded the Public Administration Medal (Silver), the Public Administration Medal (Gold) in 1981, and the MERITORIOUS SERVICE MEDAL in 1998.

Tee Yih Jia The world's biggest producer of POPIAH (spring roll) wrappers. Tee Yih Jia began operations as a labour-intensive, semi-mechanized *popiah* wrapper factory in Geylang in 1969. The business was bought over in 1977 by Sam Goi Seng Hui, who ran an electrical factory next door. Goi took charge of Tee Yih Jia in 1980 and within two years had fully automated the manufacturing process. This was eventually computerized for consistency of standards.

The privately held company has since transformed itself into a multi-million dollar, export-oriented enterprise with markets in Asia (including Japan and China), the Middle East, Australia, New Zealand, South Africa, Europe and the United States. Besides its manufacturing operations in Singapore, Tee Yih Jia has production facilities in the United States, China, Taiwan and Malaysia.

Although it made its mark with *popiah* wrappers—a feat that has earned executive chairman Goi the nickname 'Popiah King'—Tee Yih Jia has widened its product range to include crêpes, ROTI PRATA, samosas, glutinous rice balls, biscuits, noodles and other products specific to the needs of each market. Having established its presence in China in 1988, it also bought into Fuzhou's biggest brewery in May 1993.

Teh Cheang Wan (1928–1986) Civil servant and politician. Born in China, Teh Cheang Wan was educated at Lai Teck School and Chung Ling High School in Penang, and at the University of Sydney where he graduated with a degree in architecture (1956). After graduation, he worked for the Public Works Department and the Housing

Tay Kay Chin: Ghim Moh Market *(2001).*

Tay Koh Yat

Tay Koh Yat: ticket issued by Tay Koh Yat Bus Company.

Tee Yih Jia: production of popiah *wrappers.*

Teh Cheang Wan

Commission, both in New South Wales, and later for the Housing Trust in Kuala Lumpur and the Penang City Council.

In 1959, Teh came to Singapore and joined the Building Department of the SINGAPORE IMPROVEMENT TRUST (SIT) as its architect. Two months later, he was promoted to head the SIT's Building Department. When the Housing & Development Board (HDB) was created to replace the SIT in 1960, Teh became its chief executive officer, a post he held until 1979. In 1976, he was awarded the MERITORIOUS SERVICE MEDAL.

Teh also served as chairman of the Jurong Town Council (1977–79). He entered politics on the PEOPLE'S ACTION PARTY ticket in 1979, and was returned unopposed in Geylang West constituency. He was appointed minister for national development.

On 21 November 1986, a complaint of corruption against Teh was lodged with the CORRUPT PRACTICES INVESTIGATION BUREAU (CPIB). He was interviewed by the CPIB in connection with a sum of $800,000 he was said to have received in 1981 and 1982 as an inducement to allow a development company to retain part of its land which had been earmarked for compulsory acquisition by the government. On 14 December 1986, Teh committed suicide.

teh tarik Popular drink sold at hawker centres. *Teh tarik* literally means 'pulled tea' in Malay. It consists of tea with milk conventionally mixed in a steel mug; after being stirred, the tea is poured back and forth between the mug and a glass. The term 'tarik' comes from the action of the person making the drink. The mug and glass are pulled away from each other as the tea is poured until they are an arm's length apart. This is repeated until a froth is created.

Teh tarik: *vendor 'pulling tea'.*

Tekka Market One of Singapore's largest wet markets, located at the junction of Bukit Timah Road and SERANGOON ROAD. 'Tekka' is a transliteration of the Hokkien term *'tek kia kah'*, (literally 'foot of bamboo shoots'). The Chinese community referred to the area and the market simply as Tek Kah, and the Malays called it Kandang Kerbau (Malay for 'buffalo enclosures'). When the old Tek Kah market was torn down in 1981 and rebuilt across the street, it was located in the podium block of a new multi-purpose complex which the government named Zhujiao Centre. 'Zhujiao' is the Hanyu Pinyin version of 'Tek Kah'. After much criticism, the complex was renamed Tekka Market in 2000.

telecommunications Until 1974, local telephone services were the responsibility of the Singapore Telephone Board (STB); international services were the province of the Telecommunication Department. In that same year, the two were merged to form the Telecommunication Authority of

Singapore (TAS). In 1982, Singapore Telecom (SINGTEL) was created to take over the regulatory and operational functions of TAS and the Postal Services Department.

Liberalization of the telecommunication market began in 1992 when a newly reconstituted TAS took on a regulatory role and SingTel was corporatized under licence from TAS to operate telecommunications services. POSTAL SERVICES were made the responsibility of Singapore Post (SINGPOST), which remained a subsidiary of SingTel until 2003. SingTel was subsequently privatized as a publicly listed company in 1993.

Following the privatization of SingTel, the government began to introduce competition into the telecommunications sector. The mobile-phone and radio-paging markets were liberalized in 1997. MOBILEONE (M1) entered both markets to compete with SingTel. In 1998, STARHUB was awarded licences for both basic telecommunications (fixed-line) services and mobile-phone services. In response to the convergence of information and telecommunications technologies, the government formed the INFOCOMM DEVELOPMENT AUTHORITY of Singapore (IDA) in December 1999. The telecommunication market was fully liberalized by April 2000.

Since liberalization, Singapore's international services market has grown, both in the diversity of services available and in the number of operators offering international telephone services. In March 2006, the mobile-phone penetration rate exceeded 100 per cent, while the fixed-line household penetration rate fell to 97.8 per cent.

SingTel has maintained its leadership position in the local market, with a 39 per cent market share in mobile-phone services. StarHub has emerged in second place, and M1 in third place. SingTel and StarHub roughly divide the broadband INTERNET market between them.

television broadcasting Preparations for the introduction of television in Singapore began in 1956 with a feasibility study, followed by a series of test transmissions. Fifty public viewing centres were established across the island.

Singaporeans were quick to adapt to the new technology and by the start of television broadcasting in 1963—operated by

---

Tekka Market: as it was in the 1930s.

the Department of Broadcasting under the Ministry of Culture—over 8 per cent of households owned a television set. From 15 February 1963, a weekly hour-long programme was broadcast on Channel 5. In April 1963, Channel 5 extended its daily transmissions to 5 hours on weekdays and ten hours over the weekend. This regular service included programmes in English and Malay. On 23 November 1963, Channel 8 was launched with Chinese and Tamil programming. In January 1964, Channel 5 started broadcasting television commercials.

At the time of Singapore's separation from Malaysia in 1965, the government realized that television would play an important role in national development. As a result, broadcasting was consolidated under the state-run Radio and Television Singapore (RTS). In 1966, an educational service was also started for schools. Programming was guided by the government policy of MULTIRACIALISM.

A satellite earth station was set up in October 1971 to facilitate the broadcast of syndicated and international programming. In 1974, Singapore became one of the first countries in Southeast Asia to introduce colour broadcasts.. The Singapore Broadcasting Act was passed in 1979 to allow RTS greater autonomy. In February 1980, RTS was restructured as the SINGAPORE BROADCASTING CORPORATION (SBC). The new corporation faced the challenges of home video technology with innovations such as electronic news gathering and stereo sound; there was more emphasis on entertainment programmes and enhanced presentation. In January 1984, SBC introduced a new station, TV12, to fill a need for more Tamil, Malay and children's programming.

In 1994, in anticipation of competition from cable television, SBC was corporatized as the TELEVISION CORPORATION OF SINGAPORE (TCS) under the Singapore International Media (SIM) group of companies. The SIM group included TCS, Singapore Television Twelve (STV12) and Singapore International Media Communications (SIMCOM).

Singapore Cable Vision (SCV) began a cable television project in 1994. A trial in the Tampines district was held in ten residential apartment blocks in 1995. By 1997, SCV was providing 40 channels of television programming across Singapore. In 2002, SCV merged with STARHUB. By 2005, over 90 per cent of households could receive free-to-air programming via cable, and approximately 30 per cent of television households subscribed to StarHub cable television. StarHub commenced digital television services in 2004.

In 1999, SIM was renamed the Media Corporation of Singapore (MEDIACORP). In 2000, the two TV12 channels, Prime 12 and Premiere 12, were restructured, respectively, into Suria (a channel dedicated specifically to Malay-language programming) and Central, which incorporated three belts—Vasantham Central for Tamil programmes, and children's and arts programming. TCS was formally renamed MediaCorp TV in 2001, and took responsibility for Channels 5, 8 and both TV12 channels. TEMASEK HOLDINGS was appointed to manage government shares in MediaCorp TV.

In 1999, MediaCorp News launched a 24-hour news channel called ChannelNewsAsia (CNA). This channel commenced international operations in September 2000, and by 2005 it was viewed in 20 countries and territories across Asia, with 80 per cent of its production being based in Singapore. In the same year, MediaCorp launched trials for a digital television service on buses, ferries and in public spaces, and was subsequently granted a licence for TVMobile, which commenced broadcasting in 2001.

In 2000, print and broadcast media were deregulated. As a result, two television stations were licensed to SINGAPORE PRESS HOLDINGS' (SPH) MediaWorks. One was TVWorks, an English-language channel; the other was Channel U, which mainly served the Chinese-language market. In mid-2001, MediaWorks renamed TVWorks Channel i, and SPH merged the programming and production of channels U and i. In 2002, a 'ratings war' between MediaWorks' Channel U and MediaCorp's Channel 8 began. At the centre of this ratings battle was the Chinese entertainment belt, specifically dramas (see box), variety shows and movies.

The economic recession which Singapore experienced after 2001 further taxed the local free-to-air television industry, with advertising revenue falling in the 2003–04 period. MediaCorp's Channel 5 also faced the financial burden of having to re-equip its studios to prepare for digital television broadcasting. The outbreak of SEVERE ACUTE RESPIRATORY SYNDROME (SARS) in March 2003 also saw a drop in television advertising. In a newly deregulat-ed television environment, the free-to-air television industry faced a difficult situation whereby public and national interest suddenly reshaped programming, and multinational advertisers reconsidered expenditure in SARS-affected countries.

In May 2003, SARS TV, a free-to-air channel broadcasting for 12 hours per day, was launched. The channel was a collaboration between SPH, StarHub and MediaCorp. This was the first time that Singapore had used a dedicated television station to educate and inform the public. Programming was in all official languages, as well as in Chinese dialects, the use of which had not been allowed in broadcast media since the 1970s, and concentrated on news about the SARS epidemic.

In order to prevent further economic losses, MediaCorp and SPH merged their television and newspaper interests in 2004. On 1 January 2005, a new holding company, MediaCorp TV Holdings Pte Ltd, assumed the management of Channels 5, 8, U and i (although Channel i ceased operations shortly thereafter). This meant that MediaCorp gained a monopoly on free-to-air television broadcasting in Singapore, albeit one with a hybrid mission—i.e. a public broadcaster that is run as a private corporation.

Television Corporation of Singapore

The Television Corporation of Singapore (TCS) replaced the SINGAPORE BROADCASTING CORPORATION (SBC) in 1994. TCS came under the control of the Singapore International Media (SIM) group of companies, and continued to put out English-language and Chinese-language programmes on Channels 5 and 8 respectively. These two channels commenced 24-hour broadcasting in 1995. From 1997, Channel 8's Mandarin-language productions have been broadcast on Taiwanese cable television. In 1999, SIM was renamed the Media Corporation of Singapore (MEDIACORP), and in 2001, TCS was formally renamed MediaCorp TV.

TELECOMMUNICATIONS: NETWORK DEVELOPMENTS		
Submarine cable system inaugurated		Satellite earth station opened
SEACOM	1965	
	1971	Sentosa Satellite Earth Station
Philippines-Singapore	1978	
Singapore-Malaysia-Thailand	1983	
Australia-Indonesia-Singapore	1986	
SEA-ME-WE*		
	1987	Bukit Timah Satellite Earth Station
Brunei-Singapore	1991	
Asia-Pacific Cable (APC)	1993	
SEA-ME-WE 2	1994	Mobile satellite communications service Inmarsat-M introduced
	1995	Seletar Satellite Earth Station
Asia-Pacific Cable Network (APCN)	1997	
	1998	ST-1 satellite launched
SEA-ME-WE 3	1999	
China-US	2000	
APCN 2	2001	
C2C	2002	
i2i		
TIS (Thailand-Indonesia-Singapore)	2003	Optus C1 satellite launched

*South East Asia-Middle East-Western Europe
Source: Singapore Telecommunications

Telecommunications

Telok Ayer

Malay for 'water bay', Telok Ayer Bay was located at the western reaches of Sir STAMFORD RAFFLES' original Singapore town, and is part of today's CHINATOWN. Telok Ayer Street was named after the bay and was originally a coastal road, with the sea lapping at its south side. This explains why the THIAN HOCK KENG TEMPLE—a temple devoted to Mazu, patron deity of seafarers, and typically built on the waterfront—is located here.

Until the late 19th century, Telok Ayer Street was a main commercial and residential thoroughfare, and between 1850 and 1870, it was the centre of the Chinese COOLIE TRADE. Telok Ayer Bay (also known as Telok Ayer Basin) was reclaimed in the first major LAND RECLAMATION project in Singapore. Plans for the reclamation were first proposed in 1865 and works were carried out between 1879 and 1889. Earth for the reclamation came from nearby Mount Wallich, which was levelled for this purpose.

The Telok Ayer area, including Amoy Street, was given conservation area status in July 1989. The SHOPHOUSES in the area are occupied by restaurants, coffee-shops and many advertising, publishing and media firms. Many historic places of worship can be found along Telok Ayer Street, including THIAN HOCK KENG TEMPLE, FUK TAK CHI TEMPLE, NAGORE DURGHA and the AL-ABRAR MOSQUE.

See also CONSERVATION AREAS.

Telok Ayer Chinese Methodist Church

The oldest Chinese Methodist church in Singapore. From August 1889, HOKKIEN Methodists in the Telok Ayer area attended church services in a rented house in Upper Nankin Street. In 1905, services were moved to a rented shophouse at 12 Japan

Telok Ayer: reclamation in progress, 1930s

Television broadcasting: screen logos for predecessors of MediaCorp (above); digital television service on public transport

television drama serials Before the establishment of the SINGAPORE BROADCASTING CORPORATION (SBC) in 1980, television drama was limited to one-off telemovies and children's series. The 1979 Broadcasting Act reduced the amount of foreign programming permitted on television. This stimulated the production of local dramas. In 1983, SBC upgraded its TV Drama Division to include its own director and a drama training studio for actors and scriptwriters, and it recruited drama specialists from Hong Kong and Taiwan.

Chinese

Since 1983, when SBC's Chinese Drama Division was officially established, Channel 8 has produced over 400 Chinese drama serials. Its first major success was *Wu Suo Nan Yang* (The Awakening) (1984) (*1*), which told the story of Chinese immigrants in Singapore during the 19th century. By 1987, SBC Chinese dramas were being telecast five nights a week. Many of these dramas were sold overseas, including *Shuang Tian Zhi Zun* (The Unbeatables) (1993) (*2*). However, during the economic recession of the late 1990s, audiences turned away from Chinese dramas to comedies and variety programmes.

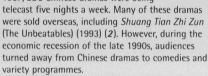
1

2

In 2001, media competition played an important role in reviving Chinese-language drama series, as actors, directors and writers from Channel 8 were recruited to MEDIAWORKS. However, when Channel U's local productions failed to attract a large audience, the channel reverted to acquiring foreign programming. MediaWorks secured the exclusive rights to broadcast successful overseas drama series such as *Zhen Qing* (A Kindred Spirit) from Hong Kong's TVB. Having lost Hong Kong's TVB as a source of dramas, MEDIACORP increased the production of local dramas.

He Lan Cun (Holland Village) (*3*) was Singapore's first 100-episode serial; its success prompted MediaCorp to plan similar series. Most local drama serials had previously only run for 20 to 30 episodes. By extending the run, MediaCorp was able to spread production expenses over more episodes, making drama more cost-efficient.

Prior to the merger of MediaWorks and MediaCorp in 2004, Channel 8 produced *Ren Wo Ao You* (The Champions) (*4*), featuring Taiwanese actress Xiao Qiao.

3

4

Tamil

During the late 1980s and early 1990s, SBC produced fortnightly Tamil dramas with contemporary Singaporean themes. *Nadaga Arangam* (Drama Showcase) was the most popular, continuing for several years. Many of SBC's Tamil programmes were aired in Sri Lanka during the 1980s. In 1988, SBC produced a six-part drama *Here is Family*, and three miniseries in 1990. Tamil drama broke new ground in 1991 with a five-part drama series, *Uravugal* (Relationship), which was shot on location in Malaysia and starred Malaysian actors. In 1992, the TV Programmes Division was restructured, and Tamil programming fell under a new unit, Entertainment Productions 8. In 1994, Prime 12 took over Tamil and Malay programming, producing programmes such as *Kalyanam* (Marriage) (2000) (*5*).

In 2001, Tamil broadcasting shifted to the newly created Vasantham Central, where dramas such as *Goal* (2006) (*6*) were produced by its subsidiary Eaglevision or private production companies.

5

6

Malay

Since the early 1980s, SBC has produced weekly Malay-language drama serials. In the late 1980s and early 1990s, *Sandiwara* (*7*), a 52-part socio-historical drama, won over local audiences and lasted several seasons. In 1986, a six-part contemporary social drama, *Yang Tersasar* (Lost), was telecast. Similar miniseries were produced in the early 1990s.

7

In 1992, the TV Programmes Division was restructured, and Malay programming came under a new unit, Entertainment Productions 5. In 1994, Malay programming came under the umbrella of Prime 12, which also assumed responsibility for Tamil programming. In 2001, MediaCorp established Eaglevision, a subsidiary of TV12, to produce quality Malay and Tamil programmes. Its early productions, such as *Jeritan Sepi* (Scream in Silence), secured unprecedentedly high ratings. In 2002, the first season of a ten-episode social drama, *Selagi Ada Kasih* (As Long as Love Remains) (*8*), also captured a large audience.

8

Many Malay dramas have been sold to Malaysia and Brunei. In 2001, MediaCorp TV12 and Radio Television Brunei jointly produced *Di Balik Jerjak Hati* (Behind Bars of Love) (*9*).

9

English

MediaCorp's English Drama Division was established in the early 1990s. *Masters of the Sea* (1994) (*10*) was the first English-language television drama series produced in Singapore. Joanne Brough, executive producer of US soap operas *Dallas* and *Falcon Crest*, developed this series with a team of expatriates. However, this epic story of a Chinese family and its shipping business failed to attract a loyal audience, and the programme's use of local actors speaking in 'Western' accents dented the public image of English-language drama in Singapore.

10

The first successful English-language drama series, *Growing Up* (*11*), was broadcast in 1996. This series, set in Singapore in 1968, was praised for its convincing performances, high-quality scriptwriting and credible depiction of Singapore in the formative post-SEPARATION years.

In the late 1990s, television drama was used to encourage Singaporeans to rise to the economic challenges of the West, and a new type of English-language drama series that valorized corporate success and 'dot.com' lifestyles emerged. Examples were *Three Rooms* (1997), *VR Man* (1998) (*12*) and *Spin* (1999). However, during the recession of the late 1990s, audiences turned away from these drama series in favour of locally produced sitcoms such as PHUA CHU KANG (1999) (*13*).

12

Following the launch of MediaWorks in 2001, MediaCorp's Channel 5 responded with *Heartlanders*, a police drama that promoted community and social values. Co-productions were also undertaken with Hong Kong broadcasters ATV and RTHK, and with NTV7.

However, MediaWorks' English-language Channel i failed to produce a successful drama series in this period. In 2001, a co-production with the Philippines, *Paradise*, was cancelled after only eight episodes. In 2003, MediaCorp's Arts Central telecast *Singapore Short Story Project*, an award-winning, experimental drama series.

The SARS crisis of the same year placed a temporary hold on drama production until more favourable advertising sales were restored. A ten-episode drama, *Shooting Stars*, which starred SINGAPORE IDOL finalists, was telecast in 2005.

13

Street (now Boon Tat Street). In 1906, this became known as the Telok Ayer Church.

In 1913, Reverend F.H. Sullivan borrowed funds to acquire land on Telok Ayer Street for the church. The first 'church' building was, in fact, a tent erected on the site in 1913. When the tent collapsed, the congregation moved to Fairfield Girls' School on Neil Road, returning to the Telok Ayer site after a wood and corrugated iron building had been erected there.

In 1921, church steward Ng Hong Guan donated $10,000 towards a new church building, and undertook to raise more funds for the church. Some of these funds went into the purchase of further land adjoining the plot upon which the tent-church had once stood. Designed by the architectural firm SWAN & MACLAREN, the new church building was constructed by the French firm BROSSARD & MOPIN at a cost of $46,000. It was completed in December 1924, and consecrated in January 1925.

The new building included many architectural features not normally found in traditional churches. It was not designed in the form of a cross, and its main door was not made to face east. It had a pavilion and ornate windows designed in an art deco style. The Chinese influences evident in the roof design were intended to reflect the cultural background of the church's Hokkien parishioners.

See also METHODISM.

Telok Ayer Market The first Telok Ayer Market, known locally as Lau Pa Sat (Hokkien for 'old market'), was opened in 1824. However, in 1838 this was replaced by a new octagonal building designed by GEORGE D. COLEMAN. The new market building came to be one of the main tourist attractions of colonial Singapore.

When reclamation of Telok Ayer Basin was undertaken in 1879, the old market was destined for closure. However, it continued to operate until a replacement building was completed on reclaimed land in March 1894. Municipal engineer JAMES MACRITCHIE supervised this project, and in a gesture to Coleman, designed the new building as an octagonal structure. William Macfarlane & Co. of Glasgow shipped 3,000 prefabricated cast iron pieces to Singapore for construction of the building, which was assembled by the firm of Riley Hargreaves & Co.

The market building was gazetted as a national monument on 6 July 1973. By this time, the area around the market had started to develop into a financial centre, and the market was turned into a hawker centre catering to local office workers. During construction of the MASS RAPID TRANSIT (MRT) system in the mid-1980s, the market building was temporarily dismantled in 1986. It was later rebuilt in 1991 as a market selling tourist goods before being converted back into a hawker centre in 1995.

Telok Ayer Chinese Methodist Church

Temasek The name Temasek appears in several Chinese, Vietnamese and Javanese texts dating from the early 14th century. According to the SEJARAH MELAYU (Malay Annals), Sri Tri Buana, the first king of the Malays, looked across the Singapore Strait from a hill and saw a beautiful white beach. Upon inquiry, the minister of the queen of Bintan, Indra Bopal, told him that the beach was 'the land called Temasek'. The king and his party travelled across the strait to the land that they had seen. There, they saw a strange animal which they believed to be a lion. Hence, when they decided to establish a city at Temasek, they named it Singapura (in Malay, '*singa*' means lion, and '*pura*' means city).

The meaning of the toponym Temasek is unclear. It was possibly derived from the Malay word *tasik* (meaning 'lake' or 'body of water'). In early Malay, Temasek might have meant 'land surrounded by water'. In the 1330s, WANG DAYUAN wrote a description of Danmaxi, which scholars agree is a Chinese transcription of the toponym Temasek. Wang used the word in reference to a general area which included two important localities: LONGYAMEN (Dragon's Tooth Strait), which was described as a place of pirates; and Banzu (from '*pancur*', literally 'spring of water' in Malay), a hill upon which traders, salt-farmers and makers of rice wine lived. Chinese sources from the Ming Dynasty, including those surviving from the early 15th-century voyages of Admiral ZHENG HE, continued to use the term Danmaxi in reference to the area.

Temasek Holdings An investment holding company for the Singapore governnment, Temasek Holdings was incorporated in 1974 to manage its investments in GOVERNMENT-LINKED COMPANIES (GLCs). It has since expanded its operations to cover key areas of business (including telecommunications, media, financial services, energy, infrastructure, engineering, pharmaceuticals and biosciences), and to manage a global portfolio worth over $103 billion in 2005.

The sole shareholder of Temasek Holdings is the MINISTRY OF FINANCE (MOF). HO CHING, wife of LEE HSIEN LOONG, was appointed executive director in 2002, and has served concurrently as chief executive officer since 2004.

Although around half of Temasek's holdings are local, the company has announced its intention to diversify outside of Singapore so that a third of its investments will be in developed markets, a third in developing countries and a third in Singapore. Some of the company's recent investments have been in Standard Chartered, ICICI Bank (India), Bank Danamon (Indonesia), Telekom Malaysia, ShinCorp (Thailand) and Amtel (Russia). Within Singapore, Temasek has shared holdings in SINGAPORE AIRLINES, SINGTEL, DBS BANK, SINGAPORE POWER and other such Temasek-linked companies (TLCs), including the SINGAPORE ZOO and JURONG BIRDPARK.

In the financial year ending March 2005, Temasek Holdings made a net profit of $7.6 billion on revenue of $68.7 billion. It has been granted an AAA credit rating by Standard and Poor's and an Aaa rating by Moody's.

See also GOVERNMENT OF SINGAPORE INVESTMENT CORPORATION.

Temasek Polytechnic Singapore's third polytechnic. Temasek Polytechnic was established on 6 April 1990. Its founding principal and chief executive officer was Dr N. Varaprasad (1990–2001).

Through its five schools—applied science, business, design, engineering and information technology—it offers 38 full-time diploma courses and 40 certified part-time courses up to advanced diploma level. Its 30-ha campus in TAMPINES overlooks Bedok Reservoir. The polytechnic is best-known for its courses in information technology, design and applied science. In 2005, the polytechnic had over 13,000 students.

In partnership with the Sentosa Leisure Group, Temasek Polytechnic established its sixth school—the Tourism Academy at Sentosa. This campus provides practical education for students in its hospitality and tourism management course; the first student intake was in May 2005.

Telok Ayer Market: popular food centre.

Maggie Teng

Teng Mah Seng

Teo Chee Hean

Teo Bee Yen: the photographer (below);
My Country, 2000.

Temenggong Daeng Ibrahim Mosque
Temenggong IBRAHIM was the successor to Temenggong ABDUL RAHMAN of Singapore and the father of Sultan ABU BAKAR of Johor. He resided at Istana Telok Blangah and set up a mosque in the vicinity. Owned and maintained by the Johor state government, the Masjid (Mosque) Temenggong Daeng Ibrahim is open daily for Muslims to pray in and attend religious classes held there. The current mosque is a single-storey white brick-and-concrete building dating from 1980. The congregation consists mainly of Muslims working and living in the Telok Blangah and Bukit Purmei areas.

Next to the mosque is a cemetery known as the TANAH KUBOR TEMENGGONG, where the graves of Temenggong Abdul Rahman, Temenggong Ibrahim and their immediate relatives are sited.

Teng, Maggie (c. 1961–) Singer. Arguably the first Singapore artiste to successfully penetrate the CHINESE POPULAR MUSIC industry in Taiwan, Maggie Teng (Deng Miaohua) entered show business and signed with White Cloud Records in 1977, releasing her first album *Xin Hua Nu Fang* (Wild With Joy). That year, she was named a Top Ten Singapore/Malaysia Singer in an event organized by REDIFFUSION. Her first English album was *A Little More Love* (1979).

While in Taiwan for vocal training, Teng recorded *Qian Yin* (Leading Along) (1981). The album sold more than 200,000 copies and topped the charts. For the next eight years, Teng was based in Taiwan and released eight albums, including *Second to No One* (1986), *Xin Ling Zhi Yue* (Promise of the Heart) (1987) and *Qing Ni Shuo Shuo Hua* (Please Say Something) (1988).

Back in Singapore, Teng played the female lead in the drama serial *Xiao Fei Yu* (The Flying Fish) (1983) and sang several television drama serial theme songs (*see* TELEVISION BROADCASTING). After an absence of 13 years, Teng returned to the scene with 'He Shui Shan' (Bukit Ho Swee) (2002) a local television serial theme song. Teng has recorded more than 50 albums, including an album each of Bahasa Indonesia and Thai songs. In 2006, she returned after a 17-year hiatus with a new

Mandarin album which was titled *Chu Fa* (A New Journey).

Teng Mah Seng (1916–1992) Musician. Born in Fujian province, China, Teng Mah Seng started working in a rice mill after a short period of formal primary-school education. At the mill, he met a master worker who introduced him to *nanyin*, a genre of CHINESE CLASSICAL MUSIC that originated in southern China. This art form became Teng's lifelong interest.

At the age of 18, Teng left China to work in Singapore. After several jobs, he formed a company in the 1940s trading RUBBER, and became a successful businessman. Over the years, he continued to be involved in promoting *nanyin*. During the 1970s, traditional art forms, including *nanyin*, were under threat in Singapore. Teng became chairman of the Siong Leng Musical Association, and was instrumental in preserving *nanyin*.

Together with composer Zhou Shengxiang, he wrote several hundred *nanyin* lyrics with a local flavour, not only injecting new expressive meaning to the ancient art form, but also expanding and developing it. These *nanyin* repertoires differ from the traditional ones in their treatment of contemporary subjects and Teng's expressions of affection for Singapore, his adopted homeland. His publications include *The Complete Book of Great Nanyin Melodies* and *The New Nanyin: A Selection of Compositions by Teng Mah Seng*.

Teng is credited with grooming *nanyin* singers and musicians through a systematic training programme. He also introduced *nanyin* to foreign audiences at the National Eisteddfod of Wales, and organized several *nanyin* conferences and musical exchanges in Asia. Teng was awarded the CULTURAL MEDALLION in 1987.

Teo, Eddie (1947–) Civil servant. Eddie Teo Chan Seng won a PRESIDENT'S SCHOLARSHIP and completed an honours degree in arts at Oxford University, graduating in 1970. He received his master's degree from the London School of Economics in 1974.

Teo worked as director of security and intelligence at the MINISTRY OF DEFENCE from 1979 to 1994, when he was named its permanent secretary. That same year, he was appointed a director and deputy company chairman of the government-owned Singapore Technologies Holdings group. He was also director of the Internal Security Department from 1982 to 1986. In 1998, he was appointed permanent secretary to the Prime Minister's Office.

Teo retired from the civil service in 2005, and was appointed High Commissioner to Australia in 2006. He was awarded the Public Administration Medal (Gold) in 1983, and the MERITORIOUS SERVICE MEDAL in 1997.

Teo Bee Yen (1950–) Photographer. Born in Fujian province, China, Teo Bee Yen settled in Singapore and became noted for his landscape photography. Rated one of the top ten photographers in the world (Colour Prints category) by the Photographic Society of America (PSA) in 1998 and in 2001, Teo also received the PSA's '5 Star' award in 2002. He was made associate of the Royal Photographic Society, United Kingdom, in 1998 and received a fellowship in 1999.

The vice-president of the Photo Art Association of Singapore, Teo has held solo exhibitions in Singapore, Malaysia and China, and has won numerous accolades including the Gold Medal (Colour Portrait) in the Scottish Salon of Photography in 2001. He was awarded the CULTURAL MEDALLION in 2004.

Teo Chee Hean (1954–) Military officer and politician. Teo Chee Hean was educated at St Michael's School and St Joseph's Institution, before going on to the University of Manchester in the United Kingdom, where he graduated in 1976 with a first-class honours degree in electrical engineering and management science.

Teo returned to Singapore to join the REPUBLIC OF SINGAPORE NAVY. In 1991, he was promoted to the rank of rear admiral and made chief of navy. In 1992, he retired from the military to enter politics on the PEOPLE'S ACTION PARTY ticket, winning a seat in Marine Parade GROUP REPRESENTATION CONSTITUENCY (GRC) during a by-election. He was immediately appointed minister of state for finance, and in 1995 was made acting minister for the environment and senior minister of state for defence. In 1996, Teo was promoted to full minister for the environment and second minister for defence. He then became minister for education (1997–2003) while continuing to serve as second minister for defence. In 1997, he was elected as a member of Parliament (MP) for Pasir Ris GRC. Since 2003, he has been minister for defence and minister in charge of the civil service. In 2006, he was re-elected as MP for Pasir Ris-Punggol GRC.

Teo Eng Seng (1938–) Artist, sculptor and educator. Teo Eng Seng studied fine arts at the Birmingham Institute of Art and Design in the United Kingdom (1963–67). His early canvases included monumental war elegies in an expressionist style, such as *Massacre in My Lai* (1970). Teo's art ranges across a broad range of social issues, such as migration, euthanasia and identity. *A Child is Born*, which addressed eugenics, won First Prize (Abstract Category) in the UOB (United Overseas Bank) Painting of the Year competition (1984).

Teo is also the creator of 'paperdyesculp' (a unique paper-based material used for relief and sculptural work), and has

Teo Soo Chuan, right, in 1969.

employed fibreglass, glass-reinforced concrete, recycled plastic and other unconventional materials in his installations and public works, such as those displayed at Outram Park North East Line station.

Teo has served as head of the United World College's Art Department (1978–96), and sat on numerous judging panels and advisory boards for the NATIONAL ARTS COUNCIL, art centres and government ministries. He has been curriculum designer and examiner for the International Baccalaureate (1992–) and the NANYANG ACADEMY OF FINE ARTS. Teo was awarded the CULTURAL MEDALLION (1986), a Fine Arts Fellowship (Birmingham Institute of Art and Design, UK) (1989) and the International Order of Merit, IBC (International Biographical Centre, Cambridge, UK) (1999).

Teo Soo Chuan (1920–) Businessman. Little is known of Teo Soo Chuan's early life. He is head of the See Hoy Chan Group, a rice- and sugar-trading company started by his father. Teo is reputedly one of the richest members of the TEOCHEW community in Singapore. He was chairman and director of Singapura Finance (1981–2002); director of Overseas Union Enterprise (1965–2001); as well as Honorary President of the SINGAPORE CHINESE CHAMBER OF COMMERCE & INDUSTRY (1995). Teo is distinguished honorary chairman of SINGAPORE KWANGTUNG HUI KUAN; and patron of Chao Yang Special School.

Teochew The term Teochew refers to the members of a Chinese dialect group as well as the language spoken by its members. The Teochew people originated from the Chaozhou region of China's Guangdong province. According to the 2000 Census of Population, they make up 21 per cent (526,197) of the Chinese population, making them the second-largest dialect group in Singapore after the Hokkiens. The first wave of Teochew migrants came in the early 19th century in search of work, and to escape poverty in their towns of origin.

They came from the districts of Jieyang, Shantou, Chaozhou, Chaoyang, Puning, Chao'an, Raoping, Huilai and Shanwei to work as labourers on PEPPER AND GAMBIER plantations. These early immigrants set sail on distinctive boats

known in Teochew as *ang tao zung* (red-headed boats), bringing with them only the bare necessities. Many were bonded as coolies (*see* COOLIE TRADE) and packed like livestock onto vessels, thus becoming known as *ter gia* ('piglets'). Most arrived at the shore along Philip Street where the WAK HAI CHENG BIO temple was built, where they would pray and give thanks for their safe arrival. They later settled in Chulia Street, spreading to BOAT QUAY and River Valley Road. While Chinese dialect groups have spread out over the island in the present day, the public housing estate of Hougang is still predominantly Teochew due to the resettlement of residents from Kampong Ponggol in the 1970s, many of whom were Teochew.

The Teochews became dominant in the local economy by trading seafood products caught in *kelongs* (palisade traps), sundry goods, rice, textiles, charcoal and porcelain. Many also worked as brokers and traders of goods stored in the many warehouses located on the banks of the SINGAPORE RIVER, and as financiers funding business transactions and ventures.

The Teochew community in Singapore counts many businessmen and community leaders among its ranks. Some prominent business personalities include SEAH EU CHIN, founder of Ngee Ann Kongsi; LIM NEE SOON, Singapore's 'Rubber and Pineapple King' and founder of the TEOCHEW POIT IP HUAY KUAN; LEE WEE NAM, founder and president of the Malayan Confederation of the Teochew Huay Kuan in 1933; and LIEN YING CHOW, founder of the Overseas Union Bank. These successful businessmen also contributed generously to education. The first school built by the Teochews was Tuan Mong School built in 1906. In 1940, Lee Wee Nam built Ngee Ann Girls' School. In 1963, Ngee Ann Kongsi started the Ngee Ann College with undergraduate programmes. In 1968, Ngee Ann College was converted into Ngee Ann Polytechnic. Teochew politicians include LIM BOON HENG, GEORGE YEO, LEE BOON YANG, YEO CHEOW TONG, TEO CHEE HEAN, LIM HNG KIANG and LOW THIA KIANG.

Teochew opera (*see* CHINESE OPERA) is a prominent aspect of Teochew culture. It is usually performed during festivals and in connection with temple worship. Teochew opera is still enjoyed in Singapore. One of the best-known troupes is Sin Yong Hua Heng Troupe, which was founded in 1827. Amateur troupes include Nam Hwa, Thau Yong and ER WOO AMATEUR MUSICAL AND DRAMATIC ASSOCIATION.

The Teochews are also known for their cuisine. As Chaozhou is a coastal region, seafood—especially fish and shark's fin—is an important part of Teochew cuisine. Popular dishes include oyster omelette, braised goose, prawn rolls and liver rolls. Well-known Teochew desserts include glutinous rice balls with sweet stuffings

Teochew Poit Ip Huay Kuan

such as red bean, yam or green bean, and *or nee* (yam paste cooked in lard and sugar).

The Teochew dialect spoken in Singapore includes borrowed lexicon from Malay and English, as well as Indian languages. For example, police are referred to as *mata* (from the Malay 'mata-mata') and nurses are called *misi* (from 'Miss' in English). There are also terms that combine two languages. An example is *loti piah* (biscuits), derived from *roti* ('bread' in Malay) and *piah* ('biscuit' in Teochew). With the introduction of BILINGUALISM and the Speak Mandarin campaign, the use of the Teochew dialect, like other dialects, has declined, although clan associations such as the TEOCHEW POIT IP HUAY KUAN conduct courses in Teochew to revive and maintain interest in the dialect.

Teochew Poit Ip Huay Kuan Clan association. The Teochew Poit Ip Huay Kuan's beginnings are linked to the Ngee Ann Kongsi, which was founded in 1845 by prominent Teochews from 12 clans, with members who originated from the districts of Chenghai and Chao'an, under the leadership of merchant SEAH EU CHIN, who came from Ngee Ann county in Guangdong, China.

The initial focus of the Ngee Ann Kongsi was the religious and funerary needs of the Teochew community. It founded the WAK HAI CHENG BIO temple on Philip Street in 1826, and also provided funerals and burials for Teochew families with the

Teo Eng Seng: the artist (below); Five Nails (1991).

*Field Marshal Count
Terauchi Hisaichi*

establishment of cemeteries at several locations around the island. These included Guang Shou Shan at Clementi (site of the present-day NGEE ANN POLYTECHNIC) and Tai Shan Ting on Orchard Road.

In 1927, a group which included businessman LIM NEE SOON expressed their unhappiness with the dominance exerted by the Seah family and members of the 12 clans who had set up the Kongsi. After a meeting with the Teochew community in 1928, the Teochew Poit Ip Huay Kuan was established. Since 1934, the Ngee Ann Kongsi has provided funding for the Huay Kuan. The formation of the SINGAPORE KWANGTUNG HUI KUAN was an inititiave of the Kongsi in 1936.

As the Teochew community grew, the Ngee Ann Kongsi's functions expanded to include educational and cultural activities. One of Singapore's earliest Teochew schools was the Tuan Mong School, which was founded in 1906 as a primary school and operated out of premises on Tank Road. The Ngee Ann Kongsi assumed management of this school in 1953. Other schools established by the Ngee Ann Kongsi were the Ngee Ann Girls' School, founded in 1940 as Singapore's first Chinese school for girls, but which was later converted into the co-educational NGEE ANN PRIMARY SCHOOL; Ngee Ann Secondary School, founded in 1994; and NGEE ANN POLYTECHNIC, founded in 1963 as Ngee Ann College at a site on Tank Road.

The Huay Kuan and Kongsi provide scholarships and student bursaries, and seek to promote Chinese and Teochew culture in the form of activities featuring Teochew opera (*see* CHINESE OPERA), calligraphy, dance, music and drama. The organizations' activities are funded by revenue from business ventures and the rental of Ngee Ann Kongsi's properties, the largest of which is NGEE ANN CITY on Orchard Road. It also owns a number of SHOPHOUSES along Balestier Road and residential properties along Grange Road. The Teochew Poit Ip Huay Kuan is the parent association of 64 Teochew corporate members with individ-

ual membership of about 8,000. As of 2006, it was Singapore's largest Chinese clan association.

Terauchi Hisaichi, Field Marshal Count (1879–1946) Japanese military officer. Terauchi Hisaichi was commander of the Southern Army, and was based in Singapore in this capacity in the period 1943–44. A close relative of the Japanese emperor, Terauchi was unable to surrender SYONAN to the Allies in September 1945 because he had suffered a stroke in April that year. He died in 1946 in Regam, Johor, where he was being held pending war crime investigations. Terauchi was cremated and some of his ashes are believed to be in the JAPANESE CEMETERY PARK on Chuan Hoe Avenue.

Teutonia Club Founded in 1856 by seven Germans (including Arnold Otto Meyer of BEHN, MEYER & CO.), the Teutonia Club built its first clubhouse on Mount Elizabeth in 1861. As membership expanded, the club outgrew these premises. It acquired an adjacent plot of land, and in 1900 commissioned the firm SWAN & MACLAREN to design what would become its landmark building on Scotts Road.

The British seized the clubhouse during WORLD WAR I. The Manasseh brothers bought it and five nearby houses in 1918, and renamed the complex Goodwood Hall, after the celebrated Goodwood Racecourse in the United Kingdom. It was used as a function room-cum-restaurant and entertainment hall until 1929, when it was converted into the GOODWOOD PARK HOTEL. The Teutonia Club never recovered its clubhouse after the war, although the club itself did survive, later becoming the German House Association.

Thaipusam Hindu festival. Thaipusam is celebrated in a number of countries in which people from south India have settled. It is held in honour of the deity Murugan, and falls in the Tamil month of Thai, usually in January or February.

In 1879, Thaipusam became the first Hindu festival to be declared a PUBLIC HOLIDAY in Singapore. In 1968, however, it lost its public holiday status in favour of DEEPAVALI. Nonetheless, it has remained an important date in Singapore's festival calendar. The Thaipusam procession has been observed annually in Singapore since the founding of the SRI THENDAYUTHAPANI TEMPLE on Tank Road in April 1859.

During Thaipusam, devotees begin their procession at SRI SRINIVASA PERUMAL TEMPLE on Serangoon Road. The site was chosen because it had adequate space in which devotees could construct their *kavadis* (semi-circular steel or wooden structures decorated with flowers and peacock feathers), and a pond which could be used for ritual baths. Devotees carry *kavadis* on their shoulders, and hooks attached to

Teutonia Club, 1902.

the *kavadis* are pierced through the flesh of devotees to keep it in place. The route to the Sri Thendayuthapani Temple is a journey of about 4 km.

In the 1940s and 1950s, reformists in India called for a ban on the use of spiked *kavadis*, and several prominent temples in Tamil Nadu banned their use. There were also calls in Singapore to ban spiked *kavadis* and the Thaipusam festival itself. However, Sri Thendayuthapani Temple and the temples controlled by the MOHAMMEDAN AND HINDU ENDOWMENT BOARD followed the wishes of most devotees by continuing to observe the festival and allowing the use of *kavadis*. The carrying of spiked *kavadis* has thus survived as a practice unique to Singapore and Malaysia. An increasing number of non-Indians and non-Hindus have started to take part in Thaipusam.

Thakral, Kartar Singh (1933–) Businessman and community leader. Born in Thailand and educated at Assumption College, Bangkok, Kartar Singh Thakral moved to Singapore in 1952 when his father, Sohan Singh Thakral, a textile merchant, sent him to establish a branch of the family's Punjab Store in the city. Since the 1960s, he has continued to head the Thakral family business.

In the late 1970s, Thakral diversified into electronics and the hospitality industry, and by the 1990s, the family company had established branches in Hong Kong, China, Vietnam, Cambodia, Laos, Myanmar, India, Australia, Dubai and Eastern Europe. The Thakral Holdings Group has become one of the largest hotel operators in Australia.

Thakral has served as patron of the Singapore Khalsa Association and the Sikh Welfare Council; director of the Trade Development Board; and trustee of the Singapore Indian Development Association, the Singapore Sikh Education Foundation and the Sri Guru Nanak Sat Sang Sabha. Thakral was named Businessman of the Year by *The Business Times* in 1995.

Tham Tuck Yen (1921–2005) Civil servant. Tham Tuck Yen first joined the Public Works Department in 1938, and earned engineering certificates under both the Japanese and the British. He worked at the

Thaipusam

ECONOMIC DEVELOPMENT BOARD from 1961 to 1968, in particular on the JURONG project, a key part of Singapore's industrialization programme. In 1968, he moved over to the newly formed JURONG TOWN CORPORATION (JTC) to help develop Singapore's first industrial estate at Jurong, putting in infrastructure such as a causeway over Jurong River.

Tham was JTC's chief administrative officer, holding the position for seven years until his retirement from the civil service in 1975. Thereafter, he continued working, with stints at the Sentosa Development Corporation and the Mass Rapid Transit Corporation. From 1989 to 1994, Tham worked in Thailand as deputy managing director of Hi-Tech Industrial Estate, a joint venture between JTC and the Royal Group of Companies.

Tharman Shanmugaratnam (1957–) Civil servant and politician. Tharman Shanmugaratnam was educated at the Anglo-Chinese School and then at the London School of Economics, where he graduated with a degree in economics. He joined the MONETARY AUTHORITY OF SINGAPORE (MAS) in 1982 as director of economics. In 1995, he joined the Administrative Service and served in the Ministry of Education as deputy secretary and later senior deputy secretary. In 1997, he returned to the MAS as deputy managing director of financial supervision. He became managing director of MAS in 2001, but quit to enter politics.

In 2001, Tharman was elected member of Parliament for Jurong Group Representation Constituency (GRC) on the People's Action Party ticket. He was immediately appointed senior minister of state for trade and industry and for education. In 2003, he became acting minister for

TheatreWorks: **Workhorse Afloat** *(1997).*

Theemidhi

education, subsequently becoming minister for education (2004–) and second minister for finance (2006–). In 2006, he was re-elected to his seat in Jurong GRC.

Thean, L.P. (1933–) Judge. Born in Kuala Lumpur, Thean Lip Ping was educated at the Methodist Boys' School there and at the University of Bristol, United Kingdom, from which he graduated with an LLB in 1955. He was called to the Bar at Lincoln's Inn the following year and went on to complete an LLM at King's College, University of London. Upon completing his studies, Thean returned to Malaya and was called to the Malayan Bar in 1958. He joined the firm of Y.S. Lee and Co. in Kuala Lumpur that year, but left to become junior partner in the firm of SHOOK LIN & BOK (1960–64).

In 1964, Thean arrived in Singapore to establish the office of Shook Lin & Bok with YONG PUNG HOW, and remained there as senior partner till 1984 when he was appointed PUISNE JUDGE. In 1993, when a permanent Court of Appeal was created, Thean was made judge of appeal.

Thean retired in February 2002, just before turning 70. After his retirement, he served on the Board of DBS Group Holdings and DBS BANK, and as chairman of the Securities Industry Council of Singapore. He was also appointed consultant to the firm of KHATTARWONG. In 2002, Bristol University conferred on him an honorary doctorate of laws.

theatre *See* CHINESE THEATRE, ENGLISH THEATRE, MALAY THEATRE and TAMIL THEATRE.

Theatre Practice, The Singapore's first bilingual theatre company. In the early 1980s, a group of theatre enthusiasts got together under legendary theatre director KUO PAO KUN for a series of productions, including three performances at the SINGAPORE ARTS FESTIVAL in 1982, 1984 and 1986. This group was the core that formed the Practice Theatre Ensemble, a company that would be renamed The Theatre Practice (TTP) in 1997. TTP's approach to theatre-making reflects the struggle between tradition and modernity and remains true to its local identity. Besides producing English and Mandarin productions, TTP established the Student Theatre Exposure Programme (STEP) in 1994. Another wing of TTP which was set up in 1996 is The Finger Players, a puppetry group focusing on performances for children. The Finger Players became an independent group in 1999.

Tharman Shanmugaratnam

TheatreWorks Established in 1985, TheatreWorks is a non-profit theatre company that promotes and produces Singapore writing and drama. In 1990, it initiated a workshop for new playwrights called the Writers' Laboratory. The group has also promoted cross-cultural productions. TheatreWorks' Flying Circus Project is a long-term research and development programme which explores Asian art, with seminars and workshops on dance, drama, music, the visual arts and film. ONG KENG SEN took over from Lim Siauw Chong as TheatreWorks' artistic director in 1989. In September 2005, TheatreWorks moved from Fort Canning Centre to new premises on MOHAMED SULTAN ROAD.

Theemidhi Hindu festival. The Fire-Walking Ceremony, as this annual festival is commonly known, was first observed in Singapore around 1842. It is celebrated at the SRI MARIAMMAN TEMPLE in October, and is always held on a Monday. The festival is dedicated to the goddess Sri Drowpathai, who is believed to be an avatar of the universal mother goddess. Drowpathai is also the central female character in the Mahabharata.

Theemidhi was introduced into Singapore by boat caulkers who had migrated from the Cuddalore district of Tamil Nadu, India. After arriving in Singapore, these people continued to worship Sri Drowpathai, their village deity, and observe the Theemidhi ceremony, just as they had done in India. The boat-caulking community continued to organize this festival well into the 1970s.

During Theemidhi, devotees walk across a bed of scorching coals barefoot in order to fulfil their religious vows. Performing this ritual is believed to purify the mind and soul. The fire-walking ceremony is but one part of a month-long series of rituals, role-playing and rites, each of which celebrates a particular event that is described in the Mahabharata. Only men are allowed to walk across the pit. However, women also throng the temple during the festivities, participating in a variety of other prayer rituals.

Shane Thio

Francis Thomas

Theemidhi celebrations are organized by the HINDU ENDOWMENTS BOARD and the management committee of the temple. To avoid disruptions to traffic, the ceremony has been held in the early hours of the morning since 1999.

Then, Anthony (1944–1995) Dancer and choreographer. Having trained at the Singapore Ballet Academy and the Rambert School of Ballet in London, Anthony Then danced with companies in Germany and the United Kingdom before switching to acting, choreography and teaching. He returned to Singapore in the 1980s and later co-directed the National Dance Company's Ballet Group with GOH SOO KHIM. Together, they co-founded the SINGAPORE DANCE THEATRE (SDT) in 1987. Then was its co-artistic director (1987–95).

Then choreographed several works for SDT, such as *Concerto for VII* (1989) and *Schumann Impressions* (1990). In 1992, he staged *The Nutcracker* as the SDT's first full-evening work; it was the biggest and most expensive local DANCE production to that date.

Theroux, Paul (1941–) Author. Paul Theroux was born in Massachusetts in the United States. After graduating from the University of Massachusetts in 1963, he taught English in Malawi, Uganda and Singapore. He worked at the Singapore University's English department from 1968 to 1971. Theroux wrote some 24 novels and short stories. One of his novels, *Saint Jack* (1976), was set in Singapore in the 1970s, and was about an American expatriate, Jack Flowers, who worked as a pimp. The book was later made into a FILM by Peter Bogdanovich in 1979. The film was banned in Singapore, however, in part because Bogdanovich, who shot the film on location in 1978, had informed the Singapore authorities that he was making a film entitled *Jack of Hearts*. The ban was lifted in 2006.

Thevet, André (1502–1590) Cleric and cartographer. André Thevet was born in Angoulême, France, and entered the monastic order of St Francis of Assisi. He was later appointed official historiographer and cosmographer of the French crown. In

Thian Hock Keng Temple: plaque with temple name (below); temple photographed in 1880.

his *Cosmographie Universelle* (Universal Cosmography) of 1575, Thevet dedicated a chapter to Cingaporla (Singapura). He based this information on the maps of Abraham Ortelius, among other authorities. Thevet understood Cingaporla to include all the lands to the south of the Muar and Pahang Rivers, and claimed that Muar was the most important port in Cingaporla.

They Call Her...Cleopatra Wong (1978) A B-grade cult movie by George Richardson, this regional co-production aimed at an international audience starred Doris Young (credited as Marrie Lee) as Cleopatra Wong, an Interpol agent tasked with smashing a drug ring covering Singapore, Manila and Hong Kong. The movie tagline ran: 'She purrs like a kitten...Makes love like a siren...Fights like a panther. This side of the Pacific, she is the deadliest, meanest and sexiest secret agent!'

Among the film's most memorable moments was an extended fight scene between Interpol agents and gangsters in nuns' habits. The character of Cleopatra Wong was revived in two sequels directed by Filipino Bobby A. Suarez: *Dynamite Johnson* (1978) and *Devil's Angels* (1980). Cleopatra Wong developed into a cult icon and source of inspiration for international film-makers. Quentin Tarantino cited the movie and its protagonist as key influences on his two *Kill Bill* films.

Thian Hock Keng Temple Chinese temple. Known in Mandarin as Tian Fu Gong, this is the oldest HOKKIEN temple in Singapore, and was once the most important place of worship for the Hokkien community. The present structure was constructed between 1839 and 1842 with funds from Hokkien donors such as TAN TOCK SENG. From 1840 to 1955, the temple also housed the SINGAPORE HOKKIEN HUAY KUAN (then known as the Thian Hock Keng Huay Kuan).

Before the advent of land reclamation, the temple stood right by the seashore. Located on Telok Ayer Street, it was built on the site of an earlier shrine dedicated to Mazu (also known as Tian Hou), the patron deity of seafarers, to whom newly arrived immigrants gave thanks for a safe voyage. Other deities enshrined within include Bao Sheng Da Di, Guan Gong, the Eight Immortals and Confucius. Since the 1970s, however, the temple has become less popular with worshippers, and has increasingly functioned as a tourist attraction and heritage site. In 1906, the temple underwent a renovation, and a wrought-iron gate from Glasgow, among other elements, was incorporated. A calligraphic panel from Emperor Guangxu can also be seen in the temple. This was presented to the temple in 1907.

The temple consists of two courtyards, with the shrine to Mazu located in

the centre of the temple. Pagodas to the left and right house Confucius and ancestral tablets of the temples' founders respectively. Architecturally, it is considered a masterpiece in the Minnan (southern Fujian) style. Artisans and materials were brought in from China for its construction. Some noteworthy features include heavily gilded and intricately carved support beams, and its colourful roof ridge decorations which use broken porcelain in keeping with the Jian Nian technique. The temple has been restored twice and was gazetted as a national monument in 1973.

In 1998, the temple underwent a major restoration. Parts of the carpentry work which were suffering from decay were repaired and replaced, and the original details in sections of the temple structure in gold leaf and paint were also restored. In 2001, it received the UNESCO Asia-Pacific Heritage Award for Cultural Heritage Conservation.

Think Centre Non-governmental organization. Registered as a business in Singapore on 16 July 1999, the Think Centre was registered as a society in October 2001. The centre was formed to examine and report on issues relating to political developments, democracy, the rule of law, human rights and civil society within a multi-partisan framework.

Thio, Shane (1959–) Musician. Shane Thio started playing piano when he was seven years old. He has emerged as one of the most active concert pianists and harpsichordists in Singapore. His performances have encompassed solo, chamber, concerto, orchestral ensemble and contemporary repertoire, as well as numerous collaborations with Singapore's musical, dance and drama groups. As an accompanist, he has partnered world-renowned singers such as Sumi Jo and Charlotte Church. He has also been responsible for many Singapore premieres, including those of works by Erwin Schulhoff, György Ligeti, Olivier Messiaen, Toru Takemitsu and other composers.

Thomas, Francis (1912–1977) Teacher and politician. Born in the United Kingdom, Francis Thomas graduated from Jesus College, Cambridge University, United Kingdom. He started teaching in Singapore at St Andrew's School (1934–48), where he was principal from 1963 to 1974. Thomas served in the bomb disposal unit in Singapore during WORLD WAR II. He was interned and put to work first on the Siam-Burma Railway, and then in a factory in Japan.

In 1948, Thomas attended the inaugural meeting of the SINGAPORE LABOUR PARTY and, much to his surprise, was elected to the leadership. In 1953, Thomas followed LIM YEW HOCK, who left the SLP to start the Singapore Socialist Party (SSP). The SSP and the SLP soon merged as the LABOUR FRONT, which won enough seats in the 1955 general election to form the government. Thomas, who was not a candidate in the election, reluctantly accepted his nomination as minister of communications and works.

Increasingly unhappy with Lim's political tactics, Thomas resigned as minister in 1958, but stayed on as a backbencher. When LEE KUAN YEW, then in the opposition PEOPLE'S ACTION PARTY, pressed Lim to investigate alleged corrupt practices in government, Thomas crossed the floor to sit with the opposition. After unsuccessfully contesting the general election in 1959, he returned to teaching and was active in community and charity work. Thomas was appointed a permanent member of the PRESIDENTIAL COUNCIL FOR MINORITY RIGHTS in 1970, and received the Public Service Star in 1971.

Thomas, Sir Shenton (1879–1962) Colonial official. Sir Shenton Whitelegge Thomas was educated at St John's Leatherhead and Queen's College, Cambridge University. Thomas was governor of Singapore from 1934 to 1942, and then after the JAPANESE OCCUPATION from 1945 to 1946. He had served in the colonial service in Africa prior to his arrival in Singapore, and had served as governor of Nyasaland (present-day Malawi) (1929–32). By 1934, when Thomas was appointed Singapore's governor, Singapore had recovered from the Great Depression. Thomas' tenure as governor was marked by his good rapport with the European and Asian communities. During his time, he oversaw the establishment of the Straits Civil Service in 1934. Shenton also directed funds to relieve unemployment, and revived schemes for public works. In 1935, he restored government grants to CHINESE and TAMIL vernacular schools (*see* CHINESE EDUCATION and TAMIL EDUCATION).

The late 1930s was a period of peace and increasing standards for the upper and middle classes in Singapore. When WORLD WAR II broke out in Europe in 1939, the British estimated that naval reinforcements would be extended to Singapore within 180 days. It was considered unlikely that the war would spread to Singapore, so Singapore was allocated the task of contributing to the United Kingdom's coffers by increasing its RUBBER and TIN output. Even after the fall of Penang on 18 December 1941, Thomas was reluctant to issue orders for evacuation so as not to cause panic amongst the populace, and also to quash local sentiments of resentment which had risen upon hearing that only Europeans had been evacuated from Penang (*see* MALAYA CAMPAIGN). Shenton's conciliatory style of government was unsuited to the climate which arose as the Japanese advanced towards Singapore, and

his inability to galvanize civilians into action during this time of conflict led to calls being made for resident minister for Far Eastern Affairs ALFRED 'DUFF' COOPER to assume a larger measure of authority.

With the British surrender of Singapore on 15 February 1942, the Japanese placed Thomas and his wife in captivity, and one of the locations where he was interned was CHANGI PRISON. They were released in 1945 after the Japanese surrender. SHENTON WAY, which lies on reclaimed land in the TELOK AYER area, is named after him.

Thomas Cup Badminton tournament. Although the Singapore Badminton Association was established as early as 1929, it was only after World War II that the sport gained significant popularity. At the end of 1948, a team of Malayan and Singaporean players entered the first Thomas Cup Badminton Tournament in Preston in the United Kingdom. Two Singaporean players, ONG POH LIM and WONG PENG SOON, were selected to take part. In the final, Malaya defeated Denmark 8-1, with Ong Poh Lim defeating Paul Holm 17-14; 15-8.

Badminton was considered Malaya's national game after the Thomas Cup victory. In 1952, the Cup was defended in both Kuala Lumpur and Singapore. There was public excitement about the prospect of the final rounds being played on home soil. India and Denmark, as the winners of the tournament's Pacific and Europe Zones respectively, met in the first inter-zone tie, with the winner, India, then playing against the United States in the Inter-Zone Final. In the final, Wong Peng Soon defeated Marten Mendez and Dick Mitchell of the American team, while Ong Poh Lim defeated Bob Williams in the singles, and combined with Ismail Marjan to defeat first Dick Mitchell and Carl Loveday, and then Wynn Rogers and Bob Williams, in the doubles. Victory was an emphatic 7-2.

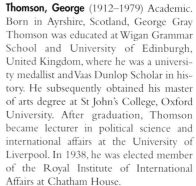
Thomas Cup: Wong Peng Soon.

They Call Her...Cleopatra Wong (1978)

In 1955, Denmark returned to play Singapore in the Challenge Round. Wong Peng Soon won both his matches—the first against J. Skaarup (15-5; 16-18; 15-4) and the second against Finn Kobberø (12-15; 15-0; 15-7). Ong Poh Lim partnered Ooi Teik Hock to win two doubles matches, and in the singles Ong defeated Ole Jensen 15-10; 15-8. The final score was an 8-1 repeat of the 1949 result. Wong Peng Soon also coached the Malayan team that defended the Cup in 1958, but that lost to the Indonesian team that same year. Since then, few players have captured the public imagintion in the way that Wong Peng Soon, Ong Poh Lim and Ismail Marjan once did. The 1955 and 1958 matches were held in the SINGAPORE BADMINTON HALL.

Sir Shenton Thomas

Thomson, George (1912–1979) Academic. Born in Ayrshire, Scotland, George Gray Thomson was educated at Wigan Grammar School and University of Edinburgh, United Kingdom, where he was a university medallist and Vaas Dunlop Scholar in history. He subsequently obtained his master of arts degree at St John's College, Oxford University. After graduation, Thomson became lecturer in political science and international affairs at the University of Liverpool. In 1938, he was elected member of the Royal Institute of International Affairs at Chatham House.

During WORLD WAR II, Thomson served as a gunner in the Royal Artillery in Kandy, Ceylon (present-day Sri Lanka), before being transferred to the BRITISH MILITARY ADMINISTRATION in Malaya in 1945. He was promoted to lieutenant-colonel and moved to Singapore as deputy director of publicity and printing. Subsequent posts he held included supervisor of elections (1950–53); director of training and director of the Singapore Civil Service (1959–69); director of the Political Study Centre (1959–69); and deputy secretary, Ministry of Foreign Affairs (1969–71). From 1971 to 1975, Thomson served as visiting professor at Nanyang University's Department of Government and Public

Anthony Then

Edwin Thumboo

Administration. Thomson became a Singapore citizen in 1957. In 1967, he received the MERITORIOUS SERVICE MEDAL.

three-quarter-tank rule In April 1989, the government introduced laws designed to discourage motorists from driving to Johor to purchase cheap petrol. Originally, the 'half-tank rule' meant that motorists whose fuel tanks were less than half full were forbidden from crossing the CAUSEWAY. This was modified to the 'three-quarter-tank rule' in February 1991. In order to enforce this rule, customs officials at road checkpoints have been tasked with checking the fuel gauges of Singapore-registered cars bound for Malaysia. Drivers are fined and asked to turn back if their fuel tanks are found to be less than three-quarters full.

Three Rifles Clothing company. Three Rifles Holdings was founded by Chong Chong Choong, who started out in the retail business at the age of 14, working at PASAR MALAM (night market) stalls in Bukit Panjang. In 1957, at the age of 20, Chong opened his own shop at 888 Bukit Panjang Road, selling shirts and other merchandise.

In 1965, Chong expanded into shirt manufacturing, opening a small factory in Geylang with a staff of only eight. After setting up his flagship Three Rifles outlet in President Shopping Centre in 1972, the company began opening outlets in People's Park Complex, People's Park Centre, Peninsula Plaza, Katong Shopping Centre and City Plaza in the 1970s and 1980s. By then, Three Rifles had also started to import other clothing brands, such as Alumo, Brado, Lonner, Portfolio and Rombert from Europe, Japan, Hong Kong and Taiwan. It became the regional manufacturer for Emporio Armani, and since 1980 Three Rifles has been the regional representative for Italian fashion label Caserini.

In 1995, the group began to diversify. It set up TV Media, a joint-venture telemarketing company based in Malaysia, and branched into commercial and residential property development in Singapore and Malaysia with the formation of Three Rifles Land. After suffering a net loss of $4.68 million in 2004—due to provisions for what it termed 'impairment of assets'—Three Rifles was bought in 2005 by TR Networks, a sister company dealing in healthcare, beauty and lifestyle products, which is also owned by the Chong family.

thumbdrive The world's smallest computer data storage drive was invented by Singapore company Trek2000 and released in 2000. Also known as a pen drive or flash drive, the thumbdrive consists of a small printed-circuit board, which operates like a floppy disk or an external hard disk. This is put in a metal or plastic casing, from which the Universal Serial Bus (USB) connector protrudes. As it has no moving

The Thunderbirds: EP from the late 1960s.

parts, it is very robust, and the data it contains will not be corrupted even if the device is dropped, scratched or gets wet. The thumbdrive is powered by plugging it into a computer's USB port, and requires no other power source.

Thumboo, Edwin (1933–) Poet and academic. After graduating in English from the University of Malaya in 1957, Edwin Nadason Thumboo worked as a civil servant before joining the university as a lecturer in 1966. His doctoral dissertation was on African poetry in English.

Thumboo is a seminal figure in the development of Singapore's literature in English. He edited some of the earliest anthologies of ENGLISH LITERATURE from Singapore and Malaysia, such as *The Flowering Tree: Selected Writings from Singapore and Malaysia* (1970), *Seven Poets: Singapore and Malaysia* (1973) and *The Second Tongue: An Anthology of Poetry from Singapore and Malaysia* (1976). He was general editor of *The Poetry of Singapore* (1985) and *The Fiction of Singapore* (1990), both multilingual anthologies sponsored by the ASEAN Committee on Culture and Information.

Thumboo has authored four volumes of poetry. *Rib of Earth* (1956) was published while Thumboo was still an undergraduate. As a member of the editorial board of *Fajar*, a publication of the University Socialist Club (*see* FAJAR TRIAL), Thumboo was among those arrested in 1954. *Gods Can Die* (1977) and *Ulysses by the Merlion* (1979) respectively won the 1978 and 1980 National Book Development Council of Singapore Book Awards for Poetry. Many of his poems are concerned with political independence, nation-building and identity. His 'Ulysses by the Merlion' has provoked a spectrum of responses by poets such as LEE TZU PHENG, ALFIAN SA'AT, Alvin Pang, Daren Shiau, Felix Cheong and Gwee Li Sui (*see* MERLION).

The first recipient of the CULTURAL MEDALLION for Literature in 1979, Thumboo also received the Southeast Asia Write Award in 1979, the ASEAN Cultural and Communication Award in 1987, the Public Service Star in 1991, and the Raja Rao Award in 2002. He was Fulbright

Professor at Pennsylvania State University (1979–80); Ida Beam Professor at the University of Iowa (1986); and George A. Miller Visiting Professor at the University of Illinois (1998). Thumboo was head of the department of English language and literature, National University of Singapore (NUS) (1977–93); dean of the faculty of arts and social sciences, NUS (1980–91); and founding director of the NUS Centre for the Arts (1993–2005). He was made emeritus professor by NUS in 1997. Thumboo was awarded the MERITORIOUS SERVICE MEDAL in 2006.

Thunderbirds, The Popular music group. The Thunderbirds were formed in 1962. Initially, the group included Harvey Fitzgerald on rhythm guitar and vocals; Derrick Fitzgerald on lead guitar; Tony Chong on vocals and bass; and Freddie Tan on drums. The band underwent various changes in personnel, with Derrick Fitzgerald being the only constant.

Philips signed a contract with the group after they won a talent competition in 1965. The Thunderbirds went on to release seven EPs and one LP. 'Little Lady' from their first EP went to number one. Their most successful recording was their second release 'My Lonely Heart'. The song on the B-side of this record, 'Hey Girl', also went to number one, and became The Thunderbirds' signature tune. In 1966, Alan Lyford joined the band on vocals. Soon thereafter, 14-year-old Heather Batchen joined the group. The Thunderbirds continued to play live and record until the end of the 1960s.

Thye Hong Biscuits and Confectionery This company was started in 1959 by Lee Gee Chong. Its products became very popular during the 1950s and 1960s, and the company became closely associated with the large round tins in which it sold its biscuits. In 1972, the company was granted the licence to produce Jacob's Cream Crackers. Thye Hong Biscuits was bought in 1982 by Nabisco. In 1990, it was acquired by the Britannia Group. Three years later, the company came under the ownership of French group, Danone, and was renamed BBM.

Thye Hong Biscuits and Confectionery, 1958.

The original red-brick Thye Hong Biscuits and Confectionery Factory was located at the junction of Alexandra Road and Leng Kee Road, and featured a distinctive lion statue on its roof. The site was later converted into an industrial and commercial complex.

Tien Wah Press The roots of Tien Wah Press (TWP) go back to 1935, when its founder Wong Lin Kwong purchased a small letterpress printing shop in Upper Cross Street from a friend for 3,000 Malayan dollars. Having survived WORLD WAR II, the management of the company was taken over by Wong's eldest son, Tik Yun, who is credited with having built the company into a major business concern. Very soon, it moved into new premises in Cecil Street, and by 1956, expansion required a further move, this time to Leng Kee Road. In 1960, a factory was started in Kuala Lumpur. Further expansion necessitated another move to Bukit Timah Road in the 1970s. In 1996, the company moved into its present premises at Pandan Crescent, which is twice the size of the Bukit Timah plant.

TWP soon became one of the two largest printers in Singapore. The company took the lead in introducing four-colour work, producing cartons, labels and commercial brochures. From there, it ventured into producing bound books, and earned the distinction of being one of only two printers in the world to have produced pop-up books in 1978. The company continued to specialize in pop-up books, board books and books with accessories. In the mid-1960s, it entered into a partnership with Rothmans of Pall Mall, and enlarged its alliance in 1970 to include the Dai Nippon Printing Group and Mitsubishi Corporation in order to take on the increasing competition. Rothmans sold its stake in 1973.

In the early 1980s, when the move of many toy manufacturers out of Singapore presaged a decline in the market for packaging, TWP shifted its strategic focus to book production for the international publishing market. A historical milestone emerged for the company when it made its first inroads into overseas markets. By the 1990s, TWP was an international business, equipped for book production with major

Tien Wah Press: early premises.

international clients and a reputation for quality. This global reach has resulted in its being a leading exporter of books with international offices opened in the United States, United Kingdom, Australia and Europe.

As it continued to carve a niche in the children's novelty book market, a new facility was established in 1984 in the industrial district of Tampoi in Johor Bahru, Malaysia. The addition of another wing to the Malaysian plant in 2004 bore testimony to the market's fast-growing demand for innovative children's books.

In 2003, the Dai Nippon Printing Group, which had bought the Wong family's equity in 1991, assumed full ownership of TWP, buying out Mitsubishi's 15 per cent share. Today, the company is a leading exporter of books, and is well-known for its educational books for adults and children. Its two plants in Singapore and Malaysia make up about a million square feet of factory space, with a workforce of over 2,000 producing a full range of books and book innovations. The company celebrated its 70th anniversary in 2005.

Tiger Balm Herbal-based ointment. Herbalist Aw Chu Kin established a pharmacy in Rangoon, Burma, in the late 1870s, where he developed and sold his own herbal balm for the relief of muscular pains. After Aw died, his son AW BOON HAW marketed the product under the Tiger Balm brand name. Aw Boon Haw and his brother, Aw Boon Par, moved production of the ointment to Singapore in the 1920s.

Tiger Balm has since developed into a global brand, although it has continued to be manufactured in Singapore as well as in several other countries under licence. The balm is closely associated with HAW PAR VILLA, also known as Tiger Balm Gardens.

Tiger Beer Malayan Breweries, predecessor of ASIA PACIFIC BREWERIES (APB), first produced Tiger Beer in Singapore in 1932. Since then, the beer has grown into an international brand, winning over 30 international medals, including Gold in the 2004 World Beer Cup from the Association of Brewers; Gold in the 1998/99 Brewing Industry International Awards from Brewing Technology Services and Grand Gold 1991, Selection Mondiale from L'Institut pour les Selections de la Qualité. In the United Kingdom, Tiger Beer was named as a CoolBrand in 2004 and 2005.

As of 2006, Tiger Beer was being brewed in seven Asian countries and available in more than 60 countries, which includes Malaysia, Vietnam, the United Kingdom, United States, Australia and New Zealand. APB (a joint venture including FRASER & NEAVE and Heineken) has recently invested in technology to further improve Tiger Beer.

tigers Tigers (*Panthera tigris*) once roamed freely in the forests of Singapore. The naturalist Alfred Russel Wallace reported hearing the roars of tigers during his visits to Singapore between 1854 and 1862, and claimed that tigers were responsible, on average, for the death of at least one person per day, with most attacks taking place in plantations. At one stage, tigers were considered such a threat that deep pitfall traps with sharpened stakes were dug in spots around Singapore. The use of these sharpened stakes was banned, however, after someone accidentally fell into one of the pits and was killed.

In the late 19th century, it was reported that tigers were still habitually swimming to Singapore across the narrow STRAIT OF JOHOR, usually by way of PULAU UBIN and PULAU TEKONG. However, by the 1890s, the tiger population had dropped drastically, due to hunting and rewards for their capture offered by the government. By the 1920s, tigers were completely gone from the forests of Bukit Timah; what is believed to have been the last tiger in Singapore was shot in 1932.

In 1997, there were rumours of a tiger living on Pulau Ubin. However, after an extensive search, the paw prints that were thought to have been those of a tiger were found to belong to a large dog.

Times the Bookshop Local bookstore chain. Times the Bookshop has been a household name ever since it opened its first outlet in 1968 at Lucky Plaza, then a new shopping centre on Orchard Road. It was the first bookstore to mount a television advertising campaign as well as to organize in-store events. It opened its first airport outlet in 1996. In 2000, it formed a joint venture with Newslink, an Australian chain specializing in books for travellers, to open a number of outlets at Changi Airport. In 2004, it also took over British company WH

Tiger Beer

Tiger Balm

Tiger: tiger-hunting, 1928.

Tien Wah Press: factory at Pandan Crescent.

Tin: floating dredge in Perak, Malaysia (above); tin smelting at Pulau Brani, 1892 (right).

Toh Chee Hung

TODAY

Smith's chain of outlets in Singapore. Times now operates over 20 shops in Singapore and Malaysia. As the retail and distribution arm of Times Publishing, it also distributes the group's own titles under the Marshall Cavendish imprint.

tin The growth of the tin mining industry in Malaya during the 19th century was a result of the development of the tin plate industry, which brought about a great change in the use of and demand for tin. Between 1874 and 1912, the United Kingdom dominated the world's tin plate industry. During this period, most of the tin imported into the United Kingdom came from Malaya. Tin was mined in Perak, Sungei Ujong and Selangor, mainly by Chinese miners.

Singapore's tin trade expanded as world demand for tin soared—primarily due to the demands of the new canning industry—and smelting became the first modern industry in Singapore. In 1890, a tin smelter was constructed on PULAU BRANI by the Straits Trading Company. It processed ore from the Malay States and the Dutch East Indies (present-day Indonesia). By the early 20th century, ore was being brought in from further afield, including Siam (present-day Thailand), Australia, Alaska and South Africa. Tin and RUBBER became the lifeblood of the Malayan economy during the first half of the 20th century. The value of Singapore's total trade—of which tin and rubber were a large component—rose from $143 million in 1883 to $975 million in 1923. By 1951, the price of tin had risen five-fold from its pre-World War II level.

Tiong Bahru First PUBLIC HOUSING estate. The Hokkien word 'tiong' means 'cemetery' and the Malay word 'bahru' (sometimes spelt baru) means 'new'. During the 19th century, there was a Chinese burial ground on what is now Tiong Bahru. It was only when the SINGAPORE IMPROVEMENT TRUST (SIT)

decided to build its first mass public housing project in the vicinity that the area was transformed from a KAMPONG into a modern housing estate. Between 1936 and 1951, the SIT built a number of low-rise, walk-up apartments in the art deco style to house some 6,000 residents. Today, Tiong Bahru is known for its architecture, wet market (see WET MARKETS) and eating places.

Toa Payoh New town. The name Toa Payoh is derived from the Hokkien word for big (toa) and a corruption of the Malay word for swamp (paya). The area was originally a Malay KAMPONG surrounded by vegetable farms. It was chosen in the 1960s by the HOUSING & DEVELOPMENT BOARD (HDB) for development as the second new town after QUEENSTOWN, and the first new town with its own facilities such as a town garden, community plaza and library. Block 52 was the first block of flats in Toa Payoh, and was completed in August 1966.

With its own 19-storey viewing gallery, Toa Payoh became a showcase estate for PUBLIC HOUSING in Singapore. Various foreign dignitaries were brought to the estate, including Queen Elizabeth II, who visited in 1972 and again in 2006. The Toa Payoh Sports Stadium was constructed for the 7th Southeast Asian Peninsular (SEAP) Games in 1973. The town also became a base for Singapore's electronics industry from the 1960s onwards, with companies such as PHILIPS ELECTRONICS SINGAPORE setting up factories there.

The HDB moved its headquarters from Bukit Merah to Toa Payoh in 2002, around the same time that the country's first 40-storey blocks were being built in the estate.

TODAY Newspaper. Launched in November 2000, TODAY is distributed free at MASS RAPID TRANSIT stations, in office buildings and selected housing estates, and has a daily readership of 550,000. The tabloid-sized paper is published by MEDIACORP Press, and was launched at the time when SINGAPORE PRESS HOLDINGS (SPH) was given a licence to broadcast two television channels as part of the government's efforts to introduce competition into the media industry. TODAY faced stiff competition from an SPH freesheet called Streats, which was dis-

Tiong Bahru

tributed at the same locations. After four years of struggle, the two companies merged their television operations in 2004, which were to be held by a new company. MediaCorp ended up with 80 per cent of the new company, called MediaCorp TV Holdings. SPH paid $10 million for the remaining 20 per cent of the company. SPH owns 40 per cent of MediaCorp Press, and Streats was subsumed under TODAY.

Toh Chee Hung (1948–) Musician. Toh Chee Hung received her musical training in London, Vienna and Milan, and developed an international reputation as a concert pianist, teacher and adjudicator. She has spent much of her career working in both the United Kingdom and Singapore, where she performs and teaches regularly. Toh married Malaysian-born pianist Dennis Lee, with whom she released Piano Music for Four Hands (2002). In 2002, she performed the world premiere of BERNARD TAN's Piano Concerto, a work dedicated to her.

Toh Chin Chye (1921–) Politician. Born in Taiping, Perak, Toh Chin Chye completed his secondary education in his home state and went on to read science at Raffles College, Singapore, but World War II interrupted his studies. After the war, he proceeded to the University of London, where he graduated with a science degree before completing a doctorate in physiology at the National Institute for Medical Research. While in London, he was drawn to the MALAYAN FORUM, a discussion group founded by GOH KENG SWEE. Toh succeeded Goh as one of the chairmen of the forum. He was also influenced by the Labour Party, which was in power in the United Kingdom at the time, and by the Fabian Society, which advocated gradual but radical social reform.

Having completed his studies, Toh returned to Singapore, where he was appointed as a lecturer (and later, reader) in physiology at the University of Malaya in Singapore (1958–64). In 1964, he was appointed research associate, and would have followed a career as a scientist had he not become one of the main players in achieving Singapore's independence.

In November 1954, Toh was one of the 14 convenors of the PEOPLE'S ACTION PARTY (PAP). He became the founding chairman of the party's 11-member central executive committee, a post he held until 1981 when he stood down from his Cabinet position. First elected to the Legislative Assembly in 1959, he represented Rochore constituency until 1988, when he left politics. On at least two occasions, his name was floated as an alternative to LEE KUAN YEW for the post of prime minister—once in 1961, when Lee offered to resign after the PAP lost the ANSON BY-ELECTION following its defeat in the Hong Lim by-election; and again in 1964, after Singapore had been rocked by RACE RIOTS. On both occasions, Toh stood by Lee.

As a Malaya-born party chairman and deputy premier (he held the latter post in 1959–68) Toh fought for merger with Malaya. In the defining Singapore general election held on 21 September 1963 (*see* GENERAL ELECTION (1963)), five days after Singapore joined Malaysia, Toh stood and won against LEE SIEW CHOH, chairman of the rival BARISAN SOSIALIS, with the slimmest majority of 89 votes. Convinced of the PAP's national mission and worried about Malaysia's ruling Alliance Party's aim to challenge the party in Singapore, Toh, together with S. RAJARATNAM and ONG PANG BOON, led the party's central executive committee in its momentous decision (taken while Lee Kuan Yew was overseas) to field a token number of candidates in the FEDERAL ELECTION (1964). Toh's announcement to this effect on 1 March 1964 immediately resulted in a serious deterioration in PAP–Alliance relations, locking both parties in combat for the first time.

The polls resulted in an almost complete rout of the PAP, save for one seat, and precipitated a series of events that set the PAP and the Alliance Party on a collision course. The search for other political allies was stepped up in anticipation of a possible clash, and Toh was one of the prime movers of the formation of the Malaysian Solidarity Convention (MSC), a PAP-led coalition of opposition parties designed to spearhead the fight for a 'Malaysian Malaysia'. These developments led Tunku ABDUL RAHMAN to decide that, in the best interest of racial harmony and to avoid bloodshed, Singapore should separate. Toh was not informed of confidential separation talks then taking place between senior representative ministers from both sides, until summoned by Lee to Kuala Lumpur and told the news. He refused to sign the separation agreement until the Tunku confirmed to him that there was no other solution.

After SEPARATION in August 1965, Toh remained deputy premier for three years.

Toh Chin Chye: led group to design the state flag.

From 1968 to 1975, he served concurrently as minister for science and technology and vice-chancellor of the University of Singapore. During his tenure, he cracked down on student union activism and took steps to depoliticize the university. He also introduced new faculties in engineering, accountancy, business administration and architecture, and streamlined existing faculties and departments with a view to transforming the university into an engine of nation-building. In August 1976, the University of Singapore conferred on him an honorary doctorate of letters. After serving as minister for health from 1975 to 1981, he left the Cabinet.

Refusing an offer of a diplomatic posting, Toh remained a backbencher in Parliament, and found himself increasingly at odds with the party he helped to form. He became one of its most outspoken MPs until his parliamentary career ended in 1988. In 1990, he was admitted into the ORDER OF NILA UTAMA. In October 2001, the National University of Singapore established a new professorship in molecular biology in Toh's honour.

Tominaga Sanemitsu (dates unknown) Japanese military officer. Tominaga Sanemitsu was educated in the United States. In April 1943, he succeeded COUNT ASAHI ISOHI as controller of enemy aliens in Singapore, Malaya and Sumatra, Indonesia during the JAPANESE OCCUPATION. His appointment marked a shift to a harsher regime. Tominaga commandeered the possessions of civilian internees and reduced food and medical supplies. Following the DOUBLE 10TH INCIDENT, conditions deteriorated further for the civilian internees under his charge.

Tong, Kelvin (1972–) Film director. Formerly a film critic with THE STRAITS TIMES, Kelvin Tong started his film career in 1995 with *Moveable Feast*, a short film about one man's obsession with food. His feature directorial debut was EATING AIR (1999), a movie about local working-class youth. In 2005, he shot his second and third features back-to-back: *The Maid*, a horror film which which featured a foreign maid (*see* MAIDS) as its protagonist, and *1942,* an independently produced Japanese horror feature set in the Malayan jungle during World War II. He was won Best Director for *Love Story* at the Silver Screen Awards (Asian Feature Film category) of the 19th SINGAPORE INTERNATIONAL FILM FESTIVAL in 2006.

Total Defence Introduced in 1984, Total Defence is a strategy which seeks to maximize resources for military defence, and also emphasizes the importance of military deterrence, economic strength, internal cohesion and stability as the foundations of security. Through Total Defence, every

Toto and 4D: tickets bearing numbers 1208 and 0812 were sold out after the announcement of a change of government leadership on 12 August 2004.

sector of society is seen as having a part to play in ensuring Singapore's security. Citizens are organized to defend the country against all forms of attack, both military and non-military. Components of Total Defence are Psychological Defence, Social Defence, Economic Defence, Civil Defence and Military Defence.

Toto and 4D Legal lotteries which are operated by SINGAPORE POOLS. For Toto, a player picks at least six numbers from 1 to 45, and matches them against the winning numbers which are drawn. Seven numbers will be announced, and if the player has at least four matching numbers, he wins a prize. With QuickPick, the computer selects the Toto numbers on the player's behalf; System Bets are variations of Toto. In November 1998, a single Toto player won the jackpot of $5.6 million—a rare occasion when a large jackpot was not shared. The largest offered to date was $12.8 million in the Chinese New Year 'Toto Hongbao Draw' in February 2002.

In 4D (4-Digit Numbers), a player selects a four-digit number from 0000 to 9999. If it corresponds with any of the 23 four-digit numbers drawn, he wins a prize. There are five ways to play 4D—Ordinary Entry, 4D Roll, System Entry, iBet and QuickPick, as well as 'big' and 'small' bets. The minimum bid amount is $1.

Tou Mu Kung Chinese temple. This Taoist temple was founded as a private family temple by businessman Ong Choo Kee in 1921 in Upper Serangoon Road. It is a centre of worship of the Nine Emperors Gods ('Kiu Ong Yah' in Hokkien), while bearing the name of the Goddess of the North Star (Tou Mu), mother of the Nine Emperor Gods.

Some accounts state that Ong was on a business trip in Penang in 1902 when he

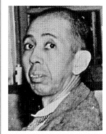

Tominaga Sanemitsu

Kelvin Tong

Tou Mu Kung

Tourism: trade fair, 1965.

heard of the Nine Emperor Gods. He visited a temple and made a vow of lifelong worship to the Nine Emperor Gods if his trip was successful. The good results from his trip led him to purchase an amulet of the Nine Emperor Gods and install it on his altar at home. From 1919 to 1921, Ong constructed a temple for the Nine Emperor Gods at Serangoon. A stage for CHINESE OPERA performances during religious festivities was located on the temple grounds, and this became a landmark until it was demolished in 1998 to make way for the expansion of Upper Serangoon Road.

Aside from the Nine Emperor Gods, the temple also has shrines dedicated to Guanyin and other lower ranking deities. Its main event is the NINE EMPEROR GODS FESTIVAL, which takes place during the first nine days of the ninth lunar month of the Chinese calender. The temple was gazetted as a national monument in 2005.

tourism Given its small size, Singapore is not a natural tourist destination, but tourism has developed into a major industry due to the city-state's prime location as a gateway to Southeast Asia. It has achieved this through its excellent communication links and world-class CHANGI AIRPORT. The growth of the Asia-Pacific outbound market and the emergence of China and India as travel destinations have also influenced the growth of tourism in Singapore.

Established in 1964, the Singapore Tourism Board (STB) is the agency responsible for the country's tourism industry. In 2005, it unveiled Tourism 2015—a ten-year plan that aims to bring $30 billion in revenue, double visitor arrivals to 17 million and create an additional 100,000 jobs in the services sector by 2015. Under Tourism

2015, three key areas of focus have been identified—strengthening Singapore's position as a leading convention and exhibition centre; developing Singapore as a major Asian leisure destination through the Uniquely Singapore campaign, and establishing Singapore as the 'services capital of Asia' in sectors such as HEALTHCARE and education. A $2-billion Tourism Development Fund was set up to develop infrastructure, attract iconic events to Singapore, and develop strategic tourism products.

In 2005, 8.94 million visitors arrived in Singapore, 7.4 per cent more than the previous year. In the same period, tourism revenue increased 10 per cent to $10.8 billion. Visitors from Asia accounted for 73 per cent of arrivals. The top five tourism markets for 2005 were Indonesia, China, Australia, Japan and India. This was the first time that India had featured among the top five countries for visitor arrivals. The market with the strongest growth was Vietnam, with visitor arrivals growing by 42 per cent.

town clubs Many town clubs—the urban equivalents of COUNTRY CLUBS—originated in the 19th century as sports or community organizations. Examples include the SINGAPORE CRICKET CLUB and SINGAPORE RECREATION CLUB at the PADANG, where Europeans used to gather for lunch, drinks or sporting competitions. Town clubs also provided accommodation in the heart of the city. Smaller clubs, most of which catered to an Asian clientele, often developed out of CLAN ASSOCIATIONS, and many were concentrated along CLUB STREET. As Singapore developed, many town clubs took on the trappings of country clubs, catering to families as well as businessmen. Examples include The Pines and Raffles Town Club.

Varying in size, scale and purpose, town clubs range from those housed in conserved buildings such as The Legends Fort Canning Park, to those housed in high-rise blocks such as the Tower Club, China Club and the Divine Society at Parkview Square on North Bridge Road.

town councils The idea of town councils was first raised in December 1984 by members of Parliament (MPs) S. CHANDRA DAS, LIM BOON HENG and S. Vasoo. In 1986, three town councils were set up as part of a pilot project. Two years later, the Town Councils Act was passed. Town councils were then set up throughout Singapore in several phases, becoming fully operational in 1989.

Town councils collect service and conservancy fees from households, and use these funds in the interests of residents. Besides maintenance of common areas—covered walkways, illuminated signboards for apartment block numbers and coin-operated taps to facilitate the washing of cars—town councils have also been tasked with upgrading local amenities.

Town clubs: Raffles Town Club.

The HOUSING & DEVELOPMENT BOARD, while continuing to sell and lease flats and commercial units, also monitors the maintenance standards of town councils. Furthermore, the government provides town councils with grants, as monthly service and conservancy fees paid by residents have become insufficient. Gradually, town councils have obtained increased powers, eventually even being able to make and enforce their own by-laws. Town councils have been granted the power to issue summonses; fine those who flout municipal laws; prescribe administrative charges for services provided; and penalize the late payment of service and conservancy fees.

Town councils are headed by a committee consisting of a chairman (who must be an MP) and up to ten appointed members for each elected MP or up to 30 members in the case of a GRC. These are volunteers who oversee full-time staff paid to look after the estate. They either belong to grassroots bodies such as RESIDENTS' COMMITTEES, or are members of the same political party as the local member of Parliament. Furthermore, two out of the three town councillors appointed to each town council are required to live in the estates in question.

Town Hall *See* VICTORIA THEATRE.

trade Singapore is a free-trade economy. In 2004, it achieved the highest trade-to-gross-domestic-product (GDP) ratio in the world, with trade in goods equivalent to 321 per cent of the country's GDP. The MINISTRY OF TRADE AND INDUSTRY (MTI) is the main body responsible for trade policy and trade-related activities in Singapore. The Singapore Trade Development Board, an agency under the ministry which was restructured in 2002 as INTERNATIONAL ENTERPRISE SINGAPORE (IE Singapore), focuses on assisting Singapore-based companies to break into the global market.

Through these bodies, the government has implemented a three-pronged trade policy—multilateral, regional and bilateral. As a result of the multilateral trading system which is embodied by the World Trade Organization, Singapore has benefited from the presence of foreign multinational corporations, the combined IMPORTS and EXPORTS of which amounted to $580 billion

TOURISM: VISITOR ARRIVALS IN 2005

Country	(000's)
Indonesia	~1800
P. R. China	~850
Australia	~620
Japan	~590
India	~580
Malaysia	~580
UK	~470
Thailand	~370
USA	~380
South Korea	~360
Philippines	~320
Hong Kong SAR	~310
Taiwan	~230
Germany	~200
Vietnam	~190

NOTE: Total number of visitor arrivals was 8,942,408.
Source: Singapore Tourism Board

in 2004. In terms of bilateral trade, Singapore has promoted FREE TRADE AGREEMENTS (FTAs), and has signed FTAs with countries such as the the United States, South Korea, New Zealand, Japan, India, Australia, Panama and Jordan. Regionally, Singapore is a core member of trading groups such as the ASSOCIATION OF SOUTH EAST ASIAN NATIONS (ASEAN), the ASIA EUROPE MEETING (ASEM) and the ASIA-PACIFIC ECONOMIC COOPERATION (APEC).

Singapore has also signed 33 Investment Guarantee Agreements (IGAs), which have helped protect investments made by Singapore-based companies in other countries. Singapore maintained a trade surplus of \$49.3 billion in 2005 and a current account surplus of \$55.4 billion, equivalent to 28.5 per cent of GDP.

trademarks The history of trademark laws in Singapore goes back to 1826, when the Second Charter of Justice imported English common law into the legal system. The common law had developed the tort of 'passing off', which prohibited one trader from misrepresenting his goods or services as those provided by another. However, it was inconvenient and time-consuming for traders to take action against others, so the authorities enacted statutes dealing specifically with trademarks, and established a public register of trademarks. The common law 'passing off' tort still exists today in Singapore and is frequently used, often in addition to the rights conferred by trademarks statutes.

On 1 February 1939, Singapore enacted its own Trade Marks Ordinance (the 1939 Act), which was based largely on the United Kingdom's Trade Marks Act of 1938. In 1991, the 1939 Act was significantly amended to make it possible for traders to register marks over services as well as goods. On 15 April 1994, Singapore acceded to the Agreement for Trade-Related Aspects of Intellectual Property Rights (the TRIPS Agreement). The TRIPS Agreement set minimum standards of intellectual property protection and imposed these as obligations on its member states. As a result, the trademark laws of Singapore were overhauled, and a new Trade Marks Act came into force on 15 January 1999.

In 2004, following the coming into force of the Trade Marks (Amendment) Act 2004 (in response to Singapore's obligations under the free trade agreement it had signed with the United States), the act was again amended substantially. One of the more significant amendments was that, for the first time in Singapore, marks did not need to be 'visually perceptible'. This meant that even sounds and smells could be registered in Singapore as trademarks.

A second amendment related to the expansion of protection accorded to 'well-known trademarks'. Trademark registrations had generally been territorial, which meant

that a trademark registered in a foreign territory did not confer on that mark any protection whatsoever in Singapore. Under this new amendment, however, any mark which was well-known in Singapore—even if it had not been registered or even used in Singapore—would be protected.

Trademarks (including service marks) are filed with the Registry of Trade Marks of the INTELLECTUAL PROPERTY OFFICE OF SINGAPORE (IPOS), which also examines and grants the registration of these marks, and maintains a public register of trademarks. A trademark registration in Singapore lasts for ten years, but such a registration may generally be indefinitely extended through the payment of a renewal fee at the expiry of every ten-year period.

In October 2000, Singapore acceded to the Protocol Relating to the Madrid Agreement Concerning the International Registration of Marks (usually referred to as the Madrid Protocol). Under the Madrid Protocol, an owner of a trademark in Singapore who has a pre-existing trademark application or registration in Singapore may elect to extend the protection over his trademark to all other signatory states of the Madrid Protocol through the payment of a fee.

Despite its relatively short history as an independent state, Singapore has created several internationally well-known trademarks such as 'DBS', 'SINGAPORE AIRLINES' and 'SINGTEL'.

traditional Chinese medicine Modern, or 'Western', medicine is the conventional medicine used in Singapore. However, many people being treated with modern medicine also seek other types of treatment, including traditional Chinese medicine (TCM), although this is confined mainly to outpatient care.

According to a survey conducted by the Ministry of Health in 1994, 45 per cent of Singaporeans have used TCM. Singaporeans go to CHINESE MEDICAL HALLS or acupuncturists for treatment with TCM. To provide some regulation, the Traditional Chinese Medicine (TCM) Practitioners Bill was passed in Parliament in November 2000. As a result, all acupuncturists have been registered with the TCM Board from 2002. From January 2004, all TCM practitioners have been registered.

There are many types of treatment that involve TCM, including acupuncture, moxibustion (heat treatment), herbal medicine, acupressure, qigong, Oriental massage and diet. Acupuncture and herbal medicine are the most popular. In acupuncture, specific areas of the skin (known as acupoints) are penetrated with thin metallic needles, which are then manipulated manually or by electrical stimulation. This technique claims to be effective for such ailments as chronic lung diseases, alcoholism, relief of pain (post-operative and back pain) and nausea.

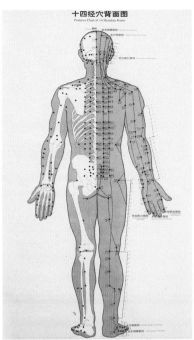

Traditional Chinese medicine: herbal tea shop (above); chart of acupoints (left); containers of herbs and other traditional medicinal products (below left).

It has been used as an adjunctive treatment for stroke rehabilitation and such conditions as asthma, osteoarthritis, carpal tunnel syndrome and menstrual cramps.

The use of moxibustion (heat treatment) is less well-known than acupuncture. In moxibustion, change of skin temperature occurs at acupoints, which are heat-stimulated by the burning of compressed herbal powders at these sites. Moxibustion is said to work through the heat-mediated neuronal release of nitric oxide and stimulation of somato-visceral reflex; 'somato' refers to muscles, bones and nerves and 'visceral' refers to the internal organs, such as the uterus, liver, heart, colon and lungs. Acumoxia is a combination of acupuncture and moxibustion.

At least three public hospitals in Singapore, namely TAN TOCK SENG HOSPITAL, ANG MO KIO-THYE HUA KWAN HOSPITAL and CHANGI GENERAL HOSPITAL—have acupuncture clinics. The latter two have gone beyond acupuncture to also allow TCM practitioners to provide *tuina* (a form of massage). At Ang Mo Kio-Thye Hua Kwan Hospital, TCM practitioners are allowed to dispense Chinese medicinal products to patients. Since 2005, Nanyang Technological University (NTU) has offered a course on biomedical sciences and TCM. Students spend the first three years at NTU and the next two years at the Beijing University of Chinese Medicine.

Trams: tramcar (right) and ticket from the late 1920s.

trams The establishment of the Singapore Electric Tramways Company (SETCo) in 1905 was the result of efforts by Singapore's municipal commissioners to modernize the city. The commissioners took over the Singapore Gas Company and granted a private company a licence to supply the city with electricity. The licence to provide electricity also included the right to run electric tramways. Until the eventual liquidation of SETCo in 1926, the company was presided over by Sir FRANK SWETTENHAM.

Tram operations commenced on 25 July 1905. Initially, five tram lines were laid. These linked the harbour area with the commercial centre of the town, then led out to the villages of Paya Lebar and Geylang. After the 1910 opening of Anderson Bridge, a sixth line was added. This linked the business district with the railway terminus at Tank Road (*see* RAILWAYS).

SETCo operated 50 tramcars and four trailers. These were operated by about 273 drivers and conductors, and services were provided from early morning until 10 p.m. Following disputes over who was entitled to sit in different sections of its trams, SETCo introduced first-class tickets for the two front benches. The company's headquarters and power station were located on McKenzie Road. Eventually, between 10 and 11 million trips were being made by passengers on SETCo's trams each year.

However, SETCo faced many challenges. The introduction of tram services brought SETCo into direct conflict with rickshaw operators (*see* RICKSHAWS), who saw trams as unwanted competition. Moreover, SETCo derived only limited profits from its tram services. Rates for electricity fell, while the price of coal to produce electricity rose. The MUNICIPAL COMMISSION declined to revise its contract with SETCo. Continued competition with rickshaws made any increase in tram fares impossible, and the company moved towards insolvency.

In the early 1920s, the Municipal Commission decided to generate and distribute electricity from its own power station at St James Park (opened in 1926), while the tram business was taken over by the Shanghai Electric Tramway Company, which replaced the trams with trolley buses

(and later with motor buses). In 1926, the last electric tram returned to the depot.

Travers, Captain Thomas (1785–1844) Colonial official. Born in Ireland, Thomas Otho Travers joined the British EAST INDIA COMPANY in 1803, and sailed for India the following year. In 1806, he was posted with his regiment to Penang, where he first met Sir STAMFORD RAFFLES.

Travers sailed with his regiment to Java in 1811 as part of an invading British force. After the capture of Java, Travers was appointed by Raffles (then lieutenant-governor of Java) as assistant secretary to the government in the Military Department. He was appointed town-major of Batavia (present-day Jakarta) in 1812, and later became one of Raffles' two aides-de-camp in Java. He also served under Raffles in West Sumatra from 1818 to 1820.

In 1820, Raffles offered Travers the position of resident and commandant in Singapore to replace Colonel WILLIAM FARQUHAR. However, Farquhar continued to retain charge of Singapore against the wishes of Raffles. After waiting in vain for Farquhar to relinquish authority, Travers and his family left Singapore for the United Kingdom in December 1820.

Travers later contributed to Lady SOPHIA RAFFLES' biography of her late husband—*Memoir of the Life and Public Services of Sir Thomas Stamford Raffles* (1830). He died at his home in County Cork, Ireland.

treaties Singapore follows the British practice under which the executive branch of government acts as the state's primary treaty-making authority. There is no requirement for treaties to be ratified, since the conduct of FOREIGN RELATIONS is considered to be the prerogative of the executive branch.

Singapore has acceded to many multilateral conventions and treaties since 1965. However, Singapore did not sign any major human rights treaties, other than those relating to slavery, until 1995. Since then, Singapore has acceded to the Genocide Convention (1948), the United Nations Convention on the Rights of the Child (1989) and the Convention on the Elimination of All Forms of Discrimination Against Women (1979). Singapore has also

signed numerous bilateral treaties, such as FREE TRADE AGREEMENTS with other countries.

tremors and earthquakes Singapore is tectonically stable, and there have been no strong earthquakes recorded during its history. The solid bedrock of the island's ancient granite core, together with an absence of any major fault lines, has left Singapore unaffected by the strong earth movements experienced in some neighbouring countries. The most significant plate boundaries in the region are the Sumatra Trench, just 400 km southwest of Singapore, and the Philippine Trench, over 1,500 km to the northeast. Along these, one tectonic plate is being dragged down under another, so there is a high level of instability.

While Singapore does not suffer from earthquakes, tall buildings in certain areas do experience tremors from earthquakes in Indonesia. After the massive earthquake off Sumatra on 26 December 2004, tremors were reported in Toa Payoh, Clementi, Beach Road, Siglap, Meyer Road and Tanjong Rhu.

The METEOROLOGICAL SERVICES DIVISION of the National Environment Agency has a network of seismological stations which monitor earth movements. These are located both in hard rock locations and at depth, in softer, new sediment on land reclaimed from the sea (*see* GEOLOGY and LAND RECLAMATION). With increasing urbanization and ever taller buildings, equipment to monitor both the effects of wind and earth movement are being built into new developments. One of the first high-rise developments to have built-in seismic equipment is Republic Plaza.

trial by jury Trial by jury has never been used in Singapore for civil cases, but from the earliest days of British colonial rule, juries did try criminal cases. The Second Charter of Justice (1826) provided for trial by jury in Singapore.

In 1960, jury trial was restricted to capital offences, and in 1970, the jury system was abolished altogether. In restricting jury trials to capital cases in 1960, Prime Minister LEE KUAN YEW noted that the jury system placed a premium on a lawyer's 'skill and agility' and that justice was often thwarted on 'pure technicalities' because jurors were ill-equipped to fully understand their role. Lee argued that judges could

Tropicana Nightclub: 1970s advertisement.

decide facts just as well as could the members of a jury.

In 1969, a bill was introduced to amend the Criminal Procedure Code to abolish juries completely. During the second reading of the bill, Law Minister E.W. BARKER argued that the jury system was unreliable and should be abolished. Again, it was Lee Kuan Yew who spoke most vehemently against the jury system. He argued that if judges were unable to decide on questions of fact better than jurymen, then 'grievous harm' was being done every day when single judges and magistrates were sitting alone in deciding questions of fact in both civil and criminal cases. Furthermore, Lee said that juries were 'overwhelmed with the responsibility of having to find a man guilty' when they knew that the death sentence was to follow.

The bill was thus referred to the Select Committee and the system was abolished. A two-judge system was then put in place to ensure that, in capital cases, the accused had the benefit of a safeguard (both judges had to be unanimous on a guilty verdict before capital punishment could be applied).

The two-judge system was then repealed in 1992. Thereafter, single High Court judges, assisted by two public prosecutors and two members of defence counsel, were given responsibility for hearing capital cases.

See also LEGAL SYSTEM.

Tropicana Nightclub. Located on Scotts Road, Tropicana was the first club to introduce topless revues when it was opened in 1968. Owned by the Shaw family (unrelated to the Shaw brothers), Tropicana proved highly popular in its first three years, and attracted substantial crowds until the 1970s. In 1972, NEPTUNE THEATRE RESTAURANT opened, and also introduced topless dancing. Tropicana thus lost much of its business, and eventually closed in 1989.

Tsuji Masanobu, Colonel (1902–1968) Japanese military officer. Tsuji Masanobu was born in Ishikawa Prefecture, Japan, received his education at the Military Academy in Tokyo, and saw action in China with the Japanese army in the 1930s.

In January 1941, Tsuji set up a secret training facility in Formosa (present-day Taiwan) to plan for the MALAYA CAMPAIGN. Tsuji also established an intelligence network in Singapore to compile lists of Chinese who had raised funds to support China's war effort against Japan, or who had supported boycotts of Japanese business and trade. During the JAPANESE OCCUPATION, Tsuji supervised the SOOK CHING operations, rounding up thousands of Chinese for interrogation, torture and execution.

During the 1947 war crimes trials (*see* WAR CRIMES COMMISSION), Tsuji was named by various defendants as having orchestrated the Sook Ching massacre. However,

Tsuji evaded arrest and disappeared, not appearing in public again until 1948. In 1950, Tsuji was cleared of war crimes charges in Japan. Tsuji later wrote about his experiences during the war, but made no mention of the Sook Ching massacres. He then entered politics, and was elected to Japan's House of Representatives in 1952 and House of Councillors in 1959. In 1961, Tsuji disappeared during a trip to Laos. He was officially declared dead in 1968.

Tuas Area in southwestern Singapore. The word 'tuas' is a corruption of the Malay word *'menuas'*, meaning 'to haul fishing nets'. This reflects the origins of Tuas as a fishing village. In the 19th century, the area was referred to by three alternative names: Tanjong Kampong, Tanjong Rawa and Tanjong Gul.

Today, Tuas stands at the westernmost end of JURONG INDUSTRIAL ESTATE and is the site of the TUAS SECOND LINK between Singapore and Johor. The customs and immigration checkpoint at the Second Link is called the Tuas Checkpoint.

Tuas Second Link Bridge at TUAS linking Singapore and Johor. The Second Link was constructed to ease traffic jams at the original Singapore–Johor CAUSEWAY at Woodlands.

In 1994, Singapore and Malaysia signed an inter-governmental agreement on the construction of a bridge linking Tuas in Singapore and Tanjung Kupang in Johor. Each country was to undertake and finance its portion of the bridge. Of the 1.9-km stretch, about 300 m would belong to Singapore, and the remainder to Malaysia. It was estimated that Singapore would spend more than $400 million on the bridge, reclamation works and customs and immigration facilities. To facilitate traffic movement, Jalan Ahmad Ibrahim was also upgraded into an expressway.

The Singapore customs checkpoint, built on 20 ha of reclaimed land, marked the start of the bridge at the Singapore end. Groundbreaking for the construction of the Second Link took place in July 1995. The bridge was opened to the public on 2 January 1998. It has six lanes and the capacity to handle 200,000 vehicles daily. It connects to the Second Link Expressway in Malaysia, which joins up with the North-South Highway.

tuberculosis This infectious disease is a major health problem around the world. Globally, it kills around 2 million people a year, and drug-resistant strains are emerging.

In Singapore, there were 400 cases of tuberculosis (TB) per 100,000 people in 1961. With improved housing, hygiene and sanitation and vaccination of all newborns since 1957, the number of cases has since dropped drastically. In 2003, there were 41 TB cases per 100,000. However, this num-

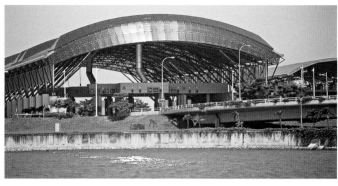

Tuas Second Link: checkpoint.

ber is not considered low when seen in the context of other developed countries.

In 1997, the MINISTRY OF HEALTH started the Singapore Tuberculosis Elimination Programme (STEP), aimed at early detection and proper treatment. Since July 2004, legal enforcement by means of the Infectious Diseases Act has been applied as a last-resort measure to ensure that recalcitrant defaulters complete their treatment. The aim is to control community transmission of the disease and prevent the emergence of drug-resistant TB. Only a very small number of patients have been served with such orders so far.

See also SINGAPORE ANTI-TUBERCULOSIS ASSOCIATION.

***tudung* issue** In early 2002, the Ministry of Education suspended two female Muslim students from a primary school for breaking school-uniform rules by wearing *tudungs* (Muslim headscarves) to class. Two other girls were later also suspended, wearing *tudungs* two weeks into the school year. Many devout Muslims consider the donning of the *tudung* obligatory once a girl reaches puberty. In these cases, however, the girls had not reached puberty.

The parents of the girls involved in this issue felt the government was denying them freedom of religion. The government's stance was that national schools were secular, and that school uniforms were an important means of building unity amongst students of different racial, religious and social backgrounds. The government also encouraged the parents to send the girls back to school in proper uniform. MAJLIS UGAMA ISLAM SINGAPURA (MUIS) issued a statement advising Muslim parents to

Tuberculosis: clinic in 1952.

12 Storeys (1997): Lum May Yee as Trixie.

prioritize their children's education. One of the girls eventually went back to school without her *tudung*, while the other three attended private schools. The issue sparked a year-long public debate about the practice of religion in a secular state.

See also ISLAM and MULTIRACIALISM.

Tuhfat al-Nafis Tuhfat al-Nafis (The Precious Gift) is a historical narrative written in Arabic of the Johor-Riau-Lingga sultanate from the perspective of its BUGIS-MALAY authors Raja Ahmad and his eldest surviving son Raja Ali Haji. Raja Ahmad was the brother of Raja Jafar, the Yam Tuan Muda (regent) of Riau, whom Colonel WILLIAM FARQUHAR met during the course of the events which led to the FOUNDING OF SINGAPORE as an entrepôt in 1819. As a court official, Raja Ahmad was aware of the developments taking place in Riau at a time when the Dutch were gaining the upper hand in the affairs of the sultanate. It was Raja Ali Haji, however, who developed what is believed to be the first drafts of the Tuhfat al-Nafis by his father, and is generally recognized as the author of the Tuhfat. Raja Ali Haji was acknowledged by both the Riau royal family and the Dutch as a great scholar, whose knowledge of genealogy and court procedure was well-respected. The Tuhfat was written with the use of a wide variety of sources such as manuscripts, anecdotes, oral accounts and recountings of incidents which both father and son had been involved in. The earliest manuscript of the text has been dated to 1866.

tuition The private tuition market is a major industry in Singapore. It was worth approximately $320 million in 2005, with an estimated 50 per cent of primary school students and 20 per cent of secondary students receiving it. A press survey conducted in 2004 revealed that more than a third of all Singapore schoolchildren (including kindergarten students) receive private tuition in some form, with the fees for such tuition ranging from $100 to $200 per month.

Private tutoring is believed to have had a major social and educational impact. Some theorists have argued that it exacerbates social inequalities, and that while it can help pupils to learn, it can also interfere with educational processes in mainstream schools.

Private tutoring in Singapore replicates daytime schooling and makes up for perceived deficiencies in daytime lessons. The practice is believed to thrive due to a desire on the part of many parents to ensure high levels of academic achievement on the part of their children.

In 1993, the Cost Review Committee reported that private, one-to-one tuition was expensive, and suggested that parents could reduce the financial burden of tuition by making use of group tuition programmes offered by community 'self-help' groups such as MENDAKI, the SINGAPORE INDIAN DEVELOPMENT ASSOCIATION (SINDA) and the CHINESE DEVELOPMENT ASSISTANCE COUNCIL (CDAC).

The CDAC Tuition Programme was launched in 1993. Since then, it has provided tuition mainly for Chinese students from lower-income families who are not performing well in school. Similarly, there were about 4,700 students enrolled in SINDA's tuition programme in 2004. Around 80 per cent of these students were from families with a monthly income of less than $2,000, and about 20 per cent of these students qualified for a waiver of tuition fees. In addition, some individual tutors and private tuition centres have been received endorsement and support from the government.

Tung On Wui Kun This clan association was established in 1870 by immigrants from Tung Kwan (present-day Dong Guan) and Po On (present-day Bao An) in Guangdong, China. It established its own school—the Tung On Free School—in 1919, and continued to maintain that institution until its closure in the mid-1960s.

Members of the Tung On Wui Kun set up a CANTONESE opera class in 1947 (*see* CHINESE OPERA). This became one of the most active Cantonese opera groups from the early 1970s, regularly staging full-length works. Led by the Chee sisters (Kin Foon, Siew Fun and Oi Fun), the group places emphasis on training. It has engaged veterans from China such as Beijing opera masters Chen Rongfang and Zhang Shijie, Cantonese actor Wang Fan Shi, and also well-known artistes from Hong Kong such as Luo Jieying and Liang Tian, to coach young members recruited by the association since the mid-1980s.

In 1991, it launched the Tung On Arts and Opera and Oriental Opera Group to present Cantonese opera productions with artistes from China, Hong Kong and Singapore, and to conduct classes for opera enthusiasts. It also has a Cantonese opera orchestra led by Chen Xiaorui. Its major productions have included *Madam White Snake*, *Dream of the Red Chamber*, *Purple Hairpin*, *Rebirth of the Red Plum* and its own original operas.

12 Storeys (1997) FILM. Directed by ERIC KHOO, *12 Storeys* was the first local feature film to have won international recognition by being screened at the Festival de Cannes. It has been widely seen as part of the renaissance in Singapore film-making sparked off by Khoo's earlier *Mee Pok Man* (1995). Starring JACK NEO, Koh Boon Pin and Lum May Yee, *12 Storeys* tackles topics as diverse as CAMPAIGNS, the phenomenon of China brides and overweening materialism. Its multilayered script features three cross-cutting stories, which come together to form a critique of Singapore society and its underlying contradictions.

Tyersall Originally the name of a house that WILLIAM NAPIER, Singapore's first law agent, built on 27 ha of land in the 'Tang Leng' district (*see* TANGLIN). Tyersall was purchased by Sultan Abu Bakar of Johor in 1860 and then demolished. In its place, Sultan ABU BAKAR built a palace, Istana Tyersall, designed by Datoh Yahya and built by Wong Ah Fook. It was completed in 1892 and its opening was a grand society event. The house stood at the top of the hill, near the corner of present-day Holland Road and Tyersall Avenue. It was rectangular in shape and measured 64 m lengthwise and 53 m deep. The architectural style was described as Corinthian, with a red-tiled roof and a tower rising nearly 21.3 m. The portico alone was 21.3 m long. There was a grand reception room, drawing room, ballroom and numerous bedrooms.

Istana Tyersall was the first residence to have electric lights, with its own generating station located away from the building. On 10 September 1905, the building was destroyed by fire caused by faulty wiring. The entire centre portion of the main back wing and the ballroom was gutted. It was never rebuilt. In August 2005, it was announced that the ruins of Istana Tyersall would be torn down. It continues to belong to the Johor sultanate.

Tyersall: Sultan of Johor's residence, 1906.

U

Ulaganathan, I. (1938–) Poet. Born in Ipoh, Perak, I. Ulaganathan began writing poetry at the age of 17. Arriving in Singapore in search of work in 1953, he assumed the editorship of literary monthly *Mathavi*, which he published from 1959 to 1964. In his role as editor, he also promoted and nurtured Tamil poets, among them Amallathasan and Paranan. His own poetry reflected his reformist aspirations for Tamil society in Singapore. His first collection of poems, *Santhana Kinnam* (Sandalwood Cup) (1966) drew the attention of the literary community in Tamil Nadu, India, whose government honoured him with the Paventhar Bharathithsan Award. Among his other works are *Makara Yazh* (1982), *Damayanthi* (1981), *Thiruppumunaikal* (Turning Points) (1982). Ulaganathan currently lives in Bangalore.

Ultimax 100 SAW Machine-gun. This locally developed 5.56-calibre light machine-gun is used by the SINGAPORE ARMED FORCES and the armies of several other countries. The Ultimax 100 Squad Automatic Weapon (SAW) was developed by Singapore Technologies Kinetics (ST Kinetics). The Ultimax is a lightweight mobile support weapon. It is a gas-operated, rotating-bolt locked, fully automatic, magazine-fed firearm that fires from an open bolt. The gas system has a three-position gas regulator. Its action design reduces recoil and improves accuracy. The current model is the Mark 3 that comes with a detachable buttstock and is available in two barrel lengths: 508 mm and 330 mm.

The Ultimax is easily controlled from the prone, hip or shoulder position and accepts 20-, 30- or 100-round drums. It uses a quick-change heavy barrel and comes with a bipod.

Umar Pulavar Tamil School This was the only Tamil-medium high school in Singapore. It was founded in 1946 by INDIAN MUSLIMS who originally came from the town of Kadayanallur, in Tamil Nadu. The school was located in a shophouse in Tanjong Pagar Road. In 1960 it was renamed the Umar Pulavar Tamil High School. The school eventually closed in 1982 because of declining enrolment but its name lives on as the Umar Pulavar Tamil Language Centre, which is now in Serangoon Road. Umar Pulavar is the name of a well-known Tamil poet of the 17th century.

Undesirable Publications Act In 1967, Parliament passed the Undesirable Publications Act, empowering the government to prohibit the importation, distribution and reproduction of undesirable publications. Publications proscribed as 'undesirable' include those thought likely to deprave and corrupt persons who are likely to be exposed to their contents. This may be because the material is obscene or is thought to deal with matters of race or religion either insensitively or in a derogatory fashion. Under the Act, the term 'publications' extends beyond printed matter and includes sound recordings and films.

Banned books are typically pornographic in nature, although there have been instances where the ban has been imposed on publications deemed to be offensive to religious groups, as in the case of Salman Rushdie's *Satanic Verses*. A blanket ban may be imposed on publications emanating from an organization that has been proscribed, such as the Watch Tower Bible and Tract Society (publishing arm of the JEHOVAH'S WITNESSES). A proscribed publication that was the subject of considerable international discussion was the magazine *Cosmopolitan*, which the government felt undesirable as it promoted promiscuous lifestyles. The ban on *Cosmopolitan* was lifted in September 2004, although copies on sale must be shrink-wrapped, and carry a warning label that its contents are 'Unsuitable for the Young'.

Unification Church The full name of the church is the Holy Spirit Association for the Unification of World Christianity. Members are popularly referred to as 'Moonies', after Korean founder Reverend Sun Myung Moon, although they prefer to call themselves 'Unificationists'. The church was founded in 1954 in Seoul and registered in Singapore in 1980. In 1982, the Ministry for Home Affairs deregistered and banned it under the Societies Act as prejudicial to public welfare and good order.

United Chinese Library The United Chinese Library was inaugurated by SUN YAT SEN on 8 August 1910 under the auspices of the Tong Teck Book and Newspaper Association. The association was founded by Teo Eng Hock, Tan Chor Nam and LIM NEE SOON in 1907 as an offshoot of Chong Shing Press which they had co-founded in July that year. Teo was the association's first president.

The library, one of more than 50 'reading rooms' set up in Singapore and Malaya between 1908 and 1911 by Chinese republicans, was originally located at the foot of Fort Canning, near River Valley Road. Like the other reading rooms, the United Chinese Library was established to disseminate revolutionary ideas and to generate support for the overthrow of the Manchu Qing dynasty in China. It later moved to 51 Armenian Street where it remained until 1987, when it shifted to 53 Cantonment Road.

United Nations The United Nations (UN) is an important platform for Singapore's foreign policy. One of Singapore's first actions as a newly-independent state was to apply for membership of the United Nations (UN). The country's admission into the UN in September 1965 signalled that Singapore had joined the community of sovereign nation states. Singapore's first permanent representative to the UN was ABU BAKAR PAWANCHEE.

In the early years, Singapore conducted much of its international diplomacy through the UN mission in New York. The UN mission was an excellent forum for maintaining contacts with countries which did not have a resident Singapore embassy. Singapore also sent many young diplomats to the annual UN General Assembly for training and exposure.

Over the years, Singapore has played an active role on many key UN issues, including the Cambodian issue, the Law of the Sea Conference, the environment, UN reforms and UN finance and budget issues.

Singapore has joined key UN bodies such as UNCITRAL (UN Commission on International Trade Law) and the UN Committee on Contributions, as well as specialized agencies where Singapore has strong national interests at stake. These include the WORLD TRADE ORGANIZATION, the International Labour Organization, the INTERNATIONAL CIVIL AVIATION ORGANIZATION, the INTERNATIONAL MARITIME ORGANIZATION, the World Health Organization, and the WORLD INTELLECTUAL PROPERTY ORGANIZATION. It also helped to form and lead key groups such as the Open-ended Working Group on UN Security Council Reforms and the Forum of Small States. Singapore also actively took part in the Non-Aligned Movement and G77 activities at the UN.

In 2001 and 2002, Singapore served on the UN Security Council for the first time.

Singapore has consistently sought to strengthen the UN's role as the enforcer of

United Nations:
S. Jayakumar speaking at
the UN Security Council.

United Nations: the Singapore flag raised for the first time at UN headquarters, 1965.

United People's Party rally, 1962.

international peace and stability and the promoter of the rule of international law. It has also taken part in PEACEKEEPING missions and has sent several Singaporeans to staff key posts within the UN Secretariat. It has also invited many UN representatives of developing countries to visit Singapore for fact-finding and educational tours and to share its developmental experiences.

United Overseas Bank

In 1935, a group of seven Chinese businessmen led by Kuching-born Wee Kheng Chiang founded the United Chinese Bank—with a paid-up capital of $1 million—to cater for the banking needs of the Chinese Hokkien community. The bank was renamed the United Overseas Bank (UOB) in 1965, as another bank in Hong Kong also bore the original name.

The bank started business in rented premises in the Bonham Building, on the corner of Bonham and Chulia Streets, before buying the building from the landlord. It was replaced in 1974 by an octagonal 30-storey building, known as the UOB Building, resembling a stack of coins. A new building, UOB Plaza 1, was completed on an adjoining site in 1993. The old UOB building was refurbished and officially re-opened in 1995 as UOB Plaza 2.

UOB acquired several other local banks in the 1970s and 1980s, including Chung Khiaw Bank in 1971, Lee Wah Bank in 1972, Far Eastern Bank in 1984, and Industrial Commercial Bank in 1987. In 2001, it took over local rival OVERSEAS UNION BANK, and so became one of the 'Big Three' local banks. By 2004, it owned UOB Radanasin and Bank of Asia in Thailand.

UOB was the first local bank to obtain an Asian Currency Unit licence. It was also the first in Singapore to introduce telephone banking.

The group has been led by WEE CHO YAW since he succeeded his father in 1974. In 2004, Wee was listed by *Forbes* magazine as one of the richest men in Singapore, with a fortune estimated at US$2.3 billion.

By 2005, UOB had 69 branches in Singapore and more than 430 offices worldwide. Listed since 1970, the bank's stock is a component of the Straits Times Index. For the financial year ending 31 December 2005, the UOB Group achieved a record net profit after tax of $1.7 billion, and group income before operating expenses was $3.8 billion. It had total assets of $145 billion and shareholders' funds of $14.9 billion.

United Overseas Land

Property company. United Overseas Land (UOL) started out as Faber Union, a subsidiary of Faber Union (Hong Kong) in 1963. UOL changed to its present name in 1975 after UNITED OVERSEAS BANK acquired a controlling interest in the company in 1973. In subsequent decades, UOL acquired a large portfolio of investment and development properties, which included office, retail, hotels and serviced apartments, and developed numerous residential properties in Singapore and overseas. Its listed subsidiary, Hotel Plaza, owns hotels in Singapore, Malaysia, Australia, Vietnam and China. UOL has also made forays into the lifestyle business, with interests in spas, furniture retailing and the distribution of health and fitness equipment.

The group has become a property conglomerate with over 40 subsidiaries and associate companies. UOL's commercial properties in Singapore include Odeon Towers, UOL Building, United Square, Faber House, Novena Square and Central Plaza. Listed in 1964, UOL's stock is a component of the Straits Times Index. In 2005, the group reported a net profit attributable to shareholders of $100.1 million on revenues of $505 million.

United People's Party

Political party. The United People's Party was founded by former People's Action Party (PAP)

United Overseas Bank: UOB Plaza.

treasurer and Singapore mayor ONG ENG GUAN in 1961. It was essentially a one-man party and won a single seat in the 1963 general election—the Hong Lim constituency. Shortly after the 1963 election, Ong resigned his seat and the party's existence was left in doubt. By the 1968 election, the party had been dissolved.

United States–Singapore relations

During the Cold War, Singapore maintained close strategic relations with the United States as a matter of geopolitical necessity. Singapore and Malaysia were critical for the control of vital sea lanes, and tin and rubber production. After Independence, leaders of both countries looked to the West, especially Britain and the US, for trade and economic assistance and for security against communism.

Singapore supported US involvement in the Vietnam War as the necessary containment of communism in the region. Furthermore, US war spending in the form of procurement orders in various Southeast Asian countries, including Singapore, helped to drive regional economic growth and trade. Singapore's early economic development was helped significantly by the US security umbrella over non-communist Southeast Asia, and the availability of US markets, technology, and investment. The late 1960s and early 1970s saw the US withdrawal from Vietnam, President Nixon's rapprochement with China, and the Paris Peace Accords. However, the role of the US was reinvigorated in the 1980s with the Reagan administration's re-engagement with Southeast Asia after Vietnam's invasion of Cambodia.

In the post-Cold War period, Singapore once again became concerned about a potential US withdrawal from the region, particularly when American bases in the Philippines were closed in 1992. Singapore supported a continued US military presence by signing a bilateral memorandum of understanding (MOU), allowing US aircraft and ships access to Singapore facilities at Paya Lebar Airbase and the Sembawang wharves. Under the MOU, the US Western Pacific logistics command centre was transferred to Singapore in 1992 from Subic Bay in the Philippines; US fighter aircraft were deployed periodically to Singapore for exercises; and a number of US military vessels visited Singapore. The MOU was amended in 1999 to permit US naval vessels, including aircraft carriers, to berth at the Changi Naval Base, completed in early 2001.

Singapore continued to view US security involvement in the region as a deterrent to potential intra-regional conflicts, and welcome in the face of uncertainties implied by an increasingly powerful China. After the terrorist attacks in the US on 11 September 2001, and the discovery of al-Qaeda-linked terrorists cells and plots in Singapore shortly afterwards, counter-terrorism became the strongest common cause in Singapore-US cooperation. Between 2003 and 2005, Singapore sent police, tank-landing ships, transport and refuelling aircraft, and about 450 troops to provide logistical support for the US war in Iraq.

In October 2003, the two countries announced their intention to expand cooperation in defence and security, and to negotiate a Framework Agreement for a Strategic Cooperation Partnership. This agreement, signed in June 2005, expanded bilateral cooperation in areas such as counter-terrorism, counter-proliferation of weapons of mass destruction, joint military exercises and training, policy dialogues, and defence technology. The two countries are not formal allies. Rather, Singapore is a 'major security cooperation partner' of the US.

The two countries enjoy very close and substantive economic relations. The US is Singapore's second largest trading partner and Singapore is the 16th-largest trading partner of the US. The US is Singapore's second largest foreign investor, with cumulative foreign direct investment amounting to $38.3 billion. Singapore is the US's fourth-largest Asian investor with cumulative direct investment of $8.9 billion. There are more than 1,300 US companies operating in Singapore. Singapore is the first Asian country with which the US has concluded a free trade agreement which came into force in January 2004.

With effect from 9 August 1999, Singapore citizens do not require a visa to enter the US, a privilege accorded to only 27 countries in the world.

United Test and Assembly Center Founded in November 1997, United Test and Assembly Center (UTAC) soon acquired the memory semiconductor test operations of Fujitsu Microelectronics Asia in 1998.

Listed on the Singapore Exchange since 15 May 2000, UTAC was ranked as the seventh-largest independent provider of semiconductor assembly and test services by Gartner Dataquest in February 2006. Headquartered in Singapore, UTAC has manufacturing facilities in Singapore and Shanghai, and a well-established sales network in Singapore, China, the United States, Italy, Japan and Israel.

UTAC's full turnkey services include wafer sort/laser repair, assembly, test, burn-in, mark-scan-pack and drop shipment, as well as value-added services such as package design and simulation, test solutions development and device characterization, failure analysis, and full reliability test.

UTAC's global customers include integrated device manufacturers, fabless companies and wafer foundries that design and manufacture semiconductors that power modern electronic devices. The company employed about 3,200 people, and turned in a profit of US$41.8 million on a turnover of US$325.5 million for the financial year 2005. The stock has been a component of the benchmark Straits Times Index since March 2006.

United World College of South East Asia International school. The United World College of South East Asia (UWCSEA) is part of the United World College movement founded in 1962 based on the philosophy of Kurt Hahn, who advocated international understanding through experiential and multicultural education. UWCSEA began in 1971 as the Singapore International School and changed to its current name in 1975. In 2005, it had nearly 2,900 students of more than 60 nationalities, ranging from 4 to 18 years of age. It is one of ten United World Colleges around the world.

universities There are three publicly-funded universities in Singapore: the NATIONAL UNIVERSITY OF SINGAPORE (NUS), NANYANG TECHNOLOGICAL UNIVERSITY (NTU) and SINGAPORE MANAGEMENT UNIVERSITY (SMU). Students with GCE 'A' Level, polytechnic or other recognized qualifications may apply for admission to these universities. The three universities currently take in about 21 per cent of the primary 1 entry cohort.

In 2004, *The Times Higher Education Supplement* included NUS in its list of the 20 best universities in the world. It is a comprehensive university offering a broad-based curriculum underpinned by multi-disciplinary courses and cross-faculty enrichment programmes. As recommended by the committee to review the University Sector and Graduate Manpower Planning in 2002, NUS will be transformed into a multi-campus university system.

A memorandum of understanding was signed in 2003, to collaborate with Duke University on the establishment of a Graduate Medical School (GMS) by 2007 and to work towards the goal of a joint NUS-Duke MD degree for graduates of the GMS.

NTU's roots go back to 1955 when it began as NANYANG UNIVERSITY (Nantah), the first Chinese-language university in Southeast Asia, through donations from ordinary citizens with the campus land donated by the SINGAPORE HOKKIEN HUAY KUAN. Nanyang Technological Institute was reborn on the same campus in 1981 with government funding to educate practice-oriented engineers for the fast-growing Singapore economy. In 1991, it became Nanyang Technological University with the absorption of the National Institute of Education.

University Cultural Centre

Incorporated in 2000, SMU holds the unique position of being Singapore's first private university funded by the government. Modelled on the Wharton School of the University of Pennsylvania, SMU's curriculum aims to groom business leaders and entrepreneurs. Its governance structure promotes innovation and flexibility.

SINGAPORE INSTITUTE OF MANAGEMENT (SIM) is one of Singapore's oldest private education organizations dating back to 1964. It is an independent, not-for-profit, professional membership organization. SIM was selected by the MINISTRY OF EDUCATION in 1992 to run the Open University Degree Programme, accredited by The Open University of the United Kingdom. In 2005, Singapore's Ministry of Education granted SIM approval to form SIM University, commencing its first student intake in 2006.

In March 2007, the University of New South Wales (UNSW), Australia will establish a full overseas campus in eastern Singapore. UNSW Asia will be Singapore's first foreign university, and the first wholly-owned and operated research and teaching campus established overseas by an Australian university.

There are many other links between local universities and overseas universities allowing for degree and post-graduate studies, such as that between NTU and Japan's Waseda University, and the NTU, NUS and Massachusetts Institute of Technology (MIT) alliance.

University Cultural Centre The largest performance and convention venue in the western part of Singapore, the University Cultural Centre is part of the NATIONAL UNIVERSITY OF SINGAPORE (NUS). It was opened in 2000 and comprises an auditorium seating 1,700 and a theatre seating 450. The auditorium is home to the National University of Singapore Symphony Orchestra and YONG SIEW TOH CONSERVATORY OF MUSIC (until 2006) and has hosted numerous formal ceremonies, concerts and performances.

Renowned performers at the venue have included Dame Kiri Te Kanawa and Tan Dun. The UCC also houses MUSEUM, NUS CENTRE FOR THE ARTS.

United World College of South East Asia

urban planning

Urban planning and coordination is undertaken by the URBAN REDEVELOPMENT AUTHORITY. Singapore's scarcity of land and natural resources presents challenges for urban planners. Broadly, the urban planning strategy involves optimizing land use for residential, business and industrial needs. Systems for transportation and communications are crucial, and policies on public health, law and order and education have a bearing. In the Singapore context it is also seen as very important that application of any urban plan must be sensitive to cultural, racial and religious differences so as to prevent social fragmentation and marginalization.

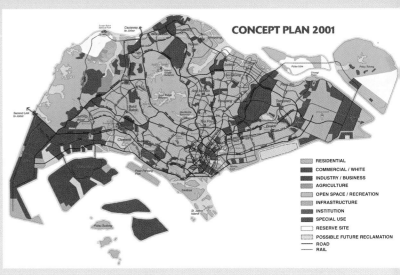

CONCEPT PLAN 2001

RESIDENTIAL
COMMERCIAL / WHITE
INDUSTRY / BUSINESS
AGRICULTURE
OPEN SPACE / RECREATION
INFRASTRUCTURE
INSTITUTION
SPECIAL USE
RESERVE SITE
POSSIBLE FUTURE RECLAMATION
ROAD
RAIL

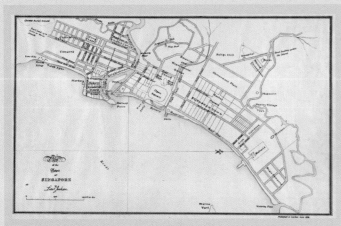

The Jackson Plan

The history of urban planning in Singapore goes back to 1822, when Sir Stamford Raffles directed Lieutenant Phillip Jackson to draw up a plan for the city. Commercial and administrative districts were demarcated. The plan located people in the settlement on the basis of the major ethnic groups, with distinct areas for Malays, Chinese, Indians and Europeans. While today racial segregation has been abandoned (indeed in public housing estates quotas are used to prevent it), areas known today as KAMPONG GLAM, CHINATOWN and LITTLE INDIA still retain something of the character of the Malay, Chinese and Indian communities respectively.

The Master Plan, 1958

As Singapore developed and the population grew, congestion, poor sanitation and over-crowding became critical problems. It was not until 1958, with the assistance of the United Nations, that the government formulated the first statutory Master Plan for the urbanization of Singapore. Housing and unemployment were seen as particularly urgent problems, and their solutions were managed respectively by the HOUSING & DEVELOPMENT BOARD (established in 1960) and the ECONOMIC DEVELOPMENT BOARD. The first Master Plan was designed to develop an urban Singapore that would not only be optimized for Singaporeans, but would also attract foreign business and investment, especially in the manufacturing and finance sectors.

TOWN MAP SHEET 1/210

The Concept Plan, 1971, 1991 and 2001

In modern Singapore's planning system, the Concept Plan maps out long-term strategy—projecting 40–50 years into the future; while the Master Plan translates this broad strategy into detailed plans that guide Singapore's physical development over the course of the next 10–15 years.

Singapore's first Concept Plan was developed in 1971, addressing the basic needs and infrastructure requirements of a new nation. The 1971 Concept Plan, also known as the 'Ring Concept Plan', visualised the development of a ring of high-density satellite towns around the central water catchment area. These towns would be linked by an inter-connected system of expressways. Most notably, the Concept Plan also proposed a Mass Rapid Transit System (MRT).

The Concept Plan 1971 was in due course reviewed and a new plan—the Concept Plan 1991—was drawn. The Concept Plan 1991 focused particularly on economic growth and providing a good quality of life. Over the next 10 years, the MRT network was expanded; a wider variety of housing types was provided; new regional centres and business parks were developed. Singapore saw more recreational options with the building of more parks and park connectors.

The Concept Plan was reviewed again in 2001 to reflect the increasingly sophisticated expectations of Singaporeans and the nation's changing strategic goals. Generally, the plan's key proposals include the provision of aesthetically satisfying and convenient urban housing, increasing choice for recreation activities, encouraging flexibility for businesses, adapting to the global economy, extending the rail network, and focusing on cultural identity.

The Master Plan 2003

The Master Plan is reviewed every five years. The Master Plan 1998 was the first to divide Singapore into 55 areas and offer detailed plans for each of the areas. The last Master Plan, presented in 2003, focuses on providing a good quality of life, enhancing the business environment, and preserving and enhancing identity to encourage a sense of 'rootedness'. It features two particular island-wide initiatives, the Parks and Waterbodies Plan and the Identity Plan. These formulations were the result of public feedback received during Concept Plan 2001, that called for enhancing greenery as well as preserving identity.

The Parks and Waterbodies Plan

This plan is designed to ensure the preservation of places for relaxation and leisure, responding to the needs of Singapore's natural heritage. Key features include making accessible to the public more areas of natural beauty, waterfronts and beaches; creating new and improved parks with pedestrian connectors between parks; creating gardens on rooftops, balconies and the sides of tall buildings; and further greening and landscaping of streets in Singapore.

The Identity Plan

Designed to foster a Singaporean identity for the benefit of both locals and visitors, among the most important features of the Identity Plan is the enhancement of distinctive upland and coastal places of interest, urban 'villages' of character, and conservation areas rich in history.

Plans for Marina Bay

In tandem with efforts to clear up slums in Singapore's city centre, making way for for commercial developments on larger plots of land, the downtown area was also enlarged through the process of land reclamation. By the 1970s, the reclaiming of 690 hectares of land southeast of the city centre had been planned to form Marina Centre, South and East for the future expansion of the city. The mid-1980s saw the development of land for a major new downtown around Marina Bay (shown in the perspective below), planned for an integrated live-work-play environment.

See also MARINA BAY.

University of Chicago Graduate School of Business

University of Chicago Graduate School of Business Founded in 1898, this is the second-oldest business school in the United States. The Singapore campus was set up in 2000 and offers an Executive Master in Business Administration Programme. It is housed within the late-19th-century HOUSE OF TAN YEOK NEE—once a traditional residence of a wealthy Chinese merchant, meticulously restored and renovated with modern facilities, and gazetted as a national monument.

University of Malaya The University of Malaya was formed in 1949 by the merger of the KING EDWARD VII COLLEGE OF MEDICINE and RAFFLES COLLEGE. The first chancellor was MALCOLM MACDONALD, the former governor-general of Malaya, Singapore and British Borneo. In 1959, two autonomous divisions were set up, one in Kuala Lumpur and one in Singapore. On January 1, 1962, the two divisions became separate, autonomous national universities. The university in Singapore was renamed the UNIVERSITY OF SINGAPORE while the one in Kuala Lumpur kept the name University of Malaya. In 1979, the Dainton report recommended that Singapore should have one strong university. The next year, the University of Singapore merged with NANYANG UNIVERSITY to become the NATIONAL UNIVERSITY OF SINGAPORE.

upgrading Improvement works to rejuvenate public housing facilities and related infrastructure. The Estate Renewal Strategy was devised to upgrade mature HOUSING & DEVELOPMENT BOARD towns, built in the 1970s and 1980s, making them as well-equipped as the newer towns. This huge undertaking, lasting several years for each mature town, can be broken down into smaller components, namely: the Selective En-bloc Redevelopment Scheme (SERS), Main Upgrading Programme (MUP) and Interim Upgrading Programme (IUP).

SERS entails the complete redevelopment of entire precincts. Old blocks are demolished, making way for new homes. Affected homeowners are compensated and resettled in flats in the same neighbourhood. The MUP involves the enhancement of precincts older than 18 years, without demolition. Residents can

expect larger flats, better lifts, better façades, and landscaping. To cater for precincts that are not as old, but still require upgrading, the IUP was conceived. Precincts that are 10–17 years old may undergo IUP. This is usually limited to the upgrading of lifts under the Lift Upgrading Programme. Precincts that have undergone IUP are still eligible for MUP when they reach maturity.

Though upgrading is subsidized by the government, residents bear part of the cost. Consequently, they have a say, by way of a poll, in whether or not their blocks undergo upgrading. However, the potential gains outweigh the initial costs as the market value of flats increases significantly after upgrading.

Another objective of upgrading is to ensure that community ties that have been established over the years are maintained. As the refurbished, modern environment meets the expectations of the grown-up children of homeowners, they are more likely to be encouraged to purchase their own flats within the neighbourhood.

Upgrading is not limited to public housing. Facilities such as retail spaces, HAWKER CENTRES, schools and sports complexes also undergo upgrading. The upgrading of housing estates has been linked to how constituencies have voted during the elections.

urban planning *See* box.

Urban Redevelopment Authority Statutory board. The Urban Redevelopment Authority (URA) is an autonomous body, responsible for land planning and development control. It was created in 1974 to take over the functions of the Urban Renewal Department of the HOUSING & DEVELOPMENT BOARD (HDB). The Urban Renewal Department had been formed in 1967 to carry out a comprehensive plan to revamp the central area.

In 1989, the URA was made the country's national conservation and central-planning authority. It acts as a co-ordinator for redevelopment plans, integrating the development of transport into these plans, and implements policies arising from laws on land-use.

See also URBAN PLANNING.

Utusan Melayu Newspaper. Two newspapers have borne this name. The first, a Malay-language newspaper launched on 7 November 1907, is not to be confused with the paper of the same name launched in 1939. The first editor of *Utusan Melayu* (Malay Mail), the Malay-language version of the SINGAPORE FREE PRESS, was MOHAMMED EUNOS ABDULLAH, the 'father of Malay journalism'. This was the first major national Malay newspaper and was circulated throughout the Malay States and the Straits Settlements. With urban Malay readers its target audience, the paper

concentrated on issues relevant to Malays, such as education, and provided a platform for Malay associations to air their views. *Utusan* was printed in Jawi (modified Arabic script), with a page in Roman script for the benefit of its PERANAKAN readers. The four-page newspaper was published three times a week, becoming a daily in 1915. However, due to financial difficulties, it closed down in 1922.

The second *Utusan Melayu* was launched in Singapore in 1939. It played an important role in the history of Malay journalism and politics in the Malay peninsula. It helped shape the intellectual development of Malay nationalists who were later to provide political leadership in Malaya's road towards independence from the British.

The paper was published by a group of Malay journalists, to counter the Arab-controlled press at the time. Founding members such as YUSOF ISHAK, who later became the first president of Singapore, raised funding from ordinary Malays as well as from the Malay elite to establish the paper. *Utusan* prided itself in being an enterprise produced wholly by and for Malays. Its first editor was Abdul Rahim Kajai (*see* MALAY LITERATURE). Many other journalists, literary figures and politicians, such as SAMAD ISMAIL, Usman Awang and Ishak Haji Muhammad (Pak Sako), worked for *Utusan*. A Sunday edition, *Utusan Zaman*, was also published in 1939.

After Malaya was granted independence in 1957, the paper moved to Kuala Lumpur in 1958. In 1961, SAID ZAHARI, its chief editor, resisted take-over attempts by the United Malays National Organisation (UMNO), the leading Malay political party in Malaysia. However, a 93-day strike failed to stop the take-over, and the company became an asset of UMNO. Kumpulan Utusan was incorporated as a public limited company in 1967 and its name changed to Utusan Melayu (Malaysia) Berhad. A new Roman-script newspaper, *Utusan Malaysia*, was launched the same year. *Utusan Melayu* and *Utusan Zaman* continued to be published in Jawi. Due to continuing financial losses and declines in readership, *Utusan Melayu* ceased to be a daily, and in 2003, it became a weekly Jawi newspaper, *Utusan Melayu Mingguan*.

Utusan Melayu: 1940 issue.

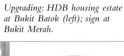

Upgrading: HDB housing estate at Bukit Batok (left); sign at Bukit Merah.

V

Lloyd Valberg: at Raffles Institution, 1950.

Valberg, Lloyd (1922–1984) Sportsman. Valberg was a versatile athlete—both a high jumper and a hurdler. At the age of 17, he cleared 1.87 m in the high jump, equalling the existing record. In 1947, he raised the mark to 1.92 m and also equalled the 120-yard hurdles record with a time of 15.5 seconds.

In 1948 Valberg became the first athlete to represent Singapore in the OLYMPIC GAMES, which were held in London that year. At the flag-raising ceremony, Valberg hoisted the Union Jack, as Singapore was then a British colony.

Known as 'Evergreen', Valberg was one of the most successful athletes in Singapore and Malaya. At the 1950 Empire Games in Auckland, New Zealand, he finished seventh in the 120-yard hurdles, and 11th in the high jump, clearing 1.83 m. In 1951, he was made captain and flag-bearer of the Singapore contingent to the 1st Asian Games in New Delhi. He won a bronze medal in the 110-yard hurdles.

Valberg later turned to coaching and again demonstrated his versatility. He helped nurture a new generation of athletes. He also organized, coached and promoted softball. He was president of the Softball Association in 1968 and vice-president of the Amateur Boxing Association (1966–68).

valleys The pattern of valleys and plains within Singapore reflects, on the one hand, GEOLOGY and relief, and on the other, rainfall and erosion. Larger river systems have been responsible for a greater amount of long-term erosion and have therefore created more extensive valley networks.

The largest area of flat land associated with river systems is found in the west of the island, where Sungei Tengah and its tributaries flow northwards into the Strait of Johor and Sungei Jurong flows southwards into the Strait of Singapore. To the east of the central hills, the northward-

Van Kleef Aquarium: young visitor; the aquarium building at River Valley (below).

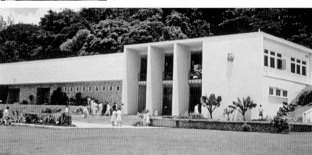

flowing Sungei Seletar and the southward-flowing Sungei Kallang carve out a natural route which is largely followed by the Central Expressway.

Smaller river systems have carved more localized valleys around the fringes of the island. In many places, these valleys have submerged with the building of estuarine barrages in order to create water storage reservoirs, such as the Tengah, Poyan, Serimbun and Murai reservoirs along the west coast. Similarly, in the centre of the island, former steep-sided river valleys, carved out by the headwaters of numerous rivers and their tributaries, have been dammed to create the Seletar, Upper Peirce and MacRitchie RESERVOIRS.

Van Kleef Aquarium Opened on 8 September 1955 in River Valley Road, the Van Kleef Aquarium was named after a former Dutch resident, Mr K.W.B. Van Kleef, who bequeathed his estate to Singapore in a will dated 7 July 1900. The Municipal Commission made plans to build the aquarium in 1933, but these were put on hold when the war broke out and only resumed in the 1950s.

In 1964, the ichthyologist A. Fraser-Brunner, curator of the aquarium, was commissioned to design the MERLION emblem for Singapore's Tourist Promotion Board.

By 1985, the aquarium housed many interesting and rare species of marine and freshwater fish, amphibians and invertebrates, including tropical fish, small sharks, poisonous lion fish and stone fish, and Amazonian piranhas. Live crocodiles were an additional attraction.

In March 1986, the aquarium had serious maintenance problems and closed for major renovation. By then, annual visitor numbers had declined drastically to 250,000, compared to around 430,000 in its heyday in 1979. After a $750,000 facelift, it re-opened on 26 August 1987 with the aim of becoming a 'public and tourist attraction' as well as a 'permanent exhibition centre for local aquarium fish farmers and exporters'. By 1 June 1991, the aquarium was considered outmoded compared to Sentosa's Underwater World and shut down.

On 1 October 1991, the Primary Production Department handed over the administration of Van Kleef Aquarium to a private company, World of Aquarium, but it too closed on 22 February 1993. Six months later, it was reopened as The Fort Canning Aquarium but this was also short-lived. It closed its doors for the last time in December 1996, and the building was eventually demolished in 1998.

van Linschoten, Jan Huyghen (1563–1611) At the age of 20, Jan Huyghen van Linschoten sailed with the Portuguese East India fleet to Goa, eventually returning to Europe in 1592. He wrote and published *Reys-Gheschrift van de Navigatiën der*

Vanda Miss Joaquim: Singapore's national flower.

Portugaloysers in Orienten (Travel Accounts of Portuguese Navigation in the Orient) in 1595 in Amsterdam. The text was a summary of the routes followed by Portuguese navigators over the last three decades of the 16th century, gathered from manuscripts of predominantly Portuguese pilots. It was subsequently translated into English and published as *Oriental Navigation*.

Chapter 20 of the text contains the sailing directions from Malacca to Macau: it is the first European mariners' sailing directions through the Old Strait (*see* VARELLA CHANNEL/OLD STRAIT) of Singapore. The information concerning the Singapore Strait is very detailed. The route begins at Karimun Island, and continues between the coast of present-day Jurong and the offshore islands south of Jurong. It then skirts Pasir Panjang, and goes through the Keppel Strait, exiting between present-day Tanjong Pagar on the mainland and Pulau Brani, before proceeding on to the eastern end of Singapore, past the entrance of the Johor Strait and then on to PEDRA BRANCA.

Although van Linschoten did not sail this route personally, the accuracy of his directions was confirmed by navigators who relied on them. Among these are the earliest English pilots who, in the 17th century, used *Oriental Navigation* as a standard reference book.

Vanda Miss Joaquim Flower. In 1981, this ORCHID was chosen as Singapore's national flower. Unlike other national flowers, the *Vanda* Miss Joaquim is a hybrid. It was the first Singapore plant hybrid to be registered.

In 1893, HENRY RIDLEY, director of the SINGAPORE BOTANIC GARDENS, first described the flower, a cross between *Vanda hookeriana* and *Vanda teres*. Ridley named it after Agnes Joaquim (1844–99), who was credited with breeding the orchid. Some controversy surrounds the origins of the orchid. One account has Joaquim stumbling upon the flower in a clump of bamboo at her home in Tanjong Pagar. However, Joaquim was herself an accomplished horticulturist who experimented with her plants. In 1899, she exhibited the orchid that bore her name at a local horticulture show and won the first prize of $12, for exhibiting the rarest breed. She had probably hybridized the orchid a decade earlier.

The flower stalk may carry up to 12 buds, usually with four flowers open at a time. Each flower is about 5 cm across and 6 cm tall, and the petals are twisted around so that the back surface faces forward. The two petals and the top sepal are rosy-violet, and the lateral sepals are a pale mauve. The lip is very large and broad and the middle lobe extends out like a fan. It is coloured violet-rose, merging into a contrasting fiery orange at the centre. Over the orange patch, the lip is finely spotted with dark purple. The orchid is free-flowering and thrives in full sunlight and high humidity.

Vanessa-Mae (1978–) Musician. Born Vanessa Mae Vanakorn in Singapore. Vanessa-Mae's mother, Pamela Tan, was a pianist and violinist active in the local classical music scene in the 1970s. Vanessa-Mae's family emigrated to the United Kingdom when she was four. A child prodigy on the violin, she performed with the London Philharmonic Orchestra at the age of 10, and at 13 became the youngest violinist to record both the Tchaikovsky and the Beethoven violin concertos. Her album, *The Violin Player* (1995), fuses different musical genres.

Varathan, S. (1934–) Playwright. Born in Singapore, S. Varathan moved to Tamil Nadu, India, shortly after his birth, returning to Singapore in 1953. The dearth of activity in the field of serious TAMIL THEATRE in Singapore led him to establish the Pagutharivu Nadaga Mandram (Rational Drama Society) in 1955, which staged a mix of social and historical dramas. He variously wrote, acted in and directed plays, including *Kasantha Karumbu* (Bitter Sugarcane), *Udaintha Valaiyal* (Broken Bangle), *Dr Sundar* and *Uyarntha Ullam* (Magnanimous Heart).

Varathan was the founder of the Singapore Indian Artiste Society, which was established in 1971 to bring stage, radio and television performers together in a single organization. He has also written two novels, *Suvadugal* (Footprints) and *Ninaivugal Maraivathillai* (Memories Never Fade), the latter published in both Tamil and English. He is also the author of *Nadagakkalai Valartha Nallavargal* (The Good Men who Promoted Theatre in Singapore). He was awarded the CULTURAL MEDALLION in 1984.

Varella Channel/Old Strait The channel between Singapore's southern coast and the island of Sentosa, formerly known as the Varella Channel or Old Strait (now called Keppel Strait), is the oldest known passage around the southern end of the Malay Peninsula. It was known as LONGYAMEN to Chinese mariners in the 14th century, and

was featured in Chinese maritime accounts until the early 17th century.

European mariners, travelling from the Indian Ocean, began using this channel in the 16th century to reach the South China Sea. The first European account of this dates to 1595, and appears in the *Reys-Gheschrift van de Navigatiën der Portugaloysers in Orienten* by JAN HUYGHEN VAN LINSCHOTEN. Portuguese and Spanish mariners noted two stone outcrops, on either side of the western entrance, which they named 'Varella'— hence the name 'Varella Channel'.

The channel was a strategic waterway. In 1585, following continued Portuguese-Johor rivalry, the sultan of Johor sank a number of junks in the channel to prevent ships from using it.

In 1586, however, another passage— south of Sentosa—was discovered, and the Varella Channel became known as the Old Strait, as indicated in the 1604 map *Descripsao Chorographica dos Estreitos de Singapura e Sabbam Ano 1604* by Manuel Godinho de Erédia, as well as a naval chart of André Pereira dos Reis dating from about 1650. By the 17th century, with the discovery of the NEW STRAIT and GOVERNOR'S STRAIT, the Old Strait fell into disuse, and from the second half of the 17th century onwards lapsed into obscurity. It was rediscovered by the English hydrographer Daniel Ross in the 19th century. It was subsequently transformed into New Harbour in the 1840s (later renamed KEPPEL HARBOUR). It now serves as one of the main cargo container terminals of PSA INTERNATIONAL.

On some late-18th-century and early-19th-century maps, the 'Old Strait' referred to Johor Strait, between the Johor coast and Singapore, and not the Varella Channel.

Venture Corporation Originally known as Venture Manufacturing (Singapore), this company was first set up in 1984 to provide contract manufacturing services to companies in the electronics and computer-related industries. It expanded its operations to Johor in Malaysia two years later and was listed on the junior board of the Singapore Exchange, Sesdaq, in 1992 with a market capitalization of $25 million. In 1997, the stock was promoted to the main board of the exchange, and within three years achieved a full-year revenue of $1 billion. By then, it had expanded its operations to Shanghai in China and established a foothold in the United States. It changed its name to Venture Corporation in May 2002.

Venture Corporation's customers include many Fortune 500 companies such as Agilent, HP, IBM, Intermec and Xerox. The group had a compound annual growth rate of 33 per cent between 1989 and 2005. Group turnover hit $3.2 billion in 2005, while earnings were $201 million. The company's stock is a component of the Straits Times Index.

Verenigde Oost-Indische Compagnie Also known as the Dutch East India Company, the Verenigde Oost-Indische Compagnie (United East India Company) or VOC, was established in 1602 by the merger of six regional trading firms. It was granted a state charter by the Netherlands Estates General to expand trade in Asia. The company was granted a monopoly on Dutch trade east of the Cape of Good Hope and west of the Strait of Magellan.

The VOC was governed by the Heeren XVII (Gentlemen Seventeen), a board of representatives from the chambers of the six major trading centres of the Netherlands—Amsterdam, Middelburg, Enkhuizen, Delft, Hoorn and Rotterdam. Representation was proportional to the amount of paid-up capital from each of these chambers, with Amsterdam having the largest representation.

The VOC was much more than a company: it could conduct diplomatic missions, wage war and conclude peace. It started as a transportation company moving spices but later evolved into a sophisticated spice marketing and distribution operation. Eventually, it went into production to ensure regular supplies.

It was arguably the first publicly listed multi-national corporation, featuring an international shareholder base and employing an international staff of soldiers, factors, administrators and crew.

In 1619, the VOC established its headquarters at Batavia (present-day Jakarta) in Java. From there, it conducted a systematic campaign of driving the Portuguese, Danes and British out of maritime Southeast Asian trade. By 1669, it had grown into the richest company in the world, with over 150 merchants, 40 warships, 50,000 employees, and a private army consisting of 10,000 soldiers; and it paid an annual dividend of 40 per cent. The company had also established its presence from the Cape of Good Hope to Japan, including Mauritius, several ports along the eastern coast of India, Sri Lanka, Arakan, Malacca, Riau-Lingga, Java, Timor, Solor, the Spice Islands, Taiwan and Deshima (in Japan).

By the second half of the 18th century, however, the VOC was experiencing serious financial problems as a result of the cost of wars and accounting irregularities. In 1799, it was declared bankrupt and dissolved. After the Napoleonic Wars, possession of the East Indies was transferred to the Dutch crown and trade conducted through the Nederlandsche Handelsmaatschappij.

Vesak Day Commemoration of three major events in the life of Siddharta Gautama Shakyamuni Buddha (563–483 BCE), namely his birth, enlightenment and death. Also called Buddha Day, it is celebrated on the full moon of the fourth lunar month. It is a PUBLIC HOLIDAY. Vesak Day is observed at all Buddhist temples.

Vanessa-Mae

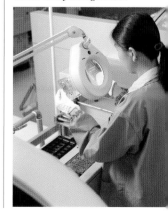

Venture Corporation: provider of contract manufacturing services.

Vesak Day: pouring water over a Buddha figurine (top); devotees prostrating themselves.

Victoria School: shown in a post-card c. 1900, when it was known as Victoria Bridge School.

Victoria Concert Hall: entrance facade to the right, the Victoria Theatre is on the left.

The circumambulation ceremony at KONG MENG SAN PHOR KARK SEE MONASTERY can be gruelling. Instead of walking around the stupa three times, some devotees walk three steps, prostrate themselves on the ground, rise and repeat the sequence. The whole procedure can take up to three hours.

The celebrations also include chanting of the holy sutras by monks, reinforcement of the Five Precepts (guidelines to being good Buddhists), and other acts of devotion and compassion. These range from pouring perfumed water over the Buddha figurine to giving gifts to the needy and releasing caged birds, and captive turtles or fish—though in recent years, temples have advised devotees to refrain from releasing animals, as the practice can upset ecosystems. Buddhists consume only vegetarian food on this day.

A candle-lit procession within the temple compound or along the street brings the day's celebrations to a close.

See also BUDDHISM.

Victoria Concert Hall Originally the Victoria Memorial Hall (VMH), this performance venue was built to commemorate Queen Victoria's death in 1901. Construction began in 1903 at Empress Place, to create a hall whose facade duplicated that of the neighbouring Town Hall (now VICTORIA THEATRE). Designed by R.A.J. BIDWELL of SWAN & MACLAREN, and completed at a cost of $340,000, the VMH was officially opened in 1905. A 54-m clock tower was later added to join the two buildings. The VMH served as a municipal building as well as a venue for concerts, public meetings and exhibitions. It was a makeshift hospital during World War II

and later the site of war crime tribunals (*see* WAR CRIMES COMMISSION). In 1954, the inaugural meeting of the People's Action Party was held there.

Following extensive renovations in 1980, the VMH was renamed Victoria Concert Hall (VCH) and became home to the SINGAPORE SYMPHONY ORCHESTRA. A Klais organ replaced the old St Clair pipe organ in 1987. With a seating capacity of 883, the auditorium of the VCH is the oldest and one of the finest concert venues in Singapore. Some of the world's great orchestras and musicians—including Benjamin Britten, Peter Pears, Claudio Arrau, Mstislav Rostropovich, Shura Cherkassky and Yo-Yo Ma—have performed there.

The Victoria Concert Hall, along with the Victoria Theatre, was gazetted as a national monument in February 1992.

Victoria School This boys' school traces its origins to an English class taught in 1876 by headmaster M. Hellier in Kampong Glam Malay School. In 1897, the school moved to Victoria Street, near the Victoria Bridge (the site of the former Kota Raja Malay School) and was known as Victoria Bridge School. It became a secondary school in 1931, and on 18 September 1933, when it moved to Tyrwhitt Road, it was given its present name. In 1993 it became an AUTONOMOUS SCHOOL, and in 2003 moved to Siglap Link. Famous alumni include presidents S.R. NATHAN, C.V. DEVAN NAIR and YUSOF ISHAK as well as journalist SAMAD ISMAIL and poet EDWIN THUMBOO.

Victoria Theatre Located at the junction of Fort Canning and Hill Street, the Victoria Theatre was originally the Town Hall. It was designed by John Bennett, a civil engineer. Construction began in 1856, but due to financial constraints, it was completed only in 1862.

Completion of the Town Hall was a milestone in Singapore's architectural history. It was the first of a number of buildings that were constructed on a scale and of a grandeur unprecedented in the colony. It was also an example of the beginning of Victorian Revivalism, reflecting a British architectural shift towards the Italian Renaissance style.

The Victoria Memorial Hall (now known as VICTORIA CONCERT HALL) was built adjacent to the Town Hall in 1905. The Town Hall itself was upgraded and re-opened as Victoria Theatre on 11 February 1909.

The Victoria Theatre, along with the Victoria Concert Hall, was gazetted as a national monument in February 1992.

void decks The Swiss-French architect Le Corbusier suggested that *pilotis* (or pillars) could be used to elevate a building's mass off the ground and free up valuable space at ground level (*Five Points of Architecture*, 1926). The uninhabited ground-floor areas

Void decks: playground at Yishun.

beneath HOUSING & DEVELOPMENT BOARD apartment blocks are known as 'void decks'.

In blocks with void decks, housing units start on the second floor. Void decks are convenient locations for wakes, funeral rites, wedding ceremonies and parties. Void decks may accomodate shops, nurseries and playgrounds. In many void decks, benches, tables and bicycle-parking facilities have been installed.

voting Singapore inherited the 'simple plurality' system, known popularly as the 'first past the post' system. The candidate securing the greatest number of votes is declared elected. This system was introduced by the British and continues to be used extensively throughout the Commonwealth.

Singapore's ELECTIONS DEPARTMENT is part of the PRIME MINISTER'S OFFICE (PMO) and reports to the PMO's permanent secretary. The Elections Department is responsible for the conduct of ELECTIONS, including the maintenance of the electoral registers. It is not, however, directly responsible for determining electoral boundaries.

Any citizen of Singapore, who is over the age of 21 and who is ordinarily resident in Singapore, is entitled to have his name entered or retained in a Register of Electors. A register is prepared for each constituency. Once the registers have been prepared, they are exhibited for people to submit claims or raise objections. The registers are then certified and will be used for the election until a new one is prepared. Voters may check their standing on the electoral register through the Internet.

A voter may be disqualified if he: owes his allegiance to another state or foreign power; is serving a jail sentence 'for an offence punishable with imprisonment for a term exceeding 12 months'; is under 'sentence of death'; is of unsound mind; is serving in 'any naval, military or air force not maintained out of moneys provided by Parliament'; or is registered as a voter in any other country.

Voting is compulsory in Singapore and each person is entitled to only one vote, which must be exercised in the electoral division for which he has been registered. Secret ballots are used in the electoral process. After the ballots are counted, the results are published in the *Government Gazette*. Singapore citizens who are living overseas may be entitled to vote if they meet certain criteria.

wage policy In 1972, the government established the NATIONAL WAGES COUNCIL (NWC), a body representing government, employers and employees. It examines wage issues and recommends wage guidelines. These guidelines, while not mandatory, are taken up by the SINGAPORE CIVIL SERVICE—Singapore's largest employer—and are largely followed by the private sector as well. During the 1970s, the NWC's recommendations prevented excessive wage increases in the face of a tight labour market.

In 1979, the government introduced a 'wage correction policy' as a means of fostering INDUSTRIALIZATION. The plan was to significantly raise wages for three years so as to hasten the economy's transition from labour intensive production towards capital intensive and high value-added industries. However, in the years that followed, wages began to escalate due to a shortage of labour. This eroded Singapore's international competitiveness and was a major factor leading to the 1985 recession. Subsequently, the NWC recommended that wages be maintained at current levels and employers' mandatory contributions to the CENTRAL PROVIDENT FUND be cut. A more responsive wage policy, known as the flexible wage system, was also implemented. Instead of quantitative recommendations, the NWC started to issue qualitatitive guidelines. Wage increases would consist of two parts—a fixed increment and a variable portion, the amount of which was left to employers to decide (this usually depended on the performance of the company). This scheme would allow employers to better weather downturns and minimize retrenchments.

Singapore does not have a minimum wage but it does have a NATIONAL TRADES UNION CONGRESS—which is represented in the NWC—that promotes workers' welfare. The Employment Act stipulates employee benefits such as vacations, sick leave and maternity leave for employees covered under the Act.

Wak Hai Cheng Bio Temple. One of the oldest Taoist temples in Singapore, this is an important place of worship for the TEOCHEW community, and is owned and managed by the Ngee Ann Kongsi (a clan association). It served as a communal and social centre for Teochew immigrants in the 19th century, when Chinese temples in Singapore still fulfilled this role.

When the present structure was built in the 1850s, it stood by the seashore, on the site of an existing shrine which had been there since 1826. Newly arrived immigrants visited the temple to give thanks for a safe journey by sea.

The temple is dedicated to the deities Xuan Tian Shang Di (also known as Shang Di Ye or Shang Di Gong) and Ma Zu (the Goddess of the Sea), who are enshrined in adjoining halls—an unusual configuration for Chinese temples. Also worshipped there are Cheng Huang Ye and the Eight Immortals.

Architecturally, the temple is noted for its internal sculptural reliefs, which depict scenes from Chinese opera, and for its heavily ornamented roof encrusted with intricate and colourful figurines. Suspended over the large forecourt are rows of incense coils. Located on Phillip Street, this temple was gazetted as a national monument in June 1996.

wakaf *Wakaf* is the giving of property by a Muslim, through will or gift, for purposes recognized by Islamic law as an act of piety or for the greater good. The original owners cannot re-acquire property given over to *wakaf*. There are two types of *wakaf*: *wakaf al-ahli* (family endowment) and *wakaf al-khairi*. The former is personal in nature and its main objective is to benefit the endower's family and descendants; the latter has various objectives and functions, with charity being the main aim.

Under the ADMINISTRATION OF MUSLIM LAW ACT, MAJLIS UGAMA ISLAM SINGAPURA (MUIS) is responsible for the proper establishment, administration and regulation of all *wakaf* properties. MUIS protects the *wakaf* against any abuse, such as illegal disposal or sale, or misuse, by ensuring that yields from *wakaf* properties are distributed to the correct beneficiaries. MUIS also defends the *wakaf* from any lawsuit by a third party.

Trustees, or *mutawallis*, appointed by MUIS manage *wakaf* properties under their care but they cannot dispose of, or purchase, *wakaf* properties without obtaining MUIS' approval. MUIS' roles include registration of all *wakaf* properties; maintenance and review of annual accounts; annual disbursement of monies generated by and as specified by the *wakaf*; record-keeping on all legal documents related to *wakaf*; and monitoring and reviewing the conditions or performance of all *wakaf* properties. Examples of *wakaf* properties include the Wisma Indah complex on Upper Changi Road and the BENCOOLEN MOSQUE complex on Bencoolen Street.

See also WAREES.

Wan Soon Bee (1939–) Politician and businessman. Wan Soon Bee was educated at Sin Nam Public School, Jurong Morning School and Raffles Institution. He graduated from the University of Pisa, Italy, with a degree in electronic engineering (1967). He started work at the Ministry of Interior and Defence as a technical officer before moving on to Olivetti (S) Pte Ltd. He entered politics in 1980 on the People's Action Party ticket, winning the Brickworks constituency seat. In 1982, Wan was appointed political secretary, and later minister of state, in the Prime Minister's Office, before retiring from politics in 2001. He has also served as chairman of Comfort Group Ltd.

Wang Dayuan (c. 1311–unknown) Author and trader. Also known as Huan-chang, Wang Dayuan was the author of a text important in the study of ancient Southeast Asia entitled *Dao Yi Zhi Lüe* (Description of the Barbarians of the Isles). He was born around 1311 in Nanchang, a port in Jiangxi province in China which prospered during the Song Dynasty (960–1279). As a young man, Wang became a trader and appears to have made two voyages to Southeast Asia (1330–34 and 1337–39). He wrote an account of his travels in 1349. Almost nothing else is known about Wang's life.

Wang's account is factual and down-to-earth, without reference to the fanciful tales found in many early Chinese works about foreign lands. The work follows a cosmological perspective. Like most early Chinese authors, Wang viewed the world as having two oceans: eastern and western. His work discusses 99 locations. LONGYAMEN (Dragon's Tooth Gate) was number 50,

Wan Soon Bee: opening union seminar in 1983.

Wak Hai Cheng Bio

Wang Sui Pick: the artist (top); calligraphy ('Love'), undated.

Wang Runhua: collection of his writings (above); the author (below).

Wang Gungwu

placing Singapore at the highly symbolic centre between east and west. Song Dynasty authors had considered the Sunda Strait, between Java and Sumatra, to be the dividing line between the eastern and western oceans. If Wang's view was shared by others, his account could mark a major shift in Chinese geographical thought.

Wang used the term 'Danmaxi' (TEMASEK) to include two inhabited areas: Longyamen and Banzu (P*ancur*, meaning 'spring' in Malay). Longyamen was a pirate lair, but he also says that Chinese lived there. This is the only trading port in the entire book which contained a Chinese population. Banzu was a hill surrounded by a town, which was governed by a local chief and where the people were simple traders. The soil was not fertile, so the inhabitants had to make a living from occupations such as salt farming and distilling alcohol.

Whereas the people of Longyamen wore their hair long and tied up in buns, and wore short shirts of dark blue cotton, the people of Banzu cut their hair short, wore satin cloth with gold patterns on their heads, and red oiled cloth (perhaps a kind of batik) around their lower bodies. Thus, two very different groups—distinguished in terms of dress, culture and economy—inhabited 14th-century Singapore.

A reference to Temasek appears in another section of the book. Wang says that the Siamese had recently attacked Temasek, but because the town was fortified with gates and a moat, the Siamese could not force their way in. This fortification was an unusual attribute for a town in Southeast Asia at that time (*see* OLD LINES).

Wang's brief record of early Singapore is unique. Archaeological and historical evidence suggests that the settlement was founded around 1300, barely 30 years before his visit.

Wang Gungwu (1930–) Academic. Born in the Dutch East Indies (present-day Indonesia), Wang Gungwu grew up in Malaya, and went to university in China, Singapore and the United Kingdom. As a historian, he has pioneered research in the fields of the Chinese Diaspora and China–Southeast Asian relations. Wang served as the head of the History Department at the University of Malaya (1963–68), head of the Department of Far Eastern History (1968–75, 1980–86) and then director of the Research School of Pacific Studies at the Australian National University (1975–80), vice-chancellor of Hong Kong University (1986–96) and director of the EAST ASIAN INSTITUTE at the National University of Singapore (1997–).

As an undergraduate in 1950s Singapore, Wang was an active participant in the literary and political activities of the day. He later edited journals and promoted public discussion on Southeast Asian issues for the South Seas Society, the Malaysian

Branch of the Royal Asiatic Society and the Singapore Society of Asian Studies. He was at the University of Malaya in Kuala Lumpur when, subscribing to the cause of nation-building and the notion of a Malayan identity, he led a curriculum review of the Nanyang University in 1965 which proved controversial, particularly in terms of its language recommendations. Before he left for Australia, he actively supported the founding of the Gerakan Ra'ayat (Malaysian People's Movement) as an expression of support for multiracialism in 1968. He returned to Singapore in 1996, after spending decades in Australia and Hong Kong, and was involved in shaping the character of public institutions such as the CHINESE HERITAGE CENTRE and Hua Song Museum at Haw Par Villa by serving either as a member of the Board of Governors or consultant.

Wang Runhua (1941–) Poet and author. Wang Runhua (Wong Yoon Wah) was chairman of the Singapore Association of Writers for many years, and professor and head of the Department of Chinese Studies at the National University of Singapore before he retired in 2003. He has often referred to childhood memories of rubber plantations and rainforests in what is now Malaysia. His works—such as *Beyond Symbols* (1984), which was written in English, and *Nanyang Xiang Tu Ji* (Nanyang, My Native Land) (1981)—offer insights into the human condition through identification with nature, and have earned him an international following.

Wang received the Epoch Poetry Award in 1974, the *China Times* Literary Award for prose in 1981, and the South East Asian Write Award in 1984. He was also made an honorary fellow by the University of Iowa in 1985. Wang was awarded the CULTURAL MEDALLION in 1986 and the Asean Award in 1993.

Wang Sa (1925–1998) Comedian. Wang Sa was the stage name of Wang Jin Qing. He began his career as a performer in the Wen Shang Acrobatic Troupe. He later moved to the Shangri-la Song Stage, a theatre that featured popular Mandarin songs and skits in the mid-1950s. Wang made a name for himself in Cao Yu's masterpiece

Wang Sa: right, with Ye Feng.

Thunderstorm. However, his greatest success came after he partnered with another comedian, YE FENG.

A Teochew from a humble background, Wang was creative in tapping his life experiences in the many comic skits he created with Ye Feng in the early 1960s. The duo regularly appeared in entertainment programmes on television with their own brand of improvisational comedy. They included Mandarin, Hokkien, Cantonese, Teochew and colloquial Malay in their banter, and often caricatured recognizable characters. Their pieces combined satire, absurdity, commentary and gross humour.

In the 1970s the duo made a number of movies in Hong Kong—the first of which was *A Niu Ru Cheng Ji* (The Crazy Bumpkins) (1974)—as part of a series of comedies. In the 1980s, Wang played the lead role in the popular local television series *Kopitiam*.

Wang Sui Pick (1904–1998) Artist. Born in Fujian province, Wang Sui Pick graduated in law from Amoy University (present-day Xiamen University). He settled in Malaya in 1954, teaching at, then becoming principal of, a primary school for more than 36 years.

A scholar steeped in classical Chinese calligraphy, Wang was admired for his command of *cao shu* (an expressive running, or cursive, script), typically executed with eloquence and vigour. Wang was a member of the San Yi Finger Painting Society, the Chinese Calligraphy Society of Singapore (CCSS) and other community associations. His works are held at the CCSS, the Singapore Art Museum and Anxi Museum, China. He received the CULTURAL MEDALLION in 1992.

Want Want Holdings Want Want Holdings started as the I Lan Foods Industrial Company in Taiwan in 1962, canning agricultural products mainly for export. It went into the rice-cracker business in 1983 when it sought a tie-up with one of the top three Japanese rice-cracker makers, Iwatsuka Confectionery Company. It became the market leader in Taiwan and explored overseas markets, starting with the huge China market in 1992 where it built up its brand name through television commercials. It opened its first plant in Changsha, Hunan, in 1994 and expanded to 24 locations in nine provinces within three years to keep up with demand from Chinese consumers. By 1997, it had captured an 80 per cent market share on the Chinese mainland.

The company was incorporated in Singapore in 1995 in anticipation of a listing on the local exchange to raise funds for expansion. It was listed in May 1996, the same year in which it officially changed its name to Want Want Holdings, and the stock became a component of the Straits Times Index.

Besides its flagship rice-cracker products, Want Want is also a manufacturer and distributor of confectionery, baby food, beverages, and Chinese and Japanese rice wines. The group reported a net profit of US$113 million on a turnover of US$688 for the financial year 2005.

War Crimes Commission The intention of Allied leaders to try war criminals was demonstrated by the setting up of a United Nations War Crimes Commission in October 1943. In November 1944, the British government argued that military courts should be set up to try persons who has committed war crimes against British subjects or in British territory. In June 1945, regulations for the trial of war criminals were introduced. Each military court would comprise a president and two other officers, one of whom would have legal training. Defendants would also be represented, initially by military personnel and later by Japanese lawyers, and a review process for all guilty verdicts and sentencing would be available. South East Asia Command (SEAC) and the Allied Land Forces South East Asia (ALFSEA) were put in charge of the minor war-crimes trials—those of Japanese nationals accused of contravening conventions dealing with the treatment of prisoners-of-war and civilians. To regain its authority, the British government saw it as essential to bring to trial those who had committed crimes against the local people.

When British forces reoccupied Malaya and Singapore, investigation teams immediately began collecting statements from victims of Japanese war crimes, and arresting suspected war criminals. Newspapers were used to appeal for information from the public, and Chinese officers of FORCE 136, a unit of the Special Operations Executive (SOE), were put in charge of investigating atrocities against civilian members of the population. Anxious to avoid delay, the British, in October 1945, authorized SEAC and ALFSEA to develop procedures for the trials, including the making of decisions on prosecution and sentencing. War-crime trials of Japanese nationals were carried out in 20 cities in five areas—Singapore, Malaya, North Borneo, Burma and Hong Kong.

A total of 919 Japanese nationals were tried for war crimes between January 1946 and December 1948, of whom 530 were imprisoned and another 280 given the death sentence. Of those tried, 550 (60 per cent) were for crimes against civilians and 227 (20 per cent) for the ill-treatment of prisoners-of-war. The majority of those accused of ill-treating and torturing civilians belonged to the KEMPEITAI, the Japanese military police. Of the 919 accused, 355 (39 per cent) were Kempeitai officers. They also accounted for 112 (40 per cent) of defendants sentenced to death.

War Crimes Commission: trial in Singapore, 1946. Indicted war criminals in dock of the Supreme Court as proceedings began.

In the first trial, which began in Singapore on 21 January 1946, ten Japanese were accused of ill-treating Indian prisoners-of-war, including causing the death of one by beheading. Eight were subsequently found guilty, and one, Lieutenant Nakamura Kaniyuki, who had carried out the execution of the Indian prisoner, received the death sentence after an 11-day trial. For the next 26 months, over half of the total number of Japanese tried for war crimes had their cases heard in Singapore. Of these 464, 269 were given prison terms (43 received life imprisonment), and 141 received the death sentence. The last trial ended on 12 March 1948.

The 'Double 10th' trial (*see* DOUBLE 10TH INCIDENT) of 21 Kempeitai officers accused of torturing and murdering civilian internees at CHANGI PRISON gripped public attention. When it ended in April 1946, eight death sentences were handed down in addition to six prison terms.

Efforts to bring to trial the Japanese responsible for the SOOK CHING massacre also engaged widespread public interest. But inconclusive evidence and uncertainty about who had issued the orders for the executions, which were carried out by ordinary soldiers of the Japanese 25th Army headed by Lieutenant-General YAMASHITA TOMOYUKI, delayed the trial until March 1947. With Yamashita already executed in February 1946 for war crimes committed in the Philippines, only seven Japanese officers were tried, and only two—Lieutenant-General KAWAMURA SABURO and Lieutenant-Colonel OISHI MASAYUKI—received death sentences, while the others escaped with prison terms, a verdict which sorely disappointed and angered the Chinese community. Colonel TSUJI MASANOBU, the man many believed to have masterminded the massacres, had disappeared and escaped retribution.

The British took a more tolerant view of collaborators, exempting those who cooperated under pressure and where no torture or murder was proved, even though public demand for punishment was strong. Dr C.J. PAGLAR, former president of the Eurasian Welfare Association, was tried for treason in January 1946 and was eventually freed, though not acquitted. Surrendered Indian National Army personnel who had taken up arms against the British were also mostly spared prosecution, and either allowed to rejoin their old units or discharged from the British army. Only a handful were tried, and their prison terms commuted to dismissal from the army.

By the time the last trial in Singapore ended, public interest had waned, overshadowed by other more pressing political and constitutional issues.

WAREES The property arm of MAJLIS UGAMA ISLAM SINGAPURA (MUIS). Its name is an abbreviation of 'WAKAF real estate'. Set up in 2001, WAREES Investments Pte Ltd provides specialist services to MUIS by managing its real estate *baitulmal* (Islamic treasury) investments and more than 100 *wakaf* properties. It also advises MUIS on optimizing land and building usage and returns. The company's portfolio includes private residential properties, commercial properties and residential apartments. It also handles the development and redevelopment of MADRASAHS and MOSQUES. One of its more prominent projects is the preservation and conservation of the ABDUL GAFFOOR MOSQUE, a designated national monument.

Warren, Stanley (1917–1992) Art teacher. Stanley Warren was taken prisoner by the Japanese while serving as a British bombardier during World War II. Warren is most famous for the Changi murals at Block 151 of Robert Barracks, Changi Camp (*see* CHANGI PRISON). Between October 1942 and May 1943, he painted five of these murals, each about 3 m long, on the walls of a chapel the Japanese had allowed to be set up in the block. The murals, depicting biblical scenes, were painted in a highly styl-

GO AND TEACH THE NATIONS
I AM WITH YOU

The Changi Museum

Stanley Warren: the artist's Resurrection mural (above); the artist, right, with fellow former POW Wally Hammond (below).

Watanabe Wataru

Water polo: Singapore's water polo team celebrating its 17th gold medal at the 1997 SEA Games.

ized manner, after European neoclassical paintings. Warren returned to the United Kingdom after the war, believing Allied bombing had destroyed the murals. However, they were rediscovered in 1958 and he made three trips to Singapore between 1963 and 1988 to restore them.

Watanabe Wataru, Colonel (unknown–1969) Japanese military officer. As chief of the Malaya Military Administration for one year, from March 1942, Watanabe devised an oppressive system for the administration of Malaya and Singapore. He was instrumental in making the Singapore and Malayan Chinese pay $50 million as a 'gift' to the Japanese war effort. His influence was reinforced by the fact that he had known Lieutenant-General YAMASHITA TOMOYUKI since 1937, when they had served together in China. Watanabe appointed retired generals as governors of the states of Malaya to enforce military discipline. With the departure of Yamashita in July 1942, Watanabe was unable to implement his hardline policies, and in March 1943 was transferred back to Tokyo. He lived for the rest of his life in retirement in Japan.

water In the early days of modern Singapore, development clustered around the SINGAPORE RIVER, and the first govern-

ment priorities in supplying water were to ships and boats. Most of the island's water needs were met by private enterprise—through wells, commercial suppliers or water mongers (*tukang ayer*). Water shortages were so bad that when a fire broke out in June 1846, there was no water for the fire brigade.

Singapore's first waterworks was funded by a municipal loan floated in London in 1864, and work began in 1867. The island obtained its first piped water in 1871 with a new main connected to the docks. At De Souza Pier off COLLYER QUAY, water was sold from metered pipes to water boats as there was great demand for water at the docks.

The waterworks at Thomson Road (later MACRITCHIE RESERVOIR) was completed in 1877. Between 1878 and 1918, some $680,000 was spent on improving Singapore's water supply. To fund it, the municipal commissioners levied annual water rates on houses and buildings. In the late 1890s, the municipality began a series of water projects to enlarge MacRitchie Reservoir (1904), and to complete Pearl's Hill Reservoir (1907) and Kallang Reservoir (later Peirce Reservoir) (1911). However, demand still outstripped supply.

On 30 January 1920, the acting water engineer wrote to the municipal commissioners to argue that a new supply from Johor had to be obtained without delay. The Johor government granted the municipality permission to conduct water surveys in southern Johor. In 1923, two schemes were presented to the municipal commissioners. The Gunong Pulai Scheme was accepted, due to the proposed reservoir's natural gravity flow and its lower cost. On 5 December 1927, a water agreement was signed between the commissioners of the City Council of Singapore and Sultan Ibrahim of Johor. The CAUSEWAY and the water mains were built at the same time.

After World War II, Singapore still faced severe water shortages. On 18 October 1946, $6.2 million, the largest item in the budget, was allocated to waterworks, compared with $5.2 million for electricity. In 1961, a severe drought hit Singapore. Islandwide water rationing was imposed, with Singapore divided into several zones, each zone going 'dry' once a week. Following this, the Singapore government spent $70 million on the Johor River Scheme and signed the 1961 Tebrau and Scudai Water Agreement (effective until 2011) and the 1962 Johor River Water Agreement (effective until 2061). These two WATER AGREEMENTS were guaranteed under the 1965 Separation Agreement with Malaysia. Under these agreements, Singapore built and maintains the waterworks in Johor (dams, pipelines, reservoirs) and has 'sole and absolute right' to a fixed amount of raw water until the agreements lapse.

In June 1988, a Memorandum of Understanding on water and gas was signed

between then Prime Minister Lee Kuan Yew of Singapore and then Prime Minister Mahathir Mohamad of Malaysia. This gave Singapore the right to build more reservoirs and to draw more water than had been previously set, for an additional 100 years. Singapore signed a 1990 agreement with Johor to build the Linggiu Dam. By the 1990s, Singapore had spent more then $1 billion on water projects in Johor.

Singapore has also begun to diversify its sources of water supply. Since September 2002, Singapore has been reclaiming used water, utilizing a combination of filtration and reverse osmosis. Around 14,000 cu m of the cleaned water, known as NEWATER, goes into Singapore's reservoirs each day. This raw water is then conventionally treated before being made available for potable use. NEWater makes up about 1 per cent of daily water consumption. NEWater is also supplied directly to industry for non-potable use. Since 2004, three NEWater factories have been set up, producing 92,000 cu m of reclaimed water each day.

Using the same technology, Singapore has started to desalinate sea water. In September 2005, Singapore's first commercial desalination plant began operations in Tuas. This plant is expected to supply 136,380 cu m of water a day. The treated water is pumped into reservoirs and goes to homes and industry in the western part of Singapore. Singapore is also expanding its water catchment areas through the creation of Marina Reservoir. This reservoir will be created by putting a barrier across the Marina Channel, turning MARINA BAY and the Kallang Basin into a freshwater body. This will create a catchment area of 10,000 ha, about a sixth the size of Singapore. The MARINA BARRAGE is expected to be completed by 2007.

water agreements *See box.*

water polo Water polo was introduced into Singapore in 1920, and was first played in the leading swimming clubs, including the SINGAPORE SWIMMING CLUB and the CHINESE SWIMMING CLUB. In the early 1950s, Singapore emerged as a regional water polo force. At the inaugural Asian Games in Delhi in 1951, the Singapore team won the silver medal. In 1954, the team—which included Kee Soon Bee (captain), TAN HWEE HOCK, Gan Eng Teck, Tan Eng Bock, Keith Mitchell, Oh Chwee Hock, Wiebe Wolters and Oh Kian Bin—won the gold medal at the 2nd Asian Games in Manila. This was the only gold medal Singapore has ever won for a team sport at that level. Many members of this team also took part in the 1956 Melbourne Olympics.

Singapore water polo teams have won five more medals (though no gold medals) at various Asian Games. The country's

Sir Archibald Wavell: left, with Brig Curtis (centre) and Major General Keith Simmons (right).

teams have been dominant at the Southeast Asian regional level. Since the introduction of water polo at the 3rd Southeast Asian Peninsular (SEAP) Games (later the SEA Games) in Bangkok in 1965, the Singapore water polo team has won 21 consecutive gold medals, a record not equalled by any other team in the region.

In 1996, the Singapore Amateur Swimming Association (SASA) was given the Excellence for Singapore Award (by the Singapore Totalisator Board) for its efforts in supporting and nurturing water polo teams.

watercolour The history of watercolour in Singapore has been shaped largely by the British watercolour tradition. A primary medium of art instruction in the colonial art-education system, watercolour was promoted by figures such as Richard Walker (Art Inspector for Singapore Schools in 1923), who taught and mentored Lim Cheng Hoe at Raffles Institution. Lim, Singapore's pioneer watercolourist, was in turn an influence on successive watercolour exponents.

Watercolour was practised in local art clubs and informal art groups in the 1920s and 1930s. Some of these groups met at the residence of architect and patron Ho Kwong Yew, who was host to many famous artists including American Dong Kingman. The illustrious Malaysian watercolourist Yong Mun Sen, sometimes referred to as the 'father of Malaysian painting', resided in Singapore briefly during this period and is said to have started an art club, retaining ties with Singapore artists and the Nanyang Academy of Fine Arts. Another notable figure instructing in watercolour was the first principal and founder of the academy, LIM HAK TAI.

The Japanese Occupation immobilized artistic practice as a whole. Watercolours were produced under very adverse circumstances by prisoners-of-war Leo Rawlings and Bill Haxworth, and have since been commemorated (and re-published). In the post-war period, watercolour supplies and materials were imported by the pioneer art supplier Straits Commercial Art. Sketching and painting clubs re-emerged and met at the British Council on Stamford Road and the Young Men's Christian Association of Singapore. Art societies such as the Chinese Art Society, Singapore Art Society and Equator Art Society embraced watercolour. Subjects included landscapes, still lifes and portraits. The most interesting paintings are those that capture the changing face of Singapore as it underwent urbanization.

A dedicated society, the Singapore Watercolour Society (SWS), was established on 18 August 1969 by 13 artists, including Lim Cheng Hoe, CHEN CHONG SWEE, Gog Sing Hooi and Ong Chye Cho. Its first exhibition was held in December 1970 at the Victoria Memorial Hall, and featured the works of 16 members. The hallmark practice of the SWS was its emphasis on *plein air* (open air) painting to achieve a sense of immediacy and spontaneity. Some of Singapore's leading watercolourists are members of the society. They include ONG KIM SENG, Leng Joon Wong, Lee Boon Wang, Tong Chin Sye, Winston Oh, Khor Ean Ghee, Lee Choon Kee, Loy Chye Chuan, Ho Yee Peng, Chan Chang How and Seah Kam Chuan. The SWS continues to define much of watercolour development in Singapore.

Wavell, Sir Archibald (1883–1950) British military officer. Field Marshal Sir Archibald Percival Wavell, the 1st Earl Wavell, came from a military family. He rose to head the Middle East Command, leading British forces in the Middle East to victory against the Italians in 1940–41, before losses to the Germans. He moved to India as commander-in-chief in July 1941, and became commander of ABDA (American-British-Dutch-Australian) Command in January 1942. Theoretically, he coordinated an area stretching from Burma, through Malaya

Watercolour: pioneer watercolourist Lim Cheng Hoe's Malay Youth, *(undated) (left);* Singapore Waterfront from Kallang *(1971).*

Wayang kulit: behind the scenes at a 1988 performance during Singapore Heritage Week.

Adelene Wee

Wee Beng Chong: with carved seals (top); Cut Wood *(undated).*

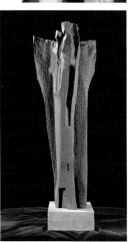

and the Dutch East Indies (present-day Indonesia) to the Philippines. In practice, however, Malaya was overwhelmed by the Japanese within days of his arrival. He moved his headquarters to Java on 15 January. On 25 February 1942, Wavell left Java for India, and ABDA was dissolved.

wayang kulit Traditional shadow puppet theatre form originating in Java. There are three main elements in *wayang kulit*: a stage and screen, puppets and gamelan music. The stage consists of a semi-transparent white screen, with a lamp or torch placed behind it. The puppets are flat, and are intricately carved by hand out of cowhide. They are stuck on banana stems and placed to the sides of the screen. Each puppet is a stylized exaggeration of the human shape and has swivelling 'arms'. The master puppeteer and storyteller, known as the *tok dalang*, sits behind the screen in the centre of the stage. He moves the puppets across the screen and their shadows can be seen by the audience. The *tok dalang* usually narrates stories based on the Hindu epics, the Ramayana and the Mahabharata. *Wayang kulit* is accompanied by a gamelan orchestra of between ten and 30 musicians. A performance can last a few hours or a whole night.

Wayang kulit was once popular among the Javanese community in Singapore. It was performed during weddings or on special occasions as entertainment. It declined in popularity over the decades and has become a vanishing art. The last reported *tok dalang* in Singapore was Taslim Harjosanojo, who performed during the 1950s. He died in 1985. Occasional performances are staged at cultural or arts festivals, usually by *wayang kulit* troupes from Malaysia.

Wee, Adelene (1965–) Sportswoman. Adelene Wee Chin Suan was Singapore's first tenpin bowling world champion, and twice Singapore Sports Council's Sportswoman of the Year (1983, 1986). At the age of 20, she won the Ladies' Masters title in the 1985 World Games in London, where she averaged 200 pinfalls. Her first

success had come three years earlier when she won the Singapore International Bowling Championships. In the same year, she broke the world record for a six-game series, totalling 1,280 pinfalls.

Wee had the rare distinction of being voted both Sportsgirl and Sportswoman of the Year in 1983. She continued her triumphs at Asian tournaments, winning gold medals in the doubles, all-events and Masters at the FIQ Youth Championships in 1983 and 1985. Over the next ten years, she represented Singapore in various international events, retiring from competition at the age of 30. She had been inducted into the SINGAPORE SPORTS COUNCIL HALL OF FAME.

Wee Beng Chong (1938–) Artist and sculptor. Wee Beng Chong was awarded a CULTURAL MEDALLION for visual arts in 1979, the first year the medallion was presented. Wee received his graduate education at the Nanyang Academy of Fine Arts (1958) and then went on to study at the Ecole Nationale Supérieure des Beaux-Arts, France (1964–69).

Wee melds Eastern and Western aesthetics, and classical and contemporary approaches. His oeuvre encompasses seal carving, calligraphy, ink and oil painting, printmaking and sculpture. He has written books on seal-carving, and also carved the signature seals of pioneer artists such as LIU KANG and CHEN WEN HSI. Wee has exhibited in Switzerland, Germany and France, winning the prestigious 17th Grand Prix Internationale de Peinture de Deauville (1966).

Wee played a pivotal role in the modern art movement in Singapore from the late 1960s, having co-founded the Modern Art Society in 1964. His contributions were recognized with the Cultural Award Pingat APAD (1974) and the Modern Art Award (1990).

Wee Cho Yaw (1929–) Banker. Born in Quemoy (present-day Kinmen) in Fujian, Wee Cho Yaw is the son of Sarawak trader and banker, Wee Kheng Chiang. In 1937, the elder Wee moved his family to Kuching and later to Singapore.

Wee attended Kong Shan Primary School in Tiong Bahru, but his studies were interrupted when the family moved to the Dutch East Indies (present-day Indonesia) for safety during the Japanese Occupation. The family returned to Singapore in 1945 and Wee attended Chinese High School for a year before transferring to Chung Cheng High School. In 1949, he left school and worked in the firm of his father, reputedly Borneo's wealthiest man.

In the 1930s, the elder Wee had extended his trading and banking empire to Singapore, and in 1935 founded the United Chinese Bank in Raffles Place. In 1958, Wee joined the board of the United

Chinese Bank. During the next year, he travelled extensively, studying the banking system of the United Kingdom. In 1960, at age 31, he was appointed managing director. The bank changed its name to UNITED OVERSEAS BANK (UOB) in 1965. Following its merger with OVERSEAS UNION BANK (OUB) in 2001, UOB became Singapore's largest local bank. Wee took over as chairman of the UOB Group when his father retired in the 1970s.

Wee has served as chairman of the Singapore Chinese Chamber of Commerce and Industry (1969–73; 1977–79); Singapore Federation of Chambers of Commerce and Industry (1978–82); Asean Federation of Chambers of Commerce and Industry (1979–81); and the Nanyang University Council (1970–80). In 1995, the Singapore Federation of Chinese Clan Associations (SFCCA) established the Chinese Heritage Centre with Wee as chairman. He has been chairman of the Singapore Hokkien Huay Kuan since 1972; and president of the SFCCA since 1986. In 2004 he was appointed pro-chancellor of Nanyang Technological University.

In 1990 and 2001, Wee won the Businessman of the Year award, presented by *The Business Times*, and was named Asean Businessman of the Year by the Asean Business Forum in 1995. His family is active in running the UOB empire, with his eldest son, Ee Cheong, serving as deputy chairman and president of UOB.

Wee Chong Jin (1917–2005) Judge. Wee Chong Jin was born in Penang and educated at the Penang Free School and later at St John's College, Cambridge University (1935–38). He was called to the Bar at Middle Temple in London. He practised as an advocate and solicitor in both Penang and Singapore from 1939 to 1957 before being appointed to the High Court in August 1957.

In 1963, Wee became chief justice, and two years later became the first chief justice of independent Singapore. In 1966, he chaired the only constitutional commission ever convened in post-independence Singapore (*see* WEE CHONG JIN COMMISSION). In 1988, Wee became the first president of the recently established Singapore Academy of Law. He retired as chief justice in 1990 after 27 years at the helm of Singapore's judiciary. He was Singapore's longest-serving chief justice.

From 1973 to 1991, Wee was chairman of the Presidential Council for Minority Rights. In 1987, Oxford University presented Wee with an honorary doctorate of civil law. In 1991 he was admitted into the DISTINGUISHED SERVICE ORDER.

Wee Chong Jin Commission This constitutional commission was set up in December 1965 to propose safeguards for minority rights and interests.

The commission issued its report in 1966, and recommended: fundamental constitutional provisions could only be amended by a vote of two-thirds majority in Parliament and two-thirds majority at a national referendum; the creation of a council of state, a purely advisory body, which would offer Parliament 'serious and weighty advice' on impending legislation and its effects on racial, linguistic, religious or cultural minorities; the appointment of an ombudsman as an 'independent check on the acts and decisions of civil servants'; the entrenching of judicial offices to maintain the independence of the judiciary; and a more appropriate method of appointing members of the Public Service Commission.

Following a brief debate in Parliament, most of these recommendations were rejected, except one—the Council of State concept was enacted as the Presidential Council in 1969. It is now known as the PRE-SIDENTIAL COUNCIL FOR MINORITY RIGHTS.

The members of the commission were WEE CHONG JIN (chairman); A.P. RAJAH (deputy chairman); C.F.J. Ess; MOHAMED JAVAD NAMAZIE; C.C. TAN; S.H.D. Elias; Syed Esa Syed Hassan Almenoar; Geoffrey Abisheganaden; Graham Starforth Hill; Abdul Manaf Ghows; Kirpal Singh; and S. Narayanaswamy (secretary).

Wee Heng Tin (1940–) Teacher and civil servant. Wee graduated from the University of Singapore with a degree in physics in 1963. The following year he joined the education service. In 1967, he won a Fulbright-Hays Scholarship.

Wee became principal of Dunearn Secondary School in 1971, and later, principal of Temasek Junior College (1977–79) and National Junior College (1980–81). He took on several senior administrative posts in the ministry headquarters before being appointed director of schools in 1987, and director of education in 1996.

For his services to education, Wee received the Public Administration Medal (Gold) (1999) and the MERITORIOUS SERVICE MEDAL (2004). He retired on 31 March 2004, but remained associated with the Ministry of Education to advise on educational issues. Wee has also served on the National University of Singapore Council, the National Institute of Education Council and the Institute of Technical Education Board of Governors.

Wee Kim Wee (1915–2005) Journalist, diplomat and head of state. Born on 4 November 1915, the son of Wee Choon Lay and Chua Lay Huan, Wee Kim Wee was educated at Pearl's Hill School and Raffles Institution. He was an avid badminton player and was junior singles badminton champion in 1937. Wee became a journalist after finishing school, joining THE STRAITS TIMES (1930) and United Press Association (1940 and 1945–59). In 1959,

Wee rejoined *The Straits Times* as deputy editor in Singapore. In 1966, Wee scored a journalistic coup as the first Singapore journalist to interview Indonesia's General Suharto, and reported on Suharto's intention to end the three-year CONFRONTATION with Malaysia.

Wee retired from journalism in 1973 and was appointed Singapore's high commissioner to Malaysia (1973–80) where he was dean of the Diplomatic Corps (1978–80). Upon his return, he was appointed ambassador to Japan (1980–84) and South Korea (1981–84). In 1984, Wee was appointed chairman of the Singapore Broadcasting Corporation. A year later, on 30 August 1985, Parliament elected Wee Singapore's fourth PRESIDENT.

During Wee's presidency, the powers of the president were substantially extended and the office transformed into a popularly elected one through amendments to the Constitution. Under transitional provisions in the Constitution, despite not actually having been elected, Wee became Singapore's 'first elected president'. He retired from office in 1993.

Wee also served as president of the Singapore Press Club, president of the Singapore Badminton Association and chairman of Cathay Organisation Holdings. In 1979, he was awarded the MERITORIOUS SERVICE MEDAL. He was admitted into the ORDER OF TEMASEK (First Class) in 1993, and received an honorary doctorate of letters from the National University of Singapore in 1994. In the United Kingdom, he was made a Knight Grand Cross, Order of the Bath (1989).

In 2004, Wee published his autobiography, *Glimpses and Reflections*. Royalties and funds raised from the book—totalling some $500,000—were donated to eight charities. Wee died on 2 May 2005 and was given a state funeral.

Wee Mon Cheng (1913–2003) Banker, businessman and diplomat. Wee Mon Cheng graduated from Amoy University (present-day Xiamen University) in China with a bachelor of law (economics) degree in 1935. He left China to seek his fortune in Burma where he sold soap and worked as a clerk. After a year, he left for Singapore.

After World War II, Wee joined Chip Hwa Shipping and Trading Co. Ltd. In 1950, Wee and other senior staff at Chip Hwa established Chip Seng Co. By 1958, Wee had stopped working with Chip Hwa and concentrated on Chip Seng, developing it into a multi-million-dollar shipping business.

In 1973, Wee was appointed ambassador to Japan (1973–80), and later ambassador to South Korea (1978–80). He also served as chairman of the Singapore Broadcasting Corporation (1981–84). In 1978, Wee was awarded the MERITORIOUS SERVICE MEDAL.

Wee Tian Siak (1921–2004) Sportsman. Wee Tian Siak, also known as Huang Tianxi, developed his basketball skills in Singapore's Chinese schools.

Wee was chosen by Nationalist Chinese selectors to be in China's delegation to the 1948 London Olympics. Four years later, he was again chosen to be in the Nationalist Chinese (Taiwan) team for the Helsinki Olympics. However, the dispute between Communist and Nationalist China over International Olympic Committee recognition led to neither side participating in the games. Wee returned to play for Singapore at the 1954 Asian Games in Manila, the 1956 Melbourne Olympics and the 1958 Asian Games in Tokyo.

Wee was nicknamed '*lao da*' (meaning 'leader' or 'big brother' in Mandarin) and was regularly selected as team captain. He played as a forward or centre and, over the course of his career, averaged nearly 20 points per game. Off the basketball court, he worked in the production department of newspaper NANYANG SIANG PAU, and also at an insurance company. He played in the newspaper's basketball squad. With Wee as captain, the squad won almost every local tournament until it was disbanded in 1956. Wee ended his basketball career as coach of the Singapore team that participated in the 1965 Southeast Asian Peninsular Games.

Wee Toon Boon (1929–) Politician. Wee Toon Boon was educated at Victoria School. He was employed in the Singapore City Council but resigned at the request of the PEOPLE'S ACTION PARTY to contest the CITY COUNCIL ELECTION in December 1957. From December 1957 to April 1959, Wee served as a city councillor. He then won a seat at the LEGISLATIVE ASSEMBLY ELECTION (1959) and was appointed parliamentary secretary in the Ministry of Labour in 1959. He served in this capacity until his appointment as minister of state for defence in September 1965.

In 1975, while serving as minister of state for the environment, Wee and his family took a trip to Indonesia. The trip was paid for by a housing developer on whose behalf Wee had made representations to civil servants. Wee also accepted a bungalow worth $500,000 from the same developer and took two overdrafts totalling $300,000 in his father's name against the developer's personal guarantee. Wee was convicted of corruption and sentenced to four-and-a-half years in prison, a term that was reduced to 18 months upon appeal. Wee resigned from his seat as member of Parliament for Sepoy Lines.

Wee Twee Kim (unknown–1945) Wee Twee Kim was the most senior Taiwanese collaborators with the Japanese military during the JAPANESE OCCUPATION. He had been a storekeeper working with Japanese firms in pre-war Singapore, and was fluent in

Wee Cho Yaw

Wee Chong Jin

Wee Kim Wee

Wee Mon Cheng

Wee Toon Boon

Sir Frederick Weld

Japanese, Mandarin and Hokkien. Wee was used as an interpreter by TAKASE TORU in negotiations to extract a $50 million 'gift' from the Chinese community in aid of the Japanese war effort in February 1942. Wee was executed by anti-Japanese Chinese guerrillas in Singapore shortly after Japan's surrender.

Weld, Sir Frederick (1823–1891) Colonial official. Appointed governor of the Straits Settlements in 1880, Sir Frederick Aloysius Weld already possessed considerable administrative experience from his stints as premier of New Zealand (1864–65), and governor of Western Australia (1869–75) and Tasmania (1875–80). He travelled to various parts of the Malay States to familiarize himself with the issues at first hand and, having observed that the Malay States were doing well economically, was of the opinion that their administration should be assimilated with that of Singapore. He therefore took steps to engender cordial relations between the Malay chiefs and British officials.

Weld was the first governor to actively support spending government funds to build a new museum in Singapore. He officially opened the Raffles Library and Museum (*see* NATIONAL MUSEUM OF SINGAPORE) on 12 October 1887. He retired later that year. He was succeeded by Sir CECIL CLEMENTI SMITH. Weld died in Dorset in the United Kingdom.

Wesley Methodist Church The Wesley Methodist Church was the first Methodist church established in Singapore. It was established by Dr James Thoburn and its first pastor was Reverend WILLIAM FITZJAMES OLDHAM, following a series of meetings in February 1885 at the Town Hall (later Victoria Memorial Hall). The church was originally known as the 'English Church'. Services were held three times a week at the Town Hall and the Christian Institute on Middle Road until December 1886, when the church moved to a building on Coleman Street—later the Anglo-Chinese Primary School (ACS) Hall. The congregation was made up mostly of Europeans and

Wesley Methodist Church

Wet markets

Eurasians, with a few English-speaking Indians and Chinese. English-speaking Chinese generally stayed away to avoid charges of 'becoming English'.

In 1907, the governor, Sir JOHN ANDERSON, granted 38,000 sq ft at Fort Canning (the church's present site) to the Methodist Mission in recognition of its contribution to missions and education, and laid the cornerstone of the new red-brick building designed in the late decorated English Gothic style. The Coleman Street building was sold to ACS. Oldham, then bishop, preached at the dedication service on 9 February 1909. The church was given its present name in 1910. In 1913, it escaped damage when an arsonist failed in an attempt to burn it down by setting fire to Bibles and hymnals piled on the floor. Membership remained small, with fewer than 100 people in 1910 and 227 in 1940.

During World War II, the church was briefly taken over by Australian troops. The last pre-Japanese Occupation service, on 8 February 1942, was interrupted by nearby bombing. Reverend Tyler Thomson stopped mid-sermon and evacuated the congregation to Wesley Hall (which had a reinforced concrete ceiling) where he continued the service. During the Occupation, the Japanese used the church as an ammunition depot. Members, including two Japanese officers who were old boys of ACS, dispersed to worship at other churches such as the Tamil Methodist Church.

After 1948, the predominantly European-Eurasian congregation gave way to a Chinese majority. Reverend (later Bishop) Yap Kim Hao was the first Asian to serve as associate pastor in 1956. In 1970, the church's first Asian pastor, Reverend Kenneth Chellappah, ended 84 years of foreign missionary pastoral leadership. In the mid-1970s, the church experienced a revival in a wave of charismatic spiritual renewal, and continued to grow. By July 2005 it was the largest Methodist church, with 6,022 members and nearly 20 worship services a week in English, Mandarin and Korean. The church runs three childcare centres, free counselling services, a Lay Training Institute with courses on Christian growth, a home-help service for

frail elderly, and a number of services for the disadvantaged and underprivileged.

wet markets Fresh produce (vegetables, meat, fruit, fish and seafood), as well as dried groceries, spices and condiments, are sold in wet markets, so named because of their perpetually wet floors. Wet markets are the descendents of the open-air markets, or *pasar*, found throughout Southeast Asia.

Singapore's early wet markets were in makeshift areas. But since the 1960s, when public housing estates were being developed, the clusters of stalls and itinerant hawkers which used to make up such markets have been moved into large, purpose-built premises fitted with electricity and piped running water. Most wet markets are located in or near public housing estates and have a hawker centre as an annexe.

Once the main channel for the distribution of fresh produce, wet markets now face competition from supermarkets, provisions shops, upmarket butchers, delicatessens and boutique food sellers.

In 2001, the government began a programme to clean up old wet markets, installing better lighting, ventilation and drainage so as to improve standards of hygiene.

Whampoa River With its source in the MACRITCHIE RESERVOIR in the Central Catchment Area, the Whampoa River is a tributary of the KALLANG RIVER. It drains into MARINA BAY. As with the Kallang and Singapore Rivers, the Whampoa was heavily polluted and was cleaned up as part of the 1977–87 Action Plan. The lower course of the Whampoa flows through a high-density urbanized area and has, in places, been straightened and given steep walled banks as a flood-prevention measure.

whip Since 1965, Singapore has had only a government whip, as there has been insufficient opposition in Parliament to require an opposition whip. The whip ensures the efficient and smooth running of the parliamentary machinery. The whip lists the speakers for each item of business and estimates the time required for each. The whip also ensures efficient communication within the party, and applies pressure to ensure that backbenchers vote in line with the party's stand. On occasion, the whip may be 'lifted' to allow party members of Parliament to vote freely. The whip is directly responsible to the LEADER OF THE HOUSE and to the prime minister.

Whiteaway, Laidlaw and Co. Department store. The firm of Whiteaway, Laidlaw and Co. established its flagship store in Singapore in November 1900 on D'Almeida Street. Later, the store moved to the corner of Hill Street and Stamford Road before moving back to Battery Road at RAFFLES PLACE, where it remained until its closure in the 1960s. The company was the leading draper of its day. In addition, the store had a boot-and-shoe department, a crockery department and a general outfitter. Whiteaways—as the store was sometimes called—was considered the biggest rival of the other two major department stores: JOHN LITTLE and ROBINSONS.

In the 1950s, Whiteaways advertised itself as 'The Department Store that Offers You Everything Under One Roof' and 'The Store of a Thousand Good Things'. Its ground-floor perfume department was legendary. It was the agent for Elizabeth Arden cosmetics, among other brands. In addition to its Singapore store, the company also had stores in India, China, Ceylon (present-day Sri Lanka), South Africa and South America.

wholesale and retail sector In 2005, the wholesale and retail trade sector amounted to about 15 per cent of Singapore's GROSS DOMESTIC PRODUCT. Wholesale and retail trade in 2005 grew at 10.5 per cent, compared to a growth of 15.6 per cent in 2004, supported by an increase in non-oil re-exports of 13 per cent, as compared to 21 per cent in 2004. Sales of most goods, including motor vehicles, increased. Supermarkets, however, recorded a decrease in sales.

The retail sector employs about 4 per cent of Singapore's workforce but this tends to fluctuate according to the seaons. Activity in the sector has a tendency to peak during the festive Christmas and Chinese New Year period. The month of June also sees a buzz in the retail sector as the annual Great Singapore Sale attracts shoppers with big discounts.

The wholesale trade industry in Singapore is dominated by petroleum, petroleum-related products, electronic accessories and equipment and, to a lesser extent, industrial machinery and telecommunications equipment.

Wicked Aura Batucada Percussion group. Made up of 13 members, this group plays its own blend of Brazilian samba batucada music infused with local ethnic rhythms.

Wicked Aura Batucada is the brainchild of local percussionist Firmann Salleh who brought in other percussionists from the local independent music circuit after being inspired by the sounds of Brazilian batucada music. Making its debut in 2003 as a five-piece band at the annual beach dance party ZoukOut (*see* ZOUK), the group then took their performances to Orchard Road where they regularly busk. It was there that regional operations director (Asia) of World of Music, Arts and Dance (WOMAD) Projects Singapore, Sarah Martin, spotted them and invited them to perform at the 2004 WOMAD festival in Singapore.

The band's performance at the festival led to invitations to perform at WOMAD festivals in the United Kingdom, Spain and Sri Lanka. In Madrid, the Spanish press described Wicked Aura Batucada as one of the best bands of the festival.

W!LD RICE Theatre company. W!LD RICE was founded in 2000 by the internationally acclaimed and award-winning theatre practitioner IVAN HENG. The theatre takes its inspiration from Singapore's diverse cultures and performance styles. By producing touring quality 'glocal' productions with a distinctively local flavour, the company creates shared experiences for audiences in Singapore and internationally. Its productions include new and original works, new productions of Singaporean repertoire and new interpretations of world classics. The company's education and outreach programme, Project Chilli Padi, reaches out to school-going children and young adults through innovative approaches to arts education.

Williams, Peter (1924–) Trade unionist and political activist. Born Peter Massillamany Williams in Ceylon (present-day Sri Lanka), he was educated at the Anglo-Chinese School, Klang, and St Joseph's Institution, Kuala Lumpur, before completing his studies at St Joseph's Institution, Singapore. He worked as a clerical worker in the Army Civil Service Union (ACSU).

Inspired by the success of the welfare-state experiment in the United Kingdom, and attracted by the prospect of winning over the large number of Indian voters in Singapore, Williams helped found the SINGAPORE LABOUR PARTY (SLP) in September 1948. He gradually assumed the leadership of the 'Indian' faction within the party, drawing on the support of white-collar office workers—largely Indians—from the ACSU and several government unions, and adopted a radical agenda. His faction was soon involved in an internal power struggle with the moderate business-professional group led by LIM YEW HOCK and FRANCIS THOMAS, over nomination of candidates for the 1952 City Council election. While Lim had control over labour support through his position as president of the SINGAPORE TRADES UNION CONGRESS, Williams controlled the general council of the party as secretary-general. In December 1952, he persuaded the council to expel Lim, causing a split in the SLP from which it never recovered.

Wing Tai Holdings Wing Tai began as a garment manufacturer in Hong Kong in 1955, before expanding into Singapore and Malaya in the early 1960s as Wing Tai Garment Manufactory. The business was incorporated in Singapore on 9 August 1963. It entered the property market in 1978. By 1987, it had become actively involved in the property business. It was listed on the stock exchange and assumed its present name in January 1989.

Wing Tai Holdings has emerged as one of Asia's leading property players in property development, investment and management. By the end of 2005, the group had developed more than 50 residential projects in Singapore, Malaysia, Hong Kong and China. It also operates boutique hotels and serviced apartments in Singapore, Kuala Lumpur, Shanghai and Hong Kong under the name Lanson Place Serviced Residences.

The group's other principal activities include apparel retailing and the trading of architectural products. Its clothing and apparel lines are sold mainly through G2000, U2, Fox Fashion and department stores. It is a distributor of Nike and Adidas sportswear. Wing Tai also operates the Yoshinoya restaurant franchise locally, which it first acquired in May 1997. The group posted a net profit of nearly $28 million on revenues of $282 million for the financial year 2005.

Winsemius, Albert (1910–1996) Dutch economist. Dr Albert Winsemius—founding father of the Dutch post-war industrialization programme—first visited Singapore in 1960 with a United Nations Survey Mission. LEE KUAN YEW reported that Winsemius 'laid two pre-conditions for Singapore's success: first, to eliminate the communists who made any economic progress impossible; second, not to remove the statue of Sir Stamford Raffles'.

We welcome you to Singapore!

Whiteaways, Laidlaw and Co.: advertisement for Whiteaways, 'the better store', 1958.

Wing Tai Holdings: garment factory, 1963.

Albert Winsemius

Alfred Wong

Aline Wong

Eleanor Wong

Winsemius became unofficial chief economic advisor to the government until 1984, visiting twice each year. He is credited with recommending an economic merger with Malaya; the INDUSTRIALIZATION of Singapore; the building of PUBLIC HOUSING; the development of the financial sector; and the establishment of Singapore as an air and sea transport hub. He urged the promotion of policies to reassure foreign investors as to the pro-business attitudes of the PEOPLE'S ACTION PARTY, despite the party's socialist stance in the 1960s. Winsemius persuaded Dutch businesses in particular to invest in Singapore.

In 1966, Winsemius was admitted into the DISTINGUISHED SERVICE ORDER. To honour his contribution to the development of Singapore, an Albert Winsemius Professorship was established at the Nanyang Technological University in 1997.

Winslow, Alfred (1916–1984) Judge. Born in Perak, Alfred Victor Winslow was educated at the Penang Free School, where he won a Queen's Scholarship to study law at Sidney Sussex College, Cambridge University, in 1935. He was called to the Bar at the Middle Temple in April 1940, after which he joined the Straits Settlements legal service as assistant official assignee. He subsequently served as deputy registrar, sheriff, district judge and first magistrate. In 1949, he was posted to the Attorney-General's Chambers as Crown Counsel and deputy public prosecutor. In 1957, he was appointed solicitor-general of Singapore. In 1959, Winslow was admitted to the Singapore Bar. He was appointed puisne judge in 1962. He retired in April 1977 due to ill health.

Women's Charter This charter was the culmination of more than five years of campaigning by the PEOPLE'S ACTION PARTY (PAP). In 1959, the PAP launched its One Man, One Wife campaign. Among the chief activists were the five women in the Legislative Assembly: Sahora Ahmat, Ho Puay Choo, Fung Yin Ching, Chan Choy Siong and Seow Peck Leng. That year, the PAP established its Women's Affairs Bureau to improve the status of women in society.

In 1960, the Legislative Assembly debated a proposal for a Women's Charter to 'enable women to have their rights safeguarded by legislation'. The Women's Charter was enacted into law in 1961.

Previously, polygamy had been legal, and often resulted in inferior treatment for secondary wives or concubines, and their offspring. The charter sought to create an equal partnership between husband and wife, and to safeguard women's rights in matters relating to marriage and divorce. It outlawed polygamy, and safeguarded matrimonial assets, maintenance and custody of children. It also protected family members from domestic violence, and women and girls from sexual offences.

Since 1961, the charter has been amended several times. The most extensive changes were made in 1996, with major amendments providing for the harmonious resolution of family disputes; more equitable distribution of matrimonial assets; mandatory counselling for perpetrators and victims of domestic violence; and the recognition of marriages of persons who have undergone sex re-assignment procedures.

Wong, Alfred (1930–) Architect. The grandson of entrepreneur and banker Wong Ah Fook, Alfred Wong Hong Kwok received a degree in architecture from Melbourne University in 1953. On his return to Singapore, he joined the firm of SWAN & MACLAREN before eventually setting up his own practice, Alfred Wong Partnership, in 1957.

His work spans more than four decades. It includes the iconic NATIONAL THEATRE (1959), the Marco Polo Hotel (1968), SINGAPORE POLYTECHNIC (1979), several Catholic parish churches, including St Francis Xavier's in Serangoon Gardens Estate and St Bernadette's in Zion Road, and the PSA Keppel Distripark (1995). Wong's buildings exhibit a crossover of modernist formal sensibilities into the local context. He sought to achieve a precision of architectural meaning without excesses of representational devices. In the early years, his style contrasted with the growing opulence and flamboyance of design which characterized the work of many architects spurred by competition and the rising influence of foreign architects. Building craft, structural virtuosity, and formal inventiveness are distinctive qualities of Wong's work.

Wong actively supported the development of the profession, its professional accreditation and its education, being especially influential in upgrading architecture as a course of study at university level. He was one of the founders of the Singapore Institute of Architects and served four terms (1962–66) as its president. In December 2003, he was made chairman of the Preservation of Monuments Board. He was the first recipient of the Singapore Institute

of Architects Gold Medal, inaugurated in 1998. He was also awarded the Public Service Star in 2005.

Wong, Aline (1941–) Academic and politician. Born in Hong Kong, Aline Wong was educated at the University of Hong Kong, and the University of California, Berkeley, where she obtained a PhD in sociology in 1970. She joined the Chinese University of Hong Kong as a lecturer in 1966 but relocated to Singapore in 1971 where she joined the University of Singapore. She was made full professor in 1991.

In 1984, Wong entered politics, on the People's Action Party (PAP) ticket for the Changkat constituency. In 1989, she founded the PAP Women's Wing and served as its first chairman until 2001. Wong served as minister of state for health (1990), minister of state for education (1994) and senior minister of state for health (1995–99) and education (1995–2001). She retired from politics in 2001. In 2003 she was appointed chairman of the Housing & Development Board.

Wong, Eleanor (1962–) Lawyer and playwright. Eleanor Wong Siew Yin's first play, *Peter's Passionate Pursuit* (1986) was joint first-prize winner in the NUS-Shell Short Play Competition. It was later adapted for television as *The Peter Project* (2005).

Often making dramatic capital from the controversial and the topical, Wong is best known for *Mergers and Accusations* (1993), *Wills and Secession* (1995) and *Jointly and Severably* (2003), a trilogy addressing bisexuality and lesbianism in a woman lawyer. In 2003, W!LD RICE Theatre Company staged the entire trilogy, also published as *Invitation to Treat* (2005).

Jackson on a Jaunt (or *Mistaken Identities*), commissioned by THEATREWORKS and sponsored by the Ministry of Health to encourage awareness of HIV/AIDS, was reworked before Theatreworks performed it two years later in 1989, the ministry having withdrawn support because of explicitly homosexual characters. Wong's political satire, *The Campaign to Confer the Public Service Star on JBJ*, was performed by W!LD RICE in August, 2006.

Wong, who was a practising lawyer, is director of the Legal Writing Progamme, National University of Singapore, and associate director of its Centre for the Development of Teaching and Learning.

Wong, James (1969–) Sportsman. James Wong Tuck Yim studied at Pasir Panjang Secondary School, then Mount San Antonio College in California before graduating from Angelo State University, Texas. Wong won seven consecutive discus gold medals at the Southeast Asian (SEA) Games between 1993 and 2005. He broke the national discus record in 1999 with a distance of 59.87 m in Germany. Wong is now

head of strength and conditioning at the Singapore Sports Council.

Wong, Mimi (c. 1939–1973) In 1966, Mimi Wong, a former cabaret queen, became the mistress of a Japanese mechanical engineer, Watanabe Hiroshi. In 1969, Watanabe's wife and children arrived in Singapore to join him, and they lived together at 55 Jalan Seaview.

On 6 January 1970, just two weeks after her arrival, Watanabe's wife Ayako was stabbed to death. Wong and her estranged husband, Sim Who Kum, were sentenced to death for the murder. Wong's appeal to the Court of Appeal—on the grounds of diminished responsibility—was handled by DAVID MARSHALL. The appeal failed, and Wong and Sim were hanged in July 1973.

Wong, Russel (1961–) Photographer. Russel Wong is particularly well known for his images of celebrities such as Jackie Chan, Aishwarya Rai, Zhang Ziyi, Isabella Rossellini and Imelda Marcos. He shot the publicity pictures for Ang Lee's *Crouching Tiger Hidden Dragon* (2000), and Zhang Yimou's *Hero* (2002) and *House of Flying Daggers* (2004). Born in Melbourne and raised in Singapore, Wong graduated from the University of Oregon in 1982. In 1988, he completed a degree in fine arts (photography) at the Art Centre College of Design, Los Angeles. Since the mid-1980s, he has done work for *Vogue*, the *New York Times* and the *Los Angeles Times*. His photographs have appeared on the cover of *TIME*. He enrolled in New York University's film programme in 1996 and his film/video projects have won awards including the Clio Award and the New York Festival Grand Award. In 2005, Wong held solo exhibitions at the Singapore Art Museum and the Singapore Tyler Print Institute.

Wong, Ruth (1918–1982) Teacher and civil servant. Ruth Wong Hie King received her doctorate in mathematics education from Harvard University, where she came under the influence of scholars such as B.F. Skinner, Jerome Bruner, Israel Scheffler and John Carroll.

Wong was the founding director of the former Institute of Education, and director of research at the Ministry of Education. She became a well-known and respected educationalist. When she was chairperson of the Advisory Committee on Curriculum Development (1969–73), she introduced the notion of an indigenized curriculum—based on local, not colonial, needs—in Singapore's schools.

Wong established a technical-rationalist approach to curriculum planning, and the notion of educational objectives in syllabus writing. Her *Unto Each Child The Best* (1990) (a collection of 23 papers) is an important source for Singaporean educators, teachers and parents. Other notable

publications include *Towards a Better Tomorrow* (1972), *Educational Innovation in Singapore* (1974) and *Called to be a Teacher: A Christian and Personal Viewpoint* (1982).

Wong Chooi Sen (1921–1998) Civil servant. Little is known of Wong Chooi Sen's early life or career. He joined the colonial civil service in 1940. After the People's Action Party came to power in 1959, he was appointed Cabinet secretary, a post he held until his retirement.

To the general public, Wong is not a well-known figure. However, he participated in many historic events and received the MERITORIOUS SERVICE MEDAL in 1963. He was the keeper of records for Cabinet meetings from 1959, and was present at the historic SEPARATION talks in 1965. It was Wong who had the task of typing the Separation Agreement, negotiated by GOH KENG SWEE, Tun Abdul Razak and E.W. BARKER. When he retired in 1997, he was made special assistant to the Cabinet Office.

Wong was a founding member of Radio Modellers Singapore—a group which builds and flies radio-controlled aircraft—in 1954.

Wong Heck Sing (1923–) Doctor. Wong Heck Sing studied at St Andrew's School, but his education was disrupted by the war. During the Japanese Occupation, he worked as a farmer on the island of Batam. He finally went to medical school in 1946. Wong entered private practice in 1953, and did voluntary work, later serving as honorary doctor at Nanyang University (1956-60).

Wong was also honorary physician to the Salvation Army Nursery Home (1956-63), the Lee Kuo Chuan Home for the Aged (1964-70), and Boys' Town (1956-70). He was corps surgeon to the St John's Ambulance Brigade (1956-70).

Wong served on the Public Service Commission (1970-73) and was deputy chairman (1973-94). He was a member of the Singapore Telephone Board (1969-71) and the Legal Service Commission (1973-94). He also chaired the Ministry of Health's committee for the selection of part-time honorary consultants for government hospitals (1974-78). A founder of the College of General Practitioners in Singapore, Wong was its president for three terms from 1973 to 1985. He has been awarded the Public Service Star (1983), and the MERITORIOUS SERVICE MEDAL (1989).

Wong Hock Boon (1923–) Doctor. Wong Hock Boon attended the Anglo-Chinese School and Raffles College and was studying to be an engineer when World War II broke out. He changed his mind during the war and went on to study at the King Edward VII College of Medicine (1946-52) to become a doctor.

Known as the 'father of paediatrics' in Singapore, Wong was the first Singaporean to be head of the Department of Paediatrics at the then University of Singapore. He initiated the setting up of a paediatric ward at Singapore General Hospital and later at National University Hospital. Besides clinical work and research, Professor Wong taught and trained successive generations of paediatricians. He started the postgraduate programme for paediatrics so that doctors would not have to go to the United Kingdom for paediatric training.

Wong's pioneering work on a defective enzyme (G6PD) in newborns resulted in a significant decrease in cases of kernicterus (brain damage in infants caused by jaundice) in Singapore and the region. For his achievements, he was awarded the MERITORIOUS SERVICE MEDAL in 1975 and the Guinness Award for Scientific Achievement in 1980. Five years later, he received the Most Outstanding Paediatrician in Asia Award from the Association of Paediatric Societies of the South East Asian Region.

Wong Hung Khim (1938–) Civil servant. Wong Hung Khim was educated at Victoria School and the University of Singapore, where he obtained an honours degree in physics. He worked as a teacher (1964–66) and then joined the Administrative Service. In 1969, he became deputy secretary in the Ministry of Labour (1969–74). Wong held several high-profile appointments, including general manager and executive director of Singapore Bus Services Ltd (1974–78) and director of the Port of Singapore Authority (1979–87).

Wong was permanent secretary, Ministry of Community Development (1984–87); president and chief executive officer of the Telecommunications Authority of Singapore (1987–95); chairman of Jurong Town Corporation (1993–97); deputy chairman, Singapore Telecommunications Ltd (1995–2000); and executive chairman, Delgro Group (1996–2002). He was awarded the MERITORIOUS SERVICE MEDAL in 1992.

Wong Kan Seng (1946–) Politician. Wong Kan Seng joined the teaching service in 1964 after completing his secondary education at Outram Secondary School. After three years, he resigned to study at the University of Singapore where he obtained an honours degree in history and English.

On graduation in 1970, he joined the Administrative Service, where he rose to the rank of deputy secretary. In 1981, he resigned from the Ministry of Defence and joined Hewlett-Packard as its personnel manager.

Wong entered politics in 1984 on the People's Action Party (PAP) ticket and became member of Parliament for Kuo Chuan constituency. The following year, he

Russel Wong

Wong Hock Boon

Wong Kan Seng

Wong Lin Ken

Michael Wong Pakshong

Joanna Wong Quee Heng

was appointed minister of state for home affairs, and then minister of state for community development and communications and information. In 1986, he was made acting minister for community development, and full minister the year after. Other government posts held by him include second minister for foreign affairs (1987–88), minister for foreign affairs (1988–94), minister for community development (1988–91), minister for home affairs (1994–) and deputy prime minister (2005–). In 2006, he was returned unopposed as member of Parliament for Bishan-Toa Payoh group representation constituency.

Wong has been the deputy chairman of the People's Association since 1992, and Leader of the House since 1987. Within the PAP, Wong has been a member of the party's Central Executive Committee since 1987 and has served as second assistant secretary general (1992–2004) and first assistant secretary-general (since 2004).

Wong Kwei Cheong (1942–) Academic, businessman and politician. Wong Kwei Cheong was educated at Gan Eng Seng School, Queenstown Secondary Technical School, Raffles Institution and the University of Singapore, on a State Scholarship. In 1966, he graduated with first class honours in physics, the top student of his year. He continued with his graduate work at Imperial College London on a Commonwealth Scholarship and graduated with a PhD in solid state physics (1969). He joined the University of Singapore in the Department of Physics. In 1973, he left the university and became chairman and managing director of Aiwa/Atlas Electronics (Singapore) Pte Ltd.

Wong entered politics in 1980 and was elected member of Parliament for Cairnhill constituency on the People's Action Party ticket. In 1981, he was appointed minister of state (labour), and then minister of state for trade and industry. He stepped down from these posts in 1985 and joined the School of Management, National University of Singapore, as associate professor. He left Singapore in 1993 to go into business in Indonesia. In late 2005 he was appointed chairman of the board of Vantage Corporation.

Wong Lin Ken (1931–1983) Academic and politician. Born in Penang, Wong Lin Ken was educated at St George's Boys' School, the Penang Free School and the University of Malaya where he obtained a first class degree in history (1954). He went on to obtain his master's degree at the same university, and his PhD at the University of London on a Queen's Scholarship. He returned to Singapore in 1959 and joined the University of Singapore's History Department as assistant lecturer. Within a decade he was Raffles Professor of History (1969).

Outside academia, Wong was active in politics. He joined the People's Action Party and contested the 1968 election, becoming member of Parliament for Alexandra constituency. He served as permanent representative to the United Nations and Singapore's first ambassador to the United States (1967–68), and as minister for home affairs (1970–72). Wong returned to become head of the NUS Department of History (1973–83). He retired from politics in 1976. On 16 February 1983, Wong, who was suffering from depression, committed suicide.

Wong Pakshong, Michael (1931–) Businessman. Born in Durban, South Africa, Michael Wong Pakshong received his honours degree in economics and accounting from the University of Bristol in the United Kingdom in 1957, and his FCA (Fellow of the Institute of Chartered Accountants in England and Wales) in 1959. He came to Singapore in 1961 as an audit assistant for Price Waterhouse and Co., becoming assistant general manager of Oversea-Chinese Banking Corporation in 1964.

In 1971, Wong became the first managing director of the Monetary Authority of Singapore (1971–81). He was a governor of the International Monetary Fund (1973–81), and chairman of Neptune Orient Lines (1970–84) and NTUC Income (1970–80). He has held multiple directorships, including the chairmanships of the Esplanade Company, Great Eastern Holdings, Robinson & Co. and Sime Singapore. His directorships have included Oversea-Chinese Banking Corporation, the Straits Trading Company, Bukit Sembawang Estates and Sime Darby.

Wong was honorary consul for the Grand Duchy of Luxembourg (1982–90), and honorary consul-general from 1990.

Wong Partnership Law firm founded as Wong Meng Meng & Partners in 1992 by Wong Meng Meng. Called to the Bar in 1972, Wong was among the first batch of Senior Counsels to be appointed (1997). Wong Partnership started out as a specialist litigation firm but broadened its practice to become a full-service law firm. In 2003, it formed a joint law venture with Clifford Chance, the world's largest law firm.

Wong Peng Soon (1918–1996) Sportsman. A member of Malaya's victorious THOMAS CUP badminton team in 1949, 1952 and 1955, and the first Asian to win the All-England Championships, Wong Peng Soon made his mark internationally after the age of 30. He won the Danish Open singles, the Indian Open singles/doubles, and the Philippines Open singles/doubles. He was the undisputed badminton singles champion in Singapore (seven times) and Malaya (eight times) during the same period. He

won the All-England singles four times—in 1950, 1951, 1952 and 1955.

Acclaimed as 'the Great Wong', he was made a member of the Order of the British Empire for his contributions to the sport. In 1962, he was awarded the Certificate of Honour (Sijil Kemuliaan) by the Singapore government, the highest National Day honour ever presented to a sportsman.

Wong Quee Heng, Joanna (1939–) Actress. Since the mid-1970s, Joanna Wong Quee Heng has been active in promoting and performing Cantonese opera. As a key member of Kong Chow Wui Koon, a Cantonese clan association, Wong was instrumental in bringing *Hong Lou Meng* (Dream of the Red Chamber) to Berlin in 1997, the first grand Cantonese opera production from Singapore to be performed in the West. The tour raised the profile of Cantonese opera as an art form. In 1981, together with her husband, Leslie Wong, a playwright and promoter, Wong founded the CHINESE THEATRE CIRCLE and became its artistic director. In the same year, she received the CULTURAL MEDALLION. In 2004, she celebrated her 50th anniversary on stage as part of the Singapore International Cantonese Opera Festival.

Woo Bih Li (1954–) Judge. Woo Bih Li was educated at the Anglo-Chinese School and the Faculty of Law, University of Singapore, where he graduated at the top of his class. He was called to the Singapore Bar in 1978 and commenced practice with the firm of Allen & Gledhill in 1980. In 1992, he established the firm of Bih Li and Lee with Anthony Lee. Woo specialized in the areas of commercial litigation, arbitration, banking and corporate insolvency. In 1997, he was among the first batch of lawyers to be appointed Senior Counsel. He was appointed judicial commissioner in 2000 and on 2

Wong Peng Soon

Leslie Woodford: back right, in 1954 with Charles Paglar, back centre, and Lord Rowallan, Chief Scout of the Commonwealth, front centre.

January 2003, became a judge of the Supreme Court.

Woodford, Leslie (1907–1976) Scout. Leslie Aubrey Woodford studied at St Joseph's Institution where he first became a Scout in 1919. He was recruited by the Catholic Church to teach at St Anthony's Boy School where he served most of his career as a teacher of English and English literature. At St Anthony's, he became assistant Scoutmaster of the 15th Singapore Troop (founded 1926).

Woodford was invested as a rover Scout and took the name Black Bear. Over the next two decades, Woodford served as assistant district commissioner, then district commissioner of the South Western District. In 1957, he succeeded R.E. Ince to become the first Singapore-born chief commissioner of the SCOUTS. He was awarded the MERITORIOUS SERVICE MEDAL in 1962. The following year, poor health caused Woodford to retire from active Scouting.

Woodhull, Sidney (1932–2003) Trade unionist, politician and lawyer. Also known as Sandy, or Sandra, his full name was Sandrasegeram Woodhull. His father had been killed by the MALAYAN PEOPLE'S ANTI-JAPANESE ARMY (MPAJA) in 1944, but Woodhull was so fervently anti-colonial that he did not renounce the use of violence as a means of overthrowing the British. Woodhull's foray into politics began when he and a group of like-minded socialists—WANG GUNGWU, JAMES PUTHUCHEARY and ONG PANG BOON—founded the University of Malaya's Socialist Club in 1953. In 1955, Woodhull and other members of the editorial board of *Fajar*, the Socialist Club's publication, were arrested and charged with sedition. D.N. PRITT and LEE KUAN YEW successfully defended the students in what became known as the FAJAR TRIAL.

Lee was impressed by Woodhull's abilities and arranged for him to be the paid secretary of the Naval Base Union. Woodhull's power base grew and he soon became active in other unions, most notably LIM CHIN SIONG's SINGAPORE FACTORY AND SHOP WORKERS' UNION. He was one of the so-called 'Big Six' of the MIDDLE ROAD UNIONS—the others being Lim Chin Siong, James Puthucheary, FONG SWEE SUAN, JAMIT SINGH and S.T. BANI.

In 1956, the British detained Woodhull, together with C.V. DEVAN NAIR, Puthucheary and several others, for leftist activities. They were released when the People's Action Party came to power in 1959. Woodhull was appointed political secretary in the Ministry of Health but was dismissed in 1961. In 1962, he joined the BARISAN SOSIALIS as vice-chairman but was again detained in 1963, under OPERATION COLD STORE, for suspected communist activities. He was released in Malaysia and quit politics.

Woodhull then studied law and practised as a partner in a Kuala Lumpur law firm until his retirement in 2001. Until 1990, he was one of nine Malaysians banned from entering Singapore because of pro-communist activities. He died in Singapore on 25 November 2003 while undergoing a medical check-up.

Woodlands The name 'Woodlands' was possibly derived from the fact that, when viewed from Johor in the 19th century, this area looked like a thick forest, with a high density of keranji trees. Until the 1970s, Woodlands was a rural part of northern Singapore—most people knew it simply as the place where the CAUSEWAY linked Singapore with Johor. This changed with the development of PUBLIC HOUSING in the area as well as in neighbouring Mandai. Woodlands has become Singapore's largest public housing estate. It comprises nine neighbourhoods and is home to several educational institutions, including the Singapore Sports School. Woodlands Town covers an area of almost 1,200 ha, with 58,000 units of public housing and a resident population of about 216,000 in 2005.

Woods, Robert Carr (1816–1875) Businessman and lawyer. Robert Carr Woods arrived in Singapore from India in the early 1840s and, in 1845, was appointed founding editor of CATCHIK MOSES' newspaper, THE STRAITS TIMES. Woods ran the newspaper single-handedly, editing and hand-pressing the first 200 copies of the first edition in a godown at 7 Commercial Square (present-day Raffles Place) on 15 July 1845. The paper was initially known as *The Straits Times and Singapore Journal of Commerce*. Woods eventually bought over the press and ran it until 1859, when he sold it to W. Wynter & Company.

Woods was called to the Bar at Gray's Inn in 1863 and admitted to the Bar in Singapore. In 1870, he was appointed attorney-general and later became senior puisne judge. Woods was responsible for the first attempt at publishing law reports. In 1869, he compiled a slim volume entitled *A Selection of Oriental Cases Decided in the Supreme Courts of the Straits Settlements*. Known more popularly as 'Wood's Oriental Cases', the book contained reports of 12 cases, the earliest of which was decided in 1835 and the latest in 1869. The volume was reprinted in London in 1911.

Woods lived on Serangoon Road and named his property Woodsville. He was a close associate of James Guthrie Davidson, who would later become a rubber magnate, and in 1861, they founded the firm of Woods and Davidson, precursor to RODYK & DAVIDSON. In 1870, when Woods became attorney-general, Davidson left to become Resident of Selangor and later Perak.

Woon Wah Siang (1916–1992) Civil servant. Woon Wah Siang was educated in Hong Kong, where he graduated with a degree in arts from Hong Kong University. He later obtained a science degree from the University of London. He worked in the War Tax and Property Tax Departments during the war. In the 1950s he was director of the Social Welfare Department, and chief administrative officer and secretary of the City Council (1960). He helped establish the Singapore Council of Social Services and the People's Association. Woon served as permanent secretary to the Ministries of Culture (1962), Foreign Affairs (1967) and Finance (1968).

Sidney Woodhull

Woon was chairman of the Jurong Town Corporation, from its inception in 1968 until he retired in 1976. As the first chairman and managing director of the JURONG BIRDPARK, Wong often requested that ambassadors and other foreign dignitaries donate birds, once explaining, 'I attended every National Day cocktail party just to ask for birds'.

Woon was awarded the MERITORIOUS SERVICE MEDAL in 1962, and an honorary doctorate by the University of Singapore in 1974. In 1977, he was admitted as an advocate and solicitor.

Woodlands: new town.

Workers' Party: rally during 1984 general election.

Workers' Party This political party was founded in 1957 by DAVID MARSHALL, Singapore's first chief minister and former LABOUR FRONT leader. Between 1957 and 1958, the Workers' Party (WP) had four members of Parliament. However, after it was routed in the LEGISLATIVE ASSEMBLY ELECTION (1959), it faded into obscurity. The party was revived by a group of professionals led by lawyer J.B. JEYARETNAM in 1972. In 1981, Jeyaretnam, the party's secretary-general, became the first opposition member of Parliament since 1968. Jeyaretnam retained his seat in the 1984 general election but was disqualified from Parliament due to a conviction in 1986. In 1987, the government labelled some of the party's members communists and they were briefly detained under the INTERNAL SECURITY ACT. They were released on condition that they would not enter politics again.

In 1988, before the general election, the BARISAN SOSIALIS and the Singapore United Front were absorbed into the WP. LEE SIEW CHOH, Barisan Sosialis' former secretary-general, stood as a WP candidate. The party failed to win any seats in the 1988 election. But as their team in the Eunos group representation constituency (GRC) was the best opposition performer, two of its members were invited to become non-constituency members of Parliament (NCMPs). Lee Siew Choh accepted the seat while the other candidate, FRANCIS SEOW, left for the United States to avoid tax evasion charges.

In 1991 the party won one seat in the Hougang constituency with its vice secretary-general, LOW THIA KIANG, who was still its only elected representative in Parliament in 2006. The two political veterans, Lee Siew Choh and Jeyaretnam, left the party in 1996 and 1997 respectively, citing irreconcilable differences. Sylvia Lim, who was appointed the party's chairman in 2003, became the first woman to lead a political party in Singapore. Following the 2006 general election, Lim was appointed as an NCMP.

Workforce Development Agency Statutory board. Established in September 2003, the Workforce Development Agency (WDA) is a statutory board which helps workers and job-seekers maintain their employability and competitiveness. The WDA works with employers, workers, labour unions, industry associations and educational institutions to develop and promote continuing education and training.

World Intellectual Property Organization In 1974, the World Intellectual Property Organization (WIPO) became one of the 16 specialized agencies of the United Nations system.

The first major international treaty dealing with intellectual property (IP) came into force in 1884. This was the Paris Convention for the Protection of Industrial Property, which covered patents, TRADE-MARKS and industrial design. In 1886, copyright issues were first addressed under the Berne Convention for the Protection of Literary and Artistic Works. Today, WIPO, with its 183 member states, administers 23 treaties that deal with the protection of IP.

WIPO is a key leverage for Singapore's progress as an IP hub in the region. With official accession to WIPO in 1990, Singapore has progressively became a signatory to international treaties and conventions. These include the Paris Convention of 1994; the Patent Cooperation Treaty and Budapest Treaty on the International Recognition of the Deposit of Microorganisms for the Purposes of Patent Procedure of 1994; the Nice Agreement Concerning the International Classification of Goods and Services for the Purpose of Registration of Marks, and the Berne Convention of 1998; the Protocol Relating to the Madrid Agreement Concerning the International Registration of Marks of 2000; the International Union for the Protection of New Varieties of Plants (UPOV) of 2004; and most recently, the WIPO Copyright Treaty, WIPO

Performances and Phonograms Treaty, Geneva (1999) Act of the Hague Agreement Concerning the International Registration of Industrial Designs, and Brussels Convention Relating to the Distribution of Programme-Carrying Signals Transmitted by Satellite of 2005.

The WIPO office for the Asia-Pacific region is based in Singapore, which was chosen for its geographical location and established communication network. In March 2006, Singapore became the first Asian country to host the Diplomatic Conference on IP. The Diplomatic Conference on the Revised Trade Mark Law Treaty saw almost 400 IP policy makers and government experts, representing the majority of the 183 WIPO member states, participating in the negotiations held at the Suntec Singapore International Convention and Exhibition Centre. The treaty was successfully concluded and named the Singapore Treaty on the Law of Trade Marks.

World Trade Organization The World Trade Organization (WTO) was established on 1 January 1995 as the successor to the General Agreement on Tariffs and Trade (Gatt), which had existed from 1 January 1948 to 31 December 1994. Singapore joined Gatt in 1973 and became a member of the WTO on 1 January 1995 as one of its founding members. The WTO is the only global international organization dealing with the rules of trade between states. The establishment of the WTO, with its strengthened dispute settlement mechanism, has brought about greater predictability and security to the conduct of trade among nations. The WTO is crucial to Singapore's economic well-being. Singapore sees the WTO as a vital institution to achieve multilateral trade liberalization and to provide an open and rules-based system for international trade.

Singapore has demonstrated a strong commitment to the multilateral trading system of the WTO. This commitment can also be seen from Singapore's role in facilitating the negotiating process in the WTO. Singapore played a key role during the Uruguay Round in pursuit of its trade interests and to move the trade liberalization process forward. Singapore hosted the first World Trade Organization Ministerial Conference in December 1996 and has since been at the forefront in facilitating the launch of the Doha Round and the post-Doha negotiating process. Singapore has taken on leadership roles to help foster agreements and move negotiations forward. Then Minister for Trade and Industry George Yeo was the facilitator of the agriculture negotiations at the Ministerial Conference in Doha in 2001 and in Cancún in 2003. Singapore's permanent representative to the WTO, Burhan Gafoor, has chaired one of the negotiating groups of the Doha Round. Singapore officials have also chaired or participated in several WTO dispute settlement panels. Singapore and the WTO signed a Memorandum of Understanding (MOU) on technical cooperation in 1996 to establish a Third Country Training Programme (TCTP) that provides for joint training in developing countries on trade and WTO-related matters. To date, the TCTP in Singapore has trained over 150 officials from 35 member countries in the Asia-Pacific region, Africa and Latin America.

World War I For Singapore, the most dramatic events of World War I were two inter-related incidents: raids by the German cruiser *Emden*; and the SEPOY MUTINY of February 1915. The *Emden* bombarded Madras, ranged across the Indian Ocean, and ran up the British ensign so as to slip into Penang Harbour unchallenged on 28 October 1914. There it sank the Russian cruiser *Zemchug* and the French destroyer *Mosquet*. It captured 18 merchantmen, before the Australian cruiser HMAS *Sydney* forced it to beach off the Cocos Islands. The *Emden*'s crew were incarcerated in Singapore, where their presence emboldened Indian SEPOYS who were guarding them to mutiny in February 1915.

The wider significance of the war lay in its impact on Japan's position in East and Southeast Asia. As a British ally since the Anglo-Japanese Alliance of 1902, Japan allowed its sailors to help quell the sepoy mutiny. It also escorted allied ships in the Indian Ocean, freeing the British to concentrate on Europe. At the same time, Japan's position as an ally allowed it to seize German concessions in China and the Pacific, leading to expectations of post-war gains. Japan's 21 Demands on China in 1915 also led to suspicions that it would attempt to gain military influence and economic control over China. This weakened the basis for the Anglo-Japanese Alliance, heralding its lapse in 1921, and the related decision that year to develop Singapore as a British naval base.

Japanese ambitions also provoked a Chinese reaction, notably in the May Fourth Movement which started with student protests in China on 4 May 1919. The protests were aimed against the Versailles Peace Conference, where Japan was demanding that it receive German concessions in the Chinese province of Shandong.

World War II: coastal defence gun, c. 1941.

World War II: coastal lookout, c. 1941.

The May Fourth Movement's boost to Chinese nationalism underpinned the growth of the Kuomintang (Chinese Nationalist Party), with cross-fertilization between Singapore and China by means of shipping and labour movements. In this way, World War I set the scene for rising Chinese nationalist sentiment in post-war Singapore, leading up to the 1920s strikes and demonstrations and, in 1930, the formation of the MALAYAN COMMUNIST PARTY.

In the shorter term, the unrest contributed to the establishment of a post-war SPECIAL BRANCH in the Straits Settlements, which would spy on and penetrate these post-war organizations. Economically, the war's impact was difficult to disentangle from normal trade cycles. A war-fuelled boom in shipping and export of commodities was followed by a post-war slump, but Singapore continued to grow economically.

World War II Singapore commands the strategic shipping lane which forms the shortest route between the Indian and Pacific Oceans. This fact persuaded the United Kingdom's Royal Navy to make Singapore its main base for the defence of the extensive British empire territories and interests in East and Southeast Asia after WORLD WAR I. The main enemy was identified as Japan. When relations did indeed sour between the United Kingdom and Japan in 1941, Singapore became a principal target for the Japanese offensive that began the war in the Pacific.

The loss of Singapore was all but guaranteed by events occurring, and decisions made, before the Japanese invaded. However, British authorities in both London and Singapore publicly insisted that the 'FORTRESS OF THE EAST' would not fall. As a result, when Singapore capitulated in February 1942, defeat escalated to

humiliation. The Fall of Singapore drove the British to the periphery of the war against Japan, leaving the brunt of the fight—and thus the ensuing credit and influence—to the United States. It also accelerated the dismantling of the British empire after the war, despite the eventual Allied victory. On the other hand, victory in Singapore perhaps fed a Japanese tendency to assume they were stronger than they really were, and thus contributed to Japan's final defeat.

World War I had left the British physically and economically battered. To avoid friction with the United States, the British government allowed their military alliance with Japan to lapse, and to accept agreements which reduced the size of the Royal Navy. Yet Japan emerged as the most likely threat to the British empire in Asia, which somehow had to be protected with smaller forces and less funds. The compromise plan finally adopted became known as the Singapore Strategy.

From 1923, the British began to build a major naval base at SEMBAWANG on the north coast of Singapore. As any Japanese attack on the empire must come first from the sea, it was accepted that the Royal Navy would take the lead in any war against Japan. The base would enable the 'main fleet' to sail out to Asia if need be, to engage any Japanese attacking force. This strategy was never militarily realistic: it was unclear what the fleet would do once it arrived; the size of the base was reduced to save costs and would not be large enough for a fleet strong enough to face the Japanese; and it was unlikely the fleet would ever be available anyway.

The British knew that Australia and New Zealand relied on the Singapore Strategy for their own defence. The United Kingdom also depended on Australia, New Zealand and India to help maintain its status as a power. The British government

World War II: arrival of British troops, 1941.

World War II: Japanese troops cycling through Kuala Lumpur during the invasion.

World War II: Lieutenant-General Yamashita Tomoyuki.

World War II: Japanese postcard depicting the British surrender in February 1942.

World War II: bombing of Victoria Memorial Hall.

Prosperity and development opened up the west and south of Malaya enough to allow an invader to advance down the peninsula and attack Singapore from the north. From 1938, military planners had to assume that, in order to defend Singapore and hold the naval base, they needed to defend all of Malaya, to keep an invader out of air-strike range. The Royal Air Force hoped to prevent an invasion by intercepting any invader far out to sea, and built airbases along the east coast and in the north of the peninsula. However when war erupted in Europe, it could not spare enough aircraft to use these bases effectively. Yet now that the bases were there, an invader could not be allowed to seize them and bring enemy aircraft close enough to cut Singapore off from all reinforcement.

In 1940, France surrendered, leaving the British without any major allies in Europe. Japan moved its forces into northern Vietnam, then a French colony, bringing them within striking distance of Singapore. The British government, led by Sir WINSTON CHURCHILL, was forced to admit there was little chance the fleet could be spared to meet any Japanese threat, but still insisted Singapore be preserved for the navy. Churchill decided to concentrate on the fight for survival. He gambled that any Japanese attack would provoke the United States to help the British, and that the powerful US fleet would prevent the Japanese from taking Singapore. Defence plans for Singapore would rest on the premise that the air force would break up any invasion, but the air force was deployed in Europe. By 1941, the army found itself in a terrible situation, required to hold a naval base for a fleet which might never arrive, and to protect an air force which was not there. The defence plans were now utterly divorced from the real military situation.

Reinforcements were sent to Malaya and Singapore during 1941. The army was built up piecemeal with whatever formations could be spared. None had combat experience. Time ran out before they could be trained in jungle warfare, or build the defences needed to hold such a large area. Planners expected the Japanese to land in neutral southern Thailand, then move into northern Malaya. Local commanders devised a plan—OPERATION MATADOR—to launch a pre-emptive strike into southern Thailand if the Japanese moved towards the peninsula. However, until the eve of the war, the British government refused to allow local commanders to trigger the plan before the Japanese moved. They feared that if the British violated Thai neutrality first, this could jeopardize US intervention.

The Japanese enjoyed the aggressor's advantage of knowing exactly when, where and how they would attack. Three of the best divisions in the Imperial Japanese Army, specially and intensively trained and equipped for jungle warfare, were assigned

feared the backlash from any confession of weakness more than the danger of relying on an unsound grand strategy. They decided to take a military, rather than a political, risk. Attention focused on how to defend the base and ensure it would be available for the fleet if needed. The length of time during which Singapore was expected to defend the base against any Japanese attack, while waiting for the fleet to arrive from Europe, was called the 'period before relief'. This steadily increased, from 42 days in mid–1939, to 180 days in 1941.

Singapore is separated from the Malay Peninsula only by the narrow Strait of Johor, but as infrastructure in southern Malaya was not well developed in the 1920s, land attack from the north appeared improbable. Attack from the sea seemed the most likely threat. The naval base was sited on the northern coast of the island, protected by a combination of heavy coastal artillery—eventually including five 15-inch guns, capable of taking on the largest battleships—supported by beach defences and four airbases, meant to hold bomber aircraft able to intercept an invader well out to sea. Unfortunately, the situation deteriorated in the 1930s.

to the attack. Lieutenant-General YAMASHITA TOMOYUKI, Japan's best field commander, was placed in command. Powerful air and naval forces supported them. When the invasion fleet set sail in early December 1941, the Japanese faced a larger army, but their troops were more experienced, better trained, better led and had far stronger air support. Even though they invaded exactly where the defenders expected them to, the fall of Singapore was all but inevitable.

The Japanese had allotted 100 days for the fall of Singapore. They took the island in 70, and captured more than 125,000 British empire troops (double their own number).

In addition to the gravely compromised position from which the defenders started, other factors contributed to the final outcome. The first setback was the successful neutralization of the Pacific Fleet by the Japanese strike on Pearl Harbor. This destroyed Churchill's gamble that US naval forces would divide Japanese strength, giving him time to reinforce Singapore. The pre-emptive advance into Thailand was called off. This left the army spread out and confused. The Japanese advance pushed the British out of their main positions in the north, and into headlong retreat, in fewer than four days. Japanese air attacks secured dominance of the air in three days. The British navy was routed. Days before the Japanese invasion, two capital ships, HMS PRINCE OF WALES and HMS REPULSE, arrived at last at the Sembawang naval base. They sailed north to contest the invasion. On the third day of the war, they were caught without air cover at sea and destroyed, northeast of Tioman Island; this was the first successful attack by air forces on capital ships at sea.

These defeats left the defenders, after only 100 hours, without any hope of help from the Pacific, with all their plans ruined, and facing an enemy with the initiative on

Woffles Wu

the ground, dominance in the air, and command of the sea. The fate of Singapore now rested on a race between the Japanese advance and the ability of the British government to dispatch reinforcements. Meanwhile, ground forces had to hold their positions, as the British insisted that Singapore would not fall.

Yamashita knew the campaign was a race. Taking calculated risks with his supplies and the fitness of his units, he drove his army forward, keeping the defenders off balance and defeating them before they could regroup. The strategy pursued by his counterpart, Lieutenant-General ARTHUR PERCIVAL, played into Yamashita's hands. Once the pre-war plans had fallen apart, Percival did not take any calculated risk to try to stem the onslaught. To carry out his orders to hold the naval base—which meant keeping the Japanese as far away as possible, and denying them the airbases—he tried to stand and fight in the north. To prevent a Japanese naval landing closer to Singapore, he kept his army divided, covering too many threats simultaneously. This allowed the Japanese to defeat his less experienced troops, one formation at a time. London might have untied Percival's hands, allowing him to destroy the naval base and fight to delay rather than hold the Japanese. However, to the end, the British government preferred the military to the political risk. The defenders were driven onto the now isolated island of Singapore on the last day of January 1942.

The siege of Singapore itself was a foregone conclusion. While some reinforcements did arrive, they were too few, too late. The island was full of refugees who had streamed down the Malay Peninsula, compromising Singapore's stocks of food and water. Singapore's defences were not designed to withstand attack from the north. Coastal defence guns were used against the attackers, and the Japanese had stretched their supply lines thin in the course of their rapid advance. But they had the island surrounded, and could land where they wanted on an all but unfortified northern coast. The final invasion began on the night of 8 February. The fighting was sometimes intense, but the defenders failed

to concentrate and coordinate their troops effectively. After a week, Percival's army unravelled and the 'impregnable fortress' collapsed. On 15 February 1942, Percival surrendered the largest British force lost in the war, under a white flag flying next to the Union Jack, in full view of Japanese newsreel cameras.

The Fall of Singapore had different implications for different principals. It drew the Japanese further into a war they could never win. For the people of Malaya and Singapore, it led to the darkest period of their history—the JAPANESE OCCUPATION—but was also the first serious step on the road to post-war independence. The contrast between public boasting and promises about 'Fortress Singapore', and the speed and disarray with which its garrison capitulated, made an indelible impression on the world. The witnessing of British weakness and humiliation at the hands of an Asian power, as well as resentment at being left to suffer a cruel occupation under that same power, fuelled the rise of nationalism in the last European colonies in Southeast Asia, including Singapore.

British forces recovered, fought back and played a contributory role in final victory in the war. But when they returned to Singapore in 1945, the British found the region no longer impressed or intimidated by European influence.

See also MALAYA CAMPAIGN and JAPANESE OCCUPATION.

Wu, Woffles (1960–) Doctor. Celebrity plastic surgeon Woffles Wu Tze-liang was named after a rabbit from Enid Blyton's *The Magic Far Away Tree* (1943). He was educated at St Andrew's School and at the Faculty of Medicine at the National University of Singapore where he obtained his MBBS in 1984. He is a fellow of the Royal College of Surgeons (General Surgery) (Edinburgh) and a fellow of the Academy of Medicine (Singapore) (plastic surgery). Wu is a well-known society figure and the plastic-surgeon-of-choice for many notables and celebrities. He pioneered the Woffles Lift, a non-surgical face-lift that leaves no scars. This patented innovation was hailed by many as the most important advancement in face-lift surgery. Wu is the only Asian plastic surgeon featured in the book, *Aesthetic Surgery* (2005) by Angelika Taschen, which features the world's top 19 cosmetic surgeons.

Wu Peng Seng (1913–) Photographer. Wu Peng Seng, also known as Goh Peng Seng, is noted for his photographic travelogues and landscapes. Born in Swatow (present-day Shantou), China, and educated in Shanghai and Hong Kong, he worked in Vietnam before settling in Singapore in the mid-1950s. He was made an associate of the Royal Photographic Society (RPS) in the United Kingdom

in 1956 and received an RPS Fellowship in 1960. Wu was granted the Honorary Excellence Distinction by the International Federation of Photographic Art (HonEFIAP)—the highest honour it can bestow—and honorary life membership of the Photographic Society of Singapore in 1997. He was awarded the CULTURAL MEDALLION in 1990.

Wubeizhi Written in the early 16th century, and presented to the Ming court in 1628, the Wubeizhi (Treatise on Military Preparation) contains information on maritime regions outside China, including geographical knowledge gathered by the Chinese over the preceding centuries.

The Wubeizhi included the Mao Kun Map. This is based on information extracted from the accounts of the early 15th-century Ming voyages, particularly those led by Admiral ZHENG HE. The map, which was probably drawn around 1422, encompassed the coastline stretching from the Yellow Sea, through Southeast Asia and the Indian Ocean littoral, to the east coast of Africa. The names of states and ports, and such navigational landmarks as hills and islands along the sailing routes, were included on the map. Sailing information, based on the Chinese magnetic compass and a time-keeping method using the burning-rate of large joss-sticks, was also marked on the map.

Three geographical landmarks pertaining to Singapore appeared on the Mao Kun Map: Jilimen (Karimun Island), Danmaxi (TEMASEK—Singapore Island) and Baijiao (PEDRA BRANCA). Jilimen and Baijiao served as navigational landmarks, while Danmaxi denotes a hill, probably present-day Fort Canning Hill. According to the sailing directions, ships had to sail past Baijiao, through LONGYAMEN (Dragon's Tooth Gate), then on to Jilimen.

Wu Peng Seng

Wubeizhi: Danmaxi is illustrated top, second from left. Longyamen is right of spine, centre.

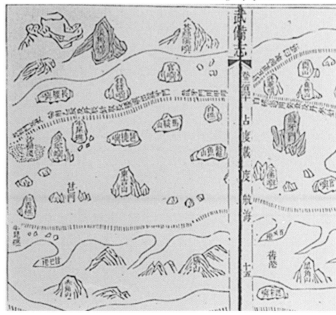

Xi Ni'er: Qing Xin Mo Yi (2001).

Xiang Yun: December Rains (1996).

Xu Fuji: Tui Kai Ge Li Men (Pushing Open the Partition) (2003).

X-Periment: psychedelic record cover.

X'Ho (unknown–) Musician, disc jockey and writer. Formerly known as Chris Ho, X'Ho (still pronounced 'Chris Ho') formed Singapore's first new wave art-punk band in 1983, Zircon Lounge. The band released an album that year called *Regal Vigor*, scoring minor hits including 'Saviour' and 'Chanachai'. He went solo in 1988 after the band broke up and recorded three solo albums: *Nite Songs In Day-glo* (1989), *PunkMonkHunk* (1994) and *X' With An X: Me All Good No Bad* (1999). *PunkMonkHunk* was named one of the year's best albums by Japanese critic Hiroshi Shinozaki, who was responsible for introducing Dick Lee to Japan. Aside from *X' With An X*, which is a spoken-word album, his solo work has all been new wave, with lyrics showing traces of punk influences such as The Sex Pistols and The Clash. Ho was a regular voice on the radio in the 1990s and wrote two books on popular culture, *Skew Me, You Rebel Meh?* (1998) and *Attack Of The SM Space Encroachers* (2002). In late 2002, he formed a new band, Zircon Gov. Pawn Starz which produces dance-driven music with lyrics that reflect socio-political concerns.

X-Periment Popular music group. Formed in October 1967, the original line-up featured Tony Shotam (guitar), Mervyn Nonis (keyboards), formerly of the Commancheros, and S. Raj and Frankie Suppiah from the Easybeats, on bass and drums respectively. The psychedelic influences of both the Commancheros and the Easybeats were brought to bear on the new group. Vocalist Joe Chandran, who had previously sung Hindustani and Tamil songs with other bands, also joined the group. The group found a mentor and lead singer in Siva Choy, who by then was no longer performing with The Cyclones and The Checkmates.

X'Ho

The group played a mix of soul and rhythm-and-blues, signing with recording label RCA and released their first EP in 1969, which featured four tracks of psychedelic music. They also made a joint LP, *Soul Sauce*, with the Idaly Sisters from Indonesia. The band switched to the EMI label in the early 1970s and played on the club circuit during that decade. A second LP, *Chinatown Rock*, was released on the WEA label in 1978, which captured their shift to a disco sound. The group disbanded in 1983.

Xi Ni'er (1957–) Author. Xi Ni'er is the pen name of Chia Hwee Pheng, who is an engineer by profession. He is also the president of the SINGAPORE ASSOCIATION OF WRITERS. A post-modernist writer, Xi Ni'er experiments with new styles, and writes about marginalized elements of Singapore society. His poetry collection *Bang Jia Sui Yue* (To Trap Time) (1989) and short story collection *Sheng Ming Li Nan Yi Cheng Shou De Zhong* (Life's Heavy Burdens) (1992) were awarded the National Book Development Council of Singapore Book Award in 1990 and 1994 respectively. Xi Ni'er also won Nanyang Siang Pau's Golden Lion Award (*Jin Shi Jiang*) in 1982 and 1983.

Xiang Yun (1961–) Actress. Born Chen Cui Chang, Xiang Yun graduated from the first batch of the Singapore Broadcasting Corporation's Drama Training Class. She started her acting career in children's drama in 1982 and went on to act in the drama serials *Chun Feng De Yi* (Double Blessings) and *Jie Jing* (All That Glitters Is Not Gold) in 1983. However, it was in the blockbuster drama serial *Wu Suo Nan Yang* (The Awakening) (1984), where she played a long-suffering wife, that she made her mark.

Aside from television, Xiang Yun performed on stage in *Yu Ji* (December Rains) in 1996 and *Hu Die Chun Qing* (Butterflies are Free) in 2001. She made her cinema debut in Jack Neo's I NOT STUPID (2001).

Xiang Yun was voted Best Supporting Actress at the 1998 and 2000 Star Awards, and was one of MediaCorp's 'Top 10 Most Popular Female Artistes' in 2000, 2001 and 2002. She is married to actor EDMUND CHEN ZHICAI.

Xingcha Shenglan In 1436, Fei Xin, a junior official who accompanied Admiral ZHENG HE on some of his maritime voyages, wrote the *Xingcha Shenglan* (literally, 'The Overall Survey of the Star Raft'). The 'star raft' refers to the Imperial Ambassador's ship. The text contains Fei Xin's travel account, and includes mention of LONGYAMEN (Dragon's Tooth Gate). He also remarked, in his account, that local pirates often attacked vessels sailing through this strait.

xinyao See CHINESE POPULAR MUSIC.

Xu Fuji (1960–) Poet and academic. Xu Fuji (Koh Hock Kiat) is associate professor in the Asian Languages and Cultures Department at the National Institute of Education and vice-president of the Singapore Association of Writers. He has also written under the pseudonym Ben Xing. Xu's writing style was influenced by modernist and post-modernist Taiwanese literature he read while studying Chinese language and literature at National Taiwan University (1982–86). His writings include *Lü Ye Kai Chuang* (Green Leaves Open the Window) (1999) and the poem 'Zhang Yu Shu' (Changi Tree) (undated).

Yaacob Ibrahim (1955–) Academic and politician. Yaacob Ibrahim was educated at Bedok Boys' School, Kembangan Primary School, Broadrick Secondary School, Tanjong Katong Technical Secondary School and the University of Singapore, where he graduated with an honours degree in civil engineering (1980). After working briefly with the Bylander Meinhardt Partnership (1980–84), he obtained a scholarship for Stanford University. After gaining his doctorate in 1989, he became a post-doctoral fellow at Cornell University.

In 1990, Yaacob returned to Singapore and joined the Department of Civil Engineering at the National University of Singapore as a research scientist. He was appointed senior lecturer there in 1993. Yaacob was council member of the MAJLIS UGAMA ISLAM SINGAPURA (MUIS) (1992–96). He became chairman of MENDAKI in 2002.

In 1997, Yaacob entered politics on the People's Action Party ticket and became a member of Parliament for Jalan Besar group representation constituency, a seat he continued to hold as of 2006. He has served as parliamentary secretary for the Ministry of Communications (1998); senior parliamentary secretary, Ministry of Communications and Information Technology (2001); minister of state for the Ministry of Community Development and Sports (2001); minister-in-charge of Muslim affairs (2002–); minister for community development and sports (2003–04); and minister for the environment and water resources (2004–).

Ya'acob Mohamed (1925–1989) Politician and diplomat. Ya'acob Mohamed was born in Kelantan. While he was still an infant, his family moved to Johor, where he later received his education. Ya'acob then moved to Singapore to continue his studies.

During World War II, Ya'acob was drawn to the MALAYAN PEOPLE'S ANTI-JAPANESE ARMY (MPAJA). After the end of the war, he joined a number of left-wing organizations, including the Malayan Nationalist Party. In 1949, he joined the United Malays National Organization (UMNO), after some of these left-wing organizations were outlawed. He soon became the head of UMNO's Bukit Panjang branch. To support himself financially, he became a barber.

By 1957, Ya'acob became disillusioned with UMNO, and decided to join the People's Action Party (PAP) in 1958. Within months, he was appointed chairman of the PAP's Bukit Panjang branch. In 1959, he contested in Bukit Timah constituency and won. He was appointed parliamentary secretary for national development. In the GENERAL ELECTION (1963), he won a seat in what was then considered the UMNO stronghold ward of Southern Islands.

In 1980, Ya'acob stepped down as member of Parliament of Kampong Ubi and was appointed Singapore's ambassador to Egypt, a post he held until 1986. He died of leukaemia in 1989. He was posthumously admitted into the DISTINGUISHED SERVICE ORDER in 1990.

Yamashita Tomoyuki, Lieutenant-General

(1885–1946) Japanese military officer. Born in Shikoku, Japan, Yamashita Tomoyuki trained to be a professional soldier in the Imperial Japanese Army. He graduated 16th in a class of 920 at the Japanese Military Academy in 1905, then sixth in a class of 56 from the War College in 1908. For these achievements, he received a sword from the emperor.

Yamashita embarked on a varied career which encompassed regimental, staff and high-command appointments, as well as diplomacy. From 1918 to 1922, Yamashita was posted to study European Affairs in Switzerland and Germany. He then served as a military attaché in Austria from February 1927 to August 1930. He led a mission to consult Japan's allies, Germany and Italy. In this role he had discussions in person with Adolf Hitler.

In China, Yamashita was chosen to command the elite 3rd Regiment of the Imperial Guards Division.

In staff postings, Yamashita helped modernize Japanese army doctrine and organization. Yet he also became involved in the factional feuds that marred the Japanese army from the 1920s onwards. This led to difficulties between Yamashita and Tojo Hideki (later Japan's wartime prime minister). On 26 February 1936, a coup d'état in the Japanese army occured. Yamashita was implicated and incurred the Japanese emperor's wrath. For the rest of his army career, Yamashita was burdened with expiating the offence that incurred the emperor's displeasure.

Yamashita's commands in China were so successful that, in late 1941, the army general staff put aside political objections and appointed him to command the most important offensive of the war at that stage—the invasion of Malaya. Yamashita took command of the 25th Army on 8 November, inheriting a broad outline plan which allowed him to decide on the details himself.

Yamashita's mission was to conquer Singapore within 100 days without suffering heavy casualties, as it was hoped that most of his ground troops could thereafter be used to reinforce other Japanese offensives. Yamashita enjoyed strong naval and air support, and these proved material to his success. Yet he himself made three decisions that were just as important.

First, because the MALAYA CAMPAIGN was a race between his advance and British efforts to reinforce defences, Yamashita decided that his forces would have to drive forward from the start of the campaign. He took the risk of running ahead of his supply lines in order to knock the British off-balance. Yamashita called this strategy *kirimomi sakusen*—'driving charge'. Second, he decided to invade northern Malaya and southern Thailand at the same time, in order to divide defenders and seize vital airbases from which ground forces could be supported. Third, he left one of his divisions in Japan in order to retain as much capacity to supply his advancing forces as possible.

Yamashita's 'driving charge' unhinged defenders within four days, and kept them disorganized and in retreat. Well before the British high command could react effectively, Yamashita's army had isolated Singapore. Yamashita drove his men relentlessly, but led from the front. And it was Yamashita's generalship that removed any chance of the British halting the Japanese advance. When Yamashita accepted the surrender of MALAYA COMMAND at the FORD MOTOR FACTORY on the evening of 15 February 1942, he became popularly known in Japan as the 'Tiger of Malaya'.

However, Yamashita was not as adept at politics as he was at warfare. A careless speech he made in April 1942, in which he said that the people of Malaya had become citizens of Imperial Japan, caused embarrassment to the Japanese government as it was out of step with government policy on the nationality of people in occupied countries. His superiors and Prime Minister Tojo saw this as evidence of Yamashita's arrogance. This faux pas was one of the reasons he was sent to Manchuria, where he was put in command of an army guarding against an unlikely Soviet attack. Yamashita

Yan Hui Chang

did not return to action until the autumn of 1944, after Tojo had been forced to resign.

Yamashita was tasked with the defence of the Philippines, which was about to be attacked by an Allied armada. The Japanese high command regarded this campaign as its last chance to keep the Allies from attacking the Japanese home islands. The high command overruled Yamashita's decision to concentrate on defending Luzon, and forced him to fight hopeless battles in Leyte.

Yamashita conducted a skilful fighting retreat into northern Luzon in 1945, and was never captured. He emerged from the jungles of the Philippines only to surrender after Japan had capitulated. A brutal rampage by a Japanese garrison in Manila (in defiance of Yamashita's direct orders to evacuate the city) resulted in the destruction of the Philippine capital.

Yamashita was tried as a war criminal by the United States. His trial remains controversial, as he was viewed as one of the few senior Japanese generals to have tried to maintain discipline amongst his troops. Yet he did oversee, and was complicit in, the SOOK CHING massacres of 1942—a fact that tarnished his career.

Yamashita was executed in Manila on 23 February 1946.

Yan Hui Chang

(1954–) Conductor and composer. Born in China, Yan Hui Chang graduated from the Shanghai Conservatory of Music (1983), after which he was appointed principal conductor-cum-artistic director of the China Central Folk Orchestra. He held concurrent positions at the Beijing Concert Hall Philharmonic and Folk Orchestra, the Department of Operatic Music of the Shaanxi Arts Academy and Kaohsiung City Chinese Orchestra.

Yan settled in Singapore in 1992 as music director of Naxos (Singapore). Since 1997, he has been the artistic director and principal conductor of the Hong Kong Chinese Orchestra. In 2001, he was awarded the CULTURAL MEDALLION.

In composition, Yan's works include symphonic poem, *The Sound of Water* and pipa solo, *Nostalgia*. Between 1992 and 1993, he wrote and recorded *Clouds*, *The Moon*, *A Music Journey on the Yellow River* and *Song of the General*. Yan is visiting professor at many music conservatories, and received Hong Kong's Bronze Bauhinia Star in 2004 for musical excellence and efforts in promoting Chinese music.

Yap, Arthur

(1943–2006) Poet. Arthur Yap Chioh Hiong graduated in 1965 from the University of Singapore with an English honours degree. He secured a master's degree in linguistics and English language teaching from Leeds University, United Kingdom, in 1975, and a PhD from the National University of Singapore in 1984.

Ya'acob Mohamed

Lieutenant-General Yamashita Tomoyuki

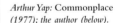

Arthur Yap: Commonplace *(1977); the author (below).*

George Yeo

Philip Yeo

Robert Yeo

Joscelin Yeo

He taught at the university's department of English language and literature from 1979 until his retirement in 1998.

Yap's first volume, *Only Lines* (1971), won the inaugural National Book Development Council of Singapore (NBDCS) Book Award for Poetry in 1979. *Down the Line* (1980) won the 1982 NBDCS Book Award for Poetry, while *Man Snake Apple and Other Poems* (1986) won the same award in 1988. *The space of city trees: selected poems* (2000) includes 121 of his published poems. Yap's pervasive interest in the commonplace is underpinned by analytical and emotional discipline and linguistic wit. Written in free verse, his poems eschew upper-case letters while observing other rules of punctuation. They resemble spoken Singaporean English in their choppy, speech-like cadences.

Yap received both the CULTURAL MEDALLION for Literature and the Southeast Asia Write Award in 1983. He died after a long battle with cancer of the larynx.

Ye Cong (1950–) Conductor. Born in China, Ye Cong began studying conducting in 1979 at the Shanghai Conservatory of Music and the Mannes College of Music in New York in 1981. In 1983, he enrolled in the master's degree program at Yale University. He joined the SINGAPORE CHINESE ORCHESTRA as music director in 2002 while holding concurrent positions as music director of the South Bend Symphony Orchestra in the United States and the conductor laureate in the Hong Kong Sinfonietta. Prior to this, he held similar positions at the Northwest Indiana Symphony Orchestra, Florida Orchestra, Albany Symphony Orchestra of New York, the Hua Xia Ensemble in Beijing and the Shanghai New Ensemble and has guest conducted in Asia, North America and Europe.

Ye Feng (1936–1995) Comedian. Ye Feng was the stage name of Xiao Tiancai. He regularly watched performances at the Broadway Song Stage in the Happy World Amusement Park in the 1950s, and his talent for singing was spotted by the manager. He soon joined Happy World as a full-time performer. In 1959, he was invited to partner WANG SA at the Xin Sheng Song Stage at the NEW WORLD Amusement Park.

The duo's comedy show was a hit, with their special blend of Mandarin and dialect.

JOSCELIN YEO: SEA GAMES MEDALS WON		
Year	Event	Medals
1991	SEA Games (Manila)	2 silver, 3 bronze
1993	SEA Games (Singapore)	9 gold
1995	SEA Games (Chiangmai)	7 gold
1997	SEA Games (Jakarta)	3 gold
1999	SEA Games (Brunei)	6 gold
2001	SEA Games (Kuala Lumpur)	3 gold
2003	SEA Games (Hanoi)	6 gold
2005	SEA Games (Manila)	6 gold
Source: Singapore Sports Council		

They appeared regularly in television variety shows and became household names in the 1960s. In the 1970s, they ventured into the Hong Kong market and made films such as *A Niu Ru Cheng Ji* (The Crazy Bumpkins) (1974) and *A Niu Qi Yu Ji* (Crazy Bumpkins in Singapore) (1976).

Yeo, George (1954–) Politician. George Yeo Yong-Boon was educated at St Joseph's Institution. He was awarded the President's Scholarship and Singapore Armed Forces (SAF) Scholarship, and studied at Cambridge University.

On his return to Singapore, he joined the Singapore Armed Forces (SAF) as a signals officer, and rose quickly through the ranks to become brigadier-general in 1988. That same year, he entered politics and won a seat on the People's Action Party ticket in the Aljunied group representation constituency, a seat he continued to hold as of 2006.

Yeo was appointed minister of state for finance and foreign affairs (1988–90). He has since served as acting minister for information and the arts (1990–91); second minister for foreign affairs (1991–94); minister for information and the arts (1991–99); minister for health (1994–97); second minister for trade and industry (1997–99); minister for trade and industry (1999–2004); and minister for foreign affairs (2004–).

Yeo, Joscelin (1981–) Sportswoman. Yeo began swimming at the age of seven. In later years, she became the first swimmer in Singapore to beat the 60-second barrier for the 100-m freestyle. She went on to win 40 gold medals at eight Southeast Asian Games. Yeo won a bronze medal at the 1994 Asian Games in Hiroshima, and another at the 2002 Asian Games in Busan; and she was the first Singaporean to compete in four separate Olympic Games—Barcelona (1992), Atlanta (1996), Sydney (2000) and Athens (2004).

Joscelin Yeo was named Sportsgirl of the Year in 1994, and Sportswoman of the Year in 1994, 1996 and 2000. She was also a recipient of the Anne Broussard Spirit Award (2002) and the Arthur Ashe Jr Sports Scholar Award (2003) at the University of Texas, United States. In 2004, she won a Rhodes Scholarship to study at Oxford University.

By 2005, Yeo was the holder of national records in six individual events: the 50-m freestyle; 50-m butterfly; 100-m freestyle; 100-m butterfly; 200-m individual medley; and 400-m individual medley.

Yeo, Philip (1946–) Civil servant. Philip Yeo Liat Kok was educated at St Joseph's Institution and then at the University of Toronto on a Colombo Plan Scholarship, graduating with a degree in industrial engineering in 1970. Yeo then joined the Administrative Service and was posted to

Ye Feng: **Crazy Bumpkins in Singapore** *(1976).*

the Ministry of Defence where he became permanent secretary in 1979. In 1980, he founded Singapore Computer Systems (SCS). He became chairman of the National Computer Board the following year, remaining there until 1987.

In 1986, Yeo was appointed chairman of the Economic Development Board (EDB), and then co-chairman of the EDB (2001). While at the EDB, Yeo also served as chairman of Chartered Industries of Singapore; Singapore Shipbuilding and Engineering; Singapore Technologies Industrial Corporation; Singapore Technologies Ventures; and Singapore Technologies Holdings (1987–93). Yeo has also held other important posts, including chairman of the Science and Engineering Research Council (2003); chairman of CapitaLand Ltd (2000); and chairman of the Agency for Science, Technology and Research (A★STAR). Yeo received the MERITORIOUS SERVICE MEDAL in 1991.

Yeo, Robert (1940–) Poet and playwright. Robert Yeo Cheng Chuan graduated from the University of Singapore and the Institute of Education, University of London. He has taught at the National Institute of Education and Nanyang Technological University. He currently teaches creative writing at Singapore Management University.

Yeo has published three collections of poetry: *Coming Home, Baby* (1971), *And Napalm Does Not Help* (1977), and *A Part of Three* (1989). *Leaving Home, Mother* (1999) is a selection of 85 published poems. Yeo's only novel, *The Adventures of Holden Heng* (1986), is concerned with the sexual education of its antihero.

One of the pioneers of Singaporean drama in English, Yeo has written six plays. *The Singapore Trilogy* (2001), comprising *Are You There, Singapore?* (1974), *One Year Back Home* (1980) and *Changi* (1996), dramatizes tensions between individual freedoms and the state. *Are You There, Singapore?* broke all box office records then for a theatre performance in Singapore. *Second Chance* (1988) is Yeo's foray into the 'Great Marriage Debate' which was initiated in 1983 when then Prime Minister Lee Kuan Yew lamented the fact that many graduate women were not marrying. His *The Eye of History* (1992) is a fantasy played out in scenes between key figures such as Munshi

Yeo Hiap Seng: members of the Yeo family, 1963.

Abdullah, Sir Stamford Raffles and Lee Kuan Yew. Yeo recently completed *Your Bed is Your Coffin*, a play, and the libretto for *Fences of the Heart*, an opera on the effects of the 1965 separation of Singapore from Malaysia. Yeo received the Public Service Medal in 1991 for his services to drama. He has begun work on his memoirs.

Yeo, Thomas (1936–) Artist. Thomas Yeo was educated at the Nanyang Academy of Fine Arts in the early 1960s, and continued his studies at the Chelsea School of Art and the Hammersmith College of Art & Architecture in London. By the time Yeo returned to Singapore in 1968, his style had moved away from the representational to the abstract. He has long been active in the arts community, serving as an advisor and judge at art competitions. He has documented the local visual arts scene in *Singapore Artists Speak* (1990) and *Change: 20 Singapore Artists—A Decade Of Their Work* (1991). He was also project director of *Young Contemporary Artists In Singapore* (2000), a book that highlights the works of 90 budding artists. Yeo was awarded the CULTURAL MEDALLION in 1984.

Yeo Cheow Tong (1947–) Politician. Yeo was educated at the Anglo-Chinese School and at the University of Western Australia, where he obtained a degree in mechanical engineering on a Colombo Plan Scholarship (1971). After graduation, he worked for the Economic Development Board (1972–75) and LeBlond Makino Asia Pte Ltd (1975–85), where he rose to become managing director.

Yeo entered politics on the People's Action Party ticket, and was elected member of Parliament for the Hong Kah constituency in 1984. He was appointed minister of state for health and foreign affairs (1985–87) and subsequently served as senior minister of state for foreign affairs (1988–90). He also served as acting minister for health (1987–90); minister for health (1990–94, 1997–99); minister for community development (1991–94); minister for trade and industry (1994–97); minister for the environment (1997–99); and minister for communications and information technology (1999–2001); and minister for transport (2001–06). Yeo

stepped down from Cabinet after the 2006 general election, but remained as a member of Parliament.

Yeo Hiap Seng Food and beverage manufacturer and distributor. Yeo Hiap Seng Ltd produces more than 200 varieties of traditional Asian drinks and sauces, canned food and instant noodles sold in more than 60 countries. Its non-carbonated beverages are marketed under the Yeo's, Pink Dolphin, Justea and H-Two-O brands. While Yeo's chrysanthemum tea and soya bean drinks continue to be its flagship drinks, new offerings include flavoured green tea, wheatgrass, black soy and isotonic drinks. The company is also the bottler and distributor for international brands such as Pepsi, 7-Up, Mug and Mountain Dew. It is the distributor for Evian and Volvic mineral water.

The history of Yeo Hiap Seng (YHS) dates back to 1900 when its founder Yeo Keng Lian, started a small soy-sauce operation in Changchow (present-day Zhangzhou) in Fujian province, China. The Yeo Hiap Seng factory in Singapore was started in 1935 by his two eldest sons, Yeo Thian In and Yeo Thian Kiew, at Havelock Road.

In 1950, YHS began making and selling other products, including its popular canned curry chicken, under the Yeo's brand. The factory moved to a new nine-acre site at Dunearn Road on Bukit Timah. It pioneered the bottling of soya bean milk in 1955.

YHS was listed on the Stock Exchange of Singapore in 1969. A failed attempt in 1989 to carve out a share of the US market through the purchase of American canned-food maker Chun King proved costly for the Yeo family. It led to heavy losses and a highly publicized family feud that ended in 1995, when control of the group was ceded to property tycoon NG TENG FONG. Ng's real estate company, FAR EAST ORGANIZATION, was interested in using the YHS factory site for residential development projects, and subsequently built the Garden Vista condominium there.

Ng's son, Philip Ng, became managing director and chief executive officer of YHS, which is now one of the two Singapore-listed vehicles under the Far East Organization. Group revenue was $366.7 million for the financial year 2005, posting a pre-tax loss of $4.3 million.

Yeo Ning Hong (1943–) Academic and politician. Yeo Ning Hong graduated from the University of Singapore on a state scholarship with a first class honours degree in chemistry in 1966. He subsequently obtained a PhD from Cambridge University, winning the Charles Darwin Memorial Prize there in 1970. From 1971 to 1974, Yeo lectured at the University of Singapore, before leaving to join the private sector.

Yeo entered politics in 1980 on the People's Action Party ticket, and was elect-

ed member of Parliament for Kim Seng constituency. In 1981, he was made minister of state for defence, and subsequently served as minister for communications (1981–83); minister for communications and information (1983–85); and minister for defence (1991–94).

From 1995 to 1997, Yeo served as executive chairman of Singapore Technologies Pte Ltd and, from 1994 to 2002, executive chairman of the Port of Singapore Authority. Other positions he has held include president, then patron, of the Singapore National Olympic Council; chairman of the Singapore Tourism Board; chairman of the Singapore Symphony Orchestra Trust Fund; and honorary president of the Southeast Asian Games Federation. In 1994, he was appointed chairman of the Singapore Totalisator Board.

For his contributions, Yeo was admitted into the DISTINGUISHED SERVICE ORDER in 2002.

Yeo Tiam Siew (1904–2000) Businessman and philanthropist. Yeo Tiam Siew was the son of Yeo Cheow Tock and Khoo Ngaw Neo. His original name was Yeo Chiang Seng, but his parents changed this to Yeo Tiam Siew because he was constantly ill as a child—it is a traditional Chinese belief that a change of name can bring a change of fortune.

Yeo was educated at the Anglo-Chinese School, Ai Tong School and Tong Nam School, but was forced to discontinue his studies due to financial difficulties. He took up part-time teaching and studied to pass the Junior and Senior Cambridge Examinations.

In 1923, Yeo graduated from Raffles Institution. He then worked as an apprentice junior clerk at the Ho Hong Bank, and was promoted to assistant secretary in 1927. Three years later, he was appointed secretary. When Ho Hong Bank merged with the Chinese Commercial Bank and the Oversea-Chinese Bank to form the Oversea-Chinese Banking Corporation (OCBC) in 1932, Yeo was appointed manager of the Kuala Lumpur branch. Yeo then rose through the ranks to become general manager of the Foreign

Thomas Yeo: the artist (above); Earth Spray (left).

Yeo Cheow Tong

Yeo Ning Hong

Yeoh Ghim Seng: at the opening of Parliament, 1985.

Ying E Ding

Ying Peian: the author;
An Xian Sheng De Shi Jie
(The World of Mr An)
(1974) (top).

Ying Fo Fui Kun: as it looked in the 1950s.

Exchange Department and branch manager of OCBC's London branch. He retired in 1969.

Yeo is widely known for his charitable works. He helped found the Association of the Blind (of which he was later president) and also served on the boards of numerous organizations, such as the Burial Grounds Committee; the KWAN IM THONG HOOD CHO Temple; the Silver Jubilee Fund; the Rotary Trust Fund; and the Parole Board. For these efforts, he was awarded the Public Service Star (1967) and the MERITORIOUS SERVICE MEDAL (1985).

Yeoh Ghim Seng (1918–1993) Doctor and politician. Yeoh Ghim Seng was born in Ipoh, Perak. He was educated at St Michael's Institution in Ipoh and then at the Penang Free School before leaving for Cambridge University to study medicine. He came to Singapore as a consultant surgeon at the Singapore General Hospital in 1951, and was the first Asian to be appointed professor of surgery at the University of Malaya.

Yeoh stood for election on the People's Action Party ticket in 1966; he was appointed deputy Speaker (1968–70), and Speaker in 1970. He stepped down as Speaker in 1989. He succumbed to cancer in 1993.

Ying E Ding (1947–) Dancer and choreographer. Born in Shanghai, Ying E Ding trained in ballet and folk dancing at the Shanghai Dance Academy, with which he later danced principal roles. Bridging balletic-contemporary and Chinese folk influences in his choreography, he created some 20 major works in China before moving to Singapore in the 1980s. One of his more ambitious creations was *Moon Flight* (1991) for the Singapore Dance Theatre, with sets by visual artist TAN SWIE HIAN. He also collaborated with Tan on *Two Wings* and *Suchness* (1992).

Ying was awarded the CULTURAL MEDALLION in 1992. After leaving Singapore in the 1990s, he served as artistic director of the Hong Kong Dance Company. In 2001, he choreographed *The Macau Bride*, the Macau Cultural Institute's first large-scale production.

Yip Cheong Fun: Rowing at Dawn *(1980).*

Ying Fo Fui Kun Chinese clan association. The Ying Fo Fui Kun was founded in 1822 by HAKKA immigrants from Guangdong province. The association was established to promote the welfare of early Hakka immigrants by addressing their needs for accommodation and jobs, and by attending to their funeral arrangements.

Liu Yun Teck and other early Hakka clansmen obtained a 999-year lease in Telok Ayer Street and the clan house was constructed in 1881–82. The association founded the Yin Sin School in 1905 to provide education for Hakka children. The school functioned for 65 years within the association's premises until 1970.

Today, the Ying Fo Fui Kun continues to serve the Hakka community by promoting Hakka heritage and identity. This includes the provision of scholarships, organization of Hakka language classes, and the celebration of important Hakka festivals. The Ying Fo Fui Kun building at Telok Ayer Street was renovated in 1997 and gazetted as a national monument in 1998.

Ying Peian (1947–) Poet and author. Ying Peian has written essays, poetry, short stories and plays. He first appeared as a modernist poet with the publication of two collections of poetry including *Shou Shu Tai Shang* (On the Operating Table) (1968), which was followed by two volumes of short stories. Most of his essays, such as *An Xian Sheng De Shi Jie* (The World of Mr An) (1974) are social criticisms. Ying uses all literary forms as vehicles for speaking the truth and exposing the illnesses of postcolonial society. Since 1980, Ying has been writing (mainly essays of social criticism), running a bookstore, and publishing a number of magazines that champion the power of reason, the value of the individual, and freedom of speech and expression. He was awarded the CULTURAL MEDALLION in 2003.

Yingya Shenglan Ma Huan, a translator who accompanied Admiral ZHENG HE on some of his voyages during the early 15th century, wrote the *Yingya Shenglan* (literally, 'Description of the Coasts of the Ocean') in 1451. The text comprises entries on ports visited by Zheng He's fleet. It includes an entry on LONGYAMEN (Dragon's Tooth Gate). Ma Huan recorded that vessels sailing from the South China Sea into the Strait of Malacca and the Indian Ocean had to sail through Longyamen. He also noted that vessels sailing through this strait were often attacked by local pirates.

Yip, John (1937–) Teacher and civil servant. John Yip Soon Kwong was educated at St Joseph's Institution and then at the University of Malaya, where he won a teaching bursary. In 1960, Yip joined the education service and taught chemistry for five years, first at Raffles Institution and then at Tanjong Katong Technical School. He obtained an honorary doctorate from Loughborough University in United Kingdom.

In 1969, Yip was made principal of Kim Seng Technical Secondary School and, a year later, he was made principal of New Town Secondary School. In 1973, Yip suffered nerve damage that affected his voice and was unable to teach. He was then posted to the Ministry of Education as assistant director of education. He was eventually appointed director of schools, and director of education (1987–96).

Yip was responsible for a number of administrative initiatives, such as the gradual devolution of authority in the management of schools to principals; the training of vice-principals and principals; and the introduction of the school appraisal system. For his services to education, Yip was awarded the Public Administration Medal (Silver) (1973); the Public Administration Medal (Gold) (1981); and the MERITORIOUS

Yishun: new town developed in the 1980s.

SERVICE MEDAL (1991). Yip retired from the education service in 1996, and was appointed chief executive officer of the Singapore Institute of Management.

Yip Cheong Fun (1903–1989) Photographer. Yip Cheong Fun took up photography in 1954, and soon began winning accolades for his phographs of landscapes. He became an associate of the Royal Photographic Society (RPS) in the United Kingdom in 1957, and a fellow of the RPS in 1961.

The New York Photographic Society named Yip 'Honorary Outstanding Photographer of the Century (Seascapes)' in 1980 for *Rowing at Dawn*. He received an honorary excellence distinction (HEFIAP) from the International Federation of Photographic Art in 1984. The PHOTOGRAPHIC SOCIETY OF SINGAPORE named a memorial award after Yip. He was a recipient of the CULTURAL MEDALLION in 1984.

Yishun This area was named after LIM NEE SOON, Singapore's 'rubber and pineapple king'. 'Yishun' is Mandarin for 'Nee Soon'. In 1930, the authorities designated three villages in the area Nee Soon Village. It was at Yishun, including Yishun Road and Yishun Ring Road, that Lim owned large rubber and pineapple plantations. Other roads in Yishun associated with Lim are Thong Aik Road, Thong Soon Road and Bah Soon Pah Road. Thong Aik Rubber was the name of Lim's company while Thong Soon is a combination of Thong Aik and Nee Soon. Bah Soon Pah is derived from a local nickname for Lim—being PERANAKAN, he was referred to as 'Baba Soon', later shortened to 'Bah Soon', while 'Pah' is a colloquial reference to the outlying area. The rural area of Yishun was transformed in the 1980s with the building of Yishun Town, a public housing estate covering some 810 ha. About 55 per cent of the land is used for residential purposes. By 2005, around 46,600 flats in Yishun housed some 157,600 residents.

Yong Nyuk Lin (1918–) Businessman, politician and diplomat. Yong Nyuk Lin was born in Seremban, Negri Sembilan. He moved to Singapore to study at Raffles College. He graduated with a diploma in science in 1937, and returned to Seremban to teach science there.

In 1941, Yong joined Overseas Assurance Company (OAC) as a management trainee. In 1949, Yong became the first Singaporean to qualify as an associate of the Chartered Insurance Institute in London. He worked in the insurance industry for the next ten years, and eventually became general manager of OAC.

In 1959, he resigned from his position at OAC and contested the Geylang West constituency on the People's Action Party ticket during the Legislatve Assembly Election that year. Yong won a seat and served as minister for education (1959–63); minister for health (1963–68); and minister for communications (1968–75). He then served as Singapore's high commissioner to the United Kingdom (1975–76). In 1990, he was admitted into the ORDER OF NILA UTAMA.

Yong Pung How (1926–) Businessman and judge. Yong Pung How was born in Kuala Lumpur, the only son of lawyer Yong Shook Lin. He was educated at Victoria Institution in Kuala Lumpur, and later read law at Downing College, Cambridge University, where he was an Exhibitioner. Yong graduated in 1950 was called to the Bar at the Inner Temple in 1951.

From 1952 to 1970, Yong practised at SHOOK LIN & BOK, a firm his father had co-founded. Yong then moved into the corporate sector, becoming chairman of Malayan Airways Ltd and Malaysia-Singapore Airlines Ltd (1964–69); chairman and managing director of Singapore International Merchant Bankers Ltd (1971–74); vice-chairman of the Oversea Chinese Banking Corporation (1976–81); managing director of the Government of Singapore Investment Corporation (1981–83); managing director of the Monetary Authority of Singapore (1982–83); chairman of the Singapore Broadcasting Corporation (1985–89) and founder chairman of the Institute of Policy Studies.

In 1989, he was appointed to the High Court Bench. A year later, upon the retirement of WEE CHONG JIN, Yong became

Yong Nyuk Lin: visiting conservancy centre, 1963.

Yong Siew Toh Conservatory of Music

chief justice. He was also appointed president of the Singapore Academy of Law; president of the Legal Service Commission; and chairman of the Presidential Council for Minority Rights. In recognition of his achievements, Yong was admitted into the DISTINGUISHED SERVICE ORDER (1989) and the ORDER OF TEMASEK (First Class) (1999). In 1997, he was appointed honorary Bencher of the Inner Temple. In 2001, the National University of Singapore awarded him an honorary doctorate of laws. Yong retired from his position as chief justice in April 2006 and was succeeded by CHAN SEK KEONG.

Yong Pung How

Yong Siew Toh Conservatory of Music The Yong Siew Toh Conservatory of Music was established in 2003 as a collaborative project by the National University of Singapore (NUS) and the Peabody Institute of the Johns Hopkins University. Founded as the Singapore Conservatory of Music in 2001, it was renamed in recognition of a $25 million gift from the family of the late music teacher, Yong Siew Toh who died in 2000. As a faculty of NUS, the conservatory offers bachelor of music degrees, with majors in orchestral instruments, piano and composition. The faculty includes leading members of the SINGAPORE SYMPHONY ORCHESTRA, as well as international musicians and members of the Singapore musical establishment. Its students, many of whom receive full scholarships, are selected from Singapore, Asia and the rest of the world. The conservatory building, due to be completed in 2006, will house a 600-seat concert hall, recording studios, practice rooms and other facilities.

yong tau foo Popular hawker dish. The name means 'stuffed tofu' in Chinese. This is a dish where diners choose the specific ingredients. Many of the ingredients—such as tofu, bittergourd slices, brinjal slices, whole chillis and ladies' fingers—are stuffed with fish paste. Other ingredients include fishcake, fishballs, cuttlefish slices, seaweed and leafy vegetables. The ingredients are cut into pieces and blanched in a clear, boiling soup. They are then served in the soup or dry, with the soup in a separate bowl. The

Yong tau foo

Young Men's Christian Association of Singapore, 1955.

soup uses soy beans as a base. Diners can eat this dish on its own or with noodles of their choice. *Yong tau foo* is served with a sweet, reddish-brown dipping sauce as well as chilli sauce. A variant of the more common type of *yong tau foo* is HAKKA *yong tau foo*, which uses minced meat instead of fish paste as a stuffing for the ingredients.

You Jin (1950–) Author. You Jin is the pen name of Tham Yew Chin. She is best-known for her essays and travel books. In the 1980s, You Jin started writing about her travel to foreign places, including remote villages in the Middle East and Africa. Her work became popular especially among readers in China. You Jin has published 116 books, 50 of which have been published in Singapore, and 66 in China and Taiwan. Among the best-known are her short-story collection *Sha Mo De E Meng* (Nightmare in the Desert) (1987); travel writings *Sha Mo Li De Xiao Bai Wu* (The Little White Hut in the Desert) (1981) and *Hei Se De Dao Mi* (Uncooked Black Rice) (2000).

You Jin: Tiao Wu De Xiang Ri Kui (Dancing Sunflower) (1992) (top).

Young, Sir Arthur (1854–1938) Colonial official. Appointed governor of the Straits Settlements in 1911, Sir Arthur Henderson Young introduced an income tax and war tax during WORLD WAR I. Excise and other duties were also introduced to increase revenue. These resulted in a marked inflow to the coffers of the colonial authorities.

Young's term in office was one of quiet construction: he was able to contribute to the war cause and yet build new facilities in Singapore without being adversely affected by the war. He achieved a significant break-through in Singapore's port development. The port was in need of large-scale mod-ernization to cope with the volume of traf-fic and to counter competition from Hong Kong and even some Javanese ports. During

Young's governorship, the port was mod-ernized, old wharves replaced and new roads and GODOWNS built. The newly reclaimed Telok Ayer Basin was developed and a wet dock constructed. In 1913, the Tanjong Pagar Dock Board was trans-formed into the Singapore Harbour Board. In the same year, the graving dock—the second largest in the world—was complet-ed. The great dock scheme was completed by the Empire Dock, opened in 1917. Young also presided over the unveiling of the Raffles statue (originally at the PADANG) at its new home in front of the Victoria Memorial Hall on Centenary Day, marking the 100th anniversary of the FOUNDING OF SINGAPORE.

Of all the colonial governors of Singapore, Young was one of the most sports-minded and sportsmanlike. He played polo, cricket, lawn tennis and golf, and served as president of the Singapore Golf Club for 11 years.

Young, Grace (1962–) Sportswoman. Young represented Singapore as a tenpin bowler for 15 years (1985-2000). During that time, she won seven gold medals, two silver medals and four bronze medals at the Southeast Asian Games (*see* table).

Young was named Sportswoman of the Year in 1990, 1992 and 1993, and was an Asian Games bronze medallist on two occa-sions (Hiroshima, 1994; Bangkok, 1998). In 1991, she was made a member of the Five Ladies Team that set a one-game world record at the World Fédération Internationale des Quilleurs (FIQ) Tournament in Singapore. In 1995, she received a National Day Award for her con-tributions to sport.

Young has also worked as a television news presenter; a master of ceremonies; and a fund-raiser for youth and health cam-paigns, and for the Red Cross. In 1999, she became an advocate for the Women and Sport Movement, and a member of the Sports Advisory Sub-Committee of the Singapore Broadcasting Authority. She has also served as a volunteer at the Assisi Home Hospice and Children's Centre.

Grace Young

GRACE YOUNG: SEA GAMES MEDALS WON		
Location	Year	Medals
Jakarta	1987	1 gold; 1 bronze
Kuala Lumpur	1989	2 gold; 1 silver; 2 bronze
Manila	1991	2 gold
Singapore	1993	1 gold
Rayong, Thailand	1995	1 gold; 1 silver; 1 bronze
Source: Singapore Sports Council		

Sir Arthur Young

Young Artist Award Conferred by the NATIONAL ARTS COUNCIL, this award was first introduced in 1992 with the aim of boosting the growth of artistic talent in Singapore. It is presented to artists aged 35 or less. The scheme is divided into four broad categories: literary arts, performing arts, visual arts and film. While awards were given to artists of traditional art forms such as painting, writing, photography and the-atre, artists in popular music and multi-media art have been considered during award deliberations in recent years.

The award takes the form of a grant of up to $10,000, allowing the young artists to embark on a major project or to further their studies. Recipients have included Noni Kaur, S. Chandrasekaran, KEN SEET and Raymond Lau.

Young Men's Christian Association of Singapore Not-for-profit organization. The Young Men's Christian Association (YMCA) is a non-sectarian movement that originated in London in 1844. It aims to develop character through activities and training. The YMCA of Singapore (now commonly referred to simply as 'The Y') was set up in 1902 and was located at Armenian Street. In 1911, the YMCA moved to a three-storey Orchard Road building. In 1913, it started the YMCA Technical Education Unit and offered courses in subjects such as building con-struction and surveying. In 1919, the YMCA Commercial Education Unit was formed, offering courses on secretarial skills. By 1931, both units were merged to form YMCA Classes.

During the JAPANESE OCCUPATION, the YMCA building was used as the headquar-ters of the Eastern Branch of the KEMPEITAI. It became a notorious torture and deten-tion centre. War heroine ELIZABETH CHOY and her husband Choy Koon Heng were among those detained there.

After the war, YMCA activities resumed in 1947. A new building was built at the

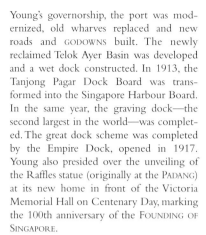

same premises and was opened in 1984. The new building houses the YMCA School, and the YMCA International House.

See also METROPOLITAN YOUNG MEN'S CHRISTIAN ASSOCIATION.

Young Women's Christian Association
First formed in London in 1855 with the aim of providing secure housing for young women, the Young Women's Christian Association (YWCA) opened its Singapore chapter in 1875. The chapter was founded by British missionary Sophia Cooke. It began by organizing self-improvement classes for Chinese women. By the late 20th century, the YWCA had broadened its activities and facilities to cover child development, care for the elderly and community projects, as well as providing accommodation. The YWCA is located on Outram Road and also manages the Fort Canning Lodge, a 175-room guest house.

Yu, Ovidia (1961–) Playwright and author. Ovidia Yu Tsin Yuen graduated from the National University of Singapore in 1982. Yu's *A Dream of China* won the 1984 Asiaweek Short Story Competition. Her first published works were in fiction: *Miss Moorthy Investigates* (1989), *The Mouse Marathon* (1993) and a collection of short stories, *Mistress and Other Creative Takeoffs* (1990), co-authored with Mary Loh Chieu Kwuan and Desmond Sim. From the late 1980s, Yu turned to drama. Her *Dead on Cue* won second prize in the 1987 NUS-Shell Short Play Competition.

Yu is one of the most prolific and versatile of Singaporean playwrights. Her plays are given to farce, satire and wit. Many of her plays deal with gender issues from the viewpoint of women, such as *The Woman in a Tree on the Hill*, which won an Edinburgh Fringe First at the 1992 Festival, *Mistress* (1990), *Three Fat Virgins* (1992), *Six Lonely Oysters* (1994; 1996) and *Breast Issues* (1997). *Viva Viagra* (1999) won an Audience Award at ACTION Theatre's First 42 Theatre Festival. Her satire, *The Silence of the Kittens* (2006), was performed at the Singapore Theatre Festival by W!LD RICE. Yu has also written musicals, such as *Haunted* (1999), co-written with Mark Chan, and *A Twist of Fate* (1987; 2005).

In 1990, a Fulbright Scholarship enabled Yu to join the Iowa International Writers' Program. In 1996, she received the Japan Chamber of Commerce and Industry Young Artist Award, as well as the National Arts Council's Young Artist Award for Literature. She received the Singapore Youth Award (Arts and Culture) in 1997.

Yu-Foo Yee Shoon (1950–) Trade unionist and politician. Yu-Foo Yee Shoon was educated at Nanyang Girls' High School and Nanyang University, where she graduated with a degree in commerce in 1971.

She began work as trainee audit assistant at the NATIONAL TRADES UNION CONGRESS (NTUC) in 1970, and worked her way up through the ranks of that union. In 1999, she was appointed deputy secretary-general of the NTUC.

Yu-Foo entered politics in 1984 on the People's Action Party (PAP) ticket, winning the Yuhua constituency seat. In 1999, she was appointed senior parliamentary secretary of community development and sports, a post she held until 2001. Yu-Foo also served as vice-chairman of the PAP Women's Wing Executive Committee; chairman of the NTUC Foodfare Cooperative; and chairman of the NTUC Club Jurong. In 2001, she was appointed mayor for South West District, which made her the first woman to hold mayoral office in Singapore.

yusheng Raw fish salad. '*Yu*' means 'fish' in Mandarin, but is also a homonym for 'abundant', while '*sheng*', which means 'raw', also means 'vitality'. This dish is thus considered auspicious. Traditionally, fishermen in Guangdong feasted on their catch to celebrate the seventh day of CHINESE NEW YEAR. Chinese migrants in Singapore modified this practice, dipping raw fish slices in hot rice porridge and consuming it. In the 1960s, four chefs, Hooi Kok Wai, Lau Yoke Pui, Sin Leong and Tham Yui Kai, combined the raw fish slices with other ingredients to create a new dish.

Today's *yusheng* consists of raw fish slices, shredded carrot, radish, pomelo, ginger, crackers and crushed peanuts, all laid out on a large dish. A dressing of plum sauce, vegetable oil, pepper, five spice powder and lime juice is added. Diners then gather round the dish, armed with chopsticks, and mix the ingredients together by tossing them high in the air to cries of '*lo hei*' (which in Cantonese sounds like 'to prosper more and more') or utterances of auspicious sayings. Traditionally, *ikan parang* (wolf herring) is used, but popular variations include carp, salmon or even lobster. The dish is served throughout the Chinese New Year period.

Yusof Ishak (1910–1970) Journalist and head of state. Yusof Ishak was the first PRESIDENT of the Republic of Singapore. Born in Padang Gajah, Perak, Yusof was the eldest son in a family of nine. He was educated at the Malay School at Kurau, Perak, and later at the Malay School in Taiping. In 1921, he began his studies in English at the King Edward VII School in Taiping.

In 1923, Yusof's father, Ishak Ahmad, a civil servant, was posted to Singapore. Yusof then enrolled briefly in Victoria Bridge School (1923–24) before gaining admittance to Raffles Institution (RI). He passed his Cambridge School Certificate with distinction (1927) and spent two further years in the Queen's Scholarship class.

Yusheng: dish traditionally eaten during Chinese New Year.

At school, Yusof was an avid sportsman, playing hockey, cricket, waterpolo and boxing. He was Singapore's lightweight boxing champion in 1933. He was active in the RI Cadet Corps, being the first student ever to be commissioned second lieutenant in that corps. He was also a prefect, and co-editor of the school's magazine, *The Rafflesian*.

When Yusof left school in 1929, he and two friends established a fortnightly sports magazine called *Sportsman*. In 1932, then joined the staff of *Warta Malaya*, then the leading Malay newspaper. Within a few years, he was made acting editor of that newspaper. In 1938, Yusof and some of his associates decided to start their own newspaper. Yusof resigned from *Warta Malaya* and established the UTUSAN MELAYU Press Ltd, serving as managing director of this company. The first issue of the newspaper *Utusan Melayu* was published in May 1939.

During the Japanese Occupation, Yusof remained in Malaya, although his newspaper ceased publication. After the Japanese surrender in 1945, Yusof resumed the publication of *Utusan Melayu*. In 1957, Yusof decided to move *Utusan*'s operations to Kuala Lumpur. While there, he was elected president of the Press Club of Malaya.

Beyond journalism, Yusof was active in public affairs. In 1959, he was appointed chairman of the PUBLIC SERVICE COMMISSION. In December 1959, he was appointed self-governing Singapore's first non-European head of state or Yang di-Pertuan Negara. On 9 August 1965, after Separation, Yusof became Singapore's first president.

During his last years in office, Yusof was often ill. He died of heart failure on 23 November 1970, and was buried at Kranji War Memorial, following a state funeral. Yusof was survived by his wife, Toh Puan NOOR AISHAH, and three children. Since 1999, his face has adorned Singapore's currency notes.

Zainal Abidin (1961–) Sportsman. Between 1979 and 1990, Zainal won the national squash title on eight occasions; and between 1980 and 1989, he won the East Asian squash title nine times. His most memorable match was in the 1985 World Team Championships in Cairo (in which Singapore came sixth), when he defeated Egyptian Gamal el-Amir. Zainal was also the winner of the World Plate in 1987,

Ovidia Yu

Yu-Foo Yee Shoon

Yusof Ishak

Zapin: Sri Warisan performers.

Zainal Abidin: Ascot Squash Championship Final, 1987.

Admiral Zheng He: statue of Zheng He in Nanjing, China (top); model of a ship in Zheng He's fleet.

defeating Egyptian Amir Wagih in Birmingham, United Kingdom.

Zainal was a member of the Singapore squash team that, in world rankings, finished 12th in 1981; ninth in 1983; sixth in 1985; and seventh in 1987. He was appointed national coach in 1983, and was voted Sportsman of the Year in 1987.

zapin Musical genre that originated in the Middle East and is believed to have been introduced into Southeast Asia around the 13th century. There are two types: *Zapin Arab* and *Zapin Melayu*. The main musical instruments are the *oud* or *gambus* (a stringed instrument) and *gendang* (drum). It can also be accompanied by the violin, accordion or *rebana* (drum). The tempo in most *zapin* music ranges from moderate to fast. Musicians usually exchange instrument solos with one another, showcasing individual styles. Lyrics, in the form of PANTUN, can be sung solo or in pairs. *Zapin* is usually performed at social ceremonies such as weddings or feasts. *Zapin* is also associated with dance, previously performed only by men. Singers in Singapore and Malaysia have recorded *zapin* or *zapin*-influenced songs, and the genre continues to be performed in cultural programmes. In 2001, Majlis Pusat and Sri Warisan (an arts group) organized a *zapin* festival in Singapore, which included a seminar, workshops and a gala concert. *Zapin* groups from Indonesia, Malaysia and Brunei also participated.

Zhang Hui (1942–) Born Cheong Weng Yatt, Zhang Hui's works, such as 'Zai Jian, Lao Shi!' (Goodbye, Teacher!) (1976) and 'Shi Meng Lu' (Memoirs of Ten Dreams) (1992), are considered to be some of the best Chinese short stories ever written by a Singaporean writer. His story *He Tang Li de Qing Ting* (The Dragonfly in the Lotus Pond) is a work of magic realism, showing social awareness, historical sense and artistic form. Cheong won the National Book Development Council Book Award and the Southeast Asia Write Award in 1992.

Zhang Xina (1958–) Journalist and author. A columnist in the Chinese press, Zhang

Xina has also published three collections of short stories: *Lüe Guo De Feng* (The Moving Wind) (1987), *Bian Diao* (Changing Tones) (1990) and *Jing Hua* (Mirror Flower) (1999). A sense of crisis afflicting Chinese cultural traditions, and tensions between the Chinese-educated and English-educated are dominant themes in her works. Zhang has won more prizes in short story writing competitions than any other writer in Singapore. In addition to prizes in the National Short Story Writing Competition and the Golden Lion Literary Award, she has received the Southeast Asia Write Award (2000).

Zhang Zhenquan (dates unknown) Musician and teacher. Born in Fujian, Zhang Zhenquan started learning various traditional Chinese instruments in his childhood and later decided to concentrate on the *erhu*. He became principal of a public school on Pulau Ubin but in his spare time promoted CHINESE CLASSICAL MUSIC. In the 1950s, he founded the Gong Shang Alumni Association Chinese Orchestra.

In the early 1960s, Zhang became an active member of the Central Cultural Board Chinese Orchestra. When the National Theatre Chinese Orchestra was formed in May 1968, he was appointed principal leader. In 1969, together with LI XUELING, Zhang gathered several senior and experienced musicians from the National Theatre Chinese Orchestra and founded the Yang Chun Chinese Orchestra, a chamber ensemble devoted to performing Chinese orchestral music on a smaller scale, as well as to providing music accompaniment for folk songs. In addition, he was the co-founder of Xin Yun Traditional Music Association. Zhang was constantly featured as an *erhu* soloist or ensemble player in concerts, both locally and overseas.

Zheng He, Admiral (1371–1435) Chinese explorer and diplomat. Zheng He (or Cheng Ho) was born into a Muslim family in 1371 in Kunyang, Yunnan, China. In 1382, after Ming troops conquered Yunnan (one of the last strongholds of Mongol support in China), young boys, including Zheng He, were castrated as punishment for the local people's defiance of Ming rule. Those who survived this ordeal were taken captive, and put into the service of officials of the Ming court. Zheng He was taken captive and sent to Nanjing. At the age of 11, he was put into the service of Zhu Di, the Prince of Yan. Zheng and Zhu developed a close relationship, and when Zhu Di ascended the imperial throne as Emperor Yong Le, Zheng also rose to prominence in the Ming court.

In 1403, Emperor Yong Le ordered that an imperial fleet be built to explore Southeast Asia and the Indian Ocean. The fleet, consisting of several hundred vessels, was completed in 1405.

Zheng was appointed to head this naval expedition, and was accorded the title admiral of the Western Seas. He was instructed to establish diplomatic relations with the states that he encountered in these maritime regions. Between 1405 and 1433, Zheng led a total of seven major voyages and a number of other minor voyages.

The voyages undertaken by Zheng greatly increased China's knowledge of Southeast Asia and the Indian Ocean, including the anthropology, economy, geography and zoology of these regions. Confucian loyalists who opposed the Ming court's policy of supporting these expensive maritime voyages later destroyed most of Zheng's travelogues. However, information pertaining to his voyages survived in two accounts—the YINGYA SHENGLAN and the XINGCHA SHENGLAN.

Zheng died at sea in 1435, while the Ming fleet—which had dispersed into smaller expeditions and had headed separately to East Africa and the Middle East—was returning to China. However, posthumously, Zheng became an important figure in coastal Chinese and Southeast Asian folklore. Chinese who migrated to Southeast Asia from the 15th century onwards began to deify Zheng, and a number of temples dedicated to him, such as the Sam Poh Kong Temple in Penang, were built throughout Southeast Asia.

Zhong Qiu Jie Chinese festival. Also known as the 'Mooncake Festival' or 'Lantern Festival', it is celebrated on the 15th day of the the eighth month in the Chinese lunar calendar (mid–late September). It has its origins in the Yuan dynasty (1280–1368), when China was ruled by the Mongols. Unhappy with Mongol rule, Chinese rebels planned a revolt, communicating their plans via notes stuffed in round cakes. To commemorate the revolt, the day has been celebrated ever since with the consumption of mooncakes—small, round cakes filled with egg yolk and a variety of other sweet or savoury fillings.

In Singapore, families celebrate this festival by taking evening strolls in parks and gardens, with children bearing Chinese lanterns. An exhibition of Chinese lanterns is also often held in conjunction with the festival at the CHINESE GARDENS in Jurong. New varieties of mooncake have been developed in Singapore in recent years, with ice-cream,

Zhong Qiu Jie: children with lanterns.

durian, banana, chocolate and kaya-paste mooncakes all proving to be popular.

Zhong Yuan Jie Festival celebrated on the 15th day of the seventh lunar month of the Chinese calendar, although festivities take place throughout the month. It is also known in Singapore as the 'Hungry Ghost Festival'. This festival is steeped in Chinese beliefs of filial piety, ancestor worship and ghosts.

On the last evening of the sixth lunar month, replica paper money—commonly known as 'hell money'—is burnt and joss sticks lit for the ghosts who will be released from the netherworld for a month from the following day. In Singapore, cylindrical receptacles resembling large oil drums are placed at housing estates in preparation for the burnt offerings. People who do not use these communal receptacles delineate their private spaces with white chalk. Offerings are seldom made inside the house, for fear of inviting unwanted spirits in.

The seventh lunar month is marked by lively events such as auctions, operas and GETAI (stage performances). The auction is marked by the booming voice of the auctioneer, and competitive bidding for 'auspicious items', ranging from figurines to plants and ornaments.

The opera and *getai* performances are free and are held on makeshift stages in open spaces. In recent years, *getai* performances have become something of a flesh parade, featuring scantily-clad women in flamboyant makeup. However, there remains a handful of *getai* performances featuring witty hosts and talented performers. A talented host can earn up to $8,000 per show. A common practice is for performers to rush from one performance venue to the next, where they wait in line for their turn on stage.

The 15th day of the month is Zhong Yuan. The Chinese observe it by 'sending' to the netherworld material possessions such as money, clothes, houses, cars and even credit cards and the latest electronic gadgets, by burning paper replicas. Families honour their ancestors with a sumptuous feast comprising roasted meats, vegetables, fruit, cakes, cookies and wine. These are usually placed on a table outside the house. Those without an altar look up at the sky when praying, clasping joss sticks between their hands. Priests may also be called upon to chant the sutras, petitioning the gods to assist loved ones in the netherworld. Huge joss sticks, some up to 3 m in height, are burnt, usually in the common areas of housing estates or in temple compounds.

The Chinese consider the seventh lunar month to be an inauspicious time for important events such as weddings, and for moving house or starting a business.

Zhou Can (1934–) Author and poet. Zhou Can, born Chew Kok Chang, received his

Zhong Yuan Jie: auctioning 'auspicious items'.

bachelor's degree at Nanyang University and his master's degree at the University of Singapore. He then lectured at the Institute of Education, and worked as a school inspector for the Ministry of Education.

Zhou Can published his first collection of poems, *Hai Zi De Meng* (The Dream of a Child) (1953), when he was only 16 years old. Thereafter, he went on to publish some 77 volumes of poetry, essays, short stories, critical essays and children's books.

Poetry is perhaps Zhou Can's strongest genre. He writes on a variety of topics, and has broadened the scope of Chinese literature by writing about local street scenes, as in *Qi Lou Di Xia* (At the Five-Foot Way), which describes the life of an old sweet-seller in downtown Singapore. He was awarded the CULTURAL MEDALLION in 1990.

Zhuang Xuefang (unknown–) Actress. Zhuang began her career in the 1940s as a stage singer. In the 1950s, she sang at the Shangri-la Song Stage at the NEW WORLD Amusement Park. She co-starred with Lu Ding in many stage plays, such as *Thunderstorm* and *The Wilderness*. In the 1960s she toured extensively in Malaysia. She later moved to Hong Kong and made many Hokkien movies. She moved to Taiwan in the 1970s. Her most successful movie was *Long Shan Si Zhi Lian* (Longshan Temple Romance) (1962). In 2005, Zhuang had a highly successful concert tour in Taiwan and Singapore.

Zouk Nightclub. Zouk opened in March 1991 in three converted GODOWNS built in 1919 on the banks of the Singapore River. The name 'Zouk' is derived from a French Caribbean term for 'party'.

This 2,000-capacity nightclub comprises four distinct spaces: Zouk, Phuture, Velvet Underground and the Wine Bar. Zouk is where the main dance floor is located, and is the central part of the club; Phuture, which was opened in 1996, has a long bar, and has windows overlooking the main dance floor; Velvet Underground was launched in 1994, caters to young executives, and has its own sound system; the Wine Bar provides both indoor and outdoor seating.

In 2000, the club started hosting ZoukOut—an outdoor dance party featur-

ing international disc-jockeys. This annual event has been held at SENTOSA most years. The 2005 ZoukOut event was attended by about 18,000 people.

In 2004, Zouk opened an outlet in Kuala Lumpur—Zouk KL. And in October 2005, the original nightclub in Singapore underwent major refurbishment costing $7 million. A new sound system was installed, the club's interior was expanded, bar tops were overhauled and the building's facade was transformed with the installation of modular, curved concrete shapes.

Zouk

Zubir Said (1907–1987) Composer. Zubir Said composed Singapore's NATIONAL ANTHEM, *Majulah Singapura* (Onward Singapore). He wrote about 1,000 other songs, including *Semoga Bahagia* (To Be Happy), the theme song for Children's Day and the Singapore Youth Festival.

Born in Sumatra, Zubir left home in 1928 to join a BANGSAWAN troupe in Singapore. He later won great acclaim as a songwriter when he worked at CATHAY-KERIS FILMS. He was awarded the Sijil Kemuliaan (Certificate of Honour) in 1963 and the Asean Cultural and Communications Award in 1987. After his retirement in 1964, Zubir taught music until his death in 1987.

Zhou Can

Zuellig Group Pharmaceuticals distributor. Started in Manila in the early 20th century as one of many European trading houses in the region, the Zuellig Group is one of the largest privately held business groups in Asia. In the 1930s, founder Frederick Eduard Zuellig saw the need to regionalize and opened an office in Singapore in 1938, focusing on textiles. After World War II, the Singapore company continued with textiles before it branched into the manufacture and distribution of scientifically prepared animal feed in the 1950s. This was the beginning of the Gold Coin Group, one of Asia's most successful feed-manufacturing operations. Frederick Zuellig also moved into the pharmaceuticals sector in the 1930s. Today, the Zuellig Group is the leading distributor of pharmaceuticals in Singapore and most Asian markets.

Zhuang Xuefang

Zulkifli Mohammed (1948–) Politician. Zulkifli Mohammed was educated at Monk's Hill School, Swiss Cottage Secondary School and the University of Singapore, where he graduated with an honours degree in social science (1970). He then joined Shell Eastern Petroleum, where he worked until 1985. Zulkifi entered politics in 1984 when he contested the Eunos constituency on the People's Action Party ticket. After being elected as a member of Parliament, he was appointed political secretary to the Ministry of Community Development (1986). He was also president of the Central Council of Malay Cultural Organisations Singapore (Majlis Pusat) (1983). He retired from politics in 1996.

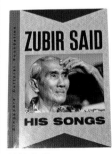

Zubir Said

Zulkifli Mohammed

PERMANENT SECRETARIES

By date of first appointment 1965–2006

1960s

Oon Khye Kiang	*Treasury*	1959
Hon Sui Sen	*Finance*	1961
Lee Siow Mong	*PMO*	1965
Abu Bakar Pawanchee	*Foreign Affairs*	Aug 1965
George Edwin Bogaars	*Interior and Defence*	Aug 1965
Kwan Sai Kheong	*Education*	Dec 1966
Ho Guan Lim	*Health*	Dec 1966
Sim Kee Boon	*Finance*	Dec 1966
Pang Tee Pow	*Labour*	Dec 1966
Woon Wah Siang	*Foreign Affairs*	Jun 1967
Harry Chan Keng How	*Foreign Affairs*	Apr 1968
K.P.R. Chandra	*Law and National Development*	Jan 1969
Howe Yoon Chong	*National Development*	Jan 1969
Lee Keng Tuan	*Finance*	Jan 1969
Stanley Toft Stewart	*Foreign Affairs*	Nov 1969

1970s

Ngiam Tong Dow	*Communications*	1970
Lim Joo Hock	*Labour*	1970
Wong Keng Sam	*Communications*	1970
Lee Ek Tieng	*Health*	1971
William Cheng	*Labour*	Sep 1972
Cheng Tong Fatt	*National Development*	Sep 1972
Kwa Soon Chuan	*Culture*	Sep 1972
S.R. Nathan	*Defence*	Sep 1972
J.Y. Pillay	*Finance*	Sep 1972
Tan Chok Kian	*National Development*	Sep 1972
Tay Seow Huah	*Home Affairs*	Sep 1972
Chia Cheong Fook	*Foreign Affairs*	Jul 1975
Herman Hochstadt	*Communications*	Jan 1977
Cheong Quee Wah	*Defence*	Nov 1977
Han Cheng Fong	*Labour*	1977
Lum Choong Wah	*Home Affairs*	1977
Andrew Chew	*Health*	1978
Hsu Tse Kwang	*Inland Revenue*	1979
Koh Cher Siang	*National Development*	1979
Philip Yeo	*Defence*	1979

1980s

F.J. D'Costa	*Social Affairs*	1980
Goh Kim Leong	*Education*	1980
Lim Siong Guan	*Defence*	Jul 1981
Tan Chin Tiong	*Home Affairs*	1982
Peter Chan	*Foreign Affairs*	Sep 1983
Kwa Soon Bee	*Health*	Feb 1984
Lam Chuan Leong	*Communications and Information*	Feb 1984
Moh Siew Meng	*Labour*	Sep 1984
Wong Hung Khim	*Community Development*	1984
Tan Guong Ching	*Communications and Information*	Jan 1987
Er Kwong Wah	*Education*	Apr 1987
Koh Yong Guan	*Defence*	May 1989

1990s

Chuang Kwong Yong	*Labour*	Nov 1991
Teo Ming Kian	*Defence*	Sep 1992
Tjong Yik Min	*Communications*	Mar 1993
Kishore Mahbubani	*Foreign Affairs*	Oct 1993
Eddie Teo	*Defence*	Jun 1994
Moses Lee	*Labour*	Nov 1994
Khaw Boon Wan	*Trade and Industry*	Mar 1995
Tan Gee Paw	*Environment*	Apr 1995
Peter Ho Hak Ean	*Defence*	Nov 1995
Niam Chiang Meng	*Information and the Arts*	Apr 1997
Tan Chin Nam	*Labour*	Dec 1997
Alan Chan	*Communications*	Jun 1999
Chiang Chie Foo	*Defence*	Jun 1999
Lim Soo Hoon	*Community Development and Sports*	Oct 1999

2000s

Liew Heng San	*Law*	Jan 2001
Peter Ong	*Defence*	Apr 2001
Bilahari Kausikan	*Foreign Affairs*	Aug 2001
Heng Swee Keat	*Trade and Industry*	Oct 2001
Yong Ying-I	*Manpower*	Jan 2002
Lim Chuan Poh	*Education*	Jul 2003
Tan Kim Siew	*Defence*	Nov 2003
Benny Lim	*Home Affairs*	Jan 2004
Tan Ching Yee	*Education*	Jan 2005
Chan Lai Fung	*Law*	Mar 2006

AMBASSADORS, HIGH COMMISSIONERS, PERMANENT REPRESENTATIVES AND TRADE REPRESENTATIVES

By date of first appointment

1960s

Ko Teck Kin	*Kuala Lumpur*	Sep 1965
Abu Bakar Pawanchee	*New York*	Sep 1965
Lien Ying Chow	*Kuala Lumpur*	Jul 1966
A.P. Rajah	*London*	Aug 1966
Ernest Monteiro	*Phnom Penh*	Aug 1966
Tan Siak Kew	*Bangkok*	Aug 1966
Stanley Toft Stewart	*Canberra*	Aug 1966
K.M. Byrne	*Wellington*	Aug 1966
Wong Lin Ken	*Washington DC*	Mar 1967
Ahmad Ibrahim	*Cairo*	Apr 1967
Maurice Baker	*New Delhi*	Jul 1967
Ho Rih Hwa	*Bangkok*	Sep 1967
Lim Kee Chin	*Hong Kong*	Sep 1967
Ang Kok Peng	*Tokyo*	Jun 1968
P.S. Raman	*Jakarta*	Jun 1968
Lee Khoon Choy	*Cairo*	Jun 1968
Tommy Koh	*New York*	Jul 1968
Ya'acob Mohamed	*Manila*	Sep 1969
Chan Keng Howe	*Phnom Penh*	Nov 1969

1970s

Chandra Das	*Moscow*	Jan 1970
Punch Coomaraswamy	*New Delhi*	Jan 1970
S. Jayakumar	*New York*	Jun 1971
Lee Yong Leng	*London*	Jul 1971
Chiang Hai Ding	*Kuala Lumpur*	Jul 1971
Chi Owyang	*Bangkok*	Aug 1971
Loy Keng Foo	*Tokyo*	Aug 1971
Cheam Kim Seang	*Manila*	Sep 1971
Wee Mon Cheng	*Tokyo*	Jun 1973
Wee Kim Wee	*Kuala Lumpur*	Sep 1973
A. Rahim Ishak	*Jakarta*	Dec 1974
Kirpa Ram Vij	*Cairo*	May 1975
Yong Nyuk Lin	*London*	Sep 1975
Lim Kim Kuay	*Hong Kong*	Jun 1976
See Chak Mun	*Canberra*	Sep 1976
Othman bin Wok	*Jakarta*	Jun 1977
J.F. Conceicao	*Moscow*	Jul 1977
Jek Yeun Thong	*London*	Oct 1977
Hwang P.Y.	*Brussels*	Apr 1978
David Marshall	*Paris*	Oct 1978
William Cheng	*Taipei*	Jun 1979

1980s

Koh Lian Hwi	*Hong Kong*	Sep 1980
Kwan Sai Kheong	*Manila*	Oct 1980
Low Choon Ming	*Canberra*	Nov 1980
Ho Guan Lim	*Moscow*	Sep 1981
Tan Song Chuan	*Beijing*	Sep 1981
Chew Tai Soo	*Geneva*	May 1982
Abdul Aziz Mahmood	*Manila*	Jul 1982
Edward Lee Kwong Foo	*Bandar Seri Begawan*	Sep 1982
Kemal Siddique	*Moscow*	Aug 1984
Kishore Mahbubani	*New York*	Aug 1984
Stephen Sim	*Hong Kong*	Apr 1985
Lee Ying Chuen	*Beijing*	Feb 1986
Peter Sung	*Manila*	Aug 1986
Francis Yeo	*Brussels*	Sep 1986
Tan Keng Jin	*Cairo*	Sep 1986
Barry Desker	*Jakarta*	Nov 1986
Chia Cheong Fook	*Wellington*	Aug 1987
Tan Seng Chye	*Bangkok*	Mar 1988
S.R. Nathan	*Kuala Lumpur*	Apr 1988
Wong Meng Quang	*Beijing*	Apr 1988
Gordon Seow Li Ming	*Hong Kong*	May 1988
Tan Chok Kian	*Taipei*	Jun 1988
Cheng Tong Fatt	*Tokyo*	Jul 1988
Chan Heng Chee	*New York*	Feb 1989
Michael Cheok	*New Delhi*	Mar 1989
Jayalekshimi Mohideen	*Brussels*	Nov 1989

1990s

Chin Siat Yoon	*Bangkok*	Sep 1990
Raymond Wong	*Seoul*	Oct 1990
Chai Chong Yii	*Taipei*	Jun 1991
V.K. Rajan	*Wellington*	Jul 1991
Lim Chin Beng	*Tokyo*	Jul 1991
K. Kesavapany	*Geneva*	Dec 1991
Lam Peck Heng	*New Delhi*	Jan 1993
Mary Seet-Cheng	*Brussels*	Jan 1993
Toh Hock Ghim	*Hanoi*	Jan 1994
Michael Teo	*Wellington*	Feb 1994
Anthony Chng	*Bandar Seri Begawan*	Mar 1994
Winston Choo	*Canberra*	Mar 1994
Bilahari Kausikan	*Moscow*	Mar 1994
Foo Meng Tong	*Paris*	Apr 1994

Calvin Eu Mun Hoo	*Yangon*	Jun 1994	**2000s**			
Pang Eng Fong	*Seoul*	Nov 1994	Seetoh Hoy Cheng	*Vientiane*	Mar 2000	
Wong Kwok Pun	*Bangkok*	Jan 1995	Verghese Mathews	*Phnom Penh*	Jul 2000	
Mushahid Ali	*Phnom Penh*	Jun 1995	Ashok Kumar Mirpuri	*Canberra*	Jul 2000	
Mark Hong Tat Soon	*Moscow*	Oct 1995	Vanu Gopala Menon	*Geneva*	Dec 2001	
J.Y. Pillay	*London*	Mar 1996	Hirubalan V.P.	*Bandar Seri Begawan*	Jan 2002	
Simon Tensing de Cruz	*Manila*	Apr 1996	Ker Sin Tze	*Taipei*	Oct 2002	
Joseph Koh	*Taipei*	Jul 1996	Michael Tay Cheow Ann	*Moscow*	Jan 2003	
Ong Keng Yong	*New Delhi*	Aug 1996	Lim Kheng Hua	*Manila*	Mar 2003	
Patrick Choy Choong Tow	*Yangon*	Oct 1996	Karen Tan	*Vientiane*	Feb 2004	
Chan Heng Wing	*Hong Kong*	Mar 1997	Lawrence Anderson	*Phnom Penh*	Mar 2004	
T. Jasudasen	*Paris*	Jul 1997	Burhan Gafoor	*Geneva*	Sep 2004	
Tee Tua Ba	*Bandar Seri Begawan*	Aug 1997	Tan Chin Tiong	*Tokyo*	Oct 2004	
Walter Woon	*Berlin*	Feb 1998	Eddie Teo	*Canberra*	Feb 2006	
A. Selverajah	*Brussels*	Sep 1999	Robert Chua	*Yangon*	May 2006	
Jacky Foo	*Manila*	Dec 1999				

NON-RESIDENT AMBASSADORS

By date of first appointment

Lee Chiong Giam	*Papua New Guinea*	Oct 1982	Chua Yong Hai	*Namibia*	Jan 2000
Ridzwan Dzafir	*Argentina, Chile, Brazil, Panama*	Jan 1986	Ng Ser Miang	*Hungary*	Feb 2000
Foo Kok Swee	*Nigeria, Ghana*	Aug 1989	Abdul Aziz Mahmood	*Oman*	Mar 2000
Herman Hochstadt	*Tanzania, Mauritius*	Aug 1989	Winston Choo	*Papua New Guinea*	Mar 2000
Gopinath Pillay	*Iran*	Aug 1989	Jayalekshimi Mohideen	*Czech Republic*	Apr 2000
Hsu Tse-Kwang	*Poland*	Aug 1991	Giam Chin Toon	*Peru*	May 2000
Tan Boon Teik	*Hungary, Austria, Slovak Republic*	Sep 1992	Philip Eng Heng Nee	*Nigeria*	Jul 2000
Kemal Siddique	*Norway*	May 1993	Chen Choong Joong	*Austria*	Nov 2000
H.M. Sithawalla	*Tanzania, Mauritius*	Oct 1994	Michael Hwang	*Switzerland*	Jan 2004
Brian Lee Chang Leng	*Oman, Kuwait*	Dec 1996	Lua Cheng Eng	*Panama*	Mar 2004
Tan Kah Hoe	*Maldives, Sri Lanka*	Dec 1996	Philip Ng Chee Tat	*Chile*	Mar 2004
Charlie Phua Kok Peng	*Peru*	Dec 1996	Quek Poh Huat	*Sweden*	Mar 2004
Lee Ying Cheun	*Brazil*	Mar 1997	Choo Chiau Beng	*Brazil*	Sep 2004
Pang Cheng Lian	*Italy*	Mar 1997	S. Chandra Das	*Turkey*	Jan 2006
Sim Cheok Lim	*Kazakhstan*	Mar 1999	Wong Kwok Pun	*Qatar*	Feb 2006
Victor Loh Kwok Hoong	*Poland*	Jan 2000	Loo Choon Yong	*Italy*	Mar 2006
			K. Kesavapany	*Jordan*	Jun 2006

CONSULS GENERAL
By date of appointment

Chew Tai Soo	*Osaka*	Nov 1975	Robert Chua Hian Kong	*Ho Chi Minh City*	Jan 2001
Lim Eng Hoe	*Xiamen*	Jan 1996	Toh Hock Ghim	*Hong Kong*	Feb 2002
Ang Chay Chuan	*Shanghai*	Aug 1996	Bernard William Baker	*Vancouver*	Jun 2002
Foo Chin Kwok	*Ho Chi Minh City*	Mar 1997	Chia Tuck Keong	*Shanghai*	Nov 2002
Chan Heng Wing	*Hong Kong*	Jul 1997	Jai Sohan Singh	*San Francisco*	Aug 2003
Ong Lu King	*Shanghai*	Mar 1998	Jimmy Chua Tin Chew	*Ho Chi Minh City*	May 2005
Rengaraju Raj Kumar	*San Francisco*	Dec 1999	Dileep Nair	*Dubai*	Aug 2005
Ng Yew Kang	*Xiamen*	Dec 2000	Ajit Singh	*Chennai*	Apr 2006

HONORARY CONSULS GENERAL
By date of appointment

Joseph Salim Habis	*Beirut*	Oct 1974	Yehoshua Gleitman	*Tel Aviv*	Apr 1999
Amin Mohammed Lakhani	*Karachi*	Mar 1989	Emile Yousef Koro	*Amman*	Apr 1999
Minos Xen Kyriakou	*Athens*	Nov 1989	Cedric Ritchie	*Toronto*	Sep 1999
Jose Maria Nin Ros	*Barcelona*	May 1990	Jozsef Toth	*Budapest*	Feb 2000
Arturo Alessandri-Cohn	*Santiago*	Sep 1990	Ronald J. Bolger	*Dublin*	May 2000
Pinar Aran	*Istanbul*	Jan 1991	Luca M Birindelli	*Rome*	Jul 2000
Toshikage Tanida	*Nagoya*	Mar 1991	Krister Harry Ahlstrom	*Helsinki*	Aug 2000
Dieter Lorenz-Meyer	*Hamburg*	Jan 1993	Newton N. Minow	*Chicago*	Feb 2001
Augusto Hector Spinazzola	*Buenos Aires*	Jan 1994	Henry F. Chow	*Port Moresby*	Mar 2001
Fernando Armbrust Lohmann	*Sao Paulo*	Mar 1994	F. Javier De Oraa Y. Moyua	*Madrid*	Jul 2001
Arne Simonsen	*Copenhagen*	May 1994	Hans Peter Stihl	*Stuttgart*	Jun 2002
Eduardo A. Henkel Perez-Castro	*Mexico City*	Jul 1995	Martin Plachy	*Prague*	Aug 2002
Walter Rothensteiner	*Vienna*	Jul 1996	Steven J. Green	*Miami*	Jul 2003
Miklos Konkoly-Thege	*Oslo*	Jun 1997	Sven Aaser	*Oslo*	Sep 2003
Erik Belfrage	*Stockholm*	Oct 1997	Josep M. Basanez	*Barcelona*	Sep 2003
Deshamanya Lalith Kotelawala	*Colombo*	Mar 1998	Antonio Horta-Osorio	*Lisbon*	Aug 2004
Larry Lim Tiong Soon	*Port Moresby*	Mar 1998	Winston Merchor	*Lima*	Feb 2005
Jon M. Huntsman Jr	*Salt Lake City*	Jun 1998	George Emile Ibrahim Haddad	*Amman*	Mar 2005
Jose F. Oulman Bensaude Carp	*Lisbon*	Dec 1998	Alfonso Vegara	*Madrid*	Apr 2005
Tan Chek Feng	*San Francisco*	Jan 1999	Kay Segler	*Munich*	Mar 2006
Carel Juliaan van den Driest	*Rotterdam*	Mar 1999	Grigory Marchenko	*Almaty*	Mar 2006
Robert Van Dine	*Los Angeles*	Mar 1999			

Abdul Rahman Napiah. *Sastera Singapura dan Malaysia: Di Era Pascamoden.* Singapore: Persama Enterprise, 2003.

Abdul Samad Ahmad. *Sulalatus Salatin, Sejarah Melayu.* Kuala Lumpur: DBP, 1979.

Acharya, Amitav. *Constructing a Security Community in Southeast Asia: ASEAN and the Problem of Regional Order.* London and New York: Routledge, 2001.

———. *Regionalism and Multilateralism: Essays on Cooperative Security in Asia Pacific.* Second ed. Singapore: Eastern Universities Press, 2003.

Ahmad Ibrahim. *Legal Status of Muslims In Singapore.* Singapore: Malayan Law Journal, 1965.

———. *Towards a History of Law in Malaysia and Singapore.* Singapore: Stamford College Press, 1970.

Ahmad Sarji. *P. Ramlee: Erti Yang Sakti.* Subang Jaya. Malaysia: Pelanduk Publications, 1999.

Ahmad Zakaria Haji (volume editor). *The Encyclopedia of Malaysia Vol 11: Government and Politics (1940–the present).* Singapore: Archipelago Press, 2005.

Akashi Yoji. "Bureaucracy and the Japanese Military Administration, with Specific Reference to Malaya." In *Japan in Asia: 1942–1945,* edited by Newell, William H. Singapore: Singapore University Press, 1981.

———. "Watanabe Wataru: The Architect of the Malaya Military Administration, December 1941 – March 1943." In *New Perspectives in Malaysian Studies,* edited by Mohd Hazim Shah, Jomo, K. S. and Phua Kai Lit. Kuala Lumpur: Persatuan Sains Sosial Malaysia, 2002.

Al-Attas, Syed Muhammad Naguib. *The Mysticism of Hamza Fansuri.* Malaysia: University of Malaya Press, 1970.

Alfian Sa'at and Aidli 'Alin' Mosbit (editors). *Bisik.* Singapore: Ethos Books, 2002.

Ampalavanar Rajeswary. "Social and political developments in the Indian community of Malaya 1920–41." Unpublished B.A. Hons. dissertation. Department of History, University of Malaya, 1969.

Andaya, B. W. and Andaya, L. Y. *A History of Malaya.* London: MacMillan Press, 1982.

Aplin, Nicholas. *To The Finishing Line: Champions of Singapore.* Singapore: SNP Editions, SNP Corporation, 2002.

Aplin, Nicholas, Waters, David and Leong May Lai. *Singapore Olympians: The Complete Who's Who 1936–2004.* Singapore: SNP International, 2005.

Arasaratnam, S. *Indian Festivals in Malaya.* Department of Indian Studies, University of Malaya, Kuala Lumpur, 1966.

Archives and Oral History Department, Singapore. *The Land Transport of Singapore: From Early Times to the Present.* Singapore: Educational Publications Bureau, 1981

Arensmeyer, Elliott Campbell. "British Merchant Enterprise and the Chinese Coolie Labour Trade, 1850–1874." Unpublished Ph.D dissertation. University of Hawaii, 1979.

Asian Civilisations Museum. *The Asian Civilisations Museum A-Z Guide.* Singapore: Asian Civilisations Museum, 2003.

Asmah Haji Omar. *The Linguistic Scenery in Malaysia.* Kuala Lumpur: Dewan Bahasa dan Pustaka, 1992.

Atin Amat, "Menyusuri Teater Melayu Singapura." In *Selves: The State of the Arts in Singapore,* edited by Kwok Kian Woon, Arun Mahizhnan, and T. Sasitharan, Singapore: National Arts Council, 2002.

Babb, Lawrence A. *Walking on flowers in Singapore: A Hindu festival cycle.* Department of Sociology, Working Paper No. 27, University of Singapore, 1974.

Ban Kah Choon. *Absent History: The Untold Story of Special Branch Operations in Singapore, 1915–1942.* Singapore: Raffles, 2001.

Ban Kah Choon and Yap Hong Kuan. *Rehearsal For War.* Singapore: Horizon Books, 2002.

Barker, Ralph. *One Man's Jungle: A Biography of F. Spencer Chapman DSO.* London: Chatto and Windus, 1975.

Barnard, Timothy P. "Confrontation on a River: Singapore as an 18th Century Battleground in Malay Historiography." In *Early Singapore – Evidence in Maps, Text and Artefacts,* edited by J. Miksic and C. Low. Singapore: Singapore History Museum, 2004.

———. "Vampires, Heroes and Jesters: A History of Cathay Keris." In *The Cathay Story,* edited by Wong Ain-ling. Hong Kong: Hong Kong Film Archive, 2002.

Bastin, J. and Winks, R.W. (compilers). *Malaysia – Selected Historical Readings.* Kuala Lumpur: Oxford University Press, 1966.

Beamish, Jane and Jane Ferguson. *The Making of a City.* Singapore: Graham Brash, 1985.

Beauchamp, Ken. *History of Telegraphy.* London: The Institution of Electrical Engineers, 2001.

Beckett, Ian. "The Singapore Mutiny of February, 1915." *The Journal of the Society for Army Historical Research,* 62 (1984).

Bedlington, Stanley S. "Political Integration and the Singapore Malay Community." *Journal of the History Society (University of Singapore)* (1970/71).

Bellows, Thomas J. "The Singapore Polity: Community, Leadership and Institutions." *Asian Journal of Political Science* 1, No. 1 (1993).

Birch, David. "Staging Crises: Media and Citizenship." In *Singapore Changes Guard: Social, Political and Economic Directions in the 1990s,* edited by Gary Rodan. New York: St Martin's Press, 1993.

Blackburn, Kevin. "Changi: A Place of Personal Pilgrimages and Collective Histories." *Australian Historical Studies* 3, No.112 (1999).

———. "The Collective Memory of the Sook Ching Massacre and the Creation of the Civilian War Memorial of Singapore." *Journal of the Malaysian Branch of the Royal Asiatic Society* 73, Part 2, (2000).

Blackburn, Kevin and Chew Ju Ern, Daniel. "Dalforce at the Fall of Singapore in 1942: An Overseas Chinese Heroic Legend." *Journal of the Chinese Overseas* 1, No. 2 (2005).

Blagden, C. O. "Historical Singapore prior to 1819." In *One Hundred Years of Singapore,* edited by W. Makepeace, G.E. Brooke, Roland T. J. Braddell, London: J. Murray, 1921.

Blakeley, Brian L. *The Colonial Office 1868–1892.* Durham: Duke University Press, 1972.

Blomqvist, Hans C. "State and Development Policy: The Case of Singapore." *Asian Profile* 29, No. 3 (2001).

Bloodworth, Dennis. *The Tiger and the Trojan Horse.* Singapore: Times Books International, 1986.

Board of Commissioners of Currency Singapore. *Annual Report.* Singapore: BCCS (various).

Booth, Gregory D. "The Madras Corporation Band: A Story of Social Change and Indigenization." *Asian Music* 28, no.1, (1996/7).

Borell, B. "Money in 14th Century Singapore." In *Southeast Asian Archaeology 1998,* edited by W. Lobo and S. Reimann. Hull: Centre for South-East Asian Studies, University of Hull, 2000.

Bose, Romen. *The End of the War: Singapore's Liberation and the Aftermath of the Second World War.* Singapore: Marshall Cavendish, 2005.

Braddell, Roland St John. *Law of the Straits Settlements: A Commentary.* Kuala Lumpur: Oxford University Press, 1982.

Brazil, David. *Insider's Singapore.* Singapore: Times Editions, 2001.

———. *Street Smart Singapore.* Singapore: Times Books, 1991.

Brown, C. C. (translator and editor) *Sejarah Melayu or Malay Annals.* Kuala Lumpur: Oxford University Press, 1970.

Buckley, Charles Burton. *An Anecdotal History of Old Times in Singapore.* Malaysia: University of Malaya Press, 1965.

Busch, Peter A. *Legitimacy and Ethnicity: A Case Study of Singapore.* Lexington, MA: Lexington Books, 1974.

Butcher, John G. "Revenue Farming and the Changing State in Southeast Asia." In *The Rise and Fall of Revenue Farming,* edited by John Butcher and Howard Dick. London: Macmillan Press, 1993.

———. "The Demise of the Revenue Farm System in the Federated Malay States." *Modern Asian Studies* 17, no.3 (1983).

Callender, Guy and Johnston, Judy. "Governments and Governance: Examining Social and Economic Autonomy in Malaysia and Singapore." *Asian Journal of Public Administration* 20, No. 2 (1998).

Carter, Lionel. *Chronicles of British business in Asia, 1850–1960: A Bibliography of Printed Company Histories with Short Accounts of the Concerns.* New Delhi: Manohar Publishers & Distributors, 2002.

Central Provident Fund. *Annual Report.* Singapore: CPF (various).

Ch'en, Kenneth K. S. *Buddhism in China: A Historical Survey.* New Jersey: Princeton University Press, 1964.

———. *The Chinese Transformation of Buddhism.* NJ: Princeton University Press, 1973.

Chan Heng Chee. *In Middle Passage: The PAP Faces the Eighties.* Singapore: Chopmen Enterprises, 1979.

———. "Political Developments, 1965–1979." In *A History of Singapore,* edited by Chew, Ernest C. T. and Edwin Lee. Singapore: Oxford University Press, 1991.

———. *The Role of Parliamentary Politicians in Singapore.* Singapore: Department of Political Science, University of Singapore, 1975.

Chan Kwee Sung. *One More Story to Tell: Memories of Singapore, 1930s-1950s.* Singapore: Landmark Books, 2005.

Chan Kwok Bun and Tong Chee Kiong. *Past Times: A Social History of Singapore.* Singapore: Times Editions, 2003.

Chan Siok Fong and Ovidia Yu. *Guiding in Singapore.* Singapore: Landmark Books, 1990.

Chan Wing Cheong and Phang, Andrew. *The Development of Criminal Law and Criminal Justice in Singapore.* Singapore: Singapore Journal of Legal Studies, 2001.

Chapman, F. Spencer. *The Jungle is Neutral.* London: Chatto and Windus, 1950.

Cheah Boon Kheng (compiler and ed.). *A. Samad Ismail: Journalism and Politics.* Malaysia: Singamal Publishing Bureau, 1987.

——— (volume ed.). *The Encyclopedia of Malaysia Vol. 7: Early Modern History (1800–1940).* Singapore: Archipelago Press, 2001.

———. *Red Star Over Malaya: Resistance and Social Conflict During and After the Japanese Occupation, 1941–1946.* Singapore: Singapore University Press, 1987.

Cheah, Philip, "Starting Over." In *Being and Becoming. The Cinemas of Asia,* edited by Vasudev Aruna, Pagaonkar Latika and Doraiwamy Rahsmi. New Delhi: MacMillan India Limited, 2002.

Chew Ju Ern, Daniel. "Reassessing the Overseas Legend of Dalforce at the Fall of Singapore." Unpublished dissertation. National Institute of Education, Nanyang Technological University, 2005.

Chew, Ernest and Lee, Edwin (ed.). *A History of Singapore.* Oxford: Oxford University Press, 1991.

Chew, Ernest C. T. "Dr John Crawford (1783–1868): The Scotsman Who Made Singapore British." *Raffles Town Club* 8 (July–Sept 2002).

———. "The Singapore Identity: Its Historical Evolution and Emergence." In *A History of Singapore,* edited by Chew, Ernest C. T. and Edwin Lee. Singapore: Oxford University Press, 1991.

Chiang Hai Ding. *A History of Straits Settlements Foreign Trade 1870–1915.* Singapore: National Museum, 1978.

Chiang Ming Shun. "Military Defences and Threat Perceptions in Nineteenth Century Singapore, 1854–1891." Unpublished B.A. Hons. dissertation. Department of History, National University of Singapore, 1993.

Chiew Seen Kong. "Nation-building in Singapore: A Historical Perspective." In *In Search of Singapore's National Values,* edited by Jon S.T. Quah, Singapore: Times Academic Press for the Institute of Policy Studies, 1990.

Chin Soo Fang. "Xinyao is back in style" in *The Straits Times.* Sep 2, 1994.

Chin, C.C. and Hack, Karl (eds). *Dialogues with Chin Peng: New Light on the Malayan Communist Party.* Singapore: Singapore University Press, 2004.

Chua Beng Huat. "Arrested Development: Democratisation in Singapore." *Third World Quarterly* 15, No. 4 (1994).

———. "Pragmatism of the People's Action Party Government in Singapore: A Critical Assessment." *Southeast Asian Journal of Social Science* 13, No. 2 (1985).

———. "Re-opening Ideological Discussion in Singapore: A New Theoretical Direction." *Southeast Asian Journal of Social Science* 11 No. 2 (1983).

———. *Communitarian Ideology and Democracy in Singapore.* New York: Routledge, 1995.

———. *Life is Not Complete without Shopping: Consumption Culture in Singapore.* Singapore: Singapore University Press, 2003.

———. *That Imagined Space: Nostalgia for the Kampung in Singapore.* Department of Sociology Working Papers, No.122, National University of Singapore: 1994.

Chua Soo Pong. "Dance in Singapore: The Multicultural Heritage." In *ASEAN Dance Symposium at the 4th ASEAN Dance Festival, Singapore: 8th–12th Dec 1996,* edited by Chua Soo Pong, Singapore: National Arts Council, 1997.

———. "Singapore." In *The Dances of ASEAN,* edited by Zainal Abiddin Tinggal. Brunei Darussalam: ASEAN Committee on Culture and Information, 1998.

Chung Chee Kit. *Longyamen is Singapore – the Final Proof?* Singapore: Friends of Admiral Zheng He, 2003.

Chung May Khuen. "Shipping in the Straits of Malacca in the 19th Century." Unpublished B.A. Hons. dissertation. Department of History, National University of Singapore, 1997.

Collins, J. T. *Malay, World Language: A Short History.* Kuala Lumpur: Dewan Bahasa dan Pustaka, 1998.

Collins, Marie Elizabeth. *Murugan's lance: power and ritual: the Hindu Tamil festival of Thaipusam in Penang, Malaysia.* Ann Arbor, Michigan: University Microfilms International. 1992.

Connelly, Mark. "Battleships and British Society, 1920–1960." *International Journal of Naval History* 3, 2/3 (August–December 2004).

Corner, E. J. H. *The Marquis: A Tale of Syonan-To.* Singapore: Heinemann Asia, 1981.

Cotton, James. "Political Innovation in Singapore: The Presidency, the Leadership and the Party." In *Singapore Changes Guard: Social, Political and Economic Directions in the 1990s,* edited by Gary Rodan. New York: St Martin's Press, 1993.

Cowan, C.D (ed.) *The Economic Development of Southeast Asia: Studies in Economic History and Political Economy.* London: George Allen & Unwin Ltd, 1968.

Danaraj, T. J. *Japanese Invasion of Malaya and Singapore: Memoirs of a Doctor.* Kuala Lumpur: T. J. Danaraj, 1990.

Darton, Mike and John Clark. *The Macmillan Dictionary of Measurement.* New York: Macmillan Publishing Company, 1994.

Davies, John D. "The Growth and Development of Local Government in Singapore 1848–1887." Unpublished B.A. Hons. dissertation. Department of History, University of Malaya, 1954.

Department of Statistics, Ministry of Trade and Industry. *Yearbook of Statistics Singapore, 2004.* Singapore: Department of Statistics, Ministry of Trade and Industry, Republic of Singapore, 2004.

———. *Yearbook of Statistics Singapore, 2005.* Singapore: Department of Statistics, Ministry of Trade and Industry, Republic of Singapore, 2005.

Devasahayam, Patricia. "Geylang Serai: The Malay Emporium of Singapore." Unpublished B.A. Hons. dissertation. Sociology Department, National University of Singapore, 1985.

Development Bank of Singapore. *Annual Report.* Singapore: DBS (various).

Dobbs, Stephen. *The Singapore River: A Social History, 1809–2002.* Singapore: Singapore University Press, 2003.

Doran, C. "Gender Matters in the Singapore Mutiny." *Sojourn* 17, 1 (2002).

Edwards, Norman and Keys, Peter. *Singapore: A Guide to Buildings, Streets, Places.* Singapore: Times Books International, 1988.

Elias, Rahita. *Beyond Boundaries: The First 35 years of the NOL Story.* Singapore: Neptune Orient Lines, 2004.

Emmerson, Donald K. "Singapore and the 'Asian Values' Debate." *Journal of Democracy* 6, No. 4 (1995).

Farrell, Brian P. *The Defence and Fall of Singapore 1940–1942.* Stroud: Tempus, 2005.

Foong Choon Hon (ed.). *He Ping de Dai Jia: Malai ban dao lun xian qi jian 136 Bu Dui ji qi ta fan qin lue sji li ji shi.* Singapore: Chinese Chamber of Commerce, 1995.

———. *The Price of Peace: True Accounts of the Japanese Occupation.* Singapore: Asiapac, 1995.

Gan Hui Cheng. "Dancing Bodies: Culture and Modernity." In *Selves: The State of the Arts in Singapore,* edited by Kwok Kian Woon, Arun Mahizhnan, and T. Sasitharan, Singapore: National Arts Council, 2002.

Ganesan, N. "Democracy in Singapore." *Asian Journal of Political Science* 4, No. 2 (1996).

———. "Singapore: Entrenching a City-state Dominant Party System." *Southeast Asian Affairs.* Singapore: Institute of Southeast Asian Studies, 1998.

Gasmier, Mary Rose. "Death in the wings." *The Straits Times,* March 6, 1990.

George, Cherian. "A Healthy Dose of Idealism Can Create One United People." *The Straits Times,* May 9, 1999.

———. *Singapore: The Air-conditioned Nation: Essays on the Politics of Comfort and Control 1990–2000.* Singapore: Landmark Books, 2000.

Gibson-Hill, C. A. "Singapore Old Strait and New Harbour 1300-1870." *Memoirs of the Raffles Museum* 3 (1956).

———. "The Master Attendants at Singapore, 1819–67." *Journal of the Malayan Branch of the Royal Asiatic Society,* 33(1).

Goh Chok Tong. *Agenda for Action: Goals and Challenges.* Singapore: Singapore National Printers, 1988.

———. *The Gordian Knot: Is There an Upper Limit To Our Prosperity?* Singapore: Information Division, Ministry of Communications and Information, 1985.

Goh Chor Boon. *Serving Singapore: A Hundred Years of Cold Storage 1903–2003.* Singapore: Cold Storage Singapore, 2003

Gomez, James. *Internet Politics: Surveillance and Intimidation in Singapore.* Singapore: Think Centre, 2002.

Gordon, Alijah (ed.). *The Real Cry of Syed Shaykh al-Hady.* Malaysia: Malaysian Sociological Research Institute, 1999.

Haas, Michael. "The Politics of Singapore in the 1980s." *Journal of Contemporary Asia* 19, No. 1, (1989).

———. *The Singapore Puzzle.* Westport, CT: Praeger, 1999.

Hack, Karl. *Defence and Decolonisation in Southeast Asia: Britain, Malaya and Singapore, 1941 to 1968.* Richmond: Curzon, 2001.

Hack, Karl and Blackburn, Kevin. *Did Singapore Have to Fall? Churchill and the Impregnable Fortress.* London: Routledge, 2004.

Hack, Karl and Rettig, Tobias. *Colonial Armies in Southeast Asia.* London: Routledge, 2006.

Hadijah Rahmat. *Kilat Senja-Sejarah Sosial dan Budaya Kampung-kampung di Singapura.* Singapore: HS Yang Publishing, 2005.

Hadijah Rahmat, "Lukisan Sastera Melayu–Antara Keunggulan dan Kenyataan." In *Sastera Melayu Warisan Jati Diri dan Jagat,* edited by Mohamed Pitchay Gani Mohamed Abdul Aziz, Singapore: NLB & ASAS 50, 2003.

Hadijah Rahmat, Dewani Abbas and Azhar Ibrahim (eds.), *Prisma Pentas: Antologi Skrip Drama Teater.* Singapore: Majlis Bahasa Melayu Singapura, MITA, 2004.

Hall, D. G. E. *A History of Southeast Asia.* London: MacMillan Education, 1981.

Hancook, T. H. H. *Coleman's Singapore.* Kuala Lumpur: Malaysian Branch of the Royal Asiatic Society, 1986.

Hao Yen-Ping. *The Comprador in Nineteenth Century China: Bridge between East and West.* Cambridge: Harvard University Press, 1970.

Harding, James and Ahmad Sarji. *P. Ramlee. The Bright Star.* Kuala Lumpur: Pelanduk Publications, 2002.

Harfield, Alan. *British and Indian Armies in the East Indies 1685–1935.* Chippenham: Picton Publishing, 1984.

Harper, R. W. E and Harry Miller. *Singapore Mutiny.* Singapore: Oxford University Press, 1984.

Hassan Kamal, M. and Ghazali Basri (volume editor). *The Encyclopedia of Malaysia Vol 10: Religions and Beliefs.* Singapore: Archipelago Press, 2005.

Heussler, Robert. *British Rule in Malaya: The Malayan Civil Service and its Predecessors, 1867–1942.* Oxford: Clio Press, 1981.

Hew, Denis and Rahul Sen. *Towards an ASEAN Economic Community.* Singapore: Institute of Southeast Asian Studies, 2004.

Hill, Michael and Lian Kwen Fee. *The Politics of Nation Building and Citizenship in Singapore.* London: Routledge, 1995.

Ho Khai Leong. "Citizen Participation and Policy Making in Singapore." *Asian Survey* 40, No. 3, (2000).

———. "Prime Ministerial Leadership and Policy-making Style in Singapore: Lee Kuan Yew and Goh Chok Tong Compared." *Asian Journal of Political Science* 8, No. 1 (2000).

———. *The Politics of Policy-making in Singapore.* Singapore: Oxford University Press, 2000.

Hsü Yün-Ts'iao. "Singapore in the Remote Past." *Journal of the Malaysian Branch of the Royal Asiatic Society* 45, No. 1, (1973).

Hu Tie Jun. *Xinghua Yi Yong Jun Zhan Dou Shi (A Military History of the Singapore Overseas Chinese anti-Japanese Army).* Singapore: Singapore Chinese Publishers, 1945.

Huang Jianli. "The Head of State in Singapore: An Historical Perspective." In *Managing Political Change in Singapore: The Elected Presidency,* edited by Tan, Kevin Y. L. and Lam Peng Er. London: Routledge, 1997.

Hussin Hamzah. *Memoir Hamzah Hussin: Dari Keris Film ke Studio Merdeka.* Bangi, Malaysia: Universiti Kebangsaan Malaysia, 1991.

Hussin Mutalib. "Illiberal Democracy and the Future of Opposition in Singapore." *Third World Quarterly* 21, No. 2 (2000).

Huxley, Tim. "Singapore's Politics in the 1980s and 90s." *Asian Affairs* 23, No. 3 (1992).

In the Spotlight: Stories of Singapore Sports Celebrities. Singapore: Candid Creation Publishing, 2005.

Jackson, R.N. *Pickering: Protector of Chinese.* Kuala Lumpur: Oxford University Press, 1965.

Jamil Sulong. *Kaca Permata: Memoir Seorang Pengarah.* Kuala Lumpur: Dewan Bahasa and Pustaka Kementrian Pendidikan, 1990.

Jayasuriya, Kaniska. "Rule of Law and Capitalism in East Asia." *Pacific Review* 9, No. 3 (1996).

Jeffries, Charles. *The Colonial Office.* London: George Allen & Unwin, 1937.

Jesudason, James V. "The Resilience of One-party Dominance in Malaysia and Singapore." In *The Awkward Embrace: One-party Domination and Democracy,* edited by Giliomee, H. and C. Simkins. Amsterdam: Harwood Academic, 1999.

John, Alan. *Unholy Trinity: The Adrian Lim 'Ritual' Child Killings.* Singapore: Times Books International, 1989.

Jones, David M. and David Brown. "Singapore and the Myth of the Liberalizing Middle Class." *Pacific Review* 7, No. 1, 1994.

Josey, Alex (compiler.). *The Crucial Years Ahead: Republic of Singapore General Election 1968.* Singapore: Donald Moore Press, 1968.

———. *Democracy in Singapore: The 1970 By-elections.* Singapore: Donald Moore, 1970.

———. *Golf in Singapore.* Singapore: Benson & Hedges, 1969.

———. *Pulau Senang: The Experiment that Failed.* Singapore: Times Books International, 1980.

———. *The Singapore General Elections, 1972.* Singapore: Eastern Universities Press, 1972.

Julita Mohd Hussen. "A Study of an Urban Malay Village: Jalan Eunos Malay Settlement." Unpublished B.A. Hons. dissertation. Department of Sociology, National University of Singapore, 1982.

Kartini Yayit. "Vanishing Landscape: Malay Kampungs in Singapore." Unpublished B.A. Hons. dissertation. Department of Geography. National University of Singapore, 1987.

Kathiravelu, S. "Fortifications of Singapore." Unpublished B. A. Hons. dissertation. Department of History, University of Malaya in Singapore, 1957.

Keith, Patrick. *Ousted!.* Singapore: Media Masters, 2005.

Kirby, S. Woodburn. *The War Against Japan, Volume I: The Loss of Singapore.* London: HMSO, 1957.

Koh, Eddie. "Meanings in Place: Recapturing The Kampung In Singapore." Unpublished B.A. Hons. dissertation. Department of Sociology, National University of Singapore, 1999.

Kong, Lily. "Making Music at the Margins? A Social and Cultural Analysis of Xinyao in Singapore." *Asian Studies Review* 19, no. 3 (1996).

Kumaraguru, V. "Rubber in Malaya, 1914–1941." Unpublished B.A. Hons. dissertation. Department of History. University of Malaya in Singapore, 1961.

Kwee Hui Kian. "Dao yi zhi lue as a maritime traders' guide-book: a contribution to the study of private enterprise in maritime trade during the Yuan period, 1279-1368." Unpublished B.A. Hons. dissertation. Southeast Asian Studies Programme, National University of Singapore, 1997.

Kwok Kian Chow. *Channels and Confluences: A History of Singapore Art.* Singapore: Singapore Art Museum, 1996.

Kwok Kian Woon, Arun Mahizhnan, T Sasitharan (eds). *Selves: The State of the Arts in Singapore*. Singapore: National Arts Council, 2002.

Laidlay, J W. "Note on the inscriptions from Singapore and Province Wellesley." *Journal of the Asiatic Society of Bengal* 17, No. 2 (1848).

Lam Peng Er. "The Elected Presidency: Towards the Twenty-first Century." In *Managing Political Change in Singapore: The Elected Presidency*, edited by Tan, Kevin Y. L. and Lam Peng Er, London: Routledge, 1997.

Lam Peng Er and Tan, Kevin Y. L.(eds.). *Lee's Lieutenants: Singapore's Old Guard*. St. Leonards, NSW: Allen & Unwin, 1999.

Lau, Albert. *A Moment of Anguish: Singapore in Malaysia and the Politics of Disengagement*. Singapore: Times Academic Press, 1998.

Lee Geok Boi. *The Syonan Years: Singapore Under Japanese Rule 1942–1945*. Singapore: National Archives of Singapore and Epigram, 2005.

Lee Hsien Loong. *Core Principles of Government*. Singapore: Resource Centre, Ministry of Information and the Arts, 1992.

Lee Khoon Choy. *On the Beat to the Hustings: An Autobiography*. Singapore: Times Books International, 1988.

Lee Kuan Yew. *From Third World to First: The Singapore Story: 1965–2000*. Singapore: Times Editions and The Straits Times Press, 2000.

———. *The Singapore Story*. Singapore: Times Editions and The Straits Times Press, 1998.

Lee Lai-To. "China's Relations with ASEAN: Partners in the 21st Century?" *Pacific Review* 13, no. 1 (2001).

Lee Poh Ping. *Chinese Society in Nineteenth Century Singapore*. London: Oxford University Press, 1968.

Lee Yong Kiat. *The Medical History of Early Singapore*. Tokyo: South East Asia Medical Centre, 1978.

Lee, Edwin. "Singapore 1867–1914: British Rule in a Multi-racial Society." Unpublished Ph.D. Thesis. Department of History, National University of Singapore, 1983.

Lee, Joanne. "The Singapore Dance Theatre." In *Selves: The State of the Arts in Singapore,* edited by Kwok Kian Woon, Arun Mahizhnan, and T. Sasitharan, Singapore: National Arts Council, 2002.

Lenzi, Iola. *Museums of Southeast Asia*. Singapore: Editions Didier Millet, 2004.

Leow Bee Geok. *Census of Population 2000: Demographic Characteristics*. Singapore: Department of Statistics, Ministry of Trade and Industry, Republic of Singapore, 2001.

———. *Census of Population 2000: Economic Statistics*. Singapore: Department of Statistics, Ministry of Trade and Industry, Republic of Singapore, 2001.

———. *Census of Population 2000: Education, Language and Religion*. Singapore: Department of Statistics, Ministry of Trade and Industry, Republic of Singapore, 2001.

Leow Wah Ping, Amy. "Music and Gender in Singapore." Unpublished B.A. Hons. dissertation. Department of Sociology, National University of Singapore, 1998.

Lewis, T. P. M. *Changi: The Lost Years: A Malayan Diary 1941–1945*. Kuala Lumpur: Malaysian Historical Society, 1984.

Leyden, John. *John Leyden's Malay Annals*. Malaysia: Malaysian Branch of the Royal Asiatic Society, 2001.

Li Chuan Siu. *Ikhtisar Sejarah Pergerakan dan Kesusasteraan Melayu Moden, 1945–1965*. Kuala Lumpur: Pustaka Antara, 1986.

Lim Huck Tee. "The Malayan Civil Service, 1896–1941." Unpublished B.A. Hons. dissertation. Department of History, University of Malaya, 1960.

Lim Jim Koon. *Our 70 Years History of Leading Chinese Newspapers in Singapore*. Singapore: Chinese Newspaper Division, Singapore Press Holdings Ltd, 1993.

Lim Kay Tong. *Cathay – 55 Years of Cinema*. Singapore: Landmark Books, 1991.

Lim Kim Seng. *Birds: An Illustrated Field Guide to the Birds of Singapore. Singapore:* Sun Tree Publishing, 2003.

Lim Thau Ping, Raymond, "'Coal Imperialism' in The History of Labuan, 1849 – 1911." Unpublished B.A. Hons. Dissertation. Department of History, National University of Singapore, 1994.

Lim, Shirley, Ng, Peter, Tan, Leo and Wee Yeow Chin. *Rhythm of the Sea: The Life and Times of Labrador Beach*. Singapore: Division of Biology, School of Science, Nanyang Technological University & Department of Zoology, the National University of Singapore, 1994.

Lin Wan Ying, Mindy. "An Analysis of Selected Singapore Ballads (Xinyao), 1980–1990." Unpublished dissertation. National Institute of Education, Nanyang Technological University, 2004.

Linehan, W. "The Kings of 14th Century Singapore." *Journal of the Malayan Branch of the Royal Asiatic Society* 20, No. 2 (1947).

Lingle, Christopher. *Singapore's Authoritarian Capitalism: Asian Values, Free Market Illusions and Political Dependency*. Barcelona: Edicions Sirocco, 1996.

Liu, Gretchen, *Singapore: A Pictorial History, 1819–2000*. Singapore: Archipelago Press and National Heritage Board, 2000

———. *In Granite and Chunam: The National Monuments of Singapore*. Singapore: Landmark Books, 1996.

———. *The Singapore Foreign Service: The First 40 Years*. Singapore: Editions Didier Millet, 2005.

Lo Tien Yin. "Dance is a love-hate relationship for Han." *The New Paper*, May 15, 1991.

Logan, J. R. (ed), "Cinnamon Cultivation in the Straits of Malacca." *The Journal of the Indian Archipelago and Eastern Asia* 5 (1851).

Loh Wen Fong. "The Singapore Houses of Agency, 1819–1900." Unpublished B.A. Hons. dissertation. Department of History, University of Malaya, 1958.

Low Kar Tiang (ed.). *Who's Who in Singapore*. Singapore: Who's Who Publishing, 2003.

Low Mei Gek, C-A. "Sawankhalok-Sukhothai Wares from the Empress Place Site, Singapore." In *Sangkhalok-Sukhothai-Ayutthaya and Asia,* edited by Charnvit Kasetsiri. Bangkok: The Foundation for the Promotion of Social Science and Humanities Textbooks Project, 2002.

Low, Linda. *The Political Economy of a City-state: Government-made Singapore*. Singapore: Oxford University Press, 1998.

Low, Linda and Toh Mun Heng (eds.). *Public Policies in Singapore: Changes in the 1980s and Future Signposts*. Singapore: Times Academic Press, 1992.

Maintenance of Religious Harmony. Singapore: Singapore National Printers, 1989.

Majlis Pusat. *Dinamika Budaya*. Singapore: Majlis Pusat, 1991.

Makepeace, Walter, Gilbert E. Brooke and Roland St J Braddell. *One Hundred Years of Singapore*. Singapore: Oxford University Press, 1991.

Mani, A. "Indians in Singapore Society." In *Indian Communities in Southeast Asia,* edited by K. S. Sandhu and A. Mani. Singapore: Institute of Southeast Asian Studies, 1993.

———. "The Changing caste-structure amongst the Singapore Indians." Unpublished M.Soc. Sci. dissertation, Department of Sociology, University of Singapore, 1978.

Manson, Joy. *Festivals of Malaya*. Singapore: Eastern Universities Press Ltd. 1965.

Marder, Arthur J. *Old Enemies, Old Friends: The Royal Navy and the Imperial Japanese Navy, Strategic Illusions, 1936–1941*. Oxford: Clarendon, 1981.

Mariam Mohd. Ali. "Orang Baru and Orang Lama: Ways of Being Malay in Singapore's North Coast." Unpublished B.Soc.Sci Hons. dissertation. Department of Sociology, National University of Singapore, 1984.

———. "Singapore's Orang Seletar, Orang Kallang, and Orang Selat: The Last Settlements." In *Tribal Communities in the Malay World: Historical, Cultural and Social Perspectives,* edited by Geoffrey Benjamin and Cynthia Chou. Leiden and Singapore: International Institute for Asian Studies and Institute of Southeast Asian Studies, 2002.

Masuri S.N. "Sastera Melayu Baru dalam Gelombang Kosmopolitanisme di Singapura," in *Pemikiran Sastera Nusantara,* edited by Hamzah Hamdani. Kuala Lumpur: DBP, 1988.

Menon, Vilasini. "The Singapore Houses of Agency, 1900–1940." Unpublished B.A. Hons. dissertation. Department of History, University of Malaya, 1958.

Middlebrook, Martin and Mahoney, Patrick. *Battleship: The Sinking of the Prince of Wales and Repulse*. New York: Charles Scribner's, 1979.

Miksic, John N. *Archaeological Research on the 'Forbidden Hill' of Singapore: Excavations at Fort Canning, 1984*. Singapore: National Museum, 1985.

Miksic, John N. and Low Mei Gek, Cheryl-Ann (general editors). *Early Singapore 1300s–1819: Evidence in Maps, Texts and Artefacts*. Singapore: Singapore History Museum, 2004.

Millet, Raphaël. *Singapore Cinema*. Singapore: Editions Didier Millet, 2006.

Mills, L. A. "British Malaya 1824–67." *Journal of the Malayan Branch, Royal Asiatic Society*, 33 (3), 1960.

Milne, R. S. and Diane K Mauzy. *Singapore: The Legacy of Lee Kuan Yew*. Boulder, Colorado: Westview Press, 1990.

Ministry of Community Development. *Singapore A Pro-Family Society*. Singapore: Ministry of Community Development, 1995.

Ministry of Culture. *One Year of Independence*. Singapore: Ministry of Culture, 1966.

———. *Singapore Festival of Dance 83: 4–10 December 1983*. Singapore: Ministry of Culture, 1983.

Ministry of Finance. *Budget 2006: Building on our Strengths, Creating our Best Home*. Singapore: Ministry of Finance, 2006.

Mitton, Roger. "Maverick Politician: Ong Teng Cheong is out But Not Down." *Asiaweek*, 10 March 2000.

Mohamed Pitchay Gani Mohamed Abdul Aziz, (ed.) *Leksikon: Direktori Penulis Melayu Singapura Pasca 1965*. Singapore: ASAS '50 & NLB, 2005.

Mohammad Rashidi Pakri. "Between The Malay Peasants and a Beautiful Theory: Romanticism and the Imperialist Agenda in Hugh Clifford's Early Fiction." *Journal of the Malaysian Branch of the Royal Asiatic Society* 77, No. 2 (2004).

Mohd Taib Osman. *An Introduction to the Development of Modern Malay Language and Literature*. Singapore: Times Books International, 1986.

Monetary Authority of Singapore. *Annual Report*. Singapore: MAS (various).

Montgomery, Brian. *Shenton of Singapore: Governor and Prisoner of War*. Singapore: Times, 1984.

Moore, Donald and Moore, Joanna. *The First 150 Years of Singapore*. Singapore: Donald Moore Press, 1969.

Morais, J. Victor (ed.). *Who's Who in Malaysia (1975–1976) and Guide to Singapore*. Kuala Lumpur: J Victor Morais, 1975.

Muhammad Haji Salleh. *Syair Tantangan Singapura Abad Kesembilan Belas*. Kuala Lumpur: DBP, 1994.

Mullaiselvi, K. "The Singapore Indian Chamber of Commerce 1935–1980." Unpublished B.A. Hons. dissertation. Department of History, National University of Singapore, 1989.

Murfett Malcolm H., John N. Miksic, Farrell, Brian P. and Chiang Ming Shun. *Between Two Oceans: A Military History of Singapore from First Settlement to Final British Withdrawal*. Singapore: Oxford University Press, 1999.

Nair, Vasandalumari. "Tamils Reform Association, Singapore (1932–61)." Unpublished B.A. Hons. dissertation. Department of History, University of Singapore, 1973.

Nam Tae Yul. "Singapore's One-party System: Its Relationship to Democracy and Political Stability." *Pacific Affairs* 42, No. 4 (1970).

National Heritage Board. *Singapore's 100 Historic Places*. Singapore: National Heritage Board and Archipelago Press, 2002.

Ng Beng Yeong. "How the Mental Hospital was Renamed Woodbridge Hospital in 1951." *Annals Academy of Medicine* 28 (1999).

———. *Till the Break of Day: A History of Mental Health Services in Singapore, 1841–1993*. Singapore: Singapore University Press, 2001.

Ng Beng Yeong and Cheah Jin Seng. "Milestones of the Medical School and Medical Progress of Singapore over the Past 100 years", in *Annals Academy of Medicine* 34, No. 6 (2005).

Ng Siew Eng (ed.). *Touches: 10 Years of the Singapore Dance Theatre*. Singapore: Singapore Dance Theatre, 1998.

Ng Wai-ming, Benjamin. "Japanese Popular Music in Singapore and the Hybridisation of Asian Music." *Asian Music* 34, no.1 (2002/3).

Ng, Tisa. *Ong Teng Cheong: Planner, Politician, President*. Singapore: Editions Didier Millet, 2005.

Nik Hassan Shuhaimi Nik Abdul Rahman (volume ed.). *The Encyclopedia of Malaysia Vol. 4: Early History*. Singapore: Archipelago Press, 1998.

Nilavu Mohammad Ali. "Mother-goddess worship: Practice and Practitioners in Three Hindu Temples." In *New Place, Old Ways: Essays on Indian Society and Culture in Modern Singapore,* edited by Anthony R. Walker. New Delhi: Hindustan Pub. Corp., 1994.

Noor Aisha Abdul Rahman and Lai Ah Eng. *Secularism and Spirituality*. Singapore: Marshall Cavendish Academic, 2006.

Omar Asmah Haji (volume editor). *The Encyclopedia of Malaysia Vol 9: Languages and Literature*. Singapore: Archipelago Press, 2004.

Ong Chit Chung. *Operation Matador: Britain's War Plans Against the Japanese*. Singapore: Times, 1997.

Ong Choo Suat and Tan Beng Luan. *Five-foot-way Traders*. Singapore: Archives & Oral History Department, 1985.

Ong Kah Kuan. *We Were Great: Thomas Cup Badminton*. Malaysia: Federal Publications, 1984.

Ooi Giok Ling. *Town Councils in Singapore: Self-determination for Public Housing Estates*. Singapore: Times Academic Press for the Institute of Policy Studies, 1990.

Ooi Giok Ling, Tan Ern Ser and Koh, Gillian. "Political Participation in Singapore: Findings from a National Survey." *Asian Journal of Political Science* 7, No. 2 (1999).

Oon, Desmond. *Government Involvement in Sport: Singapore*. Unpublished PhD Dissertation. University of Queensland, Australia, 1984.

Oriental Telephone Company. *The Story of the Telephone in Singapore*. Singapore: Oriental Telephone Company. 1951.

Overseas Union Bank, *Building a Singapore Bank: the OUB Story*. Singapore: OUB 1999.

Pan, Lynn (general ed.). *The Encyclopedia of Chinese Overseas*. North America: Harvard University Press, 1998.

Pandian Hannah. "Standing tall." *The Straits Times*, May 21, 1991.

Partridge, J. *Alexandra Hospital: From British Military to Civilian Institution*

Pearson, H. F. *People of Early Singapore*. London: University of London Press, 1955

Peebles, Gavin and Wilson, Peter. *Economic Growth and Development in Singapore: Past and Future*. Cheltenham, UK: Edward Elgar, 2002.

People's Action Party. *People's Action Party 1954–1984: Petir 30th Anniversary Issue*. Singapore: Central Executive Committee, People's Action Party, 1984.

———. *People's Action Party, 1954–1979*. Singapore: Central Executive Committee, People's Action Party, 1979.

Pereira, Joseph C. *Legends of the Golden Venus*. Singapore: Times Editions, 1999.

Peters, Joseph, "Singapore." In *The Musics of ASEAN*, edited by Santos, Ramon P. Philippines: ASEAN Committee on Culture and Information, 1995.

Pinsler, Jeffrey. *Civil Justice in Singapore: Developments in the Course of the 20th Century*. Singapore: Butterworths Asia, 2000.

Prema Nadesan. "The social and cultural significance of Hindu weddings." Unpublished B.Soc.Sci Hons. dissertation. Department of Sociology, National University of Singapore. 1992.

Prevots, Naima. *Dance for Export: Cultural Diplomacy and the Cold War*. Middletown: Wesleyan University Press, 1998.

Probert, H. A. *A History of Changi*. Singapore: Changi Museum, 2006.

Proud, Edward B. *The Postal History of British Malaya, Vol 1*. Heathfield, Sussex: Proud-Bailey Co., 1985.

PSA Corporation. *PSA: Full Ahead*. Singapore: PSA Corporation Ltd, 2003.

Pugalenthi, S. R. *Elections in Singapore*. Singapore: VJ Times, 1996.

Purcell, Victor. *The Chinese in Southeast Asia*. Second edition. London: Oxford University Press, 1965.

Quah, Jon S. T. "Government Policies and Nation-building." In *In Search of Singapore's National Values*, edited by Quah, Jon S.T. Singapore: Times Academic Press for the Institute of Policy Studies, 1990.

——— (ed.). *In Search of Singapore's National Values*. Singapore: Times Academic Press for the Institute of Policy Studies, 1990.

———. "The 1980s: A Review of Significant Political Developments." In *A History of Singapore*, edited by Chew, Ernest C. T. and Edwin Lee. Singapore: Oxford University Press, 1991.

Quah, Jon S.T., Chan Heng Chee and Seah Chee Meow (eds.). *Government and Politics of Singapore*. Rev. ed. Singapore: Oxford University Press, 1987.

Quah, Stella R. *Family in Singapore: Sociological Perspectives*. Singapore: Times Academic Press, 1994.

Raj Kumar Rengaraju. "Public and private rituals: an interpretation of Indian ceremonies in Singapore." Unpublished B.A. Hons. dissertation. Department of Sociology, University of Singapore, 1979.

Ramesh, M. "Economic Globalization and Policy Choices: Singapore." *Governance* 8, No. 2 (1995).

Rasiah Bee Abdul Halil. "Post-War Malay Novelists: An Analysis of Their Awareness and Approach to Societal Problems." Unpublished M.A. thesis. Department of Malay Studies, National University of Singapore, 1985.

Reid, Anthony. "The Origins of Revenue Farming in Southeast Asia." In *The Rise and Fall of Revenue Farming*, edited by John Butcher and Howard Dick. London: Macmillan Press, 1993.

Report of the Constitutional Commission, 1966. Singapore: Singapore National Printers, 1966.

Robert, G. *The Malaysia Cup*. Singapore: 2A Project Consultants, 1991.

Rockhill, W. W. "Notes on the Relations and Trade of China with the Eastern Archipelago and the Coast of the Indian Ocean During the Fourteenth Century", in *T'oung Pao* 15, (1914).

Rodan, Gary. "Elections Without Representation: The Singapore Experience under the PAP." In *The Politics of Elections in Southeast Asia*, edited by Taylor, R. H. New York: Woodrow Wilson Center Press and Cambridge University Press, 1996.

———. "Singapore in 1996: Extended Election Fever." *Asian Survey* 37, No. 2 (1997).

———. "The Internet and Political Control in Singapore." *Political Science Quarterly* 113, No. 1, 1998.

Roff, William R. *The Origin of Malay Nationalism*. Second Edition. Kuala Lumpur: Penerbit Universiti Oxford, 1994

Rudolph, Jürgen. *Reconstructing Identities: A Social History of the Babas in Singapore*. London: Ashgate Publishing, 1998.

Rush, James R. "Glossary and Opium Weights." In *Opium to Java: Revenue Farming and Chinese Enterprise in Colonial Indonesia, 1860–1910*. Ithaca: Cornell University Press, 1990.

Sam, Jackie (ed.). *The First Twenty Years of the People's Association*. Singapore: The People's Association, 1980.

Sandhu, K. S. and Mani, A. (eds). *Indian Communities in Southeast Asia*. Singapore: Institute of Southeast Asian Studies, 1993.

Sandhu, K. S. and Wheatley, Paul. "The Entrepot of Achievement," in *Management of Success: The Molding of Modern Singapore*. Singapore: Institute of Southeast Asian Studies, 1989.

Santos, Ramon P (ed.). *The Musics of ASEAN*. Philippines: ASEAN Committee on Culture and Information, 1995.

Sareen, Tilak Raj. *Secret documents on Singapore Mutiny, 1915*. New Delhi: Mounto Pub. House, 1995.

Savage, Victor R. and Yeoh, Brenda S. A. . *Toponymics: A Study of Singapore Street Names*. Singapore: Eastern Universities Press, 2003.

Savage, Victor R., Huang, Shirlena and Chang Tou Chuang. "Historical Study of the Singapore River." (Part I), (unpublished study prepared for the Singapore Tourism Board) Singapore: Centre for Business Research and Development, Faculty of Business Administration, National University of Singapore, July 1998.

Saw Chu-thong. "Transported Indian Convicts in Singapore, 1825–1873." Unpublished B.A. Hons. dissertation. Department of History, University of Malaya, Singapore, 1956.

Saw Swee Hock. *Population Policies and Programmes in Singapore*. Singapore: Institute of Southeast Asian Studies, 2005.

Schergen, Janek. *Goh Choo San: Master Craftsman in Dance*. Singapore: Singapore Dance Theatre, 1997.

Schweizer-Iten, Hans. *One Hundred Years of the Swiss Club and the Swiss Community of Singapore 1871–1971*. Singapore: Swiss Club, 1971.

Seow, Francis T. "The Judiciary." In *The Singapore Puzzle*, edited by Haas, Michael. Westport, Connecticut: Praeger, 1999.

Severino, Rodolfo C. *ASEAN Today and Tomorrow*. Jakarta: ASEAN Secretariat, 2002.

———. *Southeast Asia in Search of an ASEAN Community*. Singapore: Institute of Southeast Asian Studies, forthcoming.

Shaharuddin Maaruf and Sharifah Maznah Syed Omar. "Modern Literature of Singapore: Singapore Malay Litarature." In *Modern literature of ASEAN*, edited by Budi Darma. Jakarta: ASEAN Committee on Culture and Information, 2000.

Shaharuddin Maaruf. "Materialism as an Ideology in Malay Literature." In *Crossing Borders: Transmigration in Asia Pacific*, edited by Ong Jin Hui, Chan Kwok Bun, Chew Soon Beng, Singapore: Simon & Schuster, 1995.

Sharp, Ilsa. *The First 21 Years: The Singapore Zoological Gardens Story*. Singapore: Singapore Zoological Gardens, 1994.

———. *The Journey: Singapore's Land Transport Story*. Singapore: SNP International Publishing, 2005.

Shee Poon Kim. "The Evolution of the Political System." In *Government and Politics of Singapore* edited by Quah, S. T. Jon, Chan Heng Chee and Seah Chee Meow. Singapore: Oxford University Press, 1987.

Shekaran, Kana. "Respectable dancer." *The Straits Times*, Oct 25, 1992

Sheridan, L. A. "The Constitutional and Legal Implications and Problems in the Separation of Singapore from Malaysia." *Fiat Justitia* 1, No. 1 (1966).

Shinozaki Mamoru. *My Wartime Experiences in Singapore*. Singapore: Institute of Southeast Asian Studies, 1973.

Siew Nim Chee. "*Labour in the Chinese Tin Mining Industry of Malaya*." Unpublished B.A. Hons. dissertation. Department of Economics. University of Malaya in Singapore, 1951.

Silver, Lynette and Hall, Tom. *The Heroes of Rimau*. Sydney: Sally Milner Publishing, 1990.

Simson, Ivan. *Singapore: Too Little, Too Late – The Failure of Malaya's Defences in 1942*. London: Leo Cooper, 1970.

Singapore 21 Committee. *Singapore 21: Together We Make the Difference*. Singapore: Singapore 21 Committee, 1999.

Singapore Federation of Chinese Clan Associations. *Chinese Customs and Festivals in Singapore*. Singapore: Singapore Federation of Chinese Clan Associations, 1992.

———. *History of Clan Associations in Singapore Vol 1*. Singapore: Singapore Federation of Chinese Clan Associations, 2005.

———. *History of Clan Associations in Singapore Vol 2*. Singapore: Singapore Federation of Chinese Clan Associations, 2005.

Singh, Bachan. "*A History of Tin Mining in Perak 1896–1926*." Unpublished B.A. Hons. dissertation. Department of History, University of Malaya in Singapore, 1960.

Singh, Bilveer. *Whither PAP's Dominance?: An Analysis of Singapore's 1991 General Elections*. Petaling Jaya: Pelanduk Publications, 1992.

Singh, Param Ajeet. "The Civil Service in the Straits Settlements 1819–1867." Unpublished B.A. Hons. dissertation. Department of History, University of Malaya, 1960.

Sinha, Vineeta. *A New God in the Diaspora? Muneeswaran Worship in Contemporary Singapore*. Singapore: Singapore University Press, 2005.

———. "Hinduism in Singapore: A Sociological and Ethnographic Perspective." Unpublished M. Soc. Sci dissertation. Department of Sociology, National University of Singapore. 1987.

Skeat, Walter William. *Malay Magic: Being an Introduction to the Folklore and Popular Religion of the Malay Peninsular*. London: MacMillan, 1984.

Sleeman, Colin and Silkin, S C (eds.). *Trial of Sumida Haruzo and Twenty Others (The "Double Tenth" Trial)*. London: William Hodge, 1951.

Soh, Felix. *Phoenix: The Story of the Home Team*. Singapore: Times Editions, 2003.

Song Ong Siang. *One Hundred Years' History of the Chinese in Singapore*. London: John Murray, 1923.

Sopher, David E. *The Sea Nomads: A Study of the Maritime Boat People of Southeast Asia*. Singapore: National Museum, 1977.

Srinivas, M.N. *Caste in Modern India and Other Essays*. Bombay: Asia Publishing House. 1962.

Starr, Peter. *Citibank: A Century in Asia*. Singapore: Editions Didier Millet, 2002.

Straits Times, "A Hag to Beauty Then Kampong Vampire", May 3, 1957.

Straits Times, "A Time when Life was a Cabaret," Jun 9, 1995.

Straits Times, "Close Up – Jalan Besar," Feb 9, 1990.

Straits Times, "Peace – through dancing," April 9, 1967.

Straits Times, "Remembering life in the 1950s and 60s," July 16, 1998.

Straits Times, "Three Worlds," Jun 9, 1995.

Sulaiman Jeem & Abdul Ghani Hamid. *Aktivis Melayu/Islam di Singapura*. Singapore: Persatuan Wartawan Melayu Singapura, 1997.

Sullivan, Margaret. *Can Survive, La: Cottage Industries in High-rise Singapore*. Singapore: Graham Brash, 1993.

Supreme Court. *Supreme Court Singapore: Excellence into the Next Millennium*. Singapore: Supreme Court, 1999.

———. *Supreme Court Singapore: The Re-organisation of the 1990s.* Singapore: Supreme Court, 1994.

Surain Subramaniam. "The Dual Narrative of 'Good Governance': Lessons for Understanding Political and Cultural Change in Malaysia and Singapore." *Contemporary Southeast Asia* 23, no. 1 (2001).

Suratman Markasan. "Sastera Melayu Singapura Mutakhir Dalam Dua Jalur Kritik Sosial." In *Pemikiran Sastera Nusantara,* edited by Hamzah Hamdani. Kuala Lumpur: DBP, 1988.

Suryadinata, Leo. "Patterns of Chinese Political Participation in Four ASEAN States." *Contemporary Southeast Asia* 15, No. 3 (1993).

Syed Husin Ali. "Pertubuhan-pertubuhan bahasa dan sastera Melayu di Singapura selepas Perang Dunia II (Khasnya Asas 50)." Unpublished B.A. Hons. dissertation. University of Malaya, Singapore, 1959.

TalkingCock.com. *The Coxford Singlish Dictionary.* Singapore: Angsana Books, 2003.

Tan Chong Tee. *Force 136.* Singapore: Asiapac, 1995.

———. *Upholding the Tradition: Singapore Badminton.* Singapore: Asiapac Publication, 2002.

Tan Chun Lim (ed.). *Singapore Postage Stamps Catalogue.* Singapore: C S Philatelic Agency, 2005.

Tan Chwee Huat. *Financial Markets and Institutions in Singapore.* Singapore: Singapore University Press, 2005.

Tan Lai Kim, Hao Xiaoming and Chen Yaniu. "The Singapore Press as a Mediator Between the Government and the Public." *Media Asia* 15, No. 4 (1998).

Tan Tock Seng Hospital. *150 Years of Caring – The Legacy of Tan Tock Seng Hospital.* Singapore: Tan Tock Seng Hospital, 1994.

Tan Wah Piow. *Frame-up: A Singapore Court on Trial.* Oxford: TWP Pub., 1987.

Tan Wei Ping. "Xinyao (Singapore ballads) and the construction of Singaporean Identities." Unpublished dissertation. National Institute of Education, Nanyang Technological University, 2003.

Tan Yew Soon and Soh Yew Peng. *The Development of Singapore's Modern Media Industry.* Singapore: Times Academic Press, 1994.

Tan, Kevin Y. L. "Economic Development, Legal Reform and Rights in Singapore and Taiwan." In *The East Asian Challenge for Human Rights,* edited by Bauer, Joanna R. and Daniel A. Bell. Cambridge: Cambridge University Press, 1999.

Tan, Kevin Y. L. "Fifty Years of the UDHR [Universal Declaration of Human Rights]: A Singaporean Reflects." In *Human Rights Perspectives,* edited by Tan Ngoh Tiong and Kripa Sridharan. Singapore: United Nations Association of Singapore, 1999.

Tan, Kevin Y. L. "Is Singapore's Electoral System in Need of Reform?" *Commentary,* 14 (1997).

Tan, Kevin Y. L. "The Presidency in Singapore: Constitutional Developments." In *Managing Political Change in Singapore: The Elected Presidency,* edited by Tan, Kevin Y. L. and Lam Peng Er. London: Routledge, 1997.

Tan, Kevin Y. L. (ed.). *The Singapore Legal System.* Second edition. Singapore: Singapore University Press, 1999.

Tan, Kevin and George, Cherian. "Civil Society and the Societies Act." *The Straits Times,* Mar 27, 2001.

Tan, Kevin Y. L. and Lam Peng Er (eds.). *Managing Political Change in Singapore: The Elected Presidency.* London: Routledge, 1997.

Tan, Ria and Yeo, Alan. *Chek Jawa Guidebook. Singapore: Simply Green, 2003.*

Tan, Sumiko. *The Singapore Parliament: The House We Built.* Singapore: Times Media, 2000.

Tan, Thomas T. W. *Chinese Dialect Groups: Traits and Trades.* Singapore: Opinion Books, 1990.

Tang, K. F. *Kampong Days-Village Life and Times in Singapore Revisited.* Singapore: National Archive, 1993.

Tate, D. J. M. *The RGA History of the Plantation Industry in the Malay Peninsula.* New York: Oxford University Press, 1996.

Tay, Simon. "Govt Pay: Too Much and Not Enough.*" The Straits Times,* July 13, 2000.

———. "Human Rights, Culture, and the Singapore Example." *McGill Law Journal* 4 (1996).

———. "Towards a Singaporean Civil Society." *Southeast Asian Affairs.* Singapore: Institute of Southeast Asian Studies, 1998.

Telecommunication Authority of Singapore. *Hundred Years of Dedicated Telephone Service in Singapore, 1879–1979.* Singapore: Public Relations Department, Telecommunication Authority of Singapore, 1979.

Teo, Peggy, Yeoh, Brenda S. A., Ooi Giok Ling and Lai, Karen P.Y. *Changing Landscapes of Singapore.* Singapore: McGraw-Hill Education, 2004.

Teo Siew-Eng and Savage, Victor R. "Singapore Landscape: A Historical Overview of Housing Image." In *A History of Singapore* edited Chew, Ernest C.T. and Lee, Edwin. Singapore: Oxford University of Singapore, 1991.

Tham Seong Chee (ed.). *Essays on Literature and Society in Southeast Asia: Political and Sociological Perspectives.* Singapore: Singapore University Press, 1981.

The National Archives. *The Japanese Occupation: Singapore 1942–1945.* Singapore: Federal Publications, 1985.

The Principles for Determining and Safeguarding the Accumulated Reserves of the Government and the Fifth Schedule Statutory Boards and Government Companies. Singapore: Government Printers, 1999.

The Singapore and Malaysia Overseas-Returned Chinese Association (ed.). *Selected Historical Materials of the Malayan People's Anti-Japanese Army.* Hong Kong: Witness, 1992.

Thio Li-Ann. "The Post-colonial Constitutional Evolution of the Singapore Legislature: A Case Study." *Singapore Journal of Legal Studies* (1993).

Travers, Thomas, "The Journal of Thomas Otho Travers, 1813–1829." *Memoirs of the National Museum* No. 4, (1957).

Tremewan, Christopher. *The Political Economy of Social Control in Singapore.* New York: St. Martin's Press, 1994.

Trocki, Carl A. "Weights and Measures." In *Opium, Empire and the Global Political Economy: A study of the Asian opium trade 1750–1950.* London: Routledge, 1999.

———. "The Collapse of Singapore's Great Syndicate", in *The Rise and Fall of Revenue Farming,* edited by John Butcher and Howard Dick. London: Macmillan Press, 1993.

——— *Prince of Pirates Temenggongs of Johor, 1784–1885.* Singapore: Singapore University Press, 1979.

Turnbull, C. M. "Constitutional Development of Singapore, 1819–1968." In *Modern Singapore,* edited by Ooi Jin Bee and Chiang Hai Ding. Singapore: University of Singapore, 1969.

———. "Trade." In *The Straits Settlements, 1826–1867: Indian Presidency to Crown Colony.* Singapore: Oxford University Press, 1972.

———. *A History of Singapore 1819–1975.* London: Oxford University Press, 1982.

———. *A History of Singapore 1819–1988.* Singapore: Oxford University Press, 1989.

———. *Dateline Singapore: 150 Years of The Straits Times.* Singapore: Singapore Press Holdings, 1995.

———. *The Straits Settlements 1826–67.* London: Oxford University Press, 1972.

Tyers, Ray. *Singapore, Then and Now.* Edition 1 Volume 2, Singapore: University Education Press, 1976.

———. *Singapore, Then and Now.* Edition 2, Singapore: Landmark Books, 1993.

Uhde, Jan and Ng, Yvonne Uhde. *Latent Images – Film in Singapore.* Singapore: Oxford University Press in collaboration with Ngee Ann Polytechnic, 2000.

Ungku Maimunah Mohd Tahir. *Modern Malay Literary Culture: A Historical Perspective.* Singapore: Institute of Southeast Asian Studies, 1987

United Overseas Bank Group. *60 Years of Progress.* Singapore: UOB, 1995.

Urban Redevelopment Authority. *Architectural Heritage Singapore.* Singapore: Urban Redevelopment Authority, 2004.

———. *The Concept Plan 2001.* Singapore: Urban Redevelopment Authority, 2001.

Van Cuylenburg, John Bertram. *Singapore Through Sunshine and Shadow.* Singapore: Heinemann Asia, 1982.

Van Der Heide, William. *Malaysian Cinema, Asian Film, Border Crossings and National Cultures.* Amsterdam: Amsterdam University Press, 2002.

Vasil, Raj K. *Asianising Singapore: The PAP's Management of Ethnicity.* Singapore: Heinemann Asia, 1995.

———. *Governing Singapore: Democracy and National Development.* Singapore: Allen & Unwin, 2000.

———. *Governing Singapore: Interviews with the New Leaders.* Rev. ed. Singapore: Times Books International, 1988.

Venka Purushothaman (ed.). *Narratives: Notes on a Cultural Journey – Cultural Medallion Recipients, 1979–2001.* Singapore: National Arts Council, 2002.

Wakeman Jr, Frederic. *The Fall of Imperial China.* New York: The Free Press, 1977.

Warren, Allen. *Singapore 1942.* Singapore: Talisman, 2002.

Warren, James Francis. *Ah Ku and Karayuki-San: Prostitution in Singapore 1870–1940.* Singapore: Singapore University Press, 2003.

Warren, James Francis. *Rickshaw Coolie: A People's History of Singapore 1880–1940.* Singapore: Singapore University Press, 2003.

Wee Yeow Chin. *Ferns of the Tropics.* Singapore: Timber Press,1998.

Wight, Martin. *British Colonial Constitutions 1947.* Oxford: Clarendon Press, 1952.

Wilkinson, Barry. "Social Engineering in Singapore." *Journal of Contemporary Asia* 18, No. 2 (1988).

Williams, Jeremy B. "Capitalist Development and Human Rights: Singapore under Lee Kuan Yew." *Journal of Contemporary Asia* 22, No. 3 (1992).

Williams, Jeremy B. "Rapid Economic Development in Singapore and the Future of the PAP." *Journal of Contemporary Asia* 26, No. 2 (1996).

Winslow, Valentine S. "The Election of a President in a Parliamentary System." In *Managing Political Change in Singapore: the Elected Presidency,* edited by Tan, Kevin Y. L. and Lam Peng Er, London: Routledge, 1997.

Winstedt, R. O. *A History of Malaya.* Kuala Lumpur: Marican & Sons, 1982

———. "Gold Ornaments Dug up at Fort Canning, Singapore." *Journal of the Malaysian Branch, Royal Asiatic Society* 42, No. 1 (1969).

———. *History of Johore (1365 – 1895).* Kuala Lumpur: Malayan Branch of the Royal Asiatic Society, 1979.

Wong Lin Ken, "The Trade of Singapore, 1819–1969." *Journal of the Malayan Branch, Royal Asiatic Society* 33, Pt 4 (No. 192).

Wong Lin Ken. *The Malayan Tin Industry to 1914.* Tucson: The University of Arizona Press, 1965.

Wong, Douglas. *HSBC: Its Malaysian Story.* Kuala Lumpur: Editions Didier Millet, 2004.

Wong, John. "China's Emerging Economic Relationship with Southeast Asia." *Southeast Asian Studies* 25, no. 3 (1987).

———. *The Political Economy of China's Changing Relations with Southeast Asia.* London: Macmillan Press, 1984.

Woon, Walter (ed.). *The Singapore Legal System.* Singapore: Longman Singapore, 1989.

Wu Teh Yao (ed.). *Political and Social Change in Singapore.* Singapore: Institute of Southeast Asian Studies in co-operation with the Department of Political Science, University of Singapore, 1975.

Wurtzburg, C. E. *Raffles of the Eastern Isles.* London: Hodder and Stoughton, 1954.

Yap Siang Yong, Bose, Romen and Pang, Angeline. *Fortress Singapore: The Battlefield Guide.* Singapore: Times Books International, 1995.

Yen Ching-Hwang. *Coolies and Mandarins: China's Protection of Overseas Chinese during the Late Ch'ing Period (1851–1911).* Singapore: Singapore University Press, 1985.

Yeo Kim Wah and Shee Poon Kim. "Singapore." In *Political Parties of Asia and the Pacific,* edited by Fukui Haruhiro. Westport, CT: Greenwood Press, 1985.

Yong, C. F. "British Attitudes Towards the Chinese Community Leaders in Singapore, 1819–1941.*" Journal of the South Seas Society* 40, No. 1 (1985).

York, F. W. and Phillips, A.R. *Singapore: A History of its Trams Trolleybuses and Buses. Volume 1 1880s–1960s.* Surrey: DTS Publishing, 1996.

Yousof Ghulam-Sarwar (volume ed.). *The Encyclopedia of Malaysia Vol.8: Performing Arts.* Singapore: Archipelago Press, 2004.

Yu Yun. *A Life in Dance: Lee Shu Fen.* Singapore: Lee Shu Fen & Dancers Society, 1995.

PICTURE CREDITS

Thanks are due to all the organizations and individuals listed below for permission to reproduce images. Particular acknowledgement is due to the National Archives of Singapore and the National Museum of Singapore.

Special thanks are due also to the following for their support:
Asian Civilisations Museum, Civil Aviation Authority of Singapore, Housing & Development Board, Ministry of Defence, Ministry of Foreign Affairs, Monetary Authority of Singapore, Nanyang Technological University, National Arts Council, National Institute of Education, National Library Board, National Parks Board, National University of Singapore, PUB, Public Service Commission, Singapore Art Museum, Singapore Civil Defence Force, Singapore Police Force, Singapore Press Holdings, Singapore Sports Council, Singapore Tourism Board, The Raffles Museum of Biodiversity Research and Urban Redevelopment Authority.

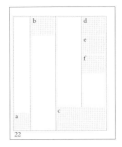

The list below gives the page numbers on which images appear. The letter after the page number identifies which image on that page is being referred to. As demonstrated in the diagram (left), the images on each page are identified by *a*, *b*, *c*, etc.; the sequence runs down from top to bottom in each column in turn, starting with the column furthest to the left. Where an image spans two columns, the column to the left is the one that matters. Pictures within special features are identified by their page number plus a description or number.

Every effort has been made to trace copyright holders. In the event of errors or omissions, appropriate credit will be made in future printings of the Encyclopedia.

20th century impressions of British Malaya 24a; 29c; 38 (pic. 1); 155c–d; 183c; 203c; 529c; 542a–b

Abdul Aleem Siddique Mosque 18a

Action for Aids 22e; 233c

Action Theatre 182 (*Autumn Tomyam*)

Agni Kootthu 536 (*Talaq* poster)

Agung Rai Museum 44 (Adrien-Jean Le Mayeur)

Ai Tong School 170b

Aidah Bridal 325c

Alkaff Mosque Kampong Melayu 172a

Alliance Entertainment and Glen Goei 202c

Arkib Negara Malaysia 313b; 327a

Asia Pacific Breweries 47a; 565d

Asian Civilisations Museum 44 (Xu Beihong's portrait of Lim Hak Tai); 48 (all pics); 372 (Drawing of the Raffles Library and Museum)

Asian Women's Welfare Association 49a

Aspidistra Fly 180 (*The Ghost of Things*)

Astreal and Wallwork Records 180 (*Fragment of the Same Dead Star*)

Timothy Auger 27b; 136b; 153a; 160c; 162c; 196a; 196d; 244c; 331a; 400b; 442 (eastwards 1920s); 461e; 472e; 519d; 524b; 570c; 589c

Australian War Memorial 328 (Japanese troops enter Kuala Lumpur, Europeans evacuated from Penang, Australian troops at Muar, Japanese troops enter Johor Baru, Rubber plantations destroyed); 394b–c; 394e

Automobile Association of Singapore 50a

Banyan Tree Hotels and Resorts 234c

Bee Cheng Hiang 59c

Boku Films 167c; 567e

Buddha Tooth Relic Temple 74c

Canadian International School, Singapore 256a

Cathay Organisation 83b–c; 228e; 234a; 284a; 313a; 345a; 417b

Celvi Store Trading (Cinkappur) 534 (*Ippadikku Naan*)

Wendy Chan 169c

Noreen Chan 140a

Chang Tou Liang 106 (album cover); 133 (all album covers); 272b

Changi General Hospital 91a–b

Chartered Semiconductor Manufacturing 94d

Cheah Jin Seng 29b; 38 (pic. 7–8); 39 (pic 18–19); 134b; 169d; 272a; 441c; 521 (all pics except pic. 6–8)

Chinatown Heritage Centre 103a

Chinese Heritage Centre 108c

Chinese Theatre Circle 115a; 592c

Peter Chong 451a

Chou Loke Ming 147a–d

Chung Cheng High School (Main) 125a

Cinkappur Tamil Eluttalar Kalakam 479b; 534 (*Pullangkuzhal, Tamizhar Thalaivar*)

Citibank Singapore 529b

Citigroup Art Collection 127c

Civil Aviation Authority of Singapore 92 (all pics except Departure Display, Singapore Visitor Centre, Budget Terminal, Terminal One 1970s)

ComfortDelgro 137a–b; 340 (SBS Transit MRT: North East Line)

Concorde-New Horizons Corp. 194 (*Saint Jack*)

Babes Conde 140e

Martin Cross 20c

Crystal Jade 152a

Richard Curtis 331b

Dance Ensemble Singapore cover (pic. 33); 156a

Dewan Bahasa dan Pustaka 323 (Usman Awang)

Drama Box 163c–d; 118 (forum performance, *Shithole*); 282a

Manesh Dutt 60a

Easternworld Holdings 114 (Paul and Peter Li); 302f

ECNAD 155a; 167a

Editions Didier Millet (publisher's collection) cover (pic. 43); 23a; 38 (pic. 2–4, 6); 39 (pic. 13, 20); 55a; 56a; 67 (1960 riverfront); 70a; 72b; 79c; 84d; 86c; 93b; 102d; 103c; 105a; 108b; 126c; 140b; 150b; 153 (back of $100 Ship series note, back of $100 Portrait series note, Banana note); 166d; 169a; 172b; 173b; 174b; 178 (*Raffles Place Ragtime, Stand Alone*); 187a; 187c; 194 (all pics except poster for *Singapore*, poster for *Road to Singapore, Saint Jack*, STB brochures); 208b; 229a; 240a; 254a; 266a; 280b; 320b; 322 (Abdul Rahim Kajai); 325a; 329 (propaganda leaflet); 340 (MRT train on overhead viaduct, MRT card); 342a; 359b; 387c; 401b; 404 (pic. 4); 416a; 424b; 433c; 446b; 459a; 461a; 487b; 488b; 493a; 496b; 515c; 521 (pic. 6–7); 532c; 532e; 549d; 565e; 571a

Editions Didier Millet (KL) 142a; 151a

Elangovan 24d; 172d

Electrico 174c

Eng Leong Medallic Industries Pte Ltd 397d–e

Eng Wah Organisation 176a–b; 210a

Er Woo Amateur Musical and Dramatic Association 112 (pamphlet); 183b

Eugene Dairiananthan and Ocean Butterflies Music 114 (all cassette covers)

ExxonMobil Asia Pacific Pte Ltd 271a

John Falconer 181a; 221a; 221b; 268c; 414 (George S. Michael ad, GR Lambert, Wilson & Co.)

Foo Tee Jun 199a; 199c

Francis and Joyce Foo 115c–d

Frontier Danceland 206d

Gan Eng Seng School 208d

Johnny Gao Yuxian 40 (pic. 5, 15–17); 41 (pic. 12); 126a; 129a

Genome Institute of Singapore 211a

Girl Guides Singapore 213b

Global Music GMP 558a

Goh Geok Yian 37 (map)

Goh Hak Su 216c

Gong Zhiyuan 214b

William Gwee 163b, 410a

Han Kee Juan 227d

Hang Chang Chieh 228a

Haw Par Corporation Ltd 51c

Health Promotion Board 362d

Heinemann Asia 217c

Herwan Samat 258a

Ho Minfong 235c

Kirsten Holst 498d

Home Nursing Foundation 237a

Housing & Development Board 32d; 39 (pic. 16); 40 (pic. 4); 76c; 209a–b; 251a; 251c; 271b; 272e; 290a; 428–429 (all pics except pic. 1–2, 6–7); 436b; 593b; 603a

HSBC Group Archives, London 153 (HSBC banknotes); 345b

Hwa Chong Institution 108d

Hyflux Ltd 243a

Ibrahim Tahir 264c; 321b; 323 (*Satu Bumi, Subuh Hilang Senja, Ziarah Rindu*)

Institute of Bioengineering and Nanotechnology 253c

Institute of Contemporary Art Singapore 253a

Institute of Molecular and Cell Biology 253b

Institute of Technical Education 254b

International Islamic University Malaysia/ISTAC Illuminated 20b; 322 (*Hikayat Abdullah*)

J Team Productions Pte Ltd 379a

Roger Jenkins 265b

Jewish Welfare Board 266b

Jiao Yu Chu Ban She 312b

Keppel Corporation 306a

Khong Guan Biscuit Factory (S) Pte Ltd 278c–e

Khoo Swee Chiow 279a

Stella Kon 282b

KP Bhaskar 62a, c

Kwong Wai Siew Peck San Theng 286e; 435c

Land Transport Authority 340 (system map, construction of Raffles Place station); 341 (Dhoby Ghaut station escalators)

Dennis Lee and Toh Chee Hung 566b

Lee Huei Min 294c

Lee Wen 298a

Leong Kwok Peng 197 (Eagle ray)

Les Amis 301c

Leslie Low 180 (*Pain-Stained Morning*)

Leung Kai Fook Medical Company (Pte) Ltd 51a–b

Arthur Lim 303e

William Lim 139a; 304e

Lim Fei Shen cover (pic. 17); 307a

Livonia and Little Orange 180 (*Zerofeel*)

M1 316b

Kishore Mahbubani 318b

MakanTime.com 94a; 152c; 237d; 289b; 367d; 454b

Malaysian Sociological Research Institute 530d; 532b

Macutu, Mu. A. 534 (*Puthiya Minnalgal*)

Maraimalai Patippakam Veliyitu 402b

S.N. Masuri 322 (ASAS 50)

Prakash Mayparol 233a

MediaCorp Pte Ltd 438c (all logos except Dongli 88.3FM and Power 98FM); 555b (all logos)

MediaCorp Raintree Pictures 193b; 244e; 343a (*Chicken Rice War, I Not Stupid Too, The Best Bet*)

MediaCorp Studios Pte Ltd 97b; 99a; 189b; 242b; 413a; 551b; 556 (pic. 1–4, 10–13); 598b

MediaCorp TV 12 556 (pic. 5–9)

Memories at Old Ford Factory 262 (rice and tools of Endau)

John Miksic 36 (pic. 1–2); 37 (pic. 5–7)

Jerome Ming 415 (Jerome Ming)

Ministry for National Development 318a

Ministry of Community Development, Youth and Sports 53d; 353a

Ministry of Defence 353b; 382a; 558c

Ministry of Education 353c; 561c

Ministry of Finance 353e

Ministry of Foreign Affairs 22b; 53c; 89b; 90d; 98a; 100a; 101b; 138a; 235d; 281b; 286b; 294d; 298b; 314c; 353f; 392e; 400d; 445a; 451d; 478b; 587d; 592a; 600a

Ministry of Health 353g

Ministry of Home Affairs 354a; 591c

Ministry of Information, Communications and Arts 292c; 354b

Ministry of Law 354c

Ministry of Manpower 354d

Ministry of National Development 354e

Ministry of the Environment and Water Resources 353d

Ministry of Transport 354f

Miror Theatre 536 (*Shanmugan* poster)

Mohd Zakaria-Ismail 197 (Puffer-fish)

Monetarium Singapore Pte Ltd (www.monetarium.com.sg) 153 (Straits dollar, Malayan dollar, Malaya and British Borneo dollar, front and back of $100 Orchid series note)

Monetary Authority of Singapore 153 (front and back of British trade dollars)

Jeremy Monteiro 358a

Museum, NUS Centre for the Arts 165b; 220b; 362c

Nan Chiau High School 364a–b

Nanyang Academy of Fine Arts 365c

Nanyang Girls' High School 170a; 365a

INDEX